THE WORLD SERIES

COMPLETE PLAY-BY-PLAY
OF EVERY GAME, 1903–1985
COMPILED BY THE ORIGINATORS OF
THE BASEBALL ENCYCLOPEDIA
RICHARD M. COHEN
and
DAVID S. NEFT

COLLIER BOOKS
MACMILLAN PUBLISHING COMPANY
New York

OTHER BOOKS BY SPORTS PRODUCTS INC.
The Sports Encyclopedia: Baseball
Pro Football: The Early Years
Pro Football: The Modern Era
The Sports Encyclopedia: Pro Basketball
The Scrapbook History of Baseball
The Scrapbook History of Pro Football
The All-Sports World Record Book
The Notre Dame Football Scrapbook
The Ohio State Football Scrapbook
The University of Michigan Football Scrapbook
Monday Morning Quarterback
The Complete All-Time Baseball Register
The Complete All-Time Pro Football Register
The World Book of Odds
Beat the Spread
Pro Football Weekly Almanac, 1981
Pro Football Weekly Almanac, 1982
The Pro Football Bettor's Companion, 1983

Macmillan Publishing Company
866 Third Avenue, New York, N.Y. 10022
Collier Macmillan Canada, Inc.

Library of Congress Cataloging-in-Publication Data
Cohen, Richard M., 1938–
  The World Series.
  1. World series (Baseball)—History. 2. Baseball—
United States—Records. I. Neft, David S.
II. Title.
[GV863.A1C59 1986b]   796.357′782   86–9702
ISBN 0–02–028040–8 (pbk.)

Macmillan books are available at special discounts for bulk purchases for sales
promotions, premiums, fund-raising, or educational use. For details, contact:
Special Sales Director
Macmillan Publishing Company
866 Third Avenue
New York, N.Y. 10022
10 9 8 7 6 5 4 3 2 1

The World Series is also published in a hardcover edition by Macmillan Publishing
Company.

Printed in the United States of America

Contents

Preface   iv

Yearly Results   1

1903 Phillippe: Five Times Over   3

1905 Christy's Three Golden Goose Eggs   9

1906 The Winningest Loser of Them All   13

1907 Grand Theft   18

1908 The Cub's Overall   23

1909 Surprise from Start to Finish   27

1910 Coombs: Thirty-one Plus Three   32

1911 The Origin of Home Run Baker   36

1912 The "$30,000 Muff"   41

1913 Oh-for-Three   48

1914 Cleanly Capping the Miracle   52

1915 Hopping Harry Hooper   57

1916 The Longest Duel in the Sun   61

1917 Ulcers in the Afternoon   66

1918 The Early Birds   71

1919 Bad Company   76

1920 Coveleski, Smith, & Wambsganss   82

1921 Shaming the Tenants   87

1922 The Generous Judge   93

1923 Home Sweet Home   97

1924 Eighteen Years and Six Games Later   102

1925 Peckinpaugh's Eight Errors   108

1926 Alexander vs. Lazzeri   114

1927 By Reputation Alone   120

1928 Double Devastation   124

1929 Late Lightning   128

1930 Earnshaw & Grove & Earnshaw   132

1931 Peppering the Opposition   137

1932 The Year Chicago Died   142

1933 A Man's Game   147

1934 A Victory in the Garbage   151

1935 Bedlam in Detroit   157

1936 Back to the Subways   162

1937 No Contest   167

1938 Gloating for a Second Time   171

1939 Fours Are Wild   175

1940 Encore Amongst the Sorrow   179

1941 The One That Got Away   184

1942 Trauma in the Bronx   188

1943 Repaying a Year-Old Debt   192

1944 Happily Settling for a Pennant   196

1945 Borowy's Weary Wing   201

1946 Play-off: Brecheen to the Rescue   207

1946 Slaughter's Sprint   208

1947 The Ninth Inning of the Fourth Game   213

1948 Play-off: Haunted by the Green Monster   219

1948 Not Enough Rain   220

1949 Reynolds and Page   225

1950 Spanking the Whiz Kids   230

1951 Play-off: One for the Books   234

1951 Washing Out the Miracle   235

1952 Martin's Desperate Dash   240

1953 Five Times Five Equals Five   245

1954 460 Feet of Frustration   250

1955 This Is Next Year   254

1956 A Perfect October   259

1957 Burdette's Twenty-Game Season   265

1958 Comeback   270

1959 Play-off: Rallying to the Top   275

1959 Serving Sherry All Around   276

1960 Mazeroski's Capper   281

1961 Maris: 62; Ford: 32   287

1962 Play-off: Shades of '51   292

1962 Terry to McCovey to Richardson   293

1963 White Shirts and Humiliation   298

1964 The Fireworks After   302

1965 Los Angeles 2, Minnesota 0   307

1966 Sunspots   312

1967 Awakening One Game Too Early   316

1968 Lolich: Twenty the Hard Way   321

1969 Lunar Dust   326

1970 The Vacuum Cleaner at Third Base   330

1971 Lights On, Orioles Off   335

1972 Forty Years Later . . .   340

1973 Mike Andrews: Hitless but Supreme   345

1974 Finley's Unhappy Heroes   351

1975 Game Six   355

1976 Almost All the Way Back   361

1977 Leaving the Squabbles Behind   365

1978 Many Comebacks in One   371

1979 Once Again Walking the Plank   377

1980 After the Dues, Redemption   383

1981 Despite Everything, It Mattered   388

1982 Herzog's Potent Brew   393

1983 The Rise of the Stooges   398

1984 A Logical Conclusion   402

1985 Brett and Bret: The I-70 Series   407

Preface

The World Series is the culmination of the baseball season for the pennant winners in baseball's best of seven "fall classic." It is the windup of a season (or of many seasons) of strategies on and off the field. Management has built the teams, always aiming at this moment. On the field the players, the coaches, and the managers have also aimed and worked hard. The World Series is the end of the season. There is only one winner. Certainly the team defeated should not be considered a loser since it did win the pennant—no small accomplishment.

Every year as October approaches, the excitement and anticipation of the World Series eclipses all sports attention. Each series, each game, has its own character, its own reality. We have tried to preserve these stories in the best possible way by creating a book that describes each game separately, as no other book has. Along with the box score of each game comes the main and unique feature of this book: We cover every game, every inning, every player completely—play-by-play. What isn't covered in the play-by-play, we do with a narrative that goes behind the scenes to cover such things as what made Pepper Martin the crowd favorite in 1931 or Willie Davis's trouble with the sun in 1966. It gives the personal side to bring these stats into a better perspective. Also included for each Series is a very comprehensive composite box. Not only have we listed the Series stats, but also, for all eligible players, their entire season stats. In addition we have listed all the men who played for the team during the year but were not eligible for the Series.

A book of this magnitude could not be possible without the help of others, and we therefore wish to thank publicly and personally all of the following: John Hogrogian, independent consultant and researcher; Jordan A. Deutsch, text and research (former associate for Sports Products); Roland Johnson, researcher (former associate for Sports Products); Cliff Kachline, former historian at the Baseball Hall of Fame; Jack Redding, former librarian at the Baseball Hall of Fame; Rick Cerrone, Baseball Commissioner's office; Steve Hirdt, Elias Sports Bureau; Bert Randolph Sugar; the membership of the Society for American Baseball Research (SABR) for their continuous efforts to keep baseball records as accurate as possible; and Jeff Neuman, editor, Macmillan. A special thanks to our wives for their faith and understanding during this project: Nancy Cohen and Naomi Neft.

Since we are all fallible human beings, some errors may be found among these six million–plus facts. We would like to thank our many correspondents who've written to correct errors, and we would appreciate any further corrections, additions, deletions, or comments in order to keep future editions as complete and accurate as possible. Please send correspondence to:

Sports Products, Inc.
P.O. Box 392
Ridgefield, CT 06877

YEARLY RESULTS

Year	Games	Team	Wins	Manager
1903	8 Games	Boston (A)	5 wins	Jimmy Collins
		Pittsburgh (N)	3 wins	Fred Clarke
1904	No Series held			
1905	5 Games	New York (N)	4 wins	John McGraw
		Philadelphia (A)	1 win	Connie Mack
1906	6 Games	Chicago (A)	4 wins	Fielder Jones
		Chicago (N)	2 wins	Frank Chance
1907	5 Games 1 tie	Chicago (N)	4 wins	Frank Chance
		Detroit (A)	0 wins	Hughie Jennings
1908	5 Games	Chicago (N)	4 wins	Frank Chance
		Detroit (A)	1 win	Hughie Jennings
1909	7 Games	Pittsburgh (N)	4 wins	Fred Clarke
		Detroit (A)	3 wins	Hughie Jennings
1910	5 Games	Philadelphia (A)	4 wins	Connie Mack
		Chicago (N)	1 win	Frank Chance
1911	6 games	Philadelphia (A)	4 wins	Connie Mack
		New York (N)	2 wins	John McGraw
1912	8 games 1 tie	Boston (A)	4 wins	Jake Stahl
		New York (N)	3 wins	John McGraw
1913	5 games	Philadelphia (A)	4 wins	Connie Mack
		New York (N)	1 win	John McGraw
1914	4 games	Boston (N)	4 wins	George Stallings
		Philadelphia (A)	0 wins	Connie Mack
1915	5 games	Boston (A)	4 wins	Bill Carrigan
		Philadelphia (N)	1 win	Pat Moran
1916	5 games	Boston (A)	4 wins	Bill Carrigan
		Brooklyn (N)	1 win	Wilbert Robinson
1917	6 games	Chicago (A)	4 wins	Pants Rowland
		New York (N)	2 wins	John McGraw
1918	6 games	Boston (A)	4 wins	Ed Barrow
		Chicago (N)	2 wins	Fred Mitchell
1919	8 games	Cincinnati (N)	5 wins	Pat Moran
		Chicago (A)	3 wins	Kid Gleason
1920	7 games	Cleveland (A)	5 wins	Tris Speaker
		Brooklyn (N)	2 wins	Wilbert Robinson
1921	8 games	New York (N)	5 wins	John McGraw
		New York (A)	3 wins	Miller Huggins
1922	5 games 1 tie	New York (N)	4 wins	John McGraw
		New York (A)	0 wins	Miller Huggins
1923	6 games	New York (A)	4 wins	Miller Huggins
		New York (N)	2 wins	John McGraw
1924	7 games	Washington (A)	4 wins	Bucky Harris
		New York (N)	3 wins	John McGraw
1925	7 games	Pittsburgh (N)	4 wins	Bill McKechnie
		Washington (A)	3 wins	Bucky Harris
1926	7 games	St. Louis (N)	4 wins	Rogers Hornsby
		New York (A)	3 wins	Miller Huggins
1927	4 games	New York (A)	4 wins	Miller Huggins
		Pittsburgh (N)	0 wins	Donie Bush
1928	4 games	New York (A)	4 wins	Miller Huggins
		St. Louis (N)	0 wins	Bill McKechnie
1929	5 games	Philadelphia (A)	4 wins	Connie Mack
		Chicago (N)	1 win	Joe McCarthy
1930	6 games	Philadelphia (A)	4 wins	Connie Mack
		St. Louis (N)	2 wins	Gabby Street
1931	7 games	St. Louis (N)	4 wins	Gabby Street
		Philadelphia (A)	3 wins	Connie Mack
1932	4 games	New York (A)	4 wins	Joe McCarthy
		Chicago (N)	0 wins	Charlie Grimm
1933	5 games	New York (N)	4 wins	Bill Terry
		Washington (A)	1 win	Joe Cronin
1934	7 games	St. Louis (N)	4 wins	Frankie Frisch
		Detroit (A)	3 wins	Mickey Cochrane
1935	6 games	Detroit (A)	4 wins	Mickey Cochrane
		Chicago (N)	2 wins	Charlie Grimm
1936	6 games	New York (A)	4 wins	Joe McCarthy
		New York (N)	2 wins	Bill Terry
1937	5 games	New York (A)	4 wins	Joe McCarthy
		New York (N)	1 win	Bill Terry
1938	4 games	New York (A)	4 wins	Joe McCarthy
		Chicago (N)	0 wins	Gabby Hartnett
1939	4 games	New York (A)	4 wins	Joe McCarthy
		Cincinnati (N)	0 wins	Bill McKechnie
1940	7 games	Cincinnati (N)	4 wins	Bill McKechnie
		Detroit (A)	3 wins	Del Baker
1941	5 games	New York (A)	4 wins	Joe McCarthy
		Brooklyn (N)	1 win	Leo Durocher
1942	5 games	St. Louis (N)	4 wins	Billy Southworth
		New York (A)	1 win	Joe McCarthy
1943	5 games	New York (A)	4 wins	Joe McCarthy
		St. Louis (N)	1 win	Billy Southworth
1944	6 games	St. Louis (N)	4 wins	Billy Southworth
		St. Louis (A)	2 wins	Luke Sewell
1945	7 games	Detroit (A)	4 wins	Steve O'Neill
		Chicago (N)	3 wins	Charlie Grimm
1946	7 games	St. Louis (N) defeated Brooklyn in playoffs (2 wins to none)	4 wins	Eddie Dyer
		Boston (A)	3 wins	Joe Cronin
1947	7 games	New York (A)	4 wins	Bucky Harris
		Brooklyn (N)	3 wins	Burt Shotten
1948	6 games	Cleveland (A) defeated Boston in one game playoff	4 wins	Lou Boudreau
		Boston (N)	2 wins	Billy Southworth
1949	5 games	New York (A)	4 wins	Casey Stengel
		Brooklyn (N)	1 win	Burt Shotten
1950	4 games	New York (A)	4 wins	Casey Stengel
		Philadelphia (N)	0 wins	Eddie Sawyer
1951	6 games	New York (A)	4 wins	Casey Stengel
		New York (N) defeated Brooklyn in playoffs (2 wins to one)	2 wins	Leo Durocher
1952	7 games	New York (A)	4 wins	Casey Stengel
		Brooklyn (N)	3 wins	Chuck Dressen
1953	6 games	New York (A)	4 wins	Casey Stengel
		Brooklyn (N)	2 wins	Chuck Dressen
1954	4 games	New York (N)	4 wins	Leo Durocher
		Cleveland (A)	0 wins	Al Lopez
1955	7 games	Brooklyn (N)	4 wins	Walter Alston
		New York (A)	3 wins	Casey Stengel
1956	7 games	New York (A)	4 wins	Casey Stengel
		Brooklyn (N)	3 wins	Walter Alston
1957	7 games	Milwaukee (N)	4 wins	Fred Haney
		New York (A)	3 wins	Casey Stengel
1958	7 games	New York (A)	4 wins	Casey Stengel
		Milwaukee (N)	3 wins	Fred Haney
1959	6 games	Los Angeles (N) defeated Milwaukee in playoffs (2 wins to none)	4 wins	Walter Alston
		Chicago (A)	2 wins	Al Lopez
1960	7 games	Pittsburgh (N)	4 wins	Danny Murtaugh
		New York (A)	3 wins	Casey Stengel
1961	5 games	New York (A)	4 wins	Ralph Houk
		Cincinnati (N)	1 win	Fred Hutchinson
1962	7 games	New York (A)	4 wins	Ralph Houk
		San Francisco (N) defeated Los Angeles in playoffs (2 wins to one)	3 wins	Al Dark
1963	4 games	Los Angeles (N)	4 wins	Walter Alston
		New York (A)	0 wins	Ralph Houk
1964	7 games	St. Louis (N)	4 wins	Johnny Keane
		New York (A)	3 wins	Yogi Berra
1965	7 games	Los Angeles (N)	4 wins	Walter Alston
		Minnesota (A)	3 wins	Sam Mele
1966	4 games	Baltimore (A)	4 wins	Hank Bauer
		Los Angeles (N)	0 wins	Walter Alston
1967	7 games	St. Louis (N)	4 wins	Red Schoendienst
		Boston (A)	3 wins	Dick Williams
1968	7 games	Detroit (A)	4 wins	Mayo Smith
		St. Louis (N)	3 wins	Red Schoendienst
1969	5 games	New York (N) Won championship series over Atlanta (3 games to none)	4 wins	Gil Hodges
		Baltimore (A) Won championship series over Minnesota (3 games to none)	1 win	Earl Weaver
1970	5 games	Baltimore (A) Won championship series over Minnesota (3 games to none)	4 wins	Earl Weaver
		Cincinnati (N) Won championship series over Pittsburgh (3 games to none)	1 win	Sparky Anderson
1971	7 games	Pittsburgh (N) Won championship series over San Francisco (3 games to one)	4 wins	Danny Murtaugh
		Baltimore (A) Won championship series over Oakland (3 games to none)	3 wins	Earl Weaver
1972	7 games	Oakland (A) Won championship series over Detroit (3 games to two)	4 wins	Dick Williams
		Cincinnati (N) Won championship series over Pittsburgh (3 games to two)	3 wins	Sparky Anderson
1973	7 games	Oakland (A) Won championship series over Baltimore (3 games to two)	4 wins	Dick Williams
		New York (N) Won championship series over Cincinnati (3 games to two)	3 wins	Yogi Berra
1974	5 games	Oakland (A) Won championship series over Baltimore (3 games to one)	4 wins	Al Dark
		Los Angeles (N) Won championship series over Pittsburgh (3 games to one)	1 win	Walter Alston
1975	7 games	Cincinnati (N) Won championship series over Pittsburgh (3 games to none)	4 wins	Sparky Anderson
		Boston (A) Won championship series over Oakland (3 games to none)	3 wins	Darrell Johnson
1976	4 games	Cincinnati (N) Won championship series over Philadelphia (3 games to none)	4 wins	Sparky Anderson
		New York (A) Won championship series over Kansas City (3 games to two)	0 wins	Billy Martin
1977	6 games	New York (A) Won championship series over Kansas City (3 games to two)	4 wins	Billy Martin
		Los Angeles (N) Won championship series over Philadelphia (3 games to one)	2 wins	Tommy Lasorda
1978	6 games	New York (A) Won championship series over Kansas City (3 games to one)	4 wins	Bob Lemon
		Los Angeles (N) Won championship series over Philadelphia (3 games to none)	2 wins	Tommy Lasorda
1979	7 games	Pittsburgh (N) Won championship series over Cincinnati (3 games to none)	4 wins	Chuck Tanner
		Baltimore (A) Won championship series over California (3 games to one)	3 wins	Earl Weaver
1980	6 games	Philadelphia (N) Won championship series over Houston (3 games to two)	4 wins	Dallas Green
		Kansas City (A) Won championship series over New York (3 games to none)	2 wins	Jim Frey

YEARLY RESULTS

Managers

1981 6 games
Los Angeles (N)   4 wins   Tommy Lasorda
Won championship series over Montreal
(3 games to two)
New York (A)   2 wins   Bob Lemon
Won championship series over Oakland
(3 games to none)

1982 7 games
St. Louis (N)   4 wins   Whitey Herzog
Won championship series over Atlanta
(3 games to none)
Milwaukee (A)   3 wins   Harvey Kuenn
Won championship series over California
(3 games to two)

1983 5 games
Baltimore (A)   4 wins   Joe Altobelli
Won championship series over Chicago
(3 games to one)
Philadelphia (N)   1 win   Paul Owens
Won championship series over Los Angeles
(3 games to one)

1984 5 games
Detroit (A)   4 wins   Sparky Anderson
Won championship series over Kansas City
(3 games to none)
San Diego (N)   1 win   Dick Williams
Won championship series over Chicago
(3 games to two)

1985 7 games
Kansas City (A)   4 wins   Dick Howser
Won championship series over Toronto
(4 games to three)
St. Louis (N)   3 wins   Whitey Herzog
Won championship series over Los Angeles
(4 games to two)

1903
Phillippe: Five Times Over

All it took was a handshake, and the first World Series was on. The twenty-eight-year-old National League and the three-year-old American League reached a peace settlement in the winter after two years of player raids and open hostility, but no provision had been made for any postseason championship series. By August, the Pittsburgh Pirates and the Boston Pilgrims were comfortably out in front of the National and American Leagues, and Pirate owner Barney Dreyfuss issued a challenge to the Pilgrims to a postseason confrontation. Pilgrim owner Henry Killilea picked up the gauntlet, and a best-of-nine series was set up for October. Although there had been a variety of postseason playoffs in the nineteenth century, this first meeting of National and American League champs was recognized as the first modern World Series.

Both clubs had famous player-managers: Fred Clarke of the Pirates and Jimmy Collins of the Pilgrims. Later known as the Red Sox, the Pilgrims had a strong offense and an excellent pitching staff, led by thirty-six-year-old Cy Young, a 28-game winner. The Pirates had just won their third straight pennant with a solid all-around team, but injuries weakened the club for its postseason engagement. Premier shortstop Honus Wagner was limping on a painfully injured right leg. Top utilityman Otto Krueger was out of action after a late-season beaning. The fine pitching trio of Sam Leever, Deacon Phillippe and Ed Doheny was thinned out, as Doheny had been hospitalized with a mental disorder and Leever was sporting a bad shoulder picked up in a trapshooting contest.

So when the Series opened on October 1 in Boston, Phillippe was the automatic choice to start for Pittsburgh against Cy Young. The Pirates jumped all over Young in the top of the first and tallied four times, and Phillippe, who won 24 games during the regular season, went all the way to pick up a 7–3 victory. A highlight of this first Series game ever was a home run, a shot by Pittsburgh outfielder Jimmy Sebring. The clubs met again the next day, with Boston's Bill Dinneen facing the sore-shouldered Leever. The Pilgrims touched up Leever for two quick runs in the bottom of the first, while Dinneen spun a neat three-hitter for a 3–0 Boston win. Pirate manager Clarke called on Phillippe to take the mound again for game three after only one day of rest, and the hurler responded with a complete game 4–2 victory, a contest spiced by seven ground-rule doubles into the overflow crowd lining the outfield.

Sunday was a day of travel to Pittsburgh, and Monday was a day of rain, so Clarke felt confident in sending Phillippe back out to the mound on two days' rest. The Deacon again went all the way and survived a three-run Boston rally in the ninth inning to take a 5–4 victory. The Pirates seemed firmly in control of the Series, but had run fatally low of pitching. Boston started Young in the fifth game, while Pittsburgh countered with Brickyard Kennedy, a thirty-five-year-old righty at the tag end of a fine career. Kennedy shut the Pilgrims out for five innings, but two errors by the limping Wagner triggered a six-run Boston outburst in the sixth inning that led to an 11–2 victory. Boston came out on top of a 6–3 score in game six, with Dinneen besting Leever. A postponement for cold weather on Friday gave Phillippe three days of rest before trying for his fourth win of the Series, but although he again went the distance, he came out a loser by a 7–3 count to Young.

The teams traveled back to Boston on Sunday, with the Pilgrims now one win away from the championship. Rain canceled the game on Monday, and a tired Phillippe took the mound for the Pirates on Tuesday. He went the distance for the fifth time in the Series and allowed only three runs, but Dinneen spun a shutout for the Pilgrims to win his third game and give Boston the honor of capturing the first modern World Series.

Game 1 October 1 at Boston

Pit.	4 0 1	1 0 0	1 0 0
Bos.	0 0 0	0 0 0	2 0 1

Pittsburgh	Pos	AB	R	H	RBI	PO	A	E
Beaumont	cf	5	1	0	0	3	0	0
Clarke	lf	5	0	2	0	4	0	0
Leach	3b	5	1	4	1	0	1	1
Wagner	ss	3	1	1	1	1	2	1
Bransfield	1b	5	2	1	0	7	0	0
Ritchey	2b	4	1	0	0	1	2	0
Sebring	rf	5	1	3	4	1	0	0
Phelps	c	4	0	1	0	10	0	0
Phillippe	p	4	0	0	0	0	2	0
Totals		40	7	12	6	27	7	2

Pitching	IP	H	R	ER	BB	SO
Pittsburgh						
Phillippe (W)	9	6	3	2	0	10
Boston						
Young (L)	9	12	7	3	3	5

Boston	Pos	AB	R	H	RBI	PO	A	E
Dougherty	lf	4	0	0	0	0	1	0
Collins	3b	4	0	0	0	2	3	0
C. Stahl	cf	4	0	1	0	2	0	0
Freeman	rf	4	2	2	0	3	0	0
Parent	ss	4	1	2	1	4	4	0
La chance	1b	4	0	0	2	8	0	0
Ferris	2b	3	0	1	0	2	4	2
Criger	c	3	0	0	0	6	1	2
a O'Brien		1	0	0	0	0	0	0
Young	p	3	0	0	0	0	1	0
b Farrell		1	0	0	0	0	0	0
Totals		35	3	6	3	27	14	4

a Struck out for Criger in 9th.
b Grounded out for Young in 9th.

Triples—Bransfield, Freeman, Leach 2, Parent. Home Run—Sebring. Stolen Bases—Bransfield, Ritchey, Wagner. Hit by Pitcher—Ferris (by Phillippe). Passed Ball—Criger. Left on Bases—Pittsburgh 9, Boston 6, Umpires—O'Day (N), Connolly (A). Attendance—16,242. Time of Game—1:55.

1st Inning
Pittsburgh
1 Beaumont flied to center.
2 Clarke fouled to Criger.
  Leach tripled into the right field crowd, allowed third by the umpire.
  Wagner singled to left, scoring Leach. Wagner stole second.
  Bransfield safe on Ferris' fumble, Wagner going to third.
  Bransfield stole second and on a delayed double steal Criger threw the ball away allowing Wagner to score and Bransfield to go to third.
  Ritchey walked.
  Ritchey stole second as Criger threw to third to try to get Bransfield.
  Sebring singled to left, scoring Bransfield and Ritchey.
  Phelps struck out but was safe at first on Criger's error, Sebring going to third.
3 Phillippe struck out.
Boston
1 Dougherty struck out.
2 Collins struck out.
  Stahl blooped a Texas League single to short left.
3 Freeman flied to right.

2nd Inning
Pittsburgh
1 Beaumont struck out.
  Clarke singled to left but out trying
2 to stretch it into a double, Dougherty to Ferris.
3 Leach flied to right.
Boston
1 Parent struck out.
2 La Chance struck out.
3 Ferris struck out.

3rd Inning
Pittsburgh
1 Wagner popped to third.
  Bransfield tripled on a low line drive past Freeman.
2 Ritchey struck out.
  Sebring singled to right, scoring Bransfield.
3 Phelps grounded back to the mound.
Boston
1 Criger grounded to third.
2 Young grounded to second.
3 Dougherty flied to center.

4th Inning
Pittsburgh
1 Phillippe popped to short.
  Beaumont safe at first when Ferris fumbled his grounder.
  Clarke singled to left, Beaumont going to second.
  Leach singled to center, Beaumont scoring as Clarke stopped at second.
2 Wagner popped to short.
3 Bransfield forced Leach at second, Ferris making a great stop to Parent.
Boston
1 Collins flied to left.
2 Stahl flied to center.
  Freeman beat out a hit to first.
  Parent got safely to second and Freeman to third on Leach's low throw to first.
3 La Chance bounced back to the mound.

5th Inning
Pittsburgh
1 Ritchey grounded to third, La Chance making a great scoop of a low throw.
2 Sebring grounded to third.
  Phelps singled to right.
3 Phillippe popped to second.
Boston
1 Ferris again struck out.
2 Criger grounded to short.
3 Young flied to left.

6th Inning
Pittsburgh
1 Beaumont fouled to Collins.
2 Clarke struck out.
  Leach beat out a bouncer to third. Wagner walked.
3 Bransfield forced Wagner at second, Ferris to Parent.
Boston
1 Dougherty popped to Ritchey, making a good catch near the foul line.
2 Collins grounded to second.
3 Stahl called out on strikes

7th Inning
Pittsburgh
1 Ritchey grounded to short.
  Sebring blasted a home run into center.
2 Phelps flied to right.
3 Phillippe grounded to short.
Boston
  Freeman tripled to right.
  Parent tripled to left, scoring Freeman.
1 La Chance flied to deep left, Parent scoring after the pitch.
  Ferris hit by a pitch.
2 Criger struck out.
3 Young struck out.

8th Inning
Pittsburgh
1 Beaumont grounded to short.
2 Clarke flied to right.
  Leach tripled to right, his second of the game.
  Wagner walked.
3 Leach out on a double steal, Criger to Ferris to Parent to Criger.
Boston
1 Dougherty popped to short.
2 Collins grounded to short.
3 Stahl flied to center.

9th Inning
Pittsburgh
1 Bransfield flied to center.
2 Ritchey grounded to third.
3 Sebring grounded to second.
Boston
  Freeman safe on Wagner's error.
  Parent singled to left, Freeman going to third.
1 LaChance flied to deep left, Freeman scoring after the catch.
  Ferris beat out a hopper to third, Parent going to second.
2 O'Brien, batting for Criger, struck out.
3 Farrell, batting for Young, grounded back to the mound.

Game 2 October 2 at Boston

Pittsburgh	Pos	AB	R	H	RBI	PO	A	E
Beaumont	cf	3	0	0	0	3	0	0
Clarke	lf	3	0	1	0	3	0	0
Leach	3b	3	0	0	0	0	2	0
Wagner	ss	3	0	0	0	3	6	0
Bransfield	1b	3	0	0	0	9	1	0
Ritchey	2b	3	0	1	0	3	3	0
Sebring	rf	3	0	1	0	1	0	0
Smith	c	3	0	0	0	2	1	1
Leever	p	0	0	0	0	0	0	0
Veil	p	2	0	0	0	0	0	1
a Phelps		1	0	0	0	0	0	0
Totals		27	0	3	0	24	13	2

a Struck out for Veil in 9th.

Pit.	0 0 0	0 0 0	0 0 0					
Bos.	2 0 0	0 0 1	0 0 x					

Boston	Pos	AB	R	H	RBI	PO	A	E
Dougherty	lf	4	2	3	2	0	1	0
Collins	3b	4	0	1	0	1	1	0
C. Stahl	cf	4	1	1	0	1	0	0
Freeman	rf	4	0	2	1	0	0	0
Parent	ss	3	0	1	0	2	3	0
La Chance	1b	2	0	0	0	8	1	0
Ferris	2b	2	0	0	0	4	0	0
Criger	c	3	0	0	0	11	0	0
Dinneen	p	2	0	1	0	0	3	0
Totals		30	3	9	3	27	9	0

Pitching	IP	H	R	ER	BB	SO
Pittsburgh						
Leever (L)	1	3	2	2	1	0
Veil	7	6	1	1	5	1
Boston						
Dinneen (W)	9	3	0	0	2	11

Double—C. Stahl. Home Runs—Dougherty 2. Stolen Bases—Collins 2. Sacrifice Hits—Dinneen, LaChance. Double Plays—Ferris (unassisted), Ritchey to Wagner to Bransfield, Wagner to Ritchey to Bransfield. Hit by Pitcher—Dougherty (by Veil). Left on Bases—Pittsburgh 2, Boston 11. Umpires—O'Day, Connolly. Attendance—9,415. Time of Game—1:47.

1st Inning
Pittsburgh
1 Beaumont called out on strikes.
Clarke walked.
2 Clarke picked off, Dinneen to La Chance.
3 Leach struck out.
Boston
Dougherty got an inside-the-park home run to deep right-center.
1 Collins flied to left.
Stahl doubled to center.
Freeman singled to center, scoring Stahl.
2 Parent flied to left.
La Chance walked.
3 Ferris forced La Chance at second, Wagner to Ritchey.

2nd Inning
Pittsburgh
1 Wagner popped to second.
2 Bransfield grounded to short.
3 Ritchey called out on strikes.
Boston
For Pittsburgh—Vail came in to pitch.
1 Criger grounded to third.
Dinneen walked.
Dougherty was hit by a pitch.
2 Collins flied to center.
3 Stahl popped to short.

3rd Inning
Pittsburgh
1 Sebring struck out.
2 Smith fouled to Collins.
3 Veil struck out.
Boston
1 Freeman flied to center.
Parent singled to center.
2 La Chance flied to center.
3 Ferris forced Parent at second, Wagner to Ritchey.

4th Inning
Pittsburgh
Beaumont walked.
Clarke singled to center, Beaumont going to second. The first Pittsburgh hit of the game.
1 Leach grounded back to Dinneen, moving up both runners.
2,3 Wagner lined into a double play, Ferris unassisted.
Boston
1 Criger grounded to short.
Dinneen again walked.
2 Dougherty forced Dinneen at second, Bransfield to Wagner.
Collins singled by first into right, Dougherty going to third.
Collins stole second.
3 Stahl grounded to short.

5th Inning
Pittsburgh
1 Bransfield called out on strikes.
2 Ritchey also called out on strikes.
Sebring singled to left.
3 Smith popped to short.
Boston
Freeman singled to left.
Parent walked.
LaChance safe when Veil fumbled his sacrifice bunt, loading the bases.
1 Ferris forced Freeman at the plate, Leach to Smith
2,3 Criger hit into a double play, Ritchey to Wagner to Bransfield.

6th Inning
Pittsburgh
1 Veil struck out.
2 Beaumont grounded to short, Parent making a nice play.
3 Clarke struck out.
Boston
1 Dinneen grounded to first.
Dougherty got his second homer of the game, a blast over the left field fence.
Collins walked.
Collins stole second and continued to third on Smith's poor throw.
2 Stahl struck out.
3 Freeman fouled to Bransfield.

7th Inning
Pittsburgh
1 Leach flied to center.
2 Wagner popped to first.
3 Bransfield grounded to third.
Boston
1 Parent flied to left.
2 La Chance grounded to second.
3 Ferris flied to right.

8th Inning
Pittsburgh
Ritchey singled to left, but out trying
1 for second, Dougherty to Ferris, a real great play.
2 Sebring struck out.
3 Smith bounced back to the mound.
Boston
Criger walked.
1 Dinneen sacrificed Criger to second, Smith to Bransfield.
Dougherty beat out a hit to third, his third of the game, Criger holding at second.
2,3 Collins hit into a double play, Wagner to Ritchey to Bransfield.

9th Inning
Pittsburgh
1 Phelps, pinch-hitting for Veil, struck out.
2 Beaumont popped to short.
3 Clarke grounded to short.

Game 3 October 3 at Boston

Pittsburgh	Pos	AB	R	H	RBI	PO	A	E
Beaumont	cf	4	1	0	0	1	0	0
Clarke	lf	4	0	1	0	0	0	0
Leach	3b	4	1	1	1	0	1	0
Wagner	ss	3	1	1	0	0	7	0
Bransfield	1b	3	0	0	0	15	0	4
Ritchey	2b	4	1	1	2	2	2	0
Sebring	rf	3	1	0	0	4	0	0
Phelps	c	4	0	2	1	5	1	0
Phillippe	p	4	0	0	0	0	4	0
Totals		33	4	7	3	27	15	1

Pit.	0 1 2	0 0 0	0 1 0					
Bos.	0 0 0	1 0 0	0 1 0					

Boston	Pos	AB	R	H	RBI	PO	A	E
Dougherty	lf	4	0	0	0	1	1	0
Collins	3b	4	2	2	0	3	6	0
C. Stahl	cf	3	0	1	1	2	0	0
Freeman	rf	3	0	0	0	1	0	0
Parent	ss	4	0	0	1	0	6	1
La Chance	1b	3	0	1	0	14	0	0
Ferris	2b	4	0	0	0	2	3	0
Criger	c	3	0	0	0	4	1	0
Hughes	p	0	0	0	0	0	0	0
Young	p	3	0	0	0	0	2	1
Totals		31	2	4	2	27	19	2

Pitching	IP	H	R	ER	BB	SO
Pittsburgh						
Phillippe (W)	9	4	2	2	3	6
Boston						
Hughes (L)	*2	4	3	2	2	0
Young	7	3	1	1	0	2

*Pitched to three batters in 3rd.

Doubles—Clarke, Collins, LaChance, Phelps 2, Ritchey, Wagner. Sacrifice Hit—Bransfield. Double Play—Dougherty to Collins. Passed Ball—Criger. Hit by Pitcher—Wagner (by Young). Left on Bases—Pittsburgh 6; Boston 5. Umpires—O'Day, Connolly. Attendance—18,801. Time of Game—1:50.

1st Inning
Pittsburgh
1 Beaumont grounded to third.
2 Clarke grounded to third.
3 Leach grounded to short.
Boston
1 Dougherty grounded to short.
2 Collins grounded to second.
3 Stahl flied to deep right.

2nd Inning
Pittsburgh
1 Wagner grounded to second.
2 Bransfield grounded to third.
Ritchey doubled into the center field crowd.
Sebring walked.
Phelps also doubled into the center field crowd, scoring Ritchey with Sebring going to third.
3 Phillippe grounded to short.
Boston
1 Freeman grounded to short.
2 Parent grounded to short.
La Chance doubled to right-center.
3 Ferris grounded to third, Leach making a nice stop.

3rd Inning
Pittsburgh
Beaumont walked.
Clarke doubled into the left field crowd, Beaumont going to third.
Leach singled to left, scoring Beaumont as Clarke stopped at third.
For Boston—Young relieved Hughes.
Wagner was hit by a pitch, loading the bases.
1 Bransfield fouled to La Chance.
2 Ritchey forced Clarke at the plate, Collins to Criger.
Sebring safe on a fumble by Parent, Leach scoring but Wagner was out also
3 trying to score, Parent to Collins to Criger.
Boston
1 Criger flied to right.
2 Young struck out.
3 Dougherty struck out.

4th Inning
Pittsburgh
Phelps doubled again, this time into the center field crowd.
1 Phillippe grounded to Young who threw to Collins getting Phelps at third.
2 Beaumont flied to center.
3 Clarke forced Phillippe at second, Parent to Ferris.
Boston
Collins singled to center
Stahl walked.
1 Freeman bounced back to the mound, advancing both runners.
2 Parent flied to right, Collins scoring after the catch.
La Chance walked.
La Chance safe on a pick-off play when Bransfield muffed Phelps' throw.
3 Ferris struck out.

5th Inning
Pittsburgh
1 Leach popped to second.
2 Wagner lined to third.
3 Bransfield grounded to short.
Boston
1 Criger bounced back to the mound.
2 Young struck out.
3 Dougherty grounded to first, Bransfield making a great stop behind first.

6th Inning
Pittsburgh
1 Ritchey struck out.
2 Sebring struck out.
3 Phelps flied to center.
Boston
1 Collins grounded back to the mound.
2 Stahl grounded to second.
Freeman walked.
3 Parent grounded back to the mound.

7th Inning
Pittsburgh
1 Phillippe grounded to third.
2 Beaumont grounded to second.
3 Clarke grounded to short.
Boston
1 La Chance grounded to short.
2 Ferris flied to center.
3 Criger flied to right.

8th Inning
Pittsburgh
1 Leach flied to right.
Wagner doubled to right.
Bransfield safe on Young's fumble, Wagner going to third.
Ritchey singled to third, scoring Wagner and Bransfield going to second.
2,3 Sebring flied to Dougherty who threw to Collins getting Bransfield.
Boston
1 Young grounded to short.
2 Dougherty struck out.
Collins doubled to right.
Stahl singled to left, scoring Collins.
3 Freeman forced Stahl at second, Wagner to Ritchey.

9th Inning
Pittsburgh
1 Phelps grounded back to the mound.
2 Phillippe rolled out, Criger to La Chance.
3 Beaumont grounded to second.
Boston
1 Parent popped to Ritchey.
2 La Chance grounded to short.
3 Ferris struck out, and thrown out Phelps to Bransfield.

Game 4 October 6 at Pittsburgh

Bos. 000 010 003
Pit. 100 010 30x

Boston	Pos	AB	R	H	RBI	PO	A	E
Dougherty	lf	4	0	0	0	3	0	1
Collins	3b	4	1	1	0	1	0	0
C. Stahl	cf	4	1	2	0	3	1	0
Freeman	rf	4	0	1	1	0	0	0
Parent	ss	4	1	1	1	1	3	0
La Chance	1b	4	1	2	0	5	0	0
Ferris	2b	4	0	1	0	3	1	0
Criger	c	3	0	1	1	8	1	0
a Farrell		1	0	0	1	0	0	0
Dinneen	p	3	0	0	0	0	1	0
b O'Brien		1	0	0	0	0	0	0
Totals		36	4	9	4	24	7	1

Pitching	IP	H	R	ER	BB	SO
Boston						
Dinneen (L)	8	12	5	5	1	7
Pittsburgh						
Phillippe (W)	9	9	4	4	0	2

Pittsburgh	Pos	AB	R	H	RBI	PO	A	E
Beaumont	cf	4	2	3	0	3	0	0
Clarke	lf	4	1	1	0	1	0	0
Leach	3b	4	1	2	3	2	5	0
Wagner	ss	4	0	3	1	1	1	0
Bransfield	1b	4	0	1	1	9	1	1
Ritchey	2b	3	0	0	0	5	5	0
Sebring	rf	4	0	1	0	1	0	0
Phelps	c	4	0	1	0	4	1	0
Phillippe	p	3	1	0	0	1	0	0
Totals		34	5	12	5	27	13	1

a Flied out for Criger in 9th.
b Flied out for Dinneen in 9th.

Triples—Beaumont, Leach. Stolen Base—Wagner. Double Plays—Ritchey to Bransfield, Criger to Parent. Left on Bases—Boston 5, Pittsburgh 6. Umpires—O'Day, Connolly. Attendance—7,600. Time of Game—1:30.

1st Inning
Boston
1 Dougherty grounded to second.
2 Collins popped to Ritchey, making a nice catch back of second.
3 Stahl popped to third.
Pittsburgh
Beaumont singled to center.
1 Clarke forced Beaumont at second, Parent to Ferris.
2 Leach flied to center.
Wagner singled to left-center, Clarke going to second.
Bransfield singled to center, scoring
3 Clarke but Wagner out trying for third, Stahl to Collins.

2nd Inning
Boston
1 Freeman fouled to Phelps.
Parent singled to left.
2 La Chance forced Parent at second, Ritchey to Wagner.
3 Ferris grounded out, Bransfield to Phillippe.
Pittsburgh
1 Ritchey flied to center.
2 Sebring struck out.
Phelps beat out a bunt to third.
3 Phillippe flied to left.

3rd Inning
Boston
1 Criger fouled to Sebring.
2 Dinneen grounded to second.
3 Dougherty struck out.
Pittsburgh
1 Beaumont grounded to first.
Clarke singled to center.
2 Leach popped to second.
Wagner singled to right-center, Clarke stopping at second.
Wagner stole second.
3 Bransfield struck out.

4th Inning
Boston
1 Collins flied to Beaumont, making a great running catch.
2 Stahl grounded to second.
3 Freeman flied to deep center.
Pittsburgh
1 Ritchey flied to center.
2 Sebring grounded to short.
3 Phelps struck out.

5th Inning
Boston
1 Parent grounded to third.
La Chance singled to left.
2 Ferris grounded to third, La Chance going to second.
Criger singled to right, scoring La Chance with Criger going to second on the throw.
3 Dinneen grounded to Leach, who tagged Criger coming in to third.
Pittsburgh
1 Phillippe struck out.
Beaumont tripled over Stahl's head.
2 Clarke fouled to Criger.
Leach singled beyond first, scoring Beaumont.
3 Wagner struck out.

6th Inning
Boston
1 Dougherty fouled to Phelps, making a good one handed catch.
2 Collins flied to center.
Stahl singled to center.
3 Freeman rolled back to the mound.
Pittsburgh
1 Bransfield struck out.
Ritchey walked.
2 Sebring flied to left.
3 Phelps out on a bunt, Ferris to La Chance.

7th Inning
Boston
Parent safe when Bransfield dropped Leach's throw. (Leach gets an assist).
1,2 La Chance lined into a double play, Ritchey to Bransfield.
3 Ferris grounded to third.
Pittsburgh
Phillippe singled to left and went to second on Dougherty's fumble. Beaumont beat out a bunt to third, Phillippe going to third. Beaumont took second on the throw home to keep Phillippe on third.
1 Clarke flied to short left.
Leach tripled to deep right, scoring Phillippe and Beaumont.
Wagner singled to center, scoring Leach.
2,3 Bransfield struck out for the third time and Wagner was doubled trying to steal, Criger to Parent.

8th Inning
Boston
1 Criger struck out.
2 Dinneen popped to second.
3 Dougherty grounded to third.
Pittsburgh
1 Ritchey grounded back to the pitcher.
2 Sebring popped to second.
3 Phelps grounded to short.

9th Inning
Boston
Collins singled to center.
Stahl singled to left, Collins going to third.
Freeman singled to right, scoring Collins as Stahl raced to third.
1 Parent forced Freeman at second, Wagner to Ritchey as Stahl scored.
La Chance singled moving Parent to second.
Ferris singled to right, loading the bases.
2 Farrell, pinch-hitting for Criger, flied to left, Parent scoring after the catch.
3 O'Brien, batting for Dinneen, popped to second.

Game 5 October 7 at Pittsburgh

Bos. 000 006 410
Pit. 000 000 020

Boston	Pos	AB	R	H	RBI	PO	A	E
Dougherty	lf	6	0	3	3	3	0	0
Collins	3b	6	0	2	0	0	3	0
C. Stahl	cf	5	2	1	0	2	0	0
Freeman	rf	4	2	2	1	2	0	0
Parent	ss	5	1	2	0	1	3	1
La Chance	1b	4	2	1	1	13	0	1
Ferris	2b	5	2	1	2	1	4	0
Criger	c	3	1	0	0	5	0	0
Young	p	5	1	2	3	0	3	0
Totals		43	11	14	10	27	13	2

Pitching	IP	H	R	ER	BB	SO
Boston						
Young (W)	9	6	2	0	0	4
Pittsburgh						
Kennedy (L)	7	11	10	4	3	3
Thompson	2	3	1	1	0	1

Pittsburgh	Pos	AB	R	H	RBI	PO	A	E
Beaumont	cf	4	1	1	0	0	0	0
Clarke	lf	4	1	0	0	3	0	1
Leach	3b	4	0	2	2	2	0	1
Wagner	ss	4	0	0	0	1	3	2
Bransfield	1b	4	0	0	0	9	1	0
Ritchey	2b	4	0	1	0	1	4	0
Sebring	rf	4	0	0	0	2	0	0
Phelps	c	3	0	0	0	9	0	0
Kennedy	p	2	0	1	0	0	1	0
Thompson		1	0	0	0	0	1	0
Totals		34	2	6	2	27	10	4

Double—Kennedy. Triples—Collins, Dougherty 2, Leach, C. Stahl, Young. Stolen Bases—Collins, C. Stahl. Sacrifice Hits—Criger, Phelps. Left on Bases—Boston 9, Pittsburgh 6. Umpires—Connolly, O'Day. Attendance—12,322. Time of Game—2:00.

1st Inning
Boston
1 Dougherty popped to Phelps.
Collins tripled to right.
2 Stahl grounded to Wagner who threw Collins out at the plate.
Stahl stole second.
Freeman walked.
Parent beat out a bouncer to third, loading the bases.
3 La Chance popped to third.
Pittsburgh
1 Beaumont flied to left.
2 Clarke grounded to third, La Chance making a good catch on Collins' bad throw.
Leach singled to center.
3 Wagner grounded to second.

2nd Inning
Boston
1 Ferris struck out.
2 Criger grounded to first.
3 Young flied to deep right.
Pittsburgh
1 Bransfield flied to La Chance.
Ritchey beat out a hit to third.
2 Sebring bounced back to the mound, Ritchey going to second.
3 Phelps grounded to second.

3rd Inning
Boston
1 Dougherty grounded back to the mound.
Collins singled to center.
2 Stahl popped to Phelps.
Collins stole second.
3 Freeman struck out.
Pittsburgh
Kennedy doubled over Stahl's head.
1 Beaumont fouled to Criger.
2 Clarke grounded to second, Kennedy holding second.
3 Leach flied to left.

4th Inning
Boston
1 Parent flied to left.
2 La Chance also flied to left.
3 Ferris fouled to Phelps.
Pittsburgh
1 Wagner struck out.
2 Bransfield flied to center.
3 Ritchey grounded to third.

5th Inning
Boston
1 Criger struck out.
Young safely to second as Leach threw high over first.
2 Dougherty grounded to second, Young going to third.
3 Collins flied to left.
Pittsburgh
Sebring safely to second when La Chance lost Parent's throw.
1 Phelps sacrificed Sebring to third, Young to La Chance.
2 Kennedy out on a liner off Young's fingers to Parent who threw to first.
3 Beaumont grounded to third.

6th Inning
Boston
Stahl safe when Clarke dropped his fly fearing a collision with Wagner. Freeman singled to left, Stahl going to second. Parent safe on a bunt when Wagner dropped Leach's throw to third, loading the bases. La Chance walked, forcing Stahl home. Ferris grounded to Wagner and was safe when Wagner threw to second with no one covering second. Freeman and Parent both scoring as La Chance safe at second.
1 Criger sacrificed La Chance to third and Ferris to second, Bransfield to Ritchey.
Young tripled to left, scoring both La Chance and Ferris.
Dougherty also tripled to deep left, scoring Young.
2 Collins popped to first.
3 Stahl grounded to short.
Pittsburgh
1 Clarke popped to second.
2 Leach flied to left.
3 Wagner grounded to short.

7th Inning
Boston
Freeman beat out a hit to second.
Parent singled to left, Freeman going to second.
1 La Chance forced Parent at second, Ritchey to Wagner as Freeman went to third.
Ferris singled to center, Freeman scoring and La Chance going to second.
Criger walked, loading the bases.
2 Young grounded to second, La Chance and advancing Ferris and Criger.
Dougherty tripled to center, his second of the game, scoring Ferris and Criger.
3 Collins grounded to short.
Pittsburgh
1 Bransfield struck out.
2 Ritchey flied to center.
3 Sebring flied to deep right.

8th Inning
Boston
For Pittsburgh—Thompson pitching.
Stahl tripled to right for Boston's fifth triple.
1 Freeman grounded to second, scoring Stahl.
2 Parent fouled to Leach.
La Chance flied to left.
3 Ferris struck out.
Pittsburgh
1 Phelps called out on strikes.
2 Thompson popped to short.
Beaumont beat out a dribbler to second.
Clarke safe on Parent's fumble, Beaumont going to second.
Leach tripled to right, scoring Beaumont and Clarke.
3 Wagner grounded to short.

9th Inning
Boston
1 Criger grounded back to the mound.
2 Young flied to right.
Dougherty singled to center.
3 Collins fouled to Phelps.
Pittsburgh
1 Bransfield flied to right.
2 Ritchey struck out.
Sebring singled to center.
3 Phelps grounded to second.

Game 6 October 8 at Pittsburgh

Boston	Pos	AB	R	H	RBI	PO	A	E
Dougherty	lf	3	1	1	0	1	0	0
Collins	3b	5	1	1	1	0	2	0
C. Stahl	cf	5	1	2	1	4	0	0
Freeman	rf	5	0	0	1	2	0	0
Parent	ss	4	2	1	0	4	2	0
La Chance	1b	4	0	1	1	8	3	0
Ferris	2b	4	0	2	0	2	3	0
Criger	c	4	0	1	0	6	0	1
Dinneen	p	4	1	1	0	2	2	0
Totals		38	6	10	4	27	12	1

Pitching	IP	H	R	ER	BB	SO
Boston						
Dinneen (W)	9	10	3	3	3	3
Pittsburgh						
Leever (L)	9	10	6	4	2	2

Bos. 003 020 100
Pit. 000 000 300

Pittsburgh	Pos	AB	R	H	RBI	PO	A	E
Beaumont	cf	5	1	4	1	5	0	0
Clarke	lf	5	0	2	2	5	0	0
Leach	3b	5	0	0	0	1	2	1
Wagner	ss	3	0	0	0	2	5	1
Bransfield	1b	3	0	1	0	12	0	0
Ritchey	2b	3	0	0	0	0	4	0
Sebring	rf	4	1	2	0	2	0	0
Phelps	c	4	1	1	0	3	0	0
Leever	p	4	0	0	0	0	2	0
Totals		36	3	10	3	27	13	3

Doubles—Clarke, La Chance. Triples—Parent, C. Stahl. Stolen Bases—Beaumont 2, Clarke, Leach, C. Stahl. Double Plays—Ritchey to Wagner to Bransfield, Parent to La Chance. Hit by Pitcher—Parent (by Leever). Left on Bases—Boston 8, Pittsburgh 9. Umpires—O'Day, Connolly. Attendance—11,556. Time of Game—2:02.

1st Inning
Boston
1 Dougherty grounded to second.
2 Collins flied to right.
3 Stahl popped to third.
Pittsburgh
1 Beaumont grounded to second.
   Clarke singled to second.
2 Leach forced Clarked at second, Parent unassisted.
   Leach stole second and continued to third on Criger's throwing error.
3 Wagner popped to short.

2nd Inning
Boston
1 Freeman grounded to short.
   Parent safe on Leach's wild throw.
2,3 La Chance hit into a double play, Ritchey to Wagner to Bransfield.
Pittsburgh
1 Bransfield flied to right.
2 Ritchey popped to third.
   Sebring beat out a hit to deep short.
3 Phelps struck out.

3rd Inning
Boston
1 Ferris bounced back to the mound.
2 Criger fouled to Phelps.
   Dinneen singled through short.
   Dougherty walked.
   Collins singled to center, Dinneen scoring as Dougherty stopped at second.
   Stahl singled to center, Dougherty scored as Collins raced to third.
   Stahl stole second.
   Freeman safe on Leach's fumble, scoring Collins as Stahl went to third.
3 Parent bounced back to the mound.
Pittsburgh
1 Leever grounded to third, Collins making a great play charging in for the ball.
   Beaumont beat out a single to second.
2 Clarke struck out.
   Beaumont stole second.
3 Leach popped to second.

4th Inning
Boston
1 La Chance grounded to third.
   Ferris beat out a chopper to the mound.
   Criger singled to left, Ferris going to second.
2 Dinneen called out on strikes.
   Dougherty beat out a liner to short, loading the bases.
3 Collins forced Dougherty at second, Wagner unassisted.
Pittsburgh
1 Wagner grounded back to the pitcher.
   Bransfield singled to left.
   Ritchey walked.
2 Sebring forced Ritchey at second, La Chance to Parent, Bransfield going to third.
3 Phelps grounded to second.

5th Inning
Boston
Stahl tripled into the crowd in left.
1 Freeman flied to center, Stahl scoring after the catch.
   Parent hit by a pitched ball.
2 La Chance flied to deep center.
   Ferris singled to center and on a wild relay throw by Wagner, Parent scored and Ferris went to second.
3 Criger grounded to short.
Pittsburgh
1 Leever grounded back to the mound.
   Beaumont singled to center.
   Beaumont stole second, his second of the game.
2 Clarke struck out.
3 Leach flied to center.

6th Inning
Boston
1 Dinneen grounded to third.
   Dougherty walked.
2 Collins flied to center.
3 Stahl flied to left.
Pittsburgh
1 Wagner grounded out, La Chance to Dinneen.
2 Bransfield fouled to Criger.
3 Ritchey also fouled to Criger.

7th Inning
Boston
1 Freeman struck out.
   Parent tripled to left.
   La Chance doubled to left, scoring Parent.
2 Ferris flied to right.
3 Criger flied to center.
Pittsburgh
   Sebring singled to right.
   Phelps singled to center, Sebring going to second.
1 Leever grounded to second, advancing both runners.
   Beaumont singled to center, scoring Sebring as Phelps went to third.
   Clarke doubled to left, scoring Phelps and Beaumont.
2 Leach flied to right.
   Clarke stole third.
   Wagner walked.
   Bransfield walked, loading the bases.
3 Ritchey forced Bransfield at second, Parent to Ferris

8th Inning
Boston
1 Dinneen grounded to second.
2 Dougherty grounded to short.
3 Collins flied to center.
Pittsburgh
1 Sebring flied to deep left.
2 Phelps grounded to third.
3 Leever grounded out, La Chance to Dinneen.

9th Inning
Boston
1 Stahl grounded to second.
2 Freeman flied to left.
3 Parent grounded to short.
Pittsburgh
   Beaumont singled to center.
1,2 Clarke lined into a double play, Parent to La Chance.
3 Leach fouled to Criger.

Game 7 October 10 at Pittsburgh

Boston	Pos	AB	R	H	RBI	PO	A	E
Dougherty	lf	5	0	1	0	2	0	0
Collins	3b	5	1	1	0	0	1	1
C. Stahl	cf	4	1	2	1	1	0	0
Freeman	rf	4	1	1	0	0	0	0
Parent	ss	4	2	2	1	3	5	1
La Chance	1b	4	0	0	2	11	0	2
Ferris	2b	3	1	2	0	4	5	0
Criger	c	4	0	2	0	6	2	0
Young	p	4	0	0	0	0	2	0
Totals		36	7	11	5	27	15	4

Pitching	IP	H	R	ER	BB	SO
Boston						
Young (W)	9	10	3	3	1	6
Pittsburgh						
Phillippe (L)	9	11	7	4	0	2

Bos. 200 202 010
Pit. 000 101 001

Pittsburgh	Pos	AB	R	H	RBI	PO	A	E
Beaumont	cf	5	0	1	0	2	0	0
Clarke	lf	5	1	1	0	1	0	0
Leach	3b	5	0	0	0	0	1	0
Wagner	ss	3	0	0	1	2	5	1
Bransfield	1b	4	1	3	0	13	2	0
Ritchey	2b	4	0	0	1	5	8	0
Sebring	rf	4	1	2	0	0	0	0
Phelps	c	3	0	2	0	3	1	1
Phillippe	p	4	0	2	1	1	0	1
Totals		37	3	10	3	27	19	3

Triples—Bransfield, Clarke, Collins, Ferris, Freeman, Parent, C. Stahl. Sacrifice Hits—Feris, LaChance, Wagner. Double Plays—Wagner to Ritchey to Bransfield, Ferris to LaChance. Wild Pitch—Phillippe. Left on Bases—Boston 4, Pittsburgh 9. Umpires—Connolly, O'Day. Attendance—17,038. Time of Game—1:45.

1st Inning
Boston
1 Dougherty grounded to second.
   Collins tripled to right.
   Stahl tripled to center into the crowd, scoring Collins.
   Freeman grounded to Ritchey who threw to the plate but Phelps dropped the ball allowing Stahl to score.
2 Freeman out trying to steal second, Phelps to Ritchey.
3 Parent grounded to short.
Pittsburgh
   Beaumont beat out a hit to short.
   Clarke safe on La Chance's fumble, Beaumont going to second.
1,2 Leach hit into a double play, Ferris to La Chance, Beaumont going to third.
3 Wagner struck out.

2nd Inning
Boston
1 La Chance grounded to second.
   Ferris singled to center.
2 Criger forced Ferris, Wagner unassisted.
3 Young forced Criger, Wagner to Ritchey.
Pittsburgh
1 Bransfield grounded to second.
2 Ritchey struck out.
   Sebring singled past second.
3 Sebring caught trying to steal second, Criger to Parent.

3rd Inning
Boston
1 Dougherty flied to left.
2 Collins grounded to second.
3 Stahl tapped out, Phelps to La Chance.
Pittsburgh
1 Phelps grounded to second.
   Phillippe singled to left.
2 Beaumont grounded to second, Phillippe going to second.
   Clarke safe on Collins' bad throw to first, Phillippe going to third.
3 Leach struck out.

4th Inning
Boston
   Freeman tripled to center.
1 Parent grounded to Short, Freeman scoring.
2 La Chance struck out.
   Ferris tripled to left-center.
   Criger singled to right, scoring Ferris.
3 Young flied to center.
Pittsburgh
1 Wagner grounded to short.
   Bransfield tripled to left.
2 Ritchey grounded to third, scoring Bransfield.
3 Sebring popped to third.

5th Inning
Boston
   Dougherty beat out a bunt.
1 Collins grounded to short, Dougherty going to second.
2 Stahl grounded to second, Dougherty going to third.
3 Freeman grounded out, Bransfield to Phillippe.
Pittsburgh
   Phelps safe on Parent's bad throw.
1 Phillippe forced Phelps, Parent to Ferris.
2 Beaumont forced Phillippe, also Parent to Ferris.
3 Beaumont picked off first, Young to La Chance.

6th Inning
Boston
   Parent beat out a slow roller to first.
   La Chance sacrificed and was safe on Phillippe's error, Parent going to second.
1 Ferris sacrificed up both runners, Bransfield to Ritchey.
   Criger singled to right, scoring Parent and La Chance.
2,3 Young hit into a double play, Wagner to Ritchey to Bransfield.
Pittsburgh
   Clarke tripled to right.
1 Leach struck out.
2 Wagner bounced back to the mound, scoring Clarke.
   Bransfield singled to right.
3 Ritchey forced Bransfield, Parent to Ferris.

7th Inning
Boston
1 Dougherty grounded to second.
2 Collins lined to second.
   Stahl beat out a hit to first.
3 Stahl caught stealing second, Phelps to Wagner.
Pittsburgh
1 Sebring grounded to short.
   Phelps walked.
2 Phillippe struck out, but thrown out.
3 Beaumont flied to center.

8th Inning
Boston
1 Freeman fouled to Bransfield.
   Parent tripled into the right field crowd.
   Parent scored on a wild pitch.
2 La Chance grounded to second.
3 Ferris flied to center.
Pittsburgh
   Clarke safe on La Chance's bobble.
1 Leach struck out for the third time
2 Wagner fouled to Criger.
   Bransfield singled to center, sending Clarke to second.
3 Ritchey lined to left.

9th Inning
Boston
1 Criger grounded to third.
   Young safe on Wagner's high throw to first.
2 Dougherty struck out.
3 Collins flied to right.
Pittsburgh
   Sebring beat out a hit to deep short.
   Phelps singled to center, Sebring stopping at second.
   Phillippe singled to center, scoring Sebring with Phelps going to second.
1 Beaumont popped to short.
2 Clarke flied to left.
3 Leach forced Phillippe, Ferris to Parent.

1903

Game 8 October 13 at Boston

		Pit.	000	000	000
		Bos.	000	201	00x

Pittsburgh	Pos	AB	R	H	RBI	PO	A	E
Beaumont	cf	4	0	0	0	4	0	0
Clarke	lf	4	0	1	0	4	0	0
Leach	3b	3	0	0	0	0	3	0
Wagner	ss	4	0	1	0	2	1	1
Bransfield	1b	3	0	0	0	7	1	1
Ritchey	2b	2	0	0	0	3	1	0
Sebring	rf	3	0	1	0	1	1	0
Phelps	c	3	0	0	0	3	0	1
Phillippe	p	3	0	1	0	0	2	0
Totals		29	0	4	0	24	9	3

Pitching	IP	H	R	ER	BB	SO
Pittsburgh						
Phillippe (L)	8	8	3	2	0	2
Boston						
Dinneen (W)	9	4	0	0	2	7

Boston	Pos	AB	R	H	RBI	PO	A	E
Dougherty	rf	4	0	0	0	3	0	0
Collins	3b	4	0	1	0	0	2	0
C. Stahl	cf	4	0	0	0	2	0	0
Freeman	lf	4	1	1	0	2	0	0
Parent	ss	4	1	0	0	1	1	0
La Chance	1b	3	1	1	0	11	0	0
Ferris	2b	4	0	2	3	0	3	0
Criger	c	3	0	2	0	8	2	0
Dinneen	p	3	0	1	0	0	3	0
Totals		33	3	8	3	27	17	0

Triples—Freeman, La Chance, Sebring.
Stolen Base—Wagner. Sacrifice Hit—
La Chance. Double Play—Criger to
La Chance. Left on Bases—Pittsburgh 4,
Boston 7. Umpires—O'Day, Connolly.
Attendance—7,455. Time of Game—1:35.

1st Inning
Pittsburgh
1 Beaumont struck out.
2 Clarke popped to short.
3 Leach flied to center.
Boston
1 Dougherty flied to center.
 Collins singled to left.
2 Stahl flied to center.
3 Freeman flied to left.

2nd Inning
Pittsburgh
1 Wagner flied to left.
2 Bransfield flied to right.
3 Ritchey struck out.
Boston
1 Parent grounded to third.
2 La Chance grounded back to the mound.
 Ferris safe on Bransfield's error.
 Criger singled to left, Ferris going
 to second.
3 Dinneen struck out.

3rd Inning
Pittsburgh
1 Sebring grounded to the mound.
2 Phelps also grounded to the mound.
3 Phillippe grounded to short.
Boston
1 Dougherty struck out.
2 Collins flied to right.
3 Stahl flied to center.

4th Inning
Pittsburgh
1 Beaumont grounded to second.
2 Clarke struck out.
 Leach walked.
 Wagner singled to left, Leach to third.
3 On delayed double steal, Leach was
 out, Criger to Collins to Criger
Boston
 Freeman tripled to center.
 Parent safe as Phelps fumbled his
 roller in front of the plate,
 Freeman holding at third.
1 La Chance sacrificed Parent to second as
 Freeman held third, Bransfield to
 Ritchey.
 Ferris singled to center, scoring
 both Freeman and Parent.
2 Criger grounded back to the mound,
 Ferris to second.
 Dinneen singled to right and Ferris
3 was out at the plate, Sebring to
 Phelps.

5th Inning
Pittsburgh
1 Bransfield struck out.
2 Ritchey grounded to third.
 Sebring tripled to left.
3 Phelps struck out.
Boston
1 Dougherty grounded to first.
2 Collins grounded to third, a great
 catch of a poor throw by Bransfield.
3 Stahl flied to left.

6th Inning
Pittsburgh
 Phillippe singled to left.
1,2 Beaumont struck out and Criger threw
 to La Chance doubling Phillippe off
 of first.
 Clarke beat out a roller to third.
3 Leach flied to left.
Boston
1 Freeman fouled to Wagner.
2 Parent flied to center.
 La Chance tripled to right.
 Ferris singled to center, scoring
 La Chance.
 Criger singled to center, Ferris
 going to second.
3 Dinneen forced Criger at second,
 Ritchey to Wagner.

7th Inning
Pittsburgh
1 Wagner grounded to second.
2 Bransfield flied to center.
 Ritchey walked.
3 Sebring grounded back to the mound.
Boston
1 Dougherty popped to second.
2 Collins bunted out to third.
 Stahl safe on Wagner's wild throw.
3 Freeman flied to left.

8th Inning
Pittsburgh
1 Phelps grounded to second.
2 Phillippe grounded to first.
3 Beaumont grounded to first.
Boston
1 Parent flied to left.
2 La Chance grounded to short.
3 Ferris popped to second.

9th Inning
Pittsburgh
1 Clarke flied to left.
2 Leach flied to right.
3 Wagner struck out.

	Wins	Composite Line Score		Manager	W	L	Pct.	Regular Season G. Ahead
Boston Pilgrims (A.L.)	5	4 0 3 5 3 10 7 3 4 – 39		Jimmy Collins	91	47	.659	14½
Pittsburgh Pirates (N.L.)	3	5 1 3 2 1 1 7 3 1 – 24		Fred Clarke	91	49	.650	6½

BATTING AND FIELDING

WORLD SERIES STATISTICS

BOSTON PILGRIMS	Pos	G	AB	R	H	2B	3B	HR	RBI	BB	SO	SB	BA	SA	PO	A	E
Candy LaChance	1b	8	27	5	6	2	1	0	4	3	2	0	.222	.370	78	4	3
Hobe Ferris	2b	8	31	3	9	0	1	0	5	0	6	0	.290	.355	18	23	2
Freddy Parent	ss	8	32	8	9	0	3	0	4	1	1	0	.281	.469	16	27	3
Jimmy Collins	3b	8	36	5	9	1	2	0	1	1	1	3	.250	.389	8	18	1
Buck Freeman	rf	8	32	6	9	0	3	0	4	2	2	0	.281	.469	10	0	0
Chick Stahl	cf	8	33	6	10	1	3	0	3	1	2	2	.303	.515	14	1	0
Patsy Dougherty	lf	8	34	3	8	0	2	2	5	2	6	0	.235	.529	13	3	1
Lou Criger	c	8	26	1	6	0	0	0	4	2	3	0	.231	.231	54	7	3
Jack O'Brien	ph	2	2	0	0	0	0	0	0	0	1	0	.000	.000			
Duke Farrell	ph	2	2	0	0	0	0	0	1	0	0	0	.000	.000			
Jake Stahl		Did not play															
Cy Young	p	4	15	1	2	0	1	0	3	0	3	0	.133	.267	0	8	1
Bill Dinneen	p	4	12	1	3	0	0	0	0	2	2	0	.250	.250	2	9	0
Long Tom Hughes	p	1	0	0	0	0	0	0	0	0	0	0	—	—	0	0	0
George Winter		Did not play															
Norwood Gibson		Did not play															
team total		8	282	39	71	4	16	2	34	14	29	5	.252	.401	213	100	14

Double Plays– 5
Left on Bases– 55

PITTSBURGH PIRATES	Pos	G	AB	R	H	2B	3B	HR	RBI	BB	SO	SB	BA	SA	PO	A	E
Kitty Bransfield	1b	8	29	3	6	0	2	0	1	6	1	.207	.345	81	6	3
Claude Ritchey	2b	8	27	2	3	1	0	0	2	4	7	1	.111	.148	20	29	0
Honus Wagner	ss	8	27	2	6	1	0	0	3	3	4	3	.222	.259	12	30	6
Tommy Leach	3b	8	33	3	9	0	4	0	7	1	4	1	.273	.515	5	14	4
Jimmy Sebring	rf	8	30	3	11	0	1	1	3	1	4	0	.367	.533	13	1	0
Ginger Beaumont	cf	8	34	6	9	1	0	0	1	2	4	2	.265	.324	21	0	0
Fred Clarke	lf	8	34	3	9	2	1	0	2	1	5	1	.265	.382	18	0	1
Eddie Phelps	c-ph	8	26	1	6	2	0	0	1	1	6	0	.231	.308	36	4	2
Harry Smith	c	1	3	0	0	0	0	0	0	0	0	0	.000	.000	2	1	1
Otto Krueger		Did not play															
Art Weaver		Did not play															
Joe Marshall		Did not play															
Fred Carisch		Did not play															
Deacon Phillippe	p	5	18	1	4	0	0	0	1	0	3	0	.222	.222	2	9	1
Sam Leever	p	2	4	0	0	0	0	0	0	0	0	0	.000	.000	0	2	0
Brickyard Kennedy	p	1	2	0	1	1	0	0	0	0	0	0	.500	1.000	0	1	0
Bucky Veil	p	1	2	0	0	0	0	0	0	0	2	0	.000	.000	0	0	1
Gus Thompson	p	1	1	0	0	0	0	0	0	0	0	0	.000	.000	0	1	0
Ed Doheny		Did not play—illness															
Kaiser Wilhelm		Did not play															
Jack Pfiester		Did not play															
team total		8	270	24	64	7	9	1	21	14	45	9	.237	.341	210	99	19

Double Plays–5
Left on Bases–51

REGULAR SEASON STATISTICS

Main Pos	G	AB	R	H	2B	3B	HR	RBI	BB	SO	SB	BA	SA
1b	141	522	60	134	22	6	1	53	28		12	.257	.328
2b	141	525	69	132	19	7	9	66	25		11	.251	.366
ss	139	560	83	170	31	17	4	80	13		24	.304	.441
3b	130	541	87	160	34	17	5	72	24		22	.296	.449
of	141	565	74	161	39	21	13	104	30		4	.285	.497
of	78	298	60	83	11	6	2	44	28		14	.279	.376
of	139	590	106	195	19	12	4	59	33		35	.331	.404
c	96	317	41	61	7	10	3	31	26		5	.192	.306
of	96	338	44	71	14	4	3	38	21		10	.210	.302
c	17	52	5	21	5	1	0	8	5		1	.404	.538
c	40	92	14	22	3	5	2	8	4		1	.239	.446
p	41	137	21	44	6	3	1	14	4		2	.321	.431
p	37	106	6	17	2	1	0	8	11		1	.160	.198
p	33	93	14	26	4	2	1	13	3		1	.280	.398
p	24	66	7	7	2	0	1	3	3		1	.106	.136
p	25	64	8	17	2	2	0	4	5		0	.266	.359
*141	4919	707	1336	222	113	48	609	262		141	.272	.392	

Broadway Aleck Smith (c), Harry Gleason (3b), George Stone (ph), Nick Altrock (p) also played for the Somersets during the season.

Main Pos	G	AB	R	H	2B	3B	HR	RBI	BB	SO	SB	BA	SA
1b	127	505	69	134	23	7	2	57	33		13	.265	.350
2b	138	506	66	145	28	10	0	59	55		15	.287	.381
ss	129	512	97	182	30	19	5	101	44		46	.355	.518
3b	124	507	97	151	16	17	7	87	40		22	.298	.438
of	124	506	71	140	16	13	4	64	32		20	.277	.383
of	141	613	137	209	30	6	7	68	44		23	.341	.444
of	104	427	88	150	32	5	5	70	41		21	.351	.532
c	81	273	32	77	1	3	2	31	17		2	.282	.352
c	61	212	15	37	3	2	0	19	12		2	.175	.208
ss-of-3b	80	256	42	63	6	8	1	28	21		5	.246	.344
a c-1b	16	48	8	11	0	1	0	3	2		0	.229	.271
of-ss	10	23	2	6	1	2	0	2	0		0	.261	.478
c	5	18	4	6	4	0	1	5	0		0	.333	.722
p	37	124	20	26	4	0	0	16	5		0	.210	.274
p	36	115	11	19	0	1	0	12	4		0	.165	.183
p	23	58	7	21	4	3	0	10	2		0	.362	.534
p	12	29	2	6	1	0	0	1	0		0	.207	.241
p	5	16	0	4	0	0	0	3	0		0	.250	.250
p	27	91	11	19	1	0	0	6	3		1	.209	.220
p	13	34	1	3	0	0	0	0	0		0	.088	.088
p	3	6	0	0	0	0	0	0	0		0	.000	.000
*141	4991	792	1430	208	110	34	650	364		172	.287	.393	

a—from St. Louis (N)

Eude Curtis (of), Ernie Diehl (of), Lou Gertenrich (of), Bill Gray (of), Solly Hofman (of), Hans Lobert (3b), George Merritt (of-p), Cy Falkenberg (p), Lew Moren (p), Doc Scanlan (p), Lafe Wintham (p) also played for the Pirates during the season.

PITCHING

WORLD SERIES STATISTICS

BOSTON PILGRIMS	G	GS	CG	IP	H	R	ER	BB	SO	W	L	SV	ERA
Bill Dinneen	4	4	4	35	29	8	8	8	28	3	1	0	2.06
Cy Young	4	3	3	34	31	13	7	4	17	2	1	0	1.85
Long Tom Hughes	1	1	0	2	4	3	2	2	0	0	1	0	9.00
Norwood Gibson		Did not play											
George Winter		Did not play											
team total	8	8	7	71	64	24	17	14	45	5	3	0	2.15

PITTSBURGH PIRATES	G	GS	CG	IP	H	R	ER	BB	SO	W	L	SV	ERA
Deacon Phillippe	5	5	5	44	38	19	14	3	22	3	2	0	2.86
Sam Leever	2	2	1	10	13	8	6	3	2	0	2	0	5.40
Brickyard Kennedy	1	1	0	7	11	10	4	3	3	0	1	0	5.14
Bucky Veil	1	0	0	7	6	1	1	5	1	0	0	0	1.29
Gus Thompson	1	0	0	2	3	1	1	0	1	0	0	0	4.50
Ed Doheny		Did not play—illness											
Kaiser Wilhelm		Did not play											
Jack Pfiester		Did not play											
team total	8	8	6	70	71	39	29	14	29	3	5	0	3.73

REGULAR SEASON STATISTICS

G	GS	CG	IP	H	ER	BB	SO	W	L	Pct.	SV	ShO	ERA
37	35	32	299	255	74	66	148	21	11	.656	1	6	2.23
40	35	34	342	294	79	37	176	28	9	.757	2	7	2.08
33	31	25	245	232	70	60	112	20	7	.741	0	5	2.57
24	21	17	183	166	65	65	76	13	11	.542	0	2	3.20
24	18	14	178	182	61	37	64	9	8	.529	0	3	3.08
*141	141	123	1255	1142	357	269	579	91	47	.659	3	20	2.56

G	GS	CG	IP	H	ER	BB	SO	W	L	Pct.	SV	ShO	ERA
36	33	31	289	269	78	29	123	24	9	.727	2	4	2.43
36	34	30	284	255	65	60	90	25	7	.781	1	7	2.06
18	15	10	125	130	48	57	39	9	6	.600	0	0	3.46
12	6	4	71	70	30	36	20	5	3	.625	0	0	3.80
5	4	3	43	52	17	16	22	2	2	.500	0	0	3.56
27	25	22	223	209	79	89	75	16	8	.667	2	2	3.19
12	9	7	86	88	31	25	20	5	3	.625	0	1	3.24
3	3	2	19	26	13	10	15	0	3	.000	0	0	6.16
*141	141	117	1251	1215	405	384	454	91	49	.650	5	15	2.91

Total Attendance—100,420   Average Attendance—12,553   Winning Player's Share—$1,182   Losing Player's Share—$1,316

Note: The Pittsburgh owner gave his share to the team; therefore, the losers earned more than the winners.

Note: For all composite boxes, the bold face indicates leader in that category.

*All regular season totals include those of players not eligible for Series.

1905
Christy's Three Golden Goose Eggs

New York Giant manager John McGraw hated American League president Ban Johnson for their many run-ins during McGraw's year and a half as player-manager of the Baltimore Orioles in the young circuit. New York Giant owner John T. Brush hated the American League for putting a new club in New York in 1903 to rival his own. These two hatreds added together explained the pennant-winning Giants' refusal to meet the Boston Pilgrims in any postseason series in 1904. But the public outcry against the Giants was so great, Brush reversed his field and proposed a code making the World Series a best-of-seven annual affair. These rules were adopted and govern the fall classic to this day, and the New York Giants and Philadelphia Athletics met in October of 1905 as the first contestants in the permanently established Series.

The Giants had stayed in front of the National League from April 23 on, while the Athletics, managed by Connie Mack, reached first place only in August and hung on despite a late slump. The Giants had more hitting clout in their lineup than the Athletics, but both clubs had deep pitching staffs headed up by outstanding stars. Christy Mathewson, a gentlemanly twenty-six-year-old graduate of Bucknell University, used his pinpoint control and puzzling screwball to log a 32–8 record with a 1.27 ERA for the Giants. While Matty was a righty, his opposite number on the A's was a lefty with a matching reputation for flakiness. Rube Waddell had little formal education, but he did possess a blazing fast ball and a cartload of eccentricities. Fire engines, parades, marbles, fishing, and drinking were only some of the passions which occasionally lured him away from the ballpark on days when he should have been in uniform, but the likable Rube toed the line enough this year to lead the majors with 287 strikeouts and post a 26–11 record. Fans eagerly anticipated the match-up of these two contrasting but equally outstanding hurlers.

The match-up never materialized, however, as Waddell hurt his left shoulder late in the season during some typical horseplay. Although Mack had a full cupboard of outstanding pitchers, he badly missed the arm of the eccentric southpaw to throw up against Mathewson. With the Giants wearing specially tailored black uniforms with white trim, Matty took the mound in game one in Philadelphia, with the Athletics pitting 25-game-winner Eddie Plank against him. Plank pitched well, but was touched for three runs; Mathewson blanked the A's on four hits to put the Giants one game in front. Iron Man Joe McGinnity, a veteran submariner who got his nickname pitching both ends of doubleheaders, got the nod from McGraw for game two in New York, with young Chief Bender pitching for the A's. This time it was Philadelphia's turn to shut the Giants out, with Bender allowing only four hits en route to a crisp 3–0 victory. Little did the Athletics realize it, but that was the end of their scoring for the Series.

After a day off, the teams met for game three in Philadelphia. McGraw sent Mathewson back to the mound on two days' rest, and Mack sent 20-game-winner Andy Coakley out to meet him. To beat Mathewson, the A's needed an almost flawless performance, but their play in game three was poor; they made four errors and gave up seven unearned runs, while Matty spun another four-hit shutout. After an overnight train ride, the Series resumed the next day in New York, with McGinnity pitching for New York and Plank for Philadelphia. The A's had beaten the Iron Man in game two, but the veteran hurler had their number this time and shut them out on five hits for a 1–0 win. An enormous Saturday crowd of 24,187 came out to the Polo Grounds for game five and went away completely satisfied. They saw Mathewson best Chief Bender for a 2–0 victory. It was Matty's third whitewash of the Series—a phenomenal performance which gave the World Championship to the Giants and ended what was the best display of pitching ever witnessed in a Series, five shutouts in five games.

Game 1 October 9 at Philadelphia

		N.Y.	000 020 001
		Phi.	000 000 000

New York	Pos	AB	R	H	RBI	PO	A	E
Bresnahan	c	3	1	1	1	6	1	0
Browne	rf	5	0	0	0	1	0	0
Donlin	cf	5	1	2	1	1	0	1
McGann	1b	3	0	1	0	14	0	0
Mertes	lf	4	0	1	1	0	0	0
Dahlen	ss	4	0	0	0	2	5	0
Devlin	3b	4	0	1	0	0	3	0
Gilbert	2b	4	1	3	0	3	4	0
Mathewson	p	3	0	1	0	0	3	0
Totals		35	3	10	3	27	16	1

Doubles—Davis, McGann, Mertes, Murphy, Schreckengost. Stolen Bases—Bresnahan, Devlin, Donlin, Gilbert. Sacrifice Hit—Mathewson. Double Play—Dahlen to McGann. Hit by Pitch—Bresnahan (by Plank). Left on Bases—New York 9, Philadelphia 4. Umpires—Sheridan (A), O'Day (N). Attendance—17,955. Time of Game—1:46.

Philadelphia	Pos	AB	R	H	RBI	PO	A	E
Hartsel	lf	4	0	1	0	1	0	0
Lord	cf	4	0	0	0	2	0	0
Davis	1b	4	0	1	0	14	0	0
L. Cross	3b	4	0	0	0	0	1	0
Seybold	rf	3	0	0	0	0	0	0
Murphy	2b	3	0	1	0	1	4	0
M. Cross	ss	3	0	0	0	4	6	0
Schreckengost	c	3	0	1	0	5	1	0
Plank	p	3	0	0	0	0	1	0
Totals		31	0	4	0	27	13	0

Pitching	IP	H	R	ER	BB	SO
New York						
Mathewson (W)	9	4	0	0	0	6
Philadelphia						
Plank (L)	9	10	3	3	2	5

1st Inning
New York
  Bresnahan hit by a pitch.
1 Browne forced Bresnahan at second, M. Cross to Murphy.
2 Donlin popped to first.
  McGann got a ground-rule double into the right field crowd, Browne going to third.
3 Mertes struck out.
Philadelphia
1 Hartsel grounded to second.
2 Lord flied to center.
3 Davis bounced to the mound.

2nd Inning
New York
1 Dahlen struck out.
  Devlin beat out a bunt to third.
  Gilbert also beat out a bunt, Devlin going to second.
  Devlin and Gilbert pulled a perfect double steal.
2 Mathewson struck out.
  Bresnahan intentionally walked, loading the bases.
3 Browne grounded to short.
Philadelphia
1 L. Cross grounded to short.
2 Seybold popped to short.
3 Murphy grounded to second.

3rd Inning
New York
1 Donlin grounded to first.
2 McGann grounded to third.
3 Mertes grounded to second.
Philadelphia
1 M. Cross grounded to third.
  Schreckengost safe when Donlin dropped his fly after losing it in the sun.
2,3 Plank grounded into a double play, Dahlen to McGann.

4th Inning
New York
1 Dahlen grounded to second.
2 Devlin struck out.
3 Gilbert grounded to short.
Philadelphia
  Hartsel singled to right-center. The first hit off of Mathewson.
1 Lord forced Hartsel at second on a bunt, Gilbert unassisted.
2 Davis forded Lord at second, Dahlen to Gilbert.
3 L. Cross grounded to short.

5th Inning
New York
  Mathewson singled over second.
1 Bresnahan forced Mathewson at second, M. Cross unassisted.
  Bresnahan stole second.
2 Browne popped to short.
  Donlin lined a single to left, Bresnahan scoring as Donlin took second on the throw to the plate.
  McGann walked.
  Mertes hit a ground-rule double into the center field crowd, scoring Donlin with McGann going to third.
3 Dahlen flied to deep left.
Philadelphia
1 Seybold grounded back to the mound.
2 Murphy struck out.
3 M. Cross grounded to second.

6th Inning
New York
1 Devlin flied to deep center.
  Gilbert singled to left.
2 Gilbert caught trying to steal second, Schreckengost to M. Cross.
3 Mathewson grounded to short.
Philadelphia
  Schreckengost doubled to deep left.
1 Plank struck out on a wild pitch, and was thrown out Schreckengost to McGann as Schreckengost went to third.
2 Hartsel grounded into a double play but Schreckengost was out at the plate, Mathewson to Bresnahan.
3 Lord forced Hartsel at second, Dahlen to Gilbert.

7th Inning
New York
1 Bresnahan flied to center.
2 Browne grounded to short.
  Donlin beat out a bunt to third.
  Donlin stole second.
3 McGann grounded to short.
Philadelphia
1 Davis struck out.
2 L. Cross grounded to second.
3 Seybold grounded to third.

8th Inning
New York
1 Mertes grounded to second.
2 Dahlen popped to short.
3 Devlin struck out.
Philadelphia
  Murphy doubled into the crowd in right field.
1 M. Cross struck out.
2 Schreckengost flied to right.
3 Plank struck out.

9th Inning
New York
  Gilbert singled over short, his third hit of the game.
1 Mathewson sacrificed Gilbert to second, Plank to Davis.
  Bresnahan singled over second, Gilbert scoring, and taking second on the throw to the plate.
2 Browne grounded to first, Bresnahan going to third.
3 Donlin grounded to second.
Philadelphia
1 Hartsel grounded to short.
2 Lord struck out.
  Davis doubled into the crowd in right-center.
3 L. Cross grounded to third.

Game 2 October 10 at New York

Philadelphia	Pos	AB	R	H	RBI	PO	A	E
Hartsel	lf	4	1	2	0	0	0	0
Lord	cf	4	0	2	2	3	0	0
Davis	1b	4	0	0	0	9	0	0
L. Cross	3b	3	0	0	0	1	1	0
Seybold	rf	4	0	0	0	0	0	0
Murphy	2b	4	0	1	0	0	3	1
M. Cross	ss	4	0	0	0	4	1	1
Schreckengost	c	4	2	1	0	10	2	0
Bender	p	2	0	0	0	0	0	0
Totals		33	3	6	2	27	7	2

Pitching	IP	H	R	ER	BB	SO
Philadelphia						
Bender (W)	9	4	0	0	3	9
New York						
McGinnity (L)	8	5	3	0	0	2
Ames	1	1	0	0	1	1

| | | | Phi. | 0 0 1 | 0 0 0 | 0 2 0 |
| | | | N.Y. | 0 0 0 | 0 0 0 | 0 0 0 |

New York	Pos	AB	R	H	RBI	PO	A	E
Bresnahan	c	4	0	1	0	3	1	0
Browne	rf	4	0	0	0	2	0	0
Donlin	cf	4	0	2	0	4	0	0
McGann	1b	3	0	0	0	13	0	1
Mertes	lf	4	0	0	0	1	0	0
Dahlen	ss	3	0	0	0	1	6	0
Devlin	3b	3	0	0	0	1	6	0
Gilbert	2b	3	0	0	0	2	1	1
McGinnity	p	2	0	0	0	0	2	0
a Strang		1	0	0	0	0	0	0
Ames	p	0	0	0	0	0	1	0
Totals		31	0	4	0	27	16	2

a Struck out for McGinnity in 8th.

Doubles—Bresnahan, Donlin, Hartsel. Stolen Bases—Dahlen, Devlin. Sacrifice Hit—Bender. Left on Bases—Philadelphia 5, New York 7. Umpires—O'Day, Sheridan. Attendance—24,992. Time of Game—1:55.

1st Inning
Philadelphia
  Hartsel singled past third.
1 Lord forced Hartsel at second, Dahlen unassisted.
2 Davis popped to third.
3 L. Cross grounded to short.
New York
  Bresnahan doubled to deep left.
1 Brown bunt popped to Davis.
2 Donlin fouled to M. Cross.
3 McGann struck out.

2nd Inning
Philadelphia
1 Seybold flied to deep center.
2 Murphy tapped back to the mound.
3 M. Cross flied to right.
New York
1 Mertes struck out.
  Dahlen walked.
  Dahlen stole second.
  Devlin walked.
2 On a double steal, Devlin stole second but Dahlen was out at third, Schreckengost to L. Cross.
3 Gilbert grounded to short.

3rd Inning
Philadelphia
  Schreckengost safe when McGann dropped Gilbert's throw.
1 Bender sacrificed Schreckengost to third, Bresnahan to McGann.
2 Hartsel grounded to second, Schreckengost going to third.
  Lord singled to left, Schreckengost scoring.
3 Davis grounded to short.
New York
1 McGinnity struck out.
2 Bresnahan popped to first.
3 Browne popped to short.

4th Inning
Philadelphia
1 L. Cross popped to second.
2 Seybold flied to deep center, Donlin making a great catch.
3 Murphy struck out.
New York
  Donlin singled to right.
1 McGann struck out for the third time.
2 Mertes struck out.
3 Donlin caught stealing second, Schreckengost to M. Cross.

5th Inning
Philadelphia
1 M. Cross grounded to short.
2 Schreckengost also grounded to short.
3 Bender bounced back to the mound.
New York
1 Dahlen flied to deep center.
2 Devlin grounded to third.
3 Gilbert called out on strikes.

6th Inning
Philadelphia
1 Hartsel grounded to short.
2 Lord lined to center.
3 Davis grounded to second.
New York
1 McGinnity struck out.
2 Bresnahan popped to first.
3 Browne grounded to second.

7th Inning
Philadelphia
1 L. Cross grounded to second.
2 Seybold popped to third.
3 Murphy grounded to third.
New York
  Donlin doubled into the right field crowd.
1 McGann struck out.
2 Mertes flied to center, Donlin going to third after the catch.
3 Dahlen fouled to Schreckengost.

8th Inning
Philadelphia
1 M. Cross struck out.
  Schreckengost singled over McGinnity's head.
2 Bender fouled to Browne.
  Hartsel singled to left, Schreckengost scored when Bresnahan dropped Devlin's relay.
  Lord singled past short, scoring Hartsel.
3 Davis forced Lord at second, Dahlen to Gilbert.
New York
  Devlin singled to center.
1 Gilbert flied to center.
2 Strang, pinch-hitting for McGinnity, struck out.
  Bresnahan safe on M. Cross' fumble, Devlin going to second.
3 Browne grounded to second.

9th Inning
Philadelphia
  For New York—Ames came in to pitch.
  L. Cross walked.
1 Seybold lined to center.
  Murphy singled to left, L. Cross going to third. Murphy went to second on the throw to third.
2 M. Cross struck out.
3 Schreckengost grounded back to the mound.
New York
  Donlin safe on Murphy's fumble.
  McGann walked.
1 Mertes popped to short.
2 Dahlen grounded to second, advancing both runners.
3 Devlin grounded to second.

Game 3 October 12 at Philadelphia

New York	Pos	AB	R	H	RBI	PO	A	E
Bresnahan	c	3	2	0	0	8	4	0
Browne	rf	5	2	1	0	2	0	0
Donlin	cf	3	3	1	0	4	0	0
McGann	1b	5	1	3	4	9	0	0
Mertes	lf	3	0	1	1	1	0	0
Dahlen	ss	3	1	0	1	3	0	0
Devlin	3b	3	0	1	1	0	6	1
Gilbert	2b	4	0	0	0	2	0	0
Mathewson	p	4	0	1	0	0	3	0
Totals		34	9	8	7	27	13	1

Pitching	IP	H	R	ER	BB	SO
New York						
Mathewson (W)	9	4	0	0	1	8
Philadelphia						
Coakley (L)	9	8	9	2	5	2

| | | | N.Y. | 2 0 0 | 0 5 0 | 0 0 2 |
| | | | Phi. | 0 0 0 | 0 0 0 | 0 0 0 |

Philadelphia	Pos	AB	R	H	RBI	PO	A	E
Hartsel	lf	4	0	0	0	2	0	1
Lord	cf	4	0	0	0	2	0	0
Davis	1b	4	0	1	0	11	0	0
L. Cross	3b	4	0	1	0	1	1	0
Seybold	rf	3	0	1	0	1	1	0
Murphy	2b	3	0	0	0	2	4	2
M. Cross	ss	3	0	1	0	2	4	2
Schreckengost	c	1	0	0	0	2	1	0
Powers	c	1	0	0	0	2	3	0
Coakley	p	2	0	0	0	0	2	0
Totals		30	0	4	0	27	12	4

Double—McGann. Stolen Bases—Browne 2, Dahlen, Devlin, Donlin. Double Plays—Coakley to Schreckengost to Davis, Seybold to Davis, Bresnahan to Dahlen. Hit by Pitchers—Coakley (by Mathewson), Bresnahan (by Coakley). Left on Bases—New York 5, Philadelphia 5. Umpires—Sheridan, O'Day. Attendance—10,991. Time of Game—1:55.

1st Inning
New York
  Bresnahan hit by a pitch.
1 Browne fouled to L. Cross.
  Donlin singled off the right field fence, Breanahan going to third.
  McGann also singled off the right field fence, Bresnahan scoring as Donlin went to third.
  Mertes safe on Murphy's fumble, Donlin scoring with McGann going to second.
  Dahlen walked loading the bases.
2,3 Devlin hit into a double play, Coakley to Schreckengost to Davis.
Philadelphia
  Hartsel safe on Devlins error.
1 Lord struck out, but had to be thrown out, Bresnahan to McGann.
2 Davis hit into a fielder's choice, Hartsel out in a run-down Mathewson to Devlin to Dahlen.
3 L. Cross grounded to first.

2nd Inning
New York
1 Gilbert grounded to third.
2 Mathewson grounded to first.
3 Bresnahan lined to first.
Philadelphia
  Seybold walked.
1 Murphy forced Seybold at second, Devlin to Gilbert.
2 Murphy out trying to steal, Bresnahan to Dahlen.
3 M. Cross struck out.

3rd Inning
New York
1 Browne struck out.
2 Donlin grounded to short.
  McGann safe by Hartsell's muff in left-center.
3 Mertes popped to short.
Philadelphia
1 Schreckengost flied to center.
2 Coakley struck out on three pitches.
3 Hartsel flied to left.

4th Inning
New York
1 Dahlen flied to deep left.
2 Devlin popped to first.
3 Gilbert bounced back to the mound.
Philadelphia
1 Lord struck out again.
2 Davis grounded to Mathewson, making a great stop.
3 L. Cross flied to center.

5th Inning
New York
1 Mathewson grounded to short.
  Bresnahan walked.
  Browne singled to left, Bresnahan going to second.
  Donlin walked, loading the bases.
  McGann safe on Murphy's error, scoring Bresnahan.
  Mertes singled off the right field fence, scoring Browne.
2 Dahlen forced Mertes at second, Murphy unassisted, Donlin scoring as McGann went to third.
  Dahlen stole second.
  Devlin singled to center, McGann scoring with Dahlen going to third.
  Devlin stole second and on the delay Dahlen scored.
3 Gilbert flied to center.

5th Inning (continued)
Philadelphia
1 Seybold flied to center.
2 Murphy flied to center.
  M. Cross lined a single to left.
3 Schreckengost flied to center.

6th Inning
New York
  For Philadelphia—Powers catching.
  Mathewson singled to center.
1 Bresnahan fouled to Powers.
2,3 Browne flied to Seybold who threw to Davis doubling Mathewson.
Philadelphia
1 Coakley rolled out, Bresnahan to McGann.
2 Hartsel struck out.
3 Lord grounded to third.

7th Inning
New York
1 Donlin grounded to second.
  McGann beat out a roller to third.
2 McGann out trying to steal, Powers to M. Cross.
  Mertes walked.
3 Mertes out trying to steal, Powers to Murphy.
Philadelphia
  Davis singled to left.
1,2 L. Cross fouled to Bresnahan making a fantastic catch and threw to Dahlen doubling Davis trying to advance after the catch.
  Seybold singled to center.
3 Murphy grounded to first.

8th Inning
New York
1 Dahlen flied to center.
2 Devlin popped to short.
3 Gilbert struck out.
Philadelphia
1 M. Cross struck out.
2 Powers grounded to third.
  Coakley hit by a pitch.
3 Hartsel grounded back to the mound.

9th Inning
New York
1 Mathewson grounded to second.
2 Bresnahan flied to left.
  Browne singled to right.
  Browne stole second.
  Donlin walked.
  Browne stole third and Donlin safe at second on Murphy's error.
  McGann doubled to center, scoring Browne and Donlin.
3 McGann picked-off, Powers to M. Cross.
Philadelphia
1 Lord struck out for the third time.
2 Davis grounded to third.
  L. Cross singled to left.
3 Seybold struck out.

Game 4 October 13 at New York

Philadelphia	Pos	AB	R	H	RBI	PO	A	E
Hartsel	lf	1	0	0	0	2	0	0
Lord	cf	4	0	0	0	2	0	0
Davis	1b	4	0	1	0	8	1	0
L. Cross	3b	4	0	1	0	2	1	0
Seybold	rf	3	0	0	0	0	1	0
Murphy	2b	3	0	1	0	0	1	1
M. Cross	ss	4	0	1	0	0	0	0
Powers	c	3	0	0	0	6	0	0
a Hoffman		1	0	0	0	0	0	0
Plank	p	3	0	1	0	1	5	0
Totals		30	0	5	0	24	8	1

a Struck out for Powers in 9th.

Double—Devlin. Stolen Base—Hartsel. Sacrifice Hits—Donlin, Hartsel, McGann, Murphy. Wild Pitch—Plank. Left on Bases—Philadelphia 8, New York 7. Umpires—O'Day, Sheridan. Attendance—13,598. Time of Game—1:55.

New York	Pos	AB	R	H	RBI	PO	A	E
Bresnahan	c	2	0	1	0	5	0	0
Browne	rf	4	0	2	0	0	0	0
Donlin	cf	3	0	0	0	6	0	0
McGann	1b	3	0	0	0	10	0	0
Mertes	lf	4	1	0	0	1	0	0
Dahlen	ss	3	0	0	1	1	2	0
Devlin	3b	3	0	1	0	4	2	0
Gilbert	2b	3	0	0	1	0	2	0
McGinnity	p	3	0	0	0	0	4	0
Totals		28	1	4	1	27	10	0

Pitching	IP	H	R	ER	BB	SO
Philadelphia						
Plank (L)	8	4	1	0	2	6
New York						
McGinnity (W)	9	5	0	0	3	4

Phi. 000 000 000
N.Y. 000 100 00x

1st Inning
Philadelphia
1 Hartsel grounded to third.
2 Lord grounded to the mound.
   Davis singled to center.
3 L. Cross fouled to Devlin.
New York
   Bresnahan walked.
1 Browne struck out, bunting foul on the third strike.
2 Donlin sacrificed Bresnahan to second, Plank to Davis. Bresnahan went to third on a wild pitch.
3 McGann called out on strikes.

2nd Inning
Philadelphia
   Seybold walked.
1 Murphy sacrificed Seybold to second, McGinnity to McGann.
2 M. Cross struck out.
3 Powers grounded to short.
New York
1 Mertes struck out.
2 Dahlen grounded to third.
   Devlin doubled to left.
3 Gilbert popped to third.

3rd Inning
Philadelphia
   Plank singled through short.
1 Hartsel sacrificed Plank to second, Devlin to McGann.
2 Lord grounded to second, Plank going to third.
3 Davis flied to center.
New York
1 McGinnity lined to Seybold, making a beautiful catch. Bresnahan singled past short. Browne singled to left, Bresnahan going to second.
2 Donlin popped to first.
3 McGann flied to center.

4th Inning
Philadelphia
1 L. Cross flied to center.
2 Seybold lined to center. Murphy singled to center. M. Cross beat out a bunt, Murphy going to second.
3 Powers flied to center.
New York
   Mertes safe on M. Cross' fumble.
1 Dahlen flied to right.
2 Bender flied out to the mound, Mertes going to second. Gilbert singled to left, Mertes scoring. Gilbert took second on the throw to the plate.
3 McGinnity flied to center.

5th Inning
Philadelphia
1 Plank fouled to Devlin. Hartsel walked.
2 Lord fouled to Bresnahan. Hartsel stole second.
3 Davis flied to center.
New York
1 Bresnahan flied to left.
2 Browne flied to left.
3 Donlin grounded to first.

6th Inning
Philadelphia
1 Lave Cross bounced back to the mound.
2 Seybold grounded to short.
3 Murphy grounded to second.
New York
1 McGann struck out.
2 Mertes struck out.
3 Dahlen grounded out, Davis to Plank.

7th Inning
Philadelphia
1 M. Cross lined to short.
2 Powers popper to third.
3 Plank rolled back to the mound.
New York
1 Devlin called out on strikes.
2 Gilbert rolled to second.
3 McGinnity flied to right.

8th Inning
Philadelphia
   Hartsel walked.
1 Lord flied to center.
2 Davis fouled to Devlin. L. Cross singled to center, Hartsel going to third.
3 Seybold struck out.
New York
   Bresnahan walked. Browne beat out an infield hit, Bresnahan to second.
1 Donlin forced Bresnahan at third on a bunt, Plank to L. Cross.
2 McGann sacrificed Browne to third and Dohlin to second, Plank to Davis.
3 Mertes grounded back to the mound.

9th Inning
Philadelphia
1 Murphy flied to deep left, at the bleachers.
2 M. Cross struck out.
3 Hoffman, pinch-hitting for Powers, struck out.

Game 5 October 14 at New York

Philadelphia	Pos	AB	R	H	RBI	PO	A	E
Hartsel	lf	4	0	2	0	4	1	0
Lord	cf	4	0	0	0	3	0	0
Davis	1b	4	0	1	0	10	0	0
L. Cross	3b	4	0	0	0	1	2	0
Seybold	rf	3	0	1	0	0	0	0
Murphy	2b	3	0	0	0	0	1	0
M. Cross	ss	3	0	1	0	5	2	0
Powers	c	3	0	1	0	4	0	0
Bender	p	3	0	0	0	0	4	0
Totals		31	0	6	0	24	13	0

Doubles—Bresnahan, Powers. Sacrifice Hits—Devlin, Mathewson. Double Play—Dahlen to McGann. Left on Bases—Philadelphia 4, New York 4. Umpires—Sheridan, O'Day. Attendance—24,187. Time of Game—1:35.

New York	Pos	AB	R	H	RBI	PO	A	E
Bresnahan	c	4	0	2	0	5	2	0
Browne	rf	4	0	1	1	0	0	0
Donlin	cf	4	0	0	0	1	0	0
McGann	1b	3	0	0	0	12	1	0
Mertes	lf	2	1	1	0	1	0	0
Dahlen	ss	2	0	0	0	3	5	0
Devlin	3b	2	0	0	0	1	3	0
Gilbert	2b	3	0	1	1	3	5	0
Mathewson	p	1	1	0	0	1	3	2
Totals		25	2	5	2	27	19	2

Pitching	IP	H	R	ER	BB	SO
Philadelphia						
Bender (L)	8	5	2	2	3	4
New York						
Mathewson (W)	9	6	0	0	0	4

Phi. 000 000 000
N.Y. 000 010 01x

1st Inning
Philadelphia
   Hartsel lined a single past short.
1 Lord popped a bunt to Bresnahan in front of the plate.
2 Davis forced Hartsel at second, Dahlen to Gilbert.
3 L. Cross grounded to second.
New York
1 Bresnahan grounded to short.
2 Browne grounded to short.
3 Donlin hit back to the mound.

2nd Inning
Philadelphia
   Seybold singled to left.
1,2 Murphy hit into a double play, Dahlen to McGann. M. Cross beat out a high bouncer to third.
3 M. Cross out trying to steal second, Bresnahan to Gilbert.
New York
1 McGann called out on strikes. Mertes singled to left.
2 Mertes caught trying to steal second, Powers to M. Cross.
3 Dahlen struck out.

3rd Inning
Philadelphia
   Powers safe on Mathewson's fumble.
1 Bender forced Powers at second, Mathewson to Dahlen.
2 Hartsel forced Bender at second, Devlin to Gilbert.
3 Lord struck out.
New York
1 Devlin fouled to Powers. Gilbert singled over short.
2 Mathewson sacrificed Gilbert to second, L. Cross to Davis.
3 Bresnahan flied to deep left.

4th Inning
Philadelphia
1 Davis grounded to second.
2 L. Cross struck out.
3 Seybold lined to center.
New York
1 Browne flied to short left.
2 Donlin bounced to the mound.
3 McGann bounced to the mound.

5th Inning
Philadelphia
1 Murphy grounded to short.
2 M. Cross popped to first. Powers doubled into the left field crowd.
3 Bender hit into a fielder's choice Powers run-down, Devlin to Gilbert to Devlin.
New York
   Mertes walked. Dahlen walked.
1 Devlin sacrificed, L. Cross to Davis.
2,3 Gilbert flied to left, Mertes scoring. Dahlen out trying for third, Hartsel to Powers to L. Cross.

6th Inning
Philadelphia
   Hartsel safe on Mathewson's fumble.
1 Lord forced Hartsel at second, Gilbert to Dahlen.
2 Lord picked off first, Bresnahan to McGann. Davis singled to left.
3 L. Cross grounded to third.
New York
1 Mathewson flied to center. Bresnahan beat out a bunt. Browne also beat out a bunt, Bresnahan going to second.
2 Donlin flied to center.
3 McGann struck out.

7th Inning
Philadelphia
1 Seybold struck out.
2 Murphy grounded to second.
3 M. Cross grounded to short.
New York
1 Mertes rolled back to the mound.
2 Dahlen grounded to short.
3 Devlin flied to deep left.

8th Inning
Philadelphia
1 Powers flied to left.
2 Bender struck out.
3 Hartsel grounded out, McGann to Mathewson.
New York
1 Gilbert lined to center. Mathewson walked. Bresnahan doubled into the crowd in left, Mathewson going to third.
2 Browne grounded to second, scoring Mathewson with Bresnahan going to third.
3 Donlin struck out.

9th Inning
Philadelphia
1 Lord grounded to Mathewson.
2 Davis grounded to Mathewson.
3 L. Cross grounded to short.
   Mathewson completing his third shutout of the Series. Each game of the Series ended in a shut out.

1905 WORLD SERIES COMPOSITE BOX

	Wins	Composite Line Score			Manager	W	L	Pct.	Regular Season G. Ahead
New York Giants (N.L.)	4	2 0 0 1 8 0 0 0 1 3 – 15			John McGraw	105	48	.686	9
Philadelphia Athletics (A.L.)	1	0 0 1 0 0 0 0 2 0 – 3			Connie Mack	92	56	.622	2

BATTING AND FIELDING

NEW YORK GIANTS

	Pos	G	AB	R	H	2B	3B	HR	RBI	BB	SO	SB	BA	SA	PO	A	E
Dan McGann	1b	5	17	1	4	2	0	0	4	2	7	0	.235	.353	58	1	1
Billy Gilbert	2b	5	17	1	4	0	0	0	0	0	1	0	.235	.235	10	15	0
Bill Dahlen	ss	5	15	1	0	0	0	0	1	3	2	1	.000	.000	10	18	0
Art Devlin	3b	5	16	0	4	1	0	0	1	3	3	3	.250	.313	7	15	2
George Browne	rf	5	22	2	4	0	0	0	1	1	3	3	.182	.182	3	0	0
Mike Donlin	cf	5	19	4	5	1	0	0	1	2	2	2	.263	.316	16	0	1
Sam Mertes	lf	5	17	3	3	1	0	0	2	2	5	0	.176	.235	3	1	0
Roger Bresnahan	c	5	16	3	5	2	0	0	1	4	0	1	.313	.438	27	8	0
Sammy Strang	ph	1	1	0	0	0	0	0	0	0	0	0	.000	.000			
Frank Bowerman		Did not play									1	0	.000	.000			
Boileryard Clarke		Did not play															
Christy Mathewson	p	3	8	1	2	0	0	0	0	1	1	0	.250	.250	1	9	2
Joe McGinnity	p	2	5	0	0	0	0	0	0	0	2	0	.000	.000	0	6	0
Red Ames	p	1	0	0	0	0	0	0	0	0	0	0	—	—	0	1	0
Hooks Wiltse		Did not play															
Dummy Taylor		Did not play															
Claude Elliott		Did not play															
team total		5	153	15	31	7	0	0	13	15	26	12	.203	.248	135	74	6

Double Plays—3
Left on Bases—32

Main Pos	G	AB	R	H	2B	3B	HR	RBI	BB	SO	SB	BA	SA
1b	136	491	88	147	23	14	5	75	55		22	.299	.434
2b	115	376	45	93	11	3	0	24	41		11	.247	.293
ss	148	520	67	126	20	4	7	81	62		37	.242	.337
3b	153	525	74	129	14	7	2	61	66		59	.246	.310
of	127	536	95	157	16	14	4	43	20		26	.293	.397
of	150	606	124	216	31	16	7	80	56		33	.356	.495
of	150	551	81	154	27	17	5	108	56		52	.279	.417
c	104	331	58	100	18	3	0	46	50		11	.302	.375
2b-of	111	294	51	76	9	4	3	29	58		23	.259	.347
c-1b	98	297	37	80	8	1	3	41	12		6	.260	.333
1b-c	31	50	2	9	0	0	1	4	4		1	.180	.240
p	44	127	15	30	5	0	2	16	10		2	.236	.323
p	46	120	11	28	6	1	0	11	7		4	.233	.300
p	34	97	6	14	0	3	0	7	4		0	.144	.206
p	33	72	13	20	2	0	0	12	12		2	.278	.306
p	32	69	10	9	1	1	0	4	4		0	.130	.174
p	10	16	2	3	0	0	0	0	0		1	.188	.188
	155	5094	780	1392	191	88	39	642	517		291	.273	.368

Moonlight Graham (of), Bob Hall (of), Offa Neal (3b) also played for the Giants during the season.

PHILADELPHIA ATHLETICS

	Pos	G	AB	R	H	2B	3B	HR	RBI	BB	SO	SB	BA	SA	PO	A	E
Harry Davis	1b	5	20	0	4	1	0	0	0	0	1	0	.200	.250	52	1	0
Danny Murphy	2b	5	16	0	3	1	0	0	0	0	2	0	.188	.250	3	11	4
Monte Cross	ss	5	17	0	3	0	0	0	0	2	7	0	.176	.176	13	12	2
Lave Cross	3b	5	19	0	2	0	0	0	0	1	0	0	.105	.105	13	12	2
Socks Seybold	rf	5	16	0	2	0	0	0	2	1	3	0	.125	.125	4	1	0
Bris Lord	cf	5	20	0	2	0	0	0	0	5	1	0	.100	.100	12	0	0
Topsy Hartsel	lf	5	17	1	5	1	0	0	0	2	5	0	.294	.353	9	1	1
Ossee Schreckengost	c	3	9	2	2	1	0	0	2	1	2	2	.222	.333	17	4	0
Mike Powers	c	3	7	0	1	1	0	0	0	0	0	0	.143	.286	13	5	0
Danny Hoffman	ph	1	1	0	0	0	0	0	0	0	0	0	.000	.000			
Jack Knight		Did not play															
Harry Barton		Did not play															
Eddie Plank	p	2	6	0	1	0	0	0	0	0	2	0	.167	.167	1	6	0
Chief Bender	p	2	5	0	0	0	0	0	0	0	2	0	.000	.000	4	0	0
Andy Coakley	p	1	2	0	0	0	0	0	0	0	1	0	.000	.000	2	0	0
Rube Waddell		Did not play—shoulder injury															
Weldon Henley		Did not play															
Jimmy Dygert		Did not play															
team total		5	155	3	25	5	0	0	2	5	25	2	.161	.194	129	53	7

Double Plays—2
Left on Bases—26

Main Pos	G	AB	R	H	2B	3B	HR	RBI	BB	SO	SB	BA	SA
1b	149	602	92	171	47	6	8	83	43		36	.284	.422
2b	150	533	71	148	36	4	6	71	42		23	.278	.394
ss	78	248	28	67	17	2	0	24	19		8	.270	.355
3b	147	583	68	155	26	5	0	77	26		8	.266	.328
of	132	488	64	132	36	5	6	59	42		5	.270	.402
of	66	238	38	57	14	0	0	13	14		9	.239	.298
of	148	533	87	147	22	8	0	28	121		36	.276	.347
c	121	416	30	113	19	6	0	45	3		9	.272	.346
a c	40	121	8	18	0	0	0	10	3		4	.149	.149
of	119	454	64	119	10	10	1	35	33		46	.262	.335
ss	88	325	28	66	12	1	3	29	9		4	.203	.274
c	29	60	5	10	2	1	0	3	3		2	.167	.233
p	41	26	12	29	3	0	5	7			0	.230	.254
p	38	92	11	20	3	0	14	3			3	.217	.293
p	35	90	2	13	1	0	1	3			1	.144	.178
p	46	116	4	20	1	0	10	4			0	.172	.216
p	25	65	4	11	3	0	2	1			0	.169	.215
p	6	15	1	4	0	0	0	1			0	.267	.267
	152	5107	617	1300	256	51	24	511	376		189	.255	.339

a—to and from New York (A)
Joe Myers (p) also played for the Athletics during the season.

PITCHING

NEW YORK GIANTS

	G	GS	CG	IP	H	R	ER	BB	SO	W	L	SV	ERA
Christy Mathewson	3	3	3	27	14	0	0	1	18	3	0	0	0.00
Joe McGinnity	2	2	1	17	10	3	0	3	6	1	1	0	0.00
Red Ames	1	0	0	1	1	0	0	1	1	0	0	0	0.00
Dummy Taylor		Did not play											
Hooks Wiltse		Did not play											
Claude Elliott		Did not play											
team total	5	5	4	45	25	3	0	5	25	4	1	0	0.00

G	GS	CG	IP	H	ER	BB	SO	W	L	Pct.	SV	ShO	ERA
43	37	32	339	252	48	64	206	32	8	.800	2	8	1.27
46	38	26	320	289	102	71	125	22	16	.579	3	2	2.87
34	31	21	263	220	80	105	198	22	8	.733	2	2	2.74
32	28	18	213	200	63	51	91	15	9	.625	0	4	2.66
32	19	18	197	158	54	61	120	14	6	.700	5	1	2.47
10	2	2	38	41	17	12	20	0	1	.000	6	0	4.03
155	155	117	1370	1160	364	364	760	105	48	.686	15	17	2.39

PHILADELPHIA ATHLETICS

	G	GS	CG	IP	H	R	ER	BB	SO	W	L	SV	ERA
Eddie Plank	2	2	2	17	14	4	3	4	11	0	2	0	1.59
Chief Bender	2	2	2	17	9	2	2	6	13	1	1	0	1.06
Andy Coakley	1	1	1	9	8	9	2	5	2	0	1	0	2.00
Rube Waddell		Did not play—shoulder injury											
Weldon Henley		Did not play											
Jimmy Dygert		Did not play											
team total	5	5	5	43	31	15	7	15	26	1	4	0	1.47

G	GS	CG	IP	H	ER	BB	SO	W	L	Pct.	SV	ShO	ERA
41	41	35	347	287	87	75	210	25	12	.676	0	4	2.26
35	23	18	229	193	72	90	142	16	11	.593	3	4	2.83
35	31	21	255	227	52	73	145	20	7	.741	0	3	1.84
46	34	27	329	231	54	90	287	26	11	.703	4	7	1.48
25	13	184	155	53	67	82	4	12	.250	0	2	2.59	
6	3	2	35	41	17	11	24	1	3	.250	0	0	4.37
152	152	117	1383	1137	337	409	895	92	56	.622	7	20	2.19

Total Attendance—91,723   Average Attendance—18,345   Winning Player's Share—$1,142   Losing Player's Share—$832

1906
The Winningest Loser of Them All

The two contestants in this Series both came from Chicago, but they followed radically different paths into the first one-city Series. The Cubs had stacked up a record 116 victories in blasting away any opposition in the National League. A team of impeccable class and flawless balance, the Cubs had the game's top double-play combination in shortstop Joe Tinker, second baseman Johnny Evers, and first baseman-manager Frank Chance. These three have been immortalized in baseball lore, but it was unheralded third baseman Harry Steinfeldt, whose name was too unwieldy for poetry, who spearheaded the Cub attack with 83 runs batted in and a .327 average. The tight infield defense royally supported a pitching staff deeper than any in baseball. Three Finger Brown, who lost most of his index finger in a childhood accident and developed a sharp drop pitch as a result of his unorthodox grip, paced the staff with 26 wins and a microscopic 1.04 ERA. To the naked eye, the Cubs had no weaknesses.

The White Sox, on the other hand, had a glaring weakness, a .230 team-batting average that was the worst in the American League. But strong pitching and a clean defense kept the Sox in the pennant race through the summer, with a 19-game winning streak in August catapulting them into first place and earning them the title of "The Hitless Wonders." The Cubs had pitching and defense too, however, and with all their hitting power, the National League champs came into the Series as three-to-one betting favorites.

Those who had put their money on the White Sox saw their investment immediately take on a rosy color. With snow flurries blowing throughout the game, lefty Nick Altrock bested Three Finger Brown 2–1 in an opening match of four-hitters. The Sox's first run came in the fifth inning, when utility infielder George Rohe, playing only because of an injury to regular shortstop George Davis, tripled and came home on an error by Brown. The teams traded runs in the sixth inning, but the White Sox triumphed 2–1. Freezing winds bore in hard on the field the next day, making hitting an unpleasant task on the hands. The White Sox kept their hands in good shape by only troubling to notch one hit and one run off of Ed Reulbach, but the Cubs persevered to score seven runs off of Doc White and Frank Owen and even the Series at one game apiece.

With no unnecessary days off between games for traveling, the two teams met again the next day in the continuing autumn cold. Ed Walsh, the Sox's spitball expert, and Jack Pfiester locked horns in a pitchers' duel which kept home plate untarnished through five innings. But in the top of the sixth, the White Sox loaded the bases with no outs, then watched two batters go out without scoring a run. Utilityman Rohe again rose to the occasion by dropping a ball down the left-field line that went for a bases-clearing triple. No more runs would score that day, and the 3–0 win put the Sox one game up. Brown and Altrock locked up the next day in another pitchers' battle, with the Cubs coming out on top of a 1–0 score.

The cold spell let up for game five, and a capacity crowd of 23,257 spilled over onto the deep part of the outfield. With the outfielders' range cut down by the crowd, both teams unleashed the bats which had stayed silent through most of the coldness of the last four days. The Cubs reached Ed Walsh for six runs, a not unexpected outburst by the Bruin attack, but the "Hitless Wonders" opened the eyes of the crowd by shelling three Cub pitchers for eight runs. On Sunday, a healthy contingent of gate-crashers pushed the total attendance into the area of 25,000 for game six. Cub manager Chance sent Brown back to the mound on one day's rest, but the ace pitcher's arm evidently still felt the strain of his two earlier Series appearances. The Sox hit him for three runs in the bottom of the first and then shelled him from the box in the midst of a four-run second inning. Those two innings sealed the game, which ended 8–3, as the White Sox thoroughly savored their World Series triumph over the winningest team in history.

Game 1 October 9 at West Side Park

White Sox	Pos	AB	R	H	RBI	PO	A	E
Hahn	rf	3	0	0	0	1	0	0
Jones	cf	4	1	1	0	3	0	0
Isbell	2b	4	0	1	0	1	1	1
Rohe	3b	4	1	1	0	1	4	0
Donahue	1b	4	0	0	0	12	2	0
Dougherty	lf	3	0	0	0	1	0	0
Sullivan	c	3	0	0	0	5	2	0
Tannehill	ss	3	0	0	0	1	2	0
Altrock	p	2	0	1	0	3	3	0
Totals		30	2	4	1	27	14	1

Pitching	IP	H	R	ER	BB	SO
White Sox						
Altrock (W)	9	4	1	1	1	3
Cubs						
Brown (L)	9	4	2	1	1	7

Sox		000	011	000					
Cubs		000	001	000					

Chicago Cubs	Pos	AB	R	H	RBI	PO	A	E
Hofman	cf	3	0	0	0	1	1	0
Sheckard	lf	3	0	0	0	1	0	0
a Moran		1	0	0	0	0	0	0
Schulte	rf	4	0	1	0	1	0	0
Chance	1b	4	0	1	0	13	0	0
Steinfeldt	3b	4	0	0	0	0	2	0
Tinker	ss	3	0	0	0	1	3	0
Evers	2b	3	0	0	0	1	3	0
Kling	c	3	0	0	0	2	3	0
Brown	p	2	0	1	0	0	6	1
Totals		29	1	4	0	27	16	2

a Flied out for Sheckard in 9th.

Triple—Rohe. Stolen Bases—Dougherty, Isbell. Sacrifice Hits—Brown, Hahn, Hofman. Passed Balls—Kling 2. Wild Pitches—Altrock, Brown. Left on Bases—White Sox 3, Cubs 4. Umpires—Johnstone (N), O'Loughlin (A). Attendance—12,693. Time of Game—1:45.

1st Inning
White Sox
1 Hahn struck out.
2 Jones flied to center.
3 Isbell struck out.
Cubs
1 Hofman grounded to third.
2 Sheckard grounded out, Donahue to Altrock.
3 Schulte grounded to third.

2nd Inning
White Sox
1 Rohe bounced back to the mound.
2 Donahue struck out.
3 Dougherty grounded to first.
Cubs
1 Chance grounded to first.
2 Steinfeldt tagged out by Altrock on a roller near the first base line.
3 Tinker flied to right.

3rd Inning
White Sox
1 Sullivan grounded to second.
2 Tannehill struck out.
3 Altrock struck out.
Cubs
1 Evers grounded to the mound.
2 Kling grounded to third.
3 Brown struck out.

4th Inning
White Sox
1 Hahn grounded to second.
2 Jones grounded back to the mound.
3 Isbell popped to first.
Cubs
1 Hofman struck out.
2 Sheckard grounded out, Donahue to Altrock.
  Schulte beat out a high bounder to second for the first hit of the game. Schulte safe at second when Isbell dropped Sullivan's throw on a stolen base attempt.
3 Chance grounded back to the mound.

5th Inning
White Sox
  Rohe tripled to deep left.
1 Donahue struck out.
  Dougherty hit back to Brown who threw to the plate but Kling dropped the ball allowing Rohe to score, Dougherty went to second on a passed ball.
2 Sullivan grounded to short.
3 Tannehill grounded to short.
Cubs
1 Steinfeldt grounded to short.
2 Tinker fouled to Sullivan.
3 Evers struck out.

6th Inning
White Sox
  Altrock walked.
1 Hahn sacrificed Altrock to second, Steinfeldt to Chance.
  Jones singled to right-center and
2 Altrock was out at the plate, Hofman to Kling, as Jones took second. Jones went to third on a passed ball.
  Isbell singled to left, scoring Jones. Isbell stole second.
3 Rohe bounced out to the mound.
Cubs
  Kling walked.
  Brown singled on a bouncer over the mound, Kling going to second.
1 Hofman sacrificed up both runners, Altrock to Donahue.
  Kling scored and Brown went to third on a wild pitch.
2 Sheckard popped to third.
3 Schulte struck out short, Donohue, making a great catch of Tannehill's wild throw.

7th Inning
White Sox
  Donahue safe on Brown's error. Donahue went to second on a wild pitch.
1 Dougherty grounded to Brown and Donahue was out in a run-down, Brown to Steinfeldt to Tinker. Dougherty stole second.
2 Sullivan flied to left.
3 Tannehill grounded to short.
Cubs
1 Chance lined to left.
2 Steinfeldt lined to short.
3 Tinker fouled to Sullivan.

8th Inning
White Sox
  Altrock singled past third.
1 Hahn bunted and forced Altrock at second, Brown to Tinker.
2 Hahn caught stealing, Kling to Evers.
3 Jones grounded to first.
Cubs
1 Evers grounded to second. Kling singled to center.
2 Brown sacrificed Kling to second, Sullivan to Donahue.
3 Hofman flied to center.

9th Inning
White Sox
1 Isbell grounded to second.
2 Rohe flied to right.
3 Donahue struck out for the third time.
Cubs
1 Moran, batting for Sheckard, flied to center.
2 Schulte grounded to third. Chance singled to center.
3 Steinfeldt flied to center.

Game 2 October 10 at South Side Park

| | | | Cubs | 031 | 001 | 020 | |
| | | | Sox | 000 | 010 | 000 | |

Chicago Cubs	Pos	AB	R	H	RBI	PO	A	E
Hofman	cf	4	0	1	1	2	0	0
Sheckard	lf	4	0	0	0	3	1	0
Schulte	rf	4	0	1	0	1	0	0
Chance	1b	5	2	1	0	12	0	0
Steinfeldt	3b	3	1	3	1	0	2	0
Tinker	ss	3	3	2	1	0	3	1
Evers	2b	4	1	1	0	4	6	1
Kling	c	2	0	1	0	5	1	0
Reulbach	p	3	0	0	1	0	2	0
Totals		32	7	10	4	27	15	2

Pitching	IP	H	R	ER	BB	SO
Cubs						
Reulbach (W)	9	1	1	0	6	3
White Sox						
White (L)	3	4	4	0	2	1
Owen	6	6	3	2	3	2

White Sox	Pos	AB	R	H	RBI	PO	A	E
Hahn	rf	3	0	0	0	0	0	0
Jones	cf	3	0	0	0	1	0	0
Isbell	2b	4	0	0	0	6	2	1
Rohe	3b	2	0	0	0	0	3	0
Donahue	1b	3	0	1	0	12	1	0
Dougherty	lf	2	1	0	0	1	0	0
Sullivan	c	4	0	0	0	7	2	2
Tannehill	ss	3	0	0	0	0	1	0
White	p	0	0	0	0	0	1	0
a Towne		1	0	0	0	0	0	0
Owen	p	2	0	0	0	0	4	0
Totals		27	1	1	0	27	15	3

a Flied out for White in 3rd.

Double—Kling. Stolen Bases—Chance 2, Evers, Hofman, Tinker 2 Sacrifice Hits—Reulbach, Sheckard, Steinfeldt. Double Plays—Sheckard to Kling, Evers to Chance. Hit by Pitcher—Rohe (by Reulbach). Wild Pitches—Owen, Reulbach. Left on Bases—Cubs 6, White Sox 6. Umpires—O'Loughlin, Johnstone. Attendance—12,595. Time of Game—1:58.

1st Inning
Cubs
1 Hofman flied to center.
2 Sheckard grounded to first.
3 Schulte grounded to third.
White Sox
1 Hahn grounded to third.
2 Jones grounded to short.
3 Isbell grounded to the mound.

2nd Inning
Cubs
1 Chance struck out.
Steinfeldt singled to left.
Tinker beat out a bunt to third.
Evers safe as Isbell threw wide to Tannehill for the force on Tinker, Steinfeldt scoring as Tinker got to third and Evers to second.
Kling intentionally walked, loading the bases.
2 Reulbach laid down a beautiful bunt, scoring Tinker and advancing Evers and Kling, Reulbach out, Isbell to Donahue.
Hofman beat out an infield hit to short,
3 scoring Evers but Kling was out trying to also score, Donahue to Sullivan.
White Sox
1 Rohe bounced back to the mound.
2 Donahue grounded to second.
Dougherty walked.
3 Sullivan flied to left.

3rd Inning
Cubs
1 Sheckard bounced to the pitcher.
Schulte walked.
2 Chance forced Schulte, Tannehill to Isbell.
Chance stole second and went to third on Sullivan's bad throw.
Steinfeldt singled past third, scoring Chance.
3 Steinfeldt caught stealing, Sullivan to Isbell.
White Sox
1 Tannehill grounded to second.
2 Towne, batting for White, flied to center.
3 Hahn grounded to short.

4th Inning
Cubs
For the White Sox—Owen pitching.
Tinker walked.
1 Evers popped to second.
Kling doubled to right-center off Hahn's glove, Tinker going to third.
2 Reulbach struck out.
3 Hofman lined to left.
White Sox
Jones safely to second when Evers kicked his grounder into the right field crowd for an error.
1 Isbell grounded to second, Jones going to third.
2,3 Rohe flied to Sheckard who threw to Kling, doubling Jones trying to score.

5th Inning
Cubs
1 Sheckard popped to second.
2 Schulte fouled to Sullivan.
3 Chance grounded to short.
White Sox
Donahue walked.
1 Dougherty forced Donahue, Steinfeldt to Evers.
Dougherty went to second on a wild pitch.
2 Sullivan fouled to Kling.
Tannehill safe on Tinker's fumble, Dougherty scoring.
3 Owen flied to left.

6th Inning
Cubs
Steinfeldt singled to left.
1 Tinker forced Steinfeldt at second, Owen to Isbell.
Evers singled to left, Tinker advancing to second.
Tinker stole third while Evers stole second and when Sullivan's throw went into the crowd behind third Tinker scored and Evers went to third
2 Kling struck out.
3 Reulbach grounded to third.
White Sox
Hahn walked.
1 Hahn out trying to steal second, Kling to Tinker.
2 Jones struck out.
3 Isbell grounded to second.

7th Inning
Cubs
1 Hofman grounded to the mound.
2 Sheckard fouled to Sullivan.
Schulte singled to right.
3 Schulte caught trying to steal, Sullivan to Isbell.
White Sox
Rohe walked.
Donahue singled to center, Rohe going to second. **The first hit allowed by Reulbach.**
1 Dougherty flied to right.
2 Sullivan struck out.
3 Tannehill forced Donahue at second, Tinker to Evers.

8th Inning
Cubs
Chance beat out an infield single to short.
1 Steinfeldt sacrificed Chance to second, Donahue unassisted.
Chance stole third.
Tinker singled to center, scoring Chance.
Tinker stole second.
2 Evers grounded to third, Tinker going to third.
Kling walked, the fourth ball being a wild pitch with Tinker scoring and Kling getting to second.
3 Reulbach grounded to the pitcher.
White Sox
1 Owen struck out.
2 Hahn grounded to second.
Jones walked.
3 Isbell grounded to first.

9th Inning
Cubs
Hofman walked.
1 Sheckard sacrificed Hofman to second, Owen to Donahue.
Hofman stole third.
2 Schulte grounded to second, Hofman holding at third.
3 Chance fouled to Sullivan.
White Sox
Rohe hit by a pitch.
1,2 Donahue grounded into a double play, Evers to Chance.
Dougherty walked.
3 Sullivan flied to center.

Game 3 October 11 at West Side Park

| | | | Sox | 000 | 003 | 000 | |
| | | | Cubs | 000 | 000 | 000 | |

White Sox	Pos	AB	R	H	RBI	PO	A	E
Hahn	rf	2	0	0	0	0	0	0
a O'Neill	rf	1	1	0	0	1	0	0
Jones	cf	4	0	0	0	1	0	0
Isbell	2b	4	0	0	0	4	1	0
Rohe	3b	3	0	1	3	0	1	0
Donahue	1b	3	0	2	0	13	0	0
Dougherty	lf	4	0	0	0	0	0	0
Sullivan	c	3	0	0	0	11	2	0
Tannehill	ss	3	1	1	0	0	4	0
Walsh	p	2	1	0	0	0	3	0
Totals		29	3	4	3	27	14	1

a Ran for Hahn in 6th.
b Safe on error for Pfiester in 9th.

Double—Schulte. Triples—Donahue, Rohe. Stole Base—Rohe. Sacrifice Hits—Donahue, Sullivan. Hit by Pitch—Hahn (by Pfiester). Wild Pitch—Walsh. Left on Bases—White Sox 4, Cubs 3. Umpires—Johnstone, O'Loughlin. Attendance—13,667. Time of Game—2:10.

Chicago Cubs	Pos	AB	R	H	RBI	PO	A	E
Hofman	cf	4	0	1	0	1	0	0
Sheckard	lf	4	0	0	0	1	0	0
Schulte	rf	4	0	1	0	1	0	0
Chance	1b	3	0	0	0	7	1	0
Steinfeldt	3b	3	0	0	0	1	2	0
Tinker	ss	3	0	0	0	2	2	1
Evers	2b	3	0	0	0	2	2	1
Kling	c	3	0	0	0	11	2	0
Pfiester	p	2	0	0	0	0	2	1
b Gessler		1	0	0	0	0	0	0
Totals		29	0	2	0	27	11	2

Pitching	IP	H	R	ER	BB	SO
White Sox						
Walsh (W)	9	2	0	0	1	12
Cubs						
Pfiester (L)	9	4	3	3	2	9

1st Inning
White Sox
1 Hahn grounded to third.
Jones beat out a hit off Pfiester's hand.
2 Isbell struck out.
3 Jones out stealing, Kling to Tinker.
Cubs
Hofman singled to center.
1 Sheckard struck out.
2 Hofman out trying to steal second, Sullivan to Isbell.
Schulte doubled to the bleachers in left.
3 Chance grounded to second.

2nd Inning
White Sox
1 Rohe grounded to short.
Donahue safe on Pfiester's fumble.
2 Dougherty struck out.
3 Donahue caught stealing, Kling to Tinker.
Cubs
1 Steinfeldt grounded to short.
2 Tinker struck out.
3 Evers flied to center.

3rd Inning
White Sox
1 Sullivan struck out.
2 Tannehill struck out.
3 Walsh flied to center.
Cubs
1 Kling struck out.
2 Pfiester struck out.
3 Hofman grounded to short.

4th Inning
White Sox
1 Hahn popped to Evers, making a great catch behind first.
2 Jones struck out.
3 Isbell struck out.
Cubs
1 Sheckard grounded to short.
2 Schulte struck out.
Chance walked.
3 Steinfeldt grounded to short.

5th Inning
White Sox
1 Rohe grounded to second.
Donahue tripled to right.
2 Dougherty fouled to Kling.
3 Sullivan struck out.
Cubs
1 Tinker grounded to second.
2 Evers struck out but had to be thrown out, Sullivan to Donahue.
3 Kling grounded to second.

6th Inning
White Sox
Tannehill singled past third.
Walsh walked.
Hahn hit by a pitch, loading the bases.
O'Neill ran for Hahn.
1 Jones fouled to Kling.
2 Isbell struck out.
Rohe tripled to left, clearing the bases.
3 Donahue popped to second.
Cubs
For the White Sox—O'Neill playing right field.
1 Pfiester grounded to the mound.
2 Hofman called out on strikes.
3 Sheckard flied to right.

7th Inning
White Sox
Dougherty safe on Tinker's error.
1 Sullivan sacrificed Dougherty to second, Pfiester to Chance.
2 Tannehill flied to right, Dougherty going to third after the catch.
3 Walsh struck out.
Cubs
1 Schulte struck out.
2 Chance bounced back to Walsh.
3 Steinfeldt grounded to third.

8th Inning
White Sox
1 Hahn popped to third.
2 Jones flied to left.
3 Isbell grounded to second.
Cubs
1 Tinker struck out.
2 Evers struck out.
3 Kling hit back to Walsh.

9th Inning
White Sox
Rohe walked.
Rohe stole second.
1 Donahue sacrificed Rohe to third, Pfiester to Chance.
2 Dougherty hit into a fielder's choice Donahue being run-down, Chance to Steinfeldt to Tinker to Steinfeldt to Chance.
3 Sullivan flied to left.
Cubs
Gessler, batting for Pfiester, safe on Isbell's fumble.
1 Hofman grounded to second, Gessler going to second.
Gessler advanced to third on a passed ball.
2 Sheckard struck out.
3 Schulte struck out.

Game 4 October 12 at South Side Park

Chicago Cubs	Pos	AB	R	H	RBI	PO	A	E
Hofman	cf	4	0	2	0	1	0	0
Sheckard	lf	3	0	0	0	1	0	0
Schulte	rf	4	0	0	0	1	0	0
Chance	1b	4	1	2	0	12	1	0
Steinfeldt	3b	2	0	1	0	1	1	1
Tinker	ss	3	0	0	0	2	3	0
Evers	2b	3	0	1	1	2	4	0
Kling	c	3	0	0	0	6	3	0
Brown	p	3	0	1	0	1	4	0
Totals		27	1	7	1	27	16	1

Pitching	IP	H	R	ER	BB	SO
Cubs						
Brown (W)	9	2	0	0	2	5
White Sox						
Altrock (L)	9	7	1	1	1	2

Cubs	000	000	100
Sox	000	000	000

White Sox	Pos	AB	R	H	RBI	PO	A	E
Hahn	rf	4	0	1	0	1	0	0
Jones	cf	4	0	0	0	0	0	0
Isbell	2b	4	0	0	0	1	3	0
Rohe	3b	3	0	0	0	0	3	0
Donahue	1b	1	0	0	0	13	3	0
Dougherty	lf	3	0	1	0	2	0	0
Davis	ss	3	0	0	0	4	3	1
Sullivan	c	3	0	0	0	3	1	0
Altrock	p	2	0	0	0	3	8	0
a McFarland		1	0	0	0	0	0	0
Totals		27	0	2	0	27	21	1

a Grounded out for Altrock in 9th.

Double—Hofman. Stolen Base—Sheckard. Sacrifice Hits—Donahue, Steinfeldt 2, Tinker 3. Double Plays—Kling to Evers, Altrock to Donahue to Sullivan. Passed Ball—Kling. Left on Bases—Cubs 5, White Sox 3. Umpires—O'Loughlin, Johnstone. Attendance—18,385. Time of Game—1:36.

1st Inning
Cubs
Hofman grounded to third.
Sheckard walked.
2 Schulte flied to left.
Sheckard stole second when no one covered second after a perfect pick off play, Sullivan to Donahue.
3 Chance grounded to Rohe and Sheckard was caught in a run-down, Rohe to Davis to Altrock.
White Sox
1 Hahn grounded to short.
2 Jones popped to Kling.
3 Isbell grounded out Kling to Chance

2nd Inning
Cubs
Steinfeldt singled to center.
1 Tinker sacrificed Steinfeldt to second, Altrock to Donahue.
2 Evers grounded to short, Steinfeldt going to third.
3 Kling hit a wide pitch of an intentional pass to Hahn in deep right. Hahn made a fantastic catch bending into the crowd.
White Sox
1 Rohe grounded to short.
Donahue walked.
2 Donahue out trying to steal, Kling to Evers.
3 Dougherty struck out.

3rd Inning
Cubs
1 Brown strike out.
2 Hofman grounded to second.
3 Sheckard grounded to third.
White Sox
1 Davis grounded to second.
2 Sullivan struck out.
3 Altrock grounded out, Chance to Brown.

4th Inning
Cubs
Schulte safe on Davis' fumble.
1 Chance popped to the pitcher.
2 Schulte picked off, Altrock to Donahue to Isbell to Donahue.
3 Steinfeldt flied to left.
White Sox
1 Hahn flied to center.
2 Jones grounded to short.
3 Isbell grounded to second.

5th Inning
Cubs
1 Tinker grounded out, Donahue to Altrock.
2 Evers grounded back to the mound.
3 Kling popped to short.
White Sox
Rohe safe on Steinfeldt's poor throw to first.
1 Donahue sacrificed Rohe to second, Brown to Chance.
2 Dougherty grounded to second, Rohe going to third.
3 Davis struck out.

6th Inning
Cubs
1 Brown struck out.
Hofman singled to center.
2 Sheckard forced Hofman at second, Altrock to Davis.
3 Schulte popped to short.
White Sox
1 Sullivan flied to left.
2 Altrock grounded to second.
Hahn singled through the box. **The first hit off of Brown.**
3 Jones flied to right.

7th Inning
Cubs
Chance singled to left as Hahn lost the ball in the sun.
1 Steinfeldt sacrificed Chance to second, Altrock to Donahue.
2 Tinker sacrificed chance to third, Altrock to Donahue.
Evers singled over third, scoring Tinker.
3 Evers caught trying to steal, Sullivan to Davis.
White Sox
1 Isbell struck out.
2 Rohe popped to third.
3 Donahue grounded back to the mound.

8th Inning
Cubs
1 Kling grounded to short.
Brown singled to center.
Hofman doubled to left, Brown going to third.
2 Sheckard grounded to second.
3 Schulte popped to second.
White Sox
Dougherty singled to right.
1 Davis forced Dougherty at second, Brown to Tinker.
2,3 Sullivan struck out and Davis doubled trying for second, Kling to Evers.

9th Inning
Cubs
Chance singled.
1 Steinfeldt sacrificed Chance to second, Altrock to Donahue.
2,3 Tinker sacrificed Chance to third (his third of the game), but Chance was doubled up trying to score, Altrock to Donahue to Sullivan.
White Sox
1 McFarland, batting for Altrock, grounded to third.
2 Hahn popped to short.
Jones walked.
Jones moved up to second on a passed ball.
3 Isbell viciously grounded back to the mound.

Game 5 October 13 at West Side Park

White Sox	Pos	AB	R	H	RBI	PO	A	E
Hahn	rf	5	2	1	0	1	0	0
Jones	cf	4	1	1	0	1	0	0
Isbell	2b	5	3	4	2	2	2	2
Davis	ss	5	2	2	3	2	2	2
Rohe	3b	4	0	3	1	0	2	2
Donahue	1b	3	0	1	1	15	2	0
Dougherty	lf	5	0	0	0	0	0	0
Sullivan	c	4	0	0	0	6	2	0
Walsh	p	2	0	0	0	0	2	1
White	p	2	0	0	0	0	0	0
Totals		37	8	12	7	27	18	6

Pitching	IP	H	R	ER	BB	SO
White Sox						
Walsh (W)	**6	5	6	2	5	5
Cubs						
Reulbach	*2	5	3	3	2	1
Pfiester (L)	1⅓	3	4	4	1	2
Overall	5⅔	4	1	1	1	5

*Pitched to two batters in 3rd.
**Pitched to one batter in 7th.

Sox	102	401	000
Cubs	300	102	000

Chicago Cubs	Pos	AB	R	H	RBI	PO	A	E
Hofman	cf	3	2	1	0	2	0	0
Sheckard	lf	4	0	0	1	0	0	0
Schulte	rf	5	1	3	2	2	1	0
Chance	1b	4	0	1	0	8	0	0
Steinfeldt	3b	5	1	1	1	1	2	0
Tinker	ss	4	1	0	2	3	4	0
Evers	2b	3	0	0	0	2	4	0
a Moran		1	0	0	0	0	0	0
Kling	c	3	0	0	0	9	0	0
Reulbach	p	0	0	0	0	0	2	0
Pfiester	p	0	0	0	0	0	0	0
Overall	p	2	1	0	0	0	1	0
Totals		34	6	6	3	27	13	0

a Hit into force out for Evers in 9th.

Doubles—Chance, Davis 2, Donahue, Isbell 4, Rohe, Schulte, Steinfeldt. Stolen Bases—Davis, Dougherty, Evers, Tinker. Sacrifice Hits—Jones, Reulbach, Sheckard. Double Play—Schulte to Evers to Kling. Passed Ball—Sullivan. Hit by Pitches—Chance (by Walsh), Donahue (by Pfiester). Wild Pitch—Overall. Left on Bases—White Sox 8, Cubs 9. Umpires—Johnstone, O'Loughlin. Attendance—23,257. Time of Game—2:40.

1st Inning
White Sox
Hahn singled to center.
1 Jones sacrificed, Reulbach to Chance. Isbell doubled to right, Hahn scoring.
2 Davis hit into a fielder's choice, Isbell out, Reulbach to Steinfeldt to Tinker.
Rohe doubled to left, Davis to third.
Donahue walked, loading the bases.
3 Dougherty grounded to second.
Cubs
Hofman grounded to right.
1 Sheckard sacrificed, Donahue unassisted. Schulte beat out a bouncer to third, Hofman holding at second.
Chance hit by a pitch, loading the bases.
2 Steinfeldt forced Chance at second, Davis to Isbell but Isbell's relay to first was wild, Steinfeldt to second after Hofman and Schulte had scored on the error.
Tinker safe when Walsh threw his bunt wild to first as Schulte scored but
3 Tinker out trying for second, Walsh to Donahue to Davis.

2nd Inning
White Sox
1 Sullivan struck out.
Walsh walked.
2 Hahn popped to first.
3 Jones grounded to second.
Cubs
1 Evers bounced back to Walsh.
Kling walked.
2 Reulbach, sacrificed, Sullivan to Donahue.
3 Hofman struck out, but had to be thrown out, Sullivan to Donahue.

3rd Inning
White Sox
Isbell doubled into the crowd in left.
Davis doubled into the crowd in right, scoring Isbell.
For the Cubs—Pfiester now pitching.
1 Rohe struck out.
Donahue hit by a pitch.
2 Dougherty forced Donahue at second, Tinker to Evers, Davis going to third. Davis and Dougherty worked a perfect delayed double steal.
3 Sullivan struck out.
Cubs
1 Sheckard struck out.
Schulte safely to second when Davis threw into the crowd.
2 Chance grounded to short, Schulte going to third.
3 Steinfeldt grounded to short.

4th Inning
White Sox
Walsh again walked.
1 Hahn forced Walsh at second, Steinfeldt to Tinker.
Jones singled to left, Hahn going to second.
Isbell got his third double to right-center, scoring Hahn as Jones went to third.
Davis doubled to left, scoring Jones and Isbell.
For the Cubs—Overall came in to pitch.
Rohe walked.
Donahue doubled to left, scoring Davis as Rohe stopped at third.
2,3 Dougherty flied to Schulte who doubled Rohe at the plate to Evers to Kling.
Cubs
Tinker safe at second when Rohe threw into the crowd.
Evers walked.
1 Kling struck out.
Tinker and Evers worked a double steal.
2 Overall struck out.

4th Inning (continued)
Tinker and Evers both scored on a wild pitch.
Hoffman walked.
3 Sheckard struck out.

5th Inning
White Sox
1 Sullivan grounded to short.
2 Walsh struck out.
3 Hahn flied to right.
Cubs
1 Schulte popped to Sullivan.
Chance singled and went to second on Isbell's error.
2 Steinfeldt flied to center.
3 Tinker grounded to short.

6th Inning
White Sox
1 Jones struck out.
Isbell's fourth double of the game was to right.
2 Davis grounded to second, Isbell going to third.
Rohe singled, scoring Isbell.
Rohe went to second on a wild pitch.
3 Donahue bounced back to the mound.
Cubs
1 Evers grounded to short.
2 Kling grounded to short.
Overall singled.
Hofman walked.
Sheckard safe on Rohe's error, loading the bases.
Schulte doubled into the center field crowd, scoring Overall and Kling as Sheckard went to third.
3 Chance grounded to second.

7th Inning
White Sox
1 Dougherty flied to center.
2 Sullivan popped to second.
3 Walsh struck out.
Cubs
Steinfeldt doubled to left.
For the White Sox—White now pitching.
1 Tinker fouled to Donahue.
2 Evers grounded to short.
3 Kling grounded to third.

8th Inning
White Sox
1 Hahn flied to center.
2 Jones fouled to Steinfeldt.
3 Isbell finally out, as he struck out.
Cubs
1 Overall grounded to second.
2 Hofman struck out.
Sheckard safe on Isbell's fumble.
3 Schulte beat out a hit to deep short, Sheckard out trying for third, Donahue to Davis.

9th Inning
White Sox
1 Davis flied to left.
Rohe beat out a bunt to third.
2 Donahue grounded to short, Rohe going to second.
3 Dougherty struck out.
Cubs
1 Chance flied to right.
2 Steinfeldt grounded to third.
Tinker walked.
3 Moran, pinch-hitting for Evers, forced Tinker at second, Davis to Isbell.

Game 6 October 14 at South Side Park

Chicago Cubs	Pos	AB	R	H	RBI	PO	A	E
Hofman	cf	5	1	2	1	3	0	0
Sheckard	lf	3	0	0	1	2	0	0
Schulte	rf	5	0	1	1	0	0	0
Chance	1b	2	0	0	0	9	0	0
Steinfeldt	3b	3	0	0	0	0	0	0
Tinker	ss	4	0	1	0	2	6	0
Evers	2b	4	1	1	0	2	0	0
Kling	c	4	1	1	0	6	2	0
Brown	p	1	0	0	0	0	1	0
Overall	p	2	0	1	0	0	1	0
a Gessler		0	0	0	0	0	0	0
Totals		33	3	7	3	24	10	0

a Walked for Overall in 9th.

Doubles—Davis, Donahue, Evers, Overall, Schulte. Stolen Base—Rohe. Sacrifice Hits—Jones, Sheckard. Double Play—Davis to Donahue. Hit by Pitcher—Chance (by White). Left on Bases—Cubs 9, White Sox 9. Umpires—O'Loughlin, Johnstone. Attendance—19,249. Time of Game—1:55.

	1 2 3	4 5 6	7 8 9
Cubs	1 0 0	0 1 0	0 0 1
Sox	3 4 0	0 0 0	0 1 x

White Sox	Pos	AB	R	H	RBI	PO	A	E
Hahn	rf	5	2	4	0	0	0	0
Jones	cf	3	2	0	0	3	0	0
Isbell	2b	5	1	3	1	1	4	0
Davis	ss	5	2	2	3	1	4	0
Rohe	3b	5	1	2	0	3	4	1
Donahue	1b	4	0	2	3	15	1	1
Dougherty	lf	3	0	1	0	1	0	1
Sullivan	c	4	0	0	0	3	1	0
White	p	3	0	0	0	1	2	0
Totals		37	8	14	8	27	16	3

Pitching	IP	H	R	ER	BB	SO
Cubs						
Brown (L)	1⅓	8	6	6	1	0
Overall	6⅔	6	2	2	2	3
White Sox						
White (W)	9	7	3	3	4	2

1st Inning
Cubs
Hofman singled to left, and continued to second on Dougherty's fumble.
1 Sheckard sacrificed Hofman to third, Rohe to Donahue.
Schulte doubled into the right field crowd, scoring Hofman.
2 Chance grounded to White who threw to Rohe getting Schulte going to third.
Steinfeldt walked.
3 Tinker flied to center.
White Sox
Hahn beat out a smasher to second.
1 Jones forced Hahn at second, Kling to Tinker.
Isbell singled to right, Jones going to second.
Davis doubled to right, scoring Jones as Isbell went to third.
2 Rohe grounded to Tinker who threw to Kling getting Isbell at the plate, as Davis went to third.
Rohe stole second.
Donahue doubled to left, scoring Davis and Rohe.
3 Dougherty grounded to first.

2nd Inning
Cubs
Evers safe on Donahue's fumble.
1,2 Kling hit into a double play, Davis to Donahue.
3 Brown struck out.
White Sox
1 Sullivan grounded to short.
2 White bounced back to the mound.
Hahn singled to left.
Jones walked.
Isbell beat out a roller to second, loading the bases.
Davis lined a single over short, Hahn and Jones scoring as Isbell stopped at second.
Rohe beat out a hit to short, loading the bases again.
For the Cubs—Overall relieves Brown on the mound.
Donahue singled to second, scoring Isbell.
Dougherty walked forcing in Davis.
3 Sullivan struck out.

3rd Inning
Cubs
1 Hofman grounded out, Donahue to White.
2 Sheckard grounded to second.
3 Schulte popped to first.
White Sox
1 White bounced back to the mound.
2 Hahn flied to left.
3 Jones popped to short.

4th Inning
Cubs
Chance walked on four pitches.
1 Steinfeldt flied to center.
2 Tinker forced chance at second, Davis to Isbell.
3 Evers grounded to second.
White Sox
1 Isbell grounded to short.
2 Davis fouled to Kling.
Rohe singled to right-center.
3 Donahue flied to deep center.

5th Inning
Cubs
Kling beat out a little roller in front of the plate.
Overall doubled to right, Kling going to third.
1 Hofman struck out.
2 Sheckard grounded to second, scoring Kling as Overall went to third.
3 Schulte grounded to short.
White Sox
1 Dougherty lined to second.
2 Sullivan again struck out.
White walked.
Hahn singled to left, White going to second.
3 Jones forced Hahn at second, Tinker to Evers.

6th Inning
Cubs
Chance was hit by a pitch.
1 Steinfeldt popped to third.
Tinker singled to center, Chance going to second.
2 Evers fouled to Sullivan.
3 Chance out trying to steal third, Sullivan to Rohe.
White Sox
1 Isbell fouled to Chance.
2 Davis fouled to Kling.
3 Rohe grounded to short.

7th Inning
Cubs
1 Kling grounded to the mound.
2 Overall grounded to third.
3 Hofman grounded to second.
White Sox
1 Donahue struck out.
Dougherty beat out a bunt to third.
2 Sullivan flied to center.
3 White flied to left.

8th Inning
Cubs
Sheckard walked.
1 Schulte grounded to first, Sheckard going to second.
2 Chance grounded to short, Sheckard going to third.
3 Steinfeldt flied to Jones in deep left-center.
White Sox
Hahn singled to left, **his fourth hit of the game.**
1 Jones sacrificed Hahn to second, Kling to Chance.
Isbell singled to center, scoring Hahn and took second on the throw to the plate.
2 Davis grounded to short, Isbell going to third.
3 Rohe lined to center.

9th Inning
Cubs
1 Tinker grounded to third.
Evers doubled to right.
2 Kling grounded to third, Evers going to third.
Gessler, pinch-hitting for Overall, walked.
Hofman singled to left, scoring Evers as Gessler stopped at second.
Sheckard safe on Rohe's fumble, loading the bases.
3 Schulte grounded to first.

1906 WORLD SERIES COMPOSITE BOX

	Wins	Composite Line Score		Regular Season
Chicago White Sox (A.L.)	4	4 4 2 4 2 5 0 1 0 – 22		
Chicago Cubs (N.L.)	2	4 3 1 1 1 4 1 2 1 – 18		

Manager	W	L	Pct.	G. Ahead
Fielder Jones	93	58	.616	3
Frank Chance	116	36	.763	20

BATTING AND FIELDING

WORLD SERIES STATISTICS

CHICAGO WHITE SOX	Pos	G	AB	R	H	2B	3B	HR	RBI	BB	SO	SB	BA	SA	PO	A	E
Jiggs Donahue	1b	6	18	0	6	2	1	0	4	3	3	0	.333	.556	80	9	1
Frank Isbell	2b	6	26	4	8	4	0	0	4	0	6	1	.308	.462	11	16	5
George Davis	ss	3	13	4	4	3	0	0	6	0	1	1	.308	.538	7	15	2
George Rohe	3b	6	21	2	7	1	2	0	4	3	1	2	.333	.571	4	17	3
Eddie Hahn	rf	6	22	4	6	0	0	0	0	1	1	0	.273	.273	3	0	0
Fielder Jones	cf	6	21	4	2	0	0	0	0	3	3	0	.095	.095	9	0	0
Patsy Dougherty	lf	6	20	1	2	0	0	0	1	3	4	2	.100	.100	4	0	1
Billy Sullivan	c	6	21	0	0	0	0	0	0	0	9	0	.000	.000	35	10	2
Lee Tannehill	ss	3	9	1	1	0	0	0	0	0	2	0	.111	.111	1	8	0
Bill O'Neill	rf	1	1	1	0	0	0	0	0	0	0	0	.000	.000	1	0	0
Babe Towne	ph	1	1	0	0	0	0	0	0	0	0	0	.000	.000			
Ed McFarland	ph	1	1	0	0	0	0	0	0	0	0	0	.000	.000			
Gus Dundon		Did not play															
Hub Hart		Did not play															
Nick Altrock	p	2	4	0	1	0	0	0	0	1	1	0	.250	.250	6	11	0
Ed Walsh	p	2	4	1	0	0	0	0	0	3	3	0	.000	.000	0	5	1
Doc White	p	3	3	0	0	0	0	0	0	1	0	0	.000	.000	1	3	0
Frank Owen	p	1	2	0	0	0	0	0	0	0	1	0	.000	.000	0	4	0
Roy Patterson		Did not play															
Frank Smith		Did not play															
Lou Fiene		Did not play															
team total		6	187	22	37	10	3	0	19	18	35	6	.198	.283	162	98	15

Double Plays—2
Left on Bases—33

CHICAGO CUBS	Pos	G	AB	R	H	2B	3B	HR	RBI	BB	SO	SB	BA	SA	PO	A	E
Frank Chance	1b	6	21	3	5	1	0	0	0	2	1	2	.238	.286	61	2	0
Johnny Evers	2b	6	20	2	3	1	0	0	1	1	3	2	.150	.200	13	19	1
Joe Tinker	ss	6	18	4	3	0	0	0	0	2	2	3	.167	.167	10	20	1
Harry Steinfeldt	3b	6	20	2	5	1	0	0	2	1	0	0	.250	.300	3	9	1
Wildfire Schulte	rf	6	26	1	7	3	0	0	3	1	3	0	.269	.385	6	1	0
Solly Hofman	cf	6	23	3	7	1	0	0	2	3	5	1	.304	.348	10	1	0
Jimmy Sheckard	lf	6	21	0	0	0	0	0	1	2	4	1	.000	.000	10	1	0
Johnny Kling	c	6	17	2	3	1	0	0	0	4	3	0	.176	.235	45	9	1
Pat Moran	ph	2	2	0	0	0	0	0	0	0	0	0	.000	.000			
Doc Gessler	ph	2	2	0	0	0	0	0	0	1	0	0	.000	.000			
Jimmy Slagle		Did not play															
Tom Walsh		Did not play															
Three Finger Brown	p	3	6	0	2	0	0	0	0	0	4	0	.333	.333	1	11	1
Orvie Overall	p	2	4	1	1	1	0	0	0	1	1	0	.250	.500	0	4	0
Ed Reulbach	p	2	3	0	0	0	0	0	0	1	0	0	.000	.000	4	0	0
Jack Pfiester	p	2	2	0	0	0	0	0	0	0	1	0	.000	.000	0	2	1
Carl Lundgren		Did not play															
Jack Taylor		Did not play															
Jack Harper		Did not play															
team total		6	184	18	36	9	0	0	11	18	28	9	.196	.245	159	81	7

Double Plays—4
Left on Bases—36

REGULAR SEASON STATISTICS

Main Pos	G	AB	R	H	2B	3B	HR	RBI	BB	SO	SB	BA	SA
1b	154	556	70	143	17	6	1	57	48		36	.257	.315
2b	143	549	71	153	18	11	0	57	30		37	.279	.352
ss	133	484	63	134	25	6	0	80	41		27	.277	.353
3b	75	225	14	58	5	1	0	25	16		8	.258	.289
a rf	130	484	80	110	7	5	0	27	69		19	.227	.262
cf	144	496	77	114	22	4	2	34	83		26	.230	.302
b lf	75	253	30	59	9	4	1	27	19		11	.233	.312
c	118	387	37	83	18	4	1	33	22		10	.214	.289
3b	116	378	26	69	8	3	0	33	31		7	.183	.220
of	94	330	37	82	4	1	1	21	22		19	.248	.276
c	7	22	0	3	1	0	0	3	3		0	.136	.182
c	13	36	3	10	0	0	0	6	7		0	.278	.278
2b-ss	33	96	7	13	1	0	0	4	11		4	.135	.146
c	17	37	1	6	0	0	0	0	2		0	.162	.162
p	38	100	4	16	2	0	0	3	8		2	.160	.180
p	42	99	12	14	3	2	0	4	3		3	.141	.212
p	28	65	11	12	1	1	0	3	13		3	.185	.231
p	42	103	7	14	1	0	0	7	8		0	.136	.175
p	21	49	4	3	2	0	0	1	0		1	.061	.102
p	20	41	6	12	2	2	0	6	3		0	.293	.439
p	6	10	0	2	1	0	0	1	0		0	.200	.300
	154	4921	570	1132	152	52	6	444	453		214	.230	.286

a—from New York (A)
b—from New York (A)
Frank Hemphill (of), Lee Quillen (ss), Frank Roth (c), Rube Vinson (of) also played for the White Sox during the season.

Main Pos	G	AB	R	H	2B	3B	HR	RBI	BB	SO	SB	BA	SA
1b	136	474	103	151	24	10	3	71	70		57	.319	.430
2b	154	533	65	136	17	6	1	51	36		49	.255	.315
ss	148	523	75	122	18	4	1	64	43		30	.233	.289
3b	151	539	81	176	27	10	3	83	47		29	.327	.430
of	146	563	77	158	18	13	7	60	31		25	.281	.396
c	149	549	90	144	27	10	1	45	67		30	.262	.353
c	107	343	45	107	15	6	2	46	23		14	.312	.420
c	70	226	22	57	13	1	0	35	7		6	.252	.319
c of	34	83	8	21	3	0	0	10	12		4	.253	.289
of	127	498	71	119	8	6	0	33	63		25	.239	.273
c	2	1	0	0	0	0	0	0	0		0	.000	.000
p	36	98	11	20	1	0	0	4	6		0	.204	.214
d p	18	53	6	9	1	0	0	3	2		1	.170	.189
p	34	83	4	13	0	0	0	1	3		0	.157	.157
p	31	84	5	4	0	0	0	1	3		0	.048	.048
p	28	67	4	12	3	0	0	3	4		0	.179	.224
e p	17	53	5	11	3	0	0	3	4		0	.208	.264
f p	1	0	0	0	0	0	0	0	0		0	—	—
	154	5018	704	1316	181	71	20	539	448		283	.262	.339

c—from Brooklyn
d—from Cincinnati
e—from St. Louis (N)
f—from Cincinnati
Pete Noonan (1b), Bull Smith (ph), Fred Beebe (p), Bob Wicker (p) also played for the Cubs during the season.

PITCHING

WORLD SERIES STATISTICS

CHICAGO WHITE SOX	G	GS	CG	IP	H	R	ER	BB	SO	W	L	SV	ERA
Nick Altrock	2	2	2	18	11	2	2	2	5	1	1	0	1.00
Ed Walsh	2	2	1	15	7	6	2	6	17	2	0	0	1.20
Doc White	3	2	1	15	12	7	3	7	4	1	1	1	1.80
Frank Owen	1	0	0	6	6	3	2	3	2	0	0	0	3.00
Roy Patterson	Did not play												
Frank Smith	Did not play												
Lou Fiene	Did not play												
Team total	6	6	4	54	36	18	9	18	28	4	2	1	1.50

CHICAGO CUBS	G	GS	CG	IP	H	R	ER	BB	SO	W	L	SV	ERA
Three Finger Brown	3	3	2	19⅓	14	8	7	4	12	1	2	0	3.20
Orvie Overall	2	0	0	12	10	3	3	3	8	0	0	0	2.25
Ed Reulbach	2	1	1	11	6	4	3	8	4	1	0	0	2.45
Jack Pfiester	2	1	1	10⅓	7	7	7	3	11	0	2	0	6.10
Carl Lundgren	Did not play												
Jack Taylor	Did not play												
Jack Harper	Did not play												
team total	6	6	4	53	37	22	20	18	35	2	4	0	3.40

REGULAR SEASON STATISTICS

	G	GS	CG	IP	H	ER	BB	SO	W	L	Pct	SV	ShO	ERA
	38	30	25	288	269	66	42	99	20	13	.606	1	4	2.06
	41	31	24	278	215	58	58	171	17	13	.567	3	10	1.88
	28	24	20	219	160	37	38	95	18	6	.750	0	7	1.52
	42	36	27	293	289	76	54	66	22	13	.629	2	7	2.33
	21	18	12	142	119	33	17	45	10	7	.588	1	2	2.09
	20	13	8	122	124	46	37	53	5	5	.500	2	1	3.39
	0	2	1	31	35	10	9	12	1	1	.500	0	0	2.90
	154	154	117	1375	1212	326	255	543	93	58	.616	9	32	2.13
	36	32	27	277	198	32	61	144	26	6	.813	3	9	1.04
d	18	14	13	144	116	30	51	94	12	3	.800	1	2	1.88
	33	24	20	218	129	40	92	94	19	4	.826	3	6	1.65
	31	29	20	242	173	42	63	153	20	8	.714	0	4	1.56
	27	24	21	208	160	51	89	103	17	6	.739	2	5	2.21
e	17	16	15	147	116	30	39	34	12	3	.800	0	2	1.84
f	1	1	0	1	0	0	0	0	0	0	—	0	0	0.00
	154	154	125	1379	1018	270	446	702	116	36	.763	40	28	1.76

Total Attendance—99,845 Average Attendance—16,641 Winning Player's Share—$1,874 Losing Player's Share—$440

1907
Grand Theft

Their upset loss in last year's Series kept the Chicago Cubs hungry for a return shot at the World Championship, and they once again ran away from the rest of the National League to earn a second straight Series appearance. The Cubs brought essentially the same team into the classic, but last year's opposition, the crosstown rival White Sox, finished third with the same personnel that won the 1906 title. This year's American League representative, the Detroit Tigers, had four top-flight starting pitchers and a solid infield, but their greatest strength lay in the outfield. Davy Jones was a competent left fielder, and mates Ty Cobb and Sam Crawford ranked among the batting stars of baseball. At the ripe age of 20, Cobb blossomed into stardom this season with fine hitting skills and an uncompromising desire to do anything possible to win. Known for his feisty personal unpleasantness and razor-sharp spikes, the Georgia Peach led the A.L. with a .350 batting average, 119 runs batted in, and 49 hard-earned stolen bases. Batting in the clean-up spot behind Cobb, Crawford hit a cool .323 with 81 RBI's. The Tigers had a weakness in the catching department, but it had not prevented them from winning the A.L. crown in a tight race.

But that weakness did catch up with the Tigers in game one of the Series, on October 8 at Chicago. Detroit held a 3–1 lead going into the bottom of the ninth, with pitcher Wild Bill Donovan three outs from the win. Frank Chance led off with a single, and then Harry Steinfeldt got hit with a pitch to put the tying runs aboard. Jimmy Kling popped out, but then Johnny Evers's grounder was muffed by third baseman Bill Coughlin to load the bases. Wildfire Schulte was retired on a grounder, with Chance scoring to cut the Detroit lead to 3–2. Del Howard pinch-hit for Joe Tinker and struck out on an outside pitch, but when the ball got past Tiger catcher Boss Schmidt, Howard made it to first base and Steinfeldt scored the tying run. Pat Moran then pinch-hit for the Cubs in an attempt to win it, but before he could swing, Evers tried to steal home and was cut down. The Cubs almost won the game in the tenth inning, when Jimmy Slagle scored from third on a Schmidt passed ball but was ruled out because of interference by batter Steinfeldt. The Cubs threatened again in the eleventh, when singles by Kling, Evers, and Schulte loaded the bases with one out, but Donovan managed to retire the N.L. champs before a run scored. After 12 innings, darkness ended the contest in a 3–3 stalemate. To add to catcher Schmidt's embarrassment, the Cubs stole seven bases during the course of the game.

That sudden slipping away of a victory may have hurt the Tigers' morale, but the strong Chicago pitching staff probably did more to depress the Tigers than did any memory. Left-hander Jack Pfiester scattered nine hits in game two but allowed only one Tiger to cross the plate, as the Cubs captured a 3–1 victory spiced by four stolen bases against the Detroit battery of George Mullin and Freddie Payne. Schmidt returned to the Detroit lineup as catcher in game three and allowed no Cub stolen bases. Chicago pitcher Ed Reulbach, however, allowed only one Tiger run, as the Cubs batted out a 5–1 win to take a 2–0 edge in the Series.

The clubs traveled to Detroit that night and found the fans there totally convinced that their Tigers were going to lose. A disappointing crowd of 11,306 showed up in rainy weather to witness a sloppy 6–1 Cub victory in which the victors stole two bases and scored three runs in the seventh inning without even hitting the ball out of the infield. The attendance dropped to 7,370 on Saturday afternoon, and the Tigers dropped their fourth straight game to the Cubs by a 2–0 count. It was easy to point a finger at the Detroit catching, which allowed 16 stolen bases and cost the team a first-game victory, but the Chicago pitching staff deserved more credit than the Tiger receivers deserved blame. Pfiester, Reulbach, Overall, and Brown hurled four straight complete-game victories for the Cubs, and they held Cobb down to a measly .200 average and Crawford to a .238 mark.

Game 1 October 8 at Chicago

Det. 000 000 030 000*
Chi. 000 100 002 000

Detroit	Pos	AB	R	H	RBI	PO	A	E
Jones	lf	5	1	3	0	3	1	0
Schaefer	2b	6	1	1	0	7	4	0
Crawford	cf	5	1	3	2	1	0	0
Cobb	rf	5	0	0	0	0	0	0
Rossman	1b	4	0	0	1	9	3	0
Coughlin	3b	5	0	0	0	1	0	1
Schmidt	c	5	0	2	0	13	2	2
O'Leary	ss	4	0	0	0	0	3	0
Donovan	p	5	0	0	0	2	2	0
Totals		44	3	9	3	36	15	3

Pitching	IP	H	R	ER	BB	SO
Detroit						
Donovan	12	10	3	1	3	12
Chicago						
Overall	9	9	3	1	2	5
Reulbach	3	0	0	0	0	2

Chicago	Pos	AB	R	H	RBI	PO	A	E
Slagle	cf	6	0	2	0	2	0	0
Sheckard	lf	5	0	1	0	2	0	0
Chance	1b	4	2	1	0	15	0	0
Steinfeldt	3b	3	1	1	0	1	2	1
Kling	c	4	0	2	1	7	4	1
Evers	2b-ss	4	0	2	0	4	2	2
Schulte	rf	5	0	1	1	2	0	0
Tinker	ss	3	0	0	0	3	5	1
a Howard		1	0	0	0	0	0	0
Zimmerman	2b	1	0	0	0	2	0	0
Overall	p	3	0	0	0	0	2	0
b Moran		0	0	0	0	0	0	0
Reulbach	p	2	0	0	0	0	2	0
Totals		41	3	10	2	36	17	5

* Game called on account of Darkness.
a Struck out for Tinker in 9th but safe on dropped third strike.
b Announced for Overall in 9th.

Stolen Bases—Chance, Evers, Howard, Jones 2, Sheckard, Slagle 2, Steinfeldt. Sacrifice Hits—Evers, O'Leary, Steinfeldt. Double Plays—Evers to Tinker, Schaefer to Rossman. Left on Bases—Detroit 8, Chicago 8. Hit by Pitcher—Sheckard and Steinfeld (by Donovan). Umpires—O'Day (N), Sheridan (A). Attendance—24,377. Time of Game—2:40.

1st Inning
Detroit
   Jones walked.
1 Schaefer forced Jones at second, Steinfeldt to Evers.
2 Crawford flied to center.
3 Schaefer out trying to steal second, Kling to Evers.
Chicago
1 Slagle fouled to Jones.
   Sheckard singled past third.
2 Chance struck out.
   Sheckard stole second and continued to third on Schmidt's wild throw.
3 Steinfeldt bounced back to the mound.

2nd Inning
Detroit
1 Cobb grounded to first.
2 Rossman grounded to short.
3 Coughlin struck out.
Chicago
   Kling walked.
1 Evers sacrificed Kling to second, Donovan to Rossman.
2 Schulte grounded to second, Kling going to third.
3 Tinker struck out.

3rd Inning
Detroit
   Schmidt singled to center.
1 O'Leary sacrificed Schmidt to second, Chance unassisted.
2 Donovan struck out.
   Jones singled over second, Schmidt going to third.
3 Schaefer grounded to short.
Chicago
1 Overall struck out.
2 Slagle popped to second.
3 Sheckard fouled to third.

4th Inning
Detroit
   Crawford singled to left.
1 Cobb sacrificed Crawford to second, Kling to Chance.
   Rossman walked.
2,3 Coughlin lined into a double play, Evers to Tinker.
Chicago
   Chance walked.
1 Steinfeldt sacrificed Chance to second, Rossman to Schaefer.
   Kling singled to left, Chance scoring
2 but Kling was out trying to stretch his hit into a double, Jones to Schmidt to Schaefer.
   Evers singled to left-center.
   Evers stole second.
3 Schulte struck out.

5th Inning
Detroit
   Schmidt singled to left.
1 O'Leary grounded to third, Schmidt going to second.
2 Donovan struck out.
   Jones beat out an infield hit, Schmidt going to third.
3 Jones stole second but Schmidt was caught napping Kling to Steinfeldt.
Chicago
1 Tinker again struck out.
2 Overall grounded out, Rossman to Donovan.
   Slagle singled to second.
3 Slagle out trying to steal, Schmidt to Schaefer.

6th Inning
Detroit
   Schaefer singled to left.
   Crawford singled to left, Schaefer going to second.
1 Cobb popped to short.
2 Rossman forced Crawford at second, Tinker to Evers, Schaefer going to third.
3 Schaefer picked off third, Kling to Steinfeldt to Kling to Tinker.
Chicago
1 Scheckard grounded to short.
2 Chance struck out.
   Steinfeldt singled to center.
   Steinfeldt stole second.
3 Kling struck out.

7th Inning
Detroit
1 Coughlin grounded to short.
2 Schmidt bounced back to the mound.
3 O'Leary struck out.
Chicago
1 Evers flied to left.
2 Schulte grounded to second.
3 Tinker struck out for the third time.

8th Inning
Detroit
1 Donovan grounded back to the mound.
   Jones got an infield single.
   Jones stole second.
   Schaefer safe on Tinker's fumble, Jones going to third.
   Crawford doubled to right, Jones and Schaefer scoring, and Crawford went to third when Kling fumbled the throw-in.
   Cobb grounded to Overall who threw to the plate and Crawford safely back to third and Cobb to second when Steinfeldt dropped Kling's throw.
2 Rossman flied to center, Crawford scoring after the catch.
3 Coughlin struck out.
Chicago
1 Overall flied to center.
2 Slagle flied to left.
3 Sheckard struck out.

9th Inning
Detroit
   Schmidt safe on Evers' fumble.
1 O'Leary grounded to second, Schmidt going to second.
2 Donovan flied to short.
3 Jones grounded to short.
Chicago
   Chance singled to right.
   Steinfeldt hit by a pitch.
1 Kling popped a bunt to Rossman.
   Evers safe on Coughlin's fumble, loading the bases.
2 Schulte grounded out, Rossman to Donovan, Chance scoring as the other runners advanced.
   Howard, batting for Tinker, struck out but was safe on Schmidt's error of dropping the third strike, Steinfeldt scored as Evers went to third.
   Howard stole second.
3 Moran announced to bat for Overall, but Evers was out trying to steal home, Schmidt unassisted.

10th Inning
Detroit
   For Chicago—Reulbach pitching, Zimmerman playing second as Evers moves to short.
1 Schaefer grounded to second.
2 Crawford struck out.
3 Cobb grounded to first.
Chicago
1 Reulbach grounded to second.
   Slagle singled past second.
2 Sheckard struck out as Slagle stole second.
   Chance walked.
   Slagle and Chance worked a double steal.
3 On a short passed ball Slagle tried to score but Steinfeldt interferred and Slagle declared out.

11th Inning
Detroit
1 Rossman flied to left.
2 Coughlin popped to first.
   Schmidt safe on Evers' low throw.
3 O'Leary flied to right.
Chicago
1 Steinfeldt popped to second.
   Kling singled past third.
   Evers beat out a bunt, Kling going to second.
   Schulte also beat out a bunt, loading the bases.
2 Zimmerman struck out.
3 Reulbach forced Schulte at second, O'Leary to Schaefer.

12th Inning
Detroit
1 Donovan struck out.
2 Jones flied to left.
3 Schaefer grounded to second.
Chicago
1 Slagle grounded to short.
   Sheckard hit by a pitch.
2,3 Chance lined into a double play, Schaefer to Rossman.

Game 2 October 9 at Chicago

Det.	010	000	000				
Chi.	010	200	00x				

Detroit	Pos	AB	R	H	RBI	PO	A	E
Jones	lf	4	0	2	0	1	0	0
Schaefer	2b	4	0	1	0	2	2	0
Crawford	cf	4	0	0	0	1	1	0
Cobb	rf	3	0	1	0	0	0	0
Rossman	1b	4	1	3	0	12	1	0
Coughlin	3b	4	0	0	0	2	1	0
Payne	c	4	0	1	1	5	1	1
O'Leary	ss	2	0	1	0	0	6	0
Mullin	p	3	0	0	0	1	2	0
Totals		32	1	9	1	24	14	1

Chicago	Pos	AB	R	H	RBI	PO	A	E
Slagle	cf	3	1	2	1	3	0	0
Sheckard	lf	3	0	1	1	2	0	0
Chance	1b	3	0	1	0	6	0	0
Steinfeldt	3b	3	0	0	0	3	0	0
Kling	c	4	1	1	0	5	4	0
Evers	2b	4	0	2	0	2	0	0
Schulte	rf	4	0	1	0	1	0	0
Tinker	ss	2	1	1	1	5	5	1
Pfiester	p	2	0	0	0	0	1	0
Totals		28	3	9	3	27	10	1

Double—Sheckard. Triple—Rossman. Stolen Bases—Chance, Evers, Slagle 2, Payne. Sacrifice Hits—Pfiester, Sheckard. Double Plays—Tinker to Chance 2, Crawford to Schaefer. Passed Ball—Kling. Hit by Pitchers—Cobb (by Pfiester), Steinfeldt (by Mullin). Left on Bases—Detroit 6, Chicago 7. Umpires—Sheridan, O'Day. Attendance—21,901. Time of Game—2:13.

Pitching	IP	H	R	ER	BB	SO
Detroit						
Mullin (L)	8	9	3	3	3	6
Chicago						
Pfiester (W)	9	9	1	1	1	3

1st Inning
Detroit
Jones singled over third.
Schaefer singled past second, Jones going to second.
1 Crawford struck out.
2,3 Cobb hit into a double play, Tinker to Chance.
Chicago
Slagle walked.
Slagle stole second and went to third on Payne's poor throw hitting Mullin on the head.
1 Sheckard struck out.
2 Slagle picked off third, Mullin to Coughlin.
Chance walked.
Chance stole second.
3 Steinfeldt struck out.

2nd Inning
Detroit
Rossman tripled on a wicked grounder past Tinker.
1 Coughlin struck out.
Payne singled on a short fly to left, scoring Rossman.
2 O'Leary fouled to Steinfeldt.
Payne stole second.
3 Mullin flied to center.
Chicago
Kling singled to left.
Evers beat out a roller to short, Kling going to second.
Schulte beat out a hard liner to the mound, too hot to handle, loading the bases.
Tinker walked forcing in Kling.
1 Pfiester struck out.
2 Slagle struck out.
3 Sheckard grounded to second.

3rd Inning
Detroit
Jones safe on Tinker's fumble.
1 Schaefer forced Jones, Tinker unassisted.
2 Schaefer caught trying to steal second, Kling to Tinker.
3 Crawford fouled to Kling.
Chicago
Chance walked.
Steinfeldt hit by a pitch.
1,2 Kling flied to Crawford, who threw to Schaefer doubling Chance at second.
Evers singled, Steinfeldt to third.
Evers stole second.
3 Schulte struck out.

4th Inning
Detroit
Cobb singled to center.
Rossman singled to right, Cobb going to
1 third but Rossman was out on a great throw by Schulte to Tinker.
2 Coughlin flied to center.
3 Payne lined to center.
Chicago
Tinker singled to center.
1 Pfiester sacrificed, Coughlin to Rossman.
Slagle singled past short, scoring Tinker.
Slagle stole second.
Sheckard doubled to right, Slagle scoring.
2 Sheckard caught trying to steal third, Payne to Coughlin.
3 Chance popped to Rossman.

5th Inning
Detroit
O'Leary singled to center.
1 Mullin flied to Sheckard, making a great catch against the fence.
2 Jones popped to third.
3 Schaefer bunted and was tagged out by Kling.
Chicago
1 Steinfeldt grounded to short.
2 Kling grounded to short.
3 Evers bounced back to the mound.

6th Inning
Detroit
1 Crawford lined fiercely to first.
2 Cobb grounded to short.
Rossman singled to left.
3 Coughlin forced Rossman at second, Tinker to Evers.
Chicago
1 Schulte grounded to short.
2 Tinker grounded to short.
3 Pfiester grounded out, Rossman to Mullin.

7th Inning
Detroit
1 Payne flied to Sheckard, making a shoestring catch.
O'Leary walked.
2 Mullin struck out.
3 O'Leary out trying to steal second, Kling to Evers.
Chicago
Slagle singled to left.
1 Sheckard sacrificed, Mullin to Rossman.
2 Chance grounded to short, Slagle going to third.
3 Steinfeldt grounded to short.

8th Inning
Detroit
Jones singled to center.
1 Schaefer grounded to short, Jones going to second.
2 Crawford flied to right.
Cobb hit by a pitched ball.
3 Jones out trying to steal third, Kling to Steinfeldt.
Chicago
1 Kling struck out.
2 Evers fouled to Jones.
3 Schulte grounded to second.

9th Inning
Detroit
Rossman singled to left.
1,2 Coughlin lined into a double play, Tinker to Chance.
3 Payne out bunting, Kling to Chance.

Game 3 October 10 at Chicago

Det.	000	001	000				
Chi.	010	310	00x				

Detroit	Pos	AB	R	H	RBI	PO	A	E
Jones	lf	3	0	0	0	2	0	1
Schaefer	2b	4	0	1	0	0	2	0
Crawford	cf	4	0	1	1	3	1	0
Cobb	rf	4	0	1	0	1	0	0
Rossman	1b	4	0	2	0	0	0	0
Coughlin	3b	3	0	0	0	4	1	0
Schmidt	c	3	0	0	0	3	1	0
O'Leary	ss	4	0	0	0	4	3	0
Siever	p	1	0	0	0	0	0	0
Killian	p	2	1	1	0	0	0	0
Totals		32	1	6	1	24	8	1

Chicago	Pos	AB	R	H	RBI	PO	A	E
Slagle	cf	4	0	0	0	3	0	0
Sheckard	lf	4	0	1	0	4	0	0
Chance	1b	4	1	1	0	12	1	0
Steinfeldt	3b	3	1	2	1	0	2	0
Kling	c	3	1	1	0	3	1	0
Evers	2b	4	0	3	1	3	2	1
Schulte	rf	4	1	1	1	0	0	0
Tinker	ss	4	1	0	0	2	7	0
Reulbach	p	3	0	1	1	0	1	0
Totals		33	5	10	4	27	15	1

Doubles—Chance, Evers 2, Sheckard, Steinfeldt. Sacrifice Hit—Kling. Double Plays—Tinker (unassisted), Steinfeldt to Evers to Chance. Left On Bases—Detroit 7, Chicago 6. Umpires—O'Day, Sheridan. Attendance—13,114. Time of Game—1:35.

Pitching	IP	H	R	ER	BB	SO
Detroit						
Siever (L)	4	7	4	2	0	1
Killian	4	3	1	1	1	1
Chicago						
Reulbach (W)	9	6	1	1	3	2

1st Inning
Detroit
1 Jones grounded to second.
2 Schaefer grounded to short.
3 Crawford grounded to first.
Chicago
1 Slagle flied to right.
2 Sheckard grounded to short.
3 Chance flied to center.

2nd Inning
Detroit
1 Cobb struck out.
2 Rossman flied to left.
3 Coughlin grounded to short.
Chicago
Steinfeldt doubled to left.
1 Kling sacrificed Steinfeldt to third, Schmidt to Rossman.
Evers doubled to right, scoring Steinfeldt.
2 Schulte grounded to second, Evers going to third.
3 Tinker grounded to short.

3rd Inning
Detroit
1 Schmidt flied to center.
2 O'Leary grounded to short.
3 Siever bounced back to the mound.
Chicago
1 Reulbach flied to center.
2 Slagle struck out.
Sheckard doubled to right.
3 Chance popped to short.

4th Inning
Detroit
1 Jones flied to left.
Schaefer beat out a hit to Reulbach, he knocked it down but couldn't hold it.
2 Crawford grounded to third, Schaefer going to second.
3 Cobb hit back to the mound.
Chicago
1 Steinfeldt flied to left.
Kling singled to right.
Evers singled to right, Kling going to second.
Schulte singled to center, scoring
2 Kling but Evers was out trying for third, Crawford to Coughlin to O'Leary.
Tinker got all the way to third on Jones' error in left, scoring Schulte.
Reulbach singled to right, scoring Tinker.
3 Slagle popped to third.

5th Inning
Detroit
Rossman beat out a hot smash to third.
Coughlin walked.
1 Schmidt sacrificed up both runners, Chance to Reulbach.
2,3 O'Leary lined into a double play, Tinker unassisted.
Chicago
For Detroit—Killian pitching.
1 Sheckard grounded to second.
Chance doubled to center.
Steinfeldt singled to center, Chance scoring.
2 Kling flied to center.
Evers got a ground-rule double to right, Steinfeldt going to third.
3 Schulte popped to third.

6th Inning
Detroit
Killian singled to center.
Jones walked.
1,2 Schaefer hit into a double play, Steinfeldt to Evers to Chance, Killian going to third.
Crawford singled over second, scoring Killian.
Cobb singled, Crawford to second.
3 Rossman flied to deep center.
Chicago
1 Tinker popped to short.
2 Reulbach fouled to Schmidt.
3 Slagle grounded to first.

7th Inning
Detroit
1 Coughlin hit a hot one off Reulbach's shins to Tinker who threw to first.
Schmidt walked.
2 O'Leary struck out.
Siever safe on Evers' error.
3 Jones grounded to second.
Chicago
1 Sheckard struck out.
2 Chance flied to left.
Steinfeldt walked.
3 Kling popped to third.

8th Inning
Detroit
1 Schaefer grounded to short.
2 Crawford flied to deep center.
3 Cobb flied to left.
Chicago
1 Evers popped to third.
2 Schulte grounded to short.
3 Tinker popped to short.

9th Inning
Detroit
Rossman singled to center.
1 Coughlin forced Rossman at second, Tinker to Evers.
2 Schmidt popped to second.
3 O'Leary flied to left.

Game 4 October 11 at Detroit

Chi. 000 020 301
Det. 000 100 000

Chicago	Pos	AB	R	H	RBI	PO	A	E
Slagle	cf	5	1	1	2	2	0	1
Sheckard	lf	5	0	2	1	1	0	0
Chance	1b	3	0	0	0	11	0	0
Steinfeldt	3b	4	0	2	0	3	1	0
Kling	c	4	0	0	0	6	0	0
Evers	2b	4	1	0	0	0	2	0
Schulte	rf	3	2	1	0	1	1	0
Tinker	ss	1	2	0	0	3	3	1
Overall	p	2	0	1	2	0	4	0
Totals		31	6	7	5	27	11	2

Pitching	IP	H	R	ER	BB	SO
Chicago						
Overall (W)	9	5	1	1	2	6
Detroit						
Donovan (L)	9	7	6	3	2	4

1st Inning
Chicago
1 Slagle popped to short.
  Sheckard singled.
2 Sheckard out stealing, Schmidt to
  O'Leary.
  Chance hit by a pitch.
  Chance stole second.
3 Steinfeldt flied to right.
Detroit
  Jones walked.
1 Schaefer sacrificed, Overall to Chance.
2 Crawford popped to short.
3 Cobb grounded to short.

2nd Inning
Chicago
1 Kling struck out.
2 Evers flied to right.
3 Schulte flied to center.
Detroit
1 Rossman grounded back to the mound.
  Coughlin singled to left.
2,3 Schmidt hit into a double play,
  Tinker unassisted.

3rd Inning
Chicago
1 Tinker flied to right.
2 Overall grounded to second.
3 Slagle grounded to short.
Detroit
1 O'Leary grounded to short.
2 Donovan grounded past first and on a
  fine scoop by Schulte; Donovan was
  out at first.
3 Jones bunted out to the mound.

4th Inning
Chicago
1 Sheckard flied to right.
2 Chance grounded to short.
  Steinfeldt singled to center.
3 Kling flied to left.
Detroit
1 Schaefer flied to left.
2 Crawford fouled to Steinfeldt.
  Cobb tripled to left.
  Rossman singled to left, scoring Cobb.
  Coughlin singled, Rossman to second.
  Schmidt walked, loading the bases.
3 O'Leary struck out.

5th Inning
Chicago
  Evers safe on O'Leary's wild throw
  to first.
    Game called for 15 minutes due to
    heavy rain.
  Schulte walked.
1 Tinker sacrificed both runners,
  Rossman unassisted.
  Overall singled to right, scoring
  Evers and Schulte.
2 Slagle flied to left.
3 Sheckard forced Overall at second,
  O'Leary unassisted.
Detroit
1 Donovan flied to center.
2 Jones grounded to second.
3 Schaefer struck out.

6th Inning
Chicago
1 Chance popped to third.
  Steinfeldt singled to left.
2 Kling struck out.
3 Evers lined to right.
Detroit
1 Crawford grounded to second.
2 Cobb grounded to short.
3 Rossman flied to center.

7th Inning
Chicago
  Schulte beat out a bunt to the mound.
  Tinker bunted into a good sacrifice.
  Donovan throwing to second too late to
  get Schulte.
1 Overall sacrificed up both runners,
  Schmidt to Rossman.
  Slagle grounded to O'Leary, who threw
  wildly to the plate, Schulte scoring
  as Tinker went to third.
  Sheckard safe on a bunt to Rossman when
  no one covered first, Tinker scoring
  as Slagle went to second.
2 Chance forced Sheckard at second,
  Coughlin to O'Leary as Slagle went to
  third.
    On a clever double steal Chance
    intentionally caught in a rundown
3   so Slagle could steal home, Chance
    out, Schmidt to Schaefer to Rossman.
Detroit
1 Coughlin struck out.
2 Schmidt flied to right.
3 O'Leary grounded to third.

8th Inning
Chicago
1 Steinfeldt struck out.
2 Kling lined to second.
3 Evers struck out.
Detroit
  Donovan safe on Tinker's fumble.
1 Jones sacrificed Donovan to second,
  Overall to Chance.
2 Schaefer struck out.
3 Crawford struck out.

9th Inning
Chicago
1 Schulte flied to left.
  Tinker walked.
2 Overall sacrificed Tinker to second,
  Donovan to Rossman.
  Slagle singled to center, scoring
  Tinker and took second on the
  throw home.
3 Sheckard grounded to second.
Detroit
1 Cobb popped to third.
  Rossman safe on Slagle's muff.
  Coughlin singled to left, Rossman
  going to second.
2 Schmidt struck out.
3 O'Leary popped to third.

Detroit	Pos	AB	R	H	RBI	PO	A	E
Jones	lf	2	0	0	0	3	0	0
Schaefer	2b	3	0	0	0	1	3	0
Crawford	cf	4	0	0	0	1	0	0
Cobb	rf	4	1	1	0	5	0	0
Rossman	1b	4	0	1	1	8	0	0
Coughlin	3b	4	0	3	0	1	1	0
Schmidt	c	3	0	0	0	4	3	0
O'Leary	ss	4	0	0	0	4	2	2
Donovan	p	3	0	0	0	0	1	0
Totals		31	1	5	1	27	10	2

Triple—Cobb. Stolen Bases—Chance, Slagle.
Sacrifice Hits—Jones, Overall 2, Schaefer,
Tinker 2. Double Play—Tinker (unassisted).
Hit by Pitcher—Chance (by Donovan). Left
on Bases—Chicago 4, Detroit 7.
Umpires—Sheridan, O'Day.
Attendance—11,306. Time of Game—1:45.

Game 5 October 12 at Detroit

Chi. 110 000 000
Det. 000 000 000

Chicago	Pos	AB	R	H	RBI	PO	A	E
Slagle	cf	4	1	1	0	3	0	0
Sheckard	lf	4	0	0	0	1	0	0
Howard	1b	4	0	1	0	10	1	0
Steinfeldt	3b	4	0	3	1	2	0	0
Kling	c	4	0	0	0	5	1	0
Evers	2b	4	1	0	0	2	6	0
Schulte	rf	4	0	1	0	0	0	1
Tinker	ss	3	0	1	0	3	3	0
Brown	p	3	0	0	0	1	1	0
Totals		34	2	7	2	27	12	1

Pitching	IP	H	R	ER	BB	SO
Chicago						
Brown (W)	9	7	0	0	1	4
Detroit						
Mullin (L)	9	7	2	1	3	2

1st Inning
Chicago
  Slagle walked.
1 Sheckard flied to left.
2 Howard struck out.
  Slagle stole second (Slagle's sixth
  steal in the Series).
  Steinfeldt singled to center, scoring
  Slagle.
3 Kling flied to right.
Detroit
  Jones walked.
1 Schaefer flied to center.
2 Crawford grounded to first, Jones
  going to second.
3 Cobb grounded to second.

2nd Inning
Chicago
  Evers safe on Rossman's muff of
  Coughlin's throw.
1 Schulte fouled to Archer.
  Tinker singled to right, Evers going
  to second.
    Tinker and Evers walked a double
    steal.
  Brown walked, loading the bases.
2 Slagle forced Brown at second,
  Schaefer to O'Leary as Evers
  scored.
3 Sheckard flied to right.
Detroit
1 Rossman grounded out, Howard to Brown.
  Coughlin singled to center.
2 Archer forced Coughlin at second,
  Evers to Tinker.
3 O'Leary bounced back to the mound.

3rd Inning
Chicago
1 Howard grounded to second.
  Steinfeldt tripled into the crowd in
  left field.
2 Kling grounded to Coughlin, who threw
  Steinfeldt out at the plate.
3 Evers grounded to second.
Detroit
1 Mullin lined to short.
2 Jones grounded to second.
3 Schaefer popped to third.

4th Inning
Chicago
1 Schulte flied to right.
2 Tinker grounded to second.
3 Brown popped to short.
Detroit
  Crawford doubled into the right
  field crowd.
1 Cobb struck out.
  Rossman singled to left, Crawford
  going to third.
  Rossman stole second.
2 Coughlin fouled to Kling.
3 Archer flied to left.

Detroit	Pos	AB	R	H	RBI	PO	A	E
Jones	lf	3	0	1	0	1	1	0
Schaefer	2b	4	0	0	0	1	6	0
Crawford	cf	4	0	1	0	0	0	0
Cobb	rf	4	0	1	0	4	0	0
Rossman	1b	4	0	2	0	12	0	1
a Payne		0	0	0	0	0	0	0
Coughlin	3b	4	0	2	0	1	2	1
Archer	c	3	0	0	0	4	1	0
b Schmidt		1	0	0	0	0	0	0
O'Leary	ss	3	0	0	0	4	2	0
Mullin	p	3	0	0	0	0	3	0
Totals		33	0	7	0	27	15	2

a Ran for Rossman in 9th.
b Flied out for Archer in 9th.

Double—Crawford. Triple—Steinfeldt.
Stolen Bases—Coughlin, Evers, Jones,
Rossman, Slagle, Tinker.
Left on Bases—Chicago 8, Detroit 7.
Umpires—O'Day, Sheridan.
Attendance—7,370. Time of Game—1:42.

5th Inning
Chicago
1 Slagle rolled back to the mound.
2 Sheckard grounded to third.
  Howard singled to left.
3 Steinfeldt singled to left, Howard out
  going to third, Jones to Coughlin.
Detroit
1 O'Leary grounded to short.
2 Mullin flied to center.
  Jones singled to center.
  Jones stole second.
3 Schaefer grounded to short.

6th Inning
Chicago
1 Kling grounded to second.
2 Evers grounded to the mound.
3 Schulte popped to second.
Detroit
1 Crawford grounded to second.
  Cobb singled to right and continued
  to second on Schulte's fumble.
2 Cobb out trying to steal third,
  Kling to Steinfeldt.
3 Rossman flied to center.

7th Inning
Chicago
1 Tinker flied to right.
2 Brown popped to short.
  Slagle singled to center.
3 Slagle caught trying to steal
  second, Archer to O'Leary.
Detroit
  Coughlin singled to right.
  Coughlin stole second.
1 Archer struck out.
2 O'Leary grounded to short, Coughlin
  going to third.
3 Mullin popped to second.

8th Inning
Chicago
1 Sheckard grounded to second.
2 Howard lined to second.
3 Steinfeldt grounded to third.
Detroit
1 Jones grounded to second.
2 Schaefer struck out.
3 Crawford grounded to second.

9th Inning
Chicago
1 Kling grounded to short.
2 Evers grounded to second.
  Schulte singled to right.
  Tinker walked.
  Brown safe on Coughlin's fumble,
  loading the bases.
3 Slagle struck out.
Detroit
1 Cobb struck out.
  Rossman singled to right.
  Payne ran for Rossman.
2 Coughlin popped to second.
3 Schmidt, batting for Archer, flied to
  Tinker in short left.

1907 WORLD SERIES COMPOSITE BOX

	Wins	Composite Line Score
Chicago Cubs (N.L.)	4	1 3 0 6 3 0 3 0 3 0 0 0 – 19
Detroit Tigers (A.L.)	0	0 1 0 1 0 1 0 3 0 0 0 0 – 6

	Regular Season			
Manager	W	L	Pct.	G. Ahead
Frank Chance	107	45	.704	17
Hughie Jennings	92	58	.613	1½

BATTING AND FIELDING

CHICAGO CUBS

	Pos	WORLD SERIES STATISTICS																REGULAR SEASON STATISTICS											
		G	AB	R	H	2B	3B	HR	RBI	BB	SO	SB	BA	SA	PO	A	E	Pos	G	AB	R	H	2B	3B	HR	RBI	BB	SO	SB	BA	SA
Frank Chance	1b	4	14	3	3	1	0	0	3	2	3	.214	.286	44	1	0	1b	111	382	58	112	19	2	1	50	51		35	.293	.361
Johnny Evers	2b-ss	5	20	2	7	2	0	0	1	0	1	3	.350	.450	11	12	3	2b	151	508	66	127	18	4	2	51	39		46	.250	.313
Joe Tinker	ss	5	13	4	2	0	0	0	1	3	3	1	.154	.154	16	23	3	ss	117	402	36	89	11	3	1	36	25		20	.221	.271
Harry Steinfeldt	3b	5	17	2	8	1	1	0	2	1	2	1	.471	.647	9	5	1	3b	152	542	52	144	25	5	1	70	37		19	.266	.336
Wildfire Schulte	rf	5	20	3	5	0	0	0	2	1	2	0	.250	.250	4	2	1	of	97	342	44	98	14	7	2	32	22		7	.287	.386
Jimmy Slagle	cf	5	22	3	6	0	0	0	4	2	3	6	.273	.273	13	0	1	of	136	489	71	126	6	6	0	32	76		28	.258	.294
Jimmy Sheckard	lf	5	21	0	5	2	0	0	2	0	4	1	.238	.333	10	0	0	of	143	484	76	129	23	1	1	36	76		31	.267	.324
Johnny Kling	c	5	19	2	4	0	0	0	1	1	4	0	.211	.211	25	9	1	c	104	334	44	95	15	8	1	43	27		9	.284	.386
Del Howard	ph-1b	2	5	0	1	0	0	0	0	0	2	0	.200	.200	10	1	0	a 1b	51	148	10	34	0	0	0	13	6		3	.230	.270
Heinie Zimmerman	2b	1	1	0	0	0	0	0	0	0	1	0	.000	.000	0	2	0	2b	5	9	0	2	1	0	0	1	0		0	.222	.333
Pat Moran	ph	1	0	0	0	0	0	0	0	0	0	0	—	—	0	0	0	c	65	198	8	45	5	1	1	19	10		5	.227	.278
Solly Hofman		Did not play																of-ss-1b	134	470	67	126	11	3	1	36	41		29	.268	.311
Orvie Overall	p	2	5	0	1	0	0	0	0	0	1	0	.200	.200	0	6	0	p	35	92	6	19	4	2	0	9	3		0	.207	.293
Ed Reulbach	p	2	5	0	1	0	0	0	1	0	0	0	.200	.200	1	3	0	p	27	63	4	11	1	0	1	3	1		0	.175	.238
Three Finger Brown	p	1	3	0	0	0	0	0	0	0	1	0	.000	.000	1	1	0	p	36	85	6	13	0	2	1	7	1		0	.153	.235
Jack Pfiester	p	1	2	0	0	0	0	0	0	0	1	0	.000	.000	0	0	0	p	30	64	4	6	1	0	0	1	5		0	.094	.109
Carl Lundgren		Did not play																p	28	66	4	7	0	0	0	3	4		0	.106	.106
Chick Fraser		Did not play																p	22	45	3	3	0	0	0	2	2		0	.067	.067
Kid Durbin		Did not play																p-of	11	18	2	6	0	0	0	0	1		0	.333	.333
Team total		5	167	19	43	6	1	0	16	12	26	16	.257	.305	144	65			156	4892	571	1224	162	48	13	450	435		235	.250	.311

Double Plays—6
Left on Bases—33

a—from Boston (N)
Jack Hardy (c), Mike Kahoe (c), Newt Randall (of), Bill Sweeney (ss), Jack Taylor (p) also played for the Cubs during the season.

DETROIT TIGERS

	Pos	WORLD SERIES STATISTICS																REGULAR SEASON STATISTICS											
		G	AB	R	H	2B	3B	HR	RBI	BB	SO	SB	BA	SA	PO	A	E	Pos	G	AB	R	H	2B	3B	HR	RBI	BB	SO	SB	BA	SA
Claude Rossman	1b	5	20	1	8	0	1	0	2	1	0	1	.400	.500	48	4	1	1b	153	571	60	158	21	8	0	69	33		20	.277	.342
Germany Schaefer	2b	5	21	1	3	0	0	0	0	0	3	0	.143	.143	11	17	0	2b-ss-3b	109	372	45	96	12	3	1	32	30		21	.258	.315
Charley O'Leary	ss	5	17	0	1	0	0	0	1	0	3	0	.059	.059	12	16	2	ss	139	465	61	112	19	1	0	34	32		11	.241	.286
Bill Coughlin	3b	5	20	0	5	0	0	0	1	4	1	1	.250	.250	9	5	2	3b	134	519	80	126	10	2	0	46	35		15	.243	.270
Ty Cobb	rf	5	20	1	4	0	1	0	0	0	3	0	.200	.300	10	0	0	of	150	605	97	212	29	15	5	119	24		49	.350	.473
Sam Crawford	cf	5	21	1	5	1	0	0	3	0	0	0	.238	.286	6	2	0	of	144	582	102	183	34	17	4	81	37		18	.323	.460
Davy Jones	lf	5	17	1	6	0	0	0	0	4	0	3	.353	.353	10	2	1	of	126	491	101	134	10	6	0	27	60		30	.273	.318
Boss Schmidt	c-ph	4	12	0	2	0	0	0	2	1	0		.167	.167	20	6	2	c	104	349	32	85	6	6	0	23	5		8	.244	.295
Freddie Payne	c-pr	2	4	0	1	0	0	0	1	0	1	1	.250	.250	5	1	1	c	53	169	17	28	2	2	0	14	7		4	.166	.201
Jimmy Archer	c	1	3	0	0	0	0	0	0	0	1	0	.000	.000	4	1	0	c	18	42	6	5	0	0	0	1	0		0	.119	.119
Red Downs		Did not play																2b-of	105	374	28	82	13	5	1	42	13		3	.219	.289
Matty McIntyre		Did not play																of	20	81	6	23	1	1	0	9	7		3	.284	.321
Bobby Lowe		Did not play																3b	17	37	2	9	2	0	0	5	4		0	.243	.297
Wild Bill Donovan	p	2	8	0	0	0	0	0	0	0	3	0	.000	.000	2	3	0	p	37	109	20	29	7	2	0	19	6		4	.266	.367
George Mullin	p	2	6	0	0	0	0	0	0	1	0	0	.000	.000	1	5	0	p-ph	70	157	16	34	5	3	0	13	12		4	.217	.287
Ed Killian	p	1	2	1	1	0	0	0	0	0	0	0	.500	.500	0	0	0	p	46	122	16	39	5	3	0	11	4		3	.320	.410
Ed Siever	p	1	1	0	0	0	0	0	0	0	0	0	.000	.000	0	0	0	p	39	91	5	14	2	1	0	4	0		1	.154	.198
Ed Willett		Did not play																p	10	13	1	1	0	0	0	1	1		0	.077	.077
team total		5	172	6	36	1	2	0	6	9	22	6	.209	.238	138	70	9		153	5201	696	1382	179	75	11	551	315		192	.266	.335

Double Plays—2
Left on Bases—35

Tex Erwin (c), Red Killefer (of), John Eubank (p), Elijah Jones (p), Herm Malloy (p) also played for the Tigers during the season.

PITCHING

CHICAGO CUBS

	WORLD SERIES STATISTICS													REGULAR SEASON STATISTICS												
	G	GS	CG	IP	H	R	ER	BB	SO	W	L	SV	ERA	G	GS	CG	IP	H	ER	BB	SO	W	L	Pct.	SV	ShO	ERA
Orvie Overall	2	2	1	18	14	4	2	4	11	1	0	0	1.00	36	31	26	268	201	50	69	141	23	8	.742	3	8	1.68
Ed Reulbach	2	1	1	12	6	1	1	3	4	1	0	0	0.75	27	22	16	192	147	36	96	17	4		.810	0	4	1.69
Three Finger Brown	1	1	1	9	7	0	0	1	4	1	0	0	0.00	34	27	20	233	180	36	40	107	20	6	.769	3	6	1.39
Jack Pfiester	1	1	1	9	9	1	1	1	3	1	0	0	1.00	30	22	13	195	143	25	48	90	15	9	.625	0	1	1.15
Carl Lundgren	Did not play													28	25	21	207	130	27	92	84	18	7	.720	0	7	1.17
Chick Fraser	Did not play													22	15	9	138	112	35	46	41	8	5	.545	1	2	2.28
Kid Durbin	Did not play													5	1	1	17	14	10	10	5	0	1	.000	0	0	5.29
team total	5	5	4	48	36	6	4	9	22	4	0	0	0.75	156	156	114	1373	1054	264	402	586	101	45	.704	7	30	1.73

DETROIT TIGERS

	WORLD SERIES STATISTICS													REGULAR SEASON STATISTICS												
	G	GS	CG	IP	H	R	ER	BB	SO	W	L	SV	ERA	G	GS	CG	IP	H	ER	BB	SO	W	L	Pct.	SV	ShO	ERA
Wild Bill Donovan	2	2	2	21	17	9	4	5	16	0	1	0	1.71	32	28	27	271	222	66	82	123	25	4	.862	1	3	2.19
George Mullin	2	2	2	17	16	5	4	6	8	0	2	0	2.12	46	42	35	357	346	103	106	146	20	20	.500	3	5	2.60
Ed Killian	1	0	0	4	3	1	1	1	0	0	0	0	2.25	41	34	29	314	286	62	91	96	25	13	.658	0	3	1.78
Ed Siever	1	1	0	4	7	4	2	0	1	0	1	0	4.50	39	33	22	275	256	66	52	88	19	10	.655	1	3	2.16
Ed Willett	Did not play													10	6	1	49	47	20	20	27	1	5	.167	0	0	3.67
team total	5	5	4	46	43	19	11	12	26	0	4	0	2.15	153	153	120	1371	1281	355	380	512	92	58	.613	6	15	2.33

Total Attendance—78,068 Average Attendance—15,614 Winning Player's Share—$2,143 Losing Player's Share—$1,946

1908
The Cubs Overall

Both the Chicago Cubs and the Detroit Tigers made it back to the World Series this year, but neither club had an easy time of it on the way. The Cubs won their third straight pennant only with the help of a famous mistake by Fred Merkle, a young substitute first baseman for the New York Giants. The Cubs and Giants battled into the closing stages of the season, and met in a key confrontation on September 23. The Giants apparently won the game in the bottom of the ninth on a two-out single by Al Bridwell with men on first and third, which broke a 1–1 tie. But Merkle, the runner on first, didn't bother to touch second base and simply sprinted for the clubhouse when he saw the winning run score. The Cubs picked up on his blunder and managed to get the ball in to second base and make a force out with the crowd already mobbing the players and the field. The umpire declared the game a tie, and when the two clubs finished in a dead heat for first place, the tied match was rescheduled for October 8. Three Finger Brown beat Christy Mathewson 4–2 to send the disappointed Giants home for the winter. The Tigers encountered no such famous bloopers in the A.L., but they too went down to the final day of the season before icing away a half-game margin of victory over the Cleveland Indians.

Only two days after the Cubs beat the Giants for the N.L. flag, the Series opened up on a rainy Saturday in Detroit. The Cubs knocked Tiger starter Ed Killian out of the box with four runs in the third inning to take a 4–1 lead. Trailing 5–1 in the seventh, the Tigers scored three in the bottom of the seventh and then took a 6–5 lead with two more runs in the bottom of the eighth. Just like last year, the Tigers had an opening game victory within grasp but failed to grab it. Knuckleballer Ed Summers, a 24-game winner during the regular season, was pitching well in relief of Killian but suddenly came unglued in the ninth. The Cubs broke the game open with six straight hits and five runs to take a 10–6 lead, which the Tigers could not change with their final turn at bat.

The scene shifted on Sunday to Chicago, where a larger crowd could be expected than in Detroit. An audience of 17,760 saw a pitchers' battle between Chicago's Orvie Overall and Detroit's Wild Bill Donovan, with neither side scoring through the first seven innings. But in the bottom of the eighth, a wind-blown home run to right field by Joe Tinker gave the Cubs a 2–0 lead and immediately unnerved Donovan, who proceeded to give up four more runs before he could retire the side. The final score was 6–1, and the Tigers were down 2–0 in the Series and facing a quick elimination. But the A.L. champions bounced back to take an 8–3 decision in the third game. The Cubs had taken a 3–1 lead by tallying three times off George Mullin in the bottom of the fourth, but the Tigers retaliated with five runs in the sixth inning which gave them a lead they never lost. Ty Cobb had his best Series game to date, going 4-for-5, driving in two runs, and stealing two bases.

As the Tigers entertained new-found hope during their train trip back from Chicago for game four, the Cub pitchers shut the door on the Detroit batters, just as they did last year. Three Finger Brown shut the Tigers out on four hits in the fourth game, as the Cubs took a 3–0 victory and a commanding 3–1 lead in the Series. With that loss, the Detroit fans gave their club up as a lost cause, and only 6,210 of them showed up on a chilly Wednesday to watch game five. Veteran mound ace Donovan pitched in fine fashion for the Tigers, allowing only solo Cub tallies in the first and fifth innings. But Chicago pitcher Orvie Overall, the winner of game two, spun a three-hit shutout which made the Cubs world champs for the second straight year. The Tigers couldn't blame subpar catching for their defeat this year, nor could they complain about a poor Series by Ty Cobb, as he rebounded from last year's disappointing performance to hit .368 in this classic. The clearest explanation lay in the failure of Detroit pitchers Summers, Donovan, and Killian and in the strong work of Chicago pitchers Brown and Overall.

Game 1 October 10 at Detroit

Chicago	Pos	AB	R	H	RBI	PO	A	E
Sheckard	lf	6	1	3	0	1	0	0
Evers	2b	4	1	2	0	2	2	1
Schulte	rf	4	2	2	1	1	1	0
Chance	1b	4	2	1	0	12	0	1
Steinfeldt	3b	3	2	2	2	0	0	0
Hofman	cf	4	1	1	2	4	0	0
Tinker	ss	5	1	2	2	0	4	0
Kling	c	3	0	1	2	7	1	0
Reulbach	p	3	0	0	0	0	4	0
Overall	p	1	0	0	0	0	0	0
Brown	p	0	0	0	0	0	1	0
Totals		37	10	14	9	27	13	2

Pitching	IP	H	R	ER	BB	SO
Chicago						
Reulbach	6⅔	8	4	4	0	5
Overall	*⅓	0	1	1	1	0
Brown (W)	2	2	1	0	1	1
Detroit						
Killian	2⅓	5	4	3	3	1
Summers (L)	6⅔	9	6	5	1	2

*Pitched to one batter in 8th.

Chi.	004	000	105
Det.	100	000	320

Detroit	Pos	AB	R	H	RBI	PO	A	E
McIntyre	lf	3	1	2	0	3	0	1
O'Leary	ss	4	0	1	0	1	3	0
b Thomas		1	0	1	0	0	0	0
c Winter		0	0	0	0	0	0	0
Crawford	cf	4	1	0	0	4	0	0
Cobb	rf	4	2	2	1	0	0	0
Rossman	1b	4	1	2	1	12	0	0
Schaefer	3b	3	0	0	0	1	2	1
Schmidt	c	4	0	0	1	4	1	0
Downs	2b	4	1	1	1	2	4	1
Killian	p	0	0	0	0	0	1	0
Summers	p	3	0	1	1	0	5	0
a Jones		1	0	0	0	0	0	0
Totals		35	6	10	5	27	16	3

a Struck out for Summers in 9th.
b Singled for O'Leary in 9th.
c Ran for Thomas in 9th.

Doubles—Downs, Sheckard 2. Stolen Bases—Chance 2, Hofman, McIntyre, Tinker 2. Sacrifice Hits—Brown, Cobb, Evers, Kling, Schaefer, Schulte, Steinfeldt. Hit by Pitcher—McIntyre (by Overall). Wild Pitch—Brown. Left on Bases—Chicago 9, Detroit 7. Umpires—Sheridan (A), O'Day (N). Attendance—10,812. Time of Game—2:10.

1st Inning
Chicago
Sheckard got a double to right when Cobb fell chasing the ball.
1 Evers struck out.
2 Schulte grounded to third, Sheckard advancing to third.
Chance walked.
Chance stole second.
3 Steinfeldt flied to center.
Detroit
McIntyre singled to right.
1 O'Leary struck out.
2 Crawford struck out.
McIntyre stole second.
Cobb singled to right, scoring McIntyre,
3 but out trying for a double, Schulte to Evers.

2nd Inning
Chicago
1 Hofman grounded to second.
2 Tinker flied to Crawford, making a great catch at the crowd.
Kling walked.
3 Reulbach forced Kling at second, O'Leary to Downs.
Detroit
1 Rossman grounded to short.
2 Schaefer flied to center.
3 Schmidt bounced back to the mound.

3rd Inning
Chicago
Sheckard again doubled to right.
Evers beat out a bunt to third, Sheckard going to third.
Schulte singled, Sheckard scoring as Evers stopped at second.
1 Chance forced Evers at third on a sacrifice bunt, Killian to Schaefer.
Steinfeldt singled to left, scoring Schulte as Chance got to third and Steinfeldt to second on McIntyre's poor throw to third.
Hofman walked loading the bases.
For Detroit—Summers now pitching.
2 Tinker forced Hofman, Downs to O'Leary, scoring Chance as Steinfeldt moved up.
Tinker stole second.
Kling safe on Schaefer's fumble, Steinfeldt scoring as Tinker went to third.
3 Kling out trying to steal, Summers to Downs to Rossman.
Detroit
1 Downs grounded to short.
2 Summers struck out.
3 McIntyre fouled to Kling.

4th Inning
Chicago
1 Reulbach struck out.
Sheckard singled to left, his third hit.
2 Evers sacrificed, Summers to Rossman.
3 Schulte flied to left.
Detroit
1 O'Leary grounded to short.
2 Crawford lined to second.
3 Cobb grounded to second.

5th Inning
Chicago
1 Chance fouled to Schmidt.
Steinfeldt walked.
2 Hofman forced Steinfeldt at second, O'Leary to Downs.
3 Tinker grounded to third.
Detroit
1 Rossman struck out.
2 Schaefer flied to left.
3 Schmidt flied to center.

6th Inning
Chicago
1 Kling flied to deep left.
2 Reulbach grounded to second.
3 Sheckard flied to left.
Detroit
1 Downs bunted out to the mound.
2 Summer bounced to the mound.

6th Inning (continued)
McIntyre beat out a bunt when Kling fell down.
O'Leary singled over third, McIntyre going to second.
3 Crawford bounced back to the mound.

7th Inning
Chicago
Evers beat out a bouncer to first.
1 Schulte sacrificed Evers to second, Summers to Rossman.
Chance safe on Down's fumble, Evers going to third.
Chance stole second.
2 Steinfeldt flied to center, Evers scoring after the catch.
3 Hofman bounced back to the mound.
Detroit
Cobb singled off of Reulbach's body.
Rossman singled to center, Cobb going to third and Rossman going to second on the throw to third.
1 Schaefer struck out on a 3–2 count.
2 Schmidt grounded to short, Cobb scoring as Rossman held second.
Downs got a ground rule double to left, scoring Rossman.
Summers blooped a Texas League single into left, scoring Downs.
For Chicago—Overall came in to pitch.
McIntyre was hit by a pitch.
3 O'Leary flied to right.

8th Inning
Chicago
Tinker doubled to right.
1 Kling sacrificed Tinker to third, Summers to Rossman.
2 Overall struck out.
3 Sheckard grounded to short.
Detroit
Crawford walked.
For Chicago—Brown relieved Overall.
Crawford to second on a wild pitch.
Cobb safe as Chance dropped Brown's throw on his bunt, Crawford to third.
Rossman singled to center, Crawford scoring. Cobb also scored and Rossman got to second on Evers wild relay to third.
1 Schaefer sacrificed Rossman to third, Kling to Chance.
2 Schmidt grounded to second.
3 Downs flied to center.

9th Inning
Chicago
1 Evers grounded to first.
Schulte beat out a hit to deep short.
Chance singled to center, Schulte to second.
Steinfeldt singled to short left, loading the bases.
Hofman singled to center, scoring Schulte and Chance, Steinfeldt to third.
Tinker beat out a bunt, Steinfeldt scoring as Hofman stopped at second.
Hofman and Tinker worked a double steal.
Kling singled to center, scoring Hofman and Tinker.
2 Brown sacrificed, Schmidt to Rossman.
3 Sheckard flied to center.
Detroit
1 Jones, batting for Summers, struck out.
McIntyre walked.
Thomas, batting for O'Leary, singled to left, McIntyre going to second.
Winter ran for Thomas.
2 Crawford flied to center, McIntyre taking third after the catch.
3 Cobb grounded back to the mound.

Game 2 October 11 at Chicago

Detroit	Pos	AB	R	H	RBI	PO	A	E
McIntyre	lf	4	0	0	0	3	0	0
O'Leary	ss	3	0	0	0	1	1	0
a Jones		0	1	0	0	0	0	0
Crawford	cf	4	0	0	0	4	0	0
Cobb	rf	4	0	1	1	1	0	0
Rossman	1b	4	0	0	0	8	1	0
Schaefer	3b	3	0	2	0	0	4	0
Schmidt	c	3	0	1	0	7	0	0
Downs	2b	2	0	0	0	0	4	0
Donovan	p	2	0	0	0	0	1	1
Totals		29	1	4	1	24	8	1

a Walked for O'Leary in 9th.

Double—Kling. Triple—Schulte. Home Run—Tinker. Stolen Bases—Chance, Evers, Schaefer, Sheckard. Sacrifice—Donovan. Double Plays—Downs to O'Leary to Rossman, Tinker to Chance. Wild Pitch—Donovan. Left on Bases—Detroit 4, Chicago 2. Umpires—Klem (N), Connolly (A). Attendance—17,760. Time of Game—1:30.

	Det.	000 000 001
	Chi.	000 000 06x

Chicago	Pos	AB	R	H	RBI	PO	A	E
Sheckard	lf	4	1	1	1	3	0	0
Evers	2b	4	1	1	0	6	0	0
Schulte	rf	4	1	1	1	1	0	0
Chance	1b	3	0	0	0	12	0	0
Steinfeldt	3b	4	0	0	0	1	1	0
Hofman	cf	3	1	1	0	4	0	0
Tinker	ss	3	1	1	2	2	3	0
Kling	c	3	1	1	0	8	0	0
Overall	p	3	0	1	0	0	2	0
Totals		31	6	7	5	27	12	0

Pitching	IP	H	R	ER	BB	SO
Detroit						
Donovan (L)	9	7	6	6	1	7
Chicago						
Overall (W)	9	4	1	1	2	5

1st Inning
Detroit
1 McIntyre lined to short.
2 O'Leary grounded to short.
3 Crawford grounded to short.
Chicago
1 Sheckard flied to left.
2 Evers flied to center.
3 Schulte struck out.

2nd Inning
Detroit
1 Cobb fouled to Kling.
2 Rossman grounded to second.
3 Schaefer fouled to Kling.
Chicago
1 Chance grounded to second.
2 Steinfeldt flied to center.
3 Hofman struck out.

3rd Inning
Detroit
1 Schmidt grounded to the mound.
   Downs walked.
2 Donovan sacrificed Downs to second,
   Steinfeldt to Chance.
3 McIntyre struck out.
Chicago
1 Tinker grounded to second.
2 Kling struck out.
   Overall safe when Donovan dropped
   Rossman's throw at first.
3 Sheckard flied to center.

4th Inning
Detroit
1 O'Leary struck out.
2 Crawford flied to right.
3 Cobb bounced to the pitcher.
Chicago
1 Evers popped to first.
2 Schulte flied to right.
3 Chance flied to left.

5th Inning
Detroit
1 Rossman flied to left.
   Schaefer singled to center for
   the first hit of the game.
   Schmidt singled to right,
   Schaefer going to second.
2 Downs struck out.
3 Donovan popped to third.
Chicago
1 Steinfeldt struck out.
2 Hofman grounded to third.
3 Tinker flied to center.

6th Inning
Detroit
1 McIntyre struck out.
2 O'Leary grounded to second.
3 Crawford grounded to second.
Chicago
1 Kling struck out.
   Overall singled to center for the
   Cubs' first hit.
2,3 Sheckard hit into a double play,
   Downs to O'Leary to Rossman.

7th Inning
Detroit
1 Cobb flied to left.
2 Rossman flied to left.
   Schaefer safe on a bunt single.
   Schaefer stole second.
3 Schmidt grounded to second.
Chicago
1 Evers grounded to second.
2 Schulte grounded to first.
3 Chance struck out.

8th Inning
Detroit
1 Downs struck out.
2 Donovan popped to Kling.
3 McIntyre grounded to second.
Chicago
1 Steinfeldt struck out.
   Hofman scratched an infield single.
   Tinker hit a two-run homer into the
   right field bleachers.
   Kling doubled into the crowd in left.
2 Overall grounded back to the mound,
   Kling moving to third.
   Sheckard singled to center, scoring
   Kling.
   Sheckard stole second.
   Evers singled, scoring Sheckard.
   Evers stole second.
   Schulte tripled to left-center,
   scoring Evers.
   Schulte scored on a wild pitch.
   Chance walked.
   Chance stole second.
3 Steinfeldt flied to left.

9th Inning
Detroit
   Jones, pinch-hitting for O'Leary,
   walked.
1 Crawford grounded to second, Jones
   going to second.
   Cobb singled to center, scoring Jones.
2,3 Rossman hit into a double play,
   Tinker to Chance.

Game 3 October 12 at Chicago

Detroit	Pos	AB	R	H	RBI	PO	A	E
McIntyre	lf	4	1	1	0	1	0	0
O'Leary	ss	4	2	0	1	3	3	1
Crawford	cf	5	1	2	1	3	0	0
Cobb	rf	5	1	4	2	0	0	0
Rossman	1b	4	2	2	2	9	0	2
Schaefer	2b	4	0	0	0	4	4	0
Thomas	c	3	0	1	1	9	2	0
Coughlin	3b	3	0	0	1	0	1	1
Mullin	p	3	1	1	0	1	0	0
Totals		35	8	11	8	27	11	4

Pitching	IP	H	R	ER	BB	SO
Detroit						
Mullin (W)	9	7	3	0	1	8
Chicago						
Pfiester (L)	8	10	8	7	3	1
Reulbach	1	1	0	0	1	0

	Det.	100 005 020
	Chi.	000 300 000

Chicago	Pos	AB	R	H	RBI	PO	A	E
Sheckard	lf	4	0	0	0	1	0	0
Evers	2b	3	0	1	0	1	6	0
Schulte	rf	4	0	1	0	1	0	0
Chance	1b	4	1	2	1	14	0	0
Steinfeldt	3b	4	1	1	0	1	4	1
Hofman	cf	4	0	2	1	3	1	0
Tinker	ss	3	0	0	0	3	2	0
Kling	c	3	0	0	0	3	2	0
Pfiester	p	2	0	0	0	0	0	0
a Howard		1	0	0	0	0	0	0
Reulbach	p	0	0	0	0	0	1	0
Totals		32	3	7	2	27	15	1

a Grounded out for Pfiester in 8th.

Doubles—Cobb, Thomas. Triple—Hofman. Stolen Bases—Chance, Cobb 2, Rossman, Steinfeldt. Sacrifice Hits—Coughlin, O'Leary. Double Plays—Schaefer to Rossman, Schaefer to O'Leary to Rossman, Evers to Chance, Hofman to Kling. Left on Bases—Detroit 6, Chicago 3. Umpires—O'Day, Sheridan. Attendance—14,543. Time of Game—2:10.

1st Inning
Detroit
1 McIntyre grounded to second.
   O'Leary safe on Steinfeldt's fumble.
2 Crawford rolled out, Kling to Chance,
   O'Leary going to second.
   Cobb singled to center, O'Leary scoring.
3 Rossman grounded to third.
Chicago
1 Sheckard struck out.
2 Evers fouled to left.
   Schulte singled to left.
3 Schulte out trying to steal second,
   Thomas to O'Leary.

2nd Inning
Detroit
1 Schaefer grounded to third.
2 Thomas grounded to second.
3 Coughlin grounded to second.
Chicago
1 Chance popped to Schaefer.
2 Steinfeldt struck out.
3 Hofman struck out.

3rd Inning
Detroit
1 Mullin grounded to third.
2 McIntyre popped to first.
3 O'Leary fouled to Kling.
Chicago
   Tinker singled to right-center.
1 Tinker caught trying to steal
   second, Thomas to Schaefer.
2 Kling grounded to first.
3 Pfiester struck out.

4th Inning
Detroit
   Crawford singled to center.
1 Cobb forced Crawford at second,
   Evers to Tinker.
2,3 Rossman popped into a hit and run
   double play, Evers to Chance.
Chicago
1 Sheckard struck out.
   Evers walked.
   Evers safe at second on Rossman's
   wild throw on a stolen base attempt.
2 Schulte fouled to Thomas.
   Chance singled to center, scoring Evers.
   Chance stole second.
   Steinfeldt safe on Coughlin's poor throw
   to first, Chance going to third.
   Rossman's return throw was also wild
   and Chance scored with Steinfeldt
   going to second.
   Hofman tripled to left, scoring
   Steinfeldt.
3 Tinker grounded out, O'Leary to
   Rossman.

5th Inning
Detroit
1 Schaefer popped to short.
2 Thomas grounded to short.
3 Coughlin struck out.
Chicago
   Kling safe on O'Leary's fumble.
1 Pfiester struck out, foul bunting on
   the third strike.
2,3 Sheckard hit into a double play,
   Schaefer to Rossman.

6th Inning
Detroit
   Mullin walked.
   McIntyre singled to left, Mullin
   going to second.
   O'Leary beat out a bunt, loading the
   bases.
   Crawford singled through first, Mullin
   scoring with the bases still loaded.
   Cobb beat out a roller to short,
   scoring McIntyre.
   Rossman singled to right, scoring
   O'Leary and Crawford as Cobb raced
   to third.
1,2 Schaefer flied to Hofman who threw
   to Kling getting Cobb trying to
   score.
   Thomas doubled to right-center,
   scoring Rossman.
3 Coughlin grounded to second.
Chicago
1 Evers grounded to third.
2 Schulte bounced back to the mound.
   Chance stole second.
3 Steinfeldt struck out.

7th Inning
Detroit
1 Mullin popped to short.
   McIntyre walked.
2 O'Leary grounded to first, McIntyre
   going to second.
3 Crawford flied to center.
Chicago
   Hofman singled to right.
1 Tinker struck out.
2,3 Kling grounded into a double play,
   O'Leary to Schaefer to Rossman.

8th Inning
Detroit
   Cobb doubled to left, his third hit.
   Rossman beat out a bunt, Cobb going
   to third.
1 Schaefer flied to right, Rossman going
   to second on the throw to the plate
   to hold Cobb.
   Thomas walked loading the bases.
2 Coughlin flied to left, Cobb scoring
   after the catch.
   Mullin singled through first, scoring
   Rossman as Thomas went to third.
3 McIntyre grounded to third.
Chicago
1 Howard, batting for Pfiester,
   grounded to second.
2 Sheckard also grounded to second.
3 Evers flied to center.

9th Inning
Detroit
   For Chicago—Reulbach pitching.
1 O'Leary popped to first.
2 Crawford flied to center.
   **Cobb singled to left, his fourth
   hit of the game.**
   Cobb stole second.
   Cobb stole third.
   Rossman walked.
3 On a double steal attempt, Cobb was
   out Reulbach to Kling to Steinfeldt,
   however Rossman credited for
   stealing second.
Chicago
1 Schulte flied to center.
2 Chance flied to center.
   Steinfeldt singled to left.
   Steinfeldt stole second.
3 Hofman grounded to short.

Game 4 October 13 at Detroit

Chicago	Pos	AB	R	H	RBI	PO	A	E
Sheckard	lf	4	0	0	0	0	0	0
Evers	2b	5	1	1	0	0	3	0
Schulte	rf	3	1	2	0	0	0	0
Chance	1b	4	1	2	0	17	0	0
Steinfeldt	3b	3	0	1	1	2	3	0
Hofman	cf	4	0	2	1	1	0	0
Tinker	ss	4	0	0	0	2	8	0
Kling	c	4	0	2	0	5	1	0
Brown	p	4	0	0	0	0	4	0
Totals		35	3	10	2	27	19	0

Pitching	IP	H	R	ER	BB	SO
Chicago						
Brown (W)	9	4	0	0	0	4
Detroit						
Summers (L)	8	9	2	2	3	5
Winter	1	1	1	0	1	0

Chi. 0 0 2 0 0 0 0 0 1
Det. 0 0 0 0 0 0 0 0 0

Detroit	Pos	AB	R	H	RBI	PO	A	E
McIntyre	lf	4	0	0	0	1	0	0
O'Leary	ss	4	0	2	0	2	3	0
Crawford	cf	4	0	2	0	2	0	0
Cobb	rf	3	0	0	0	1	0	1
Rossman	1b	3	0	0	0	12	1	0
Schaefer	2b	3	0	0	0	2	3	0
Schmidt	c	3	0	0	0	6	2	0
Coughlin	3b	2	0	0	0	1	4	0
Summers	p	2	0	0	0	0	2	0
a Jones		1	0	0	0	0	0	0
Winter	p	0	0	0	0	0	0	0
Totals		29	0	4	0	27	15	1

a Grounded out for Summers in 8th.

Double—Crawford. Stole Bases—Evers, Hofman, Schulte 2. Sacrifice Hit—Steinfeldt. Double Play—Brown to Tinker to Chance. Hit by Pitcher—Coughlin (by Brown). Left on Bases—Chicago 10, Detroit 3. Passed Balls—Kling, Schmidt. Umpires—Connolly, Klem. Attendance—12,907. Time of Game—1:35.

1st Inning
Chicago
1 Sheckard grounded to first.
2 Evers flied to right.
  Schulte singled to center.
  Schulte stole second.
  Chance singled to center, Schulte going to third.
  Chance took second on a short passed ball.
3 Steinfeldt grounded to third.
Detroit
1 McIntyre grounded to short.
2 O'Leary bounced back to the mound.
  Crawford doubled into the right field crowd.
  Crawford to third on a passed ball.
3 Cobb grounded to short.

2nd Inning
Chicago
1 Hofman grounded to the mound.
2 Tinker grounded to short.
  Kling singled to center.
3 Brown struck out.
Detroit
1 Rossman grounded to second.
2 Schaefer struck out.
3 Schmidt flied to center.

3rd Inning
Chicago
1 Sheckard grounded to second.
2 Evers grounded to short.
  Schulte walked.
  Schulte stole second.
  Chance walked.
  Steinfeldt singled to left, scoring Schulte as Chance stopped at second.
  Hofman singled to right, scoring Chance as Steinfeldt went to third and Hofman to second on the throw home.
3 Tinker grounded to short.
Detroit
1 Coughlin grounded to third.
2 Summers struck out.
3 McIntyre bounced back to the mound.

4th Inning
Chicago
1 Kling grounded to third.
2 Brown grounded to second.
  Sheckard walked.
3 Evers flied to center.
Detroit
  O'Leary singled to left,
  Crawford singled to right, O'Leary going to second.
1 Cobb bunted into a force out of O'Leary at third, Brown to Steinfeldt.
2 Crawford was picked off second, Kling to Tinker.
3 Rossman struck out.

5th Inning
Chicago
  Schulte singled to deep second.
  Chance beat out a bunt, Schulte taking second.
1 Steinfeldt sacrificed up both runners, Rossman to Schaefer.
2 Hofman flied to short left.
3 Tinker grounded to third.
Detroit
1 Schaefer grounded to second.
2 Schmidt grounded to Tinker, making a fantastic stop.
  Coughlin hit by a pitch.
3 Summers grounded to first.

6th Inning
Chicago
  Kling singled through the box.
1 Brown struck out.
2 Kling caught stealing, Schmidt to O'Leary.
3 Sheckard struck out.
Detroit
1 McIntyre fouled to Kling.
  O'Leary singled to center.
2,3 Crawford hit into a double play, Brown to Tinker to Chance.

7th Inning
Chicago
1 Evers struck out.
2 Schulte bounced back to the mound.
3 Chance flied to center.
Detroit
1 Cobb struck out.
2 Rossman grounded to short.
3 Schaefer fouled to Steinfeldt.

8th Inning
Chicago
1 Steinfeldt grounded to third.
  Hofman singled to center.
  Hofman stole second.
2 Tinker struck out.
3 Kling fouled to Coughlin.
Detroit
1 Schmidt grounded to second.
2 Coughlin grounded to third.
3 Jones, batting for Summers, grounded to short.

9th Inning
Chicago
For Detroit—Winter now pitching.
1 Brown popped to short.
2 Sheckard popped to second.
  Evers singled to right.
  Evers stole second.
  Schulte walked.
  Chance safe as Cobb muffed his fly, Evers scoring and Schulte going to third.
3 Schulte out on an attempted double steal, Schmidt to Schaefer to Schmidt.
Detroit
1 McIntyre grounded to short.
2 O'Leary grounded to third.
3 Crawford grounded to short.

Game 5 October 14 at Detroit

Chicago	Pos	AB	R	H	RBI	PO	A	E
Sheckard	lf	3	0	1	0	2	0	0
Evers	2b	4	1	3	1	2	3	0
Schulte	rf	3	0	1	0	1	0	0
Chance	1b	3	0	1	1	11	0	0
Steinfeldt	3b	2	0	0	0	0	3	0
Hofman	cf	4	0	0	0	1	4	0
Tinker	ss	4	0	1	0	1	4	0
Kling	c	3	1	2	0	9	2	0
Overall		3	0	0	0	0	3	0
Totals		29	2	10	2	27	12	0

Pitching	IP	H	R	ER	BB	SO
Chicago						
Overall (W)	9	3	0	0	4	10
Detroit						
Donovan (L)	9	10	2	2	3	3

Chi. 1 0 0 0 1 0 0 0 0
Det. 0 0 0 0 0 0 0 0 0

Detroit	Pos	AB	R	H	RBI	PO	A	E
McIntyre	lf	3	0	1	0	2	0	0
O'Leary	ss	4	0	0	0	2	2	0
Crawford	cf	4	0	1	0	3	0	0
Cobb	rf	3	0	0	0	1	0	0
Rossman	1b	4	0	0	0	7	3	0
Schaefer	2b	4	0	0	0	5	4	0
Schmidt	c	4	0	0	0	5	2	0
Coughlin	3b	3	0	1	0	2	1	0
Donovan	p	2	0	0	0	1	1	0
Totals		30	0	3	0	*26	12	0

* Overall out, hit by batted ball.

Doubles—Evers, McIntyre, Stolen Base—Donovan. Sacrifice Hits—Overall, Schulte, Steinfeldt. Double Plays—Schmidt to Schaefer to Schmidt, O'Leary to Rossman to Coughlin. Wild Pitch—Overall. Left on Bases—Chicago 6, Detroit 7. Umpires—Sheridan, O'Day. Attendance—**6,210 (record low)**. Time of Game—**1:25 (shortest in Series history)**.

1st Inning
Chicago
1 Sheckard popped to second.
  Evers singled to center.
  Schulte singled to right, Evers going to second.
  Chance singled to center, Evers scoring as Schulte stopped at second.
2 Steinfeldt flied to center.
3 Hofman forced Schulte at third, Coughlin unassisted.
Detroit
  McIntyre walked.
1 O'Leary struck out.
  Coughlin singled to center, McIntyre going to second.
2 Cobb struck out.
  Rossman struck out but safe on a wild pitch, loading the bases.
3 Schaefer struck out.

2nd Inning
Chicago
1 Tinker grounded to third.
2 Kling fouled to Schmidt.
3 Overall grounded out, Rossman to Donovan.
Detroit
1 Schmidt struck out, Overall's fifth strikeout.
2 Coughlin grounded to short.
  Donovan walked.
  Donovan stole second.
3 McIntyre flied to center.

3rd Inning
Chicago
1 Sheckard popped to first.
2 Evers popped to short.
3 Schulte flied to left.
Detroit
1 O'Leary grounded to third.
2 Crawford grounded to second.
3 Cobb flied to left.

4th Inning
Chicago
1 Chance flied to right.
  Steinfeldt walked.
2 Steinfeldt out trying to steal, Schmidt to Schaefer.
3 Hofman struck out.
Detroit
1 Rossman struck out.
  Schaefer walked.
2 Schmidt struck out.
3 Schaefer caught trying to steal, Kling to Tinker.

5th Inning
Chicago
1 Tinker popped to short.
  Kling walked.
2 Overall sacrificed, Schmidt to Rossman.
  Sheckard walked.
  Evers doubled to center, Kling scoring as Sheckard stopped at third.
3 Schulte grounded to short.
Detroit
  Coughlin singled on a bad hop over Steinfeldt.
1 Donovan struck out.
  McIntyre doubled to right, Coughlin stopping at third.
2 O'Leary flied to shallow center.
3 Crawford struck out.

6th Inning
Chicago
  Chance beat out a bunt.
1 Steinfeldt sacrificed Chance to second, Rossman unassisted.
2 Hofman flied to left.
3 Tinker lined to center.
Detroit
  Cobb walked.
1 Rossman forced Cobb at second, Tinker to Evers.
2 Schaefer struck out.
3 Schmidt popped to second.

7th Inning
Chicago
1 Kling flied to center.
  Overall singled to center.
2 Sheckard gets an automatic single when his grounder hit Overall for an automatic out.
3 Sheckard picked off, Donovan to Rossman to Schaefer.
Detroit
1 Coughlin grounded to third.
2 Donovan grounded to short.
3 McIntyre flied to left.

8th Inning
Chicago
  Evers beat out a smasher to first for his third hit of the game.
1 Schulte sacrificed Evers to second, Schmidt to Rossman.
  Chance singled to left for his third hit of the game, Evers going to third.
2,3 Steinfeldt struck out and on an attempted double steal Evers was out, Schmidt to Schaefer to Schmidt.
Detroit
1 O'Leary popped to first.
2 Crawford grounded to second.
3 Cobb grounded to short.

9th Inning
Chicago
1 Hofman struck out.
  Tinker singled past first.
2,3 Kling grounded out, O'Leary to Rossman and as Tinker tried to go to third he was out, Rossman to Coughlin.
Detroit
1 Rossman grounded to second.
2 Schaefer grounded to third.
3 Schmidt grounded out, Kling to Chance.

1908 WORLD SERIES COMPOSITE BOX

	Wins	Composite Line Score
Chicago Cubs (N.L.)	4	1 0 6 3 1 0 1 6 6 – 24
Detroit Tigers (A.L.)	1	2 0 0 0 0 5 3 4 1 – 15

Manager	W	L	Pct.	G. Ahead
	Regular Season			
Frank Chance	99	55	.643	1
Hughie Jennings	90	63	.588	½

BATTING AND FIELDING

CHICAGO CUBS

	WORLD SERIES STATISTICS Pos	G	AB	R	H	2B	3B	HR	RBI	BB	SO	SB	BA	SA	PO	A	E	REGULAR SEASON STATISTICS Main Pos	G	AB	R	H	2B	3B	HR	RBI	BB	SO	SB	BA	SA
Frank Chance	1b	5	19	4	**8**	0	0	0	2	**3**	1	**5**	**.421**	.421	**66**	0	1	1b	129	452	65	123	27	4	2	55	37		27	.272	.363
Johnny Evers	2b	5	20	**5**	7	1	0	0	2	1	2	2	.350	.400	5	**20**	1	2b	126	416	83	125	19	6	0	37	66		36	.300	.375
Joe Tinker	ss	5	19	2	5	0	0	**1**	**4**	0	2	2	.263	.421	8	**20**	0	ss	157	548	67	146	23	14	6	68	32		30	.266	.392
Harry Steinfeldt	3b	5	16	3	4	0	0	0	3	2	**5**	1	.250	.250	4	11	1	3b	150	539	63	130	20	6	1	62	36		12	.241	.306
Wildfire Schulte	rf	5	18	4	7	0	**1**	0	2	2	1	2	.389	**.500**	3	1	0	of	102	386	42	91	20	2	1	43	29		15	.236	.306
Solly Hofman	cf	5	19	2	6	0	**1**	0	**4**	1	4	2	.316	.421	10	1	0	of-3b-2b	120	411	55	100	15	5	2	42	33		15	.243	.319
Jimmy Sheckard	lf	5	**21**	2	5	**2**	0	0	1	2	3	1	.238	.333	7	0	0	of	115	403	54	93	18	3	2	22	62		18	.231	.305
Johnny Kling	c	5	16	2	4	1	0	0	2	2	2	0	.250	.313	32	6	0	c	126	424	51	117	23	5	4	59	21		16	.276	.382
Del Howard	ph	1	1	0	0	0	0	0	0	0	0	0	.000	.000				of	96	315	42	88	7	3	1	26	23		11	.279	.330
Jimmy Slagle		Did not play																of	104	352	38	78	4	1	0	26	43		17	.222	.239
Pat Moran		Did not play																c	50	150	12	39	5	1	0	12	13		6	.260	.307
Heinie Zimmerman		Did not play																2b-of	46	113	17	33	4	1	0	9	1		2	.292	.345
Kid Durbin		Did not play																of	14	28	3	7	1	0	0	0	2		0	.250	.286
Doc Marshall		Did not play																a co-f	12	20	4	6	0	1	0	3	0		0	.300	.400
Orvie Overall	p	3	6	0	2	0	0	0	0	0	1	0	.333	.333	0	2	0	p	38	70	3	9	1	1	0	9	5		1	.129	.171
Three Finger Brown	p	2	4	0	0	0	0	0	0	0	2	0	.000	.000	0	5	0	p	46	121	5	25	0	0	0	4	2		2	.207	.207
Ed Reulbach	p	2	3	0	0	0	0	0	0	0	1	0	.000	.000	0	5	0	p	46	99	10	23	6	2	0	9	6		1	.232	.333
Jack Pfiester	p	1	2	0	0	0	0	0	0	0	2	0	.000	.000	0	0	0	p	33	79	2	8	1	0	0	2	3		1	.101	.114
Chick Fraser		Did not play																p	26	50	3	6	1	0	0	1	2		1	.120	.140
Carl Lundgren		Did not play																p	23	47	2	7	0	0	0	1	0		0	.149	.149
Rube Kroh		Did not play																p	2	4	0	0	0	0	0	0	1		0	.000	.000
team total		5	164	24	48	4	2	1	20	13	26	15	.293	.360	135	71	3		158	5085	625	1267	**197**	56	19	492	418		**212**	.249	.321

Double Plays—4
Left on Bases—30

a—from St. Louis (N)
Vin Campbell (ph), Jack Hayden (of), Andy Coakley (p), Bill Mack (p), Carl Spongberg (p) also played for the Cubs during the season.

DETROIT TIGERS

	WORLD SERIES STATISTICS Pos	G	AB	R	H	2B	3B	HR	RBI	BB	SO	SB	BA	SA	PO	A	E	REGULAR SEASON STATISTICS Main Pos	G	AB	R	H	2B	3B	HR	RBI	BB	SO	SB	BA	SA
Claude Rossman	1b	5	19	3	4	0	0	0	3	1	4	1	.211	.211	48	5	**2**	1b	138	524	45	154	33	13	2	71	27		8	.294	.418
Germany Schaefer	2b-3b	5	16	0	2	0	0	0	0	1	4	1	.125	.125	10	11	1	ss-2b-3b	153	584	96	151	20	10	3	52	37		40	.259	.342
Charley O'Leary	ss	5	19	2	3	0	0	0	0	0	3	0	.158	.158	7	12	1	ss	65	211	21	53	9	3	0	17	9		4	.251	.322
Bill Coughlin	3b	3	8	0	1	0	0	0	1	0	1	0	.125	.125	3	6	1	3b	119	405	32	87	5	1	0	23	23		10	.215	.232
Ty Cobb	rf	5	19	3	7	1	0	0	**4**	1	2	2	.368	.421	3	0	1	of	150	581	88	**188**	**36**	**20**	4	**108**	34		39	**.324**	**.475**
Sam Crawford	cf	5	**21**	2	5	1	0	0	1	1	2	0	.238	.286	16	0	0	of	152	**591**	102	184	33	16	7	80	37		15	.311	.457
Matty McIntyre	lf	5	18	2	4	1	0	0	0	**3**	2	1	.222	.278	10	0	1	of	151	569	**105**	168	24	13	0	28	83		20	.295	.383
Boss Schmidt	c	4	14	0	1	0	0	0	1	0	2	0	.071	.071	22	7	0	c	122	419	45	111	14	3	1	38	16		5	.265	.320
Red Downs	2b	2	6	1	1	1	0	0	1	1	2	0	.167	.333	2	8	1	2b	84	289	29	64	10	3	1	35	5		2	.251	.322
Ira Thomas	ph-c	2	4	0	2	1	0	0	1	1	0	0	.500	.750	9	2	0	c	40	101	6	31	1	0	0	8	5		0	.307	.317
Davy Jones	ph	3	2	1	0	0	0	0	0	1	1	0	.000	.000				of	56	121	17	25	2	1	0	10	13		11	.207	.240
Red Killefer		Did not play																2b-ss-3b	28	75	9	16	1	0	0	11	3		4	.213	.227
Ed Summers	p	2	5	0	1	0	0	0	1	0	2	0	.200	.200	0	7	0	p	40	113	6	14	2	0	0	5	0		0	.124	.142
Wild Bill Donovan	p	2	4	0	0	0	0	0	0	1	1	1	.000	.000	1	2	1	p	30	82	5	13	1	0	0	2	10		2	.159	.171
George Mullin	p	1	3	1	1	0	0	0	1	1	0	0	.333	.333	0	1	0	p-ph	55	125	13	32	2	2	1	8	7		2	.256	.328
Ed Killian	p	1	0	0	0	0	0	0	0	0	0	0	—	—	0	1	0	p	28	73	5	10	3	0	0	6	0		0	.137	.178
George Winter	pr-p	2	0	0	0	0	0	0	0	0	0	0	—	—	0	0	0	b p	7	18	0	2	0	0	0	0	0		0	.111	.111
Ed Willett		Did not play—ankle injury																p	30	67	4	11	1	0	0	8	0		0	.164	.179
George Suggs		Did not play																p	6	10	1	2	1	0	0	1	1		0	.200	.300
team total		5	158	15	32	5	0	0	14	12	26	6	.203	.234	131	62	9		153	5109	**645**	**1347**	**199**	86	19	**520**	320		165	**.264**	**.347**

Double Plays—5
Left on Bases—27

b—from Boston (A)
Donie Bush (ss) Freddie Payne (c), Clay Perry (3b), Herm Malloy (p), Ed Siever (p) also played for the Tigers during the season.

PITCHING

CHICAGO CUBS

	WORLD SERIES STATISTICS G	GS	CG	IP	H	R	ER	BB	SO	W	L	SV	ERA	REGULAR SEASON STATISTICS G	GS	CG	IP	H	ER	BB	SO	W	L	Pct	SV	ShO	ERA
Orvie Overall	**3**	**2**	**2**	18 1/3	7	2	2	**7**	**15**	**2**	0	0	0.98	37	27	16	225	165	48	78	167	15	11	.577	4	4	1.92
Three Finger Brown	2	1	1	11	6	1	0	1	5	**2**	0	0	**0.00**	44	31	27	312	214	51	49	123	29	9	.763	**5**	9	1.47
Jack Pfiester	1	1	0	8	10	**8**	7	3	1	0	1	0	7.88	33	29	18	252	204	56	70	117	12	10	.565	0	3	2.00
Ed Reulbach	2	1	0	7 2/3	9	4	4	1	5	0	0	0	4.70	46	35	25	298	227	67	106	133	24	7	**.774**	1	7	2.02
Chick Fraser	Did not play													26	17	11	163	141	41	61	66	11	9	.550	2	2	2.26
Carl Lundgren	Did not play													23	15	9	139	149	65	56	38	6	9	.400	0	1	4.21
Rube Kroh	Did not play													2	1	0	12	9	2	4	11	0	0	—	0	0	1.50
team total	5	5	3	45	32	15	13	12	26	4	1	0	2.60	158	158	108	**1434**	1137	341	437	**668**	**99**	55	**.643**	12	**27**	2.14

DETROIT TIGERS

	WORLD SERIES STATISTICS G	GS	CG	IP	H	R	ER	BB	SO	W	L	SV	ERA	REGULAR SEASON STATISTICS G	GS	CG	IP	H	ER	BB	SO	W	L	Pct	SV	ShO	ERA
Wild Bill Donovan	2	**2**	**2**	17	17	**8**	**8**	4	10	0	**2**	0	4.24	29	28	25	243	210	56	53	141	18	7	.720	0	6	2.07
Ed Summers	2	1	0	14 2/3	**18**	**8**	7	4	7	0	2	0	4.30	40	32	24	301	271	55	55	103	24	12	.667	1	4	1.64
George Mullin	1	1	1	9	1	3	0	1	8	1	0	0	**0.00**	39	30	26	291	301	100	71	121	17	12	.586	1	1	3.09
Ed Killian	1	1	0	2 1/3	5	4	3	3	1	0	0	0	11.57	27	23	15	181	170	60	53	47	11	10	.524	1	0	2.98
George Winter	1	0	0	1	1	1	0	1	0	0	0	0	0.00	b 7	6	5	56	49	10	7	25	2	5	.286	1	0	1.61
Ed Willett	Did not play—ankle injury													30	22	18	197	186	50	60	77	15	9	.625	1	2	2.28
George Suggs	Did not play													6	1	1	27	32	5	2	8	1	0	1.000	1	0	1.67
team total	5	5	3	44	48	24	18	13	26	1	4	0	3.68	153	153	**120**	1374	**1313**	367	318	553	**90**	63	**.588**	6	14	2.40

Total Attendance—62,232 Average Attendance—12,446 Winning Player's Share—$1,318 Losing Player's Share—$870

1909
Surprise from Start to Finish

When the Detroit Tigers won their third straight American League pennant and the Pittsburgh Pirates dethroned the Chicago Cubs in the National League, it set the stage for the confrontation of the world's two best players, Ty Cobb and Honus Wagner. Cobb was an established superstar at the age of twenty-two, leading the A.L. with a .377 batting average, 9 home runs, 107 runs batted in, and 76 stolen bases. At the more mature age of thirty-five, Wagner had been the heart of the Pirates since the turn of the century and had just won his fourth straight N.L. batting title with a .339 mark, garnished with a league-leading total of 100 RBI's. Both men excelled on the base paths, and while Cobb had a weak throwing arm from the outfield, Wagner's big hands and long arms made him a human vacuum cleaner at shortstop with a shotgun throwing arm. Both the Tigers and Pirates had other fine talents besides these two stars, but Cobb and Wagner dominated the public images of their teams.

The hero of the Series, however, would be neither of them, but instead a twenty-seven-year-old reserve pitcher for the Pirates by the name of Babe Adams. The Pirates had three ace hurlers in Howie Camnitz, Vic Willis, and Lefty Leifield, but manager Fred Clarke named the unheralded Adams to start the opening game, no doubt impressed by his 12–3 record during the season. With the first contest staged in Pittsburgh's newly opened Forbes Field, the Tigers scored a run off Adams in the top of the first but failed to score the rest of the game; the Pirates meanwhile scored four runs off 29-game-winner George Mullin, with playing-manager Clarke showing the way with a home run. Clarke started 25-game-winner Camnitz in game two, but the Tigers shelled the ace pitcher from the mound en route to a 7–2 win behind Wild Bill Donovan, with Cobb causing a stir by stealing home in the third inning.

The clubs took Sunday off and reassembled in Detroit on Monday for game three. The Pirates kayoed Tiger starter Ed Summers with a five-run first inning, then had to withstand a late Tiger rally fueled by two errors to hang on to an 8–6 win. Wagner starred in this contest, getting three hits, two RBI's, and three stolen bases, and Nick Maddox, another lesser light on the pitching staff, got credit for the win. The Tigers then drew even with the Pirates on the strength of a five-hit shutout by Mullin, with the Detroit batters freely hitting Pittsburgh starter Leifield en route to the 5–0 win.

Game five in Pittsburgh matched knuckleballer Summers against Babe Adams. The score stood at 3–3 after six innings, but the Pirates jumped ahead with four runs in the seventh, three of them coming on another homer by manager Clarke. The Tigers went down to an 8–4 defeat and wasted home runs by Sam Crawford and Davy Jones.

The clubs went back to Detroit for games six and seven, and a small crowd of 10,535 turned out with the Tigers trailing 3–2 in the Series. But this Detroit club refused to fold as did the 1907 and 1908 Tiger teams. The Pirates scored three times in the top of the first inning off Mullin, but the Tigers chipped away against Willis and Camnitz to take a 5–4 win and send the Series into a seventh game for the first time ever.

The top Pirate pitchers had not won through the Series, so Pittsburgh pilot Clarke entrusted his team's fate to Adams, his surprisingly effective second-liner. Tiger manager Hughie Jennings picked Wild Bill Donovan, a veteran ace who had won only eight games during the regular season. Donovan gave up two runs in three shaky innings and was replaced by Mullin, still tired from his nine innings of work in game six two days ago. The Pirates greeted him with two runs in the fourth, added three more in the sixth and a final marker in the eighth, and took the World Championship with an 8–0 victory behind Adams's six-hitter. In retrospect, Wagner came out on top in his match-up with Cobb; while Cobb hit only .231, Wagner hit .333 and drove in six runs. The Detroit catching again hurt their cause, allowing the Pirates to steal a record-equaling 18 bases. But that weakness was common knowledge, while Babe Adams's step out of the shadows into the limelight with three victories provided heroics in a surprise package.

Game 1 October 8 at Pittsburgh

| | | Det. | 1 0 0 | 0 0 0 | 0 0 0 |
| Pit. | | | 0 0 0 | 1 2 1 | 0 0 x |

Detroit	Pos	AB	R	H	RBI	PO	A	E
D. Jones	lf	3	0	2	0	5	0	0
Bush	ss	2	0	0	0	1	0	1
Cobb	rf	3	1	0	0	2	0	1
Crawford	cf	4	0	1	0	1	0	0
Delahanty	2b	4	0	1	1	0	4	1
Moriarty	3b	4	0	1	0	0	1	0
T. Jones	1b	3	0	0	0	10	0	0
a McIntyre		1	0	0	0	0	0	0
Schmidt	c	3	0	0	0	5	1	1
Mullin	p	4	0	1	0	0	4	0
Totals		31	1	6	1	24	10	4

Pittsburgh	Pos	AB	R	H	RBI	PO	A	E
Byrne	3b	3	0	0	0	2	3	0
Leach	cf	3	0	0	1	4	0	0
Clarke	lf	4	1	1	1	2	0	0
Wagner	ss	3	1	1	0	4	0	0
Miller	2b	4	0	1	0	6	0	0
Abstein	1b	3	1	0	1	8	1	0
Wilson	rf	3	0	1	0	0	0	0
Gibson	c	3	1	1	1	4	0	0
Adams	p	3	0	0	0	0	2	0
Totals		29	4	5	4	*26	12	0

* Delahanty out, hit by batted ball.
a Flied out for T. Jones in 9th.

Doubles—Gibson, Wagner. Home Run—Clarke. Stolen Bases—Cobb, Miller, Wilson. Sacrifice Hit—Bush. Sacrifice Fly—Leach. Hit by Pitcher—Byrne and Wagner (by Mullin). Passed Ball—Schmidt. Left on Bases—Detroit 8, Pittsburgh 5. Umpires—Johnstone (N), O'Loughlin (A). Attendance—29,264. Time of Game—1:55.

Pitching	IP	H	R	ER	BB	SO
Detroit						
Mullin (L)	8	5	4	1	1	4
Pittsburgh						
Adams (W)	9	6	1	1	4	2

1st Inning
Detroit
 D. Jones walked on four pitches.
1 Bush sacrificed D. Jones to second, Abstein to Miller.
 Cobb walked.
2 Crawford forced D. Jones at third, Adams to Byrne.
 Delahanty singled to left, Cobb scoring.
3 Moriarty got an automatic single as his grounder hit Delahanty for an automatic out.
Pittsburgh
1 Byrne popped to short.
2 Leach grounded to second.
3 Clarke grounded back to the mound.

2nd Inning
Detroit
1 T. Jones grounded to third.
2 Schmidt grounded to third, Byrne making a play from deep third.
 Mullin singled over second.
3 D. Jones lined to third.
Pittsburgh
1 Wagner grounded to second.
2 Miller flied to right.
 Abstein walked.
3 Abstein picked off, Mullin to T. Jones.

3rd Inning
Detroit
1 Bush bunted out, Adams to Abstein.
2 Cobb grounded to short.
 Crawford singled off Adams' glove.
3 Delahanty flied to Clarke.
Pittsburgh
1 Wilson grounded to third.
2 Gibson grounded to second.
3 Adams flied to left.

4th Inning
Detroit
1 Moriarty grounded to third.
2 T. Jones flied to center.
 Schmidt walked.
3 Mullin forced Schmidt at second, Wagner to Miller.
Pittsburgh
1 Byrne grounded back to the mound.
2 Leach struck out.
 Clarke hit a home run into the right field bleachers.
 Wagner was hit by a pitch.
3 Miller flied to right.

5th Inning
Detroit
 D. Jones singled to right.
1 Bush forced D. Jones at second, Wagner to Miller.
2 Cobb forced Bush at second, Wagner to Miller.
 Cobb stole second.
3 Crawford fouled to Gibson.

5th Inning (continued)
Pittsburgh
 Abstein safely to third on errors by Delahanty and Cobb.
1 Wilson struck out.
 Gibson doubled to center, scoring Abstein.
 Adams safe on Bush's error, Gibson going to third.
 Byrne hit by a pitch, loading the bases.
2 Leach flied to left, Gibson scoring after the catch.
3 Clarke grounded to second.

6th Inning
Detroit
1 Delahanty called out on strikes.
2 Moriarty grounded to short.
3 T. Jones robbed of a Texas Leaguer just behind second by Leach.
Pittsburgh
 Wagner doubled to left.
 Wagner went to third as Schmidt's pickoff throw went into center.
1 Miller fouled to Schmidt.
2 Abstein bounced out, Schmidt to T. Jones as Wagner scored.
 Wilson singled to center.
 Wilson stole second on a short passed ball.
3 Gibson flied to left.

7th Inning
Detroit
1 Schmidt popped to second.
2 Mullin grounded to short.
 D. Jones singled to left.
 Bush walked.
3 Cobb flied to deep center.
Pittsburgh
1 Adams flied to deep left.
2 Byrne struck out.
3 Leach lined to center.

8th Inning
Detroit
1 Crawford grounded to first.
2 Delahanty popped to Miller behind first.
3 Moriarty fouled to Gibson.
Pittsburgh
1 Clarke flied to left.
2 Wagner bounced back to Mullin.
 Miller singled to center.
 Miller stole second.
3 Abstein struck out.

9th Inning
Detroit
1 McIntyre, pinch-hitting for T. Jones, flied to left.
2 Schmidt flied to center.
3 Mullin struck out.

Game 2 October 9 at Pittsburgh

Detroit	Pos	AB	R	H	RBI	PO	A	E
D. Jones	lf	5	1	1	0	1	0	0
Bush	ss	3	1	1	0	0	2	0
Cobb	rf	3	1	1	0	0	0	0
Crawford	cf	4	1	1	0	3	0	0
Delahanty	2b	3	1	1	2	3	1	1
Moriarty	3b	3	1	1	0	3	1	0
T. Jones	1b	3	1	1	0	8	1	0
Schmidt	c	4	0	2	4	9	1	1
Donovan	p	4	0	0	0	0	4	1
Totals		32	7	9	6	27	10	3

Pitching	IP	H	R	ER	BB	SO
Detroit						
Donovan (W)	9	5	2	2	2	7
Pittsburgh						
Camnitz (L)	2⅔	6	4	3	1	2
Willis	6⅓	3	3	3	4	2

Det.	0 2 3	0 2 0	0 0 0
Pit.	2 0 0	0 0 0	0 0 0

Pittsburgh	Pos	AB	R	H	RBI	PO	A	E
Byrne	3b	3	1	0	0	4	2	0
Leach	cf	4	1	2	1	2	1	0
Clarke	lf	3	0	0	0	3	0	0
Wagner	ss	4	0	1	0	1	2	0
Miller	2b	4	0	1	1	0	5	0
Abstein	1b	4	0	1	0	12	1	1
Wilson	rf	4	0	0	0	0	0	0
Gibson	c	2	0	0	0	4	2	0
Camnitz	p	1	0	0	0	0	1	0
Willis	p	2	0	0	0	1	2	0
Totals		31	2	5	2	27	16	1

Doubles—Crawford, Leach 2, Miller, Schmidt. Stolen Bases—Cobb, Gibson, Wagner. Sacrifice Hits—Bush, Clarke. Double Plays—Bush to T. Jones to Moriarty; Miller to Abstein to Byrne. Left on Bases—Detroit 4, Pittsburgh 5. Umpires—Evans (A), Klem (N). Attendance—30,915. Time of Game—1:45.

1st Inning
Detroit
D. Jones beat out a bunt.
1 Bush sacrificed D. Jones to second, Camnitz to Abstein.
2 D. Jones caught trying to steal third, Gibson to Byrne.
3 Cobb grounded to second.
Pittsburgh
Byrne walked.
Leach doubled to left, scoring Byrne.
1 Clarke sacrificed Leach to third, Donovan to T. Jones.
2 Wagner struck out.
Miller doubled to right, scoring Leach.
3 Abstein called out on strikes.

2nd Inning
Detroit
1 Crawford called out on strikes.
2 Delahanty grounded to short.
Moriarty singled to left.
T. Jones singled to left, Moriarty going to third.
Schmidt doubled to center, scoring Moriarty and T. Jones.
3 Donovan struck out.
Pittsburgh
1 Wilson bounced back to the mound.
Gibson walked.
2 Camnitz fouled to Moriarty.
Gibson stole second.
3 Byrne struck out.

3rd Inning
Detroit
D. Jones safe on a bunt when Abstein dropped Byrne's throw.
Bush singled to left, D. Jones going to second.
Cobb walked, loading the bases.
1 Crawford flied to left.
Delahanty doubled to center, scoring D. Jones and Bush as Cobb stopped at third.
For Pittsburgh—Willis relieved Camnitz.
Cobb stole home.
Moriarty walked.
2 T. Jones forced Delahanty at third, Willis to Byrne.
3 Schmidt flied to left.
Pittsburgh
Leach doubled to left.
1 Clarke flied to center.
2 Wagner popped to Schmidt.
3 Miller struck out.

4th Inning
Detroit
1 Donovan grounded to second.
2 D. Jones grounded to third.
3 Bush struck out.
Pittsburgh
Abstein singled to right.
1 Wilson fouled to Schmidt.
2 Gibson flied to left.
3 Willis lined to second.

5th Inning
Detroit
1 Cobb grounded to Abstein, making a great stop.
Crawford doubled to left.
Delahanty walked.
2 Moriarty popped to first.
T. Jones walked, loading the bases.
Schmidt singled to center, scoring Crawford and Delahanty but T. Jones
3 was out trying for third, Leach to Byrne.
Pittsburgh
1 Byrne flied to center.
2 Leach grounded to third.
3 Clarke grounded back to the mound.

6th Inning
Detroit
1 Donovan grounded to second.
2 D. Jones flied to deep center.
Bush walked.
3 Bush caught stealing second, Gibson to Wagner.
Pittsburgh
Wagner safe on Donovan's wild throw to first.
1 Miller grounded to short, Wagner going to second.
2 Abstein called out on strikes.
3 Wagner caught trying to steal third, Schmidt to Moriarty.

7th Inning
Detroit
Cobb singled past short.
1,2 Crawford grounded into a double play, Miller to Abstein to Byrne.
3 Delahanty struck out.
Pittsburgh
Wilson safe on Delahanty's fumble.
1,2 Gibson hit into a double play, Bush to T. Jones to Moriarty.
3 Willis struck out.

8th Inning
Detroit
1 Moriarty flied to deep left.
2 T. Jones grounded to short.
3 Schmidt grounded to second.
Pittsburgh
1 Byrne popped to second.
2 Leach grounded back to the mound.
3 Clarke popped to second.

9th Inning
Detroit
1 Donovan bounced back to the mound.
2 D. Jones popped to the pitcher.
3 Bush lined to deep center.
Pittsburgh
Wagner singled to right.
Wagner stole second.
1 Miller grounded to second, Wagner going to third.
2 Abstein struck out for the third time.
3 Wilson flied to center.

Game 3 October 11 at Detroit

Pittsburgh	Pos	AB	R	H	RBI	PO	A	E
Byrne	3b	5	1	2	0	2	2	0
Leach	cf	4	3	2	0	1	0	0
Clarke	lf	3	1	0	1	5	0	0
Wagner	ss	5	1	3	2	3	4	0
Miller	2b	4	1	0	0	3	6	0
Abstein	1b	4	1	2	0	8	0	2
Wilson	rf	4	0	1	1	0	0	0
Gibson	c	4	0	0	0	5	1	0
Maddox	p	4	0	0	0	0	1	0
Totals		37	8	10	4	27	14	2

Pitching	IP	H	R	ER	BB	SO
Pittsburgh						
Maddox (W)	9	10	6	1	2	4
Detroit						
Summers (L)	⅓	3	4	0	1	0
Willett	6⅔	3	2	0	0	0
Works	2	4	2	2	0	2

Pit.	5 1 0	0 0 0	0 0 2
Det.	0 0 0	0 0 0	4 0 2

Detroit	Pos	AB	R	H	RBI	PO	A	E
D. Jones	lf	5	2	1	0	0	0	0
Bush	ss	5	1	3	2	4	4	2
Cobb	rf	5	0	2	2	3	0	0
Crawford	cf	5	0	0	1	5	0	1
Delahanty	2b	5	1	3	0	3	1	0
Moriarty	3b	3	1	0	0	0	4	0
T. Jones	1b	3	1	1	1	7	0	0
Schmidt	c	4	0	0	0	4	2	1
Summers	p	0	0	0	0	0	1	0
Willett	p	2	0	0	0	1	3	1
a McIntyre		1	0	0	0	0	0	0
Works	p	0	0	0	0	0	1	0
b Mullin		1	0	0	0	0	0	0
Totals		39	6	10	6	27	16	5

a Struck out for Willett in 7th.
b Struck out for Works in 9th.

Doubles—Abstein, Cobb, Delahanty 2, Leach. Stolen Bases—Wagner 3. Sacrifice Hit—Clarke. Hit by Pitcher—Clarke and Leach (by Willett). Left on Bases—Pittsburg 6, Detroit 8. Wild Pitch—Summers. Umpires—O'Loughlin, Johnstone, Evans, Klem. Attendance—18,277. Time of Game—1:56.

1st Inning
Pittsburgh
Byrne beat out a bunt.
Leach singled to center, Byrne going to third.
1 Clarke hit to Summers who threw to Moriarty who relayed to Bush and Byrne was out in a rundown. Leach got to third and Clarke to second.
Wagner safe on Bush's error, Leach scoring as Clarke went to third.
Wagner stole second and on Schmidt's throwing error Clarke scored and Wagner continued to third.
Wagner scored on a wild pitch.
Miller walked.
Abstein singled to center, Crawford threw wildly to third, Miller scoring as Abstein went to third.
For Detroit—Willett now pitching.
Wilson singled past short, scoring Abstein.
2 Gibson grounded to second, Wilson advancing to second.
3 Maddox fouled to Schmidt.
Detroit
1 D. Jones flied to center.
Bush singled to center.
2 Cobb called out on strikes.
3 Crawford forced Bush at second, Miller to Wagner.

2nd Inning
Pittsburgh
1 Byrne grounded to third.
Leach was hit by a pitch.
Clarke also hit by a pitch.
2 Wagner forced Clarke at second, Bush to Delahanty as Leach went to third.
On a double steal attempt, Wagner stole but Leach was trapped however, he scored when Willett dropped Moriarty's throw, Wagner going to third. The play went Schmidt to Delahanty to Moriarty to Willett. No steals.
3 Miller popped to second.
Detroit
Delahanty doubled over third.
1 Moriarty struck out.
2 T. Jones popped to third.
3 Schmidt grounded to second.

3rd Inning
Pittsburgh
1 Abstein popped to second.
2 Wilson lined to center.
3 Gibson grounded to third.
Detroit
1 Willett flied to deep left.
2 D. Jones flied to left.
3 Bush grounded to third.

4th Inning
Pittsburgh
1 Maddox bounced back to the mound.
2 Byrne grounded to short.
3 Leach robbed of a hit by Crawford, who ran into the crowd to make the catch.
Detroit
1 Cobb bounced back to the mound.
2 Crawford flied to deep left.
Delahanty singled to left.
3 Moriarty forced Delahanty at second, a great play by Wagner to Miller.

5th Inning
Pittsburgh
Clarke safe on Bush's fumble.
Wagner singled to left, Clarke going to second.
1 Miller fouled to Willett, making a fine catch.
2 Abstein flied to center, Clarke going to third after the catch.
Wagner stole second.
3 Wilson lined to short.
Detroit
1 T. Jones popped to second.
2 Schmidt grounded to second.
3 Willett grounded to third.

6th Inning
Pittsburgh
1 Gibson lined to deep center.
2 Maddox flied to right.
3 Byrne grounded out, off Willett to Bush who threw to first.
Detroit
1 D. Jones popped to Gibson.
Bush singled over short.
2 Cobb forced Bush at second, Wagner to Miller.
3 Crawford forced Cobb at second, Miller to Wagner.

7th Inning
Pittsburgh
1 Leach flied to center.
2 Clarke grounded back to the mound.
Wagner singled to left.
3 Wagner finally out trying to steal, Schmidt to Bush.
Detroit
Delehanty doubled over Leach's head, his second double of the game.
Moriarty safe at first when Abstein dropped Miller's throw to first, Delahanty going to third.
T. Jones singled to right, Delahanty scoring as Moriarty stopped at second.
1 Schmidt fouled to Byrne.
2 McIntyre, batting for Willett, struck out.
D. Jones beat out a beautiful bunt, loading the bases.
Bush singled on a liner over short, scoring Moriarty and T. Jones as D. Jones stopped at second.
Cobb singled to center, scoring D. Jones with Bush going to second.
3 Crawford popped to first.

8th Inning
Pittsburgh
For Detroit—Works pitching.
1 Miller took a called third strike.
Abstein doubled into the crowd in right.
2 Wilson bounced back to the mound, Abstein going to third.
3 Gibson fouled to Schmidt.
Detroit
1 Delahanty grounded to second.
Moriarty walked.
2 Moriarty out trying to steal, Gibson to Wagner, who made a great catch of a poor throw.
T. Jones walked.
3 Schmidt flied to left.

9th Inning
Pittsburgh
1 Maddox called out on strikes.
Byrne singled to center.
Leach doubled into the left field crowd, Byrne going to third.
2 Clarke lined to right, Byrne scoring with Leach going to third after the catch.
Wagner singled to right, scoring Leach.
Wagner stole second, **his third steal of the game.**
3 Miller out on a low liner to Cobb, making a good catch.
Detroit
1 Mullin, pinch-hitting for Works, struck out.
D. Jones safe when Abstein dropped Wagner's throw.
Bush beat out a hit to third, D. Jones going to second.
Cobb doubled into the right field crowd, D. Jones scoring with Bush going to third.
2 Crawford grounded to short, Bush scoring with Cobb stopping at second.
3 Delahanty lined to left.

Game 4 October 12 at Detroit

Pit.	000 000 000
Det.	020 300 00x

Pittsburgh	Pos	AB	R	H	RBI	PO	A	E
Byrne	3b	4	0	1	0	0	2	0
Leach	cf	3	0	0	0	3	0	0
Clarke	lf	4	0	0	0	1	0	0
Wagner	ss	3	0	0	0	2	3	1
Miller	2b	4	0	1	0	3	1	1
Abstein	1b	4	0	1	0	12	1	2
Wilson	rf	4	0	1	0	0	0	0
Gibson	c	3	0	1	0	3	3	0
Leifield	p	1	0	0	0	0	5	0
a O'Connor		1	0	0	0	0	0	0
Phillippe	p	1	0	0	0	0	2	2
Totals		32	0	5	0	24	17	6

a Struck out for Leifield in 5th.

Doubles—Bush, Byrne, Cobb. Stolen Bases—Byrne, Leach. Sacrifice Hits—T. Jones, Stanage. Double Play—Wagner to Abstein. Hit by Pitcher—Cobb and Delahanty (by Leifield). Left on Bases—Pittsburgh 7, Detroit 9. Umpires—Klem, Evans, Johnstone, O'Loughlin. Attendance—17,036. Time of Game—1:57.

Detroit	Pos	AB	R	H	RBI	PO	A	E
D. Jones	lf	4	1	1	0	0	0	0
Bush	ss	3	1	1	0	1	0	0
Cobb	rf	3	0	1	2	1	0	0
Crawford	cf	4	0	1	0	2	0	0
Delahanty	2b	3	0	0	0	1	3	0
Moriarty	3b	3	0	1	0	1	3	0
T. Jones	1b	3	1	1	0	13	0	0
Stanage	c	3	0	1	2	9	1	0
Mullin	p	3	1	0	1	0	4	0
Totals		32	5	8	5	27	12	0

Pitching	IP	H	R	ER	BB	SO
Pittsburgh						
Leifield (L)	4	7	5	5	1	0
Phillippe	4	1	0	0	1	1
Detroit						
Mullin (W)	9	5	0	0	2	10

1st Inning
Pittsburgh
1 Byrne grounded to second.
2 Leach grounded to short.
3 Clarke grounded to second.
Detroit
1 D. Jones flied to center.
2 Bush grounded back to the mound.
  Cobb hit by a pitch.
  Cobb got to second on a stolen base attempt when Abstein dropped the ball during a run-down.
3 Crawford flied to center.

2nd Inning
Pittsburgh
  Wagner walked.
1 Miller struck out.
  Abstein beat out a hit to third, Wagner taking second.
2 Wilson forced Wagner at third, Mullin to Moriarty.
3 Gibson bounced back to the mound.
Detroit
  Delahanty hit by a pitch.
  Moriarty blooped a single into short left, Delahanty going to third.
1 T. Jones bounced back to Leifield, who threw to Gibson getting Delahanty on a close play at the plate as Moriarty went to third, and T. Jones to second.
  Stanage singled to right-center, scoring Moriarty and T. Jones.
2 Mullin forced Stanage at second, Wagner unassisted but got to second on a wild throw to first trying for a double play.
3 D. Jones bounced back to the mound.

3rd Inning
Pittsburgh
1 Leifield called out on strikes.
  Byrne doubled along the left field foul line.
  Leach walked.
2 Clarke struck out as Byrne and Leach pulled off a double steal.
3 Wagner called out on strikes.
Detroit
1 Bush lined to left.
2 Cobb bunted out, Leifield to Abstein.
  Crawford singled to center.
  Delahanty safe on Abstein's fumble, Crawford going to second.
3 Moriarty forced Delahanty at second, Wagner to Miller.

4th Inning
Pittsburgh
1 Miller grounded to third.
2 Abstein struck out.
  Wilson singled past third.
3 Gibson grounded to third.
Detroit
  T. Jones beat out a bunt to third.
1,2 Stanage hit into a double play, Wagner to Abstein.
  Mullin walked.
  D. Jones singled to left, Mullin going to second.
  Bush doubled to left, scoring Mullin with D. Jones stopping at third.
  Cobb doubled to left, scoring D. Jones and Bush.
3 Crawford bounced back to the mound.

5th Inning
Pittsburgh
1 O'Connor, pinch-hitting for Leifield, struck out.
2 Byrne struck out but had to be thrown out at first.
3 Leach grounded to first.
Detroit
  For Pittsburgh—Phillippe pitching.
1 Delahanty popped to Gibson.
2 Moriarty flied to center.
3 T. Jones grounded to third.

6th Inning
Pittsburgh
1 Clarke struck out.
2 Wagner lined to first after Umpire Johnstone disallowed a hit by pitch because Wagner tried to get hit.
3 Miller struck out.
Detroit
1 Stanage grounded to second.
  Mullin safe on Miller's error.
2 D. Jones forced Mullin at second, Wagner to Miller.
3 D. Jones caught stealing, Gibson to Miller, as Miller was spiked on the elbow.

7th Inning
Pittsburgh
1 Abstein flied to center.
2 Wilson bounced back to the mound.
  Gibson singled to left.
3 Phillippe struck out.
Detroit
1 Bush out on a bunt, Phillippe to Abstein.
2 Cobb out on a bunt, Gibson to Abstein.
  Crawford safe when Phillippe covering first dropped Abstein's throw.
3 Delahanty bounced back to the mound.

8th Inning
Pittsburgh
1 Byrne flied to Crawford, making a fine catch of a short fly.
2 Leach popped to second.
3 Clarke flied to right.
Detroit
  Moriarty singled off Phillippe's knee.
  T. Jones sacrificed and was safe when Phillippe fumbled the bunt.
1 Stanage sacrificed up both runners, Gibson to Abstein.
2 Mullin struck out.
  D. Jones walked, loading the bases.
3 Bush grounded to third.

9th Inning
Pittsburgh
1 Wagner grounded to third.
  Miller beat out a bunt to the mound.
2 Abstein grounded to the mound, Miller going to second.
3 Wilson grounded to first.

Game 5 October 13 at Pittsburgh

Det.	100 002 010
Pit.	111 000 41x

Detroit	Pos	AB	R	H	RBI	PO	A	E
D. Jones	lf	4	1	1	1	3	0	0
Bush	ss	3	1	0	0	1	4	0
Cobb	rf	4	1	1	0	2	0	0
Crawford	cf	4	2	3	2	1	0	0
Delahanty	2b	4	0	0	0	0	1	0
Moriarty	3b	4	0	0	0	1	3	0
T. Jones	1b	4	0	1	0	12	0	0
Stanage	c	2	0	0	0	3	1	0
a McIntyre		1	0	0	0	0	0	0
Schmidt	c	1	0	0	0	3	1	1
Summers	p	3	0	0	0	0	1	0
Willett	p	0	0	0	0	0	0	0
b Mullin		1	0	0	0	0	0	0
Totals		35	4	6	3	24	11	1

a Grounded out for Stanage in 7th.
b Flied out for Willett in 9th.

Doubles—Crawford, T. Jones, Wilson. Home Runs—Clarke, Crawford, D. Jones. Stolen Bases—Clarke, Crawford, Gibson, T. Jones, Wagner 2. Sacrifice Hits—Adams, Clarke. Hit by Pitcher—Wagner (by Summers). Wild Pitch—Summers. Left on Bases—Detroit 5, Pittsburgh 5. Umpires—Johnstone, O'Loughlin, Klem, Evans. Attendance—21,706. Time of Game—1:46.

Pittsburgh	Pos	AB	R	H	RBI	PO	A	E
Byrne	3b	5	2	2	0	1	3	0
Leach	cf	4	1	2	0	3	0	0
Clarke	lf	2	2	1	3	2	0	0
Wagner	ss	2	1	0	1	1	2	2
Miller	2b	4	0	1	0	1	0	0
Abstein	1b	3	0	1	1	11	0	0
Wilson	rf	4	1	1	0	1	0	0
Gibson	c	4	1	2	1	8	0	0
Adams	p	3	0	0	0	0	2	0
Totals		31	8	10	6	27	7	2

Pitching	IP	H	R	ER	BB	SO
Detroit						
Summers (L)	7	10	8	7	3	4
Willett	1	0	0	0	0	1
Pittsburgh						
Adams (W)	9	6	4	3	1	8

1st Inning
Detroit
  D. Jones homered over the temporary fence in center.
  Bush walked.
1 Cobb flied to center.
  Crawford singled to left, Bush going to third.
2 Delahanty called out on strikes.
  Crawford stole second.
3 Moriarty popped to first.
Pittsburgh
  Byrne singled past short.
  Leach beat out a bunt, Byrne going to second.
1 Clarke sacrificed up both runners, Stanage to T. Jones.
  Wagner walked loading the bases.
2 Miller struck out.
  Abstein walked forcing in Byrne.
3 Wilson struck out.

2nd Inning
Detroit
1 T. Jones flied to right.
2 Stanage struck out.
3 Summers struck out.
Pittsburgh
  Gibson singled through short.
1 Adams sacrificed Gibson to second, Summers to T. Jones.
2 Byrne grounded to second, Gibson going to third.
  Gibson scored on a wild pitch.
3 Leach flied to center.

3rd Inning
Detroit
1 D. Jones flied to center.
2 Bush struck out.
3 Cobb grounded to third.
Pittsburgh
  Clarke walked.
  Wagner singled past short, Clarke going to third.
1 Miller grounded to short, Clarke scoring with Wagner going to second.
2 Abstein grounded to third, Wagner going to third.
3 Wilson grounded to short.

4th Inning
Detroit
1 Crawford grounded to short.
2 Delahanty struck out.
3 Moriarty grounded to second.
Pittsburgh
1 Gibson grounded to third.
2 Adams fouled to Schmidt.
3 Byrne flied to left.

5th Inning
Detroit
  T. Jones doubled to left.
1 Stanage struck out.
2 Summers struck out.
3 D. Jones flied to left.
Pittsburgh
1 Leach flied to left.
  Clarke beat out an infield hit.
  Clarke stole second.
2 Wagner grounded to short, Clarke going to third.
3 Miller grounded to third.

6th Inning
Detroit
1 Bush struck out.
  Cobb singled to left.
  Crawford doubled to left-center, Cobb scoring.
  Delahanty safe on Wagner's throw off the temporary fence, Crawford scoring with Delahanty going to second.
2 Moriarty flied to left.
3 T. Jones popped to first.
Pittsburgh
1 Abstein popped to short.
2 Wilson grounded to short.
3 Gibson grounded to short.

7th Inning
Detroit
1 McIntyre, batting for Stanage, grounded to first.
2 Summers grounded to first.
3 D. Jones grounded to third.
Pittsburgh
  For Detroit—Schmidt catching.
1 Adams struck out.
  Byrne singled past third.
  Leach singled to left, Byrne going to third.
  Clarke hit a three-run homer over the temporary center field fence.
  Wagner hit by a pitch.
2 Miller flied to left.
  Wagner stole second.
  Wagner stole third, and also scored Schmidt's throw into left.
3 Abstein struck out.

8th Inning
Detroit
1 Bush lined to center.
2 Cobb grounded to the mound.
  Crawford homered over the temporary fence in right.
3 Delahanty grounded to third.
Pittsburgh
  Wilson doubled to left.
  Gibson singled to right, Wilson scoring.
  For Detroit—Willett pitching.
1 Adams popped to first.
  Gibson stole second.
2 Byrne struck out.
3 Gibson out trying to steal third, Schmidt to Moriarty.

9th Inning
Detroit
1 Moriarty popped to third.
  T. Jones safe on Wagner's fumble.
  T. Jones stole second.
2 Schmidt grounded to short.
3 Mullin, pinch-hitting for Willett, popped to short.

Game 6 October 14 at Detroit

Pit. 300 000 001
Det. 100 211 00x

Pittsburgh	Pos	AB	R	H	RBI	PO	A	E
Byrne	3b	4	1	1	0	2	4	0
Leach	cf	4	1	1	0	3	0	0
Clarke	lf	3	1	1	1	2	0	1
Wagner	ss	4	0	1	2	3	2	0
Miller	2b	3	1	2	0	2	1	1
Abstein	1b	4	0	1	0	9	1	0
Wilson	rf	3	0	0	0	0	1	0
Gibson	c	4	0	1	0	2	0	0
Willis	p	2	0	0	0	0	1	0
Camnitz	p	0	0	0	0	0	0	0
a Hyatt		1	0	0	0	0	0	0
Phillippe	p	0	0	0	0	1	0	0
b Abbaticchio		1	0	0	0	0	0	0
Totals		33	4	8	3	24	10	2

a Grounded out for Camnitz in 7th.
b Struck out for Phillippe in 9th.

Doubles—Cobb, Crawford, Delahanty, Mullin, Wagner. Stolen Bases—Bush, D. Jones, Miller. Sacrifice Hits—Clarke, Wilson. Double Plays—Byrne to Abstein, Schmidt to Bush, Schmidt to Moriarty. Hit by Pitcher—Bush (by Willis). Left on Bases—Pittsburgh 5, Detroit 9. Umpires—Evans, Klem, O'Loughlin, Johnstone. Attendance—10,535. Time of Game—2:00.

Detroit	Pos	AB	R	H	RBI	PO	A	E
D. Jones	lf-cf	5	1	0	0	2	0	0
Bush	ss	4	2	1	0	2	3	1
Cobb	rf	4	0	1	1	1	0	0
Crawford	cf-1b	3	1	1	1	1	4	0
Delahanty	2b	4	0	2	1	0	4	0
Moriarty	3b	3	1	1	1	1	3	0
T. Jones	1b	4	0	1	0	13	0	1
McIntyre	lf	4	0	0	0	0	0	0
Schmidt	c	3	0	1	0	7	3	0
Mullin	p	4	0	2	0	0	2	0
Totals		32	5	10	5	27	16	2

Pitching	IP	H	R	ER	BB	SO
Pittsburgh						
Willis (L)	5	7	4	2	4	1
Camnitz	1	2	1	1	1	0
Phillippe	2	1	0	0	0	1
Detroit						
Mullin (W)	9	8	4	3	1	5

1st Inning
Pittsburgh
Byrne singled to third.
Leach singled to right, Byrne going to third.
Clarke singled to right, scoring Byrne as Leach went to third.
Wagner singled to left, Leach and Clarke scoring.
1 Miller grounded to second, Wagner going to third.
2 Abstein struck out.
3 Wilson grounded back to the mound.
Detroit
1 D. Jones lined to second.
Bush walked.
2 Cobb called out on strikes.
Crawford doubled to center, Bush scoring on a low relay throw by Miller. Crawford going to third.
3 Delahanty flied to center.

2nd Inning
Pittsburgh
1 Gibson struck out, but had to be thrown out at first.
2 Willis bounced back to the mound.
3 Byrne grounded to third.
Detroit
1 Moriarty grounded to third.
2 T. Jones grounded to short.
3 Schmidt flied to center.

3rd Inning
Pittsburgh
Leach safe on Bush's fumble.
1 Clarke sacrificed Leach to second, Moriarty to T. Jones.
2 Wagner grounded to second, Leach going to third.
Miller walked.
Miller stole second.
3 Abstein struck out.
Detroit
Mullin singled to center.
1,2 D. Jones lined into a double play, Byrne to Abstein.
Bush hit by a pitch.
Bush stole second.
3 Cobb popped to second.

4th Inning
Pittsburgh
1 Wilson grounded to short.
2 Gibson grounded to third.
3 Willis grounded to second.
Detroit
Crawford walked.
Delahanty singled to center, Crawford going to second.
Moriarty singled to right, Crawford scoring but Delahanty out trying for third, Wilson to Wagner. Moriarty went to second on the play.
T. Jones singled to left, Moriarty scoring and T. Jones got to third on Clarke's error.
Schmidt walked.
2 Mullin flied to short left.
3 D. Jones flied to left.

5th Inning
Pittsburgh
1 Byrne grounded to short.
2 Leach flied to left.
3 Clarke grounded to short.
Detroit
Bush singled to center.
1 Cobb grounded to first, Bush going to second.
2 Crawford grounded to short, Bush going to third.
Delahanty doubled over third, Bush scoring.
Moriarty walked.
3 T. Jones popped to Byrne near the mound.

6th Inning
Pittsburgh
1 Wagner flied to left.
Miller singled to center.
2,3 Abstein fouled to Schmidt making a real nice catch and threw to Bush doubling Miller trying to go to second after the catch.
Detroit
For Pittsburgh—Camnitz pitching.
Schmidt doubled into the crowd in right.
1 Mullin bunted back to Camnitz, who threw to Wagner getting Schmidt running for third.
2 D. Jones forced Mullin at second, Abstein to Wagner.
D. Jones stole second.
Bush walked.
Cobb doubled into the right field crowd, scoring D. Jones as Bush went to third.
3 Crawford flied to center.

7th Inning
Pittsburgh
1 Wilson flied to right.
Gibson beat out a chopper past the mound.
2 Hyatt, batting for Camnitz, grounded to second, Gibson going to second.
3 Byrne lined to short.
Detroit
For Pittsburgh—Phillippe pitching.
1 Delahanty struck out.
2 Moriarty grounded to third.
3 T. Jones popped out a bunt to the mound.

8th Inning
Pittsburgh
1 Leach fouled to Schmidt.
2 Clarke struck out.
3 Wagner flied to center.
Detroit
1 Schmidt grounded to second.
Mullin doubled to center.
2 D. Jones grounded to third, Mullin going to third.
3 Bush popped up on a bunt to Abstein.

9th Inning
Pittsburgh
Miller singled to right.
Abstein singled to center, Miller advancing to second.
Wilson safe on a bunt when he collided with T. Jones who dropped the ball, Miller scoring and Abstein going to third.
For Detroit—T. Jones carried off on a stretcher and replaced by Crawford, D. Jones moves to center, and McIntyre moves to left.
1 Gibson grounded to Crawford who threw Abstein out at the plate.
2,3 Abbaticchio, batting for Phillippe, struck out and Wilson was doubled up trying for third, Schmidt to Moriarty.

Game 7 October 16 at Detroit

Pit. 020 203 010
Det. 000 000 000

Pittsburgh	Pos	AB	R	H	RBI	PO	A	E
Byrne	3b	0	0	0	0	0	0	0
Hyatt	cf	3	1	0	0	0	0	0
Leach	cf-3b	3	2	2	0	4	2	0
Clarke	lf	2	1	0	1	4	0	0
Wagner	ss	3	1	1	2	3	4	0
Miller	2b	5	0	2	2	2	0	0
Abstein	1b	4	1	1	0	10	0	0
Wilson	rf	4	1	0	0	2	0	0
Gibson	c	5	0	1	0	2	3	0
Adams	p	3	0	0	0	0	2	0
Totals		30	8	7	6	27	11	0

Pitching	IP	H	R	ER	BB	SO
Pittsburgh						
Adams (W)	9	6	0	0	1	1
Detroit						
Donovan (L)	3	2	2	2	6	0
Mullin	6	5	6	4	4	1

Detroit	Pos	AB	R	H	RBI	PO	A	E
D. Jones	lf	4	0	1	0	3	0	1
Bush	ss	3	0	0	0	2	5	1
Cobb	rf	4	0	0	0	1	0	0
Crawford	cf	4	0	0	0	4	0	1
Delahanty	2b	3	0	2	0	3	3	0
Moriarty	3b	1	0	1	0	0	0	0
O'Leary	3b	3	0	0	0	1	1	0
T. Jones	1b	4	0	1	0	9	0	0
Schmidt	c	3	0	1	0	3	2	0
Donovan	p	0	0	0	0	0	1	0
Mullin	p	3	0	0	0	0	2	0
Totals		32	0	6	0	27	14	3

Doubles—Abstein, Delahanty, Gibson, Leach, Moriarty, Schmidt. Triple—Wagner. Stolen Bases—Abstein, Clarke 2, Miller. Sacrifice Hits—Adams, Clarke, Hyatt, Leach, Wilson. Double Play—Bush to Schmidt to Delahanty. Hit by Pitchers—Bush (by Adams), Byrne (by Donovan). Left on Bases—Pittsburgh 11, Detroit 7. Umpires—O'Loughlin, Johnstone, Evans, Klem. Attendance—17,562. Time of Game—2:10.

1st Inning
Pittsburgh
Byrne hit by a pitched ball.
1 Leach sacrificed Byrne to second, Donovan to T. Jones.
2 Byrne out trying to steal, Schmidt to Moriarty and Byrne was spiked.
Clarke walked.
Clarke stole second.
Wagner walked.
3 Miller forced Wagner at second, Bush to Delahanty.
Detroit
For Pittsburgh—Leach playing third, and Hyatt in center.
1 Jones fouled to Leach.
Bush hit by a pitched ball.
2 Cobb flied to right.
3 Bush caught stealing, Gibson to Miller.

2nd Inning
Pittsburgh
Abstein walked.
Abstein stole second.
Wilson sacrificed Abstein to third and safe when Schmidt threw late to try to get Abstein.
1 Gibson popped to short.
Adams walked, loading the bases.
2 Hyatt flied to center, Abstein scoring after the catch.
Leach walked, again loading the bases.
Clarke also walked, forcing in Wilson.
3 Wagner flied to right.
Detroit
1 Crawford grounded to first.
Delahanty walked.
Moriarty doubled to right, Delahanty going to third.
O'Leary ran for the injured Moriarty.
2 T. Jones popped to short.
3 Schmidt rolled out, Gibson to Abstein.

3rd Inning
Pittsburgh
For Detroit—O'Leary playing third.
Miller singled to center.
Abstein doubled to left, Miller going to second.
1,2 Wilson grounded to Bush who threw to Schmidt getting Miller who threw to Delahanty getting a confused Abstein off of second.
3 Gibson forced Wilson at second, Bush to Delahanty.
Detroit
1 Mullin, batting for Donovan, flied to right.
D. Jones beat out a bunt to the mound.
2 Bush sacrificed D. Jones to second, Gibson to Abstein.
3 Cobb bounced back to the mound.

4th Inning
Pittsburgh
For Detroit—Mullin pitching.
1 Adams flied to left.
Hyatt walked.
Leach singled over short, Hyatt going to second.
2 Clarke sacrificed up both runners, Mullin to T. Jones.
Wagner walked, loading the bases.
Miller singled to right, scoring Hyatt and Leach with Wagner racing to third.
Miller stole second.
3 Abstein struck out.
Detroit
1 Crawford grounded to third.
Delahanty singled to right.
2 O'Leary popped to short.
T. Jones singled to right, Delahanty going to second.
3 Schmidt forced Delahanty at third, Wagner to Leach.

5th Inning
Pittsburgh
1 Wilson flied to center.
2 Gibson grounded to short.
3 Adams grounded to second.
Detroit
1 Mullin grounded to third.
2 D. Jones struck out.
3 Bush grounded to short.

6th Inning
Pittsburgh
1 Hyatt grounded to second.
Leach doubled to left.
Clarke walked, for the third time.
Wagner tripled to the deep left field foul line, scoring Leach and Clarke. Wagner scored on D. Jones' error of a poor throw to third.
2 Miller flied to center.
3 Abstein popped to short.
Detroit
1 Cobb bounced back to the mound.
2 Crawford flied to left.
3 Delahanty fouled to Leach.

7th Inning
Pittsburgh
1 Wilson flied to left.
Gibson doubled to left.
2 Adams grounded out, O'Leary to Bush to T. Jones, Gibson going to third.
3 Hyatt grounded to second.
Detroit
1 O'Leary fouled to Gibson.
2 T. Jones grounded to short.
Schmidt doubled to left.
3 Mullin flied to left.

8th Inning
Pittsburgh
1 Leach grounded back to the mound.
Clarke walked for the fourth time of the game.
Clarke stole second.
2 Wagner flied to center.
Miller safe at second when Crawford dropped his deep fly, Clarke scoring.
3 Abstein flied to left.
Detroit
1 D. Jones popped to second.
2 Bush popped to second.
3 Clarke flied to left.

9th Inning
Pittsburgh
1 Wilson popped to third.
Gibson safe on Bush's bobble.
2 Adams sacrificed Gibson to second, T. Jones unassisted.
3 Hyatt fouled to Schmidt.
Detroit
1 Crawford grounded to short.
Delahanty doubled.
2 Moriarty fouled to Leach.
3 T. Jones flied to left.

1909 WORLD SERIES COMPOSITE BOX

	Wins	Composite Line Score										Manager	Regular Season W	L	Pct.	G. Ahead
Pittsburgh Pirates (N.L.)	4	11	4	1	3	2	4	4	2	3	- 34	Fred Clarke	110	42	.724	6½
Detroit Tigers (A.L.)	3	3	4	3	5	3	3	4	1	2	- 28	Hughie Jennings	98	54	.645	3½

BATTING AND FIELDING

PITTSBURGH PIRATES

	WORLD SERIES STATISTICS Pos	G	AB	R	H	2B	3B	HR	RBI	BB	SO	SB	BA	SA	PO	A	E		REGULAR SEASON STATISTICS Main Pos	G	AB	R	H	2B	3B	HR	RBI	BB	SO	SB	BA	SA
Bill Abstein	1b	7	26	3	6	2	0	0	2	3	9	1	.231	.308	70	4	5		1b	137	512	51	133	20	10	1	70	27		16	.260	.344
Dots Miller	2b	7	28	2	7	1	0	0	4	2	5	3	.250	.286	16	14	2		2b	151	560	71	156	31	13	3	87	39		14	.279	.396
Honus Wagner	ss	7	24	4	8	2	1	0	6	4	2	6	.333	.500	13	23	3		ss	137	495	92	168	39	10	5	100	66		35	.339	.489
Bobby Byrne	3b	7	24	5	6	1	0	0	0	1	4	1	.250	.292	11	16	0	a	3b	46	168	31	43	6	2	0	7	32		8	.256	.315
Owen Wilson	rf	7	26	2	4	1	0	0	1	0	2	1	.154	.192	3	1	0		of	154	569	64	155	22	12	4	59	19		17	.272	.374
Tommy Leach	cf-3b	7	25	8	9	4	0	0	2	2	1	1	.360	.520	20	3	0		of	151	587	126	153	29	8	6	43	66		27	.261	.368
Fred Clarke	lf	7	19	7	4	0	0	2	7	5	3	3	.211	.526	19	0	1		of	152	550	97	158	16	11	3	68	80		31	.287	.373
George Gibson	c	7	25	2	6	2	0	0	2	1	1	2	.240	.320	28	9	0		c	150	510	42	135	25	9	2	52	44		9	.265	.361
Ham Hyatt	ph-cf	2	4	1	0	0	0	0	1	1	0	0	.000	.000	0	0	0		of	48	67	9	20	3	4	0	7	3		1	.299	.463
Ed Abbaticchio	ph	1	1	0	0	0	0	0	0	0	1	0	.000	.000					ss	36	87	13	20	0	0	1	16	19		2	.230	.264
Paddy O'Connor	ph	1	1	0	0	0	0	0	0	0	1	0	.000	.000					c	9	16	1	5	1	0	0	3	0		0	.313	.375
Mike Simon	Did not play																		c	11	18	2	3	0	0	0	2	1		0	.167	.167
Babe Adams	p	3	9	0	0	0	0	0	0	1	1	0	.000	.000	0	5	0		p	25	39	0	2	0	1	0	1	2		0	.051	.103
Vic Willis	p	2	4	0	0	0	0	0	0	0	1	0	.000	.000	1	2	0		p	39	103	6	14	1	1	0	2	7		0	.136	.165
Nick Maddox	p	1	4	0	0	0	0	0	0	0	1	0	.000	.000	0	1	0		p	31	67	6	15	1	2	0	7	7		2	.224	.299
Deacon Phillippe	p	2	1	0	0	0	0	0	0	0	1	0	.000	.000	1	2	2		p	22	42	1	3	1	0	0	4	1		0	.071	.095
Lefty Leifield	p	1	1	0	0	0	0	0	0	0	1	0	.000	.000	0	5	0		p	32	73	2	14	1	3	0	8	3		1	.192	.288
Howie Camnitz	p	2	1	0	0	0	0	0	0	0	0	0	.000	.000	0	2	0		p	41	87	8	12	1	0	0	6	12		0	.138	.149
Sam Leever	Did not play																		p	19	24	2	4	0	0	0	1	3		0	.167	.167
Sammy Frock	Did not play																		p	8	14	1	2	0	0	0	1	0		0	.143	.143
Chick Brandom	Did not play																		p	13	10	2	1	0	0	0	0	0		0	.100	.100
Bill Powell	Did not play																		p	3	3	0	1	0	0	0	0	0		0	.333	.333
Gene Moore	Did not play																		p	1	1	0	0	0	0	0	0	0		0	.000	.000
team total		7	223	34	50	13	1	2	25	20	34	18	.224	.328	182	87	13			154	5129	701	1332	218	92	25	585	479		185	.260	.353

Double Plays—3
Left on Bases—44

a—from St. Louis (N)
Jap Barbeau (3b), Kid Durbin (pr), Ward Miller (of), Alan Storke (1b-3b), Harry Camnitz (p), Charlie Wacker (p) also played for the Pirates during the season.

DETROIT TIGERS

	WORLD SERIES STATISTICS Pos	G	AB	R	H	2B	3B	HR	RBI	BB	SO	SB	BA	SA	PO	A	E		REGULAR SEASON STATISTICS Main Pos	G	AB	R	H	2B	3B	HR	RBI	BB	SO	SB	BA	SA
Tom Jones	1b	7	24	3	6	1	0	0	2	2	0	1	.250	.292	72	1	1	b	1b	44	153	13	43	9	0	0	18	5		9	.281	.340
Jim Delahanty	2b	7	26	2	9	4	0	0	4	2	5	0	.346	.500	10	17	2	c	2b	46	150	29	38	10	1	0	20	17		9	.253	.333
Donie Bush	ss	7	23	5	6	1	0	0	3	5	3	1	.261	.304	10	19	5		ss	157	532	114	145	18	2	0	33	88		53	.273	.314
George Moriarty	3b	7	22	4	6	1	0	0	1	3	1	0	.273	.318	7	15	0		3b-1b	133	473	43	129	20	4	1	39	24		34	.273	.338
Ty Cobb	rf	7	26	3	6	3	0	0	5	2	2	2	.231	.346	8	0	1		of	156	573	116	216	33	10	9	107	48		76	.377	.517
Sam Crawford	cf-1b	7	28	4	7	3	0	1	4	1	1	1	.250	.464	17	1	2		of	156	589	83	185	35	14	6	97	47		30	.314	.452
Davy Jones	lf-cf	7	30	6	7	0	0	1	1	3	1	1	.233	.333	14	0	1		of	69	204	44	57	2	2	0	10	28		12	.279	.309
Boss Schmidt	c	6	18	0	4	2	0	0	4	2	0	0	.222	.333	31	10	4		c	84	253	21	53	8	2	1	28	7		7	.209	.269
Oscar Stanage	c	2	5	0	1	0	0	0	2	0	2	0	.200	.200	12	2	0		c	77	252	17	66	8	6	0	21	11		2	.262	.341
Matty McIntyre	ph-lf	4	3	0	0	0	0	0	0	0	1	0	.000	.000	0	0	0		of	125	476	65	116	18	9	1	34	54		13	.244	.326
Charley O'Leary	3b	1	3	0	0	0	0	0	0	0	0	0	.000	.000	1	1	0		3b-2b	76	261	29	53	10	0	0	13	6		9	.203	.241
Heinie Beckendorf	Did not play																		c	15	27	1	7	1	0	0	1	2		0	.259	.296
George Mullin	p-ph	6	16	1	3	1	0	0	0	1	3	0	.188	.250	0	12	0		p-ph	53	126	13	27	7	0	0	17	13		2	.214	.270
Wild Bill Donovan	p	2	4	0	0	0	0	0	0	0	1	0	.000	.000	0	5	1		p	22	45	6	9	0	0	0	1	2		0	.200	.200
Ed Summers	p	2	3	0	0	0	0	0	0	0	2	0	.000	.000	0	2	0		p	35	94	4	10	1	0	0	3	4		0	.106	.117
Ed Willett	p	2	2	0	0	0	0	0	0	0	0	0	.000	.000	1	3	1		p	42	112	10	22	5	3	0	10	3		0	.196	.295
Ralph Works	p	1	0	0	0	0	0	0	0	0	0	0	—	—	0	1	0		p	16	17	2	1	0	0	0	0	0		0	.059	.059
Ed Killian	Did not play																		p	25	62	4	10	0	0	0	0	2		0	.161	.161
Kid Speer	Did not play																		p	13	25	1	3	1	0	0	2	2		0	.120	.160
team total		7	233	28	55	16	0	2	26	20	22	6	.236	.330	183	89	18			158	5095	666	1360	209	58	19	521	397		280	.267	.342

Double Plays—4
Left on Bases—50

b—from St. Louis (A)
c—from Washington
Joe Casey (c), Del Gainer (1b), Red Killefer (2b), Claude Rossman (1b), Germany Schaefer (2b), Elijah Jones (p), Ed Lafitte (p), Bill Lelivelt (p), George Suggs (p) also played for the Tigers during the season.

PITCHING

PITTSBURGH PIRATES

	WORLD SERIES STATISTICS G	GS	CG	IP	H	R	ER	BB	SO	W	L	SV	ERA	REGULAR SEASON STATISTICS G	GS	CG	IP	H	ER	BB	SO	W	L	Pct	SV	ShO	ERA
Babe Adams	3	3	3	27	18	5	4	6	11	3	0	0	1.33	25	12	7	130	88	16	23	65	12	3	.800	2	3	1.11
Vic Willis	2	1	0	11⅓	10	7	5	8	3	0	1	0	3.97	39	35	24	290	243	72	83	95	22	11	.667	1	4	2.23
Nick Maddox	1	1	1	9	10	6	1	2	4	1	0	0	1.00	31	27	17	203	173	50	39	56	13	8	.619	0	4	2.22
Deacon Phillippe	2	0	0	6	2	0	0	1	2	0	0	0	0.00	22	12	7	132	121	34	14	38	8	3	.727	0	1	2.32
Lefty Leifield	1	1	0	4	7	5	5	1	0	0	1	0	11.25	32	27	13	202	172	53	54	43	19	8	.704	0	3	2.36
Howie Camnitz	2	1	0	3⅔	8	5	4	2	2	0	1	0	9.82	41	30	20	283	207	51	68	133	25	6	.806	3	5	1.62
Sam Leever	Did not play													19	4	2	70	74	22	14	23	8	1	.889	2	0	2.83
Sammy Frock	Did not play													13	2	0	41	33	5	10	21	1	0	1.000	2	0	1.10
Chick Brandom	Did not play													8	4	3	36	44	10	4	11	2	1	.667	1	0	2.50
Bill Powell	Did not play													3	1	0	7	7	3	6	2	0	1	.000	0	0	3.86
Gene Moore	Did not play													1	0	0	2	4	4	3	2	0	0	—	0	0	18.00
team total	7	7	4	61	55	28	19	20	22	4	3	0	2.80	154	154	93	1402	1174	322	320	490	110	42	.724	11	20	2.07

DETROIT TIGERS

	WORLD SERIES STATISTICS G	GS	CG	IP	H	R	ER	BB	SO	W	L	SV	ERA	REGULAR SEASON STATISTICS G	GS	CG	IP	H	ER	BB	SO	W	L	Pct	SV	ShO	ERA
George Mullin	4	3	3	32	23	14	8	8	20	2	1	0	2.25	40	35	29	304	258	75	78	124	29	9	.763	1	3	2.22
Wild Bill Donovan	2	2	1	12	7	4	4	8	7	1	1	0	3.00	21	17	13	140	121	36	60	76	8	7	.533	2	4	2.31
Ed Summers	2	2	0	7⅓	13	12	7	4	4	0	2	0	8.59	35	32	24	282	243	70	52	107	19	9	.679	1	3	2.23
Ed Willett	2	0	0	7⅔	3	2	0	0	1	0	0	0	0.00	41	34	25	293	239	76	76	89	22	9	.710	1	3	2.33
Ralph Works	1	0	0	2	4	2	2	0	2	0	0	0	9.00	16	4	4	64	62	14	17	31	3	1	.750	3	0	1.97
Ed Killian	Did not play													25	19	14	173	150	33	49	54	11	9	.550	1	3	1.72
Kid Speer	Did not play													12	8	4	76	88	24	13	12	3	3	.500	2	0	2.84
team total	7	7	4	61	50	34	21	20	34	3	4	0	3.10	158	158	117	1420	1254	357	359	528	98	54	.645	14	16	2.26

Total Attendance—145,807 Average Attendance—20,830 Winning Player's Share—$1,825 Losing Player's Share—$1,275

1910
Coombs: Thirty-one Plus Three

A campaign of 104 victories gave the Chicago Cubs their fourth National League pennant in five years and reasserted their title as king-pins of the Senior Circuit after finishing behind Pittsburgh last year. Joe Tinker, Johnny Evers, and Frank Chance still patrolled the infield for the Cubs, but outfielders Solly Hofman and Wildfire Schulte had now blossomed into the team's top offensive threats. Three Finger Brown still paced the mound staff with his 25 wins, but he got surprise support from rookie King Cole, who won 20 games. Even with second baseman Evers on crutches with a broken leg, the Cubs figured to beat the young Philadelphia Athletics.

Connie Mack had led his A's to their third American League pennant and second World Series trip with a league record of 102 wins. Mack's young club on the field revolved around twenty-three-year-old second baseman Eddie Collins, a Columbia University product. He had great range and hands, and excelled as pivot man on the double play. Not a power hitter, Collins used an even stroke to bat .322 and drive in 81 runs, and once he got on base, he used his speed and instincts to steal 81 bases. Veteran hurlers Chief Bender and Eddie Plank were still around from Mack's 1905 champs, and they were joined on the hill by 18-game-winner Cy Morgan and staff ace Jack Coombs. A product of Colby College in Maine, Coombs worked through four mediocre seasons before blooming this year into a 31-game winner with a 1.30 ERA. But even with Mack's favored collegians, the Athletics shaped up as no match for the battle-hardened Cubs, especially with outfielder Rube Oldring out with a broken leg and pitcher Plank out with a sore arm.

But the A's ignored the experts and surprised the Cubs in the bargain. Chief Bender, whom Mack considered his best money pitcher, started game one in Philadelphia and threw a three-hitter as the A's beat Orvie Overall 4–1. Game two matched aces Coombs and Brown. Although Coombs's control was unreliable and he had to struggle all game—giving up eight hits and nine walks—he gamely stranded 14 Cubs on base. The A's held a slim 3–2 lead going into the bottom of the seventh, but they then jumped on a tiring Brown for six runs to sew the game up. With their 9–3 triumph, the Athletics headed to Chicago with a two-game lead.

After the travel day, Mack pulled a surprise by starting Coombs on only one day's rest. Chicago manager Chance relied on veteran Ed Reulbach, but his faith didn't pay off. Both clubs scored once in the first inning and twice in the second inning. Chance lifted Reulbach for a pinch hitter in the bottom of the second, so he sent righty Harry McIntire to the mound for the third. Left fielder Jimmy Sheckard hauled in Bris Lord's long drive for the first out, and then the roof fell in. Collins singled, Frank Baker singled and made it all the way to third when Schulte botched the play in right field, Harry Davis was hit by a pitch, and Danny Murphy launched a three-run homer. Chance was ejected from the game after protesting that Murphy's hit should have been a ground-rule double, and his last act before departing the premises was replacing McIntire with Jack Pfiester. Coombs settled down behind his big lead, however, and the A's coasted to a 12–5 victory and a 3–0 edge in the Series. Faced with insurmountable odds, the old-pro Cubs salvaged the fourth game by scoring the tying run in the bottom of the ninth and then tallying the winning run in the tenth for a 4–3 triumph. The Sunday crowd of 27,374 would have the privilege of seeing the clincher. Coombs once again faced Brown, and the A's held a tenuous 2–1 lead after seven innings. But Brown again tired, and a combination of solid Philadelphia hitting and sloppy Chicago fielding allowed five A's across the plate in the eighth and cinched a 7–2 Series-ender for the Mackmen. The most telling statistic of the Series was the Philadelphia team batting average of .316; Collins batted .429, Baker hit .409, and Coombs hit .385 in addition to winning three games on the mound.

Game 1 October 17 at Philadelphia

Chi. 000 000 001
Phi. 021 000 01x

Chicago	Pos	AB	R	H	RBI	PO	A	E
Sheckard	lf	4	0	0	0	2	0	0
Schulte	rf	2	0	1	0	0	0	0
Hofman	cf	4	0	0	0	2	0	0
Chance	1b	3	0	0	0	11	2	0
Zimmerman	2b	3	0	0	0	3	3	0
Steinfeldt	3b	3	0	0	0	0	3	0
Tinker	ss	3	1	1	0	2	2	0
Kling	c	3	0	1	1	4	3	0
Overall	p	1	0	0	0	0	0	0
McIntire	p	1	0	0	0	0	1	1
a Beaumont		1	0	0	0	0	0	0
Totals		28	1	3	1	24	14	1

a Grounded out for McIntire in 9th.

Doubles—Baker 2, Lord. Stolen Base—Murphy. Sacrifice Hits—Collins, Davis. Left on Bases—Chicago 2, Philadelphia 4. Umpires—Connolly (A), O'Day (N), Rigler (N), Sheridan (A). Attendance—26,891. Time of Game—1:54.

Philadelphia	Pos	AB	R	H	RBI	PO	A	E
Strunk	cf	3	0	0	0	1	0	1
Lord	lf	4	1	1	0	0	0	0
Collins	2b	2	1	1	0	2	5	0
Baker	3b	4	1	3	2	3	2	0
Davis	1b	3	0	0	0	11	0	0
Murphy	rf	3	1	1	1	1	0	0
Barry	ss	3	0	0	0	1	4	0
Thomas	c	1	0	0	0	8	2	1
Bender	p	3	0	1	1	0	0	0
Totals		26	4	7	4	27	13	2

Pitching	IP	H	R	ER	BB	SO
Chicago						
Overall (L)	3	6	3	3	1	1
McIntire	5	1	1	0	3	3
Philadelphia						
Bender (W)	9	3	1	0	2	8

1st Inning
Chicago
1 Sheckard struck out.
  Schulte singled to left.
2 Schulte caught trying to steal second, Thomas to Collins.
3 Hofman grounded to second.
Philadelphia
1 Strunk grounded to third.
2 Lord flied to center.
  Collins singled to left.
3 On a pitch-out Collins was caught going to second, Kling to Tinker.

2nd Inning
Chicago
1 Chance grounded to short.
2 Zimmerman fouled to Baker.
3 Steinfeldt grounded to third, Davis making a leaping catch of Baker's throw.
Philadelphia
  Baker hit a double to deep left, the ball rolling into the crowd.
1 Davis sacrificed Baker to third, Chance to Zimmerman.
  Murphy singled to left, Baker scoring. Murphy stole second.
2 Barry grounded to third. Murphy going to third.
  Thomas walked.
  Bender got a bad hop single over second, scoring Murphy as Thomas went to second.
3 Strunk flied to left.

3rd Inning
Chicago
1 Tinker grounded to second.
2 Kling popped to the mound.
3 Overall grounded to short, Barry doing a good job in his left.
Philadelphia
  Lord doubled into the crowd in center.
1 Collins sacrificed Lord to third, Chance to Zimmerman.
  Baker singled to left, scoring Lord.
2 Baker caught stealing second, Kling to Tinker.
3 Davis struck out.

4th Inning
Chicago
1 Sheckard grounded to short.
  Schulte walked.
2 Schulte out trying to steal second, Thomas to Collins.
3 Hofman struck out.
Philadelphia
  For Chicago—McIntire pitching.
1 Murphy grounded to short.
2 Barry grounded to third.
3 Thomas struck out.

5th Inning
Chicago
1 Chance grounded to second.
2 Zimmerman called out on strikes.
3 Steinfeldt also took a called third strike.
Philadelphia
1 Bender struck out.
  Strunk walked.
2 Strunk also caught trying to steal, Kling to Zimmerman.
3 Lord struck out.

6th Inning
Chicago
1 Tinker flied to center.
2 Kling flied to right.
3 McIntire struck out.
Philadelphia
1 Collins grounded to second.
2 Baker grounded to short.
3 Davis grounded to second.

7th Inning
Chicago
1 Sheckard grounded to short.
2 Schulte struck out.
3 Hofman grounded to third, Baker making a great play of a hard smash.
Philadelphia
1 Murphy flied to deep left.
2 Barry grounded to first.
  Thomas walked.
3 Bender grounded to first.

8th Inning
Chicago
1 Chance grounded to second.
2 Zimmerman struck out.
3 Steinfeldt popped to Baker.
Philadelphia
1 Strunk grounded to second.
2 Lord flied to center.
  Collins walked.
  Collins got to third on McIntire's wild pick off throw.
  Baker got a double one foot from the top of the right field wall, Collins scoring.
3 Davis bounced back to the mound.

9th Inning
Chicago
  Tinker got a reprieve when Thomas dropped his foul.
  Tinker singled to center and went to second on Strunk's fumble.
  Kling singled to center, scoring Tinker.
  Kane ran for Kling.
1 Beaumont, batting for McIntire, grounded to second, Kane going to second.
2 Sheckard struck out.
  Schulte walked.
3 Hofman forced Kane at third, Baker unassisted.

Game 2 October 18 at Philadelphia

Chi.	100	000	101						
Phi.	002	010	60x						

Chicago	Pos	AB	R	H	RBI	PO	A	E
Sheckard	lf	1	1	1	0	0	1	1
Schulte	rf	3	1	0	0	0	0	0
Hofman	cf	2	1	1	0	1	0	0
Chance	1b	5	0	2	1	14	0	0
Zimmerman	2b	3	0	1	2	1	2	0
Steinfeldt	3b	5	0	1	0	0	2	2
Tinker	ss	4	0	2	0	3	4	0
Kling	c	4	0	0	0	5	2	0
Brown	p	3	0	0	0	0	2	0
a Beaumont		1	0	0	0	0	0	0
Richie	p	0	0	0	0	0	0	0
Totals		31	3	8	3	24	13	3

Philadelphia	Pos	AB	R	H	RBI	PO	A	E
Strunk	cf	5	1	2	1	4	0	0
Lord	lf	5	1	1	0	1	0	0
Collins	2b	4	2	3	1	4	6	0
Baker	3b	4	1	1	0	1	1	0
Davis	1b	5	1	2	2	7	0	2
Murphy	rf	4	1	1	2	1	1	0
Barry	ss	3	0	1	0	3	1	0
Thomas	c	3	2	2	1	6	1	0
Coombs	p	4	0	1	0	0	1	2
Totals		37	9	14	7	27	11	4

Pitching	IP	H	R	ER	BB	SO
Chicago						
Brown (L)	7	13	9	7	4	6
Richie	1	1	0	0	0	0
Philadelphia						
Coombs (W)	9	8	3	3	9	5

a Struck out for Brown in 8th.

Doubles—Collins 2, Davis, Murphy, Sheckard, Steinfeldt, Strunk, Tinker, Zimmerman. Stolen Bases—Collins 2. Sacrifice Hits—Barry, Schulte 2, Sheckard, Zimmerman. Double Plays—Collins to Davis 2, Murphy to Thomas, Tinker to Chance. Left on Bases—Chicago 14, Philadelphia 9. Umpires—Rigler, Sheridan, O'Day, Connolly. Attendance—24,597. Time of Game—2:25.

1st Inning
Chicago
Sheckard walked.
1 Schulte forced Sheckard at second, Collins to Barry.
Hofman walked after an 0–2 count.
Chance beat out a hard smash to third, loading the bases.
2 Zimmerman flied to center, Schulte scoring after the catch. Strunk foolishly threw to the plate allowing both runners to advance.
3 Steinfeldt struck out.
Philadelphia
1 Strunk struck out on a wild pitch and Kling threw him out at first.
2 Lord grounded to third.
Collins blooped a Texas Leaguer into center.
Collins stole second.
3 Baker bounced back to the mound.

2nd Inning
Chicago
Tinker safe at first when Davis dropped Baker's throw to first.
1,2 Kling lined into a double play, Collins to Davis.
3 Brown grounded to second.
Philadelphia
1 Davis flied to center.
Murphy walked.
2,3 Barry hit into a double play, Tinker to Chance.

3rd Inning
Chicago
Sheckard again walked.
Schulte sacrificed and was safe as Davis dropped Coombs throw to first.
1 Hofman bunt popped to Davis.
2 Chance struck out.
3 Zimmerman lined to left.
Philadelphia
Thomas safe on Steinfeldt's fumble.
1 Coombs struck out.
Strunk beat out a bunt to the mound, Thomas going to second.
2 Lord forced Strunk at second, Zimmerman to Tinker, Thomas going to third.
Collins doubled to left, scoring Thomas and Lord also scored when Steinfeldt fumbled Sheckard's throw.
3 Baker grounded to second.

4th Inning
Chicago
1 Steinfeldt flied to center.
Tinker singled to center.
2 Tinker out trying to steal second, Thomas to Collins.
3 Kling took a called third strike.
Philadelphia
1 Davis grounded to short.
2 Murphy fouled to first.
Barry got a bad hop single over short.
Thomas singled sending Barry to third.
3 Coombs again struck out.

5th Inning
Chicago
Brown safe when Coombs fumbled his bunt.
Sheckard sacrificed and safe on another fumble by Coombs.
1 Schulte sacrificed, Davis unassisted.
Hofman walked loading the bases.
2,3 Chance flied to right, and Murphy threw to Thomas doubling Brown who tried to score after the catch.
Philadelphia
1 Strunk struck out.
Lord got a Texas League single to Short right-center.

5th Inning (continued)
2 Collins forced Lord at second, Tinker to Zimmerman.
Collins stole second, the second time in the game.
Baker walked.
Davis singled to left, scoring Collins.
Baker took third and Davis second on the throw to the plate.
3 Murphy grounded to short.

6th Inning
Chicago
Zimmerman walked.
1,2 Steinfeldt lined into a double play, Collins to Davis.
Tinker doubled into the left field crowd.
3 Kling flied to deep center.
Philadelphia
1 Barry called out on strikes.
Thomas walked.
Coombs got a bad hop single to second, Thomas moving over to third.
2 Strunk struck out for the third time.
3 Lord fouled to Chance.

7th Inning
Chicago
1 Brown struck out.
Sheckard doubled into the crowd in right.
2 Schulte flied to center.
Hofman walked for the third time.
Chance singled to center, scoring Sheckard as Hofman stopped at second.
3 Zimmerman forced Chance at second, Collins to Barry.
Philadelphia
Collins walked.
Baker singled to right, Collins going to third.
Davis doubled into the left field crowd, Collins scoring and Baker going to third.
Murphy also doubled into the crowd in left, scoring Baker and Davis.
1 Barry sacrificed Murphy to third, Brown to Chance.
Thomas singled to left, scoring Murphy.
2 Coombs grounded to first, Thomas going to second.
Strunk doubled to right **(the A's fourth double of the inning)**, scoring Thomas.
Lord safe on Sheckard's error, scoring Strunk.
3 Lord out trying to steal second, Kling to Tinker.

8th Inning
Chicago
Steinfeldt doubled into the left field crowd.
1 Tinker popped to third.
Kling walked.
2 Beaumont, pinch-hitting for Brown, struck out.
Sheckard walked for the third time.
3 Schulte popped to second.
Philadelphia
For Chicago—Richie now pitching.
Collins doubled into the right field crowd, for his third hit of the game.
1 Baker grounded to first, Collins advancing to third.
2 Davis grounded to first, Collins holding at third.
3 Murphy grounded to third.

9th Inning
Chicago
Hofman singled to left.
1 Chance grounded to second, Hofman advancing to second.
Zimmerman doubled into the left field crowd, scoring Hofman. The ninth double in the game.
2 Steinfeldt grounded to short, Zimmerman holding at second.
Tinker walked.
3 Kling forced Tinker at second, Barry unassisted.

Game 3 October 20 at Chicago

Phi.	125	000	400
Chi.	120	000	020

Philadelphia	Pos	AB	R	H	RBI	PO	A	E
Strunk	cf	5	1	1	0	1	0	0
Lord	lf	4	0	1	0	3	0	0
Collins	2b	5	1	1	0	1	1	0
Baker	3b	5	2	2	2	2	4	1
Davis	1b	3	3	3	0	8	0	0
Murphy	rf	5	2	1	3	3	1	0
Barry	ss	5	3	3	3	1	2	0
Thomas	c	4	0	0	0	8	1	0
Coombs	p	5	0	3	3	0	0	0
Totals		41	12	15	11	27	9	1

Pitching	IP	H	R	ER	BB	SO
Philadelphia						
Coombs (W)	9	6	5	5	4	8
Chicago						
Reulbach	2	3	3	2	2	0
McIntire (L)	$\frac{1}{3}$	3	4	4	0	0
Pfiester	$6\frac{2}{3}$	9	5	0	1	1

Chicago	Pos	AB	R	H	RBI	PO	A	E
Sheckard	lf	1	2	0	0	2	0	0
Schulte	rf	4	0	2	2	2	0	1
Hofman	cf	3	1	1	1	2	0	1
Chance	1b	1	0	0	0	3	0	0
Archer	1b	3	0	0	0	9	0	0
Zimmerman	2b	4	0	0	0	4	6	0
Steinfeldt	3b	4	0	0	0	0	2	1
Tinker	ss	4	1	3	0	3	4	2
Kling	c	4	0	0	0	2	2	0
Reulbach	p	0	0	0	0	0	1	0
a Beaumont		0	1	0	0	0	0	0
McIntire	p	0	0	0	0	0	0	0
Pfiester	p	2	0	0	0	0	1	0
b Needham		1	0	0	0	0	0	0
Totals		31	5	6	3	27	16	5

a Walked for Reulbach in 2nd.
b Fouled out for Pfiester in 9th.

Doubles—Barry 2, Coombs, Davis, Schulte 2, Tinker. Home Run—Murphy. Stolen Base—Tinker. Sacrifice Hits—Hofman, Lord. Double Plays—Zimmerman to to Tinker to Archer, Barry to Collins to Davis, Murphy to Davis. Wild Pitch—Coombs. Hit by Pitcher—Davis (by McIntire). Left on Bases—Philadelphia 7, Chicago 4. Umpires—O'Day, Sheridan, Rigler, Connolly. Attendance—26,210. Time of Game—2:07.

1st Inning
Philadelphia
Strunk walked.
1 Lord sacrificed Strunk to second, Reulbach to Chance.
2 Collins flied to left.
Baker singled to center, scoring Strunk.
3 Baker out trying to steal second, Kling to Tinker.
Chicago
Sheckard walked.
Schulte doubled into the crowd in right, Sheckard going to third.
1 Hofman flied to left, Sheckard scoring and Schulte going to third after the catch.
2 Chance struck out.
3 Zimmerman flied to left.

2nd Inning
Philadelphia
Davis walked.
1 Murphy grounded to third, Davis advancing to second.
Barry doubled to left, scoring Davis.
2 Thomas flied to right.
Coombs doubled to right, scoring Barry.
3 Strunk grounded to second.
Chicago
1 Steinfeldt popped to short.
Tinker doubled to right.
2 Kling grounded to third, Tinker going to third.
Beaumont, pinch-hitting for Reulbach, walked.
Sheckard again walked, loading the bases.
Schulte doubled to left, scoring Tinker and Beaumont as Sheckard stopped at third.
3 Hofman struck out.

3rd Inning
Philadelphia
For Chicago—McIntire pitching.
1 Lord flied to deep left.
Collins beat out an infield grounder.
Baker tripled to deep right, scoring Collins.
Davis was hit by a pitched ball.
Murphy blasted a three-run home run into the right field bleachers.
For Chicago—Chance was thrown out of the game for arguing the homer should have been a ground-rule double but to no avail. He was replaced by Archer as Pfiester came in to relieve McIntire.
Barry doubled to right.
Thomas safe on Tinker's poor throw to first, Barry scoring.
2,3 Coombs hit into a double play, Zimmerman to Tinker to Chance.
Chicago
1 Archer grounded to third.
2 Zimmerman flied to center.
3 Steinfeldt struck out.

4th Inning
Philadelphia
1 Strunk flied to center.
Lord singled to right.
2 Collins forced Lord at second, Pfiester to Zimmerman.
3 Collins caught attempting to steal second, Kling to Tinker.
Chicago
Tinker singled to right.
1,2 Kling grounded into a double play, Barry to Collins to Davis.
3 Pfiester grounded to third.

5th Inning
Philadelphia
1 Baker grounded to second.
Davis singled to left.
2 Murphy flied to center.
3 Barry forced Murphy at second, Tinker to Zimmerman.
Chicago
Sheckard singled to left.
1 Schulte struck out.
2,3 Hofman flied to right, Murphy's throw to Davis doubled Sheckard.

6th Inning
Philadelphia
1 Thomas grounded to short.
2 Coombs popped to second.
3 Strunk struck out.
Chicago
1 Archer bounced out, Thomas to Davis.
2 Zimmerman struck out.
3 Steinfeldt popped to third.

7th Inning
Philadelphia
1 Lord lined to second, Zimmerman making a good catch.
2 Collins grounded to third.
Baker safe on Steinfeldt's fumble.
Davis singled to right, Baker going to second.
Murphy beat out an infield chopper, loading the bases.
Barry singled to left, scoring Baker and Davis as Murphy went to third and Barry to second on the throw-in.
Thomas walked, again loading the bases.
Coombs singled to center, scoring Murphy and Barry with Thomas stopping at second.
Strunk got an infield hit, again loading the bases.
3 Lord grounded to second.
Chicago
1 Tinker grounded to third.
2 Kling grounded to short.
3 Pfiester struck out.

8th Inning
Philadelphia
1 Collins flied to right.
2 Baker grounded to second.
Davis doubled to left.
3 Murphy grounded to short.
Chicago
Sheckard walked for the third time
1 Schulte flied to right.
Hofman singled to left, Sheckard going to third. Hofman to second on the throw to third.
2 Archer struck out.
Sheckard and Hofman both scored on a wild pitch, to the backstop.
3 Zimmerman flied to Murphy, a good running catch against the fence.

9th Inning
Philadelphia
1 Barry fouled to Kling.
2 Thomas grounded to first.
Coombs got a Texas League single to short center.
3 Strunk grounded to second.
Chicago
1 Steinfeldt flied to left.
Tinker singled to left.
2 Kling struck out.
Tinker stole second.
3 Needhaam, batting for Pfiester, fouled to Baker.

Game 4 October 22 at Chicago

Philadelphia	Pos	AB	R	H	RBI	PO	A	E
Strunk	cf	5	0	2	1	1	0	0
Lord	lf	5	0	0	0	2	0	0
Collins	2b	5	1	1	0	6	1	1
Baker	3b	4	1	3	0	2	4	1
Davis	1b	3	0	1	0	9	0	1
Murphy	rf	4	0	2	2	1	0	0
Barry	ss	4	0	0	0	2	1	0
Thomas	c	4	0	1	0	5	4	0
Bender	p	3	1	1	0	4	2	0
Totals		37	3	11	3	*28	12	3

Pitching	IP	H	R	ER	BB	SO
Philadelphia						
Bender (L)	9⅔	9	4	4	2	6
Chicago						
Cole	8	10	3	3	3	5
Brown (W)	2	1	0	0	0	1

Phi.	001 200 000 0
Chi.	100 100 001 1

Chicago	Pos	AB	R	H	RBI	PO	A	E
Sheckard	lf	4	1	1	1	3	1	0
Schulte	rf	4	2	2	0	2	0	0
Hofman	cf	3	0	2	1	1	0	0
Chance	1b	4	0	2	2	11	1	0
Zimmerman	2b	4	0	1	0	2	0	0
Steinfeldt	3b	4	0	0	0	2	4	0
Tinker	ss	3	0	0	0	1	3	0
Archer	c	4	1	1	0	8	4	0
Cole	p	2	0	0	0	1	3	0
a Kling		1	0	0	0	0	0	0
b Kane		0	0	0	0	0	0	0
Brown	p	1	0	0	0	0	1	1
Totals		34	4	9	4	30	19	1

* Chance declared out in first on Hofman's interference—two outs when winning run scored.
a Reached first on error for Cole in 8th.
b Ran for Kling in 8th.

Doubles—Archer, Baker, Davis, Murphy, Schulte. Triples—Chance, Strunk. Stolen Base—Sheckard. Sacrifice Hits—Davis, Hofman, Murphy. Double Plays—Bender to Baker to Davis, Cole to Archer to Chance. Hit by Pitcher—Barry (by Cole). Left on Bases—Philadelphia 10, Chicago 4. Umpires—Connolly, Rigler, Sheridan, O'Day. Attendance—19,150. Time of Game—2:14.

1st Inning
Philadelphia
1 Strunk grounded to third.
2 Lord flied to deep left.
3 Collins grounded out, Chance to Cole.
Chicago
Sheckard walked (his seventh in the Series so far).
1 Schulte struck out as Sheckard was stealing second.
Hofman singled to left, scoring Sheckard.
2,3 Chance hit into a double play, Baker to Collins to Davis. Chance declared out by Umpire Rigler when Hofman interfered with Collins. (Not counted as a double play.)

2nd Inning
Philadelphia
Baker singled past second.
1 Davis struck out.
2 Murphy flied to right.
3 Baker caught trying to steal second, Archer to Tinker.
Chicago
1 Zimmerman flied to right.
2 Steinfeldt grounded to third. Tinker walked.
3 Tinker out trying to steal, Thomas to Collins.

3rd Inning
Philadelphia
1 Barry grounded to third.
2 Thomas grounded back to the mound. Bender walked. Strunk tripled to right, scoring Bender,
3 but out as he over-ran third, Sheckard to Tinker to Steinfeldt.
Chicago
1 Archer struck out.
2 Cole struck out, but had to be thrown out, Thomas to Davis.
3 Sheckard flied to left.

4th Inning
Philadelphia
1 Lord struck out after a 3-0 count. Collins beat out a single to second. Baker doubled into the left field crowd, Collins automatically to third. The hit would have easily been a triple, but only a ground-rule double.
2 Davis struck out. Murphy got a double when Sheckard could not hold the ball as he hit the fence, scoring both Collins and Baker.
3 Barry struck out.
Chicago
Schulte singled to left. Hofman signaled to right, sending Schulte to third. Chance singled to left, Schulte scoring as Hofman stopped at second.
1,2 Zimmerman hit into a double play, Bender to Baker to Davis as Chance went to second.
3 Steinfeldt flied to left.

5th Inning
Philadelphia
1 Thomas grounded to second. Bender singled to right. Strunk singled on a bunt to first as no one covered the bag.
2 Lord flied to left.
3 Collins flied to left.
Chicago
1 Tinker struck out.
2 Archer grounded to third.
3 Cole again struck out.

6th Inning
Philadelphia
Baker walked.
1 Davis sacrificed, Cole to Chance. Murphy singled to left, Baker going to third.
2 Barry grounded to Steinfeldt who threw to Archer getting Baker trying to score. Thomas chopped a single over the mound, loading the bases.
3 Bender flied to right.
Chicago
1 Sheckard lined to short. Schulte beat out a hit to second.
2 Hofman popped to third.
3 Schulte out stealing, Thomas to Collins.

7th Inning
Philadelphia
1 Strunk struck out, and thrown out Archer to Chance.
2 Lord grounded to second.
3 Collins flied to center.
Chicago
1 Chance bounced back to the mound. Zimmerman singled to left. Davis got an error dropping Steinfeldt's foul.
2 Steinfeldt struck out.
3 Zimmerman caught trying to steal second, Thomas to Collins.

8th Inning
Philadelphia
Baker got a single to first. Davis walked.
1 Murphy sacrificed up both runners, Archer to Chance. Barry was hit by a pitch, loading the bases.
2,3 Thomas hit into a double play, Cole to Archer to Chance.
Chicago
1 Tinker popped to short.
2 Archer grounded to second. Kling, batting for Cole, was safe on Baker's low throw. Kane ran for Kling.
3 Sheckard flied to center.

9th Inning
Philadelphia
For Chicago—Brown pitching.
1 Bender grounded to third. Strunk safe when Brown muffed his pop as Archer ran into him.
2 Lord forced Strunk at second, Tinker To Zimmerman.
3 Collins bounced back to the mound.
Chicago
Schulte doubled to right.
1 Hofman sacrificed Schulte to third, Davis unassisted. Chance tripled to center, scoring Schulte.
2 Zimmerman popped to Collins.
3 Steinfeldt fouled to Barry.

10th Inning
Philadelphia
1 Baker fouled to Archer. Davis doubled to right.
2 Murphy grounded to Tinker who threw to Steinfeldt getting Davis at third.
3 Barry struck out.
Chicago
1 Tinker popped to short. Archer doubled to left.
2 Brown grounded to short, Archer going to third. Sheckard singled to center, Archer scoring the game-winning run.

Game 5 October 23 at Chicago

Philadelphia	Pos	AB	R	H	RBI	PO	A	E
Hartsel	lf	5	2	1	0	2	0	0
Lord	cf	4	1	1	1	5	0	0
Collins	2b	5	0	3	2	4	4	0
Baker	3b	5	1	0	0	0	0	1
Davis	1b	4	1	0	0	9	2	0
Murphy	rf	4	2	2	1	0	0	0
Barry	ss	2	0	0	0	2	4	0
Lapp	c	4	0	1	1	4	2	0
Coombs	p	4	0	1	0	1	2	0
Totals		36	7	9	5	27	14	1

Pitching	IP	H	R	ER	BB	SO
Philadelphia						
Coombs (W)	9	9	2	2	1	4
Chicago						
Brown (L)	9	9	7	4	3	7

Phi.	100 010 050
Chi.	010 000 010

Chicago	Pos	AB	R	H	RBI	PO	A	E
Sheckard	lf	4	1	2	0	0	0	0
Schulte	rf	4	0	1	0	0	0	0
Hofman	cf	4	0	0	0	3	0	0
Chance	1b	4	1	2	1	13	0	0
Zimmerman	2b	3	0	2	0	5	1	0
Steinfeldt	3b	4	0	1	0	1	1	1
Tinker	ss	4	0	1	0	1	1	0
Archer	c	4	0	0	0	2	5	1
Brown	p	3	0	0	0	0	7	0
a Kling		1	0	0	0	0	0	0
Totals		34	2	9	2	27	14	2

a Grounded out for Brown in 9th.

Doubles—Chance, Collins 2, Lord, Murphy, Sheckard. Stolen Bases—Collins 2, Hartsel 2, Zimmerman. Sacrifice Hits—Barry, Zimmerman. Wild Pitch—Brown. Left on Bases—Philadelphia 6, Chicago 7. Umpires—O'Day, Sheridan, Rigler, Connolly. Attendance—27,374. Time of Game—2:06.

1st Inning
Philadelphia
Hartsel singled to center.
1 Lord struck out after two foul bunts. Hartsel stole second. Collins singled to center, scoring Hartsel.
2 Baker fouled to Archer. Collins stole second.
3 Davis struck out.
Chicago
1 Sheckard grounded out, Davis to Coombs.
2 Schulte grounded to second.
3 Hofman grounded to second.

2nd Inning
Philadelphia
1 Murphy grounded to third.
2 Barry popped to short.
3 Lapp struck out.
Chicago
Chance doubled into the crowd in left.
1 Zimmerman sacrificed, Davis to Collins. Steinfeldt beat out a hard smash to third, scoring Chance.
2 Tinker fouled to Davis.
3 Archer flied to center

3rd Inning
Philadelphia
1 Coombs struck out.
2 Hartsel grounded to second.
3 Lord bounced high to Brown.
Chicago
1 Brown bunted back to the mound.
2 Sheckard grounded to second. Schulte singled to center.
3 Schulte caught trying to steal second, Lapp to Collins.

4th Inning
Philadelphia
1 Collins grounded to first.
2 Baker struck out.
3 Davis grounded to second.
Chicago
Hofman walked.
1 Chance forced Hofman at second on a bunt, Coombs to Barry. Zimmerman singled to left, Chance going to second. Steinfeldt safe on a smash to Baker, who bobbled to load the bases.
2 Tinker struck out.
3 Archer struck out.

5th Inning
Philadelphia
Murphy safe on Steinfeldt's fumble.
1 Barry sacrificed Murphy to second, Brown to Chance. Lapp singled to left-center, scoring Murphy.
2 Coombs grounded back to the mound, Lapp taking second.
3 Hartsel struck out.
Chicago
1 Brown grounded to Collins, making a nice running stop. Sheckard singled to center.
2 Schulte forced Sheckard at second, Barry to Collins.
3 Schulte again caught trying to steal, Lapp to Collins.

6th Inning
Philadelphia
1 Lord fouled to Archer.
2 Collins popped to Zimmerman.
3 Baker grounded to second.
Chicago
1 Hofman grounded to short.
2 Chance flied to center. Zimmerman singled to right. Zimmerman stole second.
3 Steinfeldt flied to deep center.

7th Inning
Philadelphia
1 Davis grounded out, off Brown to Zimmerman who made the throw to first. Murphy doubled to left.
2 Barry flied to center, Murphy going to third after the catch.
3 Lapp struck out.
Chicago
1 Tinker flied to left.
2 Archer struck out.
3 Brown grounded to short.

8th Inning
Philadelphia
Coombs singled to right.
1 Hartsel forced Coombs at second, Tinker to Zimmerman. Hartsel stole second. Lord doubled to right, scoring Hartsel. Collins also doubled to right, Scoring Lord. Collins stole third for his fourth steal of the Series.
2 Baker grounded to Zimmerman who threw to Archer getting Collins at the plate. Davis walked. Murphy singled past second into center, Baker scoring. Davis also scored and Murphy got to third on Zimmerman's wild throw to the plate to get Baker. Murphy scored on a wild pitch. Barry walked.
3 Lapp grounded back to the mound.
Chicago
Sheckard doubled to left.
1 Schulte grounded to short, Sheckard going to third.
2 Hofman struck out. Chance singled to right, scoring Sheckard.
3 Zimmerman flied to left.

9th Inning
Philadelphia
1 Coombs grounded to the mound.
2 Hartsel also grounded to Brown. Lord walked. Collins doubled to the center field wall, Lord going to third. Collins' third hit of the game and fourth double of the Series.
3 Baker fouled to Chance.
Chicago
1 Steinfeldt flied to center.
2 Tinker flied to deep center. Archer singled to right.
3 Kling, pinch-hitting for Brown, forced Archer at second, Barry unassisted.

1910 WORLD SERIES COMPOSITE BOX

	Wins	Composite Line Score										
Philadelphia Athletics (A.L.)	4	2	4	9	2	2	0	10	6	0	0	- 35
Chicago Cubs (N.L.)	1	3	3	0	1	0	0	1	3	3	1	- 15

	Regular Season			
Manager	W	L	Pct.	G. Ahead
Connie Mack	102	48	680	14½
Frank Chance	104	50	.675	13

BATTING AND FIELDING

WORLD SERIES STATISTICS

	Pos	G	AB	R	H	2B	3B	HR	RBI	BB	SO	SB	BA	SA	PO	A	E
PHILADELPHIA ATHLETICS																	
Harry Davis	1b	5	17	5	6	3	0	0	2	3	4	0	.353	.529	44	2	3
Eddie Collins	2b	5	21	5	**9**	**4**	0	0	3	2	2	**4**	**.429**	.619	17	11	1
Jack Barry	ss	5	17	3	4	2	0	0	3	1	3	0	.235	.353	8	12	0
Frank Baker	3b	5	**22**	**6**	**9**	3	0	0	4	2	1	0	.409	.545	8	11	3
Danny Murphy	rf	5	20	**6**	7	3	0	1	**9**	1	0	1	.350	**.650**	6	2	0
Amos Strunk	cf	4	18	2	5	1	1	0	2	2	5	0	.278	.444	17	0	1
Bris Lord	lf-cf	5	**22**	3	4	2	0	0	1	1	3	0	.182	.273	11	0	0
Ira Thomas	c	4	12	2	3	0	0	0	1	4	1	0	.250	.250	27	8	1
Topsy Hartsel	lf	1	5	2	1	0	0	0	0	0	1	2	.200	.200	2	0	0
Jack Lapp	c	1	4	0	1	0	0	0	1	0	2	0	.250	.250	4	2	0
Rube Oldring		Did not play—injured															
Paddy Livingston		Did not play															
Stuffy McInnis		Did not play															
Ben Houser		Did not play															
Pat Donahue		Did not play															
Claude Derrick		Did not play															
Jack Coombs	p	3	13	0	5	1	0	0	3	0	1	0	.385	.462	1	3	2
Chief Bender	p	2	6	1	2	0	0	0	1	1	1	0	.333	.333	1	2	0
Cy Morgan		Did not play															
Eddie Plank		Did not play															
Harry Krause		Did not play															
Jimmy Dygert		Did not play															
Tommy Atkins		Did not play															
team total		5	177	35	56	19	1	1	30	17	24	7	.316	.452	136	59	11

Double Plays—6
Left on Bases—36

	Pos	G	AB	R	H	2B	3B	HR	RBI	BB	SO	SB	BA	SA	PO	A	E
CHICAGO CUBS																	
Frank Chance	1b	5	17	1	6	1	**1**	0	4	0	3	0	.353	.529	**52**	3	0
Heinie Zimmerman	2b	5	17	0	4	1	0	0	2	1	3	1	.235	.294	11	**18**	1
Joe Tinker	ss	5	18	2	6	2	0	0	0	2	2	1	.333	.444	10	14	2
Harry Steinfeldt	3b	5	20	0	2	1	0	0	1	0	4	0	.100	.150	2	12	4
Wildfire Schulte	rf	5	17	3	6	3	0	0	2	2	3	0	.353	.529	4	0	1
Solly Hofman	cf	5	15	2	4	0	0	0	2	4	3	0	.267	.267	7	0	1
Jimmy Sheckard	lf	5	14	5	4	2	0	0	1	**7**	2	1	.286	.429	7	2	1
Johnny Kling	c-ph	5	13	0	1	0	0	0	1	1	2	0	.077	.077	11	7	0
Jimmy Archer	1b-c	3	11	1	2	1	0	0	0	0	3	0	.182	.273	27	4	0
Ginger Beaumont	ph	3	2	1	0	0	0	0	0	1	1	0	.000	.000			
Tom Needham	ph	1	1	0	0	0	0	0	0	0	0	0	.000	.000			
John Kane	pr	1	0	0	0	0	0	0	0	0	0	0	—	—			
Johnny Evers		Did not play—injured															
Three Finger Brown	p	3	7	0	0	0	0	0	0	0	1	0	.000	.000	0	10	1
King Cole	p	1	2	0	0	0	0	0	0	0	2	0	.000	.000	1	3	0
Jack Pfiester	p	1	2	0	0	0	0	0	0	0	1	0	.000	.000	0	1	0
Harry McIntire	p	2	1	0	0	0	0	0	0	0	1	0	.000	.000	0	1	1
Orvie Overall	p	1	1	0	0	0	0	0	0	0	0	0	.000	.000	0	0	0
Ed Reulbach	p	1	0	0	0	0	0	0	0	0	0	0	—	—	0	1	0
Lew Richie	p	1	0	0	0	0	0	0	0	0	0	0	—	—	0	0	0
Big Jeff Pfeffer		Did not play															
Orlie Weaver		Did not play															
Bill Foxen		Did not play															
team total		5	158	15	35	11	1	0	13	18	31	3	.222	.304	132	76	12

Double Plays—3
Left on Bases—31

REGULAR SEASON STATISTICS

		Main Pos	G	AB	R	H	2B	3B	HR	RBI	BB	SO	SB	BA	SA
PHILADELPHIA ATHLETICS															
Harry Davis		1b	139	492	61	122	19	4	1	41	53		17	.248	.309
Eddie Collins		2b	153	583	81	188	16	15	3	81	49		**81**	.322	.417
Jack Barry		ss	145	487	64	126	19	5	3	60	52		14	.259	.337
Frank Baker		3b	146	561	83	159	25	15	2	74	34		21	.283	.392
Danny Murphy		of	151	560	70	168	28	18	4	64	31		18	.300	.436
Amos Strunk		of	16	48	9	16	0	1	0	2	3		4	.333	.375
Bris Lord	a	of	72	288	55	80	16	12	1	20	23		6	.278	.427
Ira Thomas		c	60	180	14	50	8	2	1	19	6		2	.278	.361
Topsy Hartsel		of	90	285	45	63	10	3	0	22	58		11	.221	.277
Jack Lapp		c	71	192	18	45	4	3	0	17	20		0	.234	.286
Rube Oldring		of	134	546	79	168	27	14	4	57	23		17	.308	.430
Paddy Livingston		c	37	120	11	25	4	3	0	9	6		2	.208	.292
Stuffy McInnis		ss	38	73	10	22	2	4	0	12	7		3	.301	.438
Ben Houser		1b	34	69	9	13	3	2	0	7	7		0	.188	.290
Pat Donahue	b	c	15	37	2	6	0	0	0	4	3		1	.162	.162
Claude Derrick		ss	1	1	0	0	0	0	0	0	0		0	.000	.000
Jack Coombs		p	46	132	20	29	3	0	0	9	7		3	.220	.242
Chief Bender		p	36	93	6	25	3	2	0	16	6		0	.269	.344
Cy Morgan		p	36	99	10	14	1	0	0	9	3		0	.141	.152
Eddie Plank		p	38	86	6	11	2	0	0	8	2		0	.128	.151
Harry Krause		p	16	38	4	8	1	0	0	0	1		0	.211	.237
Jimmy Dygert		p	19	36	1	3	1	0	0	2	3		0	.083	.111
Tommy Atkins		p	15	17	0	2	0	0	0	0	0		0	.118	.118
team total			155	5167	672	**1376**	**194**	**106**	19	541	409		207	**.266**	**.356**

a—from Cleveland
b—from Boston to and from Cleveland
Heinie Heifmuller (of), Earle Mack (c), Morrie Rath (3b), Lefty Russell (p) also played for the Athletics during the season.

		Main Pos	G	AB	R	H	2B	3B	HR	RBI	BB	SO	SB	BA	SA
CHICAGO CUBS															
Frank Chance		1b	88	295	54	88	12	8	0	36	37	15	16	.298	.393
Heinie Zimmerman		2b-ss-3b	99	335	35	95	16	6	3	38	20	36	7	.284	.394
Joe Tinker		ss	133	473	48	136	25	9	3	69	24	35	20	.288	.397
Harry Steinfeldt		3b	129	448	70	113	21	1	2	58	36	29	10	.252	.317
Wildfire Schulte		of	151	559	93	168	29	15	**10**	68	39	57	22	.301	.460
Solly Hofman		of-1b	136	477	83	155	24	16	3	86	65	34	29	.325	.461
Jimmy Sheckard		of	144	507	82	130	27	6	5	51	83	53	22	.256	.363
Johnny Kling		c	91	297	31	80	17	2	2	32	37	27	3	.269	.360
Jimmy Archer		c-1b	98	313	36	81	17	6	2	41	14	49	6	.259	.371
Ginger Beaumont		of	76	172	30	46	5	1	2	22	28	14	4	.267	.343
Tom Needham		c	31	76	9	14	3	1	0	10	10	10	1	.184	.250
John Kane		of-2b-3b	32	62	11	15	0	0	1	12	9	10	2	.242	.290
Johnny Evers		2b	125	433	87	114	11	7	0	28	108	18	28	.263	.326
Three Finger Brown		p	46	103	9	18	1	2	0	6	6	17	1	.175	.223
King Cole		p	34	91	7	21	2	1	0	9	3	25	1	.231	.275
Jack Pfiester		p	14	33	1	3	0	0	0	2	2	12	0	.091	.091
Harry McIntire		p	30	60	3	17	2	0	1	8	4	13	0	.258	.333
Orvie Overall		p	25	41	4	5	1	0	0	1	5	6	0	.122	.146
Ed Reulbach		p	24	56	4	6	0	0	0	2	3	20	1	.107	.107
Lew Richie	c	p	30	40	6	9	4	1	0	1	3	8	0	.225	.375
Big Jeff Pfeffer		p	14	17	1	3	1	1	0	2	1	1	0	.176	.353
Orlie Weaver		p	7	13	1	2	0	0	0	0	0	2	0	.154	.154
Bill Foxen	d	p	2	2	0	0	0	0	0	0	0	1	0	.000	.000
team total			154	4977	711	1333	219	**84**	**34**	586	542	501	173	.268	.366

c—from Boston (N)
d—from Philadelphia (N)
Fred Luderus (1b), Doc Miller (ph), Alex Carson (p), Rube Kroh (p) also played for the Cubs during the season.

PITCHING

WORLD SERIES STATISTICS

	G	GS	CG	IP	H	R	ER	BB	SO	W	L	SV	ERA
PHILADELPHIA ATHLETICS													
Jack Coombs	**3**	**3**	**3**	**27**	**23**	10	10	**14**	**17**	**3**	0	0	3.33
Chief Bender	2	2	2	18⅔	12	5	4	4	14	1	1	0	**1.93**
Cy Morgan	Did not play												
Eddie Plank	Did not play												
Harry Krause	Did not play												
Jimmy Dygert	Did not play												
Tommy Atkins	Did not play												
team total	5	5	5	45⅔	35	15	14	18	31	4	1	0	2.76
CHICAGO CUBS													
Three Finger Brown	**3**	2	1	18	**23**	**16**	**11**	7	14	1	**2**	0	5.50
King Cole	1	1	0	8	10	3	3	3	5	0	0	0	3.38
Jack Pfiester	1	0	0	6⅔	9	5	0	1	1	0	0	0	0.00
Harry McIntire	2	0	0	5⅓	4	5	4	3	3	0	1	0	6.75
Orvie Overall	1	1	0	3	6	3	3	1	1	0	1	0	9.00
Ed Reulbach	1	1	0	2	3	3	2	2	0	0	0	0	9.00
Lew Richie	1	0	0	1	1	0	0	0	0	0	0	0	0.00
Big Jeff Pfeffer	Did not play												
Orlie Weaver	Did not play												
Bill Foxen	Did not play												
team total	5	5	1	44	56	35	23	17	24	1	4	0	4.70

REGULAR SEASON STATISTICS

		G	GS	CG	IP	H	ER	BB	SO	W	L	Pct	SV	ShO	ERA
PHILADELPHIA ATHLETICS															
Jack Coombs		**45**	38	35	353	248	51	115	224	**31**	9	.775	2	**13**	1.30
Chief Bender		30	28	25	250	182	44	47	155	23	5	**.821**	1	3	1.58
Cy Morgan		36	34	23	291	214	50	**117**	134	18	12	.600	0	3	1.55
Eddie Plank		38	32	22	250	218	56	55	123	16	10	.615	2	1	2.02
Harry Krause		16	11	9	112	99	36	42	60	6	6	.500	0	2	2.89
Jimmy Dygert		19	8	6	99	81	28	49	59	4	4	.500	1	1	2.55
Tommy Atkins		15	3	2	57	53	17	23	29	3	2	.667	2	0	2.68
team total		155	155	**123**	1422	1103	282	450	**789**	**102**	48	**.680**	8	**24**	**1.78**
CHICAGO CUBS															
Three Finger Brown		46	31	**27**	295	256	61	64	143	25	13	.658	**7**	**7**	1.86
King Cole		33	29	21	240	174	48	130	114	20	4	**.833**	1	4	1.80
Jack Pfiester		14	13	5	100	82	20	26	34	6	3	.667	0	2	1.80
Harry McIntire		28	19	10	176	152	60	50	65	13	9	.591	0	2	3.07
Orvie Overall		23	21	11	145	106	43	54	92	12	6	.667	1	4	2.67
Ed Reulbach		24	23	13	173	161	60	49	55	12	8	.600	0	1	3.12
Lew Richie	c	30	11	8	130	117	39	51	53	11	4	.733	4	3	2.70
Big Jeff Pfeffer		13	1	1	41	43	15	16	11	1	0	1.000	0	0	3.29
Orlie Weaver		7	2	2	32	34	13	15	22	1	2	.333	0	0	3.66
Bill Foxen	d	2	0	0	5	7	5	3	2	0	0	—	0	0	9.00
team total		154	154	99	1379	1171	384	474	609	**104**	50	**.675**	13	**25**	**2.51**

Total Attendance—124,222 Average Attendance—24,844 Winning Player's Share—$2,068 Losing Player's Share—$1,375

1911
The Origin of Home Run Baker

Home runs were still an exotic rarity in 1911, with the outburst of the Babe Ruth era still years away. Wildfire Schulte of the Chicago Cubs led the National League with 21 clouts, while Frank Baker of the Philadelphia Athletics paced the American League with 11 homers. Baker's fame rested less on his home-run power than on his holding down third base in the "$100,000 infield" which Connie Mack had assembled on the A's. That astronomical preinflation sum described the worth of first baseman Stuffy McInnis, second baseman Eddie Collins, shortstop Jack Barry, and third baseman Baker. All four starred in the field, and their batting averages read .365 for Collins, .334 for Baker, .321 for McInnis, and a more modest .265 for Barry. With these four backing them up, the talented Athletic pitchers won 101 games and a second straight A.L. pennant for Mack.

Mack's opposite number in the fall classic this year was the feisty John McGraw of the New York Giants. It had not been an easy year for the Giants, as they had to rebuild their infield in midseason and also rebuild the Polo Grounds after fire swept the grounds on April 14. But the Giants moved back into the Polo Grounds in August with their rebuilt infield and put together a closing drive which dethroned Frank Chance's Cubs. Fred Merkle, Larry Doyle, and Chief Meyers swung the biggest bats in the lineup, while shortstop Art Fletcher and third baseman Buck Herzog tightened the infield after winning their positions during the summer. Christy Mathewson still was McGraw's mound ace with 26 wins, and behind him was lefty Rube Marquard, a 24-game winner in his first season as a regular starter. Besides the strong pitching of Mathewson and Marquard, the Giants' distinguishing trait was McGraw's frequent steal sign, leading to 347 stolen bases during the season.

But the Giants had little opportunity to run in game one, as a record crowd of 38,281 filled the Polo Grounds to view a pitchers' duel between Mathewson and Chief Bender. After six innings the score stood at 1–1, and then the Giants pulled ahead in the bottom of the seventh on a double by Meyers and a double by Josh Devore. Matty made the run stand up and the 2–1 win put the Giants on top in the Series. After a day of travel to Philly, Marquard faced Eddie Plank in the second game in another mound duel. Again the score was 1–1 when the Athletics broke it open in the bottom of the sixth. Marquard retired the first two batters, then Collins smashed a double to left. Baker then caught hold of an inside fastball and drove it over the right-field fence. The game ended 3–1, and the Series was knotted at 1–1. McGraw brought back Mathewson for game three in New York, while Mack used 28-game-winner Jack Coombs. Matty nursed a 1–0 lead into the ninth inning when, with one out, Baker drilled another home run to right. The Athletics then scored twice in the eleventh inning on three hits and two errors, and the Giants' one run in the bottom of the inning wasn't enough. After this 3–2 Philadelphia win, Frank Baker won the nickname "Home Run Baker," the label he has carried into history.

After six days of rain, the two teams reappeared in Philly on October 24, with Mathewson facing Bender. Instead of home runs, Baker hit two doubles, the first one in a three-run fourth inning and the second one driving in a run in the fifth. Bender allowed two New York runs in the first and none thereafter en route to a 4–2 win.

Down 3–1 in the Series, McGraw sent Marquard against Coombs before a Sunday crowd of 33,228 in New York. The Giants trailed 3–1 in the ninth, but they scored twice off Coombs to tie the score, then won the game in the tenth against Plank when Larry Doyle scored on a sacrifice fly; umpire Bill Klem later said that Doyle had missed home plate in his slide, an omission that went unnoticed by the A's. But the Athletics weren't about to let the Giants off the hook, and while Chief Bender held them to two runs in game six, the A's blasted three Giant pitchers for 13 runs. The hero of the Series had to be Baker, whose .375 average led both teams and whose two homers guaranteed his place in baseball folklore.

Game 1 October 14 at New York

| | Phi. | 010 000 000 |
| | N.Y. | 000 100 10x |

Philadelphia	Pos	AB	R	H	RBI	PO	A	E
Lord	lf	4	0	0	0	2	0	0
Oldring	cf	4	0	2	0	1	0	0
Collins	2b	3	0	0	0	5	1	0
Baker	3b	4	1	2	0	1	0	1
Murphy	rf	3	0	0	0	1	0	0
Davis	1b	4	0	1	1	8	0	0
Barry	ss	3	0	0	0	0	1	0
Thomas	c	3	0	0	0	12	2	0
Bender	p	3	0	1	0	0	1	0
Totals		31	1	6	1	24	10	2

New York	Pos	AB	R	H	RBI	PO	A	E
Devore	lf	3	0	1	1	3	0	0
Doyle	2b	3	0	1	0	1	0	0
Snodgrass	cf	2	1	0	0	2	0	0
Murray	rf	3	0	0	0	1	0	0
Merkle	1b	3	0	0	0	11	1	0
Herzog	3b	3	0	0	0	0	2	0
Fletcher	ss	4	0	0	0	2	3	0
Meyers	c	3	1	1	1	7	1	0
Mathewson	p	3	0	1	0	0	4	0
Totals		28	2	5	1	27	11	0

Doubles—Devore, Meyers, Oldring 2. Stolen Base—Doyle. Sacrifice Hits—Murphy, Murray. Passed Ball—Meyers. Hit by Pitcher—Snodgrass (by Bender). Left on Bases—Philadelphia 5, New York 8. Umpires—Klem (N), Dinneen (A), Brennan (N), Connolly (A). Attendance—**38,281.** Time of Game—2:12.

Pitching	IP	H	R	ER	BB	SO
Philadelphia						
Bender (L)	8	5	2	1	4	11
New York						
Mathewson (W)	9	6	1	1	1	5

1st Inning
Philadelphia
1 Lord struck out on three pitches.
2 Oldring struck out on three pitches.
3 Collins flied to left.
New York
1 Devore grounded back to the mound. Doyle singled to right.
2 Snodgrass struck out. Doyle stole second.
3 Murray called out on strikes.

2nd Inning
Philadelphia
1 Baker singled to right.
Murphy grounded out to the mound, Baker going to second. Baker went to third on a passed ball. Davis singles, scoring Baker.
2 Barry grounded to the mound, Davis going to second.
3 Thomas grounded to third.
New York
1 Merkle grounded to second.
2 Herzog grounded to second.
3 Fletcher struck out on three pitches.

3rd Inning
Philadelphia
1 Bender bunted out to the mound.
2 Lord flied to right. Oldring doubled to left. Collins walked on a full count.
3 Baker struck out on three pitches.
New York
1 Meyers flied to center.
2 Mathewson struck out on a full count. Devore walked on a full count.
3 Doyle flied to left.

4th Inning
Philadelphia
1 Murphy fouled to Meyers.
2 Davis grounded to short.
3 Barry popped to short.
New York
Snodgrass walked.
1 Murray grounded to Collins, making a good play. Snodgrass goes to second.
2 Merkle struck out on three pitches. Herzog safe on Collins' fumble, Snodgrass scoring as Herzog went to second on the throw to the plate.
3 Fletcher struck out on three pitches.

5th Inning
Philadelphia
1 Thomas flied to deep center. Bender singled to center.
2 Lord forced Bender at second on a sacrifice attempt, Merkle to Fletcher. Oldring doubled, sending Lord to third.
3 Collins grounded to first.
New York
1 Meyers grounded to short. Mathewson singled to center.
2 Devore struck out.
3 Doyle grounded to Collins, making a great play.

6th Inning
Philadelphia
Baker singled to center.
1 Murphy flied to center.
2 Baker out trying to steal second, Meyers to Doyle.
3 Davis grounded to third.
New York
Snodgrass hit by a pitch.
1 Murray grounded to second, Baker to Davis.
2 Merkle struck out. Snodgrass safe at third when Baker dropped the ball. (Thomas assist). Herzog walked on a full count.
3 Snodgrass out on a double steal attempt, Thomas to Collins to Thomas.

7th Inning
Philadelphia
1 Barry struck out.
2 Thomas flied to center.
3 Bender grounded to short.
New York
1 Fletcher grounded to first. Meyers doubled to left.
2 Mathewson struck out, becoming Bender's ninth victim. Devore doubled to deep left, Meyers scoring. Doyle walked.
3 Snodgrass fanned, Bender's tenth strikeout victim.

8th Inning
Philadelphia
1 Lord struck out on three pitches.
2 Oldring flied to Devore, making a good catch.
3 Collins bounced back to the mound.
New York
1 Murray flied to left. Merkle beat out a bunt to the mound.
2 Herzog became Bender's eleventh Strikeout victim.
3 Fletcher flied to right.

9th Inning
Philadelphia
1 Baker grounded to first.
2 Murphy popped to Meyers in front of the plate.
3 Davis grounded to short.

Game 2 October 16 at Philadelphia

New York	Pos	AB	R	H	RBI	PO	A	E
Devore	lf	4	0	0	0	5	0	1
Doyle	2b	4	0	0	0	1	2	0
Snodgrass	cf	3	0	2	0	1	0	0
Murray	rf	4	0	0	0	0	0	1
Merkle	1b	3	0	1	0	7	0	1
Herzog	3b	3	1	1	0	1	1	0
Fletcher	ss	3	0	0	0	1	1	0
Meyers	c	3	0	1	1	8	1	0
Marquard	p	2	0	0	0	0	2	0
Crandall	p	1	0	0	0	0	0	0
Totals		30	1	5	1	24	7	3

Philadelphia	Pos	AB	R	H	RBI	PO	A	E
Lord	lf	4	1	1	0	2	1	0
Oldring	cf	3	1	0	0	1	0	0
Collins	2b	3	1	2	0	2	4	0
Baker	3b	3	1	1	2	1	1	0
Murphy	rf	3	0	0	0	0	0	0
Davis	1b	3	0	0	0	10	0	0
Barry	ss	3	0	0	0	2	2	0
Thomas	c	3	0	0	0	9	0	0
Plank	p	3	0	0	0	0	2	0
Totals		28	3	4	2	27	10	0

N.Y.   010 000 000
Phi.   100 002 00x

Pitching	IP	H	R	ER	BB	SO
New York						
Marquard (L)	7	4	3	2	0	4
Crandall	1	0	0	0	0	2
Philadelphia						
Plank (W)	9	5	1	1	0	8

Doubles—Collins, Herzog. Home Run—Baker. Sacrifice Hit—Oldring. Hit by Pitcher—Snodgrass (by Plank). Wild Pitch—Marquard. Left on Bases—New York 3, Philadelphia 2. Umpires—Connolly, Brennan, Klem, Dineen. Attendance—26,286. Time of Game—1:52.

1st Inning
New York
1 Devore struck out.
2 Doyle flied to left.
   Snodgrass hit by a pitch.
3 Murray lined to second.
Philadelphia
   Lord singled to right and continued to second on Murray's bobble.
   1 Oldring sacrificed Lord to third, Marquard to Merkle.
   Lord scored on Marquard's wild pitch.
   Collins beat out a hit to third.
2 Baker struck out.
3 Murphy flied to left.

2nd Inning
New York
1 Merkle grounded to third.
   Herzog doubled to left.
2 Fletcher grounded to second, Herzog going to third.
   Meyers singled to center, scoring Herzog
3 Marquard struck out.
Philadelphia
1 Davis grounded to second.
   Barry safe when Devore dropped his deep fly, Barry getting to second.
2 Thomas lined to left.
3 Plank rolled out, Meyers to Merkle.

3rd Inning
New York
1 Devore again struck out.
2 Doyle flied to left.
   Snodgrass singled to right.
3 Murray bounced back to the mound.
Philadelphia
1 Lord struck out.
2 Oldring fouled to Meyers.
3 Collins flied to left.

4th Inning
New York
1 Merkle grounded to second.
2 Herzog popped to short.
3 Fletcher grounded to short.
Philadelphia
1 Baker grounded to second.
2 Murphy flied to left.
3 Davis fouled to Meyers.

5th Inning
New York
1 Meyers grounded to third.
2 Marquard struck out.
3 Devore struck out for the third time.
Philadelphia
1 Barry bounced back to the mound.
2 Thomas grounded to short.
3 Plank struck out.

6th Inning
New York
1 Doyle grounded to first.
   Snodgrass singled down the left field
2 line but thrown out trying for second, Lord to Barry.
3 Murray struck out.
Philadelphia
1 Lord flied to center.
2 Oldring flied to left.
   Collins doubled down the left field line.
   Baker blasted a two-run homer over the right field wall.
3 Murphy fanned.

7th Inning
New York
   Merkle singled to center.
1 Herzog flied to center.
2 Fletcher popped to third.
3   Merkle picked off first, Plank to Davis.
Philadelphia
1 Davis lined to second.
2 Barry lined to third.
3 Thomas popped to Fletcher, making a real good catch.

8th Inning
New York
1 Meyers lined to second.
2 Crandall, pinch-hitting for Marquard, grounded to second.
3 Devore struck out, **his fourth strikeout of the game.**
Philadelphia
   For New York—Crandall pitching.
1 Plank struck out.
   Merkle got an error dropping Lord's foul pop.
2 Lord struck out.
3 Oldring grounded to third.

9th Inning
New York
1 Doyle fouled to Thomas.
2 Snodgrass struck out.
3 Murray grounded to second.

Game 3 October 17 at New York

Philadelphia	Pos	AB	R	H	RBI	PO	A	E
Lord	lf	5	0	0	0	5	0	0
Oldring	cf	5	0	0	0	0	0	0
Collins	2b	5	1	2	0	5	4	2
Baker	3b	5	2	2	1	2	1	0
Murphy	rf	5	0	0	1	2	0	0
Davis	1b	5	0	2	1	10	0	0
Barry	ss	3	0	2	0	1	3	0
Lapp	c	4	0	1	0	8	6	0
Coombs	p	4	0	0	0	0	1	0
Totals		41	3	9	3	33	15	2

New York	Pos	AB	R	H	RBI	PO	A	E
Devore	lf	4	0	0	1	0	0	0
Doyle	2b	4	0	0	0	5	5	0
Snodgrass	cf	3	0	0	0	1	0	0
Murray	rf	2	0	0	0	2	1	0
Merkle	1b	3	0	0	0	11	1	0
Herzog	3b	3	1	1	0	4	3	3
Fletcher	ss	4	0	0	0	3	4	2
Meyers	c	4	1	1	0	4	4	0
Mathewson	p	3	0	1	0	1	4	0
a Becker		1	0	0	0	0	0	0
Totals		31	2	3	1	33	22	5

Phi.   000 000 001 02
N.Y.   001 000 000 01

Pitching	IP	H	R	ER	BB	SO
Philadelphia						
Coombs (W)	11	3	2	1	4	7
New York						
Mathewson (L)	11	9	3	1	0	3

a Safe on error for Mathewson in 11th.

Doubles—Barry, Herzog. Home Run—Baker. Stolen Bases—Barry, Collins. Sacrifice Hits—Barry, Murray. Double Play—Doyle to Fletcher. Left on Bases—Philadelphia 6, New York 2. Umpires—Brennan, Connolly, Klem, Dineen. Attendance—37,216. Time of Game—2:25.

1st Inning
Philadelphia
1 Lord grounded out off Mathewson's glove to Doyle who made the throw to first.
2 Oldring grounded to short.
3 Collins grounded out, Merkle to Mathewson.
New York
1 Devore struck out.
2 Doyle grounded to first.
3 Snodgrass struck out.

2nd Inning
Philadelphia
1 Baker grounded to second.
2 Murphy lined to third.
3 Davis flied to center.
New York
1 Murray flied to left.
2 Merkle grounded to short.
3 Herzog struck out.

3rd Inning
Philadelphia
   Barry singled to left.
   Barry stole second.
1,2 Lapp lined into a double play, Doyle to Fletcher.
3 Coombs popped to Doyle.
New York
1 Fletcher flied to right.
   Meyers singled off Baker's glove.
   Mathewson singled to right, Meyers going to third.
2 Devore forced Mathewson at second, Baker knocking down a hard smash to Collins, Meyers scoring.
3   Devore caught trying to steal second, Lapp to Barry.

4th Inning
Philadelphia
1 Lord flied to center.
2 Oldring popped to short.
   Collins beat out a hit to third.
   Collins stole second.
3 Baker grounded back to the mound.
New York
1 Doyle grounded to second.
2 Snodgrass flied to left.
3 Murray flied to right.

5th Inning
Philadelphia
   Murphy safe on Herzog's fumble.
   Davis singled past second, Murphy to second.
1 Barry sacrificed up both runners, Mathewson to Merkle.
2 Lapp hit to Mathewson as Murphy was caught in a run-down, Mathewson to Meyers to Herzog.
3 Coombs popped to short.
New York
1 Merkle flied to Lord making a good catch.
   Herzog walked.
2   Herzog out trying to steal second, Lapp to Collins as he overslid second.
3 Fletcher grounded to short.

6th Inning
Philadelphia
1 Lord flied to right.
2 Collins flied to center.
3 Oldring struck out.
New York
1 Meyers fouled to Lapp.
2 Mathewson popped to second.
3 Devore grounded to third.

7th Inning
Philadelphia
1 Baker flied to right.
2 Murphy popped to second.
3 Davis fanned.
New York
1 Doyle grounded to second.
2 Snodgrass struck out.
   Murray walked.
3 Merkle grounded to second.

8th Inning
Philadelphia
   Barry doubled down the left field line.
   Lapp beat out a roller to short, Barry going to third.
1 Coombs grounded to Doyle who threw out Barry at the plate.
   Lord hit to Doyle who threw to Fletcher to get Coombs but Fletcher dropped the ball. On the play Lapp
2 raced for the plate and was out, Fletcher to Doyle to Meyers to Herzog.
3 Oldring struck out.
New York
1 Herzog flied to left.
2 Fletcher grounded to short.
3 Meyers struck out.

9th Inning
Philadelphia
1 Collins grounded to third.
   Baker hit his second homer of the Series into the right field stands to tie the score.
   Murphy safe on Herzog's fumble, and went to second on Herzog's wild throw.
2 Davis rolled out in front of the plate, Meyers to Merkle as Murphy went to third.
3 Barry grounded to short.
New York
1 Mathewson struck out.
2 Devore popped for third.
3 Doyle struck out.

10th Inning
Philadelphia
1 Lapp grounded to short.
2 Coombs popped to second.
3 Lord grounded to short.
New York
   Snodgrass walked.
1 Murray sacrificed Snodgrass to second, Coombs to Davis.
   On a short passed ball, Snodgrass
2 was out trying to get to third, Lapp to Baker, Snodgrass intentionally spiking Baker.
   Merkle walked.
3   Merkle out trying to steal second, Lapp to Collins.

11th Inning
Philadelphia
1 Oldring grounded to third.
   Collins singled to left.
   Baker beat out a hit to third, Collins to third and Baker to second on Herzog's wild throw for his third error of the game.
   Murphy safe on Fletcher's fumble, Collins scoring as Baker got to third.
   Davis singled to right, scoring Baker
2 but Murphy was out trying for third, Murray to Herzog.
3   Davis out trying to steal second, Meyers to Doyle.
New York
   Herzog doubled to left.
1 Fletcher flied to left.
2 Meyers grounded to second, Herzog going to third.
   Becker, batting for Mathewson, safe on a fumble by Collins, Herzog scoring.
3   Becker out on a steal attempt, Lapp to Collins.

Game 4 October 24 at Philadelphia

New York	Pos	AB	R	H	RBI	PO	A	E
Devore	lf	4	1	2	0	0	0	0
Doyle	2b	3	1	1	1	2	0	0
Snodgrass	cf	3	0	0	1	0	0	0
Murray	rf	4	0	0	0	1	0	1
Merkle	1b	4	0	1	0	12	2	0
Herzog	3b	4	0	0	0	1	5	0
Fletcher	ss	4	0	2	0	0	4	1
Meyers	c	4	0	1	0	7	2	0
Mathewson	p	1	0	0	0	0	1	1
a Becker		1	0	0	0	0	0	0
Wiltse	p	0	0	0	0	0	0	0
Totals		32	2	7	2	24	14	3

a Grounded out for Mathewson in 8th.

Doubles—Baker 2, Barry 2, Davis, Merkle, Meyers, Murphy 2. Triple—Doyle. Sacrifice Hits—Collins, Oldring, Snodgrass, Thomas. Double Play—Baker to Davis. Left on Bases—New York 6, Philadelphia 8. Umpires—Dinneen, Klem, Connolly, Brennan. Attendance—24,355. Time of Game—1:49.

1st Inning
New York
Devore singled off of Bender's hand.
Doyle tripled to right-center, scoring Devore.
1 Snodgrass flied to deep left, Doyle scoring after the catch.
2 Murray grounded to first.
3 Merkle struck out on three pitches.
Philadelphia
1 Lord struck out on three pitches.
2 Oldring also struck out on three pitches.
Collins lined a single to center.
3 Baker struck out.

2nd Inning
New York
1 Herzog lined to center.
Fletcher lined a single to center, his first hit of the series.
2 Meyers forced Fletcher at second when his pop fell safely, Fletcher out Thomas to Collins.
3 Mathewson bounced back to the mound.
Philadelphia
Murphy doubled to deep right, also his first hit of the Series.
On a pick off attempt Murphy went to third when Fletcher couldn't get Mathewson's poor throw.
1 Davis out bunting, Mathewson to Merkle.
2 Murphy out on a broken squeeze play, Meyers unassisted.
Barry beat out a bunt towards third.
3 Thomas fouled to Meyers.

3rd Inning
New York
1 Devore flied to center.
2 Doyle fouled to Baker.
3 Snodgrass grounded to short.
Philadelphia
1 Bender grounded to short.
Lord singled to right.
2 Oldring forced Lord at second, Fletcher to Doyle.
3 Collins struck out.

4th Inning
New York
1 Murray popped to third.
2 Merkle again struck out.
3 Herzog bunted out to Davis unassisted.
Philadelphia
Baker doubled to left-center.
Murphy also doubled to left-center, Scoring Baker.
Davis doubled down the right field line, scoring Murphy.
1 Barry grounded to third, Davis going to third.
2 Thomas flied to right, Davis scoring after the catch.
3 Bender grounded to Fletcher, making a great stop and throw.

5th Inning
New York
1 Fletcher grounded to third.
Meyers doubled to right.
2 Meyers was out at third on a short passed ball, Thomas to Baker.
Mathewson walked.
3 Devore flied to left.
Philadelphia
1 Lord grounded out, Merkle to Mathewson.
2 Oldring grounded to third.
Collins singled over Doyle's head.
Baker doubled to right, Collins scoring and Baker to third on the throw-in.
3 Murphy struck out but Meyers dropped the ball and threw to first for the out.

6th Inning
New York
Doyle walked.
1 Snodgrass struck out.
2,3 Murray fouled to Baker who easily doubled Doyle at first.
Philadelphia
1 Davis grounded to Herzog, who made a sensational stop and throw.
Barry doubled over Snodgrass' head.
2 Thomas grounded to short, Barry going to third.
3 Bender grounded to third.

7th Inning
New York
1 Merkle struck out for the third time in the game.
2 Herzog flied to center.
Fletcher singled to center.
3 Meyers grounded to second.
Philadelphia
Lord safe on Fletcher's error.
1 Oldring sacrificed Lord to second, Merkle to Doyle.
2 Collins sacrificed Lord to third, Merkle unassisted.
Baker intentionally passed.
3 Murphy grounded to Merkle, coming up with a remarkable play.

8th Inning
New York
1 Becker, pinch-hitting for Mathewson, grounded to second.
Devore singled to left.
2 Doyle forced Devore at second, Collins to Barry.
Snodgrass safe on Baker's wild throw to first.
3 Murray fouled to Thomas.
Philadelphia
For New York—Wiltse now pitching.
1 Davis struck out.
Barry got a Texas League double to short right and went to third on Murray's wild throw to Fletcher.
Thomas grounded to Herzog and Barry was
2 run-down, Herzog to Meyers to Herzog, Thomas going to second.
3 Bender grounded to first.

9th Inning
New York
Merkle doubled to right.
1 Herzog grounded to Baker in front of Barry, Merkle going to third.
2 Fletcher popped to second.
3 Meyers grounded to second.

N.Y. / Phi. Line Score (Game 4)

N.Y.	200	000	000
Phi.	000	310	00x

Philadelphia	Pos	AB	R	H	RBI	PO	A	E
Lord	lf	4	0	1	0	2	0	0
Oldring	cf	3	0	0	0	3	0	0
Collins	2b	3	1	2	0	2	4	0
Baker	3b	3	1	2	1	4	3	1
Murphy	rf	4	1	2	1	0	0	0
Davis	1b	4	1	1	1	10	0	0
Barry	ss	4	0	3	0	1	1	0
Thomas	c	3	0	0	1	5	2	0
Bender	p	4	0	0	0	0	1	0
Totals		32	4	11	4	27	11	1

Pitching	IP	H	R	ER	BB	SO
New York						
Mathewson (L)	7	10	4	4	1	5
Wiltse	1	1	0	0	0	1
Philadelphia						
Bender (W)	9	7	2	2	2	4

Game 5 October 25 at New York

Philadelphia	Pos	AB	R	H	RBI	PO	A	E
Lord	lf	5	0	0	0	2	0	0
Oldring	cf	5	1	2	3	3	0	0
Collins	2b	3	0	0	0	2	1	1
Baker	3b	4	0	0	0	1	1	0
Murphy	rf	4	0	1	0	4	0	0
Davis	1b	4	0	0	0	7	2	0
Barry	ss	4	0	1	0	2	4	0
Lapp	c	4	1	1	0	10	2	0
Coombs	p	4	1	2	0	1	1	0
b Strunk		0	0	0	0	0	0	0
Plank	p	0	0	0	0	0	0	0
Totals		37	3	7	3	x29	11	1

Pitching	IP	H	R	ER	BB	SO
Philadelphia						
Coombs	9	8	3	2	2	9
Plank (L)	⅓	1	1	1	0	0
New York						
Marquard	3	3	3	0	1	2
Ames	4	2	0	0	0	2
Crandall (W)	3	2	0	0	0	0

1st Inning
Philadelphia
1 Lord flied to Devore, making a brilliant shoe top catch.
2 Oldring rolled out, second to first.
3 Collins flied to center.
New York
1 Devore grounded to short.
2 Doyle fouled to third.
3 Snodgrass grounded to third.

2nd Inning
Philadelphia
1 Baker struck out.
Murphy singled to left.
2,3 Davis struck out as Murphy was doubled trying for second, Meyers to Doyle.
New York
1 Murray struck out.
2 Merkle struck out.
Herzog singled to left.
Herzog stole second.
3 Fletcher struck out.

3rd Inning
Philadelphia
1 Barry grounded to third.
Lapp singled to center.
Coombs grounded to Herzog who threw to Doyle, but Doyle dropped the ball.
2 Lord popped to second.
Oldring blasted a three-run homer into the left field stands.
Collins walked.
Collins stole second.
3 Baker grounded to first.
New York
Meyers punched a single past third.
1 Becker, pinch-hitting for Marquard, lined to Barry, a good lunging catch
Barry threw to Davis but Davis dropped the throw.
2,3 Devore struck out and Meyers was doubled trying to steal, Lapp to Collins.

4th Inning
Philadelphia
For New York—Ames pitching.
1 Murphy fouled to Meyers.
2 Davis grounded to first.
3 Barry grounded to short.
New York
Doyle doubled to left.
1 Snodgrass struck out.
2 Murray struck out.
Merkle hit by a pitcher.
3 Herzog fouled to Lapp.

5th Inning
Philadelphia
1 Lapp grounded to second.
Coombs singled to left.
2 Lord forced Coombs at second, Fletcher to Doyle.
3 Oldring grounded to short.
New York
1 Fletcher flied to left.
2 Meyers struck out.
3 Ames struck out.

6th Inning
Philadelphia
1 Collins fouled to Merkle.
2 Baker grounded to second.
3 Murphy struck out.
New York
1 Devore grounded to second.
Doyle singled to right.
Doyle stole second.
2 Snodgrass flied to right.
3 Murray lined to left.

Phi. / N.Y. Line Score (Game 5)

Phi.	003	000	000	0
N.Y.	000	000	102	1

New York	Pos	AB	R	H	RBI	PO	A	E
Devore	lf	5	0	1	1	3	0	0
Doyle	2b	5	1	4	0	3	3	1
Snodgrass	cf	4	0	0	0	2	0	0
Murray	rf	5	0	0	0	2	0	0
Merkle	1b	2	1	0	1	12	0	0
Herzog	3b	4	0	1	0	1	1	0
Fletcher	ss	4	1	1	0	4	4	1
Meyers	c	3	0	1	1	5	3	0
Marquard	p	1	0	0	0	0	0	0
a Becker		1	0	0	0	0	0	0
Ames	p	1	0	0	0	0	1	0
Crandall	p	1	1	1	1	1	2	0
Totals		35	4	9	4	30	14	2

a Lined out for Marquard in 3rd.
b Ran for Coombs in 10th.
x Two outs when winning run scored.

Doubles—Crandall, Doyle 2, Fletcher. Home Run—Oldring. Stolen Bases—Barry, Collins, Doyle, Herzog. Sacrifice Hits—Merkle, Meyers, Snodgrass. Double Plays—Meyers to Doyle, Lapp to Collins. Hit by Pitcher—Merkle (by Coombs). Wild Pitch—Crandall. Left on Bases—Philadelphia 5, New York 8. Umpires—Klem, Dinneen, Connolly, Brennan. Attendance—33,228. Time of Game—2:33.

7th Inning
Philadelphia
1 Davis grounded to short.
Barry singled to right.
Barry stole second.
2 Lapp struck out.
3 Coombs popped to short.
New York
Merkle walked.
Herzog hit into a fielder's choice, Collins dropping Barry's throw.
1 Fletcher forced Herzog at second, Davis to Barry, Merkle going to third.
2 Meyers flied to right, Merkle scoring after the catch.
Crandall, pinch-hitting for Ames, walked.
3 Devore grounded out, Davis to Coombs.

8th Inning
Philadelphia
For New York—Crandall pitching.
1 Lord flied to center.
Oldring singled off Herzog's glove.
Oldring went to second on a wild pitch.
2 Collins flied to left.
3 Baker fouled to Herzog.
New York
Doyle singled to right.
1 Snodgrass sacrificed Doyle to second, Coombs to Davis.
2 Murray struck out for the third time.
3 Merkle grounded to Barry, making a spectacular stop and throw.

9th Inning
Philadelphia
Murphy safe on Fletcher's fumble.
1 Davis forced Murphy at second, Crandall to Fletcher.
2 Barry forced Davis at second, Herzog to Fletcher.
3 Barry out trying to steal second, Meyers to Fletcher.
New York
1 Herzog grounded to short.
Fletcher blooped a double to left.
2 Meyers grounded to short, Fletcher going to third.
Crandall doubled the center, Fletcher scoring.
Devore singled to left, scoring Crandall tying the score.
3 Devore out stealing, Lapp to Collins.

10th Inning
Philadelphia
1 Lapp bounced back to the mound.
Coombs beat out a bunt in front of the plate.
Strunk ran for Coombs who pulled a groin muscle.
2 Lord flied to left.
3 Oldring bunted out, Meyers to Merkle.
New York
For Philadelphia—Plank now pitching.
Doyle doubled to left.
Snodgrass bunted to Plank who threw too late to third to get Doyle.
1 Murray flied to short right.
2 Merkle flied deep to right, Doyle scoring the winning run after the catch.

Game 6 October 26 at Philadelphia

N.Y.	1 0 0	0 0 0	0 0 1			
Phi.	0 0 1	4 0 1	7 0 x			

New York	Pos	AB	R	H	RBI	PO	A	E
Devore	lf	4	0	0	0	5	0	0
Doyle	2b	4	1	1	0	1	4	0
Snodgrass	cf	4	0	0	0	1	0	0
Murray	rf	3	0	0	0	0	0	1
Merkle	1b	4	0	0	0	9	0	1
Herzog	3b	4	1	1	0	0	0	0
Fletcher	ss	4	0	0	1	1	2	0
Meyers	c	3	0	1	0	6	1	0
Wilson	c	1	0	0	0	1	0	0
Ames	p	1	0	1	0	0	2	1
a Crandall		0	0	0	0	0	0	0
Wiltse	p	1	0	0	0	0	1	0
Marquard	p	0	0	0	0	0	0	0
Totals		33	2	4	1	24	10	3

a Walked for Ames in 5th.

Doubles—Barry, Doyle, Lord 2, Murphy. Stolen Base—Herzog. Sacrifice Hits—Barry 2, Collins. Wild Pitches—Bender, Marquard. Left on Bases—New York 6, Philadelphia 3. Umpires—Connolly, Brennan, Klem, Dinneen. Attendance—20,485. Time of Game—2:12.

Philadelphia	Pos	AB	R	H	RBI	PO	A	E
Lord	lf	5	1	3	1	1	0	0
Oldring	cf	5	1	1	0	3	0	1
Collins	2b	4	1	0	1	2	4	0
Baker	3b	5	2	2	1	2	2	0
Murphy	rf	4	3	4	1	1	0	1
Davis	1b	4	2	1	2	9	1	0
McInnis	1b	0	0	0	0	1	0	0
Barry	ss	2	2	1	2	2	1	3
Thomas	c	3	1	1	0	5	1	0
Bender	p	4	0	0	0	1	4	0
Totals		36	13	13	8	27	13	5

Pitching	IP	H	R	ER	BB	SO
New York						
Ames (L)	4	4	5	2	1	4
Wiltse	2⅓	7	8	7	0	1
Marquard	1⅔	2	0	0	0	2
Philadelphia						
Bender (W)	9	4	2	0	2	5

1st Inning
New York
1 Devore grounded back to the mound.
   Doyle hit a ground-rule double, bouncing into the right field crowd.
2 Snodgrass lined to left.
   Murray safe when Murphy dropped his fly in right, Doyle scoring.
3   Murray picked off first, Bender to Davis.
Philadelphia
1 Lord grounded to second.
2 Oldring struck out.
3 Collins struck out.

2nd Inning
New York
1 Merkle flied to center.
   Herzog safe when Barry dropped his liner.
   Herzog stole second.
2 Fletcher struck out.
3 Meyers grounded to second.
Philadelphia
1 Baker lined to left.
   Murphy beat out a hard smash to second.
2 Davis grounded back to the mound, Murphy going to second.
3 Barry struck out.

3rd Inning
New York
   Ames singled to left.
1 Devore forced Ames at second, Bender to Barry.
2   Devore out trying to steal second, Thomas to Collins.
3 Doyle fouled to Baker.
Philadelphia
   Thomas walked.
1 Bender grounded to short, Thomas to second.
   Lord doubled to right, scoring Thomas.
2 Oldring grounded to short, Lord going to third.
3 Collins flied to left.

4th Inning
New York
1 Snodgrass flied to center.
2 Murray flied to right.
3 Merkle grounded to second.
Philadelphia
   Baker singled to center.
   Murphy singled to left, Baker going to third.
   Davis grounded to Doyle, who threw to Meyers but Baker beat the throw. Barry's attempted sacrifice was picked up by Ames whose throw hit Barry in the head and bounced to right, Murphy scoring. Murray threw wild to third to get Davis, allowing both Davis and Barry to score.
1 Thomas struck out.
2 Bender grounded to second.
3 Lord flied to Devore making a good running catch in left-center.

5th Inning
New York
1 Herzog struck out.
2 Fletcher grounded back to the mound.
   Meyers singled to center.
   Crandall, pinch-hitting for Ames, walked.
3 Devore struck out.
Philadelphia
   For New York—Wiltse pitching.
1 Oldring flied to left.
2 Collins grounded to the mound.
3 Baker grounded to first.

6th Inning
New York
1 Doyle fouled to Baker.
2 Snodgrass flied to center.
   Murray walked.
3 Merkle forced Murray at second, Baker to Collins.
Philadelphia
   Murphy doubled to center.
1 Davis grounded to second, Murphy going to third.
2 Barry flied to left, Murphy scoring after the catch.
3 Thomas struck out.

7th Inning
New York
   Herzog safe on Barry's fumble.
1 Fletcher fouled to Davis.
2 Meyers struck out.
3 Wiltse struck out.
Philadelphia
1 Bender popped to second.
   Lord singled through short.
   Oldring singled to center, Lord going to third.
   Collins hit a sacrifice bunt to Wiltse, but Merkle dropped the ball. Lord scored as Oldring went to second.
   Baker singled to right, scoring Oldring as Collins went to third.
   Murphy singled to center, scoring Collins with Baker going to third.
   Davis singled over Doyle's head, scoring Baker as Murphy stopped at second.
   Barry doubled to right, scoring Murphy as Davis went to third.
   For New York—Marquard came in to pitch. On a wild pitch both Davis and Barry scored as Meyers refused to chase the pitch.
   Thomas singled to right.
2   Thomas caught stealing second, Meyers to Fletcher
3 Bender struck out.

8th Inning
New York
1 Devore grounded to short.
2 Doyle grounded out, Davis to Bender.
   Snodgrass safe on Barry's fumble, his third of the game.
3 Murray grounded to second.
Philadelphia
   For New York—Wilson catching.
   Lord doubled to left.
1 Oldring flied to center.
2 Collins grounded to second, Lord going to third.
3 Baker struck out.

9th Inning
New York
1 Merkle flied to Barry in short right.
   Herzog singled to center, and went to second on Oldring's fumble.
   Herzog went to third on a wild pitch.
2 Fletcher grounded to second, scoring Herzog.
   For Philadelphia—McInnis replaced Davis at first.
3 Wilson grounded to third.

1911 WORLD SERIES COMPOSITE BOX

	Wins	Composite Line Score	Manager	W	L	Regular Season Pct.	G. Ahead
Philadelphia Athletics (A.L.)	4	1 1 4 7 1 3 7 0 1 0 2 — 27	Connie Mack	101	50	.669	13½
New York Giants (N.L.)	2	3 1 1 1 0 0 2 0 3 1 1 — 13	John McGraw	99	54	.647	7½

BATTING AND FIELDING

PHILADELPHIA ATHLETICS

	Pos	G	AB	R	H	2B	3B	HR	RBI	BB	SO	SB	BA	SA	PO	A	E		Main Pos	G	AB	R	H	2B	3B	HR	RBI	BB	SO	SB	BA	SA
Harry Davis	1b	6	24	3	5	1	0	0	5	0	3	0	.208	.250	54	3	0		1b	57	183	27	36	9	1	1	22	24		2	.197	.273
Eddie Collins	2b	6	21	4	6	1	0	0	1	2	2	2	.286	.333	13	22	4		2b	132	493	92	180	22	13	3	73	62	38	.365	.481
Jack Barry	ss	6	19	2	7	4	0	0	2	0	2	2	.368	.579	8	12	3		ss	127	442	73	117	18	7	1	63	38	30	.265	.344
Frank Baker	3b	6	24	7	9	2	0	2	5	1	5	0	.375	.708	10	9	2		3b	148	592	96	198	38	4	11	115	40	38	.334	.468
Danny Murphy	rf	6	23	4	7	3	0	0	3	0	3	0	.304	.435	8	0	1		of	141	508	104	167	27	11	6	66	50	22	.329	.461
Rube Oldring	cf	6	25	2	5	2	0	1	3	0	5	0	.200	.400	8	0	1		of	121	495	84	147	11	14	3	59	21	21	.297	.394
Bris Lord	lf	6	27	2	5	2	0	0	1	0	5	0	.185	.259	14	1	0		of	134	574	92	178	36	11	3	55	35	15	.310	.427
Ira Thomas	c	4	12	1	1	0	0	0	1	1	2	0	.083	.083	31	5	0		c	103	297	33	81	14	3	0	39	23		.273	.340
Jack Lapp	c	2	8	1	2	0	0	0	0	0	1	0	.250	.250	18	8	0		c	68	167	35	59	10	3	1	26	24	4	.353	.467
Stuffy McInnis	1b	1	0	0	0	0	0	0	0	0	0	0	—	—	1	0	0		1b-ss	126	468	76	150	20	10	3	77	25	23	.321	.425
Amos Strunk	ph	1	0	0	0	0	0	0	0	0	0	0	—	—					of	74	215	42	55	7	2	1	21	35	13	.256	.321
Claude Derrick		Did not play																	2b	36	100	14	23	1	2	0	5	7	7	.230	.280
Paddy Livingston		Did not play																	c	27	71	9	17	4	0	0	8	7	1	.239	.296
Topsy Hartsel		Did not play																	of	25	38	9	9	2	0	0	1	8	0	.237	.289
Chief Bender	p	3	11	0	1	0	0	0	0	0	1	0	.091	.091	1	6	0		p	32	79	9	13	0	0	0	8	2	2	.165	.165
Jack Coombs	p	2	8	1	2	0	0	0	0	0	0	0	.250	.250	1	2	0		p	52	141	31	45	6	1	2	23	8	5	.319	.418
Eddie Plank	p	2	3	0	0	0	0	0	0	0	2	0	.000	.000	0	2	0		p	40	94	7	18	2	0	0	10	5	0	.191	.213
Cy Morgan		Did not play																	p	38	94	7	15	1	0	0	7	0	0	.160	.170
Harry Krause		Did not play																	p	27	59	9	15	2	1	0	7	2	0	.254	.322
Doc Martin		Did not play																	p	11	14	1	3	1	0	0	1	0	0	.214	.286
Dave Danforth		Did not play																	p	14	6	1	1	0	0	0	0	0	0	.167	.167
team total		6	205	27	50	15	0	3	21	4	31	4	.244	.361	167	70	11			152	5199	861	1540	233	93	35	692	424	226	.296	.397

Double Plays—2
Left on Bases—29

Chester Emerson (of), Willie Hogan (of), Earle Mack (3b), Howard Armstrong (p), Boardwalk Brown (p), Allan Collamore (p), Elmer Leonard (p), Lep Long (p), Lefty Russell (p) also played for the Athletics during the season.

NEW YORK GIANTS

	Pos	G	AB	R	H	2B	3B	HR	RBI	BB	SO	SB	BA	SA	PO	A	E		Pos	G	AB	R	H	2B	3B	HR	RBI	BB	SO	SB	BA	SA
Fred Merkle	1b	6	20	1	3	1	0	0	1	2	6	0	.150	.200	62	4	2		1b	149	541	80	153	24	10	12	84	43	60	49	.283	.431
Larry Doyle	2b	6	23	3	7	3	1	0	1	2	1	2	.304	.522	13	14	1		2b	143	526	102	163	25	25	13	77	39	38	.310	.527
Art Fletcher	ss	6	23	1	3	1	0	0	1	0	4	0	.130	.174	11	18	4		ss-3b-2b	112	326	73	104	17	8	1	37	30	27	20	.319	.429
Buck Herzog	3b	6	21	3	4	2	0	0	2	3	2	0	.190	.286	7	13	3		a 3b	69	247	37	66	16	4	1	26	14	19	22	.267	.368
Red Murray	rf	6	21	0	0	0	0	0	02	5	0	.000	.000	4	1	3		of	140	488	76	142	27	15	3	78	37	48	.291	.426
Fred Snodgrass	cf	6	19	1	2	0	0	0	1	2	7	0	.105	.105	9	0	0		of	151	584	83	157	27	10	1	77	72	59	51	.294	.388
Josh Devore	lf	6	24	1	4	1	0	0	3	1	8	0	.167	.208	16	0	1		of	149	565	96	158	19	10	3	50	81	69	61	.280	.365
Chief Meyers	c	6	20	2	6	2	0	0	0	3	0	0	.300	.400	37	12	0		c	133	391	48	130	18	9	1	61	25	33	7	.332	.432
Beals Becker	ph	3	3	0	0	0	0	0	0	0	0	0	.000	.000					of	88	172	28	45	11	1	1	20	26	22	19	.262	.355
Art Wilson	c	1	1	0	0	0	0	0	0	0	0	0	.000	.000	1	0	0		c	66	109	17	33	9	1	1	17	19	12	6	.303	.431
Art Devlin		Did not play																	3b	95	260	42	71	16	2	0	25	42	19	9	.273	.350
Grover Hartley		Did not play																	c	11	18	1	4	2	0	0	1	0	1	0	.222	.333
Gene Paulette		Did not play																	1b	10	12	1	2	0	0	0	1	0	1	0	.167	.167
Christy Mathewson	p	3	7	0	2	0	0	0	1	3	0	0	.286	.286	2	9	1		p	45	112	12	22	2	0	0	12	5	13	2	.196	.214
Rube Marquard	p	3	2	0	0	0	0	0	0	0	2	0	.000	.000	0	2	0		p	45	104	9	17	1	2	1	10	2	23	0	.163	.240
Red Ames	p	2	2	0	1	0	0	0	0	0	1	0	.500	.500	0	2	1		p	34	64	2	6	0	1	0	5	5	12	0	.094	.125
Doc Crandall	p-ph	3	2	1	1	1	0	0	2	0	0	.500	1.000	2	3	0		p-ss-2b	61	113	12	27	1	4	2	21	8	16	2	.239	.372
Hooks Wiltse	p	2	1	0	0	0	0	0	0	0	1	0	.000	.000	0	1	0		p	31	69	5	13	1	0	0	14	1	12	0	.188	.203
Louis Drucke		Did not play																	p	16	23	1	2	0	0	0	3	6	0	.087	.087
team total		6	189	13	33	11	1	0	10	14	44	4	.175	.243	162	78	16			154	5006	756	1399	225	103	41	651	530	506	347	.279	.390

Double Plays—2
Left on Bases—33

a—from Boston (N)
Al Bridwell (ss), George Burns (of), Mike Donlin (of), Hank Gowdy (1b), Admiral Schlei (ph), Charlie Faust (p), Bert Maxwell (p), Bugs Raymond (p), Dick Rudolph (p) also played for the Giants during the season.

PITCHING

PHILADELPHIA ATHLETICS

	G	GS	CG	IP	H	R	ER	BB	SO	W	L	SV	ERA		G	GS	CG	IP	H	ER	BB	SO	W	L	Pct.	SV	ShO	ERA
Chief Bender	3	3	3	26	16	6	3	8	20	2	1	0	1.04		31	24	16	216	198	52	58	114	17	5	.773	4	3	2.17
Jack Coombs	2	2	1	20	11	5	3	6	16	1	0	0	1.35		47	40	26	337	360	132	119	185	28	12	.700	3	1	3.53
Eddie Plank	2	1	1	9⅓	6	2	2	0	8	1	1	0	1.86		40	30	24	257	237	60	77	149	22	8	.733	5	6	2.10
Cy Morgan	Did not play														38	30	15	250	217	75	113	136	15	7	.682	1	2	2.70
Harry Krause	Did not play														27	19	12	169	155	57	47	85	11	8	.579	2	1	3.04
Doc Martin	Did not play														11	3	1	38	40	19	17	21	1	2	.333	0	0	4.50
Dave Danforth	Did not play														14	2	1	34	29	14	17	21	5	2	.714	0	0	3.71
team total	6	6	5	55⅓	33	13	8	14	44	4	2	0	1.29		152	152	97	1376	1343	460	487	739	101	50	.669	15	13	3.01

NEW YORK GIANTS

	G	GS	CG	IP	H	R	ER	BB	SO	W	L	SV	ERA		G	GS	CG	IP	H	ER	BB	SO	W	L	Pct.	SV	ShO	ERA
Christy Mathewson	3	3	2	27	25	8	6	2	13	1	2	0	2.00		45	37	29	307	303	68	38	141	26	13	.667	3	5	1.99
Rube Marquard	3	2	0	11⅓	9	6	2	1	8	0	1	0	1.54		45	33	22	278	221	77	106	237	24	7	.774	3	5	2.49
Red Ames	2	1	0	8	6	5	2	1	6	0	1	0	2.25		34	23	13	205	170	61	54	118	11	10	.524	2	1	2.68
Doc Crandall	2	0	0	4	2	2	0	0	2	1	0	0	0.00		41	5	9	199	199	58	51	94	15	5	.750	5	2	2.62
Hooks Wiltse	2	0	0	3⅓	8	8	7	0	2	0	0	0	18.90		30	24	11	187	177	68	39	92	12	9	.571	0	4	3.27
Louis Drucke	Did not play														15	10	4	76	83	34	41	42	4	4	.500	0	0	4.02
team total	6	6	2	54	50	27	17	4	31	2	4	0	2.83		154	154	95	1368	1267	409	369	771	99	54	.647	13	18	2.69

Total Attendance—179,851   Average Attendance—29,975   Winning Player's Share—$3,655   Losing Player's Share—$2,436

1912
The "$30,000 Muff"

Fresh from two straight Series triumphs, Connie Mack considered his 1912 Athletics to be his strongest club. "They had everything that year, skill and experience and confidence that comes with winning." Unfortunately for Mack, it was also a combination which spelled complacency as the A's finished a distant third. In their place were the Boston Red Sox, who won the American League pennant in time to celebrate their newly opened Fenway Park. Boston's mound ace was 34-game-winner Smokey Joe Wood, a young fireballer who benefited from the greatest defensive outfield in history: Duffy Lewis, Tris Speaker, and Harry Hooper. All three covered ground like deer, and all three could gun runners down from the deepest reaches of the field. Hooper also was the leadoff batter, Lewis drove in 109 runs from his clean-up slot, and Speaker combined several talents in the third slot, hitting .383, knocking in 90 runs, swatting 10 home runs, and stealing 52 bases. The Red Sox's Series opponent, the New York Giants, fielded a lineup of steady hitters who consistently turned singles into doubles with stolen bases. Christy Mathewson and Rube Marquard again headed the Giant hill staff. Mathewson won 23 games in his usual quiet manner, but Marquard set the baseball world buzzing by winning 19 straight games en route to a 26–11 season.

But manager John McGraw started neither Mathewson nor Marquard in the opening game in New York, nominating instead rookie Jeff Tesreau to face Wood. Holding his aces back for the next two games in Boston, McGraw only got himself into a hole when the Sox got to Tesreau for one run in the sixth and three in the seventh for a 4–3 win. Mathewson pitched the second game up in Boston, but five New York errors undermined him and made the Giants lucky to slip away with a 6–6 tie called after 11 innings for darkness. But Marquard won the third game 2–1 to even the Series at 1–1 heading back to New York.

The Red Sox climbed back into command with 3–1 and 2–1 wins in the next two games. Tesreau and Mathewson pitched well for the Giants, but Wood and Hugh Bedient did better for the Red Sox. But the Boston pitchers would fare worse in games six and seven. The Giants socked Buck O'Brien for five runs in the bottom of the first inning in game six, and Marquard hung on for a 5–2 win. The next day in Boston, the New York batters teed off on Wood, scoring six times in the first to send Tesreau on his way to an 11–4 triumph which evened the Series at three games apiece.

A Wednesday afternoon crowd of 17,034 assembled in Fenway Park to watch the deciding match, with Mathewson and Bedient the mound opponents. The Giants scored a run off Bedient in the third, then were robbed of another in the fifth when Harry Hooper raced into right-center, leaped high at the short fence before the temporary bleachers, and caught Larry Doyle's line shot while landing atop the fans packed in there. Bedient held the line through seven innings, and the Sox evened the score in the bottom of that frame on a run driven in by Olaf Henriksen, batting for the pitcher. Smokey Joe Wood took over on the mound and battled Mathewson to a 1–1 deadlock after nine innings. In the top of the tenth, the Giants apparently won it on a double by Red Murray and a run-scoring single by Fred Merkle. But the Red Sox would make their final turn at bat count, with a little aid from the Giants. Pinch hitter Clyde Engle led off by lofting a high fly to center field. Fred Snodgrass settled under the ball and amazingly dropped it, allowing Engel to reach second base. Snodgrass then made some amends with a fine catch on Hooper's drive to deep center, but it was now Mathewson's turn to show his humanity, walking the weak-hitting Steve Yerkes. With Matty bearing down, the dangerous Speaker set up an easy pop near the first-base coach's box. But first baseman Merkle stood transfixed at his position, and a last-second dash by catcher Meyers couldn't prevent the ball from dropping. Thus reprieved, Speaker singled home Engle and sent Yerkes to third. After Lewis was intentionally walked, Larry Gardner's long fly to left was caught by Devore, but Yerkes tore down the line with the championship run after the catch. Although Snodgrass's misplay was dubbed the "$30,000 muff," Merkle's daydreaming at first also aided greatly in denying the Giants the winners' share of the pot.

Game 1 October 8 at New York

| Bos. | 0 0 0 | 0 0 1 | 3 0 0 |
| N.Y. | 0 0 2 | 0 0 0 | 0 0 1 |

Boston	Pos	AB	R	H	RBI	PO	A	E
Hooper	rf	3	1	1	1	1	0	0
Yerkes	2b	4	0	1	2	0	1	0
Speaker	cf	3	1	1	0	0	1	0
Lewis	lf	4	0	0	1	2	0	0
Gardner	3b	4	0	0	0	1	1	0
Stahl	1b	4	0	0	0	6	1	0
Wagner	ss	3	1	2	0	5	3	1
Cody	c	3	0	1	0	11	1	0
Wood	p	3	1	0	0	1	1	0
Totals		31	4	6	4	27	9	1

Pitching	IP	H	R	ER	BB	SO
Boston						
Wood (W)	9	8	3	3	2	11
New York						
Tesreau (L)	7	5	4	4	4	4
Crandall	2	1	0	0	0	2

New York	Pos	AB	R	H	RBI	PO	A	E
Devore	lf	3	1	0	0	0	0	0
Doyle	2b	4	1	2	0	2	7	0
Snodgrass	cf	4	0	1	0	2	0	0
Murray	rf	3	0	1	2	12	0	0
Merkle	1b	4	1	1	0	12	0	0
Herzog	3b	4	0	2	0	1	1	0
Meyers	c	3	0	1	1	6	1	0
b Becker		0	0	0	0	0	0	0
Fletcher	ss	4	0	0	0	3	1	1
Tesreau	p	2	0	0	0	0	2	0
a McCormick		1	0	0	0	0	0	0
Crandall	p	1	0	0	0	0	1	0
Totals		33	3	8	3	27	13	1

a Flied out for Tesreau in 7th.
b Ran for Meyers in 9th.

Doubles—Doyle, Hooper, Wagner. Triple—Speaker. Sacrifice Hits—Cady, Hooper. Double Play—Stahl to Wood. Hit by Pitcher—Meyers (by Wood). Left on Bases—Boston 6, New York 6. Umpires—Klem (N), Evans (A), Rigler (N), O'Loughlin (A). Attendance—35,730. Time of Game—2:10.

1st Inning
Boston
Hooper walked.
1 Yerkes grounded to second, Hooper going to second.
2 Speaker also grounded to second, Hooper moving to third.
3 Lewis flied to center.
New York
1 Devore struck out.
2 Doyle grounded to short. Snodgrass bounced a single over Wood's head.
Murray walked.
3 Merkle popped to short.

2nd Inning
Boston
Gardner safe on Fletcher's fumble.
1 Stahl forced Gardner at second when he bunted too hard, Tesreau to Fletcher.
2 Stahl caught trying to steal second, Meyers to Doyle.
Wagner walked.
3 Cady flied to right.
New York
1 Herzog popped to first.
2 Meyers struck out.
3 Fletcher struck out.

3rd Inning
Boston
Wood walked after an 0–2 count.
1 Hooper sacrificed Wood to second, Tesreau to Merkle.
2 Yerkes grounded to second, Wood going to third.
Speaker walked on four pitches.
3 Lewis popped to short.
New York
1 Tesreau called out on strikes.
Devore walked.
Doyle got a Texas League single to left, Devore racing to third. Doyle took second on the throw to third.
2 Snodgrass struck out on three pitches.
Murray singled to center, scoring
3 Devore and Doyle, but was out trying to get to second on the throw to the plate, Speaker to Cady to Wagner.

4th Inning
Boston
1 Gardner fouled to Herzog at the stands.
2 Stahl struck out.
3 Wagner fouled to Merkle.
New York
1 Merkle struck out.
Herzog singled on a bad hop over Wagner's head.
2 Meyers bounced back to the mound, Herzog going to second.
3 Fletcher struck out again.

5th Inning
Boston
1 Cady grounded to second.
2 Wagner grounded to first.
3 Hooper struck out.
New York
1 Tesreau again called out on strikes.
2 Devore flied to left.
Doyle singled off of Gardner, but was
3 out trying to take second, Gardner to Wagner as he overslid second.

6th Inning
Boston
1 Yerkes flied to Snodgrass in right-center.
Speaker tripled to deep center when Snodgrass cut in front of Devore to make the catch, which Devore could have made.
2 Lewis grounded to second, scoring Speaker.
3 Gardner struck out.
New York
Snodgrass safe on Wagner's error.
1,2 Murray popped into a double play on a bunt, Stahl to Wood.
3 Merkle popped to short.

7th Inning
Boston
1 Stahl grounded to second.
Wagner singled to center.
Cady also singled to center, Wagner going to second.
2 Wood forced Cady at second, Doyle to Fletcher as Wagner got to third. Hooper doubled over the first base line all the way to the wall, scoring Wagner as Wood stopped at third. Yerkes singled to left, scoring both Wood and Hooper.
3 Speaker struck out on three pitches.
New York
1 Herzog struck out. Meyers was hit by a pitch.
2 Fletcher forced Meyers at second, Yerkes to Wagner.
3 McCormick, batting for Tesreau, flied to left.

8th Inning
Boston
For New York—Crandall pitching.
1 Lewis grounded to short.
2 Gardner grounded to second.
3 Stahl struck out.
New York
1 Devore grounded to short.
2 Doyle also grounded to short.
3 Snodgrass popped to third.

9th Inning
Boston
Wagner doubled down the left field line.
1 Cady sacrificed Wagner to third, Herzog to Merkle.
2 Wood grounded back to the mound, Wagner holding third.
3 Hooper lined to second.
New York
1 Murry flied to right.
Merkle singled past short.
Herzog blooped a Texas Leaguer into short right, Merkle taking second.
Meyers singled past third, scoring Merkle and Herzog going to third. Meyers took second on the throw to the plate.
2 Fletcher struck out for the third time.
3 Crandall struck out on a full count to become Wood's eleventh strikeout victim.

Game 2 October 9 at Boston

N.Y.	010	100	030	10	*		
Bos.	300	010	010	10			

New York	Pos	AB	R	H	RBI	PO	A	E
Snodgrass	lf-rf	4	1	1	0	0	0	0
Doyle	2b	5	0	1	0	2	5	1
Becker	cf	4	1	0	0	0	0	0
Murray	rf-lf	5	2	3	2	3	0	0
Merkle	1b	5	1	1	0	19	0	0
Herzog	3b	4	1	3	2	2	4	0
Meyers	c	4	0	2	1	5	0	0
a Shafer	ss	0	0	0	0	0	3	0
Fletcher	ss	4	0	0	0	1	3	3
b McCormick		0	0	0	1	0	0	0
Wilson	c	0	0	0	0	0	1	1
Mathewson	p	5	0	0	0	1	6	0
Totals		40	6	11	6	33	23	5

Boston	Pos	AB	R	H	RBI	PO	A	E
Hooper	rf	5	1	3	0	3	0	0
Yerkes	2b	5	1	1	1	2	4	0
Speaker	cf	5	2	2	0	2	0	0
Lewis	lf	5	2	3	0	2	0	1
Gardner	3b	4	0	0	1	2	0	0
Stahl	1b	5	0	1	2	9	0	0
Wagner	ss	5	0	0	0	6	5	0
Carrigan	c	5	0	0	0	7	3	0
Collins	p	3	0	0	0	0	1	0
Hall	p	1	0	0	0	0	0	0
Bedient	p	1	0	0	0	0	0	0
Totals		44	6	10	4	33	13	1

Pitching	IP	H	R	ER	BB	SO
New York						
Mathewson	11	10	6	2	0	4
Boston						
Collins	7⅓	9	5	3	0	5
Hall	2⅔	2	1	1	4	0
Bedient	1	0	0	0	1	1

a Ran for Meyers in 10th.
b Hit sacrifice fly for Fletcher in 10th.
* Game called due to darkness.

Doubles—Herzog, Hooper, Lewis 2, Murray, Snodgrass. Triples—Herzog, Merkle, Murray, Speaker, Yerkes. Stolen Bases—Herzog, Hooper 2, Snodgrass, Stahl. Sacrifice Hits—Gardner, Herzog, McCormick. Double Play—Fletcher to Herzog. Hit by Pitcher—Snodgrass (by Bedient). Left on Bases—New York 9, Boston 6. Umpires—O'Loughlin, Rigler, Klem, Evans. Attendance—30,148. Time of Game—2:38.

1st Inning
New York
Snodgrass doubled into the left field bleachers.
1 Doyle struck out.
2 Becker grounded to second, Snodgrass going to third.
3 Murray grounded back to the mound.
Boston
Hooper singled off Mathewson's glove. Hooper stole second.
Yerkes safe on Fletcher's fumble, Hooper to third.
Speaker bunted for a hit, loading the bases.
1 Lewis forced Hooper at the plate, Herzog to Meyers.
2 Gardner grounded out off Mathewson's glove to Doyle who made the throw to first, Yerkes scoring with Speaker and Lewis advancing.
Stahl singled past third, scoring Speaker and Lewis.
3 Wagner popped to second.

2nd Inning
New York
1 Merkle struck out on three pitches.
Herzog tripled off the top railing of the right field temporary seats.
Meyers singled off Gardner's face, scoring Herzog.
2 Fletcher flied to right.
3 Mathewson forced Meyers at second, Yerkes to Wagner.
Boston
1 Carrigan grounded to third.
2 Collins grounded to Doyle near the right field line.
Hooper doubled to right.
3 Yerkes grounded to short.

3rd Inning
New York
1 Snodgrass flied to right.
2 Doyle fouled to Gardner.
3 Becker grounded to short.
Boston
1 Speaker hit a high liner which Merkle knocked down and got to the bag first.
2 Lewis flied to right.
3 Gardner grounded to second. Mathewson retiring the side on only six pitches.

4th Inning
New York
Murray tripled to deep right-center.
1 Merkle fouled to Gardner.
2 Herzog flied to deep center, Murray scoring.
Meyers singled through short.
3 Fletcher flied to right.
Boston
1 Stahl struck out.
2 Wagner flied to Murray in right-center.
3 Carrigan grounded to short.

5th Inning
New York
1 Mathewson struck out on three pitches.
2 Snodgrass struck out on four pitches.
3 Becker flied to left on the first pitch.
Boston
1 Collins struck out.
Hooper singled to center for his third hit of the game.
For New York—Snodgrass and Murray exchanged positions.
Hooper safely at second when Fletcher dropped Meyers' throw.
Yerkes tripled to deep center, scoring Hooper.
2,3 Speaker lined into a double play, Fletcher to Herzog.

6th Inning
New York
1 Becker grounded to second.
Murray singled to center.
2 Merkle singled to center, Murray just beating Speaker's throw back to first.
3 Murray was out trying to steal second, Carrigan to Wagner.
Boston
Lewis beat out a single to short.
1 Gardner sacrificed Lewis to second, Mathewson to Merkle.
2 Stahl rolled to Mathewson, Lewis going to third.
3 Wagner also rolled back to Mathewson, who made the putout.

7th Inning
New York
Herzog singled to right.
1 Meyers popped to second. Herzog stole second.
2 Fletcher grounded to second.
3 Mathewson struck out.
Boston
1 Carrigan grounded to third.
2 Collins struck out.
3 Hooper grounded to second.

8th Inning
New York
Snodgrass safe when Lewis dropped his easy fly ball.
Doyle singled past second, Snodgrass stopping at second.
1 Becker forced Doyle at second, Yerkes to Wagner, Snodgrass going to third.
Murray doubled into the left field bleachers, his third hit of the game, Snodgrass scoring as Becker had to stop at third.
For Boston—Hall came in to pitch.
2 Merkle fouled to Carrigan.
Herzog got a second life when Carrigan dropped his foul over the rail in the stands. Herzog now doubled into the left field stands, scoring Becker and Murray.
3 Meyers grounded to short.
Boston
1 Yerkes flied to left.
2 Speaker grounded to Mathewson.
Lewis blasted a double into the left field stands.
Gardner safe and Lewis scoring when Fletcher let Gardner's grounder through his legs for his third error.
Stahl safe at first and Gardner to third on Doyle's fumble.
Stahl stole second.
3 Wagner struck out.

9th Inning
New York
1 Fletcher grounded to short, Wagner making an excellent stop.
2 Mathewson popped to first.
Snodgrass walked.
Doyle intentionally walked.
Becker walked, loading the bases.
3 Murray forced Becker at second, Wagner to Yerkes.
Boston
1 Carrigan bounced back to the mound.
2 Hall fouled to Herzog.
3 Hooper popped to second.

10th Inning
New York
Merkle tripled to deep center.
1 Herzog grounded to Wagner making a great stop who held Merkle at third.
Meyers intentionally walked.
Shafer ran for Meyers.
2 McCormick, batting for Fletcher, flied to left, scoring Merkle.
3 Mathewson popped to second.
Boston
For New York—Shafer stays in to play short and Wilson catching.
1 Yerkes rolled out, Wilson to Merkle.
Speaker tripled to deep center, he headed for the plate when Shafer lost the ball, but got the ball in time to Wilson who dropped the throw.
Lewis doubled to center.
2 Gardner grounded to second.
3 Stahl grounded to third.

11th Inning
New York
For Boston—Bedient pitching.
Snodgrass was hit by a pitch.
1 Snodgrass was out trying to steal, Carrigan to Wagner.
2 Doyle struck out.
Becker walked.
3 Becker out trying to steal, Carrigan to Wagner.
Boston
1 Wagner grounded to short.
2 Carrigan grounded to short.
3 Bedient grounded to the mound.
*The Game called due to darkness.

Game 3 October 10 at Boston

N.Y. 0 1 0   0 1 0   0 0 0
Bos. 0 0 0   0 0 0   0 0 1

New York	Pos	AB	R	H	RBI	PO	A	E
Devore	rf	4	0	2	0	2	0	0
Doyle	2b	3	0	0	0	3	1	0
Snodgrass	cf	4	0	1	0	1	0	0
Murray	lf	4	1	1	0	5	0	0
Merkle	1b	3	0	0	0	5	0	1
Herzog	3b	2	1	1	1	1	3	0
Meyers	c	4	0	1	0	8	1	0
Fletcher	ss	3	0	1	1	3	2	0
Marquard	p	1	0	0	0	0	2	0
Totals		28	2	7	2	27	9	1

Pitching	IP	H	R	ER	BB	SO
New York						
Marquard (W)	9	7	1	1	1	6
Boston						
O'Brien (L)	8	6	2	2	3	3
Bedient	1	1	0	0	0	0

Boston	Pos	AB	R	H	RBI	PO	A	E
Hooper	rf	3	0	0	0	1	0	0
Yerkes	2b	4	0	1	0	3	1	0
Speaker	cf	4	0	1	0	3	1	0
Lewis	lf	4	1	2	0	4	0	0
Gardner	3b	3	0	1	1	0	2	0
Stahl	1b	4	0	2	0	11	1	0
c Henriksen		0	0	0	0	0	0	0
Wagner	ss	4	0	0	0	1	3	0
Carrigan	c	2	0	0	0	3	1	0
a Engle		1	0	0	0	0	0	0
O'Brien	p	2	0	0	0	1	5	0
b Ball		1	0	0	0	0	0	0
Cady	c	1	0	0	0	0	1	0
Bedient	p	0	0	0	0	0	0	0
Totals		33	1	7	1	27	15	0

a Flied out for Carrigan in 8th.
b Struck out for O'Brien in 8th.
c Ran for Stahl in 9th.

Doubles—Gardner, Herzog, Murray, Stahl.
Stolen Bases—Devore, Fletcher, Wagner.
Sacrifice Hits—Gardner, Herzog, Marquard,
Merkle. Double Play—Speaker to Stahl.
Hit by Pitcher—Herzog (by Bedient).
Left on Bases—New York 7, Boston 7.
Umpires—Evans, Klem, O'Loughlin, Rigler.
Attendance—34,624. Time of Game—2:15.

1st Inning
New York
Devore singled through short.
1 Doyle flied to center.
2 Devore out trying to steal second,
   Carrigan to Wagner.
3 Snodgrass lined to center.
Boston
1 Hooper popped to short.
2 Yerkes called out on strikes.
3 Speaker out when Doyle knocked down his
   liner and threw him out at first.

2nd Inning
New York
Murray doubled to center.
1 Merkle sacrificed Murray to third,
   O'Brien to Stahl.
2 Herzog flied to left, Murray scoring
   after the catch.
3 Meyers grounded to third.
Boston
Lewis lined a single over Doyle's head.
1 Gardner sacrificed Lewis to second,
   Herzog to Merkle.
2 Stahl flied to right.
3 Wagner struck out.

3rd Inning
New York
Fletcher walked.
1 Marquard sacrificed Fletcher to second,
   O'Brien to Stahl.
2 Devore called out on strikes.
3 Doyle lined to first.
Boston
1 Carrigan fouled to Meyers.
2 O'Brien struck out.
3 Hooper struck out.

4th Inning
New York
1 Snodgrass grounded to second.
2 Murray out bunting to the mound.
3 Merkle bounced back to the mound.
Boston
1 Yerkes popped to short.
   Speaker singled to left.
2 Lewis forced Speaker at second,
   Herzog to Doyle.
3 Gardner flied to left.

5th Inning
New York
Herzog doubled to left.
1 Meyers bounced back to the mound,
   Herzog going to third.
   Fletcher singled, scoring Herzog.
   Fletcher stole second.
   Marquard walked.
2 Devore forced Marquard at second,
   Wagner to Yerkes, Fletcher to third.
   Devore stole second.
   Doyle walked, loading the bases.
3 Snodgrass flied to left.
Boston
Stahl only got a single on a liner to
   right-center as he fell rounding
   first.
   When Marquard's pitch bounced out of
   Meyers' hands, Stahl raced to second
1 but was out, Meyers to Doyle.
2 Wagner robbed of a hit by a great
   leaping catch by Murray.
3 Carrigan grounded back to the mound.

6th Inning
New York
1 Murray flied to left.
2 Merkle called out on strikes.
3 Herzog grounded to short.
Boston
1 O'Brien struck out on three pitches.
2 Hooper popped to Doyle in short right.
   Yerkes singled past second.
3 Speaker popped to Meyers in front of
   the plate.

7th Inning
New York
1 Meyers struck out.
2 Fletcher grounded to third, Stahl making
   a great catch of a poor throw.
3 Marquard grounded out, Stahl to O'Brien.
Boston
1 Lewis grounded to short.
2 Gardner fouled to Murray.
   Stahl doubled off the left field fence.
3 Wagner flied to right.

8th Inning
New York
Devore singled.
1 Doyle flied to left.
   Snodgrass singled past short, Devore
   going to second.
2 Murray flied to left.
3 Merkle forced Snodgrass at second,
   Wagner to Yerkes.
Boston
1 Engle, batting for Carrigan, flied to
   left.
2 Ball, batting for O'Brien, struck out.
   Hooper walked.
3 Yerkes grounded to short.

9th Inning
New York
For Boston—Bedient pitching and Cady
   catching.
1 Herzog out at second on his roller,
   Cady to Wagner.
   Meyers singled past short.
2,3 Fletcher flied to Speaker making a
   good running catch in right-center
   and threw to Stahl easily doubling
   Meyers.
Boston
1 Speaker popped to short.
   Lewis beat out a hit to first.
   Gardner doubled inside of first,
   scoring Lewis.
2 Stahl grounded to Marquard who making
   a good stop threw to Herzog, getting
   Gardner at third.
   Henricksen ran for Stahl.
   Wagner safe when Merkle muffs Fletcher's
   throw to first as Henricksen raced to
   third.
   Wagner stole second, unopposed.
3 Cady lined to Devore in right-center.

Game 4 October 11 at New York

Bos. 0 1 0   1 0 0   0 0 1
N.Y. 0 0 0   0 0 0   1 0 0

Boston	Pos	AB	R	H	RBI	PO	A	E
Hooper	rf	4	0	1	0	1	0	0
Yerkes	2b	3	0	1	0	2	4	0
Speaker	cf	4	0	1	0	2	0	0
Lewis	lf	4	0	0	0	1	0	0
Gardner	3b	3	2	2	0	0	3	0
Stahl	1b	3	1	0	0	9	0	0
Wagner	ss	3	0	0	0	2	3	1
Cady	c	4	0	1	0	10	0	0
Wood	p	4	0	2	1	0	2	0
Totals		32	3	8	2	27	12	1

Pitching	IP	H	R	ER	BB	SO
Boston						
Wood (W)	9	9	1	1	0	8
New York						
Tesreau (L)	7	5	2	2	2	5
Ames	2	3	1	1	2	0

New York	Pos	AB	R	H	RBI	PO	A	E
Devore	lf	4	0	1	0	0	0	0
Doyle	2b	4	0	1	0	4	1	0
Snodgrass	cf	4	0	0	0	2	0	0
Murray	rf	4	0	1	0	3	0	0
Merkle	1b	4	1	2	0	2	1	0
Herzog	3b	4	1	2	0	2	1	0
Meyers	c	3	0	0	0	5	1	1
Fletcher	ss	4	0	1	1	3	6	0
Tesreau	p	2	0	1	0	0	2	0
a McCormick		1	0	1	0	0	0	0
Ames	p	0	0	0	0	0	1	0
Totals		35	1	9	1	27	12	1

a Singled for Tesreau in 7th.

Doubles—Fletcher, Speaker. Triple—
Gardner. Stolen Bases—Merkle, Stahl.
Sacrifice Hits—Stahl, Yerkes. Double
Play—Fletcher to Merkle. Wild
Pitch—Tesreau. Left on Bases—Boston 7,
New York 6. Umpires—Rigler, O'Loughlin,
Evans, Klem. Attendance—36,502.
Time of Game—2:06.

1st Inning
Boston
Hooper singled to center.
Yerkes sacrificed but safe as Meyers
   threw into center, trying to force
   Hooper at second.
1,2 Speaker grounded into a double play,
   Fletcher to Merkle, Hooper going to
   third.
3 Lewis grounded to short.
New York
1 Devore struck out.
   Doyle singled over Gardner's head.
2 Snodgrass forced Doyle at second,
   Gardner to Yerkes.
3 Snodgrass got picked off first,
   Wood to Stahl.

2nd Inning
Boston
Gardner tripled on a blast high over
   Murray's head.
   Gardner scored on Tesreau's
   wild pitch.
1 Stahl popped to second.
2 Wagner flied to center.
3 Cady struck out on a foul tip third
   strike.
New York
1 Murray called out on strikes after
   getting a 3-0 count.
   Merkle lined a single over first.
   Merkle stole second as Cady's
   throw was high.
2 Herzog grounded to second, Merkle
   going to third.
3 Meyers robbed of a hit by a leaping
   catch by Lewis.

3rd Inning
Boston
Wood singled.
   Hooper walked.
1 Yerkes forced Wood at third, Tesreau
   to Herzog.
2 Speaker grounded to second, moving up
   both runners.
3 Lewis grounded to short.
New York
1 Fletcher bounced back to the mound.
2 Tesreau struck out on three pitches.
3 Devore grounded to third.

4th Inning
Boston
Gardner walked on four pitches.
1 Stahl forced Gardner at second on a
   bunt, Tesreau to Fletcher.
   Stahl stole second.
2 Wagner grounded to first, Stahl
   going to third.
   Cady singled past short, scoring Stahl.
3 Wood flied to right.
New York
1 Doyle rolled to third.
2 Snodgrass struck out.
3 Murray also struck out.

5th Inning
Boston
1 Hooper robbed of a sure extra-base hit
   as Murray against the concrete wall
   made a sensational leaping catch.
   Yerkes lined a single just over
   Herzog's head.
2 Speaker forced Yerkes at second,
   Herzog to Doyle.
3 Speaker out trying to steal second,
   Meyers to Doyle.

5th Inning (continued)
New York
1 Merkle grounded to short, Wagner
   making a difficult stop and throw.
   Herzog singled off Stahl's glove.
2 Meyers struck out on three pitches.
3 Fletcher grounded to short.

6th Inning
Boston
1 Lewis struck out.
2 Gardner fouled to Herzog.
3 Stahl struck out.
New York
Tesreau singled over Wagner's head.
   Devore lined a single off Wood's knee,
   Tesreau going to second.
1 Doyle popped to third.
2 Snodgrass forced Devore at second,
   Yerkes to Wagner as Tesreau took
   third.
3 Murray forced Snodgrass at second,
   Yerkes to Wagner.

7th Inning
Boston
1 Wagner struck out.
2 Cady struck out on three pitches.
3 Wood flied to right.
New York
1 Merkle struck out.
   Herzog singled past short.
2 Meyers flied to center.
   Fletcher doubled to the right field
   wall, scoring Herzog.
   McCormick, pinch-hitting for Tesreau,
   singled past Yerkes and Fletcher who
   got third continued toward the plate.
3 but was out, Yerkes to Cady. Even
   though bowled over by Fletcher, Cady
   held on to the ball.

8th Inning
Boston
For New York—Ames pitching.
1 Hooper popped to short.
2 Yerkes grounded to second.
   Speaker drove a double near the left
   field stands.
3 Lewis grounded to short.
New York
1 Devore grounded to short.
2 Doyle flied to right.
   Snodgrass safe on Wagner's fumble.
   Murray singled to right-center,
   Snodgrass going to third.
3 Merkle struck out.

9th Inning
Boston
Gardner singled to center.
1 Stahl sacrificed Gardner to second,
   Ames to Merkle.
   Wagner walked on four pitches.
2 Cady forced Wagner at second, Fletcher
   to Doyle, Gardner taking third.
   Wood singled over first, scoring
   Gardner as Cady went to third.
3 Hooper flied to center.
New York
1 Herzog flied to center.
2 Meyers fouled to Cady.
3 Fletcher popped to first.

1912

Game 5 October 12 at Boston

N.Y.	000	000	100
Bos.	002	000	00x

New York	Pos	AB	R	H	RBI	PO	A	E
Devore	lf	2	0	0	0	0	0	0
Doyle	2b	4	0	0	0	0	3	1
Snodgrass	cf	4	0	0	0	2	0	0
Murray	rf	3	0	0	0	0	1	0
Merkle	1b	4	1	1	0	15	0	0
Herzog	3b	4	0	0	0	2	3	0
Meyers	c	3	0	1	0	2	0	0
Fletcher	ss	2	0	0	0	2	2	0
a McCormick		1	0	0	0	0	0	0
b Shafer	ss	0	0	0	0	1	1	0
Mathewson	p	3	0	1	0	0	3	0
Totals		30	1	3	0	24	13	1

Boston	Pos	AB	R	H	RBI	PO	A	E
Hooper	rf	4	1	2	0	4	0	0
Yerkes	2b	4	1	1	0	3	3	0
Speaker	cf	3	0	1	1	3	0	0
Lewis	lf	3	0	0	0	1	0	0
Gardner	3b	3	0	0	0	2	2	1
Stahl	1b	3	0	0	0	7	0	0
Wagner	ss	3	0	1	0	2	1	0
Cody	c	3	0	0	0	5	0	0
Bedient	p	3	0	0	0	0	0	0
Totals		29	2	5	2	27	6	1

Pitching	IP	H	R	ER	BB	SO
New York						
Mathewson (L)	8	5	2	0	0	2
Boston						
Bedient (W)	9	3	1	1	3	4

a Safe on error for Fletcher in 7th.
b Ran for McCormick in 7th.

Double—Merkle. Triples—Hooper, Yerkes.
Double Play—Wagner to Yerkes to Stahl.
Left on Bases—New York 5, Boston 3.
Umpires—O'Loughlin, Rigler, Klem, Evans.
Attendance—34,683. Time of Game—1:43.

1st Inning
New York
Devore walked on four pitches.
1 Doyle fouled to Lewis.
2,3 Snodgrass hit into a double play,
   Wagner to Yerkes to Stahl.
Boston
   Hooper lined a single over Doyle's head.
1 Yerkes popped to short.
   Speaker singled to left, Hooper going
   to second.
2 Lewis forced Hooper at third, Herzog
   unassisted.
3 Gardner struck out.

2nd Inning
New York
   Murray walked on four pitches.
1 Merkle grounded to third.
2 Herzog popped to second.
3 Meyers flied to right.
Boston
1 Stahl grounded to short.
   Wagner lined a single over second.
2 Cady rolled to the mound, Wagner
   going to second.
3 Bedient grounded to second.

3rd Inning
New York
1 Fletcher flied to right.
   Mathewson singled to center.
   Devore walked.
2 Doyle flied to center.
3 Snodgrass fouled to Cady.
Boston
   Hooper tripled down the left field line.
   Yerkes also tripled to deep center,
   scoring Hooper.
   Speaker safe as his grounder went
   through Doyle, Yerkes scoring. Speaker
1 tried to get to second but was out,
   Murray to Fletcher.
2 Lewis rolled back to the mound.
3 Gardner grounded to first.

4th Inning
New York
1 Murray popped to second.
2 Merkle struck out on three pitches.
3 Herzog popped to first.
Boston
1 Stahl grounded to third.
2 Wagner struck out on three pitches.
3 Cady flied to center.

5th Inning
New York
   Meyers lined a single to left.
1 Fletcher flied to right.
2 Mathewson struck out.
3 Devore flied to right.
Boston
1 Bedient lined to first.
2 Hooper grounded to second.
3 Yerkes grounded to Fletcher, who made
   a brilliant stop.

6th Inning
New York
1 Doyle grounded to Yerkes near the
   right field foul line.
2 Snodgrass popped to third.
3 Murray fouled to Gardner.
Boston
1 Speaker grounded to second.
2 Lewis rolled to third.
3 Gardner grounded to first.

7th Inning
New York
   Merkle doubled just into the left
   field bleachers.
1 Herzog popped to Wagner near the mound.
2 Meyers flied to deep center, Merkle
   going to third after the catch.
   McCormick, batting for Fletcher, was
   safe as his roller got through Gardner,
   as Merkle scored.
   Shafer ran for McCormick.
3 Mathewson grounded to third.
Boston
   For New York—Shafer playing short.
1 Stahl bounced back to the mound.
2 Wagner grounded to short.
3 Cady grounded to third.

8th Inning
New York
1 Devore called out on strikes.
2 Doyle grounded to first.
3 Snodgrass struck out.
Boston
1 Bedient flied to center.
2 Hooper popped to short.
3 Yerkes lined to third, Mathewson
   retiring 17 in a row.

9th Inning
New York
1 Murray popped to short.
2 Merkle flied to center.
3 Herzog grounded to second.

Game 6 October 14 at New York

Bos.	020	000	000
N.Y.	500	000	00x

Boston	Pos	AB	R	H	RBI	PO	A	E
Hooper	rf	4	0	1	0	2	2	0
Yerkes	2b	4	0	2	0	3	1	1
Speaker	cf	3	0	0	0	5	0	0
Lewis	lf	4	0	0	0	0	0	0
Gardner	3b	4	1	0	0	0	1	0
Stahl	1b	4	1	2	0	8	0	0
Wagner	ss	4	0	0	0	3	0	0
Cady	c	3	0	1	0	3	2	1
O'Brien	p	0	0	0	0	0	1	0
a Engle		1	0	1	2	0	0	0
Collins	p	0	0	0	0	0	1	0
Totals		33	2	7	2	24	9	2

New York	Pos	AB	R	H	RBI	PO	A	E
Devore	lf	4	0	1	0	3	0	0
Doyle	2b	4	1	1	0	1	1	0
Snodgrass	cf	4	0	1	0	6	0	0
Murray	rf	3	1	2	0	4	1	0
Merkle	1b	3	1	2	1	4	1	0
Herzog	3b	3	1	1	1	1	1	0
Meyers	c	3	1	2	0	6	0	0
Fletcher	ss	3	0	1	1	0	2	0
Marquard	p	3	0	0	0	0	2	1
Totals		30	5	11	3	27	7	1

Pitching	IP	H	R	ER	BB	SO
Boston						
O'Brien (L)	1	6	5	3	0	1
Collins	7	5	0	0	0	1
New York						
Marquard (W)	9	7	2	0	1	3

a Doubled for O'Brien in 2nd.

Doubles—Engle, Herzog, Merkle.
Triple—Meyers. Stolen Bases—Doyle,
Herzog, Meyers, Speaker. Double
Plays—Fletcher to Doyle to Merkle,
Hooper to Stahl. Balk—O'Brien. Left
on Bases—Boston 5, New York 1.
Umpires—Klem, Evans, O'Loughlin, Rigler.
Attendance—30,622. Time of Game—1:58.

1st Inning
Boston
   Hooper singled to deep second.
1   Hooper picked off first, Marquard
   to Merkle to Fletcher to Merkle.
2 Yerkes flied to center.
   Speaker walked.
   Speaker stole second.
3 Lewis flied to left.
New York
1 Devore grounded to third.
   Doyle beat out a hit to deep second.
   Doyle stole second.
2 Snodgrass struck out.
   Murray beat out a slow roller to short,
   Doyle going to third.
   Doyle scored and Murray went to
   second on a balk.
   Merkle doubled off the right field
   wall, scoring Murray.
   Herzog doubled to deep left, scoring
   Merkle.
   Meyers lined a single to left, Herzog
   to third.
   A double steal was started, Cady
   threw to Yerkes, but Yerkes' return
   was poor, Herzog scoring as Meyers
   went to third but both get stolen bases.
   Fletcher beat out a bunt to third,
   scoring Meyers.
3   O'Brien picked Fletcher off of
   first.

2nd Inning
Boston
   Gardner safe at first on Marquard's
   fumble.
   Stahl singled to center, Gardner
   taking second.
1 Wagner struck out.
2 Cady fouled to Meyers.
   Engle, pinch-hitting for O'Brien,
   doubled to deep left, scoring
   Gardner and Stahl.
3 Hooper popped to Meyers.
New York
   For Boston—Collins pitching.
1 Marquard popped to first.
2 Devore struck out on three pitches.
3 Doyle flied to center.

3rd Inning
Boston
   Yerkes singled past second.
1 Speaker flied to center.
2 Lewis fouled to Devore.
3 Gardner flied to left.
New York
1 Snodgrass popped to Yerkes in short
   right.
   Murray singled to right but was out
2 trying for second, Hooper to Yerkes.
   Merkle beat out a roller to third.
3   Merkle out trying to steal second,
   Cady to Wagner.

4th Inning
Boston
   Stahl beat out a roller to third.
1 Wagner flied to Snodgrass, who made a
   wonderful running-catch far back to
   the bleachers.
   Cady singled on a Texas Leaguer to
   short right, Stahl going to third.
2,3 Collins hit into a double play,
   Fletcher to Doyle to Merkle.
New York
1 Herzog flied to center.
   Meyers tripled to deep center.
2 Fletcher flied to short center.
3 Marquard grounded to second.

5th Inning
Boston
1 Hooper flied to deep right.
2 Yerkes flied to right.
3 Speaker popped to third.
New York
   Devore singled past second.
1 Doyle popped to second.
2,3 Snodgrass flied to deep right,
   Hooper throwing to Stahl doubling
   Devore off third.

6th Inning
Boston
1 Lewis popped to Meyers in front of
   the plate.
2 Gardner struck out.
3 Stahl struck out.
New York
1 Murray flied to right.
2 Merkle popped to first.
3 Herzog got a second chance when Cady
   muffed his foul, but only popped to
   second.

7th Inning
Boston
1 Wagner grounded back to the mound.
2 Cady flied to Snodgrass in deep
   right-center.
3 Collins flied to right.
New York
1 Meyers bounced back to the pitcher.
2 Fletcher flied to short center.
3 Marquard flied to Speaker in
   left-center.

8th Inning
Boston
1 Hooper flied to center.
   Yerkes singled past second.
2 Speaker flied to right.
3 Lewis flied to right.
New York
1 Devore bunted out to the mound.
2 Doyle fouled to Cady.
   Snodgrass beat out a grounder to
   second.
3   Snodgrass out stealing second,
   Cady to Wagner.

9th Inning
Boston
1 Gardner flied to short center.
2 Stahl flied to right.
3 Wagner grounded to third.

1912

Game 7 October 15 at Boston

N.Y.	6 1 0 0 0 2 1 0 1
Bos.	0 1 0 0 0 0 2 1 0

New York	Pos	AB	R	H	RBI	PO	A	E
Devore	rf	4	2	1	0	3	1	1
Doyle	2b	4	3	3	2	2	3	2
Snodgrass	cf	5	1	2	2	1	0	0
Murray	lf	4	0	0	0	1	0	0
Merkle	1b	5	1	2	1	10	0	1
Herzog	3b	4	2	1	0	0	2	0
Meyers	c	4	1	3	1	6	0	0
Wilson	c	1	0	1	0	2	0	0
Fletcher	ss	5	1	1	0	2	4	0
Tesreau	p	4	0	2	2	0	6	0
Totals		40	11	16	8	27	16	4

Boston	Pos	AB	R	H	RBI	PO	A	E
Hooper	rf	3	0	1	1	1	0	0
Yerkes	2b	4	0	0	0	1	4	0
Speaker	cf	4	1	1	0	4	0	1
Lewis	lf	4	1	1	1	3	0	0
Gardner	3b	4	1	1	1	2	0	1
Stahl	1b	5	0	1	0	11	1	0
Wagner	ss	5	0	1	0	4	4	0
Cady	c	4	1	0	0	1	1	0
Wood	p	0	0	0	0	0	1	0
Hall	p	3	0	3	0	0	5	1
Totals		36	4	9	3	27	16	3

Pitching	IP	H	R	ER	BB	SO
New York						
Tesreau (W)	9	9	4	2	5	6
Boston						
Wood (L)	1	7	6	4	0	0
Hall	8	9	5	3	5	1

Doubles—Hall, Lewis, Snodgrass. Home Runs—Doyle, Gardner. Stolen Bases—Devore 2, Doyle. Sacrifice Hits—Hooper, Murray. Double Plays—Devore to Meyers, Speaker (unassisted). Hit by Pitcher—Gardner (by Tesreau). Wild Pitches—Tesreau 2. Left on Bases—New York 8, Boston 12. Umpires—Evans, Klem, O'Loughlin, Rigler. Attendance—32,694. Time of Game—2:21.

1st Inning
New York
Devore singled off Wagner's glove.
Doyle singled over second, Devore stopping at second.
Devore and Doyle worked a perfect double steal.
Snodgrass doubled past Hooper, scoring Devore and Doyle.
1 Murray sacrificed Snodgrass to third, Stahl unassisted.
Merkle singled to left, Snodgrass scoring and Merkle took second on the throw to the plate.
2 Herzog bounced to Wood, who got Merkle caught between the bases, Wood to Wagner to Gardner. Herzog got to second on the play.
Meyers singled to left, scoring Herzog.
Fletcher singled past first, Meyers going to third.
Tesreau singled off Wood's glove, Meyers scoring as Fletcher went to third on the throw-in.
On an attempted double steal Cady threw to Yerkes who held the ball to long to get Fletcher but Tesreau
3 was thrown out, Yerkes to Stahl to Wagner.
Boston
1 Hooper struck out.
Yerkes walked.
2 Speaker flied to left.
3 Lewis grounded to third.

2nd Inning
New York
For Boston—Hall now pitching.
Devore walked.
Devore stole second.
Doyle also walked.
1 Devore was picked off second, Hall to Wagner.
Snodgrass singled to right, sending Doyle to second.
Hall threw wildly to second on a pick-off attempt. Before Hooper returned the ball, Doyle scored and Snodgrass got to third.
2 Murray flied to Wagner in short left.
3 Merkle grounded to short.
Boston
Gardner got a ground-rules home run as his blast to right bounced into the stands.
1 Stahl fouled to Meyers.
2 Wagner grounded out off Tesreau's glove to Fletcher who made the throw to first.
3 Cady took a called third strike.

3rd Inning
New York
Herzog lined a single to center, past Hall.
Meyer's singled over Wagner's head, Herzog taking second.
1 Fletcher forced Herzog at third on a bunt, Hall to Gardner.
2 Tesreau bounced back to the mound, Meyers and Fletcher both advancing.
3 Devore flied to right, Hooper making a good catch.
Boston
Hall got a slow roller single to Merkle and went to second on Merkle's wild throw to Tesreau covering first.
Hooper singled past second, Hall going to third.
1 Yerkes struck out.
2,3 Speaker flied to Devore in right-center who threw to Meyers doubling Hall at the plate.

4th Inning
New York
1 Doyle grounded to first.
2 Snodgrass popped to short.
3 Murray grounded to second.
Boston
1 Lewis flied to right.
Gardner was hit by a pitched ball.
Stahl singled to left, Gardner stopping at second.
2 Wagner forced Stahl at second, Doyle to Fletcher as Gardner got to third.
3 Cady grounded back to the mound.

5th Inning
New York
1 Merkle grounded to the mound.
2 Herzog struck out.
Meyers singled past third, his third hit of the game.
3 Fletcher forced Meyers at second, Wagner to Yerkes
Boston
Hall doubled to center.
Hooper walked.
1 Yerkes forced Hooper at second, off Doyle's arm to Fletcher as Hall went to third.
Speaker walked, loading the bases.
2 Lewis fouled to Merkle.
3 Gardner rolled to the mound.

6th Inning
New York
1 Tesreau grounded to second.
Devore walked.
Doyle hit a two-run homer on a bouncer into the right field stands.
2 Snodgrass flied to left.
3 Murray grounded back to the mound.
Boston
1 Stahl lined to right.
Wagner singled past second.
Wagner went to third on a wild pitch.
2 Cady grounded back to the mound, Wagner holding third.
Hall walked.
3 Hooper struck out.

7th Inning
New York
Merkle singled over second.
1 Herzog flied to left.
Meyers safe on a fielder's choice as Wagner's throw to Yerkes was too late to get Merkle.
2 Fletcher flied to center.
Tesreau singled off Yerkes' glove, Merkle scoring as Meyers stopped at second.
3 Devore flied to left.
Boston
For New York—Wilson catching.
1 Yerkes grounded to short.
Speaker lined a single over second.
Lewis doubled off the left field fence, Speaker going to third.
2 Gardner grounded to short, Speaker scoring and Lewis going to third. Stahl safe when his grounder went through Doyle's legs, scoring Lewis.
3 Wagner struck out.

8th Inning
New York
Doyle singled to right for his third hit of the game.
1 Snodgrass grounded to first, Doyle taking second.
2 Murray robbed of a hit by a great catch by Speaker in deep left-center.
3 Merkle grounded to short.
Boston
Cady safe when Doyle dropped his pop near the mound.
Hall singled to right, his third hit of the game and when Devore fumbled Cady went to third.
1 Hooper flied to center, Cady scoring after the catch.
2 Yerkes forced Hall at second, off Tesreau's glove to Fletcher to Doyle Yerkes went to second on a wild pitch.
3 Speaker grounded to second.

9th Inning
New York
Herzog walked.
Wilson singled to center, Herzog going to third. On Speaker's poor throw to third Herzog scored and Wilson went to second.
1,2 Fletcher lined to Speaker, racing in to short center. He ran and touched second for an unassisted double play.
Tesreau walked.
3 Devore grounded to second.
Boston
Lewis walked.
1 Gardner struck out.
2 Stahl forced Lewis at second, Herzog to Doyle.
3 Wagner grounded to the mound.

Game 8 October 16 at Boston

N.Y.	001	000	000	1
Bos.	000	000	100	2

New York	Pos	AB	R	H	RBI	PO	A	E
Devore	rf	3	1	1	0	3	1	0
Doyle	2b	5	0	0	0	1	5	1
Snodgrass	cf	4	0	1	0	4	1	1
Murray	lf	5	1	2	1	3	0	0
Merkle	1b	5	0	1	1	10	0	0
Herzog	3b	5	0	2	0	2	1	0
Meyers	c	3	0	0	0	4	1	0
Fletcher	ss	3	0	1	0	2	3	0
b McCormick		1	0	0	0	0	0	0
Shafer	ss	0	0	0	0	0	0	0
Mathewson	p	4	0	1	0	0	3	0
Totals		38	2	9	2	*29	15	2

Boston	Pos	AB	R	H	RBI	PO	A	E
Hooper	rf	5	0	0	0	4	0	0
Yerkes	2b	4	1	1	0	3	3	0
Speaker	cf	4	0	2	1	2	0	1
Lewis	lf	4	0	0	0	0	0	0
Gardner	3b	3	0	1	1	1	4	2
Stahl	1b	4	1	2	0	15	0	1
Wagner	ss	3	0	1	0	3	5	1
Cady	c	4	0	0	0	5	3	0
Bedient	p	2	0	0	0	0	1	0
a Henriksen		1	0	1	1	0	0	0
Wood	p	0	0	0	0	0	2	0
c Engel		1	1	0	0	0	0	0
Totals		35	3	8	3	30	18	5

Pitching	IP	H	R	ER	BB	SO
New York						
Mathewson (L)	9⅔	8	3	2	5	4
Boston						
Bedient	7	6	1	1	3	2
Wood (W)	3	3	1	1	1	2

a Doubled for Bedient in 7th.
b Flied out for Fletcher in 9th.
c Reached on error for Wood in 10th.
* Two out when winning run scored.

Doubles—Gardner, Henriksen, Herzog, Murray 2, Stahl. Stolen Base—Devore. Sacrifice Hits—Gardner, Meyers. Left on Bases—New York 11, Boston 9. Umpires—O'Loughlin, Rigler, Klem, Evans. Attendance—17,034. Time of Game—2:37.

1st Inning
New York
1 Devore grounded to short on a full count.
2 Doyle also grounded to short.
Snodgrass walked.
Snodgrass got safely to second when Wagner dropped Cady's perfect throw.
3 Murray grounded to Gardner making a good stop in front of Wagner.
Boston
1 Hooper bunted out to first.
2 Yerkes struck out.
Speaker singled to right and was safe at second when Doyle dropped the throw.
3 Lewis struck out on three pitches.

2nd Inning
New York
1 Merkle struck out.
2 Herzog flied to center.
Meyers safe when his grounder got through Gardner for an error.
Fletcher lined a single over second, Meyers going to second.
Cady threw to Wagner to get Meyers who ran for third. Wagner threw to Gardner who dropped the ball for another error, Fletcher in the meantime took second.
3 Mathewson flied to deep center.
Boston
Gardner walked, the first pass off Mathewson in his twenty-first inning of the series.
1 Stahl forced Gardner at second, Doyle to Fletcher.
Wagner lined a single to left, Stahl stopping at second.
2 Cady popped to first.
3 Bedient grounded to second.

3rd Inning
New York
Devore walked on four pitches.
1 Doyle grounded to third, Devore getting to second.
2 Snodgrass grounded to first, Devore advancing to third.
Murray doubled past Speaker in left-center, scoring Devore.
3 Merkle grounded to short.
Boston
1 Hooper grounded to second.
2 Yerkes rolled back to the mound.
3 Speaker struck out.

4th Inning
New York
Herzog got a ground-rule double into the passage between the stands. His fourth double of the Series.
1 Meyers sacrificed Herzog to third, Gardner to Stahl.
2 Fletcher popped to third.
3 Mathewson flied to short right.
Boston
1 Lewis grounded to short.
Gardner doubled to center but was out
2 trying to stretch it into a triple, Snodgrass to Doyle to Herzog.
3 Stahl struck out.

5th Inning
New York
Devore beat out a hit off Bedient's shin.
1 Devore out trying to steal second, Cady to Wagner.
2 Doyle flied to Hooper in deep right, making a remarkable catch as the ball was going over the fence.
Snodgrass singled past third.
3 Murray fouled to Cady.
Boston
1 Wagner flied to deep left on the first pitch.
2 Cady flied to left also on the first pitch.
3 Bedient flied to right again on the first pitch.

6th Inning
New York
1 Merkle flied to right.
2 Herzog grounded to short, Stahl pulling Wagner's low throw out of the ground. Meyers walked.
3 Fletcher struck out.
Boston
1 Hooper popped to first.
Yerkes singled to right.
Speaker walked.
2 Lewis forced Speaker at second, Fletcher to Doyle as Yerkes went to third.
3 Yerkes was caught off third, Meyers to Mathewson to Herzog.

7th Inning
New York
Mathewson lined a single over second.
1 Devore forced Mathewson at second on an attempted sacrifice, Bedient to Wagner.
2 Doyle popped to short.
Devore stole second, his 4th steal of the Series.
3 Snodgrass grounded to third.
Boston
1 Gardner flied to center.
Stahl got a Texas League single into short left-center.
Wagner walked on four pitches.
2 Cady popped to short.
Henriksen, batting for Bedient, doubled down the left field line, scoring Stahl as Wagner went to third.
3 Hooper flied to center.

8th Inning
New York
For Boston—Wood pitching.
1 Murray grounded to first.
2 Merkle grounded to second.
Herzog lined a single over Yerke's head. His twelfth hit of the Series.
3 Meyers grounded to second.
Boston
1 Yerkes grounded out off Mathewson's leg to Herzog who made the throw to first.
2 Speaker grounded to second.
3 Lewis grounded to Fletcher, making a good stop behind second.

9th Inning
New York
1 McCormick, pinch-hitting for Fletcher, flied to right.
2 Mathewson struck out on three pitches.
Devore walked.
3 Doyle grounded to second.
Boston
For New York—Shafer playing short.
1 Gardner flied to center.
Stahl doubled to deep left-center.
2 Wagner flied to deep right.
3 Cady flied to left.

10th Inning
New York
1 Snodgrass bounced back to the mound.
Murray doubled to left for his fourth double of the Series.
Merkle lined a single past second, the ball being juggled by Speaker, allowing Murray to score and Merkle to get to second.
2 Herzog struck out on three pitches.
3 Meyers grounded back to the mound.
Boston
Engle, pinch-hitting for Wood, was safe at second as Snodgrass dropped his easy fly ball.
1 Hooper robbed of a hit by Snodgrass, making a great catch, Engle going to third after the catch.
Yerkes walked.
Speaker lined a single to right, Engle scoring as Yerkes took third and Speaker second on the throw-in.
Lewis intentionally walked, loading the bases.
2 Gardner hit a long sacrifice fly to right, Yerkes scoring the Series-ending run after the catch.

1912 WORLD SERIES COMPOSITE BOX

	Wins	Composite Line Score
Boston Red Sox (A.L.)	4	3 4 2 1 1 1 6 2 2 2 1 – 25
New York Giants (N.L.)	3	1 1 3 3 1 1 2 3 3 2 1 1 – 31

Manager	W	L	Pct.	G. Ahead
Jake Stahl	105	47	.691	14
John McGraw	103	48	.682	10

Regular Season (G. Ahead column)

BATTING AND FIELDING

BOSTON RED SOX

	WORLD SERIES STATISTICS																	REGULAR SEASON STATISTICS												
	Pos	G	AB	R	H	2B	3B	HR	RBI	BB	SO	SB	BA	SA	PO	A	E	Main Pos	G	AB	R	H	2B	3B	HR	RBI	BB	SO	SB	BA	SA
Jake Stahl	1b	8	32	3	8	2	0	0	2	0	6	2	.250	.313	76	3	1	1b	95	326	40	98	21	6	3	60	31		13	.301	.429
Steve Yerkes	2b	8	32	3	8	0	2	0	4	2	3	0	.250	.375	14	21	1	2b	131	523	73	132	22	6	0	42	41		4	.252	.317
Heinie Wagner	ss	8	30	1	5	1	0	0	0	3	6	1	.167	.200	26	24	3	ss	144	504	75	138	25	6	2	68	62		21	.274	.359
Larry Gardner	3b	8	28	4	5	2	1	1	4	2	5	1	.179	.429	8	13	4	3b	143	517	88	163	24	18	3	86	56		25	.315	.449
Harry Hooper	rf	8	31	3	9	2	1	0	2	4	4	2	.290	.419	17	2	0	of	147	590	98	143	20	12	3	53	66		29	.242	.327
Tris Speaker	cf	8	30	4	9	1	2	0	4	2	1	1	.300	.467	21	2	0	of	153	580	136	222	53	12	10	90	82		52	.383	.567
Duffy Lewis	lf	8	32	4	6	3	0	0	2	2	2	0	.188	.281	13	0	1	of	154	581	85	165	36	9	6	109	52		9	.284	.408
Hick Cady	c	7	22	1	3	0	0	0	1	0	3	0	.136	.136	35	8	1	c	47	135	19	35	13	2	0	19	9		0	.259	.385
Bill Carrigan	c	2	7	0	0	0	0	0	0	0	0	0	.000	.000	10	4	0	c	87	266	24	70	7	1	0	24	38		7	.263	.297
Clyde Engle	ph	3	3	1	1	1	0	0	2	0	0	0	.333	.667				1b-2b-3b	57	171	32	40	5	3	0	18	28		12	.234	.298
Olaf Henriksen	pr-ph	2	1	0	1	0	0	0	0	1	0	0	1.000	2.000				of	37	56	20	18	3	1	0	8	14		5	.321	.411
Neal Ball	ph	1	1	0	0	0	0	0	0	0	1	0	.000	.000				a 2b	18	45	10	9	2	0	0	6	3		5	.200	.244
Hugh Bradley	Did not play																	1b	40	137	16	26	11	1	1	19	15		3	.190	.307
Les Nunamaker	Did not play																	c	35	103	15	26	5	2	0	6	6		2	.252	.340
Marty Krug	Did not play																	ss-2b	16	39	6	12	3	1	0	7	5		2	.308	.410
Pinch Thomas	Did not play																	c	12	30	0	6	0	0	0	0	5	2	1	.200	.200
Smokey Joe Wood	p	4	7	1	2	0	0	0	0	1	0	0	.286	.286	1	6	0	p	43	124	17	36	13	1	1	13	11		0	.290	.435
Hugh Bedient	p	4	6	0	0	0	0	0	0	0	1	0	.000	.000	0	1	0	p	41	73	11	14	0	0	0	7	13		0	.192	.192
Ray Collins	p	2	5	0	0	0	0	0	0	0	2	0	.000	.000	0	3	0	p	27	65	8	11	1	0	0	2	12		0	.169	.185
Charley Hall	p	2	4	0	3	1	0	0	1	0	0	0	.750	1.000	0	5	1	p	34	75	10	20	4	2	1	14	4		0	.267	.413
Buck O'Brien	p	2	2	0	0	0	0	0	0	0	0	0	.000	.000	1	6	0	p	37	94	4	13	1	1	0	6	6		0	.138	.170
Larry Pape	Did not play																	p	13	17	1	4	1	0	0	1	2		0	.235	.294
team total		8	273	25	60	14	6	1	21	19	36	6	.220	.326	222	98	14		154	5071	800	1404	269	84	29	654	565		185	.277	.380

Double Plays—5
Left on Bases—55

a—from Cleveland
Jack Bushelman (p), Eddie Cicotte (p), Casey Hageman (p), Doug Smith (p), Ben Van Dyke (p) also played for the Red Sox during the season.

NEW YORK GIANTS

	WORLD SERIES STATISTICS																	REGULAR SEASON STATISTICS												
	Pos	G	AB	R	H	2B	3B	HR	RBI	BB	SO	SB	BA	SA	PO	A	E	Main Pos	G	AB	R	H	2B	3B	HR	RBI	BB	SO	SB	BA	SA
Fred Merkle	1b	8	33	5	9	2	1	0	3	0	7	1	.273	.394	83	1	2	1b	129	479	82	148	22	6	11	84	42	70	37	.309	.449
Larry Doyle	2b	8	33	1	6	1	0	1	2	3	2	2	.242	.364	15	26	5	2b	143	558	98	184	33	8	10	90	56	20	36	.330	.471
Art Fletcher	ss	8	28	1	5	1	0	0	3	1	4	1	.179	.214	16	23	4	ss	129	419	64	118	17	9	1	57	16	29	16	.263	.355
Buck Herzog	3b	8	30	6	12	4	1	0	4	1	3	2	.400	.600	11	16	0	3b	140	482	72	127	20	9	2	47	51	34	38	.277	.413
Red Murray	rf-lf	8	31	5	10	4	1	0	5	2	2	1	.323	.516	22	1	0	of	143	539	83	152	26	20	3	92	27	45	38	.282	.413
Fred Snodgrass	cf-lf-rf	8	33	2	7	2	0	0	2	2	5	1	.212	.273	17	1	1	of-1b	146	535	91	144	24	9	3	69	70	65	43	.269	.364
Josh Devore	lf	7	24	4	6	0	0	0	0	7	5	4	.250	.250	11	2	1	of	106	327	66	90	14	6	2	37	51	43	27	.275	.373
Chief Meyers	c	8	28	2	10	0	1	0	3	2	3	1	.357	.429	42	4	1	c	126	371	60	133	16	5	6	54	47	20	1	.358	.477
Beals Becker	pr-cf	2	4	1	0	0	0	0	0	2	0	0	.000	.000	0	0	0	of	125	402	66	106	18	8	6	58	54	35	30	.264	.393
Moose McCormick	ph	5	4	0	1	0	0	0	0	0	0	0	.250	.250				of	42	39	4	13	4	1	0	8	6	9	1	.333	.487
Art Wilson	c	2	1	0	1	0	0	0	0	0	0	0	1.000	1.000	2	1	1	c	65	121	17	35	6	0	3	19	13	14	2	.289	.413
Tillie Shafer	ss	3	0	0	0	0	0	0	0	0	0	0	—	—	1	4	0	ss-2b	78	163	48	47	4	1	0	23	30	19	22	.288	.325
George Burns	Did not play																	of	29	51	11	15	4	0	0	3	8	7	9	.294	.373
Heinie Groh	Did not play																	2b-ss-3b	27	48	8	13	2	1	0	3	8	7	6	.271	.354
Grover Hartley	Did not play																	c	25	34	3	8	2	1	0	7	8	4	2	.235	.353
Christy Mathewson	p	3	12	0	2	0	0	0	0	0	4	0	.167	.167	1	12	0	p	43	110	14	29	4	1	0	10	6	8	2	.264	.318
Jeff Tesreau	p	3	8	0	3	0	0	0	2	1	3	0	.375	.375	0	10	0	p	36	82	1	12	1	2	0	6	4	12	0	.146	.207
Rube Marquard	p	2	4	0	0	0	0	0	0	0	0	1	.000	.000	0	4	1	p	43	96	14	21	2	0	0	8	7	17	2	.219	.240
Doc Crandall	p	1	1	0	0	0	0	0	0	0	1	0	.000	.000	0	1	0	p-ph	50	80	9	25	6	2	0	19	6	7	0	.313	.438
Red Ames	p	1	1	0	0	0	0	0	0	0	0	0	—	—	0	1	0	p	33	58	6	13	3	0	0	3	2	5	1	.224	.276
Hooks Wiltse	Did not play																	p	28	46	5	15	2	0	0	3	2	5	1	.326	.370
team total		8	274	31	74	14	4	1	25	22	39	12	.270	.361	221	107	16		154	5067	823	1451	231	89	47	702	522	497	319	.286	.393

Double Plays—4
Left on Bases—53

Dave Robertson (1b), Lore Bader (p), Al Demaree (p), Louis Drucke (p), Tel Goulait (p), LaRue Kirby (p), Ernie Shore (p) also played for the Giants during the season.

PITCHING

BOSTON RED SOX

	WORLD SERIES STATISTICS													REGULAR SEASON STATISTICS													
	G	GS	CG	IP	H	R	ER	BB	SO	W	L	SV	ERA	G	GS	CG	IP	H	ER	BB	SO	W	L	Pct	SV	ShO	ERA
Smokey Joe Wood	4	3	2	22	27	11	9	3	21	3	1	0	3.68	43	38	35	344	267	73	82	258	34	5	.872	1	10	1.91
Hugh Bedient	4	2	1	18	10	2	2	7	7	1	0	0	1.00	41	28	19	231	206	75	55	122	20	9	.690	3	0	2.92
Ray Collins	2	1	0	14⅓	14	5	3	0	6	0	0	0	1.88	27	23	17	199	192	56	42	82	14	8	.636	0	4	2.53
Charley Hall	2	0	0	10⅔	11	6	4	9	1	0	0	0	3.38	34	21	10	191	178	63	70	83	15	8	.658	2	5	3.02
Buck O'Brien	2	2	0	9	12	7	5	3	4	0	2	0	5.00	37	34	26	276	237	79	90	115	19	13	.594	1	2	2.58
Larry Pape	Did not play													13	2	1	49	74	27	16	17	1	1	.500	1	0	4.96
team total	8	8	3	74	74	31	23	22	39	4	3	0	2.80	154	154	110	1362	1243	416	385	712	105	47	.691	8	18	2.75

NEW YORK GIANTS

	WORLD SERIES STATISTICS													REGULAR SEASON STATISTICS													
	G	GS	CG	IP	H	R	ER	BB	SO	W	L	SV	ERA	G	GS	CG	IP	H	ER	BB	SO	W	L	Pct	SV	ShO	ERA
Christy Mathewson	3	3	3	28⅔	23	11	4	5	10	0	2	0	1.26	43	34	27	310	311	73	34	134	23	12	.657	4	0	2.12
Jeff Tesreau	3	3	1	23	19	10	8	11	15	1	2	0	3.13	36	28	19	243	177	53	106	119	17	7	.708	1	3	1.96
Rube Marquard	2	2	2	18	14	3	1	2	9	2	0	0	0.50	43	38	22	295	286	84	80	175	26	11	.703	1	1	2.56
Doc Crandall	1	0	0	2	0	0	0	0	2	0	0	0	0.00	37	10	7	162	181	65	35	60	13	9	.650	2	1	3.61
Red Ames	1	0	0	2	3	1	1	1	0	0	0	0	4.50	33	22	9	179	184	49	35	83	11	5	.688	2	2	2.46
Hooks Wiltse	Did not play													28	17	5	134	140	47	28	58	9	6	.600	3	0	3.16
team total	8	8	6	73⅓	60	25	14	19	36	3	4	0	1.71	154	154	93	1372	1352	393	338	652	103	48	.682	15	8	2.58

Total Attendance—252,037   Average Attendance—31,505   Winning Player's Share—$4,025   Losing Player's Share—$2,566

1913
Oh-for-Three

Victory had always been the highest value for New York Giant manager John McGraw, so while this year's third straight National League pennant fueled his self-satisfaction, defeats in the 1911 and 1912 World Series did nothing to bolster his over-active ego. A victory over the Philadelphia Athletics in this fall's classic would vindicate those two losses and satisfy McGraw's desire to be the best. The A's had made it back to the top of the American League despite the loss of pitching ace Jack Coombs to illness, as manager Connie Mack skillfully replaced him with a platoon of young hurlers. McGraw, however, headed into the Series with injury problems of the gravest severity. Centerfielder Fred Snodgrass was hobbling on a bad charley horse, while first baseman Fred Merkle was limping on a bad leg. McGraw's bench was notoriously thin to begin with, so the Giants were hurting with two regulars unable to properly move.

When the Series opened at the Polo Grounds on a dark, overcast October 7, McGraw sent utilityman Tillie Shafer to center in place of Snodgrass and sent Merkle into the fray, trying to hide him in the eighth batting position. Lefty Rube Marquard, a 23-game winner, took the mound for New York against Philadelphia's Chief Bender, who had won 21 games doubling as both a starter and reliever. The Giants scored a solo run in the bottom of the third inning, but the Mackmen touched up Marquard for three runs in the fourth and another pair in the fifth, coming on a four-base clout by Home Run Baker. Ahead 5–1, Bender perhaps relaxed a bit and allowed three Giant runs in the bottom of the fifth. But the veteran righty shut the Giants out the rest of the way, and the A's had a 6–4 first-game triumph.

The next day in Philly, not only were the Giants down a game but their injury situation got worse. Regular catcher Chief Meyers broke a finger in the pregame practice, and Merkle's leg simply wouldn't allow him to carry on. So McGraw plugged the gaps by using second-stringer Larry McLean behind the plate, leaving utilityman Shafer in center field, and asking the lame Snodgrass to give first base a try. The Giants had their money pitcher Christy Mathewson on the mound to face veteran southpaw Eddie Plank. Both men had faced each other during their college days before the turn of the century, and both of them hurled shutout ball through nine innings. Earlier, in the third inning, McGraw had to further scramble his lineup when Snodgrass reached first on a hit and couldn't go any farther; McGraw gambled by sending in veteran pitcher Hooks Wiltse to run, then leaving him in to make his World Series debut at first base. The unorthodox move paid off in the bottom of the ninth after the A's put men on second and third with no outs. Jack Lapp hit a grounder to Wiltse, who fielded it cleanly and gunned Amos Strunk, the potential winning run, down at the plate. Then Plank came to bat, and he hit a grounder to first. Wiltse again came up with it and threw Jack Barry out at home. Matty then coaxed Eddie Murphy to bounce back to the box, and the game went into extra innings. Buoyed up by their "goal-line stand," the Giants promptly scored three times in the tenth to sew up a 3–0 win and even the Series at a game apiece.

McGraw felt the momentum swing to his team, but the Athletic pitching staff quickly swung it back. Mack started twenty-year-old Bullet Joe Bush in game three, and the youngster bested 22-game-winner Jeff Tesreau in an 8–2 decision. Chief Bender came back for game four and was staked to a 6–0 lead after five innings against starter Al Demaree and Marquard in relief. The Giants came back to score five runs, but it wasn't enough. Down 3–1 in the Series, McGraw sought to stave off the inevitable defeat by starting Mathewson in game five against Plank. Matty gave up three early runs to the A's, and Plank's two-hitter brought the Athletics a 3–1 win and the World Championship in five games. For McGraw, there was the solace that the outcome may have been different if he had had all his men in top condition. Still, it was not enough comfort in which to carry so proud a man through a winter with the memory of three straight Series defeats.

Game 1 October 7 at New York

Philadelphia	Pos	AB	R	H	RBI	PO	A	E
E. Murphy	rf	4	0	1	0	2	0	0
Oldring	lf	4	0	1	0	2	0	0
Collins	2b	3	3	3	0	4	6	0
Baker	3b	4	1	3	3	1	3	0
McInnis	1b	3	0	1	1	10	0	0
Strunk	cf	4	1	0	0	3	0	0
Barry	ss	4	1	1	0	1	3	1
Schang	c	4	0	1	2	4	1	0
Bender	p	4	0	0	0	0	2	0
Totals		34	6	11	6	27	15	1

Pitching	IP	H	R	ER	BB	SO
Philadelphia						
Bender (W)	9	11	4	3	0	4
New York						
Marquard (L)	5	8	5	5	1	1
Crandall	*2	3	1	1	0	1
Tesreau	2	0	0	0	1	1

*Pitched to three batters in 8th.

New York	Pos	AB	R	H	RBI	PO	A	E
Shafer	cf	5	0	1	0	3	0	0
Doyle	2b	4	1	2	2	2	2	0
Fletcher	ss	4	0	2	2	2	4	0
Burns	lf	4	0	1	0	3	0	0
Herzog	3b	4	0	2	0	1	2	0
Murray	rf	4	0	2	0	1	0	0
Meyers	c	4	0	0	0	4	2	0
Merkle	1b	4	2	2	0	11	0	0
Marquard	p	0	0	0	0	0	6	0
a McCormick		1	1	1	0	0	0	0
Crandall	p	1	0	0	0	0	0	0
Tesreau	p	0	0	0	0	0	1	0
b McLean		1	0	0	0	0	0	0
Totals		36	4	11	4	27	15	0

a Singled for Marquard in 5th.
b Popped out for Tesreau in 9th.

Phi.	0 0 0	3 2 0	0 1 0					
N.Y.	0 0 1	0 3 0	0 0 0					

Doubles—Barry, Burns, McInnis. Triples—Collins, Schang. Home Run—Baker. Stolen Base—Collins. Sacrifice Hits—Marquard, McInnis. Double Play—Barry to Collins to McInnis. Left on Bases—Philadelphia 4, New York 6. Umpires—Klem (N), Egan (A), Rigler (N), Connolly (A). Attendance—36,291. Time of Game—2:06.

1st Inning
Philadelphia
1 Murphy flied to right.
  Oldring singled to right.
2   Oldring was picked off first, Marquard to Merkle.
  Collins singled.
3 Baker flied to left.
New York
1 Shafer flied to right on a 3-2 count.
2 Doyle flied to Strunk in right-center.
  Fletcher singled.
3   Fletcher caught attempting to steal second, Schang to Collins.

2nd Inning
Philadelphia
1 McInnis grounded to third.
2 Strunk struck out.
3 Barry bounced to short.
New York
1 Burns called out on strikes on a full count.
2 Herzog grounded to first, also on a full count.
  Murray singled to left.
3 Meyers flied to short left.

3rd Inning
Philadelphia
1 Schang flied to left.
2 Bender grounded to short, only jogging toward first as Fletcher poorly threw to Merkle who still had plenty of time to make the out.
  Murphy singled over Doyle's head.
3 Oldring forced Murphy at second, Fletcher unassisted.
New York
  Merkle beat out a hit to short.
1 Marquard sacrificed Merkle to second, Collins to McInnis.
2 Shafer flied to center.
  Doyle singled to right easily scoring Merkle.
3 Fletcher flied to right.

4th Inning
Philadelphia
  Collins tripled to deep right center.
  Baker singled off of Doyle's glove, scoring Collins.
1 McInnis sacrificed Baker to second, Marquard to Merkle.
2 Strunk bounced to Marquard who threw to Herzog getting Baker going into third.
  Barry doubled down the third base line, Strunk stopping at third.
  Schang boomed a triple to right-center just out of reach of Shafer, scoring Strunk and Barry.
3 Bender grounded back to the mound.
New York
  Burns doubled past third.
1 Herzog hit to Bender who threw to Baker getting Burns heading for third.
2 Murray struck out.
3 Meyers flied to left.

5th Inning
Philadelphia
1 Murphy bunted out to the mound.
2 Oldring bounced back to the mound.
  Collins walked.
  Collins stole second.
  "Home-Run" Baker blasted a two-run homer into the right field bleachers.
3 McInnis popped to short.

5th Inning (continued)
New York
  Merkle singled to center.
  McCormick, pinch-hitting for Marquard, singled past second, Merkle stopping at second.
1 Shafer grounded to second, advancing Merkle to third and McCormick to second.
  Doyle safe at first on Barry's poor throw to first, Merkle scoring and McCormick going to third.
  Fletcher singled to right, McCormick scoring with Doyle going to third.
2 Burns forced Fletcher at second, Baker to Collins, as Doyle scored.
3 Herzog popped to second.

6th Inning
Philadelphia
  For New York—Crandall now pitching.
1 Strunk flied to Shafer in right-center.
2 Barry flied to Shafer in left-center.
3 Schang flied to left.
New York
1 Murray grounded to second.
2 Meyers grounded back to the mound.
3 Merkle struck out on a full count.

7th Inning
Philadelphia
1 Bender struck out.
2 Murphy grounded to second.
3 Oldring lined to short center.
New York
1 Crandall grounded to short.
  Shafer singled to center.
  Doyle singled to right, Shafer racing to third.
2,3 Fletcher hit into a double play, Barry to Collins to McInnis.

8th Inning
Philadelphia
  Collins beat out a bunt for his third hit of the game.
  Baker singled to left-center, also his third hit of the game, sending Collins to third.
  McInnis doubled to left, scoring Collins with Baker moving to third.
  For New York—Tesreau came in to pitch.
1 Strunk struck out on three pitches.
  Meyers tried for McInnis off of second but was safe and Baker was
2   out going for the plate, Doyle to Meyers.
3 Barry popped to second.
New York
1 Burns grounded to third.
2 Herzog grounded to third.
  Murray beat out a hit off of Baker.
3 Meyers flied to Strunk making a nice catch in right-center

9th Inning
Philadelphia
1 Schang bounced to third.
2 Bender grounded to the mound.
  Murphy walked.
3   Murphy out trying to steal second, Meyers to Doyle.
New York
1 Merkle grounded to second.
2 McLean, batting for Tesreau, popped to second.
3 Shafer struck out.

Game 2 October 8 at Philadelphia

New York	Pos	AB	R	H	RBI	PO	A	E
Herzog	3b	5	1	0	0	1	3	0
Doyle	2b	4	0	0	0	3	5	2
Fletcher	ss	5	0	2	2	1	3	0
Burns	lf	4	0	0	0	4	0	0
Shafer	cf	5	0	0	0	0	0	0
Murray	rf	4	0	0	0	0	0	0
McLean	c	4	0	2	0	6	0	0
b Grant		0	1	0	0	0	0	0
Wilson	c	0	0	0	0	0	0	0
Snodgrass	1b	1	0	1	0	1	1	0
a Wiltse	1b	2	0	0	0	13	3	0
Mathewson	p	3	1	2	1	0	3	0
Totals		37	3	7	3	30	18	2

a Ran for Snodgrass in 3rd.
b Ran for McLean in 10th.
Sacrifice Hits—Collins, Wiltse. Hit by Pitcher—Doyle (by Plank). Left on Bases—New York 8, Philadelphia 10. Umpires—Connolly, Rigler, Klem, Egan. Attendance—20,563. Time of Game—2:22.

1st Inning
New York
1 Herzog flied to Collins in right field.
2 Doyle flied to center.
3 Fletcher struck out.
Philadelphia
Murphy safe on Doyle's fumble. Oldring singled to left, Murphy stopping at second.
1 Collins sacrificed up both runners, Snodgrass to Doyle.
2 Baker struck out.
3 McInnis flied to left.

2nd Inning
New York
1 Burns struck out.
2 Shafer flied to right.
3 Murray struck out.
Philadelphia
1 Strunk bounced to second.
2 Barry flied to left.
3 Lapp fanned on three pitches.

3rd Inning
New York
1 McLean popped to short. Snodgrass lined a single to left. Matty singled to center, Snodgrass limping to third as Mathewson took second on the throw to third. Wiltse ran for the injured Snodgrass.
2 Herzog hit to Plank who threw to Lapp, getting Wiltse as Mathewson went to third and Herzog to second.
3 Doyle flied to left.
Philadelphia
For New York—Wiltse, the pitcher, playing first.
1 Plank grounded to second.
2 Murphy bunted out to the mound.
3 Oldring grounded to third.

4th Inning
New York
1 Fletcher grounded to short.
2 Burns struck out on three pitches. Shafer safe on Baker's poor throw.
3 Shafer out trying to steal, Lapp to Collins.
Philadelphia
1 Collins bounced back to the mound. Baker singled to right.
2 McInnis grounded to second, Baker taking second. Strunk intentionally walked.
3 Barry forced Strunk at second, Doyle unassisted.

5th Inning
New York
1 Murray flied to left. McLean singled past first.
2 Wiltse struck out. Mathewson walked.
3 Herzog grounded to second.
Philadelphia
1 Lapp grounded to second. Plank singled off Doyle's glove.
2 Murphy flied to deep left.
3 Oldring forced Plank at second, Fletcher to Doyle.

6th Inning
New York
1 Doyle grounded back to the pitcher.
2 Fletcher fouled to McInnis.
3 Burns flied to right.
Philadelphia
1 Collins struck out.
2 Baker robbed of a hit by Fletcher who made a great gloved hand stop and got Baker on the throw to first.
3 McInnis struck out on three pitches.

N.Y.	000 000 000 3
Phi.	000 000 000 0

Philadelphia	Pos	AB	R	H	RBI	PO	A	E
E. Murphy	rf	5	0	0	0	4	0	0
Oldring	lf	5	0	1	0	4	0	0
Collins	2b	4	0	1	0	2	2	1
Baker	3b	5	0	2	0	0	0	1
McInnis	1b	4	0	0	0	5	0	0
Strunk	cf	3	0	1	0	5	0	0
Barry	ss	4	0	1	0	2	3	0
Lapp	c	4	0	1	0	7	1	0
Plank	p	4	0	1	0	1	2	0
Totals		38	0	8	0	30	6	2

Pitching	IP	H	R	ER	BB	SO
New York						
Mathewson(W)	10	8	0	0	1	5
Philadelphia						
Plank (L)	10	7	3	2	2	6

7th Inning
New York
1 Shafer flied to center.
2 Murray popped to short.
3 McLean flied to deep left.
Philadelphia
1 Strunk flied to Burns making a nice shoestring catch.
2 Barry grounded to third. Lapp singled off Wiltse's glove.
3 Plank lined to short.

8th Inning
New York
1 Wiltse grounded to second.
2 Mathewson flied to right.
3 Herzog flied to Strunk, making a great catch in right-center.
Philadelphia
1 Murphy grounded to Wiltse, making a spectacular stop.
2 Oldring grounded to short. Collins singled to left. Baker singled to left, Collins going to second.
3 McInnis forced Collins at third, Herzog unassisted.

9th Inning
New York
1 Doyle flied to deep center. Fletcher singled past short. Burns walked on four pitches.
2 Shafer flied to left.
3 Murray flied to center.
Philadelphia
Strunk singled past second. Barry singled on a bunt to Doyle who threw to second. The ball went to the stands, Strunk going to third and Barry to second.
1 Lapp hit to Wiltse making a beautiful stop and quick throw to McLean getting Strunk at the plate as Barry went to third.
2 Plank grounded to Wiltse who again threw to McLean, this time getting Barry at the plate as Lapp got to third and Plank to second.
3 Murphy grounded back to the mound.

10th Inning
New York
McLean singled to right. Grant ran for McLean.
1 Wiltse sacrificed Grant to second, Plank unassisted. Mathewson singled to left-center, scoring Grant. Herzog grounded to Collins who throwing to second bounced the ball off of Mathewson's shoulder. Mathewson got to third and Herzog to second. Doyle was hit by a pitch, loading the bases. Fletcher lined a single over Baker's head, scoring Mathewson and Herzog as Doyle went to third.
2 Burns struck out for the third time.
3 Shafer flied to right.
Philadelphia
For New York—Wilson catching.
1 Oldring grounded to third.
2 Collins called out on strikes.
3 Baker grounded out, Wiltse to Doyle to Wiltse, as the ball bounced off Wiltse to Doyle.

Game 3 October 9 at New York

Philadelphia	Pos	AB	R	H	RBI	PO	A	E
E. Murphy	rf	5	1	2	0	2	0	0
Oldring	lf	5	0	1	0	4	0	0
Collins	2b	5	2	3	3	5	4	0
Baker	3b	4	1	2	2	3	1	0
McInnis	1b	4	0	0	0	9	0	0
Strunk	cf	4	0	0	0	1	0	0
Barry	ss	4	0	1	0	2	3	0
Schang	c	4	1	1	1	5	2	1
Bush	p	4	0	1	0	1	2	0
Totals		39	8	12	6	27	11	1

Pitching	IP	H	R	ER	BB	SO
Philadelphia						
Bush (W)	9	5	2	1	4	3
New York						
Tesreau (L)	6⅓	11	7	6	0	3
Crandall	2⅔	1	1	1	0	1

1st Inning
Philadelphia
1 Murphy grounded to short. Oldring lined a single over second. Collins singled to center, Oldring racing to third. Baker singled past short, scoring Oldring as Collins stopped at second. Collins stole third and Baker stole second on a perfect double steal.
2 McInnis struck out. Strunk grounded to Fletcher who threw high over Merkle's head, Collins and Baker scored as Strunk got to second.
3 Barry popped to short.
New York
1 Herzog grounded to short on a 3-2 count. Doyle bounced a single off of Bush's glove. Fletcher was hit by a pitched ball.
2,3 Burns lined into a double play, Collins to Barry.

2nd Inning
Philadelphia
1 Schang struck out.
2 Bush flied to right. Murphy singled between third and short. Oldring singled to right, Murphy racing to third. Oldring stole second. Collins singled to center, Murphy and Oldring scoring.
3 Baker forced Collins at second, Doyle unassisted.
New York
1 Shafer flied to second.
2 Murray popped to second.
3 McLean fouled to Schang.

3rd Inning
Philadelphia
1 McInnis flied to left.
2 Strunk flied to Burns in deep left-center.
3 Barry fouled to McLean.
New York
1 Merkle flied to Strunk in right.
2 Tesreau struck out on three pitches.
3 Herzog popped to second.

4th Inning
Philadelphia
1 Schang struck out on three pitches. Bush singled to center.
2 Murphy flied to center.
3 Oldring rolled to second.
New York
1 Doyle fouled to Baker. Fletcher beat out a hit to second.
2 Burns struck out on three pitches. Fletcher stole second.
3 Shafer grounded to second.

5th Inning
Philadelphia
1 Collins lined to right.
2 Baker popped to Fletcher at the third base foul line.
3 McInnis flied to right.
New York
Murray walked. Murray stole second, error on Schang. McLean singled past third, Murray scoring. Cooper ran for McLean.
1 Merkle flied to right. Cooper stole second.
2 Tesreau grounded to third, Cooper going to third.
3 Herzog rolled out, Schang to McInnis.

Phi.	320 000 210
N.Y.	000 010 100

New York	Pos	AB	R	H	RBI	PO	A	E
Herzog	3b	4	0	0	0	1	0	0
Doyle	2b	4	0	1	0	5	1	0
Fletcher	ss	2	0	1	0	2	2	1
Burns	lf	4	0	0	0	3	0	0
Shafer	cf	3	1	1	0	4	0	0
Murray	rf	3	1	1	1	4	0	0
McLean	c	2	0	1	1	3	1	0
a Cooper		0	0	0	0	0	0	0
Wilson	c	2	0	0	0	2	0	0
Merkle	1b	2	0	0	0	3	0	0
b Wiltse	1b	0	0	0	0	0	0	0
Tesreau	p	2	0	0	0	0	0	0
Crandall	p	1	0	0	0	0	2	0
Totals		29	2	5	2	27	6	1

a Ran for McLean in 5th.
b Ran for Merkle in 7th.
Double—Shafer. Triple—Collins. Home Run—Schang. Stolen Bases—Baker, Collins, Cooper, Fletcher, Murray, Oldring. Double Plays—Bush to Barry to McInnis, Schang to Collins, Collins to Barry, Doyle (unassisted). Hit by Pitcher—Fletcher (by Bush). Left on Bases—Philadelphia 4, New York 5. Umpires—Rigler, Connolly, Klem, Egan. Attendance—36,896. Time of Game—2:11.

6th Inning
Philadelphia
For New York—Wilson catching.
1 Strunk flied to Burns in left-center. Barry singled to right.
2 Schang fouled to Wilson.
3 Bush popped to Doyle in short center.
New York
1 Doyle grounded to first. Fletcher walked.
2,3 Burns grounded into a double play, Bush to Barry to McInnis.

7th Inning
Philadelphia
Murphy singled between Doyle and Merkle.
1 Oldring forced Murphy at second, Fletcher to Doyle. Collins tripled against the right field wall, scoring Oldring. His third hit of the game. Baker singled past second, scoring Collins. For New York—Crandall relieved Tesreau on the mound.
2,3 McInnis lined into a double play, Doyle unassisted.
New York
Shafer doubled past third. Murray singled to left-center, Shafer scoring.
1,2 Wilson struck out and Shafer was doubled up trying to steal second, Schang to Collins. Merkle walked. Wiltse ran for Merkle.
3 Crandall grounded to second.

8th Inning
Philadelphia
For New York—Wiltse playing first base.
1 Strunk grounded back to the mound.
2 Barry also grounded back to the mound. Schang hit a home run deep into the right field bleachers.
3 Bush called out on strikes with a 3-2 count.
New York
1 Herzog lined to third.
2 Doyle grounded to first.
3 Fletcher fouled to Schang on a bunt attempt.

9th Inning
Philadelphia
1 Murphy flied to right.
2 Oldring fouled to Herzog.
3 Collins flied to deep center.
New York
1 Burns flied to right. Shafer walked.
2 Murray forced Shafer at second, Barry to Collins.
3 Wilson fouled to Baker.

Game 4 October 10 at Philadelphia

New York	Pos	AB	R	H	RBI	PO	A	E
Snodgrass	cf	2	0	0	0	2	0	0
Herzog	3b	2	0	1	0	2	0	0
Doyle	2b	4	0	0	0	2	4	0
Fletcher	ss	4	0	0	0	1	0	0
Burns	lf	4	2	2	1	1	0	0
Shafer	3b-cf	4	1	1	1	1	0	0
Murray	rf	2	1	1	0	2	0	0
McLean	c	2	0	2	0	1	1	0
a Cooper		0	0	0	0	0	0	0
Wilson	c	1	0	0	0	1	1	0
c Crandall		1	0	0	0	0	0	0
Merkle	1b	4	1	1	3	10	1	2
Demaree	p	1	0	0	0	0	2	0
b McCormick		1	0	0	0	0	0	0
Marquard	p	1	0	0	0	0	2	0
d Grant		1	0	0	0	0	0	0
Totals		34	5	8	5	24	11	2

a Ran for McLean in 5th.
b Flied out for Demaree in the 5th.
c Grounded out for Wilson in 9th.
d Fouled out for Marquard in 9th.

Doubles—Barry 2, Burns. Triples—Oldring, Shafer. Home Run—Merkle. Stolen Bases—Burns, Collins, Murray. Sacrifice Hit—Strunk. Hit by pitcher—Murray (by Bender). Passed Ball—McLean. Left on Bases—New York 4, Philadelphia 7. Umpires—Egan, Klem, Connolly, Rigler. Attendance—20,568. Time of Game—2:09.

1st Inning
New York
1 Snodgrass popped to third.
2 Doyle flied to center.
3 Fletcher grounded to short.
Philadelphia
1 Murphy flied to center.
Oldring tripled to the right field fence.
2 Collins hit to Merkle who threw Oldring out at the plate. Collins stole second.
3 Baker fouled to Shafer.

2nd Inning
New York
1 Burns flied to right.
2 Shafer struck out.
Murray was hit by a pitched ball. McLean singled to right-center, sending Murray to third.
3 Merkle fouled to McInnis.
Philadelphia
McInnis singled to center.
1 Strunk sacrificed McInnis to second, Demaree to Merkle.
Barry got a second chance when Merkle muffed his foul pop and doubled into the left field corner scoring McInnis. Schang walked.
2 Bender flied to left.
3 Murphy flied to center.

3rd Inning
New York
1 Demaree flied to right.
2 Snodgrass bunted back to Bender.
3 Doyle flied to center.
Philadelphia
For New York—Shafer goes to center as Herzog comes in to play third.
1 Oldring bounced back to the mound.
2 Collins fouled to Burns in left.
3 Baker grounded to second.

4th Inning
New York
1 Fletcher flied to Collins in short right.
2 Burns popped to third.
3 Shafer again struck out.
Philadelphia
1 McInnis grounded to second.
Strunk beat out a hard smash to third. Barry lined a single to left-center, Strunk racing to third. Barry took second on the throw to third. Schang singled past second, scoring Strunk and Barry and took second on the throw to the plate. Schang went to third on a passed ball.
Bender safe at first and Schang scoring as Merkle lost his slow roller for his second error of the game.
2 Murphy popped to second. Oldring singled to center, Bender stopping at second.
3 Collins out on a bunt, McLean to Merkle.

5th Inning
New York
Murray walked on four pitches.
McLean singled off of Collins' foot, Murray racing to third.
Cooper ran for McLean.

5th Inning (continued)
1 Merkle struck out.
2 McCormick, batting for Demaree, lined to the fast on-rushing Oldring.
3 Cooper caught trying to steal second, Schang to Collins.
Philadelphia
For New York—Wilson catching and Marquard on the mound.
1 Baker struck out.
2 McInnis grounded back to the mound. Strunk walked on four pitches. Barry doubled to left, putting Strunk on third. Schang again singled past second, scoring both Strunk and Barry.
3 Bender bounced back to the mound.

6th Inning
New York
1 Herzog bounced to short.
2 Doyle struck out.
3 Fletcher flied to center.
Philadelphia
1 Murphy grounded to second.
2 Oldring struck out, but had to be thrown out at first when Wilson dropped the third strike.
3 Collins popped to short.

7th Inning
New York
Burns beat out a slow roller to short.
1 Shafer popped to Collins.
Murray singled over Baker's head, Burns stopping at second.
2 Wilson struck out as Burns and Murray executed a perfect double steal. Merkle blasted a three-run homer into the left-field bleachers. The ball went into the stands on one bounce but a homer due to the ground rules in effect for the game.
3 Marquard rolled back to the mound.
Philadelphia
1 Baker popped to third.
2 McInnis fouled to Herzog.
3 Strunk grounded to second.

8th Inning
New York
Herzog singled for his first hit of the Series.
1 Doyle forced Herzog at second on a pretty stop by Collins, who threw to Barry.
2 Fletcher forced Doyle at second, Bender to Barry who made a fine catch of Bender's poor throw. Burns doubled down the left field line, scoring Fletcher all the way from first. Shafer tripled to deep right, scoring Burns.
3 Murray grounded to second.
Philadelphia
1 Barry flied to deep right. Schang walked.
2 Bender flied to right.
3 Murphy forced Schang at second, Doyle unassisted.

9th Inning
New York
1 Crandall, pinch-hitting for Wilson, grounded to second.
2 Merkle flied to right.
3 Grant, pinch-hitting for Marquard, fouled to Schang on a full count.

N.Y.   000 000 320
Phi.   010 320 00x

Philadelphia	Pos	AB	R	H	RBI	PO	A	E
E. Murphy	rf	5	0	0	0	3	0	0
Oldring	lf	4	0	2	0	1	0	0
Collins	2b	4	0	0	0	3	3	0
Baker	3b	4	0	0	0	0	2	0
McInnis	1b	4	1	1	0	7	0	0
Strunk	cf	2	2	1	0	3	0	0
Barry	ss	4	2	3	2	3	2	0
Schang	c	2	1	2	3	6	1	0
Bender	p	4	0	0	1	0	3	0
Totals		33	6	9	6	27	9	0

Pitching	IP	H	R	ER	BB	SO
New York						
Demaree (L)	4	7	4	2	1	0
Marquard	4	2	2	2	2	2
Philadelphia						
Bender (W)	9	8	5	5	1	5

Game 5 October 11 at New York

Philadelphia	Pos	AB	R	H	RBI	PO	A	E
E. Murphy	rf	3	1	2	0	3	0	0
Oldring	lf	4	2	0	0	1	0	0
Collins	2b	3	0	1	0	2	3	0
Baker	3b	3	0	2	2	0	2	0
McInnis	1b	2	0	0	1	14	0	0
Strunk	cf	4	0	0	0	2	0	0
Barry	ss	4	0	0	0	2	7	0
Schang	c	4	0	1	0	1	0	0
Plank	p	3	0	0	0	0	1	1
Totals		30	3	6	3	27	13	1

Pitching	IP	H	R	ER	BB	SO
Philadelphia						
Plank (W)	9	2	1	0	1	1
New York						
Mathewson (L)	9	6	3	2	1	2

1st Inning
Philadelphia
Murphy singled past short.
1 Oldring forced Murphy at second on a sacrifice bunt, Mathewson to Fletcher. Collins lined a single to right, Oldring going to third.
2 Baker hit a sacrifice fly to left, Oldring scoring after the catch. Collins took second on the poor throw to the plate.
3 McInnis grounded to Herzog who threw to Doyle, getting Collins trying to return to second.
New York
1 Herzog flied to right.
2 Doyle grounded to short, Barry making a beautiful stop.
3 Fletcher flied to Oldring at the left field fence.

2nd Inning
Philadelphia
1 Strunk grounded to second.
2 Barry flied to right. Schang grounded a single off of Mathewson's glove.
3 Plank popped to short.
New York
1 Burns grounded to third.
2 Shafer lined to McInnis.
3 Murray bounced back to the mound.

3rd Inning
Philadelphia
Murphy singled to left. Oldring safe at first and Murphy at second on Doyle's fumble.
1 Collins sacrificed Murphy to third and Oldring to second, Merkle unassisted. Baker got a bunt single to Merkle who ran into tag Baker but seeing Murphy trying to score threw to McLean, just too late as Baker got to first and Oldring to third.
2 McInnis hit a sacrifice fly to left, Oldring scoring after the catch.
3 Strunk grounded to second.
New York
1 McLean flied to short left.
2 Merkle lined to second.
3 Mathewson grounded to short.

4th Inning
Philadelphia
1 Barry grounded to short.
2 Schang flied to right.
3 Plank popped to Fletcher, off balance behind second.
New York
1 Herzog called out on strikes.
2 Doyle bounced out to first.
3 Fletcher flied to center.

Phi.   102 000 000
N.Y.   000 010 000

New York	Pos	AB	R	H	RBI	PO	A	E
Herzog	3b	4	0	0	0	1	2	0
Doyle	2b	4	0	0	0	1	7	1
Fletcher	ss	3	0	0	0	2	3	0
Burns	lf	3	0	0	0	2	0	1
Shafer	cf	2	1	0	0	2	0	0
Murray	rf	3	0	0	0	2	0	0
McLean	c	3	0	1	1	3	1	0
Merkle	1b	3	0	0	0	14	0	0
Mathewson	p	2	0	1	0	0	2	0
a Crandall		1	0	0	0	0	0	0
Totals		28	1	2	1	27	15	2

a Grounded out for Mathewson in 9th.

Sacrifice Hits—Baker, Collins, McInnis 2. Double Plays—Collins to Barry to McInnis, Barry to Collins to McInnis. Left on Bases—Philadelphia 5, New York 1. Umpires—Klem, Egan, Rigler, Connolly. Attendance—36,632. Time of Game—1:39.

5th Inning
Philadelphia
1 Murphy grounded to second.
2 Oldring also grounded to second.
3 Collins flied to center.
New York
1 Burns lined to first. Shafer walked to become the first Giant base-runner. Murray safe when Plank dropped his pop fly after a collision with Baker, Shafer getting to second. McLean singled to left-center for the Giants first hit, scoring Shafer as Murray stopped at second.
2,3 Merkle grounded into a double play, Collins to Barry to McInnis.

6th Inning
Philadelphia
Baker singled, his ninth hit of the Series.
1 McInnis sacrificed Baker to second, McLean to Merkle.
2 Strunk grounded to second, Baker going to third.
3 Barry grounded to short, Merkle making a great pick-up of Fletcher's low throw.
New York
Mathewson singled over Collins' head.
1,2 Herzog hit into a double play, Barry to Collins to McInnis.
3 Doyle flied to deep right.

7th Inning
Philadelphia
1 Schang struck out.
2 Plank rolled to second. Murphy walked.
3 Oldring fouled to McLean.
New York
1 Fletcher flied to center.
2 Burns grounded to short.
3 Shafer also grounded to short.

8th Inning
Philadelphia
1 Collins grounded to second.
2 Baker rolled back to the mound.
3 McInnis grounded to deep short.
New York
1 Murray grounded to third.
2 McLean flied to left.
3 Merkle grounded to short.

9th Inning
Philadelphia
1 Strunk flied to center.
2 Barry grounded to third.
3 Schang again struck out.
New York
1 Crandall, batting for Matthewson, grounded to second.
2 Herzog popped to Barry in short left.
3 Doyle flied to right.

1913 WORLD SERIES COMPOSITE BOX

	Wins	Composite Line Score
Philadelphia Athletics (A.L.)	4	4 3 2 6 4 0 2 2 0 0 – 23
New York Giants (N.L.)	1	0 0 1 0 5 0 4 2 0 3 – 15

	Regular Season			
Manager	W	L	Pct.	G. Ahead
Connie Mack	96	57	.627	6½
John McGraw	101	51	.664	12½

BATTING AND FIELDING

WORLD SERIES STATISTICS

PHILADELPHIA ATHLETICS

	Pos	G	AB	R	H	2B	3B	HR	RBI	BB	SO	SB	BA	SA	PO	A	E
Stuffy McInnis	1b	5	17	1	2	1	0	0	2	0	2	0	.118	.176	**45**	0	0
Eddie Collins	2b	5	19	**5**	8	0	**2**	0	3	1	2	**3**	.421	.632	16	18	1
Jack Barry	ss	5	20	3	6	**3**	0	0	2	0	0	0	.300	.450	9	16	1
Frank Baker	3b	5	20	2	**9**	0	0	**1**	**7**	0	2	1	.450	.600	6	6	1
Eddie Murphy	rf	5	**22**	2	5	0	0	0	0	**2**	0	0	.227	.227	14	0	0
Amos Strunk	cf	5	17	3	2	0	0	0	0	**2**	2	0	.118	.118	14	0	0
Rube Oldring	lf	5	**22**	**5**	6	0	1	0	0	0	1	1	.273	.364	10	0	0
Wally Schang	c	4	14	2	5	0	1	**1**	6	**2**	4	0	.357	**.714**	16	3	1
Jack Lapp	c	1	4	0	1	0	0	0	0	0	1	0	.250	.250	7	1	0
Jimmy Walsh		Did not play															
Tom Daley		Did not play															
Bill Orr		Did not play															
Danny Murphy		Did not play															
Ira Thomas		Did not play															
Harry Davis		Did not play															
Doc Lavan		Did not play															
Chief Bender	p	2	8	0	0	0	0	0	0	0	1	0	.000	.000	0	5	0
Eddie Plank	p	2	7	0	1	0	0	0	1	0	0	0	.143	.143	1	3	1
Bullet Joe Bush	p	1	4	0	1	0	0	0	0	0	1	0	.250	.250	0	1	0
Boardwalk Brown		Did not play															
Duke Houck		Did not play															
Bob Shawkey		Did not play															
Weldon Wyckoff		Did not play															
Herb Pennock		Did not play															
Jack Coombs		Did not play—illness															
team total		5	174	23	46	4	4	2	21	7	16	5	.204	.368	138	53	5

Double Plays—6
Left on Bases—30

REGULAR SEASON STATISTICS

PHILADELPHIA ATHLETICS

		Main Pos	G	AB	R	H	2B	3B	HR	RBI	BB	SO	SB	BA	SA
Stuffy McInnis		1b	148	543	79	177	30	4	4	90	45	31	16	.326	.418
Eddie Collins		2b	148	534	**125**	184	23	13	3	73	85	37	54	.345	.453
Jack Barry		ss	134	455	62	125	20	6	3	85	44	32	15	.275	.365
Frank Baker		3b	149	565	116	190	34	9	**12**	**117**	63	31	34	.336	.492
Eddie Murphy		of	136	508	105	150	14	7	1	30	70	44	21	.295	.356
Amos Strunk		of	93	292	30	89	11	12	0	46	29	23	14	.305	.425
Rube Oldring		of	136	538	101	152	27	9	5	71	34	37	40	.283	.394
Wally Schang		c	76	207	32	55	16	3	3	30	34	44	4	.266	.415
Jack Lapp		c	81	238	23	54	4	4	1	20	37	26	1	.227	.290
Jimmy Walsh		of	94	303	56	77	16	5	0	27	38	40	15	.254	.340
Tom Daley		of	59	141	13	36	2	1	0	11	13	28	4	.255	.284
Bill Orr		ss	27	67	6	13	1	1	0	7	4	10	1	.194	.239
Danny Murphy		of	40	59	3	19	5	1	0	6	4	8	0	.322	.441
Ira Thomas		c	21	53	3	15	4	1	0	6	4	8	0	.283	.396
Harry Davis		1b	7	17	2	6	2	0	0	4	1	4	0	.353	.471
Doc Lavan	a	ss	5	14	1	1	0	1	0	1	0	0	0	.071	.214
Chief Bender		p	48	78	7	12	3	1	0	10	6	17	1	.154	.218
Eddie Plank		p	41	76	8	8	1	0	0	6	11	16	0	.105	.118
Bullet Joe Bush		p	39	70	8	11	3	1	0	1	2	21	0	.157	.229
Boardwalk Brown		p	43	82	5	13	1	0	1	6	1	30	0	.159	.207
Duke Houck		p	41	60	1	5	1	0	0	3	3	19	0	.083	.100
Bob Shawkey		p	18	44	3	6	1	0	0	5	1	10	0	.136	.159
Weldon Wyckoff		p	17	21	2	4	1	0	0	1	0	7	0	.190	.238
Herb Pennock		p	14	9	0	1	0	0	0	0	1	2	0	.111	.111
Jack Coombs		p	2	3	1	1	1	0	0	0	0	2	0	.333	.667
team total			153	5044	**794**	**1412**	**223**	80	**33**	**660**	**534**	547	221	**.280**	**.375**

a—from St. Louis (A)

George Brickley (of), Press Cruthers (2b), Harry Fritz (3b), Joe Giebel (c), Wickey McAvoy (c), Monte Peffer (ss), Charlie Boardman (p), Pat Bohen (p), Dick Cottrell (p), Dave Morey (p), John Taff (p) also played for the Athletics during the season.

WORLD SERIES STATISTICS

NEW YORK GIANTS

	Pos	G	AB	R	H	2B	3B	HR	RBI	BB	SO	SB	BA	SA	PO	A	E
Fred Merkle	1b	4	13	3	3	0	0	**1**	3	1	2	0	.231	.462	38	1	2
Larry Doyle	2b	5	20	1	3	0	0	0	2	0	1	0	.150	.150	13	**19**	**3**
Art Fletcher	ss	5	18	1	5	0	0	0	4	1	1	1	.278	.278	8	10	1
Buck Herzog	3b	5	19	1	1	0	0	0	0	0	1	0	.053	.053	6	7	0
Red Murray	rf	5	16	2	4	0	0	0	1	**2**	2	2	.250	.250	9	0	0
Tillie Shafer	cf-3b	5	19	2	3	1	1	0	1	**2**	3	0	.158	.316	8	0	0
George Burns	lf	5	19	2	3	2	0	0	1	1	**5**	1	.158	.263	14	0	1
Larry McLean	ph-c	5	12	0	6	0	0	0	2	0	0	0	**.500**	.500	13	3	0
Chief Meyers	c	1	4	0	0	0	0	0	0	0	0	0	.000	.000	4	2	0
Art Wilson	c	3	3	0	0	0	0	0	0	0	2	0	.000	.000	4	1	0
Fred Snodgrass	1b-cf	2	3	0	1	0	0	0	0	0	0	0	.333	.333	3	1	0
Moose McCormick	ph	2	2	1	1	0	0	0	0	0	0	0	.500	.500			
Eddie Grant	pr-ph	2	1	1	0	0	0	0	0	0	0	0	.000	.000			
Claude Cooper	pr	2	0	0	0	0	0	0	0	0	0	1	—	—			
Jim Thorpe		Did not play															
Grover Hartley		Did not play															
Christy Mathewson	p	2	5	1	3	0	0	0	1	1	0	0	.600	.600	0	5	0
Doc Crandall	p-ph	4	4	0	0	0	0	0	0	0	0	0	.000	.000	0	2	0
Jeff Tesreau	p	2	2	0	0	0	0	0	0	1	0	0	.000	.000	0	1	0
Rube Marquard	p	2	1	0	0	0	0	0	0	0	0	0	.000	.000	0	8	0
Al Demaree	p	1	1	0	0	0	0	0	0	0	0	0	.000	.000	0	2	0
Hooks Wiltse	pr-1b	2	2	0	0	0	0	0	0	0	1	0	.000	.000	15	3	0
Art Fromme		Did not play															
team total		5	164	15	33	3	1	1	15	8	19	5	.201	.250	135	65	7

Double Plays—1
Left on Bases—24

REGULAR SEASON STATISTICS

NEW YORK GIANTS

		Main Pos	G	AB	R	H	2B	3B	HR	RBI	BB	SO	SB	BA	SA
Fred Merkle		1b	153	563	78	147	30	12	3	69	41	60	35	.261	.373
Larry Doyle		2b	132	482	67	135	25	6	5	73	59	29	38	.280	.388
Art Fletcher		ss	136	538	76	160	20	9	4	71	24	35	32	.297	.390
Buck Herzog		3b	96	290	46	83	15	3	3	31	22	12	23	.286	.390
Red Murray		of	147	520	70	139	21	3	2	59	34	28	35	.267	.331
Tillie Shafer		3b-2b-ss-of	138	508	74	146	17	12	5	52	61	55	32	.287	.398
George Burns		of	150	605	81	173	37	4	2	54	58	**74**	40	.286	.370
Larry McLean	b	c	30	75	3	24	4	0	0	9	4	4	1	.320	.373
Chief Meyers		c	120	378	37	118	18	5	3	47	37	22	7	.312	.410
Art Wilson		c	54	79	5	15	0	1	0	8	11	11	1	.190	.215
Fred Snodgrass		of	141	457	65	133	21	6	3	49	53	44	27	.291	.383
Moose McCormick		of	32	57	9	22	2	3	0	15	5	13	0	.275	.375
Eddie Grant	c	3b-2b	27	20	8	4	1	0	0	1	2	2	1	.200	.250
Claude Cooper		of	27	30	11	9	4	0	0	4	4	6	3	.300	.433
Jim Thorpe		of	19	35	6	5	0	0	1	2	1	9	2	.143	.229
Grover Hartley		c	23	19	4	6	0	0	0	0	1	2	4	.316	.316
Christy Mathewson		p	40	103	7	19	0	0	0	9	8	13	1	.184	.184
Doc Crandall	d	p	46	47	7	15	4	1	0	4	3	8	0	.319	.447
Jeff Tesreau		p	41	95	7	21	2	2	0	7	2	15	1	.221	.284
Rube Marquard		p	42	105	5	23	1	0	0	6	4	14	1	.219	.229
Al Demaree		p	31	66	5	7	0	1	0	1	3	22	0	.106	.136
Hooks Wiltse		p-1b	20	24	2	5	1	0	0	2	0	1	1	.208	.250
Art Fromme	e	p	26	35	2	6	2	0	0	3	1	8	0	.171	.229
team total			156	5218	684	1427	226	70	31	580	444	501	**296**	**.273**	.361

b—from St. Louis (N)
c—from Cincinnati
d—to and from St. Louis (N)
e—from Cincinnati

Josh Devore (of), Joe Evers (pr), Heinie Groh (3b), Howard Merritt (of), Milt Stock (ss), Red Ames (p), Bunny Hearn (p), Rube Schauer (p), Ferdie Schupp (p) also played for the Giants during the season.

PITCHING

WORLD SERIES STATISTICS

	G	GS	CG	IP	H	R	ER	BB	SO	W	L	SV	ERA
PHILADELPHIA ATHLETICS													
Eddie Plank	**2**	**2**	**2**	**19**	9	4	2	3	7	1	**1**	0	**0.95**
Chief Bender	**2**	**2**	**2**	18	**19**	**9**	**8**	1	**9**	**2**	0	0	4.00
Bullet Joe Bush	1	1	1	9	5	2	1	**4**	3	1	0	0	1.00
Boardwalk Brown	Did not play												
Duke Houck	Did not play												
Bob Shawkey	Did not play												
Weldon Wyckoff	Did not play												
Herb Pennock	Did not play												
Jack Coombs	Did not play—illness												
team total	5	5	5	46	33	15	11	8	19	4	1	0	2.15
NEW YORK GIANTS													
Christy Mathewson	**2**	**2**	**2**	**19**	14	3	2	2	7	1	**1**	0	**0.95**
Rube Marquard	**2**	1	0	9	10	7	7	3	3	0	**1**	0	7.00
Jeff Tesreau	**2**	1	0	8⅓	11	7	6	1	4	0	**1**	0	6.48
Doc Crandall	**2**	0	0	4⅔	4	2	2	0	2	0	0	0	3.86
Al Demaree	1	1	0	4	7	4	2	1	0	0	**1**	0	4.50
Hooks Wiltse	Did not pitch												
Art Fromme	Did not play												
team total	5	5	2	45	46	23	19	7	16	1	4	0	3.80

REGULAR SEASON STATISTICS

		G	GS	CG	IP	H	ER	BB	SO	W	L	Pct	SV	ShO	ERA
PHILADELPHIA ATHLETICS															
Eddie Plank		41	29	18	243	211	70	57	151	18	10	.643	4	7	2.59
Chief Bender		48	22	16	237	208	58	59	135	21	10	.677	**12**	2	2.20
Bullet Joe Bush		39	15	5	200	199	85	66	81	14	6	.700	3	1	3.83
Boardwalk Brown		43	35	11	235	200	77	87	70	17	11	.607	1	3	2.95
Duke Houck		41	19	4	176	147	81	122	71	14	6	.700	0	1	4.14
Bob Shawkey		18	15	8	111	92	29	50	52	8	5	.615	0	1	2.35
Weldon Wyckoff		17	7	3	62	56	30	46	31	2	4	.333	0	0	4.36
Herb Pennock		14	4	1	33	30	19	22	17	2	1	.667	0	0	5.18
Jack Coombs		2	2	0	5	5	6	6	0	0	0	—	0	0	10.80
team total		153	153	69	1351	1200	479	**532**	630	**96**	57	**.627**	21	15	3.19
NEW YORK GIANTS															
Christy Mathewson		40	35	25	306	**291**	70	21	93	25	11	.694	2	4	**2.06**
Rube Marquard		42	33	20	288	248	80	49	151	23	10	.697	3	4	2.50
Jeff Tesreau		41	**38**	17	282	222	68	119	167	22	13	.629	0	1	2.17
Doc Crandall	d	35	3	2	98	102	31	24	42	4	4	.500	6	0	2.85
Al Demaree		31	24	11	200	176	49	38	76	13	4	.765	2	2	2.21
Hooks Wiltse		17	2	0	58	53	10	8	25	0	0	—	3	0	1.55
Art Fromme	e	26	12	3	112	112	50	29	50	11	6	.644	0	0	4.02
team total		156	156	82	1420	1276	385	315	651	**101**	51	**.664**	**17**	11	**2.44**

Total Attendance—150,992 Average Attendance—30,198 Winning Player's Share—$3,246 Losing Player's Share—$2,164

1914
Cleanly Capping the Miracle

A third major circuit, the Federal League, cracked the baseball market this year, but the World Series stayed an affair between the American and National Leagues. The A.L. pennant stayed put in Philadelphia, where the Athletics finished first for the fourth time in five years. The New York Giants also seemed a sure repeat champion in the N.L., with a comfortable lead built up by June. But a major miracle was about to overtake the Giants, with the supernatural magic blessing the efforts of the Boston Braves. Mid-July saw the Braves mired in last place, apparently for the duration of the season, when the club suddenly caught fire. The hot streak continued through the summer, with the Braves reaching fourth place on July 21, second place on August 12, and finally passed the Giants for keeps on September 8. The closing drive of 34 wins in 44 games made a legend out of a collection of odds and ends managed by George Stallings, a one-time medical student with a furious temper and a politely gentle manner mixed together in unusual fashion. Stallings platooned at most positions, having only three full-time regulars in first baseman Butch Schmidt, second baseman Johnny Evers, and shortstop Rabbit Maranville. The sparkplugs of the club were Evers, the scrappy pivot man of the Chicago Cub champions of a few years back, and Maranville, a 5' 5" fielding whiz with a very large competitive will. Stallings had three pitching aces to rely on, Dick Rudolph, Bill James, and Lefty Tyler. Rudolph won 27 games with control and a sharp curve, James used speed to win 26 games, and Tyler held up the southpaw end of the staff with 16 wins. The club earned the title of the Miracle Braves, and they were the darlings of the press. But the Athletics had been to the Series before and had the more proven players; the A's were the overwhelming choice to take the Series.

But the Braves charged into the Series like a freight train, and the Athletics simply couldn't put the brake to them. With the first two games scheduled for Philadelphia, the Series opened there with a duel between Rudolph and veteran Chief Bender. Rudolph scattered five hits to the Mackmen, but the Boston hitters chipped away at Bender for two runs in the second inning, one in the fifth, then knocked him out of the box with three in the sixth. The biggest surprise of the 7–1 Boston win was the single, double, and triple collected by catcher Hank Gowdy, a .243 hitter during the season. The Athletics now knew that the Braves were for real, but that realization did them no good. Bill James blew the ball past the A's all afternoon in the second game, giving up only two hits. Philadelphia pitcher Eddie Plank was less untouchable, and kept the plate undented until the top of the ninth. After Maranville went out, Charlie Deal, a .210 hitter playing third base every game only because Red Smith broke his ankle in the last week of the season, hit a long fly to center which Amos Strunk misplayed into a double. After James fanned, Les Mann, a .247 swinger, dropped a Texas League fly past second baseman Eddie Collins to score the only run of the game.

After their two wins in Philly, the Braves took over the favorite's role. The Braves' usual home park was South End Grounds, a shabby, run-down stadium, so the team borrowed Fenway Park from the Red Sox. The third game there drew 35,520 fans to see a mound duel between Lefty Tyler and Joe Bush. After nine innings, the score was knotted at 2–2. The A's got to Tyler for two runs in the top of the tenth, but the Braves sent the game on by answering with two runs. James relieved Tyler for the eleventh inning, and the Braves won it in the twelfth on a double by Gowdy and a throwing error by Bush which sent pinch runner Mann home. The Braves now had the force of a tidal wave, and nothing could stop the four-game sweep, which happened as Rudolph won the next game 3–1. For the Braves, it was the cap to an unbelievable season, with an unbelievable .545 Series batting mark for catcher Gowdy leading all batters. For the A's, their team batting average of .172 told the story.

Game 1 October 9 at Philadelphia

Boston	Pos	AB	R	H	RBI	PO	A	E
Moran	rf	5	0	0	0	0	0	1
Evers	2b	4	1	1	0	2	2	1
Connolly	lf	3	1	1	0	1	1	0
Whitted	cf	3	2	1	2	1	0	0
Schmidt	1b	4	1	2	1	11	1	0
Gowdy	c	3	2	3	1	9	1	0
Maranville	ss	4	0	2	2	2	3	0
Deal	3b	4	0	0	0	1	2	0
Rudolph	p	4	0	1	0	0	3	0
Totals		34	7	11	6	27	13	2

Pitching	IP	H	R	ER	BB	SO
Boston						
Rudolph (W)	9	5	1	0	3	8
Philadelphia						
Bender (L)	5⅓	8	6	6	2	3
Wyckoff	3⅔	3	1	1	1	2

Bos.	020	013	010	
Phi.	010	000	000	

Philadelphia	Pos	AB	R	H	RBI	PO	A	E
Murphy	rf	4	0	1	0	0	0	0
Oldring	lf	3	0	0	0	2	0	0
Collins	2b	3	0	0	0	2	2	0
Baker	3b	4	0	1	0	3	4	0
McInnis	1b	2	1	0	0	10	1	0
Strunk	cf	4	0	2	0	0	0	0
Barry	ss	4	0	0	0	3	5	0
Schang	c	2	0	0	0	3	0	0
Lapp	c	1	0	0	0	2	1	0
Bender	p	2	0	0	0	1	3	0
Wyckoff		1	0	1	0	1	0	0
Totals		30	1	5	0	27	14	0

Doubles—Baker, Gowdy, Wyckoff. Triples—Gowdy, Whitted. Stolen Bases—Gowdy, Moran, Schmidt. Sacrifice Hit—Oldring. Double Plays—Schmidt to Deal, Barry to Collins to McInnis, Bender to Barry to McInnis, Bender to Barry to McInnis. Left on Bases—Boston 3, Philadelphia 6. Umpires—Dinneen (A), Klem (N), Byron (N), Hildebrand (A). Attendance—20,562. Time of Game—1:58.

1st Inning
Boston
1 Moran fouled to McInnis.
2 Evers flied to Collins in short right.
3 Connolly struck out on three pitches.
Philadelphia
  Murphy singled to center.
1 Oldring sacrificed Murphy to second, Gowdy to Schmidt.
  Collins walked.
2,3 Baker fouled to Schmidt close to the stands and Murphy was doubled trying to go to third, Schmidt to Deal.

2nd Inning
Boston
  Whitted walked.
1 Schmidt flied to left.
  Gowdy lined a double over short, scoring Whitted.
  Maranville singled over second, Gowdy scoring.
2,3 Deal grounded into a double play, Barry to Collins to McInnis.
Philadelphia
  McInnis walked on four pitches.
  Strunk singled to right and when Moran let it go through, McInnis scored and Strunk got to third.
1 Barry struck out.
2 Schang hit to Evers, who threw Strunk out at the plate.
3 Bender forced Schang at second, Maranville to Evers.

3rd Inning
Boston
1 Rudolph grounded back to the mound.
2 Moran struck out on a full count.
3 Evers flied to short left.
Philadelphia
1 Murphy called out on strikes.
2 Oldring struck out.
3 Collins grounded back to the pitcher.

4th Inning
Boston
  Connolly singled to right.
1,2 Whitted hit into a double play, Bender to Barry to McInnis.
3 Schmidt grounded to second.
Philadelphia
1 Baker struck out.
2 McInnis struck out.
3 Strunk singled to left-center but was out trying for second, Connolly to Maranville.

5th Inning
Boston
  Gowdy tripled to deep right-center.
  Maranville singled to right, scoring Gowdy.
1,2 Deal bunted to Bender on a fly and Maranville was doubled off first.
3 Rudolph struck out.
Philadelphia
1 Barry popped to Maranville in short left, making a magnificent catch.
2 Schang called out on strikes.
3 Bender flied to center.

6th Inning
Boston
1 Moran fouled to Barry.
  Evers singled to center.
  Connolly walked.
  Whitted tripled to deep right-center, scoring Evers and Connolly.
  Schmidt singled through short, scoring Whitted.
  For Philadelphia—Wyckoff relieved Bender on the mound.
  Gowdy walked.
  Maranville safe when Wyckoff threw his grounder to third too late, loading the bases.
2,3 Deal grounded into a double play, Baker to McInnis.
Philadelphia
1 Murphy rolled to second.
2 Oldring grounded to third.
3 Collins rolled back to the mound.

7th Inning
Boston
  For Philadelphia—Lapp catching.
  Rudolph singled over second.
1 Moran forced Rudolph at second on a bunt, Baker to Barry.
2 Evers' struck out as Moran was stealing second.
3 Connolly grounded out, McInnis to Wyckoff.
Philadelphia
  Baker safe on Evers' fumble.
  McInnis walked on four pitches.
1 Strunk grounded to first, advancing both runners.
2 Barry struck out.
3 Lapp grounded back to the mound.

8th Inning
Boston
1 Whitted popped to third.
  Schmidt singled over short.
  Gowdy singled to left-center, his third hit, Schmidt racing to third.
2 Maranville struck out, Gowdy started to steal second, Schmidt scored when Collins' throw to the plate was high. Gowdy continued for third and was
3 out, Lapp to Baker, Both get steals.
Philadelphia
  Wyckoff lined a double into right-center.
1 Murphy grounded to short, Wyckoff going to third.
2 Oldring struck out.
3 Collins flied to center.

9th Inning
Boston
1 Deal grounded to third.
2 Rudolph grounded to short.
3 Moran grounded to third.
Philadelphia
  Baker doubled to right-center.
1 McInnis grounded to third.
2 Strunk popped to second.
3 Barry grounded to short.

Game 2 October 10 at Philadelphia

Bos.	000 000 001
Phi.	000 000 000

Boston	Pos	AB	R	H	RBI	PO	A	E
Mann	rf	5	0	2	1	0	0	0
Evers	2b	4	0	2	0	0	3	0
Cather	lf	5	0	0	0	2	0	0
Whitted	cf	3	0	0	0	1	0	0
Schmidt	1b	4	0	1	0	12	1	0
Gowdy	c	2	0	0	0	8	1	0
Maranville	ss	2	0	1	0	2	4	1
Deal	3b	4	1	1	0	2	2	0
James	p	4	0	0	0	0	3	0
Totals		33	1	7	1	27	14	1

Pitching	IP	H	R	ER	BB	SO
Boston						
James (W)	9	2	0	0	3	8
Philadelphia						
Plank (L)	9	7	1	1	4	6

Philadelphia	Pos	AB	R	H	RBI	PO	A	E
Murphy	rf	3	0	0	0	2	0	0
Oldring	lf	3	0	0	0	0	0	0
Collins	2b	3	0	1	0	5	2	0
Baker	3b	3	0	0	0	2	3	0
McInnis	1b	3	0	0	0	7	0	0
Strunk	cf	3	0	0	0	4	0	0
Barry	ss	2	0	0	0	2	5	1
Schang	c	3	0	1	0	5	2	0
Plank	p	2	0	0	0	0	1	0
a Walsh		0	0	0	0	0	0	0
Totals		25	0	2	0	27	13	1

a Walked for Plank in 9th

Doubles—Deal, Schang. Stolen Bases—Barry, Deal 2. Sacrifice hit—Maranville. Double Play—Maranville to Schmidt. Passed Ball—Schang. Hit by Pitcher—Maranville (by Plank). Left on Bases—Boston 11, Philadelphia 1. Umpires—Hildebrand, Byron, Klem, Dinneen. Attendance—20,562. Time of Game—1:56.

1st Inning
Boston
1 Mann grounded to second.
 Evers beat out a roller to third.
2 Cather called out on strikes.
 Whitted walked.
3 Schmidt flied to short center.
Philadelphia
 Murphy walked.
1 On a pick-off attempt James threw wild to first, Murphy heading for second was thrown out, Schmidt to Maranville (no error on play).
2 Oldring grounded to third.
3 Collins grounded to third.

2nd Inning
Boston
 Gowdy walked.
1 Maranville sacrificed Gowdy to second, Baker to McInnis.
2 Deal grounded to Plank and Gowdy was out, Plank to Baker to Collins. Deal stole second.
3 James struck out.
Philadelphia
1 Baker fouled to Schmidt.
2 McInnis struck out.
3 Strunk also struck out.

3rd Inning
Boston
1 Mann bounced to short.
 Evers singled to center.
2 Cather popped to third.
3 Evers caught trying to steal second, Schang to Collins.
Philadelphia
1 Barry flied to left.
2 Schang flied to deep left.
3 Plank struck out.

4th Inning
Boston
1 Whitted flied to center.
 Schmidt singled to right.
2 Gowdy flied to right.
 Maranville singled to right, Schmidt stopping at second.
3 Deal forced Maranville at second, Barry unassisted, Barry leaped and got the ball as it was bouncing high over his head.
Philadelphia
1 Murphy grounded back to the mound.
2 Oldring struck out.
3 Collins grounded to short.

5th Inning
Boston
1 James struck out.
 Mann lined a single to center.
2 Evers flied to center on a full count.
3 Cather forced Mann at second, Barry to Collins.
Philadelphia
1 Baker flied to center.
2 McInnis struck out.
3 Strunk struck out.

6th Inning
Boston
1 Whitted popped to second.
2 Schmidt flied to right.
 Gowdy walked.
 Maranville was hit by a pitch.
3 Deal forced Gowdy at third, Baker unassisted.
Philadelphia
1 Barry grounded to deep short.
 Schang doubled down the third base line for the A's first hit.
2 Schang was out trying to go to third on a short passed ball, Gowdy to Deal.
3 Plank grounded to short.

7th Inning
Boston
1 James struck out for his third time.
2 Mann struck out, Schang throwing to first for the out.
3 Evers grounded to third.
Philadelphia
1 Murphy struck out.
2 Oldring rolled out to second.
 Collins beat out a bouncer to second.
3 Collins picked off first, James to Schmidt.

8th Inning
Boston
1 Cather grounded to Barry who threw wild to first but McInnis made a great one-handed catch for the out.
 Whitted safe on Barry's fumble.
2 Schmidt forced Whitted at second, Collins to Barry.
3 Gowdy flied to center.
Philadelphia
1 Baker bounced to second.
 Maranville muffed a foul pop by McInnis
2 McInnis popped to third.
3 Strunk grounded to second.

9th Inning
Boston
1 Maranville grounded to short.
 Deal doubled to center when Strunk lost the ball in the sun.
 Deal stole third.
2 James struck out, his fourth strikeout in the game.
 Mann singled on a liner over second, scoring Deal.
 Mann got to second on a passed ball.
 Evers walked.
3 Cather forced Evers at second, Barry to Collins.
Philadelphia.
 Barry walked.
1 Schang struck out and Barry went to second when Gowdy dropped the ball.
 Walsh, pinch-hitting for Plank, walked.
2,3 Murphy hit into a game-ending double play, Maranville to Schmidt.

Game 3 October 12 at Boston

Phi. 1 0 0 1 0 0 0 0 0 2 0 0
Bos. 0 1 0 1 0 0 0 0 0 2 0 1

Philadelphia	Pos	AB	R	H	RBI	PO	A	E
Murphy	rf	5	2	2	0	2	0	0
Oldring	lf	5	0	0	0	1	0	0
Collins	2b	4	0	1	1	1	4	0
Baker	3b	5	0	2	2	4	4	0
McInnis	1b	5	1	1	0	18	0	0
Walsh	cf	4	0	1	1	1	0	0
Barry	ss	5	0	0	0	0	7	0
Schang	c	4	1	1	0	6	1	1
Bush	p	5	0	0	0	0	5	1
Totals		42	4	8	4	*33	21	2

Pitching	IP	H	R	ER	BB	SO
Philadelphia						
Bush (L)	11	9	5	4	4	4
Boston						
Tyler	10	8	4	4	3	4
James (W.)	2	0	0	0	3	1

Boston	Pos	AB	R	H	RBI	PO	A	E
Moran	rf	4	1	0	0	2	0	0
Evers	2b	5	0	3	0	3	5	0
Connolly	lf	4	0	0	1	1	0	1
Whitted	cf	5	0	0	0	2	0	0
Schmidt	1b	5	1	1	0	17	1	0
Deal	3b	5	0	1	0	2	3	0
Maranville	ss	4	1	1	1	2	3	0
Gowdy	c	4	1	3	2	6	0	0
b Mann		0	1	0	0	0	0	0
Tyler	p	3	0	0	0	1	5	0
a Devore		1	0	0	0	0	0	0
James	p	0	0	0	0	0	2	0
c Gilbert		0	0	0	0	0	0	0
Totals		40	5	9	4	36	19	1

* None out when winning run scored.
a Struck out for Tyler in 10th.
b Ran for Gowdy in 12th.
c Walked for James 12th.

Doubles—Baker, Deal, Gowdy 2, McInnis, Murphy 2. Home Run—Gowdy. Stolen Bases—Collins, Evers, Maranville 2. Sacrifice Hits—Collins, Connolly, Moran, Oldring. Double Plays—Evers to Maranville to Schmidt. Left on Bases—Philadelphia 10, Boston 8.
Umpires—Klem, Dinneen, Byron, Hildebrand.
Attendance—35,520. Time of Game—3:06.

1st Inning
Philadelphia
Murphy doubled just inside of third.
1 Oldring sacrificed Murphy to third, Tyler to Schmidt.
Collins safe as Connolly muffed his fly ball, scoring Murphy.
2 Baker struck out.
Collins stole second.
McInnis walked.
3 Collins picked off second, Tyler to Evers.
Boston
1 Moran popped to second on the tenth pitch with many fouls.
Evers lined a single to left.
2 Connolly fouled to Baker, very close to the bench.
Evers stole second.
3 Whitted struck out on a wide pitch with a 3-2 count.

2nd Inning
Philadelphia
1 Walsh bounced back to the mound.
2 Barry fouled to Schmidt.
3 Schang flied to Evers in short right.
Boston
1 Schmidt struck out.
2 Deal popped to third.
Maranville walked.
Maranville stole second.
Gowdy doubled to the left field fence, scoring Maranville.
3 Tyler grounded to short.

3rd Inning
Philadelphia
1 Bush fouled to Schmidt.
2 Murphy bounced to second.
3 Oldring grounded to short.
Boston
1 Moran grounded to third.
2 Evers grounded back to the mound.
3 Connolly lined to right.

4th Inning
Philadelphia
1 Collins lined to second.
2 Baker called out on strikes.
McInnis doubled into the left field stand.
Walsh singled past short, scoring McInnis.
3 Barry bounced to third.
Boston
1 Whitted grounded out off Bush to Collins who made the throw to first.
Schmidt bounced a single over second.
2 Deal grounded to second, Schmidt going to second.
Maranville singled to center, Schmidt scoring.
Maranville stole second and went to third on Schang's bad throw to Collins.
Gowdy walked.
3 Maranville caught off third on an attempted double steal, Schang to Collins to Baker.

5th Inning
Philadelphia
1 Schang flied to deep right.
2 Bush grounded to third.
Murphy got his second double of the game a liner to left-center.
3 Oldring struck out on three pitches.
Boston
1 Tyler bounced back to the mound, Bush making a remarkable one-handed stop.
2 Moran grounded to short.
Evers lined a single over Barry's head.
3 Connolly grounded to second.

6th Inning
Philadelphia
Collins beat out a fierce smash to third.
1,2 Baker grounded into a double play, Evers to Maranville to Schmidt.
3 McInnis but bunting, Deal to Schmidt.
Boston
1 Whitted hit back to the mound.
2 Schmidt flied to short left.
Deal lined a double into the leftfield stands.
3 Maranville popped to Schang near the mound.

7th Inning
Philadelphia
1 Walsh fouled to Deal.
2 Barry grounded back to the mound.
3 Schang rolled to second.
Boston
1 Gowdy grounded to short.
2 Tyler called out on strikes.
3 Moran bounced to short.

8th Inning
Philadelphia
1 Bush grounded out, Schmidt to Tyler. A great stop by Schmidt.
2 Murphy flied to center.
3 Oldring flied to short right.
Boston
1 Evers bounced back to the mound.
2 Connolly grounded to short.
3 Whitted also grounded to short.

9th Inning
Philadelphia
1 Collins grounded to Maranville, making a brilliant stop.
Baker doubled to right.
2 McInnis flied to left.
Walsh walked on four pitches, ball four being intentional.
3 Barry fouled to Gowdy.
Boston
1 Schmidt grounded to third.
2 Deal bunted to third.
3 Maranville grounded to short.

10th Inning
Philadelphia
Schang singled past third.
1 Bush struck out trying to sacrifice.
Murphy hit back to Tyler who threw to second too late to get Schang.
2 Oldring grounded off of Tyler to Evers, who made the throw to first, both runners advancing.
Collins walked, loading the bases.
Baker singled off of Ever's shin, scoring Schang and Murphy.
3 McInnis flied to center.
Boston
Gowdy homered deep over Walsh's head, the ball bouncing into the center field stand.
1 Devore, batting for Tyler, struck out.
Moran walked.
Evers singled to right, Moran going to third.
2 Connolly flied to center, Moran scoring after the catch.
3 Whitted popped to third.

11th Inning
Philadelphia
For Boston—James pitching.
1 Walsh grounded back to the mound.
2 Barry grounded to first.
Schang walked.
3 Bush struck out.
Boston
1 Schmidt fouled to Schang.
2 Deal flied to right.
3 Maranville grounded to third.

12th Inning
Philadelphia
Murphy walked.
1 Oldring bounced back to the mound, Murphy going to second.
2 Collins popped to third.
Baker intentionally walked.
3 McInnis forced Baker at second, Evers to Maranville.
Boston
Gowdy lined a double into the left field stand.
Mann ran for Gowdy.
Gilbert, batting for James, got an intentional pass.
Moran bunted to Bush, who threw wildly past Baker to get Mann, and Mann scored.

1914

Game 4 October 13 at Boston

Phi. 000 010 000
Bos. 000 120 00x

Philadelphia	Pos	AB	R	H	RBI	PO	A	E
Murphy	rf	4	0	0	0	0	0	0
Oldring	lf	4	0	1	0	3	0	0
Collins	2b	4	0	1	0	1	4	1
Baker	3b	4	0	1	0	1	4	0
McInnis	1b	4	0	1	0	15	1	0
Walsh	cf	2	0	1	0	1	0	0
Barry	ss	3	1	1	0	0	5	0
Schang	c	3	0	0	0	3	0	0
Shawkey	p	2	0	1	1	0	3	0
Pennock	p	1	0	0	0	0	1	0
Totals		31	1	7	1	24	18	1

Boston	Pos	AB	R	H	RBI	PO	A	E
Moran	rf	4	1	1	0	0	0	0
Evers	2b	3	1	1	2	3	6	0
Connolly	lf	2	0	0	0	1	0	0
a Mann	lf	2	0	0	0	1	0	0
Whitted	cf	3	0	2	0	1	0	0
Schmidt	1b	4	0	1	1	12	0	0
Gowdy	c	2	0	0	0	8	2	0
Maranville	ss	3	0	0	0	1	3	0
Deal	3b	3	0	0	0	1	4	0
Rudolph	p	2	1	1	0	0	0	0
Totals		28	3	6	3	27	16	0

Pitching	IP	H	R	ER	BB	SO
Philadelphia						
Shawkey (L)	5	4	3	2	2	0
Pennock	3	2	0	0	2	3
Boston						
Rudolph (W)	8	7	1	1	1	7

a Lined out for Connolly in 6th.

Doubles—Moran, Shawkey, Walsh. Stolen Base—Whitted, Double Play—Gowdy to Evers. Passed Ball—Schang. Wild Pitch—Rudolph. Left on Bases—Philadelphia 4, Boston 5. Umpires—Byron, Hildebrand, Klem, Dinneen. Attendance—34,365. Time of Game—1:49.

1st Inning
Philadelphia
1 Murphy bounced to second.
2 Oldring fouled to Gowdy.
   Collins lined a single to center.
3 Baker flied to center.
Boston
1 Moran hit hard to Baker, who made a one-handed stop.
2 Evers grounded to third.
3 Connolly flied to left.

2nd Inning
Philadelphia
1 McInnis bounced to third.
   Walsh lined a double off the left field fence.
2 Barry grounded to short, Walsh holding second.
3 Schang struck out on three pitches.
Boston
1 Whitted lined to left.
2 Schmidt grounded back to the mound. Gowdy walked after hitting a long foul into the bleachers.
3 Maranville forced Gowdy at second, Barry to Collins.

3rd Inning
Philadelphia
1 Shawkey struck out on three pitches.
2 Murphy grounded to Deal, making a great stop.
   Oldring bounced a single past short.
3 Oldring out trying to steal second, Gowdy to Maranville.
Boston
1 Deal flied to left.
2 Rudolph grounded to short.
3 Moran also grounded to short.

4th Inning
Philadelphia
1 Collins grounded to second.
   Baker beat out a smasher to first. McInnis singled to left, Baker going to third. McInnis was out
2 trying to go to second, Connolly to Deal to Evers.
3 Walsh struck out.
Boston
   Evers walked on a full count.
1 Connolly bounced to second, Evers going to second.
   Whitted safe on Collins' fumble, Evers going to third.
2 Schmidt bounced to short, Evers scoring as Whitted got to second.
3 Gowdy bounced back to the mound.

5th Inning
Philadelphia
   Barry beat out a high bouncer over Deal's head which Maranville fielded.
1 Schang grounded to second, Barry advancing to second.
   Shawkey doubled to left-center, scoring Barry.
2 Murphy grounded to second, Shawkey going to third.
3 Oldring struck out.
Boston
1 Maranville grounded to short.
2 Deal grounded to third.
   Rudolph singled over second.
   Moran doubled to left-center, Rudolph stopping at third.
   Evers singled over second, scoring Rudolph and Moran.
3 Evers picked off, Shawkey to McInnis.

6th Inning
Philadelphia
1 Collins grounded to short, Maranville and Schmidt both making excellent plays
2 Baker fouled to Deal.
3 McInnis grounded to short.
Boston
   For Philadelphia—Pennock came in to pitch.
1 Mann, batting for Connolly, lined to center.
   Whitted bounced a hit over third.
   Schmidt singled off Collins' leg, Whitted going to third.
2 Gowdy called out on strikes.
3 Schmidt out on a double steal attempt, Schang to Collins to McInnis, before Whitted could score.

7th Inning
Philadelphia
   For Boston—Mann playing left.
   Walsh walked.
   Walsh went to second on a wild pitch.
1,2 Barry struck out and Walsh was caught off of second, Gowdy to Evers.
3 Schang called out on strikes.
Boston
1 Maranville grounded to second.
2 Deal grounded to third.
   Rudolph walked.
3 Moran fouled to Baker.

8th Inning
Philadelphia
1 Pennock grounded to Evers, who fumbled but recovered in time to throw for the out at first.
2 Murphy flied to Mann, making a great running catch in left-center.
3 Oldring popped to second.
Boston
1 Evers called out on strikes.
2 Mann bounced to second.
   Whitted walked.
   Whitted stole second.
   Whitted went to third on a passed ball.
3 Schmidt struck out.

9th Inning
Philadelphia
1 Collins struck out.
2 Baker grounded to second.
3 McInnis grounded to third.

1914 WORLD SERIES COMPOSITE BOX

	Wins	Composite Line Score				
Boston Braves (N.L.)	4	0 3 0	2 3 3	0 1 1	2 0 1	– 16
Philadelphia Athletics (A.L.)	0	1 1 0	1 1 0	0 0 0	2 0 0	– 6

Manager	W	L	Pct.	G. Ahead
	Regular Season			
George Stallings	94	59	.614	10½
Connie Mack	99	53	.651	8½

BATTING AND FIELDING

	WORLD SERIES STATISTICS																			REGULAR SEASON STATISTICS													
	Pos	G	AB	R	H	2B	3B	HR	RBI	BB	SO	SB	BA	SA	PO	A	E		Main Pos	G	AB	R	H	2B	3B	HR	RBI	BB	SO	SB	BA	SA
BOSTON BRAVES																																
Butch Schmidt	1b	4	**17**	2	5	0	0	0	2	0	2	1	.294	.294	**52**	3	0		1b	147	537	67	153	17	9	1	71	43	55	14	.285	.356
Johnny Evers	2b	4	16	2	**7**	0	0	0	2	2	2	1	.438	.438	8	16	**1**		2b	139	491	81	137	20	3	1	40	87	26	12	.279	.338
Rabbit Maranville	ss	4	13	1	4	0	0	0	**3**	1	1	**2**	.308	.308	7	13	**1**		ss	156	586	74	144	23	6	4	78	45	56	28	.246	.326
Charlie Deal	3b	4	16	1	2	2	0	0	0	0	0	**2**	.125	.250	6	11	0		3b	79	257	17	54	13	2	0	23	20	23	4	.210	.276
Herbie Moran	rf	3	13	2	1	1	0	0	0	1	1	1	.077	.154	2	0	**1**	a	of	41	154	24	41	3	1	0	4	17	11	4	.266	.299
Possum Whitted	cf	4	14	2	3	0	**1**	0	2	3	1	1	.214	.357	5	0	0	b	of–2b	66	218	36	57	11	4	2	31	18	18	10	.261	.376
Joe Connolly	lf	3	9	1	1	0	0	0	1	1	1	0	.111	.111	2	2	**1**		of	120	399	64	122	28	10	9	65	49	36	12	.306	.494
Hank Gowdy	c	4	11	**3**	6	**3**	**1**	**1**	**3**	**5**	1	1	**.545**	**1.273**	31	4	0		c	128	366	42	89	17	6	3	46	48	40	14	.243	.347
Les Mann	rf-pr-ph-lf	3	7	1	2	0	0	0	1	0	1	0	.286	.286	1	0	0		of	126	389	44	96	16	11	4	40	24	50	9	.247	.375
Ted Cather	lf	1	5	0	0	0	0	0	0	0	1	0	.000	.000	2	0	0	c	of	50	145	19	43	4	0	1	27	7	28	7	.297	.400
Josh Devore	ph	1	1	0	0	0	0	0	0	0	1	0	.000	.000				d	of	51	128	22	29	2	0	1	5	18	14	2	.227	.281
Larry Gilbert	ph	1	0	0	0	0	0	0	0	1	0	0	—	—					of	72	224	32	60	6	1	5	25	26	34	3	.268	.371
Red Smith		Did not play—broken ankle.																e	3b	60	207	30	65	17	1	3	37	28	24	4	.314	.449
Bert Whaling		Did not play																	c	60	172	18	36	7	0	0	12	21	28	2	.209	.250
Oscar Dugey		Did not play																	of-2b	58	109	17	21	2	0	1	10	10	15	10	.193	.239
Billy Martin		Did not play																	ss	1	3	0	0	0	0	0	0	0	0	0	.000	.000
Dick Rudolph	p	2	6	1	2	0	0	0	0	1	1	0	.333	.333	0	3	0		p	43	120	10	15	4	1	0	8	11	19	1	.125	.175
Bill James	p	2	4	0	0	0	0	0	0	0	4	0	.000	.000	0	5	0		p	49	129	9	33	3	0	0	9	0	20	0	.256	.279
Letty Tyler	p	1	3	0	0	0	0	0	0	0	1	0	.000	.000	1	5	0		p	38	94	6	19	1	0	0	4	4	20	0	.202	.213
Dick Crutcher		Did not play																	p	33	54	5	8	1	0	0	3	4	15	1	.148	.167
Otto Hess		Did not play																	p-1b	31	47	5	11	1	0	1	6	1	11	0	.234	.319
Paul Strand		Did not play																	p	18	24	2	8	2	0	0	3	0	2	0	.333	.417
George Davis		Did not play																	p	9	18	1	3	0	0	0	2	2	6	0	.167	.167
Gene Cooreham		Did not play																	p	15	10	0	1	0	0	0	0	1	6	0	.100	.100
Dick Cottrell		Did not play																	p	1	0	0	0	0	0	0	0	0	0	0	—	—
team total		4	135	16	33	6	2	1	14	15	18	9	.244	.341	117	62	4			158	**5206**	657	1307	213	60	35	**572**	**502**	617	139	.251	.335

Double Plays—4
Left on Bases—27

a—from Cincinnati
b—from St. Louis (N)
c—from St. Louis (N)
d—from Philadelphia (N)
e—from Brooklyn
Wilson Collins (of), Tommy Griffith (of), Clarence Kraft (lb), Jim Murray (of), Clancy Tyler (c), Tom Hughes (p), Dolf Luque (p), Hub Perdue (p) also played for the Braves during the season

	Pos	G	AB	R	H	2B	3B	HR	RBI	BB	SO	SB	BA	SA	PO	A	E		Main Pos	G	AB	R	H	2B	3B	HR	RBI	BB	SO	SB	BA	SA
PHILADELPHIA ATHLETICS																																
Stuffy McInnis	1b	4	14	2	2	1	0	0	0	3	3	0	.143	.214	50	2	0		1b	149	576	74	181	12	8	1	95	19	27	25	.314	.368
Eddie Collins	2b	4	14	0	3	0	0	0	1	2	1	1	.214	.214	9	12	**1**		2b	152	526	**122**	181	23	14	2	85	97	31	58	.344	.452
Jack Barry	ss	4	14	1	1	0	0	0	0	1	3	1	.071	.071	5	**20**	**1**		ss	140	467	57	113	12	0	0	42	53	34	22	.242	.268
Frank Baker	3b	4	16	0	4	2	0	0	2	1	3	0	.250	.375	10	15	0		3b	150	570	84	182	23	10	**9**	89	53	37	19	.319	.442
Eddie Murphy	rf	4	16	2	3	2	0	0	0	2	2	0	.188	.313	4	0	0		of	148	573	101	156	12	9	3	43	87	46	36	.272	.340
Amos Strunk	cf	2	7	0	2	0	0	0	0	0	2	0	.286	.286	4	0	0		of	122	404	58	111	15	3	2	45	57	38	25	.275	.342
Rube Oldring	lf	4	15	0	1	0	0	0	0	0	**5**	0	.067	.067	6	0	0		of	119	466	68	129	21	7	3	49	18	35	14	.277	.371
Wally Schang	c	4	12	1	2	1	0	0	0	1	4	0	.167	.250	17	3	**1**		c	107	307	44	88	11	8	3	45	32	33	7	.287	.404
Jimmy Walsh	ph-cf	3	6	0	2	1	0	0	1	3	1	0	.333	.500	2	0	0	f	of	67	216	35	51	11	6	3	36	30	27	6	.236	.384
Jack Lapp	c	1	1	0	0	0	0	0	0	0	0	0	.000	.000	2	1	0		c	69	199	22	46	7	2	0	19	31	14	1	.231	.286
Larry Kopf		Did not play																	ss-3b-2b	35	69	8	13	2	2	0	12	8	14	6	.188	.275
Chick Davies		Did not play																	of-p	19	46	6	11	3	1	0	5	5	13	1	.239	.348
Shag Thompson		Did not play																	of	16	29	3	5	0	1	0	2	7	8	1	172	.241
Wickey McAvoy		Did not play																	c	18	16	1	2	0	1	0	0	0	4	0	.125	.250
Harry Davis		Did not play																	1b	5	7	0	3	0	0	0	2	1	0	0	.429	.429
Ira Thomas		Did not play																	c	2	3	0	0	0	0	0	0	0	0	0	.000	.000
Bullet Joe Bush	p	1	5	0	0	0	0	0	0	0	2	0	.000	.000	0	5	**1**		p	38	74	6	14	4	0	1	8	2	25	0	.189	.284
Eddie Plank	p	1	2	0	0	0	0	0	0	0	1	0	.000	.000	0	1	0		p	34	60	6	9	2	0	0	5	4	14	1	.150	.183
Chief Bender	p	1	2	0	0	0	0	0	0	0	0	0	.000	.000	1	3	0		p	28	62	4	9	1	0	1	8	4	13	0	.145	.210
Bob Shawkey	p	1	2	0	1	1	0	0	1	0	1	0	.500	1.000	0	3	0		p	38	83	6	17	2	0	0	5	4	22	0	.205	.229
Weldon Wyckoff	p	1	1	0	1	1	0	0	0	0	0	0	1.000	2.000	1	0	0		p	34	75	7	11	0	0	1	6	4	15	3	.147	.187
Herb Pennock	p	1	1	0	0	0	0	0	0	0	0	0	.000	.000	0	0	0		p	28	56	7	12	0	2	0	9	2	11	0	.214	.286
Rube Bressler		Did not play																	p	29	51	6	11	1	1	0	4	6	7	0	.216	.275
Jack Coombs		Did not play																	p-of	5	11	0	3	1	0	0	2	1	1	0	.273	.364
team total		4	128	6	22	9	0	0	5	13	28	2	.172	.242	111	65	4			157	5126	**749**	**392**	165	80	**29**	**627**	545	512	231	**.272**	**.352**

Double Plays—4
Left on Bases—21

f—from New York (A)
John Coyle (3b), Sam Crane (ss), Press Cruthers (2b), Tom Daley (of), Earle Mack (1b), Ferdie Moore (1b), Bill Orr (ss), Ben Rochefort (1b), Dean Sturgis (c), Charlie Sweeney (of), Charlie Boardman (p), Boardwalk Brown (p), Duke Houck (p), Bill Jensen (p), Fred Worden (p), also played for the Athletics during the season.

PITCHING

	WORLD SERIES STATISTICS													REGULAR SEASON STATISTICS													
	G	GS	CG	IP	H	R	ER	BB	SO	W	L	SV	ERA	G	GS	CG	IP	H	ER	BB	SO	W	L	Pct	SV	ShO	ERA
BOSTON BRAVES																											
Dick Rudolph	**2**	**2**	**2**	**18**	**12**	2	1	4	**15**	**2**	0	0	0.50	42	36	31	336	288	88	61	138	**27**	10	.730	0	6	2.36
Bill James	**2**	1	1	11	2	0	0	**6**	9	**2**	0	0	**0.00**	46	37	30	332	261	70	118	156	26	7	**.788**	2	4	1.90
Letty Tyler	1	1	0	10	8	4	4	3	4	0	0	0	3.60	38	34	21	271	247	81	101	140	16	14	.533	2	5	2.69
Dick Crutcher	Did not play													33	15	5	159	169	61	66	48	5	6	.455	0	1	3.45
Otto Hess	Did not play													14	11	7	89	89	30	33	24	5	6	.455	1	1	3.03
George Davis	Did not play													9	6	4	56	42	21	26	26	3	3	.500	0	1	3.38
Paul Strand	Did not play													16	3	1	55	47	15	23	33	6	2	.750	0	0	2.45
Gene Cocreham	Did not play													15	3	1	45	48	24	27	15	3	4	.429	0	0	4.80
Dick Cottrell	Did not play													1	1	0	1	2	1	3	1	0	1	.000	0	0	9.00
team total	4	4	3	39	22	6	5	13	28	4	0	0	1.15	158	158	**104**	1421	1272	433	477	606	**94**	59	**.614**	5	18	2.74
PHILADELPHIA ATHLETICS																											
Bullet Joe Bush	1	1	1	11	9	5	4	4	4	0	**1**	0	3.27	38	22	14	206	184	70	81	109	17	12	.586	2	2	3.06
Eddie Plank	1	1	1	9	7	1	1	4	6	0	**1**	0	1.00	34	22	11	185	178	59	42	110	15	7	.682	2	4	2.87
Chief Bender	1	1	0	$5\frac{1}{3}$	8	**6**	**6**	2	3	0	**1**	0	10.13	28	23	14	179	159	45	55	107	17	3	**.850**	0	7	2.26
Bob Shawkey	1	1	0	5	4	3	2	2	0	0	**1**	0	3.60	38	31	18	237	223	72	75	89	16	8	.667	2	5	2.73
Weldon Wyckoff	1	0	0	$3\frac{2}{3}$	3	1	1	1	2	0	0	0	2.45	32	20	11	185	153	62	103	86	11	8	.579	2	0	3.02
Herb Pennock	1	0	0	3	2	0	0	2	3	0	0	0	0.00	28	14	8	152	136	47	65	90	11	4	.733	3	3	2.78
Rube Bressler	Did not play													29	10	8	148	112	29	56	96	10	3	.769	2	1	1.76
Chick Davies	Did not play													1	1	1	9	8	1	3	4	1	0	1.000	0	0	1.00
Jack Coombs	Did not play													2	2	0	8	8	4	3	1	0	1	.000	0	0	4.50
team total	4	4	2	37	33	16	14	15	18	0	4	0	3.41	157	157	88	1404	1264	433	521	720	**99**	53	**.651**	13	22	2.78

Total Attendance—111,009 Average Attendance—27,752 Winning Player's Share—$2,812 Losing Player's Share—$2,032

1915
Hopping Harry Hooper

It was Philadelphia against Boston again in this year's World Series, only it was the Phillies against the Red Sox instead of the Athletics against the Braves. With the Federal League still operating and bidding player salaries up, Connie Mack's slim budget dictated that he sell off most of the Athletics' star players to other clubs for cash. He fielded a club of mostly untried youngsters and finished a resounding last, 58½ games out of first. The Braves didn't fall so far, dropping only to second place. But the fans in both Boston and Philadelphia had new champions to root for. The Red Sox moved up from second place to succeed the A's on top of the American League. Manager Bill Carrigan still had the star-studded outfield of Harry Hooper, Tris Speaker, and Duffy Lewis which carried the club into the 1912 Series, but his pitching staff had been almost completely reupholstered. A bad arm had turned Smokey Joe Wood into an occasional starter who still won 14 games. The right-handed starters since 1912 were 20-game-winner Rube Foster and 19-game-winner Ernie Shore. The lefties among the starters were a twenty-year-old rookie named Babe Ruth, who won 18 games, and 14-game-winner Dutch Leonard. In addition to his pitching skills, Ruth showed some talent with the bat and led the Sox in home runs with four. The National League-champion Phillies, in contrast, had the greatest home-run hitter in baseball in outfielder Gavvy Cravath, who socked 24 circuit clouts during the year and drove in 115 runs. The Phillies' long suits, however, were defense and pitching. Rookie shortstop Dave Bancroft tied the defense together into a tight unit, while twenty-eight-year-old Grover Cleveland Alexander, usually known as "Pete," spearheaded the strong pitching staff with 31 wins.

Phillie manager Pat Moran made Alexander his natural choice to open the Series on October 8 in Philadelphia's Baker Bowl, a tiny bandbox which owner Bill Baker made even smaller by installing 400 temporary bleacher seats on the field in right-center. The reduced dimensions of the park didn't bother Alexander at all, as he took a 3–1 decision behind two Phillie runs in the eighth inning without a hit leaving the infield. Ruth made what would be his only appearance of the Series by lining out as a pinch hitter in the ninth inning. Boston hurler Rube Foster took the lead in the Red Sox's 2–1 second-game win, pitching a three-hitter and driving in the winning run in the ninth. President Woodrow Wilson spent the day at the ballpark, the first Chief Executive to see a World Series game.

When the clubs reassembled in Boston after a day of travel, they weren't at Fenway Park, the home of the Red Sox. The Braves had celebrated their 1914 championship by building a new stadium, and the Red Sox decided to borrow spanking new Braves Field for their Series games. With a record crowd of 42,300 in attendance, Alexander took the mound for the Phils on only two days' rest, and the ace held the Sox to only six hits and two runs. Red Sox hurler Dutch Leonard went him one better, however, coughing up only three hits and one run. The winning run came in the bottom of the ninth when Lewis singled Hooper home. The Red Sox took the fourth game by the identical score of 2–1, with Ernie Shore besting George Chalmers.

With their backs to the wall, the Phils wanted Alexander to pitch in game five in Baker Bowl, but the star hurler came up with a sore arm and had to pass. Manager Moran instead started 21-game-winner Erskine Mayer against Rube Foster. The Phils scored twice in the bottom of the first, and the Red Sox retaliated with a run in the top of the second. With one out in the top of the third, Hooper sent a shot to right-center which bounced up into the temporary bleachers for a home run under the rules in effect. That knocked Mayer out and brought Eppa Rixey on in relief. A homer by Fred Luderus put the Phils ahead 3–2 and put Rixey in a position to earn the win, but the long ball and near bleachers would do him in. Duffy Lewis smashed a long two-run homer in the eighth to tie it up, and then Harry Hooper duplicated his earlier shot by driving a ball in the ninth which hopped the short fence in front of the bleachers and gave the Red Sox a 5–4 win and the Series title.

Game 1 October 8 at Philadelphia

Boston	Pos	AB	R	H	RBI	PO	A	E
Hooper	rf	5	0	1	0	0	0	0
Scott	ss	3	0	1	0	2	2	0
Speaker	cf	2	1	0	0	1	0	0
Hoblitzell	1b	4	0	1	0	12	0	0
Lewis	lf	4	0	2	1	2	0	0
Gardner	3b	3	0	1	0	0	1	0
Barry	2b	4	0	1	0	4	4	0
Cady	c	2	0	0	0	3	2	0
a Henriksen		1	0	0	0	0	0	0
Shore	p	3	0	1	0	0	4	1
b Ruth		1	0	0	0	0	0	0
Totals		32	1	8	1	24	13	1

a Safe on error for Cady in 9th.
b Grounded out for Shore in 9th.

Stolen Bases—Hoblitzell, Whitted. Sacrifice Hits—Cady, Cravath, Gardner, Scott. Left on Bases—Boston 9, Philadelphia 5. Umpires—Klem (N), O'Loughlin (A), Evans (A), Rigler (N). Attendance—19,343. Time of Game—1:58.

Bos.	0 0 0	0 0 0	0 1 0					
Phi.	0 0 0	1 0 0	0 2 x					

Philadelphia	Pos	AB	R	H	RBI	PO	A	E
Stock	3b	3	1	0	0	0	2	0
Bancroft	ss	4	1	1	0	4	1	0
Paskert	cf	3	1	1	0	2	0	0
Cravath	rf	2	0	0	1	1	0	0
Luderus	1b	4	0	1	1	10	0	1
Whitted	lf	2	0	1	0	3	0	0
Niehoff	2b	3	0	0	0	1	2	0
Burns	c	3	0	0	0	7	0	0
Alexander	p	3	0	1	0	0	5	0
Totals		27	3	5	3	27	12	1

Pitching	IP	H	R	ER	BB	SO
Boston						
Shore (L)	8	5	3	3	4	2
Philadelphia						
Alexander (W)	9	8	1	1	2	6

1st Inning
Boston
Hooper singled to center.
1 Scott sacrificed Hooper to second, Alexander to Luderus. Speaker walked.
2 Hoblitzell forced Speaker at second, Bancroft to Niehoff as Hooper went to third.
3 Hoblitzell was picked off first, Alexander to Luderus.
Philadelphia
1 Stock fouled to Cady.
2 Bancroft popped to second.
3 Paskert fouled to Hoblitzell.

2nd Inning
Boston
Lewis singled to left.
1 Gardner sacrificed Lewis to second, Alexander to Luderus.
2 Barry grounded to the mound and Lewis was caught in a run-down, Alexander to Stock to Bancroft. Barry got to second on the play.
3 Cady struck out on a full count.
Philadelphia
Cravath walked.
1 Luderus forced Cravath at second, Barry unassisted.
2 Luderus caught trying to steal second, Cady to Barry. Whitted walked.
3 Niehoff struck out.

3rd Inning
Boston
1 Shore grounded to second.
2 Hooper flied to deep left. Scott lined a single to left-center.
3 Speaker flied to left.
Philadelphia
1 Burns flied to short. Alexander beat out a slow dribbler to third.
2 Stock forced Alexander at second, Gardner to Barry.
3 Bancroft rolled out to first.

4th Inning
Boston
1 Hoblitzell grounded to second.
2 Lewis struck out on a 3–2 count. Gardner singled over second.
3 Barry flied to short right.
Philadelphia
Paskert singled to right.
1 Cravath sacrificed Paskert to second, Shore to Hoblitzell.
2 Luderus grounded to second, Paskert moving to third. Whitted hit a slow roller to Barry, just beating it out as Paskert scored. Whitted stole second.
3 Niehoff grounded to short.

5th Inning
Boston
1 Cady grounded to second. Shore singled to center.
2 Hooper popped to short.
3 Scott forced Shore at second, Niehoff to Bancroft.
Philadelphia
1 Burns struck out.
2 Alexander flied to left. Stock safe when Shore dropped his popup.
3 Bancroft grounded back to the mound.

6th Inning
Boston
1 Speaker lined to left. Hoblitzell singled to right.
2 Lewis struck out as Hoblitzell was stealing second.
3 Gardner popped to Burns.
Philadelphia
1 Paskert bounced back to the mound.
2 Cravath flied to center.
3 Luderus grounded to second.

7th Inning
Boston
Barry singled through short.
1 Cady sacrificed Barry to second, Alexander to Luderus.
2 Shore struck out.
3 Hooper also struck out.
Philadelphia
1 Whitted flied to deep left.
2 Niehoff hit back to the pitcher.
3 Burns grounded to second.

8th Inning
Boston
1 Scott blooped to short. Speaker walked.
2 Hoblitzell grounded to third, Speaker going to second. Lewis singled to left, scoring Speaker and took second on the throw to the plate.
3 Gardner flied to Paskert, making a fine running catch.
Philadelphia
1 Alexander grounded to second. Stock walked. Bancroft beat out a hit to Barry when Scott failed to cover the bag, Stock going to second. Paskert walked, loading the bases.
2 Cravath grounded to short, scoring Stock and advancing Bancroft and Paskert. Luderus beat out a bounder to Shore, Bancroft scoring and Paskert going to third.
3 Luderus out trying to steal second, Cady to Scott.

9th Inning
Boston
1 Barry struck out. Henriksen, batting for Cady, was safe on Luderus' fumble.
2 Ruth, pinch-hitting for Shore, grounded to first as Henriksen went to second.
3 Hooper popped to first.

1915

Game 2 October 9 at Philadelphia

Boston	Pos	AB	R	H	RBI	PO	A	E
Hooper	rf	3	1	1	0	2	0	0
Scott	ss	3	0	0	0	0	3	0
a Henriksen		1	0	0	0	0	0	0
Cady	c	0	0	0	0	3	0	0
Speaker	cf	4	0	1	0	3	0	0
Hoblitzell	1b	4	0	1	0	8	3	0
Lewis	lf	4	0	1	0	1	0	0
Gardner	3b	4	1	2	0	0	2	0
Barry	2b	4	0	1	0	3	0	0
Thomas	c	3	0	0	0	6	0	0
Janvrin	ss	1	0	0	0	1	0	0
Foster	p	4	0	3	1	3	0	0
Totals		35	2	10	1	27	11	0

a Popped out for Scott in 7th.

Doubles—Cravath, Foster, Luderus. Left on Bases—Boston 8, Philadelphia 2. Umpires—Rigler, Evans, O'Loughlin, Klem. Attendance—20,306. Time of Game—2:05.

Bos.	1 0 0	0 0 0	0 0 1
Phi.	0 0 0	0 1 0	0 0 0

Philadelphia	Pos	AB	R	H	RBI	PO	A	E
Stock	3b	4	0	0	0	0	2	0
Bancroft	ss	4	0	1	0	2	2	0
Paskert	cf	4	0	1	0	1	0	0
Cravath	rf	3	1	1	0	1	0	0
Luderus	1b	3	0	1	1	9	1	0
Whitted	lf	3	0	0	0	3	0	0
Niehoff	2b	3	0	0	0	4	1	0
Burns	c	3	0	0	0	6	3	1
Mayer	p	3	0	0	0	1	3	0
Totals		30	1	3	1	27	12	1

Pitching	IP	H	R	ER	BB	SO
Boston						
Foster (W)	9	3	1	1	0	8
Philadelphia						
Mayer (L)	9	10	2	1	2	7

1st Inning
Boston
Hooper walked.
1 Scott popped to Luderus on an attempted sacrifice.
Speaker singled to right, Hooper advancing to third.
2 Speaker was out trying to steal second, Burns to Niehoff, Hooper was safe at the plate when Burns dropped Niehoff's throw (Niehoff gets an assist).
Hoblitzell singled to center.
3 Hoblitzell was also caught trying to steal second, Burns to Niehoff.
Philadelphia
1 Stock grounded to short.
2 Bancroft struck out.
3 Paskert grounded out, Hoblitzell fumbling but right to Barry who threw to Foster for the out, saving Hoblitzell from being charged with an error.

2nd Inning
Boston
1 Lewis struck out.
Gardner singled to left.
2 Barry struck out.
3 Thomas grounded back to Mayer.
Philadelphia
1 Cravath struck out on four pitches.
2 Luderus also fanned.
3 Whitted rolled to short.

3rd Inning
Boston
1 Foster struck out but had to be thrown out at first when Burns dropped the third strike.
2 Hooper also struck out.
3 Scott became Mayer's fifth strikeout victim.
Philadelphia
1 Niehoff struck out.
2 Burns grounded out, Hoblitzell to Foster.
3 Mayer struck out.

4th Inning
Boston
1 Speaker popped to short.
2 Hoblitzell grounded to first.
Lewis singled to short center.
3 Gardner flied to left.
Philadelphia
1 Stock flied to center.
2 Bancroft grounded out, Hoblitzell to Foster.
3 Paskert flied to deep right.

5th Inning
Boston
1 Barry grounded to third.
2 Thomas rolled out to Stock, making a pretty play.
Foster doubled off the right field wall.
Hooper walked.
3 Scott flied to left.
Philadelphia
Cravath doubled to left.
Luderus doubled to right-center, Cravath scoring.
1 Whitted grounded to short, Luderus going to third.
2 Niehoff lined to first.
3 Burns struck out.

6th Inning
Boston
1 Speaker popped to short.
2 Hoblitzell popped to second.
3 Lewis struck out on three pitches.
Philadelphia
1 Mayer grounded to second.
2 Stock grounded to Barry in short right.
Bancroft singled to center.
3 Paskert grounded to third.

7th Inning
Boston
1 Gardner flied to left.
Barry singled to left.
2 Thomas forced Barry at second, off Mayer's glove to Bancroft who flipped to Niehoff.
Foster singled to left, sending Thomas to second.
Hooper beat out a bouncer just past Mayer, loading the bases.
3 Henriksen, batting for Scott, popped to first.
Philadelphia
For Boston—Cady catching and batting second while Janvrin came in to play short and batting eighth.
1 Cravath struck out.
2 Luderus flied to right.
3 Whitted fouled to Cady.

8th Inning
Boston
1 Speaker rolled out, Luderus to Mayer.
2 Hoblitzell flied to deep right.
3 Lewis grounded to short, Bancroft making a phenomenal stop.
Philadelphia
1 Hoblitzell grounded to third.
2 Burns popped to short.
3 Mayer flied to center.

9th Inning
Boston
Gardner singled to left.
1 Barry flied to center.
2 Janvrin bounced back to the mound, Gardner taking second.
Foster singled to center, scoring Gardner and took second on the throw to the plate.
3 Hooper struck out.
Philadelphia
1 Stock flied to left.
2 Bancroft struck out.
3 Paskert flied to center.

Game 3 October 11 at Boston

Philadelphia	Pos	AB	R	H	RBI	PO	A	E
Stock	3b	3	0	1	0	1	0	0
Bancroft	ss	3	0	1	1	4	1	0
Paskert	cf	4	0	0	0	7	0	0
Cravath	rf	4	0	0	0	2	0	0
Luderus	1b	3	0	0	0	3	1	0
Whitted	lf	3	0	0	0	2	0	0
Niehoff	2b	3	0	0	0	0	2	0
Burns	c	3	1	1	0	5	2	0
Alexander	p	2	0	0	0	2	0	0
Totals		28	1	3	1	x26	6	0

x Two outs when winning run scored.

Double—Stock. Triple—Speaker. Sacrifice Hits—Alexander, Bancroft, Hoblitzell, Scott, Stock. Double Play—Burns to Bancroft to Luderus. Left on Bases—Philadelphia 3, Boston 4. Umpires—O'Loughlin, Klem, Rigler, Evans. Attendance—42,300 (new Series Record). Time of Game—1:48.

Phi.	0 0 1	0 0 0	0 0 0
Bos.	0 0 0	1 0 0	0 0 1

Boston	Pos	AB	R	H	RBI	PO	A	E
Hooper	rf	4	1	1	0	2	0	0
Scott	ss	3	0	0	0	2	1	0
Speaker	cf	3	1	2	0	2	0	0
Hoblitzell	1b	3	0	0	1	9	0	1
Lewis	lf	4	0	3	1	1	0	0
Gardner	3b	3	0	0	0	1	5	0
Barry	2b	3	0	0	0	8	0	0
Carrigan	c	2	0	0	0	8	0	0
Leonard	p	3	0	0	0	0	2	0
Totals		28	2	6	2	27	9	1

Pitching	IP	H	R	ER	BB	SO
Philadelphia						
Alexander (L)	8⅓	6	2	2	2	4
Boston						
Leonard (W)	9	3	1	1	0	6

1st Inning
Philadelphia
Stock doubled to center when Speaker lost the ball in the sun.
1 Bancroft sacrificed Stock to third, Gardner to Hoblitzell.
2 Paskert fouled to Gardner.
3 Cravath struck out.
Boston
1 Hooper flied to right.
2 Scott struck out on three pitches.
3 Speaker flied to center.

2nd Inning
Philadelphia
1 Luderus struck out.
2 Whitted popped to first.
3 Niehoff lifted to short.
Boston
1 Hoblitzell rolled to Alexander, who tagged him on the baseline.
Lewis singled over third.
2 Lewis out trying to steal, Burns to Bancroft.
3 Gardner flied to left.

3rd Inning
Philadelphia
Burns singled over Barry's head.
Alexander credited with a sacrifice and safe when Hoblitzell dropped Gardner's throw.
1 Stock sacrificed Burns to third and Alexander to second, Gardner to Barry.
Bancroft singled to center, scoring Burns. Alexander went to third and Bancroft to second on the throw-in.
2 Paskert popped to Barry, making a great backward catch in short right.
3 Cravath flied to very deep left.
Boston
1 Barry flied to center.
Carrigan walked.
2 Leonard struck out.
3 Hooper popped to Stock who ran over in front of Bancroft to make the catch.

4th Inning
Philadelphia
1 Luderus again struck out.
2 Whitted flied to deep right.
3 Niehoff popped to short.
Boston
1 Scott flied to center.
Speaker tripled deep along the right field foul line.
2 Hoblitzell flied to center, Speaker scoring after the catch.
3 Lewis flied to center.

5th Inning
Philadelphia
1 Burns bounced back to the mound.
2 Alexander also bounced to the mound.
3 Stock flied to a running Hooper in short right.
Boston
1 Gardner flied to center.
2 Barry flied to left.
3 Carrigan flied to center.

6th Inning
Philadelphia
1 Bancroft popped to Carrigan near the pitcher's mound.
2 Paskert grounded to second.
3 Cravath grounded to third.
Boston
1 Leonard struck out.
2 Hooper grounded out, Luderus to Alexander.
3 Scott fouled to Burns.

7th Inning
Philadelphia
1 Luderus struck out for the third time.
2 Whitted grounded to short.
3 Niehoff struck out.
Boston
Speaker singled to left.
1,2 Hoblitzell bounced into a lightning fast double play, Burns to Bancroft to Luderus.
Lewis beat out an infield roller.
3 Gardner flied to deep right.

8th Inning
Philadelphia
1 Burns flied to center.
2 Alexander struck out.
3 Stock flied to center.
Boston
1 Barry popped to short.
2 Carrigan struck out.
3 Leonard lined to short.

9th Inning
Philadelphia
1 Bancroft grounded to third.
2 Paskert fouled to Carrigan.
3 Cravath grounded to third. Leonard setting down 20 Phils in a row.
Boston
Hooper singled to right.
1 Scott sacrificed, Niehoff to Luderus. Speaker intentionally walked.
2 Hoblitzell grounded to second, moving up both runners.
Lewis singled over second for his third hit of the game, Hooper scoring the game-winning run.

58

Game 4 October 12 at Boston

Phi.			
Phi.	000	000	010
Bos.	001	001	00x

Philadelphia	Pos	AB	R	H	RBI	PO	A	E
Stock	3b	4	0	1	0	0	3	0
Bancroft	ss	2	0	0	0	0	0	0
Paskert	cf	4	0	0	0	5	0	0
Cravath	rf	4	1	1	0	0	0	0
Luderus	1b	4	0	3	1	5	0	0
a Dugey		0	0	0	0	0	0	0
Becker	lf	0	0	0	0	0	0	0
Whitted	lf-1b	3	0	0	0	4	0	0
Niehoff	2b	3	0	0	0	3	1	0
Burns	c	3	0	1	0	7	2	0
Chalmers	p	3	0	1	0	0	4	0
b Byrne		1	0	0	0	0	0	0
Totals		31	1	7	1	24	10	0

a Ran for Luderus in 8th.
b Flied out for Chalmers in 9th.

Double—Lewis. Triple—Cravath. Stolen Base—Dugey. Sacrifice Hits—Lewis, Shore, Whitted. Double Plays—Scott to Barry to Hoblitzell to Barry, Chalmers to Burns to Whitted. Left on Bases—Philadelphia 8, Boston 7. Umpires—Evans, Rigler, O'Laughlin, Klem. Attendance—41,096. Time of Game—2:05.

Boston	Pos	AB	R	H	RBI	PO	A	E
Hooper	rf	4	0	1	1	2	0	0
Scott	ss	4	0	0	0	2	4	0
Speaker	cf	3	0	1	0	1	0	0
Hoblitzell	1b	4	1	3	0	5	2	0
Lewis	lf	2	0	1	1	6	1	0
Gardner	3b	4	0	0	0	2	2	0
Barry	2b	2	1	0	0	3	1	1
Cady	c	3	0	2	0	6	1	0
Shore	p	2	0	0	0	0	1	0
Totals		28	2	8	2	27	12	1

Pitching	IP	H	R	ER	BB	SO
Philadelphia						
Chalmers (L)	8	8	2	2	3	6
Boston						
Shore (W)	9	7	1	1	4	4

1st Inning
Philadelphia
Stock singled down the left field line,
1 but was out trying for second by a good throw from Lewis to Scott.
Bancroft walked on four pitches. Bancroft safe at second on a steal attempt when Barry dropped Cady's perfect throw.
2 Paskert struck out.
3 Cravath also struck out.
Boston
1 Hooper struck out.
2 Scott struck out.
Speaker walked.
3 Speaker caught trying to steal second, Burns to Niehoff.

2nd Inning
Philadelphia
Luderus singled to right.
1 Whitted sacrificed Luderus to second, Hoblitzell to Barry.
2 Niehoff lined to Cady.
Burns walked on four pitches.
3 Chalmers struck out.
Boston
1 Hoblitzell struck out on a full count.
2 Lewis grounded back to the mound.
3 Gardner flied to center.

3rd Inning
Philadelphia
1 Stock grounded to third.
Bancroft again walked.
2 Paskert again struck out.
3 Cravath flied to the fence in left.
Boston
Barry walked.
Cady beat out a bunt when Chalmers fell trying to field it, moving Barry to second.
1 Shore sacrificed Barry to third and Cady to second on a beautiful bunt, Stock to Niehoff.
Hooper was safe on a very slow roller to Niehoff, Barry scoring and Cady going to third.
2 Scott fouled to Whitted, both runners holding.
3 Speaker grounded to first.

4th Inning
Philadelphia
1 Luderus flied to right.
2 Whitted grounded to short.
Niehoff walked, reaching first for the first time in the Series.
Burns singled to right, Niehoff advancing to second.
3 Chalmers forced Niehoff at third, Scott to Gardner.
Boston
Hoblitzell singled to center.
1 Lewis sacrificed Hoblitzell to second, Chalmers to Niehoff.
2 Gardner flied to left.
3 Barry flied to center.

5th Inning
Philadelphia
1 Stock flied to left.
2 Bancroft flied to right on a 3-2 count.
3 Paskert flied to left.
Boston
Cady singled to center.
1 Shore struck out on three pitches.
2 Hooper flied to center.
3 Scott flied to center on a full count.

6th Inning
Philadelphia
1 Cravath flied to center.
Luderus singled to center.
2 Whitted popped to Cady near the pitcher's mound.
3 Niehoff flied to left.
Boston
1 Speaker grounded to second.
Hoblitzell singled to center.
Lewis doubled to the left field fence, scoring Hoblitzell.
2 Gardner flied to center.
3 Barry bounced back to the mound.

7th Inning
Philadelphia
1 Burns grounded to short.
Chalmers hit a Texas League single into short center.
2,3 Stock grounded to Scott who threw to Barry to force Chalmers at second, but Barry's throw to first was low and the ball went toward the stands. With Stock streaking for second Hoblitzell threw to Barry getting Stock.
Boston
1 Cady struck out.
2 Shore struck out.
3 Hooper grounded to third.

8th Inning
Philadelphia
1 Bancroft flied to left.
2 Paskert popped to third.
Cravath blasted a triple over Speaker's head.
Luderus lined his third single of the game to center, scoring Cravath.
Dugey ran for Luderus.
Dugey stole second.
3 Whitted grounded back to the mound.
Boston
For Philadelphia—Whitted moves in to play first with Becker playing left.
1 Scott grounded to short.
Speaker beat out a hit to third.
Hoblitzell got his third single of the game, a bouncer to right, sending Speaker to third.
Lewis walked, loading the bases.
2,3 Gardner bounced into a double play, Chalmers to Burns to Whitted.

9th Inning
Philadelphia
1 Niehoff grounded to third.
2 Burns popped to short.
3 Byrne, batting for Chalmers, flied to left.

Game 5 October 13 at Philadelphia

Bos.	011	000	021
Phi.	200	200	000

Boston	Pos	AB	R	H	RBI	PO	A	E
Hooper	rf	4	2	3	2	2	0	1
Scott	ss	5	0	0	0	2	4	0
Speaker	cf	5	0	1	0	3	0	0
Hoblitzell	1b	1	0	0	0	1	0	0
a Gainer	1b	3	1	1	0	9	0	0
Lewis	lf	4	1	2	0	0	0	0
Gardner	3b	3	1	1	0	2	3	0
Barry	2b	4	0	1	1	1	0	0
Thomas	c	2	0	1	0	4	3	0
b Cady	c	1	0	0	0	2	1	0
Foster	p	4	0	1	0	1	3	0
Totals		36	5	10	5	27	12	1

Pitching	IP	H	R	ER	BB	SO
Boston						
Foster (W)	9	9	4	3	2	5
Philadelphia						
Mayer	2⅓	6	2	2	0	0
Rixey (L)	6⅔	4	3	3	2	2

Philadelphia	Pos	AB	R	H	RBI	PO	A	E
Stock	3b	3	0	0	0	0	1	0
Bancroft	ss	4	1	2	0	3	6	1
Paskert	cf	4	1	2	0	3	0	0
Cravath	rf	3	0	0	0	1	0	0
c Dugey		0	0	0	0	0	0	0
Becker		0	0	0	0	0	0	0
Luderus	1b	2	1	2	3	12	2	0
Whitted	lf	4	0	0	0	2	0	0
Niehoff	2b	4	1	1	0	2	2	0
Burns	c	4	0	1	0	3	1	0
Mayer	p	1	0	0	0	1	0	0
Rixey	p	2	0	1	0	0	1	0
d Killefer		1	0	0	0	0	0	0
Totals		32	4	9	3	27	13	1

a Hit into double play for Hoblitzell in 3rd.
b Walked for Thomas in 6th.
c Ran for Cravath in 8th.
d Grounded out for Rixey in 9th.

Double—Luderus. Triple—Gardner. Home Runs—Hooper 2, Lewis, Luderus. Double Plays—Foster to Thomas to Hoblitzell, Bancroft to Luderus. Hit by Pitchers—Stock and Luderus (by Foster), Hooper (by Rixey). Left on Bases—Boston 7, Philadelphia 5. Umpires—Klem, O'Loughlin, Evans, Rigler. Attendance—20,306. Time of Game—2:15.

1st Inning
Boston
Hooper singled to center.
1 Scott popped to Luderus on a bunt.
2 Speaker forced Hooper at second, Luderus to Bancroft.
3 Speaker was out trying to steal, Burns to Bancroft. The fifth time Burns threw out a runner trying to steal.
Philadelphia
Stock was hit by a pitch.
Bancroft singled to left, Stock going to second.
Paskert beat out a bunt, loading the bases.
1,2 Cravath rolled into a double play, Foster to Thomas to Hoblitzell. Bancroft and Paskert both advanced.
Luderus doubled to left-center, scoring Bancroft and Paskert.
3 Whitted flied to center.

2nd Inning
Boston
1 Hoblitzell grounded out, Luderus to Mayer.
2 Lewis grounded to short.
Gardner tripled to the fence in center.
Barry blooped a Texas League single to short left, scoring Gardner.
Thomas singled over second. Barry going to second.
3 Foster popped to first.
Philadelphia
1 Niehoff struck out on three pitches.
2 Burns flied to third.
3 Mayer also struck out.

3rd Inning
Boston
Hooper drove a home run over the center field fence.
1 Scott flied to center.
Speaker singled to right.
For Philadelphia—Rixey replaced Mayer on the mound.
2,3 Gainer, pinch-hitting for Hoblitzell, hit into a double play, Bancroft to Luderus.
Philadelphia
For Boston—Gainer playing first base.
1 Stock grounded to third.
2 Bancroft flied to right.
Paskert singled over second.
3 Paskert caught trying to steal second, Thomas to Scott.

4th Inning
Boston
1 Lewis flied to left.
Gardner walked.
2 Barry forced Gardner at second, Stock to Niehoff.
3 Thomas flied to right.
Philadelphia
1 Cravath struck out.
Luderus hit a home run over the right field wall.
2 Whitted popped to third.
Niehoff singled to center, his first hit of the Series.
Burns singled to right, Niehoff racing for third. Hooper's throw to third was wild allowing Niehoff to beat Gardner's throw to the plate.
3 Rixey grounded to third.

5th Inning
Boston
Foster singled to center.
Hooper was hit by a pitched ball.
1 Scott flied to left.
2 Speaker bounced back to the pitcher, advancing both runners.
3 Gainer popped to second.
Philadelphia
1 Stock grounded to third.
Bancroft singled to center.
2 Paskert flied to left.
3 Bancroft out trying to steal second, Thomas to Scott.

6th Inning
Boston
1 Lewis grounded to short.
2 Gardner fouled to Burns.
Barry got safely to second as Bancroft threw his grounder very wild to first.
Cady, batting for Thomas, walked.
3 Foster grounded to second.
Philadelphia
For Boston—Cady catching.
1 Cravath again struck out.
Luderus walked.
2 Luderus thrown out trying to steal second. Cady to Barry.
3 Whitted flied to center.

7th Inning
Boston
1 Hooper grounded to second.
2 Scott popped to Luderus near the pitcher's box.
3 Speaker grounded to short.
Philadelphia
1 Niehoff grounded to the mound.
2 Burns fouled to Foster.
Rixey singled to left.
3 Stock flied to right.

8th Inning
Boston
Gainer beat out a hit to third.
Lewis hit a two-run homer into the center field bleachers.
1 Gardner flied to center.
2 Barry grounded to short.
3 Cady flied to center.
Philadelphia
1 Bancroft grounded to short.
2 Paskert popped to first.
Cravath walked.
Dugey ran for Cravath.
Luderus was hit by a pitched ball.
3 Whitted grounded back to the pitcher.

9th Inning
Boston
For Philadelphia—Becker in right field.
1 Foster struck out.
Hooper got his second homer of the game into the center field bleachers.
2 Scott grounded to short.
3 Speaker struck out.
Philadelphia
1 Niehoff struck out.
2 Burns grounded to first.
3 Killefer, batting for Rixey, grounded to short.

1915 WORLD SERIES COMPOSITE BOX

	Wins	Composite Line Score			Regular Season			
			Manager	W	L	Pct.	G. Ahead
Boston Red Sox (A.L.)	4	1 1 2 1 0 1 0 3 3 – 12	Bill Carrigan	101	50	.669	2½
Philadelphia Phillies (N.L.)	1	2 0 1 3 1 0 0 0 3 0 – 10	Pat Moran	90	62	.592	7

BATTING AND FIELDING

BOSTON RED SOX

	Pos	G	AB	R	H	2B	3B	HR	RBI	BB	SO	SB	BA	SA	PO	A	E		Main Pos	G	AB	R	H	2B	3B	HR	RBI	BB	SO	SB	BA	SA
Dick Hoblitzell	1b	5	16	1	5	0	0	0	1	0	1	1	.313	.313	35	5	1		1b	124	399	54	113	15	12	2	61	38	26	9	.283	.396
Jack Barry	2b	5	17	1	3	0	0	0	1	1	2	0	.176	.176	10	9	1	a	2b	78	248	30	65	13	2	0	26	24	11	0	.262	.331
Everett Scott	ss	5	18	0	1	0	0	0	0	0	3	0	.056	.056	8	12	0		ss	100	359	25	72	11	0	0	28	17	21	4	.201	.231
Larry Gardner	3b	5	17	2	4	0	1	0	1	1	0	0	.235	.353	5	13	0		3b	127	430	51	111	14	6	1	55	39	24	11	.258	.326
Harry Hooper	rf	5	20	4	7	0	0	2	3	2	4	0	.350	.650	8	0	1		of	149	566	90	133	20	13	2	51	89	36	22	.235	.327
Tris Speaker	cf	5	17	2	5	0	1	0	0	4	1	0	.294	.412	10	0	0		of	150	547	108	176	25	12	0	69	81	14	29	.322	.411
Duffy Lewis	lf	5	18	1	8	1	0	1	5	1	4	0	.444	.667	10	1	0		of	152	557	69	162	31	7	2	76	45	63	14	.291	.382
Hick Cady	c-ph	4	6	0	2	0	0	0	0	0	2	0	.333	.333	14	4	0		c	78	205	25	57	10	2	0	17	19	25	0	.278	.346
Pinch Thomas	c	2	5	0	1	0	0	0	0	0	0	0	.200	.200	10	3	0		c	86	203	21	48	4	4	0	21	13	20	3	.236	.296
Del Gainer	ph-1b	1	3	1	1	0	0	0	0	0	0	0	.333	.333	9	0	0		1b	82	200	30	59	5	8	1	29	21	31	7	.295	.415
Olaf Henriksen	ph	2	2	0	0	0	0	0	0	0	0	0	.000	.000					of	73	92	9	18	2	2	0	13	18	7	1	.196	.261
Bill Carrigan	c	1	2	0	0	0	0	0	0	1	1	0	.000	.000	8	0	0		c	46	95	10	19	3	0	0	7	16	12	0	.200	.232
Hal Janvrin	ss	1	1	0	0	0	0	0	0	0	0	0	.000	.000	1	0	0		ss-3b	99	316	41	85	9	1	0	37	14	27	8	.269	.304
Heinie Wagner		Did not play																	2b	84	267	38	64	11	2	0	29	37	34	8	.240	.296
Mike McNally		Did not play																	3b	23	53	7	8	0	1	0	3	7	0	.151	.189
Rube Foster	p	2	8	0	4	1	0	0	1	0	2	0	.500	.625	4	3	0		p	40	83	10	23	7	0	1	9	6	18	0	.277	.398
Ernie Shore	p	2	5	0	1	0	0	0	0	0	3	0	.200	.200	0	5	1		p	38	79	3	8	4	1	0	10	5	29	0	.101	.177
Dutch Leonard	p	1	3	0	0	0	0	0	0	0	2	0	.000	.000	0	2	0		p	32	53	8	14	1	1	0	3	9	12	0	.264	.321
Babe Ruth	ph	1	1	0	0	0	0	0	0	0	0	0	.000	.000					p-ph	42	92	16	29	10	1	4	21	9	23	0	.315	.576
Smokey Joe Wood		Did not play																	p	29	54	6	14	1	1	1	7	5	10	1	.259	.370
Carl Mays		Did not play																	p	38	38	3	9	1	0	0	3	7	0	.237	.263
Ray Collins		Did not play																	p	25	28	3	8	2	0	0	4	9	10	0	.286	.357
Vean Gregg		Did not play																	p	18	20	2	7	0	0	0	2	2	0	.350	.350
team total		5	159	12	42	2	2	3	11	11	25	1	.264	.358	132	57	4			155	5024	668	1308	202	76	14	575	527	476	118	.260	.339

Double Plays—2
Left on Bases—35

a—from Philadelphia (A)

Pat Haley (c), Wally Rehg (of), Bill Rodgers (2b), Chick Shorten (of), Ralph Comstock (p), Guy Cooper (p), Herb Pennock (p) also played for the Red Sox during the season.

PHILADELPHIA PHILLIES

	Pos	G	AB	R	H	2B	3B	HR	RBI	BB	SO	SB	BA	SA	PO	A	E		Main Pos	G	AB	R	H	2B	3B	HR	RBI	BB	SO	SB	BA	SA
Fred Luderus	1b	5	16	1	7	2	0	1	6	1	4	0	.438	.750	39	4	1		1b	141	499	55	157	36	7	7	62	42	36	9	.315	.457
Bert Viehoff	2b	5	16	1	1	0	0	0	0	1	5	0	.063	.063	10	10	0		2b	148	529	61	126	27	2	4	49	30	63	21	.238	.308
Dave Bancroft	ss	5	17	2	5	0	0	0	1	2	2	0	.294	.294	13	10	1		ss	153	563	85	143	18	2	7	30	77	62	15	.254	.330
Milt Stock	3b	5	17	2	1	0	0	0	0	1	2	0	.118	.176	1	8	0		3b	69	227	37	59	7	3	1	15	22	26	6	.260	.330
Gavvy Cravath	rf	5	16	2	2	1	1	0	1	2	6	0	.125	.313	5	0	0		of	150	522	89	149	31	7	24	115	86	77	11	.285	.510
Dode Paskert	cf	5	19	2	3	0	0	0	0	1	2	0	.158	.158	17	0	0		of	109	328	51	80	17	4	3	39	35	38	9	.244	.348
Possum Whitted	lf-1b	5	15	0	1	0	0	0	1	0	1	0	.067	.067	14	0	0		of	128	448	46	126	17	3	1	43	29	47	24	.281	.339
Ed Burns	c	5	16	1	3	0	0	0	0	1	2	0	.188	.188	28	8	1		c	67	174	11	42	5	0	0	16	20	12	1	.241	.270
Bobby Byrne	ph	1	1	0	0	0	0	0	0	0	0	0	.000	.000					3b	105	387	50	81	6	4	0	21	39	28	4	.209	.245
Bill Killefer	ph	1	1	0	0	0	0	0	0	0	0	0	.000	.000					c	105	320	26	76	9	2	0	24	18	14	5	.238	.278
Beals Becker	lf	2	0	0	0	0	0	0	0	0	0	0	—	—	0	0	0		of	112	338	38	83	16	4	11	35	26	48	12	.246	.414
Oscar Dugey	pr	2	0	0	0	0	0	0	0	0	0	1	—	—					of	42	39	4	6	1	0	0	7	5	2	1	.154	.179
Bud Weiser		Did not play																	of	37	64	6	9	2	0	0	8	7	12	2	.141	.172
Jack Adams		Did not play																	c	24	27	1	3	0	0	0	2	2	3	0	.111	.111
Pete Alexander	p	2	5	0	1	0	0	0	0	0	1	0	.200	.200	2	5	0		p	49	130	9	22	3	0	1	8	6	23	0	.169	.215
Erskine Mayer	p	2	4	0	0	0	0	0	0	0	2	0	.000	.000	2	3	0		p	43	88	7	21	2	1	1	7	4	24	0	.239	.318
George Chalmers	p	1	3	0	1	0	0	0	0	0	1	0	.333	.333	0	4	0		p	26	59	0	10	3	0	0	6	1	20	0	.169	.220
Eppa Rixey	p	1	2	0	1	0	0	0	0	0	0	0	.500	.500	0	1	0		p	29	55	3	9	1	0	0	2	3	13	0	.164	.182
Al Demaree		Did not play																	p	32	68	6	12	1	0	0	4	4	32	0	.176	.191
George McQuillan		Did not play																b	p	9	23	1	1	0	0	0	0	1	3	0	.043	.043
Stan Baumgartner		Did not play																	p	18	12	1	1	0	0	0	0	1	7	0	.083	.083
Ben Tincup		Did not play																	p	11	9	1	0	0	0	0	0	0	0	0	.000	.000
team total		5	148	10	27	4	1	1	9	10	25	2	.182	.243	131	53	3			153	4916	589	1216	202	39	58	486	460	600	121	.247	.340

Double Plays—3
Left on Bases—23

b—from Pittsburgh

Joe Oeschger (p) also played for the Phillies during the season.

PITCHING

BOSTON RED SOX

	G	GS	CG	IP	H	R	ER	BB	SO	W	L	SV	ERA		G	GS	CG	IP	H	ER	BB	SO	W	L	Pct.	SV	ShO	ERA
Rube Foster	2	2	2	18	12	5	4	2	13	2	0	0	2.00		37	33	22	255	217	60	86	82	20	8	.714	1	5	2.12
Ernie Shore	2	2	2	17	12	4	4	8	6	1	1	0	2.12		38	32	17	247	207	45	66	102	19	8	.704	0	4	1.64
Dutch Leonard	1	1	1	9	3	1	1	0	6	1	0	0	1.00		32	21	10	183	130	48	67	116	14	7	.667	1	2	2.36
Babe Ruth	Did not pitch														32	28	16	218	166	59	85	112	18	6	.750	0	1	2.44
Smokey Joe Wood	Did not play														25	16	10	157	120	26	44	63	14	5	.737	4	3	1.49
Carl Mays	Did not play														38	6	2	132	119	38	21	65	6	5	.400	6	0	2.04
Ray Collins	Did not play														25	9	5	105	101	50	31	43	5	7	.417	1	0	4.29
Vean Gregg	Did not play														18	9	3	75	71	28	32	43	5	3	.625	1	1	3.36
team total	5	5	5	44	27	10	9	10	25	4	1	0	1.84		155	155	82	1397	1164	371	446	634	101	50	.669	16	16	2.39

PHILADELPHIA PHILLIES

	G	GS	CG	IP	H	R	ER	BB	SO	W	L	SV	ERA		G	GS	CG	IP	H	ER	BB	SO	W	L	Pct.	SV	ShO	ERA
Pete Alexander	2	2	2	17⅔	3	3	4	10	1	1	0	0	1.53		49	42	36	376	253	51	64	241	31	10	.756	3	12	1.22
Erskine Mayer	2	2	1	11⅓	16	4	3	2	7	0	1	0	2.38		43	33	20	275	240	72	59	114	21	15	.583	2	2	2.36
George Chalmers	1	1	1	8	8	2	2	3	6	0	1	0	2.25		26	20	13	170	159	47	45	82	8	9	.471	1	1	2.49
Eppa Rixey	1	0	0	6⅔	4	3	3	2	2	0	1	0	4.05		29	22	10	177	163	47	64	88	11	12	.478	1	2	2.39
Al Demaree	Did not play														32	26	13	210	201	71	58	69	14	11	.560	1	3	3.04
George McQuillan	Did not play													b	9	8	5	64	60	15	11	13	4	3	.571	0	0	2.11
Stan Baumgartner	Did not play														16	1	0	48	38	13	23	27	0	0	.000	0	0	2.44
Ben Tincup	Did not play														10	0	0	31	26	7	9	10	0	0	—	0	0	2.03
team total	5	5	4	43⅔	42	12	11	21	25	1	4	0	2.30		153	153	98	1374	1161	332	342	652	90	62	.592	8	20	2.17

Total Attendance—143,351 Average Attendance—28,670 Winning Player's Share—$3,780 Losing Player's Share—$2,520

1916
The Longest Duel in the Sun

With the collapse of the Federal League into a dim bad memory this past winter, club owners in the National and American Leagues were looking to cut back on the player salaries inflated by financial war with the departed third league. Star center fielder Tris Speaker of the champion Boston Red Sox would not hear of any cut in his salary, so team owner Joe Lannin stamped his foot and sold him to Cleveland for $50,000 and two young prospects. Lannin apparently cut off his nose to spite his face, but he had the last laugh when his Red Sox repeated as A.L. champs with journeyman Tilly Walker in center field between stars Harry Hooper and Duffy Lewis. Pitcher Smokey Joe Wood also found Lannin's salary offer unacceptable and sat out the entire season, but he was hardly missed as twenty-one-year-old Babe Ruth blossomed into the A.L.'s top lefty with 23 wins, 9 shutouts, and a 1.75 ERA. Another pitching bonus for the Sox was the work of sub-mariner Carl Mays, who unexpectedly won 18 games. The experts predicted an easy Series for the Red Sox over the Brooklyn Robins, who were making their first appearance in the fall classic after taking the N.L. pennant for the first time since 1900. Manager Wilbert Robinson had batting stars in Zack Wheat and Jake Daubert and a 25-game winner in right-hander Jeff Pfeffer, but the bulk of the squad was a collection of well-orchestrated castoffs who just edged past the defending champion Philadelphia Phillies.

Manager Robinson's strategy was to pitch southpaws against the Red Sox, so he moved his ace Pfeffer back into the bullpen and opened the Series in Boston's Braves Field with Rube Marquard, the former Giant star whom John McGraw had cut loose after several bad seasons and whom Robinson had rehabilitated into a solid starter. Boston manager Bill Carrigan answered with righty Ernie Shore, who looked very sharp through eight innings as the Red Sox piled up a 6–1 lead. But the Robins got the tiring Shore's number in the top of the ninth, and Carl Mays relieved him with the bases loaded, two outs, and the score now 6–4. Hy Myers greeted Mays with a single that made the score 6–5, but Daubert's hard grounder was handled by shortstop Everett Scott to end the rally and the game. The second game in Boston matched southpaws Ruth and Sherry Smith in the most tenacious pitching duel in Series history. Hy Myers hit a long drive to right-center in the first inning which went for an inside-the-park home run when both Hooper and Walker slipped in chasing it. Boston answered with a run in the third on a triple by Scott and an infield out by Ruth. From that point on, the pitchers shut the door. At the end of nine innings, it was still 1–1. At the end of 13 innings, it was still 1–1, with Ruth and Smith both still going strong. Ruth got the Robins out in the fourteenth, then Smith faltered by walking Dick Hoblitzell for the fourth time in the game and then giving up a double to pinch hitter Del Gainor which ended the game at 2–1.

The scene shifted to Brooklyn with the Robins down 2–0 and Robinson's left-handed plan a failure. This time he started righty Jack Coombs, another Robin retread who had starred in earlier Series with the Philadelphia Athletics. The Robins gave Coombs a 4–0 cushion after five innings, but the Red Sox started chipping away at the lead. When Larry Gardner's home run in the seventh inning made the score 4–3, Robinson lifted Coombs and brought in his ace, Pfeffer. Eight men came to bat against Pfeffer, and he retired all eight in order to save the win for Coombs. With their hopes raised, the Robins went down to a 6–2 defeat in game four before the five-hit pitching of Boston's Dutch Leonard. The teams moved back to Boston for game five, and a record crowd of 43,620 came out on Columbus Day to see Ernie Shore fire a three-hitter and wrap up the Series with a 4–1 triumph. Although the Series was a relatively easy victory for the Red Sox, the Robins had the Series' leading batter in right fielder Casey Stengel, a refreshingly eccentric character who hit .364. The two straight Series championships evidently fulfilled all the challenges baseball offered Boston manager Carrigan, for he retired to a banker's life in Lewiston, Maine, during the winter.

Game 1 October 7 at Boston

| Bkn. | 000 100 004 |
| Bos. | 001 010 31x |

Brooklyn	Pos	AB	R	H	RBI	PO	A	E
Myers	cf	5	0	2	1	1	0	0
Daubert	1b	4	0	0	0	5	1	0
Stengel	rf	4	2	2	0	1	0	1
Wheat	lf	4	1	2	1	3	0	0
Cutshaw	2b	3	1	0	0	5	2	1
Mowrey	3b	3	1	1	1	1	2	0
Olson	ss	4	0	1	0	2	1	2
Meyers	c	4	0	1	0	6	3	0
Marquard	p	2	0	0	0	0	0	0
a Johnston		1	0	1	0	0	0	0
Pfeffer	p	0	0	0	0	0	0	0
b Merkle		0	0	0	1	0	0	0
Totals		34	5	10	4	24	9	4

a Singled for Marquard in 8th.
b Walked for Pfeffer in 9th.

Doubles—Hooper, Janvrin, Lewis.
Triples—Myers, Janvrin, Walker, Wheat.
Sacrifice Hits—Janvrin, Lewis, Scott 2.
Double Plays—Janvrin to Scott to Hoblitzell, Hooper to Cady, Gardner to Janvrin to Hoblitzell, Shore to Scott to Janvrin to Hoblitzell. Passed Ball—Meyers. Hit by Pitcher—Cutshaw (by Shore). Left on Bases—Brooklyn 6, Boston 11.
Umpires—Connolly (A), O'Day (N), Quigley (N), Dinneen (A). Attendance—36,117. Time of Game—2:16.

Boston	Pos	AB	R	H	RBI	PO	A	E
Hooper	rf	4	2	1	0	1	1	0
Janvrin	2b	4	1	2	0	2	8	1
Walker	cf	4	1	2	1	0	0	0
Hoblitzell	1b	5	2	1	1	14	0	0
Lewis	lf	3	0	1	1	0	0	0
Gardner	3b	4	0	1	1	1	3	0
Scott	ss	2	0	1	2	4	0	0
Cady	c	1	0	0	0	7	0	0
Thomas	c	0	0	0	0	0	0	0
Shore	p	4	0	0	0	0	3	0
Mays	p	0	0	0	0	0	0	0
Totals		31	6	8	5	27	19	1

Pitching	IP	H	R	ER	BB	SO
Brooklyn						
Marquard (L)	7	7	5	4	4	6
Pfeffer	1	1	1	0	2	0
Boston						
Shore (W)	8⅔	9	5	3	3	5
Mays (SV)	⅓	1	0	0	0	0

1st Inning
Brooklyn
1 Myers fouled to Cady.
2 Daubert struck out.
3 Stengel rolled to second.
Boston
1 Hooper struck out.
2 Janvrin struck out.
   Walker tripled to deep left-center.
3 Hoblitzell rolled to second.

2nd Inning
Brooklyn
   Wheat beat out an infield hit to second.
1,2 Cutshaw grounded into a double play, Janvrin to Scott to Hoblitzell. Mowery walked.
3 Olson struck out.
Boston
   Lewis walked on a full count.
   Gardner beat out a sacrifice bunt down the third base line.
1 Scott sacrificed Lewis to third and Gardner to second, Meyers to Daubert. Cady walked on four pitches, loading the bases.
2 Shore called out on strikes.
3 Hooper flied to Myers in deep left-center.

3rd Inning
Brooklyn
1 Meyers bounced back to the mound.
2 Marquard called out on strikes. Myers singled over second.
3 Daubert struck out on three pitches.
Boston
1 Janvrin called out on strikes, but had to be thrown out at first when Meyers dropped the third strike.
2 Walker struck out.
   Hoblitzell tripled to the right field fence.
   Lewis doubled over third, scoring Hoblitzell.
3 Lewis picked off second, Meyers to Olson.

4th Inning
Brooklyn
   Stengel singled past second.
   Wheat singled to right, scoring Stengel.
1,2 Cutshaw flied to Hooper who made a fantastic catch in right, then threw out Wheat trying to score.
3 Mowrey grounded to second.
Boston
1 Gardner struck out.
2 Scott lined to left.
   Cady walked.
3 Shore fouled to Meyers.

5th Inning
Brooklyn
1 Olson grounded to third.
   Meyers tripled to deep center after Walker lost the hit in the sun.
2 Marquard grounded to second as Meyers was held at third.
3 Myers popped to short.

5th Inning (continued)
Boston
   Hooper doubled to center.
1 Janvrin sacrificed Hooper to third, Daubert to Cutshaw.
   Walker singled to left, Hooper scoring.
2 Hoblitzell grounded to first, Walker going to second.
3 Lewis grounded to third, Mowery tagging Walker as he came into the base.

6th Inning
Brooklyn
1 Daubert grounded to third.
2 Stengel struck out.
3 Wheat grounded to second.
Boston
   Gardner safe at first on Olson's error.
1 Scott forced Gardner at second, Mowrey to Cutshaw.
   Scott to second on a passed ball. Cady walked for the third time.
2 Shore popped to first.
3 Hooper fouled to Olson outside of the third base line.

7th Inning
Brooklyn
1 Cutshaw bounced to second. Mowery singled to right.
2,3 Olson hit into a double play, Gardner to Janvrin to Hoblitzell.
Boston
   Janvrin doubled down the left field line.
   Walker safe and Janvrin to third on Olson's second fumble.
   Hoblitzell safe on Cutshaw's fumble, Janvrin scoring.
1 Lewis sacrificed, Mowrey to Cutshaw. Gardner hit to Cutshaw whose throw to the plate failed to get Walker, Hoblitzell getting to third.
2 Scott flied to right, Hoblitzell scoring after the catch.
3 Cady grounded to second.

8th Inning
Brooklyn
1 Meyers grounded to short.
   Johnston, batting for Marquard, singled to right.
2,3 Myers hit into a double play, off of Shore to Scott to Janvrin to Hoblitzell.
Boston
   For Brooklyn—Pfeffer pitching.
1 Shore flied to deep left.
   Hooper walked.
   Janvrin singled to right, Hooper going to third and scoring on Stengel's wild throw to third, Janvrin got to second.
   Walker walked on four pitches.
2 Hoblitzell flied to left.
3 Lewis forced Walker, Olson to Cutshaw.

9th Inning
Brooklyn
   Daubert walked.
   Stengel singled to right, Daubert stopping at second.
1 Wheat forced Daubert, Shore to Gardner. Cutshaw hit by a pitched ball. Mowrey safe on Janvrin's boot, scoring Stengel and Wheat. Olson beat out a hit to third, again loading the bases.
2 Meyers popped to first. Merkle, batting for Pfeffer, walked on a full count, forcing in Cutshaw. For Boston—Mays came in to pitch. Myers just beat out a hit to second, Mowrey scoring.
3 Daubert grounded to deep short.

Game 2 October 9 at Boston

Brooklyn	Pos	AB	R	H	RBI	PO	A	E
Johnston	rf	5	0	1	0	1	0	0
Daubert	1b	5	0	0	0	17	0	0
Myers	cf	6	1	1	1	5	1	0
Wheat	lf	5	0	0	0	2	0	0
Cutshaw	2b	5	0	0	0	5	5	1
Mowrey	3b	5	0	1	0	3	5	1
Olson	ss	2	0	1	0	2	4	0
Miller	c	5	0	1	0	4	1	0
Smith	p	5	0	1	0	1	6	0
Totals		43	1	6	1	*40	22	2

Pitching	IP	H	R	ER	BB	SO
Brooklyn						
Smith (L)	14	7	2	2	6	2
Boston						
Ruth (W)	13⅓	6	1	1	3	4

Bkn. 1 0 0 0 0 0 0 0 0 0 0 0 0 0
Bos. 0 0 1 0 0 0 0 0 0 0 0 0 0 1

Boston	Pos	AB	R	H	RBI	PO	A	E
Hooper	rf	6	0	1	0	2	1	0
Janvrin	2b	6	0	1	0	4	5	0
Walker	cf	3	0	0	0	2	1	0
a Walsh	cf	3	0	0	0	1	0	0
Hoblitzell	1b	2	0	0	0	22	1	0
b McNally		0	0	0	0	0	0	0
Lewis	lf	3	0	1	0	1	0	0
Gardner	2b	5	0	0	0	2	8	1
c Gainer		1	0	1	1	0	0	0
Scott	ss	4	1	2	0	1	8	0
Thomas	c	4	0	1	0	5	4	0
Ruth	p	5	0	0	1	2	4	0
Totals		42	2	7	2	42	32	1

* One out when winning run scored.
a Hit into fielder's choice for Walker in 9th.
b Ran for Hoblitzell in 14th.
c Singled for Gardner in 14th.

Doubles—Janvrin, Smith. Triples—Scott, Thomas. Home Run—Myers. Sacrifice Hits—Lewis 2, Olson 2, Thomas. Double Plays—Mowrey to Cutshaw to Daubert, Myers to Miller, Scott to Janvrin to Hoblitzell. Left on Bases—Brooklyn 5, Boston 9. Umpires—Dinneen, Quigley, Connolly, O'Day. Attendance—**47,373.** Time of Game—2:32.

1st Inning
Brooklyn
1 Johnston flied deep to center.
2 Daubert grounded to third.
  Myers got an inside-the-park home run past Walker in deep right-center.
3 Wheat flied to right.
Boston
1 Hooper grounded back to the mound.
2 Janvrin lined to center.
3 Walker fouled to Daubert.

2nd Inning
Brooklyn
1 Cutshaw's hard grounder deflected off Ruth's leg to Gardner who made the throw to first.
2 Mowrey lined to second.
3 Olson struck out.
Boston
1 Hoblitzell bounced to short.
  Lewis singled to center.
2 Gardner forced Lewis at second, Mowrey to Cutshaw.
3   Gardner picked off first, Miller to Daubert.

3rd Inning
Brooklyn
1 Miller grounded to short.
  Smith doubled to the right field fence,
2 but was thrown out trying for third, Hooper to Walker to Gardner. Johnston singled to center.
3   Johnston caught trying for second, Thomas to Scott.
Boston
  Scott tripled deep between Myers and Wheat.
1 Thomas grounded to second, Scott being held at third.
2 Ruth grounded to second, Scott scoring the tying run.
  Hooper safe on Cutshaw's error.
3 Janvrin forced Hooper at second, Olson to Cutshaw.

4th Inning
Brooklyn
  Daubert walked.
1,2 Myers hit into a double play, Scott to Janvrin to Hoblitzell.
3 Wheat grounded back to the mound.
Boston
1 Walker tapped back to the pitcher. Hoblitzell walked.
2,3 Lewis rapped into Brooklyn's first double play of the Series, Mowrey to Cutshaw to Daubert.

5th Inning
Brooklyn
1 Cutshaw struck out on three pitches.
2 Mowrey tapped to second. Olson singled to left.
3 Miller flied to right.
Boston
1 Gardner grounded to second.
2 Scott grounded to third. Thomas tripled to deep left. Umpire Quigley giving him the third base when Olson tripped him as he was running toward the bag.
3 Ruth struck out.

6th Inning
Brooklyn
1 Smith grounded to short. Johnston walked on four pitches.
2   Johnston thrown out at second, Thomas to Janvrin.
3 Daubert grounded to third.
Boston
1 Hooper robbed of a hit by a great shoestring catch by Myers.
2 Janvrin flied to center.
3 Walker rolled to second.

7th Inning
Brooklyn
1 Myers just out on a slow grounder to second.
2 Wheat grounded to second.
3 Cutshaw popped to first.
Boston
  Hoblitzell again walked.
1 Lewis sacrificed Hoblitzell to second, Smith to Daubert.
2 Gardner popped to Olson.
3 Scott hit to Mowrey who tagged Hoblitzell coming into third.

8th Inning
Brooklyn
  Mowrey singled to left.
1 Olson sacrificed Mowrey to second, Thomas to Hoblitzell. Miller singled to center, Mowrey going to third. Smith grounded to Scott and Mowrey was
2 caught in a run-down, Scott to Thomas to Gardner to Ruth. Miller got to third and Smith to second on the play.
3 Johnston grounded to Ruth.
Boston
1 Thomas grounded to first.
2 Ruth flied to left.
3 Hooper flied to deep right.

9th Inning
Brooklyn
1 Daubert grounded to third.
2 Myers lined to center.
3 Wheat grounded out, Hoblitzell to Ruth.
Boston
  Janvrin doubled to left, Wheat just missing the fly after a long run. Walsh, batting for Walker after a one strike count, grounded to Smith who threw to Mowrey getting Janvrin at third, but Mowrey dropped the ball putting runners on first and third.
1,2 Hoblitzell lined to Myers in center who threw perfectly to Miller doubling Janvrin trying to score, Walsh to second on the play. Lewis intentionally passed.
3 Gardner fouled to Miller.

10th Inning
Brooklyn
  For Boston—Walsh playing center.
1 Cutshaw grounded to second.
2 Mowrey grounded to deep short. Olson walked.
3 Miller bounced to third.
Boston
  Scott singled.
1 Thomas sacrificed Scott to second, Olson to Smith.
2 Ruth struck out. Hooper singled off Mowrey's glove, Scott getting to third but was then
3 out Mowrey to Olson just off of third.

11th Inning
Brooklyn
1 Smith grounded to third.
2 Johnston also grounded to third.
3 Daubert struck out.
Boston
1 Janvrin popped to first.
2 Walsh fouled to Daubert. Hoblitzell walked for the third time in the game.
3 Lewis grounded to third.

12th Inning
Brooklyn
1 Myers struck out.
2 Wheat popped to third.
3 Cutshaw grounded to short.
Boston
1 Gardner flied to left. Scott walked.
2 Thomas forced Scott at second, Olson to Cutshaw.
3 Ruth bunted out to the mound.

13th Inning
Brooklyn
  Mowrey safe at first on Gardner's wild throw.
1 Olson sacrificed Mowrey to second, Ruth to Janvrin.
2 Miller popped to Thomas.
3 Smith flied to Lewis in short left, making a great running catch.
Boston
1 Hooper bounced back to the pitcher.
2 Janvrin fouled to Mowrey.
3 Walsh fouled to Mowrey.

14th Inning
Brooklyn
1 Johnson grounded to short.
2 Daubert flied to center.
3 Myers grounded to short.
Boston
  Hoblitzell walked for the fourth time in the game.
1 Lewis sacrificed Hoblitzell to second, Smith to Cutshaw. McNally ran for Hoblitzell. Gainer, batting for Gardner, singled over Mowrey's head, scoring McNally with the winning run.

Game 3 October 10 at Brooklyn

| Bos. | 000 002 100 |
| Bkn. | 001 120 00x |

Boston	Pos	AB	R	H	RBI	PO	A	E
Hooper	rf	4	1	2	1	1	0	0
Janvrin	2b	4	0	0	0	1	0	0
Shorten	cf	4	0	3	1	0	0	0
Hoblitzell	1b	4	0	1	0	12	2	0
Lewis	lf	4	0	0	0	1	1	0
Gardner	3b	3	1	1	1	2	0	1
Scott	ss	3	0	0	1	7	0	0
Thomas	c	3	0	0	0	5	0	0
Mays	p	1	0	0	0	0	4	0
a Henriksen		0	1	0	0	0	0	0
Foster	p	1	0	0	0	1	2	0
Totals		31	3	7	3	24	16	1

a Walked for Mays in 6th.

Triples—Daubert, Hooper, Olson. Home Run—Gardner, Stolen Base—Wheat. Sacrifice Hits—Miller, Myers, Stengel. Hit by Pitcher—Myers (by Mays). Wild Pitch—Foster. Left on Bases—Boston 2, Brooklyn 9. Umpires—O'Day, Connolly, Quigley, Dinneen. Attendance—21,087. Time of Game—2:01.

Brooklyn	Pos	AB	R	H	RBI	PO	A	E
Myers	cf	3	0	0	0	3	0	0
Daubert	1b	4	1	3	0	7	0	0
Stengel	rf	3	0	1	0	2	1	0
Wheat	lf	2	1	1	0	4	0	0
Cutshaw	2b	4	0	1	1	4	0	0
Mowrey	3b	3	1	0	0	2	1	0
Olson	ss	4	1	2	2	1	2	0
Miller	c	3	0	0	0	4	2	0
Coombs	p	3	0	1	0	0	2	0
Pfeffer	p	1	0	1	0	0	1	0
Totals		30	4	10	4	27	9	0

Pitching	IP	H	R	ER	BB	SO
Boston						
Mays (L)	5	7	4	3	3	2
Foster	3	3	0	0	0	1
Brooklyn						
Coombs (W)	6⅓	7	3	3	1	1
Pfeffer (SV)	2⅔	0	0	0	0	3

1st Inning

Boston
1 Hooper flied to left, after his previous hit over the right field wall was foul by just inches.
2 Janvrin grounded to third.
   Shorten singled to center.
   Hoblitzell singled to right, but Shorten
3 was out trying for third, Stengel to Mowrey.

Brooklyn
   Myers was hit by a pitch.
   Daubert beat out a bunt to the mound, Myers going to second.
1 Stengel sacrificed Myers to third and Daubert to second, Mays to Hoblitzell.
   Wheat intentionally passed, loading the bases.
2 Cutshaw forced Myers at the plate, Hoblitzell to Thomas.
3 Mowrey took a called third strike on a full count.

2nd Inning

Boston
1 Lewis flied to short center.
2 Gardner popped to Cutshaw.
3 Scott flied to deep left.

Brooklyn
1 Olson grounded to short.
2 Miller struck out.
3 Coombs grounded to short.

3rd Inning

Boston
1 Thomas popped to second.
2 Mays called out on strikes.
   Hooper lined a single to center.
3 Hooper out trying to steal second, Miller to Cutshaw.

Brooklyn
1 Myers grounded to short.
   Daubert singled to right.
   Stengel singled past third, sending Daubert to second.
2 Wheat lined to left.
   Cutshaw singled to right, scoring Daubert as Stengel got to third and Cutshaw to second on the throw to the plate.
3 Mowrey grounded to short, a real good play by Scott.

4th Inning

Boston
1 Janvrin flied to right.
   Shorten singled over Mowrey's head.
2   Shorten was cut down trying for second, Miller to Olson.
3 Hoblitzell flied to center.

Brooklyn
   Olson beat out a bunt towards third and continued to second on Gardner's wild throw past first.
1 Miller sacrificed Olson to third, Mays to Janvrin.
   Coombs singled to right, scoring Olson.
2 Myers sacrificed Coombs to second, Mays to Hoblitzell.
3 Daubert grounded to short.

5th Inning

Boston
1 Lewis lined to left.
2 Gardner popped to third.
3 Scott tapped back to the mound.

Brooklyn
1 Stengel fouled to Gardner who had to reach into the boxes to make a beautiful catch.
   Wheat walked.
2 Cutshaw bounced back to the mound, Wheat moving to second.
   Mowrey walked.
   Olson tripled off the temporary bleachers in left, scoring Wheat and Mowrey.
3 Miller grounded to short.

6th Inning

Boston
1 Thomas grounded to short.
   Henriksen, pinch-hitting for Mays, walked on four pitches.
   Hooper tripled to deep right-center, scoring Henriksen.
2 Janvrin popped to second.
   Shorten singled for his third straight hit, scoring Hooper.
3 Hoblitzell tapped back to the mound.

Brooklyn
   For Boston—Foster now pitching.
1 Coombs lined to short.
2 Myers popped to third.
   Daubert tripled to deep left, his third hit of the game, but Daubert was out at the plate when he started his slide
3 much too early. The play went Lewis to Scott to Thomas.

7th Inning

Boston
1 Lewis grounded to first.
   Gardner homered completely over the right field fence.
   For Brooklyn—Pfeffer now pitching.
2 Scott flied deep to Myers at the fence.
3 Thomas struck out.

Brooklyn
1 Stengel flied to right.
   Wheat singled to right.
   Wheat stole second, aided by a short wild pitch.
2 Cutshaw popped to Hoblitzell in short right.
3 Mowrey bounced back to the mound, Hoblitzell making a great play of Foster's low throw.

8th Inning

Boston
1 Foster struck out.
2 Hooper bounced back to the mound.
3 Janvrin struck out.

Brooklyn
1 Olson grounded back to the mound, Foster making a good leaping pick-up of the ball.
2 Miller grounded out, Hoblitzell to Foster.
   Pfeffer singled to deep right.
3 Myers struck out.

9th Inning

Boston
1 Shorten fouled to Wheat almost tumbling into the bleachers to make the catch.
2 Hoblitzell grounded to deep short.
3 Lewis flied to right.

Game 4 October 11 at Brooklyn

Boston	Pos	AB	R	H	RBI	PO	A	E
Hooper	rf	4	1	2	0	3	0	0
Janvrin	2b	5	1	0	0	1	2	1
Walker	cf	4	0	1	0	2	0	0
Hoblitzell	1b	3	1	2	0	7	0	0
Lewis	lf	4	2	2	0	6	0	0
Gardner	3b	3	1	1	3	2	3	0
Scott	ss	4	0	0	0	3	3	0
Carrigan	c	3	0	2	1	3	1	0
Leonard	p	3	0	0	0	0	1	0
Totals		33	6	10	5	27	10	1

Pitching	IP	H	R	ER	BB	SO
Boston						
Leonard (W)	9	5	2	1	4	3
Brooklyn						
Marquard (L)	4	5	4	4	2	3
Cheney	3	4	2	1	1	5
Rucker	2	1	0	0	0	3

Bos.	030 110 100
Bkn.	200 000 000

Brooklyn	Pos	AB	R	H	RBI	PO	A	E
Johnston	rf	4	1	1	0	0	0	1
Myers	cf	4	1	1	1	0	0	0
Merkle	1b	3	0	1	0	9	1	1
Wheat	lf	4	0	1	0	5	0	0
Cutshaw	2b	4	0	1	1	3	2	0
Mowrey	3b	3	0	0	0	1	4	0
Olson	ss	3	0	0	0	2	2	0
Meyers	c	3	0	0	0	11	2	0
c Stengel		0	0	0	0	0	0	0
Marquard	p	1	0	0	0	0	2	0
a Pfeffer		1	0	0	0	0	0	0
Cheney	p	0	0	0	0	0	0	1
b O'Mara		1	0	0	0	0	0	0
Rucker	p	0	0	0	0	0	0	0
d Getz		1	0	0	0	0	0	0
Totals		32	2	5	2	27	13	4

a Struck out for Marquard in 4th.
b Struck out for Cheney in 7th.
c Ran for Meyers in 9th.
d Grounded out for Rucker in 9th.

Doubles—Cutshaw, Hoblitzell, Lewis. Triple—Johnston. Home Run—Gardner. Stolen Base—Hooper. Sacrifice Hits—Carrigan, Gardner. Passed Ball—Meyers. Wild Pitch—Leonard. Left on Bases—Boston 5, Brooklyn 7. Umpires—Quigley, Dinneen, O'Day, Connolly. Attendance—21,662. Time of Game—2:30.

1st Inning
Boston
1 Hooper tapped back to the mound.
2 Janvrin struck out on a 3-2 count.
3 Walker called out on strikes.
Brooklyn
Johnston tripled to deep right-center.
Myers singled to right, Johnston scoring.
Merkle walked.
1 Wheat forced Merkle at second, Gardner to Janvrin as Myers went to third.
Wheat went to second on a wild pitch.
Cutshaw safe at first as Janvrin booted his grounder allowing Myers to score and Wheat to get to third.
2 On a double steal after Cutshaw made second, Wheat was out, Carrigan to Janvrin to Gardner.
3 Mowrey struck out.

2nd Inning
Boston
Hoblitzell walked on four pitches.
Lewis doubled off the right field wall, Hoblitzell stopping at third.
Gardner got a three run inside-the-park homer in deep left-center.
Scott safely to second when Wheat dropped his fly ball.
1 Carrigan sacrificed Scott to third, Marquard to Merkle.
2 Leonard struck out.
3 Hooper grounded to first.
Brooklyn
1 Olson fouled to Gardner in left.
Meyers walked.
2 Marquard grounded to the pitcher, Meyers going to second.
3 Johnston grounded to short.

3rd Inning
Boston
1 Janvrin grounded to Cutshaw who made a splendid pick up and throw.
Walker beat out a hit toward third.
2 Hoblitzell lined to center.
3 Walker out trying to steal second, Meyers to Cutshaw.
Brooklyn
1 Myers flied to center.
2 Merkle flied high to Scott in short left.
3 Wheat flied to left.

4th Inning
Boston
Lewis singled to left.
1 Gardner sacrificed Lewis to second, Mowery to Merkle.
2 Scott grounded to third, Lewis getting to second.
Carrigan singled, scoring Lewis.
Leonard walked.
On a short passed ball Leonard broke for second but Carrigan stayed there, Meyers threw to Merkle to get the retreating Leonard who again broke for second as Carrigan went for
3 third but was out on a toss from Merkle to Cutshaw.
Brooklyn
Cutshaw doubled to right.
Mowrey walked.
1 Olson sacrifice popped to first.
2 Meyers flied to Scott at deep short.
3 Pfeffer, batting for Marquard, struck out.

5th Inning
Boston
For Brooklyn—Cheney pitching.
Hooper walked.
1 Janvrin struck out as Hooper stole second.
2 Walker popped to short.
Hoblitzell doubled past third, scoring Hooper.
3 Lewis struck out.

5th Inning (continued)
Brooklyn
1 Johnston flied to left.
2 Myers flied to right.
Merkle singled over second.
Wheat singled past third, Merkle stopping at second.
3 Cutshaw flied to left.

6th Inning
Boston
1 Gardner struck out.
2 Scott struck out.
Carrigan singled to left.
3 Leonard struck out.
Brooklyn
1 Mowrey flied to left.
2 Olson grounded to short.
3 Meyers popped to first.

7th Inning
Boston
Hooper singled past short.
1 Janvrin forced Hooper on a sacrifice attempt, Mowrey to Olson.
2 Walker grounded to short, Janvrin moving to second.
Hoblitzell got a hit just out of Cheney's reach but Cheney's throw to first hit Hoblitzell in the back and rolled to the stands, Janvrin scoring.
3 Lewis forced Hoblitzell at second, Mowrey to Cutshaw.
Brooklyn
1 O'Mara, batting for Cheney, struck out.
2 Johnston flied to deep left.
3 Myers flied to right.

8th Inning
Boston
For Brooklyn—Rucker pitching.
1 Gardner grounded to second, a great stop and throw by Cutshaw.
2 Scott grounded to short after Merkle was given an error for dropping his foul pop-up.
3 Carrigan called out on strikes.
Brooklyn
1 Merkle robbed of a hit by a sensational stop by Scott behind third (backing up Gardner) and a perfect throw to first.
2 Wheat flied to center.
3 Cutshaw lined to right.

9th Inning
Boston
1 Leonard called out on strikes.
Hooper singled to right and continued to second as Johnston fumbled the hit.
2 Hooper out trying to steal third, Meyers to Mowrey.
3 Janvrin called out on strikes.
Brooklyn
1 Mowrey flied to left.
Olson walked.
2 Meyers forced Olson at second, Gardner to Scott.
Stengel ran for Meyers.
3 Getz, pinch-hitting for Rucker, grounded to third.

Game 5 October 12 at Boston

Brooklyn	Pos	AB	R	H	RBI	PO	A	E
Myers	cf	4	0	0	0	0	0	0
Daubert	1b	4	0	0	0	10	1	0
Stengel	rf	4	0	0	0	1	0	0
Wheat	lf	4	0	1	0	5	0	0
Cutshaw	2b	3	1	0	0	2	3	0
Mowrey	3b	3	0	1	0	1	3	1
Olson	ss	3	0	0	0	2	3	2
Meyers	c	3	0	1	0	4	2	0
Pfeffer	p	2	0	0	0	0	1	0
a Merkle		1	0	0	0	0	0	0
Dell	p	0	0	0	0	0	0	0
Totals		31	1	3	0	24	13	3

a Flied out for Pfeffer in 8th.

Double—Janvrin. Triple—Lewis. Sacrifice Hits—Gardner, Lewis, Mowrey, Shorten. Passed Ball—Cady. Wild Pitches—Pfeffer 2. Left on Bases—Brooklyn 5, Boston 4. Umpires—Connolly, O'Day, Dinneen, Quigley. Attendance—43,620. Time of Game—1:43.

Bkn.	010 000 000
Bos.	012 010 00x

Boston	Pos	AB	R	H	RBI	PO	A	E
Hooper	rf	3	2	1	0	1	0	0
Janvrin	2b	4	0	2	1	0	1	0
Shorten	cf	3	0	1	1	3	0	0
Hoblitzell	1b	3	0	0	0	14	1	0
Lewis	lf	3	1	2	0	1	0	0
Gardner	3b	2	0	0	1	0	5	0
Scott	ss	3	0	0	0	4	2	2
Cady	c	3	1	1	0	4	1	0
Shore	p	3	0	0	0	0	4	0
Totals		27	4	7	3	27	14	2

Pitching	IP	H	R	ER	BB	SO
Pfeffer (L)	7	6	4	2	2	2
Dell	1	1	0	0	0	0
Boston						
Shore (W)	9	3	1	0	1	4

1st Inning
Brooklyn
1 Myers called out on strikes on three pitches.
2 Daubert tapped out, Cady to Hoblitzell.
Stengel safely to first on Scott's fumble and then threw high to first.
3 Wheat fouled to Hoblitzell.
Boston
1 Hooper grounded to second after taking Pfeffer to a full count.
2 Janvrin bounced to third.
3 Shorten flied to short left.

2nd Inning
Brooklyn
Cutshaw walked on four pitches.
1 Mowrey sacrificed Cutshaw to second, Hoblitzell to Shore.
2 Olson bounced high to third, Cutshaw getting to third.
Cutshaw scored on a passed ball by Cady.
3 Meyers rolled to short.
Boston
1 Hoblitzell tapped to the pitcher.
Lewis tripled on a bad hop bounce over Wheat's head.
2 Gardner flied to short left, Lewis scoring after the catch.
3 Scott fouled to Meyers after Mowrey had erred by dropping his foul.

3rd Inning
Brooklyn
1 Pfeffer struck out.
2 Myers rolled to third.
3 Daubert tapped to the mound.
Boston
Cady lined a single over Daubert's head.
1 Shore fouled to Meyers on a sacrifice attempt.
Hooper walked on four pitches.
Janvrin safe at first as Olson fumbled his double play grounder, then Olson got another error throwing into right trying to get Hooper, Cady scoring, Hooper going to third as Janvrin stayed at first.
2 Janvrin was out trying to steal second, Meyers to Olson, as Hooper held third.
Shorten singled over second, scoring Hooper.
3 Shorten was also thrown out trying to steal second, Meyers to Olson.

4th Inning
Brooklyn
1 Stengel flied to center.
2 Wheat struck out.
3 Cutshaw bounced back to the pitcher.
Boston
Hoblitzell walked on four pitches.
1 Lewis sacrificed Hoblitzell to second, Daubert to Cutshaw.
2 Gardner grounded to second, Hoblitzell advancing to third.
3 Scott bounced to short with a great scoop of a low throw by Daubert.

5th Inning
Brooklyn
1 Mowrey bounced high to Gardner, who made a fantastic stop and throw just getting Mowrey at first.
2 Olson flied to center.
Meyers bounced a single just over Shore's outstretched glove, ruining Shore's no-hit attempt.
3 Pfeffer grounded to third.
Boston
1 Cady grounded to short.
2 Shore robbed of an extra-base-hit by a marvelous shoe-string catch by Wheat.
Hooper singled to right.
Janvrin doubled to center, scoring Hooper.
Janvrin went to third on a wild pitch.
3 Shorten struck out.

6th Inning
Brooklyn
1 Meyers flied to Shorten in left-center.
2 Daubert grounded to third.
3 Stengel popped to short.
Boston
1 Hoblitzell grounded to first.
Lewis singled to left.
2 Gardner forced Lewis at second, Olson to Cutshaw.
Gardner went to second on a wild pitch.
3 Scott grounded to third.

7th Inning
Brooklyn
1 Wheat flied to right.
2 Cutshaw bounced back to the mound.
Mowrey blasted a clean single past third.
Olson safely to second and Mowrey to third on Scott's throw high over first.
3 Meyers tapped back to the mound.
Boston
1 Cady fouled to Mowrey.
2 Shore struck out.
3 Hooper grounded to second.

8th Inning
Brooklyn
1 Merkle, pinch-hitting for Pfeffer, flied deep to Lewis, making a sensational catch in front of the bleachers.
2 Myers blooped a bunt to Shore.
3 Daubert grounded to short.
Boston
For Brooklyn—Dell pitching.
Janvrin lined a single over third.
1 Shorten sacrificed Janvrin to second, Mowrey to Daubert.
2 Hoblitzell lined to left.
3 Lewis flied to left.

9th Inning
Brooklyn
Stengel singled to left-center.
1 Wheat struck out.
2 Cutshaw grounded to second, moving up Stengel.
3 Mowrey popped to short.

1916 WORLD SERIES COMPOSITE BOX

	Wins	Composite Line Score					Manager	Regular Season W	L	Pct.	G. Ahead
Boston Red Sox (A.L.)	4	0 4 4	1 2 5	1 0 0	0 0 0	0 1 – 21	Bill Carrigan	91	63	.591	2
Brooklyn Robins (N.L.)	1	3 1 1	2 2 0	0 0 4	0 0 0	0 0 – 13	Wilbert Robinson	94	60	.610	2½

BATTING AND FIELDING

BOSTON RED SOX

	WORLD SERIES STATISTICS Pos	G	AB	R	H	2B	3B	HR	RBI	BB	SO	SB	BA	SA	PO	A	E		REGULAR SEASON STATISTICS Main Pos	G	AB	R	H	2B	3B	HR	RBI	BB	SO	SB	BA	SA
Dick Hoblitzell	1b	5	17	3	4	1	1	0	2	**6**	0	0	.235	.412	**69**	3	0		1b	130	417	57	108	17	1	0	39	47	28	10	259	.305
Hal Janvrin	2b	5	**23**	2	5	**3**	0	0	1	0	**6**	0	.217	.348	8	17	2		ss-2b	117	310	26	69	11	4	0	26	32	32	6	.223	.284
Everett Scott	ss	5	16	1	2	0	1	0	1	1	1	0	.125	.250	9	**24**	2		ss	123	366	37	85	19	2	0	27	23	24	8	.232	.295
Larry Gardner	3b	5	17	2	3	0	0	**2**	**6**	0	2	0	.176	.529	7	19	2		3b	148	493	47	152	19	7	2	62	48	27	12	.308	.387
Harry Hooper	rf	5	21	**6**	**7**	1	1	0	1	3	1	**1**	.333	.476	9	2	0		of	151	575	75	156	20	11	1	37	80	35	27	.271	.350
Tilly Walker	cf	3	11	1	3	0	1	0	1	1	2	0	.273	.455	4	1	0		of	128	467	68	124	29	11	3	46	23	45	14	.266	.394
Duffy Lewis	lf	5	17	3	6	2	1	0	1	2	1	0	.353	**.588**	9	1	0		of	152	563	56	151	29	5	1	56	33	56	16	.268	.343
Pinch Thomas	c	3	7	0	1	0	1	0	0	0	1	0	.143	.429	10	4	0		c	99	216	21	57	10	1	1	21	33	13	4	.264	.333
Chick Shorten	cf	2	7	0	4	0	0	0	2	0	1	0	.571	.571	3	0	0		of	53	112	14	33	2	1	0	11	10	8	1	.295	.330
Hick Cady	c	2	4	1	1	0	0	0	0	3	0	0	.250	.250	11	1	0		c	78	162	5	31	6	3	0	13	15	16	0	.191	.265
Bill Carrigan	c	1	3	0	2	0	0	0	1	0	1	0	.667	.667	3	1	0		c	33	63	7	17	2	1	0	11	11	3	2	.270	.333
Jimmy Walsh	cf	1	3	0	0	0	0	0	0	0	0	0	.000	.000	1	0	0	a	of	13	16	5	2	0	0	0	2	4	2	3	.125	.125
Del Gainer	ph	1	1	0	1	0	0	0	1	0	0	0	1.000	1.000					1b	56	142	14	36	6	0	3	18	10	24	5	.254	.359
Olaf Henriksen	ph	1	0	1	0	0	0	0	0	1	0	0	—	—					of	68	99	13	20	2	2	0	11	19	15	2	.202	.263
Mike McNally	pr	1	0	1	0	0	0	0	0	0	0	0	—	—					2b-3b-ss	87	135	28	23	0	0	0	9	10	19	9	.170	.170
Jack Barry	Did not play																		2b	94	330	28	67	6	1	0	20	17	24	8	.203	.227
Sam Agnew	Did not play																		c	40	67	4	14	2	1	0	7	6	4	0	.209	.269
Heinie Wagner	Did not play																		3b	6	8	2	4	1	0	0	0	3	0	2	.500	.625
Ernie Shore	p	2	7	0	0	0	0	0	0	0	2	0	.000	.000	2	7	0		p	38	77	3	7	2	0	0	3	3	31	0	.091	.117
Babe Ruth	p	1	5	0	0	0	0	0	1	0	2	0	.000	.000	2	4	0		p-ph	67	136	18	37	5	3	3	15	10	23	0	.272	.419
Dutch Leonard	p	1	3	0	0	0	0	0	0	1	3	0	.000	.000	0	1	0		p	48	85	2	17	3	0	0	10	6	16	0	.200	.235
Carl Mays	p	2	1	0	0	0	0	0	0	0	1	0	.000	.000	0	4	0		p	48	77	8	18	1	2	0	8	16	19	0	.234	.299
Rube Foster	p	1	1	0	0	0	0	0	0	0	1	0	.000	.000	1	2	0		p	38	62	3	11	3	0	0	2	3	10	0	.177	.226
Vean Gregg	Did not play																		p	21	18	0	2	1	0	0	0	0	3	0	.111	.167
Sad Sam Jones	Did not play																		p	13	6	0	2	0	0	0	0	0	2	0	.333	.333
Weldon Wyckoff	Did not play																	b	p	8	6	1	1	0	0	0	0	0	1	0	.167	.167
team total		5	164	21	39	7	6	2	18	18	25	1	.238	.390	147	91	6			156	5017	548	1245	196	56	14	454	464	482	129	.248	.318

Double Plays–5
Left on Bases–28

a—from Philadelphia (A)
b—from Philadelphia (A)
Pat Haley (ph), Marty Monale (p), Herb Pennock (p) also played for the Red Sox during the season.

BROOKLYN ROBINS

	WORLD SERIES STATISTICS Pos	G	AB	R	H	2B	3B	HR	RBI	BB	SO	SB	BA	SA	PO	A	E		REGULAR SEASON STATISTICS Main Pos	G	AB	R	H	2B	3B	HR	RBI	BB	SO	SB	BA	SA
Jake Daubert	1b	4	17	1	3	0	1	0	0	2	3	0	.176	.294	39	2	0		1b	127	478	75	151	16	7	3	33	38	39	21	.316	.397
George Cutshaw	2b	5	19	2	2	1	0	0	2	1	1	0	.105	.158	19	12	2		2b	154	581	58	151	21	4	2	63	25	32	27	.260	.320
Ivy Olson	ss	5	16	1	4	0	1	0	2	2	2	0	.250	.375	9	12	**4**		ss	108	351	29	89	13	4	1	38	21	27	14	.254	.322
Mike Mowrey	3b	5	17	2	3	0	0	0	1	3	2	0	.176	.176	8	15	2		3b	144	495	57	121	22	6	0	60	50	60	16	.244	.313
Casey Stengel	rf-ph	4	11	2	4	0	0	0	0	0	1	0	**.364**	.364	3	1	1		of	127	462	66	129	27	8	8	53	33	51	11	.279	.424
Hy Myers	cf	5	22	2	4	0	0	1	3	0	3	0	.182	.318	10	1	0		of	113	412	54	108	12	14	3	36	21	35	17	.262	.381
Zack Wheat	lf	5	19	2	4	0	1	0	1	2	2	1	.211	.316	14	0	1		of	149	568	76	177	32	13	9	73	43	49	19	.312	**.461**
Chief Meyers	c	3	10	0	2	0	1	0	0	1	0	0	.200	.400	21	7	0		c	80	239	21	59	10	3	0	21	26	15	2	.247	.314
Jimmy Johnston	ph-rf	3	10	1	3	0	1	0	0	1	0	0	.300	.500	1	0	1		of	118	425	58	107	13	8	1	26	35	38	22	.252	.327
Otto Miller	c	2	8	0	1	0	0	0	0	0	1	0	.125	.125	8	3	0		c	73	216	16	55	9	2	1	17	7	29	6	.255	.329
Fred Merkle	ph-1b	3	4	0	1	0	0	0	1	2	0	0	.250	.250	9	1	1	c	1b	23	69	6	16	1	0	0	2	7	4	2	.232	.246
Ollie O'Mara	ph	1	1	0	0	0	0	0	0	0	1	0	.000	.000					ss	72	193	18	39	5	2	0	15	12	20	10	.202	.249
Gus Getz	ph	1	1	0	0	0	0	0	0	0	0	0	.000	.000					3b-ss	40	96	9	21	1	2	0	8	0	5	9	.219	.271
Sherry Smith	p	1	5	0	1	1	0	0	0	0	0	0	.200	.400	1	6	0		p	38	77	4	21	1	2	0	7	4	18	1	.273	.338
Jeff Pfeffer	p-ph	4	4	0	1	0	0	0	0	0	2	0	.250	.250	0	2	0		p	43	122	5	34	2	2	0	12	4	32	2	.279	.328
Rube Marquard	p	2	3	0	0	0	0	0	0	0	1	0	.000	.000	0	2	0		p	36	63	·3	9	0	1	0	5	4	17	1	.143	.175
Jack Coombs	p	1	3	0	1	0	0	0	1	0	0	0	.333	.333	0	2	0		p	27	61	2	11	2	6	0	3	2	10	0	.180	.213
Larry Cheney	p	1	0	0	0	0	0	0	0	0	0	0	—	—	0	0	1		p	41	79	4	9	2	0	0	2	5	29	2	.114	.139
Nap Rucker	p	1	0	0	0	0	0	0	0	0	0	0	—	—					p	9	11	1	1	0	0	0	2	0	2	0	.09	.091
Wheezer Dell	p	1	0	0	0	0	0	0	0	0	0	0	—	—					p	32	44	1	4	0	0	0	3	1	14	0	.091	.091
Ed Appleton	Did not play																		p	14	12	1	2	0	0	0	0	0	0	0	.167	.167
Duster Mails	Did not play																		p	11	4	1	1	0	0	0	0	0	2	0	.250	.250
team total		5	170	13	34	2	5	1	11	14	19	1	.200	.288	142	66	13			156	5234	585	**1366**	195	80	28	493	355	550	187	**.261**	**.345**

Double Plays—2
Left on Bases—30

c—from New York (N)
Artie Dede (c), Bunny Fabrique (ss), Dave Hickman (of), John Kelleher (3b-ss), Lew McCarty (c-1b), Hack Miller (of), Al Nixon (of), Red Smyth (2b), Mack Wheat (c), Leon Cadore (p) also played for the Robins during the season.

PITCHING

BOSTON RED SOX

	WORLD SERIES STATISTICS G	GS	CG	IP	H	R	ER	BB	SO	W	L	SV	ERA	REGULAR SEASON STATISTICS G	GS	CG	IP	H	ER	BB	SO	W	L	Pct	SV	ShO	ERA
Ernie Shore	2	**2**	1	**17⅔**	12	6	3	4	**9**	**2**	0	0	1.53	38	27	10	226	221	66	49	62	17	10	.630	1	3	2.63
Babe Ruth	1	1	1	14	6	1	1	3	4	1	0	0	**0.64**	44	**40**	23	324	230	63	118	170	23	12	.657	1	**9**	**1.75**
Dutch Leonard	1	1	1	9	5	2	1	4	3	1	0	0	1.00	48	34	17	274	244	72	66	144	18	11	.621	5	6	2.36
Carl Mays	2	1	0	5⅓	8	4	3	3	2	0	1	**1**	5.06	44	25	14	245	208	65	74	76	18	13	.581	3	2	2.39
Rube Foster	1	0	0	3	3	0	0	0	1	0	0	0	0.00	33	20	9	182	173	62	86	53	13	8	.619	3	3	3.07
Vean Gregg	Did not play													21	7	3	78	71	26	30	41	2	5	.286	0	0	3.00
Sad Sam Jones	Did not play													12	0	0	27	25	11	10	7	0	1	.000	1	0	3.67
Weldon Wyckoff	Did not play													8	0	0	23	19	12	18	18	0	0	—	1	0	4.70
team total	5	5	3	49	34	13	8	14	19	4	1	1	1.47	156	156	76	1411	1221	388	463	584	**91**	63	**.591**	16	**23**	2.47

BROOKLYN ROBINS

	WORLD SERIES STATISTICS G	GS	CG	IP	H	R	ER	BB	SO	W	L	SV	ERA	REGULAR SEASON STATISTICS G	GS	CG	IP	H	ER	BB	SO	W	L	Pct	SV	ShO	ERA
Sherry Smith	1	1	1	13⅓	7	2	2	**6**	2	0	1	0	1.35	36	23	15	219	193	57	48	67	14	10	.583	1	4	2.34
Rube Marquard	2	**2**	0	11	**12**	**9**	**8**	**6**	**9**	0	**2**	0	6.55	36	20	15	205	169	36	38	107	13	6	.684	5	2	1.58
Jeff Pfeffer	**3**	1	0	10⅔	7	5	2	4	5	0	1	**1**	1.69	41	37	30	329	274	70	63	128	25	11	.694	1	6	1.91
Jack Coombs	1	1	0	6⅓	7	3	3	1	1	1	0	0	4.26	27	21	10	159	136	47	44	47	13	8	.619	0	3	2.66
Larry Cheney	1	0	0	3	4	2	1	1	5	0	0	0	3.00	41	32	15	253	178	54	105	166	18	12	.600	0	5	1.92
Nap Rucker	1	0	0	2	1	0	0	0	3	0	0	0	0.00	9	4	1	37	34	7	7	14	2	1	.667	0	0	1.70
Wheezer Dell	1	0	0	1	1	0	0	0	0	0	0	0	0.00	32	16	9	155	143	39	43	76	8	9	.471	1	2	2.26
Ed Appleton	Did not play													14	3	1	47	49	16	18	14	1	2	.333	1	0	3.06
Duster Mails	Did not play													11	0	0	17	15	7	9	13	0	1	.000	0	0	3.71
team total	5	5	1	47⅓	39	21	16	18	25	1	4	1	3.04	156	156	96	**1427**	1201	336	372	634	**94**	60	**.610**	9	22	**2.12**

Total Attendance—162,859 Average Attendance—32,572 Winning Player's Share—$3,910 Losing Player's Share—$2,835

1917
Ulcers in the Afternoon

The White Sox hadn't been in a World Series since the Hitless Wonders of 1906, but this year's championship squad had a full cupboard of hitters. Eddie Collins, Joe Jackson, and Happy Felsch packed the middle of the Chicago lineup with three of the most dangerous, respect-inducing bats in baseball. Manager Pants Rowland also had the game's top defensive catcher in Ray Schalk and a deep pitching staff headed by 28-game-winner Eddie Cicotte. Dissension split the White Sox into two exclusive cliques, but the team still had enough talent to take the American League pennant.

The National League champion Giants had no such cliques, but they were united in their fear and respect for manager John McGraw. When his team fell apart after winning the 1913 pennant, McGraw ripped the club apart, finishing in last place in 1915. But with a combination of youths, experienced pickups, and a few holdovers, McGraw pieced together a squad that took the pennant by an easy 10 games. McGraw's offensive aces were holdovers Dave Robertson and George Burns, ex-Cub Heinie Zimmerman, and Federal League product Benny Kauff. Five solid starters made the New York staff a strong point, with 21-game-winner Ferdie Schupp the standard-bearer.

But McGraw held Schupp out of game one in Chicago and instead started 18-game-winner Slim Sallee, a veteran left-hander. The White Sox entrusted the ball to Cicotte, and the shine-ball expert scattered seven hits in taking a 2–1 win, backed by a fourth-inning homer by Felsch. McGraw then called on Schupp in game two, but the ace lefty was knocked out in the second inning; three Giant relievers couldn't stem the tide, and the White Sox pounded out a 7–2 victory behind Red Faber's spitball. A fourth consecutive Series loss stared McGraw and his Giants in the eye, but Rube Benton, the third southpaw on the New York staff, bested Cicotte 2–0 in the third game in the Polo Grounds. Schupp, so rudely handled by the White Sox in game two, came back in game four to blank the Sox 5–0, with Benny Kauff smashing two homers off Faber to pin him with the loss.

With the Series tied at 2–2, the site shifted to Chicago for game five, with Slim Sallee facing the White Sox's Reb Russell. A walk and two base hits chased Russell from the mound in the first inning before he could retire anybody, and manager Rowland brought on Cicotte to put the fire out. The Giants came out of that inning with two runs, then kept chipping away at Cicotte and Lefty Williams, who came in the game in the seventh, to run their lead to 5–2 after six and a half innings. But Sallee was running low on gas, and the Sox scored three times in the bottom of the seventh to knot the score at 5–5. McGraw stubbornly stayed with Sallee into the eighth and lived to regret it; before he could rush Pol Perritt into the game in relief, the White Sox had broken the game open with three runs. Credit for the 8–5 Chicago win went to Faber, who pitched the last two innings in relief.

Now the teams traveled back to New York, and the final act was set. With Faber and Benton pitching, neither team scored through the first three innings. In the fourth, though, the Giants made the sort of mistakes which could only set McGraw fuming in the dugout and contribute to a good case of ulcers. Leadoff batter Eddie Collins reached second when third baseman Zimmerman fielded his easy grounder and heaved the ball past first baseman Walter Holke. Then Jackson hit an easy fly to right field which Robertson dropped, putting Collins on third and Jackson on first. Felsch then hit back to the mound, and Collins was caught in a rundown between third and home. Somehow, Collins sprinted past catcher Bill Rariden when Zimmerman had the ball, and since neither Benton nor Holke had bothered backing up the play, the third baseman had no alternative but to chase Collins down the line, easily losing the footrace. Unnerved by the support he was getting in the field, Benton then coughed up a two-run single to Chick Gandil. Faber didn't need any more than that, and he took the decisive game 4–2. Fans berated Zimmerman for "chasing" Collins across the plate, but he often pointed out that the only person he could have thrown the ball to was home-plate umpire Bill Klem.

Game 1 October 6 at Chicago

New York	Pos	AB	R	H	RBI	PO	A	E
Burns	lf	3	0	1	0	2	0	0
Herzog	2b	4	0	1	0	3	1	0
Kauff	cf	4	0	0	0	0	0	0
Zimmerman	3b	4	0	0	0	1	3	0
Fletcher	ss	4	0	0	0	2	3	0
Robertson	rf	4	0	1	0	0	1	0
Holke	1b	3	0	2	0	14	0	0
McCarty	c	3	1	1	0	2	1	1
Sallee	p	3	0	1	1	0	6	0
Totals		32	1	7	1	24	15	1

Pitching	IP	H	R	ER	BB	SO
New York						
Sallee (L)	8	7	2	2	0	2
Chicago						
Cicotte (W)	9	7	1	1	1	2

Chicago	Pos	AB	R	H	RBI	PO	A	E
S. Collins	rf	4	1	3	0	1	0	0
McMullin	3b	3	0	1	1	0	3	0
E. Collins	2b	3	0	0	0	2	1	0
Jackson	lf	3	0	0	0	5	0	0
Felsch	cf	3	1	1	1	4	0	0
Gandil	1b	3	0	0	0	10	1	0
Weaver	ss	3	0	0	0	2	1	1
Schalk	c	3	0	0	0	3	0	0
Cicotte	p	3	0	1	0	0	4	0
Totals		28	2	7	2	27	10	1

Doubles—S. Collins, McMullin, Robertson. Triple—McCarty. Home Rum—Felsch. Stolen Bases—Burns, Gandil. Sacrifice Hit—McMullin. Double Play—Weaver to E. Collins to Gandil. Left on Bases—New York 5, Chicago 3. Umpires—O'Loughlin (A), Klem (N), Rigler (N), Evans (A). Attendance—32,000. Time of Game—1:48.

N.Y. 000 010 000
Chi. 001 100 00x

1st Inning
New York
Burns singled through the box
1 Herzog flied to Jackson in left-center.
2 Kauff flied to left.
Burns stole second.
3 Zimmerman flied to center.
Chicago
S. Collins singled to right.
1 McMullin sacrificed S. Collins to second, Sallee to Holke.
2 E. Collins grounded to short, S. Collins going to third.
3 Jackson popped to Herzog, making an over the shoulder catch in short center.

2nd Inning
New York
1 Fletcher fouled to Gandil.
2 Robertson rolled out down the first base line, Cicotte to Gandil.
Holke beat out an infield hit between first and second as Cicotte failed to cover first.
3 Holke was picked off first, Cicotte to Gandil.
Chicago
1 Felsch popped to Fletcher in short left.
2 Gandil lined to Zimmerman who after dropping the ball still threw Gandil out at first.
3 Weaver bounced back to the mound.

3rd Inning
New York
1 McCarty flied to center.
2 Sallee popped to short.
Burns walked.
Herzog singled to short right, Burns going to second.
3 Kauff fouled to Gandil.
Chicago
1 Schalk grounded to third.
Cicotte singled to center.
S. Collins hit a long single to the right field corner, but Cicotte was
2 out trying for third, Robertson to Zimmerman as S. Collins took second. McMullin doubled to center, S. Collins scoring the first run of the Series.
3 E. Collins fouled to Fletcher just outside the left field foul line.

4th Inning
New York
1 Zimmerman fouled to Schalk.
2 Fletcher grounded to third.
Robertson lined a double over E. Collins' head into right-center.
3 Holke grounded to third.
Chicago
1 Jackson flied to left.
Felsch hit a home-run into the left-center field bleachers.
2 Gandil bounced back to the mound.
3 Weaver flied to left.

5th Inning
New York
McCarty tripled to the right-center field bleacher wall.
Sallee singled to right, scoring McCarty.
1,2 Burns bounced into a double play, Weaver to E. Collins to Gandil.
3 Herzog struck out on three pitches.
Chicago
1 Schalk dribbled out to third.
2 Cicotte bounced back to the mound on a full count.
3 S. Collins rolled to first.

6th Inning
New York
1 Kauff struck out.
2 Zimmerman popped to Gandil, between first and second.
3 Fletcher flied to left.
Chicago
1 McMullin grounded to second.
2 E. Collins struck out.
3 Jackson grounded to first.

7th Inning
New York
1 Robertson grounded to third.
Holke singled inside of first.
2 McCarty flied to Jackson, making a great diving catch, rolling over but not dropping the ball.
3 Sallee flied to center.
Chicago
1 Fetsch bounced back to the mound.
Gandil beat out a hard smash to third.
2 Weaver struck out on three pitches.
Gandil stole second and continued on to third on McCarty's wild throw.
3 Schalk grounded to short.

8th Inning
New York
1 Burns lined to center.
2 Herzog flied to Jackson in left-center.
Kauff beat out a bunt to short.
3 Kauff was out trying to steal second, Cicotte to Gandil to E. Collins.
Chicago
1 Cicotte grounded to short on a 3–2 count.
S. Collins doubled over third for his third hit of the game.
2 McMullin grounded to Sallee who caught S. Collins at third, Sallee to Zimmerman to Herzog.
3 McMullin out trying to steal second, McCarty to Herzog.

9th Inning
New York
1 Zimmerman bounced back to the mound.
2 Fletcher flied to Weaver in short left.
3 Robertson flied to right.

Game 2 October 7 at Chicago

New York	Pos	AB	R	H	RBI	PO	A	E
Burns	lf	3	0	1	0	1	0	0
Herzog	2b	4	0	0	0	2	0	0
Kauff	cf	4	0	0	0	1	0	0
Zimmerman	3b	4	0	0	0	4	2	0
Fletcher	ss	4	0	1	0	2	2	1
Robertson	rf	3	1	2	0	2	0	0
Holke	1b	3	1	1	0	6	0	0
McCarty	c	1	0	1	1	5	0	0
Rariden	c	2	0	1	0	1	3	0
Schupp	p	1	0	0	0	0	1	0
Anderson	p	0	0	0	0	0	1	0
Perritt	p	1	0	1	0	0	0	0
b Wilhoit		1	0	0	0	0	0	0
Tesreau	p	0	0	0	0	0	0	0
Totals		31	2	8	1	24	9	1

a Struck out for S. Collins in 2nd.
b Lined into double play for Perritt in 8th.
Stolen Bases—E. Collins 2, Jackson. Double Plays—Herzog (unassisted), Faber to Weaver to Gandil, Felsch to E. Collins to Weaver, Weaver to Gandil. Passed Ball—McCarty. Left on Bases—New York 3, Chicago 7. Umpires—Evans, Rigler, Klem, O'Loughlin. Attendance—32,000. Time of Game—2:13.

1st Inning
New York
Burns singled over E. Collins' head into short right.
1 Herzog forced Burns at second, Gandil to Weaver.
Kauff forced Herzog at second on a fly
2 to S. Collins in right but he dropped the ball and Herzog out, S. Collins to Weaver.
3 Zimmerman grounded to second.
Chicago
1 S. Collins popped to Zimmerman in front of the plate.
2 McMullin called out on strikes.
3 E. Collins also called out on strikes.

2nd Inning
New York
1 Fletcher grounded to short.
Robertson beat out a smash to second.
Holke singled over second, Robertson stopping at second.
McCarty singled to left, Robertson scoring and when Schalk lost Jackson's throw Holke also scored and McCarty went to second. (An assist to Jackson.)
2 Schupp grounded back to the mound, McCarty going to third.
3 Burns grounded to short.
Chicago
Jackson singled to center.
Felsch singled to right, sending Jackson to third.
Gandil singled off Schupp's glove, Jackson scoring with Felsch going to third.
Weaver singled to short left, Felsch scoring as Gandil stopped at second.
1 Schalk forced Gandil at third on a bunt, Schupp to Zimmerman.
Faber walked, loading the bases.
2 Leibold, batting for S. Collins, struck out.
3 McMullin grounded to short.

3rd Inning
New York
For Chicago—Leibold playing right.
1 Herzog struck out.
2 Kauff rolled out to Faber, who made the putout.
3 Zimmerman bounced back to the mound.
Chicago
1 E. Collins rolled back to the pitcher.
Jackson singled just out of Herzog's reach.
2 Felsch struck out.
Jackson stole second.
3 Gandil struck out.

4th Inning
New York
1 Fletcher flied to Weaver in short left.
Robertson singled over Faber's head.
2 Holke forced Robertson at second, McMullin to E. Collins.
3 Holke was out attempting to steal second, Schalk to E. Collins.
Chicago
Weaver beat out a bunt which Herzog raced in on and just missed the play.
Schalk singled to right, Weaver holding up at second.
1 Faber fouled to Zimmerman near the boxes.
Leibold singled between short and second, Weaver scoring as Schalk got to third.
McMullin singled to short center, Schalk scoring as Leibold stopped at second.
For New York—Perritt came in to pitch.
E. Collins singled to right, Leibold scoring with McMullin going to third.

Chicago

Chicago	Pos	AB	R	H	RBI	PO	A	E
S. Collins	rf	3	0	0	0	1	0	0
a Leibold	rf	3	1	1	1	0	0	0
McMullin	3b	5	1	1	1	0	3	0
E. Collins	2b	4	1	2	1	4	2	0
Jackson	lf	3	1	3	2	0	1	0
Felsch	cf	4	1	1	0	2	1	0
Gandil	1b	4	0	1	1	12	1	0
Weaver	ss	4	1	3	1	7	6	0
Schalk	c	4	1	1	0	1	2	1
Faber	p	3	0	1	0	1	4	0
Totals		35	7	14	7	27	21	1

Pitching	IP	H	R	ER	BB	SO
New York						
Schupp	1⅓	4	2	2	1	2
Anderson (L)	2	5	4	4	0	3
Perritt	3⅔	5	1	1	1	0
Tesreau	1	0	0	0	1	1
Chicago						
Faber (W)	9	8	2	2	1	1

4th Inning (continued)
For New York—McCarty was injured on the play at the plate and Rariden took his place.
Jackson singled to right, McMullin and E. Collins scoring, Jackson going to second on the throw to the plate.
2,3 Felsch lined out to Herzog who nailed Jackson for an unassisted double play.

5th Inning
New York
1 Rariden bounced to third.
Perritt singled over Faber's head into short center.
2,3 Burns grounded into a double play, Faber to Weaver to Gandil.
Chicago
1 Gandil flied to right.
Weaver safe at first when Fletcher booted his grounder.
2 Schalk grounded to third, Weaver taking second.
Faber singled to right, Robertson's good throw holding Weaver to third.
Faber took second on the throw in.
3 Faber was out as he went to third however Weaver was still there, Rariden to Zimmerman.

6th Inning
New York
1 Herzog grounded to short.
2 Kauff flied to center.
3 Zimmerman flied to E. Collins in short right, Faber using only four pitches to retire the side.
Chicago
1 Leibold flied to right.
2 McMullin grounded to short.
E. Collins safe at first on a grounder to Holke.
E. Collins stole second.
Jackson walked.
E. Collins stole again.
3 Felsch grounded to first.

7th Inning
New York
Fletcher singled to left.
1 Robertson tapped out, Schalk to Gandil, Fletcher taking second.
2,3 Holke lined to Felsch, throwing to E. Collins to Weaver to double Fletcher.
Chicago
1 Gandil grounded to third.
Weaver beat out a hit to deep short.
2 Weaver out stealing, Rariden to Fletcher.
3 Schalk flied to center.

8th Inning
New York
Rariden singled to center.
1,2 Wilhoit, batting for Perritt, lined into a double play, Weaver to Gandil.
Burns walked.
3 Herzog forced Burns at second, McMullin to E. Collins.
Chicago
For New York—Tesreau the new pitcher.
1 Faber struck out.
Leibold walked.
2 Leibold out stealing, Rariden to Fletcher.
3 McMullin flied to Burns.

9th Inning
New York
1 Kauff popped to short.
2 Zimmerman bounced out, Faber to Gandil.
3 Fletcher grounded to short.

Game 3 October 10 at New York

Chicago	Pos	AB	R	H	RBI	PO	A	E
S. Collins	rf	4	0	0	0	1	0	2
McMullin	3b	4	0	0	0	0	1	0
E. Collins	2b	4	0	2	0	3	2	0
Jackson	lf	4	0	2	0	1	0	0
Felsch	cf	3	0	1	0	5	0	0
Gandil	1b	3	0	0	0	6	0	0
Weaver	ss	3	0	2	0	2	0	0
Schalk	c	3	0	0	0	9	0	0
Cicotte	p	3	0	0	0	0	1	1
Totals		31	0	5	0	24	6	3

Pitching	IP	H	R	ER	BB	SO
Chicago						
Cicotte (L)	8	8	2	2	0	8
New York						
Benton (W)	9	5	0	0	0	5

1st Inning
Chicago
1 S. Collins popped to Rariden.
2 McMullin struck out on a bad pitch.
E. Collins singled to center.
3 Jackson bounced back to the mound.
New York
1 Burns struck out.
2 Herzog flied to center.
Kauff safely to second as S. Collins dropped his fly to right.
Zimmerman beat out a roller to third, Kauff going to third.
3 Fletcher grounded to third.

2nd Inning
Chicago
1 Felsch fouled to Holke.
2 Gandil fouled to Holke.
Weaver singled to right.
Weaver safe at second when Fletcher dropped Rariden's throw.
3 Schalk robbed of a hit by Burns in deep left.
New York
Robertson singled past the mound.
1 Holke forced Robertson at second, E. Collins unassisted.
Rariden singled to center, Holke racing to third.
2 Benton flied to short center, Felsch threw to the plate to hold Holke at third and allowed Rariden to get to second on the throw.
3 Burns again struck out.

3rd Inning
Chicago
1 Cicotte fouled to Rariden.
S. Collins got a second life when Holke dropped his foul for an error.
2 S. Collins grounded to second.
3 McMullin fouled to Rariden.
New York
1 Herzog struck out.
Kauffman safely to second as S. Collins dropped his long fly in left-center.
2 Zimmerman grounded to short, Kauff getting to third.
3 Fletcher grounded to second.

4th Inning
Chicago
1 E. Collins grounded to third.
2 Jackson bounced over Benton's head directly to Fletcher.
Felsch singled to left.
3 Gandil robbed of a hit by a fielding gem by Robertson in deep right.
New York
Robertson boomed a triple to deep right.
Holke lined a double to left, scoring Robertson.
1 Rariden sacrificed Holke to third, Cicotte to E. Collins.
2 Benton struck out.
Burns blooped a little single down the third base line, Cicotte threw to first wildly and over Gandil's head. Burns on second by way of a hit and an error.
3 Herzog fouled to Gandil at the right field wall.

New York

New York	Pos	AB	R	H	RBI	PO	A	E
Burns	lf	4	0	1	1	1	0	0
Herzog	2b	4	0	1	0	1	1	0
Kauff	cf	4	0	0	0	0	0	0
Zimmerman	3b	4	0	1	0	0	3	0
Fletcher	ss	4	0	0	0	1	4	1
Robertson	rf	4	1	3	0	1	0	0
Holke	1b	4	1	1	1	15	0	1
Rariden	c	2	0	1	0	7	4	0
Benton	p	3	0	0	0	1	2	0
Totals		33	2	8	2	27	14	2

Doubles—Holke, Weaver. Triple—Robertson. Stolen Base—Robertson. Sacrifice Hit—Rariden. Double Play—Rariden to Herzog. Left on Bases—Chicago 4, New York 8. Umpires—Klem, O'Loughlin, Evans, Rigler. Attendance—33,616. Time of Game—1:55.

5th Inning
Chicago
1 Weaver rolled to short.
2 Schalk struck out but Rariden had to throw him out, dropping the third strike.
3 Cicotte struck out.
New York
1 Kauff fouled to Schalk.
2 Zimmerman flied to center.
3 Fletcher struck out.

6th Inning
Chicago
1 S. Collins grounded to short.
2 McMullin bounced back to the mound.
3 Collins grounded to first.
New York
1 Robertson flied to center.
2 Holke struck out.
3 Rariden bounced to second.

7th Inning
Chicago
1 Jackson grounded to second.
2 Felsch called out on strikes.
3 Gandil grounded to third.
New York
1 Benton struck out on a very high pitch.
2 Burns bounced to short on a full count.
Herzog looped a Texas League single just beyond the infield.
3 Kauff flied to center.

8th Inning
Chicago
Weaver got a Texas League double just out of Burns and Fletcher's reach.
1 Schalk grounded to Benton, who ran to third and tagged out Weaver.
2,3 Cicotte struck out on a full count, as Schalk was out trying for second, Rariden to Herzog.
New York
1 Zimmerman lined to second.
2 Fletcher lined to right, this time S. Collins catching the ball without dropping it.
Robertson lined a single through the box, his third hit of the game.
Robertson stole second.
3 Holke became Cicotte's eighth strike-out victim as he was called out on strikes.

9th Inning
Chicago
1 S. Collins rolled out, Rariden to Holke.
2 McMullin grounded to short.
E. Collins beat out a hit down the first base line.
3 Jackson fouled to Fletcher, behind third.

Game 4 October 11 at New York

Chicago	Pos	AB	R	H	RBI	PO	A	E
S. Collins	rf	4	0	2	0	0	0	0
McMullin	3b	4	0	1	0	1	2	0
E. Collins	2b	3	0	1	0	1	6	0
Jackson	lf	4	0	0	0	0	0	0
Felsch	cf	4	0	0	0	2	1	0
Gandil	1b	4	0	1	0	15	0	0
Weaver	ss	3	0	0	0	0	1	0
Schalk	c	3	0	2	0	6	3	0
Faber	p	2	0	0	0	0	4	0
a Risberg		1	0	0	0	0	0	0
Danforth	p	0	0	0	0	0	1	0
Totals		32	0	7	0	24	18	0

a Flied out for Faber in 8th.

Double—E. Collins. Triple—Zimmerman. Home Runs—Kauff 2. Stolen Base—E. Collins. Sacrifice Hit—Herzog. Double Plays—Herzog to Fletcher to Holke, Faber to Schalk to Gandil. Hit by Pitcher—Holke (by Faber). Wild Pitch—Faber. Left on Bases—Chicago 6, New York 3. Umpires—Rigler, Evans, O'Loughlin, Klem. Attendance—27,746. Time of Game—2:09.

Chi.   000 000 000
N.Y. 000 110 12 x

New York	Pos	AB	R	H	RBI	PO	A	E
Burns	lf	4	0	1	0	2	0	0
Herzog	2b	3	1	1	0	3	4	1
Kauff	cf	4	2	2	3	1	0	0
Zimmerman	3b	4	0	1	0	2	2	0
Fletcher	ss	4	1	2	0	1	3	0
Robertson	rf	3	1	1	0	1	0	0
Holke	1b	2	0	1	0	9	0	0
Rariden	c	3	0	0	1	7	1	0
Schupp	p	3	0	1	1	1	3	0
Totals		30	5	10	5	27	13	1

Pitching	IP	H	R	ER	BB	SO
Chicago						
Faber (L)	7	7	3	3	0	3
Danforth	1	3	2	2	0	2
New York						
Schupp (W)	9	7	0	0	1	7

1st Inning
Chicago
1 S. Collins bounced to third. McMullin singled on a bouncer past Zimmerman.
2 E. Collins called out on strikes.
3 Jackson grounded to second.
New York
1 Burns flied to Felsch in deep right-center.
2 Herzog grounded to second.
3 Kauff grounded to third.

2nd Inning
Chicago
1 Felsch grounded to short.
2 Gandil bounced back to the mound.
3 Weaver struck out on a pitch over his head.
New York
1 Zimmerman grounded to second.
2 Fletcher grounded to third.
3 Robertson grounded back to the mound.

3rd Inning
Chicago
Schalk singled to left.
1 Faber blooped a bunt to Schupp.
2 S. Collins singled to right.
3 McMullin struck out on a very foolish pitch, way to the outside.
New York
1 Holke struck out, but had to be thrown out at first.
2 Rariden fouled to McMullin.
3 Schupp struck out.

4th Inning
Chicago
E. Collins doubled on a grounder past third and into left.
1 Jackson popped to second after fouling off two bunt attempts.
2 E. Collins was picked off second, Schupp to Herzog to Zimmerman.
3 Felsch struck out.
New York
1 Burns struck out.
2 Herzog grounded to second. Kauff got his first hit of the Series, an inside-the-park home run deep into center over Felsch's head.
3 Zimmerman grounded to second.

5th Inning
Chicago
Gandil singled to left-center.
1,2 Weaver dribbled into a double play Herzog to Fletcher to Holke. Schalk singled past second.
3 Faber rolled back to the mound.
New York
Fletcher singled to right. Robertson beat out a bunt to third, Fletcher going to second. Holke also beat out a bunt to third, loading the bases.
1,2 Rariden forced Fletcher at the plate, Faber to Schalk who threw to Gandil doubling Rariden at first.
3 Schupp rolled a single just past second, Robertson scoring but as Holke also tried to score he was an easy out, Felsch to Schalk.

6th Inning
Chicago
S. Collins singled to left.
1 McMullin called out on strikes. S. Collins safe at second on Herzog's error, losing Rariden's throw.
2 E. Collins flied to left.
3 Jackson grounded to second.
New York
Burns beat out a hard hit to second.
1 Herzog sacrificed Burns to second, Faber to Gandil.
2 Kauff flied to deep center, Burns going to third after the catch.
3 Zimmerman grounded to second for the third consecutive time.

7th Inning
Chicago
1 Felsch called out on strikes.
2 Gandil grounded to short.
3 Weaver popped to Herzog near the pitcher's box.
New York
Fletcher pounced on the first pitch for a single. On a wild pitch Fletcher went all the way to third.
1 Robertson bounced back to the mound, Fletcher holding at third.
2 Rariden grounded to second, Fletcher scoring.
3 Schupp grounded to short.

8th Inning
Chicago
1 Schalk lined to Burns.
2 Risberg, batting for Faber, flied to right on a full count.
S. Collins singled to left.
3 McMullin popped to second.
New York
For Chicago—Danforth pitching.
1 Burns called out on strikes. Herzog singled to center. Kauff got his second homer of the game, a two-run shot into the lower tier of the right field stands. Zimmerman tripled to the right field fence.
2 Fletcher struck out, but had to be thrown out at first as Zimmerman was held on third.
3 Zimmerman was out trying to steal home, Danforth to Schalk.

9th Inning
Chicago
E. Collins walked, the first pass given up in the game.
1 Jackson grounded to third on a full count, E. Collins moving up to second. E. Collins stole third.
2 Felsch fouled to Zimmerman.
3 Gandil flied to center.

Game 5 October 13 at Chicago

New York	Pos	AB	R	H	RBI	PO	A	E
Burns	lf	4	2	1	1	3	0	0
Herzog	2b	5	0	0	1	0	1	1
Kauff	cf	5	0	2	0	2	0	0
Zimmerman	3b	5	1	1	0	1	2	1
Fletcher	ss	5	1	1	0	2	3	1
Thorpe	rf	0	0	0	0	0	0	0
a Robertson	rf	5	0	3	1	2	0	0
Holke	1b	5	0	0	0	11	0	0
Rariden	c	3	1	3	1	3	1	0
Sallee	p	3	0	0	0	0	2	0
Perritt	p	0	0	0	0	0	0	0
Totals		40	5	12	5	24	9	3

Pitching	IP	H	R	ER	BB	SO
New York						
Sallee (L)	7⅓	13	8	7	4	2
Perritt	⅓	1	0	0	0	0
Chicago						
Russell	*0	2	2	1	1	0
Cicotte	6	8	2	2	1	3
Williams	1	2	1	1	0	3
Faber (W)	2	0	0	0	0	1

*Pitched to three batters in 1st.

1st Inning
New York
Burns walked on four pitches. Herzog singled to right-center, Burns going to third. Kauff doubled to the right field wall, Burns scoring as Herzog stopped at third. For Chicago—Cicotte came in to pitch.
1 Zimmerman grounded to Weaver who threw to Schalk getting Herzog at the plate as Kauff went to third.
2 Fletcher grounded to McMullin who threw to Schalk getting Kauff at the plate. Robertson, batting for Jim Thorpe the listed right fielder, singled to center, scoring Zimmerman. Fletcher went to third and Robertson to second on the throw to the plate.
3 Holke grounded back to the mound.
Chicago
1 S. Collins popped to third. McMullin walked. E. Collins singled to center, McMullin stopping at second.
2 Jackson flied to left. Felsch safe at first and loading the bases as Fletcher booted his grounder.
3 Gandil popped to first.

2nd Inning
New York
Rariden singled past second.
1 Sallee forced Rariden on a bunt, Gandil to Weaver.
2 Burns struck out. Herzog safe on Weaver's fumble, Sallee getting to second.
3 Kauff grounded to second.
Chicago
1 Weaver out, Fletcher to Holke.
2 Schalk was out, short to first. Cicotte walked.
3 S. Collins fouled to Rariden.

3rd Inning
New York
Zimmerman blooped a single to right-center. Zimmerman safely to third base on a pick-off after Weaver dropped Gandil's throw.
1,2 Fletcher lined into a double play, McMullin to Gandil. Robertson beat out a slowroller to the mound.
3 Holke struck out.
Chicago
1 McMullin flied to right. E. Collins walked.
2 Jackson to short right. Felsch doubled to left, scoring E. Collins.
3 Gandil flied to center.

4th Inning
New York
Rariden singled between first and second.
1 Sallee sacrificed Rariden to second, Gandil unassisted. Burns singled to right, scoring Rariden and took second on S. Collins' fumble. Herzog safe at first on Weaver's fumble as Burns got to third. Kauff safe on Gandil's throwing error to Cicotte, Burns scoring and Herzog getting to third.
2,3 Zimmerman hit into a double play, McMullin to E. Collins to Gandil.
Chicago
1 Weaver bounced to third.
2 Schalk grounded to first.
3 Cicotte flied to left.

5th Inning
New York
1 Fletcher lined to left. Robertson singled to right.
2 Holke popped to short. Rariden was intentionally walked.
3 Sallee struck out.

N.Y. 200 200 100
Chi.   001 001 33 x

Chicago	Pos	AB	R	H	RBI	PO	A	E
S. Collins	rf	5	1	1	0	1	0	1
McMullin	3b	3	0	0	1	1	4	0
E. Collins	2b	3	2	1	1	4	0	0
Jackson	lf	5	2	3	0	3	0	0
Felsch	cf	5	1	2	3	3	0	0
Gandil	1b	5	1	2	1	10	1	1
Weaver	ss	4	1	1	0	2	2	3
Schalk	c	3	0	1	0	9	0	0
Russell	p	0	0	0	0	0	0	0
Cicotte	p	1	0	0	0	0	1	0
b Risberg		1	0	1	1	0	0	0
Williams	p	0	0	0	0	0	0	1
c Lynn		1	0	0	0	0	0	0
Faber	p	0	0	0	0	0	1	0
Totals		37	8	14	6	27	13	6

a Singled to center for Thorpe in 1st.
b Singled for Cicotte in 6th.
c Struck out for Williams in 7th.

Doubles—Felsch, Fletcher, Gandil, Kauff. Stolen Bases—Kauff, Robertson, Schalk. Sacrifice Hits—McMullin, Sallee. Double Plays—McMullin to Gandil, McMullin to E. Collins to Gandil. Left on Bases—New York 11, Chicago 10. Umpires—O'Loughlin, Klem, Rigler, Evans. Attendance—27,323. Time of Game—2:37.

5th Inning (continued)
Chicago
1 S. Collins struck out.
2 McMullin flied to Kauff in right-center. E. Collins lined a single to left. Jackson singled off Sallee's glove, E. Collins going to second.
3 Felsch rolled out to the pitcher.

6th Inning
New York
1 Burns flied to left.
2 Herzog grounded to left. Kauff singled to left. Kauff stole second.
3 Zimmerman grounded to second.
Chicago
1 Gandil bounced back to the mound. Weaver singled to left. Schalk singled to right-center, Weaver going to third. Risberg, pinch-hitting for Cicotte, singled to right, scoring Weaver as Schalk stopped at second.
2 S. Collins grounded to first, advancing both runners.
3 McMullin grounded to second.

7th Inning
New York
For Chicago—Williams now pitching. Fletcher doubled over Jackson's head in deep left. Robertson safe at first when Williams dropped his liner bunt.
1 Holke struck out. Rariden singled to right, Fletcher scoring and Robertson stopping at second.
2 Sallee struck out.
3 Burns struck out.
Chicago
1 E. Collins popped to short. Jackson singled to left. Felsch singled to center, Jackson going to second. Gandil doubled to right-center, scoring Jackson and Felsch.
2 Weaver grounded to short, Gandil going to third. Schalk walked. Schalk stole second, Herzog muffed Sallee's throw, Gandil scoring and Schalk taking third.
3 Lynn, pinch-hitting for Williams, struckout.

8th Inning
New York
For Chicago—Faber the fourth pitcher.
1 Herzog struck out.
2 Kauff grounded back to the mound.
3 Zimmerman lined to right.
Chicago
S. Collins singled to short right.
1 McMullin sacrificed S. Collins to second, Zimmerman to Holke. E. Collins singled to center, scoring S. Collins with the tie-breaking run. Jackson singled to center, E. Collins going to third. Kauff threw to Zimmerman but missed Collins; then Zimmerman threw wildly to get Jackson and E. Collins scored as Jackson got to third. For New York—Perritt came in to pitch. Felsch singled to center, scoring Jackson.
2 Gandil flied to left.
3 Felsch caught stealing, Rariden to Fletcher.

9th Inning
New York
1 Fletcher grounded to short.
2 Robertson flied to left.
3 Holke bounced to third.

Game 6 October 15 at New York

Chi.   000 300 001
N.Y.   000 020 000

Chicago	Pos	AB	R	H	RBI	PO	A	E
S. Collins	rf	3	0	0	0	1	0	0
b Leibold	rf	2	0	1	1	1	0	0
McMullin	3b	5	0	0	0	0	1	0
E. Collins	2b	4	1	1	0	1	8	0
Jackson	lf	4	1	1	0	1	0	0
Felsch	cf	3	1	0	0	3	0	0
Gandil	1b	4	0	2	2	14	0	0
Weaver	ss	4	1	1	0	2	2	0
Schalk	c	3	0	1	0	4	1	1
Faber	p	2	0	0	0	0	0	0
Totals		34	4	7	3	27	12	1

Pitching	IP	H	R	ER	BB	SO
Chicago						
Faber (W)	9	6	2	1	2	4
New York						
Benton (L)	5	4	3	0	1	3
Perritt	4	3	1	1	2	3

New York	Pos	AB	R	H	RBI	PO	A	E
Burns	lf	4	1	0	0	2	0	0
Herzog	2b	4	0	2	2	2	5	0
Kauff	cf	4	0	0	0	2	0	1
Zimmerman	3b	4	0	0	0	1	2	1
Fletcher	ss	4	0	1	0	1	2	0
Robertson	rf	3	0	1	0	0	1	1
Holke	1b	4	0	1	0	12	0	0
Rariden	c	3	1	0	0	7	1	0
Benton	p	1	0	0	0	0	0	0
a Wilhoit		0	0	0	0	0	0	0
Perritt	p	1	0	1	0	0	1	0
c McCarty		1	0	0	0	0	0	0
Totals		33	2	6	2	27	12	3

a Walked for Benton in 5th.
b Popped out for S. Collins in 7th.
c Grounded out for Perritt in 9th.

Double—Holke. Triple—Herzog. Sacrifice Hit—Faber. Hit by Pitcher—Robertson (by Faber). Passed Ball—Schalk. Left on Bases—Chicago 7, New York 7. Umpires—Klem, O'Loughlin, Evans, Rigler. Attendance—33,969. Time of Game—2:18.

1st Inning
Chicago
1 S. Collins rolled to short.
2 McMullin fouled to Rariden.
  E. Collins lined a single to right.
3 Jackson rolled to second.
New York
1 Burns grounded to second on the first pitch by Faber appearing in his fourth game as a pitcher.
  Herzog singled to left.
2 Kauff struck out.
3 Zimmerman flied to left.

2nd Inning
Chicago
1 Felsch struck out.
  Gandil singled to center.
2 Weaver grounded to second, Gandil getting to second.
3 Schalk grounded to Zimmerman, who made an excellent fielding play.
New York
1 Fletcher topped a blooper onto the first base line and was out, Schalk to Gandil
2 Robertson grounded to second.
  Holke doubled deep over Jackson's head to the left field wall.
3 Rariden grounded to second.

3rd Inning
Chicago
1 Faber struck out.
2 S. Collins popped to second.
3 McMullin called out on strikes.
New York
1 Benton struck out.
2 Burns flied to center.
3 Herzog flied to center.

4th Inning
Chicago
  E. Collins got safely to second as Zimmerman threw very high to first. Jackson was safe when Robertson dropped his fly, E. Collins going to third. Felsch grounded to Benton who threw to Zimmerman since Collins was midway between third and home. Zimmerman threw to Rariden pushing Collins closer to third and fired to Zimmerman who foolishly raced after Collins to make the tag. He chased him totally across the plate. Jackson got to third and Felsch to second while the sprint race took place.
  Gandil singled over first, scoring
1 Jackson and Felsch, but was out trying for second, Robertson to Herzog.
2 Weaver flied to left.
  Schalk singled to center.
  Faber walked.
3 S. Collins grounded to short.

4th Inning (continued)
New York
1 Kauff grounded to second.
2 Zimmerman, with the boos ringing in his ears, flied to right.
  Fletcher just beat out a hit to deep short.
3 Robertson flied to center.

5th Inning
Chicago
1 McMullin lined to Kauff, making a good running catch in short center.
2 E. Collins flied to left.
3 Jackson grounded to Herzog, who after fumbling was able to make the play to first, just beating Jackson.
New York
1 Holke called out on strikes.
  Rariden walked.
  Wilhoit, pinch-hitting for Benton, also walked.
2 Burns forced Wilhoit at second, Weaver to E. Collins as Rariden went to third.
  Herzog got a triple on a fly which S. Collins tried to make a shoe-string catch on. He missed and it went to the wall, Rariden and Burns scoring.
3 Kauff fouled to Gandil.

6th Inning
Chicago
  For New York—Perritt pitching.
  Felsch walked.
1   Felsch out trying to steal second, Rariden to Fletcher.
2 Gandil struck out on three pitches.
3 Weaver grounded to second.
New York
1 Zimmerman grounded to his usual spot, E. Collins to Gandil as Zimmerman did not even run out the grounder.
2 Fletcher fouled to Gandil.
  Robertson singled to right (his eleventh hit of the series).
3 Holke grounded to second.

7th Inning
Chicago
  Schalk walked.
1 Faber struck out.
2 Leibold, batting for Shano Collins, popped to Herzog who intentionally dropped the ball, but the umpires ruled Leibold out as Schalk remained on first. Putout goes to Holke.
3 McMullin called out on strikes.
New York
1 Rariden grounded to first.
  Perritt lined a single to center.
2 Burns popped to short.
  Perritt went to second on a short passed ball and when Schalk threw wildly to Weaver, he continued on to third.
3 Herzog popped to short.

8th Inning
Chicago
1 E. Collins grounded to first.
  Jackson singled to right.
2 Felsch popped to first.
3 Gandil flied to center.
New York
1 Kauff flied to right.
2 Zimmerman bounced a beauty over Faber's head but a great fielding play and throw by Weaver ruined Zimmerman's hope for atonement.
3 Fletcher grounded to third.

9th Inning
Chicago
  Weaver dropped a Texas League single just out of Fletcher's reach.
1 Schalk fouled to Zimmerman.
2 Faber sacrificed Weaver to second, Perritt to Holke.
  Leibold singled to center, Weaver scoring and took second on the throw to the plate.
3 McMullin grounded to third.
New York
  Robertson was hit by a pitched ball.
1 Holke grounded to second, Robertson going to second.
2 Rariden called out on strikes with a 3–2 count on him.
3 McCarty, pinch-hitting for Perritt, grounded to second.

1917 WORLD SERIES COMPOSITE BOX

	Wins	Composite Line Score				Manager	W	L	Pct.	G. Ahead
Chicago White Sox (A.L.)	4	0 2 2	9 0 1	3 3 1	- 21	Pants Rowland	100	54	.649	9
New York Giants (N.L.)	2	2 2 0	5 4 0	2 2 0	- 17	John McGraw	98	56	.636	10

(The Manager, W, L, Pct. and G. Ahead columns are headed "Regular Season".)

BATTING AND FIELDING

CHICAGO WHITE SOX

World Series Statistics

	Pos	G	AB	R	H	2B	3B	HR	RBI	BB	SO	SB	BA	SA	PO	A	E
Chick Gandil	1b	6	23	1	6	1	0	0	**5**	0	2	1	.261	.304	**67**	3	1
Eddie Collins	2b	6	22	**4**	9	1	0	0	2	**2**	3	**3**	.409	.455	11	**23**	0
Buck Weaver	ss	6	21	3	7	1	0	0	1	0	2	0	.333	.381	13	14	**4**
Fred McMullin	3b	6	24	1	3	1	0	0	2	1	**6**	0	.125	.167	2	14	0
Shano Collins	rf	6	21	2	6	1	0	0	0	0	2	0	.286	.333	4	1	3
Happy Felsch	cf	6	22	**4**	6	1	0	1	3	1	5	0	.273	.455	16	2	0
Joe Jackson	lf	6	23	**4**	7	0	0	0	2	1	0	1	.304	.304	9	1	0
Ray Schalk	c	6	19	1	5	0	0	0	0	**2**	1	1	.263	.263	32	6	2
Nemo Leibold	ph-rf	2	5	1	2	0	0	0	2	1	1	0	.400	.400	1	0	0
Swede Risberg	ph	2	2	0	1	0	0	0	1	0	0	0	.500	.500			
Byrd Lynn	ph	1	1	0	0	0	0	0	0	0	1	0	.000	.000			
Eddie Murphy		Did not play															
Ted Jourdan		Did not play															
Joe Jenkins		Did not play															
Ziggy Hasbrouck		Did not play															
Bobby Byrne		Did not play															
Red Faber	p	4	7	0	1	0	0	0	0	**2**	3	0	.143	.143	1	9	0
Eddie Cicotte	p	3	7	0	1	0	0	0	0	1	2	0	.143	.143	0	6	1
Lefty Williams	p	1	0	0	0	0	0	0	0	0	0	0	—	—	0	0	1
Dave Danforth	p	1	0	0	0	0	0	0	0	0	0	0	—	—	0	1	0
Reb Russell	p	1	0	0	0	0	0	0	0	0	0	0	—	—	0	0	0
Jim Scott		Did not play															
Joe Benz		Did not play															
Mellie Wolfgang		Did not play															
team total		6	197	21	54	6	0	1	18	11	28	6	.274	.315	156	79	12

Double Plays—6
Left on Bases—39

Regular Season Statistics

		Main Pos	G	AB	R	H	2B	3B	HR	RBI	BB	SO	SB	BA	SA
Chick Gandil		1b	149	553	53	151	9	7	0	57	30	36	16	.273	.315
Eddie Collins		2b	156	564	91	163	18	12	0	67	89	16	53	.289	.363
Buck Weaver		3b	118	447	64	127	16	5	3	32	27	29	19	.284	.362
Fred McMullin		3b	59	194	35	46	2	1	0	12	27	17	9	.237	.258
Shano Collins		of	82	252	38	59	13	3	1	14	10	27	14	.234	.321
Happy Felsch		of	152	575	75	177	17	10	6	102	33	52	26	.308	.403
Joe Jackson		of	146	538	91	162	20	17	5	75	57	25	13	.301	.429
Ray Schalk		c	140	424	48	96	12	5	2	51	59	27	19	.226	.292
Nemo Leibold		of	125	428	59	101	12	6	0	29	74	34	27	.236	.292
Swede Risberg		ss	149	474	59	96	20	8	1	45	59	65	16	.203	.285
Byrd Lynn		c	35	72	7	16	2	0	0	5	7	11	1	.222	.250
Eddie Murphy		of	53	51	9	16	2	1	0	16	5	1	4	.314	.392
Ted Jourdan		1b	17	34	2	5	0	1	0	2	1	3	0	.147	.206
Joe Jenkins		ph	10	9	0	1	0	0	0	2	0	5	0	.111	.111
Ziggy Hasbrouck		2b	2	1	1	0	0	0	0	0	0	0	0	.000	.000
Bobby Byrne	a	2b	1	1	0	0	0	0	0	0	0	0	0	.000	.000
Red Faber		p	41	69	1	4	1	0	0	2	10	38	0	.058	.072
Eddie Cicotte		p	49	112	6	20	2	0	0	8	12	23	1	.179	.196
Lefty Williams		p	45	67	5	6	0	1	0	2	8	19	0	.090	.119
Dave Danforth		p	50	46	3	6	2	1	0	5	6	19	1	.130	.217
Reb Russell		p	39	68	5	19	3	3	0	9	2	10	0	.279	.412
Jim Scott		p	24	42	1	5	0	0	0	0	4	9	0	.119	.119
Joe Benz		p	19	30	4	5	1	0	0	0	0	11	0	.167	.200
Mellie Wolfgang		p	5	4	0	0	0	0	0	0	0	1	0	.000	.000
team total			156	5057	**657**	1281	152	**81**	18	**535**	522	479	**219**	.253	.326

a—from Philadelphia (N)
Jack Fournier (ph). Zeb Terry (ss) also played for the White Sox during the season.

NEW YORK GIANTS

World Series Statistics

	Pos	G	AB	R	H	2B	3B	HR	RBI	BB	SO	SB	BA	SA	PO	A	E
Walter Holke	1b	6	21	2	6	**2**	0	0	1	0	**6**	0	.286	.381	**67**	0	1
Buck Herzog	2b	6	24	1	6	0	**1**	0	2	1	4	0	.250	.333	11	12	2
Art Fletcher	ss	6	**25**	2	5	1	0	0	0	0	2	0	.200	.240	9	17	3
Heinie Zimmerman	3b	6	**25**	1	3	0	**1**	0	0	0	0	0	.120	.200	9	14	2
Dave Robertson	rf	6	22	3	**11**	1	**1**	0	1	0	0	2	**.500**	**.636**	6	2	1
Benny Kauff	cf	6	**25**	2	4	1	0	**2**	**5**	0	2	1	.160	.440	6	0	1
George Burns	lf	6	22	3	5	0	0	0	2	**2**	6	1	.227	.227	11	0	0
Bill Rariden	c	5	13	2	5	0	0	0	2	**2**	1	0	.385	.385	25	10	0
Lew McCarty	c-ph	3	5	1	2	0	1	0	1	0	0	0	.400	.800	7	1	1
Joe Wilhoit	ph	2	1	0	0	0	0	0	0	1	0	0	.000	.000			
Jim Thorpe	rf	1	0	0	0	0	0	0	0	0	0	0	—	—	0	0	0
Jimmy Smith		Did not play															
George Gibson		Did not play															
Hans Lobert		Did not play															
Al Baird		Did not play															
Red Murray		Did not play															
Jack Onslow		Did not play															
Slim Sallee	p	2	6	0	1	0	0	0	1	0	2	0	.167	.167	0	8	0
Rube Benton	p	2	4	0	0	0	0	0	0	0	3	0	.000	.000	1	2	0
Ferdie Schupp	p	2	4	0	1	0	0	0	1	0	1	0	.250	.250	1	4	0
Pol Perritt	p	3	2	0	2	0	0	0	0	0	0	0	1.000	1.000	0	1	0
Fred Anderson	p	1	0	0	0	0	0	0	0	0	0	0	—	—	0	1	0
Jeff Tesreau	p	1	0	0	0	0	0	0	0	0	0	0	—	—	0	0	0
Al Demaree		Did not play															
team total		6	199	17	51	5	4	2	16	6	27	4	.256	.352	153	72	1

Double Plays—3
Left on Bases—37

Regular Season Statistics

		Main Pos	G	AB	R	H	2B	3B	HR	RBI	BB	SO	SB	BA	SA
Walter Holke		1b	153	527	55	146	12	7	2	55	34	54	13	.277	.338
Buck Herzog		2b	114	417	69	98	10	8	2	31	31	36	12	.235	.312
Art Fletcher		ss	151	557	70	145	24	5	4	56	23	28	12	.260	.343
Heinie Zimmerman		3b	150	585	61	174	22	9	5	**102**	16	43	13	.297	.391
Dave Robertson		of	142	532	64	138	16	9	**12**	54	10	47	17	.259	.391
Benny Kauff		of	153	559	89	172	22	4	5	68	59	54	30	.308	.388
George Burns		of	152	597	**103**	180	25	13	5	45	**75**	55	40	.302	.412
Bill Rariden		c	101	266	20	72	10	1	0	25	42	17	3	.271	.316
Lew McCarty		c	56	162	15	40	3	2	2	19	14	6	1	.247	.327
Joe Wilhoit		of	34	50	9	17	2	2	0	8	8	5	0	.340	.460
Jim Thorpe	b	of	26	57	12	11	3	2	0	4	8	10	1	.193	.316
Jimmy Smith		2b	36	96	12	22	5	1	0	2	9	18	6	.229	.302
George Gibson		c	35	82	1	14	3	0	0	5	7	2	1	.171	.207
Hans Lobert		3b	35	52	4	10	1	0	1	5	5	5	2	.192	.269
Al Baird		2b-ss	18	24	1	7	0	0	0	4	2	2	2	.292	.292
Red Murray		of	22	22	1	1	1	0	0	3	4	3	0	.045	.091
Jack Onslow		c	9	8	1	2	1	0	0	0	0	1	0	.250	.375
Slim Sallee		p	34	77	7	17	0	0	0	11	2	12	0	.221	.221
Rube Benton		p	35	72	1	12	1	1	0	2	2	18	0	.167	.208
Ferdie Schupp		p	36	93	6	15	2	1	0	4	8	35	0	.161	.204
Pol Perritt		p	35	70	4	11	1	0	0	3	0	20	0	.157	.171
Fred Anderson		p	38	42	2	3	0	0	0	1	3	14	0	.071	.071
Jeff Tesreau		p	33	61	4	14	0	1	0	5	1	9	1	.230	.262
Al Demaree	c	p	15	18	2	2	0	0	0	2	1	6	1	.111	.111
team total			158	5211	**635**	1360	170	71	**39**	**537**	373	533	**162**	.261	.343

b—from Cincinnati
c—from Chicago (A)
Ed Hemingway (3b), Pete Kilduff (2b), Ernie Krueger (c), Joe Rodriguez (1b), Ross Youngs (of), George Kelly (p), Jim Middleton (p), George Smith (p), Ad Swigler (p) also played for the Giants during the season.

PITCHING

CHICAGO WHITE SOX

World Series Statistics

	G	GS	CG	IP	H	R	ER	BB	SO	W	L	SV	ERA
Red Faber	**4**	**3**	**2**	**27**	21	7	7	3	9	**3**	1	0	2.33
Eddie Cicotte	3	2	**2**	23	**23**	6	5	2	**13**	1	1	0	1.95
Lefty Williams	1	0	0	1	2	1	1	0	3	0	0	0	9.00
Dave Danforth	1	0	0	1	3	2	2	0	2	0	0	0	18.00
Reb Russell	1	1	0	0	2	1	1	1	0	0	0	0	∞
Jim Scott	Did not play												
Joe Benz	Did not play												
Mellie Wolfgang	Did not play												
team total	6	6	4	52	51	17	16	6	27	4	2	0	2.77

Regular Season Statistics

		G	GS	CG	IP	H	ER	BB	SO	W	L	Pct	SV	ShO	ERA
Red Faber		41	29	17	248	224	53	85	84	16	13	.552	3	3	1.92
Eddie Cicotte		49	35	29	**347**	246	59	70	150	**28**	12	.700	4	7	**1.53**
Lefty Williams		45	29	8	230	221	76	81	85	11	8	.680	1	1	2.47
Dave Danforth		**50**	9	1	173	155	51	74	79	11	6	.647	**11**	1	2.65
Reb Russell		35	24	11	189	170	41	32	54	15	5	.750	4	5	1.95
Jim Scott		24	17	6	125	126	26	42	37	6	7	.462	0	2	1.87
Joe Benz		19	13	7	95	76	26	23	25	7	3	.700	0	2	2.46
Mellie Wolfgang		5	0	0	18	18	10	6	3	0	0	—	0	0	5.00
team total		156	156	79	**1424**	1236	342	413	517	**100**	54	**.649**	**23**	**21**	**2.16**

NEW YORK GIANTS

World Series Statistics

	G	GS	CG	IP	H	R	ER	BB	SO	W	L	SV	ERA
Slim Sallee	2	2	1	15⅓	20	**10**	**9**	**4**	4	0	**2**	0	5.28
Rube Benton	2	2	1	14	9	3	0	1	8	1	1	0	**0.00**
Ferdie Schupp	2	2	1	10⅓	11	2	2	2	9	1	0	0	1.74
Pol Perritt	3	0	0	8⅓	9	2	2	3	3	0	0	0	2.16
Fred Anderson	1	0	0	2	5	4	4	0	3	0	1	0	18.00
Jeff Tesreau	1	0	0	1	0	0	0	1	1	0	0	0	0.00
Al Demaree	Did not play												
team total	6	6	3	51	54	21	17	11	28	2	4	0	3.00

Regular Season Statistics

		G	GS	CG	IP	H	ER	BB	SO	W	L	Pct	SV	ShO	ERA
Slim Sallee		34	24	18	216	199	52	34	54	18	7	.720	**4**	1	2.17
Rube Benton		35	25	14	215	190	65	41	70	15	9	.625	3	3	2.72
Ferdie Schupp		36	32	25	272	202	59	70	147	21	7	**.750**	0	6	1.95
Pol Perritt		35	26	14	215	186	45	45	72	17	7	.708	1	5	1.88
Fred Anderson		38	18	8	162	122	26	34	69	8	8	.500	3	1	1.44
Jeff Tesreau		33	20	11	184	168	63	58	85	13	8	.619	2	1	3.08
Al Demaree	c	15	11	1	78	70	23	17	23	4	5	.449	0	0	2.65
team total		158	158	92	**1427**	1221	360	327	551	**98**	56	**.631**	**14**	17	**2.27**

Total Attendance—186,654 Average Attendance—31,109 Winning Players's Share—$3,669 Losing Player's Share—$2,442

1918
The Early Birds

The United States had entered the Great War in Europe last year, but the 1917 World Series went on entirely unaffected by the hostilities. This year was another story. Players were drafted into the armed service in bunches, and others went to work in war-production factories to beat the draft. General Enoch Crowder, the provost marshal of the United States, issued in June his famous "work or fight" order, forcing all able-bodied men of draft age into either essential work or into the military. Baseball was classified nonessential, and the government gave the American and National Leagues until Labor Day to finish their seasons. An additional two-week period of grace was granted to play the World Series, so the fall classic this year was played in the heat of early September rather than the true autumn of October.

The war ruined the Chicago White Sox and New York Giants, both of whom lost key men to the military effort. Taking over the top spot in the A.L. were the Boston Red Sox, the best example of war-time patchwork in the majors. Manager Jack Barry marched off into the service, so stern Ed Barrow was hired to take charge of the team. A master stroke in plugging holes was the purchase of Stuffy McInnis, Amos Strunk, Wally Schang, and Bullet Joe Bush from Connie Mack's Philadelphia Athletics. With star left fielder Duffy Lewis in the military, Barrow replaced him with an incipient legend, using pitcher Babe Ruth in the outfield against right-hand pitching on days when he himself was not pitching. This offspring of necessity worked out splendidly, as the burly Ruth hit .300, socked a league-leading 11 homers, and won 13 games on the mound. While Ruth was splitting his attention between the mound and left field, underhand pitcher Carl Mays devoted full attention to his pitching and won 21 games in the abbreviated season. The Chicago Cubs had no spectacular stars like Ruth, but their first N.L. pennant since 1910 was enough in itself to excite Chicago fans. Shortstop Charlie Hollocher was the only .300 hitter in the lineup, but the pitching trio of Hippo Vaughn, Claude Hendrix, and Lefty Tyler was the strongest in baseball this year.

Cub manager Fred Mitchell thought it best to pitch lefties against the Red Sox, so southpaws Vaughn and Tyler started all the games for Chicago. The first game in Chicago's Comiskey Park pitted Vaughn against Ruth, who confined himself mostly to pitching in this Series. McInnis singled Dave Shean home in the fourth inning, and that was all Ruth needed, as he spun a six-hit 1–0 shutout. The good pitching continued the next day, as a three-run second inning off Joe Bush gave Lefty Tyler an easy cushion to drive to a 3–1 victory to even the Series. Travel restrictions because of the war caused the first three games to be scheduled for Chicago, and Vaughn once again pitched superbly only to lose, this time 2–1 to Carl Mays. George Whiteman, a veteran minor-leaguer who played left field for Boston against lefties, starred with a circus catch which robbed Dode Paskert of a fourth-inning homer. The game ended on a dramatic note, with Charlie Pick out stealing home with two down in the ninth.

The Red Sox now returned to Fenway Park with a 2–1 lead and Ruth scheduled to pitch against Tyler. Ruth tripled in two runs in the fourth and held the Cubs scoreless until he gave up two tying runs in the eighth; his streak of scoreless innings pitched in Series play stopped at a record 29 2/3. But the Red Sox went ahead again in the bottom of the eighth on a single, a passed ball, and a throwing error, and Bush pitched the ninth to preserve the win for Ruth. Before the fifth game, the players threatened to strike, since poor attendance and a new plan to cut all first-division teams in on the Series money insured that this year's player shares would be minuscule compared to the recent past. The game nevertheless went on as scheduled, with Hippo Vaughn pitching well and finally winning a game 3–0 over Sad Sam Jones. An intimate sixth-game gathering of 15,238 saw the Red Sox take the Series behind a 2–1 Carl Mays three-hitter. The players' predictions about their shares came absolutely true; after an agreed-upon deduction for war charities, each Red Sox player netted $1,108, while each Cub got only $671.

Game 1 September 5 at Chicago

Bos.	000	100	000				
Chi.	000	000	000				

Boston	Pos	AB	R	H	RBI	PO	A	E
Hooper	rf	4	0	1	0	4	0	0
Shean	2b	2	1	1	0	0	3	0
Strunk	cf	3	0	0	0	2	0	0
Whiteman	lf	4	0	2	0	5	0	0
McInnis	1b	2	0	1	1	10	0	0
Scott	ss	4	0	0	0	0	3	0
Thomas	3b	3	0	0	0	1	1	0
Agnew	c	3	0	0	0	5	0	0
Ruth	p	3	0	0	0	0	1	0
Totals		28	1	5	1	27	8	0

Pitching	IP	H	R	ER	BB	SO
Boston						
Ruth (W)	9	6	0	0	1	4
Chicago						
Vaughn (L)	9	5	1	1	3	6

Chicago	Pos	AB	R	H	RBI	PO	A	E
Flack	rf	3	0	1	0	2	0	0
Hollocher	ss	3	0	0	0	2	1	0
Mann	lf	4	0	1	0	2	0	0
Paskert	cf	4	0	2	0	2	0	0
Merkle	1b	3	0	0	0	9	2	0
Pick	2b	3	0	0	0	1	1	0
a O'Farrell		1	0	0	0	0	0	0
Deal	3b	4	0	1	0	1	3	0
b McCabe		0	0	0	0	0	0	0
Killefer	c	4	0	0	0	7	2	0
Vaughn	p	3	0	0	0	3	5	0
Totals		32	0	6	0	27	14	0

a Popped out for Pick in 9th.
b Ran for Deal in 9th.

Sacrifice hits—Hollocher, McInnis, Strunk. Hit by Pitcher—Flack (by Ruth). Left on Bases—Boston 5, Chicago 8. Umpires—O'Day (N), Hildebrand (A), Klem (N), Owens (A). Attendance—19,274. Time of Game—1:50.

1st Inning
Boston
1 Hooper grounded out, Merkle to Vaughn. Shean singled on a Texas Leaguer to right.
2 Strunk forced Shean at second, Deal to Pick.
3 Strunk thrown out at second on a short passed ball, Killefer to Hollocher.
Chicago
1 Flack took a called third strike.
2 Hollocher grounded to second. Mann singled on a bad hopper over Shean's head. Paskert singled to left, Mann racing to third. Paskert took second on the throw to third. Merkle walked on a full count, loading the bases.
3 Pick flied to left.

2nd Inning
Boston
Whiteman singled to center.
1 McInnis sacrificed Whiteman to second, Vaughn to Merkle.
2 Scott flied to right.
3 Thomas bounced out, Merkle to Vaughn.
Chicago
1 Deal grounded back to the mound.
2 Killefer grounded to second.
3 Vaughn fouled to Agnew.

3rd Inning
Boston
1 Agnew fouled to Killefer on a 3–2 count.
2 Ruth lined to center. Hooper singled to left.
3 Hooper caught attempting to steal second, Killefer to Hollocher.
Chicago
Flack singled to short center.
1 Hollocher sacrificed Flack to second, Thomas to McInnis.
2 Mann grounded to second, Flack moving to third.
3 Paskert grounded to short.

4th Inning
Boston
Shean walked.
1 Strunk popped to Vaughn on a sacrifice attempt. Whitehead singled over Hollocher's glove, Shean going to second. McInnis singled to left, scoring Shean with Whitehead stopping at second.
2 Scott popped to Deal on a bunt attempt.
3 Thomas struck out.
Chicago
1 Merkle flied to right.
2 Pick struck out.
3 Deal flied to right.

5th Inning
Boston
1 Agnew grounded to third.
2 Ruth struck out.
3 Hooper bounced back to the mound.
Chicago
1 Killefer flied to left.
2 Vaughn struck out. Flack was hit by a pitch.
3 Hollocher flied to center.

6th Inning
Boston
1 Shean called out on strikes on a full count.
2 Strunk grounded back to the mound.
3 Whiteman fouled to Flack.
Chicago
1 Mann flied to right. Paskert singled to center. Merkle singled over second, Paskert advancing to second.
2 Pick grounded to first, Paskert going to third and Merkle to second.
3 Deal flied to left.

7th Inning
Boston
1 McInnis flied to short center.
2 Scott grounded to short.
3 Thomas struck out on three pitches.
Chicago
1 Killefer flied to center.
2 Vaughn grounded to short, Scott making a great stop and throw.
3 Flack grounded to short

8th Inning
Boston
1 Agnew grounded to third.
2 Ruth struck out again.
3 Hooper grounded to second.
Chicago
1 Hollocher grounded to first.
2 Mann flied to left.
3 Paskert took a called third strike.

9th Inning
Boston
Shean walked.
1 Strunk sacrificed Shean to second, Vaughn to Merkle.
2 Whiteman struck out, on a foul tip. McInnis intentionally walked.
3 Scott ground back to the mound.
Chicago
1 Merkle flied to left.
2 O'Farrell, pinch-hitting for Pick, popped to third on a full count. Deal beat out a hit to third. McCabe ran for Deal.
3 Killefer flied to right.

Game 2 September 6 at Chicago

Boston	Pos	AB	R	H	RBI	PO	A	E
Hooper	rf	3	0	1	0	1	0	0
Shean	2b	4	0	1	0	5	2	0
Strunk	cf	4	1	1	0	1	2	0
Whiteman	lf	3	0	1	1	3	0	1
McInnis	1b	4	0	1	0	7	0	0
Scott	ss	2	0	0	0	3	3	0
Thomas	3b	3	0	0	0	1	1	0
b Dubuc		1	0	0	0	0	0	0
Agnew	c	2	0	0	0	2	4	0
a Schang		2	0	1	0	1	0	0
Bush	p	2	0	0	0	0	3	0
Totals		30	1	6	1	24	15	1

a Singled for Agnew in 8th.
b Struck out for Thomas in 9th.

Double—Killefer. Triples—Hollocher, Strunk, Whiteman. Sacrifice Hits—Deal, Scott. Double Plays—Killefer to Hollocher. Hollocher to Pick to Merkle. Left on Bases—Boston 7, Chicago 4. Umpires—Hildebrand, Klem, Owens, O'Day. Attendance—20,040. Time of Game—1:58.

	Bos.	000 000 001
	Chi.	030 000 00x

Chicago	Pos	AB	R	H	RBI	PO	A	E
Flack	rf	4	0	2	0	4	1	0
Hollocher	ss	4	0	1	0	4	4	0
Mann	lf	4	0	0	0	0	0	0
Paskert	cf	4	0	0	0	2	0	0
Merkle	1b	2	1	1	0	6	1	0
Pick	2b	2	1	1	0	4	4	0
Deal	3b	2	0	0	0	2	1	1
Killefer	c	2	1	1	1	4	2	0
Tyler	p	3	0	1	2	1	2	0
Totals		27	3	7	3	27	15	1

Pitching	IP	H	R	ER	BB	SO
Boston						
Bush (L)	8	7	3	3	3	0
Chicago						
Tyler (W)	9	6	1	1	4	2

1st Inning
Boston
  Hooper walked.
1,2 Shean struck out, but he interfered with Killefer. Umpire Hildebrand ruled Hooper out at second. A double play Killefer and Hollocher.
3 Strunk popped to third.
Chicago
  Flack lined a single to left.
1 Hollocher forced Flack at second, Bush to Scott.
2 Mann forced Hollocher, Strunk purposely dropping a pop up and throwing to Shean at second.
3 Paskert flied to left.

2nd Inning
Boston
  Whiteman walked on four pitches. McInnis beat out a bunt when Tyler and Killefer collided.
1 Scott sacrificed up both runners, Killefer to Pick.
2 Thomas hit to Pick who threw to Killefer getting Whiteman at the plate, as McInnis went to third.
3 Agnew fouled to Flack.
Chicago
  Merkle walked.
  Pick beat out a bunt down the third base line.
1 Deal popped to second.
  Killefer doubled to right, Merkle scoring as Pick stopped at third.
  Tyler singled over second, Pick and
2 Killefer scoring. Tyler was out trying for second on the throw to the plate, Strunk to Agnew to Scott.
  Flack beat out a bouncer to first.
3 Flack stole second, but overslid the bag and was out, Agnew to Shean.

3rd Inning
Boston
  Bush walked.
1 Hooper forced Bush at second, Tyler to Hollocher.
2 Shean forced Hooper at second, Hollocher to Pick.
3 Strunk fouled to Killefer.
Chicago
1 Hollocher grounded to second.
2 Mann bunted out, McInnis unassisted.
3 Paskert popped to second.

4th Inning
Boston
1 Whiteman popped to second.
2 McInnis grounded to short.
3 Scott grounded to second, Pick making a great stop.
Chicago
  Merkle safely to second as Whiteman dropped his fly ball.
1 Pick bunted to Bush who threw to Thomas getting Merkle going into third.
2 Deal flied to right.
3 Pick out trying to steal second, Agnew to Scott.

5th Inning
Boston
1 Thomas grounded to third.
2 Agnew flied to right.
  Bush safe at first on Deal's fumble.
3 Bush flied to deep right.
Chicago
1 Killefer grounded to third.
2 Tyler fouled to Agnew near third.
3 Flack bounced back to the mound.

6th Inning
Boston
  Shean singled to center.
1 Strunk forced Shean at second, Pick to Hollocher.
2,3 Whiteman grounded into a double play, Hollocher to Pick to Merkle.
Chicago
  Hollocher tripled down the right field line.
1 Mann grounded to short, Hollocher holding at third.
2 Paskert grounded to Scott who threw to Agnew getting Hollocher trying to score.
  Merkle singled to center, Paskert racing to third.
3 Merkle out trying to steal, Agnew to Scott to McInnis.

7th Inning
Boston
1 McInnis grounded to deep short.
2 Scott flied to center.
3 Thomas flied to right.
Chicago
  Pick walked.
1 Deal sacrificed, McInnis unassisted.
  Killefer walked.
2 Tyler flied to left.
3 Flack flied to center.

8th Inning
Boston
  Schang, pinch-hitting for Agnew, singled off Hollocher's glove.
1 Bush flied to center.
  Hooper singled to right but Schang was
2 out at third on a great throw by Flack to Deal.
3 Shean grounded out, Merkle to Tyler.
Chicago
  For Boston—Schang catching.
1 Hollocher popped to Shean behind first.
2 Mann flied to left.
3 Paskert fouled to Schang.

9th Inning
Boston
  Strunk tripled to right.
  Whiteman also tripled to right, scoring Strunk.
1 McInnis bounced back to the mound, Whiteman holding third.
  Scott walked.
2 Dubuc, pinch-hitting for Thomas, struck out.
3 Schang popped to short.

Game 3 September 7 at Chicago

Boston	Pos	AB	R	H	RBI	PO	A	E
Hooper	rf	3	0	1	0	3	0	0
Shean	2b	4	0	0	1	2	0	0
Strunk	cf	4	0	0	0	1	0	0
Whiteman	lf	3	1	1	0	3	0	0
McInnis	1b	4	1	1	0	12	0	0
Schang	c	4	0	2	1	6	3	0
Scott	ss	4	0	1	1	1	5	0
Thomas	3b	3	0	1	0	0	2	0
Mays	p	3	0	0	0	0	2	0
Totals		32	2	7	2	27	14	0

Pitching	IP	H	R	ER	BB	SO
Boston						
Mays (W)	9	7	1	1	1	4
Chicago						
Vaughn (L)	9	7	2	2	1	7

	Bos.	000 200 000
	Chi.	000 010 000

Chicago	Pos	AB	R	H	RBI	PO	A	E
Flack	rf	3	0	0	0	3	1	0
Hollocher	ss	3	0	0	0	1	3	1
Mann	lf	4	0	2	0	1	0	0
Paskert	cf	4	0	1	0	1	0	0
Merkle	1b	4	0	0	0	9	2	0
Pick	2b	4	1	2	0	4	4	0
Deal	3b	3	0	1	0	1	1	0
a Barber		0	0	0	0	0	0	0
Killefer	c	3	0	1	1	8	0	0
Vaughn	p	3	0	0	0	3	3	0
Totals		31	1	7	1	27	10	1

a Announced for Deal in 9th.

Doubles—Mann, Pick. Stolen Bases—Pick, Schang, Whiteman. Sacrifice Hit—Hollocher. Double Plays—Hollocher to Merkle, Vaughn to Merkle. Passed Ball—Schang. Hit by Pitcher—Whiteman (by Vaughn). Left on Bases—Boston 5, Chicago 5. Umpires—Klem, Owens, O'Day, Hildebrand. Attendance—27,054. Time of Game—1:57.

1st Inning
Boston
  Hooper singled on a Texas Leaguer behind third.
1 Shean flied to left.
2,3 Strunk lined into a double play, Hollocher to Merkle.
Chicago
  Flack walked.
1 Hollocher sacrificed Flack to second, Schang to McInnis.
2 Mann flied to right.
3 Paskert struck out.

2nd Inning
Boston
  Whiteman singled to left.
1 McInnis struck out, bunting foul on the third strike.
2 Schang struck out and Whiteman stole second.
  Scott safe when Hollocher fumbled his grounder, Whiteman going to third.
3 Thomas flied to right.
Chicago
1 Merkle lined to right on a 3–2 count.
2 Pick popped to second.
3 Deal grounded to third.

3rd Inning
Boston
1 Mays grounded to short.
2 Hooper grounded out, Merkle to Vaughn.
3 Shean grounded back to the mound.
Chicago
1 Killefer grounded to second.
2 Vaughn grounded to second.
3 Flack grounded to first.

4th Inning
Boston
1 Strunk fanned on three pitches.
  Whiteman was hit by a pitched ball.
  McInnis singled to left, Whiteman stopping at second.
  Schang singled over second, scoring Whiteman as McInnis raced to third.
  Scott beat out a bouncer to the mound, McInnis scoring and Schang going to second.
  Thomas singled to right, but Schang
2 was out at the plate, Flack to Killefer with both Scott and Thomas moving up on the throw.
3 Mays lined to center.
Chicago
1 Hollocher flied to right.
  Mann doubled to left.
2 Paskert flied to deep left.
3 Merkle grounded to short.

5th Inning
Boston
  Hooper walked.
1,2 Shean lined into a double play, Vaughn to Merkle.
3 Strunk struck out.
Chicago
  Pick doubled past short.
1 Deal flied to left.
  Killefer singled to left, scoring Pick.
2 Vaughn struck out.
3 Killefer out trying to steal second, Schang to Scott.

6th Inning
Boston
1 Whiteman lined to first.
2 McInnis popped to third.
3 Schang struck out.
Chicago
1 Flack foul bunted to Schang.
2 Hollocher grounded to short.
  Mann singled to right.
  Paskert singled to center, Mann stopping at second.
3 Merkle struck out.

7th Inning
Boston
1 Scott flied to right.
2 Thomas grounded out, Merkle to Vaughn.
3 Mays bounced back to the mound.
Chicago
1 Pick grounded to short.
  Deal beat out a roller to third.
2 Killefer grounded back to the pitcher, Deal moving to second.
3 Vaughn flied to left.

8th Inning
Boston
1 Hooper struck out.
2 Shean fouled to Merkle.
3 Strunk flied to right.
Chicago
1 Flack flied to center.
2 Hollocher struck out.
3 Mann grounded to Scott, making a great stop.

9th Inning
Boston
1 Whiteman grounded to third.
2 McInnis grounded to short.
  Schang singled to right.
  Schang stole second as Hollocher got an error dropping Killefer's throw.
3 Scott struck out.
Chicago
1 Paskert grounded to short.
2 Merkle grounded back to the mound.
  Pick beat out a slow roller to second.
  Barber, batting for Deal.
  Pick stole second.
  On a passed ball Pick went to
3 third but was out trying for the plate, Schang to Thomas to Schang.

Game 4 September 9 at Boston

Chicago	Pos	AB	R	H	RBI	PO	A	E
Flack	rf	4	0	1	0	3	0	0
Hollocher	ss	4	0	1	1	2	0	0
Mann	lf	4	0	0	0	3	0	0
Paskert	cf	4	0	0	0	3	0	0
Merkle	1b	3	0	1	0	9	1	0
Pick	2b	2	0	2	0	0	2	0
a Zeider	3b	0	0	0	0	1	2	0
Deal	3b	2	0	1	0	1	3	0
b O'Farrell		1	0	0	0	0	0	0
Wortman	2b	1	0	0	0	1	0	0
Killefer	c	2	1	0	0	1	0	0
e Barber		1	0	0	0	0	0	0
Tyler	p	0	0	0	0	1	4	0
c Hendrix		1	0	1	0	0	0	0
d McCabe		0	1	0	0	0	0	0
Douglas	p	0	0	0	0	0	0	1
Totals		29	2	7	2	24	12	1

a Walked for Pick in 7th.
b Hit in to double play for Deal in 7th.
c Singled for Tyler in 8th.
d Ran for Hendrix in 8th.
e Hit into double play for Killefer in 9th.

Double—Shean. Triple—Ruth. Stolen. Base—Shean. Sacrifice Hits—Hooper, Ruth. Double Plays—Ruth to Scott to McInnis, Scott to Shean to McInnis 2. Passed Balls—Killefer 2. Wild Pitch—Ruth. Left on Bases—Chicago 6, Boston 4. Umpires—Owens, O'Day, Hildebrand, Klem. Attendance—22,183. Time of Game—1:50.

Chi.	000 000 020
Bos.	000 200 01x

Boston	Pos	AB	R	H	RBI	PO	A	E
Hooper	rf	3	0	0	0	1	0	0
Shean	2b	3	0	1	0	4	4	0
Strunk	cf	4	0	0	0	0	0	0
Whiteman	lf	3	1	0	0	1	0	0
Bush	p	0	0	0	0	0	0	0
McInnis	1b	3	1	1	0	16	1	0
Ruth	p-lf	3	1	2	2	0	4	0
Scott	ss	3	0	0	0	3	8	0
Thomas	3b	3	0	0	0	2	3	0
Agnew	c	2	0	0	0	0	1	0
Schang	c	1	1	1	0	0	0	0
Totals		27	3	4	2	27	21	0

Pitching	IP	H	R	ER	BB	SO
Chicago						
Tyler	7	3	2	2	2	1
Douglas (L)	1	1	1	0	0	0
Boston						
Ruth (W)	*8	7	2	2	6	0
Bush (SV)	1	0	0	0	0	0

*Pitched to two batters in 9th.

1st Inning
Chicago
Flack singled to right.
1 Hollocher lined to short.
2 Flack picked off first, Agnew to McInnis.
3 Mann fouled to McInnis.
Boston
1 Hooper flied to right on a 3-2 count.
   Shean doubled against the left field fence.
2 Strunk struck out on a full count.
3 Whiteman flied to right.

2nd Inning
Chicago
1 Paskert grounded back to the mound.
2 Merkle grounded to short.
   Pick beat out a hit to third.
   Deal singled past third, Pick stopping at second.
3 Killefer forced Pick at third, Scott to Thomas.
Boston
1 McInnis popped to short.
2 Ruth grounded to second.
3 Scott grounded to third.

3rd Inning
Chicago
Tyler walked.
1 Flack forced Tyler at second, Scott to Shean.
2 Hollocher grounded to first, Flack moving to second.
3 Flack picked off second, Ruth to Scott.
Boston
1 Thomas popped to short.
2 Agnew flied to deep left.
3 Hooper grounded out, Merkle to Tyler.

4th Inning
Chicago
1 Mann grounded to third.
2 Paskert grounded to short, Scott making a great running stop.
3 Merkle flied to left.
Boston
Shean walked.
1 Strunk flied to center.
   Shean went to second on a passed ball, but given a stolen base by the official scorer.
   Whiteman walked.
2 McInnis forced Shean at third, Tyler to Deal.
   Ruth tripled to deep right-center on a full count, scoring Whiteman and McInnis.
3 Scott flied to center.

5th Inning
Chicago
Pick singled over Ruth's head.
1 Deal flied to short right.
2,3 Killefer hit into a double play, Ruth to Scott to McInnis.
Boston
1 Thomas dribbled back to the mound.
2 Agnew out on a slow hopper to third.
3 Hooper flied to right.

6th Inning
Chicago
Tyler again walked.
1 Flack forced Tyler at second, Ruth to Shean
2 Hollocher grounded to second, Flack going to second.
3 Mann grounded to third.
Boston
1 Shean grounded to third.
2 Strunk grounded to second.
3 Whiteman grounded back to Tyler.

7th Inning
Chicago
1 Paskert grounded to short.
   Merkle walked.
   Zeider, pinch-hitting for Pick, walked.
2,3 O'Farrell, batting for Deal, hit into a double play, Scott to Shean to McInnis.
Boston
For Chicago—Zeider playing third, and Wortman playing second.
McInnis singled to left.
1 Ruth sacrificed McInnis to second, Zeider to Merkle.
2 Scott grounded to Tyler who threw to Zeider getting McInnis going into third.
3 Thomas popped to second.

8th Inning
Chicago
Killefer walked.
Hendrix, pinch-hitting for Tyler, singled to left, Killefer going to second.
Killefer to third and Hendrix to second on a wild pitch.
1 Flack grounded to first as both runners held their bases.
   McCabe ran for Hendrix.
2 Hollocher grounded to second, scoring Killefer as McCabe went to third.
   Mann singled to left, scoring McCabe.
3 Paskert grounded to third.
Boston
For Chicago—Douglas now pitching.
Schang, pinch-hitting for Agnew, singled over second.
Schang went to second on a short passed ball.
Hooper sacrificed Schang to third, but when Douglas threw the ball away Schang scored and Hooper went to second.
1 Shean flied to left.
2 Strunk flied to center.
3 Whiteman grounded to third.

9th Inning
Chicago
For Boston—Schang catching.
Merkle singled over second.
Zeider again walked.
For Boston—Ruth went to left and Bush came in to pitch.
1 Wortman forced Merkle at third on a bunt, McInnis to Thomas.
2,3 Barber, batting for Killefer, hit into a double play, Scott to Shean to McInnis.

Game 5 September 10 at Boston

Chicago	Pos	AB	R	H	RBI	PO	A	E
Flack	rf	2	1	0	0	1	0	0
Hollocher	ss	3	2	3	0	2	5	0
Mann	lf	3	0	1	1	2	0	0
Paskert	cf	3	0	1	2	3	0	0
Merkle	1b	3	0	1	0	11	1	0
Pick	2b	4	0	1	0	4	3	0
Deal	3b	4	0	0	0	0	0	0
Killefer	c	4	0	0	0	4	0	0
Vaughn	p	4	0	0	0	0	3	0
Totals		30	3	7	3	27	12	0

Pitching	IP	H	R	ER	BB	SO
Chicago						
Vaughn (W)	9	5	0	0	1	4
Boston						
Jones (L)	9	7	3	3	5	5

Chi.	001 000 020
Bos.	000 000 000

Boston	Pos	AB	R	H	RBI	PO	A	E
Hooper	rf	4	0	1	0	1	0	0
Shean	2b	3	0	1	0	3	2	0
Strunk	cf	4	0	1	0	4	0	0
Whiteman	lf	3	0	1	0	1	2	0
McInnis	1b	3	0	0	0	9	0	0
Scott	ss	3	0	0	0	1	4	0
Thomas	3b	3	0	0	0	1	4	0
Agnew	c	2	0	0	0	5	1	0
a Schang	c	1	0	0	0	1	0	0
Jones	p	1	0	0	0	1	3	0
b Miller		1	0	0	0	0	0	0
Totals		28	0	5	0	27	13	0

a Struck out for Agnew in 8th.
b Flied out for Jones in 9th.

Doubles—Mann, Paskert, Strunk. Stolen Base—Hollocher. Sacrifice Hits—Mann, Shean. Double Plays—Merkle to Hollocher, Hollocher to Pick to Merkle 2, Whiteman to Shean. Left on Bases—Chicago 6, Boston 3. Umpires—O'Day, Hildebrand, Klem, Owens. Attendance—24,694. Time of Game—1:42.

1st Inning
Chicago
Flack walked.
Hollocher singled over second, Flack stopping at second.
1 Mann sacrificed up both runners, Jones to Shean.
2,3 Paskert lined to Whiteman who threw to Shean doubling Hollocher off of second.
Boston
Hooper singled over second.
1 Shean sacrificed Hooper to second, Vaughn to Pick.
2 Strunk struck out.
3 Whiteman fouled deep to Flack at the fence.

2nd Inning
Chicago
Merkle walked on a full count.
1 Pick grounded to first, Merkle going to second.
2 Deal popped to short.
3 Killefer grounded back to the mound.
Boston
1 McInnis flied to Pick in short center.
2 Scott grounded to short.
3 Thomas grounded to Vaughn making a good bare-handed stop.

3rd Inning
Chicago
1 Vaughn grounded to short.
2 Flack also grounded hard to short.
   Hollocher walked on four pitches.
   Hollocher stole second.
   Mann doubled to left, scoring Hollocher.
3 Paskert grounded to short.
Boston
1 Agnew grounded to short.
   Jones walked.
2 Hooper struck out.
3 Shean flied to center.

4th Inning
Chicago
1 Merkle lined to center.
2 Pick popped to third.
3 Deal flied to center.
Boston
   Strunk doubled to deep right.
1 Whiteman popped to first.
2,3 McInnis lined to Merkle who threw to Hollocher doubling Strunk at second.

5th Inning
Chicago
1 Killefer flied to short right.
2 Vaughn struckout.
3 Flack grounded to Shean who had to race the ball behind second. His throw just beating Flack.
Boston
1 Scott flied to left.
   Thomas singled to right.
2,3 Agnew grounded into a double play, Hollocher to Pick to Merkle.

6th Inning
Chicago
Hollocher singled to center.
1 Mann flied to center.
   Paskert walked.
   Merkle singled to left and Hollocher
2 Was caught at the plate, Whiteman to Agnew. Paskert got to third and Merkle to second on the play.
3 Pick flied to center.
Boston
1 Jones flied to center.
2 Hooper flied to center.
3 Shean grounded back to the mound.

7th Inning
Chicago
1 Deal struck out on three pitches.
2 Killefer lined to Jones.
3 Vaughn struck out.
Boston
1 Strunk lined to Pick, who knocked it down and threw to first.
   Whiteman singled to left.
2,3 McInnis hit into a double play, Hollocher to Pick to Merkle.

8th Inning
Chicago
Flack walked.
Hollocher beat out a bunt to third, his third hit of the game, as Flack went to second.
1 Mann popped to second.
   Paskert doubled to deep left-center, scoring both Flack and Hollocher.
2 Merkle struck out.
   Pick beat out a hard grounder to
3 second, but Paskert was out in a run-down, Shean to Agnew to Thomas to McInnis.
Boston
1 Scott grounded to short.
2 Thomas fouled to Merkle.
3 Schang, pinch-hitting for Agnew (who has not gotten a hit in the Series), struck out.

9th Inning
Chicago
For Boston—Schang catching.
1 Deal grounded to short.
2 Killefer grounded back to the mound.
3 Vaughn struck out for the third time.
Boston
1 Miller, batting for Jones, flied to left, Mann making a great catch up the steep enbankment.
2 Hooper flied to Hollocher.
   Shean beat out a hit to deep short.
3 Strunk struck out.

Game 6 September 11 at Boston

Chi.	0 0 0	1 0 0	0 0 0
Bos.	0 0 2	0 0 0	0 0 x

Chicago	Pos	AB	R	H	RBI	PO	A	E
Flack	rf	3	1	1	0	1	0	1
Hollocher	ss	4	0	0	0	0	4	0
Mann	lf	3	0	0	0	2	0	0
Paskert	cf	2	0	0	0	6	0	0
Merkle	1b	3	0	1	1	8	2	0
Pick	2b	3	0	1	0	3	1	0
Deal	3b	2	0	0	0	2	1	0
a Barber		1	0	0	0	0	0	0
Zeider	3b	0	0	0	0	0	0	0
Killefer	c	2	0	0	0	2	2	0
b O'Farrell	c	1	0	0	0	0	0	0
Tyler	p	2	0	0	0	0	3	1
c McCabe		1	0	0	0	0	0	0
Hendrix	p	0	0	0	0	0	0	0
Totals		27	1	3	1	24	13	2

a Lined out for Deal in 8th.
b Popped out for Killefer in 8th.
c Fouled out for Tyler in 8th.

Stolen Base—Flack. Sacrifice Hits—Hooper, Thomas. Hit by Pitcher—Mann (by Mays). Left on Bases—Chicago 2, Boston 8. Umpires—Hildebrand, Klem, Owens, O'Day. Attendance—15,238. Time of Game—1:46.

Boston	Pos	AB	R	H	RBI	PO	A	E
Hooper	rf	3	0	0	0	1	0	0
Shean	2b	3	1	0	0	2	4	0
Strunk	cf	4	0	2	0	0	0	0
Whiteman	lf	4	0	0	0	2	0	0
Ruth	lf	0	0	0	0	1	0	0
McInnis	1b	4	0	1	0	16	1	0
Scott	ss	4	0	1	0	3	3	0
Thomas	3b	2	0	0	0	1	2	0
Schang	c	1	0	0	0	1	2	0
Mays	p	2	1	1	0	0	6	0
Totals		27	2	5	0	27	18	0

Pitching	IP	H	R	ER	BB	SO
Chicago						
Tyler (L)	7	5	2	0	5	1
Hendrix	1	0	0	0	0	0
Boston						
Mays (W)	9	3	1	1	2	1

1st Inning
Chicago
1 Flack grounded to third.
2 Hollocher grounded to second.
3 Mann grounded to short.
Boston
1 Hooper grounded to short.
2 Shean struck out.
Strunk got a Texas Leaguer just over Hollocher's head.
3 Whiteman flied to center.

2nd Inning
Chicago
1 Paskert grounded to second.
2 Merkle struck out.
Pick singled to left.
3 Pick caught off first, Mays to McInnis.
Boston
1 McInnis grounded to Tyler.
2 Scott also hit back to the pitcher.
Thomas walked.
3 Schang grounded to Hollocher who threw too late to Pick, however, Thomas overslid the base and was out.

3rd Inning
Chicago
1 Deal flied to left.
2 Killefer grounded to short.
3 Tyler also grounded to short.
Boston
Mays walked on four pitches.
1 Hooper sacrificed Mays to second, Tyler to Merkle.
Shean walked.
2 Strunk grounded to second, both runners advancing.
Whiteman safe when Flack dropped his liner, allowing Mays and Shean to score.
McInnis beat out a hit to deep short
3 but Whiteman was out trying for third, Hollocher to Merkle to Deal.

4th Inning
Chicago
Flack singled over second.
1 Hollocher grounded to first, Flack going to second.
Mann was hit by a pitched ball.
2 Mann picked off first, Schang to McInnis.
Paskert walked.
Flack stole third.
Merkle singled to left, Flack scoring as Paskert stopped at second.
3 Pick lined to right.
Boston
Scott beat out a hard smash to third.
1 Thomas sacrificed Scott to second, Killefer to Pick.
Schang walked.
Mays beat out a bunt towards third, loading the bases.
2 Hooper forced Scott at the plate, Merkle to Killefer.
3 Shean forced Mays at third, Deal unassisted.

5th Inning
Chicago
1 Deal bounced back to the mound.
2 Killefer also grounded to Mays.
3 Tyler grounded to second.
Boston
1 Strunk flied to left.
2 Whiteman grounded to short.
McInnis beat out a hit which Tyler just knocked down, however the official scorer charged Tyler with an error and no hit for McInnis.
3 Scott flied to right.

6th Inning
Chicago
Flack walked.
1 Hollocher forced Flack at second, McInnis to Scott.
2 Mann forced Hollocher at second, Mays to Shean.
3 Mann out trying to steal second, Schang to Shean.
Boston
1 Thomas flied to short center.
Schang walked.
2 Mays flied to center.
3 Schang out trying to steal second, Killefer to Pick.

7th Inning
Chicago
1 Paskert grounded to Mays.
2 Merkle grounded to third, Thomas robbing Merkle of a hit.
3 Pick grounded to Mays.
Boston
1 Hooper grounded to first.
2 Shean grounded to third.
Strunk singled over second.
3 Whiteman flied to center.

8th Inning
Chicago
1 Barber, pinch-hitting for Deal, lined to Whiteman making a great somersault catch and hurting his shoulder.
2 O'Farrell, batting for Killefer, popped to short.
For Boston—Ruth playing left.
3 McCabe, batting for Tyler, fouled to Scott.
Boston
For Chicago—O'Farrell stays in to catch, Zeider playing third and Hendrix pitching.
1 McInnis fouled to Mann.
2 Scott flied to center.
3 Thomas flied to center.

9th Inning
Chicago
1 Flack fouled to Thomas.
2 Hollocher flied to left.
3 Mann grounded to second.

1918 WORLD SERIES COMPOSITE BOX

	Wins	Composite Line Score
Boston Red Sox (A.L.)	4	0 0 2 5 0 0 0 1 1 – 9
Chicago Cubs (N.L.)	2	0 3 1 1 1 0 0 4 0 –10

Manager	Regular Season			
	W	L	Pct.	G. Ahead
Ed Barrow	75	51	.595	2½
Fred Mitchell	84	45	.651	10½

BATTING AND FIELDING

WORLD SERIES STATISTICS

BOSTON RED SOX

	Pos	G	AB	R	H	2B	3B	HR	RBI	BB	SO	SB	BA	SA	PO	A	E
Stuffy McInnis	1b	6	20	2	5	0	0	0	1	1	1	0	.250	.250	70	2	0
Dave Shean	2b	6	19	2	4	1	0	0	0	4	3	1	.211	.263	15	17	0
Everett Scott	ss	6	21	0	2	0	0	0	1	1	1	2	.095	.095	11	26	0
Fred Thomas	3b	6	16	0	2	0	0	0	0	1	1	0	.125	.125	6	10	0
Harry Hooper	rf	6	20	0	4	0	0	0	0	2	2	0	.200	.200	11	0	0
Amos Strunk	cf	6	23	1	4	1	1	0	0	0	5	1	.174	.304	8	2	0
George Whiteman	lf	6	20	2	5	0	1	0	1	2	1	1	.250	.350	15	2	1
Sam Agnew	c	4	9	0	0	0	0	0	0	0	0	0	.000	.000	12	6	0
Wally Schang	ph-c	5	9	1	4	0	0	0	1	2	3	1	.444	.444	9	5	0
Hack Miller	ph	1	1	0	0	0	0	0	0	0	0	0	.000	.000			
George Cochran		Did not play															
Wally Mayer		Did not play															
Jack Coffey		Did not play															
Heinie Wagner		Did not play															
Babe Ruth	p-lf	3	5	0	1	0	1	0	2	0	2	0	.200	.600	1	5	0
Carl Mays	p	2	5	1	1	0	0	0	0	0	2	0	.200	.200	0	3	0
Bullet Joe Bush	p	2	2	0	0	0	0	0	0	0	1	0	.000	.000	0	3	0
Sad Sam Jones	p	1	1	0	0	0	0	0	0	0	1	0	.000	.000	1	3	0
Jean Dubuc	ph	1	1	0	0	0	0	0	0	0	0	0	.000	.000			
Walt Kinney		Did not play															
Bill Pertica		Did not play															
team total		6	172	9	32	2	3	0	6	16	21	3	.186	.233	159	89	1

Double Plays—4
Left on Bases—32

CHICAGO CUBS

	Pos	G	AB	R	H	2B	3B	HR	RBI	BB	SO	SB	BA	SA	PO	A	E
Fred Merkle	1b	6	18	1	5	0	0	0	1	4	3	0	.278	.278	52	9	0
Charlie Pick	2b	6	18	2	7	1	0	0	0	1	1	1	.389	.444	12	11	0
Charlie Hollocher	ss	6	21	2	4	0	1	0	1	1	1	1	.190	.286	11	17	1
Charlie Deal	3b	6	17	0	3	0	0	0	0	1	1	0	.176	.176	7	10	1
Max Flack	rf	6	19	2	5	0	0	0	0	4	1	1	.263	.263	14	2	1
Dode Paskert	cf	6	21	0	4	1	0	0	2	2	2	0	.190	.238	17	0	0
Les Mann	lf	6	22	0	5	2	0	0	2	0	0	0	.227	.318	7	0	0
Bill Killefer	c	6	17	2	2	1	0	0	0	2	2	0	.118	.176	26	6	0
Bob O'Farrell	ph-c	3	3	0	0	0	0	0	0	0	0	0	.000	.000	0	0	0
Turner Barber	ph	3	2	0	0	0	0	0	0	0	0	0	.000	.000			
Chuck Wortman	2b	3	1	1	0	0	0	0	0	0	0	0	.000	.000	1	0	0
Bill McCabe	pr-ph	3	1	1	0	0	0	0	0	0	0	0	—	—	1	2	0
Rollie Zeider	ph-3b	2	1	0	0	0	0	0	0	0	2	0	.000	.000			
Tommy Clarke		Did not play															
Hippo Vaughn	p	3	10	0	0	0	0	0	0	0	5	0	.000	.000	6	11	0
Lefty Tyler	p	3	5	0	1	0	0	0	2	2	0	0	.200	.200	2	9	1
Claude Hendrix	p-ph	2	1	0	1	0	0	0	0	0	0	0	1.000	1.000	0	0	0
Phil Douglas	p	1	0	0	0	0	0	0	0	0	0	0	—	—	0	0	1
Paul Carter		Did not play															
Speed Martin		Did not play															
Roy Walker		Did not play															
team total		6	176	10	37	5	1	0	10	18	14	3	.210	.250	156	17	5

Double Plays—7
Left on Bases—31

REGULAR SEASON STATISTICS

BOSTON RED SOX

Main Pos	G	AB	R	H	2B	3B	HR	RBI	BB	SO	SB	BA	SA
1b-3b	117	423	40	115	11	5	0	56	19	10	10	.272	.322
2b	115	425	58	112	16	3	0	34	40	25	11	.264	.315
ss	126	443	40	98	11	5	0	43	12	16	11	.221	.269
3b	44	144	19	37	2	1	1	11	15	20	4	.257	.306
of	126	474	81	137	26	13	1	44	75	25	24	.289	.405
of	114	413	50	106	18	9	0	35	36	13	20	.257	.344
c	72	199	11	33	4	0	0	6	11	26	0	.166	.206
c-of	88	225	36	55	7	1	0	20	46	35	4	.244	.284
of	12	29	2	8	2	0	0	4	0	4	3	.276	.345
3b	25	63	8	8	0	0	0	3	11	7	3	.127	.127
a 3b	15	44	5	7	1	0	1	2	3	2	1	.159	.250
2b-3b	3	8	0	1	0	0	0	0	0	0	0	.125	.125
of-p-1b	95	317	50	95	26	11	11	66	57	58	6	.300	.555
p	38	104	10	30	3	0	0	5	9	15	1	.288	.375
p	36	98	8	27	3	2	0	14	6	11	0	.276	.347
p	24	57	6	10	1	0	1	13	14	0	1	.175	.193
p	5	6	0	1	0	0	0	1	2	0	0	.167	.167
p	6	5	0	0	0	0	0	0	0	0	0	.000	.000
	126	3982	473	990	159	54	15	390	406	324	110	.249	.327

a—from Detroit

Walter Barbare (3b), Red Bluhm (ph), Eusebio Gonzalez (ss), Dick Hoblitzell (1b), Jack Stansbury (3b), Frank Truesdale (2b), Lore Bader (p), Dutch Leonard (p), Dick McCabe (p), Vince Molyneaux (p), Weldon Wyckoff (p) also played for the Red Sox during the season.

CHICAGO CUBS

	G	AB	R	H	2B	3B	HR	RBI	BB	SO	SB	BA	SA
1b	129	482	55	143	25	5	3	65	35	36	21	.297	.388
2b-3b	29	89	13	29	4	1	0	12	14	4	7	.326	.393
ss	131	509	72	161	23	6	2	38	47	30	26	.316	.397
3b	119	414	43	99	9	3	2	34	21	13	11	.239	.290
of	123	478	74	123	17	10	4	41	56	19	17	.257	.360
of	127	461	69	132	24	3	1	59	53	49	20	.286	.371
of	129	489	69	141	27	7	2	55	38	45	21	.288	.384
c	104	331	30	77	10	3	0	22	17	10	5	.233	.281
c	52	113	9	32	7	1	1	14	10	15	0	.283	.425
of	55	123	11	29	3	2	0	10	9	16	3	.236	.293
2b-ss	17	17	4	2	0	0	0	1	3	1	2	.118	.294
2b-of	29	45	9	8	0	1	0	5	4	7	2	.222	.222
2b	82	251	31	56	3	2	0	26	23	20	16	.223	.251
c	1	0	0	0	0	0	0	0	0	0	0	—	—
p	35	96	13	23	3	2	0	8	6	21	4	.240	.313
p	38	100	9	21	0	0	0	8	9	15	0	.210	.220
p	35	91	14	24	3	3	3	17	4	11	1	.264	.462
p	25	55	12	14	1	0	0	5	0	5	2	.255	.273
p	21	25	2	6	0	0	0	0	2	0	0	.240	.240
p	9	16	0	3	0	0	0	1	0	5	0	.188	.250
p	13	11	0	0	0	0	0	0	1	5	0	.000	.000
	131	4325	538	1147	164	53	21	438	358	343	159	.265	.342

Tom Daly (c), Rowdy Elliott (c), Pete Kilduff (2b), Fred Lear (ph), Vic Aldridge (p), Pete Alexander (p), Buddy Napier (p), Harry Weaver (p) also played for the Cubs during the season.

PITCHING

WORLD SERIES STATISTICS

BOSTON RED SOX

	G	GS	CG	IP	H	R	ER	BB	SO	W	L	SV	ERA
Carl Mays	2	2	2	18	10	2	2	3	5	2	0	0	1.00
Babe Ruth	2	2	1	17	13	2	2	7	4	2	0	0	1.06
Bullet Joe Bush	2	1	1	9	7	3	3	3	0	0	1	1	3.00
Sad Sam Jones	1	1	1	9	7	3	3	3	5	0	1	0	3.00
Jean Dubuc		Did not pitch											
Walt Kinney		Did not pitch											
Bill Pertica		Did not play											
team total	6	6	5	53	37	10	10	18	14	4	2	1	1.70

CHICAGO CUBS

	G	GS	CG	IP	H	R	ER	BB	SO	W	L	SV	ERA
Hippo Vaughn	3	3	3	27	17	3	3	5	17	1	2	0	1.00
Lefty Tyler	3	3	1	23	14	5	3	11	4	1	1	0	1.17
Claude Hendrix	1	0	0	1	0	0	0	0	0	0	0	0	0.00
Phil Douglas	1	0	0	1	1	1	0	0	0	0	1	0	0.00
Paul Carter		Did not play											
Speed Martin		Did not play											
Roy Walker		Did not play											
team total	6	6	4	52	32	9	6	16	21	2	4	0	1.04

REGULAR SEASON STATISTICS

BOSTON RED SOX

G	GS	CG	IP	H	ER	BB	SO	W	L	Pct	SV	ShO	ERA
35	33	30	293	230	72	81	114	21	13	.618	0	8	2.21
20	19	18	166	125	41	40	13	7	7	.650	0	1	2.22
36	31	26	273	241	64	91	125	15	15	.500	2	1	2.11
24	21	16	184	151	46	70	44	16	5	.762	0	5	2.25
2	1	1	11	11	5	5	1	0	1	.000	0	0	4.09
5	0	0	15	5	3	8	5	1	0	—	0	0	1.80
3	0	0	3	3	1	1	0	0	0	—	0	0	3.00
126	126	105	1120	931	287	380	392	75	51	.595	2	25	2.31

CHICAGO CUBS

G	GS	CG	IP	H	ER	BB	SO	W	L	Pct	SV	ShO	ERA
35	33	27	290	216	56	76	148	22	10	.688	0	8	1.74
33	30	22	269	218	60	67	102	19	8	.704	1	3	2.01
32	27	21	233	229	72	54	86	20	7	.741	0	3	2.78
25	19	11	157	145	37	31	51	10	9	.526	2	2	2.12
21	4	1	73	78	22	19	13	3	2	.600	2	0	2.71
9	5	4	54	47	11	14	16	5	2	.714	1	0	1.83
13	7	2	43	50	13	15	20	1	3	.250	1	0	2.72
131	131	92	1197	1150	290	296	472	84	45	.651	8	23	2.18

Total Attendance—128,483   Average Attendance—21,414   Winning Player's Share—$1,103   Losing Player's Share—$671

1919
Bad Company

Sordid rumors were making the rounds in the days before the 1919 Series started, but they were unproven and dismissed as slanderous gossip by the sporting public. In fact, interest in the Series was so high that it was lengthened to a best-of-nine affair. Time, however, would bare the rumors as cold, cruel truth. The Cincinnati Reds had a good team, led by center fielder Edd Roush and a strong pitching staff, but the Chicago White Sox clearly outclassed them on paper. Shoeless Joe Jackson's .351 batting average spearheaded the best attack in baseball, Eddie Collins and Ray Schalk glued together an outstanding defense, and the mound staff had two aces in Eddie Cicotte and Lefty Williams. The tightfisted money policies of Charley Comiskey fueled dissension and dissatisfaction in the ranks, but the Sox still shaped up as a 3–1 betting favorite a few days before the Series. But then, suddenly, by the day of the opening game, the betting odds shifted dramatically to make the Reds 8–5 favorites. That didn't seem right.

What had happened was that bettors were putting massive money down on Cincinnati, causing the books to shift their odds to cover themselves. Big money came in from a group including prominent New York gambler Arnold Rothstein; this group knew they had a sure thing, because they had bought off seven White Sox players. In secret negotiations begun in midseason, Jackson, Cicotte, Williams, Happy Felsch, Chick Gandil, Swede Risberg, and Fred McMullin agreed to dump the Series for $100,000. Buck Weaver knew of the fix, had even sat in on several of the negotiation meetings, but he wouldn't go in on the deal. He kept his mouth shut about it, however, and has been linked to the fix ever since because of his silence.

The gamblers and players agreed upon a signal to show that the fix was on; the first Cincinnati player was to get hit with a pitch. Cicotte, an excellent control pitcher, plunked leadoff man Morrie Rath in the back in the bottom of the first, and a new flood of Cincinnati money poured in. Cicotte gave up five straight hits and five runs in the fourth inning, and the Reds were on their way to a 9–1 victory. After the game, catcher Schalk wondered why Cicotte kept crossing up his signals, while the fixers wondered why the scheduled payments from the Rothstein group were not arriving as planned. As it turned out, the players never got the full $100,000 from the gamblers, but the fix went on as scheduled. Lefty Williams, another control pitcher, started the second game; in the fourth inning, he walked three men and then gave up a triple. The Reds won again 4–2. Schalk again was amazed at how his signals were ignored. He informed manager Kid Gleason, who told owner Comiskey, who told National League president John Heydler. American League president Ban Johnson dismissed the fix rumors as nonsense.

The next three games in Chicago began with a courageous performance by White Sox hurler Dickie Kerr, a rookie left-hander not in on the fix. He shut the Reds out 3–0 despite the efforts of five crooked players behind him. But the Sox went back on their losing track the next day as Cicotte made two fielding errors in the fifth inning to allow the only two runs of the game. Williams pitched game five and gave up four runs in the sixth inning, including an error by Felsch.

Down four games to one, the White Sox made moves like they might come back. Kerr pitched game six in Cincinnati and beat the Reds 5–4 in 10 innings, with Gandil driving in the winning run on an infield hit. Then Cicotte pitched like his normal self and captured game seven 4–1. Why he pitched to win has never been solidly established.

The eighth game was set for Cincinnati, with Williams pitching for the Sox. One gambler told writer Hugh Fullerton before the game, "All the betting's on Cincinnati. It's going to be the biggest first inning you ever saw." The Reds got five hits and four runs in the first inning, and their 10–5 win wrapped up the Series five games to three. Despite the persistence of some rumors, the public digested the Series as an entertaining upset and turned its attention to football.

Game 1 October 1 at Cincinnati

Chicago	Pos	AB	R	H	RBI	PO	A	E
S. Collins	rf	4	0	1	0	0	0	0
E. Collins	2b	4	0	1	0	3	3	0
Weaver	3b	4	0	1	0	0	1	0
Jackson	lf	4	1	0	0	3	0	0
Felsch	cf	3	0	0	0	4	0	0
Gandil	1b	4	0	2	1	7	0	1
Risberg	ss	2	0	0	0	5	6	0
Schalk	c	3	0	0	0	2	2	0
Cicotte	p	1	0	0	0	0	2	0
Wilkinson	p	1	0	0	0	0	0	0
a McMullin		1	0	1	0	0	0	0
Lowdermilk	p	1	0	0	0	0	1	0
Totals		32	1	6	1	24	15	1

Cincinnati	Pos	AB	R	H	RBI	PO	A	E
Rath	2b	3	2	1	1	4	2	0
Daubert	1b	4	1	3	1	9	0	0
Groh	3b	3	1	1	2	0	3	0
Roush	cf	4	0	2	1	1	0	0
Duncan	lf	4	0	2	1	1	0	0
Kopf	ss	3	0	0	0	8	0	0
Neale	rf	4	2	3	0	3	0	0
Wingo	c	3	1	1	1	1	2	0
Ruether	p	3	1	3	3	0	2	0
Totals		31	9	14	9	27	12	1

Pitching	IP	H	R	ER	BB	SO
Chicago						
Cicotte (L)	3⅔	7	6	6	2	1
Wilkinson	3⅓	5	2	1	0	1
Lowdermilk	1	2	1	1	1	0
Cincinnati						
Ruether (W)	9	6	1	0	1	1

Chi.   010 000 000
Cin.   100 500 21x

a Singled for Wilkinson in 8th.

Double—Rath. Triples—Daubert, Ruether 2. Stolen Base—Roush. Sacrifice Hits—Felsch, Groh, Rath, Roush, Wingo. Double Plays—Risberg to E. Collins, Risberg to E. Collins to Gandil. Hit by Pitchers—Rath (by Cicotte), Daubert (by Lowdermilk). Left on Bases—Chicago 5, Cincinnati 7. Umpires—Rigler (N), Evans (A), Nallin (N), Quigley (A). Attendance—30,511. Time of Game—1:42.

1st Inning
Chicago
S. Collins lined a single to center.
1 E. Collins forced S. Collins at second on a bunt, Ruether to Kopf.
2 E. Collins out attempting to steal second, Wingo to Rath.
3 Weaver flied to Roush, making a one-handed catch in left-center.
Cincinnati
Rath was hit by a pitch.
Daubert singled to right-center, Rath racing to third.
1 Groh flied to Jackson in deep left, Rath scoring after the catch.
2 Daubert out trying to steal second, Schalk to Risberg.
Roush walked.
Roush stole second.
3 Duncan grounded to short.

2nd Inning
Chicago
Jackson safely to second on Kopf's wild throw to first.
1 Felsch sacrificed Jackson to third, Ruether to Daubert.
Gandil blooped a Texas Leaguer into short left, Jackson scoring.
2 Gandil out stealing second, Wingo to Rath.
Risberg walked.
3 Schalk flied to center.
Cincinnati
1 Kopf struck out.
2 Neale grounded to second.
3 Wingo flied to center.

3rd Inning
Chicago
1 Cicotte called out on strikes.
2 S. Collins flied to center.
3 E. Collins grounded to short.
Cincinnati
Ruether walked.
1 Rath sacrificed Ruether to second, Cicotte to Gandil.
2 Daubert flied to left.
3 Groh flied to left.

4th Inning
Chicago
1 Weaver out on a bunt to third.
2 Jackson grounded to short.
3 Felsch grounded to short.
Cincinnati
1 Roush flied to deep center.
Duncan singled over E. Collin's head.
2 Kopf forced Duncan at second, Cicotte to Risberg.
Neale singled deep to short, Kopf going to second.
Wingo singled to right, Kopf scoring as Neale went to third. Wingo took second on the throw to third.
Ruether tripled to the fence in left-center, scoring Neale and Wingo.
Rath doubled to left, scoring Ruether.
Daubert singled to right, Rath scoring.
Daubert took second on the throw to the plate.
For Chicago—Wilkinson relieved Cicotte.
3 Groh flied to center.

5th Inning
Chicago
Gandil singled to center.
1 Risberg forced Gandil in deep right-center.
2 Schalk forced Gandil at second, Groh to Rath.
3 Wilkinson forced Schalk at second, Rath unassisted.
Cincinnati
1 Roush flied to deep center.
Duncan singled to center.
2 Duncan out stealing second, Schalk to Risberg.
3 Kopf grounded to Risberg, making a spectacular stop.

6th Inning
Chicago
1 S. Collins flied to Roush in left-center.
E. Collins singled off Ruether's glove.
Weaver blasted a Texas League single to right, E. Collins going to second.
2 Jackson grounded to first, advancing both runners.
3 Felsch flied to short right.
Cincinnati
Neale singled to right-center.
1 Wingo called out on strikes.
Ruether singled to right, Neale going to second.
2,3 Rath lined into a double play, Risberg to E. Collins.

7th Inning
Chicago
1 Gandil flied to short right.
2 Risberg grounded to second.
3 Schalk grounded to third.
Cincinnati
Daubert bounced a ground-rule triple into the crowd in right.
Groh singled to center, scoring Daubert.
Roush sacrificed and was safe when Gandil dropped Weaver's throw, Groh going to third. (Assist to Weaver).
1 Duncan forced Roush at second, Risberg to E. Collins, Groh scoring.
2,3 Kopf grounded into a double play, Risberg to E. Collins to Gandil.

8th Inning
Chicago
McMullen, batting for Wilkinson, singled to center.
1 S. Collins flied to left.
2 E. Collins flied to center.
3 Weaver flied to center.
Cincinnati
For Chicago—Lowdermilk pitching.
Neale singled to left.
1 Wingo sacrificed Neale to second, Lowdermilk to Gandil.
Ruether tripled to deep center, Neale scoring. Ruether's second triple of the game.
2 Rath grounded to short, Ruether holding third.
Daubert hit by a pitch.
Groh walked, loading the bases.
3 Roush forced Groh at second, E. Collins to Risberg.

9th Inning
Chicago
1 Jackson flied to deep right.
2 Felsch flied to Roush.
3 Gandil grounded to second.

Game 2 October 2 at Cincinnati

Chicago	Pos	AB	R	H	RBI	PO	A	E
S. Collins	rf	4	0	0	0	2	0	0
E. Collins	2b	3	0	0	0	2	3	0
Weaver	3b	4	0	2	0	3	0	0
Jackson	lf	4	0	3	0	1	0	0
Felsch	cf	2	0	0	0	5	1	0
Gandil	1b	4	0	1	0	7	0	0
Risberg	ss	4	1	1	0	2	2	1
Schalk	c	4	1	2	0	4	2	0
Williams	p	3	0	1	0	0	2	0
a McMullin		1	0	0	0	0	0	0
Totals		33	2	10	0	24	10	1

a Grounded out for Williams in 9th.

Doubles—Jackson, Weaver. Triple—Kopf.
Stolen Base—Gandil. Sacrifice
Hits—Daubert, Duncan, Felsch 2.
Double Plays—Kopf to Daubert, E. Collins
to Gandil, Felsch to E. Collins to
Gandil, Rath to Kopf to Daubert.
Balk—Sallee. Left on Bases—Chicago 7,
Cincinnati 3. Umpires—Evans, Quigley,
Nallin, Rigler. Attendance—29,698.
Time of Game—1:42.

1st Inning
Chicago
1 S. Collins grounded back to the mound.
  E. Collins walked.
2,3 Weaver lined into a double play,
  Kopf to Daubert.
Cincinnati
1 Rath flied to center on a full count.
2 Daubert grounded to short, also on a
  full count.
3 Groh lined to right, S. Collins making
  a real nice catch.

2nd Inning
Chicago
  Jackson lined a double into center.
1 Felsch sacrificed Jackson to third,
  Sallee to Daubert.
2 Gandil grounded to short, Jackson
  holding at third.
3 Risberg flied to right.
Cincinnati
  Roush walked.
1,2 Duncan lined into a double play,
  E. Collins to Gandil.
3 Kopf flied to center.

3rd Inning
Chicago
1 Schalk flied to Roush in right-center.
  Williams singled over short.
2 S. Collins lined to short left.
3 E. Collins grounded to first.
Cincinnati
1 Neale struck out.
2 Rariden flied to Jackson in left-center.
3 Sallee popped to third.

4th Inning
Chicago
  Weaver singled over second.
  Jackson singled to left, Weaver going
  to second.
1 Felsch sacrificed up both runners,
  Sallee to Rath.
2 Gandil safe on a fielder's choice,
  Daubert getting his grounder and
  throwing to Rariden, Weaver out at the
  plate. Jackson went to third.
  Gandil stole second.
3 Risberg popped to Daubert in short
  right.
Cincinnati
  Rath walked.
1 Daubert sacrificed Rath to second,
  Williams to Gandil.
  Groh walked.
  Roush lined a single over second, Rath
  scoring as Groh took third on the throw
  to the plate.
2 Roush out trying to steal second,
  Schalk to Risberg.
  Duncan walked.
  Kopf tripled to the fence in left,
  scoring Groh and Duncan.
3 Neale grounded to second.

5th Inning
Chicago
1 Schalk popped to Roush in short left.
2 Williams grounded to short.
3 S. Collins grounded to short.
Cincinnati
  Rariden singled to left.
1 Sallee flied to center.
  Rath safe when Risberg got an error,
  missing his pop near the mound, as
  Rariden got to second.
2 Daubert popped to second.
3 Groh lined to center.

6th Inning
Chicago
1 E. Collins lined to short.
  Weaver doubled to the left field fence.
2 Jackson called out on strikes.
  Weaver to third on a balk.
3 Felsch flied to Roush, making a superb
  running one-handed catch in deep
  center.
Cincinnati
  Roush walked.
1 Duncan sacrificed Roush to second,
  Williams to Gandil.
2 Kopf fouled to Weaver.
  Neale singled to left, Roush scoring.
3 Neale out attempting to steal
  second, Schalk to Risberg.

7th Inning
Chicago
1 Gandil grounded out, Daubert to Sallee.
  Risberg singled to left.
  Schalk singled to right, Neale's throw
  went over Kopf's head all the way to
  the left field fence. Risberg scored
  as Schalk dashed for third and then
  also raced for the plate and scored
  when Groh's throw hit Schalk in the
  back.
2 Williams struck out.
3 S. Collins flied to center.
Cincinnati
1 Rariden fouled to Schalk down the
  third base line.
2 Sallee flied to right.
3 Rath lined to Weaver.

8th Inning
Chicago
1 E. Collins flied to center.
2 Weaver grounded to short.
  Jackson singled to short right and got
  to second on Daubert's throwing error.
3 Felsh lined to Groh, who knocked it
  down and threw to first.
Cincinnati
1 Daubert grounded to short.
  Groh walked.
2,3 Roush flied to Felsch in short center
  a real good catch and threw to Gandil
  to double up Groh.

9th Inning
Chicago
  Gandil singled over second.
1,2 Risberg grounded into a double play,
  Rath to Kopf to Daubert.
  Schalk singled to center.
3 McMullin, batting for Williams,
  grounded to second.

Chi.	000 000 200
Cin.	000 301 00x

Cincinnati	Pos	AB	R	H	RBI	PO	A
Rath	2b	3	1	0	0	1	2
Daubert	1b	3	0	0	0	12	2
Groh	3b	2	1	0	0	0	1
Roush	cf	2	1	1	1	5	0
Duncan	lf	1	1	0	1	0	0
Kopf	ss	3	0	1	2	3	6
Neale	rf	3	0	1	1	1	0
Rariden	c	3	0	1	0	3	0
Sallee	p	3	0	0	0	1	3
Totals		23	4	4	4	27	14

Pitching	IP	H	R	ER	BB	SO
Chicago						
Williams (L)	8	4	4	4	6	
Cincinnati						
Sallee (W)	9	10	2	0	1	

Game 3 October 3 at Chicago

Cincinnati	Pos	AB	R	H	RBI	PO	A	E
Rath	2b	4	0	0	0	3	3	0
Daubert	1b	4	0	0	0	14	1	0
Groh	3b	3	0	0	0	2	5	0
Roush	cf	3	0	0	0	0	0	0
Duncan	lf	3	0	1	0	0	0	0
Kopf	ss	3	0	1	0	1	1	0
Neale	rf	3	0	0	0	1	0	0
Rariden	c	3	0	0	0	2	3	0
Fisher	p	2	0	1	0	0	5	1
a Magee		1	0	0	0	0	0	0
Luque	p	0	0	0	0	0	1	0
Totals		29	0	3	0	24	18	1

a Flied out for Fisher in 8th.

Triple—Risberg. Double Plays—Groh to
Rath to Daubert, Risberg to E. Collins.
Left on Bases—Cincinnati 3, Chicago 3.
Umpires—Quigley, Nallin, Rigler, Evans.
Attendance—29,126. Time of Game—1:30.

1st Inning
Cincinnati
1 Rath grounded to short.
2 Daubert flied to center.
3 Groh fanned.
Chicago
1 Leibold flied to Neale, making a
  circus catch.
2 E. Collins grounded back to the mound.
3 Weaver popped to first.

2nd Inning
Cincinnati
1 Roush grounded to short.
  Duncan singled to right-center.
2 Kopf grounded to short, Duncan
  going to second.
3 Neale grounded to second.
Chicago
  Jackson singled to left.
  Felsch safe of Fisher's wild throw
  to second, Jackson getting to third
  and Felsch to second.
  Gandil singled to right, scoring
  Jackson and Felsch, Gandil going to
  second on the throw-in.
  Risberg walked.
1 Schalk forced Gandil at third, Fisher
  to Groh.
2 Kerr forced Risberg at third, Fisher
  to Groh.
3 Leibold grounded to third.

3rd Inning
Cincinnati
1 Rariden grounded to third.
  Fisher beat out an infield hit to the
  mound.
2 Rath popped to short.
3 Daubert forced Fisher at second, E.
  Collins to Risberg.
Chicago
  E. Collins singled over short.
  Weaver also singled over short, E.
  Collins stopping at second.
1 Jackson popped to first on a sacrifice
  attempt.
2,3 Felsch grounded into a double play,
  Groh to Rath to Daubert.

4th Inning
Cincinnati
  Groh walked.
1 Roush grounded to short, Groh going to
  second.
2,3 Duncan lined into a double play,
  Risberg to E. Collins.
Chicago
1 Gandil grounded to third.
  Risberg tripled to right.
  Schalk beat out a bunt, Risberg scoring.
2 Schalk out trying to steal second,
  Rariden to Rath.
3 Kerr grounded to short.

Cin.	000 000 000
Chi.	020 100 00x

Chicago	Pos	AB	R	H	RBI	PO	A	E
Leibold	rf	4	0	0	0	2	0	0
E. Collins	2b	4	0	1	0	1	5	0
Weaver	3b	4	0	1	0	0	4	0
Jackson	lf	3	1	2	0	1	0	0
Felsch	cf	3	1	0	0	1	0	0
Gandil	1b	3	0	1	2	14	1	0
Risberg	ss	2	1	1	0	4	6	0
Schalk	c	3	0	1	1	4	0	0
Kerr	p	3	0	0	0	0	0	0
Totals		28	3	7	3	27	16	0

Pitching	IP	H	R	ER	BB	SO
Cincinnati						
Fisher (L)	7	7	3	2	2	1
Luque	1	0	0	0	0	1
Chicago						
Kerr (W)	9	3	0	0	1	4

5th Inning
Cincinnati
  Kopf singled to right.
1 Neale forced Kopf at second, Gandil
  to Risberg.
2 Rariden grounded to second, Neale
  going to second.
3 Fisher grounded to third.
Chicago
1 Leibold grounded to first.
2 E. Collins grounded back to the mound.
3 Weaver grounded back to the mound.

6th Inning
Cincinnati
1 Rath grounded to short.
2 Daubert lined to second.
3 Groh grounded to third.
Chicago
  Jackson singled behind short.
1 Jackson out trying to steal second,
  Rariden to Kopf.
  Felsch walked.
2 Felsch out stealing, Rariden to
  Rath.
3 Gandil struck out.

7th Inning
Cincinnati
1 Roush popped to first.
2 Duncan struck out.
3 Kopf flied to right.
Chicago
1 Risberg grounded to third.
2 Schalk also grounded to third.
3 Kerr grounded to second.

8th Inning
Cincinnati
1 Neale fanned.
2 Rariden grounded to second.
3 Magee, pinch-hitting for Fisher,
  flied to right.
Chicago
  For Cincinnati—Luque now pitching.
1 Leibold fanned.
2 E. Collins grounded out, Daubert to
  Luque.
3 Weaver grounded to second.

9th Inning
Cincinnati
1 Rath grounded to second.
2 Daubert fanned.
3 Groh grounded to third.

Game 4 October 4 at Chicago

Cin.	000 020 000
Chi.	000 000 000

Cincinnati	Pos	AB	R	H	RBI	PO	A	E
Rath	2b	4	0	1	0	5	1	1
Daubert	1b	4	0	0	0	9	1	0
Groh	3b	4	0	0	0	2	3	1
Roush	cf	3	0	0	0	2	0	0
Duncan	lf	3	1	0	0	1	0	0
Kopf	ss	3	1	1	1	1	1	0
Neale	rf	3	0	1	1	4	0	0
Wingo	c	3	0	2	0	2	0	0
Ring	p	3	0	0	0	1	2	0
Totals		30	2	5	2	27	8	2

Pitching	IP	H	R	ER	BB	SO
Cincinnati						
Ring (W)	9	3	0	0	3	2
Chicago						
Cicotte (L)	9	5	2	0	0	2

Chicago	Pos	AB	R	H	RBI	PO	A	E
Leibold	rf	5	0	0	0	0	0	0
E. Collins	2b	3	0	0	0	3	5	0
Weaver	3b	4	0	0	0	0	3	0
Jackson	lf	4	0	1	0	3	0	0
Felsch	cf	3	0	1	0	1	0	0
Gandil	1b	4	0	1	0	14	0	0
Risberg	ss	3	0	0	0	3	4	0
Schalk	c	1	0	0	0	4	3	0
Cicotte	p	3	0	0	0	0	2	2
a Murphy		1	0	0	0	0	0	0
Totals		31	0	3	0	27	17	2

a Flied out for Cicotte in 9th.

Doubles—Jackson, Neale. Stolen Base—Risberg. Sacrifice Hit—Felsch. Double Plays—Cicotte to Risberg to Gandil, E. Collins to Risberg to Gandil. Hit by Pitcher—E. Collins and Schalk (by Ring). Left on Bases—Cincinnati 1, Chicago 10. Umpires—Nallin, Rigler, Evans, Quigley. Attendance—34,363. Time of Game—1:37.

1st Inning
Cincinnati
Rath singled to left.
1,2 Daubert hit into a double play, E. Collins to Risberg to Gandil.
3 Groh popped to short.
Chicago
1 Leibold popped to Daubert in short right.
2 E. Collins popped to second.
3 Weaver flied to right.

2nd Inning
Cincinnati
1 Roush flied to left.
2 Duncan popped to E. Collins in short right.
3 Kopf struck out.
Chicago
Jackson doubled to right-center as Roush misjudged the fly.
1 Felsch sacrificed Jackson to second, Ring to Rath.
2 Gandil popped to Groh in front of the plate.
Risberg walked.
Risberg stole second.
Schalk walked, loading the bases.
3 Cicotte grounded to second.

3rd Inning
Cincinnati
1 Neale grounded to third.
Wingo singled to center.
2 Ring struck out.
3 Wingo out stealing second, Schalk to E. Collins.
Chicago
1 Leibold flied to right.
E. Collins hit by a pitch.
2 Weaver grounded to first, E. Collins to second.
Jackson safe on error by Rath, E. Collins going to third.
3 Felsch grounded to third.

4th Inning
Cincinnati
1 Rath flied to left.
2 Daubert bunted out, Schalk to Gandil.
3 Groh lined to second.
Chicago
1 Gandil fouled to Daubert.
2 Risberg flied to right.
3 Schalk popped to short.

5th Inning
Cincinnati
1 Roush grounded out in front of the plate, Schalk to Gandil.
Duncan got safely to second when Cicotte threw his grounder into the stands.
Kopf singled to left, Duncan scoring as Kopf went to second when Cicotte dropped Jackson's throw even though Schalk was in position to take the throw.
Neale doubled to left, Kopf scoring.
2 Wingo grounded to second, Neale advancing to third.
3 Ring grounded to second.

5th Inning (continued)
Chicago
1 Cicotte grounded out, Daubert to Ring. Leibold safe on Groh's throwing error, Leibold getting to second on the error.
2 E. Collins grounded to Groh and Leibold was caught between second and third, Groh to Rath.
3 Weaver grounded to first.

6th Inning
Cincinnati
1 Rath grounded to short.
2 Daubert grounded to second.
3 Groh grounded to third.
Chicago
1 Jackson grounded to short.
2 Felsch flied to deep left.
Gandil singled to center.
3 Risberg flied to right.

7th Inning
Cincinnati
1 Roush grounded to second.
2 Duncan grounded to Weaver making a great stop and throw.
3 Kopf grounded to short.
Chicago
Schalk hit by a pitch.
1 Cicotte popped to second.
2 Leibold flied to center.
3 E. Collins grounded to third.

8th Inning
Cincinnati
1 Neale bounced back to the mound. Wingo singled through the box.
2,3 Ring hit into a double play, Cicotte to Risberg to Gandil.
Chicago
1 Weaver popped to Rath, making a great running catch near the right field foul line.
2 Jackson struck out.
Felsch singled to left.
3 Gandil struck out.

9th Inning
Cincinnati
1 Rath fouled to Schalk.
2 Daubert flied to left.
3 Groh fouled to Schalk.
Chicago
1 Risberg grounded back to the mound.
Schalk walked.
2 Murphy, pinch-hitting for Cicotte, flied to center.
3 Leibold lined to third.

Game 5 October 6 at Chicago

Cin.	000 004 001
Chi.	000 000 000

Cincinnati	Pos	AB	R	H	RBI	PO	A	E
Rath	2b	3	1	1	0	3	0	0
Daubert	1b	2	0	0	0	11	0	0
Groh	3b	3	1	0	0	1	2	0
Roush	cf	4	2	1	2	2	0	0
Duncan	lf	2	0	0	1	2	0	0
Kopf	ss	3	0	1	0	0	4	0
Neale	rf	4	0	0	1	1	0	0
Rariden	c	4	0	0	0	10	0	0
Eller	p	3	1	1	0	0	2	0
Totals		28	5	4	5	27	11	0

Pitching	IP	H	R	ER	BB	SO
Cincinnati						
Eller (W)	9	3	0	0	1	9
Chicago						
Williams (L)	8	4	4	4	2	3
Mayer	1	0	1	0	1	0

Chicago	Pos	AB	R	H	RBI	PO	A	E
Leibold	rf	3	0	0	0	1	0	0
E. Collins	2b	4	0	0	0	1	2	1
Weaver	3b	4	0	2	0	1	2	0
Jackson	lf	4	0	0	0	3	0	0
Felsch	cf	3	0	0	0	7	0	1
Gandil	1b	4	0	0	0	8	1	0
Risberg	ss	3	0	0	0	1	2	1
Schalk	c	2	0	1	0	3	2	0
Lynn	c	1	0	0	0	1	0	0
Williams	p	2	0	0	0	1	0	0
a Murphy		1	0	0	0	0	0	0
Mayer	p	0	0	0	0	0	0	0
Totals		30	0	3	0	27	9	3

a Struck out for Williams in 8th.

Double—Eller. Triples—Roush, Weaver. Stolen Base—Roush. Sacrifice Hits—Daubert 2, Duncan, Kopf. Passed Ball—Schalk. Left on Bases—Cincinnati 3, Chicago 4. Umpires—Rigler, Evans, Quigley, Nallin. Attendance—34,379. Time of Game—1:45.

1st Inning
Cincinnati
Rath walked.
1 Daubert sacrificed Rath to second, Schalk to Gandil.
2 Groh flied to center.
3 Roush grounded out, Gandil to Williams.
Chicago
Leibold walked.
1 E. Collins grounded to short, Leibold going to second.
Weaver beat out a smash too hard for Eller to handle, Leibold taking third.
2 Jackson popped to third.
3 Felsch flied to left.

2nd Inning
Cincinnati
1 Duncan struck out.
2 Kopf fouled to Schalk.
3 Neale struck out.
Chicago
1 Gandil struck out.
2 Risberg called out on strikes on a full count.
3 Schalk also called out on strikes.

3rd Inning
Cincinnati
1 Rariden grounded to first.
2 Eller popped to Weaver in front of the plate.
3 Rath fouled to Gandil.
Chicago
1 Williams called out on strikes.
2 Leibold also called out on strikes, Eller's fifth consecutive victim.
3 E. Collins struck out on a 3-2 count, becoming Eller's sixth consecutive strikeout.

4th Inning
Cincinnati
1 Daubert flied to center.
2 Groh flied to center.
Roush safe on a fumble by Risberg. Roush stole second, aided by a short passed ball.
3 Duncan flied to left.
Chicago
1 Weaver bounced back to the mound, breaking up Eller's string of strike outs.
2 Jackson also bounced back to Eller.
3 Felsch struck out.

5th Inning
Cincinnati
Kopf singled to right-center.
1 Neale forced Kopf at second, Risberg to E. Collins.
2 Neale caught trying to steal second, Schalk to Risberg.
3 Rariden flied to center.
Chicago
1 Gandil grounded to second.
2 Risberg grounded to third.
Schalk singled to left.
3 Williams again struck out.

6th Inning
Cincinnati
Eller doubled to left-center, and went to third on Felsch's wild throw to Risberg.
Rath singled to right, scoring Eller.
1 Daubert sacrificed Rath to second, Weaver to Gandil.
Groh walked.
Roush tripled to deep center, scoring Rath and Groh. The play at the plate for Groh was very close. Schalk was thrown out of the game by Umpire Rigler.
For Chicago—Lynn came in to catch.
2 Duncan flied to left, Roush scoring after the catch.
3 Kopf flied to center.
Chicago
1 Leibold grounded to third.
2 E. Collins flied to deep center.
3 Weaver grounded to short.

7th Inning
Cincinnati
1 Neale grounded to second.
2 Rariden flied to right.
3 Eller struck out.
Chicago
1 Jackson grounded to second.
2 Felsch fouled to Rariden.
3 Gandil flied to center.

8th Inning
Cincinnati
1 Rath lined to left.
2 Daubert flied to center.
3 Groh flied to center.
Chicago
1 Risberg flied to right.
2 Lynn flied to left.
3 Murphy, pinch-hitting for Williams, struck out.

9th Inning
Cincinnati
For Chicago—Mayer pitching.
Roush safe on an error by E. Collins.
Duncan walked.
1 Kopf sacrificed up both runners, Weaver to Gandil.
2 Neale grounded to short, Roush scoring as Duncan went to third.
3 Rariden grounded to second.
Chicago
1 Leibold grounded to second.
2 E. Collins grounded to short.
Weaver tripled to deep right-center.
3 Jackson grounded to short.

Game 6 October 7 at Cincinnati

Chicago	Pos	AB	R	H	RBI	PO	A	E
S. Collins	rf	3	0	0	0	2	0	0
a Leibold	rf	1	0	0	0	0	0	0
E. Collins	2b	4	0	0	1	4	6	0
Weaver	3b	5	2	3	0	2	1	0
Jackson	lf	5	0	2	0	2	0	0
Felsch	cf	5	1	2	1	2	0	1
Gandil	1b	4	1	1	11	0	0	0
Risberg	ss	4	1	0	0	3	5	2
Schalk	c	2	0	1	1	4	2	0
Kerr	p	3	0	1	0	1	4	0
Totals		35	5	10	5	30	19	3

a Grounded out for S. Collins in 7th.

Cincinnati	Pos	AB	R	H	RBI	PO	A	E
Rath	2b	5	0	1	0	4	1	0
Daubert	1b	4	1	2	0	8	0	0
Groh	3b	4	0	1	0	2	2	0
Roush	cf	4	1	1	0	7	2	0
Duncan	lf	5	0	1	2	2	0	0
Kopf	ss	4	0	0	0	1	5	0
Neale	rf	4	1	3	0	3	0	0
Rariden	c	4	0	1	0	3	0	0
Ruether	p	2	1	1	1	0	0	0
Ring	p	2	0	0	0	0	1	0
Totals		38	4	11	3	30	11	0

Chicago Pitching	IP	H	R	ER	BB	SO
Kerr (W)	10	11	4	3	2	2

Cincinnati	IP	H	R	ER	BB	SO
Ruether	*5	6	4	3	0	2
Ring (L)	5	4	1	1	3	2

*Pitched to three batters in 6th.

Chi.   000 013 000 1
Cin.   002 200 000 0

Doubles—Duncan, Felsch, Groh, Ruether, Weaver 2. Triple—Neale. Stolen Bases—Daubert, Leibold, Rath, Schalk. Sacrifice Hits—E. Collins, Daubert, Kerr. Double Plays—Jackson to Schalk, Roush to Groh, Risberg to E. Collins to Gandil, Roush to Rath, Kopf to Rath. Hit by Pitcher—Roush (by Kerr). Left on Bases—Chicago 8, Cincinnati 8. Umpires—Evans, Quigley, Nallin, Rigler. Attendance—32,006. Time of Game—2:06.

1st Inning
Chicago
1 S. Collins flied to Rath in short center.
2 E. Collins lined to center.
  Weaver singled through short.
3 Jackson popped to third.
Cincinnati
1 Rath popped to short.
2 Daubert bounced back to the mound.
  Groh doubled to center.
  Roush beat out a hit to short, but
3 Groh was out overrunning third, Risberg to Weaver.

2nd Inning
Chicago
1 Felsch flied to deep right.
2 Gandil grounded to short.
3 Risberg flied to right.
Cincinnati
  Duncan safe on Risberg's bobble.
  Kopf walked.
1 Neale forced Duncan at third, Kerr to Weaver.
2 Rariden forced Duncan at second, E. Collins to Risberg, Kopf to third.
3 Ruether grounded back to the mound.

3rd Inning
Chicago
  Schalk walked.
1 Kerr sacrificed, Groh to Rath.
2 S. Collins flied to center.
3 E. Collins lined to Duncan, racing in to make a spectacular catch.
Cincinnati
1 Rath grounded to second
  Daubert singled to right.
2 Groh struck out, as Daubert stole second.
  Rousch was hit by a pitch.
  Duncan doubled to right-center, scoring Daubert and Roush.
3 Kopf flied to deep center.

4th Inning
Chicago
1 Weaver flied to left.
2 Jackson fouled to Rariden.
  Felsch singled to center.
3 Gandil grounded to short.
Cincinnati
  Neale tripled to deep right.
1 Rariden grounded to second, Neale holding third.
  Ruether doubled to left, scoring Neale. Rath hit to Risberg who throwing to third hit Ruether in the back as the ball rolled to the stand, allowing Ruether to score and Rath to go to second.
  Rath stole third.
2,3 Daubert flied to left and Rath was doubled trying to score, Jackson to Schalk.

5th Inning
Chicago
  Risberg walked.
  Schalk walked.
  Kerr singled off Kopf's glove, loading the bases.
1 S. Collins flied to center, Roush firing to the plate to hold Risberg at third.
2,3 E. Collins flied to center, Risberg scoring after the catch. Kerr ran to second which Schalk still held and was doubled on Roush's throw to Groh tagging out Kerr.
Cincinnati
1 Groh flied to center.
2 Roush flied to right.
  Duncan safely at third on Felsch's muff of his deep fly.
3 Kopf grounded to short.

6th Inning
Chicago
  Weaver got a Texas League double to short left.
  Jackson singled to center, scoring Weaver.
  Felsch doubled to left-center, scoring Jackson.
  For Cincinnati—Ring came in to pitch.
1 Gandil popped to first.
2 Risberg grounded to short, Felsch going to third.
  Schalk singled through short, Felsch scoring.
  Schalk stole second.
3 Kerr grounded to the mound.
Cincinnati
  Neale singled off Kerr's glove.
1 Rariden flied to right.
2 Ring struck out.
3 Neale out on a steal attempt, Schalk to Risberg.

7th Inning
Chicago
1 Leibold, batting for S. Collins, grounded to short.
2 E. Collins flied to center.
3 Weaver grounded to second.
Cincinnati
  For Chicago—Leibold playing in right. Rath got a Texas League single to center.
1 Daubert sacrificed, Kerr to Gandil.
  Groh walked.
2,3 Roush hit into a double play, Risberg to E. Collins to Gandil.

8th Inning
Chicago
  Jackson walked.
1 Felsch flied to right.
2,3 Risberg flied to Roush making a spectacular catch and throwing to Rath doubling Jackson at second.
Cincinnati
1 Duncan fouled to Gandil.
2 Kopf lined to Kerr.
  Neale singled through first.
  Rariden singled off Kerr's glove, Neale going to second.
3 Ring forced Rariden at second, Risberg to E. Collins.

9th Inning
Chicago
1 Schalk struck out.
2 Kerr bounced to the mound.
  Leibold walked.
  Leibold stole second.
3 E. Collins flied to center.
Cincinnati
1 Rath grounded to the mound.
  Daubert singled to center.
2 Groh forced Daubert at second, Risberg to E. Collins.
3 Groh out trying to steal second, Schalk to E. Collins.

10th Inning
Chicago
  Weaver doubled to left.
  Jackson beat out a bunt, Weaver going to third.
1 Felsch struck out.
  Gandil singled over second, scoring Weaver and sending Jackson to third.
2,3 Risberg lined into a double play, Kopf to Rath.
Cincinnati
1 Roush grounded to second.
2 Duncan fouled to Schalk.
3 Kopf grounded to second.

Game 7 October 8 at Cincinnati

Chicago	Pos	AB	R	H	RBI	PO	A	E
S. Collins	cf-rf	5	2	3	0	1	0	0
E. Collins	2b	4	1	2	0	3	6	1
Weaver	3b	4	1	0	0	2	2	0
Jackson	lf	4	0	2	2	2	0	0
Felsch	rf-cf	4	0	2	2	2	0	0
Gandil	1b	4	0	0	0	9	0	0
Risberg	ss	4	0	0	0	3	2	0
Schalk	c	4	0	1	0	4	1	0
Cicotte	p	4	0	0	0	0	2	0
Totals		37	4	10	4	27	13	1

Pitching	IP	H	R	ER	BB	SO
Chicago						
Cicotte (W)	9	7	1	1	3	4
Cincinnati						
Sallee (L)	4⅓	9	4	2	0	0
Fisher	⅔	0	0	0	0	1
Luque	4	1	0	0	0	5

Cincinnati	Pos	AB	R	H	RBI	PO	A	E
Rath	2b	5	0	1	0	3	2	1
Daubert	1b	4	0	0	0	10	0	1
Groh	3b	4	1	1	0	0	1	1
Roush	cf	4	0	0	0	3	1	1
Duncan	lf	4	0	1	1	1	0	0
Kopf	ss	4	0	1	0	2	5	0
Neale	rf	4	0	1	0	3	0	0
Wingo	c	1	0	1	0	5	1	0
Sallee	p	1	0	0	0	0	1	0
Fisher	p	0	0	0	0	1	0	0
a Ruether		1	0	0	0	0	0	0
Luque	p	1	0	0	0	0	0	0
b Magee		1	0	1	0	0	0	0
c Smith		0	0	0	0	0	0	0
Totals		34	1	7	1	27	12	4

a Fouled out for Fisher in 5th.
b Singled for Luque in 9th.
c Ran for Magee in 9th.

Chi.   101 020 000
Cin.   000 001 000

Doubles—S. Collins, Groh. Sacrifice Hit—E. Collins. Double Play—Kopf to Daubert. Left on Bases—Chicago 7, Cincinnati 9. Umpires—Quigley, Nallin, Rigler, Evans. Attendance—13,923. Time of Game—1:47.

1st Inning
Chicago
  S. Collins singled to center.
1 E. Collins sacrificed S. Collins to second, Sallee to Daubert.
2 Weaver flied to center.
  Jackson singled to left, scoring S. Collins. Jackson was hung up between first and second but Daubert dropped the throw for an error, as Jackson safely returned to first.
  Felsch beat out a bunt down the third base line on the first pitch, Jackson going to second.
3 Gandil forced Felsch at second, Kopf to Rath.
Cincinnati
  Rath safe on E. Collins' error.
1 Daubert popped to E. Collins.
2 Groh struck out.
3 Roush forced Rath at second, E. Collins to Risberg.

2nd Inning
Chicago
1 Risberg grounded to short.
2 Schalk lined to Neale in right-center.
3 Cicotte grounded to third.
Cincinnati
1 Duncan flied to center.
  Kopf singled to left-center.
2 Neale fouled to Weaver.
3 Kopf out trying to steal second, Schalk to Risberg.

3rd Inning
Chicago
  S. Collins singled off Sallee's glove.
  E. Collins beat out a hit to deep short, S. Collins going to second.
1,2 Weaver lined into a double play, Kopf to Daubert.
  Jackson singled to left, scoring S. Collins.
3 Felsch forced Jackson at second, Kopf to Rath.
Cincinnati
  Wingo walked.
1 Sallee flied to right.
2 Rath forced Wingo at second, Risberg to E. Collins.
3 Daubert bounced back to the mound.

4th Inning
Chicago
1 Gandil flied to right.
2 Risberg fouled to Daubert, making a spectacular catch leaning into the stands.
  Schalk singled to third.
3 Cicotte flied to center.
Cincinnati
1 Groh grounded to second.
2 Roush grounded to second.
3 Duncan grounded to third.

5th Inning
Chicago
1 S. Collins flied to right.
  E. Collins singled to center.
  Weaver safe on Groh's error, E. Collins going to second.
  Jackson safe on Rath's error, loading the bases.
  Felsch singled to center, scoring E. Collins and Weaver as Jackson stopped at second.
  For Cincinnati—Fisher relieved Sallee.
2 Gandil bounced back to the mound, advancing both runners.
3 Risberg struck out.

5th Inning (continued)
Cincinnati
1 Kopf flied to left.
  Neale singled to center.
  Wingo walked.
2 Ruether, batting for Fisher, fouled to Weaver.
3 Rath grounded to third

6th Inning
Chicago
  For Cincinnati—Luque now pitching.
1 Schalk flied to left.
2 Cicotte struck out.
  S. Collins doubled down the left field line, for his third hit.
3 E. Collins struck out, but had to be thrown out by Wingo.
Cincinnati
1 Daubert struck out.
  Groh got a ground-rule double over the left field railing.
2 Roush grounded back to the mound, Groh advancing to third.
  Duncan singled to center, scoring Groh.
3 Kopf forced Duncan at second, E. Collins to Risberg.

7th Inning
Chicago
1 Weaver struck out.
2 Jackson grounded to second.
3 Felsch struck out.
Cincinnati
1 Neale struck out.
  Wingo walked for the third time.
2 Luque struck out.
  Rath singled over second, Wingo going to second.
3 Daubert grounded to second.

8th Inning
Chicago
1 Gandil flied to Kopf racing into left.
  Risberg safe on Roush's error, but
2 out as he tried to make second, Roush to Kopf.
3 Schalk grounded to short.
Cincinnati
1 Groh flied to left.
2 Roush grounded to second.
3 Duncan grounded to short.

9th Inning
Chicago
1 Cicotte struck out.
2 S. Collins flied to center.
3 E. Collins grounded to second.
Cincinnati
1 Kopf fouled to E. Collins.
2 Neale flied to left
  Wingo singled over second.
  Magee, pinch-hitting for Luque, singled to right, Wingo stopping at second.
  Smith ran for Magee.
3 Rath flied to Felsch in right-center.

Game 8 October 9 at Chicago

Cin.   4 1 0   0 1 3   0 1 0
Chi.   0 0 1   0 0 0   0 4 0

Cincinnati	Pos	AB	R	H	RBI	PO	A	E
Rath	2b	4	1	2	0	2	2	0
Daubert	1b	4	2	2	0	8	0	0
Groh	3b	6	2	2	0	1	1	0
Roush	cf	5	2	3	4	4	0	1
Duncan	lf	4	1	2	3	1	0	0
Kopf	ss	3	1	1	0	1	3	0
Neale	rf	3	0	1	1	3	0	0
Rariden	c	5	0	2	2	7	0	1
Eller	p	4	1	1	0	0	0	0
Totals		38	10	16	10	27	6	2

Pitching	IP	H	R	ER	BB	SO
Cincinnati						
Eller (W)	9	10	5	4	1	6
Chicago						
Williams (L)	⅓	4	4	4	0	0
James	*4⅔	8	4	3	3	2
Wilkinson	4	4	2	0	4	2

*Pitched to two batters in 6th.

Chicago	Pos	AB	R	H	RBI	PO	A	E
Leibold	cf	5	0	1	0	2	0	0
E. Collins	2b	5	1	3	0	4	1	0
Weaver	3b	5	1	2	0	1	5	0
Jackson	lf	5	2	2	3	1	0	0
Felsch	rf	4	0	0	0	2	0	0
Gandil	1b	4	1	1	1	9	0	0
Risberg	ss	3	0	0	0	2	3	0
Schalk	c	4	0	1	0	6	3	1
Williams	p	0	0	0	0	0	0	0
James	p	2	0	0	0	0	0	0
Wilkinson	p	1	0	0	0	0	2	0
a Murphy		0	0	0	0	0	0	0
Totals		38	5	10	4	27	16	1

a Hit by pitcher for Wilkinson in 9th.

Doubles—E. Collins, Duncan, Jackson, Roush 2, Weaver. Triples—Gandil, Kopf. Home Run—Jackson. Stolen Bases—E. Collins, Neale, Rariden, Rath. Sacrifice Hits—Daubert, Duncan. Hit by Pitchers—Eller (by James), Murphy (by Eller), Roush (by Wilkinson). Left on Bases—Cincinnati 12, Chicago 8. Umpires—Nallin, Rigler, Evans, Quigley. Attendance—32,930. Time of Game—2:27.

1st Inning
Cincinnati
1 Rath popped to Risberg in short left.
Daubert singled to center.
Groh singled to right, Daubert stopping at second.
Roush doubled over first into right, scoring Daubert as Groh raced to third.
Duncan doubled over Weaver's head into left, scoring Groh and Roush.
For Chicago—James replaced Williams on the mound.
Kopf walked.
2 Neale struck out.
Rariden lined a single to right, scoring Duncan and putting Kopf on third.
Rariden stole second.
3 Eller flied to Felsch in short right-center.
Chicago
Leibold singled to left.
E. Collins lined a double off of Duncan's glove, Leibold stopping at third.
1 Weaver called out on strikes.
2 Jackson popped to Kopf near the left field foul line.
3 Felsch struck out.

2nd Inning
Cincinnati
1 Rath called out on strikes.
2 Daubert flied to left.
Groh beat out a roller to first.
Roush doubled off Jackson's glove in deep left, scoring Groh. Roush overran
3 second and was caught, Leibold to Risberg to Schalk to Weaver to E. Collins.
Chicago
1 Gandil lined to first.
Risberg walked.
Rariden got an error dropping Schalk's foul.
Schalk singled to left, Risberg going to second.
2 James fouled to Groh.
3 Leibold struck out.

3rd Inning
Cincinnati
1 Duncan grounded to third.
2 Kopf grounded to Weaver, making a remarkable scoop and throw to first.
Neale walked.
3 Neale caught stealing, Schalk to E. Collins.
Chicago
1 E. Collins lined to left.
2 Weaver popped to Rath in short right-center.
Jackson hit the first home run of the Series into the right field bleachers.
3 Felsch grounded to short.

4th Inning
Cincinnati
1 Rariden lined to first.
Eller was hit by a pitch.
Rath beat out a smash to second, Eller going to second.
Daubert singled to deep center, but
2 Eller was out trying to score, Leibold to Schalk. Rath went to third and Daubert to second on the play at the plate.
3 Groh popped to second.
Chicago
1 Gandil flied to Roush in right-center.
2 Risberg struck out.
3 Schalk grounded to third.

5th Inning
Cincinnati
1 Roush grounded to second.
2 Duncan lined to second.
Kopf tripled to the right-center field fence.
Neale singled past short, scoring Kopf.
Neale stole second.
3 Rariden grounded to short.
Chicago
1 James struck out.
2 Leibold grounded to short.
3 E. Collins grounded to short.

6th Inning
Cincinnati
Eller singled through the box.
Rath walked.
For Chicago—Wilkinson came in to pitch.
Daubert bunted and was safe when Schalk threw low to Weaver trying to get Eller. This loaded the bases.
1 Groh struck out on three pitches.
Roush singled off E. Collins' glove into right, Eller and Rath scoring as Daubert got to third. Roush's third hit.
Duncan singled to second, scoring Daubert with Roush stopping at second.
Roush went to third and Duncan to second on Leibold's slow throw into third.
Kopf walked, loading the bases.
2 Neale forced Roush at the plate, Weaver to Schalk.
3 Kopf was picked off second, Schalk to Risberg.
Chicago
Weaver singled over first.
1 Jackson flied to deep center.
2 Felsch flied to center.
3 Gandil flied to right.

7th Inning
Cincinnati
1 Rariden flied to right.
2 Eller struck out.
Rath walked.
Rath stole second.
Daubert walked.
3 Groh flied to center.
Chicago
1 Risberg popped to Rath in short right-center.
2 Schalk fouled to Rariden.
3 Wilkinson struck out.

8th Inning
Cincinnati
Roush hit by a pitched ball.
1 Duncan sacrificed Roush to second, Wilkinson to Gandil.
2 Kopf popped to Weaver between third and home.
Neale walked.
Rariden singled to left, scoring Roush as Neale went to third. Rariden took second on the throw to the plate.
3 Eller grounded to short.
Chicago
1 Leibold flied to deep right.
E. Collins singled to center.
Weaver doubled over first into right, his fourth double of the Series, as E. Collins stopped at third.
Jackson doubled to deep right, E. Collins and Weaver scoring.
2 Felsch popped to first.
Gandil tripled to the right field fence, after Neale lost the ball in the sun, Jackson scoring.
Risberg safe when Roush muffed his fly in short right-center, Gandil scoring.
3 Schalk bounced to second.

9th Inning
Cincinnati
Rath beat out an infield hit to Risberg.
1 Daubert sacrificed Rath to second, Wilkinson to Gandil.
2 Groh flied to center.
3 Roush grounded to third.
Chicago
Murphy, batting for Wilkinson, was hit by a pitched ball.
1 Leibold flied to Roush making a spectacular catch in deep center.
E. Collins singled to center, his third hit of the game, Murphy going to second.
2 Weaver flied to deep right, Murphy going to third after the catch.
E. Collins stole second.
3 Jackson grounded to second.

1919 WORLD SERIES COMPOSITE BOX

	Wins	Composite Line Score										
Cincinnati Reds (N.L.)	5	5	1	2	10	3	9	2	2	1	0	- 35
Chicago White Sox (A.L.)	3	1	3	2	1	3	3	2	4	0	1	- 20

	Regular Season			
Manager	W	L	Pct.	G. Ahead
Pat Moran	96	44	.686	9
Kid Gleason	88	52	.629	3½

BATTING AND FIELDING

WORLD SERIES STATISTICS

	Pos	G	AB	R	H	2B	3B	HR	RBI	BB	SO	SB	BA	SA	PO	A	E
CINCINNATI REDS																	
Jake Daubert	1b	8	29	4	7	0	1	0	1	1	2	1	.241	.310	**81**	4	2
Morrie Rath	2b	8	31	5	7	1	0	0	2	4	1	**2**	.226	.258	22	16	2
Larry Kopf	ss	8	27	3	6	0	**2**	0	3	3	2	0	.222	.370	10	28	1
Heinie Groh	3b	8	29	**6**	5	2	0	0	2	**6**	4	0	.172	.241	8	18	2
Greasy Neale	rf	8	28	3	10	1	1	0	4	2	**5**	1	.357	.464	19	0	1
Edd Roush	cf	8	28	**6**	6	2	1	0	7	3	0	**2**	.214	.357	31	3	2
Pat Duncan	lf	8	26	3	7	2	0	0	**8**	2	2	0	.269	.346	9	0	0
Bill Rariden	c	5	19	0	4	0	0	0	2	0	0	1	.211	.211	25	3	1
Ivy Wingo	c	3	7	1	4	0	0	0	1	3	1	0	.571	.571	8	3	0
Sherry Magee	ph	2	2	0	1	0	0	0	0	0	0	0	.500	.500			
Jimmy Smith	pr	1	0	0	0	0	0	0	0	0	0	0	—	—			
Rube Bressler		Did not play															
Hank Schreiber		Did not play															
Nick Allen		Did not play															
Charlie See		Did not play															
Hod Eller	p	2	7	2	2	1	0	0	0	0	2	0	.286	.429	0	2	0
Dutch Ruether	p-ph	3	6	2	4	1	**2**	0	4	1	0	0	.667	1.500	0	2	0
Jimmy Ring	p	2	5	0	0	0	0	0	0	0	2	0	.000	.000	1	3	0
Slim Sallee	p	2	4	0	0	0	0	0	0	0	0	0	.000	.000	1	4	0
Ray Fisher	p	2	2	0	1	0	0	0	0	0	0	0	.500	.500	0	6	1
Dolf Luque	p	2	1	0	0	0	0	0	0	0	1	0	.000	.000	1	0	0
Roy Mitchell		Did not play															
Ed Gerner		Did not play															
team total		8	251	35	64	10	7	0	34	25	22	7	.255	.351	216	92	12
CHICAGO WHITE SOX																	
Chick Gardil	1b	8	30	1	7	0	1	0	5	1	3	1	.233	.300	79	2	1
Eddie Collins	2b	8	31	2	7	1	0	0	1	1	2	1	.226	.258	21	**31**	2
Swede Risberg	ss	8	25	3	2	0	1	0	0	5	3	1	.080	.160	23	30	**4**
Buck Weaver	3b	8	**34**	4	11	**4**	1	0	0	0	2	0	.324	.500	9	18	0
Nemo Leibold	rf-ph-cf	5	18	0	1	0	0	0	0	2	3	1	.056	.056	5	2	0
Happy Felsch	cf-rf	8	26	2	5	1	0	0	3	1	4	0	.192	.231	23	1	2
Joe Jackson	lf	8	32	5	**12**	3	0	**1**	6	1	2	0	**.375**	**.563**	16	1	0
Ray Schalk	c	8	23	1	7	0	0	0	2	4	2	1	.304	.304	29	15	1
Shano Collins	rf-cf	4	16	2	4	1	0	0	0	0	0	0	.250	.313	5	0	0
Fred McMullin	ph	2	2	0	1	0	0	0	0	0	0	0	.500	.500			
Eddie Murphy	ph	3	2	0	0	0	0	0	0	0	1	0	.000	.000			
Byrd Lynn	c	1	1	0	0	0	0	0	0	0	0	0	.000	.000	1	0	0
Joe Jenkins		Did not play															
Hervey McClellan		Did not play															
Eddie Cicotte	p	3	8	0	0	0	0	0	0	0	3	0	.000	.000	0	6	2
Dickie Kerr	p	2	6	0	1	0	0	0	0	0	0	0	.167	.167	1	4	0
Lefty Williams	p	3	5	0	1	0	0	0	0	0	3	0	.200	.200	1	2	0
Roy Wilkinson	p	2	2	0	0	0	0	0	0	0	1	0	.000	.000	0	2	0
Bill James	p	1	2	0	0	0	0	0	0	0	1	0	.000	.000	0	0	0
Grover Lowdermilk	p	1	0	0	0	0	0	0	0	0	0	0	—	—	0	1	0
Erskine Mayer	p	1	0	0	0	0	0	0	0	0	0	0	—	—	0	0	0
Red Faber		Did not play															
John Sullivan		Did not play															
team total		8	263	20	59	10	3	1	17	15	30	5	.224	.297	213	115	12

Cincinnati Reds: Double Plays—7, Left on Bases—46

Chicago White Sox: Double Plays—9, Left on Bases—52

REGULAR SEASON STATISTICS

	Main Pos	G	AB	R	H	2B	3B	HR	RBI	BB	SO	SB	BA	SA
CINCINNATI REDS														
Jake Daubert	1b	140	537	79	148	10	12	2	44	35	23	11	.276	.350
Morrie Rath	2b	138	537	77	142	13	1	1	29	64	24	17	.264	.298
Larry Kopf	ss	135	503	51	136	18	5	0	58	28	27	18	.270	.326
Heinie Groh	3b	122	448	79	139	17	11	5	63	56	26	21	.310	.431
Greasy Neale	of	139	500	57	121	10	12	1	54	47	51	28	.242	.316
Edd Roush	of	133	504	73	162	19	12	4	71	42	19	20	**.321**	.431
Pat Duncan	of	31	90	9	22	3	3	2	17	8	7	2	.244	.411
Bill Rariden	c	74	218	16	47	6	3	1	24	17	19	4	.216	.284
Ivy Wingo	c	76	245	30	67	12	6	0	27	23	19	4	.273	.371
Sherry Magee	of	56	163	11	35	6	1	0	21	26	19	4	.215	.264
Jimmy Smith	3b-ss-2b-of	28	40	9	11	1	3	1	10	4	8	1	.275	.525
Rube Bressler	of-p	61	165	22	34	3	4	2	17	23	15	2	.206	.309
Hank Schreiber	3b	19	58	5	13	4	0	0	4	0	12	0	.224	.293
Nick Allen	c	15	25	7	8	0	1	0	5	2	6	0	.320	.400
Charlie See	of	8	14	1	4	0	0	0	1	1	0	0	.286	.286
Hod Eller	p	38	93	10	26	3	3	1	13	0	16	2	.280	.409
Dutch Ruether	p	42	92	8	24	2	3	0	6	4	18	1	.261	.348
Jimmy Ring	p	32	62	3	6	1	0	0	1	1	20	0	.097	.113
Slim Sallee	p	29	74	5	14	2	2	0	7	6	20	1	.189	.270
Ray Fisher	p	26	59	11	16	1	0	0	5	4	7	1	.271	.288
Dolf Luque	p	31	32	3	4	1	1	0	2	3	1	0	.125	.219
Roy Mitchell	p	7	10	0	0	0	0	0	0	0	0	0	.000	.000
Ed Gerner	p	6	6	1	1	1	0	0	3	0	2	1	.167	.333
team total		140	4577	578	1204	135	**83**	20	489	**405**	368	143	.263	.342
CHICAGO WHITE SOX														
Chick Gardil	1b	115	441	54	128	24	7	1	60	20	20	10	.290	.383
Eddie Collins	2b	140	518	87	165	19	7	4	80	68	27	**33**	.319	.405
Swede Risberg	ss-1b	119	414	48	106	19	6	2	38	35	38	19	.256	.345
Buck Weaver	3b-ss	140	**571**	89	169	33	9	3	75	11	21	22	.296	.401
Nemo Leibold	of	122	434	81	131	18	2	0	26	72	30	17	.302	.353
Happy Felsch	of	135	502	68	138	34	11	7	86	40	35	19	.275	.428
Joe Jackson	of	139	516	79	181	31	14	7	96	60	10	9	.351	.506
Ray Schalk	c	131	394	57	111	9	3	0	34	51	25	11	.282	.320
Shano Collins	of	63	179	21	50	6	3	1	16	7	11	3	.279	.363
Fred McMullin	3b	60	170	31	50	8	4	0	19	11	18	4	.294	.388
Eddie Murphy	of	30	35	8	17	4	0	0	5	7	0	0	.486	.600
Byrd Lynn	c	29	66	4	15	4	0	0	4	4	9	0	.227	.288
Joe Jenkins	c	11	19	0	3	1	0	0	1	1	1	1	.158	.211
Hervey McClellan	3b-ss	7	12	2	4	0	0	0	1	1	1	0	.333	.333
Eddie Cicotte	p	38	86	5	14	0	1	0	8	9	18	0	.202	.222
Dickie Kerr	p	39	68	12	17	3	1	0	4	9	8	1	.250	.324
Lefty Williams	p	41	94	10	17	2	2	0	10	9	28	0	.181	.245
Roy Wilkinson	p	4	8	1	3	2	0	0	2	1	3	0	.375	.625
Bill James	a p	5	14	2	2	0	0	0	0	0	2	0	.143	.143
Grover Lowdermilk	b p	20	34	1	3	0	0	0	1	0	19	1	.088	.088
Erskine Mayer	c p	6	7	0	0	0	0	0	0	0	3	0	.000	.000
Red Faber	p	25	54	8	10	0	0	0	4	6	20	0	.185	.185
John Sullivan	p	4	3	0	0	0	0	0	1	1	3	0	.000	.000
team total		140	4675	**668**	**1343**	218	70	25	**571**	427	358	**150**	**.287**	.380

Manuel Cueto (of), Wally Rehg (of), Billy Zitzmann (of), Mike Regan (p) also played for the Reds during the season.

a—from St. Louis (A)
b—from Detroit and Boston (A)
c—from Pittsburgh (N)

Joe Benz (p), Dave Danforth (p), Tom McGuire (p), Win Noyes (p), Pat Ragan (p), Charlie Robertson (p), Reb Russell (p), Frank Shellenback (p) also played for the White Sox during the season.

PITCHING

WORLD SERIES STATISTICS

	G	GS	CG	IP	H	R	ER	BB	SO	W	L	SV	ERA
CINCINNATI REDS													
Hod Eller	2	2	**2**	18	13	5	4	2	**15**	**2**	0	0	2.00
Dutch Ruether	2	2	1	14	12	5	4	4	1	1	0	0	2.57
Jimmy Ring	2	1	1	14	7	1	1	6	4	1	1	0	**0.64**
Slim Sallee	2	2	1	13 1/3	**19**	6	2	1	2	1	1	0	1.35
Ray Fisher	2	1	0	7 2/3	7	3	2	2	2	0	1	0	2.35
Dolf Luque	2	0	0	5	1	0	0	0	6	0	0	0	0.00
Rube Bressler	Did not play												
Roy Mitchell	Did not play												
Ed Gerner	Did not play												
team total	8	8	5	72	59	20	13	15	30	5	3	0	1.62
CHICAGO WHITE SOX													
Eddie Cicotte	**3**	**3**	**2**	21 2/3	19	9	7	5	7	1	2	0	2.91
Dickie Kerr	2	2	**2**	19	14	4	3	3	6	**2**	0	0	1.42
Lefty Williams	**3**	**3**	1	16 1/3	12	**12**	**12**	**8**	4	0	**3**	0	6.61
Roy Wilkinson	2	0	0	7 1/3	9	4	1	4	3	0	0	0	1.23
Bill James	1	0	0	4 2/3	8	4	3	3	2	0	0	0	5.79
Grover Lowdermilk	1	0	0	1	2	1	1	1	0	0	0	0	9.00
Erskine Mayer	1	0	0	1	0	1	0	1	0	0	0	0	0.00
Red Faber	Did not play												
John Sullivan	Did not play												
team total	8	8	5	71	64	35	27	25	22	3	5	0	3.42

REGULAR SEASON STATISTICS

		G	GS	CG	IP	H	ER	BB	SO	W	L	Pct	SV	ShO	ERA
CINCINNATI REDS															
Hod Eller		38	30	16	248	216	66	50	137	20	9	.690	2	7	2.40
Dutch Ruether		33	29	22	243	195	49	**83**	78	19	6	**.760**	0	3	1.81
Jimmy Ring		32	18	12	183	150	46	51	61	10	9	.526	3	2	2.26
Slim Sallee		29	28	22	228	221	52	20	24	21	7	.750	0	4	2.05
Ray Fisher		26	20	12	174	141	42	38	41	14	5	.737	1	5	2.17
Dolf Luque		30	9	6	106	89	31	36	40	9	3	.750	3	2	2.63
Rube Bressler		13	4	1	42	37	16	8	13	2	4	.333	0	0	3.43
Roy Mitchell		7	1	0	31	32	8	9	10	0	1	.000	0	0	2.32
Ed Gerner		5	1	0	17	22	6	3	2	1	0	1.000	0	0	3.18
team total		140	140	89	1274	1104	316	298	407	**96**	44	**.686**	9	**23**	2.23
CHICAGO WHITE SOX															
Eddie Cicotte		40	35	**29**	**307**	256	62	49	110	**29**	7	**.806**	1	5	1.82
Dickie Kerr		39	17	10	212	208	68	64	79	13	8	.619	0	1	2.89
Lefty Williams		41	**40**	27	297	265	87	58	125	23	11	.676	0	5	2.64
Roy Wilkinson		4	1	1	22	21	5	10	5	1	1	.500	0	1	2.05
Bill James	a	5	5	3	39	39	11	14	11	3	1	.750	0	2	2.54
Grover Lowdermilk	b	20	11	5	97	95	30	43	43	5	5	.500	0	0	2.78
Erskine Mayer	c	6	2	0	24	30	22	11	9	1	3	.250	0	0	8.25
Red Faber		25	20	9	162	185	69	45	45	11	9	.500	0	0	3.83
John Sullivan		4	2	1	15	24	7	8	9	0	1	.000	0	0	4.20
team total		140	140	**87**	1266	1245	427	342	468	**88**	52	**.629**	2	14	3.04

Total Attendance—236,928 Average Attendance—29,616 Winning Player's Share—$5,207 Losing Player's Share—$3,254

1920
Coveleski, Smith, & Wambsganss

This baseball season produced a new American hero in Babe Ruth, who slugged the outrageous total of 54 home runs after being sold to the New York Yankees over the winter, and the American League produced a torrid pennant race between the Chicago White Sox and Cleveland Indians. Then the whole thing went bad, with an unavoidable stink. The story of the 1919 Series fix broke in September, and every baseball game suddenly had to be thought about and looked at with a suspicious eye. The crooked White Sox players were immediately suspended, with the result that the Indians took the A.L. pennant by two games.

But the Indians too had encountered tragedy along the way, although not of a sordid nature. Shortstop Ray Chapman had been hit in the head by a Carl Mays pitch on August 16, and he died the next day without ever regaining consciousness. Managed by center fielder Tris Speaker, who was his own best player with a .388 batting average, the Indians had a powerful batting order and three mound stars in Jim Bagby, Stan Coveleski, and Ray Caldwell, but the gaping hole at shortstop threatened to do the team in until rookie Joe Sewell was brought up from the minors in September to fill the breach. Their opposite numbers in the Series, the Brooklyn Robins, had a star outfielder in Zack Wheat, but their long suit was a deep pitching staff headed by 23-game-winner Burleigh Grimes, a spitball master. The two opposing mound staffs were to be the outstanding feature of the Series, which was well attended in Brooklyn and Cleveland despite the recent scandals.

The top-flight pitching began in game one in Brooklyn, with Rube Marquard going for the Robins and Coveleski for the Indians. Former Giant star Marquard allowed five hits and three runs before leaving for a pinch hitter in the sixth inning, while Coveleski used his spitball to go all the way for a 3–1 five-hit victory. The Robins used the spitball to win the second game, with Burleigh Grimes winning a 3–0 shutout over Bagby, who led the majors this season with 31 wins. Brooklyn then captured game three 2–1 behind a three-hitter by Sherry Smith. The Robins scored twice in the first off Ray Caldwell, but then were shut out for 6 2/3 innings by reliever Duster Mails and one inning by George Uhle.

The scene then shifted to Cleveland for the next four games, all of which the Indians took behind strong pitching to come from behind to win the championship. Coveleski won game four 5–1 with another five-hitter; the losing pitcher was Leon Cadore, whose claim to fame will always be pitching the entire 26-inning game against Boston on May 1. Game five was an 8–1 Cleveland runaway, but it produced a trio of firsts in Series competition. Elmer Smith smacked the first grand slam in Series history off Grimes in the first inning with no one out. With that four-run cushion behind him, Bagby made his job even easier by connecting for a three-run homer in the fourth, the first pitcher to hit one out in the fall classic. Minor trouble then loomed on the horizon for Bagby when Pete Kilduff and Otto Miller reached safely to start the fifth. With men on first and second and no outs, Robin relief pitcher Clarence Mitchell stepped into the batter's box. A good hitter who often filled in at first base, Mitchell lined a shot headed for right field. Indian second baseman Bill Wambsganss leapt high into the air and speared the ball with both runners on their way around the diamond. Wambsganss instantly turned the play into a double play by stepping on second, then he completed a triple play by tagging the surprised Miller near second base. The unassisted triple play, happening for the first and only time in Series play, quickly forged Wambsganss's name into baseball history. The easy 8–1 win put the Indians on top in the Series three games to two. Speaker then nominated Duster Mails, 7–0 after his late-season recall and the relief star of the third-game loss, to start game six, and he lived up to his promise with a 1–0 three-hit shutout. Coveleski wrapped up the Series the next day with his third five-hitter in a row, a 3–0 triumph over Grimes. Although the eight-game Series victory seemed quite easy, the fans at least believed that it was on the level.

Game 1 October 5 at Brooklyn

Cleveland	Pos	AB	R	H	RBI	PO	A	E
Evans	lf	2	0	0	0	1	0	0
b Jamieson	lf	1	0	0	0	0	0	0
Wambsganss	2b	3	0	0	0	0	2	0
Speaker	cf	4	0	0	0	4	0	0
Burns	1b	3	1	1	0	9	1	0
e E. Smith	rf	1	0	0	0	0	0	0
Gardner	3b	4	0	0	0	1	3	0
Wood	rf	2	2	1	0	4	0	0
f D. Johnston	1b	1	0	0	0	0	1	0
Sewell	ss	3	0	1	0	3	4	0
O'Neill	c	3	0	2	2	3	0	0
Coveleski	p	3	0	0	0	2	2	0
Totals		30	3	5	2	27	13	0

Pitching	IP	H	R	ER	BB	SO
Cleveland						
Coveleski (W)	9	5	1	1	1	3
Brooklyn						
Marquard (L)	6	5	3	1	2	4
Manaux	2	0	0	0	0	3
Cadore	1	0	0	0	0	0

Cle.	0 2 0	1 0 0	0 0 0						
Bkn.	0 0 0	0 0 0	1 0 0						

Brooklyn	Pos	AB	R	H	RBI	PO	A	E
Olson	ss	3	0	2	0	3	0	0
J. Johnston	3b	3	0	0	0	1	3	0
Griffith	rf	4	0	1	0	1	0	0
Wheat	lf	4	1	1	0	4	0	0
Myers	cf	4	0	0	0	1	0	0
Konetchy	1b	4	0	0	1	12	1	1
Kilduff	2b	4	0	0	0	1	3	0
Krueger	c	3	0	0	0	7	1	0
Marquard	p	1	0	0	0	0	0	0
a Lamar		1	0	0	0	0	0	0
Manaux	p	0	0	0	0	0	1	0
c Mitchell		1	0	1	0	0	0	0
d Neis		0	0	0	0	0	0	0
Cadore	p	0	0	0	0	0	1	0
Totals		31	1	5	1	27	13	1

a Popped out for Marquard in 6th.
b Grounded out for Evans in 8th.
c Singled for Mamaux in 8th.
d Ran for Mitchell in 8th.
e Grounded out for Burns in 9th.
f Grounded out for Wood in 9th.

Doubles—O'Neill 2, Wheat, Wood. Sacrifice Hits—J. Johnston, Wambsganss. Double Play—Konetchy to Krueger to J. Johnston. Left on Bases—Cleveland 3, Brooklyn 5. Umpires—Klem (N), Connolly (A), O'Day (N), Dinneen (A). Attendance—23,573. Time of Game—1:41.

1st Inning
Cleveland
1 Evans grounded to short.
2 Wambsganss flied to left.
3 Speaker called out on strikes.
Brooklyn
1 Olson flied to short right.
2 J. Johnston called out on strikes.
3 Griffith grounded to short.

2nd Inning
Cleveland
  Burns got a Texas League single into short right and scored when Konetchy threw wildly to get him at second. The ball went all the way to the left field stands.
1 Gardner grounded to short, Olson making a good play.
  Wood walked.
  Sewell singled to right-center, Wood racing to second.
  O'Neill doubled to left, Wood scoring as Sewell stopped at third.
2,3 Coveleski grounded to Konetchy, who stepped on the bag, then got Sewell hung-up between third and home, Konetchy to Krueger to J. Johnston.
Brooklyn
1 Wheat flied to Speaker in short left-field.
2 Myers flied to deep right.
3 Konetchy grounded to short.

3rd Inning
Cleveland
  Evans walked on four pitches.
1 Wambsganss sacrificed Evans to second, J. Johnston to Konetchy.
2 Speaker flied to left.
3 Burns grounded to J. Johnston who threw to Kilduff getting Evans between the bases.
Brooklyn
1 Kilduff grounded to Sewell near the left field line.
2 Krueger rolled to third.
3 Marquard bunted out to third.

4th Inning
Cleveland
1 Gardner grounded to second.
  Wood doubled high off the wall in left-center, just missing a home run.
2 Sewell flied to center.
  O'Neill got his second double, a drive off the right field wall, scoring Wood.
3 Coveleski grounded to second.
Brooklyn
  Olson singled over second, for Brooklyn's first hit.
1 J. Johnston forced Olson at second, Wambsganss to Sewell.
  Griffith singled to left-center, J. Johnston stopping at second.
2 Wheat flied to Evans in short left-center.
3 Myers again flied to deep right.

5th Inning
Cleveland
1 Evans flied to left.
2 Wambsganss struck out.
3 Speaker flied to Griffith in right, making a great jumping catch against the wall.
Brooklyn
1 Konetchy flied to deep center.
2 Kilduff flied to right.
3 Krueger grounded to third.

6th Inning
Cleveland
1 Burns struck out.
2 Gardner flied to short left.
3 Wood struck out.
Brooklyn
1 Lamar, batting for Marquard, was robbed of a hit when Sewell jumped high and got his liner in his gloved hand, Olson lined a single over Sewell's head.
2 J. Johnston sacrificed Olson to second, Coveleski to Burns.
3 Griffith bounced back to the mound.

7th Inning
Cleveland
For Brooklyn—Mamaux now pitching.
1 Sewell struck out.
2 O'Neill struck out after a deep foul to right which might have given him his third double.
3 Coveleski took a called third strike.
Brooklyn
  Wheat doubled to the wall in right-center.
1 Myers grounded to short, Wheat moving to third.
2 Konetchy grounded out, Burns to Coveleski as Wheat scored.
3 Kilduff struck out.

8th Inning
Cleveland
1 Jamieson, pinch-hitting for Evans, grounded to Short.
2 Wambsganss bunted back to the pitcher.
3 Speaker grounded to third, just out on a close play.
Brooklyn
For Cleveland—Jamieson playing left.
1 Krueger flied to Speaker, making a shoestring catch in deep left-center.
  Mitchell, pinch-hitting for Mamaux, singled down the right field line.
  Neis ran for Mitchell.
  Olson walked.
2 J. Johnston popped to third.
3 Griffith forced Olson at second, Wambsganss making a great stop to Sewell.

9th Inning
Cleveland
For Brooklyn—Cadore pitching.
1 E. Smith, pinch-hitting for Burns, grounded to second.
2 Gardner grounded to first.
3 D. Johnston, pinch-hitting for Wood, grounded back to the mound.
Brooklyn
For Cleveland—D. Johnston playing first and E. Smith in right.
1 Wheat grounded out, D. Johnston to Coveleski.
2 Myers flied to Speaker in deep right-center.
3 Konetchy struck out.

Game 2 October 6 at Brooklyn

Cle.		000	000	000					
Bkn.		101	010	00x					

Cleveland	Pos	AB	R	H	RBI	PO	A	E
Jamieson	lf	4	0	1	0	2	0	0
Wambsganss	2b	3	0	0	0	3	0	0
b Burns		0	0	0	0	0	0	0
Lunte	2b	0	0	0	0	0	0	0
Speaker	cf	3	0	2	0	2	0	0
E. Smith	rf	4	0	0	0	3	0	0
Gardner	3b	3	0	2	0	1	2	0
D. Johnston	1b	4	0	0	0	3	3	0
Sewell	ss	4	0	0	0	1	1	0
O'Neill	c	4	0	1	0	7	2	0
Bagby	p	2	0	0	0	2	1	1
a Graney		1	0	0	0	0	0	0
Uhle	p	0	0	0	0	0	0	0
c Nunamaker		1	0	1	0	0	0	0
Totals		33	0	7	0	24	9	1

a Struck out for Bagby in 7th.
b Walked for Wambsganss in 8th.
c Singled for Uhle in 9th.

Doubles—Gardner, Griffith, Speaker, Wheat. Stolen Base—J. Johnston. Double Play—Gardner to O'Neill to D. Johnston. Left on Bases—Cleveland 10, Brooklyn 4. Umpires—Connolly, O'Day, Dinneen, Klem. Attendance—22,559. Time of Game—1:55.

Brooklyn	Pos	AB	R	H	RBI	PO	A	E
Olson	ss	4	1	1	0	3	2	0
J. Johnston	3b	4	1	1	0	0	1	0
Griffith	rf	4	0	2	2	3	0	0
Wheat	lf	3	1	1	3	0	0	0
Myers	cf	3	0	1	0	2	0	0
Konetchy	1b	3	0	0	0	10	1	0
Kilduff	2b	3	0	0	0	2	3	0
Miller	c	3	0	0	0	3	1	0
Grimes	p	3	1	1	0	4	4	0
Totals		30	3	7	3	27	12	0

Pitching	IP	H	R	ER	BB	SO
Cleveland						
Bagby (L)	6	7	3	2	1	0
Uhle	2	0	0	0	0	3
Brooklyn						
Grimes (W)	9	7	0	0	4	2

1st Inning
Cleveland
1 Jamieson grounded out, Konetchy to Grimes.
2 Wambsganss grounded to third. Speaker singled past first.
3 E. Smith struck out.
Brooklyn
1 Olson popped to second. J. Johnston beat out a hit to deep short. J. Johnston stole second.
2 Griffith grounded out, D. Johnston to Bagby as J. Johnston went to third. Wheat lined a double over second, J. Johnston scoring.
3 Myers bounced to third.

2nd Inning
Cleveland
Gardner doubled off of J. Johnston's bare hand.
1 D. Johnston grounded to Grimes who threw to Olson getting Gardner off of second.
2 Sewell popped to Olson in short left.
3 D. Johnston out trying to steal second, Miller to Kilduff.
Brooklyn
1 Konetchy flied to deep left.
2 Kilduff lined to third.
3 Miller fouled to O'Neill.

3rd Inning
Cleveland
1 O'Neill bounced back to the mound.
2 Bagby also grounded back to Grimes. Jamieson singled over second.
3 Wambsganss flied to short left.
Brooklyn
Grimes singled over second. Olson bunted to Bagby, who threw wide to Wheat, both runners being safe.
1 J. Johnston foul bunted to O'Neill. Griffith doubled off Wambsganss' glove, Grimes scoring and Olson stopping at third. Wheat got an intentional pass, loading the bases.
2,3 Myers grounded to Gardner who threw to O'Neill forcing Olson at the plate. O'Neill's throw to first hit Myers in the back, but D. Johnston retrieved it and threw back to O'Neill getting Griffith who was also trying to score on the play.

4th Inning
Cleveland
Speaker walked on a full count.
1 E. Smith grounded to first, Speaker going to second.
2 Gardner flied to center.
3 D. Johnston flied to Wheat in left-center.
Brooklyn
1 Konetchy popped to second.
2 Kilduff flied to Speaker running into left for the catch.
3 Miller bounced back to the mound.

5th Inning
Cleveland
1 Sewell grounded back to the mound.
2 O'Neill bounced to short.
3 Bagby flied to center.
Brooklyn
1 Grimes grounded to deep short. Olson singled past second.
2 J. Johnston grounded out, D. Johnston to Bagby as Olson went to second. Griffith singled past short, Olson scoring.
3 Griffith was out trying to steal second, O'Neill to Wambsganss.

6th Inning
Cleveland
1 Jamieson grounded to second.
2 Wambsganss flied to Griffith in short right-center. Speaker lined a double over Olson's head.
3 E. Smith grounded to first.
Brooklyn
1 Wheat flied to Speaker in deep right-center. Myers beat out a bunt towards third.
2 Konetchy flied to right.
3 Kilduff flied to deep right.

7th Inning
Cleveland
Gardner singled past the box.
1 D. Johnston forced Gardner at second, Olson to Kilduff.
2 Sewell flied to deep right, Griffith making the catch at the wall. O'Neill got a Texas League single to short left, D. Johnston going to second.
3 Graney, pinch-hitting for Bagby, struck out.
Brooklyn
For Cleveland—Uhle pitching.
1 Miller called out on strikes.
2 Grimes flied to right.
3 Olson struck out, foul tipping the third strike to O'Neill.

8th Inning
Cleveland
Jamieson walked on a full count. Burns, pinch-hitting for Wambsganss, also walked on a full count.
1 Speaker grounded to second, Jamieson going to third and Burns to second.
2 E. Smith fouled to Miller. Gardner walked on four pitches, loading the bases.
3 D. Johnston again forced Gardner at second, Kilduff to Olson.
Brooklyn
For Cleveland-Lunte playing second.
1 J. Johnston popped to short.
2 Griffith took a called third strike.
3 Wheat flied to short left.

9th Inning
Cleveland
1 Sewell grounded to first.
2 O'Neill lined to right. Nunamaker, batting for Uhle, singled to center.
3 Jamieson flied to short left on a 3–2 count.

Game 3 October 7 at Brooklyn

Cle.		000	100	000					
Bkn.		200	000	00x					

Cleveland	Pos	AB	R	H	RBI	PO	A	E
Evans	lf	4	0	0	0	2	0	0
Wambsganss	2b	3	0	0	0	2	2	0
Speaker	cf	4	1	1	0	2	0	0
Burns	1b	3	0	0	0	12	0	0
Gardner	3b	3	0	0	0	0	0	0
Wood	rf	3	0	0	0	1	0	0
Sewell	ss	2	0	0	0	2	3	1
O'Neill	c	3	0	2	0	2	2	0
b Jamieson		0	0	0	0	0	0	0
Uhle	p	0	0	0	0	0	1	0
Caldwell	p	0	0	0	0	0	0	0
Mails	p	2	0	0	0	1	3	0
c Nunamaker		1	0	0	0	0	0	0
Totals		28	1	3	0	24	11	1

a Grounded out for Griffith in 3rd.
b Ran for O'Neill in 8th.
c Hit into double play for Mails in 8th.

Double—Speaker. Sacrifice Hits—J. Johnston, Kilduff, Miller. Double Plays—Mails to Burns, Olson to Kilduff to Konetchy, Wambsganss to Sewell to Burns, J. Johnston to Kilduff to Konetchy. Left on Bases—Cleveland 2, Brooklyn 7. Umpires—O'Day, Dinneen, Klem, Connolly. Attendance—25,088. Time of Game—1:47.

Brooklyn	Pos	AB	R	H	RBI	PO	A	E
Olson	ss	2	1	1	0	0	6	0
J. Johnston	3b	3	0	0	0	0	4	0
Griffith	rf	1	1	0	0	2	0	0
a Neis	rf	3	0	0	0	0	0	0
Wheat	lf	4	0	3	1	1	0	1
Myers	cf	4	0	2	1	1	0	0
Konetchy	1b	3	0	0	0	17	2	0
Kilduff	2b	1	0	0	0	2	6	0
Miller	c	1	0	0	0	2	0	0
S. Smith	p	3	0	0	0	2	2	0
Totals		25	2	6	2	27	20	1

Pitching	IP	H	R	ER	BB	SO
Cleveland						
Caldwell (L)	⅓	2	2	1	1	0
Mails	6⅔	3	0	0	4	2
Uhle	1	1	0	0	0	0
Brooklyn						
S. Smith (W)	9	3	1	0	2	2

1st Inning
Cleveland
1 Evans grounded to short. Wambsganss walked on a full count.
2 Speaker grounded to third, Wambsganss going to second.
3 Burns grounded to short on a 3–2 count.
Brooklyn
Olson walked on a full count.
1 J. Johnston sacrificed Olson to second, O'Neill to Burns. Griffith safe on Sewell's fumble, Olson going to third. Wheat singled to left, scoring Olson with Griffith stopping at second. Myers singled off Burns' glove, scoring Griffith as Wheat stopped at second. For Cleveland—Mails replaced Caldwell on the mound.
2 Konetchy popped to second.
3 Kilduff fouled to Wood near the right field corner.

2nd Inning
Cleveland
1 Gardner flied to right.
2 Wood robbed of a hit by Griffith by a fantastic shoestring catch.
3 Sewell grounded out, Konetchy to S. Smith.
Brooklyn
Miller walked on a full count.
1,2 S. Smith popped a bunt attempt to Mails throwing to Burns for a double play. Olson lined a single to center.
3 Olson caught trying to steal second, O'Neill to Wambsganss.

3rd Inning
Cleveland
1 O'Neill grounded out, Kilduff to S. Smith after the ball bounced away from Konetchy but he gets an assist.
2 Mails flied to center.
3 Evans grounded to second.
Brooklyn
1 J. Johnston grounded to second.
2 Neis, batting for Griffith, grounded to short. Wheat got a Texas Leaguer over second.
3 Myers popped to short.

4th Inning
Cleveland
For Brooklyn—Neis playing right.
1 Wambsganss grounded to deep short. Speaker doubled along the left field line, but the ball went through Wheat and Speaker got all the way to the plate.
2 Burns grounded to third.
3 Gardner also grounded to third.
Brooklyn
Konetchy walked on a full count.
1 Kilduff sacrificed Konetchy to second, Mails to Burns.
2 Miller flied to deep left.
3 S. Smith grounded to first.

5th Inning
Cleveland
1 Wood struck out on a full count. Sewell walked on four pitches. O'Neill singled just out of Olson's reach with Sewell going to second.
2,3 Mails hit into a double play, Olson making a fine stop to Kilduff to Konetchy.
Brooklyn
1 Olson flied to center.
2 J. Johnston struck out.
3 Neis popped to first.

6th Inning
Cleveland
1 Evans flied to left.
2 Wambsganss grounded back to the mound.
3 Speaker fouled to Konetchy.
Brooklyn
1 Wheat fouled to Burns, reaching into the stands for a good catch. Myers singled to left.
2,3 Konetchy grounded into a double play, Wambsganss to Sewell to Burns.

7th Inning
Cleveland
1 Burns struck out on three pitches.
2 Gardner grounded to second.
3 Wood grounded to second.
Brooklyn
Kilduff walked.
1 Miller sacrificed Kilduff to second, Mails to Burns.
2 S. Smith struck out. Olson walked on a full count.
3 J. Johnston grounded to short, also on a full count.

8th Inning
Cleveland
1 Sewell grounded to first. O'Neill blooped a hit to short left. Jamieson ran for O'Neill.
2,3 Nunamaker, pinch-hitting for Mails, grounded into a double play, J. Johnston to Kilduff to Konetchy.
Brooklyn
For Cleveland—Uhle pitching, Nunamaker catching.
1 Neis flied to left. Wheat got a bad hop single off of Sewell's chest.
2 Myers grounded back to the mound, Wheat going to second.
3 Konetchy flied to center.

9th Inning
Cleveland
1 Evans grounded back to the pitcher.
2 Wambsganss grounded to deep short.
3 Speaker grounded to short.

Game 4 October 9 at Cleveland

Bkn.	000	100	000
Cle.	202	001	00x

Brooklyn	Pos	AB	R	H	RBI	PO	A	E
Olson	ss	4	0	1	0	1	2	0
J. Johnston	3b	4	1	2	0	1	0	0
f Neis		0	0	0	0	0	0	0
Griffith	rf	4	0	1	1	1	0	0
Wheat	lf	4	0	0	0	0	0	1
Myers	cf	3	0	0	0	6	1	0
Konetchy	1b	2	0	0	0	5	0	0
Kilduff	2b	3	0	1	0	2	4	0
Miller	c	3	0	0	0	7	0	0
Cadore	p	0	0	0	0	1	0	0
Mamaux	p	1	0	0	0	0	0	0
Marquard	p	0	0	0	0	0	1	0
d Lamar		1	0	0	0	0	0	0
Pfeffer	p	1	0	0	0	0	0	0
Totals		30	1	5	1	24	8	1

Cleveland	Pos	AB	R	H	RBI	PO	A	E
Jamieson	lf	2	0	0	0	1	0	0
c Evans	lf	3	0	1	0	0	0	0
Wambsganss	2b	4	2	2	1	4	6	0
Speaker	cf	5	2	2	0	3	0	0
E. Smith	rf	1	0	1	1	1	0	0
a Burns	1b	2	0	1	1	7	0	1
Gardner	3b	3	0	1	1	2	3	0
D. Johnston	1b	1	0	0	0	4	0	0
b Wood	rf	2	0	0	0	0	0	0
e Graney	rf	1	0	0	0	0	0	0
Sewell	ss	4	0	2	0	1	7	1
O'Neill	c	2	0	1	0	4	0	0
Coveleski	p	4	1	1	0	0	2	0
Totals		34	5	12	4	27	18	2

Pitching	IP	H	R	ER	BB	SO
Brooklyn						
Cadore (L)	*1	4	2	2	1	1
Mamaux	**1	2	2	2	0	1
Marquard	3	2	0	0	1	2
Pfeffer	3	4	1	1	2	1
Cleveland						
Coveleskie (W)	9	5	1	1	1	4

*Pitched to two batters in 2nd.
**Pitched to two batters in 3rd.

a Singled for E. Smith in 3rd.
b Flied out for D. Johnston in 3rd.
c Flied out for Jamieson in 4th.
d Grounded out for Marquard in 6th.
e Hit into force play for Wood in 7th.
f Ran for J. Johnston in 9th.

Double—Griffith. Sacrifice Hit—Gardner. Double Plays—Myers to Olson to Kilduff, Sewell to Wambsganss to Burns, Gardner to Wambsganss to Burns. Passed Ball—Miller. Wild Pitch—Pfeffer. Left on Bases—Brooklyn 3, Cleveland 10. Umpires—Dinneen, Klem, Connolly, O'Day. Attendance—25,734. Time of Game—1:54.

1st Inning
Brooklyn
1 Olson grounded to third.
2 J. Johnston grounded to deep short.
3 Griffith popped to third.
Cleveland
1 Jamieson lined to Cadore.
Wambsganss walked on a full count.
Speaker singled past second, Wambsganss stopping at second.
E. Smith singled to center, Wambsganss scoring with Speaker racing to third.
Smith took second on the throw to third.
2 Gardner flied to center, Speaker scoring after the catch.
3 D. Johnston struck out.

2nd Inning
Brooklyn
1 Wheat flied to deep left.
2 Myers flied to E. Smith in deep right-center.
3 Konetchy grounded to second.
Cleveland
Sewell singled off the right field wall.
O'Neill singled past third, Sewell stopping at second.
For Brooklyn—Mamaux came in to pitch.
1 Coveleski struck out.
2,3 Jamieson flied to Myers racing into short left-center. Myers threw to Olson who threw to Kilduff doubling Sewell.

3rd Inning
Brooklyn
1 Kilduff struck out on three pitches.
2 Miller bounced back to the mound.
3 Mamaux struck out.
Cleveland
Wambsganss singled to right.
Speaker singled to center, Wambsganss going to third and Speaker took second on the throw to third.
For Brooklyn—Marquard relieved Mamaux.
Burns, batting for E. Smith, singled to left, scoring both runners and went to second on Wheat's fumble.
1 Gardner called out on strikes.
2 Wood, batting for D. Johnston, lined to center.
Sewell beat out a roller to first, Burns getting to third.
O'Neill intentionally walked, loading the bases.
3 Coveleski forced O'Neill at second, Kilduff unassisted.

4th Inning
Brooklyn
For Cleveland—Burns playing first and Wood to right.
1 Olson flied to short center.
J. Johnston lined a single to left, Brooklyn's first hit of the game.
Griffith doubled to right-center, scoring J. Johnston.
2 Wheat flied to deep center, Griffith going to third after the catch.
3 Myers grounded to short.
Cleveland
1 Evans, batting for Jamieson, flied to Myers making a fantastic catch.
2 Wambsganss bunted out to the pitcher.
3 Speaker grounded to second.

5th Inning
Brooklyn
For Cleveland—Evans playing left field.
Konetchy walked.
1 Kilduff struck out.
2,3 Miller hit into a double play, Sewell to Wambsganss to Burns.
Cleveland
1 Burns struck out.
2 Gardner flied to Myers in deep right.
3 Wood grounded to short.

6th Inning
Brooklyn
1 Lamar, pinch-hitting for Marquard, grounded to short.
Olson singled to left.
2 J. Johnston forced Olson at second, Sewell to Wambsganss.
3 Griffith hit to Wambsganss who flipped to Sewell, who lost the ball for an error, but J. Johnston was out trying for third, Sewell to Gardner.
Cleveland
For Brooklyn—Pfeffer pitching.
1 Sewell popped to third.
2 O'Neill struck out.
Coveleski singled to center.
Coveleski went to second on a wild pitch.
Evans singled to right, Coveleski going to third.
Wambsganss beat out a hit to short, scoring Coveleski.
3 Speaker fouled to Miller.

7th Inning
Brooklyn
1 Wheat grounded to short.
2 Myers struck out.
3 Konetchy lined to deep center.
Cleveland
Burns walked on a full count.
Gardner singled to deep right, Burns going to third.
Gardner took second on a short passed ball.
Graney batting for Wood with a 1-1 count, grounded to Kilduff who chased Gardner
1 toward third, Burns staying there. Miller tagged out both and Gardner was therefore out as Graney took second.
2 Sewell popped to short.
O'Neill intentionally passed, loading the bases.
3 Coveleski flied to deep right.

8th Inning
Brooklyn
Kilduff singled over second.
1,2 Miller hit into a double play, Gardner to Wambsganss to Burns.
3 Pfeffer rolled to Coveleski
Cleveland
1 Evans grounded to second.
2 Wambsganss flied to short center.
3 Speaker grounded to second.

9th Inning
Brooklyn
1 Olson grounded to second.
J. Johnston singled off of Coveleski's shins.
Neis ran for J. Johnston.
2 Griffith forced Neis at second, Wambsganss to Sewell.
3 Wheat forced Griffith at second, Sewell to Wambsganss.

Game 5 October 10 at Cleveland

Bkn.	000	000	001
Cle.	400	310	00x

Brooklyn	Pos	AB	R	H	RBI	PO	A	E
Olson	ss	4	0	2	0	3	5	0
Sheehan	3b	3	0	1	0	1	1	1
Griffith	rf	4	0	0	0	0	0	0
Wheat	lf	4	1	2	0	3	0	0
Myers	cf	4	0	2	0	0	0	0
Konetchy	1b	4	0	2	1	9	2	0
Kilduff	2b	4	0	1	0	5	6	0
Miller	c	2	0	2	0	0	1	0
Krueger	c	2	0	1	0	2	1	0
Grimes	p	1	0	0	0	0	1	0
Mitchell	p	2	0	0	0	1	0	0
Totals		34	1	13	1	24	17	1

Cleveland	Pos	AB	R	H	RBI	PO	A	E
Jamieson	lf	4	1	2	0	2	1	0
a Graney	lf	1	0	0	0	0	0	0
Wambsganss	2b	5	1	1	0	7	2	0
Speaker	cf	3	2	1	0	1	0	0
E. Smith	rf	4	1	3	4	0	0	0
Gardner	3b	4	0	1	1	2	2	1
D. Johnston	1b	3	1	2	0	9	1	0
Sewell	ss	3	0	0	0	2	4	0
O'Neill	c	2	1	0	0	23	1	1
Thomas	c	0	0	0	0	1	0	0
Bagby	p	4	1	2	3	0	2	0
Totals		33	8	12	8	27	13	2

Pitching	IP	H	R	ER	BB	SO
Brooklyn						
Grimes (L)	3⅓	9	7	7	1	0
Mitchell	4⅔	3	1	0	3	1
Cleveland						
Bagby (W)	9	13	1	1	0	3

a Struck out for Jamieson in 8th.

Triples—Konetchy, E. Smith. Home Runs—Bagby, E. Smith. Sacrifice Hits—D. Johnston, Sheehan. Double Plays—Olson to Kilduff to Konetchy, Jamieson to O'Neill, Gardner to Wambsganss to D. Johnston, D. Johnston to Sewell to D. Johnston. Triple Play—**Wambsganss (unassisted).** Passed Ball—Miller. Wild Pitch—Bagby. Left on Bases—Brooklyn 7, Cleveland 6. Umpires—Klem, Connolly, O'Day, Dinneen. Attendance—26,884. Time of Game—1:49.

1st Inning
Brooklyn
Olson singled to left.
1 Sheehan sacrificed Olson to second, Bagby to D. Johnston.
2 Griffith grounded to first.
3 Wheat flied to left.
Cleveland
Jamieson singled to right.
Wambsganss singled to center, Jamieson stopping at second.
Speaker beat out a bunt as Grimes fell while chasing it, loading the bases.
E. Smith hit the first Grand Slam home run in Series' history. A blast over the right field fence and screen.
1 Gardner popped to short.
D. Johnston singled to center.
2,3 Sewell hit into a double play, Olson to Kilduff to Konetchy.

2nd Inning
Brooklyn
1 Myers grounded to third.
Konetchy tripled to center.
2,3 Kilduff flied to Jamieson whose throw to O'Neill doubled Konetchy.
Cleveland
1 O'Neill grounded to short.
2 Bagby flied to left.
3 Jamieson grounded back to the mound.

3rd Inning
Brooklyn
Miller singled to left.
1,2 Grimes grounded into a double play, Gardner to Wambsganss to D. Johnston.
Olson singled to right.
Sheehan singled to right, Olson stopping at second.
3 Griffith popped to third.
Cleveland
1 Wambsganss grounded to second.
2 Speaker grounded to second.
Smith tripled to deep center.
3 Gardner grounded to second.

4th Inning
Brooklyn
1 Wheat struck out.
Myers singled to center.
Myers took second on a wild pitch.
2 Myers out trying to steal third, O'Neill to Gardner.
3 Konetchy grounded to short.
Cleveland
D. Johnston singled to center.
D. Johnston went to second on Miller's passed ball.
1 Sewell grounded to third, D. Johnston going to third.
O'Neill intentionally walked.
Bagby hit a three-run homer into the center field stands.
Jamieson singled to right.
For Brooklyn—Mitchell relieved Grimes.
2 Wambsganss flied to left.
3 Jamieson out trying to steal second, Miller to Olson, Olson making the tag after Jamieson overslid the bag.

5th Inning
Brooklyn
Kilduff singled to left-center.
Miller singled to center, Kilduff stopping at second, after a good throw to third by Speaker.
1,2,3 Mitchell lined towards right but Wambsganss got the ball in one hand, touched second and tagged Miller for an unassisted triple play.

5th Inning (continued)
Cleveland.
Speaker safely to second on Sheehan's wild throw to first.
Smith singled to center, sending Speaker to third.
Gardner singled to left, scoring Speaker as Smith stopped at second.
1 D. Johnston sacrificed up both runners, Konetchy to Kilduff.
2 Sewell fouled to Sheehan.
O'Neill walked, loading the bases.
3 Bagby forced O'Neill, Olson to Kilduff.

6th Inning
Brooklyn
1 Olson popped to short.
2 Sheehan grounded to second.
3 Griffith flied to center.
Cleveland
1 Jamieson grounded out, Konetchy to Mitchell.
2 Wambsganss flied to left.
Speaker walked.
3 Smith forced Speaker at second, Kilduff to Olson.

7th Inning
Brooklyn
Wheat singled to center.
1 Myers forced Wheat at second, Sewell to Wambsganss.
2 Konetchy struck out and Myers safe at second on O'Neill's wild throw.
3 Kilduff grounded to short.
Cleveland
For Brooklyn—Krueger catching.
1 Gardner fouled to Krueger.
2 D. Johnston grounded to second.
Sewell walked.
3 Sewell caught attempting to steal second, Krueger to Kilduff.

8th Inning
Brooklyn
Krueger singled to center.
1,2 Mitchell hit into a double play, D. Johnston to Sewell to D. Johnston.
Olson safe on Gardner's fumble.
3 Sheehan grounded to first.
Cleveland
1 O'Neill grounded to short.
Bagby singled to center.
2 Graney, pinch-hitting for Jamieson, struck out.
3 Wambsganss forced Bagby at second, Olson to Kilduff.

9th Inning
Brooklyn
For Cleveland—Graney playing left, and Thomas catching.
1 Griffith struck out.
Wheat singled to right.
Myers singled to center, Wheat stopping at second.
Konetchy singled to right, scoring Wheat with Myers racing to third.
2 Kilduff grounded back to the mound, Myers holding third as Konetchy went to second.
3 Krueger popped to second.

Game 6 October 11 at Cleveland

Bkn.	000 000 000
Cle.	000 001 00x

Brooklyn	Pos	AB	R	H	RBI	PO	A	E
Olson	ss	4	0	1	0	4	1	0
Sheehan	3b	4	0	0	0	0	3	0
Neis	rf	2	0	0	0	3	0	0
a Krueger		1	0	0	0	0	0	0
Griffith	rf	0	0	0	0	0	0	0
Wheat	lf	4	0	0	0	2	0	0
Myers	cf	4	0	1	0	1	0	0
Konetchy	1b	3	0	1	0	9	1	0
b McCabe		0	0	0	0	0	0	0
Kilduff	2b	4	0	0	0	2	2	0
Miller	c	3	0	0	0	3	3	0
S. Smith	p	3	0	0	0	0	3	0
Totals		32	0	3	0	24	13	0

a Hit into force play for Neis in 8th.
b Ran for Konetchy in 9th.

Doubles—Burns, Olson. Left on Bases—Brooklyn 7, Cleveland 4. Umpires—Connolly, O'Day, Dinneen, Klem. Attendance—27,194. Time of Game—1:34.

Cleveland	Pos	AB	R	H	RBI	PO	A	E
Evans	lf	4	0	3	0	4	0	0
Wambsganss	2b	4	0	0	0	1	2	0
Speaker	cf	3	1	1	0	3	0	0
Burns	1b	2	0	1	1	10	0	0
Gardner	3b	3	0	0	0	2	2	1
Wood	rf	3	0	1	0	2	0	0
Sewell	ss	3	0	1	0	2	3	2
O'Neill	c	3	0	0	0	3	2	0
Mails	p	3	0	0	0	0	1	0
Totals		28	1	7	1	27	10	3

Pitching	IP	H	R	ER	BB	SO
Brooklyn						
S. Smith (L)	8	7	1	1	1	1
Cleveland						
Mails (W)	9	3	0	0	2	4

1st Inning
Brooklyn
1 Olson flied to deep left.
2 Sheehan called out on strikes.
3 Neis bounced to second.
Cleveland
Evans singled hard to third.
1 Evans out trying for second, Miller to Olson.
2 Wambsganss flied to short right.
3 Speaker fouled to Miller.

2nd Inning
Brooklyn
1 Wheat took a called third strike.
2 Myers flied to right.
Konetchy singled to right.
Kilduff safe at first with Konetchy to second on Sewell's fumble.
Miller safe on Gardner's fumble, loading the bases.
3 S. Smith flied to short center.
Cleveland
Burns walked on a full count after a just fouled home run.
1 Gardner forced Burns at second, Konetchy to Olson. The return throw just missed a double play.
Wood singled off Sheehan's glove into left, Gardner racing to third as Wood took second on the play at third.
2 Sewell grounded to Kilduff, who threw to Miller getting Gardner at the plate with Wood going to third.
3 O'Neill forced Sewell at second, Kilduff unassisted.

3rd Inning
Brooklyn
1 Olson lined to short.
2 Sheehan flied to center.
3 Neis popped to short.
Cleveland
1 Mails grounded to third.
Evans singled over Olson's head.
2 Wambsganss forced Evans at second on a bunt, Miller to Kilduff.
3 Speaker bounced to first.

4th Inning
Brooklyn
1 Wheat popped to first.
Myers singled to right.
Konetchy walked.
2 Kilduff flied to short right.
3 Miller flied to left.
Cleveland
1 Burns popped to Olson in short left.
2 Gardner flied to left.
3 Wood flied to right.

5th Inning
Brooklyn
1 S. Smith took a called third strike.
2 Olson flied to center.
3 Sheehan grounded to short.
Cleveland
Sewell singled over Kilduff's head.
1 Sewell out trying for second, Miller to Olson.
2 O'Neill bounced to Kilduff, robbing O'Neill of a sure hit.
3 Mails grounded to third.

6th Inning
Brooklyn
Neis walked on four pitches.
1 Neis out, O'Neill to Burns.
2 Wheat grounded to short.
3 Myers grounded to Sewell making a great gloved stop behind second.
Cleveland
1 Evans popped to Konetchy in short right.
2 Wambsganss bounced to short.
Speaker singled to left.
Burns doubled to the low fence in left, scoring Speaker all the way from first.
3 Gardner flied to right.

7th Inning
Brooklyn
1 Konetchy bounced back to the mound.
2 Kilduff struck out and was thrown out at first.
3 Miller flied to left.
Cleveland
1 Wood flied to deep center.
2 Sewell grounded to S. Smith.
3 O'Neill bounced to third after a foul into the stands.

8th Inning
Brooklyn
1 S. Smith grounded to third.
Olson doubled into the left field corner.
2 Sheehan popped to third.
3 Krueger, pinch-hitting for Neis, grounded to Gardner who tagged Olson on the way to third.
Cleveland
For Brooklyn—Griffith playing right.
1 Mails singled to left.
Evans singled over short, his third hit of the game.
2 Evans was picked off first, S. Smith to Konetchy.
3 Wambsganss flied to deep left.

9th Inning
Brooklyn
1 Wheat grounded to second.
Myers safe at first on Sewell's throwing error.
2 Konetchy forced Myers at second, Gardner to Wambsganss.
McCabe ran for Konetchy.
3 Kilduff flied to deep left.

Game 7 October 12 at Cleveland

Bkn.	000 000 000
Cle.	000 110 10x

Brooklyn	Pos	AB	R	H	RBI	PO	A	E
Olson	ss	4	0	0	0	1	1	0
Sheehan	3b	4	0	1	0	2	1	1
Griffith	rf	4	0	0	0	3	0	0
Wheat	lf	4	0	2	0	2	0	0
Myers	cf	4	0	0	0	4	0	0
Konetchy	1b	4	0	1	0	8	0	0
Kilduff	2b	3	0	0	0	1	4	0
Miller	c	2	0	0	0	2	1	0
b Lamar		1	0	0	0	0	0	0
Krueger	c	0	0	0	0	1	0	0
Grimes	p	2	0	1	0	0	2	1
c Schmandt		1	0	0	0	0	0	0
Mamaux	p	0	0	0	0	0	0	0
Totals		33	0	5	0	24	9	2

a Olson hit by batted ball in third.
b Grounded out for Miller in 7th.
c Grounded out for Grimes in 8th.

Doubles—Jamieson, O'Neill. Triple—Speaker. Stolen Bases—Jamieson, D. Johnston. Left on Bases—Brooklyn 6, Cleveland 8. Umpires—O'Day, Dinneen, Klem, Connolly. Attendance—27,525. Time of Game—1:55.

Cleveland	Pos	AB	R	H	RBI	PO	A	E
Jamieson	lf	4	1	2	1	3	0	0
Wambsganss	2b	4	0	1	0	4	3	0
Speaker	cf	3	1	1	1	3	0	0
E. Smith	rf	3	0	0	0	3	1	0
Gardner	3b	4	1	1	0	1	3	0
D. Johnston	1b	2	0	1	0	11	1	0
Sewell	ss	4	0	0	0	0	6	2
O'Neill	c	4	0	1	0	1	0	0
Coveleski	p	3	1	0	0	1	1	1
Totals		31	3	7	2	a26	15	3

Pitching	IP	H	R	ER	BB	SO
Brooklyn						
Grimes (L)	7	7	3	2	4	2
Mamaux	1	0	0	0	0	1
Cleveland						
Coveleski (W)	9	5	0	0	0	1

1st Inning
Brooklyn
1 Olson popped to third.
2 Sheehan flied to short left.
Griffith safe when Coveleski took D. Johnston's throw but failed to touch first for an error.
3 Wheat popped to second.
Cleveland
1 Jamieson bounced to first.
2 Wambsganss flied to left.
3 Speaker popped to third.

2nd Inning
Brooklyn
1 Myers bounced to short.
2 Konetchy bounced to third.
3 Kilduff bounced to short.
Cleveland
1 E. Smith bounced to Kilduff, making a brilliant play.
Gardner safely to second when Sheehan threw wildly past first.
D. Johnston walked on a full count.
2 Sewell lined to right.
3 O'Neill grounded to second.

3rd Inning
Brooklyn
1 Miller was called out on strikes.
Grimes blooped a Texas Leaguer into short left.
Olson safe at first and Grimes at second on Sewell's fumble.
Sheehan got a single when his grounder
2 hit Olson on the leg for an automatic out.
3 Griffith flied to right.
Cleveland
1 Coveleski struck out.
2 Jamieson grounded back to the mound.
Wambsganss beat out a bounder to Grimes.
3 Speaker grounded to second.

4th Inning
Brooklyn
Wheat slammed a single high off the
1 right field wall but was out trying for second, E. Smith to Wambsganss.
2 Myers out on a slow hopper to third.
3 Konetchy flied to deep left.
Cleveland
1 E. Smith grounded to first.
Gardner singled off Kilduff's glove.
D. Johnston lined a single over Kilduff's head, Gardner going to third.
2 Sewell lined to short left.
On a double steal Grimes throw to third rolled into center, Gardner scoring as D. Johnston halted at second on a stolen base.
3 O'Neill flied to right.

5th Inning
Brooklyn
1 Kilduff lined to center.
2 Miller grounded to short, Sewell making a phenomenal stop.
3 Grimes grounded back to the mound.
Cleveland
1 Coveleski called out on strikes.
Jamieson singled in front of the plate.
2 Wambsganss flied to right.
Jamieson stole second.
Speaker tripled into the deep right field corner, scoring Jamieson.
3 E. Smith flied to deep center.

6th Inning
Brooklyn
1 Olson flied to center.
2 Sheehan bounced to second.
3 Griffith flied to deep center.
Cleveland
1 Gardner bounced to first on a 3–2 count.
D. Johnston walked also on a full count.
2 Sewell flied to Myers in right-center.
3 D. Johnston out stealing second, Miller to Kilduff.

7th Inning
Brooklyn
1 Wheat lined to right.
2 Myers grounded to second.
Konetchy singled to short.
Kilduff safe and Konetchy to second on Sewell's fumble.
3 Lamar, batting for Miller, grounded to second.
Cleveland
For Brooklyn—Krueger catching.
O'Neill doubled to deep left-center.
Coveleski bunted to Grimes and O'Neill
1 was hung up between second and third, Grimes to Sheehan to Olson to Konetchy, Coveleski got to second on the play.
Jamieson doubled over Konetchy's head into right, scoring Coveleski.
2 Wambsganss flied to center on a full count.
Speaker walked.
Smith also walked, loading the bases.
3 Gardner forced Smith at second, Kilduff to Olson.

8th Inning
Brooklyn
1 Schmandt, batting for Grimes, grounded to short.
2 Olson rolled to third.
3 Sheehan flied to right.
Cleveland
For Brooklyn—Mamaux pitching.
1 D. Johnston fouled to Sheehan.
2 Sewell flied to center.
3 O'Neill struck out.

9th Inning
Brooklyn
1 Griffith flied to left.
Wheat singled past second.
2 Myers forced Wheat at second, Sewell to Wambsganss.
3 Konetchy forced Myers at second, Sewell to Wambsganss.

1920 WORLD SERIES COMPOSITE BOX

	Wins	Composite Line Score
Cleveland Indians (A.L.)	5	6 2 2 6 2 2 1 0 0 – 21
Brooklyn Robins (N.L.)	2	3 0 1 1 1 0 1 0 1 – 8

Manager	Regular Season W	L	Pct.	G. Ahead
Tris Speaker	98	56	.636	2
Wilbert Robinson	93	61	.604	7

BATTING AND FIELDING

	World Series Statistics																		Regular Season Statistics													
	Pos	G	AB	R	H	2B	3B	HR	RBI	BB	SO	SB	BA	SA	PO	A	E		Main Pos	G	AB	R	H	2B	3B	HR	RBI	BB	SO	SB	BA	SA
CLEVELAND INDIANS																																
Doc Johnston	ph-1b	5	11	1	3	0	0	0	0	2	1	**1**	.273	.273	27	6	0		1b	147	535	68	156	24	10	2	71	28	32	13	.292	.385
Bill Wambsganss	2b	7	26	3	4	0	0	0	1	2	1	0	.154	.154	21	17	0		2b	153	565	83	138	16	11	1	55	54	26	9	.244	.317
Joe Sewell	ss	7	23	0	4	0	0	0	0	2	1	0	.174	.174	11	**28**	**6**		ss	22	70	14	23	4	1	0	12	9	4	1	.329	.414
Larry Gardner	3b	7	24	1	5	1	0	0	2	1	1	0	.208	.250	9	15	2		3b	154	597	72	185	31	11	3	118	53	25	3	.310	.414
Elmer Smith	ph-rf	5	13	1	4	0	**1**	**1**	**5**	1	1	0	.308	**.692**	7	1	0		of	129	456	82	144	37	10	12	103	53	35	5	.316	.520
Tris Speaker	cf	7	25	**6**	8	2	**1**	0	1	3	1	0	.320	.480	18	0	0		of	150	552	137	214	**50**	11	8	107	97	13	10	.388	.562
Charlie Jamieson	ph-lf	6	15	2	5	1	0	0	1	1	0	**1**	**.33**	.400	8	1	0		of	108	370	69	118	17	7	1	40	41	26	2	.319	.411
Steve O'Neill	c	7	21	1	7	**3**	0	0	2	**4**	3	0	**.333**	.476	23	7	1		c	149	489	63	157	39	5	3	55	69	39	3	.321	.440
Joe Evans	lf-ph	4	13	0	4	0	0	0	0	1	0	0	.308	.308	7	0	0		of	56	172	32	60	9	9	0	23	15	3	6	.349	.506
George Burns	lb-ph	5	10	1	3	1	0	0	2	3	3	0	.300	.400	38	1	1	a	1b	44	56	7	15	4	1	0	13	4	3	1	.268	.375
Smokey Joe Wood	rf-ph	4	10	2	2	1	0	0	0	1	2	0	.200	.300	7	0	0		of	61	137	25	37	11	2	1	30	25	16	1	.270	.401
Jack Graney	ph-rf-lf	3	3	0	0	0	0	0	0	0	2	0	.000	.000	0	0	0		of	62	152	31	45	11	1	0	13	27	21	4	.296	.382
Les Nunamaker	ph-c	2	2	0	1	0	0	0	0	0	0	0	.500	.500	0	0	0		c	34	54	10	18	3	3	0	14	4	5	1	.333	.500
Harry Lunte	2b	1	0	0	0	0	0	0	0	0	0	0	—	—	0	0	0		ss	23	71	6	14	0	0	0	7	5	6	0	.197	.197
Pinch Thomas	c	1	0	0	0	0	0	0	0	0	0	0	—	—	1	0	0		c	9	9	2	3	1	0	0	0	3	1	0	.333	.444
Stan Coveleski	p	3	10	2	1	0	0	0	0	0	**4**	0	.100	.100	2	5	1		p	41	111	13	25	4	2	0	17	11	28	0	.225	.297
Jim Bagby	p	2	6	1	2	0	0	**1**	3	0	0	0	.333	.833	2	3	1		p	49	131	17	33	7	3	1	14	6	17	0	.252	.374
Duster Mails	p	2	5	0	0	0	0	0	0	0	1	0	.000	.000	1	4	0		p	9	20	3	4	1	0	0	0	2	6	0	.200	.250
George Uhle	p	2	0	0	0	0	0	0	0	0	0	0	—	—	0	1	0		p	27	32	4	11	0	0	0	2	2	2	1	.344	.344
Ray Caldwell	p	1	0	0	0	0	0	0	0	0	0	0	—	—	0	0	0		p	41	89	17	19	3	0	0	7	10	13	0	.213	.247
Guy Morton		Did not play																	p	29	46	1	10	0	0	0	2	1	9	0	.217	.217
Bob Clark		Did not play																	p	11	10	0	2	0	0	0	0	0	0	0	.200	.200
George Ellison		Did not play																	p	1	0	0	0	0	0	0	0	0	0	0	—	—
team total		7	217	21	53	9	2	2	17	21	21	2	.244	.332	182	89	12			154	5196	**857**	1574	**300**	**95**	35	**758**	**576**	379	73	.303	.417

Double Plays—8 Triple Play—1 (Wambsganss unassisted)
Left on Bases—43

a—from Philadelphia (A)
Joe Boehling (p), Tony Faeth (p), Tim Murchison (p), Elmer Myers (p), Dick Niehaus (p) also played for the Indians during the season. Ray Chapman (ss) died August 17th after being hit in the head by a pitch.

	World Series Statistics																		Regular Season Statistics													
	Pos	G	AB	R	H	2B	3B	HR	RBI	BB	SO	SB	BA	SA	PO	A	E		Main Pos	G	AB	R	H	2B	3B	HR	RBI	BB	SO	SB	BA	SA
BROOKLYN ROBINS																																
Ed Konetchy	1b	7	23	0	4	0	1	0	2	3	2	0	.174	.261	**70**	7	1		1b	131	497	62	153	22	12	5	63	33	18	3	.308	.431
Pete Kilduff	2b	7	21	0	2	0	0	0	0	1	**4**	0	.095	.095	15	**28**	0		2b	141	478	62	130	26	8	0	58	58	43	2	.272	.360
Ivy Olson	ss	7	25	2	8	1	0	0	0	3	1	0	.320	.360	12	20	0		ss	143	637	71	162	13	11	1	46	20	19	4	.254	.314
Jimmy Johnston	3b	4	14	2	3	0	0	0	0	0	2	**1**	.214	.214	2	8	0		3b	155	635	87	185	17	12	1	52	43	23	19	.291	.361
Tommy Griffith	rf	7	21	1	4	2	0	0	3	0	2	0	.190	.286	10	0	0		of	93	334	41	87	9	4	2	30	15	18	3	.260	.329
Hy Myers	cf	7	26	0	6	0	0	0	1	0	1	0	.231	.231	15	1	0		of	154	582	83	177	36	**22**	4	80	35	54	9	.304	.462
Zack Wheat	lf	7	**27**	2	**9**	2	0	0	2	1	2	0	**.333**	.407	15	0	2		of	148	583	89	191	26	13	9	73	48	21	8	.328	.463
Otto Miller	c	6	14	0	2	0	0	0	0	1	2	0	.143	.143	17	6	0		c	90	301	16	87	9	2	0	33	9	18	0	.289	.332
Jack Sheehan	3b	3	11	0	2	0	0	0	0	0	1	0	.182	.182	3	5	2		ss-3b	3	5	0	2	1	0	0	0	1	0	0	.400	.600
Ernie Krueger	c-ph	4	6	0	1	0	0	0	0	0	0	0	.167	.167	10	2	0		c	52	146	21	42	4	2	1	17	16	13	2	.288	.363
Bernie Neis	pr-rf	4	5	0	0	0	0	0	0	1	0	0	.000	.000	3	0	0		of	95	249	38	63	11	2	2	22	26	35	9	.253	.337
Bill Lamar	ph	3	3	0	0	0	0	0	0	0	0	0	.000	.000					of	24	44	5	12	4	0	0	4	0	1	0	.273	.364
Ray Schmandt	ph	1	1	0	0	0	0	0	0	0	0	0	.000	.000					1b	28	63	7	15	2	1	0	7	3	4	1	.238	.302
Bill McCabe	pr	1	0	0	0	0	0	0	0	0	0	0	—	—				b	ss-of	41	68	10	10	0	0	0	3	2	6	1	.147	.147
Rowdy Elliott		Did not play																	c	41	112	13	27	4	0	1	13	3	6	0	.241	.314
Chuck Ward		Did not play																	ss	19	71	7	11	1	0	0	4	3	3	1	.155	.169
Zack Taylor		Did not play																	c	9	13	3	5	2	0	0	5	0	2	0	.385	.538
Burleigh Grimes	p	3	6	1	2	0	0	0	0	0	0	0	.333	.333	1	7	1		p	43	111	9	34	8	3	0	16	8	21	2	.306	.432
Sherry Smith	p	2	6	0	0	0	0	0	0	0	2	0	.000	.000	2	5	0		p	33	43	6	10	2	2	0	3	1	9	1	.233	.372
Clarence Mitchell	p-ph	2	3	0	1	0	0	0	0	0	0	0	.333	.333	1	0	0		p-1b	55	107	9	25	2	2	0	11	8	9	1	.234	.290
Rube Marquard	p	2	1	0	0	0	0	0	0	0	0	0	.000	.000	0	1	0		p	28	59	2	10	1	0	0	0	5	12	1	.169	.186
Al Mamaux	p	3	1	0	0	0	0	0	0	0	1	0	.000	.000	0	1	0		p	41	60	5	10	2	0	0	5	8	14	0	.167	.200
Jeff Pfeffer	p	1	1	0	0	0	0	0	0	0	0	0	.000	.000	0	0	0		p	30	74	5	18	0	1	0	8	2	12	0	.243	.270
Leon Cadore	p	2	0	0	0	0	0	0	0	0	0	0	—	—	1	1	0		p	35	91	4	20	2	1	2	11	3	22	1	.220	.330
George Mohart		Did not play																	p	13	8	0	1	0	0	0	0	2	2	0	.125	.125
Johnny Miljus		Did not play																	p	10	6	0	2	0	1	0	0	1	0	0	.333	.667
team total		7	215	8	44	5	1	0	8	10	20	1	.205	.237	177	91	6			155	5399	660	1493	205	**99**	28	566	359	391	70	.277	.367

Double Plays—5
Left on Bases—39

b—from Chicago (N)
Doug Baird (3b), Wally Hood (of), Red Sheridan (ss) also played for the Robins during the season.

PITCHING

	World Series Statistics													Regular Season Statistics													
	G	GS	CG	IP	H	R	ER	BB	SO	W	L	SV	ERA	G	GS	CG	IP	H	ER	BB	SO	W	L	Pct	SV	ShO	ERA
CLEVELAND INDIANS																											
Stan Coveleski	**3**	**3**	**3**	**27**	15	2	2	2	**8**	**3**	0	0	0.67	41	37	26	315	284	87	65	**133**	24	14	.632	2	3	2.49
Duster Mails	2	1	1	$15\frac{2}{3}$	6	0	0	6	6	1	0	0	**0.00**	9	8	6	63	54	13	18	25	7	0	1.000	0	2	1.86
Jim Bagby	2	2	1	15	20	4	3	1	3	1	1	0	1.80	**48**	**39**	**30**	**340**	**338**	109	79	73	**31**	12	**.721**	0	3	2.89
George Uhle	2	0	0	3	1	0	0	0	3	0	0	0	0.00	27	6	4	85	98	49	29	27	4	5	.444	1	0	5.19
Ray Caldwell	1	1	0	$\frac{1}{3}$	2	2	1	1	0	0	1	0	27.00	34	33	20	238	286	102	63	80	20	10	.667	0	0	3.86
Guy Morton	Did not play													29	17	5	137	140	68	57	72	8	6	.571	1	1	4.47
Bob Clark	Did not play													11	2	2	42	59	16	13	8	1	2	.333	0	1	3.43
George Ellison	Did not play													1	0	0	1	0	0	2	1	0	0	—	0	0	0.00
team total	7	7	5	61	44	8	6	10	20	5	2	0	0.89	154	154	93	1376	1448	522	401	466	**98**	56	**.636**	7	10	3.41
BROOKLYN ROBINS																											
Burleigh Grimes	**3**	**3**	1	$19\frac{1}{3}$	**23**	**10**	**9**	**9**	4	1	**2**	0	4.19	40	33	25	304	271	75	67	131	23	11	**.676**	2	5	2.22
Sherry Smith	2	2	2	17	10	2	1	3	3	1	1	0	0.53	33	12	6	136	134	28	27	33	11	9	.550	3	2	1.85
Rube Marquard	2	1	0	9	7	3	3	3	6	0	1	0	3.00	28	26	10	190	181	68	35	89	10	7	.588	0	1	3.22
Clarence Mitchell	1	0	0	$4\frac{2}{3}$	3	1	0	3	1	0	0	0	0.00	19	7	3	79	85	27	23	18	5	2	.714	1	1	3.08
Al Mamaux	**3**	0	0	4	2	2	2	0	5	0	0	0	4.50	41	18	9	191	172	57	63	101	12	8	.600	4	2	2.69
Jeff Pfeffer	1	0	0	3	4	1	1	2	1	0	0	0	3.00	30	28	20	215	225	72	45	80	16	9	.640	0	2	3.01
Leon Cadore	2	1	0	2	4	2	2	1	1	0	1	0	9.00	35	30	16	254	256	74	56	79	15	14	.517	0	4	2.62
George Mohart	Did not play													13	1	0	36	33	7	7	13	0	1	.000	0	0	1.75
Johnny Miljus	Did not play													9	0	0	23	24	8	4	9	1	0	1.000	0	0	3.13
team total	7	7	3	59	53	21	18	21	21	2	5	0	2.75	155	155	89	**1427**	1381	416	327	**553**	**93**	61	**.604**	10	17	**2.62**

Total Attendance—178,737 Average Attendance—25,534 Winning Player's Share—$4168 Losing Player's Share—$2,419

1921
Shaming the Tenants

John McGraw thought this the greatest effrontery yet. His Giants always had ruled the hearts of New York baseball fans, and his team was indisputably number one in the Big Apple. The Yankees had only come to town in 1903 and had spent most of their existence among the also-rans in the American League and among the lesser sports stories in the local newspapers. The Giants considered their younger rivals so little a threat that they gladly took them into the Polo Grounds as tenants starting in 1913. But the postwar years caused McGraw to regret his team's welcome mat. The Yanks had blossomed into a winning club in 1919 under the direction of Miller Huggins, and then the purchase of Babe Ruth from the Boston Red Sox that winter changed the New York sports picture. Ruth celebrated his first year in New York by swatting 54 homers, a preposterous total greater than any major-league team's composite amount. The moon-faced Babe exuded color and made great newspaper copy, overnight finding the baseball world beating a path to his door. Now the Yankees were outdrawing the Giants, a bitter pill for McGraw to swallow. Building around Ruth, the Yankees constructed a championship team and won their first A.L. pennant. The public expected the World Series to be a showcase for Ruth's slugging, but McGraw could take direct steps to stop that, since his Giants took the National League pennant with a late-summer drive. Although the fans were looking for Ruth, both clubs were chock-full of hitters, as the Yanks had a team batting average of .300, slightly better than the Giants' .298 belting of the new lively ball. But the pitchers would do better than expected at keeping the ball within the bounds of the Polo Grounds, where all eight games would be played due to New York's good fortune in baseball teams.

Yankee hurler Carl Mays dished out some of that good pitching in the first game, using his sweeping submarine delivery to shoot the ball in at the Giants' knee level all afternoon. Frankie Frisch solved Mays for four hits, but the Giants went down to a 3–0 loss. Waite Hoyt started for the Yanks the next day and kept the diet of zeros coming, sending the Giants down to another 3–0 defeat. Ruth had only one hit in the two games, but the Yankee pitching was carrying the Series by itself.

The Yanks jumped out to an early third-game lead with four runs in the top of the third inning, but then the strong pitching vanished. The Giants knocked out Bob Shawkey in a four-run bottom of the third, then broke the game wide open with eight runs in a long seventh inning. The Giants' 13–5 victory came with a healthy serving of 20 hits off four Yankee pitchers. With opening-day pitchers Mays and Phil Douglas again matched, the fourth game remained close. After seven shutout innings, Mays lost his touch and coughed up three runs in the eighth and another one in the ninth, winding up the loser in a 4–2 decision. Ruth finally broke into the Series homer column with a majestic shot in the ninth inning with no one aboard the bases. Ruth's home run brought his legion of admirers to their feet, but his key play the next day in game five was beating out a bunt to start a two-run fourth inning which gave Waite Hoyt all the runs he needed to capture a 3–1 win.

But the 3–2 Series lead the Yankees had built suddenly looked small when Chick Fewster went to left field in game six instead of Babe Ruth. An infected arm and bad knee forced the Babe out of the lineup and made the Yanks seem like a much more ordinary team. The hitters showed heart by scoring three times in the first, but the pitchers fell down on the job and allowed 13 hits en route to an 8–5 loss. The Yankee pitchers wouldn't fail again, but then the hitters would not do the job without Ruth. With their star still out, the Yanks bowed 2–1 in game seven, with Mays losing to Douglas. Waite Hoyt allowed only one unearned run in the eighth game, coming in the first inning on an error by shortstop Roger Peckinpaugh, but Giant hurler Art Nehf needed no more than that and took a 1–0 victory. Ruth pinch-hit in the ninth and grounded out, but that appearance in itself was too little, too late to arouse the sleeping Yankee bats.

Game 1 October 5 at New York (N)

New York-A	Pos	AB	R	H	RBI	PO	A	E
Miller	cf	4	1	1	0	0	0	0
Peckinpaugh	ss	3	1	1	0	1	9	0
Ruth	lf	3	0	1	1	4	0	0
B. Meusel	rf	4	0	0	1	1	0	0
Pipp	1b	2	0	0	0	17	0	0
Ward	2b	3	0	1	0	3	5	0
McNally	3b	4	1	2	0	0	4	0
Schang	c	2	0	0	0	1	0	0
Mays	p	3	0	1	0	0	4	0
Totals		28	3	7	2	27	18	0

Pitching	IP	H	R	ER	BB	SO
Yankees						
Mays (W)	9	5	0	0	0	1
Giants						
Douglas (L)	8	5	3	3	4	6
Barnes	1	2	0	0	0	1

NY-A	1 0 0	0 1 1	0 0 0			
NY-N	0 0 0	0 0 0	0 0 0			

New York-N	Pos	AB	R	H	RBI	PO	A	E
Burns	cf	4	0	0	0	0	0	0
Bancroft	ss	4	0	0	0	1	2	0
Frisch	3b	4	0	4	0	1	4	0
Youngs	rf	3	0	0	0	0	0	0
Kelly	1b	4	0	0	0	13	1	0
I. Meusel	lf	3	0	0	0	0	1	0
Rawlings	2b	2	0	1	0	3	5	0
Snyder	c	3	0	0	0	7	1	0
Douglas	p	2	0	0	0	1	1	0
a Smith		1	0	0	0	0	0	0
Barnes	p	0	0	0	0	0	0	0
Totals		30	0	5	0	*26	15	0

a Flied out for Douglas in 8th.
* Schang out, hit by batted ball in 7th.

Double—McNally. Triple—Frisch. Stolen Bases—Frisch, McNally 2. Sacrifice Hits—Peckinpaugh, Pipp, Schang, Youngs. Double Plays—Frisch to Rawlings to Kelly, Peckinpaugh to Ward to Pipp. Passed Ball—Snyder. Hit by Pitcher—Rawlings (by Mays). Left on Bases—Yankees 5, Giants 5. Umpires—Rigler (N), Moriarty (A), Quigley (N), Chill (A). Attendance—30,203. Time of Game—1:38.

1st Inning
Yankees
Miller singled to center.
1 Peckinpaugh sacrificed Miller to second, Kelly to Douglas.
Ruth singled to center, scoring Miller.
2,3 B. Meusel grounded into a double play, Frisch to Rawlings to Kelly.
Giants
1 Burns grounded to short.
2 Bancroft grounded to second.
Frisch singled to center.
3 Youngs grounded back to the mound.

2nd Inning
Yankees
1 Pipp grounded to second.
Ward walked.
2 McNally grounded to third, Ward advancing to second.
3 Schang struck out.
Giants
1 Kelly flied to left.
2 I. Meusel flied to right.
Rawlings was hit by a pitch.
3 Snyder bounced back to the mound.

3rd Inning
Yankees
1 Mays grounded to second.
2 Miller grounded to short.
3 Peckinpaugh struck out.
Giants
1 Douglas flied to left.
2 Burns grounded to short.
3 Bancroft grounded to second.

4th Inning
Yankees
Ruth walked.
1 B. Meusel popped to third.
2 Pipp sacrificed Ruth to second, Frisch to Kelly.
3 Ward grounded to short.
Giants
Frisch singled to right.
Frisch stole second.
1 Youngs sacrificed Frisch to third, Mays to Pipp.
2 Kelly struck out.
3 I. Meusel grounded to short.

5th Inning
Yankees
McNally doubled to left.
1 Schang sacrificed McNally to third, Douglas to Kelly.
2 Mays struck out.
McNally stole home.
3 Miller grounded to third.
Giants
1 Rawlings grounded to short.
2 Snyder grounded to short.
3 Douglas grounded to first.

6th Inning
Yankees
Peckinpaugh beat out a slow roller to short.
Peckinpaugh went to second on a passed ball.
1 Ruth struck out.
B. Meusel tripled to deep left, scoring Peckinpaugh but I. Meusel threw the ball to Kelly and B.
2 Meusel was declared out for failing to touch first base.
Pipp walked.
3 Pipp out trying to steal second, Snyder to Rawlings.
Giants
1 Burns grounded to the pitcher.
2 Bancroft grounded to first.
Frisch tripled to left.
3 Youngs grounded to short.

7th Inning
Yankees
1 Ward struck out.
2 McNally grounded to second.
Schang walked.
3 Mays' grounder hit Schang for an automatic out.
Giants
1 Kelly popped to second.
2 I. Meusel grounded to second.
Rawlings singled to right.
3 Snyder forced Rawlings at second, Peckinpaugh to Ward.

8th Inning
Yankees
1 Miller popped to short.
2 Peckinpaugh grounded to second.
3 Ruth struck out.
Giants
1 Smith, pinch-hitting for Douglas, flied to left.
2 Burns grounded to second.
3 Bancroft flied to left.

9th Inning
Yankees
For the Giants—Barnes pitching.
1 B. Meusel popped to second.
2 Pipp grounded to first.
Ward singled to right.
McNally singled to left, Ward going to third.
McNally stole second.
3 Schang struck out.
Giants
Frisch singled to right.
1 Youngs forced Frisch at second, Ward to Peckinpaugh.
2,3 Kelly grounded into a double play, Peckinpaugh to Ward to Pipp.

Game 2 October 6 at New York (A)

| | | | NY-N | | | | 000 000 000 |
| NY-A | | | | | | | 000 100 02 x |

New York-A	Pos	AB	R	H	RBI	PO	A	E
Miller	cf	3	0	0	0	1	0	0
Peckinpaugh	ss	3	0	0	0	3	1	0
Ruth	lf	1	1	0	0	0	0	0
B. Meusel	rf	4	1	1	0	1	0	0
Pipp	1b	3	0	0	1	14	0	0
Ward	2b	4	1	1	0	4	7	0
McNally	3b	3	0	0	0	0	4	0
Schang	c	2	0	0	0	4	1	0
Hoyt	p	3	0	1	1	0	2	0
Totals		26	3	3	2	27	15	0

Pitching	IP	H	R	ER	BB	SO
Yankees						
Hoyt (W)	9	2	0	0	5	5
Giants						
Nehf (L)	8	3	3	1	7	0

New York-N	Pos	AB	R	H	RBI	PO	A	E
Burns	cf	3	0	0	0	1	0	0
Bancroft	ss	3	0	0	0	3	3	0
Frisch	3b	4	0	1	0	3	2	1
Youngs	rf	2	0	0	0	2	0	0
Kelly	1b	4	0	0	0	12	2	0
I. Meusel	lf	2	0	0	0	0	0	0
Rawlings	2b	3	0	1	0	2	2	0
Smith	c	3	0	0	0	1	1	1
Nehf	p	2	0	0	0	0	3	1
Totals		26	0	2	0	24	13	3

Stolen Bases—B. Meusel, Ruth 2.
Double Plays—McNally to Ward to Pipp,
Frisch to Rawlings. Passed Ball—Smith.
Left on Bases—Yankees 6, Giants 5.
Umpires—Moriarty, Quigley, Chill, Rigler.
Attendance—34,939. Time of Game—1:55.

1st Inning
Giants
1 Burns struck out.
2 Bancroft bounced back to the mound.
3 Frisch grounded to second
Yankees
 Miller walked.
1 Peckinpaugh grounded to the pitcher,
 Miller going to second.
 Ruth walked.
2,3 B. Meusel lined to Frisch who threw to
 Rawlings doubling Miller off second.

2nd Inning
Giants
1 Youngs grounded to first.
2 Kelly struck out.
3 I. Meusel grounded to first.
Yankees
 Pipp walked.
1 Ward grounded to short, Pipp
 going to second.
2 McNally grounded to Frisch who made a
 great stop and tagged Ward going
 into third.
3 McNally caught trying to steal
 second, Smith to Rawlings.

3rd Inning
Giants
 Rawlings singled to left.
1 Smith popped to short.
2 Nehf struck out.
3 Burns forced Rawlings at second,
 Peckinpaugh unassisted.
Yankees
1 Schang popped to short.
 Hoyt singled to right.
2 Miller flied to center.
 Peckinpaugh walked.
 Ruth walked, loading the bases.
3 B. Meusel popped to short.

4th Inning
Giants
1 Bancroft struck out.
2 Frisch grounded to short.
3 Youngs grounded to third.
Yankees
1 Pipp flied to right.
 Ward singled to right.
 McNally safe at first on Nehf's poor
 throw to second.
 Schang walked, loading the bases.
2 Hoyt grounded to second,
 Ward scoring but McNally was out
3 trying to score from second,
 Kelly to Smith.

5th Inning
Giants
1 Kelly struck out, but Schang dropping
 the third strike had to throw him out.
 I. Meusel walked.
2 Rawlings flied to right.
3 Smith flied to center.
Yankees
1 Miller grounded to third.
2 Peckinpaugh grounded to short.
 Ruth walked for the third time.
 Ruth stole second.
 Ruth stole third.
3 B. Meusel grounded to short.

6th Inning
Giants
 Nehf walked.
1 Burns popped to second.
2 Bancroft bounced back to the mound,
 sending Nehf to second.
3 Frisch grounded to first.
Yankees
1 Pipp thrown out by the pitcher.
2 Ward grounded to first.
3 McNally fouled to Frisch.

7th Inning
Giants
 Youngs walked.
1 Kelly forced Youngs at second,
 McNally to Ward.
2 I. Meusel forced Kelly at second,
 Ward to Peckinpaugh.
3 Rawlings grounded to second.
Yankees
1 Schang flied to right.
2 Hoyt popped to first.
3 Miller thrown out by the pitcher.

8th Inning
Giants
1 Smith grounded to second.
2 Nehf grounded to second.
 Burns walked.
3 Burns out stealing, Schang to Ward.
Yankees
 Peckinpaugh safe at first as Frisch
 dropped his pop.
1 Ruth forced Peckinpaugh at second,
 Kelly to Bancroft.
 B. Meusel singled to center and on the
 throw-in, Ruth scored and B. Meusel
 went to second.
2 Pipp grounded to second, B. Meusel
 moving to third.
 B. Meusel stole home.
3 Ward fouled to Kelly.

9th Inning
Giants
1 Bancroft grounded to second.
 Frisch singled to right.
 Youngs walked.
2,3 Kelly hit into a double play,
 McNally to Ward to Pipp.

Game 3 October 7 at New York (N)

| | | | NY-A | | | | 004 000 010 |
| NY-N | | | | | | | 004 000 81 x |

New York-A	Pos	AB	R	H	RBI	PO	A	E
Miller	cf	5	1	1	1	2	0	0
Peckinpaugh	ss	3	1	0	0	4	2	0
Ruth	lf	3	0	1	2	1	0	0
a Fewster	lf	0	0	0	0	0	0	0
B. Meusel	rf	3	0	2	0	1	0	0
Pipp	1b	3	0	0	1	12	0	0
Ward	2b	4	1	1	1	5	0	0
McNally	3b	3	0	0	0	2	0	0
Schang	c	2	1	1	0	2	2	0
DeVormer	c	1	0	0	0	1	0	0
Shawkey	p	1	1	1	0	0	0	0
Quinn	p	2	0	0	0	0	1	0
Collins	p	0	0	0	0	0	0	0
Rogers	p	0	0	0	0	0	1	0
b Baker		1	0	0	0	0	0	0
Totals		31	5	8	5	24	13	0

a Ran for Ruth in 8th.
b Flied out for Rogers in 9th.

Doubles—Burns, B. Meusel, I. Meusel, Youngs.
Triples—Burns, Youngs. Stolen Bases—Burns,
Frisch, I. Meusel. Sacrifice Hits—Pipp,
Bancroft. Double Plays—Ward to Pipp,
Quinn to Peckinpaugh to Pipp. Hit by
Pitcher—McNally (by Barnes). Wild
Pitch—Barnes. Left on Bases—Yankees 5,
Giants 10. Umpires—Quigley, Chill,
Rigler, Moriarty. Attendance—36,509.
Time of Game—2:40.

1st Inning
Yankees
1 Miller popped to third.
2 Peckinpaugh grounded to second.
3 Ruth struck out.
Giants
1 Burns flied to right.
2 Bancroft tapped to second.
 Frisch singled to right.
 Youngs walked.
3 Kelly grounded to third.

2nd Inning
Yankees
 B. Meusel doubled to left-center.
1 Pipp sacrificed B. Meusel to third,
 Toney to Kelly.
2 Ward hit to Rawlings who threw out
 B. Meusel trying to score.
3 McNally forced Ward at second,
 Bancroft to Rawlings.
Giants
 I. Meusel singled to center.
1,2 Rawlings lined to Ward who made a
 spectacular leaping catch and threw
 to Pipp doubling I. Meusel at first.
 Snyder singled to left.
3 Snyder thrown out stealing, Schang
 to Peckinpaugh.

3rd Inning
Yankees
 Schang walked.
 Shawkey singled to right.
 Miller singled to right, Schang scoring.
 Peckinpaugh walked, loading the bases.
 Ruth singled to center, scoring Shawkey
 and Miller with Peckinpaugh going
 to third.
 For the Giants—Barnes came in to pitch.
1 Ruth out trying to steal second,
 Snyder to Rawlings.
 B. Meusel walked.
2 Pipp grounded to second, scoring
 Peckinpaugh.
3 Ward struck out.
Giants
 Barnes singled to left.
1 Burns flied to center.
 Bancroft singled to right.
 Frisch walked, loading the bases.
 Youngs walked forcing home Barnes.
 Kelly walked forcing home Bancroft.
 For the Yankees—Quinn pitching.
2 I. Meusel grounded to first, Frisch
 scoring.
 Rawlings beat out an infield hit,
 scoring Youngs.
3 Snyder fouled to Pipp.

4th Inning
Yankees
1 McNally was hit by a pitched ball.
 Schang singled to right but was out
 trying for second, Youngs to Bancroft.
2 Quinn struck out.
3 Miller struck out.
Giants
1 Barnes grounded to second.
 Burns tripled to deep right.
2 Bancroft struck out.
 Frisch walked.
 Frisch stole second.
3 Youngs grounded to short.

5th Inning
Yankees
1 Peckinpaugh flied to left.
2 Ruth struck out.
 B. Meusel singled to left.
3 B. Meusel out stealing, Snyder to
 Bancroft.

New York-N	Pos	AB	R	H	RBI	PO	A	E
Burns	cf	6	1	4	0	1	0	0
Bancroft	ss	5	1	1	1	3	2	0
Frisch	3b	2	3	2	0	1	1	0
Youngs	rf	3	2	2	4	0	0	0
Kelly	1b	3	1	0	1	7	1	0
I. Meusel	lf	5	2	3	3	2	0	0
Rawlings	2b	5	0	3	3	5	0	0
Snyder	c	5	1	4	1	9	2	0
Toney	p	0	0	0	0	0	1	0
Barnes	p	5	2	2	0	1	1	0
Totals		39	13	20	13	27	14	0

Pitching	IP	H	R	ER	BB	SO
Yankees						
Shawkey	2⅓	5	4	4	4	0
Quinn (L)	**3⅓	8	4	4	2	2
Collins	⅓	4	4	4	1	0
Rogers	1⅓	3	1	1	0	1
Giants						
Toney	*2	4	4	4	2	1
Barnes (W)	7	4	1	1	2	7

*Pitched to 5 batters in 3rd.
**Pitched to 4 batters in 7th.

5th Inning (continued)
Giants
1 Kelly struck out.
2 I. Meusel flied to center.
3 Rawlings grounded to third.

6th Inning
Yankees
1 Pipp grounded out, Kelly making a
 good stop to Barnes.
 Ward singled to right.
2 McNally struck out.
3 Schang popped to second.
Giants
 Snyder singled to right.
1,2 Barnes hit into a quick double play,
 Quinn to Peckinpaugh to Pipp.
 Burns singled to left.
 Burns stole second.
3 Bancroft grounded to second.

7th Inning
Yankees
1 Quinn flied to center.
2 Miller struck out.
3 Peckinpaugh grounded to short.
Giants
 Frisch singled to center.
 Youngs doubled to deep right,
 Frisch stopping at third.
 Kelly walked, loading the bases.
 I. Meusel doubled to right, scoring
 Frisch and Youngs as Kelly went to
 third.
 For the Yankees—Collins pitching.
 Rawlings singled to center, scoring
 Kelly and I. Meusel.
1 Rawlings caught trying to steal
 second, Schang to Peckinpaugh.
 Snyder singled to center.
 Barnes singled to center.
 Burns singled to center, again
 loading the bases.
2 Bancroft hit a sacrifice fly to left,
 Snyder scoring after the catch.
 Frisch walked for the third time.
 Youngs tripled to deep center, Barnes,
 Burns and Frisch scoring.
 For the Yankees—Rogers pitching.
3 Kelly grounded back to the mound.

8th Inning
Yankees
 Ruth walked.
 Fewster ran for Ruth.
 Fewster to second on a wild pitch.
1 B. Meusel struck out.
2 Pipp grounded back to the mound,
 Fewster going to third.
 Ward singled to center, scoring
 Fewster.
3 McNally forced Ward at second,
 Rawlings to Bancroft.
Giants
 For the Yankees—Fewster playing left,
 DeVormer catching.
 I. Meusel singled to center.
 I. Meusel stole second.
1 Rawlings struck out.
 Snyder singled to left (his 4th hit),
 scoring I. Meusel.
2 Barnes popped to short.
 Burns doubled to left (his 4th hit),
 Snyder stopping at third.
3 Bancroft grounded to second.

9th Inning
Yankees
1 DeVormer grounded to second.
2 Baker, pinch-hitting for Rogers,
 flied to left.
3 Miller grounded to third.

Game 4 October 9 at New York (A)

New York-N	Pos	AB	R	H	RBI	PO	A	E
Burns	cf	4	0	2	2	0	0	0
Bancroft	ss	4	0	0	0	4	1	1
Frisch	3b	4	0	0	0	1	3	0
Youngs	rf	4	0	1	0	1	0	0
Kelly	1b	4	1	1	0	9	0	0
I. Meusel	lf	4	1	2	0	0	0	0
Rawlings	2b	4	1	2	1	1	4	0
Snyder	c	4	1	1	0	10	2	0
Douglas	p	2	0	0	0	1	2	0
Totals		34	4	9	4	27	12	1

Doubles—Burns, Kelly. Triples—I. Meusel, Schang. Home Run—Ruth. Sacrifice Hits—Douglas, Ward. Double Play—Ward to Peckinpaugh to Pipp. Left on Bases—Giants 4, Yankees 3. Umpires—Chill, Rigler, Moriarty, Quigley. Attendance—36,372. Time of Game—1:38.

NY-N 000 000 031
NY-A 000 010 001

New York-A	Pos	AB	R	H	RBI	PO	A	E
Miller	cf	4	0	0	0	1	0	0
Peckinpaugh	ss	4	0	1	0	2	6	0
Ruth	lf	4	1	2	1	2	0	0
B. Meusel	rf	4	0	0	0	1	0	0
Pipp	1b	4	0	1	0	16	0	0
Ward	2b	2	0	0	0	2	7	0
McNally	3b	3	1	1	0	1	2	1
Schang	c	3	0	2	1	2	1	0
Mays	p	3	0	0	0	0	3	0
Totals		31	2	7	2	27	19	1

Pitching	IP	H	R	ER	BB	SO
Giants						
Douglas (W)	9	7	2	2	0	8
Yankees						
Mays (L)	9	9	4	4	0	1

1st Inning
Giants
1 Burns struck out.
2 Bancroft grounded to second.
3 Frisch flied to center.
Yankees
1 Miller struck out.
2 Peckinpaugh grounded to short.
3 Ruth grounded to first.

2nd Inning
Giants
1 Youngs flied to left.
2 Kelly grounded to third.
3 I. Meusel grounded to second.
Yankees
1 B. Meusel grounded to third.
2 Pipp popped to short.
3 Ward tapped back to the mound.

3rd Inning
Giants
1 Rawlings grounded to short. Snyder safe on McNally's fumble.
2 Douglas grounded to second, Snyder going to second.
3 Burns grounded to short.
Yankees
1 McNally singled to right.
  McNally caught trying to steal second, Snyder to Bancroft.
2 Schang struck out.
3 Mays popped to short.

4th Inning
Giants
1 Bancroft grounded to short.
2 Frisch grounded to short.
3 Youngs flied to right.
Yankees
1 Miller grounded to third.
2 Peckinpaugh grounded to first.
  Ruth singled to right.
3 B. Meusel struck out.

5th Inning
Giants
1 Kelly grounded to third.
2 I. Meusel bounced back to the mound.
3 Rawlings grounded to short.
Yankees
  Pipp singled to left.
1 Ward sacrificed, Douglas to Kelly. McNally grounded to third and Pipp
2 was run down between second and third. Assists to Frisch and Rawlings with the putout to Frisch. Schang tripled to deep left, McNally scoring.
3 Mays grounded to second.

6th Inning
Giants
1 Snyder popped to third.
2 Douglas grounded to second. Burns singled to center.
3 Bancroft grounded to second.
Yankees
1 Miller fouled to Snyder. Peckinpaugh singled to left.
2 Peckinpaugh out trying to steal second, Snyder to Rawlings.
3 Ruth struck out.

7th Inning
Giants
1 Frisch grounded to second. Youngs singled to center.
2,3 Kelly grounded into a double play, Ward to Peckinpaugh to Pipp.
Yankees
1 B. Meusel flied to left.
2 Pipp struck out.
3 Ward struck out.

8th Inning
Giants
1 I. Meusel tripled deep to left-center. Rawlings singled to right, I. Meusel scoring.
Snyder beat out a bunt as Mays fell trying to field it, Rawlings stopping at second.
1 Douglas sacrificed up both runners, Mays to Ward.
Burns doubled just beyond Peckinpaugh, scoring Rawlings and Snyder.
2 Bancroft flied to left.
3 Frisch fouled to Schang.
Yankees
1 McNally struck out. Schang singled to right.
2 Mays forced Schang at second, Rawlings to Bancroft. Bancroft's wild throw to first allowed Mays to get to second.
3 Miller struck out.

9th Inning
Giants
1 Youngs grounded back to the mound. Kelly doubled to left. I. Meusel singled to left, scoring Kelly.
2 I. Meusel caught trying to steal second, Schang to Peckinpaugh. Rawlings singled to right.
3 Snyder popped to second.
Yankees
1 Peckinpaugh grounded to second. Ruth homered into the right field bleachers.
2 B. Meusel fouled to Snyder.
3 Pipp grounded to Douglas who made the put out.

Game 5 October 10 at New York (N)

New York-A	Pos	AB	R	H	RBI	PO	A	E
Miller	cf	3	0	1	1	2	0	0
Peckinpaugh	ss	4	0	1	0	3	3	0
Ruth	lf	4	1	1	0	2	0	0
B. Meusel	rf	4	1	2	1	1	2	0
Pipp	1b	3	0	0	0	6	1	0
Ward	2b	3	0	0	1	5	3	0
McNally	3b	2	1	0	0	1	1	1
Schang	c	3	0	1	0	7	1	0
Hoyt	p	3	0	0	0	0	1	0
Totals		29	3	6	3	27	12	1

Pitching	IP	H	R	ER	BB	SO
Yankees						
Hoyt (W)	9	10	1	0	2	6
Giants						
Nehf (L)	9	6	3	3	1	5

NY-A 001 200 000
NY-N 100 000 000

New York-N	Pos	AB	R	H	RBI	PO	A	E
Burns	cf	5	0	1	0	2	0	0
Bancroft	ss	4	1	1	0	3	1	0
Frisch	3b	4	0	2	0	1	6	1
Youngs	rf	3	0	1	0	0	0	0
Kelly	1b	4	0	3	1	11	1	0
I. Meusel	lf	4	0	1	0	3	0	0
Rawlings	2b	4	0	1	0	0	2	0
Smith	c	3	0	0	0	6	1	0
Nehf	p	3	0	0	0	1	1	0
a Snyder		1	0	0	0	0	0	0
Totals		35	1	10	1	27	12	1

a Struck out for Nehf in 9th.

Doubles—B. Meusel, I. Meusel, Miller, Rawlings, Schang. Sacrifice Hits—Miller, Pipp, Ward. Double Play—Schang to Ward. Umpires—Rigler, Moriarty, Quigley, Chill. Attendance—35,758. Time of Game—1:52.

1st Inning
Yankees
1 Miller popped to short.
2 Peckinpaugh grounded to third.
3 Ruth struck out.
Giants
  Burns safe at first on McNally's fumble.
1 Bancroft forced Burns at second, Peckinpaugh to Ward.
  Frisch singled to center.
  Youngs walked, loading the bases. Kelly singled to center, scoring Bancroft.
2 I. Meusel struck out.
3 Rawlings forced Kelly at second, Peckinpaugh to Ward.

2nd Inning
Yankees
  B. Meusel singled to right.
1 Pipp sacrificed B. Meusel to second, Frisch to Kelly.
  B. Meusel safe at third as Frisch dropped the throw but B. Meusel
2 was out trying to score on the error Frisch to Smith.
3 Ward struck out.
Giants
1 Smith flied to center.
2 Nehf flied to short. Burns singled to right. Bancroft singled to right but was trapped when he overran first. In
3 the rundown Burns was out at the plate (assists to B. Meusel, Pipp and Peckinpaugh).

3rd Inning
Yankees
  McNally walked. Schang doubled to left. McNally stopping at third.
1 Hoyt grounded to short, both runners holding.
2 Miller hit a sacrifice fly to left, McNally scoring after the catch.
3 Peckinpaugh grounded to first.
Giants
  Frisch singled to center.
1 Youngs forced Frisch at second, McNally to Ward.
2 Kelly struck out. I. Meusel doubled to left, Youngs stopping at third.
3 Rawlings popped to third.

4th Inning
Yankees
  Ruth beat out a bunt toward third. B. Meusel doubled to left, scoring Ruth.
1 Pipp grounded to second, B. Meusel going to third.
2 Ward hit a sacrifice fly to center, B. Meusel scoring after the catch.
3 McNally flied to center.
Giants
  Smith walked.
1 Smith out stealing, Schang to Ward.
2 Nehf struck out.
3 Burns struck out.

5th Inning
Yankees
1 Schang fouled to Frisch.
2 Hoyt grounded to third. Miller doubled to left.
3 Peckinpaugh flied to left.
Giants
1 Bancroft flied to right.
2 Frisch popped to short.
3 Youngs grounded to first.

6th Inning
Yankees
1 Ruth struck out.
2 B. Meusel fouled to Kelly.
3 Pipp bounced back to the mound.
Giants
  Kelly singled to center.
1 I. Meusel forced Kelly at second, Ward to Peckinpaugh.
2 Rawlings flied to center.
3 Smith grounded to second.

7th Inning
Yankees
1 Ward popped to short.
2 McNally popped to short.
3 Schang flied to left.
Giants
1 Nehf flied to left.
2 Burns bounced back to the mound.
3 Bancroft grounded to third.

8th Inning
Yankees
1 Hoyt struck out.
2 Miller grounded to third. Peckinpaugh singled to left.
3 Ruth struck out.
Giants
1 Frisch popped to first. Youngs singled to left. Kelly singled to right, Youngs going
2 to third but Kelly was out trying for second, B. Meusel to Ward.
3 I. Meusel fouled to Pipp.

9th Inning
Yankees
1 B. Meusel grounded to third.
2 Pipp grounded out, Kelly to Nehf.
3 Ward grounded to second.
Giants
  Rawlings doubled to left.
1 Smith popped to second.
2 Snyder, pinch-hitting for Nehf, struck out.
3 Burns struck out.

Game 6 October 11 at New York (A)

New York-N	Pos	AB	R	H	RBI	PO	A	E
Burns	cf	3	1	1	0	0	0	0
Bancroft	ss	5	0	2	0	2	0	0
Frisch	3b	4	2	0	1	1	2	0
Youngs	rf	5	0	1	0	2	0	0
Kelly	1b	4	1	3	2	7	0	0
I. Meusel	lf	4	1	2	2	2	0	0
Rawlings	2b	5	0	0	0	5	2	0
Snyder	c	4	2	2	1	10	0	0
Toney	p	0	0	0	0	0	0	0
Barnes	p	4	1	2	0	0	0	0
Totals		38	8	13	8	27	6	0

Pitching	IP	H	R	ER	BB	SO
Giants						
Toney	⅓	3	3	3	1	0
Barnes (W)	8⅓	4	2	2	4	10
Yankees						
Harper	1⅓	3	3	3	2	1
Shawkey (L)	6⅔	8	5	3	2	5
Piercy	1	2	0	0	0	2

NY-N   030 401 000
NY-A   320 000 000

New York-A	Pos	AB	R	H	RBI	PO	A	E
Fewster	lf	3	2	1	2	5	0	0
Peckinpaugh	ss	5	0	2	0	3	2	0
Miller	cf	5	1	1	0	1	0	0
B. Meusel	rf	4	0	1	0	2	0	0
Pipp	1b	4	0	1	0	2	0	0
Ward	2b	4	0	1	2	3	1	1
McNally	3b	4	0	0	0	3	0	1
Schang	c	2	0	1	0	8	3	0
Harper	p	0	0	0	0	0	0	0
Shawkey	p	3	1	1	0	0	0	0
a Baker		1	0	0	0	0	0	0
Piercy	p	0	0	0	0	0	0	0
Totals		35	4	7	5	27	6	2

a Grounded out for Shawkey in 8th.

Home Runs—Fewster, I. Meusel, Snyder.
Stolen Bases—Frisch, Pipp.
Sacrifice Hit—Burns. Double
Plays—Schang to McNally, Schang to Ward.
Left on Bases—Giants 8, Yankees 7.
Umpires—Moriarty, Quigley, Chill,
Rigler. Attendance—34,283.
Time of Game—2:31.

1st Inning
Giants
Burns walked.
1 Bancroft flied to left.
2 Frisch struck out.
3 Youngs fouled to Fewster in the left field corner.
Yankees
Fewster walked.
1 Peckinpaugh fouled to Frisch.
Miller singled to left, Fewster going to third.
B. Meusel singled to left-center, scoring Fewster with Miller going to third.
2 Pipp popped to second.
Ward singled to center, scoring Miller and B. Meusel.
For the Giants—Barnes now pitching.
3 McNally flied to right.

2nd Inning
Giants
Kelly walked.
I. Meusel hit a two-run homer into the lower stand in right field.
1 Rawlings flied to center.
Snyder also hit a home run into the left field bleachers.
Barnes singled to center.
For the Yankees—Shawkey pitching.
Burns singled to right, Barnes stopping at second.
2 Bancroft struck out.
3 Frisch flied to right.
Yankees
1 Schang struck out.
Shawkey singled to left.
Fewster hit a two-run homer into the left field bleachers.
2 Peckinpaugh grounded to third.
3 Miller grounded to first.

3rd Inning
Giants
1 Youngs flied to right.
Kelly singled to left.
2 I. Meusel flied to left.
3 Rawlings struck out.
Yankees
1 B. Meusel grounded to third.
Pipp singled to center.
Pipp stole second.
2 Ward struck out.
3 McNally struck out.

4th Inning
Giants
Snyder singled to left.
Barnes singled to left, Snyder stopping at second.
Burns safe at first on McNally's fumble, loading the bases.
Bancroft singled to left, scoring Snyder and Barnes with Burns stopping at second.
1 Frisch forced Bancroft at second, Peckinpaugh unassisted as Burns went to third.
Frisch stole second.
2 Youngs struck out.
Kelly singled to right, scoring Burns and Frisch.
3 Kelly out trying to steal second, Schang to Ward.

4th Inning (continued)
Yankees
Schang walked.
1 Shawkey struck out.
Fewster walked.
2 Peckinpaugh struck out.
3 Miller struck out.

5th Inning
Giants
I. Meusel walked.
Rawlings safe at first on Ward's poor throw as I. Meusel went to second.
1 Snyder popped to third.
2 Barnes fouled to McNally.
3 Burns forced Rawlings at second, Peckinpaugh to Ward.
Yankees
B. Meusel walked.
1 Pipp struck out.
2 Ward struck out.
3 McNally flied to left.

6th Inning
Giants
Bancroft singled to left.
Frisch walked.
1,2 Youngs struck out and Bancroft was doubled trying to steal third, Schang to McNally.
Kelly singled to center, scoring Frisch.
3 I. Meusel flied to left.
Yankees
Schang singled to center.
1 Shawkey forced Schang at second, Bancroft to Rawlings.
2 Fewster struck out.
3 Peckinpaugh flied to left.

7th Inning
Giants
1 Rawlings popped to short.
2 Snyder grounded to short.
3 Barnes grounded to second.
Yankees
1 Miller flied to right.
2 B. Meusel struck out.
3 Pipp grounded to second.

8th Inning
Giants
1 Burns flied to left.
2 Bancroft popped to second.
3 Frisch struck out.
Yankees
1 Ward grounded to short.
2 McNally popped to first.
Schang walked.
3 Baker, pinch-hitting for Shawkey, grounded to second.

9th Inning
Giants
For the Yankees—Piercy pitching.
Youngs singled to left.
1,2 Kelly struck out and Youngs was doubled trying to steal second, Schang to Peckinpaugh.
I. Meusel singled to right.
3 Rawlings struck out.
Yankees
1 Fewster popped to second.
2 Peckinpaugh popped to second.
3 Miller popped to second.

Game 7 October 12 at New York (N)

New York-A	Pos	AB	R	H	RBI	PO	A	E
Fewster	lf	4	0	1	0	0	0	0
Peckinpaugh	ss	4	0	2	0	4	0	0
Miller	cf	3	0	0	0	2	1	0
B. Meusel	rf	4	0	0	1	0	0	0
Pipp	1b	4	1	1	0	13	0	0
Ward	2b	3	0	0	0	3	3	1
McNally	3b	1	0	1	1	2	0	0
Baker	3b	3	0	2	0	1	0	0
a DeVormer		0	0	0	0	0	0	0
Schang	c	4	0	1	0	7	0	0
Mays	p	3	0	0	0	0	2	0
Totals		33	1	8	1	24	12	1

a Ran for Baker in 9th.

Doubles—Bancroft, Burns 2, Pipp,
Peckinpaugh, Snyder. Stolen Base—Youngs.
Sacrifice Hit—Ward. Wild Pitch—Douglas.
Left on Bases—Yankees 7, Giants 4.
Umpires—Quigley, Chill, Rigler, Moriarty.
Attendance—36,503. Time of Game—1:40.

NY-A   010 000 000
NY-N   000 100 10x

New York-N	Pos	AB	R	H	RBI	PO	A	E
Burns	cf	4	0	2	0	2	0	0
Bancroft	ss	4	0	1	0	2	2	0
Frisch	3b	4	0	0	0	2	3	0
Youngs	rf	3	1	1	0	2	0	0
Kelly	1b	3	0	0	0	13	0	0
I. Meusel	lf	3	0	1	1	0	1	0
Rawlings	2b	3	1	0	0	2	3	0
Snyder	c	3	0	1	1	3	0	0
Douglas	p	3	0	0	0	1	5	0
Totals		30	2	6	2	27	14	0

Pitching	IP	H	R	ER	BB	SO
Yankees						
Mays (L)	8	6	2	1	0	7
Giants						
Douglas (W)	9	8	1	1	1	3

1st Inning
Yankees
1 Fewster flied to right.
Peckinpaugh doubled to left.
2 Miller grounded to third.
3 B. Meusel bounced back to the mound.
Giants
1 Burns flied to right.
Bancroft doubled to center.
2 Frisch flied to center.
3 Youngs grounded to the pitcher.

2nd Inning
Yankees
Pipp doubled to left.
1 Ward sacrificed Pipp to third, Frisch to Kelly.
McNally singled to right, scoring Pipp.
2 Schang forced McNally at second, Bancroft to Rawlings.
3 Mays lined to Rawlings.
Giants
1 Kelly struck out.
2 I. Meusel grounded to third.
3 Rawlings grounded to third.

3rd Inning
Yankees
Fewster singled to left, but was out
1 trying for two bases, I. Meusel to Bancroft.
Peckinpaugh singled to center.
2 Miller popped to short.
3 B. Meusel struck out.
Giants
For the Yankees—Baker playing third.
1 Snyder grounded to short.
2 Douglas struck out.
Burns doubled to left.
3 Bancroft struck out.

4th Inning
Yankees
1 Pipp grounded to first.
2 Ward grounded back to the mound.
3 Baker popped to third.
Giants
1 Frisch grounded to the pitcher.
Youngs beat out a hard single to second.
Youngs stole second.
2 Kelly struck out.
I. Meusel singled to center, scoring Youngs.
3 Rawlings grounded to first.

5th Inning
Yankees
1 Schang bounced back to the mound.
2 Mays grounded to second.
3 Fewster struck out.
Giants
1 Snyder flied to center.
2 Douglas grounded to first.
Burns doubled to center but was out
3 trying for third, Miller to Baker.

6th Inning
Yankees
1 Peckinpaugh fouled to Frisch.
2 Miller grounded to third.
3 B. Meusel flied to deep right.
Giants
1 Bancroft grounded to second.
2 Frisch grounded to second.
3 Youngs grounded to second.

7th Inning
Yankees
1 Pipp popped to Douglas.
2 Ward flied to center.
Baker singled to center.
Schang singled to center, Baker stopping at second.
Both moved up on a wild pitch.
3 Mays grounded to second.
Giants
1 Kelly grounded to short.
2 I. Meusel flied to center.
Rawlings was safe at first on Ward's error.
Snyder doubled to left-center, scoring Rawlings.
3 Douglas struck out.

8th Inning
Yankees
1 Fewster grounded to the pitcher.
2 Peckinpaugh struck out.
Miller walked (the first walk given up in the game).
3 B. Meusel grounded to short.
Giants
1 Burns grounded to short.
2 Bancroft grounded to second.
3 Frisch struck out.

9th Inning
Yankees
1 Pipp grounded to second.
2 Ward flied to center.
Baker singled to right.
DeVormer ran for Baker.
3 Schang grounded to the mound.

Game 8 October 13 at New York (A)

NY-N	1 0 0	0 0 0	0 0 0
NY-A	0 0 0	0 0 0	0 0 0

New York-N	Pos	AB	R	H	RBI	PO	A	E
Burns	cf	4	0	1	0	3	0	0
Bancroft	ss	3	1	0	0	0	4	0
Frisch	3b	2	0	0	0	2	3	0
Youngs	rf	2	0	1	0	0	0	0
Kelly	1b	4	0	0	0	13	1	0
I. Meusel	lf	4	0	1	0	1	0	0
Rawlings	2b	4	0	3	0	4	4	0
Snyder	c	2	0	0	0	4	0	0
Nehf	p	4	0	0	0	0	0	0
Totals		31	1	6	0	27	12	0

Pitching	IP	H	R	ER	BB	SO
Giants						
Nehf (W)	9	4	0	0	5	3
Yankees						
Hoyt (L)	9	6	1	0	4	7

New York-A	Pos	AB	R	H	RBI	PO	A	E
Fewster	lf	3	0	0	0	2	0	0
Peckinpaugh	ss	2	0	0	0	2	2	1
Miller	cf	4	0	1	0	1	0	0
B. Meusel	rf	4	0	0	0	2	0	0
Pipp	1b	3	0	1	0	11	0	0
a Ruth		1	0	0	0	0	0	0
Ward	2b	3	0	1	0	0	2	0
Baker	3b	3	0	0	0	1	3	0
Schang	c	3	0	0	0	8	1	0
Hoyt	p	3	0	1	0	0	3	0
Totals		29	0	4	0	27	11	1

a Grounded out for Pipp in 9th.

Doubles—Rawlings 2. Stolen Base—Youngs. Sacrifice Hits—Snyder 2. Double Plays—Bancroft to Rawlings to Kelly, Rawlings to Kelly to Frisch. Wild Pitch—Nehf. Left on Bases—Giants 9, Yankees 7. Umpires—Chill, Rigler, Moriarty, Quigley. Attendance—25,410. Time of Game—1:57.

1st Inning
Giants
1 Burns grounded to third.
 Bancroft walked.
2 Frisch fouled to Pipp.
 Youngs walked.
 Kelly safe at first when his grounder went throug Peckinpaugh's legs to the outfield, Bancroft scoring.
3 I. Meusel grounded back to the mound.
Yankees
1 Fewster struck out.
 Peckinpaugh walked.
 Miller singled to right, Peckinpaugh stopping at second.
 Both runners advanced on a wild pitch.
2 B. Meusel popped to first.
3 Pipp struck out.

2nd Inning
Giants
 Rawlings doubled to left.
1 Snyder sacrificed Rawlings to third, Hoyt to Pipp.
2 Nehf grounded to Peckinpaugh who threw Rawlings out at the plate.
 Burns singled to right, Nehf going to third.
3 Bancroft grounded to short.
Yankees
1 Ward fouled to Snyder.
2 Baker grounded to second.
3 Schang grounded to short.

3rd Inning
Giants
1 Frisch flied to center.
 Youngs walked.
 Youngs stole second.
2 Kelly popped to short.
3 I. Meusel struck out.
Yankees
1 Hoyt grounded to third.
 Fewster walked.
2,3 Peckinpaugh grounded into a double play, Bancroft to Rawlings to Kelly.

4th Inning
Giants
 Rawlings again doubled.
1 Snyder again sacrificed Rawlings to third, Baker to Pipp.
2 Nehf flied to right.
3 Burns struck out.
Yankees
1 Miller grounded to third.
2 B. Meusel flied to center.
 Pipp singled to left.
 Ward singled to center.
 Baker walked, loading the bases.
3 Schang flied to center.

5th Inning
Giants
1 Bancroft flied to left.
2 Frisch grounded to second.
 Youngs singled to center.
3 Kelly struck out.
Yankees
1 Hoyt fouled to Kelly.
2 Fewster fouled to Kelly.
 Peckinpaugh walked.
3 Miller forced Peckinpaugh at second, Frisch to Rawlings.

6th Inning
Giants
1 I. Meusel singled to center.
1 I. Meusel caught trying to steal second, Schang to Peckinpaugh.
 Rawlings singled to right.
2 Snyder struck out.
3 Nehf fouled to Baker.
Yankees
1 B. Meusel popped to second.
2 Pipp grounded to short.
3 Ward grounded to short.

7th Inning
Giants
 Burns walked.
1 Bancroft struck out.
2 Frisch flied to right.
3 Youngs flied to left.
Yankees
1 Baker fouled to Frisch.
2 Schang flied to left.
 Hoyt singled to center.
3 Fewster forced Hoyt at second, Rawlings unassisted.

8th Inning
Giants
1 Kelly struck out.
2 I. Meusel grounded to first.
3 Rawlings grounded to second.
Yankees
1 Peckinpaugh grounded to second.
2 Miller flied to center.
3 B. Meusel struck out.

9th Inning
Giants
1 Snyder grounded to third.
2 Nehf struck out.
3 Burns grounded back to the mound.
Yankees
1 Ruth, pinch-hitting for Pipp, grounded to first.
 Ward walked.
2,3 Baker was robbed of a hit by Rawlings making a fantastic stop throwing the batter out at first. Ward trying to make third was out, Kelly to Frisch.

1921 WORLD SERIES COMPOSITE BOX

	Wins	Composite Line Score				Manager	Regular Season W	L	Pct.	G. Ahead
New York Giants (N.L.)	5	2 3 4	5 0 1	9 4 1	- 29	John McGraw	94	59	.614	4
New York Yankees (A.L.)	3	4 3 5	3 2 1	0 3 1	- 22	Miller Huggins	98	55	.641	4½

BATTING AND FIELDING

NEW YORK GIANTS

WORLD SERIES STATISTICS

	Pos	G	AB	R	H	2B	3B	HR	RBI	BB	SO	SB	BA	SA	PO	A	E
George Kelly	1b	8	30	3	7	1	0	0	4	3	**10**	0	.233	.267	85	6	0
Johnny Rawlings	2b	8	30	2	10	3	0	0	4	0	3	0	.333	.433	20	27	0
Dave Bancroft	ss	8	**33**	3	5	1	0	0	3	1	5	0	.152	.182	16	17	1
Frankie Frisch	3b	8	30	**5**	9	0	**1**	0	1	4	3	**3**	.300	.367	12	24	2
Ross Youngs	rf	8	25	3	7	1	**1**	0	4	**7**	2	2	.280	.400	7	1	0
George Burns	cf	8	**33**	2	**11**	**4**	**1**	0	2	3	5	1	.333	.515	9	0	0
Irish Meusel	lf	8	29	4	10	2	**1**	**1**	**7**	2	3	1	.345	**.586**	8	2	0
Frank Snyder	c-ph	7	22	4	8	1	0	**1**	3	0	2	0	**.364**	.545	43	5	0
Earl Smith	ph-c	3	7	0	0	0	0	0	0	1	0	0	.000	.000	7	2	1
Eddie Brown		Did not play															
Bill Cunningham		Did not play															
Mike Gonzalez		Did not play															
Casey Stengel		Did not play															
Alex Gaston		Did not play															
Wally Kopf		Did not play															
Art Nehf	p	3	9	0	0	0	0	0	0	1	3	0	.000	.000	1	4	1
Jesse Barnes	p	3	9	3	4	0	0	0	0	0	0	0	.444	.444	1	1	0
Phil Douglas	p	3	7	0	0	0	0	0	0	0	2	0	.000	.000	3	8	0
Fred Toney	p	2	0	0	0	0	0	0	0	0	0	0	—	—	0	1	0
Rosy Ryan		Did not play															
Slim Sallee		Did not play															
Red Shea		Did not play															
Red Causey		Did not play															
team total		8	264	29	71	13	4	2	28	22	38	7	.269	.371	212	98	5

Double Plays—4
Left on Bases—54

REGULAR SEASON STATISTICS

		Main Pos	G	AB	R	H	2B	3B	HR	RBI	BB	SO	SB	BA	SA
George Kelly		1b	149	587	95	181	42	9	**23**	122	40	73	4	.308	.528
Johnny Rawlings	a	2b	86	307	40	82	8	1	1	30	18	19	4	.267	.309
Dave Bancroft		ss	153	606	121	193	26	15	6	67	66	23	17	.318	.441
Frankie Frisch		3b-2b	153	618	121	211	31	17	8	100	42	28	**49**	.341	.485
Ross Youngs		of	141	504	90	165	24	16	3	102	71	47	21	.327	.456
George Burns		of	149	605	111	181	28	9	4	61	**80**	24	19	.299	.395
Irish Meusel	b	of	62	243	37	80	12	6	2	36	15	12	5	.329	.453
Frank Snyder		c	108	309	36	99	13	2	8	45	27	24	3	.320	.453
Earl Smith		c	89	229	35	77	8	4	10	51	27	8	4	.336	.537
Eddie Brown		of	70	128	16	36	6	2	0	12	4	11	1	.281	.359
Bill Cunningham		of	40	76	10	21	2	1	1	12	3	3	0	.296	.368
Mike Gonzalez		1b-c	13	24	3	9	1	0	0	0	1	0	0	.375	.417
Casey Stengel	c	of	18	22	4	5	1	0	0	2	1	5	0	.227	.273
Alex Gaston		c	20	22	1	5	1	1	0	3	1	9	0	.227	.364
Wally Kopf		3b	2	3	0	1	0	0	0	0	1	1	0	.333	.333
Art Nehf		p	42	82	9	18	2	0	0	5	7	10	0	.202	.225
Jesse Barnes		p	42	92	8	19	0	1	0	6	3	3	1	.207	.228
Phil Douglas		p	40	81	7	16	2	0	1	10	3	12	1	.198	.259
Fred Toney		p	42	86	11	18	1	0	3	12	2	13	1	.209	.326
Rosy Ryan		p	36	45	2	9	1	0	0	1	5	11	0	.200	.222
Slim Sallee		p	37	22	2	8	1	0	0	0	0	2	0	.364	.409
Red Shea		p	9	9	0	1	0	0	0	1	0	2	0	.111	.111
Red Causey	d	p	9	3	1	1	0	0	0	0	0	0	0	.333	.333
team total			153	5278	**840**	1575	237	93	75	**748**	**469**	390	**137**	.298	.421

a—from Philadelphia
b—from Philadelphia
c—from Philadelphia
d—from Philadelphia

Howard Berry (2b), Joe Connolly (of), Bud Heine (2b), Butch Henline (ph), Lee King (of), Jim Mahady (2b), John Monroe (2b), Bill Patterson (3b-ss), Goldie Rapp (3b), Hank Schreiber (2b-ss-3b), Curt Walker (of), Rute Benton (p), Claude Jonnard (p), Pol Perritt (p), Walt Zink (p) also played with the Giants during the season.

NEW YORK YANKEES

WORLD SERIES STATISTICS

	Pos	G	AB	R	H	2B	3B	HR	RBI	BB	SO	SB	BA	SA	PO	A	E
Wally Pipp	1b	8	26	1	4	1	0	0	2	2	3	1	.154	.192	**91**	1	0
Aaron Ward	2b	8	26	1	6	0	0	0	4	2	6	0	.231	.231	18	**33**	2
Roger Peckinpaugh	ss	8	28	2	5	1	0	0	0	4	3	0	.179	.214	18	29	1
Mike McNally	3b	7	20	3	4	1	0	0	1	1	3	2	.200	.250	5	11	**3**
Bob Meusel	rf	8	30	3	6	2	0	0	3	2	5	1	.200	.267	10	2	0
Elmer Miller	cf	8	31	3	5	1	0	0	2	2	5	0	.161	.194	10	1	0
Babe Ruth	lf-ph	6	16	3	5	0	0	**1**	4	5	8	2	.313	.500	9	0	0
Wally Schang	c	8	21	1	6	1	**1**	0	1	5	4	0	.286	.429	39	9	0
Chick Fewster	pr-lf	4	10	3	2	0	0	**1**	2	3	3	0	.200	.500	7	0	0
Frank Baker	ph-3b	4	8	0	2	0	0	0	0	1	0	0	.250	.250	2	3	0
Al DeVormer	pr-c	2	1	0	0	0	0	0	0	0	0	0	.000	.000	1	0	0
Bragg Roth		Did not play															
Chicken Hawks		Did not play															
Johnny Mitchell		Did not play															
Waite Hoyt	p	3	9	0	2	0	0	0	1	0	1	0	.222	.222	0	6	0
Carl Mays	p	3	9	0	1	0	0	0	0	0	1	0	.111	.111	0	9	0
Bob Shawkey	p	2	4	2	2	0	0	0	0	0	1	0	.500	.500	0	0	0
Jack Quinn	p	1	2	0	0	0	0	0	0	0	1	0	.000	.000	0	1	0
Harry Harper	p	1	0	0	0	0	0	0	0	0	0	0	—	—	0	0	0
Tom Rogers	p	1	0	0	0	0	0	0	0	0	0	0	—	—	0	1	0
Bill Piercy	p	1	0	0	0	0	0	0	0	0	0	0	—	—	0	0	0
Rip Collins	p	1	0	0	0	0	0	0	0	0	0	0	—	—	0	0	0
		Did not play															
team total		8	241	22	50	7	1	2	20	27	44	6	.207	.270	210	106	6

Double Plays–8
Left or Bases–43

REGULAR SEASON STATISTICS

	Main Pos	G	AB	R	H	2B	3B	HR	RBI	BB	SO	SB	BA	SA
Wally Pipp	1b	153	588	96	174	35	9	8	97	45	28	17	.296	.427
Aaron Ward	2b-3b	153	556	77	170	30	10	5	75	42	68	6	.306	.423
Roger Peckinpaugh	ss	149	577	128	166	25	7	8	71	84	44	2	.288	.397
Mike McNally	3b	71	215	36	56	4	2	1	24	14	15	5	.260	.312
Bob Meusel	of	149	598	104	190	40	16	24	135	34	**88**	17	.318	.559
Elmer Miller	of	56	242	41	72	9	8	4	36	39	16	2	.298	.450
Babe Ruth	of	152	540	**177**	204	44	16	**59**	**171**	**144**	81	17	.378	**.546**
Wally Schang	c	134	424	77	134	30	5	6	55	78	35	7	.316	.453
Chick Fewster	of-2b	66	207	44	58	19	0	1	19	28	43	4	.280	.386
Frank Baker	3b	94	330	46	97	16	2	9	71	26	12	8	.294	.436
Al DeVormer	c	22	49	6	17	4	0	0	7	2	4	2	.347	.429
Bragg Roth	of	43	152	29	43	9	2	2	10	19	20	1	.283	.408
Chicken Hawks	of	41	73	16	21	2	3	2	15	5	12	0	.288	.479
Johnny Mitchell	ss-2b	13	42	4	11	1	0	0	2	4	4	1	.262	.286
Waite Hoyt	p	43	99	8	22	1	1	0	7	2	17	0	.222	.253
Carl Mays	p	51	143	18	49	5	1	2	22	4	7	0	.343	.434
Bob Shawkey	p	38	90	13	27	2	1	1	11	2	3	0	.300	.378
Jack Quinn	p	33	41	4	9	2	0	1	4	3	9	0	.220	.341
Harry Harper	p	8	16	1	2	0	0	0	1	1	4	0	.125	.125
Tom Rogers	p	6	3	1	1	1	0	0	0	0	0	0	.333	.667
Bill Piercy	p	14	28	2	6	2	0	0	2	1	7	0	.214	.286
Rip Collins	p	28	56	4	11	0	1	0	6	3	18	0	.196	.232
	p	17	19	1	4	0	0	0	2	0	5	0	.211	.211
team total		153	5249	**948**	1576	285	87	**134**	**861**	588	**567**	89	.300	**.464**

Ping Bodie (of), Tom Connelly (of), Fred Hofmann (c), Tom Sheehan (p) also played for the Yankees during the season.

PITCHING

NEW YORK GIANTS

WORLD SERIES STATISTICS

	G	GS	CG	IP	H	R	ER	BB	SO	W	L	SV	ERA
Art Nehf	**3**	**3**	**3**	26	13	6	4	**13**	8	1	**2**	0	1.38
Phil Douglas	**3**	**3**	2	26	**20**	6	6	5	17	**2**	1	0	2.07
Jesse Barnes	**3**	0	0	16 1/3	10	3	3	6	**18**	**2**	0	0	1.65
Fred Toney	2	2	0	2 2/3	7	7	7	3	1	0	0	0	23.63
Rosy Ryan	Did not play												
Slim Sallee	Did not play												
Red Shea	Did not play												
Red Causey	Did not play												
team total	8	8	5	71	50	22	20	27	44	5	3	0	2.53

REGULAR SEASON STATISTICS

		G	GS	CG	IP	H	ER	BB	SO	W	L	Pct	SV	ShO	ERA
Art Nehf		41	34	18	261	266	105	55	67	20	10	.667	1	2	3.62
Phil Douglas		40	27	13	222	266	104	55	55	15	10	.600	2	3	4.22
Jesse Barnes		42	31	15	259	298	89	44	56	15	9	.625	6	1	3.09
Fred Toney		42	32	16	249	274	100	65	63	18	11	.621	3	1	3.61
Rosy Ryan		36	16	5	147	140	61	32	58	7	10	.412	3	0	3.73
Slim Sallee		37	0	0	96	115	39	14	23	6	4	.600	2	0	3.66
Red Shea		9	2	1	32	28	11	2	10	5	2	.714	0	0	3.09
Red Causey	d	7	1	0	15	13	4	6	1	1	1	.500	0	0	2.40
team total		163	153	71	1372	1497	542	295	357	**94**	59	**.614**	**18**	9	3.56

NEW YORK YANKEES

WORLD SERIES STATISTICS

	G	GS	CG	IP	H	R	ER	BB	SO	W	L	SV	ERA
Waite Hoyt	**3**	**3**	**3**	**27**	18	2	0	11	**18**	**2**	1	0	**0.00**
Carl Mays	**3**	**3**	**3**	26	**20**	6	5	0	9	1	**2**	0	1.73
Bob Shawkey	2	1	0	9	13	9	7	6	5	0	1	0	7.00
Jack Quinn	1	0	0	3 2/3	8	4	4	2	2	0	1	0	9.82
Harry Harper	1	1	0	1 1/3	3	3	3	2	1	0	0	0	20.25
Tom Rogers	1	0	0	1 1/3	3	1	1	0	1	0	0	0	6.75
Bill Piercy	1	0	0	1	2	0	0	0	2	0	0	0	0.00
Rip Collins	1	0	0	2/3	4	4	4	1	0	0	0	0	54.00
Alex Ferguson	Did not play												
team total	8	8	6	70	71	29	24	22	38	3	5	0	3.09

REGULAR SEASON STATISTICS

	G	GS	CG	IP	H	ER	BB	SO	W	L	Pct	SV	ShO	ERA
Waite Hoyt	44	32	21	282	301	97	81	102	19	13	.594	3	1	3.10
Carl Mays	**49**	38	30	**337**	332	114	76	70	**27**	9	**.750**	**7**	1	3.04
Bob Shawkey	38	31	18	245	245	111	86	126	18	12	.600	2	3	4.08
Jack Quinn	33	13	6	129	158	50	32	44	8	7	.533	0	0	3.49
Harry Harper	8	7	4	53	52	22	25	22	4	3	.571	0	0	3.74
Tom Rogers	5	0	0	11	12	9	9	0	0	1	.000	1	0	7.36
Bill Piercy	14	10	5	82	82	26	28	35	5	4	.556	0	1	2.85
Rip Collins	28	16	7	137	158	83	78	64	11	5	.688	0	1	5.45
Alex Ferguson	17	4	1	56	64	37	37	9	3	1	.750	1	0	5.95
team total	153	153	**92**	1374	1461	578	470	**481**	**98**	55	**.641**	15	7	**3.79**

Total Attendance—269,976 Average Attendance—33,747 Winning Player's Share—$5,265 Losing Player's Share—$3,510

1922
The Generous Judge

Cut back to seven games after a three-year experiment with nine games, the Series returned to the same ballpark in the same city with the same teams and the same superstars. The Yankees and Giants, both inhabitants of New York's Polo Grounds, repeated as the league champions, the Yanks by one game in a dogfight, the Giants easily by seven games. The Yankee triumph in the American League gave Babe Ruth a chance to lengthen his season into October to make up for the opening month of the season which he missed. Ruth and Bob Meusel, the heart of the Yankee attack, sat on the sidelines until May 20 under a suspension meted out by Commissioner Kenesaw M. Landis for making an unauthorized barnstorming trip last fall after the Series. The Yanks nevertheless held on to first place in the absence of the two stars, a tribute to the deals which brought Everett Scott, Joe Dugan, Joe Bush, and Sad Sam Jones from the Red Sox and Whitey Witt from the Athletics. Although the new personnel helped and holdover Wally Pipp led the club with a .329 batting average, the heart of the club still was Ruth. The darling of the fans and the men who sold the tickets, the Babe recovered from his late start to sock 35 homers, only four shy of league-leader Ken Williams of St. Louis. While the free-swinging Ruth symbolized the style of the Yankees, Frankie Frisch symbolized the Giants of John McGraw. A tough, aggressive second baseman with a good batting eye and a knack for leadership, Frisch hit .327, stole 31 bases, and capitalized on practically every chance he found to inch the Giants to victory. While Ruth captured the public with his home-run swing, Frisch won fans with his slides and hustle. Frisch had good company in the starting lineup, with future Hall of Famers George Kelly, Dave Bancroft, Ross Youngs, and Casey Stengel all hitting .321 or better. The pitching staff was less illustrious, but the Giants' team batting mark of .304 blessed Art Nehf with 19 wins and Rosy Ryan with 17.

Although underrated, the Giant mound staff rose to the occasion and cut Ruth off by limiting him to a miserable .118 average with not a single home run to count. With their big gun silenced, the Yanks never scored over three runs in any game. They got two off Nehf in the opening game on October 4, a margin that Joe Bush protected until he gave up four hits and three runs in the bottom of the eighth. Credit for the 3–2 Giant win went to Ryan in relief.

The second game got the fans excited, but it was the umpires and Judge Landis who were at the center of the outburst rather than any player. The Giants jumped out to a 3–0 lead in the first inning, only to see the Yankees chip away and send the game into extra innings at 3–3. After a scoreless tenth inning, umpires George Hildebrand and Bill Klem decided to call the game because of darkness. With the hour not yet five o'clock and with 45 minutes of sunlight yet remaining, the fans in attendance were infuriated by this overcautious decision to end the game in a tie. A rain of bottles and seat cushions was heaved onto the field at the announcement, and a group of fans who assumed that the word had come from Landis ran over to the commissioner's box and barraged him with some choice New York insults. Landis in actuality had nothing to do with the decision to call the game, and the crowd's anger moved him to donate the entire receipts of $120,000 from the game to military hospitals for disabled veterans. With that outburst thus placated, the Series resumed with a 3–0 four-hitter by Giant righty Jack Scott, a tantalizing control pitcher who had been released in midseason by Cincinnati with a seemingly hopeless sore arm. Unable to score against Scott, the Yanks got two runs off Hugh McQuillan in the first inning of game four, but Carl Mays couldn't hold the lead and wound up the loser in a 4–3 game. Ruth went 0-for-3 against McQuillan, just as he did against Scott. The Yanks simply didn't figure to take four straight games to win the Series, and they proved that out by giving up three runs in the eighth inning to lose game five 5–3. Ruth again went hitless in three at-bats to finish with a two-hit Series performance and a temporary fall from grace.

Game 1 October 4 at New York-N

New York-A	Pos	AB	R	H	RBI	PO	A	E
Witt	cf	4	0	1	0	1	0	0
Dugan	3b	4	1	1	0	0	1	0
Ruth	rf	4	0	1	1	1	0	0
Pipp	1b	4	0	1	0	10	0	0
B. Meusel	lf	4	1	2	0	0	0	0
Schang	c	2	0	1	0	7	1	0
Ward	2b	1	0	0	1	5	4	0
E. Scott	ss	3	0	0	0	0	4	0
Bush	p	3	0	0	0	0	0	0
Hoyt	p	0	0	0	0	0	0	0
Totals		29	2	7	2	24	10	0

Pitching	IP	H	R	ER	BB	SO
Yankees						
Bush (L)	*7	11	3	3	1	3
Hoyt	1	0	0	0	0	2
Giants						
Nehf	7	6	2	1	1	3
Ryan (W)	2	1	0	0	0	2

*Pitched to four batters in 8th.

New York-N	Pos	AB	R	H	RBI	PO	A	E
Bancroft	ss	4	1	1	0	3	2	0
Groh	3b	3	1	3	0	2	3	0
Frisch	2b	4	1	2	0	2	4	0
I. Meusel	lf	4	0	1	2	0	0	0
Youngs	rf	3	0	0	1	1	1	2
Kelly	1b	4	0	2	0	9	0	0
Stengel	cf	4	0	1	0	4	0	0
Snyder	c	3	0	1	0	6	2	0
Nehf	p	2	0	0	0	0	1	1
a Earl Smith		1	0	0	0	0	0	0
Ryan	p	0	0	0	0	0	0	0
Totals		32	3	11	3	27	13	3

a Hit into double play for Nehf in 7th.

Triples—Groh, Witt. Sacrifice Hits—Schang 2, Ward, Youngs. Double Plays—Snyder to Bancroft, Youngs to Frisch, Scott to Ward to Pipp, Frisch to Kelly. Passed Ball—Schang. Left on Bases—Yankees 4, Giants 7. Umpires—Klem (N), Hildebrand (A), McCormick (N), Owens (A). Attendance—36,514. Time of Game—2:08.

1st Inning
Yankees
1 Witt flied to center.
2 Dugan grounded to third.
3 Ruth struck out on four pitches.
Giants
1 Bancroft bounced to second. Groh singled to left. Frisch singled to left, Groh stopping at second. Groh and Frisch both advanced one base on a passed ball.
2 I. Meusel fouled to Schang.
3 Youngs popped to first.

2nd Inning
Yankees
1 Pipp grounded to first.
2 B. Meusel struck out on four pitches. Schang singled over Groh's head.
3 Ward grounded to third.
Giants
1 Kelly struck out on three pitches.
2 Stengel bounced to third.
3 Snyder grounded to second.

3rd Inning
Yankees
1 Scott popped to third.
2 Bush flied to Bancroft in left field, a beautiful running catch over his shoulder.
3 Witt grounded to second.
Giants
1 Nehf grounded to first.
2 Bancroft grounded to second. Groh tripled for his second hit, deep to the left field fence.
3 Frisch popped to second.

4th Inning
Yankees
Dugan singled to left.
1 Ruth forced Dugan at second, Frisch to Bancroft.
2,3 Pipp struck out on a full count and Ruth was doubled up trying to steal second, Snyder to Bancroft.
Giants
1 I. Meusel grounded to short.
2 Youngs struck out. Kelly singled to left.
3 Stengel popped to second.

5th Inning
Yankees
B. Meusel beat out a hard smash to short.
1 Schang sacrificed Meusel to second, Nehf to Kelly. Ward walked.
2,3 Scott robbed of a hit by Youngs, who made a lunging catch on his shoe tops and easily doubled B. Meusel at second with a throw to Frisch.
Giants
1 Snyder grounded to short.
2 Nehf popped to second.
3 Bancroft grounded to short.

6th Inning
Yankees
1 Bush grounded to short. Witt tripled down the left field line. Dugan grounded to Bancroft and Witt
2 was caught in a run-down, Bancroft to Snyder to Groh to Snyder, Dugan got to second on the play. Ruth singled to right, Dugan scoring the first run of the Series. Ruth got to second on Youngs' fumble.
3 Pipp grounded to first.
Giants
Groh walked.
1 Frisch fouled to Schang.
2 Groh out trying to steal second, Schang to Ward.
3 I. Meusel struck out.

7th Inning
Yankees
B. Meusel singled to left. Schang sacrificed, but Nehf trying for the play at second threw past Frisch into left, B. Meusel going to third.
1 Ward flied to center, B. Meusel scoring and Schang going to second after the catch.
2 Scott flied to center.
3 Bush grounded to Groh and he tagged Schang coming into the base.
Giants
1 Youngs flied to right. Kelly got a hit in front of the plate as Bush fell down. Stengel singled to left, Kelly stopping at second. Snyder beat out a hit to short, loading the bases.
2,3 Earl Smith, batting for Nehf, hit into a double play, Scott to Ward to Pipp.

8th Inning
Yankees
For the Giants—Ryan pitching.
1 Witt struck out.
2 Dugan flied to center.
3 Ruth called out on strikes.
Giants
Bancroft singled to right. Groh singled to right, Bancroft stopping at second. Frisch singled to left, loading the bases. I. Meusel singled through the box into center, Bancroft and Groh scoring as Frisch raced to third. For the Yankees—Hoyt came in to pitch.
1 Youngs flied to center, Frisch scoring after the catch.
2 Kelly struck out.
3 Stengel struck out.

9th Inning
Yankees
Pipp singled to left.
1,2 B. Meusel lined to Frisch who threw to Kelly doubling Pipp at first.
3 Schang grounded to short.

NY-A 000 001 100
NY-N 000 000 03x

Game 2 October 5 at New York-A

| | | NY-N | 3 0 0 | 0 0 0 | 0 0 0 | 0* |
| | | NY-A | 1 0 0 | 1 0 0 | 0 1 0 | 0 |

New York-N	Pos	AB	R	H	RBI	PO	A	E
Bancroft	ss	5	0	1	0	1	0	1
Groh	3b	4	1	1	0	1	3	0
Frisch	2b	4	1	2	0	1	4	0
I. Meusel	lf	4	1	1	3	0	0	0
Youngs	rf	3	0	1	0	1	0	0
Kelly	1b	4	0	0	0	15	0	0
Stengel	cf	1	0	1	0	0	0	0
a Cunningham	cf	2	0	0	0	2	0	0
b Earl Smith		1	0	0	0	0	0	0
King	cf	0	0	0	0	0	0	0
Snyder	c	4	0	1	0	9	1	0
J. Barnes	p	4	0	0	0	0	4	0
Totals		36	3	8	3	30	12	1

New York-A	Pos	AB	R	H	RBI	PO	A	E
Witt	cf	5	0	1	0	1	1	0
Dugan	3b	5	1	2	0	1	3	0
Ruth	rf	4	1	1	0	5	0	0
Pipp	1b	5	0	1	1	11	0	0
B. Meusel	lf	4	0	1	1	1	0	0
Schang	c	3	0	1	0	5	0	0
Ward	2b	4	1	1	1	3	5	0
E. Scott	ss	4	0	0	0	1	3	0
Shawkey	p	4	0	0	0	2	0	0
Totals		39	3	8	3	30	11	0

Pitching	IP	H	R	ER	BB	SO
Giants						
J. Barnes	10	8	3	2	2	6
Yankees						
Shawkey	10	8	3	3	2	4

a Ran for Stengel in 2nd.
b Struck out for Cunningham in 9th.

Doubles—Dugan, B. Meusel, Ruth. Home Runs—I. Meusel, Ward. Stolen Base—Frisch. Double Play—Scott to Ward to Pipp. Wild Pitches—Shawkey 2. Left on Bases—Giants 5, Yankees 8. Umpires—Hildebrand, McCormick, Owens, Klem. Attendance—37,020. Time of Game—2:40.

*Game called at end of ten innings, due to darkness.

1st Inning
Giants
1 Bancroft grounded to second.
  Groh singled through short.
  Frisch singled on a Texas Leaguer behind short, Groh stopping at second.
2 Youngs flied to center.
  I. Meusel hit a three-run homer into the left field bleachers.
2 Youngs flied to center.
3 Kelly fouled to Schang.
Yankees
1 Witt rolled to third.
  Dugan grounded to Bancroft who threw wildly over Kelly's head allowing Dugan to reach second safely.
2 Ruth grounded to first, Dugan moving over to third.
  Pipp got a lucky bounce single over Kelly, scoring Dugan.
3 B. Meusel flied to right.

2nd Inning
Giants
  Stengel beat out a slow roller to short.
  Snyder bounced a single to right, Stengel going to second.
  Cunningham ran for Stengel, who hurt his leg.
1,2 Barnes hit into a double play, Scott to Ward to Pipp, Cunningham going to third.
3 Bancroft flied to deep right.
Yankees
  For the Giants—Cunningham in center.
1 Schang grounded to second.
2 Ward grounded to third.
3 Scott robbed of a sure hit by Frisch, who made a sensational diving stop and throw to first.

3rd Inning
Giants
  Groh walked.
1 Frisch flied to right.
2 I. Meusel also flied to right.
  Youngs walked.
3 Kelly struck out.
Yankees
1 Shawkey grounded to third.
2 Witt fouled to Groh.
  Dugan doubled over third.
  Ruth walked.
3 Pipp grounded back to the mound.

4th Inning
Giants
1 Cunningham struck out.
2 Snyder fouled to Dugan.
3 Barnes struck out.
Yankees
1 B. Meusel fouled to Snyder.
2 Schang struck out, but Snyder dropped the ball and had to throw Schang out at first.
  Ward hit a home run over the left field fence.
3 Scott popped to Frisch, making another sparkling play.

5th Inning
Giants
1 Bancroft lined to first.
2 Groh was out for the first time in the Series on a grounder to short.
  Frisch beat out a pretty bunt.
  Frisch stole second.
  On a wild pitch Frisch went to third.
3 I. Meusel grounded to short.

5th Inning (continued)
Yankees
1 Shawkey flied to center.
2 Witt grounded out to the mound.
  Dugan singled to left.
3 Ruth grounded to second.

6th Inning
Giants
  Youngs beat out a hit to short.
1 Kelly forced Youngs at second, Shawkey to Ward.
2 Cunningham flied to right.
3 Snyder flied to right.
Yankees
1 Pipp fouled to Snyder.
  B. Meusel walked.
2 Schang grounded to second, moving B. Meusel to second.
3 Ward called out on strikes.

7th Inning
Giants
1 Barnes grounded to second.
2 Bancroft rolled to first.
3 Groh popped to second.
Yankees
1 Scott rolled to first.
2 Shawkey called out on strikes.
3 Witt struck out.

8th Inning
Giants
1 Frisch popped to third.
2 I. Meusel fouled to Pipp.
3 Youngs flied to left.
Yankees
1 Dugan bunted out, Barnes to Kelly.
  Ruth doubled to the wall in left.
2 Pipp flied to deep center, Ruth taking third after the catch.
  B. Meusel doubled to left-center, Ruth scoring the tying run.
3 Schang grounded to first.

9th Inning
Giants
1 Kelly popped to third.
2 Earl Smith, pinch-hitting for Cunningham, struck out.
3 Snyder grounded to second.
Yankees
  For the Giants—King playing center.
1 Ward struck out.
  Scott singled to center.
2 Shawkey forced Scott on a sacrifice attempt, Barnes to Bancroft.
  Witt singled to left, Shawkey stopping at second.
3 Dugan struck out.

10th Inning
Giants
1 Barnes tapped back to the mound.
  Bancroft singled to center, but was out
2 trying to stretch it, Witt to Scott.
3 Groh grounded to second.
Yankees
1 Ruth fouled to Snyder.
2 Pipp grounded to first.
3 B. Meusel fouled to Snyder.
Game called because of darkness.

Game 3 October 6 at New York-N

| | | NY-A | 0 0 0 | 0 0 0 | 0 0 0 | |
| | | NY-N | 0 0 2 | 0 0 0 | 1 0 x | |

New York-A	Pos	AB	R	H	RBI	PO	A	E
Witt	cf	3	0	0	0	1	0	0
Dugan	3b	4	0	0	0	2	4	0
Ruth	rf	3	0	0	0	0	0	0
Pipp	1b	4	0	1	0	10	1	0
B. Meusel	lf	4	0	1	0	1	1	0
Schang	c	3	0	1	0	2	2	0
Ward	2b	2	0	0	0	2	4	1
a Elmer Smith		1	0	0	0	0	0	0
McNally	2b	0	0	0	0	1	1	0
E. Scott	ss	3	0	0	0	4	1	0
Hoyt	p	2	0	1	0	1	2	0
b Baker		1	0	0	0	0	0	0
Jones	p	0	0	0	0	0	1	0
Totals		30	0	4	0	24	17	1

New York-N	Pos	AB	R	H	RBI	PO	A	E
Bancroft	ss	3	2	0	0	0	4	0
Groh	3b	4	1	2	0	2	3	0
Frisch	2b	2	0	2	2	1	5	1
I. Meusel	lf	4	0	1	1	1	0	0
Youngs	rf	4	0	3	0	2	0	0
Kelly	1b	3	0	1	0	15	1	0
Cunningham	cf	3	0	1	0	3	0	0
Earl Smith	c	4	0	1	0	2	1	0
J. Scott	p	4	0	1	0	1	1	0
Totals		31	3	12	3	27	15	1

Pitching	IP	H	R	ER	BB	SO
Yankees						
Hoyt (L)	7	11	3	1	2	2
Jones	1	1	0	0	1	0
Giants						
J. Scott (W)	9	4	0	0	1	2

a Struck out for Ward in 7th.
b Grounded out for Hoyt in 8th.

Double—Schang. Stolen Base—Pipp. Sacrifice Hits—Frisch, Kelly. Double Play—Ward to Pipp. Hit by Pitcher—Ruth (by J. Scott). Left on Bases—Yankees 5, Giants 9. Umpires—McCormick, Owens, Klem, Hildebrand. Attendance—37,630. Time of Game—1:48.

1st Inning
Yankees
1 Witt bunted out to third.
2 Dugan flied to right.
3 Ruth bounced to second.
Giants
1 Bancroft grounded to Hoyt, who tagged him on the base line.
  Groh singled to right.
  Frisch singled to center, Groh stopping at second.
2,3 I. Meusel lined into a double play, Ward to Pipp.

2nd Inning
Yankees
  Pipp singled to right.
1 B. Meusel fouled to Kelly.
2 Schang flied to center.
  Pipp stole second.
3 Ward grounded to short.
Giants
  Young got a Texas League single to
1 left but was out trying for a double, B. Meusel to Ward.
2 Kelly grounded to second.
  Cunningham safe on a hit to first.
3 Smith forced Cunningham at second, Ward to E. Scott.

3rd Inning
Yankees
1 E. Scott flied to right.
2 Hoyt grounded to second.
  Witt walked.
3 Witt was picked off first, Smith to Kelly.
Giants
  J. Scott singled.
  Bancroft safe as Ward booted his grounder into left, J. Scott going to third.
1 Groh grounded to Hoyt who ran J. Scott down, Hoyt to Dugan to Pipp to Dugan, Bancroft getting to third and Groh to second.
2 Frisch flied to center, Bancroft scoring and Groh going to third after the catch.
  I. Meusel singled to right, scoring Groh.
3 Youngs forced I. Meusel at second, Ward to E. Scott.

4th Inning
Yankees
1 Dugan grounded to third.
  Ruth was hit by a pitch.
2 Pipp struck out.
3 B. Meusel was safe on Frisch's error, but Ruth was out trying for third, Frisch to Groh.
Giants
  Kelly beat out a hit to second.
1 Kelly out trying to steal, Schang to E. Scott.
2 Cunningham grounded to third.
  Smith singled over third.
3 E. Scott called out on strikes.

5th Inning
Yankees
1 Schang grounded out, Kelly to J. Scott.
2 Ward flied to center.
3 E. Scott fouled to Groh.
Giants
1 Bancroft struck out.
2 Groh bunted out to third.
  Frisch walked.
3 Frisch out stealing, Schang to E. Scott.

6th Inning
Yankees
  Hoyt singled to right-center.
1 Witt forced Hoyt at second, J. Scott to Frisch.
2 Dugan flied to left.
3 Ruth grounded to first.
Giants
1 I. Meusel flied to brother Bob.
  Youngs lined a single to left.
2 Kelly fouled to Pipp.
3 Cunningham grounded to second.

7th Inning
Yankees
1 Pipp grounded to second.
  B. Meusel bounced a single over the box.
  Schang doubled down the right field line, B. Meusel stopping at third.
2 Elmer Smith, batting for Ward, struck out.
3 E. Scott bounced to short.
Giants
  For the Yankees—McNally playing second.
1 Earl Smith bounced back to the mound.
2 J. Scott grounded to second.
  Bancroft walked.
  Groh singled to right, Bancroft racing to third.
  Frisch singled to right, scoring Bancroft as Groh stopped at second.
3 I. Meusel grounded to second.

8th Inning
Yankees
1 Baker, pinch-hitting for Hoyt, grounded to first.
2 Witt flied to center.
3 Dugan grounded to third.
Giants
  For the Yankees—Jones pitching.
  Youngs singled.
1 Kelly sacrificed Youngs to second, Jones to Pipp.
  Cunningham walked.
2 Smith popped to second.
3 J. Scott fouled to Dugan.

9th Inning
Yankees
1 Ruth grounded to second.
2 Pipp grounded to short.
3 B. Meusel grounded to short.

Game 4 October 7 at New York-A

NY-N	0 0 0	0 4 0	0 0 0
NY-A	2 0 0	0 0 0	1 0 0

New York-N	Pos	AB	R	H	RBI	PO	A	E
Bancroft	ss	3	1	2	2	3	5	0
Groh	3b	4	1	1	0	0	3	0
Frisch	2b	4	0	0	0	4	3	0
I. Meusel	lf	4	0	1	1	1	0	0
Youngs	rf	4	0	2	1	3	0	0
Kelly	1b	4	0	0	0	8	0	0
Cunningham	cf	3	0	0	0	3	2	0
Snyder	c	4	1	2	0	5	0	1
McQuillan	p	4	1	1	0	0	0	0
Totals		33	4	9	4	27	13	1

Pitching	IP	H	R	ER	BB	SO
Giants						
McQuillan (W)	9	8	3	2	2	4
Yankees						
Mays (L)	8	9	4	4	2	1
Jones	1	0	0	0	0	0

New York-A	Pos	AB	R	H	RBI	PO	A	E
Witt	cf	4	1	2	0	4	0	0
Dugan	3b	4	1	1	0	0	3	0
Ruth	rf	3	0	0	0	1	0	0
Pipp	1b	4	0	2	1	12	3	0
B. Meusel	lf	4	0	1	1	5	0	0
Schang	c	4	0	1	0	1	1	0
Ward	2b	4	1	1	1	0	2	0
E. Scott	ss	2	0	0	0	4	2	0
Mays	p	2	0	0	0	0	4	0
a Elmer Smith		1	0	0	0	0	0	0
Jones		0	0	0	0	0	0	0
Totals		32	3	8	3	27	15	0

a Struck out for Mays in 8th.

Doubles—McQuillan, Pipp, Witt. Home Run—Ward. Stolen Base—B. Meusel. Sacrifice Hit—Frisch. Double Plays—Frisch to Bancroft to Kelly, Pipp to E. Scott. Left on Bases—Giants 5, Yankees 4. Umpires—Owens, Klem, Hildebrand, McCormick. Attendance—36,242. Time of Game—1:41.

1st Inning
Giants
Bancroft bounced a single over the box.
1 Groh grounded back to the mound, Bancroft going to second.
2 Frisch flied to left.
3 I. Meusel grounded to short.
Yankees
Witt singled over second.
Dugan singled to left, Witt stopping at second.
1 Ruth flied to Cunningham who made a sensational catch in deep center, Witt going to third.
Pipp singled to right, scoring Witt but
2 was out trying for second, Cunningham to Frisch, as Dugan got to third.
B. Meusel singled to right, scoring Dugan.
B. Meusel stole second and continued to third on Snyder's low throw.
3 Schang called out on strikes.

2nd Inning
Giants
1 Youngs flied to left.
2 Kelly tapped out, Mays to Pipp. Cunningham walked.
3 Snyder bounced to third.
Yankees
1 Ward flied to deep right.
2 Scott grounded to short.
3 Mays grounded to second.

3rd Inning
Giants
1 McQuillan bunted out, Schang to Pipp. Bancroft walked.
2 Groh flied to left.
3 Frisch flied to right.
Yankees
1 Witt flied to center.
2 Dugan grounded to third. Ruth walked.
3 Pipp flied to right.

4th Inning
Giants
1 I. Meusel grounded to third. Youngs singled to right.
2 Kelly forced Youngs at second, Pipp to Scott.
3 Cunningham forced Kelly at second, Ward to Scott.
Yankees
1 B. Meusel struck out.
2 Schang flied to right.
3 Ward struck out.

5th Inning
Giants
Snyder beat out a hit to short.
McQuillan doubled down the left field line, Snyder stopping at third.
Bancroft bounced a single over Ward's head, scoring Snyder and McQuillan. Groh beat out a dribbler to the mound, Bancroft to second.
1 Frisch sacrificed Bancroft to third and Groh to second, Mays to Pipp.
2 I. Meusel grounded to second, Bancroft scoring with Groh going to third. Youngs singled to left, Groh scoring.
3 Youngs run-down off of first, Mays to Pipp to Scott to Pipp.
Yankees
Scott walked.
1 Mays fouled to Kelly.
2,3 Witt hit into a double play, Frisch to Bancroft to Kelly.

6th Inning
Giants
1 Kelly flied to center.
2 Cunningham grounded to Dugan, rushing in to make a great stop and throw. Snyder singled over third.
3 McQuillan struck out.
Yankees
1 Dugan popped to Snyder.
2 Ruth popped to Snyder.
3 Pipp grounded to short.

7th Inning
Giants
1 Bancroft flied to left.
2 Groh bunted out to first.
3 Frisch flied to center.
Yankees
1 B. Meusel grounded to third.
2 Schang grounded to second. Ward hit his second home run of the Series into the left field bleachers.
3 Scott popped to Bancroft in short left.

8th Inning
Giants
I. Meusel singled to center.
1 Youngs flied to left.
2,3 Kelly hit to Pipp who touched first and threw to Scott who tagged I. Meusel.
Yankees
1 Elmer Smith, batting for Mays, took a called third strike. Witt lined a double down the left field line.
2 Dugan flied to center.
3 Ruth popped high to Frisch in short right.

9th Inning
Giants
For the Yankees—Jones came in to pitch.
1 Cunningham flied to center.
2 Snyder popped to Scott in short left.
3 McQuillan flied to center.
Yankees
Pipp doubled over first.
1 B. Meusel grounded to Groh who ran down Pipp between second and third, Groh to Kelly to Groh to Bancroft. Schang singled to center, B. Meusel
2 racing to third but was out trying for second, Cunningham to Bancroft to Frisch.
3 Ward flied to left.

Game 5 October 8 at New York-N

NY-A	1 0 0	0 1 0	1 0 0
NY-N	0 2 0	0 0 0	0 3 x

New York-A	Pos	AB	R	H	RBI	PO	A	E
Witt	cf	2	0	0	0	0	0	0
a McMillan	cf	2	0	0	0	1	0	0
Dugan	3b	3	1	1	0	0	1	0
Ruth	rf	3	0	0	0	2	0	0
Pipp	1b	4	0	1	1	8	0	0
B. Meusel	lf	4	1	1	0	4	0	0
Schang	c	3	0	0	0	4	0	0
Ward	2b	2	1	0	0	3	1	0
E. Scott	ss	2	0	1	1	5	5	0
Bush	p	3	0	1	1	1	3	0
Totals		28	3	5	3	24	10	0

Pitching	IP	H	R	ER	BB	SO
Yankees						
Bush (L)	9	10	5	5	4	3
Giants						
Nehf (W)	9	5	3	3	2	3

New York-N	Pos	AB	R	H	RBI	PO	A	E
Bancroft	ss	4	0	0	0	2	5	0
Groh	3b	4	0	2	0	1	3	0
Frisch	2b	4	1	2	0	2	4	0
I. Meusel	lf	4	2	1	0	1	0	0
Youngs	rf	2	2	0	0	2	1	0
Kelly	1b	3	0	2	2	14	0	0
Cunningham	cf	2	0	1	2	2	0	0
b Earl Smith		1	0	0	0	0	0	0
King	cf	1	0	1	1	0	0	0
Snyder	c	4	0	1	0	3	2	0
Nehf	p	3	0	0	0	0	2	0
Totals		30	5	10	5	27	17	0

a Grounded out for Witt in 5th.
b Struck out for Cunningham in 7th.

Double—Frisch. Sacrifice Hits—Kelly, Ruth, Schang, Scott. Double Plays—Bush to Scott to Pipp 2, Ward to Scott to Pipp. Hit by Pitcher—Dugan (by Nehf). Wild Pitch—Nehf. Left on Bases—Yankees 4, Giants 6. Umpires—Klem, Hildebrand, McCormick, Owens. Attendance—38,551. Time of Game—2:00.

1st Inning
Yankees
1 Witt lined to short. Dugan singled through short.
2 Ruth sacrificed Dugan to second, Groh to Kelly. Pipp singled between second and short, scoring Dugan.
3 B. Meusel forced Pipp at second, Frisch unassisted.
Giants
1 Bancroft grounded to third. Groh singled to right.
2,3 Frisch grounded into a double play, Bush to Scott to Pipp.

2nd Inning
Yankees
1 Schang fouled to I. Meusel.
2 Ward flied to center.
3 Scott grounded to short.
Giants
I. Meusel beat out a slow roller to third. Youngs walked.
1 Kelly sacrificed I. Meusel to third and Youngs to second, tagged out by Bush. Cunningham singled past short, both runners scoring. Snyder singled to left, Cunningham stopping at second. Nehf walked, loading the bases.
2 Bancroft lined to second.
3 Groh struck out.

3rd Inning
Yankees
1 Bush grounded to short.
2 Witt grounded to short.
3 Dugan grounded to short.
Giants
1 Frisch rolled to first.
2 I. Meusel flied to right.
3 Youngs popped to first.

4th Inning
Yankees
1 Ruth struck out.
2 Pipp grounded to second.
3 B. Meusel struck out.
Giants
Kelly singled over the box.
1,2 Cunningham hit into a double play, Bush to Scott to Pipp.
3 Snyder popped to short.

5th Inning
Yankees
1 Schang struck out, but Snyder dropped the ball and threw to Kelly for the putout. Ward walked. Scott singled to right, Ward stopping at second. Bush singled to center, scoring Ward
2 but Scott was caught off third Youngs to Frisch to Snyder to Groh to Snyder. Bush got to second on the play.
3 McMillan, pinch-hitting for Witt, rolled back to the mound.

5th Inning (continued)
Giants
For the Yankees—McMillan stays in to play center. Nehf again walked.
1,2 Bancroft banged into a double play, Ward to Scott to Pipp.
3 Groh grounded to first.

6th Inning
Yankees
1 Dugan grounded to short.
2 Ruth grounded back to the pitcher.
3 Pipp lined to Groh, making a great leaping catch.
Giants
Frisch singled through the middle.
1 I. Meusel flied to right.
2 Youngs forced I. Meusel at second, Bush to Scott.
3 Kelly forced Youngs at second, Scott to Ward.

7th Inning
Yankees
B. Meusel beat out a hit to third.
1 Schang sacrificed, Groh to Frisch. B. Meusel went to third on a wild pitch. Ward intentionally passed.
2 Scott flied to center, B. Meusel scored after the catch and Ward went to second on the throw to the plate.
3 Bush grounded to second.
Giants
1 Earl Smith, pinch-hitting for Cunningham, struck out on three pitches.
2 Snyder struck out.
3 Nehf popped to second.

8th Inning
Yankees
For the Giants—King playing center.
1 McMillan grounded to third. Dugan was hit by a pitch.
2 Ruth grounded to first, Dugan going to second.
3 Pipp grounded to second.
Giants
1 Bancroft grounded to first. Groh singled through short. Frisch doubled to center, Groh stopping at third.
2 I. Meusel grounded to Scott who threw to Schang getting Groh, as Frisch got to third and I. Meusel to second. Young intentionally passed Kelly singled to left-center, Frisch and I. Meusel scoring as Youngs went to third. King got a Texas League single in short left, scoring Youngs.
3 Snyder flied to center.

9th Inning
Yankees
1 B. Meusel flied to Bancroft in short left.
2 Schang flied to right.
3 Ward flied to right.

1922 WORLD SERIES COMPOSITE BOX

	Wins	Composite Line Score
New York Giants (N.L.)	4	3 2 2 0 4 0 1 6 0 0 – 18
New York Yankees (A.L.)	0	4 0 0 1 1 1 3 1 0 0 – 11

Manager	Regular Season W	L	Pct.	G. Ahead
John McGraw	93	61	.604	7
Miller Huggins	94	60	.610	1

BATTING AND FIELDING

NEW YORK GIANTS

WORLD SERIES STATISTICS

Player	Pos	G	AB	R	H	2B	3B	HR	RBI	BB	SO	SB	BA	SA	PO	A	E
George Kelly	1b	5	18	0	5	0	0	0	2	0	**3**	0	.278	.278	**61**	1	0
Frankie Frisch	2b	5	17	3	8	**1**	0	0	2	1	0	**1**	.471	.529	10	**20**	1
Dave Bancroft	ss	5	19	**4**	4	0	0	0	2	2	1	0	.211	.211	9	16	1
Heinie Groh	3b	5	19	**4**	**9**	0	**1**	0	0	2	1	0	**.474**	.579	6	15	0
Ross Youngs	rf	5	16	2	6	0	0	0	2	**3**	1	0	.375	.375	9	2	**2**
Bill Cunningham	pr-cf	4	10	0	2	0	0	0	2	2	1	0	.200	.200	10	2	0
Irish Meusel	lf	5	20	3	5	0	0	1	**7**	0	1	0	.250	.400	3	0	0
Frank Snyder	c	4	15	1	5	0	0	0	0	0	1	0	.333	.333	23	5	1
Earl Smith	ph-c	4	7	0	1	0	0	0	0	0	2	0	.143	.148	2	1	0
Casey Stengel	cf	2	5	0	2	0	0	0	0	0	1	0	.400	.400	4	0	0
Lee King	cf	2	1	0	1	0	0	0	1	0	0	0	1.000	1.000	0	0	0
Johnny Rawlings	Did not play																
Dave Robertson	Did not play																
Alex Gaston	Did not play																
Jesse Barnes	p	1	4	0	0	0	0	0	0	0	1	0	.000	.000	0	4	0
Jack Scott	p	1	4	0	1	0	0	0	0	0	1	0	.250	.250	1	1	0
Hugh McQuillan	p	1	4	1	1	**1**	0	0	0	0	1	0	.250	.500	0	0	0
Art Nehf	p	2	3	0	0	0	0	0	0	2	0	0	.000	.000	0	3	1
Rosy Ryan	p	1	0	0	0	0	0	0	0	0	0	0	—	—	0	0	0
Claude Jonnard	Did not play																
Virgil Barnes	Did not play																
Carmen Hill	Did not play																
Clint Blume	Did not play																
team total		5	162	18	50	2	1	1	18	12	15	1	.309	.352	138	70	6

Double Plays—4
Left on Bases—32

REGULAR SEASON STATISTICS

Player	Note	Main Pos	G	AB	R	H	2B	3B	HR	RBI	BB	SO	SB	BA	SA
George Kelly		1b	151	592	96	194	33	8	17	107	30	65	12	.328	.497
Frankie Frisch		2b-3b	132	514	101	168	16	13	5	51	47	13	31	.327	.438
Dave Bancroft		ss	156	651	117	209	41	5	4	60	79	27	16	.321	.418
Heinie Groh		3b	115	426	63	113	21	3	3	51	53	21	5	.265	.350
Ross Youngs		of	149	559	105	185	34	10	7	86	55	50	17	.331	.465
Bill Cunningham		of	85	227	37	75	15	2	2	33	7	9	4	.328	.437
Irish Meusel		of	154	617	100	204	28	17	16	132	35	33	12	.331	.509
Frank Snyder		c	104	318	34	109	21	5	5	51	23	25	1	.343	.487
Earl Smith		c	90	234	29	65	11	4	9	39	37	12	1	.278	.474
Casey Stengel		of	84	250	48	92	8	10	7	48	21	17	4	.368	.564
Lee King	a	of-1b	20	34	6	6	3	0	0	2	5	2	1	.176	.265
Johnny Rawlings		2b	88	308	46	87	13	8	1	30	23	15	7	.282	.386
Dave Robertson		of	42	47	5	13	2	0	1	3	3	7	0	.277	.383
Alex Gaston		c	16	26	1	5	0	0	0	1	0	3	1	.192	.192
Jesse Barnes		p	37	77	9	14	0	1	0	10	5	4	0	.182	.208
Jack Scott	b	p	17	30	2	8	0	0	0	4	1	2	0	.267	.267
Hugh McQuillan	c	p	15	37	2	7	1	0	0	4	0	7	0	.189	.216
Art Nehf		p	37	98	9	25	0	0	1	11	6	7	0	.255	.286
Rosy Ryan		p	46	62	3	12	2	0	0	3	7	13	0	.194	.226
Claude Jonnard		p	33	24	3	1	0	0	0	0	1	16	0	.042	.042
Virgil Barnes		p	22	12	1	2	0	0	0	0	0	5	0	.167	.167
Carmen Hill		p	8	11	0	2	0	0	0	0	0	4	0	.182	.182
Clint Blume		p	1	2	1	1	0	0	0	0	2	0	0	.500	.500
team total			156	5455	852	1661	253	90	80	756	448	421	116	.304	.428

a—from Philadelphia (N)
b—from Cincinnati
c—from Boston (N)

Howard Berry (pr), Ike Boone (ph), Cozy Dolan (ph), Mahlon Higbee (of), Travis Jackson (ss), Waddy MacPhee (3b), Freddie Maguire (2b), Ralph Shinners (of), Red Causey (p), Mike Cvengros (p), Phil Douglas (p), Fred Johnson (p), Red Shea (p), Fred Toney (p) also played for the Giants during the season.

NEW YORK YANKEES

WORLD SERIES STATISTICS

Player	Pos	G	AB	R	H	2B	3B	HR	RBI	BB	SO	SB	BA	SA	PO	A	E
Wally Pipp	1b	5	**21**	0	6	**1**	0	0	3	0	2	**1**	.286	.333	51	4	0
Aaron Ward	2b	5	13	3	2	0	0	**2**	3	**3**	**3**	0	.154	**.615**	13	16	1
Everett Scott	ss	5	14	0	2	0	0	0	1	1	0	0	.143	.143	14	15	0
Joe Dugan	3b	5	20	**4**	5	**1**	0	0	0	0	1	0	.250	.300	5	8	0
Babe Ruth	rf	5	17	1	2	**1**	0	0	1	2	**3**	0	.118	.176	9	0	0
Whitey Witt	cf	5	18	1	4	**1**	**1**	0	0	1	2	0	.222	.389	7	1	0
Bob Meusel	lf	5	20	2	6	**1**	0	0	2	1	**3**	**1**	.300	.350	7	1	0
Wally Schang	c	5	16	0	3	**1**	0	0	0	0	**3**	0	.188	.250	19	4	0
Norm McMillan	ph-cf	1	2	0	0	0	0	0	0	0	0	0	.000	.000	1	0	0
Elmer Smith	ph	2	2	0	0	0	0	0	0	0	2	0	.000	.000			
Frank Baker	ph	1	1	0	0	0	0	0	0	0	0	0	.000	.000			
Mike McNally	2b	1	0	0	0	0	0	0	0	0	0	0	—	—	1	1	0
Fred Hofmann	Did not play																
Al DeVormer	Did not play																
Camp Skinner	Did not play																
Bullet Joe Bush	p	2	6	0	1	0	0	0	1	0	0	0	.167	.167	1	3	0
Bob Shawkey	p	1	4	0	0	0	0	0	0	0	1	0	.000	.000	0	2	0
Waite Hoyt	p	2	2	0	1	0	0	0	0	0	0	0	.500	.500	1	2	0
Carl Mays	p	1	2	0	0	0	0	0	0	0	0	0	.000	.000	0	4	0
Sad Sam Jones	p	2	0	0	0	0	0	0	0	0	0	0	—	—	0	1	0
George Murray	Did not play																
Lefty O'Doul	Did not play																
team total		5	158	11	32	6	1	2	11	8	20	2	.203	.291	129	62	1

Double Plays—7
Left on Bases—25

REGULAR SEASON STATISTICS

Player	Note	Main Pos	G	AB	R	H	2B	3B	HR	RBI	BB	SO	SB	BA	SA
Wally Pipp		1b	152	577	96	190	32	10	9	90	56	32	7	.329	.466
Aaron Ward		2b	154	558	69	149	19	5	7	68	45	64	7	.267	.357
Everett Scott		ss	154	557	64	150	23	5	3	45	23	22	2	.269	.345
Joe Dugan	d	3b	60	252	44	72	9	1	3	25	13	21	1	.286	.365
Babe Ruth		of	110	406	94	128	24	8	35	99	84	80	2	.315	**.672**
Whitey Witt		of	140	528	98	157	11	6	4	40	**89**	29	5	.297	.364
Bob Meusel		of	121	473	61	151	26	11	16	84	40	58	13	.319	.522
Wally Schang		c	124	408	46	130	21	7	1	53	53	36	12	.319	.412
Norm McMillan		of	33	78	7	20	1	2	0	11	6	10	4	.256	.321
Elmer Smith	e	of	21	27	1	5	0	0	1	5	3	5	0	.185	.296
Frank Baker		3b	69	234	30	65	12	3	7	36	15	14	1	.278	.444
Mike McNally		3b	52	143	20	36	2	2	0	18	16	14	2	.252	.294
Fred Hofmann		c	37	91	13	27	5	3	2	10	9	12	0	.297	.484
Al DeVormer		c	24	59	8	12	4	1	0	11	1	6	0	.203	.305
Camp Skinner		of	27	33	1	6	0	0	0	2	0	4	1	.182	.182
Bullet Joe Bush		p	39	95	15	31	6	2	0	12	3	11	0	.326	.432
Bob Shawkey		p	39	115	12	21	2	0	1	12	2	18	0	.183	.226
Waite Hoyt		p	37	92	4	20	2	2	0	6	5	12	0	.217	.283
Carl Mays		p	35	92	7	23	1	1	0	7	2	10	0	.250	.283
Sad Sam Jones		p	45	87	14	23	9	0	1	8	6	28	1	.264	.402
George Murray		p	22	18	1	5	0	1	1	4	0	5	0	.278	.556
Lefty O'Doul		p	8	9	0	3	1	0	0	4	0	2	0	.333	.444
team total			154	5245	758	1504	220	75	95	674	497	532	62	.287	.412

d—from Boston (A)
e—from Boston (A)

Chick Fewster (of), Elmer Miller (of), Johnny Mitchell (ss), Clem Llewellyn (p) also played for the Yankees during the season.

PITCHING

NEW YORK GIANTS

WORLD SERIES STATISTICS

Player	G	GS	CG	IP	H	R	ER	BB	SO	W	L	SV	ERA
Art Nehf	**2**	**2**	**1**	**16**	11	5	4	3	**6**	**1**	0	0	2.25
Jesse Barnes	1	1	**1**	10	8	3	2	2	**6**	0	0	0	1.80
Jack Scott	1	1	**1**	9	4	0	0	1	2	**1**	0	0	**0.00**
Hugh McQuillan	1	1	**1**	9	8	3	3	2	4	**1**	0	0	3.00
Rosy Ryan	1	0	0	2	1	0	0	0	2	**1**	0	0	0.00
Claude Jonnard	Did not play												
Virgil Barnes	Did not play												
Carmen Hill	Did not play												
Clint Blume	Did not play												
team total	5	5	4	46	32	11	9	8	20	4	0	0	1.76

REGULAR SEASON STATISTICS

Player	Note	G	GS	CG	IP	H	ER	BB	SO	W	L	Pct	SV	ShO	ERA
Art Nehf		35	35	20	268	286	98	64	60	19	13	.594	1	3	3.29
Jesse Barnes		37	30	14	213	236	83	38	52	13	8	.619	0	2	3.51
Jack Scott	b	17	10	5	80	83	39	23	37	8	2	.800	2	0	4.39
Hugh McQuillan	c	15	13	5	94	111	40	34	24	6	5	.545	1	0	3.83
Rosy Ryan		46	20	12	192	194	64	74	75	17	12	.586	3	1	**3.00**
Claude Jonnard		33	0	0	96	96	41	28	44	6	1	.857	**5**	0	3.84
Virgil Barnes		22	3	1	52	46	20	5	6	1	0	1.000	2	0	3.46
Carmen Hill		8	4	0	28	33	15	34	13	2	1	.667	1	0	4.82
Clint Blume		1	1	1	9	7	1	1	2	1	0	1.000	0	0	1.00
team total		156	156	76	1396	1454	536	393	388	**93**	61	**.604**	**15**	7	**3.45**

NEW YORK YANKEES

WORLD SERIES STATISTICS

Player	G	GS	CG	IP	H	R	ER	BB	SO	W	L	SV	ERA
Bullet Joe Bush	**2**	**2**	**1**	15	**21**	**8**	**8**	**5**	**6**	0	**2**	0	4.80
Bob Shawkey	1	1	**1**	10	8	3	3	2	4	0	0	0	2.70
Waite Hoyt	**2**	1	0	8	11	3	1	2	4	0	1	0	1.13
Carl Mays	1	1	0	8	9	4	4	2	1	0	1	0	4.50
Sad Sam Jones	**2**	0	0	2	1	0	0	1	0	0	0	0	0.00
George Murray	Did not play												
Lefty O'Doul	Did not play												
team total	5	5	2	43	50	18	16	12	15	0	4	0	3.35

REGULAR SEASON STATISTICS

Player	G	GS	CG	IP	H	ER	BB	SO	W	L	Pct	SV	ShO	ERA
Bullet Joe Bush	39	30	20	255	240	94	85	92	26	7	**.788**	3	0	3.32
Bob Shawkey	39	33	19	300	286	97	98	130	20	12	.625	1	3	2.91
Waite Hoyt	37	31	17	265	271	101	76	95	19	12	.613	0	3	3.43
Carl Mays	34	29	21	240	257	96	50	41	12	14	.462	2	1	3.60
Sad Sam Jones	45	28	21	260	270	106	76	81	13	13	.500	**8**	0	3.67
George Murray	22	3	0	57	53	25	26	14	4	2	.667	0	0	3.95
Lefty O'Doul	6	0	0	16	24	6	12	5	0	0	—	0	0	3.38
team total	154	154	**98**	1394	1402	525	423	458	**94**	60	**.610**	14	7	3.39

Total Attendance—185,947 Average Attendance—37,189 Winning Player's Share—$4,470 Losing Player's Share—$3,225

1923
Home Sweet Home

The newly opened Yankee Stadium drew fans and tourists in a rapid stream and served to heighten the growing legend of Babe Ruth. Dubbed "The house that Ruth built," the 62,000-seat stadium sat in the Bronx in plain sight of the Polo Grounds across the Harlem River, and Yankee-owner Jacob Ruppert had the smug satisfaction of seeing his team continue to outdraw the Giants, who had forced him into building a new park by evicting him from the Polo Grounds. Not only was the team financially successful but the Yankees christened their new home with a pennant-winning campaign, their third in a row. At center stage throughout this triumphant Yankee season was the exuberant Ruth, riding the crest of unparalleled popularity, and also riding American League pitchers for 41 homers, 130 RBI's, and a .393 batting average. Ruth soaked up most of the attention of the fans and writers alike, but a solid lineup and deep pitching staff made Ruth a member of the pennant-winning team rather than a jewel mounted on a tin ring. Across the Harlem River, the Giants enjoyed the Polo Grounds by themselves and won their third straight National League pennant. For manager John McGraw, whose Giants were now the lesser lights in New York, he had two World Series triumphs over his rivals in which to console himself.

The Series this fall opened in Yankee Stadium, with Waite Hoyt opposing Mule Watson, a surprising choice by McGraw to start. Watson lasted only two innings, but reliever Ryan, who had also come on in the third, dueled reliever Bullet Joe Bush into the ninth with the score tied 4–4. Then giant center fielder Casey Stengel caught a Bush change-up in the top of the inning and drove it into deepest left-center. Rounding second base, his shoe came undone and he kept going in more of a hobble than a gallop. But Bob Meusel's throw from the outfield arrived at the plate just after Casey did, and the Giants took a 5–4 opening-game win. Home runs also played the key role in game two, this time not by Stengel but by Ruth. Twice he rode his pitch out of the park, supplying the margin of victory in a 4–2 win for lefty Herb Pennock. Art Nehf and Sam Jones hooked up in a pitchers' battle in game three, with the only run of the contest coming in the seventh inning when Casey Stengel drove a pitch into the close right-field seats in the Stadium. While circling the bases in a slow strut, Casey thumbed his nose at the Yankee bench. The crowd treated to this spectacle totaled 62,430, the largest audience ever to view a game of baseball.

McGraw seemed on his way to a third straight Series title, but the Yankee power that had been peacefully sleeping in the autumn cool the past two years suddenly came alive. The Yanks clubbed 16-game-winner Jack Scott and two Giant relievers for six runs in the second inning of game four en route to an 8–4 win. With the Series evened at two games apiece, the Yankees now kept up the heat. They drove across three runs in the first and four in the second to ice away game five quickly, coasting to an 8–1 victory. Needing a win to stay alive, the Giants used Art Nehf, their most reliable hurler, on the mound in game six against Herb Pennock. Things looked bad for the Giants when Ruth connected for a home run in the top of the first, but the Giants responded with a run in the bottom of the inning to even the score. Pennock's superb control was missing today, so the Giants built a 4–1 lead after seven innings. But in the top of the eighth, after Aaron Ward made the first out, Wally Schang and Everett Scott singled, and a walk to Fred Hofmann loaded the bases. The tiring Nehf then forced across a run by walking Joe Bush, a good-hitting pitcher batting for Whitey Witt. McGraw then lifted Nehf and brought in Rosy Ryan, who immediately threw gasoline on the fire by walking Dugan to cut the score to 4–3. Ryan bore down and fanned Ruth for the second out, but then Bob Meusel hit a single up the middle on which all three runners scored when center fielder Bill Cunningham threw wildly to the plate. The 6–4 victory made the Yankees the World Champions for the first time, with the home-run hitting of Babe Ruth and Casey Stengel the enduring memories of the Series.

Game 1 October 10 at Yankee Stadium

NY-N		004	000	001			
NY-A		120	000	100			

New York-N	Pos	AB	R	H	RBI	PO	A	E
Bancroft	ss	4	1	1	1	3	0	0
Groh	3b	4	1	2	1	3	0	
Frisch	2b	4	0	1	1	2	2	0
Youngs	rf	3	0	0	0	1	0	0
I. Meusel	lf	4	0	0	0	6	0	0
Stengel	cf	3	1	2	1	2	0	0
Cunningham	cf	0	0	0	0	1	0	0
Kelly	1b	4	1	1	0	5	2	0
Gowdy	c	0	0	0	0	1	0	0
a Maguire		0	1	0	0	0	0	0
Snyder	c	2	0	0	0	4	1	0
Watson	p	0	0	0	0	0	1	0
b Bentley		1	0	1	0	0	0	0
c Gearin		0	0	0	0	0	0	0
Ryan	p	2	0	0	0	1	2	0
Totals		31	5	8	5	27	11	0

a Ran for Gowdy in 3rd.
b Singled for Watson in 3rd.
c Ran for Bentley in 3rd.
d Flied out for Scott in 8th.

New York-A	Pos	AB	R	H	RBI	PO	A	E
Witt	cf	5	0	1	2	5	0	0
Dugan	3b	4	0	1	1	0	3	0
Ruth	rf	4	1	1	0	3	0	0
B. Meusel	lf	4	0	1	1	0	0	0
Pipp	1b	4	0	2	0	10	0	0
Ward	2b	4	1	2	0	6	3	0
Schang	c	3	1	2	0	2	2	1
E. Scott	ss	2	0	0	0	1	6	0
d Hendrick		1	0	0	0	0	0	0
Johnson	ss		0	0	0	0	1	0
Hoyt	p	1	0	0	0	0	0	0
Bush	p	3	1	2	0	0	2	0
Totals		35	4	12	4	27	17	1

Pitching	IP	H	R	ER	BB	SO
Giants						
Watson	2	4	3	3	1	1
Ryan (W)	7	8	1	1	1	2
Yankees						
Hoyt	2⅓	4	4	4	1	0
Bush (L)	6⅔	4	1	1	2	2

Doubles—Bush, B. Meusel, Schang. Triples—Dugan, Groh, Ruth. Home Run—Stengel. Stolen Base—Bancroft. Sacrifice Hit—E. Scott. Double Plays—Scott to Ward to Pipp 2, Ryan to Groh to Frisch, Frisch to Snyder. Wild Pitch—Ryan. Left on Bases—Giants 2, Yankees 7. Umpires—Evans (A), O'Day (N), Nallin (A), Hart (N). Attendance—**55,307**. Time of Game—2:05.

1st Inning
Giants
1 Bancroft flied to right.
   Groh singled to center.
2 Frisch forced Groh at second, Scott to Ward.
3 Frisch out trying to steal second, Schang to Ward.
Yankees
1 Witt lined to short.
   Dugan walked.
2 Ruth forced Dugan at second, Groh to Bancroft.
   B. Meusel doubled to center, Ruth scoring.
3 Pipp flied to left.

2nd Inning
Giants
1 Youngs grounded to third.
2 I. Meusel popped to first.
3 Stengel flied to Ruth deep in the right field corner.
Yankees
   Ward singled to left.
   Schang singled to center, Ward stopping at second.
1 Scott sacrificed Ward to third and Schang to second, Kelly unassisted.
2 Hoyt struck out.
   Witt singled over second, scoring Ward and Schang.
3 Dugan rolled back to the box.

3rd Inning
Giants
   Kelly singled to center.
   Gowdy walked.
   Maguire ran for Gowdy.
   Bentley, batting for Watson, singled to center, loading the bases.
   Gearin ran for Bentley.
1 Bancroft forced Gearin at second, Scott to Ward, Kelly scoring and Maguire going to third.
   Bancroft stole second.
   Groh tripled down the right field line, Maguire and Bancroft scoring.
   For New York—Bush relieved Hoyt.
   Frisch singled to right, scoring Groh.
2 Youngs forced Frisch at second, Scott to Ward.
3 Youngs out trying for second on a short passed ball, Schang to Scott.
Yankees
   For the Giants—Ryan pitching and Snyder catching.
1 Ruth flied to I. Meusel in left-center.
2 B. Meusel flied to center.
   Pipp beat out a roller past the mound.
3 Ward struck out.

4th Inning
Giants
1 I. Meusel grounded to short.
   Stengel walked.
2,3 Kelly hit into a double play, Scott to Ward to Pipp.
Yankees
   Schang walked.
1 Scott struck out.
   Bush doubled down the left field line, Schang stopping at third.
2,3 Witt hit to Ryan who threw to Groh getting Schang off the bag, meanwhile Bush got to third, but Witt was out trying for second, Groh to Frisch.

5th Inning
Giants
1 Snyder flied to center.
2 Ryan struck out.
3 Bancroft flied to center.
Yankees
1 Dugan flied to left.
   Ruth tripled along the left field foul line.
2,3 B. Meusel flied to Frisch, making a great catch in short right, turned and cut down Ruth trying to score after the catch.

6th Inning
Giants
1 Groh's grounder deflected by Bush to Ward, who made the throw to first.
2 Frisch flied to right.
   Youngs walked.
   Youngs went to second on a wild throw by Schang trying to pick him off of first.
3 I. Meusel bounced back to the mound.
Yankees
1 Pipp grounded out Kelly to Ryan.
2 Ward flied to left.
   Schang doubled down the right field, line and just slid in under Youngs throw to second.
3 Scott grounded to second.

7th Inning
Giants
   Stengel singled to right.
1,2 Kelly hit into a double play, Scott to Ward to Pipp.
3 Snyder struck out.
Yankees
   Bush singled to center.
1 Witt flied to left.
   Dugan tripled to right, scoring Bush.
2 Ruth grounded to Kelly making a great stop behind the bag and threw out Dugan trying to score.
3 B. Meusel flied to right.

8th Inning
Giants
1 Ryan flied to center.
   Bancroft singled to right.
2 Groh grounded to third, Bancroft going to second.
3 Frisch flied to center.
Yankees
   Pipp beat out a roller down the first base line.
   Pipp went to second on a wild pitch.
1 Pipp picked off second, Snyder to Bancroft.
   Ward singled to center.
2 Schang bounced back to the mound, Ward going to second.
3 Hendrick, batting for Scott, flied to center.

9th Inning
Giants
   For the Yankees—Johnson playing short.
1 Youngs lined to center.
2 I. Meusel grounded to third.
   Stengel hit an inside-the-park home run in deep left-center.
3 Kelly grounded to short.
Yankees
   For the Giants—Cunningham playing center.
1 Bush grounded to third.
2 Witt flied to center.
3 Dugan flied to left.

Game 2 October 11 at Polo Grounds

NY-A	010	210	000
NY-N	010	001	000

New York-A	Pos	AB	R	H	RBI	PO	A	E
Witt	cf	5	0	0	0	1	0	0
Dugan	3b	4	0	1	0	2	3	0
Ruth	rf	3	2	2	2	3	0	0
B. Meusel	lf	4	0	1	0	4	0	0
Pipp	1b	3	1	1	0	13	0	0
Ward	2b	4	1	2	1	3	4	0
Schang	c	4	0	1	0	1	0	0
E. Scott	ss	4	0	1	0	6	6	0
Pennock	p	3	0	0	0	0	1	0
Totals		34	4	10	4	27	14	0

Pitching	IP	H	R	ER	BB	SO
Yankees						
Pennock (W)	9	9	2	2	1	1
Giants						
McQuillan (L)	3⅓	5	3	3	2	1
Bentley	5⅓	5	1	1	2	0

New York-N	Pos	AB	R	H	RBI	PO	A	E
Bancroft	ss	4	0	0	0	0	6	0
Groh	3b	4	1	1	0	0	1	0
Frisch	2b	4	0	2	0	2	6	0
Youngs	rf	4	0	2	1	0	0	2
I. Meusel	lf	4	1	2	1	4	0	0
Cunningham	cf	3	0	0	0	1	0	0
a Gowdy		1	0	0	0	0	0	0
Stengel	cf	0	0	0	0	1	0	0
Kelly	1b	4	0	1	0	16	1	0
Snyder	c	4	0	0	0	3	1	0
McQuillan	p	1	0	0	0	0	0	0
Bentley	p	2	1	0	0	0	2	0
b Jackson		1	0	0	0	0	0	0
Totals		35	2	9	2	27	17	2

a Flied out for Cunningham in 8th.
b Flied out for Bentley in 9th.

Doubles—Bentley, Dugan. Home Runs—I. Meusel, Ruth 2, Ward. Double Plays—Bancroft to Frisch to Kelly 2, Scott to Ward to Pipp. Hit by Pitcher—Pennock (by Bentley). Left on Bases—Yankees 8, Giants 7. Umpires—O'Day, Nallin, Hart, Evans. Attendance—40,402. Time of Game—2:08.

1st Inning
Yankees
1 Witt grounded to second.
 Dugan walked on four pitches.
 Ruth also walked.
2,3 B. Meusel grounded into a double play, Bancroft to Frisch to Kelly.
Giants
1 Bancroft grounded to short.
2 Groh grounded back to the mound.
3 Frisch grounded to second.

2nd Inning
Yankees
1 Pipp grounded to third.
 Ward homered into the upper deck of the left field stands.
2 Schang popped to Snyder in front of the pitcher's box.
3 Scott flied to left.
Giants
1 Youngs popped to third.
 I. Meusel hit a home run into the upper deck of the left field stands.
2 Cunningham flied to right.
 Kelly singled to right.
3 Snyder popped to second.

3rd Inning
Yankees
1 Pennock grounded to second.
2 Witt grounded to second.
3 Dugan flied to I. Meusel in the left field corner.
Giants
1 McQuillan out on a bunt to third.
2 Bancroft flied to left.
 Groh walked on a full count.
 Frisch singled to center, Groh stopping at second.
3 Youngs lined to right.

4th Inning
Yankees
 Ruth homered over the roof of the right field stands.
1 B. Meusel called out on strikes.
 Pipp got a Texas League single in right.
2 Ward popped to first.
 Schang singled to right, and when Youngs fumbled the hit Ward went to third.
 Scott singled to left, Ward scoring as Schang stopped at second.
 For the Giants—Bentley relieved McQuillan. Pennock was hit by pitched ball, loading the bases.
3 Witt flied to center.
Giants
1 I. Meusel rolled to second.
2 Cunningham flied to right.
3 Kelly struck out.

5th Inning
Yankees
1 Dugan grounded to short.
 Ruth hit his second homer of the game, this one a liner into the lower tier of the right field stands.
 B. Meusel singled to right and got to second on Youngs' fumble.
2 Pipp grounded to first, B. Meusel racing to third.
3 Ward fouled to Kelly.
Giants
1 Snyder flied to left.
2 Bentley grounded to second.
3 Bancroft grounded to short.

6th Inning
Yankees
1 Schang grounded to short.
 Scott singled to center.
2,3 Pennock hit into a double play, Bancroft to Frisch to Kelly.
Giants
 Groh singled to center.
 Frisch singled to left, Groh stopping at second.
 Youngs also singled to left, Groh scoring as Frisch took second.
1 I. Meusel forced Youngs at second, Scott to Ward with Frisch going to third.
2,3 Cunningham hit into a double play, Scott to Ward to Pipp.

7th Inning
Yankees
1 Witt bounced to Bentley making a fine one-handed catch and throwing him out at first.
2 Dugan also bounced out to Bentley, Ruth walked.
3 Ruth was trapped off first, Snyder to Kelly to Bancroft to Kelly.
Giants
1 Kelly fouled to Pipp.
2 Snyder flied to left.
 Bentley doubled down the left field line.
3 Bancroft fouled to Dugan near the boxes in left field.

8th Inning
Yankees
1 B. Meusel fouled to Snyder.
 Pipp walked on four pitches.
 Ward singled to center, Pipp stopping at second.
2 Schang flied to left.
3 Scott flied to left.
Giants
1 Groh grounded to Dugan running in front of Scott for the ball.
2 Frisch grounded to short.
 Youngs singled to center.
 I. Meusel singled to left-center, Youngs stopping at second.
3 Gowdy, batting for Cunningham, flied to center.

9th Inning
Yankees
 For the Giants—Stengel playing center.
1 Pennock grounded to short.
2 Witt grounded to second.
 Dugan lined a double to center, Stengel just missing a shoe-string catch.
3 Ruth flied to deep center.
Giants
1 Kelly rolled to third.
2 Snyder grounded to short.
3 Jackson, batting for Bentley, flied to left.

Game 3 October 12 at Yankee Stadium

NY-N	000	000	100
NY-A	000	000	000

New York-N	Pos	AB	R	H	RBI	PO	A	E
Bancroft	ss	3	0	0	0	3	5	0
Groh	3b	4	0	0	0	1	5	0
Frisch	2b	4	0	2	0	4	4	0
Youngs	rf	4	0	0	0	2	0	0
I. Meusel	lf	4	0	0	0	1	0	0
Stengel	cf	3	1	1	1	1	0	0
Kelly	1b	3	0	0	0	10	0	0
Snyder	c	3	0	0	0	5	0	0
Nehf	p	3	0	1	0	0	1	0
Totals		31	1	4	1	27	15	0

Pitching	IP	H	R	ER	BB	SO
Giants						
Nehf (W)	9	6	0	0	3	4
Yankees						
Jones (L)	8	4	1	1	2	3
Bush	1	0	0	0	0	0

New York-A	Pos	AB	R	H	RBI	PO	A	E
Witt	cf	4	0	1	0	3	0	0
Dugan	3b	4	0	1	0	1	0	0
Ruth	rf-1b	2	0	1	0	4	0	0
B. Meusel	lf	4	0	0	0	5	0	0
Pipp	1b	2	0	0	0	8	0	0
Haines	rf	1	0	0	0	0	0	0
Ward	2b	4	0	1	0	0	3	0
Schang	c	4	0	1	0	3	0	0
E. Scott	ss	3	0	1	0	3	4	1
Jones	p	2	0	0	0	0	2	0
a Hofmann		1	0	0	0	0	0	0
Bush	p	0	0	0	0	0	0	0
Totals		31	0	6	0	27	9	1

a Popped out for Jones in 8th.

Double—Dugan. Home Run—Stengel. Double Plays—Bancroft to Frisch to Kelly, Jones to Scott to Pipp, Frisch to Bancroft to Kelly. Left on Bases—Giants 5, Yankees 7. Umpires—Nallin, Hart, Evans, O'Day. Attendance—**62,430.** Time of Game—2:05.

1st Inning
Giants
1 Bancroft flied to B. Meusel in the left field corner.
 Groh safe at first when Scott fumbled his grounder.
2 Frisch flied to center.
3 Youngs flied to center.
Yankees
1 Witt grounded to second.
2 Dugan grounded to short.
 Ruth singled to center.
3 B. Meusel flied to his brother.

2nd Inning
Giants
1 I. Meusel flied to brother Bob.
2 Stengel lined to center.
3 Kelly popped to short.
Yankees
1 Pipp fouled to Kelly.
2 Ward popped to Snyder near the mound.
3 Schang flied to Bancroft in short left.

3rd Inning
Giants
1 Snyder grounded to short.
2 Nehf called out on strikes.
3 Bancroft grounded to second.
Yankees
1 Scott grounded to short.
2 Jones called out on strikes.
3 Witt struck out.

4th Inning
Giants
1 Groh grounded to short.
 Frisch beat out a bunt towards third.
2 Youngs flied to Ruth in right-center.
3 I. Meusel flied to deep right.
Yankees
 Dugan doubled to center.
 Ruth walked on four pitches.
1,2 B. Meusel grounded into a double play, Bancroft to Frisch to Kelly, Dugan going to third.
3 Pipp grounded to second.

5th Inning
Giants
 Stengel walked.
1,2 Kelly hit the first pitch and grounded into a double play, Jones to Scott to Pipp.
3 Snyder grounded to short.
Yankees
 Ward singled to left.
1 Schang forced Ward at second on a bunt, Groh to Bancroft.
 Scott bounced a hit off Nehf, Schang going to second.
2,3 Jones hit into a double play, Frisch to Bancroft to Kelly.

6th Inning
Giants
1 Nehf grounded to first.
 Bancroft walked.
2 Groh fouled to Dugan.
 Frisch singled to right, Bancroft stopping at second.
3 Youngs grounded to short.
Yankees
1 Witt grounded to third.
2 Dugan flied to right.
3 Ruth called out on strikes.

7th Inning
Giants
1 I. Meusel lined to left.
 Stengel got his second homer of the Series, a blast into the right field bleachers.
2 Kelly flied to left.
3 Snyder grounded to second.
Yankees
1 B. Meusel flied to right.
 Pipp walked on a full count.
2 Ward's bouncer deflected by Nehf to Bancroft who threw to Frisch forcing Pipp at second. Schang singled to left, Ward stopping at second.
3 Scott forced Ward at third, Groh unassisted.

8th Inning
Giants
 For the Yankees—Ruth replaced Pipp at first and Haines playing right.
 Nehf blooped a single into short left.
1 Bancroft struck out.
2 Groh also struck out.
3 Frisch rolled back to the box.
Yankees
1 Hofmann, batting for Jones, popped to second.
 Witt singled to deep short.
2 Dugan forced Witt at second, Groh to Frisch.
 Ruth walked again.
3 B. Meusel flied to center.

9th Inning
Giants
 For the Yankees—Bush pitching.
1 Youngs fouled to B. Meusel.
2 I. Meusel popped to Scott in short left.
3 Stengel grounded to first.
Yankees
1 Haines grounded to third.
2 Ward called out on strikes.
3 Schang grounded to third.

Game 4 October 13 at Polo Grounds

	NY-A	061	100	000
	NY-N	000	000	031

New York-A	Pos	AB	R	H	RBI	PO	A	E
Witt	cf	4	0	3	2	1	0	0
Dugan	3b	5	1	0	0	2	3	0
Ruth	rf	3	2	1	0	2	0	1
B. Meusel	lf	5	0	1	2	3	0	0
Pipp	1b	4	1	2	0	9	1	0
Ward	2b	4	2	2	1	2	5	0
Schang	c	3	1	1	0	5	0	0
E. Scott	ss	5	1	2	2	2	1	0
Shawkey	p	3	0	1	1	1	2	0
Pennock	p	1	0	0	0	0	0	0
Totals		37	8	13	8	27	12	1

New York-N	Pos	AB	R	H	RBI	PO	A	E
Bancroft	ss	5	0	1	0	2	3	0
Groh	3b	3	0	0	0	1	2	0
Frisch	2b	5	0	2	0	4	0	0
Youngs	rf	5	2	4	1	0	0	0
I. Meusel	lf	5	1	1	0	1	0	0
Stengel	cf	2	1	2	1	4	0	0
d Cunningham		1	0	0	0	0	0	0
Kelly	1b	5	0	2	1	7	0	0
Snyder	c	4	0	0	1	8	1	0
J. Scott	p	0	0	0	0	0	0	1
Ryan	p	0	0	0	0	0	0	0
McQuillan	p	2	0	0	0	0	1	0
a Bentley		1	0	1	0	0	0	0
b Maguire		0	0	0	0	0	0	0
Jonnard	p	0	0	0	0	0	0	0
c O'Connell		0	0	0	0	0	0	0
Barnes	p	0	0	0	0	0	0	0
Totals		38	4	13	4	27	7	1

Pitching	IP	H	R	ER	BB	SO
Yankees						
Shawkey (W)	7⅔	12	3	3	4	2
Pennock (SV)	1⅓	1	1	1	0	1
Giants						
J. Scott (L)	*1	4	4	3	0	1
Ryan	⅓	2	2	0	1	0
McQuillan	5⅓	6	2	2	2	2
Jonnard	1	1	0	0	1	0
Barnes	1	0	0	0	0	2

*Pitched to four batters in 2nd.

a Singled for McQuillan in 7th.
b Ran for Bentley in 7th.
c Hit by pitch for Jonnard in 8th.
d Struck out for Stengel in 9th.

Doubles—Ruth, Witt 2. Triple—B. Meusel.
Home Run—Youngs. Sacrifice Hits—Schang 2,
Shawkey, Witt. Double Plays—Shawkey to
Dugan to Pipp, Dugan to Pipp. Left on
Bases—Yankees 10, Giants 12. Hit by
Pitcher—O'Connell (by Shawkey).
Umpires—Hart, Evans, O'Day, Nallin.
Attendance—46,302. Time of Game—2:32.

1st Inning
Yankees
Witt singled to center.
1 Dugan popped a foul to Snyder
on an attempted sacrifice.
2 Ruth called on strikes.
3 B. Meusel forced Witt at second,
Bancroft to Frisch.
Giants
1 Bancroft flied to left.
2 Groh popped to Ward in short center.
Frisch singled to center.
Youngs singled between Dugan and
E. Scott, Frisch stopping at second.
3 I. Meusel forced Youngs at second,
Ward unassisted.

2nd Inning
Yankees
Pipp singled to center.
Ward singled to center, Pipp
stopping at second.
Schang safe at first and loading the
bases when J. Scott fumbled his bunt.
E. Scott singled to left, scoring Pipp
and Ward as Schang raced to third.
For the Giants—Ryan relieved J. Scott.
1 Shawkey flied to center, Schang
scoring after the catch.
Witt doubled to left-center, E. Scott
scoring.
2 Dugan hit into a fielder's choice, a
grounder to Groh tagging Witt coming
into third.
Ruth walked.
B. Meusel tripled to deep left, scoring
Dugan and Ruth.
For the Giants—McQuillan came in to
pitch.
3 Pipp flied to center.
Giants
Stengel walked.
Kelly singled to short right, Stengel
stopping at second.
1 Snyder fouled to Schang.
2 McQuillan grounded out, Pipp to
Shawkey, advancing both runners.
3 Bancroft flied to left.

3rd Inning
Yankees
Ward walked.
1 Schang sacrificed, McQuillan to Kelly.
E. Scott singled to center, Ward
going to third.
2 Shawkey fouled to Snyder.
Witt got another double into the left
field corner, scoring Ward with E.
Scott stopping at third.
3 Dugan flied to center.
Giants
1 Groh grounded to second.
Frisch singled to center.
2 Youngs fouled to Schang.
3 I. Meusel struck out.

4th Inning
Yankees
Ruth walked.
1 B. Meusel struck out.
Pipp singled to the left field corner,
Ruth going to third.
Ward singled to left, Ruth scoring
as Pipp stopped at second.
2 Schang popped to second.
3 E. Scott popped to short.
Giants
Stengel again walked.
Kelly singled to left, putting
Stengel on second.
1,2 Snyder grounded into a double play,
Shawkey to Dugan to Pipp, as Kelly
got to second.
3 McQuillan called out on strikes.

5th Inning
Yankees
Shawkey singled to left.
1 Witt sacrificed Shawkey to second,
Snyder to Kelly.
2 Dugan flied to left.
3 Ruth struck out.
Giants
1 Bancroft grounded to Ward who fumbled
but recovered in time to make the
play at first.
2 Groh flied to left.
3 Frisch flied to Ruth in short right-center.

6th Inning
Yankees
1 B. Meusel fouled to Kelly.
2 Pipp fouled to Snyder.
3 Ward lined to second.
Giants
Youngs blooped a single into short
right.
1 I. Meusel rolled back to the box,
Youngs going to second.
Stengel lined a single to left, but
B. Meusel made a one-handed pick-up
holding Youngs at second.
2 Kelly flied to deep right, Youngs
going to third after the catch.
3 Snyder forced Stengel at second,
Dugan to Scott.

7th Inning
Yankees
Schang singled to center.
1 Scott grounded to first, Schang
going to second.
2 Shawkey flied to center.
3 Witt grounded to short.
Giants
Bentley, pinch-hitting for McQuillan,
singled to short left.
Maguire ran for Bentley.
1,2 Bancroft lined into a double play,
Dugan who made a great leaping catch
to Pipp.
Groh walked.
3 Frisch fouled to Pipp.

8th Inning
Yankees
For the Giants—Jonnard pitching.
1 Dugan grounded to third.
Ruth doubled to right.
2 B. Meusel fouled to Bancroft.
Pipp walked.
3 Ward forced Pipp at second, Bancroft
to Frisch.
Giants
Youngs beat out a grounder to third.
I. Meusel singled on a bouncer over
Scott's head, Youngs racing to third.
Stengel singled to right, scoring
Youngs as I. Meusel stopped at second,
but both runners advanced on Ruth's
wild throw to third.
1 Kelly grounded to second, I. Meusel
scoring and Stengel taking third,
2 Snyder grounded to short, Stengel
scoring.
O'Connell, batting for Jonnard, was
hit by a pitch.
Bancroft singled to right, O'Connell
going to second.
Groh again walked, loading the bases.
For the Yankees—Pennock replaced
Shawkey.
3 Frisch, on a full count, popped to
Scott in short left.

9th Inning
Yankees
For the Giants—Barnes pitching.
1 Schang struck out.
2 Scott grounded to third.
3 Pennock struck out.
Giants
Youngs got an inside-the-park home run
to deep right **(his fourth hit of the
game).**
1 I. Meusel grounded to second.
2 Cunningham, pinch-hitting for Stengel,
struck out.
3 Kelly flied to deep center.

Game 5 October 14 at Yankee Stadium

NY-N	010	000	000				
NY-A	340	100	00x				

New York-N	Pos	AB	R	H	RBI	PO	A	E
Bancroft	ss	4	0	0	0	2	3	0
Groh	3b	4	0	0	0	0	2	0
Frisch	2b	4	0	0	0	4	1	1
Youngs	rf	3	0	0	0	2	1	0
I. Meusel	lf	4	1	3	0	0	0	0
Stengel	cf	3	0	0	1	3	0	0
Kelly	1b	2	0	0	0	6	1	1
Gowdy	c	3	0	0	0	6	0	0
Bentley	p	0	0	0	0	0	0	0
J. Scott	p	1	0	0	0	0	0	0
Barnes	p	1	0	0	0	1	2	0
a O'Connell		1	0	0	0	0	0	0
Jonnard	p	0	0	0	0	0	1	0
Totals		30	1	3	1	24	11	2

a Struck out for Barnes in 8th.

Double—I. Meusel. Triples—B. Meusel,
I. Meusel. Home Run—Dugan. Stolen
Base—Ward. Sacrifice Hit—Pipp.
Double Play—Bancroft to Frisch. Left
on Bases—Giants 4, Yankees 9.
Umpires—Evans, O'Day, Nallin, Hart.
Attendance—62,817. Time of Game—1:55.

New York-A	Pos	AB	R	H	RBI	PO	A	E
Witt	cf	4	1	1	0	5	0	0
Dugan	3b	5	3	4	3	0	3	0
Ruth	rf	4	2	1	0	4	0	0
B. Meusel	lf	5	1	3	3	1	0	0
Pipp	1b	3	0	0	2	11	2	0
Ward	2b	4	0	0	0	5	0	0
Schang	c	4	0	1	0	3	0	0
E. Scott	ss	4	0	1	0	1	1	0
Bush	p	4	1	1	0	2	1	0
Totals		37	8	14	8	27	12	0

Pitching	IP	H	R	ER	BB	SO
Giants						
Bentley (L)	1⅓	5	7	6	2	1
J. Scott	2	5	1	1	1	1
Barnes	3⅔	4	0	0	0	2
Jonnard	1	0	0	0	0	1
Yankees						
Bush (W)	9	3	1	1	2	3

1st Inning
Giants
1 Bancroft grounded to second.
2 Groh flied to right.
3 Frisch grounded to second.
Yankees
1 Witt fouled to Gowdy.
  Dugan singled to right.
  Ruth walked on a full count.
  B. Meusel tripled to left-center,
    scoring Dugan and Ruth.
2 Pipp flied to deep right, B. Meusel
    scoring after the catch.
  Ward singled to left.
    Ward stole second.
3 Schang called out on strikes.

2nd Inning
Giants
1 Youngs grounded to short.
  I. Meusel tripled to left-center.
2 Stengel bounced out, Pipp to Bush,
    I. Meusel scoring.
3 Kelly flied to center.
Yankees
1 E. Scott flied to center.
  Bush singled to center.
  Witt walked.
  Dugan hit an inside-the-park home
    run past Stengel, scoring Bush and
    Witt ahead of himself.
  Ruth safe on Kelly's error.
  For the Giants—Jack Scott relieved
    Bentley on the mound.
  B. Meusel singled to center, Ruth
    going to third.
  Pipp grounded hard to Frisch who
    after making an excellent pick-up
    threw wide to the plate as Ruth
    scored, B. Meusel stopped at
    second on the play.
2,3 Ward lined into a double play,
    Bancroft to Frisch.

3rd Inning
Giants
1 Gowdy flied to right.
2 J. Scott fouled to Pipp.
3 Bancroft flied to center on a
    3—2 count.
Yankees
1 Schang popped to short.
  E. Scott singled to right.
2 Bush struck out on three pitches.
3 Witt forced E. Scott at second,
    Bancroft to Frisch.

4th Inning
Giants
1 Groh grounded to third.
2 Frisch grounded to second.
  Youngs walked.
  I. Meusel doubled down the right field
    line, Youngs stopping at third.
3 Stengel rolled back to the mound.
Yankees
  Dugan singled off Frisch's shins.
  Ruth singled to right, Dugan to third.
  Ruth had stumbled rounding first and
1 was out Youngs to Kelly.
  B. Meusel singled to right, Dugan scoring.
  Pipp walked.
  For the Giants—Barnes came into pitch.
2 Ward called out on strikes.
3 Schang forced Pipp, Groh to Frisch.

5th Inning
Giants
1 Kelly grounded to third.
2 Gowdy flied to center.
3 Barnes called out on strikes.
Yankees
1 E. Scott grounded to third.
2 Bush flied to Stengel in left-center.
  Witt beat out a hit to first.
  Dugan singled to right, Witt to second.
  **(This was Dugan's fourth consecutive
  hit.)**
3 Ruth struck out.

6th Inning
Giants
1 Bancroft flied to deep left.
2 Groh flied to right.
3 Frisch flied to deep right.
Yankees
1 B. Meusel rolled back to the box.
2 Pipp grounded out, Kelly to Barnes.
  Ward singled to left-center.
  Schang beat out a hit to third,
    Ward moving to second.
3 E. Scott forced Schang at second,
    Bancroft to Frisch.

7th Inning
Giants
1 Youngs bunted out, Pipp to Bush.
  I. Meusel singled to center. His third
    hit and the only hits off of Bush.
2 Stengel flied to Stengel.
  Kelly walked.
3 Gowdy forced Kelly, Ward to Scott.
Yankees
1 Bush flied to right.
2 Witt bunted out, Barnes to Kelly.
3 Dugan grounded to third.

8th Inning
Giants
1 O'Connell, batting for Barnes, called
    out on strikes.
2 Bancroft struck out on a full count.
3 Groh grounded to first.
Yankees
  For the Giants—Jonnard pitching.
1 Ruth flied to deep center.
2 B. Meusel bounced back to the mound.
3 Pipp called out on strikes.

9th Inning
Giants
1 Frisch grounded to third.
2 Youngs flied to center.
3 I. Meusel grounded to second.

Game 6 October 15 at Polo Grounds

NY-A	100	000	050				
NY-N	100	111	000				

New York-A	Pos	AB	R	H	RBI	PO	A	E
Witt	cf	3	0	0	0	3	1	0
c Bush		0	1	0	1	0	0	0
d Johnson		0	1	0	0	0	0	0
Jones	p	0	0	0	0	0	0	0
Dugan	3b	3	1	0	1	2	1	0
Ruth	rf	3	1	1	1	1	0	0
B. Meusel	lf	4	0	1	2	1	0	0
Pipp	1b	4	0	0	0	12	0	0
Ward	2b	4	0	1	0	0	7	0
Schang	c	4	1	1	0	7	0	0
E. Scott	ss	4	1	1	0	1	2	0
Pennock	p	2	0	0	0	0	1	0
a Hofmann		0	0	0	0	0	0	0
b Haines	cf	0	1	0	0	0	0	0
Totals		31	6	5	5	27	13	0

a Walked for Pennock in 8th.
b Ran for Hofmann in 8th.
c Walked for Witt in 8th.
d Ran for Bush in 8th.
e Fouled out for Cunningham in 8th.
f Grounded out for Ryan in 9th.

Triple—Frisch. Home Runs—Ruth, Snyder.
Double Play—Nehf to Bancroft to Kelly.
Left on Bases—Yankees 2, Giants 5.
Umpires—O'Day, Nallin, Hart, Evans.
Attendance—34,172. Time of Game—2:05.

New York-N	Pos	AB	R	H	RBI	PO	A	E
Bancroft	3b	4	0	0	0	1	7	0
Groh	ss	4	1	1	0	1	2	0
Frisch	2b	4	2	3	0	1	5	0
Youngs	rf	4	0	2	1	0	0	0
Cunningham	cf	3	0	1	0	0	0	1
e Stengel	cf	1	0	0	0	1	0	0
Kelly	1b	4	0	0	0	19	0	0
Snyder	c	4	1	2	1	4	0	0
Nehf	p	3	0	0	0	0	5	0
Ryan	p	0	0	0	0	0	0	0
f Bentley		1	0	0	0	0	0	0
Totals		36	4	10	4	27	19	1

Pitching	IP	H	R	ER	BB	SO
Yankees						
Pennock (W)	7	9	3	3	0	6
Jones (SV)	2	1	1	1	0	0
Giants						
Nehf (L)	7⅓	4	5	5	3	1
Ryan	1⅔	1	1	1	0	1

1st Inning
Yankees
1 Witt popped to third.
2 Dugan grounded to second.
  Ruth hit his third homer of the Series
    on a 3-2 count, a blast into the
    upper deck of the right field stands.
3 B. Meusel called out on strikes, also
    on a 3-2 count.
Giants
1 Bancroft flied to center.
  Groh singled to left.
  Frisch singled off Pennock's shins,
    Groh going to second.
  Youngs singled to center, scoring
2 Groh but Frisch was out trying for
    third, Witt to Dugan.
3 I. Meusel struck out.

2nd Inning
Yankees
1 Pipp rolled out to the box.
  Ward singled to left.
2,3 Schang hit into a double play,
    Nehf to Bancroft to Kelly.
Giants
1 Cunningham flied to center.
2 Kelly fouled to Schang.
3 Snyder struck out.

3rd Inning
Yankees
1 Scott out on a bunt, Nehf to Kelly.
2 Pennock bounced back to the mound.
3 Witt flied to left.
Giants
1 Nehf struck out.
2 Bancroft grounded to third.
3 Groh flied to left.

4th Inning
Yankees
1 Dugan popped to Frisch, who made an
    astonishing running catch in
    short right.
  Ruth walked.
2 B. Meusel grounded to short, Ruth
    going to second.
3 Pipp grounded to third.
Giants
  Frisch beat out a bunt towards first.
1 Youngs bounced to second, Frisch
    advancing to second.
2 I. Meusel flied to center.
  Cunningham singled to right,
    scoring Frisch.
3 Kelly grounded to second.

5th Inning
Yankees
1 Ward grounded to short.
2 Schang grounded to second.
3 Scott slowly rolled to second.
Giants
  Snyder homered into the upper deck
    of the left field stands, for his
    first hit of the Series.
1 Nehf struck out.
2 Bancroft grounded to short.
3 Groh flied to right.

6th Inning
Yankees
1 Pennock struck out.
2 Witt bounced back to the mound.
3 Dugan grounded to third.
Giants
  Frisch tripled to left-center.
1 Youngs grounded to second, Frisch
    holding at third.
  I. Meusel singled past second,
    scoring Frisch.
2 Cunningham grounded to first,
    I. Meusel to second.
3 Kelly struck out.

7th Inning
Yankees
1 Ruth struck out.
2 B. Meusel grounded to third.
3 Pipp grounded to short.
Giants
  Snyder singled to left.
1 Nehf called out on strikes.
2 Bancroft's grounder deflected by
    Pennock who made the throw
    to first, Snyder taking second.
3 Groh grounded to short.

8th Inning
Yankees
1 Ward popped to Kelly in short right.
  Schang singled down the left field
    line, the first hit off Nehf since
    the second inning.
  Scott singled into the right field
    corner, Schang getting to second.
  Hofmann, batting for Pennock, walked
    on four pitches, loading the bases.
  Haines ran for Hofmann.
  Bush, pinch-hitting for Witt, also
    walked on four pitches, forcing in
    Schang.
  For the Giants—Ryan replaced Nehf on
    the pitching rubber.
  Johnson ran for Bush.
  Dugan also walked on four pitches,
    forcing in Scott.
2 Ruth struck out.
  B. Meusel singled to center, scoring
    Haines and Johnson. Dugan also scored
    and B. Meusel went to third when
    Cunningham's throw was wild and went
    past Groh.
3 Pipp grounded to second.
Giants
  For the Yankees—Haines stays in playing
    center, and Jones pitching.
1 Frisch grounded to second.
  Youngs singled to center.
2 I. Meusel forced Youngs at second,
    Ward to Scott.
3 Stengel, batting for Cunningham,
    fouled to Dugan.

9th Inning
Yankees
  For the Giants—Stengel playing center.
1 Ward grounded to short.
2 Schang grounded to second.
3 Scott bounced to short.
Giants
1 Kelly popped to first.
2 Snyder grounded back to the pitcher.
3 Bentley, batting for Ryan, ended the
    Series on a grounder to second.

1923 WORLD SERIES COMPOSITE BOX

	Wins	Composite Line Score
New York Yankees (A.L.)	4	5 13 1 4 1 0 1 5 0 - 30
New York Giants (N.L.)	2	1 2 4 1 1 2 1 3 2 - 17

Manager	W	L	Pct.	G. Ahead
Miller Huggins	98	54	.645	16
John McGraw	95	58	.621	4½

(Regular Season)

BATTING AND FIELDING

NEW YORK YANKEES — WORLD SERIES STATISTICS

	Pos	G	AB	R	H	2B	3B	HR	RBI	BB	SO	SB	BA	SA	PO	A	E
Wally Pipp	1b	6	20	2	5	0	0	0	2	4	1	0	.250	.250	63	3	0
Aaron Ward	2b	6	24	4	10	0	0	1	2	1	3	1	.417	.542	11	27	0
Everett Scott	ss	6	22	2	7	0	0	0	3	0	1	0	.318	.318	8	20	1
Joe Dugan	3b	6	25	5	7	2	1	1	5	3	0	0	.280	.560	7	13	0
Babe Ruth	rf-1b	6	19	8	7	1	1	3	3	8	6	0	.368	1.000	17	0	1
Whitey Witt	cf	6	25	1	6	2	0	0	4	1	1	0	.240	.320	18	1	0
Bob Meusel	lf	6	26	1	7	1	2	0	8	0	3	0	.269	.462	14	0	0
Wally Schang	c	6	22	3	7	1	0	0	0	1	2	0	.318	.364	21	2	1
Hinkey Haines	rf-cf-ph	2	1	1	0	0	0	0	0	0	0	0	.000	.000	0	0	0
Fred Hofmann	ph	2	1	0	0	0	0	0	0	1	0	0	.000	.000			
Harvey Hendrick	ph	1	1	0	0	0	0	0	0	0	0	0	.000	.000			
Ernie Johnson	ss-pr	2	0	1	0	0	0	0	0	0	0	0	—	—	0	1	0
Elmer Smith	Did not play																
Benny Bengough	Did not play																
Mike McNally	Did not play																
Mike Gazella	Did not play																
Bullet Joe Bush	p-ph	4	7	2	3	1	0	0	1	1	1	0	.429	.571	2	3	0
Herb Pennock	p	3	6	0	0	0	0	0	0	0	2	0	.000	.000	0	2	0
Bob Shawkey	p	1	3	0	1	0	0	0	1	0	0	0	.333	.333	1	2	0
Sad Sam Jones	p	2	2	0	0	0	0	0	0	0	1	0	.000	.000	0	3	0
Waite Hoyt	p	1	1	0	0	0	0	0	0	0	1	0	.000	.000	0	0	0
Carl Mays	Did not play																
George Pipgras	Did not play																
Oscar Roettger	Did not play																
team total		6	205	30	60	8	4	5	29	20	22	1	.293	.444	162	77	3

Double Plays—6
Left on Bases—43

NEW YORK YANKEES — REGULAR SEASON STATISTICS

		Main Pos	G	AB	R	H	2B	3B	HR	RBI	BB	SO	SB	BA	SA
Wally Pipp		1b	144	569	79	173	19	8	6	108	36	28	6	.304	.397
Aaron Ward		2b	152	567	79	161	26	11	10	82	56	65	8	.284	.422
Everett Scott		ss	152	533	48	131	16	4	6	60	13	19	1	.246	.325
Joe Dugan		3b	146	644	111	182	30	7	7	17	25	41	4	.283	.384
Babe Ruth		of	152	522	151	205	45	13	41	131	170	93	17	.393	.764
Whitey Witt		of	146	596	113	187	18	10	6	56	67	42	2	.314	.408
Bob Meusel		of	132	460	59	144	29	10	9	91	31	52	13	.313	.478
Wally Schang		c	84	272	39	75	8	2	2	29	27	17	3	.276	.342
Hinkey Haines		of	28	25	9	4	2	0	0	3	4	5	3	.160	.240
Fred Hofmann		c	72	238	24	69	10	4	3	26	18	27	2	.290	.403
Harvey Hendrick		of	37	66	9	18	3	1	3	12	2	8	3	.273	.485
Ernie Johnson	a	ss	19	38	6	17	1	1	1	8	1	1	0	.447	.605
Elmer Smith		of	70	183	30	56	6	2	7	35	21	21	3	.306	.475
Benny Bengough		c	19	53	1	7	2	0	0	3	4	2	0	.132	.170
Mike McNally		ss-3b-2b	30	38	5	8	0	0	0	1	3	4	2	.211	.211
Mike Gazella		ss-2b-3b	8	13	2	1	0	0	0	1	2	3	0	.077	.077
Bullet Joe Bush		p	38	113	12	31	5	3	2	19	3	8	0	.274	.425
Herb Pennock		p	35	83	11	16	3	0	0	7	9	8	0	.193	.229
Bob Shawkey		p	36	99	8	20	1	1	0	10	0	15	0	.202	.232
Sad Sam Jones		p	39	85	13	19	3	0	0	6	10	28	0	.224	.259
Waite Hoyt		p	37	84	7	16	0	1	0	4	3	15	0	.190	.214
Carl Mays		p	23	27	2	4	0	1	1	3	3	4	0	.148	.333
George Pipgras		p	8	9	0	0	0	0	0	0	1	4	0	.000	.000
Oscar Roettger		p	5	2	0	0	0	0	0	0	0	0	0	.000	.000
team total			152	5347	823	1554	231	79	105	770	521	516	69	.291	.422

a—from Chicago (A)
Lou Gehrig (1b) also played for the Yankees during the season.

NEW YORK GIANTS — WORLD SERIES STATISTICS

	Pos	G	AB	R	H	2B	3B	HR	RBI	BB	SO	SB	BA	SA	PO	A	E
George Kelly	1b	6	22	1	4	0	0	0	1	1	2	0	.182	.182	63	4	1
Frankie Frisch	2b	6	25	2	10	0	1	0	1	0	0	0	.400	.480	17	18	1
Dave Bancroft	ss	6	24	1	2	0	0	0	1	1	2	1	.083	.083	11	24	0
Heinie Groh	3b	6	22	3	4	0	1	0	2	3	1	0	.182	.273	4	15	0
Ross Youngs	rf	6	23	2	8	0	0	1	3	2	0	0	.348	.478	5	1	2
Casey Stengel	cf-ph	6	12	3	5	0	0	2	4	4	0	0	.417	.917	11	0	0
Irish Meusel	lf	6	25	3	7	1	1	1	2	0	2	0	.280	.520	13	0	0
Frank Snyder	c	5	17	1	2	0	0	1	2	0	2	0	.118	.294	24	3	0
Bill Cunningham	cf-ph	4	7	0	1	0	0	0	1	0	1	0	.143	.143	2	0	1
Hank Gowdy	c	3	4	0	0	0	0	0	0	1	0	0	.000	.000	7	0	0
Jimmy O'Connell	ph	2	1	0	0	0	0	0	0	0	1	0	.000	.000			
Travis Jackson	ph	1	1	0	0	0	0	0	0	0	0	0	.000	.000			
Freddie Maguire	pr	2	0	1	0	0	0	0	0	0	0	0	—	—			
Alex Gaston	Did not play																
Ralph Shinners	Did not play																
Art Nehf	p	2	6	0	1	0	0	0	0	0	4	0	.167	.167	0	6	0
Jack Bentley	p-ph	5	5	0	3	1	0	0	0	0	0	0	.600	.800	0	2	0
Hugh McQuillan	p	2	3	0	0	0	0	0	0	0	1	0	.000	.000	0	1	0
Rosy Ryan	p	3	2	0	0	0	0	0	0	0	1	0	.000	.000	1	2	0
Virgil Barnes	p	2	1	0	0	0	0	0	0	0	1	0	.000	.000	1	2	0
Jack Scott	p	2	1	0	0	0	0	0	0	0	1	0	.000	.000	0	0	1
Claude Jonnard	p	2	0	0	0	0	0	0	0	0	0	0	—	—	0	1	0
Mule Watson	p	1	0	0	0	0	0	0	0	0	0	0	—	—	0	1	0
Dinty Gearin	pr	1	0	0	0	0	0	0	0	0	0	0	—	—	0	1	0
team total		6	201	17	47	2	3	5	17	12	18	1	.234	.348	159	80	6

Double Plays—8
Left on Bases—35

NEW YORK GIANTS — REGULAR SEASON STATISTICS

		Main Pos	G	AB	R	H	2B	3B	HR	RBI	BB	SO	SB	BA	SA
George Kelly		1b	145	560	82	172	23	5	16	103	47	64	14	.307	.452
Frankie Frisch		2b	151	641	116	223	32	10	12	111	46	12	29	.348	.485
Dave Bancroft		ss	107	444	80	135	33	3	1	31	62	23	8	.304	.399
Heinie Groh		3b	123	465	91	135	22	5	4	48	60	22	3	.290	.385
Ross Youngs		of	152	596	121	200	33	12	3	87	73	36	13	.336	.446
Casey Stengel		of	75	218	39	74	11	5	5	43	20	18	6	.339	.505
Irish Meusel		of	146	595	102	177	22	14	19	125	38	16	8	.297	.477
Frank Snyder		c	120	402	37	103	13	6	5	63	24	29	5	.256	.356
Bill Cunningham		of	79	203	22	55	7	1	5	27	10	9	5	.271	.389
Hank Gowdy	b	c	53	122	13	40	6	3	1	18	21	9	2	.328	.451
Jimmy O'Connell		of	87	252	42	63	9	2	6	39	34	32	7	.250	.373
Travis Jackson		ss-3b	96	327	45	90	12	7	4	37	22	40	3	.275	.391
Freddie Maguire		2b	41	30	11	6	1	0	0	2	2	4	1	.200	.233
Alex Gaston		c	22	39	3	8	2	0	1	5	0	6	0	.205	.333
Ralph Shinners		of	33	13	5	2	1	0	0	0	2	1	0	.154	.231
Art Nehf		p	34	63	5	12	2	0	0	8	6	2	0	.190	.222
Jack Bentley		p-ph	52	89	9	38	6	2	1	14	3	4	0	.427	.573
Hugh McQuillan		p	41	82	9	14	2	0	0	5	3	19	1	.171	.195
Rosy Ryan		p	45	53	3	11	2	0	0	4	2	11	0	.208	.245
Virgil Barnes		p	22	14	0	0	0	0	0	0	0	3	0	.000	.000
Jack Scott		p	40	79	12	25	4	0	1	10	3	5	1	.316	.405
Claude Jonnard		p	45	26	1	1	0	0	0	0	2	16	0	.038	.038
Mule Watson	c	p	17	46	3	8	3	0	0	4	0	13	0	.174	.239
Dinty Gearin		p	6	7	0	2	0	0	0	0	0	0	0	.286	.286
team total			153	5452	854	1610	248	76	85	790	487	406	106	.295	.415

b—from Boston (N)
c—from Boston (N)
Earl Smith (c), Moe Solomon (of), Bill Terry (1b), Hack Wilson (of), Jesse Barnes (p), Clint Blume (p), Walter Huntzinger (p), Fred Johnson (p), Red Lucas (p), Rube Walberg (p) also played for the Giants during the season.

PITCHING

NEW YORK YANKEES — WORLD SERIES STATISTICS

	G	GS	CG	IP	H	R	ER	BB	SO	W	L	SV	ERA
Herb Pennock	3	2	1	17⅓	19	7	7	1	8	2	0	1	3.63
Bullet Joe Bush	3	1	1	16⅔	1	2	2	4	5	1	1	0	1.08
Sad Sam Jones	2	1	0	10	5	1	1	2	3	0	1	1	0.90
Bob Shawkey	1	1	0	7⅔	12	3	3	4	2	1	0	0	3.52
Waite Hoyt	1	1	0	2⅓	4	4	4	1	0	0	0	0	15.43
Carl Mays	Did not play												
George Pipgras	Did not play												
Oscar Roettger	Did not play												
team total	6	6	2	54	47	17	17	12	18	4	2	2	2.83

NEW YORK YANKEES — REGULAR SEASON STATISTICS

		G	GS	CG	IP	H	ER	BB	SO	W	L	Pct	SV	ShO	ERA
Herb Pennock		35	27	21	224	235	83	68	93	19	6	.760	3	1	3.34
Bullet Joe Bush		37	30	23	276	263	105	117	125	19	15	.559	0	3	3.42
Sad Sam Jones		39	27	18	243	239	98	69	68	21	8	.724	4	3	3.63
Bob Shawkey		36	31	17	259	232	101	102	125	16	11	.593	1	1	3.51
Waite Hoyt		37	28	19	239	227	80	66	60	17	9	.654	1	1	3.01
Carl Mays		23	7	2	81	119	56	32	16	5	2	.714	0	0	6.22
George Pipgras		8	2	2	33	34	22	25	12	1	3	.250	0	0	6.00
Oscar Roettger		5	0	0	12	16	11	12	7	0	0	—	1	0	8.25
team total		152	152	102	1367	1365	556	491	506	98	54	.645	10	9	3.66

NEW YORK GIANTS — WORLD SERIES STATISTICS

	G	GS	CG	IP	H	R	ER	BB	SO	W	L	SV	ERA
Art Nehf	2	2	1	16⅓	10	5	5	6	7	1	1	0	2.76
Rosy Ryan	3	0	0	9⅓	11	4	1	3	3	1	0	0	0.96
Hugh McQuillan	2	1	0	9	11	5	5	4	3	0	1	0	5.00
Jack Bentley	2	1	0	6⅔	10	8	7	4	1	0	1	0	9.45
Virgil Barnes	2	0	0	4⅔	4	0	0	0	4	0	0	0	0.00
Jack Scott	2	1	0	3	9	5	4	1	2	0	1	0	12.00
Claude Jonnard	2	0	0	2	1	0	0	1	1	0	0	0	0.00
Mule Watson	1	1	0	2	4	3	3	1	1	0	0	0	13.50
Dinty Gearin	Did not pitch												
team total	6	6	1	53	60	30	25	20	22	2	4	0	4.25

NEW YORK GIANTS — REGULAR SEASON STATISTICS

		G	GS	CG	IP	H	ER	BB	SO	W	L	Pct	SV	ShO	ERA
Art Nehf		34	27	7	196	219	98	49	50	13	10	.565	2	1	4.50
Rosy Ryan		45	15	7	173	169	67	46	58	16	5	.762	4	0	3.49
Hugh McQuillan		38	32	15	230	224	87	66	75	15	14	.517	0	5	3.40
Jack Bentley		31	26	12	183	198	91	67	80	13	8	.619	3	1	4.48
Virgil Barnes		22	2	0	53	59	23	19	6	2	3	.400	1	0	3.91
Jack Scott		40	25	9	220	223	95	65	79	16	7	.696	1	3	3.89
Claude Jonnard		45	1	1	96	105	35	35	45	4	3	.571	5	0	3.28
Mule Watson	c	17	15	8	108	117	41	21	26	8	5	.615	0	0	3.42
Dinty Gearin		6	2	1	24	23	9	10	9	1	1	.500	0	0	3.38
team total		153	153	62	1377	1440	597	424	453	95	58	.621	18	10	3.90

Total Attendance—301,430 Average Attendance—50,238 Winning Player's Share—$6,143 Losing Player's Share—$4,113

1924
Eighteen Years and Six Games Later

The Washington Senators had built up an impressive reputation for ineptitude, crowned by the gag line, "First in war, first in peace, and last in the American League." But his team's reputation was swept away when owner Clark Griffith appointed twenty-seven-year-old second baseman Bucky Harris manager at the start of this season. Harris earned himself the title of "The Boy Wonder" by leading the Senators to their first A.L. pennant in a tight race with the New York Yankees. Harris didn't have any slugger on the order of Babe Ruth; in fact, his Senators ranked last in the majors with a team total of 22 homers. But he did have high-average hitters in outfielders Goose Goslin and Sam Rice, both destined to join Harris and pitcher Walter Johnson in the Hall of Fame. A first-class gentleman, Walter also had a first-class fast ball which many have called the hardest of all time. Now thirty-six years old, Johnson still relied on his fast ball to capture 23 games and lead the A.L. with 158 strikeouts. In his 18 years with the Senators, he had won 373 games with an often horrendous team behind him, and now he was getting his first chance to pitch a World Series game. Baseball fans everywhere rooted for the popular Johnson and the Senators, but the New York Giants were the betting favorites after winning their fourth straight National League pennant.

President Calvin Coolidge knew nothing of the Senators or Giants, as he found baseball a bore, but he showed up at the first game to throw out the first ball. After Silent Cal made his throw, Walter Johnson and Art Nehf took over and battled to a 2–2 deadlock after nine innings. The Giants paid no heed to the sentiment backing Johnson and scored twice in the twelfth inning to take a 4–3 victory. Home runs by Goslin and manager Harris paced the Senators to a 4–3 win the next day to send the Series to New York tied at one-all.

The third game saw each team use four pitchers, with the Giants coming out of it 6–4 victors. Again the Senators came back, winning game four 7–4 behind Goslin's 4-for-4 day with a three-run homer. Walter Johnson took the mound again in game five, but his age showed badly. Trailing 3–2 after seven and a half innings, he gave up three runs in the bottom of the eighth to put the game out of reach at 6–2. The fans mourned for Walter, as the pitching rotation for the last two games did not include him and he had not won a Series game.

But the Senators could not worry about Johnson; they had to worry about staying alive in the Series. Tom Zachary spun a 2–1 beauty in game six to send the Series into a seventh game. Virgil Barnes started the decisive game for the Giants, while Bucky Harris began righty Curly Ogden, then switched to lefty George Mogridge after only two batters. The 31,667 fans in Griffith Stadium then saw an avalanche of strategic moves, but the score stayed 0–0 until manager Harris put his team ahead in the fourth inning with a homer. The Giants stormed ahead with three runs in the sixth and seemed on their way to the World Championship. But fate smiled on the Senators in the bottom of the eighth. With two men in scoring position, Harris hit a routine grounder which took a sudden high hop over third baseman Fred Lindstrom's head, and the score just as suddenly was 3–3. Harris then brought in his best pitcher and the people's choice, Walter Johnson. The Giants kept putting men on base, but Walter emerged from the ninth and from three extra innings without allowing a run. In the bottom of the twelfth, fate again blessed the Senators. After Ralph Miller made the first out, Muddy Ruel launched an easy foul pop-up behind the plate; Giant catcher Hank Gowdy tripped over his mask and dropped the ball. Given a second chance, Ruel socked a double to left, only his second hit of the Series. Johnson came to bat for himself and reached first on an error by shortstop Travis Jackson. Now Earl McNeely batted and hit an easy grounder to third. But just as in the eighth inning, the ball suddenly careened over Lindstrom's head into left field, and Ruel raced home with the winning run. Walter Johnson had the Series victory everyone had wanted for him, and the Washington Senators had their first World Championship.

Game 1 October 4 at Washington

New York	Pos	AB	R	H	RBI	PO	A	E
Lindstrom	3b	5	0	0	0	1	3	0
a Bentley		0	0	0	0	0	0	0
b Southworth	cf	0	1	0	0	1	0	0
Frisch	2b-3b	5	0	2	0	3	3	0
Youngs	rf	6	0	2	1	2	0	0
Kelly	cf-2b	5	1	1	2	4	1	0
Terry	1b	5	1	3	1	15	0	0
Wilson	lf	6	0	2	0	4	0	0
Jackson	ss	3	0	0	0	2	6	1
Gowdy	c	3	0	1	0	4	1	0
Nehf	p	5	1	3	0	0	2	0
Totals		43	4	14	4	36	17	1

a Walked for Lindstrom in 12th.
b Ran for Bentley in 12th.
c Safe on error for Johnson in 12th.

Doubles—Frisch, McNeely, Peckinpaugh, Youngs. Home Runs—Kelly, Terry. Stolen Bases—Frisch, Peckinpaugh, Rice. Sacrifice Hits—Jackson, Kelly. Double Plays—Peckinpaugh to Harris, Jackson to Frisch to Terry, Bluege to Harris to Judge. Wild Pitch—Johnson. Left on Bases—New York 11, Washington 10. Umpires—Connolly (A), Klem (N), Dinneen (A), Quigley (N). Attendance—35,760. Time of Game—3:07.

N.Y.	010	100	000	002
Was.	000	001	001	001

Washington	Pos	AB	R	H	RBI	PO	A	E
McNeely	cf	5	1	1	0	3	0	1
Harris	2b	6	2	1	3	3	3	0
Rice	rf	5	0	2	1	0	1	0
Goslin	lf	6	0	1	0	3	0	0
Judge	1b	4	0	1	0	6	0	0
Bluege	3b	4	0	1	0	2	2	0
Peckinpaugh	ss	5	0	2	1	4	4	0
Ruel	c	3	0	0	0	15	2	0
Johnson	p	4	0	0	0	0	1	0
c Shirley		1	1	0	0	0	0	0
Totals		44	3	10	3	36	13	1

Pitching	IP	H	R	ER	BB	SO
New York						
Nehf (W)	12	10	3	2	5	3
Washington						
Johnson (L)	12	14	4	3	6	12

1st Inning
New York
1 Lindstrom flied to center.
2 Frisch popped to third.
3 Youngs called out on strikes.
Washington
1 McNeely flied to left.
2 Harris grounded to short.
3 Rice fouled to Lindstrom.

2nd Inning
New York
  Kelly homered into the left field stands.
  Terry singled over Johnson's head.
1 Wilson struck out.
  Jackson walked.
2,3 Gowdy lined into a double play, Peckinpaugh to Harris.
Washington
1 Goslin grounded to short.
  Judge singled.
2 Bluege struck out.
3 Peckinpaugh flied to left.

3rd Inning
New York
1 Nehf grounded back to the mound.
2 Lindstrom struck out.
  Frisch doubled to left-center.
3 Frisch caught off second, Ruel to Peckinpaugh.
Washington
  Ruel walked.
1,2 Johnson hit into a double play, Jackson to Frisch to Terry.
  McNeely walked.
3 Harris popped to short.

4th Inning
New York
1 Youngs struck out.
2 Kelly struck out.
  Terry homered into the left field stands.
3 Wilson struck out again.
Washington
1 Rice flied to short center.
2 Goslin grounded to second.
  Judge singled to right.
3 Bluege grounded to third.

5th Inning
New York
1 Jackson also struck out.
  Gowdy singled to right-center.
2 Nehf forced Gowdy at second, Harris to Peckinpaugh.
3 Lindstrom flied to center.
Washington
1 Peckinpaugh fouled to Terry.
2 Ruel flied to left.
3 Johnson grounded to short.

6th Inning
New York
  Frisch walked.
1 Youngs struck out for the third time.
2 Kelly flied to left.
3 Terry fouled to Ruel near third.
Washington
  McNeely doubled down the left field foul line.
1 Harris grounded to short, McNeely going to third.
2 Rice grounded to second, McNeely scoring. Goslin beat out a hit to second.
3 Goslin caught stealing, Gowdy to Frisch.

7th Inning
New York
  Wilson singled over first.
1,2 Jackson hit into a double play, Bluege to Harris to Judge.
  Gowdy walked.
  Nehf singled to right, Gowdy to second. Both advanced on a wild pitch.
3 Lindstrom grounded to short.

7th Inning (continued)
Washington
1 Judge flied to right.
2 Bluege bounced back to the mound. Peckinpaugh singled through third. Peckinpaugh stole second. Ruel walked.
3 Johnson lined to second.

8th Inning
New York
1 Frisch popped to short. Youngs doubled down the third base line.
2 Kelly grounded to short, Youngs going to third. Terry intentionally passed.
3 Youngs out on an attempted double steal, Ruel to Bluege.
Washington
1 McNeely rolled to short.
2 Harris flied to deep left. Rice walked. Rice stole second.
3 Goslin called out on strikes.

9th Inning
New York
  Wilson singled to right.
1 Jackson sacrificed, Bluege to Judge.
2 Gowdy struck out. Nehf singled to right, but Wilson out
3 at the plate, Rice to Ruel.
Washington
1 Judge called out on strikes. Bluege singled off Jackson's glove. Peckinpaugh doubled off the left field wall, scoring Bluege.
2 Ruel grounded to short, Peckinpaugh taking third.
3 Johnson flied to center.

10th Inning
New York
1 Lindstrom struck out. Frisch singled to left.
2 Youngs popped to second. Frisch stole second.
3 Kelly struck out.
Washington
1 McNeely grounded to third. Harris singled through third. Rice singled to right, Harris stopping at second.
2 Goslin popped to short.
3 Judge flied to deep right.

11th Inning
New York
1 Terry flied to center.
2 Wilson called out on strikes.
3 Jackson grounded to short.
Washington
1 Bluege flied to center.
2 Peckinpaugh fouled to Gowdy.
3 Ruel grounded back to the mound.

12th Inning
New York
  Gowdy walked.
  Nehf singled to center, Gowdy took third and Nehf second on McNeely's wild throw to second.
  Bentley, batting for Lindstrom, walked loading the bases.
  Southworth ran for Bentley.
1 Frisch forced Gowdy at the plate, Harris to Ruel. Youngs singled to center, Nehf scoring.
2 Kelly flied to left, Southworth scoring after, the catch. Terry singled, again loading the bases.
3 Wilson flied to left.
Washington
  For New York—Kelly shifts to second, Frisch shifts to third, and Southworth playing center.
  Shirley, batting for Johnson, safely to second as Jackson muffed his fly.
1 McNeely flied to center. Harris singled to center, scoring Shirley. Rice singled to center, Harris going
2 to third, but Rice out trying for a double, Southworth to Kelly.
3 Goslin grounded to Kelly who made a great bare-handed stop.

Game 2 October 5 at Washington

N.Y.	000	000	102
Was.	200	010	001

New York	Pos	AB	R	H	RBI	PO	A	E
Lindstrom	3b	3	0	1	0	0	7	0
Frisch	2b	3	1	1	0	2	2	0
Youngs	rf	4	0	1	0	0	0	0
Kelly	1b	3	2	1	1	14	1	0
Meusel	lf	4	0	1	0	1	0	0
Wilson	cf	4	0	1	1	0	0	0
Jackson	ss	4	0	0	0	1	2	0
Gowdy	c	3	0	0	0	6	2	0
Bentley	p	3	0	0	0	1	2	0
Totals		31	3	6	2	*25	16	0

Washington	Pos	AB	R	H	RBI	PO	A	E
McNeely	cf	4	0	0	0	0	0	0
Harris	2b	3	1	1	1	3	5	1
Rice	rf	3	1	2	0	4	0	0
Goslin	lf	4	1	1	2	1	0	0
Judge	1b	2	1	1	0	15	0	0
Bluege	3b	3	0	0	0	0	5	0
Peckinpaugh	ss	4	0	1	1	2	6	0
Ruel	c	3	0	0	0	1	0	0
Zachery	p	2	0	0	0	1	2	0
Marberry	p	0	0	0	0	0	0	0
Totals		28	4	6	4	27	18	1

* One out when winning run scored.

Pitching	IP	H	R	ER	BB	SO
New York						
Bentley (L)	8⅓	6	4	4	4	6
Washington						
Zachary (W)	8⅔	6	3	3	3	0
Marberry (SV)	⅓	0	0	0	0	1

Double—Peckinpaugh. Home Runs—Goslin, Harris. Stolen Base—Rice. Sacrifice Hits—Bluege, Rice. Double Plays—Bluege to Harris to Judge 2, Harris to Peckinpaugh to Judge. Passed Ball—Gowdy. Left on Bases—New York 4, Washington 5. Umpires—Klem, Dinneen, Quigley, Connolly. Attendance—35,922. Time of Game—1:58.

1st Inning
New York
Lindstrom singled to right-center.
Frisch singled to center, Lindstrom stopping at second.
1 Youngs popped to Zachary on a bunt attempt.
Kelly safe when Harris threw his grounder high to Peckinpaugh, loading the bases.
2,3 Meusel grounded into a double play, Bluege to Harris to Judge.
Washington
1 McNeely grounded to third.
2 Harris grounded to second.
Rice singled over second.
Rice stole second.
Goslin hit a two-run homer into the right field bleachers.
Judge beat out a slow roller to first.
3 Bluege forced Judge at second, Lindstrom to Frisch.

2nd Inning
New York
1 Wilson grounded to second.
2 Jackson grounded to short.
3 Gowdy grounded to third.
Washington
1 Peckinpaugh grounded to third.
2 Ruel bounced out, Gowdy to Kelly.
Zachary walked.
3 McNeely fouled to Gowdy.

3rd Inning
New York
1 Bentley flied to right.
2 Lindstrom grounded to short.
3 Frisch flied to right.
Washington
Harris walked.
1 Rice sacrificed, Lindstrom to Kelly.
2 Goslin struck out but had to be thrown out by Gowdy as Harris took third.
Judge walked.
3 Judge was caught going to second, Bentley to Frisch.

4th Inning
New York
Youngs singled to right.
1,2 Kelly grounded into a double play, Harris to Peckinpaugh to Judge.
3 Meusel flied to right.
Washington
1 Bluege grounded to Lindstrom making a pretty glove-handed stop.
2 Peckinpaugh popped to Jackson behind third.
3 Ruel took a called third strike.

5th Inning
New York
1 Wilson grounded back to the mound.
2 Jackson grounded to short.
3 Gowdy grounded to third.
Washington
1 Zachary called out on strikes.
2 McNeely grounded to short.
Harris homered into the left field bleachers.
Rice singled to center.
3 Goslin struck out.

6th Inning
New York
1 Bentley grounded to third.
Lindstrom walked.
2 Frisch flied to right.
3 Youngs popped to second.
Washington
1 Judge grounded to first.
2 Bluege struck out.
3 Peckinpaugh grounded to short.

7th Inning
New York
Kelly walked.
Meusel singled through short, Kelly going to third.
1,2 Wilson bounced into a double play, Bluege to Harris to Judge, Kelly scoring.
3 Jackson flied to left.
Washington
1 Ruel flied to left.
2 Zachary called out on strikes.
3 McNeely grounded to third.

8th Inning
New York
1 Gowdy grounded to short.
2 Bentley bounced back to the mound.
3 Lindstrom grounded to short.
Washington
1 Harris grounded to Lindstrom who raced over in front of Jackson to make the play.
2 Rice rolled out, Kelly to Bentley.
3 Goslin grounded to second.

9th Inning
New York
Frisch walked on four pitches.
1 Youngs popped to short.
Kelly singled to right, Frisch scoring on a very close play
2 Meusel grounded to Harris on a great fielding gem, Kelly taking second.
Wilson singled to right, scoring Kelly with the tying run. Wilson took second on the play at the plate.
For Washington—Marberry relieved Zachary.
3 Jackson struck out.
Washington
Judge walked.
1 Bluege sacrificed Judge to second, Bentley to Kelly.
Peckinpaugh doubled past Lindstrom, scoring Judge with the game-winning run.

Game 3 October 6 at New York

Was.	000	200	011
N.Y.	021	101	01x

Washington	Pos	AB	R	H	RBI	PO	A	E
Leibold	cf	4	0	0	0	2	0	0
Harris	2b	5	1	1	0	2	4	1
Rice	rf	3	1	1	0	1	0	0
Goslin	lf	5	0	1	0	3	1	0
Judge	1b	5	1	3	0	5	0	0
Bluege	3b-ss	3	1	1	0	2	2	0
Peckinpaugh	ss	1	0	0	0	0	0	0
Miller	3b	2	0	1	1	2	0	1
Ruel	c	3	0	0	0	7	0	0
Marberry	p	1	0	0	0	0	1	0
a Tate		0	0	0	1	0	0	0
Russell	p	0	0	0	0	0	1	0
b McNeely		1	0	0	0	0	0	0
Martina	p	0	0	0	0	0	0	0
c Shirley		1	0	1	1	0	0	0
Speece	p	0	0	0	0	0	2	0
Totals		34	4	9	3	24	11	2

a Walked for Marberry in 4th.
b Flied out for Russell in 7th.
c Singled for Martina in 8th.

New York	Pos	AB	R	H	RBI	PO	A	E
Lindstrom	3b	4	0	1	1	3	1	0
Frisch	2b	4	0	2	0	4	6	0
Youngs	rf	4	0	1	0	2	0	0
Kelly	cf	4	1	2	0	2	0	0
Southworth	cf	0	0	0	0	0	0	0
Terry	1b	4	1	2	0	10	0	0
Wilson	lf	4	0	0	0	4	0	0
Jackson	ss	4	2	1	0	0	1	0
Gowdy	c	4	1	2	2	2	0	0
McQuillan	p	0	0	0	0	0	2	0
Ryan	p	2	1	1	1	0	0	0
Jonnard	p	0	0	0	0	0	0	0
Watson	p	0	0	0	0	0	0	0
Totals		34	6	12	4	27	10	0

Pitching	IP	H	R	ER	BB	SO
Washington						
Marberry (L)	3	5	3	1	2	4
Russell	3	4	2	1	0	0
Martina	1	0	0	0	0	1
Speece	1	3	1	1	0	0
New York						
McQuillan (W)	3⅔	2	2	2	5	0
Ryan	4⅔	7	2	2	3	2
Jonnard	*0	0	0	0	1	0
Watson (SV)	⅔	0	0	0	0	0

*Pitched to one batter in 9th.

Doubles—Judge, Lindstrom. Home Run—Ryan. Stolen Base—Jackson. Sacrifice Hits—Miller, Ryan. Double Plays—McQuillan to Frisch to Terry, Marberry to Bluege to Harris to Judge. Hit by Pitcher—Frisch (by Marberry). Wild Pitch—Marberry. Left on Bases—Washington 13, New York 8. Umpires—Dinneen, Quigley, Connolly, Klem. Attendance—47,608. Time of Game—2:25.

1st Inning
Washington
1 Leibold grounded to second.
2 Harris flied to right.
Rice walked.
3 Goslin grounded to second.
New York
1 Lindstrom took a called third strike.
2 Frisch flied to left.
Youngs singled beyond short.
3 Kelly grounded to second.

2nd Inning
Washington
Judge singled to the left of second base.
1,2 Bluege bounced into a double play, McQuillan to Frisch to Terry.
3 Peckinpaugh grounded to third.
New York
Terry singled to right.
1 Wilson struck out.
Jackson, safe at first as Harris dropped Bluege's throw for the force out.
Gowdy singled to left, scoring Terry with Jackson going to third as Gowdy
2 was run down trying for second, Goslin to Bluege to Harris, to Bluege.
Jackson scored on a wild pitch.
McQuillan walked.
Lindstrom walked.
Frisch hit by a pitch.
3 Youngs called out on strikes.

3rd Inning
Washington
Ruel walked.
1 Marberry forced Ruel, McQuillan to Frisch.
2 Leibold flied to left.
3 Harris fouled to Terry.
New York
For Washington—Miller playing third as Bluege moves to short.
Kelly singled to center.
Terry singled to right, Kelly to third.
1,2 Wilson hit into a double play, off Marberry to Bluege to Harris to Judge, as Kelly scored.
3 Jackson struck out.

4th Inning
Washington
Rice walked.
1 Goslin flied to Frisch in short center.
Judge doubled to left, Rice to third.
Bluege walked, loading the bases.
2 Miller flied to left, Rice scoring after the catch.
Ruel walked, again loading the bases.
For New York—Ryan pitching.
Tate, batting for Marberry, walked forcing in Judge.
3 Leibold flied to left.
New York
For Washington—Russell now pitching.
1 Gowdy flied to center.
Ryan homered into the right field stands.
2 Lindstrom flied to Rice making a great catch against the right field wall.
Frisch singled to center.
3 Youngs flied to left.

5th Inning
Washington
1 Harris flied to center.
2 Rice grounded to second.
3 Goslin robbed of a hit as Frisch got his Texas League pop in right.
New York
Kelly singled to left.
1 Terry popped to short.
2 Wilson forced Kelly at second, Harris unassisted,
3 Jackson popped to third.

6th Inning
Washington
1 Judge flied to center.
2 Bluege struck out.
Miller beat out a hard smash to short.
3 Ruel flied to short right.
New York
Gowdy safe as his grounder got through Miller for an error.
1 Ryan sacrificed Gowdy to second, Russell to Judge.
Lindstrom doubled along the right field foul line, scoring Gowdy.
2 Frisch fouled to Miller.
3 Youngs grounded to second.

7th Inning
Washington
1 McNeely, pinch-hitting for Russell, flied to left.
Leibold walked on a full count.
2 Harris took a called third strike.
Rice singled towards second, advancing Leibold to second.
3 Goslin grounded to Frisch who made a marvelous stop.
New York
For Washington—Martina pitching
1 Kelly took a called third strike.
2 Terry fouled to Ruel making a nice catch in front of the Giant dugout.
3 Wilson flied to left.

8th Inning
Washington
1 Judge grounded to first.
Bluege singled to left.
Miller walked.
2 Ruel grounded to short, Bluege going to third and Miller to second.
Shirley, pinch-hitting for Martina, singled to Lindstrom as he raced in front of Jackson and was unable to make a play. Bluege scored and Miller went to third.
3 Leibold grounded to second.
New York
For Washington—Speece now pitching.
Jackson beat out a roller towards third.
Jackson stole second.
Gowdy singled to right with Jackson stopping at third.
1 Ryan grounded back to the pitcher, Jackson scoring and Gowdy going to second.
2 Lindstrom flied to center, Gowdy going to third after the catch.
Frisch credited with a hit on a perfect bunt to third which Speece
3 pounced on and threw to Ruel getting Gowdy at the plate. Frisch got the hit since he would have beaten it out and Gowdy was not forced to run.

9th Inning
Washington
Harris singled on a Texas League blooper to center.
1 Rice popped to third.
Goslin beat out a bunt fielded by Ryan as Harris went to second.
Judge singled to right, loading the bases.
For New York—Jonnard pitching and Southworth playing center.
Bluege walked, forcing, in Harris.
For New York—Watson replaced Jonnard on the mound.
2 Miller fouled to Lindstrom.
3 Ruel forced Judge at third, Lindstrom unassisted, Lindstrom made all three putouts for the inning.

Game 4 October 7 at New York

Washington	Pos	AB	R	H	RBI	PO	A	E
McNeely	cf	5	2	3	0	3	0	0
Harris	2b	5	2	2	0	2	8	0
Rice	rf	5	0	0	0	1	1	1
Goslin	lf	4	2	4	4	3	0	0
Judge	1b	4	1	1	0	11	1	0
Bluege	ss	4	0	3	2	2	3	1
Ruel	c	3	0	0	0	5	0	0
Miller	3b	4	0	0	0	0	2	1
Mogridge	p	4	0	0	0	0	0	0
Marberry	p	0	0	0	0	0	0	0
Totals		38	7	13	6	27	15	3

Pitching	IP	H	R	ER	BB	SO
Washington						
Mogridge (W)	$7\frac{1}{3}$	3	3	2	5	2
Marberry (SV)	$1\frac{2}{3}$	3	1	0	1	2
New York						
Barnes (L)	5	9	5	5	0	3
Baldwin	2	1	0	0	0	1
Dean	2	3	2	1	0	2

Was.	003	020	020
N.Y.	100	001	011

New York	Pos	AB	R	H	RBI	PO	A	E
Lindstrom	3b	4	1	3	1	1	2	0
Frisch	2b	4	0	0	0	3	3	0
Youngs	rf	4	1	0	1	0	0	0
Kelly	1b	5	1	1	0	11	1	0
Meusel	lf	2	0	0	0	2	0	1
Wilson	cf	4	0	1	2	3	0	0
Jackson	ss	4	0	0	0	0	3	0
Gowdy	c	4	1	1	0	6	1	0
Barnes	p	0	0	0	0	1	1	0
a Terry		1	0	0	0	0	0	0
Baldwin	p	0	0	0	0	0	0	0
b Southworth		1	0	0	0	0	0	0
Dean	p	0	0	0	0	0	0	0
c Bentley		1	0	0	0	0	0	0
Totals		34	4	6	4	27	11	1

a Grounded out for Barnes in 5th.
b Safe on error for Baldwin in 7th.
c Struck out for Dean in 9th.

Doubles—Kelly, McNeely, Wilson. Home Run—Goslin. Sacrifice Hit—Ruel. Wild Pitch—Barnes. Left on Bases—Washington 5, New York 9. Umpires—Quigley, Connolly, Klem, Dinneen. Attendance—49,243. Time of Game—2:10.

1st Inning
Washington
1 McNeely grounded to short.
2 Harris called out on strikes.
3 Rice grounded to second.
New York
Lindstrom walked.
1 Frisch bounced to second, Lindstrom going to second.
Youngs was safe at first as Bluege threw his grounder wildly past Judge, Lindstrom scoring.
2 Kelly flied to center, Youngs racing to second after the catch.
Meusel walked on a full count.
3 Wilson out on a slow roller to second.

2nd Inning
Washington
Goslin singled past second.
1 Judge popped to Kelly.
Bluege beat out a roller to third, Goslin going to second.
2 Ruel grounded to third, advancing both runners.
3 Miller grounded to third.
New York
1 Jackson flied to center.
2 Gowdy grounded to second.
Barnes walked.
Lindstrom singled to right, Barnes going to second.
3 Frisch popped to second.

3rd Inning
Washington
1 Mogridge struck out.
McNeely singled to left.
Harris singled to right, McNeely stopping at second.
2 Rice grounded to deep second, both runners moving up.
Goslin blasted the first pitch for a three-run homer into the lower tier of the right field grandstand.
3 Judge grounded out, Kelly to Barnes.
New York
1 Youngs took a called third strike.
2 Kelly also called out on strikes.
3 Meusel flied to left.

4th Inning
Washington
Bluege singled to left.
1 Ruel sacrificed Bluege to second, Barnes to Kelly.
2 Miller flied to left.
3 Mogridge called out on strikes.
New York
1 Wilson flied to left.
2 Jackson grounded to third.
3 Gowdy flied to left.

5th Inning
Washington
McNeely singled to left.
Harris singled to left, McNeely racing to third.
McNeely scored and Harris went to second on a wild pitch by Barnes.
1 Rice popped to Lindstrom near the pitcher's box.
Goslin got his third hit, a single to left, scoring Harris.
2 Judge flied to center.
3 Goslin caught trying to steal second, Gowdy to Frisch.
New York
1 Terry, batting for Barnes, bounced to second.
Lindstrom beat out a bunt toward third.
2 Frisch flied to right.
3 Youngs forced Lindstrom at second, Harris unassisted.

6th Inning
Washington
For New York—Baldwin came into pitch.
1 Bluege popped to second.
2 Ruel grounded to short.
3 Miller flied to center.
New York
Kelly doubled to deep right-center.
1 Meusel grounded to short, Kelly going to third.
2 Wilson also grounded to short, scoring Kelly.
3 Jackson also grounded to short.

7th Inning
Washington
1 Mogridge struck out for the third time.
McNeely's third hit of the game was a double to left-center.
2 Harris flied to center, McNeely racing to third after the catch.
3 Rice flied to left.
New York
1 Gowdy grounded to Harris, making a great stop and throw.
Southworth, pinch-hitting for Baldwin, reached first when Miller fumbled his bunt.
2 Lindstrom forced Southworth at second, Miller to Harris.
3 Frisch bounced to second.

8th Inning
Washington
For New York—Dean pitching.
Goslin singled to left-center for his **fourth hit of the game.**
Judge singled to left and got to second and Goslin to third on Meusel's fumble.
Bluege singled to center, scoring Goslin and Judge. Bluege taking second on the throw to the plate.
1 Ruel fouled to Kelly.
2 Miller popped to second.
3 Mogridge struck out **for the fourth time.**
New York
Youngs walked on four pitches.
1 Kelly flied to center.
Meusel walked on four pitches.
For Washington—Marberry replaced Mogridge with a 2–0 count to Wilson.
Wilson doubled to right, Youngs scoring
2 with Meusel out also trying to score, Rice to Harris to Ruel.
3 Jackson grounded to first.

9th Inning
Washington
1 McNeely struck out.
2 Harris grounded to short.
3 Rice grounded to second.
New York
Gowdy blooped a single just inside the right field foul line. Rice threw the ball back to first and it hit the bag and rolled to the grandstand, Gowdy going all the way to third.
1 Bentley, pinch-hitting for Dean, struck out.
Lindstrom beat out a bouncer to second, his third hit, scoring Gowdy.
Frisch walked.
2 Youngs forced Frisch at second, Judge to Harris as Lindstrom went to third.
3 Kelly struck out on three pitches.

Game 5 October 8 at New York

Washington	Pos	AB	R	H	RBI	PO	A	E
McNeely	cf	4	0	1	0	1	0	0
Harris	2b	5	0	1	0	8	2	0
Rice	rf	4	0	0	0	1	2	0
Goslin	lf	4	1	2	1	1	0	0
Judge	1b	4	1	3	0	3	2	0
Bluege	ss	3	0	0	0	0	2	0
Ruel	c	2	0	0	0	6	2	0
Miller	3b	3	0	1	1	3	1	0
a Leibold		1	0	0	0	0	0	0
Johnson	p	3	0	1	0	1	2	1
b Tate		0	0	0	0	0	0	0
c Taylor		0	0	0	0	0	0	0
Totals		33	2	9	2	24	13	1

a Flied out for Miller in 9th.
b Walked for Johnson in 9th.
c Ran for Tate in 9th.

Double—Frisch. Triple—Terry. Home Runs—Bentley, Goslin. Sacrifice Hits—Bluege, Jackson, Wilson. Double Plays—Rice to Johnson to Ruel, Bluege to Harris to Judge. Hit by Pitcher—Youngs (by Johnson). Left on Bases—Washington 9, New York 8. Umpires—Connolly, Klem, Dinneen, Quigley. Attendance—49,271. Time of Game—2:30.

Was.	000	100	010
N.Y.	001	020	03x

New York	Pos	AB	R	H	RBI	PO	A	E
Lindstrom	3b	5	0	4	2	1	1	0
Frisch	2b	5	0	1	0	1	6	0
Youngs	rf	3	0	1	0	1	1	0
Kelly	cf	4	1	1	0	2	0	0
Terry	1b	2	1	1	0	12	1	0
Wilson	lf	3	0	0	0	3	1	0
Jackson	ss	3	1	1	1	1	2	0
Gowdy	c	4	2	1	0	6	0	0
Bentley	p	3	1	2	2	0	1	0
McQuillan	p	1	0	1	1	0	0	0
Totals		33	6	13	6	27	13	0

Pitching	IP	H	R	ER	BB	SO
Washington						
Johnson (L)	8	13	6	3	2	3
New York						
Bentley (W)	$7\frac{1}{3}$	9	2	2	3	4
McQuillan (SV)	$1\frac{2}{3}$	0	0	0	1	1

1st Inning
Washington
1 McNeely robbed of a hit by a fantastic leaping catch by Lindstrom of his high liner.
2 Harris flied to deep left.
3 Rice popped to first.
New York
Lindstrom singled to left.
1 Frisch fouled to Miller.
2 Youngs flied to center.
3 Lindstrom caught attempting to steal second, Ruel to Harris.

2nd Inning
Washington
Goslin beat out an infield hit to first.
1 Judge flied to left.
Bluege popped behind first but Terry
2 dropped the ball. Frisch pounced on it and threw to Jackson forcing Goslin at second and saving Terry an error.
3 Miller grounded to second.
New York
1 Kelly fouled to Miller.
2 Terry grounded to first.
3 Wilson fouled to Judge.

3rd Inning
Washington
Johnson singled against the left field wall but fell after rounding first
1 and was out Wilson to Frisch to Judge.
McNeely beat out a bunt to third.
Harris beat out a hit to first, McNeely going to second.
2 Rice popped to Gowdy, in front of the plate.
3 Goslin grounded to second.
New York
Jackson beat out a slow roller to short.
1 Gowdy struck out on a 3–2 count.
Bentley singled to right, Jackson racing to third.
Lindstrom beat out a roller to third, scoring Jackson as Bentley went to second.
Frisch safe on a fielder's choice as Bluege took his grounder and threw to Miller who missed getting Bentley at third, loading the bases.
2,3 Youngs lined to Rice in right and Bentley was doubled up trying to score, Rice to Johnson to Ruel.

4th Inning
Washington
Judge singled off the right field wall.
1 Bluege sacrificed Judge to second, Bentley to Terry.
2 Ruel grounded to short, Judge going to third.
Miller singled along the right field
3 foul line, scoring Judge but was out trying for second, Youngs to Frisch.
New York
1 Kelly struck out.
Terry tripled to deep right.
Wilson bounced to the mound and Terry
2 was out in a run-down. Johnson getting the assist and Miller the putout.
Wilson meanwhile got to second.
3 Jackson popped to short.

5th Inning
Washington
1 Johnson grounded to short.
2 McNeely popped to first.
3 Harris struck out.
New York
Gowdy singled to right.
Bentley hit a two-run homer into the upper tier of the right field stands.
1 Lindstrom fouled to Ruel.
Frisch doubled to center.
Youngs was hit by a pitch.
2,3 Kelly grounded into a double play, Bluege to Harris to Judge.

6th Inning
Washington
1 Rice struck out.
2 Goslin struck out on three pitches.
Judge singled to right.
3 Bluege struck out on three pitches.
New York
Terry walked.
1 Wilson struck out.
Jackson hit a fly to center but McNeely lost it in the wind. Terry holding since he thought it would be
2 caught was out at second, Rice to Harris.
3 Gowdy popped to second.

7th Inning
Washington
Ruel walked.
1 Miller grounded to first, Ruel going to second.
2 Johnson flied to short center.
McNeely walked.
3 Harris flied to deep right.
New York
1 Bentley grounded out, Judge to Johnson.
Lindstrom singled to center.
2 Frisch popped to second.
Youngs singled over Judge's head, Lindstrom racing to third.
3 **Lindstrom was out at the plate on an attempted double steal Ruel to Harris to Judge to Harris to Ruel.**

8th Inning
Washington
1 Rice rolled out to second.
Goslin hit his third homer of the Series against the upper tier of the right field grandstand.
Judge singled to right.
For New York—McQuillan relieved Bentley.
2 Bluege grounded to second.
3 Ruel grounded to third.
New York
Kelly singled to left.
Terry walked.
Wilson safe as Johnson fumbled his bunt, loading the bases.
1 Jackson flied to left, Kelly scoring after the catch.
2 Gowdy forced Wilson at second, Miller to Harris, Terry going to third.
McQuillan blooped a single into short left, scoring Terry with Gowdy stopping at second.
Lindstrom singled to left, Gowdy scoring with McQuillan stopping at second. **His fourth hit in the game.**
3 Frisch forced Lindstrom at second, Bluege to Harris.

9th Inning
Washington
1 Leibold, pinch-hitting for Miller, flied to center.
Tate, pinch-hitting for Johnson, walked.
Taylor ran for Tate.
Taylor went to second, unmolested.
2 McNeely struck out.
3 Harris flied to left.

Game 6 October 9 at Washington

New York	Pos	AB	R	H	RBI	PO	A	E
Lindstrom	3b	4	0	0	0	1	1	0
Frisch	2b	4	0	2	0	1	2	0
Youngs	rf	4	1	0	0	1	0	0
Kelly	1b	4	0	2	1	11	1	1
b Southworth		0	0	0	0	0	0	0
Meusel	lf	4	0	0	0	1	0	0
Wilson	cf	4	0	2	0	1	0	0
Jackson	ss	3	0	0	0	3	2	0
Gowdy	c	3	0	1	0	5	1	0
Nehf	p	2	0	0	0	0	4	0
a Snyder		1	0	0	0	0	0	0
Ryan	p	0	0	0	0	0	1	0
Totals		33	1	7	1	24	12	1

a Flied out for Nehf in 8th.
b Ran for Kelly in 9th.

Doubles—Frisch 2. Stolen Bases—Bluege, McNeely. Sacrifice Hit—Ruel. Double Play—Harris to Peckinpaugh to Judge. Left on Bases—New York 5, Washington 7. Umpires—Klem, Dinneen, Quigley, Connolly. Attendance—34,254. Time of Game—1:57.

N.Y.   1 0 0   0 0 0   0 0 0
Was.   0 0 0   0 2 0   0 0 0

Washington	Pos	AB	R	H	RBI	PO	A	E
McNeely	cf	2	1	0	0	1	0	0
Harris	2b	4	0	1	2	4	5	0
Rice	rf	4	0	1	0	4	0	0
Goslin	lf	4	0	0	0	1	0	0
Judge	1b	3	0	0	0	11	0	0
Bluege	3b-ss	3	0	0	1	3	0	0
Peckinpaugh	ss	2	1	2	0	1	4	0
Taylor	3b	0	0	0	0	0	0	0
Ruel	c	2	0	0	0	4	1	0
Zachary	p	3	0	0	0	0	2	0
Totals		27	2	4	2	27	15	0

Pitching	IP	H	R	ER	BB	SO
New York						
Nehf (L)	7	4	2	2	4	4
Ryan	2	0	0	0	1	1
Washington						
Zachary (W)	9	7	1	1	0	3

1st Inning
New York
1 Lindstrom bunted out to third.
Frisch doubled down the right field foul line.
Youngs bounced to the mound and Frisch
2 was run-down between second and third, Zachary to Bluege to Harris. Youngs got to second on the play.
Kelly singled to center, scoring Youngs.
3 Meusel flied to Rice, making a nice one-handed catch.
Washington
McNeely walked on four pitches.
1 Harris forced McNeely at second, Lindstrom to Frisch.
2 Harris was picked off, Nehf to Kelly to Jackson.
Rice singled to right.
Goslin safe at first on Kelly's fumble, Rice going to second.
3 Judge struck out on three pitches.

2nd Inning
New York
1 Wilson struck out.
2 Jackson grounded to second.
Gowdy blooped a single into short left-center.
3 Nehf flied to center.
Washington
1 Bluege grounded to second.
Peckinpaugh singled off Lindstrom's shoe.
2 Ruel flied to left.
3 Zachary took a called third strike.

3rd Inning
New York
1 Lindstrom lined to right.
Frisch again doubled down the right field line.
2 Youngs grounded to second, Frisch going to third.
3 Kelly grounded to third.
Washington
1 McNeely popped to short.
2 Harris grounded to short.
3 Rice fouled to Lindstrom.

4th Inning
New York
1 Meusel grounded to short.
Wilson singled to right.
2,3 Jackson hit into a double play, Harris to Peckinpaugh to Judge.
Washington
1 Goslin flied to right.
2 Judge popped to short.
3 Bluege grounded to short.

5th Inning
New York
1 Gowdy grounded to short.
2 Nehf flied to Rice racing in to make a great catch in short right.
3 Lindstrom bounced back to the mound.
Washington
Peckinpaugh singled to left.
1 Ruel sacrificed, Nehf to Kelly.
2 Zachary grounded to first, Peckinpaugh going to third.
McNeely walked on four pitches.
McNeely stole second.
Harris singled to right, Peckinpaugh and McNeely scoring, and going to second on the throw to the plate.
3 Rice called out on strikes.

6th Inning
New York
1 Frisch fouled to Ruel.
2 Youngs tapped out, Ruel to Judge.
3 Kelly grounded to second.
Washington
1 Goslin struck out on three pitches.
2 Judge rolled out to the mound.
Bluege walked.
Bluege stole second.
Peckinpaugh walked.
3 Ruel bounced back to the mound.

7th Inning
New York
1 Meusel flied to Harris in short right.
Wilson lined a single to right, Rice just missing a shoe-string catch.
2 Jackson flied to left.
3 Gowdy popped to second.
Washington
1 Zachary bunted out, Gowdy to Kelly.
2 McNeely fouled to Kelly.
3 Harris flied to center.

8th Inning
New York
1 Snyder, batting for Nehf, flied to right.
2 Lindstrom struck out.
3 Frisch grounded to second.
Washington
For New York—Ryan now pitching.
1 Rice grounded to second.
2 Goslin called out on strikes.
Judge walked on four pitches.
3 Bluege rolled out to the mound.

9th Inning
New York
1 Youngs popped to third.
Kelly singled past first.
Southworth ran for Kelly.
2 Meusel forced Southworth at second, Peckinpaugh to Harris.
For Washington—Peckinpaugh's leg again went out and Bluege moved to short as Taylor came in to play third.
3 Wilson struck out.

Game 7 October 10 at Washington

N.Y. 000 003 000 000
Was. 000 100 020 001

New York	Pos	AB	R	H	RBI	PO	A	E
Lindstrom	3b	5	0	1	0	0	3	0
Frisch	2b	5	0	2	0	3	4	0
Youngs	rf-lf	2	1	0	0	2	0	0
Kelly	cf-1b	6	1	1	0	8	1	0
Terry	1b	2	0	0	0	6	1	0
a Meusel	lf-rf	3	0	1	1	1	0	0
Wilson	lf-cf	5	1	1	0	4	0	0
Jackson	ss	6	0	0	0	1	4	2
Gowdy	c	6	0	1	0	8	0	1
Barnes	p	4	0	0	0	1	2	0
Nehf	p	0	0	0	0	0	0	0
McQuillan	p	0	0	0	0	0	0	0
e Groh		1	0	1	0	0	0	0
f Southworth		0	0	0	0	0	0	0
Bentley	p	0	0	0	0	0	0	0
Totals		45	3	8	1	x34	15	3

Pitching	IP	H	R	ER	BB	SO
New York						
Barnes	7⅔	6	3	3	1	6
Nehf	⅓	1	0	0	0	0
McQuillan	1⅔	0	0	0	0	1
Bentley (L)	1⅓	3	1	1	1	0
Washington						
Ogden	⅓	0	0	0	1	1
Mogridge	*4⅓	4	2	1	1	3
Marberry	3	1	1	0	1	3
Johnson (W)	4	3	0	0	3	5

*Pitched to two batters in 6th.

Washington	Pos	AB	R	H	RBI	PO	A	E
McNeely	cf	6	0	1	1	0	0	0
Harris	2b	5	1	3	3	4	1	0
Rice	rf	5	0	0	0	2	0	0
Goslin	lf	5	0	2	0	3	0	0
Judge	1b	4	0	1	0	11	1	1
Bluege	ss	5	0	0	0	1	7	2
Taylor	3b	2	0	0	0	0	3	1
b Leibold		1	1	1	0	0	0	0
Miller	3b	2	0	0	0	1	1	0
Ruel	c	5	2	2	0	13	0	0
Ogden	p	0	0	0	0	0	0	0
Mogridge	p	1	0	0	0	0	0	0
Marberry	p	1	0	0	0	1	0	0
c Tate		0	0	0	0	0	0	0
d Shirley		0	0	0	0	0	0	0
Johnson	p	2	0	0	0	0	1	0
Totals		44	4	10	4	36	14	4

x One out when winning run scored.
a Flied out for Terry in 6th.
b Doubled for Taylor in 8th.
c Walked for Marberry in 8th.
d Ran for Tate in 8th.
e Singled for McQuillan in 11th.
f Ran for Groh in 11th.

Doubles—Goslin, Leibold, Lindstrom, McNeely, Ruel. Triple—Frisch. Home Run—Harris. Stolen Base—Youngs. Sacrifice Hits—Lindstrom, Meusel. Double Plays—Kelly to Jackson, Jackson to Frisch to Kelly, Johnson to Bluege to Judge. Left on Bases—New York 10, Washington 8. Umpires—Dinneen, Quigley, Connolly, Klem. Attendance—31,667. Time of Game—3:00.

1st Inning
New York
1 Lindstrom struck out on three pitches.
  Frisch walked.
  For Washington—Mogridge relieved Ogden.
2 Youngs struck out.
3 Kelly grounded to third.
Washington
1 McNeely bounced to third.
2 Harris struck out.
3 Rice grounded to the mound.

2nd Inning
New York
1 Terry grounded to second.
2 Wilson grounded to short.
  Jackson safe at first on Taylor's high, throw to Judge.
  Gowdy singled to left, Jackson stopping at second.
3 Barnes struck out.
Washington
1 Goslin struck out.
2 Judge robbed of a hit as Frisch made a leaping catch of his liner.
3 Bluege grounded to short.

3rd Inning
New York
1 Lindstrom rolled to third.
  Frisch beat out a bunt.
2 Youngs popped to first.
3 Kelly forced Frisch at second, Bluege to Harris.
Washington
1 Taylor struck out.
2 Ruel bounced back to Barnes.
3 Mogridge called out on strikes (the fifth consecutive time Mogridge struck out).

4th Inning
New York
1 Terry called out on strikes.
2 Wilson grounded to short.
3 Jackson grounded to short.
Washington
1 McNeely struck out.
  Harris homered over the left field wall, for the first hit off of Barnes.
2 Rice robbed of a hit by Wilson, with a diving catch.
3 Goslin grounded to first.

5th Inning
New York
1 Gowdy popped to second.
2 Barnes grounded to short.
  Lindstrom doubled over Taylor's head.
3 Frisch flied to left.
Washington
1 Judge grounded out, Terry to Barnes.
2 Bluege grounded to short.
3 Taylor called out on strikes.

6th Inning
New York
  Youngs walked.
  Kelly singled through short, Youngs going to third.
  Meusel, pinch-hitting for Terry.
  For Washington—Marberry now pitching.
1 Meusel flied to right, Youngs scoring after the catch.
  Wilson singled over second, Kelly racing to third.
  Jackson safe at first on Judge's fumble, Kelly scoring and Wilson going to second.
  Gowdy safe at first as Bluege let the ball get through him for an error, Wilson scoring and Jackson going to third.
2 Barnes flied to short right.
3 Lindstrom struck out.
Washington
  For New York—Meusel in left, Kelly moves to first and Wilson to center.
1 Ruel grounded to third.
2 Marberry grounded to third.
3 McNeely flied to right.

7th Inning
New York
1 Frisch fouled to Ruel leaning over the field boxes to make the catch.
  Youngs walked again.
2 Kelly grounded to third, Youngs going to second.
3 Meusel grounded to Marberry who tagged him out on the base line.
Washington
  Harris beat out a hit to deep short.
1,2 Rice hit into a double play, Kelly touching first to Jackson tagging Harris.
  Goslin singled to right.
3 Judge flied to center.

8th Inning
New York
1 Wilson struck out on three pitches.
  Jackson safe on Bluege's fumble.
2 Gowdy flied to left.
3 Barnes struck out.
Washington
1 Bluege fouled to Gowdy.
  Leibold, batting for Taylor, doubled down the third base line.
  Ruel singled off Kelly's glove (his first hit of the Series), Leibold stopping at third.
  Tate, pinch-hitting for Marberry, walked to load the bases.
  Shirley ran for Tate.
2 McNeely flied to left, all runners holding.
  Harris singled over Lindstrom's head, scoring Leibold and Ruel, Shirley stopping at second.
  For New York—Nehf relieved Barnes.
3 Rice grounded to first.

9th Inning
New York
  For Washington—Johnson pitching and Miller playing third.
1 Lindstrom popped to third.
  Frisch tripled to deep center.
  Youngs intentionally passed.
2 Kelly struck out on three pitches.
  Youngs stole second.
3 Meusel grounded to third.
Washington
1 Goslin grounded to second.
  Judge singled to center.
  Bluege safe as Jackson dropped Kelly's throw, Judge getting to third.
  For New York—McQuillan came in to pitch.
2,3 Miller hit into a double play, Jackson to Frisch to Kelly.

10th Inning
New York
  Wilson walked.
1 Jackson called out on strikes.
2,3 Gowdy bounced into a double play, Johnson to Bluege to Judge.
Washington
1 Ruel grounded to second.
2 Johnson flied to Wilson in deep left-center.
3 McNeely struck out.

11th Inning
New York
  Groh, batting for McQuillan, singled to right.
  Southworth ran for Groh.
1 Lindstrom sacrificed, Judge to Harris.
2 Frisch struck out.
  Youngs again intentionally walked, **(his fourth walk in the game).**
3 Kelly again struck out.
Washington
  For New York—Bentley pitching.
1 Harris flied to right.
2 Rice flied to Wilson in deep left-center.
  Goslin dropped a Texas League double into left-center.
  Judge got an intentional walk.
  For New York—Youngs and Meusel exchanged positions.
3 Bluege forced Judge at second, Jackson to Frisch.

12th Inning
New York
  Meusel singled to right.
1 Wilson struck out.
2 Jackson forced Meusel at second, Bluege to Harris.
3 Gowdy flied to left.
Washington
  For New York—Youngs and Meusel returned to their original positions.
1 Miller grounded to second.
  Ruel got a new life, Gowdy dropping his foul fly.
  Ruel doubled past third.
  Johnson safe on Jackson's fumble, Ruel holding second.
  McNeely singled over Lindstrom's head, scoring Ruel with the Series-ending run.

1924 WORLD SERIES COMPOSITE BOX

	Wins	Composite Line Score				
Washington Senators (A.L.)	4	2 0 3	4 5 1	0 6 3	0 0 2	– 26
New York Giants (N.L.)	3	2 4 1	2 2 5	1 5 3	0 0 2	– 27

	Regular Season			
Manager	W	L	Pct.	G. Ahead
Bucky Harris	92	62	.597	2
John McGraw	93	60	.608	1½

BATTING AND FIELDING

WASHINGTON SENATORS

WORLD SERIES STATISTICS

	Pos	G	AB	R	H	2B	3B	HR	RBI	BB	SO	SB	BA	SA	PO	A	E
Joe Judge	1b	7	26	4	10	1	0	0	0	5	2	0	.385	.423	**62**	4	1
Bucky Harris	2b	7	**33**	5	**11**	0	0	2	**7**	1	4	0	.333	.515	26	**28**	2
Roger Peckinpaugh	ss	4	12	1	5	2	0	0	2	1	0	1	.417	.583	7	14	0
Ossie Bluege	3b-ss	7	26	2	5	0	0	0	2	3	4	1	.192	.192	8	24	**3**
Sam Rice	rf	7	29	2	6	0	0	0	1	3	2	**2**	.207	.207	13	4	1
Earl McNeely	cf-ph	7	27	4	6	3	0	0	1	4	4	1	.222	.333	8	0	1
Goose Goslin	lf	7	32	4	**11**	1	0	**3**	**7**	0	7	0	.344	.656	15	1	0
Muddy Ruel	c	7	21	2	2	1	0	0	0	**6**	1	0	.095	.143	51	5	0
Ralph Miller	3b	4	11	0	2	0	0	0	2	1	0	0	.182	.182	6	4	2
Nemo Leibold	cf-ph	3	6	1	1	1	0	0	0	1	0	0	.167	.333	2	0	0
Tommy Taylor	pr-3b	3	2	0	0	0	0	0	0	0	2	0	.000	.000	0	3	1
Mule Shirley	ph-pr	3	2	1	1	0	0	0	1	0	0	0	.500	.500			
Bennie Tate	ph	3	0	0	0	0	0	0	1	3	0	0	—	—			
Showboat Fisher		Did not play															
Pinky Hargrave		Did not play															
Walter Johnson	p	3	9	0	1	0	0	0	0	0	0	0	.111	.111	1	4	1
Tom Zachary	p	2	5	0	0	0	0	0	0	1	3	0	.000	.000	1	4	0
George Mogridge	p	2	5	0	0	0	0	0	0	0	5	0	.000	.000	0	0	0
Firpo Marberry	p	4	2	0	0	0	0	0	0	0	0	0	.000	.000	1	1	0
Allen Russell	p	1	0	0	0	0	0	0	0	0	0	0	—	—	0	1	0
Joe Martina	p	1	0	0	0	0	0	0	0	0	0	0	—	—	0	0	0
By Speece	p	1	0	0	0	0	0	0	0	0	0	0	—	—	0	2	0
Curly Ogden	p	1	0	0	0	0	0	0	0	0	0	0	—	—	0	0	0
Paul Zahniser		Did not play															
team total		7	248	26	61	9	0	5	24	29	34	5	.246	.343	201	99	12

Double Plays–10
Left on Bases–57

REGULAR SEASON STATISTICS

		Main Pos	G	AB	R	H	2B	3B	HR	RBI	BB	SO	SB	BA	SA
Joe Judge		1b	140	516	71	167	38	9	3	79	53	21	13	.324	.450
Bucky Harris		2b	143	544	88	146	28	9	1	58	56	41	19	.268	.358
Roger Peckinpaugh		ss	155	523	72	142	20	5	2	73	72	45	11	.272	.340
Ossie Bluege		3b	117	402	59	113	15	4	2	49	39	36	7	.281	.353
Sam Rice		of	154	**646**	106	**216**	38	14	1	76	46	24	24	.334	.441
Earl McNeely		of	43	179	31	59	5	6	0	15	5	21	3	.330	.425
Goose Goslin		of	154	579	100	199	30	17	12	**129**	68	29	16	.344	.516
Muddy Ruel		c	149	501	50	142	20	2	0	57	62	20	7	.283	.331
Ralph Miller		2b	9	15	1	2	2	1	0	0	1	1	0	.133	.133
Nemo Leibold		of	84	246	41	72	6	4	0	20	42	10	6	.293	.350
Tommy Taylor		3b	26	73	11	19	3	1	0	10	2	8	2	.260	.329
Mule Shirley		1b	30	77	12	18	2	2	0	16	3	7	0	.234	.312
Bennie Tate		c	21	43	2	13	2	0	0	7	1	2	0	.302	.349
Showboat Fisher		of	15	41	7	9	1	0	0	6	6	6	2	.220	.244
Pinky Hargrave		c	24	33	3	5	1	1	0	5	1	4	0	.152	.242
Walter Johnson		p	39	113	18	32	9	0	1	14	3	11	0	.283	.389
Tom Zachary		p	33	72	7	22	1	0	0	8	5	8	0	.306	.319
George Mogridge		p	30	74	7	13	3	0	0	5	2	16	0	.176	.216
Firpo Marberry		p	50	59	6	8	0	1	0	1	0	12	0	.136	.169
Allen Russell		p	37	18	2	5	1	0	0	0	4	10	0	.278	.333
Joe Martina		p	25	43	2	14	2	0	0	6	2	7	0	.326	.372
By Speece		p	21	20	1	3	1	1	0	1	0	5	0	.150	.300
Curly Ogden	a	p	17	47	3	13	2	1	0	6	1	3	0	.277	.362
Paul Zahniser		p	24	30	2	4	0	0	0	2	3	13	0	.133	.133
team total			156	5304	755	1558	255	**88**	22	688	513	392	117	.294	.387

a—from Philadelphia (A)

Carl East (of), Chick Gagnon (ss), Bert Griffith (of), Wade Lefler (of), Wid Matthews (of), Doc Prothro (3b), Lance Richbourg (of), Carr Smith (of), Nick Altrack (p), Slim McGrew (p), Ted Wingfield (p) also played for the Senators during the season.

NEW YORK GIANTS

WORLD SERIES STATISTICS

	Pos	G	AB	R	H	2B	3B	HR	RBI	BB	SO	SB	BA	SA	PO	A	E
Bill Terry	1b-ph	5	14	3	6	0	**1**	1	1	3	1	0	**.429**	**.786**	43	2	0
Frankie Frisch	2b-3b	7	30	1	10	**4**	**1**	0	0	4	1	1	.333	.533	17	26	0
Travis Jackson	ss	7	27	3	2	0	0	0	1	1	4	1	.074	.074	8	20	**3**
Fred Lindstrom	3b	7	30	1	10	2	0	0	4	3	6	0	.333	.400	7	18	0
Ross Youngs	rf-lf	7	27	3	5	1	0	0	2	5	6	1	.185	.222	8	1	0
George Kelly	cf-2b-1b	7	31	**7**	9	1	0	1	4	1	8	0	.290	.419	52	5	1
Hack Wilson	lf-cf	7	30	1	7	1	0	0	3	1	**9**	0	.233	.267	19	1	0
Hank Gowdy	c	7	27	4	7	0	0	0	2	2	2	0	.259	.259	37	5	1
Irish Meusel	lf-rf	4	13	0	2	0	0	0	1	2	0	0	.154	.154	5	0	1
Billy Southworth	pr-cf-ph	5	1	1	0	0	0	0	0	0	0	0	.000	.000	1	1	0
Heinie Groh	ph	1	1	0	1	0	0	0	0	0	0	0	1.000	1.000			
Frank Snyder	ph	1	1	0	0	0	0	0	0	0	0	0	.000	.000			
Jimmy O'Connell		Did not play															
Art Nehf	p	3	7	1	3	0	0	0	0	0	0	0	.429	.429	0	6	0
Jack Bentley	p-ph	5	7	1	2	0	0	1	2	1	1	0	.286	.714	1	3	0
Virgil Barnes	p	2	4	0	0	0	0	0	0	1	2	0	.000	.000	2	3	0
Rosy Ryan	p	2	2	1	1	0	0	1	1	0	0	0	.500	2.000	0	1	0
Hugh McQuillan	p	3	1	0	1	0	0	0	1	1	0	0	1.00	1.000	0	2	0
Harry Baldwin	p	1	0	0	0	0	0	0	0	0	0	0	—	—	0	0	0
Wayland Dean	p	1	0	0	0	0	0	0	0	0	0	0	—	—	0	0	0
Mule Watson	p	1	0	0	0	0	0	0	0	0	0	0	—	—	0	0	0
Claude Jonnard	p	1	0	0	0	0	0	0	0	0	0	0	—	—	0	0	0
Walter Huntzinger		Did not play															
Ernie Maun		Did not play															
team total		7	253	27	66	9	2	4	22	25	40	3	.261	.360	200	94	6

Double Plays–4
Left on Bases–59

REGULAR SEASON STATISTICS

	Main Pos	G	AB	R	H	2B	3B	HR	RBI	BB	SO	SB	BA	SA
Bill Terry	1b	77	163	26	39	7	2	5	24	17	18	1	.239	.399
Frankie Frisch	2b	145	603	**121**	198	33	15	7	69	56	24	22	.328	.468
Travis Jackson	ss	151	596	81	180	26	8	11	76	21	56	6	.302	.428
Fred Lindstrom	2b-3b	52	79	19	20	3	1	0	4	6	10	3	.253	.316
Ross Youngs	of	133	526	112	187	33	12	10	74	77	31	11	.355	.521
George Kelly	1b	144	571	91	185	37	9	21	**136**	38	52	7	.324	.531
Hack Wilson	of	107	383	62	113	19	12	10	57	44	46	4	.295	.486
Hank Gowdy	c	87	191	25	62	9	1	4	37	26	11	1	.325	.445
Irish Meusel	of	139	549	75	170	26	9	6	102	33	18	11	.310	.423
Billy Southworth	of	94	281	40	72	13	0	3	36	32	16	1	.256	.335
Heinie Groh	3b	145	559	82	157	32	3	2	46	52	29	8	.281	.360
Frank Snyder	c	118	354	37	107	18	3	5	53	30	43	3	.302	.412
Jimmy O'Connell	of	52	104	24	33	4	2	2	18	11	16	2	.317	.452
Art Nehf	p	33	57	11	13	1	0	5	13	6	4	1	.228	.509
Jack Bentley	p-ph	46	98	12	26	5	1	0	6	3	13	0	.265	.337
Virgil Barnes	p	35	77	8	14	0	0	0	4	6	26	0	.182	.182
Rosy Ryan	p	37	36	3	5	1	0	0	3	3	12	0	.139	.167
Hugh McQuillan	p	35	67	9	14	1	1	0	2	1	15	0	.209	.254
Harry Baldwin	p	11	11	4	4	0	0	0	0	0	2	0	.364	.364
Wayland Dean	p	26	40	5	8	0	0	2	4	1	9	0	.200	.350
Mule Watson	p	22	35	4	9	0	2	2	11	2	11	0	.257	.543
Claude Jonnard	p	34	22	0	1	0	0	0	2	1	11	0	.045	.045
Walter Huntzinger	p	12	8	0	4	0	0	0	1	0	3	0	.500	.500
Ernie Maun	p	22	3	1	2	0	0	0	0	0	0	0	.667	.667
team total		154	**5445**	**857**	**1634**	269	81	**95**	**781**	467	479	82	**.300**	**.432**

Eddie Arnsmith (c), Buddy Crump (of), Grover Hartley (c), Leon Cadore (p), Dinty Gearin (p), Kent Greenfield (p), Joe Oeschger (p) also played for the Giants during the season.

PITCHING

WASHINGTON SENATORS

WORLD SERIES STATISTICS

	G	GS	CG	IP	H	R	ER	BB	SO	W	L	SV	ERA
Walter Johnson	3	**2**	**2**	**24**	**30**	**10**	6	**11**	**20**	1	**2**	0	2.25
Tom Zachary	2	**2**	1	17⅔	13	4	4	3	3	**2**	0	0	2.04
George Mogridge	2	1	0	12	7	5	3	6	5	1	0	0	2.25
Firpo Marberry	**4**	1	0	8	9	5	1	4	10	0	1	**2**	**1.13**
Allen Russell	1	0	0	3	4	2	1	0	0	0	0	0	3.00
Joe Martina	1	0	0	1	0	0	0	0	1	0	0	0	0.00
By Speece	1	0	0	1	3	1	1	0	0	0	0	0	9.00
Curly Ogden	1	1	0	⅓	0	0	0	1	1	0	0	0	0.00
Paul Zahniser	Did not play												
team total	7	7	3	67	66	27	16	25	40	4	3	2	2.15

REGULAR SEASON STATISTICS

		G	GS	CG	IP	H	ER	BB	SO	W	L	Pct	SV	ShO	ERA
Walter Johnson		38	**38**	20	278	233	84	77	**158**	**23**	7	.767	0	6	2.72
Tom Zachary		33	27	13	203	198	62	53	45	15	9	.625	2	1	2.75
George Mogridge		30	30	13	213	217	89	61	48	16	11	.593	0	2	3.76
Firpo Marberry		**50**	15	6	195	190	67	70	68	11	12	.478	15	0	3.09
Allen Russell		37	0	0	82	83	40	45	17	5	1	.833	8	0	4.39
Joe Martina		24	13	8	125	129	65	56	57	6	8	.429	0	0	4.68
By Speece		21	1	0	54	60	16	27	15	2	1	.667	0	0	2.67
Curly Ogden	a	16	16	9	108	83	31	51	23	9	5	.643	0	3	2.58
Paul Zahniser		24	14	5	92	98	45	49	28	5	7	.417	0	1	4.40
team total		156	156	74	1383	1329	514	505	469	**92**	62	**.597**	**25**	**13**	**3.34**

NEW YORK GIANTS

WORLD SERIES STATISTICS

	G	GS	CG	IP	H	R	ER	BB	SO	W	L	SV	ERA
Art Nehf	3	**2**	1	19⅔	15	5	4	9	7	1	1	0	1.83
Jack Bentley	3	**2**	1	17	18	7	7	8	10	1	**2**	0	3.71
Virgil Barnes	2	**2**	0	12⅔	15	8	**8**	1	9	0	1	0	5.68
Hugh McQuillan	3	1	0	7	2	2	2	6	2	1	0	1	2.57
Rosy Ryan	2	0	0	5⅔	7	2	2	4	3	0	0	0	3.18
Harry Baldwin	1	0	0	2	1	0	0	0	1	0	0	0	0.00
Wayland Dean	1	0	0	2	3	2	1	0	2	0	0	0	4.50
Mule Watson	1	0	0	⅔	0	0	0	0	0	0	0	1	0.00
Claude Jonnard	1	0	0	0	0	0	0	1	0	0	0	0	0.00
Walter Huntzinger	Did not play												
Ernie Maun	Did not play												
team total	7	7	2	66⅔	61	26	24	29	34	3	4	2	3.24

REGULAR SEASON STATISTICS

	G	GS	CG	IP	H	ER	BB	SO	W	L	Pct	SV	ShO	ERA
Art Nehf	30	20	11	172	167	70	42	72	14	4	.778	2	0	3.66
Jack Bentley	28	24	13	188	196	79	56	60	16	5	.762	1	1	3.78
Virgil Barnes	35	29	15	229	239	78	57	59	16	10	.615	3	1	3.07
Hugh McQuillan	27	23	14	184	179	55	43	49	14	8	.636	3	1	2.69
Rosy Ryan	37	9	2	125	137	59	37	36	8	6	.571	5	0	4.25
Harry Baldwin	10	2	1	34	42	16	11	5	3	1	.750	0	0	4.23
Wayland Dean	26	20	6	126	139	70	45	39	6	12	.333	0	0	5.00
Mule Watson	22	16	6	100	122	42	24	18	7	4	.636	0	1	3.78
Claude Jonnard	34	3	1	90	80	24	24	40	4	5	.444	5	0	2.40
Walter Huntzinger	12	2	0	32	41	16	9	6	1	1	.500	1	0	4.50
Ernie Maun	22	0	0	35	46	23	10	5	1	1	.500	1	0	5.91
team total	154	154	71	1379	1464	555	392	406	**93**	60	**.608**	**21**	4	3.62

Total Attendance—283,665 Average Attendance—40,524 Winning Player's Share—$5,970 Losing Player's Share—$3,820

1925
Peckinpaugh's Eight Errors

Babe Adams was back for his second World Series. He had starred in the 1909 classic for the Pittsburgh Pirates, winning three games against the Detroit Tigers, and now he was back in the Series as a forty-three-year-old reserve pitcher and sole link between the Pirate pennant-winners of 1909 and 1925. The first Pirate championship club in 16 years dethroned the New York Giants with a murderous batting attack, averaging .307 as a team. Pie Traynor, Kiki Cuyler, and Max Carey all were on the road to eventual membership in the Hall of Fame, while Glenn Wright, Clyde Barnhart, and George Grantham swung potent bats just as dangerous. Manager Bill McKechnie had no immortals on his pitching staff, but he did have a corps of competent hurlers in Lee Meadows, Ray Kremer, Johnny Morrison, Emil Yde, and Vic Aldridge, plus old-man Adams for spot work. Facing the Pirates in the Series were the Washington Senators, repeat winners in the American League. Walter Johnson had enough fast ball left at age thirty-seven to win 20 games, and he was matched in the win column by newly acquired spitballer Stan Coveleski. Sam Rice and Goose Goslin again filled the heart of the batting order, Bucky Harris again managed the club from his second-base position, but the unexpected star of the season was veteran shortstop Roger Peckinpaugh, whose .294 batting average and steady fielding earned him the A.L.'s Most Valuable Player award. The Series, however, would bring Peckinpaugh only trouble.

The Series started well enough for Peckinpaugh and the Senators, as Walter Johnson beat Lee Meadows 4–1 in the opening game at Forbes Field with a masterful five-hitter. The players on both teams wore black armbands for game two, mourning the death of all-time-great pitcher Christy Mathewson during the night. Coveleski and Aldridge both pitched games worthy of Matty, but a 1–1 tie was broken up in the eighth inning when Peckinpaugh muffed an easy grounder and Cuyler then hit one out into the right-field stands. The Senators came back to score once in the ninth but absorbed a 3–2 loss.

After a day of travel to Washington, the Senators took a 4–3 squeaker in which Rice made a disputed catch of an apparent home run by disappearing over the fence and coming up with the ball, and in which Senator reliever Firpo Marberry hit out of turn unnoticed by the Pirates. Walter Johnson came back in game four with a six-hitter which home runs by Goslin and Joe Harris turned into a 4–0 win. No club had ever come back from a 3–1 deficit in a seven-game Series, but the Pirates started on that road with a 6–3 fifth-game victory behind Vic Aldridge.

The Pirates kept fighting back, taking the sixth game 3–2 in Forbes Field behind Ray Kremer, with a key error by Peckinpaugh prolonging a two-run rally in the third inning. Now the entire outcome rested on the seventh game, and a day of rain on October 14 enabled the managers to start Walter Johnson and Vic Aldridge in the drizzle and mud in the deciding game. The Senators blasted Aldridge and reliever Morrison with a four-run first inning that put them firmly in the driver's seat. But Johnson was having trouble with the wet ball and gave up three Pirate runs in the third inning. The Senators then lengthened their lead out to 6–3 in the fourth inning and watched the Pirates cut it to 6–4 with a run in the fifth. In the bottom of the seventh, a muffed pop-up by Peckinpaugh fueled a two-run Pirate rally that tied the score at 6–6. Peckinpaugh took matters into his own hands in the top of the eighth by smacking a homer into the left-field seats, apparently insuring a hero's role for himself after all. But after the struggling Johnson retired the first two batters in the bottom of the eighth, back-to-back Pirate doubles again tied the score. Manager Harris resisted a temptation to remove the tiring pitcher, and Johnson got Max Carey to hit a grounder to shortstop. The unfortunate Peckinpaugh couldn't make the play, and Kiki Cuyler then doubled home two runs which were the margin of victory in a 9–7 win. For Pittsburgh, it was the first World Championship after 16 years. For Peckinpaugh, it was an embarrassing total of eight errors.

Game 1 October 7 at Pittsburgh

Was. 010 020 001
Pit. 000 010 000

Washington	Pos	AB	R	H	RBI	PO	A	E
Rice	cf-rf	4	0	2	2	3	0	0
B. Harris	2b	3	0	0	0	1	0	0
Goslin	lf	4	1	1	0	0	0	0
Judge	1b	4	0	0	0	5	2	0
J. Harris	rf	4	2	2	1	4	0	0
McNeely	cf	0	0	0	0	1	0	0
Bluege	3b	4	1	2	1	0	2	0
Peckinpaugh	ss	4	0	1	0	3	2	1
Ruel	c	3	0	0	0	10	2	0
Johnson	p	3	0	0	0	0	0	0
Totals		32	4	8	4	27	8	1

Pitching	IP	H	R	ER	BB	SO
Washington						
Johnson (W)	9	5	1	1	1	10
Pittsburgh						
Meadows (L)	8	6	3	3	0	4
Morrison	1	2	1	1	0	1

Pittsburgh	Pos	AB	R	H	RBI	PO	A	E
Moore	2b	4	0	0	0	1	1	0
Carey	cf	2	0	0	0	3	0	0
Cuyler	rf	4	0	1	0	0	0	0
Barnhart	lf	4	0	1	0	0	0	0
Traynor	3b	4	1	2	1	1	3	0
Wright	ss	4	0	0	0	1	5	0
Grantham	1b	3	0	0	0	15	1	0
Smith	c	3	0	1	0	5	0	0
a Bigbee		0	0	0	0	0	0	0
Gooch	c	0	0	0	0	1	0	0
Meadows	p	1	0	0	0	0	2	0
b McInnis		1	0	0	0	0	0	0
Morrison	p	0	0	0	0	0	1	0
Totals		30	1	5	1	27	13	0

a Ran for Smith in 8th.
b Struck out for Meadows in 8th.

Home Runs—J. Harris, Traynor. Stolen Bases—Bigbee, Grantham. Sacrifice Hit—Judge. Double Plays—Peckinpaugh to Judge, Grantham (unassisted). Hit by Pitchers—Carey 2 (by Johnson 2), B. Harris (by Meadows). Left on Bases—Washington 3, Pittsburgh 5. Umpires—Rigler (N), Owens (A), McCormick (N), Moriarty (A). Attendance—41,723. Time of Game—1:57.

1st Inning
Washington
1 Rice grounded to short.
2 B. Harris grounded to third.
3 Goslin grounded to first.
Pittsburgh
1 Moore flied to short center.
  Carey was hit by a pitch.
2 Carey caught trying to steal second, Ruel to Peckinpaugh.
3 Cuyler struck out.

2nd Inning
Washington
1 Judge grounded to short.
  J. Harris homered over the low fence in right-center.
2 Bluege struck out.
3 Peckinpaugh flied to center.
Pittsburgh
1 Barnhart flied to center.
  Traynor singled to right.
2 Wright forced Traynor at second, Judge to Peckinpaugh.
3 Grantham struck out on a full count.

3rd Inning
Washington
1 Ruel lined to third.
2 Johnson grounded to short.
  Rice singled to right.
3 Rice was picked off first, Meadows to Grantham.
Pittsburgh
1 Smith flied to right.
  Meadows walked.
2,3 Moore grounded into a double play, Peckinpaugh to Judge.

4th Inning
Washington
  B. Harris hit by a pitched ball.
1,2 Goslin lined viciously to Grantham stepping on first to double up B. Harris.
3 Judge grounded to second.
Pittsburgh
1 Carey called out on strikes.
  Cuyler singled over second.
2 Cuyler trapped off first, Ruel to Judge to Peckinpaugh to Judge to B. Harris.
3 Barnhart called out on strikes.

5th Inning
Washington
  J. Harris beat out a grounder over second.
  Bluege singled to left, J. Harris stopping at second.
  Peckinpaugh poked a single to left, loading the bases.
1 Ruel struck out.
2 Johnson struck out.
  Rice singled to center, scoring J. Harris and Bluege with Peckinpaugh taking second.
3 B. Harris grounded to third.
Pittsburgh
  Traynor hit a home run into the temporary bleachers in right.
1 Wright called out on strikes.
  Grantham safe at first on Peckinpaugh's high throw.
2 Smith flied to right.
  Grantham stole second.
3 Meadows called out on strikes.

6th Inning
Washington
1 Goslin fouled to Smith.
2 Judge flied to center.
3 J. Harris flied to center.
Pittsburgh
1 Moore grounded to third.
2 Carey grounded to first.
3 Cuyler flied to right.

7th Inning
Washington
1 Bluege struck out.
2 Peckinpaugh grounded to third.
3 Ruel bunted out to the mound.
Pittsburgh
1 Barnhart fanned.
2 Traynor flied to deep center.
3 Wright struck out.

8th Inning
Washington
1 Johnson lined to short.
2 Rice grounded to short.
3 B. Harris grounded to short.
Pittsburgh
1 Grantham flied to right.
  Smith singled to center.
  Bigbee ran for Smith.
  McInnis batted for Meadows.
  Bigbee stole second.
2 McInnis struck out.
3 Moore grounded to third.

9th Inning
Washington
  For Pittsburgh—Morrison pitching with Gooch catching.
  Goslin singled along the right field foul line.
1 Judge sacrificed Goslin to second, Grantham to Moore.
2 J. Harris took a called third strike.
  Bluege singled to center, scoring Goslin.
3 Peckinpaugh grounded back to the pitcher.
Pittsburgh
  For Washington—McNeely playing center as Rice replaced J. Harris in right.
  Carey was hit by a pitched ball for the second time in the game.
1 Cuyler took a called third strike.
  Barnhart singled to left, Carey stopping at second.
2 Traynor flied to center.
3 Wright popped to first.

Game 2 October 8 at Pittsburgh

Was.	010	000	001	
Pit.	000	100	02x	

Washington	Pos	AB	R	H	RBI	PO	A	E
Rice	cf	5	0	2	0	2	0	0
B. Harris	2b	3	0	0	0	4	4	0
Goslin	lf	4	0	0	0	0	0	0
Judge	1b	4	1	1	1	11	0	0
J. Harris	rf	3	0	2	0	0	0	0
b McNeely		0	1	0	0	0	0	0
Bluege	3b	2	0	0	0	0	1	0
a Myer	3b	1	0	1	0	1	0	0
Peckinpaugh	ss	3	0	1	0	1	7	2
Ruel	c	3	0	1	0	5	0	0
c Veach		0	0	0	1	0	0	0
Coveleski	p	2	0	0	0	0	2	0
d Ruether		1	0	0	0	0	0	0
Totals		31	2	8	2	24	14	2

Pittsburgh	Pos	AB	R	H	RBI	PO	A	
Moore	2b	4	1	0	0	3	1	0
Carey	cf	4	0	2	0	4	0	0
Cuyler	rf	3	1	1	2	1	0	0
Barnhart	lf	4	0	1	0	3	0	0
Traynor	3b	3	0	0	0	0	2	0
Wright	ss	4	1	2	1	1	5	0
Grantham	1b	4	0	0	0	9	1	0
Smith	c	3	0	1	0	6	2	0
Aldridge	p	3	0	0	0	0	2	0
Totals		32	3	7	3	27	13	0

Pitching	IP	H	R	ER	BB	SO
Washington						
Coveleski (L)	8	7	3	2	1	3
Pittsburgh						
Aldridge (W)	9	8	2	2	2	4

a Ran for Bluege in 6th.
b Ran for J. Harris in 9th.
c Sacrificed for Ruel in 9th.
d Struck out for Coveleski in 9th.

Home Runs—Cuyler, Judge, Wright. Sacrifice Hits—Coveleski, Cuyler, B. Harris, Veach. Hit by Pitcher—Bluege (by Aldridge). Passed Ball—Ruel. Balk—Aldridge. Left on Bases—Washington 8, Pittsburgh 7. Umpires—Owens, McCormick, Moriarty, Rigler. Attendance—43,364. Time of Game—2:04.

1st Inning
Washington
1 Rice grounded to second.
2 B. Harris struck out.
3 Goslin flied to center.
Pittsburgh
1 Moore grounded to short.
2 Carey called out on strikes.
3 Cuyler grounded to second.

2nd Inning
Washington
Judge homered into the temporary right field bleachers.
J. Harris singled to left.
1 J. Harris out trying to steal second, Smith to Moore.
2 Bluege flied to left.
3 Peckinpaugh grounded to third, Grantham making a fine catch of a low throw.
Pittsburgh
1 Barnhart flied to center.
2 Traynor grounded to third.
Wright singled to right.
Wright went to second on a passed ball.
3 Grantham grounded to second.

3rd Inning
Washington
1 Ruel called out on strikes.
2 Coveleski also called out on strikes.
Rice singled to center.
Rice went to second on Aldridge's balk.
3 B. Harris grounded to short.
Pittsburgh
Smith singled to left.
1 Aldridge forced Smith at second, Coveleski to B. Harris.
2 Moore struck out.
Carey singled to right, Aldridge stopping at second.
3 Cuyler forced Carey at second, Peckinpaugh to B. Harris.

4th Inning
Washington
1 Gostin grounded to short.
2 Judge lined to deep left.
J. Harris singled over Traynor's head.
3 Bluege flied to right.
Pittsburgh
1 Barnhart flied to center.
2 Traynor grounded to short.
Wright blasted a homer over the fence in left.
3 Grantham fouled to Ruel.

5th Inning
Washington
Peckinpaugh singled to left.
Ruel singled to center, Peckinpaugh stopping at second.
Coveleski credited with a sacrifice when Aldridge fielded his bunt to third too late to catch Peckinpaugh.
1 Rice forced Peckinpaugh at the plate, Aldridge to Smith.
2 B. Harris forced Ruel at the plate, Wright to Smith.
3 Goslin grounded to first.
Pittsburgh
1 Smith called out on strikes.
2 Aldridge grounded to short.
3 Moore grounded to short.

6th Inning
Washington
1 Judge flied to center.
2 J. Harris flied to short center.
Bluege was hit by a pitch on the head.
Myer ran for Bluege.
3 Myer caught stealing, Smith to Wright.
Pittsburgh
For Washington—Myer playing third.
Carey beat out a bunt to the mound.
1 Cuyler sacrificed, Coveleski to B. Harris.
2 Barnhart grounded to short, Carey going to third.
Traynor walked.
3 Wright forced Traynor at second, Peckinpaugh to B. Harris.

7th Inning
Washington
1 Peckinpaugh grounded to short.
2 Ruel flied to left.
3 Coveleski grounded to third.
Pittsburgh
1 Grantham grounded to second.
2 Smith grounded to first.
3 Aldridge popped to short, Coveleski retiring the side on 3 pitched balls.

8th Inning
Washington
Rice singled through the box.
1 B. Harris sacrificed, Grantham to Moore.
2 Goslin bounced back to the mound, Rice going to third.
3 Judge flied to Moore in short right.
Pittsburgh
Moore safe at first as Peckinpaugh dropped his grounder. The first error of the game.
1 Carey out on a chopper to second, Moore going to second.
Cuyler hit a two-run homer into the right field bleachers.
Barnhart singled to center.
Traynor safe with Barnhart going to second on Peckinpaugh's fumble.
2 Wright fouled to Myer.
3 Grantham fouled to Ruel.

9th Inning
Washington
J. Harris walked.
McNeely ran for J. Harris.
Myer singled to left.
Peckinpaugh walked, loading the bases.
1 Veach, batting for Ruel, hit a sacrifice fly to center, scoring McNeely.
2 Ruether, batting for Coveleski, struck out.
3 Rice grounded to second.

Game 3 October 10 at Washington

Pit.	010	101	000	
Was.	001	001	20x	

Pittsburgh	Pos	AB	R	H	RBI	PO	A	E
Moore	2b	3	0	1	0	2	2	0
Carey	cf	4	0	2	0	3	0	1
Cuyler	rf	4	1	1	0	1	0	0
Barnhart	lf	5	0	1	1	2	0	0
Traynor	3b	4	1	1	0	1	3	0
Wright	ss	3	1	0	1	1	2	1
Grantham	1b	4	0	0	0	8	1	0
Smith	c	3	0	1	0	5	2	1
Kremer	p	3	0	1	1	0	1	0
c Bigbee		1	0	0	0	0	0	0
Totals		34	3	8	3	x23	11	3

Pitching	IP	H	R	ER	BB	SO
Pittsburgh						
Kremer (L)	8	10	4	4	3	5
Washington						
Ferguson (W)	7	6	3	2	4	5
Marberry (SV)	2	2	0	0	0	2

Washington	Pos	AB	R	H	RBI	PO	A	E
Rice	cf-rf	5	1	2	0	2	0	0
B. Harris	2b	3	1	1	0	2	1	0
Goslin	lf	4	1	2	1	3	0	0
Judge	1b	3	0	1	2	8	0	0
J. Harris	rf	4	0	2	1	0	0	0
Marberry	p	0	0	0	0	0	0	0
Myer	3b	3	0	0	0	0	1	0
Peckinpaugh	ss	4	0	1	0	2	3	1
Ruel	c	3	0	1	0	8	2	0
Ferguson	p	2	0	0	0	0	0	0
a Leibold		0	0	0	0	0	0	0
b McNeely	cf	0	1	0	0	2	0	0
Totals		31	4	10	4	27	7	1

a Walked for Ferguson in 7th.
b Ran for Leibold in 7th.
c Flied out for Kremer in 9th.
x Myer out, hit by own batted ball in 7th.

Doubles—Carey, Cuyler, Judge. Triple—Traynor. Home Run—Goslin. Sacrifice Hits—B. Harris, Marberry. Sacrifice Flies—Judge, Wright. Double Plays—Peckinpaugh to B. Harris to Judge, Moore to Grantham. Hit by Pitchers—Carey (by Ferguson), Cuyler (By Marberry). Left on Bases—Pittsburgh 11, Washington 9. Passed Ball—Smith. Umpires—McCormick, Moriarty, Rigler, Owens. Attendance—36,495. Time of Game—2:10.

1st Inning
Pittsburgh
Moore walked.
Carey was hit by a pitch.
1 Cuyler flied to left.
2,3 Barnhart grounded into a double play, Peckinpaugh to B. Harris to Judge.
Washington
1 Rice grounded to third.
2 B. Harris flied to center.
Goslin struck out but was safe as Smith let the third strike get past him.
3 Judge popped to first.

2nd Inning
Pittsburgh
Traynor tripled on a low liner to second that B. Harris tried to get but the ball rolled through him.
1 Wright hit a sacrifice fly to left, scoring Traynor.
2 Grantham popped to short.
3 Smith popped to short.
Washington
1 J. Harris struck out.
2 Myer's liner hit Kremer and bounced to Moore who made the play to first.
Peckinpaugh safe when Carey muffed his easy fly.
Ruel walked.
3 Ferguson struck out.

3rd Inning
Pittsburgh
1 Kremer struck out.
2 Moore fouled to Ruel.
3 Carey bunted out, Ruel to Judge.
Washington
Rice singled over second.
1 B. Harris sacrificed, Traynor to Grantham.
2 Goslin flied to deep right, Rice going to third after the catch.
Judge doubled inside first, scoring Rice.
J. Harris safe on Wright's low throw but
3 Judge was out trying to score, Grantham to Smith.

4th Inning
Pittsburgh
Cuyler doubled between Goslin and Rice to the bleachers in left-center.
Barnhart singled to left, scoring Cuyler and took second on the throw to the plate.
Traynor walked.
1 Wright grounded to short, advancing both runners.
2 Grantham popped to first.
Smith intentionally walked, loading the bases.
3 Kremer struck out.
Washington
Myer walked on a full count.
1 Peckinpaugh forced Myer at second, Wright to Moore.
2 Peckinpaugh thrown out trying to steal second, Smith to Wright.
3 Ruel flied to left.

5th Inning
Pittsburgh
1 Moore struck out.
Carey doubled on a slow grounder over second, which Rice fielded slowly.
2 Cuyler grounded to third, Carey moving to third.
3 Barnhart fouled to Judge.
Washington
1 Ferguson struck out.
Rice beat out a slow roller to third.
2,3 B. Harris lined into a double play, Moore to Grantham.

6th Inning
Pittsburgh
1 Traynor flied to Rice deep at the bleacher fence.
Wright safe at first on Peckinpaugh's bad throw to first.
2 Grantham struck out.

6th Inning (continued)
Smith singled to right, Wright racing to third.
Kremer got a freak hop single over second, Wright scoring as Smith stopped at second.
Moore walked, loading the bases.
3 Carey struck out, but Ruel dropped the third strike and threw him out at first.
Washington
Goslin punched a homer into the right-center field bleachers.
1 Judge flied to center.
J. Harris singled just out of Moore's reach near second.
2 Myer struck out.
Peckinpaugh singled to left, J. Harris stopping at second.
3 Ruel forced J. Harris at third, Traynor unassisted.

7th Inning
Pittsburgh
1 Cuyler grounded to short.
2 Barnhart flied to Goslin making a racing catch in left-center.
3 Traynor popped to second.
Washington
Leibold, batting for Ferguson, walked.
McNeely ran for Leibold.
1 Rice flied to Barnhart making a fine running catch at the foul line.
B. Harris beat out a roller in front of the plate, McNeely taking second.
Goslin surprised all by bunting to third and beat it out, loading the bases.
2 Judge hit a sacrifice fly to center, scoring McNeely.
J. Harris singled to left, scoring B. Harris as Goslin stopped at second.
3 Myer declared out, being hit by his own batted ball.

8th Inning
Pittsburgh
For Washington—Marberry pitching and batting fifth, McNeely in center as Rice moves to right.
1 Wright struck out.
2 Grantham also struck out.
3 Smith flied out on a very controversial play to Rice in the right-center field bleachers. Rice leaned over the fence, threw up his glove, and speared the ball. However, it looked like a homer as Rice failed to immediately return the ball. Umpire Rigler called the batter out as the Pirates argued that a fan must have given Rice the ball.
Washington
1 Peckinpaugh grounded to short.
Ruel singled to left.
2 Marberry (batting out of turn) sacrificed Ruel to second, Smith to Grantham. The Pirates did not notice McNeely should have been batting.
3 Rice grounded to short.

9th Inning
Pittsburgh
1 Bigbee, pinch-hitting for Kremer, flied to center.
Moore singled to left-center.
Carey singled to right, Moore racing to third.
Cuyler was hit by a pitch, loading the sacks.
2 Barnhart popped to Ruel in fair territory.
3 Traynor flied to center on a 3-2 count.

Game 4 October 11 at Washington

Pittsburgh	Pos	AB	R	H	RBI	PO	A	E
Moore	2b	4	0	1	0	3	3	0
Carey	cf	3	0	1	0	0	0	0
Cuyler	rf	4	0	0	0	0	0	0
Barnhart	lf	3	0	0	0	2	1	0
Traynor	3b	4	0	2	0	0	3	0
Wright	ss	4	0	0	0	3	4	1
Grantham	1b	3	0	2	0	10	3	0
Gooch	c	3	0	0	0	6	3	0
Yde	p	1	0	0	0	0	0	0
Morrison	p	1	0	0	0	0	2	0
a Bigbee		1	0	0	0	0	0	0
Adams	p	0	0	0	0	0	0	0
Totals		31	0	6	0	24	19	1

a Popped out for Morrison in 8th.

Double—Ruel. Home Runs—Goslin, J. Harris. Stolen Bases—Carey, Peckinpaugh. Double Plays—Traynor to Moore to Grantham, B. Harris to Judge 2. Left on Bases—Pittsburgh 6, Washington 9. Umpires—Moriarty, Rigler, Owens, McCormick. Attendance—38,701. Time of Game—2:00.

Pit.	000	000	000
Was.	004	000	00x

Washington	Pos	AB	R	H	RBI	PO	A	E
Rice	cf	5	1	2	0	2	0	0
B. Harris	2b	3	1	1	0	6	7	0
Goslin	lf	3	1	2	3	3	0	0
J. Harris	rf	4	1	1	1	2	0	0
Judge	1b	3	0	0	0	9	0	0
Peckinpaugh	ss	4	0	1	0	0	2	0
Ruel	c	3	0	3	0	5	0	0
Myer	3b	4	0	1	0	0	0	0
Johnson	p	4	0	1	0	0	1	0
Totals		33	4	12	4	27	10	0

Pitching	IP	H	R	ER	BB	SO
Pittsburgh						
Yde (L)	$2\frac{1}{3}$	5	4	3	3	1
Morrison	$4\frac{2}{3}$	5	0	0	1	4
Adams	1	2	0	0	0	0
Washington						
Johnson (W)	9	6	0	0	2	2

1st Inning
Pittsburgh
1 Moore flied to center.
Carey walked.
2 Cuyler grounded to second, Carey going to second.
3 Barnhart struck out.
Washington
1 Rice grounded to short.
B. Harris walked.
Goslin walked.
2,3 J. Harris grounded into a double play, Traynor to Moore to Grantham.

2nd Inning
Pittsburgh
Traynor beat out a liner to third.
1 Wright forced Traynor at second, Peckinpaugh to B. Harris.
Grantham beat out an infield hit to third, Wright stopping at second.
2 Gooch rolled out to short, advancing both runners.
3 Yde bounced to second.
Washington
1 Judge popped to short.
2 Peckinpaugh grounded to third.
Ruel singled to center.
3 Myer took a called third strike.

3rd Inning
Pittsburgh
1 Moore lined to left.
2 Carey flied to right.
3 Cuyler grounded to second.
Washington
Johnson singled down the left field
1 line but was out trying to stretch it, Barnhart to Wright.
Rice beat out an infield hit to second.
B. Harris safe at first when Wright dropped Grantham's throw to second.
Goslin hit a three-run homer into the left-center field bleachers.
J. Harris boomed a home run high into the left field bleachers.
Judge walked.
For Pittsburgh—Morrison replaced Yde on the mound.
2 Judge was out trying to steal second, Gooch to Moore.
Peckinpaugh singled to left.
Peckinpaugh stole second.
Ruel walked.
3 Myer forced Ruel at second, Moore to Wright.

4th Inning
Pittsburgh
1 Barnhart fouled to Ruel.
2 Traynor bunted out to the mound.
3 Wright grounded to second.
Washington
1 Johnson called out on strikes.
Rice beat out a hit to third.
2 B. Harris flied to left.
3 Goslin called out on strikes.

5th Inning
Pittsburgh
1 Grantham fouled to Ruel.
2 Gooch flied to left.
3 Morrison flied to center.
Washington
1 J. Harris struck out, but had to be thrown out by Gooch, who dropped the third strike.
2 Judge grounded back to the pitcher.
3 Peckinpaugh struck out.

6th Inning
Pittsburgh
1 Moore flied to left.
Carey beat out a bunt down the first base line.
2 Cuyler called out on strikes, as Carey stole second.
3 Barnhart fouled to Ruel.
Washington
Ruel singled to left.
1 Myer popped to Grantham on a bunt attempt.
2 Johnson tapped in front of the plate, Gooch throwing to Wright but missing the force at second. Johnson was out on Wright's throw to first.
3 Rice grounded to second.

7th Inning
Pittsburgh
Traynor singled to center.
1,2 Wright lined high to B. Harris who threw to Judge doubling Traynor at first.
Grantham singled off Judge's glove.
3 Gooch popped to second.
Washington
B. Harris singled to left.
Goslin blooped a Texas League single into short center, B. Harris stopping at second.
1 J. Harris flied to deep left.
2 Judge forced Goslin at second, Grantham to Wright, B. Harris going to third.
3 Judge was trapped off first and B. Harris was out trying to sneak home, Morrison to Grantham to Gooch.

8th Inning
Pittsburgh
1 Bigbee, pinch-hitting for Morrison, popped to second.
Moore singled to left.
2 Carey popped to B. Harris behind first.
3 Cuyler flied to right.
Washington
For Pittsburgh—Adams pitching.
1 Peckinpaugh grounded to third.
Ruel bounced a double over third, his third hit of the game.
Myer beat out a hit to first when Adams failed to cover first, Ruel to third.
2 Johnson's squeeze bunt resulted in an out as Gooch tagged Ruel coming to the plate.
3 Rice forced Johnson at second, Wright to Moore.

9th Inning
Pittsburgh
Barnhart walked.
1,2 Traynor hit into a double play, B. Harris to Judge.
3 Wright grounded to second, putting Washington up 3 games to 1.

Game 5 October 12 at Washington

Pit.	002	000	211
Was.	100	100	100

Pittsburgh	Pos	AB	R	H	RBI	PO	A	E
Moore	2b	4	1	1	0	3	2	0
Carey	cf	4	2	2	0	0	0	0
Cuyler	rf	4	1	2	1	4	0	0
Barnhart	lf	4	1	2	2	1	0	0
Traynor	3b	3	0	1	1	2	0	0
Wright	ss	5	1	2	1	1	3	0
McInnis	1b	5	0	1	1	11	2	0
Smith	c	3	0	2	0	5	2	0
Aldridge	p	4	0	0	0	0	2	0
Totals		36	6	13	6	27	11	0

Pitching	IP	H	R	ER	BB	SO
Pittsburgh						
Aldridge (W)	9	8	3	3	4	5
Washington						
Coveleski (L)	$6\frac{1}{3}$	9	4	4	4	0
Ballou	$\frac{2}{3}$	0	0	0	0	1
Zachary	$1\frac{2}{3}$	3	2	2	1	0
Marberry	$\frac{1}{3}$	1	0	0	0	0

Washington	Pos	AB	R	H	RBI	PO	A	E
Rice	cf	5	1	2	1	3	0	0
B. Harris	2b	3	0	0	0	2	3	0
Goslin	lf	4	0	1	1	5	0	0
Judge	1b	3	0	0	0	11	0	0
J. Harris	rf	3	1	2	1	0	0	0
Peckinpaugh	ss	3	0	0	0	4	3	1
Ruel	c	3	0	1	0	1	1	0
Bluege	3b	4	0	1	0	1	5	0
Coveleski	p	1	0	0	0	0	2	0
Ballou	p	0	0	0	0	0	0	0
a Leibold		1	1	1	0	0	0	0
Zachary	p	0	0	0	0	0	3	0
Marberry	p	0	0	0	0	0	0	0
b Adams		1	0	0	0	0	0	0
Totals		31	3	8	3	27	17	1

a Doubled for Ballou in 7th.
b Grounded out for Mayberry in 9th.

Doubles—Bluege, Goslin, Leibold, Wright. Home Run—J. Harris. Stolen Bases—Barnhart, Carey. Sacrifice Hits—B. Harris 2, Peckinpaugh, Smith, Traynor. Double Plays—Bluege to B. Harris to Judge, Coveleski to Peckinpaugh to Judge, Smith to Traynor. Left on Bases—Pittsburgh 10, Washington 8. Umpires—Rigler, Owens, McCormick, Moriarty. Attendance—35,899. Time of Game—2:26.

1st Inning
Pittsburgh
1 Moore fouled to Peckinpaugh.
Carey singled to left.
Cuyler got a Texas League single into short left, Carey going to second.
2 Barnhart flied to deep left.
Traynor walked, loading the bases.
3 Wright's bouncer deflected by Coveleski to B. Harris who made the throw to first.
Washington
Rice lined a single to right.
1 B. Harris sacrificed Rice to second, McInnis to Moore.
Goslin blooped a double near the left field foul line, scoring Rice.
2 Judge struck out.
J. Harris walked.
3 Peckinpaugh forced Goslin at third, Traynor unassisted.

2nd Inning
Pittsburgh
1 McInnis flied to left.
Smith singled to center.
2,3 Aldridge bounced into a double play, Bluege to B. Harris to Judge.
Washington
1 Ruel popped to second.
2 Bluege struck out.
Coveleski walked.
3 Rice grounded to first.

3rd Inning
Pittsburgh
1 Moore grounded to third.
Carey walked.
Carey stole second.
Cuyler walked.
Barnhart singled to left-center, Carey scoring as Cuyler went to third.
Barnhart stole second after being almost trapped.
2 Traynor hit a sacrifice fly to center, Cuyler scoring.
3 Wright grounded to short.
Washington
1 B. Harris bunted out to the mound.
2 Goslin grounded to second.
3 Judge flied to right.

4th Inning
Pittsburgh
1 McInnis grounded to short.
Smith singled past second.
2 Aldridge lined to left.
Moore singled to right, Smith racing to third.
3 Carey was robbed of a sure hit by a diving Judge making a great stop of Carey's grounder.
Washington
J. Harris homered into the left field bleachers.
1 Peckinpaugh struck out.
Ruel singled to left.
Bluege doubled to left center, Ruel stopping at third.
2 Coveleski called out on strikes.
3 Rice grounded to first.

5th Inning
Pittsburgh
1 Cuyler flied to center.
2 Barnhart popped to short.
3 Traynor lined to second.
Washington
1 B. Harris grounded to second.
2 Goslin flied to right.
3 Judge popped to short.

6th Inning
Pittsburgh
1 Wright flied to left.
McInnis safe at first on Peckinpaugh's fifth error of the Series.
2,3 Smith grounded into a double play, Coveleski to Peckinpaugh to Judge.
Washington
J. Harris singled to left.
1 Peckinpaugh sacrificed J. Harris to second, McInnis to Moore.
Ruel walked.
2,3 Bluege struck out and J. Harris was doubled trying to steal third, Smith to Traynor.

7th Inning
Pittsburgh
1 Aldridge grounded to third.
Moore walked.
Carey singled to left.
Cuyler singled off Bluege's glove, Moore scoring and Carey racing to third.
Barnhart singled past second, Carey scoring as Cuyler went to third.
For Washington—Ballou came into pitch.
2 Traynor struck out.
3 On an attempted double steal, Cuyler was trapped off third, Ruel to Bluege to Ruel to Bluege.
Washington
Leibold, batting for Ballou, bounced a ground rule double into the right field stands.
Rice singled over second, scoring Leibold.
1 B. Harris sacrificed Rice to second, Smith to McLnnis.
2 Goslin flied to right, Rice going to third after the catch.
Judge walked.
3 J. Harris flied to right.

8th Inning
Pittsburgh
For Washington—Zachary pitching.
Wright doubled down the left field line.
McInnis singled over first, scoring Wright.
1 Smith sacrificed, Zachary to Judge.
2 Aldridge grounded to Zachary and McInnis out in a run-down, Zachary to B. Harris to Bluege to Peckinpaugh.
3 Moore flied to center.
Washington
1 Peckinpaugh grounded to short.
2 Ruel grounded to short.
3 Bluege fouled to McInnis.

9th Inning
Pittsburgh
1 Carey grounded back to the mound.
2 Cuyler grounded to first.
Barnhart walked.
Traynor singled to left, Barnhart stopping at second.
For Washington—Marberry now pitching.
Wright singled to left, Barnhart scoring as Traynor stopped at second.
3 McInnis flied to left.
Washington
1 S. Adams, pinch-hitting for Marberry, grounded back to the pitcher.
2 Rice grounded to short.
3 B. Harris lined to left.

1925

Game 6 October 13 at Pittsburgh

	Was.	1 1 0	0 0 0	0 0 0
	Pit.	0 0 2	0 1 0	0 0 x

Washington	Pos	AB	R	H	RBI	PO	A	E
Rice	cf	4	0	0	0	2	0	0
B. Harris	2b	3	0	0	0	3	0	0
c Veach		1	0	0	0	0	0	0
Ballou	p	0	0	0	0	0	0	0
Goslin	lf	3	1	1	1	2	0	0
J. Harris	lf	4	0	1	0	2	0	0
Judge	1b	4	0	1	0	9	0	0
Bluege	3b	4	1	1	0	0	6	0
Peckinpaugh	ss	3	0	1	1	0	3	1
Severeid	c	3	0	1	0	6	0	1
a McNeely		0	0	0	0	0	0	0
S. Adams	2b	0	0	0	0	0	0	0
Ferguson	p	2	0	0	0	0	1	0
b Leibold		1	0	0	0	0	0	0
Ruel	c	0	0	0	0	0	0	0
Totals		32	2	6	2	24	10	2

Pittsburgh	Pos	AB	R	H	RBI	PO	A	E
Moore	2b	3	2	2	1	2	4	0
Carey	cf	2	1	0	0	0	0	0
Cuyler	rf	3	0	0	0	2	0	0
Barnhart	lf	3	0	1	1	2	0	0
Traynor	3b	4	0	2	1	1	4	0
Wright	ss	3	0	0	0	3	2	0
McInnis	1b	4	0	1	0	12	1	0
Smith	c	4	0	1	0	3	1	0
Kremer	p	3	0	0	0	2	3	1
Totals		29	3	7	3	27	15	1

Pitching	IP	H	R	ER	BB	SO
Washington						
Ferguson (L)	7	7	3	3	2	6
Ballou	1	0	0	0	1	0
Pittsburgh						
Kremer (W)	9	6	2	2	1	3

a Ran for Severeid in 8th.
b Popped out for Ferguson in 8th.
c Grounded out for B. Harris in 8th.

Doubles—Barnhart, J. Harris, Peckinpaugh. Home Runs—Goslin, Moore. Stolen Bases—McNeely, Traynor. Sacrifice Hits—Carey 2, Cuyler. Double Play—Judge (unassisted). Left on Bases—Washington 4, Pittsburgh 8. Umpires—Owens, McCormick, Moriarty, Rigler. Attendance—43,810. Time of Game—1:57.

1st Inning
Washington
1 Rice grounded to Moore who fumbling momentarily still made the play.
2 B. Harris grounded out, Smith to McInnis. Goslin smashed a long home run deep into the right field stands.
3 J. Harris bounced back to the mound.
Pittsburgh
Moore singled through third.
1 Carey sacrificed Moore to second, Bluege to Judge.
2 Cuyler flied to right.
3 Barnhart grounded to third.

2nd Inning
Washington
Judge singled to right.
1 Bluege forced Judge at second on an attempted sacrifice, Kremer to Wright. Peckinpaugh lined a double over McInnis' head, scoring Bluege. Peckinpaugh got to third on Kremer's wild pick off throw for an error.
2 Severeid flied to short left.
3 Ferguson flied to right.
Pittsburgh
Traynor singled to center.
1 Wright forced Traynor at second, Peckinpaugh to B. Harris.
2 McInnis called out on strikes. Smith singled over second, Wright going to third.
3 Kremer called out on strikes.

3rd Inning
Washington
1 Rice lined hard to the mound.
2 B. Harris grounded to third.
3 Goslin popped to short.
Pittsburgh
Moore walked on a full count. Carey safe at first on a fielder's choice, a bouncer over the mound to Peckinpaugh who failed to touch second.
1 Cuyler advanced both runners on a neat sacrifice, Bluege to Judge.
2 Barnhart bounced to third, Moore scoring and Carey going to third. Traynor singled past Ferguson into center, Carey scoring. Traynor stole second and continued to third when Severeid's throw went into the outfield.
3 Wright grounded to third.

4th Inning
Washington
1 J. Harris struck out.
2 Judge struck out. Bluege singled to left-center.
3 Bluege trapped off first, Kremer to McInnis to Moore to McInnis to Kremer.
Pittsburgh
1 McInnis flied to right.
2 Smith struck out.
3 Kremer called out on strikes, again.

5th Inning
Washington
1 Peckinpaugh popped to Traynor.
2 Severeid grounded to short.
3 Ferguson called out on strikes.
Pittsburgh
Moore homered over the temporary fence in front of the scoreboard in left.
1 Carey lined to right.
2 Cuyler grounded to short. Barnhart doubled against the screen in left-center.
3 Traynor flied to left.

6th Inning
Washington
1 Rice grounded to Traynor making a good stop behind the bag.
2 B. Harris grounded to short. Goslin walked.
3 J. Harris grounded to second.
Pittsburgh
1 Wright called out on strikes. McInnis singled to center.
2 Smith lined to right.
3 Kremer struck out on three pitches, his third strike out in the game.

7th Inning
Washington
1 Judge flied to deep right.
2 Bluege grounded to Traynor.
3 Peckinpaugh flied to left.
Pittsburgh
Moore safe at first on Peckinpaugh's sixth error of the Series, a low throw to first.
1 Carey sacrificed Moore to second, Ferguson to Judge.
2 Cuyler flied to left. Barnhart walked.
3 Traynor forced Barnhart at second, Peckinpaugh to B. Harris.

8th Inning
Washington
Severeid singled to left-center. McNeely ran for Severeid. Leibold, batted for Ferguson. McNeely stole second.
1 Leibold popped to second.
2 Rice grounded to first, McNeely advancing to third.
3 Veach, pinch-hitting for B. Harris, grounded to second.
Pittsburgh
For Washington—Ballou pitching and batting third, Ruel catching and batting ninth, S. Adams playing third and batting eighth. Wright walked.
1,2 McInnis popped to Judge on the hit-and-run play. Judge doubled Wright stepping on the bag.
3 Smith grounded to third.

9th Inning
Washington
1 Goslin popped to second after one ball and five fouls, all very deep. J. Harris doubled off the screen in deep center.
2 Judge popped to short.
3 Bluege grounded to third.

Game 7 October 15 at Pittsburgh

	Was.	4 0 0	2 0 0	0 1 0
	Pit.	0 0 3	0 1 0	2 3 x

Washington	Pos	AB	R	H	RBI	PO	A	E
Rice	cf	5	2	2	0	3	0	0
B. Harris	2b	5	0	0	0	6	3	0
Goslin	lf	4	2	1	0	2	0	0
J. Harris	rf	3	1	1	2	1	1	0
Judge	1b	3	1	1	0	6	0	0
Bluege	3b	4	0	1	1	0	0	0
Peckinpaugh	ss	*3	1	1	2	0	2	2
Ruel	c	4	0	0	1	6	0	0
Johnson	p	4	0	0	0	0	3	0
Totals		35	7	7	6	24	9	2

Pitching	IP	H	R	ER	BB	SO
Washington						
Johnson (L)	8	15	9	5	1	3
Pittsburgh						
Aldridge	⅓	2	4	4	3	0
Morrison	3⅔	4	2	2	0	2
Kremer (W)	4	1	1	1	0	1
Oldham (SV)	1	0	0	0	0	2

Pittsburgh	Pos	AB	R	H	RBI	PO	A	E
Moore	2b	4	3	1	1	2	0	1
Carey	cf	5	3	4	2	4	0	0
Cuyler	rf	4	0	2	3	4	0	1
Barnhart	lf	5	0	1	1	2	0	0
Oldham	p	0	0	0	0	0	0	0
Traynor	3b	4	0	1	1	1	3	0
Wright	ss	4	0	1	0	1	3	0
McInnis	1b	4	0	2	0	7	0	0
Smith	c	4	0	1	0	4	0	0
b Yde		0	1	0	0	0	0	0
Gooch	c	0	0	0	0	2	0	0
Aldridge	p	0	0	0	0	0	0	0
Morrison	p	1	1	1	0	0	0	0
a Grantham		1	0	0	0	0	0	0
Kremer	p	1	0	0	0	0	1	0
c Bigbee	lf	1	1	1	1	0	0	0
Totals		38	9	15	9	27	7	2

*Awarded first on catcher interference.
a Flied out for Morrison in 4th.
b Ran for Smith in 8th.
c Doubled for Kremer in 8th.

Doubles—Bigbee, Carey 3, Cuyler 2, J. Harris, Moore, Smith. Triple—Traynor. Home Run—Peckinpaugh. Stolen Base—Carey. Sacrifice Hit—Cuyler. Double Play—B. Harris to Judge. Wild Pitches—Aldridge 2. Left on Bases—Washington 5, Pittsburgh 7. Umpires—McCormick, Moriarty, Rigler, Owens. Attendance—42,856. Time of Game—2:31.

1st Inning

Washington
Rice singled over second.
1 B. Harris flied to left.
Rice took second on a wild pitch.
Goslin walked.
Rice went to third and Goslin to second on another wild pitch.
J. Harris walked, loading the bases.
Judge walked on a full count, forcing in Rice.
Bluege singled to left, Goslin scoring and the bases still filled.
For Pittsburgh—Morrison replaced Aldridge on the mound.
Peckinpaugh was awarded first after grounding into a force out. The umpire ruling Smith had interferred with the batter. This scored J. Harris and the sacks were still full.
Ruel was safe on Moore's fumble, Judge scoring and the bases still full.
2 Johnson struck out.
3 Rice flied to left.

Pittsburgh
1 Moore bunted out to the mound.
Carey doubled to right-center.
2 Cuyler struck out.
3 Barnhart struck out.

2nd Inning

Washington
1 B. Harris flied to right.
2 Goslin flied to Carey in deep left-center.
3 J. Harris grounded to short.

Pittsburgh
1 Traynor grounded to Johnson who was saved of an error by a fantastic fielding gem on his throw by Judge.
Wright singled over second.
McInnis singled through the box, Wright stopping at second.
2,3 Smith grounded into a double play, B. Harris to Judge.

3rd Inning

Washington
Judge singled to center.
1 Bluege popped to second after bunting foul.
2 Peckinpaugh got robbed of a hit by a diving shoe-lace catch by Cuyler in short right-center. He tried to double Judge but the throw went through McInnis and Judge went to second.
3 Ruel flied to center.

3rd Inning (continued)

Pittsburgh
Morrison blooped a single into short center.
Moore doubled off the bleacher fence in left-center, scoring Morrison,
Carey singled beyond second, Moore scoring.
1 Cuyler grounded to short, Carey moving to second.
Carey stole third.
Barnhart dropped a single into short right-center, scoring Carey.
2 Traynor forced Barnhart at second, Peckinpaugh to B. Harris.
3 Wright popped to second.

4th Inning

Washington
1 Johnson flied to Carey in left-center.
Rice singled to right.
2 B. Harris called out on strikes.
Goslin singled through short, Rice racing to third as Goslin took second on the throw-in to third.
J. Harris doubled to center, scoring Rice and Goslin.
3 Judge flied to right.

Pittsburgh
McInnis singled to left.
1 Smith flied to short center.
2 Grantham, pinch-hitting for Morrison, flied to right.
3 Moore flied to left.

5th Inning

Washington
For Pittsburgh—Kremer pitching.
1 Bluege bounced to third.
2 Peckinpaugh grounded to deep short.
3 Ruel lined to Carey in left-center.

Pittsburgh (starting to rain).
Carey got another double to right-center.
Cuyler doubled down the left field line, scoring Carey.
1 Barnhart struck out.
2 Traynor fouled to Ruel.
3 Wright popped to second.

6th Inning

Washington
1 Johnson popped to Wright.
2 Rice grounded to short.
3 B. Harris struck out.

Pittsburgh
1 McInnis flied to left.
2 Smith flied to center.
3 Kremer fouled to Ruel.

7th Inning (raining hard now)

Washington
1 Goslin grounded to third.
2 J. Harris fouled to Traynor.
3 Judge flied to right.

Pittsburgh
Moore got all the way to second as Peckinpaugh muffed his pop in short left. His seventh error of the Series.
Carey doubled down the left field line, his third double and fourth hit in the game, Moore scoring.
1 Cuyler sacrificed Carey to third, Johnson to B. Harris covering first.
2 Barnhart grounded to second, Carey holding at third.
Traynor tripled to the fence in right-center, scoring Carey with the tying run. Traynor was out trying for
3 a homer, J. Harris to B. Harris to Ruel.

8th Inning

Washington
1 Bluege grounded to third.
Peckinpaugh homered over the low fence in left.
2 Ruel grounded to Traynor, making a dazzling fielding play.
3 Johnson fouled to Smith.

Pittsburgh
1 Wright fouled to Judge.
2 McInnis flied to center.
Smith doubled to right-center.
Yde ran for Smith.
Bigbee, batting for Kremer, doubled over Goslin's head, scoring Yde with the tying run.
Moore walked.
Carey safe on Peckinpaugh's poor throw to second, trying for the force.
(Peckinpaugh's 8th error of the Series).
Cuyler got a ground-rule double into the crowd in right, scoring Bigbee and Moore with Carey having to stop at third.
3 Barnhart popped to second.

9th Inning

Washington
For Pittsburgh—Oldham pitching, Gooch catching, and Bigbee replacing Barnhart in left.
1 Rice called out on strikes.
2 B. Harris lined to second.
3 Goslin called out on strikes.

1925 WORLD SERIES COMPOSITE BOX

	Wins	Composite Line Score
Pittsburgh Pirates (N.L.)	4	0 1 7 2 3 1 4 6 1 - 25
Washington Senators (A.L.)	3	6 3 5 3 2 1 3 1 2 - 26

Manager	W	L	Pct.	G. Ahead
	Regular Season			
Bill McKechnie	95	58	.621	8½
Bucky Harris	96	55	.636	8½

BATTING AND FIELDING

PITTSBURGH PIRATES

	WORLD SERIES STATISTICS																
	Pos	G	AB	R	H	2B	3B	HR	RBI	BB	SO	SB	BA	SA	PO	A	E
George Grantham	1b-ph	5	15	0	2	0	0	0	0	0	3	1	.133	.133	42	6	0
Eddie Moore	2b	7	26	**7**	6	1	0	1	2	**5**	2	0	.231	.385	16	13	1
Glenn Wright	ss	7	27	3	5	1	0	1	3	1	4	0	.185	.333	11	**24**	2
Pie Traynor	3b	7	26	2	9	0	**2**	1	4	3	1	1	.346	.615	6	18	0
Kiki Cuyler	rf	7	26	3	7	3	0	1	**6**	1	4	0	.269	.500	12	0	1
Max Carey	cf	7	24	6	11	**4**	0	0	2	2	3	**3**	**.458**	.625	14	0	1
Clyde Barnhart	lf	7	28	1	7	1	0	0	5	3	**5**	1	.250	.286	12	1	0
Earl Smith	c	6	20	0	7	1	0	0	0	1	2	0	.350	.400	28	7	1
Stuffy McInnis	ph-1b	4	14	0	4	0	0	0	1	0	2	0	.286	.286	30	3	0
Johnny Gooch	c	3	3	0	0	0	0	0	0	0	0	0	.000	.000	9	3	0
Carson Bigbee	pr-ph-lf	4	3	1	1	1	0	0	1	0	0	1	.333	.667	0	0	0
Johnny Rawlings	Did not play																
Fresco Thompson	Did not play																
Roy Spencer	Did not play																
Jewel Ens	Did not play																
Mule Haas	Did not play																
Ray Kremer	p	3	7	0	1	0	0	0	1	0	**5**	0	.143	.143	2	5	1
Vic Aldridge	p	3	7	0	0	0	0	0	0	0	0	0	.000	.000	0	4	0
Johnny Morrison	p	3	2	1	1	0	0	0	0	0	0	0	.500	.500	0	3	0
Lee Meadows	p	1	1	0	0	0	0	0	0	1	1	0	.000	.000	0	2	0
Emil Yde	p-pr	2	1	1	0	0	0	0	0	0	0	0	.000	.000	0	0	0
Babe Adams	p	1	0	0	0	0	0	0	0	0	0	0	—	—	0	0	0
Red Oldham	p	1	0	0	0	0	0	0	0	0	0	0	—	—	0	0	0
Tom Sheehan	Did not play																
Bud Culloton	Did not play																
team total		7	230	25	61	12	2	4	25	17	32	7	.265	.387	182	89	7

Double Plays–4
Left on Bases–54

		REGULAR SEASON STATISTICS													
		Main Pos	G	AB	R	H	2B	3B	HR	RBI	BB	SO	SB	BA	SA
George Grantham		1b	114	359	74	117	24	6	8	52	50	29	14	.326	.493
Eddie Moore		2b	142	547	106	163	29	8	6	77	73	26	19	.298	.413
Glenn Wright		ss	153	614	97	189	32	10	18	121	31	32	3	.308	.430
Pie Traynor		3b	150	591	114	189	39	14	6	106	52	19	15	.320	.464
Kiki Cuyler		of	153	617	**144**	220	43	**26**	18	102	58	56	41	.357	.598
Max Carey		of	133	542	109	186	39	13	5	44	66	19	**46**	.343	.491
Clyde Barnhart		of	142	539	85	175	32	11	4	114	59	25	9	.325	.447
Earl Smith		c	109	329	34	103	22	3	8	64	31	13	4	.313	.471
Stuffy McInnis		1b	59	155	19	57	10	4	0	24	17	1	1	.368	.484
Johnny Gooch		c	79	215	24	64	8	4	0	30	20	16	1	.298	.372
Carson Bigbee		of	66	126	31	30	7	0	0	8	7	8	2	.238	.294
Johnny Rawlings		2b	36	110	17	31	7	0	2	13	8	8	0	.282	.400
Fresco Thompson		2b	14	37	4	9	2	1	0	8	4	3	2	.243	.351
Roy Spencer		c	14	28	1	6	1	0	0	2	1	1	1	.214	.250
Jewel Ens		1b	3	5	2	1	0	0	1	2	0	1	0	.200	.000
Mule Haas		of	4	3	1	0	0	0	0	0	0	1	0	.000	.000
Ray Kremer		p	40	71	9	14	5	1	0	7	5	25	0	.197	.296
Vic Aldridge		p	30	86	3	20	0	0	1	10	0	4	0	.233	.267
Johnny Morrison		p	44	73	4	13	0	2	0	8	1	17	0	.178	.233
Lee Meadows		p	35	97	10	17	3	0	1	7	7	21	0	.175	.237
Emil Yde		p	47	89	11	17	4	1	0	11	2	13	1	.191	.258
Babe Adams		p	33	31	3	7	1	0	0	1	3	6	0	.226	.258
Red Oldham		p	11	18	2	6	0	1	0	1	2	4	0	.333	.444
Tom Sheehan	a	p	24	20	0	3	0	0	0	1	1	6	0	.150	.150
Bud Culloton		p	9	3	0	0	0	0	0	0	0	3	0	.000	.000
team total			153	5372	**912**	**1651**	**316**	**105**	78	**820**	**499**	363	**159**	**.307**	**.449**

a—from Cincinnati

Al Niehaus (1b), Lou Koupal (p), Don Songer (p) also played for the Pirates during the season.

WASHINGTON SENATORS

	WORLD SERIES STATISTICS																
	Pos	G	AB	R	H	2B	3B	HR	RBI	BB	SO	SB	BA	SA	PO	A	E
Joe Judge	1b	7	23	2	4	1	0	1	3	3	2	0	.174	.348	**59**	2	0
Bucky Harris	2b	7	23	2	2	0	0	0	0	1	3	0	.087	.087	24	18	0
Roger Peckinpaugh	ss	7	24	1	6	1	0	1	3	1	2	1	.250	.417	10	22	**8**
Ossie Bluege	3b	5	18	2	5	1	0	0	2	0	4	0	.278	.333	1	14	0
Joe Harris	rf	7	25	5	11	2	0	**3**	**6**	3	4	0	.440	**.880**	10	1	0
Sam Rice	cf-rf	7	**33**	5	**12**	0	0	0	3	0	1	0	.364	.364	17	0	0
Goose Goslin	lf	7	26	6	8	1	0	**3**	**6**	3	3	0	.308	.692	15	0	0
Muddy Ruel	c	7	19	0	6	1	0	0	1	3	2	0	.316	.368	35	5	0
Buddy Myer	3b	3	8	0	2	0	0	0	0	1	2	0	.250	.250	1	1	0
Hank Severeid	c	1	3	0	1	0	0	0	0	0	0	0	.333	.333	6	0	1
Nemo Leibold	ph	3	2	1	1	1	0	0	0	1	0	0	.500	1.000			
Spence Adams	ph-2b	2	1	0	0	0	0	0	0	0	0	0	.000	.000	0	0	0
Bobby Veach	ph	2	1	0	0	0	0	0	1	0	0	0	.000	.000			
Earl McNeely	cf-pr	4	0	2	0	0	0	0	0	0	0	1	—	—	2	0	0
Everett Scott	Did not play																
Bennie Tate	Did not play																
Tex Jeanes	Did not play																
Walter Johnson	p	3	11	0	1	0	0	0	0	0	3	0	.091	.091	0	4	0
Alex Ferguson	p	2	4	0	0	0	0	0	0	0	3	0	.000	.000	0	1	0
Stan Coveleski	p	2	3	0	0	0	0	0	0	1	2	0	.000	.000	0	4	0
Firpo Marberry	p	2	0	0	0	0	0	0	0	0	0	0	—	—	0	0	0
Win Ballou	p	2	0	0	0	0	0	0	0	0	0	0	—	—	0	0	0
Tom Zachary	p	1	0	0	0	0	0	0	0	0	0	0	—	—	0	3	0
Dutch Ruether	ph	1	1	0	0	0	0	0	0	0	1	0	.000	.000			
Allen Russell	Did not play																
team total		7	225	26	59	8	0	8	25	17	32	2	.262	.369	180	75	9

Double Plays—8
Left on Bases—46

		REGULAR SEASON STATISTICS													
		Main Pos	G	AB	R	H	2B	3B	HR	RBI	BB	SO	SB	BA	SA
Joe Judge		1b	112	376	65	118	31	5	8	66	55	21	7	.314	.487
Bucky Harris		2b	144	551	91	158	30	3	1	66	64	21	14	.287	.358
Roger Peckinpaugh		ss	126	422	67	124	16	4	4	64	49	23	13	.294	.379
Ossie Bluege		3b	145	522	77	150	27	4	4	79	59	56	16	.287	.377
Joe Harris	b	1b-of	100	300	60	97	21	9	12	59	51	28	5	.323	.573
Sam Rice		of	152	649	111	227	31	13	1	87	37	10	26	.350	.442
Goose Goslin		of	150	601	116	201	34	**20**	18	113	53	50	26	.334	.547
Muddy Ruel		c	127	393	55	122	9	2	0	54	63	16	4	.310	.346
Buddy Myer		ss	4	8	1	2	0	0	0	0	0	1	0	.250	.250
Hank Severeid	c	c	50	110	11	39	8	1	0	14	11	6	0	.355	.445
Nemo Leibold		of	56	84	14	23	1	1	0	7	8	7	1	.274	.310
Spence Adams		2b-ss	39	55	11	15	4	1	0	4	5	4	1	.273	.382
Bobby Veach	d	of	18	37	4	9	3	0	0	8	3	3	0	.243	.324
Earl McNeely		of	122	385	76	110	14	2	3	37	48	54	14	.286	.356
Everett Scott	e	ss	33	103	10	28	6	1	0	18	4	4	1	.272	.350
Bennie Tate		c	16	27	0	13	3	0	0	7	2	2	0	.481	.593
Tex Jeanes		of	15	19	2	5	1	0	1	4	3	2	1	.263	.474
Walter Johnson		p	36	97	12	42	6	1	2	20	3	6	0	.433	.577
Alex Ferguson	f	p	7	20	2	1	0	0	0	0	1	10	0	.050	.050
Stan Coveleski		p	32	81	3	9	0	0	0	7	1	25	0	.111	.111
Firpo Marberry		p	55	19	3	5	0	0	0	4	2	1	1	.263	.263
Win Ballou		p	10	7	1	1	1	0	0	0	0	3	0	.143	.286
Tom Zachary		p	38	69	5	12	0	1	1	5	2	20	0	.174	.246
Dutch Ruether		p-ph	55	108	18	36	3	2	1	15	10	8	0	.333	.426
Allen Russell		p	32	14	2	2	0	0	0	1	1	5	0	.143	.143
team total			152	5206	829	1577	251	72	56	747	533	427	**140**	.303	.411

b—from Boston (A)
c—from St. Louis (A)
d—from Boston and New York (A)
e—from Boston and New York (A)

Roy Carlyle (of), Pinky Hargrave (c), Wid Matthews (of), Tubby McGee (1b), Mike McNally (3b), Mule Shirley (1b), Stuffy Stewart (3b), Vean Gregg (p), Harry Kelley (p), Jim Lyle (p), George Mogridge (p), Curly Ogden (p), Spence Pumpelly (p), Lefty Thomas (p) also played for the Senators during the season.

PITCHING

PITTSBURGH PIRATES

	WORLD SERIES STATISTICS											
	G	GS	CG	IP	H	R	ER	BB	SO	W	L	SV	ERA
Ray Kremer	**3**	2	2	21	17	7	7	4	9	**2**	1	0	3.00
Vic Aldridge	**3**	**3**	2	18 1/3	18	9	**9**	**9**	9	**2**	0	0	4.42
Johnny Morrison	**3**	1	0	9 1/3	11	3	3	1	7	0	0	0	2.89
Lee Meadows	1	0	0	8	6	3	3	0	4	0	1	0	3.38
Emil Yde	1	1	0	2 1/3	5	4	3	3	1	0	1	0	11.57
Babe Adams	1	0	0	1	2	0	0	0	0	0	0	0	0.00
Red Oldham	1	0	0	1	0	0	0	0	2	0	0	**1**	0.00
Tom Sheehan	Did not play												
Bud Culloton	Did not play												
team total	7	7	4	61	59	26	25	17	32	4	3	1	3.69

		REGULAR SEASON STATISTICS													
		G	GS	CG	IP	H	ER	BB	SO	W	L	Pct	SV	ShO	ERA
Ray Kremer		40	27	14	215	232	88	47	62	17	8	.680	2	0	3.68
Vic Aldridge		30	26	14	213	218	86	74	88	15	7	.682	0	1	3.63
Johnny Morrison		**44**	26	10	211	245	91	60	60	17	14	.548	**4**	0	3.88
Lee Meadows		35	31	20	255	272	104	67	87	19	10	.655	1	1	3.67
Emil Yde		33	28	13	207	254	95	75	41	17	9	.654	0	0	4.13
Babe Adams		33	10	3	101	129	61	17	18	6	5	.545	3	0	5.44
Red Oldham		11	4	3	53	66	23	18	10	3	2	.600	1	0	3.91
Tom Sheehan	a	23	0	0	57	63	17	13	13	1	1	.500	2	0	2.68
Bud Culloton		9	1	0	21	19	6	1	3	0	1	.000	0	0	2.57
team total		153	153	77	1355	1526	583	387	386	**95**	58	**.621**	**13**	2	3.87

WASHINGTON SENATORS

	WORLD SERIES STATISTICS											
	G	GS	CG	IP	H	R	ER	BB	SO	W	L	SV	ERA
Walter Johnson	**3**	**3**	**3**	**26**	**26**	**10**	6	4	**15**	**2**	1	0	**2.08**
Stan Coveleski	2	2	0	14 1/3	16	7	6	5	3	0	**2**	0	3.77
Alex Ferguson	2	2	1	14	13	6	5	6	11	1	1	0	3.21
Firpo Marberry	2	0	0	2 1/3	3	0	0	0	2	0	0	**1**	0.00
Win Ballou	2	0	0	1 2/3	0	0	0	1	1	0	0	0	0.00
Tom Zachary	1	0	0	1 2/3	3	2	2	1	0	0	0	0	10.80
Dutch Ruether	Did not pitch												
Allen Russell	Did not play												
team total	7	7	4	60	61	25	19	17	32	3	4	1	2.85

		REGULAR SEASON STATISTICS													
		G	GS	CG	IP	H	ER	BB	SO	W	L	Pct	SV	ShO	ERA
Walter Johnson		30	29	16	229	211	78	78	108	20	7	.741	0	3	3.07
Stan Coveleski		32	32	15	241	230	76	73	58	20	5	**.800**	0	3	**2.84**
Alex Ferguson	f	7	6	3	55	52	20	23	24	5	1	.833	0	0	3.27
Firpo Marberry		**55**	0	0	93	84	36	45	53	8	6	.571	**15**	0	3.48
Win Ballou		10	1	1	28	38	14	13	13	1	1	.500	0	0	4.50
Tom Zachary		38	33	11	218	247	93	74	58	12	15	.444	2	1	3.84
Dutch Ruether		30	29	16	223	241	96	105	68	18	7	.720	0	1	3.87
Allen Russell		32	2	0	69	85	44	37	25	2	4	.333	2	0	5.74
team total		152	152	69	1358	1426	554	543	464	**96**	55	**.636**	**21**	9	**3.67**

Total Attendance—282,848 Average Attendance—40,407 Winning Player's Share—$5,333 Losing Player's Share—$3,735

1926
Alexander vs. Lazzeri

A St. Louis team had not won a pennant since 1888, but this year's Cardinals educated the city's younger generation of baseball fans in the joys of winning by taking the National League flag by two games over Cincinnati. Manager Rogers Hornsby played second base and, enduring an off-season with the bat, still hit .317 and drove in 93 runs. The big production men in the lineup instead were first baseman Sunny Jim Bottomley, who hit .299 and drove in 120 runs, and third baseman Les Bell, a .325 hitter with 100 RBI's. Twenty-game-winner Flint Rhem, top southpaw Bill Sherdel, and veteran Jesse Haines, whose newly learned knuckle ball earned him a 13–4 record and rejuvenated his failing career, headed up a pitching staff which also included thirty-nine-year-old Pete Alexander, the one-time Philly whiz whom Hornsby picked up cheap in midseason from the Cubs. The American League champion New York Yankees, on the other hand, had only been away from the top for two years, but they reappeared in the Series with many impressive new faces. Babe Ruth, Bob Meusel, Joe Dugan, Herb Pennock, Waite Hoyt, Sam Jones, and Bob Shawkey all returned from the 1923 squad, but manager Miller Huggins supplemented them with Lou Gehrig, a twenty-three-year-old first baseman who joined Ruth as the most feared power combo in history; Tony Lazzeri, a powerful second baseman who consistently drove in over 100 runs per season; shortstop Mark Koenig, a steady fielder and tough out; center fielder Earle Combs, a superfast fielder and leadoff man supreme; and veteran pitcher Urban Shocker, a 19-game winner this season. The Yanks seemed on the threshold of a dynasty, but the Cards were to hold off the coronation for a year.

The Yanks got off to a strong start with a 2–1 opening game victory, with Herb Pennock treating the Yankee Stadium crowd to a three-hit masterpiece. Old-timer Pete Alexander entertained the crowd the next day, facing Shocker in game two. A shaky start by Alexander gave the Yanks two runs in the second inning, but after Combs opened the third with a single, Pete hit his stride and set the next 21 Yankee batters down. His four-hitter earned him a 6–2 victory to even the Series at 1–1.

With the scene shifted to St. Louis, the Yankee bats remained cold as Haines spun a five-hitter and the Cards won a 4–0 game. Babe Ruth personally took it upon himself to awaken the Yankee bats in game four, swatting three homers to pace his mates to a 10–5 victory to square the Series at two games apiece. Pennock and Sherdel locked horns in game five, with the Yankees winning in ten innings 3–2 to take an identical 3–2 lead in the Series, heading back to New York.

With no margin left for losing, the Cards blasted three New York pitchers for 10 runs in the sixth game, with Pete Alexander going the distance in the 10–2 victory. Legend has it that old Pete celebrated long and hard into the night and came out to the seventh game in dire need of some rest on the bullpen bench. Jesse Haines and Waite Hoyt took the mound in this decisive match, which was played in a steady drizzle. Ruth picked out a flat Haines delivery and smacked it into the seats in the third for a 1–0 lead. But shoddy Yankee fielding in the fourth squandered that lead and put them in a 3–1 hole. After getting a run back in the sixth, the Yanks loaded the bases with two outs in the seventh against Haines, who had worn a blister on his index finger. Manager Hornsby saw Haines losing his touch and decided to bring in his most battle-hardened pitcher, Pete Alexander. The veteran hurler strode out of the Cardinal bullpen, ignoring any hangover he may have had. He worked carefully to Tony Lazzeri, going to a 1–1 count before laying in a fat one which Lazzeri drilled down the left-field line just foul. Saved by a few inches, Alexander then struck Lazzeri out on the next pitch to end the rally. Old Pete came out for the eighth inning and set the Yankees down in order. With the 3–2 lead and the World Series on the line, Alexander retired Combs and Koenig to start the ninth, then walked Ruth. Slugging Bob Meusel came to the plate, but then Ruth decided, completely on his own, to steal second. Catcher Bob O'Farrell gunned the ball down to Hornsby, who slapped the tag on the Babe in plenty of time to end the game and make the Cards the Series champs, and old Pete the Series hero.

Game 1 October 2 at New York

St. Louis	Pos	AB	R	H	RBI	PO	A	E
Douthit	cf	3	1	1	0	1	0	0
Southworth	rf	3	0	0	0	1	0	0
b Holm	rf	1	0	0	0	0	0	0
Hornsby	2b	4	0	0	0	3	3	0
Bottomley	1b	4	0	2	1	10	0	0
L. Bell	3b	3	0	0	0	1	1	1
Hafey	lf	4	0	0	0	5	1	0
O'Farrell	c	2	0	0	0	1	1	0
Thevenow	ss	2	0	0	0	1	7	0
Sherdel	p	2	0	0	0	1	2	0
a Flowers		1	0	0	0	0	0	0
Haines	p	0	0	0	0	0	0	0
Totals		29	1	3	1	24	14	1

a Flied out for Sherdel in 8th.
b Flied out for Southworth in 8th.

Double—Douthit. Sacrifice Hits—Meusel, Pennock, Thevenow. Double Play—Thevenow to Hornsby to Bottomley. Left on Bases—St. Louis 5, New York 7. Umpires—Dinneen (A), O'Day (N), Hildebrand (A), Klem (N).
Attendance—61,658 Time of Game—1:48.

New York	Pos	AB	R	H	RBI	PO	A	E
Combs	cf	3	1	1	0	2	0	0
Koenig	ss	4	0	1	0	0	4	0
Ruth	rf	3	1	1	0	1	0	0
Meusel	lf	4	0	0	0	3	0	0
Gehrig	1b	4	0	1	2	14	0	0
Lazzeri	2b	4	0	1	0	0	4	0
Dugan	3b	3	0	1	0	1	3	0
Severeid	c	3	0	0	0	6	1	0
Pennock	p	2	0	0	0	0	3	0
Totals		27	2	6	2	27	15	0

Pitching	IP	H	R	ER	BB	SO
St. Louis						
Sherdel (L)	7	6	2	2	3	1
Haines	1	0	0	0	1	0
New York						
Pennock (W)	9	3	1	1	3	4

1st Inning
St. Louis
Douthit doubled past Ruth to the right field bleacher fence.
1 Southworth grounded to second, Douthit advancing to third.
2 Hornsby bounced back to the box, Douthit holding at third. Bottomley looped a single behind Dugan, Douthit scoring.
3 L. Bell flied to short right.
New York
Combs walked.
1 Koenig flied to right. Ruth walked on four pitches. Meusel also walked, loading the bases.
2 Gehrig forced Meusel at second, Thevenow to Hornsby as Gehrig beat the throw to first, Combs scoring and Ruth going to third.
3 Lazzeri grounded to short.

2nd Inning
St. Louis
1 Hafey grounded to short.
2 O'Farrell grounded to short.
3 Thevenow grounded to second.
New York
Dugan singled to center.
1 Severeid flied to left.
2 Pennock sacrificed Dugan to second, Sherdel making the tag along the first base line.
3 Combs flied to center.

3rd Inning
St. Louis
1 Sherdel struck out.
2 Douthit was just nipped on a bunt, Pennock to Gehrig.
3 Southworth fouled to Severeid.
New York
Koenig singled to left.
1 Ruth forced Koenig at second on a bunt, O'Farrell to Thevenow.
2 Meusel bounced back to the mound, Ruth going to second.
3 Gehrig flied to left.

4th Inning
St. Louis
1 Hornsby grounded to short.
2 Bottomley called out on strikes. L. Bell walked.
3 Hafey grounded to short.
New York
1 Lazzeri struck out.
2 Dugan grounded to short.
3 Severeid flied to left.

5th Inning
St. Louis
1 O'Farrell flied to deep left.
2 Thevenow bunted out, Severeid to Gehrig.
3 Sherdel flied to left.
New York
1 Pennock grounded to short. Combs singled to left.
2,3 Koenig hit into a double play, Thevenow to Hornsby to Bottomley.

6th Inning
St. Louis
1 Douthit grounded to third.
2 Southworth flied to left.
3 Hornsby rolled out to third.
New York
Ruth singled through short.
1 Meusel sacrificed Ruth to second, Sherdel to Bottomley. Gehrig singled to right, scoring Ruth. Lazzeri singled to left but Gehrig was
2 out going for third, Hafey to L. Bell. Lazzeri taking second on the throw. Dugan safe at first on L. Bell's fumble as Lazzeri slid safely into third.
3 Severeid forced Dugan at second, Thevenow to Hornsby.

7th Inning
St. Louis
1 Bottomley grounded to first.
2 L. Bell fouled to Severeid.
3 Hafey struck out.
New York
1 Pennock grounded to short.
2 Combs grounded to second.
3 Koenig flied to center.

8th Inning
St. Louis
O'Farrell walked.
1 Thevenow sacrificed O'Farrell to second, Dugan to Gehrig.
2 Flowers, pinch-hitting for Sherdel, bounced to Pennock and O'Farrell got run-down, Pennock to Lazzeri to Dugan. Flowers got to second. Douthit walked on four pitches.
3 Holm, batting for Southworth, flied to an on-rushing Combs in very short center.
New York
For St. Louis—Holm stays in playing right and Haines pitching.
1 Ruth grounded to third. Meusel walked.
2 Gehrig flied to left.
3 Lazzeri grounded to first.

9th Inning
St. Louis
1 Hornsby flied to center. Bottomley singled to right. The first hit off Pennock since the first.
2 L. Bell struck out.
3 Hafey grounded to second.

Game 2 October 3 at New York

| St L. | 0 0 2 | 0 0 0 | 3 0 1 |
| N.Y. | 0 2 0 | 0 0 0 | 0 0 0 |

St. Louis	Pos	AB	R	H	RBI	PO	A	E
Douthit	cf	4	1	1	0	0	0	0
Southworth	rf	5	2	3	3	0	0	0
Hornsby	2b	3	0	1	0	1	5	0
Bottomley	1b	5	0	2	2	13	0	0
L. Bell	3b	4	0	0	0	0	4	0
Hafey	lf	4	0	0	0	1	0	0
O'Farrell	c	4	1	2	0	10	1	0
Thevenow	ss	4	2	3	1	2	4	0
Alexander	p	4	0	0	0	0	4	1
Totals		37	6	12	6	27	18	1

Pitching	IP	H	R	ER	BB	SO
St. Louis						
Alexander (W)	9	4	2	1	1	10
New York						
Shocker (L)	*7	10	5	5	0	2
Shawkey	1	0	0	0	0	2
Jones	1	2	1	1	2	1

*Pitched to one batter in 8th.

New York	Pos	AB	R	H	RBI	PO	A	E
Combs	cf	4	0	1	0	1	0	0
Koenig	ss	4	0	0	0	1	3	0
Ruth	rf	4	0	0	0	1	0	0
Meusel	lf	4	1	1	0	3	0	0
Gehrig	1b	3	0	0	0	12	0	0
Lazzeri	2b	3	1	1	1	2	2	0
Dugan	3b	4	0	1	0	1	1	0
Severeid	c	2	0	0	0	5	1	0
a Paschal		1	0	0	0	0	0	0
Collins	c	0	0	0	0	1	0	0
Shocker	p	2	0	0	0	0	2	0
Shawkey	p	0	0	0	0	0	0	0
b Ruether		1	0	0	0	0	0	0
Jones	p	0	0	0	0	0	0	0
Totals		30	2	4	1	27	9	0

a Struck out for Severeid in 8th.
b Grounded out for Shawkey in 8th.

Doubles—Hornsby, O'Farrell. Home Runs—Southworth, Thevenow. Sacrifice Hit—Hornsby. Double Play—Alexander to Thevenow to Hornsby to Bottomley. Left on Bases—St. Louis 7, New York 2. Umpires—O'Day, Hildebrand, Klem, Dinneen. Attendance—**63,600**. Time of Game—1:57.

1st Inning
St. Louis
1 Douthit called out on strikes.
2 Southworth fouled to Severeid. Hornsby doubled into the right field corner.
3 Bottomley grounded to short.
New York
Combs walked.
1,2 Koenig hit into a double play, the ball deflected off Alexander to Thevenow to Hornsby to Bottomley.
3 Ruth called out on strikes.

2nd Inning
St. Louis
1 L. Bell flied to left.
2 Hafey grounded to second. O'Farrell singled a single into short left. Thevenow singled off Shocker's glove past Lazzeri as O'Farrell went to third.
3 Alexander popped to Koenig near the left field foul line.
New York
Meusel lined a single to center.
1 Gehrig grounded back to the mound, Meusel going to second. Lazzeri lined the first pitch to left for a single, scoring Meusel. Dugan blooped a single into right center, Lazzeri racing to third.
2 Severeid struck out. On an attempted double steal Dugan drew O'Farrell's throw to Thevenow and Lazzeri got hung up between third and the plate. Alexander threw the ball past L. Bell for an error allowing Lazzeri to score and Dugan to get to second.
3 Shocker struck out.

3rd Inning
St. Louis
Douthit beat out a slow roller to short. Southworth singled hard to left with Meusel just missing a force on Douthit at second.
1 Hornsby sacrificed up both runners, Shocker to Gehrig. Bottomley singled to right, both Douthit and Southworth scoring.
2 L. Bell fouled to Severeid.
3 Hafey flied to left.
New York
Combs singled to right.
1 Koenig struck out.
2 Ruth popped to short.
3 Meusel grounded to third.

4th Inning
St. Louis
1 O'Farrell popped to third.
2 Thevenow fouled to Gehrig.
3 Alexander called out on strikes.
New York
1 Gehrig struck out.
2 Lazzeri also struck out.
3 Dugan struck out.

5th Inning
St. Louis
1 Douthit flied to right.
2 Southworth tapped back to the mound.
3 Hornsby grounded to third.
New York
1 Severeid grounded to third.
2 Shocker took a called third strike.
3 Combs grounded to second.

6th Inning
St. Louis
1 Bottomley grounded to first.
2 L. Bell grounded to short.
3 Hafey fouled to Gehrig.
New York
1 Koenig grounded to second.
2 Ruth grounded to second.
3 Meusel called out on strikes leaving Combs as the only Yankee yet to strike out.

7th Inning
St. Louis
O'Farrell doubled to left-center. Thevenow singled to left, O'Farrell stopping at third.
1 Alexander popped to second.
2 Douthit flied to short left. Southworth hit a three-run homer into the right field bleachers.
3 Hornsby grounded to short.
New York
1 Gehrig bounced back to the box.
2 Lazzeri grounded to short.
3 Dugan grounded to third.

8th Inning
St. Louis
Bottomley singled to right. For New York—Shawkey came into pitch.
1 L. Bell struck out.
2 Hafey struck out.
3 Bottomley caught trying to steal second, Severeid to Lazzeri.
New York
1 Paschal, batting for Severeid, struck out.
2 Ruether, batting for Shawkey, rolled back to the mound.
3 Combs flied to left, the first putout by Cardinal outfielders in the game.

9th Inning
St. Louis
For New York—Jones pitching and Collins catching.
1 O'Farrell grounded to second. Thevenow got a home run to right which Ruth dropped while running at full speed and just beating Ruth's throw to the plate.
2 Alexander struck out. Douthit walked. Southworth singled to right, Douthit going to third. Hornsby walked, loading the bases.
3 Bottomley flied to center.
New York
1 Koenig grounded to second.
2 Ruth lined to second.
3 Meusel grounded to short.

Game 3 October 5 at St. Louis

| N.Y. | 0 0 0 | 0 0 0 | 0 0 0 |
| St L. | 0 0 0 | 3 1 0 | 0 0 x |

New York	Pos	AB	R	H	RBI	PO	A	E
Combs	cf	3	0	1	0	4	0	0
Koenig	ss	4	0	0	0	2	3	1
Ruth	rf	3	0	1	0	1	0	0
Meusel	lf	4	0	0	0	1	0	0
Gehrig	1b	4	0	2	0	10	0	0
Lazzeri	2b	3	0	0	0	4	6	0
Dugan	3b	3	0	1	0	2	1	0
Severeid	c	2	0	0	0	3	0	0
Ruether	p	2	0	0	0	0	2	0
Shawkey	p	0	0	0	0	0	1	0
a Paschal		0	0	0	0	0	0	0
Thomas	p	0	0	0	0	0	0	0
Totals		29	0	5	0	24	13	1

a Walked for Shawkey in 8th.

Double—Hafey. Home Run—Haines. Sacrifice Hits—Hafey, Severeid, Southworth. Double Plays—Hornsby to Thevenow to Bottomley, Koenig to Lazzeri to Gehrig, Thevenow to Hornsby to Gehrig, St. Louis 5. Umpires—Hildebrand, Klem, Dinneen, O'Day. Attendance—37,708. Time of Game—1:41.

St. Louis	Pos	AB	R	H	RBI	PO	A	E
Douthit	cf	3	0	0	0	1	0	0
Southworth	rf	3	1	2	0	1	0	0
Hornsby	2b	4	0	1	0	1	5	0
Bottomley	1b	4	0	1	1	13	0	0
L. Bell	3b	4	1	1	0	0	4	0
Hafey	lf	3	0	1	0	4	0	0
O'Farrell	c	2	0	0	0	5	0	0
Thevenow	ss	3	1	0	0	1	2	0
Haines	p	3	1	2	2	0	2	0
Totals		29	4	8	3	27	13	0

Pitching	IP	H	R	ER	BB	SO
New York						
Ruether (L)	4⅓	7	4	2	2	1
Shawkey	2⅔	0	0	0	0	1
Thomas	1	1	0	0	0	0
St. Louis						
Haines (W)	9	5	0	0	3	3

1st Inning
New York
1 Combs flied to deep left.
2 Koenig struck out.
3 Ruth grounded to second.
St. Louis
1 Douthit flied to left. Southworth singled over second.
2 Hornsby popped to second.
3 Bottomley grounded to second.

2nd Inning
New York
1 Meusel flied to deep right.
2 Gehrig flied to left.
3 Lazzeri struck out.
St. Louis
1 L. Bell struck out. Hafey doubled deep down the left field foul line.
2 O'Farrell grounded to second, Hafey taking third.
3 Thevenow lined to center.

3rd Inning
New York
Dugan singled to left.
1 Severeid sacrificed Dugan to second, Haines to Bottomley.
2 Ruether fouled to O'Farrell. Combs walked.
3 Koenig grounded to first.
St. Louis
Haines beat out an infield hit to first. Douthit walked.
1 Southworth sacrificed both runners up a base, Ruether to Gehrig.
2 Hornsby fouled to Severeid.
3 Bottomley lined to center.

4th Inning
New York
Ruth singled to short center.
1 Meusel bounced back to the mound, Ruth going to second. The game was halted due to rain for just over thirty minutes.
2 Gehrig popped to O'Farrell in front of the plate.
3 Lazzeri grounded to second.
St. Louis
L. Bell singled over second.
1 Hafey sacrificed L. Bell to second, Ruether to Lazzeri. O'Farrell walked.
2 Thevenow forced O'Farrell at second, Lazzeri to Koenig, but Koenig's throw to first was wild and L. Bell scored. Haines hit a two-run homer into the right field bleachers.
3 Douthit lined to short.

5th Inning
New York
1 Dugan flied to deep left.
2 Severeid flied to deep right.
3 Ruether flied to left.
St. Louis
Southworth singled to left. Hornsby singled over second, Southworth going to third.
1 Bottomley rolled out to second, Southworth scoring and Hornsby going to second. For New York—Shawkey came in to pitch.
2 L. Bell grounded to short, Hornsby taking third.
3 Hafey grounded to third.

6th Inning
New York
Combs singled to left.
1,2 Koenig hit into a double play, Hornsby to Thevenow to Bottomley. Ruth walked.
3 Meusel grounded to third.
St. Louis
1 O'Farrell flied to center.
2 Thevenow flied to center.
3 Haines grounded to short.

7th Inning
New York
Gehrig singled to center.
1 Lazzeri grounded to third, moving Gehrig to second.
2 Dugan flied to deep center.
3 Severeid grounded to third.
St. Louis
1 Douthit struck out.
2 Southworth grounded to second.
3 Hornsby popped to second.

8th Inning
New York
Paschal, batting for Shawkey, walked.
1 Combs struck out.
2 Koenig grounded to first, Paschal going to second.
3 Ruth grounded to second.
St. Louis
For New York—Thomas pitching. Bottomley singled to right-center.
1,2 L. Bell hit into a double play, Koenig to Lazzeri to Gehrig.
3 Hafey grounded to third.

9th Inning
New York
1 Meusel grounded to third. Gehrig singled to right between Bottomley and Hornsby.
2,3 Lazzeri hit into a game-ending double play, Thevenow to Hornsby to Bottomley.

1926

Game 4 October 6 at St. Louis

N.Y.	1 0 1	1 4 2	1 0 0			
St L.	1 0 0	3 0 0	0 0 1			

New York	Pos	AB	R	H	RBI	PO	A	E
Combs	cf	5	2	2	1	4	0	0
Koenig	ss	6	1	1	1	1	3	1
Ruth	lf	3	4	3	4	1	1	0
Meusel	rf	2	1	1	0	1	0	0
Gehrig	1b	3	0	2	1	8	0	0
Lazzeri	2b	3	1	1	1	1	3	0
Dugan	3b	4	0	1	2	1	2	0
Severeid	c	4	1	3	0	10	0	0
Hoyt	p	4	0	0	0	0	0	0
Totals		34	10	14	10	27	9	1

Pitching	IP	H	R	ER	BB	SO
New York						
Hoyt (W)	9	14	5	2	1	8
St. Louis						
Rhem	4	7	3	3	2	4
Reinhart (L)	*0	1	4	4	4	0
H. Bell	2	4	2	2	1	1
Hallahan	2	2	1	1	3	1
Keen	1	0	0	0	0	

*Pitched to 5 batters in 5th.

St. Louis	Pos	AB	R	H	RBI	PO	A	E
Douthit	cf	5	1	2	1	2	2	0
Southworth	rf	5	0	3	0	1	2	0
Hornsby	2b	5	1	2	0	3	4	0
Bottomley	1b	4	0	1	0	6	1	0
L. Bell	3b	4	0	1	1	3	0	0
Hafey	lf	5	1	1	0	0	0	0
O'Farrell	c	4	1	2	0	8	1	0
Thevenow	ss	4	1	2	1	3	2	0
Rhem	p	1	0	0	0	0	1	0
a Toporcer		0	0	0	1	0	0	0
Reinhart	p	0	0	0	0	0	0	0
H. Bell	p	0	0	0	0	0	0	0
b Flowers		1	0	0	0	0	0	0
Hallahan	p	0	0	0	0	1	0	0
c Holm		1	0	0	0	0	0	0
Keen	p	0	0	0	0	0	1	0
Totals		39	5	14	5	27	14	0

a Hit sacrifice fly for Rhem in 4th.
b Struck out for H. Bell in 6th.
c Struck out for Hallahan in 8th.

Doubles—Combs, Douthit, Dugan, Gehrig, Koenig, Lazzeri, Thevenow. Home Runs—Ruth 3. Stolen Base—Hornsby. Sacrifice Hits—L. Bell, Gehrig, Hoyt, Lazzeri, Toporcer. Balk—H. Bell. Left on Bases—New York 10, St. Louis 10. Umpires—Klem, Dinneen, O'Day, Hildebrand. Attendance—38,825. Time of Game—2:38.

1st Inning
New York
1 Combs struck out.
2 Koenig struck out.
Ruth hit the first pitch over the right field bleacher roof for a home run.
Meusel walked.
Gehrig singled past first, but Meusel
3 tried to score all the way from first and was out Southworth to Hornsby to O'Farrell.
St. Louis
Douthit singled just beyond Dugan's reach.
Southworth singled over second, Douthit going to third.
Hornsby singled between Gehrig and Lazzeri, Douthit scoring with Southworth stopping at second.
1 Bottomley flied to left.
2 L. Bell hit a sacrifice fly to center, Southworth going to third after the catch.
Hornsby stole second.
3 Hafey struck out.

2nd Inning
New York
Lazzeri doubled to the left field wall, but was out trying to stretch the hit
1 to a triple, Douthit to Thevenow to L. Bell.
2 Dugan popped to Thevenow in short center.
Severeid singled over second.
3 Hoyt popped to Hornsby in right.
St. Louis
1 O'Farrell grounded to Lazzeri who made a very good play of the difficult hit.
2 Thevenow popped to first.
3 Rhem took a called third strike.

3rd Inning
New York
1 Combs flied to center.
2 Koenig grounded to second.
Ruth hit another homer, a boomer over the right-center field bleacher roof.
3 Meusel grounded back to the mound.
St. Louis
1 Douthit grounded to short.
Southworth got a Texas League single between Ruth, Combs and Koenig.
2 Hornsby struck out.
3 Bottomley bounced to second.

4th Inning
New York
1 Gehrig took a called third strike.
Lazzeri walked.
Dugan doubled into short left-center as Douthit and Hafey collided and L. Bell came out to retrieve the ball with Lazzeri scoring.
Severeid singled to center, but Dugan
2 was cut down at the plate, Douthit to O'Farrell.
3 Hoyt struck out.
St. Louis
1 L. Bell flied to Koenig in left.
Hafey singled through the box.
O'Farrell safely to first with Hafey to second as Koenig booted O'Farrell's grounder.
Thevenow doubled down the right field foul line, Hafey scoring as O'Farrell stopped at third.
2 Toporcer, batting for Rhem, hit a sacrifice fly to center, O'Farrell scoring after the catch.
Douthit doubled off the right-center field wall, Thevenow scoring.
Southworth singled to left, but Ruth
3 uncorked a great throw getting Douthit at the plate.

5th Inning
New York
For St. Louis—Reinhart pitching.
Combs walked.
Koenig blooped a double to short right, Combs scoring.
Ruth walked.
Meusel walked, loading the bases.
Gehrig walked, forcing in Koenig.
For St. Louis—H. Bell pitching.
1 Lazzeri hit a sacrifice fly to right, Ruth scoring and Meusel going to third after the catch.
2 Dugan bounced out, O'Farrell to Bottomley, Meusel scoring and Gehrig taking second. Gehrig to third on a balk.
Severeid walked.
3 Hoyt forced Severeid at second, Hornsby to Thevenow.
St. Louis
1 Hornsby grounded to second.
Bottomley walked.
2 L. Bell grounded to third, Bottomley going to second.
3 Hafey struck out.

6th Inning
New York
Combs beat out a hit to deep short.
1 Koenig struck out.
Ruth with a 3–2 count hit a two-run homer into the deep center field bleachers. **His third of the game and fourth run scored in the game.**
Meusel singled to right but was out
2 trying for second, Southworth to Hornsby.
Gehrig doubled off the left field fence.
3 Lazzeri popped to short.
St. Louis
O'Farrell beat out a hit to deep short.
Thevenow singled to left, O'Farrell stopping at second.
1 Flowers, batting for H. Bell, struck out.
2 Douthit flied to right.
3 Southworth grounded to short.

7th Inning
New York
For St. Louis—Hallahan pitching.
1 Dugan grounded to second.
Severeid singled through the box.
2 Hoyt sacrificed Severeid to second, being tagged by Hallahan.
Combs doubled just inside the third base line, Severeid scoring.
3 Koenig struck out for the third time in the game.
St. Louis
1 Hornsby struck out.
Bottomley beat out a single to first as Hoyt failed to cover the bag.
2 L. Bell forced Bottomley at second, Koenig to Lazzeri.
3 Hafey fouled to Dugan.

8th Inning
New York
Ruth walked on four pitches.
Meusel also walked.
1 Gehrig sacrificed up both runners, Bottomley to Hornsby.
2 Lazzeri safe at first when L. Bell fielded his grounder and tagged out Ruth who was off the bag.
Dugan walked, loading the bases.
3 Severeid fouled to L. Bell.
St. Louis
O'Farrell singled past second.
1 Thevenow struck out.
2 Holm, batting for Hallahan, took a called third strike.
3 Douthit flied to center.

9th Inning
New York
For St. Louis—Keen pitching.
1 Hoyt grounded to deep short.
2 Combs flied to center.
3 Koenig grounded back to the mound.
St. Louis
1 Southworth flied to center.
Hornsby singled to right.
2 Bottomley grounded to third, Hornsby going to second.
L. Bell singled to center, Hornsby scoring.
3 Hafey fouled to Severeid.

Game 5 October 7 at St. Louis

N.Y.	000 001 001	1
St L.	000 100 100	0

New York	Pos	AB	R	H	RBI	PO	A	E
Combs	cf	4	0	1	0	2	0	0
Koenig	ss	5	1	2	1	3	6	1
Ruth	lf	3	0	0	0	3	0	0
Meusel	rf	3	0	0	0	0	0	0
Gehrig	1b	3	1	2	0	14	0	0
Lazzeri	2b	4	0	2	1	3	2	0
Dugan	3b	3	0	0	0	0	1	0
a Paschal		1	0	1	1	0	0	0
Gazella	3b	0	0	0	0	1	2	0
Severeid	c	5	0	0	0	4	1	0
Pennock	p	4	1	1	0	0	2	0
Totals		35	3	9	3	30	14	1

St. Louis	Pos	AB	R	H	RBI	PO	A	E
Holm	cf	4	0	0	0	1	0	0
Southworth	rf	4	0	0	0	2	0	0
Hornsby	2b	4	0	0	0	3	3	0
Bottomley	1b	4	1	1	0	12	0	0
L. Bell	3b	4	1	2	1	2	3	0
Hafey	lf	4	0	0	0	6	0	0
O'Farrell	c	4	0	3	1	2	3	0
Thevenow	ss	4	0	1	0	1	3	1
Sherdel	p	3	0	0	0	1	3	0
b Flowers		1	0	0	0	0	0	0
Totals		36	2	7	2	30	15	1

Pitching	IP	H	R	ER	BB	SO
New York						
Pennock (W)	10	7	2	2	1	4
St. Louis						
Sherdel (L)	10	9	3	2	5	2

a Singled for Dugan in 9th.
b Popped out for Sherdel in 10th.

Doubles—L. Bell, Bottomley, Gehrig, Pennock. Stolen Base—Southworth. Sacrifice Hits—Lazzeri, Meusel 2. Double Plays—Hornsby to Bottomley, Lazzeri to Koenig to Gehrig. Hit by Pitcher—Gazella (by Sherdel). Wild Pitch—Sherdel. Passed Ball—Severeid. Left on Bases—New York 11, St. Louis 5. Umpires—Dinneen, O'Day, Hildebrand, Klem. Attendance—39,552. Time of Game—2:28.

1st Inning
New York
1 Combs flied to left.
2 Koenig grounded to short.
3 Ruth grounded to second.
St. Louis
1 Holm grounded to short.
Southworth safe at first on Koenig's fumble of his grounder.
Southworth stole second.
On the next pitch Severeid was charged with a passed ball.
2 Hornsby grounded to the pitcher, Southworth going to third.
3 Bottomley grounded to second.

2nd Inning
New York
1 Meusel grounded to third.
Gehrig singled over second.
Lazzeri singled to right, Gehrig racing to third.
2,3 Dugan grounded into a double play, Hornsby to Bottomley.
St. Louis
1 L. Bell struck out.
2 Hafey grounded to third, Gehrig making the tag after Dugan's poor throw.
O'Farrell singled off Pennock's glove.
3 Thevenow flied to center.

3rd Inning
New York
1 Severeid flied to center.
2 Pennock lined hard back to the mound.
3 Combs rolled out, O'Farrell to first.
St. Louis
1 Sherdel rolled out to short.
2 Holm took a called third strike.
3 Southworth flied to left.

4th Inning
New York
1 Koenig flied to left.
Ruth walked.
2 Meusel flied to left.
3 Gehrig struck out.
St. Louis
1 Hornsby rolled weakly to the mound.
Bottomley doubled to left.
L. Bell singled over Lazzeri's head, Bottomley scoring.
2 Hafey fouled to Ruth making a fantastic catch leaning into the left field boxes.
3 L. Bell was caught trying to steal second, Severeid to Koenig.

5th Inning
New York
1 Lazzeri grounded to third.
2 Dugan popped to first.
3 Severeid flied to left.
St. Louis
O'Farrell lined a single off Koenig's bare hand.
1 Thevenow grounded to short, O'Farrell going to second.
2 Sherdel struck out.
3 Holm grounded to short.

6th Inning
New York
Pennock doubled to left, Hafey losing the ball in the sun.
Pennock was trapped off second, but Thevenow dropped O'Farrell's throw for an error. O'Farrell got an assist on the play.
Combs walked.
Koenig singled to left, scoring Pennock as Combs stopped at second.
1 Ruth struck out.
2 Meusel hit a sacrifice fly to deep right as Combs went to third after the catch.
Gehrig walked, loading the bases.
3 Lazzeri flied to right.
St. Louis
1 Southworth rolled to first.
2 Hornsby flied to center.
3 Bottomley struck out.

7th Inning
New York
1 Dugan popped to third.
2 Severeid grounded to short.
3 Pennock dribbled back to the box.
St. Louis
L. Bell doubled to left.
1 Hafey flied to left.
O'Farrell singled over Koenig's head, his third hit of the game, scoring L. Bell.
2 Thevenow popped to second.
3 Sherdel tapped to first.

8th Inning
New York
Combs singled off of Hornsby's fingers.
1 Koenig flied to left.
2 Ruth forced Combs at second, Sherdel to Thevenow.
3 Meusel grounded to third.
St. Louis
Holm walked.
1 Southworth forced Holm at second, Koenig to Lazzeri.
2,3 Hornsby hit into a double play, Lazzeri to Koenig to Gehrig.

9th Inning
New York
Gehrig got a Texas-League double to short left.
Lazzeri beat out a bunt to third, Gehrig going to third.
Paschal, batting for Dugan, singled to center, Gehrig scoring as Lazzeri stopped at second.
1 Severeid forced Lazzeri at third on a bunt, O'Farrell to L. Bell.
2 Pennock forced Severeid at second, Thevenow to Hornsby with Paschal going to third.
3 Combs rolled out to second.
St. Louis
For New York—Gazella playing third.
1 Bottomley flied to Lazzeri in right.
2 L. Bell grounded to third.
3 Hafey popped to short.

10th Inning
New York
Koenig singled through short.
Koenig went to second on a wild pitch.
Ruth walked.
1 Meusel advanced both runners with a sacrifice, Sherdel to Bottomley.
Gehrig intentionally passed, loading the bases.
2 Lazzeri hit a long sacrifice fly to left, scoring Koenig
Gazella was hit by a pitched ball, again loading the bases.
3 Severeid popped to second.
St. Louis
1 O'Farrell fouled to Gazella.
Thevenow singled to right.
2 Flowers, pinch-hitting for Sherdel, popped to first.
3 Holm grounded to third.

Game 6 October 9 at New York

St L.	
St L.	300 010 501
N.Y.	000 100 100

St. Louis	Pos	AB	R	H	RBI	PO	A	E
Holm	cf	5	1	2	1	4	0	0
Southworth	rf	5	3	2	1	2	1	0
Hornsby	2b	4	1	1	3	0	1	0
Bottomley	1b	5	2	2	1	11	0	0
L. Bell	3b	4	1	3	4	1	1	1
Hafey	lf	3	0	1	0	2	0	0
O'Farrell	c	4	0	0	0	6	0	0
Thevenow	ss	3	1	2	0	1	5	1
Alexander	p	2	1	0	0	0	2	0
Totals		35	10	13	10	27	10	2

Pitching	IP	H	R	ER	BB	SO
St. Louis						
Alexander (W)	9	8	2	2	2	6
New York						
Shawkey (L)	6⅓	8	7	6	2	4
Shocker	⅔	3	2	2	0	1
Thomas	2	2	1	1	0	0

New York	Pos	AB	R	H	RBI	PO	A	E
Combs	cf	5	0	2	1	2	0	0
Koenig	ss	5	0	0	0	3	2	0
Ruth	rf	3	0	0	0	0	1	0
Meusel	lf	3	1	2	0	2	0	0
Gehrig	1b	4	0	1	1	9	1	0
Lazzeri	2b	4	0	0	0	2	1	1
Dugan	3b	4	1	2	0	3	2	0
Severeid	c	3	0	1	0	6	3	0
a Adams		0	0	0	0	0	0	0
Collins	c	1	0	0	0	0	0	0
Shawkey	p	2	0	0	0	0	1	0
Shocker	p	0	0	0	0	0	0	0
b Paschal		1	0	0	0	0	0	0
Thomas	p	0	0	0	0	0	2	0
c Ruether		1	0	0	0	0	0	0
Totals		36	2	8	2	27	13	1

a Ran for Severeid in 7th.
b Struck out for Shocker in 7th.
c Grounded out for Thomas in 9th.

Doubles—Bottomley 2, Combs, Hafey, Meusel, Southworth. Triples—Meusel, Southworth. Home Run—L. Bell. Stolen Base—Ruth. Sacrifice Hits—Alexander 2, Hafey. Double Plays—Gehrig to Koenig, Southworth to Thevenow. Hit by Pitcher—Thevenow (by Thomas). Left on Bases—New York 9, St. Louis 4. Umpires—O'Day, Hildebrand, Klem, Dinneen. Attendance—48,615. Time of Game—2:05.

1st Inning
St. Louis
Holm singled to right.
1 Southworth forced Holm at second, Koenig to Lazzeri.
Hornsby walked.
Bottomley doubled down the left field line, scoring Southworth as Hornsby stopped at third.
L. Bell singled over Dugan's head, Hornsby and Bottomley scoring.
2 Hafey struck out.
3 O'Farrell struck out.
New York
1 Combs' grounder was deflected by Alexander to Thevenow who made the throw to first.
2 Koenig struck out.
3 Ruth grounded to first.

2nd Inning
St. Louis
1 Thevenow flied to Combs in deep right-center.
2 Alexander flied to deep left.
3 Holm fouled to Severeid.
New York
Meusel hit a Texas League double between Thevenow and Hafey.
1 Gehrig grounded to short, Meusel holding second.
2 Lazzeri was robbed of a sure hit on a great stop and throw by Thevenow, as Meusel went to third.
3 Dugan grounded to third.

3rd Inning
St. Louis
1 Southworth lined to center.
2 Hornsby grounded to short.
3 Bottomley popped to first.
New York
Severeid singled over second.
Shawkey safe at first and Severeid to second as a grounder went through Thevenow's legs for an error.
1 Combs forced Severeid at third, Alexander to L. Bell.
2 Koenig flied to right.
3 Ruth grounded to first.

4th Inning
St. Louis
L. Bell walked.
1 Hafey sacrificed L. Bell to second, Shawkey to Gehrig.
2 L. Bell out attempting to steal third, Severeid to Dugan.
3 O'Farrell flied to left.
New York
Meusel tripled on a hard grounder over third as it got past Hafey all the way to the bleacher fence.
1 Gehrig grounded to first, Meusel scoring.
2 Lazzeri grounded to short.
Dugan singled to center.
3 Severeid struck out.

5th Inning
St. Louis
Thevenow singled through the hole between Koenig and Dugan.
1 Alexander sacrificed Thevenow to second, Gehrig tagging Alexander.
Holm singled to center, Thevenow scoring.
2 Southworth grounded to third, Holm moving to second.
3 Hornsby grounded to second.
New York
1 Shawkey struck out.
2 Combs flied to left.
3 Koenig flied to center.

6th Inning
St. Louis
Bottomley doubled off the bleacher fence in right center.
1 L. Bell struck out, after fouling a pitch by inches high into the left field bleachers.
2 Hafey struck out.
3 O'Farrell popped to third.

6th Inning (continued)
New York
Ruth walked.
1 Meusel flied to center.
2 Gehrig struck out as Ruth stole second.
3 Lazzeri flied to center.

7th Inning
St. Louis
Thevenow singled to left.
Alexander got credit for a sacrifice when Lazzeri dropped Severeid's throw for an error, also credit Severeid with an assist.
1 Holm attempting to sacrifice, forced Thevenow at third, Severeid to Dugan.
Southworth doubled to center with Meusel losing the ball in the sun, Alexander scoring, Holm stopping at third.
For New York—Shocker replaced Shawkey.
Hornsby singled over second, scoring Holm and Southworth.
2 Bottomley forced Hornsby at first, Koenig unassisted.
L. Bell hit a two-run homer into the left field bleachers.
Hafey lined a double to left.
3 O'Farrell struck out.
New York
Dugan singled through short.
Severeid safe at first and Dugan to third, as L. Bell threw over Bottomley's head on Severeid's grounder.
Adams ran for Severeid.
1 Paschal, batting for Shocker, struck out.
Combs singled to center, Dugan scoring as Adams stopped at second.
2 Koenig grounded to first, both runners advancing.
3 Ruth grounded to short.

8th Inning
St. Louis
For New York—Collins catching and Thomas pitching.
Thevenow was hit by a pitched ball.
1 Alexander forced Thevenow at second on a bunt, Thomas to Koenig.
2,3 Holm hit into a reverse double play, Gehrig to Koenig.
New York
Meusel walked.
Gehrig beat out a single past first, Meusel going to second.
1 Lazzeri flied to left.
2,3 Dugan robbed of a hit by Southworth making a diving catch of his sinking liner, and threw to Thevenow doubling Meusel at second.

9th Inning
St. Louis
Southworth tripled on a liner to center that took a bad hop past Combs.
1 Hornsby's grounder bounced off Thomas' shins to Dugan who made the play at first as Southworth scored.
2 Bottomley grounded to first.
3 L. Bell singled to right, but was out trying to stretch it into a double, Ruth to Lazzeri.
New York
1 Collins struck out.
2 Ruether, pinch-hitting for Thomas, grounded to second.
Combs doubled to right-center, Southworth just missing another diving catch.
3 Koenig flied to center.

Game 7 October 10 at New York

St L.	
St L.	000 300 000
N.Y.	001 001 000

St. Louis	Pos	AB	R	H	RBI	PO	A	E
Holm	cf	5	0	0	0	2	0	0
Southworth	rf	4	0	0	0	0	0	0
Hornsby	2b	4	0	2	0	4	1	0
Bottomley	1b	3	1	1	0	14	0	0
L. Bell	3b	4	1	0	0	0	4	0
Hafey	lf	4	1	2	0	3	0	0
O'Farrell	c	3	0	0	1	3	2	0
Thevenow	ss	4	0	2	2	1	3	0
Haines	p	2	0	1	0	0	4	0
Alexander	p	1	0	0	0	0	0	0
Totals		34	3	8	3	27	14	0

Pitching	IP	H	R	ER	BB	SO
St. Louis						
Haines (W)	6⅔	8	2	2	5	2
Alexander (SV)	2⅓	0	0	0	1	1
New York						
Hoyt (L)	6	5	3	0	0	2
Pennock	3	3	0	0	0	0

New York	Pos	AB	R	H	RBI	PO	A	E
Combs	cf	5	0	2	0	2	0	0
Koenig	ss	4	0	0	0	2	3	1
Ruth	rf	1	1	1	1	2	0	0
Meusel	lf	4	0	1	0	3	0	1
Gehrig	1b	2	0	0	0	11	0	0
Lazzeri	2b	4	0	0	0	3	1	0
Dugan	3b	4	1	2	0	1	3	1
Severeid	c	3	0	2	1	3	1	0
a Adams		0	0	0	0	0	0	0
Collins	c	1	0	0	0	0	0	0
Hoyt	p	2	0	0	0	0	1	0
b Paschal		1	0	0	0	0	0	0
Pennock	p	1	0	0	0	0	1	0
Totals		32	2	8	2	27	10	3

a Ran for Severeid in 6th.
b Grounded out for Hoyt in 6th.

Double—Severeid. Home Run—Ruth. Sacrifice Hits—Bottomley. Haines, Koenig, O'Farrell. Left on Bases—St. Louis 7, New York 10. Umpires—Hildebrand, Klem, Dinneen, O'Day. Attendance—38,093. Time of Game—2:15.

1st Inning
St. Louis
1 Holm grounded to first.
2 Southworth flied to left.
Hornsby singled to center.
3 Bottomley fouled to Gehrig.
New York
1 Combs lined to center.
2 Koenig grounded to first.
Ruth walked for the eighth time in the series tying his own record set in 1923 in 6 games.
Meusel singled to center, Ruth racing to third.
3 Gehrig grounded to second.

2nd Inning
St. Louis
1 L. Bell lined to third.
2 Hafey struck out.
3 O'Farrell flied to Ruth in right-center making a great running one-handed catch.
New York
1 Lazzeri struck out.
Dugan lined a single to center.
2 Dugan was out trying to steal second, O'Farrell to Hornsby.
Severeid singled along the left field foul line.
3 Hoyt grounded back to the mound.

3rd Inning
St. Louis
Thevenow singled to left.
1 Haines sacrificed Thevenow to second, Gehrig unassisted.
2 Holm fouled to Severeid.
3 Southworth flied to left.
New York
1 Combs grounded to first.
2 Koenig flied to Hafey in left-center.
Ruth homered into the right-center field bleachers, his fourth home run of the Series.
3 Meusel flied to left.

4th Inning
St. Louis
1 Hornsby bounced back to the mound.
Bottomley singled to left.
L. Bell safe at first with Bottomley to second on Koenig's fumble, his fourth error of the Series.
Hafey dropped a Texas League single into short left, loading the bases.
O'Farrell safe as Meusel muffed his easy fly, Bottomley scoring as the bases remained loaded.
Thevenow singled to right, scoring L. Bell and Hafey as O'Farrell stopped at second.
2 Haines struck out.
3 Holm forced Thevenow at second, Koenig unassisted.
New York
Gehrig walked on a full count.
1 Lazzeri flied to Holm in deep right-center.
2 Dugan bounced back to the box, Gehrig taking second.
3 Severeid lined to Thevenow, making a marvelous one-handed leaping catch.

5th Inning
St. Louis
1 Southworth fouled to Gehrig.
2 Hornsby flied to center.
3 Bottomley grounded to second.
New York
1 Hoyt grounded to short.
Combs singled to center.
2 Koenig flied to left.
Ruth walked **setting a new Series record with his ninth walk.**
3 Meusel rolled back to the box.

6th Inning
St. Louis
1 L. Bell flied to left.
Hafey safe at first on Dugan's wide throw to Gehrig.
2 O'Farrell popped to second.
3 Hafey was caught attempting to steal second, Severeid to Koenig.
New York
1 Gehrig grounded to short.
2 Lazzeri struck out.
Dugan singled to left-center.
Severeid doubled on a liner to short left, Hafey just missing a shoetop catch as Dugan scored.
Adams ran for Severeid.
3 Paschal, batting for Hoyt, grounded back to the mound.

7th Inning
St. Louis
For New York—Pennock now pitching, and Collins catching.
1 Thevenow grounded to third.
Haines singled to left.
2 Holm forced Haines at second, Dugan to Lazzeri.
3 Southworth's grounder deflected by Pennock to Koenig who made the throw to first.
New York
Combs singled on a line drive over Thevenow's head.
1 Koenig sacrificed Combs to second, L. Bell to first.
Ruth was intentionally passed for his tenth base on balls.
2 Meusel forced Ruth at second, L. Bell to Hornsby with Combs going to third.
Gehrig walked, loading the bases.
For St. Louis—Alexander replaced Haines on the mound.
3 Lazzeri struck out.

8th Inning
St. Louis
Hornsby singled to left-center.
1 Bottomley sacrificed Hornsby to second, Dugan to Gehrig.
2 L. Bell flied to center.
Hafey bounced a single off Dugan's glove, Hornsby going to third.
3 O'Farrell forced Hafey at second, Koenig to Lazzeri.
New York
1 Dugan grounded to short.
2 Collins fouled to Bottomley.
3 Pennock popped to second.

9th Inning
St. Louis
1 Thevenow flied to right on a full count.
2 Alexander grounded to short.
3 Holm grounded to first.
New York
1 Combs grounded to third.
2 Koenig grounded to third.
Ruth walked on a full count, **his eleventh walk of the Series.**
3 Ruth was out trying to steal second, O'Farrell to Hornsby.

1926 WORLD SERIES COMPOSITE BOX

	Wins	Composite Line Score
St. Louis Cardinals (N.L.)	4	5 0 2 10 2 0 9 0 3 0 – 31
New York Yankees (A.L.)	3	2 2 2 2 4 5 2 0 1 1 – 21

Regular Season	Manager	W	L	Pct.	G. Ahead
	Rogers Hornsby	89	65	.578	2
	Miller Huggins	91	63	.591	3

BATTING AND FIELDING

ST. LOUIS CARDINALS

WORLD SERIES STATISTICS

	Pos	G	AB	R	H	2B	3B	HR	RBI	BB	SO	SB	BA	SA	PO	A	E
Jim Bottomley	1b	7	29	4	10	3	0	0	5	1	2	0	.345	.448	79	1	0
Rogers Hornsby	2b	7	28	2	7	1	0	0	4	2	2	1	.250	.286	15	21	0
Tommy Thevenow	ss	7	24	5	10	1	0	1	4	0	1	0	.417	.583	10	26	2
Les Bell	3b	7	27	4	7	1	0	1	6	2	5	0	.259	.407	7	17	2
Billy Southworth	rf	7	29	6	10	1	1	1	4	0	2	0	.345	.552	8	3	0
Taylor Douthit	cf	7	15	3	4	2	0	0	1	3	2	0	.267	.400	4	2	0
Chick Hafey	lf	7	27	2	5	2	0	0	0	7	0	1	.185	.259	21	1	0
Bob O'Farrell	c	7	23	2	7	1	0	0	2	2	2	0	.304	.348	35	8	0
Wattie Holm	ph-rf-cf	5	16	1	2	0	0	0	1	1	2	0	.125	.125	7	0	0
Jake Flowers	ph	3	3	0	0	0	0	0	0	0	1	0	.000	.000			
Specs Toporcer	ph	1	0	0	0	0	0	0	0	1	0	0	—	—			
Ray Blades		Did not play-injured															
Ernie Vick		Did not play															
Pete Alexander	p	3	7	1	0	0	0	0	0	0	2	0	.000	.000	0	6	1
Bill Sherdel	p	2	5	0	0	0	0	0	0	0	2	0	.000	.000	2	5	0
Jesse Haines	p	3	5	1	3	0	0	1	2	0	1	0	.600	1.200	0	6	0
Flint Rhem	p	1	1	0	0	0	0	0	0	1	0	0	.000	.000	0	0	0
Hi Bell	p	1	0	0	0	0	0	0	0	0	0	0	—	—	0	0	0
Wild Bill Hallahan	p	1	0	0	0	0	0	0	0	0	0	0	—	—	0	1	0
Vic Keen	p	1	0	0	0	0	0	0	0	0	0	0	—	—	0	1	0
Art Reinhart	p	1	0	0	0	0	0	0	0	0	0	0	—	—	0	0	0
Allan Sothoron		Did not play															
Syl Johnson		Did not play															
Ed Clough		Did not play															
team total		7	239	31	65	12	1	4	30	11	30	2	.272	.381	189	98	5

Double Plays–6
Left on Bases–43

REGULAR SEASON STATISTICS

	Main Pos	G	AB	R	H	2B	3B	HR	RBI	BB	SO	SB	BA	SA
	1b	154	603	98	180	40	14	19	120	58	52	4	.299	.506
	2b	134	527	96	167	34	5	11	93	61	39	3	.317	.463
	ss	156	563	64	144	15	5	2	63	27	26	8	.256	.311
	3b	155	581	85	189	33	14	17	100	54	62	9	.325	.518
a	of	99	391	76	124	22	6	11	69	26	9	13	.317	.488
	of	139	530	96	163	20	4	3	52	55	46	23	.308	.377
	of	78	225	30	61	19	2	4	38	11	36	2	.271	.427
	c	147	492	63	144	30	9	7	68	61	44	1	.293	.433
	of	55	144	18	41	5	1	0	21	18	14	3	.285	.333
	2b	40	74	13	20	1	0	3	9	5	4	1	.270	.405
	2b	64	88	13	22	3	0	0	8	9	8	1	.250	.330
	of	107	416	81	127	17	12	8	43	62	57	6	.305	.462
	c	24	51	6	10	2	0	0	4	3	4	0	.196	.235
b	p	23	50	1	6	1	0	0	3	2	14	0	.120	.140
	p	36	90	9	22	5	1	1	8	1	9	0	.244	.356
	p	33	61	4	13	1	0	0	1	3	5	0	.213	.230
	p	34	96	11	18	1	0	1	12	4	36	0	.188	.229
	p	27	25	3	3	0	0	0	1	3	5	0	.120	.120
	p	19	16	0	4	1	0	0	0	0	7	0	.250	.313
	p	26	53	2	3	0	0	0	1	2	15	0	.057	.057
	p	40	63	7	20	2	2	0	11	3	3	1	.317	.413
	p	15	13	2	3	0	0	0	0	0	1	0	.231	.231
	p	19	12	0	0	0	0	0	0	0	5	0	.000	.000
team total		156	5381	817	1541	259	82	90	756	478	518	83	.286	.415

a—from New York (N)
b—from Chicago (N)
Heinie Mueller (of), Jack Smith (ph), Bill Warwick (c), Eddie Dyer (p), Walter Huntzinger (p), Duster Mails (p) also played for the Cardinals during the season.

NEW YORK YANKEES

WORLD SERIES STATISTICS

	Pos	G	AB	R	H	2B	3B	HR	RBI	BB	SO	SB	BA	SA	PO	A	E
Lou Gehrig	1b	7	23	1	8	2	0	0	4	5	4	0	.348	.435	78	1	0
Tony Lazzeri	2b	7	26	2	5	1	0	0	3	1	6	0	.192	.231	15	19	1
Mark Koenig	ss	7	32	2	4	1	0	0	2	0	6	0	.125	.156	12	24	4
Joe Dugan	3b	7	24	2	8	1	0	0	2	1	1	0	.333	.375	7	14	1
Babe Ruth	rf-lf	7	20	6	6	0	0	4	5	11	2	1	.300	.900	8	2	0
Earle Combs	cf	7	28	3	10	2	0	0	1	3	2	0	.357	.429	17	0	0
Bob Meusel	lf-rf	7	21	3	5	1	0	0	6	1	0	0	.238	.381	13	0	1
Hank Severeid	c	7	22	1	6	1	0	0	1	1	2	0	.273	.318	37	7	0
Ben Paschal	ph	5	4	0	1	0	0	0	1	1	2	0	.250	.250			
Pat Collins	c	3	2	0	0	0	0	0	0	1	0	0	.000	.000	1	0	0
Mike Gazella	3b	1	0	0	0	0	0	0	0	0	0	0	—	—	1	2	0
Spence Adams	pr	2	0	0	0	0	0	0	0	0	0	0	—	—			
Benny Bengough		Did not play—shoulder injury															
Roy Carlyle		Did not play															
Aaron Ward		Did not play															
Herb Pennock	p	3	7	1	1	1	0	0	0	0	2	0	.143	.286	0	6	0
Waite Hoyt	p	2	6	0	0	0	0	0	0	0	1	0	.000	.000	0	1	0
Dutch Ruether	p-ph	3	4	0	0	0	0	0	0	1	0	0	.000	.000	0	0	0
Bob Shawkey	p	3	2	0	0	0	0	0	0	0	1	0	.000	.000	0	1	0
Urban Shocker	p	2	2	0	0	0	0	0	0	0	2	0	.000	.000	0	2	0
Myles Thomas	p	2	0	0	0	0	0	0	0	0	0	0	—	—	0	2	0
Sad Sam Jones	p	1	0	0	0	0	0	0	0	0	0	0	—	—	0	0	0
Walter Beall		Did not play															
Garland Braxton		Did not play															
Herb McQuaid		Did not play															
team total		7	223	21	54	10	1	4	20	31	31	1	.242	.350	189	83	7

Double Plays–3
Left on Bases–55

REGULAR SEASON STATISTICS

	Main Pos	G	AB	R	H	2B	3B	HR	RBI	BB	SO	SB	BA	SA
	1b	155	572	135	179	47	20	16	107	105	72	6	.313	.549
	2b	155	589	79	162	28	14	18	114	54	96	16	.275	.462
	ss	147	617	93	167	26	8	5	62	43	37	4	.271	.363
	3b	123	434	39	125	19	5	1	64	25	16	2	.288	.362
	of	152	495	139	184	30	5	47	145	144	76	11	.372	.737
	of	145	606	113	181	31	12	8	56	47	23	8	.299	.429
	of	108	413	73	130	22	3	12	81	37	32	16	.315	.470
	c	41	127	13	34	8	1	0	13	13	4	1	.268	.346
	of	96	258	46	74	12	3	7	33	26	35	7	.287	.438
	c	102	290	41	83	11	3	7	35	73	55	3	.286	.417
	3b	66	168	21	39	6	0	0	21	25	24	2	.232	.268
	2b	28	25	7	3	1	0	1	3	7	1	1	.120	.160
	of	36	84	9	32	6	0	0	14	7	4	1	.381	.452
d	of	35	53	3	20	5	1	0	11	4	9	0	.377	.509
	2b	22	31	5	10	2	0	0	3	2	6	0	.323	.387
	p	40	85	8	18	2	0	0	6	10	8	0	.212	.235
	p	40	76	4	16	3	0	0	4	0	8	0	.211	.250
e	p-ph	13	21	2	2	0	0	0	0	8	2	0	.095	.095
	p	29	35	4	9	1	0	0	3	3	6	0	.257	.286
	p	41	76	6	13	1	0	0	4	10	20	0	.171	.184
	p	33	43	1	5	0	0	0	1	1	7	0	.116	.116
	p	44	49	3	10	1	0	0	4	3	16	1	.204	.224
	p	20	22	3	3	0	0	0	1	5	7	0	.136	.136
	p	37	30	6	9	0	0	0	1	1	5	0	.300	.300
	p	17	7	0	0	0	0	0	0	0	1	0	.000	.000
team total		155	5221	847	1508	262	75	121	794	642	580	79	.289	.437

c—from Washington
d—from Boston (A)
e—from Washington
Honey Barnes (c), Nick Cullop (ph), Kiddo Davis (of), Fred Merkle (1b), Bill Skiff (c), Hank Johnson (p) also played for the Yankees during the season.

PITCHING

ST. LOUIS CARDINALS

WORLD SERIES STATISTICS

	G	GS	CG	IP	H	R	ER	BB	SO	W	L	SV	ERA
Pete Alexander	3	2	2	20⅓	12	4	3	4	17	2	0	1	1.33
Bill Sherdel	2	2	1	17	15	5	4	8	3	0	2	0	2.12
Jesse Haines	3	2	1	16⅔	13	2	2	9	5	2	0	0	1.08
Flint Rhem	1	1	0	4	7	3	3	2	4	0	0	0	6.75
Hi Bell	1	0	0	2	4	2	2	1	1	0	0	0	9.00
Wild Bill Hallahan	1	0	0	2	2	1	1	3	1	0	0	0	4.50
Vic Keen	1	0	0	2	1	0	0	0	0	0	0	0	0.00
Art Reinhart	1	0	0	0	1	4	4	4	0	0	1	0	∞
Syl Johnson		Did not play											
Allan Sothoron		Did not play											
Ed Clough		Did not play											
team total	7	7	4	63	54	21	19	31	31	4	3	1	2.71

REGULAR SEASON STATISTICS

	G	GS	CG	IP	H	ER	BB	SO	W	L	Pct.	SV	ShO	ERA
b	23	16	11	148	136	48	24	35	9	7	.563	2	2	2.92
	34	29	17	235	255	91	49	59	16	12	.571	0	3	3.49
	33	21	14	183	186	66	48	46	13	4	.765	1	3	3.25
	34	34	20	258	241	92	75	72	20	7	.741	0	1	3.21
	27	7	3	85	82	30	17	27	6	6	.500	2	0	3.18
	19	3	0	57	45	23	32	28	1	4	.200	0	0	3.63
	26	21	12	152	179	77	47	29	10	9	.526	0	1	4.56
	27	11	9	143	159	67	47	26	10	5	.667	0	1	4.22
	19	6	1	49	54	23	15	10	0	3	.000	1	0	4.22
	15	4	1	43	37	20	16	19	3	3	.500	0	0	4.19
	1	0	0	2	5	5	3	0	0	0	—	0	0	22.50
team total	156	156	90	1399	1423	570	397	365	89	65	.578	6	10	3.67

NEW YORK YANKEES

WORLD SERIES STATISTICS

	G	GS	CG	IP	H	R	ER	BB	SO	W	L	SV	ERA
Herb Pennock	3	2	2	22	13	3	3	4	8	2	0	0	1.23
Waite Hoyt	2	2	1	15	19	8	2	1	10	1	1	0	1.20
Bob Shawkey	3	1	0	10	8	7	6	2	3	0	1	0	5.40
Urban Shocker	2	1	0	7⅔	13	7	5	0	3	0	1	0	5.87
Dutch Ruether	1	1	0	4⅓	7	4	2	2	1	0	0	0	4.16
Myles Thomas	2	0	0	3	3	1	1	0	0	0	0	0	3.00
Sad Sam Jones	1	0	0	1	2	1	1	2	1	0	0	0	9.00
Walter Beall		Did not play											
Garland Braxton		Did not play											
Herb McQuaid		Did not play											
team total	7	7	3	63	65	31	20	11	30	3	4	0	2.86

REGULAR SEASON STATISTICS

	G	GS	CG	IP	H	ER	BB	SO	W	L	Pct.	SV	ShO	ERA
	40	33	19	266	294	107	43	78	23	11	.676	2	1	3.62
	40	32	12	218	224	93	62	79	16	12	.571	4	1	3.84
	29	10	3	104	102	42	37	63	8	7	.522	3	1	3.63
	41	33	19	258	272	97	71	59	19	11	.633	2	0	3.38
e	5	5	1	36	32	14	18	8	2	3	.400	0	0	3.50
	33	13	3	140	140	66	65	38	6	6	.500	0	0	4.24
	39	23	11	161	186	89	80	69	9	8	.529	5	1	4.98
	20	9	1	82	71	32	68	56	2	4	.333	1	0	3.51
	37	1	0	67	71	20	19	30	5	1	.833	2	0	2.69
	17	1	0	38	48	26	13	6	1	0	1.000	0	0	6.16
team total	155	155	64	1372	1442	588	478	486	91	63	.591	20	4	3.86

Total Attendance—328,051   Average Attendance—46,864   Winning Player's Share—$5,585   Losing Player's Share—$3,418

1927
By Reputation Alone

An established baseball folktale states that the Pittsburgh Pirates watched the New York Yankees take batting practice the day before the 1927 World Series started and were immediately psyched out. The Pirate players supposedly saw Babe Ruth, Lou Gehrig, Bob Meusel, Tony Lazzeri, and all the rest of the Murderer's Row rocket the ball to all corners and depths of Forbes Field and on the spot lost their nerve and confidence in beating such a powerful foe. A look at their records confirms the power in the bats of the Yankee sluggers; Ruth hit his record 60 homers, batted .356, and drove in 164 runs along the way; Gehrig drove in 175 runs with 47 homers and a .373 average; Lazzeri hit .309 and drove in 102 runs; and Meusel batted .337 with 103 RBI's. But the legend of the batting practice psyche ignores the fact that the Pirates were champions and tough batsmen in their own right, a team of high-average hitters who strung together hits rather than going for the long ball. Although the Pirates had won the Series only two years ago, they came into this fall classic with a much revised outfit. New manager Donie Bush had a falling-out with star outfielder Kiki Cuyler and had him riding the bench through the later stages of the season. But Bush had two new outfield stars in brothers Paul and Lloyd Waner, two devastating batters known as Big Poison and Little Poison. Big Poison Paul hit .380 with 131 RBI's in his second big-league season, while Little Poison Lloyd broke into the majors this year with a .355 average. Pie Traynor and Glenn Wright, both heavy hitters and sure fielders, anchored the infield for the Bucs, while the top pitchers on the team were Carmen Hill, Ray Kremer, Lee Meadows, and Vic Aldridge, all righties. They had the dubious privilege of facing the toughest left-hand batters in the game in Babe Ruth and Lou Gehrig. Whether or not the batting practice of the Yankee sluggers weighed heavily on the Pirates is unknown, but the plain fact is that the Yanks made short order of the Bucs in the Series.

The first game in Forbes Field matched Ray Kremer and Waite Hoyt on the mound, and while the Yankee power took on less than a gargantuan shape, some poor fielding by the Pirates put the New Yorkers ahead 4–1 after two and a half innings. The Pittsburgh batters kept chipping away at Hoyt and lowered the count to 5–4 in the eighth. But Yankee manager Miller Huggins waved into the game Wilcy Moore, a thirty-year-old rookie pitcher who enjoyed a high degree of success in his main role as a late-inning reliever, one of the first such specialists. Moore shut the door at 5–4 and kept it shut there. With the first game lost, the Pirates took a large step toward losing the second game by giving up three runs in the third inning. Yankee pitcher George Pipgras settled into an easy groove after giving up a first-inning run, and a three-run eighth inning made him a 6–2 victor and sent the Yankees back to New York with a 2–0 edge in the Series and a world of confidence bordering on assurance.

When the Yanks counted twice in the first inning off Lee Meadows in game three, the Pirates found themselves in a hole which they couldn't battle out of. Control ace Herb Pennock shut the Pirates out through seven innings, and the Yanks then broke the game open with six runs in the bottom of that inning. Easily out in front, Pennock then gave up a run and finished with an 8–1 three-hit victory. The Pirates showed heart in the fourth game, scoring twice in the seventh to knot the score at 3–3. But the Yankees moved relentlessly to win the game and complete the sweep in the bottom of the ninth. With Johnny Miljus pitching for Pittsburgh, Earle Combs led off with a walk and moved to second when Mark Koenig beat out a bunt. A wild pitch moved the runners up, so Ruth was intentionally passed to set up a force situation at the plate. Miljus then fanned Gehrig and Meusel, and with Lazzeri at the plate, he uncorked a wild pitch which sent the winning run scurrying across the plate and sent the Pirates into winter with their embarrassment.

Game 1 October 5 at Pittsburgh

New York	Pos	AB	R	H	RBI	PO	A	E
Combs	cf	4	0	0	0	4	0	0
Koenig	ss	4	2	1	0	2	2	0
Ruth	rf	4	2	3	0	5	0	0
Gehrig	1b	2	1	1	2	9	1	0
Meusel	lf	3	0	0	1	2	0	1
Lazzeri	2b	4	0	1	1	2	5	0
Dugan	3b	3	0	0	0	0	0	0
Collins	c	2	0	0	0	3	0	0
Hoyt	p	3	0	0	0	0	0	0
Moore	p	1	0	0	0	0	2	0
Totals		30	5	6	4	27	10	1

Pitching	IP	H	R	ER	BB	SO
New York						
Hoyt (W)	7⅓	8	4	4	1	2
Moore (SV)	1⅔	1	0	0	0	0
Pittsburgh						
Kremer (L)	5	5	5	2	3	1
Miljus	4	1	0	0	1	3

N.Y.	1 0 3	0 1 0	0 0 0						
Pit.	1 0 1	0 1 0	0 1 0						

Pittsburgh	Pos	AB	R	H	RBI	PO	A	E
L. Waner	cf	4	2	1	0	1	0	0
Barnhart	lf	5	0	1	1	3	0	0
P. Waner	rf	4	0	3	1	3	0	0
Wright	ss	2	1	1	1	1	5	0
Traynor	3b	4	0	1	0	1	2	0
Grantham	2b	3	0	0	0	5	3	1
Harris	1b	4	0	1	1	8	2	0
Smith	c	4	0	0	0	4	1	1
Kremer	p	2	1	1	0	0	0	0
Miljus	p	1	0	0	0	1	2	0
a Brickell		1	0	0	0	0	0	0
Totals		34	4	9	4	27	15	2

a Grounded out for Miljus in 9th.

Doubles—Koenig, Kremer, Lazzeri, L. Waner, P. Waner. Triple—Gehrig. Sacrifice Hits—Dugan, Gehrig, Wright 2. Double Plays—Lazzeri to Gehrig, Wright to Grantham to Harris. Hit by Pitcher—L. Waner (by Hoyt). Left on Bases—New York 4, Pittsburgh 7. Umpires—Quigley (N), Nallin (A), Moran (N), Ormsby (A) Attendance—41,467. Time of Game—2:04.

1st Inning
New York
1 Combs flied to deep left.
2 Koenig struck out.
   Ruth lined a single to right.
   Gehrig tripled on a short fly to right, as P. Waner missed a shoestring catch and the ball bounced past him, Ruth scoring.
3 Meusel flied to P. Waner in right-center.
Pittsburgh
   L. Waner was hit by a pitched ball.
1 Barnhart flied to right.
   P. Waner doubled down the right field foul line, brother Lloyd stopping at third.
2 Wright hit a sacrifice fly to center, L. Waner scoring and P. Waner going to third after the catch.
3 Traynor flied to right.

2nd Inning
New York
1 Lazzeri fouled to Traynor.
2 Dugan popped to second.
   Collins walked.
3 Hoyt grounded to second.
Pittsburgh
   Grantham walked.
1,2 Harris grounded to Lazzeri who tagged Grantham running towards second, but threw the ball to Gehrig in the dirt. Gehrig made a remarkable one-handed pickup to complete the double play.
3 Smith grounded to second.

3rd Inning
New York
1 Combs grounded to second.
   Koenig safe as Grantham booted his grounder for an error.
   Ruth singled to right again on the first pitch, Koenig going to third.
   Gehrig walked, loading the bases.
   Meusel walked, forcing in Koenig.
2 Lazzeri forced Meusel at second, Wright to Grantham, Ruth scoring as Gehrig got to third.
   Gehrig was almost picked off first, Smith to Traynor but Gehrig scored when Smith dropped Traynor's return throw to the plate. Lazzeri got all the way to third.
3 Dugan flied to left.
Pittsburgh
   Kremer doubled against the right field grandstand wall.
1 L. Waner flied to left.
   Barnhart safe as Meusel dropped his fly ball as Kremer was held at second.
   P. Waner lined a single to center, Kremer scoring and Barnhart going to second.
2 Wright forced P. Waner at second, Lazzeri to Koenig as Barnhart went to third.
3 Traynor forced Wright at second, Koenig to Lazzeri.

4th Inning
New York
1 Collins flied to right.
2 Hoyt flied to short right.
3 Combs lined to deep center.
Pittsburgh
1 Grantham grounded to first.
2 Harris grounded to Koenig, who threw poorly to Gehrig, but Gehrig made a great stop and stretch for the out.
3 Smith popped to Collins in front of the plate.

5th Inning
New York
   Koenig doubled to center.
1 Ruth grounded to Grantham who made a fantastic stop between first and second and just beat Ruth to the bag. Koenig went to third on the play.
2 Gehrig hit a sacrifice fly to right, Koenig scoring after the catch.
3 Meusel popped to short.
Pittsburgh
1 Kremer called out on strikes.
   L. Waner doubled down the left field line.
   Barnhart singled to left, L. Waner scoring.
   P. Waner singled off Hoyt's glove, Barnhart stopping at second.
2 Wright hit a sacrifice fly to center, Barnhart taking third after the catch as P. Waner held first.
3 Traynor popped to Combs in short left-center.

6th Inning
New York
   Lazzeri lined a double over Barnhart's head.
   For Pittsburgh—Miljus came in to pitch.
1 Dugan sacrificed Lazzeri to third, Smith to Grantham covering first.
   Collins walked.
2,3 Hoyt grounded into a double play, Wright to Grantham to Harris.
Pittsburgh
1 Grantham grounded to first.
2 Harris flied to right.
3 Smith flied to short right.

7th Inning
New York
1 Combs struck out.
2 Koenig grounded out, Harris to Miljus.
   Ruth singled to center.
3 Ruth was picked off first, Miljus to Harris to Wright to Harris.
Pittsburgh
1 Miljus struck out.
2 L. Waner grounded to second.
3 Barnhart flied to deep right.

8th Inning
New York
1 Gehrig bounced back to the pitcher.
2 Meusel called out on strikes.
3 Lazzeri grounded to third, Traynor throwing wild to first but Harris making a good pickup tagged out Lazzeri
Pittsburgh
1 P. Waner flied to left.
   Wright singled over Lazzeri's head.
   Traynor lined a single to center, Wright stopping at second.
   For New York—Moore now pitching.
2 Grantham forced Traynor at second, Gehrig to Koenig, Wright going to third.
   Harris singled to center, scoring Wright, Grantham racing to third.
3 Smith grounded to first.

9th Inning
New York
1 Dugan bounced to short.
2 Collins grounded to short.
3 Moore took a called third strike.
Pittsburgh
1 Brickell, batting for Miljus, bounced back to the mound.
2 L. Waner lined to center.
3 Barnhart bounced out off Moore's glove to Lazzeri who made the throw to first.

Game 2 October 6 at Pittsburgh

New York	Pos	AB	R	H	RBI	PO	A	E
Combs	cf	4	1	1	1	5	0	0
Koenig	ss	5	1	3	1	3	1	0
Ruth	rf	3	0	0	1	3	0	0
Gehrig	1b	3	1	1	0	6	0	0
Meusel	lf	5	1	2	0	2	0	0
Lazzeri	2b	4	0	2	1	2	2	0
Dugan	3b	5	1	1	0	1	0	0
Bengough	c	3	1	0	0	4	0	0
Pipgras	p	3	0	1	0	1	2	0
Totals		35	6	11	4	27	5	0

Pitching	IP	H	R	ER	BB	SO
New York						
Pipgras (W)	9	7	2	2	1	2
Pittsburgh						
Aldridge (L)	7⅓	10	6	6	4	4
Cvengros	⅔	1	0	0	0	0
Dawson	1	0	0	0	0	0

N.Y.	003	000	030
Pit.	100	000	010

Pittsburgh	Pos	AB	R	H	RBI	PO	A	E
L. Waner	cf	3	2	1	0	7	0	1
Barnhart	lf	3	0	2	1	1	0	0
P. Waner	rf	3	0	1	1	5	0	0
Wright	ss	4	0	0	0	0	0	1
Traynor	3b	4	0	1	0	3	0	0
Grantham	2b	4	0	2	0	1	2	0
Harris	1b	4	0	0	0	3	0	0
Gooch	c	3	0	0	0	7	1	0
Aldridge	p	2	0	0	0	0	2	0
Cvengros	p	0	0	0	0	0	0	0
a Smith		1	0	0	0	0	0	0
Dawson	p	0	0	0	0	0	0	0
Totals		31	2	7	2	27	5	2

a Grounded out for Cvengros in 8th.

Doubles—Gehrig, Grantham, Traynor. Triple—L. Waner. Stolen Base—Meusel. Sacrifice Hits—Barnhart, Gehrig, Lazzeri, Ruth, P. Waner. Double Play—Lazzeri to Koenig. Hit by Pitcher—Combs (by Cvengros). Wild Pitch—Aldridge. Left on Bases—New York 10, Pittsburgh 5. Umpires—Nallin, Moran, Ormsby, Quigley. Attendance—41,634. Time of Game—2:20.

1st Inning
New York
1 Combs flied to deep left.
Koenig singled between first and second.
2 Ruth struck out.
Gehrig walked.
3 Meusel bounced back to the mound.
Pittsburgh
L. Waner tripled down the left field foul line.
1 Barnhart hit a sacrifice fly to Ruth at the wall, L. Waner scoring after the catch.
2 P. Waner was called out on strikes.
3 Wright flied to right.

2nd Inning
New York
Lazzeri singled off Aldridge's glove.
1 Dugan fouled to Gooch.
2 Bengough fouled to Gooch.
3 Pipgras lined to second.
Pittsburgh
1 Traynor bounced back to the mound.
Grantham singled to short center.
2 Harris grounded to first, Grantham going to second.
3 Gooch fouled to Bengough.

3rd Inning
New York
Combs singled between first and second.
Koenig singled over second, Combs racing to third. On L. Waner's fumble Combs scored and Koenig went to third.
1 Ruth hit a sacrifice fly to center, Koenig scoring after the catch.
Gehrig doubled to right-center.
Meusel singled to short, Wright making a phenominal stop but could not make a play as Gehrig went to third.
2 Lazzeri hit a sacrifice fly to left, Gehrig scoring and Meusel going to second after the catch.
3 Dugan flied to short right.
Pittsburgh
1 Aldridge lined to second.
2 L. Waner grounded to second.
Barnhart singled over second.
3 P. Waner flied to left.

4th Inning
New York
1 Bengough flied to second.
2 Pipgras struck out.
3 Combs struck out.
Pittsburgh
1 Wright flied to center.
Traynor doubled to center.
2 Grantham fouled to Dugan who gloved the ball out of a spectator's lap over the low fence at the third base boxes.
3 Harris flied to right.

5th Inning
New York
1 Koenig flied to right.
Ruth walked on four pitches.
2 Gehrig got a sacrifice on his deep fly to center near the flagpole, as Ruth went to second after the catch.
3 Meusel struck out.
Pittsburgh
1 Gooch rolled back to the box.
2 Aldridge fouled to Bengough.
3 L. Waner flied to center.

6th Inning
New York
1 Lazzeri flied to deep right.
Dugan singled to left.
2 Bengough flied to center.
Pipgras blooped a single to short right, Dugan stopping at second.
3 Combs flied to very deep center.
Pittsburgh
1 Barnhart flied to center.
P. Waner singled to left.
2 Wright flied to center.
3 Traynor forced P. Waner at second, Koenig unassisted.

7th Inning
New York
1 Koenig flied to P. Waner in right-center.
2 Ruth grounded to first.
3 Gehrig grounded back to the pitcher.
Pittsburgh
Grantham doubled off the right field wall, Ruth's fast fielding and bullet throw held the hit to a double.
1 Harris grounded to short, Grantham held at second.
2,3 Gooch lined into a double play, Lazzeri jumping in short right to spear the liner and flipping to Koenig.

8th Inning
New York
Meusel singled over second.
Lazzeri blooped a single into short right, Meusel going to third.
Meusel scored and Lazzeri took second on a wild pitch.
1 Dugan on an attempted sacrifice put Lazzeri out at third, Gooch to Traynor.
Bengough walked.
Pipgras also walked, loading the bases.
For Pittsburgh—Cvengros now pitching.
Combs was hit by a pitched ball, forcing in Dugan.
Koenig singled to left, scoring Bengough.
2 Ruth forced Pipgras at the plate, Grantham to Gooch.
3 Gehrig forced Koenig at third, Traynor unassisted.
Pittsburgh
1 Smith, pinch-hitting for Cvengros, grounded to first.
L. Waner walked.
Barnhart singled over second, L. Waner going to third.
2 P. Waner hit a sacrifice fly to left, L. Waner scoring after the catch.
3 Wright forced Barnhart at second, Koenig unassisted.

9th Inning
New York
For Pittsburgh—Dawson pitching.
Meusel safe when Wright fumbled his grounder.
1 Lazzeri flied to center.
2 Dugan flied to center.
3 Meusel stole second but was out trying for third as Gooch's throw got past Wright. Grantham threw to Traynor for the out. No error on the play.
Pittsburgh
1 Traynor flied to center.
2 Grantham struck out.
3 Harris bounced out, Pipgras unassisted.

Game 3 October 7 at New York

Pittsburgh	Pos	AB	R	H	RBI	PO	A	E
L. Waner	cf	4	0	1	0	1	1	0
Rhyne	2b	4	0	0	0	0	6	0
P. Waner	rf	4	0	0	0	0	0	0
Wright	ss	3	0	0	0	3	2	0
Traynor	3b	3	1	1	0	0	3	1
Barnhart	lf	3	0	1	1	0	1	0
Harris	1b	3	0	0	0	11	0	0
Gooch	c	2	0	0	0	9	0	0
b Spencer	c	1	0	0	0	0	0	0
Meadows	p	2	0	0	0	0	1	0
Cvengros	p	0	0	0	0	0	0	0
c Groh		1	0	0	0	0	0	0
Totals		30	1	3	1	24	14	1

a Grounded out for Grabowski in 7th.
b Grounded out for Gooch in 8th.
c Popped out for Cvengros in 9th.

Doubles—Barnhart, Gehrig, Koenig. Triple—Gehrig. Home Run—Ruth. Sacrifice Hit—Dugan. Left on Bases—Pittsburgh 2, New York 4. Umpires—Moran, Ormsby, Quigley, Nallin. Attendance—60,695. Time of Game—2:04.

Pit.	000	000	010
N.Y.	200	000	60x

New York	Pos	AB	R	H	RBI	PO	A	E
Combs	cf	4	2	2	1	5	0	0
Koenig	ss	4	2	2	1	1	2	0
Ruth	rf	4	1	1	3	1	0	0
Gehrig	1b	3	0	2	2	12	0	0
Meusel	lf	4	0	0	0	2	0	0
Lazzeri	2b	4	1	1	0	1	7	0
Dugan	3b	3	1	1	0	1	2	0
Grabowski	c	2	0	0	0	3	0	0
a Durst		1	0	0	0	0	0	0
Bengough	c	1	0	0	0	0	0	0
Pennock	p	4	1	0	1	1	1	0
Totals		34	8	9	8	27	12	0

Pitching	IP	H	R	ER	BB	SO
Pittsburgh						
Meadows (L)	6⅓	7	7	7	1	6
Cvengros	1⅔	2	1	1	0	2
New York						
Pennock (W)	9	3	1	1	0	1

1st Inning
Pittsburgh
1 L. Waner grounded to short.
2 Rhyne flied to left.
3 P. Waner flied to short left.
New York
Combs singled over second.
Koenig beat out a hit off Meadows' glove, Combs stopping at second.
1 Ruth popped to Wright behind second.
Gehrig hit a booming triple to the base of the wall in left-center, scoring Combs and Koenig. Gehrig
2 was out trying for a home run, L. Waner to Wright to Gooch.
3 Meusel struck out.

2nd Inning
Pittsburgh
1 Wright flied to short center.
2 Traynor grounded to second.
3 Barnhart grounded to second.
New York
1 Lazzeri took a called third strike.
2 Dugan grounded to short.
3 Grabowski grounded to Traynor, almost in at the pitcher's box.

3rd Inning
Pittsburgh
1 Harris flied to center.
2 Gooch called out on strikes.
3 Meadows grounded to second.
New York
1 Pennock grounded to second.
2 Combs flied to center.
3 Koenig popped to Wright in short center.

4th Inning
Pittsburgh
1 L. Waner rolled to second.
2 Rhyne popped to Koenig in short left.
3 P. Waner lined to third.
New York
1 Ruth struck out.
Gehrig walked on four pitches.
Meusel safe at second and Gehrig to third as Traynor threw Meusel's grounder over Harris' head.
2 Lazzeri took a called third strike.
3 Dugan rolled out, third to first.

5th Inning
Pittsburgh
1 Wright popped to Grabowski in front of the plate.
2 Traynor fouled to Grabowski.
3 Barnhart flied to Combs in very deep left-center.
New York
1 Grabowski popped to short.
2 Pennock called out on strikes.
3 Combs grounded back to the mound.

6th Inning
Pittsburgh
1 Harris bounced back to the pitcher.
2 Gooch flied to right.
3 Meadows flied to short center.
New York
1 Koenig grounded to second.
2 Ruth rolled out to second.
Gehrig doubled to deep right-center, the Yanks' first hit since the first inning.
3 Meusel struck out.

7th Inning
Pittsburgh
1 L. Waner grounded to second.
2 Rhyne bunted out to third, as Dugan made a fantastic play.
3 P. Waner grounded to second.
New York
Lazzeri singled to short center.
Dugan sacrificed Lazzeri to second as Lazzeri beat Meadows to the bag and Dugan safe on the fielder's choice.
1 Durst, pinch-hitting for Grabowski, grounded to second as Lazzeri went to third and Dugan to second.
Pennock safe on a fielder's choice, as Rhyne's throw to the plate was too late to get Lazzeri as Dugan went to third.
Combs singled into right-center, Dugan scoring with Pennock going to third.
Koenig doubled to the right field bleachers, scoring Pennock as Combs stopped at third.
For Pittsburgh—Cvengros replaced Meadows on the mound.
Ruth hit a three-run homer into the right-field bleachers.
2 Gehrig struck out.
3 Meusel struck out.

8th Inning
Pittsburgh
For New York—Bengough catching.
1 Wright grounded to deep short.
Traynor singled to left **breaking up Pennock's perfect game.**
Barnhart doubled to right-center, scoring Traynor.
2 Harris rolled to third, Barnhart holding second.
3 Spencer, batting for Gooch, grounded to Lazzeri who made a remarkable stop and throw.
New York
For Pittsburgh—Spencer catching.
1 Lazzeri bounced to second.
Dugan singled past second.
2 Bengough grounded to second, Dugan advancing to second.
3 Pennock grounded to third.

9th Inning
Pittsburgh
1 Groh, batting for Cvengros, popped to the pitcher.
L. Waner singled behind third.
2 Rhyne flied to center.
L. Waner went to second, unmolested therefore no stolen base.
3 P. Waner popped to second.

Game 4 October 8 at New York

Pit.	1 0 0	0 0 0	2 0 0
N.Y.	1 0 0	0 2 0	0 0 1

Pittsburgh	Pos	AB	R	H	RBI	PO	A	E
L. Waner	cf	4	1	3	0	0	0	1
Barnhart	lf	5	0	1	1	2	0	0
P. Waner	rf	4	0	1	1	0	0	0
Wright	ss	4	0	1	1	1	6	0
Traynor	3b	4	0	0	0	1	4	0
Grantham	2b	4	0	2	0	0	2	0
Harris	1b	4	0	2	0	13	0	0
Smith	c	3	0	0	0	6	0	0
a Yde		0	1	0	0	0	0	0
Gooch	c	0	0	0	0	3	0	0
Hill	p	1	0	0	0	0	0	0
b Brickell		1	1	0	0	0	0	0
Miljus	p	1	0	0	0	0	0	0
Totals		35	3	10	3	x26	12	1

New York	Pos	AB	R	H	RBI	PO	A	E
Combs	cf	4	3	2	0	2	0	0
Koenig	ss	5	0	3	0	0	3	0
Ruth	rf	4	1	2	3	1	0	0
Gehrig	1b	5	0	0	0	14	2	0
Meusel	lf	5	0	0	0	2	0	0
Lazzeri	2b	3	0	0	0	5	4	1
Dugan	3b	4	0	1	0	1	4	0
Collins	c	3	0	3	0	2	1	0
Moore	p	4	0	1	0	0	3	1
Totals		37	4	12	3	27	17	2

Pitching	IP	H	R	ER	BB	SO
Pittsburgh						
Hill	6	9	3	3	1	6
Miljus (L)	2⅓	3	1	1	3	3
New York						
Moore (W)	9	10	3	1	2	2

x two out when winning run scored.
a Ran for Smith in 7th.
b Safe on error for Hill in 7th.

Double—Collins. Home Run—Ruth.
Sacrifice Hits—L. Waner, P. Waner.
Stolen Base—Ruth. Double Plays—Lazzeri
to Gehrig, Dugan to Lazzeri to Gehrig,
Traynor to Wright to Harris.
Wild Pitches—Miljus 2. Left on
Bases—Pittsburgh 9, New York 11.
Umpires—Ormsby, Quigley, Nallin, Moran.
Attendance—57,909. Time of Game—2:15.

1st Inning
Pittsburgh
  L. Waner singled off Moore's glove, Koenig just missing the play at first.
1 Barnhart grounded to short, L. Waner moving over to second.
2 P. Waner grounded to third, L. Waner being held at second.
  Wright singled to right, L. Waner scoring and Wright taking second on the throw to the plate.
3 Traynor grounded to Dugan who tagged Wright coming to third.
New York
  Combs singled to right.
  Koenig blooped a single to right, Combs stopping at second.
  Ruth singled to right, scoring Combs with Koenig going to third.
1 Gehrig struck out.
  Ruth stole second.
2 Meusel called out on strikes.
3 Lazzeri also struck out.

2nd Inning
Pittsburgh
1 Grantham bunted out to third.
  Harris beat out an infield single to deep short.
2 Smith lined to right.
  Hill walked.
  L. Waner beat out a roller down the first base line as Moore fell trying to field the ball, loading the bases.
3 Barnhart forced L. Waner at second, Lazzeri unassisted.
New York
1 Dugan grounded to Wright near third as it went by Traynor.
  Collins doubled down the left field line.
2 Moore grounded to short, Collins holding at second.
3 Combs grounded to short.

3rd Inning
Pittsburgh
  P. Waner singled to left.
1,2 Wright hit into a double play, Lazzeri to Gehrig.
3 Traynor flied to deep left.
New York
1 Koenig grounded to Grantham who made a great play and throw to Harris.
2 Ruth grounded to first.
3 Gehrig grounded to second.

4th Inning
Pittsburgh
1 Grantham grounded to first.
  Harris blooped a single into short right.
2 Smith forced Harris at second, Koenig to Lazzeri.
3 Hill bounced out, Collins to Gehrig.
New York
1 Meusel grounded to third.
2 Lazzeri grounded to third.
  Dugan singled to left.
  Collins singled to left-center and when L. Waner fumbled the ball Dugan went to third.
3 Moore struck out.

5th Inning
Pittsburgh
  L. Waner singled through the hole between short and second.
1,2 Barnhart smashed hard into a double play, Dugan to Lazzeri to Gehrig.
3 P. Waner grounded to short.
New York
  Combs singled into short center.
1 Koenig struck out.
  Ruth hit a towering two-run homer into the right-center field bleachers.
2 Gehrig grounded to short.
3 Meusel also grounded to short.

6th Inning
Pittsburgh
1 Wright bounced high back to Moore.
2 Traynor struck out.
  Grantham beat out a hit down the first base line, Gehrig making a sensational stop but could make no play.
3 Harris lined to center.
New York
1 Lazzeri struck out.
2 Dugan fouled to Traynor.
  Collins walked.
  Moore slashed a single to right, sending Collins to third.
3 Combs flied to deep left.

7th Inning
Pittsburgh
  Smith safe at first when Gehrig fielded his grounder to Moore who dropped the ball for an error.
  Yde ran for Smith.
  Brickell, batting for Hill, was safe at first on Lazzeri's fumble with Yde going to second.
1 L. Waner sacrificed Yde to third and Brickell to second, Gehrig to Lazzeri.
  Barnhart singled over second, scoring Yde with Brickell going to third.
2 P. Waner hit a sacrifice fly to center, Brickell scoring after the catch.
3 Wright bounced back to the mound.
New York
  For Pittsburgh—Miljus pitching and Gooch catching.
  Koenig beat out a hit behind second.
1,2 Ruth hit into a double play, Traynor to Wright to Harris.
3 Gehrig flied to deep left.

8th Inning
Pittsburgh
1 Traynor grounded to third.
  Grantham lined a single to right.
2 Harris grounded to second, Grantham going to second.
  Gooch intentionally passed.
3 Miljus struck out.
New York
1 Meusel grounded to third.
  Lazzeri walked on four pitches.
2 Dugan popped to first.
  Collins singled over second, Lazzeri racing to third.
3 Moore struck out.

9th Inning
Pittsburgh
1 L. Waner grounded to second.
2 Barnhart flied to left.
3 P. Waner bounced back to the mound.
New York
  Combs walked on four pitches.
  Koenig beat out a bunt down the third base line, Combs stopping at second. Combs went to third and Koenig to second on a wild pitch.
  Ruth was purposely walked, loading the bases.
1 Gehrig struck out.
2 Meusel struck out.
  With a one strike count on Lazzeri Miljus uncorked his second wild pitch of the inning as Combs scored the game and Series ending winning run.

1927 WORLD SERIES COMPOSITE BOX

	Wins	Composite Line Score										Manager	Regular Season W	L	Pct.	G. Ahead
New York Yankees (A.L.)	4	4	0	6	0	3	0	6	3	1	- 23	Miller Huggins	110	44	.714	19
Pittsburgh Pirates (N.L.)	0	3	0	1	0	1	0	2	3	0	- 10	Donie Bush	94	60	.610	1½

BATTING AND FIELDING

	WORLD SERIES STATISTICS																	REGULAR SEASON STATISTICS													
	Pos	G	AB	R	H	2B	3B	HR	RBI	BB	SO	SB	BA	SA	PO	A	E	Main Pos	G	AB	R	H	2B	3B	HR	RBI	BB	SO	SB	BA	SA
NEW YORK YANKEES																															
Lou Gehrig	1b	4	13	2	4	2	2	0	4	3	3	0	.308	.769	41	3	0	1b	155	584	149	218	52	18	47	175	109	84	10	.373	.765
Tony Lazzeri	2b	4	15	1	4	1	0	0	2	1	4	0	267	.333	10	18	1	2b-ss	153	570	92	176	29	8	18	102	69	82	22	.309	.482
Mark Koenig	ss	4	18	5	9	2	0	0	2	0	2	0	.500	.611	6	8	0	ss	123	526	99	150	20	11	3	62	25	21	3	.285	.382
Joe Dugan	3b	4	15	2	3	0	0	0	0	0	0	0	200	.200	3	6	0	3b	112	387	44	104	24	3	2	43	27	37	1	.269	.362
Babe Ruth	rf	4	15	4	6	0	0	2	7	2	2	1	.400	.800	10	0	0	of	151	540	158	192	29	8	60	164	138	89	7	.356	.772
Earle Combs	cf	4	16	6	5	0	0	0	2	1	2	0	.313	.313	16	0	0	of	152	648	137	231	36	23	6	64	62	31	15	.356	.511
Bob Meusel	lf	4	17	1	2	0	0	0	1	1	7	1	.118	.118	8	0	1	of	135	516	75	174	47	9	8	103	45	58	24	.337	.510
Pat Collins	c	2	5	0	3	1	0	0	0	3	0	0	.600	.800	5	1	0	c	92	251	38	69	9	3	7	36	54	24	0	.275	.418
Benny Bengough	c	2	4	1	0	0	0	0	0	1	0	0	.000	.000	4	0	0	c	31	85	6	21	3	3	0	10	4	4	0	.247	.353
Johnny Grabowski	c	1	2	0	0	0	0	0	0	0	0	0	.000	.000	3	0	0	c	70	195	29	54	2	4	0	25	20	15	0	.277	.328
Cedric Durst	ph	1	1	0	0	0	0	0	0	0	0	0	.000	.000				2b	73	129	18	32	4	3	0	25	6	7	0	.248	.326
Ray Morehart		Did not play																of	65	195	45	50	7	2	1	20	29	18	4	.256	.328
Mike Gazella		Did not play																3b	54	115	17	32	8	4	0	9	23	16	4	.278	.417
Ben Paschal		Did not play																of	50	82	16	26	9	2	2	16	4	10	0	.317	.549
Julie Wera		Did not play																3b	38	42	7	10	3	0	1	8	1	5	0	.239	.381
Wilcy Moore	p	2	5	0	1	0	0	0	0	0	3	0	.200	.200	0	5	1	p	50	75	5	6	0	0	1	2	4	38	0	.080	.120
Herb Pennock	p	1	4	1	0	0	0	0	1	0	1	0	.000	.000	1	1	0	p	34	69	6	15	2	0	0	6	3	10	0	.217	.246
George Pipgras	p	1	3	0	1	0	0	0	0	1	1	0	.333	.333	1	2	0	p	29	67	4	16	1	1	1	6	2	17	0	.239	.328
Waite Hoyt	p	1	3	0	0	0	0	0	0	0	0	0	.000	.000	0	0	0	p	36	99	10	22	2	1	0	9	3	8	0	.222	.263
Dutch Ruether		Did not play																p	35	80	7	21	3	0	1	10	8	15	0	.263	.338
Urban Shocker		Did not play																p	31	54	6	13	1	0	0	10	7	12	0	.241	.259
Myles Thomas		Did not play																p	21	27	5	9	0	0	0	3	0	2	0	.333	.333
Bob Shawkey		Did not play																p	19	11	1	1	0	0	0	0	0	3	0	.091	.091
Joe Giard		Did not play																p	16	7	2	2	0	0	0	0	1	4	0	.286	.286
team total		4	136	23	38	6	2	2	19	13	25	2	.279	.397	108	44	3		155	5347	975	1644	291	103	158	908	635	605	90	.307	.489

Double Plays—4
Left on Bases—29

Walter Beall (p) also played for the Yankees during the season.

	WORLD SERIES STATISTICS																	REGULAR SEASON STATISTICS													
	Pos	G	AB	R	H	2B	3B	HR	RBI	BB	SO	SB	BA	SA	PO	A	E	Main Pos	G	AB	R	H	2B	3B	HR	RBI	BB	SO	SB	BA	SA
PITTSBURGH PIRATES																															
Joe Harris	1b	4	15	0	3	0	0	0	1	0	0	0	.200	.200	35	2	0	1b	129	411	57	134	27	9	5	73	48	19	0	.326	.472
George Grantham	2b	3	11	0	4	1	0	0	0	1	1	0	.364	.455	6	7	1	2b	151	531	96	162	33	11	8	66	74	39	9	.305	.454
Glenn Wright	ss	4	13	1	2	0	0	0	2	0	0	0	.154	.154	5	13	1	ss	143	570	78	160	26	4	9	105	39	46	4	.281	.388
Pie Traynor	3b	4	15	1	3	1	0	0	0	0	1	0	.200	.267	5	9	1	3b	149	573	93	196	32	9	5	106	22	11	11	.342	.455
Paul Waner	rf	4	15	0	5	1	0	0	3	0	1	0	.333	.400	8	0	0	of	155	623	113	237	40	17	9	131	60	14	5	.380	.543
Lloyd Waner	cf	4	15	5	6	1	1	0	0	1	0	0	.400	.600	9	1	2	of	150	629	133	223	17	6	2	27	37	23	14	.355	.410
Clyde Barnhart	lf	4	16	0	5	1	0	0	4	0	0	0	.313	.375	6	1	0	of	108	360	66	115	25	5	3	54	37	19	2	.319	.442
Earl Smith	c-ph	3	8	0	0	0	0	0	0	0	0	0	.000	.000	10	1	1	c	66	189	16	51	3	1	5	25	21	11	0	.270	.376
Johnny Gouch	c	3	5	0	0	0	0	0	0	1	1	0	.000	.000	19	1	0	c	101	291	22	75	17	2	2	48	19	21	0	.258	.351
Hal Rhyne	2b	1	4	0	0	0	0	0	0	0	0	0	.000	.000	0	6	0	2b	62	168	21	46	5	0	0	17	14	9	0	.274	.304
Fred Brickell	ph	2	2	1	0	0	0	0	0	0	0	0	.000	.000				of	32	21	6	6	1	0	1	4	1	0	0	.286	.476
Roy Spencer	ph-c	1	1	0	0	0	0	0	0	0	0	0	.000	.000	0	0	0	c	38	92	9	26	3	1	0	13	3	3	0	.283	.337
Heinie Groh	ph	1	1	0	0	0	0	0	0	0	0	0	.000	.000				3b	14	35	2	10	1	0	0	3	2	2	0	.286	.314
Kiki Cuyler		Did not play																of	85	285	60	88	13	7	3	31	37	36	20	.309	.435
Joe Cronin		Did not play																2b-ss	12	22	2	5	1	0	0	3	2	3	0	.227	.273
Vic Aldridge	p	1	2	0	0	0	0	0	0	0	0	0	.000	.000	0	2	0	p	35	96	5	21	5	0	0	9	1	3	0	.219	.271
Johnny Miljus	p	2	2	0	0	0	0	0	0	0	2	0	.000	.000	1	2	0	p	19	28	2	5	1	0	0	2	0	7	0	.179	.214
Lee Meadows	p	1	2	0	0	0	0	0	0	0	0	0	.000	.000	0	1	0	p	40	115	3	18	0	1	0	6	4	20	0	.157	.174
Ray Kremer	p	1	2	1	1	1	0	0	0	0	1	0	.500	1.000	0	0	0	p	35	83	3	14	1	0	2	10	2	19	0	.169	.253
Carmen Hill	p	1	1	0	0	0	0	0	0	1	0	0	.000	.000	0	0	0	p	44	104	10	22	3	3	0	10	5	30	0	.212	.298
Mike Cvengros	p	2	0	0	0	0	0	0	0	0	0	0	—	—	0	0	0	p	23	19	2	3	1	0	0	3	1	1	0	.158	.211
Joe Dawson	p	1	0	0	0	0	0	0	0	0	0	0	—	—	0	0	0	p	20	25	1	5	0	0	0	1	0	3	0	.200	.200
Emil Yde	pr	1	0	1	0	0	0	0	0	0	0	0	—	—				p	23	18	8	3	0	1	0	1	0	1	0	.167	.278
team total		4	130	10	29	6	1	0	10	4	7	0	.223	.285	104	46	6		156	5397	817	1648	258	78	54	759	437	355	65	.305	412

Double Plays—2
Left on Bases—23

Dick Bartell (ss), Herman Layne (of), Eddie Sicking (2b), Bullet Joe Bush (p), Roy Mahaffey (p), Johnny Morrison (p), Chet Nichols (p), Red Peery (p), Don Songer (p) also played for the Pirates during the season.

PITCHING

	WORLD SERIES STATISTICS													REGULAR SEASON STATISTICS													
	G	GS	CG	IP	H	R	ER	BB	SO	W	L	SV	ERA	G	GS	CG	IP	H	ER	BB	SO	W	L	Pct	SV	ShO	ERA
NEW YORK YANKEES																											
Wilcy Moore	2	1	1	$10\frac{2}{3}$	11	3	1	2	2	1	0	1	0.84	50	12	6	213	185	54	59	75	19	7	.731	13	1	2.28
Herb Pennock	1	1	1	9	3	1	1	0	1	1	0	0	1.00	34	26	18	210	225	70	48	51	19	8	.704	2	1	3.00
George Pipgras	1	1	1	9	7	2	2	1	2	1	0	0	2.00	29	21	9	166	148	76	77	81	10	3	.769	0	1	4.12
Waite Hoyt	1	1	0	$7\frac{1}{3}$	8	4	4	1	2	1	0	0	4.91	36	32	23	256	242	75	54	86	22	7	.759	1	3	2.64
Urban Shocker	Did not play													31	27	13	200	207	63	41	35	18	6	.750	0	2	2.84
Dutch Ruether	Did not play													27	26	12	184	202	69	52	45	13	6	.684	0	3	3.38
Myles Thomas	Did not play													21	9	1	89	111	78	43	25	7	4	.636	0	0	4.85
Bob Shawkey	Did not play													19	2	0	44	44	14	16	23	2	3	.400	4	0	2.86
Joe Giard	Did not play													16	0	0	27	38	24	19	10	0	0	—	0	0	8.00
team total	4	4	3	36	29	10	8	4	7	4	0	1	2.00	155	155	82	1390	1403	494	409	431	110	44	.714	20	11	3.20
PITTSBURGH PIRATES																											
Vic Aldridge	1	1	0	$7\frac{1}{3}$	10	6	6	4	4	0	1	0	7.36	35	34	17	239	248	113	74	86	15	10	.600	1	1	4.26
Johnny Miljus	2	0	0	$6\frac{2}{3}$	4	1	1	4	6	0	1	0	1.35	19	6	3	76	62	16	17	24	8	3	.727	0	2	1.89
Lee Meadows	1	1	0	$6\frac{1}{3}$	7	7	7	1	6	0	1	0	9.95	40	38	25	299	315	113	66	84	19	10	.655	0	2	3.40
Carmen Hill	1	1	0	6	9	3	3	1	6	0	0	0	4.50	43	31	22	278	260	100	80	95	22	11	.667	3	2	3.24
Ray Kremer	1	1	0	5	5	5	2	3	1	0	1	0	3.60	35	28	18	226	205	62	53	63	19	8	.704	2	3	2.47
Mike Cvengros	2	0	0	$2\frac{1}{3}$	3	1	1	0	2	0	0	0	3.86	23	4	0	54	55	20	24	21	2	1	.667	1	0	3.33
Joe Dawson	1	0	0	1	0	0	0	0	0	0	0	0	0.00	20	7	4	81	80	40	32	17	3	7	.300	0	0	4.44
Emil Yde	Did not pitch													9	2	0	30	45	32	15	9	1	3	.250	0	0	9.60
team total	4	4	0	$34\frac{2}{3}$	38	23	20	13	25	0	4	0	5.19	156	156	90	1385	1400	563	418	435	94	60	.610	10	10	3.66

Total Attendance—201,105   Average Attendance—50,276   Winning Player's Share—$5,592   Losing Player's Share—$3,728

1928
Double Devastation

Bill McKechnie had played a competent third base in the prewar years, but his chief baseball talent was an ability to manage clubs to National League pennants. He had taken the Pittsburgh Pirates to the top of the N.L. in 1925 and had beaten the Washington Senators in the World Series. Yet when his club fell off to third place in 1926, McKechnie was canned by the Pirate management. But his talents put him in demand as a big-league skipper, and he had a new mount in 1928, taking command of the St. Louis Cardinals. The Cards had beaten the Yankees for the World Championship in 1926, but team owner Sam Breadon broke up that club immediately after the Series by trading manager Rogers Hornsby to the Giants for Frankie Frisch. While the hustling Frisch lacked the batting power of Hornsby, he gave nothing away in fielding and leadership and got along much better with Breadon than the arrogant Hornsby. McKechnie got productive seasons out of Jim Bottomley and Chick Hafey, a .337-hitting outfielder with one of the strongest throwing arms in baseball, and installed veteran Rabbit Maranville at shortstop to cement the infield. The mound staff showed age, with thirty-one-year-old Bill Sherdel, thirty-four-year-old Jesse Haines, and forty-one-year-old Pete Alexander the top winners. McKechnie took this hodgepodge collection into the Series by beating out the New York Giants in a close pennant race. After beating out one New York team, the Cards now took on the Yankees in the Series. The Yanks still flexed enough muscle to make any opponent careful, but injuries weakened the defending champs coming into the fall classic. A bad arm had pitcher Herb Pennock in dry dock, a broken finger limited center fielder Earle Combs to pinch hitting, a bad arm dictated a late-inning fielding replacement for second baseman Tony Lazzeri whenever possible, and a bad ankle slowed down Babe Ruth. But his injury evidently did not hamper the Babe from moving around the bases, as he and Lou Gehrig ran out hits almost nonstop throughout the Series.

The opening-game crowd in Yankee Stadium saw the Bambino belt two doubles and a single in support of Waite Hoyt, who spun a three-hitter to beat Bill Sherdel 4–1. Gehrig joined the fun with two hits and two RBI's. Pete Alexander took the mound for the Cards in game two, but he could not call back the heroics of the 1926 Series. He was pummeled for three runs in the first, one in the second, and four more while being knocked from the box in the third. Yankee hurler George Pipgras practically coasted to the 9–3 victory, with Ruth collecting a double and a single in the contest, while Gehrig drove in three runs with a home run. Manager Miller Huggins's success in the first two games, however, was not solely dependent on his two sluggers: The pitching staff ably replaced the injured Pennock, rookie infielder Leo Durocher handled the late-inning duties at second base in competent manner, and youngsters Cedric Durst and Ben Paschal filled in admirably in center field. Huggins was also fortunate that Ruth's bad ankle had not at all affected his ability to swing the bat.

The Cardinals hoped to turn the Series around in St. Louis, coming alive before their hometown fans. But the liveliest items in the third game were the bats of Ruth and Gehrig. Ruth contented himself with two singles, but Gehrig rocketed a pair of homers to lead the Yanks to a 7–3 triumph that practically wrapped up the Series. The clincher came quickly the next day in game four. Ruth hit the peak of a marvelous Series by hitting three home runs, and Gehrig capped his Series performance with another home run. With the 7–3 victory completing a second straight Yankee sweep of the Series, the total statistics gave substance to the incredible impressions Ruth and Gehrig had made. The Babe had hit .625 for the four games with three homers and four RBI's. Gehrig, on the other hand, hit only .545 but belted four homers and drove in nine runs. McKechnie's Cardinals had no tools at hand to stop such an avalanche of power, but team owner Sam Breadon figured that his pennant-winning club should have made a better showing in the Series. The problem, he figured, lay in the manager, so he fired McKechnie.

Game 1 October 4 at New York

St. Louis	Pos	AB	R	H	RBI	PO	A	E
Douthit	cf	3	0	0	0	2	0	0
High	3b	4	0	0	0	0	1	0
Frisch	2b	4	0	0	0	1	6	0
Bottomley	1b	3	1	2	1	10	0	0
Hafey	lf	4	0	0	0	3	0	0
Harper	rf	3	0	1	0	2	0	0
Wilson	c	3	0	0	0	3	0	0
Maranville	ss	2	0	0	0	2	0	1
a Orsatti		0	0	0	0	0	0	0
Thevenow	ss	0	0	0	0	1	0	0
Sherdel	p	2	0	0	0	0	3	0
b Holm		1	0	0	0	0	0	0
Johnson	p	0	0	0	0	0	0	0
Totals		29	1	3	1	24	10	1

New York	Pos	AB	R	H	RBI	PO	A	E
Paschal	cf	4	0	0	0	4	0	0
Durst	cf	0	0	0	0	0	0	0
Koenig	ss	4	1	1	0	2	3	0
Ruth	rf	4	2	3	0	3	0	0
Gehrig	1b	4	0	2	2	6	0	0
Meusel	lf	4	1	1	2	2	0	0
Lazzeri	2b	2	0	0	0	2	0	0
Durocher	2b	1	0	0	0	0	0	0
Dugan	3b	3	0	0	0	2	0	0
Bengough	c	3	0	0	0	8	1	0
Hoyt	p	3	0	0	0	0	1	0
Totals		32	4	7	4	27	7	0

St L.	0 0 0	0 0 0	1 0 0
N.Y.	1 0 0	2 0 0	0 1 x

Pitching	IP	H	R	ER	BB	SO
St. Louis						
Sherdel (L)	7	4	3	3	0	2
Johnson	1	3	1	1	0	0
New York						
Hoyt (W)	9	3	1	1	3	6

a Walked for Maranville in 8th.
b Lined out for Sherdel in 8th.

Doubles—Gehrig, Ruth 2. Home Runs—Bottomley, Meusel. Left on Bases—St. Louis 4, New York 4. Umpires—Owens (A), Rigler (N), McGowan (A), Pfirman (N). Attendance—61,425. Time of Game—1:49.

1st Inning
St. Louis
1 Douthit grounded to second.
2 High flied to center.
3 Frisch grounded to short.
New York
1 Paschal flied to left.
2 Koenig flied to left.
  Ruth doubled to right-center.
  Gehrig doubled into the right field corner, scoring Ruth.
3 Meusel popped to Frisch in short right.

2nd Inning
St. Louis
  Bottomley walked on a full count.
1 Hafey called out on strikes.
2 Harper flied to center.
3 Wilson rolled back to the mound.
New York
1 Lazzeri flied to left.
2 Dugan grounded to second.
3 Bengough grounded to second.

3rd Inning
St. Louis
1 Maranville flied to right.
2 Sherdel fouled to Dugan.
3 Douthit fouled to Bengough.
New York
1 Hoyt fouled to Maranville making a running one-handed catch near the left field stands.
2 Paschal flied to Douthit in left-center.
3 Koenig grounded to second.

4th Inning
St. Louis
1 High struck out on a full count.
2 Frisch fouled to Bengough.
3 Bottomley grounded to first.
New York
  Ruth got his second double a smash into center.
1 Gehrig bounced back to the mound, Ruth holding second.
  Meusel hit a two-run home run into the right field bleachers.
2 Lazzeri fouled to Wilson.
3 Dugan popped to Maranville in short left.

5th Inning
St. Louis
1 Hafey again struck out.
  Harper singled to center for the Cards' first hit.
2 Wilson forced Harper at second, Lazzeri to Koenig.
3 Wilson out trying to steal second, Bengough to Koenig
New York
1 Bengough rolled out to second.
2 Hoyt grounded to second.
3 Paschal flied to right.

6th Inning
St. Louis
1 Maranville flied to right.
2 Sherdel struck out.
  Douthit walked on a full count.
3 High flied to left.
New York
1 Koenig grounded back to the pitcher.
2 Ruth called out on strikes with a full count.
3 Gehrig grounded to second.

7th Inning
St. Louis
  For New York—Durocher replaced Lazzeri at second.
1 Frisch grounded to short.
  Bottomley drove a home run into the right field bleachers.
2 Hafey flied to deep left.
3 Harper fouled to Dugan.
New York
1 Meusel bounced back to the mound.
2 Durocher struck out.
  Dugan safe at first when Maranville fumbled his grounder to short.
3 Bengough lined to right.

8th Inning
St. Louis
1 Wilson lined to center.
  Orsatti, pinch-hitting for Maranville, walked.
2 Holm, pinch-hitting for Sherdel, flied to center.
3 Douthit took a called third strike.
New York
  For St. Louis—Thevenow playing short and Johnson pitching.
1 Hoyt flied to center.
2 Paschal grounded to third.
  Koenig singled to center.
  Ruth singled through short, his third hit of the game, with Koenig stopping at second.
  Gehrig singled to right, Koenig scoring with Ruth stopping at second.
3 Meusel popped to short.

9th Inning
St. Louis
  For New York—Durst replaced Paschal in center.
1 High struck out.
2 Frisch grounded to short.
  Bottomley lined a single to right.
3 Hafey flied to right.

Game 2 October 5 at New York

St. Louis	Pos	AB	R	H	RBI	PO	A	E
Douthit	cf	4	0	0	1	2	1	0
High	3b	3	0	0	0	0	1	0
Frisch	2b	3	0	2	0	2	3	0
Bottomley	1b	4	0	0	0	9	0	0
Hafey	lf	4	0	0	0	3	0	0
Harper	rf	3	1	0	0	1	0	0
Wilson	c	4	1	1	1	5	2	0
Maranville	ss	3	1	1	0	1	3	0
Alexander	p	1	0	0	1	0	1	0
Mitchell	p	2	0	0	0	0	1	1
c Orsatti		1	0	0	0	0	0	0
Totals		32	3	4	3	24	10	1

Pitching	IP	H	R	ER	BB	SO
St. Louis						
Alexander (L)	2⅓	6	8	8	4	1
Mitchell	5⅔	2	1	1	2	2
New York						
Pipgras (W)	9	4	3	3	4	8

St L. 030 000 000
N.Y. 314 000 10x

New York	Pos	AB	R	H	RBI	PO	A	E
Durst	cf	2	1	2	1	0	0	0
a Paschal	cf	2	0	1	1	2	0	0
Koenig	ss	5	0	0	0	1	2	1
Ruth	rf	3	2	2	0	1	0	0
Gehrig	1b	3	2	1	3	9	0	0
Meusel	lf	3	2	1	1	2	0	0
Lazzeri	2b	3	0	0	0	1	1	1
Durocher	2b	0	0	0	0	1	1	0
Robertson	3b	1	0	0	0	2	1	0
b Dugan	3b	0	0	0	1	1	0	0
Bengough	c	3	1	1	1	9	0	0
Pipgras	p	2	0	0	0	0	1	0
Totals		28	9	8	9	27	5	2

a Singled for Durst in 3rd.
b Hit sacrifice fly for Robertson in 7th.
c Grounded out for Mitchell in 9th.

Doubles—Meusel, Ruth, Wilson, Home Run—Gehrig. Stolen Bases—Frisch 2, Meusel. Sacrifice Hits—Lazzeri, Pipgras. Sacrifice fly—Dugan. Double Plays—Frisch to Maranville to Bottomley, Koenig to Lazzeri to Gehrig. Hit by Pitcher—Pipgras (by Mitchell). Left on Bases—St. Louis 6, New York 5. Umpires—Rigler, McGowan, Pfirman, Owens. Attendance—60,714. Time of Game—2:04.

1st Inning
St. Louis
1 Douthit grounded to first.
  High walked on a full count.
  Frisch walked on a full count.
2 Bottomley fouled to Bengough, also on a full count.
3 Hafey struck out.
New York
  Durst lined a single over Frisch's head.
1 Koenig flied to left.
  Ruth walked on four pitches.
  Gehrig boomed a three-run homer deep into the right field bleachers on the first pitch.
2 Meusel took a called third strike.
3 Lazzeri tapped back to the mound.

2nd Inning
St. Louis
  Harper walked.
  Wilson doubled to right-center, Harper scoring.
  Maranville singled to right, Wilson stopping at third.
  Alexander safe at first on Lazzeri's high throw to first, Wilson scoring as Maranville got to third.
1,2 Douthit hit into a double play, Koenig to Lazzeri to Gehrig, as Maranville was scoring.
3 High popped to third.
New York
1 Robertson bounced to first.
  Bengough walked.
2 Pipgras sacrificed Bengough to second, Wilson to Bottomley.
  Durst singled to center, Bengough scoring.
3 Koenig popped to second.

3rd Inning
St. Louis
  Frisch singled through the box.
  Frisch stole second.
1 Bottomley struck out.
2 Hafey grounded to short, Frisch going to third.
3 Harper took a called third strike.
New York
  Ruth singled to center.
  Gehrig walked.
  Meusel doubled just inside the left field foul line, scoring Ruth with Gehrig stopping at third.
1 Lazzeri grounded to third, Meusel going to second as Gehrig held third. Robertson walked, loading the bases. Bengough blooped a single into short right, scoring Gehrig as the bases remained filled.
  For St. Louis—Mitchell came in to pitch. Pipgras was hit by a pitch, forcing in Meusel with the bases still full.
  Paschal, batting for Durst, singled to center, Robertson scoring but Bengough
2 was out at the plate, Douthit to Frisch to Wilson.
3 Koenig popped to first.

4th Inning
St. Louis
  For New York—Paschal playing center.
1 Wilson bounced back to the mound.
  Maranville safe at first on Koenig's fumble.
2 Mitchell popped to Koenig near the left field foul line.
3 Douthit fouled to Gehrig.

4th Inning (continued)
New York
  Ruth doubled to deep center.
1 Gehrig flied to center.
2 Meusel flied to left.
3 Lazzeri smashed a grounder back to the mound.

5th Inning
St. Louis
1 High grounded to third.
2 Frisch was called out on strikes.
3 Bottomley struck out.
New York
1 Robinson grounded to second.
2 Bengough popped to Frisch in short center.
3 Pipgras popped to short.

6th Inning
St. Louis
1 Hafey flied to left.
2 Harper flied to right.
3 Wilson grounded to first.
New York
  Paschal walked.
1 Koenig struck out.
2 Ruth took a called third strike.
3 Gehrig flied to center.

7th Inning
St. Louis
1 Maranville struck out.
2 Mitchell popped to third.
3 Douthit flied to center.
New York
  Meusel walked.
  Meusel stole second.
  Lazzeri safe on an error by Mitchell, Meusel to third with Lazzeri credited with a sacrifice.
1 Dugan, batting for Robertson, hit a sacrifice fly to right, Meusel scoring.
2,3 Bengough hit into a double play, Frisch to Maranville to Bottomley.

8th Inning
St. Louis
  For New York—Dugan playing third and Durocher playing second.
1 High popped to first.
  Frisch singled to center, first hit off Pipgras since the third inning.
2 Bottomley struck out for the third time as Frisch stole second.
3 Hafey flied to deep left.
New York
1 Pipgras struck out but had to be thrown out, Wilson to Bottomley.
2 Paschal popped to Wilson in front of the plate.
3 Koenig flied to deep left.

9th Inning
St. Louis
1 Harper popped to third.
2 Wilson struck out.
  Maranville walked.
3 Orsatti, batting for Mitchell, grounded to first.

Game 3 October 7 at St. Louis

New York	Pos	AB	R	H	RBI	PO	A	E
Durst	cf	5	1	0	0	3	0	0
Koenig	ss	5	0	1	0	1	4	0
Ruth	lf	4	2	2	0	2	1	0
Gehrig	1b	3	2	2	3	11	0	0
Meusel	rf	3	1	0	0	1	0	0
Lazzeri	2b	3	0	0	0	0	2	1
Durocher	2b	0	0	0	0	1	1	0
Robertson	3b	4	0	1	0	0	0	1
Bengough	c	4	0	1	0	8	0	0
Zachary	p	4	0	0	1	0	1	0
Totals		34	7	7	4	27	9	2

Pitching	IP	H	R	ER	BB	SO
New York						
Zachary (W)	9	9	3	3	1	7
St. Louis						
Haines (L)	6	6	6	3	3	3
Johnson	1	1	1	0	1	1
Rhem	2	2	0	0	0	1

N.Y. 010 203 100
St L. 200 010 000

St. Louis	Pos	AB	R	H	RBI	PO	A	E
Douthit	cf	4	1	1	0	2	0	0
High	3b	5	1	2	1	2	2	0
Frisch	2b	2	1	1	0	2	3	0
Bottomley	1b	4	0	1	2	6	1	0
Hafey	lf	4	0	2	0	1	0	1
Holm	rf	4	0	1	0	4	0	0
Wilson	c	4	0	0	0	6	0	2
Maranville	ss	4	0	1	0	4	1	0
Haines	p	2	0	0	0	0	1	0
Johnson	p	0	0	0	0	0	0	0
a Blades		1	0	0	0	0	0	0
Rhem	p	0	0	0	0	0	0	0
b Orsatti		1	0	0	0	0	0	0
Totals		35	3	9	3	27	8	3

a Struck out for Johnson in 7th.
b Struck out for Rhem in 9th.

Doubles—High, Triple—Bottomley. Home Runs—Gehrig 2. Stolen Bases—Lazzeri, Meusel. Sacrifice Hit—Frisch. Double Plays—Koenig to Durocher to Gehrig, High to Frisch to Bottomley. Hit by Pitcher—Douthit (by Zachary). Left on Bases—New York 4, St. Louis 8. Umpires—McGowan, Pfirman, Owens, Rigler. Attendance—39,602. Time of game—2:09.

1st Inning
New York
1 Durst lined to third.
2 Koenig fouled to High.
3 Ruth grounded to first.
St. Louis
1 Douthit tapped back to the mound. High singled off Koenig's glove. Frisch singled off Zachary's glove, High moving to second. Bottomley lined a triple to center as Durst misjudged the ball, scoring High and Frisch.
2 Hafey grounded to second as Bottomley held third.
3 Holm struck out.

2nd Inning
New York
  Gehrig hit a booming homer on top of the right field pavilion.
  Meusel walked.
1,2 Lazzeri grounded into a double play, High to Frisch to Bottomley.
3 Robertson flied to center.
St. Louis
1 Wilson struck out.
  Maranville safe as Robertson fumbled his grounder.
2 Haines flied to center.
  Douthit safe at first on Lazzeri's wild throw to second for the force on Maranville.
3 High struck out.

3rd Inning
New York
1 Bengough struck out.
2 Zachary struck out.
3 Durst popped to Wilson at the pitcher's box.
St. Louis
1 Frisch flied to Meusel behind second.
2 Bottomley took a called third strike. Hafey beat out a single to third.
3 Holm grounded to short.

4th Inning
New York
1 Koenig grounded to first. Ruth singled to right center. Gehrig got his second home-run of the game, a two-run shot lined past Douthit who missed a shoe-string catch.
2 Meusel called out on strikes.
3 Lazzeri grounded to short.
St. Louis
1 Wilson grounded to first. Maranville blooped a single to short
2 right but was out trying for a double, Ruth to Koenig.
3 Haines flied to right.

5th Inning
New York
1 Robertson flied to right. Bengough singled to center.
2 Zachary forced Bengough at second, Haines to Maranville.
3 Durst flied to deep center.
St. Louis
  Douthit was hit by a pitched ball. High doubled into the right field corner, Douthit scoring.
1 Frisch sacrificed High to third, Gehrig unassisted.
2 Bottomley fouled to Bengough.
3 Hafey lined to center.

6th Inning
New York
  Koenig singled to left.
1 Ruth forced Koenig at second, Frisch to Maranville. Gehrig walked.
2 Meusel forced Gehrig at second, High to Frisch, Ruth went all the way home as Wilson dropped Bottomley's throw to the plate. Meusel got all the way to third as Wilson threw into center for his second error. Lazzeri walked. Meusel stole home as Lazzeri stole second, a perfect double steal. Robertson singled to center, scoring Lazzeri.
3 Bengough flied to right.
St. Louis
1 Holm grounded to short.
2 Wilson took a called third strike on a full count.
3 Maranville grounded to second.

7th Inning
New York
  For St. Louis—Johnson pitching.
1 Zachary popped to short. Durst got safely into second when Hafey dropped his high deep fly for an error.
2 Koenig lined to third. Ruth singled to right, Durst scoring. Gehrig again walked.
3 Meusel struck out.
St. Louis
1 Blades, pinch-hitting for Johnson, struck out. Douthit singled to left.
2 High flied to center. Frisch walked.
3 Bottomley grounded to first.

8th Inning
New York
  For St. Louis—Rhem pitching.
1 Lazzeri flied to second.
2 Robertson popped to short.
3 Bengough grounded to second.
St. Louis
  For New York—Durocher replaced Lazzeri at second.
  Hafey singled to left. Holm singled to right, Hafey stopping at second.
1,2 Wilson hit into a double play, Koenig to Durocher to Gehrig as Hafey went to third.
3 Maranville fouled to Gehrig in front of the stands.

9th Inning
New York
1 Zachary grounded to first.
2 Durst struck out.
3 Koenig flied to left.
St. Louis
1 Orsatti, pinch-hitting for Rhem, struck out.
2 Douthit grounded to short.
3 High lined to right.

Game 4 October 9 at St. Louis

			N.Y.	000	100	420
			St L.	001	100	001

New York	Pos	AB	R	H	RBI	PO	A	E
Paschal	cf	4	0	1	0	3	0	0
Durst	cf	1	1	1	1	0	0	0
Koenig	ss	5	0	1	0	4	2	1
Ruth	lf	5	3	3	3	2	0	0
Gehrig	1b	2	1	1	1	7	0	0
Meusel	rf	5	1	1	0	0	0	0
Lazzeri	2b	4	1	3	0	1	2	0
Durocher	2b	1	0	0	0	0	0	0
Dugan	3b	3	0	1	0	0	0	0
Robertson	3b	2	0	1	0	0	0	0
Bengough	c	3	0	1	0	8	1	0
a Combs		0	0	0	1	0	0	0
Collins	c	1	0	1	0	2	0	0
Hoyt	p	4	0	1	0	0	2	1
Totals		40	7	15	7	27	7	2

St. Louis	Pos	AB	R	H	RBI	PO	A	E
Orsatti	cf	5	1	2	0	4	0	0
High	3b	5	0	3	0	0	1	0
Frisch	2b	4	0	0	1	3	3	0
Bottomley	1b	3	0	0	0	11	1	0
Hafey	lf	3	0	1	0	1	0	0
Harper	rf	3	0	0	0	2	0	0
Smith	c	4	0	3	0	3	1	0
b Martin		0	1	0	0	0	0	0
Maranville	ss	4	1	2	0	3	1	0
Sherdel	p	3	0	0	0	0	0	0
Alexander	p	0	0	0	0	0	3	0
c Holm		1	0	0	1	0	0	0
Totals		35	3	11	2	27	8	0

Pitching	IP	H	R	ER	BB	SO
New York						
Hoyt (W)	9	11	3	2	3	8
St. Louis						
Sherdel (L)	6⅓	11	4	4	3	1
Alexander	2⅔	4	3	3	0	1

a Hit sacrifice fly for Bengough in 7th.
b Ran for Smith in 9th.
c Grounded out for Alexander in 9th.

Doubles—Collins, High, Lazzeri, Maranville, Orsatti. Home Runs—Durst, Gehrig, Ruth 3. Stolen Bases—Lazzeri, Maranville. Sacrifice Hit—Hoyt. Sacrifice Flies—Combs, Frisch. Double Plays—Koenig to Gehrig, Bottomley to Maranville. Left on Bases—New York 11, St. Louis 9. Umpires—Pfirman, Owens, Rigler, McGowan. Attendance—37,331. Time of Game—2:25.

1st Inning
New York
1 Paschal fouled to Smith.
Koenig singled to left.
2,3 Ruth grounded into a double play, Bottomley to Maranville.
St. Louis
1 Orsatti took a called third strike on a full count.
High doubled to left after Ruth lost the ball in the sun.
2 Frisch also struck out on a full count.
Bottomley walked on a full count.
3 Hafey bunted out to the mound.

2nd Inning
New York
Gehrig walked for the third successive time.
1 Meusel struck out.
2 Lazzeri popped to short.
3 Dugan popped to second.
St. Louis
1 Harper grounded to second.
Smith singled past Hoyt into center.
2 Smith was out trying to steal second, Bengough to Koenig.
Maranville doubled to right.
3 Sherdel grounded to first.

3rd Inning
New York
Bengough got a long single off the bleacher wall.
1 Hoyt sacrificed Bengough to second, Smith to Bottomley.
2 Paschal grounded to third, Bengough taking third.
3 Koenig grounded to second.
St. Louis
Orsatti got a Texas League double behind second on another full count.
High beat out a bunt to Hoyt, Orsatti going to third.
1 Frisch hit a sacrifice fly to center, Orsatti scoring.
2 Bottomley fouled to Bengough.
Hafey walked also on a full count.
3 Harper struck out.

4th Inning
New York
Ruth lined a home run over the right field pavilion.
Gehrig walked on a full count for the fourth successive time.
1 Meusel flied to deep left-center.
Lazzeri singled to left, Gehrig stopping at second.
2 Dugan lined to center.
3 Bengough flied to Hafey racing into make the catch in short left.
St. Louis
Smith singled over Lazzeri's head.
1 Maranville forced Smith at second, Lazzeri to Koenig but Koenig's throw to Gehrig sailed over his head with Maranville going to second.
2 Sherdel flied to center.
Hoyt threw to second to catch Maranville but the ball sailed into center as no one covered the base, with Maranville coming all the way home on the error.
3 Orsatti struck out.

5th Inning
New York
Hoyt lined a single over Bottomley's head.
Paschal dropped a single to center, Hoyt stopping at second.
1 Koenig popped to second.
2 Ruth tapped back to the mound, advancing both runners.
Gehrig again walked.
3 Meusel forced Gehrig at second, Maranville making a great stop and throwing to Frisch.
St. Louis
1 High flied to center.
2 Frisch rolled back to the mound.
3 Bottomley took a called third strike.

6th Inning
New York
Lazzeri singled to left.
Dugan beat out a bunt past the mound, Lazzeri going to second.
1 Bengough popped a bunt to Bottomley. Lazzeri stole third.
2 Hoyt fouled to Bottomley.
3 Paschal popped to Orsatti, racing in behind short.
St. Louis
1 Hafey struck out.
Harper walked.
2 Smith popped to second.
Maranville singled to right-center, Harper going to third.
Maranville stole second.
3 Sherdel struck out on a full count.

7th Inning
New York
1 Koenig popped to short.
Ruth boomed his second homer of the game, a high one over the right field pavilion.
Gehrig homered onto the roof of the right field pavilion (**his fourth homer of the Series tying the record set by Ruth in 1926 in 6 games). Also his ninth RBI breaking Meusel's record of 8 set in 6 games in 1923.**
Meusel singled to left.
For St. Louis—Alexander now pitching.
Lazzeri doubled to left-center as Hafey lost the ball in the sun, Meusel stopping at second.
Dugan safe on a fielder's choice as Frisch, fielding his grounder, just missed Meusel at the plate. Lazzeri took third on the play.
2 Combs, batting for Bengough, lined a sacrifice fly to right, Lazzeri scoring.
3 Hoyt bounced back to the mound.
St. Louis
For New York—Durst playing center, Durocher playing second, Robertson playing third, and Collins catching.
1 Orsatti bunted a pop-up to Collins.
2 High lined to left.
3 Frisch fouled to Gehrig.

8th Inning
New York
Durst lined a homer just over the right field bleacher wall.
1 Koenig grounded to first.
Ruth hit third homer of the game on top of the right field pavilion. **His 10th hit breaking the 4 game record set by Koenig with 9 in 1927, also his 9th run breaking the record held by Leach in 1909 in 7 games and Ruth in 1923 of 6 games. This was also the Yankee's 9th homer a new record, surpassing Washington's 8 in 1925's 7 game series.**
2 Gehrig was finally out, bouncing back to the mound.
3 Meusel struck out.
St. Louis
1 Bottomley struck out.
Hafey beat out a liner to Koenig.
2,3 Harper rolled into a double play, Koenig to Gehrig.

9th Inning
New York
1 Durocher flied to right.
2 Robertson topped back to the mound.
Collins doubled to center.
3 Hoyt flied to center.
St. Louis
Smith singled off the right field wall.
Martin ran for Smith.
Martin to second, unmolested (no stolen base since no play made).
1 Maranville popped to short.
2 Holm, batting for Alexander, grounded to short, Martin scoring from second.
Orsatti singled off Koenig's glove.
High singled over Koenig's head, Orsatti racing to third.
3 Frisch fouled to Ruth, making a great running-catch in front of the grandstand.

1928 WORLD SERIES COMPOSITE BOX

	Wins	Composite Line Score
New York Yankees (A.L.)	4	4 2 4 5 0 3 6 3 0 – 27
St. Louis Cardinals (N.L.)	0	2 3 1 2 0 0 1 0 1 – 10

Manager	Regular Season W	L	Pct.	G. Ahead
Miller Huggins	101	53	.656	2½
Bill McKechnie	95	59	.617	2

BATTING AND FIELDING

NEW YORK YANKEES

Player	Pos	G	AB	R	H	2B	3B	HR	RBI	BB	SO	SB	BA	SA	PO	A	E		Main Pos	G	AB	R	H	2B	3B	HR	RBI	BB	SO	SB	BA	SA
	WORLD SERIES STATISTICS																		REGULAR SEASON STATISTICS													
Lou Gehrig	1b	4	11	5	6	1	0	**4**	**9**	**6**	0	0	.545	**1.727**	33	0	0		1b	154	562	139	210	**47**	13	27	**142**	95	69	4	.374	.648
Tony Lazzeri	2b	4	12	2	3	1	0	0	0	1	0	**2**	.250	.333	2	7	**2**		2b	116	404	62	134	30	11	10	82	43	50	15	.332	.535
Mark Koenig	ss	4	**19**	1	3	0	0	0	0	0	1	0	.158	.158	8	11	**2**		ss	132	533	89	170	19	10	4	63	32	19	3	.319	.415
Gene Robertson	3b-ph	3	8	1	1	0	0	0	2	1	0	0	.125	.125	2	1	1		3b	83	251	29	73	9	0	1	36	14	6	2	.291	.339
Babe Ruth	rf-lf	4	16	**9**	**10**	**3**	0	3	4	1	2	0	**.625**	1.375	8	1	0		of	154	536	**163**	173	29	8	**54**	**142**	**135**	**87**	4	.323	**.709**
Ben Paschal	cf-ph	3	10	0	2	0	0	0	1	1	0	0	.200	.200	8	0	0		of	65	79	12	25	6	1	1	15	8	11	1	.316	.456
Bob Meusel	lf-rf	4	15	5	3	1	0	1	3	2	5	**2**	.200	.467	5	0	0		of	131	518	77	154	45	5	11	113	39	56	6	.297	.467
Benny Bengough	c	4	13	1	3	0	0	0	1	1	1	0	.231	.231	33	2	0		c	58	161	12	43	3	1	0	9	7	8	0	.267	.298
Cedric Durst	cf	4	8	3	3	0	0	1	2	0	1	0	.375	.750	3	0	0		of	74	135	18	34	2	1	2	10	7	9	1	.252	.326
Joe Dugan	3b	3	6	0	1	0	0	0	1	0	0	0	.167	.167	3	0	0		3b	94	312	33	86	15	0	6	34	16	15	1	.276	.381
Leo Durocher	2b	4	2	0	0	0	0	0	0	0	1	0	.000	.000	1	1	0		2b-ss	102	296	46	80	8	6	0	31	22	52	1	.270	.338
Pat Collins	c	1	1	0	1	1	0	0	0	0	0	0	1.000	2.000	2	0	0		c	70	136	18	30	5	0	6	14	35	16	0	.221	.390
Earle Combs	ph	1	0	0	0	0	0	0	1	0	0	0	—	—					of	149	626	118	194	33	**21**	7	56	77	33	10	.310	.463
Johnny Grabowski	Did not play																		c	75	202	21	48	7	1	1	21	10	21	0	.238	.297
Mike Gazella	Did not play																		3b	32	56	11	13	0	0	0	2	6	7	2	.232	.232
Bill Dickey	Did not play																		c	10	15	1	3	1	1	0	2	0	2	0	.200	.400
Waite Hoyt	p	2	7	0	1	0	0	0	0	0	0	0	.143	.143	0	3	1		p	42	109	15	28	1	0	0	12	1	5	0	.257	.266
Tom Zachary	p	1	4	0	0	0	0	0	0	0	1	0	.000	.000	0	1	0	a	p	7	15	1	2	0	0	1	4	0	5	0	.133	.333
George Pipgras	p	1	2	0	0	0	0	0	1	0	0	0	.000	.000	0	1	0		p	46	115	7	18	4	0	0	5	4	28	0	.157	.191
Herb Pennock	Did not play—illness																		p	28	74	1	15	0	0	0	9	3	7	0	.203	.203
Fred Heimach	Did not play																		p	18	30	2	5	0	0	0	2	2	6	0	.167	.167
Myles Thomas	Did not play																		p	13	10	1	4	0	0	0	0	0	0	0	.400	.400
Rosy Ryan	Did not play																		p	3	4	0	0	0	0	0	0	0	1	0	.000	.000
team total		4	134	27	37	7	0	9	25	13	12	4	.276	.530	108	28	6			154	5337	**894**	**1578**	269	79	**133**	**817**	**562**	**544**	51	**.296**	**.450**

Double Plays—3
Left on Bases—24

a—from Washington
George Burns (1b), Archie Campbell (p), Stan Coveleski (p), Hank Johnson (p), Wilcy Moore (p), Al Shealy (p) also played for the Yankees during the season. Urban Shocker (p) died of pneumonia on September 9th.

ST. LOUIS CARDINALS

Player	Pos	G	AB	R	H	2B	3B	HR	RBI	BB	SO	SB	BA	SA	PO	A	E		Main Pos	G	AB	R	H	2B	3B	HR	RBI	BB	SO	SB	BA	SA
	WORLD SERIES STATISTICS																		REGULAR SEASON STATISTICS													
Jim Bottomley	1b	4	14	1	3	0	**1**	1	3	2	**6**	0	.214	.571	**36**	2	0		1b	149	576	123	187	42	**20**	**31**	**136**	71	54	10	.325	.628
Frankie Frisch	2b	4	13	1	3	0	0	0	1	2	2	**2**	.231	.231	8	**13**	0		2b	141	547	107	164	29	9	10	86	64	17	29	.300	.441
Rabbit Maranville	ss	4	13	2	4	1	0	0	0	1	1	1	.308	.385	11	3	1		ss	112	366	40	88	14	10	1	34	36	27	3	.240	.342
Andy High	3b	4	17	1	5	2	0	0	1	1	3	0	.294	.412	2	5	0		3b	111	368	58	105	14	3	6	37	37	10	2	.285	.389
George Harper	rf	3	9	1	1	0	0	0	0	2	2	0	.111	.111	5	0	0	b	of	99	272	41	83	8	2	17	58	51	15	2	.305	.537
Taylor Douthit	cf	3	11	1	1	0	0	0	1	1	1	0	.091	.091	6	1	0		of	154	648	111	191	35	3	3	43	84	36	11	.295	.372
Chick Hafey	lf	4	15	0	3	0	0	0	0	1	4	0	.200	.200	8	0	1		of	138	520	101	175	46	6	27	111	40	53	8	.337	.604
Jimmie Wilson	c	3	11	1	1	1	0	0	1	0	3	0	.091	.182	14	2	**2**	c	c	120	411	45	106	26	2	2	50	45	24	9	.258	.345
Ernie Orsatti	ph-cf	4	7	1	2	1	0	0	0	1	3	0	.286	.429	4	0	0		of	27	69	10	21	6	0	3	15	10	11	0	.304	.522
Wattie Holm	ph-rf	3	6	0	1	0	0	0	1	0	1	0	.167	.167	4	0	0		3b	102	386	61	107	24	6	3	47	32	27	1	.277	.394
Earl Smith	c	1	4	0	3	0	0	0	0	0	0	0	.750	.750	3	1	0	d	c	24	58	3	13	2	0	0	7	5	4	0	.224	.259
Ray Blades	ph	1	1	0	0	0	0	0	0	0	1	0	.000	.000					of	51	85	9	20	7	1	1	19	20	26	0	.235	.376
Pepper Martin	pr	1	0	1	0	0	0	0	0	0	0	0	—	—					of	39	13	11	4	0	0	0	0	1	2	2	.308	.308
Tommy Thevenow	ss	1	0	0	0	0	0	0	0	0	0	0	—	—	1	0	0		ss	69	171	11	35	8	3	0	13	20	12	0	.205	.287
Wally Roettger	Did not play—broken leg																		of	68	261	27	89	17	4	6	44	10	22	2	.341	.506
Howie Williamson	Did not play																		ph	10	9	0	2	0	0	0	0	1	4	0	.222	.222
Bill Sherdel	p	2	5	0	0	0	0	0	0	0	2	0	.000	.000	0	3	0		p	38	84	10	19	5	0	1	8	8	10	1	.226	.321
Jesse Haines	p	1	2	0	0	0	0	0	0	0	0	0	.000	.000	0	1	0		p	33	87	4	16	2	0	0	10	4	13	0	.184	.207
Clarence Mitchell	p	1	2	0	0	0	0	0	0	0	0	0	.000	.000	0	1	1	e	p	19	56	0	7	1	0	0	1	0	3	0	.125	.143
Pete Alexander	p	2	1	0	0	0	0	0	1	0	0	0	.000	.000	0	4	0		p	34	86	13	25	2	0	1	11	4	8	0	.291	.349
Syl Johnson	p	2	0	0	0	0	0	0	0	0	0	0	—	—	0	0	0		p	34	38	5	6	1	0	0	1	3	18	0	.158	.184
Flint Rhem	p	1	0	0	0	0	0	0	0	0	0	0	—	—	0	0	0		p	28	67	4	11	0	0	1	6	2	23	0	.164	.209
Fred Frankhouse	Did not play																		p	22	27	3	5	2	0	0	2	3	4	0	.185	.259
Art Reinhart	Did not play																		p	27	24	1	4	0	0	0	1	2	4	0	.167	.167
Hal Haid	Did not play																		p	27	8	0	3	0	0	0	1	1	2	0	.375	.375
team total		4	131	10	27	5	1	1	9	11	29	3	.207	.282	102	36	5			154	5357	807	1505	**292**	70	113	749	**568**	438	82	.281	.425

Double Plays—3
Left on Bases—27

b—from New York (N)
c—from Philadelphia (N)
d—from Pittsburgh
e—from Philadelphia (N)
Spud Davis (c), Gus Mancuso (c), Specs Toporcer (2b-1b), Tony Kaufmann (p), Carlisle Littlejohn (p) also played for the Cardinals during the season.

PITCHING

NEW YORK YANKEES

Player	G	GS	CG	IP	H	R	ER	BB	SO	W	L	SV	ERA		G	GS	CG	IP	H	ER	BB	SO	W	L	Pct	SV	ShO	ERA
	WORLD SERIES STATISTICS														REGULAR SEASON STATISTICS													
Waite Hoyt	**2**	**2**	**2**	**18**	14	4	3	**6**	**14**	**2**	0	0	**1.50**		42	31	19	273	279	102	60	67	23	7	.767	**8**	3	3.36
George Pipgras	1	1	1	9	4	3	2	4	8	1	0	0	2.00		46	**38**	22	**301**	**314**	113	103	139	**24**	13	.649	3	4	3.38
Tom Zachary	1	1	1	9	9	3	3	1	7	1	0	0	3.00	a	7	6	3	46	54	20	15	7	3	3	.500	1	0	3.91
Herb Pennock	Did not play—illness														28	24	18	211	215	60	40	53	17	6	.739	3	**5**	2.56
Fred Heimach	Did not play														13	9	5	68	66	25	16	25	2	3	.400	0	0	3.31
Myles Thomas	Did not play														12	1	0	32	33	12	9	10	1	0	1.000	0	0	3.38
Rosy Ryan	Did not play														3	0	0	6	17	11	1	5	0	0	—	0	0	16.50
team total	4	4	4	36	27	10	8	11	29	4	0	0	2.00		154	154	82	1375	1466	571	452	487	**101**	53	**.656**	**21**	13	3.74

ST. LOUIS CARDINALS

Player	G	GS	CG	IP	H	R	ER	BB	SO	W	L	SV	ERA		G	GS	CG	IP	H	ER	BB	SO	W	L	Pct	SV	ShO	ERA
Bill Sherdel	**2**	**2**	0	13⅓	**15**	7	7	3	3	0	**2**	0	4.73		38	27	20	249	251	79	56	72	21	10	.677	**5**	0	2.86
Jesse Haines	1	1	0	6	6	6	3	3	3	0	1	0	4.50		33	28	20	240	238	85	72	77	20	8	.714	0	1	3.19
Clarence Mitchell	1	0	0	5⅔	2	1	1	2	2	0	0	0	1.59	e	19	18	9	150	149	55	38	31	8	9	.471	0	1	3.30
Pete Alexander	**2**	1	0	5	10	**11**	**11**	4	2	0	1	0	19.80		34	31	18	244	262	91	37	59	16	9	.640	2	1	3.36
Syl Johnson	**2**	0	0	2	4	2	1	1	1	0	0	0	4.50		34	6	2	120	117	52	33	66	8	4	.667	3	0	3.90
Flint Rhem	1	0	0	2	0	0	0	0	1	0	0	0	0.00		28	22	9	170	199	78	71	47	11	8	.579	3	0	4.13
Fred Frankhouse	Did not play														21	10	1	84	91	37	36	29	3	2	.600	1	0	3.96
Art Reinhart	Did not play														23	9	3	75	80	24	27	12	4	6	.400	2	1	2.88
Hal Haid	Did not play														27	0	0	47	39	12	11	21	2	2	.500	**5**	0	2.30
team total	4	4	0	34	37	27	23	13	12	0	4	0	6.09		154	154	83	**1415**	1470	531	399	422	**95**	59	**.617**	**21**	4	3.38

Total Attendance—199,072 Average Attendance—49,768 Winning Player's Share—$5,532 Losing Player's Share—$4,197

1929
Late Lightning

Fifteen years ago, Connie Mack had dismantled the best club in the American League with an eye toward financial retrenchment and a desire to build again from scratch. Mack scratched around for players during most of those fifteen years while his Philadelphia Athletics grew accustomed to the atmosphere of the second division of the A.L. But at last he had found the combination again, piecing together with great care a balanced unit that ran away from the second-place New York Yankees by 18 games. Three players of All-Star proportions formed the heart of the Athletic lineup. Jimmie Foxx, a powerful man with massive arms, played first base and hit .354, gathering 33 homers and 117 RBI's along the way. Left fielder Al Simmons had a most unorthodox swing, striding away from the plate as the pitcher threw the ball, but that swing resulted in a .365 average with 34 homers and 157 RBI's. Catcher Mickey Cochrane excelled behind the plate and as a leader, and he contributed a .331 average to the lineup. Although these three men won reputations as the best at their positions, the other slots in the Athletic lineup were filled by most talented players, including Jimmy Dykes, Max Bishop, Mule Haas, and Bing Miller. The pitching staff had two aces in righty George Earnshaw, a 24-game winner, and Lefty Grove, a temperamental fast-baller who won 20 games. Lesser lights Rube Walberg, Eddie Rommel, and Jack Quinn all won over 10 games and figured to contribute to defeating the Chicago Cubs, their Series opponents.

But Mack passed over all of his main pitchers to start Howard Ehmke in the opening game at Wrigley Field. A seldom-used control pitcher with no fast ball and apparently very little future in the major leagues, the thirty-five-year-old Ehmke figured in no one's analysis of the Series. But his tantalizing off-speed pitches and near-perfect control befuddled the Cub batters, who had expected to see Grove's fast ball. By the end of the afternoon, the Chicago crowd of 50,740 had seen Ehmke strike out 13 Cubs and defeat the National League champs 3–1. Mack sent Earnshaw out to face the Cubs the next day, with the Athletic batters staking him to a 6–0 lead after four and a half innings. When the Cubs touched Earnshaw for three runs in the bottom of the fifth, Mack quickly brought on Grove to shut the Cubs off. The final Athletic victory margin was 9–3, with Earnshaw and Grove combining to fan 13 more Cub batters.

When the two teams resumed play in Philadelphia after a day of travel, the Cubs suddenly came alive. They won game three 3–1 behind the pitching of Guy Bush; then they took an 8–0 lead after six and a half innings in game four. But Al Simmons began the bottom of the seventh with a homer to left off starter Charlie Root, spoiling his shutout. When Jimmie Foxx, Bing Miller, Jimmy Dykes, and Joe Boley all singled in succession, the score read 8–3 and manager Joe McCarthy started some action in the Cub bullpen. Root got pinch hitter George Burns to pop up, but a single by Max Bishop cut the lead to 8–4 and convinced McCarthy to bring in veteran lefty Art Nehf. Mule Haas greeted Nehf with a fly to center, but when center fielder Hack Wilson lost the ball in the sun, Haas circled the bases and the score was 8–7. When the shaken Nehf walked Mickey Cochrane, McCarthy sent in Sheriff Blake to stop the oncoming wave. Blake gave up singles to Simmons and Foxx, and left in favor of staff ace Pat Malone with the score tied 8–8. But even Malone couldn't stop the A's this day as Miller was hit with a pitch and Dykes doubled to put the A's ahead 10–8. The next two men fanned, but the damage had been done. Grove came on to protect the lead, and the Cubs were effectively dead. In the next game, 22-game-winner Malone protected a 2–0 lead and kept the Cubs' hopes alive by tossing shutout ball through eight innings. Then lightening struck again. With one out in the bottom of the ninth, Bishop singled and Haas drilled a home run to tie the score. With the A's sensing the kill, Cochrane grounded out, but then Simmons doubled, Foxx was intentionally walked, and Miller doubled to end the game 3–2 and crown Connie Mack once again king of the baseball hill.

Game 1 October 8 at Chicago

| Phi. | 000 000 102 |
| Chi. | 000 000 001 |

Philadelphia	Pos	AB	R	H	RBI	PO	A	E
Bishop	2b	4	0	0	0	2	1	0
Haas	cf	3	0	0	0	1	0	0
Cochrane	c	3	1	1	0	14	1	0
Simmons	lf	4	1	0	0	2	0	0
Foxx	1b	4	1	2	1	4	0	0
Miller	rf	4	0	1	2	3	0	0
Dykes	3b	4	0	1	0	1	1	1
Boley	ss	4	0	0	0	0	0	0
Ehmke	p	4	0	1	0	0	2	0
Totals		34	3	6	3	27	5	1

Pitching	IP	H	R	ER	BB	SO
Philadelphia						
Ehmke (W)	9	8	1	0	1	13
Chicago						
Root (L)	7	3	1	1	2	5
Bush	2	3	2	0	0	0

Chicago	Pos	AB	R	H	RBI	PO	A	E
McMillan	3b	4	0	1	0	1	2	0
English	ss	4	0	2	0	1	3	2
Hornsby	2b	4	0	0	0	1	3	0
Wilson	cf	4	0	0	0	3	0	0
Cuyler	rf	4	1	1	0	1	0	0
Stephenson	lf	4	0	2	1	4	0	0
Grimm	1b	2	0	2	0	8	0	0
Taylor	c	2	0	0	0	6	0	0
a Heathcote		1	0	0	0	0	0	0
Gonzalez	c	0	0	0	0	2	0	0
c Blair		1	0	0	0	0	0	0
Root	p	2	0	0	0	0	0	0
b Hartnett		1	0	0	0	0	0	0
Bush	p	0	0	0	0	0	2	0
d Tolson		1	0	0	0	0	0	0
Totals		34	1	8	1	27	10	2

a Flied out for Taylor in 7th.
b Struck out for Root in 7th.
c Hit into force out for Gonzalez in 9th.
d Struck out for Bush in 9th.

Double—English. Home Run—Foxx. Sacrifice Hit—Grimm. Double Play—English to Hornsby to Grimm. Left on Bases—Philadelphia 6, Chicago 8. Umpires—Klem (N), Dinneen (A), Moran (N), Van Graflan (A). Attendance—50,740. Time of Game—2:03.

1st Inning
Philadelphia
1 Bishop grounded to first.
2 Haas called out on strikes. Cochrane walked on a full count.
3 Simmons struck out.
Chicago
1 McMillan fouled to Cochrane. English singled off Ehmke's glove.
2 Hornsby flied to deep right.
3 Wilson flied to right.

2nd Inning
Philadelphia
  Foxx singled to left.
1 Miller struck out. Dykes singled to left, Foxx stopping at second.
2,3 Boley grounded into a double play, English to Hornsby to Grimm.
Chicago
1 Cuyler struck out on a full count.
2 Stephenson took a called third strike, also on a full count. Grimm singled to left-center.
3 Taylor popped to first.

3rd Inning
Philadelphia
1 Ehmke fouled to McMillan.
2 Bishop lined to short. Haas walked.
3 Cochrane grounded to third.
Chicago
1 Root struck out. McMillan singled to center. English doubled to right, McMillan stopping at third.
2 Hornsby struck out.
3 Wilson struck out.

4th Inning
Philadelphia
1 Simmons flied to left.
2 Foxx grounded to second.
3 Miller grounded to second.
Chicago
1 Cuyler again struck out.
2 Stephenson lined to Dykes, who made a fantastic diving catch. Grimm walked.
3 Grimm out trying to steal second, Cochrane to Bishop.

5th Inning
Philadelphia
1 Dykes struck out.
2 Boley struck out.
3 Ehmke flied to short left.
Chicago
1 Taylor flied to deep left, Simmons making a great one-handed catch at the fence in the left field corner.
2 Root struck out.
3 McMillan struck out.

6th Inning
Philadelphia
1 Bishop grounded to short.
2 Haas flied to Wilson in deep left-center.
3 Cochrane fouled to Taylor.
Chicago
1 English struck out.
2 Hornsby struck out.
3 Wilson struck out, becoming Ehmke's fifth consecutive victim and his eleventh of the game.

7th Inning
Philadelphia
1 Simmons lined to Wilson, who made a great diving catch. Foxx homered into the left-center field bleachers.
2 Miller flied to right.
3 Dykes flied to left.
Chicago
  Cuyler singled off of Boley's glove. Stephenson singled to left, Cuyler stopping at second.
1 Grimm sacrificed Cuyler to third and Stephenson to second, Ehmke to Foxx.
2 Heathcote, pinch-hitting for Taylor, flied to short left as both runners held.
3 Hartnett, pinch-hitting for Root, struck out.

8th Inning
Philadelphia
For Chicago—Bush pitching and Gonzalez catching.
1 Boley grounded to short. Ehmke looped a single to right.
2 Bishop flied to left.
3 Haas flied to Wilson in short right-center.
Chicago
1 McMillan flied to center.
2 English flied to right.
3 Hornsby grounded to second.

9th Inning
Philadelphia
  Cochrane singled to right. Simmons safe at first when English booted his grounder. Foxx also safe, loading the bases, when English dropped his grounder. Miller singled through the box, Cochrane and Simmons scoring as Foxx went to third.
1 Dykes bounced back to Bush and Foxx was run down, Bush to Gonzalez with Miller going to third and Dykes to second on the play.
2 Boley also bounced to Bush who threw Miller out at the plate as Dykes got to third.
3 Ehmke grounded to third.
Chicago
1 Wilson's liner was knocked down by Ehmke and he threw him out at first. Cuyler got safely to second on Dykes' wild throw. Stephenson singled to center, Cuyler scoring. Grimm singled to right, Stephenson stopping at second.
2 Blair, pinch-hitting for Gonzalez, forced Grimm at second, Dykes to Bishop as Stephenson went to third.
3 Tolson, batting for Bush, struck out. **Ehmke's thirteenth victim setting a new single game Series' record.**

Game 2 October 9 at Chicago

Philadelphia	Pos	AB	R	H	RBI	PO	A	E
Bishop	2b	4	0	0	0	0	4	0
Haas	cf	5	1	1	1	1	0	0
Cochrane	c	2	2	1	0	14	0	0
Simmons	lf	4	2	2	4	2	0	0
Foxx	1b	5	2	3	3	7	0	0
Miller	rf	4	0	1	0	0	0	0
Dykes	3b	4	1	3	1	1	0	0
Boley	ss	3	0	1	0	2	3	0
Earnshaw	p	3	1	0	0	0	0	0
Grove	p	2	0	0	0	0	1	0
Totals		36	9	12	9	27	8	0

Pitching	IP	H	R	ER	BB	SO
Philadelphia						
Earnshaw (W)	$4\frac{2}{3}$	8	3	3	4	7
Grove (SV)	$4\frac{1}{3}$	3	0	0	1	6
Chicago						
Malone (L)	$3\frac{2}{3}$	5	6	3	5	5
Blake	$1\frac{1}{3}$	2	0	0	0	1
Carlson	3	5	3	3	1	2
Nehf	1	0	0	0	0	0

Phi.	0 0 3	3 0 0	1 2 0
Chi.	0 0 0	0 3 0	0 0 0

Chicago	Pos	AB	R	H	RBI	PO	A	E
McMillan	3b	4	0	0	0	1	0	0
English	ss	5	0	1	0	2	3	1
Hornsby	2b	4	1	1	0	3	2	0
Wilson	cf	3	1	3	0	4	0	0
Cuyler	rf	4	0	0	0	1	0	0
Stephenson	lf	5	1	1	1	2	0	0
Grimm	1b	4	0	2	1	6	1	0
Taylor	c	4	0	2	1	8	1	0
Malone	p	1	0	0	0	0	1	0
Blake	p	1	0	1	0	0	0	0
a Heathcote		0	0	0	0	0	0	0
b Hartnett		1	0	0	0	0	0	0
Carlson	p	0	0	0	0	0	1	0
c Gonzalez		1	0	0	0	0	0	0
Nehf	p	0	0	0	0	0	0	0
Totals		37	3	11	3	27	9	1

a Announced for Blake in 5th.
b Struck out for Heathcote in 5th.
c Struck out for Carlson in 8th.

Doubles—English, Foxx. Home Runs—Foxx, Simmons. Sacrifice Hits—Boley 2, Miller. Double Plays—English to Hornsby to Grimm, Bishop to Boley to Foxx. Left on Bases—Philadelphia 9, Chicago 12. Umpires—Dinneen, Moran, Van Graflan, Klem. Attendance—49,987. Time of Game—2:29.

1st Inning
Philadelphia
1 Bishop struck out on a full count.
2 Haas struck out.
Cochrane walked on a full count.
3 Simmons called out on strikes on only three pitches.
Chicago
1 McMillan grounded to short.
English doubled into the left field corner.
2 Hornsby struck out.
Wilson walked.
3 Cuyler struck out.

2nd Inning
Philadelphia
1 Foxx grounded to short.
2 Miller popped to first.
Dykes walked.
Boley singled to right, Dykes going to third.
3 Earnshaw struck out.
Chicago
1 Stephenson grounded to second.
Grimm singled down the left field line.
2 Taylor struck out.
3 Malone struck out.

3rd Inning
Philadelphia
1 Bishop flied to left.
2 Haas fouled to McMillan.
Cochrane singled to right.
Simmons walked.
Foxx hit a three-run homer deep into the temporary seats behind the left field wall.
3 Miller struck out.
Chicago
McMillan walked.
1 English struck out.
2 Hornsby again struck out.
Wilson again walked.
Cuyler also walked, loading the bases.
3 Stephenson flied to short left.

4th Inning
Philadelphia
Dykes singled to right.
1 Boley sacrificed, Malone to Grimm.
Earnshaw safe at first and Dykes to third on English's fumble.
Bishop walked, loading the bases.
2 Haas forced Bishop at second, English unassisted, Dykes scoring and Earnshaw going to third.
Cochrane again walked, to load the bases again.
Simmons singled over second, Earnshaw and Haas scoring as Cochrane went to third.
For Chicago—Blake came in to pitch.
3 Foxx flied to short right.
Chicago
1 Grimm fouled to Simmons.
2 Taylor flied to short center.
Blake beat out a hit to deep short.
3 McMillan forced Blake, Bishop to Boley.

5th Inning
Philadelphia
Miller singled to left.
Dykes singled to left, Miller stopping at second.
1 Boley sacrificed up both runners, Grimm to Hornsby, covering first.
2 Earnshaw struck out.
3 Bishop flied to center.
Chicago
1 English popped to Dykes almost in front of the plate.
Hornsby singled to center.
Wilson singled to right, Hornsby stopping at second.
2 Cuyler struck out.

5th Inning (continued)
Stephenson singled to right, scoring Hornsby as Wilson stopped at second.
Grimm singled over Boley's head, Wilson scoring and Stephenson going to third.
Taylor singled off Earnshaw's glove, Stephenson scoring as Grimm stopped at second.
Heathcote announced to bat for Blake.
For Philadelphia—Grove came in to pitch.
3 Hartnett, pinch-hitting for Heathcote, struck out.

6th Inning
Philadelphia
For Chicago—Carlson now pitching.
Haas singled to center.
1,2 Cochrane hit into a double play, English to Hornsby to Grimm.
3 Simmons grounder deflected by Carlson to English who threw to first for the out.
Chicago
1 McMillan struck out.
2 English struck out (the second game in a row 10 or more Cubs have struck out).
3 Hornsby grounded to first.

7th Inning
Philadelphia
Foxx singled to left.
1 Miller sacrificed Foxx to second, Taylor to Hornsby.
Dykes singled over third, scoring Foxx.
2 Boley flied to center.
3 Grove took a called third strike.
Chicago
Wilson singled to center.
1 Cuyler called out on strikes.
2,3 Stephenson grounded into a double play, Bishop to Boley to Foxx.

8th Inning
Philadelphia
1 Bishop struck out.
2 Haas popped to short.
Cochrane walked.
Simmons blasted a two-run homer over the right field screen just inside the foul pole.
Foxx doubled over third.
3 Miller flied to Wilson who made a good running catch in right-center.
Chicago
1 Grimm grounded to second.
Taylor lined a single to right.
2 Gonzales, pinch-hitting for Carlson, struck out.
3 McMillan struck out to become the Cubs' thirteenth strikeout victim.

9th Inning
Philadelphia
For Chicago—Nehf pitching.
1 Dykes grounded to second.
2 Boley flied to left.
3 Grove flied to center.
Chicago
1 English grounded to short.
Hornsby walked.
Wilson singled for his third hit, Hornsby going to third.
2 Cuyler hit into a fielder's choice, Grove throwing to Cochrane getting Hornsby at the plate. **Cochrane's new record of 14 putouts set in Game 1 was tied today.**
3 Stephenson popped to first.

Game 3 October 11 at Philadelphia

Chicago	Pos	AB	R	H	RBI	PO	A	E
McMillan	3b	4	0	0	0	1	1	0
English	ss	4	1	0	0	0	2	1
Hornsby	2b	4	1	2	1	2	1	0
Wilson	cf	3	0	2	0	3	0	0
Cuyler	rf	4	0	1	2	3	0	0
Stephenson	lf	4	0	1	0	4	0	0
Grimm	1b	4	0	0	0	9	0	0
Taylor	c	4	0	0	0	5	2	0
Bush	p	3	1	0	0	0	1	0
Totals		34	3	6	3	27	7	1

Pitching	IP	H	R	ER	BB	SO
Chicago						
Bush (W)	9	9	1	1	2	4
Philadelphia						
Earnshaw (L)	9	6	3	1	2	10

Chi.	0 0 0	0 0 3	0 0 0
Phi.	0 0 0	0 1 0	0 0 0

Philadelphia	Pos	AB	R	H	RBI	PO	A	E
Bishop	2b	4	0	1	0	3	4	0
Haas	cf	5	0	2	0	0	0	0
Cochrane	c	3	1	2	0	12	0	0
Simmons	lf	3	0	0	0	0	0	0
Foxx	1b	4	0	0	0	9	0	0
Miller	rf	4	0	1	1	2	0	0
Dykes	3b	4	0	1	0	1	0	1
Boley	ss	4	0	2	0	0	2	0
Earnshaw	p	2	0	0	0	0	2	0
a Summa		1	0	0	0	0	0	0
Totals		34	1	9	1	27	8	1

a Struck out for Earnshaw in 9th.

Doubles—Hornsby, Stephenson. Triple—Wilson. Sacrifice Hits—Earnshaw, Simmons. Wild Pitch—Bush. Left on Bases—Chicago 6, Philadelphia 10. Umpires—Moran, Van Graflan, Klem, Dinneen. Attendance—29,921. Time of Game—2:09.

1st Inning
Chicago
1 McMillan struck out.
2 English grounded to second.
3 Hornsby called out on strikes.
Philadelphia
1 Bishop popped to first.
Haas singled past the box.
2 Cochrane flied to short left.
3 Simmons forced Haas at second, English unassisted.

2nd Inning
Chicago
Wilson tripled far over Haas' head in deep center.
1 Cuyler grounded to short, Wilson holding.
2 Stephenson grounded to Bishop who threw out Wilson at the plate.
3 Grimm struck out.
Philadelphia
1 Foxx took a called third strike.
2 Miller flied to right.
Dykes singled to left.
Boley singled to right, Dykes going to third, as Boley went to second on the play at third.
3 Earnshaw called out on strikes.

3rd Inning
Chicago
1 Taylor popped to third.
2 Bush struck out.
3 McMillan popped to second.
Philadelphia
1 Bishop popped to first.
Haas singled over Grimm's head.
Cochrane singled past Bush, Haas stopping at second.
2 Simmons popped to third.
Foxx safe at first on English's fumble, loading the bases.
3 Miller flied to left.

4th Inning
Chicago
1 English fouled to Foxx.
2 Hornsby called out on strikes.
Wilson got his fifth consecutive hit, a single between Foxx and Bishop.
3 Cuyler called out on strikes.
Philadelphia
1 Dykes flied to Wilson in short left-center.
Boley singled to left-center.
2 Earnshaw sacrificed Boley to second, McMillan to Grimm.
Bishop got the first pass of the game.
3 Haas flied to right.

5th Inning
Chicago
1 Stephenson grounded to second.
2 Grimm popped to second.
3 Taylor struck out.
Philadelphia
Cochrane beat out a hit to short.
1 Simmons lined to center.
2 Foxx rolled back to the pitcher, Cochrane going to second.
Miller singled to center, scoring Cochrane.
3 Miller caught attempting to steal second, Taylor to Hornsby.

6th Inning
Chicago
Bush walked.
1 McMillan fouled to Cochrane on an attempted sacrifice.
English safely at first on Dykes' error as Bush went to second.
Hornsby singled to left, scoring Bush with English stopping at second.
2 Wilson grounded to second, both runners advancing.
Cuyler bounced a single into center, English and Hornsby scoring.
3 Stephenson flied to right.
Philadelphia
1 Dykes flied to left.
2 Boley fouled to Grimm.
3 Earnshaw struck out.

7th Inning
Chicago
1 Grimm grounded back to the pitcher.
2 Taylor flied to right.
3 Bush struck out.
Philadelphia
Bishop singled past second.
Bishop went to second on a wild pitch.
1 Haas fouled to Taylor.
Cochrane walked.
2 Simmons flied to deep center, Bishop going to third and Cochrane to second after the catch.
3 Foxx bounced out near the plate, Taylor to Grimm.

8th Inning
Chicago
1 McMillan grounded to short.
2 English struck out.
Hornsby lined a double to right as Miller missed a shoestring catch.
Wilson walked.
3 Cuyler fouled to Foxx.
Philadelphia
1 Miller grounded to short.
2 Dykes flied to deep left.
3 Boley flied to right.

9th Inning
Chicago
Stephenson doubled off the left field wall.
1 Grimm out on a broken-bat roller to the mound, Stephenson holding second.
2 Taylor popped to second.
3 Bush struck out for the third time in the game and another 10 strikeout game (or more) for the A's.
Philadelphia
1 Summa, batting for Earnshaw, fanned on three pitches.
2 Bishop grounded to first.
3 Haas grounded to second.

Game 4 October 12 at Philadelphia

Chi.	000	205	100		
Phi.	000	000	100	x	

Chicago	Pos	AB	R	H	RBI	PO	A	E
McMillan	3b	4	0	0	0	1	3	0
English	ss	4	0	0	0	2	1	0
Hornsby	2b	5	2	2	0	1	1	0
Wilson	cf	3	1	2	0	3	0	1
Cuyler	rf	4	2	3	2	0	0	1
Stephenson	lf	4	1	1	1	2	1	0
Grimm	1b	4	2	2	2	7	0	0
Taylor	c	3	0	0	1	8	1	0
Root	p	3	0	0	0	0	0	0
Nehf	p	0	0	0	0	0	0	0
Blake	p	0	0	0	0	0	0	0
Malone	p	0	0	0	0	0	0	0
b Hartnett		1	0	0	0	0	0	0
Carlson	p	0	0	0	0	0	1	0
Totals		35	8	10	6	24	8	2

a Popped out and struck out for Rommel in 7th.
b Struck out for Malone in 8th.

Doubles—Cochrane, Dykes. Triple—Hornsby. Home Runs—Grimm, Haas, Simmons. Sacrifice Hits—Boley, Haas, Taylor. Double Play—Dykes to Bishop to Foxx. Hit by Pitcher—Miller (by Malone). Left on Bases—Chicago 4, Philadelphia 6. Umpires—Van Graflan, Klem, Dinneen, Moran. Attendance—29,921. Time of Game—2:12.

Philadelphia	Pos	AB	R	H	RBI	PO	A	E
Bishop	2b	5	1	2	1	2	3	0
Haas	cf	4	1	1	3	2	0	0
Cochrane	c	4	1	2	0	9	0	0
Simmons	lf	5	2	2	1	0	0	0
Foxx	1b	4	2	2	1	10	0	0
Miller	rf	3	1	2	0	3	0	1
Dykes	3b	4	1	3	3	0	2	0
Boley	ss	3	1	1	1	1	5	0
Quinn	p	2	0	0	0	0	0	0
Walberg	p	0	0	0	0	0	0	1
Rommel	p	0	0	0	0	0	0	0
a Burns		2	0	0	0	0	0	0
Grove	p	0	0	0	0	0	0	0
Totals		36	10	15	10	27	10	2

Pitching	IP	H	R	ER	BB	SO
Chicago						
Root	6⅓	9	6	6	0	3
Nehf	**0	1	2	2	1	0
Blake (L)	***0	2	2	2	0	0
Malone	⅔	1	0	0	0	2
Carlson	1	2	0	0	0	1
Philadelphia						
Quinn	*5	7	6	5	2	2
Walberg	1	1	1	0	0	2
Rommel (W)	1	2	1	1	1	0
Grove (SV)	2	0	0	0	0	4

*Pitched to 4 batters in 6th.
**Pitched to 2 batters in 7th.
***Pitched to 2 batters in 7th.

1st Inning
Chicago
McMillan walked.
1 English fouled to Miller.
2 Hornsby struck out on a full count.
Wilson singled to right, McMillan stopping at second.
3 Cuyler called out on strikes.
Philadelphia
1 Bishop flied to short left.
2 Haas rolled to third.
3 Cochrane popped to short.

2nd Inning
Chicago
1 Stephenson grounded to second.
2 Grimm fouled to Cochrane.
3 Taylor grounded to second.
Philadelphia
1 Simmons struck out.
2 Foxx grounded to short.
3 Miller grounded to third.

3rd Inning
Chicago
1 Root grounded to short.
2 McMillan fouled to Foxx.
English walked.
3 Hornsby grounded to short.
Philadelphia
Dykes singled to right, and went to second on Cuyler's error.
1 Boley sacrificed, Grimm unassisted.
2 Quinn struck out.
3 Bishop grounded to first.

4th Inning
Chicago
1 Wilson flied to deep right.
Cuyler singled past first and went all the way to third when Miller let the ball get through him for an error.
2 Stephenson popped to short.
Grimm hit a two-run homer over the right field wall.
3 Taylor grounded to short.
Philadelphia
1 Haas popped to Taylor in fair territory.
Cochrane looped a double to left.
2 Simmons grounded to McMillan and Cochrane was caught in a run-down, McMillan to Hornsby.
3 Foxx flied to Wilson in deep left-center.

5th Inning
Chicago
1 Root grounded to third.
2 McMillan grounded to short.
3 English lined to second.
Philadelphia
Miller singled off Root's glove.
Dykes was safe when Wilson muffed his fly ball, Miller going to second.
1 Miller was out trying to steal third, Taylor to McMillan.
2 Boley flied deep to Wilson making a running one-handed catch near the scoreboard.
3 Quinn called out on strikes.

6th Inning
Chicago
Hornsby singled to center.
Wilson singled to right, Hornsby stopping at second.
Cuyler singled, scoring Hornsby and sending Wilson to third.
Stephenson singled to second, Wilson scoring and Cuyler stopping at second.
For Philadelphia—Walberg replaced Quinn on the mound.
Grimm's bunt went for a single and Cuyler and Stephenson scored on Quinn's throwing error to the stands past Foxx. Grimm went to third on the error.

6th Inning (continued)
1 Taylor flied to center, Grimm scoring after the catch.
2 Root struck out.
3 McMillan struck out.
Philadelphia
1 Bishop flied to left.
2 Haas grounded to second.
3 Cochrane flied to center.

7th Inning
Chicago
For Philadelphia—Rommel pitching.
1 English flied to Haas in short, center.
Hornsby tripled deep over Haas' head.
Wilson walked.
Cuyler singled to left (his third hit of the game), scoring Hornsby.
2,3 Stephenson hit into a double play, Dykes to Bishop to Foxx.
Philadelphia
Simmons homered onto the roof of the left field stands.
Foxx singled to right.
Miller singled to center, Wilson losing the ball in the sun.
Dykes singled to left, scoring Foxx as Miller stopped at second.
Boley singled to right, Miller scoring and Dykes going to third.
1 Burns, batting for Rommel, popped to short.
Bishop singled over Root's head, Dykes scoring and Boley going to third.
For Chicago—Nehf came in to pitch.
Haas hit a three-run homer past Wilson, who lost the ball in the sun.
Cochrane walked.
For Chicago—Blake replaced Nehf on the mound.
Simmons bounced a single over McMillan's head, Cochrane stopping at second.
Foxx singled, scoring Cochrane with the tying run.
For Chicago—Malone now pitching.
Miller was hit by a pitch, loading the bases.
Dykes doubled to the left field wall, Simmons and Foxx scoring with Miller stopping at third.
2 Boley struck out.
3 Burns up as a pinch-hitter for the second time, struck out.

8th Inning
Chicago
For Philadelphia—Grove pitching.
1 Grimm grounded to short.
2 Taylor struck out.
3 Hartnett, batting for Malone, also struck out.
Philadelphia
For Chicago—Carlson pitching.
Bishop singled to left.
1 Haas sacrificed, Carlson to Grimm.
Cochrane singled to left, but Bishop was
2 out at the plate, Stephenson to Taylor. Cochrane going to second on the play.
3 Simmons took a called third strike.

9th Inning
Chicago
1 McMillan struck out.
2 English took a called third strike **(the 44th strikeout of the Series tying the record set by the NY Giants of 1910 and the NY Yankees of 1921).**
3 Hornsby flied to right.

Game 5 October 14 at Philadelphia

Chi.	000	200	000	
Phi.	000	000	003	

Chicago	Pos	AB	R	H	RBI	PO	A	E
McMillan	3b	4	0	1	0	2	3	0
English	ss	4	0	1	0	3	3	0
Hornsby	2b	4	0	0	0	2	4	1
Wilson	cf	4	0	1	0	1	0	0
Cuyler	rf	4	1	1	0	3	0	0
Stephenson	lf	2	1	1	0	1	0	0
Grimm	1b	4	0	1	1	10	0	0
Taylor	c	4	0	1	1	4	0	0
Malone	p	3	0	1	0	0	0	0
Totals		33	2	8	2	x26	10	1

Pitching	IP	H	R	ER	BB	SO
Chicago						
Malone (L)	8⅔	6	3	3	2	4
Philadelphia						
Ehmke	3⅔	6	2	2	2	0
Walberg (W)	5⅓	2	0	0	0	6

Philadelphia	Pos	AB	R	H	RBI	PO	A	E
Bishop	2b	4	1	1	0	2	1	0
Haas	cf	4	1	1	2	1	0	0
Cochrane	c	3	0	0	0	10	1	0
Simmons	lf	4	1	2	0	0	0	0
Foxx	1b	3	0	0	0	8	1	0
Miller	rf	4	0	2	1	5	0	0
Dykes	2b	3	0	0	0	0	1	0
Boley	ss	3	0	0	0	1	2	0
Ehmke	p	1	0	0	0	0	2	0
Walberg	p	1	0	0	0	0	1	0
a French		1	0	0	0	0	0	0
Totals		31	3	6	3	27	9	0

x two out when winning run scored.
a Struck out for Walberg in 9th.

Doubles—Cuyler, Malone, Miller, Simmons, Home Run—Haas. Stolen Base—McMillan. Double Plays—Hornsby to Grimm, English to Hornsby to Grimm. Left on Bases—Chicago 6, Philadelphia 4. Umpires—Klem, Dinneen, Moran, Van Graflan. Attendance—29,921. Time of Game—1:42

1st Inning
Chicago
1 McMillan grounded to third.
English beat out a roller to the mound.
2 Hornsby popped to first.
3 English was out attempting to steal second, Cochrane to Bishop.
Philadelphia
1 Bishop took a called third strike.
2 Haas flied to left.
3 Cochrane grounded to short.

2nd Inning
Chicago
Wilson singled to left.
1 Cuyler forced Wilson at second, Ehmke to Boley.
2 Cuyler was trapped off first and out in a run-down, Ehmke to Foxx to Bishop to Cochrane.
Stephenson walked.
3 Grimm grounded to first.
Philadelphia
Simmons singled to left.
1,2 Foxx lined into a double play, Hornsby to Grimm.
3 Miller grounded to third.

3rd Inning
Chicago
1 Taylor was tagged out by Cochrane, hitting into the dirt in front of the plate.
Malone slashed a double just over first.
2 McMillan grounded to short, Malone moving to third.
3 English flied to right.
Philadelphia
1 Dykes popped to English in short left-center.
2 Boley grounded to short.
3 Ehmke flied to right.

4th Inning
Chicago
1 Hornsby grounded to short.
2 Wilson fouled to Cochrane.
Cuyler lined a double over Bishop's head into left-center.
Stephenson again walked.
Grimm blooped a single into right-center, scoring Cuyler with Stephenson going to third.
Taylor singled to left-center, scoring Stephenson with Grimm stopping at second.
For Philadelphia—Walberg replaced Ehmke on the mound.
3 Malone struck out **(a new Series record for team strikeouts).**
Philadelphia
1 Bishop grounded to third.
2 Haas grounded to third.
3 Cochrane grounded to first.

5th Inning
Chicago
1 McMillan fouled to Foxx.
2 English popped to Bishop in right.
3 Hornsby called out on strikes.
Philadelphia
1 Simmons flied to Cuyler who made a leaping-catch near the wall in right.
Foxx safe on Hornsby's fumble.
Miller singled past third, Foxx stopping at second.
2 Dykes flied to right.
3 Boley popped to McMillan near the mound.

6th Inning
Chicago
1 Wilson lined to right.
2 Cuyler bounced back to the mound.
3 Stephenson struck out.
Philadelphia
1 Walberg popped to short.
2 Bishop grounded to second.
3 Haas struck out.

7th Inning
Chicago
1 Grimm flied to center.
2 Taylor flied to right.
3 Malone fouled to Cochrane, as Walberg retired the Cubs on just three pitched balls.
Philadelphia
Cochrane walked.
1 Simmons popped to third.
2,3 Foxx hit into a double play, English to Hornsby to Grimm.

8th Inning
Chicago
McMillan blooped a single into short right-center.
1 English struck out.
2 Hornsby flied to right.
McMillan stole second, the first successful steal in the Series.
3 Wilson struck out.
Philadelphia
1 Miller popped to short.
2 Dykes flied to center.
3 Boley struck out.

9th Inning
Chicago
1 Cuyler grounded to first.
Stephenson singled to left.
2 Grimm struck out **for the Cubs' fiftieth strike out.**
3 Taylor flied to short right.
Philadelphia
1 French, batting for Walberg, fanned.
Bishop singled over third.
Haas hit a two-run homer over the right-field wall.
2 Cochrane grounded to second.
Simmons doubled off the scoreboard.
Foxx intentionally walked.
Miller slashed a double to the scoreboard, scoring Simmons with the Series-winning run.

1929 WORLD SERIES COMPOSITE BOX

	Wins	Composite Line Score
Philadelphia Athletics (A.L.)	4	0 0 3 3 1 0 12 2 5 – 26
Chicago Cubs (N.L.)	1	0 0 0 4 3 8 1 0 1 – 17

Manager	Regular Season W	L	Pct.	G. Ahead
Connie Mack	104	46	.693	18
Joe McCarthy	98	54	.645	10½

BATTING AND FIELDING

PHILADELPHIA ATHLETICS

WORLD SERIES STATISTICS	Pos	G	AB	R	H	2B	3B	HR	RBI	BB	SO	SB	BA	SA	PO	A	E
Jimmie Foxx	1b	5	20	5	7	1	0	**2**	5	1	1	0	.350	**.700**	38	1	0
Max Bishop	2b	5	**21**	2	4	0	0	0	1	2	3	0	.190	.190	9	**13**	0
Joe Boley	ss	5	17	1	4	0	0	0	1	0	3	0	.235	.235	4	12	0
Jimmy Dykes	3b	5	19	2	**8**	1	0	0	4	1	1	0	.421	.474	3	4	2
Bing Miller	rf	5	19	1	7	1	0	0	4	0	2	0	.368	.421	13	0	1
Mule Haas	cf	5	**21**	3	5	0	0	**2**	**6**	1	3	0	.238	.524	5	0	0
Al Simmons	lf	5	20	**6**	6	1	0	**2**	5	1	4	0	.300	.650	4	0	0
Mickey Cochrane	c	5	15	5	6	1	0	0	0	**7**	0	0	.400	.467	**59**	2	0
George Burns	ph	1	2	0	0	0	0	0	0	0	1	0	.000	.000			
Walt French	ph	1	1	0	0	0	0	0	0	0	1	0	.000	.000			
Homer Summa	ph	1	1	0	0	0	0	0	0	0	1	0	.000	.000			
Sammy Hale		Did not play															
Cy Perkins		Did not play															
Jim Cronin		Did not play															
Bevo LeBourveau		Did not play															
Eddie Collins		Did not play															
George Earnshaw	p	2	5	1	0	0	0	0	0	0	4	0	.000	.000	0	2	0
Howard Ehmke	p	2	5	0	1	0	0	0	0	0	0	0	.200	.200	0	4	0
Lefty Grove	p	2	2	0	0	0	0	0	0	0	1	0	.000	.000	0	1	0
Jack Quinn	p	1	2	0	0	0	0	0	0	0	2	0	.000	.000	0	0	0
Rube Walberg	p	2	1	0	0	0	0	0	0	0	0	0	.000	.000	0	1	1
Eddie Rommel	p	1	0	0	0	0	0	0	0	0	0	0	—	—	0	0	0
Bill Shores		Did not play															
Carroll Yerkes		Did not play															
Bill Breckinridge		Did not play															
team total		5	171	26	48	5	0	6	26	13	27	0	.281	.415	135	40	4

Double Plays—2
Left on Bases—35

REGULAR SEASON STATISTICS		Main Pos	G	AB	R	H	2B	3B	HR	RBI	BB	SO	SB	BA	SA
Jimmie Foxx		1b	149	517	123	183	23	9	33	117	103	**70**	9	.354	.625
Max Bishop		2b	129	475	102	110	19	6	3	36	**128**	44	1	.232	.316
Joe Boley		ss	91	303	36	76	17	6	2	47	24	16	1	.251	.366
Jimmy Dykes		ss-3b	119	401	76	131	34	6	13	79	51	25	8	.327	.539
Bing Miller		of	147	556	84	186	32	16	8	93	40	25	24	.335	.493
Mule Haas		of	139	578	115	181	41	9	16	82	34	38	0	.313	.498
Al Simmons		of	143	581	114	212	41	9	34	**157**	31	38	4	.365	.642
Mickey Cochrane		c	135	514	113	170	37	8	7	95	69	8	7	.331	.475
George Burns	a	1b	29	49	5	13	5	0	1	11	2	3	1	.265	.429
Walt French		of	45	45	7	12	1	0	1	9	2	3	0	.267	.356
Homer Summa		of	37	81	12	22	4	0	0	10	2	1	1	.272	.321
Sammy Hale		3b	101	379	51	105	14	3	1	40	12	18	6	.277	.338
Cy Perkins		c	38	76	4	16	4	0	0	9	5	4	0	.211	.263
Jim Cronin		2b-ss	25	56	7	13	2	1	0	4	5	7	0	.232	.304
Bevo LeBourveau		of	12	16	1	5	0	1	0	2	5	1	0	.313	.438
Eddie Collins		ph	9	7	0	0	0	0	0	0	2	0	0	.000	.000
George Earnshaw		p	44	87	6	15	2	0	1	10	2	21	0	.172	.230
Howard Ehmke		p	11	19	0	2	1	0	0	0	0	2	0	.105	.158
Lefty Grove		p	42	102	13	22	3	0	1	15	6	33	0	.216	.275
Jack Quinn		p	35	60	3	8	2	0	0	3	0	20	0	.133	.167
Rube Walberg		p	40	103	11	23	2	0	1	11	3	17	0	.223	.272
Eddie Rommel		p	32	39	2	8	1	0	0	4	2	7	0	.205	.231
Bill Shores		p	39	40	5	5	0	0	0	0	6	16	0	.125	.125
Carroll Yerkes		p	19	10	1	0	0	0	0	0	0	4	0	.000	.000
Bill Breckinridge		p	3	4	0	0	0	0	0	0	0	1	0	.000	.000
team total			151	5204	901	1539	288	76	122	845	543	440	63	.296	.451

a—from New York (A)
Doc Cramer (of), Joe Hassler (ss), Cloy Mattox (c), Eric McNair (ss), Rudy Miller (3b), Bud Morse (2b), Ossie Orwoll (p-of) also played for the Athletics during the season.

CHICAGO CUBS

WORLD SERIES STATISTICS	Pos	G	AB	R	H	2B	3B	HR	RBI	BB	SO	SB	BA	SA	PO	A	E
Charlie Grimm	1b	5	18	2	7	0	0	1	4	1	2	0	.389	.556	40	1	0
Rogers Hornsby	2b	5	**21**	4	5	1	**1**	0	1	1	**8**	0	.238	.381	9	11	1
Woody English	ss	5	**21**	1	4	**2**	0	0	0	1	6	0	.190	.286	8	12	**4**
Norm McMillan	3b	5	20	0	2	0	0	0	0	2	6	**1**	.100	.100	6	9	0
Kiki Cuyler	rf	5	20	4	6	1	0	0	4	1	7	0	.300	.350	8	0	1
Hack Wilson	cf	5	17	2	**8**	0	**1**	0	0	4	3	0	**.471**	.588	14	0	1
Riggs Stephenson	lf	5	19	3	6	1	0	0	3	2	2	0	.316	.368	13	1	0
Zack Taylor	c	5	17	0	3	0	0	0	3	0	3	0	.176	.176	31	4	0
Gabby Hartnett	ph	3	3	0	0	0	0	0	0	0	3	0	.000	.000			
Mike Gonzalez	c-ph	2	1	0	0	0	0	0	0	0	1	0	.000	.000	2	0	0
Cliff Heathcote	ph	2	1	0	0	0	0	0	0	0	0	0	.000	.000			
Chuck Tolson	ph	1	1	0	0	0	0	0	0	0	1	0	.000	.000			
Footsie Blair	ph	1	1	0	0	0	0	0	0	0	0	0	.000	.000			
Clyde Beck		Did not play															
Johnny Schulte		Did not play															
Johnny Moore		Did not play															
Charlie Root	p	2	5	0	0	0	0	0	0	0	3	0	.000	.000	0	0	0
Pat Malone	p	3	4	0	1	1	0	0	0	0	2	0	.250	.500	0	1	0
Guy Bush	p	2	3	1	0	0	0	0	0	1	3	0	.000	.000	0	3	0
Sheriff Blake	p	2	1	0	1	0	0	0	0	0	0	0	1.000	1.000	0	0	0
Hal Carlson	p	2	0	0	0	0	0	0	0	0	0	0	—	—	0	2	0
Art Nehf	p	2	0	0	0	0	0	0	0	0	0	0	—	—	0	0	0
Mike Cvengros		Did not play															
Ken Penner		Did not play															
Hank Grampp		Did not play															
team total		5	173	17	43	6	2	1	15	13	50	1	.249	.324	131	44	7

Double Plays—4
Left on Bases—36

REGULAR SEASON STATISTICS		Main Pos	G	AB	R	H	2B	3B	HR	RBI	BB	SO	SB	BA	SA
Charlie Grimm		1b	120	463	66	138	28	3	10	91	42	25	3	.298	.436
Rogers Hornsby		2b	156	602	**156**	229	47	8	39	149	87	65	2	.380	**.679**
Woody English		ss	144	608	131	168	29	3	1	52	68	50	13	.276	.339
Norm McMillan		3b	124	495	77	134	35	5	5	55	36	43	13	.271	.392
Kiki Cuyler		of	139	509	111	183	29	7	15	102	66	56	**43**	.360	.532
Hack Wilson		of	150	574	135	198	30	5	39	**159**	78	**83**	3	.345	.618
Riggs Stephenson		of	136	495	91	179	36	6	17	110	67	21	10	.362	.562
Zack Taylor	b	c	64	215	29	59	16	3	1	31	19	18	0	.274	.391
Gabby Hartnett		c	25	22	2	6	2	1	1	9	5	5	1	.273	.591
Mike Gonzalez		c	60	167	15	40	3	0	0	18	18	14	1	.240	.257
Cliff Heathcote		of	82	224	45	70	17	0	2	31	25	17	9	.313	.415
Chuck Tolson		1b	32	109	13	28	5	0	1	19	9	16	0	.257	.330
Footsie Blair		3b-1b	26	72	10	23	5	0	1	8	3	4	1	.319	.431
Clyde Beck		3b-ss	54	190	28	40	7	0	0	9	19	24	3	.211	.247
Johnny Schulte		c	31	69	6	18	3	0	0	9	7	11	0	.261	.304
Johnny Moore		of	37	63	13	18	1	0	2	8	4	6	0	.286	.397
Charlie Root		p	43	96	8	15	3	4	1	15	4	28	0	.156	.302
Pat Malone		p	40	105	8	22	3	0	2	11	4	23	0	.210	.295
Guy Bush		p	50	91	5	15	0	0	0	3	3	19	1	.165	.165
Sheriff Blake		p	38	81	11	14	2	0	0	4	4	10	0	.173	.198
Hal Carlson		p	31	39	4	9	2	0	0	8	2	7	0	.231	.282
Art Nehf		p	32	45	3	13	3	0	0	5	5	3	0	.289	.356
Mike Cvengros		p	33	15	5	6	1	0	0	1	2	1	0	.400	.467
Ken Penner		p	5	4	0	1	0	0	0	1	0	1	0	.250	.250
Hank Grampp		p	1	0	0	0	0	0	0	0	0	0	0	—	—
team total			156	5471	**982**	1655	**310**	46	139	**933**	**589**	**567**	103	.303	.452

b—from Boston (N)
Earl Grace (c), Tom Angley (c), Danny Taylor (of), Trader Horne (p), Claude Jonnard (p), Bos Osborne (p) also played for the Cubs during the season.

PITCHING

PHILADELPHIA ATHLETICS

WORLD SERIES STATISTICS	G	GS	CG	IP	H	R	ER	BB	SO	W	L	SV	ERA
George Earnshaw	2	**2**	**1**	**$13\frac{2}{3}$**	**14**	6	4	6	**17**	**1**	1	0	2.63
Howard Ehmke	2	**2**	**1**	$12\frac{2}{3}$	**14**	3	2	3	13	**1**	0	0	1.42
Lefty Grove	2	0	0	$6\frac{1}{3}$	3	0	0	1	10	0	0	**2**	0.00
Rube Walberg	2	0	0	$6\frac{1}{3}$	3	1	0	0	8	**1**	0	0	0.00
Jack Quinn	1	1	0	5	7	6	5	2	2	0	0	0	9.00
Eddie Rommel	1	0	0	1	2	1	1	1	0	**1**	0	0	9.00
Bill Shores	Did not play												
Carroll Yerkes	Did not play												
Bill Breckinridge	Did not play												
team total	5	5	2	45	43	17	12	13	50	4	1	2	2.40

REGULAR SEASON STATISTICS	G	GS	CG	IP	H	ER	BB	SO	W	L	Pct	SV	ShO	ERA
George Earnshaw	44	33	13	255	233	93	**125**	149	**24**	8	.750	1	2	3.28
Howard Ehmke	11	8	2	55	48	20	15	20	1	2	.778	0	0	3.27
Lefty Grove	42	**37**	21	275	278	86	81	**170**	20	6	**.769**	4	2	**2.82**
Rube Walberg	40	33	20	268	256	107	99	94	18	11	.621	4	3	3.59
Jack Quinn	35	18	7	161	182	71	39	41	11	9	.550	2	0	3.97
Eddie Rommel	32	6	4	114	135	36	34	25	12	2	.857	4	0	2.84
Bill Shores	39	13	5	153	150	61	59	49	11	6	.647	7	1	3.59
Carroll Yerkes	19	2	0	37	47	19	13	11	1	0	1.000	1	0	4.62
Bill Breckinridge	3	1	0	10	10	9	16	2	0	0	—	0	0	8.10
team total	151	151	72	1357	1371	518	487	**573**	**104**	46	**.693**	**24**	8	**3.44**

CHICAGO CUBS

WORLD SERIES STATISTICS	G	GS	CG	IP	H	R	ER	BB	SO	W	L	SV	ERA
Charlie Root	2	**2**	0	$13\frac{1}{3}$	12	7	7	2	8	0	1	0	4.73
Pat Malone	**3**	**2**	**1**	13	12	9	6	**7**	11	0	**2**	0	4.15
Guy Bush	2	1	**1**	11	12	3	1	2	4	**1**	0	0	**0.82**
Hal Carlson	2	0	0	4	7	3	3	1	3	0	0	0	6.75
Sheriff Blake	2	0	0	$1\frac{1}{3}$	4	2	2	0	1	0	1	0	13.50
Art Nehf	2	0	0	1	1	2	2	1	0	0	0	0	18.00
Mike Cvengros	Did not play												
Ken Penner	Did not play												
Hank Grampp	Did not play												
team total	5	5	2	$43\frac{2}{3}$	48	26	21	13	27	1	4	0	4.33

REGULAR SEASON STATISTICS	G	GS	CG	IP	H	ER	BB	SO	W	L	Pct	SV	ShO	ERA
Charlie Root	43	31	19	272	286	105	83	124	19	6	**.760**	5	4	3.47
Pat Malone	40	30	19	267	283	106	102	**166**	**22**	10	.688	2	**5**	3.57
Guy Bush	**50**	29	18	271	277	110	107	82	18	7	.720	**8**	2	3.65
Hal Carlson	31	14	6	112	131	64	31	35	11	5	.688	2	2	5.14
Sheriff Blake	35	30	13	218	244	104	**130**	70	14	13	.519	1	1	4.29
Art Nehf	32	15	4	121	148	75	39	27	8	5	.615	1	0	5.58
Mike Cvengros	32	2	0	64	82	33	29	23	5	4	.556	2	0	4.64
Ken Penner	5	0	0	13	14	4	6	3	0	1	.000	0	0	2.77
Hank Grampp	1	1	0	2	4	6	3	0	0	1	.000	0	0	27.00
team total	156	156	79	**1399**	1542	646	564	548	**98**	54	**.645**	21	**14**	4.16

Total Attendance—190,490 Average Attendance—38,098 Winning Player's Share—$5,621 Losing Player's Share—$3,782

1930
Earnshaw & Grove & Earnshaw

The stock market was down and the economy was failing, but batting averages in both leagues were healthy and heading higher than ever before. With the spitball outlawed and the slider not yet popular, with the lively ball and the home-run swing now essential elements in the game, hitters prospered in almost unbelievable fashion, as the National League as a whole averaged .303 and the American League .288. The St. Louis Cardinals shared in this trend fully, with .300 hitters at all eight starting positions. With this battery of hitters leading the way, the Cards came back from 12 games down in August to run through September at a torrid 21-4 pace and nose out the defending-champion Chicago Cubs. Managed by Gabby Street, the third Cardinal skipper to win the N.L. pennant in five years, the Redbirds had a .314 team-batting average and sent dangerous batters like Frankie Frisch, Chick Hafey, Jim Bottomley, and George Watkins to the plate to menace enemy pitchers. Street had no star pitchers, with his leading hurlers being lefty Bill Hallahan, spitballer Burleigh Grimes, and knuckleballer Jesse Haines. Over in the A.L., the Philadelphia Athletics repeated as champs with an impressive array of hitters featuring Al Simmons, Jimmie Foxx, and Mickey Cochrane, but Connie Mack had an edge over the Cardinals in holding two pitching aces, 28-game-winner Lefty Grove and 22-game-winner George Earnshaw. These two were among the few hurlers who could hold their heads above the constant batting barrages, and they gave the Athletics the favorite's role in the Series.

But even with rising ERA's, the pitchers on both sides surprisingly kept the batters under reasonable control throughout the Series, although the long ball came through for the A's. In game one in Philadelphia, Lefty Grove matched his fast ball with the spitball of Burleigh Grimes, one of the few active hurlers exempt from the 1920 banning of the wet one. The Cards actually outhit the A's 9-5, but the final tally of runs put Philadelphia on top 5-2. Each of those five hits came in different innings and led to a run, with Dykes hitting a double, Foxx and Haas triples, and Cochrane and Simmons homers. The A's kept the long ball coming the next day and beat Flint Rhem 6-1 with only seven hits; four of the hits went for extra bases, including a home run by Cochrane. Earnshaw gave the Cards six hits but scattered them harmlessly rather than allowing them in bunches.

Mack started Rube Walberg in game three in St. Louis against Bill Hallahan, the Cardinals' leading winner with 15 victories this season. The Athletic batters collected seven hits, the same amount as in game two, but six of them were singles and none of them produced any runs. The 5-0 Cardinal victory gave manager Street hope of climbing back into the Series, and a 3-1 victory in game four, with Haines throwing a four-hitter to beat Grove, evened the Series at two games apiece and swung the momentum over to the Cardinals.

But the Philadelphia duo of Grove and Earnshaw would bail the A's out and end the baseball season with a final gesture of assertion from the pitchers. Old man Grimes again cranked up his archaic spitball to face big George Earnshaw. Through seven innings the pitchers held sway and kept the plate untouched by runners. Mack used a pinch hitter for Earnshaw in the top of the eighth, but Lefty Grove came in to pitch in the bottom of the inning with the score still tied at 0-0. After eight innings Grimes had given up only four hits to the A's, but a leadoff walk to Cochrane boded ill in the bottom of the ninth. The Cardinal fans breathed easier when Simmons popped out, but Jimmie Foxx then rocketed a shot into the left-field stands for a 2-0 triumph. Ahead 3-2 in the Series going back to Philly, the A's were back in control and moving in for the kill. Rather than go with any of his lesser pitchers, Mack gambled on using Earnshaw again. Pitching on only one day of rest, the 6'4" Earnshaw ignored his fatigue and beat the Cards 7-1. Sharing the glory with Earnshaw were the Athletic batters, whose seven hits were all for extra bases.

Game 1 October 1 at Philadelphia

St L.		002	000	000				
Phi.		010	101	11x				

St. Louis	Pos	AB	R	H	RBI	PO	A	E
Douthit	cf	4	0	0	1	0	0	0
Adams	3b	3	0	1	1	1	2	0
Frisch	2b	4	0	2	0	1	2	0
Bottomley	1b	4	0	0	0	12	0	0
Hafey	lf	4	0	1	0	2	0	0
Blades	rf	3	0	0	0	2	0	0
Mancuso	c	4	1	1	0	6	1	0
Gelbert	ss	4	1	2	0	0	4	0
Grimes	p	3	0	2	0	0	3	0
a Puccinelli		1	0	0	0	0	0	0
Totals		34	2	9	2	24	12	0

a Fouled out for Grimes in 9th.

Philadelphia	Pos	AB	R	H	RBI	PO	A	E
Bishop	2b	3	1	0	0	2	3	0
Dykes	3b	4	0	1	1	1	1	0
Cochrane	c	3	1	1	1	7	0	0
Simmons	lf	3	1	1	1	2	0	0
Foxx	1b	3	1	1	0	8	0	0
Miller	rf	2	0	0	1	2	0	0
Haas	cf	3	1	1	0	3	0	0
Boley	ss	2	0	0	1	2	3	0
Grove	p	3	0	0	0	0	0	0
Totals		26	5	5	5	27	7	0

Pitching	IP	H	R	ER	BB	SO
St. Louis						
Grimes (L)	8	5	5	5	3	6
Philadelphia						
Grove (W)	9	9	2	2	1	5

Doubles—Dykes, Frisch, Hafey. Triples—Foxx, Haas. Home Runs—Cochrane, Simmons. Sacrifice Hits—Adams, Boley, Douthit, Miller. Left on Bases—St. Louis 8, Philadelphia 2. Umpires—Moriarty (A), Rigler (N), Geisel (A), Reardon (N). Attendance—32,295. Time of Game—1:48.

1st Inning
St. Louis
1 Douthit grounded to Bishop on a smash headed for right.
2 Adams struck out.
3 Frisch grounded to second.
Philadelphia
1 Bishop struck out.
2 Dykes rolled out to first. Cochrane walked.
3 Cochrane was out trying to steal second, Mancuso to Frisch.

2nd Inning
St. Louis
1 Bottomley struck out.
2 Hafey fouled to Dykes.
3 Blades struck out.
Philadelphia
1 Simmons grounded back to the mound. Foxx tripled on a liner against the right field wall.
2 Miller flied to right, Foxx scoring after the catch.
3 Haas lined to left.

3rd Inning
St. Louis
Mancuso singled to right. Gelbert singled to right, Mancuso stopping at second. Grimes beat out a bunt as Grove fell down, the bases loaded.
1 Douthit lined to center, Mancuso scoring and Gelbert getting to third, after the catch.
2 Adams flied to right, Gelbert scoring after the catch as Grimes still held at first. Frisch beat out a bouncer past Grove, Grimes going to second.
3 Bottomley fouled to Foxx.
Philadelphia
1 Boley flied to left.
2 Grove called out on strikes.
3 Bishop grounded back to the mound.

4th Inning
St. Louis
1 Hafey flied to center. Blades walked.
2 Mancuso lined to left. Gelbert singled to left, Blades stopping at second.
3 Grimes struck out.
Philadelphia
1 Dykes grounded to third.
2 Cochrane flied to right. Simmons hit a booming home run over the right field wall.
3 Foxx struck out.

5th Inning
St. Louis
1 Douthit lined to short.
2 Adams flied to Simmons in left-center. Frisch lined a double over Miller's head.
3 Bottomley grounded to first.
Philadelphia
1 Miller grounded to short.
2 Haas grounded to short.
3 Boley grounded to third.

6th Inning
St. Louis
1 Hafey grounded to short.
2 Blades grounded to short.
3 Mancuso flied to right.
Philadelphia
1 Grove struck out. Bishop walked. Dykes bounced a double against the left-center field stands, scoring Bishop.
2 Cochrane struck out. Simmons intentionally passed.
3 Foxx struck out again.

7th Inning
St. Louis
1 Gelbert grounded to third. Grimes singled to right.
2 Douthit forced Grimes at second, Boley making a phenomenal stop and throw to Bishop. Adams singled to left, Douthit stopping at second.
3 Frisch lined to Bishop making a leaping one-handed catch.
Philadelphia
1 Miller popped to third. Haas lined a triple over first, the ball going to the right field fence.
2 Boley hit a perfect bunt to squeeze in Haas, Boley out Grimes to first.
3 Grove grounded to second.

8th Inning
St. Louis
1 Bottomley grounded to second. Hafey lined a double through short.
2 Blades flied to center.
3 Mancuso fouled to Cochrane.
Philadelphia
1 Bishop grounded to second.
2 Dykes grounded to short. Cochrane hit a line-drive homer over the right field wall.
3 Simmons grounded to short.

9th Inning
St. Louis
1 Gelbert called out on strikes.
2 Puccinelli, batting for Grimes, fouled to Cochrane.
3 Douthit popped to short.

Game 2 October 2 at Philadelphia

St. L.	010	000	000						
Phi.	202	200	00x						

St. Louis	Pos	AB	R	H	RBI	PO	A	E
Douthit	cf	4	0	0	0	4	0	0
Adams	3b	4	0	1	0	0	1	0
Frisch	2b	4	0	1	0	1	1	1
Bottomley	1b	4	0	0	0	8	0	0
Hafey	lf	4	0	0	0	2	0	0
Watkins	rf	4	1	1	1	0	0	0
Mancuso	c	3	0	1	0	6	0	0
Gelbert	ss	3	0	1	0	3	1	0
Rhem	p	1	0	0	0	0	0	1
Lindsey	p	1	0	1	0	0	0	0
a Fisher		1	0	0	0	0	0	0
Johnson	p	0	0	0	0	0	0	0
Totals		33	1	6	1	24	3	2

a Struck out for Lindsey in 7th.

Philadelphia	Pos	AB	R	H	RBI	PO	A	E
Bishop	2b	2	1	0	0	3	0	0
Dykes	3b	3	0	1	2	4	2	0
Cochrane	c	3	2	1	1	9	0	1
Simmons	lf	4	2	2	1	3	0	0
Foxx	1b	3	0	1	1	3	2	0
Miller	rf	4	0	1	1	1	0	0
Haas	cf	4	0	0	0	2	0	0
Boley	ss	4	1	1	0	1	1	1
Earnshaw	p	3	0	0	0	1	0	0
Totals		30	6	7	6	27	5	2

Pitching	IP	H	R	ER	BB	SO
St. Louis						
Rhem (L)	$3\frac{1}{3}$	7	6	4	2	3
Lindsey	$2\frac{2}{3}$	0	0	0	0	2
Johnson	2	0	0	0	2	2
Philadelphia						
Earnshaw (W)	9	6	1	1	1	8

Doubles—Dykes, Foxx, Frisch, Simmons. Home Runs—Cochrane, Watkins. Stolen Base—Frisch. Sacrifice Hit—Dykes. Double Plays—Gelbert (unassisted), Dykes to Foxx. Left on Bases—St. Louis 6, Philadelphia 5. Umpires—Rigler, Geisel, Reardon, Moriarty. Attendance—32,295. Time of Game—1:47.

1st Inning
St. Louis
1 Douthit popped to third.
2 Adams flied to left.
Frisch doubled on a liner against the left field stands, **Frisch now has the most hits in World Series history with 43, one ahead of Eddie Collins with 42.**
3 Bottomley flied to center.
Philadelphia
1 Bishop flied to Douthit in deep right-center.
2 Dykes grounded to third.
Cochrane drove a high home run over the right field wall.
Simmons singled to center.
Foxx doubled to left-center, scoring Simmons.
3 Miller grounded to first.

2nd Inning
St. Louis
1 Hafey popped to second.
Watkins homered over the right field wall.
Mancuso beat out a hit to deep short.
Gelbert singled on a bouncer over Bishop's head into center, Mancuso taking third.
2 Rhem struck out.
3 Douthit popped to second.
Philadelphia
1 Haas struck out.
2 Boley blooped to second.
3 Earnshaw flied to left.

3rd Inning
St. Louis
1 Adams flied to right.
Frisch safe at first on Boley's fumble.
2 Bottomley struck out, after Bishop dropped his foul (no error charged).
Frisch stole second and continued on to third as Cochrane's throw was wild and bounced into center.
3 Hafey took a called third strike as his foul was missed by Dykes who fell.
Philadelphia
1 Bishop grounded to first.
2 Dykes took a called third strike.
Cochrane safe at first on Frisch's fumble.
Simmons doubled to right, when Watkins missed a shoestring catch, Cochrane scoring.
Foxx walked, the fourth ball was intentional.
Miller singled to left, Simmons scoring as Foxx went to third and Miller to second on Hafey's good throw which was deflected by Rhem into the stands for an error.
3 Haas lined out hard to center.

4th Inning
St. Louis
1 Watkins flied to short left.
2 Mancuso struck out.
3 Gelbert struck out.
Philadelphia
Boley singled past short.
1 Earnshaw struck out.
Bishop walked.
Dykes doubled to left-center, Boley and Bishop scoring.
For St. Louis—Lindsey came into pitch.
2,3 Cochrane lined into a double play, Gelbert (unassisted).

5th Inning
St. Louis
Lindsey singled to right.
1 Douthit popped to Cochrane.
2 Adams flied to center.
3 Frisch popped to third.
Philadelphia
1 Simmons flied to center.
2 Foxx grounded to short.
3 Miller lined to center.

6th Inning
St. Louis
1 Bottomley popped to second.
2 Hafey grounded to third.
3 Watkins grounded out, Foxx to Earnshaw.
Philadelphia
1 Haas struck out.
2 Boley fouled to Bottomley.
3 Earnshaw struck out.

7th Inning
St. Louis
Mancuso walked.
1 Gelbert forced Mancuso at second, Foxx to Boley.
2 Fisher, pinch-hitting for Lindsey, struck out.
3 Douthit flied to left.
Philadelphia
For St. Louis—Johnson pitching.
Bishop walked.
1 Dykes sacrificed, Bottomley unassisted.
Cochrane walked.
2 Simmons grounded to second, advancing Bishop and Cochrane.
3 Foxx struck out.

8th Inning
St. Louis
Adams singled to right.
1,2 Frisch lined into a double play, Dykes to Foxx.
3 Bottomley fouled to Dykes.
Philadelphia
1 Miller struck out.
2 Haas flied to short.
3 Boley flied to deep left-center.

9th Inning
St. Louis
1 Hafey grounded to short.
2 Watkins struck out.
3 Mancuso struck out.

Game 3 October 4 at St. Louis

Phi.	000	000	000
St L.	000	110	21x

Philadelphia	Pos	AB	R	H	RBI	PO	A	E
Bishop	2b	4	0	3	0	0	2	0
Dykes	3b	4	0	0	0	1	1	0
Cochrane	c	2	0	0	0	6	0	0
Simmons	lf	4	0	2	0	1	1	0
Foxx	1b	4	0	1	0	11	1	0
Miller	rf	4	0	0	0	1	0	0
Haas	cf	3	0	0	0	1	0	0
a Moore		1	0	1	0	0	0	0
Boley	ss	4	0	0	0	3	5	0
Walberg	p	2	0	0	0	0	0	0
Shores	p	0	0	0	0	0	0	0
Quinn	p	0	0	0	0	0	1	0
b McNair		1	0	0	0	0	0	0
Totals		33	0	7	0	24	11	0

a Singled for Haas in 9th.
b Flied out for Quinn in 9th.

St. Louis	Pos	AB	R	H	RBI	PO	A	E
Douthit	cf	4	1	2	1	3	0	0
Adams	3b	4	0	0	0	0	0	0
Frisch	2b	4	0	0	0	2	5	0
Bottomley	1b	4	1	1	0	14	0	0
Hafey	lf	4	1	2	1	0	0	0
Blades	rf	2	1	1	0	1	0	0
Watkins	rf	2	1	1	0	1	0	0
Wilson	c	4	0	2	2	6	0	0
Gelbert	ss	3	0	1	1	0	4	0
Hallahan	p	2	0	0	0	0	1	0
Totals		33	5	10	5	27	10	0

Pitching	IP	H	R	ER	BB	SO
Philadelphia						
Walberg (L)	$4\frac{2}{3}$	4	2	2	1	3
Shores	*$1\frac{1}{3}$	3	2	2	0	0
Quinn	2	3	1	1	0	1
St. Louis						
Hallahan (W)	9	7	0	0	5	6

*Pitched to 3 batters in 7th.

Doubles—Bottomley, Hafey, Simmons. Home Run—Douthit. Double Play—Gelbert to Frisch to Bottomley. Left on Bases—Philadelphia 11, St. Louis 5. Umpires—Geisel, Reardon, Moriarty, Rigler. Attendance—36,944. Time of Game—1:55.

1st Inning
Philadelphia
Bishop singled to right.
1 Dykes struck out.
Cochrane walked.
2 Simmons struck out.
Foxx singled to short, loading the bases.
3 Miller struck out.
St. Louis
1 Douthit fouled to Foxx.
2 Adams flied to left.
3 Frisch flied to right.

2nd Inning
Philadelphia
1 Haas grounded to first.
2 Boley flied to right.
3 Walberg grounded to second.
St. Louis
1 Bottomley called out on strikes.
2 Hafey also called out on strikes.
3 Blades flied to very deep center.

3rd Inning
Philadelphia
1 Bishop grounded to first.
Dykes walked.
Cochrane again walked.
2,3 Simmons grounded into a double play, Gelbert to Frisch to Bottomley.
St. Louis
1 Wilson fouled to Cochrane.
2 Gelbert grounded to short.
3 Hallahan popped to short.

4th Inning
Philadelphia
1 Foxx grounded back to the pitcher.
2 Miller bounced to first.
3 Haas struck out.
St. Louis
Douthit hit a booming homer into the left field bleachers.
1 Adams fouled to Cochrane.
2 Frisch grounded to short.
3 Bottomley again struck out.

5th Inning
Philadelphia
1 Boley flied to center.
2 Walberg struck out.
Bishop hit a long single off the right field pavilion wall as Blades played the rebound perfectly.
3 Dykes flied to short center.
St. Louis
1 Hafey grounded to short.
Blades singled to center.
Wilson singled to right, Blades racing to third.
Gelbert singled to left, scoring Blades
2 but Wilson was out trying for third, Simmons to Dykes.
Hallahan walked.
For Philadelphia—Shores came in to pitch.
3 Douthit grounded to second.

6th Inning
Philadelphia
For St. Louis—Watkins playing right.
1 Cochrane grounded to second.
Simmons doubled to right-center.
2 Foxx fouled to Bottomley, who made a spectacular catch at the boxes reaching in over the heads of the fans.
3 Miller flied to center.
St. Louis
1 Adams grounded to third.
2 Frisch fouled to Foxx.
3 Bottomley grounded to second.

7th Inning
Philadelphia
1 Haas grounded to second.
2 Boley grounded to short.
Shores walked.
Bishop singled to center, his third hit of the game as Shores stopped at second.
3 Dykes grounded to first.
St. Louis
Hafey singled to right.
Watkins singled to center, Hafey beating the throw to third, with Watkins going to second on the play at third.
Wilson singled to left, scoring Hafey and Watkins.
For Philadelphia—Quinn replaced Shores.
1 Gelbert forced Wilson at second, Foxx to Boley.
2 Hallahan struck out.
Douthit singled over third, Gelbert going to third.
3 Adams bounced back to the mound.

8th Inning
Philadelphia
1 Cochrane grounded to short.
Simmons singled to right.
2 Foxx grounded to second, Simmons going to second.
3 Miller grounded to short.
St. Louis
1 Frisch grounded to short.
Bottomley doubled over first.
Hafey doubled to right-center, scoring Bottomley.
2 Watkins popped to short.
3 Wilson grounded to short.

9th Inning
Philadelphia
Moore, pinch-hitting for Haas, singled to left.
1 Boley fouled to Frisch.
2 McNair, batting for Quinn, flied to right.
Bishop walked.
3 Dykes called out on strikes.

Game 4 October 5 at St. Louis

Phi.	1 0 0	0 0 0	0 0 0					
St L.	0 0 1	2 0 0	0 0 x					

Philadelphia	Pos	AB	R	H	RBI	PO	A	E
Bishop	2b	3	1	1	0	2	2	0
Dykes	3b	2	0	0	0	1	0	1
Cochrane	c	4	0	0	0	3	0	0
Simmons	lf	3	0	2	1	0	0	0
Foxx	1b	4	0	1	0	6	0	0
Miller	rf	4	0	0	0	7	0	0
Haas	cf	3	0	0	0	4	0	0
Boley	ss	4	0	0	0	1	1	0
Grove	p	3	0	0	0	0	0	0
Totals		30	1	4	1	24	3	1

Pitching	IP	H	R	ER	BB	SO
Philadelphia						
Grove (L)	8	5	3	1	1	3
St. Louis						
Haines (W)	9	4	1	1	4	2

St. Louis	Pos	AB	R	H	RBI	PO	A	E
Douthit	cf	4	0	0	0	0	0	0
Adams	3b	4	0	0	0	2	2	0
Frisch	2b	4	0	0	0	3	2	1
Bottomley	1b	4	0	0	0	9	0	0
Hafey	lf	3	1	1	0	3	0	0
Blades	rf	3	1	0	0	7	0	0
Wilson	c	3	0	1	0	3	0	0
Gelbert	ss	2	1	2	1	0	4	0
Haines	p	2	0	1	1	0	1	0
Totals		29	3	5	2	27	9	1

Double—Hafey. Triple—Gelbert. Sacrifice Hits—Dykes, Haines. Double Play—Gelbert to Frisch to Bottomley. Left on Bases—Philadelphia 7, St. Louis 4. Wild Pitch—Haines. Umpires—Reardon, Moriarty, Rigler, Geisel. Attendance—39,946. Time of Game—1:41.

1st Inning
Philadelphia
Bishop singled over first.
1 Dykes sacrificed Bishop to second, Haines to Bottomley.
2 Cochrane fouled to Adams. Bishop went to third on a wild pitch. Simmons singled to right, scoring Bishop. Foxx beat out a hit to second, Simmons going to second.
3 Miller grounded to short.
St. Louis
1 Douthit struck out.
2 Adams popped to short.
3 Frisch popped to first.

2nd Inning
Philadelphia
1 Haas lined to left.
2 Boley flied to right. Grove safe on Frisch's fumble. Bishop walked.
3 Dykes forced Grove at third, Adams unassisted.
St. Louis
1 Bottomley popped to third.
2 Hafey grounded to second.
3 Blades flied to deep center

3rd Inning
Philadelphia
1 Cochrane flied to Blades in right-center Simmons beat out a roller to short.
2,3 Foxx hit into a double play, Gelbert to Frisch to Bottomley.
St. Louis
1 Wilson lined to right. Gelbert tripled on a liner over first going all the way to the right field boxes. Haines singled to center, Gelbert scoring.
2 Douthit fouled to Foxx.
3 Adams struck out.

4th Inning
Philadelphia
1 Miller grounded to third.
2 Haas grounded to second.
3 Boley lined to left.
St. Louis
1 Frisch flied to right.
2 Bottomley struck out. Hafey hit a ground-rule double, the ball lodging behind the screen in right. Blades was safe on Dykes' wild throw to first, Hafey scoring. Wilson singled to right, Blades racing to third. Gelbert singled off Grove's glove, Blades scoring with Wilson stopping at second.
3 Haines flied to deep right.

5th Inning
Philadelphia
1 Grove fouled to Frisch.
2 Bishop grounded to first.
3 Dykes fouled to Wilson.
St. Louis
1 Douthit popped to second.
2 Adams flied to right.
3 Frisch flied to center.

6th Inning
Philadelphia
1 Cochrane flied to left. Simmons walked.
2 Foxx grounded to third, Simmons going to second.
3 Miller took a called third strike.
St. Louis
1 Bottomley grounded to short in a very close play at first.
2 Hafey grounded to second.
3 Blades flied to right.

7th Inning
Philadelphia
Haas walked.
1 Boley popped to second on a full count.
2 Grove struck out.
3 Bishop flied to deep right.
St. Louis
1 Wilson flied to Miller in deep right-center. Gelbert walked.
2 Haines sacrificed Gelbert to second, Foxx unassisted.
3 Douthit flied to Bishop making a great catch over his shoulder.

8th Inning
Philadelphia
Dykes walked.
1 Cochrane flied to right.
2 Simmons grounded to Gelbert rushing in behind the mound to make a great stop and throw getting Simmons, as Dykes went to second.
3 Foxx flied to right.
St. Louis
1 Adams flied to Miller in right-center.
2 Frisch flied to Miller in right-center.
3 Bottomley flied to Haas in right-center.

9th Inning
Philadelphia
1 Miller flied to right.
2 Haas grounded to short.
3 Boley flied to right.

Game 5 October 6 at St. Louis

Phi.	0 0 0	0 0 0	0 0 2					
St L.	0 0 0	0 0 0	0 0 0					

Philadelphia	Pos	AB	R	H	RBI	PO	A	E
Bishop	2b	4	0	0	0	1	0	0
Dykes	3b	3	0	0	0	0	1	0
Cochrane	c	3	1	1	0	7	1	0
Simmons	lf	4	0	0	0	3	0	0
Foxx	1b	4	1	2	2	12	0	0
Miller	rf	4	0	0	0	0	0	0
Haas	cf	4	0	1	0	2	0	0
Boley	ss	3	0	1	0	2	1	0
Earnshaw	p	2	0	0	0	0	4	0
a Moore		0	0	0	0	0	0	0
Grove	p	0	0	0	0	0	1	0
Totals		31	2	5	2	27	8	0

a Walked for Earnshaw in 8th.
b Walked for Watkins in 9th.

Double—Wilson. Home Run—Foxx. Sacrifice Hit—Grimes. Double Play—Adams to Frisch to Bottomley. Left on Bases—Philadelphia 5, St. Louis 8. Umpires—Moriarty, Rigler, Geisel, Reardon. Attendance—38,844. Time of Game—1:58.

St. Louis	Pos	AB	R	H	RBI	PO	A	E
Douthit	cf	4	0	0	0	2	0	0
Adams	3b	4	0	1	0	0	1	0
Frisch	2b	4	0	1	0	3	3	1
Bottomley	1b	4	0	0	0	9	1	0
Hafey	lf	3	0	0	0	1	0	0
Watkins	rf	3	0	0	0	1	0	0
b Blades		0	0	0	0	0	0	0
Wilson	c	4	0	1	0	9	0	0
Gelbert	ss	2	0	0	0	2	8	0
Grimes	p	2	0	0	0	0	0	0
Totals		30	0	3	0	27	13	1

Pitching	IP	H	R	ER	BB	SO
Philadelphia						
Earnshaw	7	2	0	0	3	5
Grove (W)	2	1	0	0	1	2
St. Louis						
Grimes (L)	9	5	2	2	3	7

1st Inning
Philadelphia
1 Bishop called out on strikes.
2 Dykes grounded to short. Cochrane bounced a single to center.
3 Simmons popped to short.
St. Louis
1 Douthit bunted out to first. Adams singled to center.
2 Frisch popped to short.
3 Bottomley grounded to first.

2nd Inning
Philadelphia
1 Foxx flied to left.
2 Miller flied to center.
3 Haas flied to center.
St. Louis
1 Hafey flied to left.
2 Watkins struck out.
3 Wilson lined to Simmons in left-center.

3rd Inning
Philadelphia
1 Boley struck out.
2 Earnshaw grounded to second.
3 Bishop again called out on strikes.
St. Louis
Gelbert walked.
1 Grimes sacrificed Gelbert to second, Earnshaw to Foxx. Douthit safe on a fielder's choice, Dykes trying for Gelbert who got safely back to second.
2 Adams flied to Boley in short left.
3 Frisch grounded to first.

4th Inning
Philadelphia
1 Dykes grounded to short.
2 Cochrane struck out.
3 Simmons bounced to short.
St. Louis
1 Bottomley struck out, but had to be thrown out as Cochrane dropped the third strike. Hafey walked.
2 Watkins flied to Haas in right-center.
3 Wilson grounded back to the mound.

5th Inning
Philadelphia
Foxx singled to center.
1 Miller forced Foxx at second, Gelbert to Frisch.
2,3 Haas grounded into a double play, Adams to Frisch to Bottomley.
St. Louis
1 Gelbert popped to first.
2 Grimes bounced back to the mound.
3 Douthit grounded to short.

6th Inning
Philadelphia
1 Boley grounded to short.
2 Earnshaw struck out.
3 Bishop grounded to second.
St. Louis
1 Adams struck out.
2 Frisch was out on a close play, Earnshaw fielding his bunt and flipping to Foxx.
3 Bottomley again struck out.

7th Inning
Philadelphia
Dykes walked.
1 Cochrane popped to Wilson in front of the plate.
2 Simmons flied to deep right.
3 Foxx struck out.
St. Louis
1 Hafey called out on strikes.
2 Watkins flied to left. Wilson doubled to left-center. Gelbert was intentionally passed.
3 Grimes flied to center.

8th Inning
Philadelphia
1 Miller grounded to short. Haas beat out a bunt toward third. Haas safe trying to steal second as Frisch missed the tag for an error. Boley singled off Grimes' glove, Haas going to third. Moore, pinch-hitting for Earnshaw, walked to load the bases.
2 Bishop forced Haas at the plate, Bottomley to Wilson.
3 Dykes forced Bishop at second, Gelbert to Frisch.
St. Louis
For Philadelphia—Grove pitching.
1 Douthit popped to second.
2 Adams grounded to short. Frisch singled to center.
3 Bottomley struck out for the third straight time.

9th Inning
Philadelphia
Cochrane walked.
1 Simmons flied to Gelbert in short left. Foxx smashed a two-run homer deep into the left field bleachers.
2 Miller took a called third strike.
3 Haas grounded to short.
St. Louis
1 Hafey popped to Cochrane. Blades, batting for Watkins, walked.
2 Wilson bounced hard back to the mound, Blades taking second.
3 Gelbert called out on strikes.

Game 6 October 8 at Philadelphia

St L.	000	000	001				
Phi.	201	211	00x				

St. Louis	Pos	AB	R	H	RBI	PO	A	E
Douthit	cf	4	0	0	0	5	0	0
Adams	3b	2	0	0	0	1	1	0
c High	3b	2	1	1	0	0	0	0
Watkins	rf	3	0	0	0	3	0	1
Frisch	2b	4	0	1	0	3	1	0
Hafey	lf	4	0	2	1	1	0	0
Bottomley	1b	2	0	0	0	6	1	0
Wilson	c	4	0	0	0	5	0	0
Gelbert	ss	3	0	0	0	2	0	0
Hallahan	p	0	0	0	0	0	0	0
a Fisher		1	0	1	0	0	0	0
Johnson	p	0	0	0	0	0	0	0
b Blades		1	0	0	0	0	0	0
Lindsey	p	0	0	0	0	0	1	0
d Orsatti		1	0	0	0	0	0	0
Bell	p	0	0	0	0	0	1	0
Totals		31	1	5	1	24	7	1

Philadelphia	Pos	AB	R	H	RBI	PO	A	E
Bishop	2b	2	2	0	0	0	2	0
Dykes	3b	2	2	2	2	1	1	0
Cochrane	c	3	1	1	2	8	0	0
Simmons	cf-lf	4	1	1	1	3	0	0
Foxx	1b	3	1	1	0	12	0	0
Miller	rf	3	0	2	1	1	0	0
Moore	lf	2	0	0	0	0	0	0
Haas	cf	1	0	0	1	2	0	0
Boley	ss	4	0	0	0	0	2	0
Earnshaw	p	4	0	0	0	0	2	0
Totals		28	7	7	7	27	7	0

Pitching	IP	H	R	ER	BB	SO
St. Louis						
Hallahan (L)	2	2	2	2	3	2
Johnson	3	4	4	4	1	2
Lindsey	2	1	1	1	1	0
Bell	1	0	0	0	0	0
Philadelphia						
Earnshaw (W)	9	5	1	1	3	6

a Doubled for Hallahan in 3rd.
b Struck out for Johnson in 6th.
c Grounded out for Adams in 6th.
d Grounded out for Lindsey in 8th.

Doubles—Cochrane, Dykes, Fisher, Foxx, Hafey 2, Miller 2. Home Runs—Dykes, Simmons. Sacrifice Hits—Cochrane, Haas, Miller. Double Play—Foxx (unassisted). Passed Ball—Wilson. Hit by Pitcher—Bishop (by Hallahan). Left on Bases—St. Louis 6, Philadelphia 6. Umpires—Rigler, Geisel, Reardon, Moriarty. Attendance—32,295. Time of Game—1:46.

1st Inning
St. Louis
1 Douthit struck out.
2 Adams grounded to first.
3 Watkins struck out.
Philadelphia
1 Bishop popped to second.
  Dykes walked.
  Cochrane doubled down the right field foul line, scoring Dykes and took third when Watkins over-ran the ball.
2 Simmons struck out.
  Foxx walked.
  Miller lined a double to the scoreboard in right-center, scoring Cochrane with Foxx stopping at third.
3 Moore flied to center.

2nd Inning
St. Louis
1 Frisch flied to Simmons in deep center.
2 Hafey flied to center.
3 Bottomley struck out.
Philadelphia
1 Boley grounded to short.
2 Earnshaw struck out.
  Bishop was hit by a pitch.
    Bishop took second on a passed ball.
  Dykes again walked.
3 Cochrane fouled to Adams.

3rd Inning
St. Louis
1 Wilson grounded to third.
2 Gelbert flied to center.
  Fisher, batting for Hallahan, lined a double over Boley's head.
3 Douthit bounced to short.
Philadelphia
For St. Louis—Johnson pitching.
  Simmons homered into the upper tier of the left field stands.
1 Foxx popped to second.
  Miller doubled again, a hot grounder over third into left.
2 Moore struck out.
3 Boley lined to right.

4th Inning
St. Louis
For Philadelphia—Haas playing center as Simmons moved over to left.
1 Adams struck out.
2 Watkins popped to third.
  Frisch singled to left.
3 Hafey flied to center.
Philadelphia
1 Earnshaw struck out.
  Bishop walked.
  Dykes hit a two-run homer into the lower left field stands.
2 Cochrane robbed of a hit when Frisch knocked down his liner, heading for right, with a headlong dive and getting Cochrane by a step at first.
3 Simmons grounded to third.

5th Inning
St. Louis
1 Bottomley grounded to second.
2 Wilson struck out.
3 Gelbert flied to center.
Philadelphia
  Foxx doubled off Frisch's glove into center.
1 Miller sacrificed Foxx to third, Bottomley to Frisch.
2 Haas flied to center, Foxx scoring after the catch.
3 Boley flied to right.

6th Inning
St. Louis
1 Blades, batting for Johnson, struck out.
2 Douthit fouled to Cochrane.
3 High, batting for Adams, grounded back to the mound.
Philadelphia
For St. Louis—High playing third and Lindsey, pitching
1 Earnshaw flied to left.
  Bishop walked.
  Dykes doubled to left-center, Bishop stopping at third.
2 Cochrane flied to Douthit in right-center, Bishop scoring after the catch.
3 Simmons flied to right.

7th Inning
St. Louis
1 Watkins grounded to second.
2 Frisch bounced back to the mound.
  Hafey doubled over third.
  Bottomley walked.
3 Wilson fouled to Cochrane.
Philadelphia
1 Foxx flied to center.
2 Miller fouled to Wilson.
3 Haas grounded back to the pitcher.

8th Inning
St. Louis
1 Gelbert bunted out to Foxx.
2 Orsatti, batting for Lindsey, grounded to first.
3 Douthit bounced to short.
Philadelphia
For St. Louis—Bell pitching.
1 Boley grounded to short.
2 Earnshaw flied to deep center.
3 Bishop bounced back to the pitcher.

9th Inning
St. Louis
  High lined a single near the right field wall.
  Watkins walked.
1,2 Frisch lined to Foxx, who stepped on first doubling up Watkins.
  Hafey got his second double of the game over third, scoring High (the first Cardinal run after 21 shutout innings). **For Hafey his fifth double setting a new World Series record.**
3 Wilson flied to right.

1930 WORLD SERIES COMPOSITE BOX

	Wins	Composite Line Score										Manager	Regular Season W	L	Pct.	G. Ahead
Philadelphia Athletics (A.L.)	4	5	1	3	5	1	2	1	1	2	-21	Connie Mack	102	52	.662	8
St. Louis Cardinals (N.L.)	2	0	1	3	3	1	0	2	1	1	-12	Gabby Street	92	62	.597	2

BATTING AND FIELDING

PHILADELPHIA ATHLETICS

	WORLD SERIES STATISTICS																		REGULAR SEASON STATISTICS													
	Pos	G	AB	R	H	2B	3B	HR	RBI	BB	SO	SB	BA	SA	PO	A	E		Main Pos	G	AB	R	H	2B	3B	HR	RBI	BB	SO	SB	BA	SA
Jimmie Foxx	1b	6	21	3	7	2	1	1	3	2	4	0	.333	.667	53	3	0		1b	153	562	127	188	33	13	37	156	93	**66**	7	.335	.637
Max Bishop	2b	6	18	**5**	4	0	0	0	0	**7**	3	0	.222	.222	8	9	0		2b	130	441	117	111	27	6	10	38	128	60	3	.252	.408
Joe Boley	ss	6	21	1	2	0	0	0	1	0	1	0	.095	.095	9	13	1		ss	121	420	41	116	22	2	4	55	32	26	0	.276	.367
Jimmy Dykes	3b	6	18	2	4	3	0	1	**5**	5	3	0	.222	.556	8	6	1		3b	125	435	69	131	28	4	6	73	74	53	3	.301	.425
Bing Miller	rf	6	21	0	3	2	0	0	3	0	4	0	.143	.238	12	0	0		of	154	585	89	177	38	7	9	100	47	22	13	.303	.438
Mule Haas	cf	6	18	1	2	0	**1**	0	1	1	3	0	.111	.222	14	0	0		of	132	532	91	159	33	7	2	68	43	33	2	.299	.398
Al Simmons	lf-cf	6	22	4	**8**	2	0	**2**	4	2	2	0	**.364**	**.727**	12	1	0		of	138	554	**152**	211	41	16	36	165	39	34	9	**.381**	.708
Mickey Cochrane	c	6	18	**5**	4	1	0	**2**	4	5	2	0	.222	.611	39	1	1		c	130	487	110	174	42	5	10	85	55	18	5	.357	.526
Jim Moore	ph-lf	3	3	0	1	0	0	0	0	1	1	0	.333	.333	0	0	0	a	of	15	50	10	19	3	0	2	12	2	4	1	.380	.560
Eric McNair	ph	1	1	0	0	0	0	0	0	0	0	0	.000	.000					ss-3b	78	237	27	63	12	2	0	34	9	19	5	.266	.333
Dib Williams		Did not play																	2b-ss	67	191	24	50	10	3	3	22	15	19	2	.262	.393
Wally Schang		Did not play																	c	45	92	16	16	4	1	1	9	17	15	0	.174	.272
Homer Summa		Did not play																	of	25	54	10	15	2	1	1	5	4	1	0	.278	.407
Cy Perkins		Did not play																	c	20	38	1	6	2	0	0	4	2	3	0	.158	.211
Pinky Higgins		Did not play																	3b	14	24	1	6	2	0	0	0	4	5	0	.250	.333
Eddie Collins		Did not play																	ph	3	2	1	1	2	0	0	0	0	0	0	.500	.500
George Earnshaw	p	3	9	0	0	0	0	0	0	0	5	0	.000	.000	1	6	0		p	49	114	11	26	8	1	0	10	5	21	0	.228	.316
Lefty Grove	p	3	6	0	0	0	0	0	0	0	3	0	.000	.000	0	1	0		p	50	110	11	22	3	2	2	17	7	46	0	.200	.318
Rube Walberg	p	1	2	0	0	0	0	0	0	0	1	0	.000	.000	0	0	0		p	38	73	5	12	2	2	0	9	4	13	0	.164	.247
Jack Quinn	p	1	0	0	0	0	0	0	0	0	0	0	—	—	0	1	0		p	35	34	2	9	0	0	1	4	1	9	0	.265	.353
Bill Shores	p	1	0	0	0	0	0	0	0	1	0	0	—	—	0	0	0		p	31	57	6	11	1	0	0	3	2	20	0	.193	.211
Roy Mahaffey		Did not play																	p	33	59	2	7	1	0	1	7	0	21	0	.119	.186
Eddie Rommel		Did not play																	p	35	38	8	10	3	1	0	6	7	5	0	.263	.395
Charlie Perkins		Did not play																	p	8	8	0	1	0	0	0	0	0	3	0	.125	.125
team total		6	178	21	35	10	2	6	21	24	32	0	.197	.376	156	41	3			154	5345	951	1573	319	74	125	895	599	531	50	.294	.452

Double Plays—2
Left on Bases—36

a-from Chicago (A)
Doc Cramer (of), Spence Harris (of), Jim Keesey (1b), Howard Ehmke (p), Glenn Liebhardt (p), Al Mahon (p) also played for the Athletics during the season.

ST. LOUIS CARDINALS

	WORLD SERIES STATISTICS																		REGULAR SEASON STATISTICS													
	Pos	G	AB	R	H	2B	3B	HR	RBI	BB	SO	SB	BA	SA	PO	A	E		Main Pos	G	AB	R	H	2B	3B	HR	RBI	BB	SO	SB	BA	SA
Jim Bottomley	1b	6	22	1	1	1	0	0	0	2	**9**	0	.045	.091	**57**	2	0		1b	131	487	92	148	33	7	15	97	44	36	5	.304	.493
Frankie Frisch	2b	6	**24**	0	5	2	0	0	0	0	0	**1**	.208	.292	13	14	**3**		2b	133	540	121	187	46	9	10	114	55	16	15	.346	.520
Charlie Gelbert	ss	6	17	2	6	0	1	0	2	3	3	0	.353	.471	5	**23**	0		ss	139	513	92	156	39	11	3	72	43	41	6	.304	.441
Sparky Adams	3b	6	21	0	3	0	0	0	1	0	4	0	.143	.143	4	7	0		3b	137	570	98	179	36	9	0	55	45	27	7	.314	.409
George Watkins	rf	4	12	2	2	0	0	1	1	1	3	0	.167	.417	5	0	1		of	119	391	85	146	32	7	17	87	24	49	5	.373	.621
Taylor Douthit	cf	6	**24**	1	2	0	0	1	2	0	2	0	.083	.208	14	0	0		of	154	**664**	109	201	41	10	7	93	60	38	4	.303	.426
Chick Hafey	lf	6	22	2	6	**5**	0	0	2	1	3	0	.273	.500	9	0	0		of	120	446	108	150	39	12	26	107	46	51	12	.336	.652
Jimmie Wilson	c	4	15	0	4	1	0	0	2	0	1	0	.267	.333	23	0	0		c	107	362	54	115	25	7	1	58	28	17	8	.318	.434
Ray Blades	rf-ph	5	9	2	1	0	0	0	0	2	2	0	.111	.111	10	0	0		of	45	101	26	40	6	2	4	25	21	15	1	.396	.614
Gus Mancuso	c	2	7	1	2	0	0	0	0	1	2	0	.286	.286	13	1	0		c	76	227	39	83	17	2	7	59	18	16	1	.366	.551
Andy High	ph-3b	1	2	1	1	0	0	0	0	0	0	0	.500	.500	0	0	0		3b	72	215	34	60	12	2	2	29	23	6	1	.279	.381
Showboat Fisher	ph	2	2	0	1	1	0	0	0	0	1	0	.500	1.000					of	92	254	49	95	18	6	8	61	25	21	4	.374	.587
Ernie Orsatti	ph	1	1	0	0	0	0	0	0	0	0	0	.000	.000					1b-of	48	131	24	42	8	4	1	15	12	18	1	.321	.466
George Puccinelli	ph	1	1	0	0	0	0	0	0	0	0	0	.000	.000					of	11	16	5	9	1	0	3	8	0	1	0	.563	1.188
Burleigh Grimes	p	2	5	0	2	0	0	0	0	0	1	0	.400	.400	0	3	0	b	p	23	57	9	15	4	0	0	10	5	12	0	.263	.333
Wild Bill Hallahan	p	2	2	0	0	0	0	0	0	1	1	0	.000	.000	0	1	0		p	35	81	8	10	1	0	0	4	5	41	0	.123	.136
Jesse Haines	p	1	2	0	1	0	0	0	1	0	0	0	.500	.500	0	1	0		p	29	65	3	16	3	0	0	12	4	15	0	.246	.292
Jim Lindsey	p	2	1	0	1	0	0	0	0	0	0	0	1.000	1.000	0	1	0		p	39	28	2	8	1	0	0	4	0	7	0	.286	.321
Flint Rhem	p	1	1	0	0	0	0	0	0	0	1	0	.000	.000	0	0	1		p	26	52	7	12	2	0	0	6	0	7	0	.231	.269
Syl Johnson	p	2	0	0	0	0	0	0	0	0	0	0	—	—	0	0	0		p	32	70	9	15	4	0	0	5	4	28	1	.214	.271
Hi Bell	p	1	0	0	0	0	0	0	0	0	0	0	—	—	0	1	0		p	39	26	1	2	0	0	0	0	2	11	0	.077	.077
Al Grabowski		Did not play																	p	35	33	7	12	2	0	0	5	0	11	0	.364	.424
team total		6	190	12	38	10	1	2	11	11	33	1	.200	.295	153	54	5			154	5512	**1004**	1732	**373**	89	104	**942**	479	496	72	.314	.471

Double Plays—4
Left on Bases—37

b-from Boston (N)
Doc Farrell (ss), Pepper Martin (pr-ph), Homer Peel (of), Earl Smith (c), Dizzy Dean (p), Fred Frankhouse (p), Hal Haid (p), Carmen Hill (p), Tony Kaufmann (p), Clarence Mitchell (p), Bill Sherdel (p) also played for the Cardinals during the season.

PITCHING

PHILADELPHIA ATHLETICS

	WORLD SERIES STATISTICS													REGULAR SEASON STATISTICS													
	G	GS	CG	IP	H	R	ER	BB	SO	W	L	SV	ERA		G	GS	CG	IP	H	ER	BB	SO	W	L	Pct	SV	ShO	ERA
George Earnshaw	**3**	**3**	**2**	**25**	13	2	2	7	**19**	**2**	0	0	**0.72**		49	**39**	20	296	299	146	**139**	193	22	13	.629	2	**3**	4.44
Lefty Grove	**3**	2	**2**	19	**15**	5	3	3	10	**2**	1	0	1.42		**50**	32	22	291	273	82	60	**209**	**28**	5	**.848**	**9**	2	**2.54**
Rube Walberg	1	1	0	$4\frac{2}{3}$	4	2	2	1	3	0	1	0	3.86		38	30	12	205	207	107	85	100	13	12	.520	1	2	4.10
Jack Quinn	1	0	0	2	3	1	1	0	1	0	0	0	4.50		35	7	0	90	109	44	22	28	9	7	.563	6	0	4.40
Bill Shores	1	0	0	$1\frac{1}{3}$	3	2	2	0	0	0	0	0	13.50		31	19	7	159	169	74	70	48	12	4	.750	0	1	4.19
Roy Mahaffey	Did not play														33	16	6	153	186	85	53	38	9	5	.643	0	0	5.00
Eddie Rommel	Did not play														35	9	5	130	142	62	27	35	9	4	.692	3	0	4.29
Charlie Perkins	Did not play														8	1	0	24	25	17	15	15	0	0	—	0	0	6.37
team total	6	6	4	52	38	12	10	11	33	4	2	0	1.73		154	154	72	1371	1457	652	488	**672**	**102**	52	**.662**	**21**	**8**	4.28

ST. LOUIS CARDINALS

	WORLD SERIES STATISTICS													REGULAR SEASON STATISTICS													
	G	GS	CG	IP	H	R	ER	BB	SO	W	L	SV	ERA		G	GS	CG	IP	H	ER	BB	SO	W	L	Pct	SV	ShO	ERA
Burleigh Grimes	2	2	**2**	17	10	**7**	**7**	6	13	0	**2**	0	3.71	b	22	19	10	152	174	51	43	58	13	6	.684	0	1	3.02
Wild Bill Hallahan	2	2	1	11	9	2	2	**8**	8	1	1	0	1.64		35	32	13	237	233	123	**126**	**177**	15	9	.625	2	2	4.67
Jesse Haines	1	1	1	9	4	1	1	4	2	1	0	0	1.00		29	24	14	182	215	87	54	68	13	8	.619	1	0	4.30
Syl Johnson	2	0	0	5	4	4	4	3	4	0	0	0	7.20		32	24	9	188	215	97	38	92	12	10	.545	2	2	4.64
Jim Lindsey	2	0	0	$4\frac{2}{3}$	1	1	1	1	2	0	0	0	1.93		39	6	3	106	131	52	46	50	7	5	.583	5	0	4.42
Flint Rhem	1	1	0	$3\frac{1}{3}$	7	6	4	2	3	0	1	0	10.80		26	19	9	140	173	69	37	47	12	8	.600	0	0	4.44
Hi Bell	1	0	0	1	0	0	0	0	0	0	0	0	0.00		39	9	2	115	143	50	23	42	4	3	.571	**8**	0	3.91
Al Grabowski	Did not play														33	8	1	106	121	57	50	45	6	4	.600	1	0	4.84
team total	6	6	4	51	35	21	19	24	32	2	4	0	3.35		154	154	63	1380	1595	674	477	**641**	**92**	62	**.597**	**21**	5	4.40

Total Attendance—212,619 Average Attendance—35,437 Winning Player's Share—$5,038 Losing Player's Share—$3,537

1931
Peppering the Opposition

The man on the street hustling to try to make a living could identify with Pepper Martin. A stocky 5′ 8″ outfielder from rural Oklahoma, Martin grabbed at everything with a Depression type of despair. Making up for a limited store of talent with an endless pool of effort, he stole bases with headfirst slides on his stomach, and he stood up against pitchers bigger in size than he was and hit .300 in his first full season in the majors. His craggy face and dirty uniform made this twenty-seven-year-old buccaneer a crowd favorite, and, together with hitters Frankie Frisch, Chick Hafey, and Jim Bottomley, easily helped the St. Louis Cardinals to a repeat National League pennant by 13 games over the Giants. Jimmie Foxx, Al Simmons, Mickey Cochrane and Mule Haas did likewise for the Philadelphia Athletics in the American League. This quartet, plus the pitching arms of Lefty Grove and George Earnshaw, branded the A's as favorites to repeat their Series victory of last year. Martin's regular-season exploits, at least according to the experts, would carry little weight in the Series.

But Martin outshone everyone, turning the Series into a stage for his baseball dramatics. The opening day crowd at Sportsman's Park in St. Louis saw the Cardinals lose to the A's and Lefty Grove 6–2, but Martin gave the fans something to cheer about with two singles, a double, and a stolen base. His individual exploits couldn't salvage game one, but the brash Pepper took a direct hand in winning game two 2–0. Both George Earnshaw and Bill Hallahan pitched splendid ball, but Hallahan lucked out in having Martin on his side. Pepper stretched a routine single into a double with a belly slide in the second inning, then stole third just ahead of Cochrane's throw, and came home on Jimmie Wilson's fly to center. He reached first on a single in the seventh inning and started moving again. He stole second, went to third on an infield out, and dived across home plate on a squeeze bunt by Charlie Gelbert.

Pepper had gone 5-for-7 and stolen three bases in St. Louis, and the fans in Philadelphia gave him a hand before the third game. Thus encouraged, he led his mates to a 5–2 victory to go ahead in the Series. Against Grove, who was pitching on three days of rest because of a rain-out the day before, Martin went 2-for-4 and scored twice. Helping Martin slightly with the victory was thirty-seven-year-old Burleigh Grimes, whose legal spitball moved well enough to limit the A's to only two hits. Earnshaw returned the compliment to the Cards with a two-hitter in game four for a 3–0 victory, but Martin kept in high gear with both St. Louis hits and another stolen base. Cardinal manager Gabby Street brought back his ace Bill Hallahan in game five, while Connie Mack rested Grove and Earnshaw and tried Waite Hoyt, the former Yankee star, on the mound. Hallahan scattered nine hits and allowed one run, while Hoyt and two relievers had to deal with Martin. He beat out a bunt in the fourth inning, smacked a home run in the sixth inning, singled in the eighth inning, and drove in four runs in a 5–1 St. Louis triumph. Pepper was the toast of the country with a 12-for-18 batting record, and the Cards were riding high with a 3–2 edge in games, going back to St. Louis for the final two.

Martin stopped hitting in game six, and the Cardinals lost. He went 0-for-3 against Lefty Grove and could not prevent an 8–1 loss which threw the Series into a deciding seventh game. Martin again went hitless, but the other Cardinal hitters took up the slack. The Cards scratched across two runs against Earnshaw in the bottom of the first, then added two more in the third on George Watkins's home run. Burleigh Grimes stingily protected this 4–0 lead until he ran out of gas in the top of the ninth. A pinch single by Doc Cramer scored two runs, and with two men on and two outs, manager Street lifted Grimes and called in Hallahan to get the last out. He faced scrappy second baseman Max Bishop, who socked a low liner to center. With the ball apparently dropping in for a hit, Pepper Martin tore in and gloved it for the final out of the Series. His offensive statistics for the seven games included a .500 batting average with 12 hits and 5 stolen bases. This Series made a national hero out of him, and it also marked the last fall classic for another baseball great, Connie Mack.

Phi.   004 000 200
St L. 200 000 000

Game 1 October 1 at St. Louis

Philadelphia	Pos	AB	R	H	RBI	PO	A	E
Bishop	2b	5	1	1	0	0	3	0
Haas	cf	5	1	1	1	2	0	0
Cochrane	c	4	2	2	0	7	0	0
Simmons	lf	4	1	1	3	3	0	0
Foxx	1b	4	0	2	2	9	0	0
Miller	rf	4	0	0	0	0	0	0
Dykes	3b	3	0	2	0	1	1	0
Williams	ss	4	1	2	0	2	5	0
Grove	p	4	0	0	0	0	0	0
Totals		37	6	11	6	27	9	0

Pitching	IP	H	R	ER	BB	SO
Philadelphia						
Grove (W)	9	12	2	2	0	7
St. Louis						
Derringer (L)	7	11	6	6	3	9
Johnson	2	0	0	0	0	2

St. Louis	Pos	AB	R	H	RBI	PO	A	E
High	3b	4	0	1	0	0	1	0
c Mancuso		1	0	0	0	0	0	0
Roettger	rf	5	1	2	0	1	0	0
Frisch	2b	4	0	2	0	5	1	0
Bottomley	1b	4	0	1	1	6	1	0
Hafey	lf	4	0	1	0	3	0	0
Martin	cf	4	0	3	1	2	0	0
Wilson	c	4	0	0	0	12	2	0
Gelbert	ss	4	0	2	0	1	5	0
Derringer	p	2	0	0	0	0	0	0
a Flowers		1	0	0	0	0	0	0
Johnson	p	0	0	0	0	0	0	0
b Blades		1	0	0	0	0	0	0
Totals		38	2	12	2	27	10	0

a Grounded out for Derringer in 7th.
b Struck out for Johnson in 9th.
c Fouled out for High in 9th.

Doubles—Gelbert, Haas, Martin. Home Run—Simmons. Stolen Bases—Hafey, Martin. Double Plays—Bottomley (unassisted), Bishop to Williams to Foxx. Left on Bases—Philadelphia 7, St. Louis 9. Umpires—Klem (N), Nallin (A), Stark (N), McGowan (A). Attendance—38,529. Time of Game—1:55.

1st Inning
Philadelphia
1 Bishop struck out.
2 Haas struck out.
3 Cochrane grounded to short.
St. Louis
1 High struck out.
Roettger lined a single over second.
Frisch singled along the right field foul line, Roettger going to third.
Bottomley beat out an infield bouncer over Grove's head, Roettger scoring with Frisch stopping at second.
2 Hafey struck out.
Martin doubled to right, Frisch scoring with Bottomley stopping at third.
3 Wilson grounded to short.

2nd Inning
Philadelphia
1 Simmons grounded to short.
2 Foxx took a called third strike.
3 Miller struck out.
St. Louis
1 Gelbert flied to deep right.
2 Derringer bounced to short.
High bounced a single to right.
3 Roettger flied to Haas in deep right-center.

3rd Inning
Philadelphia
Dykes beat out a high bouncer to third.
Williams singled to right, Dykes going to third.
1 Grove struck out.
2 Bishop safe as Dykes was run down trying to score, Bottomley to Wilson to High to Wilson, Williams stopping at second.
Haas doubled, Williams scoring with Bishop stopping at third.
Cochrane walked, loading the bases.
Simmons walked, forcing in Bishop.
Foxx singled to center, scoring Haas and Cochrane with Simmons stopping at second.
3 Miller grounded out, Wilson to Bottomley.
St. Louis
1 Frisch flied to deep right.
2 Bottomley flied to short right.
3 Hafey struck out.

4th Inning
Philadelphia
Dykes singled on a Texas Leaguer.
1 Williams struck out.
2 Grove again struck out.
Bishop singled to right, Dykes stopping at second.
3 Haas grounded to second.
St. Louis
Martin singled over Williams' head.
1,2 Wilson hit into a double play, Bishop to Williams to Foxx.
Gelbert singled to center.
3 Derringer struck out.

5th Inning
Philadelphia
Cochrane singled to right-center.
1 Simmons took a called third strike.
2 Foxx forced Cochrane at second, Gelbert to Frisch.
3 Miller forced Foxx at second, Gelbert to Frisch.
St. Louis
1 High flied to left.
2 Roettger struck out.
3 Frisch grounded to second.

6th Inning
Philadelphia
Dykes walked.
Williams beat out a bunt to the mound, Dykes going to second.
1 Grove called out on strikes, his third consecutive strikeout.
2,3 Bishop lined into a double play, Bottomley unassisted.
St. Louis
1 Bottomley grounded to Williams making a remarkable play.
Hafey singled to center.
Martin singled into the hole between second and third, Hafey stopping at second. (Martin's third hit.)
2 Wilson flied to left.
Hafey stole third, while Dykes was arguing the call, Martin stole second as time was not called.
3 Gelbert grounded to short.

7th Inning
Philadelphia
1 Haas popped to second.
Cochrane singled to right.
Simmons hit a two-run homer high into the left field bleachers.
Foxx singled when his liner bounced off the rubber into center field.
2 Miller forced Foxx at second, Gelbert to Frisch.
3 Dykes flied to very deep center.
St. Louis
1 Flowers, pinch-hitting for Derringer, bounced to third.
2 High fouled to Dykes.
Roettger singled to center.
Frisch hit a Texas League single into short right-center, Roettger racing to third.
3 Bottomley rolled out to second.

8th Inning
Philadelphia
For St. Louis—Johnson now pitching.
1 Williams struck out.
2 Grove flied to right.
3 Bishop popped to second.
St. Louis
1 Hafey popped to short.
2 Martin took a called third strike.
3 Wilson flied deep to Simmons who made a spectacular leaping catch against the fence.

9th Inning
Philadelphia
1 Haas flied to center.
2 Cochrane fouled to Gelbert.
3 Simmons struck out.
St. Louis
Gelbert doubled to left center hitting the bleacher fence on the first bounce.
1 Blades, batting for Johnson, struck out.
2 Mancuso, batting for High, fouled to Foxx near the right field boxes.
3 Roettger flied to deep center.

Game 2 October 2 at St. Louis

Philadelphia	Pos	AB	R	H	RBI	PO	A	E
Bishop	2b	5	0	0	0	1	5	0
Haas	cf	4	0	1	0	5	0	0
Cochrane	c	2	0	0	0	5	0	0
Simmons	lf	4	0	0	0	1	0	0
Foxx	1b	2	0	1	0	11	1	0
Miller	rf	4	0	1	0	0	0	0
Dykes	3b	2	0	0	0	0	2	0
Williams	ss	2	0	0	0	1	2	0
Earnshaw	p	3	0	0	0	0	2	0
a Moore		1	0	0	0	0	0	0
Totals		29	0	3	0	24	12	0

a Struck out but safe at first on error
for Earnshaw in 9th.

Doubles—Frisch, Martin, Watkins. Stolen
Bases—Martin 2. Sacrifice Hits—Dykes,
Gelbert, Hallahan. Double Play—Frisch
to Gelbert to Bottomley. Wild
Pitch—Hallahan. Left on Bases—
Philadelphia 10, St. Louis 6.
Umpires—Nallin, Stark, McGowan, Klem.
Attendance—35,947. Time of Game—1:49.

	Phi.	000 000 000
	St L.	010 000 10x

St. Louis	Pos	AB	R	H	RBI	PO	A	E
Flowers	3b	4	0	0	0	2	1	0
Watkins	rf	4	0	2	0	1	0	0
Frisch	2b	4	0	1	0	4	4	0
Bottomley	1b	3	0	0	0	7	0	0
Hafey	lf	4	0	0	0	4	0	0
Martin	cf	3	1	1	0	2	0	0
Wilson	c	3	0	1	0	7	0	1
Gelbert	ss	2	0	1	1	2	3	0
Hallahan	p	2	0	0	0	0	0	0
Totals		29	2	6	2	27	8	1

Pitching	IP	H	R	ER	BB	SO
Philadelphia						
Earnshaw (L)	8	6	2	2	1	5
St. Louis						
Hallahan (W)	9	3	0	0	7	8

1st Inning
Philadelphia
1 Bishop grounded to second.
2 Haas struck out.
3 Cochrane struck out.
St. Louis
1 Flowers grounded to second.
 Watkins doubled on a Texas Leaguer
 to center, getting second on
 excellent base-running.
2 Frisch flied to center.
3 Bottomley flied to center.

2nd Inning
Philadelphia
1 Simmons lined to deep left.
2 Foxx grounded to second.
3 Miller struck out.
St. Louis
1 Hafey bounced back to the mound.
 Martin doubled over Dykes' head
 as Simmons slipped trying to
 field the ball.
 Martin stole third.
2 Wilson flied to deep center,
 Martin scoring after the catch.
 Gelbert singled to right-center.
3 Hallahan struck out.

3rd Inning
Philadelphia
1 Dykes popped to Flowers on the left
 field grass.
2 Williams struck out.
3 Earnshaw rolled slowly to second.
St. Louis
1 Flowers flied to deep center.
 Watkins got a single on a blooper
 to short center.
2 Frisch popped to short.
3 Bottomley's grounder deflected off
 Earnshaw's glove to Bishop who threw
 Bottomley out at first.

4th Inning
Philadelphia
1 Bishop fouled to Flowers.
2 Haas flied to left.
 Cochrane walked, the first A's
 base-runner in the game.
3 Simmons forced Cochrane at second,
 Gelbert to Frisch.
St. Louis
1 Hafey struck out.
2 Martin grounded to third.
3 Wilson grounded to short.

5th Inning
Philadelphia
1 Foxx walked.
 Miller singled to right (the A's first
 hit), as Foxx stopped at second.
 Dykes sacrificed up both runners being
 tagged out by Bottomley.
 Williams intentionally walked, loading
 the bases.
2,3 Earnshaw hit into a double play,
 Frisch to Gelbert to Bottomley.
St. Louis
1 Gelbert bounced to first.
2 Hallahan took a called third strike.
3 Flowers fouled to Foxx.

6th Inning
Philadelphia
1 Bishop struck out.
 Haas lined a single just out of
 Gelbert's reach, into left.
2 Cochrane flied to deep right.
3 Simmons forced Haas at second,
 Flowers to Frisch.
St. Louis
1 Watkins, rolled to second.
 Frisch doubled just inside the
 third base line.
2 Bottomley struck out.
3 Hafey grounded to third.

7th Inning
Philadelphia
 Foxx lined a single to right-center.
1 Miller forced Foxx at second, Gelbert
 to Frisch.
2 Dykes fouled to Bottomley at the A's
 dugout.
 Williams walked.
 Miller went to third on a wild
 pitch as Williams held first.
3 Earnshaw struck out.
St. Louis
 Martin singled to left.
 Martin stole second.
1 Wilson grounded to second, Martin
 going to third.
 Gelbert sacrifice squeezed Martin in
 beating Earnshaw's throw to Cochrane.
2 Hallahan sacrificed Gelbert to second,
 Foxx to Williams missing Gelbert back
 to Bishop, covering first.
3 Flowers rolled out to second.

8th Inning
Philadelphia
1 Bishop popped to second.
2 Haas flied to left.
 Cochrane walked.
3 Simmons popped to Gelbert in short left.
St. Louis
1 Watkins struck out.
2 Frisch flied to Simmons, who made a
 fantastic one-handed leaping catch at
 the bleacher wall.
 Bottomley walked.
3 Hafey flied to Haas in deep left-center.

9th Inning
Philadelphia
 Foxx walked.
1 Miller flied to left.
 Dykes walked.
2 Williams took a called third strike.
 Moore, batting for Earnshaw, apparently
 missed a third strike but a big rhubarb
 began when Umpire Nallin declared the
 pitched ball had hit the ground before
 Wilson scooped it up. Wilson was
 charged with an error. On the play
 Moore was declared safe when he ran to
 first because of Wilson's error.
3 Bishop fouled to Bottomley, who made a
 sensational catch diving head first over
 the Athletics' bull pen bench.

Game 3 October 5 at Philadelphia

St. Louis	Pos	AB	R	H	RBI	PO	A	E
Adams	3b	3	0	0	0	0	1	0
Flowers	3b	1	0	0	0	1	0	0
Roettger	rf	5	0	1	0	1	0	0
b Watkins	rf	0	1	0	0	0	0	0
Frisch	2b	5	0	1	0	4	3	0
Bottomley	1b	4	1	1	1	11	0	0
Hafey	lf	5	1	1	1	4	0	0
Martin	cf	4	2	2	0	2	0	0
Wilson	c	4	0	3	1	5	0	0
Gelbert	ss	4	0	1	1	1	6	0
Grimes	p	4	0	2	0	2	0	0
Totals		39	5	12	5	27	12	0

Pitching	IP	H	R	ER	BB	SO
St. Louis						
Grimes (W)	9	2	2	2	4	5
Philadelphia						
Grove (L)	8	11	4	2	1	2
Mahaffey	1	1	1	1	0	0

1st Inning
St. Louis
1 Adams popped to Foxx.
2 Roettger grounded to second.
3 Frisch grounded to first.
Philadelphia
1 Bishop took a called third strike.
2 Haas popped to Frisch in short center.
3 Cochrane fouled to Roettger near the
 stands.

2nd Inning
St. Louis
 Bottomley walked.
1 Hafey fouled to Foxx.
 Martin lined a single over second,
 Bottomley going to third.
 Wilson singled to right, Bottomley
 scoring as Martin went to third.
2 Gelbert lined to right, Martin
 scoring after the catch.
 Grimes dribbled a single between
 short and third, Williams stopping
 at second.
3 Adams struck out.
Philadelphia
1 Simmons flied to Martin in left-center.
2 Foxx rolled out to short.
3 Miller bounced to short.

3rd Inning
St. Louis
1 Roettger grounded to short.
2 Frisch, grounded out on a bouncer over
 Grove's head, Williams coming in fast
 and with a perfect throw to Foxx, just
 beat Frisch at first.
3 Bottomley grounded to second.
Philadelphia
1 Dykes grounded to second.
2 Williams popped to Gelbert in left.
3 Grove bounced to first.

4th Inning
St. Louis
 Hafey singled to center.
 Martin doubled off the scoreboard in
 right-center, missing a home run by
 just inches as Hafey stopped at third.
1 Wilson grounded to third, both runners
 holding their bases.
2 Gelbert took a called third strike.
 Grimes singled to right, scoring Hafey
 and Martin.
3 Adams popped to Bishop in right.
Philadelphia
 Bishop walked, becoming the A's first
 base runner.
1 Haas flied to left.
2 Cochrane called out on strikes.
3 Simmons grounded to second.

5th Inning
St. Louis
1 Roettger grounded to short.
2 Frisch grounded to second.
3 Bottomley flied to left.
Philadelphia
 Foxx walked.
1 Miller forced Foxx at second,
 Adams to Frisch.
2,3 Dykes grounded into a double play,
 Gelbert to Frisch to Bottomley.

	St L.	020 200 001
	Phi.	000 000 002

Philadelphia	Pos	AB	R	H	RBI	PO	A	E
Bishop	2b	3	0	0	0	2	3	0
Haas	cf	4	0	0	0	0	0	0
Cochrane	c	3	0	0	0	2	0	0
c McNair		0	1	0	0	0	0	0
Simmons	lf	4	1	1	2	3	0	0
Foxx	1b	2	0	0	0	16	0	0
Miller	rf	3	0	1	0	2	0	0
Dykes	3b	3	0	0	0	1	4	0
Williams	ss	3	0	0	0	1	6	0
Grove	p	2	0	0	0	0	1	0
a Cramer		1	0	0	0	0	0	0
Mahaffey	p	0	0	0	0	0	1	0
Totals		28	2	2	2	27	14	0

a Popped out for Grove in 8th.
b Ran for Roettger in 9th.
c Ran for Cochrane in 9th.

Doubles—Bottomley, Martin, Roettger.
Home Run—Simmons. Double Play—Gelbert
to Frisch to Bottomley. Left on
Bases—St. Louis 9, Philadelphia 3.
Umpires—Stark, McGowan, Klem, Nallin.
Attendance—32,295. Time of Game—2:10.

6th Inning
St. Louis
1 Hafey grounded to third.
2 Martin grounded to short.
 Wilson singled to right.
3 Gelbert flied to right.
Philadelphia
 For St. Louis—Flowers replaced Adams,
 who had injured his ankle.
1 Williams struck out.
2 Grove took a called third strike.
3 Bishop flied to center.

7th Inning
St. Louis
1 Grimes grounded to short.
2 Flowers grounded to short.
 Roettger doubled into right-center.
 Frisch singled to right, Roettger only
 getting to third.
3 Bottomley popped to second.
Philadelphia
1 Haas bounced out, Grimes to Bottomley.
2 Cochrane bounced to deep short.
3 Simmons grounded to short.

8th Inning
St. Louis
1 Hafey lined to a diving Dykes at
 third.
2 Martin grounded to third.
 Wilson beat out a perfect bunt
 towards third (his third hit of
 the game).
 Gelbert singled over Williams' head,
 Wilson stopping at second.
3 Grimes lined to deep left.
Philadelphia
 Foxx walked.
 Miller got a clean single to center,
 Foxx taking second. Miller's hit
 broke up Grimes' no-hitter.
1 Dykes popped to third.
2 Williams flied to left.
3 Cramer, batting for Grove, lined to a
 leaping Frisch on the right field
 grass.

9th Inning
St. Louis
 For Philadelphia—Mahaffey pitching.
 Flowers grounded out.
1 Roettger bunted into a force out at
 second, Mahaffey to Williams.
 Watkins, running for Roettger.
2 Frisch bounced out to third, Watkins
 going to second.
 Bottomley doubled to right-center,
 scoring Watkins.
3 Hafey flied to deep left.
Philadelphia
 For St. Louis—Watkins playing right.
1 Bishop grounded to first.
2 Haas grounded out off Grimes' bare
 hand to Gelbert to Bottomley.
 Cochrane walked.
 McNair, ran for Cochrane.
 Simmons hit a two-run homer over the
 right field wall.
3 Foxx struck out.

Game 4 October 6 at Philadelphia

St. Louis	Pos	AB	R	H	RBI	PO	A	E
Flowers	3b	1	0	0	0	0	1	0
High	3b	3	0	0	0	0	1	0
Watkins	rf	4	0	0	0	2	0	0
Frisch	2b	3	0	0	0	1	2	0
Bottomley	1b	3	0	0	0	7	0	1
Hafey	lf	3	0	0	0	0	0	0
Martin	cf	3	0	2	0	4	0	0
Wilson	c	3	0	0	0	6	0	0
Gelbert	ss	3	0	0	0	4	4	0
Johnson	p	2	0	0	0	0	1	0
Lindsey	p	0	0	0	0	0	0	0
a Collins		1	0	0	0	0	0	0
Derringer	p	0	0	0	0	0	0	0
Totals		29	0	2	0	24	10	1

a Struck out for Lindsey in 8th.

Doubles—Martin, Miller, Simmons. Home Run—Foxx. Stolen Bases—Frisch, Martin. Sacrifice Hit—Haas. Double Play—Frisch to Gelbert to Bottomley. Left on Bases—St. Louis 3, Philadelphia 8. Umpires—McGowan, Klem, Nallin, Stark. Attendance—32,295. Time of Game—1:58.

1st Inning
St. Louis
1 Flowers flied to right.
2 Watkins popped back to the pitcher.
3 Frisch lined to left.
Philadelphia
  Bishop lined a single over second.
1 Haas sacrificed Bishop to second, Flowers to Bottomley.
2 Cochrane bounced to first, Bishop going to third.
  Simmons doubled off the pavilion wall in left-center, scoring Bishop.
  Foxx walked.
3 Miller fouled to Wilson.

2nd Inning
St. Louis
1 Bottomley fouled to Foxx.
2 Hafey grounded to third.
3 Martin struck out.
Philadelphia
  For St. Louis—High replaced Flowers at third.
  Dykes singled to left-center.
1 Williams struck out.
2 Earnshaw grounded back to the mound, Dykes going to second.
3 Bishop lined to Martin just catching the ball before it hit the ground.

3rd Inning
St. Louis
1 Wilson flied to left.
2 Gelbert rolled to first.
3 Johnson fanned.
Philadelphia
  Haas lined a single over Frisch, who just touched the ball as it went into right.
1 Cochrane forced Haas at second, Frisch to Gelbert but Cochrane was safe when Bottomley lost Gelbert's throw for an error as Cochrane was easily beaten.
2,3 Simmons hit into a double play, Frisch to Gelbert to Bottomley.

4th Inning
St. Louis
1 High's liner was knocked down by Earnshaw and he had plenty of time to throw to first.
2 Watkins lined to right.
  Frisch walked to become the first Cardinal base-runner, walking on a full count.
  Frisch stole second.
3 Bottomley struck out.
Philadelphia
1 Foxx grounded to short.
2 Miller popped to short.
3 Dykes grounded to third.

(Game 4 — continued, right column)

St. L.			
St L.	000	000	000
Phi.	100	002	00x

Philadelphia	Pos	AB	R	H	RBI	PO	A	E
Bishop	2b	4	1	2	0	0	0	0
Haas	cf	3	0	1	0	1	0	0
Cochrane	c	3	1	0	0	9	0	0
Simmons	lf	4	0	2	1	5	0	0
Foxx	1b	3	1	1	1	7	0	0
Miller	rf	4	0	2	1	4	0	0
Dykes	3b	4	0	2	1	0	1	0
Williams	ss	4	0	1	0	1	1	0
Earnshaw	p	3	0	0	0	0	3	0
Totals		32	3	10	3	27	5	0

Pitching	IP	H	R	ER	BB	SO
St. Louis						
Johnson (L)	5⅔	9	3	3	1	2
Lindsey	1⅓	1	0	0	1	2
Derringer	1	0	0	0	0	1
Philadelphia						
Earnshaw (W)	9	2	0	0	1	8

5th Inning
St. Louis
1. Hafey grounded to short.
  Martin got the first hit off of Earnshaw, a low liner to left.
2 Wilson struck out.
  Martin stole second.
3 Gelbert struck out.
Philadelphia
1 Williams struck out.
2 Earnshaw popped to short.
  Bishop singled off Bottomley's chest.
3 Haas forced Bishop at second, Gelbert to Frisch.

6th Inning
St. Louis
1 Johnson struck out.
2 High tapped back to the mound.
3 Watkins flied to Simmons in short left-center.
Philadelphia
1 Cochrane lined to Martin in right-center.
2 Simmons flied to Martin in deep right-center.
  Foxx boomed a homer over the second tier of the left field pavilion.
  Miller lined a double off the scoreboard in right-center.
  Dykes singled to left, scoring Miller.
  Williams singled to left, Dykes stopping at second.
  For St. Louis—Lindsey came in to pitch.
3 Earnshaw struck out.

7th Inning
St. Louis
1 Frisch out on a bunt back to the mound.
2 Bottomley struck out.
3 Hafey flied to right.
Philadelphia
1 Bishop flied to right.
2 Haas struck out.
  Cochrane walked.
  Simmons singled to center, Cochrane sliding safely into third, as Simmons took second on the play.
3 Foxx flied high and deep to center.

8th Inning
St. Louis
  Martin doubled close to the left field pavilion wall (his and the Cards' second hit).
1 Wilson flied to short right.
2 Gelbert fouled to Cochrane.
3 Collins, pinch-hitting for Lindsey, struck out.
Philadelphia
  For St. Louis—Derringer pitching.
1 Miller struck out.
2 Dykes bounced back to the mound.
3 Williams flied to right.

9th Inning
St. Louis
1 High flied to an on-rushing Simmons.
2 Watkins flied to right.
3 Frisch flied to left.

Game 5 October 7 at Philadelphia

St. Louis	Pos	AB	R	H	RBI	PO	A	E
Adams	3b	1	0	1	0	0	0	0
a High	3b	4	1	0	0	2	3	0
Watkins	rf	3	1	0	0	3	0	0
Frisch	2b	4	1	3	4	6	1	0
Martin	cf	4	1	3	4	3	0	0
Hafey	lf	4	1	0	1	0	0	0
Bottomley	1b	4	1	2	0	7	1	0
Wilson	c	4	0	2	0	7	0	0
Gelbert	ss	4	0	1	1	1	2	0
Hallahan	p	4	0	0	0	0	0	0
Totals		36	5	12	5	27	7	0

Pitching	IP	H	R	ER	BB	SO
St. Louis						
Hallahan (W)	9	9	1	1	1	4
Philadelphia						
Hoyt (L)	6	7	3	3	0	1
Walberg	2	2	1	1	1	2
Rommel	1	3	1	1	0	0

1st Inning
St. Louis
  Adams singled over third.
  High pinch-ran for Adams, whose injured leg again gave out on him.
1 Watkins flied to left.
  Frisch singled to left-center, High racing to third beating Haas' throw as Frisch raced over to second on the play.
2 Martin flied to Simmons, two steps from the wall, High scoring after the catch.
3 Hafey grounded to deep short.
Philadelphia
  For St. Louis—High stays in at third.
1 Bishop flied to Watkins in short right-center.
2 Haas struck out.
3 Cochrane popped to Frisch behind the pitcher's mound.

2nd Inning
St. Louis
  Bottomley lined a single to right.
1 Wilson flied to Miller in short right-center.
2 Gelbert forced Bottomley at second, Williams to Bishop.
3 Hallahan grounded to short.
Philadelphia
  Simmons doubled off the right center field scoreboard.
1 Foxx grounded to third, Simmons holding second.
2,3 Miller's high bouncer was fielded by Gelbert who threw to Bottomley for the out and he threw to Wilson to nab Simmons trying to score.

3rd Inning
St. Louis
1 High grounded to second.
2 Watkins flied to Bishop in short right.
3 Frisch flied to center.
Philadelphia
1 Dykes grounded to first.
2 Williams fouled to High.
3 Hoyt bounced to third.

4th Inning
St. Louis
  Martin beat out a bunt to first (his tenth hit of the Series).
1 Hafey struck out.
  Bottomley singled to right, Martin racing to third.
2,3 Wilson lined to Bishop who threw to Foxx, doubling Bottomley off of first.
Philadelphia
1 Bishop popped to Bottomley in right, who held the ball after colliding with Frisch.
2 Haas lined to left.
3 Cochrane fouled to Wilson.

5th Inning
St. Louis
1 Gelbert grounded to third.
2 Hallahan grounded to short.
3 High lined to left.
Philadelphia
  Simmons singled to left, the ball bouncing off Hallahan's shin.
  Foxx walked.
1 Miller fouled to Bottomley.
2 Dykes fouled to Bottomley.
3 Williams struck out.

6th Inning
St. Louis
1 Watkins flied to short right.
  Frisch lined a double over third.
  Martin hit a two-run homer into the upper tier of the left field pavilion.
2 Hafey flied to left.
3 Bottomley flied to Haas in short right-center.

(Game 5 — continued, right column)

St. L.			
St L.	100	002	011
Phi.	000	000	100

Philadelphia	Pos	AB	R	H	RBI	PO	A	E
Bishop	2b	2	0	0	0	3	2	0
b McNair	2b	2	0	0	0	1	1	0
Haas	cf	2	0	0	0	2	0	0
c Moore	lf	2	0	1	0	0	0	0
Cochrane	c	4	0	1	0	3	2	0
Simmons	lf–cf	4	1	3	0	5	0	0
Foxx	1b	3	0	2	0	8	1	0
Miller	rf	4	0	1	2	0	0	0
Dykes	3b	4	0	1	0	0	1	0
Williams	ss	4	0	1	0	2	5	0
Hoyt	p	2	0	0	0	0	0	0
Walberg	p	0	0	0	0	0	0	0
d Heving		1	0	0	0	0	0	0
Rommel	p	0	0	0	0	0	0	0
e Boley		1	0	0	0	0	0	0
Totals		35	1	9	1	27	12	0

a Ran for Adams in 1st.
b Fouled out for Bishop in 6th.
c Flied out for Haas in 6th.
d Flied out for Walberg in 8th.
e Struck out for Rommel in 9th.

Doubles—Frisch, Simmons. Home Run—Martin. Stolen Base—Watkins. Double Plays—Bishop to Foxx, Gelbert to Bottomley to Wilson. Left on Bases—St. Louis 5, Philadelphia 8. Umpires—Klem, Nallin, Stark, McGowan. Attendance—32,295. Time of Game—1:56.

6th Inning (continued)
Philadelphia
1 Hoyt popped to second.
2 McNair, batting for Bishop, fouled to Wilson.
3 Moore, pinch-hitting for Haas, flied to right.

7th Inning
St. Louis
  For Philadelphia—Simmons moves to center, Moore in playing right and McNair in to play second, as Walberg came in to pitch.
  Wilson singled to left.
1 Wilson was out trying to steal second, Cochrane to Williams.
2 Gelbert grounded to short.
3 Hallahan took a called third strike.
Philadelphia
1 Cochrane popped to second.
  Simmons lined a single to left-center, his third straight hit.
  Foxx bounced a single off Hallahan's hip the ball going to right, Simmons going to third.
2 Miller forced Foxx at second, High to Frisch as Simmons scored.
  Dykes beat out a single to third, Miller stopping at second.
3 Williams flied to Frisch in right-center.

8th Inning
St. Louis
1 High took a called third strike.
  Watkins walked.
  Watkins stole second.
2 Frisch fouled to Moore.
  Martin singled to left, scoring Watkins.
  Martin's twelfth hit ties the Series record held by 3 men.
3 Martin was caught stealing for the first time in the Series, Cochrane to McNair.
Philadelphia
1 Heving, batting for Walberg, flied to right.
2 McNair fanned.
  Moore bounced a high single toward third as Hallahan could not make a play.
  Cochrane singled off Bottomley's shoulder, Moore taking second.
3 Simmons forced Moore at third, High unassisted.

9th Inning
St. Louis
  For Philadelphia—Rommel now pitching.
  Hafey beat out an infield hit.
1 Bottomley forced Hafey at second, Foxx to Williams.
  Wilson singled to center, Bottomley going to third.
  Gelbert singled to left, Bottomley scoring as Wilson stopped at second.
2 Hallahan flied to center.
3 High grounded to second.
Philadelphia
  Foxx beat out a bunt in front of the plate.
1 Miller forced Foxx at second, Gelbert to Frisch.
2 Dykes forced Miller at second, Frisch to Gelbert.
  Williams got a Texas League single into short center, Dykes racing to third.
3 Boley, batting for Rommel, struck out.

Game 6 October 9 at St. Louis

| Phi. | 000 040 400 |
| St L. | 000 001 000 |

Philadelphia	Pos	AB	R	H	RBI	PO	A	E
Bishop	2b	4	2	1	0	4	4	0
Haas	cf	2	0	0	1	5	0	0
Cochrane	c	5	0	1	1	6	0	1
Simmons	lf	4	1	1	2	0	0	0
Foxx	1b	5	2	2	0	7	0	0
Miller	rf	3	1	1	0	1	0	0
Dykes	3b	3	1	0	1	1	0	0
Williams	ss	4	1	2	1	1	3	0
Grove	p	4	0	0	0	0	0	0
Totals		34	8	8	6	27	7	1

Pitching	IP	H	R	ER	BB	SO
Philadelphia						
Grove (W)	9	5	1	1	1	7
St. Louis						
Derringer (L)	4⅓	3	4	0	4	4
Johnson	1⅓	1	0	0	0	2
Lindsey	2	3	4	2	2	0
Rhem	1	1	0	0	0	1

St. Louis	Pos	AB	R	H	RBI	PO	A	E
Flowers	3b	4	1	1	0	0	2	1
Roettger	rf	4	0	1	0	2	0	0
Frisch	2b	4	0	1	1	1	4	0
Martin	cf	3	0	0	0	1	0	0
Hafey	lf	4	0	1	0	1	0	1
Bottomley	1b	4	0	0	0	11	0	0
Wilson	c	3	0	0	0	6	0	0
Mancuso	c	0	0	0	0	2	0	0
Gelbert	ss	3	0	1	0	3	5	0
Derringer	p	0	0	0	0	0	1	0
Johnson	p	0	0	0	0	0	0	0
a Blades		1	0	0	0	0	0	0
Lindsey	p	0	0	0	0	0	0	0
b Collins		1	0	0	0	0	0	0
Rhem	p	0	0	0	0	0	0	0
Totals		31	1	5	1	27	12	2

a Struck out for Johnson in 6th.
b Grounded out for Lindsey in 8th.

Doubles—Flowers, Williams. Sacrifice Hits—Derringer, Haas, Miller. Double Plays—Bishop to Williams to Foxx, Frisch to Gelbert to Bottomley. Hit by Pitcher—Miller (by Lindsey). Wild Pitch—Derringer. Left on Bases—Philadelphia 8, St. Louis 5. Umpires—Nallin, Stark, McGowan, Klem. Attendance—39,401. Time of Game—1:57.

1st Inning
Philadelphia
1 Bishop called out on strikes.
2 Haas grounded to short.
3 Cochrane lined to short.
St. Louis
1 Flowers grounded to second.
Roettger lined a single to center.
2,3 Frisch grounded into a double play, Bishop to Williams to Foxx.

2nd Inning
Philadelphia
1 Simmons bounced to second.
Foxx singled to right.
2 Miller forced Foxx at second, Gelbert to Frisch.
Miller went to second on a wild pitch.
3 Dykes grounded to third.
St. Louis
1 Martin fouled to Foxx.
2 Hafey flied to short center.
3 Bottomley lined to very deep right.

3rd Inning
Philadelphia
1 Williams grounded to short.
2 Grove called out on strikes.
3 Bishop lined to Roettger, making a desperate one-handed catch against the wall.
St. Louis
1 Wilson, flied to center.
Gelbert's liner fell for a single in short center.
2 Derringer sacrificed Gelbert to second on a fantastic stop and throw by Bishop to Foxx.
3 Flowers grounded to short.

4th Inning
Philadelphia
1 Haas took a called third strike.
2 Cochrane grounded to second.
3 Simmons lined to Roettger in right-center.
St. Louis
1 Roettger struck out.
2 Frisch struck out.
3 Martin lined to center.

5th Inning
Philadelphia
Foxx safe at first when Flowers after fielding his easy grounder, threw wildly to first.
1 Miller sacrificed Foxx to second, Derringer to Bottomley.
Dykes walked.
Williams singled to right-center, Foxx scoring with Dykes stopping at second.
2 Grove again struck out.
Bishop walked, loading the bases.
Haas also walked, forcing in Dykes with a run.
Cochrane lined a single to right off of Frisch's glove, scoring Williams.
Simmons walked on a full count, Bishop scoring.
For St. Louis—Johnson replaced Derringer on the mound.
3 Foxx popped to Gelbert in short left.
St. Louis
Hafey singled to second even though Bishop made a good bare-handed stop.
1 Bottomley popped to Dykes near the pitcher's box.
2 Wilson lined to second.
3 Gelbert popped to second.

6th Inning
Philadelphia
1 Miller struck out.
2 Dykes flied to Martin in left-center.
Williams doubled over Hafey's head.
3 Grove struck out for the third time.
St. Louis
1 Blades, batting for Johnson, struck out.
Flowers doubled to the bleachers in left-center.
2 Roettger flied to deep left, Flowers going to third after the catch.
Frisch lined a single to right, scoring Flowers.
3 Martin popped to Bishop near the right field foul line.

7th Inning
Philadelphia
For St. Louis—Lindsey now pitching.
Bishop singled to right.
1 Haas sacrificed Bishop to second, Flowers to Bottomley.
2 Cochrane flied to left.
Simmons singled to center, Bishop scoring.
Foxx singled to left, Simmons stopping at second.
Miller was hit by a pitched ball, loading the bases.
Dykes walked, forcing home Simmons.
Williams pop fly into short left was dropped by Hafey for an error, scoring Foxx and Miller as Dykes went to third.
3 Grove grounded to second.
St. Louis
1 Hafey struck out.
2 Bottomley flied to center.
3 Wilson grounded to short.

8th Inning
Philadelphia
1 Bishop grounded to short.
Haas walked.
2,3 Cochrane hit into a double play, Frisch to Gelbert to Bottomley.
St. Louis
1 Gelbert struck out.
2 Collins, batting for Lindsey, grounded to second.
3 Flowers flied to left.

9th Inning
Philadelphia
For St. Louis—Rhem now pitching with Mancuso catching.
1 Simmons fouled to Mancuso.
2 Foxx called out on strikes.
Miller singled to left.
3 Dykes fouled to Bottomley.
St. Louis
Roettger struck out, but got safely to first as Cochrane muffed the third strike for an error.
1 Frisch struck out.
Martin walked.
2 Hafey flied to left.
3 Bottomley popped to second.

Game 7 October 10 at St. Louis

| Phi. | 000 000 002 |
| St L. | 202 000 00x |

Philadelphia	Pos	AB	R	H	RBI	PO	A	E
Bishop	2b	4	0	0	0	2	1	0
Haas	cf	3	0	0	0	2	0	0
Cochrane	c	4	0	0	0	8	2	0
Simmons	lf	3	0	1	0	0	0	0
Foxx	1b	4	0	0	0	11	0	1
Miller	rf	4	1	3	0	0	0	0
Dykes	3b	3	1	0	0	1	3	0
Williams	ss	4	0	2	0	0	2	0
Earnshaw	p	2	0	0	0	0	2	0
a Todt		0	0	0	0	0	0	0
Walberg	p	0	0	0	0	0	0	0
b Cramer		1	0	1	2	0	0	0
Totals		32	2	7	2	24	10	1

a Walked for Earnshaw in 8th.
b Singled for Walberg in 9th.

Home Run—Watkins. Stolen Base—Martin. Sacrifice Hit—Frisch. Double Plays—Dykes to Bishop to Foxx, Gelbert to Frisch to Bottomley. Wild Pitch—Earnshaw. Left on Bases—Philadelphia 8, St. Louis 3. Umpires—Stark, McGowan, Klem, Nallin. Attendance—20,805. Time of Game—1:57.

St. Louis	Pos	AB	R	H	RBI	PO	A	E
High	3b	4	2	3	0	1	4	0
Watkins	rf	3	2	2	2	2	0	0
Frisch	2b	3	0	0	0	2	4	0
Martin	cf	3	0	0	0	1	0	0
Orsatti	lf	3	0	0	0	1	0	0
Bottomley	1b	3	0	0	0	12	0	0
Wilson	c	2	0	0	0	7	1	0
Gelbert	ss	3	0	0	0	1	4	0
Grimes	p	3	0	0	0	0	1	0
Hallahan	p	0	0	0	0	0	0	0
Totals		27	4	5	2	27	14	0

Pitching	IP	H	R	ER	BB	SO
Philadelphia						
Earnshaw (L)	7	4	4	3	2	7
Walberg	1	1	0	0	1	2
St. Louis						
Grimes (W)	8⅔	7	2	2	5	6
Hallahan (SV)	⅓	0	0	0	0	0

1st Inning
Philadelphia
1 Bishop fouled to High.
2 Haas grounded to second.
3 Cochrane grounded to second.
St. Louis
High popped a single into short left between Simmons and Williams.
Watkins also hit a Texas Leaguer into left for a single, High taking second.
1 Frisch sacrificed High to third and Watkins to second, Dykes to Foxx.
On a wild pitch, High scored and Watkins went to third.
Martin walked.
Martin stole second, just beating Cochrane's throw.
Orsatti struck out on a low pitch, which bounced out of Cochrane's glove.
2 Cochrane threw Orsatti out at first while Watkins dashed home and scored when Foxx's throw was low. Martin took third on the error, which was strangely only given to Foxx.
3 Bottomley struck out.

2nd Inning
Philadelphia
Simmons singled to right center.
1 Foxx flied to right.
Miller singled to left, Simmons stopping at second.
2 Dykes forced Miller at second, High to Frisch.
3 Williams, bounced to Gelbert behind the pitcher's box.
St. Louis
Wilson walked.
1,2 Gelbert hit into a double play, Dykes to Bishop to Foxx.
3 Grimes struck out.

3rd Inning
Philadelphia
1 Earnshaw grounded to third.
Bishop walked.
2 Bishop was nabbed off first, Wilson to Bottomley.
3 Haas flied to deep right.
St. Louis
High singled a single to center.
Watkins hit a two-run homer over the right field pavilion.
1 Frisch flied to center.
2 Martin popped to second.
3 Orsatti struck out but again Cochrane dropped the third strike and threw to Foxx for the putout.

4th Inning
Philadelphia
1 Cochrane grounded to second.
2 Simmons grounded to short.
3 Foxx struck out.
St. Louis
1 Bottomley again struck out.
2 Wilson grounded to short.
3 Gelbert popped to first.

5th Inning
Philadelphia
Miller singled to center.
1 Dykes grounded to first, Miller taking second.
William's beat out a bouncer to the left of the pitcher's box, Miller taking third.
2,3 Earnshaw hit into a double play, Frisch to Gelbert to Bottomley.
St. Louis
1 Grimes grounded to second.
2 High tapped back to the mound.
3 Watkins grounded to first.

6th Inning
Philadelphia
1 Bishop took a called third strike.
2 Haas flied to deep center.
3 Cochrane grounded to third.
St. Louis
1 Frisch bunted back to the mound.
2 Martin bounced to short.
3 Orsatti took a called third strike.

7th Inning
Philadelphia
1 Simmons struck out.
2 Foxx called out on strikes.
Miller singled to center for his third hit of the game.
3 Dykes struck out.
St. Louis
1 Bottomley popped to Cochrane toward first.
2 Wilson flied to center.
3 Gelbert struck out.

8th Inning
Philadelphia
1 Williams struck out.
Todt, pinch-hitting for Earnshaw, walked on a full count.
2 Bishop rolled to third, Todt taking second.
Haas walked.
3 Cochrane was out when Grimes knocked down his liner and threw him out.
St. Louis
For Philadelphia—Walberg now pitching.
1 Grimes struck out.
High got his third hit, a scratch single over second.
Watkins walked.
2 Frisch popped to third.
3 Martin struck out.

9th Inning
Philadelphia
Simmons walked on a full count.
1 Foxx fouled to Wilson.
2 Miller forced Simmons at second, Gelbert to Frisch and just missing the double play at first.
Dykes walked.
Williams bounced a single over High's head, loading the bases.
Cramer, pinch-hitting for Walberg, singled to center, scoring Miller and Dykes with Williams stopping at second.
For St. Louis—Hallahan came in to pitch.
3 Bishop flied to center.

1931 WORLD SERIES COMPOSITE BOX

	Wins	Composite Line Score
St. Louis Cardinals (N.L.)	4	5 3 2 2 0 3 1 1 2 – 19
Philadelphia Athletics (A.L.)	3	1 0 4 0 4 2 7 0 4 – 22

	Regular Season			
Manager	W	L	Pct.	G. Ahead
Gabby Street	101	53	.656	13
Connie Mack	107	45	.704	13½

BATTING AND FIELDING

WORLD SERIES STATISTICS

ST. LOUIS CARDINALS	Pos	G	AB	R	H	2B	3B	HR	RBI	BB	SO	SB	BA	SA	PO	A	E
Jim Bottomley	1b	7	25	2	4	1	0	0	2	2	5	0	.160	.200	61	2	**1**
Frankie Frisch	2b	7	**27**	2	7	2	0	0	1	1	2	1	.259	.333	23	19	0
Charlie Gelbert	ss	7	23	0	6	1	0	0	3	0	4	0	.261	.304	13	**29**	0
Andy High	3b-pr	4	15	3	4	0	0	0	0	0	2	0	.267	.267	3	9	0
George Watkins	rf-pr	5	14	4	4	1	0	1	2	2	1	1	.286	.571	8	0	0
Pepper Martin	cf	7	24	**5**	**12**	**4**	0	1	5	2	3	**5**	**.500**	**.792**	10	0	0
Chick Hafey	lf	6	24	1	4	0	0	0	0	0	5	1	.167	.167	8	0	**1**
Jimmie Wilson	c	7	23	0	5	0	0	0	2	1	1	0	.217	.217	50	3	**1**
Wally Roettger	rf	3	14	1	4	1	0	0	0	0	3	0	.286	.357	4	0	0
Jake Flowers	ph-3b	5	11	1	1	1	0	0	0	1	0	0	.091	.182	3	4	**1**
Sparky Adams	3b	2	4	0	1	0	0	0	0	0	1	0	.250	.250	0	1	0
Ernie Orsatti	lf	1	3	0	0	0	0	0	0	0	3	0	.000	.000	1	0	0
Ray Blades	ph	2	2	0	0	0	0	0	0	0	2	0	.000	.000			
Ripper Collins	ph	2	2	0	0	0	0	0	0	0	1	0	.000	.000			
Gus Mancuso	ph-c	2	1	0	0	0	0	0	0	0	0	0	.000	.000	2	0	0
Mike Gonzalez		Did not play															
Burleigh Grimes	p	2	7	0	2	0	0	0	2	0	2	0	.286	.286	0	3	0
Wild Bill Hallahan	p	3	6	0	0	0	0	0	0	0	3	0	.000	.000	0	0	0
Paul Derringer	p	3	2	0	0	0	0	0	0	0	1	0	.000	.000	0	2	0
Syl Johnson	p	3	2	0	0	0	0	0	0	0	2	0	.000	.000	0	1	0
Jim Lindsey	p	2	0	0	0	0	0	0	0	0	0	0	—	—	0	0	0
Flint Rhem	p	1	0	0	0	0	0	0	0	0	0	0	—	—	0	0	0
Jesse Haines		Did not play															
Allyn Stout		Did not play															
Tony Kaufmann		Did not play															
team total		7	229	19	54	11	0	2	17	9	41	8	.236	.310	186	73	4

Double Plays—7
Left on Bases—40

REGULAR SEASON STATISTICS

ST. LOUIS CARDINALS		Main Pos	G	AB	R	H	2B	3B	HR	RBI	BB	SO	SB	BA	SA
Jim Bottomley		1b	108	382	73	133	34	5	9	75	34	24	3	.348	.534
Frankie Frisch		2b	131	518	96	161	24	4	4	82	45	13	**28**	.311	.396
Charlie Gelbert		ss	131	447	61	129	29	5	1	62	54	31	1	.289	.383
Andy High		3b-2b	63	131	20	35	6	1	0	19	24	4	0	.267	.328
George Watkins		of	131	503	93	145	30	13	13	51	31	66	15	.288	.477
Pepper Martin		of	123	413	68	124	32	8	7	75	30	40	16	.300	.467
Chick Hafey		of	122	450	94	157	35	8	16	95	39	43	11	**.349**	.569
Jimmie Wilson		c	115	383	45	105	20	2	0	51	28	15	5	.274	.337
Wally Roettger	a	of	45	151	16	43	12	2	0	17	9	14	0	.285	.391
Jake Flowers	b	ss-2b	45	137	19	34	11	1	2	19	9	6	7	.248	.387
Sparky Adams		3b	143	608	97	178	**46**	5	1	40	42	24	16	.293	.390
Ernie Orsatti		of	70	158	27	46	16	6	0	19	14	16	1	.291	.468
Ray Blades		of	35	67	10	19	4	0	1	5	10	7	1	.284	.388
Ripper Collins		1b	89	279	34	84	20	10	4	59	18	24	1	.301	.487
Gus Mancuso		c	67	187	13	49	16	1	1	23	18	13	2	.262	.374
Mike Gonzalez		c	15	19	1	2	0	0	0	3	0	3	0	.105	.105
Burleigh Grimes		p	29	76	4	14	0	0	0	8	1	10	0	.184	.184
Wild Bill Hallahan		p	37	81	5	8	2	0	0	5	7	34	0	.099	.123
Paul Derringer		p	35	72	2	7	0	0	0	1	1	18	0	.097	.097
Syl Johnson		p	32	60	4	14	2	1	0	7	3	16	0	.233	.300
Jim Lindsey		p	35	9	1	1	0	0	0	0	1	4	0	.111	.111
Flint Rhem		p	33	69	4	9	1	0	0	6	0	21	0	.130	.145
Jesse Haines		p	19	45	3	6	1	0	0	4	0	6	0	.133	.156
Allyn Stout		p	30	19	1	2	0	0	0	1	0	9	0	.105	.105
Tony Kaufmann		p	20	18	1	2	0	0	0	0	1	3	0	.111	.111
team total			154	5435	815	1554	**353**	74	60	751	432	475	**114**	.286	.411

a—from Cincinnati
b—from Brooklyn
Joe Benes (ss), Ray Cunningham (3b), Eddie Delker (3b), Taylor Douthit (of), Joel Hunt (of) also played for the Cardinals during the season.

WORLD SERIES STATISTICS

PHILADELPHIA ATHLETICS	Pos	G	AB	R	H	2B	3B	HR	RBI	BB	SO	SB	BA	SA	PO	A	E
Jimmie Foxx	1b	7	23	3	8	0	0	1	3	**6**	5	0	.348	.478	**69**	2	**1**
Max Bishop	2b	7	**27**	4	4	0	0	0	0	3	5	0	.148	.148	12	18	0
Dib Williams	ss	7	25	2	8	1	0	0	1	2	**9**	0	.320	.360	7	24	0
Jimmy Dykes	3b	7	22	2	5	0	0	0	2	5	1	0	.227	.227	4	12	0
Bing Miller	rf	7	26	3	7	1	0	0	1	0	4	0	.269	.308	12	0	0
Mule Haas	cf	7	23	1	3	1	0	0	2	3	5	0	.130	.174	17	0	0
Al Simmons	lf-cf	7	**27**	4	9	2	0	**2**	**8**	3	3	0	.333	.630	19	0	0
Mickey Cochrane	c	7	25	2	4	0	0	0	1	5	2	0	.160	.160	40	4	**1**
Jim Moore	ph-lf	2	3	0	1	0	0	0	0	0	1	0	.333	.333	1	0	0
Eric McNair	pr-ph-2b	2	2	1	0	0	0	0	0	0	1	0	.000	.000	1	1	0
Doc Cramer	ph	2	2	0	1	0	0	0	2	0	0	0	.500	.500			
Joe Boley	ph	1	1	0	0	0	0	0	0	0	1	0	.000	.000			
Johnnie Heving	ph	1	1	0	0	0	0	0	0	0	0	0	.000	.000			
Phil Todt	ph	1	0	0	0	0	0	0	0	1	0	0	—	—			
Joe Palmisano		Did not play															
Lefty Grove	p	3	10	0	0	0	0	0	0	0	7	0	.000	.000	0	0	0
George Earnshaw	p	3	8	0	0	0	0	0	0	0	2	0	.000	.000	1	7	0
Waite Hoyt	p	1	2	0	0	0	0	0	0	0	0	0	.000	.000	0	0	0
Rube Walberg	p	2	0	0	0	0	0	0	0	0	0	0	—	—	0	0	0
Roy Mahaffey	p	1	0	0	0	0	0	0	0	0	0	0	—	—	0	1	0
Eddie Rommel	p	1	0	0	0	0	0	0	0	0	0	0	—	—	0	0	0
Hank McDonald		Did not play															
Jim Peterson		Did not play															
Lew Krausse		Did not play															
team total		7	227	22	50	5	0	3	20	28	46	0	.220	.282	183	69	2

Double Plays—4
Left on Bases—52

REGULAR SEASON STATISTICS

PHILADELPHIA ATHLETICS		Main Pos	G	AB	R	H	2B	3B	HR	RBI	BB	SO	SB	BA	SA
Jimmie Foxx		1b	139	515	93	150	32	10	30	120	73	**84**	4	.291	.567
Max Bishop		2b	130	497	115	146	30	4	5	37	112	51	3	.294	.400
Dib Williams		ss	86	294	41	79	12	2	6	40	19	21	2	.269	.384
Jimmy Dykes		3b	101	355	48	97	28	2	3	46	49	47	1	.273	.389
Bing Miller		of	137	534	75	150	43	5	8	77	36	16	5	.281	.425
Mule Haas		of	102	440	82	142	29	7	8	56	30	29	0	.323	.475
Al Simmons		of	128	513	105	200	37	13	22	128	47	45	3	**.390**	.641
Mickey Cochrane		c	122	459	87	160	31	6	17	89	56	21	2	.349	.553
Jim Moore		of	49	143	18	32	5	1	2	21	11	13	0	.223	.315
Eric McNair		3b	79	280	41	76	10	1	5	33	11	19	1	.271	.368
Doc Cramer		of	65	223	37	58	8	2	2	20	11	15	2	.260	.341
Joe Boley		ss	67	224	26	51	9	3	0	20	15	13	1	.228	.295
Johnnie Heving		c	42	113	8	27	3	2	1	12	6	8	0	.239	.327
Phil Todt		1b	62	197	23	48	14	2	5	44	8	22	1	.244	.411
Joe Palmisano		c	19	44	5	10	2	0	0	4	6	3	0	.227	.273
Lefty Grove		p	41	115	8	23	3	0	0	12	3	48	0	.200	.226
George Earnshaw		p	43	114	12	30	7	1	2	13	5	23	0	.263	.395
Waite Hoyt	c	p	16	43	5	13	3	0	0	4	2	8	0	.302	.372
Rube Walberg		p	45	105	6	13	1	1	0	6	5	16	0	.124	.152
Roy Mahaffey		p	30	63	7	12	2	0	2	8	4	25	0	.190	.317
Eddie Rommel		p	29	54	6	14	1	1	0	4	6	5	0	.259	.315
Hank McDonald		p	19	21	1	2	0	0	0	0	4	10	0	.095	.095
Jim Peterson		p	6	2	0	1	1	0	0	0	1	0	0	.500	1.000
Lew Krausse		p	3	2	1	0	0	0	0	0	1	0	0	.000	.000
team total			153	5377	858	1544	311	64	118	798	526	543	27	.287	.435

c—from Detroit
Lou Finney (of), Sol Carter (p), Bill Shores (p) also played for the Athletics during the season.

PITCHING

WORLD SERIES STATISTICS

ST. LOUIS CARDINALS	G	GS	CG	IP	H	R	ER	BB	SO	W	L	SV	ERA
Wild Bill Hallahan	**3**	2	**2**	18 1/3	12	1	1	8	12	**2**	0	**1**	**0.49**
Burleigh Grimes	2	2	1	17 2/3	9	4	4	**9**	11	**2**	0	0	2.04
Paul Derringer	**3**	2	0	12 2/3	14	**10**	6	7	14	0	**2**	0	4.26
Syl Johnson	**3**	1	0	9	10	3	3	1	6	0	1	0	3.00
Jim Lindsey	2	0	0	3 1/3	4	4	2	3	2	0	0	0	5.40
Flint Rhem	1	0	0	1	1	0	0	0	1	0	0	0	0.00
Jesse Haines	Did not play												
Allyn Stout	Did not play												
Tony Kaufmann	Did not play												
team total	7	7	3	62	50	22	16	28	46	4	3	1	2.32

REGULAR SEASON STATISTICS

ST. LOUIS CARDINALS		G	GS	CG	IP	H	ER	BB	SO	W	L	Pct	SV	ShO	ERA
Wild Bill Hallahan		37	30	16	249	242	91	**112**	**159**	**19**	9	.679	4	3	3.29
Burleigh Grimes		29	28	17	212	240	86	59	67	17	9	.654	0	3	3.65
Paul Derringer		35	23	15	212	225	79	65	134	18	8	**.692**	2	4	3.35
Syl Johnson		32	24	12	186	186	62	29	82	11	9	.550	2	2	3.00
Jim Lindsey		35	2	1	75	77	23	45	32	6	4	.600	7	1	2.76
Flint Rhem		33	26	10	207	214	82	60	72	11	10	.524	1	2	3.57
Jesse Haines		19	17	8	122	134	41	28	27	12	3	.800	0	2	3.02
Allyn Stout		30	3	1	73	87	34	34	40	6	0	1.000	3	0	4.19
Tony Kaufmann		15	1	0	49	65	33	17	13	1	1	.500	1	0	6.06
team total		54	154	80	1385	1470	531	449	**626**	**101**	53	**.656**	**20**	**17**	3.45

WORLD SERIES STATISTICS

PHILADELPHIA ATHLETICS	G	GS	CG	IP	H	R	ER	BB	SO	W	L	SV	ERA
Lefty Grove	**3**	**3**	**2**	**26**	**28**	7	**7**	2	16	**2**	1	0	2.42
George Earnshaw	**3**	**3**	**2**	24	12	6	5	4	**20**	1	**2**	0	1.88
Waite Hoyt	1	1	0	6	7	3	3	0	1	0	1	0	4.50
Rube Walberg	2	0	0	3	3	1	1	2	4	0	0	0	3.00
Roy Mahaffey	1	0	0	1	1	1	1	1	0	0	0	0	9.00
Eddie Rommel	1	0	0	1	3	1	1	0	0	0	0	0	9.00
Hank McDonald	Did not play												
Jim Peterson	Did not play												
Lew Krausse	Did not play												
team total	7	7	4	61	54	19	18	9	41	3	4	0	2.66

REGULAR SEASON STATISTICS

PHILADELPHIA ATHLETICS		G	GS	CG	IP	H	ER	BB	SO	W	L	Pct	SV	ShO	ERA
Lefty Grove		41	30	**27**	289	249	66	62	**175**	**31**	4	**.886**	5	**3**	**2.06**
George Earnshaw		43	30	23	282	255	115	75	152	21	7	.750	6	**3**	3.67
Waite Hoyt	c	16	14	9	111	130	52	37	30	10	5	.667	0	2	4.22
Rube Walberg		44	35	19	**291**	298	121	109	106	20	12	.625	3	0	3.74
Roy Mahaffey		30	20	8	162	161	76	82	59	15	4	.789	2	0	4.22
Eddie Rommel		25	10	8	118	136	39	27	18	7	5	.583	0	1	2.97
Hank McDonald		19	10	1	70	62	29	41	23	2	4	.333	0	1	3.73
Jim Peterson		6	1	1	13	18	9	4	7	0	1	.000	0	0	6.23
Lew Krausse		3	1	1	11	6	5	6	1	1	0	1.000	0	0	4.09
team total		153	153	**97**	1366	1342	526	457	574	**107**	45	**.704**	16	**12**	**3.47**

Total Attendance—231,567 Average Attendance—33,081 Winning Player's Share—$4,468 Losing Player's Share—$3,023

1932
The Year Chicago Died

The legend of Babe Ruth pointing to the distant center-field stands and then belting a home run to that very area has always overshadowed the play of the 1932 World Series. In reality, this classic tale about one of baseball's gods had evidence both confirming it and junking it as the imaginative misinterpretations of a corps of hero-building reporters. But whether Ruth did or did not call his shot should not hide the fact that the 1932 Series dripped bitterness on both sides, with the tone approaching the style of an Ozark feud more than a professional sporting event. The New York Yankees, back as American League champs after a three-year absence, reached the Series by finishing 13 games in front of the dethroned Philadelphia A's. Babe Ruth, Lou Gehrig, Tony Lazzeri, and Earle Combs linked the 1928 and 1932 squads, but newcomers like catcher Bill Dickey, shortstop Frankie Crosetti, left fielder Ben Chapman, and pitchers Lefty Gomez, Red Ruffing, and Johnny Allen gave this Yankee squad a distinctive look of its own. Another Yankee newcomer partly explained the bad blood between the two Series contestants. Yankee manager Joe McCarthy had won the National League pennant with the Chicago Cubs in 1929, only to get canned in 1930 for finishing in second place. McCarthy wanted nothing better than the sweet revenge of beating the Cubs in the World Series, and that sentiment seeped down into the player ranks.

The Cubs made their rendezvous with the Yanks only after some midseason readjustments. With his team holding first place on August 2, Cub manager Rogers Hornsby was fired because of a severe disagreement with team president William Veeck. Veteran first baseman Charlie Grimm was told he was the new manager and was directed to keep the team in first place. With first-rate hitters like Gabby Hartnett, Kiki Cuyler, Billy Herman, and Riggs Stephenson and four tough pitchers in Lon Warneke, Guy Bush, Charlie Root, and Pat Malone, Grimm was able to fulfill his mission and bring the Cubs home ahead of the pack. One weak spot on the club improved markedly when the Cubs picked up ex-Yankee shortstop Mark Koenig in late August. Although his .353 batting average and reliable glove certainly put the Cubs over the hump, Koenig was voted only a half share of the pennant and Series money by his teammates. Koenig's pals on the Yankees jumped all over the Cubs for this move, with Ruth openly calling them cheapskates. The Cubs answered with a savage round of shouted insults from the field and dugout throughout the Series, and hatred ruled on both sides, with both players and fans.

Unfortunately for the Cubs and their supporters, the Yankees shoved their insults right back down their throats. The Cubs jumped off to an optimistic start with two runs off Red Ruffing in the top of the first inning in the opening game at Yankee Stadium, but the big New York bats unloaded on starter Guy Bush and two relievers to instigate a 12–6 Yankee win. The match-up of Lefty Gomez and Lon Warneke in game two also went to the Yankees, with the 5–2 triumph putting the New Yorkers up 2–0 in the Series.

When the Series resumed in Chicago, the ugly mood on the field was reflected in the feisty conduct of the fans at Wrigley Field. The Yanks scored three runs in the first off Charlie Root, but then the Cubs came back to tie the score at 4–4 after four innings. Then, in the top of the fifth with one out, Ruth came to the plate. He took a strike, pointed out into the field, took another strike, again pointed, and then belted a Root change-up into the center-field seats. The reporters at the game wrote that he had called his shot. Ruth sometimes denied this story and sometimes confirmed it. Other witnesses have vigorously denied it. Charlie Grimm's version of the incident is that pitcher Guy Bush was needling Ruth from the bench, and that the Bambino was pointing at the pitcher's mound and telling Bush something to the effect of "You'll be out there tomorrow." At any rate, Bush was out there the next day and got clobbered, the Cubs going down to a 13–6 loss and an ignominious Series sweep. Lost in the hubbub over Ruth's "called shot" was the fabulous Series of Lou Gehrig. He hit .529 over the four games with three homers, nine runs scored, and eight runs driven in. In fact, Gehrig swatted a homer only seconds after Ruth's celebrated clout. But for all Gehrig's heroics, this Series belonged to the Babe. It was his last.

Game 1 September 28 at New York

Chi.	200	000	220	
N.Y.	000	305	31x	

Chicago	Pos	AB	R	H	RBI	PO	A	E
Herman	2b	5	2	2	1	1	2	0
English	3b	4	1	1	0	2	1	1
Cuyler	rf	5	1	1	0	2	0	0
Stephenson	lf	5	0	3	3	2	0	0
Moore	cf	4	0	0	0	1	0	0
Grimm	1b	3	0	0	0	8	1	0
Hartnett	c	5	1	2	0	4	2	0
Koenig	ss	4	1	1	1	4	3	0
Bush	p	1	0	0	0	0	2	0
Grimes	p	1	0	0	0	0	0	0
a Gudat		1	0	0	0	0	0	0
Smith	p	0	0	0	0	0	0	0
Totals		38	6	10	5	24	11	1

a Struck out for Grimes in 8th.

Doubles—Combs, Hartnett 2. Triple—Koenig. Home Run—Gehrig. Stolen base—Cuyler. Sacrifice Hit—Crosetti. Double Play—Herman to Koenig to Grimm. Hit by Pitcher—Dickey (by Grimes). Wild Pitch—Grimes. Left on Bases—Chicago 11, New York 4. Umpires—Dinneen (A), Klem (N), Van Graflan (A), Magerkurth (N). Attendance—41,459. Time of Game—2:31.

New York	Pos	AB	R	H	RBI	PO	A	E
Combs	cf	4	2	2	2	3	0	0
Sewell	3b	4	1	1	2	1	0	0
Ruth	rf	3	3	1	1	1	0	1
Gehrig	1b	4	3	2	2	7	1	0
Lazzeri	2b	4	1	1	1	2	2	0
Dickey	c	3	0	1	2	11	0	0
Chapman	lf	4	1	0	1	1	0	0
Crosetti	ss	2	1	0	0	0	3	1
Ruffing	p	4	0	0	0	1	3	0
Totals		32	12	8	11	27	7	2

Pitching	IP	H	R	ER	BB	SO
Chicago						
Bush (L)	5⅓	3	8	8	5	2
Grimes	1⅔	3	3	3	1	0
Smith	1	2	1	1	0	1
New York						
Ruffing (W)	9	10	6	4	6	10

1st Inning
Chicago
Herman singled to center.
English singled to right, Ruth slipped and the ball went by him to the bleachers for an error, allowing Herman to score and English to get to third.
1 Cuyler struck out.
Stephenson singled to center, English scoring.
2 Moore struck out.
3 Grimm struck out.
New York
1 Combs took a called third strike.
2 Sewell fouled to Grimm.
3 Ruth bounced to first.

2nd Inning
Chicago
1 Hartnett struck out.
2 Koenig went out, Ruffing to Gehrig (the first non-strikeout for Ruffing).
3 Bush grounded to first.
New York
1 Gehrig grounded to second.
2 Lazzeri rolled back to the mound.
3 Dickey flied to right.

3rd Inning
Chicago
1 Herman bounced back to the pitcher.
2 English grounded to third.
Cuyler singled to left-center.
Cuyler stole second.
3 Stephenson flied to short center.
New York
1 Chapman flied to left.
2 Crosetti struck out.
3 Ruffing flied to left.

4th Inning
Chicago
1 Moore popped to third.
2 Grimm again struck out.
Hartnett doubled against the left field stands.
Koenig intentionally passed.
Bush walked, loading the bases.
3 Herman flied to Chapman, who made a good running catch at the foul line.
New York
Combs walked (the first Yankee baserunner).
1 Sewell grounded to first, Combs going to second.
Ruth singled to right, scoring Combs.
Gehrig lined a two-run homer into the right field bleachers.
2 Lazzeri rolled to third.
3 Dickey rolled out, Bush to Grimm along the first base line.

5th Inning
Chicago
1 English struck out.
2 Cuyler struck out.
3 Stephenson flied to Combs in deep left-center.
New York
Chapman safe at first when English fumbled his grounder.
Crosetti got a sacrifice and fielder's choice when Hartnett threw his bunt too late to get Chapman at second.
1 Ruffing bunted into a force-out, Hartnett to English getting Chapman at third.
2,3 Combs grounded into a double play, Herman to Koenig to Grimm.

6th Inning
Chicago
1 Moore popped to Sewell near the mound.
Grimm walked.
2 Hartnett struck out.
3 Koenig grounded to second.
New York
Sewell walked.
Ruth walked.
Gehrig walked, loading the bases.
1 Lazzeri popped to short.
Dickey singled past second, Sewell and Ruth scoring as Gehrig went to third.
Chapman's grounder went as a fielder's choice when Herman's throw to the plate missed Gehrig as Dickey got to second.
Crosetti walked, again filling the bases.
For Chicago—Grimes came in to pitch.
2 Ruffing forced Dickey at the plate, Koenig to Hartnett.
Combs singled to center, scoring Chapman and Crosetti with Ruffing going to third.
3 Sewell forced Combs at second, Grimm to Koenig.

7th Inning
Chicago
1 Grimes struck out (Ruffing's ninth strikeout victim).
Herman singled to center.
2 English lined to Combs in short right-center.
Cuyler got safely to second and Herman to third when Crosetti missed Cuyler's slow roller which went into left-center.
Stephenson singled to left-center, scoring Herman and Cuyler.
Moore walked.
3 Grimm bounced back to the mound.
New York
Ruth again walked.
Gehrig singled to left, Ruth going to third and Gehrig to second on the throw to third.
Lazzeri beat out a hit to second, Ruth scoring and Gehrig going to third.
Dickey was hit by a pitch.
1 Chapman flied to center, Gehrig scoring after the catch.
2 Crosetti forced Dickey, Koenig to Herman, Lazzeri going to third.
Lazzeri scored on a wild pitch and
3 as Crosetti tried for third he was declared out for running out of the base line.

8th Inning
Chicago
Hartnett hit his second double, a bouncer to the left field grandstand wall.
Koenig tripled to the bleacher fence in right-center, scoring Hartnett.
1 Gudat, batting for Grimes, took a called third strike.
2 Herman grounded out, Gehrig to Ruffing, Koenig scoring.
3 English popped to second.
New York
For Chicago—Smith pitching.
1 Ruffing struck out.
Combs doubled to center on a high fly when Moore lost the ball in the sun.
Sewell singled to left-center, Combs scoring.
2 Ruth popped to short.
3 Gehrig flied out to Cuyler in deep right only a few feet from the bleacher screen.

9th Inning
Chicago
Stephenson singled to right for his third hit of the game.
1 Moore fouled to Dickey close to the Yankee dugout.
Grimm walked.
2 Hartnett flied to deep right.
3 Koenig grounded to second.

Game 2 September 29 at New York

Chi.	101	000	000
N.Y.	202	010	00x

Chicago	Pos	AB	R	H	RBI	PO	A	E
Herman	2b	4	1	1	0	1	6	0
English	3b	4	0	1	0	0	0	0
Cuyler	rf	4	0	1	0	1	0	0
Stephenson	lf	4	1	2	1	0	0	0
Demaree	cf	4	0	1	1	1	0	0
Grimm	1b	4	0	2	0	8	0	0
Hartnett	c	3	0	1	0	9	2	0
Jurges	ss	3	0	0	0	4	3	0
Warneke	p	3	0	0	0	0	2	0
a Hemsley		1	0	0	0	0	0	0
Totals		34	2	9	2	24	13	0

a Struck out for Warneke in 9th.

Doubles—Herman, Stephenson. Triple—
Cuyler. Sacrifice Hit—Jurges. Double
Plays—Warneke to Hartnett to Jurges, .
Hartnett to Herman, Herman to Jurges to
Grimm 2. Left on Bases—Chicago 7,
New York 5. Umpires—Klem, Van Graflan,
Magerkurth, Dinneen. Attendance—50,709.
Time of Game—1:46.

New York	Pos	AB	R	H	RBI	PO	A	E
Combs	cf	3	1	1	0	4	0	0
Sewell	3b	3	1	1	0	0	1	0
Ruth	rf	3	1	1	0	3	0	0
Gehrig	1b	4	2	3	1	5	0	0
Lazzeri	2b	4	0	1	0	3	1	0
Dickey	c	3	0	2	2	8	0	0
Chapman	lf	4	0	1	2	1	1	0
Crosetti	ss	3	0	0	0	3	3	1
Gomez	p	3	0	0	0	0	3	0
Totals		30	5	10	5	27	9	1

Pitching	IP	H	R	ER	BB	SO
Chicago						
Warneke (L)	8	10	5	5	4	7
New York						
Gomez (W)	9	9	2	1	1	8

1st Inning
Chicago
  Herman doubled on a grounder past third.
1 English flied to short center.
  Cuyler was safe when Crosetti fumbled
  his grounder, Herman taking third.
2 Stephenson flied to center, Herman
  scoring after the catch.
3 Demaree flied to right.
New York
  Combs walked.
  Sewell walked.
1 Ruth struck out.
  Gehrig singled to right, Combs scoring
  with Sewell stopping at second.
2 Lazzeri fouled to Hartnett at the
  third base coaching box.
  Dickey singled to short right, Sewell
  scoring with Gehrig racing to third.
3 Chapman was called out on strikes.

2nd Inning
Chicago
  Grimm singled to center.
  Hartnett walked.
1 Jurges sacrificed Grimm to third and
  Hartnett to second, Gomez (near first)
  to Lazzeri.
2 Warneke struck out.
3 Herman took a called third strike.
New York
1 Crosetti popped to short.
2 Gomez struck out.
3 Combs lined to right.

3rd Inning
Chicago
1 English flied to right.
2 Cuyler grounded to second.
  Stephenson bounced a double into right.
  Demaree singled to right, Stephenson
  scoring just before Ruth's throw.
3 Demaree was picked off first,
  Gomez to Gehrig.
New York
1 Sewell grounded to second.
  Ruth walked.
  Gehrig singled, Herman making a great
  stop and just missed getting Ruth at
  second.
2 Lazzeri grounded to Jurges, robbing
  Lazzeri of a hit as Ruth went to
  third and Gehrig to second.
  Dickey intentionally passed, loading
  the bases.
  Chapman singled to right, Ruth and
  Gehrig scoring as Dickey stopped at
  second.
3 Crosetti took a called third strike.

4th Inning
Chicago
  Grimm singled off Sewell's chest.
1 Hartnett took a called third strike.
2 Jurges forced Grimm at second, Crosetti
  making a fine stop and throw to
  Lazzeri.
3 Warneke called out on strikes.
New York
1 Gomez tapped back to the mound.
  Combs singled to left.
  Sewell singled to left, Combs going
  to third.
2,3 Ruth hit into a strange double play,
  Warneke to Hartnett who tagged Combs
  just before he returned to third to
  Jurges who tagged Sewell between
  second and third.

5th Inning
Chicago
1 Herman struck out.
2 English took a called third strike.
  Cuyler tripled into the deepest corner
  of right field, Ruth nearly catching
  the ball on the fly.
3 Sewell grounded to very deep third.
New York
  Gehrig got his third consecutive hit,
  a single to right.
1 Lazzeri grounded to second, Gehrig
  taking second.
  Dickey singled over short into left-
  center, scoring Gehrig.
2,3 Chapman struck out, and Dickey was
  doubled up trying for second,
  Hartnett to Herman.

6th Inning
Chicago
1 Demaree flied to Chapman, who made a
  good running catch almost at the
  grandstand.
2 Grimm grounded to first.
3 Hartnett grounded to short.
New York
1 Crosetti flied to Demaree at the
  running-track in deep left-center.
2 Gomez struck out.
3 Combs grounded to second.

7th Inning
Chicago
1 Jurges flied to right.
2 Warneke took a called third strike,
  his third strikeout in the game.
3 Herman popped to Combs in very
  short center.
New York
1 Sewell grounded to second.
  Ruth hit a long single off the
  bleacher fence.
2,3 Gehrig hit into a double play,
  Herman to Jurges to Grimm.

8th Inning
Chicago
  English singled to right.
1 Cuyler flied to short center.
  Stephenson singled to left, English
  stopping at second.
2 Demaree forced Stephenson at second,
  Gomez to Crosetti, as English went
  to third.
3 Grimm forced Demaree at second,
  Crosetti to Lazzeri.
New York
  Lazzeri singled past third.
1,2 Dickey rolled into a double play,
  Chicago's fourth of the game,
  Herman to Jurges to Grimm.
3 Chapman struck out.

9th Inning
Chicago
  Hartnett boomed a single down the
  left field foul line but Chapman
1 played the rebound perfectly and
  threw to Crosetti getting Hartnett
  at second.
2 Jurges popped to Crosetti in
  short left.
3 Hemsley, pinch-hitting for Warneke,
  did no better from the ninth slot
  as he also struck out.

Game 3 October 1 at Chicago

N.Y.   3 0 1   0 2 0   0 0 1
Chi.   1 0 2   1 0 0   0 0 1

New York	Pos	AB	R	H	RBI	PO	A	E
Combs	cf	5	1	0	0	1	0	0
Sewell	3b	2	1	0	0	2	2	0
Ruth	lf	4	2	2	4	2	0	0
Gehrig	1b	5	2	2	2	13	1	0
Lazzeri	2b	4	1	0	0	3	4	1
Dickey	c	4	0	1	0	2	1	0
Chapman	lf	4	0	2	1	0	0	0
Crosetti	ss	4	0	1	0	4	4	0
Pipgras	p	5	0	0	0	0	0	0
Pennock	p	0	0	0	0	0	1	0
Totals		37	7	8	7	27	13	1

Pitching	IP	H	R	ER	BB	SO
New York						
Pipgras (W)	*8	9	5	4	3	1
Pennock (SV)	1	0	0	0	0	1
Chicago						
Root (L)	4⅓	6	6	5	3	4
Malone	2⅔	1	0	0	4	4
May	1⅓	1	1	0	0	1
Tinning	⅔	0	0	0	0	1

*Pitched to 2 batters in 9th.

Chicago	Pos	AB	R	H	RBI	PO	A	E
Herman	2b	4	1	0	0	1	2	1
English	3b	4	0	0	0	0	3	0
Cuyler	rf	4	1	3	2	1	0	0
Stephenson	lf	4	0	1	0	1	0	0
Moore	cf	3	1	0	0	3	0	0
Grimm	1b	4	0	1	1	8	0	0
Hartnett	c	4	1	1	1	10	1	1
Jurges	ss	4	1	3	0	3	3	2
Root	p	2	0	0	0	0	0	0
Malone	p	0	0	0	0	0	0	0
a Gudat		1	0	0	0	0	0	0
May	p	0	0	0	0	0	0	0
Tinning	p	0	0	0	0	0	0	0
b Koenig		0	0	0	0	0	0	0
c Hemsley		1	0	0	0	0	0	0
Totals		35	5	9	4	27	9	4

a Popped out for Malone in 7th.
b Announced to bat for Tinning in 9th.
c Struck out for Koenig in 9th.

Doubles—Chapman, Cuyler, Grimm, Jurges. Home Runs—Cuyler, Gehrig 2, Hartnett, Ruth 2. Stolen Base—Jurges 2. Double Plays—Sewell to Lazzeri to Gehrig, Herman to Jurges to Grimm. Hit by Pitcher—Sewell (by May). Left on Bases—New York 11, Chicago 6. Umpires—Van Graflan, Magerkurth, Dinneen, Klem. Attendance—49,986. Time of Game—2:11.

1st Inning
New York
    Combs got safely to second as Jurges' throw of his grounder went into the Yankee dugout.
    Sewell walked.
    Ruth hit a three-run homer deep into the right-center field bleachers. His fourteenth World Series homer.
1 Gehrig grounded to second.
2 Lazzeri called out on strikes.
    Dickey singled over first.
    Chapman singled to left, Dickey stopping at second.
3 Crosetti flied to deep left.
Chicago
    Herman walked.
1 English flied to left.
    Cuyler doubled over Chapman's head, scoring Herman.
2 Stephenson grounded to short, Cuyler holding second.
    Moore walked.
3 Grimm bounced to short.

2nd Inning
New York
1 Pipgras struck out.
2 Combs flied to Moore in deep left-center.
    Sewell walked.
3 Ruth flied to Cuyler up against the right field bleachers.
Chicago
1 Hartnett grounded to short.
    Jurges singled to left.
2 Root struck out.
    Jurges stole second.
3 Herman flied to left.

3rd Inning
New York
    Gehrig homered into the right field bleachers.
1 Lazzeri grounded to short.
2 Dickey flied to Moore in left-center.
    Chapman walked.
3   Chapman was out trying to steal second, Hartnett to Jurges.
Chicago
1 English bounced to short.
    Cuyler hit a home run high into the right field bleachers.
    Stephenson singled on a Texas Leaguer to right-center.
2 Moore forced Stephenson at second, Gehrig to Crosetti.
    Grimm bounced a double to right, Moore scoring.
3 Hartnett fouled to Sewell.

4th Inning
New York
1 Crosetti grounded to third.
2 Pipgras took a called third strike.
3 Combs also called out on strikes.
Chicago
    Jurges doubled to right, Ruth just missing a shoe-string catch and still almost threw Jurges out at second.
1 Root grounded to third, Jurges holding second.
2 Herman popped to Lazzeri in center.
    English beat out an infield roller, scoring Jurges from second.
3   English was out attempting to steal second, Dickey to Lazzeri.

5th Inning
New York
1 Sewell grounded to Jurges making a brilliant play.
    Ruth hit his second homer of the game, a blast over the bleacher screen in deep center at the base of the flag pole.
    Gehrig also hit his second homer of the game, a blast into the temporary bleachers built outside the right field wall.
    For Chicago—Malone replaced Root on the mound.
    Lazzeri walked.
    Dickey walked.
2 Chapman rolled to third, advancing both runners.
    Crosetti was intentionally walked, loading the bases.
3 Pipgras was again called out on strikes.
Chicago
    Cuyler beat out a bouncer to second, his third hit of the game.
1,2 Stephenson hit into a double play, Sewell to Lazzeri to Gehrig.
3 Moore grounded to second.

6th Inning
New York
1 Combs lined to first.
2 Sewell flied to Moore in right-center.
    Ruth walked.
3 Gehrig took a called third strike.
Chicago
1 Grimm rolled out to second.
2 Hartnett fouled to Sewell.
3 Jurges grounded to second, the first 1-2-3 inning for Pipgras.

7th Inning
New York
1 Lazzeri grounded to third.
    Dickey safe at first on Jurges' low throw to Grimm, the second error in the game on Jurges.
2 Chapman struck out.
    Crosetti singled to left, Dickey stopping at second.
3 Pipgras again took a called strike, his fourth strikeout of the game.
Chicago
1 Gudat, batting for Malone, popped to short.
2 Herman slowly rolled to first.
    English walked.
3 Cuyler forced English at second, Crosetti unassisted.

8th Inning
New York
    For Chicago—May pitching, the Cubs' only southpaw.
1 Combs struck out.
    Sewell was hit by a pitched ball.
2,3 Ruth rolled into a double play, Herman to Jurges to Grimm.
Chicago
1 Stephenson flied to deep center.
2 Moore popped to Crosetti in shallow left.
3 Grimm grounded to first.

9th Inning
New York
1 Gehrig popped to Hartnett at the pitcher's mound.
    Lazzeri safe at first as Hartnett muffed his pop-up near the mound.
    Dickey safe at first and Lazzeri at second when Herman muffed a pop-up in right.
    Chapman doubled over third, Lazzeri scoring and Dickey stopping at third.
    For Chicago—Tinning came in to pitch.
2 Crosetti popped to second.
3 Pipgras struck out (**a new Series record striking out 5 times in the game**).
Chicago
    Hartnett homered into the left field bleachers.
    Jurges singled to left.
    Koenig announced to bat for Tinning.
    For New York—Pennock replaced Pipgras on the mound.
1 Hemsley, batting for Koenig, struck out.
2 Herman rolled back to the mound, Jurges going to second.
    Jurges stole third.
3 English grounded to first.

Game 4 October 2 at Chicago

N.Y.	1 0 2	0 0 2	4 0 4
Chi.	4 0 0	0 0 1	0 0 1

New York	Pos	AB	R	H	RBI	PO	A	E
Combs	cf	4	4	3	2	2	0	0
Sewell	3b	6	1	3	2	0	2	1
Ruth	lf	5	0	1	1	2	0	0
Byrd	lf	0	0	0	0	0	0	0
Gehrig	1b	4	2	2	3	12	0	1
Lazzeri	2b	5	2	3	4	1	4	0
Dickey	c	6	2	3	0	4	0	0
Chapman	rf	5	0	2	1	4	0	0
Crosetti	ss	6	1	1	0	2	5	2
Allen	p	0	0	0	0	0	0	0
W. Moore	p	3	0	1	0	0	1	0
a Ruffing		0	0	0	0	0	0	0
b Hoag		0	1	0	0	0	0	0
Pennock	p	1	0	0	0	0	0	0
Totals		45	13	19	13	27	12	4

Pitching	IP	H	R	ER	BB	SO
New York						
Allen	⅓	5	4	3	0	0
W. Moore (W)	5⅔	2	1	0	0	1
Pennock (SV)	3	2	1	1	1	3
Chicago						
Bush	⅓	2	1	1	1	0
Warneke	*2⅔	5	2	2	1	1
May (L)	3⅓	8	6	6	3	3
Tinning	1⅓	0	0	0	0	2
Grimes	1	4	4	4	1	0

*Pitched to two batters in 4th.

Chicago	Pos	AB	R	H	RBI	PO	A	E
Herman	2b	5	1	1	0	2	2	0
English	3b	5	1	1	1	1	0	0
Cuyler	rf	5	0	0	0	1	0	0
Stephenson	lf	5	1	2	0	1	0	0
Demaree	cf	3	1	1	3	3	0	1
Grimm	1b	4	2	2	0	4	2	0
Hartnett	c	4	0	1	0	8	0	0
c Hack		0	0	0	0	0	0	0
Grimes	p	0	0	0	0	0	0	0
Jurges	ss	4	0	1	1	5	2	0
Bush	p	0	0	0	0	0	0	0
Warneke	p	1	0	0	0	1	0	0
May	p	2	0	0	0	1	0	0
Tinning	p	0	0	0	0	0	1	0
d Hemsley	c	1	0	0	0	0	0	0
Totals		39	6	9	5	27	7	1

a Walked for W. Moore in 7th.
b Ran for Ruffing in 7th.
c Ran for Hartnett in 8th.
d Struck out for Tinning in 8th.

Doubles—Chapman, Crosetti, Gehrig, Grimm, Sewell. Home Runs—Combs, Demaree, Lazzeri 2. Double Play—Herman to Jurges to Grimm. Hit by Pitchers—Ruth (by Bush), Gehrig (by May). Left on Bases—New York 13, Chicago 7. Umpires—Magerkurth, Dinneen, Klem, Van Graflan. Attendance—49,844. Time of Game—2:27.

1st Inning
New York
Combs singled on a liner off Bush's glove as the ball went into center.
Sewell singled to right, Combs stopping at second.
Ruth was hit by a pitch, loading the bases on only four pitches.
1 Gehrig was robbed of a homer by Demaree catching the fly as he crashed into the bleachers, all runners advancing a base after the catch.
Lazzeri walked on a full count, again loading the bases.
For Chicago—Warneke came in to pitch.
2 Dickey forced Sewell at the plate, Jurges to Hartnett.
3 Chapman grounded to second.
Chicago
1 Herman popped to short.
English singled over Allen's head.
2 Cuyler flied to deep right, Chapman catching the ball at the bleacher screen.
Stephenson singled to center, English racing to third.
Demaree hit a three-run homer high into the left field bleachers.
Grimm safe at first on Crosetti's fumble.
Hartnett singled to left, Grimm going to third.
Jurges singled to center, scoring Grimm with Hartnett stopping at second.
For New York—W. Moore came in to pitch.
3 Warneke flied to center.

2nd Inning
New York
1 Crosetti popped to short.
2 W. Moore took a called third strike.
3 Combs lined to right.
Chicago
1 Herman flied to center.
2 English grounded to third.
3 Cuyler grounded to short.

3rd Inning
New York
1 Sewell grounded out, Grimm to Warneke.
2 Ruth popped to Herman in short right.
Gehrig lined a double to the wall at the end of the left field foul line.
Lazzeri hit a two-run homer, the ball just clearing the right field bleacher screen.
Dickey singled to center.
Chapman singled to left, Dickey stopping at second.
3 Crosetti forced Dickey at third, English unassisted.
Chicago
1 Stephenson grounded to short.
2 Demaree grounded to second.
Grimm lined a double to the wall in left-center.
3 Hartnett bounced back to the mound.

4th Inning
New York
Moore singled to center.
Combs walked.
For Chicago—May now pitching.
1 Sewell popped to short.
2 Ruth took a called third strike.
3 Gehrig grounded out, Grimm to May.
Chicago
1 Jurges bounced to short.
2 May flied to left.
3 Herman flied to deep left.

5th Inning
New York
Lazzeri singled to left.
1 Dickey lined to center.
Chapman walked.
2,3 Crosetti bounced into a double play, Herman to Jurges to Grimm.
Chicago
1 English fouled to Crosetti who made the catch crashing into the left field grandstand.
2 Cuyler hit a high bouncer over Moore's head, taken by Crosetti with his bare hand and the throw to first just barely beat Cuyler.
3 Stephenson lined to second.

6th Inning
New York
1 Moore struck out.
Combs walked.
Sewell doubled to left-center, Combs stopping at third.
2 Ruth again struck out.
Gehrig singled to center, scoring both Combs and Sewell.
3 Lazzeri flied deep to Demaree almost at the bleachers in left-center.
Chicago
1 Demaree grounded to short.
Grimm got a single and went to second on Gehrig's throwing error to Moore, covering first.
Hartnett got safely to second with Grimm scoring when his hard smash bounced off Sewell's chest to Crosetti who threw over Gehrig's head into the Yankee dugout.
2 Jurges fanned.
3 May grounded to second.

7th Inning
New York
Dickey singled over second.
1 Chapman flied to left.
Crosetti doubled to deep left-center, Dickey stopping at third.
Ruffing, batting for Moore, was passed intentionally, loading the bases.
Hoag, pinch-running for Ruffing.
Combs blooped a Texas-League single to left, scoring Dickey.
Sewell singled to right, Crosetti and Hoag scoring as Combs went to third.
Ruth singled to right, scoring Combs with Sewell stopping at second.
Gehrig was hit by a pitch, again loading the bases.
For Chicago—Tinning relieved May.
2 Lazzeri forced Sewell at the plate, Tinning to Hartnett.
3 Dickey took a called third strike.
Chicago
For New York—Pennock pitching.
1 Herman struck out on three pitches.
2 English grounded to deep short.
3 Cuyler grounded to second.

8th Inning
New York
1 Chapman popped to Jurges racing into left.
2 Crosetti took a called third strike.
3 Pennock lined to second.
Chicago
Stephenson singled over Sewell's head.
Demaree walked.
1 Grimm flied to Chapman in right-center.
Hartnett safe at first and loading the bases as Sewell fumbled his grounder.
Hack in for Hartnett as a pinch-runner.
2 Jurges flied to second.
3 Hemsley, batting for Tinning, struck out.

9th Inning
New York
For Chicago—Hemsley stays in to catch, Grimes pitching (batting 7th).
Combs homered over the right field bleacher screen.
1 Sewell grounded to first.
2 Ruth grounded to first.
Gehrig walked.
Lazzeri hit a two-run homer, his second of the game, into the bleachers in left-center.
Dickey singled to center and continued to second on Demaree's fumble.
Chapman doubled off the left field wall, scoring Dickey.
3 Crosetti fouled to Jurges.
Chicago
For New York—Byrd replaced Ruth in left.
Herman singled to center.
Herman took second and then third unmolested on strikes.
1 English grounded to second, scoring Herman.
2 Cuyler struck out.
3 Stephenson flied to right.

1932 WORLD SERIES COMPOSITE BOX

	Wins	Composite Line Score	
New York Yankees (A.L.)	4	6 0 5 3 3 7 7 1 5	– 37
Chicago Cubs (N.L.)	0	8 0 3 1 0 1 2 2 2	– 19

Manager	Regular Season W	L	Pct.	G. Ahead
Joe McCarthy	107	47	.695	13
Rogers Hornsby, Charlie Grimm	90	64	.584	4

BATTING AND FIELDING

WORLD SERIES STATISTICS

	Pos	G	AB	R	H	2B	3B	HR	RBI	BB	SO	SB	BA	SA	PO	A	E
NEW YORK YANKEES																	
Lou Gehrig	1b	4	17	**9**	**9**	1	0	**3**	**8**	2	1	0	**.529**	**1.118**	**37**	2	1
Tony Lazzeri	2b	4	17	4	5	0	0	2	5	2	1	0	.294	.647	8	11	1
Frankie Crosetti	ss	4	15	2	2	1	0	0	0	2	3	0	.133	.200	9	**12**	**4**
Joe Sewell	3b	4	15	4	5	1	0	0	3	**4**	0	0	.333	.400	4	6	1
Babe Ruth	rf-lf	4	15	6	5	0	0	2	6	**4**	3	0	.333	.733	8	0	1
Earle Combs	cf	4	16	8	6	1	0	1	4	**4**	3	0	.375	.625	10	0	0
Ben Chapman	lf-rf	4	17	1	5	**2**	0	0	6	2	4	0	.294	.412	6	1	0
Bill Dickey	c	4	16	2	7	0	0	0	4	2	1	0	.438	.438	25	1	0
Sammy Byrd	lf	1	0	0	0	0	0	0	0	0	0	0	—	—	0	0	0
Myril Hoag	pr	1	0	1	0	0	0	0	0	0	0	0	—	—			
Lyn Lary		Did not play															
Art Jorgens		Did not play															
Doc Farrell		Did not play															
Geoge Pipgras	p	1	5	0	0	0	0	0	0	0	5	0	.000	.000	0	0	0
Red Ruffing	p-ph	2	4	0	0	0	0	0	0	1	1	0	.000	.000	1	3	0
Lefty Gomez	p	1	3	0	0	0	0	0	0	0	2	0	.000	.000	0	3	0
Wilcy Moore	p	1	3	0	1	0	0	0	0	0	2	0	.333	.333	0	1	0
Herb Pennock	p	2	1	0	0	0	0	0	0	0	0	0	.000	.000	0	1	0
Johnny Allen	p	1	0	0	0	0	0	0	0	0	0	0	—	—	0	0	0
Danny MacFayden		Did not play															
Jumbo Brown		Did not play															
Ed Wells		Did not play															
Charlie Devens		Did not play															
team total		4	144	37	45	6	0	8	36	23	26	0	.313	.521	108	41	8

Double Plays—1
Left on Bases—33

	Pos	G	AB	R	H	2B	3B	HR	RBI	BB	SO	SB	BA	SA	PO	A	E
CHICAGO CUBS																	
Charlie Grimm	1b	4	15	2	5	**2**	0	0	1	2	2	0	.333	.467	28	3	0
Billy Herman	2b	4	**18**	5	4	1	0	0	1	1	3	0	.222	.278	5	**12**	1
Billy Jurges	ss	3	11	1	4	1	0	0	1	0	1	**2**	.364	.455	12	8	2
Woody English	3b	4	17	2	3	0	0	0	1	2	2	0	.176	.176	3	4	1
Kiki Cuyler	rf	4	**18**	2	5	1	**1**	1	2	0	3	1	.278	.611	5	0	0
Johnny Moore	cf	2	7	1	0	0	0	0	0	2	1	0	.000	.000	4	0	0
Riggs Stephenson	lf	4	**18**	2	8	1	0	0	4	0	0	0	.444	.500	4	0	0
Gabby Hartnett	c	4	16	2	5	**2**	0	1	1	1	3	0	.313	.625	31	5	1
Frank Demaree	cf	2	7	1	2	0	0	1	4	1	0	0	.286	.714	4	0	1
Mark Koenig	ss-ph	2	4	1	1	0	1	0	1	1	0	0	.250	.750	4	3	0
Rollie Hemsley	ph-c	3	3	0	0	0	0	0	0	0	3	0	.000	.000	0	0	0
Marv Gudat	ph	2	2	0	0	0	0	0	0	0	1	0	.000	.000			
Stan Hack	pr	1	0	0	0	0	0	0	0	0	0	0	—	—			
Zack Taylor		Did not play															
Lon Warneke	p	2	4	0	0	0	0	0	0	0	3	0	.000	.000	1	2	0
Jakie May	p	2	2	0	0	0	0	0	0	0	0	0	.000	.000	1	0	0
Charlie Root	p	1	2	0	0	0	0	0	0	0	1	0	.000	.000	0	0	0
Guy Bush	p	2	1	0	0	0	0	0	0	1	0	0	.000	.000	0	2	0
Burleigh Grimes	p	2	1	0	0	0	0	0	0	0	1	0	.000	.000	0	0	0
Pat Malone	p	1	0	0	0	0	0	0	0	0	0	0	—	—	0	0	0
Bud Tinning	p	2	0	0	0	0	0	0	0	0	0	0	—	—	0	1	0
Bob Smith	p	1	0	0	0	0	0	0	0	0	0	0	—	—	0	0	0
Leroy Herrmann		Did not play															
team total		4	146	19	37	8	2	3	16	11	24	3	.253	.397	102	40	6

Double Plays—7
Left on Bases—31

REGULAR SEASON STATISTICS

		Main Pos	G	AB	R	H	2B	3B	HR	RBI	BB	SO	SB	BA	SA
NEW YORK YANKEES															
Lou Gehrig		1b	155	596	138	208	42	9	34	151	108	38	4	.349	.621
Tony Lazzeri		2b	141	510	79	153	28	16	15	113	82	64	11	.300	.506
Frankie Crosetti		ss-3b	115	398	47	96	20	9	5	57	51	51	3	.241	.374
Joe Sewell		3b	124	503	95	137	21	3	11	68	56	3	0	.272	.392
Babe Ruth		of	132	457	120	156	13	5	41	137	**130**	62	2	.341	.661
Earle Combs		of	143	591	143	190	32	10	9	65	81	16	3	.321	.455
Ben Chapman		of	150	581	101	174	41	15	10	107	71	55	**38**	.299	.473
Bill Dickey		c	108	423	66	131	20	4	15	84	34	13	2	.310	.482
Sammy Byrd		of	104	209	49	62	12	1	9	30	30	20	1	.297	.478
Myril Hoag		of	46	54	18	20	5	0	1	7	7	13	1	.370	.519
Lyn Lary		ss	91	280	56	65	14	4	3	39	52	28	9	.232	.343
Art Jorgens		c	55	151	13	33	7	1	2	19	14	11	0	.219	.318
Doc Farrell		2b	26	63	4	11	1	1	0	4	2	8	0	.175	.222
Geoge Pipgras		p	32	82	4	18	1	1	0	10	2	19	0	.220	.256
Red Ruffing		p	55	124	20	38	6	1	3	19	6	10	0	.306	.444
Lefty Gomez		p	37	104	9	18	2	0	0	15	6	36	0	.173	.192
Wilcy Moore	a	p	10	8	0	0	0	0	0	0	0	4	0	.000	.000
Herb Pennock		p	22	53	4	8	2	0	0	6	7	5	0	.151	.189
Johnny Allen		p	33	73	5	9	2	1	1	5	4	22	0	.123	.219
Danny MacFayden	b	p	17	49	7	5	3	0	0	2	2	15	0	.102	.163
Jumbo Brown		p	19	23	3	4	1	0	0	1	0	8	0	.174	.217
Ed Wells		p	24	6	1	0	0	0	0	0	1	1	0	.000	.000
Charlie Devens		p	1	2	0	0	0	0	0	0	1	0	0	.000	.000
team total			155	5477	**1002**	1564	279	82	160	**955**	**766**	527	77	.286	.454

a—from Boston (A)
b—from Boston (A)
Dusty Cooke (ph-pr), Joe Glenn (c), Eddie Phillips (c), Jack Saltzgaver (2b), Roy Schalk (2b), Ivy Andrews (p), Hank Johnson (p), Johnny Murphy (p), Gordon Rhodes (p) also played for the Yankees during the season

	Main Pos	G	AB	R	H	2B	3B	HR	RBI	BB	SO	SB	BA	SA
CHICAGO CUBS														
Charlie Grimm	1b	149	570	66	175	42	2	7	80	35	22	2	.307	.425
Billy Herman	2b	154	656	102	206	42	7	1	51	40	33	14	.314	.404
Billy Jurges	ss	115	396	40	100	24	4	2	52	19	26	1	.253	.348
Woody English	3b-ss	127	522	70	142	23	7	3	47	55	73	5	.272	.360
Kiki Cuyler	of	110	446	58	130	19	9	10	77	29	43	9	.291	.442
Johnny Moore	of	119	443	59	135	24	5	13	64	22	38	4	.305	.470
Riggs Stephenson	of	147	583	86	189	49	4	4	85	54	27	3	.324	.443
Gabby Hartnett	c	121	406	52	110	25	3	12	52	51	59	0	.271	.436
Frank Demaree	of	23	56	4	14	3	0	0	6	2	7	0	.250	.304
Mark Koenig	ss	33	102	15	36	5	1	3	11	3	5	0	.353	.510
Rollie Hemsley	c	60	151	27	36	10	3	4	20	10	16	2	.238	.424
Marv Gudat	of-1b	60	94	15	24	4	1	1	15	16	10	0	.255	.351
Stan Hack	3b	72	178	32	42	5	6	2	19	17	16	5	.236	.365
Zack Taylor	c	21	30	2	6	1	0	0	3	1	4	0	.200	.233
Lon Warneke	p	35	99	8	19	7	1	0	9	3	20	0	.192	.222
Jakie May	p	35	8	0	1	0	0	0	0	1	1	0	.125	.125
Charlie Root	p	39	76	4	13	1	0	1	10	0	29	0	.171	.224
Guy Bush	p	40	84	6	15	2	1	0	1	4	12	0	.179	.226
Burleigh Grimes	p	30	44	4	11	1	0	0	5	0	9	1	.250	.273
Pat Malone	p	37	78	7	14	2	0	1	7	3	17	0	.179	.244
Bud Tinning	p	24	23	3	2	1	0	0	1	3	12	0	.087	.130
Bob Smith	p	36	42	5	10	4	1	0	4	0	2	1	.238	.381
Leroy Herrmann	p	7	2	0	1	0	0	0	0	0	1	0	.500	.500
team total		154	5462	720	1519	296	60	69	665	398	514	48	.278	.392

Vince Barton (of), Rogers Hornsby (of-3b), Lance Richbourg (of), Danny Taylor (of), Harry Taylor (1b), Ed Baecht (p), Bobo Newsom (p), Carroll Yerkes (p) also played for the Cubs during the season.

PITCHING

WORLD SERIES STATISTICS

	G	GS	CG	IP	H	R	ER	BB	SO	W	L	SV	ERA
NEW YORK YANKEES													
Red Ruffing	1	1	**1**	9	10	6	4	**6**	**10**	**1**	0	0	4.00
Lefty Gomez	1	1	**1**	9	9	2	1	1	8	**1**	0	0	**1.00**
George Pipgras	1	1	0	8	9	5	4	3	1	**1**	0	0	4.50
Wilcy Moore	1	0	0	5 1/3	2	1	0	0	1	**1**	0	0	0.00
Herb Pennock	**2**	0	0	4	2	1	1	1	4	0	0	**2**	2.25
Johnny Allen	1	1	0	1/3	5	4	3	0	0	0	0	0	40.50
Danny MacFayden	Did not play												
Jumbo Brown	Did not play												
Ed Wells	Did not play												
Charlie Devens	Did not play												
team total	4	4	2	36	37	19	13	11	24	4	0	2	3.25
CHICAGO CUBS													
Lon Warneke	**2**	1	**1**	**10 2/3**	15	7	7	5	8	0	**1**	0	5.91
Guy Bush	**2**	**2**	0	5 2/3	5	**9**	**9**	**6**	2	0	**1**	0	14.29
Jakie May	**2**	0	0	4 2/3	9	7	6	3	4	0	**1**	0	11.57
Charlie Root	1	1	0	4 1/3	6	6	5	3	4	0	**1**	0	10.38
Pat Malone	1	0	0	2 2/3	1	0	0	4	4	0	0	0	0.00
Burleigh Grimes	**2**	0	0	2 2/3	7	7	7	2	0	0	0	0	23.63
Bud Tinning	**2**	0	0	2 1/3	0	0	0	0	3	0	0	0	0.00
Bob Smith	1	0	0	1	2	1	1	0	1	0	0	0	9.00
Leroy Herrmann	Did not play												
team total	4	4	1	34	45	37	35	23	26	0	4	0	9.26

REGULAR SEASON STATISTICS

		G	GS	CG	IP	H	ER	BB	SO	W	L	Pct	SV	ShO	ERA
NEW YORK YANKEES															
Red Ruffing		35	29	22	259	219	89	115	**190**	18	7	.720	2	3	3.09
Lefty Gomez		37	31	21	265	266	124	105	116	24	7	.774	1	1	4.21
George Pipgras		32	27	14	219	235	102	87	111	16	9	.640	0	2	4.19
Wilcy Moore	a	10	1	0	25	27	7	6	8	2	0	1.000	4	0	2.52
Herb Pennock		22	21	9	147	191	75	38	54	9	5	.643	0	1	4.59
Johnny Allen		33	21	13	192	162	79	76	109	17	4	**.810**	4	3	3.70
Danny MacFayden	b	17	14	8	121	137	53	37	33	7	5	.583	1	0	3.94
Jumbo Brown		19	3	3	56	58	28	30	31	5	2	.714	1	1	4.50
Ed Wells		22	0	0	32	38	15	12	13	3	3	.500	2	0	4.22
Charlie Devens		1	1	1	9	6	2	7	4	1	0	1.000	0	0	2.00
team total		155	155	**95**	**1409**	1425	623	561	**780**	**107**	47	**.695**	15	**11**	**3.98**
CHICAGO CUBS															
Lon Warneke		35	32	25	277	247	73	64	106	**22**	6	**.786**	0	**4**	**2.37**
Guy Bush		40	30	15	239	262	85	70	73	19	11	.633	0	1	3.20
Jakie May		35	0	0	54	61	26	19	20	2	2	.500	1	0	4.33
Charlie Root		39	23	11	216	211	86	55	96	15	10	.600	3	0	3.58
Pat Malone		37	33	17	237	222	89	78	120	15	17	.469	0	2	3.38
Burleigh Grimes		30	18	5	141	174	75	50	36	6	11	.353	1	1	4.79
Bud Tinning		24	7	2	93	93	29	24	30	5	3	.625	0	0	2.81
Bob Smith		34	11	4	119	148	61	36	35	4	3	.571	2	1	4.61
Leroy Herrmann		7	0	0	13	18	9	9	5	2	1	.667	0	0	6.23
team total		154	154	79	1401	1444	536	409	527	**90**	64	**.584**	7	9	**3.44**

Total Attendance—191,998 Average Attendance—48,000 Winning Player's Share—$5,232 Losing Player's Share—$4,245

1933
A Man's Game

Clark Griffith, the Washington Senators owner, had appointed twenty-seven-year-old Bucky Harris the team manager in 1924, and the "Boy Wonder" had taken the Senators to two straight American League pennants. The years following 1925 were disappointing, and Griffith replaced Harris in 1929 with former pitching ace Walter Johnson. The Nats came close several times under Johnson, but Griffith decided to return to "The Boy Wonder" theme this year by putting Joe Cronin in charge of the team. A twenty-six-year-old shortstop with a steady glove and a powerful bat, Cronin led his men with brains, aggressiveness, and 118 runs batted in. Griffith brought in a bunch of veteran players in off-season trades, and Cronin brought this rebuilt club home first ahead of the New York Yankees, whose pitching fell down, and the Philadelphia Athletics, whom Connie Mack was already dismantling through Depression-motivated sales. The batting leaders for the Senators were Cronin, first baseman Joe Kuhel, and left fielder Heinie Manush, with General Crowder and Earl Whitehill combining for 46 wins at the head of the pitching staff. The Senators in this Series faced the New York Giants, whose manager was a "boy wonder" only in comparison with his predecessor. John McGraw had quit as Giant manager early last season because of health problems, and he left his mantle to thirty-four-year-old first baseman Bill Terry, a strong, silent leader with a murderous bat. Terry and young outfielder Mel Ott posed the only serious threats in the New York lineup, but strong pitching spurred the Giants into the National League title. Lanky Carl Hubbell used his left-handed screwball to win 23 games, pitch 10 shutouts, and notch a league-low 1.66 ERA. The most effective pitcher in baseball, Hubbell was backed by young 19-game-winner Hal Schumacher and veteran 16-game-winner Freddie Fitzsimmons. The Giants' pitchers definitely matched up against the Senators' pitching, but the easy superiority of the Washington bats made the A.L. champs pre-Series favorites.

But those heavy Senator hitters accomplished very little against Hubbell in game one at the Polo Grounds. The Giant ace scattered five hits, and a two-run homer by Mel Ott in the first inning got the New Yorkers off to an early lead en route to a 4–2 victory. Cronin's gamble to start Lefty Stewart instead of aces Crowder or Whitehill didn't pay off, but then Crowder was knocked out the next day by a six-run Giant sixth inning as Schumacher allowed only five hits in the 6–1 triumph.

The highly touted Washington batters showed very little in the two games at the Polo Grounds, but they hoped to get untracked as the Series moved to Washington's Griffith Stadium. With president Franklin D. Roosevelt in attendance, the Senators capitalized on Fat Freddie Fitzsimmons's early shakiness while Earl Whitehill dominated the Giant batters. Their 4–0 third-game victory got the Senators back into contention, but they had to face Hubbell again in game four. Cronin this time sent Monty Weaver up against Hubbell, and the Senator pitcher battled the New York ace to a standstill, the score reading 1–1 after nine innings. The Giants broke through in the top of the eleventh on a bunt single by Travis Jackson, a sacrifice by Gus Mancuso, and a single by Blondy Ryan, and Hubbell hung on for the 2–1 decision. Down three games to one, the Senators fell behind 3–0 against Hal Schumacher in the fifth game before Fred Schulte's three-run homer tied it up for the Senators. Relievers Dolph Luque for New York and Jack Russell for Washington pitched the late innings of the game and kept the 3–3 tie intact. But in the top of the tenth, Ott smacked a homer to center field, and the Giants cliched a 4–3 triumph and the World Championship in five games. The Series victory was the first for the Giants since 1922, and the thrill of triumph was John McGraw's as well as Bill Terry's. McGraw still thought of the Giants as his team even though he wasn't well enough to be on the field. Before the 1934 season would start, McGraw would be dead at the age of sixty.

Game 1 October 3 at New York

Was.	000	100	001					
N.Y.	202	000	00x					

Washington	Pos	AB	R	H	RBI	PO	A	E
Myer	2b	4	1	1	0	2	2	3
Goslin	rf	4	0	0	0	1	0	0
Manush	lf	4	1	0	0	2	0	0
Cronin	ss	4	0	2	1	0	2	0
Schulte	cf	4	0	2	0	4	0	0
Kuhel	1b	4	0	0	1	8	1	0
Bluege	3b	4	0	0	0	0	2	0
Sewell	c	3	0	0	0	6	1	0
Stewart	p	1	0	0	0	0	0	0
Russell	p	1	0	0	0	1	2	0
a Harris		1	0	0	0	0	0	0
Thomas		0	0	0	0	0	0	0
Totals		33	2	5	2	24	10	3

a Walked for Russell in 8th.

Home Run—Ott. Double Play—Mancuso to Ryan. Left on Bases—Washington 6, New York 7. Umpires—Moran (N), Moriarty (A), Pfirman (N), Ormsby (A). Attendance—46,672. Time of Game—2:07.

New York	Pos	AB	R	H	RBI	PO	A	E
Moore	lf	4	1	0	0	1	0	0
Critz	2b	4	1	1	0	2	2	1
Terry	1b	4	1	1	0	9	0	0
Ott	rf	4	1	4	3	0	0	0
Davis	cf	4	0	2	0	0	0	0
Jackson	3b	4	0	1	0	4	0	0
Mancuso	c	4	0	0	0	12	1	0
Ryan	ss	4	0	1	0	3	3	1
Hubbell	p	3	0	1	0	0	1	0
Totals		35	4	10	4	27	11	2

Pitching	IP	H	R	ER	BB	SO
Washington						
Stewart (L)	*2	6	4	2	0	0
Russell	5	4	0	0	0	3
Thomas	1	0	0	0	0	2
New York						
Hubbell (W)	9	5	2	0	2	10

*Pitched to 3 batters in 3rd.

1st Inning
Washington
1 Myer struck out.
2 Goslin struck out.
3 Manush struck out but had to be tagged by Mancuso who dropped the ball.
New York
  Moore safe on Myer's fumble.
1 Critz flied to right.
2 Terry fouled to Sewell.
  Ott hit a two-run homer into the lower right field stands.
  Davis singled to center.
3 Jackson flied to deep center.

2nd Inning
Washington
  Cronin singled to left.
1 Schulte forced Cronin at second, Hubbell to Ryan.
2,3 Kuhel struck out and Schulte was doubled trying for second, Mancuso to Ryan.
New York
1 Mancuso lined to center.
  Ryan singled to short right, and went to second on Myer's throwing error after a sensational stop of the hit.
2 Hubbell popped to second.
3 Moore grounded to third.

3rd Inning
Washington
1 Bluege struck out.
2 Sewell grounded to third.
3 Stewart struck out.
New York
  Critz singled off the right-field wall.
  Terry singled to right, Critz going to third.
  Ott singled to right, scoring Critz as Terry went to third.
  For Washington—Russell relieved Stewart.
1 Davis struck out.
2 Jackson grounded out off Kuhel's glove to Myer who threw to Russell covering, scoring Terry as Ott took second.
3 Mancuso flied to center.

4th Inning
Washington
  Myer singled to center.
1 Goslin grounded to first, Myer going to second.
  Manush safe when Critz fumbled his grounder, Myer going to third.
2 Cronin forced Manush at second, Jackson to Critz as Myer scored.
  Schulte singled off Hubbell's glove, Cronin going to second.
3 Kuhel grounded to second.
New York
1 Ryan struck out.
2 Hubbell bounced back to the mound.
3 Moore grounded to short.

5th Inning
Washington
1 Bluege grounded to short.
2 Sewell grounded to third.
3 Russell struck out.
New York
1 Critz grounded to second.
2 Terry bounced out, Russell to Kuhel.
  Ott singled to center.
  Davis singled to center, Ott going to second.
3 Jackson tapped back to the pitcher.

6th Inning
Washington
1 Myer fouled to Mancuso.
2 Goslin also fouled to Mancuso.
3 Manush popped to short.
New York
1 Mancuso flied to left.
2 Ryan popped to first.
  Hubbell singled to left.
3 Moore forced Hubbell at second, Bluege to Myer.

7th Inning
Washington
1 Cronin flied to Moore in short left, making a phenomenal running catch.
2 Schulte struck out.
3 Kuhel grounded to second.
New York
1 Critz grounded to short.
2 Terry flied to center.
  Ott singled off Russell's arm. **Ott's fourth hit of the game.**
  Ott safely to second when Myer dropped Sewell's throw for Myer's third error of the game.
3 Davis called out on strikes.

8th Inning
Washington
1 Bluege called out on strikes.
  Sewell walked. The first walk given up in the game.
  Harris, batting for Russell, walked.
2 Myer forced Harris at second, Ryan to Critz, Sewell going to third.
3 Goslin robbed of an extra-base-hit when Terry made a miraculous catch of his liner.
New York
  For Washington—Thomas now pitching.
1 Jackson struck out.
2 Mancuso flied to left.
3 Ryan struck out.

9th Inning
Washington
  Manush safe on Ryan's error.
  Cronin singled to right, Manush stopping at second.
  Shulte beat out a scorcher to third, loading the bases.
1 Kuhel grounded to short, Manush scoring, Cronin to third and Schulte going to second.
2 Bluege struck out for the third time.
3 Sewell grounded to third.

Game 2 October 4 at New York

Was.   0 0 1 0 0 0 0 0 0
N.Y.   0 0 0 0 0 6 0 0 x

Washington	Pos	AB	R	H	RBI	PO	A	E
Myer	2b	3	0	0	0	1	2	0
Goslin	rf	4	1	2	1	0	0	0
Manush	lf	3	0	1	0	1	0	0
Cronin	ss	4	0	0	0	3	4	0
Schulte	cf	4	0	0	0	1	0	0
Kuhel	1b	3	0	0	0	15	1	0
Bluege	3b	2	0	0	0	0	3	0
c Harris		1	0	0	0	0	0	0
Sewell	c	3	0	0	0	3	0	0
d Bolton		1	0	0	0	0	0	0
Crowder	p	2	0	1	0	0	1	0
Thomas	p	1	0	0	0	0	0	0
b Rice		1	0	1	0	0	0	0
McColl	p	0	0	0	0	0	1	0
Totals		31	1	5	1	24	12	0

a Singled for Davis in 6th.
b Singled for Thomas in 7th.
c Grounded out for Bluege in 9th.
d Grounded out for Sewell in 9th.

Double—Terry. Home Run—Goslin.
Sacrifice Hit—Jackson. Double
Plays—Cronin to Myer to Kuhel,
Jackson to Critz to Terry. Wild
Pitch—Schumacher. Left on Bases—
Washington 7, New York 6.
Umpires—Moriarty, Pfirman, Ormsby, Moran.
Attendance—35,461. Time of Game—2:09.

New York	Pos	AB	R	H	RBI	PO	A	E
Moore	lf	4	0	2	1	4	0	0
Critz	2b	3	1	1	0	1	3	0
Terry	1b	4	1	1	0	10	0	0
Ott	rf	2	1	0	0	4	0	0
Davis	cf	2	0	1	0	1	0	0
a O'Doul		1	1	1	2	0	0	0
Peel	cf	1	0	0	0	0	0	0
Jackson	3b	3	1	1	1	1	5	0
Mancuso	c	4	1	1	1	4	1	0
Ryan	ss	4	0	1	0	2	3	0
Schumacher	p	4	0	1	1	0	2	0
Totals		32	6	10	6	27	14	0

Pitching	IP	H	R	ER	BB	SO
Washington						
Crowder (L)	5⅓	9	6	6	3	3
Thomas	⅔	1	0	0	0	0
McColl	2	0	0	0	0	0
New York						
Schumacher (W)	9	5	1	1	4	2

1st Inning
Washington
Myer walked.
1 Goslin grounded to short, Myer taking
   second.
2 Manush flied to center.
3 Cronin struck out.
New York
1 Moore struck out.
2 Critz bunted out to Kuhel.
3 Terry popped to Cronin in short left.

2nd Inning
Washington
1 Schulte bounced back to the mound.
2 Kuhel popped to Ryan in short left.
   Bluege walked.
3 Sewell flied to left.
New York
Ott walked.
   Davis singled to center, Ott going
   to second.
1 Jackson sacrificed Ott to third and
   Davis to second, Bluege to Kuhel.
2 Mancuso grounded to third, both runners
   holding.
3 Ryan rolled out to Kuhel.

3rd Inning
Washington
1 Crowder grounded to third.
2 Myer bounced to short.
   Goslin homered into the upper right
   field stands.
3 Manush flied to left.
New York
1 Schumacher struck out.
2 Moore grounded back to the pitcher.
   Critz walked.
3 Terry flied to center.

4th Inning
Washington
1 Cronin flied to right.
2 Schulte grounded to third.
3 Kuhel bounced to second.
New York
1 Ott popped to first.
2 Davis fouled to Kuhel.
3 Jackson grounded to short.

5th Inning
Washington
1 Bluege flied to left.
2 Sewell grounded to short.
   Crowder singled to center.
3 Myer forced Crowder, Critz to Ryan.
New York
1 Mancuso grounded to third, Kuhel
   making a good tag from a poorly
   thrown ball.
   Ryan singled to center.
2,3 Schumacher grounded into a double play,
   Cronin to Myer to Kuhel.

6th Inning
Washington
Goslin singled to center.
   Manush walked.
1 Cronin fouled to Mancuso.
   Goslin to third and Mancuso to
   second on a wild pitch.
   Schulte safe on a fielder's choice as
2 Goslin was out in a run-down, Jackson
   to Mancuso to Jackson, with Manush
   going to third.
   Kuhel walked loading the bases.
3 Bluege struck out.
New York
Moore singled to left.
1 Critz forced Moore at second on a bunt,
   Kuhel to Cronin.
   Terry doubled to left, Critz going to
   third.
   Ott was given an intentional pass,
   loading the bases.
   O'Doul batting for Davis, singled over
   second, scoring Critz and Terry with
   Ott stopping at second.
   Jackson singled to right-center, Ott
   scoring as O'Doul went to third.
   Mancuso beat out a bunt down the third
   base line, O'Doul scoring with Jackson
   going to second.
2 Ryan called out on strikes.
   Schumacher singled to left, Jackson
   scoring with Mancuso going to second.
   Moore singled to center, scoring Mancuso
   with Schumacher stopping at second.
   For Washington—Thomas relieved Crowder.
   Critz beat out a bouncer to short, again
   loading the bases.
3 Terry forced Critz at second, Myer to Cronin.

7th Inning
Washington
For New York—Peel playing center.
1 Sewell flied to deep right.
   Rice, batting for Thomas, singled
   to center.
2 Myer flied to center.
3 Goslin flied to right.
New York
For Washington—McColl pitching.
1 Ott grounded to short.
2 Peel bounced to second.
3 Jackson bounced to short.

8th Inning
Washington
   Manush singled past first.
1,2 Cronin hit into a double play,
   Jackson to Critz to Terry.
3 Schulte fouled to Mancuso.
New York
1 Mancuso flied to left.
2 Ryan grounded back to the mound.
3 Schumacher grounded to first.

9th Inning
Washington
1 Kuhel flied to left.
2 Harris, batting for Bluege, grounded
   to third.
3 Bolton, batting for Sewell, grounded
   back to the mound.

Game 3 October 5 at Washington

N.Y.   0 0 0 0 0 0 0 0 0
Was.   2 1 0 0 0 0 1 0 x

New York	Pos	AB	R	H	RBI	PO	A	E
Moore	lf	4	0	0	0	2	1	0
Critz	2b	4	0	1	0	2	4	0
Terry	1b	4	0	0	0	9	0	0
Ott	rf	3	0	0	0	1	0	0
Davis	cf	4	0	1	0	3	0	0
Jackson	3b	3	0	1	0	0	2	0
Mancuso	c	4	0	0	0	4	1	0
Ryan	ss	3	0	1	0	3	3	0
Fitzsimmons	p	2	0	1	0	0	1	0
a Peel		1	0	1	0	0	0	0
Bell	p	0	0	0	0	0	0	0
Totals		32	0	6	0	24	12	0

a Singled for Fitzsimmons in 8th.

Doubles—Bluege, Goslin, Jackson, Myer,
Schutte. Stolen Base—Sewell. Double
Plays—Cronin to Myer to Kuhel, Moore
to Mancuso. Wild Pitch—Whitehill.
Left on Bases—New York 7, Washington 4.
Umpires—Pfirman, Ormsby, Moran, Moriarty.
Attendance—25,727. Time of Game—1:55.

Washington	Pos	AB	R	H	RBI	PO	A	E
Myer	2b	4	1	3	2	3	3	0
Goslin	rf	4	1	1	0	2	0	0
Manush	lf	4	0	0	0	3	0	0
Cronin	ss	4	0	1	0	2	1	1
Schulte	cf	4	0	2	1	1	0	0
Kuhel	1b	3	0	0	0	15	0	0
Bluege	3b	3	1	1	0	0	6	0
Sewell	c	3	1	1	0	3	0	0
Whitehill	p	3	0	0	0	0	4	0
Totals		32	4	9	4	27	15	1

Pitching	IP	H	R	ER	BB	SO
New York						
Fitzsimmons (L)	7	9	4	4	0	2
Bell	1	0	0	0	0	0
Washington						
Whitehill (W)	9	6	0	0	2	2

1st Inning
New York
1 Moore flied to right.
2 Critz grounded to third.
3 Terry grounded to second.
Washington
   Myer singled to left.
   Goslin doubled off the top of the
   fence, Myer stopping at third.
1 Manush popped to Ryan in short left.
2 Cronin grounded back to the mound, Myer
   scoring and Goslin going to third.
   Schulte doubled to right, scoring
   Goslin.
3 Kuhel grounded to Jackson and Schulte was
   caught in a run-down, Jackson to Critz.

2nd Inning
New York
1 Ott flied deep to left.
   Davis singled to left.
   Davis went to second on a wild pitch.
   Jackson walked.
2,3 Mancuso grounded into a double play,
   Cronin to Myer to Kuhel.
Washington
   Bluege doubled down the third base line.
1 Sewell grounded to second, Bluege going to
   third.
   Whitehill safe on a fielder's choice as
   Fitzsimmons fielding his bouncer threw
   to third but not in time to catch
   Bluege off the bag.
   Myer doubled down the first base line,
   scoring Bluege and moving Whitehill
   to third.
2,3 Goslin flied to left and Whitehill
   was doubled up trying to score after the
   catch, Moore to Mancuso.

3rd Inning
New York
1 Ryan robbed of a hit by Myer making an
   impossible gloved hand catch of his liner.
   Fitzsimmons singled off Cronin's glove.
2 Moore forced Fitzsimmons, Cronin to
   Myer.
   Critz singled to center, sending Moore
   to third.
3 Terry grounded to first.
Washington
1 Manush grounded to short.
2 Cronin grounded to second.
   Schulte singled past Terry into right.
3 Kuhel forced Schulte at second,
   Jackson to Critz.

4th Inning
New York
1 Ott struck out on three pitches.
2 Davis rolled out to second.
   Jackson doubled to left.
3 Mancuso flied to center.
Washington
1 Bluege grounded to short.
2 Sewell flied to center.
3 Whitehill fouled to Mancuso.

5th Inning
New York
1 Ryan bounced back to the mound.
2 Fitzsimmons grounded to third.
3 Moore bunted out to the mound, as
   Whitehill retired the side on only
   four pitches.
Washington
1 Myer called out on strikes.
2 Goslin flied to Davis in right-center.
3 Manush flied to right.

6th Inning
New York
1 Critz grounded to third.
2 Terry grounded to first.
3 Ott again struck out on three pitches.
Washington
   Cronin singled to right.
1 Schulte fouled to Terry.
2 Kuhel forced Cronin at second, Critz
   to Ryan.
3 Kuhel out trying to steal second,
   Mancuso to Ryan.

7th Inning
New York
1 Davis bounced back to the mound.
2 Jackson flied to deep left.
3 Mancuso grounded to third.
Washington
1 Bluege popped to Terry in short right.
   Sewell beat out a hit to short.
   Sewell stole second.
2 Whitehill grounded to second, Sewell
   going to third.
   Myer singled to right, scoring Sewell.
3 Goslin struck out.

8th Inning
New York
1 Ryan flied to right.
   Peel, pinch-hitting for Fitzsimmons,
   singled to left-center. Whitehill had retired
   eleven in a row.
   Moore safe at first and Peel to
   second on Cronin's fumble of Moore's
   grounder.
2 Critz grounded back to the pitcher,
   both runners advancing.
3 Terry popped to Sewell in front of
   the plate.
Washington
For New York—Bell now pitching.
1 Manush flied to left.
2 Cronin grounded to short.
3 Schulte flied to deep center.

9th Inning
New York
   Ott walked on four pitches.
1 Davis grounded to third, Ott
   taking second.
2 Jackson grounded to third, Ott
   taking third.
3 Mancuso flied to left.

Game 4 October 6 at Washington

N.Y.	000	100	000	01
Was.	000	000	100	00

New York	Pos	AB	R	H	RBI	PO	A	E
Moore	lf	5	0	2	0	3	0	0
Critz	2b	6	0	0	0	9	5	0
Terry	1b	5	1	2	1	9	0	0
Ott	rf	4	0	2	0	4	0	0
Davis	cf	4	0	1	0	1	0	0
Jackson	3b	5	1	1	0	0	2	0
Mancuso	c	2	0	0	0	5	0	0
Ryan	ss	5	0	2	1	1	5	0
Hubbell	p	4	0	1	0	1	3	1
Totals		40	2	11	2	33	15	1

Pitching	IP	H	R	ER	BB	SO
New York						
Hubbell (W)	11	8	1	0	4	5
Washington						
Weaver (L)	$10\frac{1}{3}$	11	2	2	4	3
Russell	$\frac{2}{3}$	0	0	0	0	1

Washington	Pos	AB	R	H	RBI	PO	A	E
Myer	2b	4	0	2	0	6	4	0
Goslin	rf-lf	4	0	1	0	1	0	0
Manush	lf	2	0	0	0	1	0	0
Harris	rf	1	0	0	0	2	0	0
Cronin	ss	5	0	1	0	1	4	0
Schulte	cf	5	0	1	0	2	0	0
Kuhel	1b	5	1	1	0	14	1	0
Bluege	3b	3	0	0	0	2	1	0
Sewell	c	4	0	2	1	4	1	0
Weaver	p	4	0	0	0	0	6	0
Russell	p	0	0	0	0	0	0	0
a Bolton		1	0	0	0	0	0	0
Totals		38	1	8	1	33	17	0

a Hit into double play for Russell in 11th.

Double—Moore. Home Run—Terry. Sacrifice Hits—Bluege 2, Davis, Goslin, Hubbell, Mancuso. Double Plays—Myer to Kuhel, Ryan to Critz to Terry. Left on Bases—New York 12, Washington 11. Umpires—Ormsby, Moran, Moriarty, Pfirman. Attendance—26,762. Time of Game—2:59.

1st Inning
New York
Moore walked.
1,2 Critz lined into a double play, Myer to Kuhel.
Terry beat out a hit over second.
3 Ott popped to third.
Washington
1 Myer flied to left.
2 Goslin flied to right.
3 Manush grounded to second.

2nd Inning
New York
1 Davis grounded to third.
2 Jackson struck out.
3 Mancuso flied to Goslin, who made a spectacular running catch.
Washington
1 Cronin popped to first.
2 Schulte flied to right.
3 Kuhel flied to center.

3rd Inning
New York
1 Ryan flied to left.
2 Hubbell grounded to third.
3 Moore grounded to short.
Washington
1 Bluege flied to deep left.
2 Sewell popped to Critz, racing into center.
3 Weaver grounded to second.

4th Inning
New York
1 Critz grounded to short.
Terry hit a home run into the far center field bleachers.
Ott walked on four pitches.
Davis beat out a roller to third, Ott going to second.
2 Jackson fouled to third.
Mancuso walked on four pitches, loading the bases.
3 Ryan struck out.
Washington
1 Myer out on a bunt, Hubbell to Terry.
Goslin singled past Terry becoming the Senator's first base runner.
Manush walked on four pitches.
2 Cronin flied to right, Goslin racing to third after the catch.
3 Schulte forced Manush at second, Ryan to Critz.

5th Inning
New York
1 Hubbell lined to short.
Moore singled to left.
2 Critz popped to Myer in short right.
3 Terry flied to deep center.
Washington
1 Kuhel struck out on three pitches.
2 Bluege flied to Moore making a great catch.
Sewell singled to right.
3 Weaver struck out.

6th Inning
New York
Ott singled to right-center.
1 Davis sacrificed Ott to second, Kuhel to Myer.
2 Jackson popped to Myer in short right.
Mancuso got an intentional pass.
3 Ryan tapped back to the mound.
Washington
Myer beat out a hit behind second.
1 Goslin sacrificed Myer to second, Jackson to Terry.
2 Manush grounded to Critz, making a great stop in the hole and throwing to Hubbell at first, Myer going to third.
3 Cronin struck out.

7th Inning
New York
For Washington—Manush thrown out of the game by Umpire Moran, Goslin moving to left as Harris came into play right.
1 Hubbell grounded to short.
Moore doubled to left-center.
2 Critz grounded to short, Moore moving to third.
3 Terry popped back to the mound.

7th Inning (continued)
Washington
1 Schulte popped to Terry.
Kuhel safe at first as Hubbell fumbled his bunt.
2 Bluege sacrificed Kuhel to second, Hubbell to Critz.
Sewell singled to center, Kuhel scoring.
3 Weaver popped to Critz in short right.

8th Inning
New York
Ott singled off Cronin's glove.
1 Davis struck out.
2 Jackson grounded to second, Ott going to second.
3 Mancuso rapped back to the box.
Washington
Myer walked.
1 Goslin forced Myer at second on an attempted sacrifice, Hubbell to Ryan.
2 Harris forced Goslin at second, Ryan to Critz.
Cronin hit a Texas League single into short right, Harris going all the way to third.
3 Schulte popped to second.

9th Inning
New York
Ryan singled over Kubel's head.
1 Hubbell sacrificed Ryan to second, Sewell to Myer who covered first.
2 Moore tapped back to the mound, Ryan going to third.
3 Critz flied to Harris in left.
Washington
1 Kuhel struck out.
2 Bluege flied to right.
3 Sewell grounded to short.

10th Inning
New York
1 Terry bounced back to the mound.
2 Ott flied to left.
3 Davis grounded to second.
Washington
1 Weaver struck out.
Myer singled to left on the first pitch.
2 Goslin grounded to second, Myer advancing to second.
Harris walked on four pitches.
3 Cronin forced Harris at second, Ryan to Critz.

11th Inning
New York
Jackson beat out a surprise bunt down the third base line.
1 Mancuso sacrificed Jackson to second, Weaver to Myer, covering first.
Ryan singled to left, scoring Jackson with the go-ahead run.
Hubbell singled over Cronin's head into left-center, Ryan stopping at second.
For Washington—Russell relieved Weaver on the mound.
2 Moore struck out on three pitches.
3 Critz flied to center on the first pitch.
Washington
Schulte singled over Jackson's head into left.
Kuhel safe on a bunt as Terry let it roll down the line, but it did not go foul, Schulte taking second.
1 Bluege sacrificed Schulte to third and Kuhel to second, Jackson to Critz, who covered first.
Sewell was intentionally walked, loading the bases.
2,3 Bolton, pinch-hitting for Russell, hit into a game-ending double play, Ryan to Critz to Terry.

Game 5 October 7 at Washington

N.Y.	020	001	000	1
Was.	000	003	000	0

New York	Pos	AB	R	H	RBI	PO	A	E
Moore	lf	5	0	1	0	3	0	0
Critz	2b	5	0	0	0	2	4	0
Terry	1b	5	0	2	0	13	1	0
Ott	rf	5	1	1	1	1	0	0
Davis	cf	5	1	2	0	1	0	0
Jackson	3b	3	1	1	0	2	4	1
Mancuso	c	3	1	1	1	7	1	0
Ryan	ss	2	0	1	0	0	5	0
Schumacher	p	3	0	1	2	0	0	0
Luque	p	1	0	1	0	1	0	0
Totals		37	4	11	4	30	15	1

Pitching	IP	H	R	ER	BB	SO
New York						
Schumacher	$5\frac{2}{3}$	8	3	3	1	1
Luque (W)	$4\frac{1}{3}$	2	0	0	2	5
Washington						
Crowder	$5\frac{1}{3}$	7	3	3	2	4
Russell (L)	$4\frac{2}{3}$	4	1	1	0	3

Washington	Pos	AB	R	H	RBI	PO	A	E
Myer	2b	5	0	0	0	3	1	0
Goslin	rf	4	0	1	0	4	1	0
Manush	lf	5	1	1	0	3	0	0
Cronin	ss	5	1	3	0	3	3	0
Schulte	cf	4	1	2	3	1	0	0
a Kerr		0	0	0	0	0	0	0
Kuhel	1b	5	0	2	0	7	0	0
Bluege	3b	4	0	1	0	1	1	0
Sewell	c	4	0	0	0	7	0	0
Crowder	p	2	0	0	0	0	2	0
Russell	p	1	0	0	0	1	1	0
Totals		39	3	10	3	30	9	0

a Ran for Schulte in 10th.

Doubles—Davis, Mancuso. Home Runs—Ott, Schulte. Sacrifice Hits—Jackson, Ryan. Double Plays—Jackson to Terry, Cronin to Kuhel. Wild Pitches—Crowder, Schumacher. Left on Bases. New York 7, Washington 9. Umpires—Moran, Moriarty, Pfirman, Ormsby. Attendance—28,454. Time of Game—2:38.

1st Inning
New York
Moore singled to left.
1 Critz flied to right.
Terry singled over second, Moore racing to third.
2 Ott struck out.
3 Davis forced Terry at second, Cronin to Myer.
Washington
1 Myer flied to deep left.
Goslin singled past Ryan into left-center.
2,3 Manush lined into a double play, Jackson to Terry.

2nd Inning
New York
Jackson singled to left.
Mancuso walked.
1 Ryan sacrificed Jackson to third and Mancuso to second, Crowder to Myer.
Schumacher singled to center, scoring Jackson and Mancuso.
2 Moore flied to right.
3 Critz flied to right.
Washington
1 Cronin flied to short right.
2 Schulte grounded to second.
3 Kuhel flied to left.

3rd Inning
New York
Terry singled to right.
1 Ott again struck out.
2 Davis popped to Cronin in short left.
3 Jackson struck out.
Washington
1 Bluege bounced to short.
2 Sewell grounded to short.
3 Crowder grounded to short.

4th Inning
New York
1 Mancuso fouled to Kuhel.
Ryan walked.
Ryan went to second on a wild pitch.
2 Schumacher struck out.
3 Moore grounded back to the mound.
Washington
1 Myer tapped out, Mancuso to Terry.
Goslin walked.
2 Manush forced Goslin at second, Jackson to Critz.
3 Cronin fouled to Mancuso.

5th Inning
New York
1 Critz flied to right.
2 Terry lined to third.
3 Ott flied to left.
Washington
Schulte beat out a slow roller to third.
Kuhel singled to left, Schulte stopping at second.
1 Bluege bunted foul on the third strike to be a strike out victim.
2 Sewell lined to left.
Schulte went to third but Kuhel held first on a wild pitch.
3 Crowder grounded to short.

6th Inning
New York
Davis doubled down the left field line.
1 Jackson sacrificed, Bluege to Kuhel.
Mancuso doubled to deep center, Davis scoring.
For Washington—Russell came in to pitch.
2 Ryan struck out on three pitches.
3 Schumacher struck out on four pitches.
Washington
1 Myer popped to third.
2 Goslin grounded to second.
Manush singled to right.
Cronin singled to left, sending Manush to third.
Schulte hit a three-run homer into the left field pavilion.
Kuhel singled off Critz's legs.
Bluege beat out a smash to third, Jackson recovered and got the ball but threw wildly to Terry as Kuhel went to third.
For New York—Luque now pitching.
3 Sewell grounded to second.

7th Inning
New York
1 Moore bounced back to the mound.
2 Critz grounded to short.
3 Terry flied to center.
Washington
1 Russell struck out on three pitches, but had to be tagged by Mancuso.
2 Myer took a called third strike.
3 Goslin struck out.

8th Inning
New York
1 Ott flied to deep left.
Davis singled to center.
2,3 Jackson hit into a double play, Cronin to Kuhel.
Washington
1 Manush grounded to third.
Cronin singled over Ryan's head.
2 Schulte flied to Davis in deep left-center.
3 Kuhel grounded to third.

9th Inning
New York
1 Mancuso popped to second.
Ryan blooped a single to right, but
2 was out trying for second, Goslin to Cronin.
Luque singled to center.
3 Moore struck out, tagged by Sewell who dropped the third strike.
Washington
1 Bluege called out on strikes.
2 Sewell grounded to short.
Russell walked.
3 Myer grounded to second.

10th Inning
New York
1 Critz flied to left.
2 Terry grounded to second.
Ott homered into the center field bleachers.
3 Davis bounced back to the mound.
Washington
1 Goslin grounded out, Terry to Luque.
2 Manush lined to second.
Cronin singled to left.
Schulte walked on four pitches.
Kerr ran for Schulte.
3 Kuhel struck out on three pitches.

1933 WORLD SERIES COMPOSITE BOX

	Wins	Composite Line Score				
New York Giants (N.L.)	4	2 2 2	1 0 7	0 0 0	1 1	– 16
Washington Senators (A.L.)	1	2 1 1	1 0 3	2 0 1	0 0	– 11

Manager	Regular Season W	L	Pct.	G. Ahead
Bill Terry	91	61	.599	5
Joe Cronin	99	53	.651	7

BATTING AND FIELDING

WORLD SERIES STATISTICS

	Pos	G	AB	R	H	2B	3B	HR	RBI	BB	SO	SB	BA	SA	PO	A	E
NEW YORK GIANTS																	
Bill Terry	1b	5	**22**	3	6	**1**	0	1	1	0	0	0	.273	.455	50	1	0
Hughie Critz	2b	5	**22**	2	3	0	0	0	0	1	0	0	.136	.136	16	18	1
Blondy Ryan	ss	5	18	0	5	0	0	0	1	1	5	0	.278	.278	10	**20**	1
Travis Jackson	3b	5	18	**3**	4	**1**	0	0	2	1	3	0	.222	.278	3	16	1
Mel Ott	rf	5	18	**3**	**7**	0	0	**2**	**4**	**4**	4	0	**.389**	**.722**	10	0	0
Kiddo Davis	cf	5	19	1	**7**	**1**	0	0	0	0	3	0	.368	.421	6	0	0
Jo-Jo Moore	lf	5	**22**	1	5	**1**	0	0	1	1	3	0	.227	.273	13	1	0
Gus Mancuso	c	5	17	2	2	**1**	0	0	2	3	0	0	.118	.176	31	4	0
Homer Peel	cf-ph	2	2	0	1	0	0	0	0	0	0	0	.500	.500	0	0	0
Lefty O'Doul	ph	1	1	1	1	0	0	0	2	0	0	0	1.000	1.000			
Johnny Vergez		Did not play-appendicitis															
Bernie James		Did not play															
Paul Richards		Did not play															
Chuck Dressen		Did not play															
Harry Danning		Did not play															
Carl Hubbell	p	2	7	0	2	0	0	0	0	0	0	0	.286	.286	1	4	1
Hal Schumacher	p	2	7	0	2	0	0	0	3	0	3	0	.286	.286	0	2	0
Freddie Fitzsimmons	p	1	2	0	1	0	0	0	0	0	0	0	.500	.500	0	1	0
Dolf Luque	p	1	1	0	1	0	0	0	0	0	0	0	1.000	1.000	1	0	0
Hi Bell	p	1	0	0	0	0	0	0	0	0	0	0	—	—	0	0	0
Roy Parmalee		Did not play															
Glenn Spencer		Did not play															
Watty Clark		Did not play															
Jack Salveson		Did not play															
team total		5	176	16	47	5	0	3	16	11	21	0	.267	.347	141	67	4

Double Plays-5
Left on Bases-39

REGULAR SEASON STATISTICS

		Main Pos	G	AB	R	H	2B	3B	HR	RBI	BB	SO	SB	BA	SA
Bill Terry		1b	123	475	68	153	20	5	6	58	40	23	3	.322	.423
Hughie Critz		2b	133	558	68	137	18	5	2	33	23	24	4	.246	.306
Blondy Ryan		ss	146	525	47	125	10	5	3	48	15	62	0	.238	.293
Travis Jackson		3b-ss	53	122	11	30	5	0	0	12	8	11	2	.246	.287
Mel Ott		of	152	580	98	164	36	1	23	103	**75**	48	1	.283	.467
Kiddo Davis		of	126	434	61	112	20	4	7	37	25	30	10	.258	.371
Jo-Jo Moore		of	132	524	56	153	16	5	0	42	21	27	4	.292	.342
Gus Mancuso		c	144	481	39	127	17	2	6	56	48	21	0	.264	.345
Homer Peel		of	84	148	16	38	1	1	1	12	14	10	0	.257	.297
Lefty O'Doul	a	of	78	229	31	70	9	1	9	35	29	17	1	.306	.472
Johnny Vergez		3b	123	458	57	124	21	6	16	72	39	66	1	.271	.448
Bernie James		2b	60	125	22	28	2	1	1	10	8	12	5	.224	.280
Paul Richards		c	51	87	4	17	3	0	0	10	3	12	0	.195	.230
Chuck Dressen		3b	16	45	3	10	4	0	0	3	1	4	0	.222	.311
Harry Danning		c	3	2	0	0	0	0	0	0	1	0	0	.000	.000
Carl Hubbell		p	45	109	6	20	2	1	1	12	2	18	0	.183	.248
Hal Schumacher		p	39	98	8	21	1	0	0	10	2	20	0	.214	.224
Freddie Fitzsimmons		p	36	95	3	19	3	1	2	6	1	14	0	.200	.316
Dolf Luque		p	35	19	0	5	0	0	0	1	0	2	0	.263	.263
Hi Bell		p	38	29	5	4	0	0	0	0	2	8	0	.138	.138
Roy Parmalee		p	33	81	6	19	4	0	1	8	2	22	0	.235	.321
Glenn Spencer		p	17	12	0	2	0	0	0	0	0	2	0	.167	.167
Watty Clark	b	p	16	11	1	3	0	0	0	0	1	1	0	.273	.273
Jack Salveson		p	8	9	0	1	0	0	0	0	0	1	0	.111	.111
team total			156	**5461**	636	1437	204	41	**82**	598	377	477	31	.263	.361

a—from Brooklyn
b—from Brooklyn
Hank Leiber (of), Sam Leslie (1b), Joe Malay (1b), Phil Weintraub (of), Watty Clark (p), Roy Parmalee (p), Jack Salveson (p), Glenn Spencer (p) also played for the Giants during the season.

WORLD SERIES STATISTICS

	Pos	G	AB	R	H	2B	3B	HR	RBI	BB	SO	SB	BA	SA	PO	A	E
WASHINGTON SENATORS																	
Joe Kuhel	1b	5	20	1	3	0	0	0	1	1	4	0	.150	.150	**59**	3	0
Buddy Myer	2b	5	20	2	6	**1**	0	0	2	2	3	0	.300	.350	15	12	**3**
Joe Cronin	ss	5	**22**	1	**7**	0	0	0	2	0	2	0	.318	.318	7	15	1
Ossie Bluege	3b	5	16	1	2	**1**	0	0	0	1	**6**	0	.125	.188	3	13	0
Goose Goslin	rf-lf	5	20	2	5	**1**	0	1	1	1	3	0	.250	.450	8	1	0
Fred Schulte	cf	5	21	1	**7**	**1**	0	1	**4**	1	1	0	.333	.524	9	0	0
Heinie Manush	lf	5	18	2	2	0	0	0	0	2	1	0	.111	.111	10	0	0
Luke Sewell	c	5	17	1	3	0	0	0	1	2	0	**1**	.176	.176	23	2	0
Dave Harris	ph-rf	3	2	0	0	0	0	0	0	2	0	0	.000	.000	2	0	0
Cliff Bolton	ph	2	2	0	0	0	0	0	0	0	0	0	.000	.000			
Sam Rice	ph	1	1	0	1	0	0	0	0	0	0	0	1.000	1.000			
John Kerr	pr	1	0	0	0	0	0	0	0	0	0	0	—	—			
Bob Boken		Did not play															
Moe Berg		Did not play															
General Crowder	p	2	4	0	1	0	0	0	0	0	0	0	.250	.250	0	3	0
Monty Weaver	p	1	4	0	0	0	0	0	0	0	2	0	.000	.000	0	6	0
Earl Whitehill	p	1	3	0	0	0	0	0	0	0	0	0	.000	.000	0	4	0
Jack Russell	p	3	2	0	0	0	0	0	0	1	2	0	.000	.000	2	3	0
Lefty Stewart	p	1	1	0	0	0	0	0	0	0	1	0	.000	.000	0	0	0
Alex McColl	p	1	0	0	0	0	0	0	0	0	0	0	—	—	0	1	0
Tommy Thomas	p	2	0	0	0	0	0	0	0	0	0	0	—	—	0	1	0
Ed Chapman		Did not play															
team total		5	173	11	37	4	0	2	11	13	25	1	.214	.272	138	63	4

Double Plays—4
Left on Bases—37

REGULAR SEASON STATISTICS

	Main Pos	G	AB	R	H	2B	3B	HR	RBI	BB	SO	SB	BA	SA
Joe Kuhel	1b	153	602	89	194	84	10	11	107	59	48	17	.322	.467
Buddy Myer	2b	131	530	95	160	29	15	4	61	60	29	6	.302	.436
Joe Cronin	ss	152	602	89	186	**45**	11	5	118	87	49	5	.309	.445
Ossie Bluege	3b	140	501	63	131	14	0	6	71	55	34	6	.261	.325
Goose Goslin	of	132	549	97	163	35	10	10	64	42	32	5	.297	.452
Fred Schulte	of	144	550	98	162	30	7	5	87	61	27	10	.295	.402
Heinie Manush	of	153	658	115	**221**	32	**17**	5	95	36	18	6	.336	.459
Luke Sewell	c	141	474	64	125	30	4	2	61	48	24	7	.264	.357
Dave Harris	of	82	177	33	46	9	2	5	38	25	26	3	.260	.418
Cliff Bolton	c	33	39	4	16	1	1	0	6	6	3	0	.410	.487
Sam Rice	of	73	85	19	25	4	3	1	12	3	7	0	.294	.447
John Kerr	2b	28	40	5	8	0	0	0	0	3	2	0	.200	.200
Bob Boken	2b-3b-ss	55	133	19	37	5	2	3	26	9	16	0	.278	.414
Moe Berg	c	40	65	8	12	3	0	2	9	4	5	0	.185	.323
General Crowder	p	52	102	7	19	3	0	0	7	9	8	0	.186	.216
Monty Weaver	p	23	56	6	7	1	0	0	4	2	14	0	.125	.143
Earl Whitehill	p	40	108	7	24	2	1	0	11	6	14	0	.222	.259
Jack Russell	p	50	34	5	5	0	0	0	3	3	13	0	.147	.147
Lefty Stewart	p	35	77	9	11	1	2	0	4	12	9	0	.143	.208
Alex McColl	p	4	6	2	2	1	0	0	2	0	1	0	.333	.500
Tommy Thomas	p	35	42	5	10	0	0	0	2	4	4	0	.238	.238
Ed Chapman	p	6	3	0	0	0	0	0	0	0	1	0	.000	.000
team total		153	**5524**	850	**1586**	281	**86**	60	793	539	395	65	**.287**	.402

Cecil Travis (3b), Bobby Burke (p), John Campbell (p), Ed Linke (p), Bill McAfee (p), Ray Prim (p), Bud Thomas (p) also played for the Senators during the season.

PITCHING

WORLD SERIES STATISTICS

	G	GS	CG	IP	H	R	ER	BB	SO	W	L	SV	ERA
NEW YORK GIANTS													
Carl Hubbell	2	**2**	**2**	**20**	13	3	0	**6**	**15**	**2**	0	0	**0.00**
Hal Schumacher	2	**2**	1	14⅔	13	4	4	5	3	1	0	0	2.45
Freddie Fitzsimmons	1	1	0	7	9	4	4	0	2	0	**1**	0	5.14
Dolf Luque	1	0	0	4⅓	2	0	0	2	5	1	0	0	0.00
Hi Bell	1	0	0	1	0	0	0	0	0	0	0	0	0.00
Roy Parmalee	Did not play												
Glenn Spencer	Did not play												
Watty Clark	Did not play												
Jack Salveson	Did not play												
team total	5	5	3	47	37	11	8	13	25	4	1	0	1.53
WASHINGTON SENATORS													
General Crowder	2	**2**	0	11	**16**	**9**	**9**	5	7	0	**1**	0	7.36
Monty Weaver	1	1	0	10⅓	11	2	2	4	3	0	**1**	0	1.74
Jack Russell	**3**	0	0	10⅓	8	1	1	0	7	0	**1**	0	0.87
Earl Whitehill	1	1	1	9	5	0	0	2	2	1	0	0	**0.00**
Lefty Stewart	1	1	0	2	6	4	2	0	0	0	**1**	0	9.00
Alex McColl	1	0	0	2	0	0	0	0	0	0	0	0	0.00
Tommy Thomas	2	0	0	1⅓	1	0	0	0	2	0	0	0	0.00
Ed Chapman	Did not play												
team total	5	5	1	46	47	16	14	11	21	1	4	0	2.74

REGULAR SEASON STATISTICS

		G	GS	CG	IP	H	ER	BB	SO	W	L	Pct	SV	ShO	ERA
NEW YORK GIANTS															
Carl Hubbell		45	33	22	**309**	256	57	47	156	**23**	12	.657	5	**10**	**1.66**
Hal Schumacher		35	33	21	259	199	62	84	96	19	12	.613	1	7	2.15
Freddie Fitzsimmons		36	**35**	13	252	243	81	72	65	16	11	.593	0	1	2.89
Dolf Luque		35	0	0	80	75	24	19	23	8	2	.800	4	0	2.70
Hi Bell		38	7	1	105	100	24	20	24	6	5	.545	5	1	2.06
Roy Parmalee		32	32	14	218	191	77	77	132	13	8	.619	0	3	3.18
Glenn Spencer		17	3	1	47	52	27	26	14	0	2	.000	0	0	5.17
Watty Clark	b	16	5	0	44	58	23	11	11	3	4	.429	0	0	4.70
Jack Salveson		6	2	0	31	30	13	14	8	0	2	.000	0	0	3.77
team total		156	156	75	**1409**	1280	424	400	555	**91**	61	**.599**	15	**23**	**2.71**
WASHINGTON SENATORS															
General Crowder		**52**	35	17	299	**311**	132	81	110	**24**	15	.615	4	0	3.97
Monty Weaver		23	21	12	152	147	55	53	45	10	5	.667	0	1	3.26
Jack Russell		50	3	2	124	119	37	32	28	12	6	.667	**13**	0	2.69
Earl Whitehill		39	**37**	19	270	271	100	100	96	22	8	.733	1	2	3.33
Lefty Stewart		34	31	11	231	227	98	60	69	15	6	.714	0	1	3.82
Alex McColl		4	1	1	17	13	5	7	5	1	0	1.000	0	0	2.65
Tommy Thomas		35	14	2	135	149	72	49	35	7	7	.500	3	0	4.80
Ed Chapman		6	1	0	9	10	8	0	4	0	0	—	0	0	8.00
team total		153	153	68	1390	1415	590	452	447	**99**	53	**.651**	**26**	5	3.82

Total Attendance—164,076 Average Attendance—32,815 Winning Player's Share—$4,257 Losing Player's Share—$3,010

1934
A Victory in the Garbage

Although they didn't get the name until next year, the 1934 St. Louis Cardinals were the Gashouse Gang. A collection of brash, fast-talking free spirits, the Cardinals rushed into first place on the last two days of the season with a club both good and colorful. They always played hard, never ducked a fight, started countless commotions in hotel lobbies, and fielded an excellent hillbilly band called the Mississippi Mudcats. The cast included veteran hustler Frankie Frisch, the manager and second baseman; shortstop Leo Durocher, a competant fielder and great Lip; third baseman Pepper Martin, the scrappy hero of the 1931 Series; first baseman Ripper Collins, the top power hitter in the National League; left fielder Joe Medwick, aggressive with the bats and in his personal manner; center fielder Ernie Orsatti, a former Hollywood stunt man and stand-in for Buster Keaton; and the incomparable Dizzy Dean. The possessor of a blazing fast ball and sharp curve, Dean never hesitated to beat his own drum, predicting this spring that he and his brother Paul would win 50 games between them; as it turned out, Dizzy won 30 and Paul won 19.

Facing this swashbuckling group were the more conservative Detroit Tigers. Connie Mack had a good deal to do with the Tigers' success, since he had peddled catcher Mickey Cochrane to Detroit during the winter. Installed as manager, Cochrane led the Tigers to their first American League pennant since 1909. A team batting average of .300 aptly summed up the murderous Detroit offense, led by powerful Hank Greenberg, consistent Charlie Gehringer, newly acquired veteran Goose Goslin, and Cochrane himself. Cochrane had two pitching aces in Schoolboy Rowe and Tommy Bridges, both winning over 20 games, and the second-line duo of veteran Firpo Marberry and submariner Eldon Auker each won 15 games.

But Cochrane passed over all his top starters and picked General Crowder, a late-season pickup from Washington, to start game one in Detroit against Dizzy Dean. Crowder had been knocked out twice by the Giants in last year's Series, and the Cards repeated the feat en route to an 8–3 victory. The Tigers also trailed the second game 2–1 going into the bottom of the ninth, but they sent it into extra innings and won it in the twelfth on walks to Gehringer and Greenberg and a single by Goslin.

Back in St. Louis, the Cards went back ahead in the Series behind Paul Dean's 4–1 third-game victory. Game four was tied at 4–4 after six innings, but the Tigers belted the St. Louis bullpen in the late innings and won 10–4. Dizzy Dean pinch-ran in the fourth inning, failed to slide while running to second, and caught shortstop Billy Rogell's throw right on the head. They carried Diz off the field on a stretcher, X-rayed his head, and found nothing wrong. He came out the next day and pitched game five, but lost 3–1 to Tommy Bridges.

Now the Tigers led the Series 3–2 and had the final two games in their home park. They had Rowe, their 24-game winner, up against Paul Dean in game six. Both pitchers went all the way, with Dean singling in Durocher in the seventh inning with the winning run in a 4–3 victory that kept the Cards alive into a seventh game. Frisch naturally sent Dizzy Dean to the mound in this all-or-nothing situation, while Cochrane settled upon Auker, the winner of the fourth game. Dean's fast ball and Auker's underhand deliveries kept the game scoreless through two innings, but then the Cardinals jumped all over Auker and three relievers to score seven times in the third inning and effectively wrap up the game. With Dean pitching superbly, the Cards ran the score up to 9–0 in the sixth inning, when Joe Medwick slid hard into third base on a triple and briefly wrestled with Tiger third baseman Marv Owen. When Medwick took his position in left field in the bottom of the inning, the frustrated fans pelted him with garbage of all sorts. He went to the field three times and retreated to the dugout each time under a barrage of refuse. Commissioner Kenesaw M. Landis, at a field-level box, weighed the pending riot and the possibility of finishing the game against the score, and he decided to order Medwick from the game. With the Cards ahead 9–0, it was not a vital loss; at the end of nine innings, the Cards had won 11–0 and were World Champions.

Game 1 October 3 at Detroit

| St. L. | 0 2 1 | 0 1 4 | 0 0 0 |
| Det. | 0 0 1 | 0 0 1 | 0 1 0 |

St. Louis	Pos	AB	R	H	RBI	PO	A	E
Martin	3b	5	1	1	1	1	1	0
Rothrock	rf	4	0	2	2	2	0	0
Frisch	2b	4	0	0	0	2	4	0
Medwick	lf	5	2	4	2	2	0	0
Collins	1b	4	2	1	0	13	1	0
DeLancey	c	5	0	1	2	7	1	0
Orsatti	cf	4	1	2	0	1	0	2
Fullis	cf	1	0	1	0	0	0	0
Durocher	ss	5	0	0	0	0	4	0
D. Dean	p	5	2	1	0	1	2	0
Totals		42	8	13	7	27	13	2

Pitching	IP	H	R	ER	BB	SO
St. Louis						
D. Dean (W)	9	8	3	3	2	6
Detroit						
Crowder (L)	5	6	4	1	1	1
Marberry	⅓	4	4	4	0	0
Hogsett	3⅔	3	0	0	0	1

Detroit	Pos	AB	R	H	RBI	PO	A	E
White	cf	2	1	0	0	7	0	0
Cochrane	c	4	0	1	0	2	0	0
Gehringer	2b	4	0	2	1	2	3	1
Greenberg	1b	4	2	1	1	8	1	1
Goslin	lf	4	0	2	1	3	0	0
Rogell	ss	4	0	1	0	1	4	1
Owen	3b	4	0	0	0	2	1	2
Fox	rf	4	0	0	0	2	0	0
Crowder	p	1	0	0	0	0	0	0
a Doljack		1	0	0	0	0	0	0
Marberry	p	0	0	0	0	0	1	0
Hogsett	p	1	0	0	0	0	0	0
b G. Walker		1	0	0	0	0	0	0
Totals		34	3	8	3	27	11	5

a Flied out for Crowder in 5th.
b Struck out for Hogsett in 9th.

Doubles—D. Dean, DeLancey. Home Runs—Greenberg, Medwick. Sacrifice Hits—Frisch, Rothrock. Double Play—DeLancey to Frisch. Left on Bases—St. Louis 10, Detroit 6. Umpires—Owens (A), Klem (N), Geisel (A), Reardon (N). Attendance—42,505. Time of Game—2:13.

1st Inning
St. Louis
1 Martin grounded to third.
2 Rothrock flied to center.
 Frisch was safe at first on Owen's error.
 Medwick singled to left, Frisch stopping at second.
3 Collins flied to center.
Detroit
1 White grounded to short.
2 Cochrane grounded to second.
 Gehringer singled to left.
3 Greenberg grounded to third.

2nd Inning
St. Louis
1 DeLancey flied to deep left.
 Orsatti singled to left.
2 Durocher flied to center.
 Dean got safely to first on Gehringer's fumble as Orsatti went to second.
 Martin safe at first on Owen's low throw to Greenberg, loading the bases.
 Rothrock singled to left-center, Orsatti and Dean scoring with Martin going to third.
3 Frisch grounded to second.
Detroit
 Goslin singled to left.
1,2 Rogell struck out and Goslin was doubled up trying for second, Delancey to Frisch.
3 Owen struck out.

3rd Inning
St. Louis
 Medwick singled to left.
1 Collins forced Medwick at second, Greenberg to Rogell but Rogell's return throw for a DP went into the Cardinal dugout and Collins went to second.
 DeLancey was safe at first when Greenberg let the ball go through his legs, Collins scoring.
 (Detroit's 5th error in 2 1/3 innings).
2 Orsatti flied to right.
3 Durocher flied to right.
Detroit
1 Fox fouled to Collins.
2 Crowder bounced back to the mound.
 White walked.
 Cochrane singled to left, White stopping at second.
 Gehringer singled to center, White scoring and as Orsatti fumbled the hit, Cochrane took third and Gehringer got to second.
3 Greenberg struck out.

4th Inning
St. Louis
1 Dean flied to deep left.
2 Martin struck out.
3 Rothrock popped to third.
Detroit
1 Goslin grounded to second.
2 Rogell flied to left.
3 Owen popped to Frisch in short right.

5th Inning
St. Louis
1 Frisch flied to Fox in front of the right field bleachers.
 Medwick hit a home-run into the left field bleachers.
 Collins walked.
2 DeLancey flied to center.
 Orsatti singled to left, Collins stopping at second.
3 Durocher flied to center.
Detroit
1 Fox fouled to Collins.
2 Doljack, pinch-hitting for Crowder, flied to center.
 White walked again.
3 Cochrane grounded to second.

6th Inning
St. Louis
 For Detroit—Marberry now pitching.
 Dean doubled to left center.
 Martin singled to center, Dean scoring.
1 Rothrock singled to second, Marberry to Greenberg.
2 Frisch fouled to Owen in left.
 Medwick got his fourth straight hit, a single to right, scoring Martin.
 Collins singled to right, advancing Medwick to third.
 For Detroit—Hogsett took Marberry's place on the mound.
 DeLancey lined a double off the left field wall, Medwick and Collins both scoring.
3 Orsatti grounded to second.
Detroit
1 Gehringer grounded out, Collins to Dean.
 Greenberg singled to center, and went to second when Orsatti kicked the ball for his second error.
 Goslin singled to left, scoring Greenberg.
2 Rogell grounded to second, Goslin advancing to second.
3 Owen struck out.

7th Inning
St. Louis
1 Durocher grounded out to Rogell, who made a marvelous stop and throw.
2 Dean struck out.
3 Martin grounded to short.
Detroit
1 Fox fouled to DeLancey.
2 Hogsett grounded to short.
3 White took a called third strike.

8th Inning
St. Louis
 Rothrock singled to right-center.
1 Frisch sacrificed Rothrock to second, Hogsett to Greenberg.
2 Medwick flied to center, Rothrock going to third, after the catch.
3 Collins grounded to second.
Detroit
 For St. Louis—Fullis playing center.
1 Cochrane grounded to short.
2 Gehringer flied to left.
 Greenberg homered deep into the left field bleachers.
3 Goslin grounded to short.

9th Inning
St. Louis
1 DeLancey flied to left.
 Fullis singled to center.
2 Durocher forced Fullis at second, Rogell to Gehringer.
3 Dean forced Durocher at second, Gehringer unassisted.
Detroit
 Rogell singled to left.
1 Owen grounded out off Dean's leg to Collins, Rogell going to second.
2 Fox hit a hard smash to Martin for a fielder's choice, as Martin tagged Rogell on his run to third.
3 G. Walker, batting for Hogsett, struck out on a full count.

1934

Game 2 October 4 at Detroit

St L. 011 000 000 000
Det.   000 000 100 001

St. Louis	Pos	AB	R	H	RBI	PO	A	E
Martin	3b	5	1	2	0	1	1	1
Rothrock	rf	4	0	0	0	4	0	0
Frisch	2b	5	0	1	0	3	6	1
Medwick	lf	5	0	1	1	0	0	0
Collins	1b	5	0	1	0	12	2	0
DeLancey	c	5	1	1	0	10	0	0
Orsatti	cf	4	0	1	1	2	0	0
Durocher	ss	4	0	0	0	1	3	0
Hallahan	p	3	0	0	0	1	3	1
B. Walker	p	1	0	0	0	0	1	0
Totals		41	2	7	2	x34	16	3

Pitching	IP	H	R	ER	BB	SO
St. Louis						
Hallahan	8⅓	6	2	2	4	6
B. Walker (L)	3	1	1	1	3	2
Detroit						
Rowe (W)	12	7	2	2	0	7

Detroit	Pos	AB	R	H	RBI	PO	A	E
White	cf	4	0	0	0	4	0	0
a G. Walker		1	0	1	1	0	0	0
Doljack	cf	1	0	0	0	1	0	0
Cochrane	c	4	0	0	0	8	0	0
Gehringer	2b	4	1	1	0	3	6	0
Greenberg	1b	4	0	0	0	13	1	0
Goslin	lf	6	0	2	1	3	1	0
Rogell	ss	4	1	1	0	1	2	0
Owen	3b	4	0	0	0	0	1	0
Fox	rf	5	1	2	1	2	0	0
Rowe	p	4	0	0	0	1	1	0
Totals		42	3	7	3	36	12	0

a Singled for white in 9th.
x one out when winning run scored.

Doubles—Fox, Martin, Rogell.
Triple—Orsatti. Stolen Base—Gehringer.
Sacrifice Hits—Rothrock, Rowe. Left
on Bases—St. Louis 4, Detroit 13.
Umpires—Klem, Geisel, Reardon, Owens.
Attendance—43,451. Time of Game—2:49.

1st Inning
St. Louis
1 Martin lined out to center.
2 Rothrock grounded to second.
 Frisch singled off Owen's glove.
3 Medwick took a called third strike.
Detroit
1 White grounded out, Collins to
 Hallahan.
2 Cochrane grounded to first.
 Gehringer safe at first when Hallahan
 dropped Collins' throw for an error.
3 Greenberg grounded to third.

2nd Inning
St. Louis
1 Collins flied to deep center.
 DeLancey singled off Gehringer's
 shins into right field.
 Orsatti tripled over Goslin's head to
 the left field fence, scoring
 DeLancey.
2 Durocher popped to first.
3 Hallahan lined to right.
Detroit
 Goslin singled on a high bouncer
 behind second.
1 Rogell fouled to DeLancey.
2 Owen called out on strikes.
3 Fox fouled to DeLancey.

3rd Inning
St. Louis
 Martin singled through the box on
 a full count.
1 Rothrock sacrificed Martin to second,
 Rowe to Greenberg.
2 Frisch flied to center.
 Medwick singled to left, scoring
 Martin and took second on the
 throw to the plate.
 Collins singled to left but Medwick
3 was out trying to score, a perfect
 throw from Goslin to Cochrane.
Detroit
1 Rowe struck out on three pitches.
2 White grounded to second.
 Cochrane walked.
 Gehringer singled to right, Cochrane
 racing to third.
3 Greenberg struck out on a 2–2 count.

4th Inning
St. Louis
1 DeLancey flied to left.
2 Orsatti bunted out to first.
3 Durocher grounded to third.
Detroit
1 Goslin grounded out off Hallahan to
 Durocher who made the throw to first.
 Rogell doubled to center.
2 Owen grounded to second, Rogell
 moving over to third.
 Fox doubled down the left field line,
 scoring Rogell.
3 Rowe struck out on a full count.

5th Inning
St. Louis
1 Hallahan struck out on three pitches.
2 Martin grounded to short.
3 Rothrock lined to second.
Detroit
1 White lined to second.
 Cochrane again walked.
2 Gehringer flied to right.
 Greenberg walked.
3 Goslin flied to center.

6th Inning
St. Louis
1 Frisch grounded to first.
2 Medwick flied to center.
3 Collins grounded out, Greenberg
 to Rowe.
Detroit
 Rogell got all the way to second
 when Martin after cleanly fielding
 his grounder, threw the ball over
 Collins' head all the way to the
 grandstand.
1 Owen bunted into a fielder's choice,
 Rogell out going into third,
 Hallahan to Martin.
2 Fox popped to second.
3 Rowe called out on strikes, (his third
 consecutive strikeout).

7th Inning
St. Louis
1 DeLancey lined to Rogell, making a
 headlong diving catch in the dirt.
2 Orsatti grounded to second.
3 Durocher fouled to Gehringer behind
 first.
Detroit
1 White popped to Durocher in short left.
2 Cochrane grounded to second.
 Gehringer walked.
3 Greenberg took a called third strike.

8th Inning
St. Louis
1 Hallahan popped to second.
2 Martin grounded to short.
3 On only the seventh pitch of the inning,
 Rothrock grounded to second.
Detroit
1 Goslin grounded to Frisch in short right, for a
 brilliant play.
2 Rogell flied to right.
3 Owen grounded to second. Hallahan also
 getting through the inning on only
 seven pitches.

9th Inning
St. Louis
1 Frisch fouled to Goslin.
2 Medwick called out on strikes on
 three pitches.
3 Collins also called out on strikes.

9th Inning (continued)
Detroit
 Fox singled to right.
1 Rowe sacrificed Fox to second,
 Hallahan to Collins.
 G. Walker, batting for White, singled to
 center, scoring Fox with the tying run.
 For St. Louis—B. Walker came in to pitch.
2 G. Walker was picked off first, B.
 Walker to Collins to Frisch to
 Durocher to Frisch.
3 Cochrane took a called third strike.

10th Inning
St. Louis
 For Detroit—Doljack playing center.
1 DeLancey flied to left.
2 Orsatti grounded to second.
3 Durocher flied to right.
Detroit
 Gehringer was safe when Frisch juggled
 his easy grounder.
1 Greenberg flied to Rothrock in deep
 right-center.
2 Goslin flied to right.
 Gehringer stole second.
 Rogell walked.
3 Owen lined to center.

11th Inning
St. Louis
1 B. Walker struck out.
 Martin doubled to left-center, the
 first Cardinal base-runner since
 the third inning.
2 Rothrock struck out.
3 Frisch out on a high bouncer to second.
Detroit
1 Fox fouled to Collins.
2 Rowe again struck out (the fourth time
 he struck out in the game only one shy
 of the Series record of 5).
3 Doljack fouled to Collins.

12th Inning
St. Louis
1 Medwick grounded to second.
2 Collins flied to Doljack, making a nice
 running catch at the flagpole.
3 DeLancey took a called third strike.
Detroit
1 Cochrane grounded to short.
 Gehringer walked.
 Greenberg also walked.
 Goslin singled sharply to center,
 scoring Gehringer with the winning run.

Game 3 October 5 at St. Louis

Det.	000	000	001						
St L.	110	020	00x						

Detroit	Pos	AB	R	H	RBI	PO	A	E
White	cf	5	1	2	0	4	0	0
Cochrane	c	3	0	0	0	6	3	0
Gehringer	2b	5	0	2	0	3	3	0
Greenberg	1b	4	0	1	1	6	0	0
Goslin	lf	4	0	1	0	2	0	0
Rogell	ss	4	0	1	0	1	2	2
Owen	3b	3	0	0	0	1	0	0
Fox	rf	4	0	1	0	1	0	0
Bridges	p	1	0	0	0	0	0	0
Hogsett	p	2	0	0	0	0	1	0
Totals		35	1	8	1	24	9	2

St. Louis	Pos	AB	R	H	RBI	PO	A	E
Martin	3b	3	2	2	0	2	1	0
Rothrock	rf	4	1	1	2	5	0	1
Frisch	2b	4	0	2	1	2	1	0
Medwick	lf	4	0	1	0	3	0	0
Collins	1b	4	1	2	0	3	0	0
DeLancey	c	4	0	1	0	9	0	0
Orsatti	cf	2	0	0	0	1	0	0
Durocher	ss	3	0	0	0	2	1	0
P. Dean	c	3	0	0	1	0	0	0
Totals		31	4	9	4	27	3	1

Pitching	IP	H	R	ER	BB	SO
Detroit						
Bridges (L)	*4	8	4	4	1	3
Hogsett	4	1	0	0	1	2
St. Louis						
P. Dean (W)	9	8	1	1	5	7

*Pitched to three batters in 5th.

Doubles—DeLancey, Gehringer, Martin. Triples—Greenberg, Martin, Rothrock. Double Plays—Cochrane to Gehringer, Rogell to Gehringer to Greenberg. Hit by Pitchers—Orsatti (by Bridges), Owen (by P. Dean). Left on Bases—Detroit 13, St. Louis 6. Umpires—Geisel, Reardon, Owens, Klem. Attendance—34,073. Time of Game—2:07.

1st Inning
Detroit
1 White fouled to Medwick, spearing the ball in deep left.
2 Cochrane struck out on a full count.
Gehringer singled to left.
3 Greenberg fouled to DeLancey.
St. Louis
Martin tripled off the right field pavilion screen.
1 Rothrock flied to deep center, Martin scoring after the catch.
Frisch singled to right.
2,3 Medwick struck out on a full count, and Frisch was out trying to steal second, Cochrane to Gehringer.

2nd Inning
Detroit
Goslin singled over Frisch's head, and took second on Rothrock's fumble.
1 Rogell flied to left.
Owen was hit by a pitch.
2 Fox popped to third.
3 Bridges was called out on strikes on only three pitches.
St. Louis
Collins singled to right.
DeLancey doubled off the right field screen, Collins stopping at third.
Orsatti was hit by a pitch, loading the bases.
1 Durocher fouled to Greenberg.
2 P. Dean flied to right, Collins scoring and DeLancey going to third, after the catch.
3 Martin flied to center.

3rd Inning
Detroit
1 White lined to deep right.
Cochrane walked.
Gehringer doubled to left, Cochrane stopping at third after Medwick nearly made a diving shoe-string catch.
2 Greenberg struck out on four pitches.
Goslin intentionally walked, loading the bases.
3 Rogell flied to center.
St. Louis
1 Rothrock flied to deep center.
2 Frisch fouled to Cochrane.
Medwick singled to center.
3 Collins flied to left.

4th Inning
Detroit
1 Owen grounded to short.
Fox singled to left.
Bridges walked.
2 White fouled to DeLancey.
Cochrane walked, loading the bases.
3 Gehringer grounded to second.
St. Louis
1 DeLancey struck out.
Orsatti walked.
2 Durocher popped to short.
3 Dean struck out.

5th Inning
Detroit
Greenberg walked on a full count.
1 Goslin flied to left on a full count.
Rogell singled to center, moving Greenberg to third.
2 Owen struck out on a 2–2 count.
3 Fox struck out on four pitches.
St. Louis
Martin doubled off the right field pavilion screen.
Rothrock tripled deep over Goslin's head, scoring Martin.
Frisch singled over Gehringer's head, scoring Rothrock.
For Detroit—Hogsett came in to pitch.
1,2 Medwick grounded into a double play, Rogell to Gehringer to Greenberg.
Collins was safe when Rogell threw low to first.
3 Collins was caught trying to steal second, Cochrane to Gehringer.

6th Inning
Detroit
1 Hogsett struck out.
White singled to center.
2 Cochrane lined to right.
3 Gehringer flied to right.
St. Louis
1 DeLancey fouled to Greenberg.
2 Orsatti called out on strikes on a full count.
3 Durocher flied to center.

7th Inning
Detroit
1 Greenberg grounded to third.
2 Goslin struck out with the count 2 and 2.
3 Rogell popped to short on a full count.
St. Louis
1 Dean grounded to second.
Martin walked on a full count.
Rothrock was safe on his DP grounder when Rogell dropped Gehringer's throw at second for an error.
2 Martin was caught at third on an attempted double steal as Rochrock got to second, Martin out—Cochrane to Owen.
3 Frisch grounded back to the mound.

8th Inning
Detroit
1 Owen flied to right.
2 Fox flied to right.
3 Hogsett fouled to Martin.
St. Louis
1 Medwick struck out on three pitches.
Collins beat out a hit back of second.
2 DeLancey grounded to short, Collins advancing to second.
3 Orsatti flied to left.

9th Inning
Detroit
White singled to right.
1 Cochrane popped to Durocher in short right.
2 Gehringer popped to second.
Greenberg tripled over Orsatti's head in deep center, scoring White.
3 Goslin popped to second.

Game 4 October 6 at St. Louis

Det.	003	100	150
St L.	011	200	000

Detroit	Pos	AB	R	H	RBI	PO	A	E
White	cf	4	2	1	0	2	0	0
Cochrane	c	5	2	1	0	1	0	0
Gehringer	2b	4	2	2	0	3	3	1
Goslin	lf	3	2	0	0	3	0	0
Rogell	ss	5	1	2	4	5	3	0
Greenberg	1b	5	1	4	3	10	2	0
Owen	3b	5	0	2	1	1	2	0
Fox	rf	4	0	1	0	2	0	0
Auker	p	4	0	0	0	0	2	0
Totals		39	10	13	8	27	12	1

Pitching	IP	H	R	ER	BB	SO
Detroit						
Auker (W)	9	10	4	3	4	1
St. Louis						
Carleton	$2\frac{2}{3}$	4	3	3	2	2
Vance	$1\frac{1}{3}$	2	1	0	1	3
B. Walker (L)	$3\frac{1}{3}$	5	6	4	3	0
Haines	$\frac{2}{3}$	1	0	0	0	2
Mooney	1	1	0	0	0	0

St. Louis	Pos	AB	R	H	RBI	PO	A	E
Martin	3b	4	0	1	1	1	2	3
Rothrock	rf	5	0	0	0	3	0	0
Frisch	2b	5	1	1	0	3	4	0
Medwick	lf	3	1	2	0	0	0	0
Collins	1b	4	0	2	1	8	1	0
DeLancey	c	2	0	0	0	7	1	1
Orsatti	cf	4	1	2	1	3	1	0
Durocher	ss	4	1	1	0	2	1	0
Carleton	p	1	0	0	0	0	0	0
Vance	p	0	0	0	0	0	0	0
a Davis		1	0	1	1	0	0	0
b D. Dean		0	0	0	0	0	0	0
B. Walker	p	1	0	0	0	0	0	1
Haines	p	0	0	0	0	0	0	0
c Crawford		1	0	0	0	0	0	0
Mooney	p	0	0	0	0	0	1	0
Totals		35	4	10	4	27	11	5

a Singled for Vance in 4th.
b Ran for Davis in 4th.
c Grounded out for Haines in 8th.

Doubles—Collins, Cochrane, Fox, Greenberg 2. Stolen Bases—Greenberg, Owen, White. Sacrifice Hits—Auker, Cochrane, Gehringer, Goslin. Double Plays—Greenberg to Rogell, Rogell to Greenberg, Auker to Rogell to Greenberg. Wild Pitch—Vance. Left on Bases—Detroit 12, St. Louis 8. Umpires—Reardon, Owens, Klem, Geisel. Attendance—37,492. Time of Game—2:43.

1st Inning
Detroit
1 White flied to center.
2 Cochrane grounded to second.
Gehringer singled to left-center.
3 Goslin flied to right.
St. Louis
Martin walked.
1,2 Rothrock hit into a double play, Auker to Rogell to Greenberg.
3 Frisch flied to left.

2nd Inning
Detroit
1 Rogell called out on strikes.
Greenberg singled off Durocher's glove into short left.
2 Owen popped to second.
3 Fox popped to short.
St. Louis
Medwick singled to center.
Collins doubled off the pavilion screen in right, Medwick stopping at third.
DeLancey walked, loading the bases.
1 Orsatti flied to left, Medwick scoring after the catch.
2 Durocher flied to right.
3 Carleton forced DeLancey at second, Rogell to Gehringer.

3rd Inning
Detroit
1 Auker flied to Orsatti in right-center.
2 White struck out.
Cochrane doubled to right.
Gehringer walked.
Goslin walked, loading the bases.
Rogell singled to center, scoring Cochrane and Gehringer, as Goslin went to third.
For St. Louis—Vance now pitching.
Greenberg again singled off Durocher's glove, Goslin scoring with Rogell stopping at second.
Owen singled to third, loading the bases.
3 Fox struck out.
St. Louis
1 Martin grounded to third.
2 Rothrock grounded to second.
Frisch bounced a single into center.
Medwick walked.
Collins singled to center, Frisch scoring and Medwick racing to third.
3 DeLancey grounded back to the mound.

4th Inning
Detroit
1 Auker took a called third strike.
White walked.
White stole second, and went to third as DeLancey's throw went into center. Martin also erred letting Orsatti's return throw get away.
White scored on a wild pitch.
2 Cochrane took a called third strike.
3 Gehringer grounded to second.
St. Louis
Orsatti singled to center.
Durocher safe on his grounder to Owen as Gehringer dropped Owen's throw.
Davis, batting for Vance, singled to right, scoring Orsatti as Durocher went to third.
D. Dean, pinch-running for Davis.
1 Martin forced Dean at second, Gehringer to Rogell, but Rogell's throw to first hit Dean and Durocher scored.
2 Rothrock flied to left.
3 Frisch forced Martin at second, Gehringer unassisted.

5th Inning
Detroit
For St. Louis—B. Walker pitching.
1 Goslin grounded to second.
2 Rogell flied to center.
3 Greenberg grounded to third.
St. Louis
Medwick singled to right.
1 Collins flied to center.
DeLancey walked.
2,3 Orsatti lined to Greenberg and threw to Rogell doubling Martin off second.

6th Inning
Detroit
Fox doubled off the left field bleacher wall.
1 Auker sacrificed Fox to third, DeLancey to Frisch.
2 White fouled to Martin.
3 Cochrane flied to right.
St. Louis
Durocher singled to left.
1 B. Walker struck out, trying to bunt.
2 Martin popped to Gehringer near the right field foul line.
3 Rothrock grounded to second.

7th Inning
Detroit
Gehringer singled to center.
1 Goslin sacrificed Gehringer to second, Martin to Collins.
Rogell safe when Martin dropped Durocher's throw at third.
Greenberg doubled as Orsatti misplayed his fly, Gehringer scoring with Rogell stopping at third.
2 Owen lined to right.
Fox intentionally walked.
3 Auker grounded to second.
St. Louis
1 Frisch flied to right.
2 Medwick grounded to first.
3 Collins also grounded to first.

8th Inning
Detroit
White walked.
Cochrane safe on a sacrifice as B. Walker threw wildly to second.
1 Gehringer sacrificed both runners up a base, Collins to Frisch.
Goslin intentionally walked, loading the bases.
Rogell singled to center, White and Cochrane scoring with Goslin going to third.
Greenberg hit a ground-rule double to right when a fan touched the ball, Goslin scoring as Rogell was held up at third.
For St. Louis—Haines came in to pitch.
Owen singled to right, Rogell scoring with Greenberg going to third.
2 As Fox struck out, the double steal was on and Owen beat the throw to second but on Frisch's throw, DeLancey let the throw get away as Greenberg scored and Owen went to third.
3 Auker took a called third strike.
St. Louis
1 DeLancey lined to third.
Orsatti singled to center.
2 Durocher forced Orsatti on a muffed pop by Greenberg to Rogell.
3 Crawford, hitting for Haines, grounded to second.

9th Inning
Detroit
For St. Louis—Mooney now pitching.
White singled to center.
1 Cochrane sacrificed White to second, Mooney to Collins.
2 Gehringer popped to short.
3 Goslin grounded to first.
St. Louis
Martin beat out a hit to deep short.
1 Rothrock flied to center.
2,3 Frisch grounded into a game-ending double play, Rogell to Greenberg

Game 5 October 7 at St. Louis

	Det.	St L.
	0 1 0 0 0 2 0 0 0	0 0 0 0 0 0 1 0 0

Detroit	Pos	AB	R	H	RBI	PO	A	E
White	cf	2	0	0	0	2	0	0
Cochrane	c	4	0	1	0	10	0	0
Gehringer	2b	4	1	1	1	4	1	0
Goslin	lf	4	0	1	0	1	0	0
Rogell	ss	4	1	0	0	0	2	0
Greenberg	1b	3	1	0	1	6	0	0
Owen	3b	4	0	0	0	1	0	0
Fox	rf	4	0	1	1	3	0	0
Bridges	p	4	0	1	0	0	2	0
Totals		33	3	7	3	27	5	0

Pitching	IP	H	R	ER	BB	SO
Detroit						
Bridges (W)	9	7	1	1	0	7
St. Louis						
D. Dean (L)	8	6	3	2	3	6
Carleton	1	1	0	0	0	0

St. Louis	Pos	AB	R	H	RBI	PO	A	E
Martin	3b	4	0	2	0	0	1	0
Rothrock	rf	4	0	0	0	2	0	0
Frisch	2b	4	0	1	0	2	3	0
Medwick	lf	4	0	0	0	3	0	0
Collins	1b	4	0	1	0	5	1	0
DeLancey	c	4	1	1	1	6	0	0
Fullis	cf	3	0	0	0	5	0	1
d Orsatti		1	0	0	0	0	0	0
Durocher	ss	2	0	1	0	3	2	0
a Davis		1	0	1	0	0	0	0
b Whitehead		0	0	0	0	1	0	0
D. Dean	p	2	0	0	0	0	0	0
c Crawford		1	0	0	0	0	0	0
Carleton	p	0	0	0	0	0	0	0
Totals		34	1	7	1	27	7	1

a Singled for Durocher in 8th.
b Ran for Davis in 8th.
c Fouled out for D. Dean in 8th.
d Hit into force out for Fullis in 9th.

Doubles—Fox, Goslin, Martin. Home Runs—DeLancey, Gehringer. Stolen Base—Rogell. Double Play—Collins to Durocher to Collins. Hit by Pitcher—White (by D. Dean). Wild Pitch—Bridges. Left on Bases—Detroit 7, St. Louis 6. Umpires—Owens, Klem, Geisel, Reardon. Attendance—38,536. Time of Game—1:58.

1st Inning
Detroit
White walked.
1 Cochrane flied to left.
2 Gehringer lined to center.
3 Goslin grounded to second.
St. Louis
Martin singled to center.
1 Rothrock fouled to Cochrane.
2 Frisch flied to deep right.
Martin went to second on a wild pitch.
3 Medwick popped to Greenberg, near the box.

2nd Inning
Detroit
1 Rogell took a called third strike.
Greenberg walked.
2 Owen flied to center.
Fox doubled past Fullis in center, scoring Greenberg.
3 Bridges struck out.
St. Louis
1 Collins flied to center.
2 DeLancey struck out.
3 Fullis fouled to Cochrane.

3rd Inning
Detroit
White again walked.
1,2 Cochrane grounded into a double play, Collins to Durocher to Collins.
3 Gehringer grounded to second.
St. Louis
Durocher singled to left.
1 D. Dean forced Durocher at second, Rogell to Gehringer.
2 Martin forced D. Dean at second, Gehringer unassisted.
3 Rothrock was called out for interference when his bat was intentionally in Cochrane's way trying to throw out Martin trying to steal second.

4th Inning
Detroit
Goslin blooped a double to short left.
Rogell beat out a bunt down the first base line, Goslin taking third.
1 Greenberg struck out on just four pitches.
2 Owen popped to Durocher in short left. Rogell stole second.
3 Fox struck out on three pitches.
St. Louis
1 Frisch struck out on a full count.
2 Medwick struck out on four pitches.
3 Collins grounded to first.

5th Inning
Detroit
1 Bridges called out on strikes with a full count.
2 White lined to second.
3 Cochrane flied to left.
St. Louis
1 DeLancey struck out on four pitches.
2 Fullis grounded to second.
3 Durocher flied to left.

6th Inning
Detroit
Gehringer hit a home run onto the right field pavilion roof.
1 Goslin flied to left.
Rogell singled to center and went all the way to third when the ball got through Fullis.
2 Greenberg flied to right, Rogell scoring after the catch.
3 Owen called out on strikes.
St. Louis
1 D. Dean struck out. Martin doubled off the right field pavilion wall.
2 Rothrock popped to Gehringer in short right.
3 Frisch popped to first.

7th Inning
Detroit
1 Fox grounded to short.
2 Bridges flied to center. White was hit by a pitch. Cochrane singled to right, White moving to third.
3 Gehringer flied to right.
St. Louis
1 Medwick struck out.
2 Collins fouled to Owen. DeLancey homered onto the roof of the right field pavilion.
3 Fullis bounced back to the mound.

8th Inning
Detroit
1 Goslin flied to center.
2 Rogell popped to Frisch in short right.
3 Greenberg fouled to Durocher in left field.
St. Louis
Davis, pinch-hitting for Durocher, singled to right.
Whitehead ran for Davis.
1 Crawford, pinch-hitting for D. Dean, fouled to Fox.
2 Martin lined to White, making a spectacular running catch in deep left-center.
3 Rothrock bounced back to the pitcher.

9th Inning
Detroit
For St. Louis—Carleton pitching and Whitehead playing short.
1 Owen flied to center.
2 Fox bunted out to third. Bridges singled to right.
3 White forced Bridges at second, Frisch to Whitehead.
St. Louis
Frisch singled to right.
1 Medwick flied to right. Collins hit a long single off the right field pavilion screen, Frisch going to third.
2 DeLancey called out on three straight called strikes.
3 Orsatti, batting for Fullis, forced Collins at second, Rogell to Gehringer.

Game 6 October 8 at Detroit

	St L.	Det.
	1 0 0 0 2 0 1 0 0	0 0 1 0 0 2 0 0 0

St. Louis	Pos	AB	R	H	RBI	PO	A	E
Martin	3b	5	1	1	1	1	2	0
Rothrock	rf	4	1	2	1	1	0	0
Frisch	2b	4	0	0	0	2	3	1
Medwick	lf	4	0	2	1	0	0	0
Collins	1b	4	0	0	0	8	0	0
DeLancey	c	4	0	0	0	6	4	0
Orsatti	cf	4	0	1	0	7	0	0
Durocher	ss	4	2	3	0	2	2	0
P. Dean	p	3	0	1	1	0	1	1
Totals		36	4	10	4	27	11	2

Pitching	IP	H	R	ER	BB	SO
St. Louis						
P. Dean (W)	9	7	3	1	2	4
Detroit						
Rowe (L)	9	10	4	3	0	5

Detroit	Pos	AB	R	H	RBI	PO	A	E
White	cf	2	0	0	0	0	0	0
Cochrane	c	4	0	3	1	7	0	0
Gehringer	2b	4	1	1	0	4	0	0
Goslin	lf	4	0	1	0	4	0	1
Rogell	ss	4	0	0	0	1	4	0
Greenberg	1b	4	1	1	1	10	0	0
Owen	3b	4	0	0	0	3	3	0
Fox	rf	4	0	1	0	2	0	0
Rowe	p	3	0	0	0	0	9	0
Totals		33	3	7	2	27	9	1

Doubles—Durocher, Fox, Rothrock. Sacrifice Hits—P. Dean, Rowe. Left on Bases—St. Louis 6, Detroit 6. Umpires—Klem, Geisel, Reardon, Owens. Attendance—44,551. Time of Game—1:58.

1st Inning
St. Louis
1 Martin popped to third.
Rothrock doubled to right.
2 Frisch lined to third.
Medwick singled to right, scoring Rothrock, Medwick going to second on the throw to the plate.
3 Collins flied to right.
Detroit
1 White struck out on a 2-2 count. Cochrane beat out a hit to second.
2 Gehringer grounded to second, Cochrane advancing to second.
3 Goslin hit a vicious liner to Martin, knocking it down and throwing Goslin out at first.

2nd Inning
St. Louis
1 DeLancey flied to Goslin in deep left, who made a leaping catch in front of the screen.
2 Orsatti grounded to third.
3 Durocher grounded to Owen, who made a fantastic pick-up and throw.
Detroit
1 Rogell struck out on a full count.
2 Greenberg called out on strikes on just three pitches.
3 Owen grounded to third.

3rd Inning
St. Louis
1 P. Dean grounded to first.
2 Martin grounded to second. Rothrock beat out a bouncer over Rowe's head.
3 Frisch grounded to second.
Detroit
1 Fox popped to short.
2 Rowe struck out. White walked. White went all the way to third when Frisch dropped the ball on a steal attempt, White was actually beaten so does not get credit for a stolen base.
Cochrane beat out a hit to first, scoring White.
3 Gehringer flied to right.

4th Inning
St. Louis
Medwick singled over second.
1 Collins forced Medwick at second, Gehringer to Rogell.
2 DeLancey struck out.
3 Orsatti flied to left.
Detroit
1 Goslin grounded to second.
2 Rogell fouled to DeLancey.
3 Greenberg fouled to Durocher in left.

5th Inning
St. Louis
Durocher singled past second.
1 P. Dean sacrificed Durocher to second, Greenberg unassisted.
Martin singled to left, scoring Durocher. Martin took second on the throw to the plate and continued to third when Goslin's poor throw got by Cochrane.
2 Rothrock grounded to short, scoring Martin.
3 Frisch fouled to Cochrane.
Detroit
1 Owen flied to center.
2 Fox flied to center.
3 Rowe lined to Orsatti in left-center.

6th Inning
St. Louis
1 Medwick struck out on a 2-2 count.
2 Collins also struck out.
3 DeLancey flied to left.
Detroit
White walked.
Cochrane lined a single over first as White raced to third.
Gehringer was safe at first as Dean let his grounder go through his legs for an error, White scoring and Cochrane going to second.
1 Goslin forced Cochrane at third on an attempted sacrifice, DeLancey to Martin.
2 Rogell flied to center, Gehringer going to third after the catch. Greenberg singled to left, scoring Gehringer with Goslin stopping at second.
3 Owen grounded to short.

7th Inning
St. Louis
1 Orsatti flied to left. Durocher doubled to deep center. P. Dean singled to right, scoring Durocher.
2 Martin flied to right.
3 Rothrock grounded to third.
Detroit
Fox blooped a Texas League double into short left.
1 Rowe sacrificed Fox to third, DeLancey to Frisch.
2 White grounded into a fielder's choice, Fox out at the plate, Durocher to DeLancey.
3 White was caught trying to steal second, DeLancey to Frisch.

8th Inning
St. Louis
1 Frisch grounded to short.
2 Medwick grounded to first.
3 Collins popped to Owen in short left.
Detroit
1 Cochrane grounded to second. Gehringer beat out a bouncer to second for a single. Goslin singled to right, Gehringer racing to third.
2 Rogell flied to center, both runners holding.
3 Greenberg fouled to Collins, making an almost impossible catch behind first.

9th Inning
St. Louis
1 DeLancey struck out on three pitches. Orsatti singled to center. Durocher singled to center, Orsatti racing to third and Durocher took second on the play for Orsatti at third.
2 P. Dean hit into a fielder's choice, Orsatti out at the plate, Gehringer to Cochrane as Durocher moved over to third.
3 Martin struck out.
Detroit
1 Owen fouled to Collins.
2 Fox flied to Orsatti in left-center.
3 Rowe flied to deep center.

Game 7 October 9 at Detroit

St. L.	0 0 7	0 0 2	2 0 0					
Det.	0 0 0	0 0 0	0 0 ʋ					

St. Louis	Pos	AB	R	H	RBI	PO	A	E
Martin	3b	5	3	2	1	0	1	0
Rothrock	rf	5	1	2	1	4	0	0
Frisch	2b	5	1	1	3	3	6	0
Medwick	lf	4	1	1	1	1	0	0
Fullis	lf	1	0	1	0	1	0	0
Collins	1b	5	1	4	2	7	1	1
DeLancey	c	5	1	1	1	5	0	0
Orsatti	cf	3	1	1	0	2	0	0
Durocher	ss	5	1	2	0	3	4	0
D. Dean	p	5	1	2	1	1	0	0
Totals		43	11	17	10	27	12	1

Pitching	IP	H	R	ER	BB	SO
St. Louis						
D. Dean (W)	9	6	0	0	0	5
Detroit						
Auker (L)	2⅓	6	4	4	1	1
Rowe	⅓	2	2	2	0	0
Hogsett	*0	2	1	1	2	0
Bridges	4⅓	6	4	2	0	2
Marberry	1	1	0	0	1	0
Crowder	1	0	0	0	0	1

*Pitched to four batters in 3rd.

Detroit	Pos	AB	R	H	RBI	PO	A	E
White	cf	4	0	0	0	3	0	1
Cochrane	c	4	0	0	0	2	2	0
Hayworth	c	0	0	0	0	1	0	0
Gehringer	2b	4	0	2	0	3	5	1
Goslin	lf	4	0	0	0	4	0	1
Rogell	ss	4	0	1	0	3	2	0
Greenberg	1b	4	0	1	0	7	0	0
Owen	3b	4	0	0	0	1	2	0
Fox	rf	3	0	2	0	3	0	0
Auker	p	0	0	0	0	0	0	0
Rowe	p	0	0	0	0	0	0	0
Hogsett	p	0	0	0	0	0	0	0
Brides	p	2	0	0	0	0	0	0
Marberry	p	0	0	0	0	0	0	0
a G. Walker		1	0	0	0	0	0	0
Crowder	p	0	0	0	0	0	0	0
Totals		34	0	6	0	27	11	3

a Flied out for Marberry in 8th.

Doubles—D. Dean, DeLancey, Fox 2,
Frisch, Rothrock 2. Triples—Durocher,
Medwick. Stolen Bases—Martin 2.
Double Play—Owen to Gehringer to
Greenberg. Left on Bases—St. Louis 9,
Detroit 7. Umpires—Geisel, Reardon,
Owens, Klem. Attendance—40,902.
Time of Game—2:19.

1st Inning
St. Louis
1 Martin struck out on a full count (after
   a 3–0 count).
   Rothrock doubled to left-center.
2 Frisch popped to Rogell in short
   center.
3 Medwick fouled to Owen.
Detroit
1 White grounded to second.
2 Cochrane grounded to second.
3 Gehringer flied to right.

2nd Inning
St. Louis
   Collins singled to center.
1,2 DeLancey grounded into a double play,
   Owen to Gehringer to Greenberg.
   Orsatti singled to right.
3   Orsatti out trying to steal,
   Cochrane to Gehringer.
Detroit
1 Goslin grounded out, Collins to Dean.
   Rogell bounced to short, but was safe
   when Collins dropped Durocher's
   perfect throw.
2 Greenberg struck out on four pitches.
3 Owen forced Rogell at second,
   Martin to Frisch.

3rd Inning
St. Louis
1 Durocher flied to center.
   D. Dean doubled to left just sliding in
   under Goslin's throw.
   Martin beat out a very slow roller to
   first, D. Dean going to third.
   Martin stole second.
   Rothrock walked, loading the bases.
   Frisch doubled to right (after four
   fouls), scoring D. Dean, Martin
   and Rothrock.
   For Detroit—Rowe replaced Auker on
   the mound.
2 Medwick grounded to short on Rowe's
   first pitch, Frisch going to third.
   Collins singled to left, also on the
   first pitch, scoring Frisch.
   DeLancey doubled off the right field
   screen, Collins scoring.
   For Detroit—Hogsett came in to pitch.
   Orsatti walked on a full count.
   Durocher singled to right, loading
   the bases.
   Dean beat out a bouncer to third,
   scoring DeLancey.
   Martin walked on four pitches, forcing
   in Orsatti.
   For Detroit—Bridges came in to replace
   Hogsett on the mound.
3 Rothrock forced Martin at second,
   Gehringer to Rogell.
Detroit
1 Fox flied to center.
2 Bridges grounded to second.
3 White flied to Orsatti in left-center.

4th Inning
St. Louis
1 Frisch grounded to second.
2 Medwick flied to right.
   Collins singled to right.
3 DeLancey forced Collins at second,
   Gehringer to Rogell.
Detroit
1 Cochrane popped to second.
   Gehringer singled to right (the first
   hit off of D. Dean).
2 Goslin flied to left.
3 Rogell forced Gehringer at second,
   Frisch to Durocher.

5th Inning
St. Louis
1 Orsatti flied to left.
2 Durocher flied to left.
3 D. Dean struck out on three pitches.
Detroit
   Greenberg singled to right.
1 Owen flied to center.
   Fox doubled to right, Greenberg
   stopping at third.
2 Bridges struck out on four pitches.
3 White grounded to Durocher, making a
   marvelous play and throwing to Collins
   while still in the air.

6th Inning
St. Louis
   Martin singled to left, and continued
   to second when Goslin fumbled the hit.
1 Rothrock flied to left.
2 Frisch flied to center.
   Medwick bounced a triple off the right-
   center field bleachers, Martin
   scoring.
   Collins got his **4th straight hit**, a
   single to center, scoring Medwick,
   and taking second on White's fumble.
3 DeLancey struck out but Cochrane dropped
   the ball and threw to Greenberg
   for the out.
Detroit
   Medwick after his near fight with
   Owen was pelted by fruit and soda
   bottles when he took the field. After
   a 5-minute delay Medwick attempted to
   again take left but more bottles and
   fruit fell to his feet. Finally
   Fullis replaced Medwick in left, and
   play resumed after a total 20
   minute delay.
1 Cochrane flied to right.
2 Gehringer grounded to short.
3 Goslin fouled to Collins.

7th Inning
St. Louis
1 Orsatti flied to center.
   Durocher tripled to the front of the
   right-center field bleachers,
2 Dean grounded to third, as
   Durocher held third.
   Martin was safe at first on Gehringer's
   fumble as Durocher scored.
   Martin stole second.
   Rothrock got a double to left-center,
   his second of the game, scoring
   Martin.
3 Frisch flied to right.
Detroit
1 Rogell popped to short.
2 Greenberg struck out.
3 Owen grounded to second.

8th Inning
St. Louis
   For Detroit—Marberry now pitching.
   Fullis singled to left-center.
1 Collins was finally retired on a fly to
   deep right.
2 DeLancey grounded to second, Fullis
   advancing to second.
   Orsatti walked.
3 Durocher forced Orsatti at second,
   Rogell to Gehringer.
Detroit
   Fox doubled to the left field bleacher
   wall, his second double of the game.
1 G. Walker, pinch-hitting for Marberry,
   flied to left.
2 White struck out.
3 Cochrane fouled to Rothrock.

9th Inning
St. Louis
   For Detroit—Crowder pitching and
   Hayworth catching.
1 Dean flied to left.
2 Martin fouled to Greenberg.
3 Rothrock struck out.
Detroit
   Gehringer singled to left.
1 Goslin forced Gehringer at second,
   Collins to Durocher.
   Rogell singled to right, Goslin
   stopping at second.
2 Greenberg struck out for the third
   time in the game and his ninth in
   the Series.
3 Owen forced Rogell at second,
   Durocher to Frisch.

1934 WORLD SERIES COMPOSITE BOX

	Wins	Composite Line Score												
St. Louis Cardinals (N.L.)	4	2	5	10	2	5	6	4	0	0	0	0	0	- 34
Detroit Tigers (A.L.)	3	0	1	5	2	0	5	1	6	2	0	0	1	- 23

Manager	W	L	Pct.	G. Ahead
	Regular Season			
Frankie Frisch	95	58	.621	2
Mickey Cochrane	101	53	.656	7

BATTING AND FIELDING

ST. LOUIS CARDINALS

WORLD SERIES STATISTICS	Pos	G	AB	R	H	2B	3B	HR	RBI	BB	SO	SB	BA	SA	PO	A	E
Ripper Collins	1b	7	30	4	**11**	1	0	0	3	1	2	0	.367	.400	56	6	1
Frankie Frisch	2b	7	**31**	2	6	1	0	0	4	0	1	0	.194	.226	17	**27**	2
Leo Durocher	ss	7	27	4	7	1	**1**	0	0	0	0	0	.259	.370	13	17	0
Pepper Martin	3b	7	**31**	**8**	**11**	3	**1**	0	4	3	3	**2**	.355	.516	6	9	**3**
Jack Rothrock	rf	7	30	3	7	3	**1**	0	6	1	2	0	.233	.400	19	0	1
Ernie Orsatti	cf-ph	7	22	3	7	0	**1**	0	2	3	1	0	.318	.409	16	1	2
Joe Medwick	lf	7	29	4	**11**	0	**1**	**1**	5	1	7	0	**.379**	.552	9	0	0
Bill DeLancey	c	7	29	3	5	3	0	**1**	4	2	8	0	.172	.379	50	6	2
Chick Fullis	cf-lf	3	5	0	2	0	0	0	0	0	0	0	.400	.400	6	0	1
Spud Davis	ph	2	2	0	2	0	0	0	1	0	0	0	1.000	1.000			
Pat Crawford	ph	2	2	0	0	0	0	0	0	0	0	0	.000	.000			
Burgess Whitehead	pr-ss	1	0	0	0	0	0	0	0	0	0	0	—	—	1	0	0
Francis Healy		Did not play															
Dizzy Dean	p-pr	4	12	3	3	2	0	0	1	0	3	0	.250	.417	2	2	0
Paul Dean	p	2	6	0	1	0	0	0	2	0	1	0	.167	.167	0	0	1
Wild Bill Hallahan	p	1	3	0	0	0	0	0	0	0	1	0	.000	.000	1	3	1
Bill Walker	p	2	2	0	0	0	0	0	0	0	2	0	.000	.000	0	1	1
Tex Carleton	p	2	1	0	0	0	0	0	0	0	0	0	.000	.000	0	0	0
Dazzy Vance	p	1	0	0	0	0	0	0	0	0	0	0	—	—	0	0	0
Jim Mooney	p	1	0	0	0	0	0	0	0	0	0	0	—	—	0	1	0
Jesse Haines	p	1	0	0	0	0	0	0	0	0	0	0	—	—	0	0	0
team total		7	262	34	73	14	5	2	32	11	31	2	.279	.393	196	73	15

Double Plays—2
Left on Bases—49

REGULAR SEASON STATISTICS		Main Pos	G	AB	R	H	2B	3B	HR	RBI	BB	SO	SB	BA	SA
Ripper Collins		1b	154	600	116	200	40	12	**35**	128	57	50	2	.333	**.615**
Frankie Frisch		2b	140	550	74	168	30	6	3	75	45	10	11	.305	.398
Leo Durocher		ss	146	500	62	130	26	5	3	70	33	40	2	.260	.350
Pepper Martin		3b	110	454	76	131	25	11	5	49	32	41	23	.289	.425
Jack Rothrock		of	154	**647**	106	184	35	3	11	72	49	56	10	.284	.399
Ernie Orsatti		of	105	337	39	101	14	4	0	31	27	31	6	.300	.365
Joe Medwick		of	149	620	110	198	40	**18**	18	106	21	83	3	.319	.529
Bill DeLancey		c	93	253	41	80	18	3	13	40	41	37	1	.316	.565
Chick Fullis	a	of	69	199	21	52	9	1	0	26	14	11	4	.261	.317
Spud Davis		c	107	347	45	104	22	4	9	65	34	27	0	.300	.464
Pat Crawford		3b	61	70	3	19	2	0	0	16	5	3	0	.271	.300
Burgess Whitehead		2b-ss-3b	100	332	55	92	13	5	1	24	12	19	5	.277	.355
Francis Healy		c	15	13	1	4	1	0	0	1	0	2	0	.308	.385
Dizzy Dean		p	51	118	15	29	3	1	2	9	1	15	1	.246	.339
Paul Dean		p	39	83	6	20	4	0	0	3	1	12	0	.241	.289
Wild Bill Hallahan		p	32	55	3	10	1	0	0	6	2	16	0	.182	.200
Bill Walker		p	24	54	2	5	1	0	0	1	1	26	0	.093	.111
Tex Carleton		p	41	88	7	17	2	1	1	10	5	27	0	.193	.273
Dazzy Vance	b	p	19	15	1	2	0	0	1	1	0	6	0	.133	.333
Jim Mooney		p	32	19	0	1	0	0	0	2	0	1	0	.053	.053
Jesse Haines		p	37	19	1	3	0	0	0	0	1	5	0	.158	.158
team total			154	**5502**	**799**	**1582**	**294**	75	104	**748**	392	535	**69**	**.288**	**.425**

a—from Philadelphia (N)
b—from Cincinnati
Kiddo Davis (of), Buster Mills (of), Gene Moore (of), Lew Riggs (ph), Red Worthington (ph), Burleigh Grimes (p), Clarence Heise (p), Jim Lindsey (p), Flint Rhem (p), Jim Winford (p) also played for the Cardinals during the season.

DETROIT TIGERS

WORLD SERIES STATISTICS	Pos	G	AB	R	H	2B	3B	HR	RBI	BB	SO	SB	BA	SA	PO	A	E
Hank Greenberg	1b	7	28	4	9	2	**1**	**1**	**7**	4	**9**	1	.321	**.571**	**60**	4	1
Charlie Gehringer	2b	7	29	5	**11**	1	0	**1**	2	3	0	1	**.379**	.517	19	24	**3**
Billy Rogell	ss	7	29	3	8	1	0	0	4	1	4	1	.276	.310	11	18	**3**
Marv Owen	3b	7	29	0	2	0	0	0	1	0	5	1	.069	.069	9	9	2
Pete Fox	rf	7	28	1	8	**6**	0	0	2	1	4	0	.286	.500	15	0	0
Jo-Jo White	cf	7	23	6	3	0	0	0	0	**8**	4	1	.130	.130	22	0	1
Goose Goslin	lf	7	29	2	7	1	0	0	2	3	1	0	.241	.276	20	1	2
Mickey Cochrane	c	7	28	2	6	1	0	0	1	4	3	0	.214	.250	36	5	0
Gee Walker	ph	3	3	0	1	0	0	0	1	0	1	0	.333	.333			
Frank Doljack	ph-cf	2	2	0	0	0	0	0	0	0	0	0	.000	.000	1	0	0
Ray Hayworth	c	1	0	0	0	0	0	0	0	0	0	0	—	—	1	0	0
Flea Clifton		Did not play															
Heinie Schuble		Did not play															
Schoolboy Rowe	p	3	7	0	0	0	0	0	0	0	5	0	.000	.000	1	1	0
Tommy Bridges	p	3	7	0	1	0	0	0	0	1	4	0	.143	.143	0	2	0
Eldon Auker	p	2	4	0	0	0	0	0	0	0	2	0	.000	.000	0	2	0
Chief Hogsett	p	3	3	0	0	0	0	0	0	0	1	0	.000	.000	0	2	0
General Crowder	p	2	1	0	0	0	0	0	0	0	0	0	.000	.000	0	0	0
Firpo Marberry	p	2	0	0	0	0	0	0	0	0	0	0	—	—	0	1	0
Vic Sorrell		Did not play															
Carl Fischer		Did not play															
Luke Hamlin		Did not play															
team total		7	250	23	56	12	1	2	20	25	43	5	.224	.304	195	69	12

Double Plays—6
Left on Bases—64

REGULAR SEASON STATISTICS		Main Pos	G	AB	R	H	2B	3B	HR	RBI	BB	SO	SB	BA	SA
Hank Greenberg		1b	153	593	118	201	**63**	7	26	139	63	93	9	.339	.600
Charlie Gehringer		2b	154	601	**134**	**214**	50	7	11	127	99	25	11	.356	.517
Billy Rogell		ss	154	592	114	175	32	8	3	100	74	36	13	.296	.392
Marv Owen		3b	154	565	79	179	34	9	8	96	59	37	3	.317	.451
Pete Fox		of	128	516	101	147	31	2	2	45	49	53	25	.285	.364
Jo-Jo White		of	115	384	97	120	18	5	0	44	69	39	28	.313	.385
Goose Goslin		of	151	614	106	187	38	7	13	100	65	38	5	.305	.453
Mickey Cochrane		c	129	437	74	140	32	1	2	76	78	26	8	.320	.412
Gee Walker		of	98	347	54	104	19	2	6	39	19	20	20	.300	.418
Frank Doljack		of	56	120	15	28	7	1	1	19	13	15	2	.233	.333
Ray Hayworth		c	54	167	20	49	5	2	0	27	16	22	0	.293	.347
Flea Clifton		3b	24	16	3	1	0	0	0	1	1	2	0	.063	.063
Heinie Schuble		ss-3b	27	15	2	4	2	0	0	2	1	4	0	.267	.400
Schoolboy Rowe		p	51	109	15	33	8	1	2	22	6	20	0	.303	.450
Tommy Bridges		p	36	98	7	12	2	0	0	10	7	25	0	.122	.143
Eldon Auker		p	43	74	3	11	2	0	0	8	4	28	0	.149	.176
Chief Hogsett		p	26	13	0	3	0	0	0	1	0	5	0	.231	.231
General Crowder	c	p	9	30	1	4	0	0	0	0	0	4	0	.133	.133
Firpo Marberry		p	38	55	7	12	4	0	0	9	4	4	0	.218	.291
Vic Sorrell		p	28	37	1	4	0	0	0	0	5	9	0	.108	.108
Carl Fischer		p	20	31	1	2	0	0	0	3	1	6	0	.065	.065
Luke Hamlin		p	20	26	1	6	0	0	0	2	0	8	0	.231	.231
team total			154	**5475**	**958**	**1644**	**349**	53	74	**872**	639	528	**124**	**.300**	.424

c—from Washington
Cy Perkins (ph), Frank Reiber (ph), Icehouse Wilson (ph), Rudy York (c), Vic Frasier (p), Steve Larkin (p), Red Phillips (p) also played for the Tigers during the season.

PITCHING

ST. LOUIS CARDINALS

WORLD SERIES STATISTICS	G	GS	CG	IP	H	R	ER	BB	SO	W	L	SV	ERA
Dizzy Dean	**3**	**3**	**2**	**26**	20	6	5	5	**17**	**2**	1	0	1.73
Paul Dean	2	2	**2**	18	15	4	2	**7**	11	**2**	0	0	**1.00**
Wild Bill Hallahan	1	1	0	8 1/3	6	2	2	4	6	0	0	0	2.16
Bill Walker	2	0	0	6 1/3	6	7	5	6	2	0	**2**	0	7.11
Tex Carleton	2	1	0	3 2/3	5	3	3	2	2	0	0	0	7.36
Dazzy Vance	1	0	0	1 1/3	2	1	0	1	3	0	0	0	0.00
Jim Mooney	1	0	0	1	1	0	0	0	0	0	0	0	0.00
Jesse Haines	1	0	0	2/3	1	0	0	0	2	0	0	0	0.00
team total	7	7	4	65 1/3	56	23	17	25	43	4	3	0	2.34

REGULAR SEASON STATISTICS		G	GS	CG	IP	H	ER	BB	SO	W	L	Pct	SV	ShO	ERA
Dizzy Dean		50	33	24	312	288	92	75	**195**	**30**	7	**.811**	7	7	2.65
Paul Dean		39	26	16	233	225	89	52	150	19	11	.633	2	5	3.44
Wild Bill Hallahan		32	26	10	163	195	77	66	70	8	12	.400	0	2	4.25
Bill Walker		24	19	10	153	160	53	66	76	12	4	.750	0	1	3.12
Tex Carleton		40	31	16	241	260	114	52	103	16	11	.593	2	0	4.26
Dazzy Vance	b	19	4	1	59	62	24	14	33	1	1	.500	1	0	3.66
Jim Mooney		32	7	1	82	114	50	49	27	2	4	.333	1	0	5.49
Jesse Haines		37	6	0	90	86	35	19	17	4	4	.500	1	0	3.50
team total		154	154	**78**	**1387**	1463	568	411	**689**	**95**	58	**.621**	16	**15**	3.69

DETROIT TIGERS

WORLD SERIES STATISTICS	G	GS	CG	IP	H	R	ER	BB	SO	W	L	SV	ERA
Schoolboy Rowe	**3**	2	**2**	21 1/3	19	8	**7**	0	12	1	1	0	2.95
Tommy Bridges	**3**	2	1	17 1/3	**21**	**9**	**7**	1	12	1	1	0	3.63
Eldon Auker	2	2	1	11 1/3	16	8	**7**	5	2	1	1	0	5.56
Chief Hogsett	**3**	0	0	7 1/3	6	1	1	3	3	0	0	0	1.23
General Crowder	2	1	0	6	6	4	1	1	2	0	1	0	1.50
Firpo Marberry	2	0	0	1 2/3	5	4	4	1	0	0	0	0	21.60
Vic Sorrell	Did not play												
Carl Fischer	Did not play												
Luke Hamlin	Did not play												
team total	7	7	4	65	73	34	27	11	31	3	4	0	3.74

REGULAR SEASON STATISTICS		G	GS	CG	IP	H	ER	BB	SO	W	L	Pct	SV	ShO	ERA
Schoolboy Rowe		45	30	20	266	259	102	81	149	24	8	.750	1	3	3.45
Tommy Bridges		36	**35**	23	275	249	112	104	151	22	11	.667	1	3	3.67
Eldon Auker		43	18	10	205	234	78	56	86	15	7	.682	1	2	3.42
Chief Hogsett		26	0	0	50	61	24	19	23	3	2	.600	3	0	4.32
General Crowder	c	9	9	3	67	81	31	20	30	5	1	.833	0	1	4.16
Firpo Marberry		38	19	6	156	174	79	48	64	15	5	.750	3	1	4.56
Vic Sorrell		28	19	6	130	146	69	45	46	6	9	.400	2	0	4.78
Carl Fischer		20	15	4	95	107	46	38	39	6	4	.600	1	1	4.36
Luke Hamlin		20	5	1	75	87	45	44	30	2	3	.400	1	0	5.40
team total		154	154	74	1370	1467	618	488	640	**101**	53	**.656**	14	11	4.06

Total Attendance—281,510 Average Attendance—40,216 Winning Player's Share—$5,390 Losing Player's Share—$3,355

1935
Bedlam in Detroit

The Detroit Tigers and Chicago Cubs both had impressive reigns as league champions in the first decade of this century. The Tigers of Ty Cobb and Sam Crawford won the American League pennant in 1907, 1908, and 1909 but lost all three World Series. The Cubs of Frank Chance, Johnny Evers, and Joe Tinker took the National League crown in 1906, 1907, 1908, and 1910, winning the Series in 1907 and 1908 from the Tigers. Since then, both clubs went through times of depression only to reemerge in recent seasons as powers. The Tigers had taken their first pennant since 1909 last season under the managership of catcher Mickey Cochrane, and the ex-Athletics catcher hit .319 this year while leading his men back to the top despite the challenge of the New York Yankees, who were playing without Babe Ruth for the first time since 1919. Hank Greenberg, Charlie Gehringer, and Goose Goslin paced the Tiger offense, while the quartet of Tommy Bridges, Schoolboy Rowe, Eldon Auker, and General Crowder handled most of the pitching chores in competent fashion.

The Cubs, on the other hand, had a deeper pitching staff headed by 20-game-winners Bill Lee and Lon Warneke. This hill staff and the Cub offense, featuring Gabby Hartnett and Billy Herman, jelled in late summer most spectacularly, as the Cubs won 21 straight games in September and charged past the defending-champion St. Louis Cardinals. Now the old rivals were to meet in the World Series for the first time in 27 years.

The Chicago pitching corps shaped up as the strongest staff in the Series, and that expectation held up in game one as Lon Warneke shut the Tigers out on four hits and beat Schoolboy Rowe 3–0. With the home park advantage lost, the Tigers set out to even things up in game two. They wasted no time, as Jo-Jo White singled, Cochrane doubled, Gehringer singled, and Greenberg homered to run the score up to 4–0 and chase Charlie Root from the game without retiring a batter. Detroit pitcher Tommy Bridges nursed the lead through the afternoon and came away with an 8–3 decision. The Tiger victory was a costly one, however, as Greenberg broke a wrist and was lost for the rest of the Series. The Tigers would have to go to Chicago without their 36-homer and 170-RBI big gun.

But the Tiger attack had enough bite to come up with a four-run eighth inning to take a 5–3 lead in game three, only to see the Cubs tie the game at 5–5 in the bottom of the ninth. With Schoolboy Rowe and Larry French both in relatively rare relief appearances, the game moved into the eleventh inning, when the Tigers finally scored a run on Jo-Jo White's single and captured a 6–5 decision. The Tigers moved even closer to the title on Cub turf when Crowder beat Tex Carleton 2–1 in the fourth game. Now the Cubs had lost two in a row at Wrigley Field and faced the embarrassing prospect of getting swept out of the Series before the hometown audience. Lon Warneke was given a 2–0 lead by his mates in game five, and he protected that edge until a shoulder injury forced him out of the game in the seventh; Bill Lee then took over and saved a 3–1 win for Warneke. The victory also saved some pride for the Cubs and fanned a little hope for coming back in the Series.

The sixth game in Detroit matched Larry French and Tommy Bridges, with both men still in the game after eight innings with the score tied at 3–3. In the top of the ninth, Chicago third baseman Stan Hack led off with a triple. With the potential winning run on the table, Bridges then struck out Billy Jurges, got French to bounce back to the mound, and retired Augie Galan on a fly ball. With that threat met, the Tigers moved quickly to win the game and the Series. After Flea Clifton made the first out of the Detroit ninth, Cochrane singled and moved to second on Gehringer's infield out. Given the chance to win the game with two out in the ninth, Goslin came through with a single that scored Cochrane and set off an impromptu celebration in the streets of Detroit, a rollicking party that began when the game ended and which lasted until dawn the morning after.

Game 1 October 2 at Detroit.

Chicago	Pos	AB	R	H	RBI	PO	A	E
Galan	lf	4	1	1	0	2	0	0
Herman	2b	3	1	0	0	0	3	0
Lindstrom	cf	3	0	1	0	2	0	0
Hartnett	c	4	0	2	1	1	0	0
Demaree	rf	4	1	2	1	1	0	0
Cavarretta	1b	3	0	0	0	17	0	0
Hack	3b	4	0	0	0	1	3	0
Jurges	ss	4	0	1	0	2	2	0
Warneke	p	3	0	0	0	1	8	0
Totals		32	3	7	2	27	16	0

Detroit	Pos	AB	R	H	RBI	PO	A	E
White	cf	4	0	1	0	2	0	0
Cochrane	c	4	0	0	0	8	1	0
Gehringer	2b	3	0	0	0	3	4	0
Greenberg	1b	3	0	0	0	9	0	1
Goslin	lf	3	0	0	0	1	0	1
Fox	rf	4	0	2	0	1	0	0
Rogell	ss	4	0	0	0	3	0	0
Owen	3b	3	0	0	0	0	0	0
Rowe	p	3	0	1	0	0	4	1
Totals		31	0	4	0	27	9	3

Chi. 2 0 0 0 0 0 0 0 1
Det. 0 0 0 0 0 0 0 0 0

Doubles—Fox, Galan, Rowe. Home Run—Demaree. Sacrifice Hits—Cavarretta, Herman, Lindstrom. Double Play—Cochrane to Gehringer. Passed Ball—Cochrane. Left on Bases—Chicago 5, Detroit 8. Umpires—Moriarty (A), Quigley (N), McGowan (A), Stark (N). Attendance—47,391. Time of Game—1:51.

Pitching	IP	H	R	ER	BB	SO
Chicago						
Warneke (W)	9	4	3	2	4	1
Detroit						
Rowe (L)	9	7	0	0	0	8

1st Inning
Chicago
Galan doubled to center.
Herman hit a roller to Rowe who threw past first, Galan scoring on the error.
1 Lindstrom sacrificed Herman to second, Rowe to Greenberg.
Hartnett singled to right, scoring Herman.
2 Demaree popped to short.
3 Cavarretta forced Hartnett, Gehringer to Rogell.
Detroit
1 White was called out on strikes.
2 Cochrane flied to left.
3 Gehringer popped to short.

2nd Inning
Chicago
1 Hack popped to second.
Jurges singled to left and went to second when Goslin fumbled the ball.
2 Warneke flied to right.
3 Galan struck out.
Detroit
1 Greenberg grounded to third.
2 Goslin grounded to the pitcher.
Fox doubled to right.
3 Rogell flied to left.

3rd Inning
Chicago
1 Herman lined to first.
Lindstrom singled to left.
2,3 Hartnett struck out with Lindstrom caught at second, Cochrane to Gehringer.
Detroit
1 Owen grounded to the pitcher.
2 Rowe grounded to the pitcher.
White singled to right.
3 Cochrane grounded to the pitcher.

4th Inning
Chicago
Demaree singled to left.
1 Cavarretta sacrificed Demaree to second, Rowe to Greenberg.
2 Hack grounded to second, Demaree advancing to third.
3 Jurges struck out.
Detroit
1 Gehringer grounded to the pitcher.
Greenberg walked.
Goslin also walked.
2 Fox grounded to short advancing both runners.
3 Rogell grounded to first.

5th Inning
Chicago
1 Warneke grounded to first.
2 Galan grounded to second.
3 Herman flied to left.
Detroit
1 Owen lined to right.
Rowe doubled past second.
2 White grounded to second, Rowe moving to third.
3 Cochrane hit to Warneke who made the putout.

6th Inning
Chicago
1 Lindstrom popped to second.
Hartnett singled to left.
2 Demaree flied to left.
3 Cavarretta struck out.
Detroit
1 Gehringer grounded to second.
2 Greenberg popped to third.
3 Goslin grounded out off Warneke's glove, thrown out by Herman.

7th Inning
Chicago
1 Hack struck out.
2 Jurges popped to short.
3 Warneke grounded to second.
Detroit
1 Fox grounded to Warneke.
2 Rogell fouled to Jurges.
Owen walked.
3 Rowe flied to center.

8th Inning
Chicago
Galan got to first on Greenberg's error.
1 Herman sacrificed Galan to second, Rowe to Greenberg.
Galan to third on a passed ball.
2 Lindstrom grounded to Rowe, Galan holding third.
3 Hartnett flied to center.
Detroit
1 White thrown out by Hack on a bunt.
2 Cochrane grounded to the pitcher.
Gehringer walked.
3 Greenberg grounded to third.

9th Inning
Chicago
Demaree homered into the left field seats.
1 Cavarretta struck out.
2 Hack lined to center.
3 Jurges struck out.
Detroit
1 Goslin flied to center.
Fox singled to center.
2 Rogell grounded to first.
3 Owen grounded out to short.

Game 2 October 3 at Detroit

Chicago	Pos	AB	R	H	RBI	PO	A	E
Galan	lf	4	0	0	0	3	1	0
Herman	2b	4	0	1	1	2	6	0
Lindstrom	cf	3	0	0	0	1	0	0
Hartnett	c	4	0	1	0	4	2	0
Demaree	rf	4	0	1	0	4	0	0
Cavarretta	1b	4	1	0	0	9	0	0
Hack	3b	3	0	1	0	2	1	0
Jurges	ss	3	1	1	1	3	1	0
Root	p	0	0	0	0	0	0	0
Henshaw	p	1	0	0	0	0	1	0
Kowalik	p	2	1	1	0	0	2	1
a Klein		1	0	0	0	0	0	0
Totals		33	3	6	2	24	15	1

a Flied out for Kowalik in 9th.

Doubles—Cochrane, Demaree, Rogell.
Home Run—Greenberg. Sacrifice Hit—Owen.
Double Plays—Bridges to Rogell to
Greenberg, Rogell to Gehringer to
Greenberg, Herman to Cavarretta, Jurges
to Herman to Cavarretta.
Hit Batsman—Owen (by Henshaw), Greenberg
(by Kowalik). Wild Pitch—Henshaw.
Left on Bases—Chicago 7, Detroit 5.
Umpires—Quigley, McGowan, Stark,
Moriarty. Attendance—46,742.
Time of Game—1:59.

Chi.	0 0 0	0 1 0	2 0 0
Det.	4 0 0	3 0 0	1 0 x

Detroit	Pos	AB	R	H	RBI	PO	A	E
White	cf	3	2	1	0	3	0	0
Cochrane	c	2	1	1	1	2	0	0
Gehringer	2b	3	2	2	3	2	5	0
Greenberg	1b	3	1	1	2	8	2	2
Goslin	lf	3	0	0	0	2	0	0
Fox	rf	4	0	1	1	4	0	0
Rogell	ss	4	0	2	0	3	2	0
Owen	3b	2	1	0	0	2	0	0
Bridges	p	4	1	1	0	1	2	0
Totals		28	8	9	7	27	11	2

Pitching	IP	H	R	ER	BB	SO
Chicago						
Root (L)	*0	4	4	4	0	0
Henshaw	3⅓	2	3	3	5	2
Kowalik	4⅓	3	1	1	1	1
Detroit						
Bridges (W)	9	6	3	2	4	2

*Pitched to four batters in 1st.

Game 3 October 4 at Chicago

Detroit	Pos	AB	R	H	RBI	PO	A	E
White	cf	5	1	2	1	5	0	0
Cochrane	c	5	0	0	0	4	2	1
Gehringer	2b	5	1	0	0	4	7	0
Goslin	lf	5	2	3	2	2	0	0
Fox	rf	5	1	2	0	4	0	0
Rogell	ss	5	0	3	2	2	4	0
Owen	1b	5	1	0	0	15	0	0
Clifton	3b	4	0	0	0	0	5	1
Auker	p	2	0	0	0	0	2	0
a Walker		1	0	0	0	0	0	0
Hogsett	p	0	0	0	0	0	1	0
Rowe	p	2	0	0	0	0	0	0
Totals		44	6	12	6	33	20	2

Pitching	IP	H	R	ER	BB	SO
Detroit						
Auker	6	6	3	2	2	1
Hogsett	1	0	0	0	1	0
Rowe (W)	4	4	2	2	0	3
Chicago						
Lee	7⅓	7	4	4	3	3
Warneke	1⅓	2	1	1	0	2
French (L)	2	3	1	0	0	1

Det.	0 0 0	0 0 1	0 4 0	0 1
Chi.	0 2 0	0 1 0	0 0 2	0 0

Chicago	Pos	AB	R	H	RBI	PO	A	E
Galan	lf	4	0	2	1	1	0	0
Herman	2b	5	0	1	1	3	2	1
Lindstrom	cf-3b	5	2	3	2	1	1	1
Hartnett	c	4	0	0	0	8	3	0
Demaree	rf-cf	4	1	1	1	2	0	0
Cavarretta	1b	5	0	0	0	10	1	1
Hack	3b-ss	5	2	2	0	3	2	0
Jurges	ss	1	1	1	0	3	4	0
b Klein	rf	2	1	1	0	1	0	0
Lee	p	1	0	1	0	1	0	0
Warneke	p	0	0	0	0	0	0	0
c O'Day		1	0	1	1	0	0	0
French	p	0	0	0	0	0	1	0
d Stephenson		1	0	0	0	0	0	0
Totals		38	5	10	5	33	14	3

a Hit into double play for Auker in 7th.
b Singled for Jurges in 9th.
c Singled for Warneke in 9th.
d Struck out for French in 11th.

Doubles—Gehringer, Goslin, Lindstrom.
Triple—Fox. Home Run—Demaree.
Sacrifice Hits—Hartnett, Lee 2. Stolen
Base—Hack. Double plays—Rogell to
Gehringer to Owen, Gehringer to Rogell
to Owen, Jurges to Herman to Cavarretta.
Hit by Pitcher—Jurges (by Hogsett).
Left on Bases—Detroit 8, Chicago 7.
Umpires—McGowan, Stark, Moriarty,
Quigley. Attendance—45,532.
Time of Game—2:27.

1st Inning
Chicago
· Galan walked.
1,2 Herman grounded into a double play,
Bridges to Rogell to Greenberg.
3 Lindstrom struck out.
Detroit
White singled to left.
Cochrane doubled to right scoring White.
Gehringer singled to center scoring
Cochrane.
Greenberg hit a two-run homer into the
left field stands.
For Chicago—Henshaw pitching.
Goslin walked.
1,2 Fox lined to Herman who threw to first
to double up Goslin who was off first.
3 Rogell grounded to the pitcher.

2nd Inning
Chicago
1 Hartnett grounded to second.
2 Demaree grounded to second.
3 Cavarretta grounded out, Greenberg to
Bridges covering first.
Detroit
1 Owen struck out.
2 Bridges grounded out to third.
White walked.
3 Cochrane flied to left.

3rd Inning
Chicago
Hack walked.
1 Jurges flied to right.
2 Henshaw flied to left.
3 Galan lined to center.
Detroit
Gehringer walked.
1,2 Greenberg grounded into a double play,
Jurges to Herman to Cavarretta.
3 Goslin flied to left.

4th Inning
Chicago
1 Herman called out on strikes.
2 Lindstrom popped to second.
Hartnett singled to center.
3 Demaree flied to center.
Detroit
1 Fox popped to third.
2 Rogell looked at a called third strike.
Owen was hit by a pitched ball.
Bridges singled off Henshaw's glove.
White walked filling the bases.
Owen scored, Bridges went to third,
and White went to second on a wild
pitch.
Cochrane walked to again fill the bases.
Gehringer singled to right, scoring
Bridges and White and sending Cochrane
to third.
For Chicago—Kowalik pitching.
3 Greenberg grounded out to the pitcher.

5th Inning
Chicago
Cavarretta got to first when Greenberg
fumbled his grounder.
1 Hack grounded back to the pitcher.
Jurges singled to center scoring
Cavarretta.
2 Kowalik forced Jurges, Greenberg to
Rogell.
Galan got to first when Greenberg
dropped Cochrane's throw.
3 Herman lined to third.
Detroit
1 Goslin grounded out to second.
2 Fox flied to center.
3 Rogell singled to left but was out
trying to stretch it to a double,
Galan to Jurges.

6th Inning
Chicago
Lindstrom walked.
1,2 Hartnett grounded into a double play,
Rogell to Gehringer to Greenberg.
Demaree doubled to left center.
3 Cavarretta grounded to second.
Detroit
1 Owen popped to third.
2 Bridges grounded back to the pitcher.
White safely to first on Kowalik's
3 throwing error but out trying for
second, Cavarretta to Herman.

7th Inning
Chicago
1 Hack flied to center.
Jurges walked.
Kowalik beat out a dribbler to third.
2 Galan grounded to second advancing both
runners.
Herman singled, scoring Jurges and
Kowalik and took second on the throw
to the plate.
3 Lindstrom popped to first.
Detroit
Cochrane walked.
1 Gehringer forced Cochrane, Herman to
Jurges.
Greenberg was hit by a pitched ball.
2 Goslin flied to left.
Fox singled to right, scoring Gehringer,
3 Greenberg also trying to score was out
at the plate, Herman to Hartnett.

8th Inning
Chicago
1 Hartnett flied to right.
2 Demaree fouled to third.
3 Cavarretta flied to left.
Detroit
Rogell doubled to right.
1 Owen sacrificed, Hartnett to Cavarretta.
2 Bridges struck out.
3 White thrown out by Hartnett on a bunt.

9th Inning
Chicago
Hack singled.
1 Jurges popped to short.
2 Klein, batting for Kowalik, flied to left.
3 Galan flied to right.

1st Inning
Detroit
1 White struck out (Hartnett to Cavarretta).
Cochrane safe on Herman's error.
2 Gehringer grounded to third.
3 Goslin popped to short.
Chicago
Galan singled to right.
1 Herman struck out.
Lindstrom singled along the third base line.
2,3 Hartnett hit into double play, Rogell
to Gehringer to Owen.

2nd Inning
Detroit
1 Fox fouled to the catcher.
Rogell singled on a roller to Cavarretta
who fumbled allowing Rogell to go to
second.
2 Owen grounded to short, Rogell to third.
3 Clifton bounced to the pitcher.
Chicago
Demaree homered in right field bleachers.
1 Cavarretta lined to center.
Hack singled over second.
Hack stole second.
Jurges safe on Clifton's error, Hack
going to third.
2 Lee grounded to second, scoring Hack.
3 Galan flied to left.

3rd Inning
Detroit
1 Auker fouled to the catcher.
2 White grounded to second.
Cochrane walked.
Gehringer singled beyond first.
3 Goslin lined to left.
Chicago
1 Herman grounded to third.
2 Lindstrom grounded to third.
3 Hartnett grounded to second.

4th Inning
Detroit
1 Fox popped to short.
2 Rogell popped to second.
3 Owen grounded to short.
Chicago
1 Demaree flied to center.
2 Cavarretta grounded to second.
3 Hack rolled to first.

5th Inning
Detroit
1 Clifton lined to center.
2 Auker struck out.
White singled past short.
3 Cochrane lined to right.
Chicago
Jurges walked.
1 Lee sacrificed, Auker to Gehringer.
Galan singled, scoring Jurges, and Galan
got to second when Cochrane dropped
the throw from the outfield.
Herman singled Galan to third.
2,3 Lindstrom hit into a double play,
Gehringer to Rogell to Owen.

6th Inning
Detroit
1 Gehringer popped to short.
Goslin singled to right.
Fox tripled, scoring Goslin.
2 Fox picked off, Hartnett to Hack.
3 Rogell looked at a third strike.
Chicago
1 Hartnett grounded to second.
Demaree walked.
2 Cavarretta forced Demaree, Auker to
Rogell.
3 Cavarretta caught stealing, Cochrane
to Gehringer.

7th Inning
Detroit
1 Owen flied to right.
Clifton walked
2,3 Walker, batting for Auker, hit into a
double play, Jurges to Herman to
Cavarretta.

7th Inning (continued)
Chicago
For Detroit—Hogsett pitching.
1 Hack grounded to short.
Jurges hit by a pitched ball.
2 Lee sacrificed, tagged by Hogsett.
Galan walked.
3 Herman rolled to third.

8th Inning
Detroit
White walked.
1 Cochrane popped to short.
Gehringer doubled, White to third.
Goslin singled, scoring White and
Gehringer.
For Chicago—Warneke pitching.
Fox singled, Goslin to second.
Rogell singled, scoring Goslin and
moving Fox to third.
2 Rogell on an attempted steal was
trapped between first and second
Hartnett to Herman to Jurges to
Cavarretta, Fox scoring meanwhile.
3 Owen lined to first.
Chicago
For Detroit—Rowe pitching.
1 Lindstrom flied to left.
2 Hartnett lined to center.
3 Demaree strike out.

9th Inning
Detroit
1 Clifton struck out.
2 Rowe rolled to third.
3 White struck out.
Chicago
1 Cavarretta flied out to center.
Hack singled past short.
Klein, batting for Jurges, singled.
O'Dea, batting for Warneke, singled,
scoring Hack and moving Klein to 3rd.
2 Galan flew to center, scoring Klein.
3 Herman grounded to third.

10th Inning
Detroit
For Chicago—French pitching, Klein to
right, Demaree to center, Lindstrom
to third and Hack to short.
1 Cochrane fouled to third.
2 Gehringer fouled to right.
Goslin doubled to right.
3 Fox popped to first.
Chicago
Lindstrom doubled.
1 Hartnett sacrificed Lindstrom to third,
Cochrane to Gehringer.
2 Demaree grounded to short, Lindstrom
holding at third.
3 Cavarretta grounded to second.

11th Inning
Detroit
Rogell singled past third.
1 Owen forced Rogell in an attempted
sacrifice, Lindstrom to Hack.
Clifton safe on Lindstrom's error Owen
stopping at second.
2 Rowe struck out.
White singled to center, scoring Owen
and sending Clifton to third, White
taking second on throw to the plate.
3 Cochrane fouled to Hartnett.
Chicago
1 Hack grounded to third.
2 Klein struck out.
3 Stephenson, pinch hitting for French,
struck out.

Game 4 October 5 at Chicago

Det.	001	001	000				
Chi.	010	000	000				

Detroit	Pos	AB	R	H	RBI	PO	A	E
White	cf	3	0	1	0	0	0	0
Cochrane	c	4	0	1	0	6	0	0
Gehringer	2b	4	0	2	1	3	3	0
Goslin	lf	3	0	1	0	1	0	0
Fox	rf	5	0	1	0	0	0	0
Rogell	ss	3	0	0	0	2	2	0
Owen	1b	4	0	0	0	13	1	0
Clifton	3b	4	1	0	0	0	4	0
Crowder	p	3	1	1	0	2	2	0
Totals		33	2	7	1	27	12	0

Pitching	IP	H	R	ER	BB	SO
Detroit						
Crowder (W)	9	5	1	1	3	5
Chicago						
Carleton (L)	7	6	2	1	7	4
Root	2	1	0	0	1	2

Chicago	Pos	AB	R	H	RBI	PO	A	E
Galan	lf	4	0	0	0	2	0	1
Herman	2b	4	0	1	0	4	1	0
Lindstrom	cf	4	0	0	0	3	0	0
Hartnett	c	4	1	1	1	7	0	0
Demaree	rf	4	0	1	0	4	0	0
Cavarretta	1b	4	0	2	0	3	1	0
Hack	3b	4	0	0	0	0	0	0
Jurges	ss	1	0	0	0	4	2	1
Carleton	p	1	0	0	0	0	2	0
a Klein		1	0	0	0	0	0	0
Root	p	0	0	0	0	0	1	0
Totals		31	1	5	1	27	7	2

a Grounded out for Carleton in 7th.

Doubles—Fox, Gehringer, Herman. Home Run—Hartnett. Sacrifice Hit—Gehringer. Stolen Base—Gehringer. Double Plays—Jurges to Herman, Rogell to Gehringer to Owen. Balk—Carleton. Left on Bases—Detroit 13, Chicago 6. Umpires—Stark, Moriarty, Quigley, McGowan. Attendance—49,350. Time of Game—2:28.

1st Inning
Detroit
1 White called out on strikes.
2 Cochrane grounded to second.
3 Gehringer struck out.
Chicago
1 Galan rolled out to first.
2 Herman grounded out Owen to Crowder.
3 Lindstrom fouled to first.

2nd Inning
Detroit
Goslin singled to second.
Fox doubled down the left field line.
Rogell walked to load the bases.
1 Owen popped to second.
2,3 Clifton lined to Jurges who threw to Herman doubling Fox at second.
Chicago
Hartnett homered into the right field stands.
1 Demaree struck out.
2 Cavarretta struck out.
3 Hack called out on strikes.

3rd Inning
Detroit
Crowder singled to right.
White singled past first, moving
1 Crowder to third, but White was out trying for second Demaree to Jurges.
Cochrane walked.
Gehringer doubled to right center, scoring Crowder with Cochrane stopping at third.
Goslin intentionally walked.
2 Fox forced Cochrane at the plate, Cavarretta to Hartnett.
3 Rogell struck out.
Chicago
1 Jurges grounded to third.
Carleton walked.
2 Galan popped to short.
3 Herman popped to first.

4th Inning
Detroit
1 Owen flied to center.
2 Clifton flied to center.
Crowder walked.
White walked.
3 Cochrane flied out to right.
Chicago
1 Lindstrom grounded to short.
2 Hartnett grounded to third.
3 Demaree fouled to Cochrane.

5th Inning
Detroit
1 Gehringer grounded to short.
2 Goslin popped to short.
3 Fox popped to short.
Chicago
Cavarretta singled to right.
1 Hack attempting to sacrifice popped to the pitcher.
Jurges walked.
2 Carleton struck out.
3 Galan flied to left.

6th Inning
Detroit
1 Rogell flied to right.
2 Owen flied to right.
Clifton got all the way to second on Galan's error of dropping his long fly.
Crowder got to first on Jurges' error with Clifton scoring.
Carleton's balk moved Crowder to second.
White walked.
3 Cochrane flew out to left.
Chicago
Herman doubled to left.
1 Lindstrom fouled to Gehringer, Herman going to third after the catch.
2 Hartnett struck out.
3 Demaree popped to second.

7th Inning
Detroit
Gehringer singled past second.
1 Goslin flied to left.
Gehringer stole second.
2 Fox struck out.
Rogell walked.
3 Owen grounded back to the pitcher.
Chicago
1 Cavarretta rolled out to first.
2 Hack grounded to third.
Jurges walked.
3 Klein, pitch hitting for Carleton, bounced back to the pitcher.

8th Inning
Detroit
For Chicago—Root pitching.
1 Clifton flied to center.
2 Crowder flied to left.
3 White struck out.
Chicago
1 Galan grounded to second.
2 Herman grounded to third.
3 Lindstrom grounded to second.

9th Inning
Detroit
Cochrane singled to center.
1 Gehringer sacrificed Cochrane to second, Root to Herman.
Goslin intentionally walked for the second time in the game.
2 Fox popped to second.
3 Rogell fanned.
Chicago
1 Hartnett lined to short, Rogell making a fine leaping catch.
Demaree singled to right.
Cavarretta singled to left, Demaree stopping at second.
2,3 Hack into a double play, Rogell to Gehringer to Owen.

Game 5 October 6 at Chicago

Det.	000	000	001				
Chi.	002	000	10x				

Detroit	Pos	AB	R	H	RBI	PO	A	E
White	cf	4	0	0	0	4	0	0
Cochrane	c	4	1	1	0	5	0	0
Gehringer	2b	4	1	1	0	2	2	0
Goslin	lf	3	0	1	0	1	0	0
Fox	rf	4	0	2	1	0	1	0
Rogell	ss	4	0	0	0	1	1	0
Owen	1b	3	0	0	0	5	4	1
Clifton	3b	3	0	0	0	0	4	0
Rowe	p	3	0	1	0	3	1	0
a Walker		1	0	0	0	0	0	0
Totals		33	1	7	1	24	9	1

a Grounded out for Owen in 9th.

Double—Herman. Triple—Herman. Home Run—Klein. Sacrifice Hit—Lee. Double Play—Jurges to Cavarretta. Left on Bases—Detroit 7, Chicago 6. Umpires—Moriarty, Quigley, McGowan, Stark. Attendance—49,237. Time of Game—1:49.

Chicago	Pos	AB	R	H	RBI	PO	A	E
Galan	lf	4	1	0	0	2	0	0
Herman	2b	4	1	2	0	3	3	0
Klein	cf	4	1	2	2	3	0	0
Hartnett	c	4	0	1	0	4	0	0
Demaree	rf	4	0	1	0	4	0	0
Cavarretta	1b	4	0	0	0	11	1	0
Hack	3b	2	0	0	0	0	4	0
Jurges	ss	3	0	1	0	1	4	0
Warneke	p	2	0	0	0	1	1	0
Lee	p	0	0	0	0	0	0	0
Totals		31	3	8	3	27	9	0

Pitching	IP	H	R	ER	BB	SO
Detroit						
Rowe (L)	8	8	3	2	1	3
Chicago						
Warneke (W)	6	3	0	0	0	2
Lee (SV)	3	4	1	1	2	2

1st Inning
Detroit
1 White was called out on strikes.
Cochrane singled to right.
2 Gehringer grounded to second as Cochrane stopped at second.
3 Goslin also grounded to second.
Chicago
1 Galan flied out to center.
2 Herman grounded to the pitcher.
Klein walked.
Hartnett singled to right, moving Klein to third.
3 Demaree grounded out, Owen to Rowe.

2nd Inning
Detroit
1 Fox popped to second.
2 Rogell popped to second.
3 Owen grounded to short.
Chicago
1 Cavarretta popped to Owen, trying to bunt.
Hack walked.
2 Jurges struck out.
Warneke singled to right, moving Hack to second.
3 Galan popped to short.

3rd Inning
Detroit
1 Clifton popped to second.
2 Rowe rolled out to Warneke, unassisted.
3 White grounded to first.
Chicago
Herman tripled to left center.
Klein hit a two-run homer into the right field bleachers.
1 Hartnett grounded to second.
2 Demaree flew to left.
3 Cavarretta flied to right.

4th Inning
Detroit
Cochrane singled to center.
1 Gehringer flied to left.
2 Goslin flied to center.
Fox singled to center, Cochrane stopping at second.
3 Rogell grounded to first.
Chicago
1 Hack flied to left.
2 Jurges fouled to the catcher.
3 Warneke grounded to second.

5th Inning
Detroit
1 Owen grounded to short.
2 Clifton struck out.
3 Rowe grounded to short.
Chicago
1 Galan flied to left.
2 Herman flied to left.
3 Klein looked at a third strike.

6th Inning
Detroit
1 White grounded out to the pitcher.
2 Cochrane flied out to left.
3 Gehringer lined to center.
Chicago
1 Hartnett fouled to first.
Demaree singled to right.
2 Cavarretta flied deep to center.
3 Hack forced Demaree at second, Rogell to Gehringer.

7th Inning
Detroit
For Chicago—Lee pitching replacing Warneke who hurt his shoulder in the sixth inning.
Goslin walked.
1 Fox flied to right.
2,3 Rogell hit into a double play, Jurges to Cavarretta.
Chicago
Jurges singled to left.
1 Lee sacrificed Jurges to second, Owen to Gehringer.
Galan reached first on Owen's error,
2 Jurges was out trying to score, Fox to Cochrane (Galan moved to second on the play at the plate).
Herman doubled to right-center, scoring Galan.
3 Klein grounded out, Owen to Rowe.

8th Inning
Detroit
1 Owen struck out.
Clifton walked.
Rowe singled to right, moving Clifton to second.
2 White struck out.
3 Cochrane grounded out, Cavarretta to Lee.
Chicago
1 Hartnett flied to right.
2 Demaree grounded out, Owen to Rowe.
3 Cavarretta struck out.

9th Inning
Detroit
Gehringer singled to third.
Goslin singled by first, advancing Gehringer to third.
Fox singled to left-center, scoring Gehringer, Goslin stopping at second.
1 Rogell flied to center.
2 Gee Walker, batting for Owen, grounded to second, advancing both runners
3 Clifton fouled to Cavarretta.

1935

Game 6 October 7 at Detroit

	Chi.	0 0 1	0 2 0	0 0 0
	Det.	1 0 0	1 0 1	0 0 1

Chicago	Pos	AB	R	H	RBI	PO	A	E
Galan	lf	5	0	1	0	2	0	0
Herman	2b	4	1	3	3	3	4	0
Klein	rf	4	0	1	0	0	0	0
Hartnett	c	4	0	2	0	9	1	0
Demaree	cf	4	0	0	0	0	0	0
Cavarretta	1b	4	0	1	0	8	0	0
Hack	3b	4	0	2	0	0	4	0
Jurges	ss	4	1	1	0	3	2	0
French	p	4	1	1	0	1	2	0
Totals		37	3	12	3	*26	13	0

Detroit	Pos	AB	R	H	RBI	PO	A	E
Clifton	3b	5	0	0	0	2	0	0
Cochrane	c	5	2	3	0	7	0	0
Gehringer	2b	5	0	2	0	0	4	0
Goslin	lf	5	0	1	1	2	0	0
Fox	rf	4	0	2	1	3	1	1
Walker	cf	2	1	1	0	0	0	0
Rogell	ss	4	1	2	0	2	3	0
Owen	1b	3	0	1	1	11	0	0
Bridges	p	4	0	0	1	0	3	0
Totals		37	4	12	4	27	11	1

* two outs when winning run was scored.

Doubles—Fox, Gehringer, Hack, Rogell.
Triple—Hack. Home Run—Herman.
Sacrifice Hit—Walker. Double
Play—Gehringer to Rogell to Owen.
Left on Bases—Chicago 7, Detroit 10.
Umpires—Quigley, McGowan, Stark,
Moriarty. Attendance—48,420.
Time of Game—1:57.

Pitching	IP	H	R	ER	BB	SO
Chicago						
French (L)	8⅔	12	4	4	2	7
Detroit						
Bridges (W)	9	12	3	3	0	7

1st Inning
Chicago
1 Galan's grounder was deflected off Bridges to Rogell who threw to Owen for the out.
2 Herman grounded back to Bridges.
3 Klein popped to first.
Detroit
1 Clifton grounded to third. Cochrane singled to left. Gehringer singled to right, advancing Cochrane to second.
2 Goslin popped to short. Fox doubled by third, scoring Cochrane and advancing Gehringer to third. Walker intentionally walked, loading the bases.
3 Rogell forced Gehringer at the plate on a roller, French to Hartnett.

2nd Inning
Chicago
1 Hartnett looked at a third strike.
2 Demaree flied to right. Cavarretta singled over first and got to second on Fox's fumble.
3 Hack grounded to second.
Detroit
1 Owen struck out.
2 Bridges grounded to second.
3 Clifton struck out.

3rd Inning
Chicago
Jurges singled over second.
1 French struck out. Galan singled off Gehringer's glove, moving Jurges to third. Herman singled, scoring Jurges, but
2 Galan out trying for third, Fox to Clifton.
3 Klein flied deep to right.
Detroit
1 Cochrane grounded out, Cavarretta to French. Gehringer doubled to left-center.
2 Goslin hit a roller to French and Gehringer got trapped in a run-down but got back to second, Goslin out French to Hack to Herman to Cavarretta.
3 Fox flied to left.

4th Inning
Chicago
Hartnett singled through the box.
1 Demaree took a called third strike.
2 Cavarretta popped to short.
3 Hack grounded to second.
Detroit
Walker singled to right. Rogell singled to left, advancing Walker to second.
1 Owen bunting forced Rogell, Hack to Jurges, Walker getting to third.
2 Bridges forced Owens at second scoring Walker, Hack to Herman.
3 Clifton forced Bridges at second, Jurges to Herman.

5th Inning
Chicago
1 Jurges flied to right. French singled to right.
2 Galan looked at a third strike. Herman hit a two-run homer over the left field screen. Klein singled to center.
3 Hartnett flew to left.
Detroit
1 Cochrane took a called third strike.
2 Gehringer grounded to second.
3 Goslin popped in front of the plate to Hartnett.

6th Inning
Chicago
1 Demaree grounded to short.
2 Cavarretta rolled out to second. Hack doubled to right.
3 Jurges grounded to Clifton who reached out to tag Hack coming into third, Hack was out for running out of the base-line.
Detroit
1 Fox flied to left.
2 Walker popped to short. Rogell hit a ground-rule double to the left field corner. Owen singled to left, scoring Rogell.
3 Bridges struck out.

7th Inning
Chicago
1 French struck out.
2 Galan grounded to first. Herman singled to left.
3 Klein grounded to first.
Detroit
1 Clifton grounded to short. Cochrane blooped a single to center.
2 Gehringer popped to first.
3 Goslin grounded to second.

8th Inning
Chicago
Hartnett singled to left.
1,2 Demaree grounded into a double play, Gehringer to Rogell to Owen.
3 Cavarretta struck out.
Detroit
Fox singled past first.
1 Walker sacrificed Fox to second, Hartnett to Herman.
2 Rogell struck out. Owen intentionally walked.
3 Bridges took a called third strike.

9th Inning
Chicago
Hack tripled over Walker's head.
1 Jurges struck out.
2 French bounced to the pitcher, Hack holding third.
3 Galan flied to left.
Detroit
1 Clifton struck out. Cochrane singled off Herman's glove.
2 Gehringer grounded to first, moving Cochrane to second. Goslin singled to right, scoring Cochrane with the winning run.

1935 WORLD SERIES COMPOSITE BOX

	Wins	Composite Line Score													Manager	Regular Season W	L	Pct.	G. Ahead
Detroit Tigers (A.L.)	4	5	0	1	4	0	3	1	4	2	0	1	–	21	Mickey Cochrane	93	58	.616	3
Chicago Cubs (N.L.)	2	2	3	3	0	4	0	3	0	3	0	0	–	18	Charlie Grimm	100	54	.649	4

BATTING AND FIELDING

WORLD SERIES STATISTICS

	Pos	G	AB	R	H	2B	3B	HR	RBI	BB	SO	SB	BA	SA	PO	A	E
DETROIT TIGERS																	
Marv Owen	3b-1b	6	20	2	1	0	0	0	1	2	3	0	.050	.050	46	5	1
Charlie Gehringer	2b	6	24	**4**	9	**3**	0	0	4	2	1	**1**	.375	.500	14	**25**	0
Billy Rogell	ss	6	24	1	7	2	0	0	1	2	5	0	.292	.375	13	12	0
Flea Clifton	3b	4	16	1	0	0	0	0	0	2	4	0	.000	.000	2	9	1
Pete Fox	rf	6	**26**	1	**10**	**3**	**1**	0	4	0	1	0	**.385**	.577	8	2	1
Jo-Jo White	cf	5	19	3	5	0	0	0	1	**5**	**7**	0	.263	.263	14	0	0
Goose Goslin	lf	6	22	2	6	1	0	0	3	**5**	0	0	.273	.318	12	0	1
Mickey Cochrane	c	6	24	3	7	1	0	0	1	4	1	0	.292	.333	32	3	1
Hank Greenberg	1b	2	6	1	1	0	0	1	2	1	0	0	.167	.667	17	2	**3**
Gee Walker	ph-cf	3	4	1	1	0	0	0	0	1	0	0	.250	.250	0	0	0
Ray Hayworth		Did not play															
Heinie Schuble		Did not play															
Frank Reiber		Did not play															
Hugh Shelley		Did not play															
Schoolboy Rowe	p	3	8	0	2	1	0	0	0	0	1	0	.250	.375	3	5	1
Tommy Bridges	p	2	8	1	1	0	0	0	1	0	3	0	.125	.125	1	5	0
General Crowder	p	1	3	1	1	0	0	0	0	1	0	0	.333	.333	2	1	0
Eldon Auker	p	1	2	0	0	0	0	0	0	0	1	0	.000	.000	0	2	0
Chief Hogsett	p	1	0	0	0	0	0	0	0	0	0	0	—	—	1	0	0
Joe Sullivan		Did not play															
Vic Sorrell		Did not play															
Roxie Lawson		Did not play															
team total		6	206	21	51	11	1	1	18	25	27	1	.249	.325	165	71	9

Double Plays—7
Left on Bases—51

REGULAR SEASON STATISTICS

	Main Pos	G	AB	R	H	2B	3B	HR	RBI	BB	SO	SB	BA	SA
DETROIT TIGERS														
Marv Owen	3b	134	483	52	127	24	5	2	71	43	37	1	.263	.346
Charlie Gehringer	2b	150	610	123	201	32	8	19	108	79	16	11	.330	.502
Billy Rogell	ss	150	560	88	154	23	11	6	71	80	29	3	.275	.388
Flea Clifton	3b	43	110	15	28	5	0	0	9	5	13	2	.255	.300
Pete Fox	of	131	517	116	166	38	8	15	73	45	52	14	.321	.513
Jo-Jo White	of	114	412	82	99	13	12	2	32	68	42	19	.240	.345
Goose Goslin	of	147	590	88	172	34	6	9	109	56	31	5	.292	.415
Mickey Cochrane	c	115	411	93	131	33	3	5	47	96	15	5	.319	.450
Hank Greenberg	1b	152	619	121	203	46	16	**36**	**170**	87	91	4	.328	.628
Gee Walker	of	98	362	52	109	22	6	7	53	15	21	6	.301	.453
Ray Hayworth	c	51	175	22	54	14	2	0	22	9	14	0	.309	.411
Heinie Schuble	ph-inf	11	8	3	2	0	0	0	0	1	0	0	.250	.250
Frank Reiber	c	8	11	3	3	0	0	0	1	3	3	0	.273	.273
Hugh Shelley	of	7	8	1	2	0	0	0	1	2	1	0	.250	.250
Schoolboy Rowe	p	45	109	19	34	3	2	3	28	12	12	0	.312	.459
Tommy Bridges	p	36	109	9	26	5	1	0	10	6	24	0	.239	.303
General Crowder	p	33	93	6	17	0	1	0	8	5	3	0	.183	.204
Eldon Auker	p	36	74	8	16	3	2	0	8	2	17	0	.216	.311
Chief Hogsett	p	40	23	4	6	0	0	2	4	0	5	0	.261	.522
Joe Sullivan	p	25	43	6	7	1	0	0	5	4	9	0	.163	.186
Vic Sorrell	p	12	18	0	0	0	0	0	0	0	7	0	.000	.000
Roxie Lawson	p	7	13	1	4	1	0	0	3	1	2	0	.308	.385
team total		152	5423	**919**	1573	301	83	106	**837**	**627**	456	70	**.290**	**.435**

Chet Morgan (of), Hub Walker (of), Clyde Hatter (p), Firpo Marberry (p), and Carl Fischer (p) also played for the Tigers during the season.

WORLD SERIES STATISTICS

	Pos	G	AB	R	H	2B	3B	HR	RBI	BB	SO	SB	BA	SA	PO	A	E
CHICAGO CUBS																	
Phil Cavarretta	1b	6	24	1	3	0	0	0	0	0	5	0	.125	.125	**58**	3	1
Billy Herman	2b	6	24	3	8	2	**1**	1	**6**	0	2	0	.333	**.625**	15	19	1
Billy Jurges	ss	6	16	3	4	0	0	0	1	4	4	0	.250	.250	16	15	1
Stan Hack	3b-ss	6	22	2	5	1	**1**	0	0	2	2	1	.227	.364	6	10	0
Frank Demaree	rf-cf	6	24	2	6	1	0	**2**	2	1	4	0	.250	.542	8	1	0
Fred Lindstrom	cf-3b	4	15	0	3	1	0	0	0	1	1	0	.200	.267	8	1	1
Augie Galan	lf	6	25	2	4	1	0	0	2	2	2	0	.160	.200	12	1	1
Gabby Hartnett	c	6	24	1	7	0	0	1	2	0	3	0	.292	.417	33	6	0
Chuck Klein	ph-rf-cf	5	12	2	4	0	0	1	2	0	2	0	.333	.583	4	0	0
Ken O'Dea	ph	1	1	0	1	0	0	0	1	0	0	0	1.000	1.000			
Walter Stephenson	ph	1	1	0	0	0	0	0	0	1	0	0	.000	.000			
Tuck Stainback		Did not play															
Woody English		Did not play															
Charlie Grimm		Did not play															
Lon Warneke	p	3	5	0	1	0	0	0	0	0	0	0	.200	.200	2	9	0
Larry French	p	2	4	1	1	0	0	0	0	0	2	0	.250	.250	1	2	0
Fabian Kowalik	p	1	2	1	1	0	0	0	0	0	0	0	.500	.500	0	2	1
Roy Henshaw	p	1	1	0	0	0	0	0	0	0	0	0	.000	.000	0	1	0
Bill Lee	p	2	1	0	0	0	0	0	1	0	0	0	.000	.000	1	1	0
Tex Carleton	p	1	1	0	0	0	0	0	0	1	1	0	.000	.000	0	2	0
Charlie Root	p	2	0	0	0	0	0	0	0	0	0	0	—	—	0	1	0
Clyde Shoun		Did not play															
Hugh Casey		Did not play															
team total		6	202	18	48	6	2	5	17	11	29	1	.238	.362	164	74	6

Double Plays—5
Left on Bases—38

REGULAR SEASON STATISTICS

	Main Pos	G	AB	R	H	2B	3B	HR	RBI	BB	SO	SB	BA	SA
CHICAGO CUBS														
Phil Cavarretta	1b	146	589	85	162	28	12	8	82	39	61	4	.275	.404
Billy Herman	2b	154	666	113	**227**	**57**	6	7	83	42	29	6	.341	.476
Billy Jurges	ss	146	519	69	125	33	1	1	59	42	39	3	.241	.314
Stan Hack	3b	124	427	75	133	23	9	4	64	65	17	14	.311	.436
Frank Demaree	of	107	385	60	127	19	4	2	66	26	23	6	.325	.410
Fred Lindstrom	of-3b	90	342	49	94	22	4	3	62	10	13	1	.275	.389
Augie Galan	of	154	646	**133**	203	41	11	12	79	87	53	**22**	.314	.467
Gabby Hartnett	c	116	413	67	142	32	6	13	91	41	46	1	.344	.545
Chuck Klein	of	119	434	71	127	14	4	21	73	41	42	4	.293	.488
Ken O'Dea	c	76	202	30	52	13	2	6	38	26	18	0	.257	.431
Walter Stephenson	c	16	26	2	10	1	1	0	2	1	5	0	.385	.500
Tuck Stainback	of	47	94	16	24	4	0	3	11	0	13	1	.255	.394
Woody English	3b-ss	34	84	11	17	2	0	2	8	20	4	1	.202	.298
Charlie Grimm	1b	2	8	0	0	0	0	0	0	0	1	0	.000	.000
Lon Warneke	p	44	91	9	20	1	0	0	15	3	9	0	.220	.231
Larry French	p	42	85	4	12	1	0	0	5	1	14	0	.141	.153
Fabian Kowalik	p	20	15	1	3	0	0	0	1	0	2	0	.200	.200
Roy Henshaw	p	31	51	5	13	1	0	0	2	1	11	0	.255	.275
Bill Lee	p	39	102	8	24	3	0	0	11	2	15	0	.235	.265
Tex Carleton	p	31	62	4	8	0	0	0	2	2	12	0	.129	.129
Charlie Root	p	38	69	8	14	2	1	1	7	3	22	0	.203	.304
Clyde Shoun	p	5	3	0	0	0	0	0	0	0	0	0	.000	.000
Hugh Casey	p	13	6	1	1	0	0	0	0	0	3	0	.167	.167
team total		154	5486	**847**	1581	**303**	62	88	**782**	**464**	471	66	**.288**	.414

Kiki Cuyler (of), Johnny Gill (ph), Clay Bryant (p) and Roy Joiner (p) also played for the Cubs during the season.

PITCHING

WORLD SERIES STATISTICS

	G	GS	CG	IP	H	R	ER	BB	SO	W	L	SV	ERA
DETROIT TIGERS													
Schoolboy Rowe	**3**	**2**	**2**	**21**	**19**	**8**	**6**	1	**14**	1	**2**	0	2.57
Tommy Bridges	2	**2**	**2**	18	18	6	5	4	9	**2**	0	0	2.50
General Crowder	1	1	1	9	5	1	1	3	5	1	0	0	1.00
Eldon Auker	1	1	0	6	6	3	2	2	1	0	0	0	3.00
Chief Hogsett	1	0	0	1	0	0	0	1	0	0	0	0	0.00
Joe Sullivan	Did not play												
Vic Sorrell	Did not play												
Roxie Lawson	Did not play												
team total	6	6	5	55	48	18	14	11	29	4	2	0	2.29
CHICAGO CUBS													
Lon Warneke	**3**	**2**	1	$16\frac{2}{3}$	9	1	1	4	5	**2**	0	0	**0.54**
Larry French	2	1	1	$10\frac{2}{3}$	15	5	4	2	8	0	**2**	0	3.38
Bill Lee	2	1	0	$10\frac{1}{3}$	11	5	4	5	5	0	0	**1**	3.48
Tex Carleton	1	1	0	7	6	2	1	**7**	4	0	1	0	1.29
Fabian Kowalik	1	0	0	$4\frac{1}{3}$	3	1	1	1	1	0	0	0	2.10
Roy Henshaw	1	0	0	$3\frac{2}{3}$	2	3	3	5	2	0	0	0	7.36
Charlie Root	2	1	0	2	5	4	4	1	2	0	1	0	18.00
Clyde Shoun	Did not play												
Hugh Casey	Did not play												
team total	6	6	2	$54\frac{1}{3}$	51	21	18	25	27	2	4	1	2.96

REGULAR SEASON STATISTICS

	G	GS	CG	IP	H	ER	BB	SO	W	L	Pct	SV	ShO	ERA
DETROIT TIGERS														
Schoolboy Rowe	42	34	21	276	272	113	68	140	19	13	.594	3	**6**	3.68
Tommy Bridges	36	34	23	274	277	107	113	**163**	21	10	.677	1	4	3.51
General Crowder	33	32	16	241	269	114	67	59	16	10	.615	0	2	4.26
Eldon Auker	36	25	13	195	213	83	61	63	18	7	**.720**	0	2	3.83
Chief Hogsett	40	0	0	97	109	38	49	39	6	6	.500	5	0	3.53
Joe Sullivan	25	12	5	126	119	49	71	53	6	6	.500	0	0	3.50
Vic Sorrell	12	6	4	51	65	23	25	22	4	3	.571	0	0	4.06
Roxie Lawson	1	4	4	40	34	7	24	16	3	1	.750	2	2	1.58
team total	152	152	**87**	1364	1440	665	579	522	**93**	53	**.616**	11	**16**	3.82
CHICAGO CUBS														
Lon Warneke	42	30	20	262	257	89	50	120	20	13	.606	4	1	3.06
Larry French	42	30	16	246	279	81	44	90	17	10	.630	2	**4**	2.96
Bill Lee	39	32	18	254	241	83	84	100	20	6	**.769**	1	3	2.96
Tex Carleton	31	22	8	171	169	74	60	84	11	8	.579	1	0	3.89
Fabian Kowalik	20	2	1	55	60	27	19	20	2	2	.500	1	0	4.42
Roy Henshaw	31	18	7	143	135	52	68	53	13	5	.722	1	3	3.27
Charlie Root	38	18	11	201	193	69	47	94	15	8	.652	2	1	3.09
Clyde Shoun	5	1	0	13	14	4	5	5	1	0	1.000	0	0	2.77
Hugh Casey	13	0	0	26	29	11	14	10	0	0	—	0	0	3.81
team total	154	154	81	1394	1417	505	400	589	**100**	54	**.649**	14	12	**3.26**

Total Attendance—286,672   Average Attendance—47,779   Winning Player's share—$6,545   Losing Player's Share—$4,199

1936
Back to the Subways

For the first time ever, the New York Yankees made it to the World Series without Babe Ruth. The legendary slugger led the Yanks to their first American League title in 1921 and played on a total of seven pennant-winning Yankee squads. But the Sultan of Swat began to show his age in 1933, and he definitely looked past his prime at age thirty-nine in 1934. Faced with the erosion of Ruth's skills, his high salary, and his frustrated desire to manage the Yankees, team owner Jacob Ruppert released the Babe so he could join the Boston Braves in 1935 as assistant manager and part-time outfielder. Ruth had pitifully little left as a player, and when he retired in June, the assistant manager's job went up in smoke. But the Yankee team that he had for so long personified deftly built back up to powerhouse status under the direction of general manager Ed Barrow and manager Joe McCarthy. Lou Gehrig, Tony Lazzeri, and Bill Dickey furnished a core of holdover power, Frankie Crosetti continued at shortstop, and Red Ruffing and Lefty Gomez still spearheaded the pitching staff. But a cohort of recent newcomers pushed the Yankees into a class of their own in the world of baseball. George Selkirk and Jake Powell moved into outfield slots, Red Rolfe played a slick third base, Monte Pearson and Bump Hadley joined the mound staff, and Joe DiMaggio started his own legend in center field. Breaking into the majors this season with a .323 batting average with 29 homers and 125 RBI's, DiMaggio played a gracefully splendid center field and joined Gehrig in a new one-two batting punch just as potent as the old one of Ruth and Gehrig.

New York's good fortune with the Yanks and DiMaggio continued with the resurgence of the New York Giants. With Bill Terry troubled by a bad knee, Mel Ott pretty much carried the Giant attack with his powerful bat, while Carl Hubbell paced the team's pitchers. Known as the King, Hubbell threw his screwball past batters regularly, winning his last 16 decisions of the season to lodge a 26–6 record with a 2.31 ERA. With Ott and Hubbell leading the way, the unheralded Giants fought down the stretch and took the National League flag in a tight race.

The first Subway Series in 13 years began at the Polo Grounds in bad weather with a mound duel between Hubbell and Ruffing. Although there was a light rain falling which seemed to favor the pitchers, Selkirk got the Yankees on the board in the third inning with a homer. Dick Bartell squared it in the fifth with a homer, and another run in the sixth gave Hubbell a 2–1 lead. That score stood up until the eighth inning, when the Giants broke through for four runs to ice away a 6–1 victory and to keep Hubbell's streak going.

But the Yankees were about to give a demonstration on how to win games with either overwhelming power or stiffling pitching. The Yankee power barraged the Giant hurlers in game two, banging out an 18–4 win on 17 hits against five pitchers. Featured in the onslaught was a seven-run third inning in which Tony Lazzeri hit the second grand-slammer in Series history. The scene shifted to Yankee Stadium for game three, and pitchers Bump Hadley and Freddie Fitzsimmons took the upper hand. Each allowed a solo homer in the early going and took a 1–1 game into the eighth. The Yanks scored in the bottom of the eighth on Crosetti's infield single off Fitzsimmons's glove, and relief work by Pat Malone saved the 2–1 victory for Hadley. Hubbell returned to the mound in game four and was pinned with his first loss in several months. A solo run counted against the King in the second, and then three more scored in the third on Crosetti's double, Rolfe's single, and Gehrig's homer. Monte Pearson got credit for the 5–2 win which practically sewed up the Series. The Giants did take the fifth game 5–4 in ten innings, scoring the winning run off reliever Malone on a double by Jo-Jo Moore, a sacrifice by Dick Bartell, and Bill Terry's long fly ball. But that victory only postponed the end. Back in the Polo Grounds for game six, the Yanks again unleashed their power and scored seven runs in the top of the ninth for a 13–5 wrap-up of the Series. Jake Powell got three hits in the game, and his .455 average for the six games was good enough to place him in the top spot in the Series.

Game 1 September 30 at Polo Grounds

NY Yankees	Pos	AB	R	H	RBI	PO	A	E
Crosetti	ss	4	0	1	0	1	3	1
Rolfe	3b	3	0	1	0	2	1	0
DiMaggio	cf	4	0	1	0	3	0	0
Gehrig	1b	3	0	0	0	7	0	0
Dickey	c	4	0	0	0	8	0	1
Powell	lf	4	0	3	0	2	0	0
Lazzeri	2b	3	0	0	0	1	2	0
Selkirk	rf	4	1	1	1	0	0	0
Ruffing	p	3	0	0	0	0	1	0
Totals		32	1	7	1	24	7	2

Doubles—Crosetti, Ott, Powell.
Home Runs—Bartell, Selkirk.
Sacrifice Hits—Ripple 2, Rolfe.
Double Play—Whitehead to Terry.
Hit by Pitcher—Gehrig (by Hubbell).
Left on Bases—Yankees 7, Giants 7.
Umpires—Pfirman (N), Geisel (A), Magerkurth (N), Summers (A).
Attendance—39,419. Time of Game—2:40.

NY Y	0 0 1	0 0 0	0 0 0
NY G	0 0 0	0 1 1	0 4 x

NY Giants	Pos	AB	R	H	RBI	PO	A	E
Moore	lf	5	0	0	0	0	0	0
Bartell	ss	4	1	2	1	1	2	0
Terry	1b	4	2	2	0	12	2	0
Ott	rf	2	2	2	0	0	0	0
Ripple	cf	2	0	0	0	0	0	0
Mancuso	cf	3	1	1	1	9	1	0
Whitehead	2b	4	0	0	1	3	4	0
Jackson	3b	4	0	0	1	1	1	0
Hubbell	p	4	0	2	1	1	2	1
Totals		31	6	9	5	27	12	1

Pitching	IP	H	R	ER	BB	SO
Yankees						
Ruffing (L)	8	9	6	4	4	5
Giants						
Hubbell (W)	9	7	1	1	1	8

1st Inning
Yankees
1 Crosetti grounded to third.
2 Rolfe grounded to first.
3 DiMaggio grounded to short.
Giants
1 Moore flied to left.
2 Bartell lined to left.
Terry singled beyond short.
Ott walked.
3 Ripple popped to short.

2nd Inning
Yankees
1 Gehrig grounded out, Terry to Hubbell.
2 Dickey grounded to second.
Powell singled to center.
3 Lazzeri struck out.
Giants
1 Mancuso struck out.
2 Whitehead grounded to short.
3 Jackson struck out.

3rd Inning
Yankees
Selkirk homered into the upper right field stands.
1 Ruffing grounded back to the pitcher.
2 Crosetti popped to second.
Rolfe singled past second.
DiMaggio singled to right with Rolfe falling after rounding second (he got back safely).
3 Gehrig grounded back to Hubbell.
Giants
Hubbell singled to center.
1 Moore struck out.
Bartell singled to right, advancing Hubbell to third.
2 Terry fouled out to Dickey.
Ott walked to load the bases.
3 Ripple struck out.

4th Inning
Yankees
1 Dickey struck out.
Powell doubled to left.
Lazzeri walked.
2 Powell was caught attempting to steal third, Mancuso to Jackson with Lazzeri going to second.
3 Selkirk struck out.
Giants
1 Mancuso popped to third.
2 Whitehead struck out.
3 Jackson grounded to second.

5th Inning
Yankees
1 Ruffing struck out.
2 Crosetti fouled to Mancuso.
3 Rolfe popped to second.
Giants
1 Hubbell grounded to second.
2 Moore fouled to Dickey.
Bartell homered into the left field stands.
3 Terry grounded to second.

6th Inning
Yankees
1 DiMaggio struck out.
2 Gehrig struck out.
3 Dickey grounded to first.
Giants
Ott doubled to left.
1 Ripple sacrificed Ott to third, Ruffing to Lazzeri.
Mancuso singled beyond third, scoring Ott.
2 Whitehead popped to third.
3 Jackson flied to center.

7th Inning
Yankees
Powell singled to left.
1 Lazzeri struck out.
2 Selkirk forced Powell at second, Terry to Bartell.
3 Ruffing struck out.
Giants
1 Hubbell fouled to Gehrig.
2 Moore flied to center.
3 Bartell popped to Dickey.

8th Inning
Yankees
Crosetti doubled to left.
Rolfe bunted and was safe on Hubbell's error with Crosetti stopping at second.
1,2 DiMaggio lined to Whitehead who threw to Terry to double up Rolfe with Crosetti still holding second.
Gehrig was hit by a pitched ball.
3 Dickey grounded to first.
Giants
Terry singled to right.
Ott singled to right, Terry to second.
1 Ripple sacrificed Terry to third and Ott to second, Rolfe to Gehrig.
Mancuso intentionally walked to load the bases.
Whitehead walked forcing in Terry with a run, bases still jammed.
2 Jackson flied to DiMaggio, Ott scoring after the catch.
Hubbell singled past Lazzeri scoring Mancuso and when Crosetti made a bad throw to the plate Whitehead scored, Dickey threw wildly to catch Hubbell who reached third on the two errors.
3 Moore grounded to Short.

9th Inning
Yankees
1 Powell grounded to short.
2 Lazzeri grounded to second.
3 Selkirk also grounded to second.

Game 2 October 2 at Polo Grounds

NY Y	207	001	206
NY G	010	300	000

NY Yankees	Pos	AB	R	H	RBI	PO	A	E
Crosetti	ss	5	4	3	0	0	1	0
Rolfe	3b	4	3	2	1	2	0	0
DiMaggio	cb	5	2	3	2	6	0	0
Gehrig	1b	5	1	2	3	6	0	0
Dickey	c	5	3	2	5	8	0	0
Selkirk	rf	5	1	1	0	2	0	0
Powell	lf	3	2	0	2	2	0	0
Lazzeri	2b	4	1	1	5	1	3	0
Gomez	p	5	1	1	2	0	0	0
Totals		41	18	17	18	27	4	0

Pitching	IP	H	R	ER	BB	SO
Yankees						
Gomez (W)	9	6	4	4	7	8
Giants						
Schumacher(L)	*2	3	5	4	4	1
Smith	1	2	3	3	1	0
Coffman	1⅓	2	1	1	0	1
Gabler	4	5	3	3	3	0
Gumbert	1	6	6	1	1	1

*Faced 3 batters in the 3rd.

NY Giants	Pos	AB	R	H	RBI	PO	A	E
Moore	lf	5	0	0	0	2	0	0
Bartell	ss	3	0	1	1	2	2	0
Terry	1b	5	0	2	2	6	1	0
Leiber	cf	4	0	0	0	7	1	0
Ott	rf	4	0	0	0	4	0	0
Mancuso	c	2	2	1	0	3	2	0
Whitehead	2b	4	0	0	0	2	1	0
Jackson	3b	4	1	1	0	0	2	1
Schumacher	p	0	0	0	0	0	0	0
Smith	p	0	0	0	0	0	0	0
Coffman	p	0	0	0	0	0	1	0
a Davis		1	1	1	0	0	0	0
Gabler	p	0	0	0	0	1	0	0
b Danning		1	0	0	0	0	0	0
Gumbert	p	0	0	0	0	0	0	0
Totals		33	4	6	3	27	10	1

a Singled for Coffman in 4th.
b Struck out for Gabler in 8th.

Doubles—Bartell, DiMaggio, Mancuso. Home Runs—Dickey, Lazzeri. Sacrifice Hit—DiMaggio. Stolen Base—Powell. Double Play—Leiber to Jackson to Bartell. Wild Pitches—Gomez, Schumacher. Left on Bases—Yankees 6, Giants 9. Umpires—Geisel (A), Magerkurth (N), Summers (A), Pfirman (N). Attendance—43,543. Time of Game—2:49.

1st Inning
Yankees
Crosetti singled to center.
Rolfe walked.
DiMaggio singled on a bunt to fill the bases.
1 Gehrig flied to right, Crosetti scoring after the catch and Rolfe going to third on the throw to the plate. DiMaggio to third on a wild pitch, Rolfe holding.
2,3 Dickey flied to Leiber scoring Rolfe but DiMaggio was doubled up trying for third, Leiber to Jackson to Bartell.
Giants
1 Moore struck out.
2 Bartell struck out.
Terry singled over second.
Leiber walked.
3 Ott flied to center.

2nd Inning
Yankees
Selkirk walked.
1 Powell lined to right.
2 Selkirk was caught stealing, Mancuso to Whitehead. Lazzeri walked.
3 Gomez struck out.
Giants
Mancuso walked.
1 Whitehead flied to right.
2 Jackson flew out to right.
Schumacher walked.
On a wild pitch Mancuso scored and Schumacher reached third.
3 Moore fouled to Rolfe.

3rd Inning
Yankees
Crosetti singled to left.
Rolfe walked.
DiMaggio was safe at first on Jackson's error filling the bases.
For the Giants—Smith pitching.
Gehrig singled over first, scoring Crosetti and Rolfe and moving DiMaggio to third.
Dickey singled to right, scoring DiMaggio and moving Gehrig to third.
1 Selkirk flied to Leiber in short left.
Powell walked loading the bases again.
For the Giants—Coffman pitching.
Lazzeri hit a grand slam into the lower right field stands (only the second in Series history tying Elmer Smith's mark of 1920).
2 Gomez struck out.
3 Crosetti grounded to short.
Giants
Bartell walked.
1 Terry struck out.
2 Leiber struck out.
3 Ott popped to third.

4th Inning
Yankees
1 Rolfe was tossed out by Coffman on a bunt to the mound.
2 DiMaggio flied to Moore. Gehrig singled past first.
3 Gehrig was caught stealing, Mancuso to Bartell.
Giants
Mancuso walked.
1 Whitehead fanned.
Jackson singled beyond second.
Davis, batting for Coffman, singled over second filling the bases.
2 Moore fanned.
Bartell walked forcing in Mancuso.
Terry singled to left, scoring Jackson and Davis, Bartell stopped at second.
3 Leiber lined to left.

5th Inning
Yankees
For the Giants—Gabler pitching.
1 Dickey rolled out to first.
2 Selkirk flied to left.
Powell singled off the left field wall.

5th Inning (continued)
3 Lazzeri flied to center.
Giants
1 Ott grounded to second.
2 Mancuso struck out.
3 Whitehead grounded to second.

6th Inning
Yankees
1 Gomez grounded to short.
Crosetti walked.
Rolfe singled, sending Crosetti to third.
2 DiMaggio flied to left, scoring Crosetti.
3 Gehrig flied to right.
Giants
1 Jackson popped to second.
Gabler walked.
2 Moore lined to center.
3 Bartell lined to left.

7th Inning
Yankees
Dickey walked.
Selkirk singled to center, Dickey stopping at second.
Powell singled to left, filling the bases.
1 Lazzeri flied to deep center, Dickey scored and Selkirk went to third after the catch.
2 Gomez grounded to second, scoring Selkirk.
3 Crosetti flied to center.
Giants
1 Terry grounded to second.
2 Leiber grounded to short.
3 Ott flied to center.

8th Inning
Yankees
1 Rolfe popped to second.
DiMaggio doubled off the left field wall.
Gehrig walked.
2 Dickey flied to right.
3 Terry grounded out, Terry to Gabler.
Giants
Mancuso doubled to left.
1 Whitehead fouled to Gehrig.
2 Jackson fouled to Gehrig.
3 Danning, pinch hitting for Gabler, struck out.

9th Inning
Yankees
For the Giants—Gumbert pitching.
Powell walked.
Powell stole second.
1 Lazzeri flied deep to center, advancing Powell to third.
Gomez singled to center, scoring Powell.
Crosetti singled to left, moving Gomez to second.
Rolfe singled off Jackson's glove, scoring Gomez, Crosetti moved to second.
DiMaggio only singled off the left field wall, scoring Crosetti with Rolfe stopping at second.
2 Gehrig grounded to third, advancing both base-runners.
Dickey hit a three run homer into the lower right field stands.
3 Selkirk struck out.
Giants
1 Moore flew out to center.
Bartell doubled to left.
2 Terry flew out to center.
3 Leiber also flew to DiMaggio who got all three putouts in the final inning.

Game 3 October 3 at Yankee Stadium

NY G	000	010	000
NY Y	010	000	01x

NY Giants	Pos	AB	R	H	RBI	PO	A	E
Moore	lf	5	0	1	0	2	0	0
Bartell	ss	3	0	1	0	1	0	0
Terry	1b	4	0	1	0	5	1	0
Ott	rf	4	0	2	0	4	0	0
Ripple	cf	4	1	1	1	2	0	0
Mancuso	c	4	0	1	0	7	0	0
Whitehead	2b	4	0	0	0	3	4	0
Jackson	3b	2	0	1	0	0	2	0
a Koenig		1	0	0	0	0	0	0
Fitzsimmons	p	3	0	2	0	1	1	0
b Leslie		1	0	1	0	0	0	0
c Davis		0	0	0	0	0	0	0
Totals		35	1	11	1	24	8	0

a Grounded out for Jackson in 9th.
b Singled for Fitzsimmons in 9th.
c Ran for Leslie in 9th.
d Hit into fielders choice for Hadley in 8th.
e Ran for Ruffing in 8th.

NY Yankees	Pos	AB	R	H	RBI	PO	A	E
Crosetti	ss	4	0	1	1	4	5	0
Rolfe	3b	4	0	0	0	3	1	0
DiMaggio	cf	3	0	1	0	2	0	0
Gehrig	1b	3	1	1	1	10	1	0
Dickey	c	2	0	0	0	3	2	0
Selkirk	rf	3	0	1	0	3	2	0
Powell	lf	2	1	0	1	1	0	0
Lazzeri	2b	2	0	0	0	2	2	0
Hadley	p	2	0	0	0	0	3	0
d Ruffing		1	0	0	0	0	0	0
e Johnson		0	0	0	0	0	0	0
Malone	p	0	0	0	0	0	0	0
Totals		26	2	4	2	27	14	0

Pitching	IP	H	R	ER	BB	SO
Giants						
Fitzsimmons (L)	8	2	2	2	2	5
Yankees						
Hadley (W)	8	10	1	1	1	2
Malone (SV)	1	1	0	0	0	1

Double—DiMaggio. Home Runs—Gehrig, Ripple. Sacrifice Hits—Bartell, Lazzeri. Double Plays—Grosetti to Gehrig, Bartell to Whitehead to Terry. Umpires—Magerkurth, Summers, Pfirman, Geisel. Left on Bases—Giants 9, Yankees 3. Attendance—64,842. Time of Game—2:01.

1st Inning
Giants
Moore singled past third.
1 Bartell sacrificed Moore to second, Hadley to Gehrig.
Terry singled to center with Moore stopping at third.
2,3 Ott grounded to Crosetti who stepped on second to force Terry and threw to Gehrig to get Ott in a double play.
Yankees
1 Crosetti flied to right.
2 Rolfe grounded to first.
3 DiMaggio popped to second.

2nd Inning
Giants
1 Ripple flied to right.
2 Mancuso flied to center.
3 Whitehead grounded to second.
Yankees
Gehrig homered into the right field stands.
Dickey walked.
1 Selkirk fouled to Mancuso.
2,3 Powell grounded into a double play, Bartell to Whitehead to Terry.

3rd Inning
Giants
1 Jackson grounded to third.
2 Fitzsimmons struck out.
3 Moore flied to right.
Yankees
1 Lazzeri struck out.
2 Hadley flied to right.
3 Crosetti struck out.

4th Inning
Giants
1 Bartell fouled to Rolfe.
2 Terry grounded to short.
3 Ott fouled to Rolfe.
Yankees
1 Rolfe grounded to second.
DiMaggio doubled to left-center.
2 Gehrig flied to right.
3 Dickey grounded to second.

5th Inning
Giants
Ripple homered into the right field bleachers.
Mancuso blooped a single over short.
1 Whitehead forced Mancuso at second, Gehrig to Crosetti.
2 Whitehead caught stealing Dickey to Crosetti.
Jackson walked.
Fitzsimmons bounced a single over Rolfe's head, advancing Jackson to third.
3 Moore grounded back to the pitcher.

5th Inning (continued)
Yankees
1 Selkirk struck out.
2 Powell struck out.
3 Lazzeri flied to left.

6th Inning
Giants
1 Bartell fouled to Rolfe.
2 Terry flied to center.
Ott singled over second.
3 Ripple struck out.
Yankees
1 Hadley struck out.
2 Crosetti flied to center.
3 Rolfe lined to center.

7th Inning
Giants
1 Mancuso grounded to short.
2 Whitehead bunted and was out, Dickey to Gehrig.
Jackson singled to center.
Fitzsimmons singled to left, Jackson stopping at second.
3 Moore lined to second.
Yankees
1 DiMaggio lined to left.
2 Gehrig flied to right.
3 Dickey grounded to second.

8th Inning
Giants
Bartell singled to left.
1 Terry bunted but forced Bartell, Hadley to Crosetti.
Ott singled to center, Terry to second.
2 Ripple grounded to second, both runners advancing.
3 Mancuso flied to left.
Yankees
Selkirk singled to right.
Powell walked.
1 Lazzeri sacrificed Selkirk to third and Powell to second, Jackson to Whitehead.
Ruffing, batting for Hadley, tapped to
2 Fitzsimmons and Selkirk was trapped at the plate, Fitzsimmons to Mancuso. Johnson ran for Ruffing.
Crosetti singled off Fitzsimmons' glove, scoring Powell with Johnson stopping at second.
3 Rolfe grounded out, Terry to Fitzsimmons.

9th Inning
Giants
For the Yankees—Malone pitching.
1 Whitehead struck out.
2 Koenig, batting for Jackson, grounded to short.
Leslie, batting for Fitzsimmons, singled to center.
Davis ran for Leslie.
3 Moore forced Davis, Crosetti to Lazzeri.

Game 4 October 4 at Yankee Stadium

NY G	000 100 010
NY Y	013 000 01x

NY Giants	Pos	AB	R	H	RBI	PO	A	E
Moore	lf	3	1	1	0	2	0	0
Bartell	ss	4	0	1	0	3	4	0
Terry	1b	3	0	0	1	10	1	0
Ott	rf	4	0	0	0	1	0	0
Ripple	cf	4	0	2	1	3	0	0
Mancuso	c	4	0	0	0	3	0	0
Whitehead	2b	3	0	0	0	2	5	0
c Koenig		1	0	1	0	0	0	0
Jackson	3b	4	0	1	0	0	3	1
Hubbell	p	2	0	0	0	1	0	0
a Leslie		1	0	1	0	0	0	0
b Davis		0	1	0	0	0	0	0
Gabler	p	0	0	0	0	0	0	0
Totals		33	2	7	2	24	13	1

a Singled for Hubbell in the 8th.
b Ran for Leslie in the 8th.
c Singled for Whitehead in the 9th.

Doubles—Crosetti, Gehrig, Pearson. Home Run—Gehrig. Double Play—Bartell to Whitehead to Terry. Wild Pitch—Hubbell. Left on Bases—Giants 6, Yankees 7. Umpires—Summers, Pfirman, Geisel, Magerkurth. Attendance—**66,669 (New Series record).** Time of Game—2:12.

NY Yankees	Pos	AB	R	H	RBI	PO	A	E
Crosetti	ss	4	1	2	0	4	1	0
Rolfe	3b	3	1	2	1	1	2	0
DiMaggio	cf	4	0	0	0	1	0	0
Gehrig	1b	4	2	2	2	7	0	0
Dickey	c	4	0	0	0	8	2	0
Powell	lf	4	1	1	0	2	0	0
Lazzeri	2b	4	0	0	0	3	4	0
Selkirk	rf	3	0	1	1	0	1	1
Pearson	p	4	0	2	0	1	2	0
Totals		34	5	10	5	27	11	1

Pitching	IP	H	R	ER	BB	SO
Giants						
Hubbell (L)	7	8	4	3	1	2
Gabler	1	2	1	1	1	0
Yankees						
Pearson (W)	9	7	2	2	2	7

1st Inning
Giants
Moore walked.
1 Bartell struck out.
2 Terry struck out.
3   Moore was out attempting to steal, Dickey to Crosetti.
Yankees
1 Crosetti grounded to third.
  Rolfe singled past Jackson.
2 DiMaggio popped to first.
3 Gehrig grounded to second.

2nd Inning
Giants
1 Ott struck out.
  Ripple singled between first and second.
2   Ripple caught trying for second, Dickey to Crosetti.
3 Mancuso fanned.
Yankees
1 Dickey fanned.
  Powell to first on Jackson's error.
2 Lazzeri grounded to second with Powell going to second.
  Selkirk singled to left, scoring Powell.
3 Pearson flied to center.

3rd Inning
Giants
  Whitehead safe at first as Selkirk dropped his short fly.
1 Jackson flied to center.
2 Hubbell grounded to the pitcher, Whitehead advancing to second.
3 Moore fouled to Rolfe.
Yankees
  Crosetti doubled to right.
  Rolfe singled to center, scoring Crosetti.
1 DiMaggio fouled to Mancuso.
  Rolfe went to third on a wild pitch.
  Gehrig hit a two-run homer into the right field bleachers.
2 Dickey lined to left.
3 Powell lined to Ripple who made a good low catch.

4th Inning
Giants
  Bartell singled to right.
  Terry walked.
1 Ott forced Terry at second, Crosetti to Lazzeri with Bartell going to third.
  Ripple singled to left, scoring Bartell with Ott stopping at second.
2 Mancuso forced Ripple at second Ott to third, Lazzeri to Crosetti.
3 Whitehead popped to short.
Yankees
1 Lazzeri flied to center.
2 Selkirk fanned.
  Pearson singled to left.
3 Crosetti forced Pearson at second, Bartell to Whitehead.

5th Inning
Giants
  Jackson beat out a bunt.
1 Hubbell flew out to left.
2 Moore struck out.
3 Bartell popped to short.
Yankees
  Rolfe walked.
1 DiMaggio flied to left.
2 Gehrig forced Rolfe at second, Whitehead to Bartell.
3 Dickey forced Gehrig at second, Bartell unassisted.

6th Inning
Giants
1 Terry struck out.
2 Ott flied to left.
3 Ripple popped to short.
Yankees
1 Powell grounded to third.
2 Lazzeri grounded to short.
3 Selkirk grounded out, Terry to Hubbell.

7th Inning
Giants
1 Mancuso popped to Dickey.
2 Whitehead grounded to the pitcher.
3 Jackson struck out.
Yankees
  Pearson doubled to right-center.
  Crosetti singled to right, advancing Pearson to third.
1 Rolfe popped to short.
2,3 DiMaggio hit into a double play, Bartell to Whitehead to Terry.

8th Inning
Giants
  Leslie, pinch hitting for Hubbell, singled to left.
  Davis ran for Leslie.
  Moore singled to left, moving Davis to second.
1 Bartell grounded out, Lazzeri to Pearson both runners advancing.
2 Terry grounded to second, scoring Davis and Moore going to third.
3 Ott grounded to third.
Yankees
  For the Giants—Gabler pitching.
  Gehrig doubled to left.
1 Dickey grounded to short, moving Gehrig to third.
  Powell singled to left, scoring Gehrig.
2 Lazzeri grounded to second, advancing Powell to second.
  Selkirk walked.
3 Pearson grounded to third.

9th Inning
Giants
1 Ripple grounded to short.
2 Mancuso grounded to third.
  Koenig, pinch hitting for Whitehead, singled to right center.
3 Jackson fouled to Gehrig.

Game 5 October 5 at Yankee Stadium

NY G	300 001 000 1
NY Y	011 002 000 0

NY Giants	Pos	AB	R	H	RBI	PO	A	E
Moore	lf	5	2	2	0	1	0	0
Bartell	ss	4	1	1	1	2	2	1
Terry	1b	5	0	0	1	6	2	0
Ott	rf	5	1	1	0	1	0	1
Ripple	cf	2	1	1	2	0	0	0
Mancuso	c	3	0	2	0	14	2	0
Whitehead	2b	4	0	1	1	3	4	0
Jackson	3b	4	0	0	0	1	1	1
Schumacher	p	4	0	0	0	2	2	0
Totals		36	5	8	4	30	13	3

Pitching	IP	H	R	ER	BB	SO
Giants						
Schumacher(W)	10	10	4	3	6	10
Yankees						
Ruffing	6	7	4	3	1	7
Malone (L)	4	1	1	1	1	1

NY Yankees	Pos	AB	R	H	RBI	PO	A	E
Crosetti	ss	5	0	0	1	2	3	1
Rolfe	3b	5	0	2	0	3	1	0
DiMaggio	cf	4	0	1	0	4	0	0
Gehrig	1b	4	0	0	0	5	1	0
Dickey	c	5	0	1	0	8	0	0
b Seeds		0	0	0	0	0	0	0
Selkirk	rf	4	2	1	1	2	0	0
Powell	lf	4	1	1	0	2	0	0
Lazzeri	2b	3	1	1	1	3	1	0
Ruffing	p	1	0	0	0	1	2	0
a Johnson		1	0	0	0	0	0	0
Malone	p	1	0	1	0	0	2	0
Totals		37	4	10	3	30	10	1

a Struck out for Ruffing in 6th.
b Ran for Dickey in 10th.

Doubles—Bartell, DiMaggio, Mancuso, Moore 2. Home Run—Selkirk. Sacrifice Hits—Bartell, Mancuso. Double Plays—Schumacher to Terry to Mancuso, Bartell to Whitehead to Terry, Mancuso to Whitehead, Crosetti to Lazzeri to Gehrig. Wild Pitch—Schumacher. Left on Bases—Giants 5, Yankees 9. Umpires—Pfirman, Geisel, Magerkurth, Summers. Attendance—50,024. Time of Game—2:45.

1st Inning
Giants
  Moore doubled to left.
  Bartell doubled to right, scoring Moore.
1 Terry struck out.
2 Ott grounded to short, moving Bartell to third.
  Ripple singled to left, scoring Bartell.
  Mancuso singled to right, moving Ripple to third.
  Whitehead singled to right, scoring Ripple with Mancuso stopping at second.
3 Jackson flied to center.
Yankees
1 Crosetti struck out.
2 Rolfe flied to center.
3 DiMaggio grounded to third.

2nd Inning
Giants
1 Schumacher flied to second.
2 Moore popped to third.
3 Bartell struck out.
Yankees
  Gehrig singled to right and got all the way to third as Ott erred.
1,2 Dickey was thrown out by Schumacher to Terry who pegged to Mancuso getting Gehrig trying to score for a double play.
  Selkirk homered into the right field seats.
3 Powell flied to center.

3rd Inning
Giants
1 Terry grounded out to short.
2 Ott flied to left.
3 Ripple looked at a called third strike.
Yankees
  Lazzeri walked.
  Ruffing walked.
  Lazzeri went to third and Ruffing to second on a wild pitch.
  Crosetti was safe on Bartell's low throw scoring Lazzeri with Ruffing holding second.
  Rolfe bunted for a single, loading the bases.
1 DiMaggio struck out.
2 Gehrig struck out.
3 Dickey flied to right.

4th Inning
Giants
  Mancuso doubled to left.
1 Whitehead hit back to the pitcher who caught Mancuso off second throwing to Crosetti.
2 Jackson popped to short.
3 Schumacher struck out.
Yankees
  Selkirk walked.
  Powell walked.
1 Lazzeri attempting to sacrifice forced Selkirk at third, Schumacher to Jackson.
2,3 Ruffing grounded into a double play, Bartell to Whitehead to Terry.

5th Inning
Giants
1 Moore grounded out, Gehrig to Ruffing.
2 Bartell struck out.
3 Terry fouled to Rolfe.
Yankees
1 Crosetti struck out.
  Rolfe bunted safely for a single.
2,3 DiMaggio struck out and Rolfe was doubled up going for second, Mancuso to Whitehead.

6th Inning
Giants
  Ott singled over Crosetti's head.
  Ripple walked.
1 Mancuso sacrificed both runners up, Ruffing to Lazzeri.
  Whitehead made it to first on Crosetti's fumble, Ott scoring and Ripple going to third.
2 Jackson struck out.
3 Schumacher struck out.
Yankees
1 Gehrig grounded to second.
2 Dickey struck out.
  Selkirk singled to right.
  Powell grounded to Jackson who threw over Terry's head scoring Selkirk with Powell reaching third.
  Lazzeri singled past second, scoring Powell.
3 Johnson, pinch hitting for Ruffing, struck out.

7th Inning
Giants
  For the Yankees—Malone pitching.
1 Moore flied to right.
2 Bartell flied to center.
3 Terry grounded back to the pitcher.
Yankees
1 Crosetti struck out.
2 Rolfe struck out.
  DiMaggio doubled to left-center.
  Gehrig walked.
3 Dickey fouled to Mancuso.

8th Inning
Giants
1 Ott flied to center.
  Ripple walked.
2,3 Mancuso hit into a double play, Crosetti to Lazzeri to Gehrig.
Yankees
1 Selkirk popped to Mancuso.
2 Powell struck out.
3 Lazzeri grounded to short.

9th Inning
Giants
1 Whitehead flied to right.
2 Jackson out back to the pitcher.
3 Schumacher struck out.
Yankees
  Malone singled to left.
1 Crosetti bunting forced Malone at second, Terry to Bartell.
2 Rolfe forced Crosetti, Whitehead to Bartell
  DiMaggio walked.
3 Gehrig grounded to second.

10th Inning
Giants
  Moore doubled to left.
1 Bartell sacrificed Moore to third, Rolfe to Lazzeri covering first.
2 Terry flied to center, Moore scoring after the catch.
3 Ott popped to third.
Yankees
  Dickey singled through first.
  Seeds ran for Dickey.
1 Selkirk fouled to Mancuso.
2 Powell flied to left.
3   Seeds was caught stealing Mancuso to Whitehead.

Game 6 October 6 at Polo Grounds

| NY Y | | | | | | 0 2 1 | 2 0 0 | 0 1 7 |
| NY G | | | | | | 2 0 0 | 0 1 0 | 1 1 0 |

NY Yankees	Pos	AB	R	H	RBI	PO	A	E
Crosetti	ss	4	0	0	1	0	1	0
Rolfe	3b	6	1	3	2	3	2	1
DiMaggio	cf	6	1	3	1	2	0	1
Gehrig	1b	5	1	1	1	10	0	0
Dickey	c	5	2	0	0	3	0	0
Selkirk	rf	5	2	2	0	3	0	0
Powell	lf	5	3	3	4	3	0	0
Lazzeri	2b	4	2	3	1	3	5	0
Gomez	p	3	0	1	1	0	3	0
Murphy	p	2	1	1	1	0	0	0
Totals		45	13	17	12	27	11	2

Pitching	IP	H	R	ER	BB	SO
Yankees						
Gomez (W)	6⅓	8	4	4	4	1
Murphy (SV)	2⅔	1	1	1	1	1
Giants						
Fitzsimmons (L)	3⅜	9	5	5	0	1
Castleman	4⅓	3	1	1	2	5
Coffman	*0	3	5	5	1	0
Gumbert	1	2	2	2	3	1

*Pitched to 5 batters in 9th.

NY Giants	Pos	AB	R	H	RBI	PO	A	E
Moore	lf	5	2	2	1	2	0	0
Bartell	ss	3	2	2	0	0	2	0
Terry	1b	4	0	1	1	6	0	0
Leiber	cf	2	0	0	0	6	0	0
Mayo	3b	1	0	0	0	0	0	0
Ott	rf	4	1	2	3	3	0	0
Mancuso	c	3	0	0	0	4	0	0
a Leslie		1	0	0	0	0	0	0
Danning	c	1	0	0	0	3	0	1
Whitehead	2b	2	0	0	0	1	2	0
b Ripple	cf	0	0	0	0	1	0	0
Jackson	3b	3	0	1	0	0	0	0
c Koenig	2b	1	0	0	0	1	0	0
Fitzsimmons	p	1	0	0	0	0	1	0
Castleman	p	2	0	1	0	0	0	0
d Davis		1	0	0	0	0	0	0
Coffman	p	0	0	0	0	0	0	0
Gumbert	p	0	0	0	0	0	0	0
Totals		35	5	9	5	27	5	1

a Fouled out for Mancuso in 7th.
b Walked for Whitehead in 7th.
c Struck out for Jackson in 7th.
d Flied out for Castleman in 8th.

Doubles—Bartell, Ott. Triple—Selkirk.
Home Runs—Moore, Ott, Powell.
Sacrifice Hits—Leiber, Terry.
Left on Bases—Yankees 11, Giants 10.
Umpires—Geisel, Magerkurth, Summers,
Pfirman. Attendance—38,427.
Time of Game—2:50.

1st Inning
Yankees
1 Crosetti popped to second.
2 Rolfe popped to first.
3 DiMaggio flied to center.
Giants
  Moore singled to left.
  Bartell walked.
1 Terry sacrificed Moore to third and
  Bartell to second, Rolfe to Gehrig.
  Leiber walked filling the bases.
  Ott doubled to right, scoring Moore
  and Bartell and advancing Leiber to
  third.
2 Mancuso fouled out to Rolfe.
3 Whitehead grounded to second.

2nd Inning
Yankees
1 Gehrig flied to center.
2 Dickey flied to left.
  Selkirk tripled to right-center.
  Powell homered into the upper left
  field stands.
  Lazzeri singled.
3 Gomez grounded out to the pitcher.
Giants
  Jackson singled through the box.
1 Fitzsimmons flied to right.
2 Moore flied to left.
  Bartell walked.
3 Terry flew out to center.

3rd Inning
Yankees
1 Crosetti fanned.
  Rolfe singled to left.
  DiMaggio singled to left, Rolfe
  advancing to third.
2 Gehrig flied to right, Rolfe scored
  after the catch.
3 Dickey flied to left.
Giants
1 Leiber fouled to Dickey.
2 Ott's hit was deflected by Gomez to
  Crosetti who threw him out.
  Mancuso safe at first on Rolfe's
  fumble.
3 Whitehead fouled to Selkirk.

4th Inning
Yankees
1 Selkirk flied to center.
  Powell singled between third and
  short.
  Lazzeri singled through short, Powell
  stopping at second.
  Gomez singled over Bartell's head,
  scoring Powell with Lazzeri going to
  second.
2 Crosetti flew out to center.
  Rolfe singled to right-center, scoring
  Lazzeri with Gomez going to third.
  For the Giants—Castleman pitching.
3 DiMaggio flied to right.
Giants
1 Jackson grounded to second.
  Castleman singled to right center.
2 Moore flied to right.
  Bartell beat out a bunt along the third base
  line, Castleman moving to second.
3 Terry grounded to second.

5th Inning
Yankees
1 Gehrig grounded to first.
2 Dickey grounded to second.
3 Selkirk flied to center.
Giants
1 Leiber struck out.
  Ott homered into the upper tier of
  the left field stands.
2 Mancuso flied to center.
3 Whitehead grounded back to the pitcher.

6th Inning
Yankees
1 Powell struck out.
2 Lazzeri struck out.
3 Gomez struck out.
Giants
1 Jackson popped to second.
2 Castelman grounded back to the pitcher.
3 Moore grounded to second.

7th Inning
Yankees
1 Crosetti grounded to short.
  Rolfe singled past second.
2 DiMaggio flied to center.
3 Gehrig grounded to second.
Giants
  Bartell doubled to left.
  Terry singled to center and on
  DiMaggio's bobble Bartell scored
  and Terry went to second.
1 Leiber sacrificed Terry to third,
  Rolfe to Lazzeri.
  Ott walked.
  For the Yankees—Murphy pitching.
2 Leslie, pinch hitting for Mancuso, fouled
  to Rolfe.
  Ripple, pinch hitting for Whitehead,
  walked to load the bases.
3 Koenig, pinch hitting for Jackson, fanned.

8th Inning
Yankees
  For the Giants—Koenig to second, Mayo
  to third (batting fifth), Ripple to
  center, Danning in as catcher (batting
  seventh).
  Dickey walked.
  Selkirk singled to right, Dickey
  stopping at second.
1 Powell fanned.
  Lazzeri singled to center, scoring Dickey
  and advancing Selkirk to second.
2 Murphy struck out.
  Crosetti walked filling the bases.
3 Rolfe flied to right.
Giants
1 Davis, pinch hitting for Castleman, flied
  to left.
  Moore homered into the upper deck of
  the right field stands.
2 Bartell popped to second.
3 Terry grounded to second.

9th Inning
Yankees
  For the Giants—Coffman pitching.
  DiMaggio singled over third.
  Gehrig singled to right, DiMaggio going
  to third.
  Dickey bounced to Terry and DiMaggio
  was trapped between third and home but
  scored when Danning dropped Mayo's
  throw to the plate, Gehrig got to
  third and Dickey to second.
  Selkirk intentionally walked loading
  the bases.
  Powell singled through the hole to score
  Gehrig and Dickey as Selkirk moved
  to third.
  For the Giants—Gumbert pitching.
  Lazzeri walked again loading the bases.
  Murphy singled to right, scoring Selkirk.
  Crosetti walked forcing in Powell **(For
  Powell his 8th run of the Series tying
  the 6 game record set by Babe Ruth in
  the 1923 Series).**
1 Rolfe forced Crosetti at second, Bartell
  to Koenig, scoring Lazzeri with Murphy
  going to third.
  DiMaggio got his second single of the
  inning, scoring Murphy and moving Lazzeri
  to second.
  Gehrig walked to again load the bases.
2 Dickey struck out.
3 Selkirk flied to center.
Giants
1 Mayo fouled to Rolfe.
2 Ott flied to left.
3 Danning bounced to Gehrig, unassisted.

1936 WORLD SERIES COMPOSITE BOX

	Wins	Composite Line Score										
NEW YORK YANKEES (A.L.)	4	2	5	13	2	0	3	2	3	13	0	– 43
NEW YORK GIANTS (N.L.)	2	5	1	0	4	3	2	1	6	0	1	– 23

Manager	Regular Season W	L	Pct.	G. Ahead
Joe McCarthy	102	51	.667	19.5
Bill Terry	92	62	.597	5

BATTING AND FIELDING

NEW YORK YANKEES

WORLD SERIES STATISTICS	Pos	G	AB	R	H	2B	3B	HR	RBI	BB	SO	SB	BA	SA	PO	A	E
Lou Gehrig	1b	6	24	5	7	1	0	**2**	**7**	3	2	0	.292	.583	**45**	2	0
Tony Lazzeri	2b	6	20	4	5	0	0	1	7	**4**	4	0	.250	.400	13	17	0
Frankie Crosetti	ss	6	26	5	7	2	0	0	3	3	**5**	0	.269	.346	11	14	2
Red Rolfe	3b	6	25	5	**10**	0	0	0	4	3	1	0	.400	.400	14	7	1
George Selkirk	rf	6	24	6	8	0	**1**	**2**	3	**4**	4	0	.333	**.667**	9	0	1
Joe DiMaggio	cf	6	26	3	9	**3**	0	0	3	1	3	0	.346	.462	18	0	1
Jake Powell	lf	6	22	**8**	**10**	1	0	1	5	**4**	4	**1**	**.455**	.636	12	0	0
Bill Dickey	c	6	25	5	3	0	0	1	5	3	4	0	.120	.240	38	4	1
Roy Johnson	pr-ph	2	1	0	0	0	0	0	0	0	1	0	.000	.000			
Bob Seeds	pr	1	0	0	0	0	0	0	0	0	0	0	—	—			
Joe Glenn		Did not play															
Jack Saltzgaver		Did not play															
Art Jorgens		Did not play															
Don Heffner		Did not play															
Lefty Gomez	p	2	8	1	2	0	0	0	3	0	3	0	.250	.250	0	3	0
Red Ruffing	p-ph	3	5	0	0	0	0	0	0	1	2	0	.000	.000	1	3	0
Monte Pearson	p	1	4	0	2	1	0	0	0	0	0	0	.500	.750	1	2	0
Johnny Murphy	p	1	2	1	1	0	0	0	1	0	1	0	.500	.500	0	0	0
Bump Hadley	p	1	2	0	0	0	0	0	0	0	1	0	.000	.000	0	3	0
Pat Malone	p	2	1	0	1	0	0	0	0	0	0	0	1.000	1.000	0	2	0
Johnny Broaca		Did not play															
Jumbo Brown		Did not play															
Kemp Wicker		Did not play															
team total		6	215	43	65	8	1	7	41	26	35	1	.302	.447	162	57	6

Double Plays—2
Left on Bases—43

REGULAR SEASON STATISTICS		Main Pos	G	AB	R	H	2B	3B	HR	RBI	BB	SO	SB	BA	SA
Lou Gehrig		1b	155	579	**167**	205	37	7	**49**	152	**130**	46	3	.354	**.696**
Tony Lazzeri		2b	150	537	82	154	29	6	14	109	97	65	8	.287	.441
Frankie Crosetti		ss	151	632	137	182	35	7	15	78	90	83	18	.288	.437
Red Rolfe		3b	135	568	116	181	39	**15**	10	70	68	38	3	.319	.493
George Selkirk		of	137	493	93	152	28	9	18	107	94	60	13	.308	.511
Joe DiMaggio		of	138	637	132	206	44	**15**	29	125	24	39	4	.323	.576
Jake Powell	a	of	87	324	62	99	13	3	7	48	33	30	16	.306	.429
Bill Dickey		c	112	423	99	153	26	8	22	107	46	16	0	.362	.617
Roy Johnson		of	63	147	21	39	8	2	1	19	21	14	3	.265	.367
Bob Seeds		of	13	42	12	11	1	0	4	10	5	3	3	.262	.571
Joe Glenn		c	44	129	21	35	7	0	1	20	20	10	1	.271	.349
Jack Saltzgaver		3b	34	90	14	19	5	0	1	13	13	18	0	.211	.300
Art Jorgens		c	31	66	5	18	3	1	0	5	2	3	0	.273	.348
Don Heffner		inf	19	48	7	11	2	1	0	6	6	5	0	.229	.313
Lefty Gomez		p	31	69	1	10	1	0	0	5	3	23	0	.145	.159
Red Ruffing		p	53	127	14	37	5	0	5	22	11	12	0	.291	.449
Monte Pearson		p	33	91	12	23	4	0	1	20	8	13	0	.253	.330
Johnny Murphy		p	27	36	4	13	1	0	0	7	1	4	0	.361	.389
Bump Hadley		p	31	68	14	16	2	0	0	1	3	12	0	.235	.265
Pat Malone		p	35	51	4	10	1	0	0	7	1	10	0	.196	.216
Johnny Broaca		p	37	82	2	9	0	0	0	5	1	40	0	.110	.110
Jumbo Brown		p	20	19	0	0	0	0	0	0	0	7	0	.000	.000
Kemp Wicker		p	7	7	0	1	1	0	0	0	0	1	0	.143	.286
team total			155	5591	**1065**	1676	315	83	**182**	**995**	**700**	594	76	.300	**.483**

a—from Washington.
Myril Hoag (of), Ben Chapman (of), Dixie Walker (of), Ted Kleinhans, and Steve Sundra (p) also played for the Yankees during the season.

NEW YORK GIANTS

WORLD SERIES STATISTICS	Pos	G	AB	R	H	2B	3B	HR	RBI	BB	SO	SB	BA	SA	PO	A	E
Bill Terry	1b	6	25	1	6	0	0	0	5	1	4	0	.240	.240	**45**	8	0
Burgess Whitehead	2b	6	21	1	1	0	0	0	2	1	3	0	.048	.048	14	**20**	0
Dick Bartell	ss	6	21	5	8	**3**	0	1	3	**4**	4	0	.381	**.667**	8	13	1
Travis Jackson	3b	6	21	1	4	0	0	0	1	1	3	0	.190	.190	2	8	**3**
Mel Ott	rf	6	23	4	7	2	0	1	3	3	1	0	.304	.522	12	0	1
Jimmy Ripple	cf-ph	5	12	2	4	0	0	1	3	3	3	0	.333	.583	8	0	0
Jo-Jo Moore	lf	6	**28**	4	6	2	0	1	1	1	4	0	.214	.393	9	0	0
Gus Mancuso	c	6	19	3	5	2	0	0	1	3	3	0	.263	.368	40	5	0
Hank Leiber	cf	2	6	0	0	0	0	0	0	2	2	0	.000	.000	13	1	0
Sam Leslie	ph	3	3	0	2	0	0	0	0	0	0	0	.667	.667			
Mark Koenig	ph-2b	3	3	0	1	0	0	0	0	0	1	0	.333	.333	1	0	0
Kiddo Davis	ph-pr	4	2	2	1	0	0	0	0	0	0	0	.500	.500			
Harry Danning	ph-c	2	2	0	0	0	0	0	0	0	1	0	.000	.000	3	0	1
Eddie Mayo	3b	1	1	0	0	0	0	0	0	0	0	0	.000	.000	0	0	0
Roy Spencer		Did not play															
Carl Hubbell	p	2	6	0	2	0	0	0	1	0	0	0	.333	.333	2	2	1
Freddie Fitzsimmons	p	2	4	0	2	0	0	0	0	0	1	0	.500	.500	1	2	0
Hal Schumacher	p	2	4	0	0	0	0	0	0	1	3	0	.000	.000	0	2	0
Slick Castleman	p	1	2	0	1	0	0	0	0	0	0	0	.500	.500	0	0	0
Dick Coffman	p	2	0	0	0	0	0	0	0	0	0	0	—	—	0	1	0
Frank Gabler	p	2	0	0	0	0	0	0	0	1	0	0	—	—	1	0	0
Harry Gumbert	p	2	0	0	0	0	0	0	0	0	0	0	—	—	0	0	0
Al Smith	p	1	0	0	0	0	0	0	0	0	0	0	—	—	0	0	0
team total		6	203	23	50	9	0	4	20	21	33	0	.246	.350	159	62	7

Double Plays—7
Left on Bases—46

REGULAR SEASON STATISTICS	Main Pos	G	AB	R	H	2B	3B	HR	RBI	BB	SO	SB	BA	SA
Bill Terry	1b	79	229	36	71	10	5	2	39	19	19	0	.310	.424
Burgess Whitehead	2b	154	632	99	176	31	3	4	47	29	32	14	.278	.358
Dick Bartell	ss	140	510	71	152	31	3	8	42	40	36	6	.298	.418
Travis Jackson	3b	126	465	41	107	8	1	7	53	18	56	0	.230	.297
Mel Ott	of	150	534	120	175	28	6	**33**	135	111	41	6	.328	**.588**
Jimmy Ripple	of	96	311	42	95	17	2	7	47	28	15	1	.305	.441
Jo-Jo Moore	of	152	649	110	205	29	9	7	63	37	27	2	.316	.421
Gus Mancuso	c	139	519	55	156	21	3	9	63	39	28	0	.301	.405
Hank Leiber	of	101	337	44	94	19	7	9	67	37	41	1	.279	.457
Sam Leslie	1b	117	417	49	123	19	5	6	54	23	16	0	.295	.408
Mark Koenig	inf	42	58	7	16	4	0	1	7	8	4	0	.276	.397
Kiddo Davis	of	47	67	6	16	1	0	0	5	6	5	0	.239	.254
Harry Danning	c	32	69	3	11	2	2	0	4	1	5	0	.159	.246
Eddie Mayo	3b	46	141	11	28	4	1	1	8	11	12	0	.199	.262
Roy Spencer	c	19	18	3	5	1	0	0	3	2	3	0	.278	.333
Carl Hubbell	p	42	110	9	25	1	0	0	8	3	14	0	.227	.236
Freddie Fitzsimmons	p	28	47	4	7	1	0	0	0	0	8	0	.149	.170
Hal Schumacher	p	46	74	9	16	3	0	1	10	3	18	0	.216	.297
Slick Castleman	p	30	39	2	5	0	0	1	5	2	12	0	.128	.205
Dick Coffman	p	42	20	1	4	0	0	0	0	1	7	0	.200	.200
Frank Gabler	p	43	48	3	10	3	1	0	9	3	15	0	.208	.313
Harry Gumbert	p	39	44	5	11	2	0	0	6	3	12	0	.250	.295
Al Smith	p	43	75	11	10	1	0	0	8	7	18	0	.137	.151
team total		154	5449	742	1529	237	48	97	687	431	452	31	.281	.395

Joe Martin (3b), Charlie English (2b), Johnny McCarthy (1b), Jim Sheehan (c), Babe Young (ph), and Firpo Marberry (p) also played for the Giants during the season.

PITCHING

NEW YORK YANKEES

WORLD SERIES STATISTICS	G	GS	CG	IP	H	R	ER	BB	SO	W	L	SV	ERA
Lefty Gomez	**2**	**2**	**1**	15⅓	14	8	**8**	**11**	9	**2**	0	0	4.70
Red Ruffing	**2**	**2**	0	14	**16**	**10**	7	5	**12**	0	1	0	4.50
Monte Pearson	1	1	**1**	9	7	2	2	2	7	1	0	0	2.00
Bump Hadley	1	1	0	8	10	1	1	1	2	1	0	0	**1.12**
Pat Malone	**2**	0	0	5	2	1	1	1	2	0	1	**1**	1.80
Johnny Murphy	1	0	0	2⅔	1	1	1	1	1	0	0	**1**	3.38
Johnny Broaca	Did not play												
Jumbo Brown	Did not play												
Kemp Wicker	Did not play												
team total	6	6	2	54	50	23	20	21	33	4	2	2	3.36

REGULAR SEASON STATISTICS	G	GS	CG	IP	H	ER	BB	SO	W	L	Pct	SV	ShO	ERA
Lefty Gomez	31	30	10	189	184	92	122	105	13	7	.650	0	0	4.38
Red Ruffing	33	33	25	271	274	116	90	102	20	12	.625	0	3	3.85
Monte Pearson	33	31	15	223	191	92	135	118	19	7	**.731**	1	1	3.71
Bump Hadley	31	17	8	174	194	84	89	74	14	4	.778	1	1	4.34
Pat Malone	35	9	5	135	144	57	60	72	12	4	.750	**9**	0	3.80
Johnny Murphy	27	5	2	88	96	33	36	34	9	3	.750	**5**	0	3.38
Johnny Broaca	37	27	12	206	235	97	66	84	12	7	.632	3	1	4.24
Jumbo Brown	20	3	0	64	93	42	29	19	1	4	.200	1	0	5.91
Kemp Wicker	7	0	0	20	31	17	11	5	1	2	.333	0	0	7.65
team total	155	155	77	**1401**	1474	**649**	633	**624**	**102**	51	**.667**	**21**	6	**4.17**

NEW YORK GIANTS

WORLD SERIES STATISTICS	G	GS	CG	IP	H	R	ER	BB	SO	W	L	SV	ERA
Carl Hubbell	**2**	**2**	**1**	**16**	15	5	4	2	10	1	1	0	2.25
Hal Schumacher	**2**	**2**	**1**	12	13	9	7	10	11	1	1	0	5.25
Freddie Fitzsimmons	**2**	**2**	**1**	11⅔	13	7	7	2	6	0	**2**	0	5.40
Frank Gablerman	**2**	0	0	5	7	4	4	4	0	0	0	0	7.20
Slick Castleman	1	0	0	4⅓	3	1	1	2	5	0	0	0	2.08
Harry Gumbert	**2**	0	0	2	7	8	**8**	4	2	0	0	0	36.00
Dick Coffman	**2**	0	0	1⅔	5	6	6	1	1	0	0	0	32.40
Al Smith	1	0	0	⅓	2	3	3	1	0	0	0	0	81.00
team total	6	6	3	53	65	43	40	26	35	2	4	0	6.79

REGULAR SEASON STATISTICS	G	GS	CG	IP	H	ER	BB	SO	W	L	Pct	SV	ShO	ERA
Carl Hubbell	42	34	25	304	265	78	57	123	**26**	6	**.813**	3	3	**2.31**
Hal Schumacher	35	30	9	215	234	83	69	75	11	13	.458	1	3	3.47
Freddie Fitzsimmons	28	17	7	141	147	52	39	35	10	7	.588	2	0	3.32
Frank Gablerman	43	14	5	162	170	56	34	46	9	8	.529	6	0	3.11
Slick Castleman	29	12	2	112	148	70	56	54	4	7	.364	1	1	5.63
Harry Gumbert	39	15	3	141	157	61	54	52	11	3	.786	0	0	3.89
Dick Coffman	42	2	0	102	119	44	23	26	7	5	.583	7	0	3.88
Al Smith	43	30	9	209	217	88	69	89	14	13	.519	2	**4**	3.79
team total	154	154	60	1386	1458	532	401	500	**92**	62	**.597**	22	12	**3.46**

Total Attendance—302,924 Average Attendance—50,487 Winning Player's Share—$6,431 Losing Player's Share—$4,656

1937
No Contest

New York had another Subway Series to itself, but there was really no doubt as to the better team. Giant fans beamed at their team's National League pennant, but even they had to admit that the Yankee hitters packed a lot more thunder than Bill Terry's men. Jimmy Ripple, Jo-Jo Moore, and Dick Bartell all were steady .300 hitters, but only Mel Ott swung a home-run bat. In contrast, the Yankees had power up and down the lineup. Lou Gehrig, with his consecutive game streak now over 12 years old, drove in 159 runs with a .351 batting average and 37 homers. Ahead of clean-up man Gehrig was Joe DiMaggio, who blossomed into full stardom in his second season. Statistics like a .346 average, 46 homers, and 167 RBI's told only part of the story, ignoring Joltin' Joe's superb fielding and base running. Bill Dickey and George Selkirk posed major threats in lower batting slots, and a variety of other tough hitters occupied the rest of the lineup and the bench. The pitching appeared even, with Lefty Gomez and Red Ruffing of the Yankees matching up against Carl Hubbell and Cliff Melton of the Giants. Both clubs repeated as pennant winners, but Joe McCarthy's Yanks looked like the best bet to win this Series and keep right on winning into the future.

On cue, the Yankees began winning immediately. The Giants had their meal ticket, Carl Hubbell, on the mound against Lefty Gomez in the opening contest in Yankee Stadium. A fifth-inning run gave Hubbell a 1–0 lead, and the master screwballer seemed up to the task until the bottom of the sixth. Suddenly the Yankees were paying no respect to the best pitcher in baseball; they shelled him from the box and continued to pound the Giant relief corps until seven runs crossed the plate. One oddity of the inning was that Lefty Gomez, an atrocious hitter, drew two walks. With an 8–1 first-game win against Hubbell, the Yanks looked like a sure bet, and they looked even surer after the second game. Young Cliff Melton had won 20 games in his rookie season, but he wasn't about to win another against the Yankees. Melton left in the midst of a two-run fifth inning, and relievers Harry Gumbert and Dick Coffman got the same treatment in sixth- and seventh-inning rallies good for six more tallies. With such offensive backing, Red Ruffing had no trouble taking an 8–1 decision, while contributing to the cause with two hits good for three RBI's.

For the third game, Terry stuck with practically the same lineup, seeing no benefit in radically altering the arrangement which had gotten the team into the Series. But with Hal Schumacher on the mound against Monte Pearson, the Giants went down to a third straight defeat by a 5–1 count. The Yanks had no spectacular innings this time; they simply chipped away at Schumacher until the score read 5–0 after five frames. With the Giant batters in a heavy slumber for the entire Series to date, that score was a death sentence. The Giants pushed across a run in the seventh, but Pearson allowed only five hits in going for the win with last-out help from Johnny Murphy. The Yanks seemed assured of another of their patented sweeps, but they couldn't beat Carl Hubbell in game four. Looking to save a little pride for his team, Hubbell pitched a six-hitter while his mates suddenly awoke at the plate and smashed Bump Hadley for six runs in the second inning. The 7–3 Giant victory held off the end for a day. Gomez faced Melton in the fifth game, and the young Giant southpaw departed after five innings, losing 4–2. Relievers Al Smith and Don Brennan shut the Yanks out the rest of the way, but then Gomez did the same to the Giants and ended the Series with the 4–2 complete-game victory. With the Series over, the Yankees loomed even larger than they had earlier. After knocking out Hubbell in the first game, it was easy for them. The trio of Gomez, Ruffing, and Pearson had kept the Giant batters in check, while the Yankee bats exuded power in concentrated doses. In this victory of team strength, the top batting average of the Series belonged to Tony Lazzeri, whose .400 mark ended 12 fine years with the Yanks.

Game 1 October 6 at Yankee Stadium

NY Giants	Pos	AB	R	H	RBI	PO	A	E
Moore	lf	4	0	2	0	4	0	0
Bartell	ss	4	0	1	0	1	2	1
Ott	3b	4	0	0	0	1	2	0
Leiber	cf	4	0	0	0	3	0	0
Ripple	rf	3	1	1	0	2	0	0
McCarthy	1b	4	0	1	0	8	0	0
Mancuso	c	3	0	0	1	4	1	0
Whitehead	2b	3	0	1	0	1	4	1
Hubbell	p	2	0	0	0	0	1	0
Gumbert	p	0	0	0	0	0	0	0
Coffman	p	0	0	0	0	0	0	0
a Berger		1	0	0	0	0	0	0
Smith	p	0	0	0	0	0	0	0
Totals		32	1	6	1	24	10	2

a Flied out for Whitehead in 8th.

Double—Whitehead. Home Run—Lazzeri. Double Plays—Crosetti to Lazzeri to Gehrig, Ott to Whitehead to McCarthy. Left on Bases—Giants 5, Yankees 6. Umpires—Ormsby (A), Barr (N), Basil (A), Stewart (N). Attendance—60,573. Time of Game—2:20.

	NY G	000 010 000
	NY Y	000 007 01x

NY Yankees	Pos	AB	R	H	RBI	PO	A	E
Crosetti	ss	4	1	1	0	0	2	0
Rolfe	3b	4	1	1	0	0	0	0
DiMaggio	cf	4	0	2	2	4	0	0
Gehrig	1b	3	2	1	0	9	0	0
Dickey	c	3	1	1	0	3	0	0
Hoag	lf	4	1	0	0	5	0	0
Selkirk	rf	4	1	1	2	3	0	0
Lazzeri	2b	4	1	1	1	3	2	0
Gomez	p	2	0	0	0	0	2	0
Totals		31	8	7	7	27	6	0

Pitching	IP	H	R	ER	BB	SO
NY G						
Hubbell (L)	5⅓	6	7	4	3	3
Gumbert	*0	0	0	0	0	0
Coffman	1⅓	0	0	0	4	0
Smith	1	1	1	1	0	0
NY Y						
Gomez (W)	9	6	1	1	1	2

*Pitched to one batter in 6th.

1st Inning
Giants
1 Moore grounded to first. Bartell singled beyond third.
2 Ott popped to first.
3 Leiber fanned.
Yankees
Crosetti walked.
1 Rolfe fanned. DiMaggio singled past third, advancing Crosetti to second.
2 Gehrig flied to center, runners hold.
3 Dickey flied to center.

2nd Inning
Giants
1 Ripple flied to left.
2 McCarthy lined to second.
3 Mancuso lined to right.
Yankees
1 Hoag grounded to short.
2 Selkirk grounded to second.
3 Lazzeri bounced to the pitcher.

3rd Inning
Giants
1 Whitehead grounded to short.
2 Hubbell lined to second.
3 Moore grounded back to the box.
Yankees
1 Gomez grounded to second.
2 Crosetti flied to left.
3 Rolfe flied to left.

4th Inning
Giants
1 Bartell flied to left.
2 Ott grounded to second.
3 Leiber popped to second.
Yankees
1 DiMaggio grounded to second.
2 Gehrig struck out.
3 Dickey grounded to first.

5th Inning
Giants
Ripple singled to right. McCarthy singled past second, Ripple going to third.
1,2 Crosetti hit into a double play, Crosetti to Lazzeri to Gehrig scoring Ripple. Whitehead doubled down the right field line.
3 Hubbell grounded to first.
Yankees
1 Hoag popped to short.
2 Selkirk flied to right.
3 Lazzeri struck out.

6th Inning
Giants
Moore singled through the box.
1 Bartell flied to right.
2 Ott fouled to the catcher.
3 Leiber flied to left.

6th Inning (continued)
Yankees
Gomez walked. Crosetti singled to left sending Gomez to second. Gomez trapped off second on throw from Mancuso to Bartell but Bartell dropped the ball for an error with Gomez safely returning to second. Rolfe singled to left loading the bases. DiMaggio singled to left-center, scoring Gomez and Crosetti (Rolfe advanced to third and DiMaggio to second on the throw to the plate). Gehrig intentionally walked. Dickey beat out a single to second, scoring Rolfe (bases still loaded).
1 Hoag forced DiMaggio at the plate, Ott to Mancuso. Selkirk singled, scoring Gehrig and Dickey and sending Hoag to third. For the Giants—Gumbert pitching (A mixup as Coffman came in from the bullpen but Captain Mancuso gave Gumbert's name to plate umpire Ormsby.) Lazzeri got on when Whitehead fumbled his grounder with Hoag scoring and Selkirk going to third. For the Giants—Coffman pitching. Gomez walked filling the bases.
2 Crosetti flied to short left. Rolfe walked forcing in Selkirk.
3 DiMaggio flied to center.

7th Inning
Giants
1 Ripple flied to left.
2 McCarthy grounded out to the pitcher.
3 Mancuso flied to center.
Yankees
Gehrig walked. Dickey walked.
1,2 Hoag hit into a double play, Ott to Whitehead to McCarthy, Gehrig to third.
3 Selkirk grounded to short.

8th Inning
Giants
1 Whitehead flied to center.
2 Berger pinch hit for Coffman and flied to center. Moore singled to center.
3 Bartell lined to left.
Yankees
For the Giants—Smith pitching. Lazzeri homered into the lower left field stands.
1 Gomez lined to left.
2 Crosetti lined to third.
3 Rolfe flied to left.

9th Inning
Giants
1 Ott struck out.
2 Leiber lined to center. Ripple walked.
3 McCarthy grounded to first.

1937

Game 2 October 7 at Yankee Stadium

| | | | NY G | 1 0 0 | 0 0 0 | 0 0 0 |
| | | | NY Y | 0 0 0 | 0 2 4 | 2 0 x |

NY Giants	Pos	AB	R	H	RBI	PO	A	E
Moore	lf	5	0	2	0	2	0	0
Bartell	ss	4	1	2	0	3	5	0
Ott	3b	4	0	1	1	2	1	0
Ripple	rf	4	0	0	0	1	0	0
McCarthy	1b	4	0	0	0	8	1	0
Chiozza	cf	4	0	1	0	3	0	0
Mancuso	c	4	0	0	0	4	0	0
Whitehead	2b	3	0	1	0	2	3	0
Melton	p	1	0	0	0	0	0	0
Gumbert	p	0	0	0	0	0	0	0
Coffman	p	1	0	0	0	0	1	0
a Leslie		0	0	0	0	0	0	0
Totals		34	1	7	1	24	11	0

a Walked for Coffman in 9th.

Doubles—Bartell, Crosetti, Moore, Ripple, Selkirk. Double Play—Bartell to Whitehead to McCarthy. Left on Bases—Giants 9, Yankees 6. Umpires—Barr, Basil, Stewart, Ormsby. Attendance—57,675. Time of Game—2:11.

NY Yankees	Pos	AB	R	H	RBI	PO	A	E
Crosetti	ss	5	0	0	0	1	4	0
Rolfe	3b	5	0	0	0	0	3	0
DiMaggio	cf	4	1	2	0	4	0	0
Gehrig	1b	2	1	1	0	11	0	0
Dickey	c	4	1	2	1	8	0	0
Hoag	lf	4	2	1	1	1	0	0
Selkirk	rf	4	2	2	3	1	0	0
Lazzeri	2b	3	1	2	0	1	2	0
Ruffing	p	4	0	2	3	0	2	0
Totals		35	8	12	8	27	11	0

Pitching	IP	H	R	ER	BB	SO
NY G						
Melton (L)	*4	6	2	2	1	2
Gumbert	1⅓	4	4	4	1	1
Coffmann	2⅔	2	2	2	1	1
NY Y						
Ruffing (W)	9	7	1	1	3	8

*Faced 4 men in 5th.

1st Inning
Giants
1 Moore struck out.
  Bartell doubled to left.
  Ott singled to right, scoring Bartell
  (Ott took second on the throw to plate).
2 Ripple fanned.
3 McCarthy fanned.
Yankees
1 Crosetti fanned.
2 Rolfe grounded to short.
3 DiMaggio popped to short.

2nd Inning
Giants
1 Chiozza grounded to third.
2 Mancuso grounded to short.
3 Whitehead flied to right.
Yankees
1 Gehrig grounded to short.
2 Dickey flied to center.
3 Hoag grounded to short.

3rd Inning
Giants
1 Melton grounded to third.
2 Moore grounded to short.
  Bartell singled past third.
3 Ott flied to left.
Yankees
1 Selkirk popped to third.
  Lazzeri singled.
2,3 Ruffing hit into a double play
  Bartell to Whitehead to McCarthy.

4th Inning
Giants
1 Ripple popped to short.
2 McCarthy grounded to the pitcher.
3 Ciozza grounded to second.
Yankees
1 Crosetti popped to Bartell in short
  left.
2 Rolfe grounded to first.
  DiMaggio singled to center.
  Gehrig walked.
3 Dickey took a called third strike.

5th Inning
Giants
1 Mancuso grounded to short.
2 Whitehead grounded to second.
  Melton walked.
  Moore singled to right, Melton to second.
3 Whitehead struck out.
Yankees
  Hoag doubled to right.
  Selkirk singled to right, scoring Hoag.
  Lazzeri singled to left, Selkirk to
  second.
  Ruffing singled past third, scoring
  Selkirk and moving Lazzeri to second.
  For the Giants—Gumbert pitching.
1 Crosetti flied to left.
2 Rolfe forced Ruffing, Whitehead to
  Bartell with Lazzeri moving to third.
3 DiMaggio struck out.

6th Inning
Giants
1 Ott flied to center.
2 Ripple flied to center.
3 McCarthy flied to center.
Yankees
  Gehrig singled on a roller to third.
  Dickey singled to center, Gehrig stops
  at second.
1 Hoag forced Gehrig at third on an
  attempted sacrifice, McCarthy to Ott.
  Selkirk doubled off McCarthy's leg,
  scoring Dickey and Hoag.
  Lazzeri intentionally walked.
  Ruffing doubled to left, scoring Selkirk
  and Lazzeri.
  For the Giants—Coffman pitching.
2 Crosetti flied to center moving Ruffing
  to third after the catch.
3 Rolfe grounded to second.

7th Inning
Giants
1 Chiozza struck out.
2 Mancuso grounded to the pitcher.
  Whitehead walked.
3 Coffman called out on strikes.
Yankees
  DiMaggio singled to left.
  Gehrig walked.
  Dickey singled over second, scoring
  DiMaggio and sending Gehrig to third.
1 Hoag flied to center, scoring Gehrig.
2 Selkirk forced Dickey, Bartell to
  Whitehead.
3 Lazzeri grounded to third.

8th Inning
Giants
  Moore doubled to left.
1 Bartell fanned, foul tipping his third
  strike to Dickey.
2 Ott flied to center.
3 Ripple grounded to short.
Yankees
1 Ruffing flied to left.
2 Crosetti called out on strikes.
3 Rolfe grounded to the pitcher.

9th Inning
Giants
1 McCarthy flied to left.
  Chiozza singled to left.
2 Mancuso called out on strikes.
  Whitehead singled to center moving
  Chiozza to second.
  Leslie pinch hit for Coffman and walked
  loading the bases.
3 Moore grounded to third.

Game 3 October 8 at Polo Grounds

| | | | NY Y | 0 1 2 | 1 1 0 | 0 0 0 |
| | | | NY G | 0 0 0 | 0 0 0 | 1 0 0 |

NY Yankees	Pos	AB	R	H	RBI	PO	A	E
Crosetti	ss	4	0	0	0	1	7	0
Rolfe	3b	4	1	2	0	1	1	0
DiMaggio	cf	5	0	1	0	5	0	0
Gehrig	1b	5	1	1	1	12	0	0
Dickey	c	5	1	1	1	5	0	0
Selkirk	rf	4	2	1	1	0	0	0
Hoag	lf	4	0	2	0	0	0	0
Lazzeri	2b	2	0	1	1	3	3	0
Pearson	p	3	0	0	0	0	0	0
Murphy	p	0	0	0	0	0	0	0
Totals		36	5	9	4	27	11	0

Pitching	IP	H	R	ER	BB	SO
NY Y						
Pearson (W)	8⅔	5	1	1	2	4
Murphy (SV)	⅓	0	0	0	0	0
NY G						
Schumacher (L)	6	9	5	4	4	3
Melton	2	0	0	0	2	0
Brennan	1	0	0	0	0	0

1st Inning
Yankees
  Crosetti walked.
1 Rolfe lined to right.
  Crosetti to third on wild pitch.
2 DiMaggio struck out.
3 Gehrig grounded to second.
Giants
1 Moore grounded to short.
2 Bartell flied to center.
3 Ott flied to center.

2nd Inning
Yankees
1 Dickey lined to center.
  Selkirk walked.
  Hoag singled to left, Selkirk to second.
  Lazzeri singled to center, scoring
  Selkirk and sending Hoag to third.
  Pearson walked loading the bases.
2 Crosetti forced Hoag at the plate, Ott
  to Danning.
3 Rolfe fouled to the catcher.
Giants
1 Ripple grounded to first.
2 McCarthy flew out to center.
3 Chiozza fouled to third.

3rd Inning
Yankees
1 DiMaggio flied to center.
  Gehrig singled off right field fence
  and took second on Ripple's throw to
  first.
  Dickey tripled off the left field fence,
  scoring Gehrig.
  Selkirk singled to right, scoring Dickey.
2 Hoag got a sacrifice hit, Ott to
  McCarthy.
  Lazzeri intentionally passed.
3 Pearson called out on strikes.
Giants
1 Danning popped to second.
2 Whitehead fouled to first.
3 Schumacher looked at a third strike.

4th Inning
Yankees
1 Crosetti grounded to third.
  Rolfe doubled to right.
  DiMaggio got an infield single, Rolfe
  going to third.
2 Gehrig flied to left scoring Rolfe.
3 Dickey forced DiMaggio, Whitehead to
  Bartell.
Giants
1 Moore grounded to short.
2 Bartell grounded to short.
3 Ott struck out.

5th Inning
Yankees
  McCarthy fumbled Selkirk's grounder
  then threw wild to Schumacher covering
  first, Selkirk on second (2 errors
  charged to McCarthy).
  Hoag singled to center where Chiozza
  fumbled allowing Selkirk to score.
1 Lazzeri fanned.
2 Pearson grounded to the pitcher.
3 Crosetti flew out to left.

NY Giants	Pos	AB	R	H	RBI	PO	A	E
Moore	lf	4	0	1	0	2	0	0
Bartell	ss	4	0	3	0	3	2	0
Ott	3b	4	0	1	0	1	3	0
Ripple	rf	4	1	1	0	5	0	2
McCarthy	1b	3	0	1	1	7	0	2
Chiozza	cf	3	0	1	0	3	0	1
Danning	c	4	0	0	0	5	0	0
Whitehead	2b	3	0	0	0	1	4	0
Schumacher	p	1	0	0	0	0	1	0
a Berger		1	0	0	0	0	0	0
Melton	p	0	0	0	0	0	1	0
b Leslie		1	0	0	0	0	0	0
Brennan	p	0	0	0	0	0	0	0
Totals		32	1	5	1	27	10	4

a Struck out for Schumacher in 6th.
b Fouled out for Melton in 8th.

Doubles—McCarthy, Rolfe 2. Triple—Dickey. Sacrifice Hit—Hoag. Double Play—Whitehead to Bartell to McCarthy. Left on Bases—Yankees 11, Giants 6. Wild Pitch—Schumacher. Umpires—Basil, Stewart, Ormsby, Barr. Attendance—37,385. Time of Game—2:07.

5th Inning (continued)
Giants
1 Ripple grounded to short.
2 McCarthy grounded to second.
  Chiozza singled on a bunt down the
  first base line.
3 Danning forced Chiozza, Crosetti to
  Lazzeri.

6th Inning
Yankees
  Rolfe blooped a double to short right.
1 DiMaggio grounded to short.
2 Gehrig popped to second.
3 Dickey grounded to second.
Giants
1 Whitehead grounded to second.
2 Berger, pinch-hitting for Schumacher,
  struck out.
  Moore singled to left.
3 Bartell called out on strikes.

7th Inning
Yankees
  For the Giants—Melton pitching.
1 Selkirk flied to center.
  Melton threw wildly to first on Hoag's
  hit to the box (Hoag reached second).
  Lazzeri intentionally walked.
2,3 Pearson hit into a double play,
  Whitehead to Bartell to McCarthy.
Giants
1 Ott popped to second.
  Ripple singled to right.
  McCarthy doubled off the right field
  fence, scoring Ripple.
2 Chiozza grounded to second, advancing
  McCarthy to third.
3 Danning grounded to short.

8th Inning
Yankees
1 Crosetti lined to center.
  Rolfe walked.
2 DiMaggio flied to right.
3 Gehrig flied to left.
Giants
1 Whitehead grounded to third.
2 Leslie, pinch-hitting for Melton, fouled
  out to Dickey.
3 Moore grounded to short.

9th Inning
Yankees
  For the Giants—Brennan pitching.
1 Dickey lined to right.
2 Selkirk fouled to third.
3 Hoag lined to short.
Giants
1 Bartell flied to center.
  Ott singled to left.
2 Ripple forced Ott, Crosetti unassisted.
  McCarthy walked.
  Chiozza walked loading the bases.
  For the Yankees—Murphy pitching.
3 Danning flied to center.

Game 4 October 9 at Polo Grounds

NY Yankees	Pos	AB	R	H	RBI	PO	A	E
Crosetti	ss	4	1	0	0	2	3	0
Rolfe	3b	4	1	2	0	0	2	0
DiMaggio	cf	4	0	0	1	2	0	0
Gehrig	1b	4	1	1	1	10	0	0
Dickey	c	4	0	0	0	3	1	0
Hoag	lf	4	0	2	0	3	0	0
Selkirk	rf	3	0	0	0	0	0	0
Lazzeri	2b	3	0	1	0	4	4	0
Hadley	p	0	0	0	0	0	0	0
Andrews	p	2	0	0	0	0	1	0
a Powell		1	0	0	0	0	0	0
Wicker	p	0	0	0	0	0	0	0
Totals		33	3	6	2	24	11	0

a Struck out for Andrews in 8th.

Double—Danning. Triple—Rolfe.
Home Run—Gehrig. Stolen Base—Whitehead.
Double Plays—Whitehead to Bartell,
Hubbell to Whitehead to McCarthy.
Left on Bases—Yankees 4, Giants 8.
Umpires—Stewart, Ormsby, Barr, Basil.
Attendance—44,293. Time of Game—1:57.

NY Y 101 000 001
NY G 060 000 10x

NY Giants	Pos	AB	R	H	RBI	PO	A	E
Moore	lf	5	1	1	1	1	0	0
Bartell	ss	4	1	1	1	3	2	1
Ott	3b	5	0	1	0	1	0	1
Ripple	rf	2	0	1	0	3	0	0
Leiber	cf	3	2	2	2	3	0	0
McCarthy	1b	4	1	2	0	9	0	0
Danning	c	4	0	3	2	4	0	0
Whitehead	2b	4	1	0	1	3	5	0
Hubbell	p	4	1	0	1	0	2	0
Totals		35	7	12	7	27	9	3

Pitching	IP	H	R	ER	BB	SO
NY Y						
Hadley (L)	1⅓	6	5	5	0	0
Andrews	5⅔	6	2	2	4	1
Wicker	1	0	0	0	0	0
NY G						
Hubbell (W)	9	6	3	2	1	4

1st Inning
Yankees
1 Crosetti popped to second.
Rolfe tripled past Leiber who tried and missed a shoestring catch.
2 DiMaggio flied deep to right, Rolfe scoring after the catch.
3 Gehrig fouled to first.
Giants
1 Moore flied to left.
2 Bartell popped to Dickey in front of plate.
Ott singled to right.
3 Ripple grounded to short.

2nd Inning
Yankees
1 Dickey flied to center.
Hoag singled through the box.
Selkirk walked.
2,3 Lazzeri lined into a double play, Whitehead to Bartell.
Giants
Leiber singled to center.
McCarthy singled to right, Leiber stopping at second.
Danning singled to right, scoring Leiber with McCarthy going to third.
1 Whitehead's grounder hit Danning for an automatic out (Whitehead credited with single).
Hubbell grounded to Lazzeri and was safe when Lazzeri threw to the plate to get McCarthy but throw was wide and McCarthy scored (Whitehead to second).
Moore singled to center, scoring Whitehead and moving Hubbell to second.
For the Yankees—Andrews pitching.
Bartell singled to center, scoring Hubbell and moving Moore to second.
2 Ott struck out.
Ripple walked loading the bases.
Leiber hit his second single of the inning, scoring Moore and Bartell with Ripple going to third.
3 McCarthy grounded to Lazzeri.

3rd Inning
Yankees
Andrews was safe on Bartell's throwing error to first.
1 Crosetti forced Andrews, Whitehead to Bartell but Bartell trying for the DP threw wildly to first Crosetti going to second.
2 Rolfe lined to left.
DiMaggio reached second and Crosetti scored when Ott threw wildly to first.
3 Gehrig grounded to first.
Giants
Danning beat out a hit down the third base line.
1 Whitehead forced Danning, Lazzeri to Crosetti.
Whitehead stole second.
2 Hubbell grounded to Andrews, Whitehead to third.
3 Moore popped to short.

4th Inning
Yankees
1 Dickey lined to right.
2 Hoag grounded to second.
3 Selkirk flied to center.
Giants
1 Bartell lined to center.
2 Ott grounded to first.
Ripple walked.
3 Leiber flew out to center.

5th Inning
Yankees
Lazzeri singled over second.
1 Andrews struck out.
2,3 Crosetti hit into a double play, Hubbell to Whitehead to McCarthy.
Giants
1 McCarthy grounded to second.
2 Danning grounded to third.
3 Whitehead grounded to short.

6th Inning
Yankees
Rolfe singled to right.
1 DiMaggio forced Rolfe, Whitehead to Bartell.
2 Gehrig fanned.
3 Dickey popped to first.
Giants
1 Hubbell grounded to short.
2 Moore grounded to third.
3 Bartell lined to left.

7th Inning
Yankees
1 Hoag fanned.
2 Selkirk grounded to first.
3 Lazzeri grounded to short.
Giants
1 Ott fouled to the catcher.
Ripple singled past short.
2 Ripple caught stealing, Dickey to Leiber walked.
McCarthy singled over second, Leiber moved to second.
Danning doubled to right, scoring Leiber and sending McCarthy to third.
Whitehead intentionally walked filling the bases.
3 Hubbell lined to left.

8th Inning
Yankees
1 Powell, pinch-hitting for Andrews, fanned.
2 Crosetti grounded to short.
3 Rolfe grounded to the pitcher.
Giants
For the Yankees—Wicker pitching.
1 Moore grounded to short.
2 Bartell popped to second.
3 Ott popped to second.

9th Inning
Yankees
1 DiMaggio fouled to third.
Gehrig homered into the right field stands.
2 Dickey flied to right.
Hoag singled past second.
3 Selkirk flied to center.

Game 5 October 10 at Polo Grounds

NY Yankees	Pos	AB	R	H	RBI	PO	A	E
Crosetti	ss	4	0	0	0	2	1	0
Rolfe	3b	3	0	1	0	1	0	0
DiMaggio	cf	5	1	1	1	3	0	0
Gehrig	1b	4	0	2	1	8	1	0
Dickey	c	3	0	0	0	7	0	0
Hoag	lf	4	1	1	1	3	0	0
Selkirk	rf	4	0	0	0	3	0	0
Lazzeri	2b	3	1	1	1	0	5	0
Gomez	p	4	1	1	1	0	1	0
Totals		34	4	8	4	27	8	0

Pitching	IP	H	R	ER	BB	SO
NY G						
Gomez (W)	9	10	2	2	1	6
NY G						
Melton (L)	5	6	4	4	3	5
Smith	2	1	0	0	0	1
Brennan	2	1	0	0	1	1

NY Y 011 020 000
NY G 002 000 000

NY Giants	Pos	AB	R	H	RBI	PO	A	E
Moore	lf	5	0	3	0	4	0	0
Bartell	ss	4	1	1	0	1	3	0
Ott	3b	3	1	1	2	0	3	0
Ripple	rf	4	0	2	0	1	0	0
Leiber	cf	4	0	2	0	1	0	0
McCarthy	1b	4	0	0	0	6	0	0
Danning	c	4	0	1	0	11	1	0
Whitehead	2b	4	0	1	0	1	1	0
Melton	p	1	0	0	0	0	0	0
a Ryan		1	0	0	0	0	0	0
b Mancuso		1	0	0	0	0	0	1
Smith	p	0	0	0	0	0	1	0
Brennan	p	0	0	0	0	0	0	0
c Berger		1	0	0	0	0	0	0
Totals		36	2	10	2	27	6	0

a Struck out for Melton in 5th.
b Flied out for Smith in 7th.
c Grounded out for Brennan in 9th.

Doubles—Gehrig, Whitehead.
Triples—Gehrig, Lazzeri.
Home Runs—DiMaggio, Hoag, Ott.
Sacrifice Hit—Rolfe. Double Play—Gehrig (unassisted). Left on Bases—Yankees 9, Giants 8. Wild Pitch—Melton.
Hit by Pitcher—Lazzeri (by Smith).
Umpires—Ormsby, Barr, Basil, Stewart.
Attendance—38,216. Time of Game—2:06.

1st Inning
Yankees
1 Crosetti flied deep to Moore.
Rolfe singled to left.
2 DiMaggio popped to Whitehead in short center field.
Rolfe took second on a wild pitch.
3 Dickey struck out.
Giants
Moore singled to left.
1 Bartell flied to left.
2 Ott struck out.
Ripple singled to right-center, moving Moore to third.
3 Leiber fouled to first.

2nd Inning
Yankees
Hoag homered into the right field bleachers.
1 Selkirk grounded to second.
2 Lazzeri called out on strikes.
3 Gomez also took a called third strike.
Giants
1 McCarthy grounded to second.
2 Danning struck out.
Whitehead doubled into right.
3 Melton struck out.

3rd Inning
Yankees
1 Crosetti grounded to third.
2 Rolfe called out on strikes.
DiMaggio homered over the left field stand.
3 Gehrig struck out.
Giants
1 Moore popped to short.
Bartell singled to left.
Ott hit a two-run homer into the upper deck of the right field stands.
2 Ripple popped to short.
3 Leiber lined to center.

4th Inning
Yankees
1 Dickey fouled to the catcher.
2 Hoag flied to deep left.
3 Selkirk fouled to the catcher.
Giants
1 McCarthy fanned.
2 Danning fouled to the catcher.
3 Whitehead lined to right.

5th Inning
Yankees
Lazzeri tripled to center.
Gomez singled off Whitehead's glove, scoring Lazzeri.
1 Crosetti flied to short right.
Rolfe walked.
2 DiMaggio popped to the catcher.
Gehrig doubled to center, scoring Gomez, Rolfe advancing to third.
Dickey walked, loading the bases.
3 Hoag fouled to the catcher.

5th Inning (continued)
Giants
1 Ryan, batting for Melton, struck out.
Moore singled to center.
2 Bartell flied to center.
3 Ott grounded to second.

6th Inning
Yankees
For the Giants—Smith pitching.
1 Selkirk grounded to first.
Lazzeri was hit by a pitched ball.
2 Gomez attempting to sacrifice forced Lazzeri, Ott to Bartell.
3 Crosetti bounced back to the pitcher.
Giants
Ripple singled to left.
Leiber singled to right-center, Ripple going to second.
1 McCarthy attempting to sacrifice forced Ripple at third, Gomez to Rolfe.
2 Danning struck out.
3 Whitehead grounded out to second.

7th Inning
Yankees
1 Rolfe grounded to third.
2 DiMaggio struck out.
Gehrig tripled (Ripple fell going for his hit).
3 Dickey flied to center.
Giants
1 Mancuso, pinch-hitting for Smith, flied to right.
Moore singled to left (his 9th hit of a 5 game series tying the record held by 4 others).
2 Bartell popped to Crosetti who deliberately dropped the ball and threw to Lazzeri forcing Moore.
Ott walked.
3 Ripple grounded to second.

8th Inning
Yankees
For the Giants—Brennan pitching.
1 Hoag flew deep to Moore at the left center field wall.
Selkirk singled to right.
2 Lazzeri flied to Bartell in short left.
3 Gomez flied to left.
Giants
Leiber singled to left.
1 McCarthy flied to right.
2,3 Danning lined to Gehrig who stepped on first doubling up Leiber.

9th Inning
Yankees
Crosetti walked
1 Rolfe sacrificed, Danning to McCarthy.
2 DiMaggio popped to short.
3 Gehrig struck out.
Giants
1 Whitehead lined to center.
2 Berger batted for Brennan and grounded to second.
3 Moore grounded out, Gehrig to Gomez.

1937 WORLD SERIES COMPOSITE BOX

	Wins	Composite Line Score									
NEW YORK YANKEES (A.L.)	4	1	2	4	1	5	11	2	1	1	- 28
NEW YORK GIANTS (N.L.)	1	1	6	2	0	1	0	2	0	0	- 12

	Regular Season			
Manager	W	L	Pct.	G. Ahead
Joe McCarthy	102	52	.662	13
Bill Terry	95	67	.625	- 3

BATTING AND FIELDING

NEW YORK YANKEES

	WORLD SERIES STATISTICS																		REGULAR SEASON STATISTICS													
	Pos	G	AB	R	H	2B	3B	HR	RBI	BB	SO	SB	BA	SA	PO	A	E		Main Pos	G	AB	R	H	2B	3B	HR	RBI	BB	SO	SB	BA	SA
Lou Gehrig	1b	5	17	4	5	1	**1**	**1**	3	**5**	**4**	0	.294	.647	**50**	1	0		1b	157	569	138	200	37	9	37	159	**127**	49	4	.351	.643
Tony Lazzeri	2b	5	15	3	6	0	**1**	**1**	2	3	3	0	**.400**	**.733**	11	16	0		2b	106	362	48	109	21	3	14	70	71	76	7	.244	.399
Frankie Crosetti	ss	5	21	2	1	0	0	0	0	3	2	0	.048	.048	6	**17**	0		ss	149	611	127	143	29	5	11	49	86	**105**	13	.234	.352
Red Rolfe	3b	5	20	3	6	**2**	**1**	0	1	3	2	0	.300	.500	2	6	0		3b	154	648	143	179	34	10	4	62	90	53	4	.276	.378
George Selkirk	rf	5	19	**5**	5	1	0	0	**6**	2	0	0	.263	.316	7	0	0		of	78	256	49	84	13	5	18	68	34	24	8	.328	.629
Joe DiMaggio	cf	5	22	2	6	0	0	**1**	4	0	3	0	.273	.409	18	0	0		of	151	621	**151**	215	35	15	**46**	167	64	37	3	.346	**.673**
Myril Hoag	lf	5	20	4	6	1	0	**1**	2	0	1	0	.300	.500	11	0	0		of	126	446	56	109	19	8	3	46	33	33	4	.301	.423
Bill Dickey	c	5	19	3	4	0	**1**	0	3	2	2	0	.211	.316	26	1	0		c	140	530	87	176	35	2	29	133	73	22	3	.332	.570
Jake Powell	ph	1	1	0	0	0	0	0	0	0	1	0	.000	.000					of	97	365	54	96	22	3	3	45	25	36	7	.263	.364
Tommy Henrich	Did not play—injured																		of	67	206	39	66	14	5	8	42	35	17	4	.320	.553
Don Heffner	Did not play																		2b	60	201	23	50	6	5	0	21	19	19	1	.249	.328
Joe Glenn	Did not play																		c	25	53	6	15	2	2	0	4	10	11	0	.283	.396
Jack Saltzgaver	Did not play																		1b	17	11	6	2	0	0	0	0	3	4	0	.182	.182
Art Jorgens	Did not play																		c	13	23	3	3	1	0	0	3	2	5	0	.130	.174
Lefty Gomez	p	2	6	2	1	0	0	0	1	2	1	0	.167	.167	1	3	0		p	34	105	8	21	2	0	0	4	5	22	1	.200	.219
Red Ruffing	p	1	4	0	2	1	0	0	3	0	0	0	.500	.750	0	2	0		p	54	129	11	26	3	0	1	10	13	24	0	.202	.248
Monte Pearson	p	1	3	0	0	0	0	0	0	1	1	0	.000	.000	0	0	0		p	22	51	6	11	2	0	0	7	3	5	0	.216	.255
Ivy Andrews	p	1	2	0	0	0	0	0	0	0	1	0	.000	.000	0	1	0	a	p	11	15	2	1	1	0	0	0	0	4	0	.067	.133
Bump Hadley	p	1	0	0	0	0	0	0	0	0	0	0	—	—	0	0	0		p	29	65	7	11	0	1	0	4	11	12	0	.169	.200
Johnny Murphy	p	1	0	0	0	0	0	0	0	0	0	0	—	—	0	0	0		p	39	35	2	8	3	0	0	6	2	14	0	.229	.314
Kemp Wicker	p	1	0	0	0	0	0	0	0	0	0	0	—	—	0	0	0		p	16	35	4	4	0	0	0	7	1	6	0	.114	.114
Pat Malone	Did not play																		p	28	33	0	1	0	0	0	1	0	10	0	.030	.030
Frank Makosky	Did not play																		p	26	16	2	5	0	0	0	2	1	4	0	.313	.313
Spud Chandler	Did not play																		p	12	30	2	4	0	0	0	6	1	7	0	.133	.133
team total		5	169	28	42	6	4	4	25	21	21	0	.249	.402	132	47	0			157	5487	**979**	1554	282	73	**174**	**922**	**709**	607	60	.283	**.456**

Double Plays—2
Left on Bases—36

a—from Cleveland
Babe Dahlgren (ph), Roy Johnson (of), Johnny Broaca (p), and Joe Vance (p) also played for the Yankees during the season.

NEW YORK GIANTS

	WORLD SERIES STATISTICS																		REGULAR SEASON STATISTICS													
	Pos	G	AB	R	H	2B	3B	HR	RBI	BB	SO	SB	BA	SA	PO	A	E		Main Pos	G	AB	R	H	2B	3B	HR	RBI	BB	SO	SB	BA	SA
Johnny McCarthy	1b	5	19	1	4	1	0	0	1	1	2	0	.211	.263	38	1	2		1b	114	420	53	117	19	3	10	65	24	37	2	.279	.410
Burgess Whitehead	2b	5	16	1	4	**2**	0	0	0	2	0	1	.250	.375	8	**17**	1		2b	152	574	64	164	15	6	5	52	28	20	7	.286	.359
Dick Bartell	ss	5	21	3	5	1	0	0	1	0	3	0	.238	.286	13	11	**3**		ss	128	516	91	158	38	2	14	62	40	38	5	.306	.469
Mel Ott	3b	5	20	1	4	0	0	**1**	3	1	**4**	0	.200	.350	5	9	1		of-3b	151	545	99	160	28	2	**31**	95	**102**	69	7	.294	.523
Jimmy Ripple	rf	5	17	2	5	0	0	0	0	3	1	0	.294	.294	11	0	0		of	121	426	70	135	23	3	5	66	29	20	3	.317	.420
Hank Leiber	cf	3	11	2	4	0	0	0	2	1	1	0	.364	.364	7	0	0		of	51	184	24	54	7	3	4	32	15	27	1	.293	.429
Jo-Jo Moore	lf	5	**23**	1	**9**	1	0	0	1	0	1	0	.391	.435	13	0	0		of	142	580	89	180	37	10	6	57	46	37	7	.310	.440
Harry Danning	c	3	12	0	3	1	0	0	2	0	2	0	.250	.333	20	1	0		c	93	292	30	84	12	4	8	51	18	20	0	.288	.438
Gus Mancuso	c-ph	3	8	0	0	0	0	0	1	0	1	0	.000	.000	8	1	0		c	86	287	30	80	17	1	4	39	17	20	1	.279	.387
Lou Chiozza	cf	2	7	0	2	0	0	0	0	1	1	0	.286	.286	6	0	1		3b	117	439	49	102	11	2	4	29	20	30	6	.232	.294
Wally Berger	ph	3	3	0	0	0	0	0	0	0	1	0	.000	.000				b	of	59	199	40	58	11	2	12	43	18	30	3	.291	.548
Sam Leslie	ph	2	1	0	0	0	0	0	0	1	0	0	.000	.000					1b	72	191	25	59	7	2	3	30	20	12	1	.309	.414
Blondy Ryan	ph	1	1	0	0	0	0	0	0	0	1	0	.000	.000					ss	21	75	10	18	3	1	1	13	6	8	0	.240	.347
Mickey Haslin	Did not play																		ss	27	42	8	8	1	0	0	5	9	3	1	.190	.214
Ed Madjeski	Did not play																		c	5	15	0	3	0	0	0	2	0	2	0	.200	.200
Carl Hubbell	p	2	6	1	0	0	0	0	1	0	0	0	.000	.000	0	3	0		p	39	97	4	21	4	0	0	6	0	13	0	.216	.258
Cliff Melton	p	3	2	0	0	0	0	0	0	1	1	0	.000	.000	0	0	1		p	46	82	3	10	0	0	0	5	1	21	0	.122	.122
Dick Coffman	p	2	1	0	0	0	0	0	0	0	1	0	.000	.000	0	1	0		p	42	19	1	7	2	0	0	2	0	8	0	.368	.474
Hal Schumacher	p	1	1	0	0	0	0	0	0	0	1	0	.000	.000	0	1	0		p	45	81	9	18	2	0	2	7	3	16	0	.222	.321
Don Brennan	p	2	0	0	0	0	0	0	0	0	0	0	—	—	0	0	0	c	p	6	1	0	0	0	0	0	0	1	1	0	.000	.000
Harry Gumbert	p	2	0	0	0	0	0	0	0	0	0	0	—	—	0	0	0		p	34	72	3	13	0	0	1	5	1	15	0	.181	.222
Al Smith	p	2	0	0	0	0	0	0	0	0	0	0	—	—	0	1	0		p	33	25	1	3	0	0	0	0	0	9	0	.120	.120
Slick Castleman	Did not play—arm injury																		p	23	57	4	4	1	0	0	0	2	22	0	.070	.088
Tom Baker	Did not play																	d	p	13	9	0	2	0	0	0	0	0	2	0	.222	.222
team total		5	169	12	40	6	0	1	12	11	21	1	.237	.299	129	46	9			152	5329	732	1484	251	41	**111**	677	412	492	45	.278	.403

Double Plays—5
Left on Bases—36

b—from Boston
c—from Cincinnati
d—from Brooklyn
Kiddo Davis (of), Phil Weintraub (of), Jumbo Brown (p), Ben Cantwell (p), Freddie Fitzsimmons (p), Frank Gabler (p), Bill Lohrman (p), and Hy Vandenberg (p) also played for the Giants during the season.

PITCHING

NEW YORK YANKEES

	WORLD SERIES STATISTICS														REGULAR SEASON STATISTICS													
	G	GS	CG	IP	H	R	ER	BB	SO	W	L	SV	ERA		G	GS	CG	IP	H	ER	BB	SO	W	L	Pct	SV	ShO	ERA
Lefty Gomez	2	**2**	**2**	**18**	**16**	3	3	2	**8**	**2**	0	0	1.50		34	34	25	278	233	72	93	**194**	**21**	11	.656	0	**6**	**2.33**
Red Ruffing	1	1	1	9	7	1	1	3	**8**	1	0	0	**1.00**		31	31	22	256	242	85	68	131	20	7	.741	0	4	2.99
Monte Pearson	1	1	0	$8\frac{2}{3}$	5	1	1	2	4	1	0	0	1.04		22	20	7	145	145	51	64	71	9	3	.750	1	1	3.17
Ivy Andrews	1	0	0	$5\frac{2}{3}$	6	2	2	4	1	0	0	0	3.18	a	11	5	3	49	49	17	17	17	3	2	.600	1	1	3.12
Bump Hadley	1	1	0	$1\frac{1}{3}$	6	5	5	0	0	0	1	0	33.75		29	25	6	178	199	105	83	70	11	8	.579	0	0	5.31
Kemp Wicker	1	0	0	1	0	0	0	0	0	0	0	0	0.00		16	10	6	88	107	43	26	14	7	3	.700	0	1	4.40
Johnny Murphy	1	0	0	$\frac{1}{3}$	0	0	0	0	0	0	0	**1**	0.00		39	4	0	110	121	51	50	36	13	4	.765	10	0	4.17
Pat Malone	Did not play														28	9	3	92	109	56	35	49	4	4	.500	6	0	5.48
Spud Chandler	Did not play														12	10	6	82	79	26	20	31	7	4	.636	0	2	2.85
Frank Makosky	Did not play														26	1	1	58	64	32	24	27	5	2	.714	3	0	4.97
team total	5	5	3	44	40	12	12	11	21	4	1	1	2.45		157	157	**82**	1396	1417	**566**	506	652	**102**	52	**.662**	**21**	**15**	**3.65**

NEW YORK GIANTS

	WORLD SERIES STATISTICS														REGULAR SEASON STATISTICS													
	G	GS	CG	IP	H	R	ER	BB	SO	W	L	SV	ERA		G	GS	CG	IP	H	ER	BB	SO	W	L	Pct	SV	ShO	ERA
Carl Hubbell	2	**2**	1	$14\frac{1}{3}$	12	**10**	**6**	4	7	1	1	0	3.77		39	32	18	262	261	93	55	**159**	**22**	8	**.733**	4	4	3.19
Cliff Melton	**3**	**2**	0	11	12	6	**6**	**6**	7	0	**2**	0	4.91		46	27	14	248	216	72	55	142	20	9	.690	**7**	2	2.61
Hal Schumacher	1	1	0	6	9	5	4	4	3	0	1	0	6.00		38	29	10	218	222	87	89	100	13	12	.520	1	1	3.59
Dick Coffman	2	0	0	$4\frac{1}{3}$	2	2	2	5	1	0	0	0	4.15		42	1	0	80	93	27	31	30	8	3	.727	3	0	3.04
Don Brennan	2	0	0	3	1	0	0	1	1	0	0	0	0.00	c	6	0	0	9	12	7	9	1	1	0	1.000	0	0	7.00
Al Smith	2	0	0	3	2	1	1	0	1	0	0	0	3.00		33	9	2	86	91	40	30	41	5	4	.556	0	0	4.19
Harry Gumbert	2	0	0	$1\frac{1}{3}$	4	4	4	1	1	0	0	0	27.00		34	24	10	200	194	82	62	65	10	11	.476	1	1	3.69
Slick Castleman	Did not play—arm injury														23	23	10	160	148	59	33	78	11	6	.647	0	2	3.32
Tom Baker	Did not play													d	13	0	0	31	30	14	16	11	1	0	1.000	0	0	4.06
team total	5	5	1	43	42	28	23	21	21	1	4	0	4.81		152	152	67	1361	1341	518	404	**653**	**95**	57	**.625**	17	11	3.43

Total Attendance—238,142   Average Attendance—47,628   Winning Player's Share—$6,471   Losing Player's Share—$4,490

1938
Gloating for a Second Time

Unlike the Yankees, the Cubs couldn't coast to a pennant. In fact, their hardest fighting came in the last days of September, when the Pirates came into Wrigley Field for a three-game set that would decide the National League title. On September 27, sore-armed Dizzy Dean, whom the Cubs had purchased from the Cardinals last winter as damaged goods, used a variety of slow stuff to beat the Bucs 2–1. The next day's game went into the ninth inning tied at 5–5, and with darkness setting in and threatening to call the game, manager Gabby Hartnett belted a home run with two out to put the Cubs in first place. A 10–1 win the next day put the Cubs on easy street and ran their stretch-drive winning streak to 10 games. The late pennant run came too late to save the job of Charlie Grimm, who was fired as manager in July with the Cubs treading water in the middle of the pack. With catcher Hartnett running the team, the Cubs jelled and finally reached first place in the confrontation with the Pirates. The batting order had little power and only two .300 hitters in Stan Hack and Carl Reynolds, but the pitching duo of Bill Lee and Clay Bryant, with some spot help from Dean, kept the Cubs alive down the stretch.

The Yankees, who had waltzed through the later stages of the season with a big edge over second-place Boston, fielded the same strong club with two new starters, Joe Gordon at second base and Tommy Henrich in right field. The power these two new men brought to the lineup supplemented the core of Joe DiMaggio, Lou Gehrig, and Bill Dickey, while Red Ruffing and Lefty Gomez continued to lead the mound staff in wins behind such comfortable support.

So when the clubs squared off in the first game at Wrigley Field, the similarities between 1932 and 1938 were striking. The Cubs had won the pennant once again after changing managers in midseason, and they once again faced the New York Yankees and manager Joe McCarthy. The 1932 Yankee sweep fostered revenge in the Cubs' heart, but this year's result was just another similarity to the Series six years ago. Red Ruffing and Bill Lee squared off on the mound in game one, and each did a fine job. Ruffing did a slightly better job, however, and the Yankees won a 3–1 game spiced by Bill Dickey's 4-for-4 performance. The second game was played in the cold rawness of a Chicago autumn, with Dizzy Dean facing Lefty Gomez. With his fast ball only a memory because of his bad arm, Dean pitched to spots and changed speeds to keep the Yankee batters off-stride through the early innings. The Cubs led 3–2 after seven innings, with Dean still in full command of the situation. But Dizzy's deception could go on only so long, and the Yanks finally caught up in the eighth. George Selkirk led off with a single, and Joe Gordon and pinch hitter Myril Hoag hit into force plays. But then Frankie Crosetti, the least powerful man in the Yankee lineup, timed one of Dean's deliveries and drove it into the left-field seats, putting the Yanks ahead 4–3. DiMaggio knocked Dean out of the box with another two-run homer in the ninth, and Dizzy's last flirtation with glory went unanswered.

But not only was Dean disappointed, the Cubs were also going rapidly down the drain. After a day of travel, the clubs met in game three in Yankee Stadium. Dickey and Gordon socked homers, and Gordon also contributed a two-run single to a 5–2 victory, with Monte Pearson hurling a five-hitter. Just like 1932, the Cubs were down 3–0 in games, and just like in 1932, they could not stop the stampede. After two were out in the bottom of the second in the fourth game, the Yankees struck against Bill Lee. Hoag reached first on an error by shortstop Billy Jurges, Gordon singled, Ruffing singled, and then Crosetti again unsheathed his power by smashing a bases-clearing triple. In their frantic catch-up attempts, the Cubs used six pitchers in the game, but a four-run Yankee eighth decided the issue by a score of 8–3. The sweep was bitter medicine for the Cubs to swallow, as their string of unsuccessful Series was now run up to six straight. The only disquieting note for the Yankees was the poor hitting bat of Lou Gehrig, who lacked the power of earlier years and contributed only four singles to the Yankee cause.

Game 1 October 5 at Chicago

NY Y	0 2 0	0 0 1	0 0 0					
Chi.	0 0 1	0 0 0	0 0 0					

NY Yankees	Pos	AB	R	H	RBI	PO	A	E
Crosetti	ss	4	0	1	0	4	6	0
Rolfe	3b	5	0	1	0	0	1	0
Henrich	rf	4	1	2	0	0	0	1
DiMaggio	cf	4	0	0	0	2	0	0
Gehrig	1b	3	1	1	0	10	0	0
Dickey	c	4	1	4	1	6	3	0
Selkirk	lf	4	0	1	1	1	0	0
Gordon	2b	4	0	2	1	4	2	0
Ruffing	p	3	0	0	0	0	1	0
Totals		35	3	12	3	27	13	1

Pitching	IP	H	R	ER	BB	SO
Yankees						
Ruffing (W)	9	9	1	1	0	5
Chicago						
Lee (L)	8	11	3	3	1	6
Russell	1	1	0	0	0	0

Chicago	Pos	AB	R	H	RBI	PO	A	E
Hack	3b	4	0	3	1	1	1	0
Herman	2b	4	0	1	0	2	5	1
Demaree	lf	4	0	0	0	2	0	0
Cavarretta	rf	4	0	2	0	1	1	0
Reynolds	cf	4	0	0	0	3	0	0
Hartnett	c	3	0	1	0	6	2	0
Collins	1b	3	0	1	0	10	1	0
Jurges	ss	3	0	1	0	1	3	0
Lee	p	2	0	0	0	1	0	0
a O'Dea		1	0	0	0	0	0	0
Russell	p	0	0	0	0	0	0	0
Totals		32	1	9	1	27	13	1

a Hit into force play for Lee in 8th.

Doubles—Crosetti, Gordon, Henrich. Triple—Hartnett. Sacrifice Hit—Ruffing. Stolen Base—Dickey. Double Plays—Crosetti to Gehrig, Gordon to Crosetti to Gehrig, Jurges to Herman to Collins, Collins (unassisted). Hit by Pitcher—Crosetti (by Lee). Left on Bases—New York 8, Chicago 4. Umpires—Moran (N), Kolls (A), Sears (N), Hubbard (A). Attendance—43,642. Time of Game—1:53.

1st Inning
Yankees
1 Crosetti called out on strikes.
2 Rolfe grounded to Collins who made a great stop and threw to Lee covering first.
3 Henrich looked at a called third strike.
Chicago
Hack singled to left.
1 Hack caught stealing, Dickey to Crosetti.
2 Herman grounded to short.
3 Demaree fanned.

2nd Inning
Yankees
1 DiMaggio grounded to third.
Gehrig walked.
Dickey singled to right moving Gehrig to third, Dickey taking second on the throw to third.
Selkirk safe at first on Herman's bobble, scoring Gehrig with Dickey going to third.
Gordon singled to left, scoring Dickey with Selkirk stopping at second.
2,3 Ruffing hit into a double play, Jurges to Herman to Collins.
Chicago
1 Cavarretta grounded to first.
2 Reynolds popped to second.
3 Hartnett fouled to Dickey.

3rd Inning
Yankees
1 Crosetti flied to center.
2 Rolfe flied to left.
Henrich beat out a grounder to first.
3 Henrich caught stealing, Hartnett to Herman.
Chicago
Collins singled to right.
1 Jurges fanned.
2 Lee tapped out in front of the plate, Dickey to Gehrig moving Collins to second (not a sacrifice hit).
Hack singled to right, scoring Collins and went to second on the throw to the plate.
Herman singled off Rolfe's glove and
3 Hack trying to score was out at the plate, Crosetti to Dickey.

4th Inning
Yankees
1 DiMaggio grounded out to short where Jurges made a sensational stop.
Gehrig singled to right but was out
2 trying for a double, Cavarretta to Herman to Jurges.
Dickey singled over second.
3 Selkirk popped to Hack.
Chicago
1 Demaree grounded back to the pitcher.
2 Cavarretta fanned.
3 Reynolds popped to first.

5th Inning
Yankees
Gordon doubled to left.
1 Ruffing sacrificed Gordon to third, Hartnett to Collins.
2 Crosetti fanned.
3 Rolfe grounded to second.
Chicago
1 Hartnett fanned, but Dickey dropped the third strike, throwing Hartnett out.
2 Collins rolled out to second.
3 Jurges fanned.

6th Inning
Yankees
Henrich doubled to right.
1 DiMaggio flied to right.
2 Gehrig fanned.
Dickey singled to left, scoring Henrich. Selkirk beat out a hit down the first base line, Dickey stopping at second.
3 Gordon fanned.
Chicago
1 Lee flied to center.
Hack singled past third.
2 Herman forced Hack at second, Rolfe to Gordon.
3 Demaree popped to short.

7th Inning
Yankees
1 Ruffing flied to left.
Crosetti was hit by a pitched ball. Rolfe singled to right, advancing Crosetti to third.
2,3 Henrich lined to Collins who made a great one-handed catch then stepped on first to double up Rolfe.
Chicago
Cavarretta singled to center.
1,2 Reynolds hit into a double play, Crosetti to Gehrig.
Hartnett tripled to right as the ball rolled to the wall after Henrich missed a shoe string catch.
3 Collins grounded to short.

8th Inning
Yankees
1 DiMaggio grounded to short.
2 Gehrig called out on strikes.
Dickey singled to right (his 4th hit). Dickey stole second.
3 Selkirk flied to center.
Chicago
Jurges popped a single to right.
1 O'Dea, batting for Lee, forced Jurges at second, Crosetti to Gordon.
2,3 Hack into a double play, Gordon to Crosetti to Gehrig.

9th Inning
Yankees
For Chicago—Russell pitching.
1 Gordon flied to center.
2 Ruffing grounded to second. Crosetti doubled to right.
3 Rolfe grounded to second.
Chicago
1 Herman flied to center.
2 Demaree flied to left.
Cavarretta singled to right and took second on Henrich's fumble.
3 Reynolds popped to second.

Game 2 October 6 at Chicago

NY Yankees	Pos	AB	R	H	RBI	PO	A	E
Crosetti	ss	4	1	1	2	5	3	0
Rolfe	3b	4	0	0	0	0	2	2
Henrich	rf	4	1	1	0	2	0	0
DiMaggio	cf	4	2	2	2	4	0	0
Gehrig	1b	3	1	1	0	6	0	0
Dickey	c	4	0	0	0	6	2	0
Selkirk	lf	3	0	1	0	4	0	0
Powell	lf	0	0	0	0	0	0	0
Gordon	2b	4	0	0	2	4	3	0
Gomez	p	2	0	1	0	0	1	0
a Hoag		1	1	0	0	0	0	0
Murphy	p	0	0	0	0	0	0	0
Totals		33	6	7	6	27	11	2

Pitching	IP	H	R	ER	BB	SO
Yankees						
Gomez (W)	7	9	3	3	1	5
Murphy (SV)	2	2	0	0	1	1
Chicago						
Dean (L)	*8	7	6	6	1	2
French	1	0	0	0	1	2

*Pitched to two batters in 9th.

1st Inning
Yankees
1 Crosetti flied to deep left.
2 Rolfe bunted, thrown out by Dean.
3 Henrich popped to short.
Chicago
Hack singled to left.
1 Herman struck out.
Demaree singled to right sending Hack to third and when Rolfe fumbled the throw in Demaree got to second.
2 Marty flied to deep center, Hack scoring after the catch.
3 Reynolds struck out.

2nd Inning
Yankees
DiMaggio singled to left.
Gehrig walked.
1 Dickey popped to short.
2 Selkirk flied to center.
Gordon hit an easy roller but Jurges and Hack collided, the ball going through for a double, scoring DiMaggio and Gehrig.
3 Gomez flied to left.
Chicago
1 Hartnett flied to right.
Collins singled off Rolfe's glove.
2 Jurges forced Collins at second, Rolfe to Gordon.
3 Dean grounded to short.

3rd Inning
Yankees
1 Crosetti flied to left.
2 Rolfe grounded to second.
3 Henrich grounded to second.
Chicago
Hack beat out a bouncer to short.
Herman also beat out a hit behind second, Hack stopping at second.
1 Demaree sacrificed Hack to third and Herman to second, Dickey to Gehrig.
Marty doubled to deep center, scoring Hack and Herman.
Reynolds walked.
2 Hartnett flied to center.
3 Collins fanned.

4th Inning
Yankees
1 DiMaggio fouled to Hartnett.
Gehrig singled when Collins fell going for his grounder.
2,3 Dickey hit into a double play, Herman to Jurges to Collins.
Chicago
1 Jurges grounded to third.
Dean singled to left.
2,3 Hack grounded into a double play, Crosetti to Gordon to Gehrig.

5th Inning
Yankees
1 Selkirk fouled to Collins.
2 Gordon grounded to third.
3 Gomez grounded to second.
Chicago
1 Herman popped to second.
2 Demaree flied to center.
Marty singled to left.
3 Marty caught stealing Dickey to Crosetti

Chicago	Pos	AB	R	H	RBI	PO	A	E
Hack	3b	5	2	2	0	0	3	0
Herman	2b	4	1	1	0	1	5	0
Demaree	rf	3	0	1	0	1	0	0
Marty	cf	3	0	4	3	3	0	0
Reynolds	lf	3	0	0	0	4	0	0
Hartnett	c	4	0	0	0	5	0	0
Collins	1b	4	0	1	0	10	0	0
Jurges	ss	4	0	0	0	4	1	0
Dean	p	3	0	2	0	0	2	0
French	p	0	0	0	0	0	0	0
b Cavarretta		1	0	1	0	0	0	0
Totals		34	3	11	3	27	11	0

a Hit into a force play for Gomez in 8th.
b Singled for French in 9th.

Doubles—Gordon, Marty.
Home Runs—Crosetti, DiMaggio.
Sacrifice Hit—Demaree.
Double Plays—Crosetti to Gordon to Gehrig, Gordon to Crosetti to Gehrig, Herman to Jurges to Collins.
Left on Bases—Yankees 2, Chicago 7.
Umpires—Kolls, Sears, Hubbard, Moran.
Attendance—42,108. Time of Game—1:53.

6th Inning
Yankees
1 Crosetti flied to left.
2 Rolfe fanned.
3 Henrich grounded back to the pitcher.
Chicago
1 Reynolds popped to short.
2 Hartnett flied to deep center.
Collins made it to first on Rolfe's wild throw.
3 Jurges forced Collins at second, Crosetti unassisted.

7th Inning
Yankees
1 DiMaggio grounded to third.
2 Gehrig flied to right.
3 Dickey flied to center.
Chicago
Dean singled to right.
1 Hack called out on strikes.
2 Herman fanned.
3 Dean trapped off first, Gomez to Gordon.

8th Inning
Yankees
Selkirk singled to right.
1 Gordon forced Selkirk at second, Hack to Herman.
2 Hoag, pinch-hitting for Gomez, forced Gordon at second, Herman to Jurges.
Crosetti hit a two-run homer into the left field bleachers.
3 Rolfe called out on strikes.
Chicago
For the Yankees—Murphy pitching.
1 Demaree fanned.
Marty singled to right.
2,3 Reynolds hit into a double play, Gordon to Crosetti to Gehrig.

9th Inning
Yankees
Henrich singled to right.
DiMaggio hit a two-run homer over the left field wall.
For Chicago—French pitching.
1 Gehrig fanned.
2 Dickey grounded to first.
Selkirk walked.
3 Gordon fanned.
Chicago
For the Yankees—Powell in left.
1 Hartnett flied to right.
2 Collins grounded to second.
Jurges walked.
Cavarretta, pinch hitting for French, singled past Gordon with Jurges stopping at second.
3 Hack lined to short.

NY Y	0 2 0	0 0 0	0 2 2						
Chi.	1 0 2	0 0 0	0 0 0						

Game 3 October 8 at New York

Chicago	Pos	AB	R	H	RBI	PO	A	E
Hack	3b	3	1	1	0	2	0	0
Herman	2b	4	0	1	0	1	5	0
Cavarretta	rf	4	0	1	0	2	0	0
Marty	cf	4	1	3	2	3	0	0
Reynolds	lf	4	0	0	0	0	0	0
Hartnett	c	4	0	0	0	3	1	0
Collins	1b	4	0	0	0	8	0	0
Jurges	ss	3	0	0	0	5	3	0
b Lazzeri		1	0	0	0	0	0	0
Bryant	p	2	0	0	0	0	1	0
Russell	p	0	0	0	0	0	0	0
a Galan		1	0	0	0	0	0	0
French	p	0	0	0	0	0	2	0
c O'Dea		1	0	0	0	0	0	0
Totals		34	2	5	2	24	7	1

a Popped out for Russell in 7th.

Double—Hack. Home Runs—Dickey, Gordon, Marty. Left on Bases—Chicago 7, Yankees 8.
Umpires—Sears, Hubbard, Moran, Kolls.
Attendance—55,236. Time of Game—1:57.

1st Inning
Chicago
Hack walked.
Herman walked.
1 Cavarretta singled to center.
Marty singled to deep short, loading the bases.
2 Reynolds struck out.
3 Hartnett struck out.
Yankees
1 Crosetti struck out.
2 Rolfe popped to short.
3 Henrich flied to center.

2nd Inning
Chicago
1 Collins struck out.
2 Jurges struck out.
Bryant got all the way to second on Crosetti's wide throw to first.
3 Hack grounded to Pearson who made the putout.
Yankees
DiMaggio walked.
1 Gehrig forced DiMaggio at second, Herman to Jurges.
Dickey walked.
2 Selkirk struck out.
3 Gordon struck out.

3rd Inning
Chicago
1 Herman struck out.
Cavarretta singled to right.
Marty singled to center, sending Cavarretta to third.
2 Reynolds struck out.
3 Hartnett grounded to second.
Yankees
1 Pearson grounded to short.
Crosetti walked.
2 Rolfe flied to center.
3 Crosetti caught stealing, Hartnett to Jurges.

4th Inning
Chicago
1 Collins flied to left.
2 Jurges lined to second.
3 Bryant called out on strikes.
Yankees
1 Henrich grounded to first.
2 DiMaggio grounded to short.
3 Gehrig popped to second.

5th Inning
Chicago
Hack doubled to left.
1 Herman was called out on strikes.
Cavarretta safe on Gordon's fumble, Hack going to third.
2 Marty forced Cavarretta at second, Rolfe to Gordon scoring Hack.
3 Reynolds fouled to Dickey.

Chi.	0 0 0	0 1 0	0 1 0						
NY Y	0 0 0	0 2 2	0 1 x						

NY Yankees	Pos	AB	R	H	RBI	PO	A	E
Crosetti	ss	3	0	0	0	1	0	1
Rolfe	3b	4	0	1	1	0	1	0
Henrich	rf	4	0	0	0	1	0	0
DiMaggio	cf	3	1	1	0	1	0	0
Gehrig	1b	4	1	0	0	4	1	0
Dickey	c	3	1	1	1	12	0	0
Selkirk	lf	3	1	1	0	3	2	1
Gordon	2b	4	1	2	3	2	3	1
Pearson	p	3	1	1	0	2	0	0
Totals		31	5	7	5	27	5	2

Pitching	IP	H	R	ER	BB	SO
Chicago						
Bryant (L)	5⅓	6	4	4	3	5
Russell	⅔	0	0	0	1	0
French	2	1	1	1	0	0
Yankees						
Pearson (W)	9	5	2	1	2	9

5th Inning (continued)
Yankees
1 Dickey flied to center.
2 Selkirk grounded to second.
Gordon got the first hit off of Bryant a homer into the left field stands.
Pearson singled to right.
Crosetti walked.
Rolfe singled to center, scoring Pearson and sending Crosetti to third.
3 Henrich fouled to Hack.

6th Inning
Chicago
1 Hartnett fouled to Gehrig.
2 Collins lined to right.
3 Jurges popped to Dickey in front of the plate.
Yankees
DiMaggio singled past third.
Gehrig singled to center, advancing DiMaggio to third.
1 Dickey fouled to Hack.
Selkirk walked loading the bases.
Gordon singled to left scoring DiMaggio and Gehrig, Selkirk stopping at second.
For Chicago—Russell pitching.
Pearson walked loading the bases.
2 Crosetti flied to Jurges.
3 Rolfe popped to short.

7th Inning
Chicago
1 Galan, batting for Russell, popped to short.
2 Hack called out on strikes.
3 Herman grounded to short.
Yankees
For Chicago—French pitching.
1 Henrich flied to right.
2 DiMaggio grounded to short.
3 Gehrig flied to right.

8th Inning
Chicago
1 Cavarretta grounded out, Gehrig to Pearson.
Marty homered into the left field seats.
2 Reynolds flied to left.
3 Hartnett flied to right.
Yankees
Dickey hit a homer into the right field stands.
1 Selkirk grounded to the pitcher.
2 Gordon grounded to first.
Pearson safe on Herman's fumble.
3 Crosetti grounded to the pitcher.

9th Inning
Chicago
1 Collins fouled to Gehrig.
2 Lazzeri, pinch hitting for Jurges, grounded to second.
3 O'Dea, pinch-hitting for French, flied to right.

1938

Game 4 October 9 at New York

| Chi. | 0 0 0 | 1 0 0 | 0 2 0 |
| NY Y | 0 3 0 | 0 0 1 | 0 4 x |

Chicago	Pos	AB	R	H	RBI	PO	A	E
Hack	3b	5	0	2	0	1	0	0
Herman	2b	5	0	1	0	1	3	0
Cavarretta	rf	4	1	2	0	1	0	0
Marty	cf	4	0	0	0	2	0	0
Demaree	lf	3	1	0	0	3	0	0
O'Dea	c	3	1	1	2	5	0	0
Collins	1b	4	0	0	0	10	0	0
Jurges	ss	4	0	2	0	1	0	1
Lee	p	1	0	0	0	0	0	0
a Galan		1	0	0	0	0	0	0
Root	p	0	0	0	0	0	0	0
b Lazzeri		1	0	0	0	0	0	0
Page	p	0	0	0	0	0	1	0
French	p	0	0	0	0	0	0	0
Carleton	p	0	0	0	0	0	0	0
Dean	p	0	0	0	0	0	0	0
c Reynolds		1	0	0	0	0	0	0
Totals		36	3	8	2	24	4	1

a Struck out for Lee in 4th.
b Struck out for Root in 7th.
c Flied out for Dean in 9th.

Doubles—Cavarretta, Crosetti, Hoag, Jurges. Triple—Crosetti. Home Runs—Henrich, O'Dea. Stolen Bases—Gordon, Rolfe. Wild pitches—Carleton 2. Left on Bases—Chicago 8, Yankees 6. Umpires—Hubbard, Moran, Kolls, Sears. Attendance—59,847. Time of Game—2:11.

NY Yankees	Pos	AB	R	H	RBI	PO	A	E
Crosetti	ss	5	0	2	4	6	1	0
Rolfe	3b	5	0	1	0	0	0	0
Henrich	rf	4	1	1	1	1	0	0
DiMaggio	cf	4	1	1	0	3	0	0
Gehrig	1b	4	1	1	0	5	2	0
Dickey	c	4	0	1	0	7	0	0
Hoag	lf	4	2	2	1	2	0	0
Gordon	2b	3	2	1	0	2	4	1
Ruffing	p	3	1	1	1	2	3	0
Totals		36	8	11	7	27	10	1

Pitching	IP	H	R	ER	BB	SO
Chicago						
Lee (L)	3	4	3	0	0	2
Root	3	3	1	1	0	1
Page	1⅓	2	2	2	0	0
French	⅓	0	0	0	0	0
Carleton	*0	1	2	2	2	0
Dean	⅓	1	0	0	0	0
Yankees						
Ruffing (W)	9	8	3	2	2	6

*Pitched to three batters in 8th.

1st Inning
Chicago
 Hack singled over second.
1 Herman forced Hack at second, Gordon to Crosetti.
2 Cavarretta forced Herman at second, Ruffing to Crosetti
3 Marty fanned.
Yankees
1 Crosetti fanned.
 Rolfe singled on a blooper to center.
 Rolfe stole second.
2 Henrich grounded to first, advancing Rolfe to third.
3 DiMaggio struck out.

2nd Inning
Chicago
1 Demaree fouled to Gehrig.
2 O'Dea fouled to Dickey.
3 Collins grounded out, Gehrig to Ruffing.
Yankees
1 Gehrig popped to third.
2 Dickey grounded to first.
 Hoag safe at first on Jurges' throwing error.
 Gordon singled into left, moving Hoag to third.
 Ruffing singled to right, scoring Hoag and advancing Gordon to third.
 Crosetti lined a triple to the left field corner, scoring Gordon and Ruffing.
3 Rolfe grounded to second.

3rd Inning
Chicago
1 Jurges grounded back to the pitcher.
2 Lee fanned.
 Hack singled into left.
 Herman blooped a single into short left-center, Hack stopping at second.
3 Cavarretta popped to second.
New York
1 Henrich grounded to first.
2 DiMaggio flew to Demaree at the 415-foot sign in left-center.
3 Gehrig grounded to second.

4th Inning
Chicago
1 Marty flied to deep right.
 Demaree walked.
 O'Dea walked.
2 Collins fanned.
 Jurges grounded to Crosetti who tried for the force throwing to Gordon but Gordon lost the ball for an error Demaree scoring and O'Dea going to third.
3 Galan, pinch-hitting for Lee, fanned.
Yankees
 For Chicago—Root pitching.
1 Dickey hit a high fly to Marty in short right center.
2 Hoag lined to second.
3 Gordon flied to left.

5th Inning
Chicago
1 Hack flied to left.
2 Herman grounded to second.
 Cavarretta beat out a bunt down the third-base line for a single.
3 Marty popped to short.

5th Inning (continued)
Yankees
1 Ruffing fouled to O'Dea.
2 Crosetti flied to right.
3 Rolfe struck out.

6th Inning
Chicago
1 Demaree flied to center.
2 O'Dea popped to second.
3 Collins rolled out Gehrig to Ruffing.
Yankees
 Henrich homered into the right field stands.
1 DiMaggio fouled to O'Dea.
2 Gehrig fouled to Collins.
 Dickey singled to right.
 Hoag singled to right, Dickey stopping at second.
3 Gordon flied deep to Demaree who made a sensational leaping catch.

7th Inning
Chicago
 Jurges got a ground-rule double as his hit bounced into the right field stands.
1 Lazzeri, pinch hitting for Root, fanned.
2 Hack popped to short.
3 Herman popped to short.
Yankees
 For Chicago—Page pitching.
1 Ruffing grounded to second.
2 Crosetti bounced back to the pitcher.
3 Rolfe grounded to first.

8th Inning
Chicago
 Cavarretta lined into the left field corner for a double.
1 Marty fanned.
2 Demaree grounded to second, moving Cavarretta to third.
 O'Dea hit a two-run homer into the lower deck of the right field stands.
3 Collins flied to center.
Yankees
1 Henrich flied to center.
 DiMaggio singled to left.
 Gehrig singled to right, advancing DiMaggio to third.
 For Chicago—French pitching.
2 Dickey popped to short.
 For Chicago—Carleton pitching.
 Carleton's second pitch went wild DiMaggio scoring and Gehrig going to second.
 Hoag lined a double off the left field seats, scoring Gehrig.
 Gordon intentionally walked.
 Carleton uncorked his second wild pitch of the inning allowing Hoag to take third, Gordon held first.
 Gordon stole second.
 Ruffing walked to load the bases.
 For Chicago—Dean pitching.
 Crosetti hit a bloop double between Demaree, Marty and Jurges scoring Hoag and Gordon with Ruffing going to third.
3 Rolfe lined to first.

9th Inning
Chicago
 Jurges singled into right center.
1 Reynolds, batting for Dean, flied to center.
2 Hack forced Jurges at second, Gordon to Crosetti.
3 Herman grounded back to the pitcher for the final out. **Yankees first team ever to capture 3 championships in a row.**

173

1938 WORLD SERIES COMPOSITE BOX

	Wins	Composite Line Score
New York Yankees (A.L.)	4	0 7 0 0 2 4 0 7 2 - 22
Chicago Cubs (N.L.)	0	1 0 3 1 1 0 0 3 0 - 9

Manager	W	L	Pct.	G. Ahead
	Regular Season			
Joe McCarthy	99	53	.651	9.5
Charlie Grimm, Gabby Hartnett	89	63	.586	2

BATTING AND FIELDING

NEW YORK YANKEES

WORLD SERIES STATISTICS

	Pos	G	AB	R	H	2B	3B	HR	RBI	BB	SO	SB	BA	SA	PO	A	E
Lou Gehrig	1b	4	14	4	4	0	0	0	0	2	3	0	.286	.286	25	3	0
Joe Gordon	2b	4	15	3	6	2	0	1	6	1	3	1	.400	.733	12	12	2
Frankie Crosetti	ss	4	16	1	4	2	1	1	6	2	4	0	.250	.688	16	10	1
Red Rolfe	3b	4	18	0	3	0	0	0	1	0	3	1	.167	.167	0	4	2
Tommy Henrich	rf	4	16	3	4	1	0	1	1	0	1	0	.250	.500	6	0	1
Joe DiMaggio	cf	4	15	4	4	0	0	1	2	1	1	0	.267	.467	10	0	0
George Selkirk	lf	3	10	0	2	0	0	0	1	2	1	0	.200	.200	3	0	0
Bill Dickey	c	4	15	2	6	0	0	1	2	1	0	1	.400	.600	31	5	0
Myril Hoag	ph-lf	2	5	3	2	1	0	0	1	0	0	0	.400	.600	1	0	0
Jake Powell	lf	1	0	0	0	0	0	0	0	0	0	0	—	—	0	0	0
Bill Knickerbocker	Did not play																
Joe Glenn	Did not play																
Babe Pahlgren	Did not play																
Art Jorgens	Did not play																
Red Ruffing	p	2	6	1	1	0	0	0	1	1	0	0	.167	.167	2	4	0
Monte Pearson	p	1	3	1	1	0	0	0	0	1	0	0	.333	.333	2	0	0
Lefty Gomez	p	1	2	0	0	0	0	0	0	0	0	0	.000	.000	0	1	0
Johnny Murphy	p	1	0	0	0	0	0	0	0	0	0	0	—	—	0	0	0
Spud Chandler	Did not play																
Bump Hadley	Did not play																
Steve Sundra	Did not play																
Wes Ferrell	Did not play																
Ivy Andrews	Did not play																
team total		4	135	22	37	6	1	5	21	11	16	3	.274	.444	108	39	6

Double Plays—4
Left on Bases—24

REGULAR SEASON STATISTICS

		Main Pos	G	AB	R	H	2B	3B	HR	RBI	BB	SO	SB	BA	SA
Lou Gehrig		1b	157	576	115	170	32	6	29	114	107	75	6	.295	.523
Joe Gordon		2b	127	458	83	117	24	7	25	97	56	72	11	.255	.502
Frankie Crosetti		ss	157	631	113	166	35	3	9	55	106	97	27	.263	.371
Red Rolfe		3b	151	631	132	196	36	8	10	80	74	44	13	.311	.441
Tommy Henrich		of	131	471	109	127	24	7	22	91	92	32	6	.270	.490
Joe DiMaggio		of	145	599	129	194	32	13	32	140	59	21	6	.324	.581
George Selkirk		of	99	335	58	85	12	5	10	62	68	52	9	.254	.409
Bill Dickey		c	132	454	84	142	27	4	27	115	75	22	3	.313	.568
Myril Hoag		of	85	267	28	74	14	3	0	48	25	31	4	.277	.352
Jake Powell		of	45	164	27	42	12	1	2	20	15	20	3	.256	.378
Bill Knickerbocker		3b	46	128	15	32	8	3	1	21	11	10	0	.250	.383
Joe Glenn		c	41	123	10	32	7	2	0	25	10	14	1	.260	.350
Babe Pahlgren		3b-1b	27	43	8	8	1	0	0	1	1	7	0	.186	.209
Art Jorgens		c	9	17	3	4	2	0	0	2	3	3	0	.235	.353
Red Ruffing		p	45	107	12	24	4	1	3	17	17	21	0	.224	.364
Monte Pearson		p	28	76	8	13	4	0	0	6	7	7	1	.171	.224
Lefty Gomez		p	32	86	5	13	2	0	0	7	4	18	0	.151	.174
Johnny Murphy		p	32	32	4	2	1	0	0	2	1	13	1	.063	.094
Spud Chandler		p	23	69	10	14	1	0	3	4	1	23	0	.203	.348
Bump Hadley		p	29	54	3	5	0	0	0	4	11	15	0	.093	.093
Steve Sundra		p	25	33	4	6	1	0	1	2	3	12	0	.182	.303
Wes Ferrell	a	p	5	12	1	2	1	0	0	1	1	4	0	.167	.280
Ivy Andrews		p	19	12	1	2	0	0	0	1	1	1	0	.167	.167
team total			157	5410	966	1480	283	63	174	917	749	616	91	.274	.446

a—from Washington
Joe Beggs (p), Kemp Wicker (p), Atley Donald (p), Lee Stine (p), and Joe Vance (p) also played for the Yankees during the season.

CHICAGO CUBS

WORLD SERIES STATISTICS

	Pos	G	AB	R	H	2B	3B	HR	RBI	BB	SO	SB	BA	SA	PO	A	E
Ripper Collins	1b	4	15	1	2	0	0	0	0	0	3	0	.133	.133	38	1	0
Billy Herman	2b	4	16	1	3	0	0	0	0	1	4	0	.188	.188	5	14	2
Billy Jurges	ss	4	13	0	3	1	0	0	0	1	3	0	.231	.308	11	7	1
Stan Hack	3b	4	17	3	8	1	0	0	1	1	2	0	.471	.529	4	4	0
Phil Cavarretta	rf	4	13	1	6	1	0	0	0	0	1	0	.462	.538	4	1	0
Joe Marty	cf	3	12	1	6	1	0	1	5	0	2	0	.500	.833	7	0	0
Frank Demaree	lf-rf	3	10	1	1	0	0	0	0	1	2	0	.100	.100	6	0	0
Gabby Hartnett	c	3	11	0	1	0	1	0	0	0	2	0	.091	.273	14	3	0
Carl Reynolds	cf-lf-ph	4	12	0	0	0	0	0	0	1	3	0	.000	.000	7	0	0
Ken O'Dea	ph-c	3	5	1	1	0	0	1	2	1	0	0	.200	.800	5	0	0
Augie Galan	ph	2	2	0	0	0	0	0	0	0	1	0	.000	.000			
Tony Lazzeri	ph	2	2	0	0	0	0	0	0	0	1	0	.000	.000			
Bob Garbark	Did not play																
Jim Asbell	Did not play																
Dizzy Dean	p	2	3	0	2	0	0	0	0	0	0	0	.667	.667	0	2	0
Bill Lee	p	2	3	0	0	0	0	0	0	0	1	0	.000	.000	1	0	0
Clay Bryant	p	1	2	0	0	0	0	0	0	0	1	0	.000	.000	0	0	0
Larry French	p	3	0	0	0	0	0	0	0	0	0	0	—	—	0	2	0
Jack Russell	p	2	0	0	0	0	0	0	0	0	0	0	—	—	0	0	0
Tex Carleton	p	1	0	0	0	0	0	0	0	0	0	0	—	—	0	0	0
Vance Page	p	1	0	0	0	0	0	0	0	0	0	0	—	—	0	1	0
Charlie Root	p	1	0	0	0	0	0	0	0	0	0	0	—	—	0	0	0
team total		4	136	9	33	4	1	2	8	6	26	0	.243	.331	102	35	3

Double Plays—3
Left on Bases—26

REGULAR SEASON STATISTICS

	Main Pos	G	AB	R	H	2B	3B	HR	RBI	BB	SO	SB	BA	SA
Ripper Collins	1b	143	490	78	131	22	8	13	61	54	48	1	.267	.424
Billy Herman	2b	152	624	86	173	34	7	1	56	59	31	3	.277	.359
Billy Jurges	ss	137	465	53	114	18	3	1	47	58	53	3	.245	.303
Stan Hack	3b	152	609	109	195	34	11	4	67	94	39	16	.320	.432
Phil Cavarretta	of-1b	92	268	29	64	11	4	1	28	14	27	4	.239	.321
Joe Marty	of	76	235	32	57	8	3	7	35	18	26	0	.243	.391
Frank Demaree	of	129	476	63	130	15	7	8	62	45	34	1	.273	.384
Gabby Hartnett	c	88	299	40	82	19	1	10	59	48	17	1	.274	.445
Carl Reynolds	of	125	497	59	150	28	10	3	67	22	32	9	.302	.416
Ken O'Dea	c	86	247	22	65	12	1	3	33	12	18	1	.263	.356
Augie Galan	of	110	395	52	113	16	9	6	69	49	17	8	.286	.418
Tony Lazzeri	ss	54	120	21	32	5	0	5	23	22	30	0	.267	.433
Bob Garbark	c	23	54	2	14	0	0	0	5	1	0	0	.259	.259
Jim Asbell	of	17	33	6	6	2	0	0	3	3	9	0	.182	.242
Dizzy Dean	p	13	26	3	5	1	0	0	1	0	2	0	.192	.231
Bill Lee	p	44	101	10	20	3	1	0	13	4	20	1	.198	.248
Clay Bryant	p	50	106	16	24	2	1	3	15	2	10	0	.226	.349
Larry French	p	43	62	7	13	3	1	0	7	5	9	0	.210	.290
Jack Russell	p	42	32	4	7	1	1	0	3	2	15	0	.219	.313
Tex Carleton	p	33	65	9	15	4	1	0	7	3	10	1	.231	.323
Vance Page	p	13	26	2	4	0	0	0	1	0	7	0	.154	.154
Charlie Root	p	44	48	2	8	1	0	0	3	4	16	0	.167	.188
team total		154	5333	713	1435	242	70	65	673	522	476	49	.269	.377

Coaker Triplett (of), Steve Mesner (ss), Bobby Mattick (ss), Al Epperly (p), Kirby Higbe (p), Newt Kimball (p), Bob Logan (p) also play for the Cubs during the season.

PITCHING

NEW YORK YANKEES

WORLD SERIES STATISTICS

	G	GS	CG	IP	H	R	ER	BB	SO	W	L	SV	ERA
Red Ruffing	2	2	2	18	17	4	3	2	11	2	0	0	1.50
Monte Pearson	1	1	1	9	5	2	1	2	9	1	0	0	1.00
Lefty Gomez	1	1	0	7	9	3	3	1	5	1	0	0	3.86
Johnny Murphy	1	0	0	2	2	0	0	1	1	0	0	1	0.00
Spud Chandler	Did not play												
Bump Hadley	Did not play												
Steve Sundra	Did not play												
Wes Ferrell	Did not play												
Ivy Andrews	Did not play												
team total	4	4	3	36	33	9	7	6	26	4	0	1	1.75

REGULAR SEASON STATISTICS

		G	GS	CG	IP	H	ER	BB	SO	W	L	Pct	SV	ShO	ERA
Red Ruffing		31	31	22	247	246	91	82	127	21	7	.750	0	3	3.32
Monte Pearson		28	27	17	202	198	89	113	98	16	7	.696	0	1	3.97
Lefty Gomez		32	32	20	239	239	89	99	129	18	12	.600	0	3	3.35
Johnny Murphy		32	2	1	91	90	43	41	43	8	2	.800	11	0	4.25
Spud Chandler		23	23	14	172	183	77	47	36	14	5	.737	0	2	4.03
Bump Hadley		29	17	8	167	165	67	66	61	9	8	.529	1	1	3.61
Steve Sundra		25	8	3	94	107	50	43	33	6	4	.600	0	0	4.79
Wes Ferrell	a	5	4	1	30	52	27	18	7	2	2	.500	0	0	8.10
Ivy Andrews		19	1	1	48	51	16	17	13	1	3	.250	1	0	3.00
team total		157	157	91	1382	1436	601	566	567	99	53	.651	13	10	3.91

CHICAGO CUBS

WORLD SERIES STATISTICS

	G	GS	CG	IP	H	R	ER	BB	SO	W	L	SV	ERA
Bill Lee	2	2	0	11	15	6	3	1	8	0	2	0	2.45
Dizzy Dean	2	1	0	8⅓	8	6	6	1	2	0	1	0	6.48
Clay Bryant	1	1	0	5⅓	6	4	4	5	3	0	1	0	6.75
Larry French	3	0	0	3⅓	1	1	1	1	2	0	0	0	2.70
Charlie Root	1	0	0	3	3	1	1	0	1	0	0	0	3.00
Jack Russell	2	0	0	1⅔	1	0	0	1	0	0	0	0	0.00
Vance Page	1	0	0	1⅓	2	2	2	0	0	0	0	0	13.50
Tex Carleton	1	0	0	0	1	2	2	2	0	0	0	0	∞
team total	4	4	0	34	37	22	19	11	16	0	4	0	5.03

REGULAR SEASON STATISTICS

	G	GS	CG	IP	H	ER	BB	SO	W	L	Pct	SV	ShO	ERA
Bill Lee	44	37	19	291	281	86	74	121	22	9	.710	2	9	2.66
Dizzy Dean	13	10	3	75	63	15	8	22	7	1	.875	0	1	1.80
Clay Bryant	44	30	17	270	235	93	125	135	19	11	.633	2	3	3.10
Larry French	43	27	10	201	210	85	62	83	10	19	.345	0	3	3.81
Charlie Root	44	11	5	161	163	51	30	90	8	7	.533	8	0	2.85
Jack Russell	42	0	0	102	100	38	30	29	6	1	.857	3	0	3.35
Vance Page	13	9	3	68	90	29	13	18	5	4	.556	1	0	3.84
Tex Carleton	33	24	9	168	213	101	74	80	10	9	.526	0	0	5.41
team total	154	154	67	1397	1414	522	454	583	89	63	.586	18	16	3.37

Total Attendance—200,833 Average Attendance—50,208 Winning Player's Share—$5,783 Losing Player's Share—$4,675

1939
Fours Are Wild

The Yankee dynasty ruled baseball almost by habit, but disease bit into the cast of the game's leading club and subtracted two members. Owner Jacob Ruppert died in January of phlebitis, and Lou Gehrig came out of the lineup in May with amyotrophic lateral sclerosis gradually devastating his body. After playing in 2,130 straight games extending over 14 seasons, Gehrig sat himself down on May 2 because of his continued sloppy fielding at first base and inability to hit the ball with power. Suspicions that something was wrong with Gehrig were crushingly confirmed by the Mayo Clinic, which revealed on June 21 that the Iron Horse was suffering from a rare form of polio. Gehrig came into this Series in uniform as the nonplaying captain of the Yankees, with light-hitting Babe Dahlgren on first base. Even without Gehrig in the lineup, the Yanks had enough hitters to win the American League crown by 17 games over Boston. Joe DiMaggio, Joe Gordon, Bill Dickey, George Selkirk, Red Rolfe, and rookie Charlie Keller formed a fierce gauntlet for pitchers to run. Lefty Gomez was hampered by a sore arm, but Red Ruffing had his fourth 20-win season in a row and a platoon of competent hurlers filled in the other starting spots. Johnny Murphy kept the Yankees one-up on the baseball world by providing fine relief work in a specialist's role. The loss of Gehrig undoubtedly weakened the club, but the Yankees nevertheless won their fourth straight pennant. Less familiar with World Series pressure were the Cincinnati Reds, the winners of the National League pennant for the first time since 1919. General manager Warren Giles and manager Bill McKechnie had taken a club that finished last in 1937 to the top of the N.L. in two short years. The key blocks in the championship structure were right fielder Ival Goodman, first baseman Frank McCormick, catcher Ernie Lombardi, and pitchers Bucky Walters and Paul Derringer. The Reds rightfully exulted in their N.L. flag, but a World Series against the Yankees was a different sort of test.

The Series opener at Yankee Stadium pitted Red Ruffing against 25-game-winner Derringer, with a 1–1 tie holding into the bottom of the ninth. The Yanks unfurled their ninth-inning magic when Keller smashed a long triple to left-center that just eluded the lunge of Ival Goodman. With no one out, DiMaggio was passed and the infield drawn in, but Dickey hit the ball past second baseman Lonny Frey for a 2–1 victory. In the second game, Yankee right-hander Monte Pearson almost won immortality by spinning the first no-hitter in Series play. While his mates scored four runs off Walters, Pearson kept the Reds without a hit through seven innings. He retired Frank McCormick to start the top of the eighth, but then Ernie Lombardi smashed a clean single to spoil the masterpiece. Bill Werber hit a single in the ninth, but his two-hit performance earned Pearson a 4–0 victory and put the Yankees on the road to another Series sweep.

The role of Yankee batting power stood out more clearly in game three than in any other. The Reds collected a total of 10 hits, all singles, good for three runs; the Yanks managed only five hits off three Cincinnati pitchers, but they included two homers by Keller and one homer each by DiMaggio and Dickey. Outhit 10–5, the Yanks won the game 7–3. The Crosley Field crowd sensed the impending doom, and they saw the end come in game four in unusual fashion. The Yanks scored twice in the ninth to knot the score at 4–4, and Frankie Crosetti started the tenth with a walk and moved to second on Rolfe's sacrifice bunt. Shortstop Billy Myers then muffed a bouncer by Keller, and DiMaggio slashed a single to right. Crosetti scored, and when Goodman kicked the ball around in the outfield, Keller made a dash for home. Goodman's throw arrived simultaneously with Keller at the plate, and Keller accidently kicked catcher Lombardi in the groin in the collision. With Lombardi lying stunned behind the plate and the ball resting untouched a few feet away, DiMaggio raced home and capped the Series sweep with a single-turned-homer and a 7–4 triumph to give the Yankees an unprecedented four World Championships in four years.

Game 1 October 4 at New York

Cincinnati	Pos	AB	R	H	RBI	PO	A	E
Werber	3b	4	0	0	0	0	1	0
Frey	2b	4	0	0	0	1	2	0
Goodman	rf	2	1	0	0	4	0	0
McCormick	1b	3	0	2	1	9	1	0
Lombardi	c	3	0	0	0	7	0	0
Craft	cf	3	0	1	0	2	0	0
Berger	lf	3	0	0	0	1	0	0
Myers	ss	3	0	1	0	0	1	0
Derringer	p	3	0	0	0	1	0	0
Totals		28	1	4	1	*25	5	0

New York	Pos	AB	R	H	RBI	PO	A	E
Crosetti	ss	4	0	0	0	1	7	0
Rolfe	3b	4	0	0	0	1	2	0
Keller	rf	4	1	1	0	2	0	0
DiMaggio	cf	3	0	1	0	2	0	0
Dickey	c	4	0	1	1	4	0	0
Selkirk	lf	3	0	0	0	2	0	0
Gordon	2b	3	1	1	0	2	4	0
Dahlgren	1b	3	0	1	1	13	0	0
Ruffing	p	3	0	1	0	0	3	0
Totals		31	2	6	2	27	16	0

Cin.   000 100 000
N.Y.   000 010 001

* One out when winning run was scored.

Pitching	IP	H	R	ER	BB	SO
New York						
Ruffing (W)	9	4	1	1	1	4
Cincinnati						
Derringer (L)	8⅓	6	2	2	1	7

Double—Dahlgren. Triple—Keller.
Stolen Base—Goodman.
Double Plays—Rolfe to Gordon to Dahlgren, Ruffing to Crosetti to Gordon to Dahlgren, Gordon to Crosetti to Dahlgren.
Left on Bases—Cincinnati 1, New York 5.
Umpires—McGowan (A), Reardon (N), Summers (A), Pinelli (N). Attendance—58,541.
Time of Game—1:33.

1st Inning
Cincinnati
1 Werber flied to left.
2 Frey flied to short-center.
3 Goodman fanned.
New York
1 Crosetti popped to Goodman, in close.
2 Rolfe rolled out to second.
3 Keller flied to left.

2nd Inning
Cincinnati
McCormick singled over Crosetti's head.
1,2 Lombardi rolled into a double play, Rolfe to Gordon to Dahlgren.
3 Craft fanned.
New York
1 DiMaggio flew out to right.
2 Dickey took a called third strike.
3 Selkirk struck out.

3rd Inning
Cincinnati
1 Berger struck out.
Myers singled past second.
2,3 Derringer's grounder was deflected by Ruffing to Crosetti who threw to Gordon to force Myers and fired to Dahlgren to double up Derringer.
New York
1 Gordon fouled to McCormick.
2 Dahlgren rolled easily to second. Ruffing singled to left to be the Yankees first base runner.
3 Crosetti missed a third strike.

4th Inning
Cincinnati
1 Werber grounded to short.
2 Frey flied to deep right.
Goodman walked.
Goodman stole second.
McCormick singled past third scoring Goodman.
3 Lombardi grounded back to the pitcher.
New York
1 Rolfe flew out to right.
2 Keller took a called third strike. DiMaggio singled by third, Werber let it go thinking it would turn foul.
3 Dickey grounded to first, McCormick making a brilliant stop.

5th Inning
Cincinnati
Craft singled on a slow roller between Rolfe and Crosetti
1 Berger struck out.
2,3 Myers bounced into a double play, Gordon to Crosetti to Dahlgren.
New York
1 Selkirk grounded to first. Gordon singled past third. Dahlgren doubled down the left field line, Gordon scored when Berger threw to second.
2 Ruffing fouled to McCormick.
3 Crosetti flied to center.

6th Inning
Cincinnati
1 Derringer grounded to short.
2 Werber flied to left.
3 Frey flied to center.
New York
1 Rolfe flied to center.
2 Keller grounded out, McCormick to Derringer.
3 DiMaggio rolled out to short.

7th Inning
Cincinnati
1 Goodman grounded to third.
2 McCormick grounded to short.
3 Lombardi fouled to Dahlgren.
New York
1 Dickey popped to second.
2 Selkirk lined to short right.
3 Gordon fanned.

8th Inning
Cincinnati
1 Craft popped to third.
2 Berger grounded to second.
3 Myers grounded to short.
New York
1 Dahlgren struck out.
2 Ruffing struck out.
3 Crosetti grounded to third.

9th Inning
Cincinnati
1 Derringer tapped back to the pitcher.
2 Werber grounded to short.
3 Frey flew out to left.
New York
1 Rolfe grounded to first.
Keller tripled to the right-center field bleachers.
DiMaggio intentionally walked.
Dickey singled over second, scoring Keller with the winning run.

Game 2 October 5 at New York

Cincinnati	Pos	AB	R	H	RBI	PO	A	E
Werber	3b	3	0	1	0	0	1	0
Frey	2b	4	0	0	0	2	2	0
Goodman	rf	3	0	0	0	1	0	0
McCormick	1b	3	0	0	0	7	0	0
Lombardi	c	3	0	1	0	5	1	0
a Bordagaray		0	0	0	0	0	0	0
Hershberger	c	0	0	0	0	0	0	0
Craft	cf	3	0	0	0	3	1	0
Berger	lf	3	0	0	0	1	0	0
Myers	ss	3	0	0	0	5	3	0
Walters	p	2	0	0	0	0	3	0
b Gamble		1	0	0	0	0	0	0
Totals		28	0	2	0	24	11	0

a Ran for Lombardi in 8th.
b Fanned for Walters in 9th.

Doubles—Dahlgren, Keller. Home Run—Dahlgren. Sacrifice Hit—Pearson. Double Plays—Dickey to Crosetti, Walters to Myers to McCormick. Left on Bases—Cincinnati 2, New York 3. Umpires—Reardon, Summers, Pinelli, McGowan. Attendance—59,791. Time of Game—1:27.

Cin.	000 000 000
N.Y.	003 100 00x

New York	Pos	AB	R	H	RBI	PO	A	E
Crosetti	ss	4	0	1	1	1	2	0
Rolfe	3b	4	1	1	0	1	1	0
Keller	rf	4	1	2	1	0	0	0
DiMaggio	cf	4	0	1	0	4	0	0
Dickey	c	3	0	1	1	8	1	0
Selkirk	lf	3	0	1	0	3	0	0
Gordon	2b	3	0	0	0	2	0	0
Dahlgren	1b	3	2	2	1	8	0	0
Pearson	p	2	0	0	0	0	5	0
Totals		30	4	9	4	27	9	0

Pitching	IP	H	R	ER	BB	SO
Cincinnati						
Walters (L)	8	9	4	4	0	5
New York						
Pearson (W)	9	2	0	0	1	8

1st Inning
Cincinnati
1 Werber popped to second.
2 Frey flied to center.
3 Goodman foul popped to Rolfe.
New York
Crosetti singled over Myer's head.
1 Rolfe forced Crosetti at second, Walters to Myers.
2 Keller forced Rolfe at second, Myers to Frey.
3 DiMaggio flied out very deep to Berger in left-center.

2nd Inning
Cincinnati
1 McCormick flied to center.
2 Lombardi flied to Selkirk in center.
3 Craft struck out.
New York
1 Dickey struck out.
Selkirk blooped a single into short
2 center but was out Craft to Myers trying to get to second.
3 Gordon flied to center.

3rd Inning
Cincinnati
1 Berger lined to deep left.
2 Myers fanned.
3 Walters grounded to Rolfe.
New York
Dahlgren hit a ground rule double into the left field stands.
1 Pearson sacrificed Dahlgren to third, Walters to Frey.
2 Crosetti grounded to third, scoring Dahlgren.
Rolfe singled to right.
Keller doubled on a line drive down the left field line, scoring Rolfe.
DiMaggio beat out a slow roller down the third base line, Keller holding.
Dickey lined a single to right, scoring Keller and moving DiMaggio to third.
3 Selkirk grounded to second.

4th Inning
Cincinnati
Werber walked.
1,2 Frey struck out and Werber was doubled up trying to steal second Dickey to Crosetti.
3 Goodman fanned.
New York
1 Gordon grounded to third.
Dahlgren homered into the lower left field stands.
2 Pearson struck out.
3 Crosetti tapped in front of the plate and was thrown out by Lombardi.

5th Inning
Cincinnati
1 McCormick fanned.
2 Lombardi rolled out to the pitcher.
3 Craft struck out.
New York
1 Rolfe grounded to second.
Keller singled to left.
2,3 DiMaggio grounded into a double play, Walters to Myers to McCormick.

6th Inning
Cincinnati
1 Berger tapped back to the pitcher.
2 Myers grounded to short.
3 Walters tapped back to the pitcher.
New York
1 Dickey lined to the right field stands.
2 Selkirk took a called third strike.
3 Gordon struck out.

7th Inning
Cincinnati
1 Werber popped to short center.
2 Frey popped to center.
3 Goodman flied to DiMaggio with a nice running catch.
New York
1 Dahlgren struck out.
2 Pearson popped to short.
3 Crosetti popped to Myers in short-left.

8th Inning
Cincinnati
1 McCormick lined to deep left.
Lombardi broke up **Pearson's no-hitter** with a single over second.
Bordagaray ran for Lombardi.
2 Craft struck out (third time).
3 Berger grounded out, Pearson to Dahlgren on a tap down the first base line.
New York
For Cincinnati—Hershberger catching.
1 Rolfe flied to center.
2 Keller flied to deep center.
3 DiMaggio rolled out to short.

9th Inning
Cincinnati
1 Myers tapped back to the pitcher.
2 Gamble, pinch hitting for Walters, fanned.
Werber singled to left for the Reds' second hit.
3 Frey forced Werber at second, Crosetti to Gordon.

Game 3 October 7 at Cincinnati

New York	Pos	AB	R	H	RBI	PO	A	E
Crosetti	ss	4	1	0	0	2	2	0
Rolfe	3b	4	1	1	0	0	2	0
Keller	rf	3	2	2	4	2	0	0
DiMaggio	cf	4	1	1	2	2	0	0
Dickey	c	3	1	1	1	5	1	0
Selkirk	lf	2	0	0	0	3	0	0
Gordon	2b	4	0	0	0	3	5	0
Dahlgren	1b	4	0	0	0	9	2	0
Gomez	p	1	0	0	0	0	0	0
Hadley	p	3	0	0	0	1	1	1
Totals		32	7	5	7	27	13	1

Pitching	IP	H	R	ER	BB	SO
New York						
Gomez	1	3	1	1	0	1
Hadley (W)	8	7	2	2	3	2
Cincinnati						
Thompson (L)	4⅓	5	7	7	4	3
Grissom	1⅓	0	0	0	1	0
Moore	3	0	0	0	0	2

N.Y.	202 030 000
Cin.	120 000 000

Cincinnati	Pos	AB	R	H	RBI	PO	A	E
Werber	3b	4	1	1	1	3	2	0
Frey	2b	4	0	0	0	2	2	0
Goodman	rf	5	1	3	1	2	0	0
McCormick	1b	5	0	2	0	9	0	0
Lombardi	c	3	0	1	1	5	0	0
b Bordagaray		0	0	0	0	0	0	0
Hershberger	c	1	0	0	0	0	1	0
Craft	cf	4	0	0	0	2	0	0
Berger	lf	4	0	0	0	2	0	0
Myers	ss	3	1	2	0	1	4	0
Thompson	p	1	0	1	0	0	0	0
Grissom	p	0	0	0	0	0	0	0
a Bongiovanni		1	0	0	0	0	0	0
Moore	p	1	0	0	0	0	2	0
Totals		36	3	10	3	27	10	0

a Grounded out for Grissom in 6th.
b Ran for Lombardi in 7th.

Home Runs—Dickey, DiMaggio, Keller 2. Sacrifice Hit—Thompson. Double Play—Rolfe to Gordon to Dahlgren. Hit by Pitcher—Lombardi (by Hadley). Wild Pitch—Thompson. Left on Bases—New York 3, Cincinnati 11. Umpires—Summers, Pinelli, McGowan, Reardon. Attendance—32,723. Time of Game—2:01.

1st Inning
New York
Crosetti walked.
1 Rolfe grounded to first moving Crosetti to second.
Keller hit a two-run homer into the right field stands at the 375 foot mark.
2 DiMaggio struck out.
Dickey got all the way to third when he walked on a wild pitch with Lombardi having trouble retrieving the pitch.
3 Selkirk was out on a great pick-up and throw by Werber on his bunt.
Cincinnati
1 Werber grounded to second with Dahlgren making a great pick up of Gordon's throw which was in the dirt.
2 Frey flied to center.
Goodman singled on a high bounder.
McCormick hit a Texas League single into right, moving Goodman to third.
Lombardi singled over second, scoring Goodman with McCormick stopping at second.
3 Craft struck out.

2nd Inning
New York
1 Gordon fouled to Lombardi.
2 Dahlgren popped to second.
3 Gomez fanned.
Cincinnati
For New York—Hadley pitching.
1 Berger fanned.
Myers singled past short.
Thompson singled on a Texas Leaguer just beyond Crosetti's reach, Myers stopping at second.
Werber singled to center, scoring Myers and advancing Thompson to third.
2 Frey hit an easy grounder to Dahlgren who threw to Dickey getting Thompson at the plate, Werber to second.
Goodman singled to right, scoring Werber.
3 McCormick popped to Gordon in short right.

3rd Inning
New York
1 Crosetti fouled to Werber.
2 Rolfe fouled to right where Goodman made a sensational catch reaching into the stands for the ball.
Keller walked.
DiMaggio hit a two-run homer over the fence in dead center.
3 Dickey rolled out to second.
Cincinnati
1 Lombardi flied to Selkirk in center.
2 Craft flied to center.
3 Berger popped to short.

4th Inning
New York
Selkirk walked.
1 Gordon forced Selkirk at second, Myers to Frey.
2 Dahlgren fanned.
3 Hadley forced Gordon at second, Frey unassisted.
Cincinnati
Myers singled over second.
1 Thompson sacrificed Myers to second, Dickey to Dahlgren.
2 Werber grounded out, Dahlgren to Hadley.
3 Frey grounded to second.

5th Inning
New York
1 Crosetti grounded to short.
Rolfe singled between first and second.
Keller hit his second two-run homer to the exact spot of his first homer.
2 DiMaggio popped to third.
Dickey homered deep into the right field stands.
For Cincinnati—Grissom pitching.
Selkirk walked.
3 Gordon flied to left in front of the scoreboard.
Cincinnati
1 Goodman popped to short.
2 McCormick fouled to Dickey in front of the Yankee dugout.
Lombardi was hit by a pitch.
3 Craft flied to left.

6th Inning
New York
1 Dahlgren flied to very deep center.
2 Hadley grounded to short.
3 Crosetti grounded to Werber who made a great stop.
Cincinnati
1 Berger fanned.
Myers walked.
2 Bongiovanni, pinch-hitting for Grissom, grounded back to Hadley, who threw wide to first but Dahlgren made a sensational one-handed stab for the out.
Werber walked.
3 Frey grounded to second.

7th Inning
New York
For Cincinnati—Moore pitching.
1 Rolfe grounded to short.
2 Keller struck out swinging.
3 DiMaggio tapped back to the mound.
Cincinnati
1 Goodman flied to Selkirk in center.
McCormick singled between short and third.
Lombardi got to first on Hadley's throwing error to Gordon when the ball went into center, McCormick going to third.
Bordagaray ran for Lombardi.
2,3 Craft hit into a double play, Rolfe to Gordon to Dahlgren.

8th Inning
New York
For Cincinnati—Hershberger catching.
1 Dickey flied deep to center.
2 Selkirk flied to left.
3 Gordon popped to third.
Cincinnati
1 Berger grounded to short.
2 Myers grounded to short.
3 Moore grounded to third.

9th Inning
New York
1 Dahlgren flied to right.
2 Hadley tapped back to the mound.
3 Crosetti fanned.
Cincinnati
1 Werber grounded to second.
Frey walked.
Goodman singled to right where Keller just missed a shoe-string catch at the foul line, Frey only to second fearing the possible catch.
2 McCormick lined to right.
3 Hershberger flied out to right.

Game 4 October 8 at Cincinnati

N.Y.	000	000	202	3
Cin.	000	000	310	0

New York	Pos	AB	R	H	RBI	PO	A	E
Crosetti	ss	4	1	0	0	2	3	0
Rolfe	3b	4	0	0	0	1	3	1
Keller	rf	5	3	2	1	2	0	0
DiMaggio	cf	5	2	2	1	3	0	0
Dickey	c	5	1	1	1	10	0	0
Selkirk	lf	4	0	1	0	1	0	0
Gordon	2b	4	0	1	0	3	0	0
Dahlgren	1b	4	0	0	0	11	0	0
Hildebrand	p	1	0	0	0	0	0	0
Sundra	p	0	0	0	0	0	0	0
Murphy	p	2	0	0	0	0	3	0
Totals		38	7	7	4	30	12	1

Pitching	IP	H	R	ER	BB	SO
New York						
Hildebrand	4	2	0	0	0	3
Sundra	2⅔	4	3	0	1	2
Murphy (W)	3⅓	5	1	1	0	2
Cincinnati						
Derringer	7	3	2	2	2	2
Walters (L)	3	4	5	2	1	1

Cincinnati	Pos	AB	R	H	RBI	PO	A	E
Werber	3b	5	0	2	1	0	1	0
Frey	2b	5	0	0	0	3	4	0
Goodman	rf	5	1	2	0	3	2	1
McCormick	1b	4	1	2	0	7	2	0
Lombardi	c	5	0	1	1	4	0	1
Craft	cf	1	0	0	0	0	0	0
Simmons	lf	4	1	1	0	3	0	0
Berger	lf-cf	5	0	0	1	4	0	0
Myers	ss	3	1	1	0	5	1	2
Derringer	p	2	0	1	0	1	0	0
a Hershberger		1	0	1	1	0	0	0
Walters	p	1	0	0	0	0	0	0
Totals		41	4	11	4	30	10	4

a Singled for Derringer in 7th.

Doubles—Goodman, McCormick, Selkirk, Simmons. Triple—Myers. Home Runs—Dickey, Keller. Sacrifice Hits—McCormick, Rolfe. Left on Bases—New York 5, Cincinnati 9. Umpires—Pinelli, McGowan, Reardon, Summers. Attendance—32,794. Time of Game—2:04.

1st Inning
New York
1 Crosetti flied to right.
2 Rolfe fouled to Lombardi in front of the Reds' dugout.
3 Keller grounded to short.
Cincinnati
1 Werber grounded to short.
2 Frey grounded to second.
3 Goodman flied to left.

2nd Inning
New York
1 DiMaggio flied to right.
2 Dickey grounded out, McCormick to Derringer.
3 Selkirk grounded to second.
Cincinnati
McCormick doubled to right-center (The Reds' first extra-base hit of the Series).
1 Lombardi flied deep to center, McCormick going to third after the catch.
2 Craft fanned.
3 Berger grounded to second.

3rd Inning
New York
1 Gordon flied to deep left.
2 Dahlgren struck out.
3 Hildebrand struck out.
Cincinnati
1 Myers took a called third strike. Derringer singled to left.
2 Werber flied to center.
3 Frey fanned.

4th Inning
New York
1 Crosetti lined to short.
2 Rolfe grounded to first.
3 Keller fouled to Lombardi.
Cincinnati
1 Goodman grounded to second.
2 McCormick grounded to short.
3 Lombardi grounded to third.

5th Inning
New York
For Cincinnati—Berger moves to center, Simmonts to left (batting 6th).
1 DiMaggio grounded to third.
2 Dickey grounded to second.
Selkirk doubled off the right field fence for the Yanks' first hit.
3 Gordon flied deep to center.
Cincinnati
For New York—Sundra pitching.
1 Simmons flied to right.
2 Berger grounded to Rolfe who threw high to Dahlgren who made a jumping catch for the out.
Myers tripled down the right field line.
3 Derringer fouled to Dickey.

6th Inning
New York
1 Dahlgren flied to Frey in short right. Sundra walked.
Crosetti sent a fly to Goodman who
2 dropped it but recovered to force Sundra at second (no error).
3 Rolfe lined to second.
Cincinnati
1 Werber fouled to Dickey
2 Frey called out on strikes.
3 Goodman grounded to third.

7th Inning
New York
Keller homered into the right field bleachers.
1 DiMaggio flied to Simmons at the fence. Dickey homered into the right-center stands.
Selkirk walked.
2 Gordon fouled to Simmons in front of the stands (good catch by Simmons).
3 Dahlgren forced Selkirk at second, Frey to Myers.
Cincinnati
McCormick got safely to first on Rolfe's fumble.
1 Lombardi fanned.
Simmons doubled to the center field scoreboard, advancing McCormick to third.
2 Berger grounded to second, scoring McCormick with Simmons holding second.
Myers walked.
Hershberger, pinch hitting for Derringer, singled on a blooper to short left, scoring Simmons with Myers racing to third.
Werber singled to right scoring Myers, Hershberger stopping at second.
For New York—Murphy pitching.
3 Frey struck out for the third time.

8th Inning
New York
For Cincinnati—Walters pitching.
1 Murphy popped to second.
2 Crosetti flied to center.
3 Rolfe flied to right.
Cincinnati
Goodman doubled to left-center.
1 McCormick sacrificed Goodman to third, Murphy to Dahlgren.
Lombardi singled to center, scoring Goodman.
2 Simmons forced Lombardi at second, Murphy to Crosetti.
3 Berger grounded back to the pitcher.

9th Inning
New York
Keller singled through the box.
DiMaggio singled to left, moving Keller to third.
Dickey hit a perfect double play ball to Frey but Myers dropped the ball with Keller scoring and DiMaggio safe at second and Dickey safe at first.
1 Selkirk flied to deep right, DiMaggio going to third after the catch.
Gordon grounded to Werber who threw to the plate but DiMaggio beat it (Gordon credited with a hit on the play).
2 Dahlgren popped to first.
3 Murphy fanned.
Cincinnati
1 Myers fanned.
2 Walters flied deep to center.
Werber singled over short.
3 Frey fouled to Rolfe.

10th Inning
New York
Crosetti walked.
1 Rolfe sacrificed Crosetti to second, McCormick unassisted.
Keller was safe at first on Myers' fumble of his grounder, Crosetti going to third.
DiMaggio singled to right scoring Crosetti and when Goodman bobbled the ball Keller also scored, Lombardi dropped Goodman's throw to the plate and DiMaggio also scored (Goodman and Lombardi both got errors on the play).
2 Dickey flied deep to left.
3 Selkirk flied to center.
Cincinnati
Goodman singled to center.
McCormick singled off Crosetti's glove, moving Goodman to second.
1 Lombardi fouled to Dickey.
2 Simmons lined to right.
3 Berger lined to short, **the Yankees winning a fourth consecutive Series.**

1939 WORLD SERIES COMPOSITE BOX

	Wins	Composite Line Score
New York Yankees (A.L.)	4	2 0 5 1 4 0 2 0 3 3 – 20
Cincinnati Reds (N.L.)	0	1 2 0 1 0 0 3 1 0 0 – 8

Manager	Regular Season W	L	Pct.	G. Ahead
Joe McCarthy	106	45	.702	17
Bill McKechnie	97	57	.630	4.5

BATTING AND FIELDING

	World Series Statistics Pos	G	AB	R	H	2B	3B	HR	RBI	BB	SO	SB	BA	SA	PO	A	E		Regular Season Statistics Main Pos	G	AB	R	H	2B	3B	HR	RBI	BB	SO	SB	BA	SA
NEW YORK YANKEES																																
Babe Dahlgren	1b	4	14	2	3	**2**	0	1	2	0	4	0	.214	.571	**41**	2	0		1b	144	531	71	125	18	6	15	89	57	54	2	.235	.377
Joe Gordon	2b	4	14	1	2	0	0	0	1	0	2	0	.143	.143	7	12	0		2b	151	567	92	161	32	5	28	111	75	57	11	.284	.506
Frankie Crosetti	ss	4	16	2	1	0	0	0	1	2	2	0	.063	.063	6	**14**	0		ss	152	**656**	109	153	25	5	10	56	65	81	11	.233	.332
Red Rolfe	3b	4	16	2	2	0	0	0	0	0	0	0	.125	.125	3	8	1		3b	152	648	**139**	**213**	**46**	10	14	80	81	41	7	.329	.495
Charlie Keller	rf	4	16	**8**	**7**	1	**1**	**3**	**6**	1	2	0	**.438**	**1.188**	6	0	0		of	111	398	87	133	21	6	11	83	81	49	6	.334	.500
Joe DiMaggio	cf	4	16	3	5	0	0	1	3	1	1	0	.313	.500	11	0	0		of	120	462	108	176	32	6	30	126	52	20	3	**.381**	.671
George Selkirk	lf	4	12	0	2	1	0	0	0	**3**	2	0	.167	.250	9	0	0		of	128	418	103	128	17	4	21	101	103	49	12	.306	.517
Bill Dickey	c	4	15	2	4	0	0	2	5	1	2	0	.267	.667	27	2	0		c	128	480	98	145	23	3	24	105	77	37	5	.302	.513
Tommy Henrich		Did not play																	of	99	347	64	96	18	4	9	57	51	23	7	.217	.429
Buddy Rosar		Did not play																	c	43	105	18	29	5	1	0	12	13	10	4	.276	.343
Jake Powell		Did not play																	of	31	86	12	21	4	1	1	9	3	8	1	.244	.349
Lou Gehrig		Did not play—Illness																	1b	8	28	2	4	0	0	0	1	5	1	0	.143	.143
Bill Knickerbocker		Did not play																	2b-ss	6	13	2	2	1	0	0	1	0	0	0	.154	.231
Art Jorgens		Did not play																	c	3	0	1	0	0	0	0	0	0	0	0	.000	.000
Red Ruffing	p	1	3	0	1	0	0	0	0	0	1	0	.333	.333	0	3	0		p-ph	44	114	12	35	1	0	1	20	7	18	1	.307	.342
Bump Hadley	p	1	3	0	0	0	0	0	0	0	0	0	.000	.000	1	1	1		p	26	62	3	11	2	0	0	3	4	12	1	.177	.210
Johnny Murphy	p	1	2	0	0	0	0	0	0	0	1	0	.000	.000	0	3	0		p	38	11	1	2	0	0	0	1	3	1	0	.182	.182
Monte Pearson	p	1	2	0	0	0	0	0	0	0	1	0	.000	.000	0	5	0		p	22	53	9	17	3	1	0	7	5	6	0	.321	.415
Lefty Gomez	p	1	1	0	0	0	0	0	0	0	1	0	.000	.000	0	0	0		p	26	73	3	11	2	0	0	4	5	22	0	.151	.178
Oral Hildebrand	p	1	1	0	0	0	0	0	0	0	1	0	.000	.000	0	0	0		p	21	44	5	8	1	0	0	5	1	5	0	.182	.205
Steve Sundra	p	1	0	0	0	0	0	0	0	1	0	0	—	—	0	0	0		p	24	49	7	13	5	0	0	6	3	15	0	.265	.367
Atley Donald		Did not play																	p	24	60	7	15	1	1	0	7	4	15	0	.250	.300
Marius Russo		Did not play																	p	21	41	4	10	0	1	0	9	2	8	0	.244	.293
Spud Chandler		Did not play																	p	11	5	2	2	1	0	0	1	1	1	0	.400	.600
team total		4	131	20	27	4	1	7	18	9	20	0	.206	.412	111	50	2			152	5300	**967**	1521	259	55	**166**	**903**	**701**	543	72	.287	**.451**

Double Plays—5
Left on Bases—16

Joe Gallagher (of), Wes Ferrell (p), and Marv Breuer (p) also played for the Yankees during the Season.

	World Series Statistics Pos	G	AB	R	H	2B	3B	HR	RBI	BB	SO	SB	BA	SA	PO	A	E		Regular Season Statistics Main Pos	G	AB	R	H	2B	3B	HR	RBI	BB	SO	SB	BA	SA
CINCINNATI REDS																																
Frank McCormick	1b	4	15	1	6	1	0	0	1	0	1	0	.400	.467	32	2	0		1b	156	630	99	**209**	41	4	18	**128**	40	16	1	.332	.495
Lonny Frey	2b	4	**17**	0	0	0	0	0	0	1	4	0	.000	.000	8	10	0		2b	125	484	95	141	27	9	11	55	72	46	5	.291	.452
Billy Myers	ss	4	12	2	4	0	**1**	0	0	2	3	0	.333	.500	10	9	**2**		ss	151	509	79	143	18	6	9	56	71	90	4	.281	.393
Bill Werber	3b	4	16	1	4	0	0	0	2	2	0	0	.250	.250	3	5	0		3b	147	599	**115**	173	35	5	5	57	91	46	15	.289	.389
Ival Goodman	rf	4	15	3	5	1	0	0	1	1	2	**1**	.333	.400	10	1	1		of	124	470	85	152	37	16	7	84	54	32	2	.323	.515
Harry Craft	cf	4	11	0	1	0	0	0	0	0	**6**	0	.091	.091	7	1	0		of	134	502	58	129	20	7	13	67	27	54	5	.257	.402
Wally Berger	lf-cf	4	15	0	0	0	0	0	1	0	4	0	.000	.000	8	0	0		of	97	329	36	85	15	1	14	44	36	63	1	.258	.438
Ernie Lombardi	c	4	14	0	3	0	0	0	2	0	1	0	.214	.214	22	1	1		c	130	450	43	129	26	2	20	85	35	19	0	.287	.487
Al Simmons	lf	1	4	1	1	1	0	0	0	0	0	0	.250	.500	3	0	0	a	of	9	21	0	3	0	0	0	1	2	3	0	.143	.143
Willard Hershberger	c-ph	3	2	0	1	0	0	0	1	0	0	0	.500	.500	1	0	0		c	63	174	23	60	9	2	0	32	9	4	1	.345	.420
Frenchy Bordagaray	pr	2	0	0	0	0	0	0	0	0	0	0	—	—					of	63	122	19	24	5	1	0	12	9	10	3	.197	.254
Nino Bongiovanni	ph	1	1	0	0	0	0	0	0	0	0	0	.000	.000					of	66	159	17	41	6	0	0	16	9	8	0	.258	.296
Lee Gamble	ph	1	1	0	0	0	0	0	0	0	1	0	.000	.000					of	72	221	24	59	7	2	0	14	9	14	5	.267	.317
Eddie Joost		Did not play																	2b	42	143	23	36	6	3	0	14	12	15	1	.252	.336
Lew Riggs		Did not play																	3b	22	38	5	6	1	0	0	1	5	4	1	.158	.184
Les Scarsella		Did not play																	ph	16	14	0	2	0	0	0	2	0	2	0	.143	.143
Paul Derringer	p	2	5	0	1	0	0	0	0	0	0	0	.200	.200	2	0	0		p	38	110	10	23	3	0	0	16	1	11	0	.209	.236
Bucky Walters	p	2	3	0	0	0	0	0	0	0	0	0	.000	.000	0	3	0		p	40	120	16	39	8	1	1	16	5	12	1	.325	.433
Junior Thompson	p	1	1	0	1	0	0	0	0	0	0	0	1.000	1.000	0	0	0		p	42	48	3	11	1	0	0	1	0	11	0	.229	.250
Whitey Moore	p	1	1	0	0	0	0	0	0	0	0	0	.000	.000	0	2	0		p	42	61	4	6	1	0	0	2	2	13	0	.098	.115
Lee Grissom	p	1	0	0	0	0	0	0	0	0	0	0	—	—	0	0	0		p	33	47	5	4	0	1	0	1	2	18	0	.085	.128
Johnny Vander Meer		Did not play																	p	30	36	1	4	1	0	0	1	3	10	0	.111	.139
Johnny Niggerling		Did not play																	p	10	13	3	2	0	0	0	1	1	5	0	.154	.154
Milt Shoffner		Did not play																b	p	10	11	1	1	0	0	0	0	1	8	0	.091	.091
Hank Johnson		Did not play																	p	20	5	0	2	0	0	0	0	0	2	0	.400	.400
team totals		4	133	8	27	3	1	0	8	6	22	1	.203	.241	106	34	4			156	5378	767	1493	269	60	98	714	500	538	46	.278	.405

Double Plays—1
Left on Bases—23

a—from Boston (N)
b—from Boston (N)

Vince DiMaggio (of), Dick West (of), Bud Hafey (of), Jimmie Wilson (c), Milt Galatzer (1b), Nolen Richardson (ss), Peaches Davis (p), Red Barrett (p), Art Jacobs (p), Wes Livengood (p), Pete Naktenis (p), Elmer Riddle (p), and Jim Weaver (p) also played for the Reds during the season.

PITCHING

	World Series Statistics G	GS	CG	IP	H	R	ER	BB	SO	W	L	SV	ERA		Regular Season Statistics G	GS	CG	IP	H	ER	BB	SO	W	L	Pct	SV	ShO	ERA
NEW YORK YANKEES																												
Monte Pearson	1	1	**1**	9	2	0	0	1	8	**1**	0	0	**0.00**		22	20	8	146	151	73	70	76	12	5	.706	0	0	4.50
Red Ruffing	1	1	**1**	9	4	1	1	1	4	**1**	0	0	1.00		28	28	22	233	211	76	75	95	21	7	.750	0	**4**	2.94
Bump Hodley	1	0	0	8	7	2	2	3	2	**1**	0	0	2.25		26	18	7	154	132	51	85	65	12	6	.667	2	1	2.98
Oral Hildebrand	1	1	0	4	2	0	0	0	3	0	0	0	0.00		21	15	7	127	102	43	41	50	10	4	.714	2	1	3.05
Johnny Murphy	1	0	0	3⅓	5	1	1	0	2	**1**	0	0	2.70		38	0	0	61	57	30	28	30	3	6	.333	**19**	0	4.43
Steve Sundra	1	0	0	2⅔	4	3	0	1	2	0	0	0	0.00		24	11	8	121	110	37	56	27	11	1	.917	0	1	2.75
Lefty Gomez	1	1	0	1	3	1	1	0	1	0	0	0	9.00		26	26	14	198	173	75	84	102	12	8	.600	0	2	3.41
Atley Donald	Did not play														24	20	11	153	144	63	60	55	13	3	.813	1	1	3.71
Marius Russo	Did not play														21	11	9	116	86	31	41	55	8	3	.727	2	2	2.41
Spud Chandler	Did not play														11	0	0	19	26	6	9	4	3	0	1.000	0	0	2.84
team total	4	4	2	37	27	8	5	6	22	4	0	0	1.22		152	152	**87**	1349	1208	**496**	567	565	**106**	45	**.702**	**26**	**12**	**3.31**
CINCINNATI REDS																												
Paul Derringer	**2**	**2**	**1**	**15⅓**	9	4	4	3	**9**	0	1	0	2.35		38	35	28	301	**321**	98	35	128	25	7	**.781**	0	**5**	2.93
Bucky Walters	**2**	1	**1**	11	**13**	**9**	6	1	6	0	**2**	0	4.91		39	**36**	**31**	**319**	250	81	109	**137**	**27**	11	.711	0	2	**2.29**
Junior Thompson	1	1	0	4⅔	5	7	**7**	**4**	3	0	1	0	13.50		42	11	5	152	130	43	55	87	13	5	.722	2	3	2.55
Whitey Moore	1	0	0	3	0	0	0	0	2	0	0	0	0.00		42	24	9	188	177	72	95	81	13	12	.520	3	2	3.45
Lee Grissom	1	0	0	1⅓	0	0	0	1	0	0	0	0	0.00		33	21	3	154	145	70	56	53	9	7	.563	0	0	4.09
Johnny Vander Meer	Did not play														30	21	8	129	128	67	95	102	5	9	.357	0	0	4.67
Johnny Niggerling	Did not play														10	5	2	40	51	26	13	20	2	1	.667	0	1	5.85
Milt Shoffner	Did not play													b	10	3	0	38	43	14	11	6	2	2	.500	0	0	3.32
Hank Johnson	Did not play														20	0	0	31	30	7	13	10	0	3	.000	1	0	2.03
team total	4	4	2	35⅓	27	20	17	9	20	0	4	0	4.33		156	156	**86**	1404	1340	510	499	**637**	**97**	57	**.630**	9	13	**3.27**

Total Attendance—183,849 Average Attendance—45,962 Winning Player's Share—$5,542 Losing Player's Shares—$4,193

1940
Encore Amongst the Sorrow

Jimmie Wilson had finished a respectable career as a catcher with the Phillies and Cardinals, hitting .284 in over 15 seasons and playing in three World Series while with St. Louis. Now the forty-year-old ex-receiver had a job coaching the National League-champion Cincinnati Reds, but fate removed Wilson from his retirement and set him up in the spotlight as he never had been in his peak years. The first step was a tragic one, when reserve catcher Willard Hershberger killed himself on August 2 after the Reds lost a tough game in Boston. Shook but undaunted by the tragedy, the Reds kept up the hot pace that had put them in front of the N.L. since early July. But in mid-September, Ernie Lombardi severely sprained an ankle, taking one of the team's best bats and its only experienced catcher out of action. With a limping Lombardi available only for spot duty, manager Bill McKechnie activated Wilson, who handled the job smoothly for the final weeks of the regular season.

Their Series opponent amazingly was not the New York Yankees, who dropped off to third place after four straight American League and Series championships, but instead the Detroit Tigers. Manager Del Baker souped up the Tiger offense this year by shifting first baseman Hank Greenberg to left field and inserting backup catcher Rudy York into the lineup at first base. The defensive problems caused by the move paled in the light of Greenberg's 41 homers and 150 RBI's added to York's 33 homers and 134 RBI's. Veteran second baseman Charlie Gehringer and young center fielder Barney McCoskey set the table for the sluggers with batting averages over .300, while the pitching staff was led by righty Bobo Newsom, a colorful journeyman who settled down long enough in Detroit to win 21 games this season, and lefty Schoolboy Rowe, whose 16–3 record marked a full recovery from a sore arm.

Newsom and Paul Derringer squared off in game one in Crosley Field, but it was no contest after the Tigers got to Derringer for five runs in the second inning. Newsom pitched a masterful game and won 7-2, with his father enjoying the game from the stands, but Bobo grieved the next morning when his father died of a heart attack. Later in the day, the Reds evened the Series with a 5-3 victory, as Bucky Walters overcame early wildness to throw a three-hitter and outfielder Jimmy Ripple hit a two-run homer. Old-man Wilson contributed two hits to the Reds' cause.

The third game moved to Briggs Stadium and matched veteran pitchers Jim Turner and Tommy Bridges, both of whom relied on control and slow stuff. A 1-1 tie held after six innings, but then the Tigers broke the game open in the seventh on two-run homers by York and Pinky Higgins. After their 7–4 loss put them into a hole, the Reds climbed right back out with a 5-2 fourth-game win behind Paul Derringer's five-hitter. The seesaw continued in game five, as the Tigers went back ahead with an 8–0 triumph. The Detroit batters ripped 13 hits, including a three-run homer by Greenberg, and Newsom threw a three-hit shutout which the press turned into a memorial for his father.

The Reds went back to Cincinnati needing both of the remaining games for the Series championship, and they took the first step along that path behind Bucky Walters's performance in game six. In addition to shutting the Tigers out on five hits, the former infielder also hit a solo homer to support his cause. That brought everything down to a seventh game, Paul Derringer against Bobo Newsom, pitching on only one day of rest, since no travel days were alloted this year. Detroit scored an unearned run in the third, and Newsom made it stand up through six innings. But Frank McCormick doubled to left to open the seventh and came in on Ripple's double to right; the Tigers actually had a play of the slow-footed McCormick at home, but shortstop Dick Bartell cut the ball off. Jimmie Wilson, who already had two hits in the game, sacrificed Ripple to third, from where he scored on a long fly by Billy Myers. Derringer held the 2–1 lead the rest of the way to make the Reds World Champions. Perhaps the noblest Red in triumph was Jimmie Wilson, who hit .353 for the Series and skillfully handled the Cincinnati pitchers. He promptly accepted an offer to manage the Chicago Cubs and never played another game.

Game 1 October 2 at Cincinnati

Detroit	Pos	AB	R	H	RBI	PO	A	E
Bartell	ss	4	0	2	2	2	0	1
McCosky	cf	5	0	2	1	2	0	0
Gehringer	2b	4	0	0	0	4	3	0
Greenberg	lf	5	1	1	0	4	0	0
York	1b	4	2	2	0	7	1	0
Campbell	rf	3	1	2	2	3	0	0
Higgins	3b	4	1	1	2	0	5	0
Sullivan	c	3	1	0	0	4	2	0
Newsom	p	4	1	0	0	1	0	0
Totals		36	7	10	7	27	11	1

Pitching	IP	H	R	ER	BB	SO
Detroit						
Newsom (W)	9	8	2	2	1	4
Cincinnati						
Derringer (L)	1⅓	5	5	5	1	1
Moore	6⅔	5	2	2	4	7
Riddle	1	0	0	0	0	2

Cincinnati	Pos	AB	R	H	RBI	PO	A	E
Werber	3b	4	1	1	0	1	2	1
M. McCormick	cf	4	0	1	0	2	0	0
Goodman	rf	4	1	2	1	0	0	0
F. McCormick	1b	3	0	0	0	6	1	0
Ripple	lf	4	0	1	1	2	0	0
Wilson	c	2	0	0	0	9	1	0
a Riggs		1	0	0	0	0	0	0
Baker	c	1	0	1	0	3	0	1
Joost	2b	4	0	2	0	3	1	0
Myers	ss	4	0	0	0	0	1	1
Derringer	p	0	0	0	0	0	1	0
Moore	p	2	0	0	0	0	0	0
b Craft		1	0	0	0	0	0	0
Riddle	p	0	0	0	0	0	0	0
Totals		34	2	8	2	27	8	3

Det. 050 020 000
Cin. 000 100 010

a Struck out for Wilson in 7th.
b Fouled out for Moore in 8th.

Doubles—Goodman, M. McCormick, Werber. Triple—York. Home Run—Campbell. Sacrifice Hit—Campbell. Double Plays—Higgins to Gehringer to York, Wilson to Joost. Left on Bases—Detroit 8, Cincinnati 6. Umpires—Klem (N), Ormsby (A), Ballanfant (N), Basil (A). Attendance—31,793. Time of Game—2:09.

1st Inning
Detroit
1 Bartell struck out.
2 McCosky flied to left.
3 Gehringer bounced back to the mound.
Cincinnati
1 Werber grounded to third.
M. McCormick doubled over York's head.
2 Goodman grounded to third, M. McCormick holding second.
3 F. McCormick flied to McCosky making a fine leaping catch at the center field fence.

2nd Inning
Detroit
Greenberg singled to left.
York singled to right, Greenberg going to second.
Campbell sacrificed and was safe when Werber threw high to first.
Higgins singled to center, scoring Greenberg and York, Campbell stopping at second.
Sullivan walked, loading the bases.
1 Newsom forced Campbell at the plate, F. McCormick to Wilson.
Bartell singled to center, scoring Higgins and Sullivan as Newsom pulled up at second.
McCosky singled to left, scoring Newsom with Bartell stopping at second.
For Cincinnati—Moore came in to pitch. Moore had picked Bartell off of second on a perfect throw, but Myers dropped the ball for an error and Bartell was still at second.
2 Gehringer popped to third.
3 Greenberg grounded to third.
Cincinnati
1 Ripple grounded to second.
2 Wilson flied to short left.
Joost singled to center.
3 Myers forced Joost at second, Gehringer to Bartell.

3rd Inning
Detroit
1 York struck out.
Campbell singled to center.
2,3 Higgins struck out and Campbell was doubled attempting to steal second, Wilson to Joost.
Cincinnati
1 Moore grounded out, York to Newsom.
2 Werber flied to Campbell in right-center.
3 M. McCormick struck out, but Sullivan dropped the third strike and threw to York for the putout.

4th Inning
Detroit
1 Sullivan popped to Joost behind second.
2 Newsom struck out.
Bartell walked.
McCosky singled over second, Bartell racing to third.
3 Gehringer grounded to second.
Cincinnati
Goodman doubled to center.
1 F. McCormick popped to Gehringer in short right.
Ripple singled to right, scoring Goodman.
2,3 Wilson hit into a double play, Higgins to Gehringer to York.

5th Inning
Detroit
1 Greenberg called out on strikes.
York tripled off the right field bleacher screen.
Campbell hit a two-run homer into the right-center field bleachers.
2 Higgins flied to Ripple in deep left-center.
3 Sullivan struck out.

5th Inning (continued)
Cincinnati
Joost singled to center.
1 Myers took a called third strike.
2 Moore struck out but Joost was safe at second when Bartell dropped Sullivan's throw.
3 Werber grounded to third.

6th Inning
Detroit
1 Newsom grounded to third.
2 Bartell called out on strikes.
3 McCosky popped to first.
Cincinnati
1 M. McCormick popped to second.
2 Goodman popped to short.
F. McCormick walked.
3 Ripple fouled to Sullivan in front of the Detroit dugout.

7th Inning
Detroit
Gehringer walked.
1 Greenberg struck out.
York walked.
Campbell walked, loading the bases.
2 Higgins popped to third.
3 Sullivan lined to Goodman in front of the right field bleachers.
Cincinnati
1 Riggs, pinch-hitting for Wilson, struck out.
2 Joost flied to left.
3 Myers flied to right.

8th Inning
Detroit
For Cincinnati—Baker now catching.
1 Newsom grounded to short.
Bartell singled to right.
2 McCosky flied to deep center. Bartell went to third when Baker's throw to get him stealing second went into center.
3 Gehringer flied to right.
Cincinnati
1 Craft, pinch-hitting for Moore, fouled to Greenberg near the seats. Werber doubled to center.
2 McCormick grounded to first, Werber advancing to third.
Goodman singled to center, scoring Werber.
3 F. McCormick flied to center.

9th Inning
Detroit
For Cincinnati—Riddle now pitching.
1 Greenberg fouled to Baker nearly falling into the Red's dugout.
2 York took a called third strike.
3 Campbell struck out.
Cincinnati
1 Ripple flied to left.
Baker singled off Newsom's glove.
2 Joost forced Baker at second, Higgins to Gehringer as the throw to first just missed getting Joost.
3 Myers flied to Campbell in right-center.

Game 2 October 3 at Cincinnati

Det.	200	001	000
Cin.	022	100	00x

Detroit	Pos	AB	R	H	RBI	PO	A	E
Bartell	ss	3	1	0	0	3	2	0
McCosky	cf	2	1	0	0	4	0	0
Gehringer	2b	4	1	1	1	0	3	0
Greenberg	lf	3	0	1	1	1	0	0
York	1b	4	0	0	0	10	0	0
Campbell	rf	4	0	0	0	3	0	0
Higgins	3b	3	0	1	0	1	4	0
Tebbetts	c	3	0	0	0	2	0	1
Rowe	p	1	0	0	0	0	0	0
Gorsica	p	2	0	0	0	0	1	0
	Totals	29	3	3	2	24	10	1

Doubles—Greenberg, Higgins, Walters, Werber, Ripple. Home Run—Ripple. Double Play—Werber to Joost to F. McCormick. Left on Bases—Detroit 3, Cincinnati 5. Umpires—Ormsby, Ballanfant, Basil, Klem. Attendance—30,640. Time of Game—1:54.

1st Inning
Detroit
Bartell walked.
McCosky walked.
Gehringer singled to right, scoring Bartell and McCosky going to third.
1,2 Greenberg grounded into a double play, Werber to Joost to F. McCormick. McCosky scoring on the play.
3 York struck out.
Cincinnati
1 Werber grounded to short.
2 M. McCormick struck out being tagged by Tebbetts after dropping the third strike.
3 Goodman grounded to second.

2nd Inning
Detroit
1 Campbell fouled to Werber.
2 Higgins grounded to short.
3 Tebbetts popped to short.
Cincinnati
F. McCormick singled to left.
1 Ripple popped to Bartell in short left.
Wilson singled to right, F. McCormick stopping at second.
Joost singled to center, scoring F. McCormick with Wilson stopping at second.
Myers singled to left, scoring Wilson as Joost stopped at second.
Tebbetts threw wildly trying to pick Joost off second, Joost going to third, and Myers to second.
2 Walters flied to short center.
Werber walked, loading the bases.
3 M. McCormick popped to short.

3rd Inning
Detroit
1 Rowe struck out.
2 Bartell flied to center.
3 McCosky lined to center.
Cincinnati
Goodman beat out a bunt towards first.
1 F. McCormick lined out hard to center.
Ripple hit a two-run homer into the right field bleachers, on the first pitch.
2 Wilson popped to short.
3 Joost flied to right.

4th Inning
Detroit
1 Gehringer grounded back to the pitcher's mound.
Greenberg walked.
2 York popped to Myers in short center.
3 Campbell flied to center.
Cincinnati
1 Myers flied to right.
Walters doubled down the left field foul line.
Werber doubled down the left field corner, scoring Walters.
For Detroit—Gorsica replaced Rowe on the mound.
2 M. McCormick bounced to Higgins, who tagged Werber coming into third.
3 Goodman grounded to second.

5th Inning
Detroit
Higgins doubled into the left field corner.
1 Tebbetts flied to left.
2 Gorsica rolled out to the pitcher, Higgins advancing to third.
3 Bartell grounded to third.
Cincinnati
1 F. McCormick grounded to third.
2 Ripple flied to left.
3 Wilson grounded to third.

6th Inning
Detroit
McCosky walked.
1 Gehringer forced McCosky at second, Werber to Joost.
Greenberg doubled to deep left, scoring Gehringer.
2 York flied to deep right, Greenberg going to third after the catch.
3 Campbell grounded to second.
Cincinnati
1 Joost flied to center.
2 Myers struck out.
3 Walters rolled to the mound.

7th Inning
Detroit
1 Higgins grounded to short.
2 Tebbetts grounded to third.
3 Gorsica called out on strikes.
Cincinnati
1 Werber grounded to third.
2 M. McCormick grounded to third.
3 Goodman grounded to short.

8th Inning
Detroit
1 Bartell flied to left.
2 McCosky grounded to short.
3 Gehringer fouled to Werber.
Cincinnati
1 F. McCormick flied to center.
2 Ripple grounded to second.
Wilson singled off of Higgins' glove.
3 Joost flied to short right.

9th Inning
Detroit
1 Greenberg flied to deep left.
2 York called out on strikes.
3 Campbell popped to Myers in short left.

Cincinnati	Pos	AB	R	H	RBI	PO	A	E
Werber	3b	3	0	1	1	2	4	0
M. McCormick	cf	4	0	0	0	3	0	0
Goodman	rf	4	1	1	0	1	0	0
F. McCormick	1b	4	1	1	0	9	0	0
Ripple	lf	4	1	1	2	4	0	0
Wilson	c	4	1	2	0	4	0	0
Joost	2b	4	0	1	1	2	2	0
Meyers	ss	3	1	1	1	3	3	0
Walters	p	3	1	1	0	0	2	0
	Totals	33	5	9	5	27	11	0

Pitching	IP	H	R	ER	BB	SO
Detroit						
Rowe (L)	3⅓	8	5	5	1	1
Gorsica	4⅔	1	0	0	0	1
Cincinnati						
Walters (W)	9	3	3	3	4	4

Game 3 October 4 at Detroit

Cin.	100	000	012
Det.	000	100	42x

Cincinnati	Pos	AB	R	H	RBI	PO	A	E
Werber	3b	4	1	3	1	2	3	0
M. McCormick	cf	5	0	2	1	3	0	1
Goodman	rf	4	0	1	1	0	0	0
F. McCormick	1b	4	0	0	0	9	1	0
Ripple	lf	4	1	1	0	2	0	0
Lombardi	c	3	0	1	0	4	0	0
Baker	c	1	1	0	0	2	0	0
Joost	2b	4	0	1	1	2	2	0
Myers	ss	4	0	0	0	3	0	0
Turner	p	2	0	0	0	0	1	0
Moore	p	0	0	0	0	0	0	0
a Riggs		1	0	0	0	0	0	0
Beggs	p	0	0	0	0	0	0	0
b Frey	p	1	0	0	0	0	0	0
	Totals	37	4	10	4	24	10	1

a Hit into Force out for Moore in 8th.
b Flied out for Beggs in 9th.

Doubles—Campbell, Higgins, Lombardi, McCosky, Werber. Triple—Greenberg. Home Runs—Higgins, York. Double Plays—Werber to Joost to F. McCormick, Myers to F. McCormick to Baker. Left on Bases—Cincinnati 7, Detroit 4. Umpires—Ballanfant, Basil, Klem, Ormsby. Attendance—52,877. Time of Game—2:08.

1st Inning
Cincinnati
Werber doubled into the left field corner, on the first pitch.
1 M. McCormick struck out.
Goodman singled to center, scoring Werber.
2 F. McCormick flied to right.
3 Ripple struck out.
Detroit
1 Bartell grounded to short.
2 McCosky rolled out to second.
3 Gehringer bounced back to the mound.

2nd Inning
Cincinnati
Lombardi doubled into the right field corner.
1 Joost called out on strikes.
2 Myers popped to short.
3 Turner flied to center.
Detroit
1 Greenberg struck out.
2 York was called out on strikes.
Campbell doubled to center.
3 Higgins grounded to third.

3rd Inning
Cincinnati
1 Werber grounded to short.
2 M. McCormick grounded back to the mound.
3 Goodman flied to center.
Detroit
1 Tebbetts flied to left.
2 Bridges struck out.
3 Bartell flied to center.

4th Inning
Cincinnati
1 F. McCormick grounded to third.
2 Ripple grounded to second.
3 Lombardi grounded to third.
Detroit
McCosky singled to left-center.
Gehringer singled through first, McCosky going to third.
1,2 Greenberg hit into a double play, Werber to F. McCormick to Joost, as McCosky was scoring.
York singled to right.
3 Campbell grounded to first.

5th Inning
Cincinnati
1 Joost flied to center.
2 Myers grounded to third, a fantastic stop and throw by Higgins.
3 Turner flied to right.
Detroit
1 Higgins struck out, the third strike a foul tip which Lombardi held.
2 Tebbetts lined to third.
3 Bridges grounded to third.

6th Inning
Cincinnati
Werber walked.
1 Werber was out trying to steal second, Tebbetts to Bartell.
M. McCormick singled to center.
2 Goodman forced M. McCormick at second, Gehringer unassisted.
3 F. McCormick flied to right.
Detroit
1 Bartell flied to left.
2 McCosky flied to center.
3 Gehringer flied to deep right.

7th Inning
Cincinnati
1 Ripple grounded to second.
2 Lombardi grounded to short.
3 Joost flied to right.
Detroit
Greenberg singled to center.
York hit a two-run homer into the left field stands.
Campbell singled to left.
Higgins hit a two-run homer into the upper deck in left.
For Cincinnati—Moore now pitching.
1 Tebbetts flied to center.
2 Bridges grounded to short.
Bartell singled to center.
McCosky doubled to center, Bartell stopping at third.
3 Gehringer fouled to Werber.

8th Inning
Cincinnati
Myers singled off Bartell's glove.
1 Riggs, batting for Moore, forced Myers, Gehringer unassisted.
Werber singled to left, Riggs stopping at second.
M. McCormick singled to center, scoring Riggs as Werber stopped at second.
2 Goodman flied to left.
3 F. McCormick forced M. McCormick at second, Bartell unassisted.
Detroit
For Cincinnati—Beggs pitching, and Baker catching.
Greenberg tripled to deep center.
1 York was called out on strikes.
Campbell singled to center, scoring Greenberg. Campbell was safe at second on M. McCormick's bad throw-in.
Higgins doubled just inside the right field foul line, scoring Campbell.
2,3 Tebbetts grounded to Myers and Higgins was doubled trying to score, F. McCormick to Baker.

9th Inning
Cincinnati
Ripple bounced a single over York's head.
Baker safe at first on Higgins' error.
Joost singled over second, scoring Ripple with Baker stopping at second.
1 Myers struck out.
2 Frey, pinch-hitting for Beggs, flied to center.
Werber singled to left, scoring Baker as Joost went to third.
3 M. McCormick struck out.

Detroit	Pos	AB	R	H	RBI	PO	A	E
Bartell	ss	4	0	1	0	4	3	0
McCosky	cf	4	1	2	0	4	0	0
Gehringer	2b	4	0	1	0	1	4	0
Greenberg	lf	4	2	2	1	0	0	0
York	1b	4	1	2	2	8	0	0
Campbell	rf	4	2	3	1	4	0	0
Higgins	3b	4	1	2	3	0	3	1
Tebbetts	c	4	0	0	0	5	1	0
Bridges	p	3	0	0	0	0	1	0
	Totals	35	7	13	6	27	12	1

Pitching	IP	H	R	ER	BB	SO
Cincinnati						
Turner (L)	*6	8	5	5	0	4
Moore	1	2	0	0	0	0
Beggs	1	3	2	2	0	1
Detroit						
Bridges (W)	9	10	4	3	1	5

*Pitched to 4 batters in 6th.

Game 4 October 5 at Detroit

Cincinnati	Pos	AB	R	H	RBI	PO	A	E
Werber	3b	3	2	2	0	2	1	0
M. McCormick	cf	5	1	2	1	3	0	0
Goodman	rf	5	2	2	1	1	0	0
F. McCormick	1b	5	0	2	0	13	0	0
Ripple	lf	3	0	1	1	0	0	0
b Arnovich	lf	1	0	0	0	2	0	0
Wilson	c	5	0	1	0	4	0	0
Joost	2b	5	0	1	0	0	1	0
Myers	ss	3	0	0	0	2	5	1
Derringer	p	4	0	0	0	0	3	0
Totals		38	5	11	4	27	10	1

Pitching	IP	H	R	ER	BB	SO
Cincinnati						
Derringer (W)	9	5	2	2	6	4
Detroit						
Trout (L)	*2	6	3	2	1	1
Smith	4	1	1	1	3	1
McKain	3	4	1	1	0	0

*Pitched to 3 batters in 3rd.

Cin.	2 0 1	1 0 0	0 1 0
Det.	0 0 1	0 0 1	0 0 0

Detroit	Pos	AB	R	H	RBI	PO	A	E
Bartell	ss	4	0	0	0	1	0	0
d Fox		1	0	0	0	0	0	0
McCosky	cf	2	1	1	0	2	0	0
Gehringer	2b	4	0	0	0	5	3	0
Greenberg	lf	4	0	1	1	2	0	0
York	1b	2	0	0	0	13	1	0
Campbell	rf	4	1	1	0	1	0	0
Higgins	3b	4	0	2	1	1	9	1
Sullivan	c	2	0	0	0	2	0	0
Trout	p	1	0	0	0	0	1	0
Smith	p	1	0	0	0	0	1	0
a Averill		1	0	0	0	0	0	0
McKain	p	0	0	0	0	0	1	0
c Tebbetts		1	0	0	0	0	0	0
Totals		31	2	5	2	27	16	1

a Flied out for Smith in 6th.
b Flied out for Ripple in 7th.
c Grounded out for McKain in 9th.
d Flied out for Bartell in 9th.

Doubles—Goodman, Greenberg, M. McCormick, Ripple. Triple—Higgins. Sacrifice Hit—Arnovich. Double Plays—Myers to Joost to F. McCormick, Derringer to Myers, to F. McCormick. Wild Pitch—McKain. Left on Bases—Cincinnati 11, Detroit 8. Umpires—Basil, Klem, Ormsby, Ballanfant. Attendance—54,093. Time of Game—2:06.

1st Inning
Cincinnati
Werber walked.
1 M. McCormick forced Werber at second, York to Bartell.
Goodman doubled into the left field corner, scoring M. McCormick from first.
2 F. McCormick grounded to third, Goodman moving to third.
Ripple safe at first as Goodman scored on Higgins' error.
3 Wilson flied to center.
Detroit
1 Bartell struck out.
McCosky walked.
2,3 Gehringer grounded into a double play, Joost to Myers to F. McCormick.

2nd Inning
Cincinnati
Joost beat out a roller to third.
1 Myers forced Joost at second, Higgins to Gehringer.
2 Derringer struck out.
Werber singled to right-center, Myers moving to third.
3 M. McCormick tapped back to the mound.
Detroit
1 Greenberg flied to center.
York walked.
2 Campbell fouled to Werber.
Higgins singled to center, York going to third, as Higgins took second on the throw to third.
Sullivan intentionally walked, loading the bases.
3 Trout grounded to first.

3rd Inning
Cincinnati
Goodman singled to center.
F. McCormick singled to right, Goodman going to third.
Ripple doubled to left, Goodman scoring and F. McCormick going to third.
For Detroit—Smith came in to pitch.
1 Wilson bounced to third, the runners holding their bases.
2 Joost popped to second.
Myers intentionally passed, loading the bases.
3 Derringer forced Myers at second, Higgins to Gehringer.
Detroit
1 Bartell bounced back to the pitcher.
McCosky walked.
2 Gehringer grounded to short, McCosky going to second.
Greenberg doubled along the left field foul line, scoring McCosky.
York walked.
3 Campbell struck out.

4th Inning
Cincinnati
Werber walked.
M. McCormick doubled along the right field foul line, Werber stopping at third.
1 Goodman flied to Greenberg in deep left-center, Werber scoring and M. McCormick going to third after the catch.
2 F. McCormick popped to second.
Ripple got an intentional pass.
3 Wilson struck out.
Detroit
1 Higgins popped to first.
2 Sullivan fouled to Werber, making a one-handed catch near the stands.
3 Smith struck out.

5th Inning
Cincinnati
1 Joost grounded back to the mound.
2 Myers grounded to third.
3 Derringer rolled to third.
Detroit
1 Bartell popped to first.
McCosky singled to center.
2,3 Gehringer grounded into a double play, Derringer to Myers to F. McCormick.

6th Inning
Cincinnati
1 Werber grounded to third.
2 M. McCormick lined out to center.
3 Goodman grounded to second.
Detroit
1 Greenberg grounded to short.
2 York flied to F. McCormick near the box.
Campbell singled to right.
Higgins tripled off the right field stands, scoring Campbell.
Sullivan walked.
3 Averill, pinch-hitting for Smith, flied to right.

7th Inning
Cincinnati
For Detroit—McKain pitching.
1 F. McCormick grounded to third.
2 Arnovich, pinch-hitting for Ripple, flied to right.
Wilson singled to left.
3 Joost forced Wilson, Gehringer tagging him near second.
For Cincinnati—Arnovich playing left.
1 Bartell flied to center.
McCosky grounded to short, but was safe on Myers' error on the throw to first.
2 Gehringer flied to deep center.
3 Greenberg flied to left.

8th Inning
Cincinnati
1 Myers flied to left.
2 Derringer grounded to third **(for Higgins' 9th assist an all-time Series, single game record).**
Werber singled off McKain's glove.
Werber went to second on a wild pitch.
M. McCormick singled to left, scoring Werber.
3 Goodman fouled to Higgins.
Detroit
1 York grounded to short.
2 Campbell fanned.
3 Higgins grounded to third.

9th Inning
Cincinnati
F. McCormick singled to right.
1 Arnovich sacrificed F. McCormick to second, McKain to York.
2 Wilson grounded to second, F. McCormick going to third.
3 Joost grounded to second.
Detroit
1 Sullivan popped to first.
2 Tebbetts, batting for McKain, bounced back to the mound.
3 Fox, batting for Bartell, flied to left.

Game 5 October 6 at Detroit

Cincinnati	Pos	AB	R	H	RBI	PO	A	E
Werber	3b	4	0	1	0	0	0	0
M. McCormick	cf	4	0	1	0	5	1	0
Goodman	rf	4	0	0	0	1	0	0
F. McCormick	1b	4	0	1	0	5	0	0
Ripple	lf	2	0	0	0	4	0	0
Wilson	c	1	0	0	0	3	1	0
a Baker		1	0	0	0	0	0	0
Joost	2b	3	0	0	0	2	1	0
Myers	ss	2	0	0	0	2	0	0
Thompson	p	1	0	0	0	0	1	0
Moore	p	0	0	0	0	0	0	0
b Frey		1	0	0	0	0	0	0
Vander Meer	p	0	0	0	0	0	0	0
c Riggs		1	0	0	0	0	0	0
Hutchings	p	0	0	0	0	0	1	0
Totals		29	0	3	0	24	5	0

a Struck out for Wilson in 5th.
b Grounded out for Moore in 5th.
c Struck out for Vander Meer in 8th.

Double—Bartell. Home Run—Greenberg. Sacrifice Hit—Newson. Double Play—Bartell to Gehringer to York. Passed Ball—Wilson. Wild Pitch—Hutchings. Left on Bases—Cincinnati 4, Detroit 13. Umpires—Klem, Ormsby, Ballanfant, Basil. Attendance—55,189. Time of Game—2:26.

Cin.	0 0 0	0 0 0	0 0 0
Det.	0 0 3	4 0 0	0 1 x

Detroit	Pos	AB	R	H	RBI	PO	A	E
Bartell	ss	4	1	2	1	0	1	0
McCosky	cf	3	2	2	0	3	0	0
Gehringer	2b	4	2	0	3	2	4	0
Greenberg	lf	5	2	3	4	1	0	0
York	1b	4	0	0	0	7	0	0
Campbell	rf	4	0	3	2	2	0	0
Higgins	3b	4	0	1	0	1	3	0
Sullivan	c	4	1	1	0	11	0	0
Newsom	p	4	0	0	0	0	0	0
Totals		34	8	13	7	27	8	0

Pitching	IP	H	R	ER	BB	SO
Cincinnati						
Thompson (L)	3⅓	8	6	6	4	2
Moore	⅔	1	1	1	2	0
Vander Meer	3	2	0	0	3	2
Hutchings	1	2	1	1	1	0
Detroit						
Newsom (W)	9	3	0	0	2	7

1st Inning
Cincinnati
1 Werber grounded to third.
2 M. McCormick grounded to second.
3 Goodman fouled to Sullivan.
Detroit
Bartell singled to center.
1 McCosky grounded to second, Bartell advancing to second.
Gehringer singled to short center,
2 but Bartell was out trying to score, M. McCormick to Wilson.
Greenberg singled to left, Gehringer stopping at second.
3 York flied to center.

2nd Inning
Cincinnati
F. McCormick singled to left.
1 Ripple flied to center.
2 Wilson fouled to Sullivan.
3 Joost lined to center.
Detroit
1 Campbell struck out.
Higgins walked.
Sullivan singled to right, Higgins stopping at second.
2 Newsom flied to deep left.
3 Bartell flied to short left.

3rd Inning
Cincinnati
1 Myers flied to right.
2 Thompson took a called third strike.
3 Werber also called out on strikes.
Detroit
McCosky singled to center.
Gehringer singled to right, McCosky moving to third.
Greenberg hit a tremendous three-run homer into the upper deck of the left field stands.
1 York flied to deep center, M. McCormick making a leaping catch.
Campbell walked.
2 Campbell out trying to steal second, Wilson to Joost.
3 Higgins struck out.

4th Inning
Cincinnati
M. McCormick singled to center.
1 Goodman out on a slow roller to second, M. McCormick moving to second.
2 F. McCormick fouled to Sullivan.
3 Ripple fouled to Greenberg.
Detroit
Sullivan walked.
1 Newsom sacrificed Sullivan to second, Thompson to Joost.
Bartell doubled into the left field corner, scoring Sullivan.
Bartell went to third on a passed ball.
McCosky walked.
For Cincinnati—Moore came in to pitch.
Gehringer walked, loading the bases.
2 Greenberg flied to deep center, Bartell scoring as McCosky went to third after the catch.
York walked, again loading the bases.
Campbell singled beyond second, scoring McCosky and Gehringer with York going to third.
3 Higgins forced Campbell at second, Myers unassisted.

5th Inning
Cincinnati
1 Baker, pinch-hitting for Wilson, struck out.
2 Joost took a called third strike.
Myers walked.
3 Frey, pinch-hitting for Moore, grounded to second.
Detroit
For Cincinnati—the new battery was Baker catching and Vander Meer pitching.
1 Sullivan took a called third strike.
2 Newsom bounced out to first.
Bartell walked.
McCosky singled to center, Bartell stopping at second.
3 Gehringer popped to short.

6th Inning
Cincinnati
Werber singled to center.
1,2 M. McCormick grounded into a double play, Bartell to Gehringer to York.
3 Goodman struck out.
Detroit
1 Greenberg flied to center.
2 York was called out on strikes.
Campbell singled to left.
Higgins walked.
3 Sullivan flied to center.

7th Inning
Cincinnati
1 F. McCormick fouled to Sullivan.
Ripple walked.
2 Baker flied to Campbell in right-center.
3 Joost flied to short center.
Detroit
1 Newsom lined to first.
2 Bartell flied to right.
McCosky walked.
3 Gehringer flied to left.

8th Inning
Cincinnati
1 Myers grounded to third.
2 Riggs, pinch-hitting for Vander Meer, struck out.
3 Werber grounded to second.
Detroit
For Cincinnati—Hutchings now pitching.
Greenberg singled to center.
1 York fouled to F. McCormick on an attempted sacrifice.
Campbell singled to center, moving Greenberg to third.
Greenberg scored and Campbell went to second on a passed ball.
Higgins walked.
2 Sullivan flied to Ripple in the left field corner, making a fantastic running one-handed catch.
3 Newsom bounced back to the box.

9th Inning
Cincinnati
1 M. McCormick lined to second.
2 Goodman popped to Higgins, who held on to the ball after colliding with Bartell.
3 F. McCormick struck out.

Game 6 October 7 at Cincinnati

Detroit	Pos	AB	R	H	RBI	PO	A	E
Bartell	ss	3	0	2	0	0	4	0
b Sullivan		1	0	0	0	0	0	0
Croucher	ss	0	0	0	0	0	0	0
McCosky	cf	4	0	0	0	1	0	0
Gehringer	2b	4	0	0	0	2	1	0
Greenberg	lf	3	0	0	0	2	0	0
York	1b	4	0	2	0	10	0	0
Campbell	rf	3	0	0	0	2	0	0
Higgins	3b	3	0	1	0	1	2	0
Tebbetts	c	3	0	0	0	6	2	0
Rowe	p	0	0	0	0	0	1	0
Gorsica	p	0	0	0	0	0	5	0
a Averill		1	0	0	0	0	0	0
Hutchinson	p	0	0	0	0	0	0	0
Totals		31	0	5	0	24	15	0

a Safe at first on an error for Gorsica in 8th.
b Flied out for Bartell in 8th.

Doubles—Bartell, Werber. Home Run—Walters. Sacrifice Hits—Goodman, M. McCormick. Double Plays—Joost to Myers to F. McCormick, Werber to Joost to F. McCormick, F. McCormick to Myers to F. McCormick, Gorsica to Tebbetts to York. Left on Bases—Cincinnati 11, Detroit 6. Umpires—Ormsby, Ballanfant, Basil, Klem. Attendance—30,481. Time of Game—2:01.

Det.	000 000 000
Cin.	200 001 01x

Cincinnati	Pos	AB	R	H	RBI	PO	A	E
Werber	3b	5	1	2	0	1	3	0
M. McCormick	cf	3	0	1	0	4	0	0
Goodman	rf	4	1	2	1	2	0	0
F. McCormick	1b	4	0	1	0	10	1	1
Ripple	lf	2	0	1	2	2	0	0
Wilson	c	3	1	1	0	4	0	0
Joost	2b	3	0	0	0	2	4	0
Myers	ss	4	0	0	0	2	4	1
Walters	p	4	1	1	2	0	2	0
Totals		32	4	10	4	27	14	2

Pitching	IP	H	R	ER	BB	SO
Detroit						
Rowe (L)	1	4	2	2	0	0
Gorsica	6⅔	5	1	1	4	3
Hutchinson	1	1	1	1	1	1
Cincinnati						
Walters (W)	9	5	0	0	2	2

1st Inning
Detroit
1 Bartell flied to left.
2 McCosky fouled to Werber.
3 Gehringer flied to left.
Cincinnati
  Werber doubled off the left field wall.
1 M. McCormick sacrificed Werber to third, Rowe to York.
  Goodman beat a single to first as Rowe was slow covering the bag, Werber scoring.
  F. McCormick singled to left, Goodman stopping at second.
  Ripple singled to right, Goodman scoring with F. McCormick going to third.
  For Detroit—Gorsica replaced Rowe on the mound.
2 Wilson fanned.
3 Joost forced Ripple at second, Higgins to Gehringer.

2nd Inning
Detroit
1 Greenberg struck out.
2 York flied to right.
  Campbell walked.
  Higgins singled to left, Campbell stopping at second.
3 Tebbetts grounded back to the mound.
Cincinnati
1 Myers struck out.
2 Walters tapped back to the mound.
  Werber singled to center.
3 M. McCormick tapped out, Tebbetts to York.

3rd Inning
Detroit
1 Gorsica flied to center.
  Bartell doubled over third.
2 McCosky flied to right, Bartell going to third after the catch.
3 Gehringer fouled to Wilson.
Cincinnati
1 Goodman flied to center.
2 F. McCormick fouled to Higgins.
  Ripple walked.
3 Wilson lined to right where Campbell made a nice shoe-string catch of the low liner.

4th Inning
Detroit
1 Greenberg fouled to Wilson.
  York singled to left.
2,3 Campbell grounded into a double play, Joost to Myers to F. McCormick.
Cincinnati
1 Joost grounded to short, just being nipped at first.
2 Myers' hopper deflected off Gorsica to Bartell who made the throw to first.
3 Walters took a called third strike.

5th Inning
Detroit
1 Higgins grounded to second.
2 Tebbetts grounded to short.
3 Gorsica called out on strikes.
Cincinnati
1 Werber grounded to short.
2 M. McCormick flied to deep left.
  Goodman lined a single to left.
3 F. McCormick forced Goodman at second, Higgins to Gehringer.

6th Inning
Detroit
  Bartell singled to left.
1 McCosky forced Bartell, Werber to Joost.
2,3 Gehringer hit into a double play, F. McCormick to Myers to F. McCormick.
Cincinnati
  Ripple singled to center.
  Wilson singled to right, sending Ripple to third.
  Joost walked, loading the bases.
1 Myers forced Ripple at the plate, Gorsica to Tebbetts.
  Walters hit into a fielder's choice as Higgins threw late to the plate, Wilson scoring.
2,3 Werber grounded into a double play, Gorsica to Tebbetts forcing Joost at the plate to York getting Werber at first.

7th Inning
Detroit
1 Greenberg grounded to the mound.
  York singled to left.
2 Campbell grounded out to Joost making an amazing glove-handed stop, York going to second.
3 Higgins grounded to short.
Cincinnati
  M. McCormick singled through the box.
1 Goodman sacrificed, Gorsica to York.
2 F. McCormick grounded to short, M. McCormick holding at second.
  Ripple intentionally passed.
  Wilson walked, loading the bases.
3 Joost grounded to second.

8th Inning
Detroit
1 Tebbetts grounded to third.
  Averill, batting for Gorsica, safe at first on F. McCormick's error.
2 Sullivan, batting for Bartell, flied to center.
3 McCosky flied to center.
Cincinnati
  For Detroit—Hutchinson pitching, and Croucher playing short.
1 Myers struck out.
  Walters homered over the left field wall.
2 Werber flied to right.
  M. McCormick walked.
3 Goodman flied to left.

9th Inning
Detroit
  Gehringer safely to second as Myers' throw went over first to the stands.
  Greenberg walked.
1,2 York grounded into a double play, Werber to Joost to F. McCormick, Gehringer going to third.
3 Campbell flied to center.

Game 7 October 8 at Cincinnati

Detroit	Pos	AB	R	H	RBI	PO	A	E
Bartell	ss	4	0	0	0	3	2	0
McCosky	cf	3	0	0	0	3	0	0
Gehringer	2b	4	0	0	0	3	2	0
Greenberg	lf	4	0	2	0	1	0	0
York	1b	4	0	0	0	5	0	0
Campbell	rf	3	0	0	0	2	0	0
Higgins	3b	4	0	1	0	4	0	0
Sullivan	c	3	1	1	0	6	0	0
Newsom	p	2	0	1	0	0	0	0
c Averill		1	0	0	0	0	0	0
Totals		32	1	7	0	24	8	0

Pitching	IP	H	R	ER	BB	SO
Detroit						
Newsom (L)	9	7	2	2	1	6
Cincinnati						
Derringer (W)	8	7	1	0	3	1

Det.	001 000 000
Cin.	000 000 20x

Cincinnati	Pos	AB	R	H	RBI	PO	A	E
Werber	3b	4	0	0	0	1	3	1
M. McCormick	cf	4	0	2	0	4	0	0
Goodman	rf	3	0	0	0	3	0	0
F. McCormick	1b	4	1	1	0	6	1	0
Ripple	lf	3	1	1	1	1	0	0
Wilson	c	2	0	2	1	4	0	0
Joost	2b	0	0	0	0	5	1	0
a Lombardi		0	0	0	0	0	0	0
b Frey	2b	0	0	0	0	2	0	0
Myers	ss	3	0	1	1	5	1	0
Derringer	p	3	0	0	0	0	1	0
Totals		29	2	7	2	27	8	1

a Intentionally passed for Joost in 7th.
b Ran for Lombardi in 7th.
c Grounded out for Newsom in 9th.

Doubles—Higgins, M. McCormick, F. McCormick, Ripple. Stolen Base—Wilson. Sacrifice Hits—Newsom, Wilson. Double Play—Gehringer to Bartell to York. Left on Bases—Detroit 8, Cincinnati—5. Umpires—Ballanfant, Basil, Klem, Ormsby. Attendance—26,854. Time of Game—1:47.

1st Inning
Detroit
1 Bartell lined to short.
2 McCosky flied to center.
3 Gehringer flied to left.
Cincinnati
1 Werber flied to left.
2 M. McCormick struck out.
3 Goodman grounded to short.

2nd Inning
Detroit
  Greenberg beat out a hit to deep short.
1 York grounded to third, Greenberg going to second.
2 Campbell hit back to the box and Greenberg was trapped, Derringer to Myers to Werber to Joost as Campbell got to second.
3 Higgins grounded to second.
Cincinnati
1 F. McCormick grounded to third.
2 Ripple struck out.
  Wilson singled to left.
  Wilson stole second (the first stolen base in the Series).
3 Joost grounded to second.

3rd Inning
Detroit
  Sullivan singled back of first.
1 Newsom sacrificed Sullivan to second, F. McCormick to Joost.
2 Bartell popped to second.
  McCosky walked.
  Gehringer beat out a single to third, but Werber threw wild to first, scoring Sullivan, with McCosky racing to third.
3 Greenberg struck out.
Cincinnati
  Myers singled to left.
1 Derringer popped to Newsom on an attempted sacrifice.
2 Werber forced Myers at second, Higgins to Gehringer.
3 M. McCormick struck out.

4th Inning
Detroit
1 York fouled to Wilson.
2 Campbell flied to center.
  Higgins doubled over third.
  Sullivan got an intentional walk.
3 Newsom's grounder hit Higgins on the leg for an automatic out.
Cincinnati
1 Goodman struck out.
2 F. McCormick flied to center.
3 Ripple grounded to first.

5th Inning
Detroit
1 Bartell flied to center.
2 McCosky flied to right.
3 Gehringer popped to short.
Cincinnati
  Wilson singled to center.
1,2 Joost hit into a double play, Gehringer to Bartell to York.
3 Myers flied to right.

6th Inning
Detroit
  Greenberg singled to center.
1 York popped to second.
  Campbell walked.
2 Higgins was robbed of a hit when Myers made a great stop in the hole and raced to second forcing Campbell, as Greenberg went to third.
3 Sullivan grounded to first.
Cincinnati
1 Derringer flied to right.
2 Werber popped to short.
  M. McCormick doubled to right-center.
3 Goodman lined to deep center.

7th Inning
Detroit
1 Newsom popped to Joost in short right.
2 Bartell lined to third.
3 McCosky flied to center.
Cincinnati
  F. McCormick doubled off the left field wall.
  Ripple doubled off the screen in right, scoring F. McCormick.
1 Wilson sacrificed Ripple to third, Higgins to Gehringer.
  Lombardi, batting for Joost, was intentionally walked.
  Frey ran for Lombardi.
2 Myers flied to deep in center, Ripple scoring after the catch as Frey held first.
3 Derringer forced Frey at second, Higgins to Gehringer.

8th Inning
Detroit
  For Cincinnati—Frey playing second.
  Gehringer singled to right.
1 Greenberg lined to short, as Gehringer just got back to first avoiding a double play.
2 York flied to center.
3 Campbell flied to right.
Cincinnati
1 Werber called out on strikes.
  M. McCormick beat out a bunt to third.
2 Goodman struck out.
3 F. McCormick popped to short.

9th Inning
Detroit
1 Higgins grounded to third.
2 Sullivan grounded to first.
3 Averill, pinch-hitting for Newsom, ended Detroit's hopes by grounding to second.

1940 WORLD SERIES COMPOSITE BOX

	Wins	Composite Line Score									
Cincinnati Reds (N.L.)	4	5	2	3	3	0	1	2	4	2	– 22
Detroit Tigers (A.L.)	3	2	5	5	5	2	2	4	3	0	– 28

	Regular Season			
Manager	W	L	Pct.	G. Ahead
Bill McKechnie	100	53	.654	12
Del Baker	90	64	.584	1

BATTING AND FIELDING

WORLD SERIES STATISTICS

	Pos	G	AB	R	H	2B	3B	HR	RBI	BB	SO	SB	BA	SA	PO	A	E
CINCINNATI REDS																	
Frank McCormick	1b	7	28	2	6	1	0	0	0	1	1	0	.214	.250	58	4	1
Eddie Joost	2b	7	25	0	5	0	0	0	2	1	2	0	.200	.200	15	12	0
Billy Myers	ss	7	23	0	3	0	0	0	2	2	5	0	.130	.130	14	17	**3**
Bill Werber	3b	7	27	**5**	**10**	**4**	0	0	2	4	2	0	**.370**	.519	9	16	2
Ival Goodman	rf	7	**29**	**5**	8	2	0	0	5	0	3	0	.276	.345	10	0	0
Mike McCormick	cf	7	**29**	1	9	3	0	0	2	1	6	0	.310	.414	24	1	1
Jimmy Ripple	lf	7	21	3	7	2	0	**1**	**6**	4	2	0	.333	.571	14	0	0
Jimmie Wilson	c	6	17	2	6	0	0	0	0	1	2	**1**	.353	.353	26	2	0
Bill Baker	c	3	4	1	1	0	0	0	0	0	1	0	.250	.250	7	0	1
Ernie Lombardi	ph-c	2	3	0	1	1	0	0	0	1	0	0	.333	.667	4	0	0
Lonnie Frey	ph-pr-2b	3	2	0	0	0	0	0	0	0	0	0	.000	.000	0	1	0
Morrie Arnovich	ph-lf	1	1	0	0	0	0	0	0	0	0	0	.000	.000	2	0	0
Lew Riggs	ph	3	3	1	0	0	0	0	0	0	2	0	.000	.000			
Harry Craft	ph	1	1	0	0	0	0	0	0	0	0	0	.000	.000			
Bucky Walters	p	2	7	2	2	1	0	**1**	2	0	1	0	.286	.857	0	4	0
Paul Derringer	p	3	7	0	0	0	0	0	0	0	1	0	.000	.000	0	5	0
Whitey Moore	p	3	2	0	0	0	0	0	0	0	1	0	.000	.000	0	1	0
Jim Turner	p	1	2	0	0	0	0	0	0	0	0	0	.000	.000	0	1	0
Junior Thompson	p	1	1	0	0	0	0	0	0	0	1	0	.000	.000	0	1	0
Joe Beggs	p	1	0	0	0	0	0	0	0	0	0	0	—	—	0	0	0
Johnny Hutchings	p	1	0	0	0	0	0	0	0	0	0	0	—	—	0	1	0
Elmer Riddle	p	1	0	0	0	0	0	0	0	0	0	0	—	—	0	1	0
Johnny Vander Meer	p	1	0	0	0	0	0	0	0	0	0	0	—	—	0	0	0
Milt Shoffner		Did not play															
Witt Guise		Did not play															
team total		7	232	22	58	14	0	2	21	15	30	1	.250	.336	183	66	8

Double Plays—9
Left on Bases—49

REGULAR SEASON STATISTICS

		Main Pos	G	AB	R	H	2B	3B	HR	RBI	BB	SO	SB	BA	SA
CINCINNATI REDS															
Frank McCormick		1b	155	**618**	93	**191**	**44**	3	19	127	52	26	2	.309	.482
Eddie Joost		ss	88	278	24	60	7	2	1	24	32	40	4	.216	.266
Billy Myers		ss	90	282	33	57	14	2	5	30	30	56	0	.202	.319
Bill Werber		3b	143	584	105	162	35	5	12	48	68	40	16	.277	.416
Ival Goodman		of	136	519	78	134	20	6	12	63	60	54	9	.258	.389
Mike McCormick		of	110	417	48	125	20	0	1	30	13	36	8	.300	.355
Jimmy Ripple	a	of	32	101	15	31	10	0	4	20	13	5	1	.307	.525
Jimmie Wilson		c	16	37	2	9	2	0	0	3	2	1	1	.243	.297
Bill Baker		c	27	69	5	15	1	1	0	7	4	8	2	.217	.261
Ernie Lombardi		c	109	376	50	120	22	0	14	74	31	14	0	.319	.489
Lonnie Frey		2b	150	563	102	150	23	6	8	54	80	48	**22**	.266	.371
Morrie Arnovich	b	of	62	211	17	62	10	2	0	21	13	10	1	.284	.351
Lew Riggs		ph	41	72	8	21	7	1	1	9	2	4	0	.292	.458
Harry Craft		of	115	422	47	103	18	5	6	48	17	46	2	.244	.353
Bucky Walters		p	37	117	11	24	3	0	1	18	4	14	2	.205	.256
Paul Derringer		p	37	108	4	18	4	0	0	8	0	19	0	.167	.204
Whitey Moore		p	25	39	1	5	0	0	0	1	2	9	0	.128	.128
Jim Turner		p	25	75	7	18	5	1	0	2	0	3	0	.240	.333
Junior Thompson		p	33	79	5	18	4	1	0	11	2	26	0	.228	.308
Joe Beggs		p	37	21	1	4	0	0	0	0	0	5	0	.190	.190
Johnny Hutchings		p	19	13	2	2	0	0	0	0	2	1	0	.154	.154
Elmer Riddle		p	15	7	0	1	0	0	0	0	1	4	0	.143	.143
Johnny Vander Meer		p	12	20	6	6	2	0	0	0	1	3	0	.300	.400
Milt Shoffner		p	20	16	1	2	0	0	0	0	0	4	0	.125	.125
Witt Guise		p	2	3	0	1	0	0	0	0	0	0	0	.333	.333
team total			155	5372	707	1427	264	38	89	649	453	503	72	.266	.379

a—from Brooklyn
b—from Philadelphia
Willard Hershberger (c), Lew Gamble (of-ph), Johnny Rizzo (of), Mike Dejan (ph), Dick West (c), Wally Berger (ph), Vince DiMaggio (of), and Red Barrett (p) also played for the Reds during the season

WORLD SERIES STATISTICS

	Pos	G	AB	R	H	2B	3B	HR	RBI	BB	SO	SB	BA	SA	PO	A	E
DETROIT TIGERS																	
Rudy York	1b	7	26	3	6	0	**1**	1	2	4	**7**	0	.231	.423	**60**	2	0
Charlie Gehringer	2b	7	28	3	6	0	0	0	1	2	0	0	.214	.214	17	20	0
Dick Bartell	ss	7	26	2	7	2	0	0	3	3	3	0	.269	.346	13	12	1
Pinky Higgins	3b	7	24	2	8	3	**1**	**1**	**6**	3	3	0	.333	**.667**	4	**30**	2
Bruce Campbell	rf	7	25	4	9	1	0	**1**	5	4	4	0	.360	.520	17	0	0
Barney McCosky	cf	7	23	**5**	7	1	0	0	1	**7**	0	0	.304	.348	19	0	0
Hank Greenberg	lf	7	28	**5**	**10**	2	**1**	**1**	**6**	2	5	0	.357	.607	12	0	0
Billy Sullivan	c-ph	5	13	3	2	0	0	0	0	5	2	0	.154	.154	23	2	0
Birdie Tebbetts	c-ph	4	11	0	0	0	0	0	0	0	0	0	.000	.000	13	3	1
Frank Croucher	ss	1	0	0	0	0	0	0	0	0	0	0	—	—	0	0	0
Earl Averill	ph	3	3	0	0	0	0	0	0	0	0	0	.000	.000			
Pete Fox	ph	1	1	0	0	0	0	0	0	0	0	0	.000	.000			
Dutch Meyer		Did not play															
Tuck Stainbach		Did not play															
Bobo Newsom	p	3	10	1	1	0	0	0	0	0	1	0	.100	.100	2	0	0
Johnny Gorsica	p	2	4	0	0	0	0	0	0	0	2	0	.000	.000	0	**6**	0
Tommy Bridges	p	1	3	0	0	0	0	0	0	0	1	0	.000	.000	0	1	0
Schoolboy Rowe	p	2	1	0	0	0	0	0	0	0	1	0	.000	.000	0	1	0
Clay Smith	p	1	1	0	0	0	0	0	0	0	1	0	.000	.000	0	1	0
Dizzy Trout	p	1	1	0	0	0	0	0	0	0	0	0	.000	.000	0	1	0
Fred Hutchinson	p	1	0	0	0	0	0	0	0	0	0	0	—	—	0	0	0
Archie McKain	p	1	0	0	0	0	0	0	0	0	0	0	—	—	0	1	0
Hal Newhouser		Did not play															
Al Benton		Did not play															
Tom Seats		Did not play															
team total		7	228	28	56	9	3	4	24	30	30	0	.246	.364	180	80	4

Double Plays—4
Left on Bases—50

REGULAR SEASON STATISTICS

	Main Pos	G	AB	R	H	2B	3B	HR	RBI	BB	SO	SB	BA	SA
DETROIT TIGERS														
Rudy York	1b	155	588	105	186	46	6	33	134	89	88	3	.316	.583
Charlie Gehringer	2b	139	515	108	161	33	3	10	81	101	17	10	.313	.447
Dick Bartell	ss	139	528	76	123	24	3	7	53	76	53	12	.233	.330
Pinky Higgins	3b	131	480	70	130	24	3	13	76	61	31	4	.271	.415
Bruce Campbell	of	103	297	56	84	15	5	8	44	45	28	2	.283	.448
Barney McCosky	of	143	589	123	**200**	39	**19**	4	57	67	41	13	.340	.491
Hank Greenberg	of	148	573	129	195	**50**	8	**41**	**150**	93	75	6	.340	**.670**
Billy Sullivan	c	78	220	36	68	14	4	3	41	31	11	2	.309	.450
Birdie Tebbetts	c	111	379	46	112	24	4	4	46	35	14	4	.296	.412
Frank Croucher	ss	37	57	3	6	0	0	0	2	4	5	0	.105	.105
Earl Averill	ph	64	118	10	33	4	1	2	20	5	14	0	.280	.381
Pete Fox	of	93	350	49	101	17	4	5	48	21	30	7	.289	.403
Dutch Meyer	2b	23	58	12	15	3	0	0	6	4	10	2	.259	.310
Tuck Stainbach	of	15	40	4	9	2	0	0	1	1	9	0	.225	.275
Bobo Newsom	p	36	107	9	23	5	0	0	16	1	17	0	.215	.262
Johnny Gorsica	p	29	62	6	12	0	2	1	7	3	15	0	.194	.306
Tommy Bridges	p	29	68	5	12	2	0	0	4	3	23	0	.176	.206
Schoolboy Rowe	p	27	67	7	18	6	1	1	18	5	13	1	.269	.433
Clay Smith	p	14	7	0	0	0	0	0	0	0	4	0	.000	.000
Dizzy Trout	p	33	31	4	4	0	0	0	4	2	9	0	.129	.129
Fred Hutchinson	p	17	30	1	8	1	0	0	2	0	0	0	.267	.300
Archie McKain	p	27	7	3	1	0	0	0	0	2	4	0	.143	.143
Hal Newhouser	p	28	40	3	8	0	0	0	2	3	4	0	.200	.200
Al Benton	p	42	17	0	0	0	0	0	0	0	8	0	.000	.000
Tom Seats	p	26	12	0	1	0	0	0	0	0	2	0	.083	.083
team total		155	5418	**888**	1549	**312**	65	134	**829**	**664**	556	66	**.286**	.442

Red Kress (3b-ss), Scat Metha (2b-3b), Pat Mullin (ph), Frank Secory (ph), Floyd Giebell (p), Cotton Pippen (p), Lynn Nelson (p), Dick Conger (p), Bud Thomas (p), and Bob Uhle (p) also played for the Tigers during the season.

PITCHING

WORLD SERIES STATISTICS

	G	GS	CG	IP	H	R	ER	BB	SO	W	L	SV	ERA
CINCINNATI REDS													
Paul Derringer	**3**	**3**	2	19⅓	17	**8**	6	**10**	6	**2**	1	0	2.79
Bucky Walters	2	2	2	18	8	3	3	6	6	**2**	0	0	1.50
Whitey Moore	**3**	0	0	8⅓	8	3	3	6	7	0	0	0	3.24
Jim Turner	1	1	0	6	8	5	5	0	4	0	1	0	7.50
Junior Thompson	1	1	0	3⅓	8	6	6	4	2	0	1	0	16.20
Johnny Vander Meer	1	0	0	3	2	0	0	3	2	0	0	0	0.00
Joe Beggs	1	0	0	1	3	2	1	0	1	0	0	0	9.00
Johnny Hutchings	1	0	0	1	2	1	1	1	0	0	0	0	9.00
Elmer Riddle	1	0	0	1	0	0	0	0	2	0	0	0	0.00
Milt Shoffner	Did not play												
Witt Guise	Did not play												
team total	7	7	4	61	56	28	25	30	30	4	3	0	3.69
DETROIT TIGERS													
Bobo Newsom	**3**	**3**	**3**	**26**	**18**	4	4	4	**17**	**2**	1	0	1.38
Johnny Gorsica	2	0	0	11⅓	6	1	1	4	4	0	0	0	**0.79**
Tommy Bridges	1	1	1	9	10	4	3	1	5	1	0	0	3.00
Clay Smith	1	0	0	4	1	1	1	3	1	0	0	0	2.25
Schoolboy Rowe	2	2	0	3⅔	12	7	**7**	1	1	0	**2**	0	17.18
Archie McKain	1	0	0	3	4	1	1	0	0	0	0	0	3.00
Dizzy Trout	1	1	0	2	6	3	2	1	1	0	1	0	9.00
Fred Hutchinson	1	0	0	1	1	1	1	1	1	0	0	0	9.00
Hal Newhouser	Did not play												
Al Benton	Did not play												
Tom Seats	Did not play												
team total	7	7	4	60	58	22	20	15	30	3	4	0	3.00

REGULAR SEASON STATISTICS

	G	GS	CG	IP	H	ER	BB	SO	W	L	Pct	SV	ShO	ERA
CINCINNATI REDS														
Paul Derringer	37	**37**	26	297	280	101	48	115	20	12	.625	0	3	3.06
Bucky Walters	36	36	**29**	**305**	241	84	92	115	**22**	10	.688	0	3	**2.48**
Whitey Moore	25	15	5	117	100	47	56	60	8	8	.500	1	1	3.62
Jim Turner	24	23	11	187	187	60	32	53	14	7	.667	0	0	2.89
Junior Thompson	33	31	17	225	197	83	96	103	16	9	.640	0	3	3.32
Johnny Vander Meer	10	7	2	48	38	20	41	41	3	1	.750	1	0	3.75
Joe Beggs	37	1	0	77	68	17	21	25	12	3	.800	**7**	0	1.99
Johnny Hutchings	19	4	0	54	53	21	18	18	2	1	.667	0	0	3.50
Elmer Riddle	15	1	1	34	30	7	17	9	1	2	.333	2	0	1.85
Milt Shoffner	20	0	0	54	56	34	18	17	1	0	1.000	0	0	5.67
Witt Guise	2	0	0	8	8	1	5	1	0	0	—	0	0	1.13
team total	155	155	**91**	1408	1263	477	445	557	**100**	53	**.654**	11	10	**3.05**
DETROIT TIGERS														
Bobo Newsom	36	34	20	264	235	83	100	164	21	5	.808	0	3	2.83
Johnny Gorsica	29	20	5	160	170	77	57	68	7	7	.500	0	2	4.33
Tommy Bridges	29	28	12	198	171	74	88	133	12	9	.571	0	2	3.36
Clay Smith	14	1	0	28	32	16	13	14	1	1	.500	0	0	5.14
Schoolboy Rowe	27	23	11	169	170	65	43	61	16	3	**.842**	0	1	3.46
Archie McKain	27	0	0	51	48	16	25	24	5	0	1.000	3	0	2.82
Dizzy Trout	33	10	1	101	125	50	54	64	3	7	.300	2	0	4.46
Fred Hutchinson	17	10	1	76	85	48	26	32	3	7	.300	0	0	5.68
Hal Newhouser	28	20	7	133	149	72	76	89	9	9	.500	0	0	4.87
Al Benton	42	0	0	79	93	39	36	50	6	10	.375	**17**	0	4.44
Tom Seats	26	2	0	56	67	29	21	25	2	2	.500	1	0	4.66
team total	155	155	59	1375	1425	613	570	**752**	**90**	64	**.584**	**23**	10	4.01

Total Attendance—281,927   Average Attendance—40,275   Winning Player's Share—$5,804   Losing Player's Share—$3,532

1941
The One That Got Away

Joe DiMaggio hit safely in 56 straight games this summer and Ted Williams successfully broke through the .400 barrier with a .406 batting average, but these noteworthy achievements took a backseat in Brooklyn to the pennant drive of the Dodgers. Beating out the Cardinals with a September spurt, the Dodgers rewarded their fanatical fans with their first pennant in 21 years. Managed by thirty-five-year-old Leo Durocher, who also put in some time t shortstop, the Bums fielded a solid lineup from top to bottom. In the outfield were batting champion Pete Reiser, an extraordinary young talent who would later ruin his career with a series of collisions with outfield walls; Dixie Walker, a popular player dubbed "The People's Cherce"; and Joe Medwick, the former slugger on the Gashouse Gang Cardinals. The infield had National League MVP Dolph Camilli at first base, longtime Cub Billy Herman at second base, clutch-hitting Cookie Lavagetto at third base, and young Pee Wee Reese at shortstop. The catcher was Mickey Owen, a good glove man picked up from the Cards, and the top pitchers were 22-game-winners Kirby Higbe and Whit Wyatt, plus relief ace Hugh Casey.

The borough of Brooklyn followed every move of this bunch, while many fans in other parts of New York City enjoyed a smug satisfaction with the return of the Yankees to the top of the American League after a year off the pace. Manager Joe McCarthy still had the old bunch of Joe DiMaggio, Charlie Keller, Tommy Henrich, Joe Gordon, Bill Dickey, Red Rolfe, Red Ruffing, Lefty Gomez, and Johnny Murphy, and to them he added a rookie first baseman in Johnny Sturm and a fine rookie shortstop in little Phil Rizzuto. Five times before had the Yankees faced the Giants in the World Series, but the Subway Series this year took the train out to Brooklyn for the first time.

The Dodgers took their first look at Yankee Stadium in the Series opener, with Red Ruffing facing veteran Curt Davis on the mound. Both thirty-seven-year-old starters used their mound savvy to limit the opposition to six hits, but the Yanks used their hits to score three runs and drive Davis from the game in the sixth inning. Joe Gordon and Bill Dickey did most of the clutch hitting in the 3–2 Yankee win. The Dodgers turned the tables the next day, however, winning 3–2 behind Wyatt's nine-hitter to even the Series at 1–1.

The Yankees then got their first taste of bandbox Ebbets Field, an irregularly shaped hitters' paradise. The Yanks started 14-game-winner Marius Russo on the mound, while the Bums relied on thirty-nine-year-old Freddie Fitzsimmons, who had a good knuckle ball and a lot of heart in his repertoire. Both men pitched shutout ball through six innings, but then a line drive off Russo's bat caught Fitzsimmons flush on the left knee and broke the kneecap. Old Freddie came out, but reliever Hugh Casey couldn't do the job. Four hits in the eighth inning netted the Yanks two runs, and a single tally by the Bums in the bottom of the eighth wasn't enough to avert a 2–1 loss. Down in the Series two games to one, the Dodgers scrapped back the next day to take a 4–3 lead after eight innings. Hugh Casey had pitched shutout ball since the fifth inning and needed only three outs to wrap up a win. He quickly disposed of Sturm and Rolfe and went to a full count on Tommy Henrich. He then broke off a curve which some people have claimed was a spitter, and Henrich swung and missed. The cheer about to burst forth from the lungs of the Ebbets Field fans choked when catcher Owen let the pitch get past him and Henrich sprinted safely down to first. Casey was still only one out from victory, but he was about to make a classic goat out of Mickey Owen. DiMaggio promptly singled to left, and a crushing double to right by Keller drove two runs in and left the crowd in shocked anguish. Bill Dickey walked, Joe Gordon doubled, and the Yankees had a 7–4 victory and a 3–1 edge in the Series. The Dodgers tried to come back from that disheartening slap of fate, but Ernie Bonham threw a four-hitter in game five for a 3–1 Yankee triumph to give the Bronx Bombers their ninth World Championship.

Game 1 October 1 at New York

Bkn.		000	010	100				
N.Y.		010	101	00x				

Brooklyn	Pos	AB	R	H	RBI	PO	A	E
Walker	rf	3	0	0	0	3	0	0
Herman	2b	3	0	0	0	0	6	0
Reiser	cf	3	0	0	0	4	0	0
Camilli	1b	4	0	0	0	7	2	0
Medwick	lf	4	0	1	0	4	0	0
Lavagetto	3b	4	1	0	0	0	0	0
Reese	ss	4	1	3	0	4	2	0
Owen	c	2	0	1	1	1	0	0
a Riggs		1	0	1	1	0	0	0
Franks	c	1	0	0	0	0	1	0
Davis	p	2	0	0	0	1	0	0
Casey	p	0	0	0	0	0	0	0
b Wasdell		1	0	0	0	0	0	0
Allen	p	0	0	0	0	0	0	0
Totals		32	2	6	2	24	11	0

a Singled for Owen in 7th.
b Fouled out for Casey in 7th.

Double—Dickey. Triple—Owen. Home Run—Gordon. Double Plays—Rolfe to Rizzuto, Gordon to Rizzuto to Sturm. Hit by Pitcher—Sturm (by Allen). Left on Bases—Brooklyn 6, New York 8. Umpires—McGowan (A), Pinelli (N), Grieve (A), Goetz (N). Attendance—**68,540.** Time of Game—2:08.

New York	Pos	AB	R	H	RBI	PO	A	E
Sturm	1b	3	0	1	0	7	0	0
Rolfe	3b	3	0	1	0	2	2	0
Henrich	rf	4	0	0	0	4	0	0
DiMaggio	cf	4	0	0	0	5	0	0
Keller	lf	2	2	0	0	4	0	0
Dickey	c	4	0	2	1	6	0	0
Gordon	2b	2	1	2	2	0	2	0
Rizzuto	ss	4	0	0	0	3	5	1
Ruffing	p	3	0	0	0	0	0	0
Totals		29	3	6	3	27	9	1

Pitching	IP	H	R	ER	BB	SO
Brooklyn						
Davis (L)	5⅓	6	3	3	3	1
Casey	⅓	0	0	0	0	0
Allen	2	0	0	0	0	2
New York						
Ruffing (W)	9	6	2	1	3	5

1st Inning
Brooklyn
Walker walked.
1 Herman grounded to third.
2 Reiser flied to center.
3 Camilli struck out.
New York
Sturm singled to left.
1 Rolfe forced Sturm at second, Camilli to Reese.
2 Henrich forced Rolfe at second, Herman to Reese.
3 DiMaggio flied to left.

2nd Inning
Brooklyn
1 Medwick struck out.
2 Lavagetto grounded to short.
3 Reese flied to left.
New York
1 Keller flied to center.
2 Dickey grounded to second. Gordon homered into the lower left field stands.
3 Rizzuto flied to left.

3rd Inning
Brooklyn
1 Owen flied to left.
2 Davis flied to left.
3 Walker flied to left (Keller's 4th successive putout).
New York
1 Ruffing grounded to short.
2 Sturm grounded out, Camilli to Davis.
3 Rolfe struck out.

4th Inning
Brooklyn
1 Herman grounded to short.
2 Reiser fanned.
3 Camilli fanned.
New York
1 Henrich popped to short.
2 Medwick made a great catch of DiMaggio's fly at the low left field concrete wall. Keller walked. Dickey doubled off the right-center field wall, scoring Keller. Gordon intentionally walked.
3 Rizzuto grounded to second.

5th Inning
Brooklyn
1 Medwick flied to center.
2 Lavagetto flied to center. Reese singled to left. Owen tripled into left-center, scoring Reese.
3 Davis grounded to short.
New York
1 Ruffing flied to center.
2 Sturm grounded to second. Rolfe singled to center.
3 Henrich flied to right.

6th Inning
Brooklyn
1 Walker lined to center. Herman walked. Reiser walked.
2 Camilli struck out for the third time.
3 Medwick forced Herman at third, Rolfe unassisted.
New York
1 DiMaggio grounded to short. Keller walked. Dickey singled to center, moving Keller to third. Gordon singled to center, scoring Keller with Dickey stopping at second. For Brooklyn—Casey pitching.
2 Rizzuto flied to center.
3 Ruffing flied to right.

7th Inning
Brooklyn
Lavagetto safe at first on Rizzuto's throwing error to first. Reese singled with Lavagetto going to second. Riggs, pinch-hitting for Owen, singled to center, scoring Lavagetto with Reese going to second.
1,2 Wasdell, pinch hitting for Casey, fouled to Rolfe who threw to Rizzuto covering third to double up Reese trying to advance after the catch.
3 Walker grounded to second.
New York
For Brooklyn—Franks catching and Allen pitching. Sturm hit by a pitched ball.
1 Sturm caught stealing Franks to Reese. Rolfe walked.
2 Henrich flied to left.
3 DiMaggio flied to center.

8th Inning
Brooklyn
1 Herman grounded to short.
2 Reiser lined to center.
3 Camilli flied to center.
New York
1 Keller grounded to second.
2 Dickey flied to right. Gordon walked.
3 Rizzuto grounded to second.

9th Inning
Brooklyn
Medwick beat out an infield hit.
1 Lavagetto fouled to Dickey. Reese singled (his third) sending Medwick to second.
2,3 Franks in his first at-bat hit into a double play, Gordon to Rizzuto to Sturm.

Game 2 October 2 at New York

Brooklyn	Pos	AB	R	H	RBI	PO	A	E
Walker	rf	4	1	0	0	4	0	0
Herman	2b	4	0	1	0	4	4	0
Reiser	cf	4	0	0	0	2	1	0
Camilli	1b	3	1	1	1	8	1	0
Medwick	lf	4	1	2	0	0	0	0
Lavagetto	3b	3	0	1	0	1	1	0
Reese	ss	4	0	1	0	1	4	2
Owen	c	2	0	1	1	6	1	0
Wyatt	p	3	0	0	0	0	1	0
Totals		31	3	6	3	27	13	2

Pitching	IP	H	R	ER	BB	SO
Brooklyn						
Wyatt (W)	9	9	2	2	5	5
New York						
Chandler (L)	*5	4	3	2	2	2
Murphy	4	2	0	0	1	2

*Pitched to 2 batters in 6th.

```
Bkn.   000 021 000
N.Y.   011 000 000
```

New York	Pos	AB	R	H	RBI	PO	A	E
Sturm	1b	5	0	1	0	11	0	0
Rolfe	3b	5	0	1	0	1	2	0
Henrich	rf	4	1	1	0	4	0	0
DiMaggio	cf	3	0	0	0	4	0	0
Keller	lf	4	1	2	1	1	0	0
Dickey	c	4	0	0	0	5	1	0
a Bordagaray		0	0	0	0	0	0	0
Rosar	c	0	0	0	0	0	0	0
Gordon	2b	1	0	1	0	2	7	1
Rizzuto	ss	4	0	1	0	3	5	0
Chandler	p	2	0	1	1	0	0	0
Murphy	p	1	0	0	0	0	0	0
b Selkirk		1	0	1	0	0	0	0
Totals		34	2	9	2	27	15	1

a Ran for Dickey in 8th.
b Singled for Murphy in 9th.

Doubles—Henrich, Medwick.
Double Plays—Reese to Herman to Camilli, Gordon to Rizzuto to Sturm 2, Dickey to Gordon. Left on Bases—Brooklyn 4, New York 10. Umpires—Pinelli, Grieve, Goetz, McGowan. Attendance—66,248. Time of Game—2:31.

1st Inning
Brooklyn
1 Walker took a called third strike.
2 Herman grounded to second.
3 Reiser struck out on an outside pitch with a 3-2 count.
New York
1 Sturm looked at a third strike.
Henrich walked.
2,3 DiMaggio grounded into a double play Reese to Herman to Camilli.

2nd Inning
Brooklyn
1 Camilli flied to second.
Medwick singled to left-center.
2,3 Lavagetto bounced into a double play, Gordon to Rizzuto to Sturm.
New York
Keller singled to center.
1 Dickey looked at a called third strike.
Gordon walked.
2 Rizzuto grounded to second, advancing both runners.
Chandler beat out a bounder to third for a single, scoring Keller, Gordon
3 was out also attempting to score, Camilli to Owen.

3rd Inning
Brooklyn
1 Reese flied to left.
2 Owen grounded to second.
3 Wyatt grounded to short.
New York
1 Sturm lined to Camilli.
2 Rolfe grounded to first.
Henrich doubled off the right field wall.
DiMaggio walked.
Keller singled between first and second, scoring Henrich with DiMaggio going to third.
3 Dickey grounded to second.

4th Inning
Brooklyn
1 Walker grounded to second.
2 Herman grounded to third.
3 Reiser grounded to second.
New York
Gordon singled to left.
1 Rizzuto lined to second.
2 Chandler forced Gordon at second, Reese to Herman.
Sturm blooped a Texas League single into
3 center and Chandler was out trying for third, Reiser to Lavagetto.

5th Inning
Brooklyn
Camilli walked on five pitches.
Medwick doubled down the left field line, moving Camilli to third.
Lavagetto walked loading the bases.
1 Reese forced Lavagetto at second, Rizzuto to Gordon scoring Camilli.
Owen singled to left, scoring Medwick and sending Reese to third.
2,3 Wyatt grounded into a double play, Gordon to Rizzuto to Sturm.

5th Inning (continued)
New York
1 Rolfe grounded to first.
2 Henrich flied to center.
3 DiMaggio flied to right.

6th Inning
Brooklyn
Walker safely to first on Gordon's throwing error.
Herman singled to left, moving Walker to third.
For New York—Murphy pitching.
1 Reiser fanned.
Camilli singled to right, scoring Walker and advancing Herman to third.
Medwick hit a slow roller to Rizzuto
2 who threw to the plate to nail Herman.
3 Lavagetto flew out to center.
New York
1 Keller flied to right.
2 Dickey flied to right.
Gordon walked.
Rizzuto singled to left, Gordon stopping at second.
3 Murphy fanned.

7th Inning
Brooklyn
1 Reese popped to short.
Owen walked.
2,3 Wyatt was called out on strikes and Owen was doubled up trying to steal, Dickey to Gordon.
New York
1 Sturm fanned.
2 Rolfe grounded to short.
3 Henrich struck out.

8th Inning
Brooklyn
1 Walker grounded to second.
2 Herman lined to first.
3 Reiser fouled to Rolfe.
New York
1 DiMaggio flied to center.
2 Keller grounded back to the mound.
Dickey got all the way to second on Reese's double error, fumbling the grounder then throwing over Camilli's head.
Gordon intentionally walked.
Bordagaray ran for Dickey.
3 Rizzuto forced Gordon, Reese to Herman.

9th Inning
Brooklyn
For New York—Rosar catching.
1 Camilli flied to center.
2 Medwick flied to center.
Lavagetto singled to left.
3 Reese grounded to third.
New York
Selkirk, pinch hitting for Murphy, singled to right.
1 Sturm forced Selkirk at second on an attempted sacrifice, Owen to Reese.
2 Rolfe forced Sturm at second, Herman to Reese.
3 Henrich flied to right.

Game 3 October 4 at Brooklyn

New York	Pos	AB	R	H	RBI	PO	A	E
Sturm	1b	4	0	1	0	12	0	0
Rolfe	3b	4	1	2	0	1	2	0
Henrich	rf	3	1	1	0	2	0	0
DiMaggio	cf	4	0	2	1	2	0	0
Keller	lf	4	0	1	1	2	0	0
Dickey	c	4	0	0	0	4	1	0
Gordon	2b	3	0	1	0	2	4	0
Rizzuto	ss	3	0	0	0	2	3	0
Russo	p	4	0	0	0	0	4	0
Totals		33	2	8	2	27	14	0

Pitching	IP	H	R	ER	BB	SO
New York						
Russo (W)	9	4	1	1	2	5
Brooklyn						
Fitzsimmons	7	4	0	0	3	1
Casey (L)	⅓	4	2	2	0	0
French	⅔	0	0	0	0	0
Allen	1	0	0	0	0	

```
N.Y.   000 000 020
Bkn.   000 000 010
```

Brooklyn	Pos	AB	R	H	RBI	PO	A	E
Reese	ss	4	0	1	1	3	1	0
Herman	2b	1	0	0	0	0	1	0
Coscarart	2b	2	0	0	0	3	0	0
Reiser	cf	4	0	1	0	5	0	0
Medwick	lf	4	0	1	0	3	0	0
Lavagetto	3b	3	0	1	0	1	0	0
Camilli	1b	3	0	0	0	11	0	0
Walker	rf	3	1	1	0	2	0	0
Owens	c	3	0	0	0	2	1	0
Fitzsimmons	p	2	0	0	0	0	2	0
Casey	p	0	0	0	0	0	0	0
French	p	0	0	0	0	0	0	0
a Galan		1	0	0	0	0	0	0
Allen	p	0	0	0	0	0	0	0
Totals		30	1	4	1	27	8	0

a Struck out for French in 8th.

Doubles—Reiser, Walker. Triple—Gordon. Stolen Bases—Rizzuto, Sturm. Double Plays—Rizzuto to Sturm, Reese to Camilli. Left on Bases—New York 7, Brooklyn 4. Umpires—Grieve, Goetz, McGowan, Pinelli. Attendance—33,100. Time of Game—2:22.

1st Inning
New York
1 Sturm flied to center.
2 Rolfe flied to left.
3 Henrich popped to third.
Brooklyn
1 Reese bunted out to the mound. Herman walked on a full count.
2 Reiser forced Herman at second, Russo to Rizzuto, Reiser just beating the throw to first.
3 Medwick flied to right.

2nd Inning
New York
DiMaggio singled to left.
1 Keller grounded to first, DiMaggio going to second.
2 Dickey foul popped to Camilli.
3 Gordon was retired for the first time in the Series, flying to right.
Brooklyn
Lavagetto walked.
1,2 Camilli grounded into a double play, Rizzuto to Sturm.
3 Walker grounded to third.

3rd Inning
New York
1 Rizzuto grounded to the pitcher.
2 Russo flied to left.
3 Sturm grounded to second and the Yanks were retired on 5 pitches.
Brooklyn
1 Owen flied to center.
2 Fitzsimmons flied to left.
3 Reese grounded to short.

4th Inning
New York
Rolfe singled to center.
1 Henrich forced Rolfe at second, Reese unassisted.
2 Henrich picked off first Owen to Camilli.
3 DiMaggio popped to first.
Brooklyn
1 Herman grounded to second (Herman hurting his side on the swing).
2 Reiser lined to second.
Medwick got the first hit off Russo a tap down the third base-line which he and Rolfe let go hoping it would roll foul but it stayed fair.
3 Lavagetto lined to second.

5th Inning
New York
For Brooklyn—Coscarart playing second.
1 Keller grounded to second.
2 Dickey flied to deep center.
Gordon tripled off the lower stand in left-center.
Rizzuto intentionally walked.
Rizzuto stole second.
3 Russo fanned.
Brooklyn
1 Camilli fanned.
2 Walker grounded to second.
3 Owen flied deep to center.

6th Inning
New York
Sturm singled on a blooper to short center.
Sturm stole second.
1 Rolfe pop fouled to Owen on an attempted sacrifice.
Henrich walked.
2 DiMaggio flied to right.
3 Keller grounded weakly to first.
Brooklyn
1 Fitzsimmons grounded to short.
2 Reese flied to left.
3 Coscarart's bounder was deflected by Russo to Rolfe who threw to first for the out.

7th Inning
New York
1 Dickey grounded to second.
Gordon walked.
2 Rizzuto grounded to second, advancing Gordon to second.
3 Russo's line drive caromed off Fitzsimmons' left leg to Reese for a pop out. Fitzsimmons had to be helped from the field.
Brooklyn
Reiser doubled off the right-center screen.
1 Dickey dropped Medwick's third strike and had to throw him out.
2 Lavagetto grounded to second with Reiser going to third.
3 Camilli took a called third strike.

8th Inning
New York
For Brooklyn—Casey pitching.
1 Sturm flied to center.
Rolfe singled to right.
Henrich beat out an infield hit.
DiMaggio singled to center, scoring Rolfe with Henrich going to third.
Keller singled to center, scoring Henrich with DiMaggio going to third.
For Brooklyn—French pitching.
2,3 Dickey grounded into a double play, Reese to Camilli.
Brooklyn
Walker lined a double into right.
1 Owen bounced back to the pitcher with Walker holding second.
2 Galan, pinch hitting for French, fanned. Reese singled to right, scoring Walker.
3 Coscarart popped to third.

9th Inning
New York
For Brooklyn—Allen pitching.
1 Gordon flied to center.
2 Rizzuto flied to left.
3 Russo lined to center.
Brooklyn
1 Reiser struck out.
2 Medwick flied to short right.
3 Lavagetto grounded to second.

Game 4 October 5 at Brooklyn

New York	Pos	AB	R	H	RBI	PO	A	E
Sturm	1b	5	0	2	2	9	1	0
Rolfe	3b	5	1	2	0	0	2	0
Henrich	rf	4	1	0	0	3	0	0
DiMaggio	cf	4	1	2	0	2	0	0
Keller	lf	5	1	4	3	1	0	0
Dickey	c	2	2	0	0	7	0	0
Gordon	2b	5	1	2	2	2	3	0
Rizzuto	ss	4	0	0	0	2	3	0
Donald	p	2	0	0	0	0	1	0
Breuer	p	1	0	0	0	0	1	0
b Selkirk		1	0	0	0	0	0	0
Murphy	p	1	0	0	0	1	0	0
Totals		39	7	12	7	27	11	0

Pitching	IP	H	R	ER	BB	SO
New York						
Donald	*4	6	4	4	3	2
Breuer	3	3	0	0	1	2
Murphy (W)	2	0	0	0	0	1
Brooklyn						
Higbe	$3\frac{2}{3}$	6	3	3	2	1
French	$\frac{1}{3}$	0	0	0	0	0
Allen	$\frac{2}{3}$	1	0	0	1	0
Casey (L)	$4\frac{1}{3}$	5	4	0	2	1

*Pitched to 2 batters in 5th.

N.Y.	100	200	004
Bkn.	000	220	000

Brooklyn	Pos	AB	R	H	RBI	PO	A	E
Reese	ss	5	0	0	0	2	4	0
Walker	rf	5	1	2	0	5	0	0
Reiser	cf	5	1	2	2	1	0	0
Camilli	1b	4	0	2	0	10	1	0
Riggs	3b	3	0	0	0	0	2	0
Medwick	lf	2	0	0	0	1	0	0
Allen	p	0	0	0	0	0	0	0
Casey	p	2	0	1	0	0	3	0
Owen	c	2	1	0	0	2	1	1
Coscarart	2b	3	1	0	0	4	2	0
Higbe	p	1	0	1	0	0	1	0
French	p	0	0	0	0	0	0	0
a Wasdell	lf	3	0	1	2	2	0	0
Totals		35	4	9	4	27	14	1

a Doubled for French in 4th.
b Grounded out for Breuer in 8th.

Doubles—Camilli, Gordon, Keller 2, Walker, Wasdell. Home Run—Reiser. Double Play—Gordon to Rizzuto to Sturm. Hit by Pitcher—Henrich (by Allen). Left on Bases—New York 11, Brooklyn 8. Umpires—Goetz, McGowan, Pinelli, Grieve. Attendance—33,813. Time of Game—2:54.

1st Inning
New York
1 Sturm grounded to short.
Rolfe singled into left.
2 Henrich flied to left.
DiMaggio walked.
Keller singled beyond first, scoring Rolfe with DiMaggio going to third.
3 Dickey grounded to second.
Brooklyn
1 Reese fouled to Dickey.
2 Walker out on his bunt toward third, thrown out by Donald.
3 Reised looked at a third strike.

2nd Inning
New York
1 Gordon grounded back to the mound.
2 Rizzuto flied to center.
3 Donald popped to short.
Brooklyn
Camilli doubled off the right-center field wall.
1 Riggs flied to short right.
2 Medwick grounded to third, Sturm making a good catch on Rolfe's high throw.
Owen walked.
3 Coscarart fanned.

3rd Inning
New York
1 Sturm lined to right.
Rolfe singled to center.
2 Henrich flied deep to Walker in right-center.
3 DiMaggio forced Rolfe at second, Reese to Coscarart.
Brooklyn
Higbe singled to center.
1 Reese forced Higbe at second, Gordon to Rizzuto.
2 Walker lined to left.
Reiser singled off Gordon's glove, advancing Reese to third.
3 Camilli grounded to first.

4th Inning
New York
Keller doubled to right-center.
Dickey walked.
Gordon singled to left, loading the bases.
1 Rizzuto forced Keller at the plate, Riggs to Owen (bases still loaded).
2 Donald struck out on three pitches.
Sturm singled to left, scoring Dickey and Gordon, Rizzuto going to second.
For Brooklyn—French pitching.
3 On a passed ball both Rizzuto and Sturm ran for the next bases with Rizzuto getting caught and tagged out by Reese.
Brooklyn
1 Riggs popped to second.
2 Medwick flied to DiMaggio in left-center.
Owen walked.
Coscarart walked.
Wasdell, pinch hitting for French, doubled into the left field corner, scoring Owen and Coscarart.
3 Reese grounded to short.

5th Inning
New York
For Brooklyn—Wasdell playing left, Allen pitching (batting 6th).
1 Rolfe flied to right.
Henrich hit by a pitched ball.
2 DiMaggio lined to left.
Keller singled off Coscarart's leg, moving Henrich to third.
Dickey walked, loading the bases.
For Brooklyn—Casey pitching.
3 Gordon flied to left.
Brooklyn
Walker doubled to left.
Reiser hit a two-run homer over the scoreboard.
For New York—Breuer pitching.
1 Camilli lined to right.
2 Riggs fanned.
Casey singled to center.
3 Owen lined to center.

6th Inning
New York
1 Rizzuto fouled to Camilli.
2 Breuer flied to right.
Sturm singled to right.
3 Rolfe popped to second.
Brooklyn
1 Coscarart grounded to third.
2 Wasdell grounded back to the mound.
3 Reese popped to second.

7th Inning
New York
1 Henrich popped to second.
DiMaggio singled on an infield hit to third.
2 Keller popped to second.
3 Dickey grounded to the pitcher.
Brooklyn
Walker singled to left.
1,2 Reiser grounded into a double play, Gordon to Rizzuto to Sturm.
Camilli singled through the box.
Riggs walked.
3 Casey looked at a called third strike.

8th Inning
New York
1 Gordon flied to right.
2 Rizzuto bunted for an out to the pitcher.
3 Selkirk, pinch hitting for Breuer, grounded to short.
Brooklyn
For New York—Murphy pitching.
1 Owen grounded to second.
2 Coscarart struck out.
3 Wasdell flied to right.

9th Inning
New York
1 Sturm grounded to second.
2 Rolfe grounded to the pitcher.
Henrich got to first on a strike out as Owen dropped his third strike for an error.
DiMaggio singled into left.
Keller doubled off the right field wall, scoring Henrich and DiMaggio.
Dickey walked.
Gordon doubled over Wasdell's head, scoring Keller and Dickey.
Rizzuto walked.
3 Murphy grounded to short.
Brooklyn
1 Reese fouled to Dickey.
2 Walker grounded to short.
3 Reiser grounded out, Sturm to Murphy.

Game 5 October 6 at Brooklyn

New York	Pos	AB	R	H	RBI	PO	A	E
Sturm	1b	4	0	1	0	9	0	0
Rolfe	3b	3	0	0	0	3	0	0
Henrich	rf	3	1	1	1	1	0	0
DiMaggio	cf	4	0	1	0	6	0	0
Keller	lf	3	1	0	0	4	0	0
Dickey	c	4	1	1	0	2	0	0
Gordon	2b	3	0	1	1	0	3	0
Rizzuto	ss	3	0	1	0	2	2	0
Bonham	p	4	0	0	0	0	1	0
Totals		31	3	6	2	27	6	0

Pitching	IP	H	R	ER	BB	SO
New York						
Bonham (W)	9	4	1	1	2	2
Brooklyn						
Wyatt (L)	9	6	3	3	5	9

N.Y.	020	010	000
Bkn.	001	000	000

Brooklyn	Pos	AB	R	H	RBI	PO	A	E
Walker	rf	3	0	1	0	0	0	0
Riggs	3b	4	0	1	0	1	3	0
Reiser	cf	4	0	1	1	2	0	0
Camilli	1b	4	0	0	0	9	1	0
Medwick	lf	3	0	0	0	0	0	0
Reese	ss	3	0	0	0	2	3	1
b Wasdell		1	0	0	0	0	0	0
Owen	c	3	0	0	0	9	1	0
Coscarart	2b	2	0	0	0	3	3	0
a Galan		1	0	0	0	0	0	0
Herman	2b	0	0	0	0	0	2	0
Wyatt	p	3	1	1	0	1	1	0
Totals		31	1	4	1	27	14	1

a Fouled out for Coscarart in 7th.
b Flied out for Reese in 9th.

Double—Wyatt. Triple—Reiser. Home Run—Henrich. Double Plays—Owen to Riggs, Reese to Coscarart to Camilli, Herman to Reese to Camilli. Wild Pitch—Wyatt. Left on Bases—New York 6, Brooklyn 5. Umpires—McGowan, Pinelli, Grieve, Goetz. Attendance—34,072. Time of Game—2:13.

1st Inning
New York
Sturm singled to center.
1 Rolfe forced Sturm at second, Reese to Coscarart.
Henrich walked, the fourth ball getting away from Owen rolling into the Yankee dugout however, Rolfe held second.
2,3 As DiMaggio went down swinging, Rolfe was caught trying for third, Owen to Riggs.
Brooklyn
1 Walker flied to left.
2 Riggs grounded to second.
Reiser tripled off the center field fence.
3 Camilli popped to short.

2nd Inning
New York
Keller walked (again Owen lost the ball).
Dickey singled to center moving Keller to third.
Keller scored and Dickey went to second on Wyatt's wild pitch.
Gordon singled to right, scoring Dickey.
1 Rizzuto forced Gordon at second, Riggs to Coscarart.
2 Bonham fanned.
3 Sturm bunted out to third.
Brooklyn
Medwick walked.
1 Reese flied to center.
2 Owen flied to left.
3 Coscarart grounded to the pitcher.

3rd Inning
New York
Rolfe walked.
1 Henrich flied to center.
2 DiMaggio struck out.
3 Keller grounded to second.
Brooklyn
Wyatt doubled into the left field corner.
1 Walker flied to center.
Riggs singled off Bonham's ankle, the ball rolling toward third and advancing Wyatt to third.
2 Reiser flied to very deep right, Wyatt scoring after the catch.
3 Camilli fanned.

4th Inning
New York
1 Dickey grounded back to the mound.
Gordon walked provoking a big argument by Wyatt and Durocher on plate umpire McGowan's calls.
Rizzuto walked.
2 Bonham fanned after a big protest by McCarthy and Bonham to McGowan on the second strike call.
3 Sturm grounded to first.
Brooklyn
1 Medwick lined to center.
2 Reese lined to left.
3 Owen fouled to Rolfe.

5th Inning
New York
1 Rolfe grounded out Camilli to Wyatt.
Henrich homered over the right field wall.
2 DiMaggio flied to deep center, a fight between Wyatt and DiMaggio was averted by the umps as both dugouts emptied on to the field.
3 Keller fanned.
Brooklyn
1 Coscarart flied to DiMaggio as objects from the stands were hurled at him.
2 Wyatt also flied to DiMaggio.
Walker walked.
3 Riggs fouled to Rolfe.

6th Inning
New York
Dickey got safely to first on Reese's error.
1,2 Gordon hit into a double play, Reese to Coscarart to Camilli.
Rizzuto singled to left.
3 Bonham fanned.
Brooklyn
1 Reiser grounded to second.
2 Camilli flied to left.
3 On only the fourth pitch of the inning Medwick grounded to short.

7th Inning
New York
1 Storm grounded to second.
2 Rolfe popped to short.
3 Henrich looked at a called third strike.
Brooklyn
1 Reese popped to first.
2 Owen grounded to short.
3 Galan, pinch-hitting for Coscarart, fouled to Sturm (Bonham using only three pitches to retire the side, he only pitched seven balls in the course of two innings).

8th Inning
New York
For Brooklyn—Herman at second.
DiMaggio singled to center.
1,2 Keller grounded into a double play, Herman to Reese to Camilli.
3 Dickey grounded to second.
Brooklyn
1 Wyatt grounded to second.
Walker singled to right.
2 Riggs fouled to Storm.
3 Reiser fanned.

9th Inning
New York
1 Gordon grounded to third.
2 Rizzuto went down swinging.
3 Bonham also swung at a third strike.
Brooklyn
1 Camilli lined to short.
2 Medwick fouled to Rolfe.
3 Wasdell, pinch hitting for Reese, ended the Series flying to deep center.

1941 WORLD SERIES COMPOSITE BOX

	Wins	Composite Line Score
New York Yankees (A.L.)	4	1 4 1 3 1 1 0 2 4 – 17
Brooklyn Dodgers (N.L.)	1	0 0 1 2 5 1 1 1 0 – 11

Regular Season

Manager	W	L	Pct.	G. Ahead
Joe McCarthy	101	53	.656	17
Leo Durocher	100	54	.649	2.5

BATTING AND FIELDING

NEW YORK YANKEES

WORLD SERIES STATISTICS

	Pos	G	AB	R	H	2B	3B	HR	RBI	BB	SO	SB	BA	SA	PO	A	E
Johnny Sturm	1b	5	21	0	6	0	0	0	2	0	2	1	.286	.286	48	1	0
Joe Gordon	2b	5	14	2	7	1	1	1	5	7	0	0	.500	.929	6	19	1
Phil Rizzuto	ss	5	18	0	2	0	0	0	0	3	3	0	.111	.111	12	18	1
Red Rolfe	3b	5	20	2	6	0	0	0	0	2	1	0	.300	.300	7	8	0
Tommy Henrich	rf	5	18	4	3	1	0	1	1	3	3	0	.167	.389	6	0	0
Joe DiMaggio	cf	5	19	1	5	0	0	0	1	2	2	0	.263	.263	19	0	0
Charlie Keller	lf	5	18	5	7	2	0	0	5	3	1	0	.389	.500	12	0	0
Bill Dickey	c	5	18	3	3	1	0	0	1	3	1	0	.167	.222	24	2	0
George Selkirk	ph	2	2	0	1	0	0	0	0	0	0	0	.500	.500			
Buddy Rosar	c	1	0	0	0	0	0	0	0	0	0	0	—	—	0	0	0
Frenchy Bordagaray	pr	1	0	0	0	0	0	0	0	0	0	0	—	—			
Jerry Priddy		Did not play															
Frankie Crosetti		Did not play															
Ken Silvestri		Did not play															
Ernie Bonham	p	1	4	0	0	0	0	0	0	0	4	0	.000	.000	0	1	0
Marius Russo	p	1	4	0	0	0	0	0	0	0	1	0	.000	.000	0	4	0
Red Ruffing	p	1	3	0	0	0	0	0	0	0	1	0	.000	.000	0	0	0
Spud Chandler	p	1	2	0	1	0	0	0	1	0	1	0	.500	.500	0	0	0
Johnny Murphy	p	2	2	0	0	0	0	0	0	0	0	0	.000	.000	0	0	0
Atley Donald	p	1	2	0	0	0	0	0	0	0	0	0	.000	.000	0	1	0
Marv Breuer	p	1	1	0	0	0	0	0	0	0	0	0	.000	.000	0	0	0
Lefty Gomez		Did not play															
Steve Peek		Did not play															
Charley Stanceau		Did not play															
Norm Branch		Did not play															
team total		5	166	17	41	5	1	2	16	23	18	2	.247	.325	135	55	2

Double Plays—7
Left on Bases—42

REGULAR SEASON STATISTICS

Main Pos	G	AB	R	H	2B	3B	HR	RBI	BB	SO	SB	BA	SA
1b	124	524	58	125	17	3	3	36	37	50	3	.239	.300
2b	156	588	104	162	26	7	24	87	72	80	10	.276	.466
ss	133	515	65	158	20	9	3	46	27	36	14	.307	.398
3b	136	561	106	148	22	5	8	42	57	38	3	.264	.364
of	144	538	106	149	27	5	31	85	81	40	3	.277	.519
of	139	541	122	193	43	11	30	125	76	13	4	.357	.643
of	140	507	102	151	24	10	33	122	102	65	6	.298	.580
c	109	348	35	99	15	5	7	71	45	17	2	.284	.417
of	70	164	30	36	5	0	6	25	28	30	1	.220	.360
c	67	209	25	60	17	2	1	36	22	10	0	.287	.402
of	36	73	10	19	1	0	0	4	6	8	1	.260	.274
2b	56	174	18	37	7	0	1	26	18	16	4	.213	.270
ss	50	148	13	33	2	2	1	22	18	14	0	.223	.284
c	17	40	6	10	5	0	1	4	7	6	0	.250	.450
p	23	50	1	8	0	0	0	2	2	12	0	.160	.160
p	28	78	5	18	2	0	0	7	3	11	0	.231	.256
p-ph	38	89	10	27	8	1	2	22	4	12	0	.303	.483
p	28	60	4	11	0	0	0	4	1	18	0	.183	.183
p	35	18	1	1	0	0	0	0	1	8	0	.056	.056
p	22	62	3	5	1	0	0	2	2	22	0	.081	.097
p	26	46	1	4	0	0	0	2	2	21	0	.087	.087
p	23	59	5	9	1	0	0	4	3	12	0	.153	.169
p	17	28	0	1	0	0	0	1	1	15	0	.036	.036
p	22	12	0	0	0	0	0	0	0	5	0	.000	.000
p	27	10	0	0	0	0	0	0	1	4	0	.000	.000
	156	5444	830	1464	243	60	151	774	616	565	51	.269	.419

Johnny Lindell (ph), George Washburn (p) also played for the Yankees during the season.

BROOKLYN DODGERS

WORLD SERIES STATISTICS

	Pos	G	AB	R	H	2B	3B	HR	RBI	BB	SO	SB	BA	SA	PO	A	E
Dolph Camilli	1b	5	18	1	3	0	0	1	1	6	0	0	.167	.222	45	5	0
Billy Herman	2b	4	8	0	1	0	0	0	0	1	2	0	.125	.125	4	13	0
Pee Wee Reese	ss	5	20	1	4	0	0	0	2	0	0	0	.200	.200	13	14	3
Cookie Lavagetto	3b	3	10	1	1	0	0	0	0	0	1	0	.100	.100	2	1	0
Dixie Walker	rf	5	18	3	4	2	0	0	2	1	0	0	.222	.333	14	0	0
Pete Reiser	cf	5	20	1	4	1	1	1	3	1	6	0	.200	.500	14	1	0
Joe Medwick	lf	5	17	1	4	1	0	0	1	2	0	0	.235	.294	8	0	0
Mickey Owen	c	5	12	1	2	0	1	0	2	3	0	0	.167	.333	20	4	1
Lew Riggs	ph-3b	3	8	0	2	0	0	0	1	1	0	0	.250	.250	1	5	0
Pete Coscarart	2b	3	7	1	0	0	0	0	2	2	0	0	.000	.000	7	8	0
Jimmy Wasdell	ph-lf	3	5	0	1	1	0	0	2	0	0	0	.200	.400	2	0	0
Augie Galan	ph	2	2	0	0	0	0	0	0	0	0	0	.000	.000	1	0	0
Herman Franks	c	1	1	0	0	0	0	0	0	0	0	0	.000	.000	1	0	0
Leo Durocher		Did not play															
Whit Wyatt	p	2	6	1	1	0	0	0	0	0	4	0	.167	.167	1	2	0
Hugh Casey	p	3	2	0	1	0	0	0	0	0	0	0	.500	.500	0	3	0
Curt Davis	p	1	2	0	0	0	0	0	0	0	0	0	.000	.000	1	0	0
Freddie Fitzsimmons	p	1	2	0	0	0	0	0	0	0	0	0	.000	.000	0	1	0
Kirby Higbe	p	1	1	0	1	0	0	0	0	0	0	1	1.000	1.000	0	1	0
Johnny Allen	p	3	0	0	0	0	0	0	0	0	0	0	—	—	0	0	0
Larry French	p	2	0	0	0	0	0	0	0	0	0	0	—	—	0	0	0
Luke Hamlin		Did not play															
Newt Kimball		Did not play															
Tom Drake		Did not play															
Ed Albosta		Did not play															
team totals		5	159	11	29	7	2	1	11	14	21	0	.182	.272	132	60	4

Double Plays—5
Left on Bases—27

REGULAR SEASON STATISTICS

	Main Pos	G	AB	R	H	2B	3B	HR	RBI	BB	SO	SB	BA	SA
	1b	149	529	92	151	29	6	34	120	104	115	3	.285	.556
a	2b	133	536	77	156	30	4	3	41	58	38	1	.291	.379
	ss	152	595	76	136	23	5	2	46	68	56	10	.229	.294
	3b	132	441	75	122	24	7	1	78	80	21	7	.277	.370
	of	148	531	88	165	32	8	9	71	70	18	4	.311	.452
	of	137	536	117	184	39	17	14	76	46	71	4	.343	.558
	of	133	538	100	171	33	10	18	88	38	35	2	.318	.517
	c	128	386	32	89	15	2	1	44	34	14	1	.231	.288
	3b	77	197	27	60	13	4	5	36	16	12	1	.305	.487
	2b	43	62	13	8	1	0	0	5	7	12	1	.129	.145
	of	94	265	39	79	14	3	4	48	16	5	2	.298	.419
b	of	17	27	3	7	3	0	0	4	3	1	0	.259	.370
	c	57	139	10	28	7	0	1	11	14	13	0	.201	.273
	ss	18	42	2	12	1	0	0	5	3	3	0	.286	.310
	p	40	109	10	26	5	0	3	22	4	12	0	.239	.367
	p	45	50	4	6	1	0	0	4	0	15	0	.120	.140
	p	31	59	5	11	2	0	2	9	1	10	0	.186	.322
	p	13	28	1	4	1	0	0	1	3	1	0	.143	.179
	p	48	112	6	21	3	1	0	14	4	23	0	.188	.232
c	p	11	20	1	1	0	0	0	0	0	5	0	.050	.050
d	p	6	4	1	1	0	0	0	1	0	1	0	.250	.500
	p	30	41	3	6	1	0	0	2	1	12	0	.146	.171
	p	15	14	1	3	0	0	0	1	1	3	0	.214	.214
	p	10	5	0	2	0	0	0	0	0	1	0	.400	.400
	p	2	4	0	0	0	0	0	0	0	3	0	.000	.000
		157	5485	800	1494	286	69	101	747	600	535	36	.272	.405

a—from Chicago (N)
b—from Chicago (N)
c—from St. Louis (A)
d—from Chicago (N)

Joe Vosmik (of), Alex Kampouris (2b), Babe Phelps (c), Paul Waner (of), Tommy Tatum (of), Tony Giuliani (c), George Pfeister (c), Bill Swift (p), Mace Brown (p), Bob Chipman (p), Kemp Wicker (p), Vito Tamulis (p), Lee Grissom (p), and Van Lingle Mungo (p) also played for the Dodgers during the season.

PITCHING

NEW YORK YANKEES

WORLD SERIES STATISTICS

	G	GS	CG	IP	H	R	ER	BB	SO	W	L	SV	ERA
Ernie Bonham	1	1	1	9	4	1	1	2	2	1	0	0	1.00
Red Ruffing	1	1	1	9	6	2	1	3	5	1	0	0	1.00
Marius Russo	1	1	1	9	4	1	1	2	5	1	0	0	1.00
Johnny Murphy	2	0	0	6	2	0	0	1	3	1	0	0	0.00
Spud Chandler	1	1	0	5	4	3	2	2	0	1	0	0	3.60
Atley Donald	1	1	0	4	6	4	4	3	2	0	1	0	9.00
Marv Breuer	1	0	0	3	3	0	0	1	2	0	0	0	0.00
Lefty Gomez		Did not play											
Steve Peek		Did not play											
Charley Stanceau		Did not play											
Norm Branch		Did not play											
team total	5	5	2	45	29	11	9	14	21	4	1	0	1.80

REGULAR SEASON STATISTICS

G	GS	CG	IP	H	ER	BB	SO	W	L	Pct.	SV	ShO	ERA
23	14	7	127	118	42	31	43	9	6	.600	2	1	2.98
23	23	13	186	177	73	54	60	15	6	.714	0	2	3.53
28	27	17	210	195	72	87	105	14	10	.583	1	3	3.09
35	0	0	77	68	17	40	29	8	3	.727	15	0	1.99
28	20	11	164	146	58	60	60	10	4	.714	4	4	3.18
22	20	10	159	141	63	69	71	9	5	.643	0	3	3.57
26	18	7	141	131	64	49	77	9	7	.563	2	1	4.09
23	23	8	156	151	65	103	76	15	5	.750	0	2	3.75
17	8	2	80	85	45	39	18	4	2	.667	0	0	5.06
22	3	0	48	58	30	35	21	3	3	.500	0	0	5.60
27	0	0	47	37	15	26	28	5	1	.833	2	0	2.87
156	156	75	1396	1309	547	598	589	101	53	.656	26	13	3.53

BROOKLYN DODGERS

WORLD SERIES STATISTICS

	G	GS	CG	IP	H	R	ER	BB	SO	W	L	SV	ERA
Whit Wyatt	2	2	2	18	15	5	5	5	10	14	1	1	2.50
Freddie Fitzsimmons	1	1	0	7	4	0	0	3	1	0	0	0	0.00
Hugh Casey	3	0	0	5⅓	9	6	2	2	1	0	2	0	3.38
Curt Davis	1	1	0	5⅓	3	3	3	1	0	1	0	0	5.06
Johnny Allen	3	0	0	3⅔	1	0	0	3	0	0	0	0	0.00
Kirby Higbe	1	1	0	3⅔	8	6	3	3	2	0	1	0	7.36
Larry French	2	0	0	1	1	0	0	0	0	0	0	0	0.00
Luke Hamlin		Did not play											
Newt Kimball		Did not play											
Tom Drake		Did not play											
Ed Albosta		Did not play											
team totals	5	5	2	44	41	17	13	23	18	1	4	0	2.66

REGULAR SEASON STATISTICS

	G	GS	CG	IP	H	ER	BB	SO	W	L	Pct.	SV	ShO	ERA
	38	35	23	288	223	75	82	176	22	10	.688	1	7	2.34
	13	12	3	83	78	19	26	19	6	1	.857	0	1	2.06
	45	18	4	162	155	70	57	61	14	11	.560	7	1	3.89
	28	16	10	154	141	51	27	50	13	7	.650	2	5	2.98
c	11	4	1	57	38	16	12	23	5	1	1.000	0	2	2.53
	48	39	19	298	244	104	132	121	22	9	.710	3	2	3.14
d	6	1	0	16	16	6	4	8	0	0	—	0	0	3.38
	30	20	5	136	139	64	41	58	8	8	.500	1	1	4.24
	15	5	1	52	43	21	29	17	3	1	.750	1	0	3.63
	10	2	0	25	26	12	9	12	1	1	.500	0	0	4.32
	2	2	0	13	11	9	8	5	0	2	.000	0	0	6.23
team totals	157	157	66	1421	1236	496	495	603	100	54	.649	22	17	3.14

Total Attendance—235,773 Average Attendance—47,155 Winning Player's Share—$5,943 Losing Player's Share—$4,829

1942
Trauma in the Bronx

The Gashouse Gang had scattered to the wind, but a new flock of St. Louis Cardinals flew back to the top of the National League this year. These Redbirds were assembled by Branch Rickey, the crafty general manager who built the first farm system in baseball. In an era when the norm was for independent minor-league teams to develop players and sell them to the highest bidding major-league team, Rickey went out on a limb by signing hordes of unpolished but talented youngsters, then seasoning them on St. Louis-owned minor-league clubs. The result of this practice was a young team which streaked past the strong Brooklyn Dodgers with 43 wins in its last 51 games. Batting in key runs down the stretch were outfielders Enos Slaughter, a hustling scrapper from North Carolina, and rookie Stan Musial, a thin young man with a corkscrew stance which issued one of the smoothest swings on the big-league scene. Center fielder Terry Moore, shortstop Marty Marion, and catcher Walker Cooper provided manager Billy Southworth with strong defense up the middle, while the pitching staff had a pair of 20-game winners in Walker's brother Mort Cooper and rookie Johnny Beazley.

Their late-season burst earned these Cards the right to play the New York Yankees in the World Series. Back for their sixth Series in seven years, the Yanks lost Johnny Sturm and Tommy Henrich to the war effort, but they still had an arsenal featuring Joe DiMaggio, Charlie Keller, Joe Gordon, and Bill Dickey. Old-time aces Red Ruffing and Lefty Gomez figured less prominently on the pitching staff, as righties Ernie Bonham, Spud Chandler, and Hank Borowy took over the top winning spots. Since the Yankees had been to the Series so many times before and the Cardinals were the youngest team in the majors, the experts made the Yanks strong favorites to win.

And the first game at Sportsman's Park followed the script laid down by these experts for eight and a half innings. The jittery Cards made four errors, and got their first hit off Red Ruffing with two out in the eighth inning, on a single by Terry Moore. But in the bottom of the ninth, the Cards remembered how they had swept past the rest of the N.L. They got to old man Ruffing for four runs in the inning, and they greeted reliever Spud Chandler with two hits before Musial grounded out to end the game with the tying runs on base. Even with a 7–4 loss, the Cards came out of the game with their feet on the ground. They took an early 2–0 lead the next day on a two-run double by Walker Cooper in the first inning, upping the score to 3–0 on a run-producing triple by rookie Whitey Kurowski in the seventh. The Yankees tied the score in the top of the eighth with a three-run rally, capped by a two-run homer by Keller off Beazley, but the young Redbirds went back ahead in the bottom of the inning on a double by Slaughter and a single by Musial. A Yankee ninth-inning rally died when right fielder Slaughter gunned down Tuck Stainback at third with a bullet throw, and the Cards headed off to New York even with the Yankees at one game apiece.

That great throw by Slaughter only previewed the sort of outfield defense the Cards would get in game three. A crowd of almost 70,000 filled Yankee Stadium to watch a pitching match between Cardinal lefty Ernie White and Yankee righty Spud Chandler. With the Cards ahead 1–0 and with two out and one on in the sixth, DiMaggio lined a shot into the left-center gap, but center fielder Moore galloped after it and hauled it in with a diving catch. In the seventh, Gordon drove the ball deep to left, and Musial grabbed the ball just as it was heading into the short left-field seats. Then Keller blasted the ball to deep right, and Slaughter made a leaping catch at the fence to rob the Yanks of another homer. The Redbirds went on to a 2–0 victory in the game, and manager Southworth branded the three outfield plays in succession as the turning point of the Series. The Cards took game four 9–6 in a seesaw battle, then completed the route of the stunned Yankees with a 4–2 fifth-game win in which Kurowski belted a two-run homer with one out in the ninth. The Yanks had won eight straight Series since losing to the Cards in 1926, and now they had to relearn the empty taste of being second-best.

Game 1 September 30 at St. Louis

New York	Pos	AB	R	H	RBI	PO	A	E
Rizzuto	ss	4	0	0	0	2	2	0
Rolfe	3b	5	2	2	0	0	1	0
Cullenbine	rf	3	1	1	0	1	0	0
DiMaggio	cf	5	2	3	1	3	0	0
Keller	lf	4	0	0	0	4	0	0
Gordon	2b	5	0	0	0	2	1	0
Dickey	c	4	1	2	0	9	0	0
Hassett	1b	4	1	2	2	5	1	0
Ruffing	p	4	0	1	0	0	0	0
Chandler	p	0	0	0	0	1	0	0
Totals		38	7	11	3	27	5	0

Pitching	IP	H	R	ER	BB	SO
New York						
Ruffing (W)	$8\frac{2}{3}$	5	4	4	6	8
Chandler (SV)	$\frac{1}{3}$	2	0	0	0	0
St. Louis						
M. Cooper (L)	$7\frac{2}{3}$	10	5	3	3	7
Gumbert	$\frac{1}{3}$	0	0	0	0	0
Lanier	1	1	2	0	1	1

N.Y.	000	110	032
St L.	000	000	004

St. Louis	Pos	AB	R	H	RBI	PO	A	E
Brown	2b	4	0	1	0	1	2	1
Moore	cf	4	0	2	1	1	0	0
Slaughter	rf	3	0	1	0	1	0	1
Musial	lf	4	0	0	0	1	0	0
W. Cooper	c	4	1	1	0	8	1	0
Hopp	1b	4	0	0	0	11	1	0
Kurowski	3b	3	0	0	0	1	0	0
b Sanders		0	1	0	0	0	0	0
Marion	ss	4	1	1	2	3	2	0
M. Cooper	p	2	0	0	0	0	1	0
Gumbert	p	0	0	0	0	0	0	0
a Walker		1	0	0	0	0	0	0
Lanier	p	0	0	0	0	0	1	2
c O'Dea		1	0	1	1	0	0	0
d Crespi		0	1	0	0	0	0	0
Totals		34	4	7	4	27	8	4

a Struck out for Gumbert in 8th.
b Walked for Kurowski in 9th.
c Singled for Lanier in 9th.
d Ran for O'Dea in 9th.

Doubles—Cullenbine, Hassett.
Triple—Marion. Sacrifice Hit—Cullenbine.
Left on Bases—New York 9, St. Louis 9.
Umpires—Magerkurth (N), Summers (A), Barr (N), Hubbard (A).
Attendance—34,769. Time of Game—2:35.

1st Inning
New York
1 Rizzuto grounded to short.
2 Rolfe struck out.
Cullenbine walked.
DiMaggio singled to deep short, Cullenbine stopping at second.
3 Keller struck out.
St. Louis
1 Brown grounded to short.
Moore walked.
Slaughter walked.
2 Musial flied to right.
3 W. Cooper called out on strikes.

2nd Inning
New York
1 Gordon grounded to second.
Dickey hit a bouncer off Brown's chest who threw wildly to first but W. Cooper backing up on the play trapped
2 Dickey between first and second, W. Cooper to Hopp to Marion.
3 Hassett lined to second.
St. Louis
1 Hopp popped to Rizzuto near the left field foul line.
2 Kurowski struck out.
3 Marion struck out.

3rd Inning
New York
Ruffing singled against the right field pavilion screen.
Rizzuto walked.
1 Rolfe took a called third strike.
2 Ruffing was picked off second, M. Cooper to Marion.
3 Cullenbine rolled out to first.
St. Louis
1 M. Cooper grounded to short.
Brown walked.
2 Moore flied to deep center.
3 Slaughter struck out.

4th Inning
New York
DiMaggio singled to left.
1 Keller popped to Marion near the mound.
2 Gordon popped to Hopp near the mound.
Dickey walked.
Hassett doubled down the left field line, scoring DiMaggio with Dickey stopping at third.
3 Ruffing grounded to short.
St. Louis
1 Musial flied to deep left.
2 W. Cooper flied to DiMaggio in left-center.
3 Hopp struck out.

5th Inning
New York
1 Rizzuto bunted out to first.
Rolfe blooped a single to center.
Cullenbine doubled off the right field wall, Rolfe stopping at third.
2 DiMaggio bounced to Kurowski who tagged out Cullenbine but his throw to first was late and Rolfe scored.
3 Keller grounded to second.
St. Louis
1 Kurowski struck out.
2 Marion grounded to second.
3 M. Cooper grounded to third.

6th Inning
New York
1 Gordon struck out.
Dickey singled off the right field screen.
2 Hassett struck out.
3 Ruffing flied to deep center.

6th Inning (continued)
St. Louis
1 Brown popped to Gordon, making an over-the-shoulder catch in right-center.
2 Moore flied to deep left.
Slaughter walked.
Musial walked.
3 W. Cooper popped to Gordon.

7th Inning
New York
1 Rizzuto flied to left.
2 Rolfe flied to deep right.
3 Callenbine grounded to first.
St. Louis
1 Hopp flied to left.
2 Kurowski struck out for the third time.
3 Marion fouled to Hassett.

8th Inning
New York
DiMaggio singled to center.
1 Keller called out on strikes.
2 Gordon struck out.
Dickey singled to right, DiMaggio racing to third.
Hassett singled over Brown's glove, scoring DiMaggio with Dickey stopping at second.
Ruffing got to second on Slaughter's error as Dickey and Hassett scored.
For St. Louis—Gumbert now pitching.
3 Rizzuto bounced back to the mound.
St. Louis
1 Walker, batting for Gumpert, struck out.
2 Brown popped to Rizzuto in short left.
Moore singled to right for St. Louis' first hit in the game.
3 Slaughter flied to deep center.

9th Inning
New York
For St. Louis—Lanier pitching.
Rolfe singled to right.
Cullenbine bunted and Lanier fielding the ball threw over Hopp's head, Rolfe scoring and Cullenbine going all the way to third (a sacrifice and an error).
1 DiMaggio grounded to the mound.
Keller walked.
Lanier failed to pick Keller off first and on the return throw Lanier lost the ball for an error, Cullenbine scoring as Keller held at first.
2 Gordon struck out for the third time.
3 Dickey grounded to first.
St. Louis
1 Musial fouled to Dickey.
W. Cooper singled off Rolfe's glove.
2 Hopp flied to left.
Sanders, batting for Kurowski, walked.
Marion tripled to right, scoring W. Cooper and Sanders.
O'Dea, batting for Lanier, singled to center, scoring Marion.
Crespi ran for O'Dea.
Brown singled to center, Crespi stopping at second.
For New York—Chandler now pitching.
Moore singled to left, scoring Crespi with Brown stopping at second.
Slaughter beat out a bouncer to short, loading the bases.
3 Musial grounded out, Hassett to Chandler.

1942

Game 2 October 1 at St. Louis

New York	Pos	AB	R	H	RBI	PO	A	E
Rizzuto	ss	4	0	1	0	0	3	1
Rolfe	3b	4	0	1	0	0	2	0
Cullenbine	rf	4	1	1	0	2	0	0
DiMaggio	cf	4	1	1	2	7	0	0
Keller	lf	4	1	2	1	0	0	0
Gordon	2b	4	0	1	0	0	3	0
Dickey	c	4	0	2	0	5	0	0
a Stainback		0	0	0	0	0	0	0
Hassett	1b	4	0	1	0	9	0	1
Bonham	p	2	0	0	0	0	0	0
b Ruffing		1	0	0	0	0	0	0
Totals		35	3	10	3	24	8	2

N.Y.　000 000 030
St L.　200 000 11x

a Ran for Dickey in 9th.
b Flied out for Bonham in 9th.

Doubles—W. Cooper, Gordon, Rolfe, Slaughter. Triple—Kurowski. Home Run—Keller. Stolen Bases—Cullenbine, Rizzuto. Sacrifice Hit—Moore. Double Play—Brown to Marion to Hopp. Left on Bases—New York 7, St. Louis 4. Umpires—Summers, Barr, Hubbard, Magerkurth. Attendance—34,255. Time of Game—1:57.

1st Inning
New York
Rizzuto walked.
1 Rolfe flied to center.
　Rizzuto stole second.
2 Cullenbine struck out.
3 DiMaggio grounded to third.
St. Louis
Brown walked.
Moore safe when Bonham threw his bunt too late to second (a sacrifice and fielder's choice).
1 Slaughter flied to Keller in left-center.
2 Musial fouled to Hassett.
W. Cooper doubled to the right-center field wall, scoring Brown and Moore.
3 Hopp flied to center.

2nd Inning
New York
1 Keller flied to short center.
Gordon lined a double to left.
2 Dickey grounded to first, Gordon advancing to third.
3 Hassett rolled to second.
St. Louis
1 Kurowski grounded to short.
2 Marion fouled to Dickey.
3 Beazley took a called third strike.

3rd Inning
New York
1 Bonham grounded to first.
2 Rizzuto flied to deep left.
Rolfe doubled off the right field wall.
3 Cullenbine flied to left.
St. Louis
1 Brown flied to DiMaggio in left-center.
2 Moore fouled to Dickey.
3 Slaughter grounded to short.

4th Inning
New York
1 DiMaggio fouled to Hopp.
Keller singled past Beazley's head.
2 Gordon lined to third, Kurowski's throw just missing the double play.
Dickey singled to right, Keller stopping at second on Slaughter's excellent throw.
3 Hassett flied to deep right.
St. Louis
1 Musial grounded to Rizzuto racing in behind the mound.
2 W. Cooper grounded to third.
Hopp singled to right and continued to second when Hassett dropped Cullenbine's throw trying to get Hopp overrunning first.
3 Kurowski flied to DiMaggio in right-center.

5th Inning
New York
Bonham walked.
Rizzuto singled to left, Bonham stopping at second.
1,2 Rolfe hit into a double play, Brown to Marion to Hopp as Bonham went to third.
3 Cullenbine flied to left.
St. Louis
1 Marion flied to DiMaggio in left-center.
2 Beazley took a called third strike.
3 Brown grounded to second.

6th Inning
New York
1 DiMaggio grounded to Marion on a very slow roller at the mound.
2 Keller flied to left.
3 Gordon took a called third strike.
St. Louis
1 Moore flied to center.
2 Slaughter flied to right.
3 Musial grounded to second.

7th Inning
New York
1 Dickey popped to Hopp, halfway between home and first.
2 Hassett flied to left.
3 Bonham grounded to short.
St. Louis
1 W. Cooper flied to center.
Hopp singled to right.
Kurowski lined a triple just inside the left field foul line, scoring Hopp.
2 Marion grounded to third, Kurowski holding at third.
3 Beazley struck out for the third consecutive time.

8th Inning
New York
1 Rizzuto struck out.
2 Rolfe grounded to second.
Cullenbine beat out a smash to second.
Cullenbine stole second.
DiMaggio singled to right, scoring Cullenbine.
Keller hit a two-run homer over the right field pavilion roof.
3 Gordon struck out.
St. Louis
1 Brown grounded to second.
2 Moore flied to deep center, DiMaggio making a running catch.
Slaughter doubled into the right field corner, racing to third when Rizzuto fumbled Cullenbine's throw.
Musial singled, scoring Slaughter.
3 W. Cooper flied to right.

9th Inning
New York
Dickey singled to the left of second.
Stainback ran for Dickey.
Hassett singled to right, but Stainback
1 　was out at third on Slaughter's great throw to Kurowski.
2 Ruffing, batting for Bonham, flied to right.
3 Rizzuto grounded to short.

Game 3 October 3 at New York

St. Louis	Pos	AB	R	H	RBI	PO	A	E
Brown	2b	4	1	1	1	2	0	
Moore	cf	4	0	0	0	2	0	0
Slaughter	rf	4	0	1	0	3	0	0
Musial	lf	3	0	1	0	2	0	0
W. Cooper	c	4	0	0	0	8	0	1
Hopp	1b	4	0	0	0	8	0	0
Kurowski	3b	2	1	1	0	2	2	0
Marion	ss	3	0	1	0	0	1	0
White	p	2	0	0	0	0	0	0
Totals		30	2	5	2	27	5	1

St L.　001 000 001
N.Y.　000 000 000

Pitching

St. Louis	IP	H	R	ER	BB	SO
White (W)	9	6	0	0	0	6

New York	IP	H	R	ER	BB	SO
Chandler (L)	8	3	1	1	1	3
Breuer	*0	2	1	0	0	0
Turner	1	0	0	0	1	0

*Pitched to 3 batters in 9th.

1st Inning
St. Louis
1 Brown grounded back to the mound.
2 Moore struck out.
3 Slaughter struck out.
New York
Rizzuto beat out a perfect bunt toward third.
1 Hassett fouled to W. Cooper.
2 Cullenbine struck out.
Rizzuto stole second and went to third on W. Cooper's throw over Marion's head into center.
3 DiMaggio struck out.

2nd Inning
St. Louis
For New York—Hassett was hurt while at bat in the first and was taken out, Priddy going to first with Crosetti coming in to play third.
1 Musial grounded to short.
2 W. Cooper grounded to short.
3 Hopp grounded to short.
New York
1 Gordon struck out.
2 Keller grounded to first.
Dickey singled to right-center.
3 Priddy flied to Moore in left-center.

3rd Inning
St. Louis
Kurowski walked.
Marion beat out a bunt toward third.
1 White sacrificed up both runners, Chandler to Gordon.
2 Brown grounded to second, scoring Kurowski and Marion going to third.
3 Moore took a called third strike.
New York
1 Chandler struck out.
2 Rizzuto lined to third.
3 Crosetti struck out.

4th Inning
St. Louis
1 Slaughter grounded to first.
Musial singled to center.
2 W. Cooper popped to Gordon in short center.
3 　Musial was caught trying to steal second, Dickey to Rizzuto.
New York
1 Cullenbine fouled to Hopp.
DiMaggio singled to left.
2 Gordon flied to deep left.
3 Keller flied to short right.

New York	Pos	AB	R	H	RBI	PO	A	E
Rizzuto	ss	4	0	2	0	2	6	0
Hassett	1b	1	0	0	0	1	0	0
Crosetti	3b	3	0	0	0	1	1	0
Cullenbine	rf	4	0	1	0	0	0	0
DiMaggio	cf	4	0	2	0	2	0	0
Gordon	2b	4	0	0	0	3	3	0
Keller	lf	4	0	1	0	5	1	0
Dickey	c	3	0	1	0	5	1	0
Priddy	3b-1b	3	0	0	0	10	1	0
Chandler	p	2	0	0	0	1	2	0
a Ruffing		1	0	0	0	0	0	0
Breuer	p	0	0	0	0	0	0	1
Turner	p	0	0	0	0	0	0	0
Totals		33	0	6	0	27	15	1

a Struck out for Chandler in 8th.

Stolen Base—Rizzuto. Sacrifice Hit—White. Double Play—Keller to Dickey. Left on Bases—St. Louis 4, New York 6. Umpires—Barr, Hubbard, Magerkurth, Summers. Attendance—**69,123.** Time of Game—2:30.

5th Inning
St. Louis
1 Hopp grounded to short.
2 Kurowski lined to short.
3 Marion grounded to third.
New York
1 Dickey grounded to second.
2 Priddy fouled to Hopp.
3 Chandler grounded to third.

6th Inning
St. Louis
1 White grounded to short.
2 Brown grounded to second.
3 Moore flied to center.
New York
1 Rizzuto fouled to W. Cooper.
2 Crosetti grounded to second.
Cullenbine got a single on a Texas Leaguer to left-center.
3 DiMaggio flied deep to Moore, making a running glove-handed catch in left-center.

7th Inning
St. Louis
1 Slaughter fouled to Crosetti.
2 Musial grounded out, Priddy to Chandler.
3 W. Cooper flied to left.
New York
1 Gordon flied to very deep left.
2 Keller flied to deep right.
3 Dickey grounded to short.

8th Inning
St. Louis
1 Hopp grounded to second.
Kurowski singled past third.
2 Marion forced Kurowski at second, Rizzuto to Gordon.
3 White fouled to Dickey.
New York
1 Priddy popped to second.
2 Ruffing, batting for Chandler, struck out.
Rizzuto singled over short.
3 Crosetti grounded to third.

9th Inning
St. Louis
For New York—Breuer pitching.
Brown singled to right-center.
Moore bunted to Breuer who threw high to second, both runners safe.
Slaughter singled, scoring Brown as Moore went to third. Slaughter went to second on the throw to third.
For New York—Turner now pitching. Musial was intentionally passed, loading the bases.
1 W. Cooper flied to DiMaggio in short left-center, the runners holding.
2,3 Hopp flied to Keller in short left who fired to Dickey doubling up Moore trying to score.
New York
1 Cullenbine flied to short center.
DiMaggio singled to left.
2 Gordon fouled to Kurowski.
3 Keller flied to deep right.

Game 4 October 4 at New York

St. Louis	Pos	AB	R	H	RBI	PO	A	E
Brown	2b	6	0	2	0	1	5	0
Moore	cf	3	0	2	1	6	0	0
Slaughter	rf	4	1	0	0	1	0	0
Musial	lf	3	2	2	1	3	0	0
W. Cooper	c	5	1	2	1	2	0	0
Hopp	1b	3	2	1	0	7	0	0
Kurowski	3b	3	1	1	2	1	0	1
Marion	ss	4	1	0	1	6	4	0
M. Cooper	p	3	1	1	2	0	0	0
Gumbert	p	0	0	0	0	0	0	0
Pollet	p	0	0	0	0	0	0	0
a Sanders		1	0	0	0	0	0	0
Lanier	p	1	0	1	1	0	0	0
Totals		36	9	12	9	27	9	1

a Popped out for Pollet in 7th.
b Singled for Bonham in 9th.

Doubles—Moore, Musial, Priddy, Rolfe. Home Run—Keller. Sacrifice Hits—Hopp, Kurowski, Moore. Double Play—Marion to Brown. Left on Bases—St. Louis 10, New York 5. Umpires—Hubbard, Magerkurth, Summers, Barr. Attendance—**69,902.** Time of Game—2:28.

1st Inning
St. Louis
1 Brown grounded to short.
  Moore doubled to left-center.
2 Slaughter tapped to the mound, Moore holding second.
3 Musial flied to short center.
New York
1 Rizzuto grounded to second.
  Rolfe doubled inside the left field line.
  Cullenbine singled to left-center, scoring Rolfe.
2 DiMaggio flied to Moore in short left-center.
3 Keller flied to Musial in left-center.

2nd Inning
St. Louis
1 W. Cooper flied to DiMaggio in right-center.
2 Hopp flied to DiMaggio in left-center.
3 Kurowski flied to short left.
New York
1 Gordon popped to short.
2 Dickey flied to Musial in short left-center.
3 Priddy flied to center.

3rd Inning
St. Louis
1 Marion called out on strikes.
2 M. Cooper grounded to third.
  Brown beat out a bouncer to third.
  Moore walked.
3 Slaughter flied to short left.
New York
1 Borowy called out on strikes.
  Rizzuto beat out a bunt to third.
  Rolfe also beat out a bunt to third.
2,3 Cullenbine lined to Marion tossing to Brown doubling Rizzuto off second.

4th Inning
St. Louis
  Musial beat out a bunt to third.
  W. Cooper singled, Musial going to third. Cooper going to second on DiMaggio's throw to third.
  Hopp walked, loading the bases.
  Kurowski singled to left, scoring Musial and W. Cooper as Hopp raced to third.
  Marion walked, loading the bases.
  M. Cooper blooped a singled to short right, scoring Hopp and Kurowski with Marion going to third.
  For New York—Donald took the mound.
1 Brown flied to DiMaggio in short right-center.
  Moore singled to left, scoring Marion as M. Cooper stopped at second.
2 Slaughter forced Moore, Priddy to Rizzuto, M. Cooper going to third.
  Musial doubled to right, scoring M. Cooper.
3 W. Cooper lined to second.
New York
1 DiMaggio flied to Moore in deep left-center.
2 Keller struck out.
3 Gordon popped to Marion in short left.

5th Inning
St. Louis
1 Hopp popped to third.
2 Kurowski grounded to short.
3 Marion flied to left.
New York
1 Dickey flied to left.
2 Priddy flied to center.
3 Donald grounded to short.

New York	Pos	AB	R	H	RBI	PO	A	E
Rizzuto	ss	5	1	3	0	4	2	0
Rolfe	3b	4	2	2	0	2	2	0
Cullenbine	rf	4	1	2	2	2	0	0
DiMaggio	cf	4	0	1	0	5	0	0
Keller	lf	4	1	1	3	4	0	0
Gordon	2b	4	1	0	0	3	2	0
Dickey	c	4	0	0	0	2	0	1
Priddy	1b	4	0	1	1	7	2	0
Borowy	p	1	0	0	0	0	1	0
Donald	p	2	0	0	0	0	0	0
Bonham	p	0	0	0	0	0	2	0
b Rosar		1	0	1	0	0	0	0
Totals		37	6	10	6	27	11	1

Pitching	IP	H	R	ER	BB	SO
St. Louis						
M. Cooper	5⅓	7	5	5	1	2
Gumbert	⅓	1	1	0	0	0
Pollet	⅓	0	0	0	0	0
Lanier (W)	3	2	0	0	0	0
New York						
Borowy	*3	6	6	6	3	1
Donald (L)	**3	3	3	2	2	1
Bonham	3	3	1	1	2	0

*Pitched to 6 batters in 4th.
**Pitched to 3 batters in 7th.

6th Inning
St. Louis
1 M. Cooper struck out.
2 Brown grounded to third.
3 Moore flied to Keller, making a one-handed catch at the bullpen gate.
New York
  Rizzuto singled to left.
  Rolfe walked.
  Cullenbine singled to right, scoring Rizzuto as Rolfe stopped at second.
1 DiMaggio popped to second.
  Keller hit a three-run homer into the lower right field stands.
  For St. Louis—Gumbert pitching.
  Gordon safe at first on Kurowski's throwing error.
2 Dickey grounded to second, Gordon advancing to second.
  Priddy doubled to right-center, scoring Gordon.
  For St. Louis—Pollet came in to pitch.
3 Donald grounded to second.

7th Inning
St. Louis
  Slaughter walked.
  Musial walked, Slaughter running went to third on Dickey's wild throw.
  W. Cooper singled to center, scoring Slaughter as Musial went to second.
  For New York—Bonham took the mound.
1 Hopp sacrificed up both runners, Priddy unassisted.
  Kurowski intentionally walked, loading the bases.
2 Marion flied to center, Musial scoring and both runners advancing as DiMaggio's throw to the plate was high.
3 Sanders, batting for Pollet, popped to third.
New York
  For St. Louis—Lanier pitching.
  Rizzuto lined a single to left.
1 Rolfe forced Rizzuto at second, Brown to Marion, the DP just missed.
2 Cullenbine flied to Moore in left-center.
3 DiMaggio grounded to short.

8th Inning
St. Louis
  Brown singled to center.
1 Moore sacrificed, Bonham to Gordon.
2 Slaughter popped to short.
  Musial was intentionally passed.
3 W. Cooper forced Musial, Gordon to Rizzuto.
New York
1 Keller flied to Moore in right-center.
2 Gordon popped to Marion in short left.
3 Dickey popped to Kurowski near the mound.

9th Inning
St. Louis
  Hopp singled to left-center.
1 Kurowski sacrificed Hopp to second, Priddy to Gordon.
2 Marion grounded to short, Hopp moving to third.
  Lanier singled to right, scoring Hopp.
3 Brown forced Lanier at second, Gordon to Rizzuto.
New York
1 Priddy grounded to short.
  Rosar, batting for Bonham, singled over short.
2 Rizzuto flied to right.
3 Rolfe grounded to second.

Game 5 October 5 at New York

St. Louis	Pos	AB	R	H	RBI	PO	A	E
Brown	2b	3	0	2	0	3	4	2
Moore	cf	3	1	1	0	3	0	0
Slaughter	rf	4	1	2	1	2	0	0
Musial	lf	4	0	0	0	2	0	0
W. Cooper	c	4	1	2	1	2	1	0
Hopp	1b	3	0	0	0	9	2	1
Kurowski	3b	4	1	1	2	1	1	0
Marion	ss	4	0	0	0	3	5	0
Beazley	p	4	0	1	0	2	0	1
Totals		33	4	9	4	27	13	4

Pitching	IP	H	R	ER	BB	SO
St. Louis						
Beazley (W)	9	7	2	2	1	2
New York						
Ruffing (L)	9	9	4	4	1	3

1st Inning
St. Louis
  Brown walked.
1 Moore struck out.
2,3 Slaughter hit into a double play, Gordon to Rizzuto to Priddy.
New York
  Rizzuto homered into the lower left-field stands.
1 Rolfe grounded to second.
2 Cullenbine grounded to first.
3 DiMaggio flied to Moore in left-center.

2nd Inning
St. Louis
1 Musial popped to short.
  W. Cooper singled through the middle.
2 Hopp popped to Rizzuto on the left field grass.
3 Kurowski popped to Gordon in short right-center.
New York
1 Keller grounded to second.
2 Gordon grounded to short.
3 Dickey grounded to second.

3rd Inning
St. Louis
1 Marion fouled to Priddy with a good glove-catch at the Cardinal dugout.
2 Beazley called out on strikes, his fourth consecutive.
  Brown singled over second.
3 Moore flied to right.
New York
  Priddy walked.
1,2 Ruffing bunted into a double play on an attempted sacrifice, Hopp to Marion to Brown.
3 Rizzuto flied to Moore in deep left-center.

4th Inning
St. Louis
  Slaughter hit a home run deep into the lower right field stands.
1 Musial flied to center.
2 W. Cooper grounded to first.
3 Hopp grounded to second.
New York
  Rolfe beat out a bunt to first and continued to second on Beazley's wild throw.
1 Cullenbine flied to Moore in deep right-center, Rolfe going to third after the catch.
  DiMaggio singled to left, scoring Rolfe.
  Keller singled to right, DiMaggio going to second.
2 Gordon struck out, his 7th in the Series.
3 Dickey forced Keller at second, Marion to Brown.

5th Inning
St. Louis
1 Kurowski flied to left.
2 Marion flied to Cullenbine in short right-center.
  Beazley singled to right.
3 Brown popped to third.
New York
1 Priddy grounded to short.
  Ruffing beat out a slow roller to third.
  Rizzuto safe at first when Hopp threw his grounder into the dirt.
  Rolfe safe, loading the bases, on Brown's fumble.
2 Cullenbine popped to Marion behind third.
3 DiMaggio forced Rizzuto at third, Kurowski unassisted.

New York	Pos	AB	R	H	RBI	PO	A	E
Rizzuto	ss	4	1	2	1	7	1	0
Rolfe	3b	4	1	1	0	1	0	0
Cullenbine	rf	4	0	0	0	3	0	0
DiMaggio	cf	4	0	1	1	3	0	0
Keller	lf	4	0	1	0	3	0	0
Gordon	2b	4	0	0	0	3	3	0
Dickey	c	4	0	0	0	4	0	0
a Stainback		0	0	0	0	0	0	0
Priddy	1b	3	0	0	0	5	1	1
Ruffing	p	3	0	1	0	1	0	0
b Selkirk		1	0	0	0	0	0	0
Totals		35	2	7	2	27	6	1

a Ran for Dickey in 9th.
b Grounded out for Ruffing in 9th.

Home Runs—Kurowski, Rizzuto, Slaughter. Sacrifice Hits—Hopp, Moore. Double Plays—Gordon to Rizzuto to Priddy, Hopp to Marion to Brown. Left on Bases—St. Louis 5, New York 7. Umpires—Magerkurth, Summers, Barr, Hubbard. Attendance—69,052. Time of Game—1:58.

6th Inning
St. Louis
  Moore singled to left.
  Slaughter singled to right-center, Moore advancing to third.
1 Musial popped to Rizzuto in short left.
2 W. Cooper flied to right, Moore scoring after the catch. Priddy threw the relay wild and Slaughter went to third.
3 Hopp flied to deep center.
New York
1 Keller flied to deep left.
2 Gordon grounded to third.
3 Dickey flied to the wall in right.

7th Inning
St. Louis
1 Kurowski flied to DiMaggio in left-center.
2 Marion popped to Rizzuto in short left.
3 Beazley struck out.
New York
1 Priddy grounded to short.
2 Ruffing struck out.
  Rizzuto singled to left-center.
3 Rolfe flied to Slaughter in front of the Cardinal Bullpen.

8th Inning
St. Louis
  Brown singled to left.
1 Moore sacrificed Brown to second, Priddy to Gordon.
2 Slaughter popped to short.
3 Musial grounded to second.
New York
1 Cullenbine grounded out, Hopp to Beazley.
2 DiMaggio lined out to deep left.
3 Keller grounded to first, Beazley making the putout unassisted.

9th Inning
St. Louis
  W. Cooper lined a single to right-center.
1 Hopp sacrificed W. Cooper to second, Ruffing to Gordon.
  Kurowski hit a two-run homer into the stands just inside the left field foul pole.
2 Marion popped to Dickey, in front of the plate.
3 Beazley popped to Rizzuto in short left-center.
New York
  Gordon singled to left.
  Dickey got safely to first when Brown fumbled his grounder, for his second error of the game.
  Stainback ran for Dickey.
1 Gordon was picked off second, W. Cooper to Marion.
2 Priddy popped to Brown, racing in on the grass.
3 Selkirk, pinch-hitting for Ruffing, grounded to second.

1942 WORLD SERIES COMPOSITE BOX

	Wins	Composite Line Score										Regular Season Manager	W	L	Pct.	G. Ahead
St. Louis Cardinals (N.L.)	4	2	0	1	7	0	1	3	1	8	-23	Billy Southworth	106	48	.688	2
New York Yankees (A.L.)	1	2	0	0	2	1	5	0	6	2	-18	Joe McCarthy	103	51	.669	9

BATTING AND FIELDING

WORLD SERIES STATISTICS

	Pos	G	AB	R	H	2B	3B	HR	RBI	BB	SO	SB	BA	SA	PO	A	E
ST. LOUIS CARDINALS																	
Johnny Hopp	1b	5	17	3	3	0	0	0	0	1	1	0	.176	.176	**46**	3	1
Jimmy Brown	2b	5	20	2	6	0	0	0	1	3	0	0	.300	.300	6	**16**	**3**
Marty Marion	ss	5	18	2	2	0	**1**	0	3	1	2	0	.111	.222	13	**16**	0
Whitey Kurowski	3b	5	15	3	4	0	**1**	1	**5**	2	3	0	.267	**.600**	7	4	1
Enos Slaughter	rf	5	19	3	5	1	0	1	2	3	2	0	.263	.474	9	1	1
Terry Moore	cf	5	17	2	5	1	0	0	2	2	3	0	.294	.353	15	0	0
Stan Musial	lf	5	18	2	4	1	0	0	2	**4**	0	0	.222	.278	13	0	0
Walker Cooper	c	5	**21**	3	6	1	0	0	4	0	1	0	.286	.333	24	2	1
Ray Sanders	ph	2	1	1	0	0	0	0	0	1	0	0	.000	.000			
Ken O'Dea	ph	1	1	0	1	0	0	0	1	0	0	0	1.000	1.000			
Harry Walker	ph	1	1	0	0	0	0	0	0	0	1	0	.000	.000			
Creepy Crespi	pr	1	0	1	0	0	0	0	0	0	0	0	—	—			
Coaker Triplett		Did not play															
Sam Narron		Did not play															
Johnny Beazley	p	2	7	0	1	0	0	0	0	0	5	0	.143	.143	2	0	1
Mort Cooper	p	2	5	1	1	0	0	0	2	0	1	0	.200	.200	0	1	0
Ernie White	p	1	2	0	0	0	0	0	0	0	0	0	.000	.000	0	0	0
Max Lanier	p	2	1	0	1	0	0	0	1	0	0	0	1.000	1.000	0	1	2
Harry Gumbert	p	2	0	0	0	0	0	0	0	0	0	0	—	—	0	1	0
Howie Pollet	p	1	0	0	0	0	0	0	0	0	0	0	—	—	0	0	0
Howie Krist		Did not play															
Murry Dickson		Did not play															
Whitey Moore		Did not play															
team total		5	163	23	39	4	2	2	23	17	19	0	.239	.325	135	45	10

Double Plays—3
Left on Bases—32

	Pos	G	AB	R	H	2B	3B	HR	RBI	BB	SO	SB	BA	SA	PO	A	E
NEW YORK YANKEES																	
Jerry Priddy	3b-1b	3	10	0	1	1	0	0	1	1	0	6	.100	.200	22	4	1
Joe Gordon	2b	5	**21**	1	2	1	0	0	0	0	**7**	0	.095	.143	11	12	0
Phil Rizzuto	ss	5	**21**	2	**8**	0	0	1	1	2	1	**2**	**.381**	.524	15	14	1
Red Rolfe	3b	4	17	**5**	6	**2**	0	0	0	1	2	0	.353	.471	3	5	0
Roy Cullenbine	rf	5	19	3	5	1	0	0	2	1	2	1	.263	.316	6	0	0
Joe DiMaggio	cf	5	**21**	3	7	0	0	0	3	0	1	0	.333	.333	20	0	0
Charlie Keller	lf	5	20	2	4	0	0	**2**	**5**	1	3	0	.200	.500	12	1	0
Bill Dickey	c	5	19	1	5	0	0	0	0	1	0	0	.263	.263	25	1	1
Buddy Hassett	1b	3	9	1	3	1	0	0	2	0	1	0	.333	.444	15	1	1
Frankie Crosetti	3b	1	3	0	0	0	0	0	0	0	1	0	.000	.000	1	1	0
Buddy Rosar	ph	1	1	0	1	0	0	0	0	0	0	0	1.000	1.000			
George Selkirk	ph	1	1	0	0	0	0	0	0	0	0	0	.000	.000			
Tuck Stainback	pr	2	0	0	0	0	0	0	0	0	0	0	—	—			
Rollie Hemsley		Did not play															
Tommy Henrich		Not in series—military															
Red Ruffing	p-ph	4	9	0	2	0	0	0	0	0	2	0	.222	.222	0	1	0
Ernie Bonham	p	2	2	0	0	0	0	0	0	1	0	0	.000	.000	0	2	0
Spud Chandler	p	2	2	0	0	0	0	0	0	0	1	0	.000	.000	2	2	0
Atley Donald	p	1	2	0	0	0	0	0	0	0	0	0	.000	.000	0	0	0
Hank Borowy	p	1	1	0	0	0	0	0	0	0	1	0	.000	.000	0	1	0
Marv Brever	p	1	0	0	0	0	0	0	0	0	0	0	—	—	0	0	1
Jim Turner	p	1	0	0	0	0	0	0	0	0	0	0	—	—	0	0	0
Lefty Gomez		Did not play															
Marius Russo		Did not play															
Johnny Murphy		Did not play															
Johnny Lindell		Did not play															
team total		5	178	18	44	6	0	3	14	8	22	3	.247	.331	132	45	5

Double Plays—2
Left on Bases—34

REGULAR SEASON STATISTICS

		Main Pos	G	AB	R	H	2B	3B	HR	RBI	BB	SO	SB	BA	SA
ST. LOUIS CARDINALS															
Johnny Hopp		1b	95	314	41	81	16	7	3	37	36	40	14	.258	.382
Jimmy Brown		2b-3b	145	**606**	15	155	28	4	1	71	52	11	4	.256	.320
Marty Marion		ss	147	485	66	134	**38**	5	0	54	48	50	8	.276	.375
Whitey Kurowski		3b	115	366	51	93	17	3	9	42	33	60	7	.254	.391
Enos Slaughter		of	152	591	100	**188**	31	**17**	13	98	88	30	9	.318	.494
Terry Moore		of	130	489	80	141	26	3	6	49	56	26	10	.288	.391
Stan Musial		of	140	467	87	147	32	10	10	72	62	25	6	.315	.490
Walker Cooper		c	125	438	58	123	32	7	7	65	29	29	4	.281	.434
Ray Sanders		1b	95	282	37	71	17	2	5	39	42	31	2	.252	.379
Ken O'Dea		c	58	192	22	45	7	1	5	32	17	23	0	.234	.359
Harry Walker		of	74	191	38	60	12	2	0	16	11	14	2	.314	.398
Creepy Crespi		2b	93	292	33	71	4	2	0	35	27	29	4	.243	.271
Coaker Triplett		of	64	154	18	42	7	4	1	23	17	15	1	.273	.390
Sam Narron		ph	10	10	0	4	0	0	0	1	0	0	0	.400	.400
Johnny Beazley		p	43	73	6	10	2	2	0	9	3	37	0	.137	.219
Mort Cooper		p	37	103	6	19	1	0	0	7	3	21	0	.184	.194
Ernie White		p	27	41	5	8	0	0	0	3	3	4	0	.195	.195
Max Lanier		p	34	47	6	12	0	0	0	4	5	5	0	.255	.255
Harry Gumbert		p	38	54	2	6	2	0	0	3	1	12	0	.111	.148
Howie Pollet		p	27	31	2	7	2	0	0	7	7	7	0	.226	.290
Howie Krist		p	35	42	5	6	1	0	0	1	1	12	0	.143	.167
Murry Dickson		p	37	42	6	8	2	0	0	1	0	3	0	.190	.238
Whitey Moore	a	p	9	2	0	0	0	0	0	0	0	1	0	.000	.000
team total			156	**5421**	**755**	**1454**	**282**	**69**	60	**682**	551	507	71	**.268**	**.379**

a—from Cincinnati
Buddy Blattner (ss), Erv Dusak (of), Estel Crabtree (ph), Gus Mancuso (c), Jeff Cross (ss), Lon Warneke (p), Bill Beckmann (p), Bill Lohrman (p), and Clyde Shoun (p) also played for the Cardinals during the season.

		Main Pos	G	AB	R	H	2B	3B	HR	RBI	BB	SO	SB	BA	SA
NEW YORK YANKEES															
Jerry Priddy		3b	59	189	23	53	9	2	2	28	31	27	0	.280	.381
Joe Gordon		2b	147	538	88	173	29	4	18	103	79	**95**	12	.322	.491
Phil Rizzuto		ss	144	553	79	157	24	7	4	68	44	40	22	.284	.374
Red Rolfe		3b	69	265	42	58	8	2	8	25	23	18	1	.219	.355
Roy Cullenbine	b	of	21	77	16	28	7	0	2	17	18	2	0	.364	.532
Joe DiMaggio		of	154	610	123	186	29	13	21	114	68	36	4	.305	.498
Charlie Keller		of	152	544	106	159	24	9	26	108	114	61	14	.292	.513
Bill Dickey		c	82	268	28	79	13	1	2	37	26	11	2	.295	.373
Buddy Hassett		1b	132	538	80	153	16	6	5	48	32	16	5	.284	.364
Frankie Crosetti		3b	74	285	50	69	5	5	4	23	31	31	1	.242	.337
Buddy Rosar		c	69	209	18	48	10	0	2	34	17	20	1	.230	.306
George Selkirk		ph-of	42	78	15	15	3	0	0	10	16	8	0	.192	.231
Tuck Stainback		pr	15	10	0	2	0	0	0	0	0	2	0	.200	.200
Rollie Hemsley	d	c	31	85	12	25	3	1	0	15	5	9	1	.294	.353
Tommy Henrich		of	127	483	77	129	30	5	13	67	58	42	4	.267	.431
Red Ruffing		p	30	80	8	20	4	0	1	13	5	13	0	.250	.338
Ernie Bonham		p	28	74	4	9	0	0	0	2	3	17	0	.122	.122
Spud Chandler		p	24	71	6	15	2	0	0	5	8	14	0	.211	.239
Atley Donald		p	20	61	4	9	1	0	0	3	1	16	0	.148	.164
Hank Borowy		p	25	70	4	11	1	1	0	7	1	17	0	.157	.200
Marv Brever		p	27	54	3	3	0	1	0	0	3	24	0	.056	.093
Jim Turner	c	p	5	1	0	0	0	0	0	0	0	0	0	.000	.000
Lefty Gomez		p	13	33	4	5	0	0	0	4	1	12	0	.152	.152
Marius Russo		p	9	17	1	4	2	0	0	3	0	5	0	.235	.353
Johnny Murphy		p	31	13	1	2	2	0	0	0	0	8	0	.154	.308
Johnny Lindell		p	27	24	1	6	1	0	0	4	0	5	0	.250	.292
team total			154	5305	**801**	1429	223	57	**108**	**744**	591	556	69	.269	.394

b—from St. Louis and Washington
c & d—from Cincinnati
Ed Levy (1b), Ed Kearse (c), Mike Chartak (ph), Mel Queen (p), and Norm Branch (p) also played for the Yankees during the season.

PITCHING

WORLD SERIES STATISTICS

	G	GS	CG	IP	H	R	ER	BB	SO	W	L	SV	ERA
ST. LOUIS CARDINALS													
Johnny Beazley	**2**	**2**	**2**	**18**	**17**	5	5	3	6	**2**	0	0	2.50
Mort Cooper	**2**	**2**	0	13	**17**	10	8	4	9	0	**1**	0	5.54
Ernie White	1	1	1	9	6	0	0	0	6	1	0	0	**0.00**
Max Lanier	**2**	0	0	4	3	2	0	1	1	1	0	0	0.00
Harry Gumbert	**2**	0	0	$\frac{2}{3}$	1	1	0	0	0	0	0	0	0.00
Howie Pollet	1	0	0	$\frac{1}{3}$	0	0	0	0	0	0	0	0	0.00
Howie Krist	Did not play												
Murry Dickson	Did not play												
Whitey Moore	Did not play												
team total	5	5	3	45	44	18	13	8	22	4	1	0	2.60
NEW YORK YANKEES													
Red Ruffing	**2**	**2**	1	$17\frac{2}{3}$	14	8	8	**7**	**11**	1	**1**	0	4.08
Ernie Bonham	**2**	1	1	11	9	5	5	3	3	0	**1**	0	4.09
Spud Chandler	**2**	1	0	$8\frac{1}{3}$	5	1	1	1	3	0	**1**	**1**	1.08
Hank Borowy	1	1	0	3	6	6	6	3	1	0	0	0	18.00
Atley Donald	1	0	0	3	3	2	2	2	1	0	**1**	0	6.00
Jim Turner	1	0	0	1	0	0	0	1	0	0	0	0	0.00
Marv Brever	1	0	0	0	2	1	0	0	0	0	0	0	0.00
Lefty Gomez	Did not play												
Marius Russo	Did not play												
Johnny Murphy	Did not play												
Johnny Lindell	Did not play												
team total	5	5	2	44	39	23	22	17	19	1	4	1	4.50

REGULAR SEASON STATISTICS

		G	GS	CG	IP	H	ER	BB	SO	W	L	Pct	SV	ShO	ERA
ST. LOUIS CARDINALS															
Johnny Beazley		43	23	13	215	181	51	73	91	21	6	.778	3	3	2.14
Mort Cooper		37	35	22	270	207	55	63	152	**22**	7	.759	0	**10**	**1.77**
Ernie White		26	19	7	128	113	36	41	67	7	5	.583	2	1	2.53
Max Lanier		34	20	8	161	137	53	60	93	13	8	.619	2	2	2.96
Harry Gumbert		38	19	5	163	156	59	59	52	9	5	.643	5	0	3.26
Howie Pollet		27	13	5	109	102	35	39	42	7	5	.583	0	2	2.89
Howie Krist		34	8	3	118	103	33	43	47	13	3	.813	1	0	2.52
Murry Dickson		36	7	2	121	91	39	61	66	6	3	.667	2	0	2.90
Whitey Moore	a	9	0	0	12	10	6	11	1	0	1	.000	0	0	4.50
team total		156	156	70	1409	1192	399	473	**651**	**106**	48	**.688**	15	**18**	**2.55**
NEW YORK YANKEES															
Red Ruffing		24	24	16	194	183	69	41	80	14	7	.667	0	4	3.20
Ernie Bonham		28	27	**22**	226	199	57	24	71	21	5	**.808**	0	**6**	2.27
Spud Chandler		24	24	17	201	176	53	74	74	16	5	.762	0	3	2.37
Hank Borowy		25	21	13	178	157	50	66	85	15	4	.789	1	4	2.53
Atley Donald		20	19	10	148	133	51	45	53	11	3	.786	0	1	3.10
Jim Turner	c	5	0	0	7	4	1	1	2	1	1	.500	1	0	1.29
Marv Brever		27	19	6	164	157	56	37	72	8	9	.471	1	0	3.07
Lefty Gomez		13	13	2	80	67	38	65	41	6	4	.600	0	0	4.28
Marius Russo		9	5	2	45	41	14	14	15	4	1	.800	0	0	2.80
Johnny Murphy		31	0	0	58	66	22	23	24	4	10	.286	**11**	0	3.41
Johnny Lindell		23	2	0	53	52	22	22	28	2	1	.667	1	0	3.74
team total		154	154	**88**	1375	1259	444	431	558	**103**	51	**.669**	**17**	**18**	**2.91**

Total Attendance—277,101 Average Attendance—55,420 Winning Player's Share—$6,193 Losing Player's Share—$3,352

1943
Repaying a Year-Old Debt

Even with the military draft plucking players into World War II in large numbers and with Branch Rickey leaving St. Louis to take charge of the Brooklyn Dodgers, the Yankees and Cardinals repeated as league champions. The Yanks suffered losses that would ruin a club in normal times, as Joe DiMaggio, Phil Rizzuto, Red Ruffing, and Buddy Hassett all marched off into the armed services and Red Rolfe retired to coach at Dartmouth College. But the war effort had weakened the rest of the American League sufficiently for the Yanks to breeze to another pennant with the material left at hand. Charlie Keller, Bill Dickey, and Joe Gordon still provided the beef in the center of the lineup, and manager Joe McCarthy plugged holes by using ex-Phillie Nick Etten at first base, rookie Billy Johnson at third base, veteran Frankie Crosetti at shortstop, and converted pitcher Johnny Lindell to DiMaggio's center-field position.

Cardinal manager Billy Southworth had his own manpower problems, as Enos Slaughter, Terry Moore, Jimmy Brown, Johnny Beazley, and Howie Pollet joined the military. But the St. Louis attack kept on rolling with the blossoming of Stan Musial, who hit .357 in his second major-league season, and with solid contributions by catcher Walker Cooper and third baseman Whitey Kurowski. Shortstop Marty Marion held the defense together, Mort Cooper and Max Lanier led the pitching staff, and the farm system fashioned by the departed Rickey provided the Cards with second baseman Lou Klein and lefty pitchers Harry Brecheen and Alpha Brazle. The Cards ran away from the rest of the National League and relished the idea of again facing the Yankees in the World Series.

Last year, the Cards had lost the first game only to win the next four, so optimistic St. Louis fans took it as a good omen when their team dropped a 4–2 decision in the opener at Yankee Stadium. A 2–2 tie was broken in the sixth on singles by Crosetti, Johnson, and Dickey, plus a wild pitch by losing pitcher Lanier. The pattern held in game two, as the Cards won 4–3. Pitcher Mort Cooper and catcher Walker Cooper played the game with a special kind of concentration, as their father had died that morning. The Yanks scored twice off Mort in the bottom of the ninth but couldn't get the tying run. St. Louis fans now expected their Cards to turn it on and take the next three games, just as they had last year. With Hank Borowy and Alpha Brazle doing the pitching, the Cards led 2–1 after seven innings of game three, which was scheduled for Yankee Stadium to cut down on war-restricted travel. In the bottom of the eighth, Lindell led off with a single and moved to second when center fielder Harry Walker bobbled the ball. Pinch hitter Snuffy Stirnweiss then bunted to first baseman Ray Sanders, who slung the ball to third. The throw had Lindell beat, but he slid hard into Kurowski and knocked the ball loose. After Stirnweiss moved to second on a fly-out, the Cards passed Crosetti to set up a force play at home, but Billy Johnson turned the strategy sour by tripling home three runs. Three more hits in the inning off two relievers scored two more runs and clinched a 6–2 victory for the Yanks to put them up two games to one and cancel out last year's pattern.

When the teams reassembled in St. Louis, the even older pattern of Yankee dominance came back to life. Max Lanier and Marius Russo locked horns in game four, with the score tied at 1–1 after seven innings. After Lanier went out for a pinch hitter, Brecheen came on to pitch the eighth and ran into immediate trouble when Russo doubled. After moving to third on Tuck Stainback's bunt, Russo scored on Crosetti's fly ball. He made the run stand up and the Yankees had a 2–1 victory and a towering 3–1 edge in the Series. With the Cards up against the wall, Mort Cooper pitched brilliantly in game five, striking out the first five Yankee batters in the game. But New York starter Spud Chandler matched Cooper in brilliance, and while the Cards could not score all afternoon, Cooper slipped once and gave up a two-run homer to Dickey in the sixth inning. The victory crowned the Yankees as World Champions again, the seventh and last title for the Bronx Bombers under the direction of manager Joe McCarthy.

Game 1 October 5 at New York

| St L. | 010 010 000 |
| N.Y. | 000 202 00x |

St. Louis	Pos	AB	R	H	RBI	PO	A	E
Klein	2b	4	0	1	0	0	2	1
Walker	cf	4	0	0	0	2	0	0
Musial	rf	4	0	1	0	1	0	0
W. Cooper	c	4	1	1	0	7	1	0
Kurowski	3b	3	0	0	0	1	1	0
Sanders	1b	4	1	2	0	8	0	0
Litwhiler	lf	3	0	0	0	3	0	0
Marion	ss	3	0	1	1	2	3	0
Lanier	p	2	0	1	1	0	1	1
a Garms		1	0	0	0	0	0	0
Brecheen	p	0	0	0	0	0	1	0
Totals		32	2	7	2	24	9	2

a Fanned for Lanier in 8th.

New York	Pos	AB	R	H	RBI	PO	A	E
Stainback	rf	4	0	1	0	2	1	0
Crosetti	ss	4	2	1	0	3	3	1
Johnson	3b	4	1	2	0	0	3	0
Keller	lf	4	0	1	0	4	0	0
Gordon	2b	3	1	1	1	4	8	0
Dickey	c	4	0	1	1	4	0	0
Etten	1b	4	0	0	0	11	0	1
Lindell	cf	3	0	0	0	3	0	0
Chandler	p	3	0	1	0	0	2	0
Totals		33	4	8	2	27	17	2

Pitching	IP	H	R	ER	BB	SO
St. Louis						
Lanier (L)	7	7	4	2	0	7
Brecheen	1	1	0	0	1	1
New York						
Chandler (W)	9	7	2	1	1	3

Double—Marion. Home Run—Gordon. Sacrifice Hit—Kurowski. Stolen Base—Crosetti. Double Plays—Klein to Marion to Sanders, Gordon to Crosetti to Etten. Wild Pitch—Lanier. Left on Bases—St. Louis 5, New York 6. Umpires—Rommel (A), Reardon (N), Rue (A), Stewart (N). Attendance—68,676. Time of Game—2:07.

1st Inning
St. Louis
1 Klein flied to center.
2 Walker flied to right.
3 Musial flied to center.
New York
1 Stainback lined to third.
2 Crosetti grounded to short.
3 Johnson looked at called third strike.

2nd Inning
St. Louis
   W. Cooper singled off of Johnson's glove.
1 Kurowski sacrificed Cooper to second, Chandler to Gordon.
2 Sanders fanned.
   Litwhiler walked.
   Marion doubled off Etten's glove scoring
3 W. Cooper, but Litwhiler was thrown out at plate trying to score, Stainback to Dickey.
New York
1 Keller took a called third strike.
2 Gordon grounded back to the pitcher.
3 Dickey grounded to third.

3rd Inning
St. Louis
1 Lanier grounded to second.
2 Klein grounded to second.
3 Walker flied to right.
New York
1 Etten grounded to Marion and was out as Sanders caught Marion's wide throw.
2 Lindell fanned but had to be thrown out W. Cooper to Sanders.
   Chandler singled to left.
3 Stainback fanned.

4th Inning
St. Louis
1 Musial grounded to second.
2 W. Cooper grounded to short.
3 Kurowski grounded to second.
New York
   Crosetti was safe on Lanier's error who dropped Klein's throw as he covered first.
   Crosetti stole second.
   Johnson beat out a bunt toward first, moving Crosetti to third.
1,2 Keller grounded into a double play scoring Crosetti, Klein to Marion to Sanders.
   Gordon homered into the left field stands for a 450 footer.
3 Dickey popped to short.

5th Inning
St. Louis
   Sanders got an infield single to Gordon who made a great stop and he got to second when Etten thinking Sanders was out threw past Dickey.
1 Litwhiler flied to center, Sanders going to third after the catch.
2 Marion grounded to second, Sanders holds. Lanier singled into center, scoring Sanders.
3 Klein forced Lanier at second, Johnson to Gordon.

5th Inning (continued)
New York
   Etten safe at first on Klein's boot.
1 Lindell fanned.
2 Chandler fanned.
3 Stainback flied to left.

6th Inning
St. Louis
1 Walker fanned.
2 Musial grounded to second.
   W. Cooper got safely to first on Crosetti's fumble.
3 Kurowski grounded to second.
New York
   Crosetti singled by second.
   Johnson singled over second.
   On a wild pitch which bounced to the right Crosetti scored from second and Johnson went to third.
1 Keller flied to right.
2 Gordon fanned.
   Dickey got a Texas League single to center scoring Johnson.
3 Etten flied to left.

7th Inning
St. Louis
   Sanders singled to right.
1 Litwhiler popped to short.
2,3 Marion hit into a double play (he just missed a homer the ball being slightly foul), Gordon to Crosetti to Etten.
New York
1 Lindell flied to deep center.
2 Chandler flied to center, a great catch by Walker robbing Chandler of a long double or triple.
   Stainback singled to left.
3 Crosetti popped to first.

8th Inning
St. Louis
1 Garms, pinch hitting for Lanier, fanned.
   Klein singled to center.
2 Walker forced Klein at second, Johnson to Gordon.
   Musial singled to right with Walker stopping at second.
3 W. Cooper forced Musial at second, Johnson to Gordon.
New York
   For St. Louis—Brecheen pitching.
1 Johnson grounded back to Brecheen.
   Keller singled to right.
   Gordon walked.
2 Dickey fanned.
3 Etten flied to left.

9th Inning
St. Louis
1 Kurowski grounded to short.
2 Sanders lined to short.
3 Litwhiler grounded back to the mound.

Game 2 October 6 at New York

St. Louis	Pos	AB	R	H	RBI	PO	A	E
Klein	2b	4	0	1	0	4	4	0
Walker	cf	5	0	1	0	5	0	1
Musial	rf	4	1	1	0	2	0	0
W. Cooper	c	3	0	1	0	5	1	0
Kurowski	3b	4	1	1	1	0	1	0
Sanders	1b	3	1	1	2	8	0	0
Litwhiler	lf	3	0	0	0	3	0	0
Marion	ss	3	1	1	1	0	3	0
M. Cooper	p	3	0	0	0	0	0	0
Totals		32	4	7	4	27	8	2

Pitching	IP	H	R	ER	BB	SO
St. Louis						
M. Cooper (W)	9	6	3	3	1	4
New York						
Bonham (L)	8	6	4	4	3	9
Murphy	1	1	0	0	1	0

New York	Pos	AB	R	H	RBI	PO	A	E
Crosetti	ss	4	1	2	0	2	2	0
Methany	rf	*3	3	0	0	2	0	0
Johnson	3b	4	1	2	0	0	1	0
Keller	lf	4	1	1	2	3	0	0
Dickey	c	3	0	0	0	9	2	0
Etten	1b	4	0	0	1	4	0	0
Gordon	2b	4	0	1	0	4	0	0
Stainback	cf	3	0	0	0	3	0	0
Bonham	p	2	0	0	0	0	0	0
a Weatherly		1	0	0	0	0	0	0
Murphy	p	0	0	0	0	0	1	0
Totals		32	3	6	3	27	6	0

a Fouled out for Bonham in 8th.
* Awarded first on W. Cooper's interference in 6th.

Double—Johnson. Triple—Keller. Home Runs—Marion, Sanders. Sacrifice Hits—M. Cooper, W. Cooper. Stolen Base—Marion. Double Play—Marion to Klein to Sanders. Left on Bases—St. Louis 7, New York 4. Umpires—Reardon, Rue, Stewart, Rommel. Attendance—68,578. Time of Game—2:08.

St. L. 001 300 000
N.Y. 000 100 002

1st Inning
St. Louis
1 Klein flied to right.
2 Walker fanned.
3 Musial flied to center.
New York
1 Crosetti grounded to short.
2 Methany grounded to second.
3 Johnson lined to second.

2nd Inning
St. Louis
1 W. Cooper popped to short.
2 Kurowski fanned.
  Sanders walked.
3 Litwhiler popped to second.
New York
1 Keller flied to center.
2 Dickey flied to center.
3 Etten fanned.

3rd Inning
St. Louis
  Marion hit a 320 foot homer into the left field stands.
1 M. Cooper flied to left.
2 Klein popped to Gordon in short center.
3 Walker grounded to short.
New York
1 Gordon fanned.
2 Stainback lined to second.
3 Bonham grounded to third.

4th Inning
St. Louis
  Musial singled to center.
1 W. Cooper sacrificed Musial to second, Dickey to Etten.
  Kurowski singled to center, scoring Musial.
  Sanders hit a two-run homer into the right field stands at 350 feet.
2 Litwhiler fanned.
3 Marion flied to the right field corner where Methany made a good one-handed catch.
New York
  Crosetti bunted a single over Sanders' head to be the first Yankee baserunner.
1 Methany flied to center.
  Johnson singled to center, advancing Crosetti to third.
2 Keller flied to center, Crosetti scoring after the catch.
3 Dickey flied to left.

5th Inning
St. Louis
1 M. Cooper fanned.
  Klein walked.
  Walker got an infield single beating out a roller towards first.
2 Musial flied to left.
3 W. Cooper lined to second.

5th Inning (continued)
New York
1 Etten flied to right.
  Gordon singled to center and got to second when Walker fumbled for an error.
2 Stainback flied to Walker making a great catch.
3 Bonham grounded to short.

6th Inning
St. Louis
1 Kurowski fanned.
2 Sanders fanned.
3 Litwhiler fanned.
New York
  Crosetti singled through short.
  Methany was awarded first on catcher's interference as W. Cooper touched his bat.
1,2 Johnson grounded into a double play, Marion to Klein to Sanders.
3 Keller flied to right.

7th Inning
St. Louis
  Marion walked.
1 M. Cooper struck out as Marion stole second.
2 Klein grounded to short, Marion holding.
3 Walker rolled to third and Marion was caught in a run-down between second and third, Gordon making the putout.
New York
  Dickey walked.
1 Etten flied to left.
2 Gordon lined to left.
3 Stainback fanned.

8th Inning
St. Louis
1 Musial flied to center.
  W. Cooper singled to third as Johnson lost his high bouncer in the sun.
2 Kurowski fanned.
3 Sanders flied to left.
New York
1 Weatherly, pinch hitting for Bonham, fouled to Sanders.
2 Crosetti struck out.
3 Methany grounded to second.

9th Inning
St. Louis
  For New York—Murphy pitching.
  Litwhiler walked.
1 Marion forced Litwhiler at second on an attempted bunt, Murphy to Crosetti.
2 M. Cooper sacrificed Marion to second, Dickey to Etten.
  Klein beat out a hit to third, Marion holding second.
3 Walker flied to center.
New York
  Johnson doubled to left-center.
  Keller tripled in left, scoring Johnson.
1 Dickey lined to second.
2 Etten grounded to second scoring Keller.
3 Gordon fouled to W. Cooper.

Game 3 October 7 at New York

St. Louis	Pos	AB	R	H	RBI	PO	A	E
Klein	2b	4	0	0	0	2	2	0
Walker	cf	4	0	1	0	1	0	1
Musial	rf	3	1	1	0	1	1	0
W. Cooper	c	4	0	1	0	4	1	0
Kurowski	3b	3	1	1	0	2	2	2
b O'Dea		1	0	0	0	0	0	0
Sanders	1b	3	0	0	0	9	2	0
Litwhiler	lf	4	0	2	2	3	0	0
Marion	ss	3	0	0	0	2	4	1
Brazle	p	3	0	0	0	1	2	0
Krist	p	0	0	0	0	0	0	0
Brecheen	p	0	0	0	0	0	0	0
Totals		31	2	6	2	24	15	4

a Got on base on error for Borowy in 8th.
b Popped out for Kurowski in 9th.

Doubles—Borowy, Kurowski, Walker. Triple—Johnson. Sacrifice Hit—Crosetti. Double Plays—Crosetti to Gordon to Etten, Marion to Klein to Sanders. Left on Bases—St. Louis 5, New York 4. Umpires—Rue, Stewart, Rommel, Reardon. Attendance—**69,990 (new World Series record).** Time of Game—2:10.

St. L. 000 200 000
N.Y. 000 001 05x

New York	Pos	AB	R	H	RBI	PO	A	E
Stainback	cf	4	0	1	0	1	0	0
Crosetti	ss	2	1	0	0	2	4	0
Johnson	3b	4	1	1	3	0	1	0
Keller	lf	3	1	0	0	2	0	0
Gordon	2b	4	0	1	1	3	2	0
Dickey	c	4	0	2	0	6	1	0
Etten	1b	4	0	1	1	9	1	0
Lindell	rf	3	1	1	0	2	0	0
Borowy	p	2	1	1	0	2	0	0
a Stirnweiss		1	1	0	0	0	0	0
Murphy	p	0	0	0	0	0	0	0
Totals		31	6	8	5	27	9	0

Pitching	IP	H	R	ER	BB	SO
St. Louis						
Brazle (L)	7⅓	5	6	3	2	4
Krist	*0	1	0	0	0	0
Brecheen	⅔	2	0	0	0	0
New York						
Borowy (W)	8	6	2	2	3	4
Murphy (Sv)	1	0	0	0	0	1

*Pitched to one batter in 8th.

1st Inning
St. Louis
1 Klein flied to center.
  Walker doubled past third.
  Musial walked.
2,3 W. Cooper grounded into a double play, Crosetti to Gordon to Etten.
New York
  Stainback singled to left.
1 Crosetti sacrificed Stainback to second, Brazle to Klein.
2 Johnson hit into a fielder's choice, Marion throwing to Kurowski to get Stainback at third.
3 Keller fanned.

2nd Inning
St. Louis
1 Kurowski fouled to Dickey.
2 Sanders fanned.
  Litwhiler singled off Borowy's leg.
3 Marion foul to Keller who reached into the stands to make the catch.
New York
1 Gordon lined to left.
2 Dickey grounded to second.
3 Etten grounded to third.

3rd Inning
St. Louis
1 Brazle fanned.
2 Klein bunted out, Etten to Borowy.
3 Walker flied to right.
New York
1 Lindell flied to center at 430 feet.
2 Borowy fanned but had to be thrown out, W. Cooper to Sanders.
3 Stainback grounded to short.

4th Inning
St. Louis
  Musial singled to left.
1 W. Cooper popped to Crosetti back of the box.
  Kurowski hit a double down the left field line with Musial stopping at third.
  Sanders intentionally walked, loading the bases.
  Litwhiler hit a line-single to left, scoring Musial and Kurowski. Sanders went to third and Litwhiler to second on the throw to the plate.
  Marion got the second intentional walk of the inning, again bases loaded.
2 Brazle fouled to Etten.
3 Klein grounded to short.
New York
  Crosetti safely to first when his grounder went through Marion's legs for an error.
1,2 Johnson grounded into a double play, Marion to Klein to Sanders.
3 Keller grounded back to the mound.

5th Inning
St. Louis
1 Walker popped to Borowy.
2 Musial grounded to short.
3 W. Cooper grounded to third.

5th Inning (continued)
New York
1 Gordon grounded to third.
  Dickey singled to right.
2 Etten popped to short.
3 Lindell looked at a third strike.

6th Inning
St. Louis
1 Kurowski popped to first.
2 Sanders grounded to second.
3 Litwhiler fanned.
New York
  Borowy hit a ground-rule double into the left field stands.
1 Stainback fouled to Musial who made a great one-handed catch with Borowy going to third after the catch.
2 Crosetti flied to left. Johnson safe on first with Borowy scoring on Kurowski's fumble.
3 Keller forced Johnson at second, Marion unassisted.

7th Inning
St. Louis
1 Marion fanned.
2 Brazle grounded to short.
3 Klein popped to short.
New York
1 Gordon grounded to short.
2 Dickey rolled out, Sanders to Brazle.
3 Etten fanned.

8th Inning
St. Louis
1 Walker popped to first.
2 Musial flied to left.
  W. Cooper singled to right.
3 Cooper caught stealing, Dickey to Gordon.
New York
  Lindell singled to center and took second on Walker's fumble.
  Stirnweiss, pinch hitting for Borowy, bunted to Sanders who threw to Kurowski beating Lindell but Kurowski dropped the ball when Lindell crashed into him.
1 Stainback flied to left, Stirnweiss going to second after the catch.
  Crosetti intentionally walked loading the bases.
  Johnson tripled between Litwhiler and Walker, scoring Lindell, Stirnweiss and Crosetti.
  Keller walked.
  For St. Louis—Krist pitching.
  Gordon singled to left, scoring Johnson.
  For St. Louis—Brecheen pitching.
2 Dickey's grounder hit Gordon on the leg Gordon automatically out and Dickey credited with a single, Keller going to third.
  Etten singled to right scoring Keller
3 but Dickey was out trying for third, Musial to W. Cooper to Kurowski.

9th Inning
St. Louis
  For New York—Murphy pitching.
1 O'Dea, pinch hitting for Kurowski, popped to second.
2 Sanders flied to right.
3 Litwhiler fanned.

Game 4 October 10 at St. Louis

New York	Pos	AB	R	H	RBI	PO	A	E
Stainback	cf	3	0	0	0	1	0	0
Crosetti	ss	4	0	1	1	2	2	1
Johnson	3b	4	0	0	0	1	2	1
Keller	lf	4	0	1	0	4	0	0
Gordon	2b	4	1	1	0	3	7	0
Dickey	c	3	0	1	1	2	0	0
Etten	1b	4	0	0	0	11	0	0
Lindell	rf	3	0	0	0	3	0	0
Russo	p	3	1	2	0	0	2	0
Totals		32	2	6	2	27	13	2

Pitching	IP	H	R	ER	BB	SO
New York						
Russo (W)	9	7	1	0	1	2
St. Louis						
Lanier	7	4	1	1	1	5
Brecheen (L)	2	2	1	1	2	2

St. Louis	Pos	AB	R	H	RBI	PO	A	E
Klein	2b	5	0	0	0	1	4	1
Walker	cf	4	0	0	0	2	0	0
Musial	rf	4	0	2	0	2	1	0
W. Cooper	c	4	0	1	0	7	0	0
Kurowski	3b	4	0	1	0	0	2	0
Sanders	1b	4	1	1	0	9	1	0
Litwhiler	lf	4	0	1	0	2	0	0
Marion	ss	3	0	2	0	2	1	0
Lanier	p	2	0	0	0	0	1	0
a Demaree		1	0	0	0	0	0	0
b White		0	0	0	0	0	0	0
Brecheen	p	0	0	0	0	0	1	0
c Narron		1	0	0	0	0	0	0
Totals		36	1	7	0	27	10	1

N.Y. 000 100 010
St L. 000 000 100

a Reached first on an error for Lanier in 7th.
b Ran for Demaree in 7th.
c Grounded out for Brecheen in 9th.

Doubles—Gordon, Litwhiler, Marion, Russo 2. Sacrifice Hit—Stainback. Stolen Base—Keller. Left on Bases—New York 7, St. Louis 9. Umpires—Stewart, Rommel, Reardon, Rue. Attendance—36,196. Time of Game—2:06.

1st Inning
New York
1 Stainback fouled to Sanders.
2 Crosetti flied to right.
3 Johnson fanned.
St. Louis
1 Klein flied to right.
2 Walker grounded to second.
3 Musial lined to second.

2nd Inning
New York
1 Keller grounded to second.
2 Gordon flied to left.
3 Dickey grounded back to the pitcher.
St. Louis
1 W. Cooper fanned.
2 Kurowski flied to right.
Sanders singled to left.
3 Litwhiler forced Sanders at second, Johnson to Gordon.

3rd Inning
New York
1 Etton flied to Marion in short left.
2 Lindell grounded to third.
Russo walked.
Stainback safely to first on Klein's fumble, Russo to second.
Crosetti singled to right with Russo
3 getting caught in a rundown off of third, Musial to Sanders to Kurowski.
St. Louis
1 Marion popped to third.
2 Lanier grounded to second.
3 Klein flied to left.

4th Inning
New York
1 Johnson flied to right.
2 Keller fanned.
Gordon doubled to left-center.
Dickey singled to center, scoring Gordon.
3 Etten forced Dickey at second, Klein to Marion.
St. Louis
1 Walker flied to left.
Musial singled on a bunt in front of the plate beating Dickey's throw to first.
2 W. Cooper lined to right.
3 Kurowski lined to second.

5th Inning
New York
1 Lindell fanned.
Russo doubled past first.
2 Stainback fouled to Sanders.
3 Crosetti fanned.
St. Louis
1 Sanders fanned.
2 Litwhiler fouled to Etten.
Marion singled to left.
3 Lanier grounded back to the pitcher.

6th Inning
New York
1 Johnson grounded to second.
2 Keller took a called third strike.
3 Gordon flied to center.
St. Louis
1 Klein bounced back to the pitcher.
2 Walker grounded to second.
3 Musial grounded to second.

7th Inning
New York
1 Dickey flied to left.
2 Etten grounded to second.
3 Lindell popped to third.
St. Louis
1 W. Cooper flied to left.
2 Kurowski thrown out by Johnson after a fantastic stop.
Sanders safe on first when Crosetti dropped his pop-up for an error.
Litwhiler doubled to right with Sanders stopping at third.
Marion given an intentional pass to load the bases.
Demaree, pinch hitting for Lanier, was safe at first as Johnson bobbled his grounder with Sanders scoring.
White ran for Demaree.
3 Klein forced White at second, Gordon to Crosetti

8th Inning
New York
For St. Louis—Brecheen pitching.
Russo doubled to left.
1 Stainback sacrificed Russo to third, Brecheen to Klein.
2 Crosetti flied to center with Russo scoring after the catch.
3 Johnson grounded to short.
St. Louis
1 Walker grounded to second.
Musial beat out a high bouncer to third. W. Cooper singled to short where Crosetti made a good stop moving Musial to second.
2 Kurowski flied to deep left.
Sanders hit to Gordon whose toss to Crosetti did not get Cooper in a force
3 but Cooper tagged out by Crosetti as he overran second.

9th Inning
New York
Keller singled between first and second.
1 Gordon fanned and Keller stole second. Dickey given an intentional pass.
2 Etten grounded to first.
Lindell also got a free pass to load the bases.
3 Russo fanned.
St. Louis
1 Litwhiler grounded to short.
Marion doubled to left.
2 Narron, pinch hitting for Brecheen, grounded to short, Marion holding.
3 Klein flied to center.

Game 5 October 11 at St. Louis

New York	Pos	AB	R	H	RBI	PO	A	E
Crosetti	ss	4	0	1	0	0	5	1
Metheny	rf	4	0	1	0	1	0	0
Lindell	rf	0	0	0	0	0	0	0
Johnson	3b	4	0	1	0	1	2	0
Keller	lf	3	1	1	0	1	1	0
Dickey	c	4	1	1	2	7	0	0
Etten	1b	3	0	1	0	11	1	0
Gordon	2b	2	0	0	0	6	6	0
Stainback	cf	3	0	1	0	0	0	0
Chandler	p	3	0	0	0	0	2	0
Totals		31	2	7	2	27	17	1

Pitching	IP	H	R	ER	BB	SO
New York						
Chandler (W)	9	10	0	0	2	7
St. Louis						
M. Cooper (L)	7	5	2	2	2	6
Lanier	1⅓	2	0	0	2	1
Dickson	⅔	0	0	0	1	0

St. Louis	Pos	AB	R	H	RBI	PO	A	E
Klein	3b	5	0	1	0	3	1	0
Garms	lf	4	0	0	0	1	0	0
Musial	rf	3	0	0	0	1	0	0
W. Cooper	c	2	0	0	0	6	0	1
O'Dea	c	2	0	2	0	6	0	0
Kurowski	3b	4	0	2	0	1	3	0
Sanders	1b	3	0	1	0	7	2	0
Hopp	cf	4	0	0	0	1	0	0
Marion	ss	3	0	1	0	2	3	0
M. Cooper	p	2	0	0	0	0	1	0
a Walker		1	0	1	0	0	0	0
Lanier	p	0	0	0	0	0	1	0
Dickson	p	0	0	0	0	0	1	0
b Litwhiler		1	0	1	0	0	0	0
Totals		34	0	10	0	27	11	1

N.Y. 000 002 000
St L. 000 000 000

a Singled for M. Cooper in 7th.
b Singled for Dickson in 9th.

Home Run—Dickey. Sacrifice Hits—Chandler, Garms, Marion, Stainback. Double Plays—Crosetti to Gordon to Etten, Klein to Marion to Sanders. Wild Pitch—M. Cooper. Left on Bases—New York 9, St. Louis 11. Umpires—Rommel, Reardon, Rue, Stewart. Attendance—33,872. Time of Game—2:24.

1st Inning
New York
1 Crosetti struck out.
2 Methany struck out.
3 Johnson struck out.
St. Louis
Klein singled off Chandler's glove.
1 Garms sacrificed Klein to second, Johnson to Etten.
Musial walked.
2 W. Cooper forced Musial at second, Crosetti to Gordon with Klein moving to third.
3 Kurowski grounded to third.

2nd Inning
New York
1 Keller struck out.
2 Dickey became Mort Cooper's fifth successive strike out victim.
Etten walked.
Etten to second on Walker Cooper's bad throw to first trying to pick him off.
3 Gordon grounded to third.
St. Louis
Sanders singled between first and second.
Hopp safe on first on his grounder to Chandler who threw to Crosetti in an attempt to force Sanders but Crosetti dropped the ball for an error.
1 Marion out on a good sacrifice, Etten to Gordon advancing both runners.
2 M. Cooper fanned.
3 Klein flied to right.

3rd Inning
New York
1 Stainback rolled to first.
2 Chandler fanned.
Crosetti singled to center.
Methany singled to left-center, advancing Crosetti to third.
3 Johnson popped to third.
St. Louis
1 Garms grounded to second.
2 Musial fanned.
Walker Cooper singled to left but out
3 trying for a double, Keller to Gordon.

4th Inning
New York
1 Keller flied to Marion in short-left.
2 Dickey grounded to short.
3 Etten fouled to Kurowski.
St. Louis
Kurowski beat out a single to third.
Sanders walked.
1 Hopp fanned.
2 Marion forced Sanders at second, Crosetti to Gordon with Kurowski going to third.
3 M. Cooper forced Marion at second, Crosetti on a good stop to Gordon.

5th Inning
New York
1 Gordon grounded to third.
Stainback singled off Marion's glove.
2 Chandler sacrificed Stainback to second, M. Cooper to Klein.
Stainback to third on a wild pitch.
For St. Louis—O'Dea catching as Walker Cooper got a fractured right index finger from a foul tip.
3 Crosetti flied to left.

5th Inning (continued)
St. Louis
1 Klein grounded to short.
2 Garms fanned.
3 Musial fanned.

6th Inning
New York
1 Methany flied to right.
2 Johnson grounded to short.
Keller singled between first and second.
Dickey hit a two-run homer on top of the right field stands.
3 Etten lined to center.
St. Louis
O'Dea singled on a roller down the third base line.
1,2 Kurowski grounded into a double play, Crosetti to Gordon to Etten.
3 Sanders grounded to first.

7th Inning
New York
Gordon walked.
1 Stainback sacrificed Gordon to second, Sanders to Klein.
2 Chandler flied to center.
3 Crosetti grounded to third.
St. Louis
1 Hopp bunted back to the pitcher.
2 Marion fouled to Johnson.
Walker, pinch hitting for M. Cooper, hit a Texas League single into right.
3 Klein took a called third strike.

8th Inning
New York
For St. Louis—Lanier pitching.
1 Methany fanned.
Johnson singled to left.
Keller walked.
2,3 Dickey grounded into a double play, Klein to Marion to Sanders.
St. Louis
1 Garms grounded to second.
2 Musial grounded to second.
O'Dea singled to right-center.
Kurowski's high bounder went over Johnson's head for a single with O'Dea stopping at second.
3 Sanders grounded to second.

9th Inning
New York
Etten beat out a hit to second.
Gordon walked.
1 Stainback forced Etten at third on an attempted sacrifice, Lanier to Kurowski.
For St. Louis—Dickson pitching.
2 Chandler fouled to O'Dea.
Crosetti walked, loading the bases.
3 Methany grounded out Sanders to Dickson, covering first.
St. Louis
For New York—Lindell in right field.
1 Hopp flied to left.
Marion singled to left.
Litwhiler, pinch hitting for Dickson, singled to center, Marion stopping at second.
2 Klein fanned.
3 Garms thrown out by **Gordon who set a 5-game Series record with 43 total chances accepted. Also this became the Yankees' 10th championship.**

1943 WORLD SERIES COMPOSITE BOX

	Wins	Composite Line Score	Manager	Regular Season W	L	Pct.	G. Ahead
New York Yankees (A.L.)	4	0 0 0 4 0 5 0 6 2 – 17	Joe McCarthy	98	56	.636	13.5
St. Louis Cardinals (N.L.)	1	0 1 1 5 1 0 1 0 0 – 9	Billy Southworth	105	49	.682	18

BATTING AND FIELDING

WORLD SERIES STATISTICS

	Pos	G	AB	R	H	2B	3B	HR	RBI	BB	SO	SB	BA	SA	PO	A	E
NEW YORK YANKEES																	
Nick Etten	1b	5	19	0	2	0	0	0	2	1	2	0	.105	.105	**46**	2	1
Joe Gordon	2b	5	17	2	4	1	0	**1**	2	**3**	3	0	.235	.471	20	**23**	0
Frankie Crosetti	ss	5	18	**4**	5	0	0	0	1	2	3	**1**	.278	.278	9	16	**3**
Billy Johnson	3b	5	20	3	**6**	1	**1**	0	3	0	3	0	.300	.450	2	9	1
Johnny Lindell	cf-rf	4	9	1	1	0	0	0	0	1	4	0	.111	.111	8	0	0
Tuck Stainback	rf-cf	5	17	0	3	0	0	0	0	0	2	0	.176	.176	7	1	0
Charlie Keller	lf	5	18	3	4	0	**1**	0	2	2	**5**	**1**	.222	.333	10	1	0
Bill Dickey	c	5	18	1	5	0	0	**1**	**4**	2	2	0	.278	.444	28	3	0
Bud Methany	rf	2	8	0	1	0	0	0	0	0	2	0	.125	.125	3	0	0
Snuffy Stirnweiss	ph	1	1	1	0	0	0	0	0	0	0	0	.000	.000			
Roy Weatherly	ph	1	1	0	0	0	0	0	0	0	0	0	.000	.000			
Ken Sears		Did not play															
Rollie Hemsley		Did not play															
Oscar Grimes		Did not play															
Spud Chandler	p	2	6	0	1	0	0	0	0	0	2	0	.167	.167	0	4	0
Marius Russo	p	1	3	1	2	2	0	0	0	1	1	0	.667	1.333	0	2	0
Hank Borowy	p	1	2	1	1	1	0	0	0	0	1	0	.500	1.000	2	0	0
Ernie Bohham	p	1	2	0	0	0	0	0	0	0	0	0	.000	.000	0	0	0
Johnny Murphy	p	2	0	0	0	0	0	0	0	0	0	0	—	—	0	1	0
Butch Wensloff		Did not play															
Bill Zuber		Did not play															
Atley Donald		Did not play															
Jim Turner		Did not play															
Tommy Byrne		Did not play															
Marv Breuer		Did not play															
team total		5	159	17	35	5	2	2	14	12	30	2	.220	.314	135	62	5

Double Plays—3
Left on Bases—30

REGULAR SEASON STATISTICS

	Main Pos	G	AB	R	H	2B	3B	HR	RBI	BB	SO	SB	BA	SA
Nick Etten	1b	154	583	78	158	35	5	14	107	76	31	3	.271	.420
Joe Gordon	2b	152	543	82	135	28	5	17	69	98	75	4	.249	.413
Frankie Crosetti	ss	95	348	36	81	8	1	2	20	36	47	4	.233	.279
Billy Johnson	3b	155	592	70	166	24	6	5	94	53	30	3	.280	.367
Johnny Lindell	of	122	441	53	108	17	**12**	4	51	51	55	2	.245	.365
Tuck Stainback	of	71	231	31	60	11	2	0	10	7	16	3	.260	.325
Charlie Keller	of	141	513	97	139	15	11	31	86	**106**	60	7	.271	.524
Bill Dickey	c	85	242	29	85	18	2	4	33	41	12	2	.351	.492
Bud Methany	of	103	360	51	94	18	2	9	36	39	34	2	.261	.397
Snuffy Stirnweiss	ss	83	274	34	60	8	4	1	25	47	37	11	.219	.288
Roy Weatherly	of	77	280	37	74	8	3	7	28	18	9	4	.264	.389
Ken Sears	c	60	187	22	52	7	0	2	22	11	18	1	.278	.348
Rollie Hemsley	c	62	180	12	43	6	3	2	24	13	9	0	.239	.339
Oscar Grimes	ss	9	20	4	3	0	0	0	1	3	7	0	.150	.150
Spud Chandler	p	30	97	9	25	5	0	2	7	1	22	0	.258	.371
Marius Russo	p	24	31	4	6	1	0	0	2	4	7	0	.194	.226
Hank Borowy	p	29	74	2	15	4	1	0	7	5	17	0	.203	.284
Ernie Bohham	p	28	76	5	15	1	0	0	2	4	15	0	.197	.211
Johnny Murphy	p	37	19	1	1	0	0	0	0	0	8	0	.053	.053
Butch Wensloff	p	29	79	6	14	2	0	0	4	4	25	0	.177	.203
Bill Zuber	p	20	38	1	7	1	2	0	2	4	14	0	.184	.316
Atley Donald	p	22	47	3	6	1	0	0	5	0	7	0	.128	.149
Jim Turner	p	18	13	2	1	0	0	0	0	0	2	0	.077	.077
Tommy Byrne	p	13	11	0	1	0	0	0	0	2	3	0	.091	.091
Marv Breuer	p	5	3	0	1	0	0	0	0	0	1	0	.333	.333
team total		155	5282	**669**	1350	218	**59**	**100**	**635**	**624**	562	46	.256	**.376**

Aaron Robinson (ph) also played for the Yankees during the season.

WORLD SERIES STATISTICS

	Pos	G	AB	R	H	2B	3B	HR	RBI	BB	SO	SB	BA	SA	PO	A	E
ST. LOUIS CARDINALS																	
Ray Sanders	1b	5	17	3	5	0	0	**1**	2	**3**	4	0	.294	.471	41	5	0
Lou Klein	2b	5	**22**	0	3	0	0	0	0	1	2	0	.136	.136	10	13	2
Marty Marion	ss	5	14	1	5	**2**	0	**1**	2	**3**	1	**1**	**.357**	**.714**	8	14	1
Whitey Kurowski	3b	5	18	2	4	1	0	0	1	0	3	0	.222	.278	8	8	2
Stan Musial	rf	5	18	2	5	0	0	0	0	2	2	0	.278	.278	7	2	0
Harry Walker	cf-ph	5	18	0	3	1	0	0	0	0	2	0	.167	.222	10	0	2
Danny Litwhiler	lf-ph	5	15	0	4	1	0	0	2	2	4	0	.267	.333	11	0	0
Walker Cooper	c	5	17	1	5	0	0	0	0	0	1	0	.294	.294	28	3	2
Debs Garms	ph-lf	2	5	0	0	0	0	0	0	0	2	0	.000	.000	1	0	0
Johnny Hopp	cf	1	4	0	0	0	0	0	0	0	1	0	.000	.000	1	0	0
Ken O'Dea	ph-c	2	3	0	2	0	0	0	0	0	0	0	.667	.667	2	0	0
Frank Demaree	ph	1	1	0	0	0	0	0	0	0	0	0	.000	.000			
Sam Narron	ph	1	1	0	0	0	0	0	0	0	0	0	.000	.000			
George Fallon		Did not play															
Mort Cooper	p	2	5	0	0	0	0	0	0	0	3	0	.000	.000	0	1	0
Max Lanier	p	3	4	0	1	0	0	0	1	0	0	0	.250	.250	0	3	1
Al Brazie	p	1	3	0	0	0	0	0	0	0	1	0	.000	.000	1	2	0
Harry Brecheen	p	3	0	0	0	0	0	0	0	0	0	0	—	—	0	2	0
Murry Dickson	p	1	0	0	0	0	0	0	0	0	0	0	—	—	1	0	0
Howie Krist	p	1	0	0	0	0	0	0	0	0	0	0	—	—	0	0	0
Ernie White	pr	1	0	0	0	0	0	0	0	0	0	0	—	—			
Harry Gumbert		Did not play															
George Munger		Did not play															
team totals		5	165	9	37	5	0	2	8	11	26	1	.224	.291	129	53	10

Double Plays—4
Left on Bases—37

REGULAR SEASON STATISTICS

		Main Pos	G	AB	R	H	2B	3B	HR	RBI	BB	SO	SB	BA	SA
Ray Sanders		1b	144	478	69	134	21	5	11	73	77	33	1	.280	.414
Lou Klein		2b	154	627	91	180	28	14	7	62	50	70	9	.287	.410
Marty Marion		ss	129	418	38	117	15	3	1	52	32	37	1	.280	.337
Whitey Kurowski		3b	139	522	69	150	24	8	13	70	31	54	3	.287	.439
Stan Musial		of	157	617	108	**220**	**48**	**20**	13	81	72	18	9	**.357**	**.562**
Harry Walker		of	148	564	76	166	28	6	2	53	40	24	5	.295	.376
Danny Litwhiler	a	of	80	258	40	72	14	3	7	31	19	31	1	.279	.438
Walker Cooper		c	122	449	52	143	30	4	9	81	19	19	1	.319	.463
Debs Garms		of-3b	90	249	26	64	10	2	0	22	13	8	1	.257	.313
Johnny Hopp		of-1b	91	241	33	54	10	2	2	25	24	22	8	.224	.307
Ken O'Dea		c	71	203	15	67	11	2	3	25	19	25	0	.281	.399
Frank Demaree		of	39	86	5	25	2	0	0	9	8	4	1	.291	.314
Sam Narron		c	10	11	0	1	0	0	0	0	1	2	0	.091	.091
George Fallon		2b	36	78	6	18	1	0	0	5	2	9	0	.231	.244
Mort Cooper		p	37	100	7	17	3	0	1	11	2	14	0	.170	.230
Max Lanier		p	32	73	8	12	0	0	0	5	1	5	0	.164	.164
Al Brazie		p	13	32	4	9	1	1	0	4	0	2	0	.281	.375
Harry Brecheen		p	29	42	4	8	2	0	0	3	2	8	0	.190	.238
Murry Dickson		p	31	34	1	9	2	0	0	6	0	1	0	.265	.324
Howie Krist		p	34	60	7	10	1	0	0	2	1	13	0	.167	.183
Ernie White		p	21	28	5	6	0	0	0	0	1	2	0	.214	.218
Harry Gumbert		p	21	45	1	7	0	0	0	1	1	11	0	.156	.156
George Munger		p	32	28	3	6	2	0	0	3	1	5	0	.214	.286
team totals			157	**5438**	679	**1515**	259	72	70	638	428	438	40	**.279**	**.391**

a—from Philadelphia (N)
Jimmy Brown (inf), Coaker Triplett (of), Buster Adams (of), Howie Pollet (p), and Bud Byerly (p) also played for the Cardinals during the season.

PITCHING

WORLD SERIES STATISTICS

	G	GS	CG	IP	H	R	ER	BB	SO	W	L	SV	ERA
NEW YORK YANKEES													
Spud Chandler	2	**2**	**2**	**18**	**17**	2	1	**3**	10	**2**	0	0	0.50
Marius Russo	1	1	1	9	7	1	0	1	2	1	0	0	**0.00**
Hank Borowy	1	1	0	8	6	2	2	**3**	4	1	0	0	2.25
Ernie Bonham	1	1	0	8	6	4	4	**3**	9	0	**1**	0	4.50
Johnny Murphy	2	0	0	2	1	0	0	1	1	0	0	**1**	0.00
Butch Wensloff	Did not play												
Bill Zuber	Did not play												
Atley Donald	Did not play												
Jim Turner	Did not play												
Tommy Byrne	Did not play												
Marv Breuer	Did not play												
team total	5	5	3	45	37	9	7	11	26	4	1	1	1.46
ST. LOUIS CARDINALS													
Mort Cooper	2	**2**	1	16	11	5	**5**	**3**	10	1	**1**	0	2.81
Max Lanier	**3**	**2**	0	15 1/3	13	5	3	**3**	**13**	0	**1**	0	1.76
Al Brazle	1	1	0	7 1/3	5	**6**	3	2	4	0	**1**	0	3.68
Harry Brecheen	**3**	0	0	3 2/3	5	1	1	**3**	3	0	**1**	0	2.45
Murry Dickson	1	0	0	2/3	0	0	0	1	0	0	0	0	0.00
Howie Krist	1	0	0	0	1	0	0	0	0	0	0	0	0.00
Harry Gumbert	Did not play												
George Munger	Did not play												
Ernie White	Did not pitch												
team total	5	5	1	43	35	17	12	12	30	1	4	0	2.51

REGULAR SEASON STATISTICS

	G	GS	CG	IP	H	ER	BB	SO	W	L	Pct	SV	ShO	ERA
NEW YORK YANKEES														
Spud Chandler	30	30	**20**	253	197	46	54	134	**20**	4	**.833**	0	**5**	**1.64**
Marius Russo	24	14	5	102	89	42	45	42	5	10	.333	1	1	3.71
Hank Borowy	29	27	14	217	195	68	72	113	14	9	.609	0	3	2.82
Ernie Bonham	28	26	17	226	197	57	52	71	15	8	.652	1	4	2.27
Johnny Murphy	37	0	0	68	44	19	30	31	12	4	.750	8	0	2.51
Butch Wensloff	29	27	18	223	179	63	70	105	13	11	.542	1	1	2.54
Bill Zuber	20	13	7	118	100	51	74	57	8	4	.667	1	0	3.89
Atley Donald	22	15	2	119	134	61	38	57	6	4	.600	0	0	4.61
Jim Turner	18	0	0	43	44	17	13	15	3	0	1.000	1	0	3.56
Tommy Byrne	11	2	0	32	28	23	35	22	2	1	.667	0	0	6.47
Marv Breuer	5	1	0	14	22	13	6	6	0	1	.000	0	0	8.36
team total	155	155	**83**	1415	1229	**460**	489	653	**98**	56	**.636**	13	14	**2.93**
ST. LOUIS CARDINALS														
Mort Cooper	37	32	24	274	228	70	79	141	**21**	8	**.724**	3	6	2.30
Max Lanier	32	25	14	213	195	45	75	123	15	7	.682	3	2	1.90
Al Brazle	13	9	8	88	74	15	29	26	8	2	.800	0	1	1.53
Harry Brecheen	29	13	8	135	98	34	39	68	9	6	.600	4	1	2.27
Murry Dickson	31	7	2	116	114	46	49	44	8	2	.800	0	0	3.57
Howie Krist	34	17	9	164	141	53	62	57	11	5	.688	3	2	2.91
Harry Gumbert	21	19	7	133	115	42	32	40	10	5	.667	0	2	2.84
George Munger	32	9	5	93	101	41	42	45	9	5	.643	2	0	3.97
Ernie White	14	10	5	79	78	33	33	28	5	5	.500	0	1	3.76
team total	157	157	**94**	**1427**	1241	**407**	477	**639**	**105**	49	**.682**	15	**21**	**2.57**

Total Attendance—277,312 Average Attendance—55,462 Winning Player's Share—$6,139 Losing Player's Share—$4,322

1944
Happily Settling for a Pennant

It took a World War to make a pennant winner out of the St. Louis Browns. The Brownies had their usual squad of castoffs, which was annually good enough for the second division, but the military draft had dragged the rest of the American League clubs down to their level. Even the Yankees had been bled into feebleness, so the A.L. flag was thrown open to the club that could manage to lose the least games. Into the final week of the season chugged the Browns, Tigers, and Yankees, with the Browns grabbing their first-ever pennant by beating the Yanks on the final day of the campaign. The collection of odds and ends fielded by St. Louis manager Luke Sewell would not have made a dent in the prewar or postwar baseball scenes, but in the diluted baseball world of 1944, Sewell had stars in power-hitting short-stop Vern Stephens, thirty-six-year-old singles-hitter Mike Kreevich, and yeoman pitchers Nelson Potter and Jack Kramer.

One factor that made the Browns' pennant win even more savory for St. Louis fans was that the Cardinals, who had been winning pennants at regular intervals for years, made it an all-St. Louis Series by collecting their third straight National League championship. Manager Billy Southworth lost a few more men to the armed forces, but he still had a .347 hitter in young Stan Musial, the N.L. MVP in shortstop Marty Marion, solid hitters in Whitey Kurowski, Ray Sanders, Johnny Hopp, and Walker Cooper, reliable starters in Mort Cooper, Max Lanier, and Harry Brecheen, and a new rookie find in pitcher Ted Wilks, who had a 17–4 season. The Cards still had enough talent to resemble a prewar club and rated the favorite's role on that basis alone, but the Browns had the traditional claim of the underdog on the affections of the fans.

No travel days were needed for this Series, as all the games would be played in Sportsman's Park, the stadium which the Browns owned but in which the tenant Cards prospered. Mort Cooper took the mound for the Cardinals in the opener against nine-game winner Denny Galehouse for the Browns. While Galehouse gave up only seven hits and one run to the Cards, Cooper allowed a mere two hits to the Browns, but they were a single by Gene Moore and a homer by George McQuinn in the fourth inning, enough to lose the game 2–1. Faced with such treatment by their landlord, the Cards sent Lanier out to face Potter and won the second game 3–2 in the bottom of the eleventh on a pinch single by Ken O'Dea off reliever Bob Muncrief. Rookie Cardinal reliever Blix Donnelly got the win with four shutout innings in which he struck out seven men. Southworth started his other rookie pitcher in game three, but a four-run third inning drove Ted Wilks from the game and launched the Browns on their way to a 6–2 victory.

Ahead in the Series two games to one, the Browns were riding the highest crest in the history of the franchise, but the Cards were about to cash in on the Series experience that the Browns obviously lacked. Manager Sewell chose Sig Jakucki, who had beaten the Yankees on the last day of the season to clinch the pennant, to start game four, but the Cards rapped him hard in the first three innings and went on to a 5–1 win to even the Series. The young Browns got nine hits off Harry Brecheen, but left ten men on base. Game five saw another pitching duel between Mort Cooper and Denny Galehouse, and while Cooper relaxed his hit allotment up to seven, he was fortunate enough to scatter them around so as to prevent any runs. Galehouse gave up only six hits, but the long ball cursed him this time as Ray Sanders and Danny Litwhiler hit solo homers good enough for a 2–0 win. The Cards quickly moved in for the kill, winning game six 3–1 by scoring three runs in the fourth inning after a throwing error by Stephens opened the door. For the Cardinals, it was one more World Series banner to fly over Sportsman's Park. For the Browns, they at least had an American League pennant to hoist up the flagpole, the only championship the team won since joining the league in 1902.

Game 1 October 4 at St. Louis—N

St. Louis—A	Pos	AB	R	H	RBI	PO	A	E
Gutteridge	2b	4	0	0	0	1	2	0
Kreevich	cf	4	0	0	0	6	0	0
Laabs	lf	4	0	0	0	2	0	0
Stephens	ss	3	0	0	0	1	3	0
Moore	rf	3	1	1	0	1	0	0
McQuinn	1b	3	1	1	2	10	0	0
Christman	3b	3	0	0	0	1	1	0
Hayworth	c	3	0	0	0	5	0	0
Galehouse	p	2	0	0	0	0	2	0
Totals		29	2	2	2	27	8	0

Pitching	IP	H	R	ER	BB	SO
St. Louis—A						
Galehouse (W)	9	7	1	1	4	5
St. Louis—N						
M. Cooper (L)	7	2	2	2	3	4
Donnelly	2	0	0	0	0	2

St—A	0 0 0	2 0 0	0 0 0
St—N	0 0 0	0 0 0	0 0 1

St. Louis—N	Pos	AB	R	H	RBI	PO	A	E
Hopp	cf	5	0	1	0	1	0	0
Sanders	1b	3	0	1	0	12	0	0
Musial	rf	3	0	1	0	2	0	0
W. Cooper	c	3	0	0	0	8	0	0
Kurowski	3b	4	0	1	0	0	4	0
Litwhiler	lf	2	0	0	0	1	0	0
Fallon	2b	2	0	0	0	1	0	0
Marion	ss	4	1	2	0	1	4	0
Verban	2b	2	0	1	0	1	1	0
a Bergamo	lf	1	0	0	0	1	0	0
M. Cooper	p	2	0	0	0	0	3	0
b Garms		1	0	0	0	0	0	0
Donnelly	p	0	0	0	0	0	1	0
c O'Dea		1	0	0	1	0	0	0
Totals		32	1	7	1	27	12	0

a Walked for Verban in 7th.
b Grounded out for M. Cooper in 7th.
c Hit sacrifice fly for Donnelly in 9th.

Doubles—Marion 2. Home Run—McQuinn. Sacrifice Hit—Musial. Double Play—Gutteridge to Stephens to McQuinn. Left on Bases—Browns 3, Cardinals 9. Umpires—Sears (N), McGowan (A), Dunn (N), Pipgras (A). Attendance—33,242. Time of Game—2:05.

1st Inning
Browns
1 Gutteridge popped to Marion back of third base.
2 Kreevich struck out.
3 Laabs struck out.
Cardinals
1 Hopp flied to left.
2 Sanders struck out.
Musial singled past second.
3 W. Cooper flied to center.

2nd Inning
Browns
1 Stephens grounded back to the mound.
Moore walked.
2 McQuinn flied to left.
3 Christman called out on strikes.
Cardinals
1 Kurowski flied to deep right.
2 Litwhiler struck out.
Marion doubled down the third-base line.
Verban singled over second, Marion stopping at third.
3 M. Cooper took a called third strike.

3rd Inning
Browns
1 Hayworth grounded to third.
Galehouse walked.
2 Gutteridge flied to center.
3 Kreevich smashed a grounder back to the mound.
Cardinals
Hopp singled to right.
Sanders singled to right, Hopp stopping at second.
1 Musial sacrificed up both runners, Galehouse to McQuinn.
W. Cooper intentionally walked, loading the bases.
2 Kurowski struck out.
3 Litwhiler forced Sanders at third, Christman unassisted.

4th Inning
Browns
1 Laabs flied to deep right.
2 Stephens popped to second.
Moore singled to right.
McQuinn hit a two-run homer over the right field stands.
3 Christman grounded to short.
Cardinals
1 Marion flied to center.
2 Verban bounced back to the mound.
3 M. Cooper struck out.

5th Inning
Browns
1 Hayworth grounded to third.
2 Galehouse grounded to short.
3 Gutteridge hit back to the pitcher.
Cardinals
1 Hopp popped to second.
Sanders walked.
2,3 Musial hit into a double play, Gutteridge to Stephens to McQuinn.

6th Inning
Browns
1 Kreevich grounded to short.
2 Laabs took a called third strike.
Stephens walked.
3 Moore grounded to second.
Cardinals
1 W. Cooper grounded to third.
2 Kurowski flied to deep left.
Litwhiler singled to center.
3 Marion flied to center.

7th Inning
Browns
1 McQuinn fouled to W. Cooper.
2 Christman fouled to W. Cooper.
3 Hayworth flied to shallow right.
Cardinals
Bergamo, batting for Verban, walked.
1 Garms, batting for M. Cooper, grounded to first, Bergamo moving to second.
2 Hopp flied to short center.
3 Sanders lined to first.

8th Inning
Browns
For the Cardinals—Bergamo playing left, Fallon playing second (batting 6th) and Donnelly pitching.
1 Galehouse grounded to short.
2 Gutteridge flied to left.
3 Kreevich struck out.
Cardinals
1 Musial grounded to first.
2 W. Cooper grounded to short.
Kurowski singled to left.
3 Fallon grounded to short.

9th Inning
Browns
1 Laabs bounced back to the pitcher.
2 Stephens grounded to third.
3 Moore struck out.
Cardinals
Marion doubled to center.
1 Bergamo grounded to second, Marion moving to third.
2 O'Dea, pinch-hitting for Donnelly, flied to center, Marion scoring after the catch.
3 Hopp flied to center.

Game 2 October 5 at St. Louis—N

St. Louis—A	Pos	AB	R	H	RBI	PO	A	E
Gutteridge	2b	4	0	0	0	5	4	1
Kreevich	cf	5	0	2	0	1	0	0
Laabs	lf	4	0	0	0	1	0	0
c Zarilla	lf	1	0	0	0	0	0	0
Stephens	ss	5	0	0	0	2	5	0
McQuinn	1b	2	0	1	0	13	1	0
Christman	3b	5	0	0	0	0	5	1
Moore	rf	5	1	2	0	1	0	0
Hayworth	c	5	1	1	1	7	1	0
Potter	p	2	0	0	0	1	1	2
a Mancuso		1	0	1	1	0	0	0
b Shirley		0	0	0	0	0	0	0
Muncrief	p	1	0	0	0	0	0	0
Totals		40	2	7	2	e31	17	4

a Singled for Potter in 7th.
b Ran for Mancuso in 7th.
c Hit into force play for Laabs in 10th.
d Singled for Verban in 11th.
e One out when winning run scored.

Doubles—W. Cooper, Hayworth, Kreevich, Kurowski, McQuinn. Sacrifice Hits—W. Cooper, Kurowski, Lanier. Double Plays—Stephens to Gutteridge, Stephens to Gutteridge to McQuinn. Left on Bases—Browns 9, Cardinals 10.
Umpires—McGowan, Dunn, Pipgras, Sears.
Attendance—35,076. Time of Game—2:32.

St—A	000	000	200	00	
St—N	001	100	000	01	

St. Louis—N	Pos	AB	R	H	RBI	PO	A	E
Bergamo	lf	5	0	0	1	0	0	0
Hopp	cf	5	0	0	0	2	0	0
Musial	rf	5	0	1	0	2	0	0
W. Cooper	c	4	0	1	0	15	0	0
Sanders	1b	3	2	1	0	8	1	0
Kurowski	3b	4	0	2	0	1	4	0
Marion	ss	3	0	0	0	2	6	0
Verban	2b	3	1	1	1	3	0	0
d O'Dea		1	0	1	1	0	0	0
Lanier	p	2	0	0	0	0	0	0
Donnelly	p	1	0	0	0	0	1	0
Totals		36	3	7	3	33	12	0

Pitching	IP	H	R	ER	BB	SO
St. Louis—A						
Potter	6	4	2	0	2	3
Muncrief (L)	$4\frac{1}{3}$	3	1	1	3	4
St. Louis—N						
Lanier	*7	5	2	2	3	6
Donnelly (W)	4	2	0	0	1	7

*Pitched to one batter in 8th.

1st Inning
Browns
1 Gutteridge struck out.
2 Kreevich grounded to short.
3 Laabs flied to center.
Cardinals
1 Bergamo fouled to Hayworth.
2 Hopp flied to short center.
3 Musial grounded to second.

2nd Inning
Browns
1 Stephens grounded to short.
McQuinn walked.
2 Christman struck out.
3 Moore struck out.
Cardinals
W. Cooper doubled to left.
1 Sanders fanned.
2 Kurowski grounded to short, W. Cooper going to third.
3 Marion grounded to third.

3rd Inning
Browns
1 Hayworth popped to short.
2 Potter grounded to short.
Gutteridge walked.
3 Kreevich forced Gutteridge at second, Marion to Verban.
Cardinals
Verban singled to left.
Lanier safe when Potter fumbled his bunt, then threw wildly to first as Verban got to third (a sacrifice for Lanier and two errors on Potter).
1 Bergamo grounded to second, Verban scoring with Lanier going to second.
2 Hopp struck out.
3 Musial grounded to second.

4th Inning
Browns
1 Laabs struck out.
2 Stephens grounded to third.
McQuinn walked.
3 Christman forced McQuinn at second, Kurowski to Verban.
Cardinals
1 W. Cooper grounded to third.
Sanders walked.
Kurowski singled to left, Sanders stopping at second.
Marion safe on Christman's fumble of his grounder, loading the bases.
2 Verban flied to left, Sanders scoring after the catch as Kurowski went to third and Marion to second on the throw to the plate.
3 Lanier grounded to short.

5th Inning
Browns
Moore beat out a bunt for a hit.
1 Hayworth forced Moore at second, Marion to Verban.
2 Potter grounded to short, a good pick-up by Marion as Hayworth went to second.
3 Gutteridge flied to deep center.
Cardinals
1 Bergamo struck out.
2 Hopp flied to short right.
3 Musial grounded out, McQuinn to Potter.

6th Inning
Browns
1 Kreevich flied to right.
2 Laabs struck out but had to be tagged by W. Cooper when he dropped the third strike.
3 Stephens grounded to third.
Cardinals
1 W. Cooper popped to Stephens in back of the box.
2 Sanders popped to second.
Kurowski doubled to deep center.
Marion got an intentional pass.
3 Verban popped to first.

7th Inning
Browns
1 McQuinn struck out.
2 Christman fouled to W. Cooper.
Moore singled to center.
Hayworth doubled off the left field wall, scoring Moore.
Mancuso, pinch-hitting for Potter, singled to center, scoring Hayworth.
Shirley ran for Mancuso.
3 Gutteridge grounded to third.
Cardinals
For the Browns—Muncrief now pitching.
1 Lanier popped to second.
2 Bergamo struck out.
3 Hopp struck out.

8th Inning
Browns
Kreevich doubled off the left field wall.
For the Cardinals—Donnelly replaced Lanier on the mound.
1 Laabs struck out for the third straight time.
2 Stephens struck out.
McQuinn was intentionally passed.
3 Christman struck out.
Cardinals
Musial singled beyond second.
1 W. Cooper sacrificed Musial to second, Christman to McQuinn.
Sanders was intentionally passed.
2,3 Kurowski popped to Stephens in short left and quickly threw to Gutteridge doubling Musial at second.

9th Inning
Browns
1 Moore grounded to first.
2 Hayworth popped to W. Cooper in front of the plate.
3 Muncrief took a called third strike.
Cardinals
1 Marion grounded to short.
Verban walked.
2 Donnelly took a called third strike.
3 Bergamo struck out for the third time but Hayworth dropped the third strike and threw him out at first.

10th Inning
Browns
1 Gutteridge struck out.
Kreevich singled off Marion's leg.
2 Zarilla, batting for Laabs, forced Kreevich, Sanders to Marion.
3 Stephens struck out.
Cardinals
For the Browns—Zarilla, playing left.
1 Hopp grounded to third.
Musial safe on Gutteridge's fumble.
2,3 W. Cooper hit into a double play, Stephens to Gutteridge to McQuinn.

11th Inning
Browns
McQuinn hit a long double off the right field fence.
1 Christman bunted down the third base line and McQuinn was out at third, Donnelly to Kurowski.
2 Moore flied to Musial deep at the right field wall.
3 Hayworth struck out.
Cardinals
Sanders singled past second.
1 Kurowski sacrificed Sanders to second, Christman to Gutteridge.
Marion got an intentional pass for the second time in the game.
O'Dea, pinch-hitting for Verban, singled to right, scoring Sanders with the game-winning run.

Game 3 October 6 at St. Louis—A

St. Louis—N	Pos	AB	R	H	RBI	PO	A	E
Litwhiler	lf	5	0	0	0	0	0	0
Hopp	cf	4	1	1	0	1	0	0
Musial	rf	4	0	1	0	2	0	0
W. Cooper	c	4	0	2	1	5	0	0
Sanders	1b	3	0	1	0	11	0	0
Kurowski	3b	4	1	0	0	0	4	0
Marion	ss	4	0	2	1	2	5	0
Verban	2b	2	0	0	0	3	1	0
a Garms		1	0	0	0	0	0	0
Fallon	2b	1	0	0	0	0	0	0
Wilks	p	1	0	0	0	0	0	0
Schmidt	p	1	0	0	0	0	0	0
b Bergamo		0	0	0	0	0	0	0
Jurisich	p	0	0	0	0	0	0	0
Byerly	p	0	0	0	0	0	0	0
c O'Dea		1	0	0	0	0	0	0
Totals		35	2	7	2	24	10	0

a Flied out for Verban in 7th.
b Walked for Schmidt in 7th.
c Grounded out for Byerly in 9th.

Doubles—W. Cooper, Gutteridge, McQuinn.
Double Play—Marion to Sanders.
Passed Ball—W. Cooper, Wild Pitch—Schmidt.
Left on Bases—Cardinals 8, Browns 6.
Umpires—Dunn, Pipgras, Sears, McGowan.
Attendance—34,737. Time of Game—2:19.

St—N	100	000	100	
St—A	004	000	20x	

St. Louis—A	Pos	AB	R	H	RBI	PO	A	E
Gutteridge	2b	4	1	1	0	2	1	1
Kreevich	cf	4	0	0	0	1	0	0
Moore	rf	4	1	1	0	3	0	0
Stephens	ss	2	2	1	0	1	1	1
McQuinn	1b	3	1	3	2	6	0	0
Zarilla	lf	4	1	1	1	2	0	0
Christman	3b	4	0	1	1	1	0	0
Hayworth	c	2	0	0	0	11	0	0
Kramer	p	4	0	0	0	0	2	0
Totals		31	6	8	4	27	4	2

Pitching	IP	H	R	ER	BB	SO
St. Louis—N						
Wilks (L)	$2\frac{2}{3}$	5	4	4	3	3
Schmidt	$3\frac{1}{3}$	1	0	0	1	1
Jurisich	$\frac{2}{3}$	2	2	2	1	0
Byerly	$1\frac{1}{3}$	0	0	0	0	1
St. Louis—A						
Kramer (W)	9	7	2	0	2	10

1st Inning
Cardinals
1 Litwhiler flied to left.
Hopp safely to second as his grounder went through Stephens' legs.
2 Musial popped to Stephens behind third.
W. Cooper singled over short, scoring Hopp.
Sanders walked.
3 Kurowski struck out.
Browns
1 Gutteridge struck out.
2 Kreevich fouled to Sanders.
3 Moore grounded to second.

2nd Inning
Cardinals
1 Marion struck out.
2 Verban fouled to Hayworth.
3 Wilks called out on strikes.
Browns
Stephens walked.
McQuinn walked.
1 Zarilla flied to right.
2 Christman forced McQuinn at second, Marion to Verban, as Stephens went to third.
Hayworth walked, loading the bases.
3 Kramer struck out.

3rd Inning
Cardinals
1 Litwhiler grounded back to the mound.
2 Hopp grounded to first.
Musial singled through second.
3 W. Cooper flied to center.
Browns
1 Gutteridge took a called third strike.
2 Kreevich flied to Hopp in left-center.
Moore singled to right.
Stephens singled to left, Moore stopping at second.
McQuinn singled over short, scoring Moore with Stephens stopping at second.
Zarilla singled to left, scoring Stephens with McQuinn stopping at second.
Christman singled over short, scoring McQuinn with Zarilla going to third.
Christman went to second on the throw to the plate.
For the Cardinals—Schmidt on the mound.
Hayworth got an intentional pass, loading the bases.
Zarilla scored, Christman went to third and Hayworth to second on a wild pitch.
3 Kramer grounded to third.

4th Inning
Cardinals
1 Sanders struck out.
2 Kurowski grounded back to the pitcher.
3 Marion flied to deep right.
Browns
1 Gutteridge grounded to third.
2 Kreevich grounded to short.
3 Moore flied to right.

5th Inning
Cardinals
1 Verban popped to first.
2 Schmidt called out on strikes.
3 Litwhiler struck out.
Browns
1 Stephens grounded to third.
McQuinn singled to left.
2,3 Zarilla grounded into a double play, Marion to Sanders.

6th Inning
Cardinals
1 Hopp struck out.
2 Musial popped to Christman between third and home.
3 W. Cooper grounded to first.
Browns
1 Christman popped to second.
2 Hayworth lined to second.
3 Kramer struck out.

7th Inning
Cardinals
Sanders singled to right-center.
1 Kurowski forced Sanders to second, Stephens to Gutteridge, but trying for the double play Gutteridge threw wildly to first and Kurowski got to second.
Marion singled through second, scoring Kurowski.
2 Garms, pinch-hitting for Verban, flied to left.
Bergamo, pinch-hitting for Schmidt, walked.
3 Litwhiler popped to Gutteridge on the outfield grass.
Browns
For the Cardinals—Jurisch pitching, and Fallon playing second.
Gutteridge doubled off the right field screen.
1 Kreevich popped to short.
2 Moore grounded to first, Gutteridge going to third.
Stephens walked with Gutteridge scoring as the fourth ball got away from W. Cooper for a passed ball.
McQuinn doubled to right, scoring Stephens, McQuinn going to third on the throw-in.
For the Cardinals—Byerly now pitching.
3 Zarilla took a called third strike.

8th Inning
Cardinals
Hopp singled to center.
1 Musial flied to deep right.
W. Cooper doubled off the left field wall, Hopp stopping at third.
2 Sanders took a called third strike.
3 Kurowski flied to right.
Browns
1 Christman bounced to third.
2 Hayworth grounded to short.
3 Kramer grounded to short.

9th Inning
Cardinals
Marion singled to center.
1 Fallon struck out.
2 O'Dea, batting for Byerly, grounded to second, Marion moving to second.
3 Litwhiler struck out.

Game 4 October 7 at St. Louis—A

St.—N	2 0 2	0 0 1	0 0 0					
St.—A	0 0 0	0 0 0	0 1 0					

St. Louis—N	Pos	AB	R	H	RBI	PO	A	E
Litwhiler	lf	4	1	2	0	2	0	0
Hopp	cf	5	1	2	0	4	0	0
Musial	rf	4	2	3	2	2	0	0
W. Cooper	c	4	0	2	1	4	0	0
Sanders	1b	5	1	1	0	9	0	0
Kurowski	3b	4	0	2	1	4	0	0
Marion	ss	4	0	1	1	3	0	0
Verban	2b	4	0	1	0	4	3	0
Brecheen	p	4	0	0	0	1	3	0
Totals		38	5	12	4	27	12	0

Pitching	IP	H	R	ER	BB	SO
St. Louis—N						
Brecheen (W)	9	9	1	1	4	4
St. Louis—A						
Jakucki (L)	3	5	4	3	0	4
Hollingsworth	4	5	1	1	2	1
Shirley	2	2	0	0	1	1

St. Louis—A	Pos	AB	R	H	RBI	PO	A	E
Gutteridge	2b	4	0	2	0	3	2	1
Kreevich	cf	5	0	1	0	4	0	0
Moore	rf	3	1	0	0	1	0	0
Stephens	ss	4	0	1	0	1	6	0
Laabs	lf	4	0	2	0	1	0	0
McQuinn	1b	3	0	1	0	9	0	0
Christman	3b	4	0	1	0	0	1	0
Hayworth	c	2	0	1	0	5	0	0
Mancuso	c	2	0	1	0	3	0	0
Jakucki	p	0	0	0	0	0	1	0
a Clary		1	0	0	0	0	0	0
Hollingsworth	p	1	0	0	0	1	0	0
b Byrnes		1	0	0	0	0	0	0
Shirley	p	0	0	0	0	1	0	0
c Turner		1	0	0	0	0	0	0
Totals		34	1	9	0	27	14	1

a Flied out for Jakucki in 3rd.
b Walked for Hollingsworth in 7th.
c Flied out for Shirley in 9th.

Doubles—Laabs, Marion, Musial.
Triple—W. Cooper. Home Run—Musial.
Double Plays—Kurowski to Verban to Sanders, Marion to Verban to Sanders.
Left on Bases—Cardinals 9, Browns 10.
Umpires—Pipgras, Sears, McGowan, Dunn.
Attendance—35,455. Time of Game—2:22.

1st Inning
Cardinals
1 Litwhiler struck out.
Hopp singled back of second.
Musial hit a two-run homer over the right field pavilion.
2 W. Cooper grounded back to the mound.
3 Sanders took a called third strike.
Browns
1 Gutteridge struck out.
Kreevich singled to left.
2 Moore flied to Hopp who made a running one-handed catch near the right-center field wall.
3 Stephens grounded to short.

2nd Inning
Cardinals
1 Kurowski flied to center.
2 Marion grounded to short.
3 Verban grounded to short.
Browns
1 Laabs flied to left.
McQuinn singled over short.
Christman singled to center, McQuinn racing to third.
2,3 Hayworth grounded into a double play, Kurowski to Verban to Sanders.

3rd Inning
Cardinals
1 Brecheen struck out.
Litwhiler singled off Stephens' glove.
2 Hopp struck out.
Musial beat out a hit between the mound and second, Litwhiler stopping at second.
W. Cooper singled to left, scoring Litwhiler with Musial stopping at second.
Sanders safe at first on Gutteridge's error, allowing Musial to score and W. Cooper to get to third.
3 Kurowski grounded to short.
Browns
1 Clary, batting for Jakucki, flied to short right.
Gutteridge singled over second.
2 Kreevich flied to left.
3 Moore struck out.

4th Inning
Cardinals
For the Browns—Hollingsworth pitching.
1 Marion grounded to second.
2 Verban flied to center.
3 Brecheen grounded to third.
Browns
1 Stephens bounced back to the mound.
Laabs singled to center.
2 McQuinn grounded to the pitcher, Laabs going to second.
3 Christman called out on strikes.

5th Inning
Cardinals
1 Litwhiler grounded to short.
2 Hopp flied to left.
Musial walked.
3 W. Cooper forced Musial at second, Stephens to Gutteridge.
Browns
1 Hayworth fouled to Sanders, making a one-handed catch near the right field boxes.
2 Hollingsworth grounded to first.
Gutteridge singled to left.
3 Kreevich lined to the pitcher.

6th Inning
Cardinals
Sanders singled to center.
1 Kurowski struck out.
Marion doubled to left-center, scoring Sanders.
2 Verban flied to center.
3 Brecheen bounced back to the mound.
Browns
1 Moore flied to deep center.
2 Stephens singled to center.
Laabs doubled to left.
McQuinn walked.
3 Christman forced McQuinn at second, Kurowski to Verban.

7th Inning
Cardinals
For the Browns—Mancuso catching.
Litwhiler singled to center but was
1 out trying for second, Kreevich to Gutteridge.
Hopp singled to left.
Musial doubled down the left field line, Hopp stopping at third.
W. Cooper was intentionally passed, loading the bases.
2 Sanders popped to second.
3 Kurowski flied deep (400 feet mark) in center.
Browns
1 Mancuso flied to right.
Byrnes, batting for Hollingsworth, walked.
2 Gutteridge forced Byrnes at second, Kurowski to Verban.
3 Kreevich grounded back to the mound.

8th Inning
Cardinals
For the Browns—Shirley pitching.
1 Marion struck out.
Verban singled over Christman's head.
2 Brecheen forced Verban at second, Shirley to Stephens.
Litwhiler walked.
3 Hopp fouled to Mancuso.
Browns
Moore walked.
Stephens singled off the right field screen, Moore going to third.
1,2 Laabs grounded into a double play, Marion to Verban to Sanders as Moore scored.
3 McQuinn grounded to short.

9th Inning
Cardinals
1 Musial grounded to second.
W. Cooper tripled off the center field wall, but was out trying for a
2 home run, Kreevich to Stephens to Mancuso.
3 Sanders flied to right.
Browns
1 Christman called out on strikes.
Mancuso singled to left.
2 Turner, batting for Shirley, flied to short center.
Gutteridge walked.
3 Kreevich forced Gutteridge at second, Verban to Marion.

Game 5 October 8 at St. Louis—A

St.—N	0 0 0	0 0 1	0 1 0					
St.—A	0 0 0	0 0 0	0 0 0					

St. Louis—N	Pos	AB	R	H	RBI	PO	A	E
Litwhiler	lf	4	1	2	1	0	0	0
Hopp	cf	4	0	0	0	3	0	0
Musial	rf	3	0	1	0	1	0	1
W. Cooper	c	4	0	0	0	13	0	0
Sanders	1b	4	1	1	1	4	0	0
Kurowski	3b	4	0	1	0	3	0	0
Marion	ss	4	0	0	0	1	2	0
Verban	2b	3	0	1	0	2	0	0
M. Cooper	p	2	0	0	0	0	3	0
Totals		32	2	6	2	27	5	1

Pitching	IP	H	R	ER	BB	SO
St. Louis—N						
M. Cooper (W)	9	7	0	0	2	12
St. Louis—A						
Galehouse (L)	9	6	2	2	1	10

St. Louis—A	Pos	AB	R	H	RBI	PO	A	E
Gutteridge	2b	2	0	0	0	1	0	0
a Baker	2b	1	0	0	0	0	0	0
Kreevich	cf	4	0	2	0	5	0	0
Moore	rf	4	0	0	0	2	0	0
Stephens	ss	4	0	3	0	1	1	1
McQuinn	1b	3	0	0	0	6	0	0
Zarilla	lf	4	0	0	0	1	0	0
Christman	3b	3	0	0	0	0	1	0
b Byrnes		1	0	0	0	0	0	0
Hayworth	c	3	0	1	0	12	1	0
c Laabs		1	0	0	0	0	0	0
Galehouse	p	3	0	1	0	0	3	0
d Chartak		1	0	0	0	0	0	0
Totals		34	0	7	0	27	6	1

a Struck out for Gutteridge in 7th.
b Struck out for Christman in 9th.
c Struck out for Hayworth in 9th.
d Struck out for Galehouse in 9th.

Doubles—Kreevich, Litwhiler, Musial, Stephens. Home Runs—Litwhiler, Sanders.
Sacrifice Hit—M. Cooper. Double Play—Stephens to McQuinn.
Left on Bases—Cardinals 5, Browns 9.
Umpires—Sears, Pipgras, Dunn, McGowan.
Attendance—36,568. Time of Game—2:04.

1st Inning
Cardinals
Litwhiler doubled to left-center at the 400 foot mark.
1 Hopp struck out.
Musial walked.
2 W. Cooper struck out.
3 Sanders struck out.
Browns
Gutteridge walked.
1 Kreevich took a called third strike.
2 Moore flied to right.
Stephens singled through short, Gutteridge stopping at second.
3 McQuinn grounded to short.

2nd Inning
Cardinals
Kurowski beat out a hit to short.
1 Marion, on an attempted sacrifice, popped to Hayworth.
Verban beat out a hit through the box, Kurowski stopping at second.
2,3 M. Cooper grounded into a double play, Stephens to McQuinn.
Browns
1 Zarilla struck out.
2 Christman popped to Kurowski near the mound.
3 Hayworth flied to center.

3rd Inning
Cardinals
1 Litwhiler struck out.
2 Hopp grounded to the mound.
Musial doubled to right.
3 W. Cooper struck out.
Browns
1 Galehouse struck out.
2 Gutteridge fouled to W. Cooper.
Kreevich doubled to left.
3 Moore struck out.

4th Inning
Cardinals
1 Sanders grounded to first.
2 Kurowski bunted out, Hayworth to McQuinn.
3 Marion struck out.
Browns
1 Stephens fouled to Kurowski.
2 McQuinn struck out.
3 Zarilla grounded to the pitcher.

5th Inning
Cardinals
Verban safe at first when Stephens juggled his grounder.
1 M. Cooper sacrificed Verban to second, Galehouse to Gutteridge.
2 Litwhiler flied to deep center, Verban going to third after the catch.
3 Hopp struck out.
Browns
1 Christman popped to second.
Hayworth singled to right and went to second when Musial fumbled the ball.
2 Galehouse popped to second.
3 Gutteridge bounced back to the mound.

6th Inning
Cardinals
1 Musial bunted out to the mound.
2 W. Cooper flied to right.
Sanders homered over the right field pavilion.
3 Kurowski fouled to Hayworth.
Browns
Kreevich singled into right.
1 Moore forced Kreevich at second, M. Cooper to Marion.
Stephens singled over second, Moore going to third.
McQuinn walked, loading the bases.
2 Zarilla called put on strikes.
3 Christman called out on strikes.

7th Inning
Cardinals
1 Marion flied to left-center.
2 Verban flied to center.
3 M. Cooper grounded to third.
Browns
1 Hayworth grounded to short.
Galehouse singled through second.
2 Baker, pinch-hitting for Gutteridge, struck out.
3 Kreevich fouled to Kurowski.

8th Inning
Cardinals
For the Browns—Baker playing second.
Litwhiler homered into the right-center pavilion.
1 Hopp struck out for the third time.
2 Musial flied to center.
3 W. Cooper flied to center.
Browns
1 Moore struck out.
Stephens doubled to center.
2 McQuinn flied to short right-center.
3 Zarilla flied to short right-center.

9th Inning
Cardinals
1 Sanders struck out.
2 Kurowski struck out.
3 Marion flied to short.
Browns
1 Byrnes, pinch-hitting for Christman, took a called third strike.
2 Laabs, pinch-hitting for Hayworth, also took a called third strike.
3 Chartak, pinch-hitting for Galehouse, struck out swinging.

Game 6 October 9 at St. Louis—N

```
St—A   010 000 000
St—N   000 300 00x
```

St. Louis—A	Pos	AB	R	H	RBI	PO	A	E
Gutteridge	2b	3	0	0	0	3	2	0
b Baker	2b	1	0	0	0	1	0	0
Kreevich	cf	4	0	1	0	3	0	0
Moore	rf	3	0	0	0	0	0	0
Stephens	ss	4	0	0	0	3	3	1
Laabs	lf	2	1	1	0	1	1	0
McQuinn	1b	2	0	1	1	6	1	0
Christman	3b	3	0	0	0	1	1	0
c Byrnes		1	0	0	0	0	0	0
Hayworth	c	2	0	0	0	5	0	1
d Chartak		1	0	0	0	0	0	0
Potter	p	2	0	0	0	1	1	0
Muncrief	p	0	0	0	0	0	1	0
a Zarilla		1	0	0	0	0	0	0
Kramer	p	0	0	0	0	0	1	0
Totals		29	1	3	1	24	11	2

a Struck out for Muncrief in 7th.
b Struck out for Gutteridge in 7th.
c Struck out for Christman in 9th.
d Struck out for Hayworth in 9th.

Double—Kreevich. Triple—Laabs.
Sacrifice Hits—Marion, McQuinn, Wilks.
Wild Pitch—Lanier. Left on
Bases—Browns 7, Cardinals 10.
Umpires—McGowan, Dunn, Pipgras, Sears.
Attendance—31,630. Time of Game—2:06.

St. Louis—N	Pos	AB	R	H	RBI	PO	A	E
Litwhiler	lf	5	0	0	0	3	0	0
Hopp	cf	4	0	1	0	2	0	0
Musial	rf	4	0	0	0	2	0	0
W. Cooper	c	3	1	2	0	10	0	0
Sanders	1b	3	1	1	0	7	1	0
Kurowski	3b	3	1	1	1	0	1	0
Marion	ss	3	0	0	0	2	2	0
Verban	2b	3	0	3	1	2	2	0
Lanier	p	2	0	2	1	1	1	0
Wilks	p	1	0	0	0	0	1	0
Totals		31	3	10	3	27	8	0

Pitching	IP	H	R	ER	BB	SO
St. Louis—A						
Potter (L)	3⅓	6	3	1	1	3
Muncrief	2⅔	2	0	0	1	0
Kramer	2	2	0	0	2	2
St. Louis—N						
Lanier (W)	5⅓	3	1	1	5	5
Wilks (SV)	3⅔	0	0	0	0	4

1st Inning
Browns
1 Gutteridge fouled to Sanders.
2 Kreevich struck out.
3 Moore called out on strikes.
Cardinals
1 Litwhiler struck out.
2 Hopp popped to second.
3 Musial grounded to second.

2nd Inning
Browns
1 Stephens struck out.
  Laabs tripled to center.
  McQuinn singled through center,
    scoring Laabs.
2 Christman flied to short center.
3 Hayworth flied to short center.
Cardinals
1 Cooper lined to short.
2 Sanders popped to second.
  Kurowski singled off Christman's glove.
3 Kurowski trapped between first and
  second and was out, Potter to
  McQuinn to Gutteridge to Potter.

3rd Inning
Browns
1 Potter took a called third strike (For
  the Cards this tied the 6 game record
  of 44 by the A's in 1911).
2 Gutteridge fouled to deep right,
  Musial making a great running catch.
  Kreevich doubled to center.
  Moore walked.
3 Stephens forced Moore at second,
  Marion to Verban.
Cardinals
1 Marion grounded to third.
  Verban singled to center.
  Lanier singled to center, Verban
  stopping at second.
2 Litwhiler again struck out.
3 Hopp struck out.

4th Inning
Browns
  Laabs walked.
1 McQuinn sacrificed Laabs to second,
  Lanier to Sanders.
2 Christman grounded to second,
  Laabs moving to third.
  Hayworth intentionally walked.
3 Potter grounded to second.
Cardinals
1 Musial flied to right-center.
  W. Cooper walked.
  Sanders singled to center, W. Cooper
  going to third.
  Kurowski safe on Stephens' bad throw
  to second, scoring W. Cooper with
  Sanders stopping at second.
2 Marion fouled to Laabs.
  Verban singled to left, scoring Sanders
  with Kurowski stopping at second.
  Lanier singled through short, scoring
  Kurowski with Verban going to second.
  For the Browns—Muncrief pitching.
3 Litwhiler forced Lanier at second,
  Stephens to Gutteridge.

5th Inning
Browns
1 Gutteridge flied to left.
2 Kreevich took a called third strike.
3 Moore grounded out, Sanders to Lanier.
Cardinals
1 Hopp popped to short.
2 Musial popped to short.
  W. Cooper beat out a roller to second.
  Sanders walked.
3 Kurowski flied to deep left-center.

6th Inning
Browns
1 Stephens grounded to short.
  Laabs again walked.
  McQuinn walked.
  Laabs went to third and McQuinn to
    second on a wild pitch.
  For the Cardinals—Wilks came in to pitch.
2 Christman grounded to Kurowski who threw
  Laabs out at the plate.
3 Hayworth flied to center.
Cardinals
1 Marion popped to first.
  Verban singled through second.
2 Wilks sacrificed Verban to second,
  Muncrief to McQuinn.
3 Litwhiler flied to left-center.

7th Inning
Browns
1 Zarilla, pinch-hitting for Muncrief,
  struck out.
2 Baker, pinch-hitting for Gutteridge,
  took a called third strike. (The 88th
  strikeout of the Series surpassing the
  record set in the 1931 seven game
  Series).
3 Kreevich flied to right-center.
Cardinals
  For the Browns—Baker stays in to play
  second with Kramer now pitching.
  Hopp singled to left, but was caught
1 between first and second, Laabs to
  Stephens to McQuinn.
2 Musial fouled to Christman.
  W. Cooper singled between short and third.
3 Sanders struck out.

8th Inning
Browns
1 Moore popped to second.
2 Stephens bounced to the pitcher.
3 Laabs fouled to Sanders.
Cardinals
  Kurowski walked.
1 Marion sacrificed Kurowski to second,
  Kramer to Baker.
  Verban intentionally passed.
  Kurowski went to third and Verban to
    second on Hayworth's wild pickoff
    throw into center.
2 Wilks called out on strikes
3 Litwhiler grounded to short.

9th Inning
Browns
1 McQuinn fouled to Litwhiler.
2 Byrnes, batting for Christman,
  struck out.
3 Chartak, batting for Hayworth,
  struck out.

1944 WORLD SERIES COMPOSITE BOX

	Wins	Composite Line Score
St. Louis Cardinals (N.L.)	4	3 0 3 4 0 2 1 1 1 0 1 – 16
St. Louis Browns (A.L.)	2	0 1 4 2 0 0 4 1 0 0 0 – 12

Manager	Regular Season W	L	Pct.	G. Ahead
Billy Southworth	105	49	.682	14.5
Luke Sewell	89	65	.578	1

BATTING AND FIELDING

ST. LOUIS CARDINALS

	WORLD SERIES STATISTICS Pos	G	AB	R	H	2B	3B	HR	RBI	BB	SO	SB	BA	SA	PO	A	E	REGULAR SEASON STATISTICS Main Pos	G	AB	R	H	2B	3B	HR	RBI	BB	SO	SB	BA	SA
Ray Sanders	1b	6	21	**5**	6	0	0	**1**	1	5	**8**	0	.286	.429	52	2	0	1b	154	601	87	177	34	9	12	102	71	50	2	.295	.441
Emil Verban	2b	6	17	1	**7**	0	0	0	2	2	0	0	.412	.412	15	7	0	2b	146	498	51	128	14	2	0	43	19	14	0	.257	.293
Marty Marion	ss	6	22	1	5	**3**	0	0	2	2	3	0	.227	.364	7	**22**	0	ss	144	506	50	135	26	2	6	63	43	50	1	.267	.362
Whitey Kurowski	3b	6	23	2	5	1	0	0	1	1	4	0	.217	.261	4	15	0	3b	149	555	95	150	25	7	20	87	58	40	2	.270	.449
Stan Musial	rf	6	23	2	**7**	2	0	**1**	2	2	0	0	.304	.522	11	0	1	of	146	568	112	**197**	**51**	14	12	94	90	28	7	.347	**.549**
Johnny Hopp	cf	6	**27**	2	5	0	0	0	0	0	**8**	0	.185	.185	14	0	0	of	139	527	106	177	35	9	11	72	58	47	15	.336	.499
Danny Litwhiler	lf	5	20	2	4	1	0	**1**	1	2	7	0	.200	.400	5	0	0	of	140	492	53	130	25	5	15	82	37	56	2	.264	.427
Walker Cooper	c	6	22	1	**7**	2	**1**	0	2	3	2	0	.318	.500	**54**	0	0	c	112	397	56	126	25	5	13	72	20	19	4	.317	.504
Augie Bergamo	ph-lf	3	6	0	0	0	0	0	1	2	3	0	.000	.000	1	0	0	of	80	192	35	55	6	3	2	19	35	23	0	.286	.380
George Fallon	2b	2	2	0	0	0	0	0	0	0	1	0	.000	.000	0	0	0	2b-ss	69	141	16	28	6	0	1	9	16	11	1	.199	.262
Ken O'Dea	ph	3	3	0	1	0	0	0	2	0	0	0	.333	.333				c	85	265	35	66	11	2	6	37	37	29	1	.249	.374
Debs Garms	ph	2	2	0	0	0	0	0	0	0	0	0	.000	.000				ph-of-3b	73	149	17	30	3	0	0	5	13	8	0	.201	.221
Pepper Martin	Did not play																	of	40	86	15	24	4	0	2	4	15	11	2	.279	.395
Bob Keely	Did not play																	c	1	0	0	0	0	0	0	0	0	0	0	.000	.000
Mort Cooper	p	2	4	0	0	0	0	0	0	0	2	0	.000	.000	0	6	0	p	34	94	9	19	3	0	0	13	7	12	0	.202	.234
Max Lanier	p	2	4	0	2	0	0	0	1	0	0	0	.500	.500	1	1	0	p	33	77	11	14	1	0	0	2	4	2	0	.182	.195
Harry Brecheen	p	1	4	0	0	0	0	0	0	0	1	0	.000	.000	1	3	0	p	31	68	8	11	0	1	0	4	9	12	0	.162	.191
Ted Wilks	p	2	2	0	0	0	0	0	0	0	2	0	.000	.000	0	1	0	p	36	64	6	9	2	0	0	6	5	15	0	.141	.172
Blix Donnelly	p	2	1	0	0	0	0	0	0	0	1	0	.000	.000	0	2	0	p	27	16	0	1	0	0	0	0	3	2	0	.063	.063
Freddie Schmidt	p	1	1	0	0	0	0	0	0	0	1	0	.000	.000	0	0	0	p	37	34	3	7	0	0	0	3	1	16	0	.206	.206
Bud Byerly	p	1	0	0	0	0	0	0	0	0	0	0	—	—	0	0	0	p	9	12	1	2	0	0	0	1	0	3	0	.167	.167
Al Jurisich	p	1	0	0	0	0	0	0	0	0	0	0	—	—	0	0	0	p	30	45	2	8	1	0	0	1	1	13	0	.178	.200
George Munger	Not in series—military service																	p	21	44	2	5	1	0	0	0	0	4	0	.114	.136
team total		6	204	16	49	9	1	3	15	19	43	0	.240	.338	165	59	1		157	**5475**	**712**	**1507**	**274**	59	**100**	**720**	544	473	37	**.275**	**.402**

Double Plays—3
Left on Bases—51

John Antonelli (1b,3b), Harry Gumbert (p), Bill Trotter (p), and Mike Naymick (p) also played for the Cardinals during the season.

ST. LOUIS BROWNS

	WORLD SERIES STATISTICS Pos	G	AB	R	H	2B	3B	HR	RBI	BB	SO	SB	BA	SA	PO	A	E		REGULAR SEASON STATISTICS Main Pos	G	AB	R	H	2B	3B	HR	RBI	BB	SO	SB	BA	SA
George McQuinn	1b	6	16	2	**7**	2	0	**1**	**5**	**7**	2	0	**.438**	**.750**	50	2	0		1b	146	516	83	129	26	3	11	72	85	74	4	.250	.376
Don Gutteridge	2b	6	21	1	3	1	0	0	0	3	5	0	.143	.190	15	11	**3**		2b	148	603	89	148	27	11	3	36	51	63	20	.245	.342
Vern Stephens	ss	6	22	2	5	1	0	0	0	3	3	0	.227	.273	9	19	**3**		ss	145	559	91	164	32	1	20	**109**	62	54	2	.293	.462
Mark Christman	3b	6	22	0	2	0	0	0	1	0	6	0	.091	.091	3	9	1		3b	148	547	56	148	25	1	6	83	47	37	5	.271	.353
Gene Moore	rf	6	22	4	4	0	0	0	0	3	6	0	.182	.182	8	0	0		of	110	390	56	93	13	6	6	58	24	37	0	.238	.349
Mike Kreevich	cf	6	26	0	6	**3**	0	0	0	0	5	0	.231	.346	20	2	0		of	105	402	55	121	15	6	5	44	27	24	3	.301	.405
Chet Laabs	lf-ph	5	15	1	3	1	**1**	0	0	2	6	0	.200	.400	5	1	0		of	66	201	28	47	10	2	5	23	29	33	3	.234	.378
Red Hayworth	c	6	17	1	2	1	0	0	1	3	1	0	.118	.176	45	2	1		c	89	269	20	60	11	1	1	25	10	13	0	.223	.283
Al Zarilla	ph-lf	4	10	1	1	0	0	0	1	0	4	0	.100	.100	2	0	0		of	100	288	43	86	13	6	6	45	29	33	1	.299	.448
Frank Mancuso	ph-c	2	3	0	2	0	0	0	1	0	0	0	.667	.667	3	0	0		c	88	244	19	50	11	0	1	24	20	32	1	.205	.262
Floyd Baker	ph-2b	2	2	0	0	0	0	0	0	0	2	0	.000	.000	1	0	0		2b-ss	44	97	10	17	3	0	0	5	11	5	2	.175	.206
Milt Byrnes	ph	3	2	0	0	0	0	0	0	1	2	0	.000	.000					of	128	407	63	120	20	4	4	45	68	50	1	.295	.393
Mike Chartak	ph	2	2	0	0	0	0	0	0	0	2	0	.000	.000					ph	35	72	8	17	2	1	1	7	6	9	0	.236	.333
Ellis Clary	ph	1	1	0	0	0	0	0	0	0	0	0	.000	.000					ph-3b	25	49	6	13	2	1	0	4	12	9	1	.265	.327
Tom Turner	ph	1	1	0	0	0	0	0	0	0	0	0	.000	.000				a	c	15	25	2	8	1	0	0	4	2	5	0	.320	.360
Denny Galehouse	p	2	5	0	1	0	0	0	0	1	1	0	.200	.200	0	5	0		p	24	48	1	3	0	0	0	1	3	19	0	.063	.063
Jack Kramer	p	2	4	0	0	0	0	0	0	0	2	0	.000	.000	0	3	0		p	33	85	6	14	2	0	2	6	8	21	0	.165	.259
Nels Potter	p	2	4	0	0	0	0	0	0	0	1	0	.000	.000	2	2	2		p	32	82	4	13	1	0	0	5	4	4	0	.159	.171
Bob Muncrief	p	2	1	0	0	0	0	0	0	0	1	0	.000	.000	0	1	0		p	33	78	4	18	2	0	0	10	3	16	1	.231	.256
Al Hollingsworth	p	1	1	0	0	0	0	0	0	0	0	0	.000	.000	0	1	0		p	26	28	1	2	0	0	0	0	4	8	0	.071	.071
Sig Jakucki	p	1	0	0	0	0	0	0	0	0	0	0	—	—	0	1	0		p	36	73	9	11	1	1	1	8	1	14	0	.151	.233
Tex Shirley	pr-p	2	0	0	0	0	0	0	0	0	0	0	—	—	0	1	0		p-pr	30	28	7	4	0	0	0	1	0	9	0	.143	.143
George Caster	Did not play																		p	42	20	1	5	1	0	0	2	0	7	0	.250	.300
Willis Hudlin	Did not play																		p	1	0	0	0	0	0	0	0	1	0	0	.000	.000
Sam Zoldak	Did not play																		p	18	6	1	2	0	0	0	0	0	0	0	.333	.333
team total		6	197	12	36	9	1	1	9	23	49	0	.183	.254	163	60	10			154	5269	684	1328	223	45	72	628	531	604	44	.252	.352

Double Plays—4
Left on Bases—44

a—from Chicago (A)
Hal Epps (of), Frank Demaree (of), Tom Hafey (of), Joe Schultz (c), Babe Martin (of), Len Schulte (ph), Steve Sundra (p), and Lefty West (p) also played for the Browns during the season.

PITCHING

ST. LOUIS CARDINALS

	WORLD SERIES STATISTICS G	GS	CG	IP	H	R	ER	BB	SO	W	L	SV	ERA	REGULAR SEASON STATISTICS G	GS	CG	IP	H	ER	BB	SO	W	L	Pct	SV	ShO	ERA
Mort Cooper	**2**	**2**	1	16	9	2	2	5	**16**	**1**	**1**	0	1.13	34	33	22	252	227	69	60	97	22	7	.759	1	**7**	2.46
Max Lanier	**2**	**2**	0	$12\frac{1}{3}$	8	3	3	**8**	11	**1**	0	0	2.19	33	30	16	224	192	66	71	141	17	12	.586	0	5	2.65
Harry Brecheen	1	1	1	9	9	1	1	4	4	**1**	0	0	1.00	30	22	13	189	174	60	46	88	16	5	.762	0	3	2.86
Ted Wilks	**2**	1	0	$6\frac{1}{3}$	5	4	**4**	3	7	0	**1**	**1**	5.68	36	21	16	208	173	61	49	70	17	4	**.810**	0	4	2.64
Blix Donnelly	**2**	0	0	6	2	0	0	1	9	**1**	0	0	0.00	27	4	2	76	61	18	34	45	2	1	.667	2	1	2.13
Freddy Schmidt	1	0	0	$3\frac{1}{3}$	1	0	0	1	1	0	0	0	0.00	37	9	3	114	94	40	58	58	7	3	.700	5	2	3.16
Bud Byerly	1	0	0	$1\frac{1}{3}$	0	0	0	0	1	0	0	0	0.00	9	4	2	42	37	16	20	13	2	2	.500	0	0	3.43
Al Jurisich	1	0	0	$\frac{2}{3}$	2	2	2	1	0	0	0	0	27.00	30	14	5	130	102	49	65	53	7	9	.438	1	2	3.39
George Munger	Not in series—military service													21	12	7	121	92	18	41	55	11	3	.786	2	2	1.34
team total	6	6	2	55	36	12	12	23	49	4	2	1	1.96	157	157	89	**1427**	1228	424	468	**637**	**105**	49	.682	12	**26**	**2.67**

ST. LOUIS BROWNS

	WORLD SERIES STATISTICS G	GS	CG	IP	H	R	ER	BB	SO	W	L	SV	ERA	REGULAR SEASON STATISTICS G	GS	CG	IP	H	ER	BB	SO	W	L	Pct	SV	ShO	ERA
Denny Galehouse	**2**	**2**	**2**	**18**	**13**	3	3	5	15	**1**	**1**	0	1.50	24	19	6	153	162	64	44	80	9	10	.474	0	2	3.12
Jack Kramer	**2**	1	1	11	9	2	0	4	12	**1**	0	0	**0.00**	33	31	18	257	233	71	75	124	17	13	.567	0	1	2.49
Nels Potter	**2**	**2**	0	$9\frac{2}{3}$	10	**5**	1	3	6	0	**1**	0	0.93	32	29	16	232	211	73	70	91	19	7	.731	0	3	2.83
Bob Muncrief	**2**	0	0	$6\frac{2}{3}$	5	1	1	4	4	0	**1**	0	1.35	33	27	12	219	216	75	50	88	13	8	.619	1	3	3.08
Al Hollingsworth	1	0	0	4	5	1	1	2	1	0	0	0	2.25	26	10	3	93	108	46	37	22	5	7	.417	1	2	4.45
Sig Jakucki	1	1	0	3	5	4	3	0	4	0	**1**	0	9.00	35	24	12	198	211	78	54	67	13	9	.591	3	4	3.55
Tex Shirley	1	0	0	2	2	0	0	1	1	0	0	0	0.00	23	11	2	80	59	37	64	35	5	4	.556	0	1	4.16
George Caster	Did not play													42	0	0	81	91	22	33	46	6	6	.500	**12**	0	2.44
Willis Hudlin	Did not play													1	0	0	2	3	1	0	1	0	1	.000	0	0	4.50
Sam Zoldak	Did not play													18	0	0	39	49	16	19	15	0	0	—	0	0	3.69
team total	6	6	3	$54\frac{1}{3}$	49	16	9	19	43	2	4	0	1.49	154	154	71	1397	1392	492	469	**581**	**89**	65	**.578**	17	16	3.17

Total Attendance—206,708 Average Attendance—34,451 Winning Player's Share—$4,626 Losing Player's Share—$2,744

1945
Borowy's Weary Wing

The World War was rushing to a victorious end for the Allied armies, but hostilities dragged on deep enough into summer to keep the majority of big-league stars in the armed forces and out of baseball uniforms for this year. Symbolic of the lack of available talent was Pete Gray, the one-armed outfielder who hit .218 in 77 games for the St. Louis Browns. No All-Star game was played, obstensibly because of travel restrictions, but just as likely for a lack of stars. In this air of innovative endurance, the Detroit Tigers and Chicago Cubs won the league pennants and met in the World Series. The Tigers had a squad of older players of whom the key men were slugger Hank Greenberg, who rejoined the team from the army air corps after the war in Europe ended in May; power hitters Rudy York and Roy Cullenbine; and twenty-four-year-old lefty, Hal Newhouser, whose fast ball made him the top pitcher of the war years. Manager Steve O'Neill came into the Series with an extra bonus in pitcher Virgil Trucks, who got his discharge from the navy after the Japanese surrender in August and just in time to pitch the final game of the season which clinched the flag.

The Cubs had a similar glaze of first-rate talent. Manager Charlie Grimm, in his second tour as Cub skipper, had the National League batting leader in Phil Cavaretta; a solid third baseman in thirty-five-year-old Stan Hack; two power-hitting outfielders in Andy Pafko and Bill Nicholson; and a full house of experienced starters in Hank Wyse, Claude Passeau, Paul Derringer, Ray Prim, and midseason pickup Hank Borowy, who won 10 games for the Yankees and 11 for the Cubs in an unusual 21-win season. But the bulk of both rosters was kindly described as mediocre, and when Chicago sportswriter Warren Brown was asked about his pick for the Series, he answered, "I don't think either of them can win."

But the Series went on, with the war already over and mass discharges beginning under demobilization. The crowd of 54,637 which piled into Briggs Stadium for the opener watched in dismay as the 25-game-winner Newhouser was shelled from the box by the Cubs, giving up seven runs before leaving in the third inning. Borowy, meanwhile, scattered six hits and took a 9–0 decision. The next day, the Cubs sent their ace Wyse up against Trucks, who was less than a week out of the navy. Both teams got seven hits in the contest, but a three-run homer by Greenberg propelled the Tigers to a 4–1 victory that evened the Series at one game apiece. Chicago veteran Claude Passeau froze the Tiger hitters in game three with his curve ball and control. Only two Detroit men reached base, Rudy York on a second-inning single and Bob Swift on a sixth-inning walk, in Passeau's one-hit 3–0 victory.

After the clubs shifted to Wrigley Field, Ray Prim kept up the sterling pitching for the Cubs by turning back the first 10 Tigers to face him. But he suddenly lost the touch and gave up four runs in the fourth inning, with the Cubs going down to a 4–1 loss before Dizzy Trout's five-hitter. The fifth game again matched Newhouser against Borowy, but Newhouser came out ahead this time, going all the way in an 8–4 victory. The Cubs needed a win in game six to stay alive, and they held a 5–3 lead when starting pitcher Passeau injured his finger in knocking down a liner in the seventh. The Cubs even lengthened their lead to 7–3 in the bottom of the seventh, but relievers Wyse and Prim couldn't hold the edge and the Tigers tied the score on an eighth-inning homer by Greenberg. Hank Borowy and Dizzy Trout took on the pitching chores as the game moved into extra innings, and Borowy's four hitless innings were rewarded when a hit by Stan Hack hopped over left fielder Greenberg's head in the twelfth inning and allowed pinch runner Bill Schuster to score from first. After a day of rest, Cub manager Grimm gambled on using Borowy in the pivotal seventh game despite his extensive use in the fifth and sixth contests. Grimm gave Borowy a quick hook when the first three Tigers got hits, but the Detroit batters kept up the rally against reliever Derringer, piling up a 5–0 lead before the Cubs even came to bat. Hal Newhouser gave up 10 hits but judiciously limited the Cubs to three runs and captured a 9–3 victory, which made the Tigers the final World War II champions.

Game 1 October 3 at Detroit

| | | | | Chi. | 4 0 3 | 0 0 0 | 2 0 0 |
| | | | | Det. | 0 0 0 | 0 0 0 | 0 0 0 |

Chicago	Pos	AB	R	H	RBI	PO	A	E
Hack	3b	5	0	1	0	3	0	0
Johnson	2b	5	2	2	0	3	4	0
Lowrey	lf	4	0	0	0	1	0	0
Cavaretta	1b	4	3	3	2	8	1	0
Pafko	cf	4	3	3	1	4	1	0
Nicholson	rf	4	1	2	3	0	0	0
Livingston	c	4	0	2	2	5	0	0
Hughes	ss	3	0	0	0	2	4	0
Borowy	p	3	0	0	0	1	1	0
Totals		36	9	13	8	27	11	0

Pitching	IP	H	R	ER	BB	SO
Chicago						
Borowy (W)	9	6	0	0	5	4
Detroit						
Newhouser (L)	2⅔	8	7	7	1	3
Benton	1⅓	1	0	0	0	1
Tobin	3	4	2	2	1	0
Mueller	2	0	0	0	1	1

Detroit	Pos	AB	R	H	RBI	PO	A	E
Webb	ss	4	0	1	0	1	2	0
d McHale		1	0	0	0	0	0	0
Mayo	2b	4	0	2	0	4	1	0
Cramer	cf	3	0	1	0	6	0	0
Greenberg	lf	2	0	0	0	0	0	0
Cullenbine	rf	3	0	1	0	8	0	0
York	1b	3	0	1	0	0	0	0
Outlaw	3b	4	0	0	1	4	2	0
Richards	c	2	0	0	0	7	2	0
b Hostetler		1	0	0	0	0	0	0
Newhouser	p	1	0	0	0	0	1	0
Benton	p	0	0	0	0	0	0	0
a Eaton		1	0	0	0	0	0	0
Tobin	p	1	0	0	0	0	1	0
Mueller	p	0	0	0	0	0	0	0
c Borom		1	0	0	0	0	0	0
Totals		31	0	6	0	27	11	0

a Struck out for Benton in 4th.
b Grounded out for Richards in 9th.
c Grounded out for Mueller in 9th.
d Flied out for Webb in 9th.

Doubles—Johnson, Pafko. Triple—Nicholson. Home Run—Cavaretta. Stolen Bases—Johnson, Pafko. Sacrifice Hits—Borowy, Lowrey. Double Plays—Hughes to Johnson to Cavaretta, Johnson to Hughes to Cavaretta. Passed Balls—Richards 2. Hit by Pitcher—Greenberg (by Borowy). Left on Bases—Chicago 5, Detroit 10. Umpires—Summers (A), Jorda (N), Passarella (A), Conlan (N). Attendance—54,637. Time of Game—2:10.

1st Inning
Chicago
1 Hack grounded to third.
 Johnson singled through the box.
 Johnson stole second.
2 Lowrey flied to center.
 Cavaretta beat out a single to second, moving Johnson to third. On a Richards passed ball Johnson scored and Cavaretta got to third.
 Pafko intentionally walked.
 Nicholson tripled against the right field wall, scoring Cavaretta and Pafko.
 Livingston singled to right, scoring Nicholson.
3 Livingston was caught attempting to steal Richards to Mayo.
Detroit
 Webb singled to left.
 Mayo singled to center, Webb stopping at second.
1,2 Cramer grounded into a double play, Hughes to Johnson to Cavaretta with Webb going to third.
 Greenberg walked.
 Cullenbine walked loading the bases.
3 York fouled to Cavaretta.

2nd Inning
Chicago
1 Hughes took a called third strike.
2 Borowy fanned.
3 Hack fanned.
Detroit
1 Outlaw fouled to Cavaretta.
 Richards walked.
2,3 Newhouser grounded into a double play, Johnson to Hughes to Cavaretta.

3rd Inning
Chicago
 Johnson doubled over Cramer's glove.
1 Lowrey sacrificed Johnson to third, Newhouser to York.
 Cavaretta singled to center, scoring Johnson.
 Pafko doubled to left center, scoring Cavaretta.
2 Nicholson popped to second.
 Livingston singled to center, scoring Pafko.
 For Detroit—Benton pitching.
3 Livingston again caught stealing, Richards to Mayo.
Detroit
1 Webb grounded out Cavaretta (who made a great stop saving an extra base hit) to Borowy, covering first.
2 Mayo struck out.
 Cramer walked.
 Greenberg was hit by a pitched ball.
3 Cullenbine popped to second.

4th Inning
Chicago
1 Hughes flied to center.
2 Borowy fanned.
 Hack singled on a roller just beyond the mound.
3 Johnson grounded to third.
Detroit
 York walked.
 Outlaw singled to center, York stopping at second.
1 Richards struck out.
2 Eaton, pinch hitting for Benton, struck out.
3 Webb popped to third.

5th Inning
Chicago
 For Detroit—Tobin pitching.
1 Lowrey grounded to short.
2 Cavaretta grounded back to the mound.
 Pafko singled to left.
3 Nicholson fouled to Richards.
Detroit
 Mayo singled to left.
1 Cramer fouled to Livingston.
 Greenberg singled to center but Mayo
2 was out going for third, Pafko to Hack.
3 Cullenbine flied to left.

6th Inning
Chicago
1 Livingston flied to center.
 Hughes walked.
2 Borowy sacrificed Hughes to second, Outlaw to Mayo, covering first.
3 Hack grounded to second.
Detroit
 York singled to left-center.
 Outlaw bounced into a fielder's choice as Hack threw to second to get York in a force but was too late.
1 Richards flied to center.
2 Tobin popped to second.
3 Webb grounded to second.

7th Inning
Chicago
1 Johnson popped to Webb in short left.
2 Lowrey flied to center.
 Caverretta homered into the right field stands.
 Pafko singled to center.
 Pafko stole second.
 Pafko to third on a passed ball.
 Nicholson singled to right, scoring Pafko.
3 Livingston grounded to short.
Detroit
1 Mayo grounded to second.
2 Cramer popped to short.
3 Greenberg fanned.

8th Inning
Chicago
 For Detroit—Mueller pitching.
1 Hughes fanned.
2 Borowy lined to center.
3 Hack lined to center.
Detroit
1 Cullenbine flied to center.
2 York flied to left.
3 Outlaw fouled to Hack.

9th Inning
Chicago
1 Johnson fouled to Richards.
2 Lowrey grounded to third.
 Cavaretta walked.
3 Pafko fouled to Outlaw.
Detroit
1 Hostetler, pinch hitting for Richards, grounded to short.
2 Borom, pinch hitting for Mueller, hit off Borowy's glove to Hughes who threw Borom out.
3 McHale, pinch hitting for Webb, flied to center.

Game 2 October 4 at Detroit

Chi.	000	100	000
Det.	000	040	00x

Chicago	Pos	AB	R	H	RBI	PO	A	E
Hack	3b	3	0	3	0	0	2	0
Johnson	2b	3	0	0	0	2	4	0
Lowrey	lf	4	0	2	0	3	0	0
Cavarretta	1b	4	1	1	0	8	0	0
Pafko	cf	4	0	0	0	4	0	0
Nicholson	rf	3	0	1	1	2	0	0
Gillespie	c	4	0	0	0	3	0	0
Hughes	ss	3	0	0	0	2	2	0
Wyse	p	2	0	0	0	0	0	0
a Secory		1	0	0	0	0	0	0
Erickson	p	0	0	0	0	0	0	0
b Becker		1	0	0	0	0	0	0
Totals		32	1	7	1	24	8	0

a Flied out for Wyse in 7th.
b Struck out for Erickson in 9th.
Doubles—Cavarretta, Hack.
Home Run—Greenberg. Sacrifice Hit—Johnson.
Left on Bases—Chicago 8, Detroit 7.
Umpires—Jorda, Passarella, Conlan, Summers.
Attendance—53,636. Time of Game—1:47.

Detroit	Pos	AB	R	H	RBI	PO	A	E
Webb	ss	4	1	2	0	4	0	
Mayo	2b	3	1	0	0	3	3	0
Cramer	cf	4	1	3	1	2	0	0
Greenberg	lf	3	1	1	3	1	0	0
Cullenbine	rf	2	0	0	0	2	0	0
York	1b	4	0	0	0	11	1	0
Outlaw	3b	4	0	1	0	1	0	0
Richards	c	4	0	0	0	5	0	0
Trucks	p	3	0	0	0	1	1	0
Totals		31	4	7	4	27	10	0

Pitching	IP	H	R	ER	BB	SO
Chicago						
Wyse (L)	6	5	4	4	3	1
Erickson	2	2	0	0	1	1
Detroit						
Trucks (W)	8	7	1	1	3	4

1st Inning
Chicago
Hack beat out a single to short.
1 Johnson sacrificed Hack to second, York unassisted.
Lowrey lined a single to left and Hack
2 was nipped at the plate on a good throw by Greenberg to Richards, Lowrey to second on the out.
3 Cavarretta bounced out to first.
Detroit
1 Webb flied to left.
2 Mayo flied to left.
3 Cramer grounded to second.

2nd Inning
Chicago
1 Pafko popped to second.
2 Nicholson flied to right.
3 Gillespie popped to second.
Detroit
1 Greenberg flied to deep center. Cullenbine walked.
2 York looked at a called third strike. Outlaw singled.
3 Richards grounded to short.

3rd Inning
Chicago
1 Hughes grounded to second.
2 Wyse fanned. Hack singled on his roller to York when no one covered first.
3 Johnson fanned.
Detroit
1 Trucks grounded to short.
2 Webb flied to right.
3 Mayo grounded to second.

4th Inning
Chicago
1 Lowrey grounded to short. Cavarretta got a double to right-center as neither Cramer nor Cullenbine went for the ball.
2 Pafko grounded to short with Cavarretta holding second. Nicholson singled to right-center, scoring Cavarretta.
3 Gillespie flied to center.
Detroit
Cramer singled to center.
1 Greenberg grounded to third, moving Cramer to second. Cullenbine walked.
2 York lined to center.
3 Outlaw forced Cullenbine at second, Johnson to Hughes.

5th Inning
Chicago
1 Hughes grounded back to the pitcher.
2 Wyse grounded to short. Hack doubled to center.
3 Johnson grounded to second.

5th Inning (continued)
Detroit
1 Richards flied to deep left.
2 Trucks popped to second. Webb singled to left. Mayo walked. Cramer singled over third, scoring Webb and sending Mayo to third. Greenberg hit a three-run homer into the left field stands.
3 Cullenbine grounded to first.

6th Inning
Chicago
1 Lowrey flied to right.
2 Cavarretta flied to center.
3 Pafko popped to second.
Detroit
1 York flied deep to Pafko at the left field wall.
2 Outlaw grounded to third.
3 Richards popped to second.

7th Inning
Chicago
1 Nicholson grounded to second.
2 Gillespie flied to left. Hughes walked.
3 Secory, pinch hitting for Wyse, lined to left.
Detroit
For Chicago—Erickson pitching.
1 Trucks fanned.
Webb singled to the left of the mound.
2 Mayo popped to Lowrey in short left. Cramer singled through the box, moving Webb to third. Greenberg walked, loading the bases.
3 Cullenbine flied to deep right.

8th Inning
Chicago
Hack walked.
1 Johnson took a called third strike. Lowrey singled to left with Hack stopping at second.
2 Cavarretta bounced out York to Trucks advancing both runners.
3 Pafko grounded to short.
Detroit
1 York grounded to short.
2 Outlaw fouled to Gillespie.
3 Richards lined to short.

9th Inning
Chicago
Nicholson walked.
1 Gillespie grounded to first, moving Nicholson to second.
2 Hughes popped to third.
3 Becker, pinch hitting for Erickson, fanned.

Game 3 October 5 at Detroit

Chi.	000	200	100
Det.	000	000	000

Chicago	Pos	AB	R	H	RBI	PO	A	E
Hack	3b	5	0	2	0	1	1	0
Johnson	2b	3	0	0	0	1	1	0
Lowrey	lf	4	1	2	0	4	0	0
Cavarretta	1b	2	0	1	0	10	1	0
Pafko	cf	2	1	0	0	3	0	0
Nicholson	rf	4	0	1	1	2	0	0
Livingston	c	4	1	1	0	3	0	0
Hughes	ss	3	0	1	1	4	0	0
Passeau	p	4	0	0	1	1	2	0
Totals		33	3	8	3	27	9	0

Pitching	IP	H	R	ER	BB	SO
Chicago						
Passeau (W)	9	1	0	0	1	1
Detroit						
Overmire (L)	6	4	2	2	2	3
Benton	3	4	1	1	0	3

Detroit	Pos	AB	R	H	RBI	PO	A	E
Webb	ss	3	0	0	0	2	3	1
d McHale		1	0	0	0	0	0	0
Mayo	2b	3	0	0	0	2	1	1
Cramer	cf	3	0	0	0	4	0	0
Greenberg	lf	3	0	0	0	2	0	0
Cullenbine	rf	3	0	0	0	2	0	0
York	1b	3	0	1	0	12	0	0
Outlaw	3b	3	0	0	0	0	3	0
Swift	c	1	0	0	0	2	0	0
a Borom		0	0	0	0	0	0	0
Richards	c	1	0	0	0	3	1	0
Overmire	p	1	0	0	0	0	1	0
b Walker		1	0	0	0	0	0	0
Benton	p	0	0	0	0	0	3	0
c Hostetler		1	0	0	0	0	0	0
Totals		27	0	1	0	27	12	2

a Ran for Swift in 6th.
b Grounded into double play for Overmire in 6th.
c Grounded out for Benton in 9th.
d Fouled out for Webb in 9th.

Doubles—Hack, Livingston, Lowrey.
Sacrifice Hits—Cavarretta, Hughes, Pafko.
Double Play—Johnson to Cavarretta.
Left on Bases—Chicago 8, Detroit 1.
Umpires—Passarella, Conlan, Summers, Jorda. Attendance—55,500.
Time of Game—1:55.

1st Inning
Chicago
1 Hack lined to left.
2 Johnson grounded to third. Lowrey singled to left. Cavarretta walked.
3 Pafko forced Cavarretta at second Webb to Mayo.
Detroit
1 Webb grounded to short.
2 Mayo grounded to Hack who made a real good stop.
3 Cramer flied to deep center.

2nd Inning
Chicago
1 Nicholson rolled to second.
2 Livingston flied to right.
3 Hughes grounded to short.
Detroit
1 Greenberg fanned.
2 Cullenbine flied to short left.
York singled sharply to left (the only hit off of Passeau in the game).
3 Outlaw flied to center.

3rd Inning
Chicago
1 Passeau struck out.
2 Hack grounded to short.
3 Johnson fouled to York.
Detroit
1 Swift popped to Livingston in front of the plate.
2 Overmire grounded back to the pitcher.
3 Webb also grounded to the pitcher.

4th Inning
Chicago
Lowrey doubled against the left field wall.
1 Cavarretta sacrificed Lowrey to third, Overmire to York.
Pafko walked.
Nicholson singled just beyond short, scoring Lowrey with Pafko stopping at second.
2 Livingston flied to center. Hughes singled over Mayo's head, scoring Pafko with Nicholson stopping at second.
3 Passeau struck out.
Detroit
1 Mayo hit a smasher down the first base line on which Cavarretta made a diving stop and flipped to Passeau for the out.
2 Cramer lined to deep left.
3 Greenberg flied to left.

5th Inning
Chicago
1 Hack popped to Cramer in short left-center.
2 Johnson flied to center.
3 Lowrey popped to short.

5th Inning (continued)
Detroit
1 Cullenbine grounded to first.
2 York grounded to short.
3 Outlaw lined to short.

6th Inning
Chicago
1 Cavarretta grounded to first.
2 Pafko grounded to third.
3 Nicholson grounded to first.
Detroit
Swift became only the Tigers' second base runner by walking. Borom ran for Swift.
1,2 Walker, pinch hitting for Overmire, grounded into a double play, Johnson to Cavarretta.
3 Webb lined to right.

7th Inning
Chicago
For Detroit—Richards catching and Benton pitching.
Livingston doubled off the right field screen.
1 Hughes sacrificed Livingston to third, Outlaw to Mayo, who covered first.
2 Passeau flied to center, Livingston scoring after the catch. Hack doubled down the left field line. Johnson safely on first on Mayo's fumble while Hack moved on to third.
3 Lowrey grounded back to the pitcher.
Detroit
1 Mayo grounded to short.
2 Cramer flied deep to right.
3 Greenberg flied to left.

8th Inning
Chicago
Cavarretta singled to right.
1 Pafko sacrificed Cavarretta to second, Benton to York.
2 Nicholson fanned.
3 Livingston popped to short.
Detroit
1 Cullenbine flied to right.
2 York flied to center.
3 Outlaw popped to third.

9th Inning
Chicago
1 Hughes grounded back to the pitcher.
2 Passeau struck out. Hack singled on a bounder through the box.
Hack got to second on an attempted steal when Mayo got an error dropping Richards' perfect peg.
3 Johnson struck out.
Detroit
1 Richards fouled to Cavarretta.
2 Hostetler, pinch hitting for Benton, grounded to short.
3 McHale, pinch hitting for Webb, fouled out to Livingston.

1945

Game 4 October 6 at Chicago

Det. 000 400 000
Chi. 000 001 000

Detroit	Pos	AB	R	H	RBI	PO	A	E
Webb	ss	5	0	0	0	1	3	0
Mayo	2b	3	1	0	0	1	1	0
Cramer	cf	4	1	2	0	4	0	0
Greenberg	lf	3	1	1	1	1	0	0
Cullenbine	rf	3	1	1	1	1	0	0
York	1b	3	0	0	0	10	3	1
Outlaw	3b	4	0	1	1	0	3	0
Richards	c	4	0	1	1	7	0	0
Trout	p	4	0	1	0	2	2	0
Totals		33	4	7	4	27	12	1

Pitching	IP	H	R	ER	BB	SO
Detroit						
Trout (W)	9	5	1	0	1	6
Chicago						
Prim (L)	3⅓	3	4	4	4	1
Derringer	1⅔	2	0	0	2	1
Vandenberg	2	0	0	0	0	0
Erickson	2	2	0	0	1	2

Chicago	Pos	AB	R	H	RBI	PO	A	E
Hack	3b	4	0	0	0	2	2	0
Johnson	2b	4	1	2	0	1	3	0
Lowrey	lf	4	0	1	0	3	0	0
Cavarretta	1b	4	0	0	0	10	1	0
Pafko	cf	4	0	0	0	1	0	0
Nicholson	rf	4	0	0	0	1	0	1
Livingston	c	3	0	1	0	4	1	0
Hughes	ss	2	0	1	0	3	3	0
b Becker		1	0	1	0	0	0	0
c Merullo	ss	0	0	0	0	1	0	0
Prim	p	0	0	0	0	0	1	0
Derringer	p	0	0	0	0	0	0	0
a Secory		1	0	0	0	0	0	0
Vandenberg	p	0	0	0	0	1	0	0
d Gillespie		1	0	0	0	0	0	0
Erickson	p	0	0	0	0	0	0	0
Totals		31	1	5	0	27	11	1

a Struck out for Derringer in 5th.
b Singled for Hughes in 7th.
c Ran for Becker in 7th.
d Grounded out for Vandenberg in 7th.

Double—Cullenbine. Triple—Johnson. Sacrifice Hit—Prim. Passed Ball—Livingston. Left on Bases—Detroit 6, Chicago 5. Umpires—Conlan, Summers, Jorda, Passarella. Attendance—42,923. Time of Game—2:00.

1st Inning
Detroit
1 Webb grounded to third.
2 Mayo flied to Pafko who made a great running catch of his sinking liner behind second base.
3 Cramer grounded back to the pitcher.
Chicago
1 Hack grounded to short and was out when York made a great pick up of Webb's low throw.
2 Johnson grounded to first.
3 Lowrey lined to right.

2nd Inning
Detroit
1 Greenberg fanned.
2 Cullenbine popped to first.
3 York grounded to second.
Chicago
1 Cavarretta took a called third strike.
2 Pafko hit a real hard smash to York who threw to Trout for the out.
3 Nicholson struck out.

3rd Inning
Detroit
1 Outlaw grounded to short.
2 Richards flied deep to left.
3 Trout lined to third.
Chicago
Livingston singled to left.
1 Hughes forced Livingston on an attempted sacrifice, Trout to Webb.
2 Prim sacrificed Hughes to second, York to Mayo.
3 Hack bounced out to third.

4th Inning
Detroit
1 Webb grounded to third.
Mayo walked.
Cramer singled to right, sending Mayo to second.
Greenberg singled to left, scoring Mayo with Cramer stopping at second.
Cullenbine doubled down the left field line, scoring Cramer and advancing Greenberg to third.
For Chicago—Derringer pitching.
York intentionally walked, loading the bases.
2 Outlaw forced York at second, Johnson to Hughes with Greenberg scoring and Cullenbine going to third.
Richards singled to center, scoring Cullenbine with Outlaw stopping at second.
3 Trout forced Richards at second, Hughes to Johnson.
Chicago
Johnson singled to center.
Lowrey singled to right with Johnson stopping at second.
1 Cavarretta fanned.
2 Pafko grounded to second, advancing both runners.
3 Nicholson fanned.

5th Inning
Detroit
1 Webb took a called third strike.
2 Mayo flied to left.
Cramer singled to right and got safely to second on Nicholson's error, losing the ball.
Greenberg walked.
3 Cullenbine grounded to first.
Chicago
1 Livingston flied to center.
Hughes walked.
2 Secory, pinch hitting for Derringer, fanned.
3 Hack grounded to first.

6th Inning
Detroit
For Chicago—Vandenberg pitching.
1 York flied to deep left.
2 Outlaw popped to first.
3 Richards lined to short.
Chicago
Johnson tripled down the right field line.
1 Lowrey grounded to third, Johnson scored when York trying to catch Johnson off of third overthrew the bag for an error.
2 Cavarretta flied to left.
3 Pafko flied to center.

7th Inning
Detroit
1 Trout popped to short.
2 Webb grounded out, Cavarretta to Vandenberg.
3 Mayo grounded to short.
Chicago
1 Nicholson grounded back to the mound.
2 Livingston flew out to Cramer in left-center.
Becker, pinch hitting for Hughes, singled to left.
Merullo ran for Becker.
3 Gillespie, pinch hitting for Vandenberg, grounded out, York to Trout.

8th Inning
Detroit
For Chicago—Merullo at short, Erickson pitching.
1 Cramer popped to short.
2 Greenberg fanned.
Cullenbine walked.
3 York grounded to second.
Chicago
1 Hack grounded to short.
2 Johnson grounded to short.
3 Lowrey struck out.

9th Inning
Detroit
Outlaw singled to left.
1 Richards fanned.
Trout singled to third, Outlaw stopping at second.
2 Outlaw got caught in a rundown off of third after a passed ball, Livingston to Hack.
3 Webb flied to right.
Chicago
1 Cavarretta flied very deep to center.
2 Pafko grounded to third where Outlaw made a brilliant stop.
3 Nicholson fouled to Richards.

Game 5 October 7 at Chicago

Det. 001 004 102
Chi. 001 000 201

Detroit	Pos	AB	R	H	RBI	PO	A	E
Webb	ss	4	1	1	1	2	4	0
Mayo	2b	4	0	2	0	2	1	0
Cramer	cf	4	2	1	1	1	0	0
Greenberg	lf	4	1	3	3	0	0	0
Cullenbine	rf	4	1	2	2	1	0	0
York	1b	5	1	1	1	9	2	0
Outlaw	3b	4	0	0	1	0	3	0
Richards	c	4	0	1	0	11	1	0
Newhouser	p	3	0	0	0	1	3	0
Totals		37	8	11	8	27	14	0

Pitching	IP	H	R	ER	BB	SO
Detroit						
Newhouser (W)	9	7	4	4	2	9
Chicago						
Borowy (L)	*5	8	5	5	1	4
Vandenberg	⅔	0	0	0	2	0
Chipman	⅓	0	0	0	1	0
Derringer	2	1	1	1	0	0
Erickson	1	2	2	2	0	0

*Faced 4 batters in 6th.

Chicago	Pos	AB	R	H	RBI	PO	A	E
Hack	3b	3	0	1	1	2	2	1
Johnson	2b	3	0	0	0	2	1	0
Lowrey	lf	4	1	1	0	1	0	0
Cavarretta	1b	4	1	1	0	10	0	0
Pafko	cf	4	1	0	0	5	0	1
Nicholson	rf	4	0	1	2	1	0	0
Livingston	c	4	0	1	1	4	1	0
Merullo	ss	2	0	0	0	2	1	0
b Williams		1	0	0	0	0	0	0
Schuster	ss	0	0	0	0	1	2	0
Borowy	p	1	1	1	0	0	0	0
Vandenberg	p	0	0	0	0	0	1	0
Chipman	p	0	0	0	0	0	0	0
a Sauer		1	0	0	0	0	0	0
Derringer	p	1	0	0	0	0	1	0
c Secory		1	0	1	0	0	0	0
Erickson	p	0	0	0	0	0	1	0
Totals		32	4	7	4	27	11	2

a Struck out for Chipman in 6th.
b Struck out for Merullo in 7th.
c Singled for Derringer in 8th.

Doubles—Borowy, Cavarretta, Cullenbine, Greenberg 3, Livingston. Sacrifice Hits—Cullenbine, Johnson, Outlaw. Double Plays—Mayo to York to Webb to Mayo, Johnson to Merullo to Cavarretta. Hit by Pitcher—Cramer (by Erickson). Left on Bases—Detroit 9, Chicago 4. Umpires—Summers, Jorda, Passarella, Conlan. Attendance—43,463. Time of Game—2:18.

1st Inning
Detroit
1 Webb grounded to third.
Mayo singled down the left field line.
2 Cramer grounded to the pitcher, moving Mayo to second.
Greenberg safely on first and Cramer to third on Hack's bobble of a grounder.
3 Cullenbine fanned.
Chicago
Hack walked.
1 Johnson fanned.
2,3 Lowrey grounded into a double play, Mayo to York getting Lowrey then Hack was caught York to Webb to Mayo.

2nd Inning
Detroit
1 York struck out.
2 Outlaw flied to right.
3 Richards flied to left.
Chicago
1 Cavarretta tossed out by Richards on a bunt.
2 Pafko fanned.
3 Nicholson grounded to first.

3rd Inning
Detroit
1 Newhouser fanned.
Webb walked.
Mayo singled to right, moving Webb to third.
2 Cramer flied to deep center, Webb scoring after the catch.
3 Greenberg robbed of an extra-base hit by Pafko on a glove stab in right-center.
Chicago
1 Livingston was tagged out by Newhouser on a roller.
2 Merullo struck out.
Borowy doubled down the left field line.
Hack singled to center scoring Borowy.
3 Hack was picked off first Newhouser to York to Webb.

4th Inning
Detroit
1 Cullenbine popped to second.
2 York flied to center.
3 Outlaw struck out.
Chicago
1 Johnson flied to center.
2 Lowrey grounded to short.
3 Cavarretta called out on strikes.

5th Inning
Detroit
Richards singled through the box.
1,2 Newhouser grounded into a double play, Johnson to Merullo to Cavarretta.
Webb singled to center.
3 Mayo grounded to first.
Chicago
1 Pafko took a called third strike.
2 Nicholson grounded to third.
3 Livingston grounded to short.

6th Inning
Detroit
Cramer singled to center and went to second when Pafko let the ball go through his legs for an error.
Greenberg doubled down the left field line, scoring Cramer.
Cullenbine beat out an infield hit to first, moving Greenberg to third.
York singled to center, scoring Greenberg with Cullenbine stopping at second.
For Chicago—Vandenberg pitching.
1 Outlaw sacrificed, Vandenberg to Cavarretta, advancing both runners.

6th Inning (continued)
Richards intentionally walked.
Newhouser walked forcing in Cullenbine with the bases still loaded.
2 Webb forced Newhouser, Johnson to Merullo scoring York with Richards going to third. For Chicago—Chipman pitching. Mayo walked.
3 Cramer bounced out to second.
Chicago
1 Merullo grounded to short.
2 Sauer, pinch hitting for Chipman, struck out.
3 Hack grounded to third.

7th Inning
Detroit
For Chicago—Derringer pitching.
Greenberg got a double when his pop fell between Merullo and Lowrey.
Cullenbine sacrificed when Derringer threw to catch Greenberg at third but late so Cullenbine safe at first.
1 York flied to center.
2 Outlaw flied to center, Greenberg scoring after the catch.
3 Richards grounded to third.
Chicago
1 Johnson struck out.
Lowrey singled to center.
Cavarretta walked.
2 Pafko forced Cavarretta at second, Newhouser to Mayo with Lowrey going to third.
Nicholson hit a grounder to Outlaw whose throw to second was too late to force Pafko with Lowrey scoring.
Livingston hit a ground rule double into the right field stands, scoring Pafko with Nicholson going to third.
3 Williams, batting for Merullo, struck out.

8th Inning
Detroit
For Chicago—Schuster at short.
1 Newhouser fouled to Hack.
2 Webb lined to short.
3 Mayo grounded to short.
Chicago
Secory, pinch hitting for Derringer, singled behind second.
1 Hack forced Secory, Newhouser to Webb.
2 Johnson sacrificed, Outlaw to York.
3 Lowrey popped to Richards.

9th Inning
Detroit
For Chicago—Erickson pitching.
Cramer was hit by a pitch.
Greenberg hit his third double of the game to left, Cramer going to third.
Cullenbine doubled to center, scoring Cramer and Greenberg.
1 York lined to third.
2 Outlaw grounded to short, Cullenbine holding second.
3 Richards grounded out to the pitcher.
Chicago
Cavarretta doubled into center.
1 Pafko fanned.
Nicholson singled to center, scoring Cavarretta.
2 Livingston flied to right.
3 Schuster fouled to Richards.

Game 6 October 8 at Chicago

	Det.	010 000 240 000
	Chi.	000 041 200 001

Detroit	Pos	AB	R	H	RBI	PO	A	E
Webb	ss	3	0	0	0	3	3	0
c Hostetler		1	0	0	0	0	0	0
Hoover	ss	3	1	1	1	1	1	0
Mayo	2b	6	0	1	1	4	5	0
Cramer	cf	6	1	2	1	2	0	0
Greenberg	lf	5	2	1	1	4	0	0
Cullenbine	rf	5	1	2	1	1	0	0
York	1b	6	0	2	1	9	1	0
Outlaw	3b	5	0	1	0	2	0	0
Richards	c	0	0	0	1	4	1	1
a Maier		1	0	1	0	0	0	0
Swift	c	2	1	1	0	5	1	0
Trucks	p	1	0	0	0	0	0	0
Caster	p	0	0	0	0	0	0	0
b McHale		1	0	0	0	0	0	0
Bridges	p	0	0	0	0	0	0	0
Benton	p	0	0	0	0	0	0	0
d Walker		1	1	1	0	0	0	0
Trout	p	2	0	0	0	0	3	0
Totals		48	7	13	7	*35	15	1

Chicago	Pos	AB	R	H	RBI	PO	A	E
Hack	3b	5	1	4	3	3	3	2
Johnson	2b	4	0	0	0	2	6	1
Lowrey	lf	5	1	1	0	6	1	0
Cavarretta	1b	5	1	2	2	15	0	0
Pafko	cf	6	0	2	0	1	1	0
Nicholson	rf	5	0	0	0	1	0	0
Livingston	c	3	2	2	1	2	2	0
e Gillespie		1	0	0	0	0	0	0
Williams	c	1	0	0	0	1	1	0
Hughes	ss	4	1	3	2	4	3	0
f Becker		0	0	0	0	0	0	0
g Block		0	0	0	0	0	0	0
Merullo	ss	0	0	0	0	1	1	0
h Secory		1	0	1	0	0	0	0
i Schuster		1	0	0	0	0	0	0
Passeau	p	3	1	0	0	0	1	0
Wyse	p	1	0	0	0	0	0	0
Prim	p	0	0	0	0	0	0	0
Borowy	p	2	0	0	0	0	0	0
Totals		46	8	15	8	36	19	3

Pitching	IP	H	R	ER	BB	SO
Detroit						
Trucks	4⅓	7	4	4	2	3
Caster	0	0	0	0	0	0
Bridges	1⅓	3	3	3	0	1
Benton	⅓	1	0	0	0	1
Trout (L)	4⅓	4	1	1	2	3
Chicago						
Passeau	6⅔	5	3	3	6	2
Wyse	⅓	3	3	2	1	0
Prim		1	1	0	0	0
Borowy (W)	4	4	0	0	0	0

*Two out when winning run was scored.
a Singled for Richards in 6th.
b Struck out for Caster in 6th.
c Reached on error for Webb in 7th.
d Doubled for Benton in 8th.
e Grounded out for Livingston in 9th.
f Walked for Hughes in 9th.
g Ran for Becker in 9th.
h Singled for Merullo in 12th.
i Ran for Secory in 12th.

Doubles—Hack, Hughes, Livingston, Pafko, Walker, York. Home Run—Greenberg. Stolen Base—Cullenbine. Sacrifice Hits—Johnson 2. Double Plays—Mayo to Webb to Richards to Webb, Merullo to Johnson to Cavarretta, Mayo to Hoover to York. Left on Bases—Detroit 12, Chicago 12. Umpires—Jorda, Passarella, Conlan, Summers. Attendance—41,708. Time of Game—3:28.

1st Inning
Detroit
1 Webb grounded to second.
2 Mayo flied to the right field line.
3 Cramer ground to second.
Chicago
Hack walked.
1 Johnson sacrificed Hack to second, York to Mayo.
2 Lowrey flied to right.
3 Cavarretta grounded to short.

2nd Inning
Detroit
1 Greenberg flied to left.
Cullenbine walked.
York doubled to right-center, with Cullenbine stopping at third.
Outlaw intentionally walked to load the bases.
Richards walked forcing in Cullenbine.
2 Trucks popped to short.
3 Webb forced Richards at second, Hughes unassisted.
Chicago
Pafko singled through the box.
1 Nicholson fouled to York.
2,3 A weird double play, Livingston forced Pafko at second, Mayo to Webb. Webb's throw to first was wild and past first. Richards picking it up and throwing to second to get Livingston.

3rd Inning
Detroit
1 Mayo grounded to second.
2 Cramer popped to first.
3 Greenberg grounded to short.
Chicago
1 Hughes struck out.
2 Passeau struck out.
Hack singled to center.
3 Johnson flied to center.

4th Inning
Detroit
Cullenbine got safely to first when Johnson booted his grounder for an error.
1 York fouled to Cavarretta.
2 Outlaw grounded to second, with Cullenbine going to second.
Richards intentionally walked.
Trucks walked to load the bases.
3 Webb flied to deep center.
Chicago
1 Lowrey took a called third strike.
Cavarretta singled through the middle.
2 Pafko lined to Greenberg in left-center.
3 Nicholson popped to short.

5th Inning
Detroit
1 Mayo grounded to third.
2 Cramer flied to left.
3 Greenberg flied to left.
Chicago
Livingston singled to center.
Hughes bunted to first beating it out for a single as York fell down.
Passeau safe on a fielder's choice as Trucks took his bunt and threw to third to force Livingston but too late and the bases were loaded.
Hack singled to center, scoring Livingston and Hughes, as Passeau went to third and Hack to second as Richards let Cramer's throw-in get by him for an error.
1 Johnson grounded to second as Passeau and Hack held their bases.
Lowrey walked to load the bases again.
Cavarretta singled to center, scoring Passeau and Hack with Lowrey stopping at second.
For Detroit—Caster pitching.
2 Pafko popped to third.
3 Nicholson fanned.

6th Inning
Detroit
Cullenbine got a single past the box.
1 York struck out while Cullenbine stole second.
2 Outlaw hit a hard smash to the mound which Passeau knocked down with his bare hand and threw him out (Passeau needed attention as he ripped the nail off his middle finger).
Maier, pinch hitting for Richards, beat out a single off Passeau's glove, Cullenbine moving to third.
3 McHale, pinch hitting for Caster, took a called third strike.
Chicago
For Detroit—Swift catching and Bridges pitching.
Livingston blooped a double into short left in front of on-rushing Greenberg.
Hughes doubled inside the right field line, scoring Livingston.
1 Hughes picked off first in a run-down, Swift to Webb to Outlaw.
2 Passeau lined to second.
3 Hack grounded to short.

7th Inning
Detroit
Hostetler, batting for Webb, reached first safely when Hack fumbled his roller.
1 Mayo bounced to first, moving Hostetler to second.
Cramer singled to left and when Hostetler fell between third and home
2 he was thrown out Lowrey to Livingston to Hughes. Cramer to second on the play.
Greenberg walked.
Cullenbine singled to center, scoring Cramer with Greenberg stopping at second.
For Chicago—Wyse pitching.
York singled to left, scoring Greenberg with Cullenbine stopping at second.
3 Outlaw forced York at second, Johnson to Hughes.
Chicago
For Detroit—Hoover playing shortstop.
1 Johnson took a called third strike.
Lowrey beat out a hit to short.
Cavarretta walked.
2 Pafko flied to deep left.
Nicholson walked loading the bases.
Livingston walked forcing in Lowrey.
For Detroit—Benton pitching.
Hughes singled off Benton's leg, scoring Cavarretta.
3 Wyse fanned.

8th Inning
Detroit
Swift walked.
Walker, pinch hitting for Benton, doubled past first to the right field stands, moving Swift to third.
Hoover grounded to Hack who fumbled it for his second error, Swift scoring.
Mayo singled into center, scoring Walker and Hoover going to third but Mayo was
1 out trying for a double Pafko to Johnson.
For Chicago—Prim pitching.
2 Cramer flied deep to left with Hoover scoring after the catch.
Greenberg homered over the left field wall.
3 Cullenbine grounded to short.
Chicago
For Detroit—Trout pitching.
Hack walked.
1 Johnson sacrificed, Trout to Mayo.
2 Lowrey grounded to second, Hack going to third.
3 Cavarretta flied to left.

9th Inning
Detroit
For Chicago—Borowy pitching.
1 York grounded to third.
Outlaw singled to left.
Swift singled to center with Outlaw going to third.
Trucks grounded to Hughes and Outlaw
2 was caught in a run-down, Hughes to Livingston to Hack.
3 Hoover popped to first.
Chicago
Pafko doubled down the left field line.
1 Nicholson fanned.
2 Gillespie, batting for Livingston, grounded back to the mound.
Becker, pinch hitting for Hughes, got an intentional walk.
Block ran for Becker.
3 Borowy flied to center.

10th Inning
Detroit
For Chicago—Merullo at short, Williams catching.
1 Mayo lined to third.
Cramer singled to right.
2,3 Greenberg grounded into a double play, Merullo to Johnson to Cavarretta.
Chicago
Hack singled to left.
1 Johnson fanned.
2,3 Lowrey grounded into a double play, Mayo to Hoover to York.

11th Inning
Detroit
1 Cullenbine fouled to Hack.
2 York grounded to third.
3 Outlaw flied to left.
Chicago
1 Cavarretta grounded back to the mound.
2 Pafko popped to Mayo at the right field line.
3 Nicholson flied to left.

12th Inning
Detroit
1 Swift flied to left.
2 Trout fouled to Williams.
Hoover singled to left.
3 Hoover caught stealing, Williams to Merullo.
Chicago
1 Williams grounded to second.
Secory, pinch hitting for Merullo, singled to center.
Schuster ran for Secory.
2 Borowy struck out.
Hack hit a double in front of Greenberg with Schuster scoring the winning run.

Game 7 October 10 at Chicago

| Det. | 5 1 0 | 0 0 0 | 1 2 0 |
| Chi. | 1 0 0 | 1 0 0 | 0 1 0 |

Detroit	Pos	AB	R	H	RBI	PO	A	E
Webb	ss	4	2	1	0	0	5	0
Mayo	2b	5	2	2	1	2	1	0
Cramer	cf	5	2	3	1	2	0	0
Greenberg	lf	2	0	0	1	0	0	0
Mierkowicz	lf	0	0	0	0	0	0	0
Cullenbine	rf	2	2	0	0	2	0	0
York	1b	4	0	0	1	8	1	0
Outlaw	3b	4	1	1	1	1	2	0
Richards	c	4	0	2	4	1	0	0
Swift	c	1	0	0	0	2	0	0
Newhouser	p	4	0	0	0	1	2	1
Totals		35	9	9	9	27	11	1

Pitching	IP	H	R	ER	BB	SO
Detroit						
Newhouser (W)	9	10	3	3	1	10
Chicago						
Borowy (L)	*0	3	3	3	0	0
Derringer	1⅓	2	3	3	5	0
Vandenberg	3⅓	1	0	0	1	3
Erickson	2	2	1	1	1	2
Passeau	1	1	2	2	1	0
Wyse	1	0	0	0	0	0

*Pitched to 3 batters in first.

Chicago	Pos	AB	R	H	RBI	PO	A	E
Hack	3b	5	0	0	0	1	3	0
Johnson	2b	5	1	1	0	1	3	0
Lowrey	lf	4	1	2	0	3	0	0
Cavarretta	1b	4	1	3	1	10	0	0
Pafko	cf	4	0	1	1	6	0	0
Nicholson	rf	4	0	1	1	1	0	0
Livingston	c	4	0	1	0	4	1	0
Hughes	ss	3	0	1	0	1	1	0
Borowy	p	0	0	0	0	0	0	0
Derringer	p	0	0	0	0	0	0	0
Vandenberg	p	1	0	0	0	0	1	0
a Sauer		1	0	0	0	0	0	0
Erickson	p	0	0	0	0	0	0	0
b Secory		1	0	0	0	0	0	0
Passeau	p	0	0	0	0	0	0	0
Wyse	p	0	0	0	0	0	0	0
c Mccullough		1	0	0	0	0	0	0
Totals		37	3	10	3	27	9	0

a Struck out for Vandenberg in 5th.
b Struck out for Erickson in 7th.
c Struck out for Wyse in 9th.

Doubles—Johnson, Mayo, Nicholson, Richards 2. Triple—Pafko. Stolen Bases—Cramer, Outlaw. Sacrifice Hit—Greenberg. Double Play—Webb to Mayo to York. Wild Pitch—Newhouser. Umpires—Passarella, Conlan, Summers, Jorda. Attendance—41,590. Time of Game—2:31.

1st Inning
Detroit
   Webb singled to right.
   Mayo singled to right, moving Webb to third.
   Cramer singled to left, scoring Webb with Mayo stopping at second.
   For Chicago—Derringer pitching.
1 Greenberg sacrificed, Cavarretta unassisted.
   Cullenbine got an intentional pass, loading the bases.
2 York popped to third.
   Outlaw walked to force in Mayo.
   Richards doubled into the left field corner, scoring Cramer, Cullenbine and Outlaw.
3 Newhouser grounded to second.
Chicago
1 Hack looked at a third strike.
   Johnson doubled into left-center.
   Lowrey bunted to Newhouser who fumbled for an error, Johnson held second.
   Cavarretta singled to right, scoring Johnson and sending Lowrey to third.
2,3 Pafko grounded into a double play, Webb to Mayo to York.

2nd Inning
Detroit
1 Webb flied to center.
2 Mayo lined to center.
   Cramer singled to right.
   Greenberg walked.
   Cullenbine walked, loading the bases.
   York walked forcing in Cramer.
   For Chicago—Vandenberg pitching.
3 Outlaw bounced back to the mound.
Chicago
1 Nicholson fouled to Richards.
2 Livingston grounded to third.
3 Hughes looked at a called third strike.

3rd Inning
Detroit
1 Richards called out on strikes.
2 Newhouser grounded to second.
3 Webb grounded to short.
Chicago
1 Vandenberg flied to right.
2 Hack grounded to third.
3 Johnson bounced to short.

4th Inning
Detroit
1 Mayo took a called third strike.
2 Cramer popped to short.
   Greenberg walked.
3 Cullenbine struck out but had to be thrown out, Livingston to Cavarretta.
Chicago
1 Lowrey flied very deep to right.
   Cavarretta singled to center.
   Pafko tripled to deep center, scoring Cavarretta.
2 Nicholson grounded to the pitcher.
3 Livingston grounded to the pitcher.

5th Inning
Detroit
1 York grounded to third.
   Outlaw singled beyond short.
   Outlaw stole second.
2 Richards grounded to third.
3 Newhouser lined to left.
Chicago
1 Hughes took a called third strike.
2 Sauer, pinch hitting for Vandenberg, fanned.
3 Hack grounded to short.

6th Inning
Detroit
   For Chicago—Erickson pitching.
1 Webb flied to center.
2 Mayo flied to deep left.
   Cramer singled to center.
   Cramer stole second.
3 Greenberg struck out.
Chicago
1 Johnson fanned.
   Lowrey singled to left.
2 Cavarretta flied to center.
3 Pafko struck out.

7th Inning
Detroit
   Cullenbine walked.
1 York took a called third strike.
2 Outlaw flied to center.
   Richards doubled to the right field wall, scoring Cullenbine.
3 Newhouser lined to center.
Chicago
1 Nicholson grounded out, York to Newhouser.
   Livingston singled to left.
   Livingston went to second on a wild pitch.
   Hughes walked.
2 Secory, pinch hitting for Erickson, took a called third strike.
3 Hack bounded to third where Outlaw stepped on third to force Livingston.

8th Inning
Detroit
   For Chicago—Passeau pitching.
   Webb walked.
   Mayo doubled down the left field line, scoring Webb.
1 Cramer grounded to second, sending Mayo to third.
2 Greenberg lined to left, Mayo scoring after the catch.
3 Cullenbine popped to second.
Chicago
1 Johnson grounded to short.
   Lowrey singled to left.
   Cavarretta singled through the box, sending Lowrey to third.
2 Pafko struck out.
   For Detroit—Swift catching (Richards injured the little finger of his right hand on a foul).
   Nicholson doubled to center, scoring Lowrey and moving Cavarretta to third.
3 Livingston fanned.

9th Inning
Detroit
   For Chicago—Wyse pitching.
1 York flied to right.
2 Outlaw flied to center.
3 Swift grounded to third.
Chicago
   For Detroit—Mierkowicz playing left field.
   Hughes singled through the box.
1 McCullough, pinch hitting for Wyse, struck out (**McCullough becomes first player in Series history to appear in the Series without playing a game during the regular season**).
2 Hack flied to center.
3 Johnson forced Hughes at second, Webb to Mayo.

1945 WORLD SERIES COMPOSITE BOX

	Wins	Composite Line Score					Manager	Regular Season W	L	Pct.	G. Ahead
Detroit Tigers (A.L.)	4	5 2 1	4 4 4	4 6 2	0 0 0	– 32	Steve O'Neill	88	65	.575	1.5
Chicago Cubs (N.L.)	3	5 0 4	4 4 2	7 1 1	0 0 1	– 29	Charlie Grimm	98	56	.636	3

BATTING AND FIELDING

DETROIT TIGERS — World Series Statistics

	Pos	G	AB	R	H	2B	3B	HR	RBI	BB	SO	SB	BA	SA	PO	A	E
Rudy York	1b	7	28	1	5	1	0	0	3	3	4	0	.179	.214	67	8	1
Eddie Mayo	2b	7	28	4	7	1	0	0	2	2	2	0	.250	.286	18	13	1
Skeeter Webb	ss	7	27	4	5	0	0	0	1	3	1	0	.185	.185	9	**24**	1
Jimmy Outlaw	3b	7	28	1	5	0	0	0	3	2	1	**1**	.179	.179	5	15	0
Roy Cullenbine	rf	7	22	5	5	2	0	0	4	**8**	2	**1**	.227	.318	8	0	0
Doc Cramer	cf	7	29	**7**	**11**	0	0	0	4	1	0	**1**	.379	.379	21	0	0
Hank Greenberg	lf	7	23	**7**	7	**3**	0	**2**	7	6	5	0	.304	**.696**	8	1	0
Paul Richards	c	7	19	0	4	2	0	0	6	4	3	0	.211	.316	46	5	1
Bob Swift	c	3	4	1	1	0	0	0	0	2	0	0	.250	.250	9	1	0
Joe Hoover	ss	1	3	1	1	0	0	0	1	0	0	0	.333	.333	1	1	0
Chuck Hostetler	ph	3	3	0	0	0	0	0	0	0	0	0	.000	.000			
John McHale	ph	3	3	0	0	0	0	0	0	0	1	0	.000	.000			
Hub Walker	ph	2	2	1	1	1	0	0	0	0	0	0	.500	1.000			
Bob Maier	ph	1	1	0	1	0	0	0	0	0	0	0	1.000	1.000			
Red Borom	ph	2	1	0	0	0	0	0	0	0	0	0	.000	.000			
Ed Mierkowicz	lf	1	0	0	0	0	0	0	0	0	0	0	—	—	0	0	0
Zeb Eaton	ph	1	1	0	0	0	0	0	0	0	1	0	.000	.000			
Hack Miller		Did not play															
Hal Newhouser	p	3	8	0	0	0	0	0	1	1	1	0	.000	.000	2	6	1
Dizzy Trout	p	2	6	0	1	0	0	0	0	0	0	0	.167	.167	2	5	0
Virgil Trucks	p	2	4	0	0	0	0	0	0	1	1	0	.000	.000	1	1	0
Stubby Overmire	p	1	1	0	0	0	0	0	0	0	0	0	.000	.000	0	1	0
Jim Tobin	p	1	1	0	0	0	0	0	0	0	0	0	.000	.000	0	1	0
Al Benton	p	3	0	0	0	0	0	0	0	0	0	0	—	—	0	3	0
Tommy Bridges	p	1	0	0	0	0	0	0	0	0	0	0	—	—	0	0	0
George Caster	p	1	0	0	0	0	0	0	0	0	0	0	—	—	0	0	0
Les Mueller	p	1	0	0	0	0	0	0	0	0	0	0	—	—	0	0	0
Walter Wilson		Did not play															
Art Houtterman		Did not play															
Billy Pierce		Did not play															
team total		7	242	32	54	10	0	2	32	33	22	3	.223	.298	197	85	5

Double Plays—4
Left on Bases—53

DETROIT TIGERS — Regular Season Statistics

		Main Pos	G	AB	R	H	2B	3B	HR	RBI	BB	SO	SB	BA	SA
Rudy York		1b	155	595	71	157	25	5	18	87	59	85	6	.264	.413
Eddie Mayo		2b	134	501	71	143	24	3	10	54	48	29	7	.285	.405
Skeeter Webb		ss	118	407	43	81	12	2	0	21	30	35	8	.199	.238
Jimmy Outlaw		of	132	446	56	121	16	5	0	34	45	33	6	.271	.330
Roy Cullenbine	a	of	146	523	80	145	27	5	18	93	**101**	36	2	.277	.451
Doc Cramer		of	141	541	62	149	22	8	6	58	35	21	2	.275	.379
Hank Greenberg		of	78	270	47	84	20	2	13	60	42	40	3	.311	.544
Paul Richards		c	83	234	26	60	12	1	3	32	19	31	4	.256	.355
Bob Swift		c	95	279	19	65	5	0	0	24	25	22	1	.233	.251
Joe Hoover		ss	74	222	33	57	10	5	1	17	21	35	6	.257	.360
Chuck Hostetler		ph	42	44	3	7	3	0	0	2	7	8	0	.159	.227
John McHale		ph	19	14	0	2	0	0	0	1	1	4	0	.143	.143
Hub Walker		ph-of	28	23	4	3	0	0	0	1	9	4	1	.130	.130
Bob Maier		3b	132	486	58	128	25	7	1	34	37	32	7	.263	.350
Red Borom		2b	55	130	19	35	4	0	0	9	7	8	4	.269	.300
Ed Mierkowicz		of	10	15	0	2	2	0	0	2	1	3	0	.133	.267
Zeb Eaton		p-ph	26	32	2	8	1	0	2	10	0	7	0	.250	.469
Hack Miller		c	2	4	0	3	0	0	0	1	0	0	0	.750	.750
Hal Newhouser		p	40	109	9	28	5	1	0	17	7	10	0	.257	.321
Dizzy Trout		p	42	102	11	25	3	2	2	11	2	23	1	.245	.373
Virgil Trucks		p	1	2	1	0	0	0	0	0	1	1	0	.000	.000
Stubby Overmire		p	31	53	5	10	2	1	0	3	4	6	0	.189	.264
Jim Tobin	b	p	17	25	2	3	0	0	2	5	1	5	0	.120	.360
Al Benton		p	31	63	2	4	2	0	0	3	2	21	0	.063	.095
Tommy Bridges		p	4	3	0	0	0	0	0	0	0	0	0	.000	.000
George Caster	c	p	22	11	0	2	0	0	0	1	2	3	0	.182	.182
Les Mueller		p	26	44	5	8	3	0	1	4	2	10	0	.182	.318
Walter Wilson		p	25	19	1	1	0	0	0	0	0	9	0	.053	.053
Art Houtterman		p	13	5	0	0	0	0	0	0	0	2	0	.000	.000
Billy Pierce		p	5	2	0	0	0	0	0	0	0	1	0	.000	.000
team total			155	5257	633	1345	**227**	47	77	588	517	533	60	.256	.361

a—from Cleveland (led league in BB with 112).
b—from Boston (N) c—from St. Louis (A); Don Ross (3b), Russ Kerns (ph), Carl McNabb (ph), Milt Welch (c), Joe Orrell (p), Prince Oana (p), and Pat McLaughlin also played for the Tigers during the season.

CHICAGO CUBS — World Series Statistics

	Pos	G	AB	R	H	2B	3B	HR	RBI	BB	SO	SB	BA	SA	PO	A	E
Phil Cavarretta	1b	7	26	**7**	**11**	2	0	1	5	4	3	0	**.423**	.615	**71**	3	0
Don Johnson	2b	7	29	4	5	2	**1**	0	0	0	**8**	**1**	.172	.310	11	**24**	1
Roy Hughes	ss	6	17	1	5	1	0	0	3	4	5	0	.294	.353	13	17	0
Stan Hack	3b	7	**30**	1	**11**	**3**	0	0	4	4	2	0	.367	.467	12	13	**3**
Bill Nicholson	rf	7	28	1	6	1	**1**	0	**8**	2	5	0	.214	.321	9	0	1
Andy Pafko	cf	7	28	5	6	2	**1**	0	2	2	5	**1**	.214	.357	24	2	1
Peanuts Lowrey	lf	7	29	4	9	1	0	0	0	1	2	0	.310	.345	21	1	0
Mickey Livingston	c	6	22	3	8	**3**	0	0	4	1	1	0	.364	.500	22	4	0
Paul Gillespie	ph-c	3	6	0	0	0	0	0	0	0	0	0	.000	.000	3	0	0
Frank Secory	ph	5	5	0	2	0	0	0	0	0	2	0	.400	.400			
Heinz Becker	ph	3	2	0	1	0	0	0	0	1	1	0	.500	.500			
Lenny Merullo	ss-pr	3	2	0	0	0	0	0	0	0	1	0	.000	.000	4	2	0
Ed Sauer	ph	2	2	0	0	0	0	0	0	0	2	0	.000	.000			
Dewey Williams	ph-c	2	2	0	0	0	0	0	0	0	1	0	.000	.000	1	1	0
Bill Schuster	ss-pr	2	1	1	0	0	0	0	0	0	0	0	.000	.000	1	2	0
Clyde McCullough	ph	1	1	0	0	0	0	0	0	0	0	0	.000	.000			
Cy Block	pr	1	0	0	0	0	0	0	0	0	1	0	—	—			
Len Rice		Did not play															
Claude Passeau	p	3	7	1	0	0	0	0	1	0	4	0	.000	.000	1	3	0
Hank Borowy	p	4	6	1	1	1	0	0	0	0	3	0	.167	.333	1	2	0
Hank Wise	p	3	3	0	0	0	0	0	0	0	2	0	.000	.000	0	0	0
Hy Vandenberg	p	3	1	0	0	0	0	0	0	0	0	0	.000	.000	1	2	0
Paul Erickson	p	4	0	0	0	0	0	0	0	0	0	0	—	—	0	1	0
Paul Derringer	p	3	0	0	0	0	0	0	0	0	0	0	—	—	0	0	0
Ray Prim	p	2	0	0	0	0	0	0	0	0	0	0	—	—	0	1	0
Bob Chipman	p	1	0	0	0	0	0	0	0	0	0	0	—	—	0	0	0
Ray Starr		Did not play															
Lon Warneke		Did not play															
Walter Signer		Did not play															
Ed Hanyzsewski		Did not play															
Hi Bithorn		Did not play															
team total		7	247	29	65	16	3	1	27	19	48	2	.263	.364	195	78	6

Double Plays—5
Left on Bases—50

CHICAGO CUBS — Regular Season Statistics

		Main Pos	G	AB	R	H	2B	3B	HR	RBI	BB	SO	SB	BA	SA
Phil Cavarretta		1b	132	498	94	177	34	10	6	97	81	34	5	**.355**	.500
Don Johnson		2b	138	557	94	168	23	2	2	58	32	34	9	.302	.361
Roy Hughes		ss-2b	69	222	34	58	8	1	0	8	16	18	6	.261	.306
Stan Hack		3b	150	597	110	193	29	7	2	43	99	30	12	.323	.405
Bill Nicholson		of	151	559	82	136	28	4	13	88	92	73	4	.243	.377
Andy Pafko		of	144	534	64	159	24	12	12	110	45	36	5	.298	.455
Peanuts Lowrey		of	143	523	72	148	22	7	7	89	48	27	11	.283	.392
Mickey Livingston		c	71	224	19	57	4	2	2	23	19	6	2	.254	.317
Paul Gillespie		c	75	163	12	47	6	0	3	25	18	9	2	.288	.380
Frank Secory		ph-of	35	57	4	9	1	0	0	6	2	7	0	.158	.175
Heinz Becker		1b	67	133	25	38	8	2	2	27	17	16	0	.286	.421
Lenny Merullo		ss	121	394	40	94	18	0	2	37	31	30	7	.239	.299
Ed Sauer		of	49	93	8	24	4	1	2	11	8	23	2	.258	.387
Dewey Williams		c	59	100	16	28	2	2	2	5	13	13	0	.280	.400
Bill Schuster		ss	45	47	8	9	2	1	0	2	7	4	2	.191	.277
Clyde McCullough		was in Military Service during season													
Cy Block		3b-2b	2	7	1	1	0	0	0	1	0	0	0	.143	.143
Len Rice		c	32	99	10	23	3	0	0	7	5	8	2	.232	.263
Claude Passeau		p	34	91	10	17	2	0	2	9	2	22	0	.187	.275
Hank Borowy	d	p	15	41	5	7	1	0	0	0	4	11	0	.171	.195
Hank Wise		p	38	101	6	17	2	0	0	7	0	16	0	.168	.188
Hy Vandenberg		p	30	32	4	4	0	1	0	2	1	4	0	.125	.188
Paul Erickson		p	28	32	2	5	2	0	0	0	3	8	0	.156	.219
Paul Derringer		p	35	75	3	15	3	0	0	8	0	12	0	.200	.240
Ray Prim		p	38	51	4	13	0	0	0	1	5	9	0	.255	.255
Bob Chipman		p	25	17	1	3	1	0	0	2	2	4	0	.176	.235
Ray Starr	e	p	9	2	1	1	0	0	0	0	0	0	0	.500	.500
Lon Warneke		p	9	2	1	0	0	0	0	0	1	0	0	.000	.000
Walter Signer		p	6	1	0	0	0	0	0	0	0	1	0	.000	.000
Ed Hanyzsewski		p	2	1	0	0	0	0	0	0	1	1	0	.000	.000
Hi Bithorn		Was in Military Service during season.													
team total			155	5298	735	1465	229	52	57	674	554	462	69	**.277**	.372

d—from New York (A)
e—from Pittsburgh
Reggie Otero (1b), Johnny Moore (ph), John Ostrowski (3b), Lloyd Christopher (of), Mack Stewart (p), Jorge Corellas (p), and George Hennessy (p) also played for the Clubs during the season.

PITCHING

DETROIT TIGERS — World Series Statistics

	G	GS	CG	IP	H	R	ER	BB	SO	W	L	SV	ERA
Hal Newhouser	3	**3**	**2**	**$20\frac{2}{3}$**	**25**	**14**	**14**	4	**22**	**2**	1	0	6.10
Dizzy Trout	2	1	1	$13\frac{2}{3}$	9	2	1	3	9	1	1	0	**0.66**
Virgil Trucks	2	2	1	$13\frac{1}{3}$	14	5	5	5	7	1	0	0	3.38
Stubby Overmire	1	1	0	6	4	2	2	2	2	0	1	0	3.00
Al Benton	3	0	0	$4\frac{2}{3}$	6	1	1	0	5	0	0	0	1.93
Jim Tobin	1	0	0	3	4	2	2	1	0	0	0	0	6.00
Les Mueller	1	0	0	2	0	0	0	1	1	0	0	0	0.00
Tommy Bridges	1	0	0	$1\frac{2}{3}$	3	3	3	3	1	0	0	0	16.20
George Caster	1	0	0	$\frac{2}{3}$	0	0	0	0	1	0	0	0	0.00
Zeb Eaton	Did not pitch												
Walter Wilson	Did not play												
Art Houtterman	Did not play												
Billy Pierce	Did not play												
team total	7	7	4	$65\frac{2}{3}$	65	29	28	19	48	4	3	0	3.84

DETROIT TIGERS — Regular Season Statistics

		G	GS	CG	IP	H	ER	BB	SO	W	L	Pct	SV	ShO	ERA
Hal Newhouser		40	**36**	**29**	**313**	239	63	110	**212**	**25**	9	**.735**	2	**8**	**1.81**
Dizzy Trout		41	31	18	246	252	86	79	97	18	15	.545	2	4	3.15
Virgil Trucks		1	1	0	5	3	1	2	3	0	0	.000	0	0	1.80
Stubby Overmire		31	22	9	162	189	70	42	36	9	9	.500	4	0	3.89
Al Benton		31	27	12	192	175	43	63	76	13	8	.619	3	5	2.02
Jim Tobin	b	14	6	2	58	61	23	28	14	4	5	.444	1	0	3.57
Les Mueller		26	18	6	135	117	55	58	42	6	8	.429	1	2	3.67
Tommy Bridges		4	1	0	11	14	4	2	6	1	0	1.000	0	0	3.27
George Caster	c	22	0	0	51	47	22	27	23	5	1	.833	2	0	3.88
Zeb Eaton		17	3	0	53	48	24	40	15	4	2	.667	0	0	4.08
Walter Wilson		25	4	1	70	76	36	35	28	1	3	.250	0	0	4.63
Art Houtterman		13	0	0	25	27	15	11	9	0	2	.000	0	0	5.40
Billy Pierce		5	0	0	10	6	2	10	10	0	0	—	0	0	1.80
team total		155	155	78	1394	1305	463	538	**588**	**88**	65	**.575**	**16**	**19**	2.99

CHICAGO CUBS — World Series Statistics

	G	GS	CG	IP	H	R	ER	BB	SO	W	L	SV	ERA
Hank Borowy	**4**	**3**	1	18	21	8	8	6	8	**2**	**2**	0	4.00
Claude Passeau	3	2	1	$16\frac{2}{3}$	7	5	5	**8**	3	1	0	0	2.70
Hank Wyse	3	1	0	$7\frac{2}{3}$	8	7	6	4	1	0	1	0	7.04
Paul Erickson	**4**	0	0	7	8	3	3	3	5	0	0	0	3.86
Fly Vandenberg	3	0	0	6	1	0	0	3	3	0	0	0	0.00
Paul Derringer	3	0	0	$5\frac{1}{3}$	5	4	4	7	1	0	0	0	6.75
Ray Prim	2	1	0	4	4	5	4	1	1	0	1	0	9.00
Bob Chipman	1	0	0	$\frac{1}{3}$	0	0	0	1	0	0	0	0	0.00
Ray Starr	Did not play												
Lon Warneke	Did not play												
Walter Signer	Did not play												
Ed Hanyzewski	Did not play												
Hi Bithorn	Did not play												
team total	7	7	2	65	54	32	30	33	22	3	4	0	4.15

CHICAGO CUBS — Regular Season Statistics

		G	GS	CG	IP	H	ER	BB	SO	W	L	Pct	SV	ShO	ERA
Hank Borowy	d	15	14	11	122	105	29	47	47	11	2	.846	1	1	**2.14**
Claude Passeau		34	27	19	227	205	62	59	98	17	9	.654	1	**5**	2.46
Hank Wyse		38	34	23	278	272	83	55	77	22	10	.688	0	2	2.69
Paul Erickson		28	9	3	108	94	40	48	53	7	4	.636	3	0	3.33
Fly Vandenberg		30	7	3	95	91	37	33	35	7	3	.700	2	1	3.51
Paul Derringer		35	30	15	214	223	82	51	86	16	11	.593	4	1	3.45
Ray Prim		34	19	9	165	142	44	23	88	13	8	.619	2	2	2.40
Bob Chipman		25	10	3	72	63	28	34	29	4	5	.444	1	1	3.50
Ray Starr	e	9	1	0	13	17	11	7	5	1	0	1.000	0	0	7.62
Lon Warneke		9	1	0	14	16	6	1	6	0	1	.000	0	0	3.86
Walter Signer		6	0	0	8	11	3	5	0	0	0	—	1	0	3.38
Ed Hanyzewski		2	1	0	5	7	3	1	0	0	0	—	0	0	5.40
Hi Bithorn															
team total		155	155	**86**	1366	1301	**452**	385	541	98	56	**.636**	14	15	**2.98**

Total Attendance—333,457 Average Attendance—47,639 Winning Player's Share—$6,443 Losing Player's Share—$3,930.

1946 Play-off
Brecheen to the Rescue

By losing their games on the final day of the season, the St. Louis Cardinals and Brooklyn Dodgers created an unprecedented situation. They had come through an entire 154-game schedule only to finish in a dead heat for first place in the National League with identical 96–58 records, the first tie at the top of a major league in history. Brooklyn manager Leo Durocher and St. Louis skipper Eddie Dyer each had frazzled pitching staffs and injuries to key players. Ace Cardinal lefty Howie Pollet had a pulled muscle on his left side, shortstop Marty Marion struggled to stay in the St. Louis lineup with a bad back, and Dodger outfielder Pete Reiser, an inspirational leader and the most dangerous base stealer in baseball, was shelved with a broken ankle. With just one day off after the final day of the campaign, the Dodgers called on young Ralph Branca to pitch the opening game of the three-game set, while Dyer surprisingly chose Pollet. Although he had twice been knocked from the box in the hectic final week of the schedule, Pollet pitched a masterful game in this vital contest in Sportsman's Park. The Cards took an early lead in the first inning. Red Schoendienst struck out, Terry Moore singled, and Stan Musial fanned to open the frame. Enos Slaughter then singled and Whitey Kurowski walked to load the bases. Rookie catcher Joe Garagiola then hit a grounder which shortstop Pee Wee Reese fielded deep in the hole; a strong throw just failed to beat Garagiola, and the Cards led 1–0. A home run by Howie Schultz in the third inning tied the score at 1–1, but the Cards came right back at Branca. After Moore made out, Musial walked and Slaughter singled him to third. Musial scored on an infield out, then Garagiola and Harry Walker followed with singles to make the score 3–1.

The Dodgers made a move to tie the score in the top of the seventh. With one out, Reese and Bruce Edwards singled. Schultz then socked a single to right; Reese scored, but a great throw by Slaughter cut Edwards down at third to defuse the rally. The Cards upped the count to 4–2 in the bottom of the inning on a triple by Musial and a single by Garagiola, his third hit of the game. Aided by Marion's fine catch of a low liner in the eighth and Walker's running catch of a line drive in left-center in the ninth, Pollet wrapped up his twenty-first win of the season and gave the Cards a one-game edge to take on the train to New York.

Ebbets Field rocked with optimism when the Dodgers scored a run in the first inning of the second game off right-hander Murray Dickson. After Stanky and Dick Whitman made out, an infield hit by Augie Galan and a walk to popular Dixie Walker set up a run-scoring single through the middle by Ed Stevens. But Dickson settled into an almost perfect groove after that, while Brooklyn southpaw Joe Hatten was less sure of himself. Erv Dusak blasted a triple off the left-field wall to open the second inning for the Cards, and he scored on an outfield fly by Marion. Clyde Kluttz then hit a seemingly harmless single, but Dickson lined a triple to right-center to put the Cards ahead 2–1. With Dickson coasting through the Dodger lineup, the Cards padded their lead in the fifth. With two outs, Musial doubled and Kurowski was intentionally passed. Slaughter spoiled the strategy, however, by belting a triple to deep right, and a single by Dusak ran the score up to 5–1 and drove Hatten from the box. A squeeze bunt by Marion in the seventh and a two-run single by Kurowski in the eighth made the score 8–1 and spelled the end for Brooklyn. But the Dodgers made one last move in the bottom of the ninth, starting with Galan's double. After Walker flew out, Stevens tripled Galan home and Furillo singled Stevens home. When Dickson walked Reese, Dyer waved lefty Harry Brecheen in from the bullpen. A key man down the stretch, Brecheen immediately made matters worse by giving a single to Edwards and a walk to pinch hitter Cookie Lavagetto. Although trailing 8–4, the Dodgers now had the tying run at the plate with only one out. But Brecheen reached back for some sharp breaking pitches, and he fanned Stanky and pinch hitter Schultz to eliminate the Dodgers, who would have to wait until next year.

Game 1 Playoffs October 1 at St. Louis

Bkn.	001	000	100
St.L	102	000	10x

Brooklyn	Pos	AB	R	H	RBI	PO	A	E
Stanky	2b	3	0	1	0	3	2	0
Lavagetto	3b	3	0	0	0	2	2	0
Medwick	lf	4	0	1	0	1	0	0
c Tepsic		0	0	0	0	0	0	0
Whitman	lf	0	0	0	0	1	0	0
D. Walker	rf	4	0	0	0	0	0	0
Furillo	cf	4	0	0	0	5	0	0
Reese	ss	4	1	2	0	2	2	0
Edwards	c	4	0	2	0	5	1	0
Schultz	1b	3	1	2	2	5	0	0
Branca	p	1	0	0	0	0	0	0
Higbe	p	0	0	0	0	0	0	0
a Rojek		0	0	0	0	0	0	0
Gregg	p	0	0	0	0	0	0	0
b Ramazzotti		1	0	0	0	0	0	0
Lombardi	p	0	0	0	0	0	0	0
Melton	p	0	0	0	0	0	0	0
Totals		31	2	8	2	24	7	0

a Walked for Higbe in 5th.
b Grounded out for Edwards in 7th.
c Ran for Medwick in 8th.

St. Louis	Pos	AB	R	H	RBI	PO	A	E
Schoendienst	2b	5	0	2	0	1	7	0
Moore	cf	5	1	3	0	1	0	0
Musial	1b	4	2	1	0	10	0	0
Slaughter	rf	4	0	2	0	4	1	0
Kurowski	3b	2	1	0	1	1	2	0
Garagiola	c	4	0	3	2	2	0	0
H. Walker	lf	3	0	1	1	3	0	0
Marion	ss	4	0	0	0	5	4	0
Pollet	p	4	0	0	0	0	2	1
Totals		35	4	12	4	27	16	1

Pitching	IP	H	R	ER	BB	SO
Brooklyn						
Branca (L)	$2\frac{2}{3}$	6	3	3	2	3
Higbe	$1\frac{1}{3}$	1	0	0	0	0
Gregg	2	1	0	0	1	1
Lombardi	$\frac{1}{3}$	1	1	1	0	0
Melton	$1\frac{2}{3}$	3	0	0	1	1
St. Louis						
Pollet (W)	9	8	2	2	3	2

Triple—Musial. Home Run—Schultz. Sacrifice Hit—Schultz. Double Plays—Pollet to Marion to Musial, Schoendienst to Marion to Musial 2. Wild Pitch—Melton. Left on Bases—Brooklyn 6, St. Louis 11. Umpires—Reardon, Pinelli, Goetz, Boggess. Attendance—26,012. Time of Game—2:48.

Game 2 Playoffs October 3 at Brooklyn

St.L.	020	030	120
Bkn.	100	000	003

St. Louis	Pos	AB	R	H	RBI	PO	A	E
Schoendienst	2b	5	1	1	0	1	5	0
Moore	cf	5	1	2	0	2	0	0
Musial	1b	4	1	1	0	14	1	0
Kurowski	3b	2	2	1	2	1	1	0
Slaughter	rf	3	1	1	2	0	0	0
Dusak	lf	3	1	2	1	1	0	0
b H. Walker	lf	1	0	0	0	0	0	0
Marion	ss	3	0	1	2	4	3	0
Kluttz	c	5	1	2	0	3	2	0
Dickson	p	5	0	2	1	1	5	0
Brecheen	p	0	0	0	0	0	0	0
Totals		36	8	13	8	27	17	0

Pitching	IP	H	R	ER	BB	SO
St. Louis						
Dickson (W)	$8\frac{1}{3}$	5	4	4	5	3
Brecheen (SV)	$\frac{2}{3}$	1	0	0	1	2
Brooklyn						
Hatten (L)	$4\frac{2}{3}$	7	5	5	3	0
Behrman	$\frac{1}{3}$	1	0	0	0	0
Lombardi	$1\frac{1}{3}$	1	1	1	2	0
Higbe	1	3	2	2	2	1
Melton	$\frac{2}{3}$	0	0	0	0	0
Taylor	1	1	0	0	0	1

Brooklyn	Pos	AB	R	H	RBI	PO	A	E
Stanky	2b	5	0	0	0	3	4	0
Whitman	lf	4	0	0	0	2	0	0
e Schultz		1	0	0	0	0	0	0
Galan	3b	4	2	2	0	0	4	0
D. Walker	rf	3	0	0	0	1	0	0
Stevens	1b	4	1	2	2	11	0	0
Furillo	cf	4	1	1	1	4	0	0
Reese	ss	2	0	0	0	2	3	0
Edwards	c	2	0	1	1	3	1	0
Hatten	p	1	0	0	0	0	1	0
Behrman	p	0	0	0	0	0	0	0
a Hermanski		1	0	0	0	0	0	0
Lombardi	p	0	0	0	0	0	1	0
Higbe	p	0	0	0	0	1	0	0
Melton	p	0	0	0	0	0	0	0
c Medwick		1	0	0	0	0	0	0
Taylor	p	0	0	0	0	0	0	0
d Lavagetto		0	0	0	0	0	0	0
Totals		32	4	6	4	27	14	0

a Called out on strikes for Behrman in 5th.
b Fouled out for Dusak in 8th.
c Grounded out for Melton in 8th.
d Walked for Taylor in 9th.
e Struck out for Whitman in 9th.

Doubles—Galan, Moore, Musial. Triples—Dickson, Dusak, Slaughter, Stevens. Sacrifice Hits—Dusak, Marion, Slaughter. Double Plays—Dickson to Marion to Musial, Stanky to Reese to Stevens. Wild Pitch—Dickson. Left on Bases—St. Louis 11, Brooklyn 7. Umpires—Pinelli, Goetz, Boggess, Reardon. Attendance—31,437. Time of Game—2:44.

1946
Slaughter's Sprint

Along with millions of other returning veterans, the big-leaguers who had served in the armed forces put their military uniforms away and picked up their lives where the thread had been broken off. Those fans who had stayed on the home front and had grown accustomed to the makeshift teams of the war years once again feasted on a diet made up of the likes of Joe DiMaggio, Stan Musial, Ted Williams, Phil Rizzuto, Pete Reiser, and other ex-servicemen who resumed their starring roles in the peacetime. Perhaps the brightest stars returning were Stan Musial and Ted Williams, each of whom won the MVP award and led his club to the pennant. Musial hit .365 to spearhead the St. Louis Cardinals' drive to their fourth pennant in five years. Outfielder Enos Slaughter and pitchers Howie Pollet and Murray Dickson brought large talents back from the military, Marty Marion and Whitey Kurowski continued their fine work on the right side of the infield, and a new look on the team came from manager Eddie Dyer, young second baseman Red Schoendienst, and rookie catcher Joe Garagiola.

The Boston Red Sox won their flag with an experienced club, getting to the Series for the first time since selling Babe Ruth to the Yankees. The heavy artillery in the Boston attack came from the bat of Williams, who hit .342 with 38 homers and 123 runs batted in. Rudy York, Bobby Doerr, Dom DiMaggio, and Johnny Pesky chipped in with heavy hitting, while Boo Ferriss, Tex Hughson, and Mickey Harris won big at the head of manager Joe Cronin's pitching staff. But when these two gleaming outfits actually got down to playing the Series, MVP's Musial and Williams shriveled up and died, with Musial hitting .222 and Williams .200. The hero's laurels instead would go to a pair of lesser lights on the Cardinals, Enos Slaughter and Harry Brecheen.

The Series got off to a slow start for the Cards, as they dropped game one in St. Louis 3–2 on a tenth-inning homer by York off Pollet. Manager Dyer chose as his second-game starter Brecheen, a crafty southpaw with a hard-luck 15–15 record for the season. His teammates supported him royally in the field and at bat in this game, and "The Cat" ended the day with a four-hit shutout that squared the Series heading back to Boston.

Back in the friendly confines of Fenway Park, the Sox quickly took command of game three on a three-run homer by York in the first inning, going on to a 4–0 victory behind Ferriss's six-hit shutout. The Cardinals perhaps needed a game to get used to the invitingly close left-field wall at Fenway, for they zeroed in on the "Green Monster" and the Boston pitching staff in game four. The Cards blasted six pitchers for a 12–3 victory on 20 hits, four each by Slaughter, Kurowski, and Garagiola. But the Red Sox bounced back the next day to drive Pollet from the mound in the first inning and take a 6–3 decision behind Joe Dobson's four-hitter.

Back in St. Louis for the wrap-up, the Cards needed to win both games to take the Series. They took game six 4–1 behind Brecheen's seven-hitter to throw the Series into a seventh contest. Ferriss and Dickson started on the mound, and the Cardinal righty protected a 3–1 lead through seven innings. But in the top of the eighth, pinch hitters Rip Russell and Catfish Metkovich came through with hits and scored on Dom DiMaggio's two-out double. Brecheen relieved Dickson to get the final out, but the damage had been done and the score was tied at 3–3. But in the bottom of the eighth Enos Slaughter, ignoring a broken elbow suffered in game five, led off with a single off Bob Klinger. Kurowski and Del Rice made out, and then Harry Walker drilled a two-out single to left-center. Center fielder Leon Culberson, who came in when DiMaggio pulled a muscle in the Boston rally, fielded the ball and relayed it in to shortstop Johnny Pesky. Slaughter had dashed around to third, then threw caution to the wind and sprinted for home. Pesky had a play at the plate but he hesitated, holding the ball for a split second. When he did get his throw off to the plate, Slaughter slid in ahead of it to give the Cards a 4–3 lead, which Brecheen nailed down into a World Championship for the Cards and his third victory of the Series.

Game 1 October 6 at St. Louis

Boston	Pos	AB	R	H	RBI	PO	A	E
McBride	rf	5	0	1	1	1	0	1
Moses	rf	0	0	0	0	1	0	0
Pesky	ss	5	0	0	0	0	3	1
DiMaggio	cf	5	0	2	0	1	1	0
Williams	lf	3	0	1	0	4	0	0
York	1b	4	2	1	1	10	0	0
Doerr	2b	4	0	1	0	4	4	0
Higgins	3b	4	0	2	1	2	0	0
a Gutteridge		0	1	0	0	0	0	0
Johnson	p	1	0	0	0	0	2	0
Wagner	c	3	0	0	0	6	1	0
b Russell	3b	1	0	1	0	0	0	0
Hughson	p	2	0	0	0	0	1	0
c Partee		1	0	0	0	1	0	0
Totals		38	3	9	3	30	12	2

a Ran for Higgins in 9th.
b Singled for H. Wagner in 9th.
c Fanned for Hughson in 9th.
d Flied out for Walker in 9th.

Doubles—Garagiola, Musial. Triple—Slaughter. Home Run—York. Stolen Base—Schoendienst. Sacrifice Hits—Marion, Moore. Hit by Pitchers—York (by Pollet), Kurowski (by Hughson). Left on Bases—Boston 10, St. Louis 8. Umpires—Ballanfant (N), Hubbard (A), Barlick (N), Berry (A). Attendance—36,218. Time of Game—2:39.

		Bos.	010	000	001	1
		St L.	000	001	010	0

St. Louis	Pos	AB	R	H	RBI	PO	A	E
Schoendienst	2b	5	1	2	0	2	5	0
Moore	cf	4	0	0	0	3	1	0
Musial	1b	5	0	1	0	13	0	0
Slaughter	rf	4	0	1	0	3	0	0
Kurowski	3b	3	1	1	0	1	4	0
Garagiola	c	4	0	1	0	4	0	0
Walker	lf	2	0	1	0	3	0	0
d Dusak	lf	1	0	0	0	0	0	0
Marion	ss	3	0	0	1	1	3	0
Pollet	p	4	0	0	0	0	0	0
Totals		35	2	7	2	30	13	0

Pitching	IP	H	R	ER	BB	SO
Boston						
Hughson	8	7	2	2	2	5
Johnson (W)	2	0	0	0	0	1
St. Louis						
Pollet (L)	10	9	3	3	4	3

1st Inning
Boston
1 McBride grounded to third.
2 Pesky popped to left.
3 DiMaggio grounded to third.
St. Louis
1 Schoendienst flied to center.
2 Moore grounded to short.
3 Musial grounded to second.

2nd Inning
Boston
1 Williams grounded to second.
York was hit by a pitched ball.
Doerr walked.
Higgins singled to center, scoring York and advancing Doerr to third.
2 Wagner flied to center.
3 Hughson grounded to third.
St. Louis
1 Slaughter popped to second.
2 Kurowski fanned.
3 Garagiola lined to left.

3rd Inning
Boston
1 McBride grounded to third.
2 Pesky flied to right.
DiMaggio singled over Marion's head.
Williams walked.
3 York fouled to Walker.
St. Louis
Walker singled to center.
1 Marion grounded back to the mound, moving Walker to second.
2 Pollet grounded to second, Walker going to third.
3 Schoendienst grounded to short.

4th Inning
Boston
1 Doerr flied to deep center, at the wall.
2 Higgins flied to left.
3 Wagner popped to second.
St. Louis
1 Moore called out on strikes.
2 Musial popped to second.
Slaughter tripled between Williams and DiMaggio.
3 Kurowski flied to right.

5th Inning
Boston
1 Hughson grounded to short.
2 McBride called out on strikes.
3 Pesky grounded to second.
St. Louis
1 Garagiola flied to left.
2 Walker fanned.
3 Marion rolled out to first.

6th Inning
Boston
1 DiMaggio lined to first.
Williams singled to right-center.
2 York flied to center.
3 Doerr fouled to Kurowski.
St. Louis
1 Pollet fouled to Wagner.
Schoendienst singled beyond second.
2 Moore grounded to second, moving Schoendienst to second.
Musial doubled off the right field wall, scoring Schoendienst and took third on McBride's bad throw to the infield (McBride charged with an error).

6th Inning (continued)
Slaughter got an intentional pass.
Kurowski hit by a pitched ball to load the bases.
3 Garagiola struck out.

7th Inning
Boston
1 Higgins grounded to short.
2 Wagner grounded to second.
Hughson walked.
3 McBride grounded to second.
St. Louis
Walker walked.
1 Marion sacrificed Walker to second, Wagner to Doerr who covered first.
2 Pollet took a called third strike.
Schoendienst beat out an infield hit to the left of the mound, sending Walker to third.
Schoendienst stole second.
3 Moore flied to left.

8th Inning
Boston
1 Pesky flied to right.
DiMaggio singled to center but was out
2 trying to stretch the hit to a double, Moore to Schoendienst.
Williams walked.
3 York fouled to Garagiola.
St. Louis
1 Musial grounded to first.
2 Slaughter popped to third.
Kurowski singled past third.
Garagiola got a double when DiMaggio lost the ball in the sun with Kurowski scoring, but Garagiola was
3 out trying for three bases, DiMaggio to Pesky to Higgins.

9th Inning
Boston
1 Doerr fanned.
Higgins singled to left.
Gutteridge ran for Higgins.
Russell, pinch-hitting for Wagner, singled to center, moving Gutteridge to third.
2 Partee, pinch-hitting for Hughson, struck out.
McBride singled between short and third, scoring Gutteridge and Russell going to second.
3 Pesky flied to right.
St. Louis
For Boston—Johnson pitching, Partee catching, Russell playing third.
1 Dusak, batting for Walker, flied to left.
2 Marion fanned.
3 Pollet bunted back to the pitcher.

10th Inning
Boston
For St. Louis—Dusak playing left field.
1 DiMaggio grounded to short.
2 Williams fouled to Musial.
York homered into the left field bleachers.
Doerr singled to center.
3 Johnson forced Doerr at second, Schoendienst to Marion.
St. Louis
Schoendienst safe at first on Pesky's boot of his grounder.
1 Moore sacrificed Schoendienst to second, Johnson to Doerr.
For Boston—Moses in left field.
2 Musial grounded to second, moving Schoendienst to third.
3 Slaughter flied to right.

1946

Game 2 October 7 at St. Louis

Boston	Pos	AB	R	H	RBI	PO	A	E
McBride	rf	4	0	1	0	3	0	0
Pesky	ss	4	0	0	0	3	2	0
DiMaggio	cf	4	0	1	0	3	0	0
Williams	lf	4	0	0	0	1	0	0
York	1b	2	0	0	0	6	2	0
Doerr	2b	4	0	1	0	4	5	0
Higgins	3b	2	0	0	0	0	2	1
Partee	c	2	0	0	0	1	0	0
Wagner	c	1	0	0	0	2	0	0
Harris	p	2	0	1	0	1	0	0
a Culberson		1	0	0	0	0	0	0
Dobson	p	0	0	0	0	0	0	0
Totals		30	0	4	0	24	11	1

a Flied out for Harris in 8th.
b Grounded out for Dusak in 8th.

Doubles—Dusak, Rice. Sacrifice Hit—Schoendienst. Double Play—Marion to Musial. Left on Bases—Boston 6, St. Louis 7. Umpires—Hubbard, Barlick, Berry, Ballanfant. Attendance—35,815. Time of Game—1:56.

Bos.	000	000	000
St L.	001	020	00x

St. Louis	Pos	AB	R	H	RBI	PO	A	E
Schoendienst	2b	3	0	1	0	2	3	0
Moore	cf	3	1	0	0	3	0	0
Musial	1b	4	0	0	1	11	0	0
Kurowski	3b	4	0	1	0	1	1	0
Slaughter	rf	4	0	0	0	2	0	0
Dusak	lf	2	0	1	0	1	0	0
b Sisler		1	0	0	0	0	0	0
Walker	lf	0	0	0	0	1	0	0
Marion	ss	4	0	0	0	2	6	0
Rice	c	2	2	2	0	4	0	0
Brecheen	p	3	1	1	1	0	0	0
Totals		30	3	6	3	27	10	0

Pitching	IP	H	R	ER	BB	SO
Boston						
Harris (L)	7	6	3	2	3	3
Dobson	1	0	0	0	0	0
St. Louis						
Brecheen (W)	9	4	0	0	3	4

1st Inning
Boston
McBride singled to right.
1 Pesky called out on strikes.
2,3 DiMaggio grounded into a double play, Marion to Musial.
St. Louis
1 Schoendienst flied to center.
2 Moore popped to short.
3 Musial grounded to second.

2nd Inning
Boston
1 Williams grounded to first.
York walked.
2 Doerr grounded to second, moving York to second.
Higgins got an intentional walk.
3 Partee grounded to second.
St. Louis
Kurowski singled to left-center.
1 Slaughter popped to short.
2 Dusak fanned.
3 Marion forced Kurowski at second, Higgins to Doerr.

3rd Inning
Boston
1 Harris took a called third strike.
2 McBride grounded to short.
3 Pesky grounded to second.
St. Louis
Rice doubled to left.
Brecheen singled to right, scoring Rice.
1 Schoendienst sacrificed Brecheen to second, York to Doerr.
2 Moore grounded to third, Brecheen going to third.
3 Musial flied to center.

4th Inning
Boston
1 DiMaggio flied to center.
2 Williams fanned but Rice had to tag him out as he dropped the third strike.
York walked.
Doerr singled to right, York stopping at second.
3 Higgins forced Doerr at second, Marion to Schoendienst.
St. Louis
1 Kurowski flied to center.
2 Slaughter fouled to Doerr.
Dusak walked.
3 Marion flied to right.

5th Inning
Boston
1 Partee popped to third.
Harris singled to center.
2 McBride flied to center.
3 Pesky grounded to first.

5th Inning (continued)
St. Louis
Rice singled to left-center.
Brecheen bunted and when Higgins made a poor throw to second to get the force, Rice went to third and Brecheen got to second.
1 Schoendienst grounded to second with both runners holding their bases.
Moore singled off Doerr's glove scoring Rice and sending Brecheen to third.
2 Musial forced Moore at second, Doerr to Pesky, Brecheen scoring.
3 Kurowski grounded to short.

6th Inning
Boston
1 DiMaggio grounded to short.
2 Williams lined to second.
3 York grounded to third.
St. Louis
1 Slaughter grounded out, York to Harris.
Dusak doubled off the right field wall.
For Boston—Wagner catching (Partee got a finger injury).
2 Marion flied to right.
Rice got an intentional pass.
3 Brecheen fanned.

7th Inning
Boston
1 Doerr flied to left.
2 Higgins grounded to short.
3 Wagner took a called third strike.
St. Louis
1 Schoendienst grounded to short.
Moore walked.
2 Musial called out on strikes.
3 Kurowski flied to left.

8th Inning
Boston
1 Culberson, pinch-hitting for Harris, flied to right.
2 McBride flied to center.
3 Pesky grounded to short.
St. Louis
For Boston—Dobson pitching.
1 Slaughter flied to right.
2 Sisler, batting for Dusak, grounded to second.
3 Marion grounded to second.

9th Inning
Boston
For St. Louis—Walker playing left field.
DiMaggio singled down the third base line.
1 Williams fouled to Marion.
2 York flied to right.
3 Doerr flied to left.

Game 3 October 9 at Boston

St. Louis	Pos	AB	R	H	RBI	PO	A	E
Schoendienst	2b	4	0	0	0	3	2	1
Moore	cf	4	0	0	1	1	0	0
Musial	1b	3	0	1	0	8	1	0
Slaughter	rf	4	0	0	0	4	0	0
Kurowski	3b	3	0	0	0	1	0	0
Garagiola	c	3	0	1	0	3	1	0
Walker	lf	3	0	1	0	2	0	0
Marion	ss	3	0	1	0	2	3	0
Dickson	p	2	0	1	0	0	2	0
a Sisler		1	0	0	0	0	0	0
Wilks	p	0	0	0	0	0	1	0
Totals		30	0	6	0	24	10	1

a Hit into force play for Dickson in 8th.

Doubles—Dickson, DiMaggio, Doerr. Triple—Musial. Home Run—York. Stolen Base—Musial. Sacrifice Hit—Wagner. Double Plays—DiMaggio to Pesky, Pesky to Doerr to York. Left on Bases—St. Louis 4, Boston 8. Passed Ball—Garagiola. Umpires—Barlick, Berry, Ballanfant, Hubbard. Attendance—34,500. Time of Game—1:54.

St L.	000	000	000
Bos.	300	000	01x

Boston	Pos	AB	R	H	RBI	PO	A	E
Moses	rf	3	0	0	0	2	0	0
Pesky	ss	4	1	2	0	1	3	0
DiMaggio	cf	4	0	1	0	4	1	0
Williams	lf	3	1	1	0	2	0	0
York	1b	4	2	2	3	1	2	0
Doerr	2b	4	0	2	0	2	8	0
Higgins	3b	3	0	0	0	3	0	0
Wagner	c	3	0	0	0	3	0	0
Ferriss	p	4	0	0	0	0	3	0
Totals		32	4	8	3	27	15	0

Pitching	IP	H	R	ER	BB	SO
St. Louis						
Dickson (L)	7	6	3	3	3	4
Wilks	1	2	1	0	0	0
Boston						
Ferriss (W)	9	6	0	0	1	2

1st Inning
St. Louis
1 Schoendienst grounded to the pitcher.
2 Moore rolled to second.
Musial walked.
Musial stole second.
3 Musial taking a big lead off second was trapped, Ferriss to Higgins.
Boston
1 Moses flied to center.
Pesky singled just inside third.
2 DiMaggio grounded to first and Pesky went to second.
Williams given an intentional pass.
On a 3-2 count York hit a three-run homer over the left field wall.
3 Doerr fanned.

2nd Inning
St. Louis
1 Slaughter grounded to short.
2 Kurowski grounded to second.
3 Garagiola grounded to first.
Boston
Higgins walked.
Higgins to second on a passed ball.
1 Wagner sacrificed Higgins to third, Musial to Schoendienst.
2 Ferris fanned.
3 Moses grounded to second.

3rd Inning
St. Louis
1 Walker flied to right.
Marion singled to short.
2 Dickson flied to center.
3 Schoendienst flied to right.
Boston
1 Pesky lined to right.
2 DiMaggio grounded to short.
Williams bunted down the third base line and into left against the shift.
3 York forced Williams at second, Marion to Schoendienst.

4th Inning
St. Louis
1 Moore grounded to second.
2 Musial grounded to second.
3 Slaughter fouled to Wagner.
Boston
Doerr got a Texas League single over second.
1 Higgins grounded back to the mound, Doerr going to second.
2 Wagner popped to second.
3 Ferriss flied to right.

5th Inning
St. Louis
1 Kurowski flied to left.
Garagiola singled to right.
2 Walker flied to left.
3 Marion grounded to second.
Boston
1 Moses struck out but had to be thrown out at first, Garagiola dropping the third strike.
2 Pesky grounded back to the pitcher.
DiMaggio doubled to left.
3 Williams fanned.

6th Inning
St. Louis
Dickson doubled to left.
1,2 Schoendienst flied to short center where DiMaggio made a shoe-string catch and threw to Pesky to get Dickson in a double play.
3 Moore fanned.
Boston
1 York grounded to short.
2 Doerr popped to short.
3 Higgins popped to third.

7th Inning
St. Louis
1 Musial rolled to second.
Slaughter singled to right.
2,3 Kurowski hit into a double play, Pesky to Doerr to York.
Boston
1 Wagner flied to center.
2 Ferriss flied to left.
Moses walked.
Pesky singled to left, Moses to third.
3 DiMaggio flied to right.

8th Inning
St. Louis
1 Garagiola grounded back to the mound.
Walker singled to right.
2 Marion flied to center.
3 Sisler, pinch-hitting for Dickson, forced Walker, Pesky to Doerr.
Boston
For St. Louis—Wilks pitching.
1 Williams lined to right.
York singled to center.
Doerr doubled off the wall in left-center.
2 Higgins grounded back to the mound.
Wagner safely to first as Schoendienst bobbled his bouncer, allowing York to score and Doerr to go to third.
3 Ferriss forced Wagner at second, Schoendienst to Marion.

9th Inning
St. Louis
1 Schoendienst grounded to second.
2 Moore flied to center.
Musial tripled off the right field wall.
3 Slaughter fanned.

Game 4 October 10 at Boston

St. L.	0 3 3	0 1 0	1 0 4						
Bos.	0 0 0	1 0 0	0 2 0						

St. Louis	Pos	AB	R	H	RBI	PO	A	E
Schoendienst	2b	6	1	1	0	1	4	0
Moore	cf	4	1	1	0	3	0	0
Musial	1b	5	1	1	2	6	1	0
Slaughter	rf	6	4	4	1	5	1	0
Kurowski	3b	5	2	4	1	2	0	0
Garagiola	c	5	1	4	3	4	0	0
Walker	lf	2	1	1	1	3	0	0
Marion	ss	4	1	3	3	2	1	1
Munger	p	4	0	1	0	1	0	0
Totals		41	12	20	11	27	7	1

Pitching	IP	H	R	ER	BB	SO
St. Louis						
Munger (W)	9	9	3	1	3	2
Boston						
Hughson (L)	*2	5	6	2	0	1
Bagby	3	6	1	1	1	1
Zuber	2	3	1	1	1	1
Brown	**1	4	3	3	1	0
Ryba	$\frac{2}{3}$	2	1	1	1	0
Dreisewerd	$\frac{1}{3}$	0	0	0	0	0

*Faced 3 batters in 3rd.
**Faced 3 batters in 9th.

Boston	Pos	AB	R	H	RBI	PO	A	E
Moses	rf	5	0	4	0	1	0	0
Pesky	ss	5	0	0	0	3	2	1
DiMaggio	cf	4	1	0	0	3	1	0
Williams	lf	3	1	1	0	0	1	0
York	1b	3	0	1	1	9	1	0
Doerr	2b	3	1	2	2	4	6	0
Gutteridge	2b	0	0	0	0	0	0	0
Higgins	3b	4	0	1	0	2	1	1
Wagner	c	4	0	0	0	5	1	0
Hughson	p	0	0	0	0	0	0	1
Bagby	p	1	0	0	0	0	1	0
a Metkovich		1	0	0	0	0	0	0
Zuber	p	0	0	0	0	0	0	0
b McBride		1	0	0	0	0	0	0
Brown	p	0	0	0	0	0	0	0
Ryba	p	0	0	0	0	0	0	1
Dreisewerd	p	0	0	0	0	0	0	0
c Culberson		1	0	0	0	0	0	0
Totals		35	3	9	3	27	14	4

a Flied out for Bagby in 5th.
b Grounded out for Zuber in 7th.
c Lined out for Dreisewerd in 9th.

Doubles—Garagiola, Kurowski 2, Marion, Musial, Slaughter, York. Home Runs—Doerr, Slaughter. Sacrifice Hits—Marion, Moore, Munger, Walker. Double Plays—Slaughter to Garagiola, Doerr to Pesky to York, Schoendienst to Musial, Pesky to Doerr. Left on Bases—St. Louis 10, Boston 8. Umpires—Berry, Ballanfant, Hubbard, Barlick. Attendance—35,645. Time of Game—2:31.

1st Inning
St. Louis
1 Schoendienst grounded to first.
2 Moore popped to second.
3 Musial grounded to second.
Boston
1 Moses flied to center.
2 Pesky flied to left.
3 DiMaggio flied to right.

2nd Inning
St. Louis
Slaughter homered into the right field seats.
Kurowski doubled off the left field wall.
1 Garagiola flied to center.
Walker singled to right, scoring Kurowski.
Walker was apparently trapped trying to steal second but while scampering back to first Pesky threw wild into the Red Sox dugout and Walker was allowed to go to third on the error.
2 Marion put down a beautiful squeeze bunt, Doerr to York and Walker scored.
3 Munger fanned.
Boston
Williams walked.
1 York flied to center.
2 Doerr flied to right.
3 Higgins flied to right.

3rd Inning
St. Louis
Schoendienst singled to center.
Moore sacrificed but when Hughson threw wild to first, Schoendienst went to third and Moore to second.
Musial doubled to right-center, scoring Schoendienst and Moore.
For Boston—Bagby pitching.
1 Slaughter grounded to second, Musial going to third.
2 Kurowski fouled to York.
Garagiola singled to center, scoring Musial.
3 Walker fanned.
Boston
1 Wagner grounded to second.
2 Bagby flied to center.
Moses singled to right.
3 Pesky fanned.

4th Inning
St. Louis
Marion singled to left.
1 Munger sacrificed Marion to second, Bagby to Doerr.
2 Schoendienst flied to center.
3 Moore flied to center.
Boston
1 DiMaggio grounded to second.
Williams singled to right.
York doubled to center, scoring Williams.
Doerr walked.
2 Higgins flied to left.
3 Wagner flied to right.

5th Inning
St. Louis
1 Musial lined to third.
Slaughter doubled off the left field wall.
Kurowski also doubled off the left field wall, scoring Slaughter.
Garagiola singled to center, but as
2 Kurowski tried to score he was thrown out at the plate, DiMaggio to Wagner.
On the play Garagiola went to second.
Walker given an intentional pass.
Marion singled to left and Garagiola
3 was out at the plate, Williams to Wagner.
Boston
1 Metkovich, batting for Bagby, flied to left.
Moses singled to center.
2 Pesky lined to first.
3 DiMaggio popped to short.

6th Inning
St. Louis
For Boston—Zuber pitching.
1 Munger called out on strikes.
2 Schoendienst fouled to Higgins.
3 Moore flied to right.
Boston
1 Williams grounded to second.
York walked.
Doerr singled to left, York to second.
Higgins singled past third, bases loaded.
2,3 Wagner flied to Slaughter who threw to Garagiola getting York attempting to score.

7th Inning
St. Louis
1 Musial grounded to second.
Slaughter singled to center.
Kurowski singled to left.
Garagiola doubled to left, Slaughter scoring and Kurowski going to third.
Walker intentionally passed to load the bases.
2,3 Marion hit into a double play, Doerr to Pesky to York.
Boston
1 McBride, pinch-hitting for Zuber, grounded to short.
Moses singled to right.
2,3 Pesky lined into a double play, Schoendienst to Musial.

8th Inning
St. Louis
For Boston—Brown pitching.
Munger singled past second.
1 Schoendienst forced Munger on an attempted sacrifice, Wagner to Pesky.
Moore walked.
2,3 Musial lined into a double play, Pesky to Doerr doubling Schoendienst.
Boston
DiMaggio safe on Marion's fumble.
1 Williams grounded to third.
2 York fanned.
Doerr hit a two-run homer over the left field fence.
3 Higgins fouled to Garagiola.

9th Inning
St. Louis
Slaughter singled to center.
Kurowski singled on a bunt to third, and Slaughter got to third on Higgins' bad throw to first, for an error.
Garagiola singled to right, scoring Slaughter with Kurowski to second.
For Boston—Ryba pitching.
1 Walker sacrificed, Higgins to Doerr, both runners advancing.
Marion doubled to left, scoring Kurowski and Garagiola.
2 Munger grounded to second with Marion advancing to third.
Schoendienst safe at first and Marion scoring when Ryba taking Doerr's throw failed to touch the bag for an error.
For Boston—Gutteridge playing second.
Moore singled to center.
Musial walked loading the bases.
For Boston—Dreisewerd pitching.
3 Slaughter popped to first.
Boston
1 Wagner popped to short.
2 Culberson, pinch-hitting for Dreisewerd, lined to third.
Moses singled to first.
3 Pesky grounded out, Musial to Munger.

Game 5 October 11 at Boston

St L.	0 1 0	0 0 0	0 0 2						
Bos.	1 1 0	0 0 1	3 0 x						

St. Louis	Pos	AB	R	H	RBI	PO	A	E
Schoendienst	2b	4	0	1	0	3	1	0
Moore	cf	4	0	0	0	2	0	0
Musial	1b	3	1	1	0	7	0	0
Slaughter	rf	2	0	0	0	0	0	0
Dusak	lf	1	0	0	0	0	0	0
Kurowski	3b	4	1	0	0	3	1	0
Garagiola	c	4	1	0	0	7	1	0
Walker	lf-rf	4	0	2	3	1	0	0
Marion	ss	4	0	0	0	1	7	1
Pollet	p	0	0	0	0	0	0	0
Brazle	p	2	0	0	0	0	1	0
a Jones		1	0	0	0	0	0	0
Beazley	p	0	0	0	0	0	1	0
Totals		33	3	4	3	24	12	1

a Fanned for Brazle in 8th.

Boston	Pos	AB	R	H	RBI	PO	A	E
Gutteridge	2b	5	0	2	1	0	2	0
Pesky	ss	5	1	3	0	2	2	2
DiMaggio	cf	3	1	1	0	3	0	0
Williams	lf	5	0	1	1	4	0	0
York	1b	2	1	0	0	8	0	1
Higgins	3b	4	1	1	1	0	1	0
Culberson	rf	3	1	2	1	2	0	0
Partee	c	3	1	1	1	8	1	0
Dobson	p	3	0	0	0	0	1	0
Totals		33	6	11	5	27	7	3

Pitching	IP	H	R	ER	BB	SO
St. Louis						
Pollet	$\frac{1}{3}$	3	1	1	0	0
Brazle (L)	$6\frac{2}{3}$	7	5	4	6	4
Beazley	1	1	0	0	0	1
Boston						
Dobson (W)	9	4	3	0	1	8

Doubles—DiMaggio, Higgins, Musial, Walker. Home Run—Culberson. Stolen Bases—Culberson, Pesky, Slaughter. Sacrifice Hits—DiMaggio, Dobson. Double Plays—Partee to Pesky, Marion to Schoendienst to Musial. Hit by Pitcher—Slaughter (by Dobson). Wild Pitch—Beazley. Left on Bases—St. Louis 5, Boston 11. Umpires—Ballanfant, Hubbard, Barlick, Berry. Attendance—35,982. Time of Game—2:23.

1st Inning
St. Louis
Schoendienst singled to right.
1,2 Moore fanned and Schoendienst was doubled trying to steal second, Partee to Pesky.
3 Musial flied to left.
Boston
Gutteridge singled off Musial's glove.
Pesky singled to right, Gutteridge stopping at second.
1 DiMaggio forced Gutteridge at third, Kurowski unassisted.
Williams singled to right, scoring Pesky and DiMaggio going to third, as Williams took second on the throw to the plate.
For St. Louis—Brazle pitching.
York intentionally walked, filling the bases.
2 Higgins forced DiMaggio at the plate, Kurowski to Garagiola.
3 Culberson forced Higgins at second, Marion to Schoendienst.

2nd Inning
St. Louis
1 Slaughter grounded to second.
2 Kurowski popped to first.
Garagiola went all the way to second when his grounder went through Pesky's legs for a two-base error.
Walker doubled to left, scoring Garagiola.
3 Marion flied to right.
Boston
Partee singled over second.
Dobson sacrificed and was safe when Kurowski went for the force at second and Partee beat the throw.
Gutteridge singled to center, scoring Partee with Dobson going to second.
1 Pesky forced Dobson at third, Brazle to Kurowski.
2,3 DiMaggio grounded into a double play, Marion to Schoendienst to Musial.

3rd Inning
St. Louis
1 Brazle flied to center.
2 Schoendienst grounded to short.
3 Moore fanned.
Boston
1 Williams grounded to short.
2 York popped to short.
3 Higgins lined to left.

4th Inning
St. Louis
1 Musial flied to right.
Slaughter was hit by a pitched ball.
2 Kurowski fanned.
Slaughter stole second.
3 Garagiola struck out.
Boston
Culberson singled to right.
Culberson stole second.
1 Partee flied to center.
2 Dobson grounded to short, Culberson advancing to third.
3 Gutteridge grounded to short.

5th Inning
St. Louis
1 Walker bunted out to third.
2 Marion flied to left.
3 Brazle flied to center.
Boston
Pesky singled to center.
Pesky stole second.
DiMaggio walked.
1 Williams struck out.
On an attempted double steal, Pesky
2 was out at third, Garagiola to Kurowski with DiMaggio getting to second.
York intentionally walked.
3 Higgins bounced out to short.

6th Inning
St. Louis
1 Schoendienst grounded to second.
2 Moore flied to left.
Musial doubled to right-center.
3 Slaughter flied to center.
Boston
Culberson homered into the left field screen.
Partee walked.
1 Dobson fanned, but had to be tagged out by Garagiola.
2 Gutteridge forced Partee at second, Marion to Schoendienst.
3 Pesky fouled to Musial.

7th Inning
St. Louis
1 Kurowski was out swinging.
2 Garagiola grounded to first.
Walker safe at first on York's error, dropping Dobson's throw.
3 Marion flied to center.
Boston
For St. Louis—Dusak playing left field and Walker moving to right field.
DiMaggio doubled to left.
1 Williams called out on strikes.
York got his third intentional walk.
Higgins doubled to left-center, scoring DiMaggio and moving York to third.
Culberson also got an intentional pass to load the bases.
Partee grounded to Marion who threw wildly to second, York and Higgins scoring with Culberson ending up on third and Partee on second.
2 Dobson struck out.
3 Gutteridge flied to center.

8th Inning
St. Louis
1 Jones, pinch-hitting for Brazle, struck out.
2 Schoendienst struck out.
3 Moore grounded to short.
Boston
For St. Louis—Beazley pitching.
Pesky singled on a hit to short.
1 DiMaggio sacrificed, Beazley to Musial.
2 Williams fouled to Garagiola.
Pesky to third on a wild pitch.
3 York fanned.

9th Inning
St. Louis
Musial walked.
1 Dusak fanned.
Kurowski safe at first on Pesky's fumble.
2 Garagiola grounded to short, both runners advancing.
Walker singled to right, scoring Musial and Kurowski.
3 Marion popped to short.

Game 6 October 13 at St. Louis

Boston	Pos	AB	R	H	RBI	PO	A	E
Culberson	rf	4	0	0	0	5	0	0
Pesky	ss	3	0	1	0	2	3	0
DiMaggio	cf	4	0	1	0	5	0	0
Williams	lf	3	0	1	0	2	0	0
York	1b	4	1	1	0	4	0	0
Doerr	2b	3	0	1	1	1	1	0
Higgins	3b	3	0	1	0	1	1	0
Partee	c	3	0	0	0	4	0	0
Harris	p	1	0	0	0	0	0	0
Hughson	p	1	0	1	0	0	0	0
a McBride		1	0	0	0	0	0	0
Johnson	p	0	0	0	0	0	0	0
Totals		30	1	7	1	24	5	0

a Fouled out for Hughson in 8th.
b Lined out for Dusak in 3rd.

Doubles—Marion, Schoendienst. Triple—York. Double Plays—Kurowski to Schoendienst to Musial 2, Brecheen to Schoendienst to Marion to Musial. Left on Bases—Boston 4, St. Louis 8. Umpires—Hubbard, Barlick, Berry, Ballanfant. Attendance—35,768. Time of Game—1:56.

Bos.	000	000	100
St L.	003	000	01x

St. Louis	Pos	AB	R	H	RBI	PO	A	E
Schoendienst	2b	4	1	1	0	4	3	0
Moore	cf	4	0	1	1	2	0	0
Musial	1b	4	1	1	0	9	0	0
Kurowski	3b	4	0	1	1	2	2	0
Slaughter	rf	2	0	1	1	2	0	0
Dusak	lf	0	0	0	0	0	1	0
b Walker	lf	3	1	0	0	1	0	0
Marion	ss	4	0	2	1	2	1	0
Rice	c	3	0	1	0	5	1	0
Brecheen	p	4	1	0	0	0	2	0
Totals		32	4	8	4	27	10	0

Pitching	IP	H	R	ER	BB	SO
Boston						
Harris (L)	2⅔	5	3	3	1	2
Hughson	4⅓	2	0	0	1	2
Johnson	1	1	1	1	2	0
St. Louis						
Brecheen (W)	9	7	1	1	2	6

1st Inning
Boston
1 Culberson fanned.
Pesky singled to right.
DiMaggio singled to left.
Williams walked, loading the bases.
2,3 York hit into a double play, Kurowski to Schoendienst to Musial.
St. Louis
1 Schoendienst fouled to Higgins.
2 Moore fanned.
3 Musial grounded to short.

2nd Inning
Boston
Doerr singled off Kurowski's glove.
Higgins singled to left as Doerr was
1 caught at third Dusak to Kurowski
2 Partee fanned.
3 Harris flied to center.
St. Louis
1 Kurowski flied to left.
2 Slaughter struck out.
Dusak walked.
3 Marion flied to right.

3rd Inning
Boston
1 Culberson grounded to the mound.
2 Pesky fouled to Kurowski.
3 DiMaggio fanned but had to be thrown out at first Rice to Musial.
St. Louis
Rice singled over Pesky's head.
1 Brecheen forced Rice in an attempted sacrifice, Higgins to Pesky.
Schoendienst doubled inside the first base line, advancing Brecheen to third.
2 Moore flied to right, Brecheen scoring after the catch.
Musial singled between short and third, Schoendienst going to third.
Kurowski singled to left, scoring Schoendienst with Musial stopping at second.
Slaughter singled to center, Musial scoring and Kurowski going to third.
For Boston—Hughson pitching.
3 Walker, pinch-hitting for Dusak, flied to DiMaggio, who made a great shoestring catch to rob Walker of a hit.

4th Inning
Boston
For St. Louis—Walker playing left field.
1 Williams popped to first.
2 York popped to second.
3 Doerr popped to first.
St. Louis
1 Marion lined to right.
2 Rice flied to center.
3 Brecheen fouled to Pesky.

5th Inning
Boston
1 Higgins popped to short.
2 Partee flied to right.
Hughson singled to right.
3 Culberson flied to right.
St. Louis
1 Schoendienst grounded to second.
2 Moore struck out.
3 Musial also whiffed.

6th Inning
Boston
Pesky walked.
1,2 DiMaggio grounded into a double play, Kurowski to Schoendienst to Musial.
3 Williams fanned.
St. Louis
1 Kurowski fouled to Culberson.
Slaughter walked.
2 Walker flied to center.
Marion singled to center, Slaughter stopping at second.
3 Rice flied to deep center.

7th Inning
Boston
York tripled against the center field wall.
1 Doerr flied to left, York scoring after the catch.
2 Higgins fouled to Musial.
3 Partee popped to second.
St. Louis
1 Brecheen grounded to short.
2 Schoendienst flied to right.
Moore singled to center.
3 Musial flied to left.

8th Inning
Boston
1 McBride, pinch-hitting for Hughson, fouled to Musial.
2 Culberson struck out.
3 Pesky also struck out.
St. Louis
For Boston—Johnson pitching.
1 Kurowski flied to center.
Slaughter walked.
2 Walker forced Slaughter at second, Pesky to Doerr.
Marion doubled over York's head, scoring Walker.
Rice given an intentional pass.
3 Brecheen grounded to first.

9th Inning
Boston
1 DiMaggio lined to center.
Williams singled between second and short.
2,3 York's grounder was deflected by Brecheen to Schoendienst, who threw to Marion for the force and he relayed to Musial to get York in a double play.

Game 7 October 15 at St. Louis

Boston	Pos	AB	R	H	RBI	PO	A	E
Moses	rf	4	1	1	0	1	0	0
Pesky	ss	4	0	1	0	2	1	0
DiMaggio	cf	3	0	1	3	0	0	0
Culberson	cf	0	0	0	0	0	0	0
Williams	lf	4	0	0	0	3	1	0
York	1b	4	0	1	0	10	1	0
c Campbell		0	0	0	0	0	0	0
Doerr	2b	4	0	2	0	3	7	0
Higgins	3b	4	0	0	0	0	1	0
Wagner	c	2	0	0	0	4	0	0
a Russell		1	1	1	0	0	0	0
Partee	c	1	0	0	0	0	0	0
Ferriss	p	2	0	0	0	0	0	0
Dobson	p	0	0	0	0	0	1	0
b Metkovich		1	1	1	0	0	0	0
Klinger	p	0	0	0	0	1	0	0
Johnson	p	0	0	0	0	0	0	0
d McBride		1	0	0	0	0	0	0
Totals		35	3	8	3	24	12	0

a Singled for Wagner in 8th.
b Doubled for Dobson in 8th.
c Ran for York in 9th.
d Grounded out for Johnson in 9th.

Doubles—Dickson, DiMaggio, Kurowski, Metkovich, Musial, Walker. Sacrifice Hit—Marion. Left on Bases—Boston 3, St. Louis 4. Umpires—Barlick, Berry, Ballanfant, Hubbard. Attendance—36,143. Time of Game—2:17.

Bos.	100	000	020
St L.	010	020	01x

St. Louis	Pos	AB	R	H	RBI	PO	A	E
Schoendienst	2b	4	0	2	1	2	3	0
Moore	cf	4	0	1	0	3	0	0
Musial	1b	3	0	1	0	6	0	0
Slaughter	rf	3	1	1	0	4	0	0
Kurowski	3b	4	1	1	0	3	1	1
Garagiola	c	3	0	0	0	4	0	0
Rice	c	1	0	0	0	0	0	0
Walker	lf	3	1	2	2	3	0	0
Marion	ss	2	0	0	0	2	1	0
Dickson	p	3	1	1	1	0	1	0
Brecheen	p	1	0	0	0	0	0	0
Totals		31	4	9	4	27	6	1

Pitching	IP	H	R	ER	BB	SO
Boston						
Ferriss	4⅓	7	3	4	1	2
Dobson	2⅔	0	0	0	2	2
Klinger (L)	⅔	2	1	1	1	0
Johnson	⅓	0	0	0	0	0
St. Louis						
Dickson	*7	5	3	3	1	3
Brecheen (W)	2	3	0	0	0	1

*Faced 2 batters in 8th.

1st Inning
Boston
Moses singled to center.
Pesky singled over second, Moses to third.
1 DiMaggio flied to right, Moses scoring after the catch.
2 Williams flied to Moore in deep right-center.
3 York popped to second.
St. Louis
Schoendienst singled to left but was
1 out trying for a double, Williams to Pesky.
2 Moore popped to first.
Musial doubled to left.
3 Slaughter fanned.

2nd Inning
Boston
Doerr singled on a high bouncer to Kurowski and went to second on his bad throw to first.
1 Higgins grounded to second, Doerr moving to third.
2 Wagner flied to left.
3 Ferriss flied to left.
St. Louis
Kurowski doubled to left-center.
1 Garagiola grounded to second, sending Kurowski to third.
2 Walker lined to left, Kurowski scoring after the catch.
3 Marion grounded to second.

3rd Inning
Boston
1 Moses fouled to Kurowski.
2 Pesky grounded to second.
3 DiMaggio fanned.
St. Louis
1 Dickson struck out.
2 Schoendienst grounded to short.
3 Moore flied to left.

4th Inning
Boston
1 Williams flied to Walker in deep center.
2 York fanned.
3 Doerr flied to right.
St. Louis
Musial walked.
1 Slaughter fouled to short.
2 Kurowski flied to right.
3 Garagiola grounded to second.

5th Inning
Boston
1 Higgins flied to Moore who made a great catch near the wall.
2 Wagner fouled to Kurowski.
3 Ferriss grounded to the pitcher.
St. Louis
Walker singled past short.
1 Marion sacrificed Walker to second, York to Doerr.
Dickson doubled over third, Walker scoring.
Schoendienst singled over second, scoring Dickson.

5th Inning (continued)
Moore singled to center with Schoendienst stopping at second.
For Boston—Dobson pitching.
2 Musial grounded to second, advancing both runners.
Slaughter give an intentional pass to load the bases.
3 Kurowski forced Slaughter at second, Higgins to Doerr.

6th Inning
Boston
1 Moses grounded to first.
2 Pesky lined to third.
DiMaggio walked.
3 Williams flied to right.
St. Louis
1 Garagiola fanned.
Walker walked.
2 Marion grounded to second.
3 Dickson grounded to second.

7th Inning
Boston
1 York struck out.
2 Doerr flied to center.
3 Higgins grounded to short.
St. Louis
1 Schoendienst fanned.
2 Moore flied to Doerr who collided with Moses, but held the ball.
3 Musial grounded to the mound.

8th Inning
Boston
Russell, batting for Wagner, singled.
Metkovich, pinch-hitting for Dobson, doubled to left, moving Russell to third.
For St. Louis—Brecheen pitching.
1 Moses fanned.
2 Pesky lined to right.
DiMaggio doubled off the right-center field wall, scoring Russell and Metkovich.
Culberson ran for DiMaggio who twisted his ankle.
For St. Louis—Rice catching as Garagiola split his finger on a Williams' foul tip.
3 Williams popped to second.
St. Louis
For Boston—Klinger pitching, Partee catching and Culberson in center field.
Slaughter singled to center.
1 Kurowski popped to Klinger on an attempted sacrifice.
2 Rice flied to left.
Walker lined over Pesky's head and Slaughter scored as Pesky hesitated in relaying Culberson's throw to the plate. Walker on second with a double.
Marion intentionally walked.
For Boston—Johnson pitching.
3 Brecheen grounded to second.

9th Inning
Boston
York singled to left.
Campbell ran for York.
Doerr singled to short.
1 Higgins forced Doerr at second, Kurowski to Marion, Campbell to third.
2 Partee fouled to Musial.
3 McBride, pinch-hitting for Johnson, forced Higgins at second, Schoendienst to Marion.

1946 WORLD SERIES COMPOSITE BOX

	Wins	Composite Line Score										
St. Louis Cardinals (N.L.)	4	0	5	7	0	5	1	1	3	6	0	– 28
Boston Red Sox (A.L.)	3	5	2	0	1	0	1	4	5	1	1	– 20

Manager	W	L	Pct.	G. Ahead
Eddie Dyer	98	58	.628	Won playoff over Brooklyn
Joe Cronin	104	50	.675	12

(Regular Season)

BATTING AND FIELDING

WORLD SERIES STATISTICS

ST. LOUIS CARDINALS	Pos	G	AB	R	H	2B	3B	HR	RBI	BB	SO	SB	BA	SA	PO	A	E
Stan Musial	1b	7	27	3	6	4	1	0	4	4	2	1	.222	.444	60	2	0
Red Schoendienst	2b	7	30	3	7	1	0	0	1	0	2	1	.233	.267	17	21	1
Marty Marion	ss	7	24	1	6	2	0	0	4	1	1	0	.250	.333	12	22	2
Whitey Kurowski	3b	7	27	5	8	3	0	0	2	0	3	0	.296	.407	13	9	1
Enos Slaughter	rf	7	25	5	8	1	1	1	2	4	3	1	.320	.560	20	1	0
Terry Moore	cf	7	27	1	4	0	0	0	2	2	6	0	.148	.148	17	1	0
Harry Walker	lf-rf-ph	7	17	3	7	2	0	0	6	4	2	0	.412	.529	14	0	0
Joe Garagiola	c	5	19	2	6	2	0	0	4	0	3	0	.316	.421	22	2	0
Del Rice	c	3	6	2	3	1	0	0	0	2	0	0	.500	.667	9	1	0
Erv Dusak	ph-lf	4	4	0	1	1	0	0	0	2	2	0	.250	.500	1	1	0
Dick Sisler	ph	2	2	0	0	0	0	0	0	0	0	0	.000	.000			
Nippy Jones	ph	1	1	0	0	0	0	0	0	0	1	0	.000	.000			
Buster Adams		Did not play															
Clyde Kluttz		Did not play															
Jeff Cross		Did not play															
Bill Endicott		Did not play															
Walter Sessi		Did not play															
Harry Brecheen	p	3	8	2	1	0	0	0	1	0	1	0	.125	.250	0	2	0
Murry Dickson	p	2	5	1	2	2	0	0	1	0	1	0	.400	.800	0	3	0
George Munger	p	1	4	0	1	0	0	0	0	0	2	0	.250	.250	1	0	0
Howie Pollet	p	2	4	0	0	0	0	0	0	0	1	0	.000	.000	0	0	0
Al Brazle	p	1	2	0	0	0	0	0	0	0	0	0	.000	.000	0	1	0
Johnny Beazley	p	1	0	0	0	0	0	0	0	0	0	0	—	—	0	1	0
Ted Wilks	p	1	0	0	0	0	0	0	0	0	0	0	—	—	0	1	0
Ken Burkhart		Did not play															
Red Barrett		Did not play															
Freddy Schmidt		Did not play															
Howie Krist		Did not play															
Johnny Grodzicki		Did not play															
team totals		7	232	28	60	19	2	1	27	19	30	3	.259	.371	186	68	4

Double Plays—7
Left on Bases—50

REGULAR SEASON STATISTICS

ST. LOUIS CARDINALS		Main Pos	G	AB	R	H	2B	3B	HR	RBI	BB	SO	SB	BA	SA
Stan Musial		1b	156	624	124	228	50	20	16	103	73	31	7	.365	.587
Red Schoendienst		2b	142	606	94	170	28	5	0	34	37	27	12	.281	.343
Marty Marion		ss	146	498	51	116	29	4	3	46	59	53	1	.233	.325
Whitey Kurowski		3b	142	519	76	156	32	5	14	89	72	47	2	.301	.462
Enos Slaughter		of	156	609	100	183	30	8	18	130	69	41	9	.300	.465
Terry Moore		of	91	278	32	73	14	1	3	28	18	26	0	.263	.353
Harry Walker		of	112	346	53	82	14	6	3	27	30	29	12	.237	.338
Joe Garagiola		c	74	211	21	50	4	1	3	22	23	25	0	.237	.308
Del Rice		c	55	139	10	38	8	1	1	12	8	16	0	.273	.367
Erv Dusak		of	100	275	38	66	9	1	9	42	33	63	7	.240	.378
Dick Sisler		1b-of	83	235	17	61	11	2	3	42	14	28	0	.260	.362
Nippy Jones		2b	16	12	3	4	0	0	0	1	2	2	0	.333	.333
Buster Adams		of	81	173	21	32	6	0	5	22	29	27	3	.185	.306
Clyde Kluttz	a	c	52	136	8	36	7	0	0	14	10	10	0	.265	.316
Jeff Cross		ss	49	69	17	15	3	0	0	6	10	8	4	.217	.261
Bill Endicott		of	20	20	2	4	3	0	0	3	4	4	0	.200	.350
Walter Sessi		ph	15	14	2	2	0	0	1	2	1	4	0	.143	.357
Harry Brecheen		p	37	83	2	11	1	0	0	6	3	17	0	.133	.145
Murry Dickson		p	47	65	8	18	5	1	0	6	1	6	0	.277	.385
George Munger		p	10	16	1	4	0	0	0	3	2	3	0	.250	.250
Howie Pollet		p	40	87	2	14	4	0	0	7	6	23	0	.161	.207
Al Brazle		p	37	52	5	11	0	0	0	2	0	2	0	.212	.212
Johnny Beazley		p	19	33	2	8	1	0	0	4	2	9	0	.242	.273
Ted Wilks		p	40	24	5	5	0	0	0	1	1	5	0	.208	.208
Ken Burkhart		p	25	34	2	5	1	1	0	3	1	8	0	.147	.235
Red Barrett		p	23	17	1	1	0	0	0	1	1	4	0	.059	.059
Freddy Schmidt		p	16	1	0	0	0	0	0	0	0	1	0	.000	.000
Howie Krist		p	15	0	0	0	0	0	0	0	0	0	0	—	—
Johnny Grodzicki		p	3	0	0	0	0	0	0	0	0	0	0	—	—
team totals			156	5372	712	1426	265	56	81	665	530	537	58	.265	.381

a—from New York (N)
Lou Klein (2b), Ken O'Dea (c), Danny Litwhiler (of), Del Wilbur (c), Emil Verban (2b), Freddie Martin (p), Max Lanier (p), and Blix Donnelly (p) also played for the Cardinals during the season.

WORLD SERIES STATISTICS

BOSTON RED SOX	Pos	G	AB	R	H	2B	3B	HR	RBI	BB	SO	SB	BA	SA	PO	A	E
Rudy York	1b	7	23	6	6	1	1	2	5	6	4	0	.261	.652	59	4	1
Bobby Doerr	2b	6	22	1	9	1	0	1	3	2	2	0	.409	.591	18	31	0
Johnny Pesky	ss	7	30	2	7	0	0	0	0	1	3	1	.233	.233	13	16	4
Pinky Higgins	3b	7	24	1	5	1	0	0	2	2	0	0	.208	.250	6	6	2
Wally Moses	rf	4	12	1	5	0	0	0	0	1	2	0	.417	.417	5	0	0
Dom DiMaggio	cf	7	27	2	7	3	0	0	3	2	2	0	.259	.370	19	3	0
Ted Williams	lf	7	25	2	5	0	0	0	1	5	5	0	.200	.200	16	2	0
Hal Wagner	c	5	13	0	0	0	0	0	0	0	1	0	.000	.000	20	2	0
Tom McBride	rf-ph	5	12	0	2	0	0	0	1	0	1	0	.167	.167	4	0	1
Roy Partee	ph-c	5	10	1	1	0	0	0	1	1	2	0	.100	.100	14	1	0
Leon Culberson	rf-cf	5	9	1	2	0	0	1	1	1	2	1	.222	.556	7	0	0
Don Gutteridge	pr-2b	3	5	1	2	0	0	0	1	0	0	0	.400	.400	0	2	0
Rip Russell	ph-3b	2	2	1	2	0	0	0	0	0	0	0	1.000	1.000	0	0	0
Catfish Metkovich	ph	2	2	1	1	1	0	0	0	0	0	0	.500	1.000			
Paul Campbell	pr	1	0	0	0	0	0	0	0	0	0	0	—	—			
Johnny Lazor		Did not play															
Eddie Pellagrini		Did not play															
Ed McGah		Did not play															
Boo Ferriss	p	2	6	0	0	0	0	0	0	0	1	0	.000	.000	0	3	0
Mickey Harris	p	2	3	0	1	0	0	0	0	0	0	0	.333	.333	1	0	0
Tex Hughson	p	3	3	0	1	0	0	0	0	1	0	0	.333	.333	0	1	1
Joe Dobson	p	3	3	0	0	0	0	0	0	0	2	0	.000	.000	0	2	0
Earl Johnson	p	3	1	0	0	0	0	0	0	0	0	0	.000	.000	0	2	0
Jim Bagby	p	1	1	0	0	0	0	0	0	0	0	0	.000	.000	0	1	0
Mace Brown	p	1	0	0	0	0	0	0	0	0	0	0	—	—	0	0	0
Clem Dreisewerd	p	1	0	0	0	0	0	0	0	0	0	0	—	—	0	0	0
Bob Klinger	p	1	0	0	0	0	0	0	0	0	0	0	—	—	1	0	0
Mike Ryba	p	1	0	0	0	0	0	0	0	0	0	0	—	—	0	0	1
Bill Zuber	p	1	0	0	0	0	0	0	0	0	0	0	—	—	0	0	0
team totals		7	233	20	56	7	1	4	18	22	28	2	.240	.345	183	76	10

Double Plays—5
Left on Bases—53

REGULAR SEASON STATISTICS

BOSTON RED SOX		Main Pos	G	AB	R	H	2B	3B	HR	RBI	BB	SO	SB	BA	SA
Rudy York		1b	154	579	78	160	30	6	17	119	86	93	3	.276	.437
Bobby Doerr		2b	151	583	95	158	34	9	18	116	66	67	5	.271	.453
Johnny Pesky		ss	143	621	115	208	43	4	2	55	65	29	9	.335	.427
Pinky Higgins	b	3b	64	200	18	55	11	1	2	28	24	24	0	.275	.370
Wally Moses	c	of	48	175	13	36	11	3	2	17	14	15	2	.206	.337
Dom DiMaggio		of	142	534	85	169	24	7	7	73	66	58	10	.316	.427
Ted Williams		of	150	514	142	176	37	8	38	123	156	44	0	.342	.667
Hal Wagner		c	117	370	39	85	12	2	6	52	69	32	3	.230	.322
Tom McBride		of	61	153	21	46	5	2	0	19	9	6	0	.301	.359
Roy Partee		c	40	111	13	35	5	2	0	9	13	14	0	.315	.396
Leon Culberson		of	59	179	34	56	10	1	3	18	16	19	3	.313	.430
Don Gutteridge		2b-3b	22	47	8	11	3	0	1	6	2	7	0	.234	.632
Rip Russell		3b	80	274	22	57	10	1	6	35	13	30	1	.208	.318
Catfish Metkovich		of	86	281	42	69	15	2	4	25	36	39	8	.246	.356
Paul Campbell		1b	28	26	3	3	1	0	0	0	2	7	0	.115	.154
Johnny Lazor		of	23	29	1	4	0	0	1	4	2	11	0	.138	.241
Eddie Pellagrini		3b	22	71	7	15	3	1	2	4	3	18	1	.211	.366
Ed McGah		c	15	37	2	8	1	1	0	1	7	7	0	.216	.297
Boo Ferriss		p	45	115	12	24	6	0	0	7	7	19	0	.209	.261
Mickey Harris		p	34	78	11	18	1	0	0	5	10	21	0	.231	.244
Tex Hughson		p	39	91	5	12	1	0	0	4	8	28	0	.132	.143
Joe Dobson		p	32	50	5	5	0	0	0	2	4	28	0	.100	.100
Earl Johnson		p	29	22	4	5	2	0	0	4	4	9	0	.227	.318
Jim Bagby		p	21	42	2	5	1	0	0	2	2	9	0	.119	.143
Mace Brown		p	18	5	0	0	0	0	0	0	0	0	0	.000	.000
Clem Dreisewerd		p	20	10	0	0	0	0	0	0	1	7	0	.000	.000
Bob Klinger		p	28	16	1	5	0	0	0	2	0	2	0	.313	.313
Mike Ryba		p	9	2	0	0	0	0	0	0	0	0	0	.000	.000
Bill Zuber	d	p	15	18	1	2	0	0	0	2	1	6	0	.111	.111
team totals			156	5318	792	1441	268	50	109	736	687	661	45	.271	.402

b—from Detroit; c—from Chicago (A); d—from New York (A)
Ernie Andres (3b), Frankie Pytlak (c), Tom Carey (2b), Ben Steiner (3b), Andy Gilbert (of), Charlie Wagner (p), Bill Butland (p), Randy Heflin (p), Mel Deutsch (p), and Tim Wilson (p) also played for the Red Sox during the season.

PITCHING

WORLD SERIES STATISTICS

ST. LOUIS CARDINALS	G	GS	CG	IP	H	R	ER	BB	SO	W	L	SV	ERA
Harry Brecheen	3	2	2	20	14	1	1	5	11	3	0	0	0.45
Murry Dickson	2	2	0	14	11	6	6	4	7	0	1	0	3.86
Howie Pollet	2	2	1	10⅓	12	4	4	4	3	0	1	0	3.48
George Munger	1	1	1	9	9	3	1	3	2	1	0	0	1.00
Al Brazle	1	0	0	6⅔	7	5	4	6	4	0	1	0	5.40
Johnny Beazley	1	0	0	1	1	0	0	0	1	0	0	0	0.00
Ted Wilks	1	0	0	1	2	1	0	0	0	0	0	0	0.00
Ken Burkhart	Did not play												
Red Barrett	Did not play												
Freddie Schmidt	Did not play												
Howie Krist	Did not play												
Johnny Grodzicki	Did not play												
team totals	7	7	4	62	56	20	16	22	28	4	3	0	2.32

REGULAR SEASON STATISTICS

ST. LOUIS CARDINALS	G	GS	CG	IP	H	ER	BB	SO	W	L	Pct	SV	ShO	ERA
Harry Brecheen	36	30	14	231	212	64	67	117	15	15	.500	3	5	2.49
Murry Dickson	47	19	12	184	160	59	56	82	15	6	.714	1	2	2.89
Howie Pollet	40	32	22	266	228	62	86	107	21	10	.677	5	4	2.10
George Munger	10	7	2	49	47	18	12	28	2	2	.500	1	0	3.31
Al Brazle	37	15	6	153	152	56	55	58	11	10	.524	0	2	3.29
Johnny Beazley	19	18	5	103	109	51	55	36	7	5	.583	0	0	4.46
Ted Wilks	40	4	0	95	88	36	38	40	8	0	1.000	1	0	3.41
Ken Burkhart	25	13	5	100	111	32	36	32	6	3	.667	2	2	2.88
Red Barrett	23	9	1	67	75	30	24	22	3	2	.600	2	1	4.03
Freddie Schmidt	16	0	0	27	27	10	15	14	1	0	1.000	0	0	3.33
Howie Krist	15	0	0	19	22	14	8	3	0	1	.000	0	0	6.63
Johnny Grodzicki	3	0	0	4	4	4	4	2	0	0	—	0	0	9.00
team totals	156	156	75	1397	1326	467	493	607	98	58	.628	15	18	3.01

WORLD SERIES STATISTICS

BOSTON RED SOX	G	GS	CG	IP	H	R	ER	BB	SO	W	L	SV	ERA
Tex Hughson	3	2	0	14⅓	14	8	5	3	8	0	1	0	3.14
Boo Ferriss	2	2	1	13⅓	13	3	3	2	4	1	0	0	2.03
Joe Dobson	3	1	1	12⅔	4	3	0	3	10	1	0	0	0.00
Mickey Harris	2	2	0	9⅔	11	6	4	4	5	0	2	0	3.72
Earl Johnson	3	0	0	3⅓	1	1	1	2	1	1	0	0	2.70
Jim Bagby	1	0	0	3	6	1	1	1	1	0	0	0	3.00
Bill Zuber	1	0	0	2	3	1	1	1	1	0	0	0	4.50
Mace Brown	1	0	0	1	4	3	3	1	0	0	0	0	27.00
Mike Ryba	1	0	0	⅔	2	1	1	1	0	0	0	0	13.50
Bob Klinger	1	0	0	⅔	2	1	1	1	0	0	1	0	13.50
Clem Dreisewerd	1	0	0	⅓	0	0	0	0	0	0	0	0	0.00
team totals	7	7	2	61	60	28	20	19	30	3	4	0	2.95

REGULAR SEASON STATISTICS

BOSTON RED SOX		G	GS	CG	IP	H	ER	BB	SO	W	L	Pct	SV	ShO	ERA
Tex Hughson		39	35	21	278	252	85	51	172	20	11	.645	3	6	2.75
Boo Ferriss		40	35	26	274	274	99	71	106	25	6	.806	3	6	3.25
Joe Dobson		32	24	9	167	148	60	68	91	13	7	.650	0	1	3.23
Mickey Harris		34	30	15	223	236	90	76	131	17	9	.654	0	0	3.63
Earl Johnson		29	5	0	80	78	33	39	40	5	4	.556	3	0	3.71
Jim Bagby		21	11	6	107	117	44	49	16	7	6	.538	0	1	3.70
Bill Zuber	d	15	7	2	57	37	16	39	29	5	1	.833	0	1	2.53
Mace Brown		18	0	0	26	26	6	16	10	3	1	.750	1	0	2.08
Mike Ryba		9	0	0	13	12	5	5	5	0	1	.000	1	0	3.46
Bob Klinger		28	1	0	57	49	15	25	16	3	2	.600	9	0	2.37
Clem Dreisewerd		20	1	0	47	50	22	15	19	4	1	.800	0	0	4.21
team totals		156	156	79	1397	1359	525	501	667	104	50	.675	20	15	3.38

Total Attendance—250,071 Average Attendance—35,724 Winning Player's Share—$3,742 Losing Player's Share—$2,141

1947
The Ninth Inning of the Fourth Game

Hostilities between the New York Yankees and Brooklyn Dodgers began in the winter when the Yanks hired coach Chuck Dressen away from Leo Durocher's Brooklyn staff. Verbal attacks from both sides filled the newspapers through spring training until Commissioner Happy Chandler stepped in. He handed down a batch of penalties to both teams, coming down the hardest by suspending Durocher for the entire season for "conduct detrimental to baseball." But the Dodgers drove to the pennant anyway, with gentlemanly Burt Shotton as interim manager and with Jackie Robinson making history simply by stepping on the field, the first black man to play in the big leagues in the twentieth century. An absolute success as a racial trailblazer, Robinson also sparked the Dodgers to the pennant with his hitting, sensational base running, and solid play at first base. With stars like Pee Wee Reese, Dixie Walker, and Eddie Stanky in the lineup around Robinson, and with Ralph Branca, Joe Hatten, and Hugh Casey leading the mound corps, Shotton brought home a winner in his temporary mount. The Yankees won a pennant for their new manager, Bucky Harris, who reorganized the squad but found his biggest guns in holdovers Joe DiMaggio, Tommy Henrich, and Billy Johnson. In the four-year interval since the Yanks last made it to the Series, the pitching staff had turned over almost completely, with Allie Reynolds, Spec Shea, and reliever Joe Page now the top men.

These new-look Yankees got off to a typical old-Yankee start before a record crowd of 73,365 in Yankee Stadium for game one. After going down in order for the first four innings, they exploded against Branca for five runs in the fifth, taking a 5–3 victory behind Shea. With Reynolds pitching the next day, the Yanks made it two straight by pounding out a 10–3 win on the strength of 15 hits. With no travel days needed to move the clubs from the Bronx to Brooklyn, the Dodgers took their first game the next day at Ebbets Field 9–8, surviving a late Yankee comeback and the first Series pinch homer ever, off the bat of rookie catcher Yogi Berra.

The fourth game on October 3 stands high on the list of most dramatic baseball games ever. Yankee starter Bill Bevens, a mediocre 7–13 hurler for the season, survived persistent wildness to enter the bottom of the ninth leading 2–1 and pitching a no-hit game. Bruce Edwards flew out to start the inning, then Carl Furillo drew Brooklyn's ninth walk of the game. When Spider Jorgensen fouled out, the Bums were down to their last out. Shotton sent in reserve outfielder Al Gionfriddo to run for Furillo, and the little sub promptly stole second with pinch hitter Pete Reiser at the plate. Reiser had an ankle bad enough to prevent his running, but he concealed his limp when he walked up to the plate. With Gionfriddo on second, manager Harris chose to give Reiser an intentional walk and face the lighter-hitting Eddie Stanky. Eddie Miksis went in to run for the lame Reiser, and Cookie Lavagetto went to bat instead of Stanky. Once a regular at third base, Cookie rarely played now, but the crowning moment of his baseball career was at hand. Just one out away from history and victory, Bevens saw both vanish as Lavagetto slashed a double off the right-field wall and both Gionfriddo and Miksis scampered home for an unbelievable 3–2 triumph. But the Yankees didn't let such happenings bother them the next day, taking a 2–1 victory to head back to Yankee Stadium ahead three games to two.

The Dodgers needed game six to stay alive, and they won it 8–6 with another broad stroke of heroics. Four runs in the top of the sixth put them ahead 8–5, but the Yanks moved to come back in the bottom of the inning. The Bronx Bombers put two men on base, and with two out DiMaggio smashed a Hatten pitch on a dead line for the left-center bullpen. Little Al Gionfriddo, who had just come into the game as a defensive replacement, took off with his back to the ball, twisted his glove out and speared the ball just as he hit the bullpen fence. Foiled in that attempt, the Yanks went down to an 8–6 loss and went into a seventh game. Fate and momentum seemed to favor the Dodgers, but the old-pro Yankees went ahead in the fourth inning and called on fork-ball expert Joe Page to cement a 5–2 win with five shutout innings of relief. The Yanks again were World Champions, and while Bevens, Lavagetto, and Gionfriddo rated as Series stars, none of them ever played another major-league game.

Game 1 September 30 at New York

Bkn.	1 0 0	0 0 1	1 0 0			
N.Y.	0 0 0	0 5 0	0 0 x			

Brooklyn	Pos	AB	R	H	RBI	PO	A	E
Stanky	2b	4	0	1	0	0	4	0
J. Robinson	1b	2	1	0	0	8	1	0
Reiser	cf-lf	4	1	1	0	3	0	0
Walker	rf	4	0	2	1	1	0	0
Hermanski	lf	2	0	0	0	2	0	0
b Furillo	cf	1	0	1	1	2	0	0
Edwards	c	4	0	0	0	8	0	0
Jorgensen	3b	2	0	0	0	0	1	0
c Lavagetto	3b	2	0	0	0	0	0	0
Reese	ss	4	1	1	0	0	2	0
Branca	p	2	0	0	0	0	0	0
Behrman	p	0	0	0	0	0	1	0
d Miksis		1	0	0	0	0	0	0
Casey	p	0	0	0	0	0	0	0
Totals		32	3	6	2	24	9	0

a Walked for Shea in 5th.
b Singled for Hermanski in 6th.
c Popped out for Jorgensen in 7th.
d Struck out for Behrman in 7th.

Double—Lindell. Stolen Bases—Reese, Robinson. Double Play—Johnson to McQuinn. Hit by Pitcher—Johnson (by Branca). Wild Pitch—Page. Balk—Shea. Left on Bases—Brooklyn 5, New York 3. Umpires—McGowan (A), Pinnelli (N), Rommel (A), Goetz (N), Magerkurth (N), Boyer (A). Attendance—73,365 **(A new Series record)**. Time of Game—2:20.

New York	Pos	AB	R	H	RBI	PO	A	E
Stirnweiss	2b	4	0	0	0	3	1	0
Henrich	rf	4	0	1	2	3	0	0
Berra	c	4	0	0	0	5	0	0
DiMaggio	cf	4	1	1	0	2	0	0
McQuinn	1b	3	1	0	0	7	2	0
Johnson	3b	2	1	0	0	1	0	0
Lindell	lf	3	0	1	2	3	0	0
Rizzuto	ss	2	1	1	0	1	3	0
Shea	p	1	0	0	0	1	2	0
a Brown		0	1	0	1	0	0	0
Page	p	1	0	0	0	1	2	0
Totals		28	5	4	5	27	12	0

Pitching	IP	H	R	ER	BB	SO
Brooklyn						
Branca (L)	*4	2	5	5	3	5
Behrman	2	1	0	0	0	0
Casey	2	1	0	0	0	1
New York						
Shea (W)	5	2	1	1	2	3
Page (SV)	4	4	2	2	1	2

*Pitched to 6 batters in 5th.

1st Inning
Brooklyn
1 Stanky flied to left.
Robinson walked.
Robinson stole second.
Reiser hit back to the box and Robinson
2 was trapped on a run-down between second and third, Shea to Rizzuto. Reiser got to second on the play.
Walker singled to left, scoring Reiser.
3 Hermanski fanned.
New York
1 Stirnweiss grounded to second.
2 Henrich fanned.
3 Berra flied to center.

2nd Inning
Brooklyn
1 Edwards flied to deep center.
2 Jorgensen fanned.
3 Reese grounded to short.
New York
1 DiMaggio grounded to short.
2 McQuinn grounded to third.
3 Johnson grounded to second.

3rd Inning
Brooklyn
1 Branca grounded out, McQuinn to Shea.
2 Stanky rolled to Johnson.
Robinson walked.
Robinson went to second on Shea's balk.
3 Reiser flied to right.
New York
1 Lindell struck out.
2 Rizzuto flied to left.
3 Shea fanned.

4th Inning
Brooklyn
Walker singled past first.
1,2 Hermanski lined to Johnson who threw to McQuinn to double up Walker.
3 Edwards flied to center.
New York
1 Stirnweiss took a called third strike.
2 Henrich flied to center.
3 Berra fanned.

5th Inning
Brooklyn
1 Jorgensen flied to left.
2 Reese grounded back to the mound.
3 Branca fanned.
New York
DiMaggio was the first Yankee base-runner on a single to deep short.
McQuinn walked.
Johnson was hit by a pitch, loading the bases.
Lindell doubled to left, scoring DiMaggio and McQuinn with Johnson stopping at third.

5th Inning (continued)
Rizzuto walked to again fill the bases.
Brown, pinch-hitting for Shea, got two balls when Branca was removed;
For Brooklyn—Behrman pitching to Brown. Brown walked, forcing in Johnson.
1 Stirnweiss forced Lindell at the plate, Robinson to Edwards.
Henrich singled to left, scoring Rizzuto and Brown.
2 Berra flied to right.
3 DiMaggio flied to left.

6th Inning
Brooklyn
For New York—Page pitching.
Stanky singled through the box.
1 Robinson forced Stanky at second, Rizzuto to Stirnweiss.
Reiser singled to first when McQuinn missed the tag.
2 Walker flied to right.
Furillo, pinch-hitting for Hermanski, singled to center, scoring Robinson with Reiser moving to third.
3 Edwards forced Furillo at second, Rizzuto to Stirnweiss.
New York
For Brooklyn—Furillo in center with Reiser moving to left.
1 McQuinn fouled to Edwards.
2 Johnson flied to left.
3 Lindell grounded out, Behrman to Robinson.

7th Inning
Brooklyn
1 Lavagetto, batting for Jorgensen, popped to second.
Reese singled to right.
2 Miskis, pinch-hitting for Behrman, fanned as Reese stole second.
Reese scored from second on a wild-pitch by Page.
3 Stanky grounded out to the pitcher.
New York
For Brooklyn—Lavagetto at third, Casey pitching.
Rizzuto singled to left.
1 Page grounded to second.
2 Stirnweiss grounded to short, moving Rizzuto to third.
3 Henrich grounded to second.

8th Inning
Brooklyn
1 Robinson flied to left.
2 Reiser grounded out, McQuinn to Page.
3 Walker grounded to short.
New York
1 Berra flied to center.
2 DiMaggio flied to center.
3 McQuinn struck out.

9th Inning
Brooklyn
Furillo walked.
1 Edwards flied to right.
2 Lavagetto fanned.
3 Reese bounced back to the mound.

Game 2 October 1 at New York

Bkn.	001	100	001
N.Y.	101	121	40x

Brooklyn	Pos	AB	R	H	RBI	PO	A	E
Stanky	2b	4	0	1	0	3	2	1
J. Robinson	1b	4	0	2	1	5	0	0
Reiser	cf	4	0	1	0	4	0	1
Walker	rf	4	1	1	1	1	0	0
Hermanski	lf	3	1	0	0	3	0	0
Edwards	c	4	0	1	0	5	1	0
Reese	ss	3	1	2	0	0	0	0
Jorgensen	3b	4	0	1	1	3	5	0
Lombardi	p	2	0	0	0	0	0	0
Gregg	p	0	0	0	0	0	2	0
a Vaughan		1	0	0	0	0	0	0
Behrman	p	0	0	0	0	0	0	0
Barney	p	0	0	0	0	0	0	0
b Gionfriddo		1	0	0	0	0	0	0
Totals		34	3	9	3	24	10	2

a Flied out for Gregg in 7th.
b Grounded into force out for Barney in 9th.

New York	Pos	AB	R	H	RBI	PO	A	E
Stirnweiss	2b	4	2	3	1	1	2	0
Henrich	rf	4	1	2	1	3	0	0
Lindell	lf	4	1	2	2	2	0	0
DiMaggio	cf	4	0	1	0	4	0	0
McQuinn	1b	5	1	2	1	6	1	0
Johnson	3b	5	2	2	0	1	2	0
Rizzuto	ss	5	0	1	1	3	4	0
Berra	c	3	1	0	0	6	1	1
Reynolds	p	4	2	2	1	1	0	0
Totals		38	10	15	7	27	10	1

Pitching	IP	H	R	ER	BB	SO
Brooklyn						
Lombardi (L)	*4	9	5	5	1	3
Gregg	2	2	1	1	1	2
Behrman	⅓	3	4	4	1	0
Barney	1⅔	1	0	0	1	0
New York						
Reynolds (W)	9	9	3	3	2	6

*Pitched to 2 batters in 5th.

Doubles—Lindell, Rizzuto, Robinson. Triples—Johnson, Lindell, Stirnweiss. Home Runs—Henrich, Walker. Stolen Base—Reese. Sacrifice Hit—Henrich. Double Plays—Jorgensen to Stanky to Robinson, Stirnweiss to Rizzuto to McQuinn. Wild Pitches—Barney, Behrman. Left on Bases—Brooklyn 6, New York 9. Umpires—Pinelli, Rommel, Goetz, McGowan, Boyer, Magerkurth. Attendance—69,865. Time of Game—2:36.

1st Inning
Brooklyn
1 Stanky fanned.
2 Robinson fanned.
3 Reiser flied to left.
New York
Stirnweiss singled to right.
Henrich singled to center, Stirnweiss going to third.
1,2 Lindell grounded into a double play, scoring Stirnweiss, Jorgensen to Stanky to Robinson.
DiMaggio singled off Reese's glove.
3 McQuinn struck out.

2nd Inning
Brooklyn
1 Walker lined to center.
2 Hermanski fouled to Johnson.
3 Edwards fanned.
New York
1 Johnson flied to right.
2 Rizzuto grounded to third on a bunt.
3 Berra grounded to second.

3rd Inning
Brooklyn
Reese walked.
1 Jorgensen flied to right.
2 Lombardi flied to center.
Reese stole second.
Stanky singled through the box, Reese going to third.
Robinson singled to left, scoring Reese and Stanky going to second.
3 Reiser struck out.
New York
1 Reynolds grounded to third.
Stirnweiss tripled to right-center.
2 Henrich fouled to Jorgensen.
Lindell tripled to center, scoring Stirnweiss.
DiMaggio got an intentional pass.
3 McQuinn fanned.

4th Inning
Brooklyn
Walker homered into the lower right field stands (on the first pitch).
1 Hermanski grounded out, McQuinn to Reynolds.
2 Edwards popped to first.
Reese singled to right.
3 Reese caught stealing, Berra to Rizzuto.
New York
Johnson tripled to center.
Rizzuto's short fly to left dropped in for a double, scoring Johnson.
1 Berra flied to center, Rizzuto moving to third after the catch.
On Reynolds' hit to Jorgensen, Rizzuto
2 was trapped in a run-down between third and home, out Edwards to Jorgensen.
Reynolds took second on the play.
3 Stirnweiss fanned.

5th Inning
Brooklyn
1 Jorgensen fanned.
2 Lombardi grounded to short.
3 Stanky grounded to short.
New York
Henrich homered into the right-center field bleachers.
Lindell bounced a ground-rule double into the lower left field stands.
For Brooklyn—Gregg pitching with a 1–0 count to DiMaggio.
1 DiMaggio grounded to third, Lindell holding second.

5th Inning (continued)
McQuinn singled to center, Lindell scoring.
Johnson safe at first when Stanky dropped Gregg's throw to force McQuinn.
2 Rizzuto flied to deep center.
3 Berra fanned.

6th Inning
Brooklyn
1 Robinson flied to center.
Reiser singled to left.
2,3 Walker hit into a double play, Stirnweiss to Rizzuto to McQuinn.
New York
Reynolds singled to left.
Stirnweiss walked.
1 Henrich sacrificed, Gregg to Stanky, advancing both runners.
2 Lindell flied to left, Reynolds scoring after the catch.
3 DiMaggio took a called third strike.

7th Inning
Brooklyn
1 Hermanski called out on strikes.
Edwards singled to right.
2 Reese flied to right.
Jorgensen got to first on a single in front of the plate with Edwards going to third on Berra's wild throw.
3 Vaughan, pinch-hitting for Gregg, flied to center.
New York
For Brooklyn—Behrman pitching.
McQuinn singled to right.
McQuinn to second on a wild pitch.
Johnson singled to center, scoring McQuinn and going all the way to third as Reiser lost the ball.
1 Rizzuto popped to second.
Berra intentionally walked.
Reynolds singled on a squeeze bunt, scoring Johnson and moving Berra to third.
For Brooklyn—Barney pitching.
Stirnweiss singled to first, scoring Berra.
2 Henrich flied to center, Reynolds to third after the catch.
Reynolds scored on a wild pitch, and Stirnweiss to second.
Lindell walked.
3 DiMaggio forced Stirnweiss at third, Jorgensen unassisted.

8th Inning
Brooklyn
1 Stanky grounded to third.
Robinson doubled to left.
2 Reiser flied to right.
3 Walker rolled to short.
New York
1 McQuinn flied to left.
2 Johnson flied to center.
3 Rizzuto flied to left.

9th Inning
Brooklyn
Hermanski walked.
1 Edwards flied to left.
Reese singled past short, Hermanski moving to third.
2 Jorgensen forced Reese at second, scoring Hermanski, Stirnweiss to Rizzuto.
3 Gionfriddo, pinch-hitting for Barney, forced Jorgensen at second, Johnson to Stirnweiss.

Game 3 October 2 at Brooklyn

N.Y.	002	221	100
Bkn.	061	200	00x

New York	Pos	AB	R	H	RBI	PO	A	E
Stirnweiss	2b	5	0	2	1	2	3	0
Henrich	rf	4	0	1	1	0	0	0
Lindell	lf	4	1	2	1	0	0	0
DiMaggio	cf	4	1	2	3	3	0	0
McQuinn	1b	4	0	0	0	8	1	0
Johnson	3b	4	1	1	0	2	1	0
Rizzuto	ss	5	0	1	0	5	2	0
Lollar	c	3	2	2	1	2	1	0
e Berra	c	2	1	1	1	2	0	0
Newsom	p	0	0	0	0	0	1	0
Raschi	p	0	0	0	0	0	0	0
b Clark		0	1	0	0	0	0	0
Drews	p	0	0	0	0	0	2	0
c Phillips		1	0	0	0	0	0	0
Chandler	p	0	0	0	0	0	0	0
d Brown		1	1	1	0	0	0	0
Page	p	1	0	0	0	0	0	0
Totals		38	8	13	8	24	11	0

Brooklyn	Pos	AB	R	H	RBI	PO	A	E
Stanky	2b	4	2	1	2	4	5	0
J. Robinson	1b	4	1	2	0	10	1	0
Reiser	cf	0	0	0	0	0	0	0
a Furillo	cf	3	1	2	2	0	0	1
Walker	rf	5	0	2	1	1	0	0
Hermanski	lf	3	2	1	1	4	0	0
Edwards	c	4	1	1	1	5	0	0
Reese	ss	3	1	1	1	1	3	0
Jorgensen	3b	4	0	2	1	1	3	0
Hatten	p	2	1	1	0	0	0	0
Branca	p	1	0	0	0	0	0	0
Casey	p	1	0	0	0	1	1	0
Totals		34	9	13	9	27	13	1

Pitching	IP	H	R	ER	BB	SO
New York						
Newsom (L)	1⅔	5	5	5	2	0
Raschi	⅓	2	1	1	0	0
Drews	1	1	1	1	0	0
Chandler	2	2	2	2	3	1
Page	3	3	0	0	1	3
Brooklyn						
Hatten	4⅓	8	6	6	3	3
Branca	2	4	2	2	2	1
Casey (W)	2⅔	1	0	0	1	1

a Doubled for Reiser in 2nd.
b Walked for Raschi in 3rd.
c Flied out for Drews in 4th.
d Doubled for Chandler in 6th.
e Homered for Lollar in 7th.

Doubles—Brown, Edwards, Furillo, Henrich, Jorgensen, Lollar, Stanky. Home Runs—Berra, DiMaggio. Stolen Bases—Robinson, Walker. Sacrifice Hit—Robinson. Double Plays—Reese to Stanky to Robinson, Stanky to Robinson. Passed Ball—Lollar. Hit by Pitch—Hermanski (by Drews). Wild Pitches—Drews, Page. Left on Bases—New York 9, Brooklyn 9. Umpires—Rommel, Goetz, McGowan, Pinelli, Magerkurth, Boyer. Attendance—33,098. Time of Game—3:05.

1st Inning
New York
Stirnweiss singled to right.
1,2 Henrich grounded into a double play, Reese to Stanky to Robinson.
3 Lindell grounded to third.
Brooklyn
1 Stanky grounded back to the mound.
Robinson singled to center.
Robinson stole second on Lollar's low
2 throw but was out as he overran the bag, Stirnweiss to Rizzuto.
Reiser walked.
3 Reiser got caught stealing, Lollar to Rizzuto.

2nd Inning
New York
1 DiMaggio popped to short.
2 McQuinn called out on strikes.
Johnson singled to right.
3 Rizzuto grounded to third.
Brooklyn
1 Walker grounded to short.
Hermanski walked.
Edwards doubled, Hermanski scoring.
Reese singled to center, scoring Edwards.
2 Jorgensen flied to center.
Hatten singled to left, Reese at second.
Reese went to third and Hatten to second on Lollar's passed ball.
Stanky doubled to right, scoring Reese and Hatten.
For New York—Raschi pitching.
Robinson singled, moving Stanky to third.
Furillo, pinch-hitting for Reiser, doubled off the scoreboard, scoring Stanky and Robinson.
3 Walker grounded to short.

3rd Inning
New York
For Brooklyn—Furillo playing center.
Lollar singled to center.
Clark, batting for Raschi, walked.
1 Stirnweiss took a called third strike.
2 Henrich flied to left.
Lindell singled to center, Lollar scoring and Clark stopping at second.
DiMaggio singled, scoring Clark.
3 McQuinn fanned.
Brooklyn
For New York—Drews pitching.
Hermanski hit by a pitch.
Hermanski to second on a wild pitch.
1 Edwards grounded to Drews, Hermanski to third.
2 Reese also grounded to Drews.
Jorgensen singled, Hermanski scoring.
3 Hatten forced Jorgenson at second, Rizzuto to Stirnweiss.

4th Inning
New York
Johnson walked.
1 Rizzuto flied to left.
Lollar doubled to right, Johnson scoring.
2 Phillips, pinch-hitting for Drews, flied to left.
Stirnweiss singled to center to score Lollar and took second as Furillo threw past Edwards for an error.
3 Henrich grounded to second.
Brooklyn
For New York—Chandler pitching.
Stanky walked.
1 Robinson sacrificed Stanky to second, McQuinn to Stirnweiss.

4th Inning (continued)
Furillo walked.
Walker singled to center, Stanky scoring with Furillo going to third.
Hermanski singled to center, scoring Furillo with Walker stopping at second.
2 Edwards fanned.
Reese walked, loading the bases.
3 Jorgensen grounded easily to first.

5th Inning
New York
Lindell walked.
DiMaggio hit a two-run homer into the upper left field deck.
1 McQuinn grounded to third.
For Brooklyn—Branca pitching.
2 Johnson fanned.
Rizzuto singled past first.
3 Lollar forced Rizzuto at second, Reese to Stanky.
Brooklyn
1 Branca lined to third.
2 Stanky popped to short.
3 Robinson popped to short.

6th Inning
New York
Brown, pinch-hitting for Chandler, doubled to right.
1 Stirnweiss grounded to short, Brown moving over to third.
Henrich doubled off Stanky's glove to score Brown.
2 Lindell fouled to Jorgensen.
DiMaggio walked.
McQuinn walked to load the bases.
3 Johnson popped to second.
Brooklyn
For New York—Page is the fifth pitcher.
Furillo singled to right.
1 Walker forced Furillo in an attempted sacrifice, Johnson to Rizzuto.
2 Hermanski popped to third.
Walker stole second.
Edwards walked.
3 Reese called out on strikes.

7th Inning
New York
1 Rizzuto flied to left.
Berra, pinch-hitting for Lollar, homered into the scoreboard.
For Brooklyn—Casey pitching.
2 Page grounded to short.
3 Stirnweiss took a called third strike.
Brooklyn
For New York—Berra stayed in to catch.
Jorgensen doubled to right.
1 Casey fanned.
2 Stanky popped to first.
3 Robinson flied to center.

8th Inning
New York
Henrich walked.
Lindell singled to center, Henrich stopping at second.
1,2 DiMaggio grounded into a double play, Stanky tagging Lindell and throwing to first getting DiMaggio. Henrich to third on the double killing.
3 McQuinn grounded to first.
Brooklyn
1 Furillo grounded to short.
Walker singled to left.
Walker to second on a wild pitch.
2 Hermanski took a called third strike.
3 Edwards flied to center.

9th Inning
New York
1 Johnson grounded out, Robinson to Casey who covered first.
2 Rizzuto flied to right.
3 Berra grounded out off Casey's glove to Stanky who threw to Robinson.

Game 4 October 3 at Brooklyn

New York	Pos	AB	R	H	RBI	PO	A	E
Stirnweiss	2b	4	1	2	0	2	1	0
Henrich	rf	5	0	1	0	2	0	0
Berra	c	4	0	0	0	6	1	1
DiMaggio	cf	2	0	0	1	2	0	0
McQuinn	1b	4	0	1	0	7	0	0
Johnson	3b	4	1	1	0	3	2	0
Lindell	lf	3	0	2	1	3	0	0
Rizzuto	ss	4	0	1	0	1	2	0
Bevens	p	3	0	0	0	0	1	0
Totals		33	2	8	2	*26	7	1

* Two out when winning run was scored.
a. Walked for Gregg in 7th.
b. Ran for Furillo in 9th.
c. Walked for Casey in 9th.
d. Ran for Reiser in 9th.
e. Doubled for Stanky in 9th.

Doubles—Lavagetto, Lindell. Triple—Johnson. Stolen Bases—Gionfriddo, Reese, Rizzuto. Sacrifice Hits—Bevens, Stanky. Double Plays—Reese to Stanky to Robinson, Gregg to Reese to Robinson, Casey to Edwards to Robinson. Wild Pitch—Bevens. Left on Bases—New York 9, Brooklyn 8. Umpires—Goetz, McGowan, Pinelli, Rommel, Boyer, Magerkurth. Attendance—33,443. Time of Game—2:20.

	N.Y.	1 0 0	1 0 0	0 0 0
	Bkn.	0 0 0	0 1 0	0 0 2

Brooklyn	Pos	AB	R	H	RBI	PO	A	E
Stanky	2b	1	0	0	0	2	3	0
e Lavagetto		1	0	1	2	0	0	0
Reese	ss	4	0	1	3	5	1	
J. Robinson	1b	4	0	0	0	11	1	0
Walker	rf	2	0	0	0	1	0	0
Hermanski	lf	4	0	0	0	2	0	0
Edwards	c	4	0	0	0	7	1	1
Furillo	cf	3	0	0	0	2	0	0
b Gionfriddo		0	1	0	0	0	0	0
Jorgensen	3b	2	1	0	0	0	1	1
Taylor	p	0	0	0	0	0	0	0
Gregg	p	1	0	0	0	0	1	0
a Vaughan		0	0	0	0	0	0	0
Behrman	p	0	0	0	0	0	1	0
Casey	p	0	0	0	0	0	1	0
c Reiser		0	0	0	0	0	0	0
d Miksis		0	1	0	0	0	0	0
Totals		26	3	1	3	27	15	3

Pitching	IP	H	R	ER	BB	SO
New York						
Bevens (L)	9	1	3	3	10	5
Brooklyn						
Taylor	**0	2	1	0	1	0
Gregg	7	4	1	1	3	5
Behrman	1⅓	2	0	0	0	0
Casey (W)	⅔	0	0	0	0	0

**Pitched to four batters in 1st.

1st Inning
New York
Stirnweiss singled to left.
Henrich singled through the box with Stirnweiss stopping at second.
Berra safe at first on his hit to Robinson who tried to start a DP but Reese dropped the ball to load the bases.
DiMaggio walked, forcing in Stirnweiss.
For Brooklyn—Gregg pitching.
1 McQuinn popped to short.
2,3 Johnson hit into a double play, Reese to Stanky to Robinson.
Brooklyn
Stanky walked.
1 Reese grounded to second, with Stanky going to second.
2 Robinson grounded to third, Stanky holding.
Walker walked.
3 Hermanski fouled to Johnson.

2nd Inning
New York
1 Lindell grounded to short.
Rizzuto singled to left.
Rizzuto stole second.
2 Bevens flied to center.
3 Stirnweiss struck out.
Brooklyn
1 Edwards fanned.
2 Furillo grounded to Rizzuto.
Jorgensen walked.
3 Gregg struck out.

3rd Inning
New York
1 Henrich struck out.
2 Berra grounded to first.
DiMaggio walked.
McQuinn singled in front of the plate and went all the way to second on Edward's wild throw but DiMaggio was
3 out trying to score on the error, Walker to Edwards.
Brooklyn
Stanky walked.
1 Reese lined to left.
Stanky went to second on a wild pitch.
2 Robinson fouled deep to Lindell.
3 Walker popped to third.

4th Inning
New York
Johnson tripled to center.
Lindell doubled to right to score Johnson.
1 Rizzuto grounded to first with Lindell going to third.
2 Bevens grounded to short.
3 Stirnweiss called out on strikes.
Brooklyn
1 Hermanski flied to center.
2 Edwards took a called third strike.
3 Furillo fouled to Berra.

5th Inning
New York
1 Henrich grounded to short.
2 Berra grounded to second.
3 DiMaggio popped to second.

5th Inning (continued)
Brooklyn
Jorgensen walked.
Gregg walked.
1 Stanky sacrificed up both runners, Berra to Stirnweiss.
2 Reese safe on a fielder's choice as Rizzuto got Gregg at third with Jorgensen scoring on the play.
Reese stole second and continued on to third on Berra's wild throw.
3 Robinson fanned.

6th Inning
New York
1 McQuinn called out on strikes.
2 Johnson flied to left.
Lindell walked.
3 Rizzuto flied to center.
Brooklyn
Walker walked.
1 Hermanski popped to second.
2 Edwards fanned.
3 Furillo flied to right.

7th Inning
New York
1 Bevens fanned.
Stirnweiss walked.
2,3 Henrich grounded into a double play, Gregg to Reese to Robinson.
Brooklyn
1 Jorgensen lined to center.
Vaughan, pinch-hitting for Gregg, walked.
2 Stanky popped to short.
3 Reese grounded to first.

8th Inning
New York
For Brooklyn—Behrman pitching.
1 Berra grounded to second.
DiMaggio safe at first on Jorgensen's fumble.
2 McQuinn flied to left.
3 Johnson grounded to third.
Brooklyn
1 Robinson grounded to third.
2 Walker grounded back to the mound.
3 Hermanski flied to right.

9th Inning
New York
Lindell singled past third.
1 Rizzuto forced Lindell at second, Behrman to Reese.
Bevens sacrificed and was safe at first when Edwards' throw to get Rizzuto was not in time.
Stirnweiss singled to center, loading the bases.
For Brooklyn—Casey now pitching.
2,3 Henrich grounded into a double play on the first pitch, Casey to Edwards to Robinson.
Brooklyn
1 Edwards flied to very deep center.
Furillo walked.
2 Jorgensen fouled to McQuinn.
Gionfriddo ran for Furillo.
Reiser was batting for Casey, while Gionfriddo stole second.
Reiser intentionally walked.
Miksis ran for Reiser.
Lavagetto, pinch-hitting for Stanky, doubled off the right field wall to score Gionfriddo and Miksis with the winning runs. **The first and only hit allowed by Bevens.**

Game 5 October 4 at Brooklyn

New York	Pos	AB	R	H	RBI	PO	A	E
Stirnweiss	2b	3	0	0	0	3	4	0
Henrich	rf	4	0	2	0	1	0	0
Lindell	lf	2	0	0	0	3	0	0
DiMaggio	cf	4	1	1	1	3	0	0
McQuinn	1b	4	0	0	0	7	0	0
Johnson	3b	3	0	0	0	2	1	0
A. Robinson	c	3	1	0	0	7	0	0
Rizzuto	ss	2	0	0	0	1	1	0
Shea	p	4	0	2	1	0	1	0
Totals		29	2	5	2	27	7	0

a. Walked for Hatten in 6th.
b. Doubled for Behrman in 7th.
c. Walked for Stanky in 7th.
d. Ran for Reiser in 7th.
e. Ran for Edwards in 9th.
f. Fanned for Casey in 9th.

Doubles—Henrich, Shea, Vaughan. Home Run—DiMaggio. Sacrifice Hit—Furillo. Double Plays—Reese to Stanky to J. Robinson, Reese to Miksis to J. Robinson. Passed Balls—Edwards 2. Hit by Pitcher—Lindell (by Casey). Wild Pitch—Barney. Left on Bases—New York 11, Brooklyn 8. Umpires—McGowen, Pinelli, Rommel, Goetz, Magerkurth, Boyer. Attendance—34,379. Time of Game—2:46.

	N.Y.	0 0 0	1 1 0	0 0 0
	Bkn.	0 0 0	0 0 1	0 0 0

Brooklyn	Pos	AB	R	H	RBI	PO	A	E
Stanky	2b	3	0	0	0	2	2	0
c Reiser		0	0	0	0	0	0	0
d Miksis	2b	0	0	0	0	1	1	1
Reese	ss	4	0	0	0	2	3	0
J. Robinson	1b	4	0	1	1	9	0	0
Walker	rf	4	0	0	0	0	0	0
Hermanski	lf	4	0	1	0	2	0	0
Edwards	c	3	0	1	0	9	2	0
e Lombardi		0	0	0	0	0	0	0
Furillo	cf	3	0	0	0	2	0	0
Jorgensen	3b	4	0	0	0	3	0	0
Barney	p	1	0	0	0	0	1	0
Hatten	p	0	0	0	0	0	0	0
a Gionfriddo		0	1	0	0	0	0	0
Behrman	p	0	0	0	0	0	1	0
b Vaughan		1	0	1	0	0	0	0
Casey	p	0	0	0	0	1	0	0
f Lavagetto		1	0	0	0	0	0	0
Totals		30	1	4	1	27	10	1

Pitching	IP	H	R	ER	BB	SO
New York						
Shea (W)	9	4	1	1	5	7
Brooklyn						
Barney (L)	4⅔	3	2	2	9	3
Hatten	1⅓	0	0	0	0	1
Behrman	1	1	0	0	1	2
Casey	2	1	0	0	0	1

1st Inning
New York
Stirnweiss walked.
Henrich doubled to right-center, Stirnweiss stopping at third.
Lindell walked, loading the bases.
1 DiMaggio struck out.
2 McQuinn forced Stirnweiss at the plate, Barney to Edwards.
3 Johnson fanned.
Brooklyn
1 Stanky grounded to second.
2 Reese fouled to Johnson.
3 J. Robinson grounded to third.

2nd Inning
New York
1 A. Robinson flied to center.
Rizzuto walked.
Rizzuto went to second on a wild pitch.
2 Rizzuto out trying to steal third, Edwards to Jorgensen.
3 Shea lined to third.
Brooklyn
1 Walker lined to second.
2 Hermanski flied to left.
3 Edwards struck out.

3rd Inning
New York
1 Stirnweiss lined to center.
Henrich walked.
Lindell walked.
2,3 DiMaggio grounded into a double play, Reese to Stanky to J. Robinson.
Brooklyn
1 Furillo popped to second.
2 Jorgensen struck out.
3 Barney grounded to second.

4th Inning
New York
1 McQuinn flied to left.
2 Johnson struck out.
A. Robinson walked.
Rizzuto walked.
Shea singled to left, scoring A. Robinson with Rizzuto stopping at second.
Stirnweiss walked, loading the bases.
3 Henrich grounded to second.
Brooklyn
1 Stanky flied to center.
Reese walked.
2 J. Robinson popped to first.
3 Walker grounded to second.

5th Inning
New York
1 Lindell grounded to short.
DiMaggio homered into the left field stands.
2 McQuinn popped to second.
Johnson walked.
For Brooklyn—Hatten pitching.
3 A. Robinson popped to third.
Brooklyn
Hermanski singled to right.
1 Edwards lined to left.
2 Furillo popped to short.
3 Jorgensen fanned.

6th Inning
New York
1 Rizzuto popped to short.
2 Shea fanned.
3 Stirnweiss fouled to Edwards.
Brooklyn
Gionfriddo pinch-hitting for Hatten, walked.
1 Stanky fanned.
Reese walked.
J. Robinson singled to center, scoring Gionfriddo with Reese going to third. Robinson to second on DiMaggio's throw to third.
2 Walker fouled to Johnson.
3 Hermanski flied to center.

7th Inning
New York
For Brooklyn—Behrman pitching.
Henrich singled to center.
1 Lindell fanned.
DiMaggio walked.
2 McQuinn struck out but Edwards let the ball go through him to advance Henrich and DiMaggio (a passed ball).
3 Johnson grounded back to the mound.
Brooklyn
Edwards walked.
1 Furillo flied to center.
2 Jorgensen flied to left.
Vaughan, pinch-hitting for Behrman, doubled to right, sending Edwards to third.
Reiser, batting for Stanky, got an intentional walk.
Miksis ran for Reiser.
3 Reese took a called third strike.

8th Inning
New York
For Brooklyn—Casey pitching and Miksis playing second.
1 A. Robinson popped to short.
2 Rizzuto lined to left.
Shea doubled to left.
Shea to third on a passed ball.
3 Stirnweiss fanned.
Brooklyn
1 J. Robinson fanned.
2 Walker grounded to short.
3 Hermanski grounded to second.

9th Inning
New York
Henrich safe at first on Miksis' error.
Lindell hit by a pitched ball.
1,2 DiMaggio grounded into a double play, Reese to Miksis to J. Robinson with Henrich to third.
3 Henrich out trying to score on a passed ball, Edwards to Casey.
Brooklyn
Edwards singled to left.
Lombardi ran for Edwards.
1 Furillo sacrificed Lombardi to second, Shea to Stirnweiss.
2 Jorgensen flied to right.
3 Lavagetto, pinch-hitting for Casey, fanned.

1947

Game 6 October 5 at New York

Bkn.	202 004 000						
N.Y.	004 100 001						

Brooklyn	Pos	AB	R	H	RBI	PO	A	E
Stanky	2b	5	2	2	0	4	2	0
Reese	ss	4	2	3	2	2	1	0
J. Robinson	1b	5	1	2	1	7	1	0
Walker	rf	5	0	1	1	3	0	0
Hermanski	lf	1	0	0	0	0	0	0
b Miksis	lf	1	0	0	0	0	0	0
Gionfriddo	lf	2	0	0	0	1	0	0
Edwards	c	4	1	1	0	5	0	0
Furillo	cf	4	1	2	0	4	1	0
Jorgensen	3b	2	0	0	0	1	1	1
c Lavagetto	3b	2	0	0	1	0	1	0
Lombardi	p	1	0	0	0	0	0	0
Branca	p	1	0	0	0	0	1	0
d Bragan		1	0	1	1	0	0	0
e Bankhead		0	1	0	0	0	0	0
Hatten	p	1	0	0	0	0	0	0
Casey	p	0	0	0	0	0	1	0
Totals		39	8	12	6	27	9	1

a Singled for Phillips in 3rd.
b Popped out for Hermanski in 5th.
c Flied out for Jorgensen in 6th.
d Doubled for Branca in 6th.
e Ran for Bragan in 6th.
f Lined out for Newsom in 6th.
g Singled for Raschi in 7th.
h Hit into force out for Wensloff in 9th.

Doubles—Bragan, Furillo, Lollar, Reese, J. Robinson, Walker.
Double Play—Rizzuto to Phillips.
Passed Ball—Lollar. Wild Pitch—Lombardi.
Left on Bases—Brooklyn 6, New York 13.
Umpires—Pinelli, Rommel, Goetz, McGowan, Boyer, Magerkurth. Attendance—74,065.
(A new Series record). Time of Game—3:19.

New York	Pos	AB	R	H	RBI	PO	A	E
Stirnwieiss	2b	5	0	0	1	1	6	0
Henrich	rf-lf	5	1	2	0	1	0	0
Lindell	lf	2	1	2	1	0	0	0
Berra	rf	3	0	2	1	1	0	0
DiMaggio	cf	5	1	1	0	5	0	0
Johnson	3b	5	1	2	1	1	5	0
Phillips	1b	1	0	0	0	4	0	0
a Brown		1	0	1	1	0	0	0
McQuinn	1b	1	0	0	0	6	0	1
Rizzuto	ss	4	0	1	0	6	1	0
Lollar	c	1	1	1	0	0	0	0
A. Robinson	c	4	1	2	0	2	0	1
Reynolds	p	0	0	0	0	0	1	0
Drews	p	2	0	0	0	0	1	0
Page	p	0	0	0	0	0	0	0
Newsom	p	0	0	0	0	0	0	0
f Clark		1	0	0	0	0	0	0
Raschi	p	0	0	0	0	0	0	0
g Houk		1	0	1	0	0	0	0
Wensloff	p	0	0	0	0	0	1	0
h Frey		1	0	0	1	0	0	0
Totals		42	6	15	6	27	14	2

Pitching	IP	H	R	ER	BB	SO
Brooklyn						
Lombardi	2⅓	5	4	4	0	2
Branca (W)	2⅓	6	1	1	0	2
Hatten	*3	3	1	1	4	0
Casey (sv)	1	1	0	0	0	0
New York						
Reynolds	2⅓	6	4	3	1	0
Drews	2	1	0	0	1	0
Page (L)	1	4	4	4	0	1
Newsom	⅓	1	0	0	0	0
Raschi	1	0	0	0	0	1
Wensloff	2	0	0	0	0	0

*Pitched to two batters in 9th.

1st Inning
Brooklyn
Stanky singled to left.
Reese singled to center with Stanky stopping at second.
J. Robinson singled to left when Lindell lost the ball in the sun to load the bases.
1,2 Walker hit into a double play, Rizzuto to Phillips. Stanky scored and Reese went to third on the double play.
Reese scored on Lollar's passed ball.
Hermanski walked.
3 Edwards grounded to third.
New York
1 Stirnweiss flied to right.
2 Henrich popped to second.
Lindell singled to left.
3 DiMaggio grounded to second.

2nd Inning
Brooklyn
1 Furillo flied to center.
2 Jorgensen grounded to second.
3 Lombardi flied to center.
New York
1 Johnson fanned.
2 Phillips grounded to first.
3 Rizzuto grounded to short.

3rd Inning
Brooklyn
1 Stanky flied to center.
Reese doubled over third.
J. Robinson got a ground-rule double to left, scoring Reese.
Walker doubled to right, J. Robinson scoring.
For New York—Drews pitching.
2 Hermanski grounded to second, moving Walker to third.
3 Edwards flied to center.
New York
Lollar doubled to left.
1 Drews fanned.
Lollar went to third on a wild pitch.
Stirnweiss was safe at first on Jorgensen's fumble, Lollar scoring.
Henrich singled to center, however
2 Stirnweiss was out trying for third, Furillo to Jorgensen.
Lindell singled to center to score Henrich.
DiMaggio singled through third, Lindell stopping at second.
For Brooklyn—Branca pitching.
Johnson on a single to right scored Lindell and moved DiMaggio to third.
Brown, pinch-hitting for Phillips, singled to left, scoring DiMaggio and moving Johnson to third.
3 Rizzuto lined to second.

4th Inning
Brooklyn
For New York—McQuinn at first, A. Robinson catching, Berra in right as Henrich moves to left.
Furillo singled behind second.
1 Jorgensen forced Furillo at second, Stirnweiss to Rizzuto.
2 Branca forced Jorgensen at second, Drews to Rizzuto.
3 Stanky forced Branca at second, Stirnweiss to Rizzuto.
New York
A. Robinson singled to center.
1 Drews called out on strikes.
2 Stirnweiss took a called third strike.
Henrich singled to center with A. Robinson stopping at second.
Berra singled over first to score A. Robinson and moving Henrich to third.
3 DiMaggio forced Berra at second, Jorgensen to Stanky.

5th Inning
Brooklyn
Reese walked.
1 J. Robinson forced Reese at second, Johnson to Stirnweiss.
For New York—Page relieved Drews with a 2–1 count on Walker.
2 Walker went down swinging.
3 Miksis, batting for Hermanski, popped to short.
New York
For Brooklyn—Miksis playing left.
1 Johnson grounded back to the pitcher.
2 McQuinn popped to second.
Rizzuto singled to left.
3 A. Robinson grounded to second.

6th Inning
Brooklyn
Edwards singled to right.
Furillo doubled to left, moving Edwards to third.
1 Lavagetto, pinch-hitting for Jorgensen, flied to right, Edwards scoring after the catch.
Bragan, batting for Branca, doubled to left, Furillo scoring.
Bankhead ran for Bragan.
Stanky singled to right, Bankhead going to third. Stanky went on to second when A. Robinson lost Berra's throw to the plate.
For New York Newsom pitching.
Reese singled to left, scoring Bankhead and Stanky.
2 J. Robinson lined to left.
3 Walker fouled to Johnson.

6th Inning (continued)
New York
For Brooklyn—Hatten pitching, Lavagetto at third and Gionfriddo going to left.
1 Clark pinch-hitting for Newsom, lined to short.
Stirnweiss walked.
2 Henrich fouled to Edwards.
Berra singled to left with Stirnweiss stopping at second.
3 DiMaggio flied to left where Gionfriddo made the catch of the Series, a glove-handed catch at the 415 foot mark just in front of the bullpen.

7th Inning
Brooklyn
For New York—Raschi pitching.
1 Gionfriddo grounded to third.
2 Edwards fanned.
3 Furillo rolled to second.
New York
1 Johnson flied to right.
McQuinn walked.
Rizzuto walked.
2 A. Robinson flied to center.
Houk, pinch-hitting for Raschi, singled past the box to load the bases.
3 Stirnweiss flied to center.

8th Inning
Brooklyn
For New York—Wensloff pitching.
1 Lavagetto grounded to third.
2 Hatten rolled to the box.
3 Stanky grounded to third.
New York
1 Henrich lined to right.
2 Berra flied to center.
3 DiMaggio grounded to third.

9th Inning
Brooklyn
1 Reese grounded to second.
2 J. Robinson popped to short.
Walker safe at first on McQuinn's fumble.
3 Gionfriddo flied to center.
New York
Johnson singled to left.
McQuinn walked.
For Brooklyn—Casey pitching.
1 Rizzuto flied to center.
A. Robinson singled to left, loading the bases.
2 Frey, pinch-hitting for Wensloff, forced A. Robinson at second, J. Robinson to Reese. Johnson scored on the force out, with McQuinn going to third.
3 Stirnweiss grounded back to the mound.

Game 7 October 6 at New York

| Bkn. | 020 000 000 |
| N.Y. | 010 201 10x |

Brooklyn	Pos	AB	R	H	RBI	PO	A	E
Stanky	2b	4	0	1	0	3	1	0
Reese	ss	3	0	0	0	0	1	0
J. Robinson	1b	4	0	0	0	3	2	0
Walker	rf	3	0	0	0	3	0	0
Hermanski	lf	2	1	1	0	2	0	0
b Miksis	lf	2	0	1	0	2	0	0
Edwards	c	4	1	2	1	5	0	0
Furillo	cf	3	0	1	0	4	0	0
Jorgensen	3b	2	0	1	1	0	1	0
d Lavagetto	3b	1	0	0	0	0	0	0
Gregg	p	2	0	0	0	1	0	0
Behrman	p	0	0	0	0	1	0	0
Hatten	p	0	0	0	0	0	0	0
Barney	p	0	0	0	0	0	0	0
e Hodges		1	0	0	0	0	0	0
Casey	p	0	0	0	0	0	0	0
Totals		31	2	7	2	24	5	0

New York	Pos	AB	R	H	RBI	PO	A	E
Stirnweiss	2b	2	0	0	0	5	4	0
Henrich	lf	5	0	1	1	2	0	0
Berra	rf	3	0	0	0	1	0	0
c Clark	rf	1	0	1	1	2	0	0
DiMaggio	cf	3	0	0	0	3	0	0
McQuinn	1b	2	1	0	0	7	0	0
Johnson	3b	3	2	1	0	1	1	0
A. Robinson	c	3	0	0	1	4	2	0
Rizzuto	ss	4	2	3	1	2	2	0
Shea	p	0	0	0	0	0	0	0
Bevens	p	1	0	0	0	0	0	0
a Brown		1	0	1	1	0	0	0
Page	p	2	0	0	0	0	0	0
Totals		30	5	7	5	27	9	0

Pitching	IP	H	R	ER	BB	SO
Brooklyn						
Gregg (L)	3⅔	3	3	3	4	3
Behrman	1⅓	2	1	1	3	1
Hatten	⅓	1	0	0	0	1
Barney	⅓	0	0	0	0	0
Casey	2	1	1	1	0	0
New York						
Shea	1⅓	4	2	2	1	0
Bevens	2⅔	2	0	0	1	2
Page (W)	5	1	0	0	0	1

a Doubled for Bevens in 4th.
b Grounded out for Hermanski in 6th.
c Singled for Berra in 6th.
d Popped out for Jorgenson in 7th.
e Struck out for Barney in 7th.

Doubles—Brown, Jorgensen. Triples—Hermanski, Johnson. Stolen Base—Rizzuto. Sacrifice Hit—McQuinn. Double Play—Rizzuto to Stirnweiss to McQuinn. Left on Bases—Brooklyn 4, New York 9. Umpires—Rommel, Goetz, McGowan, Pinelli, Magerkurth, Boyer. Attendance—71,548. Time of Game—2:19.

1st Inning
Brooklyn
Stanky singled to right-center.
1 Stanky was caught stealing, A. Robinson to Stirnweiss.
Reese walked.
2 J. Robinson lined to right.
3 Reese caught stealing, A. Robinson to Rizzuto.
New York
1 Stirnweiss flied to right.
2 Henrich flied to left.
3 Berra grounded out, J. Robinson to Gregg.

2nd Inning
Brooklyn
1 Walker fouled to McQuinn.
Hermanski tripled to right.
Edwards singled to left, Hermanski scoring.
Furillo singled to center with Edwards stopping at second.
For New York—Bevens pitching.
Jorgensen doubled to right, Edwards scoring with Furillo stopping at third.
2 Gregg to first on a fielder's choice, Rizzuto took his hit and threw Furillo out at the plate.
3 Stanky popped to short.
New York
1 DiMaggio flied to center.
McQuinn walked.
2 Johnson popped to second.
A. Robinson walked.
Rizzuto singled to left, McQuinn scoring with A. Robinson stopping at second.
3 Bevens fanned.

3rd Inning
Brooklyn
1 Reese fanned.
2 J. Robinson fanned.
Walker walked.
3 Hermanski lined to third.
New York
Stirnweiss walked.
1 Henrich flied to right.
2 Berra flied to center.
3 DiMaggio flied to left.

4th Inning
Brooklyn
Edwards singled to left.
1 Furillo popped to second.
2 Jorgensen popped to second.
3 Gregg grounded to second.
New York
1 McQuinn fanned.
Johnson walked.
2 A. Robinson fanned.
Rizzuto singled to left with Johnson stopping at second.
Brown, pinch-hitting for Bevens, doubled to left to score Johnson and sending Rizzuto to third.
For Brooklyn—Behrman pitching.
Stirnweiss walked, loading the bases.
Henrich singled to right, Rizzuto scoring with the bases still loaded.
3 Berra grounded out, J. Robinson to Behrman.

5th Inning
Brooklyn
For New York—Page pitching.
1 Stanky grounded to second.
2 Reese flied to right.
3 J. Robinson lined to left.
New York
DiMaggio walked
1 McQuinn sacrificed DiMaggio to second, Jorgensen to Stanky (covering first).
2 Johnson grounded to second, moving DiMaggio to third.
3 A. Robinson flied to right.

6th Inning
Brooklyn
1 Walker lined to center.
2 Miksis, pinch-hitting for Hermanski, grounded to third.
3 Edwards flied to center.
New York
For Brooklyn—Miksis in left.
Rizzuto beat out a bunt.
Rizzuto stole second.
1 Page fanned.
Stirnweiss walked.
For Brooklyn—Hatten pitching.
2 Henrich fanned.
Clark, pinch-hitting for Berra, singled to center to score Rizzuto.
For Brooklyn—Barney pitching.
3 DiMaggio flied to center.

7th Inning
Brooklyn
For New York—Clark in right.
1 Furillo fouled to McQuinn.
2 Lavagetto, pinch-hitting for Jorgensen, popped to second.
3 Hodges, batting for Barney, fanned.
New York
For Brooklyn—Lavagetto stays in at third with Casey pitching.
1 McQuinn grounded to short.
Johnson tripled to left.
2 A. Robinson flied to left, Johnson scoring after the catch.
3 Rizzuto popped to second.

8th Inning
Brooklyn
1 Stanky flied to right.
2 Reese lined to right.
3 J. Robinson flied to center.
New York
1 Page grounded to first.
2 Stirnweiss flied to center.
3 Henrich flied to left.

9th Inning
Brooklyn
1 Walker grounded to second.
Miksis singled to center.
2,3 Edwards grounded into a double play, Rizzuto to Stirnweiss to McQuinn.

1947 WORLD SERIES COMPOSITE BOX

	Wins	Composite Line Score
New York Yankees (A.L.)	4	2 1 7 8 10 3 6 0 1 – 38
Brooklyn Dodgers (N.L.)	3	3 8 4 3 1 6 1 0 3 – 29

Manager	Regular Season W	L	Pct.	G. Ahead
Bucky Harris	97	57	.630	12
Clyde Sukeforth, Bert Shotton	94	60	.610	5

BATTING AND FIELDING

	WORLD SERIES STATISTICS Pos	G	AB	R	H	2B	3B	HR	RBI	BB	SO	SB	BA	SA	PO	A	E	REGULAR SEASON STATISTICS Main Pos	G	AB	R	H	2B	3B	HR	RBI	BB	SO	SB	BA	SA
NEW YORK YANKEES																															
George McQuinn	1b	7	23	3	3	0	0	0	1	5	8	0	.130	.130	48	4	1	1b	144	517	84	157	24	3	13	80	78	66	0	.304	.437
Snuffy Stirnweiss	2b	7	27	3	7	0	1	0	3	8	8	0	.259	.333	17	21	0	2b	148	571	102	146	18	8	5	41	89	47	5	.256	.342
Phil Rizzuto	ss	7	26	3	8	1	0	0	2	4	0	2	.308	.346	19	15	0	ss	153	549	78	150	26	9	2	60	57	31	11	.273	.364
Billy Johnson	3b	7	26	8	7	0	3	0	2	3	4	0	.269	.500	11	14	0	3b	132	494	67	141	19	8	10	95	44	43	1	.285	.417
Tommy Henrich	rf-lf	7	31	2	10	2	0	1	5	2	3	0	.323	.484	12	0	0	of	142	550	109	158	35	13	16	98	71	54	3	.287	.485
Joe DiMaggio	cf	7	26	4	6	0	0	2	5	6	2	0	.231	.462	22	0	0	of	141	534	97	168	31	10	20	97	64	32	3	.315	.522
Johnny Lindell	lf	6	18	3	9	3	1	0	7	5	2	0	.500	.778	11	0	0	of	127	476	66	131	18	7	11	67	32	70	1	.275	.412
Yogi Berra	c-ph-rf	6	19	2	3	0	0	1	2	1	2	0	.158	.316	21	2	2	c	83	293	41	82	15	3	11	54	13	12	0	.280	.464
Aaron Robinson	c	3	10	2	2	0	0	0	1	2	1	0	.200	.200	13	2	1	c	82	252	23	68	11	5	5	36	40	26	0	.270	.413
Sherm Lollar	c	2	4	3	3	2	0	0	1	0	0	0	.750	1.250	2	1	0	c	11	32	4	7	0	1	1	6	1	5	0	.219	.375
Bobby Brown	ph	4	3	2	3	2	0	0	3	1	0	0	1.000	1.667				3b	69	150	21	45	6	1	1	18	21	9	0	.300	.373
Allie Clark	ph-rf	3	2	1	1	0	0	0	1	1	0	0	.500	.500	2	0	0	of	24	67	9	25	5	0	1	14	5	2	0	.373	.493
Jack Phillips	ph-1b	2	2	0	0	0	0	0	0	0	0	0	.000	.000	4	0	0	1b	16	36	5	10	0	1	1	2	3	5	0	.278	.417
Lonnie Frey	ph	1	1	0	0	0	0	0	1	0	0	0	.000	.000				a ph-2b	24	28	10	5	2	0	0	2	10	1	3	.179	.250
Ralph Houk	ph	1	1	0	1	0	0	0	0	0	0	0	1.00	1.000				c	41	92	7	25	3	1	0	12	11	5	0	.272	.326
Charlie Keller	Did not play																	of	45	151	36	36	6	1	13	36	41	18	0	.238	.550
Spec Shea	p	3	5	0	2	1	0	0	1	0	2	0	.400	.600	1	3	0	p	27	56	8	11	2	1	0	1	5	9	0	.196	.268
Allie Reynolds	p	2	4	2	2	0	0	0	1	0	0	0	.500	.500	1	0	0	p	38	89	7	13	1	0	0	5	7	26	0	.146	.157
Joe Page	p	4	4	0	0	0	0	0	0	0	1	0	.000	.000	1	2	0	p	56	46	1	10	0	0	1	5	2	16	0	.217	.283
Bill Bevens	p	2	4	0	0	0	0	0	0	0	2	0	.000	.000	0	1	0	p	28	58	2	7	1	0	0	1	2	31	0	.121	.138
Karl Drews	p	2	2	0	0	0	0	0	0	0	2	0	.000	.000	0	3	0	p	30	27	1	1	0	0	0	0	3	6	0	.037	.037
Bobo Newsom	p	2	0	0	0	0	0	0	0	0	0	0	—	—	0	1	0	b p	17	42	0	4	0	0	0	1	0	11	0	.095	.095
Vic Raschi	p	2	0	0	0	0	0	0	0	0	0	0	—	—	0	0	0	p	15	40	5	10	2	0	0	3	1	7	0	.250	.300
Spud Chandler	p	1	0	0	0	0	0	0	0	0	0	0	—	—	0	0	0	p	17	49	5	12	3	0	2	4	1	10	1	.245	.429
Butch Wensloff	p	1	0	0	0	0	0	0	0	0	0	0	—	—	0	1	0	p	11	19	1	5	0	0	0	1	1	7	0	.263	.263
Randy Gumpert	Did not play																	p	25	14	0	1	0	0	0	0	0	7	0	.071	.071
Don Johnson	Did not play																	p	15	13	0	0	0	0	0	0	1	8	0	.000	.000
team total		7	238	38	67	11	5	4	36	38	37	2	.282	.424	185	70	4		155	5308	794	1439	230	72	115	746	610	581	27	.271	.407

Double Plays—4
Left on Bases—63

a—from Chicago (N)
b—from Washington
Frank Colman (of), Johnny Lucadello (2b), Frankie Crosetti (ss), Ken Silvestri (c), Ted Sepkowski (pr), Ray Mack (ph), Al Lyons (p), Dick Starr (p), Bill Wight (p), Mel Queen (p), Tommy Byrne (p), and Rugger Andizioa (p) also played for the Yankees during the season.

	WORLD SERIES STATISTICS Pos	G	AB	R	H	2B	3B	HR	RBI	BB	SO	SB	BA	SA	PO	A	E	REGULAR SEASON STATISTICS Main Pos	G	AB	R	H	2B	3B	HR	RBI	BB	SO	SB	BA	SA
BROOKLYN DODGERS																															
Jackie Robinson	1b	7	27	3	7	2	0	0	3	2	4	2	.259	.333	49	6	0	1b	159	590	125	175	31	5	12	48	74	36	29	.297	.427
Eddie Stanky	2b	7	25	4	6	1	0	0	2	3	2	0	.240	.280	18	19	1	2b	146	559	97	141	24	5	3	53	103	39	3	.252	.329
Pee Wee Reese	ss	7	23	5	7	1	0	0	4	6	3	3	.304	.348	8	15	1	ss	142	476	81	135	24	4	12	73	104	67	7	.284	.426
Spider Jorgensen	3b	7	20	1	4	2	0	0	3	2	4	0	.200	.300	8	12	2	3b	129	441	57	121	29	8	5	67	58	45	4	.274	.410
Dixie Walker	rf	7	27	1	6	1	0	1	4	3	1	1	.222	.370	9	1	0	of	148	529	77	162	31	3	9	94	97	26	6	.306	.427
Carl Furillo	ph-cf	6	17	2	6	2	0	0	3	3	0	0	.353	.471	14	1	1	of	124	437	61	129	24	7	8	88	34	24	7	.295	.437
Gene Hermanski	lf	7	19	4	3	0	1	0	1	3	3	0	.158	.263	15	0	0	of	79	189	36	52	7	1	7	39	28	7	5	.275	.434
Bruce Edwards	c	7	27	3	6	1	0	0	2	2	7	0	.222	.259	44	4	1	c	130	471	53	139	15	8	9	80	49	55	2	.295	.418
Pete Reiser	cf-lf-ph	5	8	1	2	0	0	0	0	3	1	0	.250	.250	7	0	1	of	110	388	68	120	23	2	5	46	68	41	14	.309	.418
Cookie Lavagetto	ph-3b	5	7	0	1	1	0	0	3	0	2	0	.143	.246	0	1	0	3b	41	67	6	18	1	0	3	11	12	5	0	.261	.406
Eddie Miksis	ph-pr-2b-lf	5	4	1	1	0	0	0	0	0	1	0	.250	.250	3	1	1	inf-of	45	86	18	23	1	0	4	10	9	8	0	.267	.419
Al Gionfriddo	ph-lf	4	3	2	0	0	0	0	0	1	0	1	.000	.000	1	0	0	c of	37	62	10	11	2	1	0	6	16	11	2	.177	.242
Arky Vaughan	ph	3	2	0	1	1	0	0	0	1	0	0	.500	1.000				of	64	126	24	41	5	2	2	25	27	11	4	.325	.444
Bobby Bragan	ph	1	1	0	1	1	0	0	1	0	0	0	1.000	2.000				c	25	36	3	7	2	0	0	3	7	3	1	.194	.250
Gil Hodges	ph	1	1	0	0	0	0	0	0	0	1	0	.000	.000				c	28	77	9	12	3	1	1	7	14	19	0	.156	.260
Stan Rojek	Did not play																	ss	32	80	7	21	0	1	0	7	7	3	1	.263	.288
Tommy Brown	Did not play																	3b	15	34	3	8	1	0	0	2	1	6	0	.235	.265
Ralph Branca	p	3	4	0	0	0	0	0	0	0	1	0	.000	.000	0	1	0	p	43	97	8	12	1	0	0	9	7	34	0	.124	.134
Joe Hatten	p	4	3	1	1	0	0	0	0	0	0	0	.333	.333	0	0	0	p	42	83	3	17	2	0	0	8	2	16	1	.205	.229
Hal Gregg	p	3	3	0	0	0	0	0	0	1	1	0	.000	.000	1	3	0	p	37	34	3	9	1	0	0	2	1	8	0	.265	.294
Vic Lombardi	p-pr	3	3	0	0	0	0	0	0	0	0	0	.000	.000	0	0	0	p	36	66	1	16	2	0	0	6	1	4	0	.242	.273
Hugh Casey	p	6	1	0	0	0	0	0	0	0	1	0	.000	.000	2	3	0	p	46	18	0	1	0	0	0	1	1	2	0	.056	.056
Rex Barney	p	3	1	0	0	0	0	0	0	0	0	0	.000	.000	0	1	0	p	28	27	3	3	1	0	0	3	0	12	0	.111	.148
Hank Behrman	p	5	0	0	0	0	0	0	0	0	0	0	—	—	1	3	0	d p	40	26	1	6	1	0	0	1	1	9	0	.231	.269
Harry Taylor	p	1	0	0	0	0	0	0	0	0	0	0	—	—	0	0	0	p	33	62	3	8	2	1	0	8	0	15	0	.129	.194
Dan Bankhead	pr	1	0	1	0	0	0	0	0	0	0	0	—	—	0	0	0	p	6	4	2	1	0	0	1	2	0	1	0	.250	1.000
Clyde King	Did not play																	p	29	26	1	3	1	0	0	4	1	12	0	.115	.154
team total:		7	226	29	52	13	1	1	26	30	32	7	.230	.314	180	71	8		155	5249	774	1428	241	50	83	719	732	561	88	.272	.384

Double Plays—8
Left on Bases—46

c—from Pittsburgh
d—to and from Pittsburgh
Duke Snider (of), Marv Rackley (of), Don Lund (of), Ed Stevens (1b), Tommy Tatum (of), Dick Whitman (cf), Howie Schultz (1b), Kirby Higbe (p), Phil Haugstad (p), Willie Ramsdell (p), Ed Chandler (p), Rube Melton (p), Jack Banta (p), Erv Palica (p), George Dockins (p), and Johnny Van Cuyk (p) also played for the Dodgers during the season.

PITCHING

	WORLD SERIES STATISTICS G	GS	CG	IP	H	R	ER	BB	SO	W	L	SV	ERA	REGULAR SEASON STATISTICS G	GS	CG	IP	H	ER	BB	SO	W	L	Pct	SV	ShO	ERA
NEW YORK YANKEES																											
Spec Shea	3	3	1	15 1/3	10	4	4	8	10	2	0	0	2.35	27	23	13	179	127	61	89	89	14	5	.737	1	3	3.07
Joe Page	4	0	0	13	12	6	6	2	7	1	1	1	4.15	56	2	0	141	105	39	72	116	14	8	.636	17	0	2.49
Bill Bevens	2	1	1	11 1/3	3	3	3	7	11	0	1	0	2.38	28	23	11	165	167	70	77	77	7	13	.350	0	1	3.82
Allie Reynolds	2	2	1	11 1/3	15	7	6	3	6	1	0	0	4.76	34	30	17	242	207	86	123	129	19	8	.704	2	4	3.20
Karl Drews	2	0	0	3	2	1	1	1	0	0	0	0	3.00	30	10	0	92	92	50	55	45	6	6	.500	1	0	4.89
Bobo Newsom	2	1	0	2 1/3	6	5	5	2	0	0	1	0	19.29	b 17	15	6	116	109	36	30	42	7	5	.583	0	2	2.79
Butch Wensloff	1	0	0	2	0	0	0	0	0	0	0	0	0.00	11	5	1	52	41	15	22	18	3	1	.750	0	0	2.60
Spud Chandler	1	0	0	2	2	2	2	3	1	0	0	0	9.00	17	16	13	128	100	35	41	68	9	5	.643	0	2	2.46
Vic Paschi	2	0	0	1 1/3	2	1	1	0	1	0	0	0	6.75	15	14	6	105	89	45	38	51	7	2	.778	0	1	3.86
Randy Gumpert	Did not play													24	6	2	56	71	34	28	25	4	1	.800	0	0	5.46
Don Johnson	Did not play													15	8	2	54	57	22	23	16	4	3	.571	0	0	3.67
team total	7	7	3	61 2/3	52	29	28	30	32	4	3	1	4.09	155	155	73	1374	1221	518	628	691	97	57	.630	21	14	3.39
BROOKLYN DODGERS																											
Hal Gregg	3	1	0	12 2/3	9	5	5	8	10	0	1	0	3.55	37	16	2	104	115	68	55	59	4	5	.444	1	1	5.88
Hugh Casey	6	0	0	10 1/3	5	1	1	1	3	2	0	1	0.87	46	0	0	77	75	34	29	40	10	4	.714	18	0	3.97
Joe Hatten	4	1	0	9	12	7	7	7	5	0	0	0	7.00	42	32	11	225	211	91	105	76	17	8	.680	0	3	3.64
Ralph Branca	3	1	0	8 1/3	12	8	8	5	8	1	1	0	8.64	43	36	15	280	251	83	98	148	21	12	.636	1	4	2.67
Rex Barney	3	1	0	6 2/3	4	2	2	10	3	0	0	0	2.70	28	9	0	78	66	43	59	36	5	2	.714	0	0	4.96
Vic Lombardi	2	2	0	6 2/3	14	9	9	1	5	0	1	0	12.15	33	20	7	175	156	58	65	72	12	11	.522	3	3	2.98
Hank Behrman	5	0	0	6 1/3	9	5	5	5	3	0	0	0	7.11	d 40	6	0	92	97	56	48	33	5	3	.625	8	0	5.48
Harry Taylor	1	1	0	0	2	1	0	1	0	0	0	0	0.00	33	20	10	162	130	56	83	58	10	5	.667	1	2	3.11
Dan Bankhead	Did not pitch													4	0	0	10	15	8	8	6	0	0	—	1	0	7.20
Clyde King	Did not play													29	9	2	88	85	27	29	31	6	5	.545	0	0	2.76
team total	7	7	0	60	67	38	37	38	37	3	4	1	5.55	155	155	47	1375	1299	583	626	592	94	60	.610	34	14	3.82

Total Attendance—389,763 Average Attendance—55,680 Winning Player's Share—$5,830 Losing Player's Share—$4,081

1948 Play-off
Haunted by the Green Monster

Going into the final weekend of the season, the Cleveland Indians had apparently won a close three-way race for the American League pennant. They led the Boston Red Sox and the New York Yankees by one and a half games on Friday morning with the schedule ending on Sunday. But with the Red Sox and Yankees off for the day, the Indians blew their Friday game to the Tigers 5–3 by allowing three runs in the ninth inning. The Red Sox eliminated the Yankees with a 5–1 decision in Boston on Saturday, but the Indians beat Detroit 8–0 behind Gene Bearden's eight-hitter to clinch at least a tie for the flag. Only a Boston victory and a Cleveland loss on Sunday could deadlock the race, and that is exactly what happened. The Red Sox clubbed the Yanks 10–5, while the Indians lost to the Tigers 7–1, with Bob Feller losing to Hal Newhouser in a battle of aces. The A.L.'s first pennant play-off, a single game on Monday in Boston, capped heroic seasons for both clubs. Indian owner Bill Veeck had boosted attendance with a series of lively promotions, while manager Lou Boudreau, an experienced skipper at age thirty, blistered the ball at a .355 clip with 106 RBI's and cemented a fine infield with his play at shortstop. Boston manager Joe McCarthy, the old Yankee mentor lured out of retirement, had an unimpeachable star in Ted Williams, who hit .369 and drove in 127 runs. With the Boston Braves champions in the National League, the Red Sox hoped to give Boston its first intercity World Series.

The one-game showdown on a cold October 4 brought together two hard-hitting clubs which had exhausted their pitching staffs in the final days of the regular campaign. The two skippers took different tacks in choosing their pitchers for the play-off. McCarthy opted for a well-rested hurler and chose thirty-six-year-old Denny Galehouse, a right-hander with an 8–8 record. Boudreau decided instead to stick with his best hurlers, and his nod went to Bearden, a twenty-eight-year-old rookie who had pitched nine shutout innings against Detroit on Saturday.

Both pitchers had shaky first innings. Galehouse retired the first two Indians, then served up a fat pitch which Boudreau sent flying over the Green Monster, the tall, invitingly close left-field wall in Fenway Park. The Red Sox came right back in the bottom of the first inning, however, with Pesky doubling and coming home on a single to left by Vern Stephens.

In the fourth inning, the Indian bats warmed up in the New England chill. Boudreau, playing an inspired game, led the inning off with a single. Joe Gordon then followed with a single, and Ken Keltner lifted a long shot over the Green Monster to put the Indians ahead 4–1 and end McCarthy's experiment with Galehouse. Into the game came Ellis Kinder, a stocky right-hander with a 10–7 mark for the year. He began his stint on the mound by giving up a double into left-center by Larry Doby. Bob Kennedy moved Doby over to third base with a sacrifice bunt, and Doby then scored on an infield grounder by Jim Hegan. Kinder got through the fourth inning smoothly and retired the first two men in the fifth. Boudreau, however, belted a pitch for his second homer of the day, putting his club ahead 6–1. Bearden, meanwhile, seemingly had the game well in hand, his fluttering knuckle ball allowing the Sox nothing more dangerous than grounders for most of the afternoon. But in the bottom of the sixth, the big right-hander ran into trouble. Ted Williams had reached base when second baseman Gordon dropped his towering pop-up because of the glare of the sun. After Stephens whiffed, Bobby Doerr parked a pitch over the left-field target to cut the score to 6–3. But that was to be the extent of the Boston scoring for the day. The Indians got another run in the eighth inning on a hit, a walk, and a dropped fly ball by Williams, then turned two hits in the ninth into a final insurance tally. The 8–3 triumph triggered a merry Indian clubhouse celebration centering around Bearden, who won his twentieth game, and Boudreau, who led his team to victory by example.

American League PLAYOFF GAME
October 4 at Boston

Cle. 1 0 0   4 1 0   0 1 1
Bos. 1 0 0   0 0 2   0 0 0

Cleveland	Pos	AB	R	H	RBI	PO	A	E
Mitchell	lf	5	0	1	0	1	0	0
Clark	1b	2	0	0	0	5	0	0
Robinson	1b	2	1	1	0	9	0	0
Boudreau	ss	4	3	4	2	3	5	0
Gordon	2b	4	1	1	0	2	3	1
Keltner	3b	5	1	3	3	0	6	0
Doby	cf	5	1	2	0	1	0	0
Kennedy	rf	2	0	0	0	0	0	0
Hegan	c	3	1	0	1	6	1	0
Bearden	p	3	0	1	0	0	2	0
Totals		35	8	13	6	27	17	1

Pitching	IP	H	R	ER	BB	SO
Cleveland						
Bearden (W)	9	5	3	3	5	6
Boston						
Galehouse (L)	*3	5	4	4	1	1
Kinder	6	8	4	3	3	2

*Pitched to 3 batters in 4th.

Boston	Pos	AB	R	H	RBI	PO	A	E
DiMaggio	cf	4	0	0	0	3	0	0
Pesky	3b	4	1	1	0	3	4	0
Williams	lf	4	1	1	0	3	0	1
Stephens	ss	4	0	1	1	2	4	0
Doerr	2b	4	1	1	2	5	2	0
Spence	rf	1	0	0	0	1	0	0
a Hitchcock		0	0	0	0	0	0	0
b Wright		0	0	0	0	0	0	0
Goodman	1b	3	0	0	0	7	1	0
Tebbetts	c	4	0	1	0	3	1	0
Galehouse	p	0	0	0	0	0	1	0
Kinder	p	2	0	0	0	0	1	0
Totals		30	3	5	3	27	14	1

a Walked for Spence in 9th.
b Ran for Hitchcock in 9th.

Doubles—Doby 2, Keltner, Pesky.
Home Runs—Boudreau 2, Doerr, Keltner.
Sacrifice Hits—Kennedy 2, Robinson.
Double Plays—Hegan to Boudreau, Gordon to Boudreau to Robinson, Bearden to Gordon to Robinson, Stephens to Doerr to Goodman 2. Wild Pitch—Kinder.
Left on Bases—Cleveland 7, Boston 5.
Umpires—McGowan, Summers, Rommel, Berry.
Attendance—33,957. Time of Game—2:24.

1948
Not Enough Rain

The Yankees, Dodgers, Cardinals, and Giants had played in more than their share of World Series, but they were upstaged this year by two clubs who had only a passing acquaintance with Series pressure. The Cleveland Indians made it to the Series for the first time since 1920 by beating the Boston Red Sox in a one-game play-off for the American League flag, while the Boston Braves brought the Series to Bean Town by winning their first pennant since 1914. The Indians had a colorful owner in Bill Veeck, who staged numerous imaginative promotions to hype attendance, and the best kind of manager in Lou Boudreau, one who aided the team's cause by playing air-tight shortstop, driving in 106 runs, and batting .355. Helping out the skipper in the infield were second baseman Joe Gordon and third baseman Ken Keltner, both with over 30 homers and 100 RBI's. Fireballing Bob Feller, the top pitcher in the majors for years, had 19 wins in his first championship season, while converted infielder Bob Lemon and rookie knuckleballer Gene Bearden each chalked up 20 wins. Veeck bolstered the club with talent out of the Negro leagues, signing powerful Larry Doby to play center field and forty-one-year-old legend Satchel Paige to pitch in spots.

The Braves lacked the power of the Indian lineup, but Boston manager Billy Southworth, who headed the war-time Cardinal champs, had five .300 hitters in his attack, featuring Mike McCormick, Jeff Heath, Tommy Holmes, and a new double-play combination of Alvin Dark and Eddie Stanky. Southworth had two excellent pitchers in righty Johnny Sain and lefty Warren Spahn, and the other starters so paled in the reputation of these two that the catchphrase of the club was "Spahn and Sain and two days of rain." When the rain did not materialize, Bob Voiselle and Vern Bickford often did the pitching and did it well.

Southworth went with 24-game-winner Sain in game one at Boston, while Bob Feller made his Series debut for the Indians. Like Walter Johnson, Feller had the affection of the fans for his years of excellence, but his superb performance today went for naught as he dropped a 1–0 heartbreaker. Bill Salkeld walked in the bottom of the eighth, and Phil Masi ran for him. After moving to second on a sacrifice, Masi was obviously picked off by Feller, but umpire Bill Stewart claimed that Masi somehow slipped past Boudreau's tag. Arguing did not change the decision, and a single by Holmes drove Masi in with the only tally of the contest. The angered Indians came back the next day to take out their frustrations on Spahn, who left the game in the fifth inning and wound up the loser in a 4–1 game. Bob Lemon got credit for the win by scattering eight hits, the same number of hits the Indians had collected.

The teams proceeded to Cleveland directly for game three, and since there was no rain, the Braves sent out Bickford to oppose Bearden, the twenty-seven-year-old freshman who had suffered serious knee and head injuries in the war when his cruiser was sunk. Both sides again got the same amount of hits, but the Indians used their five to score two runs while the Braves never crossed the plate against Bearden. The Indians the next day again got only five hits off Sain, but they strung these together into a 2–1 victory, with Steve Gromek pitching the entire game and Larry Doby clouting a long homer. The Indians now had won three straight since dropping the opener, and they sent Feller out to clinch the title. A record crowd of 86,288 turned out to root for the ace, but the Braves got hold of Feller's fast balls this day and drove him from the box in the seventh inning while rolling to an 11–5 victory, with Spahn getting the win in relief of Nelson Potter.

That triumph gave the Braves some hope of coming back, but the Indians put the heat on in game six by going ahead 4–1 behind Lemon after seven and a half innings. In the bottom of the eighth, the Braves loaded the bases with one out, and Boudreau brought in Bearden to put out the fire. One run scored on a sacrifice fly and another counted on a pinch double by Masi, but Bearden kept the tying run on third and closed the Series out in the ninth. The Indian fans savored their first World Championship in 28 years, but Bob Feller, unlike Walter Johnson, did not win a Series game.

Game 1 October 6 at Boston

Cle.	000	000	000				
Bos.	000	000	01x				

Cleveland	Pos	AB	R	H	RBI	PO	A	E
Mitchell	lf	4	0	0	0	2	0	0
Doby	cf	4	0	1	0	3	0	0
Boudreau	ss	4	0	0	0	2	1	0
Gordon	2b	4	0	1	0	1	1	0
Keltner	3b	4	0	1	0	1	1	0
Judnich	rf	4	0	0	0	2	0	0
Robinson	1b	3	0	0	0	10	1	0
Hegan	c	3	0	1	0	2	1	0
Feller	p	2	0	0	0	1	4	0
Totals		32	0	4	0	24	9	0

Pitching	IP	H	R	ER	BB	SO
Cleveland						
Feller (L)	8	2	1	1	3	2
Boston						
Sain (W)	9	4	0	0	0	6

Boston	Pos	AB	R	H	RBI	PO	A	E
Holmes	rf	4	0	1	1	5	0	0
Dark	ss	4	0	0	0	1	1	0
Torgeson	1b	2	0	0	0	4	0	0
Elliott	3b	3	0	0	1	0	2	0
Rickert	lf	3	0	1	0	5	0	0
Salkeld	c	1	0	0	0	5	1	0
a Masi	c	0	1	0	0	1	0	0
M. McCormick	cf	2	0	0	0	5	0	0
Stanky	2b	2	0	0	0	1	0	0
b Sisti	2b	0	0	0	0	0	0	0
Sain	p	3	0	0	0	0	0	0
Totals		24	1	2	1	27	3	2

a Ran for Salkeld in 8th.
b Ran for Stanky in 8th.

Sacrifice Hits—Feller, M. McCormick, Salkeld. Stolen Bases—Gordon, Hegan, Torgeson. Left on Bases—Cleveland 6, Boston 4. Umpires—Barr (N), Summers (A), Stewart (N), Grieve (A), Paparella (A), Pinelli (N). Attendance—40,135. Time of Game—1:42.

1st Inning
Cleveland
1 Mitchell flied to center.
2 Doby flied to center.
3 Boudreau fouled to Rickert.
Boston
1 Holmes flied to center.
2 Dark grounded to first.
3 Torgeson took a called third strike.

2nd Inning
Cleveland
1 Gordon called out on strikes.
  Keltner singled to left.
2 Judnich lined to right.
3 Robinson grounded to first.
Boston
1 Elliott flied to right.
2 Rickert flied to center.
3 Salkeld struck out.

3rd Inning
Cleveland
  Hegan was safe at first on Elliott's fumble.
1 Feller struck out.
2 Mitchell fouled to Elliott.
  Hegan stole second.
3 Doby grounded to short.
Boston
1 M. McCormick popped to short.
2 Stanky popped to third.
3 Sain fouled to Robinson.

4th Inning
Cleveland
1 Boudreau struck out, Salkeld holding the foul tip.
  Gordon singled to center.
2 Keltner struck out as Gordon was stealing second.
3 Judnich flied to right.
Boston
1 Holmes rolled back to the mound.
2 Dark grounded to second.
  Torgeson walked.
  Torgeson stole second.
3 Elliott flied to left.

5th Inning
Cleveland
1 Robinson flied to right.
  Hegan singled to left.
2 Feller sacrificed Hegan to second, Salkeld to Torgeson.
3 Mitchell flied to left.
Boston
  Rickert singled to left.
1 Salkeld sacrificed Rickert to second, Hegan to Robinson.
2 M. McCormick popped to second.
3 Stanky rolled back to the pitcher.

6th Inning
Cleveland
  Doby singled to center.
1 Boudreau bounced to second, Doby moving to second.
2 Gordon flied to left.
3 Keltner flied to left.
Boston
1 Sain grounded to short.
2 Holmes flied to left.
3 Dark flied to center.

7th Inning
Cleveland
1 Judnich flied to right.
2 Robinson flied to right.
3 Hegan flied to center.
Boston
1 Torgeson grounded out, Robinson to Feller.
2 Elliott grounded back to the mound.
3 Rickert popped to short.

8th Inning
Cleveland
1 Feller fanned.
2 Mitchell lined to center.
3 Doby fouled to Rickert.
Boston
  Salkeld walked.
  Masi ran for Salkeld.
1 M. McCormick sacrificed Masi to second, Feller to Robinson.
  Stanky intentionally walked.
  Sisti ran for Stanky.
  (A controversial pick-off play occurred, Feller to Boudreau to get Masi, but Ump Stewart called Masi safe. A big rhubarb ensued).
2 Sain lined to right.
  Holmes singled beyond third, scoring Masi and on the throw to the plate Sisti went to third and Holmes to second.
3 Dark grounded to third.

9th Inning
Cleveland
  For Boston—Masi now catching, Sisti at second.
1 Boudreau flied to center.
2 Gordon fouled to Dark.
  Keltner got all the way to second as Elliott threw wildly to first on his bouncer.
3 Judnich struck out.

Game 2 October 7 at Boston

Cleveland	Pos	AB	R	H	RBI	PO	A	E
Mitchell	lf	5	1	1	0	1	0	0
Clark	rf	3	0	0	0	2	0	0
Kennedy	rf	1	0	1	1	0	0	0
Boudreau	ss	5	1	2	1	4	2	0
Gordon	2b	4	1	1	1	2	3	1
Keltner	3b	4	0	0	0	0	0	0
Doby	cf	4	0	2	1	0	0	0
Robinson	1b	3	0	1	0	8	3	0
Hegan	c	3	1	0	0	7	0	0
Lemon	p	4	0	0	0	3	6	0
Totals		36	4	8	4	27	14	1

Pitching	IP	H	R	ER	BB	SO
Cleveland						
Lemon (W)	9	8	1	0	3	5
Boston						
Spahn (L)	4⅓	6	3	3	2	1
Barrett	2⅔	1	0	0	0	1
Potter	2	1	1	0	0	1

Cle.	000	210	001
Bos.	100	000	000

Boston	Pos	AB	R	H	RBI	PO	A	E
Holmes	rf	4	0	0	0	2	1	0
Dark	ss	4	1	1	0	0	2	2
Torgeson	1b	4	0	2	0	14	1	0
Elliott	3b	4	0	1	1	1	5	1
Rickert	lf	4	0	0	0	5	0	0
Salkeld	c	1	0	1	0	2	0	0
a Masi	c	1	0	0	0	1	0	0
M. McCormick	cf	4	0	1	0	0	0	0
Stanky	2b	2	0	1	0	1	3	0
Spahn	p	2	0	0	0	0	1	0
Barrett	p	0	0	0	0	0	0	0
b F. McCormick		1	0	0	0	0	0	0
Potter	p	0	0	0	0	0	0	0
c Sanders		1	0	0	0	0	0	0
Totals		32	1	8	1	27	13	3

a Ran for Salkeld in 6th.
b Struck out for Barrett in 7th.
c Grounded out for Sanders in 9th.

Doubles—Boudreau, Doby, Stanky.
Sacrifice Hits—Clark, Stanky.
Double Plays—Holmes to Torgeson, Boudreau to Gordon to Robinson, Gordon to Boudreau to Robinson.
Left on Bases—Cleveland 8, Boston 8.
Umpires—Summers, Stewart, Grieve, Barr, Pinelli, Paparella. Attendance—39,633.
Time of Game—2:14.

1st Inning
Cleveland
1 Mitchell fouled to Elliott.
2 Clark struck out.
3 Boudreau grounded to third.
Boston
1 Holmes grounded back to the mound.
 Dark safely on first when Gordon fumbled his bouncer.
 Torgeson singled to right, advancing Dark to third.
 Elliott singled to left, Dark scoring with Torgeson stopping at second.
2 Torgeson was picked off second, Lemon to Boudreau.
3 Rickert struck out.

2nd Inning
Cleveland
1 Gordon grounded to short.
2 Keltner flied to left.
 Doby doubled to left-center.
 Robinson walked.
3 Hegan flied to center.
Boston
 Salkeld singled to right.
1 M. McCormick popped to the pitcher on an attempted bunt.
 Stanky walked.
2 Spahn grounded to second, advancing both runners.
3 Holmes again tapped back to the mound.

3rd Inning
Cleveland
1 Lemon flied to left.
2 Mitchell fouled to Rickert.
3 Clark grounded to third.
Boston
 Dark singled to left.
1 Torgeson flied to right.
2 Elliott struck out.
3 Rickert grounded back to the pitcher.

4th Inning
Cleveland
 Boudreau got a double into the right field corner.
 Gordon singled to left, scoring Boudreau and going to second on the throw in.
1 Keltner fouled to Rickert.
 Doby singled to right, Gordon scoring with Doby taking second on the throw to the plate.
2 Robinson flied to left.
 Hegan got an intentional walk.
3 Lemon bounced back to the mound.
Boston
 Salkeld walked.
 M. McCormick singled to left with Salkeld stopping at second.
1 Stanky sacrificed up both runners, Robinson to Gordon.
2 Spahn grounded to the mound.
3 Holmes flied to left.

5th Inning
Cleveland
 Mitchell singled to left.
1 Clark sacrificed Mitchell to second, Torgeson to Stanky.
 Boudreau singled to center, scoring Mitchell.
 For Boston—Barrett pitching.
2 Gordon grounded to first, sending Boudreau to second.
3 Keltner grounded to third.
Boston
1 Dark struck out.
2 Torgeson grounded out, Robinson to Lemon.
3 Elliott fouled to Hegan.

6th Inning
Cleveland
1 Doby struck out.
 Robinson singled over second.
2,3 Hegan flied to Holmes who threw to Torgeson to double up Robinson.
Boston
1 Rickert popped to short.
 Salkeld walked.
 M. McCormick singled to center, Salkeld stopping at second.
 Masi ran for Salkeld.
2,3 Stanky grounded into a double play, Boudreau to Gordon to Robinson.

7th Inning
Cleveland
 For Boston—Masi catching.
1 Lemon flied to right.
2 Mitchell grounded to second.
 Clark safe at first on Dark's boot of his grounder.
 Boudreau also safe on an Elliott boot.
3 Gordon grounded to third.
Boston
1 F. McCormick, pinch-hitting for Barrett, struck out.
2 Holmes popped to short.
3 Dark flied to right.

8th Inning
Cleveland
 For Boston—Potter pitching.
1 Keltner grounded to short.
2 Doby struck out.
3 Robinson grounded to second.
Boston
 For Cleveland—Kennedy in right.
 Torgeson singled to center.
1,2 Elliott hit into a double play, Gordon to Boudreau to Robinson.
3 Rickert grounded out, Robinson to Lemon.

9th Inning
Cleveland
 Hegan safe at first on Dark's fumble.
1 Lemon grounded to first, moving Hegan to second.
2 Mitchell grounded to second, Hegan going to third.
 Kennedy singled to right, scoring Hegan.
3 Boudreau grounded to second.
Boston
1 Masi fouled to Hegan.
2 M. McCormick struck out.
 Stanky doubled to left-center.
3 Sanders, pinch-hitting for Potter, hit back to the mound.

Game 3 October 8 at Cleveland

Boston	Pos	AB	R	H	RBI	PO	A	E
Holmes	rf	4	0	0	0	2	0	0
Dark	ss	4	0	1	0	3	2	1
M. McCormick	lf	4	0	1	0	6	0	0
Elliott	3b	3	0	1	0	2	1	0
F. McCormick	1b	3	0	1	0	5	1	0
Conatser	cf	3	0	0	0	1	0	0
Masi	c	3	0	0	0	2	0	0
Stanky	2b	3	0	1	0	2	3	0
Bickford	p	0	0	0	0	0	0	0
Voiselle	p	1	0	0	0	1	0	0
a Ryan		1	0	0	0	0	0	0
Barrett	p	0	0	0	0	0	0	0
Totals		29	0	5	0	24	7	1

a Struck out for Voiselle in 8th.

Doubles—Bearden, Dark.
Sacrifice Hit—Bickford.
Double Plays—Dark to Stanky to F. McCormick, Bearden to Gordon to Robinson, Keltner to Gordon to Robinson.
Left on Bases—Boston 3, Cleveland 7.
Umpires—Stewart, Grieve, Barr, Summers, Paparella, Pinelli. Attendance—70,306.
Time of Game—1:36.

Bos.	000	000	000
Cle.	001	100	00x

Cleveland	Pos	AB	R	H	RBI	PO	A	E
Mitchell	lf	3	0	0	0	2	0	0
Doby	cf	3	0	1	0	1	0	0
Boudreau	ss	3	0	0	0	1	2	0
Gordon	2b	4	0	0	0	3	4	0
Keltner	3b	3	1	0	0	0	4	0
Judnich	rf	3	0	0	0	1	0	0
Robinson	1b	3	0	1	0	14	0	0
Hegan	c	3	0	1	1	5	0	0
Bearden	p	3	1	2	0	0	6	0
Totals		28	2	5	1	27	16	0

Pitching	IP	H	R	ER	BB	SO
Boston						
Bickford (L)	3⅓	4	2	1	5	1
Voiselle	3⅔	1	0	0	0	0
Barrett	1	0	0	0	0	0
Cleveland						
Bearden (W)	9	5	0	0	0	4

1st Inning
Boston
1 Holmes grounded to short.
2 Dark struck out.
3 M. McCormick struck out.
Cleveland
1 Mitchell lined to left.
 Doby walked.
2,3 Boudreau hit into a double play, Dark to Stanky to F. McCormick.

2nd Inning
Boston
1 Elliott grounded to third.
 F. McCormick singled to center.
2 Conatser grounded back to the mound, F. McCormick going to second.
3 Masi flied to left.
Cleveland
1 Gordon flied to left.
2 Keltner grounded to first.
 Judnich walked.
3 Robinson flied to left.

3rd Inning
Boston
 Stanky singled to right.
1 Bickford sacrificed Stanky to second, Hegan unassisted.
2 Holmes rolled to the pitcher, moving Stanky to third.
3 Dark flied to right.
Cleveland
1 Hegan fouled to Masi.
 Bearden doubled to right.
 Mitchell walked.
2 Doby forced Mitchell at second, Stanky to Dark, but Dark threw wildly to first to double Doby. Bearden scored and Doby went to second.
 Boudreau walked.
3 Gordon flied to left.

4th Inning
Boston
 M. McCormick singled to center.
1 Elliott flied to center.
2,3 F. McCormick hit into a double play, Bearden to Gordon to Robinson.
Cleveland
 Keltner walked.
1 Judnich struck out.
 Robinson singled to left, Keltner stopping at second.
 Hegan singled to center, scoring Keltner with Robinson stopping at second.
 Bearden singled to left, to load the bases.
 For Boston—Voiselle pitching.
2 Mitchell fouled to Elliott.
3 Doby grounded out, F. McCormick to Voiselle.

5th Inning
Boston
1 Conatser grounded to third.
2 Masi grounded to third.
3 Stanky flied to left.
Cleveland
1 Boudreau popped to third.
2 Gordon grounded to third.
3 Keltner flied to left.

6th Inning
Boston
1 Voiselle grounded to short.
2 Holmes grounded to second.
 Dark doubled to left.
3 M. McCormick popped to second.
Cleveland
1 Judnich flied to center.
2 Robinson popped to second.
3 Hegan flied to right.

7th Inning
Boston
 Elliott singled to left.
1 F. McCormick struck out.
2,3 Conatser grounded into a double play, Keltner to Gordon to Robinson.
Cleveland
1 Bearden grounded to short.
2 Mitchell popped to short.
 Doby singled to right.
3 Boudreau popped to short.

8th Inning
Boston
1 Masi out bunting to the pitcher.
2 Stanky bounced to the mound.
3 Ryan, pinch-hitting for Voiselle, struck out.
Cleveland
 For Boston—Barrett pitching.
1 Gordon flied to left.
2 Keltner flied to right.
3 Judnich grounded to second.

9th Inning
Boston
1 Holmes rolled to the mound.
2 Dark grounded to second.
3 M. McCormick popped to short.

Game 4 October 8 at Cleveland

Boston	Pos	AB	R	H	RBI	PO	A	E
Holmes	rf	4	0	0	0	0	1	0
Dark	ss	4	0	0	0	2	5	0
Torgeson	1b	3	0	2	0	11	2	0
Elliott	3b	4	0	0	0	2	2	0
Rickert	lf	4	1	2	1	2	0	0
M. McCormick	cf	4	0	1	0	1	0	0
Masi	c	3	0	0	0	3	1	0
a Salkeld		1	0	0	0	0	0	0
Stanky	2b	3	0	1	0	1	1	0
Sain	p	2	0	1	0	2	2	0
Totals		32	1	7	1	24	14	0

a Flied out for Masi in 9th.

Doubles—Boudreau, Torgeson 2.
Home Runs—Doby, Rickert.
Sacrifice Hits—Hegan, Sain.
Double Play—Boudreau to Gordon to Robinson. Left on Bases—Boston 6, Cleveland 2. Umpires—Grieve, Barr, Summers, Stewart, Pinelli, Paparella.
Attendance—81,897 **(a new Series record).**
Time of Game—1:31.

Bos.	000 000 100
Cle.	101 000 00x

Cleveland	Pos	AB	R	H	RBI	PO	A	E
Mitchell	lf	4	1	1	0	2	0	0
Doby	cf	3	1	1	1	2	0	0
Boudreau	ss	3	0	1	1	2	4	0
Gordon	2b	3	0	0	0	4	1	0
Keltner	3b	3	0	0	0	1	2	0
Judnich	rf	3	0	0	0	1	0	0
Kennedy	rf	0	0	0	0	1	0	0
Robinson	1b	3	0	2	0	8	1	0
Hegan	c	2	0	0	0	5	1	0
Gromek	p	3	0	0	0	1	1	0
Totals		27	2	5	2	27	10	0

Pitching	IP	H	R	ER	BB	SO
Boston						
Sain (L)	8	5	2	2	0	3
Cleveland						
Gromek (W)	9	7	1	1	1	2

1st Inning
Boston
1 Holmes flied to right.
2 Dark fouled to Hegan.
Torgeson doubled to center.
3 Elliott fouled to Hegan.
Cleveland
Mitchell singled to center.
1 Doby grounded out, Torgeson to Sain, with Mitchell going to second.
Boudreau doubled inside the first-base line, scoring Mitchell but was out
2 trying for a triple, Holmes to Dark to Elliott.
3 Gordon grounded to short.

2nd Inning
Boston
1 Rickert lined to first.
2 M. McCormick flied to left.
3 Masi popped to short.
Cleveland
1 Keltner grounded to short.
2 Judnich bounced to first.
Robinson singled to right.
3 Hegan popped to short.

3rd Inning
Boston
Stanky singled to center.
1 Sain sacrificed Stanky to second, Hegan to Robinson.
2 Holmes grounded to third.
3 Dark popped to second.
Cleveland
1 Gromek struck out.
2 Mitchell grounded to third.
Doby homered over the right field fence.
3 Boudreau grounded to short.

4th Inning
Boston
1 Torgeson grounded out, Robinson to Gromek.
2 Elliott grounded to third.
Rickert singled to center.
3 M. McCormick forced Rickert at second, Boudreau to Gordon.
Cleveland
1 Gordon grounded back to the pitcher.
2 Keltner fouled to Elliott.
3 Judnich struck out.

5th Inning
Boston
1 Masi grounded to short.
2 Stanky grounded to short.
Sain singled to left.
3 Holmes fouled to Gordon.
Cleveland
Robinson singled as Sain failed to cover first on his grounder to Torgeson.
1 Hegan sacrificed Robinson to second, Elliott to Torgeson.
2 Gromek fouled to Dark.
3 Mitchell grounded back to the mound.

6th Inning
Boston
1 Dark lined to center.
Torgeson walked.
2,3 Elliott grounded into a double play, Boudreau to Gordon to Robinson.
Cleveland
1 Doby grounded to second.
2 Boudreau flied to center.
3 Gordon fouled to Rickert.

7th Inning
Boston
Rickert homered into the right field stands.
M. McCormick singled to left.
1 Masi popped to third.
2 Stanky flied to left.
3 Sain grounded to the pitcher.
Cleveland
1 Keltner flied to left.
2 Judnich took a called third strike.
3 Robinson bounced out, Torgeson to Sain.

8th Inning
Boston
For Cleveland—Kennedy in right.
1 Holmes flied to center.
2 Dark popped to short.
Torgeson doubled to left.
3 Elliott popped to Hegan.
Cleveland
1 Hegan popped to second.
2 Gromek grounded out, Masi to Torgeson.
3 Mitchell grounded to short.

9th Inning
Boston
1 Rickert struck out.
2 M. McCormick struck out.
3 Salkeld, pinch-hitting for Masi, flied to right.

Game 5 October 10 at Cleveland

Boston	Pos	AB	R	H	RBI	PO	A	E
Holmes	rf	5	2	2	0	0	0	0
Dark	ss	4	1	1	0	1	1	0
Torgeson	1b	5	1	2	1	10	1	0
Elliott	3b	4	3	2	4	1	3	0
Rickert	lf	5	1	1	1	3	0	0
Salkeld	c	4	2	1	1	8	0	0
M. McCormick	cf	5	1	1	1	2	0	0
Stanky	2b	3	0	1	1	1	2	0
Potter	p	2	0	1	0	1	0	0
Spahn	p	2	0	0	1	0	1	0
Totals		39	11	12	10	27	8	0

Pitching	IP	H	R	ER	BB	SO
Boston						
Potter	3⅓	5	5	5	2	0
Spahn (W)	5⅔	1	0	0	1	7
Cleveland						
Feller (L)	6⅓	8	7	7	2	5
Klieman	*0	1	3	3	2	0
Christopher	**0	2	1	1	0	0
Paige	⅔	0	0	0	0	0
Muncrief	2	1	0	0	0	0

*Pitched to three batters in 7th.
**Pitched to two batters in 7th.

Bos.	301 001 600
Cle.	100 400 000

Cleveland	Pos	AB	R	H	RBI	PO	A	E
Mitchell	lf	3	1	1	1	3	0	0
Doby	cf	4	0	0	0	4	0	1
Boudreau	ss	4	0	2	0	0	3	0
Gordon	2b	3	1	1	0	2	1	0
Keltner	3b	3	1	0	0	1	1	1
Judnich	rf	3	1	1	1	3	0	0
b Boone		1	0	0	0	0	0	0
Peck	rf	0	0	0	0	0	0	0
Robinson	1b	4	0	0	0	8	2	0
Hegan	c	4	1	1	3	4	1	0
Feller	p	2	0	0	0	1	0	0
Klieman	p	0	0	0	0	0	0	0
Christopher	p	0	0	0	0	0	0	0
Paige	p	0	0	0	0	0	0	0
a Rosen		1	0	0	0	0	0	0
Muncrief	p	0	0	0	0	1	0	0
c Tipton		1	0	0	0	0	0	0
Totals		33	5	6	5	27	8	2

a Popped out for Paige in 7th.
b Struck out for Judnich in 8th.
c Struck out for Muncrief in 9th.

Double—Boudreau. Home Runs—Elliott 2, Hegan, Mitchell, Salkeld.
Sacrifice Hit—Dark. Balk—Paige.
Left on Bases—Boston 6, Cleveland 4.
Umpires—Barr, Summers, Stewart, Grieve, Paparella, Pinelli.
Attendance—86,288 **(a new Series record).**
Time of Game—2:39.

1st Inning
Boston
Holmes singled to right.
Dark singled to third.
1 Torgeson flied to right.
Elliott hit a three-run homer over the right field fence.
2 Rickert struck out.
3 Salkeld flied to center.
Cleveland
Mitchell homered over the right field fence.
1 Doby grounded to second.
Boudreau singled off Potter's glove.
Gordon walked.
2 Keltner fouled to Salkeld.
3 Judnich grounded to first.

2nd Inning
Boston
M. McCormick safe at first on Keltner's bobble.
1 Stanky flied to center.
2 Potter struck out.
3 Holmes grounded to first.
Cleveland.
1 Robinson flied to center.
2 Hegan grounded to third.
3 Feller grounded to short.

3rd Inning
Boston
1 Dark grounded to third.
2 Torgeson grounded to first.
Elliott homered over the left field fence. (His second of the game).
3 Rickert grounded out, Robinson to Feller.
Cleveland
1 Mitchell lined to left.
2 Doby grounded out, Torgeson to Potter.
3 Boudreau grounded to third.

4th Inning
Boston
1 Salkeld popped to second.
2 M. McCormick flied to right.
Stanky walked.
Potter singled to right, moving Stanky to second.
3 Holmes flied to left.
Cleveland
Gordon singled to left.
Keltner walked.
Judnich singled to center, Gordon scoring with Keltner going to third.
1 Robinson popped to short.
Hegan hit a three-run homer over the left field fence.
For Boston—Spahn pitching.
2 Feller grounded to the mound.
Mitchell walked.
3 Doby struck out.

5th Inning
Boston
1 Dark lined to center.
2 Torgeson flied to left.
3 Elliott struck out.
Cleveland
1 Boudreau grounded to third.
2 Gordon lined to third.
3 Keltner flied to center.

6th Inning
Boston
1 Rickert struck out, but Hegan tossed to Robinson as he dropped the third strike.
Salkeld homered over the right field fence.
2 M. McCormick grounded to short.
Stanky walked.
3 Spahn struck out.
Cleveland
1 Judnich popped to first.
2 Robinson grounded to second.
3 Hegan struck out.

7th Inning
Boston
Holmes singled to left-center.
1 Dark sacrificed Holmes to second, Robinson to Gordon.
Torgeson singled to center, Holmes scoring.
For Cleveland—Klieman pitching.
Elliott walked.
Rickert singled to center, scoring Torgeson. Elliott also scored when Doby's throw went past third, moving Rickert all the way to third.
Salkeld walked.
For Cleveland—Christopher pitching.
M. McCormick singled to left, Rickert scoring with Salkeld going to third.
Stanky singled to right, scoring Salkeld with M. McCormick moving to third.
For Cleveland—Paige pitching.
2 Spahn flied to center, M. McCormick scoring after the catch.
Stanky to second on Paige's balk.
3 Holmes grounded to short.
Cleveland
1 Rosen, pinch-hitting for Paige, popped to second.
2 Mitchell popped to first.
3 Doby flied to left.

8th Inning
Boston
For Cleveland—Muncrief pitching.
1 Dark grounded to short.
Torgeson singled over first.
2 Elliott flied to left.
3 Rickert flied to right.
Cleveland
Boudreau doubled to right-center.
1 Gordon struck out.
2 Keltner struck out.
3 Boone, batting for Judnich, struck out.

9th Inning
Boston
For Cleveland—Peck playing right.
1 Salkeld grounded to second.
2 M. McCormick popped to third.
3 Stanky popped to the pitcher.
Cleveland
1 Robinson flied to left.
2 Hegan struck out.
3 Tipton, pinch-hitting for Muncrief, struck out.

1948

Game 6 October 11 at Boston

Cle.	001	002	010
Bos.	000	100	020

Cleveland	Pos	AB	R	H	RBI	PO	A	E
Mitchell	lf	4	1	1	0	3	0	0
Kennedy	lf	1	0	0	0	1	0	0
Doby	rf	4	0	2	0	1	0	0
Boudreau	ss	3	0	1	1	2	2	0
Gordon	2b	4	1	1	1	3	3	0
Keltner	3b	4	1	1	0	0	3	0
Tucker	cf	3	1	1	0	3	1	0
Robinson	1b	4	0	2	1	12	0	0
Hegan	c	4	0	1	0	2	2	0
Lemon	p	3	0	0	0	0	3	0
Bearden	p	1	0	0	0	0	1	0
Totals		35	4	10	4	27	15	0

Pitching	IP	H	R	ER	BB	SO
Cleveland						
Lemon (W)	7⅓	8	3	3	4	1
Bearden (SV)	1⅔	1	0	0	1	0
Boston						
Voiselle (L)	7	7	3	3	2	2
Spahn	2	3	1	1	0	4

Boston	Pos	AB	R	H	RBI	PO	A	E
Holmes	rf	5	1	2	0	1	0	0
Dark	ss	4	0	1	0	1	0	0
Torgeson	1b	4	1	1	0	5	1	0
Elliott	3b	3	1	3	0	4	3	0
Rickert	lf	3	0	0	0	5	0	0
b Conatser	cf	1	0	0	1	0	0	0
Salkeld	c	2	0	0	0	4	1	0
c Masi	c	1	0	1	1	3	0	0
M. McCormick	cf-lf	4	0	1	1	2	0	0
Stanky	2b	1	0	0	0	3	2	0
d Ryan		0	0	0	0	0	0	0
Voiselle	p	1	0	0	0	0	0	0
a F. McCormick		1	0	0	0	0	0	0
Spahn	p	0	0	0	0	0	1	0
e Sisti		1	0	0	0	0	0	0
Totals		31	3	9	3	27	9	0

a Grounded out for Voiselle in 7th.
b Flied out for Rickert in 8th.
c Doubled for Salkeld in 8th.
d Ran for Stanky in 9th.
e Hit into double play for Spahn in 9th.

Doubles—Boudreau, Masi, Mitchell, Torgeson. Home Run—Gordon. Sacrifice Hit—Voiselle. Double Plays—Tucker to Robinson, Lemon to Boudreau to Robinson, Gordon to Boudreau to Robinson, Elliott to Stanky to Torgeson, Hegan to Gordon. Hit by Pitcher—Boudreau (by Voiselle). Balk—Lemon. Left on Bases—Cleveland 7, Boston 7. Umpires—Summers, Stewart, Grieve, Barr, Pinelli, Paparella. Attendance—40,103. Time of Game—2:16.

1st Inning
Cleveland
1 Mitchell lined to center.
Doby singled to left.
Boudreau was hit by a pitched ball.
2 Gordon flied to left.
3 Keltner grounded to short.
Boston
1 Holmes grounded to the mound.
Dark beat out a bunt down the third base line.
2,3 Torgeson flied to Tucker in center who threw to Robinson to double up Dark off of first.

2nd Inning
Cleveland
1 Tucker fouled to Elliott.
2 Robinson lined to second.
Hegan singled to left.
3 Lemon flied to left.
Boston
Elliott beat out a hit to third.
Elliott to second on a balk.
1 Rickert flied to center, Elliott to third after the catch.
2 Salkeld grounded to first, Elliott holding.
3 M. McCormick grounded to third.

3rd Inning
Cleveland
Mitchell doubled to left.
1 Doby flied to left.
Boudreau doubled to right, Mitchell scoring.
2 Gordon fouled to Elliott.
3 Keltner struck out.
Boston
Stanky walked.
1 Voiselle sacrificed Stanky to second, Hegan to Gordon.
Holmes singled to left, Stanky moving to third.
2,3 Dark grounded into a double play, Lemon to Boudreau to Robinson.

4th Inning
Cleveland
1 Tucker grounded to second.
2 Robinson lined to right.
3 Hegan struck out.
Boston
1 Torgeson flied to left.
Elliott beat out a hit down the third base line.
2 Rickert flied to left.
Salkeld walked.
M. McCormick singled to center, scoring Elliott with Salkeld stopping at second.
Stanky walked, loading the bases.
3 Voiselle grounded to second.

5th Inning
Cleveland
1 Lemon popped to first.
2 Mitchell fouled to Elliott.
Doby walked.
3 Boudreau flied to left.
Boston
1 Holmes flied to left.
2 Dark rolled to the mound.
3 Torgeson popped to second.

6th Inning
Cleveland
Gordon homered over the left field wall.
1 Keltner fouled to Elliott.
Tucker walked.
Robinson singled to right, moving Tucker to third.
2 Hegan forced Robinson at second, Elliott to Stanky, scoring Tucker.
3 Lemon grounded to first.
Boston
Elliott singled to center.
1,2 Rickert grounded into a double play, Gordon to Boudreau to Robinson.
3 Salkeld grounded to second.

7th Inning
Cleveland
1 Mitchell flied to center.
Doby singled to center.
2,3 Boudreau grounded into a double play, Elliott to Stanky to Torgeson.
Boston
1 M. McCormick struck out.
2 Stanky grounded to third.
3 F. McCormick, pinch-hitting for Voiselle, grounded to third.

8th Inning
Cleveland
For Boston—Spahn pitching.
1 Gordon lined to left.
Keltner singled off Spahn's glove.
Tucker singled to right with Keltner stopping at second.
Robinson singled to right, Keltner scoring and Tucker going to third.
2 Hegan struck out.
On an attempted pick-off play to catch Robinson off first he got back but
3 Tucker was caught trying to score, Torgeson to Salkeld to Elliott to Salkeld.
Boston
Holmes singled to center
1 Dark lined to right.
Torgeson doubled to right, Holmes holding up at third.
Elliott walked loading the bases.
For Cleveland—Bearden pitching.
2 Conatser, pinch-hitting for Rickert, flied to center, Holmes scoring and Torgeson going to third after the catch.
Masi, pinch-hitting for Salkeld, doubled to left scoring Torgeson, Elliott stopping at third.
For Cleveland—Kennedy in left.
3 M. McCormick bounced to the pitcher.

9th Inning
Cleveland
For Boston—M. McCormick moved to left, Conatser in center, Masi catching.
1 Bearden struck out.
2 Kennedy struck out.
3 Doby struck out.
Boston
Stanky walked.
Ryan, running for Stanky.
1,2 Sisti, batting for Spahn, popped into a double play, Hegan to Gordon.
3 Holmes flied to left.

1948 WORLD SERIES COMPOSITE BOX

	Wins	Composite Line Score									
Cleveland Indians (A.L.)	4	2	0	3	7	1	2	0	1	1	–17
Boston Braves (N.L.)	2	4	0	1	1	0	1	7	3	0	–17

Manager	W	L	Pct.	G. Ahead
	Regular Season			
Lou Boudreau	97	58	.626	Won playoff over Boston
Billy Southworth	91	62	.595	6.5

BATTING AND FIELDING

CLEVELAND INDIANS

WORLD SERIES STATISTICS

	Pos	G	AB	R	H	2B	3B	HR	RBI	BB	SO	SB	BA	SA	PO	A	E
Eddie Robinson	1b	6	20	0	6	0	0	0	1	1	0	0	.300	.300	60	7	0
Joe Gordon	2b	6	22	3	4	0	0	1	2	1	2	1	.182	.318	15	13	1
Lou Boudreau	ss	6	22	1	6	4	0	0	3	1	1	0	.273	.455	11	14	0
Ken Keltner	3b	6	21	3	2	0	0	0	0	2	3	0	.095	.095	3	11	1
Walt Judnich	rf	4	13	1	1	0	0	0	1	1	4	0	.077	.077	7	0	0
Larry Doby	cf-rf	6	22	1	7	1	0	1	2	2	4	0	.318	.500	11	0	1
Dale Mitchell	lf	6	23	4	4	1	0	1	1	2	0	0	.174	.348	13	0	0
Jim Hegan	c	6	19	2	4	0	0	1	5	1	4	1	.211	.368	25	5	0
Thurman Tucker	cf	1	3	1	1	0	0	0	0	1	0	0	.333	.333	3	1	0
Allie Clark	rf	1	3	0	0	0	0	0	0	0	1	0	.000	.000	2	0	0
Bob Kennedy	rf-lf	3	2	0	1	0	0	0	1	0	1	0	.500	.500	2	0	0
Hal Peck	rf	1	0	0	0	0	0	0	0	0	0	0	—	—	0	0	0
Ray Boone	ph	1	1	0	0	0	0	0	0	0	1	0	.000	.000			
Al Rosen	ph	1	1	0	0	0	0	0	0	0	0	0	.000	.000			
Joe Tipton	ph	1	1	0	0	0	0	0	0	0	1	0	.000	.000			
Johnny Berardino	Did not play																
Hank Edwards	Did not play																
Bob Lemon	p	2	7	0	0	0	0	0	0	0	0	0	.000	.000	3	9	0
Gene Bearden	p	2	4	1	2	1	0	0	0	0	1	0	.500	.750	0	7	0
Bob Feller	p	2	4	0	0	0	0	0	0	0	2	0	.000	.000	2	4	0
Steve Gromek	p	1	3	0	0	0	0	0	0	0	1	0	.000	.000	1	1	0
Russ Christopher	p	1	0	0	0	0	0	0	0	0	0	0	—	—	0	0	0
Eddie Klieman	p	1	0	0	0	0	0	0	0	0	0	0	—	—	0	0	0
Bob Muncrief	p	1	0	0	0	0	0	0	0	0	0	0	—	—	1	0	0
Satchel Paige	p	1	0	0	0	0	0	0	0	0	0	0	—	—	0	0	0
Sam Zoldak	Did not play																
Don Black	Did not play—injured																
team total		6	191	17	38	7	0	4	16	12	26	2	.199	.298	159	72	3

Double plays—9
Left on Bases—34

REGULAR SEASON STATISTICS

		Main Pos	G	AB	R	H	2B	3B	HR	RBI	BB	SO	SB	BA	SA
Eddie Robinson		1b	134	493	53	125	18	5	16	83	36	42	1	.254	.408
Joe Gordon		2b	144	550	96	154	21	4	32	124	77	68	5	.280	.507
Lou Boudreau		ss	152	560	116	199	34	6	18	106	98	9	3	.355	.534
Ken Keltner		3b	153	558	91	166	24	4	31	119	89	52	2	.297	.522
Walt Judnich		of	79	218	36	56	13	3	2	29	56	23	2	.257	.372
Larry Doby		of	121	439	83	132	23	9	14	66	54	77	9	.301	.490
Dale Mitchell		of	141	608	82	204	30	8	4	56	45	17	13	.336	.431
Jim Hegan		c	144	472	60	117	21	6	14	61	48	74	6	.248	.407
Thurman Tucker		of	83	242	52	63	13	2	1	19	31	17	11	.260	.343
Allie Clark		of	81	271	43	84	5	2	9	38	23	13	0	.310	.443
Bob Kennedy	a	of	66	73	10	22	3	2	0	5	4	6	0	.301	.397
Hal Peck		ph-of	45	63	12	18	3	0	0	8	4	8	1	.286	.333
Ray Boone		ss	6	5	0	2	1	0	0	1	0	1	0	.400	.600
Al Rosen		3b	5	5	0	1	0	0	0	0	0	2	0	.200	.200
Joe Tipton		c	47	90	11	26	3	0	1	13	4	10	0	.289	.356
Johnny Berardino		inf	66	147	19	28	5	1	2	10	27	16	0	.190	.279
Hank Edwards		of	55	160	27	43	9	2	3	18	18	18	1	.269	.406
Bob Lemon		p	52	119	20	34	9	0	5	21	8	23	0	.286	.487
Gene Bearden		p	37	90	14	23	3	0	2	14	5	9	0	.256	.356
Bob Feller		p	44	95	1	9	2	0	0	3	1	39	0	.095	.116
Steve Gromek		p	38	41	3	6	1	0	0	1	3	7	0	.146	.171
Russ Christopher		p	45	6	1	0	0	0	0	0	2	3	0	.000	.000
Eddie Klieman		p	44	14	0	2	0	0	0	0	2	9	0	.143	.143
Bob Muncrief		p	21	18	0	2	0	0	0	0	2	6	0	.111	.111
Satchel Paige		p	21	23	0	2	0	0	0	0	0	5	0	.087	.087
Sam Zoldak	b	p	23	36	0	5	1	0	0	0	1	6	1	.139	.167
Don Black		p	18	15	1	3	0	0	0	0	0	3	0	.200	.200
team total			156	**5446**	840	**1534**	242	54	**155**	802	646	**575**	54	**.283**	.431

a—from Chicago (A)
b—from St. Louis (A)
Pat Seerey (of), Ray Murray (ph), Bill Kennedy (p), Al Gettel (p), Butch Wensloff (p), Lyman Linde (p), Ernie Groth (p), Mike Garcia (p), and Les Webber (p) also played for the Indians during the season

BOSTON BRAVES

WORLD SERIES STATISTICS

	Pos	G	AB	R	H	2B	3B	HR	RBI	BB	SO	SB	BA	SA	PO	A	E
Earl Torgeson	1b	5	18	2	7	3	0	0	1	2	1	1	.389	.556	44	5	0
Eddie Stanky	2b	6	14	0	4	1	0	0	1	7	0	0	.286	.357	8	12	0
Al Dark	ss	6	24	2	4	1	0	0	0	0	2	0	.167	.208	7	12	3
Bob Elliott	3b	6	21	4	7	0	0	2	5	2	2	0	.333	.619	11	14	3
Tommy Holmes	rf	6	26	3	5	0	0	0	1	0	0	0	.192	.192	10	2	0
Mike McCormick	cf-lf	6	23	1	6	0	0	0	2	0	4	0	.261	.261	17	0	0
Marv Rickert	lf	5	19	2	4	0	0	1	2	0	4	0	.211	.368	20	0	0
Bill Salkeld	c-ph	5	9	2	2	0	0	1	1	5	1	0	.222	.556	19	2	0
Phil Masi	pr-c-ph	5	8	1	1	1	0	0	1	0	0	0	.125	.250	10	1	0
Frank McCormick	ph-1b	3	5	0	1	0	0	0	0	0	2	0	.200	.200	5	1	0
Clint Conatser	cf	2	4	0	0	0	0	0	1	0	0	0	.000	.000	1	0	0
Sibby Sisti	pr-2b-ph	2	1	0	0	0	0	0	0	0	0	0	.000	.000	0	0	0
Connie Ryan	ph-pr	2	1	0	0	0	0	0	0	0	1	0	.000	.000			
Ray Sanders	ph	1	1	0	0	0	0	0	0	0	0	0	.000	.000			
Jeff Heath	Did not play—injured																
Jim Russell	Did not play—heart illness																
Bobby Sturgeon	Did not play																
Johnny Sain	p	2	5	0	1	0	0	0	0	0	0	0	.200	.200	2	2	0
Warren Spahn	p	3	4	0	0	0	0	0	1	0	1	0	.000	.000	0	3	0
Nels Potter	p	2	2	0	1	0	0	0	0	0	1	0	.500	.500	1	0	0
Bill Voiselle	p	2	2	0	0	0	0	0	0	0	0	0	.000	.000	1	0	0
Red Barrett	p	2	0	0	0	0	0	0	0	0	0	0	—	—	0	0	0
Vern Bickford	p	1	0	0	0	0	0	0	0	0	0	0	—	—	0	0	0
Bobby Hogue	Did not play																
Clyde Shoun	Did not play																
Al Lyons	Did not play																
Ernie White	Did not play																
team total		6	187	17	43	6	0	4	16	16	19	1	.230	.326	156	54	6

Double Plays—3
Left on Bases—34

REGULAR SEASON STATISTICS

		Main Pos	G	AB	R	H	2B	3B	HR	RBI	BB	SO	SB	BA	SA
Earl Torgeson		1b	134	438	70	111	23	5	10	67	81	54	19	.253	.397
Eddie Stanky		2b	67	247	49	79	14	2	2	29	61	13	3	.320	.417
Al Dark		ss	137	543	85	175	39	6	3	48	24	36	4	.322	.433
Bob Elliott		3b	161	540	99	153	24	5	23	100	131	57	6	.283	.474
Tommy Holmes		of	139	585	85	190	35	7	6	61	46	20	1	.325	.439
Mike McCormick		of	115	343	45	104	22	7	1	39	32	34	1	.303	.417
Marv Rickert	c	of	3	13	1	3	0	1	0	2	0	1	0	.231	.385
Bill Salkeld		c	78	198	26	48	8	1	8	28	42	37	1	.242	.414
Phil Masi		c	113	376	43	95	19	0	5	44	35	26	2	.253	.343
Frank McCormick		1b	75	180	14	45	9	2	4	34	10	9	0	.250	.389
Clint Conatser		of	90	224	30	62	9	3	3	23	32	27	0	.277	.384
Sibby Sisti		2b-ss	83	221	30	54	6	2	0	21	31	34	0	.244	.290
Connie Ryan		2b	51	122	14	26	3	0	0	10	21	16	0	.213	.238
Ray Sanders		ph	5	4	0	1	0	0	0	2	1	0	0	.250	.250
Jeff Heath		of	115	364	64	116	26	5	20	76	51	46	2	.319	.582
Jim Russell		of	89	322	44	85	18	1	9	54	46	31	4	.264	.410
Bobby Sturgeon		2b	34	78	10	17	3	1	0	4	4	5	0	.218	.282
Johnny Sain		p	43	115	11	25	3	1	0	16	1	3	0	.217	.261
Warren Spahn		p	37	90	10	15	3	0	1	7	6	24	0	.167	.233
Nels Potter	d	p	18	29	0	11	1	0	0	3	0	3	0	.379	.414
Bill Voiselle		p	37	72	2	7	0	0	0	4	4	17	0	.097	.097
Red Barrett		p	34	39	0	7	0	0	0	3	0	11	0	.179	.179
Vern Bickford		p	33	49	3	10	2	0	0	7	2	12	0	.204	.245
Bobby Hogue		p	40	21	0	2	1	0	0	1	0	5	0	.095	.143
Clyde Shoun		p	36	21	2	4	2	0	0	6	0	4	0	.190	.286
Al Lyons		p-of	16	12	2	2	0	0	0	0	2	4	0	.167	.167
Ernie White		p	16	3	0	0	0	0	0	0	0	2	0	.000	.000
team total			154	5297	739	**1458**	**272**	49	95	695	**671**	536	43	**.275**	.399

c—from Cincinnati
d—from St. Louis (A) and Philadelphia (A)
Danny Litwhiler (of), Paul Burris (c), Glenn Elliott (p), Jim Prendergast (p), Johnny Beazley (p), Johnny Antonelli (p), Ed Wright (p), and Ray Martin (p) also played for the Braves during the season.

PITCHING

CLEVELAND INDIANS

WORLD SERIES STATISTICS

	G	GS	CG	IP	H	R	ER	BB	SO	W	L	SV	ERA
Bob Lemon	2	2	1	16⅓	16	4	3	7	6	2	0	0	1.65
Bob Feller	2	2	1	14⅓	10	8	8	5	7	0	2	0	5.02
Gene Bearden	2	1	1	10⅔	6	0	0	1	4	1	0	1	0.00
Steve Gromek	1	1	1	9	7	1	1	1	2	1	0	0	1.00
Bob Muncrief	1	0	0	2	1	0	0	0	0	0	0	0	0.00
Satchel Paige	1	0	0	⅔	0	0	0	0	0	0	0	0	0.00
Russ Christopher	1	0	0	0	2	1	1	0	0	0	0	0	∞
Eddie Klieman	1	0	0	0	1	3	3	2	0	0	0	0	∞
Sam Zoldak	Did not play												
Don Black	Did not play—injured												
team total	7	6	4	53	43	17	16	16	19	4	2	1	2.72

REGULAR SEASON STATISTICS

		G	GS	CG	IP	H	ER	BB	SO	W	L	Pct	SV	ShO	ERA
Bob Lemon		43	37	**20**	**294**	231	92	129	147	20	14	.588	2	**10**	2.82
Bob Feller		44	**38**	18	280	**255**	111	116	**164**	19	15	.559	3	2	3.57
Gene Bearden		37	29	15	230	187	62	106	80	20	7	.741	1	6	**2.43**
Steve Gromek		38	9	4	130	109	41	51	50	9	3	.750	2	1	2.84
Bob Muncrief		21	9	1	72	76	32	31	24	5	4	.556	0	1	4.00
Satchel Paige		21	7	3	73	61	20	25	45	6	1	.857	1	2	2.47
Russ Christopher		45	0	0	59	55	19	27	14	3	2	.600	**17**	0	2.90
Eddie Klieman		44	0	0	80	62	23	46	18	3	2	.600	4	0	2.59
Sam Zoldak	b	23	12	4	106	104	33	24	17	9	6	.600	0	1	2.80
Don Black		18	10	1	52	57	31	40	16	2	2	.500	0	0	5.37
team total		156	156	66	**1409**	1246	**505**	628	595	**97**	58	**.626**	**30**	**26**	**3.23**

BOSTON BRAVES

WORLD SERIES STATISTICS

	G	GS	CG	IP	H	R	ER	BB	SO	W	L	SV	ERA
Johnny Sain	2	2	2	17	9	2	2	0	9	1	1	0	1.06
Warren Spahn	3	1	0	12	10	4	4	3	12	1	1	0	3.00
Bill Voiselle	2	1	0	10⅔	8	3	3	2	2	0	1	0	2.53
Nels Potter	2	1	0	5⅓	6	6	5	2	1	0	0	0	8.44
Red Barrett	2	0	0	3⅔	1	0	0	0	1	0	0	0	0.00
Vern Bickford	1	1	0	3⅓	4	2	1	5	1	0	1	0	2.70
Bobby Hogue	Did not play												
Clyde Shoun	Did not play												
Al Lyons	Did not play												
Ernie White	Did not play												
team totals	7	6	2	52	38	17	15	12	26	2	4	0	2.60

REGULAR SEASON STATISTICS

		G	GS	CG	IP	H	ER	BB	SO	W	L	Pct	SV	ShO	ERA
Johnny Sain		42	**39**	**28**	**315**	**297**	91	83	137	**24**	15	.615	1	4	2.60
Warren Spahn		36	35	16	257	237	106	77	114	15	12	.556	1	3	3.71
Bill Voiselle		37	30	9	216	226	87	90	89	13	13	.500	2	2	3.63
Nels Potter	d	18	7	3	85	77	22	8	47	5	2	.714	2	0	2.33
Red Barrett		34	13	3	128	132	52	26	40	7	8	.467	0	0	3.66
Vern Bickford		33	22	10	146	125	53	63	60	11	5	.688	1	1	3.27
Bobby Hogue		40	1	0	86	88	31	19	43	8	2	.800	2	0	3.24
Clyde Shoun		36	2	1	74	77	33	20	25	5	1	.833	4	0	4.01
Al Lyons		7	0	0	13	17	11	8	5	1	0	1.000	0	0	7.62
Ernie White		15	0	0	23	13	5	17	8	0	2	.000	2	0	1.96
team totals		154	154	**70**	1389	1354	**521**	430	579	**91**	62	**.595**	17	10	**3.38**

Total Attendance—358,362 Average Attendance—59,727 Winning Player's Share—$6,772.07 Losing Player's Share—$4,570.73

1949
Reynolds and Page

The New York Yankees and Brooklyn Dodgers had met in the World Series only two years ago, yet they both showed up this year with revised squads. The Yanks had finished third last year, and that failing was enough to get manager Bucky Harris fired, with Casey Stengel coming in as the new skipper. A competent National League outfielder from 1912 to 1925, an unsuccessful manager with the Dodgers and Braves in the 1930's, and a highly successful manager with the Oakland Oaks of the Pacific Coast League in recent years, Casey came to the Yanks with a reputation more for humor than for managerial excellence. He had a fine-tuned sense of the incongruous and loved to spellbind the sportswriters with tales told in his own colorful slang, dubbed "Stengelese." But Casey turned out to be a superb manager as well as a clown, bringing the Yanks home in first place despite early-season injuries to Joe DiMaggio and Yogi Berra. His team came in the final weekend trailing Boston by one game, so they simply beat the Red Sox twice to take the flag. Around a core of DiMaggio, Berra, Phil Rizzuto, and Tommy Henrich, Stengel weaved into the lineup a fabric of younger men like Hank Bauer, Jerry Coleman, and Bobby Brown. Almost all of the important pitching was done by Vic Raschi, Allie Reynolds, Eddie Lopat, Tommy Byrne, and reliever Joe Page.

While Stengel had to juggle his lineup because of injuries, Brooklyn manager Burt Shotton had a relatively stable lineup, although one very different from the championship squad of 1947. With Shotton as full-fledged manager now that Leo Durocher had moved on to manage the Giants, the Bums still had Carl Furillo and Gene Hermanski in the outfield and Pee Wee Reese at shortstop, but other positions had new occupants. Jackie Robinson now held down second base and won the league MVP award for his efforts. Gil Hodges moved from backup catcher to first-base starter last year and blossomed into a dangerous power hitter. Young Duke Snider nailed down the center-field job for the first time, and former Negro League star Roy Campanella had gracefully moved into the top ranks of big-league catchers since joining the team last year. Spider Jorgensen still played some third base, but shared it with Billy Cox, a fine gloveman picked up from the Pirates in a deal. Lefty Preacher Roe came in the same deal and was the top southpaw on the pitching staff, while Don Newcombe, another find from black baseball, broke into the majors with 17 wins on the strength of his powerful right arm.

Shotton had a young club which would challenge for the World Championship for years to come. But they would not win it this year. The opening game at Yankee Stadium told a losing tale that would become familiar to Brooklyn fans. Don Newcombe and Allie Reynolds hooked up in a tenacious pitching duel, scoreless until Henrich led off the bottom of the ninth with a home run. Always the ace of the staff, Newcombe would never be able to win a Series game. The Bums turned the 1–0 score around the next day and beat the Yanks in game two, with Roe scattering six hits and the Dodgers scoring a run off Raschi in the second inning on a double by Robinson and a single by Hodges.

But after the scene shifted to Ebbets Field for the next three games, the Dodgers simply couldn't upset the calculated professionalism of the Yankees. The third game went into the ninth inning tied at 1–1, but the Yanks scored three times in the top of the ninth off Ralph Branca on run-producing singles by Mize and Coleman. Every one of those runs counted, because home runs by Luis Olmo and Campanella closed the gap to 4–3 before Page could get the final out. Shotton sent Newcombe into action again in game four, but the big winner was kayoed in a three-run fourth inning, and the Yanks added three more in the fifth off Joe Hatten. The Dodgers chipped away at Eddie Lopat, but Stengel brought on Reynolds to end the game by retiring the last ten men in order.

The Yanks moved in for the kill in game five, running up a 10–1 lead in the sixth inning before the Bums made a final comeback try. A four-run outburst in the seventh narrowed the score to 10–6, but it also brought Joe Page into the game to shut the door the rest of the way.

Game 1 October 5 at New York

Bkn.	000	000	000			
N.Y.	000	000	001			

Brooklyn	Pos	AB	R	H	RBI	PO	A	E
Reese	ss	4	0	1	0	2	2	0
Jorgensen	3b	3	0	1	0	0	2	0
Snider	cf	4	0	0	0	3	0	0
Robinson	2b	4	0	0	0	3	0	0
Hermanski	lf	3	0	0	0	0	0	0
Furillo	rf	3	0	0	0	0	0	0
Hodges	1b	2	0	0	0	4	0	0
Campanella	c	2	0	0	0	11	0	0
Newcombe	p	3	0	0	0	0	0	0
Totals		28	0	2	0	*24	4	0

* None out when winning run scored.

Doubles—Coleman, Jorgensen, Reynolds. Home Run—Henrich. Stolen Base—Reese. Sacrifice Hit—Hodges. Double Play—Reynolds to Coleman to Henrich. Left on Bases—Brooklyn 6, New York 4. Umpires—Hubbard (A), Reardon (N), Passarella (A), Jorda (N), Hurley (A), Barr (N). Attendance—66,224. Time of Game—2:24.

New York	Pos	AB	R	H	RBI	PO	A	E
Rizzuto	ss	4	0	0	0	1	2	0
Henrich	1b	4	1	1	1	9	0	0
Berra	c	3	0	0	0	9	0	0
DiMaggio	cf	3	0	0	0	1	0	0
Lindell	lf	3	0	1	0	0	0	0
Johnson	3b	3	0	1	0	2	3	0
Mapes	rf	3	0	0	0	4	0	0
Coleman	2b	3	0	1	0	1	2	1
Reynolds	p	3	0	2	0	0	1	0
Totals		29	1	5	1	27	8	1

Pitching	IP	H	R	ER	BB	SO
Brooklyn						
Newcombe (L)	8	5	1	1	0	11
New York						
Reynolds (W)	9	2	0	0	4	9

1st Inning
Brooklyn
1 Reese grounded to first.
Jorgensen doubled to left-center over Lindell's head.
2 Snider struck out.
3 Robinson flied to right.
New York
1 Rizzuto fouled to Hodges on an attempted bunt.
2 Henrich grounded to short.
3 Berra popped to short.

2nd Inning
Brooklyn
Hermanski walked.
Furillo walked.
1,2 Hodges grounded into a double play, Reynolds to Coleman to Henrich as Hermanski went to third.
3 Campanella flied to right.
New York
1 DiMaggio struck out.
Lindell singled to left.
2 Johnson struck out.
3 Mapes struck out.

3rd Inning
Brooklyn
1 Newcombe grounded to short.
2 Reese bunted out to third.
3 Jorgensen grounded to second.
New York
1 Coleman called out on strikes. Reynolds doubled to left.
2 Rizzuto popped to second.
3 Henrich popped to short.

4th Inning
Brooklyn
1 Snider fouled to Johnson.
2 Robinson grounded to third.
3 Hermanski flied to right.
New York
1 Berra grounded to short.
2 DiMaggio popped to second.
3 Lindell flied to center.

5th Inning
Brooklyn
Furillo safe at first when his grounder got through Coleman for an error.
1 Hodges sacrificed Furillo to second, Johnson to Henrich. Campanella walked.
2 Newcombe struck out as Berra held his foul tip.
3 Reese forced Furillo at third, Johnson unassisted.
New York
1 Johnson struck out.
2 Mapes struck out.
3 Coleman struck out.

6th Inning
Brooklyn
Jorgensen walked.
1 Snider struck out.
2 Robinson flied to center.
3 Hermanski struck out.
New York
Reynolds singled to left.
1 Rizzuto forced Reynolds at second, Jorgensen to Robinson.
2 Henrich flied to center.
3 Berra struck out.

7th Inning
Brooklyn
1 Furillo popped to first.
2 Hodges called out on strikes.
3 Campanella called out on strikes.
New York
1 DiMaggio popped to second.
2 Lindell called out on strikes.
3 Johnson grounded to third.

8th Inning
Brooklyn
1 Newcombe called out on strikes. Reese singled through the middle. Reese stole second.
2 Jorgensen struck out.
3 Snider struck out, for the third time in the game.
New York
1 Mapes struck out for the third time. Coleman doubled down the right field line.
2 Reynolds called out on strikes.
3 Rizzuto flied to center.

9th Inning
Brooklyn
1 Robinson grounded to short.
2 Hermanski popped to short.
3 Furillo flied to right.
New York
Henrich, on a 2–0 count, hit a game-winning home run into the lower right field stands.

Game 2 October 6 at New York

Bkn.	010	000	000
N.Y.	000	000	000

Brooklyn	Pos	AB	R	H	RBI	PO	A	E
Reese	ss	4	0	0	0	1	3	1
Jorgensen	3b	4	0	1	0	1	4	0
Snider	cf	4	0	1	0	3	1	0
Robinson	2b	3	1	1	0	3	1	0
Hermanski	rf	3	0	1	0	2	0	0
d Furillo		1	0	0	0	0	0	0
McCormick	rf	0	0	0	0	1	0	0
Rackley	lf	2	0	0	0	0	0	0
Olmo	lf	2	0	1	0	2	0	0
Hodges	1b	3	0	1	1	9	1	0
Campanella	c	2	0	1	0	4	0	0
Roe	p	3	0	0	0	1	1	1
Totals		31	1	7	1	27	11	2

Pitching	IP	H	R	ER	BB	SO
Brooklyn						
Roe (W)	9	6	0	0	0	3
New York						
Raschi (L)	8	6	1	1	1	4
Page	1	1	0	0	0	0

New York	Pos	AB	R	H	RBI	PO	A	E
Rizzuto	ss	3	0	1	0	0	6	0
Henrich	1b	4	0	0	0	11	1	0
Bauer	rf	4	0	1	0	1	0	0
DiMaggio	cf	4	0	1	0	1	0	0
Lindell	lf	4	0	0	0	2	1	1
Johnson	3b	4	0	1	0	0	2	0
Coleman	2b	4	0	1	0	6	3	0
Silvera	c	2	0	0	0	6	0	0
a Mize		1	0	1	0	0	0	0
b Stirnweiss		0	0	0	0	0	0	0
Niarhos	c	0	0	0	0	0	0	0
Raschi	p	2	0	0	0	0	0	0
c Brown		1	0	0	0	0	0	0
Page	p	0	0	0	0	0	0	0
Totals		33	0	6	0	27	13	1

a Singled for Silvera in 8th.
b Ran for Mize in 8th.
c Struck out for Raschi in 8th.
d Popped out for Hermanski in 9th.

Doubles—Coleman, Jorgensen, Robinson. Triple—Hermanski. Stolen Bases—Johnson, Rizzuto. Sacrifice Hits—Rizzuto, Robinson. Double Play—Rizzuto to Coleman to Henrich. Left on Bases—Brooklyn 5, New York 7. Umpires—Reardon, Passarella, Jorda, Hubbard, Hurley, Barr. Attendance—70,053. Time of Game—2:30.

1st Inning
Brooklyn
1 Reese flied to left.
2 Jorgensen grounded to first.
3 Snider grounded to short.
New York
Rizzuto singled down the left field line.
1 Henrich flied to left.
2 Bauer fouled to Robinson.
3 DiMaggio flied to center.

2nd Inning
Brooklyn
Robinson doubled to left.
1 Hermanski fouled to Coleman deep behind first, Robinson moving to third after the catch.
2 Rackley grounded to third, Robinson holding at third.
Hodges singled to left, scoring Robinson and went to second on Lindell's fumble.
Campanella intentionally walked.
3 Roe struck out.
New York
1 Lindell flied to right.
2 Johnson flied to center.
3 Coleman flied to center.

3rd Inning
Brooklyn
1 Reese grounded to short.
2 Jorgensen fouled to Silvera.
3 Snider grounded to second.
New York
1 Silvera popped to third.
2 Raschi grounded to short.
Rizzuto safe when Reese fumbled his grounder.
Rizzuto stole second.
3 Henrich grounded to short.

4th Inning
Brooklyn
1 Robinson struck out.
Hermanski tripled to center when his liner wildly bounced past DiMaggio.
2 Rackley hit into a fielder's choice, Coleman to Silvera getting Hermanski trying to score.
3 Hodges flied to right.
New York
Bauer singled to center but was out
1 trying for a double, Snider to Reese.
For Brooklyn—Olmo replaced Rackley in left.
2 DiMaggio struck out.
3 Lindell hit back to Roe.

5th Inning
Brooklyn
Campanella singled to left, trying for second on Lindell's bobble but was
1 out, Lindell to Coleman.
2 Roe called out on strikes.
3 Reese grounded to third.
New York
1 Johnson fouled to Campanella.
Coleman doubled to left.
2 Silvera grounded to short, Coleman going to third.
3 Raschi grounded to third.

6th Inning
Brooklyn
Jorgensen doubled to left.
1 Snider flied to center.
2 Robinson grounded to short, Jorgensen going to third.
3 Hermanski grounded to first.
New York
1 Rizzuto grounded to first.
2 Henrich grounded out, Hodges to Roe.
3 Bauer grounded to third.

7th Inning
Brooklyn
Olmo singled to right.
1,2 Hodges hit into a double play, Rizzuto to Coleman to Henrich.
3 Campanella flied to left.
New York
1 DiMaggio grounded to third.
2 Lindell flied to left.
Johnson singled to left.
Johnson stole second.
3 Coleman grounded to second.

8th Inning
Brooklyn
1 Roe struck out for the third time.
2 Reese grounded to short.
3 Jorgensen lined to second.
New York
Mize, pinch-hitting for Silvera, singled to right.
Stirnweiss ran for Mize.
1 Brown, pinch-hitting for Raschi, took a called third strike.
Rizzuto safe at first as Roe dropped his bunt sacrifice for an error.
2 Henrich flied to left.
3 Bauer forced Rizzuto at second, Jorgensen to Robinson.

9th Inning
Brooklyn
For New York—Page pitching and Niarhos catching.
Snider singled to left.
1 Robinson sacrificed Snider to second, Henrich to Coleman.
2 Furillo, pinch-hitting for Hermanski, popped to second.
3 Olmo bounced to short.
New York
For Brooklyn—McCormick playing right.
DiMaggio beat out a roller to third.
1 Lindell struck out.
2 Johnson popped to second.
3 Coleman flied to right.

Game 3 October 7 at Brooklyn

N.Y.	001	000	003
Bkn.	000	100	002

New York	Pos	AB	R	H	RBI	PO	A	E
Rizzuto	ss	4	0	0	1	0	0	0
Henrich	1b	3	0	0	0	10	0	0
Berra	c	3	1	0	0	7	2	0
DiMaggio	cf	4	0	0	0	4	0	0
Brown	3b	4	1	1	0	0	2	0
Woodling	lf	3	1	1	0	2	0	0
Mapes	rf	2	1	0	0	2	0	0
a Mize		1	0	1	2	0	0	0
b Bauer	rf	0	0	0	0	0	0	0
Coleman	2b	4	0	1	1	2	4	0
Byrne	p	1	0	1	0	0	0	0
Page	p	3	0	0	0	0	1	0
Totals		32	4	5	4	27	9	0

a Singled for Mapes in 9th.
b Ran for Mize in 9th.
c Struck out for Banta in 9th.

Double—Woodling. Home Runs—Campanella, Olmo, Reese. Double Play—Berra to Coleman. Hit by Pitcher—Reese (by Byrne). Left on Bases—New York 5, Brooklyn 6. Umpires—Passarella, Jorda, Hubbard, Reardon, Barr, Hurley. Attendance—32,788. Time of Game—2:30.

Brooklyn	Pos	AB	R	H	RBI	PO	A	E
Reese	ss	2	1	1	1	1	2	0
Miksis	3b	4	0	1	0	3	1	0
Furillo	rf	4	0	1	0	2	0	0
Robinson	2b	2	0	0	0	2	3	0
Hodges	1b	3	0	0	0	8	0	0
Olmo	lf	4	1	1	1	0	0	0
Snider	cf	4	0	0	0	3	0	0
Campanella	c	4	1	1	1	7	0	0
Branca	p	3	0	0	0	1	0	0
Banta	p	0	0	0	0	0	0	0
c Edwards		1	0	0	0	0	0	0
Totals		31	3	5	3	27	6	0

Pitching	IP	H	R	ER	BB	SO
New York						
Byrne	$3\frac{1}{3}$	2	1	1	2	1
Page (W)	$5\frac{2}{3}$	3	2	2	2	4
Brooklyn						
Branca (L)	$8\frac{2}{3}$	4	4	4	4	6
Banta	$\frac{1}{3}$	1	0	0	0	1

1st Inning
New York
1 Rizzuto grounded to third.
2 Henrich grounded to first.
3 Berra struck out.
Brooklyn
Reese was hit by a pitched ball.
1,2 Miksis fouled to Berra who threw to Coleman doubling Reese trying to advance after the catch.
3 Furillo flied to center.

2nd Inning
New York
1 DiMaggio struck out.
2 Brown popped to second.
3 Woodling fouled to Miksis
Brooklyn
1 Robinson popped to second.
2 Hodges fouled to Berra.
3 Olmo grounded to third.

3rd Inning
New York
Mapes walked (the first walk in the Series given up by Dodger pitchers).
1 Coleman called out on strikes.
Byrne singled to center, Mapes going to third.
2 Rizzuto flied to right, Mapes scoring after the catch.
Henrich walked.
3 Berra popped to second.
Brooklyn
1 Snider flied to left.
2 Campanella grounded to third.
3 Branca struck out and was thrown out Berra to Henrich when Berra dropped the third strike.

4th Inning
New York
1 DiMaggio struck out.
2 Brown fouled to Miksis.
Woodling doubled off the right field scoreboard.
3 Mapes rolled out, Robinson to Branca.
Brooklyn
Reese hit a home-run into the lower left-center field stands.
1 Miksis flied to center.
Furillo singled to left.
Robinson walked.
Hodges walked, loading the bases.
For New York—Page pitching.
2 Olmo fouled to Henrich.
3 Snider grounded to second.

5th Inning
New York
1 Coleman flied to center.
2 Page struck out.
3 Rizzuto grounded to short.
Brooklyn
1 Campanella grounded to second.
2 Branca took a called third strike.
3 Reese bounced back to the mound.

6th Inning
New York
1 Henrich flied to right.
2 Berra grounded to first.
3 DiMaggio popped to first.
Brooklyn
1 Miksis flied to right.
2 Furillo grounded to second.
Robinson walked.
3 Hodges flied to center.

7th Inning
New York
1 Brown grounded to second.
2 Woodling flied to center.
3 Mapes flied to center.
Brooklyn
1 Olmo fouled to Berra.
2 Snider grounded to first.
3 Campanella flied to left.

8th Inning
New York
1 Coleman called out on strikes.
2 Page grounded to short.
3 Rizzuto popped to short.
Brooklyn
1 Branca took a called third strike.
Reese walked.
Miksis singled to left, Reese stopping at second.
2 Furillo flied to right.
3 Robinson flied to center.

9th Inning
New York
1 Henrich grounded to second.
Berra walked.
2 DiMaggio fouled to Miksis.
Brown singled to right, Berra stopping at second.
Woodling walked, loading the bases.
Mize, pinch-hitting for Mapes, singled against the right field fence, scoring Berra and Brown with Woodling going to third.
For Brooklyn—Banta replaced Branca on the mound.
Bauer ran for Mize.
Coleman singled to center, scoring Woodling with Bauer going to third.
3 Page struck out.
Brooklyn
For New York—Bauer playing right.
1 Hodges grounded to second.
Olmo hit a home run into the lower left field stands.
2 Snider struck out.
Campanella hit a home run into the left field stands.
3 Edwards, pinch-hitting for Banta, was called out on strikes.

Game 4 October 8 at Brooklyn

N.Y.	000	330	000
Bkn.	000	004	000

New York	Pos	AB	R	H	RBI	PO	A	E
Rizzuto	ss	4	0	2	0	1	4	0
Henrich	1b	4	1	3	0	10	1	0
Berra	c	5	1	1	0	10	1	0
DiMaggio	cf	3	1	0	0	1	0	0
B. Brown	3b	3	1	2	3	0	3	0
Woodling	lf	3	1	0	0	2	0	0
Mapes	rf	2	1	1	2	1	0	0
a Bauer	rf	2	0	0	0	2	0	0
Coleman	2b	4	0	0	0	3	0	0
Lopat	p	3	0	1	1	0	1	0
Reynolds	p	1	0	0	0	0	0	0
Totals		34	6	10	6	27	9	0

Pitching	IP	H	R	ER	BB	SO
New York						
Lopat (W)	5⅔	9	4	4	1	4
Reynolds (SV)	3⅓	0	0	0	0	5
Brooklyn						
Newcombe (L)	3⅔	5	3	3	3	0
Hatten	1⅓	3	3	3	2	0
Erskine	1	1	0	0	0	1
Banta	3	1	0	0	1	1

Brooklyn	Pos	AB	R	H	RBI	PO	A	E
Reese	ss	4	1	2	0	0	2	0
Miksis	3b	2	0	0	0	0	2	1
c Cox	3b	2	0	1	0	1	0	0
Snider	cf	4	0	0	0	4	0	0
Robinson	2b	3	1	1	1	2	3	0
Hodges	1b	4	1	1	0	8	1	0
Olmo	lf	4	1	1	1	2	1	0
Campanella	c	4	0	1	1	5	2	0
Hermanski	rf	4	0	2	1	4	0	0
Newcombe	p	1	0	0	0	1	1	0
Hatten	p	0	0	0	0	0	0	0
b T. Brown		1	0	0	0	0	0	0
Erskine	p	0	0	0	0	0	0	0
d Jorgensen		1	0	0	0	0	0	0
Banta	p	0	0	0	0	0	0	0
e Whitman		1	0	0	0	0	0	0
Totals		35	4	9	4	27	12	1

a Flied out for Mapes in 5th.
b Flied out for Hatten in 5th.
c Singled for Miksis in 6th.
d Struck out for Erskine in 6th.
e Struck out for Banta in 9th.

Doubles—B. Brown, Lopat, Mapes, Reese. Triple—B. Brown. Double Plays—Miksis to Campanella to Robinson, Rizzuto to Henrich. Left on Bases—New York 7, Brooklyn 5. Umpires—Jorda, Hubbard, Reardon, Passarella, Hurley, Barr. Attendance—33,934. Time of Game—2:42.

1st Inning

New York
Rizzuto singled to center.
Henrich singled to right, Rizzuto racing to third.
1,2 Berra grounded to Miksis, and Rizzuto caught in a rundown was declared out running out of the base line to elude Campanella's tag. Campanella threw to Robinson to double up Henrich who had rounded second.
DiMaggio walked.
B. Brown walked, loading the bases.
3 Woodling lined to center.

Brooklyn
Reese doubled off the left-center field wall.
1 Miksis tapped out, Berra to Henrich, Reese holding second.
2 Snider grounded to third, Reese still holding second.
3 Robinson grounded to short.

2nd Inning

New York
1 Mapes grounded back to the mound.
2 Coleman fouled to Campanella
3 Lopat flied to center.

Brooklyn
1 Hodges flied to left.
2 Olmo flied to left.
3 Campanella bounced to the pitcher.

3rd Inning

New York
1 Rizzuto grounded to third.
2 Henrich grounded out, Hodges to Newcombe.
3 Berra flied to right.

Brooklyn
1 Hermanski struck out.
2 Newcombe struck out.
3 Reese popped to first.

4th Inning

New York
1 DiMaggio flied to center.
B. Brown doubled off the wall in left-center.
Woodling walked.
Mapes doubled down the left field line, scoring B. Brown and Woodling.
2 Coleman flied to left.
Lopat doubled off the wall in left-center, scoring Mapes.
For Brooklyn—Hatten replaced Newcombe on the mound.
Rizzuto singled to left, but Lopat
3 was out trying to score, Olmo to Campanella

4th Inning (continued)

Brooklyn
1 Miksis was called out on strikes.
2 Snider flied to right.
Robinson walked.
3 Hodges struck out.

5th Inning

New York
Henrich walked.
Berra singled to right, Henrich stopping at second, but when Hermanski's throw was muffed by Miksis, both runners advanced a base.
DiMaggio intentionally walked, loading the bases.
B. Brown tripled clearing the bases.
1 Woodling flied to center.
2 Bauer, batting for Mapes, lined to right.
3 Coleman grounded to short.

Brooklyn
For New York—Bauer playing right.
1 Olmo fouled to Berra.
2 Campanella grounded to short. Hermanski singled to right.
3 T. Brown, pinch-hitting for Hatten, flied to right.

6th Inning

New York
For Brooklyn—Erskine pitching
1 Lopat popped to first.
2 Rizzuto flied to left.
Henrich hit a long single off the right field wall.
3 Berra popped to second.

Brooklyn
Reese singled to center
Cox, batting for Miksis, beat out a roller to third, Reese stopping at second.
1,2 Snider hit into a double play, Rizzuto to Henrich, Reese going to third.
Robinson singled to left, scoring Reese
Hodges singled to center, Robinson going to third.
Olmo singled to center, scoring Robinson with Hodges going to third.
Campanella singled to left, scoring Hodges as Olmo stopped at second.
Hermanski singled to right, Olmo scoring as Campanella raced to third.
For New York—Reynolds replaced Lopat on the mound.
3 Jorgensen, pinch-hitting for Erskine, took a called third strike.

7th Inning

New York
For Brooklyn—Cox playing third with Banta the new pitcher.
1 DiMaggio grounded to second.
2 B. Brown grounded to second.
3 Woodling grounded to second.

Brooklyn
1 Reese lined to right.
2 Cox flied to center.
3 Snider struck out.

8th Inning

New York
1 Bauer grounded to short.
2 Coleman flied to right.
3 Reynolds fouled to Campanella.

Brooklyn
1 Robinson grounded to third.
2 Hodges grounded to short.
3 Olmo called out on strikes.

9th Inning

New York
Rizzuto walked.
Henrich singled to right, Rizzuto going to third.
1 Rizzuto was picked off third, Campanella to Cox.
2 Berra flied to right.
3 DiMaggio struck out.

Brooklyn
1 Campanella grounded to third.
2 Hermanski struck out.
3 Whitman, pinch-hitting for Banta, struck out.

Game 5 October 9 at Brooklyn

N.Y.	203	113	000
Bkn.	001	001	400

New York	Pos	AB	R	H	RBI	PO	A	E
Rizzuto	ss	3	2	0	0	3	3	0
Henrich	1b	4	2	1	0	8	0	0
Berra	c	5	0	0	1	11	0	0
DiMaggio	cf	4	1	1	2	0	0	0
B. Brown	3b	4	2	3	2	0	1	0
Woodling	lf	4	2	3	0	3	0	0
Mapes	rf	3	1	0	0	1	0	1
Coleman	2b	5	0	2	3	1	0	0
Raschi	p	3	0	1	1	0	0	0
Page	p	1	0	0	0	0	1	0
Totals		36	10	11	9	27	5	1

Pitching	IP	H	R	ER	BB	SO
New York						
Raschi (W)	6⅔	9	6	6	4	7
Page (SV)	2⅓	2	0	0	1	4
Brooklyn						
Barney (L)	2⅔	3	5	5	6	2
Banta	2⅓	3	2	2	0	2
Erskine	⅓	2	3	3	1	0
Hatten	⅓	1	0	0	0	0
Palica	2	1	0	0	1	1
Minner	1	1	0	0	0	0

Brooklyn	Pos	AB	R	H	RBI	PO	A	E
Reese	ss	5	0	2	1	1	0	0
Jorgensen	3b	3	1	0	0	0	0	0
e Miksis		1	0	1	0	0	0	0
Snider	cf	5	2	2	0	5	0	0
Robinson	2b	4	0	1	1	1	2	1
Hermanski	rf	3	1	1	1	1	0	0
Hodges	1b	5	1	2	3	9	1	0
Rackley	lf	3	0	0	0	2	0	0
c Olmo	lf	1	0	0	0	2	0	0
Campanella	c	3	1	1	0	5	0	0
Barney	p	0	0	0	0	1	1	1
Banta	p	1	0	0	0	0	1	0
a T. Brown		1	0	0	0	0	0	0
Erskine	p	0	0	0	0	0	0	0
Hatten	p	0	0	0	0	0	0	0
b Cox		1	0	0	0	0	0	0
Palica	p	0	0	0	0	0	1	0
d Edwards		1	0	1	0	0	0	0
Minner	p	0	0	0	0	0	1	0
Totals		37	6	11	6	27	7	2

a Struck out for Banta in 5th.
b Struck out for Hatten in 6th.
c Struck out for Rackley in 7th.
d Singled for Palica in 8th.
e Doubled for Jorgensen in 9th.

Doubles—Campanella, Coleman, Miskis, Snider, Woodling 2. Triple—B. Brown. Home Runs—DiMaggio, Hodges. Sacrifice Hits—Mapes, Rizzuto. Double Play—Page to Rizzuto to Henrich. Left on Bases—New York 9, Brooklyn 9. Umpires—Hubbard, Reardon, Passarella, Jorda, Barr, Hurley. Attendance—33,711. Time of Game—3:04.

1st Inning
New York
  Rizzuto walked.
  Henrich walked.
    Rizzuto went to third and Henrich to second on Barney's wild pick off attempt, the ball sailing over Reese's head into center field.
1 Berra struck out.
2 DiMaggio flied to deep center, Rizzuto scoring and Henrich going to third after the catch.
  B. Brown singled through the box, scoring Henrich.
  Woodling walked.
3 Mapes called out on strikes.
Brooklyn
1 Reese grounded to short.
2 Jorgensen grounded to third.
3 Snider struck out.

2nd Inning
New York
1 Coleman popped to short.
  Raschi walked.
2 Rizzuto sacrificed Raschi to second, Hodges unassisted.
3 Henrich grounded out, Hodges to Barney.
Brooklyn
1 Robinson lined to second.
2 Hermanski flied to right.
3 Hodges grounded to short.

3rd Inning
New York
1 Berra bounced back to the pitcher.
2 DiMaggio lined to center.
  B. Brown walked.
  Woodling singled to center, B. Brown advancing to third.
  Mapes walked, loading the bases.
  Coleman singled to left, scoring B. Brown and Woodling with Mapes stopping at second.
  For Brooklyn—Banta came in to pitch.
  Raschi singled to center, Mapes scoring and Coleman stopping at second.
3 Rizzuto flied to center.
Brooklyn
1 Rackley struck out.
  Campanella doubled to left.
2 Banta grounded to first, Campanella advancing to third.
  Reese singled to right, scoring Campanella.
3 Jorgensen popped to short.

4th Inning
New York
1 Henrich grounded to second.
2 Berra lined to first.
  DiMaggio hit a home run into the lower left field stands.
3 B. Brown struck out.
Brooklyn
1 Snider struck out.
  Robinson singled to center.
2 Hermanski flied to left.
  Hodges singled off the right field wall, Robinson going to third.
3 Rackley struck out.

5th Inning
New York
  Woodling hit a double off the scoreboard in right.
1 Mapes sacrificed Woodling to third, Banta to Hodges.
2 Coleman grounded to first, scoring Woodling.
3 Raschi took a called third strike.
Brooklyn
1 Campanella lined to short.
2 T. Brown, pinch-hitting for Banta, struck out.
  Reese singled to left.
3 Jorgensen grounded to first.

6th Inning
New York
  For Brooklyn—Erskine pitching.
  Rizzuto walked.
  Henrich singled to left, Rizzuto going to third.
1 Berra flied to deep left, Rizzuto scoring after the catch.
2 DiMaggio popped to second.
  B. Brown tripled off the right field wall, scoring Henrich and also scored on Robinson's wild relay to the plate.
  For Brooklyn—Hatten came in to pitch.
  Woodling doubled off the left-center field wall.
3 Mapes flied to left.
Brooklyn
  Snider doubled off the left-center field wall.
  Robinson walked.
  Hermanski singled to right, scoring Snider as Robinson stopped at second, but Robinson went to third on Mapes' fumble.
1 Hodges struck out.
2 Rackley bounced to first, Robinson holding and Hermanski going to second.
  Campanella walked, loading the bases.
3 Cox, pinch-hitting for Hatten, struck out.

7th Inning
New York
  For Brooklyn—Palica now pitching.
1 Coleman grounded to second.
2 Raschi grounded back to the mound.
3 Rizzuto struck out.
Brooklyn
1 Reese lined to left.
  Jorgensen walked.
  Snider singled to center, Jorgensen moving to third.
2 Robinson flied to left, Jorgensen scoring after the catch.
  Hermanski walked.
  Hodges hit a three-run homer into the lower left field stands.
  For New York—Page came in to pitch.
3 Olmo, pinch-hitting for Rackley, struck out.

8th Inning
New York
  For Brooklyn—Olmo playing left.
1 Henrich lined to Snider, making a fantastic diving catch.
2 Berra flied to center.
  DiMaggio walked.
  B. Brown singled to left, DiMaggio stopping at second.
3 Woodling flied to left.
Brooklyn
1 Campanella popped to first.
  Edwards, batting for Palica, singled to left.
2,3 Reese hit into a double play, Page to Rizzuto to Henrich.

9th Inning
New York
  For Brooklyn—Minner pitching.
1 Mapes flied to left.
  Coleman doubled off the right-center field scoreboard.
2 Page grounded to the mound.
3 Rizzuto lined to right.
Brooklyn
  Miksis, batting for Jorgensen, doubled down the left field line.
1 Snider struck out.
2 Robinson struck out.
  Hermanski walked.
3 Hodges struck out.

1949 WORLD SERIES COMPOSITE BOX

	Wins	Composite Line Score
New York Yankees (A.L.)	4	2 0 4 4 4 3 0 0 4 – 21
Brooklyn Dodgers (N.L.)	1	0 1 1 1 0 5 4 0 2 – 14

Manager	W	L	Pct.	G. Ahead
Casey Stengel	97	57	.630	1
Burt Shotton	97	57	.630	1

(Regular Season)

BATTING AND FIELDING

WORLD SERIES STATISTICS

NEW YORK YANKEES

	Pos	G	AB	R	H	2B	3B	HR	RBI	BB	SO	SB	BA	SA	PO	A	E
Tommy Henrich	1b	5	19	**4**	5	0	0	**1**	1	3	0	0	.263	.421	**48**	1	0
Jerry Coleman	2b	5	20	0	5	**3**	0	0	4	0	4	0	.250	.400	10	9	**1**
Phil Rizzuto	ss	5	18	2	3	0	0	0	1	3	1	**1**	.167	5	**15**	0	
Bobby Brown	ph-3b	4	12	**4**	**6**	1	**2**	0	**5**	2	2	0	**.500**	**.917**	0	6	0
Cliff Mapes	rf	4	10	3	1	1	0	0	2	2	4	0	.100	.200	8	0	**1**
Joe DiMaggio	cf	5	18	2	2	0	0	**1**	2	3	5	0	.111	.278	7	0	0
Gene Woodling	lf	3	10	4	4	**3**	0	0	0	3	0	0	.400	.700	7	0	0
Yogi Berra	c	4	16	2	1	0	0	0	1	1	3	0	.063	.063	37	3	0
Billy Johnson	3b	2	7	0	1	0	0	0	0	0	2	**1**	.143	.143	2	5	0
Johnny Lindell	lf	2	7	0	1	0	0	0	0	0	2	0	.143	.143	2	1	**1**
Hank Bauer	rf-pr-ph	3	6	0	1	0	0	0	0	0	0	0	.167	.167	3	0	0
Charlie Silvera	c	1	2	0	0	0	0	0	0	0	0	0	.000	.000	6	0	0
Gus Niarhos	c	1	0	0	0	0	0	0	0	0	0	0	—	—	0	0	0
Johnny Mize	ph	2	2	0	2	0	0	0	2	0	0	0	1.000	1.000			
Snuffy Stirnweiss	pr	1	0	0	0	0	0	0	0	0	0	0	—	—			
Charlie Keller		Did not play															
Vic Raschi	p	2	5	0	1	0	0	0	1	1	1	0	.200	.200	0	0	0
Joe Page	p	3	4	0	0	0	0	0	0	0	2	0	.000	.000	0	2	0
Allie Reynolds	p	2	4	0	2	1	0	0	0	0	1	0	.500	.750	0	1	0
Ed Lopat	p	1	3	0	1	1	0	0	1	0	0	0	.333	.667	0	1	0
Tommy Byrne	p	1	1	0	1	0	0	0	0	0	0	0	1.000	1.000	0	0	0
Fred Sanford		Did not play															
Cuddles Marshall		Did not play															
Duane Pillette		Did not play															
Ralph Buxton		Did not play															
team total		5	164	21	37	10	2	2	20	18	27	2	.226	.348	135	44	3

Double Plays—5
Left on Bases—32

REGULAR SEASON STATISTICS

NEW YORK YANKEES

		Main Pos	G	AB	R	H	2B	3B	HR	RBI	BB	SO	SB	BA	SA
Tommy Henrich		of-1b	115	411	90	118	20	3	24	85	86	34	2	.287	.526
Jerry Coleman		2b	128	447	54	123	21	5	2	42	63	44	8	.275	.358
Phil Rizzuto		ss	153	614	110	169	22	7	5	65	72	34	18	.275	.358
Bobby Brown		3b	104	343	61	97	14	4	6	61	38	18	4	.283	.399
Cliff Mapes		of	111	304	56	75	13	3	7	38	58	50	6	.247	.378
Joe DiMaggio		of	76	272	58	94	14	6	14	67	55	18	0	.346	.596
Gene Woodling		of	112	296	60	80	13	7	5	44	52	21	2	.270	.412
Yogi Berra		c	116	415	59	115	20	2	20	91	22	25	2	.277	.480
Billy Johnson		3b	113	329	48	82	11	3	8	56	48	44	1	.249	.374
Johnny Lindell		of	78	211	33	51	10	0	6	27	35	27	3	.242	.374
Hank Bauer		of	103	301	56	82	6	6	10	45	37	42	2	.272	.432
Charlie Silvera		c	58	130	8	41	2	0	0	13	18	5	2	.315	.331
Gus Niarhos		c	32	43	7	12	2	1	0	6	13	8	0	.279	.372
Johnny Mize	a	1b-ph	13	23	4	6	1	0	1	2	4	2	0	.261	.435
Snuffy Stirnweiss		2b	70	157	29	41	8	2	0	11	29	20	3	.261	.338
Charlie Keller		of-ph	60	116	17	29	4	1	3	16	25	15	2	.250	.379
Vic Raschi		p	38	83	7	13	1	1	0	6	13	19	0	.157	.193
Joe Page		p	60	40	2	7	0	0	0	5	1	14	0	.175	.175
Allie Reynolds		p	38	78	8	17	3	2	0	10	13	15	0	.218	.308
Ed Lopat		p	31	76	9	20	8	0	1	4	7	8	0	.263	.408
Tommy Byrne		p	35	83	8	16	4	2	0	13	2	20	0	.193	.289
Fred Sanford		p	29	34	1	4	0	0	0	1	1	9	0	.118	.118
Cuddles Marshall		p	21	9	0	1	0	0	0	0	1	2	0	.111	.111
Duane Pillette		p	12	11	0	0	0	0	0	0	2	2	0	.000	.000
Ralph Buxton		p	14	3	0	0	0	0	0	0	0	2	0	.000	.000
team total			155	5196	829	1396	215	60	115	759	731	539	58	.269	.400

a—from New York (N)

Dick Kryhoski (1b), Jack Phillips (1b), Fenton Mole (1b), Jim Delsing (of), Joe Collins (1b), Ralph Houk (c), Mickey Witek (ph), Bob Porterfield (p), Hugh Casey (p), Spec Shea (p), Frank Hiller (p), and Wally Hood also played for the Yankees during the season.

WORLD SERIES STATISTICS

BROOKLYN DODGERS

	Pos	G	AB	R	H	2B	3B	HR	RBI	BB	SO	SB	BA	SA	PO	A	E
Gil Hodges	1b	5	17	2	4	0	0	**1**	4	1	4	0	.235	.412	38	3	0
Jackie Robinson	2b	5	16	2	3	1	0	0	2	**4**	2	0	.188	.250	12	9	**1**
Pee Wee Reese	ss	5	19	2	**6**	1	0	**1**	2	1	0	**1**	.316	.526	5	9	**1**
Spider Jorgensen	3b-ph	4	11	1	2	2	0	0	0	2	2	0	.182	.364	1	6	0
Gene Hermanski	lf-rf	4	13	1	4	0	1	0	2	3	3	0	.308	.462	7	0	0
Duke Snider	cf	5	**21**	2	3	1	0	0	0	0	**8**	0	.143	.190	18	1	0
Luis Olmo	lf	4	11	2	3	0	0	**1**	2	0	2	0	.273	.545	6	1	0
Roy Campanella	c	5	15	2	4	1	0	**1**	2	3	1	0	.267	.533	32	2	0
Carl Furillo	rf-ph	3	8	0	1	0	0	0	0	1	0	0	.125	.125	2	0	0
Eddie Miksis	3b-ph	3	7	0	2	1	0	0	0	0	1	0	.286	.429	3	3	1
Marv Rackley	lf	2	5	0	0	0	0	0	0	0	2	0	.000	.000	2	0	0
Billy Cox	ph-3b	2	3	0	1	0	0	0	0	0	1	0	.333	.333	1	0	0
Mike McCormick	rf	1	0	0	0	0	0	0	0	0	0	0	—	—	1	0	0
Bruce Edwards	ph	2	2	0	1	0	0	0	0	0	1	0	.500	.500			
Tommy Brown	ph	2	2	0	0	0	0	0	0	0	1	0	.000	.000			
Dick Whitman	ph	1	1	0	0	0	0	0	0	0	1	0	.000	.000			
Don Newcombe	p	2	4	0	0	0	0	0	0	0	3	0	.000	.000	1	1	0
Ralph Branca	p	1	3	0	0	0	0	0	0	0	3	0	.000	.000	1	0	0
Preacher Roe	p	1	3	0	0	0	0	0	0	0	3	0	.000	.000	1	1	**1**
Jack Banta	p	3	1	0	0	0	0	0	0	0	0	0	.000	.000	0	1	0
Carl Erskine	p	2	0	0	0	0	0	0	0	0	0	0	—	—	0	0	0
Joe Hatten	p	2	0	0	0	0	0	0	0	0	0	0	—	—	0	0	0
Rex Barney	p	1	0	0	0	0	0	0	0	0	0	0	—	—	1	1	**1**
Erv Palica	p	1	0	0	0	0	0	0	0	0	0	0	—	—	0	1	0
Paul Minner	p	1	0	0	0	0	0	0	0	0	0	0	—	—	0	1	0
team total		5	162	14	34	7	1	4	14	15	38	1	.210	.340	132	40	5

Double Plays—1
Left on Bases—31

REGULAR SEASON STATISTICS

BROOKLYN DODGERS

		Main Pos	G	AB	R	H	2B	3B	HR	RBI	BB	SO	SB	BA	SA
Gil Hodges		1b	156	596	94	170	23	4	23	115	66	64	10	.285	.453
Jackie Robinson		2b	156	593	122	203	38	12	16	124	86	27	**37**	**.342**	.528
Pee Wee Reese		ss	155	617	**132**	172	27	3	16	73	116	59	26	.279	.410
Spider Jorgensen		3b	53	134	15	36	5	1	1	14	23	13	0	.269	.343
Gene Hermanski		of	87	224	48	67	12	3	8	42	47	21	12	.299	.487
Duke Snider		of	146	552	100	161	28	7	23	92	56	**92**	12	.292	.493
Luis Olmo		of	38	105	15	32	4	1	1	14	5	11	2	.305	.390
Roy Campanella		c	130	436	65	125	22	2	22	82	67	36	3	.287	.498
Carl Furillo		of	142	549	95	177	27	10	18	106	37	29	4	.322	.506
Eddie Miksis		2b	50	113	17	25	5	0	1	6	7	8	3	.221	.292
Marv Rackley	b	of	63	150	25	45	5	1	1	15	14	8	1	.300	.367
Billy Cox		3b	100	390	48	91	18	2	8	40	30	18	5	.233	.351
Mike McCormick		of	55	139	17	29	5	1	2	14	14	12	1	.209	.302
Bruce Edwards		c	64	148	24	31	3	0	8	25	25	15	0	.209	.392
Tommy Brown		of	41	89	14	27	2	0	3	18	6	8	0	.303	.427
Dick Whitman		ph-of	23	49	8	9	2	0	0	2	4	4	0	.184	.224
Don Newcombe		p	39	96	8	22	4	0	0	10	5	16	0	.229	.271
Ralph Branca		p	34	62	5	5	1	0	0	2	9	26	0	.081	.097
Preacher Roe		p	30	70	5	8	0	0	0	7	7	28	0	.114	.114
Jack Banta		p	48	46	2	5	1	0	0	1	3	9	0	.139	.130
Carl Erskine		p	22	26	1	3	0	0	0	1	0	5	0	.115	.115
Joe Hatten		p	39	67	4	12	1	0	0	4	1	21	0	.179	.194
Rex Barney		p	38	47	3	10	1	0	0	2	1	14	0	.213	.234
Erv Palica		p	49	19	2	3	1	0	0	2	2	6	0	.158	.211
Paul Minner		p	27	14	3	3	0	0	0	2	0	5	0	.214	.214
team total			156	5400	**879**	1477	236	47	**152**	**816**	638	570	**117**	.274	**.419**

b—to and from Pittsburgh

Cal Abrams (of), Johnny Hopp (of), Bob Ramazzotti (3b-ph), Chuck Connors (ph), George Shuba (ph), Pat McGlothlin (p), Morrie Martin (p), Bud Podbielan (p), and Johnny Van Cuyk (p) also played for the Dodgers during the season.

PITCHING

WORLD SERIES STATISTICS

	G	GS	CG	IP	H	R	ER	BB	SO	W	L	SV	ERA
NEW YORK YANKEES													
Vic Raschi	2	**2**	0	**$14\frac{2}{3}$**	**15**	**7**	**7**	5	11	**1**	1	0	4.30
Allie Reynolds	2	1	**1**	$12\frac{1}{3}$	2	0	0	4	**14**	**1**	0	**1**	**0.00**
Joe Page	**3**	0	0	9	6	2	2	3	8	**1**	0	**1**	2.00
Ed Lopat	1	1	0	$5\frac{2}{3}$	9	4	4	1	4	**1**	0	0	6.35
Tommy Byrne	1	1	0	$3\frac{1}{3}$	2	1	1	2	1	0	0	0	2.70
Fred Sanford	Did not play												
Cuddles Marshall	Did not play												
Duane Pillette	Did not play												
Ralph Buxton	Did not play												
team total	5	5	1	45	34	14	14	15	38	4	1	2	2.80
BROOKLYN DODGERS													
Don Newcombe	2	**2**	**1**	$11\frac{2}{3}$	10	4	4	3	11	0	**2**	0	3.09
Preacher Roe	1	1	**1**	9	6	0	0	0	3	**1**	0	0	**0.00**
Ralph Branca	1	1	0	$8\frac{2}{3}$	4	4	4	4	6	0	1	0	4.15
Jack Banta	**3**	0	0	$5\frac{2}{3}$	5	2	2	1	4	0	0	0	3.18
Rex Barney	1	1	0	$2\frac{2}{3}$	3	5	5	**6**	2	0	1	0	16.88
Erv Palica	1	0	0	2	1	0	0	1	1	0	0	0	0.00
Carl Erskine	2	0	0	$1\frac{2}{3}$	3	3	3	1	0	0	0	0	16.20
Joe Hatten	2	0	0	$1\frac{2}{3}$	4	3	3	2	0	0	0	0	16.20
Paul Minner	1	0	0	1	1	0	0	0	0	0	0	0	0.00
team total	5	5	2	44	37	21	21	18	27	1	4	0	4.30

REGULAR SEASON STATISTICS

	G	GS	CG	IP	H	ER	BB	SO	W	L	Pct	SV	ShO	ERA
NEW YORK YANKEES														
Vic Raschi	38	37	21	275	247	102	138	124	21	10	.677	0	3	3.34
Allie Reynolds	35	31	4	214	200	95	123	105	17	6	.739	1	2	4.00
Joe Page	**60**	0	0	135	103	39	75	99	13	8	.619	**27**	0	2.60
Ed Lopat	31	30	14	215	222	78	69	70	15	10	.600	1	4	3.27
Tommy Byrne	32	30	12	196	125	81	**179**	129	15	7	.682	0	3	3.72
Fred Sanford	29	11	3	95	100	41	57	51	7	3	.700	0	0	3.88
Cuddles Marshall	21	2	0	49	48	28	48	13	3	0	1.000	3	0	5.14
Duane Pillette	12	3	2	37	43	18	19	9	2	4	.333	0	0	4.38
Ralph Buxton	14	0	0	27	22	12	16	14	0	1	.000	2	0	4.00
team total	155	155	59	1371	1231	563	**812**	**671**	**97**	57	**.630**	**36**	12	3.70
BROOKLYN DODGERS														
Don Newcombe	38	31	19	244	223	86	73	149	17	8	.680	1	**5**	3.17
Preacher Roe	30	27	13	213	201	66	44	109	15	6	**.714**	1	3	2.79
Ralph Branca	34	27	9	187	181	91	91	109	13	5	.722	1	2	4.38
Jack Banta	48	12	2	152	125	57	68	97	10	6	.625	3	1	3.38
Rex Barney	38	20	6	141	108	69	89	80	9	8	.529	1	2	4.40
Erv Palica	49	1	0	97	93	39	49	44	8	9	.471	6	0	3.62
Carl Erskine	22	3	2	80	68	41	51	49	8	1	.889	0	0	4.61
Joe Hatten	37	29	11	187	194	87	69	58	12	8	.600	2	2	4.19
Paul Minner	27	1	0	47	49	20	18	17	3	1	.750	2	0	3.83
team total	156	156	62	**1409**	1306	595	582	**743**	**97**	57	**.630**	17	**15**	3.80

Total Attendance—236,716 Average Attendance—47,343 Winning Player's Share—$5,627 Losing Player's Share—$4,273

1950
Spanking the Whiz Kids

The New York Yankees stood for precision excellence, a tradition of superiority spanning the Ruth years of the 1920's and the new era of Casey Stengel. The pinstriped Bronx Bombers captured their second pennant in two years under Stengel, outlasting strong challenges from Detroit, Boston, and Cleveland. Yankee regulars such as Joe DiMaggio, Yogi Berra, Phil Rizzuto, Johnny Mize, and Hank Bauer conjured up intimidating images of awesome batting power, flawless fielding, and an uncanny knack for pulling games out with ninth-inning magic. The Yankee pitching staff featured four experienced workhorses in Vic Raschi, Eddie Lopat, Allie Reynolds, and Tommy Byrne, plus rookie southpaw Whitey Ford, who built a 9–1 record after his recall in June.

But while the Yankees represented established excellence, the National League-champion Philadelphia Phillies embodied the cocky rise of a nobody to challenge the neighborhood kingpin. Dubbed the Whiz Kids because of the relative youth of keymen Del Ennis, Richie Ashburn, Willie Jones, Granny Hamner, Robin Roberts, and Curt Simmons, the Phils made it into the Series only by beating the powerful Brooklyn Dodgers in extra innings on the last day of the season. The team lacked experience, both by reason of its youth and the fact that the Phillies had last played in a World Series in 1915. Ennis, Jones, and veteran catcher Andy Seminick swung long-ball bats, but the club as a whole lacked the brutal power of the Yankees. The team had the spirit of the young, but manager Eddie Sawyer's pitching staff had the doddering look of a worn-out wreck. Right-handed ace Robin Roberts was frazzled after pitching three games in the last five days of the season, a task necessitated by the late-season induction of lefty ace Curt Simmons into military service. The only other hurler rising above mediocrity on the staff was veteran Jim Konstanty, who earned himself the N.L. MVP award by relieving in a record 74 games and compiling a 16–7 record.

So when the Series opened in Philadelphia only three days after the Phils ended their season, Philly manager Sawyer went out on a limb and nominated Konstanty, who hadn't started a game all year, to face the Yankees. Stengel made a more conventional choice in Raschi, and both hurlers pitched masterful games. While Raschi efficiently disposed of the Philly batters, the Yankees broke through Konstanty's roadblock to score a run in the fourth inning on Bobby Brown's double and deep outfield flies by Bauer and Jerry Coleman. New York tried in vain to pad the lead in later innings against Konstanty, while the Phils never solved Raschi and went down to a heartbreaking 1–0 loss with only two hits. Yankee pitching rather than Yankee power won the first game, but both elements took a hand in the second contest. Burly pitcher Reynolds limited the Phils to one run, driven in by center fielder Ashburn, while powerful Robin Roberts used his rest-replenished fast ball to allow the Yanks only one run through nine innings. With the contest moving into extra innings, old pro Joe DiMaggio settled things with a tenth-inning homer that gave Reynolds a 2–1 win and the Yanks a comfortable 2–0 edge in the Series.

Now the Phillies had to meet Goliath on his own turf in the Bronx, and they had to do it with their second-line pitching. Veteran Ken Heintzelman started the third game and exceeded all of Sawyer's hopes by taking a 2–1 lead into the bottom of the eighth. But after retiring the first two men in that frame, Heintzelman walked the next three men and then handed the ball over to Konstanty. The spectacled reliever got Bobby Brown to hit an easy grounder to shortstop, but Hamner booted the play, and the tying run scored. With Russ Meyer pitching the bottom of the ninth, the Yanks won the game 3–2, on infield hits by Gene Woodling and Phil Rizzuto and a game-winning single by Coleman.

The fourth game formalized the sweep that everyone saw coming. The Yanks chased Philly starter Bob Miller from the game with a first-inning rally, then reached Konstanty for three runs in a sixth inning featured by Berra's homer. Young Whitey Ford gave up only two unearned runs in the ninth inning and got last-out help from Reynolds in preserving the 5–2 victory and the Yankees' second straight championship and thirteenth world title.

Game 1 October 4 at Philadelphia

| N.Y. | 000 100 000 |
| Phi. | 000 000 000 |

New York	Pos	AB	R	H	RBI	PO	A	E
Woodling	lf	3	0	1	0	1	0	0
Rizzuto	ss	3	0	1	0	0	2	0
Berra	c	4	0	0	0	7	0	0
DiMaggio	cf	2	0	0	0	3	0	0
Mize	1b	4	0	0	0	7	0	0
Hopp	1b	0	0	0	0	3	0	0
Brown	3b	4	1	1	0	0	0	0
Johnson	3b	0	0	0	0	0	0	0
Bauer	rf	4	0	1	0	5	0	0
Coleman	2b	4	0	1	1	2	0	0
Raschi	p	3	0	1	0	0	3	0
Totals		31	1	5	1	27	7	0

Pitching	IP	H	R	ER	BB	SO
New York						
Raschi (W)	9	2	0	0	1	5
Philadelphia						
Konstanty (L)	8	4	1	1	4	0
Meyer	1	1	0	0	0	0

Philadelphia	Pos	AB	R	H	RBI	PO	A	E
Waitkus	1b	3	0	0	0	9	2	0
Ashburn	cf	4	0	0	0	2	0	0
Sisler	lf	4	0	0	0	3	0	0
Ennis	rf	3	0	0	0	4	0	0
Jones	3b	3	0	1	0	4	3	1
Hamner	ss	3	0	0	0	0	1	0
Seminick	c	3	0	1	0	1	1	0
Goliat	2b	3	0	0	0	3	2	0
Konstanty	p	2	0	0	0	1	0	0
a Whitman		1	0	0	0	0	0	0
Meyer	p	0	0	0	0	0	1	0
Totals		29	0	2	0	27	10	1

a Flied out for Konstanty in 8th.

Double—Brown. Sacrifice Hits—Raschi, Rizzuto. Left on Bases—New York 9, Philadelphia 3. Umpires—Conlan (N), McGowan (A), Boggess (N), Berry (A), Barlick (N), McKinley (A). Attendance—30,746. Time of Game—2:17.

1st Inning
New York
Woodling walked.
Rizzuto singled between short and third, Woodling stopping at second.
1 Berra flied to deep right, Woodling going to third after the catch.
2 DiMaggio flied to Waitkus.
3 Mize flied to right.
Philadelphia
1 Waitkus fouled to Berra (previously he fouled to left where Woodling was stunned after crashing into the wall.
2 Ashburn bunted back to the mound.
3 Sisler bounced to the pitcher.

2nd Inning
New York
1 Brown flied to right.
2 Bauer grounded to short.
3 Coleman fouled to Sisler.
Philadelphia
1 Ennis grounded to second.
2 Jones popped (fair) to Berra.
3 Hamner grounded to short.

3rd Inning
New York
Raschi singled to left.
Woodling walked.
1 Rizzuto sacrificed both runners, Waitkus to Goliat, covering first.
2 Berra flied to short left.
DiMaggio got an intentional walk.
3 Mize popped to third.
Philadelphia
1 Seminick struck out.
2 Goliat flied to left.
3 Konstanty grounded back to the mound.

4th Inning
New York
Brown got a double inside the third base line.
1 Bauer flied to deep center with Brown going to third after the catch.
2 Coleman flied to deep left, Brown scoring after the catch.
3 Raschi grounded to third.
Philadelphia
1 Waitkus grounded to second.
2 Ashburn flied to center.
3 Sisler struck out.

5th Inning
New York
1 Woodling grounded out, Waitkus to Konstanty, covering first.
2 Rizzuto fouled to Seminick.
3 Berra fouled to Waitkus.
Philadelphia
1 Ennis flied to right.
Jones singled through the box.
2 Hamner flied to right.
Seminick singled to left, Jones stopping at second.
3 Goliat struck out.

6th Inning
New York
DiMaggio walked.
1 Mize popped to third.
2 Brown lined to right.
3 Bauer forced DiMaggio at second, Jones to Goliat.
Philadelphia
1 Konstanty struck out.
Waitkus walked.
2 Ashburn flied to center.
3 Sisler popped to first.

7th Inning
New York
1 Coleman grounded to third.
Raschi safe at first on Jones' low throw.
Woodling singled to left with Raschi stopping at second.
2 Rizzuto grounded to third.
3 Berra grounded to first.
Philadelphia
1 Ennis flied to right.
2 Jones lined to center.
3 Hamner flied to deep right.

8th Inning
New York
1 DiMaggio popped to third.
2 Mize grounded to second.
3 Brown grounded to second.
Philadelphia
For New York—Hopp at first, Johnson at third.
1 Seminick fouled to Hopp.
2 Goliat lined to second.
3 Whitman, pinch-hitting for Konstanty, flied to right.

9th Inning
New York
For Philadelphia—Meyer pitching.
Bauer singled off Jones' hand.
1 Coleman flied to center.
2 Raschi sacrificed Bauer to second, Meyer to Goliat, covering first.
3 Woodling out on a bouncer, Seminick to Waitkus.
Philadelphia
1 Waitkus grounded to short.
2 Ashburn bounced to first.
3 Sisler struck out.

Game 2 October 5 at Philadelphia

New York	Pos	AB	R	H	RBI	PO	A	E
Woodling	lf	5	0	2	1	2	0	0
Rizzuto	ss	4	0	0	0	2	1	0
Berra	c	5	0	1	0	7	0	0
DiMaggio	cf	5	1	1	1	3	0	0
Mize	1b	4	0	1	0	6	0	0
Johnson	3b	1	0	0	0	0	2	0
Brown	3b	4	0	2	0	0	0	0
b Hopp	1b	1	0	0	0	3	0	0
Bauer	rf	5	0	1	0	1	0	0
Coleman	2b	3	1	1	0	5	6	0
Reynolds	p	3	0	1	0	1	2	0
Totals		40	2	10	2	30	11	0

Pitching	IP	H	R	ER	BB	SO
New York						
Reynolds (W)	10	7	1	1	4	6
Philadelphia						
Roberts (L)	10	10	2	2	3	5

N.Y.	010	000	000	1
Phi.	000	010	000	0

Philadelphia	Pos	AB	R	H	RBI	PO	A	E
Waitkus	1b	4	0	2	0	8	0	0
Ashburn	cf	5	0	2	1	4	0	0
Sisler	lf	5	0	0	0	3	0	0
Ennis	rf	4	0	0	0	1	0	0
Jones	3b	4	0	0	0	3	0	0
Hamner	ss	3	0	2	0	2	2	0
Seminick	c	2	0	0	0	5	0	0
a Caballero		0	0	0	0	0	0	0
Silvestri	c	0	0	0	0	1	0	0
c Whitman		0	0	0	0	0	0	0
Lopata	c	0	0	0	0	1	0	0
Goliat	2b	4	1	1	0	2	2	0
Roberts	p	2	0	0	0	0	0	0
d Mayo		0	0	0	0	0	0	0
Totals		33	1	7	1	30	4	0

a Ran for Seminick in 7th.
b Ran for Brown in 8th.
c Intentionally walked for Silvestri in 9th.
d Walked for Roberts in 10th.

Doubles—Ashburn, Coleman, Hamner, Waitkus. Triple—Hamner. Home Run—DiMaggio. Stolen Base—Hamner. Sacrifice Hits—Roberts, Waitkus. Double Plays—Johnson to Coleman to Hopp, Rizzuto to Coleman to Hopp. Left on Bases—New York 11, Philadelphia 8. Umpires—McGowan, Boggess, Berry, Conlan, McKinley, Barlick. Attendance—32,660. Time of Game—3:06.

1st Inning
New York
Woodling beat out a slow roller to short.
1 Rizzuto fouled to Seminick.
Berra singled to left, Woodling going to third.
2 DiMaggio popped to second.
3 Mize fouled to Seminick.
Philadelphia
1 Waitkus grounded to second.
Ashburn doubled to right as Bauer missed a shoestring catch.
2 Sisler struck out.
3 Ennis grounded to second.

2nd Inning
New York
1 Brown lined to center.
2 Bauer fouled to Jones.
Coleman walked.
Reynolds singled to right, sending Coleman to third.
Woodling got another hit on a roller to short, Coleman scoring and Reynolds stopping at second.
3 Rizzuto flied to center.
Philadelphia
1 Jones called out on strikes.
Hamner tripled to right-center.
2 Seminick grounded to second, Hamner holding third.
3 Goliat flied to center.

3rd Inning
New York
1 Berra struck out.
2 DiMaggio popped to second.
Mize singled to right.
3 Brown flied to center.
Philadelphia
1 Roberts struck out.
Waitkus doubled down the right field line.
2 Ashburn fouled to Berra.
3 Sisler grounded to second.

4th Inning
New York
1 Bauer popped to short.
Coleman doubled into center.
Reynolds walked.
2 Woodling fouled to Sisler.
3 Rizzuto lined to right.
Philadelphia
1 Ennis struck out.
2 Jones popped to first.
Hamner walked.
Hamner stole second.
3 Seminick struck out.

5th Inning
New York
1 Berra popped to short.
2 DiMaggio popped to third.
3 Mize struck out.
Philadelphia
Goliat singled between first and second.
1 Roberts popped to the pitcher on an attempted sacrifice.
Waitkus singled over Coleman's head, Goliat moving to third.
2 Ashburn flied to left, Goliat scoring after the catch.
3 Sisler fouled to Mize.

6th Inning
New York
Brown singled to left-center.
1 Bauer fouled to Waitkus.
2 Coleman popped to first.
3 Reynolds struck out.
Philadelphia
1 Ennis flied out to DiMaggio in very deep right-center. A spectacular running catch.
2 Jones lined to short.
3 Hamner popped to second.

7th Inning
New York
1 Woodling flied to Sisler.
Rizzuto walked.
2 Berra flied to center.
3 DiMaggio fouled to Waitkus.
Philadelphia
Seminick walked.
Caballero ran for Seminick.
1 Goliat flied to left.
2 Roberts sacrificed Caballero to second, Reynolds to Coleman.
3 Waitkus lined to center.

8th Inning
New York
For Philadelphia—Silvestri catching.
1 Mize fouled to Waitkus.
Brown singled over third.
Bauer singled between short and third, Brown stopping at second.
Hopp ran for Brown.
2 Coleman grounded to short, advancing both runners.
3 Reynolds took a called third strike.
Philadelphia
For New York—Hopp at first (batting 6th), and Johnson playing third (batting 5th).
Ashburn singled on a bunt toward third.
1 Sisler forced Ashburn at second, on a bunt, Reynolds to Rizzuto.
2,3 Ennis hit into a double play, Johnson to Coleman to Hopp.

9th Inning
New York
1 Woodling grounded to second.
2 Rizzuto grounded to second.
3 Berra fouled to Jones.
Philadelphia
1 Jones flied to right.
Hamner doubled to right-center.
Whitman, batting for Silvestri, was given an intentional walk.
2,3 Goliat grounded into a double play, Rizzuto to Coleman to Hopp.

10th Inning
New York
For Philadelphia—Lopata catching.
DiMaggio homered into the upper left field stands.
1 Johnson struck out.
2 Hopp flied to left.
3 Bauer grounded to short.
Philadelphia
Mayo, batting for Roberts, walked.
1 Waitkus sacrificed Mayo to second, Johnson to Coleman.
2 Ashburn fouled to Hopp.
3 Sisler looked at a called third strike.

Game 3 October 6 at New York

Philadelphia	Pos	AB	R	H	RBI	PO	A	E
Waitkus	1b	5	0	1	0	8	0	0
Ashburn	cf	4	0	1	0	0	0	0
Jones	3b	3	0	1	0	1	2	0
Ennis	rf	4	1	1	0	3	0	0
Sisler	lf	4	0	1	1	2	0	0
Mayo	lf	0	0	0	0	1	0	0
Hamner	ss	4	1	3	0	2	2	1
Seminick	c	2	0	1	0	5	0	1
Goliat	2b	3	0	1	1	4	1	0
d Caballero		0	0	0	0	0	0	0
Bloodworth	2b	0	0	0	0	0	0	0
Heintzelman	p	2	0	0	0	0	2	0
Konstanty	p	0	0	0	0	0	0	0
e Whitman		1	0	0	0	0	0	0
Meyer	p	0	0	0	0	0	0	0
Totals		32	2	10	2	*26	7	2

* Two out when winning run scored.
a Popped out for Lopat in 8th.
b Safe on error for Bauer in 8th.
c Ran for Brown in 8th.
d Ran for Goliat in 9th.
e Hit into fielder's choice for Konstanty in 9th.

Doubles—Ennis, Hamner. Stolen Base—Rizzuto. Sacrifice Hits—Heintzelman, Jones, Seminick 2. Double Play—Hamner to Waitkus. Left on Bases—Philadelphia 8, New York 9. Umpires—Boggess, Berry, Conlan, McGowan, Barlick, McKinley. Attendance—64,505. Time of Game—2:35.

Phi.	000	001	100
N.Y.	001	000	011

New York	Pos	AB	R	H	RBI	PO	A	E
Rizzuto	ss	3	1	1	0	1	1	0
Coleman	2b	4	1	3	2	3	1	0
Berra	c	2	0	0	0	6	1	0
DiMaggio	cf	3	0	1	0	1	0	0
Bauer	lf	3	0	0	0	1	0	0
b Brown		1	0	0	0	0	0	0
c Jensen		0	0	0	0	0	0	0
Ferrick	p	0	0	0	0	0	0	0
Mize	1b	4	0	0	0	9	2	0
Collins	1b	0	0	0	0	1	1	0
Johnson	3b	4	0	0	0	1	3	0
Mapes	rf	4	0	0	0	3	0	0
Lopat	p	2	0	1	0	1	4	0
a Woodling	lf	2	1	1	0	0	0	0
Totals		32	3	7	2	27	13	0

Pitching	IP	H	R	ER	BB	SO
Philadelphia						
Heintzelman	$7\frac{2}{3}$	4	2	1	6	3
Konstanty	$\frac{1}{3}$	0	0	0	0	0
Meyer (L)	$\frac{2}{3}$	3	1	1	0	1
New York						
Lopat	8	9	2	2	0	5
Ferrick (W)	1	1	0	0	1	0

1st Inning
Philadelphia
Waitkus singled between first and second into right.
1 Ashburn struck out.
2 Jones rolled back to the mound, Waitkus moving to second.
3 Ennis grounded to third.
New York
Rizzuto walked.
1,2 Coleman blooped to Hamner who easily doubled Rizzuto at first.
Berra walked.
3 DiMaggio flied to right.

2nd Inning
Philadelphia
1 Sisler grounded to second.
Hamner singled off Johnson's glove.
Seminick singled to center, Hamner going to third.
2 Goliat grounded to the pitcher, Seminick to second while Hamner held third.
3 Heintzelman grounded to third.
New York
1 Bauer bounced back to the mound.
2 Mize popped to second.
3 Johnson struck out.

3rd Inning
Philadelphia
1 Waitkus flied to right.
2 Ashburn called out on strikes.
Jones singled to left.
3 Ennis popped to short.
New York
1 Mapes popped to first.
2 Lopat took a called third strike.
Rizzuto walked.
Rizzuto stole second and went to third when Seminick's throw went into center field.
Coleman singled to right, Rizzuto
3 scoring, but was out trying for a double Sisler to Hamner to Goliat.

4th Inning
Philadelphia
1 Sisler grounded to first.
2 Hamner flied to right.
3 Seminick struck out.
New York
1 Berra grounded to the pitcher.
DiMaggio singled to left.
2 Bauer flied to Ennis in deep right-center.
3 Mize grounded to first.

5th Inning
Philadelphia
1 Goliat grounded to short.
2 Heintzelman grounded out, Mize to Lopat.
3 Waitkus fouled to Johnson
New York
1 Johnson grounded to third.
2 Mapes flied to left.
Lopat singled to center.
3 Rizzuto popped to second.

6th Inning
Philadelphia
1 Ashburn struck out.
2 Jones struck out.
Ennis doubled into the left field corner.
Sisler singled over Rizzuto's head, Ennis scoring.
3 Hamner missed an attempted surprise bunt and Sisler was picked off of first, Berra to Mize.
New York
Coleman singled to left.
1 Berra fouled to Seminick.
2 DiMaggio flied to deep left.
3 Bauer popped to second.

7th Inning
Philadelphia
Hamner singled into center.
1 Seminick sacrificed Hamner to second, Lopat to Coleman.
Goliat singled to center, Hamner scoring.
2 Heintzelman sacrificed Goliat to second, Lopat to Coleman.
3 Waitkus flied to left.
New York
1 Mize flied to right.
2 Johnson struck out.
3 Mapes grounded to second.

8th Inning
Philadelphia
Ashburn singled past first.
1 Jones sacrificed Ashburn to second, Mize to Coleman.
2 Ennis flied to center.
3 Sisler popped to first.
New York
For Philadelphia—Mayo in left.
1 Woodling, pinch-hitting for Lopat, popped to short.
2 Rizzuto bounced to third.
Coleman walked.
Berra walked.
DiMaggio walked loading the bases.
For Philadelphia—Konstanty pitching.
Brown, batting for Bauer, was safe at first on Hamner's fumble, Coleman scoring.
Jensen ran for Brown.
3 Mize fouled to third.

9th Inning
Philadelphia
For New York—Woodling in left, Collins at first, Ferrick pitching.
Hamner doubled to left-center.
1 Seminick sacrificed Hamner to third, Johnson to Collins.
Goliat intentionally walked.
2 Whitman, pinch-hitting for Konstanty, hit into a fielder's choice, Collins throwing to Berra to get Hamner at the plate.
Caballera ran for Goliat.
3 Waitkus flied to right.
New York
For Philadelphia—Meyer pitching, Bloodworth at second.
1 Johnson lined to left.
2 Mapes struck out.
Woodling singled to second.
Rizzuto lined a single beyond second, Woodling stopping at second.
Coleman singled to left-center, Woodling scoring the winning run.

Game 4 October 7 at New York

Philadelphia	Pos	AB	R	H	RBI	PO	A	E
Waitkus	1b	3	0	1	0	9	1	0
Ashburn	cf	4	0	0	0	3	0	0
Jones	3b	4	1	2	0	0	4	0
Ennis	rf	3	0	1	0	1	0	0
Sisler	lf	4	0	0	0	2	0	0
b K. Johnson		0	1	0	0	0	0	0
Hamner	ss	4	0	1	0	2	2	0
Seminick	c	4	0	0	0	3	1	0
c Mayo		0	0	0	0	0	0	0
Goliat	2b	4	0	1	0	4	4	1
Miller	p	0	0	0	0	0	0	0
Konstanty	p	2	0	1	0	0	1	0
a Caballero		1	0	0	0	0	0	0
Roberts	p	0	0	0	0	0	0	0
d Lopata		1	0	0	0	0	0	0
Totals		34	2	7	0	24	13	1

a Struck out for Konstanty in 8th.
b Ran for Sisler in 9th.
c Ran for Seminick in 9th.
d Struck out for Roberts in 9th.

Doubles—DiMaggio, Jones. Triple—Brown.
Home Run—Berra. Double plays—Mize to
Berra, Coleman to Rizzuto to Mize.
Hit by Pitchers—DiMaggio (by Konstanty),
Ennis (by Ford). Wild Pitch—Miller.
Left on Bases—Philadelphia 7, New York 4.
Umpires—Berry, Conlan, McGowan, Boggess,
McKinley, Barlick. Attendance—68,098.
Time of Game—2:05.

Phi.	000 000 002
N.Y.	200 003 00x

New York	Pos	AB	R	H	RBI	PO	A	E
Woodling	lf	4	1	2	0	4	0	1
Rizzuto	ss	4	0	0	0	2	4	0
Berra	c	4	2	2	2	10	0	0
DiMaggio	cf	3	1	2	1	1	0	0
Mize	1b	3	0	1	0	5	1	0
Hopp	1b	1	0	0	0	1	1	0
Brown	3b	3	1	1	1	0	1	0
B. Johnson	3b	1	0	0	0	0	0	0
Bauer	rf	3	0	1	1	1	0	0
Coleman	2b	3	0	0	0	2	3	0
Ford	p	3	0	0	0	1	0	0
Reynolds	p	0	0	0	0	0	0	0
Totals		32	5	8	5	27	10	2

Pitching	IP	H	R	ER	BB	SO
Philadelphia						
Miller (L)	⅓	2	2	1	0	0
Konstanty	7⅔	5	3	3	0	3
Roberts	1	1	0	0	0	0
New York						
Ford (W)	8⅔	7	2	0	1	7
Reynolds (SV)	⅓	0	0	0	0	1

1st Inning
Philadelphia
  Waitkus walked
1 Ashburn flied to left.
  Jones hit a ground-rule double into the
    right field stands, Waitkus moving to
    third.
2 Ennis hit into a fielder's choice as
    Brown threw to Berra nipping Waitkus at
    the plate with Jones holding second.
3 Sisler called out on strikes.
New York
  Woodling safe at first on Goliat's
    fumble.
1 Rizzuto grounded to third, moving
    Woodling to second.
  Berra singled to right, Woodling
    scoring.
    Berra went all the way to third on
      a wild pitch.
  DiMaggio doubled to right, scoring
    Berra.
  For Philadelphia—Konstanty pitching.
2 Mize grounded to second, moving
    DiMaggio to third.
3 Brown grounded to second.

2nd Inning
Philadelphia
1 Hamner grounded to short.
2 Seminick grounded to short.
3 Goliat flied to left.
New York
1 Bauer popped to short.
2 Coleman flied to left.
3 Ford took a called third strike.

3rd Inning
Philadelphia
1 Konstanty grounded to second.
  Waitkus singled to center.
2 Ashburn struck out.
3 Jones forced Waitkus at second, Rizzuto
    to Coleman.
New York
1 Woodling flied to center.
2 Rizzuto grounded to third.
3 Berra grounded to second.

4th Inning
Philadelphia
  Ennis beat out a roller down the third
    base line.
1 Sisler flied to right.
  Hamner singled to right, sending Ennis
    to third.
2,3 Seminick bounced into a double play,
    Mize stepping on first to Berra
    getting Ennis at the plate
New York
1 DiMaggio struck out.
  Mize singled to right.
2 Brown flied to center.
3 Bauer forced Mize at second, Jones to
    Goliat.

5th Inning
Philadelphia
1 Goliat struck out.
  Konstanty singled to right.
2 Waitkus flied to left.
3 Ashburn popped to second.
New York
1 Coleman grounded to third.
2 Ford grounded to the pitcher.
  Woodling singled to right.
3 Rizzuto grounded to first.

6th Inning
Philadelphia
1 Jones called out on strikes.
  Ennis safe at first when Brown booted
    his grounder.
2,3 Sisler grounded into a double play,
    Coleman to Rizzuto to Mize.
New York
  Berra homered into the right field
    lower deck.
  DiMaggio hit by a pitched ball.
1 Mize out as his grounder went off of
    Waitkus' glove to Goliat who threw
    back to Waitkus for the out. DiMaggio
    moved to second.
  Brown tripled to deep center, DiMaggio
    scored.
2 Bauer lined to left, scoring Brown
    after the catch.
3 Coleman popped to short.

7th Inning
Philadelphia
  For New York—B. Johnson at third, Hopp
    at first.
1 Hamner took a called third strike.
2 Seminick flied to left.
3 Goliat fouled to Hopp.
New York
1 Ford struck out.
  Woodling singled to center.
2   Woodling caught stealing, Seminick
      to Goliat.
3 Rizzuto flied to center.

8th Inning
Philadelphia
1 Caballero, pinch-hitting for Konstanty,
    struck out.
2 Waitkus grounded out, Hopp to Ford.
3 Ashburn flied to center.
New York
  For Philadelphia—Roberts pitching.
1 Berra flied to right.
  DiMaggio singled off Goliat's glove.
2 Hopp forced DiMaggio at second, Hamner
    to Goliat.
3 Johnson forced Hopp at second, Hamner
    to Goliat.

9th Inning
Philadelphia
  Jones singled to left-center.
  Ennis hit by a pitched ball.
1 Sisler forced Ennis at second, Coleman
    to Rizzuto. Jones moved to third.
  K. Johnson ran for Sisler.
2 Hamner struck out.
  Seminick was safe at first when Woodling
    dropped his deep fly to score Jones and
    K. Johnson.
  Mayo ran for Seminick.
  Goliat singled to left, Mayo to second.
  For New York—Reynolds pitching.
3 Lopata, pinch-hitting for Roberts, fanned.

1950 WORLD SERIES COMPOSITE BOX

	Wins	Composite Line Score
New York Yankees (A.L.)	4	2 1 1 1 0 3 0 1 1 1 – 11
Philadelphia Phillies (N.L.)	0	0 0 0 0 1 1 1 0 2 0 – 5

Manager	W	L	Pct.	G. Ahead
	Regular Season			
Casey Stengel	98	56	.636	3
Eddie Sawyer	91	63	.591	2

BATTING AND FIELDING

	World Series Statistics																		Regular Season Statistics													
	Pos	G	AB	R	H	2B	3B	HR	RBI	BB	SO	SB	BA	SA	PO	A	E		Main Pos	G	AB	R	H	2B	3B	HR	RBI	BB	SO	SB	BA	SA
NEW YORK YANKEES																																
Johnny Mize	1b	4	15	0	2	0	0	0	0	0	1	0	.133	.133	27	3	0		1b	90	274	43	76	12	0	25	72	29	24	0	.277	.595
Jerry Coleman	2b	4	14	2	4	1	0	0	3	2	0	0	.286	.357	11	12	0		2b	153	522	69	150	19	6	6	69	67	38	3	.287	.381
Phil Rizzuto	ss	4	14	1	2	0	0	0	0	3	0	1	.143	.143	5	8	0		ss	155	617	125	200	36	7	7	66	91	38	12	.324	.439
Bobby Brown	3b-ph	4	12	2	4	1	1	0	1	0	0	0	.333	.583	0	1	1		3b	95	277	33	74	4	2	4	37	39	18	3	.267	.339
Hank Bauer	rf-lf	4	15	0	2	0	0	0	1	0	0	0	.133	.133	8	0	0		of	113	415	72	133	16	2	13	70	33	41	2	.320	.463
Joe DiMaggio	cf	4	13	2	4	1	0	1	2	3	1	0	.308	.615	8	0	0		of	139	525	114	158	33	10	32	122	80	33	0	.301	.585
Gene Woodling	lf-ph	4	14	2	6	0	0	0	1	2	0	0	.429	.429	7	0	1		of	122	449	81	127	20	10	6	60	69	31	5	.283	.412
Yogi Berra	c	4	15	2	3	0	0	1	2	2	1	0	.200	.400	30	1	0		c	151	597	116	192	30	6	28	124	55	12	4	.322	.533
Billy Johnson	3b	4	6	0	0	0	0	0	0	0	3	0	.000	.000	1	5	0		3b	108	327	44	85	16	2	6	40	42	30	1	.260	.376
Cliff Mapes	rf	1	4	0	0	0	0	0	0	0	1	0	.000	.000	3	0	0		of	108	356	60	88	14	6	12	61	47	61	1	.247	.421
Johnny Hopp	1b-pr	3	2	0	0	0	0	0	0	0	0	0	.000	.000	7	1	0	a	1b	19	27	9	9	2	1	1	8	9	1	0	.333	.593
Joe Collins	1b	1	0	0	0	0	0	0	0	0	0	0	—	—	1	1	0		1b	108	205	47	48	8	3	8	28	31	34	5	.234	.420
Jackie Jensen	pr	1	0	0	0	0	0	0	0	0	0	0	—	—					of	45	70	13	12	2	2	1	5	7	8	4	.171	.300
Billy Martin		Did not play																	2b	34	36	10	9	1	0	1	8	3	3	0	.250	.361
Charlie Silvera		Did not play																	c	18	25	2	4	0	0	0	1	1	2	0	.160	.160
Ralph Houk		Did not play																	c	10	9	0	1	1	0	0	1	0	2	0	.111	.222
Vic Raschi	p	1	3	0	1	0	0	0	0	0	0	0	.333	.333	0	3	0		p	33	86	6	17	2	0	1	8	7	14	0	.198	.256
Allie Reynolds	p	2	3	0	1	0	0	0	0	1	2	0	.333	.333	1	2	0		p	36	81	5	15	3	1	0	9	7	16	0	.185	.247
Whitey Ford	p	1	3	0	0	0	0	0	0	0	2	0	.000	.000	1	0	0		p	20	36	2	7	0	0	0	3	4	4	0	.194	.194
Ed Lopat	p	1	2	0	1	0	0	0	0	0	1	0	.500	.500	1	4	0		p	36	82	14	19	2	3	0	7	17	9	0	.232	.329
Tom Ferrick	p	1	0	0	0	0	0	0	0	0	0	0	—	—	0	0	0	b	p	30	14	2	2	1	0	0	0	2	2	0	.143	.214
Tommy Byrne		Did not play																	p	34	81	14	22	3	1	2	16	4	15	1	.272	.407
Fred Sanford		Did not play																	p	26	35	4	8	2	0	0	3	1	6	0	.229	.286
Joe Page		Did not play																	p	37	8	1	2	1	0	0	2	2	3	0	.250	.375
Joe Ostrowski		Did not play																c	p	21	9	2	1	0	0	0	1	2	1	0	.111	.111
team total		4	135	11	30	3	1	2	10	13	12	1	.222	.304	111	41	2			155	5361	914	1511	234	70	159	863	687	463	41	.282	.441

Double Plays—4
Left on Bases—33

a—from Pittsburgh
b—from St. Louis (A)
c—from St. Louis (A)
Tommy Henrich (of), Jim Delsing (ph), Johnny Lindell (of), Snuffy Stirnweiss (2b), Dick Wakefield (ph), Hank Workman (1b), Gus Niarhos (ph), Bob Porterfield (p), Don Johnson (p), Duane Pillette (p), Ernie Nevel (p), Lew Burdette (p), and Dave Madison (p), also played for the Yankees during the season.

	World Series Statistics																		Regular Season Statistics													
	Pos	G	AB	R	H	2B	3B	HR	RBI	BB	SO	SB	BA	SA	PO	A	E		Main Pos	G	AB	R	H	2B	3B	HR	RBI	BB	SO	SB	BA	SA
PHILADELPHIA PHILLIES																																
Dick Waitkus	1b	4	15	0	4	1	0	0	0	2	0	0	.267	.333	34	3	0		1b	154	641	102	182	32	5	7	44	55	29	3	.284	.359
Mike Goliat	2b	4	14	1	3	0	0	0	1	1	2	0	.214	.214	13	9	1		2b	145	483	49	113	13	6	13	64	53	75	3	.234	.366
Granny Hamner	ss	4	14	1	6	2	1	0	0	1	2	1	.429	.714	6	7	1		ss	157	637	78	172	27	5	11	82	39	35	2	.270	.380
Willie Jones	3b	4	14	1	4	1	0	0	0	0	3	0	.286	.357	8	9	1		2b	157	610	100	163	28	6	25	88	61	40	5	.267	.456
Del Ehnis	rf	4	14	1	2	1	0	0	0	0	1	0	.143	.214	9	0	0		of	153	595	92	185	34	8	31	126	56	59	2	.311	.551
Richie Ashburn	cf	4	17	0	3	1	0	0	1	0	4	0	.176	.235	9	0	0		of	151	594	84	180	25	14	2	41	63	32	14	.303	.402
Dick Sisler	lf	4	17	0	1	0	0	0	1	0	5	0	.059	.059	10	1	0		of	141	523	79	115	29	4	13	83	64	50	1	.296	.442
Andy Seminick	c	4	11	0	2	0	0	0	1	3	0	0	.182	.182	14	2	1		c	130	393	55	113	15	3	24	68	68	50	0	.288	.524
Stan Lopata	c-ph	2	1	0	0	0	0	0	0	0	1	0	.000	.000	1	0	0		c	58	129	10	27	2	2	1	11	25	25	1	.209	.279
Ken Silvestri	c	1	0	0	0	0	0	0	0	0	0	0	—	—	1	0	0		c	11	20	2	5	0	1	0	4	4	3	0	.250	.350
Jimmy Bloodworth	2b	1	0	0	0	0	0	0	0	0	0	0	—	—	0	0	0	d	2b	54	96	6	22	2	0	0	13	6	12	0	.229	.250
Dick Whitman	ph	3	2	0	0	0	0	0	0	1	0	0	.000	.000					of	75	132	21	33	7	0	0	12	10	10	1	.250	.303
Putsy Caballero	pr-ph	3	1	0	0	0	0	0	0	0	1	0	.000	.000					ph-ph	46	24	12	4	0	0	0	0	2	2	1	.167	.167
Jackie Mayo	ph-lf-pr	3	0	0	0	0	0	0	0	1	0	0	—	—	1	0	0		of	18	36	1	8	3	0	0	3	2	5	0	.222	.306
Stan Hollmig		Did not play																	of	12	1	3	2	0	0	1	0	3	0	0	.250	.417
Jim Konstanty	p	3	4	0	1	0	0	0	0	0	1	0	.250	.250	1	1	0		p	74	37	0	4	0	0	0	3	0	13	0	.108	.108
Robin Roberts	p	2	2	0	0	0	0	0	0	0	1	0	.000	.000	0	0	0		p	40	102	1	12	0	0	0	7	8	39	0	.118	.118
Ken Heintzelman	p	1	2	0	0	0	0	0	0	0	0	0	.000	.000	0	2	0		p	23	38	0	2	0	0	0	3	1	13	0	.053	.053
Russ Meyer	p	2	0	0	0	0	0	0	0	0	0	0	—	—	0	1	0		p	32	50	2	7	1	0	0	0	3	20	0	.140	.160
Bob Miller	p	1	0	0	0	0	0	0	0	0	0	0	—	—	0	0	0		p	35	61	4	11	1	0	0	6	1	11	0	.180	.197
Ken Johnson	pr	1	0	1	0	0	0	0	0	0	0	0	—	—				e	p	29	19	4	3	0	0	0	0	1	3	0	.158	.158
Bubba Church		Did not play																	p	39	44	4	8	2	0	0	1	0	9	0	.182	.227
Blix Donnelly		Did not play																	p	14	5	0	1	0	0	0	0	0	1	0	.200	.200
Milo Candini		Did not play																	p	18	6	1	1	0	0	0	0	0	1	0	.167	.167
Jocko Thompson		Did not play																	p	2	0	0	0	0	0	0	0	0	0	0	.000	.000
team total		4	128	5	26	6	1	0	3	7	24	1	.203	.266	107	35	4			157	5426	722	1440	225	55	125	673	535	569	33	.265	.396

Double Plays—1
Left on Bases—26

d—from Cincinnati
e—from St. Louis (N)
Bill Nicholson (of), Johnny Blatnik (of), Curt Simmons (p-military), Hank Borowy (p), John Brittin (p), Paul Stuffel (p), Steve Ridzik (p) also played for the Phillies during the season.

PITCHING

	World Series Statistics														Regular Season Statistics													
	G	GS	CG	IP	H	R	ER	BB	SO	W	L	SV	ERA		G	GS	CG	IP	H	ER	BB	SO	W	L	Pct	SV	ShO	ERA
NEW YORK YANKEES																												
Allie Reynolds	2	1	1	10 1/3	7	1	1	4	7	1	0	1	0.87		35	29	14	241	215	100	138	160	16	12	.571	2	2	3.73
Vic Raschi	1	1	1	9	2	0	0	1	5	1	0	0	0.00		33	32	17	257	232	114	116	155	21	8	.724	1	2	3.99
Whitey Ford	1	1	0	8 2/3	7	2	0	1	7	1	0	0	0.00		20	12	7	112	87	35	52	59	9	1	.900	1	2	2.81
Ed Lopat	1	1	0	8	9	2	2	0	5	0	0	0	2.25		35	32	15	236	244	91	65	72	18	8	.698	1	3	3.47
Tom Ferrick	1	0	0	1	1	0	0	1	0	1	0	0	0.00	b	30	0	0	57	49	23	22	20	8	4	.667	9	0	3.63
Tommy Byrne	Did not play														31	31	10	203	188	107	160	118	15	9	.625	0	2	4.74
Fred Sanford	Did not play														26	12	2	113	103	57	79	54	5	4	.556	0	0	4.54
Joe Page	Did not play														37	0	0	55	66	31	31	33	3	7	.300	13	0	5.07
Joe Ostrowski	Did not play													c	21	4	1	44	50	25	15	15	1	1	.500	3	0	5.11
team total	4	4	2	37	26	5	3	7	24	4	0	1	0.73		155	155	66	1373	1322	633	708	712	98	56	.636	31	12	4.15
PHILADELPHIA PHILLIES																												
Jim Konstanty	3	1	0	15	9	4	4	4	3	0	1	0	2.40		74	0	0	152	108	45	50	56	16	7	.696	22	0	2.66
Robin Roberts	2	1	1	11	11	2	2	3	5	0	1	0	1.64		40	39	21	304	282	102	77	146	20	11	.645	1	5	3.02
Ken Heintzelman	1	1	0	7 2/3	4	2	1	6	3	0	0	0	1.17		23	17	4	125	122	57	54	39	3	9	.250	0	1	4.10
Russ Meyer	2	0	0	1 2/3	4	1	1	0	1	0	1	0	5.40		32	25	3	160	193	94	67	74	9	11	.450	1	0	5.29
Bob Miller	1	1	0	1/3	2	2	1	0	0	0	1	0	27.00		35	22	7	174	190	69	57	44	11	6	.647	1	2	3.57
Ken Johnson	Did not pitch													e	14	8	3	61	61	27	43	32	4	1	.800	0	1	3.98
Bubba Church	Did not play														31	18	8	142	113	43	56	50	8	6	.571	1	2	2.73
Blix Donnelly	Did not play														14	1	0	21	30	10	10	10	2	4	.333	0	0	4.29
Milo Candini	Did not play														18	0	0	30	32	9	15	10	1	0	1.000	0	0	2.70
Jocko Thompson	Did not play														2	0	0	4	1	0	4	2	0	0	—	0	0	0.00
team total	4	4	1	35 2/3	30	11	9	13	12	0	4	0	2.27		157	157	57	1406	1324	546	530	620	91	63	.591	27	13	3.50

Total Attendance—196,009 Average Attendance—49,002 Winning Player's Share—$5,738 Losing Player's Share—$4,081

1951 Play-off
One for the Books

The New York Giants had engineered the greatest comeback in baseball history, driving from 13½ games behind the Brooklyn Dodgers on August 11 to cross the wire in a dead heat with the Brooklyn outfit. The Giants won 52 of their last 63 contests, including their last seven in a row, while the Dodgers let their lead melt by dropping six of their last 10 decisions. Without a day off, the play-off series began on Monday, October 1, in Ebbets Field, where 30,707 cheering fans urged the Dodgers to put an end to this growing miracle. Brooklyn manager Chuck Dressen picked hard-throwing Ralph Branca to pitch, while Giant skipper Leo Durocher settled on Jim Hearn. Both right-handers pitched well, with moments of weakness deciding the outcome. Hearn served up a fat pitch which Andy Pafko belted for a home run in the second inning, putting the Brooks ahead 1–0. Branca breezed along until he lost his stuff in the fourth inning. Don Mueller flew out to deep center to begin the frame, then Monte Irvin took first base when hit by a pitch. Whitey Lockman hit the ball deep to left-center, but Duke Snider hauled it in for the second out. Bobby Thomson came to bat, and when Branca threw him a belt-high fast ball, he drove it into the stands in left field for a 2–1 Giant lead. With the aid of four double plays, Hearn stayed out of trouble the rest of the way, and an Irvin home run in the eighth inning made the final count 3–1.

The clubs moved over to Manhattan for the second game, with the Giants one game away from wrapping up their miracle and a blanketing humiliation for the Dodgers. Dressen chose as his pitcher Clem Labine, a rookie with a modest 4–1 record, and the youngster responded with a six-hit shutout to lead the Bums back from the brink of extinction. On an afternoon punctuated by occasional showers, the Dodgers unloaded their big bats, belting four homers against three pitchers for a 10–0 slaughter.

The 34,320 fans who came to the Polo Grounds on an overcast October 3 saw the best pitchers on each team, Don Newcombe of Brooklyn and Sal Maglie of New York, take the mound for game three. Maglie misplaced his control in the top of the first inning, and walks to Pee Wee Reese and Snider coupled with a single by Jackie Robinson led to a run for Brooklyn. After that point, both Newcombe and Maglie handcuffed the opposing batters until the bottom of the seventh inning, when the Giants pieced together a run to tie the score. In the top of the eighth, however, the Giants' miracle apparently died with the fatigue in Maglie's right arm. After Carl Furillo made the first out, Reese and Snider singled. A wild pitch let Reese score and Snider reach third base, so Maglie then intentionally passed Robinson to set up a double play. But singles by Pafko and Billy Cox drove two runs in and put the Giants at a 4–1 disadvantage. Newcombe breezed through the bottom of the eighth, and Larry Jansen came into the game to pitch the ninth for New York and retired three straight men. That left the Giants with only three outs to come back from a 4–1 deficit against an overpowering Newcombe. But after 272 innings of work this season, Newk's arm didn't have three more outs left in it. Al Dark led off with a scratch single between first and second base. With first baseman Gil Hodges holding Dark on base, Mueller drove a single through the gap on the right side of the infield, sending Dark to third. Newcombe got Irvin to foul out to Hodges, but then Lockman went to the opposite field and sliced a double to left, scoring Dark and sending Mueller to third. Mueller hurt his ankle sliding and left the game in favor of pinch runner Clint Hartung. Dressen took this interlude to change pitchers, lifting Newcombe and calling in Branca to get the final two outs. The proud wearer of uniform number 13, Branca had lost a play-off game in 1946 and the first game of this series. The first batter to face him was Thomson, the power hitter who had beaten him two days ago with a home run. The first pitch was a fast ball down the middle, taken for a called strike. The second pitch was a fast ball belt-high, and Thomson jumped on it as he did two days ago. His high line drive started sinking in deep left field, but it dropped into the stands for a three-run homer, a 5–4 victory, and a practically unbelievable pennant for the Giants. The Dodgers had only a long walk to the clubhouse in center field to end the season, while the Giants had a World Series to begin against the Yankees.

Game 1 Playoffs October 1 at Brooklyn

New York	Pos	AB	R	H	RBI	PO	A	E
Stanky	2b	5	0	2	0	6	3	0
Dark	ss	4	0	1	0	0	4	1
Mueller	rf	5	0	0	0	1	0	0
Irvin	lf	4	2	1	1	2	0	0
Lockman	1b	4	0	1	0	10	1	0
Thomson	3b	2	1	1	2	2	3	0
Mays	cf	3	0	0	0	2	0	0
Westrum	c	2	0	0	0	4	3	0
Hearn	p	3	0	0	0	0	1	0
Totals		32	3	6	3	27	15	1

Pitching	IP	H	R	ER	BB	SO
New York						
Hearn (W)	9	5	1	1	2	5
Brooklyn						
Branca (L)	8	5	3	3	5	5
Podbielan	1	1	0	0	0	0

N.Y.   0 0 0   2 0 0   0 1 0
Bkn.   0 1 0   0 0 0   0 0 0

Brooklyn	Pos	AB	R	H	RBI	PO	A	E
Furillo	rf	4	0	0	0	2	0	0
Reese	ss	3	0	1	0	2	0	0
Snider	cf	4	0	1	0	6	0	1
Robinson	2b	3	0	1	0	3	0	0
Campanella	c	3	0	0	0	7	0	0
Pafko	lf	3	1	1	1	0	0	0
Hodges	1b	2	0	0	0	2	1	0
Cox	3b	3	0	1	0	3	0	0
Branca	p	2	0	0	0	0	1	0
a Russell		1	0	0	0	0	0	0
Podbielan	p	0	0	0	0	0	0	0
Totals		28	1	5	1	27	2	1

a Hit into double play for Branca in 8th.

Double—Dark. Home Runs—Irvin, Pafko, Thomson. Sacrifice Hits—Hearn, Thomson. Double Plays—Dark to Stanky to Lockman 2, Westrum to Stanky, Lockman to Dark to Stanky. Hit by Pitcher—Irvin (by Branca). Left on Bases—New York 10, Brooklyn 2. Umpires—Stewart, Goetz, Jorda, Conlan. Attendance—30,751. Time of Game—2:39.

Game 2 Playoffs October 2 at New York

Brooklyn	Pos	AB	R	H	RBI	PO	A	E
Furillo	rf	5	0	0	0	0	0	0
Reese	ss	5	1	2	0	1	7	1
Snider	cf	4	1	2	1	2	0	0
Robinson	2b	5	1	3	3	6	0	0
Pafko	lf	5	1	1	1	4	0	0
Hodges	1b	4	2	2	1	10	0	1
Cox	3b	4	0	0	4	4	0	
Walker	c	5	1	3	2	4	0	0
Labine	p	4	1	0	0	1	6	0
Totals		40	10	13	8	27	12	2

Pitching	IP	H	R	ER	BB	SO
Brooklyn						
Labine (W)	9	6	0	0	3	3
New York						
Jones (L)	2⅓	4	2	2	1	2
Spencer	3⅔	6	4	2	1	0
Corwin	3	3	4	2	2	2

Bkn.   2 0 0   0 1 3   2 0 2
N.Y.   0 0 0   0 0 0   0 0 0

New York	Pos	AB	R	H	RBI	PO	A	E
Stanky	2b	5	0	1	0	2	4	0
Dark	ss	5	0	0	0	1	1	0
Mueller	rf	4	0	1	0	3	0	0
Irvin	lf	4	0	1	0	3	0	0
Lockman	1b	3	0	0	0	11	2	0
Thomson	3b	4	0	1	0	1	4	1
Mays	cf	4	0	1	0	1	0	1
Westrum	c	3	0	0	0	5	2	0
b Williams		0	0	0	0	0	0	0
Jones	p	1	0	0	0	0	1	0
Spencer	p	1	0	1	0	0	1	2
a Rigney		1	0	0	0	0	0	0
Corwin	p	0	0	0	0	0	0	0
c Thompson		1	0	0	0	0	0	0
Totals		35	0	6	0	27	15	5

a Walked for Spencer in 6th.
b Ran for Westrum in 9th.
c Fouled out for Corwin in 9th.

Doubles—Snider, Thomson. Home Runs—Hodges, Pafko, Robinson, Walker. Sacrifice Hit—Cox. Double Play—Thomson to Stanky to Lockman. Left on Bases—Brooklyn 8, New York 11. Umpires—Goetz, Jorda, Conlan, Stewart. Attendance—38,609. Time of Game—2:44.

Game 3 Playoffs October 3 at New York

Brooklyn	Pos	AB	R	H	RBI	PO	A	E
Furillo	rf	5	0	0	0	0	0	0
Reese	ss	4	2	1	0	2	5	0
Snider	cf	3	1	2	0	4	0	0
Robinson	2b	2	1	1	1	3	2	0
Pafko	lf	4	0	1	1	4	1	0
Hodges	1b	4	0	0	0	11	1	0
Cox	3b	4	0	2	1	1	3	0
Walker	c	4	0	1	0	2	0	0
Newcombe	p	4	0	0	0	1	1	0
Branca	p	0	0	0	0	0	0	0
Totals		34	4	8	3	*25	13	0

Pitching	IP	H	R	ER	BB	SO
Brooklyn						
Newcombe	8⅓	7	4	4	2	2
Branca (L)	**0	1	1	1	0	0
New York						
Maglie	8	8	4	4	4	6
Jansen (W)	1	0	0	0	0	0

**Pitched to one batter in 9th.

Bkn.   1 0 0   0 0 0   0 3 0
N.Y.   0 0 0   0 0 0   1 0 4

New York	Pos	AB	R	H	RBI	PO	A	E
Stanky	2b	4	0	0	0	0	4	0
Dark	ss	4	1	1	0	2	2	0
Mueller	rf	4	0	1	0	0	0	0
c Hartung		0	1	0	0	0	0	0
Irvin	lf	4	1	1	0	0	0	0
Lockman	1b	3	1	2	1	11	1	0
Thomson	3b	4	1	3	4	4	1	0
Mays	cf	3	0	0	0	1	0	0
Westrum	c	0	0	0	0	7	1	0
a Rigney		1	0	0	0	0	0	0
Noble	c	0	0	0	0	0	0	0
Maglie	p	2	0	0	0	1	2	0
b Thompson		1	0	0	0	0	0	0
Jansen	p	0	0	0	0	0	0	0
Totals		30	5	8	5	27	11	0

* One out when winning run scored.
a Struck out for Westrum in 8th.
b Grounded out for Maglie in 8th.
c Ran for Mueller in 9th.

Doubles—Irvin, Lockman, Thomson. Home Run—Thomson. Sacrifice Hit—Lockman. Double Plays—Cox to Robinson to Hodges, Reese to Robinson to Hodges. Wild Pitch—Maglie. Left on Bases—Brooklyn 7, New York 3. Umpires—Jorda, Conlan, Stewart, Goetz. Attendance—34,320. Time of Game—2:28.

1951
Washing Out the Miracle

Every New York Giant fan on the planet bathed in such ecstasy at his team's National League pennant that the World Series seemed very much an anticlimax. What caused such convulsions of joy was the drive of Leo Durocher's club from 13½ games out on August 11 to catch the hated Brooklyn Dodgers at the wire in a dead heat for the flag. With Monte Irvin, Bobby Thomson, Alvin Dark, and rookie Willie Mays swinging the big bats and with Sal Maglie, Larry Jansen, and Jim Hearn pitching superbly, the Jints captured 39 of their final 47 games to melt away the big Brooklyn lead. The two rivals split the first two matches of their three-game play-off, then set a new standard in baseball drama as the Dodgers went into the bottom of the ninth leading 4–1 and the Giants came back to win the game on a three-run homer by Bobby Thomson off reliever Ralph Branca, who wore number 13. Such a glorious moment was to be savored, not to be shadowed by plans and concern for the upcoming Subway Series with the Yankees.

Casey Stengel's men won the American League title in less spectacular fashion, taking the pennant almost from habit of success. Stengel lost young Whitey Ford to the military and had to deal with an unmistakable slowing down of the great Joe DiMaggio. Yogi Berra and Phil Rizzuto starred in everyday roles, but Casey juggled at all other positions with unarguable results. Two rookies helped the cause, versatile infielder Gil McDougald and a talented but green outfielder by the name of Mickey Mantle. The three pillars of the pitching staff were veterans Eddie Lopat, Vic Raschi, and Allie Reynolds. The Yankees never could be underrated in a Series, but the aging of DiMaggio no doubt made them beatable, and the tidal wave of Giant momentum could conceivably sweep them away.

That momentum inspired the Giants in general and Dave Koslo in particular in game one at Yankee Stadium. A workman lefty with a lackluster 10–9 record, Koslo handcuffed the Yanks and limited them to seven hits and one run for the game. The Giants, meanwhile, scored twice off Reynolds in the top of the first, with the second run coming on Irvin's steal of home. Although Irvin went 4-for-5, the big hit in the 5–1 win was Dark's three-run homer in the sixth inning. After Koslo's complete game, Durocher could use his overworked top three pitchers after a day off. Jansen pitched well in game two, but dropped a 3–1 decision to Eddie Lopat's five-hitter. In the heroics column for the game were Irvin's three hits in the losing cause, while a tragic aspect of the contest was Mickey Mantle ripping up his right knee in the outfield, the first in a long series of leg injuries to haunt his career.

Across the river in the Polo Grounds, the Yankee cause was injured by a 6–2 defeat in the third game. The Giants held a 1–0 lead coming into the bottom of the fifth, when Stanky walked with one out. With the hit-and-run play on, Yankee catcher Berra called for a pitchout and gunned the ball to Rizzuto in plenty of time to nail Stanky. The Brash Brat slid hard into second and kicked the ball out of Rizzuto's glove, and that break ignited a five-run rally capped by Whitey Lockman's three-run homer. The Yankees looked to be in real trouble now, but after a day off because of rain, they regrouped and took three straight from the suddenly unmagic Giants. Allie Reynolds pitched all the way in a 6–2 fourth-game victory in which Joe DiMaggio hit a two-run homer off Maglie, the last circuit clout of his career.

The pressure-hardened Yanks hit Jansen hard in game five, including a grand-slam home run by McDougald, and Lopat used his slow stuff to pitch the 13–1 complete game. When the clubs moved back to the Polo Grounds for game six, Koslo again started and held a 1–1 tie until Hank Bauer tripled in three runs in the bottom of the sixth. Trailing 4–1, the Giants took their final shot at miracle-making in the ninth. The Giants scored two runs and had the tying run on second base with two out when pinch hitter Sal Yvars lined a low liner to right. Bauer charged in and gloved the ball only inches from the ground to end the Series.

Joe DiMaggio ended his career following the Series, saying "I'm not Joe DiMaggio anymore." Rookie outfielders Mays and Mantle performed no heroics in this Series, with Mays playing all six games and hitting a weak .182 with no home runs. Mantle played in two games and collected one hit for a .200 average.

Game 1 October 4 at New York (A)

New York-N	Pos	AB	R	H	RBI	PO	A	E
Stanky	2b	4	1	0	0	4	2	0
Dark	ss	5	1	2	3	1	2	0
Thompson	rf	3	1	0	0	3	0	1
Irvin	lf	5	1	4	0	4	0	0
Lockman	1b	4	0	1	1	4	1	0
Thomson	3b	3	0	1	0	2	2	0
Mays	cf	5	0	0	0	2	0	0
Westrum	c	3	1	2	0	5	0	0
Koslo	p	3	0	0	0	2	0	0
Totals		35	5	10	4	27	7	1

Pitching New York-N	IP	H	R	ER	BB	SO
Koslo (W)	9	7	1	1	3	3
New York-A						
Reynolds (L)	6	8	5	5	7	1
Hogue	1	0	0	0	0	0
Morgan	2	2	0	0	1	3

		NY-N	2 0 0	0 0 3	0 0 0
		NY-A	0 1 0	0 0 0	0 0 0

New York-A	Pos	AB	R	H	RBI	PO	A	E
Mantle	rf	3	0	0	0	4	0	0
Rizzuto	ss	4	0	2	0	1	2	0
Bauer	lf	4	0	0	0	0	0	0
DiMaggio	cf	4	0	0	0	3	0	0
Berra	c	4	0	1	0	5	1	0
McDougald	3b	4	1	1	0	2	1	0
Coleman	2b	3	0	1	0	3	3	0
Collins	1b	3	0	1	0	11	0	0
b Mize		1	0	0	0	0	0	0
Reynolds	p	2	0	1	0	0	3	0
Hogue	p	0	0	0	0	0	1	0
a Brown		1	0	0	0	0	0	0
Morgan	p	0	0	0	0	0	1	0
c Woodling		1	0	0	0	0	0	0
Totals		34	1	7	0	27	13	1

a Struck out for Hogue in 8th.
b Popped out for Collins in 9th.
c Struck out for Morgan in 9th.

Doubles—Lockman, McDougald. Triple—Irvin. Home Run—Dark. Stolen Base—Irvin. Sacrifice Hits—Koslo 2. Double Play—McDougald to Coleman to Collins. Left on Bases—Giants 13, Yankees 9. Umpires—Summers (A), Ballanfant (N), Paparella (A), Barlick (N), Stevens (A), Gore (N). Attendance—65,673. Time of Game—2:58.

1st Inning
Giants
1 Stanky grounded to short.
2 Dark flied to right.
   Thompson walked.
   Irvin singled to right-center, moving Thompson to third.
   Lockman bounced a ground-rule double into the left field stands, Thompson scoring and Irvin stopping at third.
      Irvin stole home, sliding in under a high pitch.
   Thomson walked.
3 Mays flied to right.
Yankees
1 Mantle flied to right.
   Rizzuto singled to left.
2 Bauer flied to Irvin in left, who made a leaping one-handed catch at the 400-foot mark.
3 DiMaggio flied to right.

2nd Inning
Giants
   Westrum walked.
1 Koslo forced Westrum at second, on a bunt, Reynolds to Rizzuto.
2,3 Stanky hit into a double play, McDougald to Coleman to Collins.
Yankees
1 Berra grounded to first.
   McDougald bounced into the left field corner.
   Coleman singled to right, McDougald going to third, but Thompson fumbled the hit allowing McDougald to score.
2 Collins forced Coleman at second, Thomson to Stanky.
   Reynolds singled to right, Collins stopping at second.
   Mantle walked, loading the bases.
3 Rizzuto grounded out, Lockman to Koslo.

3rd Inning
Giants
1 Dark struck out.
2 Thompson grounded back to the mound.
   Irvin singled to right.
   Lockman walked.
   Thomson singled to left, loading the bases.
3 Mays lined to second.
Yankees
1 Bauer popped to third.
2 DiMaggio flied to left.
3 Berra fouled to Thomson.

4th Inning
Giants
   Westrum walked.
1 Koslo sacrificed Westrum to second, Reynolds to Collins.
2 Stanky grounded to third, Westrum holding at second.
3 Dark flied to center.
Yankees
1 McDougald fouled to Westrum.
2 Coleman grounded to short.
   Collins singled to right.
3 Reynolds grounded out, Stanky to Koslo.

5th Inning
Giants
1 Thompson flied to center.
   Irvin tripled over DiMaggio's head.
2 Lockman grounded to second, Irvin holding third.
3 Thomson grounded to short.
Yankees
   Mantle walked.
1 Rizzuto struck out.
2 Bauer lined to center.
3 DiMaggio flied to deep right.

6th Inning
Giants
1 Mays flied to right.
   Westrum singled to left.
2 Koslo again sacrificed Westrum to second, Berra to Coleman.
   Stanky walked.
   Dark hit a three-run homer into the lower left field stands.
   Thompson walked.
   Irvin singled to center, Thompson going to third (Irvin's 4th hit).
3 Lockman grounded to second.
Yankees
1 Berra popped to second.
2 McDougald flied to left.
3 Coleman grounded to third.

7th Inning
Giants
   For the Yankees—Hogue now pitching.
1 Thomson bounced back to the mound.
2 Mays flied to center.
3 Westrum fouled to Berra.
Yankees
1 Collins bunted out to second.
2 Brown, pinch-hitting for Hogue, struck out.
3 Mantle flied to Westrum.

8th Inning
Giants
   For the Yankees—Morgan pitching.
1 Koslo called out on strikes.
   Stanky safe at first on McDougald's wild throw of his grounder.
   Dark singled to right, Stanky stopping at second.
2 Thompson flied to deep right, Stanky going to third after the catch.
3 Irvin was finally retired, lining out to first.
Yankees
   Rizzuto singled to right-center.
1 Bauer forced Rizzuto at second, Dark to Stanky.
2 DiMaggio flied to left.
   Berra singled to right, Bauer stopping at second.
3 McDougald popped to second.

9th Inning
Giants
1 Lockman grounded back to the mound.
   Thomson walked.
2 Mays struck out.
   Westrum singled to left, Thomson stopping at second.
3 Koslo struck out.
Yankees
   Coleman walked.
1 Mize, pinch-hitting for Collins, popped to short.
2 Woodling, pinch-hitting for Morgan, took a called third strike.
3 Mantle flied to center.

Game 2 October 5 at New York-A

| | | NY-N | 000 000 100 |
| | | NY-A | 110 000 01x |

New York-N	Pos	AB	R	H	RBI	PO	A	E
Stanky	2b	3	0	0	0	1	4	0
Dark	ss	4	0	1	0	0	4	0
Thomson	3b	4	0	0	0	2	3	0
Irvin	lf	4	1	3	0	3	0	0
Lockman	1b	4	0	1	0	11	0	1
Mays	cf	4	0	0	0	2	0	0
Westrum	c	2	0	0	0	5	0	0
b Schenz		0	0	0	0	0	0	0
Hartung	rf	1	0	0	0	0	0	0
Thompson	rf	2	0	0	0	0	0	0
a Rigney		1	0	1	0	0	0	0
Spencer	p	0	0	0	0	0	0	0
Jansen	p	2	0	0	0	0	0	0
c Noble	c	1	0	0	0	0	0	0
Totals		32	1	5	0	24	11	1

a Flied out for Thompson in 7th.
b Ran for Westrum in 7th.
c Fouled out for Jansen in 7th.

Home Run—Collins. Stolen Base—Irvin.
Double Play—Dark to Stanky to Lockman.
Left on Bases—Giants 6, Yankees 2.
Umpires—Ballanfant, Paparella, Barlick,
Summers, Gore, Stevens.
Attendance—66,018. Time of Game—2:05.

New York-A	Pos	AB	R	H	RBI	PO	A	E
Mantle	rf	2	1	1	0	0	0	0
Bauer	rf	2	0	0	1	0	0	0
Rizzuto	ss	4	0	1	0	2	2	0
McDougald	2b-3b	3	0	1	1	2	3	0
DiMaggio	cf	3	0	0	0	4	0	0
Berra	c	3	0	0	0	4	0	0
Woodling	lf	3	0	0	0	4	0	0
Brown	3b	3	0	1	0	0	4	0
d Martin		0	1	0	0	0	0	0
Coleman	2b	0	0	0	0	0	1	0
Collins	1b	3	1	1	1	9	2	0
Lopat	p	3	0	1	1	2	2	0
Totals		29	3	6	3	27	13	0

Pitching	IP	H	R	ER	BB	SO
New York-N						
Jansen (L)	6	4	2	2	0	5
Spencer	2	2	1	1	0	0
New York-A						
Lopat (W)	9	5	1	1	2	1

d Ran for Brown in 8th.

1st Inning
Giants
1 Stanky grounded to second.
2 Dark grounded to short.
3 Thomson flied to left.
Yankees
Mantle beat out a bunt past the mound.
Rizzuto also beat out a bunt past
Jansen, but Lockman fielding the ball
threw wildly past Stanky at first and
Mantle raced to third with Rizzuto
holding first.
McDougald singled to right, scoring Mantle as
Rizzuto stopped at second.
1,2 DiMaggio grounded into a double play,
Dark to Stanky to Lockman with
Rizzuto going to third.
3 Berra struck out.

2nd Inning
Giants
Irvin singled to left-center.
Irvin stole second.
1 Lockman bounced back to the mound,
Irvin holding second.
2 Mays grounded to third, Irvin
still holding at second.
3 Westrum grounded to third.
Yankees
1 Woodling flied to left.
2 Brown grounded to second.
Collins hit a home run into the
right field stands.
3 Lopat grounded to first.

3rd Inning
Giants
1 Thompson grounded out, Collins to
Lopat.
2 Jansen flied to center.
Stanky walked.
3 Dark flied to left.
Yankees
1 Mantle struck out.
2 Rizzuto flied to left.
3 McDougald lined to third.

4th Inning
Giants
1 Thomson flied to center.
2 Irvin popped to second.
3 Lockman grounded to short.
Yankees
1 DiMaggio struck out.
2 Berra grounded to short.
3 Woodling flied to center.

5th Inning
Giants
1 Mays flied to DiMaggio in right-center.
For the Yankees—Bauer replaced Mantle in
right after he wrenched his knee on the
previous play.
2 Westrum flied to left.
3 Thompson was called out on strikes.
Yankees
1 Brown grounded to short.
2 Collins fouled to Thomson.
3 Lopat took a called third strike.

6th Inning
Giants
1 Jansen popped to second.
2 Stanky bounced back to the mound.
Dark singled to left.
3 Thomson flied to DiMaggio in deep
left-center.
Yankees
1 Bauer grounded to short.
2 Rizzuto grounded to third.
3 McDougald struck out.

7th Inning
Giants
Irvin singled to center.
Lockman singled to center, Irvin
stopping at second.
1 Mays forced Lockman at second on a
bunt, Brown to Rizzuto as Irvin
went to third.
Westrum walked loading the bases.
Rigney, up batting for Thompson.
Schenz ran for Westrum.
2 Rigney flied to right, Irvin scoring
and Mays going to third after the catch.
3 Noble, batting for Jansen, fouled
to Berra.
Yankees
For the Giants—Noble stays in as catcher,
Spencer pitching (batting 8th), and
Hartung in right (batting 7th).
1 DiMaggio grounded to third.
2 Berra grounded to second.
3 Woodling grounded to short.

8th Inning
Giants
1 Stanky popped to first.
2 Dark flied to left.
3 Thomson grounded to third.
Yankees
Brown singled over second, the first
Yankee base runner since the second.
Martin ran for Brown.
1 Collins grounded to third, Martin
moving to second.
Lopat singled to center, scoring Martin.
2 Bauer flied to deep left.
3 Rizzuto flied to center.

9th Inning
Giants
For the Yankees—McDougald moved to third,
as Coleman went to second.
Irvin singled to center.
1 Lockman forced Irvin at second,
McDougald to Rizzuto.
2 Mays forced Lockman at second,
McDougald to Coleman.
3 Hartung grounded out, Collins to Lopat.

Game 3 October 6 at New York-N

| | | NY-A | 000 000 011 |
| | | NY-N | 010 050 00x |

New York-A	Pos	AB	R	H	RBI	PO	A	E
Woodling	lf	4	1	1	1	3	0	0
Rizzuto	ss	4	1	1	1	2	4	1
McDougald	2b	3	0	2	0	2	2	0
DiMaggio	cf	4	0	0	0	4	0	0
Berra	c	3	0	1	0	5	1	1
Brown	3b	3	0	0	0	1	0	0
Collins	1b	3	0	1	0	6	0	0
Bauer	rf	4	0	0	0	2	0	0
Raschi	p	1	0	0	0	0	0	0
Hogue	p	0	0	0	0	0	0	0
a Hopp		1	0	0	0	0	0	0
Ostrowski	p	0	0	0	0	0	0	0
b Mize		1	0	0	0	0	0	0
Totals		30	2	5	2	24	8	2

a Walked for Hogue in 7th.
b Flied out for Ostrowski in 9th.

Double—Thomson. Home Runs—Lockman,
Woodling. Double Plays—Stanky to Dark
to Lockman, Hearn to Lockman to Dark
to Lockman, Rizzuto to McDougald to
Collins. Hit by Pitchers—Stanky
(by Raschi), Rizzuto (by Hearn).
Left on Bases—Yankees 10, Giants 5.
Umpires—Paparella, Barlick, Summers,
Ballanfant, Stevens, Gore.
Attendance—52,035. Time of Game—2:42.

New York-N	Pos	AB	R	H	RBI	PO	A	E
Stanky	2b	2	1	1	0	2	2	0
Dark	ss	4	1	1	0	4	4	0
Thompson	rf	3	1	1	0	1	0	0
Irvin	lf	3	1	0	0	4	0	0
Lockman	1b	4	1	1	3	10	1	1
Thomson	3b	4	0	1	0	3	4	0
Mays	cf	4	0	2	1	3	0	0
Westrum	c	4	0	0	0	2	1	1
Hearn	p	3	0	0	0	1	3	0
Jones	p	0	0	0	0	0	1	0
Totals		31	6	7	5	27	15	2

Pitching	IP	H	R	ER	BB	SO
New York-A						
Raschi (L)	4⅓	5	6	1	3	3
Hogue	2⅔	1	0	0	0	0
Ostrowski	2	1	0	0	0	1
New York-N						
Hearn (W)	7⅓	4	1	1	8	1
Jones (SV)	1⅓	1	1	1	0	0

1st Inning
Yankees
1 Woodling fouled to Thomson.
Rizzuto singled to left.
2 Rizzuto was caught trying to steal
second, Westrum to Dark.
McDougald singled off the left
field wall.
3 DiMaggio flied to left.
Giants
Stanky was hit by a pitch.
1 Dark flied to center.
2 Thompson struck out.
Irvin walked.
3 Lockman grounded to second.

2nd Inning
Yankees
Berra beat out a roller to first.
1 Brown forced Berra at second, Dark
to Stanky.
2,3 Collins grounded into a double play,
Stanky to Dark to Lockman.
Giants
Thomson doubled down the left field
line.
Mays singled to right, scoring Thomson.
1 Westrum popped to short.
2 Hearn popped to second.
3 Stanky took a called third strike.

3rd Inning
Yankees
Bauer safe at first when Lockman
dropped Dark's throw.
1,2 Raschi, on a bunt, forced Bauer at
second, Hearn to Dark but Dark's throw
to first was wild and Raschi tried
for second. He was out, Lockman to
Dark for a weird double play.
Woodling walked.
3 Rizzuto grounded to first.
Giants
1 Dark flied to right.
Thompson walked.
2 Irvin lined to center.
3 Lockman flied to left.

4th Inning
Yankees
McDougald walked.
1 DiMaggio forced McDougald at second,
Thomson to Stanky.
2 Berra fouled to Thomson.
3 Brown flied to left.
Giants
1 Thompson flied to left.
2 Mays grounded to second.
3 Westrum flied to center.

5th Inning
Yankees
1 Collins grounded to first.
2 Bauer grounded to third.
Raschi walked.
3 Woodling flied to deep center.

5th Inning (continued)
Giants
1 Hearn struck out.
Stanky walked.
Stanky went all the way to third
when Stanky kicked the ball thrown
by Berra out of Rizzuto's hands.
Dark singled to left, scoring Stanky.
Thompson singled to right, Dark
going to third.
Irvin safe when Berra dropped Brown's
throw getting Dark at the plate as
Thompson stopped at second.
Lockman lined a three-run homer into
the lower right field stands.
For the Yankees—Hogue took Raschi's
place on the mound.
2 Thomson fouled to Berra.
3 Mays flied to center.

6th Inning
Yankees
1 Rizzuto grounded to third.
McDougald walked.
2 DiMaggio struck out.
McDougald went to second on
Westrum's error, dropping a pitch.
Berra walked.
3 Brown grounded to second.
Giants
1 Westrum fouled to Collins.
2 Hearn flied to right.
Stanky singled to left.
3 Dark flied to left.

7th Inning
Yankees
1 Collins flied to deep center.
2 Bauer flied to Westrum.
Hopp, batting for Hogue, walked.
3 Woodling grounded to second.
Giants
For the Yankees—Ostrowski pitching.
1 Thompson grounded to short.
2 Irvin grounded to short.
3 Lockman struck out.

8th Inning
Yankees
Rizzuto was hit by a pitch.
McDougald singled to center, Rizzuto
stopping at second.
1 DiMaggio popped to third.
2 Berra grounded back to the mound,
advancing both runners.
Brown walked, loading the bases.
Collins walked, forcing Rizzuto over
the plate.
For the Giants—Jones came in to pitch.
3 Bauer bounced back to the mound.
Giants
1 Thompson popped to short.
Mays singled to right.
2,3 Westrum hit into a double play,
Rizzuto to McDougald to Collins.

9th Inning
Yankees
1 Mize, batting for Ostrowski, flied
to right.
Woodling homered into the lower
right field stands.
2 Rizzuto flied to deep center.
3 McDougald fouled to Lockman.

1951

Game 4 October 8 at New York-N

NY-A	010	120	200
NY-N	100	000	001

New York-A	Pos	AB	R	H	RBI	PO	A	E
Bauer	rf	4	0	2	0	0	0	0
Rizzuto	ss	5	1	1	0	5	5	0
Berra	c	5	1	1	0	8	1	0
DiMaggio	cf	5	1	2	2	2	0	0
Woodling	lf	4	2	1	0	1	0	0
McDougald	2b-3b	4	0	1	1	3	2	0
Brown	3b	4	1	2	0	0	0	0
Coleman	2b	0	0	0	0	1	1	0
Collins	1b	3	0	1	1	7	0	0
Reynolds	p	4	0	1	1	0	2	0
Totals		38	6	12	5	27	11	0

Pitching	IP	H	R	ER	BB	SO
New York-A						
Reynolds (W)	9	8	2	2	4	7
New York-N						
Maglie (L)	5	8	4	4	2	3
Jones	3	4	2	0	1	2
Kennedy	1	0	0	0	0	2

New York-N	Pos	AB	R	H	RBI	PO	A	E
Stanky	2b	4	0	1	0	3	0	1
Dark	ss	4	1	3	0	2	1	0
Thompson	rf	3	1	0	0	1	0	0
Irvin	lf	4	0	2	1	3	0	0
Lockman	1b	4	0	0	0	4	0	0
Thomson	3b	4	0	2	1	2	3	1
Mays	cf	4	0	0	0	5	1	0
Westrum	c	2	0	0	0	7	1	0
Maglie	p	1	0	0	0	1	0	0
a Lohrke		1	0	0	0	0	0	0
Jones	p	0	0	0	0	0	0	0
b Rigney		1	0	0	0	0	0	0
Kennedy	p	0	0	0	0	0	0	0
Totals		30	2	8	2	27	6	2

a Popped out for Maglie in 5th.
b Struck out for Jones in 8th.

Doubles—Brown, Dark 3, Woodling. Home Run—DiMaggio. Double Plays—Rizzuto to McDougald to Collins, Reynolds to Rizzuto to Collins 2, Rizzuto to Coleman to Collins. Left on Bases—Yankees 8, Giants 5. Umpires—Barlick, Summers, Ballanfant, Paparella, Gore, Stevens. Attendance—49,010. Time of Game—2:57.

1st Inning
Yankees
  Bauer walked.
1 Rizzuto struck out.
2 Berra lined to center.
3 DiMaggio called out on strikes.
Giants
1 Stanky lined to short.
  Dark doubled off the left field wall.
2 Thompson grounded to second, Dark going to third.
  Irvin singled to left, scoring Dark.
3 Irvin caught trying to steal second, Berra to Rizzuto.

2nd Inning
Yankees
  Woodling doubled down the left field foul line.
  McDougald safe at first on Thomson's fumble as Woodling held second.
1 Brown flied to deep center, Woodling moving to third after the catch.
  Collins singled to right, Woodling scoring with McDougald stopping at second.
2 Reynolds flied to left.
3 Bauer's grounder hit McDougald giving Bauer an automatic single with an automatic out on McDougald with Dark getting credit for the putout.
Giants
1 Lockman struck out.
  Thomson walked.
2,3 Mays hit into a double play, Rizzuto to McDougald to Collins.

3rd Inning
Yankees
1 Rizzuto grounded to third.
2 Berra lined to third.
  DiMaggio singled to left.
3 Woodling flied to left.
Giants
1 Westrum struck out.
2 Maglie called out on strikes.
3 Stanky fouled to Berra.

4th Inning
Yankees
1 McDougald flied to center.
  Brown beat out a hit to deep short.
  Collins walked.
  Reynolds singled to center, Brown scoring and Collins going to third,
2 but Reynolds was trapped after rounding first and was out Mays to Dark to Lockman.
3 Bauer grounded to third.
Giants
  Dark again doubled off the left field wall.
1 Thompson popped to second.
2 Irvin struck out.
3 Lockman flied to deep center.

5th Inning
Yankees
1 Rizzuto popped to second.
  Berra singled to right.
  DiMaggio blasted a two-run homer into the upper deck of the left field stands.
2 Woodling popped to short.
3 McDougald struck out.
Giants
  Thomson walked.
1,2 Mays again hit into a double play, Reynolds to Rizzuto to Collins.
  Westrum walked.
3 Lohrke, batting for Maglie, popped to second.

6th Inning
Yankees
  For the Giants—Jones pitching.
  Brown doubled to left-center.
1 Collins flied to left.
2 Reynolds grounded to third, Brown holding at third.
3 Bauer popped to second.
Giants
1 Stanky lined to short.
  Dark got his third consecutive double, this one down the left field line.
2 Thompson popped to short.
3 Irvin fouled to Collins.

7th Inning
Yankees
  Rizzuto singled to right.
1 Berra flied to center.
2 DiMaggio popped to second.
  Woodling walked.
  Westrum trapped Rizzuto off second throwing to Stanky but Rizzuto was racing for third and Stanky's throw hit Rizzuto in the back for an error enabling Rizzuto to score and Woodling to get to second.
  McDougald singled to left, scoring Woodling, and took second on the throw to the plate.
3 Brown flied to center.
Giants
  For the Yankees—Coleman came in to play second as McDougald moved to third.
1 Lockman grounded to short.
  Thomson singled to left.
2 Mays flied to center.
3 Westrum struck out.

8th Inning
Yankees
1 Collins popped to third.
2 Reynolds struck out.
  Bauer singled to left.
3 Rizzuto called out on strikes.
Giants
1 Rigney, pinch-hitting for Jones, struck out.
  Stanky singled to left.
2,3 Dark bounced into a double play, Reynolds to Rizzuto to Collins.

9th Inning
Yankees
  For the Giants—Kennedy pitching.
1 Berra popped to third.
2 DiMaggio called out on strikes.
3 Woodling struck out.
Giants
  Thompson walked.
  Irvin singled to center, Thompson stopping at second.
1 Lockman flied to left.
  Thomson singled to left, scoring Thompson with Irvin going to third.
2,3 For the third time in the game, Mays hit into a double play, Rizzuto to Coleman to Collins.

Game 5 October 9 at New York-N

NY-A	005	202	400
NY-N	100	000	000

New York-A	Pos	AB	R	H	RBI	PO	A	E
Woodling	lf	3	3	1	0	5	0	1
Rizzuto	ss	4	2	3	3	0	6	0
Berra	c	4	2	1	0	3	0	0
DiMaggio	cf	3	1	1	1	3	0	0
Mize	1b	3	1	1	1	6	0	0
Bauer	rf	4	1	3	3	3	0	0
McDougald	2b-3b	5	1	1	4	2	2	0
Brown	3b	3	0	2	0	1	3	0
c Coleman	2b	1	1	0	0	1	0	0
Collins	rf-1b	5	1	0	0	7	0	0
Lopat	p	5	0	0	0	0	2	0
Totals		39	13	12	11	27	14	1

Pitching	IP	H	R	ER	BB	SO
New York-A						
Lopat (W)	9	5	1	0	1	3
New York-N						
Jansen (L)	2	3	5	5	4	1
Kennedy	2	3	2	2	1	2
Spencer	1⅓	4	6	6	3	0
Corwin	1⅔	1	0	0	0	1
Konikowski	1	1	0	0	0	0

New York-N	Pos	AB	R	H	RBI	PO	A	E
Stanky	2b	4	0	0	0	1	4	0
Dark	ss	4	1	2	0	2	3	0
Thomson	3b	4	0	0	0	1	3	1
Irvin	lf	4	0	2	0	2	0	1
Lockman	1b	4	0	0	0	9	3	0
Mays	cf	2	0	0	0	4	1	1
Hartung	rf	3	0	0	0	1	1	1
Westrum	c	3	0	1	0	7	0	0
Jansen	p	1	0	0	0	1	1	0
a Lohrke		1	0	0	0	0	0	0
Kennedy	p	0	0	0	0	0	1	0
b Rigney		1	0	0	0	0	0	0
Spencer	p	0	0	0	0	0	1	0
Corwin	p	0	0	0	0	1	0	0
d Williams		1	0	0	0	0	0	0
Konikowski	p	0	0	0	0	0	0	0
Totals		31	1	5	0	27	17	3

a Struck out for Jansen in 3rd.
b Flied out for Kennedy in 5th.
c Ran for Brown in 7th.
d Grounded out for Corwin in 8th.

Doubles—DiMaggio, Mize, Westrum. Triple—Woodling. Home Runs—McDouglad, Rizzuto. Double Play—Lopat to McDougald to Mize. Wild Pitch—Corwin. Left on Bases—Yankees 7, Giants 4. Umpires—Summers, Ballanfant, Paparella, Barlick, Stevens, Gore. Attendance—47,530. Time of Game—2:31.

1st Inning
Yankees
1 Woodling struck out.
2 Rizzuto grounded to second.
  Berra walked.
3 DiMaggio forced Berra, Dark to Stanky.
Giants
1 Stanky grounded to third.
  Dark singled to left.
2 Thomson flied to center.
  Irvin singled to left, Dark going to third but when Woodling fumbled the ball, Dark scored and Irvin went to second.
3 Lockman flied to center.

2nd Inning
Yankees
1 Mize flied to center.
  McDougald got safely to second when Thomson threw wildly to first.
2 Brown flied to center.
3 Collins grounded out, Lockman to Jansen.
Giants
  Mays walked.
1,2 Hartung bounced into a double play, Lopat to McDougald to Mize.
3 Westrum grounded to third.

3rd Inning
Yankees
1 Lopat bounced back to the mound.
  Woodling walked.
  Rizzuto walked.
2 Berra forced Rizzuto at second, Lockman to Dark, Woodling moving to third.
  DiMaggio singled to left, scoring Woodling and when Irvin kicked the ball, Berra went to third and DiMaggio to second.
  Mize got an intentional walk, loading the bases.
  McDougald hit a grand slam home run into the left field stands.
  Brown singled to center.
3 Collins flied to center.
Giants
1 Lohrke, pinch-hitting for Jansen, struck out.
2 Stanky bounced back to the pitcher.
  Dark singled to center.
3 Thomson flied to left.

4th Inning
Yankees
  For the Giants—Kennedy pitching.
1 Lopat called out on strikes.
  Woodling walked.
  Rizzuto hit a two-run homer into the right field stands.
2 Berra popped to short.
  DiMaggio singled to left.
3 Mize fouled to Westrum.
Giants
1 Irvin grounded to third.
2 Lockman grounded to short.
3 Mays flied to left.

5th Inning
Yankees
1 McDougald grounded to third.
  Brown singled to left.
2 Collins struck out.
3 Lopat's grounder was deflected by Kennedy to Stanky who threw to first for the out.
Giants
1 Hartung flied to deep center.
  Westrum doubled to left-center.
2 Rigney, pinch-hitting for Kennedy, flied to left.
3 Stanky flied to left.

6th Inning
Yankees
  For the Giants—Spencer pitching.
1 Woodling grounded to second.
  Rizzuto singled to left.
  Berra singled to right, Rizzuto going to third and as Hartung was fumbling the ball, Rizzuto scored and Berra got to second.
2 DiMaggio flied to right.
  Mize doubled to center, scoring Berra.
3 McDougald grounded to short.
Giants
  For the Yankees—Bauer came in to play right field as Collins moved to first replacing Mize.
1 Dark grounded to short.
2 Thomson lined to second.
  Irvin singled to center (his 11th hit of the Series).
3 Lockman grounded to short.

7th Inning
Yankees
  Brown walked.
  Collins beat out a bunt, Brown going to second.
  Coleman ran for Brown.
1 Lopat bounced back to the pitcher, advancing both runners.
  Woodling walked, his third of the game, loading the bases.
  Rizzuto walked, forcing Coleman in with a run.
  For the Giants—Corwin pitching.
  On a wild pitch, Collins scored and the other runners each advanced.
2 Berra flied to left.
  DiMaggio doubled to left, scoring Woodling and Rizzuto.
3 Bauer hit into a fielder's choice, DiMaggio being out at third, Dark to Thomson.
Giants
  For the Yankees—Coleman stays in playing second as McDougald moves to third.
1 Mays struck out.
2 Hartung grounded to second.
3 Westrum struck out.

8th Inning
Yankees
1 McDougald grounded to short.
2 Coleman struck out.
3 Collins grounded out, Lockman to Corwin.
Giants
1 Williams, batting for Corwin, grounded to short.
2 Stanky grounded to second.
3 Dark lined to third.

9th Inning
Yankees
  For the Giants—Konikowski pitching.
1 Lopat fouled to Westrum.
  Woodling tripled to right-center but
2 was out trying for a home run, Hartung to Stanky to Westrum.
3 Rizzuto grounded to third.
Giants
1 Thomson grounded to third.
2 Irvin flied to deep left.
3 Lockman grounded to short.

Game 6 October 10 at New York-A

NY-N   000 010 002
NY-A   100 003 00x

New York-N	Pos	AB	R	H	RBI	PO	A	E
Stanky	2b	5	1	1	1	3	4	0
Dark	ss	3	1	1	0	1	2	0
Lockman	1b	5	0	3	0	10	0	0
Irvin	lf	4	0	0	1	3	0	0
Thomson	3b	4	0	1	0	2	0	0
Thompson	rf	3	0	1	0	0	0	1
d Yvars		1	0	0	0	0	0	0
Westrum	c	3	0	1	0	3	0	0
b Williams		0	0	0	0	0	0	0
Jansen	p	0	0	0	0	0	1	0
Mays	cf	3	1	2	0	2	0	0
Koslo	p	2	0	0	0	0	1	0
a Rigney		1	0	1	0	0	0	0
Hearn	p	0	0	0	0	0	0	0
c Noble	c	1	0	0	0	0	1	0
Totals		35	3	11	3	24	9	2

New York-A	Pos	AB	R	H	RBI	PO	A	E
Rizzuto	ss	4	0	1	0	4	4	0
Coleman	2b	4	1	1	0	2	1	0
Berra	c	4	1	2	0	4	0	0
DiMaggio	cf	2	1	1	0	1	0	0
McDougald	3b	4	0	0	1	1	3	0
Mize	1b	2	1	1	0	6	0	0
Collins	1b	1	0	0	0	0	0	0
Bauer	rf	3	0	1	3	4	0	0
Woodling	lf	3	0	0	0	5	0	0
Raschi	p	1	0	0	0	0	0	0
Sain	p	1	0	0	0	0	0	0
Kuzava	p	0	0	0	0	0	0	0
Totals		29	4	7	4	27	8	0

Pitching	IP	H	R	ER	BB	SO
New York-N						
Koslo (L)	6	5	4	4	4	3
Hearn	1	1	0	0	0	0
Jansen	1	1	0	0	0	0
New York-A						
Raschi (W)	*6	7	1	0	5	0
Sain	**2	4	2	2	2	0
Kuzava (SV)	1	0	0	0	0	0

*Pitched to two batters in 7th.
**Pitched to three batters in 9th.

a Singled for Koslo in 7th.
b Ran for Westrum in 8th.
c Struck out for Hearn in 8th.
d Lined out for Thompson in 9th.

Doubles—Berra, DiMaggio, Lockman.
Triple—Bauer. Double Plays—Rizzuto to
Mize 2, Rizzuto to Coleman to Mize,
Dark to Stanky to Lockman. Passed
Ball—Berra. Wild Pitch—Koslo. Left
on Bases—Giants 12, Yankees 5.
Umpires—Ballanfant, Paparella, Barlick,
Summers, Gore, Stevens.
Attendance—61,711. Time of Game—2:59.

1st Inning
Giants
1 Stanky grounded to third.
2 Dark took a called third strike.
Lockman bounced a ground-rule double
into the right field stands.
3 Irvin grounded to short.
Yankees
1 Rizzuto flied to left.
Coleman singled to center.
Berra doubled off the right field
wall, Coleman stopping at third.
DiMaggio intentionally walked,
loading the bases.
2 McDougald flied to center, Coleman
scoring after the catch.
3 Mize lined to second.

2nd Inning
Giants
Thomson beat out a hit to deep short.
1 Thompson popped to short.
Westrum walked.
2 Mays lined to right.
3 Koslo popped to short.
Yankees
1 Bauer popped to short.
2 Woodling grounded to second.
3 Raschi struck out.

3rd Inning
Giants
1 Stanky flied to deep left.
Dark walked.
2,3 Lockman hit into a double play,
Rizzuto to Mize.
Yankees
1 Rizzuto fouled to Lockman.
2 Coleman flied to left.
3 Berra fouled to Lockman.

4th Inning
Giants
Irvin walked.
1 Thomson forced Irvin at second,
McDougald to Coleman.
Thompson singled to right, Thomson
going to third.
2,3 Westrum grounded into a double
play, Rizzuto to Coleman to Mize.
Yankees
1 DiMaggio flied to center.
2 McDougald popped to first.
Mize singled to right.
3 Bauer struck out.

5th Inning
Giants
Mays singled to center.
Mays took second on Berra's
passed ball.
1 Koslo flied to right, Mays going to
third after the catch.
2 Stanky flied to left, Mays scoring
after the catch.
Dark walked.
Lockman beat out a hit down the third
base line, Dark stopping at second.
3 Irvin grounded to third.
Yankees
1 Woodling bunted out to the mound.
Raschi walked.
2,3 Rizzuto bounced into a double play,
Dark to Stanky to Lockman.

6th Inning
Giants
Thomson walked.
1,2 Thompson bounced into a double play,
Rizzuto to Mize.
3 Westrum popped to Berra.
Yankees
1 Coleman called out on strikes.
Berra singled to right and went to
second on Thompson's fumble.
DiMaggio got an intentional pass.
Berra went to third and DiMaggio to
second on a wild pitch.
2 McDougald lined to third.
Mize walked, loading the bases.
Bauer tripled to deep left, scoring
Berra, DiMaggio and Mize.
3 Woodling grounded to second.

7th Inning
Giants
For the Yankees—Collins playing first.
Mays singled to center.
Rigney, pinch-hitting for Koslo, singled
to right, Mays stopping at second.
For the Yankees—Sain now pitching.
1 Stanky flied to right.
2 Dark struck out.
3 Lockman flied to center.
Yankees
For the Giants—Hearn pitching.
1 Sain grounded to short.
Rizzuto singled to deep short.
2 Coleman fouled to Lockman.
3 Berra grounded to second.

8th Inning
Giants
1 Irvin flied to left.
2 Thomson fouled to McDougald.
Thompson walked.
Westrum singled over second, Thompson
stopping at second.
Williams ran for Westrum.
Mays walked, loading the bases.
3 Noble, pinch-hitting for Hearn, was
called out on strikes.
Yankees
For the Giants—Noble stays in to catch
with Jansen pitching.
DiMaggio doubled to right.
1 McDougald bunted into a fielder's
choice as DiMaggio was out at third,
Jansen to Thomson.
2 Collins flied to left.
3 McDougald was caught attempting to
steal second, Noble to Stanky.

9th Inning
Giants
Stanky singled to left.
Dark beat out a bunt down the third
base line, for his 10th hit of the
Series. Stanky stopping at second.
Lockman singled to center, loading
the bases.
For the Yankees—Kuzava replaced Sain
on the mound.
1 Irvin flied to left, Stanky scoring
and both other runners advancing
after the catch.
2 Thomson flied to left, Dark scoring
after the catch.
3 Yvars, batting for Thompson, lined to
right.

1951 WORLD SERIES COMPOSITE BOX

	Wins	Composite Line Score
New York Yankees (A.L.)	4	2 3 5 3 2 5 6 2 1 – 29
New York Giants (N.L.)	2	4 1 0 0 6 3 1 0 3 – 18

Manager	Regular Season W	L	Pct.	G. Ahead
Casey Stengel	98	56	.636	5
Leo Durocher	98	59	.624	1 (beat Brooklyn in playoffs)

BATTING AND FIELDING

WORLD SERIES STATISTICS

NEW YORK YANKEES

	Pos	G	AB	R	H	2B	3B	HR	RBI	BB	SO	SB	BA	SA	PO	A	E
Joe Collins	1b-rf	6	18	2	4	0	0	**1**	3	2	1	0	.222	.389	39	2	0
Gil McDougald	2b-3b	6	23	2	6	1	0	**1**	**7**	2	2	0	.261	.435	10	14	1
Phil Rizzuto	ss	6	**25**	5	8	0	0	**1**	3	2	3	0	.320	.440	15	24	1
Bobby Brown	ph-3b	5	14	1	5	1	0	0	0	2	1	0	.357	.429	1	8	0
Hank Bauer	rf-lf	6	18	0	3	0	**1**	0	3	1	1	0	.167	.278	7	0	0
Joe DiMaggio	cf	6	23	3	6	2	0	**1**	5	2	**4**	0	.261	.478	17	0	0
Gene Woodling	ph-lf	6	18	**6**	3	1	**1**	**1**	1	5	3	0	.167	.500	18	0	1
Yogi Berra	c	6	23	4	6	1	0	0	0	2	1	0	.261	.304	27	3	1
Jerry Coleman	2b-pr	5	8	2	2	0	0	0	0	1	2	0	.250	.250	7	5	0
Johnny Mize	ph-1b	4	7	2	2	1	0	0	1	2	0	0	.286	.429	12	0	0
Mickey Mantle	rf	2	5	1	1	0	0	0	0	2	1	0	.200	.200	4	0	0
Johnny Hopp	ph	1	0	0	0	0	0	0	0	1	0	0	—	—			
Billy Martin	pr	1	0	1	0	0	0	0	0	0	0	0	—	—			
Charlie Silvera		Did not play															
Ralph Houk		Did not play															
Ed Lopat	p	2	8	0	1	0	0	0	1	0	2	0	.125	.125	2	4	0
Allie Reynolds	p	2	6	0	2	0	0	0	1	0	1	0	.333	.333	0	5	0
Vic Raschi	p	2	2	0	0	0	0	0	0	2	1	0	.000	.000	0	0	0
Johnny Sain	p	1	1	0	0	0	0	0	0	0	0	0	.000	.000	0	0	0
Bobby Hogue	p	2	0	0	0	0	0	0	0	0	0	0	—	—	0	1	0
Bob Kuzava	p	1	0	0	0	0	0	0	0	0	0	0	—	—	0	0	0
Tom Morgan	p	1	0	0	0	0	0	0	0	0	0	0	—	—	0	1	0
Joe Ostrowski	p	1	0	0	0	0	0	0	0	0	0	0	—	—	0	0	0
Spec Shea		Did not play															
Art Schallock		Did not play															
Stubby Overmire		Did not play															
team total		6	199	29	49	7	2	5	25	26	23	0	.246	.377	159	67	4

Double Plays—10
Left on Bases—41

REGULAR SEASON STATISTICS

NEW YORK YANKEES

		Main Pos	G	AB	R	H	2B	3B	HR	RBI	BB	SO	SB	BA	SA
Joe Collins		1b	125	262	52	75	8	5	9	48	34	23	9	.286	.458
Gil McDougald		3b-2b	131	402	72	123	23	4	14	63	56	54	14	.306	.488
Phil Rizzuto		ss	144	540	87	148	21	6	2	43	58	27	18	.274	.346
Bobby Brown		3b	103	313	44	84	15	2	6	51	47	18	1	.268	.387
Hank Bauer		of	118	348	53	103	19	3	10	54	42	39	5	.296	.454
Joe DiMaggio		of	116	415	72	109	22	4	12	71	61	36	0	.263	.422
Gene Woodling		of	120	420	65	118	15	8	15	71	62	37	0	.281	.462
Yogi Berra		c	141	547	92	161	19	4	27	88	44	20	5	.294	.492
Jerry Coleman		2b	121	362	48	90	11	2	3	43	31	36	6	.249	.315
Johnny Mize		1b	113	332	37	86	14	1	10	49	36	24	1	.259	.398
Mickey Mantle		of	96	341	61	91	11	5	13	65	43	74	8	.267	.443
Johnny Hopp		1b-ph	46	63	10	13	1	0	2	4	9	11	2	.206	.317
Billy Martin		2b-ph	51	58	10	15	1	2	0	2	4	9	0	.259	.345
Charlie Silvera		c	18	51	5	14	3	0	1	7	5	3	0	.275	.392
Ralph Houk		c	3	5	0	1	0	0	0	2	0	1	0	.200	.200
Ed Lopat		p	31	84	7	15	1	0	3	9	7	10	0	.179	.298
Allie Reynolds		p	43	76	8	14	3	0	0	11	7	18	1	.184	.224
Vic Raschi		p	35	85	5	15	2	0	0	5	6	24	0	.176	.200
Johnny Sain	a	p	7	14	3	4	1	0	0	0	0	0	0	.286	.357
Bobby Hogue	b	p	7	0	0	0	0	0	0	0	0	0	0	.000	.000
Bob Kuzava	c	p	24	22	4	3	1	0	0	2	5	10	0	.136	.182
Tom Morgan		p	27	44	6	12	2	0	1	3	0	3	0	.273	.386
Joe Ostrowski		p	34	28	2	3	0	0	0	1	3	7	0	.107	.107
Spec Shea		p	25	28	5	6	0	0	1	5	2	7	0	.214	.321
Art Schallock		p	11	17	2	5	0	0	0	2	2	8	0	.294	.294
Stubby Overmire	d	p	15	7	0	1	0	0	0	0	2	0	0	.143	.143
team total			154	5194	798	1395	208	48	**140**	741	605	547	78	.269	**.408**

a—from Boston (N)
b—from Boston (N) and St. Louis (A)
c—from Washington
d—from St. Louis (A)

Jackie Jensen (of), Cliff Mapes (of), Billy Johnson (3b), Bob Cerv (of), Jim Brideweser (ss), Clint Courtney (c), Archie Wilson (of), Tommy Byrne (p), Tom Ferrick (p), Jack Kramer (p), Bob Munceief (p), Ernie Nevel (p), Bob Porterfield (p), Bob Wiesler (p), and Fred Sanford (p) also played for the Yankees during the season.

WORLD SERIES STATISTICS

NEW YORK GIANTS

	Pos	G	AB	R	H	2B	3B	HR	RBI	BB	SO	SB	BA	SA	PO	A	E
Whitey Lockman	1b	6	**25**	1	6	2	0	**1**	4	1	2	0	.240	.440	**48**	5	**2**
Eddie Stanky	2b	6	22	3	3	0	0	0	1	3	2	0	.136	.136	14	16	1
Al Dark	ss	6	24	5	10	**3**	0	**1**	4	2	3	0	.417	**.667**	10	15	0
Bobby Thomson	3b	6	21	1	5	1	0	0	2	**5**	0	0	.238	.286	12	15	**2**
Hank Thompson	rf	5	14	3	2	0	0	0	0	**5**	2	0	.143	.143	5	0	**2**
Willie Mays	cf	6	22	1	4	0	0	0	1	2	2	0	.182	.182	16	1	0
Monte Irvin	lf	6	24	3	**11**	0	**1**	0	2	2	1	**2**	**.458**	.542	17	0	1
Wes Westrum	c	6	17	1	4	1	0	0	0	**5**	3	0	.235	.294	29	2	1
Clint Hartung	rf	2	4	0	0	0	0	0	0	0	0	0	.000	.000	1	1	1
Ray Noble	ph-c	2	2	0	0	0	0	0	0	0	1	0	.000	.000	0	1	0
Bill Rigney	ph	4	4	0	1	0	0	0	1	0	1	0	.250	.250			
Lucky Lohrke	ph	2	2	0	0	0	0	0	0	0	1	0	.000	.000			
Davey Williams	ph-pr	2	1	0	0	0	0	0	0	0	0	0	.000	.000			
Sal Yvars	ph	1	1	0	0	0	0	0	0	0	0	0	.000	.000			
Hank Schenz	pr	1	0	0	0	0	0	0	0	0	0	0	—	—			
Don Mueller		Did not play (broken ankle)															
Dave Koslo	p	2	5	0	0	0	0	0	0	0	2	0	.000	.000	2	2	0
Jim Hearn	p	2	3	0	0	0	0	0	0	0	1	0	.000	.000	0	2	0
Larry Jansen	p	3	2	0	0	0	0	0	0	0	0	0	.000	.000	1	2	0
Sal Maglie	p	1	1	0	0	0	0	0	0	0	1	0	.000	.000	0	0	0
George Spencer	p	2	0	0	0	0	0	0	0	0	0	0	—	—	0	1	0
Sheldon Jones	p	2	0	0	0	0	0	0	0	0	0	0	—	—	0	1	0
Monte Kennedy	p	2	0	0	0	0	0	0	0	0	0	0	—	—	0	1	0
Al Corwin	p	1	0	0	0	0	0	0	0	0	0	0	—	—	1	0	0
Alex Konikowski	p	1	0	0	0	0	0	0	0	0	0	0	—	—	0	0	0
team total		6	194	18	46	7	1	2	15	25	22	2	.237	.314	156	65	10

Double Plays—4
Left on Bases—45

REGULAR SEASON STATISTICS

NEW YORK GIANTS

		Main Pos	G	AB	R	H	2B	3B	HR	RBI	BB	SO	SB	BA	SA
Whitey Lockman		1b	153	614	85	173	27	7	12	73	50	32	4	.282	.407
Eddie Stanky		2b	145	515	88	127	17	2	14	43	127	63	8	.247	.369
Al Dark		ss	156	646	114	196	**41**	7	14	69	42	39	12	.303	.454
Bobby Thomson		of-3b	148	518	89	152	27	8	32	101	73	57	5	.293	.562
Hank Thompson		3b	87	264	37	62	8	4	8	33	43	23	1	.235	.386
Willie Mays		of	121	464	59	127	22	5	20	58	66	60	7	.274	.472
Monte Irvin		of	151	558	94	174	19	11	24	**121**	89	44	12	.312	.514
Wes Westrum		c	124	361	59	79	12	0	20	70	104	93	1	.219	.418
Clint Hartung		of	21	44	4	9	1	0	0	2	1	9	0	.205	.227
Ray Noble		c	55	141	16	33	6	0	5	26	6	26	0	.234	.383
Bill Rigney		ph-3b-2b	44	69	9	16	2	0	4	9	8	7	0	.232	.435
Lucky Lohrke		3b	23	40	3	8	0	0	1	3	10	2	0	.200	.275
Davey Williams		2b	30	64	17	17	1	0	2	8	5	8	1	.266	.375
Sal Yvars		c	25	41	9	13	2	0	2	3	5	7	0	.317	.512
Hank Schenz	e	pr	8	0	1	0	0	0	0	0	0	0	0	.000	.000
Don Mueller		of	122	469	58	130	10	7	16	69	19	13	1	.277	.431
Dave Koslo		p	39	50	1	5	1	0	0	1	6	18	1	.100	.120
Jim Hearn		p	34	74	7	12	0	0	1	6	4	29	0	.162	.203
Larry Jansen		p	39	96	5	9	0	0	0	5	7	33	0	.094	.094
Sal Maglie		p	42	112	9	17	1	0	1	5	1	22	0	.152	.188
George Spencer		p	57	32	2	4	0	0	0	3	3	11	0	.125	.125
Sheldon Jones		p	41	31	1	3	1	1	0	1	1	6	0	.097	.194
Monte Kennedy		p	29	15	0	3	1	0	0	1	0	5	0	.200	.267
Al Corwin		p	15	20	1	1	1	0	0	0	0	6	0	.050	.100
Alex Konikowski		p	3	0	0	0	0	0	0	0	0	0	0	.000	.000
team total			157	5360	781	1396	201	53	179	734	**671**	624	55	.260	.418

e—from Pittsburgh

Spider Jorgensen (ph-of), Artie Wilson (ph), Jack Maguire (of), Earl Rapp (ph), Roger Bowman (p), Al Gettel (p), Jack Kramer (p), George Bamberger (p), and Red Hardy (p) also played for the Giants during the season.

PITCHING

WORLD SERIES STATISTICS

	G	GS	CG	IP	H	R	ER	BB	SO	W	L	SV	ERA
NEW YORK YANKEES													
Eddie Lopat	2	**2**	**2**	**18**	10	2	1	3	4	**2**	0	0	**0.50**
Allie Reynolds	2	**2**	1	15	**16**	**7**	**7**	**11**	**8**	1	1	0	4.20
Vic Raschi	2	**2**	0	10⅓	12	**7**	1	8	4	1	1	0	0.87
Bobby Hogue	2	0	0	2⅔	1	0	0	0	0	0	0	0	0.00
Tom Morgan	1	0	0	2	2	0	0	1	3	0	0	0	0.00
Joe Ostrowski	1	0	0	2	1	0	0	0	1	0	0	0	0.00
Johnny Sain	1	0	0	2	4	2	2	2	2	0	0	0	9.00
Bob Kuzava	1	0	0	1	0	0	0	0	0	0	0	**1**	0.00
Spec Shea	Did not play												
Art Schallock	Did not play												
Stubby Overmire	Did not play												
team total	6	6	3	53	46	18	11	25	22	4	2	1	1.87
NEW YORK GIANTS													
Dave Koslo	2	**2**	1	15	12	5	5	7	6	1	1	0	3.00
Larry Jansen	**3**	**2**	0	10	8	**7**	**7**	4	6	0	**2**	0	6.30
Jim Hearn	2	1	0	8⅔	5	1	1	8	1	1	0	0	1.04
Sal Maglie	1	1	0	5	8	4	4	2	3	0	1	0	7.20
Sheldon Jones	2	0	0	4	⅓	5	3	1	1	2	0	0	**1**
George Spencer	2	0	0	3⅓	6	**7**	**7**	3	0	0	0	0	18.90
Monte Kennedy	2	0	0	3	3	2	2	1	4	0	0	0	6.00
Al Corwin	1	0	0	1⅔	1	0	0	0	1	0	0	0	0.00
Alex Konikowski	1	0	0	1	1	0	0	0	0	0	0	0	0.00
team total	6	6	1	52	49	29	27	26	23	2	4	1	4.67

REGULAR SEASON STATISTICS

		G	GS	CG	IP	H	ER	BB	SO	W	L	Pct	SV	ShO	ERA
NEW YORK YANKEES															
Eddie Lopat		31	31	20	235	209	76	71	93	21	9	.700	0	4	2.91
Allie Reynolds		40	26	16	221	171	75	100	126	17	8	.680	7	**7**	3.05
Vic Raschi		35	**34**	15	258	233	94	103	**164**	21	10	.677	0	4	3.28
Bobby Hogue	b	7	0	0	7	4	0	3	2	1	0	1.000	0	0	0.00
Tom Morgan		27	16	4	125	119	51	36	57	9	3	.750	2	2	3.67
Joe Ostrowski		34	3	2	95	103	37	18	30	6	4	.600	5	0	3.51
Johnny Sain	a	7	4	1	37	41	17	8	21	2	1	.667	1	0	4.14
Bob Kuzava	c	23	8	4	82	76	22	27	50	8	4	.667	5	1	2.41
Spec Shea		25	11	2	96	112	46	50	38	5	5	.500	0	2	4.31
Art Schallock		11	6	1	46	50	20	20	19	3	1	.750	0	0	3.91
Stubby Overmire	d	15	4	1	45	50	23	18	14	1	1	.500	0	0	4.60
team total		154	154	66	1367	1290	541	562	**664**	**98**	56	**.636**	22	24	3.56
NEW YORK GIANTS															
Dave Koslo		39	16	5	150	153	55	45	54	10	9	.526	3	2	3.30
Larry Jansen		39	34	18	279	254	94	56	145	**23**	11	.676	0	3	3.03
Jim Hearn		34	34	11	211	204	85	82	66	17	9	.654	0	0	3.63
Sal Maglie		42	37	22	298	254	97	86	146	**23**	6	.793	4	3	2.93
Sheldon Jones		2.08	12	2	120	119	57	52	58	6	11	.353	4	0	4.28
George Spencer		57	4	2	132	125	55	56	36	10	4	.714	6	0	3.75
Monte Kennedy		29	5	1	68	68	17	31	22	1	2	.333	0	0	2.25
Al Corwin		15	8	3	59	49	24	21	30	5	1	.833	1	1	3.66
Alex Konikowski		3	0	0	4	2	0	0	5	0	0	.000	0	0	0.00
team total		157	157	64	1413	1334	546	482	625	**98**	59	**.624**	18	9	**3.48**

Total Attendance—341,977 Average Attendance—56,996 Winning Player's Share—$6,446 Losing Player's Share—$4,951

1952
Martin's Desperate Dash

They were the Boys of Summer, unimpeachable heroes for Brooklyn youth and characters to be celebrated in later years. Manager Chuck Dressen had a full slate of all-around players, with Duke Snider, Carl Furillo, and Andy Pafko in the outfield, Gil Hodges, Jackie Robinson, Billy Cox, and Pee Wee Reese in the infield, and Roy Campanella behind the plate. These men exuded both color and thunder, and if the pitching staff led by Joe Black, Carl Erskine, Billy Loes, and Preacher Roe shone less brightly, it got its job done well enough to boost the Bums into the National League pennant in vindication for last year's humiliation at the hands of the Giants.

Such a crew hoped to end the string of three Series championships running for the New York Yankees of Casey Stengel. No longer did Joe DiMaggio patrol center field for the Yanks, but young Mickey Mantle excited the baseball world with his power and speed. A tested veteran cast featuring Yogi Berra, Gil McDougald, and Phil Rizzuto steered the Yanks to their fourth successive pennant, while the oldman quartet of Allie Reynolds, Vic Raschi, Johnny Sain, and Eddie Lopat answered the bulk of Stengel's pitching needs. With the intangible class of DiMaggio gone, the Yanks were as much of an unknown quantity as any champion of three years' running could be.

The Yanks got off to a bad start by dropping the opener in Ebbets Field 4–2. Dressen started big rookie Joe Black, who relieved 54 times during the season and started only two games prior to his Series debut. Backing up Black's strong pitching were home runs off the bats of Robinson, Snider, and Reese. The Yankees, however, were not ready to be counted out yet, and they rebounded to a 7–1 victory in game two, with Raschi throwing a three-hitter to even the Series.

Game three at Yankee Stadium matched two crafty pitchers who had long ago outgrown their fast balls, Eddie Lopat and Preacher Roe. The Dodgers led 3–2 going into the ninth and got a break when two men crossed the plate on a passed ball by Berra, who had homered earlier. Those runs meant the game when Johnny Mize pinch-hit a homer off Roe in the bottom of the ninth to up the final score to 5–3. Both managers brought back their opening starters on two days' rest for game four, but Reynolds this time beat Black 2–0 by throwing a four-hitter with 10 strikeouts, fanning the dangerous Robinson three times. Dressen called on Erskine to pitch game five on two days' rest, while Stengel reached farther back into the cupboard to come up with Ewell Blackwell, the one-time Cincinnati ace who had fallen on hard times with a sore arm. The Dodgers went ahead 4–0 in the top of the fifth on a two-run homer by Snider, but five runs in the bottom of the inning put the Yanks ahead. Erskine settled down and retired every Yankee from that point on, while Snider drove in the tying run in the seventh inning and the winning run in the eleventh. The 6–5 victory gave the Bums a 3–2 edge in games, with the Series going back to Brooklyn for a conclusion.

But the Yankee class came through in the battle on enemy turf. Duke Snider kept his bat humming with two homers, but an RBI single by Raschi plus solo homers by Berra and Mantle sent the Dodgers down to a tough 3–2 loss which threw the outcome of the Series into the seventh game, with Joe Black and Eddie Lopat on the mound. A 2–2 tie was broken in the top of the sixth by a solo homer by Mantle, and a run-producing single by Mickey ran the count to 4–2 in the seventh. The Dodgers loaded the bases with one out in the bottom of the inning, and then Stengel brought in southpaw Bob Kuzava to face Snider. The Duke popped up for the second out, and then Robinson did the same with a full count and all runners moving with the pitch. The short pop between the mound and first base suddenly looked like it would drop when first baseman Joe Collins lost the ball in the sun. Second baseman Billy Martin saved the day with a last-second sprint and knee-level catch to end the inning. Kuzava got the next six outs without incident, and the taste of victory that watered in Brooklyn's mouth only two days before disappeared like cotton candy on the tongue.

Game 1 October 1 at Brooklyn

N.Y. 001 000 010
Bkn. 010 002 01x

New York	Pos	AB	R	H	RBI	PO	A	E
Bauer	rf	4	0	0	1	2	0	0
Rizzuto	ss	4	0	1	0	2	1	0
Mantle	cf	4	0	2	0	2	0	0
Berra	c	4	0	0	0	7	2	0
Collins	1b	4	0	0	0	8	0	0
Noren	lf	3	0	0	0	1	0	0
McDougald	3b	2	1	1	1	0	4	1
Martin	2b	3	0	1	0	2	1	0
Reynolds	p	2	0	0	0	0	1	1
a Woodling		1	1	1	0	0	0	0
Scarborough	p	0	0	0	0	0	1	0
Totals		31	2	6	2	24	10	2

Brooklyn	Pos	AB	R	H	RBI	PO	A	E
Cox	3b	3	0	0	0	1	2	0
Reese	ss	4	2	2	1	4	1	0
Snider	cf	4	1	2	2	2	0	0
Robinson	2b	2	1	1	1	1	4	0
Campanella	c	3	0	0	0	6	0	0
Pafko	lf	3	0	0	0	3	1	0
Hodges	1b	3	0	0	0	6	3	0
Furillo	rf	3	0	0	0	3	0	0
Black	p	3	0	0	0	1	0	0
Totals		28	4	6	4	27	11	0

Pitching	IP	H	R	ER	BB	SO
New York						
Reynolds (L)	7	5	3	3	2	4
Scarborough	1	1	1	1	0	1
Brooklyn						
Black (W)	9	6	2	2	2	6

a Tripled for Reynolds in 8th.

Double—Snider. Triple—Woodling. Home Runs—McDougald, Reese, Robinson, Snider. Double Plays—Martin to Collins, Cox to Robinson to Hodges. Wild Pitch—Reynolds. Left on bases—New York 4, Brooklyn 2. Umpires—Pinelli (N), Passarella (A), Goetz (N), McKinley (A), Boggess (N), Honochick (A). Attendance—34,861. Time of Game—2:21.

1st Inning
New York
1 Bauer flied to left.
2 Rizzuto flied to left.
3 Mantle popped to short.
Brooklyn
1 Cox flied to left.
2 Reese took a called third strike.
3 Snider flied to center.

2nd Inning
New York
1 Berra grounded out the ball deflecting off of Hodges to Robinson who threw to Black for the out.
2 Collins lined to right.
3 Noren popped to short.
Brooklyn
 Robinson homered into the lower left field stands.
 Campanella singled off the right field wall.
1 Campanella caught stealing, Berra to Martin.
2 Pafko grounded to third.
3 Hodges tapped back to the pitcher.

3rd Inning
New York
 McDougald homered into the lower left field stands.
1 Martin struck out.
2 Reynolds struck out.
3 Bauer called out on strikes.
Brooklyn
1 Furillo fouled to Berra.
2 Black took a called third strike.
 Cox walked.
3 Cox caught stealing, Berra to Rizzuto.

4th Inning
New York
 Rizzuto singled to left.
 Mantle beat out a bunt down the third-base line to move Rizzuto to second.
1 Berra forced Mantle at second, Hodges to Reese, with Rizzuto advancing to third.
2 Collins lined to right, both runners holding on Furillo's great throw to the plate.
3 Noren grounded to second.
Brooklyn
1 Reese lined to center.
 Snider doubled off the right field screen.
 Robinson walked.
2,3 Campanella grounded into a double play, Martin tagging Robinson and throwing to Collins getting Campanella

5th Inning
New York
 McDougald walked.
 Martin singled down the left field
1 line, McDougald out trying for third, Pafko to Cox. Martin went to second on the throw.
2 Reynolds grounded to short, Martin holding second.
3 Bauer flied to left.
Brooklyn
1 Pafko flied to right.
2 Hodges grounded to third.
3 Furillo grounded to third.

6th Inning
New York
1 Rizzuto struck out.
 Mantle singled to left.
2 Berra forced Mantle at second, Hodges to Reese.
3 Collins grounded to first.
Brooklyn
1 Black took a called third strike.
2 Cox fouled to Berra.
 Reese singled to left.
 Reese went to second on a wild pitch.
 Snider hit a two-run homer over the right field scoreboard.
 Robinson safe on McDougald's fumble. Robinson went to second on Reynold's wild pick-off throw.
3 Campanella grounded to short.

7th Inning
New York
 Noren walked.
1,2 McDougald hit into a double play, Cox to Robinson to Hodges.
3 Martin grounded to third.
Brooklyn
1 Pafko flied to right.
2 Hodges called out on strikes.
3 Furillo lined to short.

8th Inning
New York
 Woodling, batting for Reynolds, tripled off the right-center screen.
1 Bauer flied to center, Woodling scoring after the catch.
2 Rizzuto flied to right.
3 Mantle struck out.
Brooklyn
 For New York—Scarborough pitching.
1 Black struck out.
2 Cox grounded to third.
 Reese homered into the lower left field stands.
3 Snider grounded back to the mound.

9th Inning
New York
1 Berra flied to center.
2 Collins grounded to second.
3 Noren looked at a called third strike.

Game 2 October 2 at Brooklyn

New York	Pos	AB	R	H	RBI	PO	A	E
Bauer	rf	4	0	1	0	3	0	0
Rizzuto	ss	4	0	0	0	2	2	0
Mantle	cf	5	2	3	0	2	0	0
Woodling	lf	4	1	1	0	2	0	0
Berra	c	3	0	2	1	10	2	0
Collins	1b	3	1	0	0	8	1	0
McDougald	3b	3	2	1	1	0	1	0
Martin	2b	4	1	2	4	0	1	0
Raschi	p	3	0	0	0	0	0	0
Totals		33	7	10	6	27	7	0

Pitching	IP	H	R	ER	BB	SO
New York						
Raschi (W)	9	3	1	1	5	9
Brooklyn						
Erskine (L)	*5	6	4	4	6	4
Loes	2	2	3	2	0	2
Lehman	2	2	0	0	1	0

*Pitched to three batters in 6th.

N.Y.   000 115 000
Bkn.   001 000 000

Brooklyn	Pos	AB	R	H	RBI	PO	A	E
Cox	3b	4	0	0	0	1	0	0
Reese	ss	3	1	1	0	2	5	0
Snider	cf	4	0	1	0	1	0	0
Robinson	2b	3	0	0	0	3	3	0
Campanella	c	4	0	1	1	7	3	0
Pafko	lf	4	0	0	0	2	0	0
Hodges	1b	3	0	0	0	9	0	1
Furillo	rf	3	0	0	0	2	0	0
Erskine	p	2	0	0	0	0	1	0
Loes	p	0	0	0	0	0	0	0
a Nelson		0	0	0	0	0	0	0
Lehman	p	0	0	0	0	0	1	0
Totals		30	1	3	1	27	13	1

a Walked for Loes in 7th.

Double—Mantle. Home Run—Martin. Stolen Base—McDougald. Double Play—Reese to Robinson to Hodges. Wild Pitch—Erskine. Left on Bases—New York 6, Brooklyn 7. Umpires—Passarella, Goetz, McKinley, Pinelli, Honochick, Boggess. Attendance—33,792. Time of Game—2:47.

1st Inning
New York
Bauer singled to right-center.
1 Bauer caught stealing when Rizzuto missed a pitch, Campanella to Robinson. Rizzuto walked.
2 Mantle struck out.
3 Rizzuto caught stealing, Campanella to Reese.
Brooklyn
1 Cox grounded to short.
2 Reese flied to right.
3 Snider took a called third strike.

2nd Inning
New York
Woodling walked.
Berra singled to right-center, moving Woodling to third.
1 Collins called out on strikes.
2 McDougald struck out.
3 Martin grounded to short.
Brooklyn
Robinson walked.
1 Campanella grounded to first, Robinson going to second.
2 Pafko flied to right, Robinson moved to third after the catch. Hodges walked.
Furillo walked, loading the bases.
3 Erskine flied to center.

3rd Inning
New York
Raschi walked.
1,2 Bauer grounded into a double play, Reese to Robinson to Hodges.
3 Rizzuto grounded to short.
Brooklyn
1 Cox called out on strikes.
Reese singled to left-center. Snider beat out a bunt down the third base line, moving Reese to second.
2 Robinson forced Snider at second, Collins to Rizzuto, Reese going to third. Campanella singled to left, Reese scoring and Robinson going to second.
3 Pafko struck out.

4th Inning
New York
Mantle doubled off the right-center field scoreboard.
1 Woodling grounded to second, Mantle moving on to third.
2 Berra flied to right, Mantle scoring after the catch.
3 Collins tapped back to the mound.
Brooklyn
1 Hodges fanned but Berra dropped the third strike and had to throw to Collins for the putout.
2 Furillo flied to right.
3 Erskine bunted out to third.

5th Inning
New York
McDougald walked.
McDougald stole second. Martin singled to left, McDougald scoring with Martin going to second on the throw to the plate.
1 Raschi called out on strikes. Bauer walked.
A pitch got away from Campanella, Bauer went to second but Martin was
2 out at third, Campanella to Cox.
3 Rizzuto grounded to short.

5th Inning (continued)
Brooklyn
1 Cox grounded to short.
2 Reese took a called third strike.
3 Snider struck out but Berra again dropped the ball and had to throw to Collins for the putout.

6th Inning
New York
Mantle singled on a bunt to second.
Woodling singled to center, Mantle stopping at second.
Mantle went to third and Woodling to second on a wild pitch.
Berra walked to load the bases.
For Brooklyn—Loes pitching.
1 Collins grounded to second, Robinson tagging Berra and throwing to Hodges for the DP, but Hodges dropped the ball for an error. On the play, Mantle scored with Woodling going to third. McDougald beat out a bunt toward first, Woodling scoring with Collins going to second.
Martin hit a three-run homer into the left field stands.
2 Raschi was called out on strikes.
3 Bauer fanned.
Brooklyn
1 Robinson fouled to Berra.
2 Campanella fouled behind third to Rizzuto.
3 Pafko fouled to Berra.

7th Inning
New York
1 Rizzuto grounded to first.
2 Mantle popped to short.
3 Woodling flied to right.
Brooklyn
1 Hodges flied to center.
2 Furillo struck out.
Nelson, pinch-hit for Loes and walked.
3 Cox grounded to second.

8th Inning
New York
For Brooklyn—Lehman pitching.
Berra singled to right.
Collins walked.
1 McDougald flied to center.
2 Martin lined to left.
3 Raschi grounded to the mound.
Brooklyn
Reese walked.
1 Snider struck out.
2 Robinson flied to left.
3 Campanella flied to left.

9th Inning
New York
1 Bauer grounded to short.
2 Rizzuto flied to left.
Mantle singled to left-center.
3 Woodling popped to Campanella.
Brooklyn
1 Pafko fouled to Berra.
2 Hodges grounded to first.
3 Furillo fanned.

Game 3 October 3 at New York

Brooklyn	Pos	AB	R	H	RBI	PO	A	E
Furillo	rf	5	1	1	0	0	0	0
Reese	ss	5	1	3	1	1	4	0
Robinson	2b	4	2	2	1	2	3	0
Campanella	c	5	0	1	0	9	1	0
Pafko	lf	5	0	2	1	2	0	0
Snider	cf	5	0	1	0	3	0	0
Hodges	1b	3	0	0	0	9	2	0
Cox	3b	2	1	1	0	0	2	0
Roe	p	2	0	0	0	1	0	0
Totals		36	5	11	3	27	12	0

Pitching	IP	H	R	ER	BB	SO
Brooklyn						
Roe (W)	9	6	3	3	5	5
New York						
Lopat (L)	8⅓	10	5	5	4	0
Gorman	⅔	1	0	0	0	0

Bkn.   001 010 012
N.Y.   010 000 011

New York	Pos	AB	R	H	RBI	PO	A	E
Rizzuto	ss	4	0	0	0	4	4	0
Collins	1b	4	0	0	0	7	0	0
b Sain		1	0	0	0	0	0	0
Mantle	cf	4	0	0	0	6	0	0
Woodling	lf	4	0	1	0	2	0	0
Berra	c	4	1	3	1	1	1	1
Bauer	rf	2	1	0	0	3	0	0
McDougald	3b	4	0	0	0	1	2	1
Martin	2b	4	0	0	0	3	3	0
Lopat	p	2	0	1	1	0	0	0
Gorman	p	0	0	0	0	0	0	0
a Mize		1	1	1	1	0	0	0
Totals		31	3	6	3	27	10	2

a Homered for Gorman in 9th.
b Flied out for Collins in 9th.

Doubles—Berra, Furillo. Home Runs—Berra, Mize. Stolen Bases—Reese, Robinson, Snider. Sacrifice Hits—Bauer, Roe 2. Double Plays—Rizzuto to Martin, McDougald to Collins. Passed Ball—Berra. Hit by Pitcher—Martin (by Roe). Left on Bases—Brooklyn 10, New York 8. Umpires—Goetz, McKinley, Pinelli, Passarella, Boggess, Honochick. Attendance—66,698. Time of Game—2:56.

1st Inning
Brooklyn
1 Furillo grounded to second.
2 Reese popped to short. Robinson walked.
3 Campanella flied to right.
New York
Rizzuto walked.
1 Collins struck out.
2 Mantle fouled to Campanella.
3 Woodling grounded to short.

2nd Inning
Brooklyn
1 Pafko lined to center. Snider walked to second.
2 Hodges flied to center. Snider stole second. Cox got an intentional walk.
3 Roe forced Cox at second, McDougald to Martin.
New York
1 Berra fouled to Campanella. Bauer walked.
2 McDougald grounded to third, Bauer going to second. Martin intentionally walked. Lopat singled to right-center, Bauer scoring and Martin going to third.
3 Rizzuto grounded to second.

3rd Inning
Brooklyn
Furillo hit a ground-rule double into the right field boxes. Reese beat out a bunt down the third base line, moving Furillo to third.
1 Robinson flied to deep center, Furillo scoring and Reese going to second after the catch.
2,3 Campanella lined into a double play, Rizzuto to Martin getting Reese off second.
New York
1 Collins grounded out, Hodges to Roe.
2 Mantle flied to left.
3 Woodling was called out on strikes.

4th Inning
Brooklyn
Pafko singled to left.
1,2 Snider on an attempted sacrifice, popped into a double play, McDougald to Collins.
3 Hodges flied to center.
New York
Berra doubled into the left field corner.
1 Bauer sacrificed Berra to third, Hodges to Robinson.
2 McDougald fanned. Martin walked.
Lopat walked, filling the bases.
3 Rizzuto forced Lopat at second, Reese to Robinson.

5th Inning
Brooklyn
Cox singled to left.
1 Roe sacrificed Cox to second, Berra to Martin.
2 Furillo grounded to short, Cox holding second. Reese singled to right, Cox scoring.
3 Robinson flied to left.
New York
1 Collins grounded to second.
2 Mantle popped to Campanella. Woodling singled to left-center. Berra singled to center, Woodling stopping at second.
3 Bauer grounded to second.

6th Inning
Brooklyn
1 Campanella grounded to short.
2 Pafko flied to right.
3 Snider grounded to second.
New York
1 McDougald grounded to short. Martin was hit by a pitched ball.
2 Martin out trying to steal second, Campanella to Reese.
3 Lopat called out on strikes.

7th Inning
Brooklyn
Hodges safe at first on McDougald's low throw to first.
1 Cox flied to center. Roe sacrificed Hodges to second, and was safe when Lopat's throw to second was too late to get Hodges.
2 Furillo flied to left.
3 Reese flied to right.
New York
1 Rizzuto flied to left.
2 Collins grounded to first.
3 Mantle grounded to short.

8th Inning
Brooklyn
Robinson singled to center. Campanella singled to left, Robinson advancing to third.
1 Pafko flied to left, Robinson scoring and Campanella going to second after the catch.
Berra charged with an error when he dropped Snider's pop foul.
2 Snider popped to short. Hodges got an intentional pass. Cox also intentionally walked to load the bases.
3 Roe grounded to second.
New York
1 Woodling fanned. Berra homered into the lower left field stands.
2 Bauer grounded to third.
3 McDougald flied to center.

9th Inning
Brooklyn
1 Furillo grounded to short. Reese singled to right. Robinson singled to center, Reese stopping at second.
For New York—Gorman pitching. Reese and Robinson worked a good double steal.
2 Campanella popped to short. Both Reese and Robinson scored on a Berra passed ball. Pafko singled to right-center.
3 Snider fouled to Berra.
New York
1 Martin popped to Campanella. Mize, pinch-hitting for Gorman, homered into the lower right field stands.
2 Rizzuto flied to center.
3 Sain, batting for Collins, flied to center.

Game 4 October 4 at New York

Brooklyn	Pos	AB	R	H	RBI	PO	A	E
Cox	3b	3	0	0	0	2	2	0
b Nelson		1	0	0	0	0	0	0
Morgan	3b	0	0	0	0	0	1	0
Reese	ss	4	0	2	0	0	3	1
Snider	cf	4	0	0	0	5	0	0
Robinson	2b	4	0	0	0	0	2	0
Campanella	c	3	0	0	0	4	0	0
Pafko	lf	3	0	1	0	2	0	0
Hodges	1b	2	0	0	0	10	0	0
Furillo	rf	2	0	1	0	1	0	0
Black	p	1	0	0	0	0	2	0
a Shuba		1	0	0	0	0	0	0
Rutherford	p	0	0	0	0	0	0	0
Totals		28	0	4	0	24	10	1

a Flied out for Black in 8th.
b Struck out for Cox in 8th.
c Ran for Mize in 8th.

Doubles—Mize, Woodling. Triple—Mantle.
Home Run—Mize. Sacrifice Hit—Furillo.
Double Play—Rizzuto to Martin to Mize.
Left on Bases—Brooklyn 5, New York 8.
Umpires—McKinley, Pinelli, Passarella,
Goetz, Honochick, Boggess.
Attendance—71,787. Time of Game—2:33.

Bkn. 000 000 000
N.Y. 000 100 01x

New York	Pos	AB	R	H	RBI	PO	A	E
McDougald	3b	3	0	0	0	0	1	0
Rizzuto	ss	2	0	0	0	1	3	0
Mantle	cf	3	1	1	0	4	0	0
Mize	1b	3	1	2	1	4	2	0
c Collins	1b	0	0	0	0	1	0	0
Berra	c	4	0	0	0	12	1	0
Woodling	lf	3	0	1	0	1	0	0
Bauer	rf	4	0	0	0	1	0	0
Martin	2b	3	0	0	0	2	1	1
Reynolds	p	3	0	0	0	1	0	0
Totals		28	2	4	1	27	8	1

Pitching	IP	H	R	ER	BB	SO
Brooklyn						
Black (L)	7	3	1	1	5	2
Rutherford	1	1	1	1	1	1
New York						
Reynolds (W)	9	4	0	0	3	10

1st Inning
Brooklyn
1 Cox struck out.
  Reese singled to left-center.
  Snider safe at first on Martin's wild
  throw to Rizzuto to get the force on
  Reese who wound up on third.
2 Robinson called out on strikes.
3 Campanella struck out.
New York
1 McDougald lined to center.
2 Rizzuto lined to left.
  Mantle walked.
3 Mize grounded to second.

2nd Inning
Brooklyn
1 Pafko struck out.
2 Hodges grounded to short.
3 Furillo grounded out, Mize to Reynolds.
New York
1 Berra struck out.
  Woodling doubled over Pafko's head.
2 Bauer grounded to third, Woodling holding.
3 Martin grounded to short.

3rd Inning
Brooklyn
1 Black struck out.
2 Cox flied to center.
  Reese singled off Rizzuto's glove.
3 Reese caught stealing, Berra to
  Rizzuto.
New York
1 Reynolds grounded to short.
2 McDougald bunted out to the mound.
  Rizzuto walked.
3 Mantle flied to center.

4th Inning
Brooklyn
1 Snider grounded to first.
2 Robinson grounded to short.
3 Campanella struck out.
New York
  Mize homered into the lower left field
  stands.
1 Berra flied to Snider in right-center,
  who made a leaping one-handed catch.
2 Woodling fouled to Cox.
3 Bauer flied to left.

5th Inning
Brooklyn
  Pafko singled to left.
  Hodges walked.
1 Furillo sacrificed both runners up,
  Mize to Martin.
  On an attempted squeeze Black missed
  the pitch, Pafko tagged out at the
2 plate by Berra with Hodges going to
  third.
  Black walked.
3 Cox fouled to Berra.

5th Inning (continued)
New York
1 Martin grounded to third.
2 Reynolds grounded to second.
  McDougald walked.
  Rizzuto walked.
3 Mantle flied to center.

6th Inning
Brooklyn
1 Reese flied to right.
2 Snider flied to center.
3 Robinson looked at a called third
  strike.
New York
  Mize got a ground-rule double into
  the right field stands.
1 Berra flied to center.
  Woodling got an intentional pass.
2 Bauer forced Mize at third, Cox
  unassisted.
3 Martin fouled to Campanella.

7th Inning
Brooklyn
  Campanella walked.
1 Pafko struck out.
2,3 Hodges grounded into a double play,
  Rizzuto to Martin to Mize.
New York
1 Reynolds fanned.
2 McDougald grounded back to the mound.
3 Rizzuto grounded to short.

8th Inning
Brooklyn
  Furillo singled over Rizzuto's glove.
1 Shuba pinch-hitting for Black, flied
  to center.
2 Nelson pinch-hitting for Cox, struck
  out.
3 Reese flied to left.
New York
  For Brooklyn—Rutherford pitching,
  Morgan at third.
  Mantle tripled over Snider's head and
  scored when Reese threw Snider's relay
  into the stands trying to get Mantle
  at third.
  Mize walked.
  Collins ran for Mize.
1 Berra lined to right.
2 Woodling grounded to third, moving
  Collins to second.
3 Bauer called out on strikes.

9th Inning
Brooklyn
  For New York—Collins playing first.
1 Snider flied to center.
2 Robinson called out on strikes.
3 Campanella grounded to third.

Game 5 October 5 at New York

Brooklyn	Pos	AB	R	H	RBI	PO	A	E
Cox	3b	5	2	3	0	2	2	0
Reese	ss	5	0	1	1	1	1	0
Snider	cf	5	1	3	4	4	0	0
Robinson	2b	2	1	0	0	2	1	0
Shuba	lf	2	0	1	0	4	0	0
Furillo	rf	4	0	1	0	3	0	0
Campanella	c	5	0	0	0	6	1	0
Pafko	rf-lf	4	0	1	1	3	0	0
Holmes	lf	1	0	0	0	2	0	0
Hodges	1b	3	1	0	0	6	0	0
Erskine	p	4	1	0	0	0	1	0
Totals		40	6	10	6	33	6	0

Pitching	IP	H	R	ER	BB	SO
Brooklyn						
Erskine (W)	11	5	5	5	3	6
New York						
Blackwell	5	4	4	4	3	4
Sain (L)	6	6	2	2	3	3

Bkn. 010 030 100 01
N.Y. 000 050 000 00

New York	Pos	AB	R	H	RBI	PO	A	E
McDougald	3b	4	1	0	1	0	2	0
Rizzuto	ss	5	1	1	0	1	4	1
Mantle	cf	5	0	1	0	1	0	0
Mize	1b	5	1	1	3	9	1	0
Berra	c	4	0	0	0	10	1	0
Woodling	lf	4	0	0	0	5	0	0
Bauer	rf	3	1	1	0	1	0	0
Martin	2b	4	1	1	0	6	3	0
Blackwell	p	1	0	0	0	0	1	0
a Noren		1	0	1	1	0	0	0
Sain	p	2	0	0	0	0	2	0
Totals		38	5	5	5	33	14	1

a Singled for Blackwell in 5th.

Doubles—Furillo, Snider. Home Runs—Mize,
Snider. Stolen Base—Robinson.
Sacrifice Hits—Cox, Erskine, Reese.
Double Plays—Martin to Rizzuto to Mize,
McDougald to Berra to Mize.
Hit by Pitched Ball—Snider (by Sain).
Umpires—Pinelli, Passarella, Goetz,
McKinley, Boggess, Honochick.
Attendance—70,536. Time of Game—3:00.

1st Inning
Brooklyn
  Cox singled off McDougald's glove.
1 Reese flied to left.
2,3 Snider grounded into a double play,
  Martin to Rizzuto to Mize.
New York
1 McDougald flied to left.
2 Rizzuto lined to left.
3 Mantle fanned but had to be thrown out,
  Campanella to Hodges.

2nd Inning
Brooklyn
  Robinson walked.
  Shuba singled on a chopper off Martin's
  glove, Robinson going to second.
1 Campanella struck out.
  Pafko singled to center, scoring
  Robinson with Shuba stopping at second.
  Hodges walked, filling the bases.
2 Erskine forced Shuba at the plate on an
  attempted squeeze, Blackwell to Berra.
3 Cox forced Erskine at second, Rizzuto to
  Martin.
New York
1 Mize grounded to first.
  Berra walked.
2 Woodling was robbed of a homer by Pafko,
  who made a leaping catch in front of
  the lower right field stands.
3 Bauer flied to left.

3rd Inning
Brooklyn
1 Reese flied to left.
2 Snider took a called third strike.
3 Robinson fouled to Berra.
New York
1 Martin flied to right.
2 Blackwell flied to center.
  McDougald walked.
3 Rizzuto flied to left.

4th Inning
Brooklyn
1 Shuba fanned.
2 Campanella lined to second.
3 Pafko flied to right.
New York
  Mantle beat out a bunt to Robinson.
1 Mize struck out.
2 Berra struck out.
3 Woodling lined to right.

5th Inning
Brooklyn
  Hodges walked.
  Erskine sacrificed and was safe when
  Blackwell's throw to second was too
  late to force Hodges.
1 Cox sacrificed both runners up, Mize
  to Martin.
2 Reese flied to deep left, Hodges
  scoring after the catch.
  Snider hit a two-run homer into the
  right-center field stands.
3 Robinson struck out.
New York
  For Brooklyn—Pafko moved to left and
  Furillo came in to play right.
  Bauer walked.
  Martin singled to center, Bauer stopping
  at second.
  Noren, batting for Blackwell, singled to
  center, Bauer scoring and Martin
  advancing to third.
1 McDougald forced Noren at second, Reese
  to Robinson, Martin scoring.
  Rizzuto singled past first, moving
  McDougald to second.
2 Mantle fouled to Cox.
  Mize hit a three-run homer into the lower
  right field stands.
3 Berra flied to center.

6th Inning
Brooklyn
  For New York—Sain pitching.
  Furillo doubled to the left field
  corner.
1 Campanella popped to second.
2 Pafko popped to first.
3 Hodges struck out.
New York
1 Woodling took a called third strike.
2 Bauer flied to center.
3 Martin grounded to third.

7th Inning
Brooklyn
1 Erskine flied to center.
  Cox beat out a roller to third.
2 Reese sacrificed Cox to second, Sain
  to Mize.
  Snider singled to center, Cox
  scoring with Snider to second on the
  throw to the plate.
  Robinson given an intentional walk.
3 Furillo flied to Woodling in deep
  left-center.
New York
1 Sain popped to second.
2 McDougald fouled to Campanella.
3 Rizzuto struck out.

8th Inning
Brooklyn
1 Campanella grounded to short.
2 Pafko grounded to short.
  Hodges safe at first on Rizzuto's wide
  throw to first.
3 Erskine grounded to second.
New York
1 Mantle flied to center.
2 Mize popped to short.
3 Berra flied to deep right.

9th Inning
Brooklyn
1 Cox popped to second.
2 Reese grounded back to the pitcher.
  Snider was hit by a pitched ball.
  Robinson walked.
3 Furillo forced Robinson at second,
  McDougald to Martin.
New York
  For Brooklyn—Holmes playing left.
1 Woodling flied to left.
2 Bauer fouled to Cox.
3 Martin flied to right.

10th Inning
Brooklyn
1 Campanella struck out.
2 Holmes grounded to second.
3 Hodges flied to left.
New York
1 Sain grounded to second.
2 McDougald flied to left.
3 Rizzuto grounded to third.

11th Inning
Brooklyn
1 Erskine struck out.
  Cox singled off McDougald's glove.
  Reese singled to center, sending Cox
  to third.
  Snider doubled, Cox scoring with Reese
  stopping at third.
  Robinson intentionally walked to load
  the bases.
2,3 Furillo hit into a double play,
  McDougald to Berra (forcing Reese at
  the plate) to Mize (getting Furillo
  at first).
New York
1 Mantle rolled to Erskine.
2 Mize was robbed of a homer by Furillo,
  with a leaping catch in front of the
  barrier in right.
3 Berra took a called third strike.

Game 6 October 6 at Brooklyn

New York	Pos	AB	R	H	RBI	PO	A	E
McDougald	3b	4	0	1	0	1	2	0
Rizzuto	ss	4	0	1	0	2	2	0
Mantle	cf	3	1	1	1	0	0	0
Mize	1b	3	0	0	0	7	0	0
Collins	1b	1	0	0	0	2	0	0
Berra	c	5	1	1	1	12	0	0
Woodling	lf	3	1	2	0	3	0	0
Noren	rf	4	0	2	0	0	0	0
Bauer	rf	0	0	0	0	0	0	0
Martin	2b	4	0	0	0	0	3	0
Raschi	p	3	0	1	1	0	1	0
Reynolds	p	1	0	0	0	0	0	0
Totals		35	3	9	3	27	8	0

Pitching	IP	H	R	ER	BB	SO
New York						
Raschi (W)	$7\frac{2}{3}$	8	2	2	1	9
Reynolds (SV)	$1\frac{1}{3}$	0	0	0	1	2
Brooklyn						
Loes (L)	$8\frac{1}{3}$	9	3	3	5	3
Roe	$\frac{2}{3}$	0	0	0	1	1

N.Y.	000	000	210
Bkn	000	001	010

Brooklyn	Pos	AB	R	H	RBI	PO	A	E
Cox	3b	5	0	2	0	1	3	0
Reese	ss	4	0	0	0	5	2	1
Snider	cf	3	2	2	2	4	0	0
Robinson	2b	4	0	0	0	2	2	0
Shuba	lf	4	0	1	0	2	0	0
a Amoros		0	0	0	0	0	0	0
Holmes	lf	0	0	0	0	0	0	0
Campanella	c	4	0	1	0	5	0	0
Hodges	1b	3	0	0	0	7	1	0
b Nelson		1	0	0	0	0	0	0
Furillo	rf	3	0	1	0	1	0	0
Loes	p	3	0	1	0	0	2	0
Roe	p	0	0	0	0	0	0	0
c Pafko		1	0	0	0	0	0	0
Totals		35	2	8	2	27	10	1

a Ran for Shuba in 8th.
b Struck out for Hodges in 9th.
c Popped out for Roe in 9th.

Doubles—Cox, Shuba. Home Runs—Berra, Mantle, Snider 2. Stolen Base—Loes. Double Play—Hodges to Reese to Robinson. Balk—Loes. Left on Bases—New York 11, Brooklyn 8. Umpires—Passarella, Goetz, McKinley, Pinelli, Honochick, Boggess. Attendance—30,037. Time of Game—2:56.

1st Inning
New York
1 McDougald grounded to third.
2 Rizzuto popped to short.
Mantle walked.
3 Mize flied to center.
Brooklyn
Cox doubled inside the left field foul line.
1 Reese popped to Berra on an attempted sacrifice.
Snider walked.
2 Robinson forced Cox at third, McDougald unassisted.
3 Shuba grounded to second.

2nd Inning
New York
1 Berra popped to short.
Woodling singled to right-center.
2 Noren fanned.
3 Martin fanned.
Brooklyn
1 Campanella grounded to short.
2 Hodges struck out.
Furillo singled to left.
3 Loes fanned.

3rd Inning
New York
1 Raschi's grounder deflected off Loes to Reese who threw to Hodges for the out.
2 McDougald fouled to Campanella.
3 Rizzuto flied to center.
Brooklyn
1 Cox grounded to third.
2 Reese lined to left.
3 Snider grounded to second.

4th Inning
New York
1 Mantle popped to second.
Mize walked.
2 Berra forced Mize at second, Robinson to Reese but Reese's throw to first went beyond Hodges and Berra was safe on second.
3 Woodling flied to center.
Brooklyn
1 Robinson took a called third strike.
2 Shuba struck out.
Campanella singled to left.
3 Hodges fanned.

5th Inning
New York
Noren singled off Cox' glove.
1 Martin flied to left.
2,3 Raschi bunted into a double play, Hodges to Reese to Robinson who covered first.
Brooklyn
1 Furillo struck out.
2 Loes grounded to second.
Cox singled to left.
3 Reese forced Cox at second, Rizzuto unassisted.

6th Inning
New York
1 McDougald popped to short.
Rizzuto walked.
2 Mantle flied to left.
3 Mize grounded to second.
Brooklyn
Snider homered over the right field screen.
1 Robinson flied to left.
2 Shuba fanned.
3 Campanella tapped back to the mound.

7th Inning
New York
Berra homered over the right field screen.
Woodling singled to center.
Woodling to second on a balk.
1 Noren called out on strikes.
2 Martin popped to third.
Raschi singled on a bouncer off of Loes' leg, Woodling scoring.
McDougald walked.
3 Rizzuto grounded to third.
Brooklyn
1 Hodges fanned.
2 Furillo grounded to first.
Loes singled to right.
Loes stole second.
3 Cox struck out.

8th Inning
New York
Mantle homered into the left-center field stands.
1 Mize popped to first.
2 Berra flied to center.
Woodling walked.
Noren singled to right, moving Woodling to second.
3 Martin grounded to third.
Brooklyn
For New York—Collins at first.
1 Reese grounded to short.
Snider hit his second homer of the game over the right field screen **(his fourth of the Series tying him for the most ever in a Series).**
2 Robinson flied to left.
Shuba doubled to left-center.
For New York—Reynolds pitching.
Amoros ran for Shuba.
3 Campanella struck out.

9th Inning
New York
For Brooklyn—Holmes in left.
1 Reynolds tapped back to the pitcher.
McDougald beat out a roller to third.
Rizzuto singled down the left field line, McDougald going to third.
For Brooklyn—Roe pitching.
Mantle walked to load the bases.
2 Collins struck out.
3 Berra lined to right.
Brooklyn
For New York—Bauer playing right.
1 Nelson, pinch-hitting for Hodges, struck out.
Furillo walked.
2 Pafko, batting for Roe, popped to short.
3 Cox grounded to third.

Game 7 October 7 at Brooklyn

New York	Pos	AB	R	H	RBI	PO	A	E
McDougald	3b	5	1	2	0	2	3	2
Rizzuto	ss	4	1	1	0	1	1	0
Mantle	cf	5	1	2	2	1	0	0
Mize	1b	3	0	2	1	6	0	0
Collins	1b	0	0	0	0	1	0	0
Berra	c	4	0	0	0	7	0	0
Woodling	lf	4	1	2	1	5	0	1
Noren	rf	2	0	0	0	1	0	0
a Bauer	rf	1	0	0	0	0	0	0
Martin	2b	4	0	1	0	2	4	0
Lopat	p	1	0	0	0	0	1	0
Reynolds	p	1	0	0	0	1	0	1
b Houk		1	0	0	0	0	0	0
Raschi	p	0	0	0	0	0	0	0
Kuzava	p	1	0	0	0	0	0	0
Totals		36	4	10	4	27	9	4

Pitching	IP	H	R	ER	BB	SO
New York						
Lopat	*3	4	1	1	0	3
Reynolds (W)	3	3	1	1	0	2
Raschi	$\frac{1}{3}$	1	0	0	2	0
Kuzava (SV)	$2\frac{2}{3}$	0	0	0	0	2
Brooklyn						
Black (L)	$5\frac{1}{3}$	6	3	3	1	1
Roe	$1\frac{2}{3}$	3	1	1	0	1
Erskine	2	1	0	0	1	0

*Pitched to three batters in 4th.

N.Y.	000	111	100
Bkn.	000	110	000

Brooklyn	Pos	AB	R	H	RBI	PO	A	E
Cox	3b	5	1	2	0	2	3	1
Reese	ss	4	0	1	1	2	2	0
Snider	cf	4	1	1	0	4	0	0
Robinson	2b	4	0	1	0	0	4	0
Campanella	c	4	0	2	0	2	0	0
Hodges	1b	4	0	0	1	13	0	0
Shuba	lf	3	0	1	0	1	0	0
d Pafko		1	0	0	0	0	0	0
Holmes	lf	0	0	0	0	0	0	0
Furillo	rf	3	0	0	0	3	0	0
Black	p	2	0	0	0	0	0	0
Roe	p	0	0	0	0	0	0	0
c Nelson		1	0	0	0	0	0	0
Erskine	p	0	0	0	0	0	0	0
e Morgan		1	0	0	0	0	0	0
Totals		36	2	8	2	27	9	1

a Safe on an error for Noren in 6th.
b Grounded out for Reynolds in 7th.
c Popped out for Roe in 7th.
d Struck out for Shuba in 8th.
e Flied out for Erskine in 9th.

Doubles—Cox, Rizzuto. Home Runs—Mantle, Woodling. Sacrifice Hit—Rizzuto.
Double Plays—Robinson to Reese to Hodges, Rizzuto to Martin to Mize.
Left on Bases—New York 8, Brooklyn 9.
Umpires—Goetz, McKinley, Pinelli, Passarella, Boggess, Honochick.
Attendance—33,195. Time of Game—2:54.

1st Inning
New York
1 McDougald grounded to short.
2 Rizzuto bunted to first where Hodges tagged him out.
3 Mantle struck out.
Brooklyn
1 Cox struck out but had to be tagged by Berra who dropped the ball.
Reese safe at first on McDougald's wild throw.
2 Snider called out on strikes.
3 Robinson lined to left.

2nd Inning
New York
Mize walked.
1 Berra flied to center.
2 Woodling flied to left.
3 Noren flied to right.
Brooklyn
1 Campanella grounded back to the mound.
2 Hodges flied to center.
Shuba singled through Lopat's legs.
3 Furillo grounded to third.

3rd Inning
New York
1 Martin flied to center.
2 Lopat grounded to first.
3 McDougald grounded to third.
Brooklyn
1 Black fanned.
2 Cox grounded to third.
3 Reese flied to right.

4th Inning
New York
Rizzuto doubled down the left field line.
1 Mantle grounded to first, Rizzuto advancing to third.
Mize singled to left, scoring Rizzuto.
2,3 Berra hit into a double play, Robinson to Reese to Hodges.
Brooklyn
Snider singled to right.
Robinson beat out a bunt down the third base line, moving Snider to second.
Campanella also beat out a bunt down the third base line to load the bases.
For New York—Reynolds pitching.
1 Hodges lined to left, Snider scoring after the catch. Robinson went to third when Reynolds dropped Woodling's throw at the plate.
2 Shuba struck out.
3 Furillo grounded to third.

5th Inning
New York
Woodling homered over the right field screen.
1 Noren popped to third.
Martin singled to center.
2 Reynolds grounded to second, Martin going to second.
3 McDougald grounded to second.
Brooklyn
1 Black took a called third strike.
Cox doubled off the right-center field wall.
Reese singled to left, Cox scoring and Reese to second on Woodling's wild throw to the plate.
2 Snider grounded out, Martin to Reynolds, moving Reese to third.
3 Robinson lined to third.

6th Inning
New York
1 Rizzuto lined to short.
Mantle homered over the right field scoreboard.
Mize singled to right.
For Brooklyn—Roe pitching.
2 Berra struck out.
Woodling singled to center, Mize stopping at second.
Bauer, pinch-hitting for Noren, was safe at first on Cox' fumble, loading the bases.
3 Martin flied to center.
Brooklyn
For New York—Bauer playing right.
Campanella singled to right-center.
1,2 Hodges grounded into a double play, Rizzuto to Martin to Mize.
3 Shuba grounded to second.

7th Inning
New York
1 Houk, pinch-hitting for Reynolds, grounded to third.
McDougald singled to center.
2 Rizzuto sacrificed McDougald to second, Cox to Hodges.
Mantle singled to left, scoring McDougald.
3 Mize fouled to Furillo.
Brooklyn
For New York—Raschi pitching, Collins playing first.
Furillo walked.
1 Nelson, pinch-hitting for Roe, popped to short.
Cox singled to right, Furillo stopping at second.
Reese walked, loading the bases.
For New York—Kuzava pitching.
2 Snider popped to third.
3 Robinson popped to second.

8th Inning
New York
For Brooklyn—Erskine pitching.
1 Berra flied to right.
2 Woodling lined to first.
Bauer walked.
3 Martin flied to center.
Brooklyn
1 Campanella struck out.
Branca ejected from game by plate umpire Goetz.
Hodges safe at first on McDougald's wide throw to first.
2 Pafko, pinch-hitting for Shuba, fanned.
3 Furillo flied to left.

9th Inning
New York
For Brooklyn—Holmes playing left.
1 Kuzava grounded to second.
McDougald singled to center.
2 Rizzuto fouled to Cox.
3 Mantle grounded to first.
Brooklyn
1 Morgan, pinch-hitting for Erskine, flied to left.
2 Cox grounded to second.
3 Reese flied to left.

1952 WORLD SERIES COMPOSITE BOX

	Wins	Composite Line Score											
New York Yankees (A.L.)	4	0	1	1	3	7	6	3	4	1	0	0	– 26
Brooklyn Dodgers (N.L.)	3	0	2	2	1	5	3	1	3	2	0	1	– 20

Manager	Regular Season W	L	Pct.	G. Ahead
Casey Stengel	95	60	.617	2
Chuck Dressen	96	57	.627	4.5

BATTING AND FIELDING

WORLD SERIES STATISTICS

	Pos	G	AB	R	H	2B	3B	HR	RBI	BB	SO	SB	BA	SA	PO	A	E
NEW YORK YANKEES																	
Johnny Mize	1b-ph	5	15	3	6	1	0	3	6	3	1	0	**.400**	**1.067**	25	3	0
Billy Martin	2b	7	23	2	5	0	0	1	4	2	2	0	.217	.348	16	16	1
Phil Rizzuto	ss	7	27	2	4	1	0	0	0	5	2	0	.148	.185	13	17	1
Gil McDougald	3b	7	25	5	5	0	0	1	3	5	2	1	.200	.320	4	15	**4**
Hank Bauer	rf-ph	7	18	2	1	0	0	0	1	4	3	0	.056	.056	10	0	0
Mickey Mantle	cf	7	**29**	**5**	**10**	1	**1**	2	3	3	4	0	.345	.655	16	0	0
Gene Woodling	lf-ph	7	23	4	8	1	**1**	1	1	3	3	0	.348	.609	18	0	1
Yogi Berra	c	7	28	2	6	1	0	2	3	2	4	0	.214	.464	59	7	1
Joe Collins	1b-pr	6	12	1	0	0	0	0	0	1	3	0	.000	.000	27	1	0
Irv Noren	lf-ph-rf	4	10	0	3	0	0	0	1	1	3	0	.300	.300	2	0	0
Ralph Houk	ph	1	1	0	0	0	0	0	0	0	0	0	.000	.000			
Jim Brideweser		Did not play															
Charlie Silvera		Did not play															
Loren Babe		Did not play															
Allie Reynolds	p	4	7	0	0	0	0	0	0	0	2	0	.000	.000	2	1	2
Vic Raschi	p	3	6	0	1	0	0	0	1	1	2	0	.167	.167	0	1	0
Ed Lopat	p	2	3	0	1	0	0	0	1	1	1	0	.333	.333	0	1	0
Johnny Sain	ph-p	2	3	0	0	0	0	0	0	0	0	0	.000	.000	0	2	0
Ewell Blackwell	p	1	1	0	0	0	0	0	0	0	0	0	.000	.000	0	1	0
Bob Kuzava	p	1	1	0	0	0	0	0	0	0	0	0	.000	.000	0	0	0
Ray Scarborough	p	1	0	0	0	0	0	0	0	0	0	0	—	—	0	1	0
Tom Gorman	p	1	0	0	0	0	0	0	0	0	0	0	—	—	0	0	0
Bill Miller		Did not play															
Jim McDonald		Did not play															
Joe Ostrowski		Did not play															
team total		7	232	26	50	5	2	10	24	31	32	1	.216	.384	192	66	10

Double Plays—7
Left on Bases—48

REGULAR SEASON STATISTICS

		Main Pos	G	AB	R	H	2B	3B	HR	RBI	BB	SO	SB	BA	SA
Johnny Mize		ph-1b	78	137	9	36	9	0	4	29	11	15	0	.263	.416
Billy Martin		2b	109	363	32	97	13	3	3	33	22	31	3	.267	.344
Phil Rizzuto		ss	152	578	89	147	24	10	2	43	67	42	17	.254	.341
Gil McDougald		3b	155	555	65	146	16	5	11	78	57	73	6	.263	.369
Hank Bauer		of	141	553	86	162	31	6	17	74	50	61	6	.293	.463
Mickey Mantle		of	142	549	94	171	37	7	23	87	75	**111**	4	.311	.530
Gene Woodling		of	122	408	58	126	19	6	12	63	59	31	1	.309	.473
Yogi Berra		c	142	534	97	146	17	1	30	98	66	24	2	.273	.478
Joe Collins		1b	122	428	69	120	16	8	18	59	55	47	4	.280	.481
Irv Noren	a	of	93	272	36	64	13	2	5	21	26	34	4	.235	.353
Ralph Houk		c	9	6	0	2	0	0	0	0	1	0	0	.333	.333
Jim Brideweser		ss	42	38	12	10	0	0	0	2	3	5	0	.263	.263
Charlie Silvera		c	20	55	4	18	3	0	0	11	5	2	0	.327	.382
Loren Babe		3b	12	21	1	2	1	0	0	0	4	4	1	.095	.143
Allie Reynolds		p	41	85	6	13	0	1	0	7	5	22	0	.153	.176
Vic Raschi		p	31	69	4	13	2	0	0	2	8	27	0	.188	.217
Ed Lopat		p	20	52	7	9	2	0	0	4	3	5	0	.173	.212
Johnny Sain		p	47	71	4	19	4	1	1	14	3	5	0	.268	.394
Ewell Blackwell	b	p	5	5	0	1	0	0	0	1	0	1	0	.200	.200
Bob Kuzava		p	28	43	2	4	0	0	0	1	5	14	0	.193	.193
Ray Scarborough	c	p	9	14	1	5	1	0	0	0	0	0	0	.357	.429
Tom Gorman		p	12	23	1	2	0	0	0	1	2	14	0	.087	.087
Bill Miller		p	21	28	3	6	2	0	0	2	0	8	0	.214	.286
Jim McDonald		p	26	19	3	6	3	0	0	3	3	6	0	.316	.474
Joe Ostrowski		p	20	8	0	0	0	0	0	0	0	2	0	.000	.000
team total			154	5294	727	**1411**	221	**56**	129	672	566	652	52	**.267**	.403

a—from Washington; b—from Cincinnati; c—from Boston (A)
Bob Cerv (of), Bobby Brown (3b), Andy Carey (3b), Johnny Hopp (1b), Jerry Coleman (2b), Jackie Jensen (of), Charlie Keller (of), Kal Segrist (2b), Archie Wilson (of), Tom Morgan (p), Bobby Hogue (p), Johnny Schmitz (p), Harry Schaeffer (p), and Art Shallock also played for the Yankees during the season.

WORLD SERIES STATISTICS

	Pos	G	AB	R	H	2B	3B	HR	RBI	BB	SO	SB	BA	SA	PO	A	E
BROOKLYN DODGERS																	
Gil Hodges	1b	7	21	1	0	0	0	0	1	5	**6**	0	.000	.000	**60**	5	1
Jackie Robinson	2b	7	23	4	4	0	0	1	2	**7**	5	**2**	.174	.304	10	**20**	0
Pee Wee Reese	ss	7	**29**	4	**10**	0	0	1	4	2	2	1	.345	.448	15	18	2
Billy Cox	3b	7	27	4	8	**2**	0	0	0	3	4	0	.296	.370	9	14	1
Carl Furillo	rf	7	23	1	4	**2**	0	0	0	3	3	0	.174	.261	13	0	0
Duke Snider	cf	7	**29**	**5**	**10**	**2**	0	**4**	**8**	1	5	1	.345	.828	23	0	0
Andy Pafko	of-rf-ph	7	21	0	4	0	0	0	2	0	4	0	.190	.190	12	1	0
Roy Campanella	c	7	28	0	6	0	0	0	1	1	**6**	0	.214	.214	39	5	0
George Shuba	of-ph	4	10	0	3	1	0	0	0	0	4	0	.300	.400	7	0	0
Rocky Nelson	ph	4	3	0	0	0	0	0	0	1	2	0	.000	.000			
Tommy Holmes	lf	3	1	0	0	0	0	0	0	0	0	0	.000	.000	2	0	0
Bobby Morgan	3b-ph	2	1	0	0	0	0	0	0	0	0	0	.000	.000	0	1	0
Sandy Amoros	pr	1	0	0	0	0	0	0	0	0	0	0	—	—			
Rocky Bridges		Did not play															
Rube Walker		Did not play															
Dick Williams		Did not play															
Joe Black	p	3	6	0	0	0	0	0	0	1	**6**	0	.000	.000	1	2	0
Carl Erskine	p	3	6	1	0	0	0	0	0	0	1	0	.000	.000	0	2	0
Billy Loes	p	2	3	0	1	0	0	0	0	0	1	1	.333	.333	0	2	0
Preacher Roe	p	3	2	0	0	0	0	0	0	0	0	0	.000	.000	1	0	0
Ken Lehman	p	1	0	0	0	0	0	0	0	0	0	0	—	—	0	1	0
Johnny Rutherford	p	1	0	0	0	0	0	0	0	0	0	0	—	—	0	0	0
Ben Wade		Did not play															
Clem Labine		Did not play															
Ralph Branca		Did not play															
Clyde King		Did not play															
Ray Moore		Did not play															
Joe Landrum		Did not play															
team total		7	233	20	50	7	0	6	18	24	49	5	.215	.322	192	71	4

Double Plays—4
Left on Bases—52

REGULAR SEASON STATISTICS

		Main Pos	G	AB	R	H	2B	3B	HR	RBI	BB	SO	SB	BA	SA
Gil Hodges		1b	153	508	87	129	27	1	32	102	107	90	2	.254	.500
Jackie Robinson		2b	149	510	104	157	17	3	19	75	106	40	24	.308	.465
Pee Wee Reese		ss	149	559	94	152	18	8	6	58	86	59	**30**	.272	.365
Billy Cox		3b	116	455	56	118	12	3	6	34	25	32	10	.259	.338
Carl Furillo		of	134	425	52	105	18	1	8	59	31	33	1	.247	.351
Duke Snider		of	144	534	80	162	25	7	21	92	55	77	7	.303	.494
Andy Pafko		of	150	551	76	158	17	5	19	85	64	48	4	.287	.439
Roy Campanella		c	128	468	73	126	18	1	22	97	57	59	8	.269	.453
George Shuba		of	94	256	40	78	12	1	9	40	38	29	1	.305	.465
Rocky Nelson		ph	37	39	6	10	1	0	0	3	7	4	0	.256	.282
Tommy Holmes	d	ph	31	36	2	4	1	0	0	1	4	4	0	.111	.139
Bobby Morgan		3b	67	191	36	45	8	0	7	16	46	35	2	.236	.387
Sandy Amoros		of	20	44	10	11	3	1	0	3	5	14	1	.250	.364
Rocky Bridges		2b	51	56	9	11	3	0	0	2	7	9	0	.196	.250
Rube Walker		c	46	139	9	36	8	0	1	19	8	17	0	.259	.338
Dick Williams		of	36	68	13	21	4	1	0	11	2	10	0	.309	.397
Joe Black		p	57	36	1	5	0	0	0	5	0	15	0	.139	.139
Carl Erskine		p	34	66	7	10	1	0	0	2	3	19	0	.152	.167
Billy Loes		p	40	54	3	5	0	0	0	1	2	13	0	.093	.093
Preacher Roe		p	27	57	2	4	0	0	0	3	3	19	0	.070	.070
Ken Lehman		p	4	4	1	0	0	0	0	0	2	0	0	.000	.000
Johnny Rutherford		p	22	31	3	9	1	0	0	3	1	11	0	.290	.323
Ben Wade		p	37	60	7	7	3	0	3	6	1	22	0	.117	.317
Clem Labine		p	26	22	0	1	1	0	0	0	0	9	0	.045	.091
Ralph Branca		p	16	19	0	3	0	0	0	2	0	9	0	.158	.158
Clyde King		p	23	5	0	0	0	0	0	0	0	1	0	.000	.000
Ray Moore		p	14	3	0	0	0	0	0	0	0	1	0	.000	.000
Joe Landrum		p	9	8	0	1	0	0	0	1	0	4	0	.125	.125
team total			155	5266	**775**	1380	199	32	**153**	**725**	**663**	699	**90**	.262	**.399**

d—from Philadelphia (N)
Cal Abrams (of), Steve Lembo (c), Chris Van Cuyk (p), Jim Hughes (p), Johnny Schmitz (p), Ron Negray (p), and Bud Podbielen (p) also played for the Dodgers during the season.

PITCHING

WORLD SERIES STATISTICS

	G	GS	CG	IP	H	R	ER	BB	SO	W	L	SV	ERA
NEW YORK YANKEES													
Allie Reynolds	**4**	2	**1**	20 1/3	12	4	4	6	**18**	**2**	1	**1**	1.77
Vic Raschi	3	2	**1**	17	12	3	3	8	**18**	**2**	0	0	**1.59**
Ed Lopat	2	2	0	11 1/3	14	6	6	4	3	0	1	0	4.76
Johnny Sain	1	0	0	6	6	2	2	3	3	0	1	0	3.00
Ewell Blackwell	1	1	0	5	4	4	4	3	4	0	0	0	7.20
Bob Kuzava	1	0	0	2 2/3	0	0	0	0	2	0	0	1	0.00
Ray Scarborough	1	0	0	1	1	1	1	0	1	0	0	0	9.00
Tom Gorman	1	0	0	2/3	1	0	0	0	0	0	0	0	0.00
Bill Miller	Did not play												
Jim McDonald	Did not play												
Joe Ostrowski	Did not play												
team total	7	7	2	64	50	20	20	24	49	4	3	2	2.81
BROOKLYN DODGERS													
Joe Black	3	**3**	1	**21 1/3**	**15**	6	6	8	9	1	**2**	0	2.53
Carl Erskine	3	2	**1**	18	12	**9**	**9**	**10**	10	1	1	0	4.50
Preacher Roe	3	1	0	11 1/3	9	4	4	6	7	1	0	0	3.18
Billy Loes	2	1	0	10 1/3	11	6	5	5	5	0	1	0	4.35
Ken Lehman	1	0	0	2	2	0	0	1	0	0	0	0	0.00
Johnny Rutherford	1	0	0	1	1	1	1	1	1	0	0	0	9.00
Ben Wade	Did not play												
Clem Labine	Did not play												
Ralph Branca	Did not play												
Clyde King	Did not play												
Ray Moore	Did not play												
Joe Landrum	Did not play												
team total	7	7	2	64	50	26	25	31	32	3	4	0	3.52

REGULAR SEASON STATISTICS

		G	GS	CG	IP	H	ER	BB	SO	W	L	Pct	SV	ShO	ERA
NEW YORK YANKEES															
Allie Reynolds		35	29	24	244	194	56	97	**160**	20	8	.714	6	**6**	**2.07**
Vic Raschi		31	31	13	223	174	78	91	127	16	6	.727	0	4	2.78
Ed Lopat		20	19	10	149	127	42	53	56	10	5	.667	0	2	2.54
Johnny Sain		35	16	8	148	149	57	38	57	11	6	.647	7	0	3.47
Ewell Blackwell	b	5	2	0	16	12	1	12	7	1	0	1.000	1	0	0.56
Bob Kuzava		28	12	6	133	115	51	63	67	8	8	.500	3	1	3.45
Ray Scarborough	c	9	4	1	34	27	11	15	13	5	1	.833	0	0	2.91
Tom Gorman		12	6	1	61	63	31	22	31	6	2	.750	1	1	4.57
Bill Miller		21	13	5	88	78	34	49	45	4	6	.400	0	2	3.48
Jim McDonald		26	5	1	69	71	27	40	20	3	4	.429	0	0	3.52
Joe Ostrowski		20	1	0	40	56	25	17	17	2	2	.500	2	0	5.63
team total		154	154	72	1381	1240	**482**	581	666	**95**	50	**.617**	27	**17**	**3.14**
BROOKLYN DODGERS															
Joe Black		56	2	1	142	102	34	41	85	15	4	.789	15	0	2.15
Carl Erskine		33	26	10	207	167	72	71	131	14	6	.700	2	4	2.70
Preacher Roe		27	25	8	159	163	55	39	83	11	2	.846	0	2	3.11
Billy Loes		39	21	8	187	154	62	71	115	13	8	.619	1	4	2.70
Ken Lehman		4	3	0	15	19	9	6	7	1	2	.333	0	0	5.40
Johnny Rutherford		22	11	4	97	97	46	29	29	7	7	.500	2	0	4.27
Ben Wade		37	24	5	180	166	72	94	118	11	9	.550	3	1	3.60
Clem Labine		25	9	0	77	76	44	47	43	8	4	.667	0	0	5.14
Ralph Branca		16	7	2	61	52	26	21	26	4	2	.667	0	0	3.84
Clyde King		23	0	0	43	56	24	12	17	2	0	1.000	0	0	5.02
Ray Moore		14	2	0	28	29	15	26	11	1	2	.333	0	0	4.82
Joe Landrum		9	5	2	38	46	22	10	17	1	3	.250	0	0	5.21
team total		155	155	45	**.399**	1295	549	544	**773**	**96**	57	**.627**	24	11	3.53

Total Attendance—340,906 Average Attendance—48,701 Winning Player's Share—$5,983 Losing Player's Share—$4,201

1953
Five Times Five Equals Five

It was the clash of the gods, the New York Yankees and the Brooklyn Dodgers, far and away the best of major-league baseball. Casey Stengel's Yankees easily won an unprecedented fifth straight American League pennant and came in search of a matching fifth consecutive World Series crown. The Dodgers also had a record of excellence over the same five years, winning three pennants and losing out on the last day of the season in 1950 and 1951. But in the last four World Series, the Yankees had reigned supreme. A high-production attack centered around budding superstar Mickey Mantle and free-swinging Yogi Berra, with a variety of steady hitters setting the table for these two sluggers. Stengel still had four excellent veteran pitchers in Eddie Lopat, Johnny Sain, Vic Raschi, and Allie Reynolds, but young Whitey Ford, a stylish lefty back after two years of military service, led the staff with 18 wins.

The Dodgers of Chuck Dressen, however, had every hope of taking the Series title away from the Yanks. The Bums smashed the ball all over Ebbets Field and the other National League parks, with Duke Snider, Roy Campanella, Gil Hodges, Carl Furillo, and Jackie Robinson leading the assault on pitchers. Pee Wee Reese, Billy Cox, and rookie Jim Gilliam kept the infield air-tight in addition to contributing timely batting. Carl Erskine paced the pitching staff with 20 wins, while Russ Meyer, Billy Loes, Preacher Roe, and reliever Clem Labine followed with double-figure win totals. Summed up, the Dodgers were looking to post their first Series win ever, while the Yanks were flirting with the possibility of capturing five straight World Championships.

The Yanks got off on the right foot in game one at Yankee Stadium by scoring four runs in the first inning off Carl Erskine, with Billy Martin's three-run triple the heart of the outburst. But the Brooklyn power struck back at Allie Reynolds and reliever Sain, finally tying the score at 5–5 in the top of the seventh. But steady Joe Collins sent the Yanks back ahead in the bottom of the seventh with a solo homer off Labine, and three more Yankee runs in the eighth put the game away 9–5. Crafty veterans Lopat and Roe matched up in the second game, and while the Dodgers outhit the Yankees 9 to 5, the Bronx Bombers won the game 4–2. A solo homer by Martin tied the score at 2–2 in the seventh, and a two-run clout by Mantle in the eighth iced away the victory.

Without the need for a travel delay, the Series moved on the next day, October 2, to Ebbets Field, with Erskine facing Raschi. After lasting only one inning in game one, Erskine came back strong in the third game, fanning a Series-record 14 batters with a fine overhand curve ball. The strikeouts seemed an empty prize when the Yanks scored in the eighth to knot the score at 2–2, but a Campanella homer off Raschi in the bottom of the inning gave Erskine a 3–2 win. The Bums then evened the Series, knocking Ford out with a three-run first inning and taking a 7–3 fourth-game decision. Loes got the win, Labine got the save, and Snider got four RBI's out of two doubles and a home run. Both managers counted on second-line hurlers in game five, Johnny Podres of Brooklyn and Jim McDonald of New York. The Dodgers again outhit the Yankees but lost the game, dropping an 11–7 slugfest. Meyer relieved Podres with the bases loaded in the third and immediately served up a grand-slammer to Mantle which put the Yanks irretrievably ahead.

On the edge of defeat, the Dodgers brought back Erskine on two days' rest in game six in Yankee Stadium. The Dodger righty, however, couldn't relive his third-game gem, coughing up three runs in the first two innings. The Bums came back with one run off Ford in the sixth and a pair off Reynolds in the top of the ninth on Furillo's homer to tie the contest at 3–3, but the Yanks won it in the bottom of the ninth off Labine with a walk to Bauer, an infield hit by Mantle, and Martin's run-scoring single. Martin's inspired .500 batting average led all batters, while the .300 team average for the Dodgers could not salve the frustration of dropping their seventh straight World Series without a victory. The front office showed its annoyance by answering manager Dressen's demand for a two-year contract with a termination notice.

Game 1 September 30 at New York

Brooklyn	Pos	AB	R	H	RBI	PO	A	E
Gilliam	2b	5	1	2	1	3	3	0
Reese	ss	3	0	0	0	3	3	0
Snider	cf	5	0	2	0	3	0	0
Robinson	lf	4	0	0	0	0	0	0
Campanella	c	4	1	1	0	6	3	0
Hodges	1b	5	1	3	1	7	0	0
Furillo	rf	4	0	1	1	2	0	1
Cox	3b	5	1	2	0	0	1	0
Erskine	p	0	0	0	0	0	0	0
a Belardi		1	0	0	0	0	0	0
Hughes	p	1	0	0	0	0	0	1
b Shuba		1	1	1	2	0	0	0
Labine	p	1	0	0	0	0	1	0
Wade	p	0	0	0	0	0	0	0
Totals		39	5	12	5	24	11	2

a Struck out for Erskine in 2nd.
b Homered for Hughes in 6th.

Doubles—Cox, Sain, Snider.
Triples—Bauer, Martin. Home Runs—Berra, Collins, Gilliam, Hodges, Shuba.
Stolen Base—Martin. Hit by Pitcher—Campanella (by Reynolds).
Left on Bases—Brooklyn 12, New York 6.
Umpires—Grieve (A), Stewart (N), Hurley (A), Gore (N), Soar (A), Dascoli (N).
Attendance—69,374. Time of Game—3:10.

Bkn.	000	013	100
N.Y.	400	010	13x

New York	Pos	AB	R	H	RBI	PO	A	E
McDougald	3b	5	0	0	0	3	2	0
Collins	lb	4	2	2	2	6	0	0
Bauer	rf	5	1	2	1	4	0	0
Berra	c	4	1	2	1	8	2	0
Mantle	cf	3	1	1	0	0	0	0
Woodling	lf	3	1	1	0	4	0	0
Martin	2b	4	1	3	3	1	2	0
Rizzuto	ss	3	1	0	0	1	1	0
Reynolds	p	1	0	0	0	0	0	0
Sain	p	2	1	1	2	0	0	0
Totals		34	9	12	9	27	7	0

Pitching	IP	H	R	ER	BB	SO
Brooklyn						
Erskine	1	2	4	4	3	1
Hughes	4	3	1	1	1	3
Labine (L)	$1\frac{2}{3}$	4	1	1	0	1
Wade	$1\frac{1}{3}$	3	3	3	1	2
New York						
Reynolds	$5\frac{1}{3}$	7	4	4	3	6
Sain (W)	$3\frac{2}{3}$	5	1	1	1	0

1st Inning
Brooklyn
Gilliam singled through Reynolds' legs.
1 Reese flied to right.
2 Snider grounded to second, moving Gilliam to second.
3 Robinson grounded to short.
New York
1 McDougald popped to second.
Collins walked.
Bauer tripled to right-center, scoring Collins.
2 Berra struck out.
Mantle walked.
Woodling walked, filling the bases.
Martin cleaned the bases with a triple over Robinson's head in left-center.
3 Rizzuto grounded to third.

2nd Inning
Brooklyn
Campanella was hit by a pitched ball.
1 Hodges flied to left.
2 Furillo called out on strikes.
Cox doubled into the left field corner, Campanella going to third.
3 Belardi, pinch-hitting for Erskine, struck out.
New York
For Brooklyn—Hughes pitching.
1 Reynolds struck out.
2 McDougald grounded to short.
3 Collins popped to short.

3rd Inning
Brooklyn
1 Gilliam struck out.
Reese walked.
2 Snider fanned.
3 Robinson lined to second.
New York
1 Bauer took a called third strike.
2 Berra struck out, but had to be thrown out, Campanella to Hodges on a dropped third strike.
Mantle singled to right.
3 Mantle was caught trying to steal second, Campanella to Reese.

4th Inning
Brooklyn
1 Campanella popped to short.
2 Hodges looked at a called third strike.
Furillo walked.
3 Cox flied to right.
New York
1 Woodling flied to center.
Martin beat out a bunt and went all the way to third on a double error (Hughes' throw to first went low into right and Furillo's return throw went past third for the second error of the play).
2 Rizzuto grounded to short, Martin holding.
Reynolds walked.
3 McDougald forced Reynolds at second, Reese to Gilliam.

5th Inning
Brooklyn
1 Hughes called out on strikes.
Gilliam homered into the lower right field seats.
2 Reese flied to right.
Snider doubled to right-center.
Robinson walked.
3 Campanella flied to deep left.

5th Inning (continued)
New York
1 Collins flied to Snider who made a leaping catch in deep right-center.
2 Bauer flied to right.
Berra homered into the lower right field stands.
3 Mantle grounded to second.

6th Inning
Brooklyn
Hodges homered into the lower left field stands.
1 Furillo flied to right.
Cox singled to left-center.
Shuba, pinch-hitting for Hughes, hit a two-run homer into the lower right field stands, just out of Bauer's reach.
For New York—Sain came in to pitch.
2 Gilliam grounded to second.
Reese walked.
Snider singled to right, Reese going to third.
3 Robinson grounded to third.
New York
For Brooklyn—Labine pitching.
Woodling singled to right center.
1 Martin forced Woodling at second, Gilliam to Reese.
2 Martin out trying to steal, Campanella to Gilliam.
3 Rizzuto grounded back to the pitcher.

7th Inning
Brooklyn
Campanella singled to left.
Hodges got a single off Rizzuto's glove, moving Campanella to third.
Furillo singled to center, scoring Campanella with Hodges stopping at second.
1 Cox forced Hodges at third on a bunt, Berra to McDougald.
2 Labine forced Cox at third on a bunt, Berra to McDougald.
3 Gilliam fouled to Berra.
New York
1 Sain took a called third strike.
2 McDougald flied to center.
Collins homered into the right field stands.
Bauer singled past third.
Berra singled to right, Bauer going to second.
For Brooklyn—Wade came in to pitch.
3 Mantle called out on strikes.

8th Inning
Brooklyn
1 Reese flied to left.
2 Snider grounded to first.
3 Robinson flied to left.
New York
1 Woodling grounded to second.
Martin singled to right-center.
Martin stole second.
Rizzuto walked.
Sain doubled to right-center, scoring Martin and Rizzuto.
2 McDougald lined to right.
Collins singled to right, Sain scoring.
3 Bauer fanned.

9th Inning
Brooklyn
1 Campanella lined to third.
Hodges singled to left.
2 Furillo fouled to Berra.
3 Cox grounded to third.

Game 2 October 1 at New York

Brooklyn	Pos	AB	R	H	RBI	PO	A	E
Gilliam	2b	5	0	0	0	1	2	0
Reese	ss	3	0	2	0	1	0	0
Snider	cf	5	0	0	0	2	0	0
Robinson	lf	4	0	1	0	3	0	0
Campanella	c	4	0	0	0	5	3	0
Hodges	1b	3	1	2	0	9	1	0
Furillo	rf	4	1	2	0	3	0	1
Cox	3b	3	0	1	2	0	2	0
Roe	p	3	0	0	0	1	1	0
a Williams		1	0	1	0	0	0	0
Totals		35	2	9	2	24	10	1

a Singled for Roe in 9th.

Doubles—Cox, Furillo, Rizzuto.
Triple—Reese. Home Runs—Mantle, Martin. Stolen Base—Hodges. Sacrifice Hit—Rizzuto. Double Play—Martin to Rizzuto to Collins. Hit by Pitcher—McDougald (by Roe). Left on Bases—Brooklyn 10, New York 5. Umpires—Stewart, Hurley, Gore, Grieve, Dascoli, Soar. Attendance—66,786. Time of Game—2:42.

New York	Pos	AB	R	H	RBI	PO	A	E
Woodling	lf	3	1	0	0	1	0	0
Collins	1b	3	0	0	0	15	0	0
Bauer	rf	4	1	1	0	1	0	0
Berra	c	3	0	0	1	4	0	0
Mantle	cf	3	1	1	2	4	0	0
McDougald	3b	3	0	0	0	0	3	0
Martin	2b	3	1	1	1	1	5	0
Rizzuto	ss	2	0	1	0	1	5	0
Lopat	p	3	0	0	0	0	2	0
Totals		27	4	5	4	27	15	0

```
Bkn.  000 200 000
N.Y.  100 000 12x
```

Pitching	IP	H	R	ER	BB	SO
Brooklyn						
Roe (L)	8	5	4	4	4	4
New York						
Lopat (W)	9	9	2	2	4	3

1st Inning
Brooklyn
1 Gilliam grounded to short. Reese tripled to right when Bauer fell, Mantle retrieving the ball.
2 Snider fouled to Berra.
3 Robinson flied to center.
New York
Woodling walked.
Collins walked.
1 Bauer flied to right, Woodling going to third after the catch.
2 Berra flied to right, Woodling scoring after the catch and Collins to second on the throw to the plate. Mantle walked. McDougald was hit by a pitch, loading the bases.
3 Martin lined to Snider in very short center.

2nd Inning
Brooklyn
1 Campanella grounded to third. Hodges walked.
2 Furillo grounded to third, advancing Hodges to second. Hodges stole third. Cox intentionally walked.
3 Roe grounded off Lopat's glove to Collins who made the putout.
New York
Rizzuto doubled to right and went to third as Furillo fumbled the ball.
1 Lopat struck out.
2 Woodling hit into a fielder's choice, Gilliam to Campanella to get Rizzuto at the plate.
3 Collins grounded to first.

3rd Inning
Brooklyn
1 Gilliam popped to second.
2 Reese flied to center.
3 Snider flied to deep center.
New York
1 Bauer grounded to third.
2 Berra grounded out, Hodges to Roe.
3 Mantle grounded to third.

4th Inning
Brooklyn
1 Robinson flied to left.
2 Campanella grounded to second. Hodges singled to center. Furillo singled to right, Hodges advancing to third. Cox doubled into the left field corner, scoring both Hodges and Furillo.
3 Roe struck out.
New York
1 McDougald tapped out, Campanella to Hodges. Martin singled to right.
2 Rizzuto sacrificed Martin to second, Campanella to Hodges.
3 Lopat grounded to first.

5th Inning
Brooklyn
1 Gilliam bunted out, Lopat to Collins. Reese singled to center.
2 Snider struck out. Robinson singled to left, Reese going to second.
3 Campanella grounded to second.
New York
1 Woodling struck out.
2 Collins popped to second.
3 Bauer fanned.

6th Inning
Brooklyn
1 Hodges flied to right. Furillo doubled off the right-center field wall.
2 Cox grounded to third, Furillo holding second.
3 Roe struck out.
New York
Berra walked.
1 Mantle flied to left.
2 Berra trapped between first and second when McDougald missed a pitch. Berra was out, Campanella to Gilliam.
3 McDougald grounded back to the mound.

7th Inning
Brooklyn
1 Gilliam grounded to short. Reese walked.
2 Snider grounded to second, Reese moving to second.
3 Robinson fouled to Collins.
New York
Martin homered into the lower left field stands.
1 Rizzuto flied to left.
2 Lopat took a called third strike.
3 Woodling grounded to short.

8th Inning
Brooklyn
1 Campanella grounded to short. Hodges singled to left.
2,3 Furillo grounded into a double play, Martin to Rizzuto to Collins.
New York
1 Collins flied to right. Bauer singled to left.
2 Berra flied to center. Mantle hit a two-run homer into the lower left field stands.
3 McDougald flied to left.

9th Inning
Brooklyn
1 Cox grounded to short. Williams, pinch-hitting for Roe, singled to left.
2 Gilliam flied to center. Reese walked.
3 Snider grounded to second.

Game 3 October 2 at Brooklyn

New York	Pos	AB	R	H	RBI	PO	A	E
McDougald	3b	4	0	1	1	2	3	0
c Noren		0	0	0	0	0	0	0
Collins	1b	5	0	0	0	8	0	0
Bauer	rf	4	1	1	0	1	0	0
Berra	c	1	0	1	0	4	1	0
Mantle	cf	4	0	0	0	2	0	0
Woodling	lf	4	0	1	1	1	0	0
Martin	2b	3	1	1	0	3	4	0
Rizzuto	ss	3	0	1	0	3	3	0
a Bollweg		1	0	0	0	0	0	0
Raschi	p	2	0	0	0	1	1	0
b Mize		1	0	0	0	0	0	0
Totals		32	2	6	2	24	12	0

a Struck out for Rizzuto in 9th.
b Struck out for Raschi in 9th.
c Walked for McDougald in 9th.

Double—Robinson. Home Run—Campanella. Sacrifice Hits—Cox, Raschi. Double Play—Rizzuto to Martin to Collins. Hit by Pitcher—Berra 2 (by Erskine). Wild Pitch—Erskine. Balk—Raschi. Left on Bases—New York 9, Brooklyn 8. Umpires—Hurley, Gore, Grieve, Stewart, Soar, Dascoli. Attendance—35,270. Time of Game—3:00.

Brooklyn	Pos	AB	R	H	RBI	PO	A	E
Gilliam	2b	4	0	1	0	1	2	0
Reese	ss	4	0	1	0	1	4	0
Snider	cf	3	1	1	0	3	0	0
Hodges	1b	2	0	1	0	8	1	0
Campanella	c	4	1	1	1	14	0	0
Furillo	rf	4	0	0	0	1	0	0
Robinson	lf	4	1	3	1	1	0	0
Thompson	lf	0	0	0	0	0	0	0
Cox	3b	3	0	1	0	1	0	0
Erskine	p	3	0	1	0	1	2	0
Totals		31	3	9	3	27	10	0

```
N.Y.  000 010 010
Bkn.  000 011 01x
```

Pitching	IP	H	R	ER	BB	SO
New York						
Raschi (L)	8	9	3	3	3	4
Brooklyn						
Erskine (W)	9	6	2	2	3	14

1st Inning
New York
1 McDougald struck out.
2 Collins struck out.
3 Bauer grounded to short.
Brooklyn
Gilliam singled off Martin's chest.
1 Gilliam caught stealing second, Berra to Rizzuto.
2 Reese called out on strikes.
3 Snider grounded out, off Raschi's glove to Rizzuto who threw to Collins.

2nd Inning
New York
Berra walked and went to second as ball four was a wild pitch.
1 Mantle looked at a called third strike.
2 Woodling grounded out, Hodges to Erskine, Berra advancing to third. Martin walked.
3 Rizzuto took a called third strike.
Brooklyn
Hodges singled to left.
1 Campanella struck out.
2,3 Furillo grounded into a double play, Rizzuto to Martin to Collins.

3rd Inning
New York
1 Raschi took a called third strike.
2 McDougald flied to left.
3 Collins struck out.
Brooklyn
1 Robinson flied to right.
2 Cox grounded to third.
3 Erskine bunted out to third.

4th Inning
New York
1 Bauer grounded to short. Berra was hit by a pitched ball.
2 Mantle struck out.
3 Woodling popped to short.
Brooklyn
1 Gilliam grounded to second.
2 Reese popped to third. Snider walked. Hodges walked.
3 Campanella forced Hodges at second, Martin to Rizzuto.

5th Inning
New York
Martin singled off Reese's glove. Rizzuto singled off Gilliam's glove, Martin going to second.
1 Raschi moved both runners up with a sacrifice, Erskine to Gilliam. McDougald singled on a hard smash to third, Martin scoring with Rizzuto going to third.
2 Collins took a called third strike.
3 Bauer grounded to second.

5th Inning (continued)
Brooklyn
1 Furillo lined to center. Robinson doubled off the right field screen. Robinson went to third on a balk. Cox credited with a sacrifice on a squeeze bunt, scoring Robinson as Martin's throw to the plate was not in time. Erskine singled to left, Cox stopping at second.
2 Gilliam fouled to Berra.
3 Reese grounded to second.

6th Inning
New York
Berra singled to right.
1 Mantle struck out.
2 Woodling struck out.
3 Martin flied to right.
Brooklyn
Snider singled to right. Hodges walked.
1 Campanella popped to Raschi on an attempted sacrifice.
2 Furillo called out on strikes. Robinson singled to left, scoring Snider with Hodges going to second.
3 Cox fanned.

7th Inning
New York
1 Rizzuto grounded to short.
2 Raschi grounded to short.
3 McDougald grounded to third.
Brooklyn
1 Erskine popped to second.
2 Gilliam flied to center. Reese walked.
3 Snider popped to short.

8th Inning
New York
1 Collins struck out. Bauer singled to center. Berra hit by a pitched ball.
2 Mantle struck out. Woodling singled to center, scoring Bauer and moving Berra to third.
3 Martin grounded to second.
Brooklyn
1 Hodges grounded to short. Campanella homered into the lower left field stands.
2 Furillo grounded to third. Robinson singled to center.
3 Cox fouled to Martin.

9th Inning
New York
For Brooklyn—Thompson playing left.
1 Bollweg, batting for Rizzuto, struck out.
2 Mize, batting for Raschi, struck out. (A new Series record by Erskine of 14 strikeouts.) Noren, batting for McDougald, walked.
3 Collins grounded back to the mound.

Game 4 October 3 at Brooklyn

New York	Pos	AB	R	H	RBI	PO	A	E
Mantle	cf	5	0	1	1	1	0	0
Collins	lb	4	0	0	0	9	1	0
Bauer	rf	4	0	1	0	4	0	0
Berra	c	4	0	2	0	4	0	0
Woodling	lf	3	1	1	0	1	0	0
Martin	2b	4	1	2	0	4	2	0
McDougald	3b	3	1	1	2	0	5	0
Rizzuto	ss	4	0	1	0	0	2	0
Ford	p	0	0	0	0	0	0	0
Gorman	p	1	0	0	0	1	0	0
a Bollweg		1	0	0	0	0	0	0
Sain	p	0	0	0	0	0	0	0
b Noren		1	0	0	0	0	0	0
Schallock	p	0	0	0	0	0	1	0
c Mize		1	0	0	0	0	0	0
Totals		35	3	9	3	24	11	0

a Struck out for Gorman in 5th.
b Popped out for Sain in 7th.
c Flied out for Schallock in 9th.

Doubles—Cox, Gilliam 3, Snider 2. Triple—Martin. Home Runs—McDougald, Snider. Sacrifice Hit—Loes. Wild Pitch—Ford. Left on Bases—New York 7, Brooklyn 7. Umpires—Gore, Grieve, Stewart, Hurley, Dascoli, Soar. Attendance—36,775. Time of Game—2:46.

N.Y.	000	020	001
Bkn.	300	102	10x

Brooklyn	Pos	AB	R	H	RBI	PO	A	E
Gilliam	2b	5	1	3	2	2	2	0
Reese	ss	5	0	0	0	2	1	0
Robinson	lf	4	0	1	1	1	0	0
Thompson	lf	0	0	0	0	0	1	0
Hodges	1b	4	1	0	0	5	1	0
Campanella	c	2	2	0	0	10	0	0
Snider	cf	4	1	3	4	5	0	0
Furillo	rf	4	1	1	0	2	0	0
Cox	3b	4	1	2	0	0	1	0
Loes	p	3	0	2	0	0	0	0
Labine	p	0	0	0	0	0	0	0
Totals		35	7	12	7	27	6	0

Pitching	IP	H	R	ER	BB	SO
New York						
Ford (L)	1	3	3	3	1	0
Gorman	3	4	1	1	0	1
Sain	2	3	2	2	0	1
Schallock	2	2	1	1	1	1
Brooklyn						
Loes (W)	*8	8	3	3	2	8
Labine (SV)	1	1	0	0	0	1

*Pitched to three batters in 9th.

1st Inning
New York
1 Mantle struck out.
2 Collins flied to left.
3 Bauer fouled to Hodges.
Brooklyn
Gilliam hit a ground-rule double into the right field seats as Bauer misjudged his high fly.
1 Reese grounded to first, advancing Gilliam to third.
Robinson singled to center, Gilliam scoring.
2 Hodges forced Robinson at second, McDougald to Martin.
Hodges went to second on a wild pitch.
Campanella got an intentional pass.
Snider doubled off the right field screen, scoring Hodges and Campanella.
3 Furillo lined to right.

2nd Inning
New York
1 Berra took a called third strike.
Woodling walked.
2 Martin forced Woodling at second, Hodges to Reese.
3 McDougald forced Martin at second, Reese to Gilliam.
Brooklyn
For New York—Gorman pitching.
1 Cox struck out.
2 Loes grounded out, Collins to Gorman.
Gilliam got a Texas League double as his high pop dropped in short left.
3 Reese grounded to third.

3rd Inning
New York
1 Rizzuto flied to right.
2 Gorman struck out.
3 Mantle flied to deep center.
Brooklyn
1 Robinson grounded to third.
2 Hodges popped to second.
3 Campanella fouled to Berra.

4th Inning
New York
1 Collins called out on strikes.
2 Bauer flied to right.
Berra singled to right.
3 Woodling grounded to second.
Brooklyn
1 Snider grounded to second.
Furillo singled to center.
2 Cox flied to left.
Loes singled along the right field line, advancing Furillo to third.
Gilliam doubled off the right field screen, Furillo scoring and Loes stopping at third.
3 Reese popped to second.

5th Inning
New York
Martin tripled to the center field gate.
McDougald hit a two-run homer into the lower left field stands.
1 Rizzuto flied to center.
2 Bollweg, batting for Gorman, was called out on strikes, but Campanella had to tag him after dropping the strike.
3 Mantle took a called third strike.
Brooklyn
For New York—Sain pitching.
1 Robinson grounded to short.
2 Hodges grounded to short.
3 Campanella grounded to third.

6th Inning
New York
1 Collins flied to center.
2 Bauer grounded to third.
Berra singled to center.
3 Woodling grounded to second.
Brooklyn
Snider homered over the right field screen.
1 Furillo took a called third strike.
Cox doubled to left.
Loes singled to center, Cox stopping at third.
2 Gilliam lined to right, Cox scoring after the catch and Loes going to second on the throw to the plate.
3 Reese grounded to third.

7th Inning
New York
1 Martin struck out.
2 McDougald flied to center.
Rizzuto singled to left.
3 Noren, pinch-hitting for Sain, popped to short.
Brooklyn
For New York—Schallock pitching.
1 Robinson lined to right.
2 Hodges struck out.
Campanella walked.
Snider doubled into the left field corner, scoring Campanella.
3 Furillo grounded to second.

8th Inning
New York
1 Mantle popped to second.
2 Collins struck out.
Bauer singled to center.
3 Berra grounded to first, Hodges tagging him along the base line.
Brooklyn
Cox singled to right.
1 Loes sacrificed Cox to second, Schallock to Martin covering first.
2 Gilliam flied to deep center, Cox went to third after the catch.
3 Reese lined to right.

9th Inning
New York
For Brooklyn—Thompson playing in left.
Woodling singled to right-center.
Martin singled to left, Woodling stopping at second.
McDougald walked, loading the bases.
For Brooklyn—Labine pitching.
1 Rizzuto struck out.
2 Mize, pinch-hitting for Schallock, flied to shallow center, with all runners holding.
Mantle singled to left, scoring Woodling but Martin also attempting
3 to score was out at the plate on Thompson's good peg to Campanella.

Game 5 October 4 at Brooklyn

New York	Pos	AB	R	H	RBI	PO	A	E
Woodling	lf	3	1	1	1	2	1	0
Collins	1b	5	2	1	0	6	2	0
Bauer	rf	3	1	0	0	1	0	0
Berra	c	4	2	2	1	6	0	0
Mantle	cf	5	1	1	4	1	0	0
Martin	2b	5	1	2	2	3	2	0
McDougald	3b	5	1	2	1	0	1	0
Rizzuto	ss	3	2	1	0	4	6	1
McDonald	p	2	0	1	1	3	0	0
Kuzave	p	1	0	0	0	0	0	0
Reynolds	p	0	0	0	0	0	0	0
Totals		36	11	11	10	27	12	1

Pitching	IP	H	R	ER	BB	SO
New York						
McDonald (W)	7⅔	12	6	5	0	3
Kuzava	⅔	2	1	1	0	1
Reynolds (SV)	⅔	0	0	0	0	0
Brooklyn						
Podres (L)	2⅔	1	5	1	2	0
Meyer	4⅓	8	4	3	4	5
Wade	1	1	1	1	0	0
Black	1	1	1	1	0	2

N.Y.	105	000	311
Bkn.	010	010	041

Brooklyn	Pos	AB	R	H	RBI	PO	A	E
Gilliam	2b	4	2	2	1	4	3	0
Reese	ss	5	0	1	0	0	1	0
Snider	cf	5	0	2	1	3	0	0
Robinson	lf	5	1	1	0	0	0	0
Campanella	c	4	2	3	0	8	3	0
Hodges	1b	4	0	2	0	11	1	1
Furillo	rf	4	1	1	1	0	0	0
Cox	3b	4	1	1	3	1	4	0
Podres	p	1	0	1	0	0	1	0
Meyer	p	1	0	0	0	0	1	0
a Belardi		1	0	0	0	0	0	0
Wade	p	0	0	0	0	0	0	0
b Shuba		0	0	0	0	0	0	0
c Williams		1	0	0	0	0	0	0
Black	p	0	0	0	0	0	0	0
Totals		39	7	14	6	27	14	1

a Grounded out for Meyer in 7th.
b Announced for Wade in 8th.
c Struck out for Shuba in 8th.

Doubles—Collins, McDonald. Triple—McDougald. Home Runs—Cox, Gilliam, Mantle, Martin, McDougald, Woodling. Stolen Base—Rizzuto. Sacrifice Hits—Bauer, McDonald. Double Plays—Woodling to Berra, Rizzuto to Collins, Martin to Rizzuto to Collins. Hit by Pitchers—Bauer (by Podres), Gilliam (by McDonald). Left on Bases—New York 7, Brooklyn 6. Umpires—Grieve, Stewart, Hurley, Gore, Soar, Dascoli. Attendance—36,775. Time of Game—3:02.

1st Inning
New York
Woodling homered into the lower left field stands.
1 Collins flied to center.
2 Bauer grounded to short.
3 Berra lined to center.
Brooklyn
Gilliam singled to left.
1 Reese flied to center.
2 Snider struck out.
3 Robinson forced Gilliam at second, McDougald to Martin.

2nd Inning
New York
1 Mantle grounded to third.
2 Martin tapped out, Campanella to Hodges.
3 McDougald grounded to third.
Brooklyn
Campanella singled to center.
Hodges singled to center, Campanella stopping at second.
Furillo was safe at first on a DP grounder to Rizzuto who threw wild to second, allowing Campanella to score and Hodges to get to third.
1,2 Cox lined to Woodling who threw to Berra to double up Hodges trying to score after the catch.
Podres singled to center, Furillo going to second.
3 Gilliam grounded to second.

3rd Inning
New York
Rizzuto walked.
1 McDonald sacrificed Rizzuto to second, Campanella to Gilliam covering first.
2 Woodling grounded to the mound, advancing Rizzuto to third.
Collins' grounder bounced off Hodges' glove for an error, Rizzuto scoring.
Bauer was hit by a pitched ball.
Berra walked, loading the bases.
For Brooklyn—Meyer came in to pitch.
Mantle hit a grand-slam home run into the upper deck of the left field stands.
Martin singled to center.
3 Martin was caught stealing, Campanella to Gilliam.
Brooklyn
1 Reese grounded to short.
2 Snider grounded to first.
3 Robinson flied to right.

4th Inning
New York
1 McDougald struck out.
2 Rizzuto grounded to second.
McDonald walked.
Woodling walked.
3 Collins struck out.
Brooklyn
Campanella singled to left.
Hodges singled to center, Campanella stopping at second.
1,2 Furillo hit into a double play, Rizzuto to Collins, with Campanella going to third.
3 Cox popped to short.

5th Inning
New York
1 Bauer fanned.
Berra singled to right.
2 Mantle struck out.
3 Martin grounded back to the pitcher.
Brooklyn
1 Meyer called out on strikes.
Gilliam hit by a pitched ball.
Reese singled to left, Gilliam stopping at second.
Snider singled to center, scoring Gilliam with Reese stopping at second.
2 Robinson fouled to Berra.
3 Campanella forced Snider at second, Rizzuto to Martin.

6th Inning
New York
McDougald tripled off the left-center field wall.
Rizzuto walked.
Rizzuto stole second.
1 McDonald called out on strikes.
Woodling intentionally walked.
2 Collins forced McDougald at the plate, Cox to Campanella.
3 Bauer forced Woodling at third, Cox unassisted (a great stop).
Brooklyn
1 Hodges popped to short.
2 Furillo grounded out, Collins to McDonald.
3 Cox flied to deep center.

7th Inning
New York
Berra singled to center.
1 Mantle grounded to first. Berra just beat the throw to second.
Martin hit a two-run homer into the lower left field stands.
2 McDougald grounded to third.
Rizzuto singled to left.
McDonald doubled to left, the ball bouncing over Robinson's glove, Rizzuto scoring.
3 Woodling grounded to second.
Brooklyn
1 Belardi, pinch-hitting for Meyer, grounded to short.
2 Gilliam grounded to short.
3 Reese popped to Martin in short right.

8th Inning
New York
For Brooklyn—Wade pitching.
Collins doubled off the center field wall.
1 Bauer sacrificed Collins to third, Hodges to Gilliam covering first.
2 Berra flied to deep center, Collins scoring after the catch.
3 Mantle grounded to second.
Brooklyn
1 Snider grounded out, Collins to McDonald on a great stop.
Robinson singled to center.
Campanella singled off of McDougald's shoulder, Robinson stopping at second.
2 Hodges struck out.
Furillo singled to center, Robinson scoring and Campanella to second.
Cox hit a three-run homer into the lower left field stands.
Shuba announced as pinch-hitter for Wade.
For New York—Kuzava pitching.
3 Williams batted for Shuba and fanned.

9th Inning
New York
For Brooklyn—Black pitching.
1 Martin fanned.
McDougald homered over the rail of the lower left field stands.
2 Rizzuto popped to second.
3 Kuzava called out on strikes.
Brooklyn
Gilliam homered into the lower left field stands.
1 Reese flied to left.
Snider singled to right-center.
For New York—Reynolds now pitching.
2,3 Robinson hit into a double play, Martin to Rizzuto to Collins.

Game 6 October 5 at New York

Bkn.	000 001 002
N.Y.	210 000 001

Brooklyn	Pos	AB	R	H	RBI	PO	A	E
Gilliam	2b	4	0	0	0	4	4	1
Reese	ss	4	0	1	0	1	4	0
Robinson	lf	4	1	2	0	3	0	0
Campanella	c	4	0	1	1	4	0	0
Hodges	1b	4	0	0	0	7	0	0
Snider	cf	3	1	0	0	4	1	0
Furillo	rf	4	1	3	2	2	0	0
Cox	3b	4	0	1	0	0	1	1
Erskine	p	1	0	0	0	0	0	1
a Williams		0	0	0	0	0	0	0
Milliken	p	0	0	0	0	0	0	0
b Morgan		1	0	0	0	0	0	0
Labine	p	1	0	0	0	0	1	0
Totals		34	3	8	3	*25	11	3

New York	Pos	AB	R	H	RBI	PO	A	E
Woodling	lf	4	1	2	1	1	0	0
Collins	1b	3	0	1	0	5	1	0
c Mize		1	0	0	0	0	0	0
Bollweg	1b	0	0	0	0	0	0	0
Bauer	rf	3	2	1	0	3	0	0
Berra	c	5	0	2	1	10	0	0
Mantle	cf	4	0	1	0	5	0	0
Martin	2b	5	0	2	2	1	0	0
McDougald	3b	4	0	0	0	0	0	0
Rizzuto	ss	4	1	2	0	2	2	0
Ford	p	3	0	1	0	0	1	0
Reynolds	p	1	0	1	0	0	0	0
Totals		37	4	13	4	27	4	0

a Walked for Erskine in 5th.
b Lined out for Milliken in 7th.
c Grounded out for Collins in 8th.
* One out when winning run scored.

Doubles—Berra, Furillo, Martin, Robinson. Home Run—Furillo. Stolen Base—Robinson. Double Plays—Cox to Gilliam to Hodges, Snider to Gilliam to Campanella, Labine to Gilliam to Hodges. Left on Bases—Brooklyn 6, New York 13. Umpires—Stewart, Hurley, Gore, Grieve, Dascoli, Soar. Attendance—62,370. Time of Game—2:55.

Pitching	IP	H	R	ER	BB	SO
Brooklyn						
Erskine	4	6	3	3	3	1
Milliken	2	2	0	0	1	0
Labine (L)	2⅓	5	1	1	1	1
New York						
Ford	7	6	1	1	1	7
Reynolds (W)	2	2	2	2	1	3

1st Inning
Brooklyn
1 Gilliam popped to first.
Reese singled to left.
2 Robinson bounced to Martin, who tagged Reese out but could not make a play at first as Reese upset him. Stengel had a big argument to charge Reese with interference, but Umpire Gore denied that claim.
Campanella singled to center, Robinson stopping at second.
3 Hodges lined to short.
New York
Woodling walked.
1 Collins struck out.
Bauer singled to left, advancing Woodling to second.
Berra hit a ground-rule double past Furillo into the right field stands, Woodling scoring and Bauer going to third.
Mantle got an intentional pass, filling the bases.
Martin safe at first as his grounder bounced off Gilliam's shoe for an error, Bauer scoring (Martin given an RBI on the play).
2,3 McDougald grounded into a double play, Cox to Gilliam to Hodges (the Dodgers first DP in the Series).

2nd Inning
Brooklyn
1 Snider fanned.
Furillo singled down the right field line,
2 but he was out trying for second, Collins to Rizzuto.
3 *Cox struck out.
New York
Rizzuto singled into left-center.
Ford singled to right, advancing Rizzuto to third.
1 Woodling flied to left, Rizzuto scoring after the catch.
Collins safe on a check-swing hit down the third base line when Erskine's throw to first was wild. Ford to third and Collins to second on the error.
Bauer walked loading the bases.
2,3 Berra flied to Snider in deep center, but Ford left third too soon, went back and then was doubled at the plate, Snider to Gilliam to Campanella.

3rd Inning
Brooklyn
1 Erskine struck out.
2 Gilliam flied to deep left.
3 Reese flied to center.
New York
1 Mantle grounded to second.
2 Martin lined to left.
McDougald safe when Cox muffed his grounder.
3 Rizzuto fouled to Hodges.

4th Inning
Brooklyn
1 Robinson grounded to short.
2 Campanella fanned.
3 Hodges grounded back to the pitcher.
New York
1 Ford flied to center.
Woodling singled to center.
2 Collins flied to right.
3 Bauer forced Woodling at second, Reese to Gilliam.

5th Inning
Brooklyn
1 Snider struck out.
Furillo doubled to deep left-center.
2 Cox flied to center.
Williams, batting for Erskine, walked.
3 Gilliam called out on strikes.
New York
For Brooklyn—Milliken pitching.
1 Berra popped to second.
2 Mantle flied to center.
Martin hit a ground-rule double into the right field stands.
3 McDougald grounded to short.

6th Inning
Brooklyn
1 Reese flied to center.
Robinson doubled off the wall in the left field corner.
Robinson stole third.
2 Campanella grounded to short, scoring Robinson.
3 Hodges grounded to first.
New York
1 Rizzuto flied to center.
2 Ford grounded to short.
Woodling singled off Gilliam's glove.
Collins walked.
3 Bauer popped to short.

7th Inning
Brooklyn
1 Snider struck out.
2 Furillo flied to center.
Cox singled to left.
3 Morgan, pinch-hitting for Milliken, lined to right.
New York
For Brooklyn—Labine pitching.
Berra singled to left.
1 Mantle flied to left.
2,3 Martin grounded into a double play, Labine to Gilliam to Hodges.

8th Inning
Brooklyn
For New York—Reynolds pitching.
1 Gilliam flied to deep right.
2 Reese flied to right.
Robinson singled to left.
3 Campanella struck out.
New York
1 McDougald struck out.
Rizzuto singled off Labine's glove.
Reynolds singled to right, Rizzuto going to third.
2 Woodling hit a bouncer to Reese who threw to Campanella to get Rizzuto at the plate.
3 Mize, pinch-hitting for Collins, grounded to first.

9th Inning
Brooklyn
For New York—Bollweg at first.
1 Hodges flied to center.
Snider walked.
Furillo hit a two-run homer into the lower right field stand.
2 Cox called out on strikes.
3 Labine called out on strikes.
New York
Bauer walked.
1 Berra lined to right.
Mantle beat out a high bouncer between third and the mound, Bauer stopping at second.
Martin singled (**his 12th hit, tying a Series record**) to center, scoring Bauer with the winning run. (**The Yankees winning their 5th consecutive championship**).

1953 WORLD SERIES COMPOSITE BOX

	Wins	Composite Line Score		Manager	W	L	Pct.	G. Ahead
					Regular Season			
New York Yankees (A.L.)	4	8 1 5 0 4 0 5 7 3	- 33	Casey Stengel	99	52	.656	8.5
Brooklyn Dodgers (N.L.)	2	3 1 0 3 3 7 2 5 3	- 27	Chuck Dressen	105	49	.682	13

BATTING AND FIELDING

NEW YORK YANKEES

WORLD SERIES STATISTICS	Pos	G	AB	R	H	2B	3B	HR	RBI	BB	SO	SB	BA	SA	PO	A	E
Joe Collins	1b	6	24	4	4	1	0	1	2	3	**8**	0	.167	.333	**49**	4	0
Billy Martin	2b	6	24	5	**12**	1	**2**	**2**	**8**	1	2	**1**	**.500**	**.958**	13	15	0
Phil Rizzuto	ss	6	19	4	6	1	0	0	0	3	2	**1**	.316	.368	11	**19**	1
Gil McDougald	3b	6	24	2	4	0	1	2	4	1	3	0	.167	.500	5	14	0
Hank Bauer	rf	6	23	**6**	6	0	1	0	1	2	4	0	.261	.348	14	0	0
Mickey Mantle	cf	6	24	3	5	0	0	**2**	7	3	**8**	0	.208	.458	14	0	0
Gene Woodling	lf	6	20	5	6	0	0	1	3	**6**	2	0	.300	.450	9	1	0
Yogi Berra	c	6	21	3	9	1	0	1	4	3	3	0	.429	.619	36	3	0
Don Bollweg	ph-1b	3	2	0	0	0	0	0	0	0	2	0	.000	.000	0	0	0
Johnny Mize	ph	3	3	0	0	0	0	0	0	0	1	0	.000	.000			
Irv Noren	ph	2	1	0	0	0	0	0	0	1	0	0	.000	.000			
Bill Renna		Did not play															
Andy Carey		Did not play															
Willie Miranda		Did not play															
Charlie Silvera		Did not play															
Gus Triandos		Did not play															
Jerry Coleman		Did not play															
Whitey Ford	p	2	3	0	1	0	0	0	0	0	0	0	.333	.333	0	1	0
Ed Lopat	p	1	3	0	0	0	0	0	0	0	2	0	.000	.000	0	2	0
Allie Reynolds	p	3	2	0	1	0	0	0	0	1	1	0	.000	.000	0	0	0
Johnny Sain	p	2	2	1	1	1	0	0	2	0	1	0	.500	1.000	0	0	0
Jim McDonald	p	1	2	0	1	1	0	0	1	1	1	0	.500	1.000	3	0	0
Vic Raschi	p	1	2	0	0	0	0	0	0	0	1	0	.000	.000	1	1	0
Tom Gorman	p	1	1	0	0	0	0	0	0	0	1	0	.000	.000	1	0	0
Bob Kuzava	p	1	1	0	0	0	0	0	0	0	1	0	.000	.000	0	0	0
Art Schallock	p	1	0	0	0	0	0	0	0	0	0	0	—	—	0	1	0
Bill Miller		Did not play															
Steve Kraly		Did not play															
team total		6	201	33	56	6	4	9	32	25	43	2	.279	.483	156	61	1

Double Plays—5
Left on Bases—47

REGULAR SEASON STATISTICS		Main Pos	G	AB	R	H	2B	3B	HR	RBI	BB	SO	SB	BA	SA
Joe Collins		1b	127	387	72	104	11	2	17	44	59	36	2	.269	.439
Billy Martin		2b	149	587	72	151	24	6	15	75	43	56	6	.257	.395
Phil Rizzuto		ss	134	413	54	112	21	3	2	54	71	39	4	.271	.351
Gil McDougald		3b	141	541	82	154	27	7	10	83	60	65	3	.285	.416
Hank Bauer		of	133	437	77	133	20	6	10	57	59	45	2	.304	.446
Mickey Mantle		of	127	461	105	136	24	3	21	92	79	90	8	.295	.497
Gene Woodling		of	125	395	64	121	26	4	10	58	82	29	2	.306	.468
Yogi Berra		c	137	503	80	149	23	5	27	108	50	32	0	.296	.523
Don Bollweg		1b	70	155	24	46	6	4	6	24	21	31	1	.297	.503
Johnny Mize		ph	81	104	6	26	3	0	4	27	12	17	0	.250	.394
Irv Noren		of	109	345	55	92	12	6	6	46	42	39	3	.267	.388
Bill Renna		of	61	121	19	38	6	3	2	13	13	31	0	.314	.463
Andy Carey		3b	51	81	14	26	5	0	4	8	9	12	2	.321	.531
Willie Miranda	a	ss	48	58	12	13	0	0	1	5	5	10	1	.224	.276
Charlie Silvera		c	42	82	11	23	3	1	0	12	9	5	0	.280	.341
Gus Triandos		1b	18	51	5	8	2	0	1	6	3	9	0	.157	.255
Jerry Coleman		2b	8	10	1	2	0	0	0	0	0	2	0	.200	.200
Whitey Ford		p	33	75	10	20	2	0	0	10	9	13	0	.267	.293
Ed Lopat		p	26	63	5	12	3	0	0	1	5	13	0	.190	.238
Allie Reynolds		p	42	41	3	5	2	0	0	2	7	11	0	.122	.171
Johnny Sain		p	41	68	8	17	3	1	0	8	5	1	0	.250	.324
Jim McDonald		p	29	41	2	4	0	0	0	4	2	18	0	.098	.098
Vic Raschi		p	28	63	4	9	1	0	0	11	3	13	0	.143	.159
Tom Gorman		p	40	15	0	2	0	0	0	0	1	7	0	.133	.133
Bob Kuzava		p	33	21	3	1	0	0	0	0	4	7	0	.048	.048
Art Schallock		p	7	6	1	2	0	0	0	0	0	2	0	.333	.333
Bill Miller		p	13	10	1	2	1	0	0	1	0	1	0	.200	.300
Steve Kraly		p	5	7	0	0	0	0	0	0	0	2	0	.000	.000
team total			151	5194	**801**	1420	226	52	139	**762**	**656**	644	34	**.273**	**.417**

a—from St. Louis (A)

Ralph Houk (c), Bob Cerv (ph), Art Schult (pr), Loren Babe (3b), Jim Brideweser (ss), Frank Verdi (ss), Ewell Blackwell (p), Ray Scarborough (p), and Johnny Schmidtz (p) also played for the Yankees during the season.

BROOKLYN DODGERS

WORLD SERIES STATISTICS	Pos	G	AB	R	H	2B	3B	HR	RBI	BB	SO	SB	BA	SA	PO	A	E
Gil Hodges	1b	6	22	3	8	0	0	1	1	3	3	**1**	.364	.500	47	4	1
Jim Gilliam	2b	6	**27**	4	8	**3**	0	**2**	4	0	2	0	.296	.630	15	16	1
Pee Wee Reese	ss	6	24	0	5	0	1	0	0	4	1	0	.208	.292	7	14	0
Billy Cox	3b	6	23	3	7	3	0	1	6	1	4	0	.304	.565	1	10	1
Carl Furillo	rf	6	24	4	8	2	0	1	4	1	3	0	.333	.542	10	0	**2**
Duke Snider	cf	6	25	3	8	**3**	0	1	5	2	6	0	.320	.560	17	1	0
Jackie Robinson	lf	6	25	3	8	2	0	0	2	1	0	**1**	.320	.400	8	0	0
Roy Campanella	c	6	22	**6**	6	0	0	1	2	2	3	0	.273	.409	47	9	0
Don Thompson	lf	2	0	0	0	0	0	0	0	0	0	0	—	—	0	1	0
Dick Williams	ph	3	2	0	1	0	0	0	0	1	1	0	.500	.500			
Wayne Belardi	ph	2	2	0	0	0	0	0	0	0	1	0	.000	.000			
George Shuba	ph	2	1	1	1	0	0	1	2	0	0	0	1.000	4.000			
Bobby Morgan	ph	1	1	0	0	0	0	0	0	0	0	0	.000	.000			
Rube Walker		Did not play															
Bill Antonello		Did not play															
Carl Erskine	p	3	4	0	1	0	0	0	0	0	1	0	.250	.250	1	2	1
Billy Loes	p	1	3	0	2	0	0	0	0	0	0	0	.667	.667	0	0	0
Preacher Roe	p	1	3	0	0	0	0	0	0	0	2	0	.000	.000	1	1	0
Clem Labine	p	3	2	0	0	0	0	0	0	0	1	0	.000	.000	0	2	0
Johnny Podres	p	1	1	0	1	0	0	0	0	0	0	0	1.000	1.000	0	1	0
Jim Hughes	p	1	1	0	0	0	0	0	0	0	1	0	.000	.000	0	0	1
Russ Meyer	p	1	1	0	0	0	0	0	0	0	1	0	.000	.000	0	1	0
Ben Wade	p	2	0	0	0	0	0	0	0	0	0	0	—	—	0	0	0
Joe Black	p	1	0	0	0	0	0	0	0	0	0	0	—	—	0	0	0
Bob Milliken	p	1	0	0	0	0	0	0	0	0	0	0	—	—	0	0	0
Erv Palica		Did not pitch															
team total		6	213	27	64	13	1	8	26	15	30	2	.300	.484	154	62	7

Double Plays—3
Left on Bases—49

REGULAR SEASON STATISTICS	Main Pos	G	AB	R	H	2B	3B	HR	RBI	BB	SO	SB	BA	SA
Gil Hodges	1b	141	520	101	157	22	7	31	122	75	84	1	.302	.550
Jim Gilliam	2b	151	605	125	168	31	**17**	6	63	100	38	21	.278	.415
Pee Wee Reese	ss	140	524	108	142	25	7	13	61	82	61	22	.271	.420
Billy Cox	3b	100	327	44	95	18	1	10	44	37	21	2	.291	.443
Carl Furillo	of	132	479	82	165	38	6	21	92	34	32	1	**.344**	.580
Duke Snider	of	153	590	**132**	198	38	4	42	126	82	90	16	.336	**.627**
Jackie Robinson	of-3b	136	484	109	159	34	7	12	95	74	30	17	.329	.502
Roy Campanella	c	144	519	103	162	26	3	41	**142**	67	58	4	.312	.611
Don Thompson	of	96	153	25	37	5	0	1	12	14	13	2	.242	.294
Dick Williams	of	30	55	4	12	2	0	2	5	3	10	0	.218	.364
Wayne Belardi	1b	69	163	19	39	3	2	11	34	16	40	0	.239	.485
George Shuba	of	74	169	19	43	12	1	5	23	17	20	1	.254	.426
Bobby Morgan	3b	69	196	35	51	6	2	7	33	33	47	2	.260	.418
Rube Walker	c	43	95	5	23	6	0	3	9	7	11	0	.242	.400
Bill Antonello	of	40	43	9	7	1	1	1	4	2	11	0	.163	.302
Carl Erskine	p	43	93	12	20	2	0	0	8	1	17	0	.215	.237
Billy Loes	p	32	56	2	7	1	1	0	4	1	13	0	.125	.179
Preacher Roe	p	25	57	4	3	0	0	1	2	3	18	0	.053	.105
Clem Labine	p	37	28	1	2	1	0	0	0	3	18	0	.071	.107
Johnny Podres	p	34	36	5	11	0	0	0	1	0	1	1	.306	.306
Jim Hughes	p	48	14	1	4	0	0	0	1	0	1	0	.286	.286
Russ Meyer	p	34	75	6	11	1	0	0	2	3	21	0	.147	.160
Ben Wade	p	32	24	1	4	0	0	1	2	0	8	0	.167	.292
Joe Black	p	34	17	1	4	0	0	0	1	0	5	0	.235	.235
Bob Milliken	p	37	34	1	4	2	0	0	1	1	10	0	.118	.176
Erv Palica	p	4	1	0	1	0	0	0	0	0	0	0	1.000	1.000
team total		155	5373	**955**	**1529**	274	59	**208**	**887**	**655**	686	**90**	**.285**	**.474**

Carmen Mauro (of), Dixie Housh (ph), Dick Teed (ph), Glenn Mickens (p), Ray Moore (p), and Ralph Branca (p) also played for the Dodgers during the season.

PITCHING

NEW YORK YANKEES

WORLD SERIES STATISTICS	G	GS	CG	IP	H	R	ER	BB	SO	W	L	SV	ERA
Ed Lopat	1	1	**1**	9	9	2	2	4	3	1	0	0	**2.00**
Vic Raschi	1	1	**1**	8	9	3	3	3	4	0	1	0	3.38
Whitey Ford	2	2	0	8	9	4	4	2	7	0	1	0	4.50
Allie Reynolds	**3**	1	0	8	9	6	6	4	9	1	0	**1**	6.75
Jim McDonald	1	1	0	7 2/3	12	6	5	0	3	1	0	0	5.87
Johnny Sain	2	0	0	5 2/3	8	3	3	1	1	1	0	0	4.76
Tom Gorman	1	0	0	3	4	1	1	0	1	0	0	0	3.00
Art Schallock	1	0	0	2	2	1	1	1	1	0	0	0	4.50
Bob Kuzava	1	0	0	2/3	2	1	1	0	1	0	0	0	13.50
Bill Miller	Did not play												
Steve Kraly	Did not play												
team total	6	6	2	52	64	27	26	15	30	4	2	1	4.50

REGULAR SEASON STATISTICS	G	GS	CG	IP	H	ER	BB	SO	W	L	Pct	SV	ShO	ERA
Ed Lopat	25	24	9	178	169	48	32	50	16	4	**.800**	0	3	**2.43**
Vic Raschi	28	26	7	181	150	67	55	76	13	6	.684	1	4	3.33
Whitey Ford	32	30	11	207	187	69	110	110	18	6	.750	0	3	3.00
Allie Reynolds	41	15	5	145	140	55	61	86	13	7	.650	13	1	3.41
Jim McDonald	27	18	6	130	128	55	39	43	9	7	.563	0	2	3.81
Johnny Sain	40	19	10	189	189	63	45	84	14	7	.667	9	1	3.00
Tom Gorman	40	1	0	77	65	29	32	38	4	5	.444	6	0	3.39
Art Schallock	7	1	0	21	30	7	15	13	0	0	.000	1	0	3.00
Bob Kuzava	33	6	2	92	92	34	32	48	6	5	.545	4	2	3.33
Bill Miller	13	3	0	34	46	18	19	17	2	1	.667	1	0	4.76
Steve Kraly	5	3	0	25	19	9	16	8	0	2	.000	1	0	3.24
team total	151	151	50	1358	1286	482	500	609	**99**	52	**.656**	**39**	**16**	**3.20**

BROOKLYN DODGERS

WORLD SERIES STATISTICS	G	GS	CG	IP	H	R	ER	BB	SO	W	L	SV	ERA
Carl Erskine	**3**	**3**	1	**14**	**14**	**9**	**9**	**9**	**16**	1	0	0	5.79
Billy Loes	1	1	0	8	8	3	3	2	8	1	0	0	3.38
Preacher Roe	1	1	1	8	5	4	4	4	4	0	1	0	4.50
Clem Labine	**3**	0	0	5	10	2	2	1	3	0	**2**	**1**	3.60
Russ Meyer	1	0	0	4 1/3	8	4	3	4	5	0	0	0	6.23
Jim Hughes	1	0	0	4	3	1	1	1	3	0	0	0	2.25
Johnny Podres	1	1	0	2 2/3	1	5	1	2	0	0	1	0	3.38
Ben Wade	2	0	0	2 1/3	4	4	4	1	2	0	0	0	15.43
Bob Milliken	1	0	0	2	2	0	0	1	0	0	0	0	0.00
Joe Black	1	0	0	1	1	1	1	0	2	0	0	0	9.00
Erv Palica	Did not play												
team total	6	6	2	51 1/3	56	33	28	25	43	2	4	1	4.91

REGULAR SEASON STATISTICS	G	GS	CG	IP	H	ER	BB	SO	W	L	Pct	SV	ShO	ERA
Carl Erskine	39	33	16	247	213	97	95	187	20	6	**.769**	3	4	3.53
Billy Loes	32	25	9	163	165	82	53	75	14	8	.636	0	1	4.53
Preacher Roe	25	24	9	157	171	76	40	85	11	3	.786	0	1	4.36
Clem Labine	37	7	0	110	92	34	30	44	11	6	.647	7	0	2.78
Russ Meyer	34	32	10	191	201	97	63	106	15	5	.750	0	2	4.57
Jim Hughes	48	0	0	86	80	33	41	49	4	3	.571	9	0	3.45
Johnny Podres	33	18	3	115	126	54	64	82	9	4	.692	0	1	4.23
Ben Wade	32	0	0	90	79	38	33	65	7	5	.583	3	0	3.80
Bob Milliken	37	10	3	118	94	44	42	65	8	4	.667	2	0	3.36
Joe Black	34	3	0	73	74	43	27	42	6	3	.667	5	0	5.30
Erv Palica	4	0	0	6	10	8	8	3	0	0	—	0	0	12.00
team total	155	155	51	1381	1337	630	509	**817**	**105**	49	**.682**	29	11	4.10

Total Attendance—307,350 Average Attendance—51,225 Winning Player's Share—$8,281 Losing Player's Share—$6,178

1954
460 Feet of Frustration

Wonder of wonders, the New York Yankees did not win the American League pennant. Casey Stengel fielded a strong club which went over the 100-win level for the first time in the Old Professor's six-year reign, but the Cleveland Indians put all the pieces together this year to set an A.L. record of 111 victories and dethrone the Yankees after a five-year run at the top of the circuit. General manager Hank Greenberg and manager Al Lopez built a powerful team on the ashes of the 1948 championship squad, retaining only Larry Doby, Dale Mitchell, Jim Hegan, Bob Lemon, and Bob Feller from that unit. Doby, Al Rosen, and midseason pickup Vic Wertz clubbed the long ball in the middle of the Cleveland batting order, while second baseman Bobby Avila swung the bat at a league-leading .341 clip. The pitching staff had three right-handed aces, 23-game-winners Lemon and Early Wynn and 19-game-winner Mike Garcia, while strong second-line hurling came from Art Houtteman, fading stars Feller and Hal Newhouser, and rookie relievers Don Mossi and Ray Narleski. This deep squad clearly outclassed the National League-champion New York Giants.

Managed by Lippy Leo Durocher, the Giants had two outstanding stars in Willie Mays and Johnny Antonelli, neither of whom was with the team last year. Mays came out of two years of military service to blossom into exciting maturity, hitting .345 with 41 homers and 110 RBI's, and covering center field in magnificent style. Antonelli came from the Braves in an off-season deal and used his strong left arm to win 21 games. Other holdover Giants such as Don Mueller and Alvin Dark had good seasons, but Mays and Antonelli were considered the key men on the team.

Both men starred in the classic, joined by a little-known pinch hitter named Dusty Rhodes. The opening game in the Polo Grounds matched Bob Lemon and Sal Maglie on the mound and set the stage for Giant heroics which would start an upset rolling. A triple by the powerful Wertz got Cleveland off to a 2–0 lead in the top of the first inning, but a walk and three hits off Lemon in the third knotted the score at 2–2. The game proceeded quickly into the eighth, when the Indians threatened. Doby and Rosen reached base with one out, and manager Durocher brought in southpaw Don Liddle to face Wertz, who already had three hits. Wertz drove the ball on a line into the deepest center field of any major-league park, but Mays tore out with his back to the plate and caught the ball as it whizzed past his left shoulder, 460 feet from home. Praised as one of the best plays in Series history, Mays's catch broke the back of the Indian rally. The game went into extra innings, and the Giants moved to win it in the tenth. Mays walked and stole second with one out, and Lemon gave Hank Thompson a pass in order to face Monty Irvin. Durocher replaced the aging Irvin with Rhodes, a lefty batter who hit .341 for the season in spot roles as an outfielder and pinch hitter. Rhodes swung at Lemon's first pitch and lofted a 260-foot fly down the right-field line which dropped into the close seats for a three-run homer and a 5–2 Giant win. Rhodes's homer paled in comparison with Wertz's out, but it was placed well enough to send the Giants off on the road to victory.

Wynn faced Antonelli the next day, with a lead-off homer by Al Smith getting the Indians off to another quick lead. But the Giants struck back in the fifth. Mays walked and Thompson singled, and then Rhodes again hit for Irvin. Dusty this time dropped a Texas League single into center which tied the game, and a second run in the inning later scored on a force play. Durocher left Rhodes in the game, and Dusty responded with a seventh-inning homer to right to cap a 3–1 Giant win.

With the tide flowing against them, the Indians tried to come back in game three in Cleveland with Garcia pitching against Ruben Gomez. The Giants scored a run in the top of the first, and when they loaded the bases in the third, Durocher fingered Rhodes to again bat for Irvin. Dusty promptly singled in two runs, and the Jints were on their way to a 6–2 win which finished the Indians. The club which had pulverized the A.L. went down the drain in game four, dropping a 7–4 decision to Liddle with a save going to Antonelli. Aside from Rhodes's miraculous heroics, fans after the Series could discuss the sad failure of Bob Feller to get into any of the games, and how the odd dimensions of the old Polo Grounds vitally affected the opening game. What they could not discuss or realize was that this was the last World Series ever to be played in that venerable park.

Game 1 September 29 at New York

Cleveland	Pos	AB	R	H	RBI	PO	A	E
Smith	lf	4	1	1	0	1	0	0
Avila	2b	5	1	1	0	2	3	0
Doby	cf	3	0	1	0	3	0	0
Rosen	3b	5	0	1	0	1	3	0
Wertz	1b	5	0	4	2	11	1	0
d Regalado		0	0	0	0	0	0	0
Grasso	c	0	0	0	0	1	0	0
Philley	rf	3	0	0	0	0	0	0
a Majeski		0	0	0	0	0	0	0
b Mitchell		0	0	0	0	0	0	0
Dente	ss	0	0	0	0	0	0	0
Strickland	ss	3	0	0	0	2	3	0
c Pope	rf	1	0	0	0	0	0	0
Hegan	c	4	0	0	0	6	1	0
e Glynn	1b	1	0	0	0	0	0	0
Lemon	p	4	0	0	0	1	1	0
Totals		38	2	8	2	*28	12	0

* One out when winning run scored.
a Announced for Philley in 8th.
b Walked for Majeski in 8th.
c Struck out for Strickland in 8th.
d Ran for Wertz in 10th.
e Struck out for Hegan in 10th.
f Homered for Irvin in 10th.

Double—Wertz. Triple—Wertz. Home Run—Rhodes. Stolen Base—Mays. Sacrifice Hits—Dente, Irvin. Hit by Pitcher—Smith (by Maglie). Wild Pitch—Lemon. Left on Bases—Cleveland 13, New York 9. Umpires—Barlick(N), Berry(A), Conlan(N), Stevens(A), Warneke(N), Napp(A). Attendance—52,751. Time of Game—3:11.

Cle.	200	000	000	0
N.Y.	002	000	000	3

New York	Pos	AB	R	H	RBI	PO	A	E
Lockman	1b	5	1	1	0	9	0	0
Dark	ss	4	0	2	0	3	2	0
Mueller	rf	5	1	2	1	2	0	2
Mays	cf	3	1	0	0	2	0	0
Thompson	3b	3	1	1	1	3	3	0
Irvin	lf	3	0	0	0	5	0	1
f Rhodes		1	1	1	3	0	0	0
Williams	2b	4	0	0	0	1	1	0
Westrum	c	4	0	2	0	5	0	0
Maglie	p	3	0	0	0	0	2	0
Liddle	p	0	0	0	0	0	0	0
Grissom	p	1	0	0	0	0	0	0
Totals		36	5	9	5	30	8	3

Pitching	IP	H	R	ER	BB	SO
Cleveland						
Lemon (L)	9⅓	9	5	5	5	6
New York						
Maglie	**7	7	2	2	2	2
Liddle	⅓	0	0	0	0	0
Grissom (W)	2⅔	1	0	0	3	2

**Pitched to two batters in 8th.

1st Inning
Cleveland
Smith was hit by a pitched ball.
Avila singled to right, with Smith going to third on Mueller's fumble.
1 Doby fouled to Thompson.
2 Rosen popped to first.
Wertz tripled off the right field wall, scoring Smith and Avila.
3 Philley flied to deep right.
New York
1 Lockman bunted out to second.
Dark walked.
Mueller singled to right, moving Dark to third.
2 Mays popped to short.
3 Thompson grounded to first.

2nd Inning
Cleveland
1 Strickland struck out.
2 Hegan popped to third.
Lemon walked.
3 Smith struck out.
New York
1 Irvin fouled to Hegan.
2 Williams grounded to third.
Westrum singled to left.
3 Maglie struck out.

3rd Inning
Cleveland
1 Avila fouled to Westrum.
2 Doby grounded to second.
3 Rosen grounded to short.
New York
Lockman singled to right.
Dark singled to center, Lockman going to third.
1 Mueller forced Dark at second, Avila to Strickland, Lockman scoring.
Mays walked.
Thompson singled to right, Mueller scoring with Mays going to third.
2 Irvin struck out.
3 Williams grounded to short.

4th Inning
Cleveland
Wertz singled to left.
1 Philley bounced back to the mound, Wertz moving to second.
2 Strickland grounded to short, Wertz holding second.
On a pitchout, Westrum threw wildly to second trying to pick off Wertz, but Wertz held at second.
3 Hegan popped to short.
New York
Westrum singled beyond third into left.
1 Maglie struck out.
2 Lockman grounded to first, Westrum going to second.
Dark beat out a hit to third, with Westrum moving to third.
3 Mueller grounded to first.

5th Inning
Cleveland
1 Lemon flied to deep center.
Smith beat out a roller to third.
2 Avila flied to left.
Doby singled to right, Smith going to third.
3 Rosen flied to right.
New York
1 Mays grounded to third.
2 Thompson struck out.
3 Irvin flied to deep center.

6th Inning
Cleveland
Wertz singled to right and went to second on Mueller's wild throw into the infield (his second error).
1 Philley grounded to the mound, Maglie making a good play, Wertz moved to third.
2 Strickland popped to short.
3 Hegan grounded to third.
New York
1 Williams grounded to third.
2 Westrum lined to center.
3 Maglie grounded out, Wertz to Lemon.

7th Inning
Cleveland
1 Lemon popped to short.
2 Smith grounded to third.
3 Avila lined to third.
New York
1 Lockman grounded to short.
2 Dark fouled to Rosen.
Mueller singled to left.
3 Mays forced Mueller at second, Strickland to Avila.

8th Inning
Cleveland
Doby walked.
Rosen singled off Dark's hand, Doby stopping at second.
For New York—Liddle pitching.
1 Wertz flied out to Mays at the center field bleachers, a fantastic over-the-shoulder catch. Doby moving to third after the catch.
Majeski announced to bat for Philley.
For New York—Grissom pitching.
Mitchell, batting for Majeski, walked.
2 Pope, batting for Strickland, was called out on strikes.
3 Hegan flied to left.
New York
For Cleveland—Pope in right, Dente at short (batting 6th).
Thompson walked.
1 Irvin sacrificed Thompson to second, Hegan to Avila covering first.
2 Williams grounded to third.
Thompson to third on a wild pitch.
3 Westrum lined to center.

9th Inning
Cleveland
1 Lemon flied to left.
2 Smith flied to left.
Avila safe at second when Irvin dropped his fly.
Doby intentionally walked.
3 Rosen flied to left.
New York
1 Grissom fanned.
2 Lockman grounded to the mound.
3 Dark flied to left.

10th Inning
Cleveland
Wertz doubled to left-center.
Regalado ran for Wertz.
1 Dente sacrificed Regalado to third, Thompson to Williams.
Pope got an intentional pass.
2 Glynn, batting for Hegan, struck out.
3 Lemon lined to first.
New York
For Cleveland—Glynn stays in at first, Grasso catching (batting 5th).
1 Mueller struck out but had to be tagged out by Grasso.
Mays walked.
Mays stole second.
Thompson intentionally walked.
Rhodes, pinch-hitting for Irvin, on the first pitch homered into the lower right field stands, scoring Mays and Thompson ahead of himself.

Game 2 September 30 at New York

Cleveland	Pos	AB	R	H	RBI	PO	A	E
Smith	lf	4	1	2	1	3	0	0
Avila	2b	4	0	1	0	2	2	0
Doby	cf	5	0	0	0	2	0	0
Rosen	3b	3	0	1	0	0	0	0
b Regalado	3b	1	0	0	0	0	0	0
Wertz	1b	3	0	1	0	5	1	0
Westlake	rf	3	0	1	0	3	0	0
Strickland	ss	3	0	0	0	1	1	0
c Philley		1	0	0	0	0	0	0
Dente	ss	0	0	0	0	0	0	0
Hegan	c	4	0	1	0	7	0	0
Wynn	p	2	0	1	0	1	1	0
d Majeski		1	0	0	0	0	0	0
Mossi	p	0	0	0	0	0	1	0
Totals		34	1	8	1	24	6	0

a Singled for Irvin in 5th.
b Ran for Rosen in 7th.
c Struck out for Strickland in 8th.
d Grounded out for Wynn in 8th.

Doubles—Hegan, Wynn. Home Runs—Rhodes, Smith. Sacrifice Hit—Wynn. Wild Pitch—Wynn. Left on Bases—Cleveland 13, New York 3. Umpires—Berry, Conlan, Stevens, Barlick, Warneke, Napp. Attendance—49,099. Time of Game—2:50.

			Cle.	1 0 0	0 0 0	0 0 0	
			N.Y.	0 0 0	0 2 0	1 0 x	

New York	Pos	AB	R	H	RBI	PO	A	E
Lockman	1b	4	0	0	0	8	0	0
Dark	ss	4	0	1	0	0	6	0
Mueller	rf	4	0	0	0	1	0	0
Mays	cf	3	1	1	0	1	3	0
Thompson	3b	3	1	1	0	1	3	0
Irvin	lf	1	0	0	0	2	0	0
a Rhodes	lf	2	1	2	2	1	0	0
Williams	2b	3	0	0	0	4	0	0
Westrum	c	2	0	0	0	9	0	0
Antonelli	p	3	0	0	1	0	1	0
Totals		28	3	4	3	27	10	0

Pitching	IP	H	R	ER	BB	SO
Cleveland						
Wynn (L)	7	4	3	3	2	5
Mossi	1	0	0	0	0	0
New York						
Antonelli (W)	9	8	1	1	6	9

1st Inning
Cleveland
Smith hit a home run over the left field roof, on Antonelli's first pitch.
1 Avila grounded to short.
2 Doby called out on strikes.
Rosen singled.
Wertz walked.
Westlake singled to center, loading the bases.
3 Strickland popped to first.
New York
1 Lockman grounded back to the mound.
2 Dark lined to center.
3 Mueller grounded to second.

2nd Inning
Cleveland
Hegan doubled down the left field line.
1 Wynn sacrificed Hegan to third, Thompson to Lockman.
2 Smith fanned.
3 Avila fouled to Thompson.
New York
1 Mays flied to right.
2 Thompson flied to left.
3 Irvin took a called third strike.

3rd Inning
Cleveland
1 Doby called out on strikes.
2 Rosen grounded to short (Rosen pulled a thigh muscle).
Wertz singled to center.
Westlake singled.
3 Strickland forced Westlake at second, Dark to Williams.
New York
1 Williams struck out, but had to be tagged by Hegan.
2 Westrum flied to Smith in deep left-center.
3 Antonelli flied to right.

4th Inning
Cleveland
1 Hegan flied to center.
2 Wynn struck out, but had to be tagged by Westrum.
Smith walked.
3 Avila forced Smith at second, a fantastic stop by Thompson to Williams.
New York
1 Lockman struck out.
2 Dark grounded to short.
3 Mueller flied to deep right.

5th Inning
Cleveland
1 Doby flied to left.
Rosen singled to right.
2 Wertz flied to left.
3 Westlake fanned.

5th Inning (continued)
New York
Mays walked.
Thompson singled to right, advancing Mays to third.
Rhodes, pinch-hitting for Irvin, singled to center, Mays scoring with Thompson going to third. Rhodes went to second on Doby's throw to third.
1 Williams took a called third strike.
Westrum walked, loading the bases.
2 Antonelli forced Westrum at second, Avila to Strickland but the relay to first was too late and Thompson scored.
3 Lockman grounded out, Wertz to Wynn.

6th Inning
Cleveland
For New York—Rhodes playing left.
1 Strickland took a called third strike.
2 Hegan lined to right.
Wynn doubled off the left field wall.
3 Smith fouled to Lockman.
New York
Dark singled to right.
Dark went to second on a wild pitch.
1 Mueller flied to center.
2 Mays fanned.
3 Thompson fouled to Hegan.

7th Inning
Cleveland
Avila walked.
1 Doby grounded to first, Avila going to second.
2 Rosen grounded to Antonelli with Avila getting caught in a run-down, Antonelli to Thompson to Williams.
Wertz walked.
Regalado ran for Rosen.
3 Westlake grounded to short.
New York
For Cleveland—Regalado playing third. Rhodes homered against the right field facade.
1 Williams popped to the catcher.
2 Westrum flied to very deep left.
3 Antonelli popped to second.

8th Inning
Cleveland
1 Philley, pinch-hitting for Strickland, struck out.
2 Hegan struck out.
3 Majeski, pinch-hitting for Wynn, grounded to short.
New York
For Cleveland—Mossi pitching and Dente at short.
1 Lockman fouled to Wertz.
2 Dark lined to second.
3 Mueller tapped back to the mound.

9th Inning
Cleveland
Smith singled off Antonelli's glove.
Avila singled to left, moving Smith to second.
1 Doby struck out.
2 Regalado forced Avila at second, Dark to Williams as Smith went to third.
3 Wertz flied to deep left.

Game 3 October 1 at Cleveland

New York	Pos	AB	R	H	RBI	PO	A	E
Lockman	1b	4	1	1	0	13	0	0
Dark	ss	4	0	1	0	2	2	1
Mueller	rf	5	2	2	0	1	0	0
Mays	cf	5	1	3	2	2	0	0
Thompson	3b	3	2	1	0	0	3	0
Irvin	lf	1	0	0	0	2	0	0
a Rhodes	lf	3	0	1	2	3	0	0
Williams	2b	3	0	0	0	2	5	0
Westrum	c	4	0	1	1	4	0	0
Gomez	p	4	0	0	0	1	2	0
Wilhelm	p	0	0	0	0	0	0	0
Totals		35	6	10	6	27	12	1

Pitching	IP	H	R	ER	BB	SO
New York						
Gomez (W)	7⅓	4	2	2	3	2
Wilhelm (SV)	1⅔	0	0	0	0	2
Cleveland						
Garcia (L)	3	5	4	3	3	3
Houtteman	2	2	1	1	1	1
Narleski	3	1	1	1	1	2
Mossi	1	2	0	0	0	1

			N.Y.	1 0 3	0 1 1	0 0 0	
			Cle.	0 0 0	0 0 0	1 1 0	

Cleveland	Pos	AB	R	H	RBI	PO	A	E
Smith	lf	3	0	0	1	0	0	0
Avila	2b	2	0	0	0	4	1	0
Doby	cf	4	0	1	0	2	0	0
Wertz	1b	4	1	1	1	6	1	0
Majeski	3b	4	0	0	0	2	1	0
Philley	rf	3	0	1	0	1	0	0
Strickland	ss	3	0	0	0	3	4	1
f Pope		1	0	0	0	0	0	0
Hegan	c	2	0	0	0	8	1	0
d Glynn		1	1	1	0	0	0	0
Naragon	c	0	0	0	0	1	0	0
Garcia	p	0	0	0	0	0	1	1
b Lemon		1	0	0	0	0	0	0
Houtteman	p	1	0	0	0	0	0	0
c Regalado		1	0	0	0	0	0	0
Narleski	p	0	0	0	0	0	1	0
e Mitchell		1	0	0	0	0	0	0
Mossi	p	0	0	0	0	0	0	0
Totals		30	2	4	2	27	10	2

a Singled for Irvin in 3rd.
b Struck out for Garcia in 3rd.
c Grounded out for Houtteman in 5th.
d Doubled for Hegan in 8th.
e Grounded out for Narleski in 8th.
f Grounded out for Strickland in 9th.

Doubles—Glynn, Thompson. Home Run—Wertz. Sacrifice Hits—Avila, Dark, Williams. Double Plays—Dark to Williams to Lockman, Strickland to Wertz. Wild Pitch—Garcia. Left on Bases—New York 9, Cleveland 5. Umpires—Conlan, Stevens, Barlick, Berry, Napp, Warneke. Attendance—71,555. Time of Game—2:28.

1st Inning
New York
Lockman singled to right-center.
1 Dark struck out.
2 Mueller forced Lockman at second, Avila to Strickland but Mueller got to second on Strickland's bad throw to first.
Mays singled to right, Mueller scoring. Thompson walked.
3 Irvin fouled to Hegan.
Cleveland
Smith walked.
1 Avila sacrificed Smith to second, Gomez to Lockman.
2 Doby flied to center.
3 Wertz lined to short.

2nd Inning
New York
Williams walked.
Williams went to second on a wild pitch.
1 Westrum struck out.
2 Gomez lined to center.
3 Lockman fouled to Avila.
Cleveland
1 Majeski fouled to Lockman.
Philley walked.
2 Strickland forced Philley at second, Gomez on a very good stop to Williams.
3 Hegan grounded to third.

3rd Inning
New York
Dark singled to left-center.
Mueller singled through short, advancing Dark to third.
1 Mays grounded to Majeski and Dark was caught in a run-down, being putout by Hegan (assists to Hegan and Majeski). Mueller got to third and Mays to second.
Thompson got an intentional pass, loading the bases.
Rhodes, pinch-hitting for Irvin, singled to right, Mueller and Mays scoring with Thompson going to third.
Williams pulled a sacrifice squeeze, scoring Thompson and moving Rhodes to second. Williams safe at first when Garcia threw high to first for an error.
2 Westrum grounded back to the mound, advancing both runners.
3 Gomez was called out on strikes.
Cleveland
For New York—Rhodes playing left.
1 Lemon, pinch-hitting for Garcia, struck out.
2 Smith lined to center.
3 Avila grounded to third.

4th Inning
New York
For Cleveland—Houtteman pitching.
1 Lockman grounded to short.
2 Dark lined to right.
3 Mueller popped to second.
Cleveland
Doby singled to left.
1 Wertz forced Doby at second, Williams to Dark.
2,3 Majeski grounded into a double play, Dark to Williams to Lockman.

5th Inning
New York
1 Mays flied to deep center.
Thompson doubled to center.
Rhodes intentionally walked.
2 Williams forced Rhodes at second, Strickland to Avila.
Westrum singled to left, Thompson scoring, with Williams stopping at second.
3 Gomez took a called third strike.

5th Inning (continued)
Cleveland
Philley singled to center.
1 Strickland flied to left.
2 Hegan flied to left.
3 Regalado, batting for Houtteman, grounded to third.

6th Inning
New York
For Cleveland—Narleski pitching.
Lockman walked.
1 Dark sacrificed Lockman to second, Wertz to Avila.
2 Mueller popped to third.
Mays singled to right, scoring Lockman.
3 Thompson popped to third.
Cleveland
1 Smith grounded to short.
2 Avila flied to left.
3 Doby flied to center.

7th Inning
New York
1 Rhodes fanned.
2 Williams grounded to short.
3 Westrum struck out.
Cleveland
Wertz homered over the inner fence in right-center.
1 Majeski grounded to second.
2 Philley struck out.
3 Strickland popped to first.

8th Inning
New York
1 Gomez popped to short.
2 Lockman grounded to first.
3 Dark rolled back to the pitcher.
Cleveland
Glynn, batting for Hegan, got credit for a double when Mueller dropped his long fly to right after a long run.
1 Mitchell, pinch-hitting for Narleski, grounded to first, Glynn advancing to third.
Smith got safely to second when Dark threw his grounder wildly to first, Glynn scoring (Smith gets credit for an RBI).
Avila walked.
For New York—Wilhelm pitching.
2 Doby grounded to first, advancing both runners.
3 Wertz struck out.

9th Inning
New York
For Cleveland—Mossi pitching and Naragon catching.
Mueller singled to left.
Mays singled to left-center, sending Mueller to third.
1,2 Thompson lined to Strickland who threw to Wertz doubling up Mays.
3 Rhodes fanned.
Cleveland
1 Majeski called out on strikes.
2 Philley grounded to second.
3 Pope, pinch-hitting for Strickland, grounded to second.

1954

Game 4 October 2 at Cleveland

N.Y.	021	040	000				
Cle.	000	030	100				

New York	Pos	AB	R	H	RBI	PO	A	E
Lockman	1b	5	0	0	0	10	0	0
Dark	ss	5	2	3	0	2	2	0
Mueller	rf	4	1	3	0	0	0	0
Mays	cf	4	1	1	1	5	0	0
Thompson	3b	2	2	1	1	1	2	0
Irvin	lf	4	1	2	2	1	0	0
Williams	2b	2	0	0	0	3	3	1
Westrum	c	1	0	0	2	5	0	0
Liddle	p	3	0	0	0	0	1	1
Wilhelm	p	1	0	0	0	0	1	0
Antonelli	p	0	0	0	0	0	0	0
Totals		31	7	10	6	27	9	3

Pitching	IP	H	R	ER	BB	SO
New York						
Liddle (W)	6⅓	5	4	1	1	2
Wilhelm	⅔	1	0	0	0	1
Antonelli (SV)	1⅓	0	0	0	1	3
Cleveland						
Lemon (L)	*4	7	6	5	3	5
Newhouser	**0	1	1	1	1	0
Narleski	1	0	0	0	0	0
Mossi	2	1	0	0	0	0
Garcia	2	1	0	0	1	1

*Pitched to three batters in 5th.
**Pitched to two batters in 5th.

Cleveland	Pos	AB	R	H	RBI	PO	A	E
Smith	lf	3	0	0	0	0	0	0
c Pope	lf	1	0	0	0	0	0	0
e Mitchell		1	0	0	0	0	0	0
Avila	2b	4	0	0	0	4	4	0
Doby	cf	4	0	0	0	2	0	0
Rosen	3b	4	0	1	0	1	0	0
Wertz	1b	4	1	2	0	11	3	1
Westlake	rf	4	0	0	0	3	0	1
Dente	ss	3	1	0	0	1	1	0
Hegan	c	3	1	1	0	6	1	0
Lemon	p	1	0	0	0	1	1	0
Newhouser	p	0	0	0	0	0	0	0
Narleski	p	0	0	0	0	0	0	0
a Majeski		1	1	1	3	0	0	0
Mossi	p	0	0	0	0	0	1	0
b Regalado		1	0	1	1	0	0	0
Garcia	p	0	0	0	0	0	1	0
d Philley		1	0	0	0	0	0	0
Totals		35	4	6	4	27	12	2

a Homered for Narleski in 5th.
b Singled for Mossi in 7th.
c Grounded out for Smith in 7th.
d Struck out for Garcia in 9th.
e Fouled out for Pope in 9th.

Doubles—Irvin, Mays, Wertz. Home Run—Majeski. Sacrifice Hits—Mueller, Westrum, Williams. Sacrifice Flies—Westrum 2. Double Plays—Thompson to Williams to Lockman, Dente to Avila to Wertz. Wild Pitch—Liddle. Left on Bases—New York 7, Cleveland 6. Umpires—Stevens, Barlick, Berry, Conlan, Warneke, Napp. Attendance—78,102. Time of Game—2:52.

1st Inning
New York
1 Lockman struck out.
2 Dark flied to right.
 Mueller singled to center.
3 Mays fouled to Wertz.
Cleveland
1 Smith popped to second.
2 Avila lined to second.
3 Doby fanned.

2nd Inning
New York
 Thompson walked.
 Irvin doubled to left-center, moving Thompson to third.
1 Williams lined to Wertz who threw wildly to second trying to double up Irvin, allowing Thompson to score and Irvin to get to third.
 Westrum flied to Westlake, who dropped the ball for an error, Irvin scoring. (Westrum credited with a sacrifice fly and an RBI).
2 Liddle fanned.
3 Westrum caught stealing, Hegan to Dente.
Cleveland
1 Rosen grounded to second.
 Wertz doubled off the right-center field fence.
2 Westlake grounded to short, Wertz holding second.
 Wertz got to third on a wild-pitch.
3 Dente lined to center.

3rd Inning
New York
1 Lockman grounded out, Wertz to Lemon.
 Dark singled to left.
 Mueller singled to right, advancing Dark to third.
 Mays doubled into the left field corner, scoring Dark and moving Mueller to third.
 Thompson intentionally walked, loading the bases.
2 Irvin struck out.
3 Williams forced Mays at third, Rosen unassisted.
Cleveland
 Hegan walked.
1 Lemon popped to short.
2,3 Smith grounded into a double play, Thompson to Williams to Lockman.

4th Inning
New York
1 Westrum struck out.
2 Liddle struck out.
3 Lockman grounded back to the mound.
Cleveland
1 Avila popped to short.
2 Doby grounded to second.
3 Rosen grounded to third.

5th Inning
New York
 Dark singled to left-center.
 Mueller singled to right, Dark going to third.
 Mays walked loading the bases.
 For Cleveland—Newhouser came in to pitch.
 Thompson walked, forcing in Dark.
 Irvin singled to left, Mueller and Mays scoring with Thompson stopping at second.
 For Cleveland—Narleski now pitching.
1 Williams sacrificed up both runners, Wertz to Avila.
2 Westrum hit a sacrifice fly to right, Thompson scoring and Irvin to third.

5th Inning (continued)
3 Liddle grounded to third.
Cleveland
1 Wertz flied to center.
2 Westlake fouled to Lockman.
 Dente safe at first when Liddle covering first took Lockman's throw and missed the bag for an error.
 Hegan grounded to Williams who fumbled for an error, Dente going to second.
 Majeski, pinch-hitting for Narleski, hit a three-run homer over the left field fence.
3 Smith flied to center.

6th Inning
New York
 For Cleveland—Mossi pitching.
1 Lockman bunted out to first.
2 Dark grounded to first.
3 Mueller tapped back to the mound.
Cleveland
1 Avila flied to center.
2 Doby grounded to the pitcher.
3 Rosen grounded to third.

7th Inning
New York
1 Mays grounded to first.
 Thompson singled off Avila's glove.
2,3 Irvin grounded into a double play, Dente to Avila to Wertz.
Cleveland
 Wertz singled to center.
1 Westlake struck out.
2 Dente lined to left.
 Hegan singled to left, Wertz stopping at second.
 Regalado, pinch-hitting for Mossi, singled into center, scoring Wertz with Hegan going to third.
 For New York—Wilhelm pitching.
3 Pope, pinch-hitting for Smith, grounded back to the pitcher.

8th Inning
New York
 For Cleveland—Pope in left, Garcia came in to pitch.
 Williams walked.
1 Westrum sacrificed Williams to second, Wertz to Avila covering first.
2 Wilhelm fanned.
3 Lockman flied to right.
Cleveland
 Avila struck out but was safe at first as Wilhelm's pitch was wild for an error.
1 Doby lined to center.
 Rosen singled to left-center, Avila moving over to third.
 For New York—Antonelli came in to pitch.
2 Wertz struck out.
3 Westlake took a called third strike.

9th Inning
New York
 Dark singled to center.
1 Mueller sacrificed, Garcia to Avila.
2 Mays grounded to second, Dark moving to third.
3 Thompson grounded to third.
Cleveland
 Dente walked.
1 Hegan fouled to Lockman.
2 Philley, batting for Garcia, fanned.
3 Mitchell, batting for Pope, fouled to Thompson.

1954 WORLD SERIES COMPOSITE BOX

	Wins	Composite Line Score				
New York Giants (N.L.)	4	1 2 6	0 7 1	1 0 0	3	– 21
Cleveland Indians (A.L.)	0	3 0 0	0 3 0	2 1 0	0	– 9

	Regular Season			
Manager	W	L	Pct.	G. Ahead
Leo Durocher	97	57	.630	5
Al Lopez	111	43	.721	8

BATTING AND FIELDING

NEW YORK GIANTS

World Series Statistics

	Pos	G	AB	R	H	2B	3B	HR	RBI	BB	SO	SB	BA	SA	PO	A	E
Whitey Lockman	1b	4	**18**	2	2	0	0	0	0	1	2	0	.111	.111	**40**	0	0
Davey Williams	2b	4	11	0	0	0	0	0	1	2	2	0	.000	.000	10	9	1
Al Dark	ss	4	17	2	7	0	0	0	0	1	1	0	.412	.412	7	**12**	1
Hank Thompson	3b	4	11	**6**	4	1	0	0	2	**7**	1	0	.364	.455	5	11	0
Don Mueller	rf	4	**18**	4	7	0	0	0	1	0	1	0	.389	.389	3	0	**2**
Willie Mays	cf	4	14	4	4	1	0	0	3	4	1	**1**	.286	.357	10	0	0
Monte Irvin	lf	4	9	1	2	1	0	0	2	0	3	0	.222	.333	8	0	1
Wes Westrum	c	4	11	0	3	0	0	0	3	1	3	0	.273	.273	23	0	0
Dusty Rhodes	ph-lf	3	6	2	4	0	0	**2**	**7**	1	2	0	.667	1.667	4	0	0
Ray Katt		Did not play															
Bobby Hofman		Did not play															
Billy Gardner		Did not play															
Bill Taylor		Did not play															
Foster Castleman		Did not play															
Joey Amalfitano		Did not play															
Ruben Gomez	p	1	4	0	0	0	0	0	0	0	2	0	.000	.000	1	2	0
Sal Maglie	p	1	3	0	0	0	0	0	0	0	2	0	.000	.000	0	2	0
Johnny Antonelli	p	2	3	0	0	0	0	0	1	0	0	0	.000	.000	0	1	0
Don Liddle	p	2	3	0	0	0	0	0	0	0	2	0	.000	.000	0	1	1
Hoyt Wilhelm	p	2	1	0	0	0	0	0	0	0	1	0	.000	.000	0	1	1
Marv Grissom	p	1	1	0	0	0	0	0	0	0	1	0	.000	.000	0	0	0
Jim Hearn		Did not play															
Windy McCall		Did not play															
Al Corwin		Did not play															
Al Worthington		Did not play															
Alex Konikowski		Did not play															
Paul Giel		Did not play															
team total		4	130	21	33	3	0	2	20	17	24	1	.254	.323	111	39	7

Double Plays—2
Left on Bases—28

Regular Season Statistics

	Main Pos	G	AB	R	H	2B	3B	HR	RBI	BB	SO	SB	BA	SA
Whitey Lockman	1b	148	570	73	143	17	3	16	60	59	31	2	.251	.375
Davey Williams	2b	142	544	65	121	18	3	9	46	43	33	1	.222	.316
Al Dark	ss	154	**644**	98	118	26	6	20	70	27	40	5	.293	.446
Hank Thompson	3b	136	448	76	118	18	1	26	86	90	58	3	.263	.482
Don Mueller	of	153	619	90	**212**	35	8	4	71	22	17	2	.342	.444
Willie Mays	of	151	565	119	195	33	**13**	41	110	66	57	8	**.345**	**.667**
Monte Irvin	of	135	432	62	113	13	3	19	64	70	23	7	.262	.438
Wes Westrum	c	98	246	25	46	3	1	8	27	45	60	0	.187	.305
Dusty Rhodes	ph-of	82	164	31	56	7	3	15	50	18	25	1	.341	.695
Ray Katt	c	86	200	26	51	7	1	9	33	19	29	1	.255	.435
Bobby Hofman	ph	71	125	12	28	5	0	8	30	17	15	0	.224	.456
Billy Gardner	3b	62	108	10	23	5	0	1	7	6	19	0	.213	.287
Bill Taylor	ph	55	65	4	12	1	0	2	10	3	15	0	.185	.292
Foster Castleman	ph	13	12	0	3	0	0	0	1	0	3	0	.250	.250
Joey Amalfitano	3b	9	5	2	0	0	0	0	0	0	4	0	.000	.000
Ruben Gomez	p	39	98	6	16	0	0	2	9	4	25	0	.163	.224
Sal Maglie	p	34	63	3	8	0	0	0	1	4	16	0	.127	.127
Johnny Antonelli	p	49	81	11	14	1	0	2	6	0	8	0	.173	.259
Don Liddle	p	29	37	3	7	0	0	0	3	8	12	0	.189	.189
Hoyt Wilhelm	p	57	21	0	1	0	0	0	1	0	8	0	.048	.048
Marv Grissom	p	56	32	3	5	0	0	0	1	2	11	0	.156	.156
Jim Hearn	p	29	45	2	5	1	0	1	3	3	17	0	.111	.200
Windy McCall	p	33	11	0	0	0	0	0	1	1	4	0	.000	.000
Al Corwin	p	23	3	1	0	0	0	0	0	0	2	0	.000	.000
Al Worthington	p	10	4	0	0	0	0	0	0	0	2	0	.000	.000
Alex Konikowski	p	10	1	0	0	0	0	0	0	0	1	0	.000	.000
Paul Giel	p	6	0	0	0	0	0	0	0	0	0	0	.000	.000
team total		154	5245	732	1386	194	42	**186**	701	522	561	30	.264	.424

Ebba St. Claire (c), Hoot Evers (ph), Ron Samford (of), Joe Garagiola (c), Eric Rodin (of), Harvey Gentry (ph), Bob Lennon (ph), Larry Jansen (p), George Spencer (p), Ray Monzant (p), and Mario Picone (p) also played for the Giants during the season.

CLEVELAND INDIANS

World Series Statistics

	Pos	G	AB	R	H	2B	3B	HR	RBI	BB	SO	SB	BA	SA	PO	A	E
Vic Wertz	1b	4	16	2	**8**	**2**	**1**	1	3	2	2	0	**.500**	**.938**	33	6	1
Bobby Avila	2b	4	15	1	2	0	0	0	0	2	1	0	.133	.133	12	10	0
George Strickland	ss	3	9	0	0	0	0	0	0	0	2	0	.000	.000	6	8	1
Al Rosen	3b	3	12	0	3	0	0	0	0	1	0	0	.250	.250	2	3	0
Dave Philley	rf-ph	4	8	0	1	0	0	0	0	1	3	0	.125	.125	1	0	0
Larry Doby	cf	4	16	0	2	0	0	0	0	2	**4**	0	.125	.125	7	0	0
Al Smith	lf	4	14	2	3	0	0	1	2	2	2	0	.214	.429	4	0	0
Jim Hegan	c	4	13	1	2	1	0	0	0	1	1	0	.154	.231	27	3	0
Wally Westlake	rf	2	7	0	1	0	0	0	0	1	3	0	.143	.143	6	0	1
Hank Majeski	ph-3b	4	6	1	1	0	0	1	3	0	1	0	.167	.667	2	1	0
Rudy Regalado	pr-3b-ph	4	3	0	1	0	0	0	1	0	0	0	.333	.333	0	0	0
Sam Dente	ss	3	3	1	0	0	0	0	0	1	0	0	.000	.000	1	1	0
Dave Pope	ph-rf-lf	3	3	0	0	0	0	0	0	1	1	0	.000	.000	0	0	0
Billy Glynn	ph-1b	2	2	1	1	1	0	0	0	0	1	0	.500	1.000	0	0	0
Dale Mitchell	ph	3	2	0	0	0	0	0	0	1	0	0	.000	.000			
Mickey Grasso	c	1	0	0	0	0	0	0	0	0	0	0	—	—	1	0	0
Hal Naragon	c	1	0	0	0	0	0	0	0	0	0	0	—	—	1	0	0
Bob Lemon	p-ph	3	6	0	0	0	0	0	0	1	1	0	.000	.000	2	2	0
Early Wynn	p	1	2	0	1	1	0	0	0	0	1	0	.500	1.000	1	1	0
Don Mossi	p	3	0	0	0	0	0	0	0	0	0	0	—	—	0	2	0
Mike Garcia	p	2	0	0	0	0	0	0	0	0	0	0	—	—	0	2	1
Ray Narleski	p	2	0	0	0	0	0	0	0	0	0	0	—	—	0	1	0
Art Houtteman	p	1	0	0	0	0	0	0	0	0	0	0	—	—	0	0	0
Hal Newhouser	p	1	0	0	0	0	0	0	0	0	0	0	—	—	0	0	0
Bob Feller		Did not play															
Bob Hooper		Did not play															
team total		4	137	9	26	5	1	3	9	16	23	0	.190	.307	106	40	4

Double Plays—2
Left on Bases—37

Regular Season Statistics

	Main Pos	G	AB	R	H	2B	3B	HR	RBI	BB	SO	SB	BA	SA
Vic Wertz	a 1b	94	295	33	81	14	2	14	48	34	40	0	.275	.478
Bobby Avila	2b	143	555	112	189	27	2	15	67	59	31	9	**.341**	.477
George Strickland	ss	112	361	42	77	12	3	6	37	55	62	2	.213	.313
Al Rosen	3b	137	466	76	140	20	2	24	102	85	43	6	.300	.506
Dave Philley	of	133	452	48	102	13	3	12	60	57	48	2	.226	.347
Larry Doby	of	153	577	94	157	18	4	**32**	**126**	85	94	3	.272	.484
Al Smith	of	131	481	101	135	29	6	11	50	88	65	2	.281	.435
Jim Hegan	c	139	423	56	99	12	7	11	40	34	48	0	.234	.374
Wally Westlake	of	85	240	36	63	9	2	11	42	26	37	0	.263	.454
Hank Majeski	2b	57	121	10	34	4	0	3	17	7	14	0	.281	.388
Rudy Regalado	3b	65	180	21	45	5	0	2	24	19	16	0	.250	.311
Sam Dente	ss	68	169	18	45	7	1	1	19	14	4	0	.266	.337
Dave Pope	of	60	102	21	30	2	1	4	13	10	22	2	.294	.451
Billy Glynn	1b	111	171	19	43	3	2	5	18	12	21	3	.251	.380
Dale Mitchell	ph	53	60	6	17	1	0	1	6	9	1	0	.283	.350
Mickey Grasso	c	4	6	1	2	0	0	1	1	1	1	0	.333	.833
Hal Naragon	c	46	101	10	24	2	2	0	12	9	12	0	.238	.297
Bob Lemon	p	40	98	11	21	4	1	2	10	6	24	0	.214	.337
Early Wynn	p	40	93	10	17	3	0	0	4	7	13	0	.183	.215
Don Mossi	p	40	19	1	3	0	0	0	0	3	10	0	.158	.158
Mike Garcia	p	45	81	5	11	0	0	0	4	6	22	0	.136	.136
Ray Narleski	p	42	16	0	0	0	0	0	0	1	5	0	.000	.000
Art Houtteman	p	32	65	6	18	2	0	1	10	2	11	1	.277	.354
Hal Newhouser	p	26	13	0	2	0	0	0	1	0	0	0	.154	.154
Bob Feller	p	19	48	6	9	1	0	0	1	4	17	0	.188	.208
Bob Hooper	p	17	5	0	0	0	0	0	0	0	1	0	.000	.000
team total		156	5222	746	1368	188	39	**156**	714	637	668	30	.262	.403

a—from Baltimore
Luke Easter (ph), Rocky Nelson (1b), Joe Ginsberg (c), Jim Dyck (ph), Bob Kennedy (3b), Bob Chakales (p), Dave Hoskins (p), Jose Santiago (p), and Dick Tomanek (p) also played for the Indians during the season.

PITCHING

NEW YORK GIANTS

World Series Statistics

	G	GS	CG	IP	H	R	ER	BB	SO	W	L	SV	ERA
Johnny Antonelli	2	1	**1**	10⅔	8	1	1	7	**12**	**1**	0	**1**	**0.84**
Ruben Gomez	1	1	0	7⅓	4	2	2	3	2	**1**	0	0	2.45
Don Liddle	2	1	0	7	5	4	1	1	2	**1**	0	0	1.29
Sal Maglie	1	1	0	7	7	2	2	2	2	0	0	0	2.57
Marv Grissom	1	0	0	2⅔	1	0	0	3	2	**1**	0	0	0.00
Hoyt Wilhelm	2	0	0	2⅓	1	0	0	0	3	0	0	**1**	0.00
Jim Hearn	Did not play												
Windy McCall	Did not play												
Al Corwin	Did not play												
Al Worthington	Did not play												
Alex Konikowski	Did not play												
Paul Giel	Did not play												
team total	4	4	1	37	26	9	6	16	23	4	0	2	1.46

Regular Season Statistics

	G	GS	CG	IP	H	ER	BB	SO	W	L	Pct	SV	ShO	ERA
Johnny Antonelli	39	37	18	259	209	66	194	152	21	7	**.750**	2	**6**	**2.29**
Ruben Gomez	37	32	10	222	202	71	**109**	106	17	9	.654	0	4	2.88
Don Liddle	28	19	4	127	100	43	55	44	9	4	.692	0	3	3.05
Sal Maglie	34	32	9	218	222	79	70	117	14	6	.700	2	1	3.26
Marv Grissom	56	3	1	122	100	32	50	64	10	7	.588	19	1	2.36
Hoyt Wilhelm	57	0	0	111	77	26	52	64	12	4	.750	7	0	2.11
Jim Hearn	29	18	3	130	137	60	66	45	8	8	.500	1	2	4.15
Windy McCall	33	4	0	61	50	22	29	38	2	5	.286	2	0	3.25
Al Corwin	20	0	0	31	35	14	14	14	1	3	.250	0	0	4.06
Al Worthington	10	1	0	18	21	7	15	8	0	2	.000	0	0	3.50
Alex Konikowski	10	0	0	12	10	10	12	6	0	0	—	0	0	7.50
Paul Giel	6	0	0	4	8	4	2	4	0	0	—	0	0	9.00
team total	154	154	45	1390	1258	**478**	613	692	**47**	57	**.630**	33	19	**3.09**

CLEVELAND INDIANS

World Series Statistics

	G	GS	CG	IP	H	R	ER	BB	SO	W	L	SV	ERA
Bob Lemon	2	**2**	**1**	**13⅓**	**16**	**11**	**10**	**8**	11	0	**2**	0	6.75
Early Wynn	1	1	0	7	4	3	3	2	5	0	1	0	3.86
Mike Garcia	2	1	0	5	6	4	3	4	4	0	1	0	5.40
Don Mossi	**3**	0	0	4	3	0	0	0	1	0	0	0	0.00
Ray Narleski	2	0	0	4	1	1	1	1	2	0	0	0	2.25
Art Houtteman	1	0	0	2	2	1	1	1	1	0	0	0	4.50
Hal Newhouser	1	0	0	0	1	1	1	1	0	0	0	0	∞
Bob Feller	Did not play												
Bob Hooper	Did not play												
Team total	4	4	1	35⅓	33	21	19	17	24	0	4	0	4.84

Regular Season Statistics

	G	GS	CG	IP	H	ER	BB	SO	W	L	Pct	SV	ShO	ERA
Bob Lemon	36	33	**21**	258	228	78	92	110	**23**	7	.767	0	2	2.72
Early Wynn	40	**36**	20	**271**	225	82	83	**155**	**23**	11	.676	2	3	2.72
Mike Garcia	45	34	13	259	220	76	71	129	19	8	.704	5	**5**	**2.64**
Don Mossi	40	5	2	93	56	20	39	55	6	1	.857	7	0	1.94
Ray Narleski	42	2	1	89	59	22	44	52	3	3	.500	13	0	2.22
Art Houtteman	32	25	11	188	198	70	59	68	15	7	.682	0	1	3.35
Hal Newhouser	26	1	0	47	34	13	18	25	7	2	.778	7	0	2.49
Bob Feller	19	19	9	140	127	48	39	59	13	3	.813	0	1	3.09
Bob Hooper	17	0	0	35	39	19	16	12	0	0	—	2	0	4.89
Team total	156	156	**77**	**1419**	1220	**439**	486	678	**111**	43	**.721**	36	12	**2.78**

Total Attendance—251,507 Average Attendance—62,877 Winning Player's Share—$11,118 Losing Player's Share—$6,713

1955
This Is Next Year

The Brooklyn Dodgers came into this World Series faced with an unavoidable fact; they had lost all seven Series played in the history of the franchise. The last five of those defeats came at the hands of the New York Yankees, who again furnished the opposition this year. Both clubs returned to the Series after missing out in 1954. Casey Stengel still had Mickey Mantle and Yogi Berra as the pillars of the Yankee attack, but he also added some key newcomers since the 1953 Series, first baseman Bill Skowron and catcher-outfielder Elston Howard. Whitey Ford was the undisputed leader of the pitching staff now that Allie Reynolds, Eddie Lopat, Johnny Sain, and Vic Raschi were gone. To flesh out the mound corps, Stengel got Bob Turley, Don Larsen, and reliever Jim Konstanty in trades, and reclaimed veteran lefty Tommy Byrne from the minors.

The Dodgers had practically the same team on the field as two years ago, a bit older but still very powerful. Jackie Robinson was now past his prime, but Duke Snider, Roy Campanella, Gil Hodges, and Carl Furillo still swung big bats. The biggest additions to the team were Walt Alston, the soft-spoken manager who replaced Chuck Dressen after the 1953 Series; Don Newcombe, who recovered from two years in the army and a poor 1954 campaign to reclaim his spot as mound ace with a 20–5 record; and Sandy Amoros, a hustling little Cuban left fielder.

Any hopes this Dodger crew had of knocking off the Yanks were severely shaken by the first two games of the Series at Yankee Stadium. The opening game matched the aces, Ford vs. Newcombe. The Dodgers scored a pair in the top of the second inning, but the Yanks tied it in the bottom of the inning on a two-run homer by Howard. The Bums went ahead 3–2 in the third, but the Yanks immediately tied it up again. Ford hit his stride after that point, but Newcombe never settled down. Joe Collins put New York ahead with a solo homer in the fourth, then kayoed Newcombe with a two-run blast in the sixth. The Bums closed the gap but lost 6–5, wasting homers by Furillo and Snider. Billy Loes started the second game for Brooklyn but lost a 4–2 decision to Byrne's five-hitter. Mickey Mantle played in neither game due to a bad leg which plagued him throughout the Series.

No team had ever come back from losing the first two games, but the Bums started on the road back with an 8–3 victory in game three in Ebbets Field. Johnny Podres, a young southpaw with a mediocre 9–10 record for the year, went all the way for Brooklyn and scattered seven hits. Mantle limped through the game and hit a homer, but regular right fielder Hank Bauer sat the day out with a pulled muscle. Erskine and Larsen started game four but got early showers under pressure. Home runs by Campanella, Snider, and Hodges gave the Dodgers an 8–5 win, which Labine got credit for with his four innings of relief. Now the Dodgers had pulled even, and they went ahead in the Series in game five. Rookie Roger Craig and Labine combined on a six-hitter, and a home run by Amoros and a pair by Snider powered a 5–3 Dodger win. Looking to ride the swelling tide to the championship, the Dodgers started young Karl Spooner in game six in Yankee Stadium but suffered a 5–1 setback to set the stage for the seventh game.

The two clubs had hit a record 17 homers in the first six games, but there would be no circuit clouts in the final contest. Alston bypassed Newcombe, his ace who couldn't seem to beat the Yankees, in favor of Podres, the winner of the third game, while Stengel fingered the veteran Byrne. With Podres pitching a masterful game, Gil Hodges drove in runs in the fourth and sixth innings for a 2–0 lead. In the bottom of the sixth, Alston moved Jim Gilliam from left field to second base and sent Amoros to left, a prophetic move. Billy Martin walked and Gil McDougald bunted for a hit to put the tying runs aboard with Berra at the plate. The Dodgers played Yogi far over to right, and when he sliced a fly down the left-field line, it looked like a sure extra-base hit. But Amoros came tearing out of left-center and speared the ball with his glove extended to its fullest. He zipped the ball in to shortstop Pee Wee Reese, who relayed the ball perfectly to Hodges to double off McDougald. With the rally broken, Podres took heart and shut the Yanks out the rest of the way, and Brooklyn for once did not have to wait for next year.

Game 1 September 28 at New York

Bkn.	0 2 1	0 0 0	0 2 0				
N.Y.	0 2 1	1 0 2	0 0 x				

Brooklyn	Pos	AB	R	H	RBI	PO	A	E
Gilliam	lf	3	0	0	0	2	0	0
Reese	ss	5	0	1	0	2	5	0
Snider	cf	5	1	2	1	1	0	0
Campanella	c	5	0	0	0	5	1	0
Furillo	rf	4	2	3	1	4	0	0
Hodges	1b	4	0	1	0	12	1	0
J. Robinson	3b	4	2	1	0	0	2	0
Zimmer	2b	2	0	1	2	1	3	0
Newcombe	p	3	0	0	0	0	1	0
Bessent	p	0	0	0	0	0	1	0
b Kellert		1	0	1	0	0	0	0
c Hoak		0	0	0	0	0	0	0
Labine	p	0	0	0	0	0	0	0
Totals		36	5	10	4	24	14	0

a Batting for Rizzuto in 6th when Martin was out attempting to steal home.
b Singled for Bessent in 8th.
c Ran for Kellert in 8th.

Triples—Martin, J. Robinson.
Home Runs—Collins 2, Furillo, Howard, Snider. Stolen Base—J. Robinson.
Sacrifice Fly—Zimmer.
Double Plays—Zimmer to Hodges. Martin to Rizzuto to Collins, Hodges to Reese to Hodges. Left on Bases—Brooklyn 9, New York 2. Umpires—Summers (A), Ballanfant (N), Honochick (A), Dascoli (N), Flaherty (A), Donatelli (N).
Attendance—63,869. Time of Game—2:31.

New York	Pos	AB	R	H	RBI	PO	A	E
Bauer	rf	4	0	2	0	3	0	0
McDougald	3b	4	0	1	0	2	1	1
Noren	cf	4	0	0	1	4	0	0
Berra	c	3	1	1	0	5	0	0
Collins	1b	3	3	2	3	6	1	0
Howard	lf	3	1	1	2	4	0	0
Martin	2b	4	0	2	0	2	3	0
Rizzuto	ss	2	0	0	0	3	2	0
a E. Robinson		0	0	0	0	0	0	0
J. Coleman	ss	0	0	0	0	0	0	0
Ford	p	2	1	0	0	1	3	0
Grim	p	0	0	0	0	0	0	0
Totals		29	6	9	6	27	10	1

Pitching	IP	H	R	ER	BB	SO
Brooklyn						
Newcombe (L)	5⅓	8	6	6	2	4
Bessent	1⅓	0	0	0	0	0
Labine	1	1	0	0	1	0
New York						
Ford (W)	8	9	5	3	4	2
Grim (SV)	1	1	0	0	0	2

1st Inning
Brooklyn
1 Gilliam grounded back to the mound.
  Reese singled to left.
2 Snider struck out.
3 Campanella popped to second.
New York
  Bauer beat out a bunt past the mound.
1 McDougald called out on strikes.
2,3 Noren bounced into a double play, Zimmer tagging Bauer to Hodges.

2nd Inning
Brooklyn
  Furillo homered into the lower right field stands.
1 Hodges grounded to second.
  J. Robinson tripled to left-center.
  Zimmer singled over second, scoring J. Robinson.
2 Newcombe grounded out to the mound, advancing Zimmer to second.
  Gilliam walked.
3 Reese forced Gilliam at second, McDougald to Martin.
New York
1 Berra grounded to second.
  Collins walked.
  Howard hit a two-run homer into the lower deck of the left field stands.
2 Martin flied to right.
3 Rizzuto grounded to third.

3rd Inning
Brooklyn
  Snider homered into the third deck of the right field stands.
1 Campanella popped to third.
  Furillo walked.
2 Hodges flied to center.
3 Robinson was called out on strikes.
New York
  Ford walked.
  Bauer singled to left, moving Ford to second.
1 McDougald grounded to short, advancing both runners.
2 Noren grounded to second, Ford scoring and Bauer going to third.
3 Berra grounded back to the mound.

4th Inning
Brooklyn
  Zimmer walked.
1 Newcombe forced Zimmer at second on an attempted sacrifice bunt, Ford to Rizzuto.
  Gilliam walked.
2,3 Reese grounded into a double play, Martin to Rizzuto to Collins.
New York
  Collins hit a home run into the lower deck of the right field stands.
1 Howard took a called third strike.
  Martin singled to left.
2 Martin caught stealing, Campanella to Reese.
3 Rizzuto called out on strikes.

5th Inning
Brooklyn
1 Snider popped to short.
2 Campanella grounded to short.
  Furillo singled to center.
  Hodges singled to center, Furillo advancing to third.
3 J. Robinson flied to deep center.
New York
1 Ford struck out.
2 Bauer flied to right.
3 McDougald grounded to short.

6th Inning
Brooklyn
1 Zimmer flied to center.
2 Newcombe grounded to second.
3 Gilliam fouled to Berra.
New York
1 Noren grounded to first.
  Berra singled to right.
  Collins hit his second homer of the game, a two-run shot into the right-center field bleachers.
2 Howard grounded to short.
  Martin tripled over Gilliam's head.
  For Brooklyn—Bessent came in to pitch.
  E. Robinson batted for Rizzuto.
3 Martin was out trying to steal home, being tagged out on a close play, by Campanella.

7th Inning
Brooklyn
  For New York—Jerry Coleman at short.
1 Reese flied to right.
2 Snider grounded out, Collins to Ford.
3 Campanella flied to right.
New York
1 J. Coleman grounded to third.
2 Ford flied to center.
3 Bauer grounded to short.

8th Inning
Brooklyn
  Furillo singled to center.
1 Hodges flied to left.
  J. Robinson safe at second as his grounder bounced off McDougald's knee into left, Furillo going to third.
2 Zimmer hit a sacrifice fly to Noren in left-center, Furillo scoring with J. Robinson going to third after the catch.
  Kellert batted for Bessent, and with a 1–0 count, J. Robinson stole home in a very controversial play. Kellert then hit a Texas-League single into short right-center.
  Hoak ran for Kellert.
3 Gilliam popped to third.
New York
  For Brooklyn—Labine pitching.
  McDougald singled to left.
1,2 Noren grounded into a reverse double play, first to short to first.
  Berra walked.
3 Collins flied to Gilliam in deep left-center.

9th Inning
Brooklyn
  For New York—Grim pitching.
1 Reese took a called third strike.
  Snider singled past first into right.
2 Campanella lined to very deep right.
3 Furillo fanned on a third-strike foul tip.

Game 2 September 29 at New York

Brooklyn	Pos	AB	R	H	RBI	PO	A	E
Gilliam	lf	4	0	1	1	0	1	0
Reese	ss	4	1	2	0	2	3	0
Snider	cf	4	0	1	0	2	0	0
Campanella	c	3	0	0	0	11	2	0
Furillo	rf	3	0	0	0	0	0	0
Hodges	1b	3	0	0	0	6	1	0
J. Robinson	3b	2	1	0	0	1	1	0
Zimmer	2b	3	0	1	0	2	2	2
Loes	p	1	0	0	0	0	0	0
c Kellert		1	0	0	0	0	0	0
Bessent	p	0	0	0	0	0	1	0
Spooner	p	0	0	0	0	0	0	0
d Hoak		0	0	0	0	0	0	0
Labine	p	0	0	0	0	0	0	0
Totals		28	2	5	2	24	11	2

New York	Pos	AB	R	H	RBI	PO	A	E
Bauer	rf	1	0	1	0	3	0	0
Cerv	cf	3	0	0	0	0	0	0
McDougald	3b	4	0	1	0	1	0	0
Noren	cf-lf	3	0	0	0	4	0	0
Berra	c	3	1	2	0	6	1	0
Collins	1b	3	1	0	0	5	0	0
Howard	lf-rf	4	1	1	1	2	1	0
Martin	2b	3	1	1	1	2	3	0
Rizzuto	ss	1	0	1	0	2	1	0
a E. Robinson		0	0	0	0	0	0	0
b J. Coleman	ss	1	0	0	0	2	2	0
Byrne	p	3	0	1	2	0	0	0
Totals		29	4	8	4	27	8	0

```
Bkn.   000 110 000
N.Y.   000 400 00x
```

a Hit by pitch for Rizzuto in 4th.
b Ran for E. Robinson in 4th.
c Hit into double play for Bessent in 5th.
d Walked for Spooner in 8th.

Double—Reese. Double Plays—Campanella
to Zimmer, Zimmer to Reese to Hodges,
Hodges to Reese, J. Coleman to Martin to
Collins, Berra to Martin, J. Coleman to
Collins. Hit by Pitcher—Berra (by Loes),
E. Robinson (by Loes). Left on
Bases—Brooklyn 4, New York 5.
Umpires—Ballanfant, Honochick, Dascoli,
Summers, Flaherty, Donatelli.
Attendance—64,707. Time of Game—2:28.

Pitching	IP	H	R	ER	BB	SO
Brooklyn						
Loes (L)	3⅓	7	4	4	1	5
Bessent	⅓	0	0	0	0	0
Spooner	3	1	0	0	1	5
Labine	1	0	0	0	0	1
New York						
Byrne (W)	9	5	2	2	5	6

1st Inning
Brooklyn
1 Gilliam struck out.
2 Reese flied to right.
3 Snider flied to right.
New York
Bauer singled into left.
1,2 McDougald struck out and Bauer was
doubled up trying to steal,
Campanella to Zimmer. (Bauer pulled
a muscle while sliding into second.)
3 Noren flied to center.

2nd Inning
Brooklyn
1 Campanella fouled to McDougald.
Furillo walked.
2 Hodges flied to right.
3 Robinson popped to Rizzuto in short
left.
New York
Berra was hit by a pitched ball.
1 Collins fanned.
2 Howard struck out and Berra attempting
second was a sure out but Zimmer
dropped Campanella's throw for an
error.
3 Martin struck out.

3rd Inning
Brooklyn
For New York—Cerv in at center, Noren
moved to left and Howard to right.
1 Zimmer took a called third strike.
2 Loes grounded to short.
3 Gilliam flied to Noren in deep left-
center.
New York
Rizzuto singled to left.
1,2 Byrne hit into a double play, Zimmer
to Reese to Hodges.
3 Cerv took a called third strike.

4th Inning
Brooklyn
Reese doubled into the left field corner.
Snider singled to right but was out
1 trying for second, Howard to Rizzuto
as Reese scored.
Campanella walked.
2 Furillo flied to left.
3 Hodges flied to left.
New York
McDougald singled to right.
1,2 Noren grounded into a double play,
Hodges tagging the base to Reese who
tagged McDougald.
Berra singled to left.
Collins walked.
Howard singled to left, Berra scoring
with Collins stopping at second.
Martin singled to left, Collins scoring
with Howard stopping at second.
E. Robinson, batting for Rizzuto, was hit
by a pitch, to load the bases.
J. Coleman ran for E. Robinson.
Byrne singled into center, Howard and
Martin scoring with J. Coleman stopping
at second.
For Brooklyn—Bessent came in to pitch.
3 Cerv grounded to second on Bessent's
first pitch.

5th Inning
Brooklyn
For New York—J. Coleman playing short.
J. Robinson walked.
Zimmer singled to left, moving J.
Robinson to second.
1,2 Kellert, pinch-hitting for Bessent,
grounded into a double play, J. Coleman
to Martin to Collins. J. Robinson
moved over to third.
Gilliam singled through the hole between
short and third, scoring J. Robinson.
3 Reese took a called third strike.
New York
For Brooklyn—Spooner pitching.
1 McDougald was called out on strikes.
Noren walked.
Berra singled into left-center but
2 Noren was out at third, Gilliam to
J. Robinson.
3 Collins struck out.

6th Inning
Brooklyn
1 Snider grounded to second.
2 Campanella flied to right.
3 Furillo popped to first.
New York
1 Howard grounded to third.
2 Martin fanned.
3 J. Coleman struck out.

7th Inning
Brooklyn
Hodges walked.
1 J. Robinson flied to right.
2,3 Zimmer struck out and Hodges was out
trying for second, Berra to Martin.
New York
1 Byrne grounded back to the pitcher.
2 Cerv grounded to short.
3 McDougald struck out.

8th Inning
Brooklyn
Hoak, pinch-hitting for Spooner, walked.
1,2 Gilliam hit into a double play,
Martin to J. Coleman to Collins.
Reese singled to left.
3 Snider fanned.
New York
For Brooklyn—Labine pitching.
Noren lined to Zimmer, who dropped the
ball for an error.
1 Berra called out on strikes.
2 Collins flied to center.
3 Howard forced Noren at second, Reese
to Zimmer.

9th Inning
Brooklyn
1 Campanella popped to short.
2 Furillo flied to deep left.
3 Hodges struck out.

Game 3 September 30 at Brooklyn

New York	Pos	AB	R	H	RBI	PO	A	E
Cerv	lf-cf	4	0	0	0	3	0	0
McDougald	3b	4	0	1	0	0	3	0
Berra	c	4	0	1	0	6	1	0
Mantle	cf-rf	4	1	1	1	2	0	0
Skowron	1b	4	1	2	0	5	2	0
Howard	rf-lf	4	0	0	0	5	0	0
Martin	2b	4	0	0	0	3	0	0
Rizzuto	ss	2	1	1	0	2	1	0
Turley	p	1	0	0	0	0	0	0
Morgan	p	0	0	0	0	0	0	0
a Bauer		1	0	0	0	0	0	0
Kucks	p	0	0	0	0	0	0	0
b Carey		1	0	1	1	0	0	0
Sturdivant	p	0	0	0	0	0	1	0
Totals		33	3	7	2	24	7	0

Brooklyn	Pos	AB	R	H	RBI	PO	A	E
Gilliam	2b	3	1	1	1	2	3	0
Reese	ss	3	1	1	2	1	3	0
Snider	cf	4	1	1	0	1	0	0
Campanella	c	5	1	3	3	6	0	1
Furillo	rf	5	0	1	1	1	0	0
Hodges	1b	5	0	0	0	14	0	0
J. Robinson	3b	5	2	2	0	0	7	0
Amoros	lf	1	1	1	1	2	1	0
Podres	p	3	1	1	0	0	0	0
Totals		34	8	11	8	27	14	1

```
N.Y.   020 000 100
Bkn.   220 200 20x
```

a Flied out for Morgan in 5th.
b Tripled for Kucks in 7th.

Doubles—Campanella, Furillo, J. Robinson,
Skowron. Triple—Carey. Home
Runs—Campanella, Mantle. Sacrifice
Hit—Podres. Double Play—Reese to Gilliam
to Hodges. Hit by Pitcher—Amoros (by
Turley). Left on Bases—New York 5,
Brooklyn 11. Umpires—Honochick, Dascoli,
Summers, Ballanfant, Donatelli, Flaherty.
Attendance—34,209. Time of Game—2:20.

Pitching	IP	H	R	ER	BB	SO
New York						
Turley (L)	1⅓	3	4	4	2	1
Morgan	2⅔	3	2	2	3	1
Kucks	2	1	0	0	1	0
Sturdivant	2	4	2	2	1	0
Brooklyn						
Podres (W)	8	7	3	2	2	6

1st Inning
New York
1 Cerv grounded back to the mound.
2 McDougald flied to center.
3 Berra flied to right.
Brooklyn
1 Gilliam flied to center.
Reese walked.
2 Snider struck out.
Campanella hit a two-run homer into
the lower left-center field stands.
3 Furillo lined to center.

2nd Inning
New York
Mantle homered into the lower center
field stands.
Skowron doubled down the left field
line.
1 Howard grounded to third, Skowron holding
second.
2 Martin struck out.
Rizzuto singled to left, Skowron scoring
when Campanella dropped Amoros' throw
when Skowron crashed into him. Rizzuto
got to third on the error.
3 Turley grounded to third.
Brooklyn
For New York—Mantle's thigh was sore so
he moved to right, Howard to left and
Cerv moved to center.
1 Hodges flied to center.
J. Robinson singled to center.
Amoros was hit by a pitch.
Podres beat out a bunt down the third
base line, loading the bases.
Gilliam walked, forcing in J. Robinson.
For New York—Morgan came in to pitch.
Reese walked, forcing in Amoros.
2 Snider forced Podres at the plate,
Skowron to Berra.
3 Campanella lined to second.

3rd Inning
New York
1 Cerv fanned.
2 McDougald grounded to second.
3 Berra fouled to Hodges.
Brooklyn
Furillo doubled into the left field
corner.
1 Hodges grounded to third, Furillo
holding second.
2 J. Robinson popped to second.
Amoros got an intentional pass.
3 Podres struck out.

4th Inning
New York
1 Mantle grounded to third.
2 Skowron struck out.
3 Howard was called out on strikes.
Brooklyn
Gilliam singled to left.
1 Reese flied to center.
Snider walked.
Campanella singled to left, scoring
Gilliam with Snider going to third.
2 Furillo fouled to Howard at the left
field boxes, Snider scoring after the
catch and Campanella going to second
on Howard's throw to the plate.
3 Hodges grounded to short.

5th Inning
New York
1 Martin grounded to third on a great
stop by J. Robinson.
Rizzuto walked.
2 Bauer, pinch-hitting for Morgan, flied
to left.
3 Cerv struck out.
Brooklyn
For New York—Kucks pitching.
1 J. Robinson grounded to third.
Amoros walked.
2 Podres sacrificed Amoros to second,
Skowron to Martin who covered first.
3 Gilliam flied to left.

6th Inning
New York
McDougald singled to center.
Berra singled to center, sending
McDougald to second.
1,2 Mantle grounded into a double play,
Reese to Gilliam to Hodges, with
McDougald advancing to third.
3 Skowron grounded to short.
Brooklyn
1 Reese flied to center.
Snider singled to left.
2 Campanella flied to left.
3 Furillo grounded to third.

7th Inning
New York
1 Howard flied to the left field wall.
2 Martin grounded to third.
Rizzuto walked.
Carey, pinch-hitting for Kucks,
tripled off the left field wall,
scoring Rizzuto.
3 Cerv struck out.
Brooklyn
For New York—Sturdivant pitching.
1 Hodges robbed of a homer by a leaping-
catch by Howard in left-center.
Robinson doubled inside the third base
line and reached third on Howard's
throw to second.
Amoros singled to right, scoring
J. Robinson.
2 Podres forced Amoros at second on an
attempted sacrifice, Sturdivant to
Rizzuto.
Gilliam walked.
Reese singled to center, scoring
Podres with Gilliam going to third.
3 Snider lined to left.

8th Inning
New York
1 McDougald grounded to third.
2 Berra grounded to second.
3 Mantle grounded to third.
Brooklyn
Campanella doubled into the
left field corner.
1 Furillo fouled to Berra.
2 Hodges fouled to Rizzuto.
3 Robinson fouled to Skowron.

9th Inning
New York
Skowron singled to right.
1 Howard popped to Gilliam in
short right.
2 Martin popped to short.
3 Rizzuto popped to first.

Game 4 October 1 at Brooklyn

New York	Pos	AB	R	H	RBI	PO	A	E
Noren	cf	5	0	1	0	3	0	0
McDougald	3b	5	1	1	1	1	1	0
Mantle	rf	5	0	1	0	2	0	0
Berra	c	3	0	1	0	4	1	0
Collins	1b	2	2	0	0	11	1	0
Howard	lf	3	1	1	0	0	0	0
Martin	2b	4	1	2	2	1	3	0
Rizzuto	ss	3	0	1	1	2	2	0
Larsen	p	2	0	0	0	0	1	0
Kucks	p	0	0	0	0	0	1	0
a E. Robinson		1	0	1	1	0	0	0
b Carroll		0	0	0	0	0	0	0
R. Coleman	p	0	0	0	0	0	0	0
Morgan	p	0	0	0	0	0	0	0
c Skowron		1	0	0	0	0	0	0
Sturdivant	p	0	0	0	0	0	0	0
Totals		34	5	9	5	24	10	0

a Singled for Kucks in 6th.
b Ran for E. Robinson in 6th.
c Flied out for Morgan in 8th.

N.Y.	110	102	000
Bkn.	001	330	10x

Brooklyn	Pos	AB	R	H	RBI	PO	A	E
Gilliam	2b	4	1	2	1	1	4	0
Reese	ss	4	1	2	0	1	2	0
Snider	cf	4	1	1	3	6	0	0
Campanella	c	5	2	3	1	4	0	0
Furillo	rf	5	1	2	0	1	0	0
Hodges	1b	4	1	3	3	11	0	0
J. Robinson	3b	4	0	0	0	1	2	0
Amoros	lf	3	1	1	0	2	0	0
Erskine	p	1	0	0	0	0	1	0
Bessent	p	1	0	0	0	0	1	0
Labine	p	2	0	0	0	0	2	0
Totals		37	8	14	8	27	12	0

Pitching	IP	H	R	ER	BB	SO
New York						
Larsen (L)	**4	5	5	5	2	2
Kucks	1	3	2	2	0	1
R. Coleman	***1	5	1	1	0	1
Morgan	1	0	0	0	0	0
Sturdivant	1	1	0	0	1	0
Brooklyn						
Erskine	*3	3	3	3	2	3
Bessent	1⅔	3	0	0	1	1
Labine (W)	4⅓	3	2	2	1	0

*Pitched to two batters in 4th.
**Pitched to one batter in 5th.
***Pitched to three batters in 7th.

Doubles—Campanella, Gilliam, Martin. Home Runs—Campanella, Hodges, McDougald, Snider. Stolen Bases—Collins, Gilliam, Rizzuto, Sacrifice Hits—Howard, Reese. Double Play—J. Robinson to Gilliam to Hodges. Left on Bases—New York 7, Brooklyn 9. Umpires—Dascoli, Summers, Ballanfant, Honochick, Donatelli, Flaherty. Attendance—36,242. Time of Game—2:57.

1st Inning
New York
1 Noren struck out.
McDougald homered into the lower left field stands.
2 Mantle struck out.
3 Berra lined to center.
Brooklyn
1 Gilliam grounded to short.
2 Reese popped to Collins in short right.
3 Snider grounded to first.

2nd Inning
New York
Collins walked.
1 Howard sacrificed Collins to second, Erskine to Hodges.
2 Martin grounded to second, Collins moving over to third.
Rizzuto singled to left-center, Collins scoring.
Rizzuto stole second.
3 Larsen flied to center.
Brooklyn
1 Campanella flied to center.
2 Furillo called out on strikes.
Hodges singled to left.
3 J. Robinson flied to right.

3rd Inning
New York
1 Noren flied to left.
2 McDougald grounded to short.
3 Mantle called out on strikes.
Brooklyn
Amoros walked.
1 Erskine fouled to Rizzuto.
Gilliam doubled down the third base line, scoring Amoros.
2 Reese flied to right.
3 Snider grounded to second.

4th Inning
New York
Berra singled to center.
Collins walked
For Brooklyn—Bessent pitching.
1 Howard forced Berra at third on an attempted sacrifice, Bessent to J. Robinson.
Collins stole third.
Martin blooped a single into short right, scoring Collins and sending Howard to third.
2,3 Rizzuto hit into a double play, J. Robinson to Gilliam to Hodges.
Brooklyn
Campanella homered into the lower left field seats.
Furillo beat out a hit over Larsen's head.
Hodges hit a two-run homer over the right-center field scoreboard.
1 J. Robinson grounded to third.
2 Amoros bounced back to the mound.
3 Bessent called out on strikes.

5th Inning
New York
1 Larsen grounded to short.
Noren singled to center.
2 McDougald took a called third strike.
Mantle singled to right, Noren stopping at second.
Berra walked loading the bases.
For Brooklyn—Labine came in to pitch.
3 Collins forced Berra at second, Gilliam to Reese.

5th Inning (continued)
Brooklyn
Gilliam walked.
Gilliam stole second.
For New York—Kucks pitching with a 2–0 count to Reese.
Reese beat out an infield hit to first, moving Gilliam to third.
Snider hit a three-run homer over the right field screen.
Campanella doubled to right.
1 Furillo struck out.
2 Hodges grounded back to the mound, moving Campanella to third.
3 Robinson lined to third.

6th Inning
New York
Howard singled to left.
Martin doubled over Snider's head, scoring Howard.
1 Rizzuto fouled to Hodges.
E. Robinson, batting for Kucks, singled to right, scoring Martin.
Carroll ran for E. Robinson.
2 Noren flied to deep center.
3 McDougald lined to center.
Brooklyn
For New York—Rip Coleman pitching.
Amoros singled to right.
1 Labine took a called third strike.
2 Gilliam grounded to second, Amoros advancing to second.
Reese beat out a hit to short, moving Amoros to third.
3 Snider forced Reese at second, Collins to Rizzuto.

7th Inning
New York
1 Mantle bounced back to the mound.
2 Berra lined to left.
3 Collins grounded to second.
Brooklyn
Campanella singled to center.
Furillo singled off the right-center field wall, Campanella moving to third.
Hodges singled through the box, scoring Campanella with Furillo stopping at second.
For New York—Morgan came in to pitch.
1 J. Robinson flied to center.
2 Amoros grounded to second, advancing both runners.
3 Labine grounded to short.

8th Inning
New York
1 Howard grounded to third.
2 Martin flied to center.
Rizzuto walked
3 Skowron, batting for Morgan lined to right-center where Snider made a running one-handed catch.
Brooklyn
For New York—Sturdivant pitching.
Gilliam singled on a bunt down the third base line.
1 Reese sacrificed Gilliam to second, Berra to Collins.
Snider got an intentional pass.
2 Campanella lined to center.
3 Furillo popped to second.

9th Inning
New York
1 Noren lined to first.
2 McDougald flied to right.
3 Mantle grounded back to the pitcher.

Game 5 October 2 at Brooklyn

New York	Pos	AB	R	H	RBI	PO	A	E
Howard	lf	4	0	1	0	0	0	0
Noren	cf	4	0	0	0	2	0	0
McDougald	3b	3	0	0	0	1	2	0
Berra	c	4	2	2	1	9	1	0
Collins	rf-1b	3	0	0	0	0	0	0
E. Robinson	1b	2	0	1	0	6	0	0
c Carroll		0	0	0	0	0	0	0
Bauer	rf	0	0	0	0	0	0	0
Martin	2b	4	0	1	1	4	3	0
Rizzuto	ss	1	0	0	0	2	0	0
a Skowron		1	0	0	0	0	0	0
J. Coleman	ss	1	0	0	0	0	1	0
d Carey		1	0	0	0	0	0	0
Grim	p	2	0	0	0	0	1	0
b Cerv		1	1	1	1	0	0	0
Turley	p	0	0	0	0	0	1	0
e Byrne		1	0	0	0	0	0	0
Totals		32	3	6	3	24	9	0

a Fouled out for Rizzuto in 4th.
b Homered for Grim in 7th.
c Ran for E. Robinson in 8th.
d Grounded out for J. Coleman in 9th.
e Grounded out for Turley in 9th.

N.Y.	000	100	110
Bkn.	021	010	01x

Brooklyn	Pos	AB	R	H	RBI	PO	A	E
Gilliam	2b	3	0	1	0	1	5	0
Reese	ss	3	0	0	0	4	3	1
Snider	cf	4	2	3	2	0	0	0
Campanella	c	3	0	0	0	6	0	0
Furillo	rf	4	1	1	0	1	0	0
Hodges	1b	3	1	2	0	14	1	0
J. Robinson	3b	3	0	1	1	0	3	1
Amoros	lf	4	1	1	2	1	0	0
Craig	p	0	0	0	0	0	1	0
Labine	p	2	0	0	0	0	1	0
Totals		29	5	9	5	27	14	2

Pitching	IP	H	R	ER	BB	SO
New York						
Grim (L)	6	6	4	4	4	5
Turley	2	3	1	1	1	5
Brooklyn						
Craig (W)	*6	4	2	2	5	4
Labine (SV)	3	2	1	1	0	1

*Pitched to two batters in 7th.

Double—Snider, Home Runs—Amoros, Berra, Cerf, Snider 2. Sacrifice Hits—Craig, Hodges. Double Plays—Gilliam to Reese to Hodges, Martin to E. Robinson, J. Coleman to Martin to E. Robinson, Hodges to Reese to Hodges, J. Robinson to Gilliam to Hodges. Left on Bases—New York 7, Brooklyn 7. Umpires—Summers, Ballanfant, Honochick, Dascoli, Donatelli, Flaherty. Attendance—36,796. Time of Game—2:40.

1st Inning
New York
1 Howard struck out.
2 Noren popped to short.
McDougald safe on Reese's fumble.
3 Berra rolled out to first.
Brooklyn
1 Gilliam grounded to first.
Reese walked.
2 Snider forced Reese at second, Martin to Rizzuto.
3 Campanella took a called third strike.

2nd Inning
New York
Collins walked.
E. Robinson walked.
1 Martin grounded back to the mound, advancing both runners.
2 Rizzuto popped to first.
3 Grim grounded to third.
Brooklyn
1 Furillo lined to third.
Hodges singled to left.
2 J. Robinson lined to short.
Amoros hit a two-run homer over the right field screen.
Craig walked.
Gilliam singled to right-center advancing Craig to third.
3 Reese grounded to third.

3rd Inning
New York
1 Howard fanned.
2 Noren lined to left.
3 McDougald grounded to short.
Brooklyn
Snider homered over the right field screen.
1 Campanella lined to center.
2 Furillo struck out.
3 Hodges struck out.

4th Inning
New York
Berra singled off the right field score board.
1 Collins struck out.
E. Robinson walked.
Martin singled to left, Berra scoring with E. Robinson stopping at second.
2 Skowron, pinch-hitting for Rizzuto, fouled to Campanella.
3 Grim lined to short.
Brooklyn
For New York—J. Coleman playing short.
J. Robinson walked.
1 Amoros struck out.
2 Craig sacrificed J. Robinson to second, Grim to Martin.
3 Gilliam grounded to third.

5th Inning
New York
Howard singled to left.
1,2 Noren hit into a double play, Gilliam to Reese to Hodges.
McDougald walked.
3 Berra grounded out to Hodges unassisted on a real hard smash which Hodges was just able to knock down.

5th Inning (continued)
Brooklyn
1 Reese flied to center
Snider hit his second homer of the game over the right-center field score board. **(Also his 4th of the Series, becoming the first batter ever to hit 4 in more than one Series, having also hit 4 in 1952).**
Campanella walked.
2,3 Furillo rolled into a double play, Martin to E. Robinson.

6th Inning
New York
1 Collins grounded to second.
2 E. Robinson struck out.
Martin was safe at first on J. Robinson's low throw to first.
3 J. Coleman lined to right.
Brooklyn
Hodges beat out a single to short.
1,2 J. Robinson grounded into a double play, J. Coleman to Martin to E. Robinson.
3 Amoros struck out but Berra dropped the ball and threw to first to make the out.

7th Inning
New York
Cerv, batting for Grim, homered into the upper left field deck.
Howard walked.
For Brooklyn—Labine came in to pitch.
1,2 Noren hit into a double play for the 5th time in the Series, Hodges to Reese to Hodges.
3 McDougald grounded to the mound.
Brooklyn
For New York—Turley pitching.
1 Labine struck out.
Gilliam walked.
2 Reese took a called third strike.
Snider doubled inside the left field line, sending Gilliam to third.
3 Campanella called out on strikes.

8th Inning
New York
Berra hit a home run over the right field screen.
1 Collins struck out but had to be tagged out by Campanella.
E. Robinson singled into the right field corner.
Carroll ran for E. Robinson.
2,3 Martin bounced into a double play, J. Robinson to Gilliam to Hodges.
Brooklyn
For New York—Bauer playing right, Collins moving to first.
Furillo singled off Martin's glove.
1 Hodges sacrificed Furillo to second, Turley to Martin.
J. Robinson singled past short, scoring Furillo.
2 Amoros struck out.
3 Labine struck out.

9th Inning
New York
1 Carey, batting for J. Coleman, grounded to third.
2 Byrne, pinch-hitting for Turley, grounded to second.
3 Howard grounded to second.

Game 6 October 3 at New York

Bkn.		0 0 0	1 0 0	0 0 0
N.Y.		5 0 0	0 0 0	0 0 x

Brooklyn	Pos	AB	R	H	RBI	PO	A	E
Gilliam	2b-lf	3	0	1	0	0	0	0
Reese	ss	4	1	1	0	3	2	0
Snider	cf	1	0	0	0	1	0	0
a Zimmer	2b	2	0	0	0	1	1	0
Campanella	c	3	0	0	0	5	0	0
Furillo	rf	3	0	1	1	1	0	0
Hodges	1b	3	0	0	0	7	1	0
J. Robinson	3b	4	0	0	0	2	3	1
Amoros	lf-cf	4	0	1	0	2	0	0
Spooner	p	0	0	0	0	0	0	0
Meyer	p	2	0	0	0	0	1	0
c Kellert		1	0	0	0	0	0	0
Roebuck	p	0	0	0	0	2	0	0
Totals		30	1	4	1	24	8	1

a Struck out for Snider in 4th.
b Walked for Skowron in 5th.
c Popped out for Meyer in 7th.

Home Run—Skowron. Stolen Base—Rizzuto.
Double Plays—McDougald to Martin to
Skowron, J. Robinson to Hodges.
Hit by Pitch—Furillo (by Ford). Wild
Pitch—Ford. Left on Bases—Brooklyn 7,
New York 7. Umpires—Ballafant, Honochick,
Dascoli, Summers, Flaherty, Donatelli.
Attendance – 64,022. Time of Game—2:34.

New York	Pos	AB	R	H	RBI	PO	A	E
Rizzuto	ss	3	1	0	0	1	5	0
Martin	2b	4	1	0	0	4	2	0
McDougald	3b	3	1	0	0	0	5	0
Berra	c	3	1	2	1	8	0	0
Bauer	rf	4	1	3	1	0	0	0
Skowron	1b	2	1	1	3	6	0	0
b Collins	1b	0	0	0	0	5	1	0
Cerv	cf	4	0	1	0	2	0	0
Howard	lf	4	0	0	0	1	0	0
Noren	lf	0	0	0	0	0	0	0
Ford	p	4	0	0	0	0	1	0
Totals		32	5	8	5	27	14	0

Pitching	IP	H	R	ER	BB	SO
Brooklyn						
Spooner (L)	⅓	3	5	5	2	1
Meyer	5⅔	4	0	0	2	4
Roebuck	2	1	0	0		0
New York						
Ford (W)	9	4	1	1	4	8

1st Inning
Brooklyn
1 Gilliam lined to left.
2 Reese called out on strikes.
3 Snider took a called third strike.
New York
Rizzuto walked.
1 Martin struck out, as Rizzuto stole
second.
McDougald walked.
Berra singled over Spooner's head into
center, scoring Rizzuto while
McDougald went to second.
Bauer singled into left, scoring
McDougald with Berra going to second.
Skowron hit a three-run homer into the
lower right field stands.
For Brooklyn—Meyer pitching.
Cerv beat out a roller toward first.
2 Howard took a called third strike.
3 Ford flied to left.

2nd Inning
Brooklyn
1 Campanella flied to center.
Furillo was hit by a pitched ball.
Hodges walked.
2,3 Robinson grounded into a double play,
McDougald to Martin to Skowron.
New York
1 Rizzuto popped to third.
2 Martin fanned.
3 McDougald fouled to Reese.

3rd Inning
Brooklyn
1 Amoros grounded back to the mound.
2 Meyer struck out.
3 Gilliam grounded to third.
New York
Berra walked.
Bauer singled to left, Berra stopping
at second.
1 Skowron flied to center.
2,3 Cerv grounded into a double play,
Robinson who tagged Berra to Hodges.

4th Inning
Brooklyn
Reese singled on a high bouncer
behind second
1 Zimmer, pinch-hitting for Snider (who twisted
his knee in the 3rd), took a called
third strike.
Campanella walked.
Furillo singled to left, scoring Reese
with Campanella stopping at second.
2 Hodges forced Furillo at second,
Rizzuto to Martin, Campanella
going to third.
3 Robinson forced Hodges at second,
Rizzuto to Martin.
New York
For Brooklyn—Amoros moved to center,
Gilliam moved to left and Zimmer at
second.
1 Howard struck out.
2 Ford grounded to third.
3 Rizzuto grounded to short.

5th Inning
Brooklyn
1 Amoros grounded to first.
2 Meyer grounded to second.
Gilliam singled to left.
3 Reese grounded to third.
New York
Martin singled to left.
1 McDougald flied to center.
Berra singled to center, moving
Martin to second.
2 Bauer forced Berra at second, Robinson
to Zimmer, Martin going to third.
Collins, pinch-hitting for Skowron,
walked loading the bases.
3 Cerv popped to Reese in short
left-center.

6th Inning
Brooklyn
For New York—Collins at first.
Zimmer walked.
1 Campanella called out on strikes.
2 Furillo grounded to short, moving
Zimmer to second.
3 Hodges grounded to third.
New York
1 Howard took a called third strike.
2 Ford grounded back to the mound.
3 Rizzuto grounded to short.

7th Inning
Brooklyn
1 Robinson flied to center.
Amoros singled to center.
2 Kellert, pinch-hitting for Meyer,
popped to second.
Amoros went to third on a
wild pitch.
Gilliam walked.
3 Reese forced Gilliam at second,
Collins to Rizzuto.
New York
For Brooklyn—Roebuck pitching.
Martin safe on Robinson's error.
1 McDougald popped to the mound, on an
attempted sacrifice.
2 Berra forced Martin at second,
Hodges to Reese.
Bauer blooped a single into short-
center, Berra going to third.
3 Collins grounded to second.

8th Inning
Brooklyn
1 Zimmer called out on strikes.
2 Campanella grounded to short.
3 Furillo fanned.
New York
1 Cerv lined to the pitcher.
2 Howard flied to right.
3 Ford grounded to first.

9th Inning
Brooklyn
For New York—Noren replaced Howard
in left.
1 Hodges grounded to short.
2 Robinson grounded to third.
3 Amoros struck out.

Game 7 October 4 at New York

Bkn.		0 0 0	1 0 1	0 0 0
N.Y.		0 0 0	0 0 0	0 0 0

Brooklyn	Pos	AB	R	H	RBI	PO	A	E
Gilliam	lf-2b	4	0	1	0	2	0	0
Reese	ss	4	1	1	0	2	6	0
Snider	cf	3	0	0	0	2	0	0
Campanella	c	3	1	1	0	5	0	0
Furillo	rf	3	0	0	0	3	0	0
Hodges	1b	2	0	1	2	10	0	0
Hoak	3b	3	0	1	0	1	1	0
Zimmer	2b	2	0	0	0	0	2	0
a Shuba		1	0	0	0	0	0	0
Amoros	lf	0	0	0	0	2	1	0
Podres	p	4	0	0	0	0	1	0
Totals		29	2	5	2	27	11	0

Pitching	IP	H	R	ER	BB	SO
Brooklyn						
Podres (W)	9	8	0	0	2	4
New York						
Byrne (L)	5⅓	3	2	1	3	2
Grim	1⅔	1	0	0	1	1
Turley	2	1	0	0	1	1

New York	Pos	AB	R	H	RBI	PO	A	E
Rizzuto	ss	3	0	1	0	1	3	0
Martin	2b	3	0	1	0	1	6	0
McDougald	3b	4	0	3	0	1	1	0
Berra	c	4	0	1	0	4	1	0
Bauer	rf	4	0	0	0	1	0	0
Skowron	1b	4	0	1	0	11	1	1
Cerv	cf	4	0	0	0	5	0	0
Howard	lf	4	0	1	0	2	0	0
Byrne	p	2	0	0	0	0	2	0
Grim	p	0	0	0	0	0	1	0
b Mantle		1	0	0	0	0	0	0
Turley	p	0	0	0	0	0	0	0
Totals		33	0	8	0	27	14	1

a Grounded out for Zimmer in 6th.
b Popped out for Grim in 7th.

Doubles—Berra, Campanella, Skowron.
Sacrifice Hits—Campanella, Snider.
Sacrifice Fly—Hodges. Double
Play—Amoros to Reese to Hodges.
Wild Pitch—Grim. Left on Bases—Brooklyn
8, New York 8. Umpires—Honochick,
Dascoli, Summers, Ballanfant, Flaherty,
Donatelli. Attendance—62,465.
Time of Game—2:44.

1st Inning
Brooklyn
1 Gilliam grounded to short.
2 Reese flied to center.
3 Snider grounded to second.
New York
1 Rizzuto fouled to Campanella.
2 Martin flied to left.
3 McDougald called out on strikes.

2nd Inning
Brooklyn
1 Campanella grounded to second.
2 Furillo flied to deep left.
Hodges walked.
3 Hoak grounded to second.
New York
1 Berra lined to center.
2 Bauer grounded to second.
Skowron got a ground-rule double
into the right field stands.
3 Cerv grounded to short.

3rd Inning
Brooklyn
1 Zimmer grounded to short.
2 Podres grounded to second.
Gilliam walked.
3 Reese lined to center.
New York
1 Howard flied to center
2 Byrne took a called third strike.
Rizzuto walked.
Martin singled to right, Rizzuto
stopping at second.
3 McDougald's grounder hit Rizzuto
going to third for an automatic
out and an automatic hit for
McDougald.

4th Inning
Brooklyn
1 Snider struck out.
Campanella hit a double into the
left field corner.
2 Furillo grounded to short,
Campanella going to third.
Hodges singled to left, scoring
Campanella.
3 Hoak grounded to short.
New York
Berra got a Texas League double
in short center.
1 Bauer flied to second.
2 Skowron grounded to second, Berra
advancing to third.
3 Cerv popped to Reese in short
left-center.

5th Inning
Brooklyn
1 Zimmer fanned.
2 Podres fouled to McDougald.
3 Gilliam tapped out to second.
New York
1 Howard flied to deep left.
2 Byrne called out on strikes.
3 Rizzuto grounded to third.

6th Inning
Brooklyn
Reese singled to center.
Snider sacrificed Reese to second and
was safe at first when Skowron
dropped Byrne's throw.
1 Campanella sacrificed up both runners,
Byrne to Martin covering first.
Furillo got an intentional pass,
loading the bases.
For New York—Grim came in to pitch.
2 Hodges hit a sacrifice fly to Cerv in
deep right-center, Reese scoring and
Snider going to third after the catch.
Furillo went to second with Snider
holding third on a wild pitch.
Hoak walked again loading the bases.
3 Shuba, pinch-hitting for Zimmer,
grounded out Skowron to Grim.
New York
For Brooklyn—Amoros playing left as
Gilliam went to second.
Martin walked.
McDougald beat out a bunt inside
the third base line.
1,2 Berra was robbed of an extra-base
hit by a fantastic glove-handed
catch by Amoros who easily doubled
up McDougald at first, to Reese to
Hodges.
3 Bauer grounded to short.

7th Inning
Brooklyn
1 Podres grounded to second.
Gilliam singled to right.
2 Gilliam caught trying to steal
second, Berra to Rizzuto.
3 Reese struck out.
New York
1 Skowron grounded to short.
2 Cerv grounded to short.
Howard singled to left.
3 Mantle, pinch-hitting for Grim, popped
to short.

8th Inning
Brooklyn
For New York—Turley pitching.
1 Snider took a called third strike.
2 Campanella flied to left.
3 Furillo flied to center.
New York
Rizzuto singled to left-center.
1 Martin flied to right.
McDougald singled to left, moving
Rizzuto to third.
2 Berra flied to short-right.
3 Bauer fanned.

9th Inning
Brooklyn
1 Hodges fouled to Skowron.
Hoak singled to right-center.
Amoros walked.
2 Podres flied to center.
3 Gilliam flied to deep right.
New York
1 Skowron grounded to the mound.
2 Cerv flied to left.
3 Howard grounded to short.

1955 WORLD SERIES COMPOSITE BOX

	Wins	Composite Line Score
Brooklyn Dodgers (N.L.)	4	2 6 3 8 5 1 3 3 0 – 31
New York Yankees (A.L.)	3	6 5 1 7 0 4 2 1 0 – 26

Manager	Regular Season W	L	Pct.	G. Ahead
Walt Alston	98	55	.641	13.5
Casey Stengel	96	58	.623	3

BATTING AND FIELDING

WORLD SERIES STATISTICS

	Pos	G	AB	R	H	2B	3B	HR	RBI	BB	SO	SB	BA	SA	PO	A	E
BROOKLYN DODGERS																	
Gil Hodges	1b	7	24	2	7	0	0	1	5	3	2	0	.292	.417	**74**	4	0
Jim Gilliam	lf-2b	7	24	2	7	1	0	0	3	**8**	1	1	.292	.333	8	13	0
Pee Wee Reese	ss	7	**27**	5	8	1	0	0	2	3	5	0	.296	.333	15	**23**	1
Jackie Robinson	3b	6	22	5	4	1	**1**	0	1	2	1	1	.182	.318	4	18	**2**
Carl Furillo	rf	7	**27**	4	8	1	0	1	3	3	5	0	.296	.444	8	0	0
Duke Snider	cf	7	25	5	8	1	0	**4**	**7**	2	6	0	.320	**.840**	13	0	0
Sandy Amoros	lf-cf	5	12	3	4	0	0	1	3	4	4	0	.333	.583	9	2	0
Roy Campanella	c	7	**27**	4	7	**3**	0	2	4	3	3	0	.259	.593	42	3	1
Don Zimmer	2b-ph	4	9	0	2	0	0	0	2	2	5	0	.222	.228	4	8	**2**
Don Hoak	pr-ph-3b	3	3	0	1	0	0	0	0	2	0	0	.333	.333	1	1	0
Frank Kellert	ph	3	3	0	1	0	0	0	0	0	0	0	.333	.333			
George Shuba	ph	1	1	0	0	0	0	0	0	0	0	0	.000	.000			
Rube Walker		Did not play															
Dixie Howell		Did not play															
Johnny Podres	p	2	7	1	1	0	0	0	0	0	1	0	.143	.143	0	2	0
Clem Labine	p	4	4	0	0	0	0	0	0	0	3	0	.000	.000	0	3	0
Don Newcombe	p	1	3	0	0	0	0	0	0	0	0	0	.000	.000	0	1	0
Russ Meyer	p	1	2	0	0	0	0	0	0	0	1	0	.000	.000	0	1	0
Don Bessent	p	3	1	0	0	0	0	0	0	0	1	0	.000	.000	0	2	0
Billy Loes	p	1	1	0	0	0	0	0	0	0	0	0	.000	.000	0	1	0
Carl Erskine	p	1	1	0	0	0	0	0	0	0	0	0	.000	.000	0	1	0
Karl Spooner	p	2	0	0	0	0	0	0	0	0	0	0	—	—	0	1	0
Roger Craig	p	1	0	0	0	0	0	0	0	1	0	0	—	—	0	1	0
Ed Roebuck	p	1	0	0	0	0	0	0	0	0	0	0	—	—	2	0	0
Sandy Koufax		Did not play															
team total		7	223	31	58	8	1	9	30	33	38	2	.260	.426	180	84	6

Double Plays—12
Left on Bases—55

REGULAR SEASON STATISTICS

	Main Pos	G	AB	R	H	2B	3B	HR	RBI	BB	SO	SB	BA	SA
BROOKLYN DODGERS														
Gil Hodges	1b	150	546	75	158	24	5	27	102	80	91	2	.289	.500
Jim Gilliam	2b	147	538	110	134	20	8	7	40	70	37	15	.249	.355
Pee Wee Reese	ss	145	553	99	156	29	4	10	61	78	60	8	.282	.403
Jackie Robinson	3b	105	317	51	81	6	2	8	36	61	18	12	.256	.363
Carl Furillo	of	140	523	83	164	24	3	26	95	43	43	4	.314	.520
Duke Snider	of	148	538	**126**	166	34	6	42	**136**	104	87	9	.309	.628
Sandy Amoros	of	119	388	59	96	16	7	10	51	55	45	10	.247	.402
Roy Campanella	c	123	446	81	142	20	1	32	107	56	41	2	.318	.583
Don Zimmer	2b	88	280	38	67	10	1	15	50	19	66	5	.239	.443
Don Hoak	3b	94	279	50	67	13	3	5	19	46	50	9	.240	.362
Frank Kellert	1b	39	80	12	26	4	2	4	19	9	10	0	.325	.575
George Shuba	of	44	51	8	14	2	0	1	8	11	10	0	.275	.373
Rube Walker	c	48	103	6	26	5	0	2	13	15	11	1	.252	.359
Dixie Howell	c	16	42	2	11	4	0	0	5	1	7	0	.262	.357
Johnny Podres	p	32	60	9	11	2	0	0	5	4	5	0	.183	.217
Clem Labine	p	60	31	4	3	0	0	3	5	3	18	0	.097	.387
Don Newcombe	p-ph	57	117	18	42	9	1	7	23	6	18	1	.359	.632
Russ Meyer	p	18	27	1	1	1	0	0	2	1	10	0	.037	.074
Don Bessent	p	24	20	1	2	0	0	0	2	0	8	0	.100	.100
Billy Loes	p	22	44	2	4	0	0	0	0	3	15	1	.091	.091
Carl Erskine	p	42	74	12	15	3	0	1	11	0	12	0	.203	.284
Karl Spooner	p	29	28	3	8	3	1	0	4	2	14	0	.286	.464
Roger Craig	p	21	26	2	2	0	0	0	0	1	10	0	.077	.077
Ed Roebuck	p	47	18	0	2	0	0	0	2	0	6	0	.111	.111
Sandy Koufax	p	12	12	0	0	0	0	0	0	0	12	0	.000	.000
team total		154	5193	**857**	1406	**230**	44	**201**	**800**	**674**	718	**79**	**.271**	**.448**

Walt Moryn (of), Bob Borkowski (of), Bert Hamric (ph), Joe Black (p), Chuck Templeton (p), Jim Hughes (p), and Tom Lasorda (p) also played for the Dodgers during the season.

WORLD SERIES STATISTICS

	Pos	G	AB	R	H	2B	3B	HR	RBI	BB	SO	SB	BA	SA	PO	A	E
NEW YORK YANKEES																	
Joe Collins	1b-rf-ph	5	12	**6**	2	0	0	2	3	6	4	1	.167	.667	27	3	0
Billy Martin	2b	7	25	2	8	1	1	0	4	1	5	0	.320	.440	17	20	0
Phil Rizzuto	ss	7	15	2	4	0	0	0	1	5	1	**2**	.267	.267	13	14	0
Gil McDougald	3b	7	**27**	2	7	0	0	1	1	2	6	0	.259	.370	6	13	1
Hank Bauer	rf-ph	6	14	1	6	0	0	0	1	0	1	0	**.429**	.429	7	0	0
Irv Noren	cf-lf	5	16	0	1	0	0	0	1	1	1	0	.063	.063	13	0	0
Elston Howard	lf-rf	7	26	3	5	0	0	1	3	1	**8**	0	.192	.308	11	1	0
Yogi Berra	c	7	24	5	**10**	1	0	1	2	3	1	0	.417	.583	40	4	0
Bob Cerv	cf-lf-ph	5	16	1	2	0	0	1	1	0	4	0	.125	.313	10	0	0
Bill Skowron	1b-ph	5	12	2	4	2	0	1	3	0	1	0	.333	.750	22	3	1
Mickey Mantle	cf-rf-ph	3	10	1	2	0	0	1	1	0	2	0	.200	.500	4	0	0
Eddie Robinson	ph-1b	4	3	0	2	0	0	0	1	2	1	0	.667	.667	6	0	0
Jerry Coleman	ss-pr	3	3	0	0	0	0	0	0	0	1	0	.000	.000	2	3	0
Andy Carey	ph	2	2	0	1	0	**1**	0	1	0	0	0	.500	1.500			
Tommy Carroll	pr	2	0	0	0	0	0	0	0	0	0	0	—	—			
Charlie Silvera		Did not play															
Frank Leja		Did not play															
Tommy Byrne	p-ph	3	6	0	1	0	0	0	2	0	2	0	.167	.167	0	2	0
Whitey Ford	p	2	6	1	0	0	0	0	0	1	1	0	.000	.000	1	4	0
Bob Grim	p	3	2	0	0	0	0	0	0	0	0	0	.000	.000	1	1	0
Don Larsen	p	1	2	0	0	0	0	0	0	0	0	0	.000	.000	0	1	0
Bob Turley	p	3	1	0	0	0	0	0	0	0	0	0	.000	.000	0	1	0
Johnny Kucks	p	2	0	0	0	0	0	0	0	0	0	0	—	—	0	1	0
Tom Morgan	p	2	0	0	0	0	0	0	0	0	0	0	—	—	0	0	0
Tom Sturdivant	p	2	0	0	0	0	0	0	0	0	0	0	—	—	0	1	0
Rip Coleman	p	1	0	0	0	0	0	0	0	0	0	0	—	—	0	0	0
Bob Wiesler		Did not play															
team total		7	222	26	55	4	2	8	25	22	39	3	.248	.392	180	72	2

Double Plays—7
Left on Bases—41

REGULAR SEASON STATISTICS

	Main Pos	G	AB	R	H	2B	3B	HR	RBI	BB	SO	SB	BA	SA
NEW YORK YANKEES														
Joe Collins	1b	105	278	40	65	9	1	13	45	44	32	0	.234	.414
Billy Martin	2b	20	70	8	21	2	0	1	9	7	9	1	.300	.371
Phil Rizzuto	ss	81	143	19	37	4	1	1	9	22	18	7	.259	.322
Gil McDougald	2b	141	533	79	152	10	8	13	53	65	77	6	.285	.407
Hank Bauer	of	139	492	97	137	20	5	20	53	56	65	8	.278	.461
Irv Noren	of	132	371	49	94	15	1	8	59	43	33	5	.253	.375
Elston Howard	of	97	279	33	81	8	7	10	43	20	36	0	.290	.477
Yogi Berra	c	147	541	84	147	20	3	27	108	60	20	1	.272	.470
Bob Cerv	ph-of	55	85	17	29	4	2	3	22	7	16	4	.341	.541
Bill Skowron	1b	108	288	46	92	17	3	12	61	21	32	1	.319	.524
Mickey Mantle	of	147	517	121	158	25	**11**	**37**	99	**113**	97	8	.306	**.611**
Eddie Robinson	ph-1b	88	173	25	36	1	0	16	42	36	26	0	.208	.491
Jerry Coleman	ss	43	96	12	22	5	0	0	8	11	11	0	.229	.281
Andy Carey	3b	135	510	73	131	19	**11**	7	47	44	51	3	.257	.378
Tommy Carroll	pr-ss	14	6	3	2	0	0	0	0	0	2	0	.333	.333
Charlie Silvera	c	14	26	1	5	0	0	0	1	6	4	0	.192	.192
Frank Leja	1b	7	2	1	0	0	0	0	0	0	1	0	.000	.000
Tommy Byrne	p-ph	45	78	6	16	1	1	1	6	8	15	0	.205	.282
Whitey Ford	p	39	86	9	14	0	0	1	7	11	16	0	.163	.198
Bob Grim	p	26	25	2	3	0	0	0	1	1	9	0	.120	.120
Don Larsen	p	21	41	4	6	1	0	2	7	4	13	0	.146	.317
Bob Turley	p	36	82	7	11	4	0	0	7	6	21	0	.134	.183
Johnny Kucks	p	29	40	0	2	1	0	0	0	0	10	0	.050	.075
Tom Morgan	p	40	18	2	4	1	0	0	0	0	5	0	.222	.278
Tom Sturdivant	p	33	12	1	1	0	0	0	0	0	3	0	.083	.083
Rip Coleman	p	10	10	2	2	0	0	0	0	2	7	0	.200	.200
Bob Wiesler	p	16	14	1	2	0	0	0	1	0	3	0	.143	.143
team total		154	5161	762	1342	179	**55**	**175**	722	609	658	55	.260	.418

Bobby Richardson (2b), Enos Slaughter (ph), Lou Berberet (c), Dick Tettelbach (of), Billy Hunter (ss), Marv Throneberry (1b), Johnny Blanchard (c), Jim Konstanty (p), Ed Lopat (p), Johnny Sain (p), Art Schallock (p), Gerry Staley (p) and Ted Gray (p) also played for the Yankees during the season.

PITCHING

WORLD SERIES STATISTICS

	G	GS	CG	IP	H	R	ER	BB	SO	W	L	SV	ERA
BROOKLYN DODGERS													
Johnny Podres	2	**2**	**2**	**18**	**15**	3	2	4	**10**	**2**	0	0	**1.00**
Clem Labine	**4**	0	0	9⅓	6	3	3	2	2	1	0	**1**	2.89
Roger Craig	1	1	0	6	4	2	2	5	4	1	0	0	3.00
Russ Meyer	1	0	0	5⅔	4	0	0	2	4	0	0	0	0.00
Don Newcombe	1	1	0	5⅔	8	**6**	**6**	2	4	0	**1**	0	9.53
Billy Loes	1	1	0	3⅔	7	4	4	1	5	0	**1**	0	9.82
Don Bessent	3	0	0	3⅓	3	0	0	1	1	0	0	0	0.00
Karl Spooner	2	1	0	3⅓	4	5	5	3	6	0	**1**	0	13.50
Carl Erskine	1	1	0	3	3	3	3	2	3	0	0	0	9.00
Ed Roebuck	1	0	0	2	1	0	0	0	0	0	0	0	0.00
Sandy Koufax	Did not play												
team total	7	7	2	60	55	26	25	22	39	4	3	1	3.75
NEW YORK YANKEES													
Whitey Ford	2	**2**	1	17	13	**6**	4	**8**	**10**	**2**	0	0	2.12
Tommy Byrne	2	**2**	1	14⅓	8	4	3	**8**	8	1	1	0	1.88
Bob Grim	3	1	0	8⅔	8	4	4	5	8	0	1	**1**	4.15
Bob Turley	3	1	0	5⅓	7	5	5	4	7	0	**1**	0	8.44
Don Larsen	1	1	0	4	5	5	5	2	2	0	**1**	0	11.25
Tom Morgan	2	0	0	3⅔	3	2	2	3	1	0	0	0	4.91
Johnny Kucks	2	0	0	3	4	2	2	1	1	0	0	0	6.00
Tom Sturdivant	2	0	0	3	5	2	2	2	0	0	0	0	6.00
Rip Coleman	1	0	0	1	5	1	1	0	0	0	0	0	9.00
Bob Wiesler	Did not play												
team total	7	7	2	60	58	31	28	33	38	3	4	1	4.20

REGULAR SEASON STATISTICS

	G	GS	CG	IP	H	ER	BB	SO	W	L	Pct	SV	ShO	ERA
BROOKLYN DODGERS														
Johnny Podres	27	24	5	159	160	70	57	114	9	10	.474	0	2	3.96
Clem Labine	60	8	1	144	121	52	55	67	13	5	.722	11	0	3.25
Roger Craig	21	10	3	91	81	28	43	48	5	3	.625	2	0	2.77
Russ Meyer	18	11	2	73	86	44	31	26	6	2	.750	0	1	5.42
Don Newcombe	34	31	17	234	222	83	38	143	20	5	**.800**	0	1	3.19
Billy Loes	22	19	6	128	116	51	46	85	10	4	.714	0	0	3.59
Don Bessent	24	2	1	63	51	19	21	29	8	1	.889	3	0	2.71
Karl Spooner	29	14	2	99	79	40	41	78	8	6	.571	2	1	3.64
Carl Erskine	31	29	7	195	185	82	64	84	11	8	.579	1	2	3.78
Ed Roebuck	47	0	0	84	96	44	24	33	5	6	.455	12	0	4.71
Sandy Koufax	12	5	2	42	33	14	28	30	2	2	.500	0	2	3.00
team total	154	154	46	1378	1296	**564**	483	**773**	**98**	55	**.641**	**87**	11	**3.68**
NEW YORK YANKEES														
Whitey Ford	39	33	**18**	254	188	74	113	137	**18**	7	.720	2	5	2.62
Tommy Byrne	27	22	9	160	137	56	87	76	16	5	**.762**	2	3	3.15
Bob Grim	26	11	1	92	81	43	42	63	7	5	.583	4	1	4.21
Bob Turley	36	34	13	247	168	84	**177**	210	17	13	.567	1	6	3.06
Don Larsen	19	13	5	97	81	33	51	44	9	2	.818	2	1	3.06
Tom Morgan	40	1	0	72	72	26	24	17	7	3	.700	10	0	3.25
Johnny Kucks	29	13	3	127	122	48	44	49	8	7	.533	0	1	3.40
Tom Sturdivant	33	1	0	68	48	24	42	48	1	3	.250	0	0	3.18
Rip Coleman	10	6	0	29	40	17	16	15	2	1	.667	1	0	5.28
Bob Wiesler	16	17	0	53	39	23	49	22	0	2	.000	0	0	3.91
team total	154	154	52	1372	1163	**493**	688	732	**96**	58	**.623**	33	**19**	3.23

Total Attendance—362,310 Average Attendance—51,759 Winning Player's Share—$9,768 Losing Player's Share—$5,599

1956
A Perfect October

The passing years had chipped away at the bases of their dynasties, but the New York Yankees and Brooklyn Dodgers still had enough talent to win repeat berths in the World Series. Shortstop Phil Rizzuto hung up his spikes after a long career with the Yankees, but Casey Stengel adequately covered himself by shifting Gil McDougald to the position. Otherwise, the Yankees were in as fine shape as ever. Mickey Mantle hit a top stride of stardom by winning the Triple Crown with a .353 average, 52 homers, and 130 RBI's, while Yogi Berra, Bill Skowron, and Hank Bauer powered the ball in other lineup spots. Pitchers Whitey Ford, Johnny Kucks, and Tom Sturdivant combined for 53 wins, and Stengel topped his squad by purchasing former Cardinal star outfielder Enos Slaughter, now a ripe forty years old, to help out down the stretch.

Age also played a key role in the Dodgers' narrow first-place finish over the Braves and Reds. Manager Walt Alston used thirty-seven-year-old Jackie Robinson only part-time, and a bad finger cut thirty-four-year-old Roy Campanella's offensive production drastically. The Bums still got outstanding hitting from Duke Snider, Gil Hodges, Carl Furillo, and Jim Gilliam, steady infield play from Pee Wee Reese, and 27 wins from workhorse pitcher Don Newcombe, but the crowning touch was the purchase of thirty-nine-year-old pitcher Sal Maglie, whose 13 wins sparked his mates down a tough pennant fight. Although they had lost Series hero Johnny Podres to the navy, the Dodgers still came into the classic with the unaccustomed confidence of a defending champion.

And that confidence burst out all over in the first two games at Ebbets Field. Maglie faced Ford in the opener, and while the Yanks jumped out to an early lead on a two-run homer by Mantle in the top of the first inning, the Dodgers came back on homers by Robinson and Hodges to win 6–3. After a day of rain, the second game pitted Newcombe against Don Larsen, an 11–5 hurler for the season with an unusual "no windup" delivery. The Yankees as usual jumped all over Newcombe and shelled him from the mound in the second, taking an imposing 6–0 lead on Berra's grand-slam homer. The Brooks responded in the bottom of the second by pounding out six runs to knot the game at 6–6. Don Bessent took over the pitching for Brooklyn in the third and stemmed the Yankee tide, but the Dodgers kept up the heat and rolled on to a 13–8 victory which put the Bums in fine shape to take a second straight Series title.

The Yankees regrouped over in Yankee Stadium, however, and took game three 5–3, with Ford going all the way and Slaughter swatting a three-run homer. A six-hitter by Sturdivant and homers by Mantle and Bauer gave the Yanks a 6–2 win in game four. In the fifth game, Alston started Maglie, while Stengel took a chance on Larsen, who had been severely clubbed in the second game. But Larsen sparkled in the Yankee Stadium autumn, retiring the Dodgers in order inning after inning. With the aid of a great catch and a homer by Mantle, Larsen came into the ninth leading 2–0 and pitching a perfect game. He retired the first two men, then capped the first no-hitter in Series history by slipping a called third strike past pinch hitter Dale Mitchell.

Such a performance monopolized the press, but Clem Labine turned in a pitching gem of his own in game six. Primarily a reliever, Labine started and pitched 10 shutout innings, winning 1–0 when Slaughter misjudged Robinson's liner to left to score Gilliam. Stengel settled on Johnny Kucks for his seventh-game pitcher, while Alston went with his Cy Young award-winner, Don Newcombe. Big Newk had not won a Series game in four previous tries, and he failed again with the chips on the table. Berra rocked him for two-run homers in the first and third innings, and a solo homer by Howard in the fourth sent Newk off to a sad shower. A grand slam by Skowron in the seventh capped the 9–0 holocaust, as Kucks limited the Dodgers to three hits. For Casey Stengel and the Yankees, it was a sweet return to the pinnacle of success. For the Dodgers, things would never be the same. Jackie Robinson had played his last game, while the team itself would never play another World Series as representatives of Brooklyn.

Game 1 October 3 at Brooklyn

New York	Pos	AB	R	H	RBI	PO	A	E
Bauer	rf	5	0	2	0	3	0	0
Slaughter	lf	5	1	3	0	3	0	0
Mantle	cf	3	1	1	2	4	1	0
Berra	c	3	0	0	0	4	0	0
Skowron	1b	4	0	0	0	5	3	1
McDougald	ss	4	0	0	0	2	6	0
Martin	2b-3b	3	1	1	1	2	1	0
Carey	3b	3	0	1	0	0	1	0
c Collins		1	0	0	0	0	0	0
Turley	p	0	0	0	0	0	0	0
Ford	p	1	0	0	0	1	0	0
a Wilson		1	0	0	0	0	0	0
Kucks	p	0	0	0	0	0	0	0
b Cerv		1	0	1	0	0	0	0
Morgan	p	0	0	0	0	0	0	0
d Byrne		1	0	0	0	0	0	0
Coleman	2b	0	0	0	0	0	0	0
Totals		35	3	9	3	24	12	1

Brooklyn	Pos	AB	R	H	RBI	PO	A	E
Gilliam	2b	3	0	0	0	3	1	0
Reese	ss	4	1	2	0	1	1	0
Snider	cf	3	1	1	0	1	0	0
Robinson	3b	4	1	1	1	2	2	0
Hodges	1b	4	2	2	3	4	0	0
Furillo	rf	4	0	1	1	2	0	0
Campanella	c	4	1	1	0	11	1	0
Amoros	lf	3	0	1	1	3	0	0
Maglie	p	3	0	0	0	0	0	0
Totals		32	6	9	6	27	5	0

N.Y. 2 0 0 1 0 0 0 0 0
Bkn. 0 2 3 1 0 0 0 0 x

Pitching	IP	H	R	ER	BB	SO
New York						
Ford (L)	3	6	5	5	0	1
Kucks	2	2	1	1	0	1
Morgan	2	1	0	0	2	0
Turley	1	0	0	0	0	2
Brooklyn						
Maglie (W)	9	9	3	3	4	10

a Struck out for Ford in 4th.
b Singled for Kucks in 6th.
c Struck out for Carey in 8th.
d Fouled out for Morgan in 8th.

Doubles—Campanella, Furillo.
Home Runs—Hodges, Mantle, Martin, Robinson. Stolen Base—Gilliam.
Double Plays—Skowron to McDougald to Martin, Gilliam to Reese to Hodges.
Left on Bases—New York 9, Brooklyn 4.
Umpires—Pinelli (N), Soar (A), Boggess (N), Napp (A), Gorman (N), Runge (A).
Attendance—34,479. Time of Game—2:32.

1st Inning
New York
1 Bauer grounded to third.
  Slaughter singled off Hodges' glove.
  Mantle hit a two-run homer over the right field screen.
  Berra walked.
2 Skowron struck out.
3 McDougald struck out.
Brooklyn
1 Gilliam grounded to short.
2 Reese lined to right.
3 Snider tapped out, Skowron to Ford.

2nd Inning
New York
1 Martin fouled to Campanella.
2 Carey fanned.
3 Ford fanned.
Brooklyn
  Robinson homered into the lower left field seats.
  Hodges singled to center.
  Furillo doubled to left-center, scoring Hodges.
1 Campanella flied to right, Furillo going to third after the catch.
2 Amoros flied to shallow center.
3 Maglie struck out.

3rd Inning
New York
  Bauer singled to left.
  Slaughter singled between short and third, Bauer stopping at second.
1 Mantle called out on strikes.
2 Berra popped to third.
3 Skowron forced Slaughter at second, Robinson to Gilliam.
Brooklyn
1 Gilliam popped to third.
  Reese singled to deep short.
  Snider singled to center, Reese stopping at second.
2 Robinson lined to center.
  Hodges hit a three-run homer into the lower left field stands.
3 Furillo flied to right.

4th Inning
New York
1 McDougald flied to left.
  Martin homered into the lower left field seats.
2 Carey flied to right.
3 Wilson, pinch-hitting for Ford, fanned but had to be thrown out, Campanella to Hodges.
Brooklyn
  For New York—Kucks pitching.
  Campanella doubled off the gate in center field.
  Amoros singled to center, scoring Campanella.
1,2 Maglie bunted into a double play on an attempted sacrifice Skowron to McDougald to Martin covering first.
  Gilliam safe at first on Skowron's error.
  Gilliam stole second.
3 Reese took a called third strike.

5th Inning
New York
  Bauer singled to left.
1 Slaughter popped to third.
  Mantle walked.
2 Berra flied to left.
3 Skowron flied to left.
Brooklyn
1 Snider lined to left.
2 Robinson lined to left.
3 Hodges grounded to short.

6th Inning
New York
1 McDougald called out on strikes.
2 Martin popped to second.
  Carey singled over Maglie's head.
  Cerv, pinch-hitting for Kucks, singled to center, moving Carey to second.
3 Bauer popped to first.
Brooklyn
  For New York—Morgan pitching.
1 Furillo grounded to short.
2 Campanella lined to center.
3 Amoros flied to left.

7th Inning
New York
1 Slaughter lined to center.
  Mantle walked.
2 Berra lined to right.
3 Skowron lined to second.
Brooklyn
1 Maglie flied to center.
  Gilliam walked.
  Reese singled to center, Gilliam going
2 to third but Reese was out rounding first, Mantle to McDougald to Skowron to Martin to Skowron.
  Snider got an intentional pass.
3 Robinson forced Snider at second, Carey to Martin.

8th Inning
New York
1 McDougald struck out for the third time.
  Martin walked.
2 Collins, batting for Carey, struck out.
3 Byrne, pinch-hitting for Morgan, fouled to Campanella.
Brooklyn
  For New York—Turley pitching (batting 8th)
  Coleman at second (batting 9th)
1 Hodges struck out.
2 Furillo grounded to short.
3 Campanella looked at a called third strike.

9th Inning
New York
1 Bauer struck out.
  Slaughter singled to left.
2,3 Mantle hit into a double play, Gilliam to Reese to Hodges.

Game 2 October 5 at Brooklyn

N.Y.	1 5 0	1 0 0	0 0 1
Bkn.	0 6 1	2 2 0	0 2 x

New York	Pos	AB	R	H	RBI	PO	A	E
McDougald	ss	3	0	1	0	1	0	0
Slaughter	lf	4	3	2	1	1	0	0
Mantle	cf	4	1	1	0	2	0	0
Berra	c	4	1	2	4	10	0	0
Collins	1b	4	0	1	2	3	0	1
Bauer	rf	5	0	1	0	2	0	1
Martin	3b-2b	4	1	1	0	3	2	0
Coleman	2b	2	0	0	0	2	2	0
d Skowron		1	0	0	0	0	0	0
Carey	3b	0	0	0	0	0	1	0
Larsen	p	1	1	1	1	0	0	0
Kucks	p	0	0	0	0	0	0	0
Byrne	p	0	0	0	0	0	0	0
Sturdivant	p	0	0	0	0	0	0	0
Morgan	p	1	1	1	0	0	0	0
Turley	p	0	0	0	0	0	0	0
b Siebern		1	0	0	0	0	0	0
McDermott	p	1	0	1	0	0	0	0
Totals		35	8	12	8	24	5	2

a Fouled out for Roebuck in 2nd.
b Flied out for Turley in 6th.
c Struck out for Amoros in 7th.
d Struck out for Coleman in 8th.

Doubles—Hodges 2. Home Runs—Berra, Snider. Sacrifice Hits—Bessent, Coleman, McDougald. Sacrifice Flies—Campanella, Slaughter. Double Plays—Martin to Collins, Reese to Gilliam to Hodges. Wild Pitch—Bessent. Left on Bases—New York 7, Brooklyn 11. Umpires—Soar, Boggess, Napp, Pinelli, Runge, Gorman. Attendance—36,217. Time of Game—3:26.

Brooklyn	Pos	AB	R	H	RBI	PO	A	E
Gilliam	2b	3	1	1	2	5	3	0
Reese	ss	6	1	1	2	5	0	0
Snider	cf	4	3	2	3	6	0	0
Robinson	3b	3	2	2	0	0	2	0
Hodges	1b	3	2	3	4	6	0	0
Amoros	lf	4	1	0	0	0	0	0
c Jackson		1	0	0	0	0	0	0
Cimoli	lf	0	0	0	0	1	0	0
Furillo	rf	4	2	2	0	2	0	0
Campanella	c	3	1	0	1	5	0	0
Newcombe	p	0	0	0	0	0	1	0
Roebuck	p	0	0	0	0	0	0	0
a Mitchell		1	0	0	0	0	0	0
Bessent	p	2	0	1	1	0	0	0
Totals		35	13	12	13	27	11	0

Pitching	IP	H	R	ER	BB	SO
New York						
Larsen	1⅔	1	4	0	4	0
Kucks	*0	1	1	0	0	0
Byrne	⅓	1	1	0	0	1
Sturdivant	⅓	2	1	1	2	2
Morgan (L)	2	5	4	4	2	3
Turley	⅓	0	0	0	0	1
McDermott	3	2	2	1	3	3
Brooklyn						
Newcombe	1⅔	6	6	6	2	0
Roebuck	⅓	0	0	0	0	0
Bessent (W)	7	6	2	2	2	4

*Pitched to one batter in 2nd.

1st Inning
New York
1 McDougald grounded to short.
Slaughter singled to right.
2 Mantle flied to center.
Berra walked.
Collins singled to center, scoring Slaughter with Berra stopping at second.
3 Bauer popped to second.
Brooklyn
Gilliam walked.
1 Reese popped to short.
Snider walked.
2,3 Robinson grounded into a double play, Martin stepping on third to force Gilliam and throwing to Collins to get Robinson at first.

2nd Inning
New York
Martin singled behind second.
1 Coleman sacrificed Martin to second, Newcombe to Hodges.
Larsen singled to left, Martin scoring.
McDougald singled in the hole between first and second, Larsen stopping at second.
2 Slaughter forced McDougald at second, Reese to Gilliam, moving Larsen to third.
Mantle walked, loading the bases.
Berra hit a grand slam homer over the right field screen.
For Brooklyn—Roebuck came in to pitch.
3 Collins grounded to second.
Brooklyn
Hodges singled to right.
Amoros safe at first as Collins dropped his grounder for an error.
Furillo walked, loading the bases.
1 Campanella hit a sacrifice fly to left, Hodges scoring after the catch.
2 Mitchell, pinch-hitting for Roebuck, fouled to Martin.
Gilliam walked, again loading the bases.
For New York—Kucks now pitching.
Reese singled to left, Amoros and Furillo scoring with Gilliam stopping at second.
For New York—Byrne came in to pitch.
Snider hit a three-run homer over the right-center field screen.
3 Robinson struck out.

3rd Inning
New York
For Brooklyn—Bessent pitching.
Bauer beat out a roller to second.
1,2 Martin grounded into a double play, Reese to Gilliam to Hodges.
3 Coleman grounded to short.
Brooklyn
For New York—Sturdivant pitching.
Hodges walked.
1 Amoros struck out.
Furillo singled to left, Hodges stopping at second.
2 Campanella struck out.
Bessent singled to left, Hodges scoring and Furillo going to second.
Gilliam walked loading the bases.
For New York—Morgan became the 5th pitcher.
3 Reese popped to second.

4th Inning
New York
Morgan singled to left-center.
1 McDougald sacrificed Morgan to second, Robinson to Gilliam covering first. Morgan went to third on a wild pitch.
2 Slaughter hit a sacrifice fly to Snider in deep right-center, scoring Morgan.
3 Mantle called out on strikes.
Brooklyn
Snider singled to right-center.
Robinson singled to left-center, Snider going to third.
Hodges doubled off the wall in left, scoring Snider and Robinson.
1 Amoros struck out.
2 Furillo grounded to second, Hodges moving to third.
Campanella intentionally walked.
3 Bessent struck out.

5th Inning
New York
1 Berra flied to center.
Collins walked.
2 Bauer flied to center.
3 Martin struck out.
Brooklyn
1 Gilliam struck out.
2 Reese flied to right.
Snider walked.
Robinson singled to center, Snider stopping at second.
Hodges doubled to left-center, scoring Snider and Robinson.
For New York—Turley pitching.
3 Amoros called out on strikes, his third strikeout.

6th Inning
New York
1 Coleman flied to right.
2 Siebern, pinch-hitting for Turley, flied to center.
McDougald walked.
3 Slaughter lined to right.
Brooklyn
For New York—McDermott pitching.
1 Furillo flied to right.
2 Campanella flied to center.
Bessent walked.
3 Gilliam forced Bessent at second, Martin to Coleman.

7th Inning
New York
Mantle hit a long single off the top of the right field wall.
1 Berra forced Mantle at second, Gilliam to Reese.
2 Collins fouled to Campanella.
3 Bauer forced Berra at second, Reese unassisted.
Brooklyn
1 Reese grounded to second.
2 Snider took a called third strike.
Robinson walked.
Hodges walked.
3 Jackson, batting for Amoros, struck out.

8th Inning
New York
For Brooklyn—Cimoli playing left.
1 Martin struck out.
2 Skowron, pinch-hitting for Coleman, also struck out.
McDermott beat out a bouncer behind second.
3 McDougald grounded to third.
Brooklyn
For New York—Martin went to second and Carey came in to play third.
Furillo singled to left.
Campanella flied to Bauer who dropped the ball for an error.
1 Bessent sacrificed up both runners, Carey to Martin covering first.
Gilliam singled to center, scoring Furillo and Campanella.
2 Reese flied to center.
3 Snider struck out.

9th Inning
New York
Slaughter singled to center.
1 Mantle flied to center.
Berra singled to deep left, moving Slaughter to third.
2 Collins forced Berra at second, Reese to Gilliam. Slaughter scoring on the play.
3 Bauer flied to left.

Game 3 October 6 at New York

Brooklyn	Pos	AB	R	H	RBI	PO	A	E
Gilliam	lf	4	0	0	0	2	0	0
Reese	ss	4	1	2	0	2	3	0
Snider	cf	3	0	0	1	4	0	0
Robinson	3b	3	1	1	0	0	5	0
Hodges	1b	4	0	2	0	1	0	0
Furillo	rf	4	0	2	0	1	0	0
Campanella	c	3	0	1	1	7	0	0
Neal	2b	4	0	0	0	2	2	1
Craig	p	2	0	1	0	1	1	0
a Jackson		1	0	0	0	0	0	0
Labine	p	0	0	0	0	0	0	0
Totals		31	3	8	2	24	7	1

a Flied out for Craig in 7th.

Doubles—Berra, Furillo. Triple—Reese. Home Runs—Martin, Slaughter. Sacrifice Flies—Campanella, Snider. Double Plays—Martin to McDougald to Collins, Craig to Reese to Hodges, Neal to Reese to Hodges. Left on Bases—Brooklyn 5, New York 4. Umpires—Boggess, Napp, Pinelli, Soar, Gorman, Runge. Attendance—73,977. Time of Game—2:17.

New York	Pos	AB	R	H	RBI	PO	A	E
Bauer	rf	4	1	1	0	2	1	0
Collins	1b	4	1	0	0	8	0	0
Mantle	cf	4	0	1	0	2	0	0
Berra	c	4	1	2	1	8	1	0
Slaughter	lf	3	1	2	3	1	0	0
Martin	2b	4	1	1	1	1	3	0
McDougald	ss	2	1	0	0	4	2	0
Carey	3b	3	0	0	0	1	5	1
Ford	p	3	0	0	0	0	0	0
Totals		31	5	8	5	27	12	1

Pitching	IP	H	R	ER	BB	SO
Brooklyn						
Craig (L)	6	7	4	4	1	4
Labine	2	1	1	0	1	2
New York						
Ford (W)	9	8	3	2	2	7

Bkn. 010 001 100
N.Y. 010 003 01x

1st Inning
Brooklyn
1 Gilliam grounded to third.
2 Reese struck out.
3 Snider struck out.
New York
1 Bauer flied to right.
2 Collins flied to center.
Mantle got a single on a bunt past the mound.
3 Berra grounded to second.

2nd Inning
Brooklyn
Robinson walked.
Hodges beat out a bouncer to deep short.
1 Furillo flied to right, Robinson going to third after the catch.
Campanella hit a sacrifice fly to right, scoring Robinson.
3 Neal fouled to Berra.
New York
1 Slaughter flied to left.
Martin homered into the lower left field stands.
McDougald walked.
2 Carey struck out.
3 Ford struck out.

3rd Inning
Brooklyn
Craig singled to right.
1,2 Gilliam grounded into a double play, Martin to McDougald to Collins.
Reese singled to center.
3 Snider struck out.
New York
1 Bauer fanned.
2 Collins grounded out, Hodges to Craig.
3 Mantle fouled to Campanella.

4th Inning
Brooklyn
1 Robinson grounded to third.
2 Hodges grounded to short.
3 Furillo took a called third strike.
New York
1 Berra popped to second.
Slaughter singled to left-center.
2,3 Martin hit into a double play, Craig to Reese to Hodges.

5th Inning
Brooklyn
Campanella singled to left.
1 Neal struck out.
2 Campanella was caught stealing, Berra to McDougald.
3 Craig grounded to second.
New York
McDougald singled to right.
1 Carey struck out.
2,3 Ford grounded into a double play, Neal to Reese to Hodges.

6th Inning
Brooklyn
1 Gilliam popped to second.
Reese tripled to right-center past Mantle.
2 Snider hit a sacrifice fly to deep center, scoring Reese after the catch.
3 Robinson grounded to third.
New York
Bauer singled to left.
1 Collins flied to center.
2 Mantle popped to first.
Berra singled to right-center, Bauer advancing to third.
Slaughter hit a three-run homer into the lower left field stands.
3 Martin flied to center.

7th Inning
Brooklyn
Hodges walked.
Furillo singled off Ford's glove, Hodges going all the way to third.
1 Campanella fouled to McDougald.
Neal was safe on Carey's fumble, who threw too late to the plate as Hodges scored and Furillo moved to second.
2 Jackson, pinch-hitting for Craig, flied to left.
3 Gilliam forced Neal at second, McDougald (unassisted).
New York
For Brooklyn—Labine pitching.
1 McDougald grounded to short.
2 Carey took a called third strike.
3 Ford also called out on strikes.

8th Inning
Brooklyn
1 Reese grounded to short.
2 Snider struck out.
Robinson singled to left.
3 Hodges flied to center.
New York
1 Bauer flied to Snider in short right on a good one-handed catch.
Collins safe at first on Neal's bad throw to first.
2 Mantle popped to second.
Berra doubled to right-center, Collins scoring.
Slaughter intentionally walked.
3 Martin flied to left.

9th Inning
Brooklyn
Furillo doubled off the right-center field scoreboard, but was out trying for a triple, Bauer to Martin to Carey.
2 Campanella called out on strikes.
3 Neal grounded to third.

Game 4 October 7 at New York

Brooklyn	Pos	AB	R	H	RBI	PO	A	E
Gilliam	2b	4	0	0	0	1	4	0
Reese	ss	4	0	1	0	1	2	0
Snider	cf	4	1	1	0	3	0	0
Robinson	3b	3	0	0	0	0	2	0
Hodges	1b	4	0	1	1	10	1	0
Amoros	lf	3	0	0	0	2	0	0
Furillo	rf	3	0	0	0	4	0	0
Campanella	c	2	0	2	1	6	0	0
Erskine	p	1	0	0	0	1	2	0
a Walker		1	0	0	0	0	0	0
Roebuck	p	0	0	0	0	0	0	0
b Mitchell		1	0	0	0	0	0	0
Drysdale	p	0	0	0	0	0	0	0
c Jackson		1	0	0	0	0	0	0
Totals		31	2	6	2	24	11	0

a Hit into double play for Erskine in 5th.
b Flied out for Roebuck in 7th.
c Struck out for Drysdale in 9th.

Doubles—Collins, Robinson, Snider. Home Runs—Bauer, Mantle. Stolen Base—Mantle. Sacrifice Fly—McDougald. Double Plays—Gilliam to Reese to Hodges, Collins (unassisted), Martin to McDougald to Collins. Left on Bases—Brooklyn 8, New York 3. Umpires—Napp, Pinelli, Soar, Boggess, Runge, Gorman. Attendance—69,705. Time of Game—2:43.

New York	Pos	AB	R	H	RBI	PO	A	E
Bauer	rf	4	1	1	2	1	0	0
Collins	1b	3	1	1	0	8	2	1
Mantle	cf	3	2	1	1	4	0	0
Berra	c	4	0	1	1	8	1	0
Slaughter	lf	3	1	0	0	1	0	0
Martin	2b	4	0	1	1	0	3	0
McDougald	ss	2	0	1	1	3	3	0
Carey	3b	3	1	1	0	0	0	1
Sturdivant	p	3	0	1	0	2	0	0
Totals		29	6	7	6	27	9	2

Pitching	IP	H	R	ER	BB	SO
Brooklyn						
Erskine (L)	4	4	3	3	2	2
Roebuck	2	1	1	1	0	2
Drysdale	2	2	2	2	1	1
New York						
Sturdivant (W)	9	6	2	2	6	7

Bkn. 000 100 001
N.Y. 100 201 20x

1st Inning
Brooklyn
Gilliam walked.
1 Gilliam caught stealing, Berra to McDougald.
2 Reese called out on strikes.
3 Snider grounded out, Collins to Sturdivant.
New York
1 Bauer flied to center.
Collins doubled into the right field corner.
2 Mantle grounded out, Hodges to Erskine, with Collins going to third.
Berra singled to center, scoring Collins.
3 Slaughter grounded back to the mound.

2nd Inning
Brooklyn
Robinson walked.
1 Hodges struck out.
2 Amoros fouled to Collins. On the play Robinson was trapped off first but got back safely on Collins' bad throw to Martin covering first. Collins charged with an error.
3 Furillo grounded to first.
New York
1 Martin flied to left.
2 McDougald grounded to third.
3 Carey called out on strikes.

3rd Inning
Brooklyn
Campanella walked.
1 Erskine struck out.
2 Gilliam flied to center.
3 Reese took a called third strike.
New York
Sturdivant singled behind third.
1 Bauer fouled popped to Campanella.
2,3 Collins grounded into a double play, Gilliam to Reese to Hodges.

4th Inning
Brooklyn
Snider doubled off the right field wall.
1 Robinson fouled to Berra.
Hodges singled over second, Snider scoring.
2,3 Amoros lined to Collins who stepped on first to double up Hodges.
New York
Mantle walked.
1 Berra struck out as Mantle stole second.
Slaughter intentionally walked.
Martin singled to left, Mantle scoring with Slaughter going to third.
2 McDougald hit a sacrifice fly to center, scoring Slaughter.
3 Carey bunted out back to the mound.

5th Inning
Brooklyn
Furillo was safe on Carey's bobble.
Campanella singled to left, Furillo stopping at second.
1,2 Walker, pinch-hitting for Erskine, hit into a double play, Martin to McDougald to Collins. Furillo went to third on the play.
3 Gilliam grounded out, Collins to Sturdivant.
New York
For Brooklyn—Roebuck pitching.
1 Sturdivant flied to left.
2 Bauer fanned.
3 Collins popped to second.

6th Inning
Brooklyn
Reese beat out a roller to third.
1 Snider flied to right.
2 Robinson grounded out McDougald to Martin to Collins as Reese beat the force at second.
3 Hodges grounded to short.
New York
Mantle hit a home-run into the right-center field bleachers.
1 Berra flied to center.
2 Slaughter grounded to third.
3 Martin struck out.

7th Inning
Brooklyn
1 Amoros grounded to second.
2 Furillo flied to center.
Campanella walked.
3 Mitchell, batting for Roebuck, flied to left.
New York
For Brooklyn—Drysdale pitching.
1 McDougald grounded to short.
Carey singled to left.
2 Sturdivant struck out.
Bauer hit a two-run homer into the lower left field stands.
Collins walked.
3 Mantle grounded to second.

8th Inning
Brooklyn
1 Gilliam flied to deep center.
2 Reese popped to short.
3 Snider struck out.
New York
1 Berra grounded to first.
2 Slaughter grounded to second.
3 Martin grounded to second.

9th Inning
Brooklyn
Robinson doubled to left-center.
1 Hodges struck out.
Amoros walked.
Furillo walked, loading the bases.
Campanella singled to short left, Robinson scoring.
2 Jackson, batting for Drysdale, took a third strike.
3 Gilliam flied to center.

Game 5 October 8 at New York

Bkn.		000	000	000			
N.Y.		000	101	00x			

Brooklyn	Pos	AB	R	H	RBI	PO	A	E
Gilliam	2b	3	0	0	0	2	0	0
Reese	ss	3	0	0	0	4	2	0
Snider	cf	3	0	0	0	1	0	0
Robinson	3b	3	0	0	0	2	4	0
Hodges	1b	3	0	0	0	5	1	0
Amoros	lf	3	0	0	0	3	0	0
Furillo	rf	3	0	0	0	0	0	0
Campanella	c	3	0	0	0	7	2	0
Maglie	p	2	0	0	0	0	1	0
a Mitchell		1	0	0	0	0	0	0
Totals		27	0	0		24	10	0

New York	Pos	AB	R	H	RBI	PO	A	E
Bauer	rf	4	0	1	1	4	0	0
Collins	1b	4	0	1	0	7	0	0
Mantle	cf	3	1	1	1	4	0	0
Berra	c	3	0	0	0	7	0	0
Slaughter	lf	2	0	0	0	1	0	0
Martin	2b	3	0	1	0	3	4	0
McDougald	ss	2	0	0	0	0	2	0
Carey	3b	3	1	1	0	1	1	0
Larsen	p	2	0	0	0	0	1	0
Totals		26	2	5	2	27	8	0

a Struck out for Maglie in 9th.

Home Run—Mantle. Sacrifice Hit—Larsen. Double Plays—Reese to Hodges, Hodges to Campanella to Robinson to Campanella to Robinson. Left on Bases—Brooklyn 0, New York 3. Umpires—Pinelli, Soar, Boggess, Napp, Gorman, Runge. Attendance—64,519. Time of Game—2:06. (Note in play-by-play below, the number before the Brooklyn batters indicates the sequence of Larsen's 97 pitches).

Pitching	IP	H	R	ER	BB	SO
Brooklyn						
Maglie (L)	8	5	2	2	2	5
New York						
Larsen (W)	9	0	0	0	0	7

1st Inning
Brooklyn
1 Gilliam—(1) Ball.
(2) Foul down first base line.
(3) Ball 2.
(4) Strike 2 called.
(5) Strike 3 called.
2 Reese—(6) Strike 1 foul.
(7) Ball.
(8) Strike 2 called.
(9) Ball 2.
(10) Ball 3.
(11) Strike 3 called.
3 Snider—(12) Ball.
(13) Strike 1.
(14) Ball 2.
(15) Lined to right.
New York
1 Bauer popped to short.
2 Collins bunted out to third.
3 Mantle flied to left.

2nd Inning
Brooklyn
1 Robinson (16) Strike 1 called.
(17) Hit liner off Carey's glove to McDougald who threw to first, getting Robinson by less than a step.
2 Hodges (18) Ball.
(19) Strike 1.
(20) Strike 2 called.
(21) Fanned on low outside curve.
3 Amoros (22) Strike 1.
(23) Strike 2 foul.
(24) Ball 1.
(25) Ball 2.
(26) Popped to second.
New York
1 Berra popped to short.
2 Slaughter flied to left.
3 Martin struck out, but had to be tagged out by Campanella who dropped the third strike.

3rd Inning
Brooklyn
1 Furillo (27) Strike 1 called.
(28) Flied to right.
2 Campanella (29) Ball.
(30) Strike 1 called.
(31) Strike 2.
(32) Strike 3 swinging.
3 Maglie (33) Lined to center.
New York
1 McDougald grounded to third.
2 Carey fouled to Campanella.
3 Larsen fouled to Campanella.

4th Inning
Brooklyn
1 Gilliam (34) Grounded to second.
2 Reese (35) Tapped to second.
3 Snider (36) Ball.
(37) Ball 2.
(38) Strike, long foul into lower deck.
(39) Strike 2 called.
(40) Foul to left.
(41) Strike 3 called.
New York
1 Bauer grounded to third.
2 Collins called out on strikes.
Mantle hit a homer just inside the foul pole into the lower right field stands. (First hit off Maglie).
3 Berra lined to center where Snider made a diving shoe-string catch.

5th Inning
Brooklyn
1 Robinson (42) Ball.
(43) Strike 1 foul.
(44) Strike 2.
(45) Long foul to left.
(46) Flied deep to right.
2 Hodges (47) Strike 1 called.
(48) Strike 2 called.
(49) Ball 1.
(50) Ball 2.
(51) Flied to Mantle in deep left-center on a one-handed catch.
3 Amoros (52) Ball.
(53) Strike 1 called.
(54) Long foul into right field lower deck.
(55) Ball 2.
(56) Grounded to second.
New York
Slaughter walked.
1 Martin forced Slaughter at second, Maglie to Reese on a bunt.
2,3 McDougald lined to Reese who fired to Hodges for a double play.

6th Inning
Brooklyn
1 Furillo (57) Strike 1 foul.
(58) Popped to Martin in short right.
2 Campanella (59) Popped to Martin in short center.
3 Maglie (60) Strike 1.
(61) Strike 2.
(62) Ball.
(63) Foul.
(64) Foul.
(65) Ball 2.
(66) Struck out.
New York
Carey singled over Maglie's head.
1 Larsen sacrificed Carey to second, Campanella to Gilliam.
Bauer singled into left, scoring Carey.
Collins singled to right-center, Bauer advancing to third.
2,3 Mantle grounded to Hodges who stepped on first and threw to Campanella trapping Bauer for a double play, the DP went Hodges to Campanella to Robinson to Campanella to Robinson.

7th Inning
Brooklyn
1 Gilliam (67) Strike 1 called.
(68) Ball.
(69) Strike 2 foul to left.
(70) Grounded sharply to short.
2 Reese (71) Strike 1 fouled back on screen.
(72) Flied to deep center.
3 Snider (73) Ball.
(74) Flied to left.
New York
1 Berra fouled to Robinson.
2 Slaughter flied to left.
Martin singled past third.
McDougald walked.
3 Carey forced McDougald at second, Reese to Gilliam.

8th Inning
Brooklyn
1 Robinson (75) Strike 1 called.
(76) Strike 2 foul.
(77) Grounded back to the mound.
2 Hodges (78) Strike 1 called.
(79) Ball high.
(80) Strike 2 swinging.
(81) Ball 2 outside.
(82) Lined to third.
3 Amoros (83) Strike 1 called.
(84) Flied to deep center.
New York
1 Larsen struck out.
2 Bauer struck out.
3 Collins struck out.

9th Inning
Brooklyn
1 Furillo (85) Strike 1 foul.
(86) Strike 2 foul.
(87) Ball high.
(88) Foul into first base box seats.
(89) Foul into the right field boxes.
(90) Flied to right.
2 Campanella (91) Strike 1 foul.
(92) Grounded to second.
3 Mitchell, pinch-hitting for Maglie.
(93) Ball outside.
(94) Strike 1 called.
(95) Strike 2 swinging.
(96) Fouled into the left field stands.
(97) Strike 3 called **and a perfect game for Larsen on only 97 pitches.**

Game 6 October 9 at Brooklyn

N.Y. 000 000 000 0
Bkn. 000 000 000 1

New York	Pos	AB	R	H	RBI	PO	A	E
Bauer	rf	5	0	2	0	2	0	0
Collins	1b	5	0	2	0	4	1	0
Mantle	cf	3	0	0	0	2	0	0
Berra	c	4	0	2	0	12	0	0
Slaughter	lf	3	0	0	0	1	1	0
Martin	2b	4	0	1	0	3	1	0
McDougald	ss	4	0	0	0	3	0	0
Carey	3b	4	0	0	0	2	0	0
Turley	p	4	0	0	0	0	2	0
Totals		36	0	7	0	*29	5	0

* Two out when winning run scored.

Brooklyn	Pos	AB	R	H	RBI	PO	A	E
Gilliam	2b	3	1	1	0	0	7	0
Reese	ss	4	0	0	0	2	3	0
Snider	cf	2	0	1	0	4	0	0
Robinson	3b	4	0	1	1	1	1	0
Hodges	1b	2	0	0	0	14	0	0
Amoros	lf	3	0	0	0	2	0	0
Furillo	rf	4	0	0	0	2	0	0
Campanella	c	4	0	0	0	5	0	0
Labine	p	4	0	1	0	0	3	0
Totals		30	1	4	1	30	14	0

Pitching	IP	H	R	ER	BB	SO
New York						
Turley (L)	9⅔	4	1	1	8	11
Brooklyn						
Labine (W)	10	7	0	0	2	5

Doubles—Berra, Collins, Labine.
Sacrifice Hit—Reese. Double Play—Gilliam
to Reese to Hodges. Left on Bases—New
York 8, Brooklyn 10. Umpires—Soar,
Boggess, Napp, Pinelli, Runge, Gorman.
Attendance—33,224. Time of Game—2:37.

1st Inning
New York
  Bauer singled to center.
1,2 Collins grounded into a double play,
    Gilliam to Reese to Hodges.
3 Mantle grounded to second.
Brooklyn
1 Gilliam grounded to second.
2 Reese struck out.
  Snider singled to left.
3 Robinson lined to short.

2nd Inning
New York
  Berra singled off the right field wall.
1 Slaughter forced Berra at second,
    Gilliam to Reese.
2 Martin flied to center.
3 McDougald struck out.
Brooklyn
  Hodges walked.
1 Amoros forced Hodges at second,
    Collins to McDougald.
2 Furillo struck out.
3 Campanella struck out.

3rd Inning
New York
1 Carey flied to right.
2 Turley grounded back to the mound.
  Bauer singled to center.
  Collins beat out a bouncer to short.
3 Mantle grounded to first.
Brooklyn
1 Labine struck out.
  Gilliam singled to left when Slaughter
    lost the ball in the sun, but was out
2 trying for a double, Slaughter to
    Martin.
3 Reese lined to first.

4th Inning
New York
1 Berra grounded to second.
2 Slaughter flied to center.
  Martin singled off the
    right field wall.
3 McDougald flied to left.
Brooklyn
1 Snider struck out.
  Robinson walked.
2 Hodges flied to right.
3 Amoros popped to third.

5th Inning
New York
1 Carey flied to right.
2 Turley popped to first.
3 Bauer flied to left.
Brooklyn
1 Furillo struck out.
2 Campanella struck out.
3 Labine struck out.

6th Inning
New York
1 Collins flied to deep center.
2 Mantle grounded to second.
  Berra doubled to right-center.
  Slaughter walked.
3 Martin fouled to Robinson.
Brooklyn
  Gilliam walked.
1 Reese fouled to Berra on an
    attempted sacrifice.
  Snider walked.
2 Robinson popped to short.
3 Hodges popped to Martin.

7th Inning
New York
1 McDougald called out on strikes.
2 Carey grounded to short.
3 Turley grounded to the mound.
Brooklyn
1 Amoros took a called third strike.
2 Furillo flied to right.
3 Campanella struck out.

8th Inning
New York
1 Bauer struck out.
  Collins doubled off the right
    field scoreboard.
  Mantle intentionally passed.
2 Berra flied to center.
3 Slaughter grounded to second.
Brooklyn
  Labine hit a ground-rule double
    into the left field stands.
1 Gilliam struck out.
2 Reese flied to center.
  Snider intentionally walked.
3 Robinson popped to third.

9th Inning
New York
1 Martin grounded to third.
2 McDougald struck out.
3 Carey tapped to the mound.
Brooklyn
1 Hodges grounded back to the mound.
  Amoros walked.
2 Furillo flied to left.
3 Campanella flied to center.

10th Inning
New York
1 Turley took a called third strike.
2 Bauer grounded to short.
3 Collins grounded to second.
Brooklyn
1 Labine popped to second.
  Gilliam walked.
2 Reese sacrificed Gilliam to second,
    Turley to Collins.
  Snider again was intentionally
    walked.
  Robinson lined a single over the
    leaping Slaughter's head, scoring
    Gilliam with the winning run.

Game 7 October 10 at Brooklyn

N.Y. 202 100 400
Bkn. 000 000 000

New York	Pos	AB	R	H	RBI	PO	A	E
Bauer	rf	5	1	1	0	0	0	0
Martin	2b	5	2	2	0	2	6	0
Mantle	cf	4	1	1	0	4	0	0
Berra	c	3	3	2	4	1	1	0
Skowron	1b	5	1	1	4	16	1	0
Howard	lf	5	1	2	1	2	0	0
McDougald	ss	4	0	1	0	3	3	0
Carey	3b	3	0	0	0	2	2	0
Kucks	p	3	0	0	0	1	2	0
Totals		37	9	10	9	27	15	0

Pitching	IP	H	R	ER	BB	SO
New York						
Kucks (W)	9	3	0	0	3	1
Brooklyn						
Newcombe (L)	*3	5	5	5	1	4
Bessent	3	2	0	0	1	1
Craig	**0	3	4	4	2	0
Roebuck	2	0	0	0	0	3
Erskine	1	0	0	0	0	0

*Pitched to one batter in 4th.
**Pitched to five batters in 7th.

1st Inning
New York
  Bauer singled to left.
  Bauer stole second.
1 Martin struck out.
2 Mantle struck out.
  Berra hit a two-run homer over the
    right field screen.
3 Skowron struck out.
Brooklyn
1 Gilliam grounded to first.
  Reese walked.
  Snider singled between short and third,
    Reese stopping at second.
2,3 Robinson hit into a double play,
    Kucks to Martin to Skowron.

2nd Inning
New York
1 Howard grounded to short.
2 McDougald lined to second.
  Carey walked.
3 Kucks forced Carey at second as
    Newcombe deflected his grounder to
    Reese who stepped on second.
Brooklyn
1 Hodges grounded to third.
2 Amoros grounded to second.
3 Furillo grounded to second.

3rd Inning
New York
1 Bauer grounded to second on a bunt.
  Martin singled to center.
2 Mantle struck out.
  Berra hit a two-run homer over the
    right field scoreboard after
    Campanella dropped his foul-tipped
    third strike.
3 Skowron popped to second.
Brooklyn
1 Campanella grounded to second.
2 Newcombe grounded back to the mound.
3 Gilliam flied to left.

4th Inning
New York
  Howard homered over the right field
    scoreboard.
  For Brooklyn—Bessent pitching.
1 McDougald popped to second.
  Carey safely at first on Reese's fumble.
2 Kucks sacrificed Carey to second,
    Hodges to Gilliam covering first.
3 Bauer grounded to second.
Brooklyn
  Reese walked.
1 Snider forced Reese at second,
    Skowron to McDougald.
2 Robinson fouled to Kucks outside the
    third base line on a surprise bunt.
3 Hodges grounded to second.

5th Inning
New York
1 Martin grounded to third.
  Mantle doubled off the left field wall.
  Berra intentionally walked.
2 Skowron popped to second.
3 Howard forced Berra at second,
    Hodges to Reese.

Brooklyn	Pos	AB	R	H	RBI	PO	A	E
Gilliam	2b	4	0	0	0	6	2	0
Reese	ss	2	0	0	0	2	5	1
Snider	cf	4	0	2	0	1	0	0
Robinson	3b	3	0	0	0	0	1	0
Hodges	1b	3	0	0	0	10	2	0
Amoros	lf	3	0	0	0	2	0	0
Furillo	rf	3	0	1	0	0	0	0
Campanella	c	3	0	0	0	8	0	0
Newcombe	p	1	0	0	0	0	1	0
Bessent	p	0	0	0	0	0	0	0
a Mitchell		1	0	0	0	0	0	0
Craig	p	0	0	0	0	0	0	0
Roebuck	p	0	0	0	0	0	0	0
b Walker		1	0	0	0	0	0	0
Erskine	p	0	0	0	0	0	0	0
Totals		28	0	3	0	27	11	1

a Grounded out for Bessent in 6th.
b Grounded out for Roebuck in 8th.

Doubles—Howard, Mantle. Home Runs—Berra
2, Howard, Skowron. Stolen Base—Bauer.
Sacrifice Hit—Kucks. Double Plays—Kucks
to Martin to Skowron, McDougald to
Skowron. Wild Pitch—Craig. Left on
Bases—New York 6, Brooklyn 4.
Umpires—Boggess, Napp, Pinelli, Soar,
Gorman, Runge. Attendance—33,782.
Time of Game—2:19.

5th Inning (continued)
Brooklyn
1 Amoros flied to left.
2 Furillo grounded to third.
3 Campanella grounded to short.

6th Inning
New York
  McDougald singled to left.
1 Carey grounded to short, sending
    McDougald to second.
2 Kucks fanned.
3 Bauer fouled to Hodges.
Brooklyn
1 Mitchell, batting for Bessent,
    grounded to short.
2 Gilliam lined to second.
3 Reese popped to short.

7th Inning
New York
  For Brooklyn—Craig pitching.
  Martin singled to left.
  Mantle walked.
    A wild pitch advanced both runners.
  Berra intentionally walked, loading
    the bases.
  **Skowron hit a grand slam homer into
    the lower left field stands.**
  Howard doubled off the right-center
    field screen.
  For Brooklyn—Roebuck came in to pitch.
1 McDougald popped to first.
2 Carey struck out but had to be tagged
    by Campanella who dropped the
    third strike.
3 Kucks grounded to short.
Brooklyn
1 Snider popped to third.
  Robinson walked.
2,3 Hodges lined to McDougald who threw
    to Skowron to double up Robinson.

8th Inning
New York
1 Bauer flied to center.
2 Martin fanned.
3 Mantle fanned.
Brooklyn
1 Amoros grounded to first.
  Furillo singled to center.
2 Campanella popped to third.
3 Walker, batting for Roebuck,
    grounded to second.

9th Inning
New York
  For Brooklyn—Erskine pitching.
1 Berra lined to second.
2 Skowron grounded to short.
3 Howard grounded to short.
Brooklyn
1 Gilliam grounded to first.
2 Reese fouled to Berra, on a bunt.
  Snider singled to center.
3 Robinson struck out but Berra
    dropped the third strike and had
    to throw to first for the out.

1956 WORLD SERIES COMPOSITE BOX

	Wins	Composite Line Score										
New York Yankees (A.L.)	4	6	6	2	6	0	5	6	1	1	0	- 33
Brooklyn Dodgers (N.L.)	3	0	9	4	4	2	1	1	2	1	1	- 25

	Regular Season			
Manager	W	L	Pct.	G. Ahead
Casey Stengel	97	57	.630	9
Walt Alston	93	61	.604	1

BATTING AND FIELDING

NEW YORK YANKEES

WORLD SERIES STATISTICS

	Pos	G	AB	R	H	2B	3B	HR	RBI	BB	SO	SB	BA	SA	PO	A	E
Joe Collins	1b-ph	6	21	2	5	**2**	0	0	2	2	3	0	.238	.333	30	3	**2**
Billy Martin	2b-3b	7	27	5	8	0	0	2	3	1	6	0	.296	.519	14	20	0
Gil McDougald	ss	7	21	0	3	0	0	0	1	3	6	0	.143	.143	16	16	0
Andy Carey	3b	7	19	2	3	0	0	0	0	1	6	0	.158	.158	6	10	**2**
Hank Baver	rf	7	**32**	3	**9**	0	0	1	3	0	5	**1**	.281	.375	14	1	1
Mickey Mantle	cf	7	24	**6**	6	1	0	**3**	4	6	5	**1**	.250	.667	18	1	0
Enos Slaughter	lf	6	20	**6**	7	0	0	1	4	4	0	0	.350	.500	8	1	0
Yogi Berra	c	7	25	5	**9**	**2**	0	**3**	**10**	4	1	0	**.360**	**.800**	50	3	0
Bill Skowron	1b-ph	3	10	1	1	0	0	1	4	0	3	0	.100	.400	21	4	1
Elston Howard	lf	1	5	1	2	1	0	1	1	0	0	0	.400	1.200	2	0	0
Jerry Coleman	2b	2	2	0	0	0	0	0	0	0	0	0	.000	.000	2	2	0
Bob Cerv	ph	1	1	0	1	0	0	0	0	0	0	0	1.000	1.000			
Norm Siebern	ph	1	1	0	0	0	0	0	0	0	0	0	.000	.000			
George Wilson	ph	1	1	0	0	0	0	0	0	0	1	0	.000	.000			
Billy Hunter		Did not play															
Tommy Carroll		Did not play															
Charlie Silvera		Did not play															
Whitey Ford	p	2	4	0	0	0	0	0	0	0	3	0	.000	.000	1	0	0
Don Larsen	p	2	3	1	1	0	0	0	1	0	1	0	.333	.333	0	1	0
Tom Sturdivant	p	2	3	0	1	0	0	0	0	0	1	0	.333	.333	2	0	0
Johnny Kucks	p	3	3	0	0	0	0	0	0	0	1	0	.000	.000	1	2	0
Bob Turley	p	3	4	0	0	0	0	0	0	0	1	0	.000	.000	0	2	0
Tom Morgan	p	2	1	1	1	0	0	0	0	0	0	0	1.000	1.000	0	0	0
Mickey McDermott	p	1	1	0	1	0	0	0	0	0	0	0	1.000	1.000	0	0	0
Tommy Byrne	ph-p	2	1	0	0	0	0	0	0	0	0	0	.000	.000	0	0	0
Bob Grim		Did not play															
Rip Coleman		Did not play															
team total		7	229	33	58	6	0	12	33	21	43	2	.253	.437	185	66	6

Double Plays—7
Left on Bases—40

REGULAR SEASON STATISTICS

		Main Pos	G	AB	R	H	2B	3B	HR	RBI	BB	SO	SB	BA	SA
Joe Collins		of-1b	100	262	38	59	5	3	7	43	34	33	3	.225	.347
Billy Martin		2b	121	458	76	121	24	5	9	49	30	56	7	.264	.397
Gil McDougald		ss	120	438	79	136	13	3	13	56	68	59	3	.311	.443
Andy Carey		3b	132	422	54	100	18	2	7	50	45	53	9	.237	.339
Hank Baver		of	147	539	96	130	18	7	26	84	59	72	4	.241	.445
Mickey Mantle		of	150	533	**132**	188	22	5	**52**	**130**	112	99	10	**.353**	**.705**
Enos Slaughter	a	of	24	83	15	24	4	2	0	4	5	6	1	.289	.386
Yogi Berra		c	140	521	93	155	29	2	30	105	65	29	3	.298	.534
Bill Skowron		lb	134	464	78	143	21	6	23	90	50	60	4	.308	.528
Elston Howard		of	98	290	35	76	8	3	5	34	21	30	0	.262	.362
Jerry Coleman		2b	80	183	15	47	5	1	0	18	12	33	1	.257	.297
Bob Cerv		of	54	115	16	35	5	6	3	25	18	13	0	.304	.530
Norm Siebern		of	54	162	27	33	1	4	4	21	19	38	1	.204	.333
George Wilson	b	of	11	12	1	2	0	0	0	0	3	0	0	.167	.167
Billy Hunter		ss	39	75	8	21	3	4	0	11	2	4	0	.280	.427
Tommy Carroll		pr-3b	36	17	11	6	0	0	0	0	1	3	1	.353	.353
Charlie Silvera		c	7	9	0	2	0	0	0	0	2	3	0	.222	.222
Whitey Ford		p	31	78	9	17	2	0	0	4	9	14	0	.218	.244
Don Larsen		p	45	79	10	19	5	0	2	12	6	17	0	.241	.380
Tom Sturdivant		p	32	64	5	20	1	1	0	5	0	7	0	.313	.359
Johnny Kucks		p	34	77	7	11	1	0	0	1	7	25	0	.143	.156
Bob Turley		p	27	46	5	8	2	0	0	3	3	16	0	.174	.217
Tom Morgan		p	41	13	1	2	0	0	0	0	1	5	0	.154	.154
Mickey McDermott		p-ph	46	52	4	11	0	0	1	4	8	13	0	.212	.269
Tommy Byrne		p	44	52	8	14	1	1	3	10	2	11	0	.269	.500
Bob Grim		p	26	16	2	1	0	0	0	1	4	9	0	.163	.163
Rip Coleman		p	29	24	2	1	0	0	0	0	1	14	0	.042	.042
team total			154	5312	**857**	1433	193	55	**190**	**788**	615	755	51	.270	**.434**

a—from Kansas City
b—from New York (N)
Phil Rizzuto (ss), Irv Noren (ph-of), Eddie Robinson (lb-ph), Jerry Lumpe (ss), Lou Skizas (of), Bobby Richardson (2b), Ralph Terry (p), Sonny Dixon (p), Jim Konstanty (p), Gerry Staley (p), and Jim Coates also played for the Yankees during the season.

BROOKLYN DODGERS

WORLD SERIES STATISTICS

	Pos	G	AB	R	H	2B	3B	HR	RBI	BB	SO	SB	BA	SA	PO	A	E
Gil Hodges	1b	7	23	5	7	**2**	0	1	8	4	4	0	.304	.522	**54**	5	0
Jim Gilliam	2b-lf	7	24	2	2	0	0	0	2	**7**	3	**1**	.083	.083	19	17	0
Pee Wee Reese	ss	7	27	3	6	0	**1**	0	2	2	6	0	.222	.296	14	**21**	1
Jackie Robinson	3b	7	24	5	6	1	0	1	2	5	2	0	.250	.417	5	12	0
Carl Furillo	rf	7	25	2	6	**2**	0	0	1	2	3	0	.240	.320	7	0	0
Duke Snider	cf	7	23	5	7	1	0	1	4	6	**8**	0	.304	.478	20	0	0
Sandy Amoros	lf	6	19	1	1	0	0	0	1	2	4	0	.053	.053	10	0	0
Roy Campanella	c	7	22	2	4	1	0	0	3	3	7	0	.182	.227	49	3	0
Charlie Neal	2b	1	4	0	0	0	0	0	0	0	1	0	.000	.000	2	2	1
Gino Cimoli	of	1	0	0	0	0	0	0	0	0	0	0	—	—	1	0	0
Dale Mitchell	ph	4	4	0	0	0	0	0	0	0	1	0	.000	.000			
Randy Jackson	ph	3	3	0	0	0	0	0	0	0	2	0	.000	.000			
Rube Walker	ph	2	2	0	0	0	0	0	0	0	0	0	.000	.000			
Chico Fernandez		Did not play															
Dixie Howell		Did not play															
Sal Maglie	p	2	5	0	0	0	0	0	0	0	2	0	.000	.000	0	1	0
Clem Labine	p	2	4	0	1	1	0	0	0	0	2	0	.250	.500	0	3	0
Don Bessent	p	2	2	0	1	0	0	0	1	1	1	0	.500	.500	0	0	0
Roger Craig	p	2	2	0	1	0	0	0	0	0	0	0	.500	.500	1	1	0
Don Newcombe	p	2	1	0	0	0	0	0	0	0	0	0	.000	.000	0	2	0
Carl Erskine	p	2	1	0	0	0	0	0	0	0	1	0	.000	.000	1	2	0
Ed Roebuck	p	3	0	0	0	0	0	0	0	0	0	0	—	—	0	0	0
Don Drysdale	p	1	0	0	0	0	0	0	0	0	0	0	—	—	0	0	0
Ken Lehman		Did not play															
Sandy Koufax		Did not play															
team total		7	215	25	42	8	1	3	24	32	47	1	.195	.312	183	69	2

Double Plays—8
Left on Bases—42

REGULAR SEASON STATISTICS

		Main Pos	G	AB	R	H	2B	3B	HR	RBI	BB	SO	SB	BA	SA
Gil Hodges		1b	153	550	86	146	29	4	32	87	76	91	3	.265	.507
Jim Gilliam		2b-of	153	594	102	178	23	8	6	43	95	39	21	.300	.396
Pee Wee Reese		ss	147	572	85	147	19	2	9	46	56	69	13	.257	.344
Jackie Robinson		3b	113	357	61	98	15	2	10	43	60	32	12	.275	.412
Carl Furillo		of	149	523	66	151	30	0	21	83	57	41	1	.289	.467
Duke Snider		of	151	542	112	158	33	2	**43**	101	**99**	101	3	.292	**.598**
Sandy Amoros		of	114	292	53	76	11	8	16	58	59	51	3	.260	.517
Roy Campanella		c	124	388	39	85	6	1	20	73	66	61	1	.219	.394
Charlie Neal		2b	62	136	22	39	5	1	2	14	14	19	2	.287	.382
Gino Cimoli		of	73	36	3	4	1	0	0	4	1	8	1	.111	.139
Dale Mitchell	c	ph	19	24	3	7	1	0	0	1	0	3	0	.292	.333
Randy Jackson		3b	101	307	37	84	15	7	8	53	28	38	2	.274	.446
Rube Walker		c	54	146	5	31	6	1	3	20	7	18	0	.212	.329
Chico Fernandez		ss	34	66	11	15	2	0	1	9	3	10	2	.227	.303
Dixie Howell		c	7	13	0	3	2	0	0	1	1	3	0	.231	.385
Sal Maglie	d	p	28	70	1	9	0	0	0	2	1	29	0	.129	.129
Clem Labine		p	62	23	0	2	0	0	0	1	1	14	0	.087	.087
Don Bessent		p	38	18	0	2	0	0	0	1	0	5	0	.111	.111
Roger Craig		p	35	61	1	1	0	0	0	1	6	33	0	.016	.016
Don Newcombe		p-ph	52	111	13	26	6	0	2	16	12	18	1	.234	.342
Carl Erskine		p	32	66	1	8	1	0	0	0	0	8	0	.121	.136
Ed Roebuck		p	43	18	3	6	2	0	0	1	0	4	0	.333	.444
Don Drysdale		p	26	26	4	5	1	0	1	1	1	8	0	.192	.346
Ken Lehman		p	25	10	0	3	1	0	0	3	0	0	0	.300	.400
Sandy Koufax		p	16	17	0	2	0	0	0	0	2	12	0	.118	.118
team total			154	5098	720	1315	212	36	179	680	**649**	738	65	.258	.419

c—from Cleveland
d—from Cleveland
Rocky Nelson (1b), Don Zimmer (ss), Dick Williams (ph), Don Demeter (of), Bob Aspromonte (ph), Chuck Templeton (p), Billy Loes (p), Jim Hughes (p), Ralph Branca (p) and Bob Darnell (p) also played for the Dodgers during the season.

PITCHING

NEW YORK YANKEES

WORLD SERIES STATISTICS

	G	GS	CG	IP	H	R	ER	BB	SO	W	L	SV	ERA
Whitey Ford	2	**2**	1	12	**14**	8	7	2	8	**1**	**1**	0	5.25
Bob Turley	**3**	1	1	11	4	1	1	**8**	14	0	**1**	0	0.82
Johnny Kucks	**3**	1	1	11	6	2	1	3	2	**1**	0	0	0.82
Don Larsen	2	2	1	10 2/3	1	4	0	4	7	**1**	0	0	**0.00**
Tom Sturdivant	2	1	1	9 2/3	8	3	3	**8**	9	**1**	0	0	2.79
Tom Morgan	2	0	0	4	6	4	4	4	3	0	**1**	0	9.00
Mickey McDermott	1	0	0	3	2	2	1	3	3	0	0	0	3.00
Tommy Byrne	1	0	0	1/3	1	1	0	0	1	0	0	0	0.00
Bob Grim	Did not play												
Rip Coleman	Did not play												
team total	7	7	5	61 2/3	42	25	17	32	47	4	3	0	2.48

REGULAR SEASON STATISTICS

		G	GS	CG	IP	H	ER	BB	SO	W	L	Pct	SV	ShO	ERA
Whitey Ford		31	30	18	226	187	62	84	141	19	6	**.760**	1	2	**2.47**
Bob Turley		27	21	5	132	138	74	103	91	8	4	.667	1	1	5.05
Johnny Kucks		34	31	12	224	223	96	72	67	18	9	.667	0	3	3.86
Don Larsen		38	20	6	180	133	65	96	107	11	5	.688	1	1	3.25
Tom Sturdivant		32	17	6	158	134	58	52	110	16	8	.667	5	2	3.30
Tom Morgan		41	0	0	71	74	33	27	20	6	7	.462	11	0	4.18
Mickey McDermott		23	9	1	87	85	41	47	38	2	6	.250	0	0	4.24
Tommy Byrne		37	8	1	110	108	41	72	52	7	3	.700	6	0	3.35
Bob Grim		26	6	1	75	64	23	31	48	6	1	.857	5	0	2.76
Rip Coleman		29	9	0	88	97	36	42	42	3	5	.375	2	0	3.68
team total		154	154	50	1382	1285	559	652	732	**97**	57	**.630**	**35**	10	3.63

BROOKLYN DODGERS

WORLD SERIES STATISTICS

	G	GS	CG	IP	H	R	ER	BB	SO	W	L	SV	ERA
Sal Maglie	2	**2**	**2**	**17**	**14**	5	5	6	**15**	**1**	**1**	0	2.65
Clem Labine	2	1	1	12	8	1	0	3	7	**1**	0	0	**0.00**
Don Bessent	2	0	0	10	8	2	2	3	5	**1**	0	0	1.80
Roger Craig	2	1	0	6	10	8	8	3	4	0	**1**	0	12.00
Carl Erskine	2	1	0	5	4	3	3	2	2	0	**1**	0	5.40
Don Newcombe	2	**2**	0	4 2/3	11	**11**	**11**	3	4	0	**1**	0	21.21
Ed Roebuck	**3**	0	0	4 1/3	1	1	1	0	5	0	0	0	2.08
Don Drysdale	1	0	0	2	2	2	2	1	1	0	0	0	9.00
Ken Lehman	Did not play												
Sandy Koufax	Did not play												
team total	7	7	3	61	58	33	32	21	43	3	4	0	4.72

REGULAR SEASON STATISTICS

		G	GS	CG	IP	H	ER	BB	SO	W	L	Pct	SV	ShO	ERA
Sal Maglie	d	28	26	9	191	154	61	52	108	13	5	.722	0	3	2.87
Clem Labine		62	3	1	116	111	43	39	75	10	6	.625	**19**	0	3.34
Don Bessent		38	0	0	79	63	22	31	52	4	3	.571	9	0	2.51
Roger Craig		35	32	8	199	169	82	87	109	12	11	.522	1	2	3.71
Carl Erskine		31	28	8	186	189	88	57	95	13	11	.542	0	1	4.26
Don Newcombe		38	36	18	268	219	91	46	139	**27**	7	**.794**	0	5	3.06
Ed Roebuck		43	0	0	89	83	39	29	60	5	4	.556	1	0	3.94
Don Drysdale		25	12	2	99	95	29	31	55	5	5	.500	0	0	2.64
Ken Lehman		25	4	0	49	65	31	23	29	2	3	.400	0	0	5.69
Sandy Koufax		16	10	0	59	66	32	29	30	2	4	.333	0	0	4.88
team total		154	154	46	1369	1251	544	441	**772**	**93**	61	**.604**	**30**	**12**	3.57

Total Attendance—345,903 Average Attendance—49,415 Winning Player's Shares—$8,715 Losing Player's Share—$6,934

1957
Burdette's Twenty-Game Season

The Boston Braves had fallen on hard times both on the field and financially after their 1948 National League pennant, but owner Lou Perini revived his club by moving it to Milwaukee in 1953, the first big-league franchise shift since 1903. Wildly enthusiastic crowds inspired the Braves to leap from the second division into the ranks of contenders immediately upon their arrival in town, and the city's baseball fever hit a new peak when the Braves won this year's N.L. pennant. Manager Fred Haney had a fine lineup featuring sluggers Hank Aaron and Eddie Mathews and steady veterans Red Schoendienst and Del Crandall. Southpaw Warren Spahn, the only holdover from the 1948 squad, paced the mound staff with 21 wins, ably seconded by righties Bob Buhl and Lew Burdette. This upstart team in a new big-league city met as their World Series opponents the utmost in Establishment baseball, the New York Yankees. Manager Casey Stengel led his Yanks to their eighth American League flag in his nine-year tenure, once again surrounding stars like Mickey Mantle, Yogi Berra, Bill Skowron, and Whitey Ford with youngsters and journeymen who played their best when wearing the Yankee pinstripes.

The professional excellence of the Yankees was in full display when the Series opened in New York with Ford beating Spahn in a 3–1 decision. In the second game, the Yanks pitched southpaw Bobby Shantz while the Braves called on Burdette, a 17-game winner reputed to throw the illegal spitball. The Braves broke a 2–2 tie in the fourth inning with two runs on three hits, and whatever pitches Burdette was using baffled the Yanks enough to shut them out after the third inning for a 4–2 victory.

The rabid fans in Milwaukee planned to cheer every move of their heroes as the teams reassembled in Wisconsin, but they found an unlikely favorite in Tony Kubek, the rookie handyman of the Yankees. A native of Milwaukee, Kubek won his hometown fans over to cheering him with three hits, including two home runs good for four RBI's. The Yanks routed the Braves by a 12–3 score, with the win going to Don Larsen for his 7 1/3 innings of relief work. With Spahn on the mound, the Braves took a 4–1 lead the next day on two-run homers by Aaron and Frank Torre in the fourth inning off Tom Sturdivant. Spahn held that lead until two out in the ninth when, with two men on base, Elston Howard drilled Spahn's full-count pitch for a three-run homer to tie the game. All seemed lost when the Yankees scored in the top of the tenth on Kubek's infield hit and Hank Bauer's triple, but the Braves had a rabbit to pull out of their hats to cheer the loyal fans. Pinch hitter Nippy Jones claimed that a low pitch by Tommy Byrne hit him on the foot, and he convinced skeptical home-plate umpire Augie Donatelli by showing him a shoe-polish stain on the ball. After Schoendienst made out and Felix Mantilla went in to run for Jones, Logan tied the score with a double off reliever Bob Grim, then Mathews belted a homer to win it 7–5. The Yanks played the next day without Mantle, who sat down with a bad shoulder, and the New Yorkers never crossed the plate against Burdette. A single Milwaukee run off Ford in the sixth inning earned Burdette a 1–0 triumph and put the Braves one game short of the World Championship.

But the Yanks stayed alive with a sixth-game win in Yankee Stadium, with Bob Turley pitching a four-hitter and Bauer hitting a seventh-inning homer off the left-field foul pole for the winning run in a 3–2 game. Stengel picked Larsen to pitch the decisive seventh game, while Spahn's case of the flu made Burdette the only logical choice for Haney. Pitching on only two days of rest, Burdette completely handcuffed the Bronx Bombers while his mates strung together four hits and a New York error in the third inning into four runs. The Yanks loaded the bases in the bottom of the ninth, but Mathews fielded Skowron's hot drive to end the game 5–0, to give Burdette his third complete-game win of the Series. For the Braves, it was their first World Championship since 1914. New York fans had much to mourn this October; besides losing the World Championship, the Dodgers and Giants filed for divorce and headed west to begin new lives in 1958 in the sunny land of California.

Game 1 October 2 at New York

Mil.	000 000 100					
N.Y.	000 012 00x					

Milwaukee	Pos	AB	R	H	RBI	PO	A	E
Schoendienst	2b	4	0	1	1	1	2	0
Logan	ss	3	0	0	0	2	3	0
Mathews	3b	2	0	0	0	0	1	0
Aaron	cf	4	0	1	0	2	0	0
Adcock	1b	4	0	0	0	7	0	0
Torre	1b	0	0	0	0	1	0	0
Pafko	rf	4	0	0	0	3	0	0
Covington	lf	4	0	2	0	4	0	0
Crandall	c	4	0	1	0	4	1	0
Spahn	p	1	0	0	0	0	1	0
Johnson	p	0	0	0	0	0	1	0
a Jones		1	0	0	0	0	0	0
McMahon	p	0	0	0	0	0	0	0
Totals		31	1	5	1	24	9	0

a Grounded out for Johnson in 7th.

Doubles—Bauer, Coleman, Covington.
Sacrifice Hit—Coleman.
Double Plays—McDougald to Coleman to Howard, Crandall to Logan.
Left on Bases—Milwaukee 7, New York 7.
Umpires—Paparella (A), Conlan (N), McKinley (A), Donatelli (N), Secory (N), Chylak (A).
Attendance—69,476. Time of Game—2:10.

New York	Pos	AB	R	H	RBI	PO	A	E
Bauer	rf	4	0	1	1	1	0	0
McDougald	ss	4	0	1	0	2	6	0
Mantle	cf	4	0	2	0	2	0	0
Skowron	1b	1	0	0	0	2	0	0
Howard	1b	2	1	1	0	3	1	1
Collins	1b	1	0	0	0	5	0	0
Berra	c	3	0	1	0	5	0	0
Carey	3b	3	0	1	1	2	4	0
Coleman	2b	3	1	2	1	3	4	0
Kubek	lf	3	0	0	0	1	0	0
Ford	p	3	0	0	0	1	1	0
Totals		31	3	9	3	27	14	1

Pitching	IP	H	R	ER	BB	SO
Milwaukee						
Spahn (L)	5⅓	7	3	3	1	0
Johnson	⅔	0	0	0	0	1
McMahon	2	2	0	0	1	3
New York						
Ford (W)	9	5	1	1	4	5

1st Inning
Milwaukee
1 Schoendienst grounded to third.
2 Logan popped to second.
3 Mathews popped to third.
New York
1 Bauer flied to right.
  McDougald singled to right.
  Mantle beat out a single to short,
  McDougald going to second.
2 Skowron forced Mantle at second,
  Schoendienst to Logan, with
  McDougald going to third.
3 Berra popped to second.

2nd Inning
Milwaukee
1 Aaron grounded to second.
2 Adcock flied to right.
3 Pafko flied to left.
New York
1 Carey flied to center.
  Coleman hit a double down
  the right field line.
2 Kubek flied to left.
3 Ford flied to left.

3rd Inning
Milwaukee
For New York—Howard replaced Skowron at
  first. He injured his back in the first.
1 Covington struck out.
  Crandall singled to center.
2 Spahn forced Crandall at second,
  Coleman to McDougald.
3 Schoendienst flied to center.
New York
1 Bauer grounded to short.
2 McDougald flied to left.
3 Mantle flied to left.

4th Inning
Milwaukee
1 Logan grounded to short.
  Mathews walked.
  Aaron singled to right, Mathews
  going to third.
2,3 Adcock grounded into a double play,
  McDougald to Coleman to Howard.
New York
1 Howard grounded to first.
2 Berra flied to right.
3 Carey flied to right.

5th Inning
Milwaukee
1 Pafko grounded to short.
  Covington singled to center.
2 Crandall forced Covington at second,
  McDougald to Coleman but Howard
  dropped Coleman's throw for an error,
  and Crandall was safe at first.
  Spahn walked.
3 Schoendienst forced Crandall at third,
  Carey unassisted.

5th Inning (continued)
New York
  Coleman singled to left.
1 Kubek grounded out to the mound,
  advancing Coleman to second.
2 Ford grounded to short, Coleman
  going to third.
  Bauer doubled to center,
  scoring Coleman.
3 McDougald grounded to short.

6th Inning
Milwaukee
  Logan walked.
  Mathews walked.
1 Aaron struck out.
2 Adcock grounded out Howard to Ford,
  both runners advancing.
3 Pafko struck out.
New York
1 Mantle flied to center.
  Howard singled to center.
  Berra walked.
  Carey singled to center, Howard
  scoring with Berra going to third.
  For Milwaukee—Johnson came in to pitch.
2 Coleman out on a sacrifice squeeze,
  Johnson to Adcock scoring Berra
  and moving Carey to second.
3 Kubek struck out.

7th Inning
Milwaukee
For New York—Collins playing first.
  Covington doubled to left.
1 Crandall grounded to short,
  Covington holding second.
2 Jones, pinch-hitting for Johnson,
  grounded back to the mound, advancing
  Covington to third.
  Schoendienst singled through the
  middle, scoring Covington.
3 Logan struck out.
New York
For Milwaukee—McMahon pitching.
1 Ford grounded to second.
2 Bauer struck out.
3 McDougald struck out.

8th Inning
Milwaukee
1 Mathews bunted out to third.
2 Aaron popped to short.
3 Adcock grounded to short.
New York
For Milwaukee—Torre playing first.
  Mantle singled on a bunt past the
  mound to second.
1,2 Collins struck out and Mantle was
  doubled trying for second,
  Crandall to Logan.
  Berra singled past first into right.
  Carey walked.
3 Coleman grounded to third.

9th Inning
Milwaukee
1 Pafko popped to first.
2 Covington struck out.
3 Crandall flied to center.

Game 2 October 3 at New York

Mil.	011	200	000	
N.Y.	011	000	000	

Milwaukee	Pos	AB	R	H	RBI	PO	A	E
Schoendienst	2b	4	0	0	0	1	3	0
Logan	ss	3	1	1	1	3	3	0
Mathews	3b	4	0	0	0	1	2	0
Aaron	cf	4	1	1	0	2	0	0
Adcock	1b	4	1	2	1	8	1	0
Torre	1b	0	0	0	0	2	0	0
Pafko	rf	4	1	1	0	2	0	0
Covington	lf	4	0	2	1	3	0	0
Crandall	c	3	0	1	0	5	0	0
Burdette	p	3	0	0	0	0	4	0
Totals		33	4	8	3	27	13	0

Pitching	IP	H	R	ER	BB	SO
Milwaukee						
Burdette (W)	9	7	2	2	3	5
New York						
Shantz (L)	*3	6	4	3	1	3
Ditmar	4	1	0	0	0	1
Grim	2	1	0	0	0	2

*Pitched to three batters in 4th.

New York	Pos	AB	R	H	RBI	PO	A	E
Bauer	rf	5	1	1	1	3	0	0
McDougald	ss	4	0	0	0	2	3	0
Mantle	cf	3	0	0	0	2	0	1
Berra	c	4	0	0	0	6	0	0
Slaughter	lf	3	1	1	0	2	0	0
Simpson	1b	4	0	0	0	10	1	0
Kubek	3b	4	0	2	0	1	1	1
Coleman	2b	2	0	1	1	1	1	0
b Collins		1	0	0	0	0	0	0
Shantz	p	1	0	0	0	0	1	0
Ditmar	p	1	0	0	0	0	0	0
a Lumpe		1	0	1	0	0	0	0
Grim	p	0	0	0	0	0	0	0
c Howard		1	0	1	0	0	0	0
d Richardson		0	0	0	0	0	0	0
Totals		34	2	7	2	27	7	2

a Singled for Ditmar in 7th.
b Popped out for Coleman in 9th.
c Singled for Grim in 9th.
d Ran for Howard in 9th.

Double—Slaughter. Triple—Aaron. Home Runs—Bauer, Logan. Sacrifice Hit—Burdette. Double Play—McDougald to Simpson. Hit by Pitcher—Logan (by Ditmar). Left on Bases—Milwaukee 5, New York 8. Umpires—Conlan, McKinley, Donatelli, Paparella, Secory, Chylak. Attendance—65,202. Time of Game—2:26.

1st Inning
Milwaukee
1 Schoendienst called out on strikes.
2 Logan called out on strikes.
3 Mathews struck out.
New York
1 Bauer called out on strikes.
2 McDougald flied to right.
3 Mantle grounded out off Burdette's leg to Logan who threw him out at first.

2nd Inning
Milwaukee
Aaron tripled over Mantle's head in deep center.
Adcock singled to right-center, scoring Aaron. Adcock went to second on Mantle's fumble of his single.
1 Pafko flied to right.
2 Covington lined to third where Kubek made a good leaping catch.
Crandall walked.
3 Burdette out, Shantz to Simpson.
New York
1 Berra grounded to second.
Slaughter walked.
2 Simpson fanned.
Kubek singled to left, moving Slaughter to third.
Coleman beat out a roller to third, Slaughter scoring with Kubek going to second.
3 Shantz lined to left, Covington making a good backhanded, running catch.

3rd Inning
Milwaukee
1 Schoendienst flied to center.
Logan hit a home run into the lower left field stands.
2 Mathews flied to center.
3 Aaron popped to short.
New York
Bauer homered far into the lower left field stands.
1 McDougald flied to left.
2 Mantle flied to center.
3 Berra flied to left.

4th Inning
Milwaukee
Adcock singled to left.
Pafko singled to left, Adcock stopping at second.
Covington blooped a single over McDougald's head, Adcock scoring with Pafko going to third. Pafko scored and Covington got all the way to third as Slaughter's throw went through Kubek's legs. Charge Kubek with the error.
For New York—Ditmar came in to pitch.
1 Crandall popped to first.
2 Burdette popped to first.
3 Schoendienst grounded to short.
New York
1 Slaughter struck out.
2 Simpson flied to center.
3 Kubek grounded hard back to the mound.

5th Inning
Milwaukee
Logan was hit by a pitched ball.
1,2 Mathews bounced into a double play, McDougald to Simpson.
3 Aaron popped to first.

5th Inning (continued)
New York
Coleman walked.
1 Ditmar fanned.
2 Bauer grounded to short, moving Coleman to second.
3 McDougald grounded to second.

6th Inning
Milwaukee
1 Adcock flied to right.
2 Pafko popped to first.
3 Covington struck out.
New York
Mantle walked.
1 Berra forced Mantle at second, Adcock to Logan.
Slaughter doubled down the left field line, sending Berra to third.
2 Simpson bounced back to the mound, both runners holding.
3 Kubek grounded to second.

7th Inning
Milwaukee
Crandall singled on a bunt down the third base line.
1 Burdette sacrificed Crandall to second, Simpson to Coleman.
2 Schoendienst grounded to second, moving Crandall to third.
3 Logan flied to left.
New York
1 Coleman grounded to third.
Lumpe, batting for Ditmar, singled to right.
2 Bauer popped to short.
3 McDougald flied to right.

8th Inning
Milwaukee
For New York—Grim pitching.
1 Mathews called out on strikes.
2 Aaron struck out.
3 Adcock flied to right.
New York
For Milwaukee—Torre playing first.
1 Mantle fouled to Mathews.
2 Berra grounded to third.
3 Slaughter called out on strikes.

9th Inning
Milwaukee
1 Pafko flied to left.
Covington singled to left.
2 Crandall grounded to third, Covington going to second.
3 Burdette grounded to short.
New York
1 Simpson bounced back to the mound.
Kubek singled to right.
2 Collins, pinch-hitting for Coleman, popped to short.
Howard, pinch-hitting for Grim, beat out a grounder over second, sending Kubek to second.
Richardson ran for Howard.
3 Bauer forced Richardson at second, Logan to Schoendienst.

Game 3 October 5 at Milwaukee

N.Y.	302	200	500
Mil.	010	020	000

New York	Pos	AB	R	H	RBI	PO	A	E
Bauer	rf	5	1	1	2	3	0	0
Kubek	lf	5	3	3	4	4	0	0
Mantle	cf	3	2	2	2	1	0	0
Berra	c	4	2	1	0	7	0	0
McDougald	ss	1	2	0	1	3	3	0
Simpson	1b	1	0	1	1	0	0	0
a Howard	1b	2	0	0	0	6	0	0
Collins	1b	1	0	0	0	1	0	0
Lumpe	3b	5	0	1	2	2	3	0
Coleman	2b	4	1	0	0	0	1	0
Turley	p	1	0	0	0	0	0	0
Larsen	p	2	1	0	0	0	0	0
Totals		34	12	9	12	27	7	0

Pitching	IP	H	R	ER	BB	SO
New York						
Turley	$1\frac{2}{3}$	3	1	1	4	2
Larsen (W)	$7\frac{1}{3}$	5	2	2	4	4
Milwaukee						
Buhl (L)	$\frac{2}{3}$	2	3	2	2	0
Pizzaro	$1\frac{2}{3}$	3	2	2	2	1
Conley	$1\frac{2}{3}$	2	2	2	1	0
Johnson	2	0	0	0	1	2
Trowbridge	1	2	5	5	3	1
McMahon	2	0	0	0	2	2

Milwaukee	Pos	AB	R	H	RBI	PO	A	E
Schoendienst	2b	5	0	3	1	0	2	0
Logan	ss	4	1	2	0	0	1	0
Mathews	3b	2	0	0	0	3	6	0
Aaron	cf	5	1	2	2	2	0	0
Covington	lf	3	0	0	0	2	0	0
Adcock	1b	3	0	0	0	9	1	0
Trowbridge	p	0	0	0	0	0	0	0
d Jones		1	0	0	0	0	0	0
McMahon	p	0	0	0	0	0	1	0
f Pafko		0	0	0	0	0	0	0
Hazle	rf	4	1	0	0	1	0	0
Rice	c	3	0	1	0	5	1	0
e DeMerit		0	0	0	0	0	0	0
Crandall	c	1	0	0	0	1	0	0
Buhl	p	0	0	0	0	0	1	1
Pizzaro	p	1	0	0	0	0	0	0
Conley	p	0	0	0	0	1	0	0
b Sawatski		1	0	0	0	0	0	0
Johnson	p	0	0	0	0	0	1	0
c Torre	1b	2	0	0	0	3	0	0
Totals		35	3	8	3	27	14	1

a Walked for Simpson in 3rd.
b Struck out for Conley in 4th.
c Grounded out for Johnson in 6th.
d Grounded out for Trowbridge in 7th.
e Ran for Rice in 8th.
f Hit by pitched ball for McMahon in 9th.

Home Runs—Aaron, Kubek 2, Mantle. Stolen Base—McDougald. Sacrifice Fly—MyDougald. Double Play—Schoendienst to Torre. Passed Ball—Rice. Hit by Pitcher—Pafko (by Larsen), Wild Pitch—Turley. Left on Bases—New York 7, Milwaukee 14. Umpires—McKinley, Donatelli, Paparella, Conlan, Chylak, Secory. Attendance—45,804. Time of Game—3:18.

1st Inning
New York
1 Bauer bounced back to the pitcher.
Kubek homered over the right field wall.
Mantle walked.
Berra walked.
Buhl's pickoff throw to second went into center, for an error, both runners advancing one base.
2 McDougald hit a sacrifice fly to center, scoring Mantle after the catch.
Simpson beat out a high bouncer in back of second, scoring Berra.
For Milwaukee—Pizarro came in to pitch.
3 Lumpe flied to right.
Milwaukee
Schoendienst singled to right.
Logan walked.
1 Mathews popped to third.
2 Aaron popped to short.
Covington walked, loading the bases.
3 Adcock called out on strikes.

2nd Inning
New York
1 Coleman flied to left.
2 Turley grounded to third.
Bauer walked.
3 Kubek struck out.
Milwaukee
Hazle walked.
Rice singled through the middle, Hazle stopping at second.
1 Pizzaro flied to left.
Hazle to third on a wild pitch.
Schoendienst singled to right, scoring Hazle with Rice stopping at second.
2 Logan took a called third strike.
Mathews walked, loading the bases.
For New York—Larsen came in to pitch.
3 Aaron flied to right.

3rd Inning
New York
Mantle singled to center.
Berra singled to right, Mantle to third.
1 McDougald hit to Mathews and Mantle was run-down, Mathews to Rice to Mathews, Berra staying at second.
Howard, pinch-hitting for Simpson, walked to load the bases.
Lumpe singled to right, Berra and McDougald scoring and Howard to third.
For Milwaukee—Conley now pitching.
2 Coleman popped to third.
3 Larsen grounded to third.
Milwaukee
For New York—Howard playing first.
1 Covington struck out, but had to be tagged by Berra.
2 Adcock grounded to short.
3 Hazle grounded to short.

4th Inning
New York
1 Bauer grounded to third.
Kubek singled to left-center.
Mantle hit a two-run homer into the right-center field bullpen.
2 Berra grounded out, Adcock to Conley.
McDougald walked.
3 Howard grounded to third.
Milwaukee
1 Rice grounded to third.
2 Sawatski, batting for Conley, fanned.
3 Schoendienst flied to center.

5th Inning
New York
For Milwaukee—Johnson pitching.
1 Lumpe bunted out to the pitcher.
2 Coleman grounded to short.
3 Larsen took a called third strike.

5th Inning (continued)
Milwaukee
Logan singled through the middle.
1 Mathews flied to left.
Aaron hit a two-run homer over the right-center field screen.
Covington walked.
2 Adcock struck out.
3 Hazle flied to left.

6th Inning
New York
1 Bauer struck out.
2 Kubek grounded to second. Mantle walked.
3 Berra grounded to third.
Milwaukee
1 Rice grounded to third.
2 Torre, pinch-hitting for Johnson, grounded to second.
Schoendienst singled to right.
Logan singled into left, Schoendienst stopping at second.
Mathews walked, loading the bases.
3 Aaron grounded to third.

7th Inning
New York
For Milwaukee—Torre stays in game at first and Trowbridge pitching (batting 6th).
McDougald walked.
McDougald stole second.
1 Howard called out on strikes.
2 Lumpe flied to center.
Coleman walked.
Larsen walked, loading the bases.
Bauer singled over second, McDougald and Coleman scoring with Larsen stopping at second.
Kubek hit a three-run homer over the right field fence, his second of the game.
3 Mantle flied to left.
Milwaukee
For New York—Collins playing first.
1 Covington fouled to Lumpe.
2 Jones, pinch-hitting for Trowbridge, grounded to short.
3 Hazle flied to right.

8th Inning
New York
For Milwaukee—McMahon pitching.
1 Berra fouled to Mathews.
McDougald walked.
McDougald to second on passed ball.
2 Collins called out on strikes.
3 Lumpe grounded to the mound.
Milwaukee
Rice walked.
DeMerit ran for Rice.
1 Torre fouled to Berra.
2 Schoendienst popped to the short stop.
3 Logan lined to right.

9th Inning
New York
For Milwaukee—Crandall catching.
1 Coleman took a called third strike.
Larsen walked.
2,3 Bauer grounded to Schoendienst who threw to Torre for the out, Larsen was tagged by Torre in a run-down.
Milwaukee
Mathews walked.
Aaron singled to right-center, Mathews stopping at second.
1 Covington flied to left.
Pafko, batting for McMahon, was hit by a pitched ball, loading the bases.
2 Hazle popped to short.
3 Crandall took a called third strike.

Game 4 October 6 at Milwaukee

New York	Pos	AB	R	H	RBI	PO	A	E
Kubek	lf-cf	5	1	2	0	1	0	0
Bauer	rf	5	0	1	1	0	0	0
Mantle	cf	5	1	0	0	1	0	0
Slaughter	lf	0	0	0	0	0	0	0
Berra	c	3	1	2	0	8	0	0
McDougald	ss	4	1	2	1	1	2	0
Howard	1b	4	1	1	3	13	0	0
Collins	1b	0	0	0	0	0	1	0
Carey	3b	4	0	1	0	1	4	0
Coleman	2b	4	0	0	0	3	4	0
Sturdivant	p	1	0	0	0	0	1	0
a Simpson		1	0	0	0	0	0	0
Shantz	p	1	0	0	0	0	0	0
b Lumpe		1	0	1	0	0	0	0
Kucks	p	0	0	0	0	0	0	0
Byrne	p	1	0	0	0	0	0	0
Grim	p	0	0	0	0	0	0	0
Totals		38	5	11	5	x28	12	0

a Hit into double play for Sturdivant in 5th.
b Singled for Shantz in 8th.
c Grounded out for Torre in 9th.
d Hit by pitched ball for Spahn in 10th.
e Ran for Jones in 10th
x One out when winning run scored.

Doubles—Carey, Logan, Mathews, Schoendienst. Triple—Bauer. Home Runs—Aaron, Howard, Mathews, Torre. Stolen Base—Covington. Sacrifice Hit—Schoendienst. Double Plays—Schoendienst to Torre, Logan to Schoendienst to Torre 2. Hit by Pitcher—Jones (by Byrne). Left on Bases—New York 4, Milwaukee 4. Umpires—Donatelli, Paparella, Conlan, McKinley, Chylak, Secory. Attendance—45,804. Time of Game—2:31.

1st Inning
New York
Kubek singled on a bunt to the mound.
1 Bauer grounded to short, sending Kubek to second.
2 Mantle safe on his tap to Spahn who threw to Logan getting Kubek off of second.
Berra walked.
McDougald singled to left, Mantle scoring with Berra stopping at second.
3 Howard grounded to Mathews, who tagged Berra going into third.
Milwaukee
1 Schoendienst fouled to Carey.
2 Logan grounded to second.
3 Mathews grounded to first.

2nd Inning
New York
1 Carey flied to right.
2 Coleman grounded to third.
3 Sturdivant grounded to third.
Milwaukee
Aaron beat out a hit to deep short.
1 Covington forced Aaron at second, Carey to Coleman.
Covington stole second.
2 Torre grounded to second, moving Covington to third.
3 Hazle grounded to short.

3rd Inning
New York
1 Kubek grounded out, Torre to Spahn.
2 Bauer grounded to third.
3 Mantle bounced back to the mound.
Milwaukee
1 Crandall popped to second.
2 Spahn grounded to short.
3 Schoendienst popped to the catcher.

4th Inning
New York
1 Berra flied to right.
2 McDougald grounded to short.
3 Howard grounded to short.
Milwaukee
Logan walked.
Mathews doubled into the right field corner, Logan stopping at third.
Aaron hit a three-run homer over the left field fence.
1 Covington grounded to second.
Torre homered over the right field fence.
2 Hazle struck out.
3 Crandall grounded back to the pitcher.

5th Inning
New York
1 Carey grounded to short.
Coleman singled to right.
2,3 Simpson, batting for Sturdivant, hit into a double play, Schoendienst to Torre.
Milwaukee
For New York—Shantz pitching.
1 Spahn struck out.
2 Schoendienst popped to short.
3 Logan grounded to third.

Milwaukee	Pos	AB	R	H	RBI	PO	A	E
Schoendienst	2b	4	0	1	0	3	3	0
Logan	ss	4	2	1	1	1	10	0
Mathews	3b	4	2	2	2	1	4	0
Aaron	cf	3	1	2	3	1	0	0
Covington	lf	4	0	0	0	2	0	0
Torre	1b	3	1	1	1	15	1	0
c Adcock	1b	1	0	0	0	1	0	0
Hazle	rf	2	0	0	0	2	0	0
Pafko	rf	2	0	0	0	3	0	0
Crandall	c	4	0	0	0	2	0	0
Spahn	p	3	0	0	0	1	2	0
d Jones		0	0	0	0	0	0	0
e Mantilla		0	0	0	0	0	0	0
Totals		34	7	7	7	30	20	0

Pitching	IP	H	R	ER	BB	SO
New York						
Sturdivant	4	4	4	4	1	1
Shantz	3	0	0	0	1	4
Kucks	1	1	0	0	1	1
Byrne	*1⅓	0	1	1	0	1
Grim (L)	⅓	2	2	2	0	0
Milwaukee						
Spahn (W)	10	11	5	5	1	2

*Pitched to one batter in 10th.

N.Y.   1 0 0 0 0 0 0 0 3 1
Mil.   0 0 0 4 0 0 0 0 0 3

6th Inning
New York
1 Kubek grounded to third.
2 Bauer grounded to short.
3 Mantle struck out.
Milwaukee
Mathews walked.
1 Aaron called out on strikes.
2 Covington fanned.
3 Torre popped to first.

7th Inning
New York
For Milwaukee—Pafko playing right.
Berra singled past first.
1 McDougald flied to deep right.
2,3 Howard grounded into a double play, Logan to Schoendienst to Torre.
Milwaukee
1 Pafko grounded to third.
2 Crandall popped to the catcher.
3 Spahn called out on strikes.

8th Inning
New York
Carey doubled into left-center.
1 Coleman grounded to short, Carey holding Lumpe, pinch-hitting for Shantz, singled to center, moving Carey to third.
2,3 Kubek grounded into a double play, Logan to Schoendienst to Torre.
Milwaukee
For New York—Kucks pitching.
Schoendienst doubled to left-center.
1 Logan struck out.
2 Mathews flied to left.
Aaron walked.
For New York—Byrne came in to pitch.
3 Covington called out on strikes.

9th Inning
New York
1 Bauer flied to center.
2 Mantle grounded to short.
Berra singled to right.
McDougald singled to right, advancing Berra to second.
Howard hit a three-run homer into the left field stands.
3 Carey flied to right.
Milwaukee
1 Adcock, pinch-hitting for Torre, grounded to short.
2 Pafko grounded to third.
3 Crandall flied to deep center.

10th Inning
New York
For Milwaukee—Adcock playing first.
1 Coleman grounded to short **(Logan sets a new shortstop assist record with his 10th assist of the game).**
2 Byrne struck out, but had to be tagged by Crandall.
Kubek singled to second.
Bauer tripled off the left-field fence, scoring Kubek.
3 Mantle flied to right.
Milwaukee
For New York—Collins playing first.
Jones, pinch-hitting for Spahn, was hit by a pitched ball.
For New York—Grim came in to pitch.
Mantilla ran for Jones.
1 Schoendienst sacrificed Mantilla to second, Collins to Coleman.
For New York—Kubek moved to center and Slaughter came in to play left.
Logan doubled into the left field corner, scoring Mantilla.
Mathews hit a game-winning, two-run homer over the right field fence.

Game 5 October 7 at Milwaukee

New York	Pos	AB	R	H	RBI	PO	A	E
Bauer	rf	4	0	2	0	0	0	0
Kubek	cf	3	0	0	0	4	0	0
McDougald	ss	4	0	1	0	1	7	0
Berra	c	4	0	1	0	4	1	0
Slaughter	lf	3	0	2	0	3	0	0
Simpson	1b	3	0	0	0	8	0	0
Lumpe	3b	3	0	0	0	0	2	0
Coleman	2b	3	0	1	0	4	1	0
a Mantle		0	0	0	0	0	0	0
Turley	p	0	0	0	0	0	0	0
Ford	p	2	0	0	0	0	0	0
b Howard		1	0	0	0	0	0	0
Richardson	2b	0	0	0	0	0	0	0
Totals		30	0	7	0	24	11	0

a Ran for Coleman in 8th.
b Struck out for Ford in 8th.

Sacrifice Hits—Covington, Kubek.
Double Plays—Crandall to Logan. Mathews to Mantilla to Adcock, McDougald to Coleman to Simpson, Logan to Adcock.
Left on Bases—New York 4, Milwaukee 5.
Umpires—Paparella, Conlan, McKinley, Donatelli, Chylak, Secory.
Attendance—45,811. Time of Game—2:00.

1st Inning
New York
Bauer singled to left.
1 Kubek sacrificed Bauer to second, Burdette to Adcock.
2 McDougald lined to right.
3 Berra grounded to short.
Milwaukee
1 Schoendienst grounded to short.
2 Logan popped to second.
Mathews walked.
3 Aaron lined to left.

2nd Inning
New York
Slaughter singled to center.
1,2 Simpson struck out and Slaughter was doubled up trying for second, Crandall to Logan.
For Milwaukee—Mantilla playing second as Schoendienst strained his leg.
3 Lumpe grounded out, Crandall to Adcock.
Milwaukee
1 Adcock grounded to third.
Pafko singled to center.
2 Covington fouled to McDougald.
3 Crandall grounded to third.

3rd Inning
New York
1 Coleman grounded to second.
2 Ford grounded to second.
Bauer beat out a bouncer to short.
3 Kubek forced Bauer at second, Logan unassisted.
Milwaukee
1 Burdette grounded to short.
2 Mantilla grounded to short.
3 Logan flied to center.

4th Inning
New York
1 McDougald flied to Covington, who made a great catch bouncing off the fence.
Berra safe at first on Adcock's fumble.
Slaughter singled to left, Berra stopping at second.
2,3 Simpson hit into a double play, Mathews to Mantilla to Adcock.
Milwaukee
1 Mathews called out on strikes.
Aaron singled to left-center.
2,3 Adcock grounded into a double play, McDougald to Coleman to Simpson.

5th Inning
New York
1 Lumpe grounded to second.
2 Coleman grounded to second.
3 Ford fanned.
Milwaukee
Pafko singled to left.
1 Covington sacrificed Pafko to second, Berra to Coleman.
2 Crandall flied to left.
3 Burdette flied to center.

Milwaukee	Pos	AB	R	H	RBI	PO	A	E
Schoendienst	2b	1	0	6	0	0	0	0
Mantilla	2b	3	0	0	0	2	7	0
Logan	ss	4	0	0	0	3	3	0
Mathews	3b	3	0	1	0	1	2	0
Aaron	cf	3	0	2	0	4	0	0
Adcock	1b	3	0	1	1	13	0	1
Torre	1b	0	0	0	0	1	0	0
Pafko	rf	3	0	2	0	1	0	0
Covington	lf	2	0	0	0	2	0	0
Crandall	c	3	0	0	0	5	3	0
Burdette	p	3	0	0	0	0	2	0
Totals		28	1	6	0	27	17	1

Pitching	IP	H	R	ER	BB	SO
New York						
Ford (L)	7	6	1	1	1	2
Turley	1	0	0	0	0	2
Milwaukee						
Burdette (W)	9	7	0	0	0	5

N.Y.   0 0 0 0 0 0 0 0 0
Mil.   0 0 0 0 0 1 0 0 x

6th Inning
New York
1 Bauer grounded to third.
2 Kubek grounded to second.
3 McDougald grounded to second.
Milwaukee
1 Mantilla grounded to short.
2 Logan flied to left.
Mathews beat out a bouncer to second.
Aaron singled to right-center, sending Mathews to third.
Adcock singled to right, Mathews scoring and Aaron stopping at second.
3 Pafko forced Adcock at second, McDougald to Coleman.

7th Inning
New York
Berra singled to center.
1,2 Slaughter grounded into a double play, Logan to Adcock.
3 Simpson grounded to short.
Milwaukee
1 Covington flied to center.
2 Crandall grounded to short.
3 Burdette took a called third strike.

8th Inning
New York
For Milwaukee—Torre playing first.
1 Lumpe tapped back to the mound.
Coleman singled to right.
Mantle ran for Coleman.
2 Howard, pinch-hitting for Ford, was called out on strikes.
3 Mantle caught trying to steal second, Crandall to Mantilla.
Milwaukee
For New York—Richardson playing second (batting 9th) and Turley now pitching (batting 8th).
1 Mantilla flied to center.
2 Logan took a called third strike.
3 Mathews also called out on strikes.

9th Inning
New York
1 Bauer struck out.
2 Kubek struck out.
McDougald singled over second.
3 Berra popped to third.

Game 6 October 9 at New York

Milwaukee	Pos	AB	R	H	RBI	PO	A	E
Mantilla	2b	3	0	0	0	2	1	0
Logan	ss	4	0	0	0	2	1	0
Mathews	3b	3	0	1	0	0	0	0
Aaron	cf	4	1	1	1	1	0	0
Covington	lf	4	0	0	0	1	1	0
Torre	1b	3	1	2	1	7	1	0
Hazle	rf	3	0	0	0	0	0	0
Rice	c	3	0	0	0	10	1	0
Buhl	p	1	0	0	0	0	1	0
Johnson	p	1	0	0	0	1	2	0
a Sawatski		1	0	0	0	0	0	0
McMahon	p	0	0	0	0	0	1	0
Totals		30	2	4	2	24	9	0

a Struck out for Johnson in 8th.

Doubles—Berra, Coleman, Mathews. Home Runs—Aaron, Bauer, Berra, Torre. Sacrifice Hit—McDougald. Double Plays—Rice to Logan, Covington to Rice, Turley to McDougald to Collins. Wild Pitch—Buhl. Left on Bases—Milwaukee 3, New York 6. Umpires—Conlan, McKinley, Donatelli, Paparella, Secory, Chylak. Attendance—61,408. Time of Game—2:09.

Mil.	000	010	100
N.Y.	002	000	10x

New York	Pos	AB	R	H	RBI	PO	A	E
Bauer	rf	4	1	1	1	1	0	0
Kubek	cf	4	0	0	0	3	0	0
Slaughter	lf	2	1	0	0	0	0	0
Berra	c	4	1	3	2	10	0	0
McDougald	ss	3	0	1	0	2	2	0
Lumpe	3b	3	0	1	0	1	1	0
Simpson	1b	3	0	0	0	6	0	0
Collins	1b	0	0	0	0	1	1	0
Coleman	2b	2	0	1	0	1	3	0
Turley	p	3	0	0	0	2	2	0
Totals		28	3	7	3	27	9	0

Pitching	IP	H	R	ER	BB	SO
Milwaukee						
Buhl	$2\frac{2}{3}$	4	2	2	4	4
Johnson (L)	$4\frac{1}{3}$	2	1	1	0	5
McMahon	1	1	0	0	0	0
New York						
Turley (W)	9	4	2	2	2	8

1st Inning
Milwaukee
1 Mantilla flied to center.
2 Logan struck out.
3 Mathews grounded back to the mound.
New York
1 Bauer struck out.
2 Kubek struck out.
Slaughter walked.
Berra singled into right, Slaughter stopping at second.
Both runners moved up a base on a wild pitch.
3 McDougald struck out.

2nd Inning
Milwaukee
1 Aaron struck out.
2 Covington flied to center.
Torre singled to right.
3 Hazle fouled to Berra.
New York
Lumpe singled to right.
1,2 Simpson was called out on strikes, and Lumpe was doubled trying to steal second, Rice to Logan.
Coleman walked.
3 Turley grounded back to the mound.

3rd Inning
Milwaukee
1 Rice called out on strikes.
2 Buhl called out on strikes.
3 Mantilla flied to right.
New York
1 Bauer popped to short.
2 Kubek grounded to second.
Slaughter walked.
Berra hit a two-run homer into the lower right field stands.
McDougald singled past the mound.
Lumpe walked.
For Milwaukee—Johnson now pitching.
3 Simpson fanned.

4th Inning
Milwaukee
1 Logan fouled to Berra.
Mathews doubled off the right field auxiliary score board.
2 Aaron grounded to second, moving Mathews to third.
3 Covington fouled to Lumpe
New York
Coleman doubled inside the right field foul line.
1 Turley struck out as he bunted the third strike foul.
2 Bauer struck out.
3 Kubek grounded out, Torre to Johnson

5th Inning
Milwaukee
Torre hit a home run into the lower right field stands.
1 Hazle grounded to second.
2 Rice grounded to third.
3 Johnson called out on strikes.
New York
1 Slaughter grounded to first.
2 Berra grounded to first.
3 McDougald struck out.

6th Inning
Milwaukee
1 Mantilla grounded to short.
2 Logan popped to second.
3 Mathews grounded to second.
New York
1 Lumpe's grounder deflected off Johnson's hand to Logan who threw Lumpe out at first.
2 Simpson lined to center.
3 Coleman rolled to the mound.

7th Inning
Milwaukee
For New York—Collins playing first.
Aaron homered into the left field bullpen.
1 Covington grounded out, Collins to Turley.
2 Torre lined to the pitcher.
3 Hazle flied to center.
New York
1 Turley struck out, bunting foul on the third strike.
Bauer homered into the lower left field stands.
2 Kubek popped to second.
3 Slaughter grounded out to first.

8th Inning
Milwaukee
1 Rice struck out.
2 Sawatski, pinch-hitting for Johnson, called out on strikes.
Mantilla walked.
3 Logan popped to short.
New York
For Milwaukee—McMahon pitching.
Berra doubled down the left field line.
1 McDougald sacrificed Berra to third, McMahon to Mantilla.
2,3 Lumpe flied to Covington who threw to Rice doubling Berra trying to score.

9th Inning
Milwaukee
Mathews walked.
1 Aaron took a called third strike.
2,3 Covington grounded into a game ending double play, Turley to McDougald to Collins.

Game 7 October 10 at New York

Milwaukee	Pos	AB	R	H	RBI	PO	A	E
Hazle	rf	4	1	2	0	3	0	0
d Pafko	rf	1	0	0	0	0	0	0
Logan	ss	5	1	1	0	2	4	0
Mathews	3b	4	1	1	2	3	4	1
Aaron	cf	5	1	2	1	3	0	0
Covington	lf	3	0	1	0	2	0	0
Torre	1b	2	0	0	1	8	0	0
Mantilla	2b	4	0	0	0	2	0	0
Crandall	c	4	1	2	1	4	0	0
Burdette	p	2	0	0	0	0	3	0
Totals		33	5	9	5	27	11	1

Pitching	IP	H	R	ER	BB	SO
Milwaukee						
Burdette (W)	9	7	0	0	1	3
New York						
Larsen (L)	$2\frac{1}{3}$	3	3	2	1	2
Shantz	$\frac{2}{3}$	2	1	0	0	0
Ditmar	2	1	0	0	1	0
Sturdivant	2	2	0	0	1	0
Byrne	2	1	1	1	2	0

Mil.	004	000	010
N.Y.	000	000	000

New York	Pos	AB	R	H	RBI	PO	A	E
Bauer	rf	4	0	1	0	2	0	0
Slaughter	lf	4	0	0	0	2	0	0
Mantle	cf	4	0	1	0	2	0	0
Berra	c	3	0	0	0	4	1	1
McDougald	ss	4	0	1	0	2	1	1
Kubek	3b	4	0	1	0	3	4	1
Coleman	2b	4	0	2	0	4	3	0
Collins	1b	2	0	0	0	5	0	0
Sturdivant	p	0	0	0	0	0	0	0
c Howard		1	0	0	0	0	0	0
Byrne	p	1	0	1	0	0	0	0
Larsen	p	0	0	0	0	0	1	0
Shantz	p	0	0	0	0	0	0	0
a Lumpe		1	0	0	0	0	0	0
Ditmar	p	0	0	0	0	0	0	0
b Skowron	1b	3	0	0	0	3	2	0
Totals		35	0	7	0	27	12	3

a Struck out for Shantz in 3rd.
b Grounded into forceout for Ditmar in 5th.
c Struck out for Sturdivant in 7th.
d Fouled out for Hazle in 8th.

Doubles—Bauer, Mathews. Home Run—Crandall. Sacrifice Hits—Burdette, Covington, Mathews. Double Play—McDougald to Coleman to Skowron. Left on Bases—Milwaukee 8, New York 9. Umpires—McKinley, Donatelli, Paparella, Conlan, Chylak, Secory. Attendance—61,207. Time of Game—2:34.

1st Inning
Milwaukee
1 Hazle struck out.
2 Logan grounded to third.
3 Mathews took a called third strike.
New York
Bauer doubled down the left field line.
Slaughter tapped to Burdette who caught Bauer in a rundown but Bauer got back to second safely. In the meantime Slaughter had advanced to second and
1 he was tagged out by Logan. Assists go to Logan, Burdette and Mathews.
2 Mantle grounded back to the mound, as Bauer held second.
Berra got an intentional pass.
3 McDougald popped to third.

2nd Inning
Milwaukee
Aaron singled to left.
1 Covington sacrificed Aaron to second, Larsen to Collins.
Torre walked.
2 Mantilla flied to deep left, Aaron going to third after the catch.
3 Crandall forced Torre, Kubek to Coleman.
New York
1 Kubek grounded to third.
2 Coleman rolled out to third.
3 Collins struck out.

3rd Inning
Milwaukee
1 Burdette fouled to Kubek.
Hazle singled to left.
Logan grounded to third but was safe when Kubek's throw pulled Coleman off the bag at second trying for the force.
Mathews doubled into the right field corner, Hazle and Logan scoring.
For New York—Shantz came into pitch.
Aaron singled through the middle, Mathews scoring.
Covington singled to center, Aaron racing to third.
2 Torre forced Covington, Coleman to McDougald, Aaron scoring.
3 Mantilla flied to right.
New York
1 Lumpe, batting for Shantz, struck out.
2 Bauer flied to center.
3 Slaughter grounded to first.

4th Inning
Milwaukee
For New York—Ditmar pitching.
1 Crandall flied to left.
2 Burdette struck out.
Hazle singled into right.
Logan safe at first on McDougald's throwing error trying for the force.
3 Mathews lined to center.
New York
1 Mantle flied to right.
2 Berra lined to right.
3 McDougald flied to right.

5th Inning
Milwaukee
Aaron safe at first when Berra fumbled his bunt in front of the plate for an error.
1 Covington tapped out to third, Aaron going to second.
2 Torre grounded to first, moving Aaron to third.
3 Mantilla grounded to third.
New York
1 Kubek flied to left.
Coleman singled to right-center.
2 Collins forced Coleman at second, Logan to Mantilla.
3 Skowron, pinch-hitting for Ditmar, forced Collins at second, Logan to Mantilla.

6th Inning
Milwaukee
For New York—Skowron playing first and Sturdivant pitching (batting 8th).
Crandall singled to center.
1 Burdette sacrificed Crandall to second, Skowron to Coleman.
2 Crandall stealing third beat Berra's throw but was out oversliding the bag, Berra to Kubek.
3 Hazle flied to right.
New York
1 Bauer grounded to third.
2 Slaughter flied to center.
Mantle singled to right.
Berra safe on first as Mathews fumbled his grounder for an error.
3 McDougald forced Mantle at third, Mathews unassisted.

7th Inning
Milwaukee
Logan beat out a hit to second.
1 Mathews sacrificed Logan to second, Skowron to Coleman.
2 Aaron took a called third strike.
3 Covington lined to short.
New York
Kubek singled to left.
1 Coleman bounced back to the mound, moving Kubek to second.
2 Howard, pinch-hitting for Sturdivant, struck out.
3 Skowron grounded to short.

8th Inning
Milwaukee
For New York—Byrne pitching.
Torre walked.
1,2 Mantilla grounded into a double play, McDougald to Coleman to Skowron.
Crandall hit a home run into the lower left field stands.
Burdette walked.
3 Pafko, batting for Hazle, fouled to Skowron.
New York
For Milwaukee—Pafko in right.
1 Bauer popped to short.
2 Slaughter fouled to Crandall.
3 Mantle flied to left.

9th Inning
Milwaukee
1 Logan lined to third.
2 Mathews grounded to second.
3 Aaron flied to deep center.
New York
1 Berra popped to first.
McDougald singled to center.
2 Kubek flied to Aaron in right-center.
Coleman singled to right, McDougald stopping at second.
Byrne singled off Mantilla's glove, loading the bases.
3 Skowron grounded to Mathews, who made a fantastic stop on the line and stepped on the bag forcing McDougald.

1957 WORLD SERIES COMPOSITE BOX

	Wins	Composite Line Score
Milwaukee Braves (N.L.)	4	0 2 5 6 3 1 2 1 0 3 - 23
New York Yankees (A.L.)	3	4 1 5 2 1 2 6 0 3 1 - 25

	Regular Season			
Manager	W	L	Pct.	G. Ahead
Fred Haney	95	59	.617	8
Casey Stengel	98	56	.636	8

BATTING AND FIELDING

MILWAUKEE BRAVES

	WORLD SERIES STATISTICS																	REGULAR SEASON STATISTICS														
	Pos	G	AB	R	H	2B	3B	HR	RBI	BB	SO	SB	BA	SA	PO	A	E		Main Pos	G	AB	R	H	2B	3B	HR	RBI	BB	SO	SB	BA	SA
Joe Adcock	1b-ph	5	15	1	3	0	0	0	2	0	2	0	.200	.200	38	2	1		1b	65	209	31	60	13	2	12	38	20	51	0	.287	.541
Red Schoendienst	2b	5	18	0	5	1	0	0	2	0	1	0	.278	.333	5	10	0	a	2b	93	394	56	*122	26	4	3	32	23	7	2	.310	.434
Johnny Logan	ss	7	27	**5**	5	1	0	1	2	3	**6**	0	.185	.333	13	**25**	0		ss	129	494	59	135	19	7	10	49	31	49	5	.273	.401
Eddie Mathews	3b	7	22	4	5	**3**	0	1	4	**8**	5	0	.227	.500	9	19	1		3b	148	572	109	167	28	9	32	94	90	79	3	.292	.540
Andy Pafko	rf-ph	6	14	1	3	0	0	0	0	0	1	0	.214	.214	9	0	0		of	83	220	31	61	6	1	8	27	10	22	1	.277	.423
Hank Aaron	cf	7	28	**5**	**11**	0	**1**	**3**	**7**	1	**6**	0	**.393**	.786	11	0	0		of	151	615	**118**	198	27	6	**44**	**132**	57	58	1	.322	.600
Wes Covington	lf	7	24	1	5	1	0	0	1	2	**6**	**1**	.208	.250	13	1	0		of	96	328	51	93	4	8	21	65	29	44	4	.284	.537
Del Crandall	c	6	19	1	4	0	0	1	1	1	1	0	.211	.368	21	4	0		c	118	383	45	97	11	2	15	46	30	38	1	.253	.410
Bob Hazle	rf	4	13	2	2	0	0	0	0	1	2	0	.154	.154	6	0	0		of	41	134	26	54	12	0	7	27	18	15	1	.403	.649
Frank Torre	1b-ph	7	10	2	3	0	0	2	3	2	0	0	.300	**.900**	37	2	0		1b	129	364	46	99	19	5	5	49	29	19	0	.272	.393
Felix Mantilla	pr-2b	4	10	1	0	0	0	0	0	1	0	0	.000	.000	6	8	0		3b	71	182	28	43	9	1	4	21	14	34	2	.236	.363
Del Rice	c	2	6	0	1	0	0	0	0	1	2	0	.167	.167	15	2	0		c	54	144	15	33	1	1	9	20	17	37	0	.229	.438
Nippy Jones	ph	3	2	0	0	0	0	0	0	0	0	0	.000	.000					1b	30	79	5	21	2	1	2	8	3	7	0	.266	.392
Carl Sawatski	ph	2	2	0	0	0	0	0	0	0	2	0	.000	.000					c	58	105	13	25	4	0	6	17	10	15	0	.238	.448
John DeMerit	pr	1	0	0	0	0	0	0	0	0	0	0	—	—					ph	33	34	8	5	0	0	0	1	0	8	1	.147	.147
Mel Roach		Did not play																	2b	7	6	1	1	0	0	0	0	0	3	0	.167	.167
Lew Burdette	p	3	8	0	0	0	0	0	0	1	2	0	.000	.000	0	9	0		p	41	88	11	13	2	0	2	9	3	22	0	.148	.239
Warren Spahn	p	2	4	0	0	0	0	0	0	1	2	0	.000	.000	1	3	0		p	39	94	3	13	2	1	2	8	4	25	0	.138	.245
Ernie Johnson	p	3	1	0	0	0	0	0	0	0	1	0	.000	.000	1	4	0		p	30	17	1	6	1	0	1	7	0	3	0	.353	.588
Bob Buhl	p	2	1	0	0	0	0	0	0	0	1	0	.000	.000	0	2	1		p	34	73	4	6	0	0	0	4	6	34	0	.082	.082
Juan Pizzaro	p	1	1	0	0	0	0	0	0	0	0	0	.000	.000	0	0	0		p	25	36	5	9	1	0	1	2	1	10	0	.250	.361
Don McMahon	p	3	0	0	0	0	0	0	0	0	0	0	—	—	0	2	0		p	32	8	1	2	1	0	0	3	2	2	0	.250	.375
Gene Conley	p	1	0	0	0	0	0	0	0	0	0	0	—	—	1	0	0		p	35	46	1	9	2	0	0	2	1	14	0	.196	.239
Bob Trowbridge	p	1	0	0	0	0	0	0	0	0	0	0	—	—	0	0	0		p	32	39	1	4	0	0	0	0	2	18	0	.103	.103
Taylor Phillips		Did not play																	p	27	20	0	2	0	0	0	1	0	12	0	.100	.100
Dave Jolley		Did not play																	p	23	5	1	3	0	0	0	2	0	1	0	.600	.600
team total		7	225	23	47	6	1	8	22	22	40	1	.209	.351	186	93	3			155	5458	772	1469	221	**62**	**199**	722	461	729	35	.269	**.442**

Double Plays—10
Left on Bases—46

a—from New York (N) *leads league in hits with 200.
Bill Bruton (of-knee injury), Danny O'Connell (2b), Bobby Thomson (of), Chuck Tanner (of), Dick Cole (2b), Bobby Malkmus (2b), Hawk Taylor (c), Harry Hanebrink (3b), Ray Shearer (of), Ray Crone (p), Red Murff (p), Joey Jay (p), and Phil Paine (p) also played for the Braves during the season.

NEW YORK YANKEES

	WORLD SERIES STATISTICS																	REGULAR SEASON STATISTICS														
	Pos	G	AB	R	H	2B	3B	HR	RBI	BB	SO	SB	BA	SA	PO	A	E		Main Pos	G	AB	R	H	2B	3B	HR	RBI	BB	SO	SB	BA	SA
Elston Howard	1b-ph	6	11	2	3	0	0	1	3	1	3	0	.273	.545	22	1	1		of	110	356	33	90	13	4	8	44	16	43	2	.253	.379
Jerry Coleman	2b	7	22	2	8	2	0	0	2	3	1	0	.364	.455	16	17	0		2b	72	157	23	42	7	2	2	12	20	21	1	.268	.376
Gil McDougald	ss	7	24	3	6	0	0	0	2	3	3	**1**	.250	.250	13	24	1		ss	141	539	87	156	25	**9**	13	62	59	71	2	.289	.442
Jerry Lumpe	3b-ph	6	14	0	4	0	0	0	2	1	1	0	.286	.286	3	6	0		3b	40	103	15	35	6	2	0	11	9	13	2	.340	.437
Hank Bauer	rf	7	**31**	3	8	2	**1**	2	6	1	**6**	0	.258	.581	10	0	0		of	137	479	70	124	22	**9**	18	65	42	64	7	.259	.455
Mickey Mantle	cf-pr	6	19	3	5	0	0	1	2	3	1	0	.263	.421	8	0	1		of	144	474	**121**	173	28	6	34	94	**146**	75	16	.365	.665
Tony Kubek	1f-3b-cf	7	28	4	8	0	0	2	4	0	4	0	.286	.500	17	5	**2**		of-ss-3b	127	431	56	128	21	3	3	39	24	48	6	.297	.381
Yogi Berra	c	7	25	**5**	8	1	0	1	2	4	0	0	.320	.480	**44**	2	1		c	134	482	74	121	14	2	24	82	57	24	1	.251	.438
Enos Slaughter	1f	5	12	2	3	1	0	0	0	3	2	0	.250	.333	7	0	0		of	96	209	24	53	7	1	5	34	40	19	0	.254	.368
Harry Simpson	1b-ph	5	12	0	1	0	0	0	1	0	4	0	.083	.083	24	1	0	b	of	75	224	27	56	7	*3	7	39	19	36	1	.250	.402
Andy Carey	3b	2	7	0	2	1	0	0	1	1	0	0	.286	.429	3	6	0		3b	85	247	30	63	6	5	6	33	15	42	2	.255	.393
Joe Collins	1b-ph	6	5	0	0	0	0	0	0	0	3	0	.000	.000	12	2	0		1b-ph	79	149	17	30	1	0	2	10	24	18	2	.201	.248
Bill Skowron	1b-ph	2	4	0	0	0	0	0	0	0	0	0	.000	.000	5	2	0		1b	122	457	54	139	15	5	17	88	31	60	3	.304	.470
Bobby Richardson	pr-2b	2	0	0	0	0	0	0	0	0	0	0	—	—	0	0	0		2b	97	305	36	78	11	1	0	19	9	26	1	.256	.298
Darrell Johnson		Did not play																	c	21	46	4	10	1	0	1	8	3	10	0	.217	.304
Whitey Ford	p	2	5	0	0	0	0	0	0	0	1	0	.000	.000	1	1	0		p	24	42	4	6	0	0	0	2	3	7	0	.143	.143
Bob Turley	p	3	4	0	0	0	0	0	0	0	2	0	.000	.000	2	2	0		p	32	57	4	5	0	0	0	0	8	27	0	.088	.088
Tommy Byrne	2	2	0	1	0	0	0	0	0	1	0	.500	.500	0	0	0			p	35	37	5	7	2	0	3	8	3	11	0	.189	.486
Don Larsen	p	2	2	1	0	0	0	0	0	2	1	0	.000	.000	0	1	0		p	31	56	6	14	5	0	0	5	6	11	0	.250	.339
Tom Sturdivant	p	2	1	0	0	0	0	0	0	0	0	0	.000	.000	0	1	0		p	28	71	4	13	0	0	0	0	6	10	0	.183	.183
Bobby Shantz	p	3	1	0	0	0	0	0	0	0	0	0	.000	.000	0	1	0		p	33	56	6	10	3	0	0	6	8	16	0	.179	.232
Art Ditmar	p	2	1	0	0	0	0	0	0	0	1	0	.000	.000	0	0	0		p	46	35	3	7	0	0	0	2	0	9	0	.200	.200
Bob Grim	p	2	0	0	0	0	0	0	0	0	0	0	—	—	0	0	0		p	46	9	1	1	0	0	1	3	1	4	0	.111	.444
Johnny Kucks	p	1	0	0	0	0	0	0	0	0	0	0	—	—	0	0	0		p	37	55	4	6	0	0	0	2	5	18	0	.109	.109
Al Cicotte		Did not play																	p	20	20	0	3	1	0	0	0	0	4	0	.150	.200
team total		7	230	25	57	7	1	7	25	22	34	1	.248	.378	187	72	6			154	5271	**723**	**1412**	200	**54**	145	682	562	709	49	**.268**	**.409**

Double Plays—5
Left on Bases—45

b—from Kansas City *league leader with 9 triples.
Billy Martin (2b), Bobby Del Greco (of), Zeke Bella (of), Woodie Held (ph), Sal Maglie (p), and Ralph Terry (p) also played for the Yankees during the season.

PITCHING

MILWAUKEE BRAVES

	WORLD SERIES STATISTICS													REGULAR SEASON STATISTICS													
	G	GS	CG	IP	H	R	ER	BB	SO	W	L	SV	ERA	G	GS	CG	IP	H	ER	BB	SO	W	L	Pct	SV	ShO	ERA
Lew Burdette	**3**	**3**	**3**	**27**	**21**	2	2	4	**13**	**3**	0	0	**0.67**	37	33	14	257	260	106	59	78	17	9	.654	0	1	3.71
Warren Spahn	2	2	1	$15\frac{1}{3}$	18	**8**	**8**	2	2	1	**1**	0	4.70	39	35	**18**	271	241	81	78	111	**21**	11	.656	3	4	2.69
Ernie Johnson	3	0	0	7	2	1	1	1	8	0	**1**	0	1.29	30	0	0	65	67	28	26	44	7	3	.700	4	0	3.88
Don McMahon	**3**	0	0	5	3	0	0	3	5	0	0	0	0.00	32	0	0	47	33	8	29	46	2	3	.400	9	0	1.53
Bob Buhl	2	2	0	$3\frac{1}{3}$	6	5	4	**6**	4	0	**1**	0	10.80	34	31	14	217	191	66	121	117	18	7	**.720**	0	2	2.74
Juan Pizzaro	1	0	0	$1\frac{2}{3}$	3	2	2	2	1	0	0	0	10.80	24	10	3	99	99	51	51	68	5	6	.455	0	0	4.64
Gene Conley	1	0	0	$1\frac{2}{3}$	2	2	2	1	0	0	0	0	10.80	35	18	6	148	133	52	64	61	9	9	.500	1	1	3.16
Bob Trowbridge	1	0	0	1	2	5	5	3	1	0	0	0	45.00	32	16	3	126	118	51	52	75	7	5	.583	1	1	3.64
Taylor Phillips	Did not play													27	6	0	73	82	45	40	36	3	2	.600	2	0	5.55
Dave Jolley	Did not play													23	0	0	38	37	21	21	27	1	1	.500	1	0	4.97
team total	7	7	4	62	57	25	24	22	34	4	3	0	3.48	155	155	**60**	1411	1347	544	570	693	**95**	59	**.617**	24	9	3.47

NEW YORK YANKEES

	WORLD SERIES STATISTICS													REGULAR SEASON STATISTICS													
	G	GS	CG	IP	H	R	ER	BB	SO	W	L	SV	ERA	G	GS	CG	IP	H	ER	BB	SO	W	L	Pct	SV	ShO	ERA
Whitey Ford	2	2	1	16	11	2	2	5	7	1	**1**	0	1.13	24	17	5	129	114	37	53	84	11	5	.688	0	0	2.58
Bob Turley	**3**	2	1	$11\frac{2}{3}$	7	3	3	**6**	12	1	0	0	2.31	32	23	9	176	120	53	85	152	13	6	.684	3	4	2.71
Don Larsen	2	1	0	$9\frac{2}{3}$	8	5	4	5	6	1	**1**	0	3.72	27	20	4	140	113	58	87	81	10	4	.714	0	1	3.73
Bobby Shantz	**3**	1	0	$6\frac{2}{3}$	8	5	3	2	7	0	**1**	0	4.05	30	21	9	173	157	47	40	72	11	5	.688	5	1	**2.45**
Art Ditmar	2	0	0	6	2	0	0	0	2	0	0	0	0.00	46	11	0	127	128	46	35	64	8	3	.723	6	0	3.26
Tom Sturdivant	2	1	0	6	4	4	4	1	2	0	0	0	6.00	28	28	7	202	170	57	80	118	16	6	**.727**	0	2	2.54
Tommy Byrne	2	0	0	$3\frac{1}{3}$	1	2	2	2	1	0	0	0	5.40	30	4	1	85	70	41	60	57	4	6	.400	2	0	4.34
Bob Grim	2	0	0	$2\frac{1}{3}$	3	2	2	0	2	0	**1**	0	7.71	46	0	0	72	60	21	36	52	12	8	.600	**19**	0	2.63
Johnny Kucks	1	0	0	$\frac{2}{3}$	1	0	0	1	1	0	0	0	0.00	37	23	4	179	169	71	59	78	8	10	.444	2	1	3.57
Al Cicotte	Did not play													20	2	0	65	57	22	30	36	2	2	.500	2	0	3.05
team total	7	7	2	$62\frac{1}{3}$	47	23	20	22	40	3	4	0	2.89	154	154	41	1395	1198	**465**	580	**810**	**98**	56	**.636**	**42**	13	**3.00**

Total Attendance—394,712 Average Attendance—56,387 Winning Player's Share—$8,924 Losing Player's Share—$5,606

1958
Comeback

Traditionally divided into three camps, New York baseball fans found themselves with only one team to support this year as the Dodgers and Giants played their home games 3,000 miles away in California. But even without any competition in town, the New York Yankees suffered at the ticket window. The city's disenchantment with baseball perhaps accounted for part of the gate slump, but a more likely reason was the ridiculous ease with which the Yankees captured their fourth straight American League pennant. Casey Stengel's merry men found no serious challengers in their circuit, while the Milwaukee Braves similarly had little resistance in repeating as National League champs. Both outfits clearly outclassed the rest of the major-league clubs, making the World Series a fitting climax to a season without pennant races.

Both Stengel and Milwaukee manager Fred Haney called on ace southpaws to hurl the opening game in Milwaukee. The Yankees got home runs from Bill Skowron and Hank Bauer off Warren Spahn, but the Braves scored three times off Whitey Ford to send the game into extra innings tied at 3–3. Spahn retired the Yanks in the top of the tenth inning, but singles by Joe Adcock, Del Crandall, and Billy Bruton tagged New York reliever Ryne Duren with the loss in the 4–3 victory. The ace right-handers took over in game two, 21-game-winner Bob Turley against 20-game-winner Lew Burdette. The Yanks touched a shaky Burdette for a run in the top of the first inning, but the Braves wrapped the game up in the bottom of the inning with seven runs, beginning with Bruton's leadoff homer and ending with Burdette's three-run circuit clout. The Yanks got two homers from Mickey Mantle and another from Bauer, but wound up on the short end of a 13–5 score.

The Yanks needed a win in game three in New York to stay in striking distance of the Braves, and a finely pitched game by Don Larsen, with relief help from Duren, paced the Yanks to a 4–0 win. Bauer accounted for all four of New York's runs, including a two-run single in the fifth inning and a two-run homer in the seventh. Bauer's Series hitting streak of 17 games came to an end the next day as Spahn completely tamed the Yankees, shutting them out 3–0 on only two hits. Yankee left fielder Norm Siebern battled the sun all afternoon and lost fly balls in the sixth and seventh innings that led to Milwaukee runs. The Yankees now appeared hopelessly lost, but the intangible Yankee pride prevented any quick foldup. Turley and Burdette pitched in game five with none of the shakiness of the second game. A home run by Gil McDougald in the third inning gave the Yanks a 1–0 lead, and Turley escaped unscathed from the top of the sixth when left fielder Elston Howard made a diving catch that defused a budding rally. In the bottom of the inning, the Yanks pinned Burdette's ears back with a six-run salvo that tagged him with the 7–0 loss after winning four straight games over the past two Octobers. Turley allowed only five hits en route to the win.

The managers called on aces Spahn and Ford to pitch game six on short rest. Bauer led the game off with his fourth homer of the Series, but the clubs settled into a defensive match that produced a 2–2 tie after nine innings. Pitching mostly on heart, the tired Spahn gave up a homer to McDougald in the top of the tenth, then allowed singles to Howard and Yogi Berra before dejectedly leaving the game in favor of Don McMahon. Skowron singled in another run off McMahon, an important insurance run. A walk and two singles off Duren in the bottom of the tenth had the Braves hoping to pull it out, but Stengel brought in Turley to retire Frank Torre for the final out in the 4–3 game. That set up the seventh game, with Haney relying on Burdette and Stengel going with Larsen. The Yanks took a 2–1 lead after two innings, but two Milwaukee singles in the bottom of the third brought Stengel out to the mound to replace Larsen with an overworked Turley. The stocky Turley bore down and pitched superb ball, marred only by Crandall's sixth-inning homer which tied the game at 2–2. After Burdette retired the first two men in the bottom of the eighth, the Yanks went ahead on a double by Berra and a single by Howard. The laboring Burdette then coughed up a single to Andy Carey and a fat pitch to Skowron, which he clubbed for a three-run homer to nail down the 6–2 win and make the Yankees the first club since the 1925 Pittsburgh Pirates to fight back to victory from a 3–1 deficit in the Series.

Game 1 October 1 at Milwaukee

New York	Pos	AB	R	H	RBI	PO	A	E
Bauer	rf	5	1	2	2	0	0	0
McDougald	2b	4	0	2	0	1	2	0
Mantle	cf	3	0	0	0	3	0	0
Howard	lf	5	0	0	0	4	0	0
Berra	c	4	0	2	0	13	2	0
Skowron	1b	4	1	2	1	7	0	0
Carey	3b	4	0	0	0	0	2	0
Kubek	ss	4	0	0	0	1	1	1
Ford	p	2	1	0	0	0	0	0
Duren	p	1	0	0	0	0	0	0
Totals		36	3	8	3	*29	7	1

Pitching	IP	H	R	ER	BB	SO
New York						
Ford	**7	6	3	3	3	8
Duren (L)	2⅓	4	1	1	1	5
Milwaukee						
Spahn (W)	10	8	3	3	4	6

**Pitched to two batters in 8th.

N.Y. 000 120 000 0
Mil. 000 200 010 1

Milwaukee	Pos	AB	R	H	RBI	PO	A	E
Schoendienst	2b	4	0	0	0	2	2	0
Logan	ss	4	0	1	0	2	3	0
b Torre		1	0	0	0	0	0	0
Mantilla	ss	0	0	0	0	0	0	0
Mathews	3b	3	1	0	0	1	3	0
Aaron	rf	4	1	1	0	3	0	0
Adcock	1b	5	1	2	0	8	2	0
Covington	lf	4	0	0	1	2	1	0
Crandall	c	5	1	2	1	7	0	0
Pafko	cf	3	0	1	0	4	0	0
a Bruton	cf	2	0	1	1	1	0	0
Spahn	p	4	0	2	1	1	2	0
Totals		39	4	10	4	30	13	0

a Struck out for Pafko in 9th.
b Popped out for Logan in 9th.
* Two out when winning run scored.

Doubles—Aaron, Berra, Logan.
Home Runs—Bauer, Skowron. Sacrifice Fly—Covington. Passed Ball—Berra. Wild Pitches—Ford, Spahn. Left on Bases—New York 7, Milwaukee 11. Umpires—Barlick (N), Berry (A), Gorman (N), Flaherty (A), Jackowski (N), Umont (A). Attendance—46,367. Time of Game—3:09.

1st Inning
New York
Bauer singled to left.
1 Bauer was picked off, Spahn to Adcock to Logan.
McDougald singled off Mathew's glove.
2 Mantle fouled to Crandall.
McDougald took second on a wild pitch.
3 Howard flied to Pafko in deep left-center.
Milwaukee
1 Schoendienst flied to center.
Logan doubled into the left field corner.
2 Mathews struck out.
3 Aaron struck out.

2nd Inning
New York
Berra singled to left-center.
Skowron singled to left, but Berra was
1 out trying for third, Covington to Mathews as Skowron went to second on the out.
2 Carey flied to deep center.
3 Kubek took a called third strike.
Milwaukee
Adcock singled to right.
1 Covington fouled to Berra.
2 Crandall called out on strikes.
Adcock took second on a wild pitch.
Pafko safe at first when Kubek fumbled his grounder, Adcock going to third.
3 Spahn flied to right.

3rd Inning
New York
1 Ford called out on strikes.
2 Bauer lined to left.
McDougald walked.
3 Mantle lined to center.
Milwaukee
1 Schoendienst grounded to third.
2 Logan struck out.
3 Mathews struck out.

4th Inning
New York
1 Howard flied to right.
2 Berra popped to second.
Skowron hit a home run into the left field bleachers.
3 Carey struck out.
Milwaukee
Aaron walked.
Aaron took second on a passed ball.
1 Adcock grounded to third, Aaron holding second.
2 Covington grounded to second, sending Aaron to third.
Crandall singled to left, Aaron scoring. Pafko singled to center, Crandall stopping at second.
Spahn singled to left-center, scoring Crandall with Pafko going to third.
3 Schoendienst struck out.

5th Inning
New York
1 Kubek flied to left.
Ford walked.
Bauer hit a two-run homer into the left field bleachers.
2 McDougald grounded to short.
Mantle walked.
3 Howard forced Mantle at second, Mathews to Schoendienst.
Milwaukee
1 Logan grounded to short.
Mathews walked.
2 Aaron forced McDougald at second, McDougald unassisted.
3 Adcock flied to left.

6th Inning
New York
Berra doubled to left center.
1 Skowron grounded to third, Berra holding at second.
2 Carey grounded to third, and again Berra could not advance.
3 Kubek grounded out, Adcock to Spahn.
Milwaukee
1 Covington lined to left.
2 Crandall grounded out, Berra to Skowron.
3 Pafko flied to deep left.

7th Inning
New York
1 Ford grounded to short.
2 Bauer popped to short.
3 McDougald struck out.
Milwaukee
1 Spahn flied to center.
2 Schoendienst grounded to second.
3 Logan struck out, but had to be tagged by Berra who dropped the ball.

8th Inning
New York
1 Mantle flied to deep center.
2 Howard lined to right.
3 Berra grounded to second.
Milwaukee
Mathews walked.
Aaron hit a long double over Bauer off the right field fence, Mathews going to third.
For New York—Duren came in to pitch.
1 Adcock struck out.
2 Covington hit a sacrifice fly to Mantle in left-center, scoring Mathews with Aaron holding second.
3 Crandall called out on strikes.

9th Inning
New York
1 Skowron struck out.
2 Carey grounded to short.
3 Kubek grounded to second.
Milwaukee
1 Bruton, pinch-hitting for Pafko, struck out.
Spahn singled into right.
Schoendienst walked.
2 Torre, pinch-hitting for Logan, popped to second.
3 Mathews struck out.

10th Inning
New York
For Milwaukee—Bruton stays in to play center, and Mantilla playing short.
1 Duren grounded back to the pitcher.
2 Bauer struck out.
McDougald singled off Spahn's glove.
Mantle walked.
3 Howard flied to short.
Milwaukee
1 Aaron struck out but Berra dropped the ball and threw him out at first on a very close play.
Adcock singled to center.
2 Covington flied to left.
Crandall singled through the middle, Adcock stopping at second.
Bruton lined a single into right-center, scoring Adcock with the winning run.

1958

Game 2 October 2 at Milwaukee

			N.Y.	100	100	003
			Mil.	710	000	23 x

New York	Pos	AB	R	H	RBI	PO	A	E
Bauer	rf	4	2	2	1	1	0	0
McDougald	2b	4	1	1	0	0	6	0
Mantle	cf	3	2	2	3	3	0	0
Howard	lf	1	0	0	1	1	0	0
Siebern	lf	3	0	1	0	2	0	0
Berra	c	4	0	0	0	3	0	0
Skowron	1b	4	0	0	0	11	0	0
Carey	3b	2	0	0	0	1	2	0
c Slaughter		1	0	0	0	0	0	0
Richardson	3b	1	0	0	0	0	0	0
Kubek	ss	3	0	0	0	2	2	0
Turley	p	0	0	0	0	0	0	0
Maas	p	0	0	0	0	0	0	0
Kucks	p	1	0	1	0	0	0	0
a Lumpe		1	0	0	0	0	0	0
Dickson	p	0	0	0	0	0	0	0
d Throneberry		1	0	0	0	0	0	0
Monroe	p	0	0	0	0	0	0	0
Totals		33	5	7	5	24	10	0

Milwaukee	Pos	AB	R	H	RBI	PO	A	E
Bruton	cf	4	2	3	1	3	0	0
Schoendienst	2b	5	2	2	0	2	6	0
Mathews	3b	5	2	2	2	0	0	1
Aaron	rf	4	2	2	0	1	0	0
Covington	lf	4	1	3	2	1	0	0
b Mantilla		0	1	0	0	0	0	0
Pafko	lf	0	0	0	1	1	0	0
Torre	1b	5	0	1	1	10	1	0
Crandall	c	2	1	0	1	5	1	0
Logan	ss	4	1	1	2	3	5	0
Burdette	p	4	1	1	3	1	0	0
Totals		37	13	15	13	27	13	1

Pitching New York	IP	H	R	ER	BB	SO
Turley (L)	⅓	3	4	4	1	1
Maas	⅓	2	3	3	1	0
Kucks	3⅓	1	1	0	0	0
Dickson	3	4	2	2	0	1
Monroe	1	3	3	3	1	1
Milwaukee						
Burdette (W)	9	7	5	4	1	5

a Flied out for Kucks in 5th.
b Ran for Covington in 7th.
c Grounded out for Carey in 8th.
d Struck out for Dickson in 8th.

Doubles—Mathews, Schoendienst 2.
Home Runs—Bauer, Bruton, Burdette,
Mantle 2. Stolen Base—Mathews.
Sacrifice Flies—Crandall, Pafko.
Double Plays—Schoendienst to Logan to
Torre, Logan to Schoendienst to Torre.
Left on Bases—New York 2, Milwaukee 5.
Umpires—Berry, Gorman, Flaherty,
Barlick, Umont, Jackowski.
Attendance—46,367. Time of Game—2:43.

1st Inning
New York
Bauer singled to center.
McDougald safe at second, with Bauer
going to third on Mathew's wide throw
to first, for an error.
Mantle intentionally passed,
loading the bases.
1 Howard forced Mantle at second,
Schoendienst to Logan, Bauer scoring
with McDougald going to third.
2,3 Berra grounded into a double play,
Schoendienst to Logan to Terry.
Milwaukee
Bruton hit a home run into the
right field bleachers.
Schoendienst doubled to right.
1 Mathews took a called third strike.
Aaron walked.
Covington singled to right-center,
Schoendienst scoring with Aaron
going to third.
For New York—Maas now pitching.
2 Torre flied to left, Covington going
to second on the throw to the plate.
Crandall walked, loading the bases.
Logan singled to left, Aaron and
Covington scoring with Crandall
going to third and Logan to second
on the throw to the plate.
Burdette hit a three-run homer over
the left field fence. Howard crashed
into the fence trying for the ball.
For New York—Siebern replaced Howard
in left and Kucks came in to pitch.
3 Bruton lined to short.

2nd Inning
New York
1 Skowron flied to center.
2 Carey struck out.
3 Kubek struck out.
Milwaukee
1 Schoendienst grounded to second.
Mathews doubled off the left-
center field fence.
2 Aaron grounded to second,
Mathews going to third.
Covington singled to center,
scoring Mathews.
3 Torre grounded to second.

3rd Inning
New York
Kucks singled to right.
1,2 Bauer hit into a double play,
Logan to Schoendienst to Torre.
3 McDougald grounded to short.
Milwaukee
1 Crandall flied to left.
2 Logan grounded to short.
3 Burdette grounded to short.

4th Inning
New York
Mantle homered over the
center field fence.
1 Siebern grounded to second.
2 Berra grounded to short.
3 Skowron struck out.
Milwaukee
Bruton singled to right.
1 Schoendienst flied to left.
2 Mathews forced Bruton at second,
McDougald to Kubek.
Mathews stole second.
3 Aaron grounded to third.

5th Inning
New York
1 Carey lined to short.
2 Kubek grounded out, Torre to Burdette.
3 Lumpe, pinch-hitting for Kucks,
flied to center.
Milwaukee
For New York—Dickson pitching.
1 Covington grounded to second.
2 Torre flied to Mantle in left-center.
3 Crandall struck out.

6th Inning
New York
1 Bauer called out on strikes.
2 McDougald popped to Schoendienst
in short center.
3 Mantle popped to second.
Milwaukee
1 Logan popped to third.
2 Burdette grounded to third.
Bruton singled to center.
3 Schoendienst flied to deep right.

7th Inning
New York
1 Siebern flied to left.
2 Berra flied to Bruton making a good
running catch in right-center.
3 Skowron bounced out to short.
Milwaukee
1 Mathews grounded to first.
Aaron beat out a chopper to third.
Covington singled to right,
Aaron going to third.
Mantilla ran for Covington.
Torre singled past first, Aaron scoring
with Mantilla racing to third.
2 Crandall hit a sacrifice fly to Mantle,
Mantilla scoring after the catch.
3 Logan fouled to Skowron.

8th Inning
New York
For Milwaukee—Pafko playing in left.
1 Slaughter, pinch-hitting for Carey,
grounded to second.
2 Kubek grounded to first.
3 Throneberry, pinch-hitting for
Dickson, struck out.
Milwaukee
For New York—Richardson playing third
and Monroe pitching.
1 Burdette struck out.
Bruton walked.
Schoendienst got a ground-rule double
off Bauer into the right field stands,
Bruton going to third.
Mathews singled to left, Bruton
and Schoendienst scoring.
Aaron singled to right, moving
Mathews to third.
2 Pafko hit a sacrifice fly to center,
scoring Mathews.
3 Torre grounded to second.

9th Inning
New York
Bauer hit a home run into the
left field bleachers.
McDougald singled to left.
Mantle hit a two-run homer, his
second of the game, into the
left-center field bleachers.
Siebern singled to right.
1 Berra flied to right.
2 Skowron flied to left.
3 Richardson bunted out on a very
close play, Crandall to Torre.

Game 3 October 4 at New York

			Mil.	000	000	000
			N.Y.	000	020	20 x

Milwaukee	Pos	AB	R	H	RBI	PO	A	E
Bruton	cf	3	0	0	0	2	0	0
Schoendienst	2b	4	0	2	0	3	0	0
Mathews	3b	3	0	0	0	1	0	0
Aaron	rf	3	0	0	1	0	0	0
Covington	lf	3	0	1	0	4	0	0
Torre	1b	4	0	2	0	9	0	0
Crandall	c	4	0	1	0	4	1	0
Logan	ss	3	0	0	0	2	0	0
Rush	p	2	0	0	0	0	3	0
a Hanebrink		1	0	0	0	0	0	0
McMahon	p	0	0	0	0	1	0	0
c Wise		1	0	0	0	0	0	0
Totals		31	0	6	0	24	8	0

New York	Pos	AB	R	H	RBI	PO	A	E
Bauer	rf	4	1	3	4	2	0	0
Kubek	ss	4	0	0	0	2	2	0
Mantle	cf	2	0	0	0	4	0	0
Berra	c	4	0	0	0	9	2	0
Siebern	lf	2	1	0	0	1	0	0
Lumpe	3b	3	0	1	0	2	1	0
Richardson	3b	1	0	0	0	0	1	0
Skowron	1b	4	0	0	0	4	1	0
McDougald	2b	2	1	0	0	2	2	0
Larsen	p	1	0	0	0	1	0	0
b Slaughter		0	1	0	0	0	0	0
Duren	p	0	0	0	0	0	1	0
Totals		27	4	4	4	27	7	0

Pitching Milwaukee	IP	H	R	ER	BB	SO
Rush (L)	6	3	2	2	5	2
McMahon	2	1	2	2	2	2
New York						
Larsen (W)	7	6	0	0	3	8
Duren (SV)	2	0	0	0	3	1

a Popped out for Rush in 7th.
b Walked for Larsen in 7th.
c Struck out for McMahon in 9th.

Home Run—Bauer. Double Plays—Crandall
to Torre, Duren to Kubek to Skowron.
Wild Pitch—Duren. Left on Bases—
Milwaukee 10, New York 6. Umpires—Gorman,
Flaherty, Barlick, Berry, Jackowski,
Umont. Attendance—71,599.
Time of Game—2:42.

1st Inning
Milwaukee
1 Bruton bunted out, Berra to Skowron.
2 Schoendienst grounded to first.
3 Mathews struck out.
New York
Bauer singled to deep short.
1,2 Kubek struck out and Bauer was
doubled off the first base bag,
Crandall to Torre.
3 Mantle struck out.

2nd Inning
Milwaukee
1 Aaron struck out.
2 Covington popped to third.
Torre singled to center.
3 Crandall fanned.
New York
1 Berra fouled to Logan.
2 Siebern flied to left.
3 Lumpe grounded to Mathews who threw
wide to third but Torre was able
to make the tag.

3rd Inning
Milwaukee
1 Logan fouled to Kubek.
2 Rush struck out.
Bruton walked.
Schoendienst singled through a
hole at short, moving Bruton
to third.
3 Mathews struck out.
New York
1 Skowron bunted out back to the pitcher.
2 McDougald grounded back to the mound.
3 Larsen grounded to the mound.

4th Inning
Milwaukee
1 Aaron flied to left.
2 Covington flied to Mantle
in left-center.
Torre singled to center.
3 Crandall called out on strikes.
New York
1 Bauer fouled to Torre.
2 Kubek lined to short.
Mantle walked.
3 Berra popped to second.

5th Inning
Milwaukee
1 Logan flied to left.
2 Rush struck out.
3 Bruton fouled to Lumpe.
New York
Siebern walked.
1 Lumpe flied to short center.
2 Skowron grounded to second,
Schoendienst making a great stop
and throwing for the out at
first as Siebern took second.
McDougald intentionally walked.
Larsen walked, loading the bases.
Bauer singled to right, Siebern
and McDougald scoring with
Larsen going to third.
3 Kubek lined to center.

6th Inning
Milwaukee
Schoendienst singled into the
right field corner.
1 Mathews struck out for the third
consecutive time.
Aaron walked.
Covington singled off Skowron's glove
to the field boxes, Schoendienst
went beyond third but raced back as
Skowron retrieved the ball and threw
to the plate, however, Aaron had also
gone to third. Schoendienst was then
2 caught in a run down, Berra to Lumpe
to Larsen, as Aaron safely got back to
second.
3 Torre flied to right.
New York
1 Mantle flied to left.
2 Berra flied to left.
Siebern walked.
Lumpe singled to center, Siebern
going to third.
3 Skowron lined to right.

7th Inning
Milwaukee
Crandall singled to left.
1 Logan flied to center.
2 Hanebrink, batting for Rush, popped to
McDougald behind first.
Bruton walked.
3 Schoendienst flied to center.
New York
For Milwaukee—McMahon pitching.
1 McDougald struck out.
Slaughter, pinch-hitting for Larsen,
walked.
Bauer hit a 400 foot, two-run homer
into the left field stands.
2 Kubek flied to left.
Mantle walked.
3 Berra rolled to McMahon, who tagged
Berra out.

8th Inning
Milwaukee
For New York—Duren pitching and
Richardson playing third.
Mathews walked.
1 Aaron flied to right.
Covington walked.
2 Torre flied to center.
Both runners advanced on Duren's
wild pitch.
3 Crandall grounded to short.
New York
1 Siebern grounded to second.
2 Richardson grounded to second.
3 Skowron struck out.

9th Inning
Milwaukee
Logan walked.
1 Wise, pinch-hitting for McMahon,
struck out.
2,3 Bruton grounded into a game-ending
double play, Duren to Kubek to
Skowron.

Game 4 October 5 at New York

		Mil.	000	001	110
New York					
N.Y.		000	000	000

Milwaukee	Pos	AB	R	H	RBI	PO	A	E
Schoendienst	2b	5	1	1	0	2	2	0
Logan	ss	5	1	1	0	1	5	0
Mathews	3b	4	0	1	1	1	1	0
Aaron	cf-rf	4	0	2	0	2	0	0
Adcock	1b	3	0	0	0	9	0	0
b Torre	1b	1	0	0	0	2	0	0
Crandall	c	3	1	2	0	8	0	0
Covington	lf	3	0	0	1	0	0	0
c Bruton	cf	0	0	0	0	1	0	0
Pafko	rf-lf	4	0	1	0	0	0	0
Spahn	p	4	0	1	1	0	2	0
Totals		36	3	9	2	27	10	0

Pitching	IP	H	R	ER	BB	SO
Milwaukee						
Spahn (W)	9	2	0	0	2	7
New York						
Ford (L)	*7	8	3	2	1	6
Kucks	1	1	0	0	1	0
Dickson	1	0	0	0	1	0

*Pitched to two batters in 8th.

New York	Pos	AB	R	H	RBI	PO	A	E
Siebern	lf	3	0	0	0	1	0	0
McDougald	2b	4	0	0	0	4	4	0
Bauer	rf	4	0	0	0	2	0	0
Mantle	cf	4	0	1	0	2	0	0
Skowron	1b	3	0	1	0	10	0	0
Berra	c	3	0	0	0	7	0	0
Richardson	3b	2	0	0	0	1	0	0
a Howard		1	0	0	0	0	0	0
Carey	3b	0	0	0	0	0	1	0
Kubek	ss	2	0	0	0	2	6	1
d Slaughter		1	0	0	0	0	0	0
Dickson	p	0	0	0	0	0	0	0
Ford	p	1	0	0	0	1	1	0
Kucks	p	0	0	0	0	0	0	0
e Lumpe	ss	1	0	0	0	0	0	0
Totals		29	0	2	0	27	12	1

a Struck out for Richardson in 7th.
b Popped out for Adcock in 8th.
c Ran for Covington in 8th.
d Struck out for Kubek in 8th.
e Popped out for Kucks in 8th.

Doubles—Aaron, Logan, Mathews, Pafko.
Triples—Mantle, Schoendienst.
Double Play—McDougald to Kubek to Skowron.
Wild Pitch—Ford. Left on Bases—Milwaukee
8, New York 4. Umpires—Flaherty,
Barlick, Berry, Gorman, Umont, Jackowski.
Attendance—71,563. Time of Game—2:17.

1st Inning
Milwaukee
1 Schoendienst grounded to short.
2 Logan grounded to short.
3 Mathews was called out on strikes.
New York
Siebern walked.
1 McDougald struck out.
2 Bauer popped to first.
3 Mantle forced Siebern at second,
Logan to Schoendienst.

2nd Inning
Milwaukee
1 Aaron struck out.
2 Adcock grounded back to the mound.
Crandall singled to center.
3 Covington grounded to second.
New York
1 Skowron grounded to short.
2 Berra grounded to first.
3 Richardson flied to left.

3rd Inning
Milwaukee
1 Pafko grounded to second.
2 Spahn struck out.
3 Schoendienst grounded to short.
New York
1 Kubek flied to Aaron in left-center.
Ford walked.
2 Siebern forced Ford at second,
Schoendienst to Logan.
3 McDougald bounced back to the mound.

4th Inning
Milwaukee
1 Logan fouled to Skowron.
2 Mathews popped to McDougald
in short center.
Aaron doubled down the third base line.
Aaron went to third on a Ford
wild pitch.
3 Adcock struck out.
New York
1 Bauer grounded to short.
Mantle tripled off the scoreboard
in deep left.
2 Skowron grounded back to the mound,
Mantle holding third.
3 Berra lined sharply to Schoendienst
who leaping knocked it down and threw
Berra out at first on a very close
play.

5th Inning
Milwaukee
Crandall singled to left.
1 Covington struck out.
2 Pafko flied to deep center.
3 Spahn struck out.
New York
1 Richardson popped to Adcock in
short right.
2 Kubek lined to third.
3 Ford took a called third strike.

6th Inning
Milwaukee
Schoendienst tripled into deep left-
center the ball falling between
Mantle and Siebern.
Logan safe at first and Schoendienst
scored when Kubek let the ball go
through him for an error.
1 Mathews popped to Ford on an
attempted bunt.
2 Aaron forced Logan at second,
Kubek to McDougald.
3 Adcock forced Aaron at second,
Kubek to McDougald
New York
1 Siebern called out on strikes.
2 McDougald flied to Aaron in deep
left-center.
3 Bauer grounded to short.

7th Inning
Milwaukee
Crandall walked.
1 Covington flied to deep center.
Pafko doubled to right, Crandall
going to third.
Spahn blooped a single to short left,
Crandall scoring with Pafko holding.
2,3 Schoendienst hit into a double play,
McDougald to Kubek to Skowron.
New York
1 Mantle took a called third strike.
Skowron singled to center.
2 Berra fouled to Crandall.
3 Howard, batting for Richardson,
was called out on strikes.

8th Inning
Milwaukee
For New York—Carey playing third.
Logan got a ground-rule double into the
left field stands after Siebern had
lost the ball in the sun.
Mathews doubled off the left-center
field scoreboard, Logan scoring.
For New York—Kucks came in to pitch.
Aaron singled off Kucks' leg, moving,
Mathews to third.
1 Torre, batting for Adcock, lined to
short.
2 Crandall popped to first.
Covington walked, loading the bases.
Bruton ran for Covington.
3 Pafko forced Bruton at second,
Carey to McDougald.
New York
For Milwaukee—Torre at first, Bruton
in center, Aaron moved to right field
and Pafko moved to left field.
1 Slaughter, batting for Kubek, took
a called third strike.
2 Lumpe, batting for Kucks, popped to
second.
3 Siebern struck out.

9th Inning
Milwaukee
For New York—Dickson pitching and
Lumpe at short.
1 Spahn grounded to second.
2 Schoendienst fouled to Berra.
3 Logan flied to deep left.
New York
1 McDougald flied to Bruton in
deep right-center.
2 Bauer grounded to third.
3 Mantle grounded to short.

Game 5 October 6 at New York

| | | Mil. | 000 | 000 | 000 |
| | | N.Y. | 001 | 006 | 00x |

Milwaukee	Pos	AB	R	H	RBI	PO	A	E
Bruton	cf	3	0	2	0	2	0	0
Schoendienst	2b	3	0	1	0	0	1	0
Mathews	3b	4	0	1	0	1	3	0
Aaron	rf	4	0	1	0	1	0	0
Covington	lf	4	0	0	0	2	0	0
b Wise		0	0	0	0	0	0	0
Torre	1b	3	0	0	0	9	1	0
Crandall	c	3	0	0	0	8	1	0
Logan	ss	3	0	0	0	0	3	0
Burdette	p	2	0	0	0	1	0	0
Pizarro	p	0	0	0	0	0	1	0
a Hanebrink		1	0	0	0	0	0	0
Willey	p	0	0	0	0	0	0	0
Totals		30	0	5	0	24	10	0

a Fouled out for Pizarro in 8th.
b Ran for Covington in 9th.

Doubles—Berra, McDougald. Home
Run—McDougald. Sacrifice Hit—Schoen-
dienst. Double Plays—Mathews to Torre,
Howard to McDougald to Skowron.
Wild Pitch—Pizarro. Left on Bases—
Milwaukee 7, New York 4.
Umpires—Barlick, Berry, Gorman, Flaherty,
Jackowski, Umont. Attendance—65,279.
Time of Game—2:19.

New York	Pos	AB	R	H	RBI	PO	A	E
Bauer	rf	4	1	1	0	2	0	0
Lumpe	3b	3	0	0	0	0	1	0
Richardson	3b	1	0	0	0	0	1	0
Mantle	cf	3	1	2	0	3	0	0
Berra	c	4	1	1	1	11	0	0
Howard	lf	3	1	0	0	1	0	0
Skowron	1b	4	1	1	1	5	1	0
McDougald	2b	4	2	2	3	3	1	0
Kubek	ss	4	0	1	0	1	1	0
Turley	p	3	0	1	2	0	0	0
Totals		33	7	10	7	27	6	0

Pitching	IP	H	R	ER	BB	SO
Milwaukee						
Burdette (L)	5⅓	8	6	6	1	4
Pizarro	1⅔	2	1	1	1	3
Willey	1	0	0	0	0	2
New York						
Turley (W)	9	5	0	0	3	10

1st Inning
Milwaukee
Bruton walked.
1 Schoendienst sacrificed Bruton to
second, Skowron to McDougald.
2 Mathews flied to right.
3 Aaron flied to center.
New York
1 Bauer struck out.
2 Lumpe flied to Bruton in short
right-center.
3 Mantle struck out.

2nd Inning
Milwaukee
1 Covington flied to center.
Torre walked.
2 Crandall called out on strikes.
3 Logan also took a third strike.
New York
1 Berra grounded out, Torre to Burdette.
2 Howard flied to right.
3 Skowron grounded to short.

3rd Inning
Milwaukee
1 Burdette struck out.
2 Bruton flied to right.
Schoendienst singled over second.
3 Mathews called out on strikes.
New York
McDougald homered into the screen
next to the left field foul pole.
1 Kubek struck out.
2 Turley grounded to second.
3 Bauer grounded to short.

4th Inning
Milwaukee
1 Aaron flied to left.
2 Covington called out on strikes.
3 Torre grounded to first.
New York
Lumpe beat out a hard chopper
behind second.
Mantle singled to right, moving
Lumpe to second.
1,2 Berra grounded into a double play,
Mathews stepping on third to force
Lumpe and firing to Torre to get
Berra at first.
3 Howard flied to deep center.

5th Inning
Milwaukee
1 Crandall grounded to third.
2 Logan struck out.
3 Burdette flied to Howard
in deep left-center.
New York
1 Skowron flied to right.
2 McDougald grounded to third.
Kubek beat out a roller in front
of the plate.
3 Turley grounded to short.

6th Inning
Milwaukee
Bruton singled over Kubek's head.
1,2 Schoendienst lined to Howard in
short left, and he threw to Skowron
off of McDougald's glove to
double up Bruton.
Mathews singled to right.
3 Aaron struck out.
New York
Bauer singled to left.
1 Lumpe struck out as he bunted the
third strike foul.
Mantle singled to left-center,
advancing Bauer to third.
Berra doubled into the right field
corner, Bauer scoring with Mantle
stopping at third.
Howard got an intentional pass,
loading the bases.
Skowron singled to right, scoring
Mantle with the bases still loaded.
For Milwaukee—Pizarro came in to pitch.
McDougald hit a ground-rule double
into the Milwaukee bullpen, scoring
Berra and Howard with Skowron
going to third.
2 Kubek struck out but had to be
thrown out Crandall to Torre.
Turley singled to left, Skowron
and McDougald scoring.
Turley went to second on
Pizarro's wild pitch.
3 Bauer struck out.

7th Inning
Milwaukee
For New York—Richardson playing third.
1 Covington struck out.
2 Torre grounded to first.
Crandall walked.
3 Logan flied to right.
New York
1 Richardson grounded to the mound.
Mantle walked.
2 Berra grounded to third, moving
Mantle to second.
3 Howard was called out on strikes.

8th Inning
Milwaukee
1 Hanebrink, batting for Pizarro,
fouled to Berra.
Bruton singled to left-center.
2 Schoendienst popped to short.
3 Mathews grounded to third.
New York
For Milwaukee—Willey pitching.
1 Skowron struck out.
2 McDougald struck out.
3 Kubek flied to short left.

9th Inning
Milwaukee
1 Aaron struck out.
Covington singled off Kubek's glove.
Wise ran for Covington.
2 Torre popped to second.
3 Crandall forced Wise at second,
Kubek to McDougald.

Game 6 October 8 at Milwaukee

N.Y.	100	001	000	2
Mil.	110	000	000	1

New York	Pos	AB	R	H	RBI	PO	A	E
Carey	3b	5	0	0	0	0	1	0
McDougald	2b	5	1	2	1	6	4	0
Bauer	rf	5	1	2	1	0	0	0
Mantle	cf	5	1	1	0	0	0	0
Howard	lf	5	1	2	0	3	1	0
Berra	c	4	0	2	1	14	1	0
Skowron	1b	4	0	1	1	6	2	0
Kubek	ss	2	0	0	0	0	1	0
a Slaughter		1	0	0	0	0	0	0
Duren	p	2	0	0	0	0	0	0
Turley	p	0	0	0	0	0	0	0
Ford	p	1	0	0	0	0	0	0
Ditmar	p	1	0	0	0	1	0	1
b Lumpe	ss	1	0	0	0	0	1	0
Totals		41	4	10	4	30	11	1

a Grounded out for Kubek in 6th.
b Struck out for Ditmar in 6th.
c Ran for Adcock in 10th.
d Popped out for Crandall in 10th.

Double—Schoendienst. Home Runs—Bauer, McDougald. Sacrifice Hits—Logan 2. Sacrifice Fly—Berra. Double Plays—Howard to Berra, Crandall to Schoendienst. Left on Bases—New York 10, Milwaukee 9. Umpires—Berry, Gorman, Flaherty, Barlick, Umont, Jackowski. Attendance—46,367. Time of Game—3:07.

Milwaukee	Pos	AB	R	H	RBI	PO	A	E
Schoendienst	2b	4	1	2	0	6	2	1
Logan	ss	2	1	0	0	1	3	2
Mathews	3b	5	0	0	0	1	3	0
Aaron	rf	5	0	3	2	2	0	0
Adcock	1b	4	0	1	0	6	0	0
c Mantilla		0	0	0	0	0	0	0
Crandall	c	4	0	0	0	7	1	0
d Torre		1	0	0	0	0	0	0
Covington	lf	4	1	2	0	0	0	0
Pafko	cf	2	0	1	0	3	0	0
Bruton	cf	2	0	0	0	3	0	1
Spahn	p	4	0	1	1	1	2	0
McMahon	p	0	0	0	0	0	0	0
Totals		37	3	10	3	30	11	4

Pitching	IP	H	R	ER	BB	SO
New York						
Ford	1⅓	5	2	2	1	2
Ditmar	3⅔	2	0	0	0	2
Duren (W)	4⅔	3	1	1	2	8
Turley (SV)	⅓	0	0	0	0	0
Milwaukee						
Spahn	9⅔	9	4	4	2	5
McMahon	⅓	1	0	0	0	1

1st Inning
New York
1 Carey flied to center.
2 McDougald lined to third.
Bauer hit his 4th homer of the Series into the left field bleachers.
Mantle safe when Schoendienst booted his grounder for an error.
3 Howard forced Mantle at second, Logan to Schoendienst.
Milwaukee
Schoendienst singled to left.
1 Logan sacrificed, Berra to McDougald.
2 Mathews called out on strikes.
Aaron singled to left, Schoendienst scoring.
3 Adcock forced Aaron at second, Kubek to McDougald.

2nd Inning
New York
1 Berra grounded back to the mound.
Skowron safe at first when Logan booted his grounder for an error.
2 Kubek struck out.
3 Ford forced Skowron at second, Logan to Schoendienst.
Milwaukee
1 Crandall struck out.
Covington singled to center on a trap by Mantle.
Pafko singled to right, Covington advancing to third.
Spahn singled to right-center, scoring Covington with Pafko stopping at second.
Schoendienst walked, loading the bases.
For New York—Ditmar now pitching.
2,3 Logan flied to Howard and Pafko was doubled up trying to score by a perfect throw from Howard to Berra.

3rd Inning
New York
1 Carey flied to center.
2 McDougald grounded to short.
Bauer safe at first on Logan's fumble.
3 Mantle forced Bauer at second, Mathews to Schoendienst.
Milwaukee
1 Mathews grounded out, Skowron to Ditmar.
Aaron beat out a bunt near the mound and went to second on Ditmar's wild throw.
2 Adcock grounded to second, moving Aaron to third.
3 Crandall struck out.

4th Inning
New York
1 Howard flied to center.
Berra singled to right.
2 Skowron flied to right.
3 Kubek grounded back to the mound.
Milwaukee
1 Covington grounded to second.
2 Pafko popped to second.
3 Spahn struck out.

5th Inning
New York
1 Ditmar grounded to second.
2 Carey flied to right.
McDougald singled down the left field line.
3 Bauer fouled to Crandall.
Milwaukee
Schoendienst doubled into the left field corner.
1 Logan sacrificed Schoendienst to third, Skowron to McDougald.
2 Mathews popped to first.
3 Aaron grounded to third.

6th Inning
New York
For Milwaukee—Bruton playing center.
Mantle singled over Logan's glove.
Howard singled to center with Mantle going to third when Bruton fumbled the ball for an error.
1 Berra hit a sacrifice fly to center, Mantle scoring after the catch.
Skowron walked.
2 Slaughter, pinch-hitting for Kubek, grounded to second, advancing both runners.
3 Lumpe, pinch-hitting for Ditmar, struck out.
Milwaukee
For New York—Duren pitching (batting 8th) and Lumpe playing short (batting 9th).
1 Adcock took a called third strike.
2 Crandall also called out on strikes.
Covington singled to right.
3 Bruton struck out.

7th Inning
New York
1 Carey lined to the pitcher.
2 McDougald flied to center.
Bauer beat out a dribbler to the mound as Spahn fell down.
3 Mantle forced Bauer at second, Mathews to Schoendienst.
Milwaukee
1 Spahn struck out.
2 Schoendienst lined to left.
3 Logan lined to left.

8th Inning
New York
1 Howard took a called third strike.
2 Berra lined to second.
3 Skowron popped to short.
Milwaukee
1 Mathews fouled to Berra.
2 Aaron grounded to second.
Adcock walked.
3 Crandall forced Adcock at second, Lumpe to McDougald.

9th Inning
New York
1 Duren called out on strikes.
Lumpe walked.
2,3 Carey struck out and Lumpe was doubled as he was trying for second, Crandall to Schoendienst.
Milwaukee
1 Covington struck out.
2 Bruton struck out.
3 Spahn struck out.

10th Inning
New York
McDougald hit a home run over the left field fence.
1 Bauer flied to deep center.
2 Mantle grounded to second.
Howard singled to right.
Berra singled to right, moving Howard to third.
For Milwaukee—McMahon now pitching.
Skowron singled to right, Howard scoring with Berra stopping at second.
3 Duren struck out.
Milwaukee
1 Schoendienst grounded to second.
Logan walked.
2 Mathews took a called third strike.
Logan went to second on Duren's full wind up (not a stolen base).
Aaron singled to left, Logan scoring.
Adcock singled through the middle, Aaron going to third.
For New York—Turley pitching.
Mantilla ran for Adcock.
3 Torre, pinch-hitting for Crandall, lined to McDougald at the edge of the outfield grass.

Game 7 October 9 at Milwaukee

N.Y.	020	000	040
Mil.	100	001	000

New York	Pos	AB	R	H	RBI	PO	A	E
Bauer	rf	5	0	0	0	2	0	0
McDougald	2b	5	0	2	0	3	6	0
Mantle	cf	4	0	0	0	2	0	0
Berra	c	4	2	1	0	3	1	0
Howard	lf	3	2	2	1	3	0	0
Lumpe	3b	3	0	0	0	0	2	0
Carey	3b	1	1	1	0	1	0	0
Skowron	1b	4	1	2	4	12	0	0
Kubek	ss	2	0	0	1	1	2	0
Larsen	p	1	0	0	0	0	0	0
Turley	p	2	0	0	0	0	1	0
Totals		34	6	8	6	27	12	0

Pitching	IP	H	R	ER	BB	SO
New York						
Larsen	2⅓	3	1	1	3	1
Turley (W)	6⅔	2	1	1	3	2
Milwaukee						
Burdette (L)	8	7	6	4	2	3
McMahon	1	1	0	0	1	2

Milwaukee	Pos	AB	R	H	RBI	PO	A	E
Schoendienst	2b	5	1	1	0	5	3	0
Bruton	cf	3	0	1	0	1	0	0
Torre	1b	2	0	0	0	10	0	2
Aaron	rf	3	0	1	0	4	0	0
Covington	lf	4	0	0	1	1	0	0
Mathews	3b	1	0	0	0	1	2	0
Crandall	c	4	1	1	1	4	1	0
Logan	ss	4	0	0	0	1	5	0
Burdette	p	3	0	0	0	0	2	0
McMahon	p	0	0	0	0	0	0	0
a Adcock		1	0	1	0.	0	0	0
b Mantilla		0	0	0	0	0	0	0
Totals		30	2	5	2	27	13	2

a Singled for McMahon in 9th.
b Ran for Adcock in 9th.

Doubles—Berra, McDougald.
Home Runs—Crandall, Skowron.
Sacrifice Hits—Howard, Torre, Turley.
Sacrifice Fly—Kubek. Stolen Base—Howard.
Double Play—McDougald to Skowron.
Left on Bases—New York 7, Milwaukee 8.
Umpires—Gorman, Flaherty, Barlick, Berry, Jackowski, Umont.
Attendance—46,367. Time of Game—2:31.

1st Inning
New York
1 Bauer lined to right.
2 McDougald grounded to short.
3 Mantle grounded to first.
Milwaukee
Schoendienst singled to left.
Bruton walked.
1 Torre sacrificed up both runners, Lumpe to McDougald.
Aaron walked, loading the bases.
2 Covington grounded to first, scoring Schoendienst and advancing both other runners up one base.
Mathews got an intentional pass.
3 Crandall took a called third strike.

2nd Inning
New York
Berra walked.
Howard sacrificed and was safe at first when Torre tossed poorly to Burdette.
Lumpe grounded to Torre, who again threw too high to Burdette for another error, loading the bases.
1 Skowron forced Lumpe at second, Logan to Schoendienst, scoring Berra and moving Howard to third.
2 Kubek hit a sacrifice fly to left, Howard scoring after the catch.
3 Larsen forced Skowron at second, Logan to Schoendienst.
Milwaukee
1 Logan popped to short.
2 Burdette grounded to third.
3 Schoendienst grounded to second.

3rd Inning
New York
1 Bauer grounded to short.
McDougald doubled off the left-center field fence.
2 Mantle grounded to third, as McDougald held second.
3 Berra grounded to first.
Milwaukee
Bruton singled to right-center.
1 Torre popped to McDougald in short right.
Aaron singled to left, Bruton stopping at second.
For New York—Turley came in to pitch.
2 Covington grounded out, Berra to Skowron, advancing both runners one base.
Mathews got an intentional pass, loading the bases.
3 Crandall's grounder deflected off Turley to McDougald who threw him out at first.

4th Inning
New York
Howard singled to right.
Howard stole second.
1 Lumpe grounded to third, Howard holding at second.
2 Skowron flied to center.
Kubek got an intentional pass.
3 Turley forced Kubek at second, Logan to Schoendienst.
Milwaukee
1 Logan flied to right.
2 Burdette struck out.
3 Schoendienst grounded to short.

5th Inning
New York
1 Bauer popped to second.
2 McDougald flied to right.
3 Mantle grounded to second.
Milwaukee
1 Bruton struck out.
Torre walked.
2,3 Aaron hit into a double play, McDougald to Skowron.

6th Inning
New York
1 Berra flied to deep right.
2 Howard struck out.
3 Lumpe grounded out, off Burdette to Schoendienst who threw Lumpe out at first.
Milwaukee
For New York—Carey playing third.
1 Covington flied to deep right.
2 Mathews grounded to second.
Crandall hit a home run into the left field stands.
3 Logan lined to left.

7th Inning
New York
Skowron singled to left.
1 Kubek popped to short.
2 Turley sacrificed Skowron to second, Burdette to Schoendienst.
3 Bauer popped to third.
Milwaukee
1 Burdette grounded to short.
2 Schoendienst grounded to second.
3 Bruton grounded to first.

8th Inning
New York
1 McDougald flied to right.
2 Mantle took a called third strike.
Berra doubled off the wall in the right field corner.
Howard singled to center, scoring Berra.
Carey singled off Mathew's glove, Howard stopping at second.
Skowron hit a three-run homer into the left-center field bleachers.
3 Kubek struck out, but had to be thrown out, Crandall to Torre.
Milwaukee
1 Torre lined to McDougald, who made a sensational catch.
2 Aaron fouled to Howard.
3 Covington popped to third.

9th Inning
New York
For Milwaukee—McMahon pitching.
1 Turley struck out.
2 Bauer struck out.
McDougald singled to right.
Mantle walked.
3 Berra grounded to second.
Milwaukee
Mathews walked.
1 Crandall flied to left.
2 Logan flied to center.
Adcock, batting for McMahon, singled to left, Mathews stopping at second.
Mantilla ran for Adcock.
3 Schoendienst lined to center.

1958 WORLD SERIES COMPOSITE BOX

	Wins	Composite Line Score				
New York Yankees (A.L.)	4	2 2 1	2 4 7	2 4 3	2	- 29
Milwaukee Braves (N.L.)	3	9 2 0	2 0 2	3 5 0	2	- 25

Manager	Regular Season W	L	Pct.	G. Ahead
Casey Stengel	92	62	.597	10
Fred Haney	92	62	.597	8

BATTING AND FIELDING

WORLD SERIES STATISTICS

	Pos	G	AB	R	H	2B	3B	HR	RBI	BB	SO	SB	BA	SA	PO	A	E
NEW YORK YANKEES																	
Bill Skowron	1b	7	27	3	7	0	0	2	7	1	4	0	.259	.481	55	4	0
Gil McDougald	2b	7	28	5	9	2	0	2	4	2	4	0	.321	.607	18	23	0
Tony Kubek	ss	7	21	0	1	0	0	0	1	1	7	0	.048	.048	9	15	**2**
Jerry Lumpe	3b-ss-ph	6	12	0	2	0	0	0	0	1	2	0	.167	.167	2	5	0
Hank Bauer	rf	7	**31**	**6**	**10**	0	0	**4**	**8**	0	5	0	.323	**.7107**	0	0	
Mickey Mantle	cf	7	24	4	6	0	**1**	2	3	**7**	4	0	.250	.583	16	0	0
Elston Howard	1f-ph	6	18	4	4	0	0	0	2	1	4	**1**	.222	.222	14	2	0
Yogi Berra	c	7	27	3	6	**3**	0	0	2	1	0	0	.222	.333	**60**	6	0
Andy Carey	3b	5	12	1	1	0	0	0	0	0	3	0	.083	.083	2	6	0
Norm Siebern	1f	3	8	1	1	0	0	0	0	3	2	0	.125	.125	5	0	0
Bobby Richardson	3b	4	5	0	0	0	0	0	0	0	0	0	.000	.000	0	1	0
Enos Slaughter	ph	4	3	1	0	0	0	0	0	1	1	0	.000	.000			
Marv Throneberry	ph	1	1	0	0	0	0	0	0	0	1	0	.000	.000			
Darrell Johnson		Did not play															
Bob Turley	p	4	5	0	1	0	0	0	2	0	1	0	.200	.200	0	1	0
Whitey Ford	p	3	4	1	0	0	0	0	0	2	2	0	.000	.000	1	1	0
Ryne Duren	p	3	3	0	0	0	0	0	0	0	2	0	.000	.000	0	1	0
Don Larsen	p	2	2	0	0	0	0	0	0	1	0	0	.000	.000	1	0	0
Johnny Kucks	p	2	1	0	1	0	0	0	0	0	0	0	1.000	1.000	0	0	0
Art Ditmar	p	1	1	0	0	0	0	0	0	0	0	0	.000	.000	1	0	1
Murry Dickson	p	2	0	0	0	0	0	0	0	0	0	0	—	—	0	0	0
Duke Maas	p	1	0	0	0	0	0	0	0	0	0	0	—	—	0	0	0
Zack Monroe	p	1	0	0	0	0	0	0	0	0	0	0	—	—	0	0	0
Bobby Shantz		Did not play															
Tom Sturdivant		Did not play—sore arm															
team total		7	233	29	49	5	1	10	29	21	42	1	.210	.369	191	65	3

Double Plays—5
Left on Bases—40

REGULAR SEASON STATISTICS

		Main Pos	G	AB	R	H	2B	3B	HR	RBI	BB	SO	SB	BA	SA
Bill Skowron		1b	126	465	61	127	22	3	14	73	28	69	1	.273	.424
Gil McDougald		2b	138	503	69	126	19	1	14	65	59	75	6	.250	.376
Tony Kubek		ss	138	559	66	148	21	1	2	48	25	57	5	.265	.317
Jerry Lumpe		3b	81	232	34	59	8	4	3	32	23	21	1	.254	.362
Hank Bauer		of	128	452	62	121	22	6	12	50	32	56	3	.268	.493
Mickey Mantle		of	150	519	**127**	**158**	21	1	**42**	97	**127**	**120**	18	.304	.592
Elston Howard		c	103	376	45	118	19	5	11	66	22	60	1	.314	.479
Yogi Berra		c	122	433	60	115	17	3	22	90	35	35	3	.266	.471
Andy Carey		3b	102	315	39	90	19	4	12	45	34	43	1	.286	.486
Norm Siebern		of	134	460	79	138	19	5	14	55	66	87	5	.300	.454
Bobby Richardson		2b	73	182	18	45	6	2	0	14	8	5	1	.247	.302
Enos Slaughter		ph-of	77	138	21	42	4	1	4	19	21	16	2	.304	.435
Marv Throneberry		1b	60	150	30	34	5	2	7	19	19	40	1	.227	.427
Darrell Johnson		c	5	16	1	4	0	0	0	0	0	2	0	.250	.250
Bob Turley		p	33	88	8	12	0	0	2	6	4	35	0	.136	.205
Whitey Ford		p	30	73	10	15	1	0	0	2	5	10	0	.205	.219
Ryne Duren		p	44	13	0	1	0	0	0	1	3	8	0	.077	.077
Don Larsen		p-ph	28	49	9	15	1	0	4	13	5	9	0	.306	.571
Johnny Kucks		p	34	40	2	5	2	0	0	2	3	9	0	.125	.175
Art Ditmar		p	38	44	8	11	0	0	0	5	2	10	0	.250	.250
Murry Dickson	a	p	6	7	0	2	0	0	0	1	0	2	0	.286	.286
Duke Maas	b	p	22	34	3	3	0	0	0	1	3	11	0	.088	.088
Zack Monroe		p	21	17	2	2	1	0	0	0	0	6	0	.118	.176
Bobby Shantz		p	33	35	1	8	3	0	0	1	2	12	0	.229	.314
Tom Sturdivant		p	15	21	1	4	0	0	0	0	2	0	0	.190	.190
team total			155	**5294**	**759**	**1418**	212	39	**164**	**715**	537	**822**	48	**.268**	**.416**

a—from Kansas City
b—from Kansas City

Harry Simpson (of), Bobby Del Greco (of), Fritzie Brickell (2b), Virgil Trucks (p), Sal Maglie (p), Bob Grim (p) and Johnny James (p) also played for the Yankees during the season.

WORLD SERIES STATISTICS

	Pos	G	AB	R	H	2B	3B	HR	RBI	BB	SO	SB	BA	SA	PO	A	E
MILWAUKEE BRAVES																	
Frank Torre	1b-ph	7	17	0	3	0	0	0	1	2	0	0	.176	.176	40	2	**2**
Red Schoendienst	2b	7	30	5	9	**3**	**1**	0	0	2	1	0	.300	.467	18	19	1
Johnny Logan	ss	7	25	3	3	2	0	0	2	2	4	0	.120	.200	10	**24**	**2**
Eddie Mathews	3b	7	25	3	4	2	0	0	3	6	**11**	**1**	.160	.240	5	13	1
Hank Aaron	rf-cf	7	27	3	9	2	0	0	2	4	6	0	.333	.407	14	0	0
Bill Bruton	ph-cf-pr	7	17	2	7	0	0	1	2	5	5	0	**.412**	.588	12	0	1
Wes Covington	1f	7	26	2	7	0	0	0	4	2	4	0	.269	.269	11	1	0
Del Crandall	c	7	25	4	6	0	0	1	3	3	10	0	.240	.360	43	5	0
Joe Adcock	1b-ph	4	13	1	4	0	0	0	0	1	3	0	.308	.308	23	2	0
Andy Pafko	cf-rf-1f	4	9	0	3	1	0	0	1	0	0	0	.333	.444	8	0	0
Felix Mantilla	ss-pr	4	0	1	0	0	0	0	0	0	0	0	—	—	0	0	0
Harry Hanebrink	ph	2	2	0	0	0	0	0	0	0	0	0	.000	.000			
Casey Wise	ph-pr	2	1	0	0	0	0	0	0	0	1	0	.000	.000			
Del Rice		Did not play															
Warren Spahn	p	3	12	0	4	0	0	0	3	0	6	0	.333	.333	2	6	0
Lew Burdette	p	3	9	1	1	0	0	1	3	0	3	0	.111	.444	2	2	0
Bob Rush	p	1	2	0	0	0	0	0	0	0	2	0	.000	.000	0	3	0
Don McMahon	p	3	0	0	0	0	0	0	0	0	0	0	—	—	1	0	0
Juan Pizarro	p	1	0	0	0	0	0	0	0	0	0	0	—	—	0	1	0
Carl Willey	p	1	0	0	0	0	0	0	0	0	0	0	—	—	0	0	0
Bob Buhl		Did not play—sore arm															
Ernie Johnson		Did not play															
Humberto Robinson		Did not play															
Bob Trowbridge		Did not play															
Gene Conley		Did not play—arm injury															
team total		7	240	25	60	10	1	3	24	27	56	1	.250	.296	189	78	7

Double Plays—5
Left on Bases—58

REGULAR SEASON STATISTICS

	Main Pos	G	AB	R	H	2B	3B	HR	RBI	BB	SO	SB	BA	SA
Frank Torre	1b	138	372	41	115	22	5	6	55	42	14	2	.309	.444
Red Schoendienst	2b	106	427	47	112	23	1	1	24	31	21	3	.262	.328
Johnny Logan	ss	145	530	54	120	20	0	11	53	40	57	1	.226	.326
Eddie Mathews	3b	149	546	97	137	18	1	31	77	85	85	5	.251	.458
Hank Aaron	of	153	601	109	196	34	4	30	95	59	49	4	.326	.546
Bill Bruton	of	100	325	47	91	11	3	3	28	27	37	4	.280	.360
Wes Covington	of	90	294	43	97	12	1	24	74	20	35	0	.330	.622
Del Crandall	c	427	427	50	116	23	1	18	63	48	38	4	.272	.457
Joe Adcock	1b	105	320	40	88	15	1	19	54	21	63	0	.275	.506
Andy Pafko	of	95	164	17	39	7	1	3	23	15	17	0	.238	.348
Felix Mantilla	of	85	226	37	50	5	1	7	19	20	20	2	.221	.345
Harry Hanebrink	of	63	133	14	25	3	0	4	10	13	9	0	.188	.301
Casey Wise	2b	31	71	8	14	1	0	0	0	4	8	1	.197	.211
Del Rice	c	43	121	10	27	7	0	1	8	8	30	0	.223	.306
Warren Spahn	p	41	108	10	36	6	1	2	15	7	24	0	.333	.463
Lew Burdette	p	47	99	11	24	1	1	3	15	3	24	0	.242	.364
Bob Rush	p	28	49	2	9	1	0	0	1	3	14	0	.200	.222
Don McMahon	p	38	9	0	1	0	0	0	0	2	6	0	.111	.111
Juan Pizarro	p	16	32	4	8	2	0	0	6	3	9	0	.250	.313
Carl Willey	p	23	48	0	5	2	0	0	1	0	25	0	.104	.146
Bob Buhl	p	11	25	3	5	0	0	0	0	0	6	0	.200	.200
Ernie Johnson	p	15	2	0	0	0	0	0	1	1	1	0	.000	.000
Humberto Robinson	p	19	6	0	1	0	0	0	0	2	2	0	.167	.167
Bob Trowbridge	p	27	9	1	1	0	0	0	0	0	3	0	.111	.111
Gene Conley	p	26	16	2	3	0	0	1	2	0	4	0	.188	.375
team total		154	5225	675	1388	221	21	167	641	478	646	26	**.266**	.412

Mel Roach (2b), Bob Hazle (of), Joe Koppe (ss), Carl Sawatski (c), Eddie Haas (of), Hawk Taylor (of), John DeMerit (of), Bob Roselli (ph), Joey Jay (p) and Dick Littlefield (p) also played for the Braves during the season.

PITCHING

WORLD SERIES STATISTICS

	G	GS	CG	IP	H	R	ER	BB	SO	W	L	SV	ERA
NEW YORK YANKEES													
Bob Turley	**4**	2	1	16⅓	10	5	5	7	13	**2**	1	**1**	2.76
Whitey Ford	3	**3**	0	15⅓	19	8	7	5	16	0	1	0	4.11
Don Larsen	2	2	0	9⅓	9	1	1	6	9	1	0	0	**0.96**
Ryne Duren	3	0	0	9⅓	7	2	2	6	14	1	1	**1**	1.93
Johnny Kucks	2	0	0	4⅓	4	1	1	1	0	0	0	0	2.08
Murry Dickson	2	0	0	4	4	2	2	0	1	0	0	0	4.56
Art Ditmar	1	0	0	3⅔	2	0	0	0	2	0	0	0	0.00
Zack Monroe	1	0	0	1	3	3	3	1	1	0	0	0	27.00
Duke Maas	1	0	0	⅓	2	3	3	1	0	0	0	0	81.00
Bobby Shantz	Did not play												
Tom Sturdivant	Did not play												
team total	7	7	1	63⅔	60	25	24	27	56	4	3	2	3.39
MILWAUKEE BRAVES													
Warren Spahn	3	**3**	**2**	**28⅔**	19	7	7	**8**	**18**	**2**	1	0	2.20
Lew Burdette	3	**3**	1	22⅓	**22**	**17**	**14**	4	12	1	**2**	0	5.64
Bob Rush	1	1	0	6	3	2	2	5	2	0	1	0	3.00
Don McMahon	3	0	0	3⅓	3	2	2	3	5	0	0	0	5.40
Juan Pizarro	1	0	0	1⅔	2	1	1	1	3	0	0	0	5.40
Carl Willey	1	0	0	1	0	0	0	0	2	0	0	0	0.00
Bob Buhl	Did not play—sore arm												
Ernie Johnson	Did not play												
Humberto Robinson	Did not play												
Bob Trowbridge	Did not play												
Gene Conley	Did not play—arm injury												
team total	7	7	3	63	49	29	26	21	42	3	4	0	3.71

REGULAR SEASON STATISTICS

		G	GS	CG	IP	H	ER	BB	SO	W	L	Pct	SV	ShO	ERA
NEW YORK YANKEES															
Bob Turley		33	31	**19**	245	178	81	**128**	168	**21**	7	**.750**	1	6	2.98
Whitey Ford		30	29	15	219	174	49	62	145	14	7	.667	1	**7**	**2.01**
Don Larsen		19	19	5	114	100	39	52	55	9	6	.600	0	3	3.08
Ryne Duren		44	1	0	76	40	17	43	87	6	4	.600	**20**	0	2.01
Johnny Kucks		34	15	4	126	132	55	39	46	8	8	.500	4	1	3.93
Murry Dickson	a	6	2	0	20	18	13	12	9	1	2	.333	1	0	5.85
Art Ditmar		38	13	4	140	124	53	38	52	9	8	.529	4	0	3.41
Zack Monroe		21	6	1	58	57	21	27	18	4	2	.667	1	0	3.26
Duke Maas	b	22	13	2	101	93	43	36	50	7	3	.700	0	1	3.83
Bobby Shantz		33	13	3	126	127	47	35	80	7	6	.538	0	0	3.36
Tom Sturdivant		15	10	0	71	77	33	38	41	3	6	.333	0	0	4.18
team total		155	155	53	1379	1201	**493**	557	796	**92**	62	**.597**	33	21	3.22
MILWAUKEE BRAVES															
Warren Spahn		38	36	**23**	**290**	257	99	76	150	**22**	11	**.667**	1	2	3.07
Lew Burdette		40	36	19	275	279	89	50	113	20	10	**.667**	0	3	2.91
Bob Rush		28	20	5	147	142	56	31	84	10	6	.625	0	2	3.43
Don McMahon		38	0	0	59	50	24	29	37	7	2	.778	8	0	3.66
Juan Pizarro		16	10	7	97	75	29	47	84	6	4	.600	1	1	2.69
Carl Willey		23	19	9	140	110	42	53	74	9	7	.563	0	4	2.70
Bob Buhl		11	10	3	73	34	28	30	27	5	2	.714	1	0	3.45
Ernie Johnson		15	0	0	23	35	21	10	13	3	1	.750	1	0	8.22
Humberto Robinson		19	0	0	42	30	14	13	26	2	4	.333	1	0	3.00
Bob Trowbridge		27	4	0	55	53	24	26	31	1	3	.333	1	0	3.93
Gene Conley		26	7	0	72	89	39	17	53	0	6	.000	2	0	4.88
team total		154	154	**72**	1376	1261	**491**	426	773	**92**	62	**.597**	17	**16**	**3.21**

Total Attendance—393,909 Average Attendance—56,273 Winning Player's Share—$8,759 Losing Player's Share—$5,896

1959 Play-off
Rallying to the Top

The collapse of the San Francisco Giants, who blew a sure lead by dropping seven of their last eight games, opened the door to the Los Angeles Dodgers, who finished seventh last season, and the defending-champion Milwaukee Braves to tie for first place in the National League. Both clubs won pressure games to end the regular season on Sunday, then began the N.L.'s third pennant play-off on a rainy Monday afternoon in Milwaukee. A disappointingly small crowd of 18,297 turned out for the first game, which was held up by rain for 47 minutes and played with the lights on from the start. In this depressing weather, both managers relied on secondary pitchers from their overworked hill staffs. Milwaukee manager Fred Haney picked 5-game-winner Carl Willey to start, while Dodger skipper Walter Alston sent 10-game-winner Danny McDevitt to the mound. After the Dodgers took a 1–0 lead in the top of the first inning, the Braves got to McDevitt in the bottom of the second. With one out, Johnny Logan drew a walk. Del Crandall and Billy Bruton then followed with singles, driving one run across the plate and sending Alston to his bullpen for help. Into the contest shuffled Larry Sherry, a hard-throwing rookie who had put together a 7–2 record after coming up from Spokane during the summer. Sherry got Willey to hit an infield grounder, but rookie shortstop Maury Wills butchered the play to load the bases. The second run of the inning crossed the plate when the Dodgers failed to get a double play on Bobby Avila's grounder. Sherry ended the inning without further damage and settled into an overpowering groove.

Singles by Charley Neal, Norm Larker, and Gil Hodges tied the game up in the third, and a leadoff homer to right by Johnny Roseboro in the sixth inning gave Los Angeles a 3–2 lead. Sherry's fine relief work made that edge stand up for a victory which put the Dodgers in a fine condition heading back to Los Angeles for the rest of the series.

The Los Angeles Coliseum, the converted football stadium serving as the Dodgers' home until a new park could be built, contained 36,853 fans on a bright Tuesday afternoon to view a confrontation between Lew Burdette and Don Drysdale, the ace right-handers of each team. The Braves got up on the scoreboard almost immediately when Eddie Mathews walked, Hank Aaron doubled, and Frank Torre singled both of them home in the top of the first inning. The Dodgers scored in the bottom of the first on a triple by Neal and a single by Wally Moon, and the Braves added another run in the second inning. A home run by Neal in the fourth cut the score to 3–2, but Mathews homered in the top of the fifth to put the Braves ahead 4–2. The score held until the eighth inning, when the Braves scored a run off Chuck Churn on a triple by Del Crandall and a sacrifice fly by Felix Mantilla.

The Dodgers came into the ninth inning trailing 5–2 and facing a master pitcher in Burdette. Moon opened the frame with a single to center, and veterans Duke Snider and Gil Hodges followed with singles which brought home a run and brought Don McMahon into the game in relief of Burdette. Larker's single cut the score to 5–4 and prompted Haney to bring ace Warren Spahn into the game in relief. Carl Furillo, another veteran of the Brooklyn glory years, pinch-hit a fly to right field on which Hodges scored for the tying run. A single by Wills sent Spahn to the showers in favor of Joey Jay, who ended the inning with the aid of a fine running catch in right by Aaron. With sure defeat suddenly shattered, the Dodgers rolled into the extra innings with a world of momentum.

Big righty Stan Williams came in to pitch and hurled three scoreless and hitless innings, although walking three men in the top of the eleventh. With Bob Rush on the mound, the Dodgers moved to end the deadlock in the bottom of the twelfth. The first two men made out, but then Hodges worked out a walk. Joe Pignatano then singled, with Hodges stopping at second. Furillo, who had stayed in the game after his pinch-hitting performance, then sent a grounder up the middle. Shortstop Mantilla made a fine catch of the ball behind second, but his off-balance heave bounced past first baseman Torre into the dugout, and Hodges sprinted home to win a pennant that seemed distant three innings ago and most unlikely in the spring.

Game 1 Playoffs September 28 at Milwaukee

Los Angeles	Pos	AB	R	H	RBI	PO	A	E
Gilliam	3b	4	0	0	0	1	1	0
Moon	2b	5	1	3	0	3	4	0
Neal	lf	4	1	1	0	2	0	0
Larker	rf	4	0	3	1	0	0	0
c Lillis		0	0	0	0	0	0	0
Fairly	rf	0	0	0	0	1	0	0
Hodges	1b	3	0	1	1	7	1	0
Demeter	cf	4	0	1	0	2	0	0
Roseboro	c	4	1	1	1	8	0	0
Wills	ss	4	0	0	0	3	3	1
McDevitt	p	1	0	0	0	0	0	0
L. Sherry	p	2	0	0	0	0	0	0
Totals		35	3	10	3	27	9	1

Pitching	IP	H	R	ER	BB	SO
Los Angeles						
McDevitt	1⅓	2	2	2	2	2
L. Sherry (W)	7⅔	4	0	0	2	4
Milwaukee						
Willey (L)	6	8	3	3	2	3
McMahon	3	2	0	0	1	2

L.A. 101 001 000
Mil. 020 000 000

Milwaukee	Pos	AB	R	H	RBI	PO	A	E
Avila	2b	5	0	0	1	4	3	0
Mathews	3b	4	0	0	0	2	3	0
Aaron	rf	2	0	0	0	3	0	0
Adcock	1b	3	0	0	0	6	0	0
Pafko	lf	2	0	0	0	0	0	0
a Maye	lf	2	0	1	0	1	0	0
Logan	ss	3	1	1	0	1	3	0
Crandall	c	4	1	2	0	5	0	0
Bruton	cf	4	0	1	1	4	0	0
Willey	p	2	0	1	0	0	1	0
b Slaughter		1	0	0	0	0	0	0
McMahon	p	0	0	0	0	0	0	0
d Torre		1	0	0	0	0	0	0
Totals		33	2	6	2	27	10	0

a Singled for Pafko in 5th.
b Grounded out for Willey in 6th.
c Ran for Larker in 7th.
d Flied out for McMahon in 9th.

Home Run—Roseboro. Double Plays—Gilliam to Neal to Hodges, Mathews to Avila to Adcock 2. Left on Bases—Los Angeles 8, Milwaukee 8. Umpires—Conlan, Barlick, Boggess, Donatelli, Gorman, Jackowski. Attendance—18,297. Time of Game—2:40.

Game 2 Playoffs September 29 at Los Angeles

Milwaukee	Pos	AB	R	H	RBI	PO	A	E
Bruton	cf	6	0	0	0	4	0	0
Mathews	3b	4	2	2	1	2	2	0
Aaron	rf	4	1	2	0	3	0	0
Torre	1b	3	0	1	2	10	2	0
Maye	lf	2	0	0	0	2	0	0
a Pafko	lf	1	0	0	0	0	0	0
b Slaughter		1	0	0	0	0	0	0
DeMerit	lf	0	0	0	0	1	0	0
j Spangler	lf	0	0	0	0	3	0	0
Logan	ss	3	1	2	0	2	5	0
Schoendienst	2b	1	0	0	0	0	0	0
d Vernon		1	0	0	0	0	0	0
Cottier	2b	1	0	0	0	1	0	0
k Adcock		1	0	0	0	0	0	0
Avila	2b	0	0	0	0	1	0	0
Crandall	c	6	1	1	1	6	1	0
Mantilla	2b-ss	5	0	1	1	1	1	2
Burdette	p	4	0	1	0	0	2	0
McMahon	p	0	0	0	0	0	0	0
Spahn	p	0	0	0	0	0	0	0
Jay	p	1	0	0	0	0	0	0
Rush	p	1	0	0	0	0	0	0
Totals		44	5	10	4	x35	13	2

a Flied out for Maye in 5th.
b Popped out for Pafko in 7th.
c Lined out for Churn in 8th.
d Called out on strikes for Schoendienst in 9th.
e Ran for Snider in 9th.
f Ran for Larker in 9th.
g Hit sacrifice fly for Roseboro in 9th.
h Announced for Labine in 9th.
i Hit into force out for Essegian in 9th.
j Walked for DeMerit in 11th.
k Hit into force out for Cottier in 11th.
x Two out when winning run scored.

Double—Aaron. Triples—Crandall, Neal. Home Runs—Mathews, Neal. Sacrifice Flies—Furillo, Mantilla. Double Plays—Wills to Neal to Hodges, Torre to Logan to Mantilla. Passed Ball—Pignatano. Hit by Pitcher—Pignatano (by Jay). Wild Pitch—Podres. Left on Bases—Milwaukee 13, Los Angeles 11. Umpires—Barlick, Boggess, Donatelli, Conlan, Jackowski, Gorman. Attendance—36,853. Time of Game—4:06.

Mil. 210 010 010 000
L.A. 100 100 003 001

Los Angeles	Pos	AB	R	H	RBI	PO	A	E
Gilliam	3b	5	0	1	0	4	3	0
Neal	2b	5	3	2	1	3	2	1
Moon	rf-lf	6	1	3	1	3	1	0
Snider	cf	4	0	1	0	1	0	1
e Lillis		0	0	0	0	0	0	0
Williams	p	2	0	0	0	0	0	0
Hodges	1b	5	2	2	0	11	0	0
Larker	lf	4	0	2	2	2	0	0
f Pignatano	c	1	0	1	0	3	0	0
Roseboro	c	3	0	0	0	5	1	0
g Furillo	rf	2	0	1	1	0	0	0
Wills	ss	5	0	1	0	2	5	0
Drysdale	p	1	0	0	0	1	1	0
Podres	p	1	0	0	0	0	1	0
Churn	p	0	0	0	0	0	1	0
c Demeter		1	0	0	0	0	0	0
Koufax	p	0	0	0	0	0	3	0
Labine	p	0	0	0	0	0	0	0
h Essegian		1	0	0	0	0	0	0
i Fairly	cf	2	0	0	0	1	0	0
Totals		48	6	15	5	36	14	2

Pitching	IP	H	R	ER	BB	SO
Milwaukee						
Burdette	*8	10	5	5	0	4
McMahon	**0	1	0	0	0	0
Spahn	⅓	1	0	0	0	0
Jay	2⅓	1	0	0	1	1
Rush (L)	1	2	1	0	1	0
Los Angeles						
Drysdale	4⅓	6	4	3	2	3
Podres	2⅓	3	0	0	1	1
Churn	1⅓	1	1	1	0	0
Koufax	⅓	0	0	0	3	1
Labine	⅓	0	0	0	0	1
Williams (W)	3	0	0	0	3	3

*Pitched to three batters in 9th.
**Pitched to one batter in 9th.

1959
Serving Sherry All Around

The Dodgers needed time to adjust to their new surroundings in Los Angeles. For one thing, they had to play their games in the Los Angeles Coliseum, the vast football stadium never built with major-league baseball in mind. When the playing field was laid out, a huge right field ranging out to 440 feet and a close 251-foot left-field fence topped by a 40-foot-high screen made the place unmistakably unique. The combination of the new setting plus the ravages of age dumped the Dodgers into a dismal seventh-place finish in their first year on the Coast, but Walt Alston regrouped his club this year, and with a mixture of Brooklyn holdovers and young newcomers, won the National League pennant by beating the Milwaukee Braves in a play-off to break their season's tie.

It took the Dodgers only two years to bring the World Series to Los Angeles, while the Chicago White Sox brought the Series to their fans for the first time since 1919, when they should have won it but instead dumped it. Both clubs relied on pitching and speed, but the Go-Go Sox had the majors' best base stealer in Luis Aparicio, and expected to run on the Bums. Catchers Johnny Roseboro and Sherm Lollar, however, neutralized the base stealers with their arms, and the Series would have to be settled on the strengths of hitting and pitching.

The White Sox's shocking display of batting power in the opening game in Chicago shadowed the Dodgers' chances. The Sox scored twice off Roger Craig in the first inning, then drove him to cover in the third with a seven-run outburst featuring a home run by Ted Kluszewski, the former Cincinnati star picked up late in the season for a power lift. Big Klu socked another homer in the fourth inning to run the score up to 11–0, a lead which 22-game-winner Early Wynn and relief ace Gerry Staley protected to the end. Things looked bad for the Dodgers in game two when the White Sox scored twice in the first inning and Bob Shaw shut them out for four innings. After Charley Neal's fifth-inning homer broke the ice for the Dodgers, they took the lead with three runs in the seventh on Chuck Essegian's pinch homer, Jim Gilliam's walk, and Neal's second homer of the day. Larry Sherry, a midseason recall from the minors, pitched the last three innings and saved the 4–3 win for Johnny Podres. An eighth-inning rally for the White Sox fell short when Lollar was thrown out at the plate with the tying run.

California then got its first look at the World Series and turned out in record numbers, with crowds of 92,394, 92,650, and 92,706 attending the three contests. With the clubs tied at 1–1 in the Series, Don Drysdale faced Dick Donovan in game three. Both right-handers pitched well, shutting out the opposition through six innings. But Donovan weakened in the seventh, giving up a single to Neal and walks to Norm Larker and veteran Gil Hodges. Chicago manager Al Lopez then sent Staley in to pitch, but Carl Furillo, the Brooklyn veteran pinch hitting for Don Demeter, singled home two runs on a bouncer up the middle. The Sox rallied in the eighth, but Sherry again came in to preserve the 3–1 victory for Drysdale. The Dodgers jumped ahead in game four with four runs in the third inning off Wynn, but the White Sox came back with four in the seventh off Craig, the last three coming on a homer by Lollar. Sherry again came out of the bullpen, pitching scoreless ball in the eighth and ninth innings and getting the 5–4 win on Hodges's eighth-inning homer off Staley.

Looking to end the Series on their home turf, the Bums pitched young Sandy Koufax in game five against Shaw. The Sox scored in the fourth inning on a single by Nellie Fox, a single by Jim Landis, and a double-play ball. Shaw, meanwhile, combined with relievers Billy Pierce and Donovan to shut the Dodgers out and take the 1–0 win to keep the Series alive. But back in Chicago for game six, the Los Angeles' batters again ripped into Wynn. Duke Snider belted a two-run homer in the third, and six runs in the fourth practically wrapped the game up. But a three-run homer by Kluszewski in the bottom of the fourth caused Alston to doubt Podres, and he played it safe by bringing in Sherry. The hard-throwing youngster shut the gate the rest of the way, and Essegian's pinch homer in the ninth upped the final score to 9–3 to give Sherry an impressive two victories and two saves in the Dodgers' second World Series triumph.

Game 1 October 1 at Chicago

L.A.		000	000	000				
Chi.		207	200	00x				

Los Angeles	Pos	AB	R	H	RBI	PO	A	E
Gilliam	3b	4	0	1	0	0	1	0
Neal	2b	4	0	2	0	3	1	
Moon	lf	4	0	1	0	2	0	0
Snider	cf	2	0	0	0	2	0	2
Demeter	cf	1	0	0	0	0	0	0
Larker	rf	4	0	1	0	4	0	0
Hodges	1b	4	0	2	0	10	0	0
Roseboro	c	4	0	0	0	5	0	0
Wills	ss	3	0	1	0	1	2	0
c Furillo		1	0	0	0	0	0	0
Craig	p	1	0	0	0	0	1	0
Churn	p	0	0	0	0	0	1	0
Labine	p	0	0	0	0	0	0	0
a Essegian		1	0	0	0	0	0	0
Koufax	p	0	0	0	0	0	0	0
b Fairly		1	0	0	0	0	0	0
Klippstein	p	0	0	0	0	0	1	0
Totals		34	0	8	0	24	9	3

Chicago	Pos	AB	R	H	RBI	PO	A	E
Aparicio	ss	5	0	0	0	3	3	0
Fox	2b	4	2	1	0	2	2	0
Landis	cf	4	3	3	1	1	0	0
Kluszewski	1b	4	2	3	5	8	2	0
Lollar	c	3	1	0	1	7	0	0
Goodman	3b	2	1	1	1	0	0	0
Esposito	3b	2	0	0	0	1	0	0
Smith	lf	4	1	2	0	4	0	0
Rivera	rf	4	1	0	0	2	0	0
Wynn	p	3	0	1	1	1	1	0
Staley	p	1	0	0	0	0	1	0
Totals		36	11	11	9	27	9	0

Pitching	IP	H	R	ER	BB	SO
Los Angeles						
Craig (L)	2⅓	5	5	5	1	1
Churn	*⅔	5	6	2	0	0
Labine	1	0	0	0	0	1
Koufax	2	0	0	0	0	1
Klippstein	2	1	0	0	0	2
Chicago						
Wynn (W)	**7	6	0	0	1	6
Staley (SV)	2	2	0	0	0	1

*Pitched to two batters in 3rd.
**Pitched to one batter in 8th.

a Struck out for Labine in 5th.
b Grounded out for Koufax in 7th.
c Flied out for Wills in 9th.

Doubles—Fox, Smith 2, Wynn. Home Runs—Kluszewski 2. Stolen Base—Neal. Sacrifice Fly—Lollar. Double Play—Aparicio to Fox to Kluszewski. Left on Bases—Los Angeles 8, Chicago 3. Umpires—Summers (A), Dascoli (N), Hurley (A), Secory (N), Rice (A), Dixon (N). Attendance—48,013. Time of Game—2:35.

1st Inning
Los Angeles
1 Gilliam grounded to short.
Neal singled off Goodman's glove.
2 Moon popped to Aparicio in short left.
Neal stole second.
Snider walked.
3 Larker lined to right.
Chicago
1 Aparicio popped to short.
Fox walked.
Landis singled to right-center, Fox racing to third.
Kluszewski singled past first, Fox scoring with Landis going to third.
2 Lollar hit a sacrifice-fly to right, scoring Landis from third.
3 Goodman flied to center.

2nd Inning
Los Angeles
1 Hodges flied to deep left.
2 Roseboro popped to short.
3 Wills struck out.
Chicago
1 Smith called out on strikes.
2 Rivera fouled to Hodges.
3 Wynn grounded back to the mound.

3rd Inning
Los Angeles
1 Craig struck out.
2 Gilliam popped to second.
3 Neal grounded to short.
Chicago
1 Aparicio lined to right.
Fox doubled down the right field line.
Landis singled to right, scoring Fox.
Kluszewski hit a two-run homer into the right field stands.
For Los Angeles—Churn pitching.
Lollar safe at second when his fly to left-center was dropped by Snider.
Goodman singled into right, Lollar scoring.
Smith doubled off the left-center field wall, Goodman advancing to third, but Goodman scored and Smith went to third as Snider made another error throwing wild past second.
Rivera hit to Neal who threw to the plate in the dirt with Smith scoring and Rivera getting to second.
Wynn doubled to keep left-center, Rivera scoring.
2 Aparicio grounded back to the mound.
3 Fox grounded to short.

4th Inning
Los Angeles
For Chicago—Esposito playing third.
Moon beat out a hit to second.
1 Snider flied to right.
2 Larker flied to center.
Hodges singled to center, Moon stopping at second.
3 Roseboro struck out.
Chicago
Landis singled to left.
Kluszewski hit his second homer of the game, a two-run shot into the upper right field stands.
For Los Angeles—Labine pitching.
1 Lollar flied to center.
2 Esposito called out on strikes.
3 Smith flied to right.

5th Inning
Los Angeles
1 Wills grounded to second.
2 Essegian, batting for Labine, struck out.
3 Gilliam called out on strikes.
Chicago
For Los Angeles—Koufax pitching.
1 Rivera flied to right.
2 Wynn took a called third strike.
3 Aparicio lined to left.

6th Inning
Los Angeles
Neal singled to left.
1 Moon grounded to first, Neal going to second.
2 Snider fouled to Esposito.
3 Larker struck out.
Chicago
For Los Angeles—Demeter playing center.
1 Fox flied to left.
2 Landis grounded to short.
3 Kluszewski grounded to second.

7th Inning
Los Angeles
1 Hodges grounded back to the mound.
2 Roseboro fouled to Lollar.
Wills singled to left.
3 Fairly, pinch-hitting for Koufax, grounded out Kluszewski to Wynn.
Chicago
For Los Angeles—Klippstein pitching.
1 Lollar grounded to third.
2 Esposito grounded back to the mound.
Smith doubled to right.
3 Rivera struck out.

8th Inning
Los Angeles
Gilliam singled to left.
For Chicago—Staley relieved Wynn with a 2–0 count to Neal. Wynn's elbow had stiffened.
1,2 Neal grounded into a double play, Aparicio to Fox to Kluszewski.
3 Moon grounded back to the mound.
Chicago
1 Staley took a called third strike.
2 Aparicio grounded to second.
3 Fox grounded to second.

9th Inning
Los Angeles
1 Demeter struck out.
Larker singled to left-center.
Hodges singled off Esposito's glove, Larker stopping at second.
2 Roseboro forced Hodges at second, Kluszewski to Aparicio, with Larker going to third.
3 Furillo, pinch-hitting for Wills, flied to left.

Game 2 October 2 at Chicago

Los Angeles	Pos	AB	R	H	RBI	PO	A	E
Gilliam	3b	4	1	1	0	1	1	0
Neal	2b	5	2	2	3	2	4	0
Moon	lf	3	0	1	0	1	1	0
Snider	cf	4	0	1	0	1	0	0
Demeter	cf	0	0	0	0	0	0	0
Larker	rf	3	0	0	0	4	0	0
Sherry	p	1	0	0	0	1	1	0
Hodges	1b	4	0	0	0	10	1	0
Roseboro	c	4	0	1	0	6	0	0
Wills	ss	4	0	1	0	1	6	1
Podres	p	2	0	1	0	0	0	0
a Essegian		1	1	1	1	0	0	0
Fairly	rf	1	0	0	0	0	0	0
Totals		36	4	9	4	27	14	1

Pitching	IP	H	R	ER	BB	SO
Los Angeles						
Podres (W)	6	5	2	2	3	3
Sherry (SV)	3	3	1	1	0	1
Chicago						
Shaw (L)	6⅔	8	4	4	1	1
Lown	2⅓	1	0	0	1	3

L.A.	000	010	300
Chi.	200	000	010

Chicago	Pos	AB	R	H	RBI	PO	A	E
Aparicio	ss	5	1	2	0	3	1	0
Fox	2b	4	0	0	0	0	5	0
Landis	cf	3	1	0	0	2	0	0
Kluszewski	1b	4	0	1	1	9	0	0
b Torgeson	1b	0	1	0	0	0	0	0
Lollar	c	4	0	2	1	4	0	0
Smith	lf	3	0	1	1	2	0	0
Phillips	3b	3	0	1	0	2	0	0
c Goodman	3b	1	0	0	0	0	0	0
McAnany	rf	3	0	0	0	3	0	0
Rivera	rf	1	0	0	0	2	0	0
Shaw	p	3	0	1	0	0	1	0
Lown	p	0	0	0	0	0	0	0
d Cash		1	0	0	0	0	0	0
Totals		35	3	8	3	27	7	0

a Homered for Podres in 7th.
b Ran for Kluszewski in 8th.
c Struck out for Phillips in 8th.
d Grounded out for Lown in 9th.

Doubles—Aparicio, Phillips, Smith. Home Runs—Essegian, Neal 2. Stolen Bases—Gilliam, Moon. Left on Bases—Los Angeles 7, Chicago 8. Umpires—Dascoli, Hurley, Secory, Summers, Rice, Dixon. Attendance—47,368. Time of Game—2:21.

1st Inning
Los Angeles
1 Gilliam grounded back to the mound.
2 Neal lined to right.
Moon singled over second.
Moon stole second.
Snider singled off Shaw's glove, moving Moon to third.
3 Larker flied to right.
Chicago
Aparicio doubled down the right field line.
1 Fox flied to deep right, Aparicio advancing to third after the catch.
Landis walked.
2 Kluszewski grounded to second, scoring Aparicio with Landis going to second.
Lollar singled off Neal's glove into right, scoring Landis.
Smith safe at first when Wills fumbled his grounder, Lollar reaching second.
3 Phillips forced Lollar at third, Gilliam unassisted.

2nd Inning
Los Angeles
1 Hodges grounded to short.
2 Roseboro flied to center.
Wills singled to center.
Podres singled to center, advancing Wills to third.
3 Gilliam lined foul to Kluszewski.
Chicago
1 McAnany grounded to second.
2 Shaw took a called third strike.
Aparicio singled to left.
Fox walked.
3 Landis struck out.

3rd Inning
Los Angeles
1 Neal popped to Phillips at the mound.
2 Moon grounded to second.
3 Snider grounded to second.
Chicago
1 Kluszewski grounded to second.
2 Lollar struck out.
Smith walked.
3 Phillips forced Smith, Wills to Neal.

4th Inning
Los Angeles
1 Larker popped to third.
2 Hodges struck out.
Roseboro singled off Aparicio's glove.
3 Wills fouled to Aparicio behind third.
Chicago
1 McAnany grounded to third.
Shaw singled to right.
2 Aparicio flied to center.
3 Fox forced Shaw at second, Wills to Neal

5th Inning
Los Angeles
1 Podres flied to center.
2 Gilliam grounded to first.
Neal hit a home run into the lower left field stands.
3 Moon flied to left.
Chicago
1 Landis flied to right.
2 Kluszewski flied to right.
3 Lollar flied to left.

6th Inning
Los Angeles
1 Snider grounded to second.
2 Larker grounded to second.
3 Hodges popped to short.
Chicago
1 Smith grounded to short.
Phillips doubled inside the left field line.
2 McAnany flied to right, Phillips going to third after the catch.
3 Shaw grounded to short.

7th Inning
Los Angeles
1 Roseboro popped to short.
2 Wills grounded to second.
Essegian, pinch-hitting for Podres, hit a homer into the upper left field seats.
Gilliam walked.
Neal hit a two-run homer into the White Sox bullpen in center, his second homer of the game.
For Chicago—Lown came in to pitch.
Moon walked.
3 Snider flied to right.
Chicago
For Los Angeles—Sherry pitching (batting 5th), Fairly playing right (batting 9th) and Demeter playing center (batting 4th).
1 Aparicio popped to Wills in short center.
2 Fox grounded to first.
3 Landis bunted out, Sherry to Hodges.

8th Inning
Los Angeles
For Chicago—Rivera playing right.
1 Sherry struck out.
2 Hodges fouled to Smith.
3 Roseboro struck out.
Chicago
Kluszewski singled to center.
Lollar singled on a chopper that bounced off Gilliam's chest, moving Kluszewski to second.
Torgeson ran for Kluszewski.
Smith doubled to deep left-center,
1 scoring Torgeson but Lollar was out at the plate Moon to Wills to Roseboro with Smith taking third.
2 Goodman, pinch-hitting for Phillips, struck out.
3 Rivera fouled to Roseboro.

9th Inning
Los Angeles
For Chicago—Torgeson playing first and Goodman playing third.
1 Wills struck out, bunting foul on the third strike.
2 Fairly lined to right.
Gilliam singled to left.
Gilliam stole second.
3 Neal flied to right.
Chicago
1 Cash, pinch-hitting for Lown, grounded out Hodges to Sherry.
2 Aparicio grounded to short.
3 Fox grounded to second.

Game 3 October 4 at Los Angeles

Chicago	Pos	AB	R	H	RBI	PO	A	E
Aparicio	ss	4	0	2	0	0	3	0
Fox	2b	4	0	3	0	3	6	0
Landis	cf	5	0	1	0	2	0	0
Kluszewski	1b	3	1	1	0	11	1	0
Lollar	c	4	0	2	0	5	1	0
Goodman	3b	3	0	2	0	1	1	0
c Esposito	3b	0	0	0	0	0	0	0
Smith	lf	4	0	0	0	0	0	0
Rivera	rf	3	0	0	0	1	0	0
Donovan	p	3	0	1	0	1	1	0
Staley	p	0	0	0	0	0	0	0
d Cash		1	0	0	0	0	0	0
Totals		34	1	12	0	24	13	0

Pitching	IP	H	R	ER	BB	SO
Chicago						
Donovan (L)	6⅔	2	2	2	2	5
Staley	1⅓	3	1	1	0	0
Los Angeles						
Drysdale (W)	*7	11	1	1	4	5
Sherry (SV)	2	1	0	0	0	3

*Pitched to two batters in 8th.

Chi.	000	000	010
L.A.	000	000	21x

Los Angeles	Pos	AB	R	H	RBI	PO	A	E
Gilliam	3b	4	0	0	0	3	2	0
Neal	2b	4	1	2	1	3	2	0
Moon	rf	4	0	0	0	1	0	0
Larker	lf	2	1	0	0	1	0	0
Hodges	1b	2	0	1	0	6	1	0
Demeter	cf	2	0	0	0	0	0	0
a Furillo		1	0	1	2	0	0	0
b Fairly	cf	0	0	0	0	0	0	0
Roseboro	c	3	0	0	0	9	3	0
Wills	ss	3	1	1	0	3	2	0
Drysdale	p	2	0	0	0	1	1	0
Sherry	p	0	0	0	0	0	0	0
Totals		27	3	5	3	27	11	0

a Singled for Demeter in 7th.
b Ran for Furillo in 7th.
c Ran for Goodman in 8th.
d Struck out for Staley in 9th.

Double—Neal. Stolen Base—Landis. Sacrifice Hit—Sherry. Double Plays—Aparicio to Fox to Kluszewski, Roseboro to Neal, Gilliam to Neal to Hodges, Wills to Neal to Hodges. Hit by Pitcher—Goodman (by Sherry). Left on Bases—Chicago 11, Los Angeles 3. Umpires—Hurley, Secory, Summers, Dascoli, Dixon, Rice. Attendance—**92,394 (Series Record).** Time of Game—2:33.

1st Inning
Chicago
1 Aparicio called out on strikes.
Fox walked.
Landis singled to center, Fox going to third.
Kluszewski intentionally walked after a 3–0 count, loading the bases.
2 Lollar fouled to Gilliam.
3 Goodman grounded to first.
Los Angeles
1 Gilliam flied to Landis who made a great catch in right-center.
2 Neal lined to third.
3 Moon flied to center.

2nd Inning
Chicago
1 Smith lined to left.
Rivera walked.
2 Rivera caught stealing second, Roseboro to Wills.
Donovan singled off the left field screen.
Aparicio walked.
3 Fox grounded out, Hodges to Drysdale.
Los Angeles
1 Larker struck out.
Hodges singled to left.
2,3 Demeter grounded into a double play, Aparicio to Fox to Kluszewski.

3rd Inning
Chicago
1 Landis grounded back to the mound.
2 Kluszewski grounded to third.
Lollar singled to left-center.
Goodman singled off the left field screen, Lollar stopping at second.
3 Smith struck out.
Los Angeles
1 Roseboro bunted out to first.
2 Wills struck out.
3 Drysdale struck out.

4th Inning
Chicago
1 Rivera fouled to Gilliam
2 Donovan grounded to short.
Aparicio singled to center.
3 Aparicio caught stealing, Roseboro to Wills.
Los Angeles
1 Gilliam grounded to second.
2 Neal tapped back to the mound.
3 Moon grounded to second.

5th Inning
Chicago
Fox singled off the left field screen.
1,2 Landis struck out and Fox was caught trying for second, Roseboro to Neal.
3 Kluszewski fouled to Gilliam down the left field line.
Los Angeles
1 Larker grounded out, Kluszewski to Donovan covering first.
2 Hodges struck out.
3 Demeter grounded to third.

6th Inning
Chicago
1 Lollar flied to deep right.
Goodman singled off the left field screen.
2,3 Smith grounded into a double play, Gilliam to Neal to Hodges.
Los Angeles
1 Roseboro flied to Rivera in very deep right-center.
2 Wills grounded to second.
3 Drysdale fanned.

7th Inning
Chicago
1 Rivera lined to short.
2 Donovan called out on strikes.
Aparicio singled off the left field screen.
Fox singled to left, Aparicio stopping at second.
3 Landis struck out.
Los Angeles
1 Gilliam grounded to second.
Neal singled off the left field screen.
2 Moon grounded to second, moving Neal to second.
Larker walked.
Hodges walked, loading the bases.
For Chicago—Staley came in to pitch.
Furillo, pinch-hitting for Demeter, singled past short into center, Neal and Larker scoring with Hodges stopping at second.
Fairly ran for Furillo.
3 Roseboro lined to second.

8th Inning
Chicago
For Los Angeles—Fairly playing center.
Kluszewski singled past third.
Lollar singled on a fly to Moon, who lost the ball in the sun, Kluszewski moved to second.
For Los Angeles—Sherry now pitching.
Goodman was hit by a pitch, loading the bases.
Esposito in to run for Goodman.
1,2 Smith grounded into a double play, Wills to Neal to Hodges, as Kluszewski scored and Lollar went to third.
3 Rivera popped to the catcher.
Los Angeles
For Chicago—Esposito playing third.
Wills singled into right.
1 Sherry sacrificed Wills to second, Lollar to Fox covering first.
2 Gilliam grounded to short, Wills moving to third.
Neal doubled off Esposito's knee, scoring Wills.
3 Moon grounded to short.

9th Inning
Chicago
1 Cash, batting for Staley, struck out.
2 Aparicio took a called third strike.
Fox singled to center.
3 Landis struck out.

Game 4 October 5 at Los Angeles

Chi.	000	000	400
L.A.	004	000	01x

Chicago	Pos	AB	R	H	RBI	PO	A	E
Landis	cf	5	1	1	0	0	0	1
Aparicio	ss	3	0	1	0	0	2	1
Fox	2b	5	1	3	0	3	4	0
Kluszewski	1b	4	1	2	1	9	0	0
Lollar	c	4	1	1	3	6	2	0
Goodman	3b	4	0	0	0	0	0	0
Smith	lf	3	0	2	0	3	0	0
Rivera	rf	3	0	0	0	3	1	0
Wynn	p	1	0	0	0	0	1	0
Lown	p	0	0	0	0	0	0	0
a Cash		1	0	0	0	0	0	0
Pierce	p	0	0	0	0	0	0	1
c Torgeson		1	0	0	0	0	0	0
Staley	p	0	0	0	0	0	0	0
Totals		34	4	10	4	24	10	3

Los Angeles	Pos	AB	R	H	RBI	PO	A	E
Gilliam	3b	4	0	0	0	0	1	0
Neal	2b	4	0	0	0	4	4	0
Moon	rf-lf	4	1	2	0	3	0	0
Larker	lf	2	1	1	0	0	0	0
b Furillo	rf	1	0	0	0	0	0	0
Fairly	rf	1	0	0	0	0	0	0
Hodges	1b	4	2	2	2	10	0	0
Demeter	cf	3	1	2	0	1	0	0
Roseboro	c	3	0	1	1	7	0	0
Wills	ss	4	0	1	0	2	6	0
Craig	p	2	0	0	0	0	1	0
Sherry	p	0	0	0	0	0	0	0
Totals		32	5	9	3	27	12	0

Pitching	IP	H	R	ER	BB	SO
Chicago						
Wynn	$2\frac{2}{3}$	8	4	3	0	2
Lown	$\frac{1}{3}$	0	0	0	0	0
Pierce	3	0	0	0	1	2
Staley (L)	2	1	1	1	0	2
Los Angeles						
Craig	7	10	4	4	4	7
Sherry (W)	2	0	0	0	1	

a Struck out for Lown in 4th.
b Struck out for Larker in 5th.
c Grounded out for Pierce in 7th.

Double—Fox. Home Runs—Hodges, Lollar. Stolen Bases—Aparicio, Wills. Sacrifice Hits—Aparicio, Craig, Roseboro. Double Plays—Wills to Neal to Hodges, Neal to Wills to Hodges. Left on Bases—Chicago 9, Los Angeles 6. Passed Ball—Lollar. Umpires—Secory, Summers, Dascoli, Hurley, Dixon, Rice. Attendance—**92,650 (Series Record).** Time of Game—2:30.

1st Inning
Chicago
1 Landis flied to center.
Aparicio walked.
Aparicio stole second.
Fox blooped a Texas League double into short right, moving Aparicio to third.
Kluszewski intentionally walked, loading the bases.
2,3 Lollar grounded into a double play, Wills to Neal to Hodges.
Los Angeles
1 Gilliam popped to Fox in short right.
2 Neal bunted out, Lollar to Kluszewski.
Moon singled to center.
3 Larker called out on strikes.

2nd Inning
Chicago
1 Goodman struck out.
Smith singled between short and third.
2 Rivera flied to right.
3 Wynn popped to second.
Los Angeles
1 Hodges flied to left.
Demeter beat out a bouncer to deep short.
2 Roseboro flied to deep right, Demeter going to second after the catch.
Wills beat out a bouncer to short, Demeter advancing to third.
Wills stole second.
3 Craig struck out.

3rd Inning
Chicago
1 Landis grounded to short.
Aparicio singled to right.
Fox singled to deep short, Aparicio going to second.
2,3 Kluszewski grounded into a double play, Neal to Wills to Hodges.
Los Angeles
1 Gilliam popped to second.
2 Neal bounced out back to the mound.
Moon singled to left.
Larker singled to center, Moon racing to third. Moon scored and Larker went to second when Landis' throw to third hit Moon in the back.
Hodges singled into left, Larker scoring.
Demeter singled into center, moving Hodges to third.
Hodges scored and Demeter went to second on Lollar's passed ball.
Roseboro singled to short right, Demeter scoring. Roseboro went to second when Aparicio dropped Rivera's throw.
For Chicago—Lown now pitching.
3 Wills grounded to second.

4th Inning
Chicago
1 Lollar struck out.
2 Goodman called out on strikes.
Smith singled to left.
Rivera walked.
3 Cash, pinch-hitting for Lown, fanned.
Los Angeles
For Chicago—Pierce pitching.
1 Craig flied to right.
2 Gilliam grounded to short.
3 Neal grounded to second.

5th Inning
Chicago
1 Landis struck out.
2 Aparicio fouled to Hodges.
3 Fox struck out.
Los Angeles
1 Moon struck out.
2 Furillo, pinch-hitting for Larker, also struck out.
3 Hodges flied to left.

6th Inning
Chicago
For Los Angeles—Furillo playing right as Moon moved to left.
Kluszewski singled to right.
1 Lollar popped to Wills in short-left.
2 Goodman flied to Moon in front of the screen in left-center.
Smith walked.
3 Rivera popped to second.
Los Angeles
Demeter walked.
Roseboro sacrificed and was safe at first as Pierce fumbled the bunt.
1 Wills flied to left.
2 Craig sacrificed up both runners, Lollar to Fox covering first.
3 Gilliam popped to first.

7th Inning
Chicago
For Los Angeles—Fairly playing right.
1 Torgeson, pinch-hitting for Pierce, grounded to second.
Landis singled to center.
2 Aparicio sacrificed Landis to second, Craig to Hodges.
Fox singled off Craig's glove, moving Landis to third.
Kluszewski singled to center, Landis scoring with Fox going to third.
Lollar hit a three-run homer over the left field screen.
3 Goodman struck out.
Los Angeles
For Chicago—Staley pitching.
1 Neal grounded to short.
2 Moon grounded to second.
3 Fairly struck out.

8th Inning
Chicago
For Los Angeles—Sherry pitching.
1 Smith grounded to short.
2 Rivera grounded to second.
Staley walked.
3 Landis forced Staley at second, Gilliam to Neal.
Los Angeles
Hodges hit a home run into the left field stands.
1 Demeter struck out.
2 Roseboro flied to right.
3 Wills grounded to second.

9th Inning
Chicago
1 Aparicio grounded to short.
2 Fox grounded to short.
3 Kluszewski flied to left.

Game 5 October 6 at Los Angeles

Chi.	000	100	000
L.A.	000	000	000

Chicago	Pos	AB	R	H	RBI	PO	A	E
Aparicio	ss	4	0	2	0	3	5	0
Fox	2b	3	1	1	0	4	4	0
Landis	cf	4	0	1	0	2	0	0
Lollar	c	4	0	0	0	1	0	0
Kluszewski	1b	4	0	0	0	12	0	0
Smith	rf-lf	4	0	0	0	1	0	0
Phillips	3b	3	0	1	0	1	2	0
McAnany	lf	1	0	0	0	1	0	0
Rivera	rf	0	0	0	0	2	0	0
Shaw	p	1	0	0	0	0	3	0
Pierce	p	0	0	0	0	0	0	0
Donovan	p	0	0	0	0	0	0	0
Totals		28	1	5	0	27	14	0

Los Angeles	Pos	AB	R	H	RBI	PO	A	E
Gilliam	3b	5	0	4	0	0	3	0
Neal	2b	5	0	1	0	5	2	0
Moon	rf-cf	4	0	1	0	0	0	0
Larker	lf	4	0	0	0	3	1	0
Hodges	1b	4	0	3	0	7	1	0
Demeter	cf	3	0	0	0	4	0	0
e Fairly		0	0	0	0	0	0	0
f Repulski	rf	0	0	0	0	0	0	0
Roseboro	c	3	0	0	0	6	1	0
g Furillo		1	0	0	0	0	0	0
Pignatano	c	0	0	0	0	1	0	0
Wills	ss	2	0	0	0	1	2	0
a Essegian		0	0	0	0	0	0	0
b Zimmer	ss	1	0	0	0	0	1	0
Koufax	p	2	0	0	0	0	0	0
c Snider		1	0	0	0	0	0	0
d Podres		0	0	0	0	0	0	0
Williams	p	0	0	0	0	0	0	0
h Sherry		1	0	0	0	0	0	0
Totals		36	0	9	0	27	11	0

Pitching	IP	H	R	ER	BB	SO
Chicago						
Shaw (W)	$7\frac{1}{3}$	9	0	0	1	1
Pierce	*0	0	0	0	1	0
Donovan (SV)	$1\frac{2}{3}$	0	0	0	0	0
Los Angeles						
Koufax (L)	7	5	1	1	1	6
Williams	2	0	0	0	2	1

*Pitched to one batter in 8th.

a Walked for Wills in 7th.
b Ran for Essegian in 7th.
c Hit into force play for Koufax in 7th.
d Ran for Snider in 7th.
e Announced for Demeter in 8th.
f Intentionally walked for Fairly in 8th.
g Popped out for Roseboro in 8th.
h Grounded out for Williams in 9th.

Triple—Hodges. Stolen Base—Gilliam. Sacrifice Hits—Shaw 2. Double Play—Neal to Hodges. Wild Pitch—Shaw. Left on Bases—Chicago 5, Los Angeles 11. Umpires—Summers, Dascoli, Hurley, Secori, Pixon, Rice. Attendance—**92,706 (Series Record).** Time of Game—2:28.

1st Inning
Chicago
1 Aparicio took a called third strike.
2 Fox popped to short.
3 Landis struck out.
Los Angeles
Gilliam singled to right-center.
1 Neal fouled to Aparicio who made a good running catch at the third base boxes, Gilliam taking second after the catch.
2 Moon grounded to the mound as Gilliam held second.
3 Larker grounded back to the mound.

2nd Inning
Chicago
1 Lollar grounded to third.
2 Kluszewski flied to short left.
3 Smith flied to left.
Los Angeles
1 Hodges popped to Aparicio behind second.
2 Demeter grounded to third.
3 Roseboro grounded to second.

3rd Inning
Chicago
Phillips singled off the left field screen.
1 McAnany popped to first.
2 Shaw sacrificed Phillips to second, Roseboro to Neal.
Aparicio singled to left, Phillips stopping at third but Aparicio was
3 out trying for second, Larker to Gilliam to Neal.
Los Angeles
1 Wills grounded to short.
2 Koufax grounded to short.
Gilliam singled to right.
Neal singled off the left field screen, Gilliam going to third.
3 Moon forced Neal at second, Fox unassisted.

4th Inning
Chicago
Fox singled to right.
Landis singled to right-center, Fox advancing to third.
1,2 Lollar grounded in to a double play, Neal to Hodges, Fox scoring.
3 Kluszewski flied to deep center.
Los Angeles
1 Larker flied to Landis in left-center.
Hodges tripled to the right-center field fence.
2 Demeter tapped back to the mound as Hodges held third.
3 Roseboro popped to Aparicio in short left.

5th Inning
Chicago
1 Smith struck out.
2 Phillips grounded to short.
McAnany walked.
3 Shaw struck out.
Los Angeles
1 Wills grounded to second.
2 Koufax struck out.
Gilliam singled through the middle.
Gilliam stole second.
3 Neal popped to Fox in short right.

6th Inning
Chicago
Aparicio singled to center.
1 Fox flied to center.
2 Landis called out on strikes.
3 Lollar forced Aparicio at second, Wills to Neal.
Los Angeles
1 Moon grounded to second.
2 Larker flied to center.
Hodges singled off the left field screen.
3 Demeter forced Hodges at second, Aparicio to Fox.

7th Inning
Chicago
1 Kluszewski flied to left.
2 Smith struck out.
3 Phillips flied to center.
Los Angeles
1 Roseboro flied to left.
Essegian, pinch-hitting for Wills, walked.
Zimmer ran for Essegian.
2 Snider, pinch-hitting for Koufax, forced Zimmer at second, Aparicio to Fox.
Podres ran for Snider.
Gilliam singled off the left field screen, Podres holding up at second.
For Chicago—Smith went to left, and Rivera came in to play right.
Podres went to third and Gilliam to second on Shaw's wild pitch.
3 Neal flied to Rivera in right-center.

8th Inning
Chicago
For Los Angeles—Williams pitching and Zimmer playing short.
Rivera walked.
1 Shaw sacrificed, Hodges to Neal.
2 Aparicio grounded to second, sending Rivera to third. Fox walked.
3 Landis flied to deep center.
Los Angeles
Moon singled to center as Landis lost the ball.
1 Larker flied to right.
Hodges singled to center, advancing Moon to third, and took second on Landis' throw to third.
Fairly announced as batting for Demeter.
For Chicago—Pierce pitching.
Repulski, batted for Fairly, and got an intentional pass, loading the bases.
Furillo, pinch-hitting for Roseboro.
For Chicago—Donovan came in to pitch.
2 Furillo popped to third.
3 Zimmer flied to left.

9th Inning
Chicago
For Los Angeles—Pignatano catching, Repulski playing right and Moon shifting to center.
1 Lollar took a called third strike.
2 Kluszewski grounded to third.
3 Smith grounded to short.
Los Angeles
1 Sherry, pinch-hitting for Williams, grounded to third.
2 Gilliam grounded to second.
3 Neal grounded to short.

Game 6 October 8 at Chicago

L.A.	0 0 2	6 0 0	0 0 1
Chi.	0 0 0	3 0 0	0 0 0

Los Angeles	Pos	AB	R	H	RBI	PO	A	E
Gilliam	3b	4	1	0	0	0	2	0
Neal	2b	5	1	3	2	4	4	0
Moon	lf	4	2	1	2	3	0	0
Snider	cf-rf	3	1	1	2	2	0	0
e Essegian		1	1	1	1	0	0	0
Fairly	rf	0	0	0	0	0	0	0
Hodges	1b	5	0	1	0	10	0	0
Larker	rf	1	0	1	0	0	0	0
a Demeter	cf	3	1	1	0	4	0	0
Roseboro	c	4	0	0	0	2	0	0
Wills	ss	4	1	1	1	2	3	0
Podres	p	2	1	1	1	0	1	0
Sherry	p	2	0	2	0	0	2	0
Totals		38	9	13	9	27	12	0

Pitching	IP	H	R	ER	BB	SO
Los Angeles						
Podres	3⅓	2	3	3	3	1
Sherry (W)	5⅔	4	0	0	1	1
Chicago						
Wynn (L)	3⅓	5	5	5	3	2
Donovan	*0	2	3	3	1	0
Lown	⅓	1	0	0	0	0
Staley	3	2	0	0	0	0
Pierce	1	2	0	0	0	0
Moore	1	1	1	1	0	1

*Pitched to three batters in 4th.

Chicago	Pos	AB	R	H	RBI	PO	A	E
Aparicio	ss	5	0	1	0	1	2	1
Fox	2b	4	0	1	0	2	2	0
Landis	cf	3	1	1	0	2	0	0
Lollar	c	3	1	0	0	5	2	0
Kluszewski	1b	4	1	2	3	10	0	0
Smith	lf	2	0	0	0	2	0	0
Phillips	3b-rf	4	0	1	0	3	1	0
McAnany	rf	1	0	0	0	1	0	0
b Goodman	3b	3	0	0	0	0	1	0
Wynn	p	1	0	0	0	0	1	0
Donovan	p	0	0	0	0	0	0	0
Lown	p	0	0	0	0	0	0	0
c Torgeson		0	0	0	0	0	0	0
Staley	p	0	0	0	0	1	0	0
d Romano		1	0	0	0	0	0	0
Pierce	p	0	0	0	0	0	0	0
Moore	p	0	0	0	0	0	0	0
f Cash		1	0	0	0	0	0	0
Totals		32	3	6	3	27	9	1

a Ran for Larker in 4th.
b Struck out for McAnany 4th.
c Walked for Lown in 4th.
d Grounded out for Staley in 7th.
e Homered for Snider in 9th.
f Flied out for Moore in 9th.

Doubles—Fox, Kluszewski, Neal, Podres.
Home Runs—Essegian, Kluszewski, Moon, Snider. Sacrifice Hit—Roseboro.
Double Play—Podres to Neal to Hodges.
Hit by Pitcher—Landis (by Podres).
Left on Bases—Los Angeles 7, Chicago 7.
Umpires—Dascoli, Hurley, Secory, Summers, Rice, Dixon.
Attendance—47,653. Time of Game—2:33.

1st Inning
Los Angeles
1 Gilliam took a called third strike.
  Neal singled to center.
2 Moon flied to deep center.
  Snider walked.
3 Hodges forced Snider at second, Phillips to Fox
Chicago
1 Aparicio grounded to second.
2 Fox lined to left.
  Landis beat out a roller to third.
3 Lollar forced Landis, Wills to Neal.

2nd Inning
Los Angeles
  Larker walked.
1 Roseboro flied to right.
2 Wills grounded to second, moving Larker to second.
3 Podres flied to center.
Chicago
1 Kluszewski grounded to second.
  Smith walked.
2,3 Phillips hit into a double play, Podres to Neal to Hodges.

3rd Inning
Los Angeles
1 Gilliam flied to left.
2 Neal struck out.
  Moon walked.
  Snider hit a two-run homer into the lower stands in left-center.
3 Hodges popped to second.
Chicago
1 McAnany popped to Neal in short right.
2 Wynn struck out.
3 Aparicio grounded to short.

4th Inning
Los Angeles
  Larker singled to center.
  Demeter ran for Larker.
1 Roseboro sacrificed Demeter to second, Wynn to Kluszewski.
  Wills singled to center, scoring Demeter.
  Podres doubled off the center field fence, Wills scoring.
  For Chicago—Donovan came in to pitch.
  Gilliam walked.
  Neal doubled to right-center, both Podres and Gilliam scored.
  Moon hit a two-run homer into the lower stands in right-center.
  For Chicago—Lown now pitching.
2 Snider grounded to first.
  Hodges singled past the mound and got to second on Aparicio's low throw to first.
3 Demeter grounded to second.
Chicago
  For Los Angeles—Demeter playing center, Snider switched to right.
1 Fox fouled to Wills behind third base.
  Landis was hit by a pitch.
  Lollar walked.
  Kluszewski hit a three-run homer into the upper right field stands. **(A new 6 game RBI record of 10).**
  Smith walked.
  For Los Angeles—Sherry pitching (his 4th appearance as a pitcher).
  Phillips singled to left-center, Smith going to third.
2 Goodman, pinch-hitting for McAnany, struck out.
  Torgeson, batting for Lown, walked loading the sacks.
3 Aparicio popped to short.

5th Inning
Los Angeles
  For Chicago—Staley pitching, Goodman at third, and Phillips switched to right.
1 Roseboro flied to right. Phillips made a good leaping catch in the corner.
2 Wills grounded to third.
  Sherry singled to left-center.
3 Gilliam lined to right.
Chicago
  Fox doubled just inside the first baseline.
1 Landis flied to short right.
2 Lollar flied to center.
3 Kluszewski grounded to first.

6th Inning
Los Angeles
1 Neal popped to first.
2 Moon out on a bunt, tagged by Staley.
3 Snider tapped out, Lollar to Kluszewski.
Chicago
1 Smith grounded to second.
2 Phillips flied to center.
3 Goodman flied to center.

7th Inning
Los Angeles
1 Hodges grounded to short.
  Demeter singled to center.
2 Roseboro flied to right.
3 Demeter caught stealing, Lollar to Aparicio.
Chicago
1 Romano, pinch-hitting for Staley, grounded to short.
  Aparicio singled to left.
2 Fox lined to left.
3 Landis forced Aparicio at second, Gilliam to Neal.

8th Inning
Los Angeles
  For Chicago—Pierce pitching.
1 Wills grounded to first.
  Sherry singled to left.
2 Gilliam lined to left.
  Neal singled to right, Sherry stopping at second.
3 Moon struck out.
Chicago
1 Lollar flied to center.
  Kluszewski doubled into the left field corner.
2 Smith grounded to third, as Kluszewski held second.
3 Phillips grounded out, Sherry to Hodges.

9th Inning
Los Angeles
  For Chicago—Moore pitching.
  Essegian, pinch-hitting for Snider, homered into the lower left field stands.
1 Hodges grounded to short.
2 Demeter struck out.
3 Roseboro fouled to Lollar.
Chicago
  For Los Angeles—Fairly playing right.
1 Goodman grounded to the mound.
2 Cash, pinch-hitting for Moore, lined to center.
3 Aparicio flied to left.

1959 WORLD SERIES COMPOSITE BOX

	Wins	Composite Line Score									
Los Angeles Dodgers (N.L.)	4	0	0	6	6	1	0	5	2	1	- 21
Chicago White Sox (A.L.)	2	4	0	7	6	0	0	4	2	0	- 23

	Regular Season			
Manager	W	L	Pct.	G. Ahead
Walt Alston	88	68	.564	Won playoff over Milwaukee
Al Lopez	94	60	.610	5

BATTING AND FIELDING

LOS ANGELES DODGERS

	WORLD SERIES STATISTICS																
	Pos	G	AB	R	H	2B	3B	HR	RBI	BB	SO	SB	BA	SA	PO	A	E
Gil Hodges	1b	6	23	2	9	0	1	1	2	1	2	0	.391	.609	53	3	0
Charlie Neal	2b	6	27	4	10	2	0	2	6	0	1	1	.370	.667	18	19	1
Maury Wills	ss	6	20	2	5	0	0	0	1	0	3	1	.250	.250	10	21	1
Jim Gilliam	3b	6	25	2	6	0	0	0	0	2	2	2	.240	.240	4	10	0
Norm Larker	rf-1f	6	16	2	3	0	0	0	0	2	3	0	.188	.188	12	1	0
Don Demeter	cf-pr	6	12	2	3	0	0	0	0	1	3	0	.250	.250	9	0	0
Wally Moon	1f-rf-cf	6	23	3	6	0	0	1	2	2	2	1	.261	.391	10	1	0
Johnny Roseboro	c	6	21	0	2	0	0	0	1	0	2	0	.095	.095	35	4	0
Duke Snider	cf-rf-ph	4	10	1	2	0	0	1	2	2	0	0	.200	.500	5	0	2
Carl Furillo	ph-rf	4	4	0	1	0	0	0	2	0	1	0	.250	.250	0	0	0
Ron Fairly	ph-rf-pr-cf	6	3	0	0	0	0	0	0	0	1	0	.000	.000	0	0	0
Don Zimmer	pr-ss	1	1	0	0	0	0	0	0	0	0	0	.000	.000	0	1	0
Joe Pignatano	c	1	0	0	0	0	0	0	0	0	0	0	—	—	1	0	0
Chuck Essegian	ph	4	3	2	2	0	0	2	2	1	1	0	.667	2.667			
Rip Repulski	ph-rf	1	0	0	0	0	0	0	0	1	0	0	.000	.000	0	0	0
Larry Sherry	p-ph	5	4	0	2	0	0	0	0	0	1	0	.500	.500	1	3	0
Johnny Podres	p-pr	3	4	1	2	1	0	0	1	0	0	0	.500	.750	0	1	0
Roger Craig	p	2	3	0	0	0	0	0	0	0	2	0	.000	.000	0	2	0
Sandy Koufax	p	2	2	0	0	0	0	0	0	0	1	0	.000	.000	0	0	0
Don Drysdale	p	1	2	0	0	0	0	0	0	0	2	0	.000	.000	1	1	0
Chuck Churn	p	1	0	0	0	0	0	0	0	0	0	0	—	—	0	1	0
Johnny Klippstein	p	1	0	0	0	0	0	0	0	0	0	0	—	—	0	1	0
Clem Labine	p	1	0	0	0	0	0	0	0	0	0	0	—	—	0	0	0
Stan Williams	p	1	0	0	0	0	0	0	0	0	0	0	—	—	0	0	0
Danny McDevitt		Did not play															
team total		6	203	21	53	3	1	7	19	12	27	5	.261	.389	159	69	4

Double Plays—7
Left on Bases—42

		REGULAR SEASON STATISTICS												
		Main Pos	G	AB	R	H	2B	3B	HR	RBI	BB	SO	SB	BA	SA
Gil Hodges		1b	124	413	57	114	19	2	25	80	58	92	3	.276	.513
Charlie Neal		2b	151	616	103	177	30	11	19	83	43	86	17	.287	.464
Maury Wills		ss	83	242	27	63	5	2	0	7	13	27	7	.260	.298
Jim Gilliam		3b	145	553	91	156	18	4	3	34	96	25	23	.282	.345
Norm Larker		1b	108	311	37	90	14	1	8	49	26	25	0	.289	.418
Don Demeter		of	139	371	55	95	11	1	18	70	16	87	5	.256	.437
Wally Moon		of	145	543	93	164	26	11	19	74	81	64	15	.302	.495
Johnny Roseboro		c	118	397	39	92	14	7	10	38	52	69	7	.232	.378
Duke Snider		of	126	370	59	114	11	2	23	88	58	71	1	.308	.535
Carl Furillo		ph-of	50	93	8	27	4	0	0	13	7	11	0	.290	.333
Ron Fairly		of	118	244	27	58	12	1	4	23	31	29	0	.238	.344
Don Zimmer		ss	97	249	21	41	7	1	4	28	37	56	3	.165	.249
Joe Pignatano		c	52	139	17	33	4	1	1	11	21	15	1	.237	.302
Chuck Essegian	a	ph-of	24	46	6	14	6	0	1	5	4	11	0	.304	.500
Rip Repulski		of	53	94	11	24	4	0	2	14	13	23	0	.255	.362
Larry Sherry		p	23	32	3	7	0	0	2	5	1	6	0	.219	.406
Johnny Podres		p	34	65	4	16	1	0	0	4	6	13	0	.246	.262
Roger Craig		p	29	52	1	3	0	0	0	3	1	28	0	.058	.058
Sandy Koufax		p	35	54	3	6	3	0	0	0	2	29	0	.111	.167
Don Drysdale		p	46	91	9	15	1	1	4	12	4	31	0	.165	.330
Chuck Churn		p	14	6	1	1	1	0	0	0	0	3	0	.167	.333
Johnny Klippstein		p	28	7	0	1	0	0	0	0	0	2	0	.143	.143
Clem Labine		p	56	16	1	0	0	0	0	0	0	9	0	.000	.000
Stan Williams		p	35	36	3	7	0	0	0	3	3	15	0	.194	.194
Danny McDevitt		p	39	46	4	5	1	0	0	3	0	17	0	.109	.130
team total			156	5282	705	1360	196	46	148	667	591	891	84	.257	.396

a—from St. Louis
Bob Lillis (ss), Dick Gray (3b), Jim Baxes (3b), Frank Howard (of), Solly Drake (of), Sandy Amoros (ph), Norm Sherry (c), Tommy Davis (ph), Art Fowler (p), Gene Snyder (p), Carl Erskine (p), Fred Kipp (p), and Bill Harris (p) also played for the Dodgers during the season.

CHICAGO WHITE SOX

	WORLD SERIES STATISTICS																
	Pos	G	AB	R	H	2B	3B	HR	RBI	BB	SO	SB	BA	SA	PO	A	E
Ted Kluszewski	1b	6	23	5	9	1	0	3	10	2	0	0	.391	.826	59	3	0
Nellie Fox	2b	6	24	4	9	3	0	0	0	4	1	0	.375	.500	14	23	0
Luis Aparicio	ss	6	26	1	8	1	0	0	0	2	3	1	.308	.346	10	16	2
Billy Goodman	3b-ph	5	13	1	3	0	0	0	1	0	5	0	.231	.231	1	2	0
Jim Rivera	rf	5	11	1	0	0	0	0	0	3	1	0	.000	.000	10	1	0
Jim Landis	cf	6	24	6	7	0	0	0	1	1	7	1	.292	.292	9	0	1
Al Smith	lf-rf	6	20	1	5	3	0	1	1	4	4	0	.250	.400	10	0	0
Sherm Lollar	c	6	22	3	5	0	0	1	5	1	3	0	.227	.364	28	5	0
Bubba Phillips	3b-rf	3	10	0	3	1	0	0	0	0	0	0	.300	.400	6	3	0
Jim McAnany	rf-1f	3	5	0	0	0	0	0	0	1	0	0	.000	.000	5	0	0
Earl Torgeson	pr-1b-ph	3	1	1	0	0	0	0	0	1	0	0	.000	.000	0	0	0
Sammy Esposito	3b-pr	2	2	0	0	0	0	0	0	0	1	0	.000	.000	1	0	0
Norm Cash	ph	4	4	0	0	0	0	0	0	0	2	0	.000	.000			
Johnny Romano	ph	1	1	0	0	0	0	0	0	0	0	0	.000	.000			
Earl Battey		Did not play															
Early Wynn	p	3	5	0	1	1	0	0	1	0	2	0	.200	.400	1	3	0
Bob Shaw	p	2	4	0	1	0	0	0	0	0	2	0	.250	.250	0	4	0
Dick Donovan	p	3	3	0	1	0	0	0	0	0	1	0	.333	.333	1	1	0
Gerry Staley	p	4	1	0	0	0	0	0	0	1	1	0	.000	.000	1	1	0
Turk Lown	p	3	0	0	0	0	0	0	0	0	0	0	—	—	0	0	0
Billy Pierce	p	3	0	0	0	0	0	0	0	0	0	0	—	—	0	0	1
Ray Moore	p	1	0	0	0	0	0	0	0	0	0	0	—	—	0	0	0
Barry Latman		Did not play															
Rudy Arias		Did not play															
Ken McBride		Did not play															
team total		6	199	23	52	10	0	4	19	20	33	2	.261	.372	156	62	4

Double Plays—2
Left on Bases—43

		REGULAR SEASON STATISTICS												
		Main Pos	G	AB	R	H	2B	3B	HR	RBI	BB	SO	SB	BA	SA
Ted Kluszewski	b	1b	31	101	11	30	2	1	2	10	9	10	0	.297	.396
Nellie Fox		2b	156	624	84	191	34	6	2	70	71	13	5	.306	.389
Luis Aparicio		ss	152	612	98	157	18	5	8	51	52	40	56	.257	.332
Billy Goodman		3b	104	268	21	67	14	1	1	28	19	20	3	.250	.321
Jim Rivera		of	80	177	18	39	9	4	4	19	11	19	5	.220	.384
Jim Landis		of	149	515	76	140	26	7	5	60	78	68	20	.272	.379
Al Smith		of	129	472	65	112	16	4	17	51	46	74	7	.237	.396
Sherm Lollar		c	140	505	63	134	22	3	22	84	55	49	4	.265	.451
Bubba Phillips		3b	117	379	43	100	27	1	5	40	27	28	1	.264	.380
Jim McAnany		of	67	210	22	58	9	3	0	27	19	26	2	.276	.348
Earl Torgeson		1b	127	277	40	61	5	3	9	45	62	55	7	.220	.357
Sammy Esposito		3b	69	66	12	11	1	0	1	5	11	16	0	.167	.227
Norm Cash		1b-ph	58	104	16	25	0	1	4	16	18	9	1	.240	.375
Johnny Romano		c	53	126	20	37	5	1	5	25	23	18	0	.294	.468
Earl Battey		c	26	64	9	14	1	2	2	7	8	13	0	.219	.391
Early Wynn		p	37	90	11	22	7	0	2	8	9	18	0	.244	.389
Bob Shaw		p	47	73	7	9	1	0	0	2	5	19	0	.123	.137
Dick Donovan		p	31	61	4	8	4	0	1	5	5	32	0	.131	.246
Gerry Staley		p	67	13	2	2	0	0	0	0	3	5	0	.154	.154
Turk Lown		p	60	12	1	3	0	0	0	0	1	3	0	.250	.250
Billy Pierce		p	34	68	3	13	1	2	0	7	7	13	0	.191	.265
Ray Moore		p	29	23	0	2	1	0	0	0	1	11	0	.087	.130
Barry Latman		p	37	47	3	6	1	0	0	6	4	4	0	.128	.149
Rudy Arias			34	4	0	0	0	0	0	0	0	2	0	.000	.000
Ken McBride		p	11	6	0	1	0	0	0	0	0	2	0	.167	.167
team total			156	5297	669	1325	220	46	97	620	580	634	113	.250	.364

b—from Pittsburgh (N.L.)
Johnny Callison (of), Harry Simpson (ph), Del Ennis (of), Larry Doby (of), Ron Jackson (1b), Ray Boone (1b), Lou Skizas (of), Joe Hicks (of), Don Mueller (ph), J.C. Martin (3b), Cam Carreon (c), Joe Stanka (p), Don Rudolph (p), Claude Raymond (p), and Gary Peters (p) also played for the White Sox during the season.

PITCHING

LOS ANGELES DODGERS

	WORLD SERIES STATISTICS											
	G	GS	CG	IP	H	R	ER	BB	SO	W	L	SV	ERA
Larry Sherry	4	0	0	12⅔	8	1	1	2	5	2	0	2	0.71
Johnny Podres	2	2	0	9⅓	7	5	5	6	4	1	0	0	4.82
Roger Craig	2	2	0	9⅓	15	9	9	5	8	0	1	0	8.68
Sandy Koufax	2	1	0	9	5	1	1	1	7	0	1	0	1.00
Don Drysdale	1	1	0	7	11	1	1	4	5	1	0	0	1.29
Stan Williams	1	0	0	2	0	0	0	2	1	0	0	0	0.00
Johnny Klippstein	1	0	0	2	1	0	0	0	2	0	0	0	0.00
Clem Labine	1	0	0	1	0	0	0	0	1	0	0	0	0.00
Chuck Churn	1	0	0	⅔	5	6	2	0	0	0	0	0	27.00
Danny McDevitt	Did not play												
team total	6	6	0	53	52	23	19	20	33	4	2	2	3.23

	REGULAR SEASON STATISTICS												
	G	GS	CG	IP	H	ER	BB	SO	W	L	Pct	SV	ShO	ERA
Larry Sherry	23	9	1	94	75	23	43	72	7	2	.778	3	1	2.19
Johnny Podres	34	29	6	195	192	89	74	145	14	9	.609	0	2	4.11
Roger Craig	29	17	7	153	122	35	45	76	11	5	.688	0	4	2.06
Sandy Koufax	35	23	6	153	136	69	92	173	8	6	.571	2	1	4.06
Don Drysdale	44	36	15	271	237	104	93	242	17	13	.567	2	4	3.45
Stan Williams	35	15	2	125	102	55	86	89	5	5	.500	0	0	3.96
Johnny Klippstein	28	0	0	46	48	30	33	30	4	0	.000	2	0	5.87
Clem Labine	56	0	0	85	91	37	25	37	5	10	.333	9	0	3.92
Chuck Churn	14	0	0	31	28	17	10	24	3	2	.600	1	0	4.94
Danny McDevitt	39	22	6	145	149	64	51	106	10	8	.556	4	2	3.97
team total	156	156	43	1412	1317	595	614	1077	88	68	.564	26	14	3.79

CHICAGO WHITE SOX

	WORLD SERIES STATISTICS											
	G	GS	CG	IP	H	R	ER	BB	SO	W	L	SV	ERA
Bob Shaw	2	2	0	14	17	4	4	2	2	1	1	0	2.57
Early Wynn	3	3	0	13	19	9	8	4	10	1	1	0	5.54
Gerry Staley	4	0	0	8⅓	8	2	2	0	3	0	1	1	2.16
Dick Donovan	3	1	0	8⅓	4	5	5	3	5	0	1	1	5.40
Billy Pierce	3	0	0	4	2	0	0	2	3	0	0	0	0.00
Turk Lown	3	0	0	3⅓	2	0	0	1	3	0	0	0	0.00
Ray Moore	1	0	0	1	1	1	1	0	1	0	0	0	9.00
Barry Latman	Did not play												
Rudy Arias	Did not play												
Ken McBride	Did not play												
team total	6	6	0	52	53	21	20	12	27	2	4	2	3.46

	REGULAR SEASON STATISTICS												
	G	GS	CG	IP	H	ER	BB	SO	W	L	Pct	SV	ShO	ERA
Bob Shaw	47	26	8	231	217	69	54	89	18	6	.750	3	3	2.69
Early Wynn	37	37	14	256	202	90	119	179	22	10	.688	0	5	3.16
Gerry Staley	67	0	0	116	111	29	25	54	8	5	.615	14	0	2.25
Dick Donovan	31	29	5	180	171	23	58	71	9	10	.474	0	1	3.65
Billy Pierce	34	33	12	224	217	90	62	114	14	15	.483	0	2	3.62
Turk Lown	60	0	0	93	73	30	42	63	9	2	.818	15	0	2.90
Ray Moore	29	8	0	90	86	41	46	49	3	6	.333	0	0	4.10
Barry Latman	37	21	5	156	138	65	72	97	8	5	.615	0	2	3.75
Rudy Arias	34	0	0	44	49	20	20	28	2	0	1.000	2	0	4.09
Ken McBride	11	2	0	23	20	08	17	12	0	1	.000	1	0	3.13
team total	156	156	44	1425	1297	521	525	761	94	60	.610	36	13	3.29

Total Attendance—420,784 Average Attendance—70,131 Winning Player's Share—$11,231 Losing Player's Share—$7,275

1960
Mazeroski's Capper

The Pittsburgh Pirates hadn't made it to the World Series since 1927, when the New York Yankees of Babe Ruth and Lou Gehrig blew them out in four straight games. The batting muscle of the Yankees didn't change much over the years, as the New Yorkers set new Series records with 55 runs scored, 91 hits, 27 extra-base hits, and a .338 team-batting average. The only difference was that the Pirates this time won the Championship in seven games.

The two clubs came into the classic rated even. The Pirates, managed by Danny Murtaugh, featured Roberto Clemente, Dick Groat, Bill Mazeroski, and pitchers Vernon Law and Bob Friend. Casey Stengel's Yankees rebounded into first place after missing out in 1959. This squad featured newly acquired Roger Maris, Mickey Mantle, Bill Skowron, and a lackluster pitching staff led by Whitey Ford. Stengel chose Art Ditmar to pitch the first game against Law, but Pittsburgh scored three times in the bottom of the first to spark a 6–4 victory. The traditional Yankee power, however, came out in the second game. Pirate starter Friend left for a pinch hitter trailing 3–0 in the fourth, and then the Yankee batters feasted, smashing five relievers and rolling to a 16–3 laugher.

In game three at Yankee Stadium, the Yanks blasted away for six runs in the first inning, the unlikely knockout punch coming on a grand-slam homer by little Bobby Richardson, the smooth second baseman with only one homer for the season. Richardson singled in two more runs in the fourth inning, and Ford coasted to a four-hit 10–0 win. After two such pulverizing losses, the Pirates battled back in game four. Bill Skowron gave the Yanks a 1–0 lead with a fourth-inning homer, but the Bucs scored three times in the fifth, with pitcher Law doubling in one run and Bill Virdon singling in two. When the Yanks scored a run in the seventh, Murtaugh brought in Roy Face to protect the 3–2 lead the rest of the way. With the Series even, Stengel brought back 15-game-winner Ditmar against lefty Harvey Haddix in game five. The Pirates kayoed Ditmar, tallying three times in the second inning to ignite a 5–2 victory.

On the edge of elimination, Stengel turned to his money pitcher, Whitey Ford, while Murtaugh called on hardworking Bob Friend in the sixth game at Forbes Field. Fans hoping to see the Pirates wrap up the Series instead saw another New York massacre, with the Yanks drumming out a 12–0 win behind Ford's seven-hitter. That put the title on the line on October 13 at Forbes Field in one of the most dramatic seventh games in history, with Bob Turley and Vernon Law on the mound. A two-run homer by Rocky Nelson in the first and a two-run single by Virdon in the second kayoed Turley and staked Law to a 4–0 lead. The Yanks made it 4–1 in the fifth on a Skowron homer, then took a 5–4 lead in the sixth. Face relieved Law after two men reached base, but the little reliever gave up a run-scoring single to Mantle and a three-run homer to Yogi Berra. Two more runs in the top of the eighth ran the lead up to 7–4 and gave the Yanks the look of a winner. But Gino Cimoli led off the Pittsburgh eighth with a pinch single off Bobby Shantz, and then Virdon hit a hard grounder to shortstop which took a bad hop and hit Tony Kubek in the throat, spoiling a sure double play. Groat's single then scored Cimoli and brought tall Jim Coates into the game as the new Yankee pitcher. Coates retired Bob Skinner and Nelson, but he was slow covering first on Clemente's infield hit which cut the score to 7–6. Reserve catcher Hal Smith then made his first plate appearance of the day and sent the fans into delirium with a three-run homer to put the Bucs ahead 9–7. Stengel brought in Terry to get the final out, and the Yanks then came back in their final turn at bat. Friend came in to try and get the final three outs, but left quickly after giving up two singles. Haddix then came in, retired Maris, and gave up a run-scoring single to Mantle. Berra then drilled the ball down the first-base line; Nelson speared it, stepped on the bag, and turned to throw the ball to second for the game-ending double play. But with the force play removed, Mantle instead dove back into second base, and the tying run crossed the plate. Both clubs had now come from behind only to blow leads, but the Bucs took a final 10–9 edge when Bill Mazeroski rocketed Terry's second pitch in the bottom of the ninth over the ivy-covered wall in left. As Mazeroski circled the bases pursued by enthusiastic fans, the Yanks could only shake their heads. The Series loss ended the regime of manager Casey Stengel, who was discharged presumably for his advanced age.

Game 1 October 5 at Pittsburgh

| N.Y. | 1 0 0 | 1 0 0 | 0 0 2 |
| Pit. | 3 0 0 | 2 0 1 | 0 0 x |

New York	Pos	AB	R	H	RBI	PO	A	E
Kubek	ss	5	0	3	0	2	4	1
Lopez	lf	5	0	1	0	1	0	0
Maris	rf	4	2	3	1	3	0	0
Mantle	cf	3	0	0	0	3	0	0
Berra	c	4	0	1	0	4	1	0
Skowron	1b	4	0	2	1	9	0	0
Boyer	3b	0	0	0	0	0	0	0
a Long		1	0	0	0	0	0	0
McDougald	3b	3	0	1	0	1	1	0
Richardson	2b	4	1	0	0	2	2	1
Ditmar	p	0	0	0	0	0	0	0
Coates	p	1	0	0	0	0	0	0
b Blanchard		1	0	0	0	0	0	0
Maas	p	0	0	0	0	0	0	0
c Cerv		1	0	1	0	0	0	0
Duren	p	0	0	0	0	0	1	0
d Howard		1	1	1	2	0	0	0
Totals		37	4	13	4	24	10	2

a Flied out for Boyer in 2nd.
b Grounded out for Coates in 5th.
c Singled for Maas in 7th.
d Homered for Duren in 9th.

Doubles—Groat, Virdon. Home Runs—Maris, Mazeroski, Howard. Stolen Bases—Skinner, Virdon. Sacrifice Hit—Law. Double Plays—Mazeroski to Stuart, Skinner to Mazeroski, Mazeroski to Groat to Stuart. Hit by Pitcher—Law (by Coates), Skinner (by Duren). Wild Pitch—Law. Left on Bases—New York 7, Pittsburgh 6. Umpires—Boggess (N), Stevens (A), Jackowski (N), Chylak (A), Landes (N), Honochick (A). Attendance—36,676. Time of Game—2:29.

Pittsburgh	Pos	AB	R	H	RBI	PO	A	E
Virdon	cf	3	1	1	1	3	0	0
Groat	ss	4	1	2	1	2	3	0
Skinner	lf	3	1	1	1	3	1	0
Cimoli	lf	0	0	0	0	0	0	0
Stuart	1b	4	0	1	0	9	0	0
Clemente	rf	4	0	1	1	2	0	0
Burgess	c	4	0	0	5	0	0	0
Hoak	3b	2	1	0	0	0	0	0
Mazeroski	2b	4	2	2	2	2	3	0
Law	p	1	0	0	0	0	2	0
Face	p	1	0	0	0	0	0	0
Totals		30	6	8	6	27	9	0

Pitching	IP	H	R	ER	BB	SO
New York						
Ditmar (L)	1	3	3	3	1	0
Coates	3⅔	3	2	2	1	2
Maas	2	2	1	1	0	1
Duren	2	0	0	0	1	1
Pittsburgh						
Law (W)	*7	10	2	2	1	3
Face (SV)	2	3	2	2	0	2

*Pitched to two batters in 8th.

1st Inning
New York
Kubek singled off the third base bag.
1,2 Lopez hit into a double play, Mazeroski to Stuart.
Maris hit a home run into the upper right field deck.
3 Mantle flied to center.
Pittsburgh
Virdon walked.
Virdon stole second and went to third when nobody covered second and Berra's throw went into center. Error charged to Kubek.
Groat doubled into the right field corner, scoring Virdon.
Skinner singled to center, Groat scoring. Skinner stole second.
1 Stuart lined to right.
Clemente singled to center, Skinner scoring.
For New York—Coates came in to pitch.
2 Burgess forced Clemente at second, Richardson to Kubek.
3 Hoak grounded to short.

2nd Inning
New York
Berra singled to center.
Skowron singled to right, Berra stopping at second.
1 Long, pinch-hitting for Boyer, flied to right.
2,3 Richardson lined to Skinner whose throw to Mazeroski doubled up Berra.
Pittsburgh
For New York—McDougald playing third.
1 Mazeroski struck out.
2 Law grounded to third.
3 Virdon struck out.

3rd Inning
New York
1 Coates struck out.
2 Kubek bounced back to the mound.
3 Lopez thrown out by Law.
Pittsburgh
Groat singled to right-center.
1 Skinner lined to center.
Stuart singled to left, but Groat was
2 out trying for third, Lopez to McDougald, Stuart going to second.
3 Clemente flied to right.

4th Inning
New York
Maris singled to right-center.
Mantle walked.
1 Berra flied deep (420 feet) to the right-center field wall where Virdon made a great catch, Maris tagged up and went to third after the catch.
Skowron singled to left, Maris scoring and Mantle stopping at second.
2 McDougald fouled to Hoak.
3 Richardson flied to center.
Pittsburgh
1 Burgess flied to center.
Hoak walked.
Mazeroski hit a two-run homer, on a 2 and 0 count, over the left field scoreboard. Law was hit by a pitch.
2 Virdon fouled to Skowron.
3 Groat lined to Mantle in right-center.

5th Inning
New York
1 Blanchard, pinch-hitting for Coates, grounded to first.
Kubek singled past the mound.
2 Lopez popped to first.
3 Maris fouled to Stuart.
Pittsburgh
For New York—Maas pitching.
Skinner safe at second as Richardson booted his grounder into right.
1 Stuart grounded to short, Skinner holding second.
2 Clemente tapped to short who trapped Skinner off of second, Richardson getting the put out.
3 Burgess struck out.

6th Inning
New York
1 Mantle called out on strikes.
2 Berra flied to left.
3 Skowron struck out.
Pittsburgh
1 Hoak flied to right.
Mazeroski singled to left.
2 Law sacrificed Mazeroski to second, Skowron unassisted.
Virdon doubled off the right field screen, scoring Mazeroski.
3 Groat grounded to short

7th Inning
New York
1 McDougald grounded to short.
2 Richardson grounded to short.
Cerv, pinch-hitting for Maas, singled off Groat's glove.
Cerv took second on a wild pitch.
3 Kubek flied to deep left.
Pittsburgh
For New York—Duren pitching.
Skinner was hit by a pitched ball.
1 Stuart struck out.
2 Clemente fouled to Richardson in front of the first base stands.
3 Burgess grounded to second.

8th Inning
New York
For Pittsburgh—Cimoli playing left.
Lopez singled to right.
Maris singled to left, Lopez stopping at second.
For Pittsburgh—Face now pitching.
1 Mantle took a called third strike.
2 Berra flied to right.
3 Skowron struck out.
Pittsburgh
Hoak walked.
1 Mazeroski fouled to Skowron.
2 Hoak out going for second, Berra to Kubek.
3 Face grounded out to the mound.

9th Inning
New York
McDougald singled over Mazeroski's head.
1 Richardson forced McDougald at second, Mazeroski to Groat.
Howard, pinch-hitting for Duren, hit a two-run homer into the lower right field seats.
Kubek singled to center.
2,3 Lopez grounded into a double play, Mazeroski to Groat to Stuart.

Game 2 October 6 at Pittsburgh

	N.Y.	0 0 2	1 2 7	3 0 1
	Pit.	0 0 0	1 0 0	0 0 2

New York	Pos	AB	R	H	RBI	PO	A	E
Kubek	ss-lf	6	3	3	1	2	3	0
McDougald	3b	3	1	2	2	1	0	0
DeMaestri	ss	2	1	1	0	0	0	0
Maris	rf	5	2	1	0	3	0	0
Mantle	cf	4	3	2	5	4	0	0
Berra	lf	4	1	1	2	1	0	0
Boyer	3b	2	0	1	0	0	0	0
Skowron	1b	6	1	2	1	11	0	0
Howard	c	5	1	2	1	1	0	0
Richardson	2b	4	3	3	2	4	6	1
Turley	p	4	0	1	0	0	2	0
Shantz	p	0	0	0	0	0	1	0
Totals		45	16	19	15	27	12	1

Pittsburgh	Pos	AB	R	H	RBI	PO	A	E
Virdon	cf	5	0	0	0	2	0	0
Groat	ss	4	0	1	0	1	0	1
Gibbon	p	0	0	0	0	1	0	0
Cheney	p	0	0	0	0	0	1	0
c Christopher		0	1	0	0	0	0	0
Clemente	rf	5	0	2	0	1	0	0
Nelson	1b	5	1	2	0	4	3	0
Cimoli	lf	4	1	2	1	2	0	0
Burgess	c	4	0	2	0	11	1	0
Hoak	3b	5	0	2	1	0	0	0
Mazeroski	2b	4	0	1	0	2	2	0
Friend	p	1	0	0	0	1	1	0
a Baker		1	0	0	0	0	0	0
Green	p	0	0	0	0	0	0	0
Labine	p	0	0	0	0	0	1	0
Witt	p	0	0	0	0	0	0	0
b Schofield	ss	1	0	1	0	2	0	0
Totals		39	3	13	2	27	9	1

Pitching	IP	H	R	ER	BB	SO
New York						
Turley (W)	8⅓	13	3	2	3	0
Shantz (SV)	⅔	0	0	0	0	0
Pittsburgh						
Friend (L)	4	6	3	2	2	6
Green	*1	3	4	4	1	0
Labine	⅓	3	5	0	1	1
Witt	⅓	2	0	0	0	0
Gibbon	2	4	3	3	0	2
Cheney	1	1	1	1	1	2

*Pitched to two batters in 6th.

a Popped out for Friend in 4th.
b Singled for Witt in 6th.
c Hit by pitch for Cheney in 9th.

Doubles—Boyer, Hoak 2, Mazeroski, McDougald, Richardson. Triple—Howard. Home Runs—Mantle 2. Sacrifice Hit—Turley. Double Play—Shantz to Richardson to Skowron. Hit by Pitcher—Christopher (by Turley). Wild Pitch—Cheney. Passed Balls—Burgess 2. Left on Bases—New York 8, Pittsburgh 13. Umpires—Stevens, Jackowski, Chylak, Boggess, Landes, Honochick. Attendance—37,308. Time of Game—3:14.

1st Inning
New York
Kubek singled to left.
1 Kubek caught stealing second, Burgess to Mazeroski.
2 McDougald struck out.
Maris singled to right.
3 Mantle struck out.
Pittsburgh
1 Virdon flied to Berra, in left-center.
2 Groat grounded to second.
Clemente singled to right-center.
3 Nelson grounded to second.

2nd Inning
New York
1 Berra grounded out, Nelson to Friend.
2 Skowron struck out.
3 Howard called out on strikes.
Pittsburgh
Cimoli walked.
1 Burgess popped to second.
2 Hoak flied to deep center.
Mazeroski doubled into the left field corner, Cimoli stopping at third.
3 Friend popped to first.

3rd Inning
New York
Richardson walked.
1 Turley sacrificed Richardson to second, Friend to Mazeroski covering first.
Kubek singled into center, scoring Richardson.
McDougald doubled inside the third base line, scoring Kubek.
2 Maris grounded to first, moving McDougald to third.
Mantle walked.
3 Berra flied to center.
Pittsburgh
1 Virdon grounded out, off Turley to Kubek who threw Virdon out at first.
2 Groat grounded to short.
Clemente singled to third as McDougald hoped the ball would roll foul.
3 Nelson flied to center.

4th Inning
New York
1 Skowron took a called third strike.
2 Howard struck out.
Richardson singled to center.
Richardson went to second on a Burgess passed ball.
Turley singled to left-center, scoring Richardson.
3 Kubek flied to left.
Pittsburgh
Cimoli singled to right.
Burgess singled to right, Cimoli moving to third.
Hoak doubled off the right field wall, scoring Cimoli with Burgess going to third.
1 Mazeroski lined to third.
2 Baker, pinch-hitting for Friend, popped to second.
3 Virdon grounded to second.

5th Inning
New York
For Pittsburgh—Green now pitching.
McDougald walked.
1 Maris forced McDougald at second, Nelson to Groat.
Mantle hit a two-run homer into the lower right field seats.
2 Berra grounded to second.
3 Skowron flied to deep right.
Pittsburgh
Groat singled to center.
1 Clemente forced Groat at second, Kubek to Richardson.
Nelson singled to left, Clemente stopping at second.
2 Cimoli flied to Maris in deep right-center, Clemente going to third after the catch.
3 Burgess popped to first.

6th Inning
New York
Howard tripled off the left field wall.
Richardson doubled to left-center, scoring Howard.
For Pittsburgh—Labine pitching.
Richardson went to third on a Burgess passed ball.
1 Turley grounded back to the mound, Richardson holding third.
Kubek safe at first on Groat's fumble, Richardson holding third.
McDougald singled to left, scoring Richardson as Kubek stopped at second.
Maris walked, loading the bases.
2 Mantle took a called third strike.
Berra singled into left-center, scoring Kubek and McDougald as Maris went to third.
Skowron singled to left-center, Maris scoring and moving Berra to third.
For Pittsburgh—Witt came in to pitch.
Howard singled to left, scoring Berra with Skowron stopping at second.
Richardson singled to center, Skowron scoring as Howard stopped at second.
3 Turley flied to center.
Pittsburgh
For New York—Boyer playing third (batting 5th), DeMaestri at short (batting 2nd), as Kubek switched to left.
Hoak doubled into the left field corner.
1 Mazeroski grounded back to the mound, Hoak holding second.
Schofield, pinch-hitting for Witt, singled to right as Hoak stopped at third.
2 Virdon fouled to Howard.
3 Groat flied to right.

7th Inning
New York
For Pittsburgh—Schoefield stays in at short, Gibbon pitching (batting second).
Kubek singled to center.
DeMaestri singled to right, Kubek stopping at second.
1 Maris called out on strikes.
Mantle hit a 475 foot, three-run homer over the center field wall.
2 Boyer popped to center.
Skowron singled to center.
3 Howard forced Skowron at second, Mazeroski to Schoefield.
Pittsburgh
1 Clemente lined to Mantle in right-center.
2 Nelson grounded to second.
3 Cimoli flied to right.

8th Inning
New York
1 Richardson grounded out, Nelson to Gibbon.
2 Turley took a called third strike.
3 Kubek flied to left.
Pittsburgh
Burgess walked.
1 Hoak flied to deep center.
2 Mazeroski flied to left.
Schoefield walked.
3 Virdon grounded to second.

9th Inning
New York
For Pittsburgh—Cheney pitching.
1 DeMaestri took a called third strike.
2 Maris struck out.
Mantle walked.
Boyer doubled to left, moving Mantle to third.
Mantle scored and Boyer took third on a Cheney wild pitch.
3 Skowron grounded back to the mound.
Pittsburgh
Christopher, pinch-hitting for Cheney, was hit by a pitch.
1 Clemente flied to left.
Nelson singled to right, moving Christopher to second.
Cimoli singled to center, Christopher scoring with Nelson stopping at second.
Burgess only singled on a hit high off the right field screen as Nelson held up thinking the ball might be caught and only got to third. Richardson's relay to trap Burgess went wide past Skowron, scoring Nelson and Cimoli going to third.
For New York—Shantz pitching.
2,3 Hoak grounded into a double play, Shantz to Richardson to Skowron.

Game 3 October 8 at New York

| | | Pit. | 000 000 000 |
| | | N.Y. | 600 400 00x |

Pittsburgh	Pos	AB	R	H	RBI	PO	A	E
Virdon	cf	4	0	1	0	3	0	0
Groat	ss	4	0	1	0	1	1	0
Clemente	rf	4	0	1	0	1	0	0
Stuart	1b	4	0	1	0	6	0	0
Cimoli	lf	3	0	0	0	2	0	0
Smith	c	3	0	0	0	9	1	0
Hoak	3b	3	0	0	0	1	3	0
Mazeroski	2b	3	0	1	0	1	3	0
Mizell	p	0	0	0	0	0	1	0
Labine	p	0	0	0	0	0	1	0
Green	p	1	0	0	0	0	0	0
Witt	p	0	0	0	0	0	0	0
a Baker		1	0	0	0	0	0	0
Cheney	p	0	0	0	0	0	0	0
b Schofield		1	0	0	0	0	0	0
Gibbon	p	0	0	0	0	0	0	0
Totals		31	0	4	0	24	9	0

New York	Pos	AB	R	H	RBI	PO	A	E
Cerv	lf	5	1	2	0	3	0	0
Maris	rf	3	0	0	0	1	0	0
Berra	rf	1	0	1	0	1	0	0
Mantle	cf	5	2	4	2	2	0	0
Skowron	1b	5	2	2	1	11	3	0
McDougald	3b	4	2	1	0	0	3	0
Howard	c	4	1	2	1	3	0	0
Richardson	2b	5	1	2	6	1	4	0
Kubek	ss	3	0	1	0	2	1	1
Ford	p	4	1	1	0	3	4	0
Totals		39	10	16	10	27	15	1

Pitching	IP	H	R	ER	BB	SO
Pittsburgh						
Mizell (L)	⅓	3	4	4	1	0
Labine	⅓	4	2	2	0	0
Green	3	5	4	4	3	3
Witt	1⅓	3	0	0	2	1
Cheney	2	1	0	0	0	3
Gibbon	1	0	0	0	1	0
New York						
Ford (W)	9	4	0	0	1	0

a Grounded out for Witt in 6th.
b Lined out for Cheney in 8th.

Doubles—Mantle, Virdon. Home Runs—Mantle, Richardson. Double Play—Ford to Richardson to Skowron. Wild Pitches—Green, Witt. Left on Bases—Pittsburgh 5, New York 9. Umpires—Jackowski, Chylak, Boggess, Stevens, Honochick, Landes. Attendance—70,001. Time of Game—2:41.

1st Inning
Pittsburgh
1 Virdon tapped back to the mound.
2 Groat grounded to second.
3 Clemente struck out.
New York
Cerv singled into center.
1 Maris lined to Clemente in right-center.
Mantle singled to center, advancing Cerv to third.
Skowron singled to center, scoring Cerv and moving Mantle to third.
McDougald walked, loading the bases.
For Pittsburgh—Labine came in to pitch.
Howard beat out a slow roller to third scoring Mantle.
Richardson hit a grand slam homer into the lower left field stands just inside the foul line.
Kubek beat out a high bouncer to second.
2 Ford forced Kubek at second on a bunt, Labine to Groat.
Cerv singled into left, Ford stopping at second.
For Pittsburgh—Green now pitching.
3 Maris fouled to Smith.

2nd Inning
Pittsburgh
1 Stuart called out on strikes.
2 Cimoli flied to left.
3 Smith flied to left.
New York
Mantle singled to center.
Mantle took second on a wild pitch.
1 Skowron struck out.
2 Mantle caught trying to steal third, Smith to Hoak.
3 McDougald struck out.

3rd Inning
Pittsburgh
1 Hoak flied to Mantle in left-center.
2 Mazeroski grounded back to the mound.
3 Green lined to short.
New York
1 Howard flied to left.
2 Richardson struck out.
3 Kubek grounded to third.

4th Inning
Pittsburgh
Virdon doubled to right-center.
1 Groat grounded to the mound.
2 Clemente grounded to third, Virdon still holding at second.
3 Stuart flied to right.
New York
Ford singled to right-center.
1 Cerv grounded to third, Ford moving to second.
2 Maris grounded to second, Ford going to third.
Mantle hit his third homer of the Series, a two-run shot into the left field bullpen.
Skowron singled to right.
McDougald beat out a hit down the third base line, advancing Skowron to second.
For Pittsburgh—Witt came in to pitch.
Howard beat out a single off of Hoak's chest, loading the bases.
Richardson singled to left, Skowron and McDougald scoring with Howard stopping at second. **(A Series record of 6 RBI's for Richardson).**
Howard went to third and Richardson to second on a wild pitch.
Kubek intentionally passed, loading the bases.
3 Ford grounded to second.

5th Inning
Pittsburgh
1 Cimoli grounded to second.
2 Smith grounded to short.
3 Hoak flied to deep left.
New York
1 Cerv struck out.
Maris walked.
Mantle bounced a ground-rule double into the right field stands, sending Maris to third.
2 Skowron grounded to second and Maris was trapped, Mazeroski to Smith as Mantle went to third and Skowron to second on the run-down.
3 McDougald grounded to third.

6th Inning
Pittsburgh
Mazeroski singled to center.
1 Baker, pinch-hitting for Witt, grounded out, Skowron to Ford as Mazeroski went to second.
2 Virdon grounded to second, sending Mazeroski to third.
3 Groat grounded to third.
New York
For Pittsburgh—Cheney pitching.
1 Howard struck out.
2 Richardson flied to center.
3 Kubek flied to left.

7th Inning
Pittsburgh
For New York—Berra playing right.
1 Clemente flied to right.
Stuart singled to center.
Cimoli walked.
2,3 Smith bounced into a double play, Ford to Richardson to Skowron.
New York
1 Ford struck out.
2 Cerv flied to center.
Berra singled to left-center.
3 Mantle called out on strikes.

8th Inning
Pittsburgh
1 Hoak grounded to third.
2 Mazeroski flied to center.
3 Schoefield, pinch-hitting for Cheney, lined to short.
New York
For Pittsburgh—Gibbon now pitching.
1 Skowron grounded to short.
2 McDougald flied to center.
Howard walked.
3 Richardson popped to second.

9th Inning
Pittsburgh
1 Virdon grounded out, Skowron to Ford.
2 Groat grounded out, Skowron to Ford.
Clemente singled to center.
Stuart safe at first on Kubek's fumble, Clemente going to second.
3 Cimoli struck out.

Game 4 October 9 at New York

| | | Pit. | 000 030 000 |
| | | N.Y. | 000 100 100 |

Pittsburgh	Pos	AB	R	H	RBI	PO	A	E
Virdon	cf	4	0	1	2	0	0	0
Groat	ss	4	0	0	0	1	1	0
Clemente	rf	4	0	1	0	4	0	0
Stuart	1b	4	0	0	0	12	0	0
Cimoli	lf	4	1	1	0	0	0	0
Burgess	c	3	1	0	0	5	1	0
Oldis	c	0	0	0	0	0	0	0
Hoak	3b	4	0	1	0	1	3	0
Mazeroski	2b	3	0	1	0	2	3	0
Law	p	3	1	2	1	0	3	0
Face	p	1	0	0	0	0	1	0
Totals		34	3	7	3	27	12	0

New York	Pos	AB	R	H	RBI	PO	A	E
Cerv	lf	4	0	1	0	1	0	0
Kubek	ss	4	0	1	0	0	2	0
Maris	rf	4	0	0	0	3	0	0
Mantle	cf	3	0	0	0	3	0	0
Berra	c	4	0	0	0	7	0	0
Skowron	1b	4	2	2	1	8	1	0
McDougald	3b	4	0	1	0	1	1	0
Richardson	2b	3	0	2	1	1	6	3
c Long		1	0	0	0	0	0	0
Terry	p	2	0	0	0	0	3	0
Shantz	p	0	0	0	0	0	0	0
a Blanchard		1	0	1	0	0	0	0
b DeMaestri		0	0	0	0	0	0	0
Coates	p	0	0	0	0	1	1	0
Totals		34	2	8	2	27	11	0

Pitching	IP	H	R	ER	BB	SO
Pittsburgh						
Law (W)	6⅓	8	2	2	1	5
Face (SV)	2⅔	0	0	0	0	1
New York						
Terry (L)	6⅓	6	3	3	1	5
Shantz	⅓	0	0	0	1	0
Coates	2	1	0	0	0	1

a Singled for Shantz in 7th.
b Ran for Blanchard in 7th.
c Flied out for Richardson in 9th.

Doubles—Kubek, Law, Richardson, Skowron. Home Run—Skowron. Sacrifice Hit—Mazeroski. Double Play—Hoak to Stuart. Left on Bases—Pittsburgh 6, New York 6. Umpires—Chylak, Boggess, Stevens, Jackowski, Landes, Honochick. Attendance—67,812. Time of Game—2:29.

1st Inning
Pittsburgh
1 Virdon struck out.
2 Groat popped to second.
3 Clemente struck out.
New York
Cerv singled to center.
Kubek doubled to left, Cerv going to third.
1 Maris flied to short right.
Mantle got an intentional pass, loading the bases.
2,3 Berra hit into a double play, Hoak forcing Kubek to Stuart.

2nd Inning
Pittsburgh
1 Stuart popped to third.
2 Cimoli rapped to the mound.
Burgess walked.
3 Hoak lined to left.
New York
1 Skowron tapped back to the pitcher.
2 McDougald lined to right.
Richardson doubled down the left field line.
3 Terry grounded out, Law to Stuart.

3rd Inning
Pittsburgh
1 Mazeroski struck out.
2 Law called out on strikes.
3 Virdon grounded to second.
New York
1 Cerv grounded to second.
2 Kubek popped to Mazeroski behind first base.
3 Maris grounded to second.

4th Inning
Pittsburgh
1 Groat flied to center.
2 Clemente struck out.
3 Stuart's grounder deflected off Terry to Kubek who threw him out.
New York
1 Mantle struck out, bunting foul on the third strike.
2 Berra grounded back to the pitcher.
Skowron hit a home run into the lower right field seats.
3 McDougald struck out.

5th Inning
Pittsburgh
Cimoli singled to right.
Burgess safe on a fielder's choice when Skowron threw too late to second for the force out.
1 Hoak popped to Richardson, on a bunt attempt.
2 Mazeroski popped to first.
Law doubled off the fence in the left field corner, Cimoli scoring with Burgess going to third.
Virdon singled to center, Burgess and Law scoring. Virdon went to second on Mantle's throw to the plate.
3 Groat popped to second.
New York
Richardson singled over Stuart's head.
1 Terry struck out.
2 Cerv struck out.
3 Kubek struck out.

6th Inning
Pittsburgh
Clemente singled to right.
1 Stuart rolled to third, sending Clemente to second.
2 Cimoli grounded to second, Clemente going to third.
3 Burgess flied to deep right.
New York
1 Maris grounded to second.
2 Mantle flied to right.
3 Berra grounded to second.

7th Inning
Pittsburgh
Hoak singled to center.
1 Mazeroski sacrificed Hoak to second, Terry to Richardson.
Law singled over McDougald's glove, Hoak going to third.
For New York—Shantz came in to pitch.
2 Virdon struck out.
3 Groat forced Law at second, Kubek to Richardson.
New York
Skowron bounced a ground-rule double into the right field stands.
McDougald singled to right, moving Skowron to third.
1 Richardson forced McDougald at second, Mazeroski unassisted as Skowron scored.
Blanchard, batting for Shantz, singled past first, moving Richardson to second.
For Pittsburgh—Face came in to pitch. DeMaestri ran for Blanchard.
2 Cerv flied out at 400 feet in right-center where Virdon made a fantastic leaping catch. Richardson went to third after the catch.
3 Kubek grounded back to the mound.

8th Inning
Pittsburgh
For New York—Coates pitching.
1 Clemente tapped to second.
2 Stuart popped to second.
3 Cimoli rolled back to the mound.
New York
1 Maris flied to center.
2 Mantle struck out but Burgess had to throw him out dropping the ball.
3 Berra grounded to third.

9th Inning
Pittsburgh
1 Burgess grounded out, Skowron to Coates.
2 Hoak flied to Mantle in right-center.
Mazeroski singled to right.
3 Face struck out.
New York
For Pittsburgh—Oldis catching.
1 Skowron hit a hard grounder to Hoak who made a good back-handed stop and threw him out.
2 McDougald lined to short.
3 Long, pinch-hitting for Richardson, flied to right.

Game 5 October 10 at New York

Pittsburgh	Pos	AB	R	H	RBI	PO	A	E
Virdon	cf	5	0	1	0	1	0	0
Groat	ss	4	1	1	0	3	4	1
Clemente	rf	4	0	1	1	3	0	0
Stuart	1b	4	0	1	0	8	0	0
Nelson	1b	0	0	0	0	2	0	0
Cimoli	lf	4	1	0	0	0	0	0
Burgess	c	4	1	2	0	6	0	0
c Christopher		0	1	0	0	0	0	0
Oldis	c	0	0	0	0	0	0	0
Hoak	3b	4	1	2	2	1	1	1
Mazeroski	2b	4	0	1	2	2	5	0
Haddix	p	3	0	1	0	1	1	0
Face	p	1	0	0	0	0	0	0
Totals		37	5	10	5	27	11	2

Pitching	IP	H	R	ER	BB	SO
Pittsburgh						
Haddix (W)	$6\frac{1}{3}$	5	2	2	2	6
Face (SV)	$2\frac{2}{3}$	0	0	0	1	1
New York						
Ditmar	$1\frac{1}{3}$	3	3	1	0	0
Arroyo	* $\frac{2}{3}$	2	1	1	0	1
Stafford	5	3	0	0	0	2
Duren	2	2	1	1	0	4

*Pitched to two batters in 3rd.

Pit.	0 3 1	0 0 0	0 0 1
N.Y.	0 1 1	0 0 0	0 0 0

New York	Pos	AB	R	H	RBI	PO	A	E
McDougald	3b	4	0	0	0	2	2	1
Maris	rf	4	1	1	1	1	0	0
Cerv	lf	4	0	1	0	4	0	1
Mantle	cf	1	0	0	0	1	0	0
Skowron	1b	4	0	0	0	8	0	0
Howard	c	3	1	1	0	6	0	0
b Berra	c	1	0	0	0	2	0	0
Richardson	2b	4	0	0	0	2	2	0
Kubek	ss	4	0	1	1	1	5	0
Ditmar	p	0	0	0	0	0	0	0
Arroyo	p	1	0	0	0	0	0	0
Stafford	p	1	0	0	0	0	1	0
a Lopez		1	0	1	0	0	0	0
Duren	p	0	0	0	0	0	1	0
d Blanchard		1	0	0	0	0	0	0
Totals		33	2	5	2	27	11	2

a Singled for Stafford in 7th.
b Grounded out for Howard in 8th.
c Ran for Burgess in 9th.
d Flied out for Duren in 9th.

Doubles—Burgess, Groat, Howard, Mazeroski, Virdon. Home Run—Maris. Double Plays—Stafford to Kubek to Skowron, Mazeroski to Stuart. Wild Pitch—Duren, Left on Bases—Pittsburgh 5, New York 7. Passed Ball—Burgess. Umpires—Boggess, Stevens, Jackowski, Chylak, Landes, Honochick. Attendance—62,753. Time of Game—2:32.

1st Inning
Pittsburgh
1 Virdon fouled to Howard.
2 Groat flied to left.
3 Clemente grounded to short.
New York
1 McDougald bunted out to third.
2 Maris grounded to second.
Cerv singled on a slow roller to third and got to second on Hoak's throwing error.
Mantle got an intentional pass.
3 Skowron struck out.

2nd Inning
Pittsburgh
Stuart singled to left.
1 Cimoli forced Stuart, Richardson unassisted.
Burgess doubled into the right field corner, moving Cimoli to third.
Hoak bounced to Kubek who threw to McDougald trying to get Burgess going into third as Cimoli scored, but McDougald dropped the ball for an error allowing Hoak to get to second.
Mazeroski doubled down the left field line, Burgess and Hoak scoring.
For New York—Arroyo came in to pitch.
2 Haddix struck out.
3 Virdon fouled to McDougald.
New York
Howard doubled off the right field wall.
1 Richardson grounded out, Mazeroski to Haddix covering first, as Howard went to third.
2 Kubek grounded to first, scoring Howard.
3 Arroyo grounded to short.

3rd Inning
Pittsburgh
Groat doubled into the left field corner.
Clemente singled to left, scoring Groat.
For New York—Stafford pitching.
1 Stuart popped to third.
2 Cimoli flied to right.
3 Burgess grounded to second.
New York
1 McDougald grounded back to the mound.
Maris hit a home run into the third deck of the right field stands.
2 Cerv grounded to second.
Mantle walked.
3 Skowron flied to right.

4th Inning
Pittsburgh
Hoak singled off Kubek's chest.
1 Mazeroski forced Hoak at second, McDougald to Richardson.
2,3 Haddix hit into a double play, Stafford to Kubek to Skowron.
New York
Howard safe at first on Groat's error pulling Stuart off the bag.
1,2 Richardson lined into a double play, Mazeroski to Stuart doubling Howard.
Kubek struck out but got to first safely on a Burgess' passed ball.
3 Stafford struck out.

5th Inning
Pittsburgh
1 Virdon grounded to second.
2 Groat grounded to short.
3 Clemente grounded to short.
New York
1 McDougald flied to right.
2 Maris popped to short.
3 Cerv struck out.

6th Inning
Pittsburgh
1 Stuart grounded to third.
2 Cimoli struck out.
3 Burgess flied to center
New York
1 Mantle struck out.
2 Skowron grounded to short.
3 Howard called out on strikes.

7th Inning
Pittsburgh
1 Hoak struck out.
2 Mazeroski flied to short left.
Haddix beat out a hit behind second.
Virdon doubled off Skowron's glove down the right field line, moving Haddix to third.
3 Groat flied to left.
New York
1 Richardson lined to third.
Kubek singled to center.
Lopez, pinch-hitting for Stafford, singled to right, Kubek stopping at second.
For Pittsburgh—Face came in to pitch.
2 McDougald forced Lopez at second, Groat to Mazeroski but missing the DP, Kubek going to third.
3 Maris struck out.

8th Inning
Pittsburgh
For New York—Duren pitching.
1 Clemente struck out.
2 Stuart flied to left.
3 Cimoli called out on strikes
New York
For Pittsburgh—Nelson playing first.
1 Cerv flied to deep center.
Mantle walked.
2 Skowron popped to short.
3 Berra, pinch-hitting for Howard, grounded to second.

9th Inning
Pittsburgh
For New York—Berra catching.
Burgess singled to left and went to second on Cerv's fumble.
Christopher ran for Burgess.
Christopher to third on a wild pitch.
Hoak singled through the box, Christopher scoring.
1 Mazeroski struck out.
2 Face struck out, bunting the third strike foul.
3 Virdon grounded back to the mound.
New York
For Pittsburgh—Oldis catching.
1 Richardson grounded to short.
2 Kubek popped to short.
3 Blanchard, pinch-hitting for Duren, flied to deep right.

Game 6 October 12 at Pittsburgh

New York	Pos	AB	R	H	RBI	PO	A	E
Boyer	3b	6	1	1	0	0	5	0
Kubek	ss-lf	5	2	1	1	2	4	1
Maris	rf	5	1	3	0	1	0	0
Mantle	cf	4	2	1	2	2	0	0
Berra	lf	4	3	3	2	0	0	0
DeMaestri	ss	0	0	0	0	0	2	0
Skowron	1b	4	0	2	1	13	0	0
Howard	c	0	0	0	0	1	0	0
a Grba		0	0	0	0	0	0	0
Blanchard	c	4	2	3	1	4	1	0
Richardson	2b	5	1	2	3	4	6	0
Ford	p	4	0	1	2	0	11	0
Totals		41	12	17	12	27	19	1

Pitching	IP	H	R	ER	BB	SO
New York						
Ford (W)	9	7	0	0	1	5
Pittsburgh						
Friend (L)	*2	5	5	5	1	1
Cheney	1	2	1	1	0	1
Mizell	2	1	0	0	1	1
Green	**0	3	2	2	0	0
Labine	3	6	4	4	0	1
Witt	1	0	0	0	0	0

*Pitched to four batters in 3rd.
**Pitched to three batters in 6th.

N.Y.	0 1 5	0 0 2	2 2 0
Pit.	0 0 0	0 0 0	0 0 0

Pittsburgh	Pos	AB	R	H	RBI	PO	A	E
Virdon	cf	4	0	1	0	4	0	1
Groat	ss	4	0	1	0	1	1	0
Witt	p	0	0	0	0	0	0	0
Clemente	rf	4	0	2	0	4	0	0
Stuart	1b	4	0	0	0	10	0	0
Cimoli	lf	4	0	1	0	1	0	0
Smith	c	4	0	2	0	4	0	0
Hoak	3b	2	0	0	0	1	1	0
Mazeroski	2b	3	0	0	0	2	7	0
Friend	p	0	0	0	0	0	2	0
Cheney	p	0	0	0	0	0	0	0
b Baker		1	0	0	0	0	0	0
Mizell	p	0	0	0	0	0	0	0
c Nelson		1	0	0	0	0	0	0
Green	p	0	0	0	0	0	0	0
Labine	p	0	0	0	0	0	0	0
d Schoefield	ss	1	0	0	0	0	0	0
Totals		32	0	7	0	27	11	1

a Ran for Howard in 2nd.
b Struck out for Cheney in 3rd.
c Struck out for Mizell in 5th.
d Grounded out for Labine in 8th.

Doubles—Blanchard 2, Maris Skowron. Triples—Boyer, Richardson 2. Sacrifice Hit—Ford. Sacrifice Fly—Skowron. Double Plays—Richardson to Kubek to Skowron, Boyer to Richardson to Skowron 2, Groat to Mazeroski to Stuart, Hoak to Mazeroski to Stuart. Hit by Pitch—Howard (by Friend), Kubek (by Friend). Wild Pitch—Labine. Left on Bases—New York 8, Pittsburgh 6. Umpires—Stevens, Jackowski, Chylak, Boggess, Landes, Honochick. Attendance—38,580. Time of Game—2:38.

1st Inning
New York
1 Boyer grounded back to the mound.
2 Kubek grounded to second.
3 Maris flied to center.
Pittsburgh
Virdon singled to center.
1,2 Groat grounded into a double play, Richardson to Kubek to Skowron.
Clemente singled to right.
3 Stuart struck out.

2nd Inning
New York
1 Mantle grounded back to the mound.
Berra walked.
Skowron singled to right, Berra moving to third.
Howard was hit by a pitched ball.
Grba ran for Howard.
2 Richardson flied to short center.
Ford singled back to Friend, Berra scoring by just beating the throw.
3 Boyer struck out.
Pittsburgh
For New York—Blanchard catching.
1 Cimoli grounded to third.
Smith singled to left.
2 Hoak forced Smith at second, McDougald to Richardson.
3 Mazeroski lined to center.

3rd Inning
New York
Kubek was hit by a pitched ball.
Maris doubled off the right field screen, sending Kubek to third.
Mantle singled to right, Kubek and Maris scoring.
Berra singled to right-center, advancing Mantle to third.
For Pittsburgh—Cheney pitching.
1 Skowron hit a sacrifice fly to deep right-center, scoring Mantle.
Blanchard singled to center, Berra stopping at second.
Richardson tripled off the left field score board, Berra and Blanchard scoring. **(A new Series record of 11 RBI's for Richardson).**
2 Ford took a called third strike.
3 Boyer flied to center.
Pittsburgh
1 Baker, batting for Cheney, struck out.
2 Virdon grounded to second.
3 Groat struck out.

4th Inning
New York
For Pittsburgh—Mizell pitching.
1 Kubek flied to right.
2 Maris struck out.
Mantle walked.
3 Berra grounded to first.
Pittsburgh
1 Clemente grounded to short.
2 Stuart grounded to short.
3 Cimoli took a called third strike.

5th Inning
New York
Skowron doubled off the left-center field wall.
1 Blanchard flied to deep right, Skowron going to third after the catch.
2 Richardson lined to third.
3 Ford grounded to second.
Pittsburgh
Smith singled to center.
Hoak walked.
1,2 Mazeroski grounded into a double play, Boyer to Richardson to Skowron, as Smith went to third.
3 Nelson, pinch-hitting for Mizell, struck out.

6th Inning
New York
For Pittsburgh—Green pitching.
Boyer tripled off the right-center field wall.
Kubek singled to right, Boyer scoring.
Maris singled to right, Kubek moving to third.
For Pittsburgh—Labine pitching.
1 Mantle struck out.
Berra singled to right, scoring Kubek as Maris went to third.
2,3 Skowron hit into a double play, Groat to Mazeroski to Stuart.
Pittsburgh
1 Virdon grounded to second.
2 Groat flied to right.
Clemente singled to center.
3 Stuart bounced back to the mound.

7th Inning
New York
Blanchard doubled off the right field screen.
Richardson hit his second triple off the left center field wall, scoring Blanchard **(A Series record of 12 RBI's).**
Ford bunted and Richardson scored just ahead of Hoak's toss.
1,2 Boyer hit into a double play, Hoak to Mazeroski to Stuart.
3 Kubek lined to Virdon in right-center.
Pittsburgh
Cimoli safe on Kubek's fumble
1 Smith forced Cimoli at second, Kubek to Richardson.
2 Hoak forced Smith on a bunt, Blanchard to Kubek.
3 Mazeroski flied to center.

8th Inning
New York
Maris singled to right.
1 Mantle forced Maris at second, Mazeroski to Groat.
Mantle took second on a wild pitch.
Berra singled to center, scoring Mantle, and took second on Virdon's throwing error to the plate.
2 Skowron grounded to second, moving Berra to third.
Blanchard doubled off the right field screen, scoring Berra.
3 Richardson flied to left.
Pittsburgh
For New York—Kubek moves to left as DeMaestri comes in to play short.
1 Schoefield, pinch-hitting for Labine, grounded to third.
2 Virdon grounded to second.
Groat singled off DeMaestri's glove.
3 Clemente grounded to short.

9th Inning
New York
For Pittsburgh—Schoefield playing short, Witt pitching.
1 Ford grounded to first.
2 Boyer grounded to second.
3 Kubek lined to right.
Pittsburgh
1 Stuart grounded to short.
Cimoli singled to center.
2,3 Smith hit into a game ending double play, Boyer to Richardson to Skowron.

Game 7 October 13 at Pittsburgh

	N.Y.	000	014	022
	Pit.	220	000	051

New York	Pos	AB	R	H	RBI	PO	A	E
Richardson	2b	5	2	2	0	2	5	0
Kubek	ss	3	1	0	0	3	2	0
DeMaestri	ss	0	0	0	0	0	0	0
d Long		1	0	1	0	0	0	0
e McDougald	3b	0	1	0	0	0	0	0
Maris	rf	5	0	0	0	2	0	1
Mantle	cf	5	1	3	2	0	0	0
Berra	lf	4	2	1	4	3	0	0
Skowron	1b	5	2	2	1	10	2	0
Blanchard	c	4	0	1	1	1	1	0
Boyer	3b-ss	4	0	1	1	0	3	0
Turley	p	0	0	0	0	0	0	0
Stafford	p	0	0	0	0	0	1	0
a Lopez		1	0	1	0	0	0	0
Shantz	p	3	0	1	0	3	1	0
Coates	p	0	0	0	0	0	0	0
Terry	p	0	0	0	0	0	0	0
Totals		40	9	13	9	x24	15	1

Pittsburgh	Pos	AB	R	H	RBI	PO	A	E
Virdon	cf	4	1	2	2	3	0	0
Groat	ss	4	1	1	1	3	2	0
Skinner	lf	2	1	0	0	1	0	0
Nelson	1b	3	1	1	2	7	0	0
Clemente	rf	4	1	1	1	4	0	0
Burgess	c	3	0	2	0	0	0	0
b Christopher		0	0	0	0	0	0	0
Smith	c	1	1	1	3	1	0	0
Hoak	3b	3	1	0	0	3	2	0
Mazeroski	2b	4	2	2	1	5	0	0
Law	p	2	0	0	0	0	1	0
Face	p	0	0	0	0	0	1	0
c Cimoli		1	1	1	0	0	0	0
Friend	p	0	0	0	0	0	0	0
Haddix	p	0	0	0	0	0	0	0
Totals		31	10	11	10	27	6	0

Pitching	IP	H	R	ER	BB	SO
New York						
Turley	*1	2	3	3	1	0
Stafford	1	2	1	1	1	0
Shantz	***5	4	3	3	1	0
Coates	⅓	2	2	2	0	0
Terry (L)	*****⅓	1	1	1	0	0
Pittsburgh						
Law	**5	4	3	3	1	0
Face	3	6	4	4	1	0
Friend	****0	2	2	2	0	0
Haddix (W)	1	1	0	0	0	0

a Singled for Stafford in 3rd.
b Ran for Burgess in 7th.
c Singled for Face in 8th.
d Singled for DeMaestri in 9th.
e Ran for Long in 9th.
x No outs when winning run scored.

Double—Boyer. Home Runs—Berra, Mazeroski, Nelson, Skowron, Smith. Sacrifice Hit—Skinner. Double Plays—Stafford to Blanchard to Skowron, Richardson to Kubek, to Skowron, Kubek to Richardson to Skowron. Left on Bases—New York 6, Pittsburgh 1. Umpires—Jackowski, Chylak, Boggess, Stevens, Landes, Honochick. Attendance—36,683. Time of Game—2:36.

*Pitched to one batter in 2nd.
**Pitched to two batters in 6th.
***Pitched to three batters in 8th.
****Pitched to two batters in 9th.
*****Pitched to one batter in 9th.

1st Inning
New York
1 Richardson lined to short.
2 Kubek popped to second.
3 Maris fouled to Hoak.
Pittsburgh
1 Virdon flied to left.
2 Groat popped to short.
Skinner walked.
Nelson hit a two-run homer into the lower right field stands.
3 Clemente popped to second.

2nd Inning
New York
1 Mantle flied to center.
2 Berra grounded to third, a real good stop by Hoak.
3 Skowron grounded to short.
Pittsburgh
Burgess singled down the first base line into right.
For New York—Stafford now pitching.
Hoak walked.
Mazeroski bunted a single toward third beating Stafford's throw to load the bases.
1,2 Law grounded into a double play, Stafford to Blanchard forcing Burgess, to Skowron.
Virdon singled to right-center, scoring Hoak and Mazeroski and went to second on Maris' fumble of the hit.
3 Groat grounded to third.

3rd Inning
New York
1 Blanchard grounded back to the mound.
2 Boyer popped to second.
Lopez, pinch-hitting for Stafford, singled to left.
3 Richardson flied to left.
Pittsburgh
For New York—Shantz pitching.
1 Skinner grounded out, Skowron to Shantz.
Nelson walked.
2,3 Clemente hit into a double play, Richardson to Kubek to Skowron.

4th Inning
New York
1 Kubek popped to Groat behind third.
2 Maris lined to right.
Mantle singled to right.
3 Berra flied to right.
Pittsburgh
1 Burgess grounded to second.
2 Hoak grounded to second.
3 Mazeroski popped to short.

5th Inning
New York
Skowron hit a home run into the lower right field stands.
1 Blanchard flied to center.
2 Boyer lined to second.
3 Shantz popped to first.
Pittsburgh
1 Law grounded to third.
2 Virdon grounded to second.
3 Groat lined to the mound.

6th Inning
New York
Richardson singled to center.
Kubek walked.
For Pittsburgh—Face came into pitch.
1 Maris fouled to Hoak.
Mantle singled to center, Richardson scoring and Kubek going to third.
Berra hit a three-run homer along the foul line into the upper right field stands.
2 Skowron fouled to Hoak.
3 Blanchard grounded to first.
Pittsburgh
1 Skinner flied to right.
2 Nelson grounded out, Skowron to Shantz.
3 Clemente bounced back to the mound.

7th Inning
New York
1 Boyer flied to center.
Shantz bounced a single over Hoak's head.
2 Richardson forced Shantz at second, Hoak to Mazeroski.
3 Kubek lined to right.
Pittsburgh
Burgess singled to center.
Christopher ran for Burgess.
1 Hoak lined to left.
2,3 Mazeroski grounded into a double play, Kubek to Richardson to Skowron.

8th Inning
New York
For Pittsburgh—Smith catching.
1 Maris grounded to the mound.
2 Mantle lined to short.
Berra walked.
Skowron singled on a high bouncer to third, sending Berra to second.
Blanchard singled to right-center, scoring Berra with Skowron going to third.
Boyer doubled into the left field corner, Skowron scoring with Blanchard stopping at third.
3 Shantz flied to right.
Pittsburgh
Cimoli, pinch-hitting for Face, singled to right-center.
Virdon singled on a bad hop grounder that hit Kubek on the neck, Cimoli stopping at second.
For New York—DeMaestri replaced Kubek at short.
Groat singled past third, Cimoli scoring with Virdon stopping at second.
For New York—Coates came in to pitch.
1 Skinner sacrificed up both runners, Boyer to Skowron.
2 Nelson flied to right, the runners holding.
Clemente singled on a slow chopper to first, Virdon scoring with Groat moving to third.
Smith hit a three-run homer over the left-field wall.
For New York—Terry pitching.
3 Hoak flied to left.

9th Inning
New York
For Pittsburgh—Friend pitching.
Richardson singled to left-center.
Long, pinch-hitting for DeMaestri, singled to right, Richardson stopping at second.
For Pittsburgh—Haddix came in to pitch.
1 Maris fouled to Smith.
Mantle singled to right-center, scoring Richardson and sending Long to third.
McDougald ran for Long.
2 Berra grounded to first, scoring McDougald with Mantle going to second.
3 Skowron forced Berra, Groat to Mazeroski.
Pittsburgh
For New York—McDougald playing third as Boyer shifts to short.
Mazeroski hit Terry's second pitch for a **Series winning home run** over the left field wall.

1960 WORLD SERIES COMPOSITE BOX

	Wins	Composite Line Score
Pittsburgh Pirates (N.L.)	4	5 5 1 3 3 1 0 5 4 - 27
New York Yankees (A.L.)	3	7 2 8 7 3 13 6 4 5 - 55

Manager	W	L	Pct.	Regular Season G. Ahead
Danny Murtaugh	95	59	.617	7
Casey Stengel	97	57	.630	8

BATTING AND FIELDING

PITTSBURGH PIRATES

	Pos	G	AB	R	H	2B	3B	HR	RBI	BB	SO	SB	BA	SA	PO	A	E
Dick Stuart	1b	6	20	0	3	0	0	0	0	0	3	0	.150	.150	45	0	0
Bill Mazeroski	2b	7	25	4	8	2	0	2	5	0	3	0	.320	.640	16	23	0
Dick Groat	ss	7	28	3	6	2	0	0	2	0	1	0	.214	.286	12	12	2
Don Hoak	3b	7	23	3	5	2	0	0	3	4	1	0	.217	.304	8	10	1
Roberto Clemente	rf	7	29	1	9	0	0	0	3	0	4	0	.310	.310	19	0	0
Bill Virdon	cf	7	29	2	7	3	0	0	5	1	3	1	.241	.345	18	0	1
Gino Cimoli	1f-ph	7	20	4	5	0	0	0	1	2	4	0	.250	.250	5	0	0
Smoky Burgess	c	5	18	2	6	1	0	0	0	2	1	0	.333	.389	27	2	0
Rocky Nelson	1b-ph	4	9	2	3	0	0	1	2	1	1	0	.333	.667	13	3	0
Bob Skinner	1f	2	5	2	1	0	0	0	1	1	0	1	.200	.200	4	1	0
Hal Smith	c	3	8	1	3	0	0	1	3	0	0	0	.375	.750	14	1	0
Dick Schofield	ph-ss	3	3	0	1	0	0	0	0	1	0	0	.333	.333	2	0	0
Gene Baker	ph	3	3	0	0	0	0	0	0	0	1	0	.000	.000			
Joe Christopher	ph-pr	3	0	2	0	0	0	0	0	0	0	0	—	—			
Bob Oldis	c	2	0	0	0	0	0	0	0	0	0	0	—	—	0	0	0
Vernon Law	p	3	6	1	2	1	0	0	1	0	1	0	.333	.500	0	6	0
Roy Face	p	4	3	0	0	0	0	0	0	0	2	0	.000	.000	0	2	0
Harvey Haddix	p	2	3	0	1	0	0	0	0	0	1	0	.333	.333	1	1	0
Bob Friend	p	3	1	0	0	0	0	0	0	0	0	0	.000	.000	1	3	0
Freddie Green	p	3	1	0	0	0	0	0	0	0	0	0	.000	.000	0	0	0
Tom Cheney	p	3	0	0	0	0	0	0	0	0	0	0	—	—	0	1	0
Clem Labine	p	3	0	0	0	0	0	0	0	0	0	0	—	—	1	0	0
George Witt	p	2	0	0	0	0	0	0	0	0	0	0	—	—	0	0	0
Vinegar Bend Mizell	p	2	0	0	0	0	0	0	0	0	0	0	—	—	0	0	0
Joe Gibbon	p	2	0	0	0	0	0	0	0	0	0	0	—	—	1	0	0
team total		7	234	27	60	11	0	4	26	12	26	2	.256	.355	186	67	4

Double Plays—7
Left on Bases—42

REGULAR SEASON STATISTICS

	Main Pos	G	AB	R	H	2B	3B	HR	RBI	BB	SO	SB	BA	SA
	1b	122	438	48	114	17	5	23	83	39	107	0	.260	.479
	2b	151	538	58	147	21	5	11	64	40	50	4	.273	.392
	ss	138	573	85	186	26	4	2	50	39	35	0	.325	.394
	3b	155	553	97	156	24	9	16	79	74	74	3	.282	.445
	of	144	570	89	179	22	6	16	94	39	72	4	.314	.458
	of	120	409	60	108	16	9	8	40	44	44	8	.264	.406
	of	101	307	36	82	14	4	0	28	32	43	1	.267	.339
	c	110	337	33	99	15	2	7	39	35	13	0	.294	.412
	1b	93	200	34	60	11	1	7	35	24	15	1	.300	.470
	of	145	571	83	156	33	6	15	86	59	86	11	.273	.431
	c	77	258	37	76	18	2	11	45	22	48	1	.295	.508
	ss	65	102	9	34	4	1	0	10	16	20	0	.333	.392
	ph	33	37	5	9	0	0	4	2	9	0	0	.243	.243
	pr-of	50	56	21	13	2	0	1	3	5	8	1	.232	.321
	c	22	20	1	4	1	0	0	1	1	2	0	.200	.250
	p	35	94	10	17	5	2	1	7	2	19	0	.181	.309
	p	68	17	3	7	1	0	0	0	4	4	0	.412	.471
	p	29	67	7	17	4	0	0	7	3	15	0	.254	.313
	p	38	88	5	6	1	0	0	3	6	31	0	.068	.080
	p	45	8	3	3	0	0	2	2	1	4	0	.375	1.125
	p	11	17	2	3	1	0	0	2	1	4	0	.176	.235
a	p	15	4	0	0	0	0	0	1	0	2	0	.000	.000
	p	10	9	0	0	0	0	0	0	0	4	0	.000	.000
b	p	23	51	2	7	0	0	0	3	2	14	0	.137	.137
	p	27	19	2	4	0	0	0	2	0	5	0	.211	.211
		155	5406	734	1493	236	56	120	689	486	747	34	.276	.407

a—from Los Angeles and Detroit
b—from St. Louis
R.C. Stevens (1b), Mickey Vernon (ph), Danny Kravitz (c), Harry Bright (ph), Dick Barone (ss), Roman Mejias (pr), Paul Giel (p), Earl Francis (p), Jim Umbricht (p), Bennie Daniels (p), Don Gross (p), and Diomedes Olivo (p) also played for the Pirates during the season.

NEW YORK YANKEES

	Pos	G	AB	R	H	2B	3B	HR	RBI	BB	SO	SB	BA	SA	PO	A	E
Bill Skowron	1b	7	32	7	12	2	0	2	6	0	6	0	.375	.625	70	6	0
Bobby Richardson	2b	7	30	8	11	2	2	1	12	1	1	0	.367	.667	21	28	2
Tony Kubek	ss-lf	7	30	6	10	1	0	0	3	2	2	0	.333	.367	12	21	3
Gil McDougald	3b-pr	6	18	5	1	0	0	0	2	3	0	0	.278	.333	5	7	1
Roger Maris	rf	7	30	6	8	1	0	2	2	4	4	0	.267	.500	11	0	1
Mickey Mantle	cf	7	25	8	10	1	0	3	11	8	9	0	.400	.800	15	0	0
Yogi Berra	lf-c-rf-ph	7	22	6	7	0	0	1	8	2	0	0	.318	.455	18	1	0
Elston Howard	c-ph	5	13	4	6	1	1	1	4	1	4	0	.462	.923	11	0	0
Bob Cerv	ph-lf	4	14	1	5	0	0	0	0	0	3	0	.357	.357	8	0	1
Clete Boyer	3b-ss	4	12	1	3	2	1	0	1	0	1	0	.250	.583	4	7	0
Johnny Blanchard	ph-c	5	11	2	5	2	0	0	2	0	0	0	.455	.636	5	2	0
Hector Lopez	lf-ph	3	7	0	3	0	0	0	0	1	0	0	.429	.429	0	1	0
Joe DeMaestri	ss-pr	4	2	1	1	0	0	0	0	0	0	0	.500	.500	2	4	0
Dale Long	ph	3	3	0	1	0	0	0	0	0	1	0	.333	.333			
Eli Grba	pr	1	0	0	0	0	0	0	0	0	0	0	—	—			
Whitey Ford	p	2	8	1	2	0	0	0	2	0	2	0	.250	.250	3	5	0
Bob Turley	p	2	4	0	1	0	0	0	1	0	1	0	.250	.250	0	2	0
Bobby Shantz	p	3	3	0	1	0	0	0	0	0	0	0	.333	.333	3	2	0
Ralph Terry	p	2	2	0	0	0	0	0	0	0	1	0	.000	.000	0	3	0
Jim Coates	p	3	1	0	0	0	0	0	0	0	1	0	.000	.000	1	1	0
Bill Stafford	p	2	1	0	0	0	0	0	0	1	0	0	.000	.000	0	2	0
Luis Arroyo	p	1	1	0	0	0	0	0	0	0	0	0	.000	.000	0	0	0
Art Ditmar	p	2	0	0	0	0	0	0	0	0	0	0	—	—	0	0	0
Ryne Duren	p	2	0	0	0	0	0	0	0	0	0	0	—	—	0	0	0
Duke Maas	p	1	0	0	0	0	0	0	0	0	0	0	—	—	0	0	0
team total		7	269	55	91	13	4	10	54	18	40	0	.338	.528	183	93	8

Double Play—9
Left on Bases—51

	Main Pos	G	AB	R	H	2B	3B	HR	RBI	BB	SO	SB	BA	SA
	1b	146	538	63	166	34	3	26	91	38	95	2	.309	.528
	2b	150	460	45	116	12	3	1	26	35	19	6	.252	.298
	ss	147	568	77	155	25	3	14	62	31	42	3	.273	.401
	3b	119	337	54	87	16	4	8	34	38	45	2	.258	.401
	of	136	499	98	141	18	7	39	112	70	65	2	.283	.581
	of	153	527	119	145	17	6	40	94	111	125	14	.275	.558
	c-of	120	359	46	99	14	1	15	62	38	23	2	.276	.446
	c	107	323	29	79	11	3	6	39	28	43	3	.245	.353
c	of	87	216	32	54	11	1	8	28	30	36	0	.250	.421
	3b	124	393	54	95	20	1	14	46	23	85	2	.242	.405
	c-ph	53	99	8	24	3	1	4	14	6	17	0	.242	.414
	of	131	408	66	116	14	6	9	42	46	64	1	.284	.414
	2b-ss	49	35	4	8	1	0	0	2	0	9	0	.229	.257
d	1b-ph	26	41	6	15	3	1	3	10	5	6	0	.366	.707
	p	27	21	1	5	0	1	1	2	7	7	0	.238	.381
	p	33	53	4	8	2	0	0	3	9	14	0	.151	.189
	p	34	55	4	4	1	0	1	2	18	0	.073	.091
	p	43	10	1	1	0	0	0	1	2	0	.100	.100
	p	35	49	1	6	1	0	1	1	18	0	.122	.143
	p	35	48	10	12	4	0	0	6	2	20	0	.250	.333
	p	12	22	0	1	0	0	0	1	0	8	0	.045	.045
	p	29	5	0	0	0	0	0	1	1	0	.000	.000
	p	36	69	2	11	2	0	2	4	14	0	.159	.188
	p	42	6	0	0	0	0	0	4	0	.000	.000
	p	35	6	0	0	0	0	0	0	0	2	0	.000	.000
		155	5290	746	1377	215	40	193	699	537	818	37	.260	.426

c—from Kansas City
d—from San Francisco
Kent Hadley (1b), Ken Hunt (of), Jim Pisoni (of), Deron Johnson (3b), Elmer Valo (ph), Jesse Gonder (ph), Andy Carey (3b), Billy Shantz (c), Johnny James (p), John Gabler (p), Bill Short (p), Fred Kipp (p), and Hal Stowe (p) also played for the Yankees during the season.

PITCHING

PITTSBURGH PIRATES

	G	GS	CG	IP	H	R	ER	BB	SO	W	L	SV	ERA
Vernon Law	3	3	0	18⅓	22	7	7	3	8	2	0	0	3.44
Roy Face	4	0	0	10⅓	9	6	6	2	4	0	0	3	5.23
Harvey Haddix	2	1	0	7⅓	6	2	2	6	2	2	0	0	2.45
Bob Friend	3	2	0	6	13	10	9	3	7	0	2	0	13.50
Tom Cheney	3	0	0	4	4	2	2	1	6	0	0	0	4.50
Clem Labine	3	0	0	4	11	11	6	1	2	0	0	0	13.50
Freddie Green	3	0	0	4	11	10	10	1	3	0	0	0	22.50
Joe Gibbon	2	0	0	3	4	3	3	1	2	0	0	0	9.00
George Witt	3	0	0	2⅓	5	0	0	2	1	0	0	0	0.00
Vinegar Bend Mizell	2	1	0	2⅓	4	4	4	2	1	0	1	0	15.43
team total	7	7	0	62	91	55	49	18	40	4	3	3	7.11

NEW YORK YANKEES

	G	GS	CG	IP	H	R	ER	BB	SO	W	L	SV	ERA
Whitey Ford	2	2	2	18	11	0	0	2	8	2	0	0	0.00
Bob Turley	2	2	0	9⅓	15	6	5	4	0	1	0	0	4.82
Ralph Terry	2	1	0	6⅓	7	4	4	1	5	0	2	0	5.40
Bobby Shantz	3	0	0	6⅓	4	3	3	1	4	0	0	0	4.26
Jim Coates	3	0	0	6⅓	6	4	4	1	3	0	0	0	5.68
Bill Stafford	2	0	0	6	5	1	1	2	0	0	0	0	1.50
Ryne Duren	2	0	0	4	3	1	1	1	5	0	0	0	2.25
Duke Maas	1	0	0	2	4	1	1	0	0	0	0	0	4.50
Art Ditmar	2	2	0	1⅔	6	6	4	1	0	0	2	0	21.60
Luis Arroyo	1	0	0	⅔	2	1	1	0	1	0	0	0	13.50
Eli Grba	Did not pitch												
team total	7	7	2	61	60	27	24	12	26	3	4	1	3.54

REGULAR SEASON STATISTICS

	G	GS	CG	IP	H	ER	BB	SO	W	L	Pct.	SV	ShO	ERA
	35	35	18	272	266	93	40	120	20	9	.690	0	3	3.08
	68	0	0	115	93	37	29	72	10	8	.556	24	0	2.90
	29	28	4	172	189	76	38	101	11	10	.524	1	3	3.98
	38	37	16	276	266	92	45	183	18	12	.600	1	4	3.00
	11	8	1	52	44	23	33	35	2	2	.500	0	1	3.98
a	15	4	0	30	29	5	11	21	3	0	1.000	3	0	1.50
	45	0	0	70	61	25	33	49	8	4	.667	3	0	3.21
	27	9	0	80	87	36	31	60	4	2	.667	0	0	4.05
	10	6	0	30	33	14	12	15	1	2	.333	0	0	4.20
b	23	23	8	156	141	54	46	71	13	5	.722	0	3	3.12
	155	155	47	1400	1363	543	386	811	95	59	.617	33	11	3.49

	G	GS	CG	IP	H	ER	BB	SO	W	L	Pct.	SV	ShO	ERA
	33	29	8	193	168	66	65	85	12	9	.571	0	4	3.08
	34	24	4	173	138	63	87	87	9	3	.750	5	1	3.28
	35	23	7	167	149	63	52	92	10	8	.556	1	3	3.40
	42	0	0	68	57	21	24	54	5	4	.556	11	0	2.78
	35	18	6	149	139	71	66	73	13	3	.813	1	2	4.29
	11	8	2	60	50	15	18	36	3	1	.750	0	1	2.25
	42	1	0	49	27	27	49	67	3	4	.429	9	0	4.96
	35	1	0	70	70	32	35	28	5	1	.833	4	0	4.11
	34	28	8	200	195	68	65	55	15	9	.625	0	1	3.06
	29	0	0	41	30	13	22	29	5	1	.833	7	0	2.88
	24	9	1	81	65	33	46	32	6	4	.600	1	0	3.67
	155	155	38	1398	1225	546	609	712	97	57	.630	42	16	3.52

Total Attendance—349,813   Average Attendance—49,973   Winning Player's Share—$8,418   Losing Player's Share—$5,125

1961
Maris: 62; Ford: 32

Political puns about a battle between the Reds and Yanks surrounded this World Series confrontation between Cincinnati and New York, but more serious baseball talk still buzzed about the awesome Yankee club and the home-run extravaganza staged by Roger Maris and Mickey Mantle. The M&M boys chased Babe Ruth's ghost throughout the summer, keeping pace with Ruth's 60-homer season of 1927. Injuries in September kayoed Mantle's bid at 54, but Maris went on to hit his sixty-first homer of the season in the last game of the campaign. Commissioner Ford Frick took note of the controversy raging over Ruth's record and ruled that it would stand, as Maris's mark came in the new 162-game schedule which the American League's expansion to 10 teams this year necessitated. While Maris was earning a place in the record books with an asterisk and drawing quote-hungry reporters in droves, the Yankees made a shambles of the A.L. race and won the pennant in the first year under Ralph Houk, who succeeded Casey Stengel as manager. Houk's men hit a record 240 homers, with Bill Skowron, Yogi Berra, Elston Howard, and Johnny Blanchard all joining Maris and Mantle over the 20-homer mark. The infield defense shone with Bobby Richardson, Tony Kubek, and Clete Boyer, and the pitching staff boasted of a 25-game-winner in Whitey Ford, reliable starters in Ralph Terry and Bill Stafford, and a relief sensation in screwballing Luis Arroyo. Some writers ranked this club with the 1927 Yanks as the best in history, an honor no one conferred on the Cincinnati Reds. The Reds shuffled men at the key second-base, shortstop, and catching positions, but manager Fred Hutchinson brought his club home an upset winner with a superb season by Frank Robinson, strong batting by Vada Pinson, Gordy Coleman, Gene Freese, and Wally Post, and three top starters in Joey Jay, Jim O'Toole, and Bob Purkey. But the Reds simply didn't stack up against the Yankees, the cream of American baseball.

The Yanks took game one in Yankee Stadium, but they did it more on Ford's left arm than on Yankee power. Solo homers by Howard and Skowron gave Ford two runs to work with, and the Chairman of the Board shut the Reds out on two hits, running his string of Series shutouts to three. But the Reds came back the next day with a show of the spirit that got them into the Series. After Coleman and Berra traded two-run homers in the fourth inning, the Reds went ahead with two out in the fifth when Elio Chacon sprinted home from third on a passed ball that got no more than a dozen feet behind Howard. The Reds added four more runs against Terry, while Jay threw a four-hitter for a 6–2 victory which evened the Series going back to Cincinnati.

The Reds now hoped to pull another upset on their home turf, so Houk prevailed on Mantle, who sat out the first two games with an abscess on his right hip. Mickey went 0-for-4 against Purkey, but the Yanks still won 3–2. The Reds led 2–1 after seven innings, but pinch hitter Blanchard belted a homer in the eighth to tie the score at 2–2. Arroyo held the Reds in the bottom of the inning, and then Maris showed the Cincinnati fans what he had been doing all summer by driving a deep home run to right, his first hit of the Series. The New York win took some of the spunk out of the Reds and threw them into two embarrassing losses in front of their home fans. O'Toole lacked his usual stuff in game four and lost a 7–0 decision. The big story of the game, however, was Whitey Ford's five shutout innings before leaving with a foot injury. Those frames ran his scoreless-inning streak to 32, breaking Babe Ruth's old record of 29 2/3 innings. Mantle singled in the fourth inning and left for a pinch runner with blood soaking his uniform on the right hip. A stiff shoulder sat Berra on the bench with Mantle for game five, but substitutes Hector Lopez and Blanchard picked up in championship style. Lopez drove in five runs with a triple and home run, while Blanchard's three hits included a double and a homer. Five Yankee runs in the top of the first started a parade of eight Cincinnati pitchers to the mound, but nothing Hutchinson did could stop the tide of a 13–5 win and a quick Series elimination. Although Maris and Mantle drove in only two runs between them, the Yankees' bench strength made Houk the third manager in history to win the World Championship in his freshman year.

Game 1 October 4 at New York

| Cin. | 000 000 000 |
| N.Y. | 000 101 00x |

Cincinnati	Pos	AB	R	H	RBI	PO	A	E
Blasingame	2b	3	0	0	0	3	2	0
d Lynch		1	0	0	0	0	0	0
Kasko	ss	4	0	1	0	3	3	0
Pinson	cf	4	0	0	0	4	0	0
Robinson	lf	2	0	0	0	0	0	0
Post	rf	3	0	1	0	2	0	0
Freese	3b	3	0	0	0	1	0	0
Coleman	1b	3	0	0	0	7	0	0
D. Johnson	c	2	0	0	0	3	1	0
a Cardenas		1	0	0	0	0	0	0
Zimmerman	c	0	0	0	0	1	0	0
O'Toole	p	2	0	0	0	0	0	0
b Gernert		1	0	0	0	0	0	0
Brosnan	p	0	0	0	0	0	0	0
Totals		29	0	2	0	24	6	0

New York	Pos	AB	R	H	RBI	PO	A	E
Richardson	2b	4	0	3	0	1	4	0
Kubek	ss	3	0	0	0	2	3	0
Maris	cf-rf	4	0	0	0	2	0	0
Howard	c	4	1	1	1	6	0	0
Skowron	1b	3	1	1	1	13	0	0
Berra	lf	2	0	0	0	1	0	0
Lopez	rf	2	0	0	0	0	0	0
c Blanchard		1	0	0	0	0	0	0
Reed	cf	0	0	0	0	0	0	0
Boyer	3b	3	0	1	0	2	5	0
Ford	p	3	0	0	0	0	1	0
Totals		29	2	6	2	27	13	0

Pitching	IP	H	R	ER	BB	SO
Cincinnati						
O'Toole (L)	7	6	2	2	4	2
Brosnan	1	0	0	0	1	1
New York						
Ford (W)	9	2	0	0	1	6

a Struck out for D. Johnson in 8th.
b Grounded out for O'Toole in 8th.
c Popped out for Lopez in 8th.
d Popped out for Blasingame in 9th.

Home Runs—Howard, Skowron. Double Play—D. Johnson to Kasko to Coleman. Left on Bases—Cincinnati 3, New York 8. Umpires—Runge (A), Conlan (N), Umont (A), Donatelli (N), Crawford (N), Stewart (A). Attendance—62,397. Time of Game—2:11.

1st Inning
Cincinnati
1 Blasingame struck out.
Kasko blooped a single to left.
2 Pinson lined to deep center.
3 Robinson struck out.
New York
Richardson singled to center.
Kubek walked.
1 Maris popped to Kasko in short left.
2 Howard flied to Pinson in left-center.
Skowron walked, loading the bases.
3 Berra popped to second.

2nd Inning
Cincinnati
1 Post grounded to third.
2 Freese grounded to third.
3 Coleman grounded to the mound.
New York
1 Lopez flied to deep right.
2 Boyer popped to third.
3 Ford grounded to second.

3rd Inning
Cincinnati
1 Johnson grounded to third.
2 O'Toole took a called third strike.
3 Blasingame struck out.
New York
Richardson beat out a hopper to deep short.
1 Kubek popped to Kasko behind third.
2,3 Maris struck out and Richardson was trapped between first and second. Doubled up by Johnson to Kasko to Coleman.

4th Inning
Cincinnati
1 Kasko grounded to short.
2 Pinson grounded to second.
3 Robinson struck out.
New York
Howard hit a home run into the lower right field stands.
1 Skowron grounded to short.
Berra walked.
2 Lopez took a called third strike.
Boyer singled to right, Berra stopping at second.
3 Ford lined to short.

5th Inning
Cincinnati
Post singled to left.
1 Freese flied to left.
2 Coleman grounded to second, Post advancing to second.
3 Johnson grounded to third, Boyer tagged Post coming into third.
New York
1 Richardson was tagged out bunting by Coleman.
2 Kubek flied to center.
3 Maris grounded to first.

6th Inning
Cincinnati
1 O'Toole flied to short-center.
2 Blasingame grounded to second.
3 Kasko grounded to second.
New York
1 Howard flied to deep center.
Skowron hit a home run into the lower left field stands.
2 Berra popped to Blasingame in short right.
Lopez walked.
3 Boyer flied to Pinson in deep left-center.

7th Inning
Cincinnati
1 Pinson popped to first.
Robinson walked.
2 Post forced Robinson at second, Boyer to Richardson.
3 Freese popped to short.
New York
1 Ford grounded to second.
Richardson singled to left.
2 Kubek flied to right.
3 Maris fouled to Johnson.

8th Inning
Cincinnati
1 Coleman grounded to short.
2 Cardenas, batting for Johnson, fanned.
3 Gernert, batting for O'Toole, grounded to third, where Boyer made a fantastic play.
New York
For Cincinnati—Brosnan pitching and Zimmerman catching.
1 Howard grounded to short.
2 Skowron fanned.
Berra walked.
3 Blanchard, batting for Lopez, popped to second.

9th Inning
Cincinnati
For New York—Maris moved to right with Reed coming in to play center.
1 Lynch, pinch-hitting for Blasingame, popped to third.
2 Kasko grounded to short.
3 Pinson popped to short.

Game 2 October 5 at New York

Cincinnati	Pos	AB	R	H	RBI	PO	A	E
Chacon	2b	4	1	1	0	6	4	0
Kasko	ss	5	0	1	0	6	4	0
Pinson	cf	5	0	1	0	2	0	0
Robinson	lf	4	2	0	0	0	0	0
Coleman	1b	5	1	2	2	5	1	0
Post	rf	4	2	2	0	0	0	0
Freese	3b	2	0	0	0	1	1	0
Edwards	c	4	0	2	2	6	1	0
Jay	p	4	0	0	0	1	0	0
Totals		37	6	9	4	27	11	0

Pitching	IP	H	R	ER	BB	SO
Cincinnati						
Jay (W)	9	4	2	2	6	6
New York						
Terry (L)	7	6	4	2	2	7
Arroyo	2	3	2	1	2	1

Cin.	000	211	020					
N.Y.	000	200	000					

New York	Pos	AB	R	H	RBI	PO	A	E
Richardson	2b	4	0	1	0	2	3	0
Kubek	ss	4	0	1	0	1	2	0
Maris	cf	3	1	0	0	1	0	0
Berra	lf	4	1	2	2	4	0	1
Blanchard	rf	4	0	0	0	1	0	0
Howard	c	3	0	0	0	8	0	0
Skowron	1b	3	0	0	0	8	1	0
Boyer	3b	2	0	0	0	2	1	1
Terry	p	2	0	0	0	0	1	0
a Lopez		0	0	0	0	0	0	0
Arroyo	p	0	0	0	0	1	0	1
b Gardner		1	0	0	0	0	0	0
Totals		30	2	4	2	27	9	3

a Walked for Terry in 7th.
b Lined out for Arroyo in 9th.

Doubles—Edwards, Pinson, Post. Home Runs—Berra, Coleman. Double Plays—Chacon to Kasko to Coleman 2. Passed Ball—Howard. Left on Bases—Cincinnati 8, New York 7. Umpires—Conlan, Umont, Donatelli, Runge, Crawford, Stewart. Attendance—63,083. Time of Game—2:43.

1st Inning
Cincinnati
1 Chacon flied to deep left.
2 Kasko struck out.
3 Pinson grounded to second.
New York
Richardson singled to left.
1 Kubek forced Richardson at second, Kasko to Chacon.
2 Maris forced Kubek at second, Chacon to Kasko.
3 Berra grounded to second.

2nd Inning
Cincinnati
1 Robinson popped to Kubek in short center.
2 Coleman grounded to short.
Post singled off Boyer's glove.
3 Freese struck out.
New York
1 Blanchard popped to short.
2 Howard grounded to third.
Skowron walked.
3 Boyer forced Skowron at second, Kasko to Chacon.

3rd Inning
Cincinnati
1 Edwards grounded to the mound.
2 Jay flied to deep left.
Chacon walked.
3 Kasko struck out.
New York
1 Terry popped to second.
2 Richardson popped to Chacon in short center.
3 Kubek fanned.

4th Inning
Cincinnati
1 Pinson flied to left.
Robinson safe on Boyer's fumble.
Coleman hit a two-run homer into the right-center field bleachers.
2 Post struck out.
3 Freese grounded to short.
New York
Maris walked.
Berra hit a two-run homer into the lower right field stands.
1 Blanchard grounded out, Coleman to Jay.
Howard walked.
2,3 Skowron grounded into a double play, Chacon to Kasko to Coleman.

5th Inning
Cincinnati
1 Edwards lined to second.
2 Jay struck out.
Chacon blooped a single to center.
Kasko singled to center, advancing Chacon to third.
Chacon scored and Kasko went to second on Howard's passed ball.
3 Pinson struck out.
New York
Boyer walked.
1 Terry popped to Chacon in short right.
Richardson safe on a fielder's choice as Kasko tried for the force at second but Boyer just beat the throw.
2 Kubek struck out.
3 Maris struck out.

6th Inning
Cincinnati
1 Robinson grounded to Boyer who made another brilliant fielding play.
2 Coleman struck out.
Post doubled off the wall in the left field corner.
Freese got an intentional pass.
Edwards singled to right, Post scored and Freese went to third.
3 Jay grounded to second.
New York
Berra singled to center.
1 Blanchard popped to Kasko in short center.
2,3 Howard hit into a double play, Chacon to Kasko to Coleman.

7th Inning
Cincinnati
1 Chacon flied to deep left.
2 Kasko flied to center.
3 Pinson lined to first.
New York
1 Skowron struck out.
2 Boyer flied to deep center.
Lopez, pinch-hitting for Terry, walked.
3 Richardson forced Lopez at second, Chacon unassisted.

8th Inning
Cincinnati
For New York—Arroyo pitching.
Robinson walked.
Coleman singled on a roller between third and the mound. Arroyo threw wild to first with Robinson scoring but
1 Coleman was out trying for third, Blanchard to Boyer.
Post safe on third when Berra missed his fly for an error.
Freese again intentionally walked.
Edwards blooped a double to left, Post scoring and Freese stopping at third.
2 Jay struck out.
3 Chacon grounded to second.
New York
Kubek singled to center.
1 Maris struck out.
2 Berra flied to center.
3 Blanchard fouled to third.

9th Inning
Cincinnati
1 Kasko popped to second.
Pinson blooped a double into short left.
2 Robinson fouled to Boyer.
3 Coleman grounded out, Skowron to Arroyo.
New York
1 Howard grounded out, Edwards to Coleman.
2 Skowron struck out.
Boyer walked.
3 Gardner, pinch-hitting for Arroyo, lined to short.

Game 3 October 7 at Cincinnati

New York	Pos	AB	R	H	RBI	PO	A	E
Richardson	2b	4	0	1	0	2	2	0
Kubek	ss	4	1	1	0	1	2	0
Maris	rf	4	1	1	1	2	0	0
Mantle	cf	4	0	0	0	1	0	0
Reed	cf	0	0	0	0	0	0	0
Berra	lf	3	0	1	1	2	0	0
Howard	c	4	0	1	0	10	0	0
Skowron	1b	3	0	0	0	9	1	0
Boyer	3b	3	0	0	0	0	3	0
Stafford	p	2	0	0	0	1	0	1
Daley	p	0	0	0	0	0	0	0
c Blanchard		1	1	1	1	0	0	0
Arroyo	p	0	0	0	0	0	1	0
Totals		32	3	6	3	27	8	1

Pitching	IP	H	R	ER	BB	SO
New York						
Stafford	6⅓	7	2	2	2	5
Daley	⅓	0	0	0	0	0
Arroyo (W)	2	1	0	0	0	2
Cincinnati						
Purkey (L)	9	6	3	2	1	3

N.Y.	000	000	111					
Cin.	001	000	100					

Cincinnati	Pos	AB	R	H	RBI	PO	A	E
Chacon	2b	3	1	1	0	2	1	0
a Lynch		0	0	0	0	0	0	0
b Blasingame	2b	0	0	0	0	0	0	0
f Bell		1	0	0	0	0	0	0
Kasko	ss	4	0	2	1	3	1	0
Pinson	cf	4	0	0	0	4	0	0
Robinson	rf	4	0	1	1	1	0	0
Coleman	1b	4	0	2	0	6	3	0
Post	lf	4	0	0	0	2	0	0
Freese	3b	3	0	0	0	2	0	0
Edwards	c	3	1	1	0	3	0	0
d Cardenas		1	0	1	0	0	0	0
Purkey	p	3	0	0	0	4	2	0
e Gernert		1	0	0	0	0	0	0
Totals		35	2	8	2	27	7	0

a Intentionally walked for Chacon in 7th.
b Ran for Lynch in 7th.
c Homered for Daley in 8th.
d Doubled for Edwards in 9th.
e Grounded out for Purkey in 9th.
f Grounded out for Blasingame in 9th.

Doubles—Cardenas, Edwards, Howard, Robinson. Home Runs—Blanchard, Maris. Stolen Base—Richardson. Double Play—Kasko (unassisted). Passed Ball—Edwards. Left on Bases—New York 3, Cincinnati 8. Umpires—Umont, Donatelli, Runge, Conlan, Crawford, Stewart. Attendance—32,589. Time of Game—2:15.

1st Inning
New York
1 Richardson grounded to short.
2 Kubek grounded to second.
3 Maris popped to third.
Cincinnati
1 Chacon took a called third strike.
Kasko singled to center.
2 Pinson flied to Mantle in left-center.
3 Robinson struck out.

2nd Inning
New York
1 Mantle flied to center.
Berra walked.
2 Howard popped to second.
3 Skowron flied to right.
Cincinnati
Coleman singled off Stafford's glove.
1 Post flied to right.
Freese walked.
2 Edwards grounded to first, moving up both runners.
3 Purkey took a called third strike.

3rd Inning
New York
1 Boyer fouled to Coleman.
2 Stafford lined to Purkey.
3 Richardson grounded to the mound.
Cincinnati
Chacon beat out a bunt and went to second as Stafford threw wildly.
1 Kasko fouled to Skowron.
2 Pinson grounded to second, sending Chacon to third.
Robinson doubled off the left field wall, scoring Chacon.
3 Coleman grounded out, Skowron to Stafford.

4th Inning
New York
1 Kubek flied to left.
2 Maris grounded out, Coleman to Purkey.
3 Mantle flied to deep center.
Cincinnati
1 Post grounded to second.
2 Freese flied to Berra in left-center.
3 Edwards grounded to first.

5th Inning
New York
1 Berra struck out but had to be tagged by Edwards, who dropped strike three.
Howard doubled off the center field wall.
2,3 Skowron lined into a double play, Kasko, unassisted.
Cincinnati
1 Purkey called out on strikes.
2 Chacon grounded to third.
3 Kasko popped to second.

6th Inning
New York
1 Boyer popped to short.
2 Stafford popped to Chacon behind first base.
3 Richardson lined to left.
Cincinnati
1 Pinson fouled to Howard on an attempted bunt.
2 Robinson fouled to Howard.
Coleman singled to left.
3 Post forced Coleman at second, Boyer to Richardson.

7th Inning
New York
Kubek singled to center.
1 Maris flied to center.
Kubek went to second on a passed ball.
2 Mantle struck out.
Berra blooped a Texas League single to short right, scoring Kubek.
3 Howard fouled to Freese.
Cincinnati
1 Freese flied to left.
Edwards doubled into the right field corner.
2 Purkey struck out.
Lynch, pinch-hitting for Chacon, got an intentional pass.
Blasingame ran for Lynch.
Kasko singled to left, scoring Edwards with Blasingame stopping at second.
For New York—Daley came in to pitch.
3 Pinson flied to right.

8th Inning
New York
For Cincinnati—Blasingame playing second.
1 Skowron tapped back to the mound.
2 Boyer fouled to Coleman.
Blanchard, pinch-hitting for Daley, homered into the right field bleachers.
Richardson singled to left.
Richardson stole second.
3 Kubek flied to center.
Cincinnati
For New York—Arroyo pitching.
1 Robinson struck out.
2 Coleman fouled to Howard.
3 Post grounded to third.

9th Inning
New York
Maris hit a homer into the right field bleachers.
1 Mantle struck out.
2 Berra grounded out, Coleman to Purkey.
3 Howard grounded out, Coleman to Purkey.
Cincinnati
For New York—Reed playing center.
1 Freese struck out.
Cardenas, batting for Edwards, doubled off the left-center field scoreboard.
2 Gernert, batting for Purkey, grounded to short, Cardenas holding second.
3 Bell, pinch-hitting for Blasingame, grounded back to the mound.

Game 4 October 8 at Cincinnati

N.Y.	000 112 300
Cin.	000 000 000

New York	Pos	AB	R	H	RBI	PO	A	E
Richardson	2b	5	1	3	0	4	4	0
Kubek	ss	5	0	1	1	0	4	0
Maris	rf-cf	3	2	0	0	3	0	0
Mantle	cf	2	0	1	0	1	0	0
a Lopez	rf	3	1	1	2	3	0	0
Howard	c	4	1	1	0	3	0	0
Berra	lf	2	1	0	0	4	0	0
Skowron	1b	3	0	3	1	9	0	0
Boyer	3b	4	0	1	2	0	2	0
Ford	p	2	1	0	0	0	0	0
Coates	p	1	0	0	0	0	0	0
Totals		34	7	11	6	27	10	0

Pitching	IP	H	R	ER	BB	SO
New York						
Ford (W)	*5	4	0	0	0	1
Coates (SV)	4	1	0	0	1	2
Cincinnati						
O'Toole (L)	5	5	2	2	3	2
Brosnan	3	6	5	5	3	3
Henry	1	0	0	0	0	2

*Pitched to one batter in 6th.

Cincinnati	Pos	AB	R	H	RBI	PO	A	E
Chacon	2b	4	0	1	0	4	4	0
Kasko	ss	4	0	1	0	1	2	0
Pinson	cf	4	0	0	0	4	1	1
Robinson	rf	1	0	0	0	2	0	0
Post	lf	4	0	1	0	1	0	0
Freese	3b	4	0	0	0	1	2	0
Coleman	1b	4	0	0	0	5	0	0
Johnson	c	2	0	2	0	5	0	0
c Bell		1	0	0	0	0	0	0
Zimmerman	c	0	0	0	0	3	0	0
O'Toole	p	1	0	0	0	1	0	0
b Gernert		1	0	0	0	0	0	0
Brosnan	p	0	0	0	0	0	0	0
d Lynch		1	0	0	0	0	0	0
Henry	p	0	0	0	0	0	0	0
Totals		31	0	5	0	27	9	1

a Ran for Mantle in 4th.
b Hit into force out for O'Toole in 5th.
c Grounded out for Johnson in 7th.
d Struck out for Brosnan in 8th.

Doubles—Boyer, Howard, Richardson. Double Plays—Kasko to Chacon to Coleman, Kubek to Richardson to Skowron, Freese to Chacon to Coleman, Coleman (unassisted). Hit by Pitcher—Robinson 2 (by Ford and Coates). Wild Pitch—Brosnan. Left on Bases—New York 6, Cincinnati 7. Umpires—Donatelli, Runge, Conlan, Umont, Crawford, Stewart. Attendance—32,589. Time of Game—2:27.

1st Inning
New York
1 Richardson flied to center.
2 Kubek fanned.
3 Maris fouled to Johnson.
Cincinnati
1 Chacon struck out.
2 Kasko flied to short right.
3 Pinson flied to center.

2nd Inning
New York
1 Mantle grounded to third.
2 Howard struck out.
3 Berra flied to right.
Cincinnati
1 Robinson grounded to third.
2 Post flied to left.
3 Freese flied to deep right.

3rd Inning
New York
Skowron walked.
1 Boyer forced Skowron at second, Kasko to Chacon.
2 Ford forced Boyer at second, Chacon to Kasko.
Richardson doubled to left, moving Ford to third.
3 Kubek flied to Pinson in left-center.
Cincinnati
1 Coleman grounded to second.
Johnson singled to left.
2 O'Toole forced Johnson at second, Kubek to Richardson.
3 Chacon grounded to second. **(Ford broke Babe Ruth's record of 29 2/3 consecutive scoreless innings with his string now at 30 innings.)**

4th Inning
New York
Maris walked.
Mantle singled to left-center, moving Maris to third.
Lopez ran for Mantle.
1,2 Howard grounded into a double play, Kasko to Chacon to Coleman as Maris scored.
3 Berra rolled out, Chacon to O'Toole.
Cincinnati
For New York—Lopez playing right as Maris switched to center.
Kasko singled to left.
1 Pinson flied to Berra who made a running catch near the foul line.
Robinson was hit by a pitched ball.
2,3 Post grounded into a double play, Kubek to Richardson to Skowron.

5th Inning
New York
Skowron singled to right.
1,2 Boyer grounded into a double play, Freese to Chacon to Coleman.
Ford walked.
Richardson singled to center, Ford stopping at second.
Kubek singled to right-center, scoring Ford and moving Richardson to third.
Kubek took second on Pinson's throw to the plate.
3 Maris flied to deep right.
Cincinnati
1 Freese flied to short right.
2 Coleman grounded to short.
Johnson singled to center.
3 Gernert, pinch-hitting for O'Toole, forced Johnson at second, Boyer to Richardson.

6th Inning
New York
For Cincinnati—Brosnan pitching.
1 Lopez took a called third strike.
Howard doubled to right-center.
Berra was intentionally walked.
Skowron beat out a roller to third, loading the bases.
Boyer doubled to left, Howard and Berra scoring with Skowron going to third.
2,3 Ford grounded out to Coleman and Skowron was trapped between third and home, tagged by Coleman for an unassisted DP.
Cincinnati
Chacon singled to left.
For New York—Coates replaced Ford on the mound. Ford leaves with an ankle injury and **32 straight shutout innings.**
1 Kasko flied to left.
2 Pinson grounded to first, moving Chacon to second.
Robinson was hit again by a pitched ball.
3 Post flied to Maris in right-center.

7th Inning
New York
Richardson singled to center, and went to second on Pinson's fumble.
1 Kubek flied to left.
Maris intentionally walked.
A wild pitch advanced both runners.
Lopez singled to center, Richardson and Maris scoring with Lopez taking second on the throw to the plate.
2 Howard struck out.
Berra got an intentional pass.
Skowron singled off Brosnan's knee, scoring
3 Lopez but Berra was out trying for third, Pinson to Freese.
Cincinnati
1 Freese flied to left.
2 Coleman flied to right.
3 Bell, batting for Johnson, grounded to second.

8th Inning
New York
For Cincinnati—Zimmerman catching.
1 Boyer flied to center.
2 Coates struck out.
3 Richardson lined to second.
Cincinnati
1 Lynch, batting for Brosnan, fanned.
2 Chacon popped to second.
3 Kasko grounded to short.

9th Inning
New York
For Cincinnati—Henry pitching.
1 Kubek struck out.
2 Maris struck out.
3 Lopez flied to center.
Cincinnati
1 Pinson popped to first.
Robinson walked.
Post singled to left, Robinson stopping at second.
2 Freese struck out.
3 Coleman flied to right.

Game 5 October 9 at Cincinnati

		N.Y.	5 1 0	5 0 2	0 0 0
		Cin.	0 0 3	0 2 0	0 0 0

New York	Pos	AB	R	H	RBI	PO	A	E
Richardson	2b	6	1	1	0	1	3	0
Kubek	ss	6	2	2	0	2	1	0
Maris	cf-rf	5	0	1	1	3	1	0
Blanchard	rf	4	3	3	2	4	0	0
Reed	cf	0	0	0	0	0	0	0
Howard	c	5	3	2	0	4	0	0
Skowron	1b	5	2	2	3	7	3	0
Lopez	1f	4	2	2	5	5	0	0
Boyer	3b	3	0	2	1	2	1	0
Terry	p	1	0	0	0	1	1	0
Daley	p	1	0	0	1	0	0	1
Totals		40	13	15	13	27	10	1

Pitching	IP	H	R	ER	BB	SO
New York						
Terry	2⅓	6	3	3	0	0
Daley (W)	6⅔	5	2	0	0	3
Cincinnati						
Jay (L)	⅓	4	4	4	0	0
Maloney	⅔	4	2	2	1	1
K. Johnson	⅔	0	0	0	0	0
Henry	1⅓	4	5	5	2	1
Jones	⅔	0	0	0	0	0
Purkey	2	0	2	0	2	2
Brosnan	2	3	0	0	0	1
Hunt	1	0	0	0	1	1

Cincinnati	Pos	AB	R	H	RBI	PO	A	E
Blasingame	2b	4	1	1	0	2	2	0
e Chacon		1	0	0	0	0	0	0
Kasko	ss	5	1	2	0	0	3	1
Pinson	cf	5	0	1	0	4	0	0
Robinson	rf	4	1	2	3	2	0	0
Coleman	1b	4	1	1	0	7	0	1
Post	lf	3	1	2	2	3	0	0
Freese	3b	4	0	1	0	1	1	0
Edwards	c	4	0	1	0	8	0	0
Jay	p	0	0	0	0	0	0	0
Maloney	p	0	0	0	0	0	0	0
K. Johnson	p	0	0	0	0	0	0	0
a Bell		1	0	0	0	0	0	0
Henry	p	0	0	0	0	0	1	0
Jones	p	0	0	0	0	0	0	0
b Gernert		1	0	0	0	0	0	0
Purkey	p	0	0	0	0	0	1	1
c Cardenas		1	0	0	0	0	0	0
Brosnan	p	0	0	0	0	0	0	0
d Lynch		1	0	0	0	0	0	0
Hunt	p	0	0	0	0	0	1	0
Totals		38	5	11	5	27	9	3

a Fouled out for K. Johnson in 2nd.
b Called out on strikes for Jones in 4th.
c Flied out for Purkey in 6th.
d Grounded out for Brosnan in 8th.
e Grounded out for Blasingame in 9th.

Doubles—Blanchard, Boyer, Freese, Howard, Maris, Robinson. Triple—Lopez. Home Runs—Blanchard, Lopez, Post, Robinson. Sacrifice Hits—Daley, Lopez, Terry. Sacrifice Fly—Daley. Hit by Pitcher—Post (by Daley). Wild Pitch—Brosnan. Umpires—Runge, Conlan, Umont, Donatelli, Crawford, Stewart. Attendance—32,589. Time of Game—3:05.

1st Inning
New York
Richardson singled to left.
1 Kubek flied to deep center.
2 Maris flied to right.
Richardson went to second when Coleman dropped Jay's pickoff throw.
Blanchard hit a two-run homer into the right field bleachers.
Howard got a ground-rule double when his blast went through an opening in the left-center field scoreboard.
Skowron hit a long single off the left field fence, scoring Howard.
For Cincinnati—Maloney came in to pitch.
Lopez tripled to right, scoring Skowron.
Boyer doubled off the scoreboard, scoring Lopez.
3 Terry struck out.
Cincinnati
1 Blasingame thrown out by Terry on a bunt.
Kasko singled to left.
2 Pinson popped to Boyer near the mound.
3 Robinson flied to left.

2nd Inning
New York
1 Richardson flied to Robinson in right-center.
Kubek singled to left.
Maris doubled inside the left field line, scoring Kubek.
Blanchard walked.
For Cincinnati—K. Johnson now pitching.
2 Howard lined to third.
3 Skowron flied to deep center.
Cincinnati
1 Coleman grounded out, Skowron to Terry.
Post singled to left.
2 Freese flied to short center.
Edwards singled to right-center, moving Post to third.
3 Bell, pinch-hitting for K. Johnson, fouled to Howard.

3rd Inning
New York
For Cincinnati—Henry pitching.
1 Lopez struck out.
Boyer walked.
2 Terry sacrificed Boyer to second, Henry to Blasingame covering first.
3 Richardson grounded to short.
Cincinnati
Blasingame singled to center.
Kasko singled to left, Blasingame stopping at second.
1 Pinson flied to Blanchard in right-center, Blasingame moved on to third after the catch.
Robinson hit a three-run homer over the deep right-center field fence.
For New York—Daley came in to pitch.
Coleman beat out a bunt down the first base line.
2 Post flied to left.
Freese doubled off the scoreboard, moving Coleman to third.
3 Edwards fouled to Boyer

4th Inning
New York
Kubek singled to center.
1 Maris flied to short left.
Blanchard doubled into the right field corner, Kubek stopping at third.
Howard intentionally walked, loading the bases.
Skowron singled to center, scoring Kubek and Blanchard with Howard stopping at second.
Lopez drilled a three-run homer over the center field fence.
For Cincinnati—Jones becomes the Red's 5th pitcher.
2 Boyer popped to Edwards.
3 Daley grounded to second.
Cincinnati
1 Gernert, batting for Jones, took a called third strike.
2 Blasingame grounded to first.
3 Kasko grounded to third.

5th Inning
New York
For Cincinnati—Purkey pitching.
1 Richardson bounced back to the mound.
2 Kubek flied to left.
3 Maris struck out.
Cincinnati
Pinson singled to right-center but
1 was out trying for second, Maris to Kubek.
2 Robinson fouled to Richardson near the right field boxes.
Coleman safe at first when Daley dropped Skowron's throw.
Post hit a two-run homer over the left field wall.
3 Freese took a called third strike.

6th Inning
New York
Blanchard walked.
Howard safely to first and Blanchard to third on Kasko's error.
1 Skowron struck out.
Lopez got safely to second on a sacrifice squeeze when Purkey threw wildly to the plate, Blanchard scoring and Howard going to third. Lopez got credit for sacrifice and RBI.
Boyer got an intentional walk, loading the bases.
2 Daley hit a sacrifice fly to center, Howard scoring after the catch.
3 Richardson fouled to Edwards.
Cincinnati
1 Edwards grounded to second.
2 Cardenas, pinch-hitting for Purkey, flied to left.
3 Blasingame took a called third strike.

7th Inning
New York
For Cincinnati—Brosnan pitching.
1 Kubek flied to center.
2 Maris struck out.
Blanchard singled off Coleman's glove.
Howard singled to center, Blanchard stopping at second.
Blanchard went to third and Howard to second on a wild pitch.
3 Skowron flied to left.
Cincinnati
1 Kasko flied to left.
2 Pinson flied to right.
Robinson doubled off Boyer's glove down the left field line.
3 Coleman grounded to second.

8th Inning
New York
1 Lopez grounded to short.
Boyer singled to center.
2 Daley sacrificed Boyer to second, Freese to Blasingame covering first.
3 Richardson grounded to short.
Cincinnati
Post was hit by a pitched ball.
1 Freese flied to Maris in left-center.
2 Edwards forced Post at second, Skowron to Kubek.
3 Lynch, pinch-hitting for Brosnan, grounded to second.

9th Inning
New York
For Cincinnati—Hunt becomes the 8th pitcher for Cincinnati.
1 Kubek grounded to second.
Maris walked.
2 Blanchard grounded back to the mound, Maris advancing to second.
3 Howard took a called third strike.
Cincinnati
For New York—Reed came in to play center as Maris moved to right.
1 Chacon, pinch-hitting for Blasingame, grounded to short.
2 Kasko flied to right.
3 Pinson flied to left.

1961 WORLD SERIES COMPOSITE BOX

	Wins	Composite Line Score		Manager	W	L	Pct.	Regular Season G. Ahead
New York Yankees (A.L.)	4	5 1 0 9 1 5 4 1 1 - 27		Ralph Houk	109	53	.673	8
Cincinnati Reds (N.L.)	1	0 0 4 2 3 1 1 2 0 - 13		Fred Hutchinson	93	61	.604	4

BATTING AND FIELDING

NEW YORK YANKEES — WORLD SERIES STATISTICS

	Pos	G	AB	R	H	2B	3B	HR	RBI	BB	SO	SB	BA	SA	PO	A	E
Bill Skowron	1b	5	17	3	6	0	0	1	5	3	4	0	.353	.529	46	5	0
Bobby Richardson	2b	5	23	2	9	1	0	0	0	0	0	1	.391	.435	10	16	0
Tony Kubek	ss	5	22	3	5	0	0	0	1	1	4	0	.227	.227	5	11	0
Clete Boyer	3b	5	15	0	4	2	0	0	3	4	0	0	.267	.400	6	12	1
Johnny Blanchard	ph-rf	4	10	4	4	1	0	2	3	2	0	0	.400	1.100	2	1	0
Roger Maris	cf-rf	5	19	4	2	1	0	1	2	4	6	0	.105	.316	11	1	0
Yogi Berra	lf	4	11	2	3	0	0	1	3	5	1	0	.273	.545	4	0	1
Elston Howard	c	5	20	5	5	3	0	1	1	2	3	0	.250	.550	31	0	0
Hector Lopez	ph-rf-lf-pr	4	9	3	3	0	1	1	7	2	3	0	.333	.889	2	0	0
Mickey Mantle	cf	2	6	0	1	0	0	0	0	0	2	0	.167	.167	2	0	0
Jack Reed	cf	3	0	0	0	0	0	0	0	0	0	0	—	—	0	0	0
Billy Gardner	ph	1	1	0	0	0	0	0	0	0	0	0	.000	.000			
Joe DeMaestri		Did not play															
Bob Hale		Did not play															
Whitey Ford	p	2	5	1	0	0	0	0	0	0	1	0	.000	.000	1	2	0
Ralph Terry	p	2	3	0	0	0	0	0	0	0	1	0	.000	.000	1	0	1
Bill Stafford	p	1	2	0	0	0	0	0	0	0	0	0	.000	.000	0	0	0
Bud Daley	p	2	1	0	0	0	0	0	1	0	0	0	.000	.000	0	0	0
Jim Coates	p	1	1	0	0	0	0	0	0	0	0	0	.000	.000	0	0	1
Luis Arroyo	p	2	0	0	0	0	0	0	0	0	0	0	—	—	1	1	1
Rollie Sheldon	p	Did not play															
Bob Turley		Did not play—sore arm.															
Hal Reniff		Did not play															
Tex Clevenger		Did not play															
Al Downing		Did not play															
team total		5	165	27	42	8	1	7	26	24	25	1	.255	.442	135	50	5

Double Plays—1
Left on Bases—34

NEW YORK YANKEES — REGULAR SEASON STATISTICS

	Main Pos	G	AB	R	H	2B	3B	HR	RBI	BB	SO	SB	BA	SA
	1b	150	561	76	150	23	4	28	89	35	108	0	.267	.472
	2b	162	662	80	173	17	5	3	49	30	23	9	.261	.316
	ss	153	617	84	170	38	6	8	46	27	60	1	.276	.395
	3b	148	504	61	113	19	5	11	55	63	83	1	.224	.347
	c-ph	93	243	38	74	10	1	21	54	27	28	1	.305	.613
	of	161	590	132	159	16	4	61	142	94	67	0	.269	.620
	of	119	395	62	107	11	0	22	61	35	28	2	.271	.466
	c	129	446	64	155	17	5	21	77	28	65	0	.348	.549
	of	93	243	27	54	7	2	3	22	24	38	1	.222	.305
	of	153	514	132	163	16	6	54	112	126	112	12	.317	.687
	of	28	13	4	2	0	0	0	0	1	5	0	.154	.154
a	3b	41	99	11	21	5	0	1	2	6	18	0	.212	.293
	ss	30	41	1	6	0	0	0	2	0	13	0	.146	.146
b	ph	11	13	2	2	0	0	1	1	0	0	0	.154	.385
	p	39	96	11	17	1	0	0	10	12	17	0	.177	.188
	p	31	66	3	15	2	0	0	5	1	16	0	.227	.258
	p	36	67	5	12	2	1	0	3	4	11	0	.179	.239
c	p	23	45	3	6	1	0	0	2	1	1	0	.133	.156
	p	43	35	1	1	0	0	0	0	1	21	0	.029	.029
	p	65	25	2	7	2	0	0	0	0	4	0	.280	.360
	p	36	56	1	7	0	0	0	4	2	24	0	.125	.125
	p	15	21	1	2	0	0	0	0	3	11	0	.095	.095
	p	25	5	0	0	0	0	0	0	0	2	0	.000	.000
d	p	21	4	1	1	1	0	0	1	0	1	0	.250	.500
	p	5	1	0	0	0	0	0	0	0	0	0	.000	.000
team total		163	5559	827	1461	194	40	240	782	543	785	28	.263	.441

a—from Minnesota
b—from Cleveland
c—from Kansas City
d—from Los Angeles
Bob Cerv (of), Earl Torgeson (ph), Jesse Gonder (ph), Deron Johnson (3b), Tom Tresh (ss), Lee Thomas (ph), Art Ditmar (p), Danny McDevitt (p), Ryne Duren (p), Johnny James (p) and Duke Maas (p) also played for the Yankees during the season.

CINCINNATI REDS — WORLD SERIES STATISTICS

	Pos	G	AB	R	H	2B	3B	HR	RBI	BB	SO	SB	BA	SA	PO	A	E
Gordy Coleman	1b	5	20	2	5	0	0	1	0	1	0	0	.250	.400	30	4	1
Elio Chacon	2b-ph	4	12	2	3	0	0	0	0	1	2	0	.250	.250	12	9	0
Eddie Kasko	ss	5	22	1	7	0	0	0	1	0	2	0	.318	.318	13	13	1
Gene Freese	3b	5	16	0	1	1	0	0	3	4	4	0	.063	.125	6	4	0
Frank Robinson	rf-lf	5	15	3	3	2	0	1	4	3	4	0	.200	.533	5	0	0
Vada Pinson	cf	5	22	0	2	0	0	0	0	0	1	0	.091	.136	18	1	1
Wally Post	lf-rf	5	18	3	6	1	0	1	2	0	1	0	.333	.556	8	0	0
Johnny Edwards	c	3	11	1	4	2	0	0	2	0	0	0	.364	.545	17	1	0
Don Blasingame	2b-pr	3	7	1	1	0	0	0	0	0	3	0	.143	.143	5	4	0
Darrell Johnson	c	2	4	1	2	0	0	0	0	0	0	0	.500	.500	8	1	0
Jerry Zimmerman	c	2	0	0	0	0	0	0	0	0	0	0	—	—	4	0	0
Dick Gernert	ph	4	4	0	0	0	0	0	0	0	0	0	.000	.000			
Jerry Lynch	ph	4	3	0	0	0	0	0	0	0	0	0	.000	.000			
Gus Bell	ph	3	3	0	0	0	0	0	0	0	0	0	.000	.000			
Leo Cardenas	ph	3	3	0	1	1	0	0	0	0	0	0	.333	.667			
Joey Jay	p	2	4	0	0	0	0	0	0	0	2	0	.000	.000	1	0	0
Jim O'Toole	p	2	3	0	0	0	0	0	0	0	3	0	.000	.000	4	3	1
Bob Purkey	p	2	3	0	0	0	0	0	0	0	0	0	.000	.000	0	0	0
Jim Broshan	p	3	0	0	0	0	0	0	0	0	0	0	—	—	0	0	0
Bill Henry	p	2	0	0	0	0	0	0	0	0	0	0	—	—	0	1	0
Ken Hunt	p	1	0	0	0	0	0	0	0	0	0	0	—	—	0	0	0
Ken Johnson	p	1	0	0	0	0	0	0	0	0	0	0	—	—	0	0	0
Sherman Jones	p	1	0	0	0	0	0	0	0	0	0	0	—	—	0	0	0
Jim Maloney	p	1	0	0	0	0	0	0	0	0	0	0	—	—	0	0	0
Howie Nunn		Did not play															
Jay Hook		Did not play															
team total		5	170	13	35	8	0	3	11	8	27	0	.206	.306	132	42	4

Double Plays—7
Left on Bases—33

CINCINNATI REDS — REGULAR SEASON STATISTICS

	Main Pos	G	AB	R	H	2B	3B	HR	RBI	BB	SO	SB	BA	SA
	1b	150	520	63	149	27	4	26	87	45	67	1	.287	.504
	2b	61	132	26	35	4	2	5	21	22	22	1	.265	.371
	ss	126	469	64	127	22	1	2	27	32	36	4	.271	.335
	3b	152	575	78	159	27	4	26	87	27	78	8	.277	.466
	of	153	545	117	176	32	7	37	124	71	64	22	.323	.611
	of	154	607	101	208	34	8	16	87	39	63	23	.343	.504
	of	99	282	44	83	16	3	20	57	22	61	0	.294	.585
	c	52	145	14	27	5	0	2	14	18	28	1	.186	.262
e	2b	123	450	59	100	18	4	1	21	39	38	4	.222	.287
f	c	20	54	3	17	2	0	1	6	1	2	0	.315	.407
	c	76	204	8	42	5	0	0	10	11	21	1	.206	.230
g	1b-ph	40	63	4	19	1	0	0	7	7	9	0	.302	.317
	ph-of	96	181	33	57	13	2	13	50	27	25	2	.315	.624
	of	103	235	27	60	10	1	3	33	18	21	1	.255	.345
	ss	74	198	23	61	18	1	5	24	15	39	1	.308	.485
	p	34	89	3	8	3	0	0	5	2	29	0	.090	.124
	p	39	93	7	16	1	0	0	4	3	29	0	.172	.183
	p	36	80	6	8	0	0	1	2	2	32	0	.100	.163
	p	53	13	1	2	0	0	0	1	1	6	0	.154	.154
	p	48	5	0	0	0	0	0	0	0	3	0	.000	.000
	p	29	39	0	7	0	0	0	3	2	19	0	.179	.231
h	p	15	25	1	6	1	0	0	5	0	11	0	.240	.280
	p	24	11	0	2	0	0	0	1	3	6	0	.182	.182
	p	30	29	6	11	0	0	0	1	2	7	0	.379	.483
	p	24	8	1	2	0	0	0	0	0	5	0	.250	.250
	p	22	15	1	2	0	0	0	0	0	7	0	.133	.133
team total		154	5243	710	1414	247	35	158	675	423	761	70	.270	.421

e—from San Francisco
f—from Philadelphia
g—from Detroit (AL)
h—from Kansas City (AL)
Bob Schmidt (c), Pete Whisenant (of-ph), Ed Bailey (c), Jim Baumer (2b), Willie Jones (ph), Joe Gaines (of), Cliff Cook (ph), Harry Anderson (ph), Hal Bevan (ph), Marshall Bridges (p) and Claude Osteen (p) also played for the Reds during the season

PITCHING

NEW YORK YANKEES — WORLD SERIES STATISTICS

	G	GS	CG	IP	H	R	ER	BB	SO	W	L	SV	ERA
Whitey Ford	2	2	1	14	6	0	0	1	7	2	0	0	0.00
Ralph Terry	2	2	0	9⅓	12	7	5	2	7	0	1	0	4.82
Bud Daley	2	0	0	7	5	2	0	0	3	1	0	0	0.00
Bill Stafford	1	1	0	6⅔	7	2	2	2	5	0	0	0	2.70
Luis Arroyo	2	0	0	4	4	2	1	2	3	1	0	0	2.25
Jim Coates	1	0	0	4	1	0	0	1	2	0	0	1	0.00
Rollie Sheldon	Did not play												
Bob Turley	Did not play—sore arm												
Hal Reniff	Did not play												
Tex Clevenger	Did not play												
Al Downing	Did not play												
team total	5	5	1	45	35	13	8	8	27	4	1	1	1.60

NEW YORK YANKEES — REGULAR SEASON STATISTICS

	G	GS	CG	IP	H	ER	BB	SO	W	L	Pct.	SV	ShO	ERA
	39	39	11	283	242	101	92	209	25	4	.862	0	3	3.21
	31	27	9	188	162	66	42	86	16	3	.842	0	2	3.16
c	23	17	7	130	127	57	51	83	8	9	.471	0	3	3.95
	36	25	6	195	168	58	59	101	14	9	.609	2	3	2.68
	65	0	0	119	83	29	49	87	15	5	.750	29	0	2.19
	43	11	4	141	128	54	53	80	11	5	.688	5	1	3.45
	35	21	6	163	149	65	55	84	11	5	.688	0	2	3.59
	15	12	1	72	74	46	51	48	3	5	.375	0	0	5.75
	25	0	0	45	31	13	31	21	2	0	1.000	2	0	2.60
d	21	0	0	32	35	17	21	14	1	1	.500	0	0	4.78
	5	1	0	9	7	8	12	12	0	1	.000	0	0	8.00
team total	163	163	47	1451	1288	558	542	866	109	53	.673	39	14	3.46

CINCINNATI REDS — WORLD SERIES STATISTICS

	G	GS	CG	IP	H	R	ER	BB	SO	W	L	SV	ERA
Jim O'Toole	2	2	0	12	11	4	4	7	4	0	2	0	3.00
Bob Purkey	2	1	1	11	6	3	2	3	5	0	1	0	1.64
Joey Jay	2	2	1	9⅔	8	6	6	6	6	1	1	0	5.59
Jim Broshan	3	0	0	6	7	5	5	4	5	0	0	0	7.50
Bill Henry	2	0	0	2⅓	4	5	5	2	3	0	0	0	19.29
Ken Hunt	1	0	0	1	0	0	0	1	0	0	0	0	0.00
Ken Johnson	1	0	0	1	0	0	0	0	0	0	0	0	0.00
Sherman Jones	1	0	0	1	0	0	0	0	1	0	0	0	0.00
Jim Maloney	1	0	0	4	2	4	4	1	1	0	0	0	27.00
Howie Nunn	Did not play												
Jay Hook	Did not play												
team total	5	5	2	44	42	27	24	24	25	1	4	0	4.91

CINCINNATI REDS — REGULAR SEASON STATISTICS

	G	GS	CG	IP	H	ER	BB	SO	W	L	Pct.	SV	ShO	ERA
	39	35	11	253	229	87	93	178	19	9	.679	2	3	3.09
	36	34	13	246	245	102	51	116	16	12	.571	1	1	3.73
	34	34	14	247	217	97	92	157	21	10	.677	0	4	3.53
	53	0	0	80	77	27	18	40	10	4	.714	16	0	3.04
	47	0	0	50	13	15	53	2	1	.667	16	0	2.21
	29	22	4	136	130	60	66	75	9	10	.474	0	3	3.97
h	15	11	3	83	71	30	22	42	6	2	.750	1	1	3.25
	24	2	0	55	51	27	27	32	1	1	.500	2	0	4.42
	27	11	1	95	86	46	59	57	6	7	.462	2	0	4.36
	30	0	0	38	35	15	24	26	3	3	.500	1	0	3.55
	22	5	0	63	83	54	22	36	1	3	.250	0	0	7.71
team total	154	154	46	1370	1300	576	500	829	93	61	.604	40	12	3.78

Total Attendance—223,247 Average Attendance—44,649 Winning Player's Share—$7,389 Losing Player's Share—$5,356

1962 Play-off Shades of '51

A dead heat between the Dodgers and Giants for the National League pennant capped a most incredible season for the Los Angeles team. The Dodgers held a comfortable lead through the summer on the strength of Maury Wills's record number of stolen bases plus superb pitching, but after ace southpaw Sandy Koufax went out of action in July with a circulatory problem in his left index finger, the team began to falter. September proved disastrous, as the Dodgers lost 10 of their last 13 games and their final four in a row to blow a four-game lead in the final week of the season. A San Francisco victory and a Los Angeles loss on the final day of the campaign threw the race into a deadlock. When the three-game play-off opened in Candlestick Park, the Giants rode their galloping momentum, combined with Billy Pierce's three-hit pitching, two homers by Willie Mays, and single homers from Orlando Cepeda and Jim Davenport, to blow the Dodgers away 8–0. Los Angeles manager Walter Alston gambled that Koufax could come off the injury list to stop the Dodger skid, but the rusty mound star didn't last through the second inning.

The Dodgers hadn't scored a run in their last three games in coming to the brink of a humiliating elimination. Alston chose as his pitcher for game two Don Drysdale, who was making his fourth start in nine days, while Giant skipper Alvin Dark relied on Jack Sanford. Pitching on two days' rest, Sanford kept the sleeping Dodger bats in a deep freeze in the early innings. The Giants, meanwhile, scored a solo run off a game Drysdale in the second inning, then batted him out with four runs in the top of the sixth. Trailing 5–0 and scoreless in their last 36 innings, the Dodgers were given up as dead by the enemy and by their fans in Dodger Stadium. But in the bottom of the sixth, Jim Gilliam walked to open the frame, prompting Dark to relieve the tired Sanford with Stu Miller. Duke Snider doubled and Tommy Davis hit a deep outfield fly to break the shutout. When Wally Moon walked and Frank Howard singled in another run, Billy O'Dell came out of the Giant bullpen to pitch. Three pinch hitters came to bat against O'Dell; Doug Camilli singled to load the bases, Andy Carey was hit with a pitch to force in a run, and Lee Walls blasted a double to left-center which scored three runs. After Don Larsen came in to pitch, Walls scored on an infield play when catcher Tom Haller dropped a throw. When the inning ended, seven Dodgers had crossed the plate and hope was reborn. The Giants came back to tie the score with two runs in the eighth inning, but the Dodgers then won it in the bottom of the ninth on three walks and a short fly to center on which Wills dashed home ahead of Mays's strong throw.

The Dodgers felt that their slump was over, and 45,693 fans came out to Dodger Stadium to see their team reassert itself in game three, with Johnny Podres facing Juan Marichal. The Giants jumped out to a 2–0 lead in the third inning, practically given the runs on throwing errors by Podres, Johnny Roseboro, and Gilliam. The Dodgers cut the lead to 2–1 with a run in the fourth, then nearly got into serious trouble in the top of the sixth. Three singles loaded the bases for the Giants with no outs, but Ed Roebuck came into the game and retired the side on two grounders to Wills. Inspired by this stonewall stand, Snider singled and Tommy Davis homered in the bottom of the inning to put the Dodgers ahead 3–2. In the bottom of the seventh, Wills singled, stole second and third, and scored when catcher Ed Bailey threw the ball into left field. After eight innings the Dodgers led 4–2 and stood only three outs from vindication. Matty Alou led off the top of the ninth with a pinch single, and after Roebuck retired Harvey Kuenn, he walked Willie McCovey and Felipe Alou to load the bases. Mays then lined the ball off Roebuck's body to score one run. Stan Williams, the relief winner of yesterday's game, then entered the fray. Cepeda greeted him with a deep fly to right that scored the tying run. After wild pitching put the two runners into scoring position, Williams intentionally walked Bailey to set up a force play at the plate. But with a stunned audience looking on, the only force play came on ball four to Davenport, forcing the go-ahead run in. Ron Perranoski now relieved, getting Jose Pagan to hit a grounder to second baseman Larry Burright. A defensive replacement, Burright botched the play and the Giants led 6–4. There was no coming back from this collapse, as Pierce came in to retire the Dodgers one-two-three in the bottom of the ninth to end a series without the heroics of a Bobby Thomson but with the same dramatic result.

Game 1 Playoffs October 1 at San Francisco

L.A.	000	000	000
S.F.	210	002	03x

Los Angeles	Pos	AB	R	H	RBI	PO	A	E
Wills	ss	4	0	0	0	1	2	0
Gilliam	2b	3	0	0	0	1	2	0
T. Davis	lf	4	0	0	0	0	0	0
Howard	rf	4	0	0	0	3	0	1
Walls	1b	3	0	0	0	9	0	0
Roseboro	c	3	0	0	0	4	1	0
Carey	3b	3	0	1	0	2	3	0
W. Davis	cf	3	0	0	0	4	0	0
Koufax	p	0	0	0	0	0	0	0
Roebuck	p	1	0	0	0	0	1	0
a McMullen		1	0	1	0	0	0	0
b Tracewski		0	0	0	0	0	0	0
L. Sherry	p	0	0	0	0	0	0	0
Smith	p	0	0	0	0	0	0	0
c Camilli		1	0	1	0	0	0	0
Ortega	p	0	0	0	0	0	0	0
Perranoski	p	0	0	0	0	0	0	0
Totals		30	0	3	0	24	9	1

a Singled for Roebuck in 6th.
b Ran for McMullen in 6th.
c Doubled for Smith in 8th.

Doubles—F. Alou, Canilli, Pagan. Home Runs—Cepeda, Davenport, Mays 2. Stolen Base—Mays. Sacrifice Hit—Pagan. Double Play—Roseboro to Carey. Left on Bases—Los Angeles 4, San Francisco 5. Umpires—Conlan, Boggess, Donatelli, Landes. Attendance—32,652. Time of Game—2:39.

San Fran.	Pos	AB	R	H	RBI	PO	A	E
Kuenn	lf	5	0	0	0	2	0	0
Hiller	2b	4	0	1	0	2	0	0
F. Alou	rf	4	1	1	0	5	0	0
Mays	cf	3	3	3	3	2	0	0
Cepeda	1b	4	1	1	1	6	0	0
Davenport	3b	3	2	2	1	0	0	0
Bailey	c	2	1	1	0	6	0	0
Pagan	ss	3	0	1	2	4	4	0
Pierce	p	4	0	0	0	0	0	0
Totals		32	8	10	7	27	4	0

Pitching	IP	H	R	ER	BB	SO
Los Angeles						
Koufax (L)	*1	4	3	3	0	0
Roebuck	4	1	0	0	0	2
L. Sherry	⅓	3	2	2	1	0
Smith	1⅔	1	0	0	0	2
Ortega	⅓	0	2	2	2	0
Perranoski	⅔	1	1	0	1	0
San Francisco						
Pierce (W)	9	3	0	0	1	6

*Pitched to two batters in 2nd.

Game 2 Playoffs October 2 at Los Angeles

S.F.	010	004	020
L.A.	000	007	001

San Fran.	Pos	AB	R	H	RBI	PO	A	E
Hiller	2b	3	1	1	1	0	3	0
f Nieman		1	0	0	0	0	0	0
Bowman	2b	1	0	0	0	2	0	0
Davenport	3b	6	1	2	1	1	1	0
Mays	cf	5	0	1	0	4	1	0
McCovey	lf	2	0	1	1	2	0	0
Miller	p	0	0	0	0	0	0	0
O'Dell	p	0	0	0	0	0	0	0
Larsen	p	0	0	0	0	0	0	0
g Bailey		1	0	1	1	0	0	0
h Boles		0	1	0	0	0	0	0
Bolin	p	0	0	0	0	0	0	0
LeMay	p	0	0	0	0	0	0	0
Perry	p	0	0	0	0	0	1	0
McCormick	p	0	0	0	0	0	0	0
Cepeda	1b	5	1	1	0	6	1	0
F. Alou	rf	4	0	2	1	3	0	0
Haller	c	1	1	0	0	4	0	1
Orsino	c	1	0	1	1	3	1	0
Pagan	ss	5	1	3	0	1	1	0
Sanford	p	3	1	0	0	0	1	0
M. Alou	lf	0	0	0	0	0	0	0
e Kuenn	lf	2	0	0	0	0	0	0
Totals		40	7	13	6	x26	10	1

a Singled for Roseboro in 6th.
b Hit by pitch for W. Davis in 6th.
c Doubled for Roebuck in 6th.
d Ran for Carey in 6th.
e Hit into force out for M. Alou in 7th.
f Flied out for Hiller in 7th.
g Singled for Larsen in 8th.
h Ran for Bailey in 8th.
i Sacrificed for Snider in 9th.
x Two outs when winning run scored.

Doubles—F. Alou, Pagan, Snider, Walls. Stolen Base—Wills. Sacrifice Hit—Spencer. Sacrifice Flies—T. Davis, Fairly, Orsino. Hit by Pitchers—Hiller (by Drysdale), Carey (by O'Dell). Left on Bases—San Francisco 13, Los Angeles 7. Umpires—Barlick, Boggess, Donatelli, Conlan. Attendance—25,321. Time of Game—4:18.

Los Angeles	Pos	AB	R	H	RBI	PO	A	E
Wills	ss	4	1	0	0	3	1	0
Gilliam	2b-3b	3	1	0	0	3	2	0
Snider	lf	3	1	1	0	2	0	0
i Spencer		0	0	0	0	0	0	0
T. Davis	3b-cf	3	0	1	1	2	2	0
Moon	1b	2	1	1	0	2	0	0
Fairly	1b	1	0	1	1	3	0	0
Howard	rf	3	1	1	1	0	0	1
Roseboro	c	2	0	0	0	6	0	0
a Camilli	c	2	1	1	0	2	0	0
W. Davis	cf	2	0	0	0	3	0	0
b Carey		0	0	0	1	0	0	0
d Burright	2b	0	1	0	0	1	1	0
Drysdale	p	2	0	0	0	0	2	1
Roebuck	p	0	0	0	0	0	0	0
c Walls		1	1	1	3	0	0	0
Perranoski	p	0	0	0	0	0	0	0
Smith	p	0	0	0	0	0	0	0
Williams	p	1	0	0	0	0	0	0
Totals		29	8	7	7	27	8	2

Pitching	IP	H	R	ER	BB	SO
San Francisco						
Sanford	m5	2	1	1	3	4
Miller	⅓	2	3	3	1	0
O'Dell	n0	2	3	2	0	0
Larsen	1⅔	1	0	0	0	1
Bolin (L)	p1	0	1	1	2	2
LeMay	q0	0	0	0	1	0
Perry	⅓	0	0	0	0	0
McCormick	⅓	0	0	0	1	0
Los Angeles						
Drysdale	5⅓	7	5	3	4	4
Roebuck	⅔	1	0	0	0	0
Perranoski	o1	4	1	1	0	0
Smith	⅓	1	1	0	0	0
Williams (W)	1⅔	0	0	0	1	2

m Pitched to one batter in 6th.
n Pitched to three batters in 6th.
o Pitched to two batters in 8th.
p Pitched to one batter in 9th.
q Pitched to one batter in 9th.

Game 3 Playoffs October 3 at Los Angeles

S.F.	002	000	004
L.A.	000	102	100

San Fran.	Pos	AB	R	H	RBI	PO	A	E
Kuenn	lf	5	1	2	1	2	0	0
Hiller	2b	3	0	1	0	4	1	0
b McCovey		0	0	0	0	0	0	0
c Bowman	2b	0	1	0	0	0	0	0
F. Alou	rf	4	1	1	0	4	0	0
Mays	cf	3	1	1	1	3	0	0
Cepeda	1b	4	0	1	1	8	0	0
Bailey	c	4	0	2	0	3	0	1
Davenport	3b	4	0	1	1	2	4	0
Pagan	ss	5	1	2	0	1	1	1
Marichal	p	2	1	1	0	0	0	1
Larsen	p	0	0	0	0	0	1	0
a M. Alou		1	0	1	0	0	0	0
d Nieman		1	0	0	0	0	0	0
Pierce	p	0	0	0	0	0	0	0
Totals		36	6	13	4	27	7	3

Pitching	IP	H	R	ER	BB	SO
San Francisco						
Marichal	**7	8	4	3	1	2
Larsen (W)	1	0	0	0	2	1
Pierce (SV)	1	0	0	0	0	0
Los Angeles						
Podres	*5	9	2	1	1	0
Roebuck (L)	3⅓	4	4	3	3	0
Williams	⅓	0	0	0	2	0
Perranoski	⅓	0	0	0	0	1

*Pitched to three batters in 6th.
**Pitched to one batter in 8th.

Los Angeles	Pos	AB	R	H	RBI	PO	A	E
Wills	ss	5	1	4	0	3	6	0
Gilliam	2b-3b	5	0	0	0	3	1	1
Snider	lf	3	2	2	0	2	1	0
Burright	2b	1	0	0	0	4	2	1
e Walls		1	0	0	0	0	0	0
T. Davis	3b-lf	3	1	2	2	1	1	0
Moon	1b	3	0	0	0	7	0	0
Fairly	1b-rf	0	0	0	0	2	0	0
Howard	rf	4	0	0	1	0	0	0
Harkness	1b	0	0	0	0	0	0	0
Roseboro	c	3	0	0	0	3	1	1
W. Davis	cf	3	0	0	0	2	0	0
Podres	p	2	0	0	0	0	2	1
Roebuck	p	2	0	0	0	0	0	0
Williams	p	0	0	0	0	0	0	0
Perranoski	p	0	0	0	0	0	0	0
Totals		35	4	8	3	27	14	4

a Singled for Larsen in 9th.
b Walked for Hiller in 9th.
c Ran for McCovey in 9th.
d Struck out for M. Alou in 9th.
e Lined out for Burright in 9th.

Doubles—Hiller, Snider. Home Run—T. Davis. Stolen Bases—T. Davis, Wills 3. Sacrifice Hits—Fairly, Hiller, Marichal. Sacrifice Fly—Cepeda. Double Plays—Gilliam to Wills to Moon, Wills to Moon, Wills to Burright to Fairly. Wild Pitch—Williams. Left on Bases—S.F. 12, L.A. 8. Umpires—Boggess, Donatelli, Conlan, Barlick. Attendance—45,693. Time of Game—3:00.

1962
Terry to McCovey to Richardson

Horace Stoneham followed the lead of Walter O'Malley and the Dodgers in bringing his Giants to California in 1958, and now Stoneham's team followed the Dodgers by three years in bringing the National League pennant to the West Coast. Similar to 1951, the Giants this year caught up with the Dodgers late in the season and then beat the Bums in a play-off for the flag. Only the peerless Willie Mays remained active from the 1951 and 1954 championship squads, although Alvin Dark now managed the team. Other Giants bred in San Francisco surrounded Mays with talent, as Orlando Cepeda, Willie McCovey, and Felipe Alou all were established power hitters at young ages. The pitching staff was built around four castoff veterans in Jack Sanford, Billy O'Dell, Billy Pierce, and Stu Miller, plus a talented homegrown pitcher in Juan Marichal. These Giants faced a traditional rival in the Series, the New York Yankees. Six times before these clubs had met in Subway Series, but this was their first transcontinental affair. Even though Roger Maris and Mickey Mantle had more normal seasons and Tony Kubek was called back into the army until August, manager Ralph Houk had enough talent to come in first, with a fine rookie season by shortstop Tom Tresh and 23 wins by Ralph Terry the major surprises from the supporting cast.

At Candlestick Park, where strong winds made pitching and fielding an adventure, Whitey Ford faced Bill O'Dell in a first-game match-up of southpaws. The Yankees took a 2–0 lead in the top of the first inning on two singles and Maris's double, but the Giants came back with a run in the second, snapping Ford's record scoreless-inning streak at 33 2/3. Another San Francisco run in the third knotted the score at 2–2, and it stood that way until the seventh, when Clete Boyer socked a solo homer to put the Yanks out in front. Two more runs in the eighth and one in the ninth wrapped up the game for the Yanks and Ford by a 6–2 score. The second game pitted 23-game-winner Terry against 24-game-winner Sanford. The burly Giant right-hander came out on top, throwing a three-hit shutout to take a 2–0 win and square the Series at one game apiece.

The Giants then returned to New York, wearing the colors of San Francisco, yet still the favorites of many New Yorkers. Starting pitchers Pierce and Bill Stafford both threw shutout ball through the first six innings of game three, but singles by Tresh, Mantle, and Maris scored two runs in the seventh, prompting Dark to relieve Pierce with Don Larsen, the old Yankee hero of no-hit fame. Larsen retired the side in order, but another run scored to make the Yankee lead 3–0. Stafford breezed until the ninth, when a double by Mays and a homer by Ed Bailey cut the final score to an anxious 3–2. Young Marichal outpitched Ford in the fourth game until he injured a finger bunting in the fifth inning. Ahead 2–0 when Marichal left, the Giants lost the lead when reliever Bobby Bolin gave up two runs in the bottom of the sixth on two walks and two hits. But the Giants loaded the bases in the seventh on a walk to Jim Davenport, a double by Matty Alou, and an intentional pass to Bob Nieman; then they quickly unloaded them on a home run by Chuck Hiller, a second baseman not known for his power. This first grand slam by a National League player put the Giants ahead to stay, and the 7–3 win was credited to Larsen on the sixth anniversary of his Series perfect game. After a day off because of rain, the Yankees again went ahead in the Series, taking a 5–3 win behind Terry's complete game and Tresh's three-run homer in the bottom of the eighth inning.

The teams took a day off to travel to San Francisco, then watched the rain fall for three more days. When the weather finally did break, Pierce beat Ford by throwing a three-hitter, with the 5–2 triumph putting all the chips on the table in game seven.

Terry and Sanford both pitched masterfully, with the Yanks scoring in the fifth inning on a double play. In the bottom of the ninth, Matty Alou led off with a bunt single. Felipe Alou and Hiller struck out, but Mays then drilled a double to right, with only a perfect stop and throw by Maris holding the fast Alou at third. With memories of Bill Mazeroski in the air, McCovey lined Terry's pitch toward right field. Second baseman Bobby Richardson reached up and grabbed the ball, and the Yankees were 1–0 victors and still World Champions.

Game 1 October 4 at San Francisco

N.Y. 200 000 121
S.F. 011 000 000

New York	Pos	AB	R	H	RBI	PO	A	E
Kubek	ss	5	0	2	0	3	4	0
Richardson	2b	5	1	1	0	4	2	0
Tresh	lf	5	2	2	0	0	0	0
Mantle	cf	4	0	0	0	1	0	0
Maris	rf	4	1	2	2	2	0	0
Howard	c	3	1	2	1	6	0	0
Skowron	1b	2	0	0	0	7	0	0
Long	1b	2	0	1	1	3	0	0
Boyer	3b	3	1	1	2	1	2	0
Ford	p	3	0	0	0	0	4	0
Totals		36	6	11	6	27	12	0

Pitching	IP	H	R	ER	BB	SO
New York						
Ford (W)	9	10	2	2	2	6
San Francisco						
O'Dell (L)	7⅓	9	5	5	3	8
Larsen	1	1	1	1	1	0
Miller	⅔	1	0	0	1	0

San Francisco	Pos	AB	R	H	RBI	PO	A	E
Kuenn	lf	5	0	0	0	6	0	0
Hiller	2b	4	1	1	0	4	4	0
F. Alou	rf	4	0	1	0	4	0	0
Mays	cf	4	1	3	1	1	0	0
Cepeda	1b	4	0	0	0	6	0	0
Davenport	3b	2	0	1	0	0	2	0
Bailey	c	4	0	0	0	8	0	0
Miller	p	0	0	0	0	0	0	0
Pagan	ss	4	0	3	1	1	2	0
O'Dell	p	3	0	1	0	0	0	0
Larsen	p	0	0	0	0	0	0	0
Orsino	c	1	0	0	0	0	0	0
Totals		35	2	10	2	27	9	0

Doubles—Hiller, Maris. Home Run—Boyer. Stolen Bases—Mantle, Tresh. Sacrifice Fly—Boyer. Double Plays—Richardson to Kubek to Skowron, Boyer to Richardson to Long, Davenport to Hiller to Cepeda. Hit by Pitcher—Howard (by O'Dell). Left on Bases—New York 10, S. Francisco 8. Umpires—Barlick (N), Berry (A), Landes (N), Honochick (A), Burkhart (N), Soar (A). Attendance—43,852. Time of Game—2:43.

1st Inning
New York
1 Kubek struck out.
Richardson singled to right-center:
Tresh singled to center, Richardson stopping at second.
2 Mantle struck out.
Maris doubled to right over F. Alou's head, scoring Richardson and Tresh.
3 Howard popped to second.
San Francisco
1 Kuenn fanned.
2 Hiller popped to short.
3 F. Alou grounded out down the first base line, Ford to Skowron.

2nd Inning
New York
Skowron walked.
1 Boyer struck out.
2 Ford struck out.
Kubek singled to center, Skowron stopping at second.
3 Richardson forced Kubek at second, Pagan to Hiller.
San Francisco
Mays singled to left.
1 Cepeda took a called third strike.
Davenport singled to center, sending Mays to third.
2 Bailey fouled to Richardson behind first.
Pagan beat out a bunt between the mound and third, scoring Mays and sending Davenport to second.
(Ford's scoreless innings record stopped at 33 2/3 innings)
3 O'Dell forced Pagan at second, Kubek unassisted.

3rd Inning
New York
1 Tresh flied to F. Alou in short right-center.
Mantle walked.
2 Maris called out on strikes.
Mantle stole second.
Howard walked.
3 Skowron struck out.
San Francisco
1 Kuenn grounded to third.
Hiller doubled to left-center.
F. Alou singled to left, Hiller stopping at third.
Mays singled to center, scoring Hiller with F. Alou stopping at second.
2,3 Cepeda hit into a double play, Richardson to Kubek to Skowron.

4th Inning
New York
1 Boyer flied to Mays in left-center.
2 Ford grounded to second.
3 Kubek flied to left.
San Francisco
Davenport walked.
1 Bailey flied to right.
2 Pagan popped to second.
O'Dell singled to right, moving Davenport to second.
3 Kuenn tapped back to the mound.

5th Inning
New York
1 Richardson flied to left.
2 Tresh grounded to second.
3 Mantle took a called third strike.
San Francisco
1 Hiller struck out.
2 F. Alou struck out.
Mays singled to left.
3 Cepeda fouled to Richardson down the right field line.

6th Inning
New York
1 Maris grounded to second.
Howard singled to center.
2,3 Skowron hit into a double play, Davenport to Hiller to Cepeda.
San Francisco
1 Davenport grounded to short.
2 Bailey grounded to short.
Pagan beat out a hit to deep short.
3 O'Dell grounded back to the mound.

7th Inning
New York
Boyer hit a home run over the left-center field fence.
1 Ford took a called third strike.
Kubek singled to center.
2 Richardson flied to left.
3 Tresh forced Kubek at second, Davenport to Hiller.
San Francisco
For New York—Long playing first.
1 Kuenn grounded to the mound.
2 Hiller popped to Boyer near the mound.
3 F. Alou struck out.

8th Inning
New York
1 Mantle flied to deep left.
Maris singled to right.
Howard was hit by a pitched ball.
Long singled to right, scoring Maris and moving Howard to third.
For San Francisco—Larsen came in to pitch.
2 Boyer popped a sacrifice fly to Pagan in short left, scoring Howard with Long going to second on Pagan's throw to the plate.
Ford walked.
3 Kubek grounded to short.
San Francisco
1 Mays took a called third strike.
2 Cepeda grounded to short.
Davenport walked.
3 Bailey flied to Maris in short right-center.

9th Inning
New York
1 Richardson fouled to Kuenn near the left field boxes.
Tresh singled to left.
For San Francisco—Miller pitching (batting 8th) and Orsino catching (batting 9th).
2 Mantle flied to Kuenn in left-center.
Tresh stole second.
Maris walked.
Howard singled to right, scoring Tresh with Maris stopping at second.
3 Long grounded to the mound.
San Francisco
Pagan singled to left.
1,2 Orsino hit into a double play, Boyer to Richardson to Long.
3 Kuenn flied to center.

Game 2 October 5 at San Francisco

New York	Pos	AB	R	H	RBI	PO	A	E
Kubek	ss	4	0	0	0	1	1	1
Richardson	2b	4	0	0	0	3	3	0
Tresh	lf	3	0	1	0	0	0	0
Mantle	cf	4	0	1	0	3	0	0
Maris	rf	3	0	0	0	0	1	0
Berra	c	2	0	0	0	6	1	0
Long	1b	3	0	0	0	6	3	0
Boyer	3b	3	0	1	0	3	2	0
Terry	p	2	0	0	0	2	0	0
a Blanchard		1	0	0	0	0	0	0
Daley	p	0	0	0	0	0	0	0
Totals		29	0	3	0	24	11	1

```
N.Y.   000 000 000
S.F.   100 000 10x
```

San Francisco	Pos	AB	R	H	RBI	PO	A	E
Hiller	2b	3	1	1	0	6	0	
F. Alou	rf	2	0	1	0	0	0	0
M. Alou	lf	4	0	1	1	1	0	0
Mays	cf	4	0	0	0	3	0	0
McCovey	1b	4	1	1	1	11	1	0
Haller	c	3	0	1	0	8	1	0
Davenport	3b	3	0	0	0	1	0	0
Pagan	ss	3	0	1	0	2	4	0
Sanford	p	3	0	1	0	1	1	0
Totals		27	2	6	2	27	13	0

Pitching	IP	H	R	ER	BB	SO
New York						
Terry (L)	7	5	2	2	1	5
Daley	1	1	1	0	1	0
San Francisco						
Sanford (W)	8	3	0	0	3	6

a Struck out for Terry in 8th.

Doubles—Hiller, Mantle. Home Run—McCovey. Stolen Base—Tresh. Sacrifice Hits—F. Alou, Pagan. Double Play—Hiller to Pagan to McCovey. Hit by Pitcher—Pagan (by Terry). Left on Bases—New York 5, San Francisco 6. Umpires—Berry, Landes, Honochick, Barlick, Burkhart, Soar. Attendance—43,910. Time of Game—2:11.

1st Inning
New York
1 Kubek grounded to second.
2 Richardson grounded to short. Tresh walked.
3 Mantle popped to short.
San Francisco
Hiller doubled into the right field corner.
1 F. Alou sacrificed Hiller to third, Long unassisted.
2 M. Alou grounded to second, scoring Hiller.
3 Mays struck out.

2nd Inning
New York
Maris walked.
1,2 Berra grounded into a double play, Hiller to Pagan to McCovey.
3 Long struck out.
San Francisco
1 McCovey grounded out, Long to Terry.
2 Haller grounded to second.
3 Davenport lined to second.

3rd Inning
New York
1 Boyer flied to center.
2 Terry struck out.
3 Kubek flied to center.
San Francisco
1 Pagan flied to center.
2 Sanford took a called third strike. Hiller walked.
3 F. Alou fouled to Boyer.

4th Inning
New York
1 Richardson grounded to short. Tresh singled when his pop fly bunt fell safely in the infield.
2 Mantle fouled to Davenport. Tresh stole second.
3 Maris fouled to Haller.
San Francisco
1 M. Alou bunted out to first.
2 Mays popped to Richardson in short center.
3 McCovey struck out.

5th Inning
New York
1 Berra flied to shallow left.
2 Long fouled to Haller. Boyer singled to left.
3 Terry grounded to short.
San Francisco
1 Haller fouled to Boyer.
2 Davenport struck out. Pagan was hit by a pitched ball.
3 Sanford struck out.

6th Inning
New York
1 Kubek struck out.
2 Richardson flied to center.
3 Tresh struck out, but had to be thrown out by Haller.
San Francisco
1 Hiller grounded out, Long to Terry. F. Alou singled to left-center.
2 M. Alou flied to center.
3 Mays grounded to short.

7th Inning
New York
1 Mantle grounded out, McCovey to Sanford.
2 Maris grounded to second. Berra walked.
3 Long fouled to Haller.
San Francisco
McCovey hit a deep home run far over the right field fence. Haller singled off the first base bag. Davenport got safely to first on Kubek's fumble, Haller moving to second.
1 Pagan sacrificed up both runners, Boyer to Richardson. Haller was caught between third and home as Sanford missed the ball on a squeeze bunt attempt. Pagan was
2 out, Berra to Boyer to Long to Kubek, with Davenport holding second. Sanford singled to right, but Davenport
3 was out trying to score, Maris to Berra.

8th Inning
New York
1 Boyer struck out.
2 Blanchard, pinch-hitting for Terry, struck out.
3 Kubek grounded to second.
San Francisco
For New York—Daley pitching.
1 Hiller fouled to Boyer. F. Alou walked. M. Alou beat out a bunt down the third base line, moving brother Felipe to second.
2 Mays flied to deep center, both runners advancing after the catch.
3 McCovey grounded to second.

9th Inning
New York
1 Richardson grounded back to the mound.
2 Tresh grounded to second. Mantle doubled to right.
3 Maris grounded to second.

Game 3 October 7 at New York

San Francisco	Pos	AB	R	H	RBI	PO	A	E
F. Alou	lf	4	0	0	0	3	0	1
Hiller	2b	3	0	0	0	3	0	1
Mays	cf	4	1	1	0	6	0	0
McCovey	rf	3	0	0	0	2	0	1
Cepeda	1b	3	0	0	0	4	0	0
Bailey	c	4	1	1	2	4	0	0
Davenport	3b	4	0	1	0	1	1	1
Pagan	ss	3	0	1	0	1	2	0
Pierce	p	2	0	0	0	1	0	0
Larsen	p	0	0	0	0	0	0	0
a M. Alou		1	0	0	0	0	0	0
Bolin	p	0	0	0	0	0	0	0
Totals		32	2	4	2	24	3	3

```
S.F.   000 000 002
N.Y.   000 000 30x
```

New York	Pos	AB	R	H	RBI	PO	A	E
Kubek	ss	4	0	1	0	1	2	0
Richardson	2b	4	0	0	0	2	4	0
Tresh	lf	4	1	1	0	4	0	0
Mantle	cf	3	1	1	0	2	0	0
Maris	rf	3	1	1	2	3	0	0
Howard	c	3	0	1	0	7	0	0
Skowron	1b	2	0	0	0	7	0	0
Boyer	3b	3	0	1	1	1	2	1
Stafford	p	3	0	0	0	0	1	0
Totals		29	3	5	3	27	9	1

Pitching	IP	H	R	ER	BB	SO
San Francisco						
Pierce (L)	*6	5	3	2	0	3
Larsen	1	0	0	0	0	0
Bolin	1	0	0	0	0	1
New York						
Stafford (W)	9	4	2	2	2	5

*Pitched to three batters in 7th.

a Hit into force out for Larsen in 8th.

Doubles—Davenport, Howard, Kubek, Mays. Home Run—Bailey. Double Play—Davenport to Hiller. Hit by Pitcher—Skowron (by Larsen). Left on Bases—San Francisco 5, New York 3. Umpires—Landes, Honochick, Barlick, Berry, Soar, Burkhart. Attendance—71,434. Time of Game—2:06.

1st Inning
San Francisco
1 F. Alou lined to left-center. Hiller walked.
2 Mays popped to short. McCovey walked.
3 Cepeda grounded to second.
New York
1 Kubek lined to left.
2 Richardson flied to McCovey in right-center.
3 Tresh struck out.

2nd Inning
San Francisco
1 Bailey flied to center. Davenport doubled down the left field line.
2 Pagan grounded to second, Davenport moving to third.
3 Pierce flied to Tresh in left-center.
New York
Mantle safe on Davenport's fumble.
1 Maris flied to deep right.
2 Howard lined out at the left field wall.
3 Skowron struck out.

3rd Inning
San Francisco
1 F. Alou grounded to third.
2 Hiller took a called third strike.
3 Mays grounded to short.
New York
1 Boyer flied to center.
2 Stafford flied to center. Kubek doubled off the left field wall.
3 Richardson lined to first.

4th Inning
San Francisco
1 McCovey called out on strikes. Cepeda safe at first on Boyer's wild throw to first.
2 Bailey forced Cepeda at second, Kubek to Richardson.
3 Davenport flied to left.
New York
1 Tresh flied to center.
2 Mantle lined to left.
3 Maris grounded to first.

5th Inning
San Francisco
1 Pagan fouled to Howard.
2 Pierce called out on strikes.
3 F. Alou flied to right.
New York
Howard doubled inside the left field line.
1,2 Skowron lined to Davenport who threw to Hiller doubling Howard off of second.
3 Boyer flied to deep center.

6th Inning
San Francisco
1 Hiller flied to deep right.
2 Mays struck out.
3 McCovey flied to Tresh in short left-center.
New York
1 Stafford struck out.
2 Kubek popped to short.
3 Richardson grounded to short.

7th Inning
San Francisco
1 Cepeda popped to Howard
2 Bailey popped to Boyer.
3 Davenport struck out.
New York
Tresh singled to center. Mantle singled to left and when F. Alou fumbled the ball, Tresh went to third and Mantle went to second. Maris singled to right-center scoring Tresh and Mantle, Maris took second when McCovey booted the ball. For San Francisco—Larsen pitching.
1 Howard flied to center, Maris moving to third after the catch. Skowron was hit by a pitched ball.
2 Boyer forced Skowron at second, Pagan to Hiller as Maris scored.
3 Stafford grounded to first.

8th Inning
San Francisco
Pagan singled to left.
1 M. Alou, pinch-hitting for Larsen, forced Pagan at second, Boyer to Richardson.
2 F. Alou grounded out to the mound, moving M. Alou to second.
3 Hiller grounded to second.
New York
For San Francisco—Bolin now pitching.
1 Kubek popped to second.
2 Richardson flied to center.
3 Tresh struck out.

9th Inning
San Francisco
Mays doubled into the left field corner.
1 McCovey grounded to second, Mays going to third.
2 Cepeda flied to short-right. Bailey hit a two-run homer into the lower right field stands.
3 Davenport flied to left.

Game 4 October 8 at New York

| | | | S.F. | 020 | 000 | 401 |
| | | | N.Y. | 000 | 002 | 001 |

San Francisco	Pos	AB	R	H	RBI	PO	A	E
Kuenn	rf	3	0	0	0	3	0	0
O'Dell	p	0	0	0	0	0	0	0
Hiller	2b	5	1	2	4	3	2	0
Mays	cf	4	0	0	0	2	0	0
F. Alou	lf	4	1	1	0	1	0	0
Cepeda	1b	4	0	0	0	8	3	0
Davenport	3b	2	1	0	0	1	1	1
Haller	c	4	1	2	2	6	1	0
Pagan	ss	2	0	1	0	0	1	0
b M. Alou	rf	2	2	2	0	1	0	0
Marichal	p	2	0	0	0	0	1	0
Bolin	p	0	0	0	0	0	0	0
Larsen	p	0	0	0	0	0	1	0
c Bailey		0	0	0	0	0	0	0
d Nieman		0	0	0	0	0	0	0
e Bowman	ss	1	1	0	0	0	4	0
Totals		34	7	9	6	27	12	1

a Walked for Ford in 6th.
b Doubled for Pagan in 7th.
c Announced for Larsen in 7th.
d Intentionally walked for Bailey in 7th.
e Ran for Nieman in 7th.
f Grounded out for Bridges in 9th.

Doubles—F. Alou, M. Alou. Triple—Skowron. Home Runs—Haller, Hiller. Sacrifice Hit—O'Dell. Double Plays—Haller to Cepeda to Marichal, Boyer to Richardson to Skowron, Hiller to Cepeda. Left on Bases—San Francisco 5, NY 10. Umpires—Honochick, Barlick, Berry, Landes, Soar, Burkhart. Attendance—66,607. Time of Game—2:55.

1st Inning
San Francisco
1 Kuenn flied to left.
2 Hiller lined to short.
3 Mays grounded to third.
New York
Kubek walked.
1,2 Richardson struck out and Kubek was doubled up between first and second, Haller to Hiller to Cepeda to Marichal.
Tresh singled to center.
3 Mantle struck out.

2nd Inning
San Francisco
F. Alou doubled down the left field line.
1 Cepeda grounded to short, Alou holding.
2 Davenport struck out.
Haller hit a two-run homer into the lower left field stands.
3 Pagan grounded to first.
New York
1 Maris flied to Mays in left-center.
2 Howard grounded to short.
Skowron tripled over Mays' head in left-center.
3 Boyer flied to right.

3rd Inning
San Francisco
1 Marichal flied to right.
2 Kuenn grounded to third.
3 Hiller grounded to second.
New York
1 Ford flied to right.
2 Kubek flied to short center.
Richardson walked.
3 Tresh flied to left.

4th Inning
San Francisco
Mays singled to center.
1,2 F. Alou hit into a double play, Boyer to Richardson to Skowron.
3 Cepeda flied to right.
New York
1 Mantle struck out.
2 Maris grounded to first.
3 Howard struck out.

5th Inning
San Francisco
1 Davenport grounded to short.
Haller singled to center.
Pagan singled to left-center, Haller advancing to third.
2 Marichal struck out, bunting foul on the third strike.
Kuenn walked to load the bases.
3 Hiller struck out.
New York
For San Francisco—Bolin pitching as Marichal injured his hand batting in the top of the 5th.
Skowron beat out a bouncer to deep short.
Boyer singled to center, sending Skowron to third.
Ford bounced to first with Skowron
1 trapped and out Cepeda to Davenport. On the play Boyer went to third and Ford went to second.
Kubek safe at first on Davenport's fumble, loading the bases.
2,3 Richardson hit into a double play, Hiller to Cepeda.

6th Inning
San Francisco
1 Mays grounded to short.
2 F. Alou grounded to short.
3 Cepeda grounded to first.
New York
1 Tresh struck out.
Mantle walked.
Maris walked.
2 Howard flied to right.
Skowron singled to left, Mantle scoring and Maris going to third.
Boyer singled to left, scoring Maris with Skowron stopping at second.
For San Francisco—Larsen now pitching.
Berra, batting for Ford, walked loading the bases.
3 Kubek grounded out, Cepeda to Larsen.

7th Inning
San Francisco
For New York—Coates pitching.
Davenport walked.
1 Haller struck out.
M. Alou, pinch-hitting for Pagan, doubled down the left field line, advancing Davenport to third.
Bailey announced as pinch-hitter for Larsen.
For New York—Bridges came in to pitch.
Nieman, batting for Bailey, got an intentional pass, loading the bases.
Bowman ran for Nieman.
2 Kuenn popped to Boyer near the mound.
Hiller hit a grand slam home run into the lower right field stands.
3 Mays grounded to third.
New York
For San Francisco—M. Alou playing right, O'Dell pitching, Bowman playing short.
1 Richardson flied to left.
2 Tresh fouled to Hiller near the right field boxes.
3 Mantle popped to first.

8th Inning
San Francisco
1 F. Alou grounded to second.
2 Cepeda struck out.
Davenport walked.
3 Haller struck out.
New York
1 Maris fouled to Haller.
2 Howard grounded to short.
3 Skowron grounded to third.

9th Inning
San Francisco
M. Alou beat out a chopper to short.
1 Bowman flied to short right.
2 O'Dell sacrificed M. Alou to second, Bridges to Richardson.
Hiller beat out a slow roller to second, but when Richardson's throw bounced past first into the Yankee dugout, M. Alou scored and Hiller went to second.
3 Mays took a called third strike.
New York
1 Boyer grounded to short.
2 Lopez, pinch-hitting for Bridges, grounded to deep short.
Kubek singled to left.
Richardson singled to left-center, Kubek stopping at second.
Tresh singled to right center, scoring Kubek with Richardson stopping at second.
3 Mantle forced Tresh at second, Bowman to Hiller.

New York	Pos	AB	R	H	RBI	PO	A	E
Kubek	ss	4	1	1	0	1	4	0
Richardson	2b	4	0	1	0	2	3	1
Tresh	lf	5	0	2	1	1	0	0
Mantle	cf	4	1	0	0	4	0	0
Maris	rf	3	1	0	0	3	0	0
Howard	c	4	0	0	0	7	0	0
Skowron	1b	4	0	3	1	12	0	0
Boyer	3b	4	0	2	1	1	4	0
Ford	p	2	0	0	0	0	0	0
a Berra		0	0	0	0	0	0	0
Coates	p	0	0	0	0	0	1	0
Bridges	p	0	0	0	0	0	1	0
f Lopez		1	0	0	0	0	0	0
Totals		35	3	9	3	27	12	1

Pitching	IP	H	R	ER	BB	SO
San Francisco						
Marichal	4	2	0	0	2	4
Bolin	1⅓	4	2	2	1	1
Larsen (W)	⅓	0	0	0	1	0
O'Dell (SV)	3	3	1	1	0	0
New York						
Ford	6	5	2	2	1	3
Coates (L)	⅓	1	2	2	1	1
Bridges	2⅔	3	3	2	2	3

Game 5 October 10 at New York

| | | | S.F. | 001 | 010 | 001 |
| | | | N.Y. | 000 | 101 | 03x |

San Francisco	Pos	AB	R	H	RBI	PO	A	E
Hiller	2b	3	0	1	1	3	3	1
Davenport	3b	4	0	0	0	0	3	0
M. Alou	rf	4	0	0	0	1	0	0
Mays	cf	4	0	0	0	4	0	0
McCovey	1b	4	1	1	0	7	3	1
F. Alou	lf	4	0	2	0	1	0	0
Haller	c	4	0	1	0	10	0	0
Pagan	ss	4	2	2	1	2	2	0
Sanford	p	2	0	1	0	2	1	0
Miller	p	0	0	0	0	0	0	0
a Bailey		1	0	0	0	0	0	0
Totals		34	3	8	3	24	9	2

a Flied out for Miller in 9th.

Doubles—Haller, Hiller, Tresh. Triple—F. Alou. Home Runs—Pagan, Tresh. Stolen Base—Mantle. Sacrifice Hits—Sanford, Tresh. Double Play—Sanford to McCovey. Passed Ball—Haller. Wild Pitch—Sanford. Left on Bases—San Francisco 6, New York 4. Umpires—Barlick, Berry, Landes, Honochick, Soar, Burkhart. Attendance—63,165. Time of Game—2:42.

1st Inning
San Francisco
Hiller walked.
1 Davenport struck out.
2 M. Alou struck out.
3 Mays lined to left.
New York
Kubek singled to center.
Richardson safe at first on Hiller's fumble, moving Kubek to second.
1,2 Tresh lined to Sanford who threw to McCovey to double up Richardson.
Mantle safe on McCovey's error, Kubek moving to third.
Mantle stole second.
3 Maris flied to left.

2nd Inning
San Francisco
1 McCovey struck out.
2 F. Alou flied to center.
3 Haller grounded to second
New York
1 Howard struck out.
2 Skowron struck out.
3 Boyer grounded to short.

3rd Inning
San Francisco
Pagan singled to center.
1 Sanford sacrificed Pagan to second, Skowron to Richardson.
Hiller doubled to left, scoring Pagan.
2 Davenport grounded to third.
3 M. Alou grounded to short.
New York
1 Terry struck out.
2 Kubek popped to Pagan in short center.
3 Richardson popped to first.

4th Inning
San Francisco
1 Mays struck out.
2 McCovey grounded to second.
F. Alou tripled into the left field corner.
3 Haller lined to right.
New York
Tresh blooped a double into short center.
Mantle walked.
1 Maris forced Mantle at second, McCovey to Pagan, Tresh moving to third.
2 Howard struck out.
Tresh scored and Maris went to second on a wild pitch.
3 Skowron struck out.

5th Inning
San Francisco
Pagan homered into the lower left field stands.
1 Sanford popped to second.
2 Hiller lined to first.
3 Davenport struck out.
New York
1 Boyer grounded out, McCovey to Sanford.
2 Terry struck out.
3 Kubek struck out.

6th Inning
San Francisco
1 M. Alou grounded to first.
2 Mays flied to deep center.
3 McCovey flied to right.
New York
Richardson beat out a roller to third.
1 Tresh sacrificed Richardson to second, McCovey to Pagan covering first.
2 Mantle grounded to second, moving Richardson to third.
Richardson scored on a passed ball.
3 Maris grounded to second.

7th Inning
San Francisco
F. Alou singled to center.
1 Haller fouled to Boyer.
2 Pagan fouled to Kubek down the left field line.
Sanford singled to center, F. Alou going to third.
3 Hiller bounced back to the mound.
New York
1 Howard grounded to short.
2 Skowron again struck out.
3 Boyer struck out.

8th Inning
San Francisco
1 Davenport again struck out.
2 M. Alou flied to left.
3 Mays grounded to third.
New York
1 Terry struck out.
Kubek singled to right.
Richardson singled to left.
Tresh hit a three-run homer into the lower right field stands.
For San Francisco—Miller pitching.
2 Mantle grounded to second.
Maris walked.
3 Howard flied to center.

9th Inning
San Francisco
McCovey singled to center.
1 M. Alou struck out.
Haller doubled to left-center, scoring McCovey.
2 Pagan grounded to short.
3 Bailey, batting for Miller, lined to right.

New York	Pos	AB	R	H	RBI	PO	A	E
Kubek	ss	4	1	2	0	1	2	0
Richardson	2b	4	2	2	0	2	2	0
Tresh	lf	3	2	3	3	2	0	0
Mantle	cf	3	0	0	0	3	0	0
Maris	rf	3	0	0	0	3	0	0
Howard	c	4	0	0	0	7	0	0
Skowron	1b	3	0	0	0	9	1	0
Boyer	3b	4	0	0	0	0	3	0
Terry	p	3	0	0	0	0	1	0
Totals		30	5	6	3	27	8	0

Pitching	IP	H	R	ER	BB	SO
San Francisco						
Sanford (L)	7⅓	6	5	4	1	10
Miller	⅔	0	0	0	1	0
New York						
Terry (W)	9	8	3	3	1	7

Game 6 October 15 at San Francisco

N.Y.   000 010 010
S.F.   000 320 00x

New York	Pos	AB	R	H	RBI	PO	A	E
Kubek	ss	4	0	1	1	4	4	0
Richardson	2b	4	0	0	0	3	5	0
Tresh	lf	4	0	0	0	1	0	0
Mantle	cf	4	0	0	0	1	0	0
Maris	rf	3	1	1	1	0	0	0
Howard	c	3	0	0	0	5	1	0
Skowron	1b	3	0	0	0	11	0	0
Boyer	3b	2	1	1	0	0	2	1
Ford	p	2	0	0	0	0	0	1
Coates	p	0	0	0	0	0	0	0
a Lopez		1	0	0	0	0	0	0
Bridges	p	0	0	0	0	0	0	0
Totals		30	2	3	2	24	12	2

a Flied out for Coates in 8th

Doubles—Boyer, Cepeda. Home Run—Maris.
Stolen Base—Mays. Double Plays—Kubek to
Richardson to Skowron, Howard to Kubek,
Davenport to Hiller to Cepeda.
Left on Bases—New York 3, San Francisco 5.
Umpires—Berry, Landes, Honochick,
Barlick, Burkhart, Soar.
Attendance—43,948. Time of Game—2:00.

San Francisco	Pos	AB	R	H	RBI	PO	A	E
Kuenn	lf	4	1	1	0	2	0	0
M. Alou	lf	0	0	0	0	1	0	0
Hiller	2b	4	1	2	0	4	4	0
F. Alou	rf	4	1	2	1	1	0	0
Mays	cf	3	1	1	0	5	0	0
Cepeda	1b	4	1	3	2	9	1	0
Davenport	3b	4	0	1	1	0	4	1
Bailey	c	4	0	0	0	3	0	0
Pagan	ss	3	0	0	0	1	1	0
Pierce	p	3	0	0	0	1	0	0
Totals		33	5	10	4	27	10	1

Pitching	IP	H	R	ER	BB	SO
New York						
Ford (L)	4⅓	9	5	5	1	3
Coates	2⅔	0	0	0	0	2
Bridges	1	1	0	0	0	0
San Francisco						
Pierce (W)	9	3	2	2	2	2

1st Inning
New York
1 Kubek grounded to second.
2 Richardson popped to Pagan in
  short center.
3 Tresh grounded to short.
San Francisco
1 Kuenn grounded to third.
  Hiller beat out a hit to deep short.
  F. Alou safe at first on Boyer's fumble.
2,3 Mays grounded into a double play,
  Kubek to Richardson to Skowron.

2nd Inning
New York
1 Mantle flied to deep center.
2 Maris grounded to second.
3 Howard popped to first.
San Francisco
  Cepeda singled on a bouncer
  over Kubek's head.
1 Davenport struck out.
2,3 Bailey struck out and Cepeda was
  doubled up trying for second,
  Howard to Kubek.

3rd Inning
New York
1 Skowron flied to Mays in deep
  left-center.
2 Boyer fouled to Bailey.
3 Ford took a called third strike.
San Francisco
1 Pagan grounded to third.
2 Pierce grounded to second.
3 Kuenn popped to short.

4th Inning
New York
1 Kubek grounded to third.
2 Richardson grounded to third.
3 Tresh popped to Hiller in short center.
San Francisco
1 Hiller flied to left.
  F. Alou singled off Boyer's glove.
  Mays walked.
  F. Alou scored, and Mays went to
   third on Ford's pickoff throw which
   went into center field.
  Cepeda doubled off the right-center
   field fence scoring Mays.
  Davenport singled to center,
   scoring Cepeda.
2 Bailey took a called third strike.
3 Pagan forced Davenport at second,
  Kubek to Richardson.

5th Inning
New York
1 Mantle flied to center.
  Maris hit a home run over the
   right field screen.
  Howard safely to second on
   Davenport's wild throw to first.
2 Skowron flied to Mays in deep
  left-center.
  Boyer got an intentional pass.
3 Ford popped to second.

5th Inning (continued)
San Francisco
1 Pierce grounded to short.
  Kuenn lined a single to left.
  Hiller singled to center,
   moving Kuenn to third.
  F. Alou singled to left, scoring Kuenn
   with Hiller stopping at second.
2 Mays fouled to Skowron.
  Cepeda singled to center, scoring
   Hiller and sending F. Alou to third.
  For New York—Coates came in to pitch.
3 Davenport popped to short.

6th Inning
New York
1 Kubek grounded out, Cepeda to Pierce.
2 Richardson grounded to third.
3 Tresh grounded to second.
San Francisco
1 Bailey struck out.
2 Pagan struck out.
3 Pierce grounded to short.

7th Inning
New York
1 Mantle popped to second.
  Maris walked.
2,3 Howard grounded into a double play,
  Davenport to Hiller to Cepeda.
San Francisco
1 Kuenn grounded to first.
2 Hiller grounded to second.
3 F. Alou grounded to second.

8th Inning
New York
1 Skowron flied to left.
  Boyer doubled down the left field line.
2 Lopez, pinch-hitting for Coates, flied
  to right.
  Kubek singled to left-center,
   scoring Boyer.
3 Richardson flied to left.
San Francisco
  For New York—Bridges pitching.
  Mays beat out a wicked bouncer
   to third.
1 Cepeda popped to short.
  Mays stole second.
2 Davenport popped to second.
3 Bailey grounded to second.

9th Inning
New York
  For San Francisco—M. Alou playing left.
1 Tresh flied to M. Alou in left-center.
2 Mantle flied to center.
3 Maris struck out.

Game 7 October 16 at San Francisco

N.Y.   000 010 000
S.F.   000 000 000

New York	Pos	AB	R	H	RBI	PO	A	E
Kubek	ss	4	0	1	0	1	0	0
Richardson	2b	2	0	1	0	3	0	0
Tresh	lf	4	0	1	0	6	0	0
Mantle	cf	3	0	1	0	3	0	0
Maris	rf	4	0	0	0	0	0	0
Howard	c	4	0	0	0	5	0	0
Skowron	1b	4	1	1	0	6	0	0
Boyer	3b	4	0	2	0	2	2	0
Terry	p	3	0	1	0	1	1	0
Totals		32	1	7	0	27	3	0

Pitching	IP	H	R	ER	BB	SO
New York						
Terry (W)	9	4	0	0	0	4
San Francisco						
Sanford (L)	*7	7	1	1	4	3
O'Dell	2	2	0	0	0	1

*Pitched to three batters in 8th.

San Francisco	Pos	AB	R	H	RBI	PO	A	E
F. Alou	rf	4	0	0	0	1	0	0
Hiller	2b	4	0	0	0	1	3	0
Mays	cf	4	0	1	0	1	0	0
McCovey	lf	4	0	1	0	3	0	0
Cepeda	1b	3	0	0	0	12	0	0
Haller	c	3	0	0	0	5	0	0
Davenport	3b	3	0	0	0	3	4	0
Pagan	ss	2	0	0	0	1	2	1
a Bailey		1	0	0	0	0	0	0
Bowman	ss	0	0	0	0	0	1	0
Sanford	p	2	0	1	0	0	1	0
O'Dell	p	0	0	0	0	0	0	0
b M. Alou		1	0	1	0	0	0	0
Totals		31	0	4	0	27	11	1

a Fouled out for Pagan in 8th.
b Singled for O'Dell in 9th.

Double—Mays. Triple—McCovey.
Double Plays—Hiller to Cepeda,
Davenport to Cepeda. Left on
Bases—New York 8, San Francisco 4.
Umpires—Landes, Honochick, Barlick,
Berry, Burkhart, Soar.
Attendance—43,948. Time of Game—2:29.

1st Inning
New York
1 Kubek flied to center.
  Richardson walked.
2 Tresh fouled to Davenport.
3 Mantle flied to left.
San Francisco
1 F. Alou fouled to Skowron.
2 Hiller grounded to first.
3 Mays flied to left.

2nd Inning
New York
1 Maris lined to third.
2 Howard grounded to third.
3 Skowron grounded to short.
San Francisco
1 McCovey fouled to Howard.
2 Cepeda struck out.
3 Haller popped to short.

3rd Inning
New York
1 Boyer lined to right.
2 Terry struck out.
  Kubek singled to left.
  Richardson walked.
3 Tresh grounded to second.
San Francisco
1 Davenport popped to second.
2 Pagan grounded to third.
3 Sanford flied to center.

4th Inning
New York
1 Mantle struck out.
2 Maris grounded to third.
3 Howard popped to short.
San Francisco
1 F. Alou flied to short left.
2 Hiller flied to short center.
3 Mays flied to center.

5th Inning
New York
  Skowron singled to left.
  Boyer singled to left-center,
   moving Skowron to third.
  Terry walked, loading the bases.
1,2 Kubek hit into a double play,
  Pagan to Hiller to Cepeda,
   scoring Skowron and moving Boyer
   to third.
3 Richardson fouled to Cepeda.
San Francisco
1 McCovey flied to left.
2 Cepeda popped to second.
3 Haller grounded to the mound.

6th Inning
New York
1 Tresh fouled to Cepeda.
  Mantle walked.
2   Mantle picked off first, Sanford
   to Cepeda.
3 Maris grounded to first.
San Francisco
1 Davenport flied to left.
2 Pagan grounded to third.
  Sanford singled to right-center (the
   first Giant to get on base).
3 F. Alou grounded to third.

7th Inning
New York
1 Howard struck out.
2 Skowron flied to McCovey in
  left-center.
  Boyer singled to center.
  Terry lined to left, Boyer
   stopping at second.
3 Kubek flied to left.
San Francisco
1 Hiller lined to Terry, on a bunt.
2 Mays lined to Tresh who made a running
  one-handed catch in the left field
  corner.
  McCovey tripled over Mantle's head
   to the center field fence.
3 Cepeda struck out.

8th Inning
New York
  Richardson safe at first on Pagan's
   throwing error.
  Tresh singled off Pagan's knee,
   Richardson stopping at second.
  Mantle singled to right, loading
   the bases.
  For San Francisco—O'Dell pitching.
1 Maris forced Richardson at the plate,
   Hiller to Haller.
2,3 Howard grounded to Davenport who
   stepped on third to force Mantle
   and threw to Cepeda for a double
   play.
San Francisco
1 Haller flied to Tresh in left-center.
2 Davenport fouled to Boyer.
3 Bailey, pinch-hitting for Pagan,
   fouled to Skowron.

9th Inning
New York
  For San Francisco—Bowman playing short.
1 Skowron grounded to short.
2 Boyer grounded to third.
3 Terry struck out.
San Francisco
  M. Alou, batting for O'Dell beat out
   a bunt to second.
1 F. Alou struck out.
2 Hiller struck out.
  Mays doubled to right, M. Alou holding
   up at third.
3 McCovey lined to second.

1962 WORLD SERIES COMPOSITE BOX

	Wins	Composite Line Score	
New York Yankees (A.L.)	4	2 0 0 1 2 3 4 6 2	—20
San Francisco Giants (N.L.)	3	1 3 2 3 3 0 5 0 4	—21

Manager	W	L	Pct.	G. Ahead
	Regular Season			
Ralph Houk	96	66	.593	5
Al Dark	103	62	.624	Won playoff over Los Angeles

BATTING AND FIELDING

NEW YORK YANKEES

	WORLD SERIES STATISTICS Pos	G	AB	R	H	2B	3B	HR	RBI	BB	SO	SB	BA	SA	PO	A	E	REGULAR SEASON STATISTICS Main Pos	G	AB	R	H	2B	3B	HR	RBI	BB	SO	SB	BA	SA
Bill Skowron	1b	6	18	1	4	0	**1**	0	1	1	5	0	.222	.333	**52**	1	0	1b	140	478	63	129	16	6	23	80	36	99	0	.270	.473
Bobby Richardson	2b	7	27	3	4	0	0	0	0	3	1	0	.148	.148	19	19	1	2b	161	**692**	99	**209**	38	5	8	59	37	24	11	.302	.406
Tony Kubek	ss	7	**29**	2	8	1	0	0	1	1	3	0	.276	.310	12	17	1	ss	45	169	28	53	6	1	4	17	12	17	2	.314	.432
Clete Boyer	3b	7	22	2	7	1	0	**1**	4	1	3	0	.318	.500	9	16	2	3b	158	566	85	154	24	1	18	68	51	106	3	.272	.413
Roger Maris	rf	7	23	4	4	1	0	**1**	**5**	**5**	2	0	.174	.348	11	1	0	of	157	590	92	151	34	1	33	100	87	78	1	.256	.485
Mickey Mantle	cf	7	25	2	3	1	0	0	0	4	5	**2**	.120	.160	11	0	0	of	123	377	96	121	15	1	30	89	**122**	78	9	.321	**.605**
Tom Tresh	lf	7	28	**5**	**9**	1	0	**1**	4	1	4	**2**	.321	.464	14	0	0	ss	157	622	94	178	26	5	20	93	67	74	4	.286	.441
Elston Howard	c	6	21	1	3	1	0	0	1	1	4	0	.143	.190	37	1	0	c	136	494	63	138	23	5	21	91	31	76	1	.279	.474
Dale Long	1b	2	5	0	1	0	0	0	1	0	1	0	.200	.200	9	3	0	a 1b	41	94	12	28	4	0	4	17	18	9	1	.298	.468
Yogi Berra	c-ph	2	2	0	0	0	0	0	0	2	0	0	.000	.000	6	1	0	c-of-ph	86	232	25	52	8	0	10	35	24	18	0	.224	.388
Hector Lopez	ph	2	2	0	0	0	0	0	0	0	0	0	.000	.000				of	106	335	45	92	19	1	6	48	33	53	0	.275	.391
Johnny Blanchard	ph	1	1	0	0	0	0	0	0	0	1	0	.000	.000				of-ph	93	246	33	57	7	0	13	39	28	32	0	.232	.419
Jack Reed		Did not play																of	88	43	17	13	2	1	1	4	4	7	2	.302	.465
Phil Linz		Did not play																inf	71	129	28	37	8	0	1	14	6	17	6	.287	.372
Ralph Terry	p	3	8	0	1	0	0	0	0	1	6	0	.125	.125	3	2	0	p	43	106	6	20	0	0	0	7	2	27	0	.189	.189
Whitey Ford	p	3	7	0	0	0	0	0	0	1	3	0	.000	.000	0	4	1	p	38	85	5	10	2	0	0	5	8	22	1	.118	.141
Bill Stafford	p	1	3	0	0	0	0	0	0	0	1	0	.000	.000	0	1	0	p	35	78	5	17	4	0	0	5	2	16	0	.218	.269
Marshall Bridges	p	2	0	0	0	0	0	0	0	0	0	0	—	—	0	1	0	p	52	14	0	0	0	0	0	0	0	7	0	.000	.000
Jim Coates	p	2	0	0	0	0	0	0	0	0	0	0	—	—	0	0	0	p	50	32	1	4	0	0	0	1	1	17	0	.125	.125
Bud Daley	p	1	0	0	0	0	0	0	0	0	0	0	—	—	0	0	0	p	43	27	1	5	0	0	0	0	0	4	0	.185	.185
Jim Bouton		Did not play																p	38	32	0	2	0	0	0	1	3	10	0	.063	.063
Rollie Sheldon		Did not play																p	34	26	1	2	0	0	0	1	7	17	0	.077	.077
Bob Turley		Did not play																p	24	12	0	0	0	0	0	0	0	6	0	.000	.000
Tex Clevenger		Did not play																p	22	4	0	0	0	0	0	0	0	2	0	.000	.000
Luis Arroyo		Did not play—sore arm																p	27	4	0	2	0	0	0	0	0	1	0	.500	.500
team total		7	221	20	44	6	1	3	17	21	39	4	.199	.276	183	67	5		162	**5644**	**817**	**1509**	240	29	199	**791**	584	842	42	**.267**	**.426**

Double Plays—5
Left on Bases—43

a—from Washington
Bob Cerv (ph), Joe Pepitone (ph-of), Billy Gardner (2b-3b), Jake Gibbs (3b), Hal Brown (p), Jack Cullen (p), Hal Reniff (p), and Al Downing (p) also played for the Yankees during the season.

SAN FRANCISCO GIANTS

	WORLD SERIES STATISTICS Pos	G	AB	R	H	2B	3B	HR	RBI	BB	SO	SB	BA	SA	PO	A	E	REGULAR SEASON STATISTICS Main Pos	G	AB	R	H	2B	3B	HR	RBI	BB	SO	SB	BA	SA
Orlando Cepeda	1b	5	19	1	3	1	0	0	2	0	4	0	.158	.211	39	4	0	1b	162	625	105	191	26	1	35	114	37	97	10	.306	.518
Chuck Hiller	2b	7	26	4	7	**3**	0	**1**	**5**	3	4	0	.269	.500	16	**22**	1	2b	161	602	94	166	22	2	3	48	55	49	5	.276	.334
Jose Pagan	ss	7	19	2	7	0	0	**1**	2	0	1	0	**.368**	.526	8	14	1	ss	164	580	73	150	25	6	7	57	47	77	13	.259	.359
Jim Davenport	3b	7	22	1	3	1	0	0	1	4	**7**	0	.136	.182	6	12	**3**	3b	144	485	83	144	25	5	14	58	45	76	2	.297	.456
Felipe Alou	rf-lf	7	26	2	7	1	**1**	0	1	1	4	0	.269	.385	8	0	1	of	154	561	96	177	30	3	25	98	33	66	10	.316	.513
Willie Mays	cf	7	28	3	7	2	0	0	1	1	5	1	.250	.321	19	0	0	of	162	621	130	189	36	5	**49**	141	78	85	18	.304	.615
Harvey Kuenn	lf-rf	4	12	1	1	0	0	0	0	1	1	0	.083	.083	11	0	0	of	130	487	73	148	23	5	10	68	49	37	3	.304	.433
Tom Haller	c	4	14	1	4	1	0	**1**	3	0	2	0	.286	**.571**	29	2	0	c	99	272	53	71	13	1	18	55	51	59	1	.261	.515
Willie McCovey	1b-rf-lf	4	15	2	3	0	**1**	**1**	1	1	3	0	.200	.533	23	4	2	of	91	229	41	67	6	1	20	54	29	35	3	.293	.590
Ed Bailey	c-ph	6	14	1	1	0	0	**1**	2	0	3	0	.071	.286	15	0	0	c	96	254	32	59	9	1	17	45	42	42	1	.232	.476
Matty Alou	lf-rf-ph	6	12	2	4	1	0	0	1	0	1	0	.333	.417	3	0	0	of	78	195	28	57	8	1	3	14	14	17	3	.292	.390
Ernie Bowman	ss-pr	2	1	1	0	0	0	0	0	0	0	0	.000	.000	0	5	0	inf.	46	42	9	8	1	0	1	4	1	10	0	.190	.286
Bob Nieman	ph	1	0	0	0	0	0	0	0	1	0	0	.000	.000				b ph	30	30	1	9	2	0	1	3	1	9	0	.300	.467
John Orsino	c	1	1	0	0	0	0	0	0	0	0	0	.000	.000	0	0	0	c	18	48	4	13	2	0	0	4	5	11	0	.271	.313
Carl Boles		Did not play																ph	19	24	4	9	0	0	0	1	0	6	0	.375	.375
Jack Sanford	p	3	7	0	3	0	0	0	0	0	2	0	.429	.429	3	3	0	p	39	98	5	15	3	0	0	4	4	34	0	.153	.184
Billy Pierce	p	2	5	0	0	0	0	0	0	0	1	0	.000	.000	1	0	0	p	30	56	3	12	0	0	0	5	3	12	0	.214	.214
Billy O'Dell	p	3	3	0	1	0	0	0	0	0	0	0	.333	.333	0	0	0	p	49	90	7	12	0	0	0	6	6	29	1	.133	.133
Juan Marichal	p	1	2	0	0	0	0	0	0	0	1	0	.000	.000	1	0	0	p	38	89	13	21	1	0	0	10	4	19	0	.236	.247
Don Larsen	p	3	0	0	0	0	0	0	0	0	0	0	—	—	1	0	0	p	52	25	3	5	0	1	0	1	0	7	0	.200	.280
Bobby Bolin	p	2	0	0	0	0	0	0	0	0	0	0	—	—	0	0	0	p	41	23	3	6	2	0	0	4	1	9	0	.261	.348
Stu Miller	p	2	0	0	0	0	0	0	0	0	0	0	—	—	0	1	0	p	60	16	2	2	0	0	0	1	1	3	0	.125	.125
Mike McCormick		Did not play—sore arm																p	29	28	3	3	0	0	1	1	2	11	0	.107	.214
Jim Duffalo		Did not play																p	24	6	0	0	0	0	0	0	1	4	0	.000	.000
Bob Garibaldi		Did not play																p	9	1	0	0	0	0	0	0	0	1	0	.000	.000
team total		7	226	21	51	10	2	5	19	12	39	1	.226	.354	183	67	8		165	5588	**878**	**1552**	235	32	**204**	**807**	523	822	73	**.278**	**.441**

Double Plays—9
Left on Bases—39

b—from Cleveland
Manny Mota (of), Joe Pignatano (c), Dick Phillips (ph), Cap Peterson (ss), Gaylord Perry (p), and Dick LeMay (p) also played for the Giants during the season.

PITCHING

NEW YORK YANKEES

	WORLD SERIES STATISTICS G	GS	CG	IP	H	R	ER	BB	SO	W	L	SV	ERA	REGULAR SEASON STATISTICS G	GS	CG	IP	H	ER	BB	SO	W	L	Pct	SV	ShO	ERA
Ralph Terry	**3**	**3**	**2**	**25**	17	5	5	2	16	**2**	1	0	**1.80**	43	**39**	14	**299**	257	106	57	176	**23**	12	.657	2	3	3.19
Whitey Ford	**3**	**3**	1	19⅔	**24**	**9**	**9**	4	12	1	1	0	4.12	38	37	7	258	243	83	69	160	17	8	.680	0	0	2.90
Bill Stafford	1	1	1	9	4	2	2	2	5	1	0	0	2.00	35	33	7	213	188	87	77	109	14	9	.609	0	2	3.68
Marshall Bridges	2	0	0	3⅔	4	3	2	2	3	0	0	0	4.91	52	0	0	72	49	25	48	66	8	4	.667	18	0	3.13
Jim Coates	2	0	0	2⅔	1	2	2	1	3	0	1	0	6.75	50	6	0	118	119	58	50	67	7	6	.538	6	0	4.42
Bud Daley	1	0	0	1	1	0	0	1	0	0	0	0	0.00	43	6	0	105	105	42	21	55	7	5	.583	4	0	3.60
Jim Bouton	Did not play													36	16	3	163	124	59	59	71	7	7	.500	2	1	3.99
Rollie Sheldon	Did not play													34	16	2	118	136	72	28	54	7	8	.467	1	0	5.49
Bob Turley	Did not play													24	8	0	69	68	35	47	52	3	3	.500	1	0	4.57
Tex Clevenger	Did not play													21	0	0	38	36	12	17	11	2	0	1.000	0	0	2.84
Luis Arroyo	Did not play—Sore arm													27	0	0	34	33	18	17	21	1	3	.250	7	0	4.76
team total	7	7	4	61	51	21	20	12	39	4	3	0	2.95	162	162	33	**1470**	1375	605	499	838	**96**	66	**.593**	42	10	3.70

SAN FRANCISCO GIANTS

	WORLD SERIES STATISTICS G	GS	CG	IP	H	R	ER	BB	SO	W	L	SV	ERA	REGULAR SEASON STATISTICS G	GS	CG	IP	H	ER	BB	SO	W	L	Pct	SV	ShO	ERA
Jack Sanford	**3**	**3**	1	23⅓	16	6	5	**8**	**19**	1	**2**	0	1.93	39	38	13	265	233	101	92	147	24	7	.774	0	2	3.43
Billy Pierce	2	2	1	15	8	5	4	2	5	1	1	0	2.40	30	23	7	162	147	63	35	76	16	6	.727	1	2	3.50
Billy O'Dell	**3**	1	0	12⅓	12	6	6	3	9	0	1	**1**	4.38	43	39	20	281	**282**	110	66	195	19	14	.576	0	2	3.52
Juan Marichal	1	1	0	4	2	0	0	2	4	0	0	0	0.00	37	36	18	263	233	98	90	153	18	11	.621	1	3	3.35
Bobby Bolin	2	0	0	2⅔	4	2	2	2	2	0	0	0	6.75	41	5	2	92	84	37	35	74	7	3	.700	5	0	3.62
Don Larsen	**3**	0	0	2⅓	1	1	1	2	0	1	0	0	3.86	49	0	0	86	83	42	47	58	5	4	.556	11	0	4.40
Stu Miller	2	0	0	1⅓	1	0	0	2	0	0	0	0	0.00	59	0	0	107	107	49	42	78	5	8	.385	19	0	4.12
Mike McCormick	Did not play—sore arm													28	15	1	99	112	59	45	42	5	5	.500	0	0	5.36
Jim Duffalo	Did not play													24	2	0	42	42	17	23	29	1	2	.333	0	0	3.64
Bob Garibaldi	Did not play													9	0	0	12	13	7	5	9	0	0	—	1	0	5.25
team total	7	7	2	61	44	20	18	21	39	3	4	1	2.76	165	165	**62**	1462	1399	616	503	886	**103**	62	**.624**	39	10	3.79

Total Attendance—376,864 Average Attendance—53,838 Winning Player's Share—$9,883 Losing Player's Share—$7,291

1963
White Shirts and Humiliation

The Dodgers had built up a bit of a reputation for choking through the years. There was the 1951 collapse of the Brooklyn squad, plus all those World Series losses to the Yankees. Out in Los Angeles, the Bums had reaffirmed that negative image by dropping 10 of their final 13 games last season to allow the Giants to tie them for first place, then dropped the deciding play-off game by walking across the winning run in the ninth inning. But Walt Alston and his team went a long way toward dispelling that label by beating back a late challenge from the St. Louis Cardinals to take the National League pennant, their second while based in Los Angeles. Unlike the Dodgers of the 1950's, this outfit relied on speed and pitching more than on power. Tommy Davis and Frank Howard hit the long ball, but just as many runs were produced by the speed and finesse of Maury Wills, Jim Gilliam, and Willie Davis. At the head of the mound corps was Sandy Koufax, the brilliant lefty who developed after several mediocre seasons into the majors' top hurler. A blazing fast ball and sharp curve earned him a 25–5 record, with an average of almost one strikeout per inning. Alston's pitching wealth did not stop there, as he had a strong right-hander in Don Drysdale, a wily southpaw in veteran Johnny Podres, and a top reliever in Ron Perranoski. The Series gave the Dodgers an even greater chance to dispel the ghosts of past failures, as their opponents were the old rival New York Yankees. The Yanks made it three straight pennants under Ralph Houk, with such standbys as Roger Maris, Mickey Mantle, Tommy Tresh, Whitey Ford, Bobby Richardson, and Ralph Terry, plus top performances from new regulars Joe Pepitone, Jim Bouton, and Al Downing. The one-time Subway Series now needed coast-to-coast air flight, but the Yanks hoped to continue their mastery in this new setting.

The opening game in Yankee Stadium matched Koufax against Ford, two of the game's most eminent southpaws. Koufax served immediate notice that he had it all together by striking out the first five New York batters in the game. The Dodgers meanwhile got to Ford, thanks largely to Bill Skowron, the old Yankee star who had been traded to the Dodgers last winter and suffered through a horrible season. Alston decided to use him in the pressure Series games, and the Moose responded by driving in the first run of the game in the second inning with a single, followed closely by a three-run homer by Johnny Roseboro. Koufax kept up his strikeout pace, and despite Tresh's two-run homer in the eighth, he took a 5–2 victory with 15 strikeouts, breaking Carl Erskine's old Series record of 14 set 10 years ago to the day. The strong Dodger pitching continued the next day, with Podres confounding the Yanks with his control and change-up. Willie Davis doubled home two runs in the first, Skowron belted a solo homer in the fourth, and a triple by Tommy Davis in the eighth gave Podres a 4–0 lead. When the Yankees scored a run in the bottom of the ninth, Alston brought Perranoski on to get the final two outs in the 4–1 win. The Dodgers now were sitting pretty with two wins on the road and three home games coming up.

And when they got back to Los Angeles, the Dodgers quickly did away with the Yankees' air of invincibility. Housed in two-year-old Dodger Stadium, the Bums pitched big Don Drysdale in game three, while the Yanks relied on young Jim Bouton. Both hard throwers excelled, with Bouton giving up a run in the bottom of the first on Gilliam's single, a wild pitch, and a run-scoring hit by Tommy Davis. That one-run lead stood up all the way, with Drysdale's three-hitter good for the 1–0 win and Bouton's four-hitter tagged with the heartbreaking loss. The continued snooze of the Yankee bats ushered them out the door with a 2–1 loss in game four. Both Koufax and Ford pitched well, with the Dodgers collecting only two hits for the day. But a 1–1 tie was broken in the bottom of the seventh when first baseman Pepitone lost a throw in the background of white shirts for a three-base error, and a deep outfield fly scored the winning run. The Yanks moved Houk upstairs as general manager after the Series and made veteran catcher Yogi Berra the new manager, a sign of the passing years.

Game 1 October 2 at New York

| L.A. | 041 | 000 | 000 |
| N.Y. | 000 | 000 | 020 |

Los Angeles	Pos	AB	R	H	RBI	PO	A	E
Wills	ss	5	0	0	0	2	0	0
Gilliam	3b	4	0	1	0	1	1	0
W. Davis	cf	3	1	0	0	1	0	0
T. Davis	lf	4	0	3	0	0	0	0
F. Howard	rf	4	1	1	0	0	0	0
Fairly	rf	0	0	0	0	0	0	0
Skowron	1b	3	1	2	2	3	0	0
Tracewski	2b	4	1	1	0	2	2	0
Roseboro	c	4	1	1	3	18	0	0
Koufax	p	4	0	0	0	0	1	0
Totals		35	5	9	5	27	4	0

Pitching	IP	H	R	ER	BB	SO
Los Angeles						
Koufax (W)	9	6	2	2	3	15
New York						
Ford (L)	5	8	5	5	2	4
Williams	3	1	0	0	0	5
Hamilton	1	0	0	0	0	1

New York	Pos	AB	R	H	RBI	PO	A	E
Kubek	ss	4	1	1	0	1	5	0
Richardson	2b	3	0	0	0	2	2	0
Tresh	lf	3	1	1	2	0	0	0
Mantle	cf	3	0	0	1	0	0	0
Maris	rf	4	0	0	0	2	0	0
E. Howard	c	4	0	1	0	11	0	0
Pepitone	1b	4	0	2	0	8	0	0
Boyer	3b	4	0	1	0	1	2	0
Ford	p	1	0	0	0	1	2	0
a Lopez		1	0	0	0	0	0	0
Williams	p	0	0	0	0	0	0	0
b Linz		1	0	0	0	0	0	0
Hamilton	p	0	0	0	0	0	0	0
c Bright		1	0	0	0	0	0	0
Totals		33	2	6	2	27	11	0

a Struck out for Ford in 5th.
b Struck out for Williams in 8th.
c Struck out for Hamilton in 9th.

Double—F. Howard. Home Runs—Roseboro, Tresh. Stolen Base—T. Davis.
Sacrifice Hit—W. Davis.
Left on Bases—Los Angeles 6, New York 7.
Umpires—Paparella (A), Gorman (N), Napp (A), Crawford (N), Venzon (N), Rice (A). Attendance—69,000.
Time of Game—2:09.

1st Inning
Los Angeles
1 Wills took a called third strike.
2 Gilliam grounded to short.
3 W. Davis struck out.
New York
1 Kubek struck out.
2 Richardson struck out.
3 Tresh took a called third strike.

2nd Inning
Los Angeles
1 T. Davis grounded to short.
  F. Howard doubled off the left-center field fence.
  Skowron singled to center, scoring F. Howard.
  Tracewski singled to center, Skowron stopping at second.
  Roseboro hit a three-run homer into the upper right field deck.
2 Koufax flied to right.
3 Wills again took a called third strike.
New York
1 Mantle called out on strikes.
2 Maris struck out (5 in row).
3 E. Howard fouled to Roseboro.

3rd Inning
Los Angeles
  Gilliam singled to center.
1 W. Davis forced Gilliam at second, Richardson to Kubek.
  T. Davis singled to right, W. Davis advancing to third.
2 F. Howard fouled to E. Howard.
  Skowron singled to center, scoring W. Davis and moving T. Davis to third.
3 Tracewski forced Skowron at second, Boyer to Richardson.
New York
1 Pepitone struck out.
2 Boyer's grounder deflected off Koufax to Tracewski who threw to Skowron for the putout.
3 Ford fouled to Gilliam.

4th Inning
Los Angeles
1 Roseboro struck out.
2 Koufax grounded to third.
3 Wills lined to the mound.
New York
1 Kubek struck out.
2 Richardson struck out.
3 Tresh called out on strikes.

5th Inning
Los Angeles
  Gilliam walked.
1 W. Davis sacrificed Gilliam to second, Ford to Richardson covering first.
  T. Davis beat out a bouncer to second, Gilliam moving over to third.
2 F. Howard grounded back to the mound, moving T. Davis to second as Gilliam held third.
  Skowron intentionally walked, loading the bases.
3 Tracewski forced T. Davis at third, Boyer unassisted.
New York
1 Mantle struck out.
2 Maris fouled to Roseboro.
  E. Howard singled to right.
  Pepitone singled to right, E. Howard stopping at second.
  Boyer singled off Tracewski's glove, loading the bases.
3 Lopez, pinch-hitting for Ford, struck out.

6th Inning
Los Angeles
  For New York—Williams pitching.
1 Roseboro grounded to second.
2 Koufax flied to center.
3 Wills grounded to short.
New York
1 Kubek grounded to third.
  Richardson walked.
  Tresh walked.
2 Mantle popped to second.
3 Maris popped to short.

7th Inning
Los Angeles
1 Gilliam struck out.
2 W. Davis singled to right.
  T. Davis singled to right.
  T. Davis stole second.
3 F. Howard struck out.
New York
  For Los Angeles—Fairly in right.
1 E. Howard struck out.
2 Pepitone fouled to Roseboro.
3 Boyer popped to short.

8th Inning
Los Angeles
1 Skowron struck out.
2 Tracewski grounded to short.
3 Roseboro struck out.
New York
1 Linz, batting for Williams, fanned.
  Kubek beat out a slow roller to short.
2 Richardson struck out for the third time.
  Tresh hit a two-run homer into the left field stands.
  Mantle walked.
3 Maris grounded to second.

9th Inning
Los Angeles
  For New York—Hamilton pitching.
1 Koufax struck out.
2 Wills flied to right.
3 Gilliam grounded to short.
New York
1 E. Howard lined to second.
  Pepitone singled to right.
2 Boyer flied to center.
3 Bright, pinch-hitting for Hamilton, struck out (Koufax' 15th strikeout victim to break the Series single game record of 14 set by Carl Erskine with Brooklyn on October 2, 1953, also versus the Yankees).

Game 2 October 3 at New York

Los Angeles	Pos	AB	R	H	RBI	PO	A	E
Wills	ss	4	1	2	0	2	3	0
Gilliam	3b	4	1	1	0	1	1	0
W. Davis	cf	4	1	2	2	3	0	0
T. Davis	lf	4	0	2	1	6	0	0
F. Howard	rf	3	0	0	0	2	0	0
b Fairly	rf	0	0	0	0	0	0	0
Skowron	1b	4	1	2	1	8	1	0
Tracewski	2b	3	0	0	0	0	1	0
Roseboro	c	4	0	0	0	5	0	0
Podres	p	4	0	1	0	0	2	1
Perranoski	p	0	0	0	0	0	0	0
Totals		34	4	10	4	27	8	1

Pitching	IP	H	R	ER	BB	SO
Los Angeles						
Podres (W)	8⅓	6	1	1	1	4
Perranoski (SV)	⅔	1	0	0	0	1
New York						
Downing (L)	5	7	3	3	1	6
Terry	3	3	1	1	1	0
Reniff	1	0	0	0	0	0

L.A. 200 100 010
N.Y. 000 000 001

New York	Pos	AB	R	H	RBI	PO	A	E
Kubek	ss	4	0	0	0	2	4	0
Richardson	2b	4	0	1	0	3	5	0
Tresh	lf	4	0	2	0	1	0	0
Mantle	cf	4	0	0	0	1	0	0
Maris	rf	1	0	0	0	1	0	0
Lopez	rf	3	1	2	0	1	0	0
E. Howard	c	4	0	2	1	6	0	0
Pepitone	1b	3	0	0	0	13	1	0
Boyer	3b	4	0	0	0	0	3	0
Downing	p	1	0	0	0	0	1	0
a Bright		1	0	0	0	0	0	0
Terry	p	0	0	0	0	1	1	0
c Linz		1	0	0	0	0	0	0
Reniff	p	0	0	0	0	0	0	0
Totals		34	1	7	1	27	15	0

a Called out on strikes for Downing in 5th.
b Intentionally walked for F. Howard in 8th.
c Lined out for Terry in 8th.

Doubles—W. Davis 2, Lopez 2.
Triples—T. Davis 2. Home Run—Skowron.
Stolen Base—Wills. Double
Plays—Richardson to Kubek to Pepitone,
Kubek to Richardson to Pepitone, Terry
to Richardson to Pepitone.
Left on Bases—Los Angeles 5, New York 7.
Umpires—Gorman, Napp, Crawford, Paparella,
Venzon, Rice. Attendance—66,455.
Time of Game—2:13.

1st Inning
Los Angeles
Wills singled into center.
Wills stole second.
Gilliam singled to right, moving Wills
to third. Gilliam to second on the
throw to the plate.
W. Davis lined a double to the right
field fence, scoring Wills and Gilliam.
1 T. Davis flied to right.
2 F. Howard grounded to short, moving
W. Davis to third.
3 Skowron struck out.
New York
1 Kubek lined to center.
2 Richardson grounded to second.
Tresh struck out.
3 Mantle flied to F. Howard in deep
right-center.

2nd Inning
Los Angeles
1 Tracewski struck out.
2 Roseboro took a called third strike.
Podres singled to center.
3 Wills grounded back to the mound.
New York
1 Maris tapped back to the mound.
E. Howard singled off Tracewski's glove.
Pepitone flied to left.
2 Boyer struck out.
3 Downing struck out.

3rd Inning
Los Angeles
1 Gilliam grounded to third.
2 W. Davis took a called third strike.
T. Davis tripled to the right field
corner as Maris injured his left
knee against the railing.
For New York—Lopez replaced Maris.
3 F. Howard struck out.
New York
1 Kubek lined to T. Davis in left-center.
2 Richardson popped to short.
3 Tresh flied to center.

4th Inning
Los Angeles
Skowron homered into the lower right
field stands.
Tracewski walked.
1,2 Roseboro hit into a double play,
Richardson to Kubek to Pepitone.
3 Podres popped to short.
New York
1 Mantle grounded to short.
2 Lopez grounded back to the mound.
3 E. Howard flied to right.

5th Inning
Los Angeles
Wills beat out a bunt down the
first base line.
1,2 Gilliam hit into a double play,
Kubek to Richardson to Pepitone.
3 W. Davis took a called third strike.
New York
1 Pepitone grounded to first.
2 Boyer struck out but had to be
tagged out by Roseboro.
3 Bright, pinch-hitting for Downing,
was called out on strikes.

6th Inning
Los Angeles
For New York—Terry pitching.
1 T. Davis grounded to third.
2 F. Howard grounded to first.
Skowron singled to right.
3 Tracewski grounded to third.
New York
1 Kubek grounded to short.
2 Richardson grounded to short.
Tresh singled to left.
Tresh went to second on Podres'
wild pick-off throw.
3 Mantle flied to W. Davis in deep
left-center.

7th Inning
Los Angeles
1 Roseboro lined to right where Lopez
made a leaping catch in front of
the right field barrier.
2 Podres grounded to second.
3 Wills grounded to second.
New York
Lopez bounced a ground-rule double
into the right field stands.
1 E. Howard flied to T. Davis
in left-center.
2 Pepitone flied to left.
3 Boyer lined to left.

8th Inning
Los Angeles
1 Gilliam grounded out, Pepitone to Terry.
W. Davis doubled off the right
field fence.
T. Davis tripled to left-center,
scoring W. Davis.
Fairly, batting for F. Howard, got
an intentional pass.
2,3 Skowron grounded into a double play,
Terry to Richardson to Pepitone.
New York
For Los Angeles—Fairly playing right.
1 Linz, pinch-hitting for Terry, lined
to third.
2 Kubek flied to left.
Richardson beat out a hit to deep short.
3 Tresh grounded to third.

9th Inning
Los Angeles
For New York—Reniff pitching.
1 Tracewski grounded to short.
2 Roseboro lined to second.
3 Podres popped to first.
New York
1 Mantle flied to deep left.
Lopez bounced another ground rule
double, this time into the left
field stands.
For Los Angeles—Perranoski pitching.
E. Howard singled over Tracewski's
head, scoring Lopez.
2 Pepitone forced E. Howard at second,
Skowron to Wills.
3 Boyer struck out.

Game 3 October 5 at Dodger Stadium

New York	Pos	AB	R	H	RBI	PO	A	E
Kubek	ss	4	0	2	0	2	2	0
Richardson	2b	3	0	0	0	1	3	0
Tresh	lf	4	0	0	0	2	0	0
Mantle	cf	4	0	1	0	1	0	0
Pepitone	1b	3	0	0	0	8	2	0
E. Howard	c	3	0	0	0	7	1	0
Blanchard	rf	3	0	0	0	1	0	0
Boyer	3b	2	0	0	0	1	1	0
Bouton	p	2	0	0	0	1	2	0
a Berra		1	0	0	0	0	0	0
Reniff	p	0	0	0	0	0	0	0
Totals		29	0	3	0	24	11	0

a Lined out for Bouton in 8th.

Sacrifice Hits—W. Davis, Richardson.
Double Plays—Pepitone to Kubek to
Pepitone, Richardson to Pepitone to
Kubek. Hitt by Pitcher—Pepitone (by
Drysdale). Wild Pitches—Bouton 2.
Left on Bases—New York 5, Los Angeles 6.
Umpires—Napp, Crawford, Paparella,
Gorman, Rice, Venzon.
Attendance—55,912. Time of Game—2:05.

1st Inning
New York
1 Kubek grounded out, Skowron to Drysdale.
2 Richardson fouled to Skowron.
3 Tresh struck out.
Los Angeles
1 Wills bunted out back to the mound.
Gilliam walked.
2 W. Davis lined to right.
Gilliam took second on a wild pitch.
T. Davis singled off Richardson's glove
into short right center, scoring
Gilliam.
3 Fairly fouled to E. Howard.

2nd Inning
New York
Mantle bunted over Gilliam's head.
Pepitone was hit by a pitched ball.
1 E. Howard struck out.
2 Blanchard grounded to second, moving
up both runners.
Boyer got an intentional pass, loading
the bases.
3 Bouton struck out.
Los Angeles
Skowron singled to left.
Skowron went to second on a wild
pitch.
1 Roseboro grounded to second, sending
Skowron to third.
2 Tracewski took a called third strike.
Drysdale walked.
3 Wills flied to left.

3rd Inning
New York
Kubek safe at first on Will's error.
1 Kubek picked off first, Drysdale
to Skowron to Wills.
2 Richardson popped to first.
3 Tresh grounded to first.
Los Angeles
1 Gilliam tapped back to the mound.
2 W. Davis lined to the pitcher.
3 T. Davis struck out.

4th Inning
New York
1 Mantle took a called third strike.
2 Pepitone popped to second.
3 E. Howard called out on strikes.
Los Angeles
Fairly walked.
1 Skowron forced Fairly at second,
Boyer to Richardson.
2 Roseboro flied to left.
3 Tracewski flied to center.

N.Y. 000 000 000
L.A. 100 000 00x

Los Angeles	Pos	AB	R	H	RBI	PO	A	E
Wills	ss	4	0	0	0	1	2	1
Gilliam	3b	2	1	0	0	0	0	0
W. Davis	cf	3	0	0	0	0	0	0
T. Davis	lf	4	0	1	1	0	0	0
Fairly	rf	1	0	0	0	3	0	0
Skowron	1b	3	0	1	0	10	2	0
Roseboro	c	3	0	1	0	9	0	0
Tracewski	2b	3	0	0	0	4	3	0
Drysdale	p	1	0	0	0	0	3	0
Totals		24	1	4	1	27	10	1

Pitching	IP	H	R	ER	BB	SO
New York						
Bouton (L)	7	4	1	1	5	4
Reniff	1	0	0	0	1	1
Los Angeles						
Drysdale (W)	9	3	0	0	1	9

5th Inning
New York
1 Blanchard grounded to short.
2 Boyer grounded to short.
3 Bouton fanned.
Los Angeles
Drysdale walked.
1 Wills popped to E. Howard in front of
the plate on an attempted bunt.
2,3 Gilliam grounded into a double play,
Pepitone to Kubek to Pepitone.

6th Inning
New York
Kubek singled to right.
1 Richardson sacrificed Kubek to second,
Drysdale to Tracewski.
2 Tresh grounded to second as
Richardson went to third.
3 Mantle took a called third strike.
Los Angeles
1 W. Davis struck out.
2 T. Davis grounded to short. Fairly walked.
3 Skowron struck out.

7th Inning
New York
1 Pepitone grounded to second.
2 E. Howard tapped back to the mound.
3 Blanchard flied to right.
Los Angeles
Roseboro singled to left-center.
Tracewski singled to left, Roseboro
going to third and taking second on
the throw to third.
1,2 Drysdale grounded to second with
Richardson making a good stop and
throwing to Pepitone for the out.
Tracewski raced to third, but
Roseboro held third and Tracewski
was tagged out by Kubek who took
the throw from Pepitone.
3 Wills grounded to second.

8th Inning
New York
1 Boyer took a called third strike.
2 Berra, batting for Bouton, lined
to right.
Kubek singled to left.
3 Richardson forced Kubek at second,
Tracewski unassisted.
Los Angeles
For New York—Reniff pitching.
Gilliam walked.
1 W. Davis sacrificed Gilliam to second,
Pepitone unassisted.
2 Gilliam caught stealing third,
E. Howard to Boyer.
3 T. Davis struck out.

9th Inning
New York
1 Tresh struck out.
2 Mantle grounded to first.
3 Pepitone flied to deep right.

Game 4 October 6 at Dodger Stadium

N.Y.	000	000	100
L.A.	000	010	10x

New York	Pos	AB	R	H	RBI	PO	A	E
Kubek	ss	4	0	0	0	0	2	0
Richardson	2b	4	0	2	0	1	4	0
Tresh	lf	4	0	0	0	1	0	0
Mantle	cf	4	1	1	1	4	0	0
E. Howard	c	4	0	2	0	6	1	0
Lopez	rf	4	0	0	0	1	0	0
Pepitone	1b	3	0	0	0	8	3	1
Boyer	3b	3	0	0	0	0	2	0
Ford	p	2	0	0	0	2	0	0
a Linz		1	0	1	0	0	0	0
Reniff	p	0	0	0	0	1	0	0
Totals		33	1	6	1	24	12	1

a Singled for Ford in 8th.

Double—Richardson. Home Runs—F. Howard, Mantle. Sacrifice Fly—W. Davis. Double Plays—E. Howard to Pepitone, Kubek to Richardson to Pepitone, Tracewski to Skowron. Left on Bases—New York 5, Los Angeles 0. Umpires—Crawford, Paparella, Gorman, Napp, Rice, Venzon. Attendance—55,912. Time of Game—1:50.

Los Angeles	Pos	AB	R	H	RBI	PO	A	E
Wills	ss	2	0	0	0	0	5	0
Gilliam	3b	3	1	0	0	0	0	0
W. Davis	cf	2	0	0	1	2	0	0
T. Davis	lf	3	0	0	0	0	0	0
F. Howard	rf	3	1	2	1	2	0	0
Fairly	rf	0	0	0	0	0	0	0
Skowron	1b	3	0	0	0	9	1	0
Roseboro	c	3	0	0	0	11	0	0
Tracewski	2b	3	0	0	0	2	1	1
Koufax	p	2	0	0	0	1	2	0
Totals		24	2	2	2	27	9	1

Pitching	IP	H	R	ER	BB	SO
New York						
Ford (L)	7	2	2	1	1	4
Reniff	1	0	0	0	0	0
Los Angeles						
Koufax (W)	9	6	1	1	0	8

1st Inning
New York
1 Kubek struck out **(Koufax sets a new 4 game record with this 16th strikeout).**
2 Richardson fouled to Roseboro.
3 Tresh struck out.
Los Angeles
  Wills walked.
1,2 Gilliam attempting to sacrifice popped to E. Howard who threw to Pepitone doubling up Wills.
3 W. Davis struck out.

2nd Inning
New York
1 Mantle flied to right.
2 E. Howard flied to center.
3 Lopez flied to W. Davis in deep left-center.
Los Angeles
1 T. Davis lined to right.
  F. Howard singled to right-center.
2,3 Skowron grounded into a double play, Kubek to Richardson to Pepitone.

3rd Inning
New York
1 Pepitone struck out.
2 Boyer struck out.
3 Ford grounded out, Skowron to Koufax.
Los Angeles
1 Roseboro grounded out, Pepitone to Ford.
2 Tracewski grounded to short.
3 Koufax grounded to first.

4th Inning
New York
1 Kubek grounded back to the mound.
  Richardson blooped a double into short center when W. Davis lost the ball in the sun.
2 Tresh fouled to Roseboro.
3 Mantle grounded to short.
Los Angeles
1 Wills took a called third strike.
2 Gilliam grounded to third.
3 W. Davis fouled to E. Howard.

5th Inning
New York
  E. Howard singled to center.
1 Lopez flied to right.
2 Pepitone again struck out.
3 Boyer forced E. Howard at second, Wills to Tracewski.
Los Angeles
1 T. Davis grounded to second.
  F. Howard homered into the second deck of the left field stands.
2 Skowron lined to center.
3 Roseboro struck out.

6th Inning
New York
1 Ford fouled to Roseboro.
2 Kubek tapped back to the mound.
3 Richardson grounded to short.
Los Angeles
1 Tracewski flied to deep center.
2 Koufax took a called third strike.
3 Wills grounded to second.

7th Inning
New York
1 Tresh fouled to Skowron.
  Mantle homered into the left-center pavilion at 380 feet.
  E. Howard singled to right-center.
2 Lopez fouled to Skowron.
3 Pepitone grounded to first.
Los Angeles
  Gilliam safely to third as Pepitone lost Boyer's throw to first with the ball bouncing off his wrist all the way to the stands.
1 W. Davis hit a sacrifice fly to deep center, Gilliam scoring after the catch.
2 T. Davis grounded to second.
3 F. Howard grounded out, Pepitone to Ford.

8th Inning
New York
  For Los Angeles—Fairly playing right.
1 Boyer struck out.
  Linz, pinch-hitting for Ford, singled to left.
2,3 Kubek hit into a double play, Tracewski to Skowron.
Los Angeles
  For New York—Reniff now pitching.
1 Skowron flied to left.
2 Roseboro grounded out, Pepitone to Reniff.
3 Tracewski lined to center.

9th Inning
New York
  Richardson singled to center.
1 Tresh took a called third strike.
2 Mantle also called out on strikes.
  E. Howard safe at first on Tracewski's error of dropping Will's throw trying for the force at second.
3 Lopez grounded to short.

1963 WORLD SERIES COMPOSITE BOX

	Wins	Composite Line Score
Los Angeles Dodgers (NL)	4	3 4 1 1 1 0 1 1 0 - 12
New York Yankees (AL)	0	0 0 0 0 0 0 1 2 1 - 3

Manager	W	L	Pct.	G. Ahead
	Regular Season			
Walt Alston	99	63	.611	6
Ralph Houk	104	57	.646	10.5

BATTING AND FIELDING

LOS ANGELES DODGERS

WORLD SERIES STATISTICS

	Pos	G	AB	R	H	2B	3B	HR	RBI	BB	SO	SB	BA	SA	PO	A	E
Bill Skowron	1b	4	13	2	5	0	0	**1**	**3**	1	3	0	.385	.615	30	4	0
Dick Tracewski	2b	4	13	1	2	0	0	0	0	1	2	0	.154	.154	7	7	**1**
Maury Wills	ss	4	15	1	2	0	0	0	0	1	3	1	.133	.133	5	10	**1**
Jim Gilliam	3b	4	13	**3**	2	0	0	0	0	**3**	1	0	.154	.154	2	2	0
Frank Howard	rf	3	10	2	3	1	0	**1**	1	0	2	0	.300	**.700**	4	0	0
Willie Davis	cf	4	12	2	2	**2**	0	0	**3**	0	**6**	0	.167	.333	6	0	0
Tommy Davis	lf	4	15	0	**6**	0	**2**	0	2	0	2	**1**	**.400**	.667	6	0	0
Johnny Roseboro	c	4	14	1	2	0	0	**1**	**3**	0	4	0	.143	.357	**43**	0	0
Ron Fairly	rf-ph	4	1	0	0	0	0	0	0	**3**	0	0	.000	.000	3	0	0
Ken McMullen	Did not play																
Wally Moon	Did not play																
Lee Walls	Did not play																
Doug Camilli	Did not play																
Al Ferrara	Did not play																
Marv Breeding	Did not play																
Sandy Koufax	p	2	6	0	0	0	0	0	0	0	2	0	.000	.000	1	3	0
Johnny Podres	p	1	4	0	1	0	0	0	0	0	0	0	.250	.250	0	2	**1**
Don Drysdale	p	1	1	0	0	0	0	0	0	2	0	0	.000	.000	1	3	0
Ron Perranoski	p	1	0	0	0	0	0	0	0	0	0	0	—	—	0	0	0
Bob Miller	Did not play																
Pete Richert	Did not play																
Dick Calmus	Did not play																
Larry Sherry	Did not play																
Ken Rowe	Did not play																
team total		4	117	12	25	3	2	3	12	11	25	2	.214	.350	108	31	3

Double Plays—1
Left on Bases—17

REGULAR SEASON STATISTICS

		Main Pos	G	AB	R	H	2B	3B	HR	RBI	BB	SO	SB	BA	SA
Bill Skowron		1b	89	237	19	48	8	0	4	19	13	49	0	.203	.287
Dick Tracewski		ss	104	217	23	49	2	1	1	10	19	39	2	.226	.258
Maury Wills		ss	134	527	83	159	19	3	0	34	44	48	**40**	.302	.349
Jim Gilliam		2b	148	525	77	148	27	4	6	49	60	28	19	.282	.383
Frank Howard		of	123	417	58	114	16	1	28	64	33	116	1	.273	.518
Willie Davis		of	156	515	60	126	19	8	9	60	25	61	25	.245	.365
Tommy Davis		of	146	556	69	181	19	3	16	88	29	59	15	**.326**	.457
Johnny Roseboro		c	135	470	50	111	13	7	9	49	36	50	7	.236	.351
Ron Fairly		1b	152	490	62	133	21	0	12	77	58	69	5	.271	.388
Ken McMullen		3b	79	233	16	55	9	0	5	28	20	46	1	.236	.339
Wally Moon		of	122	343	41	90	13	2	8	48	45	43	5	.262	.382
Lee Walls		ph	64	86	12	20	1	0	3	11	7	25	0	.233	.349
Doug Camilli		c	49	117	9	19	1	1	3	10	11	22	0	.162	.265
Al Ferrara		of	21	44	2	7	0	0	1	1	6	9	0	.159	.227
Marv Breeding	a	2b	20	36	6	6	0	0	0	1	2	5	1	.167	.167
Sandy Koufax		p	40	110	3	7	0	0	1	7	6	51	0	.064	.091
Johnny Podres		p	37	64	6	9	2	0	1	8	1	11	0	.141	.219
Don Drysdale		p	42	96	5	16	1	1	0	5	9	35	0	.167	.198
Ron Perranoski		p	69	24	1	3	0	0	0	0	2	15	0	.125	.125
Bob Miller		p	42	57	1	4	0	0	0	2	2	24	0	.070	.070
Pete Richert		p	20	22	1	4	1	0	0	1	1	9	0	.182	.227
Dick Calmus		p	21	6	0	0	0	0	0	0	0	5	0	.000	.000
Larry Sherry		p	36	9	1	1	1	0	0	0	2	3	0	.111	.222
Ken Rowe		p	14	5	0	0	0	0	0	0	0	3	0	.000	.000
team total			163	5428	640	1361	178	34	110	584	453	867	**124**	.251	.357

a—from Washington
Nate Oliver (2b), Don Zimmer (3b-ph), Dick Nen (1b), Daryl Spencer (ph), Roy Gleason (ph), Derrell Griffith (2b), Nick Willhite (p), Ed Roebuck (p), Dick Scott (p), Jack Smith (p), and Phil Ortega (p) also played for the Dodgers during the season.

NEW YORK YANKEES

WORLD SERIES STATISTICS

	Pos	G	AB	R	H	2B	3B	HR	RBI	BB	SO	SB	BA	SA	PO	A	E
Joe Pepitone	1b	4	13	0	2	0	0	0	0	1	3	0	.154	.154	37	6	**1**
Bobby Richardson	2b	4	14	0	3	1	0	0	0	1	3	0	.214	.286	7	**14**	0
Tony Kubek	ss	4	**16**	1	3	0	0	0	0	0	3	0	.188	.188	5	13	0
Clete Boyer	3b	4	13	0	1	0	0	0	0	1	**6**	0	.077	.077	2	8	0
Hector Lopez	ph-rf	3	8	1	2	**2**	0	0	0	0	1	0	.250	.500	2	0	0
Mickey Mantle	cf	4	15	1	2	0	0	**1**	1	1	5	0	.133	.333	6	0	0
Tom Tresh	lf	4	15	1	3	0	0	**1**	2	1	**6**	0	.200	.400	3	0	0
Elston Howard	c	4	15	0	5	0	0	0	1	0	3	0	.333	.333	30	2	0
Roger Maris	rf	2	5	0	0	0	0	0	0	0	1	0	.000	.000	3	0	0
Johnny Blanchard	rf	1	3	0	0	0	0	0	0	0	0	0	.000	.000	1	0	0
Phil Linz	ph	3	3	0	1	0	0	0	0	0	1	0	.333	.333			
Harry Bright	ph	2	2	0	0	0	0	0	0	0	2	0	.000	.000			
Yogi Berra	ph	1	1	0	0	0	0	0	0	0	0	0	.000	.000			
Jack Reed	Did not play																
Whitey Ford	p	2	3	0	0	0	0	0	0	0	0	0	.000	.000	3	2	0
Jim Bouton	p	1	2	0	0	0	0	0	0	0	2	0	.000	.000	1	2	0
Al Downing	p	1	1	0	0	0	0	0	0	0	1	0	.000	.000	0	1	0
Hal Reniff	p	3	0	0	0	0	0	0	0	0	0	0	—	—	1	1	0
Steve Hamilton	p	1	0	0	0	0	0	0	0	0	0	0	—	—	0	0	0
Ralph Terry	p	1	0	0	0	0	0	0	0	0	0	0	—	—	1	1	0
Stan Williams	p	1	0	0	0	0	0	0	0	0	0	0	—	—	0	0	0
Bill Stafford	Did not play																
Bill Kunkel	Did not play																
Marshall Bridges	Did not play																
Tom Metcalf	Did not play																
team total		4	129	4	22	3	0	2	4	5	37	0	.171	.240	102	50	1

Double Plays—7
Left on Bases—24

REGULAR SEASON STATISTICS

		Main Pos	G	AB	R	H	2B	3B	HR	RBI	BB	SO	SB	BA	SA
Joe Pepitone		1b	157	580	79	157	16	3	27	89	23	63	3	.271	.448
Bobby Richardson		2b	151	**630**	72	167	20	6	3	48	25	22	15	.265	.330
Tony Kubek		ss	135	557	72	143	21	3	7	44	28	68	4	.257	.343
Clete Boyer		3b	152	557	59	140	20	3	12	54	33	91	4	.251	.363
Hector Lopez		of	130	433	54	108	13	4	14	52	35	71	1	.249	.395
Mickey Mantle		of	65	172	40	54	8	0	15	35	40	32	2	.314	.622
Tom Tresh		of	145	520	91	140	28	5	25	71	83	79	3	.269	.487
Elston Howard		c	135	487	75	140	21	6	28	85	35	68	0	.287	.528
Roger Maris		of	90	312	53	84	14	1	23	53	35	40	1	.269	.542
Johnny Blanchard		of	76	218	22	49	4	0	16	45	26	30	0	.225	.463
Phil Linz		ss-ph-3b	72	186	22	50	9	0	2	12	15	18	1	.269	.349
Harry Bright	b	1b	60	157	15	37	7	0	7	23	13	31	0	.236	.414
Yogi Berra		c-ph	64	147	20	43	6	0	8	28	15	17	1	.293	.497
Jack Reed		of	106	73	18	15	3	1	0	1	9	14	5	.205	.274
Whitey Ford		p	38	92	5	13	2	0	1	4	6	22	2	.141	.196
Jim Bouton		p	40	83	0	6	1	0	0	5	1	33	0	.072	.084
Al Downing		p	24	58	4	6	2	0	0	2	3	31	0	.103	.138
Hal Reniff		p	48	15	0	0	0	0	0	0	2	10	0	.000	.000
Steve Hamilton	c	p	34	14	2	4	0	1	0	2	0	3	0	.286	.429
Ralph Terry		p	40	87	2	7	0	0	0	3	2	17	0	.080	.080
Stan Williams		p	29	49	2	5	1	1	0	5	2	29	0	.102	.163
Bill Stafford		p	28	24	2	7	0	1	0	3	1	7	0	.292	.375
Bill Kunkel		p	22	6	0	2	0	0	0	1	1	3	0	.333	.333
Marshall Bridges		p	23	0	0	0	0	0	0	0	0	0	0	.000	.000
Tom Metcalf		p	8	0	0	0	0	0	0	0	0	0	0	.000	.000
team total			161	5506	714	1387	197	35	188	666	434	808	42	.252	.403

b—from Cincinnati
c—from Washington
Pedro Gonzalez (2b), Dale Long (ph), Jake Gibbs (c), Luis Arroyo (p), and Bud Daley (p) also played for the Yankees during the season.

PITCHING

LOS ANGELES DODGERS

WORLD SERIES STATISTICS

	G	GS	CG	IP	H	R	ER	BB	SO	W	L	SV	ERA
Sandy Koufax	2	**2**	**2**	**18**	**12**	3	3	3	**23**	**2**	0	0	1.50
Don Drysdale	1	1	1	9	3	0	0	1	9	1	0	0	**0.00**
Johnny Podres	1	1	0	$8\frac{1}{3}$	6	1	1	1	4	1	0	0	1.08
Ron Perranoski	1	0	0	$\frac{2}{3}$	1	0	0	0	1	0	0	**1**	0.00
Bob Miller	Did not play												
Pete Richert	Did not play												
Dick Calmus	Did not play												
Larry Sherry	Did not play												
Ken Rowe	Did not play												
team total	4	4	3	36	22	4	4	5	37	4	0	1	1.00

REGULAR SEASON STATISTICS

		G	GS	CG	IP	H	ER	BB	SO	W	L	Pct	SV	ShO	ERA
Sandy Koufax		40	40	20	311	214	65	58	**306**	**25**	5	.833	0	**11**	**1.88**
Don Drysdale		42	**42**	17	315	**287**	92	57	251	19	17	.528	0	3	2.63
Johnny Podres		37	34	10	198	196	78	64	134	14	12	.538	1	5	3.55
Ron Perranoski		**69**	0	0	129	112	24	43	75	16	3	**.842**	21	0	1.67
Bob Miller		42	23	2	187	171	60	65	125	10	8	.556	1	0	2.89
Pete Richert		20	12	1	78	80	39	28	54	5	3	.625	0	0	4.50
Dick Calmus		21	1	0	44	32	13	16	25	3	1	.750	0	0	2.66
Larry Sherry		36	3	0	80	82	33	24	47	2	6	.250	3	0	3.71
Ken Rowe		14	0	0	28	28	9	11	12	1	1	.500	1	0	2.89
team total		163	163	51	1470	1329	466	402	**1095**	**99**	63	**.611**	29	**24**	**2.85**

NEW YORK YANKEES

WORLD SERIES STATISTICS

	G	GS	CG	IP	H	R	ER	BB	SO	W	L	SV	ERA
Whitey Ford	2	**2**	0	12	10	**7**	**6**	3	8	0	**2**	0	4.50
Jim Bouton	1	1	0	7	4	1	1	**5**	4	0	1	0	1.29
Al Downing	1	1	0	5	7	3	3	1	6	0	1	0	5.40
Hal Reniff	**3**	0	0	3	0	0	0	1	1	0	0	0	0.00
Ralph Terry	1	0	0	3	3	1	1	1	0	0	0	0	3.00
Stan Williams	1	0	0	3	1	0	0	0	5	0	0	0	0.00
Steve Hamilton	1	0	0	1	0	0	0	0	1	0	0	0	0.00
Bill Stafford	Did not play												
Bill Kunkel	Did not play												
Marshall Bridges	Did not play												
Tom Metcalf	Did not play												
team total	4	4	0	34	25	12	11	11	25	0	4	0	2.91

REGULAR SEASON STATISTICS

		G	GS	CG	IP	H	ER	BB	SO	W	L	Pct	SV	ShO	ERA
Whitey Ford		38	**37**	13	**269**	240	82	56	189	**24**	7	**.774**	1	3	2.74
Jim Bouton		40	30	12	249	191	70	87	148	21	7	.750	1	6	2.53
Al Downing		24	22	10	176	114	50	80	171	13	5	.722	0	4	2.56
Hal Reniff		48	0	0	89	63	26	42	56	4	3	.571	18	0	2.63
Ralph Terry		40	**37**	**18**	268	246	96	39	114	17	15	.531	1	3	3.22
Stan Williams		29	21	6	146	137	52	57	98	9	8	.529	0	1	3.21
Steve Hamilton	c	34	0	0	62	49	18	24	63	5	1	.833	5	0	2.60
Bill Stafford		28	14	0	90	104	60	42	52	4	8	.333	3	0	6.00
Bill Kunkel		22	0	0	46	42	14	13	31	3	2	.600	0	0	2.74
Marshall Bridges		23	0	0	33	27	14	30	35	2	0	1.000	1	0	3.82
Tom Metcalf		8	0	0	13	12	4	3	3	1	0	1.000	0	0	2.77
team total		161	161	**59**	1449	1239	495	476	965	**104**	57	**.646**	31	19	3.07

Total Attendance—247,279 Average Attendance—61,820 Winning Player's Share—$12,794 Losing Player's Share—$7,874

1964
The Fireworks After

The New York Yankees stumbled through the summer like washed-up champs playing mostly on memory. The team played sluggish ball, and rumors started that new manager Yogi Berra was having a hard time maintaining control over the players. An incident over Phil Linz's harmonica playing on the team bus after a tough loss made headlines, and the team seemed to pull together after that and make a run for the pennant. Rookie pitcher Mel Stottlemeyer came up from the minors in August and played a key role with such holdovers as Mickey Mantle, Roger Maris, Elston Howard, Joe Pepitone, Whitey Ford, and Jim Bouton in powering the late New York drive to their fifth straight American League flag. The St. Louis Cardinals came back from a similar slow start to take the National League pennant, after the Phillies blew a sure lead in the last two weeks of the season. Manager Johnny Keane had a core of stars in Ken Boyer, Bill White, Dick Groat, Curt Flood, Ray Sadecki, Bob Gibson, and Curt Simmons, but he added key help by getting left fielder Lou Brock from the Cubs in a June trade and bringing knuckleballing reliever Barney Schultz back from the minors in August. Keane heard rumors all summer long that he would be replaced by Leo Durocher, but the sudden pennant made his job secure.

The Yankees came into the confrontation hurting, as Mickey Mantle was limping around on a bad leg and Tony Kubek was completely out of action with a sprained wrist. Things immediately got worse for the Bronx Bombers, as ace pitcher Whitey Ford lost the opener in St. Louis 9–5 and sat out the rest of the Series with arm trouble. Sadecki got credit for the win with relief help from Schultz's knuckleball. The second game pitted young Stottlemeyer against the hard-throwing Gibson, and the Yankee rookie came out on top of an 8–3 score. Gibson weakened late in the game and left after eight innings with the score 4–3; the Yanks put the game away with four runs in the ninth off Schultz and Gordon Richardson.

Oldster Curt Simmons and young Jim Bouton hooked up in a tight pitching duel in game three in New York. The scoreboard read 1–1 until the bottom of the ninth, when Schultz came in to pitch after Simmons left for a pinch hitter. Schultz threw one pitch, and Mantle socked it for a home run and a 2–1 Yankee win. The homer also put Mickey in first place in the all-time Series home-run totals, surpassing Babe Ruth's 15. The Yankees seemed on their way to another Series title when they kayoed Sadecki the next day with three runs in the first inning, but relievers Roger Craig and Ron Taylor shut them out the rest of the way, and a grand-slam homer by Ken Boyer off Al Downing in the sixth inning accounted for all the scoring in the 4–3 Cardinal win. Gibson and Stottlemeyer again hooked up in game five, and Gibson looked like a winner when he took a 2–0 lead into the bottom of the ninth. But after Mantle reached on an error by Groat, Tresh belted a two-run homer to send the game into overtime. Undaunted by the ninth-inning thunder, the Cards won the game 5–2 on a tenth-inning three-run homer by Tim McCarver off Pete Mikkelsen.

So the Yanks traveled back to St. Louis needing a sweep of both games, and they accomplished the first leg of that task by taking the sixth game 8–3 behind Bouton's pitching and Pepitone's grand slam. The Yanks faced a seventh-game situation for what seemed like the millionth time, with Berra picking young Stottlemeyer to pitch on short rest against the also-tired Gibson. The Cards scored three times in the fourth and three times in the fifth to run up a 6–0 lead that looked safe in Gibson's hands. But Mantle's three-run homer in the sixth put the Yankees back in hailing distance of the Cards. St. Louis added another run in the seventh and gave Gibson a 7–3 lead to take into the last frame. The Yanks went down fighting, as Clete Boyer and Phil Linz hit solo homers in the ninth before Gibson wrapped up the 7–5 victory and the Cardinals' first World Championship since 1946. The day after the Series ended, the Yankees canned Berra, and Keane quit the Cardinals, both decisions reached during the dog days of summer. To cap the irony, the Yanks later hired Keane to replace Berra.

Game 1 October 7 at St. Louis

N.Y.	030	010	010				
St L.	110	004	03x				

New York	Pos	AB	R	H	RBI	PO	A	E
Linz	ss	4	0	0	0	1	1	0
Richardson	2b	5	0	2	1	2	3	0
Maris	cf	4	0	1	0	0	0	0
Mantle	rf	5	1	2	0	1	0	1
Howard	c	4	1	2	0	5	0	0
Tresh	lf	4	1	2	3	1	0	0
Pepitone	1b	5	0	0	0	11	0	0
C. Boyer	3b	4	1	1	0	2	4	1
Ford	p	1	0	1	1	0	1	0
Downing	p	0	0	0	0	0	0	0
d Blanchard		1	0	1	0	0	0	0
e Hegan		0	1	0	0	0	0	0
Sheldon	p	0	0	0	0	1	1	0
Mikkelsen	p	0	0	0	0	0	0	0
Totals		37	5	12	5	24	10	2

Pitching	IP	H	R	ER	BB	SO
New York						
Ford (L)	5⅓	8	5	5	1	4
Downing	1⅔	2	1	1	0	1
Sheldon	⅔	2	1	0	2	0
Mikkelsen	⅓	2	1	0	1	0
St. Louis						
Sadecki (W)	6	8	4	4	5	2
Schultz (SV)	3	4	1	1	1	1

St. Louis	Pos	AB	R	H	RBI	PO	A	E
Flood	cf	5	1	2	2	5	0	0
Brock	lf	5	1	2	1	1	0	0
Groat	ss	4	0	1	0	1	4	0
K. Boyer	3b	3	1	1	1	1	4	0
White	1b	4	0	0	0	11	0	0
Shannon	rf	4	3	2	2	0	0	0
McCarver	c	3	1	2	0	4	0	0
Maxvill	2b	2	0	0	0	2	2	0
a James		1	0	0	0	0	0	0
Schultz	p	0	0	0	0	0	0	0
Sadecki	p	2	0	1	1	0	1	0
b Warwick		1	0	1	1	0	0	0
c Javier	2b	0	1	0	0	0	1	0
f Skinner		0	0	0	0	0	0	0
g Buchek	2b	0	1	0	0	0	0	0
Totals		35	9	12	9	27	13	0

a Popped out for Maxvill in 6th.
b Singled for Sadecki in 6th.
c Ran for Warwick in 6th.
d Doubled for Downing in 8th.
e Ran for Blanchard in 8th.
f Intentionally walked for Javier in 8th.
g Ran for Skinner in 8th.

Doubles—Blanchard, Brock, McCarver, Tresh. Triples—Flood, McCarver. Home Runs—Shannon, Tresh. Stolen Base—C. Boyer. Sacrifice Fly—K. Boyer. Double Plays—Groat to Maxvill to White, Sheldon to Pepitone. Left on Bases—New York 11, St. Louis 7. P. Balls—Howard 2. Umpires—Secory (N), McKinley (A), Burkhart (N), Soar (A), V. Smith (N), A. Smith (A). Attendance—30,805. Time of Game—2:42.

1st Inning
New York
1 Linz grounded to third.
2 Richardson popped to second.
  Maris walked.
3 Mantle flied to right.
St. Louis
1 Flood grounded to third.
  Brock singled to right.
  Groat singled to right, Brock racing to third.
2 K. Boyer hit a sacrifice fly to right, Brock scoring after the catch.
3 White struck out.

2nd Inning
New York
  Howard singled to left-center.
  Tresh hit a two-run homer into the left-center field bleachers.
1 Pepitone grounded to second.
  C. Boyer singled to center.
    C. Boyer stole second.
  Ford singled to right, scoring C. Boyer.
  Linz walked.
  Richardson singled to left, Ford was out
2 trying to score, Brock to McCarver.
  Linz stopped at second.
3 Maris took a called third strike.
St. Louis
  Shannon singled to left.
1 McCarver fouled to C. Boyer.
2 Maxvill tapped to the pitcher, Shannon going to second.
  Sadecki singled to right, scoring Shannon and Sadecki went to third when Mantle's throw went over Howard's head and into the stands.
3 Flood grounded to short.

3rd Inning
New York
1 Mantle struck out.
  Howard walked.
2,3 Tresh grounded into a double play, Groat to Maxvill to White.
St. Louis
1 Brock grounded to second.
2 Groat popped to second.
  K. Boyer walked.
3 White bounced out to first.

4th Inning
New York
1 Pepitone fouled to Shannon in the right field corner.
2 C. Boyer grounded to short.
  Ford walked.
3 Linz was robbed of a base hit as K. Boyer made a superb stop and threw him out.
St. Louis
1 Shannon fouled to Linz behind third.
  McCarver tripled to right-center.
2 Maxvill struck out.
3 Sadecki struck out.

5th Inning
New York
1 Richardson tapped to third.
2 Maris bounced back to the mound.
  Mantle singled to center.
  Howard singled to right-center, Mantle moving to third.
  Tresh doubled over K. Boyer's head, scoring Mantle with Howard stopping at third.
3 Pepitone flied to center.
St. Louis
1 Flood grounded to third, a fine play by C. Boyer.
2 Brock flied to short left.
3 Groat grounded to third.

6th Inning
New York
1 C. Boyer flied to deep center.
  Ford walked.
2 Linz flied to left.
3 Richardson popped to short.
St. Louis
  K. Boyer singled to left.
    K. Boyer to second on a passed ball.
1 White struck out.
  Shannon hit a booming two-run homer atop of the left field bleacher wall.
  McCarver doubled to right-center.
  James announced to hit for Maxvill.
  For New York—Downing on the mound.
2 James popped to second.
  Warwick, pinch-hitting for Sadecki, singled to left, scoring McCarver, and went to second on the throw to the plate.
  Javier ran for Warwick.
  Flood tripled to the base of the left field wall, scoring Javier.
3 Brock grounded to third.

7th Inning
New York
  For St. Louis—Schultz pitching and Javier playing second.
1 Maris flied to short center.
  Mantle singled off the screen in right.
2 Howard flied to center.
  Tresh walked.
3 Pepitone struck out.
St. Louis
1 Groat grounded to second.
2 K. Boyer struck out.
3 White grounded to second.

8th Inning
New York
1 C. Boyer grounded to short.
  Blanchard, batting for Downing, doubled into the right field corner.
  Hegan ran for Blanchard.
2 Linz grounded to third, Hegan holding second.
  Richardson singled to left, scoring Hegan.
  Maris beat out a slow roller to second, Richardson going to third.
3 Mantle grounded to second.
St. Louis
  For New York—Sheldon pitching.
  Shannon safe on C. Boyer's error.
    Shannon went to second on Howard's second passed ball.
  McCarver walked.
1,2 Schultz lined into a double play, Sheldon to Pepitone.
  Skinner, batting for Javier, was intentionally walked.
  Buchek ran for Skinner.
  For New York—Mikkelsen pitching.
  Flood singled to left, Shannon scoring and Buchek going to second.
  Brock doubled into the left field corner, scoring Buchek and Flood.
  Groat walked.
3 K. Boyer fouled to C. Boyer.

9th Inning
New York
  For St. Louis—Buchek playing second.
1 Howard grounded to short.
2 Tresh popped to third.
3 Pepitone flied to center.

Game 2 October 8 at St. Louis

New York	Pos	AB	R	H	RBI	PO	A	E
Linz	ss	4	2	3	1	1	8	0
B. Richardson	2b	5	1	2	1	4	2	0
Maris	cf	5	1	2	0	2	0	0
Mantle	rf	4	2	1	2	0	0	0
Lopez	rf	0	0	0	0	0	0	0
Howard	c	4	2	1	0	4	1	0
Pepitone	1b	4	0	2	1	14	1	0
Tresh	lf	3	0	1	2	1	0	0
C. Boyer	3b	3	0	0	1	0	3	0
Stottlemyre	p	5	0	0	0	1	3	0
Totals		37	8	12	8	27	18	0

Pitching	IP	H	R	ER	BB	SO
New York						
Stottlemyre (W)	9	7	3	3	2	4
St. Louis						
Gibson (L)	8	8	4	4	3	9
Schultz	⅓	2	2	2	0	0
G. Richardson	⅓	2	2	2	2	0
Craig	⅓	0	0	0	0	1

N.Y.	000 101 204
St L	001 000 011

St. Louis	Pos	AB	R	H	RBI	PO	A	E
Flood	cf	4	0	0	1	1	0	0
Brock	lf	4	0	0	0	1	0	0
White	1b	4	0	0	0	7	0	0
K. Boyer	3b	4	0	0	0	2	1	0
Groat	ss	4	0	1	0	2	3	0
McCarver	c	4	0	1	1	10	0	0
Shannon	rf	4	1	1	0	2	0	0
Maxvill	2b	2	0	1	0	1	3	0
a Warwick		1	1	1	0	0	0	0
Schultz	p	0	0	0	0	0	0	0
G. Richardson	p	0	0	0	0	0	0	0
Craig	p	0	0	0	0	0	0	0
d James		1	0	0	0	0	0	0
Gibson	p	3	0	1	0	1	0	0
b Skinner		1	0	1	0	0	0	0
c Buchek	2b	1	0	0	0	0	0	0
Totals		32	3	7	3	27	7	0

a Singled for Maxvill in 8th.
b Doubled for Gibson in 8th.
c Ran for Skinner in 8th.
d Struck out for Craig in 9th.

Doubles—Howard, Mantle, Pepitone, B. Richardson, Skinner. Triple—Groat. Home Run—Linz. Sacrifice Hit—Gibson. Sacrifice Flies—C. Boyer, Tresh. Double Play—Linz to B. Richardson to Pepitone. Hit by Pitcher—Pepitone (by Gibson). Wild Pitch—Gibson. P. Ball—Howard. Left on Bases—New York 10, St. Louis 5. Umpires—McKinley, Burkhart, Soar, V. Smith, A. Smith, Secory. Attendance—30,805. Time of Game—2:29.

1st Inning
New York
Linz walked.
1 Richardson took a called third strike.
2 Maris struck out.
3 Mantle struck out.
St. Louis
1 Flood took a called third strike.
2 Brock tapped back to the mound.
3 White called out on strikes.

2nd Inning
New York
1 Howard struck out.
2 Pepitone lined to third.
3 Tresh struck out.
St. Louis
1 K. Boyer grounded to short.
2 Groat rolled to third.
3 McCarver grounded to short.

3rd Inning
New York
1 C. Boyer grounded to second.
2 Stottlemyre took a called third strike.
Linz singled to right-center.
Richardson doubled to left, Linz stopping at third.
3 Maris grounded to short.
St. Louis
Shannon singled to left-center.
Maxvill singled between third and short, Shannon stopping at second.
1 Gibson sacrificed Shannon to third and Maxvill to second, Howard to Richardson.
2 Flood rolled to short, Shannon scoring with Maxvill going to third.
3 Brock bounced back to the mound.

4th Inning
New York
1 Mantle took a called third strike.
Howard doubled inside the third base line (just fair).
Pepitone got a double on a short fly to left when Brock missed a shoestring catch, Howard only getting to third.
Tresh intentionally walked.
2 C. Boyer hit a sacrifice fly to center, Howard scoring after the catch.
3 Stottlemyre struck out.
St. Louis
1 White grounded out, Pepitone to Stottlemyre.
2 K. Boyer flied to deep center.
Groat walked.
3 McCarver grounded to short.

5th Inning
New York
1 Linz grounded to short.
2 Richardson lined to Groat in short left-center with an over-the-shoulder catch.
3 Maris flied to short left.
St. Louis
1 Shannon grounded to second.
2 Maxvill grounded to third.
Gibson singled to center.
3 Flood forced Gibson at second, Richardson unassisted.

6th Inning
New York
Mantle walked.
1 Howard lined to Maxvill behind second.
Pepitone was hit by a pitch.
Tresh singled to center, scoring Mantle as Pepitone stopped at second.
2 C. Boyer flied to right.
3 Stottlemyre forced Pepitone at third, K. Boyer unassisted.
St. Louis
1 Brock out, Stottlemyre to Pepitone.
2 White flied to Tresh in left-center.
3 K. Boyer struck out.

7th Inning
New York
Linz singled to left.
On a wild pitch Linz got all the way to third.
Richardson singled to center, scoring Linz.
Maris singled over White's head, Richardson racing to third.
1 Mantle grounded to second, scoring Richardson with Maris going to second.
2 Howard grounded to short, Maris moving to third.
3 Pepitone flied to Flood in deep right-center.
St. Louis
1 Groat lined to short.
2 McCarver lined to Maris in deep right-center making an excellent one-handed catch.
3 Shannon grounded to short.

8th Inning
New York
1 Tresh grounded to second.
2 C. Boyer rolled to his brother at third.
3 Stottlemyre struck out.
St. Louis
Warwick, batting for Maxvill, singled to left.
Skinner, batting for Gibson, got a ground-rule double into the left field stands, Warwick moving to third.
Buchek ran for Skinner.
1 Flood grounded to third, both runners holding.
2 Brock grounded to short, Warwick scoring as Buchek held at second. Buchek went to third on a passed ball.
White walked.
3 K. Boyer forced White at second, Linz to Richardson.

9th Inning
New York
For St. Louis—Buchek playing second, and Schultz pitching.
Linz hit a home run into the left field bleachers.
1 Richardson lined to short.
Maris singled to center.
For St. Louis—G. Richardson pitching.
Mantle doubled down the left field line, scoring Maris.
Howard got an intentional pass.
Pepitone singled off the right field screen, Mantle scored and Howard raced to third.
2 Tresh hit a sacrifice fly to Shannon in right-center, Howard scoring after the catch and Pepitone to second on the throw to the plate.
C. Boyer intentionally walked.
For St. Louis—Craig came in to pitch.
3 Stottlemyre took a called third strike (his 4th strikeout of the game).
St. Louis
For New York—Lopez playing right field.
Groat tripled into the right field corner.
McCarver singled to center, scoring Groat.
1,2 Shannon hit into a double play, Linz to Richardson to Pepitone.
3 James, pinch-hitting for Craig, struck out.

Game 3 October 10 at New York

St. Louis	Pos	AB	R	H	RBI	PO	A	E
Flood	cf	5	0	0	0	1	0	0
Brock	lf	4	0	0	0	2	0	0
White	1b	4	0	1	0	12	0	0
K. Boyer	3b	4	0	0	0	1	3	0
Groat	ss	4	0	1	0	1	4	0
McCarver	c	2	1	1	0	3	0	0
Shannon	rf	3	0	1	0	1	0	0
Maxvill	2b	3	0	1	0	1	2	0
a Warwick		0	0	0	0	0	0	0
Buchek	2b	0	0	0	0	0	0	0
Simmons	p	2	0	1	0	1	2	0
b Skinner		1	0	0	0	0	0	0
Schultz	p	0	0	0	0	0	0	0
Totals		32	1	6	1	c24	12	0

a Walked for Maxvill in 9th.
b Flied out for Simmons in 9th.
c None out when winning run scored.

Doubles—C. Boyer, Groat, Mantle, Maxvill. Home Run—Mantle. Sacrifice Hits—Simmons, Shannon. Double Play—Maxvill to Groat to White. Left on Bases—St. Louis 9, New York 5. Umpires—Burkhart, Soar, V. Smith, A. Smith, Secory, McKinley. Attendance—67,101. Time of Game—2:16.

1st Inning
St. Louis
1 Flood flied to right.
2 Brock popped to third.
3 White lined to left.
New York
1 Linz grounded to second.
2 Richardson grounded to second.
3 Maris popped to second.

2nd Inning
St. Louis
1 K. Boyer popped to first.
2 Groat took a called third strike.
McCarver walked.
Shannon singled to center, McCarver racing to third.
3 Maxvill popped to third.
New York
1 Mantle grounded to short, Howard singled to center.
2 Tresh fouled to K. Boyer.
Pepitone walked.
C. Boyer doubled to left, scoring Howard with Pepitone stopping at third.
3 Bouton flied to left.

3rd Inning
St. Louis
1 Simmons struck out.
2 Flood flied to Maris in left-center.
3 Brock grounded to short.
New York
1 Linz grounded to short, a great play by Groat.
2 Richardson fouled to White.
3 Maris grounded out, White to Simmons.

4th Inning
St. Louis
1 White flied to left.
2 K. Boyer flied to center.
3 Groat popped to second.
New York
Mantle walked.
1,2 Howard grounded into a double play, Maxvill to Groat to White.
3 Tresh grounded to third.

5th Inning
St. Louis
McCarver singled to right, continuing to second as Mantle lost the ball for an error.
1 Shannon lined to right.
2 Maxvill grounded to second, McCarver moving to third.
Simmons singled off C. Boyer's glove, scoring McCarver.
3 Flood forced Simmons at second, Linz to Richardson.
New York
1 Pepitone rolled out, White to Simmons.
2 C. Boyer grounded to third.
3 Bouton fouled to McCarver.

St L	000 010 000
N.Y.	010 000 001

New York	Pos	AB	R	H	RBI	PO	A	E
Linz	ss	4	0	0	0	0	3	1
Richardson	2b	4	0	1	0	4	3	0
Maris	cf	4	0	0	0	4	0	0
Mantle	rf	3	1	2	1	3	0	1
Howard	c	2	1	1	0	2	0	0
Tresh	lf	3	0	0	0	4	0	0
Pepitone	1b	2	0	0	0	8	0	0
C. Boyer	3b	3	0	1	1	1	3	0
Bouton	p	3	0	0	0	1	0	0
Totals		28	2	5	2	27	9	2

Pitching	IP	H	R	ER	BB	SO
St. Louis						
Simmons	8	4	1	1	3	2
Schultz (L)	*0	1	1	1	0	0
New York						
Bouton (W)	9	6	1	0	3	2

*Pitched to one batter in 9th.

6th Inning
St. Louis
1 Brock grounded to second.
White beat out a bouncer to third.
2 K. Boyer flied to deep left.
Groat doubled to left, White stopping at third.
McCarver got an intentional walk, loading the bases.
3 Shannon forced McCarver at second, Linz to Richardson.
New York
1 Linz tapped back to the pitcher. Richardson grounded to second.
2 Maris flied to short right.
Mantle doubled to right, Richardson stopping at third.
Howard intentionally walked, loading the bases.
3 Tresh popped to White near the mound.

7th Inning
St. Louis
Maxvill doubled to left-center.
1 Simmons sacrificed Maxvill to third, C. Boyer to Richardson.
2 Flood flied to short center.
3 Brock grounded to third.
New York
1 Pepitone fouled to White.
2 C. Boyer struck out but had to be tagged by McCarver who dropped the third strike.
3 Bouton flied to left.

8th Inning
St. Louis
1 White grounded out, Richardson to Bouton who covered first.
2 K. Boyer flied to left.
3 Groat grounded to third.
New York
1 Linz flied to center.
2 Richardson grounded to short.
3 Maris struck out.

9th Inning
St. Louis
McCarver safe on Linz' fumble.
1 Shannon sacrificed McCarver to second, Pepitone unassisted.
Warwick, pinch-hitting for Maxvill, walked.
2 Skinner, pinch-hitting for Simmons, flied to deep center, McCarver going to third after the catch.
3 Flood lined to right.
New York
For St. Louis—Schultz pitching and Buchek playing second.
Mantle homered on the first pitch, deep into the right field stands.

Game 4 October 11 at New York

St. Louis	Pos	AB	R	H	RBI	PO	A	E
Flood	cf	4	1	2	0	1	0	0
Brock	lf	4	0	0	0	1	0	0
Groat	ss	4	1	1	0	1	2	0
K. Boyer	3b	4	1	1	4	0	2	1
White	1b	4	0	0	0	11	0	0
Shannon	rf	4	0	0	0	1	1	0
McCarver	c	3	0	1	0	10	1	0
Maxvill	2b	3	0	0	0	1	1	0
Sadecki	p	0	0	0	0	0	0	0
Craig	p	1	0	0	0	0	2	0
a Warwick		1	1	1	0	0	0	0
Taylor	p	1	0	0	0	0	2	0
Totals		33	4	6	4	27	11	1

Pitching	IP	H	R	ER	BB	SO
St. Louis						
Sadecki	⅓	4	3	2	0	0
Craig (W)	4⅔	2	0	0	3	8
Taylor (SV)	4	0	0	0	1	2
New York						
Downing (L)	*6	4	4	3	2	4
Mikkelsen	1	0	0	0	0	1
Terry	2	2	0	0	0	3

*Pitched to one batter in 7th.

St L.	0 0 0	0 0 4	0 0 0
N.Y.	3 0 0	0 0 0	0 0 0

New York	Pos	AB	R	H	RBI	PO	A	E
Linz	ss	4	1	1	0	0	3	0
Richardson	2b	4	1	1	1	2	1	0
Maris	cf	4	1	1	0	6	0	0
Mantle	rf	2	0	1	1	2	0	0
Howard	c	3	0	1	1	9	0	0
Tresh	lf	4	0	0	0	1	0	0
Pepitone	1b	3	0	0	0	8	0	0
C. Boyer	3b	4	0	1	0	0	3	0
Downing	p	2	0	0	0	0	1	0
Mikkelsen	p	0	0	0	0	0	0	0
b Blanchard		1	0	0	0	0	0	0
Terry	p	0	0	0	0	0	0	0
Totals		31	3	6	3	27	9	1

a Singled for Craig in 6th.
b Flied out for Mikkelsen in 7th.

Doubles—Linz, Richardson. Home Run—K. Boyer. Double Play—Linz to Richardson to Pepitone. Left on Bases—St. Louis 4, New York 5. Umpires—Soar, A. Smith, Secory, McKinley, Burkhart. Attendance—66,312. Time of Game—2:18.

1st Inning
St. Louis
1 Flood's liner deflected off Downing to Linz who threw to first for the out.
2 Brock grounded to third.
3 Groat grounded to third.
New York
Linz doubled into the right field corner.
Linz safe at third, attempting to steal, on K. Boyer's throwing error after Linz was trapped.
Richardson doubled into the left field corner, scoring Linz.
Maris singled to right, Richardson stopping at third.
Mantle singled to right, scoring Richardson with Maris going to third,
1 but Mantle out trying for a double, Shannon to Maxvill.
For St. Louis—Craig replaced Sadecki on the mound.
Howard singled to center, scoring Maris.
2 Tresh struck out.
3 Pepitone flied to right.

2nd Inning
St. Louis
1 K. Boyer took a called third strike.
2 White grounded to short.
3 Shannon struck out.
New York
1 C. Boyer struck out.
2 Downing struck out.
3 Linz called out on strikes.

3rd Inning
St. Louis
1 McCarver flied to center.
Maxvill walked.
2 Craig flied to center.
Flood singled to center, Maxvill stopping at second.
3 Brock flied to center.
New York
1 Richardson grounded to third.
2 Maris bounced back to the mound. Mantle walked.
Howard walked.
3 Mantle got picked off second on a beautiful motion from Craig to Groat.

4th Inning
St. Louis
1 Groat struck out.
2 K. Boyer flied to left.
3 White lined to right.
New York
1 Tresh struck out.
Pepitone walked.
C. Boyer lined a single to center, Pepitone stopping at second.
2 Downing struck out.
3 Linz struck out.

5th Inning
St. Louis
1 Shannon struck out.
2 McCarver grounded to first.
3 Maxvill flied to right.
New York
1 Richardson lined to third.
2 Maris flied to left.
3 Mantle struck out.

6th Inning
St. Louis
Warwick, batting for Craig, singled to left.
Flood singled to right, Warwick stopping at second.
1 Brock flied to center.
Groat safe on Richardson's fumble.
K. Boyer hit a grand-slam home run into the lower left field stands.
2 White fouled to Howard.
3 Shannon flied to Maris in left-center.
New York
For St. Louis—Taylor now pitching.
1 Howard grounded to first.
2 Tresh struck out.
3 Pepitone grounded to second.

7th Inning
St. Louis
McCarver walked.
For New York—Mikkelsen took the mound with a 2-0 count to Maxvill.
1 Maxvill grounded to second, McCarver moving to second.
2 Taylor struck out.
3 Flood grounded to third.
New York
1 C. Boyer fouled to White.
2 Blanchard, batting for Mikkelsen, flied to center.
3 Linz bunted out to third.

8th Inning
St. Louis
For New York—Terry pitching.
1 Brock struck out.
Groat singled to right.
2,3 K. Boyer grounded into a double play, Linz to Richardson to Pepitone.
New York
1 Richardson grounded to short.
2 Maris' grounder deflected by Taylor to Groat who made a great stop and threw to first to get Maris.
Mantle walked.
3 Howard struck out but McCarver dropped the third strike and had to tag Howard out.

9th Inning
St. Louis
1 White struck out.
2 Shannon flied to center.
McCarver singled to center.
3 Maxvill struck out.
New York
1 Tresh bunted back to the mound.
2 Pepitone grounded to first.
3 C. Boyer grounded to first.

Game 5 October 12 at New York

St. Louis	Pos	AB	R	H	RBI	PO	A	E
Flood	cf	4	1	1	0	1	0	0
Brock	lf	5	0	2	1	1	0	0
White	1b	4	1	0	1	7	0	0
x K. Boyer	3b	4	0	1	0	3	1	0
Groat	ss	4	1	1	0	2	2	1
McCarver	c	5	1	3	3	13	0	0
Shannon	rf	5	0	0	0	1	0	0
Maxvill	2b	4	0	1	0	2	1	0
Gibson	p	4	1	1	0	1	1	0
Totals		40	5	10	5	30	5	1

Pitching	IP	H	R	ER	BB	SO
St. Louis						
Gibson (W)	10	6	2	0	2	13
New York						
Stottlemyre	7	6	2	1	2	6
Reniff	⅓	2	0	0	0	0
Mikkelsen (L)	2⅔	2	3	3	1	3

St L.	0 0 0	0 2 0	0 0 0	3
N.Y.	0 0 0	0 0 0	0 0 2	0

New York	Pos	AB	R	H	RBI	PO	A	E
Linz	ss	5	0	0	0	1	3	0
Richardson	2b	5	0	3	0	5	3	1
Maris	cf	5	0	0	0	3	0	0
Mantle	rf	3	1	0	0	1	0	0
Howard	c	3	0	0	0	9	0	1
Pepitone	1b	4	0	0	0	8	1	0
Tresh	lf	3	1	1	2	4	0	0
C. Boyer	3b	2	0	0	0	0	3	0
a Blanchard		1	0	0	0	0	0	0
Gonzalez	3b	0	0	0	0	1	3	0
Stottlemyre	p	2	0	1	0	0	1	0
b Lopez		1	0	0	0	0	0	0
Reniff	p	0	0	0	0	0	0	0
Mikkelsen	p	0	0	0	0	0	1	0
c Hegan		1	0	0	0	0	0	0
Totals		36	2	6	2	30	14	2

x Reached first on catcher's interference.
a Popped out for C. Boyer in 7th.
b Struck out for Stottlemyre in 7th.
c Struck out for Mikkelsen in 10th.

Home Runs—McCarver, Tresh. Stolen Base—White. Double Plays—Maxvill to Groat to White, Linz to Richardson to Pepitone. Hit by Pitcher—Howard (by Gibson). Left on Bases—St. Louis 9, New York 7. Umpires—V. Smith, A. Smith, Secory, McKinley, Burkhart, Soar. Attendance—65,633. Time of Game—2:37.

1st Inning
St. Louis
Flood walked.
1 Brock took a called third strike.
2 White struck out.
K. Boyer awarded first on Howard's interference.
Groat walked, loading the bases.
3 McCarver struck out.
New York
1 Linz struck out.
Richardson singled to center.
2,3 Maris hit into a double play, Maxvill to Groat to White.

2nd Inning
St. Louis
1 Shannon grounded to third.
Maxvill singled to right.
2 Gibson struck out.
3 Flood forced Maxvill at second, Linz to Richardson.
New York
Mantle walked.
Howard was hit by a pitched ball.
1 Pepitone rolled out inside the first base line, Gibson unassisted, as both runners advanced.
Tresh intentionally walked, loading the bases.
2 C. Boyer struck out.
3 Stottlemyre struck out.

3rd Inning
St. Louis
1 Brock bunted out to first.
2 White flied to right.
3 K. Boyer grounded to brother Clete.
New York
1 Linz grounded to short.
2 Richardson popped to second.
3 Maris flied to Brock in left-center.

4th Inning
St. Louis
1 Groat grounded to short.
2 McCarver bounced back to the mound.
3 Shannon flied to deep center.
New York
1 Mantle struck out.
2 Howard grounded to first.
3 Pepitone grounded to first.

5th Inning
St. Louis
1 Maxvill took a called third strike.
Gibson singled to left.
Flood safe on Richardson's fumble.
Brock singled to right, Gibson scoring and Flood going to third.
2 White forced Brock, Richardson to Linz as Flood scored.
3 K. Boyer forced White, C. Boyer to Richardson.
New York
1 Tresh flied to right.
2 C. Boyer struck out.
Stottlemyre singled to right.
3 Linz struck out.

6th Inning
St. Louis
1 Groat flied to center.
McCarver singled to center.
2,3 Shannon grounded into a double play, Linz to Richardson to Pepitone.
New York
Richardson singled to center.
1 Maris flied to center.
2 Mantle struck out.
3 Howard struck out.

7th Inning
St. Louis
1 Maxvill grounded to second.
2 Gibson called out on strikes.
Flood singled to left.
Brock singled to left-center, Flood going to third.
3 White lined to deep left.
New York
Pepitone singled to right.
1 Tresh struck out.
2 Blanchard, batting for C. Boyer, popped to third.
3 Lopez, batting for Stottlemyre, struck out.

8th Inning
St. Louis
For New York—Gonzalez playing third, and Reniff pitching.
1 K. Boyer grounded to third.
Groat singled to right.
McCarver looped a single into short left, moving Groat to second.
For New York—Mikkelsen pitching.
2 Shannon struck out.
3 Maxvill forced McCarver at second, Gonzalez to Richardson.
New York
1 Linz grounded to third.
2 Richardson popped to short.
3 Maris grounded to first.

9th Inning
St. Louis
1 Gibson struck out for the third time.
2 Flood lined to third.
3 Brock flied to center.
New York
Mantle safe on Groat's fumble.
1 Howard struck out.
2 Pepitone bounced a smasher to the mound, Mantle moving to second.
Tresh hit a game tying two-run homer into the right-center field bleachers.
3 Gonzalez popped to first.

10th Inning
St. Louis
White walked.
K. Boyer beat out a bunt to the right of the mound.
White credited with a stolen base, going to third after being trapped off second.
1 Groat forced K. Boyer at second, Gonzalez to Richardson as White held third.
McCarver hit a three-run homer into the right field stands.
2 Shannon struck out.
3 Maxvill grounded out, Pepitone to Mikkelsen.
New York
1 Hegan, batting for Mikkelsen, took a called third strike.
2 Linz popped to K. Boyer near the mound.
Richardson singled to center.
3 Maris fouled to K. Boyer, making a good catch in the box seats behind third.

Game 6 October 14 at St. Louis

New York	Pos	AB	R	H	RBI	PO	A	E
Linz	ss	5	1	1	0	2	3	0
B. Richardson	2b	4	0	2	0	2	3	0
Maris	cf	4	1	1	1	4	0	0
Mantle	rf	3	2	1	1	3	0	0
Howard	c	4	1	1	1	5	0	0
Tresh	lf	3	2	1	0	1	0	0
Pepitone	1b	4	1	1	4	6	2	0
C. Boyer	3b	4	0	1	0	1	1	0
Bouton	p	4	0	1	1	3	0	0
Hamilton	p	0	0	0	0	0	0	0
Totals		35	8	10	8	27	9	0

Pitching	IP	H	R	ER	BB	SO
New York						
Bouton (W)	$8\frac{1}{3}$	9	3	3	2	5
Hamilton (SV)	$\frac{2}{3}$	1	0	0	0	0
St. Louis						
Simmons (L)	$6\frac{1}{3}$	7	3	3	0	6
Taylor	$\frac{2}{3}$	0	0	0	0	0
Shultz	$\frac{2}{3}$	2	4	4	2	0
G. Richardson	$\frac{1}{3}$	1	1	1	0	0
Humphreys	1	1	0	0	0	1

N.Y.	000	012	050
St L.	100	000	011

St. Louis	Pos	AB	R	H	RBI	PO	A	E
Flood	cf	3	2	1	0	1	0	0
Brock	lf	4	0	3	0	2	0	1
White	1b	4	0	0	1	8	1	0
K. Boyer	3b	4	0	0	0	0	3	0
Groat	ss	4	0	0	0	3	0	0
McCarver	c	4	0	2	0	8	0	0
Shannon	rf	4	1	1	0	3	0	0
Maxvill	2b	2	0	0	0	2	3	0
a Warwick		1	0	0	0	0	0	0
Buchek	2b	1	0	1	0	0	1	0
Simmons	p	2	0	1	0	0	0	0
Taylor	p	0	0	0	0	0	0	0
b James		1	0	0	0	0	0	0
Schultz	p	0	0	0	0	0	0	0
G. Richardson	p	0	0	0	0	0	0	0
Humphreys	p	0	0	0	0	0	0	0
c Skinner		1	0	1	1	0	0	0
Totals		35	3	10	2	27	8	1

a Fouled out for Maxvill in 7th.
b Grounded out for Taylor in 7th.
c Singled for Humphreys in 9th.

Doubles—Brock, Tresh. Home Runs—Maris, Mantle, Pepitone. Stolen Base—B. Richardson. Sacrifice Hit—B. Richardson. Double Plays—B. Richardson to Linz to Pepitone, Maxvill to Groat, Linz to B. Richardson to Pepitone. Left on Bases—New York 3, St. Louis 7. Umpires—A. Smith, Secory, McKinley, Burkhart, Soar, V. Smith. Attendance—30,805. Time of Game—2:37

1st Inning
New York
1 Linz lined to left.
B. Richardson singled to left.
B. Richardson stole second.
2 Maris struck out.
3 Mantle struck out.
St. Louis
Flood singled to left.
Brock singled to center, Flood going to third.
1,2 White hit into a double play, B. Richardson to Linz to Pepitone, scoring Flood.
3 K. Boyer flied to left.

2nd Inning
New York
1 Howard popped to Maxvill in short center.
2 Tresh grounded to third.
3 Pepitone lined to Shannon, making a leaping catch against the right field wall.
St. Louis
1 Groat took a called third strike.
McCarver singled to right.
2 Shannon struck out.
3 Maxvill flied to right.

3rd Inning
New York
1 C. Boyer flied to center.
2 Bouton struck out.
3 Linz struck out.
St. Louis
Simmons singled to center.
1 Flood flied to Maris in right-center.
2 Brock popped to Maris in short center, making a fine running catch.
3 White grounded out, Pepitone to Bouton.

4th Inning
New York
B. Richardson singled to center.
1 Maris fouled to White.
2 Mantle forced B. Richardson at second, White to Groat.
3 Howard grounded to second.
St. Louis
1 K. Boyer struck out.
2 Groat flied to Maris in right-center.
McCarver beat out a roller to short.
3 Shannon again struck out.

5th Inning
New York
Tresh bounced a ground-rule double into the left field stands.
1 Pepitone struck out.
2 C. Boyer grounded to second, Tresh advancing to third.
Bouton singled to left-center, scoring Tresh.
3 Linz flied to deep left.
St. Louis
1 Maxvill flied to right.
2 Simmons popped to short.
Flood walked.
Brock singled to center, Flood going to third.
3 White grounded out, Bouton unassisted.

6th Inning
New York
1 B. Richardson popped to short.
Maris hit a home run to the right field pavilion roof.
Mantle homered against the screen over the right field pavilion roof.
2 Howard flied to right.
3 Tresh called out on strikes.

6th Inning (continued)
St. Louis
1 K. Boyer grounded to second.
2 Groat lined to Mantle in right-center.
3 McCarver flied to center.

7th Inning
New York
1 Pepitone fouled to White.
C. Boyer singled to left and went to second on Brock's fumble.
For St. Louis—Taylor on the mound.
2,3 Bouton lined to Maxvill, throwing to Groat at second to double up C. Boyer.
St. Louis
1 Shannon struck out for the third consecutive time.
2 Warwick, pinch-hitting for Maxvill, fouled to C. Boyer.
3 James, pinch-hitting for Taylor, grounded to third.

8th Inning
New York
For St. Louis—Buchek playing second, and Schultz pitching.
Linz singled to left.
1 B. Richardson sacrificed Linz to second, being tagged out by McCarver.
2 Maris grounded to second, Linz moving to third.
Mantle intentionally passed.
Howard singled to center, Linz scoring and Mantle stopping at second.
Tresh walked, loading the bases.
For St. Louis—G. Richardson pitching.
Pepitone hit a grand-slam home run onto the right field pavilion roof.
3 C. Boyer flied to right.
St. Louis
Flood walked.
Brock doubled off the right-center field wall, Flood stopping at third.
1 White grounded out, Pepitone to Bouton, Flood scoring and Brock going to third.
2 K. Boyer fouled to Pepitone.
3 Groat grounded to short.

9th Inning
New York
For St. Louis—Humphreys pitching.
1 Bouton called out on strikes.
2 Linz grounded to third.
3 B. Richardson grounded to third.
St. Louis
1 McCarver popped to second.
Shannon singled off the right field screen.
Buchek singled to left-center, Shannon going to third.
Skinner announced to pinch-hit for Humphreys.
For New York—Hamilton came in to pitch.
Skinner singled to center, scoring Shannon with Buchek stopping at second.
2,3 Flood hit into a game-ending double play, Linz to Richardson to Pepitone.

Game 7 October 15 at St. Louis

New York	Pos	AB	R	H	RBI	PO	A	E
Linz	ss	5	1	2	1	2	0	1
Richardson	2b	5	1	2	0	1	3	0
Maris	cf	4	1	1	0	1	0	0
Mantle	rf	4	1	1	3	2	0	0
Howard	c	4	0	1	0	6	1	0
Pepitone	1b	4	0	0	0	8	2	0
Tresh	lf	2	0	1	0	2	0	0
C. Boyer	3b	4	1	1	1	1	5	1
Stottlemyre	p	1	0	0	0	1	1	0
a Hegan		0	0	0	0	0	0	0
Downing	p	0	0	0	0	0	0	0
Sheldon	p	0	0	0	0	0	0	0
b Lopez		1	0	0	0	0	0	0
Hamilton	p	0	0	0	0	0	0	0
Mikkelsen	p	0	0	0	0	0	1	0
c Blanchard		1	0	0	0	0	0	0
Totals		35	5	9	5	24	13	2

a Walked for Stottlemyre in 5th.
b Struck out for Sheldon in 7th.
c Struck out for Mikkelsen in 9th.

Doubles—K. Boyer, White. Home Runs—C. Boyer, K. Boyer, Brock, Linz, Mantle. Stolen Bases—McCarver, Shannon. Sacrifice Hit—Maxvill. Sacrifice Fly—McCarver. Double Play—Groat to Maxvill to White to Shannon to Groat. Left on Bases—New York 6, St. Louis 6. Umpires—Secory, McKinley, Burkhart, Soar, V. Smith, A. Smith. Attendance—30,346. Time of Game—2:40.

N.Y.	000	003	002
St L.	000	330	10x

St. Louis	Pos	AB	R	H	RBI	PO	A	E
Flood	cf	5	0	0	0	2	0	0
Brock	lf	4	1	2	1	0	0	0
White	1b	4	1	2	0	6	0	0
K. Boyer	3b	4	3	3	1	1	2	0
Groat	ss	3	0	0	1	1	1	1
McCarver	c	2	1	1	1	9	0	0
Shannon	rf	4	1	1	0	3	1	0
Maxvill	2b	3	0	1	1	5	3	0
Gibson	p	4	0	0	0	0	1	0
Totals		33	7	10	5	27	8	1

Pitching	IP	H	R	ER	BB	SO
New York						
Stottlemyre (L)	4	5	3	3	2	2
Downing	*0	3	3	3	0	0
Sheldon	2	0	0	0	0	2
Hamilton	$1\frac{1}{3}$	2	1	1	0	2
Mikkelsen	$\frac{2}{3}$	0	0	0	0	0
St. Louis						
Gibson (W)	9	9	5	5	3	9

*Pitched to 3 batters in 5th.

1st Inning
New York
1 Linz grounded to third.
2 Richardson struck out.
3 Maris grounded to second.
St. Louis
1 Flood grounded to third.
2 Brock thrown out on a bunt to first by Stottlemyre.
White doubled over Maris' head to the center field wall.
3 K. Boyer struck out.

2nd Inning
New York
1 Mantle struck out.
Howard singled to left.
2 Pepitone fouled to K. Boyer.
Tresh singled to left-center, Howard stopping at second.
C. Boyer safe at first on Groat's fumble, loading the bases.
3 Stottlemyre struck out.
St. Louis
1 Groat grounded out, Pepitone to Stottlemyre.
McCarver walked.
2 Shannon struck out.
3 Maxvill flied to left.

3rd Inning
New York
Linz beat out a slow roller to third.
1,2 Richardson hit into a double play, Groat to Maxvill to White.
3 Maris grounded to third.
St. Louis
1 Gibson flied to center.
2 Flood grounded to third.
Brock singled to center.
3 White grounded to second.

4th Inning
New York
1 Mantle tapped back to the mound.
2 Howard grounded to second.
3 Pepitone popped to second.
St. Louis
K. Boyer singled to center.
Groat walked.
1 McCarver forced Groat at second, Pepitone to Linz, K. Boyer going to third but K. Boyer scored when Linz threw wildly to first for the double play.
Shannon singled to right-center, McCarver going to third.
McCarver scored and Shannon got to second on a double steal.
Maxvill singled to right, scoring Shannon and took second on the throw to the plate.
2 Gibson popped to first.
3 Flood grounded to second.

5th Inning
New York
Tresh walked.
1 C. Boyer flied to center.
Hegan, pinch-hitting for Stottlemyre, walked.
2,3 Linz flied to short right where Shannon made a running catch and threw to Groat, doubling Tresh.
St. Louis
For New York—Downing pitching.
Brock homered to the roof of the pavilion in deep right-center.
White singled to center.
K. Boyer doubled to right-center, White stopping at third.
For New York—Sheldon came in to pitch.
1 Groat grounded to second, scoring White with K. Boyer going to third.
2 McCarver hit a sacrifice fly to short right, scoring K. Boyer.
3 Shannon struck out.

6th Inning
New York
Richardson beat out a roller to third.
Maris singled to right, Richardson stopping at second.
Mantle hit a three-run homer into the left-center field bleachers.
1 Howard struck out.
2 Pepitone popped to second.
Tresh walked.
3 C. Boyer struck out.
St. Louis
1 Maxvill struck out.
2 Gibson flied to left.
3 Flood flied to right.

7th Inning
New York
1 Lopez, batting for Sheldon, fanned.
2 Linz flied to right.
Richardson singled to center **(his 13th hit—a new all-time Series record).**
3 Maris lined to right.
St. Louis
For New York—Hamilton pitching.
1 Brock struck out.
2 White took a called third strike.
K. Boyer homered into the left field bleachers.
3 Groat grounded to third.

8th Inning
New York
1 Mantle flied to center.
2 Howard struck out.
3 Pepitone popped to second.
St. Louis
McCarver singled off Pepitone's glove.
Shannon safe at first on C. Boyer's fumble of his grounder.
1 Maxvill sacrificed up both runners, C. Boyer to Richardson.
For New York—Mikkelsen pitching.
2 Gibson bounced to third and McCarver got caught in a rundown, C. Boyer to Howard to C. Boyer to Mikkelsen to Linz.
3 Flood lined to third.

9th Inning
New York
1 Tresh struck out.
C. Boyer homered into the left field bleachers.
2 Blanchard, batting for Mikkelsen, struck out **(Gibson's 31st).**
Linz homered into the left field bleachers.
3 Richardson popped to second.

1964 WORLD SERIES COMPOSITE BOX

	Wins	Composite Line Score											
St. Louis Cardinals (N.L.)	4	2	1	1	3	6	8	1	5	2	3	-	32
New York Yankees (A.L.)	3	3	4	0	1	2	6	2	6	9	0	-	33

Manager	Regular Season W	L	Pct.	G. Ahead
Johnny Keane	93	69	.574	1
Yogi Berra	99	63	.611	1

BATTING AND FIELDING

ST. LOUIS CARDINALS

	WORLD SERIES STATISTICS Pos	G	AB	R	H	2B	3B	HR	RBI	BB	SO	SB	BA	SA	PO	A	E		REGULAR SEASON STATISTICS Main Pos	G	AB	R	H	2B	3B	HR	RBI	BB	SO	SB	BA	SA
Bill White	1b	7	27	2	3	1	0	0	2	2	6	**1**	.111	.148	62	3	0		1b	160	631	92	191	37	4	21	102	52	103	7	.303	.474
Dal Maxvill	2b	7	20	0	4	1	0	0	1	1	4	0	.200	.250	13	15	0		2b-ss	37	26	4	6	0	0	0	4	0	7	1	.231	.231
Dick Groat	ss	7	26	3	5	1	**1**	0	1	4	3	0	.192	.308	11	16	**2**		ss	161	636	70	186	35	6	1	70	44	42	2	.292	.371
Ken Boyer	3b	7	27	5	6	1	0	2	6	1	5	0	.222	.481	9	16	1		3b	162	628	100	185	30	10	24	**119**	70	85	3	.295	.489
Mike Shannon	rf	7	28	6	6	0	0	1	2	0	**9**	**1**	.214	.321	13	2	0		of	88	253	30	66	8	2	9	43	19	54	4	.261	.415
Curt Flood	cf	7	30	5	6	0	**1**	0	3	3	1	0	.200	.267	13	0	0		of	162	**679**	97	**211**	25	3	5	46	43	53	8	.311	.378
Lou Brock	lf	7	30	2	9	**2**	0	1	5	0	3	0	.300	.467	8	1	1	a	of	103	419	81	146	21	9	12	44	27	87	33	.348	.527
Tim McCarver	c	7	23	4	11	1	**1**	1	5	5	1	**1**	**.478**	**.739**	57	1	0		c	143	465	53	134	19	3	9	52	40	44	2	.288	.400
Jerry Buchek	pr-2b	4	1	1	1	0	0	0	0	0	0	0	1.000	1.000	0	1	0		ss	35	30	7	6	0	2	0	1	3	11	0	.200	.333
Julian Javier	pr-2b	1	0	1	0	0	0	0	0	0	0	0	—	—	0	1	0		2b	155	535	66	129	19	5	12	65	30	82	9	.241	.363
Carl Warwick	ph	5	4	2	3	0	0	0	1	1	0	0	.750	.750					of-ph	88	158	14	41	7	1	3	15	11	30	2	.259	.323
Bob Skinner	ph	4	3	0	2	1	0	0	1	1	0	0	.667	1.000				b	of-ph	55	118	10	32	5	0	1	16	11	20	0	.271	.339
Charlie James	ph	3	3	0	0	0	0	0	0	0	1	0	.000	.000					of-ph	88	233	24	52	9	1	5	17	11	58	0	.233	.335
Bob Uecker		Did not play																	c	40	106	8	21	1	0	1	6	17	24	0	.198	.236
Ed Spiezio		Did not play																	ph	12	12	0	4	0	0	0	0	0	1	0	.333	.333
Bob Gibson	p	3	9	1	2	0	0	0	0	0	3	0	.222	.222	1	2	0		p	40	96	8	15	3	1	0	4	3	38	0	.156	.208
Curt Simmons	p	2	4	0	2	0	0	0	1	0	1	0	.500	.500	2	1	0		p	34	94	6	10	0	0	0	6	4	32	0	.106	.106
Ray Sadecki	p	2	2	0	1	0	0	0	1	0	1	0	.500	.500	0	1	0		p	39	75	7	12	6	1	0	6	2	14	0	.160	.167
Barney Schultz	p	4	1	0	0	0	0	0	0	0	0	0	.000	.000	0	0	0		p	30	6	0	1	0	0	0	0	0	2	0	.167	.167
Roger Craig	p	2	1	0	0	0	0	0	0	0	0	0	.000	.000	0	2	0		p	39	48	4	10	1	0	0	3	5	24	0	.208	.229
Ron Taylor	p	2	1	0	0	0	0	0	0	0	1	0	.000	.000	0	2	0		p	63	15	0	2	0	0	0	0	0	9	0	.133	.133
Gordie Richardson	p	2	0	0	0	0	0	0	0	0	0	0	—	—	0	0	0		p	19	13	0	1	0	0	0	0	2	9	0	.077	.077
Bob Humphreys	p	1	0	0	0	0	0	0	0	0	0	0	—	—	0	0	0		p	28	4	2	1	0	0	0	1	2	1	0	.250	.250
Mike Cuellar		Did not play																	p	32	18	0	0	0	0	0	0	0	8	0	.000	.000
Ray Washburn		Did not play																	p	15	15	2	2	1	0	0	1	0	7	0	.133	.200
team total		7	240	32	61	8	3	5	29	18	39	3	.254	.375	189	64	4			162	**5625**	715	**1531**	240	53	109	654	427	925	73	**.272**	.393

Double Plays—6
Left on Bases—47

a—from Chicago (N)
b—from Cincinnati

Johnny Lewis (of), Phil Gagliano (ph-2b), Doug Clemens (of), Jeoff Long (ph), Joe Morgan (ph), Ernie Broglio (p), Lew Burdette (p), Glen Hobbie (p), Bobby Shantz (p), Harry Fanok (p), Dave Bakenhaster (p), Jack Spring (p), and Dave Darling (p) also played for the Cardinals during the season.

NEW YORK YANKEES

	WORLD SERIES STATISTICS Pos	G	AB	R	H	2B	3B	HR	RBI	BB	SO	SB	BA	SA	PO	A	E	REGULAR SEASON STATISTICS Main Pos	G	AB	R	H	2B	3B	HR	RBI	BB	SO	SB	BA	SA
Joe Pepitone	1b	7	26	1	4	1	0	1	5	2	3	0	.154	.308	**64**	5	0	1b	160	613	71	154	12	3	28	100	24	63	2	.251	.418
Bobby Richardson	2b	7	**32**	3	**13**	**2**	0	0	3	0	2	**1**	.406	.469	19	19	**2**	2b	159	**679**	90	181	25	4	4	50	28	36	11	.267	.333
Phil Linz	ss	7	31	5	7	1	0	2	2	2	5	0	.226	.452	7	21	**2**	ss-3b	112	368	63	92	21	3	5	25	43	61	3	.250	.364
Clete Boyer	3b	7	24	2	5	1	0	1	3	1	5	**1**	.208	.375	5	**22**	**2**	3b	147	510	43	111	10	5	8	52	36	93	6	.218	.304
Mickey Mantle	rf	7	24	**8**	8	**2**	0	**3**	**8**	**6**	8	0	.333	**.792**	13	0	**2**	of	143	465	92	141	25	7	35	111	99	102	6	.303	.591
Roger Maris	cf	7	30	4	6	0	0	1	1	1	4	0	.200	.300	19	0	0	of	141	513	86	144	12	2	26	71	62	78	3	.281	.464
Tommy Tresh	lf	7	22	4	6	**2**	0	2	7	**6**	7	0	.273	.636	11	0	0	of	153	533	75	131	25	5	16	73	73	110	13	.246	.402
Elston Howard	c	7	24	5	7	1	0	0	2	4	6	0	.292	.333	40	2	1	c	150	550	63	172	27	3	15	84	48	73	1	.313	.455
Hector Lopez	rf-ph	3	2	0	0	0	0	0	0	0	2	0	.000	.000	0	0	0	of	127	285	34	74	9	3	10	34	24	54	1	.260	.418
Pedro Gonzalez	3b	1	1	0	0	0	0	0	0	0	0	0	.000	.000	1	3	0	1b-of	80	112	18	31	8	1	0	5	7	22	3	.277	.366
Johnny Blanchard	ph	4	4	0	1	1	0	0	0	0	1	0	.250	.500				ph-c	77	161	18	41	8	0	7	28	24	24	1	.255	.435
Mike Hegan	pr-ph	3	1	1	0	0	0	0	0	1	1	0	.000	.000				ph-1b	5	5	0	0	0	0	0	0	1	2	0	.000	.000
Archie Moore		Did not play																ph-of	31	23	4	4	2	0	0	1	2	9	0	.174	.261
Chester Trail		Did not play																Did not play for Yankees during regular season.													
Tony Kubek		Not in series—sprained wrist																ss	106	415	46	95	16	3	8	31	26	55	4	.229	.340
Mel Stottlemyre	p	3	8	0	1	0	0	0	0	0	6	0	.125	.125	2	5	0	p	14	37	2	9	1	0	0	3	1	12	0	.243	.270
Jim Bouton	p	2	7	0	1	0	0	0	1	0	2	0	.143	.143	4	0	0	p	38	100	3	13	2	0	0	7	1	44	0	.130	.150
Al Downing	p	2	2	0	0	0	0	0	0	0	2	0	.000	.000	0	1	0	p	40	85	5	15	1	1	0	7	4	33	0	.176	.212
Whitey Ford	p	1	1	0	1	0	0	0	1	2	0	0	1.000	1.000	0	1	0	p	39	67	5	8	1	0	0	2	10	23	0	.119	.134
Pete Mikkelson	p	4	0	0	0	0	0	0	0	0	0	0	—	—	0	2	0	p	50	16	1	1	0	0	0	0	0	12	0	.063	.063
Steve Hamilton	p	2	0	0	0	0	0	0	0	0	0	0	—	—	0	0	0	p	32	20	3	4	0	0	0	1	2	4	0	.200	.200
Rollie Sheldon	p	2	0	0	0	0	0	0	0	0	0	0	—	—	1	1	0	p	19	34	0	3	0	0	0	1	0	23	0	.088	.088
Hal Reniff	p	1	0	0	0	0	0	0	0	0	0	0	—	—	0	0	0	p	44	10	2	1	0	0	0	0	0	7	0	.100	.100
Ralph Terry	p	1	0	0	0	0	0	0	0	0	0	0	—	—	0	0	0	p	27	35	2	7	1	0	0	0	3	10	0	.200	.229
Bill Stafford		Did not play																p	31	13	1	1	1	0	0	1	0	6	0	.077	.154
Stan Williams		Did not play																p	22	21	1	3	1	0	0	0	0	10	0	.143	.190
team total		7	239	33	60	11	0	10	33	25	54	2	.251	.423	186	82	9		164	**5705**	730	**1442**	208	35	162	688	520	976	54	.253	.387

Double Plays—6
Left on Bases—47

Harry Bright (1b), Elvio Jiminez (of), Jake Gibbs (c), Roger Repoz (of), Bud Daley (p), Pedro Ramos (p), and Bob Meyer (p) also played for the Yankees during the season.

PITCHING

ST. LOUIS CARDINALS

	WORLD SERIES STATISTICS G	GS	CG	IP	H	R	ER	BB	SO	W	L	SV	ERA	REGULAR SEASON STATISTICS G	GS	CG	IP	H	ER	BB	SO	W	L	Pct	SV	ShO	ERA
Bob Gibson	3	**3**	**2**	**27**	**23**	**11**	**9**	**8**	**31**	**2**	1	0	3.00	40	36	17	287	250	96	86	245	19	12	.613	1	2	3.01
Curt Simmons	2	2	0	$14\frac{1}{3}$	11	4	4	3	8	0	**1**	0	2.51	34	34	12	244	233	93	49	104	18	9	.667	0	3	3.43
Ray Sadecki	2	2	0	$6\frac{1}{3}$	12	7	6	5	2	1	0	0	8.53	37	32	9	220	232	90	60	119	20	11	.645	1	2	3.68
Roger Craig	2	0	0	5	2	0	0	3	9	1	0	0	0.00	39	19	3	166	180	60	35	84	7	9	.438	5	0	3.25
Ron Taylor	2	0	0	$4\frac{2}{3}$	0	0	0	1	2	0	0	**1**	0.00	63	2	0	101	109	52	33	69	8	4	.667	7	0	4.63
Barney Schultz	**4**	0	0	4	9	8	8	3	1	0	**1**	**1**	18.00	30	0	0	49	35	9	11	29	1	3	.250	14	0	1.65
Bob Humphreys	1	0	0	1	0	0	0	0	1	0	0	0	0.00	28	0	0	43	32	12	15	36	2	0	1.000	2	0	2.51
Gordie Richardson	2	0	0	$\frac{2}{3}$	3	3	3	2	0	0	0	0	40.50	19	6	1	47	40	12	15	28	4	2	.667	1	0	2.30
Mike Cuellar	Did not play													32	7	1	72	80	36	33	56	5	5	.500	4	0	4.50
Ray Washburn	Did not play													15	10	0	60	60	27	17	28	3	4	.429	2	0	4.05
team total	7	7	2	63	60	33	30	25	54	4	3	2	4.29	162	162	47	1445	1405	551	410	877	**93**	69	**.574**	38	10	3.43

NEW YORK YANKEES

	WORLD SERIES STATISTICS G	GS	CG	IP	H	R	ER	BB	SO	W	L	SV	ERA	REGULAR SEASON STATISTICS G	GS	CG	IP	H	ER	BB	SO	W	L	Pct	SV	ShO	ERA
Mel Stottlemyre	3	3	1	20	18	8	7	6	12	1	**1**	0	3.15	13	12	5	96	77	22	35	49	9	3	.750	0	2	2.06
Jim Bouton	2	2	1	$17\frac{1}{3}$	15	4	3	5	7	**2**	0	0	**1.56**	38	37	11	271	227	91	60	125	18	13	.581	0	4	3.02
Al Downing	3	1	0	$7\frac{2}{3}$	9	8	7	2	5	0	**1**	0	8.22	37	35	11	244	201	94	**120**	**217**	13	8	.619	2	1	3.47
Whitey Ford	1	1	0	$5\frac{1}{3}$	8	5	5	1	4	0	**1**	0	8.44	39	36	12	245	212	58	57	172	17	6	.739	1	8	2.13
Pete Mikkelsen	**4**	0	0	$4\frac{2}{3}$	4	4	3	2	4	0	**1**	0	5.79	50	0	0	86	79	34	41	63	7	4	.636	12	0	3.56
Rollie Sheldon	2	0	0	$2\frac{2}{3}$	0	2	0	2	2	0	0	0	0.00	19	12	3	102	92	41	18	57	5	2	.714	1	0	3.62
Steve Hamilton	2	0	0	2	3	1	1	0	2	0	0	**1**	4.50	30	3	1	60	55	22	15	49	7	2	.778	3	0	3.30
Ralph Terry	1	0	0	2	2	0	0	0	3	0	0	0	0.00	27	14	2	115	130	58	31	77	7	11	.389	4	1	4.54
Hal Reniff	1	0	0	$\frac{1}{3}$	2	0	0	0	0	0	0	0	0.00	41	0	0	69	47	24	30	38	6	4	.600	9	0	3.13
Bill Stafford	Did not play													31	1	0	61	50	18	22	39	5	0	1.000	4	0	2.66
Stan Williams	Did not play													21	10	1	82	76	35	38	54	1	5	.167	0	0	3.84
team total	7	7	2	62	61	32	26	18	39	3	4	1	3.77	164	164	46	**1507**	1312	528	504	989	99	63	**.611**	**45**	18	3.15

Total Attendance—321,807 Average Attendance—45,972 Winning Player's Share—$8,622 Losing Player's Share—$5,309

1965
Los Angeles 2, Minnesota 0

The dynasty crumbled to the ground, and with the long years of Yankee supremacy at an end, the American League returned to a normalcy of sorts by furnishing a World Series contender other than New York. While age and injuries dropped the Yanks into a poor sixth place, their lowest finish since 1925, the Minnesota Twins broke into championship class for the first time ever. This club had played for decades as the Washington Senators, moving to the far north in 1961 and leaving an expansion club behind in the capital city. Managed by quiet Sam Mele, the Twins earned their flag primarily through the long ball. Harmon Killebrew, Bob Allison, Don Mincher, and Jimmie Hall swung the big home-run bats, while Tony Oliva won the A.L. batting title with a .321 mark and Zoilo Versalles won the MVP award with his solid hitting and sound shortstop play. A plucky pitching staff benefited from this batting support, with 21-game-winner Mudcat Grant the ace. Unlike the Twins' offensive threat, their opponent, the Los Angeles Dodgers, had the fewest home runs of any big-league team, but operated on a string of singles, stolen bases, and superb pitching—all of which was enough to open the National League throne room for the twelfth time. Shortstop Maury Wills epitomized the Los Angeles attack, hitting a powerless .286 and stealing 94 bases. Willie Davis, Wes Parker, Jim Gilliam, and Lou Johnson kept the attack moving, while pitchers Sandy Koufax and Don Drysdale stopped enemy offenses in their tracks. Southpaw Koufax chalked up a dazzling 26–8 record, while righty Drysdale worked his way to a 23–12 mark. Dodger manager Walt Alston conceded the long ball to the Twins, hoping to win on the legs of his base runners and the arms of his pitchers.

But the Twins won the opening game in Minnesota on the bats of their sluggers. Koufax sat this game out because of a Jewish holiday, and Drysdale simply wasn't at his best. Mincher slugged a solo homer in the second inning, and then the big guns opened fire in the third. The Twins scored six times in the inning, with a three-run homer by Versalles the big shot. Grant coasted home with the 8–2 victory. Koufax took the mound the next day, facing 18-game-winner Jim Kaat. Both men pitched shutout ball through the early innings, with a great diving catch by left fielder Allison in the fifth inning helping Kaat. The Twins got to Koufax in the bottom of the sixth, scoring twice on an error by Gilliam, Oliva's double, and Killebrew's single. After Koufax left for a pinch hitter, the Twins added three runs and went on to a 5–1 victory. The Twins had pulled off a rarity, beating Drysdale and Koufax back-to-back.

The Dodgers returned to Los Angeles in bad shape, but got back into the Series with a 4–0 win, with three stolen bases and a five-hitter by Claude Osteen showing that the formula still worked. Drysdale and Grant took the mound again in game four, with solo homers by Killebrew and Oliva the only Minnesota runs of the day. The Dodgers, meanwhile, got homers from Parker and Johnson and built 10 hits into a 7–2 triumph which evened the Series at two games apiece. In game five, Koufax avenged his earlier loss by scattering four hits and striking out 10 batters in a 7–0 breeze which gave the Dodgers a sweep of the California leg of the Series.

The pattern of home-team victories held true in the sixth game with a 5–1 Minnesota win. Pitching on two days' rest, Grant scattered six hits to the Dodgers and belted a three-run homer to salt away the decision. The two teams now faced the seventh game with radically different pitching situations. Mele could use Kaat on short rest or use sore-armed Camilo Pascual, who had been ineffective in game three. Alston had a well-rested Drysdale, and a Koufax eager to pitch on two days' rest. Alston mulled over his options until the day of the game, then chose Koufax to face Kaat. A Johnson home run, Ron Fairly double, and Parker single scored two runs in the fourth inning, and that was all Sandy needed. A great play by Gilliam in the fifth snuffed out the only Minnesota rally, and Koufax rewarded his manager's confidence with a three-hit shutout for the 2–0 victory and the fourth World Championship of Walt Alston's career.

Game 1 October 6 at Minnesota

| | L.A. | 010 000 001 |
| | Min. | 016 001 00x |

Los Angeles	Pos	AB	R	H	RBI	PO	A	E
Wills	ss	5	0	2	1	3	2	0
Gilliam	3b	5	0	1	0	0	1	0
Davis	cf	4	0	1	0	2	0	0
Fairly	rf	4	1	1	1	2	0	0
Johnson	lf	4	0	1	0	4	0	0
Lefebvre	2b	4	1	0	0	0	4	1
Parker	1b	3	0	1	0	7	0	0
Roseboro	c	4	0	1	0	6	0	0
Drysdale	p	1	0	0	0	0	1	0
Reed	p	0	0	0	0	0	0	0
a Crawford		1	0	1	0	0	0	0
Brewer	p	0	0	0	0	0	0	0
b Moon		1	0	0	0	0	0	0
Perranoski	p	0	0	0	0	0	1	0
c LeJohn		1	0	0	0	0	0	0
Totals		37	2	10	2	24	9	1

a Singled for Reed in 5th.
b Fouled for Brewer in 7th.
c Struck out for Perranoski in 9th.

Minnesota	Pos	AB	R	H	RBI	PO	A	E
Versalles	ss	5	1	2	4	3	2	0
Valdespino	lf	4	1	1	0	4	0	0
Oliva	rf	4	0	0	0	7	0	0
Killebrew	3b	3	1	1	0	3	0	0
Hall	cf	3	0	1	0	1	0	0
Mincher	1b	3	2	1	1	0	0	0
Battey	c	4	0	1	2	5	0	0
Quilici	2b	4	1	2	1	1	0	0
Grant	p	3	2	1	0	0	0	0
Totals		33	8	10	8	27	3	0

Pitching	IP	H	R	ER	BB	SO
Los Angeles						
Drysdale (L)	2⅔	7	7	3	1	4
Reed	1⅓	0	0	0	0	1
Brewer	2	3	1	1	0	1
Perranoski	2	0	0	0	0	2
Minnesota						
Grant (W)	9	10	2	2	1	5

Doubles—Grant, Quilici, Valdespino.
Home Runs—Fairly, Mincher, Versalles.
Stolen Base—Versalles. Sacrifice
Hit—Grant. Double Play—Perranoski to
Wills to Parker. Wild Pitch—Brewer.
Left on Bases—Los Angeles 9, Minnesota 5.
Umpires—Hurley (A), Venzon (N), Flaherty (A),
Sudol (N), Stewart (A), Vargo (N).
Attendance—47,797. Time of Game—2:29.

1st Inning
Los Angeles
1 Wills took a called third strike.
2 Gilliam flied to short right.
3 Davis lined to Oliva, making a leaping-catch at the bleachers in right-center.
Minnesota
1 Versalles struck out.
2 Valdespino grounded to second.
3 Oliva grounded to short.

2nd Inning
Los Angeles
Fairly hit a home run into the right field bleachers.
1 Johnson struck out.
2 Lefebvre flied to left.
3 Parker struck out.
Minnesota
1 Killebrew struck out.
2 Hall struck out.
Mincher hit a home-run deep into the right field bleachers.
3 Battey flied to Johnson in short left-center.

3rd Inning
Los Angeles
1 Roseboro fouled to Killebrew.
2 Drysdale grounded to short.
3 Wills fouled to Versalles.
Minnesota
Quilici doubled inside the third base line.
Grant sacrificed and was safe at first when Lefebvre covering first dropped Drysdale's throw as Quilici went to third.
Versalles hit a three-run homer into the left field pavilion.
Valdespino doubled into the right field corner.
1 Oliva grounded to third, as Valdespino held second.
Killebrew singled to left, Valdespino advancing to third.
2 Hall struck out.
Mincher walked, loading the bases.
Battey singled to right, scoring Valdespino and Killebrew as Mincher went to third.
Quilici singled to right, scoring Mincher as Battey stopped at second.
For Los Angeles—Reed took the mound.
3 Grant grounded to second.

4th Inning
Los Angeles
Gilliam singled to left-center.
1 Davis struck out.
2 Fairly flied to short right.
3 Johnson forced Gilliam at second, Versalles unassisted.
Minnesota
1 Versalles took a called third strike.
2 Valdespino flied to center.
3 Oliva flied to deep center.

5th Inning
Los Angeles
1 Lefebvre grounded to second.
2 Parker flied to left.
Roseboro singled to right.
Crawford, pinch-hitting for Reed, singled to center, Roseboro stopping at second.
3 Wills flied to Hall, making a running-catch in left-center.
Minnesota
For Los Angeles—Brewer pitching.
1 Killebrew called out on strikes.
Hill singled off Lefebvre's glove.
2 Mincher forced Hill at second, Lefebvre (letting Mincher's pop fall) to Wills.
Mincher advanced to second on a wild pitch.
3 Battey grounded to second.

6th Inning
Los Angeles
1 Gilliam grounded to short.
Davis singled to left.
2 Fairly flied to left.
Johnson singled to left, Davis stopping at second.
3 Lefebvre lined to second.
Minnesota
1 Quilici flied to left.
Grant doubled down the third base line.
Versalles singled to center, scoring Grant.
Versalles stole second.
2 Valdespino grounded to first, Versalles going to third.
3 Oliva flied to deep left.

7th Inning
Los Angeles
Parker walked.
1 Roseboro flied to right.
2 Moon, pinch-hitting for Brewer, fouled to Killebrew.
Wills singled to left, Parker stopping at second.
3 Gilliam flied to right.
Minnesota
For Los Angeles—Perranoski pitching.
Killebrew walked.
Hall walked.
1 Mincher lined to right.
2,3 Battey hit into a double play, Perranoski to Wills to Parker.

8th Inning
Los Angeles
1 Davis lined to right.
2 Fairly flied to deep right.
3 Johnson popped to second.
Minnesota
1 Quilici lined to left.
2 Grant flied to left.
3 Versalles lined to short.

9th Inning
Los Angeles
Lefebvre singled to left.
Parker singled to center, Lefebvre going to third.
1 Roseboro fouled to Killebrew.
2 LeJohn, batting for Perranoski, struck out.
Wills beat out a bunt to first, scoring Lefebvre with Parker stopping at second.
3 Gilliam flied to left.

Game 2 October 7 at Minnesota

Los Angeles	Pos	AB	R	H	RBI	PO	A	E
Wills	ss	4	0	1	0	1	2	0
Gilliam	3b	4	0	0	0	0	0	2
Davis	cf	4	0	0	0	1	0	0
Johnson	lf	4	0	0	0	3	0	1
Fairly	rf	4	1	2	0	1	0	0
Lefebvre	2b	4	0	2	0	2	0	0
Parker	1b	1	0	1	0	3	1	0
Roseboro	c	4	0	1	1	12	1	0
Koufax	p	2	0	0	0	1	2	0
a Drysdale		1	0	0	0	0	0	0
Perranoski	p	0	0	0	0	0	0	0
Miller	p	0	0	0	0	0	0	0
b Tracewski		1	0	0	0	0	0	0
Totals		33	1	7	1	24	6	3

a Struck out for Koufax in 7th.
b Lined out for Miller in 9th.

Doubles—Allison, Oliva. Triple—Versalles. Sacrifice Hits—Nossek, Parker. Hit by Pitcher—Parker (by Kaat). Wild Pitch—Perranoski. Balk—Perranoski. Left on Bases—Los Angeles 8, Minnesota 8. Umpires—Venzon, Flaherty, Sudol, Stewart, Vargo, Hurley. Attendance—48,700. Time of Game—2:13.

	L.A.	0 0 0	0 0 0	1 0 0
	Min.	0 0 0	0 0 2	1 2 x

Minnesota	Pos	AB	R	H	RBI	PO	A	E
Versalles	ss	5	2	1	0	0	0	0
Nossek	cf	3	0	1	0	4	0	0
Oliva	rf	4	1	1	1	3	0	0
Killebrew	3b	3	0	2	1	2	1	0
Battey	c	4	0	1	0	3	1	0
Allison	lf	4	1	1	0	2	0	0
Mincher	1b	4	1	1	0	7	4	0
Quilici	2b	2	0	0	0	1	3	0
Kaat	p	4	0	1	2	5	0	0
Totals		33	5	9	4	27	9	0

Pitching	IP	H	R	ER	BB	SO
Los Angeles						
Koufax (L)	6	6	2	1	1	9
Perranoski	1⅓	3	3	3	2	1
Miller	⅔	0	0	0	0	0
Minnesota						
Kaat (W)	9	7	1	1	1	3

1st Inning
Los Angeles
1 Wills flied to short right.
2 Gilliam flied to center.
3 Davis grounded out, Mincher to Kaat.
Minnesota
1 Versalles flied to short right.
2 Nossek flied to deep left.
3 Oliva bounced back to the mound.

2nd Inning
Los Angeles
1 Johnson struck out.
2 Fairly grounded out, Mincher to Kaat.
3 Lefebvre grounded to second.
Minnesota
1 Killebrew flied to left.
2 Battey struck out.
3 Allison took a called third strike.

3rd Inning
Los Angeles
 Parker walked.
1 Roseboro lined to left.
2 Koufax grounded to second, Parker moving to second.
3 Wills flied to right.
Minnesota
1 Mincher took a called third strike.
 Quilici walked.
2 Quilici was caught trying to steal second, Roseboro to Wills.
3 Kaat took a called third strike.

4th Inning
Los Angeles
1 Gilliam flied to right.
2 Davis grounded out, Mincher to Kaat.
3 Johnson flied to Nossek at the center field fence.
Minnesota
1 Versalles struck out.
 Nossek lined a single to center for the first hit of the game.
2 Oliva struck out.
 Killebrew singled to left, Johnson fumbled the ball and Nossek went to third with Killebrew to second.
3 Battey fouled to Parker, reaching way into the boxes behind first.

5th Inning
Los Angeles
 Fairly singled to right.
1 Lefebvre lined out to Allison making a spectacular diving one-handed catch down the left field line.
 Parker beat out a roller to first, Fairly stopping at second.
2 Roseboro flied to Killebrew.
3 Koufax fouled to Mincher.
Minnesota
1 Allison struck out and was tagged by Roseboro who dropped the third strike.
 Mincher singled to left-center.
2 Quilici popped to second.
3 Kaat struck out.

6th Inning
Los Angeles
 Wills bounced a single over Killebrew's head.
1 Gilliam grounded to third, Wills going to second.
2 Davis popped to Killebrew near the mound.
3 Johnson popped to first.
Minnesota
 Versalles made it safely to second on Gilliam's error.
1 Nossek sacrificed, Koufax to Lefebvre.
 Oliva doubled to left, scoring Versalles.
 Killebrew singled to left, scoring Oliva.
 Battey singled to left, Killebrew stopping at second.
2 Allison for the third time was called out on strikes.
3 Mincher grounded out, Parker to Koufax.

7th Inning
Los Angeles
 Fairly singled to left.
 Lefebvre singled to left, Fairly stopping at second.
1 Parker sacrificed up both runners, Battey to Quilici.
 Roseboro singled to right, scoring Fairly with Lefebvre stopping at third, as Roseboro took second on the throw to the plate.
2 Drysdale, pinch-hitting for Koufax, struck out.
3 Wills flied to short center.
Minnesota
 For Los Angeles—Perranoski pitching.
1 Quilici grounded to short.
2 Kaat struck out for the third time.
 Versalles tripled into the right field corner.
 Versalles scored on a wild pitch.
 Nossek got safely to second on Gilliam's wild throw to first.
3 Oliva flied to left.

8th Inning
Los Angeles
1 Gilliam flied to center.
2 Davis grounded out, Mincher to Kaat.
3 Johnson grounded to second.
Minneapolis
 Killebrew walked.
1 Battey fouled to Roseboro on an attempted sacrifice.
 Allison doubled to right-center, Killebrew stopping at third.
2 Mincher hit into a fielder's choice, Wills to Roseboro getting Killebrew at the plate as Allison held.
 Allison went to third and Mincher to second on a balk.
 Quilici intentionally passed, loading the bases.
 Kaat singled to center, scoring Allison and Mincher as Quilici stopped at second.
 For Los Angeles—Miller now pitching.
3 Versalles flied to short center.

9th Inning
Los Angeles
1 Fairly struck out.
 Lefebvre singled to left.
 Parker was hit by a pitched ball.
2 Roseboro grounded to first, advancing both runners.
3 Tracewski, batting for Miller, lined back to the pitcher.

Game 3 October 9 at Los Angeles

Minnesota	Pos	AB	R	H	RBI	PO	A	E
Versalles	ss	3	0	2	0	3	3	0
Nossek	cf	4	0	1	0	3	0	0
Oliva	rf	4	0	1	0	2	0	0
Killebrew	3b	3	0	0	0	1	1	0
Battey	c	3	0	0	0	3	1	0
Zimmerman	c	1	0	0	0	2	0	0
Allison	lf	3	0	0	0	3	0	0
Mincher	1b	3	0	1	0	7	0	0
Quilici	2b	3	0	0	0	4	2	0
Pascual	p	1	0	0	0	0	1	0
a Rollins		1	0	0	0	0	0	0
Merritt	p	0	0	0	0	0	2	0
b Valdespino		1	0	0	0	0	0	0
Klippstein	p	0	0	0	0	0	0	0
Totals		30	0	5	0	24	10	0

a Grounded out for Pascual in 6th.
b Popped out for Merritt in 8th.

Doubles—Fairly, Gilliam, Johnson 2, Versalles, Wills. Stolen Bases—Parker, Roseboro, Wills. Sacrifice Hits—Johnson, Osteen. Double Plays—Tracewski to Parker, Zimmerman to Versalles, Wills to Parker. Left on Bases—Minnesota 5, Los Angeles 6. Umpires—Flaherty, Sudol, Stewart, Vargo, Hurley, Venzon. Attendance—55,934. Time of Game—2:06

	Min.	0 0 0	0 0 0	0 0 0
	L.A.	0 0 0	2 1 1	0 0 x

Los Angeles	Pos	AB	R	H	RBI	PO	A	E
Wills	ss	4	0	1	1	2	5	0
Gilliam	3b	4	0	1	1	1	1	0
Kennedy	3b	0	0	0	0	0	0	1
Davis	cf	4	1	1	0	2	0	0
Fairly	rf	4	1	1	0	1	0	0
Johnson	lf	2	2	1	0	1	0	0
Lefebvre	2b	2	0	1	1	1	3	0
Tracewski	2b	2	0	0	2	3	0	0
Parker	1b	3	1	1	0	14	2	0
Roseboro	c	3	0	1	2	2	2	0
Osteen	p	2	0	1	0	2	2	0
Totals		30	4	10	4	27	18	1

Pitching	IP	H	R	ER	BB	SO
Minnesota						
Pascual (L)	5	8	3	3	1	0
Merritt	2	2	1	1	0	0
Klippstein	1	0	0	0	1	1
Los Angeles						
Osteen (W)	9	5	0	0	2	2

1st Inning
Minnesota
 Versalles hit a ground-rule double into the left field corner boxes.
1 Nossek grounded out, Parker to Osteen, Versalles going to third.
2 Oliva grounded to second, Versalles holding at third.
 Killebrew walked.
3 Versalles was caught in a rundown on a delayed double steal, Roseboro to Wills to Roseboro to Gilliam.
Los Angeles
1 Wills bunted out to third.
 Gilliam doubled down the right field line.
2 Davis flied to deep left.
3 Fairly flied to deep left.

2nd Inning
Minnesota
1 Battey grounded to short.
2 Allison tapped out, Roseboro to Parker.
 Mincher singled to center.
3 Quilici forced Mincher at second, Wills to Lefebvre.
Los Angeles
 Johnson doubled to left-center.
1 Lefebvre lined to left.
2 Parker flied to deep center, Johnson going to third after the catch.
3 Roseboro grounded to second.

3rd Inning
Minnesota
1 Pascual tapped to the mound.
2 Versalles grounded to second.
3 Nossek grounded to second.
Los Angeles
 Osteen singled to left.
1 Wills forced Osteen at second, Versalles to Quilici.
 Wills stole second.
2 Gilliam grounded to short, Wills moving to third.
3 Davis grounded to first.

4th Inning
Minnesota
1 Oliva took a called third strike.
2 Killebrew grounded to short.
3 Battey grounded to short.
Los Angeles
 Fairly doubled down the left field line.
1 Johnson sacrificed Fairly to third, Pascual to Mincher.
 Lefebvre beat out a hit to deep short, Fairly holding at third.
 Parker walked, filling the bases.
 Roseboro singled to right, Fairly and Lefebvre scoring with Parker stopping at second.
2 Osteen popped to third.
 Parker and Roseboro both moved up on a double steal.
3 Wills popped to short.

5th Inning
Minnesota
 For Los Angeles—Tracewski replaced Lefebvre at second who injured his heel.
1 Allison struck out.
2 Mincher grounded to second.
3 Quilici popped to first.
Los Angeles
1 Gilliam popped to second.
 Davis singled to center.
2 Fairly grounded to second, Davis advancing to second.
 Johnson doubled to left-center, scoring Davis.
3 Tracewski grounded to short.

6th Inning
Minnesota
1 Rollins, pinch-hitting for Pascual, grounded back to the mound.
 Versalles singled to center.
2,3 Oliva grounded into a double play, Tracewski to Parker.
Los Angeles
 For Minnesota—Merritt pitching.
 Parker singled to center.
1 Roseboro flied to right.
2 Osteen sacrificed Parker to second, Merritt to Quilici.
 Wills doubled to right-center, scoring Parker.
3 Wills was picked off second, Merritt to Quilici.

7th Inning
Minnesota
1 Killebrew flied to right.
2 Battey flied to center.
3 Allison grounded to second.
Los Angeles
1 Gilliam flied to left.
 For Minnesota—Zimmerman replaced Battey who was injured running into the dugout railing in an attempt to catch a foul popup hit by Davis.
2 Davis fouled to Oliva.
3 Fairly lined to center.

8th Inning
Minnesota
 For Los Angeles—Kennedy playing third.
1 Mincher grounded out Parker to Osteen. Quilici was safe at first on Kennedy's fumble.
2 Valdespino, batting for Merritt, popped to second.
 Versalles walked.
3 Nossek popped to short.
Los Angeles
 For Minnesota—Klippstein pitching.
 Johnson walked.
1,2 Tracewski struck out and Johnson was doubled up trying to steal second, Zimmerman to Versalles.
3 Parker popped to short.

9th Inning
Minnesota
 Oliva singled to center.
1 Killebrew flied to center.
2,3 Zimmerman hit into a game-ending double play, Wills to Parker.

Game 4 October 10 at Los Angeles

Minnesota	Pos	AB	R	H	RBI	PO	A	E
Versalles	ss	4	0	1	0	3	2	0
Valdespino	lf	4	0	1	0	2	0	0
Oliva	rf	4	1	1	1	2	0	0
Killebrew	3b	2	1	1	1	1	0	0
Hall	cf	4	0	0	0	1	0	0
Mincher	1b	4	0	0	0	8	0	0
Battey	c	3	0	0	0	3	2	0
Zimmerman	c	0	0	0	0	1	0	0
Quilici	2b	3	0	0	0	3	3	1
Grant	p	2	0	0	0	0	0	0
Worthington	p	0	0	0	0	0	0	1
b Nossek		1	0	1	0	0	0	0
Pleis	p	0	0	0	0	0	1	0
Totals		31	2	5	2	24	8	2

Min.	000 101 000
L.A.	110 103 01x

Los Angeles	Pos	AB	R	H	RBI	PO	A	E
Wills	ss	4	1	2	0	1	1	0
Gilliam	3b	2	1	0	0	1	1	0
a Kennedy	3b	0	0	0	0	0	1	0
Davis	cf	4	1	2	0	3	0	0
Fairly	rf	4	1	1	3	1	0	0
Johnson	lf	4	1	2	1	1	1	0
Parker	1b	4	2	2	1	8	0	0
Roseboro	c	3	0	1	0	10	1	0
Tracewski	2b	4	0	0	0	2	3	0
Drysdale	p	3	0	0	0	0	1	0
Totals		32	7	10	5	27	10	0

Pitching	IP	H	R	ER	BB	SO
Minnesota						
Grant (L)	*5	6	5	4	1	2
Worthington	2	2	1	0	1	2
Pleis	1	2	1	1	0	0
Los Angeles						
Drysdale (W)	9	5	2	2	2	11

*Pitched to 2 batters in 6th.

a Ran for Gilliam in 7th.
b Singled for Worthington in 8th.

Home Runs—Johnson, Killebrew, Oliva, Parker. Stolen Bases—Parker, Wills. Double Play—Battey to Versalles. Hit by Pitcher—Gilliam (by Worthington). Wild Pitch—Grant. Left on Bases—Minnesota 4, Los Angeles 4. Umpires—Sudol, Stewart, Vargo, Hurley, Venzon, Flaherty. Attendance—55,920. Time of Game—2:15.

1st Inning
Minnesota
1 Versalles flied to left.
2 Valdespino singled to left but was out trying for second, Johnson to Tracewski.
3 Oliva fouled to Gilliam.
Los Angeles
Wills beat out a roller to first.
1 Gilliam flied to left.
Wills stole second.
Davis beat out a tap down the first base line, Wills going to third.
2 Fairly forced Davis at second, Quilici to Versalles, Wills scoring.
3 Johnson popped to second.

2nd Inning
Minnesota
Killebrew walked.
1 Hall took a called third strike.
2 Mincher struck out.
3 Battey took a called third strike.
Los Angeles
Parker beat out a bunt between first and the mound.
Parker stole second.
Parker went to third on a wild pitch.
Roseboro safe at second on Quilici's fumble, Parker scoring.
1 Tracewski fouled to Mincher on an attempted sacrifice.
2,3 Drysdale took a called third strike and Roseboro was doubled trying to steal second, Battey to Versalles.

3rd Inning
Minnesota
1 Quilici flied to center.
2 Grant took a called third strike.
Versalles singled to center.
3 Valdespino flied to center.
Los Angeles
Wills singled to deep short.
1 Wills caught trying to steal second, Battey to Quilici.
2 Gilliam fouled to Killebrew.
3 Davis grounded to first.

4th Inning
Minnesota
1 Oliva bounced back to the mound.
Killebrew hit a home run into the left field pavilion.
2 Hall grounded to short.
3 Mincher grounded to third.
Los Angeles
1 Fairly fouled to Mincher.
2 Johnson flied to right.
Parker hit a home run into the right field pavilion.
3 Roseboro lined to first.

5th Inning
Minnesota
1 Battey took a called third strike.
2 Quilici grounded to second.
3 Grant grounded to second.
Los Angeles
1 Tracewski grounded to second.
2 Drysdale struck out.
3 Wills grounded to short.

6th Inning
Minnesota
1 Versalles grounded to short, Wills racing in to get the slow roller.
2 Valdespino struck out and was thrown out, Roseboro to Parker when Roseboro dropped the third strike.
Oliva hit a homer into the right field stands.
3 Killebrew was called out on strikes.
Los Angeles
Gilliam walked.
Davis singled to right, Gilliam going to third. Davis went to second on the throw to third.
For Minnesota—Worthington now pitching.
Fairly singled to center, scoring both Gilliam and Davis and took second on the throw to the plate.
Johnson safe at first on a bunt (ruled as a hit) and Worthington got an error on the throw as Fairly scored. However, Quilici recovered the ball quickly and
1 Johnson was trapped off first, Quilici to Versalles to Quilici.
2 Parker struck out.
Roseboro walked.
3 Tracewski flied to Hall in short right-center.

7th Inning
Minnesota
1 Hall struck out.
2 Mincher struck out.
3 Battey flied to right.
Los Angeles
For Minnesota—Zimmerman catching.
1 Drysdale took a called third strike.
2 Wills popped to Versalles behind third.
Gilliam was hit by a pitched ball.
Kennedy ran for Gilliam.
3 Davis grounded to first.

8th Inning
Minnesota
For Los Angeles—Kennedy playing third.
1 Quilici popped to short.
Nossek, batting for Worthington, singled to center.
2 Versalles forced Nossek at second on a fantastic stop by Kennedy to Tracewski.
3 Valdespino lined to center.
Los Angeles
For Minnesota—Pleis pitching.
1 Fairly flied to right.
Johnson homered into the left field stands.
2 Parker bounced back to the mound.
Roseboro beat out a bunt.
3 Tracewski flied to deep left.

9th Inning
Minnesota
1 Oliva grounded to second.
Killebrew walked.
2 Hall took a called third strike.
3 Mincher also fanned, as Hall for the third time in the game.

Game 5 October 11 at Los Angeles

Minnesota	Pos	AB	R	H	RBI	PO	A	E
Versalles	ss	4	0	0	0	2	0	0
Nossek	cf	4	0	0	0	2	0	0
Oliva	rf	3	0	0	0	2	0	0
Killebrew	3b	3	0	1	0	1	2	0
Battey	c	3	0	0	0	7	1	0
Allison	lf	2	0	0	0	3	0	0
Mincher	1b	3	0	0	0	5	0	0
Quilici	2b	3	0	1	0	2	3	1
Kaat	p	1	0	0	0	0	1	0
Boswell	p	0	0	0	0	0	0	0
a Rollins		1	0	0	0	0	0	0
Perry	p	0	0	0	0	0	1	0
b Valdespino		1	0	1	0	0	0	0
Totals		28	0	4	0	24	8	1

Min.	000 000 000
L.A.	202 100 20x

Los Angeles	Pos	AB	R	H	RBI	PO	A	E
Wills	ss	5	2	4	1	1	7	0
Gilliam	3b	4	1	2	2	0	4	0
Kennedy	3b	1	0	0	0	0	0	0
Davis	cf	4	1	2	0	1	0	0
Johnson	lf	5	1	3	1	2	0	0
Fairly	rf	5	1	3	1	2	0	0
Parker	1b	4	0	0	0	7	0	0
Tracewski	2b	3	0	1	0	4	2	0
Roseboro	c	2	1	0	0	10	0	0
Koufax	p	4	0	1	1	0	1	0
Totals		37	7	14	6	27	10	0

Pitching	IP	H	R	ER	BB	SO
Minnesota						
Kaat (L)	2⅓	6	4	3	0	1
Boswell	2⅓	3	1	1	2	3
Perry	3	5	2	2	1	3
Los Angeles						
Koufax (W)	9	4	0	0	1	10

a Flied out for Boswell in 6th.
b Singled for Perry in 9th.

Doubles—Fairly, Wills 2. Stolen Bases—Davis 3, Wills. Sacrifice Hits—Davis, Parker. Double Plays—Wills to Tracewski to Parker 2, Wills to Tracewski. Left on Bases—Minnesota 2, Los Angeles 11. Umpires—Stewart, Vargo, Hurley, Venzon, Flaherty, Sudol. Attendance—55,801. Time of Game—2:34.

1st Inning
Minnesota
1 Versalles grounded to short.
2 Nossek grounded to Wills making a great play behind third.
3 Oliva bunted out to the mound.
Los Angeles
Wills hit a ground-rule double into the right field stands.
Gilliam singled to right-center, scoring Wills.
Davis sacrificed but was safe on Quilici's bobble of Killebrew's throw, scoring Gilliam as Davis ran to third after Quilici lost the ball.
1 Johnson popped to Quilici.
2 Fairly flied to short right.
3 Parker bounced back to the mound.

2nd Inning
Minnesota
1 Killebrew struck out.
2 Battey flied to right.
3 Allison struck out.
Los Angeles
Tracewski beat out a hit to deep short.
Roseboro was safe on a fielder's choice when Kaat threw his smasher late to second.
1 Koufax struck out.
2 Tracewski was out on an attempted double steal, Battey to Killebrew, as Roseboro went to second.
3 Wills grounded to second.

3rd Inning
Minnesota
1 Mincher flied to center.
2 Quilici popped to second.
3 Kaat struck out, bunting foul on the third strike.
Los Angeles
1 Gilliam grounded to third.
Davis singled to right.
Davis stole second.
Johnson singled to center, scoring Davis.
Fairly doubled to left-center, scoring Johnson.
For Minnesota—Boswell replaced Kaat on the mound.
2 Parker grounded to first, Fairly advancing to third.
Tracewski walked.
3 Roseboro struck out.

4th Inning
Minnesota
1 Versalles flied to right.
2 Nossek grounded to short.
3 Oliva took a called third strike.
Los Angeles
1 Koufax took a called third strike.
Wills beat out a roller to short.
Wills stole second.
Gilliam singled to right-center, scoring Wills.
2 Davis forced Gilliam at second, Quilici to Versalles.
Davis stole second.
3 Johnson grounded to second.

5th Inning
Minnesota
Killebrew blooped a single to short center to become the Twin's first base runner in the game.
1,2 Battey hit into a double play, Wills to Tracewski to Parker.
3 Allison struck out.
Los Angeles
Fairly singled to center.
1 Parker flied to deep left.
2 Tracewski lined to left.
Roseboro walked.
3 Koufax took a called third strike.

6th Inning
Minnesota
1 Mincher struck out.
2 Quilici popped to second.
3 Rollins, pinch-hitting for Boswell, flied to deep left.
Los Angeles
For Minnesota—Perry took the mound.
Wills doubled to left-center.
1 Gilliam grounded to short.
2 Davis struck out.
3 Johnson flied to right.

7th Inning
Minnesota
For Los Angeles—Kennedy playing third.
1 Versalles struck out.
Nossek beat out a hit to deep short.
2 Oliva struck out.
3 Killebrew lined to left.
Los Angeles
Fairly beat out a hit to deep short.
1 Parker sacrificed Fairly to second, Perry to Quilici.
2 Tracewski took a called third strike.
Roseboro intentionally walked.
Koufax singled to left-center, scoring Fairly as Roseboro stopped at second.
Wills got his 4th hit of the game, a single to center, scoring Roseboro as Koufax stopped at second.
3 Kennedy flied to left.

8th Inning
Minnesota
1 Battey grounded to short.
Allison walked.
2,3 Mincher grounded into a double play, Wills to Tracewski to Parker.
Los Angeles
Davis singled to center.
1 Johnson flied to deep center.
Davis stole second (**his third steal in the game tying a record set by Honus Wagner of Pittsburgh in 1909).**
2 Fairly flied to deep center, Davis advancing to third after the catch.
3 Parker took a called third strike.

9th Inning
Minnesota
Quilici singled just inside the right field foul line.
Valdespino, batting for Perry, singled to right, Quilici stopping at second.
1 Versalles struck out.
2,3 Nossek lined into a game-ending double play, Wills to Tracewski doubling Quilici at second

Game 6 October 13 at Minnesota

Los Angeles	Pos	AB	R	H	RBI	PO	A	E
Wills	ss	4	0	1	0	4	4	0
Gilliam	3b	4	0	0	0	0	3	0
Davis	cf	4	0	0	0	1	0	0
Fairly	rf	4	1	2	1	1	0	0
Johnson	lf	4	0	1	0	0	0	0
Parker	1b	4	0	0	0	10	1	0
Roseboro	c	3	0	1	0	5	0	0
Tracewski	2b	3	0	1	0	2	3	1
Osteen	p	1	0	0	0	0	1	0
a Crawford		1	0	0	0	0	0	0
Reed	p	0	0	0	0	1	0	0
b Moon		1	0	0	0	0	0	0
Miller	p	0	0	0	0	0	0	0
Totals		33	1	6	1	24	12	1

a Struck out for Osteen in 6th.
b Grounded out for Reed in 8th.

Triple—Battey. Home Runs—Allison, Fairly, Grant. Stolen Base—Allison. Double Plays—Osteen to Wills to Parker, Battey to Versalles. Left on Bases—Los Angeles 5, Minnesota 6. Umpires—Vargo, Hurley, Venzon, Sudol, Stewart. Attendance—49,578. Time of Game—2:16.

L.A.	000 000 100
Min.	000 203 00x

Minnesota	Pos	AB	R	H	RBI	PO	A	E
Versalles	ss	3	0	1	0	2	3	0
Nossek	cf	4	0	0	0	4	0	0
Oliva	rf	4	0	2	0	0	0	0
Killebrew	3b	4	0	0	0	1	1	1
Battey	c	4	1	1	0	5	1	0
Allison	lf	3	2	1	2	2	0	0
Mincher	1b	3	0	0	0	11	0	0
Quilici	2b	2	1	0	0	2	4	0
Grant	p	3	1	1	3	0	1	0
Totals		30	5	6	5	27	10	1

Pitching	IP	H	R	ER	BB	SO
Los Angeles						
Osteen (L)	5	4	2	1	3	2
Reed	2	2	3	3	2	3
Miller	1	0	0	0	0	0
Minnesota						
Grant (W)	9	6	1	1	0	5

1st Inning
Los Angeles
1 Wills grounded to first.
2 Gilliam flied to short left.
3 Davis flied to center.
Minnesota
Versalles singled to right.
1,2 Nossek hit into a double play, Osteen to Wills to Parker.
Oliva singled to left.
3 Killebrew forced Oliva at second, Gilliam to Tracewski.

2nd Inning
Los Angeles
1 Fairly lined to center.
2 Johnson fouled to Mincher.
3 Parker grounded to second.
Minnesota
Battey tripled to center when his fly got by Davis attempting a shoestring diving catch.
1 Allison struck out.
Mincher walked.
2 Quilici took a called third strike.
3 Grant popped to short.

3rd Inning
Los Angeles
Roseboro safe at first when Killebrew dropped his pop fly.
1,2 Tracewski struck out and Roseboro was doubled up trying to steal second, Battey to Versalles.
3 Osteen flied to deep left.
Minnesota
Versalles walked.
1 Nossek grounded to short, Versalles moving to second.
2 Oliva grounded to third, Versalles holding at second.
3 Killebrew grounded to short.

4th Inning
Los Angeles
1 Wills grounded to short.
2 Gilliam fouled to Quilici down the right field line.
3 Davis grounded to first.
Minnesota
Battey safe at first when Tracewski fumbled his grounder.
Allison hit a two-run homer into the left field stands.
1 Mincher grounded to second.
Quilici walked.
2 Grant grounded to third, Quilici going to second.
3 Versalles popped to short.

5th Inning
Los Angeles
Fairly singled to center.
1 Johnson forced Fairly at second, Killebrew to Quilici.
2 Parker grounded to second, Johnson moving to second.
3 Roseboro called out on strikes.
Minnesota
1 Nossek fouled to Parker.
2 Oliva grounded to short.
3 Killebrew grounded to second.

6th Inning
Los Angeles
Tracewski singled to left.
1 Crawford, pinch-hitting for Osteen, struck out.
Wills singled to center, Tracewski stopping at second.
2 Gilliam popped to Versalles in short left.
3 Davis flied to center.
Minnesota
For Los Angeles—Reed pitching.
1 Battey grounded out, Parker to Reed.
Allison walked.
2 Mincher called out on strikes as Allison was stealing second.
Quilici intentionally passed.
Grant hit a three-run homer into the left-center field stands.
3 Versalles struck out.

7th Inning
Los Angeles
Fairly hit a home run over the right-center field screen.
1 Johnson struck out, being tagged by Battey who dropped the third strike.
2 Parker bounced back to the mound. Roseboro singled to left.
3 Tracewski flied to center.
Minnesota
1 Nossek struck out.
Oliva singled to right-center.
2 Killebrew fouled to Wills down the left field line.
3 Battey flied to right.

8th Inning
Los Angeles
1 Moon, batting for Reed, grounded to second.
2 Wills took a called third strike.
3 Gilliam grounded to short.
Minnesota
For Los Angeles—Miller pitching.
1 Allison popped to Tracewski in short right-center.
2 Mincher grounded to second.
3 Quilici flied to center.

9th Inning
Los Angeles
1 Davis fouled to Killebrew.
2 Fairly grounded to short.
Johnson singled to left.
3 Parker grounded to second.

Game 7 October 14 at Minnesota

Los Angeles	Pos	AB	R	H	RBI	PO	A	E
Wills	ss	4	0	0	0	2	4	0
Gilliam	3b	5	0	2	0	2	1	0
Kennedy	3b	0	0	0	0	0	0	0
Davis	cf	2	0	0	0	1	0	0
Johnson	lf	4	1	1	1	3	0	0
Fairly	rf	4	1	1	0	0	0	0
Parker	1b	4	0	2	1	6	0	0
Tracewski	2b	4	0	0	0	1	6	0
Roseboro	c	2	0	1	0	12	0	0
Koufax	p	3	0	0	0	0	1	0
Totals		32	2	7	2	27	7	0

Pitching	IP	H	R	ER	BB	SO
Los Angeles						
Koufax (W)	9	3	0	0	3	10
Minnesota						
Kaat (L)	*3	5	2	2	1	2
Worthington	2	0	0	0	1	0
Klippstein	1⅓	2	0	0	1	2
Merritt	1⅓	0	0	0	0	1
Perry	1	0	0	0	1	1

*Pitched to 3 batters in 4th.

L.A.	000 200 000
Min.	000 000 000

Minnesota	Pos	AB	R	H	RBI	PO	A	E
Versalles	ss	4	0	1	0	2	0	0
Nossek	cf	4	0	0	0	2	0	0
Oliva	rf	3	0	0	0	4	0	1
Killebrew	3b	3	0	1	0	2	2	0
Battey	c	4	0	0	0	8	1	0
Allison	lf	4	0	1	0	2	0	0
Mincher	1b	3	0	0	0	10	0	0
Quilici	2b	3	0	1	0	1	3	0
Kaat	p	1	0	0	0	0	1	0
Worthington	p	0	0	0	0	1	1	0
a Rollins		0	0	0	0	0	0	0
Klippstein	p	0	0	0	0	0	0	0
Merritt	p	0	0	0	0	0	0	0
b Valdespino		1	0	0	0	0	0	0
Perry	p	0	0	0	0	0	0	0
Totals		30	0	3	0	27	10	1

a Walked for Worthington in 5th.
b Fouled out for Merritt in 8th.

Doubles—Fairly, Quilici, Roseboro. Triple—Parker. Home Run—Johnson. Sacrifice Hit—Davis. Hit by Pitcher—Davis (by Klippstein). Left on Bases—Los Angeles 9, Minnesota 6. Umpires—Hurley, Venzon, Flaherty, Sudol, Stewart, Vargo. Attendance—50,596. Time of Game—2:27.

1st Inning
Los Angeles
1 Wills took a called third strike.
Gilliam singled to left-center.
2 Davis sacrificed Gilliam to second, Kaat to Mincher.
3 Johnson popped to Oliva in short right who made a diving catch.
Minnesota
1 Versalles struck out.
2 Nossek grounded to short.
Oliva walked.
Killebrew walked.
3 Battey struck out.

2nd Inning
Los Angeles
1 Fairley popped to Battey in front of the plate.
2 Parker fouled to Mincher.
3 Tracewski took a called third strike.
Minnesota
1 Allison struck out.
2 Mincher took a called third strike.
3 Quilici popped to short.

3rd Inning
Los Angeles
Roseboro doubled into the right field corner.
Koufax walked.
1 Wills grounded to second, both runners advancing.
2 Gilliam lined to right.
3 Davis fouled to Battey.
Minnesota
1 Kaat struck out.
Versalles singled to center.
2 Nossek was ruled out for interfering with Roseboro's throw to second as Versalles tried to steal but on the out had to return to first.
3 Oliva struck out.

4th Inning
Los Angeles
Johnson hit a line drive home run which hit the left field foul pole.
Fairly doubled down the right field line.
Parker singled over Mincher's head, scoring Fairly. Parker took second when Oliva fumbled the ball.
For Minnesota—Worthington replaced Kaat on the mound.
1 Tracewski popped to Worthington on an attempted sacrifice.
Roseboro walked.
2 Koufax grounded back to the pitcher, both runners advancing.
3 Wills fouled to Killebrew.
Minnesota
1 Killebrew grounded to the pitcher.
2 Battey flied to center.
3 Allison grounded to third.

5th Inning
Los Angeles
1 Gilliam grounded to second.
2 Davis fouled to Killebrew.
3 Johnson flied to Oliva in deep right-center.
Minnesota
1 Mincher fouled to Gilliam.
Quilici doubled off the left-center field screen.
Rollins, batting for Worthington, walked.
2 Versalles forced Quilici at third, Gilliam unassisted after a good diving stop.
3 Nossek forced Versalles at second, Wills to Tracewski.

6th Inning
Los Angeles
For Minnesota—Klippstein pitching.
1 Fairly flied to left.
Parker tripled off the center field screen.
2 Tracewski struck out, bunting foul on the third strike.
Roseboro intentionally passed.
3 Koufax struck out.
Minnesota
1 Oliva struck out.
2 Killebrew fouled to Johnson.
3 Battey lined to short.

7th Inning
Los Angeles
1 Wills grounded to short.
Gilliam singled to right.
Davis was hit by a pitch.
2 Johnson grounded to third, advancing both runners.
For Minnesota—Merritt came in to pitch.
3 Fairly flied to right.
Minnesota
1 Allison grounded to short.
2 Mincher fouled to Roseboro.
3 Quilici struck out.

8th Inning
Los Angeles
1 Parker grounded to second.
2 Tracewski grounded to third.
3 Roseboro struck out.
Minnesota
1 Valdespino, batting for Merritt, fouled to Johnson.
2 Versalles flied to deep left.
3 Nossek grounded to short.

9th Inning
Los Angeles
For Minnesota—Perry pitching.
1 Koufax struck out.
Wills walked.
2 Wills caught trying to steal second, Battey to Quilici.
3 Gilliam grounded to short.
Minnesota
For Los Angeles—Kennedy playing third.
1 Oliva grounded to third.
Killebrew singled to left.
2 Battey took a called third strike.
3 Allison struck out.

1965 WORLD SERIES COMPOSITE BOX

	Wins	Composite Line Score									
Los Angeles Dodgers (N.L.)	4	3	2	2	6	1	4	4	1	1	- 24
Minnesota Twins (A.L.)	3	0	1	6	3	0	7	1	2	0	- 20

	Regular Season			
Manager	W	L	Pct.	G. Ahead
Walt Alston	97	65	.599	2
Sam Mele	102	60	.630	7

BATTING AND FIELDING

LOS ANGELES DODGERS

WORLD SERIES STATISTICS

	Pos	G	AB	R	H	2B	3B	HR	RBI	BB	SO	SB	BA	SA	PO	A	E
Wes Parker	1b	7	23	3	7	0	**1**	1	2	3	3	2	.304	.522	55	4	0
Dick Tracewski	ph-2b	6	17	0	2	0	0	0	0	1	5	0	.118	.118	11	11	1
Maury Wills	ss	7	**30**	3	**11**	**3**	0	0	3	1	3	**3**	.367	.467	14	**26**	0
Jim Gilliam	3b	7	28	2	6	1	0	0	2	1	0	0	.214	.250	4	7	**2**
Ron Fairly	rf	7	29	**7**	**11**	**3**	0	**2**	**6**	0	1	0	.379	**.690**	8	0	0
Willie Davis	cf	7	26	3	6	0	0	0	0	0	2	**3**	.231	.231	11	0	0
Lou Johnson	lf	7	27	3	8	2	0	**2**	4	1	3	0	.296	.593	13	1	1
Johnny Roseboro	c	7	21	1	6	1	0	0	3	5	3	1	.286	.333	**57**	4	0
Jim Lefebvre	2b	3	10	2	4	0	0	0	0	0	0	0	.400	.400	3	7	1
John Kennedy	3b-pr	4	1	0	0	0	0	0	0	0	0	0	.000	.000	0	2	1
Willie Crawford	ph	2	2	0	1	0	0	0	0	0	1	0	.500	.500			
Wally Moon	ph	2	2	0	0	0	0	0	0	0	0	0	.000	.000			
Don Le John	ph	1	1	0	0	0	0	0	0	0	1	0	.000	.000			
Jeff Torborg		Did not play															
Sandy Koufax	p	3	9	0	1	0	0	0	1	1	5	0	.111	.111	1	4	0
Don Drysdale	p-ph	3	5	0	0	0	0	0	0	0	4	0	.000	.000	0	2	0
Claude Osteen	p	2	3	0	1	0	0	0	0	0	0	0	.333	.333	2	3	0
Bob Miller	p	2	0	0	0	0	0	0	0	0	0	0	—	—	0	0	0
Ron Perranoski	p	2	0	0	0	0	0	0	0	0	0	0	—	—	0	1	0
Howie Reed	p	2	0	0	0	0	0	0	0	0	0	0	—	—	1	0	0
Jim Brewer	p	1	0	0	0	0	0	0	0	0	0	0	—	—	0	0	0
Johnny Podres		Did not play															
John Purdin		Did not play															
Nick Willhite		Did not play															
Mike Kekich		Did not play															
team total		7	234	24	64	10	1	5	21	13	31	9	.274	.389	180	72	6

Double Plays—7
Left on Bases—52

REGULAR SEASON STATISTICS

		Main Pos	G	AB	R	H	2B	3B	HR	RBI	BB	SO	SB	BA	SA
Wes Parker		1b	154	542	80	129	24	7	8	51	75	95	13	.238	.352
Dick Tracewski		3b	78	186	17	40	6	0	1	20	25	30	2	.215	.263
Maury Wills		ss	158	650	92	186	14	7	0	33	40	64	**94**	.286	.329
Jim Gilliam		3b	111	372	54	104	19	4	4	39	53	31	9	.280	.384
Ron Fairly		of	158	555	73	152	28	1	9	70	76	72	2	.274	.377
Willie Davis		of	142	558	52	133	24	3	10	57	14	81	25	.238	.346
Lou Johnson		of	131	468	57	121	24	1	12	58	24	81	15	.259	.391
Johnny Roseboro		c	136	437	42	102	10	0	8	57	34	51	1	.233	.311
Jim Lefebvre		2b	157	544	57	136	21	4	12	69	71	92	3	.250	.369
John Kennedy		3b	104	105	12	18	3	0	1	5	8	33	1	.171	.229
Willie Crawford		ph-pr	52	27	10	4	0	0	0	0	2	8	2	.148	.148
Wally Moon		ph-of	53	89	6	18	3	0	1	11	13	22	2	.202	.270
Don Le John		3b	34	78	2	20	2	0	0	7	5	13	0	.256	.282
Jeff Torborg		c	56	150	8	36	5	1	3	13	10	26	0	.240	.347
Sandy Koufax		p	43	113	4	20	2	0	0	7	10	44	0	.177	.195
Don Drysdale		p-ph	58	130	18	39	4	1	7	19	5	34	0	.300	.508
Claude Osteen		p	42	99	6	12	0	1	0	2	3	32	0	.121	.141
Bob Miller		p	61	16	0	0	0	0	0	0	0	10	0	.000	.000
Ron Perranoski		p	59	19	0	3	0	0	0	0	2	7	0	.158	.158
Howie Reed		p	38	12	0	0	0	0	0	1	4	10	0	.000	.000
Jim Brewer		p	20	10	0	0	0	0	0	0	0	2	0	.000	.000
Johnny Podres		p	27	45	1	8	0	0	0	2	1	8	0	.178	.178
John Purdin		p	11	3	0	0	0	0	0	0	0	1	0	.000	.000
Nick Willhite	a	p	15	10	1	4	1	0	0	3	3	3	0	.400	.500
Mike Kekich		p	5	2	0	0	0	0	0	0	0	0	0	.000	.000
team total			162	5425	608	1329	193	32	78	548	492	891	**172**	.245	.335

a—from Washington
Al Ferrara (of), Derrell Griffith (of-ph), Tommy Davis (of), Hec Valle (c), Dick Smith (of), Nate Oliver (pr-2b), Johnny Werhas (ph), and Bill Singer (p) also played for the Dodgers during the season.

MINNESOTA TWINS

WORLD SERIES STATISTICS

	Pos	G	AB	R	H	2B	3B	HR	RBI	BB	SO	SB	BA	SA	PO	A	E
Don Mincher	1b	7	23	3	3	0	0	1	1	2	7	0	.130	.261	51	4	0
Frank Quilici	2b	7	20	2	4	2	0	0	1	4	3	0	.200	.300	14	19	**2**
Zoilo Versalles	ss	7	28	3	8	1	**1**	1	4	2	7	1	.286	.500	13	12	0
Harmon Killebrew	3b	7	21	2	6	0	0	1	2	**6**	4	0	.286	.429	11	7	1
Tony Oliva	rf	7	26	2	5	1	0	1	2	1	6	0	.192	.346	20	0	1
Joe Nossek	cf-ph	6	20	0	4	0	0	0	0	0	1	0	.200	.200	13	0	0
Bob Allison	lf	5	16	3	2	1	0	1	2	2	**9**	1	.125	.375	11	0	0
Earl Battey	c	7	25	1	3	0	**1**	0	2	0	5	0	.120	.200	31	**6**	0
Sandy Valdespino	lf-ph	5	11	1	3	1	0	0	0	0	1	0	.273	.364	6	0	0
Jimmie Hall	cf	2	7	0	1	0	0	0	0	1	5	0	.143	.143	2	0	0
Jerry Zimmerman	c	2	1	0	0	0	0	0	0	0	0	0	.000	.000	2	1	0
Rich Rollins	ph	3	2	0	0	0	0	0	0	1	0	0	.000	.000			
Jerry Kindall		Did not play															
John Sevcik		Did not play															
Mudcat Grant	p	3	8	3	2	1	0	1	3	0	1	0	.250	.750	0	1	0
Jim Kaat	p	3	6	0	1	0	0	0	2	0	5	0	.167	.167	5	2	0
Camilio Pascual	p	1	1	0	0	0	0	0	0	0	0	0	.000	.000	0	1	0
Johnny Klippstein	p	2	0	0	0	0	0	0	0	0	0	0	—	—	0	0	0
Jim Merritt	p	2	0	0	0	0	0	0	0	0	0	0	—	—	0	2	0
Jim Perry	p	2	0	0	0	0	0	0	0	0	0	0	—	—	0	1	0
Al Worthington	p	2	0	0	0	0	0	0	0	0	0	0	—	—	1	1	1
Dave Boswell	p	1	0	0	0	0	0	0	0	0	0	0	—	—	0	0	0
Bill Pleis	p	1	0	0	0	0	0	0	0	0	0	0	—	—	0	1	0
Dick Stigman		Did not play															
Mel Nelson		Did not play															
team total		7	215	20	42	7	2	6	19	19	54	2	.195	.330	180	58	5

Double Plays—3
Left on Bases—36

REGULAR SEASON STATISTICS

	Main Pos	G	AB	R	H	2B	3B	HR	RBI	BB	SO	SB	BA	SA
Don Mincher	1b	128	346	43	87	17	3	22	65	49	73	1	.251	.509
Frank Quilici	2b	56	149	16	31	5	1	0	7	15	33	1	.208	.255
Zoilo Versalles	ss	160	**666**	**126**	182	**45**	**12**	19	77	41	**122**	27	.273	.462
Harmon Killebrew	1b-3b	113	401	78	108	16	1	25	75	72	69	0	.269	.501
Tony Oliva	of	149	576	107	**185**	40	5	16	98	55	64	19	**.321**	.491
Joe Nossek	of-ph	87	170	19	37	9	0	2	16	7	22	2	.218	.306
Bob Allison	of	135	438	71	104	14	5	23	78	73	114	10	.233	.445
Earl Battey	c	131	394	36	117	22	2	6	60	50	23	0	.297	.409
Sandy Valdespino	of-ph	108	245	38	64	8	2	1	22	20	28	7	.261	.322
Jimmie Hall	of	148	522	81	149	25	4	20	86	51	79	14	.285	.464
Jerry Zimmerman	c	83	154	8	33	1	1	1	11	12	23	0	.214	.253
Rich Rollins	3b	140	469	59	117	22	1	5	32	37	54	4	.249	.333
Jerry Kindall	2b	125	342	41	67	12	1	6	36	36	97	2	.196	.289
John Sevcik	c	12	16	1	1	1	0	0	0	1	5	0	.063	.125
Mudcat Grant	p	50	97	13	15	3	2	0	8	7	27	0	.155	.227
Jim Kaat	p	56	93	6	23	4	0	1	9	3	29	2	.247	.323
Camilio Pascual	p	27	60	7	12	1	0	2	8	2	8	0	.200	.317
Johnny Klippstein	p	56	8	0	0	0	0	0	0	1	3	0	.000	.000
Jim Merritt	p	16	22	1	3	0	0	0	3	2	14	0	.136	.136
Jim Perry	p	36	53	3	9	1	1	0	3	1	16	0	.170	.226
Al Worthington	p	62	10	1	1	0	0	0	0	2	4	0	.100	.100
Dave Boswell	p	36	38	7	12	0	1	0	1	1	6	0	.316	.368
Bill Pleis	p	41	7	0	0	0	0	0	0	0	3	0	.000	.000
Dick Stigman	p	33	15	0	2	1	0	0	0	0	7	0	.133	.200
Mel Nelson	p	28	9	0	1	0	0	0	0	0	5	0	.111	.111
team total		162	5488	**774**	**1396**	**257**	42	150	**711**	554	969	92	**.254**	.399

Andy Kosco (of), Frank Kostro (2b-3b), Bernie Allen (2b), Cesar Tovar (2b-ph), Rich Reese (1b-ph), Ted Uhlaender (ph), Jerry Fosnow (p), Garry Roggenburk (p), Dwight Siebler (p), and Pete Cimino (p) also played for the Twins during the season.

PITCHING

LOS ANGELES DODGERS

WORLD SERIES STATISTICS

	G	GS	CG	IP	H	R	ER	BB	SO	W	L	SV	ERA
Sandy Koufax	**3**	**3**	**2**	**24**	13	2	1	**5**	**29**	**2**	1	0	**0.38**
Claude Osteen	2	2	1	14	9	2	1	**5**	4	1	1	0	0.64
Don Drysdale	2	2	1	$11\frac{2}{3}$	12	**9**	5	3	15	1	1	0	3.86
Ron Perranoski	2	0	0	$3\frac{2}{3}$	3	3	3	4	1	0	0	0	7.36
Howie Reed	2	0	0	$3\frac{1}{3}$	2	3	3	2	4	0	0	0	8.10
Jim Brewer	1	0	0	2	3	1	1	0	1	0	0	0	4.50
Bob Miller	2	0	0	$1\frac{1}{3}$	0	0	0	0	0	0	0	0	0.00
Johnny Podres	Did not play												
John Purdin	Did not play												
Nick Willhite	Did not play												
Mike Kekich	Did not play												
team total	7	7	4	60	42	20	14	19	54	4	3	0	2.10

REGULAR SEASON STATISTICS

		G	GS	CG	IP	H	ER	BB	SO	W	L	Pct	SV	ShO	ERA
Sandy Koufax		43	41	**27**	**336**	216	76	71	**382**	**26**	8	**.765**	2	8	**2.04**
Claude Osteen		40	40	9	281	253	89	78	162	15	15	.500	0	1	2.79
Don Drysdale		44	**42**	20	308	**270**	95	66	210	23	12	.657	1	7	2.78
Ron Perranoski		59	0	0	105	85	26	40	53	6	6	.500	17	0	2.23
Howie Reed		38	5	0	78	73	27	27	47	7	5	.583	1	0	3.12
Jim Brewer		19	2	0	49	33	10	28	31	3	2	.600	2	0	1.84
Bob Miller		61	1	0	103	82	34	26	77	6	7	.462	9	0	2.97
Johnny Podres		27	22	2	134	126	51	39	63	7	6	.538	1	1	3.43
John Purdin		11	2	0	23	26	17	13	16	2	1	.667	0	0	6.65
Nick Willhite	a	15	6	0	42	47	25	22	28	2	2	.500	1	0	5.36
Mike Kekich		5	1	0	10	10	11	13	9	0	1	.000	0	0	9.90
team total		162	162	**58**	1476	1223	461	425	1079	**97**	65	**.599**	34	**23**	**2.81**

MINNESOTA TWINS

WORLD SERIES STATISTICS

	G	GS	CG	IP	H	R	ER	BB	SO	W	L	SV	ERA
Mudcat Grant	**3**	**3**	**2**	23	**22**	8	**7**	2	12	**2**	1	0	2.74
Jim Kaat	**3**	**3**	1	$14\frac{1}{3}$	18	7	6	2	6	1	**2**	0	3.77
Camilio Pascual	1	1	0	5	8	3	3	1	0	0	1	0	5.40
Jim Perry	2	0	0	4	5	2	2	2	4	0	0	0	4.50
Al Worthington	2	0	0	4	2	1	0	2	2	0	0	0	0.00
Jim Merritt	2	0	0	$3\frac{1}{3}$	2	1	1	0	1	0	0	0	2.70
Johnny Klippstein	2	0	0	$2\frac{2}{3}$	2	0	0	2	3	0	0	0	0.00
Dave Boswell	1	0	0	$2\frac{2}{3}$	3	1	1	2	3	0	0	0	3.38
Bill Pleis	1	0	0	1	2	1	1	0	0	0	0	0	9.00
Dick Stigman	Did not play												
Mel Nelson	Did not play												
team total	7	7	3	60	64	24	21	13	31	3	4	0	3.15

REGULAR SEASON STATISTICS

	G	GS	CG	IP	H	ER	BB	SO	W	L	Pct	SV	ShO	ERA
Mudcat Grant	41	39	14	270	252	99	61	142	**21**	7	**.750**	0	**6**	3.30
Jim Kaat	45	**42**	7	264	**267**	83	63	154	18	11	.621	2	2	2.83
Camilio Pascual	27	27	5	156	126	58	63	96	9	3	.750	0	1	3.35
Jim Perry	36	19	4	168	142	49	47	88	12	7	.632	0	2	2.63
Al Worthington	62	0	0	80	57	19	41	59	10	7	.588	21	0	2.14
Jim Merritt	16	9	1	77	68	27	20	61	5	4	.556	2	0	3.16
Johnny Klippstein	56	0	0	76	59	19	31	59	9	3	.750	5	0	2.25
Dave Boswell	27	12	1	106	77	40	46	85	6	5	.545	0	0	3.40
Bill Pleis	41	2	0	51	49	17	27	33	4	4	.500	4	0	3.00
Dick Stigman	33	8	0	70	59	34	33	70	4	2	.667	4	0	4.37
Mel Nelson	28	3	0	55	57	25	23	31	0	4	.000	3	0	4.09
team total	162	162	32	1457	1278	508	503	934	**102**	60	**.630**	45	12	3.14

Total Attendance—364,326 Average Attendance—52,047. Winning Player's Share—$10,297 Losing Player's Share—$6,634

1966
Sunspots

Even with the Yankees a last-place wreck, no tight pennant race blessed the American League this year, as the Baltimore Orioles ran off a 13-game lead by the end of July and coasted to their first pennant since coming to town with the carcass of the St. Louis Browns in 1954. Although the Orioles had stood for excellence in the nineteenth century, they were also-rans in this century until obtaining outfielder Frank Robinson from Cincinnati this past winter. An outstanding batter with the Reds, Robinson launched an all-out assault on A.L. pitchers, winning the Triple Crown with 49 homers, 122 runs batted in, and a .316 batting average. The competitive Robinson sparked a cast that included slugging first baseman Boog Powell, clutch hitter and third-base wizard Brooks Robinson, and fielding stars Luis Aparicio and Paul Blair. The pitching staff mixed strong young arms with wise old arms, with youngsters Jim Palmer and Dave McNally the top winners. The Oriole mound corps didn't have the blue-chip look of the Dodger staff that led the Bums to a repeat National League pennant. Sandy Koufax and Don Drysdale staged a joint holdout in the spring that netted them contracts over the $100,000 mark, and although Drysdale slumped to a 13–16 record, Koufax sparkled as brightly as ever en route to a 27–9 campaign with a brilliant 1.73 ERA. The same gypsy band led by Maury Wills, Willie Davis, Lou Johnson, and Jim Lefebvre returned, with some added help from Tommy Davis, who recovered from a broken ankle suffered last year. Even though the Orioles had the superior batting, the Dodger edge in pitching and speed made them the favorites to win the Series.

Since Koufax had pitched on the final day of the season to nail down the pennant, Dodger manager Walt Alston picked Drysdale to pitch the opening game in Dodger Stadium, while Oriole manager Hank Bauer chose lefty Dave McNally, a 13-game winner for the season. Just like last year, Drysdale had problems with the home run. After Russ Snyder walked in the top of the first, Frank Robinson and Brooks Robinson belted homers to give McNally a 3–0 lead before he ever took the mound. The Birds added another run in the second, but the Dodgers broke through in the bottom of the inning on a solo homer by Lefebvre. In the bottom of the third, McNally lost all track of home plate. After retiring Willie Davis, McNally walked Johnson, Tommy Davis, and Lefebvre. Bauer then lifted the young lefty and brought in well-traveled righty Moe Drabowsky in relief. Drabowsky fanned Wes Parker, walked Jim Gilliam to force in a run, then retired Johnny Roseboro to end the inning. The Orioles added another run in the top of the fourth, and Drabowsky protected the 5–2 lead the rest of the way with a brilliant relief job, fanning 11 batters in his 6 2/3 innings, including six straight men in the fourth and fifth innings. The Dodgers had Koufax ready the next day to even the Series, but twenty-year-old Jim Palmer outpitched Sandy this day, throwing a four-hit shutout. A dismal fifth inning did the Dodgers in. Powell singled, and after Dave Johnson made out, Blair hit a fly to deep center which Willie Davis lost in the sun for a two-base error. Andy Etchebarren then popped a fly to short center which Davis also lost in the sun; after picking the ball up, he heaved it wildly past third base for his third error of the inning. Aparicio doubled home the third run of the inning, and Palmer worked his way home for a 6–0 victory.

The Dodgers had hopes of staging a comeback in Baltimore after a day off, but the Orioles crushed those hopes with a 1–0 third game triumph behind twenty-one-year-old pitcher Wally Bunker, with the sole run coming on a home run by Blair. The fourth game again pitted Drysdale against McNally, and the young lefty caught the spirit of the Series by shutting the Dodgers out 1–0, with a Frank Robinson homer accounting for the run. The vaunted Dodger pitching proved no match for the younger Oriole hurlers, who shut the Dodgers out for the last 33 innings of the classic. The Dodgers left immediately after the Series for a tour of Japan, during which the club broke up. Sandy Koufax announced his retirement because of arthritis in his left elbow, Tommy Davis was traded to the Mets, and Maury Wills left the team in the middle of the tour—a move for which he was later punished by being traded to the Pirates.

Game 1 October 5 at Los Angeles

| Bal. | 3 1 0 | 1 0 0 | 0 0 0 |
| L.A. | 0 1 1 | 0 0 0 | 0 0 0 |

Baltimore	Pos	AB	R	H	RBI	PO	A	E
Aparicio	ss	5	0	0	1	4	1	0
Snyder	cf-lf	3	1	1	1	2	0	0
F. Robinson	rf	5	1	2	2	1	0	0
B. Robinson	3b	5	1	1	1	2	1	0
Powell	1b	3	0	3	0	3	0	0
Blefary	lf	3	0	1	0	2	0	0
Blair	cf	0	0	0	0	0	0	0
D. Johnson	2b	4	1	2	0	0	2	0
Etchebarren	c	3	1	1	0	13	0	0
McNally	p	0	0	0	0	0	0	0
Drabowsky	p	2	0	0	0	0	0	0
Totals		35	5	9	5	27	4	0

Pitching	IP	H	R	ER	BB	SO
Baltimore						
McNally	2⅓	2	2	2	5	1
Drabowsky (W)	6⅔	1	0	0	2	11
Los Angeles						
Drysdale (L)	2	4	4	4	2	1
Moeller	2	1	1	1	1	0
R. Miller	3	2	0	0	2	1
Perranoski	2	2	0	0	0	1

Los Angeles	Pos	AB	R	H	RBI	PO	A	E
Wills	ss	3	0	0	0	6	5	0
W. Davis	cf	4	0	1	0	1	0	0
L. Johnson	rf	3	1	0	0	3	0	0
T. Davis	lf	3	0	0	0	1	0	0
Lefebvre	2b	4	1	1	1	5	4	0
Parker	1b	4	0	1	0	9	0	0
Gilliam	3b	2	0	1	1	1	3	0
Roseboro	c	4	0	0	0	3	0	0
Drysdale	p	0	0	0	0	0	1	0
a Stuart		1	0	0	0	0	0	0
Moeller	p	0	0	0	0	0	0	0
b Barbieri		1	0	0	0	0	0	0
R. Miller	p	0	0	0	0	0	1	0
c Covington		1	0	0	0	0	0	0
Perranoski	p	0	0	0	0	0	1	0
d Fairly		1	0	0	0	0	0	0
Totals		30	2	3	2	27	14	0

a Flied out for Drysdale in 2nd.
b Struck out for Moeller in 4th.
c Struck out for R. Miller in 7th.
d Struck out for Perranoski in 9th.

Doubles—D. Johnson, Parker, Powell. Home Runs—Lefebvre, B. Robinson, F. Robinson. Stolen Base—Wills. Sacrifice Hit—McNally. Left on Bases—Baltimore 9, Los Angeles 8. Umpires—Jackowski (N), Chylak (A), Pelekoudas (N), Rice (A), Steiner (N), Drummond (A). Attendance—55,941. Time of Game—2:56.

1st Inning
Baltimore
1 Aparicio flied to right.
Snyder walked.
F. Robinson lined a two-run homer into the lower left field stands.
B. Robinson hit a home-run also into the lower left field stands.
2 Powell fouled to Gilliam.
Blefary singled to right.
3 D. Johnson struck out.
Los Angeles
Wills walked.
Wills stole second.
1 W. Davis popped to short.
2 L. Johnson flied to center.
3 T. Davis grounded to third.

2nd Inning
Baltimore
Etchebarren walked.
1 McNally sacrificed Etchebarren to second, Drysdale to Lefebvre.
2 Aparicio flied to right.
Snyder singled to left, Etchebarren scored and Snyder taking second on the throw to the plate.
3 F. Robinson flied to left.
Los Angeles
Lefebvre hit a homer into the deep left-center pavilion.
Parker doubled inside the right field line having to stop at second when a fan reached out of the stands and touched the ball.
Gilliam walked.
1 Roseboro lined to Snyder in right-center.
2 Stuart, pinch-hitting for Drysdale, flied to F. Robinson in deep right-center, Parker going to third after the catch.
3 Wills struck out.

3rd Inning
Baltimore
For Los Angeles—Moeller pitching.
1 B. Robinson grounded to third.
2 Powell grounded to short.
3 Blefary popped to short.
Los Angeles
1 W. Davis popped to short.
L. Johnson walked.
T. Davis walked.
Lefebvre walked to load the bases.
For Baltimore—Drabowski now pitching.
2 Parker fanned.
Gilliam walked, forcing in L. Johnson.
3 Roseboro fouled to Etchebarren.

4th Inning
Baltimore
D. Johnson doubled off the bullpen screen in left.
1 Etchebarren grounded to second, D. Johnson advancing to third.
Drabowsky walked.
2 Aparicio forced Drabowsky at second, Wills to Lefebvre as D. Johnson scored.
3 Snyder grounded to second.
Los Angeles
1 Barbieri, pinch-hitting for Moeller, struck out.
2 Wills struck out.
3 W. Davis also struck out.

5th Inning
Baltimore
For Los Angeles—R. Miller pitching.
1 F. Robinson flied to short center.
2 B. Robinson popped to short.
Powell doubled down the left field line.
Blefary intentionally walked after the count got to 3–0.
3 D. Johnson grounded to second.
Los Angeles
1 L. Johnson struck out.
2 T. Davis struck out.
3 Lefebvre also struck out (Drabowsky ties a Series record of six consecutive strikeouts).

6th Inning
Baltimore
Etchebarren singled to right.
1 Drabowsky forced Etchebarren at second on a sacrifice attempt, R. Miller to Wills.
2 Aparicio forced Drabowsky at second, Wills to Lefebvre. Snyder walked.
3 F. Robinson took a called third strike.
Los Angeles
1 Parker lined to left.
2 Gilliam popped to short.
3 Roseboro lined to left.

7th Inning
Baltimore
1 B. Robinson grounded to short.
2 Powell grounded to second.
3 Blefary grounded to second.
Los Angeles
1 Covington, pinch-hitting for R. Miller, fanned.
Wills walked.
W. Davis singled to left, Wills stopping at second.
2 L. Johnson fouled to B. Robinson.
3 T. Davis forced W. Davis at second, D. Johnson to Aparicio.

8th Inning
Baltimore
For Los Angeles—Perranoski pitching.
D. Johnson singled to center.
1 Etchebarren forced D. Johnson at second on an attempted sacrifice, Perranoski to Wills.
2 Drabowsky struck out, bunting the third strike foul.
3 Aparicio lined to short.
Los Angeles
1 Lefebvre popped to third.
2 Parker struck out.
3 Gilliam grounded to short.

9th Inning
Baltimore
1 Snyder grounded to second.
F. Robinson singled to left.
2 B. Robinson lined to second.
3 Powell lined to right.
Los Angeles
For Baltimore—Snyder switched to left and Blair playing center.
1 Roseboro struck out.
2 Fairly, pinch-hitting for Perranoski, fanned.
3 Wills grounded to second.

Game 2 October 6 at Los Angeles

| Bal. | 000 031 020 |
| L.A. | 000 000 000 |

Baltimore	Pos	AB	R	H	RBI	PO	A	E
Aparicio	ss	5	0	2	1	4	1	0
Blefary	lf	5	0	0	0	1	0	0
F. Robinson	rf	3	2	1	0	1	0	0
B. Robinson	3b	4	1	1	0	1	1	0
Powell	1b	3	1	2	1	8	0	0
D. Johnson	2b	4	0	2	1	2	4	0
Blair	cf	3	1	0	0	4	0	0
Etchebarren	c	3	1	0	0	6	0	0
Palmer	p	4	0	0	0	0	2	0
Totals		34	6	8	3	27	8	0

Pitching	IP	H	R	ER	BB	SO
Baltimore						
Palmer (W)	9	4	0	0	3	6
Los Angeles						
Koufax (L)	6	6	4	1	2	2
Perranoski	1⅓	2	2	2	1	1
Regan	⅔	0	0	0	1	1
Brewer	1	0	0	0	0	1

Los Angeles	Pos	AB	R	H	RBI	PO	A	E
Wills	ss	4	0	0	0	3	1	0
Gilliam	3b	4	0	0	0	2	3	1
W. Davis	cf	4	0	0	0	2	0	3
Fairly	rf	3	0	0	0	3	0	1
Lefebvre	2b	3	0	0	0	3	0	0
L. Johnson	lf	4	0	1	0	1	0	0
Roseboro	c	4	0	1	0	8	1	0
Parker	1b	2	0	1	0	5	1	0
Koufax	p	2	0	0	0	0	1	0
Perranoski	p	0	0	0	0	0	1	1
Regan	p	0	0	0	0	0	0	0
a T. Davis		1	0	1	0	0	0	0
Brewer	p	0	0	0	0	0	0	0
Totals		31	0	4	0	27	8	6

a Singled for Regan in 8th.

Doubles—Aparicio, L. Johnson. Triple—F. Robinson. Sacrifice Hit—Powell. Double Play—Gilliam to Roseboro to Parker. Wild Pitch—Regan, Palmer. Left on Bases—Baltimore 6, Los Angeles 1. Umpires—Chylak, Pelekoudas, Rice, Steiner, Drummond, Jackowski. Attendance—55,947. Time of Game—2:26.

1st Inning
Baltimore
Aparicio singled to deep short.
1 Blefary flied to short-center.
2 Aparicio breaking for second was picked off first, Koufax to Parker to Wills.
3 F. Robinson flied to left.
Los Angeles
1 Wills grounded back to the mound.
2 Gilliam popped to short.
3 W. Davis struck out.

2nd Inning
Baltimore
1 B. Robinson fouled to Roseboro.
2 Powell lined to deep right.
3 D. Johnson popped to second.
Los Angeles
Fairly walked.
1 Lefebvre struck out.
L. Johnson blooped a double into short right, Fairly stopping at third.
2 Roseboro popped to short.
Parker got an intentional pass, filling the bases.
3 Koufax popped to second.

3rd Inning
Baltimore
1 Blair lined to right.
2 Etchebarren took a called third strike.
3 Palmer popped to third.
Los Angeles
1 Wills grounded to second.
2 Gilliam grounded to short.
3 W. Davis struck out.

4th Inning
Baltimore
1 Aparicio popped to Gilliam.
2 Blefary popped to short.
F. Robinson walked.
B. Robinson safe at first on Gilliam's fumble of his grounder, but F.
3 Robinson was out rounding second, Gilliam to Lefebvre.
Los Angeles
1 Fairly flied to Blair in right-center.
2 Lefebvre grounded back to the mound.
3 L. Johnson flied to deep center.

5th Inning
Baltimore
Powell singled to left.
1 D. Johnson fouled to Roseboro on an attempted sacrifice.
Blair safely to second and Powell made third as W. Davis dropped his fly for an error (after losing the ball in the sun).
Etchebarren was safe on a short fly to center which W. Davis again lost and then dropped, Powell scored and Blair went to third. W. Davis threw wildly past third allowing Blair to score and Etchebarren going to third. **2 errors on the play by Davis for his third of the inning.**
2 Palmer struck out.
Aparicio doubled down the left field line, scoring Etchebarren.
3 Blefary flied to right.

5th Inning (continued)
Los Angeles
1 Roseboro flied to center.
Parker singled to right.
2 Koufax flied to right.
3 Wills grounded to second.

6th Inning
Baltimore
F. Robinson tripled to right-center.
1 B. Robinson fouled to Parker.
Powell singled to right-center scoring F. Robinson.
D. Johnson singled to right, Powell moving to third. D. Johnson went to second on Fairly's throwing error to Gilliam.
Blair intentionally walked, loading the bases.
2,3 Etchebarren hit into a double play, Gilliam to Roseboro to Parker.
Los Angeles
1 Gilliam grounded to second.
2 W. Davis grounded to second.
3 Fairly struck out.

7th Inning
Baltimore
For Los Angeles—Perranoski pitching.
1 Palmer grounded to third.
2 Aparicio flied to center.
3 Blefary struck out.
Los Angeles
1 Lefebvre struck out.
2 Johnson grounded to third.
Roseboro singled to right.
3 Parker fouled to B. Robinson.

8th Inning
Baltimore
F. Robinson walked.
B. Robinson singled to left, F. Robinson stopping at second.
1 Powell sacrificed up both runners, Perranoski to Parker.
D. Johnson singled off Perranoski's glove, scoring F. Robinson and moving B. Robinson to third. D. Johnson went to second and B. Robinson scored on Perranoski's wild throw to first.
For Los Angeles—Regan now pitching.
2 Blair popped to short.
Etchebarren walked.
Both runners moved up on a wild pitch.
3 Palmer took a called third strike.
Los Angeles
T. Davis, pinch-hitting for Regan, singled to right center.
1 Wills popped to second.
T. Davis to second on a wild pitch.
2 Gilliam fouled to Aparicio down the left field line.
3 W. Davis flied to center.

9th Inning
Baltimore
For Los Angeles—Brewer pitching.
1 Aparicio popped to second.
2 Blefary fanned.
3 F. Robinson grounded to short.
Los Angeles
1 Fairly struck out.
Lefebvre walked.
2 L. Johnson flied to left.
3 Roseboro popped to short.

Game 3 October 8 at Baltimore

| L.A. | 000 000 000 |
| Balt. | 000 010 00x |

Los Angeles	Pos	AB	R	H	RBI	PO	A	E
Wills	ss	3	0	1	0	1	6	0
Parker	1b	4	0	1	0	10	1	0
Regan	p	0	0	0	0	1	0	0
W. Davis	cf	4	0	0	0	2	0	0
Fairly	rf-1b	3	0	1	0	2	0	0
Lefebvre	2b	4	0	0	0	3	4	0
L. Johnson	lf-rf	4	0	2	0	1	0	0
Roseboro	c	3	0	0	0	4	0	0
Kennedy	3b	3	0	0	0	0	2	0
Osteen	p	2	0	0	0	1	0	0
a T. Davis	lf	1	0	1	0	0	0	0
Totals		31	0	6	0	24	14	0

a Singled for Osteen in 8th.

Double—Parker. Home Run—Blair. Sacrifice Hit—Wills. Double Plays—Aparicio to D. Johnson to Powell, Wills to Lefebvre to Parker, Lefebvre to Wills to Parker. Left on Bases—Los Angeles 6, Baltimore 1. Umpires—Pelekoudas, Rice, Steiner, Drummond, Jackowski, Chylak. Attendance—54,445. Time of Game—1:55.

1st Inning
Los Angeles
1 Wills struck out.
2 Parker took a called third strike.
3 W. Davis flied to Blefary, making a good running catch in the left field corner.
Baltimore
1 Aparicio grounded to second.
2 Blefary grounded to first.
3 F. Robinson struck out.

2nd Inning
Los Angeles
Fairly singled off Bunker's glove.
1 Lefebvre flied to short left.
2,3 L. Johnson grounded into a double play, Aparicio to D. Johnson to Powell.
Baltimore
1 B. Robinson flied to L. Johnson in deep left-center.
Powell singled to right.
2,3 D. Johnson grounded into a double play, Wills to Lefebvre to Parker.

3rd Inning
Los Angeles
1 Roseboro struck out.
2 Kennedy grounded to deep short, where Aparicio made a great stop.
3 Osteen fanned.
Baltimore
1 Blair flied to deep center.
2 Etchebarren grounded to short.
3 Bunker grounded to short.

4th Inning
Los Angeles
1 Wills bunted out, Bunker to Powell.
Parker got a ground-rule double when his liner to right-center bounced over the fence.
2 W. Davis flied to center.
Fairly walked.
3 Lefebvre struck out.
Baltimore
Aparicio blooped a single to left.
1 Blefary took a called third strike.
2 F. Robinson forced Aparicio at second, Kennedy to Lefebvre.
3 B. Robinson forced F. Robinson at second, Wills to Lefebvre.

5th Inning
Los Angeles
L. Johnson singled to left.
1 Roseboro popped to third.
2 Kennedy forced L. Johnson at second, B. Robinson to D. Johnson.
3 Osteen flied to deep left.
Baltimore
1 Powell fouled to Parker.
2 D. Johnson grounded out, Parker to Osteen.
Blair homered into the left field bleachers (a 430 foot smash).
3 Etchebarren grounded to short.

Baltimore	Pos	AB	R	H	RBI	PO	A	E
Aparicio	ss	3	0	1	0	1	4	0
Blefary	lf	3	0	0	0	3	0	0
Snyder	lf	0	0	0	0	0	0	0
F. Robinson	rf	3	0	0	0	1	0	0
B. Robinson	3b	2	0	0	0	1	1	0
Powell	1b	3	0	1	0	9	1	0
D. Johnson	2b	3	0	0	0	3	3	0
Blair	cf	3	1	1	1	3	0	0
Etchebarren	c	3	0	0	0	6	0	0
Bunker	p	2	0	0	0	0	3	0
Totals		25	1	3	1	27	12	0

Pitching	IP	H	R	ER	BB	SO
Los Angeles						
Osteen (L)	7	3	1	1	1	3
Regan	1	0	0	0	0	1
Baltimore						
Bunker (W)	9	6	0	0	1	6

6th Inning
Los Angeles
Wills singled to center.
1 Parker grounded to first, moving Wills to second.
2 W. Davis flied to deep center, Wills going to third after the catch.
3 Fairly bounced back to the mound.
Baltimore
1 Bunker called out on strikes.
2 Aparicio flied to center.
3 Blefary lined to first.

7th Inning
Los Angeles
1 Lefebvre lined to right.
L. Johnson singled off Aparicio's glove.
2 Roseboro flied to center.
3 Kennedy tapped back to the mound.
Baltimore
1 F. Robinson grounded to third.
B. Robinson walked.
2,3 Powell hit into a double play, Lefebvre to Wills to Parker.

8th Inning
Los Angeles
T. Davis, batting for Osteen, singled to center.
1 Wills sacrificed T. Davis to second, Powell to D. Johnson.
2 Parker popped to Aparicio in short left.
3 W. Davis grounded to second.
Baltimore
For Los Angeles—Regan pitching, T. Davis in left, L. Johnson moved to right and Fairly to first.
1 D. Johnson bounced back to the mound.
2 Blair grounded to second.
3 Etchebarren struck out.

9th Inning
Los Angeles
For Baltimore—Snyder playing left.
1 Fairly struck out.
2 Lefebvre grounded to second.
3 L. Johnson grounded to short.

Game 4 October 9 at Baltimore

L.A.   000 000 000
Balt. 000 100 00x

Los Angeles	Pos	AB	R	H	RBI	PO	A	E
Wills	ss	3	0	0	0	2	3	0
W. Davis	cf	4	0	0	0	1	0	0
L. Johnson	rf	4	0	1	0	4	0	0
T. Davis	lf	3	0	0	0	2	0	0
Lefebvre	2b	2	0	1	0	1	1	0
Parker	1b	3	0	0	0	7	0	0
Roseboro	c	3	0	0	0	7	1	0
Kennedy	3b	2	0	1	0	0	1	0
a Stuart		1	0	0	0	0	0	0
Drysdale	p	2	0	0	0	0	2	0
b Ferrara		1	0	1	0	0	0	0
c Oliver		0	0	0	0	0	0	0
Totals		28	0	4	0	24	8	0

a Struck out for Kennedy in 9th.
b Singled for Drysdale in 9th.
c Ran for Ferrara in 9th

Home Run—F. Robinson. Double Plays—Lefebvre to Wills to Parker, Aparicio to D. Johnson to Powell, B. Robinson to D. Johnson to Powell, Etchebarren to D. Johnson. Left on Bases—Los Angeles 3, Baltimore 2. Umpires—Rice, Steiner, Drummond, Jackowski, Chylak, Pelekoudas. Attendance—54,458. Time of Game—1:45.

Baltimore	Pos	AB	R	H	RBI	PO	A	E
Aparicio	ss	3	0	1	0	0	3	0
Snyder	cf-lf	3	0	0	0	0	0	0
F. Robinson	rf	3	1	1	1	3	0	0
B. Robinson	3b	3	0	1	0	0	3	0
Powell	1b	3	0	1	0	7	0	0
Blefary	lf	2	0	0	0	1	0	0
Blair	cf	0	0	0	0	2	0	0
D. Johnson	2b	3	0	0	0	7	3	0
Etchebarren	c	3	0	0	0	7	1	0
McNally	p	3	0	0	0	0	0	0
Totals		26	1	4	1	27	10	0

Pitching	IP	H	R	ER	BB	SO
Los Angeles						
Drysdale (L)	8	4	1	1	1	5
Baltimore						
McNally (W)	9	4	0	0	2	4

1st Inning
Los Angeles
1 Wills popped to second.
2 W. Davis grounded to first.
3 L. Johnson fouled to Etchebarren.
Baltimore
1 Aparicio fouled to Roseboro.
2 Snyder an automatic out when he ran into his own fair bunt. Putout goes to Roseboro.
3 F. Robinson flied out to T. Davis in the left field corner.

2nd Inning
Los Angeles
1 T. Davis lined to F. Robinson in right-center.
Lefebvre walked.
2 Parker forced Lefebvre at second, Aparicio to D. Johnson.
3 Roseboro flied to right.
Baltimore
B. Robinson singled to center.
1 Powell struck out.
Blefary walked.
2,3 D. Johnson hit into a double play, Lefebvre to Wills to Parker.

3rd Inning
Los Angeles
1 Kennedy popped to second.
2 Drysdale grounded to short.
3 Wills fouled to Etchebarren.
Baltimore
1 Etchebarren called out on strikes.
2 McNally tapped to the mound.
3 Aparicio flied to right.

4th Inning
Los Angeles
1 W. Davis fanned.
L. Johnson singled to left.
2,3 T. Davis grounded into a double play, Aparicio to D. Johnson to Powell.
Baltimore
1 Snyder popped to second.
F. Robinson hit a home run deep into the left field stands.
2 B. Robinson grounded to third.
3 Powell was robbed of a home run by W. Davis who made a one-handed leaping catch at the center field barrier

5th Inning
Los Angeles
Lefebvre lined a single to center.
1,2 Parker hit into a double play, B. Robinson to D. Johnson to Powell.
3 Roseboro took a called third strike.
Baltimore
1 Blefary flied to right.
2 D. Johnson flied to left.
3 Etchebarren struck out.

6th Inning
Los Angeles
Kennedy singled to left.
1,2 Drysdale struck out and Kennedy was doubled trying to steal second, Etchebarren to D. Johnson.
3 Wills grounded to third.
Baltimore
1 McNally took a called third strike.
Aparicio singled to center.
2 Aparicio was trapped between first and second, Roseboro to Wills to Parker.
3 Snyder grounded back to the mound.

7th Inning
Los Angeles
1 W. Davis flied to left.
2 L. Johnson fouled to Etchebarren on a bunt attempt.
3 T. Davis popped to second.
Baltimore
1 F. Robinson struck out.
2 B. Robinson grounded to short.
Powell singled to center.
3 Blefary flied to right.

8th Inning
Los Angeles
For Baltimore—Snyder shifted to left as Blair came in to play center.
1 Lefebvre robbed of an extra-base hit by Blair in left-center with a leaping one-handed catch against the fence.
2 Parker grounded to third.
3 Roseboro grounded to second.
Baltimore
1 D. Johnson flied to right.
2 Etchebarren popped to first.
3 McNally popped to short.

9th Inning
Los Angeles
1 Stuart, pinch-hitting for Kennedy, took a called third strike.
Ferrara, pinch-hitting for Drysdale, singled to center.
Oliver ran for Ferrara.
Wills walked.
2 W. Davis lined to right.
3 L. Johnson flied to center. **(LA sets a Series record being shut out 33 consecutive innings as Baltimore completes its 3rd shutout in a 4 game series).**

1966 WORLD SERIES COMPOSITE BOX

	Wins	Composite Line Score	Manager	W	L	Pct.	G. Ahead
				Regular Season			
Baltimore Orioles (AL)	4	3 1 0 2 4 1 0 2 0 – 13	Hank Bauer	97	63	.606	9
Los Angeles Dodgers (NL)	0	0 1 1 0 0 0 0 0 0 – 2	Walt Alston	95	67	.586	1.5

BATTING AND FIELDING

	WORLD SERIES STATISTICS																		REGULAR SEASON STATISTICS													
	Pos	G	AB	R	H	2B	3B	HR	RBI	BB	SO	SB	BA	SA	PO	A	E		Main Pos	G	AB	R	H	2B	3B	HR	RBI	BB	SO	SB	BA	SA
BALTIMORE ORIOLES																																
Boog Powell	1b	4	14	1	**5**	1	0	0	1	0	1	0	**.357**	.429	27	1	0		1b	140	491	78	141	18	0	34	109	67	125	0	.287	.532
Dave Johnson	2b	4	14	1	4	1	0	0	1	0	1	0	.286	.357	12	12	0		2b	131	501	48	129	20	3	7	56	31	64	3	.257	.351
Luis Aparicio	ss	4	**16**	0	4	1	0	0	2	0	0	0	.250	.313	9	8	0		ss	151	**659**	97	182	25	8	6	41	33	42	25	.276	.366
Brooks Robinson	3b	4	14	2	3	0	0	1	1	1	0	0	.214	.429	4	6	0		3b	157	620	91	167	35	2	23	100	56	36	2	.279	.444
Frank Robinson	rf	4	14	**4**	4	0	**1**	**2**	**3**	2	3	0	.286	**.857**	6	0	0		of	155	576	**122**	182	34	2	**49**	**122**	87	90	8	**.316**	**.637**
Paul Blair	cf	4	6	2	1	0	0	1	1	1	0	0	.167	.667	9	0	0		of	133	303	35	84	20	2	6	33	15	36	5	.277	.416
Curt Blefary	lf	4	13	0	1	0	0	0	0	2	3	0	.077	.077	7	0	0		of	131	419	73	107	14	3	23	64	73	56	1	.255	.468
Andy Etchebarren	c	4	12	2	1	0	0	0	0	2	**4**	0	.083	.083	**32**	1	0		c	121	412	41	91	14	6	11	50	38	106	0	.221	.364
Russ Snyder	cf-lf	3	6	1	1	0	0	0	1	2	0	0	.167	.167	2	0	0		of	117	373	66	114	21	5	3	41	38	37	2	.306	.413
Sam Bowens	Did not play																		of	89	243	26	51	9	1	6	20	17	52	9	.210	.329
Bob Johnson	Did not play																		ph-2b	71	157	13	34	5	0	1	10	12	24	0	.217	.268
Woody Held	Did not play																		ph	56	82	6	17	3	1	1	7	12	30	0	.207	.305
Vic Roznovsky	Did not play																		c	41	97	4	23	5	0	1	10	9	11	0	.237	.320
Larry Haney	Did not play																		c	20	56	3	9	1	0	1	3	1	15	0	.161	.232
Jim Palmer	p	1	4	0	0	0	0	0	0	0	2	0	.000	.000	0	2	0		p	36	73	11	7	1	0	1	5	3	33	0	.096	.151
Dave McNally	p	2	3	0	0	0	0	0	0	0	1	0	.000	.000	0	0	0		p	34	77	6	15	5	0	0	3	2	27	0	.195	.260
Wally Bunker	p	1	2	0	0	0	0	0	0	0	1	0	.000	.000	0	3	0		p	30	48	4	5	3	0	0	2	4	22	0	.104	.167
Moe Drabowsky	p	1	2	0	0	0	0	0	0	1	1	0	.000	.000	0	0	0		p	44	22	3	8	2	0	0	4	1	6	0	.364	.455
Steve Barber	Missed Series—Arm Injury																		p	25	44	1	3	0	0	0	1	0	30	0	.068	.068
Stu Miller	Did not play																		p	51	19	2	2	0	0	0	3	0	8	0	.105	.105
Eddie Watt	Did not play																		p	43	46	4	14	1	0	2	2	1	9	0	.304	.457
Dick Hall	Did not play																		p	32	12	0	2	0	0	0	2	0	5	0	.167	.167
Eddie Fisher	Did not play																	a	p	44	13	0	2	1	0	0	1	0	8	0	.154	.231
Gene Brabender	Did not play																		p	31	13	0	1	0	0	0	0	0	9	0	.077	.077
John Miller	Did not play																		p	23	34	3	4	0	0	0	1	0	11	0	.118	.118
Frank Bertaina	Did not play																		p	16	19	1	2	0	0	0	0	1	6	0	.105	.105
team total		4	120	13	24	3	1	4	10	11	17	0	.200	.342	108	33	0			160	**5529**	**755**	**1426**	**243**	35	175	**703**	514	926	55	**.258**	**.409**

Double Plays—4
Left on Bases—18

a—from Chicago (AL)
Charlie Lau (ph), Jerry Adair (2b), Mark Belanger (ss), Mike Epstein (1b), Cam Carreon (c), Tom Phoebus (p), Bill Short (p) and Ed Barnowski also played for the Orioles during the season.

	WORLD SERIES STATISTICS																		REGULAR SEASON STATISTICS													
	Pos	G	AB	R	H	2B	3B	HR	RBI	BB	SO	SB	BA	SA	PO	A	E		Main Pos	G	AB	R	H	2B	3B	HR	RBI	BB	SO	SB	BA	SA
LOS ANGELES DODGERS																																
Wes Parker	1b	4	13	0	3	**2**	0	0	0	1	3	0	.231	.385	31	2	0		1b	156	475	67	120	17	5	12	51	69	83	7	.253	.385
Jim Lefebvre	2b	4	12	1	2	0	0	1	1	**3**	**4**	0	.167	.417	10	10	0		2b	152	544	69	149	23	3	24	74	48	72	1	.274	.460
Maury Wills	ss	4	13	0	1	0	0	0	0	**3**	3	**1**	.077	.077	12	**15**	0		ss	143	594	60	162	14	2	1	39	34	60	38	.273	.308
Jim Gilliam	3b	2	6	0	0	0	0	0	1	2	0	0	.000	.000	3	4	1		3b	88	235	30	51	9	0	1	16	34	17	2	.217	.268
Lou Johnson	rf-lf	4	15	1	4	1	0	0	0	1	1	0	.267	.333	9	0	0		of	152	526	71	143	20	2	17	73	21	75	8	.272	.414
Willie Davis	cf	4	**16**	0	1	0	0	0	0	0	**4**	0	.063	.063	6	0	**3**		of	153	624	74	177	31	6	11	61	15	68	21	.284	.405
Tommy Davis	lf-ph	4	8	0	2	0	0	0	0	1	1	0	.250	.250	3	0	0		of	100	313	27	98	11	1	3	27	16	36	3	.313	.383
Johnny Roseboro	c	4	14	0	1	0	0	0	0	0	3	0	.071	.071	22	2	0		c	142	445	47	123	23	2	9	53	44	51	3	.276	.398
Ron Fairly	ph-rf-1b	3	7	0	1	0	0	0	0	2	**4**	0	.143	.143	5	0	1		of	117	351	53	101	20	0	14	61	52	38	3	.288	.464
John Kennedy	3b	2	5	0	1	0	0	0	0	0	0	0	.200	.200	0	3	0		3b	125	274	15	55	9	2	3	24	10	64	1	.201	.281
Dick Stuart	ph	2	2	0	0	0	0	0	0	0	1	0	.000	.000				b	1b	38	91	4	24	1	0	3	9	11	17	0	.264	.374
Jim Barbieri	ph	1	1	0	0	0	0	0	0	0	1	0	.000	.000					of-ph	39	82	9	23	5	0	0	3	9	7	2	.280	.341
Wes Covington	ph	1	1	0	0	0	0	0	0	0	1	0	.000	.000				c	ph	37	33	1	4	0	1	1	6	6	5	0	.121	.273
Al Ferrara	ph	1	1	0	1	0	0	0	0	0	0	0	1.000	1.000					of-ph	63	115	15	31	4	0	5	23	9	35	0	.270	.435
Nate Oliver	pr	1	0	0	0	0	0	0	0	0	0	0	—	—					2b	80	119	17	23	2	0	0	3	13	17	3	.193	.210
Jeff Torborg	Did not play																		c	46	120	4	27	3	0	1	13	10	23	0	.225	.275
Don Drysdale	p	2	2	0	0	0	0	0	0	0	1	0	.000	.000	0	3	0		p	46	106	6	20	2	0	2	8	3	28	0	.189	.264
Sandy Koufax	p	1	2	0	0	0	0	0	0	0	0	0	.000	.000	0	1	0		p	41	118	5	9	3	0	0	5	5	57	0	.076	.102
Claude Osteen	p	1	2	0	0	0	0	0	0	0	1	0	.000	.000	1	0	0		p	39	76	8	16	1	2	1	6	5	18	1	.211	.316
Ron Perranoski	p	2	0	0	0	0	0	0	0	0	0	0	—	—	0	2	1		p	55	8	1	2	1	1	0	1	0	5	0	.250	.625
Phil Regan	p	2	0	0	0	0	0	0	0	0	0	0	—	—	0	1	0		p	65	21	2	3	0	0	0	0	3	4	0	.143	.143
Jim Brewer	p	1	0	0	0	0	0	0	0	0	0	0	—	—	0	0	0		p	13	0	0	0	0	0	0	0	0	0	0	—	—
Bob Miller	p	1	0	0	0	0	0	0	0	0	0	0	—	—	0	1	0		p	46	13	0	1	0	0	0	1	0	4	0	.077	.077
Joe Moeller	p	1	0	0	0	0	0	0	0	0	0	0	—	—	0	0	0		p	29	12	1	2	0	0	0	0	2	5	0	.167	.168
Don Sutton	Did not play																		p	38	82	4	15	2	0	0	2	1	27	0	.183	.207
team total		4	120	2	17	3	0	1	2	13	28	1	.142	.192	102	44	6			162	5471	606	1399	201	27	108	565	430	830	94	.256	.362

Double Plays—4
Left on Bases—24

b—from New York (NL)
c—from Chicago (NL)
Derrell Griffith (of), Dick Schofield (3b), Bart Shirley (ss-ph), Willie Crawford (pr), Tommy Hutton (1b), Jim Campanis (ph), Nick Willhite (p), Bill Singer (p), Johnny Podres (p) and Howie Reed (p) also played for the Dodgers during the season.

PITCHING

	WORLD SERIES STATISTICS														REGULAR SEASON STATISTICS													
	G	GS	CG	IP	H	R	ER	BB	SO	W	L	SV	ERA		G	GS	CG	IP	H	ER	BB	SO	W	L	Pct	SV	ShO	ERA
BALTIMORE ORIOLES																												
Dave McNally	**2**	**2**	**1**	**11 1/3**	6	2	2	**7**	5	**1**	0	0	1.59		34	33	5	213	212	75	64	158	13	6	.684	0	1	3.17
Wally Bunker	1	1	**1**	9	6	0	0	1	6	**1**	0	0	**0.00**		29	24	3	143	151	68	48	89	10	6	.625	0	0	4.28
Jim Palmer	1	1	**1**	9	4	0	0	3	6	**1**	0	0	**0.00**		30	30	6	208	176	80	91	147	15	10	.600	0	0	3.46
Moe Drabowsky	1	0	0	6 2/3	1	0	0	2	**11**	**1**	0	0	0.00		44	3	0	96	62	30	29	98	6	0	1.000	7	0	2.81
Steve Barber	Missed Series—Arm Injury														25	22	5	133	104	34	49	91	10	5	.667	0	3	2.30
Stu Miller	Did not play														51	0	0	92	65	23	22	67	9	4	.692	18	0	2.25
Eddie Watt	Did not play														43	13	1	146	123	62	44	102	9	7	.563	4	0	3.82
Dick Hall	Did not play														32	0	0	66	59	29	8	44	6	2	.750	7	0	3.95
Eddie Fisher	Did not play													a	***44**	0	0	72	60	21	19	39	5	3	.625	13	0	2.62
Gene Brabender	Did not play														31	1	0	71	57	28	29	62	4	3	.571	2	0	3.55
John Miller	Did not play														23	16	0	101	92	53	58	81	4	8	.333	0	0	4.72
Frank Bertaina	Did not play														16	9	0	63	52	22	36	46	2	5	.286	0	0	3.14
team total	4	4	3	36	17	2	2	13	28	4	0	0	0.50		160	160	23	1466	1267	541	514	1070	**97**	63	**.606**	**51**	13	3.32
LOS ANGELES DODGERS																												
Don Drysdale	**2**	**2**	**1**	10	**8**	**5**	**5**	3	6	0	**2**	0	4.50		40	40	11	274	279	104	45	177	13	16	.448	0	0	3.42
Claude Osteen	1	1	0	7	3	1	1	1	3	0	1	0	1.29		39	38	8	240	238	76	65	137	17	14	.548	0	3	2.85
Sandy Koufax	1	1	0	6	6	4	1	2	2	0	1	0	1.50		41	**41**	**27**	**323**	241	62	77	**317**	**27**	9	.750	0	**5**	**1.73**
Ron Perranoski	**2**	0	0	3 1/3	4	2	2	1	2	0	0	0	5.40		55	0	5	82	82	30	31	50	6	7	.462	7	0	3.18
Bob Miller	1	0	0	3	2	0	0	2	1	0	0	0	0.00		46	0	0	84	70	26	29	58	4	2	.667	5	0	2.79
Joe Moeller	1	0	0	2	1	1	1	1	0	0	0	0	4.50		29	8	0	79	73	22	14	31	2	4	.333	0	0	2.51
Phil Regan	**2**	0	0	1 2/3	0	0	0	1	2	0	0	0	0.00		65	0	0	117	85	20	24	88	14	1	.933	**21**	0	1.62
Jim Brewer	1	0	0	1	0	0	0	0	1	0	0	0	0.00		13	0	0	22	17	9	11	8	0	2	.000	2	0	3.68
Don Sutton	Did not play														37	37	6	226	192	75	52	290	12	12	.500	0	2	2.99
team total	4	4	1	34	24	13	10	11	17	0	4	0	2.65		162	162	**52**	1458	1287	**425**	356	**1084**	**95**	67	**.586**	35	**20**	**2.62**

*League leader with 67.

Total Attendance—220,791 Average Attendance—55,198 Winning Player's Share—$11,683 Losing Player's Share—$8,189

1967
Awakening One Game Too Early

Like the 1914 Miracle Braves, the Red Sox made their dreams into reality by fighting into a furious pennant race and taking the American League flag with a victory on the final day of the season. In pulling off the "impossible dream," as the press so called it, the Red Sox came from a ninth-place finish last year all the way to first under the stern rule of freshman manager Dick Williams. A variety of young players and journeymen came through with unexpected heroics down the stretch, but the biggest heroes of the dream season were Carl Yastrzemski and Jim Lonborg. Yaz blossomed into stardom this year, playing an inspired left field and winning the Triple Crown with 44 home runs, 121 RBI's, and a .326 batting average. Yaz led the team by example every day, while Lonborg provided strong pitching every fourth day, logging a 22–9 record. The Red Sox represented a triumph for the underdogs of the world, and they came into the World Series in that same role against the St. Louis Cardinals, easy victors in the National League. Managed by Red Schoendienst, the Cards had a top-flight team, with a great power hitter in Orlando Cepeda, great singles hitter in Curt Flood, and great base stealer in Lou Brock. The defense was sound, and the pitching so deep that it could carry on through July and August without ace Bob Gibson, who sat out 56 games with a broken leg.

Gibson took the mound for the Cards on opening day at Fenway Park, but since Lonborg had pitched on the final day of the regular season, 12-game-winner Jose Santiago pitched for the Sox. The Cards scored a run in the third on two hits and an infield out, but the Red Sox tied it up in the bottom of the inning on a home run by Santiago. The Boston righty matched Gibson most of the way, but the Cards scored a run in the seventh on a single by Brock, his stolen base, and two infield outs. That run held up for a 2–1 St. Louis win, but the Sox now had their ace ready for game two. Lonborg overpowered the Cardinal batters, and while the Sox piled up five runs after seven innings, the Cards had not yet made a base hit. After the first two Cards went out in the eighth, Julian Javier ripped a double to left, but that was the only St. Louis hit in the 5–0 gem.

But when the Series resumed in St. Louis, the Red Sox starting pitchers got pounded. Gary Bell gave up three runs to the Cards in the first two innings of game three, as the Redbirds went on to a 5–2 triumph. Santiago was knocked out in a four-run, first-inning outburst the next day, and with Gibson blowing the Boston batters down, the Cards skated to a 6–0 win that put the Red Sox one game from elimination. But with Lonborg pitching in game five, the entire Red Sox team seemed to pick up. They scored a run off Steve Carlton in the third on an error and two singles, then added two important insurance runs in the top of the ninth on two walks and two hits. Lonborg again sparkled, throwing a three-hitter and losing a shutout only on a solo homer by ex-Yankee Roger Maris in the bottom of the ninth. The 3–1 win sent the Series back to Boston, where Red Sox manager Williams had to come up with a starting pitcher for game six. He gambled on Gary Waslewski, who won only two games during the season but pitched well in a relief role in the third game. Waslewski gave the Sox five workmanlike innings, then turned the game over to the bullpen. Home runs by Yastrzemski, Smith, and Petrocelli in the fourth inning put Boston ahead 4–2, but two runs in the seventh by the Cards tied the score at 4–4. In the bottom of the seventh, however, the Boston batters drove across four runs to spark an 8–4 victory and send the Series into a final confrontation.

The seventh game matched the aces, Bob Gibson against Jim Lonborg. Although he had popular sentiment behind him, Lonborg was pitching tired on two days' rest, while Gibson had rested three days since his last outing. From the start, it was apparent that Lonborg was struggling. Three Cardinal hits and a wild pitch put St. Louis ahead 2–0 in the third inning. Two more scored in the fifth on a home run by Gibson, Brock's single and two stolen bases, and an outfield fly by Maris. A Boston run in the fifth cut the score to 4–1, but the Red Sox dream was abruptly halted in the sixth on a three-run homer by Javier off the arm-weary Lonborg. With the 7–2 defeat, the "impossible dream" ended one game too early, thanks mostly to Brock, who hit .414 and stole a record seven bases, and Gibson, who won three outstanding games.

Game 1 October 4 at Boston

St.L.	001	000	100
Bos.	001	000	000

St. Louis	Pos	AB	R	H	RBI	PO	A	E
Brock	lf	4	2	4	0	2	0	0
Flood	cf	5	0	1	0	2	0	0
Maris	rf	4	0	1	2	3	0	0
Cepeda	1b	4	0	0	0	6	0	0
McCarver	c	3	0	0	0	11	2	0
Shannon	3b	4	0	2	0	0	1	0
Javier	2b	4	0	2	0	1	1	0
Maxvill	ss	2	0	0	0	2	2	0
Bob Gibson	p	4	0	0	0	0	0	0
Totals		34	2	10	2	27	6	0

Pitching	IP	H	R	ER	BB	SO
St. Louis						
Gibson (W)	9	6	1	1	1	10
Boston						
Santiago (L)	7	10	2	2	3	5
Wyatt	2	0	0	0	2	1

Doubles—Flood, Scott. Home Run—Santiago. Stolen Bases—Brock 2. Sacrifice hit—Howard. Double Plays—Jones to Scott; Jones to Adair to Scott. Left on Bases—St. Louis 10, Boston 5. Balk—Wyatt. Passed Ball—Gibson. Umpires—Stevens (A), Barlick (N), Umont (A), Donatelli (N), Runge (A), Pryor (N). Attendance—34,796. Time of Game—2:22.

Boston	Pos	AB	R	H	RBI	PO	A	E
Adair	2b	4	0	0	0	2	3	0
Jones	3b	4	0	1	0	2	2	0
Yastrzemski	lf	4	0	0	0	4	1	0
Harrelson	rf	3	0	0	0	1	0	0
Wyatt	p	0	0	0	0	0	0	0
c Foy		1	0	0	0	0	0	0
Scott	1b	3	0	2	0	8	0	0
Petrocelli	ss	3	0	0	0	0	0	0
d Andrews		1	0	0	0	0	0	0
Smith	cf	3	0	1	0	1	0	0
Russ Gibson	c	2	0	0	0	8	0	0
a Siebern	rf	1	0	1	0	0	0	0
b Tartabull	rf	0	0	0	0	1	0	0
Santiago	p	3	1	1	1	0	0	0
Howard	c	0	0	0	0	1	0	0
Totals		31	1	6	1	27	6	0

a At bat for Gibson when side retired in 7th.
b Ran for Siebern in 8th.
c Ground out for Wyatt in 9th.
d Flied out for Petrocelli in 9th.

1st Inning
St. Louis
  Brock singled to left.
    Brock stole second.
1 Flood fanned.
  Maris fanned.
2,3 Cepeda hit into DP (Jones to Scott).
Boston
1 Adair struck out.
2 Jones fanned.
3 Yastrzemski fouled to first.

2nd Inning
St. Louis
1 McCarver struck out.
  Shannon singled to left.
  Javier singled, Shannon to third.
  Maxvill walked, loading the bases.
2,3 Gibson grounded into DP (Jones to Adair to Scott).
Boston
1 Harrelson flied to right.
  Scott singled to left-center.
2 Petrocelli fanned.
3 Smith struck out.

3rd Inning
St. Louis
  Brock singled to center.
  Flood doubled, Brock to third.
1 Maris grounded to first, scoring Brock with Flood to third.
2 Cepeda fouled to third.
  McCarver walked.
3 Shannon popped to second.
Boston
1 Gibson struck out.
  Santiago homered in left-center.
2 Adair struck out.
3 Jones popped to Cepeda in right.

4th Inning
St. Louis
  Javier singled to center.
1 Maxvill grounded to second, Javier to second.
2 Gibson struck out.
  Brock singled to left. Javier was out
3 at the plate, Yastrzemski to Gibson.
Boston
1 Yastrzemski grounded to second.
2 Harrelson flied to center.
  Scott doubled off the left field wall.
3 Petrocelli fanned.

5th Inning
St. Louis
1 Flood flew to left (great leaping catch by Yastrzemski).
  Maris singled to right-center.
2 Cepeda popped to first.
3 McCarver fouled to the catcher.
Boston
1 Smith flied to deep right.
2 Gibson fanned.
3 Santiago struck out.

6th Inning
St. Louis
  Shannon singled to center.
  Shannon to second on Gibson's passed ball.
1 Javier struck out.
2 Maxvill fouled to the catcher.
3 Gibson flied to left.
Boston
1 Adair grounded to third.
  Jones singled to center.
2 Yastrzemski flied to short left.
3 Harrelson fouled to the catcher.

7th Inning
St. Louis
  Brock singled to right (fourth hit).
    Brock stole second.
1 Flood grounded to first, Brock to third.
2 Maris grounded to second scoring Brock.
3 Cepeda struck out.
Boston
1 Scott grounded to short.
2 Petrocelli struck out.
  Smith singled to second.
    Siebern batting for Gibson, Smith
3 out stealing McCarver to Maxvill.

8th Inning
St. Louis
  For Boston—Siebern in right, Wyatt pitching, Howard catching.
1 McCarver flied to center.
2 Shannon flied to left.
3 Javier fanned.
Boston
  Siebern singled to center.
  Tartabull ran for Siebern.
1 Howard sacrificed, McCarver to Javier.
2 Adair flied to center.
3 Jones popped to Maxvill in short left.

9th Inning
St. Louis
  For Boston—Tartabull in right.
  Maxvill walked.
1 Gibson fouled to Scott (attempting to sacrifice).
  Brock walked.
2 Flood flied to right.
  Wyatt balked advancing Maxvill to third and Brock to second.
3 Maris flied to left.
Boston
1 Yastrzemski flied to left.
2 Foy pinch hit for Wyatt and grounded to short.
  Scott walked.
3 Andrews, batting for Petrocelli, flied to right.

Game 2 October 5 at Boston

St. L.	000 000 000
Bos.	000 101 30x

St. Louis	Pos	AB	R	H	RBI	PO	A	E
Brock	lf	4	0	0	0	4	0	0
Flood	cf	3	0	0	0	3	0	0
Maris	rf	3	0	0	0	4	0	0
Cepeda	1b	3	0	0	0	1	1	0
McCarver	c	3	0	0	0	9	0	0
Shannon	3b	3	0	0	0	1	1	1
Javier	2b	3	0	1	0	0	1	0
Maxvill	ss	2	0	0	0	1	0	0
a Tolan		1	0	0	0	0	0	0
Bressoud	ss	0	0	0	0	0	0	0
Hughes	p	2	0	0	0	1	0	0
Willis	p	0	0	0	0	0	0	0
Hoerner	p	0	0	0	0	0	0	0
Lamabe	p	0	0	0	0	0	0	0
b Ricketts		1	0	0	0	0	0	0
Totals		28	0	1	0	24	3	1

a Grounded out for Maxvill in 8th.
b Popped out for Lamabe in 9th.

Double—Javier. Home Runs—Yastrzemski 2. Stolen Base—Adair. Sacrifice Fly—Petrocelli. Left on Bases—St. Louis 2, Boston 11. Umpires—Barlick, Umont, Donatelli, Runge, Pryor, Stevens. Attendance—35,188. Time of Game—2:24.

1st Inning
St. Louis
1 Brock lined to short.
2 Flood grounded to third.
3 Maris flied to right.
Boston
1 Tartabull flied to right.
2 Jones fanned.
  Yastrzemski walked.
3 Scott struck out.

2nd Inning
St. Louis
1 Cepeda flied to left.
2 McCarver grounded out, Scott to Lonborg.
3 Shannon struck out.
Boston
1 Smith fouled to the catcher.
2 Adair flied to deep left.
  Petrocelli singled to left.
3 Howard flied to deep center.

3rd Inning
St. Louis
1 Javier grounded to short.
2 Maxvill lined to first.
3 Hughes struck out.
Boston
1 Lonborg struck out.
2 Tartabull struck out.
3 Jones flied to right.

4th Inning
St. Louis
1 Brock grounded to second, out by a step.
2 Flood grounded to third.
3 Maris popped to Petrocelli.
Boston
  Yastrzemski homered into the right-field stands.
  Scott lined to deep left.
1 Smith flied to Brock.
  Adair singled on a tap down the third base line, Scott stopped at second.
2 Petrocelli fanned.
3 Howard forced Adair at second, Javier to Maxvill.

5th Inning
St. Louis
1 Cepeda grounded to third.
2 McCarver flied to left.
3 Shannon struck out.
Boston
1 Lonborg flied to short right.
2 Tartabull flied to center.
3 Jones grounded out, Cepeda to Hughes.

6th Inning
St. Louis
1 Javier flied to right.
2 Maxvill grounded to short.
3 Hughes struck out.

6th Inning (continued)
Boston
1 Yastrzemski flied to left.
  Scott walked.
  Smith walked.
  Adair grounded to Shannon who fumbled for an error, loading the bases.
  For St. Louis—Willis pitching.
2 Petrocelli flied deep to center scoring Scott with Smith advancing to third. Adair stole second.
  Howard intentionally walked to load the bases.
3 Lonborg struck out.

7th Inning
St. Louis
1 Brock grounded to second.
  Flood walked (the first Cardinal base-runner).
2 Maris flied to left.
3 Cepeda forced Flood, Petrocelli to Adair.
Boston
  Tartabull walked.
  Jones singled in the infield, Tartabull stopped at second.
  For St. Louis—Hoerner pitching.
  Yastrzemski hit a three-run homer into the right-center field stands (his second of the game).
1 Scott lined out to left.
2 Smith flied to right.
  Adair singled to center.
  Petrocelli walked.
  For St. Louis—Lamabe pitching.
3 Howard struck out.

8th Inning
St. Louis
1 McCarver grounded to second.
2 Shannon grounded to short.
  Javier doubled into the left field corner breaking up Lonborg's no-hitter.
3 Tolan, pinch hitting for Maxvill, grounded to second.
Boston
  For St. Louis—Bressoud at short.
1 Lonborg struck out.
2 Tartabull fouled to Shannon.
  Jones singled to right.
  Yastrzemski singled to right-center, Jones advancing to third.
3 Scott grounded to third.

9th Inning
St. Louis
1 Ricketts, pinch hitting for Lamabe, popped to short.
2 Brock grounded to second.
3 Flood flied to center.

Boston	Pos	AB	R	H	RBI	PO	A	E
Tartabull	rf	4	1	0	0	2	0	0
Jones	3b	5	1	2	0	0	3	0
Yastrzemski	lf	4	2	3	4	3	0	0
Scott	1b	4	1	1	0	12	1	0
Smith	cf	3	0	0	0	1	0	0
Adair	2b	4	0	2	0	1	4	0
Petrocelli	ss	2	0	1	1	3	5	0
Howard	c	3	0	0	0	4	0	0
Lonborg	p	4	0	0	0	1	0	0
Totals		33	5	9	5	27	13	0

Pitching	IP	H	R	ER	BB	SO
St. Louis						
Hughes (L)	5⅓	4	2	1	3	5
Willis	*⅔	1	2	2	2	1
Hoerner	⅔	2	1	1	1	0
Lamabe	1⅓	2	0	0	0	2
Boston						
Lonborg (W)	9	1	0	0	0	4

*Pitched to two batters in 7th.

Game 3 October 7 at St. Louis

Bos.	000 001 100
St. L.	120 001 01x

Boston	Pos	AB	R	H	RBI	PO	A	E
Tartabull	rf	4	0	0	0	3	0	0
Jones	3b	4	0	3	1	2	1	0
Yastrzemski	lf	3	0	0	0	1	0	0
Scott	1b	4	0	0	0	8	1	0
Smith	cf	4	1	2	1	2	0	0
Adair	2b	4	0	0	0	2	2	0
Petrocelli	ss	4	0	1	0	1	5	0
Howard	c	2	0	1	0	5	0	0
Bell	p	0	0	0	0	0	1	0
a Thomas		1	0	0	0	0	0	0
Waslewski	p	0	0	0	0	1	0	0
b Andrews		1	1	1	0	0	0	0
Stange	p	0	0	0	0	0	0	1
c Foy		1	0	0	0	0	0	0
Osinski	p	0	0	0	0	0	0	0
Totals		32	2	7	2	24	11	1

a Struck out for Bell in 3rd.
b Singled for Waslewski in 6th.
c Grounded out for Stange in 8th.

Double—Cepeda. Triple—Brock. Home Runs—Shannon, Smith. Double Plays—Bell to Petrocelli to Scott; Javier to Maxvill to Cepeda. Left on Bases—Boston 4, St. Louis 3. Hit by Pitcher—Yastrzemski (by Briles). Umpires—Umont, Donatelli, Runge, Pryor, Stevens, Barlick. Attendance—54,575. Time of Game—2:15.

1st Inning
Boston
1 Tartabull grounded to second.
2 Jones struck out.
  Yastrzemski was hit by a pitch.
3 Pitch rolls away for McCarver, Yastrzemski thrown out going to second, McCarver to Maxvill.
St. Louis
  Brock tripled to left-center.
  Flood singled to center, Brock scoring.
1,2 Maris grounded into a double play, Bell to Petrocelli to Scott.
3 Cepeda fouled to third.

2nd Inning
Boston
1 Scott grounded out (off Brile's leg), Javier to Cepeda.
2 Smith popped to third.
3 Adair grounded to third.
St. Louis
  McCarver singled to center.
  Shannon hit a two-run homer to left.
  Javier singled but was out trying for
1 second (Yastrzemski to Adair).
2 Maxvill fanned.
3 Briles grounded to second.

3rd Inning
Boston
1 Petrocelli flied to left.
  Howard singled down the right field line.
2 Thomas, pinch hitting for Bell, fanned.
3 Tartabull popped to center.
St. Louis
  For Boston—Waslewski pitching.
1 Brock struck out.
2 Flood grounded to second.
3 Maris flied to right.

4th Inning
Boston
  Jones singled to left.
1,2 Yastrzemski grounded into a double play, Javier to Maxvill to Cepeda.
3 Scott struck out.
St. Louis
1 Cepeda struck out.
2 McCarver grounded out, Scott to Waslewski.
3 Shannon grounded to short.

5th Inning
Boston
  Smith singled to right.
1 Adair popped to first.
2 Petrocelli flied to center.
3 Howard fanned.
St. Louis
1 Javier struck out.
2 Maxvill flied to right.
3 Briles grounded to short.

6th Inning
Boston
  Andrews, pinch hitting for Waslewski, singled to center.
1 Tartabull out bunting, Briles to Cepeda, Andrews advancing to second (not counted as a sacrifice hit).
  Jones singled to right, scoring Andrews.
2 Yastrzemski grounded to second, Jones stopping at second.
3 Scott grounded to Maxvill.
St. Louis
  For Boston—Stange pitching.
  Brock bunted for a single.
  Stange attempting to pick off Brock threw wild into right Brock going to third.
1 Flood flied to short right.
  Maris singled to right-center, scoring Brock.
2 Cepeda fouled to the catcher.
3 McCarver fouled to third.

7th Inning
Boston
  Smith homered over the fence in right.
1 Adair grounded to short.
2 Petrocelli flied to left.
3 Howard grounded to second.
St. Louis
  Shannon bunted for a single.
1 Javier grounded to short, Shannon advanced to second.
2 Maxvill flied to center.
3 Briles popped to second.

8th Inning
Boston
1 Foy, pinch hitting for Stange, grounded to short.
2 Tartabull flied to deep center. Jones singled to center.
3 Yastrzemski grounded to second.
St. Louis
  For Boston—Osinski pitching.
1 Brock flied to center.
2 Flood grounded to third.
  Maris beat out an infield tap for a single.
  Cepeda doubled off the wall in right-center, scoring Maris.
3 McCarver grounded to short.

9th Inning
Boston
1 Scott grounded to third.
2 Smith called out for interference when he ran into McCarver trying to catch his foul down the first base line (McCarver gets the putout).
3 Adair popped to third.

St. Louis	Pos	AB	R	H	RBI	PO	A	E
Brock	lf	4	2	2	0	2	0	0
Flood	cf	4	0	1	1	3	0	0
Maris	rf	4	1	2	1	0	0	0
Cepeda	1b	4	0	1	1	13	2	0
McCarver	c	4	1	1	0	5	1	0
Shannon	3b	3	1	2	2	2	2	0
Javier	2b	3	0	1	0	0	6	0
Maxvill	ss	3	0	0	0	2	4	0
Briles	p	3	0	0	0	0	2	0
Totals		32	5	10	5	27	15	0

Pitching	IP	H	R	ER	BB	SO
Boston						
Bell (L)	2	5	3	3	0	1
Waslewski	3	0	0	0	0	3
Stange	2	3	1	0	0	0
Osinski	1	2	1	1	0	0
St. Louis						
Briles (W)	9	7	2	2	0	4

Game 4 October 8 at St. Louis

Bos.	0 0 0	0 0 0	0 0 0
St.L.	4 0 2	0 0 0	0 0 x

Boston	Pos	AB	R	H	RBI	PO	A	E
Tartabull	rf	4	0	2	0	1	0	0
Jones	3b	4	0	0	0	0	2	0
Yastrzemski	lf	4	0	2	0	3	0	0
Scott	1b	4	0	1	0	9	0	0
Smith	cf	3	0	0	0	3	0	0
Adair	2b	4	0	0	0	2	2	0
Petrocelli	ss	3	0	0	0	2	4	0
Howard	c	2	0	0	0	0	0	0
Brett	p	0	0	0	0	0	0	0
Santiago	p	0	0	0	0	0	0	0
Bell	p	0	0	0	0	0	0	0
a Foy		1	0	0	0	0	0	0
Stephenson	p	0	0	0	0	0	0	0
Morehead	p	0	0	0	0	0	0	0
b Siebern		1	0	0	0	0	0	0
Ryan	c	2	0	0	0	4	0	0
Totals		32	0	5	0	24	8	0

a Struck out for Bell in 3rd.
b Flied out for Morehead in 8th.

Doubles—Maris, Cepeda, Brock, Javier, Yastrzemski. Stolen Base—Brock. Sacrifice Fly—McCarver. Left on Bases—Boston 6, St. Louis 6. Wild Pitch—Stephenson. Umpires—Donatelli, Runge, Pryor, Stevens, Barlick, Umont. Attendance—54,575. Time of Game—2:05.

St. Louis	Pos	AB	R	H	RBI	PO	A	E
Brock	lf	4	1	2	0	2	0	0
Flood	cf	4	1	1	0	3	0	0
Maris	rf	4	1	1	2	2	0	0
Cepeda	1b	4	0	1	0	11	1	0
McCarver	c	3	1	1	2	7	0	0
Shannon	3b	4	0	0	0	0	2	0
Javier	2b	4	0	2	1	0	2	0
Maxvill	ss	3	0	1	1	0	2	0
Gibson	p	3	0	0	0	2	2	0
Totals		32	6	9	6	27	9	0

Pitching	IP	H	R	ER	BB	SO
Boston						
Santiago (L)	⅔	6	4	4	0	0
Bell	1⅓	0	0	0	0	0
Stephenson	2	3	2	2	1	0
Morehead	3	0	0	0	1	2
Brett	1	0	0	0	1	1
St. L.						
Gibson (W)	9	5	0	0	1	6

1st Inning
Boston
1 Tartabull grounded out, Cepeda to Gibson.
2 Jones grounded to the pitcher. Yastrzemski singled to right.
3 Scott struck out.
St. Louis
Brock singled with a slow roller to third.
Flood singled to left, Brock stops at second.
Maris doubled into the left field corner, scoring Brock and Flood.
1 Cepeda flied to right, with Maris advancing to third.
McCarver singled to right, scoring Maris.
2 Shannon fouled to Petrocelli. Javier singled between short and third, McCarver to second.
Maxvill singled to left, scoring McCarver Javier to third and Maxvill to second on the throw to the plate.
For Boston—Bell pitching.
3 Gibson flied to left.

2nd Inning
Boston
1 Smith grounded to second.
2 Adair fanned.
3 Petrocelli fanned.
St. Louis
1 Brock flied to left.
2 Flood popped to first.
3 Maris grounded to first.

3rd Inning
Boston
1 Howard fouled to first.
2 Foy, pinch hitting for Bell, struck out.
3 Tartabull grounded to first.
St. Louis
For Boston—Stephenson pitching.
Cepeda doubled into the left field corner.
A wild pitch moves Cepeda to third.
1 McCarver hit a sacrifice fly to center, scoring Cepeda.
Shannon walked.
Javier doubled inside the third base line, scoring Shannon.
2 Maxvill grounded to short, Javier advancing to third.
3 Gibson flied to center.

4th Inning
Boston
1 Jones flied to left.
2 Yastrzemski grounded to the pitcher. Scott singled to left.
3 Smith grounded to first.
St. Louis
Brock hit an automatic double off the right-center field wall as a spectator had touched the ball (Brock had made it to third).
1 Flood grounded to second, advancing Brock to third.
2 Maris grounded to first, Brock holds third.
3 Cepeda grounded to third.

5th Inning
Boston
1 Adair grounded to third.
2 Petrocelli grounded to third.
3 Howard flied to center.
St. Louis
For Boston—Morehead pitching (batting eighth), Ryan catching (batting ninth).
1 McCarver struck out.
2 Shannon grounded to second.
3 Javier fanned.

6th Inning
Boston
1 Ryan fanned.
Tartabull singled off Gibson's glove.
2 Jones flied to left.
3 Yastrzemski grounded to short.
St. Louis
1 Maxvill grounded to third. Gibson walked.
2 Brock forced Gibson, Petrocelli to Adair.
Brock stole second.
3 Flood grounded to short.

7th Inning
Boston
1 Scott grounded to short. Smith walked.
2 Adair fouled to the catcher.
3 Petrocelli popped to the pitcher.
St. Louis
1 Maris flied to left.
2 Cepeda flied to center.
3 McCarver popped to short.

8th Inning
Boston
1 Siebern, pinch hitting for Morehead, flied deep to center.
2 Ryan flied to center.
Tartabull singled to center.
3 Jones flied to right.
St. Louis
For Boston—Brett pitching.
1 Shannon fouled to the catcher.
2 Javier struck out.
Maxvill walked.
3 Gibson forced Maxvill, Petrocelli to Adair.

9th Inning
Boston
Yastrzemski doubled to right-center.
1 Scott flied to right, Yastrzemski advancing to third.
2 Smith fanned.
3 Adair grounded to second.

Game 5 October 9 at St. Louis

Bos.	0 0 1	0 0 0	0 0 2
St.L.	0 0 0	0 0 0	0 0 1

Boston	Pos	AB	R	H	RBI	PO	A	E
Foy	3b	5	1	1	0	2	4	0
Andrews	2b	3	0	1	0	1	2	0
Yastrzemski	lf	3	0	1	0	2	0	0
Harrelson	rf	3	0	1	1	1	0	0
Tartabull	rf	0	0	0	0	1	0	0
Scott	1b	4	1	0	0	14	0	0
Smith	cf	4	1	1	0	1	0	0
Petrocelli	ss	3	0	0	0	1	2	1
Howard	c	4	0	1	1	5	0	0
Lonborg	p	4	0	0	0	0	2	0
Totals		32	3	6	2	27	10	1

Pitching	IP	H	R	ER	BB	SO
Boston						
Lonborg (W)	9	3	1	1	0	4
St. L.						
Carlton (L)	6	3	1	0	0	5
Washburn	2	1	0	0	0	2
Willis	*0	1	2	1	1	0
Lamabe	1	1	0	0	0	2

*Faced 3 batters in 9th.

St. Louis	Pos	AB	R	H	RBI	PO	A	E
Brock	lf	4	0	0	0	0	0	0
Flood	cf	4	0	0	0	3	0	0
Maris	rf	4	1	2	1	3	0	1
Cepeda	1b	4	0	0	0	5	0	0
McCarver	c	3	0	0	0	9	1	0
Shannon	3b	3	0	0	0	1	3	1
Javier	2b	3	0	0	0	4	3	0
Maxvill	ss	2	0	1	0	3	4	0
b Ricketts		1	0	0	0	0	0	0
Willis	p	0	0	0	0	0	0	0
Lamabe	p	0	0	0	0	0	1	0
a Tolan		1	0	0	0	0	0	0
Washburn	p	0	0	0	0	0	1	0
c Gagliano		1	0	0	0	0	0	0
Bressoud	ss	0	0	0	0	0	0	0
Totals		31	1	3	1	27	13	2

a Struck out for Carlton in 6th.
b Grounded out for Maxvill in 8th.
c Popped out for Washburn in 8th.

Doubles—Yastrzemski, Smith. Home Run—Maris. Sacrifice Hit—Andrews. Double Plays—Javier, Maxvill and Cepeda; McCarver, Javier, McCarver, Shannon, Lamabe and McCarver. Left on Bases—Boston 7, St. Louis 3. Wild Pitch—Carlton. Umpires—Runge, Pryor, Stevens, Barlick, Umont, Donatelli. Attendance—54,575. Time of Game—2:20.

1st Inning
Boston
1 Foy struck out.
2 Andrews popped to second. Yastrzemski walked.
3 Harrelson forced Yastrzemski, Maxvill to Javier.
St. Louis
1 Brock flied to deep right.
2 Flood grounded to third.
3 Maris grounded to first.

2nd Inning
Boston
McCarver let Scott's third strike get by and he reached first safely (ruled a wild pitch).
1 Smith flied to deep center.
2 Petrocelli flied to right.
3 Howard forced Scott, Maxvill to Javier.
St. Louis
1 Cepeda struck out.
2 McCarver flied to left.
3 Shannon fouled to the catcher.

3rd Inning
Boston
1 Lonborg struck out.
Foy singled to left.
Andrews bunted a sacrifice to Shannon who fumbled the ball and was charged with an error.
2 Yastrzemski looked at a third strike. Harrelson singled to left, scoring Foy with Andrews stopping at second.
3 Scott flied to right.
St. Louis
1 Javier bounced to the pitcher. Maxvill singled to the right of second.
2 Carlton popped to Foy on an attempted sacrifice.
3 Brock struck out.

4th Inning
Boston
1 Smith popped to short.
2 Petrocelli grounded to third.
3 Howard fouled to Maris.
St. Louis
1 Flood grounded to first. Maris singled to right.
2 Cepeda fouled to Yastrzemski.
3 McCarver grounded to the pitcher.

5th Inning
Boston
1 Lonborg fanned.
2 Foy flied to deep center. Andrews singled to right.
3 Yastrzemski forced Andrews, Javier to Maxvill.
St. Louis
1 Shannon fanned.
2 Javier fouled to third.
3 Maxvill grounded to 9th.

6th Inning
Boston
Harrelson walked.
1,2 Tartabull grounded into a double play, Javier to Maxvill to Cepeda (A great stop and throw by Javier).
3 Smith popped to second.
St. Louis
1 Tolan, pinch hitting for Carlton, looked at a called third strike.
2 Brock grounded to first.
3 Flood grounded to second.

7th Inning
Boston
For St. Louis—Washburn pitching.
1 Petrocelli fanned.
2 Howard tapped to the pitcher.
3 Lonborg fouled to third.
St. Louis
1 Maris popped to Andrews in short right.
2 Cepeda grounded to short.
3 McCarver flied to center.

8th Inning
Boston
1 Foy struck out.
2 Andrews grounded to third. Yastrzemski doubled down the left field line.
3 Harrelson grounded to short.
St. Louis
For Boston—Tartabull in right.
1 Shannon grounded to short. Javier safe on an error by Petrocelli.
2 Ricketts, pinch hitting for Maxvill, grounded to first, advancing Javier to second.
3 Gagliano, pinch hitting for Washburn, popped to short.

9th Inning
Boston
For St. Louis—Bressoud at short, Willis pitching.
Scott walked.
Smith doubled down the left field line, Scott stopping at third.
Petrocelli intentionally walked, loading the bases.
For St. Louis—Lamabe pitching after a 1–0 count on Howard.
Howard popped a single into short right scoring Scott. On high throw to the plate by Maris, Smith also scored with Petrocelli going to third.
1 Lonborg struck out on foul third strike bunt.
2,3 Foy struck out with Howard going for second, Petrocelli got trapped in a double play run-down between third and home (McCarver to Javier to McCarver to Shannon to Lamabe to McCarver).
St. Louis
1 Brock grounded to second.
2 Flood grounded to third. Maris homered over the right field fence.
3 Cepeda grounded to third.

Game 6 October 11 at Boston

St.L.	002	000	200	
Bos.	010	300	40x	

St. Louis	Pos	AB	R	H	RBI	PO	A	E
Brock	lf	5	2	2	3	2	0	0
Flood	cf	5	0	1	1	2	0	0
Maris	rf	4	0	2	0	2	0	0
Cepeda	1b	5	0	1	0	10	0	0
McCarver	c	3	0	0	0	2	0	0
Shannon	3b	4	0	1	0	1	4	0
Javier	2b	4	1	1	0	3	3	0
Maxvill	ss	3	0	0	0	2	2	0
Hughes	p	1	0	0	0	0	0	0
Willis	p	0	0	0	0	0	0	0
a Spiezio		1	0	0	0	0	0	0
Briles	p	0	0	0	0	0	2	0
b Tolan		0	1	0	0	0	0	0
Lamabe	p	0	0	0	0	0	0	0
Hoerner	p	0	0	0	0	0	0	0
Jaster	p	0	0	0	0	0	0	0
Washburn	p	0	0	0	0	0	0	0
c Ricketts		1	0	0	0	0	0	0
Woodeshick	p	0	0	0	0	0	1	0
Totals		36	4	8	4	24	12	0

a Grounded out for Willis in 5th.
b Walked for Briles in 7th.
c Flied out for Washburn in 8th.
d Singled for Wyatt in 7th.
e Hit sacrifice fly for Tartabull in 7th.

Doubles—Javier, Foy, Shannon. Home Runs—Petrocelli 2, Yastrzemski, Smith, Brock. Stolen Base—Brock. Sacrifice Hit—Foy. Sacrifice Fly—Adair. Left on Bases—St. Louis 9, Boston 7. Hit by Pitcher—Waslewski (by Briles). Umpires—Pryor, Stevens, Barlick, Umont, Donatelli, Runge. Attendance—35,188. Time of Game—2:48.

Boston	Pos	AB	R	H	RBI	PO	A	E
Foy	3b	4	1	1	1	3	3	0
Andrews	2b	5	1	2	1	0	2	0
Yastrzemski	lf	4	2	3	1	2	0	0
Harrelson	rf	3	0	0	0	1	0	0
Tartabull	rf	0	0	0	0	0	0	0
e Adair		0	0	0	1	0	0	0
Thomas	rf	1	0	0	0	1	0	0
Scott	1b	4	0	1	0	10	1	0
Smith	cf	4	1	2	2	4	0	0
Petrocelli	ss	3	2	2	2	1	3	1
Howard	c	4	0	0	0	4	0	0
Waslewski	p	1	0	0	0	1	0	0
Wyatt	p	0	0	0	0	0	0	0
d Jones		1	1	1	0	0	0	0
Bell	p	0	0	0	0	0	1	0
Totals		34	8	12	8	27	10	1

Pitching	IP	H	R	ER	BB	SO
St. Louis						
Hughes	3⅔	5	4	4	0	2
Willis	⅓	0	0	0	0	0
Briles	2	0	0	0	1	0
Lamabe (L)	⅓	2	2	2	0	0
Hoerner	*0	2	2	2	0	0
Jaster	⅓	2	0	0	0	0
Washburn	⅓	0	0	0	1	0
Woodeshick	1	1	0	0	0	0
Boston						
Waslewski	5⅓	4	2	2	2	4
Wyatt (W)	1⅔	1	2	2	1	0
Bell (SV)	2	3	0	0	1	0

*Faced 2 batters in 7th.

1st Inning
St. Louis
1 Brock struck out.
2 Flood grounded to second.
3 Maris fanned.
Boston
1 Foy popped to second.
2 Andrews flied to deep left.
Yastrzemski singled past first.
3 Harrelson struck out.

2nd Inning
St. Louis
1 Cepeda fouled to third.
2 McCarver grounded to short.
3 Shannon grounded to short.
Boston
1 Scott flied to left.
2 Smith flied to right.
Petrocelli homered over left field wall.
3 Howard grounded to second.

3rd Inning
St. Louis
Javier doubled off the left field wall.
1 Maxvill grounded to short, Javier held second.
2 Hughes fanned.
Brock singled to right, scoring Javier.
Brock stole second.
Flood singled to left, scoring Brock on a great slide.
Maris singled to right, Flood to third.
3 Cepeda grounded to third.
Boston
1 Waslewski looked at a third strike.
2 Foy popped to short.
3 Andrews fouled to third.

4th Inning
St. Louis
1 McCarver grounded to first.
Shannon to first on Petrocelli's error.
2 Javier popped to third.
3 Maxvill flied to center.
Boston
Yastrzemski homered over the wall in left-center.
1 Harrelson flied to very deep center.
2 Scott grounded to short.
Smith homered in to right field stands.
Petrocelli hit his second homer over the left field wall **(New World Series record of 3 homers in inning).**
For St. Louis—Willis pitching.
3 Howard grounded to third.

5th Inning
St. Louis
1 Spiezio, pinch hitting for Willis, grounded to third.
2 Brock grounded out, Scott to Waslewski.
3 Flood struck out.
Boston
For St. Louis—Briles pitching.
Waslewski hit by pitched ball.
1 Foy sacrificed Waslewski to second, Briles to Javier.
2 Andrews grounded to third, Waslewski held second.
Yastrzemski to first with an intentional walk.
3 Harrelson popped to second.

6th Inning
St. Louis
Maris walked.
1 Cepeda flied to right.
McCarver walked.
For Boston—Wyatt came in to pitch with a 1–0 count on Shannon.
2 Shannon popped to short.
3 Javier grounded to third.
Boston
1 Scott grounded out to the pitcher
2 Smith grounded to second.
3 Petrocelli flied to short right.

7th Inning
St. Louis
For Boston—Tartabull in right field.
1 Maxvill flied to deep center.
Tolan, batting for Briles, walked.
Brock hit a two-run homer into the right-center field bleachers.
2 Flood flied to center.
3 Maris flied to center.
Boston
For St. Louis—Lamabe pitching.
1 Howard grounded to third.
Jones, pinch hitting for Wyatt, singled to right.
Foy doubled to left, scoring Jones (went to third on throw to plate).
For St. Louis—Hoerner pitching.
Andrews singled to left, scoring Foy.
Yastrzemski singled to right, advancing Andrews to third.
For St. Louis—Jaster pitching.
2 Adair, pinch hitting for Tartabull, hit a sacrifice fly to center, scoring Andrews.
Scott singled past short.
Smith singled to left, scoring Yastrzemski, Scott going to third, Smith went to second on the throw to the plate.
For St. Louis—Washburn the fourth Cardinal pitcher in the inning.
Petrocelli intentionally walked to load the bases.
3 Howard grounded to third.

8th Inning
St. Louis
For Boston—Bell pitching (batting eighth), and Thomas in right (batting ninth).
Cepeda beat out an infield roller.
1 McCarver hit a liner to Yastrzemski (Great catch in left-center).
Shannon doubled off left field wall.
2 Javier lined to third.
Maxvill walked.
3 Ricketts, batting for Washburn, flied to left.
Boston
For St. Louis—Woodeshick pitching **(ties Series Record of 8 pitchers used and sets two team record of 11 pitchers).**
1 Thomas grounded to short.
2 Foy grounded to the pitcher.
Andrews singled off the second base bag.
3 Yastrzemski forced Andrews, Javier to Maxvill.

9th Inning
St. Louis
1 Brock flied to deep right.
2 Flood grounded to second.
Maris singled to left.
3 Cepeda tapped to the pitcher.

Game 7 October 12 at Boston

St. L.	002	023	000	
Bos.	000	010	010	

St. Louis	Pos	AB	R	H	RBI	PO	A	E
Brock	lf	4	1	2	0	1	0	0
Flood	cf	3	1	1	1	0	0	0
Maris	rf	3	0	2	1	1	0	0
Cepeda	1b	5	0	0	0	6	2	0
McCarver	c	5	1	1	0	12	0	0
Shannon	3b	4	1	0	0	0	0	0
Javier	2b	4	1	2	3	4	4	1
Maxvill	ss	4	1	1	0	3	3	0
Bob Gibson	p	4	1	1	1	0	1	0
Totals		36	7	10	6	27	10	1

Pitching	IP	H	R	ER	BB	SO
St. Louis						
Gibson (W)	9	3	2	2	3	10
Boston						
Lonborg (L)	6	10	7	6	1	3
Santiago	2	0	0	0	0	1
Morehead	⅓	0	0	0	3	1
Osinski	⅓	0	0	0	0	0
Brett	⅓	0	0	0	0	0

Boston	Pos	AB	R	H	RBI	PO	A	E
Foy	3b	3	0	0	0	2	3	1
Morehead	p	0	0	0	0	0	0	0
Osinski	p	0	0	0	0	0	0	0
Brett	p	0	0	0	0	0	0	0
Andrews	2b	3	0	0	0	1	2	0
Yastrzemski	lf	3	0	1	0	2	0	0
Harrelson	rf	4	0	0	0	3	0	0
Scott	1b	4	1	1	0	9	0	0
Smith	cf	3	0	0	0	2	0	0
Petrocelli	ss	3	1	1	0	3	2	0
Howard	c	2	0	0	0	4	1	0
b Jones	3b	0	0	0	0	0	0	0
Lonborg	p	1	0	0	0	0	0	0
a Tartabull		1	0	0	0	0	0	0
Santiago	p	0	0	0	0	0	0	0
c Siebern		1	0	0	1	0	0	0
Russ Gibson	c	0	0	0	0	1	0	0
Totals		28	2	3	1	27	8	1

a Struck out for Lonborg in 6th.
b Walked for Howard in 8th.
c Hit into force for Santiago in 8th.

Doubles—McCarver, Brock, Petrocelli. Triples—Maxvill, Scott. Home Runs—Bob Gibson, Javier. Stolen Bases—Brock 3. Sacrifice Hit—Andrews. Sacrifice Fly—Maris. Double Play—Maxvill, Javier and Cepeda. Left on Bases—St. Louis 7, Boston 3. Wild Pitches—Lonborg, Gibson. Umpires—Stevens, Barlick, Umont, Donatelli, Runge, Pryor. Attendance—35,188. Time of Game—2:23.

1st Inning
St. Louis
1 Brock flied to left (good catch).
2 Flood flied to center.
Maris singled off Lonborg's glove.
3 Cepeda grounded to second.
Boston
Foy walked.
1 Andrews sacrificed Foy to second, Cepeda to Javier.
2 Yastrzemski popped to Maxvill.
3 Harrelson looked at a third strike.

2nd Inning
St. Louis
1 McCarver popped to short.
2 Shannon struck out.
Javier singled to left.
3 Javier out attempting to steal second, Howard to Andrews.
Boston
1 Scott called out on strikes.
2 Smith grounded to second.
3 Petrocelli fanned.

3rd Inning
St. Louis
Maxvill tripled off center field wall.
1 Gibson lined to third.
2 Brock popped to short.
Flood singled to center, scoring Maxvill.
Maris singled to right, advancing Flood to third.
A wild pitch scored Flood with Maris going to second.
3 Cepeda grounded to short.
Boston
1 Howard popped to first.
2 Lonborg struck out.
3 Foy fanned.

4th Inning
St. Louis
1 McCarver grounded to second.
2 Shannon grounded to third.
3 Javier took a called third strike.
Boston
1 Andrews fanned.
2 Yastrzemski grounded to second.
3 Harrelson struck out.

5th Inning
St. Louis
1 Maxvill grounded to third.
Gibson homered.
Brock singled to left.
Brock stole second.
Flood walked as Brock stole third on the fourth ball.
2 Maris hit a sacrifice fly to right, scoring Brock.
3 Cepeda flied to left.
Boston
Scott tripled off the centerfield wall, scoring when Javier's relay to third went into the dugout.
1 Smith flied to right.
2 Petrocelli struck out.
3 Howard flied to left.

6th Inning
St. Louis
McCarver doubled to right.
Shannon safe on Foy's fumble, with McCarver staying at second.
Javier hit a three-run homer into the left field screen.
1 Maxvill flied to right.
2 Gibson grounded to third.
Brock doubled down the left field line.
3 Flood struck out.
Boston
1 Tartabull, pinch hitting for Lonborg, fanned.
2 Foy fouled to the catcher.
3 Andrews grounded to short.

7th Inning
St. Louis
For Boston—Santiago pitching.
1 Maris flied to deep center.
2 Cepeda struck out.
3 McCarver popped to Foy.
Boston
Yastrzemski walked.
1 Harrelson forced Yastrzemski, Maxvill to Javier.
2 Scott fouled to the catcher.
3 Smith popped to Javier in short right.

8th Inning
St. Louis
1 Shannon grounded to short.
2 Javier flied to deep right (one-handed catch in front of bleachers).
3 Maxvill popped to Scott in short right.
Boston
Petrocelli doubled into the left field corner.
Petrocelli to third on a wild pitch.
Jones, pinch hitting for Howard, walked.
1 Siebern, batting for Santiago, forced Jones, Javier to Maxvill and scoring Petrocelli.
2 Foy forced Siebern, Cepeda to Maxvill.
3 Andrews grounded to the pitcher.

9th Inning
St. Louis
For Boston—Jones to third (batting eighth), Russ Gibson catching (batting ninth) and Morehead pitching (batting first).
1 Gibson struck out.
Brock walked.
Brock stole second **(his 7th steal a new Series record).**
Flood walked.
Maris walked loading the bases.
For Boston—Osinski pitching.
2 Cepeda fouled to Petrocelli.
For Boston—Brett pitching.
3 McCarver grounded to first.
Boston
Yastrzemski singled to right.
1,2 Harrelson hit into a double play, Maxvill to Javier to Cepeda.
3 Scott struck out.

1967 WORLD SERIES COMPOSITE BOX

	Wins	Composite Line Score	Manager	Regular Season W	L	Pct.	G. Ahead
St. Louis Cardinals (N.L.)	4	5 2 7 0 2 4 3 1 1 – 25	Red Schoendienst	101	60	.627	10.5
Boston Red Sox (A.L.)	3	0 1 2 4 1 2 8 1 2 – 21	Dick Williams	92	70	.568	1

BATTING AND FIELDING

ST. LOUIS CARDINALS

	Pos	G	AB	R	H	2B	3B	HR	RBI	BB	SO	SB	BA	SA	PO	A	E	Main Pos	G	AB	R	H	2B	3B	HR	RBI	BB	SO	SB	BA	SA
Orlando Cepeda	1b	7	29	1	3	2	0	0	1	0	4	0	.103	.172	52	4	0	1b	151	563	91	183	37	0	25	111	62	75	11	.325	.524
Julian Javier	2b	7	25	2	9	3	0	1	4	0	6	0	.360	.600	12	20	1	2b	140	520	68	146	16	3	14	64	25	92	6	.281	.404
Dal Maxvill	ss	7	19	1	3	0	0	0	1	4	1	0	.158	.263	13	17	0	ss	152	476	37	108	14	4	1	41	48	66	0	.227	.279
Mike Shannon	3b	7	24	3	5	1	0	1	2	1	4	0	.208	.375	5	13	2	3b	130	482	53	118	18	3	12	77	37	89	2	.245	.369
Roger Maris	rf	7	26	3	10	1	0	1	7	3	1	0	.385	.538	15	0	1	of	125	410	64	107	18	7	9	55	52	61	0	.261	.405
Curt Flood	cf	7	28	2	5	0	0	0	3	3	3	0	.179	.214	15	0	0	of	134	514	68	172	24	1	5	50	37	46	2	.335	.414
Lou Brock	lf	7	29	8	12	2	1	1	3	2	3	7	.414	.655	13	0	0	of	159	689	113	206	32	12	21	76	24	109	52	.299	.472
Tim McCarver	c	7	24	3	3	1	0	0	2	2	2	0	.125	.167	55	4	0	c	138	471	68	139	26	3	14	69	54	32	8	.295	.452
																		c	52	99	11	27	8	0	1	14	4	7	0	.273	.384
Dave Ricketts	ph	3	3	0	0	0	0	0	0	0	0	0	.000	.000				of	110	265	35	67	7	3	6	32	19	43	12	.253	.370
Bobby Tolan	ph	3	2	1	0	0	0	0	0	0	1	0	.000	.000				2b-3b	73	217	20	48	7	0	2	21	19	26	0	.221	.281
Phil Gagliano	ph	1	1	0	0	0	0	0	0	0	0	0	.000	.000				3b	55	105	9	22	2	0	3	10	7	18	2	.210	.314
Ed Spiezio	ph	1	1	0	0	0	0	0	0	0	0	0	.000	.000				ss	52	67	8	9	1	1	1	9	8	18	0	.132	.224
Ed Bressoud	ss	2	0	0	0	0	0	0	0	0	0	0	—	—	0	0	0	of	81	175	20	39	9	2	1	12	9	26	6	.223	.314
Alex Johnson		Did not play																													
Bob Gibson	p	3	11	1	1	0	0	1	1	0	2	0	.091	.364	2	3	0	p	27	60	7	8	0	0	0	3	8	26	0	.133	.133
Nelson Briles	p	2	3	0	0	0	0	0	0	0	2	0	.000	.000	0	4	0	p	49	40	5	6	0	0	0	4	3	20	0	.150	.150
Dick Hughes	p	2	3	0	0	0	0	0	0	0	3	0	.000	.000	1	0	0	p	40	78	3	10	0	0	0	3	2	36	0	.128	.128
Steve Carlton	p	1	1	0	0	0	0	0	0	0	0	0	.000	.000	0	0	0	p	30	72	5	11	2	0	0	3	3	28	0	.153	.181
Jack Lamabe	p	3	0	0	0	0	0	0	0	0	0	0	—	—	0	1	0	a p	23	10	0	2	0	0	0	1	6	0	0	.200	.200
Ron Willis	p	3	0	0	0	0	0	0	0	0	0	0	—	—	0	0	0	p	65	8	0	3	1	0	0	2	0	2	0	.375	.500
Joe Hoerner	p	2	0	0	0	0	0	0	0	0	0	0	—	—	0	0	0	p	57	11	0	2	0	0	0	0	5	0	0	.182	.182
Ray Washburn	p	2	0	0	0	0	0	0	0	0	0	0	—	—	0	0	0	p	27	66	0	6	1	1	0	3	1	41	0	.091	.136
Larry Jaster	p	1	0	0	0	0	0	0	0	0	0	0	—	—	0	0	0	p	35	50	3	5	0	0	0	2	3	11	0	.100	.100
Hal Woodeshick	p	1	0	0	0	0	0	0	0	0	0	0	—	—	0	0	1	p	36	4	0	0	0	0	0	0	0	4	0	.000	.000
Al Jackson		Did not play																p	41	31	4	8	1	0	0	2	2	9	0	.258	.290
team total		7	229	25	51	11	2	5	24	17	30	7	.223	.354	183	68	4		161	5566	695	1462	225	40	115	656	443	919	102	.263	.379

Double Plays—4
Left on Bases—40

a—from Chicago (A) and New York (N)
Johnny Romano (c), Ted Savage (ph), Steve Huntz (ab), Jim Williams (ss), Jim Cosman (p), and Mike Torrez (p) also played for the Cardinals during the season

BOSTON RED SOX

	Pos	G	AB	R	H	2B	3B	HR	RBI	BB	SO	SB	BA	SA	PO	A	E	Main Pos	G	AB	R	H	2B	3B	HR	RBI	BB	SO	SB	BA	SA
George Scott	1b	7	26	3	6	1	1	0	0	3	6	0	.231	.346	70	3	0	1b	159	565	74	171	21	7	19	82	63	119	10	.303	.465
Jerry Adair	2b-ph	5	16	0	2	0	0	0	1	0	3	1	.125	.125	7	11	0	b inf	89	316	41	92	13	1	3	26	13	35	1	.291	.367
Rico Petrocelli	ss	7	20	3	4	1	0	2	3	3	8	0	.200	.550	11	21	2	ss	142	491	53	127	24	2	17	66	49	93	2	.259	.420
Dalton Jones	3b-ph	6	18	2	7	0	0	1	1	3	0	0	.389	.389	4	8	0	3b	89	159	18	46	6	2	3	25	11	23	0	.289	.409
Jose Tartabull	pr-rf-ph	7	13	1	2	0	0	0	1	0	1	0	.154	.154	7	0	0	of	115	247	36	55	1	2	0	10	23	26	6	.223	.243
Reggie Smith	cf	7	24	3	6	1	0	2	3	2	4	0	.250	.542	14	0	0	of	158	565	78	139	24	6	15	61	57	95	16	.246	.389
Carl Yastrzemski	lf	7	25	4	10	2	0	3	5	4	1	0	.400	.840	16	2	0	lf	161	579	112	189	31	4	44	121	91	69	10	.326	.622
Elston Howard	c	7	18	0	2	0	0	0	1	1	2	0	.111	.111	23	1	0	c c	42	116	9	17	3	0	1	11	9	24	0	.147	.198
Joe Foy	ph-3b	5	15	2	2	1	0	0	1	5	0	0	.133	.200	7	10	1	3b	130	446	70	112	22	4	16	49	46	87	8	.251	.426
Mike Andrews	ph-2b	5	13	2	4	0	0	0	1	0	1	0	.308	.308	2	4	0	2b	142	494	79	130	20	0	8	40	62	72	7	.263	.352
Ken Harrelson	rf	4	13	0	1	0	0	0	0	0	3	0	.077	.077	5	0	0	d of	23	80	9	16	4	1	3	14	5	12	1	.200	.388
Norm Siebern	ph-rf	3	3	0	1	0	0	0	1	0	0	0	.000	.000	0	0	0	e 1b	33	44	2	9	2	0	0	7	6	8	0	.205	.295
George Thomas	ph-rf	2	2	0	0	0	0	0	0	0	2	0	.000	.000	0	0	0	of	65	89	10	19	2	0	1	6	3	23	0	.213	.270
Russ Gibson	c	2	2	0	0	0	0	0	0	0	0	0	.000	.000	9	0	0	c	49	138	6	28	7	0	1	15	12	31	0	.203	.275
Mike Ryan	c	1	2	0	0	0	0	0	0	0	0	0	.000	.000	4	0	0	c	79	226	21	45	4	2	2	27	26	42	2	.199	.261
Jim Lonborg	p	3	9	0	0	0	0	0	0	0	7	0	.000	.000	1	2	0	p	39	99	7	14	1	1	0	8	4	52	1	.141	.172
Jose Santiago	p	3	2	1	1	0	0	1	1	0	1	0	.500	2.000	1	0	0	p	50	42	5	8	3	0	1	3	2	15	0	.190	.333
Gary Waslewski	p	2	1	0	0	0	0	0	0	0	0	0	.000	.000	0	2	0	p	12	11	0	1	0	0	0	0	0	7	0	.091	.091
Gary Bell	p	3	0	0	0	0	0	0	0	0	0	0	—	—	0	2	0	f	29	59	7	12	3	0	0	0	0	12	0	.203	.254
Ken Brett	p	2	0	0	0	0	0	0	0	0	0	0	—	—	0	0	0	p	1	0	0	0	0	0	0	0	0	0	0	.000	.000
Dave Moorehead	p	2	0	0	0	0	0	0	0	0	0	0	—	—	0	0	0	p	10	12	1	1	0	0	0	1	4	0	0	.083	.083
Dan Osinski	p	2	0	0	0	0	0	0	0	0	0	0	—	—	0	0	0	p	34	12	1	4	1	0	0	4	0	4	0	.333	.444
John Wyatt	p	2	0	0	0	0	0	0	0	0	0	0	—	—	0	0	0	p	60	12	0	1	0	0	0	0	1	4	0	.083	.083
Lee Stange	p	1	0	0	0	0	0	0	0	0	0	0	—	—	0	0	1	p	35	49	2	3	1	0	0	1	2	14	0	.061	.082
Jerry Stephenson	p	1	0	0	0	0	0	0	0	0	0	0	—	—	0	0	0	p	8	16	0	4	0	0	0	0	0	2	0	.250	.250
team total		7	222	21	48	6	1	8	19	17	49	1	.216	.360	183	66	4		162	5471	722	1394	216	39	158	666	522	1020	68	.255	.395

Double Plays—3
Left on Bases—43

b—from Chicago (A)
c—from New York (A)
d—from Washington and Kansas City
e—from San Francisco
f—from Cleveland
Tony Conigliaro (of-eye injury), Bob Tillman (c), Tony Horton (1b), Don Demeter (of), Jim Landis (of), Ken Poulsen (ss-3b), Darrell Brandon (p), Dennis Bennett (p), Billy Rohr (p), Bill Landis (p), Hank Fischer (p), Don McMahon (p), Sparkly Lyle (p), and Galen Cisco (p) also played for the Red Sox during the season.

PITCHING

ST. LOUIS CARDINALS

	G	GS	CG	IP	H	R	ER	BB	SO	W	L	SV	ERA	G	GS	CG	IP	H	ER	BB	SO	W	L	Pct.	SV	ShO	ERA
Bob Gibson	3	3	3	27	14	3	3	5	26	3	0	0	1.00	24	24	10	175	151	58	40	147	13	7	.650	0	2	2.98
Nelson Briles	2	1	1	11	7	2	2	1	4	1	0	0	1.64	49	14	4	155	139	42	40	94	14	5	.737	6	2	2.44
Dick Hughes	2	2	0	9	9	6	5	3	7	0	1	0	5.00	37	27	12	222	164	66	48	161	16	6	.727	3	3	2.68
Steve Carlton	1	1	0	6	3	1	0	2	5	0	1	0	0.00	30	28	11	193	173	64	62	168	14	9	.609	1	2	2.98
Jack Lamabe	a	3	0	0	2⅔	5	2	2	0	4	0	1	0	6.75	23	1	1	48	43	15	10	30	3	4	.429	4	1	2.81
Ray Washburn	2	0	0	2⅔	1	0	0	1	2	0	0	0	0.00	27	27	3	186	190	73	42	98	10	7	.588	0	1	3.53
Hal Woodeshick	1	0	0	1	1	0	0	0	0	0	0	0	0.00	36	0	0	42	41	24	28	20	2	1	.667	2	0	5.14
Ron Willis	3	0	0	1	2	3	3	1	0	0	0	0	27.00	65	0	0	81	76	24	43	42	6	5	.545	10	0	2.67
Joe Hoerner	2	0	0	⅓	4	3	1	0	0	0	0	0	40.50	57	0	0	66	52	19	20	50	4	4	.500	15	0	2.59
Larry Jaster	1	0	0	⅓	2	0	0	0	0	0	0	0	0.00	34	23	2	152	141	51	44	87	9	7	.563	3	1	3.02
Al Jackson		Did not play												38	11	1	107	117	47	29	43	9	4	.692	1	1	3.95
team total	7	7	4	61	48	21	18	17	49	4	3	0	2.66	161	161	44	1465	1313	496	431	956	101	60	.627	45	17	3.05

BOSTON RED SOX

	G	GS	CG	IP	H	R	ER	BB	SO	W	L	SV	ERA	G	GS	CG	IP	H	ER	BB	SO	W	L	Pct.	SV	ShO	ERA
Jim Lonborg	3	3	2	24	14	8	7	2	11	2	1	0	2.63	39	39	15	273	228	96	83	246	22	9	.710	0	2	3.16
Jose Santiago	3	2	0	9⅔	16	6	6	3	6	0	2	0	5.59	50	11	2	145	138	58	47	109	12	4	.750	5	0	3.60
Gary Waslewski	2	1	0	8⅓	4	2	2	2	7	0	0	0	2.16	12	8	0	42	34	15	20	22	2	2	.500	0	0	3.21
Gary Bell	3	1	0	5⅓	8	3	3	1	1	0	1	1	5.06	f	29	24	8	165	143	58	47	115	12	8	.600	3	0	2.81
John Wyatt	2	0	0	3⅔	1	2	2	3	1	1	0	0	4.91	60	0	0	93	71	29	39	68	10	7	.588	20	0	2.61
Dave Moorehead	2	0	0	3⅓	0	0	0	4	3	0	0	0	0.00	10	9	1	48	48	23	22	40	5	4	.556	0	1	4.31
Lee Stange	1	0	0	2	3	1	1	0	0	0	0	0	9.00	35	24	8	182	171	56	32	101	8	10	.444	1	2	2.77
Jerry Stephenson	1	0	0	1	2	1	1	2	0	0	0	0	9.00	8	6	0	40	32	17	16	24	3	1	.750	0	0	3.83
Ken Brett	2	0	0	1⅓	1	0	0	0	1	0	0	0	0.00	1	0	0	2	1	1	0	5	0	0	.000	0	0	4.50
Dan Osinski	2	0	0	1⅓	2	1	1	0	0	0	0	0	6.75	34	0	0	64	61	18	14	38	3	1	.750	2	0	2.53
team total	7	7	2	61	51	25	23	17	30	3	4	1	3.39	162	162	41	1459	1307	545	477	1010	92	70	.568	44	9	3.36

Total Attendance—304,085   Average Attendance—43,441   Winning Player's Share—$8,315   Losing Player's Share—$5,115

1968
Lolich: Twenty the Hard Way

In a year when batting averages plummeted and pitchers took charge of the game, Bob Gibson and Denny McLain stood above the rest as symbols of pitching supremacy. Gibson overpowered National League batters in compiling an incredible 1.12 ERA, winning 22 games and both the Cy Young and MVP awards. With Gibson leading the way, the St. Louis Cardinals won a repeat pennant by a wide margin. Offensive production fell off even in St. Louis, but the Cards still had feared batters in Curt Flood, Orlando Cepeda, Lou Brock, and Mike Shannon. Manager Red Schoendienst also got 19 wins out of right-hander Nelson Briles to complement Gibson on the mound corps. While the Cardinals were repeating as champs, the Detroit Tigers were winning the American League pennant for the first time since 1945. Manager Mayo Smith found his meal ticket in McLain, who captivated the sporting public with his uninhibited antics and by winning 31 games, the first 30-win season since Dizzy Dean's 1934 campaign. McLain also won his league's Cy Young and MVP awards, getting help in the pennant drive from southpaw Mickey Lolich's 17 wins and from the batting power of Willie Horton, Bill Freehan, Jim Northrup, and Norm Cash. The Tigers had a sentimental favorite in Al Kaline, a member of a championship squad for the first time in his 16-year Detroit career, and they made room in the outfield for him by shifting regular center fielder Mickey Stanley to shortstop, a big gamble which paid off when Stanley handled the infield job competently and Kaline hit .379 for the Series.

A confrontation between Gibson and McLain opened the Series in St. Louis, but it was no contest. The Cards scored three times off McLain in the fourth inning, while Gibson was practically untouchable. He shut the Tigers out on five hits and fanned a Series record of 17 men with his blazing fast ball. The Cards also stole three bases, an indication that they would be running just like in the 1967 Series. The number-two hurlers, Briles and Lolich, pitched the next day, and it was just as much a no-contest. Lolich scattered six hits and belted the first home run of his professional career, and additional homers by Horton and Cash triggered an 8–1 Detroit victory that squared the Series. Lou Brock stole two more bases in the losing cause, bringing his total up to three for the first two games.

The Cardinals pounded out a 7–3 victory in game three in Detroit, with Cepeda and Tim McCarver socking three-run homers and Brock stealing three bases. Gibson and McLain met again on a rainy day for game four, and the result was even more one-sided. The Cards knocked McLain out of the box in the third inning, while Gibson allowed only five hits and struck out 10 men. Gibson himself hit a homer and Brock stole another base in the 10–1 victory which spelled the end for the Tigers. When the Cards scored three times off Lolich in the top of the first in game five, the Series seemed all but done. But Lolich settled down, the Tigers scored twice in the fourth, and Detroit took heart when Brock tried to score standing up and was thrown out at the plate by Horton's great throw in the fifth inning. Old pro Kaline singled home two runs in the seventh, and the Tigers stayed alive with a 5–3 triumph.

Manager Mayo Smith called on McLain to pitch the sixth game, hoping for at least one good Series effort out of his ace. Denny came through with a fine-crafted performance, while the Tiger batters came through with 10 big runs in the third inning, with Northrup's grand slam the big blow. That put all the chips on the table, with a tired Lolich pitching against the invincible Gibson. Both men pitched shutout ball through the first six innings, but then disaster hit the Cardinals in the seventh. After two were out, Cash and Horton singled, then Northrup lined a shot to center. The fine-fielding Flood misjudged the ball, and it sailed past him for a triple that broke Gibson's spell. Freehan promptly doubled in Northrup, and Lolich wrapped up his third win of the Series by a 4–1 score to give the Tigers their third World Championship and finish the season with a hard-earned 20 victories.

Game 1 October 2 at St. Louis

Det.	000	000	000					
St. L.	000	300	100					

Detroit	Pos	AB	R	H	RBI	PO	A	E
McAuliffe	2b	4	0	1	0	4	0	0
Stanley	ss	4	0	2	0	3	2	0
Kaline	rf	4	0	1	0	2	0	0
Cash	1b	4	0	0	0	6	1	1
Horton	lf	4	0	0	0	2	0	1
Northrup	cf	3	0	0	0	2	0	0
Freehan	c	2	0	0	0	4	1	1
Wert	3b	2	0	1	0	0	1	0
b Mathews		1	0	0	0	0	0	0
Tracewski	3b	0	0	0	0	0	0	0
McLain	p	1	0	0	0	0	2	0
a Matchick		1	0	0	0	0	0	0
Dobson	p	1	0	0	0	0	0	0
c Brown		1	0	0	0	0	0	0
McMahon	p	0	0	0	0	1	0	0
Totals		31	0	5	0	24	7	3

St. Louis	Pos	AB	R	H	RBI	PO	A	E
Block	lf	4	1	1	1	2	0	0
Flood	cf	4	0	1	0	1	0	0
Maris	rf	3	1	0	0	1	0	0
Cepeda	1b	4	0	0	0	11	1	0
McCarver	c	3	1	1	0	17	1	0
Shannon	3b	4	1	2	1	0	1	0
Javier	2b	3	0	1	2	2	0	0
Maxvill	ss	2	0	0	0	2	0	0
Gibson	p	2	0	0	0	1	0	0
Totals		29	4	6	4	27	2	0

Pitching	IP	H	R	ER	BB	SO
Detroit						
McLain (L)	5	3	3	2	3	3
Dobson	2	2	1	1	1	0
McMahon	1	1	0	0	0	0
St. Louis						
Gibson (W)	9	5	0	0	1	17

a Grounded out for McLain in 6th.
b Struck out for Wert in 8th.
c Flied out for Dobson in 8th.

Double—Kaline. Triple—McCarver. Home Run—Brock. Stolen Bases—Brock, Flood, Javier. Sacrifice Hit—Gibson. Left on Bases—Detroit 5, St. Louis 6. Umpires—Gorman (N), Honochick (A), Landes (N), Kinnamon (A), Harvey (N), Haller (A). Attendance—54,692. Time of Game—2:29.

1st Inning
Detroit
1 McAuliffe struck out.
  Stanley singled to left.
2   Stanley caught stealing, McCarver to Javier.
3 Kaline whiffed.
St. Louis
1 Brock grounded to short.
2 Flood flied to right.
3 Maris flied to right.

2nd Inning
Detroit
1 Cash struck out.
2 Horton called out on strikes.
3 Northrup struck out.
St. Louis
1 Cepeda flied to center.
  McCarver tripled to right-center.
2 Shannon struck out.
3 Javier took a called third strike.

3rd Inning
Detroit
1 Freehan took a called third strike, becoming the fifth consecutive Tiger strikeout.
  Wert singled to center.
2 McLain struck out, bunting foul on the third strike.
3 McAuliffe grounded to first.
St. Louis
  Maxvill walked.
1 Gibson sacrificed Maxvill to second, McLain to McAuliffe covering first.
2 Brock safe on a fielder's choice when he grounded sharply to McLain who threw to Stanley getting Maxvill sliding back to the bag.
  Brock stole second and went to third when Freehan's throw went into center field.
3 Flood popped to short.

4th Inning
Detroit
1 Stanley flied to right.
2 Kaline called out on strikes.
3 Cash flied to center.
St. Louis
  Maris walked.
1 Cepeda fouled to Cash.
  McCarver walked.
  Shannon singled to left, scoring Maris and as Horton fumbled McCarver got to third and Shannon to second.
  Javier singled to right, scoring McCarver and Shannon.
  Javier stole second.
2 Maxvill flied to Horton in short left-center.
3 Gibson fanned.

5th Inning
Detroit
1 Horton popped to second.
2 Northrup lined to short.
  Freehan walked.
3 Wert called out on strikes.
St. Louis
1 Brock grounded to third.
2 Flood popped to second.
  Maris safe on Cash's error.
3 Cepeda lined to Horton making a one-handed catch in deep left-center.

6th Inning
Detroit
1 Matchick, batting for McLain, grounded out, Cepeda to Gibson.
  McAuliffe singled to right.
2 Stanley struck out.
  Kaline doubled into the left field corner, McAuliffe stopping at third.
3 Cash fanned.
St. Louis
For Detroit—Dobson pitching.
1 McCarver popped to second.
2 Shannon grounded to short.
  Javier walked.
3   Javier was out stealing, Freehan to Stanley.

7th Inning
Detroit
1 Horton lined to short.
2 Northup struck out.
3 Freehan struck out.
St. Louis
1 Maxvill fouled to Cash.
2 Gibson popped to Cash.
  Brock homered into the right-center field bleachers.
  Flood singled to center.
  Flood stole second.
3 Maris popped to second.

8th Inning
Detroit
1 Mathews, pinch-hitting for Wert, struck out.
2 Brown, pinch-hitting for Dobson, flied to left.
3 McAuliffe flied to left.
St. Louis
For Detroit—McMahon pitching and Tracewski playing third.
1 Cepeda fouled to Freehan.
2 McCarver grounded out, Cash to McMahon.
  Shannon singled to center.
3 Javier flied to center.

9th Inning
Detroit
  Stanley lined a single to center.
1 Kaline struck out for the third time.
2 Cash struck out also for the third time becoming Gibson's 16th victim. **(Breaking the old Series record of 15 set by Sandy Koufax vs. the Yankees in 1963.)**
3 Horton became Gibson's 17th victim as he took a called third strike.

Game 2 October 3 at St. Louis

| | | Det. | 0 1 1 | 0 0 3 | 1 0 2 |
| | | St. L. | 0 0 0 | 0 0 1 | 0 0 0 |

Detroit	Pos	AB	R	H	RBI	PO	A	E
McAuliffe	2b	5	0	2	2	1	5	0
Stanley	ss-cf	5	0	1	0	0	3	1
Kaline	rf	5	2	2	0	2	0	0
Cash	1b	5	2	3	1	11	0	0
Horton	lf	3	2	2	1	0	0	0
Oyler	ss	0	0	0	0	0	0	0
Northrup	cf-lf	5	1	1	0	4	0	0
Freehan	c	4	0	0	0	9	1	0
Wert	3b	2	0	0	1	0	2	0
Lolich	p	4	1	2	2	0	0	0
Totals		38	8	13	7	27	11	1

Pitching	IP	H	R	ER	BB	SO
Detroit						
Lolich (W)	9	6	1	1	2	9
St. Louis						
Briles (L)	*5	7	4	4	1	2
Carlton	**1	4	2	2	1	1
Willis	2	1	0	0	2	2
Hoerner	1	1	2	0	3	1

*Pitched to 2 batters in 6th.
**Pitched to 2 batters in 7th.

1st Inning
Detroit
1 McAuliffe grounded to first.
2 Stanley flied to right.
3 Kaline grounded to short.
St. Louis
1 Brock took a called third strike.
Javier singled over Wert's head.
Flood walked.
2 Cepeda fouled deep into the right field corner where Kaline made a one-handed catch.
3 Shannon flied to Kaline in right-center.

2nd Inning
Detroit
1 Cash fouled to Shannon.
Horton hit a home-run into the left-center field bleachers.
2 Northrup popped to short.
3 Freehan took a called third strike.
St. Louis
1 McCarver bunted out, Freehan to Cash.
2 Davis took a called third strike.
3 Maxvill flied to deep center.

3rd Inning
Detroit
1 Wert popped to Javier in short center.
Lolich hit his first major league home run into the lower left field stands.
2 McAuliffe grounded to short.
Stanley beat out a slow roller to third.
3 Kaline fouled to McCarver.
St. Louis
1 Briles took a called third strike.
2 Brock struck out.
Javier singled off Wert's glove and went to second as Stanley fumbled the ball.
3 Flood grounded to second.

4th Inning
Detroit
Cash singled to right.
1 Horton flied to Flood in deep left-center.
2 Northrup flied to center.
3 Freehan flied to Davis making a fine catch inside the foul line.
St. Louis
1 Cepeda grounded to short.
2 Shannon grounded to second.
3 McCarver grounded to second.

5th Inning
Detroit
Wert walked.
1 Lolich forced Wert on an attempted sacrifice, Shannon to Maxvill.
McAuliffe beat out a dribbler down the first base line, moving Lolich to second.
2 Stanley fanned.
3 Kaline forced McAuliffe at second, Shannon to Javier.
St. Louis
1 Davis flied to Northrup in deep left-center.
2 Maxvill grounded to short.
3 Briles struck out.

6th Inning
Detroit
Cash hit a home run into the right field stands.
Horton beat out a single to deep short.
For St. Louis—Carlton came in to pitch.
Northrup singled to center, Horton stopping at second.

6th Inning (continued)
1 Freehan popped to first.
Wert walked, loading the bases.
2 Lolich struck out.
McAuliffe lined a single to short center, scoring Horton and Northrup, with Wert going to third. McAuliffe moved to second on the throw to the plate.
3 Stanley lined to right.
St. Louis
Brock walked.
Brock stole second.
1 Javier struck out.
Flood singled when Lolich fell down, Brock advancing to third.
Cepeda blooped a single to left-center, scoring Brock and moving Flood to third.
2,3 Shannon grounded into a double play, Stanley to McAuliffe to Cash.

7th Inning
Detroit
Kaline singled to center.
Cash singled to center, advancing Kaline to third.
For St. Louis—Willis pitching.
Horton walked, loading the bases.
1,2 Northrup grounded into a double play, Maxvill to Cepeda, Kaline scoring and Cash moving to third.
3 Freehan struck out.
St. Louis
For Detroit—Oyler came in to play short, Stanley moved to center as Northrup moved to left.
1 McCarver grounded to second.
2 Davis lined to left.
3 Maxvill took a called third strike.

8th Inning
Detroit
1 Wert took a called third strike.
Lolich singled to center.
McAuliffe walked.
2,3 Stanley hit into a double play, Javier to Maxvill to Cepeda.
St. Louis
1 Gagliano, pinch-hitting for Willis, grounded to third.
Brock singled to center.
Brock stole second on a pickoff attempt beating Cash's bad throw.
2 Javier grounded to third, Brock holding second.
3 Flood struck out.

9th Inning
Detroit
For St. Louis—Hoerner pitching.
Kaline singled to left.
Cash safe on Shannon's throw of Cash's bunt pulling Maxvill off the bag at second.
1 Oyler sacrificed Kaline to third and Cash to second, Shannon to Javier.
2 Northrup fanned.
Freehan got an intentional pass, loading the bases.
Wert walked, forcing in Kaline.
Lolich walked, forcing in Cash.
3 McAuliffe fouled to Davis down the right field line.
St. Louis
Cepeda singled to left.
1 Shannon struck out.
2 McCarver flied to center.
3 Davis fouled to Cash.

St. Louis	Pos	AB	R	H	RBI	PO	A	E
Brock	lf	3	1	1	0	0	0	0
Javier	2b	4	0	2	0	3	2	0
Flood	cf	3	0	1	0	2	0	0
Cepeda	1b	4	0	2	1	6	0	0
Shannon	3b	4	0	0	0	1	3	1
McCarver	c	4	0	0	0	7	0	0
Davis	rf	4	0	0	0	4	0	0
Maxvill	ss	3	0	0	0	4	3	0
Briles	p	2	0	0	0	0	0	0
Carlton	p	0	0	0	0	0	0	0
Willis	p	0	0	0	0	0	0	0
a Gagliano		1	0	0	0	0	0	0
Hoerner	p	0	0	0	0	0	0	0
Totals		32	1	6	1	27	8	1

a Grounded out for Willis in 8th.

Home Runs—Cash, Horton, Lolich. Stolen Bases—Brock 2. Sacrifice Hit—Oyler. Double Plays—Stanley to McAuliffe to Cash, Maxvill to Cepeda, Javier to Maxvill to Cepeda. Left on Bases—Detroit 11, St. Louis 6. Umpires—Honochick, Landes, Kinnamon, Harvey, Haller, Gorman. Attendance—54,692. Time of Game—2:41.

Game 3 October 5 at Detroit

| | | St.L. | 0 0 0 | 0 4 0 | 3 0 0 |
| | | Det. | 0 0 2 | 0 1 0 | 0 0 0 |

St. Louis	Pos	AB	R	H	RBI	PO	A	E
Brock	lf	4	1	3	0	5	0	0
Flood	cf	4	2	1	0	2	0	0
Maris	rf	3	2	1	0	2	0	0
Cepeda	1b	4	1	1	3	10	0	0
McCarver	c	5	1	2	3	5	0	0
Shannon	3b	4	0	2	0	1	0	0
Javier	2b	4	0	1	0	2	5	0
Maxvill	ss	4	0	0	0	2	2	0
Washburn	p	3	0	0	0	0	1	0
Hoerner	p	2	0	1	0	0	1	0
Totals		38	7	13	7	27	9	0

Pitching	IP	H	R	ER	BB	SO
St. Louis						
Washburn (W)	5⅓	3	3	3	4	3
Hoerner (SV)	3⅔	1	0	0	1	2
Detroit						
Wilson (L)	4⅓	4	3	3	6	3
Dobson	⅔	2	1	1	0	1
McMahon	*1	3	3	3	0	0
Patterson	1	0	0	0	0	0
Hiller	2	4	0	0	1	1

*Pitched to 3 batters in 7th.

1st Inning
St. Louis
Brock awarded first on a walk as the umpire declared Wilson moistened the ball on the fourth pitch of a 3-0 count. Brock stole second.
Flood walked.
1,2 Maris struck out with Brock doubled trying to steal third, Freehan to Wert as Flood took second.
3 Cepeda grounded to short.
Detroit
1 McAuliffe grounded to first.
2 Stanley grounded to second.
3 Kaline flied to left.

2nd Inning
St. Louis
1 McCarver flied to center.
2 Shannon tapped back to the mound.
Javier walked.
3 Maxvill flied to left.
Detroit
1 Cash popped to short.
Horton walked.
2 Northrup flied to right.
Freehan walked.
3 Wert struck out.

3rd Inning
St. Louis
1 Washburn grounded to short.
Brock beat out a hit to short.
2 Flood fouled to Cash.
Brock stole second.
Maris walked.
3 Cepeda flied to center.
Detroit
1 Wilson took a called third strike.
McAuliffe singled to left.
2 Stanley grounded to second, moving McAuliffe to second.
Kaline hit a two-run homer into the upper left field stands.
3 Cash grounded to second.

4th Inning
St. Louis
McCarver singled to right.
Shannon walked.
1,2 Javier took a called third strike, McCarver was caught in a double steal attempt, Freehan to Wert as Shannon moved to second.
3 Maxvill grounded back to the mound.
Detroit
1 Horton grounded to third.
2 Northrup flied to left.
3 Freehan flied to left.

5th Inning
St. Louis
1 Washburn called out on strikes.
Brock singled to center.
Brock stole second for his third steal of the game.
Flood doubled into the left field corner, scoring Brock.
Maris walked.
For Detroit—Dobson now pitching.
2 Cepeda fouled to Freehan.
McCarver hit a three-run homer into the upper right field deck.
Shannon singled to center.
3 Javier flied to center.

Detroit	Pos	AB	R	H	RBI	PO	A	E
McAuliffe	2b	4	2	2	1	0	1	0
Stanley	ss	3	0	0	0	0	2	0
Kaline	rf	4	1	1	2	1	0	0
Cash	1b	3	0	0	0	8	1	0
Horton	lf	2	0	0	0	1	0	0
Northrup	cf	4	0	0	0	7	0	0
Freehan	c	3	0	0	0	6	2	0
Wert	3b	4	0	0	0	3	2	0
Wilson	p	1	0	0	0	0	1	0
Dobson	p	0	0	0	0	0	0	0
a Matchick		1	0	0	0	0	0	0
McMahon	p	0	0	0	0	0	0	0
Patterson	p	0	0	0	0	0	0	0
b Comer		1	0	1	0	0	0	0
Hiller	p	0	0	0	0	1	0	0
c Price		1	0	0	0	0	0	0
Totals		31	3	4	3	27	10	0

a Struck out for Dobson in 5th.
b Singled for Patterson in 7th.
c Flied out for Hiller in 9th.

Doubles—Flood, Maris. Home Runs—Cepeda, Kaline, McAuliffe, McCarver. Stolen Bases—Brock 3. Double Play—Freehan to Wert 2. Left on Bases—St. Louis 11, Detroit 6. Umpires—Landes, Kinnamon, Harvey, Haller, Gorman, Honochick. Attendance—53,634. Time of Game—3:17.

5th Inning (continued)
Detroit
1 Wert grounded to second.
2 Matchick, pinch-hitting for Dobson, struck out.
McAuliffe homered into the right field stands.
3 Stanley's grounder caromed off Washburn's leg to Cepeda.

6th Inning
St. Louis
For Detroit—McMahon pitching.
1 Maxvill grounded to second.
2 Washburn flied to right.
3 Brock struck out.
Detroit
1 Kaline grounded to short.
Cash walked.
Horton walked.
For St. Louis—Hoerner pitching.
2 Northrup popped to second.
3 Freehan flied to left.

7th Inning
St. Louis
Flood singled to right.
Maris popped a double to left, Flood stopping at third.
Cepeda hit a three-run homer into the lower left field stands.
For Detroit—Patterson pitching.
1 McCarver popped to third.
2 Shannon grounded to second.
3 Javier flied to center.
Detroit
1 Wert flied to right.
Comer, pinch-hitting for Patterson, singled to center.
2 McAuliffe popped to second.
Stanley walked.
3 Kaline forced Stanley at second, Javier to Maxvill.

8th Inning
St. Louis
For Detroit—Hiller pitching.
1 Maxvill flied to center.
Hoerner singled to left.
Brock singled to right, Hoerner stopping at second.
2 Flood flied to right.
3 Maris grounded out, Cash to Hiller.
Detroit
1 Cash took a called third strike.
2 Horton struck out.
3 Northrup grounded to first.

9th Inning
St. Louis
1 Cepeda flied to center.
2 McCarver grounded to third.
Shannon singled to center.
Javier singled to right, Shannon stopping at second.
Maxvill walked, loading the bases.
3 Hoerner struck out.
Detroit
1 Freehan flied to left.
2 Wert grounded to short.
3 Price, batting for Hiller, flied to left.

Game 4 October 6 at Detroit

St. Louis	Pos	AB	R	H	RBI	PO	A	E
Brock	lf	5	2	3	4	2	0	0
Flood	cf	5	1	1	0	3	0	0
Maris	rf	5	1	0	1	0	0	0
Cepeda	1b	4	0	1	0	9	1	0
McCarver	c	5	1	3	1	10	0	0
Shannon	3b	5	1	2	2	1	0	0
Javier	2b	4	1	2	0	0	2	0
Maxvill	ss	4	1	0	0	2	1	0
Gibson	p	3	2	1	2	0	0	0
Totals		40	10	13	10	27	4	0

Pitching	IP	H	R	ER	BB	SO
St. Louis						
Gibson (W)	9	5	1	1	2	10
Detroit						
McLain (L)	2⅔	6	4	3	1	3
Sparma	*⅓	2	2	2	0	0
Patterson	2	1	0	0	1	0
Lasher	2	1	0	0	0	1
Hiller	**0	2	4	3	2	0
Dobson	2	1	0	0	0	0

*Pitched to 2 batters in 4th.
**Pitched to 5 batters in 8th.

Detroit	Pos	AB	R	H	RBI	PO	A	E
McAuliffe	2b	4	0	0	0	2	4	0
Stanley	ss	4	0	0	0	3	3	0
Kaline	rf	4	0	2	0	3	0	0
Cash	1b	4	0	1	0	10	2	0
Horton	lf	3	0	0	0	1	0	0
Northrup	cf	4	1	1	1	5	0	1
Mathews	3b	2	0	1	0	0	1	1
Freehan	c	3	0	0	0	4	1	1
McLain	p	1	0	0	0	0	0	1
Sparma	p	0	0	0	0	0	0	0
Patterson	p	0	0	0	0	0	1	0
a Price	1	0	0	0	0	0	0	
Lasher	p	0	0	3	0	0	1	0
b Matchick	1	0	0	0	0	0	0	
Hiller	p	0	0	0	0	0	0	0
Dobson	p	0	0	0	0	0	1	0
Totals		31	1	5	1	27	13	4

a Struck out for Patterson in 5th.
b Flied out for Lasher in 7th.

Doubles—Brock, Javier, Kaline, Shannon.
Triples—Brock, McCarver. Home Runs—Brock, Gibson, Northrup. Stolen Base—Brock.
Double Play—Cepeda to Maxvill. Left on Bases—St. Louis 7, Detroit 5.
Umpires—Kinnamon, Harvey, Haller, Gorman, Honochick, Landes. Attendance—53,634.
Time of Game—2:34.

1st Inning
St. Louis
Brock hit a home run into the upper deck of the right-center field stands.
1 Flood grounded to second.
Maris safe at first when McLain dropped Cash's throw.
2 Cepeda struck out.
McCarver singled to left-center, advancing Maris to third.
Shannon beat out a high bouncer to short, scoring Maris with McCarver stopping at second.
3 Javier took a called third strike.
Detroit
1 McAuliffe grounded to first.
2 Stanley fouled to Cepeda.
Kaline doubled to right-center.
3 Cash struck out.

2nd Inning
St. Louis
1 Maxvill took a called third strike.
2 Gibson grounded to short.
3 Brock grounded to second.
Detroit
Horton walked.
1 Northrup flied to left.
Mathews singled to right, Horton stopping at second.
2 Freehan took a called third strike.
3 McLain fouled to Cepeda.

3rd Inning
St. Louis
Flood singled to right.
1 Maris lined to center.
2 Cepeda fouled to Cash down the right field line.
McCarver tripled to left-center, scoring Flood.
Shannon doubled inside the left field line, scoring McCarver.
Javier walked.
Rain delayed the game for one hour and fourteen minutes.
For Detroit—After the rain delay Sparma came in to pitch.
3 Maxvill grounded to second.
Detroit
1 McAuliffe struck out.
2 Stanley called out on strikes.
Kaline singled to center.
3 Cash lined foul to Cepeda.

4th Inning
St. Louis
Gibson homered into the lower left field stands.
Brock tripled to right-center.
For Detroit—Patterson pitching.
1 Flood flied to very shallow right.
Freehan got an error dropping Maris' pop foul as he collided with Cash.
2 Maris grounded to second, scoring Brock.
Cepeda walked.
3 Cepeda caught stealing, Freehan to Stanley.
Detroit
1 Horton struck out.
Northrup hit a towering homer into the upper deck in right-center.
2 Mathews grounded to second.
3 Freehan struck out.

5th Inning
St. Louis
1 McCarver flied to center.
2 Shannon flied to left.
Javier singled to center.
3 Javier was out trying to steal second, Patterson to Stanley.

5th Inning (continued)
Detroit
1 Price, pinch-hitting for Patterson, took a called third strike.
2 McAuliffe struck out.
3 Stanley flied to center.

6th Inning
St. Louis
For Detroit—Lasher pitching.
1 Maxvill struck out.
2 Gibson bounced back to the mound.
3 Brock grounded to short.
Detroit
1 Kaline lined to short.
2 Cash popped to third.
3 Horton struck out.

7th Inning
St. Louis
1 Flood popped to short.
2 Maris popped to McAuliffe in short center.
Cepeda singled to left.
3 McCarver flied to shallow center.
Detroit
1 Northrup grounded to first.
Mathews walked.
2 Freehan took a called third strike.
3 Matchick, batting for Lasher, flied to center.

8th Inning
St. Louis
For Detroit—Hiller pitching.
Shannon safe at first on Mathews' throwing error.
Javier doubled down the left field line moving Shannon to third.
Maxvill walked, loading the bases.
Gibson walked, forcing in Shannon.
Brock doubled over Northrup's head in deep center, clearing the bases.
For Detroit—Dobson now pitching.
Brock stole third (his 7th of the Series tying his own record of 7 set in '67).
1 Flood grounded to third, Brock holding.
2 Maris lined to second.
3 Cepeda grounded out, Cash to Dobson.
Detroit
1 McAuliffe grounded to second.
2 Stanley flied to Brock in left-center.
3 Kaline grounded to short.

9th Inning
St. Louis
McCarver blooped a singled to center and continued to second when Northrup fumbled the ball.
1 Shannon grounded to short, McCarver holding second.
2 Javier flied to center.
3 Maxvill lined to center.
Detroit
Cash lined a single to right.
1 Horton popped to center, Flood making a good running catch.
2,3 Northrup grounded to Cepeda who stepped on first and threw to Maxvill who tagged Cash for a game-ending double play.

Game 5 October 7 at Detroit

St. Louis	Pos	AB	R	H	RBI	PO	A	E
Brock	lf	5	1	3	0	2	0	0
Javier	2b	4	0	2	0	2	1	0
Flood	cf	4	1	1	1	3	0	0
Cepeda	1b	4	1	2	2	4	0	0
Shannon	3b	4	0	0	0	1	2	0
McCarver	c	3	0	1	0	6	0	0
Davis	rf	3	0	0	0	3	0	0
a Gagliano	1	0	0	0	0	0	0	
Maxvill	ss	3	0	0	0	1	2	0
b Spiezio	1	0	1	0	0	0	0	
c Schofield	0	0	0	0	0	0	0	
Briles	p	2	0	0	0	0	2	0
Hoerner	p	0	0	0	0	0	0	0
Willis	p	0	0	0	0	1	0	0
d Maris	1	0	0	0	0	0	0	
Totals		35	3	9	3	24	7	0

a Flied out for Davis in 9th.
b Singled for Maxvill in 9th.
c Ran for Spiezio in 9th.
d Struck out for Willis in 9th.

Doubles—Brock 2. Triples—Horton, Stanley. Home Run—Cepeda. Stolen Base—Flood.
Sacrifice Fly—Cash. Double Play—Shannon to Javier to Cepeda. Hit by Pitcher—Briles (by Lolich) Left on Bases—St. Louis 7, Detroit 7. Umpires—Harvey, Haller, Gorman, Honochick, Landes, Kinnamon.
Attendance—53,634. Time of Game—2:43.

Detroit	Pos	AB	R	H	RBI	PO	A	E
McAuliffe	2b	4	1	1	0	1	2	0
Stanley	ss-cf	3	2	1	0	2	3	0
Kaline	rf	4	0	2	3	3	0	0
Cash	1b	2	0	2	2	7	1	1
Horton	lf	4	1	1	0	1	1	0
Oyler	ss	0	0	0	0	1	0	0
Northrup	cf-lf	3	0	1	1	4	0	0
Freehan	c	3	0	0	0	9	1	0
Wert	3b	4	0	0	0	1	1	0
Lolich	p	4	1	1	0	1	2	0
Totals		31	5	9	5	27	11	1

Pitching	IP	H	R	ER	BB	SO
St. Louis						
Briles	6⅓	6	3	3	3	5
Hoerner (L)	*0	3	2	2	1	0
Willis	1⅔	0	0	0	0	1
Detroit						
Lolich (W)	9	9	3	3	1	8

*Pitched to 4 batters in 7th.

1st Inning
St. Louis
Brock doubled into the left field corner.
1 Javier grounded to short, Brock holding second.
Flood singled to right, scoring Brock. Flood stole second.
Cepeda hit a two-run homer into the left-center field stands.
2 Shannon flied to center.
3 McCarver took a called third strike.
Detroit
1 McAuliffe lined to center.
2 Stanley flied to center.
3 Kaline struck out.

2nd Inning
St. Louis
1 Davis grounded back to the mound.
2 Maxvill popped to short.
3 Briles struck out.
Detroit
Cash singled off the right-center field wall as Flood played the rebound perfectly.
1,2 Horton grounded into a double play, Shannon to Javier to Cepeda.
3 Northrup bounced back to the mound.

3rd Inning
St. Louis
Brock singled to center.
1 Brock was caught trying to steal second, Freehan to McAuliffe.
2 Javier grounded to short.
3 Flood grounded to short.
Detroit
1 Freehan flied to deep left.
Wert walked.
2 Lolich struck out.
3 McAuliffe out on a roller to third.

4th Inning
St. Louis
1 Cepeda fanned.
Shannon got safely to second as his ground ball got through Cash.
McCarver walked.
2 Davis flied to center.
3 Maxvill struck out.
Detroit
Stanley lined a triple into the right field corner.
1 Kaline tapped to the mound, as Stanley held third.
2 Cash hit a sacrifice fly to Brock in left-center, scoring Stanley.
Horton tripled to right-center.
Northrup singled over Javier's head, scoring Horton.
3 Freehan flied to right.

5th Inning
St. Louis
1 Briles struck out.
Brock doubled off the left-center field wall.
Javier singled to left, but Brock was 2 out at the plate, Horton to Freehan.
3 Flood flied to Horton in left-center.

5th Inning (continued)
Detroit
1 Wert popped to short.
2 Lolich flied to center.
3 McAuliffe took a called third strike.

6th Inning
St. Louis
1 Cepeda flied to right.
2 Shannon grounded to short.
3 McCarver lined to right.
Detroit
1 Stanley flied to center.
Kaline singled to left.
Cash walked.
2 Horton grounded to first, Kaline moving to third and Cash to second.
Northrup intentionally walked, loading the bases.
3 Freehan forced Northrup at second, Maxvill to Javier.

7th Inning
St. Louis
1 Davis struck out.
2 Maxvill grounded out, Cash to Lolich.
Briles was hit by a pitched ball.
3 Brock grounded to second.
Detroit
1 Wert took a called third strike.
Lolich blooped a single into short right.
For St. Louis—Hoerner pitching.
McAuliffe singled to right, Lolich stopping at second.
Stanley walked, loading the bases.
Kaline singled to right-center, scoring Lolich and McAuliffe with Stanley going to third.
Cash singled to right, scoring Stanley and sending Kaline to third.
For St. Louis—Willis came in to pitch.
2 Horton fouled to Shannon.
3 Northrup grounded to first.

8th Inning
St. Louis
For Detroit—Oyler at short, Stanley shifts to center as Northrup shifts to left.
Javier beat a tapper down the first base line.
1 Flood forced Javier at second, McAuliffe to Oyler.
2 Cepeda flied to right.
3 Shannon struck out.
Detroit
1 Freehan struck out.
2 Wert lined to the pitcher.
3 Lolich grounded to short.

9th Inning
St. Louis
McCarver singled to center.
1 Gagliano, pinch-hitting for Davis, flied to center.
Spiezio, pinch-hitting for Maxvill, singled to left, McCarver stopping at second.
Schofield ran for Spiezio.
2 Maris, pinch-hitting for Willis, struck out.
3 Brock grounded back to the mound.

Game 6 October 9 at St. Louis

Detroit	Pos	AB	R	H	RBI	PO	A	E
McAuliffe	ab	2	2	0	0	3	1	0
Stanley	ss-cf	5	2	1	0	2	1	1
Kaline	rf	4	3	3	4	7	0	0
Cash	1b	4	2	3	2	5	0	0
Horton	lf	3	2	2	2	0	0	0
Oyler	ss	0	0	0	0	0	0	0
Northrup	cf-lf	5	1	2	4	1	0	0
Freehan	c	4	0	1	1	7	0	0
Wert	3b	3	1	0	0	2	2	0
McLain	p	4	0	0	0	0	1	0
Totals		34	13	12	13	27	5	1

Pitching	IP	H	R	ER	BB	SO
Detroit						
McLain (W)	9	9	1	1	0	7
St. Louis						
Washburn (L)	*2	4	5	5	3	3
Jaster	**0	2	3	3	1	0
Willis	⅓	1	4	4	2	0
Hughes	⅔	2	0	0	0	0
Carlton	3	3	1	1	0	2
Granger	2	0	0	0	1	1
Nelson	1	0	0	0	0	1

*Pitched to 3 batters in 3rd.
**Pitched to 3 batters in 3rd.

St. Louis	Pos	AB	R	H	RBI	PO	A	E
Brock	lf	4	0	1	0	1	0	1
Flood	cf	4	0	0	0	2	0	0
Maris	rf	4	1	2	0	2	0	0
Cepeda	1b	4	0	2	0	7	2	0
McCarver	c	4	0	1	0	8	0	0
Shannon	3b	4	0	1	0	1	2	0
Javier	2b	4	0	1	1	3	2	0
Maxvill	ss	4	0	0	0	4	5	0
Washburn	p	0	0	0	0	0	0	0
Jaster	p	0	0	0	0	0	0	0
Willis	p	0	0	0	0	0	0	0
Hughes	p	0	0	0	0	0	0	0
a Ricketts		1	0	1	0	0	0	0
Carlton	p	0	0	0	0	1	1	0
b Tolan		1	0	0	0	0	0	0
Granger	p	0	0	0	0	0	1	0
c Edwards		1	0	0	0	0	0	0
Nelson	p	0	0	0	0	0	0	0
Totals		35	1	9	1	27	13	1

Det. 0 2 1 0 0 1 0 0 0 0
St. L. 0 0 0 0 0 0 0 0 1

a Singled for Hughes in 3rd.
b Struck out for Carlton in 6th.
c Struck out for Granger in 8th.

Double—Horton. Home Runs—Kaline, Northrup. Sacrifice Hit—McLain. Double Plays—Maxvill to Javier to Cepeda 2, Stanley to McAuliffe to Cash, Granger to Maxvill to Cepeda. Hit by Pitchers—Wert (by Willis), Kaline and Horton (by Granger). Left on Bases—Detroit 5, St. Louis 7. Umpires—Haller, Gorman, Honochick, Landes, Kinnamon, Harvey. Attendance—54,692. Time of Game—2:26.

1st Inning
Detroit
1 McAuliffe struck out.
2 Stanley flied to right.
3 Kaline struck out.
St. Louis
1 Brock bounced back to the mound.
2 Flood lined to short.
3 Maris grounded to third.

2nd Inning
Detroit
Cash walked.
Horton doubled to left-center, scoring Cash.
1 Northrup struck out.
Freehan singled to left, scoring Horton, and went to third as Brock lost the ball for a two-base error.
Wert walked.
2,3 McLain hit into a double play, Maxvill to Javier to Cepeda.
St. Louis
Cepeda singled to left.
1 McCarver popped to Kaline in short right.
2,3 Shannon hit into a double play, Stanley to McAuliffe to Cash.

3rd Inning
Detroit
McAuliffe walked.
Stanley singled to left, McAuliffe stopping at second.
Kaline singled to center, scoring McAuliffe with Stanley going to third.
For St. Louis—Jaster came in to pitch.
Cash singled to center, scoring Stanley with Javier racing to third.
Horton walked, filling the bases.
Northrup hit a grand-slam homer into the right field bullpen.
For St. Louis—Willis now pitching.
Freehan walked.
Wert was hit by a pitched ball.
1 McLain sacrificed, Shannon to Javier. McAuliffe got an intentional pass.
2 Stanley forced Freehan at the plate, Cepeda to McCarver.
Kaline singled to left, scoring Wert and McAuliffe with Stanley going to third.
For St. Louis—Hughes came in to pitch.
Cash singled over Cepeda's head, scoring Stanley with Kaline going to third.
Horton singled off Hughes' glove, scoring Kaline, Cash stopping at second.
3 Northrup flied to left.
St. Louis
1 Javier flied to right.
2 Maxvill flied to center.
Ricketts, pinch-hitting for Hughes, singled to center.
3 Brock flied to right.

4th Inning
Detroit
For St. Louis—Carlton pitching.
1 Freehan grounded to third.
2 Wert popped to Maxvill.
3 McLain struck out.
St. Louis
1 Flood popped to McAuliffe down the right field line.
Maris singled off McAuliffe's glove.
2 Cepeda popped to short.
3 McCarver took a called third strike.

5th Inning
Detroit
1 McAuliffe struck out.
2 Stanley grounded to short.
Kaline hit a line drive homer into the lower left field stands.
Cash singled to right.
3 Horton popped to short.

5th Inning (continued)
St. Louis
1 Shannon struck out.
2 Javier lined to third.
3 Maxvill fouled to Kaline.

6th Inning
Detroit
Northrup singled to center.
1 Freehan flied to Maris in short right.
2 Northrup out on pickoff attempt, Carlton to Cepeda to Maxvill but Northrup declared out for interference of Maxvill's throw, putout credited to Carlton.
3 Wert fouled to Cepeda.
St. Louis
1 Tolan, pinch-hitting for Carlton, struck out.
Brock bounced a single over McAuliffe's head.
2 Flood struck out.
3 Maris popped to McAuliffe in short right.

7th Inning
Detroit
For St. Louis—Granger the 6th pitcher.
1 McLain struck out.
McAuliffe walked.
2,3 Stanley hit into a double play, Maxvill to Javier to Cepeda.
St. Louis
1 Cepeda flied to right.
McCarver singled to right.
Shannon singled to deep short but when Stanley threw wildly to second, McCarver got to third and Shannon to second.
2 Javier grounded to third, as both runners held.
3 Maxvill flied to right.

8th Inning
Detroit
Kaline was hit by a pitch.
1 Cash grounded to first, moving Kaline to second.
Horton also was hit by a pitch.
2,3 Northrup hit into a double play, Granger to Maxvill to Cepeda.
St. Louis
For Detroit—Oyler playing short, Stanley in center and Northrup in left.
1 Edwards, pinch-hitting for Granger, struck out.
Rain delayed the game 49 minutes.
2 Brock struck out.
3 Flood flied to right.

9th Inning
Detroit
For St. Louis—Nelson pitching.
1 Freehan popped to Maxvill in short left.
2 Wert popped to third.
3 McLain struck out.
St. Louis
Maris singled to center.
Cepeda singled to left, Maris stopping at second.
1 McCarver popped to first.
2 Shannon popped to third.
Javier singled to right, scoring Maris with Cepeda stopping at second.
3 Maxvill took a called third strike.

Game 7 October 10 at St. Louis

Detroit	Pos	AB	R	H	RBI	PO	A	E
McAuliffe	2b	4	0	0	0	1	3	0
Stanley	ss-cf	4	0	1	0	5	2	0
Kaline	rf	4	0	0	0	2	0	0
Cash	1b	4	1	1	0	11	2	0
Horton	lf	4	1	2	0	0	0	0
b Tracewski		0	1	0	0	0	0	0
Oyler	ss	0	0	0	0	0	1	0
Northrup	cf-lf	4	1	2	2	1	0	1
Freehan	c	4	0	1	1	6	0	0
Wert	3b	3	0	1	1	0	6	0
Lolich	p	4	0	0	0	0	2	0
Totals		35	4	8	4	27	15	1

Pitching	IP	H	R	ER	BB	SO
Detroit						
Lolich (W)	9	5	1	1	3	4
St. Louis						
Gibson (L)	9	8	4	4	1	8

St. Louis	Pos	AB	R	H	RBI	PO	A	E
Brock	lf	3	0	1	0	1	0	0
Javier	2b	4	0	0	0	3	2	0
Flood	cf	4	0	2	0	3	0	0
Cepeda	1b	4	0	0	0	7	0	0
Shannon	3b	4	1	1	1	1	2	0
McCarver	c	3	0	1	0	8	1	0
Maris	rf	3	0	0	0	3	0	0
Maxvill	ss	2	0	0	0	0	1	0
a Gagliano		1	0	0	0	0	0	0
Schofield	ss	0	0	0	0	0	0	0
Gibson	p	3	0	0	0	0	1	0
Totals		30	1	5	1	27	5	0

Det. 0 0 0 0 0 0 3 0 1
St. L. 0 0 0 0 0 0 0 0 1

a Grounded out for Maxvill in 8th.
b Ran for Horton in 9th.

Double—Freehan. Triple—Northrup. Home Run—Shannon. Stolen Base—Flood. Double Play—Stanley to Cash. Left on Bases—Detroit 5, St. Louis 5. Umpires—Gorman, Honochick, Landes, Kinnamon, Harvey, Haller. Attendance—54,692. Time of Game—2:07.

1st Inning
Detroit
1 McAuliffe foul popped to Cepeda near the first base line.
2 Stanley lined to the mound.
3 Kaline took a called third strike.
St. Louis
1 Brock grounded to second.
2 Javier flied to center.
Flood singled to right-center.
Flood stole second.
3 Shannon flied to Kaline in right-center.

2nd Inning
Detroit
1 Cash flied to right.
2 Horton called out on strikes.
3 Northrup struck out.
St. Louis
McCarver walked.
1,2 Maris hit into a double play, Stanley to Cash.
3 Maxvill grounded to third.

3rd Inning
Detroit
1 Freehan flied to center.
2 Wert struck out.
3 Lolich took a called third strike.
(Gibson's 32nd strikeout in the Series breaking the record of 31 set by Gibson in 1964).
St. Louis
1 Gibson grounded to third.
2 Brock grounded to second.
3 Javier grounded to third.

4th Inning
Detroit
1 McAuliffe flied to right.
Stanley beat out a slow roller to short.
2 Kaline again called out on strikes.
3 Cash grounded to third.
St. Louis
1 Flood grounded to short.
2 Cepeda grounded to third.
3 Shannon struck out.

5th Inning
Detroit
1 Horton popped to second.
2 Northrup foul popped to Shannon, who made a fine running catch down the left field line.
3 Freehan flied to deep left.
St. Louis
McCarver singled to left.
1 Maris struck out.
2 Maxvill fouled to Cash.
3 Gibson popped to second.

6th Inning
Detroit
1 Wert flied to center.
2 Lolich grounded to second.
3 McAuliffe flied to center.
St. Louis
Brock singled to left.
1 Brock picked off first, Lolich to Cash to Stanley.
2 Javier lined to short.
Flood singled to deep short.
3 Flood picked off first, Lolich to Cash to McAuliffe to Lolich to Stanley.

7th Inning
Detroit
1 Stanley took a called third strike.
2 Kaline grounded to third.
Cash singled to right.
Horton singled to left, Cash stopping at second.
Northrup tripled to deep center, scoring Cash and Horton.
Freehan doubled on a liner to left-center, scoring Northrup.
Wert got an intentional pass.
3 Lolich took a called third strike.
St. Louis
1 Cepeda struck out.
Shannon safe at second when Northrup dropped his fly to left-center after he collided with Horton.
2 McCarver flied to right.
3 Maris popped to short.

8th Inning
Detroit
1 McAuliffe grounded to second.
2 Stanley grounded to short.
3 Kaline lined to second.
St. Louis
1 Gagliano, batting for Maxvill, grounded to third.
2 Gibson struck out.
Brock walked.
3 Javier bunted out to third.

9th Inning
Detroit
For St. Louis—Schofield playing short.
1 Cash flied to right.
Horton singled to left.
Tracewski ran for Horton.
Northrup singled to center, sending Tracewski to third.
2 Freehan fouled to Cepeda.
Wert singled to center, scoring Tracewski with Northrup going to second.
3 Lolich popped to Cepeda.
St. Louis
For Detroit—Northrup in left, Stanley in center, Oyler playing short.
1 Flood lined to short.
2 Cepeda fouled to Freehan.
Shannon hit a line-drive homer into the lower left field stands.
3 McCarver fouled to Freehan

1968 WORLD SERIES COMPOSITE BOX

	Wins	Composite Line Score
Detroit Tigers (AL)	4	0 3 1 3 3 2 3 7 0 3 - 34
St. Louis Cardinals (NL)	3	5 0 2 5 4 1 4 4 2 - 27

	Regular Season			
Manager	W	L	Pct.	G. Ahead
Mayo Smith	103	59	.636	12
Red Schoendienst	97	65	.599	9

BATTING AND FIELDING

DETROIT TIGERS

	Pos	G	AB	R	H	2B	3B	HR	RBI	BB	SO	SB	BA	SA	PO	A	E
Norm Cash	1b	7	26	5	10	0	0	1	5	3	5	0	.385	.500	58	7	2
Dick McAuliffe	2b	7	27	5	6	0	0	1	3	4	6	0	.222	.333	12	16	0
Mickey Stanley	ss-cf	7	28	4	6	0	1	0	0	2	4	0	.214	.286	15	16	2
Don Wert	3b	6	17	1	2	0	0	0	2	6	5	0	.118	.118	5	14	0
Al Kaline	rf	7	29	6	11	2	0	2	8	0	7	0	.379	.655	18	0	0
Jim Northrup	cf-lf	7	28	4	7	0	1	2	8	1	5	0	.250	.536	22	0	2
Willie Horton	lf	7	23	6	7	1	1	1	3	5	6	0	.304	.565	5	1	1
Bill Freehan	c	7	24	0	2	1	0	0	2	4	8	0	.083	.125	45	6	2
Eddie Mathews	ph-3b	2	3	0	1	0	0	0	0	1	1	0	.333	.333	0	1	1
Ray Oyler	ss	4	0	0	0	0	0	0	0	0	0	0	—	—	2	0	0
Dick Tracewski	3b-pr	2	0	1	0	0	0	0	0	0	0	0	—	—	0	0	0
Tom Matchick	ph	3	3	0	0	0	0	0	0	0	1	0	.000	.000			
Jim Price	ph	2	2	0	0	0	0	0	0	0	1	0	.000	.000			
Gates Brown	ph	1	1	0	0	0	0	0	0	0	0	0	.000	.000			
Wayne Comer	ph	1	1	1	1	0	0	0	0	0	0	0	1.000	1.000			
Mickey Lolich	p	3	12	2	3	0	0	1	2	1	5	0	.250	.500	1	4	0
Denny McLain	p	3	6	0	0	0	0	0	0	0	4	0	.000	.000	0	3	1
Earl Wilson	p	1	1	0	0	0	0	0	0	0	0	0	.000	.000	0	2	0
Pat Dobson	p	3	0	0	0	0	0	0	0	0	0	0	—	—	1	0	0
John Hiller	p	2	0	0	0	0	0	0	0	0	0	0	—	—	1	0	0
Don McMahon	p	2	0	0	0	0	0	0	0	0	0	0	—	—	1	0	0
Daryl Patterson	p	2	0	0	0	0	0	0	0	0	0	0	—	—	0	1	0
Fred Lasher	p	1	0	0	0	0	0	0	0	0	0	0	—	—	0	1	0
Joe Sparma	p	1	0	0	0	0	0	0	0	0	0	0	—	—	0	0	0
John Warden		Did not play															
team total		7	231	34	56	4	3	8	33	27	59	0	.242	.390	186	72	11

Double Plays—5
Left on Bases—44

ST. LOUIS CARDINALS

	Pos	G	AB	R	H	2B	3B	HR	RBI	BB	SO	SB	BA	SA	PO	A	E
Orlando Cepeda	1b	7	28	2	7	0	0	2	6	2	3	0	.250	.464	47	4	0
Julian Javier	2b	7	27	1	9	1	0	0	3	3	4	1	.333	.370	15	14	0
Dal Maxvill	ss	7	22	0	0	0	0	0	0	3	5	0	.000	.000	15	14	0
Mike Shannon	3b	7	29	3	8	1	0	1	4	1	5	0	.276	.414	5	10	1
Roger Maris	rf-ph	6	19	5	3	1	0	0	1	3	3	0	.158	.211	8	0	0
Curt Flood	cf	7	28	4	8	1	0	0	2	2	2	3	.286	.321	13	0	0
Lou Brock	lf	7	28	6	13	3	1	2	5	3	4	7	.464	.857	13	1	0
Tim McCarver	c	7	27	3	9	0	2	1	4	3	2	0	.333	.593	61	1	0
Ron Davis	rf	2	7	0	0	0	0	0	0	0	2	0	.000	.000	5	0	0
Dick Schofield	pr-ss	2	0	0	0	0	0	0	0	0	0	0	—	—	0	0	0
Phil Gagliano	ph	3	3	0	0	0	0	0	0	0	1	0	.000	.000			
Johnny Edwards	ph	1	1	0	0	0	0	0	0	0	0	0	.000	.000			
Dave Ricketts	ph	1	1	0	1	0	0	0	0	0	0	0	1.000	1.000			
Ed Spiezio	ph	1	1	0	1	0	0	0	0	0	0	0	1.000	1.000			
Bobby Tolan	ph	1	1	0	0	0	0	0	0	0	0	0	.000	.000			
Bob Gibson	p	3	8	2	1	0	0	1	2	1	2	0	.125	.500	2	0	0
Nelson Briles	p	2	4	0	0	0	0	0	0	0	0	0	.000	.000	0	2	0
Ray Washburn	p	2	3	0	0	0	0	0	0	0	1	0	.000	.000	0	1	0
Joe Hoerner	p	3	2	0	1	0	0	0	0	0	0	0	.500	.500	0	0	0
Ron Willis	p	3	0	0	0	0	0	0	0	0	0	0	—	—	1	0	0
Steve Carlton	p	2	0	0	0	0	0	0	0	0	0	0	—	—	1	1	0
Wayne Granger	p	1	0	0	0	0	0	0	0	0	0	0	—	—	0	1	0
Dick Hughes	p	1	0	0	0	0	0	0	0	0	0	0	—	—	0	0	0
Larry Jaster	p	1	0	0	0	0	0	0	0	0	0	0	—	—	0	0	0
Mel Nelson	p	1	0	0	0	0	0	0	0	0	0	0	—	—	0	0	0
team total		7	239	27	61	7	3	7	27	21	40	11	.255	.397	186	48	2

Double Plays—7
Left on Bases—49

DETROIT TIGERS — REGULAR SEASON STATISTICS

	Main Pos	G	AB	R	H	2B	3B	HR	RBI	BB	SO	SB	BA	SA
	1b	127	411	50	108	15	1	25	63	39	70	1	.263	.487
	2b	151	570	95	142	24	10	16	56	82	99	8	.249	.411
	of	153	583	88	151	16	6	11	60	42	57	4	.259	.364
	3b	150	536	44	107	15	1	12	37	37	79	1	.200	.299
	of	102	327	49	94	14	1	10	53	55	39	6	.287	.428
	of	154	580	76	153	29	7	21	90	50	87	4	.264	.447
	of	143	512	68	146	20	2	36	85	49	110	0	.285	.543
	c	155	540	73	142	24	2	25	84	65	64	0	.263	.454
	ph	31	52	4	11	0	0	3	8	5	12	0	.212	.385
	ss	111	215	13	29	6	1	1	12	20	59	0	.135	.186
	ss	90	212	30	33	3	1	4	15	24	51	1	.156	.236
	ss	80	227	18	46	6	2	3	14	10	46	0	.203	.286
	c	64	132	12	23	4	0	3	13	13	14	0	.174	.273
	ph	67	92	15	34	7	2	6	15	12	4	0	.370	.685
	of-ph	48	48	8	6	0	1	1	3	2	7	0	.125	.229
	p	41	70	5	8	3	0	0	3	6	25	0	.114	.157
	p	44	111	7	18	1	0	4	1	37	0		.162	.189
	p	40	88	9	20	0	1	7	17	2	35	0	.227	.489
	p	47	28	2	4	0	0	0	1	2	7	0	.143	.143
	p	39	37	1	3	0	0	0	2	0	14	0	.081	.081
a	p	20	4	0	0	0	0	0	0	0	0	0	.000	.000
	p	38	13	0	0	0	0	0	1	1	8	0	.000	.000
	p	34	9	0	1	0	0	0	0	0	0	0	.111	.111
	p	34	60	2	8	1	0	0	2	1	24	0	.133	.150
	p	28	2	0	0	0	0	0	0	0	0	0	.000	.000
		164	5490	671	1292	190	39	185	640	521	964	26	.235	.385

a—from Chicago (A.L.)

Dave Campbell (2b), Lenny Green (of), Bob Christian (1b-of), Dennis Ribant (p), Les Cain (p), John Wyatt (p), Roy Face (p) and Jim Rooker (p) also played for the Tigers during the season.

ST. LOUIS CARDINALS — REGULAR SEASON STATISTICS

	Main Pos	G	AB	R	H	2B	3B	HR	RBI	BB	SO	SB	BA	SA
	1b	157	600	71	149	26	2	16	73	43	96	8	.248	.378
	2b	139	519	54	135	25	4	4	52	24	61	10	.260	.347
	ss	151	459	51	116	8	5	1	24	52	71	0	.253	.298
	3b	156	576	62	153	29	2	15	79	37	114	1	.266	.401
	of	100	310	25	79	18	2	5	45	24	38	0	.255	.374
	of	150	618	71	186	17	4	5	60	33	58	11	.301	.366
	of	159	660	92	184	46	14	6	51	46	124	62	.279	.418
	c	128	434	35	110	15	6	5	48	26	31	4	.253	.350
b	of	33	79	11	14	4	2	0	5	17	1		.177	.278
	ss-2b	69	127	14	28	7	1	1	8	13	11	1	.220	.315
	ph-2b	53	105	13	24	4	0	2	13	7	12	0	.229	.307
	c	85	230	14	55	9	1	3	29	16	20	1	.239	.326
	ph	20	22	1	3	0	0	0	1	0	3	0	.136	.136
	ph-of	29	51	1	8	0	0	0	2	5	6	1	.157	.157
	of	92	278	28	64	12	1	5	17	13	42	9	.230	.335
	p	35	94	3	16	5	0	0	6	7	32	1	.170	.223
	p	33	80	5	11	2	0	0	5	4	21	0	.138	.163
	p	31	60	5	5	0	0	0	5	8	38	0	.083	.117
	p	47	6	0	0	0	0	0	0	0	4	0	.000	.000
	p	48	11	0	0	0	0	0	0	1	4	0	.000	.000
	p	35	73	6	12	0	1	1	2	3	25	0	.164	.274
	p	34	5	0	1	0	0	0	0	0	0	0	.200	.200
	p	25	15	0	0	0	0	0	0	1	7	0	.000	.000
	p	31	43	2	6	0	0	1	1	1	9	0	.140	.209
	p	18	12	2	2	0	0	0	2	1	4	0	.167	.167
		162	5561	583	1383	227	48	73	539	378	897	110	.249	.346

b—from Houston

Dick Simpson (of), Joe Hague (of), Floyd Wicker (ph), Ted Simmons (c), Mike Torrez (p), Hal Gilson (p) and Pete Mikkelsen (p) also played for the Cardinals during the season.

PITCHING

DETROIT TIGERS — WORLD SERIES STATISTICS

	G	GS	CG	IP	H	R	ER	BB	SO	W	L	SV	ERA
Mickey Lolich	3	3	3	27	20	5	5	6	21	3	0	0	1.67
Denny McLain	3	3	1	16⅔	18	8	6	4	13	1	2	0	3.24
Pat Dobson	3	0	0	4⅔	5	2	2	1	0	0	0	0	3.86
Earl Wilson	1	1	0	4⅓	4	3	3	6	3	0	1	0	6.23
Daryl Patterson	2	0	0	3	1	0	0	1	3	0	0	0	0.00
Fred Lasher	1	0	0	2	1	0	0	1	0	0	0	0	0.00
John Hiller	2	0	0	2	6	4	3	1	0	0	0	0	13.50
Don McMahon	2	0	0	2	4	3	3	0	1	0	0	0	13.50
Joe Sparma	1	0	0	⅓	2	2	2	0	0	0	0	0	54.00
John Warden	Did not play												
team total	7	7	4	62	61	27	24	21	40	4	3	0	3.48

DETROIT TIGERS — REGULAR SEASON STATISTICS

	G	GS	CG	IP	H	ER	BB	SO	W	L	Pct	SV	ShO	ERA
	39	32	8	220	178	78	65	197	17	9	.654	1	4	3.19
	41	41	28	336	241	73	63	280	31	6	.838	0	6	1.96
	47	10	2	125	89	37	48	93	5	8	.385	7	1	2.66
	34	33	10	224	192	71	65	168	13	12	.520	0	3	2.85
	38	1	0	68	53	16	27	49	2	3	.400	7	0	2.12
	34	0	0	49	37	18	22	32	5	1	.833	5	0	3.31
	39	12	4	128	92	34	51	78	9	6	.600	2	1	2.39
a	20	0	0	36	22	8	10	33	3	1	.750	1	0	2.00
	34	31	7	182	169	75	77	110	10	10	.500	0	1	3.71
	28	0	0	37	30	15	15	25	4	1	.800	3	0	3.65
team total	164	164	59	1490	1180	449	486	1115	103	59	.636	29	19	2.71

ST. LOUIS CARDINALS — WORLD SERIES STATISTICS

	G	GS	CG	IP	H	R	ER	BB	SO	W	L	SV	ERA
Bob Gibson	3	3	3	27	18	5	5	4	35	2	1	0	1.67
Nelson Briles	2	2	0	11⅓	13	7	7	4	7	0	1	0	5.56
Ray Washburn	2	2	0	7⅓	7	8	8	7	6	1	1	0	9.82
Joe Hoerner	3	0	0	4⅔	5	4	2	5	3	0	1	1	3.86
Ron Willis	3	0	0	4⅓	2	4	4	4	3	0	0	0	8.31
Steve Carlton	2	0	0	4	7	3	3	1	3	0	0	0	6.75
Wayne Granger	1	0	0	2	2	0	0	1	1	0	0	0	0.00
Mel Nelson	1	0	0	1	0	0	0	0	1	0	0	0	0.00
Dick Hughes	1	0	0	⅔	2	0	0	0	0	0	0	0	0.00
Larry Jaster	1	0	0	0	2	3	3	1	0	0	0	0	∞
team total	7	7	3	62	56	34	32	27	59	3	4	1	4.65

ST. LOUIS CARDINALS — REGULAR SEASON STATISTICS

	G	GS	CG	IP	H	ER	BB	SO	W	L	Pct	SV	ShO	ERA
	34	34	28	305	198	38	62	268	22	9	.710	0	13	1.12
	33	33	13	244	251	76	55	141	19	11	.633	0	4	2.80
	31	30	8	215	191	54	47	124	14	8	.636	0	4	2.26
	47	0	0	49	34	8	12	42	8	2	.800	17	0	1.47
	48	0	0	64	50	24	28	39	2	3	.400	4	0	3.38
	34	33	10	232	215	77	61	162	13	11	.542	0	5	2.99
	34	0	0	44	40	11	12	27	4	2	.667	4	0	2.25
	18	4	1	53	49	17	9	16	2	1	.667	1	0	2.89
	25	5	0	45	45	25	21	49	2	2	.500	4	0	3.52
	31	21	3	154	153	60	38	70	9	13	.409	0	1	3.51
team total	162	162	63	1479	1282	409	375	971	97	65	.599	32	30	2.49

Total Attendance—379,670 Average Attendance—54,239 Winning Player's Share—$10,937 Losing Player's Share—$7,079

1969
Lunar Dust

In a summer when Man walked on the moon for the first time, America gaped in amazement at the miracle of the New York Mets. Lovable losers since their creation in the 1962 expansion, the Mets rekindled the spirit of the Dodgers and Giants in New York fans despite the team's never finishing above ninth place until this year. But with a good young pitching staff led by Tom Seaver and Jerry Koosman and with Cleon Jones, Tommie Agee, and Bud Harrelson playing every day amidst platooning at all other spots, the Mets charged up from nine and a half games back in August with a torrid stretch run. With manager Gil Hodges orchestrating the club flawlessly, the Mets passed the slumping Chicago Cubs in early September and drummed out an amazing eight-game edge in taking the Eastern Division of the National League. Expansion to 12 clubs ushered divisional play into both leagues this season, and the Mets nailed down the N.L. pennant by beating the highly favored Atlanta Braves three straight games in the first championship play-off series between divisional winners.

The Baltimore Orioles came into the World Series similarly favored over the Mets after taking the Eastern Division of the American League by 19 games and then sweeping the Minnesota Twins in the championship series. Managed by Earl Weaver, the Orioles had an all-around squad that was the class of baseball. Frank Robinson, Boog Powell, and Brooks Robinson swung powerful bats, while Brooks also joined Mark Belanger and Paul Blair as peerless glovemen. The pitching staff which seemed so young in 1966 had grown into a seasoned corps, with Mike Cuellar, Dave McNally, and Jim Palmer three top-flight starters. Although the Mets had momentum and the hopes of millions, the Orioles objectively had the better club.

The Mets' magic seemed to turn into jitters in the Series opener in Baltimore. The Orioles got off to a flying start when Don Buford drove Seaver's second pitch over the right-field fence for a home run. The Birds added three more runs in the fourth inning, and Cuellar coasted to a 4–1 victory. The Mets broke the ice in the second game with a solo homer by Donn Clendenon in the fourth inning, but the Orioles tied the score in the seventh on a single by Blair, his stolen base, and Brooks Robinson's single. Those two singles were the only hits Koosman would allow all day, while the Mets went ahead in the top of the ninth on singles by Ed Charles, Jerry Grote, and Al Weis. When Koosman walked two men in the bottom of the inning, Hodges brought Ron Taylor out of the bullpen to finish the 2–1 victory.

When the clubs reassembled in Shea Stadium after a day of travel, the Mets had their magic back in full swing. Tommie Agee led off with a home run off Palmer in the first inning and pitcher Gary Gentry drove in two runs with a double in the second inning. The hard-throwing Gentry kept the Orioles scoreless with the help of Agee, who tore from his center-field spot deep into the left-center gap to make a diving backhand grab of Elrod Hendrick's shot in the fourth inning. Gentry walked three men in the seventh inning with two out, so Hodges relieved him with fireballing Nolan Ryan. Blair greeted him with a liner up the right-center gap, but Agee again outdid himself with a diving catch that preserved a 5–0 New York victory. Seaver and Cuellar pitched again in game four, with New York taking a 1–0 lead on Clendenon's second-inning homer. The Birds threatened to go ahead in the ninth, but a diving catch by right fielder Ron Swoboda cut the rally short with only one run. In the bottom of the tenth inning, the Met magic reappeared. Buford misplayed Grote's fly to left into a double, and after Weis got an intentional walk, Weaver brought in Pete Richert to pitch and Hodges sent up J.C. Martin to hit. Martin bunted toward the mound, and Richert's throw to first hit Martin on the wrist and caromed away, letting the winning run score for New York. Photos showed that Martin had run illegally in foul territory, but the 2–1 Met victory stood up. The will of fate was now clear, and the world waited for its manifestation. After the Orioles took an early 3–0 lead in the fifth game, the Mets came back in the sixth inning, with Cleon Jones proving he was hit on the foot with a pitch by showing a shoe-polish mark on the ball and Clendenon following that incident with a homer. Light-hitting Al Weis socked a home run in the seventh to tie it up, and then two New York doubles and two Baltimore throwing errors gave the Mets two eighth-inning runs and capped an astronomical miracle with a 5–3 triumph.

Game 1 October 11 at Baltimore

N.Y.   000 000 100
Bal.   100 300 00x

New York	Pos	AB	R	H	RBI	PO	A	E
Agee	cf	4	0	0	0	4	0	0
Harrelson	ss	3	0	1	0	0	1	0
Jones	lf	4	0	1	0	1	0	0
Clendenon	1b	4	1	2	0	9	1	0
Swoboda	rf	3	0	1	0	0	0	0
Charles	3b	4	0	0	0	1	4	0
Grote	c	4	0	1	0	6	0	0
Weis	2b	1	0	0	1	3	1	1
Seaver	p	1	0	0	0	0	0	0
a Dyer		1	0	0	0	0	0	0
Cardwell	p	0	0	0	0	0	0	0
b Gaspar		1	0	0	0	0	0	0
Taylor	p	0	0	0	0	1	0	0
c Shamsky		1	0	0	0	0	0	0
Totals		31	1	6	1	24	8	1

Baltimore	Pos	AB	R	H	RBI	PO	A	E
Buford	lf	4	1	2	2	2	0	0
Blair	cf	3	0	0	0	2	0	0
F. Robinson	rf	4	0	0	0	2	0	0
Powell	1b	4	0	1	0	11	0	0
B. Robinson	3b	4	0	0	0	0	6	0
Hendricks	c	3	1	1	0	8	0	0
Johnson	2b	2	1	0	1	1	3	0
Belanger	ss	3	1	1	1	1	3	0
Cuellar	p	3	0	1	0	0	0	0
Totals		30	4	6	4	27	12	0

Pitching	IP	H	R	ER	BB	SO
New York						
Seaver (L)	5	6	4	4	1	3
Cardwell	1	0	0	0	0	0
Taylor	2	0	0	0	1	3
Baltimore						
Cuellar (W)	9	6	1	1	4	8

a Grounded out for Seaver in 6th.
b Grounded out for Cardwell in 7th.
c Grounded out for Taylor in 9th.

Doubles—Buford, Clendenon. Home Run—Buford. Sacrifice Fly—Weis. Double Play—Belanger to Johnson to Powell. Left on Bases—New York 8, Baltimore 4. Umpires—Soar (A), Secory (N), Napp (A), Crawford (N), DiMuro (A), Weyer (N). Attendance—50,429. Time of Game—2:13.

1st Inning
New York
1 Agee grounded to third.
2 Harrelson grounded to third.
Jones singled to center.
3 Clendenon struck out.
Baltimore
Buford homered over the right field fence.
1 Blair struck out.
2 F. Robinson struck out.
Powell singled to right.
3 B. Robinson flied to deep center.

2nd Inning
New York
1 Swoboda struck out.
2 Charles struck out.
3 Grote grounded to short.
Baltimore
1 Hendricks popped to third.
2 Johnson flied to center.
3 Belanger grounded to third.

3rd Inning
New York
Weis walked.
1 Seaver struck out.
2,3 Agee hit into a double play, Belanger to Johnson to Powell.
Baltimore
1 Cuellar struck out.
Buford safe on Weis' fumble.
2 Blair flied to left.
3 F. Robinson grounded to third.

4th Inning
New York
1 Harrelson grounded to third.
2 Jones flied to left.
Clendenon doubled to left-center.
3 Swoboda flied to center.
Baltimore
1 Powell grounded to short.
2 B. Robinson popped to second.
Hendricks singled to right.
Johnson walked.
Belanger singled to right, scoring Hendricks with Johnson going to third.
Cuellar singled to left-center, scoring Johnson as Belanger stopped at second.
Buford doubled down the right field line, Belanger scoring with Cuellar going to third.
3 Blair grounded to third.

5th Inning
New York
1 Charles grounded to third.
2 Grote flied to right.
3 Weis grounded to third.
Baltimore
1 F. Robinson flied to Agee in left-center.
2 Powell grounded to second.
3 B. Robinson lined to second.

6th Inning
New York
1 Dyer, pinch-hitting for Seaver, grounded to short.
2 Agee took a called third strike.
Harrelson walked.
3 Jones fouled to Powell.
Baltimore
For New York—Cardwell pitching.
1 Hendricks grounded to first.
2 Johnson grounded to third.
3 Belanger fouled to Clendenon.

7th Inning
New York
Clendenon singled to center.
Swoboda walked.
1 Charles flied to right.
Grote singled to left, loading the bases.
2 Weis hit a sacrifice fly to left, Clendenon scoring after the catch.
3 Gaspar, batting for Cardwell, was out on a roller to third.
Baltimore
For New York—Taylor pitching.
1 Cuellar struck out.
2 Buford flied to center.
Blair walked.
3 Blair was picked off first, Taylor to Clendenon to Weis.

8th Inning
New York
1 Agee struck out.
Harrelson singled to left.
2 Jones forced Harrelson at second, Johnson to Belanger.
3 Clendenon struck out.
Baltimore
1 F. Robinson struck out.
2 Powell grounded to first.
3 B. Robinson struck out.

9th Inning
New York
Swoboda singled off Cuellar's glove.
1 Charles flied to center.
2 Grote took a called third strike.
Weis walked.
3 Shamsky, pinch-hitting for Taylor, grounded to second.

Game 2 October 12 at Baltimore

New York	Pos	AB	R	H	RBI	PO	A	E
Agee	cf	4	0	0	0	3	0	0
Harrelson	ss	3	0	0	0	3	3	0
Jones	lf	4	0	0	0	2	0	0
Clendenon	1b	3	1	1	1	7	0	0
Swoboda	rf	4	0	0	0	5	0	0
Charles	3b	4	1	2	0	0	3	0
Grote	c	4	0	1	0	4	0	0
Weis	2b	3	0	2	1	3	1	0
Koosman	p	4	0	0	0	0	1	0
Taylor	p	0	0	0	0	0	0	0
Totals		33	2	6	2	27	7	0

Pitching	IP	H	R	ER	BB	SO
New York						
Koosman (W)	$8\frac{2}{3}$	2	1	1	3	4
Taylor (SV)	$\frac{1}{3}$	0	0	0	0	0
Baltimore						
McNally (L)	9	6	2	2	3	7

N.Y.	000	100	001
Bal.	000	000	100

Baltimore	Pos	AB	R	H	RBI	PO	A	E
Buford	lf	4	0	0	0	1	0	0
Blair	cf	4	1	1	0	2	0	0
F. Robinson	rf	3	0	0	0	2	0	0
a Rettenmund		0	0	0	0	0	0	0
Powell	1b	3	0	0	0	10	1	0
B. Robinson	3b	4	0	1	1	0	2	0
Johnson	2b	2	0	0	0	1	3	0
Etchebarren	c	3	0	0	0	8	0	0
Belanger	ss	3	0	0	0	2	4	0
McNally	p	3	0	0	0	1	1	0
Totals		29	1	2	1	27	11	0

a Ran for F. Robinson in 9th.

Double—Charles. Home Run—Clendenon. Stolen Base—Blair. Wild Pitch—McNally. Left on Bases—New York 7, Baltimore 4. Umpires—Secory, Napp, Crawford, DiMuro, Weyer, Soar. Attendance—50,850. Time of Game—2:20.

1st Inning
New York
1 Agee struck out.
2 Harrelson tapped back to the mound.
3 Jones fouled to Powell.
Baltimore
1 Buford struck out.
2 Blair flied to left.
3 F. Robinson flied to Swoboda in deep right-center.

2nd Inning
New York
Clendenon walked.
1 Swoboda fouled to Powell.
2 Charles forced Clendenon at second, Johnson to Belanger.
Charles went to second on a wild pitch.
3 Grote flied to center.
Baltimore
1 Powell struck out.
2 B. Robinson popped to Harrelson in short center.
Johnson walked.
3 Etchebarren flied to center.

3rd Inning
New York
Weis singled to center.
1 Koosman struck out, bunting foul on the third strike.
2 Agee forced Weis at second, Belanger to Johnson.
Harrelson walked.
3 Jones lined to Buford making a running catch near the foul line.
Baltimore
1 Belanger flied to deep center.
2 McNally struck out.
3 Buford lined to short.

4th Inning
New York
Clendenon hit a home-run over the right field fence.
1 Swoboda struck out.
2 Charles grounded to short.
3 Grote rolled out to B. Robinson who made a good onehanded pickup and threw Grote out on a very close play.
Baltimore
1 Blair popped to short.
2 F. Robinson grounded to short.
3 Powell grounded to second.

5th Inning
New York
1 Weis called out on strikes.
2 Koosman struck out.
3 Agee called out on strikes.
Baltimore
1 B. Robinson grounded to third.
2 Johnson flied to right.
3 Etchebarren flied to very deep right.

6th Inning
New York
1 Harrelson fouled to Etchebarren on a bunt attempt.
2 Jones flied to Blair in short center.
3 Clendenon grounded to second.
Baltimore
1 Belanger flied to right.
2 McNally bounced back to the mound.
3 Buford grounded to short.

7th Inning
New York
1 Swoboda flied to deep right.
Charles doubled into the left field corner.
2 Grote popped to short.
Weis given an intentional pass.
3 Koosman grounded to second.
Baltimore
Blair singled to left **(first hit off of Koosman).**
1 F. Robinson lined to center.
2 Powell popped to short.
Blair stole second.
B. Robinson singled to center, scoring Blair.
3 Johnson forced B. Robinson at second, Charles to Weis.

8th Inning
New York
1 Agee grounded to short.
2 Harrelson rolled to third.
3 Jones flied to right.
Baltimore
1 Etchebarren lined to second.
2 Belanger took a called third strike.
3 McNally flied to deep left.

9th Inning
New York
1 Clenden struck out.
2 Swoboda grounded out, Powell to McNally.
Charles singled to left.
Grote singled to left, moving Charles to third.
Weis singled to left, scoring Charles as Grote stopped at second.
3 Koosman grounded to short.
Baltimore
1 Buford flied to short right.
2 Blair grounded to short.
F. Robinson walked.
Rettenmund ran for F. Robinson.
Powell walked.
For New York—Taylor came in to pitch.
3 B. Robinson grounded to third.

Game 3 October 14 at New York

Baltimore	Pos	AB	R	H	RBI	PO	A	E
Buford	lf	3	0	0	0	2	0	0
Blair	cf	5	0	0	0	0	0	0
F. Robinson	rf	2	0	1	0	7	0	0
Powell	1b	4	0	2	0	5	1	0
B. Robinson	3b	4	0	0	0	0	1	0
Hendricks	c	4	0	0	0	6	0	0
Johnson	2b	4	0	0	0	1	3	0
Belanger	ss	2	0	0	0	2	0	0
Palmer	p	2	0	0	0	1	0	1
a May		0	0	0	0	0	0	0
Leonhard	p	0	0	0	0	0	1	0
b Dalrymple		1	0	1	0	0	0	0
c Salmon		0	0	0	0	0	0	0
Totals		31	0	4	0	24	6	1

a Walked for Palmer in 7th.
b Singled for Leonhard in 9th.
c Ran for Dalrymple in 9th.

Doubles—Gentry, Grote. Home Runs—Agee, Kranepool. Sacrifice Hit—Garrett. Left on Bases—Baltimore 11, New York 6. Umpires—Napp, Crawford, DiMuro, Weyer, Soar, Secory. Attendance—56,335. Time of Game—2:23.

Bal.	000	000	000
N.Y.	120	001	01x

New York	Pos	AB	R	H	RBI	PO	A	E
Agee	cf	3	1	1	1	6	0	0
Garrett	3b	1	0	0	0	1	0	0
Jones	lf	4	0	0	0	0	0	0
Shamsky	rf	4	0	0	0	1	0	0
Weis	2b	0	0	0	0	0	0	0
Boswell	2b	3	1	1	0	0	1	0
Gaspar	rf	1	0	0	0	2	0	0
Kranepool	1b	4	1	1	1	7	0	0
Grote	c	3	1	1	1	7	0	0
Harrelson	ss	3	1	1	0	3	5	0
Gentry	p	3	0	1	2	0	0	0
Ryan	p	0	0	0	0	0	0	0
Totals		29	5	6	5	27	6	0

Pitching	IP	H	R	ER	BB	SO
Baltimore						
Palmer (L)	6	5	4	4	4	5
Leonhard	2	1	1	1	1	1
New York						
Gentry (W)	$6\frac{2}{3}$	3	0	0	5	4
Ryan (SV)	$2\frac{1}{3}$	1	0	0	2	3

1st Inning
Baltimore
1 Buford struck out.
2 Blair flied to center.
F. Robinson walked.
3 Powell grounded to second.
New York
Agee homered over the center field fence.
1 Garrett took a called third strike.
2 Jones flied to deep right.
3 Shamsky also flied to deep right.

2nd Inning
Baltimore
1 B. Robinson grounded to short.
2 Hendricks popped to third.
3 Johnson popped to Harrelson in short left.
New York
1 Boswell grounded out, Powell to Palmer.
2 Kranepool popped to short.
Grote walked.
Harrelson singled to center, Grote stopping at second.
Gentry doubled over Blair's head in right-center, scoring Grote and Harrelson.
3 Agee grounded to third.

3rd Inning
Baltimore
1 Belanger grounded to short.
2 Palmer fouled to Kranepool.
3 Buford fouled to Harrelson down the left field line.
New York
Garrett walked.
1 Jones struck out.
2 Shamsky grounded to first, Garrett moving to second.
3 Boswell flied to right.

4th Inning
Baltimore
1 Blair took a called third strike.
F. Robinson singled to left.
Powell singled to right, sending F. Robinson to third.
2 B. Robinson struck out.
3 Hendricks flied to deep left-center where Agee made a back-handed catch at the base of the wall.
New York
1 Kranepool flied to right.
2 Grote grounded to second.
Harrelson walked.
Harrelson to second on Palmer's wild pick-off throw to first.
3 Gentry struck out.

5th Inning
Baltimore
1 Johnson grounded to deep short.
2 Belanger grounded to short.
3 Palmer grounded to short.
New York
1 Agee lined to short.
Garrett walked.
2 Jones flied to right.
3 Shamsky grounded to second.

6th Inning
Baltimore
1 Buford struck out.
2 Blair popped to short.
F. Robinson walked.
Powell singled to right, sending F. Robinson to third.
3 B. Robinson flied to right.
New York
Boswell beat out a slow roller to second.
1 Kranepool grounded to second, advancing Boswell to second.
Grote doubled down the left field line, scoring Boswell.
2 Harrelson took a called third strike.
3 Gentry struck out.

7th Inning
Baltimore
1 Hendricks flied to Agee in deep right-center.
2 Johnson flied to center.
Belanger walked.
May, pinch-hitting for Palmer, walked.
Buford walked, loading the bases.
For New York—Ryan came in to pitch.
3 Blair was robbed of an extra-base hit when Agee made a belly sliding one-handed catch of his liner in right-center.
New York
For Baltimore—Leonhard pitching.
Agee walked.
1 Garrett sacrificed Agee to second, Leonhard to Johnson covering first.
2 Jones flied to short right.
3 Shamsky flied to left.

8th Inning
Baltimore
For New York—Weis playing second and Gaspar in right.
1 F. Robinson flied to Agee in deep left-center.
2 Powell took a called third strike.
3 B. Robinson struck out.
New York
1 Gaspar flied to short left.
Kranepool homered over the right-center field fence.
2 Grote flied to right.
3 Harrelson struck out.

9th Inning
Baltimore
1 Hendricks flied to right.
2 Johnson flied to right.
Belanger walked.
Dalrymple, pinch-hitting for Leonhard, singled to the right of second, moving Belanger to second.
Salmon ran for Dalrymple.
Buford walked, loading the bases.
3 Blair took a called third strike.

1969

Game 4 October 15 at New York

Baltimore	Pos	AB	R	H	RBI	PO	A	E
Buford	lf	5	0	0	0	2	0	0
Blair	cf	4	0	1	0	0	0	0
F. Robinson	rf	4	1	1	0	0	0	0
Powell	1b	4	0	1	0	14	0	0
B. Robinson	3b	3	0	0	1	0	3	0
Hendricks	c	3	0	0	0	7	1	0
Johnson	2b	4	0	0	0	4	6	0
Belanger	ss	4	0	1	0	0	6	0
Cuellar	p	2	0	1	0	0	1	0
a May		1	0	0	0	0	0	0
Watt	p	0	0	0	0	0	0	0
c Dalrymple		1	0	1	0	0	0	0
Hall	p	0	0	0	0	0	0	0
Richert	p	0	0	0	0	0	0	1
Totals		35	1	6	1	x27	17	1

x None out when winning run scored.
a Struck out for Cuellar in 8th.
b Grounded out for Charles in 9th.
c Singled for Watt in 10th.
d Ran for Grote in 10th.
e Sacrificed and safe on an error for Seaver in 10th.

Double—Grote. Home Run—Clendenon. Sacrifice Hit—Martin. Sacrifice Fly—B. Robinson. Double Plays—Belanger to Johnson to Powell 2, Hendricks to Johnson. Left on Bases—Baltimore 7, New York 7. Umpires—Crawford, DiMuro, Weyer, Soar, Secory, Napp. Attendance—57,367. Time of Game—2:33.

Bal.	000 000 001 0
N.Y.	010 000 000 1

New York	Pos	AB	R	H	RBI	PO	A	E
Agee	cf	4	0	1	0	2	0	0
Harrelson	ss	4	0	1	0	5	2	0
Jones	lf	4	0	1	0	1	0	0
Clendenon	1b	4	1	1	1	6	3	0
Swoboda	rf	4	0	3	0	4	0	0
Charles	3b	3	0	0	0	2	1	0
b Shamsky		1	0	0	0	0	0	0
Garrett	3b	0	0	0	0	0	0	1
Grote	c	4	0	1	0	7	2	0
d Gaspar		0	1	0	0	0	0	0
Weis	2b	3	0	2	0	1	1	0
Seaver	p	3	0	0	0	2	1	0
e Martin		0	0	0	0	0	0	0
Totals		34	2	10	1	30	10	1

Pitching	IP	H	R	ER	BB	SO
Baltimore						
Cuellar	7	7	1	1	0	5
Watt	2	2	0	0	0	2
Hall (L)	*0	1	1	0	1	0
Richert	**0	0	0	0	0	0
New York						
Seaver (W)	10	6	1	1	2	6

*Pitched to 2 batters in 10th.
**Pitched to 1 batter in 10th.

1st Inning
Baltimore
1 Buford struck out.
  Blair singled to center.
2 F. Robinson flied to Agee in deep left-center.
3 Powell took a called third strike.
New York
1 Agee grounded to third.
  Harrelson singled to left.
2,3 Jones hit into a double play, Belanger to Johnson to Powell.

2nd Inning
Baltimore
1 B. Robinson grounded to short.
  Hendricks walked.
2 Johnson forced Hendricks at second, Harrelson to Weis.
3 Johnson was caught stealing, Grote to Harrelson.
New York
  Clendenon hit a home run over the left field fence.
1 Swoboda grounded to short.
2 Charles grounded to short.
3 Grote took a called third strike.

3rd Inning
Baltimore
  Belanger singled to right.
  Cuellar blooped a single to short left-center, moving Belanger to second.
1 Buford forced Cuellar at second, Clendenon to Harrelson, with Belanger going to third.
2 Blair out on a bunt, Seaver to Clendenon, Buford advancing to second as Belanger held third.
3 F. Robinson fouled to Clendenon.
New York
  Weis singled on a bouncer off B. Robinson's chest.
1 Seaver struck out, bunting foul on the third strike.
  Agee singled to left-center, Weis stopping at second.
2 Harrelson grounded to second, both runners advancing.
3 Jones grounded to third.

4th Inning
Baltimore
1 Powell grounded to second.
2 B. Robinson fouled to Charles.
3 Hendricks grounded out, Clendenon to Seaver.
New York
1 Clendenon took a called third strike.
  Swoboda singled to center.
2,3 Charles struck out and Swoboda was doubled up trying for second, Hendricks to Johnson.

5th Inning
Baltimore
1 Johnson popped to Jones in short left.
2 Belanger tapped out, Grote to Clendenon.
3 Cuellar struck out.
New York
1 Grote struck out.
  Weis singled to left.
2,3 Seaver hit into a double play, Belanger to Johnson to Powell.

6th Inning
Baltimore
1 Buford grounded out, Clendenon to Seaver.
  Blair walked.
2 F. Robinson popped to short.
3 Powell flied to center.
New York
1 Agee grounded to third.
2 Harrelson popped to second.
3 Jones grounded to short.

7th Inning
Baltimore
1 B. Robinson grounded to third.
2 Hendricks popped to Harrelson in short left.
3 Johnson struck out.
New York
1 Clendenon bounced back to the mound.
  Swoboda singled to left.
2 Charles lined to left.
3 Grote grounded to short.

8th Inning
Baltimore
1 Belanger popped to short.
2 May, pinch-hitting for Cuellar, fanned.
3 Buford popped to third.
New York
  For Baltimore—Watt pitching.
1 Weis flied to left.
2 Seaver grounded to second.
3 Agee struck out.

9th Inning
Baltimore
1 Blair flied to right.
  F. Robinson singled to left.
  Powell singled to right, sending F. Robinson to third.
2 B. Robinson hit a sacrifice fly, being robbed of a base-hit as Swoboda made a diving onehanded catch in right-center. F. Robinson scored after the catch.
3 Hendricks lined to Swoboda who made a good running catch.
New York
1 Harrelson grounded to second.
  Jones singled to left.
2 Clendenon struck out.
  Swoboda blooped a single to right, Jones advancing to third.
3 Shamsky, pinch-hitting for Charles, grounded to second.

10th Inning
Baltimore
  For New York—Garrett playing third.
  Johnson safe on Garrett's fumble.
1 Belanger fouled to Grote.
  Dalrymple, batting for Watt, singled to center, Johnson stopping at second.
2 Buford flied to deep right, Johnson taking third after the catch.
3 Blair struck out.
New York
  For Baltimore—Hall pitching.
  Grote doubled into short left.
  Gaspar ran for Grote.
  Weis got an intentional pass.
  Martin, batting for Seaver.
  For Baltimore—Richert came in to pitch.
  Martin bunted, Richert fielded it and on the throw to first the ball hit Martin on the wrist and rolled toward the outfield. Gaspar scored the game-ending run. Martin given a sacrifice with an error to Richert.

Game 5 October 16 at New York

Baltimore	Pos	AB	R	H	RBI	PO	A	E
Buford	lf	4	0	0	0	1	0	0
Blair	cf	4	0	0	0	3	0	0
F. Robinson	rf	3	1	1	1	2	0	0
Powell	1b	4	0	1	0	6	0	1
b Salmon		0	0	0	0	0	0	0
B. Robinson	3b	4	0	0	1	1	4	0
Johnson	2b	4	0	1	0	1	0	0
Etchebarren	c	3	0	0	0	8	0	0
Belanger	ss	3	1	1	0	2	1	0
McNally	p	2	1	1	2	0	0	0
a Motton		1	0	0	0	0	0	0
Watt	p	0	0	0	0	0	0	1
Totals		32	3	5	3	24	5	2

a Grounded out for McNally in 8th.
b Ran for Powell in 9th.

Doubles—Jones, Koosman, Swoboda. Home Runs—Clendenon, McNally, F. Robinson, Weis. Stolen Base—Agee. Hit by Pitch—Jones (by McNally). Left on Bases—Baltimore 3, New York 6. Umpires—DiMuro, Weyer, Soar, Secory, Napp, Crawford. Attendance—57,397. Time of Game—2:14.

Bal.	003 000 000
N.Y.	000 002 12 x

New York	Pos	AB	R	H	RBI	PO	A	E
Agee	cf	3	0	1	0	4	0	0
Harrelson	ss	4	0	0	0	1	6	0
Jones	lf	3	2	1	0	3	0	0
Clendenon	1b	3	1	1	2	8	0	0
Swoboda	rf	4	1	2	1	5	0	0
Charles	3b	4	0	0	0	0	2	0
Grote	c	4	0	0	0	5	0	0
Weis	2b	4	1	1	1	1	2	0
Koosman	p	3	0	1	0	0	0	0
Totals		32	5	7	4	27	10	0

Pitching	IP	H	R	ER	BB	SO
Baltimore						
McNally	7	5	3	3	2	6
Watt (L)	1	2	2	1	0	1
New York						
Koosman (W)	9	5	3	3	1	5

1st Inning
Baltimore
1 Buford grounded to short.
2 Blair flied to center.
3 F. Robinson flied to short right.
New York
  Agee walked.
1 Harrelson struck out with Agee stealing second.
2 Jones flied to right, Agee racing to third after the catch.
  Clendenon walked.
3 Swoboda struck out.

2nd Inning
Baltimore
1 Powell flied to left.
2 B. Robinson grounded to short.
  Johnson singled off Charles' glove.
3 Etchebarren forced Johnson at second, Charles to Weis.
New York
1 Charles grounded to third.
2 Grote flied to center.
3 Weis popped to short.

3rd Inning
Baltimore
  Belanger singled down the right field line.
  McNally hit a two-run homer into the left-field bullpen.
1 Buford grounded to short.
2 Blair struck out.
  F. Robinson homered over the fence in left-center.
3 Powell struck out.
New York
  Koosman doubled into the left field corner.
1 Agee flied to short center.
2 Harrelson struck out.
3 Jones popped to first.

4th Inning
Baltimore
1 B. Robinson flied to Agee in left-center.
2 Johnson bounced back to the mound.
3 Etchebarren grounded to second.
New York
1 Clendenon took a called third strike.
  Swoboda singled to center.
2 Charles fouled to Etchebarren.
3 Grote forced Swoboda at second, Belanger unassisted.

5th Inning
Baltimore
1 Belanger flied to right.
2 McNally struck out.
3 Buford flied to Swoboda in right-center making a good running catch.
New York
1 Weis grounded to third.
2 Koosman struck out.
  Agee beat out a bunt down the third base line.
3 Harrelson flied to center.

6th Inning
Baltimore
1 Blair flied to deep center.
2 F. Robinson struck out.
  Powell singled to left.
3 B. Robinson flied to left.
New York
  Jones was hit by a pitch on the left foot. Shoe polish on ball was the proving factor that Jones was hit.
  Clendenon hit a two-run homer into the left field stands.
1 Swoboda popped to second.
2 Charles grounded to short.
3 Grote grounded to Short.

7th Inning
Baltimore
1 Johnson fouled to Swoboda.
2 Etchebarren struck out.
3 Belanger grounded to short.
New York
  Weis homered into the left field stands.
1 Koosman struck out.
2 Agee flied to right.
3 Harrelson lined to third.

8th Inning
Baltimore
1 Motton, pinch-hitting for McNally, grounded to short.
2 Buford flied to center.
3 Blair grounded to deep short.
New York
  For Baltimore—Watt pitching.
  Jones doubled off the left-center field fence.
1 Clendenon grounded to third, Jones holding second.
  Swoboda doubled to left, scoring Jones.
2 Charles flied to left.
  Grote safe at first as Powell fumbled his grounder for an error and when Watt fumbled Powell's late throw for another error, Swoboda scored.
3 Weis took a called third strike.

9th Inning
Baltimore
  F. Robinson walked.
1 Powell forced F. Robinson at second, Weis to Harrelson.
  Salmon ran for Powell.
2 B. Robinson flied to right.
3 Johnson flied to left.

1969 WORLD SERIES COMPOSITE BOX

	Wins	Composite Line Score	
New York Mets (N.L.)	4	1 3 0 1 0 3 2 3 1 1	- 15
Baltimore Orioles (A.L.)	1	1 0 3 3 0 0 1 0 1 0	- 9

Manager	W	L	Pct.	G. Ahead	
	Regular Season				
Gil Hodges	100	62	.617	8	(beat Atlanta in Playoffs)
Earl Weaver	109	53	.673	19	(beat Minnesota in Playoffs)

BATTING AND FIELDING

WORLD SERIES STATISTICS

	Pos	G	AB	R	H	2B	3B	HR	RBI	BB	SO	SB	BA	SA	PO	A	E
NEW YORK METS																	
Donn Clendenon	1b	4	14	**4**	5	1	0	**3**	**4**	2	**6**	0	.357	**1.071**	30	4	0
Al Weis	2b	5	11	1	5	0	0	1	3	**4**	2	0	**.455**	.727	8	5	**1**
Bud Harrelson	ss	5	17	1	3	0	0	0	0	3	4	0	.176	.176	12	**17**	0
Ed Charles	3b	4	15	1	2	1	0	0	0	0	2	0	.133	.200	3	9	0
Ron Swododa	rf	4	15	1	**6**	1	0	0	1	1	3	0	.400	.467	14	0	0
Tommie Agee	cf	5	18	1	3	0	0	1	1	2	5	1	.167	.333	19	0	0
Cleon Jones	lf	5	19	2	3	1	0	0	0	0	1	0	.158	.211	7	0	0
Jerry Grote	c	5	19	1	4	**2**	0	0	1	1	3	0	.211	.316	29	2	0
Art Shamsky	ph-rf	3	6	0	0	0	0	0	0	0	0	0	.000	.000	1	0	0
Ken Boswell	2b	1	3	1	1	0	0	0	0	0	0	0	.333	.333	0	1	0
Rod Gaspar	ph-rf-pr	3	2	1	0	0	0	0	0	0	0	0	.000	.000	2	0	0
Ed Kranepool	1b	1	4	1	1	0	0	1	1	0	0	0	.250	1.000	7	0	0
Wayne Garrett	3b	2	1	0	0	0	0	0	0	2	1	0	.000	.000	1	0	**1**
Duffy Dyer	ph	1	1	0	0	0	0	0	0	0	0	0	.000	.000			
J. C. Martin	ph	1	0	0	0	0	0	0	0	0	0	0	—	—			
Jerry Koosman	p	2	7	0	1	1	0	0	0	0	4	0	.143	.286	0	2	0
Tom Seaver	p	2	4	0	0	0	0	0	0	0	2	0	.000	.000	2	1	0
Gary Gentry	p	1	3	0	1	1	0	0	2	0	2	0	.333	.667	0	0	0
Ron Taylor	p	2	0	0	0	0	0	0	0	0	0	0	—	—	0	1	0
Don Cardwell	p	1	0	0	0	0	0	0	0	0	0	0	—	—	0	0	0
Nolan Ryan	p	1	0	0	0	0	0	0	0	0	0	0	—	—	0	0	0
Tug McGraw	Did not play																
Cal Koonce	Did not play																
Jim McAndrew	Did not play																
Jack DiLauro	Did not play																
team total		5	159	15	35	8	0	6	13	15	35	1	.220	.384	135	42	2

Double Plays—0
Left on Bases—34

REGULAR SEASON STATISTICS

		Main Pos	G	AB	R	H	2B	3B	HR	RBI	BB	SO	SB	BA	SA
NEW YORK METS															
Donn Clendenon	a	1b	72	202	31	51	5	0	12	37	19	62	3	.252	.455
Al Weis		ss-2b	103	247	20	53	9	2	2	23	15	51	3	.215	.291
Bud Harrelson		ss	123	395	42	98	11	6	0	24	54	54	1	.248	.306
Ed Charles		3b	61	169	21	35	8	1	3	18	18	31	4	.207	.320
Ron Swododa		of	109	327	38	77	10	2	9	52	43	90	1	.235	.361
Tommie Agee		of	149	565	97	153	23	4	26	76	59	137	12	.271	.464
Cleon Jones		of	137	483	92	164	25	4	12	75	64	60	16	.340	.482
Jerry Grote		c	113	365	38	92	12	3	6	40	32	59	2	.252	.351
Art Shamsky		of	100	303	42	91	9	3	14	47	36	32	1	.300	.488
Ken Boswell		2b	102	362	48	101	14	7	3	32	36	47	7	.279	.381
Rod Gaspar		of	118	215	26	49	6	1	1	14	25	19	7	.228	.279
Ed Kranepool		1b	112	353	36	84	9	2	11	49	37	32	3	.238	.368
Wayne Garrett		3b-2b	124	400	38	87	11	3	1	39	40	75	4	.218	.268
Duffy Dyer		c	29	74	5	19	3	1	3	12	4	22	0	.257	.446
J. C. Martin		c	66	177	12	37	5	1	4	21	12	32	0	.209	.316
Jerry Koosman		p	32	84	1	4	0	0	0	1	1	46	0	.048	.048
Tom Seaver		p	39	91	7	11	3	0	0	6	7	34	1	.121	.154
Gary Gentry		p	35	74	2	6	1	0	0	1	1	52	0	.081	.095
Ron Taylor		p	59	4	0	1	0	0	0	0	0	2	0	.250	.250
Don Cardwell		p	30	47	3	8	0	0	1	5	0	26	0	.170	.234
Nolan Ryan		p	25	29	3	3	0	0	0	2	0	14	0	.103	.103
Tug McGraw		p	43	24	1	4	1	0	0	3	1	6	0	.167	.208
Cal Koonce		p	40	17	1	4	0	0	0	1	0	7	0	.235	.235
Jim McAndrew		p	27	37	0	5	1	0	0	3	3	18	0	.135	.162
Jack DiLauro		p	23	12	0	0	0	0	0	0	0	9	0	.000	.000
team total			162	5427	632	1311	184	41	109	598	527	1089	66	.242	.351

a—from Montreal

Bobby Pfeil (3b), Amos Otis (of), Kevin Collins (3b), Jim Gosger (of), Bob Heise (ss), Danny Frisella (p), Jesse Hudson (p), Al Jackson (p), Bob Johnson (p), and Les Rohr (p) also played for the Mets during the season.

WORLD SERIES STATISTICS

	Pos	G	AB	R	H	2B	3B	HR	RBI	BB	SO	SB	BA	SA	PO	A	E
BALTIMORE ORIOLES																	
Boog Powell	1b	5	19	0	5	0	0	0	0	1	4	0	.263	.263	**46**	2	1
Dave Johnson	2b	5	16	1	1	0	0	0	0	2	1	0	.063	.063	8	15	0
Mark Belanger	ss	5	15	2	3	0	0	0	1	2	1	0	.200	.200	7	14	0
Brooks Robinson	3b	5	19	0	1	0	0	0	2	0	3	0	.053	.053	1	16	0
Frank Robinson	rf	5	16	2	3	0	0	1	1	**4**	3	0	.188	.375	13	0	0
Paul Blair	cf	5	**20**	1	2	0	0	0	0	2	5	**1**	.100	.100	7	0	0
Don Buford	lf	5	**20**	1	2	1	0	1	2	2	4	0	.100	.300	8	0	0
Ellie Hendricks	c	3	10	1	1	0	0	0	0	1	0	0	.100	.100	21	1	0
Andy Etchebarren	c	2	6	0	0	0	0	0	0	0	1	0	.000	.000	16	0	0
Clay Dalrymple	ph	2	2	0	2	0	0	0	0	0	0	0	1.000	1.000			
Dave May	ph	2	1	0	0	0	0	0	0	1	1	0	.000	.000			
Curt Motton	ph	1	1	0	0	0	0	0	0	0	0	0	.000	.000			
Chico Salmon	pr	2	0	0	0	0	0	0	0	0	0	0	—	—			
Merv Rettenmund	pr	1	0	0	0	0	0	0	0	0	0	0	—	—			
Bobby Floyd	Did not play																
Mike Cuellar	p	2	5	0	2	0	0	0	1	0	3	0	.400	.400	0	1	0
Dave McNally	p	2	5	1	1	0	0	1	2	0	2	0	.200	.800	1	1	0
Jim Palmer	p	1	2	0	0	0	0	0	0	0	0	0	.000	.000	1	0	**1**
Eddie Watt	p	2	0	0	0	0	0	0	0	0	0	0	—	—	0	0	**1**
Dick Hall	p	1	0	0	0	0	0	0	0	0	0	0	—	—	0	0	0
Dave Leonhard	p	1	0	0	0	0	0	0	0	0	0	0	—	—	0	1	0
Pete Richert	p	1	0	0	0	0	0	0	0	0	0	0	—	—	0	0	**1**
Tom Phoebus	Did not play																
Jim Hardin	Did not play																
Marcelino Lopez	Did not play																
team total		5	157	9	23	1	0	3	9	15	28	1	.146	.210	129	51	4

Double Plays—4
Left on Bases—29

REGULAR SEASON STATISTICS

	Main Pos	G	AB	R	H	2B	3B	HR	RBI	BB	SO	SB	BA	SA
BALTIMORE ORIOLES														
Boog Powell	1b	152	533	83	162	25	0	37	121	72	76	1	.304	.559
Dave Johnson	2b	142	511	52	143	34	1	7	57	57	52	3	.280	.391
Mark Belanger	ss	150	530	76	152	17	4	2	50	53	54	14	.287	.345
Brooks Robinson	3b	156	598	73	140	21	3	23	84	56	55	2	.234	.395
Frank Robinson	of	148	539	111	166	19	5	32	100	88	62	9	.308	.540
Paul Blair	of	150	625	102	178	32	5	26	76	40	72	20	.285	.477
Don Buford	of	144	554	99	161	31	3	11	64	96	62	19	.291	.417
Ellie Hendricks	c	105	295	36	72	5	0	12	38	39	44	0	.244	.383
Andy Etchebarren	c	73	217	29	54	9	2	3	26	28	42	1	.249	.350
Clay Dalrymple	c	37	80	8	19	1	1	3	6	13	8	0	.238	.388
Dave May	of-ph	78	120	8	29	6	0	3	10	9	23	2	.242	.367
Curt Motton	ph-of	56	89	15	27	6	0	6	21	13	10	3	.303	.573
Chico Salmon	inf	52	91	18	27	5	0	3	12	10	22	0	.297	.451
Merv Rettenmund	of	95	190	27	47	10	3	4	25	28	28	6	.247	.395
Bobby Floyd	2b-ss	39	84	7	17	4	0	0	1	6	17	0	.202	.250
Mike Cuellar	p	39	103	6	12	1	2	0	5	0	43	0	.117	.165
Dave McNally	p	41	94	4	8	2	0	1	5	8	39	0	.085	.138
Jim Palmer	p	27	64	5	13	3	0	0	6	3	30	0	.203	.250
Eddie Watt	p	56	8	0	0	0	0	0	0	2	2	0	.000	.000
Dick Hall	p	39	7	1	2	0	0	0	2	1	1	1	.286	.286
Dave Leonhard	p	38	21	2	2	1	0	0	0	2	8	0	.095	.143
Pete Richert	p	44	8	0	1	0	0	0	0	0	4	1	.125	.125
Tom Phoebus	p	35	75	8	15	2	0	0	4	3	26	0	.200	.227
Jim Hardin	p	30	45	5	7	0	0	2	6	2	15	0	.156	.289
Marcelino Lopez	p	27	14	2	3	0	0	0	0	3	5	0	.214	.214
team total		162	5518	779	1465	234	29	175	722	634	806	82	.265	.414

Terry Crowley (1b), Al Severinsen (p), Mike Adamson (p), Fred Beene (p), and Frank Bertaina (p) also played for the Orioles during the season.

PITCHING

WORLD SERIES STATISTICS

	G	GS	CG	IP	H	R	ER	BB	SO	W	L	SV	ERA
NEW YORK METS													
Jerry Koosman	**2**	**2**	**1**	**17⅔**	7	4	4	4	9	**2**	0	0	2.04
Tom Seaver	**2**	**2**	**1**	15	12	**5**	**5**	3	9	1	**1**	0	3.00
Gary Gentry	1	1	0	6⅔	3	0	0	**5**	4	1	0	0	0.00
Ron Taylor	**2**	0	0	2⅓	0	0	0	1	3	0	0	**1**	0.00
Nolan Ryan	1	0	0	2⅓	1	0	0	2	3	0	0	**1**	0.00
Don Cardwell	1	0	0	1	0	0	0	0	0	0	0	0	0.00
Tug McGraw	Did not play												
Cal Koonce	Did not play												
Jim McAndrew	Did not play												
Jack DiLauro	Did not play												
team total	5	5	2	45	23	9	9	15	28	4	1	2	1.80
BALTIMORE ORIOLES													
Mike Cuellar	**2**	**2**	**1**	16	**13**	2	2	4	**13**	1	0	0	**1.13**
Dave McNally	**2**	**2**	**1**	16	11	**5**	**5**	**5**	**13**	0	**1**	0	2.81
Jim Palmer	1	1	0	6	5	4	4	4	5	0	1	0	6.00
Eddie Watt	2	0	0	3	4	2	1	0	3	0	1	0	3.00
Dave Leonhard	1	0	0	2	1	1	1	1	1	0	0	0	4.50
Dick Hall	1	0	0	0	1	1	0	1	0	0	1	0	0.00
Pete Richert	1	0	0	0	0	0	0	0	0	0	0	0	0.00
Tom Phoebus	Did not play												
Jim Hardin	Did not play												
Marcelino Lopez	Did not play												
team total	5	5	2	43	35	15	13	15	35	1	4	0	2.72

REGULAR SEASON STATISTICS

	G	GS	CG	IP	H	ER	BB	SO	W	L	Pct	SV	ShO	ERA
NEW YORK METS														
Jerry Koosman	32	32	16	241	187	61	68	180	17	9	.654	0	6	2.28
Tom Seaver	36	35	18	273	202	67	82	208	**25**	7	.781	0	5	2.21
Gary Gentry	35	35	6	234	192	89	81	154	13	12	.520	0	3	3.42
Ron Taylor	59	0	0	76	61	23	24	42	9	4	.692	13	0	2.72
Nolan Ryan	25	10	2	89	60	35	53	92	6	3	.667	1	0	3.54
Don Cardwell	30	21	4	152	145	51	47	60	8	10	.444	0	0	3.02
Tug McGraw	42	4	1	100	89	25	47	92	9	3	.750	12	0	2.25
Cal Koonce	40	0	0	83	85	46	42	48	6	3	.667	7	0	4.99
Jim McAndrew	27	21	4	135	112	52	44	90	6	7	.462	0	2	3.47
Jack DiLauro	2	4	0	64	50	17	18	27	1	4	.200	1	0	2.39
team total	162	162	51	1468	1217	487	517	1012	**100**	62	**.617**	35	**28**	2.99
BALTIMORE ORIOLES														
Mike Cuellar	39	39	18	291	213	77	79	182	23	11	.676	0	5	2.38
Dave McNally	41	40	11	269	232	96	84	166	20	7	.741	0	4	3.21
Jim Palmer	26	23	11	181	131	47	64	123	16	4	**.800**	0	6	2.34
Eddie Watt	56	0	0	71	49	13	26	46	5	2	.714	16	0	1.65
Dave Leonhard	37	3	1	94	78	26	38	37	7	4	.636	1	1	2.49
Dick Hall	39	0	0	66	49	14	9	31	5	2	.714	6	0	1.91
Pete Richert	44	0	0	57	42	14	14	54	7	4	.636	12	0	2.21
Tom Phoebus	35	33	6	202	180	79	87	117	14	7	.667	0	2	3.52
Jim Hardin	30	20	3	138	128	55	43	64	6	7	.462	1	1	3.59
Marcelino Lopez	27	4	0	69	65	34	34	57	5	3	.625	0	0	4.43
team total	162	162	50	1474	1194	**463**	498	897	**109**	53	**.673**	36	**20**	**2.83**

Total Attendance—272,378 Average Attendance—54,472 Winning Player's Share—$13,260* Losing Player's Share—$9,350
*Including Playoff Series: Winners—$18,338 Losers—$14,904

1970
The Vacuum Cleaner at Third Base

The Baltimore Orioles went home last October with a Series loss to the New York Mets and a burning conviction that they were the better team despite the outcome. The frustration of the 1969 defeat drove the Birds through the season to an easy first place in the American League East and another three-game sweep of the Minnesota Twins in the championship series. Earl Weaver and his boys itched for another shot at the Mets, but the New York outfit had run out of magic and fell by the wayside. The National League representative in the World Series instead was the Cincinnati Reds, the Big Red Machine that flattened the Western Division and then the Pittsburgh Pirates in the play-offs for the pennant even though cooling off after setting a torrid pace for the first half of the season. While the Baltimore cast of Frank Robinson, Brooks Robinson, Boog Powell, Mike Cuellar, Dave McNally, Jim Palmer and company was familiar with October baseball, the Reds were new to it. Led by freshman manager Sparky Anderson, the Reds had a murderous lineup featuring Johnny Bench, Pete Rose, Tony Perez, Lee May, Bobby Tolan, and Bernie Carbo. The Cincinnati pitching staff, however, was hampered by injuries to Jim Merritt, Wayne Simpson, and Jim Maloney—all reasons for the second-half slump by the Reds.

Anderson started his healthiest regular starter, 18-game-winner Gary Nolan, in the opener at the new Riverfront Stadium against Jim Palmer. In this first Series ever played on artificial turf, the Reds scored a run in the first inning on two hits, then ran their lead up to 3–0 in the second on a two-run homer by Lee May. But the Orioles came back on homers by Boog Powell and Elrod Hendricks to knot the score at 3–3 after five innings. The Reds threatened in the bottom of the sixth. May led off with a shot down the line, but Brooks Robinson made the first of a series of great catches at third base, backhanding the bullet going to his right, then spinning and throwing May out with an accurate throw. Carbo then walked, and Tommy Helms singled him to third. Pinch hitter Ty Cline then bounced the ball high in front of the plate. Catcher Hendricks grabbed it, dove back to the plate and sent home-plate umpire Ken Burkhart sprawling. Burkhart had his back to the play, but claimed he saw Hendricks tag Carbo out. Brooks Robinson then took to the offensive with a home run in the seventh inning which gave Palmer and the Birds a 4–3 victory. Cuellar pitched the second game against Jim McGlothlin, a 14-game-winner for the Reds. Cincinnati again had the better of the early going, taking a 4–0 lead after three innings. But while the Oriole relief corps of Tom Phoebus, Moe Drabowsky, Marcelino Lopez, and Dick Hall cooled the Cincinnati bats, the Orioles got moving with a solo homer by Powell in the fourth, then punished McGlothlin and reliever Milt Wilcox with five runs in the fifth inning. The Birds held on for a 6–5 win and headed back to Baltimore in great shape.

The Cincinnati pitching staff now was wearing thin, as Anderson had to call on Tony Cloninger as third-game starter. Brooks Robinson had his game together, making sparkling fielding plays in the first, second, and sixth innings and starting the Baltimore scoring with a two-run double in the first inning. A grand-slam homer by pitcher Dave McNally in the sixth inning put the game out of reach, and the 9–3 win had the Orioles tasting their vindication. Brooks had another fine game the next day, going 4-for-4 including a home run. The Birds led 5–3 after seven innings behind Jim Palmer and seemed ready to complete a four-game sweep. But the Big Red Machine had one more game-winning rally left in its gears. After giving up a walk to Perez and a single to Bench, Palmer left the game in favor of Eddie Watt. Lee May drilled Watt's first pitch into the bleachers in left for a 6–5 lead which reliever Clay Carroll made stand up. The Reds opened up with three runs in the top of the first inning of game five, but their pitching staff now was finished. Sore-armed Jim Merritt gave it a try but left in the second inning after giving up four runs. The Baltimore batters built up their lead against a flow of Cincinnati relievers, and the final score of 9–3 finally made it official that the Orioles indeed were the best team in baseball, at least this year if not last.

Game 1 October 10 at Cincinnati

Baltimore	Pos	AB	R	H	RBI	PO	A	E
Buford	lf	4	0	1	0	1	0	0
Blair	cf	4	1	1	0	7	0	0
Powell	1b	3	1	1	2	6	0	0
F. Robinson	rf	4	0	0	0	2	0	0
B. Robinson	3b	4	1	1	1	3	3	1
Hendricks	c	4	1	1	1	4	1	1
Johnson	2b	3	0	1	0	2	0	0
Belanger	ss	3	0	1	0	2	3	0
Palmer	p	4	0	0	0	0	0	0
Richert	p	0	0	0	0	0	0	0
Totals		33	4	7	4	27	7	2

Pitching	IP	H	R	ER	BB	SO
Baltimore						
Palmer (W)	8⅔	5	3	3	5	2
Richert (SV)	⅓	0	0	0	0	0
Cincinnati						
Nolan (L)	6⅔	5	4	4	1	7
Carroll	2⅓	2	0	0	2	4

Cincinnati	Pos	AB	R	H	RBI	PO	A	E
Rose	rf	*3	0	0	0	3	0	0
Tolan	cf	4	2	1	0	0	0	0
Perez	3b	3	0	0	0	0	3	0
Bench	c	4	0	1	1	12	0	0
May	1b	4	1	2	2	7	1	0
Carbo	lf	2	0	0	0	2	0	0
Helms	2b	4	0	1	0	2	1	0
Woodward	ss	2	0	0	0	2	1	0
a Cline		1	0	0	0	0	0	0
Chaney	ss	0	0	0	0	0	0	0
b Stewart		1	0	0	0	0	0	0
Nolan	p	2	0	0	0	0	0	0
Carroll	p	0	0	0	0	0	0	0
c Bravo		1	0	0	0	0	0	0
Totals		31	3	5	3	27	6	0

* Awarded first base on catcher's interference.
a Grounded into fielder's choice for Woodward in 6th.
b Struck out for Chaney in 9th.
c Struck out for Carroll in 9th.

Doubles—Johnson, Tolan. Home Runs—Hendricks, May, Powell, B. Robinson. Stolen Base—Tolan. Sacrifice Hit—Nolan. Double Play—May to Woodward to May. Wild Pitch—Palmer. Left on Bases—Baltimore 5, Cincinnati 8. Umpires—Burkhart (N), Flaherty (A), Venzon (N), Stewart (A), Williams (N), Ashford (A). Attendance—51,531. Time of Game—2:24.

1st Inning
Baltimore
1 Buford fouled to Bench.
2 Blair popped to short.
3 Powell took a called third strike.
Cincinnati
1 Rose grounded to short.
 Tolan doubled to right-center.
2 Perez flied to deep right, Tolan going to third after the catch.
 Bench singled to left, scoring Tolan.
 May singled to left, Bench stopping at second.
3 Carbo lined to third

2nd Inning
Baltimore
1 F. Robinson flied to left.
2 B. Robinson grounded to third.
3 Hendricks fouled to May.
Cincinnati
1 Helms popped to third.
 Woodward safe at first on B. Robinson's wide throw.
2 Nolan sacrificed Woodward to second, B. Robinson to Johnson.
3 Rose grounded to short.

3rd Inning
Baltimore
1 Johnson popped to second.
2 Belanger fanned.
3 Palmer grounded to second.
Cincinnati
 Tolan walked.
 Tolan stole second.
1 Perez flied to center.
2 Bench popped to Johnson in short right.
 May lined a two-run homer over the left field wall.
 Carbo walked.
3 Carbo caught stealing, Hendricks, to Belanger.

4th Inning
Baltimore
1 Buford flied to right.
 Blair beat out a roller down the third base line.
 Powell hit a two-run homer over the left field wall.
2 F. Robinson flied to right.
3 B. Robinson grounded to third.
Cincinnati
1 Helms flied to center.
2 Woodward fouled to Powell.
3 Nolan flied to center.

5th Inning
Baltimore
 Hendricks lined a home run over the right field wall.
1 Johnson struck out.
2 Belanger took a called third strike.
3 Palmer struck out.
Cincinnati
 Rose to first on catcher's interference (Hendricks interfered with his swing). An error on Hendricks.
1 Tolan flied to center.
2 Perez flied to center.
3 Bench fouled to Hendricks.

6th Inning
Baltimore
 Buford singled to center.
1 Blair fanned.
2,3 Powell hit into a double play, May to Woodward to May.
Cincinnati
1 May grounded out to third, B. Robinson making a remarkable play.
 Carbo walked.
 Helms singled to center, Carbo racing to third.
2 Cline, pinch-hitting for Woodward, hit a chopper in front of the plate. Hendricks fielding the ball tagged out Carbo trying to score. However, he tagged him with an empty glove. Umpire Burkhart who blocked plate on the play still called Carbo out.
3 Nolan flied to center.

7th Inning
Baltimore
 For Cincinnati—Chaney playing short.
1 F. Robinson popped to first.
 B. Robinson hit a home run over the left field fence.
2 Hendricks fanned.
 Johnson walked.
 For Cincinnati—Carroll pitching.
 Belanger singled to right, Johnson stopping at second.
3 Palmer took a called third strike.
Cincinnati
1 Rose flied to center.
2 Tolan flied to left.
 Perez walked.
 Perez to second on a wild pitch.
3 Bench grounded to third.

8th Inning
Baltimore
1 Buford flied to Carbo in short left-center.
2 Blair grounded to third.
 Powell walked.
3 F. Robinson took a called third strike.
Cincinnati
1 May grounded to short.
2 Carbo lined to third.
3 Helms flied to center.

9th Inning
Baltimore
1 B. Robinson called out on strikes.
2 Hendricks fanned.
 Johnson doubled to center.
 Belanger intentionally walked.
3 Palmer flied to right.
Cincinnati
1 Stewart, batting for Chaney, struck out.
2 Bravo, batting for Carroll, fanned.
 Rose walked.
 For Baltimore—Richert came in to pitch.
3 Tolan lined to short.

1970

Game 2 October 11 at Cincinnati

Bal. 000 150 000
Cin. 301 001 000

Baltimore	Pos	AB	R	H	RBI	PO	A	E
Buford	lf	4	1	2	0	1	0	0
Blair	cf	5	1	2	1	6	0	1
Powell	1b	3	2	2	2	9	2	0
F. Robinson	rf	5	0	0	0	1	0	0
B. Robinson	3b	4	1	1	1	1	6	0
Hendricks	c	3	0	1	2	3	0	0
Johnson	2b	3	0	1	0	5	3	0
Belanger	ss	4	0	0	0	0	3	1
Cuellar	p	1	0	0	0	0	1	0
Phoebus	p	0	0	0	0	0	0	0
a Salmon		1	1	1	0	0	0	0
Drabowsky	p	1	0	0	0	1	0	0
Lopez	p	0	0	0	0	0	0	0
Hall	p	1	0	0	0	0	0	0
Totals		35	6	10	6	27	14	2

Cincinnati	Pos	AB	R	H	RBI	PO	A	E
Rose	rf	3	0	0	0	3	0	0
Tolan	cf	4	2	1	1	1	0	0
Perez	3b	4	1	1	0	0	3	0
Bench	c	3	1	1	1	5	0	0
May	1b	4	1	1	2	13	1	0
McRae	lf	4	0	2	1	0	0	0
Helms	2b	4	0	0	0	4	4	0
Woodward	ss	2	0	0	0	2	4	0
b Cline		1	0	1	0	0	0	0
Chaney	ss	0	0	0	0	0	1	0
d Carbo		1	0	0	0	0	0	0
McGlothlin	p	2	0	0	0	0	0	0
Wilcox	p	0	0	0	0	0	0	0
Carroll	p	0	0	0	0	0	0	0
c Bravo		0	0	0	0	0	0	0
Gullett	p	0	0	0	0	0	0	0
e Stewart		1	0	0	0	0	0	0
Totals		33	5	7	5	27	13	0

Pitching	IP	H	R	ER	BB	SO
Baltimore						
Cuellar	2⅓	4	4	4	1	1
Phoebus (W)	1⅔	1	0	0	0	0
Drabowsky	2⅓	2	1	1	1	1
Lopez	⅓	0	0	0	0	0
Hall (SV)	2⅓	0	0	0	0	0
Cincinnati						
McGlothlin	4⅓	6	4	4	2	2
Wilcox (L)	⅓	3	2	2	0	0
Carroll	2⅓	1	0	0	0	1
Gullett	2	0	0	0	3	2

a Singled for Phoebus in 5th.
b Singled for Woodward in 7th.
c Sacrificed for Carroll in 7th.
d Grounded out for Chaney in 9th.
e Flied out for Gullett in 9th.

Doubles—Hendricks, May, McRae. Home Runs—Bench, Powell, Tolan. Sacrifice Hit—Bravo. Double Plays—Woodward to Helms to May, B. Robinson to Johnson to Powell, May to Woodward to May. Left on Bases—Baltimore 7, Cincinnati 4. Umpires—Flaherty, Venzon, Stewart, Williams, Ashford, Burkhart. Attendance—51,531. Time of Game—2:26.

1st Inning
Baltimore
Buford singled over Perez' head.
1,2 Blair hit into a double play, Woodward to Helms to May.
Powell walked.
3 F. Robinson took a called third strike.
Cincinnati
Rose safe at first on Belanger's fumble.
1 Tolan forced Rose at second, B. Robinson to Johnson.
Perez singled to center, Tolan stopping at second.
2 Bench flied to right, Tolan advancing to third after the catch.
May lined a double to left-center, scoring Tolan and Perez. May went to third on Blair's bobble of the hit.
McRae safely bunted down the third base line, scoring May.
3 Helms forced McRae at second, B. Robinson to Johnson.

2nd Inning
Baltimore
1 B. Robinson popped to first.
2 Hendricks grounded to first.
Johnson singled to left.
3 Belanger fouled to May.
Cincinnati
1 Woodward flied to center.
2 McGlothlin struck out.
3 Rose grounded to third.

3rd Inning
Baltimore
1 Cuellar struck out.
2 Buford flied to deep right.
3 Blair grounded to short.
Cincinnati
Tolan hit a home run over the right field wall.
1 Perez fouled to Hendricks.
Bench walked.
For Baltimore—Phoebus came in to pitch.
2,3 May grounded into a double play, B. Robinson, making a good backhanded stop to Johnson to Powell.

4th Inning
Baltimore
Powell hit a home run into the second deck of the center field stands.
1 F. Robinson grounded to deep short.
2 B. Robinson grounded to third.
Hendricks walked.
3 Johnson forced Hendricks at second, Perez to Helms.
Cincinnati
McRae doubled down the left field line.
1 Helms grounded to second, McRae holding at second.
2 Woodward flied to center.
3 McGlothlin grounded to short.

5th Inning
Baltimore
1 Belanger popped to short.
Salmon, pinch-hitting for Phoebus, singled to center.
Buford singled to right, Salmon stopping at second.
Blair singled to left, scoring Salmon with Buford stopping at second.
For Cincinnati—Wilcox now pitching.
Powell singled to left, scoring Buford as Blair stopped at second.
2 F. Robinson flied to deep right, Blair going to third after the catch.
B. Robinson singled to right, scoring Blair with Powell stopping at second.
Hendricks lined a double into the left field corner, scoring Powell and B. Robinson.
For Cincinnati—Carroll came in to pitch.
3 Johnson grounded to second.
Cincinnati
For Baltimore—Drabowsky pitching.
1 Rose grounded out, Powell to Drabowsky.
2 Tolan grounded to second.
3 Perez struck out.

6th Inning
Baltimore
1 Belanger grounded to second.
2 Drabowsky struck out.
3 Buford grounded to second.
Cincinnati
Bench lined a homer over the left field wall.
1 May flied to center.
2 McRae grounded to third.
3 Helms flied to center.

7th Inning
Baltimore
Blair singled to center.
1,2 Powell hit into a double play, May to Woodward to May.
3 F. Robinson grounded to third.
Cincinnati
Cline, pinch-hitting for Woodward, lined a single to left.
1 Bravo, pinch-hitting for Carroll, sacrificed Cline to second, Powell to Johnson covering first.
Rose walked.
For Baltimore—Lopez came in to pitch.
2 Tolan fouled to B. Robinson.
For Baltimore—Hall came in to pitch.
3 Perez forced Rose at second, B. Robinson to Johnson.

8th Inning
Baltimore
For Cincinnati—Gullett pitching and Chaney playing short.
1 B. Robinson grounded to short.
2 Hendricks lined to second.
Johnson walked.
3 Belanger forced Johnson at second, Perez to Helms.
Cincinnati
1 Bench flied to center.
2 May grounded to short.
3 McRae flied to left.

9th Inning
Baltimore
1 Hall fanned.
Buford walked.
2 Blair flied to right.
Powell walked.
3 F. Robinson called out on strikes.
Cincinnati
1 Helms grounded to short.
2 Carbo, pinch-hitting for Chaney, grounded to first.
3 Stewart, pinch-hitting for Gullett, flied to deep center.

Game 3 October 13 at Baltimore

Cincinnati	Pos	AB	R	H	RBI	PO	A	E
Rose	rf	5	0	2	1	4	0	0
Tolan	cf	4	0	1	0	2	0	0
Perez	3b	3	0	0	0	0	2	0
Bench	c	4	0	0	0	5	2	0
May	1b	3	1	1	0	9	0	0
McRae	lf	4	1	2	0	1	1	0
Helms	2b	4	1	1	0	3	1	0
Concepcion	ss	3	0	1	2	0	2	0
Cloninger	p	2	0	0	0	0	0	0
Granger	p	0	0	0	0	0	1	0
a Woodward		1	0	1	0	0	0	0
Gullett	p	0	0	0	0	0	0	0
b Cline		1	0	0	0	0	0	0
Totals		34	3	9	3	24	9	0

a Singled for Granger in 7th.
b Grounded into force play force Gullett in 9th.

Doubles—Blair, B. Robinson 2. Home Runs—Buford, McNally, F. Robinson. Sacrifice Fly—Concepcion. Double Plays—B. Robinson to Powell, Bench to Helms. Left on Bases—Cincinnati 7, Baltimore 3. Umpires—Venzon, Stewart, Williams, Ashford, Burkhart, Flaherty. Attendance—51,773. Time of Game—2:09.

Cin.	010	000	200
Bal.	201	014	10x

Baltimore	Pos	AB	R	H	RBI	PO	A	E
Buford	lf	3	2	1	1	3	0	0
Belanger	ss	4	0	0	0	2	3	0
Powell	1b	3	1	0	0	8	0	0
F. Robinson	rf	4	2	3	1	2	0	0
Blair	cf	3	1	3	1	0	0	0
B. Robinson	3b	4	1	2	2	3	3	0
Johnson	2b	2	1	0	0	4	2	0
Etchebarren	c	4	0	0	0	5	0	1
McNally	p	4	1	1	4	0	1	0
Totals		31	9	10	9	27	9	1

Pitching	IP	H	R	ER	BB	SO
Cincinnati						
Cloninger (L)	$5\frac{1}{3}$	6	5	5	3	3
Granger	$\frac{2}{3}$	2	3	3	1	1
Gullett	2	2	1	1	1	0
Baltimore						
McNally (W)	9	9	3	3	2	5

1st Inning
Cincinnati
Rose singled to center.
Tolan beat out a bunt down the third base line, moving Rose to second.
1,2 Perez hit into a double play, B. Robinson, stepping on third forcing Rose to Powell as Tolan went to second.
3 Bench lined to third.
Baltimore
Buford walked.
1 Belanger flied to short right.
2 Powell fouled to Bench.
F. Robinson singled to right, Buford advancing to third.
Blair walked loading the bases.
B. Robinson doubled to left-center, scoring Buford and F. Robinson with Blair stopping at third.
3 Johnson flied to center.

2nd Inning
Cincinnati
1 May took a called third strike.
McRae singled to center.
2 Helms rolled to third on a good play by B. Robinson, McRae going to second.
Concepcion singled to right, scoring McRae and when Etchebarren erred on F. Robinson's throw, Concepcion went to second.
3 Cloninger took a called third strike.
Baltimore
1 Etchebarren grounded to third.
2 McNally took a called third strike.
3 Buford flied to right.

3rd Inning
Cincinnati
1 Rose lined to Johnson, making a leaping one-handed catch.
2 Tolan grounded to second.
Perez walked.
3 Bench fouled to Powell.
Baltimore
1 Belanger fouled to May.
2 Powell grounded to short.
F. Robinson hit a home run over the center field fence.
Blair singled to center.
3 Blair was caught attempting to steal second, Bench to Helms.

4th Inning
Cincinnati
1 May grounded to third.
2 McRae fanned.
3 Helms flied to Buford in deep left-center.
Baltimore
1 B. Robinson grounded to third.
Johnson walked.
2,3 Etchebarren struck out with Johnson doubled trying for second, Bench to Helms.

5th Inning
Cincinnati
1 Concepcion lined to left.
2 Cloninger bounced back to the mound.
3 Rose grounded to short.
Baltimore
1 McNally took a called third strike.
Buford hit a home run over the right field fence.
2 Belanger flied to short right.
3 Powell grounded to first.

6th Inning
Cincinnati
1 Tolan flied to left.
2 Perez struck out.
3 Bench lined to third.
Baltimore
1 F. Robinson flied to Tolan in left-center.
Blair singled to center.
For Cincinnati—Granger pitching.
B. Robinson doubled off the left field fence, Blair going to third.
Johnson got an intentional pass, loading the bases.
2 Etchebarren struck out.
McNally hit a grand slam home run into the left field bleachers.
3 Buford bounced back to the mound.

7th Inning
Cincinnati
May walked.
McRae singled to left-center, May stopping at second.
1 Helms forced McRae at second, Belanger to Johnson, May moving to third.
2 Concepcion hit a sacrifice fly to right, May scoring after the catch.
Woodward, batting for Granger, singled to short left, Helms stopping at second.
Rose singled to right, scoring Helms with Woodward stopping at second.
3 Tolan popped to Belanger behind third.
Baltimore
For Cincinnati—Gullett came on to pitch.
1 Belanger grounded to second.
Powell walked.
F. Robinson singled to left, advancing
2 Powell to third. F. Robinson was out trying for second, McRae to Helms.
Blair doubled down the left field line, scoring Powell.
3 B. Robinson fouled to May.

8th Inning
Cincinnati
1 Perez popped to first.
2 Bench took a called third strike.
May singled to left.
3 McRae popped to Johnson in short right.
Baltimore
1 Johnson flied to short right.
2 Etchebarren grounded to short.
3 McNally flied to left.

9th Inning
Cincinnati:
Helms singled to center.
1 Concepcion lined to right.
2 Cline, batting for Gullett forced Helms at second, Johnson to Belanger.
3 Rose forced Kline at second, Belanger to Johnson.

Game 4 October 14 at Baltimore

Cincinnati	Pos	AB	R	H	RBI	PO	A	E
Tolan	cf	3	1	1	0	1	0	1
Rose	rf	5	1	2	1	1	1	1
Perez	3b	4	1	0	0	0	3	1
Bench	c	4	1	1	0	8	1	0
May	1b	3	2	2	4	13	0	0
Carbo	lf	4	0	0	0	2	0	0
Helms	2b	3	0	1	0	1	3	0
Concepcion	ss	3	0	1	1	0	0	0
Carroll	p	1	0	0	0	0	0	0
Nolan	p	1	0	0	0	0	1	0
Gullett	p	1	0	0	0	0	0	0
Woodward	ss	0	0	0	0	0	0	0
a Bravo		1	0	0	0	0	0	0
Chaney	ss	1	0	0	0	1	1	0
Totals		34	6	8	6	27	10	3

a Popped out for Woodward in 7th.
b Grounded out for Belanger in 9th.
c Reached first on error for Drabowsky in 9th.

Triple—Concepcion. Home Runs—May, B. Robinson, Rose. Sacrifice Hit—Blair. Left on Bases—Cincinnati 6, Baltimore 5. Umpires—Stewart, Williams, Ashford, Burkhart, Flaherty, Venzon. Attendance—53,007. Time of Game—2:26.

Cin.	011	010	030
Bal.	013	001	000

Baltimore	Pos	AB	R	H	RBI	PO	A	E
Buford	lf	4	0	0	0	1	0	0
Blair	cf	3	0	0	0	3	0	0
Powell	1b	3	1	0	0	6	0	0
F. Robinson	rf	4	1	1	1	1	0	0
B. Robinson	3b	4	2	4	2	1	0	0
Hendricks	c	4	0	2	1	10	1	0
Johnson	2b	4	0	0	0	2	3	0
Belanger	ss	3	0	0	0	3	1	0
b Crowley		1	0	0	0	0	0	0
Palmer	p	3	1	1	0	0	0	0
Watt	p	0	0	0	0	0	0	0
Drabowsky	p	0	0	0	0	0	0	0
c Rettenmund		1	0	0	0	0	0	0
Totals		34	5	8	4	27	5	0

Pitching	IP	H	R	ER	BB	SO
Cincinnati						
Nolan	$2\frac{2}{3}$	4	4	4	2	2
Gullett	$2\frac{2}{3}$	3	1	0	0	2
Carroll (W)	$3\frac{2}{3}$	1	0	0	0	4
Baltimore						
Palmer	*7	6	5	5	4	7
Watt (L)	**1	2	1	1	1	3
Drabowsky	1	0	0	0	0	0

*Pitched to 2 batters in 8th.
**Pitched to 1 batter in 9th.

1st Inning
Cincinnati
Tolan singled to right.
1 Rose grounded to second, Tolan advancing to second.
2 Perez fanned.
3 Bench fouled to Powell.
Baltimore
Buford walked.
1 Blair sacrificed, Perez to May.
2 Powell grounded to first, Buford going over to third.
3 F. Robinson took a called third strike.

2nd Inning
Cincinnati
May walked.
1 Carbo struck out.
2 Helms struck out.
Concepcion tripled to the right field wall, scoring May.
3 Nolan grounded to second.
Baltimore
B. Robinson homered into the left field stands.
1 Hendricks grounded to second.
2 Johnson bounced back to the mound.
3 Belanger flied to center.

3rd Inning
Cincinnati
Tolan walked.
Rose singled to center, moving Tolan to third.
1 Perez struck out.
2 Bench popped to Belanger in short left.
May singled behind second, scoring Tolan with Rose stopping at second.
3 Carbo forced Rose, B. Robinson unassisted.
Baltimore
Palmer singled to center.
1 Buford grounded to first, Palmer going to second.
2 Blair struck out.
Powell walked.
F. Robinson singled to left, scoring Palmer with Powell going to second.
B. Robinson singled to center, scoring Powell and when Tolan fumbled F. Robinson went to third and B. Robinson to second.
For Cincinnati—Gullett came on to pitch.
Hendricks singled to right, scoring F. Robinson but B. Robinson was out at
3 the plate, Rose to Bench.

4th Inning
Cincinnati
1 Helms lined to right.
2 Concepcion grounded to second.
3 Gullett struck out.
Baltimore
1 Johnson flied to right.
2 Belanger grounded to second.
3 Palmer fanned.

5th Inning
Cincinnati
1 Tolan popped to Belanger in short left.
Rose homered over the left-center field fence.
2 Perez flied to deep center.
3 Bench flied to left.
Baltimore
1 Buford grounded to second.
2 Blair grounded to third.
3 Powell struck out.

6th Inning
Cincinnati
1 May grounded to short.
2 Carbo struck out.
Helms walked.
3 Concepcion lined to short.
Baltimore
1 F. Robinson lined to left.
B. Robinson singled to left.
Hendricks singled to right, Rose's throw went into the Baltimore dugout allowing B. Robinson to score and Hendricks to reach third.
For Cincinnati—Carroll pitching (batting 8th), Woodward at short (batting 9th).
2 Johnson struck out.
3 Belanger flied to left.

7th Inning
Cincinnati
1 Bravo, batting for Woodward, popped to second.
2 Tolan struck out.
3 Rose grounded to first.
Baltimore
For Cincinnati—Chaney playing short.
1 Palmer popped to second.
2 Buford struck out but had to be thrown out, Bench to May.
3 Blair took a called third strike.

8th Inning
Cincinnati
Perez walked.
Bench singled off the left field wall, advancing Perez to third.
For Baltimore—Watt came in to pitch.
May hit a three-run homer into the left field stands.
1 Carbo struck out.
Helms beat out a single to deep short.
2 Carroll struck out, bunting foul on the third strike.
3 Chaney struck out.
Baltimore
1 Powell grounded to third.
2 F. Robinson grounded to short.
B. Robinson singled to center.
3 Hendricks grounded to first.

9th Inning
Cincinnati
Tolan walked.
For Baltimore—Drabowsky pitching.
1 Rose flied to center.
2 Tolan caught trying to steal second, Hendricks to Johnson.
3 Perez flied to center.
Baltimore
1 Johnson fouled to Chaney behind third.
2 Crowley, pinch-hitting for Belanger, grounded to first.
Rettenmund, batting for Drabowsky, was safe at first on Perez' bad throw to first on his grounder.
3 Buford struck out.

Game 5 October 15 at Baltimore

Cin.	3 0 0	0 0 0	0 0 0
Bal.	2 2 2	0 1 0	0 2 x

Cincinnati	Pos	AB	R	H	RBI	PO	A	E
Tolan	cf	4	0	0	0	1	0	0
Rose	rf	4	1	1	0	3	0	0
Perez	3b	4	0	0	0	3	2	0
Bench	c	4	1	1	1	6	0	0
May	1b	4	1	1	0	6	1	0
McRae	lf	3	0	1	2	1	0	0
c Corrales		1	0	0	0	0	0	0
Helms	2b	3	0	1	0	1	4	0
Concepcion	ss	3	0	1	0	2	0	0
Merritt	p	1	0	0	0	0	0	0
Granger	p	0	0	0	0	0	0	0
Wilcox	p	0	0	0	0	0	1	0
a Bravo		0	0	0	0	0	0	0
Cloninger	p	0	0	0	0	0	1	0
b Carbo		1	0	0	0	0	0	0
Washburn	p	0	0	0	0	1	3	0
Carroll	p	0	0	0	0	0	0	0
Totals		32	3	6	3	24	12	0

Baltimore	Pos	AB	R	H	RBI	PO	A	E
Belanger	ss	5	0	1	1	4	4	0
Blair	cf	4	2	3	1	2	0	0
F. Robinson	rf	5	2	2	1	1	0	0
Powell	1b	5	1	2	1	9	0	0
Rettenmund	lf	4	2	2	2	3	0	0
B. Robinson	3b	5	0	1	0	1	2	0
Johnson	2b	4	1	3	2	2	1	0
Etchebarren	c	3	1	1	0	5	0	0
Cuellar	p	3	0	0	0	0	1	0
Totals		38	9	15	9	27	8	0

Pitching	IP	H	R	ER	BB	SO
Cincinnati						
Merritt (L)	1⅓	3	4	4	1	0
Granger	⅓	5	2	2	0	0
Wilcox	1⅓	0	0	0	0	2
Cloninger	2	4	1	1	2	1
Washburn	1⅓	2	2	2	2	0
Carroll	⅓	1	0	0	0	2
Baltimore						
Cuellar (W)	9	6	3	3	1	4

a Walked for Wilcox in 5th.
b Grounded into double play for Cloninger in 7th.
c Grounded out for McRae in 9th.

Doubles—Johnson, May, McRae, Powell, Rose. Home Runs—Rettenmund, F. Robinson. Sacrifice Hit—Cuellar. Double Play—Cuellar to Belanger to Powell. Left on Bases—Cincinnati 3, Baltimore 11. Umpires—Williams, Ashford, Burkhart, Flaherty, Venzon, Stewart. Attendance—45,341. Time of Game—2:35.

1st Inning
Cincinnati
1 Tolan struck out.
  Rose doubled down the right field line.
2 Perez flied to left.
  Bench singled to right-center, scoring Rose.
  May doubled off the left field wall, Bench stopping at third.
  McRae doubled to center, scoring Bench and May.
3 Helms grounded to short.
Baltimore
1 Belanger fouled to Perez.
  Blair singled to left.
  F. Robinson hit a two-run homer into the left field stands.
2 Powell flied to Concepcion making a backhanded catch in short left-center.
3 Rettenmund popped to Concepcion behind third.

2nd Inning
Cincinnati
1 Concepcion popped to Johnson in short right.
2 Merritt struck out.
3 Tolan grounded to first.
Baltimore
1 B. Robinson flied to left.
  Johnson walked.
  Etchebarren singled to center, Johnson stopping at second.
2 Cuellar lined to right.
  For Cincinnati—Granger now pitching.
  Belanger singled between short and third, scoring Johnson with Etchebarren stopping at second.
  Blair singled to left, scoring Etchebarren with Belanger stopping at second.
3 F. Robinson flied to center.

3rd Inning
Cincinnati
1 Rose grounded to second.
2 Perez lined to left.
3 Bench struck out.
Baltimore
  Powell lined a double to right.
  Rettenmund singled to center, scoring Powell and taking second on the throw to the plate.
1 B. Robinson bounced to second, moving Rettenmund to third.
  Johnson singled to left, scoring Rettenmund.
  For Cincinnati—Wilcox came in to pitch.
2 Etchebarren flied to right.
3 Cuellar struck out.

4th Inning
Cincinnati
1 May grounded to third.
2 McRae popped to short.
3 Helms popped to first.
Baltimore
1 Belanger grounded to second.
2 Blair fanned.
3 F. Robinson thrown out by Perez on a liner off of Wilcox' hip.

5th Inning
Cincinnati
1 Concepcion grounded to short.
  Bravo, batting for Wilcox, walked.
2 Tolan flied to left.
3 Rose flied to right.
Baltimore
  For Cincinnati—Cloninger pitching.
1 Powell popped to third.
  Rettenmund homered over the right field fence just inside the foul line.
  B. Robinson blooped a single to center.
  Johnson doubled down the left field line, B. Robinson moving to third.
  Etchebarren intentionally passed, loading the bases.
2 Cuellar forced B. Robinson at the plate, Cloninger to Bench.
3 Belanger flied to right.

6th Inning
Cincinnati
1 Perez lined to short.
2 Bench popped to second.
3 May flied to deep center.
Baltimore
  Blair walked.
1 F. Robinson struck out.
  Powell singled to left-center, Blair racing to third.
2 Rettenmund fouled to Perez.
3 B. Robinson forced Powell at second, Perez to Helms.

7th Inning
Cincinnati
1 McRae fouled to Etchebarren.
  Helms singled off Johnson's glove.
  Concepcion singled to right, Helms stopping at second.
2,3 Carbo, batting for Cloninger, grounded into a double play, Cuellar to Belanger to Powell.
Baltimore
  For Cincinnati—Washburn pitching.
1 Johnson grounded back to the mound.
  Etchebarren walked.
2 Cuellar sacrificed, Washburn to May.
3 Belanger's grounder deflected off Washburn to Helms who threw to first for the out.

8th Inning
Cincinnati
1 Tolan flied to center.
2 Rose grounded to short.
3 Perez popped to short.
Baltimore
  Blair singled to deep short.
  F. Robinson singled to right, Blair stopping at second.
1 Powell grounded out Helms to Washburn, after May fell down. Blair scored and F. Robinson went to second.
  Rettenmund walked.
  For Cincinnati—Carroll pitching.
2 B. Robinson took a called third strike.
  Johnson singled to center, F. Robinson scoring and Rettenmund stopping at second.
3 Etchebarren struck out.

9th Inning
Cincinnati
1 Bench lined to third.
2 May struck out.
3 Corrales, pinch-hitting for McRae, grounded to third.

1970 WORLD SERIES COMPOSITE BOX

	Wins	Composite Line Score
Baltimore Orioles (A.L.)	4	4 3 6 3 8 5 2 2 0 – 33
Cincinnati Reds (N.L.)	1	7 2 4 0 1 1 2 3 0 – 20

Manager	W	L	Pct.	G. Ahead	
	Regular Season				
Earl Weaver	108	54	.667	15	(beat Minnesota in playoffs)
Sparky Anderson	102	60	.630	16	(beat Pittsburgh in playoffs)

BATTING AND FIELDING

BALTIMORE ORIOLES

	WORLD SERIES STATISTICS																	REGULAR SEASON STATISTICS													
	Pos	G	AB	R	H	2B	3B	HR	RBI	BB	SO	SB	BA	SA	PO	A	E		Main Pos	G	AB	R	H	2B	3B	HR	RBI	BB	SO	SB	BA	SA
Boog Powell	1b	5	17	6	5	1	0	2	5	5	2	0	.294	.706	38	2	0		1b	154	526	82	156	28	0	35	114	104	80	1	.297	.549
Dave Johnson	2b	5	16	2	5	2	0	0	2	5	2	0	.313	.438	15	9	0		2b	149	530	68	149	27	1	10	53	66	68	2	.281	.392
Mark Belanger	ss	5	19	0	2	0	0	0	1	1	2	0	.105	.105	11	14	1		ss	145	459	53	100	6	5	1	36	52	65	13	.218	.259
Brooks Robinson	3b	5	21	5	9	2	0	2	6	0	2	0	.429	.814	9	14	1		3b	158	608	84	168	31	4	18	94	53	53	1	.276	.429
Frank Robinson	rf	5	22	5	6	0	0	2	4	0	5	0	.273	.545	7	0	0		of	132	471	88	144	24	1	25	78	69	70	2	.306	.528
Paul Blair	cf	5	19	5	9	1	0	0	3	2	4	0	.474	.526	18	0	1		of	133	480	79	128	24	2	18	65	56	93	24	.267	.438
Don Buford	lf	4	15	3	4	0	0	1	1	3	2	0	.267	.467	6	0	0		of	144	504	99	137	15	2	17	66	109	55	16	.272	.411
Ellie Hendricks	c	3	11	1	4	1	0	1	4	1	2	0	.364	.727	17	2	1		c	106	322	32	78	9	0	12	41	33	44	1	.242	.382
Andy Etchebarren	c	2	7	1	1	0	0	0	0	2	3	0	.143	.143	10	0	1		c	78	230	19	56	10	1	4	28	21	41	4	.243	.348
Merv Rettenmund	ph-lf	2	5	2	2	0	0	1	2	1	0	0	.400	1.000	3	0	0		of	106	338	60	109	17	2	18	58	38	59	13	.322	.544
Terry Crowley	ph	1	1	0	0	0	0	0	0	0	0	0	.000	.000					ph-of-1b	83	152	25	39	5	0	5	20	35	26	2	.257	.388
Chico Salmon	ph	1	1	1	1	0	0	0	0	0	0	0	1.000	1.000					ss	63	172	19	43	4	0	7	22	8	30	2	.250	.395
Curt Motton	Did not play																		pn-of	52	84	16	19	3	1	3	19	18	20	1	.226	.393
Bobby Grich	Did not play																		ss	30	95	11	20	1	3	0	8	9	21	1	.211	.284
Jim Palmer	p	2	7	1	1	0	0	0	0	0	3	0	.143	.143	0	0	0		p	44	113	13	17	0	0	1	9	2	48	0	.150	.177
Mike Cuellar	p	2	4	0	0	0	0	0	0	0	2	0	.000	.000	0	1	0		p	41	112	6	10	1	0	2	7	2	46	0	.089	.152
Dave McNally	p	1	4	1	1	0	0	1	4	0	2	0	.250	1.000	0	1	0		p	41	105	14	14	6	0	1	6	15	53	0	.133	.219
Moe Drabowsky	p	2	1	0	0	0	0	0	0	0	1	0	.000	.000	1	0	0	a	p	21	5	0	0	0	0	0	0	0	3	0	.000	.000
Dick Hall	p	1	1	0	0	0	0	0	0	0	1	0	.000	.000	0	0	0		p	32	12	2	1	0	0	0	1	0	3	0	.083	.083
Marcelino Lopez	p	1	0	0	0	0	0	0	0	0	0	0	—	—	0	0	0		p	25	13	0	1	0	0	0	0	3	11	0	.077	.077
Tom Phoebus	p	1	0	0	0	0	0	0	0	0	0	0	—	—	0	0	0		p	27	43	2	7	1	0	0	3	0	16	0	.163	.186
Pete Richert	p	1	0	0	0	0	0	0	0	0	0	0	—	—	0	0	0		p	50	4	0	0	0	0	0	0	1	3	0	.000	.000
Eddie Watt	p	1	0	0	0	0	0	0	0	0	0	0	—	—	0	0	0		p	53	8	1	1	0	0	0	0	0	3	0	.125	.125
Jim Hardin	Did not play																		p	36	45	2	3	0	1	0	4	4	21	0	.067	.111
Dave Leonhard	Did not play																		p	25	1	1	0	0	0	0	0	1	1	0	.000	.000
team total		5	171	33	50	7	0	10	32	20	33	0	.292	.509	135	43	5			162	5545	792	1424	213	25	179	748	717	952	84	.257	.401

Double Plays—3
Left on Bases—31

a—from Kansas City
Dave May (ph), Clay Dalrymple (c), Don Baylor (†of), Johnny Oates (c), Bobby Floyd (ss), Roger Freed (1b), and Fred Beene (p) also played for the Orioles during the season.

CINCINNATI REDS

	WORLD SERIES STATISTICS																	REGULAR SEASON STATISTICS													
	Pos	G	AB	R	H	2B	3B	HR	RBI	BB	SO	SB	BA	SA	PO	A	E		Main Pos	G	AB	R	H	2B	3B	HR	RBI	BB	SO	SB	BA	SA
Lee May	1b	5	18	6	7	2	0	2	8	2	2	0	.389	.833	48	3	0		1b	153	605	78	153	34	2	34	94	38	125	1	.253	.484
Tommy Helms	2b	5	18	1	4	0	0	0	0	1	1	0	.222	.222	10	13	0		2b	150	575	42	136	21	1	1	45	21	33	2	.237	.282
Dave Concepcion	ss	3	9	0	3	0	1	0	3	0	0	0	.333	.556	2	2	0		ss	101	265	38	69	6	3	1	19	23	45	10	.260	.317
Tony Perez	3b	5	18	2	1	0	0	0	0	3	4	0	.056	.056	3	13	1		3b	158	587	107	186	26	6	40	129	83	134	8	.317	.589
Pete Rose	rf	5	20	2	5	1	0	1	2	2	0	0	.250	.450	14	1	1		of	159	649	120	205	37	9	15	52	73	64	12	.316	.470
Bobby Tolan	cf	5	19	5	4	1	0	1	1	3	2	1	.211	.421	4	0	1		of	152	589	112	186	34	6	16	80	62	94	57	.316	.475
Hal McRae	lf	3	11	1	5	2	0	0	3	0	1	0	.455	.636	2	1	0		of	70	165	18	41	6	1	8	23	15	23	0	.248	.442
Johnny Bench	c	5	19	3	4	0	0	1	3	1	2	0	.211	.368	36	3	0		c	158	605	97	177	35	4	45	148	54	102	5	.293	.587
Bernie Carbo	lf-ph	4	8	0	0	0	0	0	0	2	3	0	.000	.000	4	0	0		of	125	365	54	113	19	3	21	63	94	77	10	.310	.551
Woody Woodward	ss-ph	4	5	0	1	0	0	0	0	0	0	0	.200	.200	4	5	0		ss	100	264	23	59	8	3	1	14	20	21	1	.223	.288
Darrel Chaney	ss	3	1	0	0	0	0	0	0	0	1	0	.000	.000	1	2	0		ss-2b	57	95	7	22	3	0	1	4	3	26	1	.232	.295
Ty Cline	ph	3	3	0	1	0	0	0	0	0	0	0	.333	.333				b	ph-of	48	63	13	17	7	1	0	8	12	11	1	.270	.413
Angel Bravo	ph	4	2	0	0	0	0	0	0	1	1	0	.000	.000					ph	65	65	10	18	1	1	0	3	9	13	0	.277	.323
Jimmy Stewart	ph	2	2	0	0	0	0	0	0	0	1	0	.000	.000					of-inf	101	105	15	28	3	1	1	8	8	13	5	.267	.343
Pat Corrales	ph	1	1	0	0	0	0	0	0	0	0	0	.000	.000					c	43	106	9	25	5	1	1	10	8	22	0	.236	.330
Gary Nolan	p	2	3	0	0	0	0	0	0	0	0	0	.000	.000	0	1	0		p	37	82	4	13	1	1	0	6	5	27	0	.159	.195
Tony Cloninger	p	2	2	0	0	0	0	0	0	0	1	0	.000	.000	0	1	0		p	30	47	7	10	2	0	2	3	0	16	0	.213	.383
Jim McGlothlin	p	1	2	0	0	0	0	0	0	0	1	0	.000	.000	0	0	0		p	35	66	5	8	1	1	1	6	7	26	0	.121	.212
Clay Carroll	p	4	1	0	0	0	0	0	0	0	1	0	.000	.000	0	0	0		p	65	14	1	1	0	0	0	0	1	4	0	.071	.071
Don Gullett	p	3	1	0	0	0	0	0	0	0	1	0	.000	.000	0	0	0		p	44	19	3	4	0	1	0	2	1	6	1	.211	.316
Jim Merritt	p	1	1	0	0	0	0	0	0	0	1	0	.000	.000	0	0	0		p	35	83	7	14	0	0	3	6	4	42	0	.169	.277
Wayne Granger	p	2	0	0	0	0	0	0	0	0	0	0	—	—	0	1	0		p	67	10	0	1	0	0	0	0	0	4	0	.100	.100
Milt Wilcox	p	2	0	0	0	0	0	0	0	0	0	0	—	—	0	1	0		p	5	5	0	1	0	0	0	1	0	1	0	.200	.200
Ray Washburn	p	1	0	0	0	0	0	0	0	0	0	0	—	—	1	3	0		p	35	13	0	0	0	0	0	1	1	10	0	.000	.000
Mel Behney	Did not play																		p	5	1	0	0	0	0	0	0	0	1	0	.000	.000
Wayne Simpson	Not in Series—Shoulder Injury																		p	27	64	4	6	0	0	0	1	1	34	0	.094	.094
team total		5	164	20	35	6	1	5	20	15	23	1	.213	.354	129	50	3			162	5540	775	1498	253	45	191	726	547	984	115	.270	.436

Double Plays—4
Left on Bases—28

b—from Montreal
Frank Duffy (ss), Bill Plummer (c), Jay Ward (3b), Jim Maloney (p), Pedro Borbon (p), Bo Belinsky (p), and John Noriega (p) also played for the Reds during the season.

PITCHING

BALTIMORE ORIOLES

	WORLD SERIES STATISTICS													REGULAR SEASON STATISTICS													
	G	GS	CG	IP	H	R	ER	BB	SO	W	L	SV	ERA		G	GS	CG	IP	H	ER	BB	SO	W	L	Pct	SV	ShO	ERA
Jim Palmer	2	2	0	15 2/3	11	8	8	9	9	1	0	0	4.60		39	39	17	305	263	92	100	199	20	10	.667	0	5	2.71
Mike Cuellar	2	2	1	11 1/3	10	7	4	2	5	1	0	0	3.18		40	40	21	298	273	115	69	190	24	8	.750	0	4	3.47
Dave McNally	1	1	1	9	9	3	3	2	5	1	0	0	3.00		40	40	16	296	277	106	78	185	24	9	.727	0	1	3.22
Moe Drabowsky	2	0	0	3 1/3	2	1	1	1	1	0	0	0	2.70	a	21	0	0	33	30	14	15	21	4	2	.667	1	0	3.82
Dick Hall	1	0	0	2 1/3	0	0	0	0	0	0	0	1	0.00		32	0	0	61	51	21	6	30	10	5	.667	1	0	3.82
Tom Phoebus	1	0	0	1 2/3	1	0	0	0	0	1	0	0	0.00		27	21	3	135	106	46	62	72	5	5	.500	0	0	3.07
Eddie Watt	1	0	0	1	2	1	1	1	3	0	1	0	9.00		53	0	0	55	44	20	29	33	7	7	.500	12	0	3.27
Marcelino Lopez	1	0	0	1/3	0	0	0	0	0	0	0	0	0.00		25	3	0	61	47	14	37	49	1	1	.500	0	0	2.07
Pete Richert	1	0	0	1/3	0	0	0	0	0	0	0	1	0.00		50	0	0	55	36	12	24	66	7	2	.778	13	0	1.96
Jim Hardin	Did not play														36	19	3	145	150	57	26	78	6	5	.545	1	2	3.54
Dave Leonhard	Did not play														23	0	0	28	32	16	18	14	0	0	—	1	0	5.14
team total	5	5	2	45	35	20	17	15	23	4	1	2	3.40		162	162	60	1479	1317	517	469	941	108	54	.667	31	12	3.15

CINCINNATI REDS

	WORLD SERIES STATISTICS													REGULAR SEASON STATISTICS													
	G	GS	CG	IP	H	R	ER	BB	SO	W	L	SV	ERA		G	GS	CG	IP	H	ER	BB	SO	W	L	Pct	SV	ShO	ERA
Gary Nolan	2	2	0	9 1/3	9	8	8	3	9	0	1	0	7.71		37	37	4	251	226	91	96	181	18	7	.720	0	2	3.26
Clay Carroll	4	0	0	9	5	0	0	2	11	1	0	0	0.00		65	0	0	104	104	30	27	63	9	4	.692	16	0	2.60
Tony Cloninger	2	1	0	7 1/3	10	6	6	5	4	0	1	0	7.36		30	18	0	148	136	63	78	56	9	7	.563	1	0	3.83
Don Gullett	3	0	0	6 2/3	5	2	1	4	4	0	0	0	1.35		44	2	0	78	54	21	44	76	5	2	.714	6	0	2.42
Jim McGlothlin	1	1	0	4 1/3	6	4	4	2	2	0	0	0	8.31		35	34	5	211	192	84	86	97	14	10	.583	0	3	3.58
Milt Wilcox	2	0	0	2	3	2	2	0	2	0	1	0	9.00		5	2	1	22	19	6	7	13	3	1	.750	1	1	2.45
Jim Merritt	1	1	0	1 2/3	3	4	4	1	0	0	1	0	21.60		35	35	12	234	248	106	53	136	20	12	.625	0	1	4.08
Wayne Granger	2	0	0	1 1/3	7	5	5	1	1	0	0	0	33.75		67	0	0	85	79	25	27	38	6	5	.545	35	0	2.65
Ray Washburn	1	0	0	1 1/3	2	2	2	2	0	0	0	0	13.50		35	3	0	66	90	51	48	37	4	4	.500	0	0	6.95
Mel Behney	Did not play														5	1	0	10	15	5	8	2	0	2	.000	0	0	4.50
Wayne Simpson	Not in Series—Shoulder injury														26	26	10	176	125	59	81	119	14	3	.824	0	2	3.02
team total	5	5	0	43	50	33	32	20	33	1	4	0	6.70		162	162	32	1445	1370	592	592	843	102	60	.630	60	15	3.69

Total Attendance—253,183 Average Attendance—50,637 *Winning Player's Share—$18,216 *Losing Player's Share—$13,688
*includes playoffs and world series.

1971
Lights On, Orioles Off

The World Series meant long lunch breaks and transistor radios in the office, but major-league baseball brought the game to millions of television viewers in their living rooms by experimentally scheduling the fourth contest this year for night. The two clubs who would meet under the floodlights for the first time in Series history were the Baltimore Orioles and Pittsburgh Pirates. The Birds came into this Series with a hot hand, winning their last 11 games of the regular season, then sweeping three straight play-off games from the budding Oakland A's for their third straight American League pennant. Frank Robinson, Brooks Robinson, and Boog Powell as usual paced the Oriole attack, but a novelty on this squad was the presence of four 20-game-winning pitchers. Dave McNally, Pat Dobson, Mike Cuellar, and Jim Palmer all reached that plateau in pooling 81 victories. The National League-champion Pirates had a less glamorous pitching staff, but wielded a powerful attack to win the Eastern Division and beat the San Francisco Giants three games to one in the championship series. Roberto Clemente sparkled with a .341 average, and Willie Stargell hit 48 homers and drove in 125 runs in the clean-up slot. Assisting these established stars were younger sluggers like Manny Sanguillen, Bob Robertson, Al Oliver, and Richie Hebner, all new to Series pressure.

In the opening-game match-up between McNally and 19-game-winner Dock Ellis, the Bucs took a 3–0 edge due to sloppy Baltimore fielding, then lost the lead on home runs by Frank Robinson and Merv Rettenmund. Those two blows brought manager Danny Murtaugh to the mound to relieve Ellis, but McNally's three-hit pitching prevented any Pirate comeback and sewed up a 5–3 victory. After a day off for a Maryland rain, the Birds pounded out an 11–3 laugher in game two to sweep the two contests in Baltimore.

The Pirates appeared outclassed by the coolly confident Birds, but they regrouped in the friendly confines of Three Rivers Stadium. Right-hander Steve Blass, an underrated 15-game-winner, got the Pirates into the win column with a 5–1 three-hitter, with Robertson's three-run homer in the seventh inning a big help. The fourth game was the novel night game, with Pat Dobson facing 10-game-winner Luke Walker. The Birds sent Walker to the showers with three runs in the top of the first inning, with lanky twenty-one-year-old Bruce Kison coming on in relief. The Pirates came back with two runs in the bottom of the first and tied it with another tally in the third. Kison meanwhile shut the Orioles off until the Bucs reached reliever Eddie Watt in the bottom of the seventh. After Oliver made out, Robertson and Sanguillen singled. Oriole center fielder Paul Blair dropped Vic Davalillo's liner, but recovered in time to throw Sanguillen out at second. Murtaugh now called out twenty-one-year-old Milt May to pinch-hit for Kison, and the young catcher singled home Robertson for the deciding run in a 4–3 decision which evened the Series. An estimated television audience of 61 million viewers prompted Commissioner Bowie Kuhn to schedule all weekday games at night starting next year. The wave that the Pirates were riding stayed high through the fifth game, with a two-hit gem by Nelson Briles beating the Orioles 4–0.

The Orioles now found themselves facing a tide of momentum similar to that of the 1969 Mets, but after falling behind 2–0 in the sixth game, they fought back to tie the score, then win it 3–2 in the tenth inning on some courageous base running by Frank Robinson, who moved from first to third on a single up the middle, then scored on a short outfield fly. The seventh game matched Cuellar against Blass, and both of them looked sharp in the early innings. But Roberto Clemente, who had hit safely in all six games thus far, nailed a high curve ball in the fourth inning and parked it in the center-field bleachers for a 1–0 lead. Blass protected the edge like a miser, and another run in the eighth on Stargell's single and Jose Pagan's double upped the lead to 2–0. Elrod Hendricks and Mark Belanger led off the Baltimore eighth with singles, but Blass got out of the inning with only one run scored, and he retired the Orioles in order in the ninth for the 2–1 victory and a World Championship for Pittsburgh. Clemente reveled in the national recognition his .414 batting earned, and this Series was the high point of a long and distinguished career.

Game 1 October 9 at Baltimore

Pittsburgh	Pos	AB	R	H	RBI	PO	A	E
Cash	2b	4	0	1	1	1	3	0
Clines	cf	4	0	0	0	1	0	0
Clemente	rf	4	0	2	0	2	0	0
Stargell	lf	3	0	0	0	2	0	0
Robertson	1b	3	1	0	0	8	1	0
Sanguillen	c	4	1	0	0	6	0	0
Pagan	3b	4	0	0	0	2	0	0
Hernandez	ss	2	1	0	1	0	4	0
b Oliver		1	0	0	0	0	0	0
Ellis	p	1	0	0	0	1	0	0
Moose	p	1	0	0	0	0	1	0
a Mazeroski		1	0	0	0	0	0	0
Miller	p	0	0	0	0	1	1	0
Totals		32	3	3	2	24	10	0

Baltimore	Pos	AB	R	H	RBI	PO	A	E
Buford	lf	4	2	1	1	4	0	0
Blair	cf	0	0	0	0	0	0	0
Rettenmund	cf-lf	4	1	1	3	4	0	0
Powell	1b	3	0	0	0	6	0	0
F. Robinson	rf	4	1	2	1	3	0	0
Hendricks	c	4	0	1	0	9	0	1
B. Robinson	3b	4	0	1	0	0	3	0
Johnson	2b	4	0	0	0	1	1	0
Belanger	ss	4	1	2	0	0	2	2
McNally	p	3	0	0	0	0	1	0
Totals		34	5	10	5	27	7	3

	Pit.	030 000 000
	Bal.	013 010 00x

Pitching	IP	H	R	ER	BB	SO
Pittsburgh						
Ellis (L)	2⅓	4	4	4	1	1
Moose	3⅔	3	1	1	0	4
Miller	2	3	0	0	0	1
Baltimore						
McNally (W)	9	3	3	0	2	9

a Flied out for Moose in 7th.
b Struck out for Hernandez in 9th.

Double—Clemente. Triple—Belanger. Home Runs—Buford, Rettenmund, F. Robinson. Sacrifice Hit—Hernandez. Wild Pitches—McNally, Moose. Left on Bases—Pittsburgh 5, Baltimore 6. Umpires—Chylak (A), Sudol (N), Rice (A), Vargo (N), Odom (A), Kibler (N). Attendance—53,229. Time of Game—2:06.

1st Inning
Pittsburgh
1 Cash lined to center.
2 Clines flied to short left.
Clemente doubled to right-center.
3 Stargell struck out.
Baltimore
1 Buford grounded to second.
2 Rettenmund grounded to short.
3 Powell grounded to short.

2nd Inning
Pittsburgh
Robertson walked.
Robertson went to second on a wild pitch.
Sanguillen grounded to Belanger whose throw to third hit Robertson and went into the dugout, Robertson scoring and Sanguillen safely at second.
1 Pagan grounded back to the mound, Sanguillen advancing to third.
Hernandez laid down a squeeze bunt, scoring Sanguillen and when Hendricks dropped McNally's throw Hernandez went to second.
2 Ellis struck out.
Cash singled to right-center, scoring Hernandez.
3 Clines forced Cash at second, Belanger to Johnson.
Baltimore
F. Robinson hit a home run into the left field stands.
1 Hendricks grounded to second.
2 B. Robinson flied to center.
3 Johnson lined to the mound.

3rd Inning
Pittsburgh
Clemente singled to center.
Stargell walked.
1 Robertson struck out.
2 Sanguillen struck out.
3 Pagan flied to left.
Baltimore
Belanger singled to center.
1 McNally struck out.
Buford singled between first and second, Belanger stopping at second.
Rettenmund hit a three-run homer over the left-center field fence.
Powell walked.
For Pittsburgh—Moose came in to pitch.
2 F. Robinson struck out.
Powell took second on a wild pitch.
3 Hendricks lined to Clemente in right-center.

4th Inning
Pittsburgh
1 Hernandez struck out.
2 Moose took a called third strike.
3 Cash lined to right.
Baltimore
1 B. Robinson bounced back to the mound.
2 Johnson flied to Clemente in right-center.
Belanger tripled when Clemente missed a shoestring catch in right-center.
3 McNally struck out.

5th Inning
Pittsburgh
1 Clines grounded to third.
2 Clemente flied to right.
3 Stargell grounded to short.
Baltimore
Buford hit a home-run into the right field stands.
1 Rettenmund struck out.
2 Powell popped to third.
3 F. Robinson struck out.

6th Inning
Pittsburgh
1 Robertson struck out.
2 Sanguillen flied to center.
3 Pagan grounded to third.
Baltimore
1 Hendricks grounded to short.
B. Robinson singled to center.
2 Johnson flied to deep left.
3 Belanger grounded to second.

7th Inning
Pittsburgh
1 Hernandez grounded to third.
2 Mazeroski, pinch-hitting for Moose, flied to left.
3 Cash lined to left.
Baltimore
For Pittsburgh—Miller pitching.
1 McNally struck out.
2 Buford lined to left.
3 Rettenmund bounced to the mound.

8th Inning
Pittsburgh
For Baltimore—Rettenmund moved to left with Blair playing center.
1 Clines flied to deep left.
2 Clemente grounded to second.
3 Stargell struck out.
Baltimore
1 Powell grounded out, Robertson to Miller.
F. Robinson singled to center.
Hendricks singled to second, moving F. Robinson to second.
2 B. Robinson fouled to Pagan.
Johnson beat out a roller to short, loading the bases.
3 Belanger forced Johnson at second, Hernandez to Cash.

9th Inning
Pittsburgh
1 Robertson flied to left.
Sanguillen safe at second on Belanger's wild throw of his grounder.
2 Pagan flied to F. Robinson in right-center.
3 Oliver, pinch-hitting for Hernandez, struck out.

Game 2 October 11 at Baltimore

Pit.	000 000 030
Bal.	010 361 00x

Pittsburgh	Pos	AB	R	H	RBI	PO	A	E
Cash	2b	5	0	0	0	2	6	0
Hebner	3b	3	1	1	3	0	0	0
Clemente	rf	5	0	2	0	2	0	0
Stargell	lf	3	0	1	0	2	1	0
Giusti	p	0	0	0	0	0	0	0
Oliver	cf	5	0	1	0	1	0	1
Robertson	1b	3	0	0	0	8	1	0
Sanguillen	c	5	0	1	0	4	0	0
Hernandez	ss	2	1	1	0	2	1	0
d May		1	0	0	0	0	0	0
B. Johnson	p	2	0	0	0	2	0	0
Kison	p	0	0	0	0	0	0	0
Moose	p	0	0	0	0	0	0	0
Veale	p	0	0	0	0	0	1	0
a Sands		1	0	0	0	0	0	0
Miller	p	0	0	0	0	0	0	0
c Davalillo	lf	1	1	1	0	1	0	0
Totals		36	3	8	3	24	10	1

a Struck out for Veale in 6th.
b Ran for F. Robinson in 6th.
c Singled for Miller in 8th.
d Grounded out for Hernandez in 9th.

Double—Clemente. Home Run—Hebner. Double Plays—Cash to Hernandez, Stargell to Sanguillen. Hit by Pitcher—Hendricks (by B. Johnson). Left on Bases—Pittsburgh 14, Baltimore 9. Umpires—Sudol, Rice, Vargo, Odom, Kibler, Chylak. Attendance—53,239. Time of Game—2:55.

Baltimore	Pos	AB	R	H	RBI	PO	A	E
Buford	lf	5	0	0	1	3	0	0
Rettenmund	cf-rf	5	1	2	1	3	0	0
Powell	1b	5	1	1	0	4	3	0
F. Robinson	rf	4	2	3	0	2	0	0
b Blair	cf	1	1	1	0	1	0	0
Hendricks	c	3	2	2	1	10	0	0
B. Robinson	3b	3	2	3	2	0	1	0
D. Johnson	2b	5	1	2	3	1	3	0
Belanger	ss	3	1	0	0	1	2	1
Palmer	p	2	0	0	2	2	0	0
Hall	p	0	0	0	0	1	0	0
Totals		36	11	14	10	27	8	1

Pitching	IP	H	R	ER	BB	SO
Pittsburgh						
B. Johnson (L)	3⅓	4	4	4	2	1
Kison	*0	0	2	0	0	2
Moose	1	5	5	5	0	0
Veale	⅓	1	1	1	1	0
Miller	2	3	1	1	0	1
Giusti	1	1	0	1	0	1
Baltimore						
Palmer (W)	8	7	3	3	8	10
Hall (SV)	1	1	0	0	0	0

*Pitched to 2 batters in 4th.

1st Inning
Pittsburgh
1 Cash grounded to short.
 Hebner walked.
 Clemente singled to center, Hebner going to second.
2 Stargell struck out.
3 Oliver grounded out, Powell to Palmer.
Baltimore
1 Buford grounded out, Robertson to B. Johnson.
2 Rettenmund flied to deep left.
3 Powell grounded to second.

2nd Inning
Pittsburgh
 Robertson walked.
 Sanguillen singled to right, Robertson stopping at second.
1 Hernandez flied to center.
2 B. Johnson took a called third strike.
3 Cash flied to short center.
Baltimore
 F. Robinson singled to center.
 Hendricks walked.
 B. Robinson singled to center, scoring F. Robinson as Hendricks stopped at second.
1,2 D. Johnson lined into a double play, Cash to Hernandez doubling Hendricks.
3 Belanger lined to the pitcher.

3rd Inning
Pittsburgh
1 Hebner grounded to first.
 Clemente doubled off the right field wall.
 Stargell walked.
2 Oliver flied to short left.
3 Robertson struck out.
Baltimore
1 Palmer flied to right.
2 Buford struck out.
3 Rettenmund grounded to second.

4th Inning
Pittsburgh
1 Sanguillen grounded to second.
 Hernandez singled to center.
2 B. Johnson struck out.
3 Cash flied to left.
Baltimore
1 Powell grounded to second.
 F. Robinson singled to left.
 Hendricks was hit by a pitched ball.
 B. Robinson walked to load the bases.
 D. Johnson singled to left, scoring F. Robinson and Hendricks with B. Robinson moving to second.
 For Pittsburgh—Kison pitching.
 Belanger walked filling the bases.
 Palmer walked, forcing in B. Robinson.
 For Pittsburgh—Moose pitching.
2,3 Buford flied to Stargell and his perfect throw to Sanguillen doubled D. Johnson at the plate.

5th Inning
Pittsburgh
1 Hebner struck out.
2 Clemente lined to deep right.
 Stargell walked.
3 Oliver struck out.
Baltimore
 Rettenmund singled to right.
 Powell singled to right.
1 F. Robinson flied to deep right, Rettenmund to third after the catch.
 Hendricks singled to center, scoring Rettenmund. When the ball got by Oliver Powell also scored and Hendricks got all the way to third.
 B. Robinson singled to center, scoring Hendricks.
 D. Johnson singled to center, B. Robinson stopping at second.

5th Inning (continued)
 For Pittsburgh—Veale pitching.
 Belanger walked, loading the bases.
 Palmer walked, forcing in B. Robinson.
2 Buford forced Palmer, Veale to Cash to Hernandez, as D. Johnson scored.
 Rettenmund singled to right, scoring Belanger with Buford going to third.
3 Powell grounded to second.

6th Inning
Pittsburgh
 Robertson walked.
1 Sanguillen struck out.
 Hernandez walked.
2 Sands, batting for Veale, struck out.
3 Cash grounded out, Powell to Palmer.
Baltimore
 For Pittsburgh—Miller pitching.
 F. Robinson singled to center.
 Blair ran for F. Robinson.
 Hendricks singled to left, Blair advancing to third.
 B. Robinson singled to center, scoring Blair with Hendricks stopping at second.
1 D. Johnson took a called third strike.
2 Belanger forced B. Robinson at second, Cash unassisted, Hendricks to third.
3 Palmer grounded to first.

7th Inning
Pittsburgh
 For Baltimore—Blair stays in to play center as Rettenmund moves to right.
 Hebner walked.
1 Clemente fouled to Rettenmund.
 Stargell singled to center, Hebner racing to third.
2 Oliver struck out.
3 Robertson also struck out.
Baltimore
1 Buford bounced to first.
2 Rettenmund grounded to short.
3 Powell fouled to Sanguillen.

8th Inning
Pittsburgh
1 Sanguillen grounded to third where B. Robinson made a diving stop.
 Hernandez walked.
 Davalillo, pinch-hitting for Miller, singled to left with Hernandez stopping at second.
2 Cash flied to short center.
 Hebner hit a three-run homer into the right field stands.
 Clemente got safely to first as Belanger fumbled his grounder.
3 Stargell forced Clemente at second, D. Johnson to Belanger.
Baltimore
 For Pittsburgh—Davalillo stays in to play left with Giusti pitching (batting fourth).
 Blair singled to left.
1 Hendricks flied to center.
 B. Robinson walked.
2 D. Johnson flied to left.
3 Belanger fouled to Robertson.

9th Inning
Pittsburgh
 For Baltimore—Hall pitching.
 Oliver singled to center.
1 Robertson popped to second.
2 Sanguillen forced Oliver at second, D. Johnson to Belanger.
3 May, pinch-hitting for Hernandez, grounded out, Powell to Hall.

Game 3 October 12 at Pittsburgh

Bal.	000 000 100
Pit.	100 001 30x

Baltimore	Pos	AB	R	H	RBI	PO	A	E
Buford	lf	4	0	0	0	3	0	0
Rettenmund	cf	4	0	0	0	3	0	0
Powell	1b	4	0	0	0	7	0	1
F. Robinson	rf	4	1	2	1	2	0	0
Hendricks	c	3	0	0	0	4	1	0
B. Robinson	3b	3	0	1	0	1	5	1
Johnson	2b	3	0	1	0	3	2	0
Belanger	ss	3	0	0	0	1	2	0
Cuellar	p	1	0	0	0	0	0	1
Dukes	p	0	0	0	0	0	0	0
a Shopay		1	0	0	0	0	0	0
Watt	p	0	0	0	0	0	0	0
Totals		30	1	3		24	10	3

a Grounded out for Dukes in 8th.

Doubles—Cash, Pagan, Sanguillen. Home Runs—Robertson, F. Robinson. Double Play—B. Robinson to Johnson. Left on Bases—Baltimore 4, Pittsburgh 9. Umpires—Rice, Vargo, Odom, Kibler, Chylak, Sudol. Attendance—50,403. Time of Game—2:20.

Pittsburgh	Pos	AB	R	H	RBI	PO	A	E
Cash	2b	4	1	1	0	2	2	0
Oliver	cf	4	0	0	0	2	0	0
Clemente	rf	4	1	1	1	3	0	0
Stargell	lf	1	1	0	0	2	0	0
Robertson	1b	4	1	1	3	8	1	0
Sanguillen	c	4	1	2	0	8	0	0
Pagan	3b	4	0	2	1	0	3	0
Alley	ss	2	0	0	0	1	2	0
Hernandez	ss	1	0	0	0	0	1	0
Blass	p	4	0	0	0	1	2	0
Totals		32	5	7	5	27	8	0

Pitching	IP	H	R	ER	BB	SO
Baltimore						
Cuellar (L)	*6	7	5	4	6	4
Dukes	1	0	0	0	0	0
Watt	1	0	0	0	0	1
Pittsburgh						
Blass (W)	9	3	1	1	2	8

*Pitched to 3 batters in 7th.

1st Inning
Baltimore
1 Buford flied to left.
2 Rettenmund grounded to short.
3 Powell grounded to second.
Pittsburgh
 Cash doubled down the left field line.
 Oliver safe at first on Powell's wide throw to Cuellar, Cash moving over to third.
1 Clemente forced Oliver at second, Johnson to Belanger as Cash scored.
 Stargell walked.
2,3 Robertson lined to B. Robinson who threw to Johnson doubling Clemente.

2nd Inning
Baltimore
1 F. Robinson struck out.
 Hendricks walked.
2 B. Robinson fouled to Robertson.
3 Johnson flied to center.
Pittsburgh
1 Sanguillen flied to right.
 Pagan doubled down the left field line.
2 Alley grounded to second, Pagan moving over to third.
3 Blass grounded to short.

3rd Inning
Baltimore
1 Belanger popped to second.
2 Cuellar lined to right.
3 Buford flied to left.
Pittsburgh
1 Cash lined to center.
2 Oliver fouled to Buford.
3 Clemente grounded to third.

4th Inning
Baltimore
1 Rettenmund flied to short right.
2 Powell took a called third strike.
3 F. Robinson flied to right.
Pittsburgh
 Stargell walked.
1 Robertson called out on strikes.
 Sanguillen singled to center, Stargell going to second.
2 Pagan flied to center.
 Alley walked, loading the bases.
3 Blass forced Alley at second, B. Robinson to Johnson.

5th Inning
Baltimore
1 Hendricks struck out.
 B. Robinson singled to left-center.
2 Johnson forced B. Robinson at second, Alley to Cash.
3 Belanger forced Johnson at second, Alley unassisted
Pittsburgh
1 Cash flied to center.
 Oliver walked.
 Clemente singled to center, Oliver advancing to third. Clemente went to second as the throw to third got by B. Robinson.
2 Stargell took a called third strike.
3 Robertson struck out.

6th Inning
Baltimore
 Cuellar walked.
1 Buford took a called third strike.
2 Rettenmund tapped back to the mound, Cuellar going to second.
3 Powell grounded to first.
Pittsburgh
 Sanguillen doubled to right-center.
 Pagan singled to left, scoring Sanguillen.
1 Alley grounded to short, Pagan moving over to second.
2 Blass grounded to third, Pagan holding second.
 Cash intentionally walked.
3 Oliver struck out.

7th Inning
Baltimore
 For Pittsburgh—Hernandez playing short.
 F. Robinson hit a home run into the second deck of the left field stands.
1 Hendricks struck out.
2 B. Robinson struck out.
3 Johnson grounded to short.
Pittsburgh
 Clemente safe at first on Cuellar's bad throw.
 Stargell walked for the third time.
 Robertson hit a three-run homer into the right-center field stands.
 For Baltimore—Dukes came in to pitch.
1 Sanguillen flied to right.
2 Pagan flied to left.
3 Hernandez grounded to third.

8th Inning
Baltimore
1 Belanger struck out.
2 Shopay, pinch-hitting for Dukes, grounded back to the mound.
3 Buford grounded out, Robertson to Blass.
Pittsburgh
 For Baltimore—Watt pitching.
1 Blass struck out but Hendricks dropped the third strike and had to throw him out at first.
2 Cash flied to left.
3 Oliver popped to second.

9th Inning
Baltimore
1 Rettenmund took a called third strike.
2 Powell flied to deep center where Oliver made a one-handed catch.
 F. Robinson singled to left.
3 Hendricks grounded to second.

Game 4 October 13 at Pittsburgh

Baltimore	Pos	AB	R	H	RBI	PO	A	E
Blair	cf	4	1	2	0	2	1	1
Belanger	ss	4	1	1	0	3	4	0
Rettenmund	lf	4	1	1	0	1	0	0
F. Robinson	rf	2	0	0	0	2	0	0
B. Robinson	3b	3	0	0	1	1	1	0
Powell	1b	3	0	0	1	6	0	0
Johnson	2b	3	0	0	0	3	2	0
Etchebarren	c	2	0	0	0	6	0	0
Dobson	p	2	0	0	0	0	3	0
Jackson	p	0	0	0	0	0	0	0
a Shopay		1	0	0	0	0	0	0
Watt	p	0	0	0	0	0	0	0
Richert	p	0	0	0	0	0	0	0
Totals		28	3	4	2	24	11	1

Pitching	IP	H	R	ER	BB	SO
Baltimore						
Dobson	$5\frac{1}{3}$	10	3	3	3	4
Jackson	$\frac{2}{3}$	0	0	0	1	0
Watt (L)	$1\frac{1}{3}$	4	1	1	0	1
Richert	$\frac{2}{3}$	0	0	0	0	1
Pittsburgh						
Walker	$\frac{2}{3}$	3	3	3	1	0
Kison (W)	$6\frac{1}{3}$	1	0	0	0	3
Giusti (SV)	2	0	0	0	0	1

Bal.	3 0 0	0 0 0	0 0 0
Pit.	2 0 1	0 0 0	1 0 x

Pittsburgh	Pos	AB	R	H	RBI	PO	A	E
Cash	2b	4	1	1	0	3	3	0
Hebner	3b	5	1	1	0	1	1	0
Clemente	rf	4	0	3	0	0	0	0
Stargell	lf	5	1	2	1	1	0	0
Oliver	cf	4	0	2	2	6	0	0
Robertson	1b	4	1	1	0	11	0	0
Sanguillen	c	4	0	2	0	4	0	0
Hernandez	ss	3	0	1	0	1	2	0
b Davalillo		1	0	0	0	0	0	0
Giusti	p	0	0	0	0	0	0	0
Walker	p	0	0	0	0	0	0	0
Kison	p	2	0	0	0	0	1	0
c May		1	0	1	1	0	0	0
d Alley	ss	0	0	0	0	0	2	0
Totals		37	4	14	4	27	9	0

a Hit into force play for Jackson in 7th.
b Reached base on error for Hernandez in 7th.
c Singled for Kison in 7th.
d Ran for May in 7th.

Doubles—Blair, Oliver, Stargell. Stolen Bases—Hernandez, Sanguillen. Sacrifice Flies—Powell, B. Robinson. Double Plays—Hernandez to Cash to Robertson, Belanger to Johnson to Powell. Passed Ball—Sanguillen. Hit by Pitcher—Etchebarren, Johnson, F. Robinson (all by Kison). Left on Bases—Baltimore 4, Pittsburgh 13. Umpires—Vargo, Odom, Kibler, Chylak, Sudol, Rice. Attendance—51,378. Time of Game—2:48.

1st Inning
Baltimore
Blair singled to left-center.
Belanger beat out a grounder to second.
Rettenmund beat out a hit to deep short, loading the bases.
On a passed ball by Sanguillen, Blair scored, Belanger went to third and Rettenmund to second.
F. Robinson intentionally walked, loading the bases.
1 B. Robinson hit a sacrifice fly to center, Belanger scoring after the catch. Rettenmund went to third and F. Robinson to second on the throw to the plate.
2 Powell hit a sacrifice fly to center, Rettenmund scoring after the catch.
For Pittsburgh—Kison pitching.
3 Johnson grounded to third.
Pittsburgh
Cash walked.
1 Hebner popped to Belanger in short left.
2 Clemente struck out.
Stargell doubled to right-center, scoring Cash.
Oliver doubled over the oncharging Blair's head, scoring Stargell.
3 Robertson grounded back to the mound.

2nd Inning
Baltimore
1 Etchebarren grounded to second.
2 Dobson took a called third strike.
Blair doubled to right-center.
3 Belanger popped to first.
Pittsburgh
1 Sanguillen grounded to third.
2 Hernandez lined to center.
3 Kison took a called third strike.

3rd Inning
Baltimore
1 Rettenmund grounded to short.
2 F. Robinson struck out.
3 B. Robinson bounced back to the mound.
Pittsburgh
1 Cash grounded to short.
Hebner singled to center.
Clemente singled to right, Hebner stopping at second.
2 Stargell flied to short center.
Oliver singled to right, scoring Hebner and moving Clemente to third.
3 Robertson tapped back to the mound.

4th Inning
Baltimore
1 Powell fouled to Robertson.
Johnson was hit by a pitch.
2,3 Etchebarren grounded into a double play, Hernandez to Cash to Robertson.
Pittsburgh
Sanguillen singled to left.
Sanguillen stole second.
Hernandez bounced to Dobson who got
1 Sanguillen in a run-down, Dobson to Belanger.
Kison walked.
2,3 Cash hit into a double play, Belanger to Johnson to Powell.

5th Inning
Baltimore
1 Dobson struck out.
2 Blair flied to deep center.
3 Belanger flied to center.

5th Inning (continued)
Pittsburgh
1 Hebner was called out on strikes.
Clemente singled through the box.
Stargell singled to center, Clemente moving to third with Stargell going to second on Blair's bad throw to third.
Oliver got an intentional pass, loading the bases.
2 Robertson popped to Belanger in short left.
3 Sanguillen forced Oliver at second, Belanger to Johnson.

6th Inning
Baltimore
1 Rettenmund lined to short.
F. Robinson was hit by a pitch.
2 B. Robinson flied to center.
3 Powell grounded to first.
Pittsburgh
Hernandez singled to left.
1 Kison took a called third strike.
Hernandez stole second.
Cash singled off Dobson's glove, Hernandez to third.
For Baltimore—Jackson pitching.
2 Hebner lined to third.
Clemente walked, loading the bases.
3 Stargell grounded to second.

7th Inning
Baltimore
1 Johnson flied to center.
Etchebarren was hit by a pitch.
2 Shopay, pinch-hitting for Jackson, forced Etchebarren, Cash unassisted.
3 Blair flied to deep left.
Pittsburgh
For Baltimore—Watt pitching.
1 Oliver struck out.
Robertson singled to center.
Sanguillen singled to center.
Davalillo, batting for Hernandez, safely at first when Blair dropped his fly, Robertson went to third but Sanguillen
2 overran second and was out, Blair to Belanger to Johnson.
May, batting for Kison, singled to right-center, scoring Robertson with Davalillo racing to third.
Alley ran for May.
3 Cash flied to right.

8th Inning
Baltimore
For Pittsburgh—Alley playing short and Giusti pitching.
1 Belanger took a called third strike.
2 Rettenmund grounded to second.
3 F. Robinson popped to second.
Pittsburgh
1 Hebner flied to right.
Clemente beat out a hit to deep short.
For Baltimore—Richert pitching.
2 Stargell took a called third strike.
3 Oliver flied to left.

9th Inning
Baltimore
1 B. Robinson grounded to short.
2 Powell fouled to Hebner.
3 Johnson grounded to short.

Game 5 October 14 at Pittsburgh

Baltimore	Pos	AB	R	H	RBI	PO	A	E
Buford	lf	3	0	0	0	1	0	0
Blair	cf	4	0	0	0	3	1	0
Powell	1b	3	0	1	0	8	0	0
F. Robinson	rf	3	0	0	0	1	0	0
Hendricks	c	2	0	0	0	4	3	0
B. Robinson	3b	3	0	1	0	2	2	1
Johnson	2b	3	0	0	0	3	1	0
Belanger	ss	3	0	0	0	2	3	0
McNally	p	1	0	0	0	0	1	0
Leonhard	p	0	0	0	0	0	0	0
a Shopay		1	0	0	0	0	0	0
Dukes	p	0	0	0	0	0	0	0
b Rettenmund		1	0	0	0	0	0	0
Totals		27	0	2	0	24	11	1

a Flied out for Leonhard in 6th.
b Grounded out for Dukes in 9th.

Triple—Clines. Home Run—Robertson. Stolen Bases—Clines, Sanguillen. Sacrifice Hits—Briles 2. Double Plays—Hernandez to Cash to Robertson, Pagan to Cash to Robertson. Hit by Pitch—Hernandez (by Dukes). Wild Pitch—McNally. Left on Bases—Baltimore 2, Pittsburgh 9. Umpires—Odom, Kibler, Chylak, Sudol, Rice, Vargo. Attendance—51,377. Time of Game—2:16.

Bal.	0 0 0	0 0 0	0 0 0
Pit.	0 2 1	0 1 0	0 0 x

Pittsburgh	Pos	AB	R	H	RBI	PO	A	E
Cash	2b	4	0	0	0	5	2	0
Clines	cf	3	2	1	0	3	0	0
Clemente	rf	4	0	1	1	4	0	0
Stargell	lf	4	0	1	0	2	0	0
Robertson	1b	3	1	1	1	9	0	0
Sanguillan	c	4	1	1	0	2	0	0
Pagan	3b	4	0	1	0	0	6	0
Hernandez	ss	3	0	2	0	2	1	0
Briles	p	2	0	1	1	0	1	0
Totals		31	4	9	3	27	10	0

Pitching	IP	H	R	ER	BB	SO
Baltimore						
McNally (L)	*4	7	4	3	2	3
Leonhard	1	0	0	0	1	0
Dukes	3	2	0	0	0	1
Pittsburgh						
Briles (W)	9	2	0	0	2	2

*Pitched to 2 batters in 5th.

1st Inning
Baltimore
1 Buford popped to short.
2 Blair took a called third strike.
3 Powell bounced back to the pitcher.
Pittsburgh
Cash walked.
1 Clines forced Cash at second, McNally to Belanger.
2 Clemente lined to right at the wall.
Clines stole second.
3 Stargell grounded to short.

2nd Inning
Baltimore
1 F. Robinson fouled to Robertson.
2 Hendricks flied to center.
B. Robinson singled to center.
3 Johnson popped to Clines in short center.
Pittsburgh
Robertson homered over the center field fence.
Sanguillen singled to center.
1 Pagan struck out as Sanguillen was stealing second.
2 Hernandez struck out.
Briles singled to center, scoring Sanguillen.
3 Cash forced Briles at second, B. Robinson to Johnson.

3rd Inning
Baltimore
1 Belanger flied to right.
2 McNally popped to second.
3 Buford grounded to third.
Pittsburgh
Clines walked.
1 Clemente grounded to short, Clines advancing to second.
2 Stargell flied to left.
Robertson safe on B. Robinson's boot of his grounder, Clines going to third.
Clines scored and Robertson went to second on a wild pitch.
3 Sanguillen took a called third strike.

4th Inning
Baltimore
1 Blair flied to right.
2 Powell lined to second.
3 F. Robinson struck out.
Pittsburgh
Pagan singled to left.
Hernandez singled to center with Pagan out trying for third, Blair to B. Robinson.
2 Briles sacrificed Hernandez to second, Hendricks to Johnson.
3 Cash grounded to short.

5th Inning
Baltimore
Hendricks walked.
1,2 B. Robinson hit into a double play, Hernandez to Cash to Robertson.
3 Johnson flied to short left.
Pittsburgh
Clines tripled over Blair's head.
Clemente singled through the box, scoring Clines.
For Baltimore—Leonhard pitching.
1 Stargell popped to third.
Robertson walked.
2 Sanguillen fouled to Powell.
3 Pagan flied to center.

6th Inning
Baltimore
1 Belanger grounded to third.
2 Shopay, pinch-hitting for Leonhard, flied to Clemente in right-center.
3 Buford flied to right.
Pittsburgh
For Baltimore—Dukes pitching.
Hernandez was hit by a pitched ball.
1 Briles struck out.
2 Cash grounded to third, Hernandez taking second.
3 Clines flied to center.

7th Inning
Baltimore
1 Blair flied to center.
Powell singled to right-center.
2,3 F. Robinson grounded into a double play, Pagan to Cash to Robertson.
Pittsburgh
1 Clemente grounded to second.
Stargell singled to center.
2 Robertson tapped out, Hendricks to Powell, Stargell going to second.
3 Sanguillen lined to center.

8th Inning
Baltimore
1 Hendricks grounded to first.
2 B. Robinson flied to deep left.
3 Johnson popped to short.
Pittsburgh
1 Pagan fouled to Powell.
Hernandez singled to center.
2 Briles sacrificed Hernandez to second, Hendricks to Johnson.
3 Cash lined to short.

9th Inning
Baltimore
1 Belanger grounded to third.
2 Rettenmund, pinch-hitting for Dukes, grounded to third.
Buford walked.
3 Blair forced Buford at second, Pagan to Cash.

Game 6 October 16 at Baltimore

Pit.	011	000	000	0				
Bal.	000	001	100	1				

Pittsburgh	Pos	AB	R	H	RBI	PO	A	E
Cash	2b	5	0	1	0	3	4	0
Hebner	3b	4	0	0	0	0	2	1
Clemente	rf	4	1	2	1	2	0	0
Stargell	lf	4	0	0	0	2	0	0
Oliver	cf	5	1	1	0	2	0	0
Miller	p	0	0	0	0	0	0	0
Robertson	1b	4	0	2	1	9	0	0
Sanguillen	c	4	0	3	0	8	0	0
Hernandez	ss	4	0	0	0	2	2	0
Moose	p	1	0	0	0	0	2	0
B. Johnson	p	1	0	0	0	0	0	0
Giusti	p	0	0	0	0	0	0	0
b Davalillo	cf	1	0	0	0	1	0	0
Totals		37	2	9	2	29	10	1

Baltimore	Pos	AB	R	H	RBI	PO	A	E
Buford	lf	4	1	3	1	3	1	0
D. Johnson	2b	5	0	1	1	5	1	0
Powell	1b	5	0	1	0	9	1	0
F. Robinson	rf	4	1	0	0	0	0	0
Rettenmund	cf	5	0	1	0	4	0	0
B. Robinson	3b	4	0	1	1	1	0	0
Hendricks	c	4	0	0	0	6	0	0
Belanger	ss	1	1	1	0	2	5	0
Palmer	p	2	0	0	0	0	1	0
a Shopay		1	0	0	0	0	0	0
Dobson	p	0	0	0	0	0	0	0
McNally	p	0	0	0	0	0	0	0
Totals		35	3	8	3	30	9	0

Pitching	IP	H	R	ER	BB	SO
Pittsburgh						
Moose	*5	4	1	1	2	3
B. Johnson	1 2/3	1	1	1	1	2
Giusti	2 1/3	2	0	0	1	3
Miller (L)	2/3	1	1	1	1	0
Baltimore						
Palmer	9	8	2	2	1	5
Dobson	2/3	1	0	0	1	1
McNally (W)	1/3	0	0	0	1	0

*Pitched to 3 batters in 6th.

• Two out when winning run scored.
a Flied out for Palmer in 9th.
b Lined out for Giusti in 10th.

Doubles—Buford, Oliver. Triple—Clemente. Home Runs—Buford, Clemente. Stolen Bases—Cash, Belanger. Sacrifice Hits—Moose, Palmer. Sacrifice Fly—B. Robinson. Double Play—Hebner to Cash to Robinson. Left on Base—Pittsburgh 9, Baltimore 10. Umpires—Kibler, Chylak, Sudol, Rice, Vargo, Odom. Attendance—44,174. Time of Game—2:59.

1st Inning
Pittsburgh
1 Cash fouled to Powell.
2 Hebner flied to center.
Clemente tripled off the left-center field wall.
3 Stargell struck out.
Baltimore
Buford singled to center.
1,2 D. Johnson hit into a double play, Hebner to Cash to Robertson.
3 Powell flied to right.

2nd Inning
Pittsburgh
Oliver doubled to right.
Robertson singled to left, scoring Oliver.
Sanguillen singled to left, Robertson stopping at second.
1 Hernandez forced Robertson at third, Palmer to B. Robinson.
2 Moose sacrificed up both runners, Powell to D. Johnson.
3 Cash popped to D. Johnson in short right.
Baltimore
1 F. Robinson struck out.
2 Rettenmund grounded to short.
3 B. Robinson grounded to first.

3rd Inning
Pittsburgh
1 Hebner popped to Belanger in short center.
Clemente hit a home run over the right field fence.
2 Stargell grounded to short.
3 Oliver grounded to second.
Baltimore
1 Hendricks grounded to first.
Belanger walked.
2 Palmer sacrificed Belanger to second, Moose to Cash.
3 Buford struck out.

4th Inning
Pittsburgh
Robertson singled to left.
1 Sanguillen fouled to Powell.
2 Hernandez took a called third strike.
3 Moose grounded to first.
Baltimore
1 D. Johnson bounced back to the mound.
2 Powell popped to short.
3 F. Robinson lined to right.

5th Inning
Pittsburgh
1 Cash grounded to short.
Hebner walked.
2 Clemente lined to center.
3 Stargell struck out.
Baltimore
1 Rettenmund grounded to second.
B. Robinson singled to right.
2 Hendricks lined to Oliver in left-center.
Belanger walked.
3 Palmer struck out.

6th Inning
Pittsburgh
1 Oliver flied to left.
2 Robertson lined to short.
Sanguillen beat out a slow roller to short.
3 Hernandez popped to D. Johnson in short right-center.

6th Inning (continued)
Baltimore
Buford homered into the right field seats.
D. Johnson safe at first on Hebner's fumble of his slow roller
Powell singled past first, D. Johnson going to third.
For Pittsburgh—B. Johnson pitching.
1 F. Robinson popped to short.
2 Rettenmund took a called third strike.
3 B. Robinson forced Powell at second, Hebner to Cash.

7th Inning
Pittsburgh
1 B. Johnson grounded to short.
2 Cash grounded to short.
3 Hebner grounded to short.
Baltimore
1 Hendricks flied to left.
Belanger singled to right.
2 Palmer took a called third strike.
Belanger stole second.
For Pittsburgh—Giusti came in to pitch with a 3-1 count to Buford.
Buford walked (charged to B. Johnson)
D. Johnson singled to left, Belanger scoring with Buford stopping at second.
3 Powell flied to deep left.

8th Inning
Pittsburgh
1 Clemente flied to Buford in left-center.
2 Stargell flied to deep left.
3 Oliver flied to Rettenmund in right center.
Baltimore
1 F. Robinson struck out.
2 Rettenmund struck out.
3 B. Robinson grounded to second.

9th Inning
Pittsburgh
1 Robertson struck out.
Sanguillen singled on a bouncer over
2 Belanger's head, but was out trying for second, Buford to D. Johnson.
3 Hernandez took a called third strike.
Baltimore
1 Hendrick struck out.
Belanger walked.
2 Shopay, pinch-hitting for Palmer, flied to center.
Buford doubled into the right field corner, Belanger stopping at third.
3 D. Johnson grounded to short.

10th Inning
Pittsburgh
For Baltimore—Dobson pitching.
1 Davalillo, batting for Giusti, lined to second.
Cash singled to right.
2 Hebner struck out as Cash was stealing second.
Clemente was intentionally walked.
For Baltimore—McNally pitching.
Stargell walked, loading the bases.
3 Oliver flied to center.
Baltimore
For Pittsburgh—Davalillo playing center, Miller pitching (batting 5th).
1 Powell grounded to second.
F. Robinson walked.
Rettenmund singled to center, F. Robinson advancing to third.
2 B. Robinson flied to shallow center for a sacrifice fly as F. Robinson scored after the catch.

Game 7 October 17 at Baltimore

Pit.	000	100	010
Bal.	000	000	010

Pittsburgh	Pos	AB	R	H	RBI	PO	A	E
Cash	2b	4	0	0	0	4	3	0
Clines	cf	4	0	0	0	2	0	0
Clemente	rf	4	1	1	1	2	0	0
Robertson	1b	4	0	1	0	11	1	1
Sanguillan	c	4	0	2	0	5	0	0
Stargell	lf	4	1	1	0	0	0	0
Pagan	3b	3	0	1	1	0	2	0
Hernandez	ss	3	0	0	0	2	5	0
Blass	p	3	0	0	0	1	2	0
Totals		33	2	6	2	27	13	1

Baltimore	Pos	AB	R	H	RBI	PO	A	E
Buford	lf	3	0	1	1	0	0	0
Johnson	2b	4	0	0	0	2	2	0
Powell	lb	4	0	0	0	12	0	0
F. Robinson	rf	4	0	0	0	3	0	0
Rettenmund	cf	4	0	0	0	2	0	0
B. Robinson	3b	2	0	0	0	1	5	0
Hendricks	c	3	1	2	0	7	0	0
Belanger	ss	3	0	1	0	0	3	0
Cuellar	p	2	0	0	0	0	3	0
a Shopay		0	0	0	0	0	0	0
Dobson	p	0	0	0	0	0	0	0
McNally	p	0	0	0	0	0	0	0
Totals		29	1	4	1	27	13	0

Pitching	IP	H	R	ER	BB	SO
Pittsburgh						
Blass (W)	9	4	1	1	2	5
Baltimore						
Cuellar (L)	8	4	2	2	0	6
Dobson	2/3	2	0	0	0	1
McNally	1/3	0	0	0	0	0

a Sacrificed for Cuellar in 8th.

Doubles—Hendricks, Pagan. Home Run—Clemente. Sacrifice Hit—Shopay. Double Play—Cash to Robertson. Left on Bases—Pittsburgh 4, Baltimore 4. Umpires—Chylak, Sudol, Rice, Vargo, Odom, Kibler. Attendance—47,291. Time of Game—2:10.

1st Inning
Pittsburgh
1 Cash grounded to third.
2 Clines flied to Rettenmund in left-center.
3 Clemente grounded to short.
Baltimore
Buford walked.
1 Johnson popped to Blass on an attempted bunt.
2 Powell struck out.
3 F. Robinson flied out into the right field corner.

2nd Inning
Pittsburgh
1 Robertson lined to third.
2 Sanguillen grounded to third.
3 Stargell struck out.
Baltimore
1 Rettenmund grounded to short.
B. Robinson walked.
Hendricks safe at first with B. Robinson going to second on Robertson's error.
2,3 Belanger hit into a double play, Cash to Robertson.

3rd Inning
Pittsburgh
1 Pagan grounded to third.
2 Hernandez lined to right.
3 Blass grounded to second.
Baltimore
1 Cuellar struck out.
Buford singled to right.
2 Buford was picked off first, Blass to Robertson to Cash.
3 Johnson grounded to third.

4th Inning
Pittsburgh
1 Cash lined to second.
2 Clines bunted out to the mound.
Clemente homered over the left-center field wall.
3 Robertson grounded to third.
Baltimore
1 Powell grounded to second.
2 F. Robinson struck out.
3 Rettenmund grounded to third.

5th Inning
Pittsburgh
Sanguillen singled to center.
1 Stargell struck out.
2 Pagan forced Sanguillen at second, Belanger to Johnson.
3 Hernandez struck out.
Baltimore
1 B. Robinson flied to right.
Hendricks doubled to right-center.
2 Belanger flied to center.
3 Cuellar called out on strikes.

6th Inning
Pittsburgh
1 Blass tapped back to the mound.
2 Cash struck out.
3 Clines struck out.
Baltimore
1 Buford flied to center.
2 Johnson popped to short.
3 Powell struck out.

7th Inning
Pittsburgh
1 Clemente lined to center.
2 Robertson struck out.
3 Sanguillen flied to right.
Baltimore
1 F. Robinson popped to second.
2 Rettenmund grounded to short.
3 B. Robinson grounded to short.

8th Inning
Pittsburgh
Stargell singled to left.
Pagan doubled off the left-center field fence, scoring Stargell.
1 Hernandez flied to right.
2 Blass grounded to the mound.
3 Cash grounded to third.
Baltimore
Hendricks singled to center.
Belanger singled to center, Hendricks stopping at second.
1 Shopay, pinch-hitting for Cuellar, sacrificed both runners up a base, Blass to Cash.
2 Buford grounded to first, scoring Hendricks as Belanger went to third.
3 Johnson grounded to deep short.

9th Inning
Pittsburgh
For Baltimore—Dobson pitching.
1 Clines grounded to short.
2 Clemente struck out.
Robertson singled to left.
Sanguillen beat out a hit to the left of the mound.
For Baltimore—McNally pitching.
3 Stargell grounded to short.
Baltimore
1 Powell grounded to second.
2 F. Robinson popped to short.
3 Rettenmund grounded to short.

1971 WORLD SERIES COMPOSITE BOX

	Wins	Composite Line Score	Manager	Regular Season W	L	Pct.	G. Ahead	
Pittsburgh Pirates (N.L.)	4	3 6 3 1 1 1 4 4 0 0 – 23	Danny Murtaugh	97	65	.599	7	(beat San Francisco in playoffs)
Baltimore Orioles (A.L.)	3	3 2 3 3 7 2 2 1 0 1 – 24	Earl Weaver	101	57	.639	12	(beat Oakland in playoffs)

BATTING AND FIELDING

PITTSBURGH PIRATES

World Series Statistics

	Pos	G	AB	R	H	2B	3B	HR	RBI	BB	SO	SB	BA	SA	PO	A	E
Bob Robertson	1b	7	25	4	6	0	0	**2**	**5**	4	8	0	.240	.480	**64**	4	1
Dave Cash	2b	7	**30**	2	4	1	0	0	1	3	1	1	.133	.167	20	**23**	0
Jackie Hernandez	ss	7	18	2	4	0	0	0	1	2	5	1	.222	.222	9	16	0
Jose Pagan	3b	4	15	0	4	**2**	0	0	2	0	1	0	.267	.400	2	8	0
Roberto Clemente	rf	7	29	3	**12**	**2**	**1**	**2**	4	2	2	0	**.414**	**.759**	15	0	0
Al Oliver	ph-cf	5	19	1	4	**2**	0	0	2	2	5	0	.211	.333	11	0	1
Willie Stargell	lf	7	24	3	5	1	0	0	1	**7**	**9**	0	.208	.250	11	1	0
Manny Sanguillen	c	7	29	3	11	1	0	0	0	0	3	**2**	.379	.414	37	0	0
Richie Hebner	3b	3	12	2	2	0	0	1	3	3	3	0	.167	.417	1	3	1
Gene Clines	cf	3	11	2	1	0	1	0	0	1	1	1	.091	.273	6	0	0
Vic Davalillo	ph-lf-cf	3	3	1	1	0	0	0	0	0	0	0	.333	.333	2	0	0
Gene Alley	ss-pr	2	2	0	0	0	0	0	0	1	0	0	.000	.000	1	4	0
Milt May	ph	2	2	0	1	0	0	0	1	0	0	0	.500	.500			
Bill Mazeroski	ph	1	1	0	0	0	0	0	0	0	0	0	.000	.000			
Charlie Sands	ph	1	1	0	0	0	0	0	0	0	1	0	.000	.000			
Steve Blass	p	2	7	0	0	0	0	0	0	0	1	0	.000	.000	2	4	0
Bob Johnson	p	2	3	0	0	0	0	0	0	0	2	0	.000	.000	2	0	0
Bob Moose	p	3	2	0	0	0	0	0	0	0	1	0	.000	.000	0	3	0
Bruce Kison	p	2	2	0	0	0	0	0	0	1	2	0	.000	.000	0	1	0
Nelson Briles	p	1	2	0	1	0	0	0	1	0	1	0	.500	.500	0	1	0
Dock Ellis	p	1	1	0	0	0	0	0	0	0	1	0	.000	.000	1	0	0
Dave Giusti	p	3	0	0	0	0	0	0	0	0	0	0			0	0	0
Bob Miller	p	3	0	0	0	0	0	0	0	0	0	0			1	1	0
Bob Veale	p	1	0	0	0	0	0	0	0	0	0	0			0	1	0
Luke Walker	p	1	0	0	0	0	0	0	0	0	0	0			0	0	0
team total		7	238	23	56	9	2	5	21	26	47	5	.235	.353	185	70	3

Double Plays-7
Left on Bases-63

Regular Season Statistics

		Main Pos	G	AB	R	H	2B	3B	HR	RBI	BB	SO	SB	BA	SA
Bob Robertson		1b	126	469	65	127	18	2	26	72	60	101	1	.271	.484
Dave Cash		2b	123	478	79	138	17	4	2	34	46	33	13	.289	.354
Jackie Hernandez		ss	88	233	30	48	7	3	3	26	17	45	0	.206	.300
Jose Pagan		3b	57	158	16	38	7	0	5	15	16	25	0	.241	.342
Roberto Clemente		of	132	522	82	178	29	8	13	86	26	65	1	.341	.502
Al Oliver		of	143	529	69	149	31	7	14	64	27	72	4	.282	.446
Willie Stargell		of	141	511	104	151	26	0	**48**	125	83	**154**	0	.295	.628
Manny Sanguillen		c	138	533	60	170	26	5	7	81	19	32	6	.319	.426
Richie Hebner		3b	112	388	50	105	17	8	17	67	38	68	2	.271	.487
Gene Clines		of	97	273	52	84	12	4	1	24	22	36	15	.308	.392
Vic Davalillo		of	99	295	48	84	14	6	1	33	11	31	10	.285	.383
Gene Alley		ss	114	348	38	79	8	7	6	28	35	43	9	.227	.342
Milt May		c	49	126	15	35	1	0	6	25	9	16	0	.278	.429
Bill Mazeroski		2b	70	193	17	49	3	1	1	16	15	8	0	.254	.295
Charlie Sands		ph	28	25	4	5	2	0	1	5	7	6	0	.200	.400
Steve Blass		p	34	83	5	10	0	1	0	2	1	15	0	.120	.145
Bob Johnson		p	31	48	3	3	0	0	0	2	8	33	0	.063	.063
Bob Moose		p	30	39	2	4	0	0	0	0	3	11	1	.103	.103
Bruce Kison		p	18	31	2	2	1	0	0	1	2	16	1	.065	.097
Nelson Briles		p	37	39	3	10	3	0	1	4	2	13	0	.256	.410
Dock Ellis		p	44	79	11	16	0	0	0	12	6	29	2	.203	.203
Dave Giusti		p	58	17	1	1	0	0	0	2	1	4	0	.059	.059
Bob Miller	a	p	16	1	0	0	0	0	0	0	1	1	0	.000	.000
Bob Veale		p	37	9	2	3	0	0	0	1	0	4	0	.333	.333
Luke Walker		p	28	46	1	1	0	0	0	0	6	30	0	.022	.022
team total			162	**5674**	**788**	**1555**	223	**61**	**154**	**744**	469	919	65	.274	**.416**

a—From Chicago (N0) and San Diego

Rennie Stennett (2b), Richie Zisk (of), Carl Taylor (of), Rimp Lanier (ph), Frank Taveras (pr), Mudcat Grant (p), Jim Nelson (p), Frank Brosseau (p), and John Lamb (p) also played for the Pirates during the season.

BALTIMORE ORIOLES

World Series Statistics

	Pos	G	AB	R	H	2B	3B	HR	RBI	BB	SO	SB	BA	SA	PO	A	E
Boog Powell	1b	7	27	1	3	0	0	0	1	1	3	0	.111	.111	52	4	1
Dave Johnson	2b	7	27	1	4	0	0	0	3	0	1	0	.148	.148	18	12	0
Mark Belanger	ss	7	21	4	5	0	**1**	0	0	5	2	1	.238	.333	10	20	**3**
Brooks Robinson	3b	7	22	2	7	0	0	0	**5**	3	1	0	.318	.318	6	17	2
Frank Robinson	rf	7	25	**5**	7	0	0	**2**	2	2	8	0	.280	.520	12	0	0
Merv Rettenmund	cf-rf-lf-ph	7	27	3	5	0	0	1	4	0	4	0	.185	.296	17	0	0
Don Buford	lf	6	23	3	6	1	0	**2**	4	3	3	0	.261	.565	13	1	0
Ellie Hendricks	c	6	19	3	5	1	0	0	1	3	3	0	.263	.316	40	4	1
Paul Blair	cf-pr	4	9	2	3	1	0	0	0	0	1	0	.333	.444	6	2	1
Andy Etchebarren	c	1	2	0	0	0	0	0	0	0	0	0	.000	.000	6	0	0
Tom Shopay	ph	5	4	0	0	0	0	0	0	0	0	0	.000	.000			
Chico Salmon	Did not play																
Jerry DaVanon	Did not play																
Curt Motton	Did not play																
Clay Dalrymple	Did not play																
Dave McNally	p	4	4	0	0	0	0	0	0	0	3	0	.000	.000	0	2	0
Jim Palmer	p	2	4	0	0	0	0	0	2	2	2	0	.000	.000	2	1	0
Mike Cuellar	p	2	3	0	0	0	0	0	0	1	2	0	.000	.000	0	3	1
Pat Dobson	p	3	2	0	0	0	0	0	0	0	2	0	.000	.000	0	3	0
Tom Dukes	p	2	0	0	0	0	0	0	0	0	0	0	—	—	0	0	0
Eddie Watt	p	2	0	0	0	0	0	0	0	0	0	0	—	—	0	0	0
Dick Hall	p	1	0	0	0	0	0	0	0	0	0	0	—	—	1	0	0
Grant Jackson	p	1	0	0	0	0	0	0	0	0	0	0	—	—	0	0	0
Dave Leonhard	p	1	0	0	0	0	0	0	0	0	0	0	—	—	0	0	0
Pete Richert	p	1	0	0	0	0	0	0	0	0	0	0	—	—	0	0	0
team total		7	219	24	45	3	1	5	22	20	35	1	.205	.297	183	69	9

Double Plays-2
Left on Bases-39

Regular Season Statistics

	Main Pos	G	AB	R	H	2B	3B	HR	RBI	BB	SO	SB	BA	SA
Boog Powell	1b	128	418	59	107	19	0	22	92	82	64	1	.256	.459
Dave Johnson	2b	142	510	67	144	26	1	18	72	51	55	3	.282	.443
Mark Belanger	ss	150	500	67	133	19	4	0	35	73	48	10	.266	.320
Brooks Robinson	3b	156	589	67	160	21	1	20	92	63	50	0	.272	.413
Frank Robinson	of	133	455	82	128	16	2	28	99	72	62	3	.287	.516
Merv Rettenmund	of	141	491	81	156	23	4	11	75	87	60	15	.318	.448
Don Buford	of	122	449	**99**	130	19	4	19	54	89	62	15	.290	.477
Ellie Hendricks	c	101	316	33	79	14	1	9	42	39	38	0	.250	.386
Paul Blair	of	141	516	75	135	24	8	10	44	32	94	14	.262	.397
Andy Etchebarren	c	70	222	21	60	8	0	9	29	16	40	1	.270	.428
Tom Shopay	ph	47	74	10	19	2	0	0	5	3	7	2	.257	.284
Chico Salmon	ph-inf	42	84	11	15	1	0	2	7	3	21	0	.179	.262
Jerry DaVanon	2b	38	81	14	19	5	0	0	4	12	20	0	.235	.296
Curt Motton	ph	38	53	13	10	1	0	4	8	10	12	0	.189	.434
Clay Dalrymple	c	23	49	6	10	1	0	1	6	16	13	0	.204	.286
Dave McNally	p	30	74	3	12	3	0	2	7	3	35	0	.162	.284
Jim Palmer	p	38	102	7	20	1	0	0	9	3	41	1	.196	.206
Mike Cuellar	p	38	107	7	11	1	0	1	5	2	54	0	.103	.140
Pat Dobson	p	38	91	3	10	0	0	0	4	3	28	0	.110	.110
Tom Dukes	p	28	7	1	1	1	0	0	2	0	3	0	.143	.286
Eddie Watt	p	35	5	0	0	0	0	0	0	1	2	0	.000	.000
Dick Hall	p	27	5	0	2	1	0	0	0	0	1	0	.400	.600
Grant Jackson	p	29	22	5	2	0	0	1	2	2	7	0	.091	.227
Dave Leonhard	p	13	18	1	5	0	0	0	0	0	7	0	.278	.278
Pete Richert	p	35	2	0	0	0	0	0	0	0	1	0	.000	.000
team total		158	5303	**742**	1382	207	25	158	**702**	**672**	844	66	**.261**	.398

Terry Crowley (ph-of), Bobby Grich (ss), Don Baylor (of), Dave Boswell (p), Orlando Pena (p) and Jim Hardin (p) also played for the Orioles during the season.

PITCHING

PITTSBURGH PIRATES

World Series Statistics

	G	GS	CG	IP	H	R	ER	BB	SO	W	L	SV	ERA
Steve Blass	2	**2**	**2**	**18**	7	2	2	4	13	**2**	0	0	1.00
Bob Moose	3	1	0	9⅔	12	**7**	**7**	2	7	0	0	0	6.52
Nelson Briles	1	1	1	9	2	0	0	2	2	1	0	0	**0.00**
Bruce Kison	2	0	0	6⅓	1	0	0	2	3	1	0	0	0.00
Dave Giusti	3	0	0	5⅓	3	0	0	2	4	0	0	**1**	0.00
Bob Johnson	2	1	0	5	5	5	5	3	3	0	1	0	9.00
Bob Miller	3	0	0	4⅔	7	2	2	1	2	0	1	0	3.86
Dock Ellis	1	1	0	2⅓	4	4	4	1	1	0	1	0	15.43
Bob Veale	1	0	0	⅔	1	1	1	2	0	0	0	0	13.50
Luke Walker	1	1	0	⅔	3	3	3	1	0	0	0	0	40.50
team total	7	7	3	61⅔	45	24	24	20	35	4	3	1	3.50

Regular Season Statistics

		G	GS	CG	IP	H	ER	BB	SO	W	L	Pct	SV	ShO	ERA
Steve Blass		33	33	12	240	226	76	68	136	15	8	.652	0	**5**	2.85
Bob Moose		30	18	3	140	169	64	35	68	11	7	.611	1	1	4.11
Nelson Briles		37	14	4	136	131	46	35	76	8	4	.667	1	2	3.04
Bruce Kison		18	13	2	95	93	36	36	60	6	5	.545	0	1	3.41
Dave Giusti		58	0	0	86	79	28	31	55	5	6	.455	**30**	0	2.93
Bob Johnson		31	27	7	175	170	67	55	101	9	10	.474	0	1	3.45
Bob Miller	a	16	0	0	28	20	4	13	13	1	2	.333	3	0	1.29
Dock Ellis		31	31	11	227	207	77	63	137	19	9	.679	0	2	3.05
Bob Veale		37	0	0	46	59	36	24	40	6	0	1.000	2	0	7.04
Luke Walker		28	24	4	160	157	63	53	86	10	8	.556	0	2	3.54
team total		162	162	43	1461	1426	537	470	813	**97**	65	**.599**	**48**	15	3.31

BALTIMORE ORIOLES

World Series Statistics

	G	GS	CG	IP	H	R	ER	BB	SO	W	L	SV	ERA
Jim Palmer	2	**2**	0	17	**15**	5	5	**9**	**15**	1	0	0	2.65
Mike Cuellar	2	**2**	0	14	11	**7**	6	6	10	0	**2**	0	3.86
Dave McNally	**4**	**2**	1	13⅔	10	**7**	3	5	12	**2**	1	0	1.98
Pat Dobson	3	1	0	6⅔	13	3	3	4	6	0	0	0	4.05
Tom Dukes	2	0	0	4	2	0	0	0	1	0	0	0	0.00
Eddie Watt	2	0	0	2⅓	4	1	1	0	2	0	1	0	3.86
Dick Hall	1	0	0	1	1	0	0	0	0	0	0	**1**	0.00
Dave Leonhard	1	0	0	1	0	0	0	1	0	0	0	0	0.00
Grant Jackson	1	0	0	⅔	0	0	0	1	0	0	0	0	0.00
Pete Richert	1	0	0	⅔	0	0	0	0	1	0	0	0	0.00
team total	7	7	1	61	56	23	18	26	47	3	4	1	2.66

Regular Season Statistics

	G	GS	CG	IP	H	ER	BB	SO	W	L	Pct	SV	ShO	ERA
Jim Palmer	37	37	20	282	231	84	106	184	20	9	.690	0	3	2.68
Mike Cuellar	38	38	21	292	250	100	78	124	20	9	.690	0	4	3.08
Dave McNally	30	30	11	224	188	72	58	91	21	5	**.808**	0	1	2.89
Pat Dobson	38	37	18	282	248	91	63	187	20	8	.714	1	4	2.90
Tom Dukes	28	0	0	38	40	15	8	30	1	5	.167	4	0	3.55
Eddie Watt	35	0	0	40	39	8	8	26	3	1	.750	11	0	1.80
Dick Hall	27	0	0	43	52	24	11	26	6	6	.500	1	0	5.02
Dave Leonhard	12	6	1	54	51	17	19	18	2	3	.400	1	1	2.83
Grant Jackson	29	9	0	78	72	27	20	51	4	3	.571	0	0	3.12
Pete Richert	35	0	0	36	26	14	22	35	3	5	.375	4	0	3.50
team total	158	158	**71**	1415	1257	**470**	416	793	**101**	57	**.639**	22	15	**2.99**

Total Attendance—351,091 Average Attendance—50,156 *Winning Player's Share—$18,165 *Losing Player's Share—$13,906
*includes playoffs and world series.

1972
Forty Years Later . . .

The World Series would be hard pressed to match the excitement generated by the two championship series of the leagues. The Oakland A's won the first two games of the American League series, dropped the next two to the Detroit Tigers, and captured the finale by a 2–1 score. In the National League, the Cincinnati Reds and Pittsburgh Pirates split the first four games, and the Pirates led the deciding match 3–2 only to see the Reds score twice in the bottom of the ninth, the winning run crossing the plate on a wild pitch. The Reds had been to the World Series two years ago, with Johnny Bench, Pete Rose, Tony Perez, Bobby Tolan, Gary Nolan, and Clay Carroll back from that squad. Lee May had been traded to Houston, but manager Sparky Anderson had key newcomers in Joe Morgan, Denis Menke, Cesar Geronimo, Jack Billingham, Tom Hall, and Pedro Borbon.

The A's had been away from the Series considerably longer, last making it in 1931 when stationed in Philadelphia under the ownership of Connie Mack. Now based in Oakland after an intervening period in Kansas City, the A's were owned by Charles O. Finley, a stubborn but colorful insurance tycoon who paid his players to grow modish moustaches and went through managers like potato chips. Finley kept Dick Williams on the job as the skipper because he led them to the top of the Western Division of the A.L. in both his seasons at the helm. Despite losing slugger Reggie Jackson to a pulled hamstring suffered in the play-offs, Williams brought a talented young club into this confrontation, with Sal Bando, Joe Rudi, Bert Campaneris, Mike Epstein, Catfish Hunter, Ken Holtzman, and Rollie Fingers all players of All-Star caliber.

But the A's came up with a surprise hero in second-string catcher Gene Tenace. With Gary Nolan pitching for the Reds, Tenace belted homers in the second and fifth innings to stake Holtzman to a 3–2 lead he held with relief help from Fingers and Vida Blue. The second game pitted ace right-hander Hunter against young southpaw Ross Grimsley. The A's strung together four singles for a run in the second inning, then scored in the third on a home run by Rudi. Hunter overpowered the free-swinging Reds until tiring in the ninth. Perez led off the final frame with a single, then Menke drove a liner to deep left. Rudi tore back and made a leaping backhand catch at the wall. Geronimo was retired on a hard-hit ball, and Hal McRae then singled home Perez to cut the score to 2–1. Williams then brought in Fingers to get the final out of the Oakland victory.

The clubs got an extra day off when the third game was postponed by rain; then Billingham and Blue Moon Odom hooked up in a pitchers' duel in which Cincinnati scored the only run of the game in the seventh inning on two singles and a sacrifice. The fourth game saw the A's holding a 1–0 lead after seven innings on Tenace's homer. Williams cautiously replaced Holtzman in the eighth inning, but reliever Blue walked Morgan and gave up a two-run double to Tolan to blow the Oakland lead. Pinch hitter Gonzalo Marquez singled to open the ninth, and Anderson here brought in Clay Carroll to relieve Borbon. The strategy failed when singles by Tenace, Don Mincher, and Angel Mangual made the A's 3–2 winners and shoved the Reds to the brink of extinction. After Rose opened the fifth game with a homer, the Reds fell behind 3–1 only to tie the score at 4–4 with an eighth-inning run off Fingers, then beat the ace reliever with a run in the ninth.

The Reds opened up the big guns for an 8–1 sixth-game victory and raised the possibility of battling back from a three-to-one deficit in the Series to win the title. In the deciding contest, starting pitchers Odom and Billingham each allowed one run in five innings of work, but the A's scored twice off Borbon in the sixth inning while the Reds got only one run off the star-studded relief chain of Hunter, Holtzman, and Fingers. The 3–2 victory made the A's champions for the first time since 1930, with Gene Tenace's four homers and nine RBI's making up for the absence of Reggie Jackson and helping to insure Dick Williams's job for another year.

Game 1 October 14 at Cincinnati

Oakland	Pos	AB	R	H	RBI	PO	A	E
Campaneris	ss	3	0	2	0	2	3	0
Rudi	lf	4	0	0	0	3	0	0
Alou	rf	3	0	0	0	1	0	0
Epstein	1b	3	0	0	0	6	1	0
c Lewis		0	0	0	0	0	0	0
Hegan	1b	0	0	0	0	2	0	0
Bando	3b	4	0	0	0	0	3	0
Hendrick	cf	2	1	0	0	2	0	0
Tenace	c	3	2	2	3	7	2	0
Green	2b	2	0	0	0	3	1	0
b Marquez		1	0	0	0	0	0	0
Kubiak	2b	0	0	0	0	1	2	0
Holtzman	p	2	0	0	0	0	1	0
Fingers	p	0	0	0	0	0	0	0
Blue	p	0	0	0	0	0	0	0
Totals		27	3	4	3	27	13	0

Pitching	IP	H	R	ER	BB	SO
Oakland						
Holtzman (W)	*5	5	2	2	3	2
Fingers	1⅓	1	0	0	1	3
Blue (SV)	2⅔	1	0	0	1	1
Cincinnati						
Nolan (L)	6	4	3	3	2	0
Borbon	1	0	0	0	0	0
Carroll	2	0	0	0	2	1

*Pitched to 1 batter in 6th.

Cincinnati	Pos	AB	R	H	RBI	PO	A	E
Rose	lf	4	0	0	0	3	0	0
Morgan	2b	3	0	0	0	5	5	0
Tolan	cf	4	0	1	0	2	0	0
Bench	c	3	2	2	0	1	2	0
Perez	1b	4	0	2	0	10	0	0
Menke	3b	3	0	1	1	2	2	0
Geronimo	rf	3	0	0	0	3	0	0
d McRae		1	0	1	0	0	0	0
e Foster		0	0	0	0	0	0	0
Concepcion	ss	2	0	1	1	1	1	0
Nolan	p	2	0	0	0	0	1	0
Borbon	p	0	0	0	0	0	1	0
a Uhlaender		1	0	0	0	0	0	0
Carroll	p	0	0	0	0	0	1	0
f Javier		1	0	0	0	0	0	0
Totals		31	2	7	2	27	13	0

a Struck out for Borbon in 7th.
b Popped out for Green in 8th.
c Ran for Epstein in 9th.
d Singled for Geronimo in 9th.
e Ran for McRae in 9th.
f Grounded out for Carroll in 9th.

Double—Bench. Home Runs—Tenace 2. Sacrifice Hits—Campaneris, Concepcion. Double Play—Morgan to Perez. Wild Pitch—Blue. Left on Bases—Oakland 2, Cincinnati 8. Umpires—Pelekoudas (N), Honochick (A), Steiner (N), Umont (A), Engel (N), Haller (A).
Attendance—52,918. Time of Game—2:18.

Oak.   020 010 000
Cin.   010 100 000

1st Inning
Oakland
Campaneris singled to left.
1 Rudi flied to center.
2,3 Alou popped to second and Campaneris was doubled up, Morgan to Perez.
Cincinnati
1 Rose grounded to third.
2 Morgan grounded to first.
3 Tolan grounded to deep short.

2nd Inning
Oakland
1 Epstein flied deep to the right field wall.
2 Bando flied to right.
Hendrick walked.
Tenace hit a two-run homer over the left field wall.
3 Green lined to third.
Cincinnati
Bench singled to left.
Perez singled to left, Bench stopping at second.
Menke walked, loading the bases.
1 Geronimo popped to Campaneris in short left.
2 Concepcion forced Menke at second, Campaneris to Green, as Bench scored and Perez went to third.
3 Nolan struck out.

3rd Inning
Oakland
1 Holtzman flied to left.
Campaneris singled to left.
2 Campaneris caught trying to steal second, Bench to Morgan.
3 Rudi grounded to third.
Cincinnati
1 Rose bounced out to third.
2 Morgan flied to Rudi in short left-center.
Tolan singled to left-center.
3 Tolan picked off first, Holtzman to Epstein to Green.

4th Inning
Oakland
1 Alou bounced back to the mound.
2 Epstein grounded to third.
3 Bando popped to Morgan in short right.
Cincinnati
Bench walked.
Perez singled to right-center, sending Bench to third.
1 Menke forced Perez at second, Campaneris to Green, Bench scoring.
2 Geronimo grounded to second, sending Menke to second.
Concepcion got an intentional walk.
3 Nolan struck out.

5th Inning
Oakland
1 Hendrick grounded to second.
Tenace hit his second homer of the game into the left field seats.
2 Green flied to short center.
3 Holtzman flied to left.
Cincinnati
1 Rose flied to deep center.
2 Morgan struck out and had to be thrown out, Tenace to Epstein.
3 Tolan flied to left.

6th Inning
Oakland
1 Campaneris lined to Menke making a leaping one handed catch.
2 Rudi flied to right.
Alou walked.
3 Epstein grounded to second.
Cincinnati
Bench doubled off the right field wall.
For Oakland—Fingers came into pitch.
1 Perez struck out.
2 Menke struck out.
3 Geronimo lined to left.

7th Inning
Oakland
For Cincinnati—Borbon now pitching.
1 Bando grounded to second.
2 Hendrick bounced to the mound.
3 Tenace grounded to short.
Cincinnati
Concepcion singled to left.
Uhlaender, batting for Borbon,
1 Concepcion caught stealing, Tenace to Campaneris.
2 Uhlaender struck out.
Rose walked.
For Oakland—Blue came on to pitch.
Rose went to second on a wild pitch.
Morgan walked.
3 Tolan fouled to Tenace.

8th Inning
Oakland
For Cincinnati—Carroll pitching.
1 Marquez, batting for Green, popped to Concepcion in short left.
Blue walked.
2 Campaneris sacrificed Blue to second, Carroll to Morgan covering first.
3 Rudi flied to left.
Cincinnati
For Oakland—Kubiak playing second.
1 Bench flied to right.
2 Perez lined to center.
3 Menke struck out.

9th Inning
Oakland
1 Alou grounded to second.
Epstein walked.
Lewis ran for Epstein.
2 Lewis caught trying to steal second, Bench to Morgan.
3 Bando struck out.
Cincinnati
For Oakland—Hegan playing first.
McRae, batting for Geronimo, singled to left.
Foster ran for McRae.
1 Concepcion sacrificed Foster to second, Bando to Kubiak.
2 Javier, pinch-hitting for Carroll, grounded to second, Foster going to third.
3 Rose bounced out to second.

Game 2 October 15 at Cincinnati

Oakland	Pos	AB	R	H	RBI	PO	A	E
Campaneris	ss	5	0	1	0	2	1	0
Alou	rf	4	0	1	0	4	0	0
Rudi	lf	3	1	2	1	4	0	0
Epstein	1b	2	0	0	0	2	0	1
b Lewis		0	0	0	0	0	0	0
Hegan	1b	1	0	0	0	3	0	0
Bando	3b	4	0	1	0	0	1	0
Hendrick	cf	4	1	1	0	3	0	0
Tenace	c	4	0	0	0	7	0	0
Green	2b	4	0	2	0	2	1	0
Hunter	p	3	0	1	1	0	1	1
Fingers	p	0	0	0	0	0	0	0
Totals		34	2	9	2	27	4	2

Pitching	IP	H	R	ER	BB	SO
Oakland						
Hunter (W)	8⅔	6	1	1	3	6
Fingers (SV)	⅓	0	0	0	0	0
Cincinnati						
Grimsley (L)	5	6	2	2	0	1
Borbon	2	0	0	0	1	4
Hall	2	3	0	0	2	2

Oak.	0 1 1	0 0 0	0 0 0
Cin.	0 0 0	0 0 0	0 0 1

Cincinnati	Pos	AB	R	H	RBI	PO	A	E
Rose	lf	4	0	1	0	2	1	0
Morgan	2b	4	0	0	0	0	3	0
Tolan	cf	4	0	0	0	1	0	0
Bench	c	3	0	1	0	8	1	0
Perez	1b	3	1	2	0	11	0	0
Menke	3b	4	0	0	0	0	2	0
Geronimo	rf	4	0	0	0	3	0	0
Chaney	ss	2	0	0	0	2	4	0
d McRae		1	0	1	1	0	0	0
e Concepcion		0	0	0	0	0	0	0
Grimsley	p	1	0	0	0	0	2	0
a Uhlaender		1	0	1	0	0	0	0
Borbon	p	0	0	0	0	0	0	0
c Hague		1	0	0	0	0	0	0
Hall	p	0	0	0	0	0	0	0
f Javier		1	0	0	0	0	0	0
Totals		33	1	6	1	27	13	0

a Doubled for Grimsley in 5th.
b Ran for Epstein in 6th.
c Flied out for Borbon in 7th.
d Singled for Chaney in 9th.
e Ran for McRae in 9th.
f Fouled out for Hall in 9th.

Double—Uhlaender. Home Run—Rudi. Stolen Bases—Alou, Morgan. Double Plays—Campaneris to Green to Epstein, Bench to Chaney. Left on Bases—Oakland 8, Cincinnati 8. Umpires—Honochick, Steiner, Umont, Engel, Haller, Pelekoudas. Attendance—53,224. Time of Game—2:26.

1st Inning
Oakland
1 Campaneris grounded to second.
2 Alou slow rolled to third.
Rudi singled to left.
3 Epstein struck out.
Cincinnati
1 Rose flied to Rudi in short left-center.
2 Morgan struck out.
3 Tolan struck out, but was tagged by Tenace who dropped the third strike.

2nd Inning
Oakland
Bando singled to center.
1 Hendrick forced Bando at second, ball deflected by Grimsley to Morgan to Chaney.
2 Tenace flied to short left.
Green singled through the box, Hendrick stopping at second.
Hunter singled to left, scoring Hendrick as Green stopped at second.
Campaneris singled to left, but Green
3 was out trying to score, Rose to Bench.
Cincinnati
Bench beat out a hit behind second.
Perez walked.
Bench to third and Perez to second on Hunter's wild pick off throw that went into center.
1 Menke struck out.
2 Geronimo struck out.
Chaney intentionally walked, loading the bases.
3 Grimsley struck out.

3rd Inning
Oakland
1 Alou grounded to third.
Rudi hit a home run into the left field stands.
2 Epstein grounded to first.
3 Bando grounded to short.
Cincinnati
Rose singled to center.
1 Morgan fouled to Tenace.
2 Tolan popped to short.
3 Bench flied to center.

4th Inning
Oakland
1 Hendrick hit a chopper to the mound.
2 Tenace grounded to short.
3 Green flied to short right.
Cincinnati
Perez singled to center.
1,2 Menke hit into a double play, Campaneris to Green to Epstein.
3 Geronimo grounded to first.

5th Inning
Oakland
1 Hunter rolled to second.
2 Campaneris flied to Geronimo in right-center.
3 Alou grounded to short.
Cincinnati
1 Chaney lined to Hendricks in left-center.
Uhlaender, pinch-hitting for Grimsley, doubled to left-center.
2 Rose flied to right.
Morgan safe at first as Epstein dropped his grounder, Uhlaender going to third.
Morgan stole second.
3 Tolan popped to short.

6th Inning
Oakland
For Cincinnati—Borbon pitching.
1 Rudi struck out.
Epstein walked.
Lewis ran for Epstein.
2,3 Bando struck out and Lewis was doubled trying to steal second, Bench to Chaney.
Cincinnati
For Oakland—Hegan playing first.
Bench walked.
1 Perez forced Bench at second, Bando to Green.
2 Menke rolled out on a good play by Hunter, Perez going to second.
3 Geronimo flied to Hendrick in right-center.

7th Inning
Oakland
1 Hendrick flied to Geronimo making a running one handed catch in short right.
2 Tenace struck out.
3 Green took a called third strike.
Cincinnati
1 Chaney flied to short left.
2 Hague, pinch-hitting for Borbon, flied to right.
3 Rose struck out.

8th Inning
Oakland
For Cincinnati—Hall pitching.
1 Hunter popped to first.
2 Campaneris lined to center.
Alou singled to right.
Alou stole second.
Rudi walked.
3 Hegan struck out.
Cincinnati
1 Morgan flied to left.
2 Tolan flied to right.
3 Bench flied to Alou in deep right-center.

9th Inning
Oakland
1 Bando grounded to short.
Hendrick beat out a hit to Morgan.
2 Tenace flied to short left.
Green singled to center, Hendrick stopping at second.
Hunter walked, filling the bases.
3 Campaneris struck out.
Cincinnati
Perez singled to left.
1 Menke was robbed of a hit by Rudi who made a leaping, backhanded catch of his liner, against the wall.
2 Geronimo also robbed of a hit when Hegan dove for his liner, knocked it down and won the race to first as Perez went to second.
McRae, pinch-hitting for Chaney, singled to left, scoring Perez.
Concepcion ran for McRae.
Javier, batting for Hall.
For Oakland—Fingers relieved Hunter.
3 Javier fouled to Hegan.

Game 3 October 18 at Oakland

Cincinnati	Pos	AB	R	H	RBI	PO	A	E
Rose	lf	3	0	0	0	0	0	0
Morgan	2b	3	0	0	0	3	3	1
Tolan	cf	4	0	1	0	3	0	0
Bench	c	4	0	0	0	7	1	1
Perez	1b	3	1	1	0	11	0	0
Menke	3b	2	0	1	0	0	3	0
Geronimo	rf	4	0	1	1	0	0	0
Chaney	ss	4	0	0	0	3	6	0
Billingham	p	4	0	0	0	0	1	0
Carroll	p	0	0	0	0	0	1	0
Totals		31	1	4	1	27	15	2

Pitching	IP	H	R	ER	BB	SO
Cincinnati						
Billingham (W)	*8	3	0	0	3	7
Carroll (SV)	1	0	0	0	0	0
Oakland						
Odom (L)	7	3	1	1	2	11
Blue	⅓	1	0	0	1	0
Fingers	1⅔	0	0	0	1	3

*Replaced with 3–0 count on 1st batter in 9th.

Cin.	0 0 0	0 0 0	1 0 0
Oak.	0 0 0	0 0 0	0 0 0

Oakland	Pos	AB	R	H	RBI	PO	A	E
Campaneris	ss	3	0	0	0	0	0	0
Alou	rf	3	0	0	0	0	0	0
Rudi	lf	4	0	1	0	1	0	0
Epstein	1b	2	0	0	0	8	0	1
Bando	3b	4	0	0	0	1	1	0
Hendrick	cf	4	0	0	0	1	0	0
Tenace	c	3	0	0	0	14	0	1
Green	2b	2	0	1	0	0	3	0
a Marquez		1	0	1	0	0	0	0
b Lewis		0	0	0	0	0	0	0
Kubiak	2b	0	0	0	0	2	0	0
Odom	p	2	0	0	0	0	3	0
c Hegan		1	0	0	0	0	0	0
Blue	p	0	0	0	0	0	0	0
Fingers	p	0	0	0	0	0	0	0
Totals		29	0	3	0	27	7	2

a Singled for Green in 7th.
b Ran for Marquez in 7th.
c Lined out for Odom in 7th.

Stolen Bases—Geronimo, Rose, Tolan. Sacrifice Hits—Alou, Menke. Double Play—Morgan to Chaney to Perez. Left on Bases—Cincinnati 8, Oakland 6. Umpires—Steiner, Umont, Engel, Haller, Pelekoudas, Honochick. Attendance—49,410. Time of Game—2:24.

1st Inning
Cincinnati
1 Rose called out on strikes.
2 Morgan struck out.
3 Tolan tapped back to the mound.
Oakland
1 Campaneris struck out.
2 Alou grounded to short.
3 Rudi took a called third strike.

2nd Inning
Cincinnati
1 Bench grounded to third.
2 Perez flied to Rudi in left-center.
Menke singled to left.
3 Geronimo grounded to second.
Oakland
Epstein walked.
1 Bando forced Epstein at second on a bunt, Billingham to Chaney.
2 Hendrick popped to Morgan in short center.
3 Tenace forced Bando at second, Chaney to Morgan.

3rd Inning
Cincinnati
1 Chaney struck out.
2 Billingham tapped to the mound.
Rose walked.
Rose stole second and went over to third when Tenace's throw went into center field.
3 Morgan grounded to Green who made a great stop and play.
Oakland
1 Green bunted out, Bench to Perez.
2 Odom struck out.
3 Campaneris out on a roller to short.

4th Inning
Cincinnati
1 Tolan grounded to second.
2 Bench took a called third strike.
3 Perez struck out.
Oakland
1 Alou flied to short center.
Rudi beat out a bunt.
2 Epstein forced Rudi at second, Morgan to Chaney.
3 Bando took a called third strike.

5th Inning
Cincinnati
Menke walked.
Geronimo grounded to Epstein who threw wildly to Green covering first, Geronimo safe on the error as Menke raced to third.
1 Chaney struck out.
2 Billingham struck out.
Geronimo stole second.
3 Rose called out on strikes.
Oakland
1 Hendrick took a called third strike.
2 Tenace took a called third strike.
Green beat out a roller down the third base line.
3 Odom struck out.

6th Inning
Cincinnati
1 Morgan fouled to Bando.
2 Tolan struck out.
3 Bench took a called third strike.
Oakland
Campaneris walked.
Alou sacrificed and was safe as Bench's throw pulled Morgan off the bag.
Morgan also made a throwing error to Tolan who raced in to cover second.
Campaneris went to third as Alou held at first.
1 Rudi grounded to third, Campaneris holding and Alou going to second.
Epstein intentionally walked, filling the bases.
2,3 Bando grounded into a double play, Morgan to Chaney to Perez.

7th Inning
Cincinnati
Perez singled to left.
1 Menke sacrificed Perez to second, Odom to Epstein.
Geronimo singled to center, scoring Menke.
2 Chaney lined to Hendrick in left-center.
3 Billingham struck out.
Oakland
1 Hendrick flied to Tolan in left-center.
2 Tenace grounded to short.
Marquez, pinch-hitting for Green, beat out a bounder behind second which was deflected by Billingham.
Lewis ran for Marquez.
3 Hegan, pinch-hitting for Odom, lined to center.

8th Inning
Cincinnati
For Oakland—Kubiak playing second and Blue pitching.
1 Rose lined to second.
Morgan walked.
Tolan singled to center, Morgan advancing to third.
For Oakland—Fingers now pitching.
Tolan stole second.
2 Bench, for the third time, took a called third strike.
Perez got an intentional walk, loading the bases.
3 Menke fouled to Kubiak behind first.
Oakland
1 Campaneris grounded to third.
2 Alou grounded to short.
3 Rudi grounded to third.

9th Inning
Cincinnati
1 Geronimo struck out.
2 Chaney grounded to first.
3 Billingham took a called third strike.
Oakland
For Cincinnati—Carroll replaced Billingham on the mound with a 3–0 count on Epstein.
1 Epstein grounded to second.
2 Bando lined to second.
3 Hendrick thrown out by Carroll on a roller down the first base line.

Game 4 October 19 at Oakland

Cincinnati:	Pos	AB	R	H	RBI	PO	A	E
Rose	lf	4	0	0	0	3	0	0
Morgan	2b	3	1	0	0	2	1	0
Tolan	cf	4	0	1	2	0	0	0
Bench	c	4	0	2	0	4	0	0
Perez	1b	4	0	2	0	11	0	1
McRae	rf	4	0	1	0	2	0	0
Geronimo	rf	0	0	0	0	0	0	0
Menke	3b	4	0	0	0	1	4	0
Concepcion	ss	3	1	1	0	2	5	0
Gullett	p	2	0	0	0	0	1	0
a Javier		0	0	0	0	0	0	0
Borbon	p	0	0	0	0	0	0	0
Carroll	p	0	0	0	0	0	0	0
Totals		32	2	7	2	*25	11	1

Pitching	IP	H	R	ER	BB	SO
Cincinnati						
Gullett	7	5	1	1	2	4
Borbon	1⅓	2	1	1	0	0
Carroll (L)	***0	3	1	1	0	0
Oakland						
Holtzman	7⅔	5	1	1	0	1
Blue	** ⅓	2	1	1	1	0
Fingers (W)	1	0	0	0	0	1

**Pitched to 1 batter in 9th.
***Pitched to 3 batters in 9th.

Cin.	000	000	020
Oak.	000	010	002

Oakland	Pos	AB	R	H	RBI	PO	A	E
Campaneris	ss	4	0	0	0	3	3	0
Alou	rf	3	0	0	0	2	0	0
Rudi	lf	4	0	2	0	2	0	0
Bando	3b	3	0	2	0	1	4	0
Epstein	1b	3	0	0	0	7	0	0
Hegan	1b	1	0	0	0	3	1	0
Hendrick	cf	3	0	0	0	3	0	0
b Marquez		1	0	1	0	0	0	0
c Lewis		0	1	0	0	0	0	0
Tenace	c	4	2	2	1	2	1	0
Green	2b	3	0	1	0	4	6	0
d Mincher		1	0	1	1	0	0	0
e Odom		0	0	0	0	0	0	0
Holtzman	p	3	0	0	0	0	2	1
Blue	p	0	0	0	0	0	0	0
Fingers	p	0	0	0	0	0	1	0
f Mangual		1	0	1	1	0	0	0
Totals		34	3	10	3	27	18	1

* One out when winning run scored.
a Sacrificed for Gullett in 8th.
b Singled for Hendrick in 9th.
c Ran for Marquez in 9th.
d Singled for Green in 9th.
e Ran for Mincher in 9th.
f Singled for Fingers in 9th.

Doubles—Green, Tolan. Home Run—Tenace. Stolen Base—Bench. Sacrifice Hit—Javier. Double Plays—Concepcion to Perez, Holtzman to Green to Hegan. Left on Bases—Cincinnati 5, Oakland 8. Umpires—Umont, Engel, Haller, Pelekoudas, Honochick, Steiner. Attendance—49,410. Time of Game—2:06.

1st Inning
Cincinnati
1 Rose grounded to second.
2 Morgan flied to short left.
Tolan safe at first on Holtzman's high throw of his bunt.
Bench singled to right, moving Tolan to third.
Bench stole second.
3 Perez struck out.
Oakland
1 Campaneris tapped to the pitcher.
2 Alou flied to short left.
3 Rudi popped to short.

2nd Inning
Cincinnati
McRae singled to center.
1 Menke forced McRae at second, Bando to Green.
2 Concepcion forced Menke at second, Bando to Green
3 Gullett forced Concepcion at second, Green to Campaneris.
Oakland
Bando singled to right.
1 Epstein popped to second.
2,3 Hendrick grounded into a double play, Concepcion to Perez.

3rd Inning
Cincinnati
1 Rose was thrown out bunting by Tenace.
2 Morgan grounded to second.
3 Tolan grounded to third.
Oakland
1 Tenace grounded to third.
2 Green struck out and tagged by Bench who dropped the third strike.
3 Holtzman lined to left.

4th Inning
Cincinnati
Bench singled to center.
1 Perez flied to deep center.
2 McRae forced Bench at second, Campaneris to Green.
3 Menke lined to third.
Oakland
1 Campaneris grounded to third, Menke making a fine diving stop.
Alou walked.
Alou went to second when Perez dropped Bench's pickoff throw.
2 Rudi struck out.
Bando intentionally walked.
3 Epstein grounded to the shortstop.

5th Inning
Cincinnati
1 Concepcion grounded to short.
2 Gullett flied to center.
3 Rose flied to Alou who made a one handed catch against the wall.
Oakland
1 Hendrick popped to Morgan in short right.
Tenace homered into the left field stands near the foul pole.
2 Green flied to right.
3 Holtzman grounded to short.

6th Inning
Cincinnati
1 Morgan grounded to second.
2 Tolan grounded to short.
3 Bench lined to an onrushing Alou in short right.
Oakland
1 Campaneris fouled to Rose in deep left.
2 Alou grounded to third.
Rudi singled to left.
Bando singled to left, Rudi stopping at second.
3 Epstein lined to right.

7th Inning
Cincinnati
For Oakland—Hegan playing first.
Perez singled down the right field line.
1 McRae popped to short.
2,3 Menke hit into a double play, Holtzman to Green to Hegan.
Oakland
1 Hendrick struck out.
2 Tenace struck out.
Green doubled down the left field line.
3 Holtzman popped to third.

8th Inning
Cincinnati
Concepcion singled to deep short.
1 Javier, pinch-hitting for Gullett, sacrificed, Bando to Hegan.
2 Rose's grounder deflected by Holtzman to Green who threw Rose out at first, Concepcion moving to third.
For Oakland—Blue came in to pitch.
Morgan walked.
Tolan doubled down the right field line, scoring Concepcion and Morgan.
3 Bench flied to center.
Oakland
For Cincinnati—Borbon pitching.
1 Campaneris grounded to short.
2 Alou grounded to second.
Rudi singled to right.
3 Bando grounded to short.

9th Inning
Cincinnati
Perez singled to right.
For Oakland—Fingers pitching.
1 Perez picked off first, Fingers to Hegan to Campaneris.
2 McRae struck out.
3 Menke flied to Rudi in left-center.
Oakland
1 Hegan grounded to third.
Marquez, batting for Hendrick, singled to center.
Lewis ran for Marquez.
For Cincinnati—Carroll replaced Borbon on the mound with a 2–1 count on Tenace.
Tenace singled to left, Lewis stopping at second.
Mincher, pinch-hitting for Green, singled to right-center, scoring Lewis with Tenace going to third.
Odom ran for Mincher.
Mangual, batting for Fingers, singled through the right side of a drawn-in infield, scoring Tenace with the game-winning run.

Game 5 October 20 at Oakland

Cincinnati	Pos	AB	R	H	RBI	PO	A	E
Rose	lf	5	1	3	2	2	0	0
Morgan	2b	3	2	0	0	3	2	0
Tolan	cf	4	0	2	2	2	0	0
Bench	c	4	0	0	0	6	2	0
Perez	1b	4	0	1	0	10	2	0
Menke	3b	3	1	1	1	2	3	0
Geronimo	rf	4	1	1	0	1	0	0
Chaney	ss	1	0	0	0	0	1	0
d Hague		1	0	0	0	0	0	0
Carroll	p	0	0	0	0	1	0	0
Grimsley	p	0	0	0	0	0	0	0
Billingham	p	0	0	0	0	0	0	0
McGlothlin	p	1	0	0	0	0	1	0
Borbon	p	0	0	0	0	0	1	0
c Uhlaender		1	0	0	0	0	0	0
Hall	p	0	0	0	0	0	1	0
e Concepcion	ss	2	0	0	0	0	0	0
Totals		33	5	8	5	27	13	0

Pitching	IP	H	R	ER	BB	SO
Cincinnati						
McGlothlin	*3	2	4	4	2	3
Borbon	1	1	0	0	1	0
Hall	2	0	0	0	0	1
Carroll	1⅔	3	0	0	0	1
Grimsley (W)	⅔	0	0	0	1	0
Billingham (SV)	⅔	1	0	0	0	0
Oakland						
Hunter	4⅔	5	3	3	2	2
Fingers (L)	3⅔	3	2	2	1	4
Hamilton	⅔	0	0	0	0	0

*Pitched to 2 batters in 4th.

Cin.	100	110	011
Oak.	030	100	000

Oakland	Pos	AB	R	H	RBI	PO	A	E
Campaneris	ss	5	0	0	0	2	3	0
Alou	rf	4	0	0	0	1	1	1
Rudi	lf	3	0	0	0	4	0	0
Epstein	1b	2	1	0	0	6	0	0
Hegan	1b	1	0	1	0	2	0	0
Bando	3b	3	1	1	0	0	1	1
Hendrick	cf	2	1	1	0	3	0	0
f Mincher		0	0	0	0	0	0	0
g Mangual	cf	1	0	0	0	0	0	0
Tenace	c	2	1	1	3	7	0	0
i Odom		0	0	0	0	0	0	0
Green	2b	1	0	0	0	1	0	0
a Marquez		1	0	1	1	0	0	0
b Lewis		0	0	0	0	0	0	0
Kubiak	2b	2	0	1	0	1	1	0
Hunter	p	2	0	0	0	0	2	0
Fingers	p	0	0	0	0	0	1	0
Hamilton	p	0	0	0	0	0	0	0
h Duncan		1	0	1	0	0	0	0
Totals		30	4	7	4	27	9	2

a Singled for Green in 4th.
b Ran for Marquez in 4th.
c Grounded out for Borbon in 5th.
d Grounded out for Chaney in 7th.
e Flied out for Hall in 7th.
f Announced for Hendrick in 8th.
g Grounded out for Mincher in 8th.
h Singled for Hamilton in 9th
i Ran for Tenace in 9th.

Double—Perez. Home Runs—Menke, Rose, Tenace. Stolen Bases—Morgan, Tolan 2. Sacrifice Hits—Fingers, Grimsley, Hendrick, Menke. Double Plays—Morgan to Bench, Alou to Tenace. Hit by Pitcher—Rudi (by McGlothlin). Wild Pitch—Fingers. Left on Bases—Cincinnati 6, Oakland 6. Umpires—Engel, Haller, Pelekoudas, Honochick, Steiner, Umont. Attendance—49,410. Time of Game—2:26.

1st Inning
Cincinnati
Rose homered over the right-center fence.
1 Morgan tapped back to the mound.
2 Tolan popped to short.
3 Bench struck out.
Oakland
1 Campaneris tapped to the pitcher.
2 Alou grounded to short.
3 Rudi struck out.

2nd Inning
Cincinnati
Perez doubled to left.
1 Menke sacrificed, Hunter to Epstein.
2 Geronimo fouled to Rudi in short left.
Chaney intentionally passed.
3 McGlothlin flied to short center.
Oakland
Epstein walked.
1 Bando flied to deep center.
Hendrick beat out a slow roller to the left of the mound, Epstein to second.
Tenace hit his **4th homer of the Series,** a three-run shot into the left field stands.
2 Green grounded to third.
3 Hunter struck out.

3rd Inning
Cincinnati
Rose singled to right.
1 Morgan popped to Green in short center.
2 Tolan flied to deep left.
3 Bench popped to Campaneris in short center.
Oakland
1 Campaneris struck out.
2 Alou flied to short right.
Rudi was hit by a pitch.
3 Epstein grounded to first.

4th Inning
Cincinnati
1 Perez grounded to short.
Menke homered into the left field stands.
2 Geronimo took a called third strike.
3 Chaney flied to deep center.
Oakland
Bando walked.
For Cincinnati—Borbon pitching with a 2–0 count to Hendrick.
1 Hendrick sacrificed, off Borbon's glove to Perez who threw to Morgan.
Tenace got an intentional pass.
Marquez, batting for Green, singled to center, scoring Bando and Tenace to third.
Lewis ran for Marquez.
Hunter missed a bunt and Tenace trapped
2 off third, and out, Bench to Menke.
3 Hunter flied to Tolan in left-center.

5th Inning
Cincinnati
For Oakland—Kubiak playing second.
1 Uhlaender, batting for Borbon, grounded to first.
2 Rose grounded to short.
Morgan walked.
Tolan singled to right, Morgan scoring.
For Oakland—Fingers came in to pitch.
Tolan stole second.
Tolan to third on a wild pitch.
3 Bench took a called third strike.
Oakland
For Cincinnati—Hall pitching.
1 Campaneris lined to Rose in deep left-center.
2 Alou grounded to the mound.
3 Rudi struck out.

6th Inning
Cincinnati
1 Perez grounded to short.
2 Menke struck out.
3 Geronimo flied to left.
Oakland
1 Epstein grounded to first.
2 Bando grounded to third.
3 Hendrick fouled to Menke.

7th Inning
Cincinnati
For Oakland—Hegan playing first.
1 Hague, batting for Chaney, grounded to second.
2 Concepcion, batting for Hall, flied to center.
3 Rose flied to Rudi in deep left-center.
Oakland
For Cincinnati—Concepcion stays in playing short with Carroll pitching.
1 Tenace grounded to third.
Kubiak beat out a bunt.
2 Fingers sacrificed, Bench to Morgan.
3 Campaneris struck out.

8th Inning
Cincinnati
Morgan walked.
Morgan stole second.
Tolan singled to right, scoring Morgan and went to second on Alou's fumble.
1 Bench grounded to third.
2 Perez struck out as Tolan stole third.
3 Menke struck out.
Oakland
1 Alou grounded out, Perez to Carroll.
2 Rudi lined to Rose in deep left-center.
Hegan beat out a grounder to second.
Bando singled to center, Hegan moving to third.
Mincher announced for Hendrick.
For Cincinnati—Grimsley now pitching.
3 Mangual batted for Mincher and grounded to second.

9th Inning
Cincinnati
For Oakland—Mangual playing center.
Geronimo singled to right.
1 Grimsley sacrificed, Fingers to Kubiak.
Concepcion safe and Geronimo holding second on Bando's fumble.
Rose singled to center, Geronimo scoring and Concepcion to third. Rose took second on the throw to third.
For Oakland—Hamilton pitching.
2,3 Morgan flied to Alou in short right and Concepcion was doubled up trying to score, Alou to Tenace.
Oakland
Tenace walked.
1 Kubiak popped to first, trying to bunt.
Duncan, batting for Hamilton.
Odom ran for Tenace.
For Cincinnati—Billingham pitching.
Duncan singled down the left field line, Odom racing to third.
2,3 Campaneris fouled to Morgan behind first and Odom was doubled up trying to score, Morgan to Bench.

Game 6 October 21 at Cincinnati

Oak.	000	010	000
Cin.	000	111	50x

Oakland	Pos	AB	R	H	RBI	PO	A	E
Campaneris	ss	4	0	0	0	2	4	0
Alou	rf	4	0	0	0	1	0	0
Rudi	lf	4	0	1	0	1	0	0
Epstein	1b	4	0	0	0	6	1	0
Bando	3b	4	1	2	0	0	1	0
Mangual	cf	4	0	2	0	3	0	1
Tenace	c	4	0	1	0	8	1	0
Green	2b	2	0	1	1	2	1	0
a Marquez		1	0	0	0	0	0	0
Kubiak	2b	1	0	0	0	0	0	0
Blue	p	1	0	0	0	0	1	0
Locker	p	0	0	0	0	0	0	0
b Mincher		0	0	0	0	0	0	0
c Duncan		1	0	0	0	0	0	0
Hamilton	p	0	0	0	0	0	0	0
Horlen	p	0	0	0	0	1	0	0
Totals		34	1	7	1	24	9	1

a Grounded into force out for Green in 7th.
b Announced to bat for Locker in 7th.
c Struck out for Mincher in 7th.

Cincinnati	Pos	AB	R	H	RBI	PO	A	E
Rose	lf	3	1	0	0	3	0	0
Morgan	2b	5	1	2	1	2	1	0
Tolan	cf	4	2	2	2	3	0	0
Bench	c	2	2	1	1	5	0	0
Perez	1b	3	0	1	1	10	0	0
McRae	rf	3	1	1	0	2	0	0
Geronimo	rf	1	0	1	2	0	0	0
Menke	3b	4	0	0	0	1	2	0
Concepcion	ss	3	1	2	1	1	3	0
Nolan	p	1	0	0	0	0	1	0
Grimsley	p	1	0	0	0	0	0	0
Borbon	p	0	0	0	0	0	1	0
Hall	p	2	0	0	0	0	0	0
Totals		32	8	10	8	27	8	0

Pitching	IP	H	R	ER	BB	SO
Oakland						
Blue (L)	5⅔	4	3	3	2	4
Locker	⅓	1	0	0	0	0
Hamilton	⅔	3	4	4	1	1
Horlen	1⅓	2	1	1	2	1
Cincinnati						
Nolan	4⅔	3	1	1	0	3
Grimsley (W)	1	1	0	0	1	0
Borbon	1	1	0	0	0	0
Hall (SV)	2⅓	2	0	0	0	1

Doubles—Green, McRae, Morgan. Triple—Concepcion. Home Run—Bench. Stolen Bases—Concepcion, Tolan 2. Sacrifice Fly—Concepcion. Wild Pitch—Horlen. Left on Bases—Oakland 7, Cincinnati 6. Umpires—Haller, Pelekoudas, Honochick, Steiner, Umont, Engel. Attendance—52,737. Time of Game—2:21.

1st Inning
Oakland
1 Campaneris grounded to third.
2 Alou grounded to second.
3 Rudi flied to right.
Cincinnati
1 Rose grounded to short.
Morgan doubled to right-center, and went to third on Mangual's wild throw.
2 Tolan popped to Campaneris behind third.
3 Bench lined to Rudi making a backhanded catch in the corner.

2nd Inning
Oakland
1 Epstein struck out.
Bando singled to center.
2 Mangual bounced out to third, Bando advancing to second.
3 Tenace flied to short left.
Cincinnati
1 Perez flied to short right.
2 McRae flied to center.
3 Menke lined to Mangual in left-center.

3rd Inning
Oakland
1 Green grounded to short.
2 Blue struck out.
3 Campaneris grounded out hard back to the mound.
Cincinnati
1 Concepcion took a called third strike.
2 Nolan struck out.
Rose walked.
3 Rose was out trying to steal second, Tenace to Campaneris.

4th Inning
Oakland
1 Alou flied to short right.
2 Rudi flied to left.
3 Epstein struck out.
Cincinnati
1 Morgan fouled to Tenace.
2 Tolan struck out.
Bench lined a homer into the left field stands
3 Perez grounded to third.

5th Inning
Oakland
Bando singled to left-center.
1 Mangual lined to the left field wall.
2 Tenace flied to deep center.
Green doubled to the wall in right-center, scoring Bando.
For Cincinnati—Grimsley pitching.
Blue walked.
3 Campaneris popped to second.
Cincinnati
McRae doubled off the right-center field wall.
1 Menke's grounder deflected by Blue to Campaneris who threw to first, McRae advancing to third.
2 Concepcion hit a sacrifice fly to deep center, scoring McRae.
3 Grimsley struck out.

6th Inning
Oakland
1 Alou popped to second.
Rudi singled to left.
2 Epstein grounded to first, Rudi moving to second.

6th Inning (continued)
For Cincinnati—Borbon replaced Grimsley with a 3–0 count to Bando.
3 Bando fouled to Bench.
Cincinnati
1 Rose popped to Green in short right.
2 Morgan rolled out to second.
Tolan singled to center.
For Oakland—Locker replaced Blue on the mound with a 2–0 count on Bench.
Tolan stole second.
Bench intentionally walked (charge walk to Blue).
Perez singled up the middle, scoring Tolan with Bench going to third.
3 McRae forced Perez at second, Campaneris to Green.

7th Inning
Oakland
For Cincinnati—Geronimo playing in right.
Mangual singled to right-center.
1 Tenace flied to center.
2 Marquez, batting for Green, forced Mangual, Borbon to Concepcion.
Mincher, announced to bat for Locker.
For Cincinnati—Hall came in to pitch.
3 Duncan, batting for Mincher, struck out.
Cincinnati
For Oakland—Kubiak playing second and Hamilton pitching.
1 Menke fouled to Tenace.
Concepcion singled to left.
Concepcion stole second.
2 Hall struck out.
Rose got an intentional walk.
Morgan singled to left, Concepcion scoring and Rose racing to third. On the throw to third Morgan went to second.
Tolan singled to right, scoring Rose and Morgan.
For Oakland—Horlen pitching.
Tolan stole second (his 5th steal of the Series).
Bench got an intentional walk.
On a wild pitch Tolan went to third and Bench to second.
Perez walked, loading the bases.
Geronimo singled to left, scoring Tolan and Bench with Perez stopping at second.
3 Menke grounded to short.

8th Inning
Oakland
1 Campaneris grounded to short.
2 Alou grounded to short.
3 Rudi lined to center.
Cincinnati
Concepcion tripled off the left field wall.
1 Hall lined to first.
2 Rose struck out.
3 Morgan grounded out, Epstein to Horlen, as Epstein made a diving stop.

9th Inning
Oakland
1 Epstein grounded to first.
2 Bando fouled to Perez.
Mangual singled to right.
Tenace singled to center, Mangual stopping at second.
3 Kubiak forced Mangual at third, Menke unassisted.

Game 7 October 22 at Cincinnati

Oak.	100	002	000
Cin.	000	010	010

Oakland	Pos	AB	R	H	RBI	PO	A	E
Campaneris	ss	4	1	2	0	6	1	1
Mangual	cf	4	1	0	0	3	0	0
Rudi	lf	3	0	0	0	5	0	0
Tenace	1b	3	0	2	2	3	1	0
b Lewis		0	1	0	0	0	0	0
Hegan	1b	1	0	0	0	1	0	0
Bando	3b	4	0	1	1	1	1	0
Alou	rf	3	0	0	0	2	0	0
Duncan	c	3	0	0	0	5	1	0
Green	2b	4	0	1	0	0	1	0
Odom	p	2	0	0	0	1	0	0
Hunter	p	0	0	0	0	0	0	0
Holtzman	p	0	0	0	0	0	0	0
Fingers	p	1	0	0	0	0	0	0
Totals		32	3	6	3	27	5	1

Pitching	IP	H	R	ER	BB	SO
Oakland						
Odom	4⅓	2	1	1	4	2
Hunter (W)	*2⅔	1	1	1	1	3
Holtzman	**0	1	0	0	0	0
Fingers (SV)	2	0	0	0	1	0
Cincinnati						
Billingham	5	2	1	0	1	4
Borbon (L)	⅔	3	2	2	0	0
Carroll	1	0	0	0	2	1
Grimsley	⅓	0	0	0	1	1
Hall	2	1	0	0	0	3

*Pitched to 1 batter in 8th.
**Pitched to 1 batter in 8th.

Cincinnati	Pos	AB	R	H	RBI	PO	A	E
Rose	lf	5	1	2	0	1	0	0
Morgan	2b	3	0	1	0	3	3	0
Tolan	cf	2	0	0	0	0	0	1
Foster	rf	0	0	0	0	0	0	0
d Javier		0	0	0	0	0	0	0
e Hague	rf	1	0	0	0	0	0	0
Bench	c	3	0	0	0	10	1	0
Perez	1b	2	1	1	1	10	1	0
Menke	3b	4	0	0	0	0	7	0
Geronimo	rf-cf	3	0	0	0	2	0	0
Concepcion	ss	3	0	0	0	0	2	1
Billingham	p	1	0	0	0	1	0	0
a McRae		0	0	0	1	0	0	0
Borbon	p	0	0	0	0	0	0	0
Carroll	p	0	0	0	0	0	1	0
Grimsley	p	0	0	0	0	0	0	0
c Uhlaender		1	0	0	0	0	0	0
Hall	p	0	0	0	0	0	1	0
f Chaney		0	0	0	0	0	0	0
Totals		28	2	4	2	27	16	2

a Hit a sacrifice fly for Billingham in 5th.
b Ran for Tenace in 6th.
c Flied out for Grimsley in 7th.
d Announced to bat for Foster in 8th.
e Popped out for Javier in 8th.
f Hit by pitch for Hall in 9th.

Doubles—Bando, Morgan, Perez, Tenace. Stolen Base—Bench. Sacrifice Hits—Campaneris, Mangual. Sacrifice Flies—McRae, Perez. Double Play—Campaneris to Tenace. Hit by Pitch—Chaney (by Fingers). Wild Pitch—Hunter. Left on Bases—Oakland 8, Cincinnati 8. Umpires—Pelekoudas, Honochick, Steiner, Umont, Engel, Haller. Attendance—56,040. Time of Game—2:50.

1st Inning
Oakland
1 Campaneris flied to short right.
Mangual got all the way to third on Tolan's error of his fly ball.
2 Rudi flied to short left.
Tenace singled on a bad hopper to third, scoring Mangual.
3 Bando struck out.
Cincinnati
Rose beat out a chopper to second.
1,2 Morgan hit into a double play, Campaneris to Tenace.
3 Tolan grounded out, Tenace to Odom.

2nd Inning
Oakland
1 Alou out, short to first on a bunt.
Duncan walked.
Green singled to left, Duncan stopping at second.
2 Duncan caught in a rundown off of second, Bench to Concepcion to Menke to Morgan to Billingham.
3 Odom fouled to Bench.
Cincinnati
1 Bench lined to short.
2 Perez flied to deep left.
3 Menke grounded to third.

3rd Inning
Oakland
1 Campaneris tapped to third.
2 Mangual popped to second.
3 Rudi grounded to third.
Cincinnati
1 Geronimo grounded to third.
2 Concepcion flied to left.
3 Billingham struck out.

4th Inning
Oakland
1 Tenace struck out.
2 Bando grounded to third.
3 Alou grounded to second.
Cincinnati
1 Rose lined to deep center.
Morgan walked.
2 Morgan caught stealing, Duncan to Campaneris after Odom threw to first seven times.
Tolan walked.
3 Bench fouled to Bando

5th Inning
Oakland
1 Duncan struck out.
2 Green grounded to third, Menke making a good backhanded stop.
3 Odom struck out.
Cincinnati
Perez doubled down the left field line.
1 Menke struck out.
Geronimo walked.
For Oakland—Hunter replaced Odom with a 2–1 count on Concepcion.
Concepcion walked, loading the bases. The walk charged to Odom.
2 McRae, batting for Billingham, hit a sacrifice fly to deep center, Perez scoring as the other runners held.
3 Rose flied to Mangual in deep right-center.

6th Inning
Oakland
For Cincinnati—Borbon pitching.
Campaneris singled to center.
1 Mangual sacrificed, Perez to Morgan.
2 Rudi grounded to second, Campaneris moving to third.
Tenace doubled into the left field corner, scoring Campaneris.

6th Inning (continued)
Lewis ran for Tenace.
Bando doubled over Tolan's head, scoring Lewis.
For Cincinnati—Carroll pitching.
Alou got an intentional walk.
Duncan safe at first on Concepcion's fumble, loading the bases.
3 Green struck out.
Cincinnati
For Oakland—Hegan playing first.
1 Morgan popped to short.
2 Tolan struck out.
Bench safe on Campaneris' high throw to first, for an error.
Perez walked.
Bench went to third and Perez to second on a wild pitch.
3 Menke flied to short right.

7th Inning
Oakland
For Cincinnati—Geronimo moved to center with Foster playing right.
Hunter walked.
1 Campaneris sacrificed Hunter to second, Carroll to Morgan.
2 Mangual grounded to third, Hunter holding second.
For Cincinnati—Grimsley now pitching.
Rudi was intentionally passed.
3 Hegan struck out.
Cincinnati
1 Geronimo struck out.
2 Concepcion struck out.
3 Uhlaender, pinch-hitting for Grimsley, flied to left.

8th Inning
Oakland
For Cincinnati—Hall pitching.
1 Bando struck out.
2 Alou bounced back to the mound.
3 Duncan struck out.
Cincinnati
Rose singled to center.
For Oakland—Holtzman pitching.
Morgan doubled to right, Rose stopping at third.
Javier, announced to bat for Foster.
For Oakland—Fingers pitching.
1 Hague batted for Javier and popped to Campaneris in short right.
Bench intentionally walked.
2 Perez hit a sacrifice fly to right, Alou scoring and Morgan advancing to third after the catch.
Bench stole second.
3 Menke flied to left.

9th Inning
Oakland
For Cincinnati—Hague playing right.
1 Green struck out.
2 Fingers grounded to third.
Campaneris singled to center.
3 Mangual flied to center.
Cincinnati
1 Geronimo popped to short.
2 Concepcion grounded to second.
Chaney, pinch-hitting for Hall, was hit by a pitched ball.
3 Rose flied to Rudi in left-center.

1972 WORLD SERIES COMPOSITE BOX

	Wins	Composite Line Score
Oakland Athletics (A.L.)	4	1 6 1 1 3 2 0 0 2 – 16
Cincinnati Reds (N.L.)	3	1 1 0 3 3 1 6 4 2 – 21

Manager	W	L	Pct.	G. Ahead	
Regular Season					
Dick Williams	93	62	.600	5.5	(beat Detroit in playoffs)
Sparky Anderson	95	59	.617	10.5	(beat Pittsburgh in playoffs)

BATTING AND FIELDING

WORLD SERIES STATISTICS

	Pos	G	AB	R	H	2B	3B	HR	RBI	BB	SO	SB	BA	SA	PO	A	E
OAKLAND ATHLETICS																	
Mike Epstein	1b	6	16	1	0	0	0	0	0	5	3	0	.000	.000	35	2	**2**
Dick Green	2b	7	18	0	6	**2**	0	0	1	0	4	0	.333	.444	12	13	0
Bert Campaneris	ss	7	**28**	1	5	0	0	0	0	1	4	0	.179	.179	17	15	1
Sal Bando	3b	7	26	2	7	1	0	0	1	2	5	0	.269	.308	3	12	1
Matty Alou	rf	7	24	0	1	0	0	0	0	3	0	1	.042	.042	11	1	1
George Hendrick	cf	5	15	3	2	0	0	0	0	1	2	0	.133	.133	12	0	0
Joe Rudi	lf	7	25	1	6	0	0	1	1	2	5	0	.240	.360	20	0	0
Gene Tenace	c-1b	7	23	**5**	8	1	0	**4**	**9**	2	4	0	.348	**.913**	48	5	1
Angel Mangual	ph-cf	4	10	1	3	0	0	0	1	0	0	0	.300	.300	6	0	1
Mike Hegan	1b-ph	6	5	0	1	0	0	0	0	0	2	0	.200	.200	11	1	0
Dave Duncan	ph-c	3	5	0	1	0	0	0	0	1	3	0	.200	.200	5	1	0
Ted Kubiak	2b	4	3	0	1	0	0	0	0	0	0	0	.333	.333	4	3	0
Gonzalo Marquez	ph	5	5	0	3	0	0	0	1	0	0	0	.600	.600	0	0	0
Don Mincher	ph	3	1	0	1	0	0	0	1	0	0	0	1.000	1.000	0	0	0
Allen Lewis	pr	6	0	2	0	0	0	0	0	0	0	0	—	—	0	0	0
Tim Cullen		Did not play															
Dal Maxvill		Did not play															
Reggie Jackson		Not in Series—Hamstring pull															
Catfish Hunter	p	3	5	0	1	0	0	0	1	2	1	0	.200	.200	0	3	1
Ken Holtzman	p	3	5	0	0	0	0	0	0	0	0	0	.000	.000	0	3	1
Blue Moon Odom	p-pr	4	4	0	0	0	0	0	0	0	3	0	.000	.000	1	3	0
Rollie Fingers	p	6	1	0	0	0	0	0	0	0	0	0	.000	.000	0	2	0
Vida Blue	p	4	1	0	0	0	0	0	0	2	1	0	.000	.000	0	1	0
Dave Hamilton	p	2	0	0	0	0	0	0	0	0	0	0	—	—	0	0	0
Joe Horlen	p	1	0	0	0	0	0	0	0	0	0	0	—	—	1	0	0
Bob Locker	p	1	0	0	0	0	0	0	0	0	0	0	—	—	0	0	0
Darold Knowles		Not in Series—injured															
team total		7	220	16	46	4	0	5	16	21	37	1	.209	.295	186	65	9

Double Plays—0
Left on Bases—45

REGULAR SEASON STATISTICS

		Main Pos	G	AB	R	H	2B	3B	HR	RBI	BB	SO	SB	BA	SA
OAKLAND ATHLETICS															
Mike Epstein		1b	138	455	63	123	18	2	26	70	68	68	0	.270	.490
Dick Green		2b	26	42	1	12	1	1	0	3	3	5	0	.286	.357
Bert Campaneris		ss	149	**625**	85	150	25	2	8	32	32	88	**52**	.240	.325
Sal Bando		3b	152	535	64	126	20	3	15	77	78	55	3	.236	.368
Matty Alou	a	of	32	121	11	34	5	0	1	16	11	12	2	.281	.347
George Hendrick		of	58	121	10	22	1	1	4	15	3	22	3	.182	.306
Joe Rudi		of	147	593	94	**181**	32	**9**	19	75	37	62	3	.305	.486
Gene Tenace		c	82	227	22	51	5	3	5	32	24	42	0	.225	.339
Angel Mangual		of	91	272	19	67	13	2	5	32	14	48	0	.246	.364
Mike Hegan		1b	98	79	13	26	3	1	1	5	7	20	1	.329	.430
Dave Duncan		c	121	403	39	88	13	0	19	59	34	68	0	.218	.392
Ted Kubiak	b	2b	51	94	14	17	4	1	0	8	9	11	0	.181	.245
Gonzalo Marquez		ph	23	21	2	8	0	0	0	4	3	4	1	.381	.381
Don Mincher	c	ph	47	54	2	8	1	0	0	5	10	16	0	.148	.167
Allen Lewis		pr	24	10	5	2	1	0	0	2	0	1	8	.200	.300
Tim Cullen		2b	72	142	10	37	8	1	0	15	5	17	0	.261	.331
Dal Maxvill	d	2b	27	36	2	9	1	0	0	1	1	11	0	.250	.278
Reggie Jackson		of	135	499	72	132	25	2	25	75	59	125	9	.265	.473
Catfish Hunter		p	39	105	5	23	0	0	0	5	0	16	0	.219	.219
Ken Holtzman		p	40	90	6	16	4	0	0	6	1	25	0	.178	.222
Blue Moon Odom		p-pr	59	66	16	8	1	0	2	2	1	29	4	.121	.227
Rollie Fingers		p	65	19	2	6	0	0	1	2	0	3	0	.316	.474
Vida Blue		p	27	45	4	2	0	0	0	0	5	34	0	.044	.044
Dave Hamilton		p	25	26	2	4	1	0	0	0	5	12	0	.154	.192
Joe Horlen		p	32	17	1	3	0	0	0	0	0	4	0	.176	.176
Bob Locker		p	56	6	0	0	0	0	0	0	3	4	0	.000	.000
Darold Knowles		p	54	12	0	3	0	0	0	1	1	3	0	.250	.250
team total			155	5200	604	1248	195	29	**134**	565	463	886	87	.240	.366

a—From St. Louis; b—from Texas; c—from Texas; d—from St. Louis.
Larry Brown (2b), Bill Voss (of), Marty Martinez (2b), Brant Alyea (ph), Ollie Brown (of), Bobby Brooks (of), Ron Clark (2b), Curt Blefary (ph), Bill McNulty (3b), Adrian Garrett (ph), Art Shamsky (ph), Dwain Anderson (ss), Larry Haney (c), Orlando Cepeda (ph), Denny McLain (p), Diego Degui (p), Don Shaw (p), Gary Waslewski (p), Mike Kilkenny (p), and Jim Roland (p) also played for the Athletics during the season.

WORLD SERIES STATISTICS

	Pos	G	AB	R	H	2B	3B	HR	RBI	BB	SO	SB	BA	SA	PO	A	E
CINCINNATI REDS																	
Tony Perez	1b	7	23	3	**10**	**2**	0	0	2	4	4	0	**.435**	.522	**73**	3	1
Joe Morgan	2b	7	24	4	3	**2**	0	0	1	**6**	3	2	.125	.208	18	18	1
Dave Concepcion	ss-pr-ph	6	13	2	4	0	**1**	0	2	2	2	1	.308	.462	4	11	1
Denis Menke	3b	7	24	1	2	0	0	1	2	2	**6**	0	.083	.208	6	**23**	0
Cesar Geronimo	rf-cf	7	19	1	3	0	0	0	3	1	4	1	.158	.158	9	0	0
Bobby Tolan	cf	7	26	2	7	1	0	0	6	1	4	**5**	.269	.308	11	0	1
Pete Rose	lf	7	**28**	3	6	0	0	1	2	4	4	1	.214	.321	14	1	0
Johnny Bench	c	7	23	4	6	1	0	1	1	5	5	2	.261	.435	41	7	1
Hal McRae	ph-rf	5	9	1	4	1	0	0	2	0	1	0	.444	.556	4	0	0
Darrel Chaney	ss-ph	4	7	0	0	0	0	0	0	2	2	0	.000	.000	5	11	0
Joe Hague	ph-rf	3	3	0	0	0	0	0	0	0	0	0	.000	.000	0	0	0
George Foster	pr-rf	2	0	0	0	0	0	0	0	0	0	0	—	—	0	0	0
Ted Uhlaender	ph	4	4	0	1	1	0	0	0	0	1	0	.250	.500	0	0	0
Julian Javier	ph	4	2	0	0	0	0	0	0	0	0	0	.000	.000	0	0	0
Bill Plummer		Did not play															
Jack Billingham	p	3	5	0	0	0	0	0	0	0	4	0	.000	.000	1	1	0
Gary Nolan	p	2	3	0	0	0	0	0	0	0	3	0	.000	.000	0	2	0
Ross Grimsley	p	4	2	0	0	0	0	0	0	0	2	0	.000	.000	0	2	0
Tom Hall	p	4	2	0	0	0	0	0	0	0	1	0	.000	.000	0	2	0
Don Gullett	p	1	2	0	0	0	0	0	0	0	0	0	.000	.000	0	1	0
Jim McGlothlin	p	1	1	0	0	0	0	0	0	0	0	0	.000	.000	0	1	0
Pedro Borbon	p	6	0	0					0	0	0	0	—	—	0	3	0
Clay Carroll	p	5	0	0	0	0	0	0	0	0	0	0	—	—	1	3	0
Wayne Simpson		Did not play															
Ed Sprague		Did not play															
team total		7	220	21	46	8	1	3	21	27	46	12	.209	.295	187	89	5

Double Plays—5
Left on Bases—49

REGULAR SEASON STATISTICS

		Main Pos	G	AB	R	H	2B	3B	HR	RBI	BB	SO	SB	BA	SA
CINCINNATI REDS															
Tony Perez		1b	136	515	64	146	33	7	21	90	55	121	4	.283	.497
Joe Morgan		2b	149	552	**122**	161	23	4	16	73	**115**	44	58	.292	.435
Dave Concepcion		ss	119	378	40	79	13	2	2	29	32	65	13	.209	.270
Denis Menke		3b	140	447	41	104	19	2	9	50	58	76	0	.233	.345
Cesar Geronimo		of	120	255	32	70	9	7	4	29	24	64	2	.275	.412
Bobby Tolan		of	149	604	88	171	28	5	8	82	44	88	42	.283	.386
Pete Rose		of	154	**645**	107	**198**	31	**11**	6	57	73	46	10	.307	.417
Johnny Bench		c	147	538	87	145	22	2	**40**	**125**	100	84	6	.270	.541
Hal McRae		ph	61	97	9	27	4	0	5	26	2	10	0	.278	.474
Darrel Chaney		ss	83	196	29	49	7	2	2	19	29	28	1	.250	.337
Joe Hague	e	1b-of-ph	69	138	17	34	7	1	4	20	20	18	1	.246	.399
George Foster		of	59	145	15	29	4	1	2	12	5	44	2	.200	.283
Ted Uhlaender		ph-of	73	113	9	18	3	0	0	6	13	11	0	.159	.186
Julian Javier		3b-ph	44	91	3	19	2	0	2	12	6	11	1	.209	.297
Bill Plummer		c	38	102	8	19	4	0	2	9	4	20	0	.186	.284
Jack Billingham		p	36	71	2	5	1	0	0	2	2	29	0	.070	.085
Gary Nolan		p	25	60	5	7	1	0	0	2	4	24	0	.117	.133
Ross Grimsley		p	30	66	5	8	0	0	0	1	1	29	0	.121	.121
Tom Hall		p	47	30	5	3	0	0	0	0	2	14	0	.100	.100
Don Gullett		p	31	38	7	8	1	0	0	3	2	14	0	.211	.237
Jim McGlothlin		p	31	46	6	8	1	0	1	1	5	21	0	.174	.261
Pedro Borbon		p	62	21	0	1	0	0	0	1	1	10	0	.048	.048
Clay Carroll		p	65	11	2	2	0	0	0	1	0	3	0	.182	.182
Wayne Simpson		p	24	48	2	3	1	0	0	0	1	31	0	.063	.083
Ed Sprague		p	33	7	0	0	0	0	0	0	0	5	0	.000	.000
team total			154	5241	707	1317	214	44	124	650	**606**	914	**140**	.251	.380

e—from St. Louis
Bernie Carbo (ph), Sonny Ruberto (c), Pat Corrales (c), Jim Merritt (p), Joe Gibbon (p), and Dave Tomlin (p) also played for the Reds during the season.

PITCHING

WORLD SERIES STATISTICS

	G	GS	CG	IP	H	R	ER	BB	SO	W	L	SV	ERA
OAKLAND ATHLETICS													
Catfish Hunter	3	**2**	0	**16**	**12**	**5**	**5**	**6**	11	**2**	0	0	281
Ken Holtzman	3	**2**	0	12⅔	11	3	3	3	4	1	0	0	2.13
Blue Moon Odom	2	**2**	0	11⅓	5	2	2	**6**	**13**	0	**1**	0	1.59
Rollie Fingers	**6**	0	0	10⅓	4	2	2	4	11	1	**1**	**2**	1.74
Vida Blue	4	1	0	8⅔	8	4	4	5	5	0	**1**	1	4.15
Dave Hamilton	2	0	0	1⅓	2	1	1		1	0	0	0	27.00
Joe Horlen	1	0	0	1⅓	3	4	4	1	1	0	0	0	6.75
Bob Locker	1	0	0	⅓	1	0	0	0	0	0	0	0	0.00
Darold Knowles	Not in Series—Injured												
team total	7	7	0	62	46	21	21	27	46	4	3	3	3.05
CINCINNATI REDS													
Jack Billingham	3	**2**	0	13⅔	6	1	0	4	11	1	0	1	**0.00**
Gary Nolan	2	**2**	0	10⅔	7	4	4	2	3	0	**1**	0	3.38
Tom Hall	4	0	0	8⅓	6	0	0	2	7	0	0	1	**0.00**
Pedro Borbon	**6**	0	0	7	7	3	3	2	4	0	**1**	0	3.86
Ross Grimsley	4	1	0	7	7	2	2	3	2	**2**	**1**	0	2.57
Don Gullett	1	1	0	7	5	1	1	2	4	0	0	0	1.29
Clay Carroll	5	0	0	5⅔	6	1	1	4	3	0	**1**	1	1.59
Jim McGlothlin	1	1	0	3	2	4	4	2	3	0	0	0	12.00
Wayne Simpson	Did not play												
Ed Sprague	Did not play												
team total	7	7	0	62⅓	46	16	15	21	37	3	4	3	2.17

REGULAR SEASON STATISTICS

	G	GS	CG	IP	H	ER	BB	SO	W	L	Pct	SV	ShO	ERA
OAKLAND ATHLETICS														
Catfish Hunter	38	37	16	295	200	67	70	191	21	7	**.750**	0	5	2.04
Ken Holtzman	39	37	16	265	232	74	52	134	19	11	.633	0	4	2.51
Blue Moon Odom	31	30	4	194	164	54	87	86	15	6	.714	0	2	2.51
Rollie Fingers	65	0	0	111	85	31	32	113	11	9	.550	21	0	2.51
Vida Blue	25	23	5	151	117	47	48	111	6	10	.375	0	4	2.80
Dave Hamilton	25	14	1	101	94	33	31	55	6	6	.500	0	0	2.94
Joe Horlen	32	6	0	84	74	28	20	58	3	4	.429	1	0	3.00
Bob Locker	56	0	0	78	69	23	16	47	6	1	.857	10	0	2.65
Darold Knowles	54	0	0	66	49	10	37	36	5	1	.833	11	0	1.36
team total	155	155	42	**1418**	1170	406	418	862	**93**	62	**.600**	**43**	**23**	2.58
CINCINNATI REDS														
Jack Billingham	36	31	8	218	197	77	64	137	12	12	.500	1	4	3.18
Gary Nolan	25	25	6	176	147	39	30	90	15	5	**.750**	0	2	1.99
Tom Hall	47	7	1	124	77	36	56	134	10	1	.909	8	1	2.61
Pedro Borbon	62	2	0	122	115	43	32	48	8	3	.727	11	0	3.17
Ross Grimsley	30	28	4	198	194	67	50	79	14	8	.636	1	1	3.05
Don Gullett	31	16	2	135	127	59	43	96	9	10	.474	2	0	3.93
Clay Carroll	65	0	0	96	89	24	32	51	6	4	.600	**37**	0	2.25
Jim McGlothlin	31	21	3	145	165	63	49	69	9	8	.529	0	1	3.91
Wayne Simpson	24	22	1	130	124	60	49	70	8	5	.615	0	0	4.15
Ed Sprague	33	1	0	57	55	26	26	25	3	3	.500	0	0	4.11
team total	154	154	25	1413	1313	434	435	806	**95**	59	.617	**60**	15	3.21

Total Attendance—363,149 Average Attendance—51,878 *Winning Player's Share—$20,705 *Losing Player's Share—$15,080
*includes Playoffs and World Series.

1973
Mike Andrews: Hitless but Supreme

The New York Mets graced their fans with another miracle, thanks to divisional play. The Mets stumbled through the summer in last place in the Eastern Division of the National League, with key players injured and manager Yogi Berra rumored to be on the way out. But none of the Eastern clubs got very far above the .500 level, so when the Mets got hot in September, they didn't have much ground to make up. At the end of a dramatic final week of the season, the Mets had captured first place with an 82–79 record. Then came a riotous play-off series with the Cincinnati Reds, whose 99–63 record could not prevent elimination in five games to the sky-high Mets. With the lowest percentage of any pennant-winner in history, the Mets still had Cleon Jones, Bud Harrelson, Jerry Grote, Tom Seaver, Jerry Koosman, and Tug McGraw in key positions, just like in 1969. But the club was different in several ways. Berra became manager when Gil Hodges died of a heart attack in 1972, the farm system produced power hitter John Milner and left-hand pitcher Jon Matlack, and trades brought in Rusty Staub, Felix Millan, and the legendary Willie Mays, an old man of forty-two playing out his final season. Trying to halt the Met tidal wave in the Series were the Oakland A's, who won a return berth by beating the Baltimore Orioles in five games in the American League championship series. Reggie Jackson came into this Series in fine health and joined Sal Bando, Bert Campaneris, Joe Rudi, and Gene Tenace in a formidable lineup. Manager Dick Williams had three 20-game winners in Catfish Hunter, Ken Holtzman, and Vida Blue and a superb reliever in Rollie Fingers. Two problems facing the A's were the loss of center fielder Billy North with an injury, and that with the American League using the designated-hitter rule this season the Oakland pitchers, who had not batted all year, would have to take their turn at the plate in the Series.

With a little batting practice to sharpen his eye, Holtzman doubled off Matlack in the third inning of game one in Oakland, scoring when Millan missed Campaneris's grounder on the next play and sparking a 2–1 Oakland win. Koosman and Blue started game two, but neither was around when the A's tied the score at 6–6 with two runs in the bottom of the ninth, with Mays pathetically falling down on tired legs on a double by Deron Johnson. With Fingers on the mound, Harrelson doubled and McGraw bunted for a single to open the twelfth inning. After Wayne Garrett and Millan made out, Mays pulled out the final hit of his career to drive in the go-ahead run. After Jones singled to load the bases, Paul Lindblad came in to pitch. Milner hit a grounder which went right through the legs of second baseman Mike Andrews to score two runs, and when Andrews made a throwing error on the next play, another run scored. After the 10–7 New York victory was over, A's owner Charley Finley claimed that Andrews was incapacitated by a shoulder injury and tried to replace him with another player on the roster. All the Oakland players and the sporting public rose up indignantly at Finley's tasteless attempt to "fire" Andrews for his errors. Commissioner Bowie Kuhn ordered Andrews reinstated and socked Finley with a healthy fine.

The hostility of the Oakland players toward the team's owner was not the usual background for a World Series triumph. The A's took game three in New York 3–2 in 11 innings, but they lost the fourth game 6–1, with Staub and Matlack starring for the Mets, and dropped the fifth game 2–0 to a combined three-hitter by Koosman and McGraw.

The Mets needed just one win in Oakland to take the title. Berra sent Tom Seaver against Hunter in game six, but Reggie Jackson's three hits and two RBI's sent the New York ace down to a 3–1 defeat. The key seventh game matched Matlack against Holtzman. Matlack didn't have his best stuff and met his Waterloo in the third inning, when Holtzman again doubled, Campaneris homered to right, Rudi singled, and Jackson applied the killer with a long homer to right-center. Relievers Fingers and Darold Knowles wrapped up the 5–2 victory which made the A's the first repeat World Champions since the New York Yankees of 1961–62. A lingering memory of the Series was the standing ovation New York fans gave Mike Andrews for pinch hitting in the eighth inning of the fourth game, a salute to a survivor of Charley Finley's wrath. Besides costing him a fine, the incident also cost Finley his manager, as Dick Williams announced his resignation minutes after the seventh game.

Game 1 October 13 at Oakland

| N.Y. | 000 100 000 |
| Oak. | 002 000 00x |

New York	Pos	AB	R	H	RBI	PO	A	E
Garrett	3b	5	0	0	0	0	0	0
Millan	2b	4	0	1	0	1	2	1
Mays	cf	4	0	1	0	0	0	1
Jones	lf	4	1	2	0	3	0	0
Milner	1b	4	0	2	1	11	0	0
Grote	c	4	0	0	0	5	2	0
Hahn	rf	2	0	0	0	0	0	0
c Kranepool		1	0	0	0	0	0	0
Harrelson	ss	2	0	0	0	4	6	0
d Hodges		0	0	0	0	0	0	0
e Martinez		0	0	0	0	0	0	0
Matlack	p	0	0	0	0	0	0	0
b Boswell		1	0	1	0	0	0	0
McGraw	p	0	0	0	0	0	0	0
f Staub		0	0	0	0	0	0	0
g Beauchamp		1	0	0	0	0	0	0
Totals		32	1	7	1	24	10	2

a Lined out for Holtzman in 5th.
b Singled for Matlack in 7th.
c Lined out for Hahn in 9th.
d Walked for Harrelson in 9th.
e Ran for Hodges in 9th.
f Announced for McGraw in 9th.
g Popped out for Staub in 9th.

Doubles—Holtzman, Jones. Triple—Millan. Stolen Base—Campaneris. Sacrifice Hits—Matlack, Rudi. Double Plays—Holtzman to Tenace, Green to Campaneris to Tenace. Passed Ball—Fosse. Left on Bases—New York 9, Oakland 5. Umpires—Springstead (A), Donatelli (N), Neudecker (A), Pryor (N), Goetz (A), Wendelstedt (N). Attendance—46,021. Time of Game—2:26.

Oakland	Pos	AB	R	H	RBI	PO	A	E
Campaneris	ss	4	1	1	0	3	1	0
Rudi	lf	3	1	0	0	1	0	0
Bando	3b	3	0	1	0	1	3	0
Jackson	cf-rf	3	0	0	0	4	0	0
Tenace	1b	3	0	0	0	11	0	0
Alou	rf	3	0	0	0	1	0	0
Davalillo	cf	0	0	0	0	0	0	0
Fosse	c	3	0	0	0	4	1	0
Green	2b	2	0	0	0	2	3	0
Holtzman	p	1	1	1	0	1	3	0
a Mangual		1	0	0	0	0	0	0
Fingers	p	1	0	0	0	0	0	0
Knowles	p	0	0	0	0	0	0	0
Totals		27	2	4	1	27	11	0

Pitching	IP	H	R	ER	BB	SO
New York						
Matlack (L)	6	3	2	0	2	3
McGraw	2	1	0	0	1	1
Oakland						
Holtzman (W)	5	4	1	1	3	2
Fingers	3⅓	3	0	0	1	3
Knowles (SV)	⅔	0	0	0	0	0

1st Inning
New York
1 Garrett fouled to Bando.
2 Millan grounded to second.
 Mays singled to left.
3 Jones bounced back to the pitcher.
Oakland
1 Campaneris popped to second.
2 Rudi lined to short.
3 Bando flied to left.

2nd Inning
New York
1 Milner flied to center.
2 Grote grounded to second.
3 Hahn took a called third strike.
Oakland
1 Jackson grounded to short.
2 Tenace struck out.
3 Alou fouled to Milner

3rd Inning
New York
 Harrelson walked.
1 Matlack sacrificed Harrelson to second, Holtzman to Green.
2 Garrett fouled to Tenace.
3 Millan grounded to third as Tenace made a leaping catch of Bando's high throw.
Oakland
1 Fosse fouled to Milner.
 Green walked.
2 Green caught trying to steal second, Grote to Harrelson.
 Holtzman doubled down the left field line.
 Campaneris safe at first when his grounder went through Millan's legs for an error, Holtzman scoring.
 Campaneris stole second.
 Rudi singled to right, scoring Campaneris.
 Bando singled to center, Mays fumbled for an error as Rudi went to third.
3 Jackson fouled to Harrelson down the left field line.

4th Inning
New York
1 Mays grounded to third.
 Jones doubled to left-center.
 Milner singled to center, scoring Jones and went to second on the throw to the plate.
2 Grote lined to deep center, Jackson making a running catch.
 Hahn walked.
3 Harrelson struck out.
Oakland
1 Tenace flied to short left.
2 Alou flied to deep left.
3 Fosse grounded to short.

5th Inning
New York
 Matlack walked.
1,2 Garrett, on an attempted sacrifice, popped to Holtzman who threw to Tenace doubling Matlack off first.
 Millan tripled to left when Rudi lost the ball in the sun.
3 Mays flied to right.
Oakland
1 Green struck out.
2 Mangual, pinch-hitting for Holtzman, lined to short.
3 Campaneris struck out.

6th Inning
New York
For Oakland—Fingers now pitching.
 Jones singled to center.
1 Milner rolled out, Fosse to Tenace, Jones advancing to second.
2 Grote flied to short center.
 Hahn struck out but was safe at first on Fosse's passed ball as Jones went to third.
3 Harrelson struck out.
Oakland
1 Rudi was automatically out as he was hit by his own batted ball in fair territory. Grote gets the putout.
2 Bando grounded to short.
 Jackson walked.
3 Tenace grounded to second.

7th Inning
New York
 Boswell, batting for Matlack, singled to right.
1,2 Garrett again hit into a double play, Green to Campaneris to Tenace.
3 Millan lined to short.
Oakland
For New York—McGraw pitching.
1 Alou grounded to short.
2 Fosse grounded to short.
3 Green grounded to short.

8th Inning
New York
For Oakland—Jackson moved to right as Davalillo went to center.
1 Mays took a called third strike.
2 Jones grounded to third.
 Milner singled to right.
3 Grote fouled to Tenace.
Oakland
1 Fingers struck out.
 Campaneris beat out a bunt down the first base line.
2 Rudi sacrificed Campaneris to second, Grote to Milner.
 Bando got an intentional walk.
3 Jackson grounded to second.

9th Inning
New York
1 Kranepool, batting for Hahn, lined to short.
 Hodges, batting for Harrelson, walked.
 Martinez ran for Hodges.
 Staub announced to bat for McGraw.
 For Oakland—Knowles came on to pitch.
2 Beauchamp, pinch-hitting for Staub, popped to Green in short center.
3 Garrett flied to short right.

1973

Game 2 October 14 at Oakland

N.Y. 011 004 000 004
Oak. 210 000 102 001

New York	Pos	AB	R	H	RBI	PO	A	E
Garrett	3b	6	1	1	1	1	5	0
Millan	2b	6	0	0	0	4	5	0
Staub	rf	5	0	1	0	1	0	0
g Mays	cf	3	0	1	0	1	0	0
Jones	lf	5	3	3	1	0	0	0
Milner	1b	6	1	2	0	15	0	0
Grote	c	6	1	2	0	15	2	0
Hahn	cf-rf	7	1	1	1	0	0	0
Harrelson	ss	6	1	3	1	0	4	0
Koosman	p	1	0	0	0	0	0	1
Sadecki	p	1	0	0	0	0	1	0
a Theodore		1	0	0	0	0	0	0
Parker	p	1	0	0	0	0	0	0
b Kranepool		0	0	0	0	0	0	0
c Beauchamp		1	0	0	0	0	0	0
McGraw	p	2	1	1	0	0	2	0
Stone	p	0	0	0	0	0	0	0
Totals		54	10	15	5	36	19	1

Pitching	IP	H	R	ER	BB	SO
New York						
Koosman	2⅓	6	3	3	3	4
Sadecki	1⅔	0	0	0	0	3
Parker	1	1	0	0	0	0
McGraw (W)	**6	5	4	4	3	8
Stone (SV)	1	1	0	0	1	0
Oakland						
Blue	5⅓	4	4	4	2	4
Pina	*0	2	2	0	0	0
Knowles	1⅓	1	0	0	2	2
Odom	2	2	0	0	2	2
Fingers (L)	2⅓	6	4	1	0	2
Lindblad	⅓	0	0	0	0	0

*Pitched to 3 batters in 6th.
**Pitched to 2 batters in 12th.

Oakland	Pos	AB	R	H	RBI	PO	A	E
Campaneris	ss	6	2	1	0	0	6	0
Rudi	lf	5	1	2	1	3	1	0
Bando	3b	5	2	1	1	1	4	1
Jackson	cf	6	1	2	3	0	0	0
Tenace	1b	3	0	1	1	13	0	1
Alou	rf	6	0	3	2	2	0	0
Fosse	c	5	0	0	0	11	0	0
Green	2b	2	0	0	0	2	1	0
d Mangual		1	0	0	0	0	0	0
Kubiak	2b	0	0	0	0	0	0	0
f Andrews	2b	2	0	0	1	0	2	2
Blue	p	2	0	0	0	0	0	0
Pina	p	0	0	0	0	0	0	1
Knowles	p	0	0	0	0	0	0	1
e Conigliaro		1	0	0	0	0	0	0
Odom	p	0	0	0	0	0	0	0
h Johnson		1	0	1	0	0	0	0
i Lewis		0	1	0	0	0	0	0
Fingers	p	1	0	0	0	0	1	0
Lindblad	p	0	0	0	0	0	0	0
j Davalillo		1	0	0	0	0	0	0
Totals		47	7	13	7	36	13	5

a Grounded out for Sadecki in 5th.
b Announced to bat for Parker in 6th.
c Safe on an error for Kranepool in 6th.
d Struck out for Green in 6th.
e Grounded out for Knowles in 7th.
f Grounded for Kubiak in 8th.
g Ran for Staub in 9th.
h Doubled for Odom in 9th.
i Ran for Johnson in 9th.
j Popped out for Lindblad in 12th.

Doubles—Alou, Harrelson, Jackson, Johnson, Rudi. Triples—Bando, Campaneris, Jackson. Home Runs—Garrett, Jones. Stolen Base—Campaneris. Sacrifice Hit—McGraw. Double Plays—Garrett to Millan, to Milner, Rudi to Fosse. Hit by Pitchers—Grote (by Pina), Campaneris (by McGraw), Jones (by Fingers). Left on Bases—New York 15, Oakland 12. Umpires—Donatelli, Neudecker, Pryor, Goetz, Wendelstedt, Springstead. Attendance—49,151. Time of Game—4:13 (**the longest game in Series history**).

1st Inning
New York
1 Garrett struck out.
2 Millan took a called third strike.
3 Staub grounded to short.
Oakland
1 Campaneris grounded to short.
Rudi doubled to left when Jones lost the ball in the sun.
Bando tripled to right-center, scoring Rudi.
2 Jackson struck out.
Tenace walked.
Alou doubled down the left field line, scoring Bando with Tenace stopping at third.
Fosse got an intentional walk.
3 Green struck out.

2nd Inning
New York
Jones hit a home run over the right field wall.
1 Milner grounded to second.
2 Grote popped to Green in short right.
3 Hahn grounded to first.
Oakland
1 Blue struck out.
Campaneris tripled to right-center.
Rudi singled to center, scoring Campaneris.
2 Rudi was caught trying to steal second, Grote to Millan.
3 Bando struck out.

3rd Inning
New York
1 Harrelson called out on strikes.
2 Koosman grounded to third.
Garrett hit a home run into the right field stands.
3 Millan grounded to third.
Oakland
1 Jackson grounded to short.
Tenace walked.
Alou singled to right, Tenace stopping at second.
Fosse safe at first when Koosman threw high to first on his bouncer, loading the bases.
For New York—Sadecki took the mound.
2 Tenace was trapped when Green missed a pitch, out Grote to Garrett to Milner.
3 Green took a called third strike.

4th Inning
New York
1 Staub flied to left.
Jones singled to center.
2 Milner lined to right.
Grote safe at first and Jones moving to second when Bando booted Grote's grounder for an error.
3 Hahn lined to right.
Oakland
1 Blue struck out.
2 Campaneris struck out.
3 Rudi tapped back to the mound.

5th Inning
New York
1 Harrelson flied to short center.
2 Theodore, pinch-hitting for Sadecki, grounded to short.
Garrett walked.
3 Millan forced Garrett at second, Campaneris to Green
Oakland
For New York—Parker pitching.
1 Bando fouled to Garrett.
Jackson singled to right.
2,3 Tenace hit into a double play, Garrett to Millan to Milner.

6th Inning
New York
1 Staub fanned.
Jones walked.
Milner singled to right-center, Jones going to third.
For Oakland—Pina came in to pitch.
Grote was hit by a pitch, loading the bases.
Hahn beat out a roller to third, scoring Jones. Bases still filled.
Harrelson singled to right, scoring Milner.
Kranepool, up to bat for Parker.
For Oakland—Knowles pitching.
Beauchamp, batting for Kranepool, bounced to Knowles who threw wild to the plate, scoring Grote and Hahn as Harrelson wound up on third and Beauchamp on second.
2 Garrett took a called third strike.
Millan intentionally passed, again loading the bases.
3 Staub flied to center.
Oakland
For New York—McGraw pitching.
1 Alou grounded to third.
2 Fosse grounded to second.
3 Mangual, batting for Green, struck out.

7th Inning
New York
For Oakland—Kubiak playing second.
1 Jones grounded to third.
Milner walked.
Grote singled to left, Milner racing to second.
2 Hahn struck out.
3 Harrelson flied to left.
Oakland
1 Conigliaro, batting for Knowles, grounded to second.
Campaneris was hit by a pitch.
Rudi walked.
2 Bando took a called third strike as Campaneris stole third.
Jackson doubled to right, Campaneris scoring with Rudi stopping at third.
3 Tenace struck out.

8th Inning
New York
For Oakland—Odom pitching.
1 McGraw struck out.
2 Garrett struck out.
3 Millan flied to short center.
Oakland
1 Alou grounded to second.
2 Fosse grounded to second.
3 Andrews, batting for Kubiak, tapped back to the mound.

9th Inning
New York
For Oakland—Andrews playing second.
Staub singled to center.
Mays ran for Staub.
1 Jones fouled to Tenace.
Milner singled to right, Mays stopping at second.
2 Grote fouled to Bando.
3 Hahn grounded to short.

9th Inning (continued)
Oakland
For New York—Hahn moved over to right as Mays stayed in playing center.
Johnson, pinch-hitting for Odom, doubled to center.
Lewis ran for Johnson.
1 Campaneris struck out.
2 Rudi grounded to third, Lewis holding second.
Bando walked.
Jackson singled to right, scoring Lewis and sending Bando to third.
Tenace singled to left, scoring Bando as Jackson stopped at second.
3 Alou bounced back to the mound.

10th Inning
New York
For Oakland—Fingers pitching.
Harrelson singled to center.
1 McGraw sacrificed Harrelson to second, Fingers to Campaneris to Andrews.
Garrett safe at first with Harrelson going to third on Tenace's bad throw to Fingers covering first.
2,3 Millan flied to Rudi in short left who fired the ball into Fosse doubling Harrelson trying to score.
Oakland
1 Fosse struck out.
2 Andrews took a called third strike.
3 Fingers flied to short center.

11th Inning
New York
1 Mays popped to first.
Jones was hit by a pitch.
2 Milner struck out.
Grote singled to left, Jones stopping at second.
3 Hahn grounded to short.
Oakland
1 Campaneris grounded to third.
2 Rudi struck out.
3 Bando struck out for the third time.

12th Inning
New York
Harrelson doubled to right-center.
McGraw singled on an attempted bunt over Bando's head, Harrelson racing to third.
1 Garrett was a strikeout victim for the fourth time.
2 Millan popped to first.
Mays singled over Finger's head into center, scoring Harrelson with McGraw stopping at second.
Jones singled to left, loading the bases.
For Oakland—Lindblad replaced Fingers on the mound.
Milner's grounder went through Andrews' legs, allowing McGraw and Mays to score with Jones going to third and Milner to second.
Grote safe at first on Andrews' high throw, scoring Jones as Milner went to third.
3 Hahn grounded to second.
Oakland
Jackson tripled off the left-center field wall.
Tenace walked for the third time.
For New York—Parker pitching.
Alou singled to right, scoring Jackson as Tenace stopped at second.
1 Fosse forced Alou at second, Harrelson to Millan, Tenace going to third.
Andrews walked, loading the bases.
2 Davalillo, pinch-hitting for Lindblad, popped to second.
3 Campaneris grounded to short.

1973

Game 3 October 16 at New York

Oak. 000 001 010 01
N.Y. 200 000 000 00

Oakland	Pos	AB	R	H	RBI	PO	A	E
Campaneris	ss	6	1	3	1	2	7	0
Rudi	lf	5	0	2	1	7	0	0
Bando	3b	4	1	2	0	0	1	0
Jackson	rf	5	0	0	0	2	0	0
Tenace	1b-c	3	0	1	1	4	0	0
Davalillo	cf-1b	5	0	1	0	7	0	0
Fosse	c	2	0	0	0	5	0	0
a Bourque	1b	2	0	1	0	2	0	0
e Lewis		0	0	0	0	0	0	0
Lindblad	p	1	0	0	0	0	0	0
Fingers	p	0	0	0	0	0	0	0
Green	2b	2	0	0	0	1	0	0
b Alou		1	0	0	0	0	0	0
Kubiak	2b	1	1	0	0	2	2	0
Hunter	p	2	0	0	0	0	2	1
c Johnson		1	0	0	0	0	0	0
Knowles	p	0	0	0	0	0	0	0
f Mangual	cf	2	0	0	0	1	0	0
Totals		42	3	10	3	33	12	1

New York	Pos	AB	R	H	RBI	PO	A	E
Garrett	3b	4	1	2	1	1	2	0
Millan	2b	5	1	2	0	3	2	2
Staub	rf	6	0	2	0	2	0	0
Jones	lf	5	0	0	0	2	1	0
Milner	1b	3	0	1	0	5	1	0
Grote	c	5	0	0	0	15	0	0
Hahn	cf	5	0	2	0	4	1	0
Harrelson	ss	5	0	2	0	1	3	0
Seaver	p	3	0	0	0	0	0	0
d Beauchamp		0	0	0	0	0	0	0
Sadecki	p	0	0	0	0	0	0	0
McGraw	p	0	0	0	0	0	1	0
g Mays		1	0	0	0	0	0	0
Parker	p	0	0	0	0	0	0	0
Totals		42	2	10	1	33	11	2

Pitching	IP	H	R	ER	BB	SO
Oakland						
Hunter	6	7	2	2	3	5
Knowles	2	0	0	0	1	0
Lindblad (W)	**2	3	0	0	1	0
Fingers (SV)	1	0	0	0	0	0
New York						
Seaver	8	7	2	2	1	12
Sadecki	*0	1	0	0	0	0
McGraw	2	1	0	0	1	0
Parker (L)	1	1	1	0	1	1

*Pitched to 2 batters in 9th.
**Pitched to 1 batter in 11th.

a Flied out for Fosse in 7th.
b Grounded out for Green in 7th.
c Struck out for Hunter in 7th.
d Flied out for Seaver in 8th.
e Ran for Bourque in 9th.
f Struck out for Knowles in 9th.
g Grounded into force out for McGraw in 10th.

Doubles—Bando, Hahn, Rudi, Staub, Tenace. Home Run—Garrett. Stolen Base—Campaneris. Sacrifice Hits—Bando, Millan. Passed Ball—Grote. Wild Pitch—Hunter. Left on Bases—Oakland 10, New York 14. Umpires—Neudecker, Pryor, Goetz, Wendelstedt, Springstead, Donatelli. Attendance—54,817. Time of Game—3:15.

1st Inning
Oakland
1 Campaneris fouled to Grote.
Rudi doubled to left.
2 Bando struck out.
3 Jackson was called out on strikes.
New York
Garrett hit a home run into the right field stands.
Millan singled to left.
Staub singled to left, Millan racing to third.
Millan scored and Staub went to second on a wild pitch.
1 Jones struck out.
Milner safe at first when Hunter fumbled his roller, Staub holding second.
2 Grote struck out.
3 Hahn lined to left.

2nd Inning
Oakland
1 Tenace struck out.
2 Davalillo took a called third strike.
3 Fosse struck out becoming Seaver's fifth consecutive victim.
New York
1 Harrelson flied to short center.
2 Seaver fouled to Tenace reaching into the first base seats.
Garrett walked.
3 Millan lined to short.

3rd Inning
Oakland
1 Green grounded to third.
2 Hunter lined to center.
Campaneris singled to right.
3 Rudi forced Campaneris at second, Harrelson to Millan.
New York
1 Staub flied to left.
2 Jones grounded to third.
Milner walked.
3 Grote forced Milner at second, Campaneris to Green.

4th Inning
Oakland
1 Bando lined to left.
2 Jackson struck out.
Tenace walked.
Davalillo beat out a tap in front of the plate, Tenace going to second.
3 Fosse grounded to short.
New York
Hahn hit a ground-rule double down the left field line when spectators touched the ball.
1 Harrelson flied to right.
2 Seaver took a called third strike.
Garrett got an intentional walk.
Millan singled to third, loading the bases.
3 Staub bounced back to the mound.

5th Inning
Oakland
1 Green struck out.
2 Hunter struck out.
3 Campaneris also struck out, the second inning that Seaver struck out the side.
New York
1 Jones tapped back to the mound.
Milner singled off the right field wall as Jackson fielded the rebound perfectly and fired in to second.
2 Grote flied to left.
3 Hahn flied to short left.

6th Inning
Oakland
1 Rudi flied to Hahn in deep right-center.
Bando doubled over Hahn's head in center.
2 Jackson struck out for the third time.
Tenace doubled down the left field line, scoring Bando.
3 Davalillo grounded to second.
New York
Harrelson singled to center.
1 Seaver struck out, bunting foul on the third strike.
2 Garrett took a called third strike.
3 Millan lined to Davalillo in left-center.

7th Inning
Oakland
1 Bourque, batting for Fosse flied to deep right.
2 Alou, batting for Green, grounded to short.
3 Johnson, batting for Hunter, took a called third strike.
New York
For Oakland—Bourque stays in at first, Kubiak playing second, Knowles pitching, and Tenace took over behind the plate.
1 Staub lined to left.
2 Jones grounded to short.
Milner walked.
3 Grote forced Milner at second, Campaneris to Kubiak.

8th Inning
Oakland
Campaneris singled to left.
Campaneris stole second.
Rudi singled into right, scoring Campaneris.
1 Bando sacrificed Rudi to second, Milner to Millan covering first.
2 Jackson flied to center.
3 Tenace struck out.
New York
1 Hahn grounded to short.
2 Harrelson flied to short left.
3 Beauchamp, pinch-hitting for Seaver, lined to left.

9th Inning
For New York—Sadecki pitching.
Davalillo safe at first on Millan's fumble.
Bourque beat out a bunt between the mound and first with Davalillo going to second.
Lewis ran for Bourque.
For New York—McGraw came on to pitch.
1 Kubiak forced Davalillo at third on an attempted sacrifice, McGraw to Garrett.
2 Mangual, batting for Knowles, took a called third strike.
3 Campaneris flied to center.
New York
For Oakland—Davalillo moved to first, Mangual stays in at center, Lindblad pitching.
1 Garrett popped to Campaneris in short left.
2 Millan grounded to short.
Staub got a ground-rule double when his liner bounced over the left-center field fence.
Jones got an intentional walk.
3 Milner flied to right.

10th Inning
Oakland
1 Rudi lined to left.
Bando singled off the left field wall and as he tried for second, Jones' throw had him beaten but Millan had the ball jarred out of his glove for an error.
2 Jackson grounded to second, Bando going to third.
Tenace intentionally walked.
3 Davalillo flied to right.
New York
1 Grote grounded to second.
2 Hahn grounded to second.
Harrelson singled to right.
3 Mays, pinch-hitting for McGraw forced Harrelson at second, Campaneris to Kubiak.

11th Inning
Oakland
For New York—Parker pitching.
1 Lindblad, lined to short.
Kubiak walked.
2 Mangual struck out but when the ball got by Grote for a passed ball Kubiak went to second.
Campaneris singled to center, scoring Kubiak but was out trying to take second
3 on the throw in, Hahn to Garrett to Millan.
New York
Garrett singled to center.
For Oakland—Fingers replaced Lindblad on the mound.
1 Millan sacrificed Garrett to second, Davalillo unassisted.
2 Staub flied to center.
3 Jones grounded to short.

Game 4 October 17 at New York

Oakland	Pos	AB	R	H	RBI	PO	A	E
Campaneris	ss	4	0	0	0	1	2	0
Rudi	lf	4	0	1	0	1	1	0
Bando	3b	3	1	0	0	3	4	0
Jackson	cf	4	0	1	0	0	0	0
Tenace	1b	3	0	1	1	12	0	0
Alou	rf	4	0	0	0	1	0	0
Fosse	c	4	0	1	0	4	2	0
Green	2b	1	0	0	0	1	3	1
a Mangual		1	0	0	0	0	0	0
Kubiak	2b	1	0	0	0	1	3	0
d Johnson		1	0	1	0	0	0	0
Holtzman	p	0	0	0	0	0	0	0
Odom	p	1	0	0	0	0	1	0
Knowles	p	0	0	0	0	0	1	0
b Conigliaro		1	0	0	0	0	0	0
Pina	p	0	0	0	0	0	0	0
c Andrews		1	0	0	0	0	0	0
Lindblad	p	0	0	0	0	0	0	0
e Davalillo		0	0	0	0	0	0	0
Totals		33	1	5	1	24	17	1

a Popped out for Green in 5th.
b Flied out for Knowles in 5th.
c Grounded out for Pina in 8th.
d Singled for Kubiak in 9th.
e Walked for Lindblad in 9th.

Home Run—Staub. Double Plays—Bando to Green to Tenace, Green to Campaneris to Tenace, Knowles to Fosse to Tenace, Kubiak to Tenace. Hit by Pitchers—Garrett (by Knowles), Campaneris (by Matlack). Wild Pitch—Odom. Left on Bases—Oakland 9, New York 10. Umpires—Pryor, Goetz, Wendelstedt, Springstead, Donatelli, Neudecker. Attendance—54,817. Time of Game—2:41.

Oak.	000	100	000
N.Y.	300	300	00x

New York	Pos	AB	R	H	RBI	PO	A	E
Garrett	3b	4	2	1	0	0	4	1
Millan	2b	5	1	1	0	4	1	0
Staub	rf	4	1	4	5	1	0	0
Jones	lf	3	0	1	0	2	0	0
Theodore	lf	1	0	0	0	1	0	0
Milner	1b	3	0	0	0	9	0	0
Grote	c	4	0	3	0	7	0	0
Hahn	cf	4	1	1	0	2	0	0
Harrelson	ss	2	1	1	0	1	3	0
Matlack	p	3	0	1	0	0	1	0
Sadecki	p	0	0	0	0	0	0	0
Totals		33	6	13	5	27	9	1

Pitching	IP	H	R	ER	BB	SO
Oakland						
Holtzman (L)	$\frac{1}{3}$	4	3	3	1	0
Odom	*$2\frac{2}{3}$	3	2	2	2	0
Knowles	1	1	1	0	1	1
Pina	3	4	0	0	2	0
Lindblad	1	1	0	0	0	1
New York						
Matlack (W)	8	3	1	0	2	5
Sadecki (SV)	1	2	0	0	1	2

*Pitched to 2 batters in 4th.

1st Inning
Oakland
1 Campaneris was out tagged by Milner on a bunt down the first base line.
2 Rudi lined to right.
Bando walked.
3 Jackson struck out.
New York
Garrett singled to right.
Millan beat out a bunt to third, Garrett going to second.
Staub hit a three-run homer over the left-center field fence.
1 Jones grounded to second.
Milner walked.
Grote singled to left-center, Milner racing to third.
For Oakland—Odom came in to pitch.
2,3 Hahn grounded into a double play, Bando to Green to Tenace.

2nd Inning
Oakland
1 Tenace grounded to third.
2 Alou fouled to Milner.
3 Fosse took a called third strike.
New York
1 Harrelson grounded to short.
Matlack walked.
Matlack went to second on a wild pitch.
2 Garrett grounded to third, moving Matlack to third.
3 Millan grounded to third.

3rd Inning
Oakland
1 Green struck out.
2 Odom took a called third strike.
3 Campaneris grounded to third.
New York
Staub walked.
Jones singled to right-center, moving Staub to third.
1 Milner tapped to the mound and Staub was caught in a rundown, Odom to Fosse to Bando, as Jones went to second with Milner safe at first.
2,3 Grote hit into a double play, Green to Campaneris to Tenace.

4th Inning
Oakland
1 Rudi struck out.
Bando safe on Garrett's fumble.
Jackson singled to center, Bando racing to third. Jackson to second on the throw to third.
2 Tenace grounded to short, scoring Bando with Jackson going to third.
3 Alou flied to short left.
New York
Hahn singled to right.
Harrelson singled to left, Hahn stopping at second.
For Oakland—Knowles pitching.
1 Matlack took a called third strike.
Garrett was hit by a pitched ball, loading the bases.
Millan safe at first on Green's fumble, scoring Hahn.
Staub singled to right, scoring Harrelson and Garrett with Millan going to third.

4th Inning (continued)
Jones walked.
2,3 Milner hit into a double play, Knowles to Fosse to Tenace.

5th Inning
Oakland
Fosse singled to left.
1 Mangual, batting for Green, popped to Millan in short right.
2 Conigliaro, batting for Knowles, flied to center.
3 Campaneris forced Fosse at second, Garrett to Millan.
New York
For Oakland—Kubiak at second and Pina pitching.
Grote singled to center.
1 Hahn lined to deep left.
Harrelson walked.
2,3 Matlack hit into the 4th double play, Kubiak to Tenace.

6th Inning
Oakland
1 Rudi popped to second.
2 Bando grounded to short.
3 Jackson lined to left.
New York
1 Garrett grounded to second.
2 Millan grounded to third.
Staub singled to center.
3 Jones flied to right.

7th Inning
Oakland
Tenace walked
1 Alou forced Tenace at second, Harrelson to Millan.
2 Fosse flied to Hahn in left-center.
3 Kubiak tapped back to the mound.
New York
1 Milner grounded to second.
Grote singled to center.
2 Hahn grounded to first, Grote going to second.
Harrelson got an international pass.
3 Matlack singled to left, but Grote was out trying to score, Rudi to Fosse.

8th Inning
Oakland
For New York—Theodore playing left.
1 Andrews, pinch-hitting for Pina, grounded to third.
Campaneris was hit by a pitch.
Rudi singled to left, Campaneris stopping at second.
2 Bando lined to Theodore in left-center.
3 Jackson grounded to second.
New York
For Oakland—Lindblad pitching.
1 Garrett struck out.
2 Millan lined to third.
Staub singled to left.
3 Theodore popped to third.

9th Inning
Oakland
For New York—Sadecki came in to pitch.
Tenace singled to left.
1 Alou lined to short.
2 Fosse struck out.
Johnson, pinch-hitting for Kubiak, singled to left, Tenace stopping at second.
Davalillo, batting for Lindblad, walked to load the bases.
3 Campaneris struck out.

Game 5 October 18 at New York

Oakland	Pos	AB	R	H	RBI	PO	A	E
Campaneris	ss	3	0	1	0	0	4	1
Rudi	lf	4	0	0	0	3	0	0
Bando	3b	3	0	1	0	1	1	0
Jackson	cf	3	0	0	0	1	0	0
Tenace	1b	1	0	0	0	7	2	0
d Odom		0	0	0	0	0	0	0
Bourque	1b	0	0	0	0	1	1	0
Alou	rf	4	0	0	0	0	0	0
Fosse	c	4	0	1	0	6	0	0
Green	2b	2	0	0	0	1	0	0
a Johnson		0	0	0	0	0	0	0
b Lewis		0	0	0	0	0	0	0
Kubiak	2b	1	0	0	0	2	2	0
Blue	p	2	0	0	0	2	1	0
Knowles	p	0	0	0	0	0	0	0
c Mangual		1	0	0	0	0	0	0
Fingers	p	0	0	0	0	0	0	0
e Conigliaro		1	0	0	0	0	0	0
Totals		29	0	3	0	24	11	1

a Walked for Green in 7th.
b Ran for Johnson in 7th.
c Popped out for Knowles in 7th.
d Ran for Tenace in 8th.
e Struck out for Fingers in 9th.

Doubles—Fosse, Jones. Triple—Hahn. Sacrifice Hit—Grote. Double Play—Millan to Harrelson to Milner. Wild Pitch—Blue. Left on Bases—Oakland 9, New York 10. Umpires—Goetz, Wendelstedt, Springstead, Donatelli, Neudecker, Pryor. Attendance—54,817. Time of Game—2:39.

Oak.	000	000	000
N.Y.	010	001	00x

New York	Pos	AB	R	H	RBI	PO	A	E
Garrett	3b	3	0	0	0	1	2	1
Millan	2b	4	0	0	0	2	1	0
Staub	rf	3	0	1	0	0	0	0
Jones	lf	4	1	2	0	2	0	0
Milner	1b	4	0	2	1	7	0	0
Grote	c	3	1	1	0	10	0	0
Hahn	cf	4	0	1	1	2	0	0
Harrelson	ss	2	0	0	0	3	4	0
Koosman	p	3	0	0	0	0	1	0
McGraw	p	1	0	0	0	0	0	0
Totals		31	2	7	2	27	8	1

Pitching	IP	H	R	ER	BB	SO
Oakland						
Blue (L)	$5\frac{2}{3}$	6	2	2	1	4
Knowles	$\frac{1}{3}$	0	0	0	1	1
Fingers	2	1	0	0	2	1
New York						
Koosman (W)	$6\frac{1}{3}$	3	0	0	4	4
McGraw (SV)	$2\frac{2}{3}$	0	0	0	3	3

1st Inning
Oakland
1 Campaneris grounded to third.
2 Rudi grounded to short.
Bando walked.
3 Jackson struck out.
New York
1 Garrett struck out.
2 Millan grounded out, Tenace to Blue.
3 Staub lined to left.

2nd Inning
Oakland
1 Tenace struck out.
2 Alou grounded to short.
3 Fosse grounded to short.
New York
Jones doubled to left.
Milner singled to right, scoring Jones.
1 Grote flied to center.
2 Hahn forced Milner at second, Campaneris to Green.
3 Harrelson flied to left.

3rd Inning
Oakland
1 Green flied to center.
2 Blue struck out.
Campaneris singled to center.
3 Campaneris was picked off first, Koosman to Milner.
New York
1 Koosman struck out.
2 Garrett took a called third strike.
3 Millan grounded to short.

4th Inning
Oakland
1 Rudi popped to Millan in short right.
Bando singled on a bad hop over Garrett's head.
2,3 Jackson grounded into a double play, Millan to Harrelson to Milner.
New York
Staub singled to left.
Jones singled to center, Staub stopping at second.
1 Milner forced Staub at third on a bunt, Blue to Bando.
2 Grote fouled to Tenace.
Hahn safe at first when Campaneris fumbled his bouncer, loading the bases.
3 Harrelson popped to first.

5th Inning
Oakland
Tenace walked.
1 Alou fouled to Grote.
2 Fosse popped to Millan in short right.
3 Green flied to center.
New York
1 Koosman struck out.
Garrett walked.
Garrett to second on a wild pitch.
2 Millan grounded to first, Garrett going to third.
3 Staub grounded to short.

6th Inning
Oakland
1 Blue struck out.
Campaneris walked.
2 Rudi fouled to Grote.
Bando safe on Garrett's bobble, Campaneris going to second.
3 Jackson forced Bando at second, Harrelson unassisted.
New York
1 Jones flied deep to Rudi who made a leaping backhanded catch as he crashed into the left field fence.
2 Milner bounced out, Tenace to Blue.
Grote singled to left.
Hahn tripled to left-center, scoring Grote.
For Oakland—Knowles pitching.
Harrelson got an intentional walk.
3 Koosman struck out for the third time.

7th Inning
Oakland
Tenace walked.
1 Alou fouled to Grote.
Fosse doubled to left, Tenace stopping at third.
For New York—McGraw now pitching.
Johnson, batting for Green, walked, loading the bases.
Lewis ran for Johnson.
2 Mangual, batting for Knowles, popped to short.
3 Campaneris took a called third strike.
New York
For Oakland—Kubiak playing second and Fingers pitching.
1 Garrett grounded to second.
2 Millan grounded to third.
Staub walked.
3 Jones forced Staub at second, Campaneris to Kubiak.

8th Inning
Oakland
1 Rudi grounded to third.
2 Bando flied to left.
Jackson walked.
Tenace walked for the third time.
Odom ran for Tenace.
3 Alou lined to third.
New York
For Oakland—Bourque playing first.
Milner singled to center.
1 Grote sacrificed Milner to second, Bourque to Kubiak.
2 Hahn struck out.
Harrelson again intentionally passed.
3 McGraw grounded to second.

9th Inning
Oakland
1 Fosse lined to left.
2 Kubiak took a called third strike.
3 Conigliaro, batting for Fingers, took a called third strike.

Game 6 October 20 at Oakland

New York	Pos	AB	R	H	RBI	PO	A	E
Garrett	3b	3	0	1	0	0	2	1
Millan	2b	4	0	1	1	2	1	0
Staub	rf	4	0	1	0	0	0	0
Jones	lf	4	0	0	0	1	0	0
Milner	1b	4	0	1	0	10	0	0
Grote	c	4	0	1	0	7	1	0
Hahn	cf	3	0	0	0	4	0	1
c Kranepool		1	0	0	0	0	0	0
Harrelson	ss	3	0	0	0	0	2	0
Seaver	p	2	0	0	0	0	2	0
a Boswell		1	1	0	0	0	0	0
McGraw	p	0	0	0	0	0	0	0
Totals		33	1	6	1	24	8	2

Pitching	IP	H	R	ER	BB	SO
New York						
Seaver (L)	7	6	2	2	2	6
McGraw	1	1	1	1	0	1
Oakland						
Hunter (W)	7⅓	4	1	1	1	4
Knowles	⅓	2	0	0	0	1
Fingers (SV)	1⅓	0	0	0	0	0

Oakland	Pos	AB	R	H	RBI	PO	A	E
Campaneris	ss	4	0	0	0	2	4	0
Rudi	lf	3	1	1	0	3	0	0
Bando	3b	4	1	1	0	0	0	0
Jackson	rf-cf	4	1	3	2	2	0	0
Tenace	c-1b	3	0	0	0	3	0	0
Davalillo	cf	2	0	0	0	6	0	0
b Alou	rf	0	0	1	1	0	0	0
Johnson	1b	4	0	1	0	5	1	0
Fosse	c	0	0	0	0	0	0	0
Green	2b	3	0	1	0	4	2	0
Hunter	p	3	0	0	0	1	0	0
Knowles	p	0	0	0	0	0	0	0
Fingers	p	0	0	0	0	0	0	0
Totals		30	3	7	3	27	7	0

a Singled for Seaver in 8th.
b Hit Sacrifice fly for Davalillo in 8th.
c Popped out for Hahn in 9th.

Doubles—Jackson 2. Sacrifice fly—Alou.
Double Play—Grote to Millan.
Wild Pitch—Seaver. Left on Bases—
New York 6, Oakland 7.
Umpires—Wendelstedt, Springstead,
Donatelli, Neudecker, Pryor, Goetz.
Attendance—49,333. Time of Game—2:07.

1st Inning
New York
Garrett walked.
1 Millan fouled to Green.
  Staub singled to center, Garrett
  stopping at second.
2 Jones flied to center.
3 Milner flied to short center.
Oakland
1 Campaneris flied to Hahn in short
  left-center.
  Rudi singled to right.
2 Bando struck out.
  Jackson lined a double to left-
  center, scoring Rudi.
3 Tenace struck out.

2nd Inning
New York
1 Grote flied to deep left.
2 Hahn fouled to Campaneris behind third.
3 Harrelson grounded out, Johnson
  to Hunter.
Oakland
Davalillo walked.
1 Johnson grounded to short, Davalillo
  going to second.
2 Green bounced back to the mound,
  Davalillo going to third.
3 Hunter took a called third strike.

3rd Inning
New York
1 Seaver flied to Davalillo in
  left-center.
2 Garrett popped to short.
3 Millan flied to short center.
Oakland
1 Campaneris fouled to Milner.
2 Rudi struck out.
  Bando singled to center.
  Jackson doubled to right-center,
  scoring Bando.
3 Tenace popped to first.

4th Inning
New York
1 Staub popped to second.
2 Jones grounded to short.
3 Milner grounded to first.
Oakland
1 Davalillo bounced to first.
2 Johnson grounded to short.
  Green singled to center.
3 Hunter flied to center.

5th Inning
New York
  Grote singled to left.
1 Hahn struck out.
2 Harrelson flied to center.
3 Seaver flied to deep left.
Oakland
1 Campaneris grounded to third.
2 Rudi popped to Millan in short right.
  Bando safe on Garrett's error.
3 Jackson grounded to second.

6th Inning
New York
1 Garrett flied to short center.
2 Millan grounded to short.
3 Staub grounded to second.
Oakland
1 Tenace grounded to third.
2 Davalillo flied to short center.
  Johnson singled to center.
3 Green bounced back to the mound.

7th Inning
New York
1 Jones grounded to short.
  Milner singled to right.
2 Grote lined to deep left.
3 Hahn forced Milner at second,
  Campaneris to Green.
Oakland
1 Hunter called out on strikes.
2 Campaneris struck out.
  Rudi walked.
  Rudi advanced to second on a
  wild pitch.
3 Bando flied to center.

8th Inning
New York
1 Harrelson flied to center.
  Boswell, pinch-hitting for Seaver,
  singled to right.
  For Oakland—Knowles now pitching.
  Garrett singled to left-center,
  Boswell racing to second.
  Millan singled to right, scoring
  Boswell with Garrett going to third.
2 Staub struck out.
  For Oakland—Fingers came in to pitch.
3 Jones flied to center.
Oakland
  For New York—McGraw on the mound.
  Jackson singled to center and raced to
  third when the ball got by Hahn for
  an error.
  Tenace walked.
1 Alou, pinch-hitting for Davalillo, hit
  a sacrifice fly to left, Jackson
  scoring with Tenace holding at first.
2,3 Johnson struck out and Tenace was
  doubled up trying to steal second,
  Grote to Millan.

9th Inning
New York
  For Oakland—Alou stays in playing right,
  Jackson switches to center, Tenace moves
  to first, and Fosse catching.
1 Milner flied to right.
2 Grote grounded to second.
3 Kranepool, pinch-hitting for Hahn,
  popped to Green in short center

Game 7 October 21 at Oakland

New York	Pos	AB	R	H	RBI	PO	A	E
Garrett	3b	5	0	0	0	1	4	0
Millan	2b	4	1	1	0	1	0	0
Staub	rf	4	0	2	1	2	0	0
Jones	lf	3	0	0	1	0	1	0
Milner	1b	3	1	0	0	9	0	0
Grote	c	4	0	1	0	8	0	0
Hahn	cf	4	0	3	0	1	0	0
Harrelson	ss	4	0	0	0	2	2	0
Matlack	p	1	0	0	0	0	0	0
Parker	p	0	0	0	0	0	0	0
b Beauchamp		1	0	0	0	0	0	0
Sadecki	p	0	0	0	0	0	0	0
c Boswell		1	0	1	0	0	0	0
Stone	p	0	0	0	0	0	0	0
d Kranepool		1	0	0	0	0	0	0
e Martinez		0	0	0	0	0	0	0
Totals		35	2	8	1	24	7	1

Pitching	IP	H	R	ER	BB	SO
New York						
Matlack (L)	2⅔	4	4	4	1	3
Parker	1⅓	0	0	0	1	1
Sadecki	2	2	1	0	1	0
Stone	2	3	0	0	0	3
Oakland						
Holtzman (W)	5⅓	5	1	1	1	4
Fingers	3⅓	3	1	0	1	2
Knowles (SV)	⅓	0	0	0	0	0

Oakland	Pos	AB	R	H	RBI	PO	A	E
Campaneris	ss	4	2	3	2	2	4	0
Rudi	lf	3	1	2	0	3	0	0
Bando	3b	4	0	0	0	0	1	0
Jackson	cf-rf	4	1	1	2	5	0	0
Tenace	c-1b	3	0	0	0	7	0	1
Alou	rf	1	0	0	0	0	0	0
a Davalillo	cf	3	0	0	0	3	0	0
Johnson	1b	4	0	0	0	3	0	0
Fosse	c	1	0	1	0	2	0	0
Green	2b	4	0	0	0	3	2	0
Holtzman	p	2	1	1	0	0	0	0
Fingers	p	1	0	1	0	0	1	0
Knowles	p	0	0	0	0	0	0	0
Totals		33	5	9	5	27	8	1

a Flied out for Alou in 3rd.
b Struck out for Parker in 5th.
c Singled for Sadecki in 7th.
d Safe on error for Stone in 9th.
e Ran for Kranepool in 9th.

Doubles—Holtzman, Millan, Staub.
Home Runs—Campaneris, Jackson.
Double Play—Bando to Campaneris to Green.
Left on Bases—New York 8, Oakland 6.
Umpires—Springstead, Donatelli, Neudecker,
Pryor, Goetz, Wendelstedt.
Attendance—49,333. Time of Game—2:37.

1st Inning
New York
1 Garrett took a called third strike.
2 Millan grounded to short.
3 Staub flied to Jackson in left-center.
Oakland
1 Campaneris grounded to third.
  Rudi walked.
2 Bando struck out.
3 Jackson tapped to third.

2nd Inning
New York
1 Jones flied to deep center.
2 Milner popped to Green in short right.
3 Grote lined to center.
Oakland
1 Tenace took a called third strike.
2 Alou fouled to Milner.
3 Johnson grounded to third.

3rd Inning
New York
  Hahn singled to left.
1 Harrelson flied to left.
2,3 Matlack bunted into a double play,
  Bando to Campaneris to Green who
  covered first.
Oakland
1 Green took a called third strike.
  Holtzman doubled down the left
  field line.
  Campaneris hit a two-run homer over
  the right field fence.
  Rudi singled to center.
2 Bando popped to second.
  Jackson also hit a two-run homer deep
  into the right-center field stands.
  For New York—Parker on the mound.
  Tenace walked (**his eleventh of the
  Series tying the record set by Babe
  Ruth in 1926**).
3 Davalillo, pinch-hitting for Alou,
  flied to short center.

4th Inning
New York
  For Oakland—Davalillo playing center
  with Jackson moving to right.
1 Garrett flied to center.
2 Millan fouled to Jackson making a
  running catch in the right field
  corner.
  Staub singled to center.
  Jones walked.
3 Milner grounded to second.
Oakland
1 Johnson called out on strikes.
2 Green grounded to third.
3 Holtzman fouled to Harrelson down
  the left field line.

5th Inning
New York
  Grote singled to left.
1 Hahn struck out.
2 Harrelson forced Grote at second,
  Campaneris to Green.
3 Beauchamp, batting for Parker,
  took a called third strike.

5th Inning (continued)
Oakland
  For New York—Sadecki pitching.
  Campaneris singled to left and went
  to second when the ball got by Jones.
  Rudi grounded to center, scoring
  Campaneris.
1 Bando lined to right.
2 Jackson fouled to Garrett.
3 Tenace popped to Harrelson in
  short center.

6th Inning
New York
1 Garrett struck out.
  Millan doubled to left-center.
  Staub doubled to right-center,
  scoring Millan.
  For Oakland—Fingers pitching.
2 Jones flied to deep right, Staub
  going to third after the catch.
3 Milner grounded to first.
Oakland
1 Davalillo flied to short right.
2 Johnson struck out.
3 Green grounded to short.

7th Inning
New York
  For Oakland—Fosse catching with
  Tenace moving over to play first.
1 Grote lined to left.
  Hahn singled to right.
2 Harrelson flied to Davalillo in
  left-center.
  Boswell, batting for Sadecki,
  singled to center, Hahn stopping
  at second.
3 Garrett called out on strikes (**his
  eleventh strikeout tying the Series
  record set by Eddie Mathews in 1958**).
Oakland
  For New York—Stone pitching.
  Fingers singled to right.
  Campaneris beat out a bunt to first.
1 Rudi took a called third strike.
2 Bando struck out.
3 Jackson struck out.

8th Inning
New York
1 Millan grounded to short.
2 Staub grounded to second.
3 Jones struck out.
Oakland
1 Tenace flied to Jones in left-center.
2 Davalillo grounded to second.
  Fosse singled to left.
3 Green grounded to short.

9th Inning
New York
  Milner walked.
1 Grote flied to left.
  Hahn singled to right, Milner
  stopping at second.
2 Harrelson thrown out by Fingers,
  both runners advancing.
  Kranepool, batting for Stone, safe
  at first on Tenace's fumble,
  Milner scoring and Hahn going
  to third.
  For Oakland—Knowles pitching (**his
  seventh appearance in seven games**).
  Martinez ran for Kranepool.
3 Garrett popped to short.

1973 WORLD SERIES COMPOSITE BOX

	Wins	Composite Line Score												Manager	Regular Season W	L	Pct.	G. Ahead	
Oakland Athletics (A.L.)	4	3 1 7	1 1 1	1 2 2	0 1 1	— 21								Dick Williams	94	68	.580	6	(beat Baltimore in playoffs)
New York Mets (N.L.)	3	5 2 1	4 0 6	0 1 1	0 0 4	— 24								Yogi Berra	82	79	.509	1.5	(beat Cincinnati in playoffs)

BATTING AND FIELDING

	WORLD SERIES STATISTICS Pos	G	AB	R	H	2B	3B	HR	RBI	BB	SO	SB	BA	SA	PO	A	E		REGULAR SEASON STATISTICS Main Pos	G	AB	R	H	2B	3B	HR	RBI	BB	SO	SB	BA	SA
OAKLAND ATHLETICS																																
Gene Tenace	1b-c	1	19	0	3	1	0	0	3	**11**	7	0	.158	.211	57	2	2		1b	160	510	83	132	18	2	24	84	101	94	2	.259	.443
Dick Green	2b	7	16	0	1	0	0	0	0	1	6	0	.063	.063	14	11	1		2b	133	332	33	87	17	0	3	42	21	63	0	.262	.340
Bert Campaneris	ss	7	31	**6**	9	0	**1**	1	3	1	7	**3**	.290	.452	10	**28**	1		ss	151	601	89	150	17	6	4	46	50	79	34	.250	.318
Sal Bando	3b	7	26	5	6	1	**1**	0	1	4	7	0	.231	.346	6	14	1		3b	162	592	97	170	32	3	29	98	82	84	4	.287	.498
Jesus Alou	rf-ph	7	19	0	3	1	0	0	3	0	0	0	.158	.211	5	0	0	a	of	36	108	10	33	3	0	1	11	2	6	0	.306	.361
Reggie Jackson	cf-rf	7	29	3	9	**3**	**1**	1	**6**	2	7	0	.310	.587	17	0	0		of	151	539	**99**	158	28	2	**32**	**117**	76	111	22	.293	**.531**
Joe Rudi	lf	7	27	3	9	2	0	0	4	3	4	0	.333	.407	20	2	0		of	120	437	53	118	25	1	12	66	30	72	0	.270	.414
Ray Fosse	c	7	19	0	3	1	0	0	0	1	4	0	.158	.211	32	3	0		c	143	492	37	126	23	2	7	52	25	62	2	.256	.354
Vic Davalillo	cf-ph-1b	6	11	0	1	0	0	0	0	2	1	0	.091	.091	15	0	0	b	1b-dh	38	64	5	12	1	0	0	4	3	4	0	.188	.203
Deron Johnson	ph-1b	6	10	0	3	1	0	0	0	1	4	0	.300	.400	8	1	0	c	dh	131	464	61	114	14	2	19	81	59	116	0	.246	.407
Angel Mangual	ph-cf	5	6	0	0	0	0	0	0	0	3	0	.000	.000	1	0	0		of	74	192	20	43	4	1	3	13	8	34	1	.224	.302
Ted Kubiak	2b	4	3	1	0	0	0	0	0	1	1	0	.000	.000	5	7	0		2b	106	182	15	40	6	1	3	17	12	19	1	.220	.313
Mike Andrews	ph-2b	2	3	0	0	0	0	0	0	1	1	0	.000	.000	1	0	2	d	2b	18	21	1	4	1	0	0	0	3	1	0	.190	.238
Pat Bourque	ph-1b	2	2	0	1	0	0	0	0	0	0	0	.500	.500	3	1	0	e	dh	23	42	8	8	4	1	2	9	15	10	0	.190	.476
Billy Conigliaro	ph	3	3	0	0	0	0	0	0	0	1	0	.000	.000					of	48	110	5	22	2	2	0	14	9	26	1	.200	.255
Allen Lewis	pr	3	0	1	0	0	0	0	0	0	0	0	—	—					pr	35	0	16	0	0	0	0	0	0	0	7	.000	.000
Bill North	Not in Series—Injured																		of	146	554	98	158	10	5	5	34	78	89	53	.285	.348
Catfish Hunter	p	2	5	0	0	0	0	0	0	0	3	0	.000	.000	1	2	1		p	37	1	0	1	0	0	0	0	0	0	0	1.000	1.000
Vida Blue	p	2	4	0	0	0	0	0	0	0	4	0	.000	.000	2	1	0		p	38	1	0	0	0	0	0	0	0	0	0	.000	.000
Rollie Fingers	p	6	3	0	1	0	0	0	0	0	1	0	.333	.333	0	2	0		p	62	1	0	0	0	0	0	0	0	1	0	.000	.000
Ken Holtzman	p	3	3	2	2	2	0	0	0	0	0	0	.667	1.333	1	3	0		p	41	0	0	0	0	0	0	0	1	0	0	—	—
Paul Lindblad	p	3	1	0	0	0	0	0	0	0	0	0	.000	.000	0	0	0		p	36	0	0	0	0	0	0	0	0	0	0	—	—
Blue Moon Odom	p-pr	3	1	0	0	0	0	0	0	0	1	0	.000	.000	0	1	0		p-pr	51	1	5	0	0	0	0	0	0	0	1	.000	.000
Darold Knowles	p	7	0	0	0	0	0	0	0	0	0	0	—	—	0	1	1		p	53	0	0	0	0	0	0	1	0	0	0	—	—
Horacio Pina	p	2	0	0	0	0	0	0	0	0	0	0	—	—	0	0	0		p	47	0	0	0	0	0	0	0	0	0	0	—	—
team total		7	241	21	51	12	3	2	20	28	62	3	.212	.311	198	79	9			162	5507	758	1431	216	28	147	**714**	595	919	128	.260	.389

Double Plays—8
Left on Bases—58

a—from Houston
b—from Pittsburgh
c—from Philadelphia
d—from Chicago (A)
e—from Chicago (N)

Mike Hegan (1b), Rich McKinney (ph), Dal Maxvill (ss 2b), Jay Johnstone (ph), Gonzalo Marquez (ph), Manny Trillo (2b), Tim Hosley (c), Phil Garner (3b), Rico Carty (ph), Jose Morales (dh), Larry Haney (c), Dave Hamilton (p), Glenn Abbott (p), Chuck Dobson (p),and Rod Gardner (p) also played for the Athletics during the season.

	WORLD SERIES STATISTICS Pos	G	AB	R	H	2B	3B	HR	RBI	BB	SO	SB	BA	SA	PO	A	E	REGULAR SEASON STATISTICS Main Pos	G	AB	R	H	2B	3B	HR	RBI	BB	SO	SB	BA	SA
NEW YORK METS																															
John Milner	1b	7	27	2	8	0	0	0	2	5	1	0	.296	.296	66	1	0	1b	129	451	69	108	12	3	23	72	62	84	1	.239	.432
Felix Millan	2b	7	**32**	3	6	1	**1**	0	1	1	1	0	.188	.281	16	13	**3**	2b	153	638	82	185	23	4	3	37	35	22	2	.290	.353
Bud Harrelson	ss	7	24	2	6	1	0	0	1	5	3	0	.250	.292	11	24	0	ss	106	356	35	92	12	3	0	20	48	48	5	.258	.309
Wayne Garrett	3b	7	30	4	5	0	0	**2**	2	5	**11**	0	.167	.367	4	19	**3**	3b	140	504	76	129	20	3	16	58	72	74	6	.256	.403
Rusty Staub	rf	7	26	1	**11**	2	0	1	**6**	2	2	0	**.423**	**.615**	5	0	0	of	152	585	77	163	36	1	15	76	74	52	1	.279	.421
Don Hahn	rf-cf	7	29	2	7	1	**1**	0	2	1	6	0	.241	.345	13	1	1	of	93	262	22	60	10	0	2	21	22	43	2	.229	.290
Cleon Jones	lf	7	28	5	8	2	0	1	1	4	2	0	.286	.464	11	1	1	of	92	339	48	88	13	0	11	48	28	51	1	.260	.395
Jerry Grote	c	7	30	2	8	0	0	0	0	0	1	0	.267	.267	**67**	5	0	c	84	285	17	73	10	2	1	32	13	23	0	.256	.316
Willie Mays	cf-pr-ph	3	7	1	2	0	0	0	1	0	1	0	.286	.286	1	0	1	of	66	209	24	44	10	0	6	25	27	47	1	.211	.344
George Theodore	ph-lf	2	2	0	0	0	0	0	0	0	0	0	.000	.000	1	0	0	of	45	116	14	30	4	0	1	15	10	13	1	.259	.319
Jim Beauchamp	ph	4	4	0	0	0	0	0	0	0	1	0	.000	.000				ph	50	61	5	17	1	1	0	14	7	11	1	.279	.328
Ed Kranepool	ph	4	3	0	0	0	0	0	0	0	0	0	.000	.000				1b-of	100	264	28	68	12	2	1	35	30	28	1	.239	.306
Ken Boswell	ph	3	3	1	3	0	0	0	0	0	0	0	1.000	1.000				ph	76	110	12	25	2	1	2	14	12	11	0	.227	.318
Ted Martinez	pr	2	0	0	0	0	0	0	0	0	0	0	—	—				ss-of	92	263	34	67	11	0	1	14	13	38	2	.255	.308
Ron Hodges	ph	1	0	0	0	0	0	0	0	1	0	0	—	—				c	45	127	5	33	2	0	1	18	11	19	0	.260	.299
Duffy Dyer	Did not play																	c	70	189	9	35	6	1	1	9	13	40	0	.185	.243
Tom Seaver	p	2	5	0	0	0	0	0	0	0	2	0	.000	.000	0	2	0	p	39	93	9	15	2	1	1	5	7	34	1	.161	.237
Jon Matlack	p	3	4	0	1	0	0	0	0	2	1	0	.250	.250	0	1	0	p	35	65	5	9	0	0	0	2	13	38	0	.138	.138
Jerry Koosman	p	2	4	0	0	0	0	0	0	0	3	0	.000	.000	0	1	1	p	35	78	3	8	1	0	0	3	2	37	0	.103	.115
Tug McGraw	p	5	3	1	1	0	0	0	0	0	1	0	.333	.333	0	3	0	p	60	24	0	4	0	0	0	2	2	9	0	.167	.167
Ray Sadecki	p	4	0	0	0	0	0	0	0	0	0	0	—	—	0	1	0	p	31	31	3	7	2	0	0	1	0	5	0	.226	.290
Harry Parker	p	3	0	0	0	0	0	0	0	0	0	0	—	—	0	0	0	p	38	23	0	4	0	0	0	2	0	8	0	.174	.174
George Stone	p	2	0	0	0	0	0	0	0	0	0	0	—	—	0	0	0	p	28	48	4	13	0	0	0	5	0	8	0	.271	.271
Jim McAndrew	Did not play																	p	24	15	3	2	1	0	0	2	6	7	0	.133	.200
Buzz Capra	Did not play																	p	24	2	1	0	0	0	0	0	2	0	0	.000	.000
team total		7	261	24	66	7	2	4	16	26	36	0	.253	.341	195	72	10		161	5457	608	1345	198	24	85	553	540	805	27	.246	.338

Double Plays—3
Left on Bases—72

Jim Fregosi (ss-3b), Jim Gosger (of), Dave Schneck (of), Rich Chiles (of, Jerry May (c), Brian Ostrosser (ss), Lute Barnes (ph), Greg Harts (ph), Tommy Moore (p), Craig Swan (p), Phil Hennigan (p), John Strohmayer (p), Hank Webb (p), Bob Apodaca (p), and Bob Miller (p) also played for the Mets during the season.

PITCHING

	WORLD SERIES STATISTICS G	GS	CG	IP	H	R	ER	BB	SO	W	L	SV	ERA	REGULAR SEASON STATISTICS G	GS	CG	IP	H	ER	BB	SO	W	L	Pct	SV	ShO	ERA
OAKLAND ATHLETICS																											
Rollie Fingers	6	0	0	13⅔	**13**	5	1	4	8	0	1	**2**	**0.66**	62	2	0	127	107	27	39	110	7	8	.467	22	0	1.91
Catfish Hunter	2	2	0	13⅓	11	3	3	4	6	1	0	0	2.03	36	36	11	256	222	95	69	124	21	5	**.808**	0	3	3.34
Vida Blue	2	2	0	11	10	6	**6**	3	8	0	1	0	4.91	37	37	13	264	214	96	105	158	20	9	.690	0	4	3.27
Ken Holtzman	3	**3**	0	10⅔	**13**	5	5	5	6	**2**	1	0	4.22	40	40	16	297	275	98	66	157	21	13	.618	0	4	2.97
Darold Knowles	**7**	0	0	6⅓	4	1	0	5	5	0	0	**2**	0.00	52	5	1	99	87	34	49	46	6	8	.429	9	1	3.09
Blue Moon Odom	2	0	0	4⅔	5	2	2	2	2	0	0	0	3.86	30	24	3	150	153	75	67	83	5	12	.294	0	0	4.50
Paul Lindblad	3	0	0	3⅓	4	0	0	1	1	1	0	0	0.00	36	3	0	78	89	32	28	33	1	5	.167	2	0	3.69
Horacio Pina	2	0	0	3	6	2	0	2	0	0	0	0	0.00	47	0	0	88	58	27	34	41	6	3	.667	8	0	2.76
team total	7	7	0	66	66	24	17	26	36	4	3	4	2.32	162	162	46	1457	1311	532	494	797	94	68	.580	41	16	3.29
NEW YORK METS																											
Jon Matlack	3	**3**	0	**16⅔**	10	**7**	4	5	11	1	**2**	0	2.16	34	34	14	242	210	86	99	205	14	16	.467	0	3	3.20
Tom Seaver	2	2	0	15	**13**	4	4	3	**18**	0	1	0	2.40	36	36	**18**	290	219	67	64	**251**	19	10	.655	0	3	**2.08**
Tug McGraw	5	0	0	13⅔	8	5	4	**9**	14	1	0	1	2.63	60	2	0	119	106	51	55	81	5	6	.455	25	0	3.86
Jerry Koosman	2	2	0	8⅔	9	3	3	7	8	1	0	0	3.12	35	35	12	263	234	83	76	156	14	15	.483	0	3	2.84
Ray Sadecki	4	0	0	4⅔	5	1	1	1	6	0	0	1	1.93	31	11	1	117	109	44	41	87	5	4	.556	1	0	3.38
Harry Parker	3	0	0	3⅓	2	1	0	2	2	0	1	0	0.00	38	9	0	97	79	36	36	63	8	4	.667	5	0	3.34
George Stone	2	0	0	3	4	0	0	1	3	0	0	1	0.00	27	20	2	148	157	46	31	77	12	3	.800	1	0	2.80
Jim McAndrew	Did not play													23	12	0	80	109	48	31	38	3	8	.273	1	0	5.40
Buzz Capra	Did not play													24	0	0	42	35	18	28	35	2	7	.222	**4**	0	3.86
team total	7	7	0	65	51	21	16	28	62	3	4	3	2.22	161	161	47	1465	1345	531	490	**1027**	82	79	.509	40	15	3.26

Total Attendance—358,289 Average Attendance—51,184 *Winning Player's Share—$24,618 Losing Player's Share—$14,950
*Includes Playoffs and World Series

1974
Finley's Unhappy Heroes

The Oakland A's did not exhibit the sort of solidarity that high-school coaches could use for their charges to copy. On the eve of the World Series, star pitcher Catfish Hunter was threatening to declare himself a free agent if owner Charley Finley didn't come up with some back pay owed to him, former A's player Mike Andrews filed a two million dollar libel suit against Finley for the 1973 Series incident involving them, pitchers Rollie Fingers and Blue Moon Odom punched each other out in the clubhouse the day before the first game, and star players Reggie Jackson and Vida Blue scarcely concealed their contempt for Finley. But through it all, new manager Alvin Dark stayed calm and comforted himself with reading the Bible, as the A's had battled through adversity to take the American League West and then do away with the Baltimore Orioles in four games in the A.L. championship series. The same old crew of spirited A's was back for a third straight year, with the cast of Jackson, Hunter, Blue, Fingers, Sal Bando, Bert Campaneris, Joe Rudi, Gene Tenace, and Ken Holtzman becoming fixtures to October baseball fans. The Los Angeles Dodgers had beaten the Pittsburgh Pirates in the National League play-offs to make this the first all-California World Series. The Dodgers brought a more conventional team spirit into the Series along with a host of talented players, with Steve Garvey, Jimmy Wynn, Davey Lopes, Billy Buckner, Ron Cey, Billy Russell, and Joe Ferguson shining every day in the lineup and with Andy Messersmith, Don Sutton, and rubber-armed reliever Mike Marshall spearheading the pitching staff.

Messersmith needed time to settle down in the opening game, serving up a home-run pitch to Jackson in the second inning before finding his groove. But Ken Holtzman, who didn't bat all season because of the American League's designated-hitter rule, doubled in the fifth and eventually scored on Campaneris's bunt. Errors by Campaneris and Jackson gave the Dodgers a run in the bottom of the fifth, but the A's again moved two runs in front by scoring in the eighth inning although being denied another run on a great throw by right fielder Ferguson, which cut Bando down at the plate trying to score after a fly ball. Wynn socked a home run in the ninth off Fingers, but then Dark brought in Hunter to fan Ferguson to end the game.

With Sutton pitching a superb game, the Dodgers led the second contest 3–0 after eight innings, with Ferguson's two-run homer off Blue the big offensive blow. But when Sutton hit Bando with a pitch and then gave up a double to Jackson at the start of the ninth inning, manager Walt Alston brought in Marshall. Rudi greeted him with a single that scored two runs and then, after Tenace struck out, left the game in favor of Herb Washington, a world-class sprinter signed by Finley as a pinch-running specialist. Marshall set the inexperienced Washington up with a few easy tosses to first base, then nailed him cleanly with a quick pick-off move. Marshall then fanned pinch hitter Angel Mangual to nail down the 3–2 victory.

The clubs then moved north to Oakland, where the A's would have things entirely their way. Sloppy Dodger fielding coupled with Hunter's fine performance gave the A's the 3–2 decision in game three. Despite Holtzman's home run, the A's trailed 2–1 going into the bottom of the sixth inning in game four. Messersmith walked Billy North, then let him go to second by making a wild pick-off throw. After Bando singled North in, Jackson walked, Rudi sacrificed, and young Claudell Washington got an intentional pass to load the bases. Dark sent unheralded Jim Holt up to hit for Ray Fosse, and Holt came through with a single to score two runs. The A's coasted home with a 5–2 win that put them completely in charge in the Series. The fifth game was tied 2–2 when the fans caused a six-minute delay in the bottom of the seventh inning by throwing debris on the field. As soon as play resumed, Rudi smashed a home run off Marshall to put the A's in front 3–2. The Dodgers had their last hurrah in the top of the eighth. Buckner drilled a single to center which bounced past North. After making it to second, Buckner tried to take third. Jackson, meanwhile, retrieved the ball and gunned it in to second baseman Dick Green on the edge of the outfield grass. Green spun and made a perfect throw to nail the sliding Buckner. The Dodgers went meekly to their grave after that, and the MVP award in Oakland's third straight World Series triumph went to Green, whose fine fielding throughout the classic more than offset his 0-for-13 batting.

Game 1 October 12 at Los Angeles

Oakland	Pos	AB	R	H	RBI	PO	A	E
Campaneris	ss	2	1	1	1	0	5	1
North	cf	2	0	0	0	4	0	0
Bando	3b	4	0	0	0	1	1	0
Jackson	rf	3	1	1	1	0	0	1
C. Washington	rf	0	0	0	0	0	0	0
Rudi	lf	4	0	2	0	6	0	0
Tenace	1b	3	0	1	0	6	1	0
Fosse	c	3	0	0	0	7	0	0
Green	2b	3	0	0	0	3	2	0
c Holt		1	0	0	0	0	0	0
Maxvill	2b	0	0	0	0	0	0	0
Holtzman	p	1	1	1	0	0	1	0
Fingers	p	2	0	0	0	0	0	0
Hunter	p	0	0	0	0	0	0	0
Totals		28	3	6	2	27	10	2

Los Angeles	Pos	AB	R	H	RBI	PO	A	E
Lopes	2b	5	1	0	0	5	0	0
Buckner	lf	5	0	2	0	2	0	0
Wynn	cf	4	1	1	1	1	0	0
Garvey	1b	5	0	2	0	6	1	0
d Paciorek		0	0	0	0	0	0	0
Ferguson	rf-c	3	0	0	0	2	1	0
Cey	3b	3	0	1	0	0	5	1
Russell	ss	4	0	1	0	2	0	0
Yeager	c	3	0	1	0	9	1	0
a Crawford		1	0	1	0	0	0	0
Messersmith	p	3	0	2	0	0	4	0
b Joshua		1	0	0	0	0	0	0
Marshall	p	0	0	0	0	0	0	0
Totals		37	2	11	1	27	12	1

	Oak.	L.A.
	010 010 010	000 010 001

Pitching

Oakland	IP	H	R	ER	BB	SO
Holtzman	4⅓	7	1	0	2	3
Fingers (W)	4⅓	4	1	1	1	3
Hunter (SV)	⅓	0	0	0	0	1
Los Angeles						
Messersmith (L)	8	5	3	2	3	8
Marshall	1	1	0	0	1	1

a Singled for Yeager in 8th.
b Grounded out for Messersmith in 8th.
c Popped out for Green in 9th.
d Ran for Garvey in 9th.

Double—Holtzman. Home Runs—Jackson, Wynn. Sacrifice Hits—Campaneris 2, North, Tenace. Double Plays—Campaneris to Green to Tenace to Yeager. Hit by Pitcher—Ferguson (by Fingers). Wild Pitch—Messersmith. Left on Bases—Oakland 6, Los Angeles 12. Umpires—Gorman (N), Kunkel (A), Harvey (N), Denkinger (A), Olsen (N), Luciano (A). Attendance—55,974. Time of Game—2:43.

1st Inning
Oakland
1 Campaneris flied to Wynn in deep left-center.
2 North grounded to third.
3 Bando flied to short left.
Los Angeles
1 Lopes took a called third strike. Buckner singled to left.
2 Wynn flied to short left.
3 Buckner caught off first and out, Holtzman to Tenace to Green.

2nd Inning
Oakland
Jackson hit a home run into the pavilion in left-center.
Rudi singled to center.
1 Tenace struck out.
2 Fosse forced Rudi at second, Cey to Lopes.
3 Green struck out.
Los Angeles
Garvey singled to right. Ferguson walked.
1,2 Cey hit into a double play, Campaneris to Green to Tenace, Garvey going to third.
3 Russell grounded to short.

3rd Inning
Oakland
Holtzman walked.
1 Campaneris sacrificed Holtzman to second, Messersmith to Garvey.
2 North struck out.
3 Bando struck out.
Los Angeles
Yeager singled to center. Messersmith popped a single to center, Yeager stopping at second.
1 Lopes fouled to Rudi.
2 Buckner flied to left.
3 Wynn forced Yeager at third, Bando unassisted.

4th Inning
Oakland
Jackson walked.
1 Rudi struck out.
2 Tenace forced Jackson at second, Cey to Lopes.
3 Fosse took a third strike.
Los Angeles
1 Garvey grounded to short.
2 Ferguson struck out. Cey singled to left. Russell singled off Bando, Cey racing to third.
3 Yeager forced Russell at second, Campaneris to Green.

5th Inning
Oakland
1 Green grounded to third. Holtzman doubled down the left field line. Holtzman went to third on a wild pitch.
2 Campaneris sacrifice squeezed Holtzman in, Messersmith to Garvey. North walked.
3 North was caught attempting to steal second, Yeager to Lopes.

5th Inning (continued)
Los Angeles
1 Messersmith struck out. Lopes safe on Campaneris' fumble. Buckner singled over Tenace's head and when Jackson fumbled the hit Lopes scored, Buckner holding first. Wynn walked.
For Oakland—Fingers pitching.
2 Garvey struck out. Ferguson was hit by a pitched ball, loading the bases.
3 Cey flied to left.

6th Inning
Oakland
1 Bando struck out.
2 Jackson bounced back to the mound.
3 Rudi popped to short.
Los Angeles
1 Russell grounded to third.
2 Yeager took a called third strike. Messersmith singled to left-center.
3 Lopes flied to North in short right-center.

7th Inning
Oakland
Tenace singled to left.
1 Fosse struck out, bunting foul on the third strike.
2 Green flied to left.
3 Fingers forced Tenace, Cey to Lopes.
Los Angeles
1 Buckner lined to left.
2 Wynn flied to center.
3 Garvey grounded to short.

8th Inning
Oakland
Campaneris singled to center.
1 North sacrificed Campaneris to second, Messersmith to Garvey. Bando's high chopper was thrown wildly to first by Cey allowing Campaneris to score and Bando to get to first.
2,3 Jackson flied to Ferguson in right-center, making the catch in front of Wynn, and threw perfectly to the plate to double Bando trying to score after the catch.
Los Angeles
For Oakland—C. Washington playing right.
1 Ferguson flied to short center. Cey walked.
2 Russell struck out. Crawford, batting for Yeager, singled to right, moving Cey to third.
3 Joshua, batting for Messersmith, grounded to second.

9th Inning
Oakland
For Los Angeles—Ferguson moved to catcher, Crawford in right, Marshall on the mound.
Rudi beat out a bunt to third.
1 Tenace sacrificed, Garvey to Lopes. Fosse walked.
2 Holt, batting for Green, popped to short.
3 Fingers took a called third strike.
Los Angeles
For Oakland—Maxvill at second.
1 Lopes flied to center.
2 Buckner flied to short left. Wynn homered over the left-center field wall. Garvey singled to center. Paciorek ran for Garvey. For Oakland—Hunter came in to pitch.
3 Ferguson struck out.

Game 2 October 13 at Los Angeles

Oak. 000 000 002
L.A. 010 002 00x

Oakland	Pos	AB	R	H	RBI	PO	A	E
Campaneris	ss	4	0	1	0	0	1	0
North	cf	4	0	0	0	3	0	0
Haney	c	0	0	0	0	2	0	0
Bando	3b	3	1	0	0	0	1	0
Jackson	rf	3	1	2	0	2	0	0
Rudi	lf	4	0	1	2	3	0	0
f H. Washington		0	0	0	0	0	0	0
Tenace	1b	3	0	0	0	8	0	0
Fosse	c	2	0	0	0	5	0	0
a Alou		1	0	0	0	0	0	0
Odom	p	0	0	0	0	0	0	0
e Mangual		1	0	0	0	0	0	0
Green	2b	2	0	0	0	1	2	0
b Holt		1	0	1	0	0	0	0
c Maxvill	2b	0	0	0	0	0	0	0
Blue	p	2	0	0	0	0	1	0
d C. Washington	cf	1	0	1	0	0	0	0
Totals		31	2	6	2	24	5	0

Los Angeles	Pos	AB	R	H	RBI	PO	A	E
Lopes	2b	4	0	0	0	3	2	0
Buckner	lf	4	0	0	0	3	0	0
Wynn	cf	3	0	0	0	0	0	0
Garvey	1b	4	1	2	0	7	0	0
Ferguson	rf	3	1	1	2	0	0	0
Cey	3b	3	1	0	0	2	1	0
Russell	ss	3	0	1	0	2	3	1
Yeager	c	3	0	2	1	10	1	0
Sutton	p	2	0	0	0	0	1	0
Marshall	p	0	0	0	0	0	1	0
Totals		29	3	6	3	27	9	1

Pitching	IP	H	R	ER	BB	SO
Oakland						
Blue (L)	7	6	3	3	2	5
Odom	1	0	0	0	1	2
Los Angeles						
Sutton (W)	*8	5	2	2	2	9
Marshall (SV)	1	1	0	0	0	2

*Pitched to 2 batters in 9th.

a Struck out for Fosse in 8th.
b Singled for Green in 8th.
c Ran for Holt in 8th.
d Singled for Blue in 8th.
e Struck out for Odom in 9th.
f Ran for Rudi in 9th.

Doubles—Campaneris, Jackson. Home Run—Ferguson. Stolen Base—Ferguson. Sacrifice Hit—Sutton. Double Plays—Sutton to Lopes to Garvey, Russell to Garvey. Hit by Pitcher—Bando (by Sutton). Wild Pitch—Sutton. Left on Bases—Oakland 5, Los Angeles 6. Umpires—Kunkel, Harvey, Denkinger, Olsen, Luciano, Gorman. Attendance—55,989. Time of Game—2:40.

1st Inning
Oakland
1 Campaneris struck out.
2 North struck out but Yeager threw to Garvey as third strike was in the dirt.
3 Bando fouled to Russell behind third.
Los Angeles
1 Lopes grounded to first.
2 Buckner took a called third strike.
Wynn walked.
3 Garvey popped to first.

2nd Inning
Oakland
1 Jackson fouled to Buckner.
2 Rudi struck out.
Tenace walked.
Tenace took second on a wild pitch.
3 Fosse struck out.
Los Angeles
1 Ferguson flied to North in deep left-center.
Cey walked.
Russell singled over Tenace's head, Cey going to third.
Yeager singled to center, scoring Cey as Russell stopped at second.
2 Sutton struck out.
3 Lopes struck out.

3rd Inning
Oakland
1 Green popped to Lopes in short right.
2 Blue struck out.
Campaneris doubled into the left field corner.
3 North bounced to short.
Los Angeles
1 Buckner flied to deep center.
2 Wynn took a called third strike.
Garvey beat out a chopper to deep short.
3 Ferguson flied to Jackson in right-center.

4th Inning
Oakland
1 Bando popped to third.
Jackson walked.
2 Rudi flied to short left.
3 Tenace fouled to Cey.
Los Angeles
1 Cey grounded to short.
2 Russell flied to right.
3 Yeager grounded to third.

5th Inning
Oakland
1 Fosse grounded to third.
2 Green struck out.
3 Blue called out on strikes.
Los Angeles
1 Sutton grounded to second.
2 Lopes popped to first.
3 Buckner lined to left.

6th Inning
Oakland
1 Campaneris struck out.
2 North rolled to second.
3 Bando lined to left.
Los Angeles
1 Wynn struck out.
Garvey beat out a bouncer to Campaneris behind second base.
Ferguson hit a two-run homer over the center field fence.
2 Cey fouled to Tenace.
3 Russell flied to short left.

7th Inning
Oakland
Jackson singled to center.
1 Rudi forced Jackson at second, Russell to Lopes.
2,3 Tenace hit into a double play, Sutton to Lopes to Garvey.
Los Angeles
Yeager singled to center.
1 Sutton sacrificed Yeager to second, Blue to Green covering first.
2 Lopes flied to North in deep left-center, Yeager going to third after the catch.
3 Buckner grounded to second.

8th Inning
Oakland
1 Alou, batting for Fosse, struck out.
Holt, batting for Green, singled to right.
Maxvill ran for Holt.
C. Washington, batting for Blue, singled to right, Maxvill stopping at second.
Campaneris safe at first on Russell's fumble, loading the bases.
2,3 North bounced into a double play, Russell to Garvey.
Los Angeles
For Oakland—C. Washington playing center, Haney catching (batting second), and Odom pitching (batting seventh).
1 Wynn struck out for the third time.
2 Garvey struck out.
Ferguson walked.
Ferguson stole second.
3 Cey flied to short left.

9th Inning
Oakland
Bando was hit by a pitched ball.
Jackson doubled inside the left field line, Bando stopping at third.
For Los Angeles—Marshall replaced Sutton on the mound.
Rudi lined a single to center, scoring Bando and Jackson.
1 Tenace struck out.
Mangual batted for Odom.
H. Washington ran for Rudi.
2 H. Washington was picked off first, Marshall to Garvey.
3 Mangual struck out.

Game 3 October 15 at Oakland

L.A. 000 000 011
Oak. 002 100 00x

Los Angeles	Pos	AB	R	H	RBI	PO	A	E
Lopes	2b	3	0	2	0	1	0	0
Buckner	lf	4	1	1	1	2	0	0
Wynn	cf	4	0	1	0	2	0	0
Garvey	1b	4	0	1	0	7	0	0
Crawford	rf	4	1	1	1	1	0	0
Ferguson	c	3	0	0	0	9	0	2
d Auerbach		0	0	0	0	0	0	0
Cey	3b	4	0	0	0	1	3	0
Russell	ss	4	0	0	0	0	3	0
Downing	p	1	0	0	0	0	3	0
a Lacy		1	0	0	0	0	0	0
Brewer	p	0	0	0	0	0	0	0
Hough	p	0	0	0	0	0	1	0
b Joshua		1	0	0	0	0	0	0
Marshall	p	0	0	0	0	0	1	0
Totals		33	2	7	2	24	10	2

Oakland	Pos	AB	R	H	RBI	PO	A	E
North	cf	4	1	1	0	5	0	0
Campaneris	ss	4	0	2	1	3	2	1
Bando	3b	3	1	0	0	0	1	0
Jackson	rf	3	0	0	0	2	0	0
C. Washington	rf	0	0	0	0	0	0	0
Rudi	lf	4	0	1	0	2	0	0
Tenace	1b	2	0	1	0	4	0	0
c H. Washington		0	0	0	0	0	0	0
Holt	1b	0	0	0	0	1	0	0
Fosse	c	3	0	0	0	5	0	0
Green	2b	3	1	0	0	4	4	1
Hunter	p	2	0	0	0	1	1	0
Fingers	p	0	0	0	0	0	0	0
Totals		29	3	5	2	27	8	2

Pitching	IP	H	R	ER	BB	SO
Los Angeles						
Downing (L)	3⅓	4	3	1	4	3
Brewer	⅔	0	0	0	0	1
Hough	2	0	0	0	1	0
Marshall	2	1	0	0	0	1
Oakland						
Hunter (W)	7⅓	5	1	1	2	4
Fingers	1⅔	2	1	1	0	1

a Struck out for Brewer in 5th.
b Flied out for Hough in 7th.
c Ran for Tenace in 8th.
d Ran for Ferguson in 9th.

Double—Campaneris. Home Runs—Buckner, Crawford. Stolen Bases—Jackson, Lopes 2. Sacrifice Hit—Hunter. Double Plays—Green to Campaneris, Green to Tenace, Green to Campaneris to Holt. Wild Pitch—Hough. Left on Bases—Los Angeles 6, Oakland 8. Umpires—Harvey, Denkinger, Olsen, Luciano, Gorman, Kunkel. Attendance—49,347. Time of Game—2:35.

1st Inning
Los Angeles
Lopes singled to center.
1 Buckner flied to Jackson in right-center.
Lopes stole second.
2 Wynn popped to Campaneris in short left.
Lopes stole third.
3 Garvey flied to short center.
Oakland
1 North struck out.
Campaneris doubled over Cey's head down the left field line.
2 Bando grounded to short, Campaneris holding second.
3 Jackson bounced back to the mound.

2nd Inning
Los Angeles
1 Crawford grounded to second.
2 Ferguson struck out.
3 Cey flied to left.
Oakland
1 Rudi grounded to short.
Tenace walked.
2 Fosse lined to Crawford in right-center.
3 Green struck out.

3rd Inning
Los Angeles
1 Russell popped to Hunter.
2 Downing bounced back to the pitcher.
Lopes walked.
3 Buckner grounded to first.
Oakland
1 Hunter struck out.
North singled to left.
2 Campaneris just out on a hard smash to third, as North raced all the way to third.
Bando walked.
Jackson safe at first when Ferguson fumbled his bouncer in front of the plate, North scoring with Bando going to second.
Rudi singled to center, scoring Bando as Jackson went to third.
Tenace walked, loading the bases.
3 Fosse tapped back to the mound.

4th Inning
Los Angeles
Wynn safe at first when his grounder deflected by Hunter was fumbled by Green.
Garvey singled to left, Wynn stopping at second.
1,2 Crawford lined to Green who threw to Campaneris doubling Wynn off second.
3 Ferguson struck out.
Oakland
Green walked.
1 Hunter sacrificed Green to second, Downing to Garvey.
2 North flied to left.
Campaneris singled to center, scoring Green and he went to third when Ferguson muffed Wynn's throw to the plate.
For Los Angeles—Brewer now pitching.
3 Bando struck out.

5th Inning
Los Angeles
1 Cey struck out.
2 Russell lined to center.
3 Lacy, pinch-hitting for Brewer, struck out.
Oakland
For Los Angeles—Hough pitching.
Jackson walked.
Jackson stole second.
1 Rudi struck out.
Jackson went to third on a wild pitch.
2 Tenace took a called third strike.
3 Fosse grounded to third.

6th Inning
Los Angeles
Lopes singled to center.
1 Buckner flied to right.
2 Wynn flied to North in left-center.
3 Garvey forced Lopes at second, Bando to Green.
Oakland
1 Green popped to third.
2 Hunter struck out.
3 North struck out.

7th Inning
Los Angeles
1 Crawford flied to center.
Ferguson walked.
2 Cey forced Ferguson at second, Campaneris to Green.
Russell blooped a single to left, Cey stopping at second.
3 Joshua, batting for Hough, flied to Rudi in left-center.
Oakland
For Los Angeles—Marshall pitching.
1 Campaneris grounded to short.
2 Bando grounded to short.
3 Jackson took a called third strike.

8th Inning
Los Angeles
For Oakland—C. Washington playing right.
1 Lopes lined to North making a back-handed catch near the fence.
Buckner homered into the right field stands.
For Oakland—Fingers came into pitch.
Wynn singled to left.
2,3 Garvey lined to Green who threw to Tenace doubling Wynn at first.
Oakland
1 Rudi bounced back to the mound.
Tenace singled to left.
H. Washington ran for Tenace.
2 Fosse popped to Lopes in short center.
3 Green flied to left.

9th Inning
Los Angeles
For Oakland—Holt playing first.
Crawford homered into the right-center field stands.
Ferguson safe on Campaneris' fumble.
Auerbach ran for Ferguson.
1 Cey struck out.
2,3 Russell hit into a game-ending double play, Green to Campaneris to Holt.

Game 4 October 16 at Oakland

Los Angeles	Pos	AB	R	H	RBI	PO	A	E
Lopes	2b	4	0	0	0	8	5	0
Buckner	lf	4	0	1	0	1	0	0
Wynn	cf	3	0	1	0	1	0	0
Garvey	1b	4	1	2	0	7	2	0
Ferguson	rf	3	1	0	0	0	0	0
Cey	3b	4	0	1	0	0	0	0
Russell	ss	4	0	1	2	0	4	0
Yeager	c	3	0	1	0	6	1	0
d Joshua		1	0	0	0	0	0	0
Messersmith	p	1	0	0	0	1	0	1
c Paciorek		1	0	0	0	0	0	0
Marshall	p	0	0	0	0	0	1	0
Totals		32	2	7	2	24	13	1

Pitching	IP	H	R	ER	BB	SO
Los Angeles						
Messersmith (L)	6	6	5	5	4	4
Marshall	2	1	0	0	0	2
Oakland						
Holtzman (W)	$7\frac{2}{3}$	6	2	2	2	7
Fingers (SV)	$1\frac{1}{3}$	1	0	0	0	2

L.A.	000	200	000
Oak.	001	004	00x

Oakland	Pos	AB	R	H	RBI	PO	A	E
Campaneris	ss	3	0	0	0	1	4	0
North	cf	3	1	0	0	3	0	0
Bando	3b	3	1	1	1	0	4	0
Jackson	rf	3	1	1	0	0	0	0
Rudi	1b-lf	3	0	0	0	10	0	0
C. Washington	lf	3	1	2	0	0	0	0
Tenace	1b	0	0	0	0	1	0	0
Fosse	c	2	0	1	0	6	0	0
a Holt		1	0	1	2	0	0	0
b H. Washington		0	0	0	0	0	0	0
Haney	c	0	0	0	0	4	0	0
Green	2b	2	0	0	1	2	4	0
Holtzman	p	3	1	1	1	0	2	0
Fingers	p	0	0	0	0	0	0	0
Totals		26	5	7	5	27	14	0

a Singled for Fosse in 6th.
b Ran for Holt in 6th.
c Grounded out for Messersmith in 7th.
d Hit into double play for Yeager in 9th.

Doubles—Buckner, Wynn, Yeager. Triple—Russell. Home Run—Holtzman. Sacrifice Hits—Green, Messersmith, Rudi. Double Plays—Lopes to Garvey, Russell to Lopes to Garvey, Green to Campaneris to Tenace. Hit by Pitcher—Campaneris (by Messersmith). Wild Pitch—Holtzman. Left on Bases—Los Angeles 6, Oakland 4. Umpires—Denkinger, Olsen, Luciano, Gorman, Kunkel, Harvey. Attendance—49,347. Time of Game—2:17.

1st Inning
Los Angeles
1 Lopes flied to center.
Buckner doubled out of C. Washington's glove in the left field corner.
2 Wynn struck out.
3 Garvey struck out.
Oakland
Campaneris was hit by a pitch.
1 Campaneris caught stealing, Yeager to Lopes.
2 North bunted out to second.
3 Bando struck out.

2nd Inning
Los Angeles
1 Ferguson grounded to Green, making an excellent stop behind second.
2 Cey lined to deep center.
3 Russell grounded to short.
Oakland
1 Jackson lined to Wynn, who made a running catch in left-center.
2 Rudi grounded to second.
C. Washington beat out a hit to deep short.
3 Fosse struck out.

3rd Inning
Los Angeles
Yeager doubled to the left-center field wall.
1 Messersmith sacrificed Yeager to third, Bando to Green.
2 Lopes struck out.
3 Buckner bunted out to the mound with a two strike count.
Oakland
1 Green grounded to short.
Holtzman homered over the left field fence.
2 Campaneris fouled to Messersmith between first and home on a bunt attempt.
3 North grounded to second.

4th Inning
Los Angeles
1 Wynn bounced out off Holtzman to Green who threw to first for the out.
Garvey singled to right.
Ferguson walked.
2 Cey struck out.
Russell lined a triple to the right-center field wall, scoring Garvey and Ferguson.
3 Yeager fouled to Fosse.
Oakland
Bando walked.
1 Jackson struck out.
2,3 Rudi lined to Lopes who threw to Garvey doubling Bando off of first.

5th Inning
Los Angeles
1 Messersmith called out on strikes.
2 Lopes grounded to short.
3 Buckner popped to Green in short right.
Oakland
C. Washington singled to center.
Fosse singled to left-center, C. Washington stopping at second.
1 Green sacrificed up both runners, Garvey to Lopes.
2 Holtzman struck out.
3 Campaneris flied to deep left.

6th Inning
Los Angeles
Wynn doubled to left-center.
1 Garvey grounded to third, Wynn holding at second.
2 Ferguson grounded to third, Wynn still holding at second.
Wynn went to third on a wild pitch.
3 Cey grounded to third.
Oakland
North walked.
North went to second on Messersmith's wild pickoff throw.
Bando singled to right, North scoring.
Jackson walked.
1 Rudi sacrificed up both runners, Garvey to Lopes.
C. Washington got an intentional pass, loading the bases.
Holt, pinch-hitting for Fosse, singled to right, scoring Bando and Jackson with C. Washington racing to third.
H. Washington ran for Holt.
2 Green forced H. Washington at second, Russell to Lopes as C. Washington scored.
3 Holtzman forced Green at second, Russell to Lopes.

7th Inning
Los Angeles
For Oakland—Haney catching.
1 Russell flied to North in left-center.
2 Yeager struck out.
3 Paciorek, batting for Messersmith, grounded to short.
Oakland
For Los Angeles—Marshall on the mound.
1 Campaneris is popped to second.
2 North struck out.
3 Bando tapped back to the mound.

8th Inning
Los Angeles
1 Lopes struck out.
2 Buckner grounded to second.
Wynn walked.
Garvey singled to left, Wynn stopping at second.
For Oakland—Fingers now pitching.
3 Ferguson struck out.
Oakland
Jackson singled off Russell's glove.
1,2 Rudi for the second time in the game hit into a double play, Russell to Lopes to Garvey.
3 C. Washington struck out.

9th Inning
Los Angeles
For Oakland—Rudi moves to left with Tenace coming in to play first.
Cey singled to center.
1 Russell struck out.
2,3 Joshua, batting for Yeager, hit a sharp grounder to the right of second. Green made a diving stop flipped to Campaneris who threw to Tenace for a game-ending double play.

Game 5 October 17 at Oakland

Los Angeles	Pos	AB	R	H	RBI	PO	A	E
Lopes	2b	2	1	0	0	2	2	0
Buckner	lf	3	0	1	0	3	0	0
Wynn	cf	2	0	0	1	3	0	0
Garvey	1b	4	0	1	1	4	0	0
Ferguson	rf	4	0	1	0	3	0	0
Cey	3b	3	0	1	0	2	0	0
Russell	ss	3	0	0	0	0	1	0
b Crawford		1	0	0	0	0	0	0
Yeager	c	2	0	0	0	7	1	1
c Joshua		1	0	0	0	0	0	0
Sutton	p	1	0	0	0	0	1	0
a Paciorek		1	1	1	0	0	0	0
Marshall	p	0	0	0	0	0	1	0
Totals		27	2	5	2	24	6	1

a Doubled for Sutton in 6th.
b Popped out for Russell in 9th.
c Grounded out for Yeager in 9th.

Double—Paciorek. Home Runs—Fosse, Rudi. Stolen Bases—Campaneris, North. Sacrifice Hit--Buckner. Sacrifice Flies—Bando, Wynn. Double Play—Campaneris to Green to Rudi. Left on Bases—Los Angeles 6, Oakland 3. Umpires—Olsen, Luciano, Gorman, Kunkel, Harvey, Denkinger. Attendance—49,347. Time of Game—2:23.

L.A.	000	002	000
Oak.	110	000	10x

Oakland	Pos	AB	R	H	RBI	PO	A	E
Campaneris	ss	4	0	2	0	2	4	0
North	cf	4	1	0	0	2	0	1
Bando	3b	3	0	0	1	1	3	0
Jackson	rf	2	0	0	0	2	1	0
Rudi	1b-lf	3	1	2	1	7	0	0
C. Washington	lf	3	0	1	0	3	0	0
Fingers	p	0	0	0	0	0	1	0
Fosse	c	3	1	1	1	4	1	0
Green	2b	3	0	0	0	5	2	0
Blue	p	2	0	0	0	0	2	0
Odom	p	0	0	0	0	0	0	0
Tenace	1b	1	0	0	0	1	0	0
Totals		28	3	6	3	27	14	1

Pitching	IP	H	R	ER	BB	SO
Los Angeles						
Sutton	5	4	2	2	1	3
Marshall (L)	3	2	1	1	0	4
Oakland						
Blue	$6\frac{2}{3}$	4	2	2	5	4
Odom (W)	$\frac{1}{3}$	0	0	0	0	0
Fingers (SV)	2	1	0	0	1	0

1st Inning
Los Angeles
1 Lopes grounded to third.
2 Buckner popped to Campaneris behind third.
3 Wynn fouled to Rudi
Oakland
Campaneris singled to left.
1 North forced Campaneris at second, Russell to Lopes.
North stole second and went to third when Yeager's throw went into center.
2 Bando lined a sacrifice fly to left, North scoring after the catch.
Jackson walked.
Rudi singled to center, Jackson going to third.
3 C. Washington flied to short right.

2nd Inning
Los Angeles
1 Garvey grounded to short.
Ferguson singled to center.
Cey singled to left, Ferguson stopping at second.
2 Russell flied to North in right-center, Ferguson advancing to third after the catch as Cey held at first.
3 Yeager struck out.
Oakland
Fosse homered into the left field stands.
1 Green lined to Wynn in left-center.
2 Blue took a called third strike.
3 Campaneris flied to right.

3rd Inning
Los Angeles
1 Sutton took a called third strike.
Lopes walked.
2 Lopes caught trying to steal second, Fosse to Campaneris.
3 Buckner tapped back to the mound.
Oakland
1 North popped to third.
2 Bando flied to deep center.
3 Jackson struck out.

4th Inning
Los Angeles
1 Wynn's grounder deflected by Blue to Campaneris who threw to Rudi for the out.
2 Garvey lined to right.
3 Ferguson took a called third strike.
Oakland
1 Rudi flied to deep left.
C. Washington singled to right.
2 C. Washington caught trying to steal second, Yeager to Lopes.
3 Fosse bounced back to the mound.

5th Inning
Los Angeles
Cey walked.
1,2 Russell hit into a double play, Campaneris to Green to Rudi.
3 Yeager struck out.
Oakland
1 Green flied to Ferguson in right-center.
2 Blue again called out on strikes.
3 Campaneris flied to right.

6th Inning
Los Angeles
Paciorek, pinch-hitting for Sutton, lined a double to left-center.
Lopes walked.
1 Buckner sacrificed Paciorek to third and Lopes to second, Bando to Green.
2 Wynn hit a sacrifice fly to left, Paciorek scoring after the catch with Lopes holding second.
Garvey singled to left, scoring Lopes.
3 Ferguson flied to right.
Oakland
For Los Angeles—Marshall pitching.
1 North grounded to second.
2 Bando struck out.
3 Johnson grounded to second.

7th Inning
Los Angeles
1 Cey popped to second.
2 Russell grounded to third.
Yeager walked.
For Oakland—Odom replaced Blue with a 2–0 count to Marshall.
Marshall walked (charged to Blue).
3 Lopes forced Marshall at second, Campaneris to Green.
Oakland
Rudi hit the first pitch into the left field stands for a home run.
1 C. Washington fouled to Cey.
2 Fosse struck out.
3 Green struck out.

8th Inning
Los Angeles
For Oakland—Rudi moves to left, Tenace playing first (batting 9th), and Fingers on the mound (batting 6th).
Buckner singled to right center but North lost the ball, Buckner tried to go all the way to third but was
1 out, Jackson to Green to Bando on perfect throws.
Wynn walked.
2 Garvey flied to right.
3 Ferguson flied to short center.
Oakland
1 Tenace struck out.
Campaneris beat out a bunt down the third base line.
Campaneris stole second.
2 North flied to center, Campaneris advancing to third after the catch.
3 Bando tapped back to the mound.

9th Inning
Los Angeles
1 Cey flied to deep right.
2 Crawford, pinch-hitting for Russell, popped to Green in short center.
3 Joshua, pinch-hitting for Yeager, tapped back to the mound to end the Series.

1974 WORLD SERIES COMPOSITE BOX

	Wins	Composite Line Score
Oakland Athletics (A.L.)	4	1 2 3 1 1 4 1 1 2 - 16
Los Angeles Dodgers (N.L.)	1	0 1 0 2 1 4 0 1 2 - 11

Manager	W	L	Pct.	G. Ahead	
	Regular Season				
Dick Williams	90	72	.556	5	(beat Baltimore in playoffs)
Walt Alston	102	60	.630	4	(beat Pittsburgh in playoffs)

BATTING AND FIELDING

OAKLAND ATHLETICS

	WORLD SERIES STATISTICS Pos	G	AB	R	H	2B	3B	HR	RBI	BB	SO	SB	BA	SA	PO	A	E	REGULAR SEASON STATISTICS Main Pos	G	AB	R	H	2B	3B	HR	RBI	BB	SO	SB	BA	SA
Gene Tenace	1b-c	5	9	0	2	0	0	0	0	3	4	0	.222	.222	20	1	0	1b-c	158	484	71	102	17	1	26	73	110	105	2	.211	.411
Dick Green	2b	5	13	1	0	0	0	0	1	1	4	0	.000	.000	15	14	1	2b	100	287	20	61	8	2	2	22	22	50	2	.213	.275
Bert Campaneris	ss	5	17	1	6	2	0	0	2	0	2	1	.353	.444	6	16	2	ss	134	527	77	153	18	8	2	41	47	81	34	.290	.366
Sal Bando	3b	5	16	3	1	0	0	0	2	2	5	0	.063	.063	2	10	0	3b	146	498	84	121	21	2	22	103	86	79	2	.243	.426
Reggie Jackson	rf	5	14	3	4	1	0	1	1	5	3	1	.286	.571	6	1	1	of	148	506	90	146	25	1	29	93	86	105	25	.289	.514
Bill North	cf	5	17	3	1	0	0	0	0	2	5	1	.059	.059	17	0	1	of	149	543	79	141	20	5	4	33	69	86	54	.260	.337
Joe Rudi	lf-1b	5	18	1	6	0	0	1	4	0	3	0	.333	.500	28	0	0	of	158	593	73	174	39	4	22	99	34	92	2	.293	.484
Ray Fosse	c	5	14	1	2	0	0	1	1	1	5	0	.143	.357	27	1	0	c	69	204	20	40	8	3	4	23	11	31	1	.196	.324
C. Washington	rf-ph-cf-lf	5	7	1	4	0	0	0	0	1	1	0	.571	.571	3	0	0	dh-of	73	221	16	63	10	5	0	19	13	44	6	.285	.376
Jim Holt	ph-1b	4	3	0	2	0	0	0	2	0	0	0	.667	.667	1	0	0	a 1b	30	42	1	6	0	0	0	0	1	9	0	.143	.143
Larry Haney	c	2	0	0	0	0	0	0	0	0	0	0	—	—	6	0	0	c	76	121	12	20	4	0	2	3	3	18	1	.165	.248
Dal Maxvill	2b-pr	2	0	0	0	0	0	0	0	0	0	0	—	—	2	0	0	b 2b-ss	60	52	3	10	0	0	0	2	8	10	0	.192	.192
Herb Washington	pr	3	0	0	0	0	0	0	0	0	0	0	—	—	0	0	0	pr	92	0	29	0	0	0	0	0	0	0	29	.000	.000
Jesus Alou	ph	1	1	0	0	0	0	0	0	0	1	0	.000	.000	0	0	0	dh	96	220	13	59	8	0	2	15	5	9	0	.268	.332
Angel Mangual	ph	1	1	0	0	0	0	0	0	0	1	0	.000	.000	0	0	0	of	115	365	37	85	14	4	9	43	17	59	3	.233	.367
Ted Kubiak	Did not play																	2b	99	220	22	46	3	0	0	18	18	15	1	.209	.223
Ken Holtzman	p	2	4	2	2	1	0	1	1	1	1	0	.500	1.500	0	3	0	p	39	0	0	0	0	0	0	0	0	0	0	—	—
Vida Blue	p	2	4	0	0	0	0	0	0	0	4	0	.000	.000	0	3	0	p	40	0	0	0	0	0	0	0	0	0	0	—	—
Rollie Fingers	p	4	2	0	0	0	0	0	0	0	1	0	.000	.000	0	1	0	p	76	0	0	0	0	0	0	0	0	0	0	—	—
Catfish Hunter	p	2	2	0	0	0	0	0	0	0	2	0	.000	.000	1	1	0	p	41	0	0	0	0	0	0	0	0	0	0	—	—
Blue Moon Odom	p	2	0	0	0	0	0	0	0	0	0	0	—	—	0	0	0	p-pr	43	0	3	0	0	0	0	0	0	0	0	—	—
Glenn Abbott	Did not play																	p	19	0	0	0	0	0	0	0	0	0	0	—	—
Dave Hamilton	Did not play																	p	29	0	0	0	0	0	0	0	0	0	0	—	—
Darold Knowles	Did not play																	p	45	0	0	0	0	0	0	0	0	0	0	—	—
Paul Lindblad	Did not play																	p	45	0	0	0	0	0	0	0	0	0	0	—	—
team total		5	142	16	30	4	0	4	14	16	42	3	.211	.324	132	51	5		162	5331	689	1315	205	37	132	637	568	876	164	.247	.373

Double Plays—6
Left on Bases—26

a—from Minnesota
b—from Pittsburgh

Pat Bourque (1b), Vic Davalillo (dh-of), John Donaldson (2b), Phil Garner (3b), Tim Hosley (c), Deron Johnson (dh), Rich McKinney (ph), Gaylen Pitts (3b), John Summers (of), Manny Trillo (2b), Leon Hooten (p), and Bill Parsons (p) also played for the Athletics during the season.

LOS ANGELES DODGERS

	WORLD SERIES STATISTICS Pos	G	AB	R	H	2B	3B	HR	RBI	BB	SO	SB	BA	SA	PO	A	E	REGULAR SEASON STATISTICS Main Pos	G	AB	R	H	2B	3B	HR	RBI	BB	SO	SB	BA	SA
Steve Garvey	1b	5	21	2	8	0	0	0	1	0	3	0	.381	.381	34	3	0	1b	156	642	95	200	32	3	21	111	31	66	5	.312	.469
Dave Lopes	2b	5	18	2	2	0	0	0	0	3	4	2	.111	.111	19	9	0	2b	145	530	95	141	26	3	10	35	66	71	59	.266	.383
Bill Russell	ss	5	18	0	4	0	1	0	2	0	2	0	.222	.333	4	11	1	ss	160	553	61	149	18	6	5	65	53	53	14	.269	.351
Ron Cey	3b	5	17	1	3	0	0	0	0	3	3	0	.176	.176	5	9	1	3b	159	577	88	151	20	2	18	97	76	68	1	.262	.397
Joe Ferguson	rf-c	5	16	2	2	0	0	1	2	4	6	1	.125	.313	14	1	2	c	111	349	54	88	14	1	16	57	75	73	2	.252	.436
Jim Wynn	cf	5	16	1	3	1	0	1	2	4	4	0	.188	.438	5	0	0	of	150	535	104	145	17	4	32	108	108	104	18	.271	.497
Bill Buckner	lf	5	20	1	5	1	0	1	1	0	1	0	.250	.450	11	0	0	of	145	580	83	182	30	3	7	58	30	24	31	.314	.412
Steve Yeager	c	4	11	0	4	1	0	0	1	1	4	0	.364	.455	32	4	1	c	94	316	41	84	16	1	12	41	32	77	2	.266	.437
Willie Crawford	ph-rf	3	6	1	2	0	0	1	1	0	0	0	.333	.500	1	0	0	of	139	468	73	138	23	4	11	61	64	88	7	.295	.432
Von Joshua	ph	4	4	0	0	0	0	0	0	0	0	0	.000	.000	0	0	0	ph-of	81	124	11	29	5	1	1	16	7	17	3	.234	.315
Tom Paciorek	pr-ph	3	2	1	1	1	0	0	0	0	0	0	.500	1.000	0	0	0	of	85	175	23	42	8	6	1	24	10	32	1	.240	.371
Lee Lacy	ph	1	1	0	0	0	0	0	0	0	1	0	.000	.000	0	0	0	2b	48	78	13	22	6	0	0	8	2	14	2	.282	.359
Rick Auerbach	pr	1	0	0	0	0	0	0	0	0	0	0	—	—	0	0	0	ss-2b	45	73	12	25	0	0	1	4	8	9	4	.342	.384
Gail Hopkins	Did not play																	ph	15	18	1	4	0	0	0	0	3	1	0	.222	.222
Ken McMullen	Did not play																	ph	44	60	5	15	1	0	3	12	2	12	0	.250	.417
Manny Mota	Did not play																	ph	66	57	5	16	2	0	0	16	5	4	0	.281	.316
Andy Messersmith	p	2	4	0	2	0	0	0	0	0	2	0	.500	.500	1	4	1	p	39	96	12	23	8	0	1	11	11	28	0	.240	.354
Don Sutton	p	2	3	0	0	0	0	0	0	0	2	0	.000	.000	0	2	0	p	40	98	7	18	2	0	0	7	3	22	0	.184	.204
Al Downing	p	1	1	0	0	0	0	0	0	0	0	0	.000	.000	0	3	0	p	21	29	3	5	0	0	0	2	1	11	0	.172	.172
Mike Marshall	p	5	0	0	0	0	0	0	0	1	0	0	.000	.000	0	4	0	p	106	34	2	8	0	0	0	2	0	3	0	.235	.235
Jim Brewer	p	1	0	0	0	0	0	0	0	0	0	0	—	—	0	0	0	p	24	2	0	0	0	0	0	0	0	1	0	.000	.000
Charlie Hough	p	1	0	0	0	0	0	0	0	0	0	0	—	—	0	0	0	p	49	12	0	0	0	0	0	0	1	2	0	.000	.000
Doug Rau	Did not play																	p	36	64	3	9	0	0	0	4	6	22	0	.141	.141
Eddie Solomon	Did not play																	p	4	0	0	0	0	0	0	0	0	0	0	.000	.000
Geoff Zahn	Did not play																	p	21	23	2	4	0	0	0	0	0	5	0	.174	.174
Tommy John	Not in Series—Injured																	p	22	51	0	6	2	0	0	2	2	10	0	.118	.157
team total		5	158	11	36	4	1	4	10	16	32	3	.228	.342	126	50	6		162	5557	798	1511	231	34	139	744	597	820	149	.272	.401

Double Plays—5
Left on Bases—36

Orlando Alvarez (of), Ivan DeJesus (ss), John Hale (of), Charles Manuel (ph), Kevin Pasley (c), Jerry Royster (ph), Rex Hudson (p), Rich Rhoden (p), and Greg Shanahan (p) also played for the Dodgers during the season.

PITCHING

OAKLAND ATHLETICS

	WORLD SERIES STATISTICS G	GS	CG	IP	H	R	ER	BB	SO	W	L	SV	ERA	REGULAR SEASON STATISTICS G	GS	CG	IP	H	ER	BB	SO	W	L	Pct	SV	ShO	ERA
Vida Blue	2	2	0	13⅔	10	5	5	7	9	0	1	0	3.29	40	40	12	282	246	102	98	174	17	15	.531	0	1	3.26
Ken Holtzman	2	2	0	12	13	3	2	4	10	1	0	0	1.50	39	38	9	255	273	87	51	117	19	17	.528	0	3	3.07
Rollie Fingers	4	0	0	9⅓	8	2	2	2	6	1	0	2	1.93	76	0	0	119	104	35	29	95	9	5	.643	18	0	2.65
Catfish Hunter	2	1	0	7⅔	5	1	1	2	5	1	0	1	1.17	41	41	23	318	268	88	46	143	25	12	.676	0	6	2.49
Blue Moon Odom	2	0	0	1⅓	0	0	0	1	2	1	0	0	0.00	34	5	1	87	85	37	52	52	1	5	.167	1	0	3.83
Glenn Abbott	Did not play													19	17	3	96	89	32	34	38	5	7	.417	0	0	3.00
Dave Hamilton	Did not play													29	18	1	117	104	41	48	69	7	4	.636	0	1	3.15
Darold Knowles	Did not play													45	1	0	53	61	25	35	18	3	3	.500	3	0	4.25
Paul Lindblad	Did not play													45	2	0	101	85	23	30	46	4	4	.500	6	0	2.05
team total	5	5	0	44	36	11	10	16	32	4	1	3	2.05	162	162	49	1440	1322	472	430	755	90	72	.556	28	12	2.95

LOS ANGELES DODGERS

	WORLD SERIES STATISTICS G	GS	CG	IP	H	R	ER	BB	SO	W	L	SV	ERA	REGULAR SEASON STATISTICS G	GS	CG	IP	H	ER	BB	SO	W	L	Pct	SV	ShO	ERA
Andy Messersmith	2	2	0	14	11	8	7	7	12	0	2	0	4.50	39	39	13	292	227	84	94	221	20	6	.769	0	3	2.59
Don Sutton	2	2	0	13	9	4	4	3	12	1	0	0	2.77	40	40	10	276	241	99	80	179	19	9	.679	0	5	3.23
Mike Marshall	5	0	0	9	6	1	1	1	10	0	1	1	1.00	106	0	0	208	191	56	56	143	15	12	.556	21	0	2.42
Al Downing	1	1	0	3⅔	4	3	1	4	3	0	1	0	2.45	21	16	1	98	94	40	45	63	5	6	.455	0	1	3.67
Charlie Hough	1	0	0	2	0	0	0	0	4	0	0	0	0.00	49	0	0	96	65	40	40	63	9	4	.692	1	0	3.75
Jim Brewer	1	0	0	⅓	0	0	0	0	1	0	0	0	0.00	24	0	0	39	29	11	10	26	4	4	.500	0	0	2.54
Doug Rau	Did not play													36	35	3	198	191	82	70	126	13	11	.542	0	1	3.73
Eddie Solomon	Did not play													4	0	0	6	5	1	2	2	0	0	—	1	0	1.50
Geoff Zahn	Did not play													21	10	1	80	78	18	16	33	3	5	.375	0	0	2.03
Tommy John	Not in Series—Injured													22	22	5	153	133	44	42	78	13	3	.813	0	3	2.59
team total	5	5	0	42	30	16	13	16	42	1	4	1	2.79	162	162	33	1465	1272	484	464	943	102	60	.630	23	19	2.97

Total Attendance—260,004 Average Attendance—52,000 *Winning Player's share—$22,219 *Losing Player's Share—$15,704
*Includes Playoffs and World Series.

1975
Game Six

Seventy million estimated viewers tuned in to watch the seventh game of the World Series as the underdog Boston Red Sox lost 4–3 to the Cincinnati Reds to end the most dramatic postseason play in years. For Boston, the road to the top had been difficult, but thanks to the fine play of rookies Fred Lynn and Jim Rice, the Red Sox managed to hold off Baltimore in the American League East. Although Rice, who broke his wrist on September 21, was not around at the finish, the surprising Red Sox easily dethroned Oakland in three straight to take the pennant. By contrast, the Reds' appearance in the Series was a much easier chore as they coasted to a 20-game Western title before beating Pittsburgh three straight in the play-offs.

The first game in Boston matched Luis Tiant, an 18-game winner who was rescued from the scrap heap in 1971 by Boston, against Don Gullett, who compiled a 15–4 record although out with an injury for over two months. Boston rallied for six runs in the seventh and Tiant, the cigar-smoking Cuban, kept the Reds intact to notch a five-hit 6–0 shutout. Boston seemed on their way to taking the second game, leading 2–1 in the ninth, but Bill Lee and reliever Dick Drago could no longer contain the Reds, as a double by Johnny Bench, a single by Dave Concepcion, and a double by Ken Griffey brought a 3–2 victory. The third game, which took place in Cincinnati, matched Gary Nolan, 15–9, against Boston's Rick Wise, 19–12. Although the game featured six home runs, a disputed call on a bunt proved the difference. After Dwight Evans's two-run shot in the ninth tied the game at 5–5, Cesar Geronimo opened the tenth for the Reds with a single. Ed Armbrister then batted for reliever Rawly Eastwick and bunted in front of the plate. Carlton Fisk retrieved the ball and attempted to throw to second to nail Geronimo, but with Armbrister standing in his path, Fisk threw the ball into center field. When the play was over, Geronimo was at third and Armbrister at second. Boston screamed "Interference" to home-plate umpire Larry Barnett, but the call went unchanged. Pete Rose then got an intentional pass and, after pinch hitter Merv Rettenmund struck out, Joe Morgan singled to end the controversial game at 6–5.

Tiant returned the next night against Fred Norman, 12–4 on the season, as Boston again provided Tiant with a big inning when they scored five times in the fourth. But before Tiant could claim his second win, Lynn had to come up with a great catch in the ninth with two runners on base to preserve the 5–4 equalizer. In the fifth game, Tony Perez, who had gone 0–15, came through with two home runs as the Reds won 6–2.

The Series was to return to Boston after a day off for travel, but a steady downpour postponed the sixth game for three days. With Tiant on the mound, Lynn hit a three-run homer in the first. The Reds tied the game as Lynn was shaken up on a triple off the left-field wall by Griffey which scored the Reds' first two runs. In the seventh, Cincinnati went ahead 5–3 on a double by George Foster. Geronimo's leadoff home run in the eighth spelled the end for Tiant, who left the game to a standing ovation. With all hope seemingly gone, Boston's fortunes suddenly turned in the bottom of the eighth as Bernie Carbo, who had berated manager Darrell Johnson for not playing him as a regular in the Series, fouled off a 3–2 pitch before delivering his second pinch homer to tie the score at 6–6. In the ninth, with the bases loaded for the Red Sox with no outs, Lynn flied to Foster in left. Foster caught the ball and quickly made a perfect throw down the line to Bench, who put the tag on Denny Doyle for the double play.

The game moved into extra innings and in the eleventh, with Griffey on first, Evans made a spectacular one-hand catch in front of the right-field stands on a shot by Morgan. Griffey, who had moved to third on the play, was easily doubled at first. The next inning, Wise, the game's twelfth pitcher, came in and kept the Reds from scoring. Then, in the bottom of the inning, Fisk, the first man up, took Pat Darcy's first pitch and blasted it off the left-field foul pole to give Boston an unbelievable 7–6 victory.

Game 1 October 11 at Boston

Cincinnati	Pos	AB	R	H	RBI	PO	A	E
Rose	3b	4	0	0	0	0	0	0
Morgan	2b	4	0	2	0	2	2	0
Bench	c	4	0	0	0	6	1	0
Perez	1b	4	0	0	0	9	0	0
Foster	lf	4	0	2	0	1	0	0
Concepcion	ss	4	0	0	0	2	3	0
Griffey	rf	3	0	1	0	0	0	0
Geronimo	cf	1	0	0	0	2	1	0
Gullett	p	3	0	0	0	0	0	0
Carroll	p	0	0	0	0	0	0	0
McEnaney	p	0	0	0	0	0	0	0
Totals		31	0	5	0	24	7	0

Doubles—Griffey, Morgan, Petrocelli. Sacrifice Hits—Doyle, Evans. Sacrifice Fly—Cooper. Double Plays—Geronimo to Bench, Perez (unassisted). Balk—Tiant. Left on Bases—Cincinnati 6, Boston 9. Umpires—Frantz (A), Colosi (N), Barnett (A), Stello, (N), Maloney (A), Davidson (N). Attendance—35,205. Time of Game—2:27.

Cin.	000 000 000
Bos.	000 000 60x

Boston	Pos	AB	R	H	RBI	PO	A	E
Evans	rf	4	1	1	0	4	0	0
Doyle	2b	3	1	2	0	3	3	0
Yastrzemski	lf	4	1	1	1	3	0	0
Fisk	c	3	1	0	1	4	1	0
Lynn	cf	4	0	2	0	3	0	0
Petrocelli	3b	3	1	2	1	1	3	0
Burleson	ss	3	0	3	1	1	1	0
Cooper	1b	3	0	0	1	8	0	0
Tiant	p	3	1	1	0	0	0	0
Totals		30	6	12	6	27	8	0

Pitching	IP	H	R	ER	BB	SO
Cincinnati						
Gullett (L)	*6	10	4	4	4	3
Carroll	**0	0	1	1	1	0
McEnaney	2	2	1	1	1	1
Boston						
Tiant (W)	9	5	0	0	2	3

*Pitched to four batters in 7th.
**Pitched to one batter in 7th.

1st Inning
Cincinnati
1 Rose grounded to second on a 3–2 count.
2 Morgan lined to second.
3 Bench flied to short right, also on a full count.
Boston
Evans singled between short and third.
1 Doyle sacrificed Evans to second, Perez unassisted.
Yastrzemski walked on four pitches.
2 Fisk popped to second.
Lynn beat out a bouncer to short, but
3 Evans was out trying to score, Concepcion to Bench.

2nd Inning
Cincinnati
1 Perez lined to right.
2 Foster lined to Cooper making a great leaping catch.
3 Concepcion fouled to Yastrzemski in the left field corner.
Boston
Petrocelli walked on four pitches.
Burleson lined a singled down the left field line, sending Petrocelli to third.
1 Cooper struck out.
2 Tiant also struck out.
3 Evans fouled to Griffey.

3rd Inning
Cincinnati
1 Griffey grounded to second.
2 Geronimo flied to center.
3 Gullett flied to left.
Boston
1 Doyle grounded to second.
2 Yastrzemski grounded to short.
3 Fisk flied to Foster in deep left-center.

4th Inning
Cincinnati
1 Rose grounded to second.
Morgan singled to center for the Reds' first hit.
Morgan went to second on a balk.
2 Bench fouled to Fisk.
3 Perez called out on strikes.
Boston
1 Lynn popped to short.
2 Petrocelli flied to center.
Burleson singled to right.
3 Burleson caught trying to steal second, Bench to Concepcion

5th Inning
Cincinnati
Foster singled to left.
1 Concepcion struck out.
2 Griffey grounded to third, Foster advancing to second.
Geronimo was intentionally passed.
3 Gullett fouled to Petrocelli.
Boston
1 Cooper again struck out.
Tiant walked.
2 Evans popped to second.
Doyle singled to right, Tiant going to second.
3 Yastrzemski grounded to first.

6th Inning
Cincinnati
1 Rose lined to right.
Morgan doubled inside the first base line.
2 Bench grounded to third, Morgan holding second.
3 Perez struck out.
Boston
1 Fisk grounded to short.
Lynn singled to center.
Petrocelli doubled to right, sending Lynn to third.
Burleson intentionally walked, loading the bases.
2,3 Cooper flied to Geronimo in short center and Lynn was doubled up trying to score on a throw to Bench.

7th Inning
Cincinnati
Foster singled past short.
1 Concepcion out on a fine diving catch by Yastrzemski in very short left.
2 Foster out trying to steal second, Fisk to Burleson.
Griffey doubled into the right field corner.
Geronimo intentionally walked.
3 Gullett lined to Doyle.
Boston
Tiant singled to left.
Evans sacrificed Tiant to second, and was safe on Gullett's poor throw to second.
Doyle singled to left, loading the bases.
Yastrzemski singled to right, scoring Tiant as the bases remained loaded.
For Cincinnati—Carroll pitching.
Fisk walked on a full count, forcing in Evans.
For Cincinnati—McEnaney now pitching.
1 Lynn struck out.
Petrocelli singled to left, scoring Doyle and Yastrzemski, with Fisk stopping at second.
Burleson also singled to left, scoring Fisk as Petrocelli went to third.
Burleson took second on the throw to the plate.
2 Cooper hit a sacrifice fly to right, Petrocelli scoring, and Burleson going to third, after the catch.
3 Tiant fouled to Perez.

8th Inning
Cincinnati
1 Rose flied to center.
2 Morgan flied to right.
3 Bench grounded to short.
Boston
1 Evans grounded to second.
Doyle walked on a full count.
2,3 Yastrzemski lined to Perez who stepped on first doubling Doyle on the play.

9th Inning
Cincinnati
1 Perez flied to short center.
2 Foster popped to Doyle in short center.
3 Concepcion grounded to third.

Game 2 October 12 at Boston

Cincinnati	Pos	AB	R	H	RBI	PO	A	E
Rose	3b	4	0	2	0	1	0	0
Morgan	2b	3	1	0	0	1	4	0
Bench	c	4	1	2	0	9	1	0
Perez	1b	3	0	0	1	8	0	0
Foster	lf	4	0	1	0	2	0	0
Concepcion	ss	4	1	1	1	1	3	1
Griffey	rf	4	0	1	1	2	0	0
Geronimo	cf	3	0	0	0	3	0	0
Billingham	p	2	0	0	0	0	2	0
Borbon	p	0	0	0	0	0	0	0
McEnaney	p	0	0	0	0	0	0	0
a Rettenmund		1	0	0	0	0	0	0
Eastwick	p	1	0	0	0	0	0	0
Totals		33	3	7	3	27	10	1

a Fouled out for McEnaney in 8th.
b Lined out for Drago in 9th.

Doubles—Bench, Cooper, Griffey. Stolen Base—Concepcion. Double Play—Billingham to Concepcion to Bench to Rose to Bench. Hit by Pitch—Evans (by Billingham). Left on Bases—Cincinnati 6, Boston 8. Umpires—Colosi, Barnett, Stello, Maloney, Davidson, Frantz. Attendance—35,205. Time of Game—2:38.

1st Inning
Cincinnati
1 Rose struck out on three pitches.
2 Morgan grounded to second.
3 Bench flied to center.
Boston
Cooper doubled to left.
Doyle beat out a hit off of Billingham's glove, Cooper going to third.
1,2 Yastrzemski hit into a double play, Billingham to Concepcion (forcing Doyle) to Bench to Rose to Bench (getting Cooper trying to score).
Yastrzemski went to second.
Fisk singled to right, scoring Yastrzemski.
3 Lynn grounded to second.

2nd Inning
Cincinnati
1 Perez struck out.
2 Foster also struck out.
3 Concepcion grounded to short.
Boston
1 Petrocelli struck out.
Evans was hit by a pitch.
Burleson singled past second, Evans stopping at second.
2 Evans out trying to steal, Bench to Concepcion to Rose as Burleson advanced to second.
3 Lee struck out.

3rd Inning
Cincinnati
1 Griffey grounded to first.
2 Geronimo struck out.
3 Billingham grounded to short.
Boston
1 Cooper grounded to second.
2 Doyle grounded to second.
Yastrzemski walked.
3 Fisk struck out.

4th Inning
Cincinnati
1 Rose grounded to second.
Morgan walked.
Rose singled to center, the Reds' first hit, Morgan going to third.
2 Perez forced Bench at second, Burleson to Doyle as Morgan scored.
Foster blooped a single to left, Perez stopping at second.
3 Concepcion flied to shallow center.
Boston
1 Lynn flied to left.
2 Petrocelli grounded to short.
3 Evans struck out.

5th Inning
Cincinnati
1 Griffey grounded to first.
2 Geronimo flied to right.
3 Billingham grounded to second.
Boston
1 Burleson struck out.
2 Lee bunted out on a great play by Bench to Perez.
3 Cooper bounced back to the mound.

Cin.	000	100	002
Bos.	100	001	000

Boston	Pos	AB	R	H	RBI	PO	A	E
Cooper	1b	5	0	1	0	10	1	0
Doyle	2b	4	0	1	0	2	4	0
Yastrzemski	lf	3	2	1	0	1	0	0
Fisk	c	3	0	1	1	5	1	0
Lynn	cf	4	0	0	0	5	0	0
Petrocelli	3b	4	0	2	1	0	0	0
Evans	rf	2	0	0	0	2	0	0
Burleson	ss	4	0	1	0	2	3	0
Lee	p	3	0	0	0	0	0	0
Drago	p	0	0	0	0	0	0	0
b Carbo		1	0	0	0	0	0	0
Totals		33	2	7	2	27	9	0

Pitching	IP	H	R	ER	BB	SO
Cincinnati						
Billingham	$5\frac{2}{3}$	6	2	1	2	5
Borbon	$\frac{1}{3}$	0	0	0	0	0
McEnaney	1	0	0	0	0	2
Eastwick (W)	2	1	0	0	1	1
Boston						
Lee	8	5	2	2	2	5
Drago (L)	1	2	1	1	1	0

6th Inning
Cincinnati
Rose singled to left.
1 Morgan forced Rose at second, Cooper to Burleson.
2 Morgan caught trying to steal second, Fisk to Doyle.
3 Bench flied to Lynn who made a great diving catch.
Boston
1 Doyle grounded to second.
Yastrzemski singled to right.
Fisk safe on Concepcion's fumble. Yastrzemski going to second.
2 Lynn flied to right.
Petrocelli singled up the middle, Yastrzemski scoring as Fisk raced to third.
Evans walked on a full count, loading the bases.
For Cincinnati—Borbon came in to pitch.
3 Burleson flied to center.

7th Inning
Cincinnati
Perez walked on a 3–2 pitch.
1 Foster flied to Lynn in left-center.
2 Concepcion flied to short right.
3 Griffey struck out on a foul tip.
Boston
For Cincinnati—McEnaney replaced Borbon on the mound. Rain delayed the game 27 minutes.
1 Lee struck out.
2 Cooper grounded to short.
3 Doyle was called out on strikes.

8th Inning
Cincinnati
1 Geronimo flied to center.
2 Rettenmund, pinch-hitting for McEnaney, fouled to Cooper.
Rose singled over Doyle's head.
3 Morgan grounded to second.
Boston
For Cincinnati—Eastwick now pitching.
1 Yastrzemski flied to Geronimo in deep left-center.
Fisk walked.
2 Lynn flied to Geronimo in short right-center.
Petrocelli singled to right, Fisk stopping at second.
3 Evans took a called third strike.

9th Inning
Cincinnati
Bench doubled into the right field corner.
For Boston—Drago came in to pitch.
1 Perez grounded to short, Bench moving to third.
2 Foster flied to shallow left, Bench holding at third.
Concepcion beat out a hard grounder to second, scoring Bench.
Concepcion stole second.
Griffey doubled into left-center, scoring Concepcion.
Geronimo intentionally walked.
3 Eastwick forced Geronimo at second, Doyle to Burleson.
Boston
1 Burleson fouled to Griffey.
2 Carbo, batting for Drago, lined to left.
3 Cooper popped to short.

Game 3 October 14 at Cincinnati

Boston	Pos	AB	R	H	RBI	PO	A	E
Cooper	1b	5	0	0	0	14	0	0
Doyle	2b	5	0	1	0	0	7	0
Yastrzemski	lf	4	1	0	0	1	0	0
Fisk	c	3	1	1	1	5	0	2
Lynn	cf	3	0	1	1	6	0	0
Petrocelli	3b	4	1	2	0	1	5	0
Evans	rf	4	1	2	2	1	0	0
Burleson	ss	4	0	2	0	0	2	0
Wise	p	2	0	0	0	0	0	0
Burton	p	0	0	0	0	0	0	0
Cleveland	p	0	0	0	0	0	0	0
a Carbo		1	1	1	1	0	0	0
Willoughby	p	0	0	0	0	0	0	0
Moret	p	0	0	0	0	0	0	0
Totals		35	5	10	5	x28	14	2

Pitching	IP	H	R	ER	BB	SO
Boston						
Wise	$4\frac{1}{3}$	4	5	5	2	1
Burton	$\frac{1}{3}$	0	0	0	1	0
Cleveland	$1\frac{1}{3}$	0	0	0	0	2
Willoughby (L)	3	2	1	0	0	1
Moret	$\frac{1}{3}$	1	0	0	1	1
Cincinnati						
Nolan	4	3	1	1	1	0
Darcy	2	2	1	1	2	0
Carroll	$\frac{2}{3}$	1	1	0	0	0
McEnaney	$1\frac{2}{3}$	1	1	1	0	2
Eastwick (W)	$1\frac{2}{3}$	3	1	1	0	0

1st Inning
Boston
1 Cooper grounded to first.
2 Doyle also grounded to first.
3 Yastrzemski grounded to second.
Cincinnati
1 Rose grounded to second.
2 Griffey grounded to second.
3 Morgan flied to center.

2nd Inning
Boston
Fisk homered into the left field seats.
1 Lynn flied to shallow center.
Petrocelli singled to left.
2 Evans fouled to Griffey.
3 Burleson forced Petrocelli at second, Concepcion to Morgan.
Cincinnati
1 Perez flied to center.
2 Bench grounded to third.
Foster walked.
Foster stole second and continued to third when Fisk's throw went into center.
3 Concepcion flied to right.

3rd Inning
Boston
1 Wise flied to deep left.
2 Cooper flied to shallow left.
3 Doyle popped to third.
Cincinnati
1 Geronimo bounced to second.
2 Nolan grounded to first.
3 Rose grounded to second.

4th Inning
Boston
1 Yastrzemski grounded to first.
Fisk walked.
Lynn singled to right, Fisk going
2 to third. Lynn was thrown out having slipped after rounding first, Griffey to Concepcion to Perez.
3 Petrocelli grounded to second.
Cincinnati
1 Griffey flied to center.
2 Morgan flied to deep center.
Perez walked.
Perez stole second.
Bench hit a two-run homer off the facade in left.
3 Foster grounded to third.

5th Inning
Boston
For Cincinnati—Darcy replaced Nolan who developed a stiff neck.
1 Evans grounded to short.
Burleson singled to left.
2 Wise forced Burleson at second, Rose to Morgan.
3 Cooper grounded to second.
Cincinnati
Concepcion homered just over the yellow line in left-center.
Geronimo homered into the lower deck in right.
1 Darcy struck out.
Rose tripled to the center field wall.
For Boston—Burton came in to pitch.
Griffey walked.
2 Morgan hit a sacrifice fly to center, scoring Rose.
Griffey stole second.
For Boston—Cleveland now pitching.
3 Perez struck out.

6th Inning
Boston
1 Doyle fouled to Rose.
Yastrzemski walked on four pitches.
Fisk walked on a 3–2 pitch.
Yastrzemski and Fisk both advanced on Darcy's wild pitch.

Bos.	010	001	102	0
Cin.	000	230	000	1

Cincinnati	Pos	AB	R	H	RBI	PO	A	E
Rose	3b	4	1	1	0	2	2	0
Griffey	rf	3	0	0	0	1	1	0
c Rettenmund		1	0	0	0	0	0	0
Morgan	2b	4	0	1	2	2	6	0
Perez	1b	3	1	0	0	14	0	0
Bench	c	4	1	1	2	2	3	0
Foster	lf	3	0	0	0	3	0	0
Concepcion	ss	4	1	1	1	3	6	0
Geronimo	cf	4	2	2	1	3	0	0
Nolan	p	1	0	0	0	0	0	0
Darcy	p	1	0	0	0	0	0	0
Carroll	p	0	0	0	0	0	0	0
McEnaney	p	1	0	1	0	0	0	0
Eastwick	p	0	0	0	0	0	0	0
b Armbrister		1	0	0	0	0	0	0
Totals		34	6	7	6	30	18	0

a Homered for Cleveland in 7th.
b Safe on error for Eastwick in 10th.
c Called out on strikes for Griffey in 10th.
x One out when winning run scored.

Triple—Rose. Home Runs—Bench, Carbo, Concepcion, Evans, Fisk, Geronimo. Stolen Bases—Foster, Griffey, Perez. Sacrifice Hit—Willoughby. Sacrifice Flies—Lynn, Morgan. Double Plays—Morgan to Concepcion to Perez, Morgan to Perez, Petrocelli to Cooper. Wild Pitch—Darcy. Left on Bases—Boston 5, Cincinnati 5. Umpires—Barnett, Stello, Maloney, Davidson, Frantz, Colosi. Attendance—55,392. Time of Game—3:03.

6th Inning (continued)
2 Lynn hit a sacrifice fly to Foster in short left-center, Yastrzemski scoring as Fisk held second.
3 Petrocelli grounded to short.
Cincinnati
1 Bench struck out.
2 Foster flied to left.
3 Concepcion grounded to first.

7th Inning
Boston
Evans singled up the middle
For Cincinnati—Carroll replaced Darcy.
1,2 Burleson hit into a double play, Morgan to Concepcion to Perez.
Carbo, pinch-hitting for Cleveland, hit a home run into the lower deck in left.
For Cincinnati—McEnaney came in to pitch.
3 Cooper popped to short.
Cincinnati
For Boston—Willoughby pitching.
1 Geronimo flied to deep center.
McEnaney beat out a bouncer over the mound.
2,3 Rose lined into a double play, Petrocelli to Cooper.

8th Inning
Boston
1 Doyle grounded to first.
2 Yastrzemski called out on strikes.
3 Fisk dribbled out, Bench to Perez.
Cincinnati
1 Griffey grounded to second.
2 Morgan bounced to second.
3 Perez again struck out.

9th Inning
Boston
1 Lynn took a called third strike.
Petrocelli singled to center.
For Cincinnati—Eastwick now pitching.
Evans hit a two-run homer into the lower deck in left, to tie the score.
Burleson blooped a single into center.
2 Willoughby sacrificed Burleson to second, Perez to Morgan.
3 Cooper flied to shallow center.
Cincinnati
1 Bench grounded to third.
2 Foster grounded to short.
3 Concepcion grounded to third.

10th Inning
Boston
Doyle beat out a bouncer over the mound.
1 Yastrzemski flied to deep center.
2,3 Fisk grounded into a double play, Morgan to Perez.
Cincinnati
Geronimo singled to right.
Armbrister, batting for Eastwick safe on a bunt in front of the plate when Fisk threw into center trying for the play at second. Geronimo got to third and Armbrister to second. Fisk argued Armbrister interfered but the decision by Barnett went unchanged.
For Boston—Moret replaced Willoughby on the mound.
Rose was given an intentional pass, loading the bases.
1 Rettenmund, pinch-hitting for Griffey, took a called third strike.
Morgan singled over Lynn's head, Geronimo scoring the game-winning run.

Game 4 October 15 at Cincinnati

Boston	Pos	AB	R	H	RBI	PO	A	E
Beniquez	lf	4	0	1	1	3	0	0
Miller	lf	1	0	0	0	1	0	0
Doyle	2b	5	0	1	0	2	3	1
Yastrzemski	1b	4	0	2	1	8	0	0
Fisk	c	5	1	1	0	4	0	0
Lynn	cf	4	1	1	0	4	1	0
Petrocelli	3b	4	0	1	0	1	2	0
Evans	rf	4	1	2	2	4	0	0
Burleson	ss	4	1	1	1	0	2	0
Tiant	p	3	1	1	0	0	2	0
Totals		38	5	11	5	27	10	1

Pitching	IP	H	R	ER	BB	SO
Boston						
Tiant (W)	9	9	4	4	4	4
Cincinnati						
Nolan (L)	3⅓	7	4	4	1	2
Borbon	⅔	2	1	0	0	0
Carroll	2	2	0	0	0	2
Eastwick	3	0	0	0	1	0

Bos. 000 500 000
Cin. 200 200 000

Cincinnati	Pos	AB	R	H	RBI	PO	A	E
Rose	3b	3	1	1	0	1	3	0
Griffey	rf	5	0	1	0	0	0	0
Morgan	2b	3	1	0	0	2	7	0
Perez	1b	4	0	0	0	12	1	1
Bench	c	4	0	1	1	4	0	0
Foster	lf	4	1	2	0	4	1	0
Concepcion	ss	4	1	1	1	3	4	0
Geronimo	cf	4	0	3	1	4	0	0
Norman	p	1	0	0	0	0	0	0
Borbon	p	0	0	0	0	0	0	0
a Crowley		1	0	0	0	0	0	0
Carroll	p	0	0	0	0	1	0	0
b Chaney		1	0	0	0	0	0	0
Eastwick	p	0	0	0	0	0	0	0
c Armbrister		0	0	0	0	0	0	0
Totals		34	4	9	4	27	15	1

a Struck out for Borbon in 4th.
b Struck out for Carroll in 6th.
c Sacrificed for Eastwick in 9th.

Doubles—Bench, Burleson, Concepcion, Griffey. Triples—Evans, Geronimo. Sacrifice Hit—Armbrister. Double Play—Morgan to Concepcion to Perez. Wild Pitch—Norman. Left on Bases—Boston 8, Cincinnati 8. Umpires—Stello, Maloney, Davidson, Frantz, Colosi, Barnett. Attendance—55,667. Time of Game—2:52.

1st Inning
Boston
1 Beniquez flied to center.
2 Doyle bounced to second. Yastrzemski singled to right.
3 Fisk struck out.
Cincinnati
Rose singled up the middle. Griffey doubled into the left-center field gap, Rose scoring. Griffey was
1 out trying for a triple Lynn to Burleson to Petrocelli. Morgan walked.
2 Perez grounded to short, Morgan advancing to second. Bench doubled to deep right-center, Morgan scoring.
3 Foster grounded to third.

2nd Inning
Boston
1 Lynn struck out. Petrocelli singled to left.
2 Evans forced Petrocelli at second, Concepcion to Morgan.
3 Burleson grounded to third.
Cincinnati
1 Concepcion grounded to third.
2 Geronimo grounded to second.
3 Norman flied to left.

3rd Inning
Boston
Tiant walked on four pitches. Beniquez singled into right, Tiant stopping at second.
1 Doyle flied to center.
2,3 Yastrzemski hit into a double play, Morgan to Concepcion to Perez.
Cincinnati
1 Rose flied to center.
2 Griffey bounced back to the mound.
3 Morgan flied to right.

4th Inning
Boston
Fisk singled to left-center. Lynn singled to right, Fisk stopping at second.
1 Petrocelli popped to short. Fisk went to third and Lynn to second on a wild pitch. Evans tripled to the right field wall, scoring Fisk and Lynn. Burleson doubled over short, scoring Evans. For Cincinnati—Borbon relieved Norman on the mound. Tiant singled up the middle, Burleson going to third. Beniquez safe when Perez fumbled his dribbler, Burleson scoring as Tiant went to second.
2 Doyle fouled to Rose. Yastrzemski singled to right, scoring Tiant as Beniquez went to third.
3 Fisk flied to center.
Cincinnati
1 Perez struck out.
2 Bench flied to left. Foster beat out a hit to Doyle and continued to second on Doyle's wild throw to first. Concepcion blooped a Texas League double into short left-center, Foster scoring. Geronimo tripled into the right field corner, scoring Concepcion.
3 Crowley, pinch-hitting for Borbon, struck out.

5th Inning
Boston
For Cincinnati—Carroll pitching.
1 Lynn grounded to second.
2 Petrocelli took a called third strike. Evans lined a single off Carroll's hip.
3 Burleson forced Evans at second, Concepcion to Morgan
Cincinnati
Rose walked.
1 Griffey flied to deep right. Morgan walked on a 3-2 pitch.
2 Perez grounded to second, advancing both runners.
3 Bench flied to left.

6th Inning
Boston
1 Tiant took a called third strike.
2 Beniquez grounded to third. Doyle singled to center.
3 Yastrzemski grounded out, Perez to Carroll.
Cincinnati
For Boston—Miller playing left.
1 Foster flied to center.
2 Concepcion flied to short right. Geronimo blooped a single to center.
3 Chaney, batting for Carroll, struck out.

7th Inning
Boston
For Cincinnati—Eastwick pitching.
1 Fisk popped to first.
2 Lynn grounded to second.
3 Petrocelli also grounded to second.
Cincinnati
1 Rose lined to second.
2 Griffey grounded to second.
3 Morgan flied to deep center.

8th Inning
Boston
1 Evans flied to deep center.
2 Burleson grounded to third.
3 Tiant grounded to short.
Cincinnati
1 Perez flied to Miller in left-center.
2 Bench struck out on three pitches. Foster singled up the middle
3 Concepcion flied to shallow right.

9th Inning
Boston
1 Miller grounded to second.
2 Doyle grounded to second. Yastrzemski walked on a 3-2 pitch.
3 Fisk flied to Concepcion in short left.
Cincinnati
Geronimo singled to right.
1 Armbrister, pinch-hitting for Eastwick, sacrificed Geronimo to second, Tiant to Doyle. Rose walked.
2 Griffey lined to Lynn in deep left, making an over-the-shoulder catch.
3 Morgan popped to first.

Game 5 October 16 at Cincinnati

Boston	Pos	AB	R	H	RBI	PO	A	E
Beniquez	lf	3	0	0	0	2	1	0
Doyle	2b	4	1	1	0	1	1	0
Yastrzemski	1b	3	1	1	1	6	0	0
Fisk	c	4	0	1	0	6	0	0
Lynn	cf	4	0	1	0	1	2	0
Petrocelli	3b	4	0	0	0	2	1	0
Evans	rf	3	0	1	0	3	0	0
Burleson	ss	3	0	0	0	1	2	0
Cleveland	p	2	0	0	0	1	0	0
Willoughby	p	0	0	0	0	1	0	0
a Griffin		1	0	0	0	0	0	0
Pole	p	0	0	0	0	0	0	0
Segui	p	0	0	0	0	0	0	0
Totals		31	2	5	2	24	5	0

a Lined out for Willoughby in 8th.

Doubles—Lynn, Rose. Triple—Doyle. Home Run—Perez 2. Stolen Bases—Concepcion, Morgan. Sacrifice Flies—Concepcion, Yastrzemski. Double Plays—Beniquez to Fisk, Burleson to Yastrzemski. Hit by Pitcher—Concepcion (by Willoughby) Left on Bases—Boston 4, Cincinnati 5. Umpires—Maloney, Davidson, Frantz, Barnett, Stello. Attendance—56,393. Time of Game—2:23.

Bos. 100 000 001
Cin. 000 113 01x

Cincinnati	Pos	AB	R	H	RBI	PO	A	E
Rose	3b	3	0	2	1	1	0	0
Griffey	rf	4	0	1	0	2	0	0
Morgan	2b	3	1	1	0	3	2	0
Bench	c	3	2	1	0	8	1	0
Perez	1b	3	2	2	4	5	0	0
Foster	lf	4	0	0	0	2	0	0
Concepcion	ss	2	0	1	1	0	0	0
Geronimo	cf	3	0	0	0	6	0	0
Gullett	p	3	1	1	0	0	0	0
Eastwick	p	0	0	0	0	0	0	0
Totals		29	6	8	6	27	3	0

Pitching	IP	H	R	ER	BB	SO
Boston						
Cleveland (L)	5	7	5	5	2	3
Willoughby	2	1	0	0	0	1
Pole	*0	0	1	1	2	0
Segui	1	0	0	0	0	0
Cincinnati						
Gullett (W)	8⅓	5	2	2	1	7
Eastwick (SV)	⅔	0	0	0	0	1

*Pitched to two batters in 8th.

1st Inning
Boston
1 Beniquez grounded to third. Doyle tripled down the right field line.
2 Yastrzemski hit a sacrifice fly to right, scoring Doyle.
3 Fisk took a called third strike.
Cincinnati
Rose singled to left.
1 Griffey struck out. Morgan singled to right-center, Rose going to third.
2,3 Bench flied to Beniquez who threw to Fisk doubling Rose trying to score after the catch.

2nd Inning
Boston
1 Lynn popped to third.
2 Petrocelli struck out.
3 Evans flied to left.
Cincinnati
1 Perez struck out.
2 Foster fouled to Fisk.
3 Concepcion bounced to short.

3rd Inning
Boston
1 Burleson popped to second.
2 Cleveland called out on strikes.
3 Beniquez flied to left.
Cincinnati
1 Geronimo flied to center.
2 Gullett struck out. Rose walked.
3 Griffey lined to second.

4th Inning
Boston
1 Doyle bounced out, Bench to Perez.
2 Yastrzemski flied to Geronimo in right-center.
3 Fisk struck out.
Cincinnati
1 Morgan flied to shallow right.
2 Bench lined to Petrocelli, making a leaping catch. Perez homered into the lower deck of the left-center field stands (this was the first hit for Perez in the Series).
3 Foster popped to first.

5th Inning
Boston
1 Lynn struck out.
2 Petrocelli flied to Geronimo in shallow right-center.
3 Evans flied to Geronimo in deep left-center.
Cincinnati
1 Concepcion grounded to third.
2 Geronimo grounded to second. Gullett lined a single up the middle. Rose doubled into the left field corner, scoring Gullett.
3 Griffey fouled to Petrocelli.

6th Inning
Boston
1 Burleson flied to right.
2 Cleveland struck out on a 3-2 pitch. Beniquez walked.
3 Doyle grounded to first.
Cincinnati
Morgan walked on a full count. Bench singled to right, Morgan going to third. Bench went to second on the throw to third. Perez hit a three-run homer into the lower deck in left-center. His second of the game. For Boston—Willoughby replaced Cleveland on the mound.
1 Foster lined back to the mound. Concepcion was hit by a pitch. Concepcion stole second.
2 Geronimo grounded to first, Concepcion going to third.
3 Gullett struck out.

7th Inning
Boston
1 Yastrzemski fouled to Perez.
2 Fisk lined to deep left.
3 Lynn popped to short center.
Cincinnati
1 Rose lined to deep left. Griffey beat out a hit to second.
2,3 Morgan lined into a double play, Burleson (making a spectacular catch over second) to Yastrzemski.

8th Inning
Boston
1 Petrocelli flied to Geronimo in front of the left-center field wall. Evans singled up the middle for the second hit off of Gullett, the first since the first inning.
2 Burleson flied to center.
3 Griffin, pinch-hitting for Willoughby, lined to center.
Cincinnati
For Boston—Pole now pitching. Bench walked on four pitches. Perez also walked on four pitches. For Boston—Segui replaced Pole on the mound.
1 Foster flied to right, Bench going to third after the catch.
2 Concepcion hit a sacrifice fly to right, scoring Bench.
3 Geronimo flied to center.

9th Inning
Boston
1 Beniquez struck out on a full count.
2 Doyle grounded to second. Yastrzemski singled to right-center. Fisk singled to left, Yastrzemski going to second. Lynn doubled into the right field corner, scoring Yastrzemski as Fisk went to third. For Cincinnati—Eastwick relieved Gullett.
3 Petrocelli struck out on three pitches.

1975

Game 6 October 21 at Boston

Cin.	000	030	210	000					
Bos.	300	000	030	001					

Cincinnati	Pos	AB	R	H	RBI	PO	A	E
Rose	3b	5	1	2	0	0	2	0
Griffey	rf	5	2	2	2	0	0	0
Morgan	2b	6	1	1	0	5	3	0
Bench	c	6	0	1	1	8	0	0
Perez	1b	6	0	2	0	10	3	0
Foster	lf	6	0	2	2	4	1	0
Concepcion	ss	6	0	1	0	3	4	0
Geronimo	cf	6	1	2	1	2	0	0
Nolan	p	0	0	0	0	1	0	0
a Chaney		1	0	0	0	0	0	0
Norman	p	0	0	0	0	0	0	0
Billingham	p	0	0	0	0	0	0	0
b Armbrister		0	1	0	0	0	0	0
Carroll	p	0	0	0	0	0	0	0
c Crowley		1	0	1	0	0	0	0
Borbon	p	1	0	0	0	0	0	0
Eastwick	p	0	0	0	0	0	0	0
McEnaney	p	0	0	0	0	1	0	0
e Driessen		1	0	0	0	0	0	0
Darcy	p	0	0	0	0	0	1	0
Totals		50	6	14	6	x33	14	0

Boston	Pos	AB	R	H	RBI	PO	A	E
Cooper	1b	5	0	0	0	8	0	0
Drago	p	0	0	0	0	0	0	0
f Miller		1	0	0	0	0	0	0
Wise	p	0	0	0	0	0	0	0
Doyle	2b	5	0	1	0	0	2	0
Yastrzemski	lf-1b	6	1	3	0	7	1	0
Fisk	c	4	2	2	1	9	1	0
Lynn	cf	4	2	2	3	2	0	0
Petrocelli	3b	4	1	0	0	1	1	0
Evans	rf	5	0	1	0	3	1	0
Burleson	ss	3	0	0	0	5	2	1
Tiant	p	2	0	0	0	0	2	0
Moret	p	0	0	0	0	0	1	0
d Carbo	lf	2	1	1	3	1	0	0
Totals		41	7	10	7	36	11	1

Pitching	IP	H	R	ER	BB	SO
Cincinnati						
Nolan	2	3	3	3	0	2
Norman	⅔	1	0	0	2	0
Billingham	1⅓	1	0	0	1	1
Carroll	1	1	0	0	0	0
Borbon	2	1	2	2	2	1
Eastwick	1⅓	2	1	1	1	2
McEnaney	⅔	0	0	0	1	0
Darcy (L)	2	1	1	1	0	1
Boston						
Tiant	*7	11	6	6	2	5
Moret	1	0	0	0	0	0
Drago	3	1	0	0	0	1
Wise (W)	1	2	0	0	0	1

*Pitched to one batter in 8th.

a Flied out for Nolan in 3rd.
b Walked for Billingham in 5th.
c Singled for Carroll in 6th.
d Homered for Moret in 8th.
e Flied out for McEnaney in 10th.
f Flied out for Drago in 11th.
x None out when winning run scored.

Doubles—Doyle, Evans, Foster. Triple—Griffey. Home Runs—Carbo, Fisk, Geronimo, Lynn. Stolen Base—Concepcion. Sacrifice Hit—Tiant. Double Plays—Foster to Bench, Evans to Yastrzemski to Burleson. Hit by Pitcher—Rose (by Drago). Left on Bases—Cincinnati 11, Boston 9. Umpires—Davidson, Frantz, Colosi, Barnett, Stello, Maloney. Attendance—35,205. Time of Game—4:01.

1st Inning

Cincinnati
1 Rose flied to Yastrzemski, who made a sliding catch.
Griffey walked on a full count.
2 Morgan fouled to Fisk.
3 Bench struck out.

Boston
1 Cooper flied to center.
2 Doyle grounded out, Perez to Nolan.
Yastrzemski lined a single to right.
Fisk singled to left, Yastrzemski stopping at second.
Lynn hit a three-run home run into the right-center field bleachers.
3 Petrocelli flied to Geronimo in deep left-center.

2nd Inning

Cincinnati
1 Perez struck out.
2 Foster fouled to Cooper.
3 Concepcion flied to center.

Boston
1 Evans took a called third strike.
2 Burleson grounded to first.
3 Tiant called out on strikes.

3rd Inning

Cincinnati
1 Geronimo struck out.
2 Chaney, batting for Nolan, flied to Yastrzemski in deep left-center.
Rose lined a single to center.
3 Griffey's grounder deflected off Tiant's glove to Doyle who made the throw to first.

Boston
For Cincinnati—Norman now pitching.
1 Cooper popped to Concepcion behind third base.
Doyle doubled down the right field line.
2 Yastrzemski popped to second.
Fisk was intentionally passed.
Lynn walked on a full count, loading the bases.
For Cincinnati—Billingham relieved Norman on the mound.
3 Petrocelli struck out.

4th Inning

Cincinnati
1 Morgan grounded to second.
2 Bench took a called third strike.
Perez lined a single to right.
Foster safe on Burleson's wild throw to second as Perez got to third.
3 Concepcion fouled to Cooper.

Boston
Evans bounced a ground-rule double into the right field seats.
Burleson walked on four pitches.
1 Tiant sacrificed up both runners, Perez to Morgan.
2 Cooper grounded to first, both runners holding.
3 Doyle grounded second.

5th Inning

Cincinnati
1 Geronimo flied to right.
Armbrister, batting for Billingham, walked.
Rose singled to center, Armbrister going to third.
Griffey tripled off the wall in left-center, scoring Armbrister and Rose. Lynn was shaken up as he bounced off the wall on the hit.
2 Morgan popped to third.
Bench singled off the left field wall, scoring Griffey.
3 Perez struck out.

Boston
For Cincinnati—Carroll now pitching.
Yastrzemski singled to left.
1 Fisk forced Yastrzemski at second, Rose to Morgan.
2 Lynn flied to shallow left.
3 Petrocelli forced Fisk at second, Concepcion to Morgan.

6th Inning

Cincinnati
1 Foster bounced back to the mound.
2 Concepcion flied to right.
Geronimo singled past third.
Crowley, batting for Carroll, beat out an infield bouncer to short, Geronimo going to second.
3 Rose forced Crowley at second, Burleson unassisted.

Boston
For Cincinnati—Borbon now pitching.
1 Evans grounded to second.
Burleson walked.
2 Tiant struck out, bunting the third strike foul.
3 Cooper grounded to second.

7th Inning

Cincinnati
Griffey bounced a single to right.
Morgan singled to left, Griffey stopping at second.
1 Bench flied to deep left.
2 Perez flied to right, Griffey going to third after the catch.
Foster doubled off the center field wall, scoring Griffey and Morgan.
3 Concepcion grounded to short.

Boston
1 Doyle popped to short.
2 Yastrzemski grounded to second.
3 Fisk grounded to short.

8th Inning

Cincinnati
Geronimo hit a home run into the right field seats.
For Boston—Moret came in to pitch.
1 Borbon grounded to first.
2 Rose grounded back to the mound.
3 Griffey flied to center.

Boston
Lynn singled off Borbon's leg.
Petrocelli walked.
For Cincinnati—Eastwick relieved Borbon on the mound.
1 Evans struck out.
2 Burleson lined to short left.
Carbo, pinch-hitting for Moret, blasted a three-run homer into the center field bleachers. His second pinch homer of the Series.
3 Cooper struck out.

9th Inning

Cincinnati
For Boston—Carbo stays in playing left, Yastrzemski moved to first and Drago now pitching.
1 Morgan fouled to Yastrzemski.
2 Bench grounded to third.
3 Perez fouled to Yastrzemski.

Boston
Doyle walked.
Yastrzemski singled to right, Doyle going to third.
For Cincinnati—McEnaney became the Reds' seventh pitcher.
Fisk intentionally passed, loading the bases.
1,2 Lynn flied to Foster who threw to Bench doubling up Doyle trying to score after the catch.
3 Petrocelli grounded to third.

10th Inning

Cincinnati
1 Foster grounded to short.
Concepcion singled to center.
Concepcion stole second.
2 Geronimo struck out.
3 Driessen, pinch-hitting for McEnaney, flied to Carbo in shallow left.

Boston
For Cincinnati—Darcy now pitching. **The eighth Reds' pitcher used, tying a Series' record.**
1 Evans was out, Darcy to Perez.
2 Burleson popped to short.
3 Carbo struck out.

11th Inning

Cincinnati
Rose was hit by a pitch.
1 Griffey forced Rose at second on a bunt, Fisk to Burleson.
2,3 Morgan was robbed of a probable home-run by Evans, making a spectacular leaping one-handed catch in front of the stands. He threw to Yastremski who threw to Doyle, doubling Griffey who was already to third.

Boston
1 Miller, pinch-hitting for Drago, flied to left.
2 Doyle grounded to short.
3 Yastrzemski grounded to short.

12th Inning

Cincinnati
For Boston—Wise came into pitch. **The twelfth pitcher in the game.**
1 Bench fouled to Fisk, leaning into the crowd.
Perez singled up the middle.
Foster blooped a single to left, Perez going to second.
2 Concepcion flied to right.
3 Geronimo called out on strikes for his third strike out in the game.

Boston
Fisk blasted the second pitch high off the left field foul pole for a game-ending home run.

Game 7 October 22 at Boston

| | | | Cin. | 000 002 101 | |
| | | | Bos. | 003 000 000 | |

Cincinnati	Pos	AB	R	H	RBI	PO	A	E
Rose	3b	4	0	2	1	2	3	0
Morgan	2b	4	0	2	1	2	4	0
Bench	c	4	1	0	0	7	0	0
Perez	1b	5	1	1	2	8	1	0
Foster	lf	4	0	1	0	1	0	0
Concepcion	ss	4	0	1	0	0	3	0
Griffey	rf	2	2	1	0	3	0	0
Geronimo	cf	3	0	0	0	3	0	0
Gullett	p	1	0	1	0	0	0	0
a Rettenmund		1	0	0	0	0	0	0
Billingham	p	0	0	0	0	0	0	0
b Armbrister		0	0	0	0	0	0	0
Carroll	p	0	0	0	0	1	0	0
d Driessen		1	0	0	0	0	0	0
McEnaney	p	0	0	0	0	0	0	0
Totals		33	4	9	4	27	11	0

Boston	Pos	AB	R	H	RBI	PO	A	E
Carbo	lf	3	1	1	0	0	1	0
Miller	lf	1	0	0	0	0	0	0
e Beniquez		1	0	0	0	0	0	0
Doyle	2b	4	1	1	0	4	3	2
f Montgomery		1	0	0	0	0	0	0
Yastrzemski	1b	5	1	1	1	10	0	0
Fisk	c	3	0	0	0	4	0	0
Lynn	cf	2	0	0	0	1	0	0
Petrocelli	3b	3	0	1	1	1	2	0
Evans	rf	2	0	0	1	5	0	0
Burleson	ss	3	0	0	0	2	8	0
Lee	p	3	0	1	0	0	1	0
Moret	p	0	0	0	0	0	0	0
Willoughby	p	0	0	0	0	0	0	0
c Cooper		1	0	0	0	0	0	0
Burton	p	0	0	0	0	0	0	0
Cleveland	p	0	0	0	0	0	0	0
Totals		31	3	5	3	27	15	2

Pitching	IP	H	R	ER	BB	SO
Cincinnati						
Gullett	4	4	3	3	5	5
Billingham	2	1	0	0	2	1
Carroll (W)	2	0	0	0	1	1
McEnaney (SV)	1	0	0	0	0	0
Boston						
Lee	6⅓	7	3	3	1	2
Moret	⅓	1	0	0	2	0
Willoughby	1⅓	0	0	0	0	2
Burton (L)	⅓	1	1	1	2	0
Cleveland	⅔	0	0	0	1	0

a Ground into double play for Gullett in 5th.
b Walked for Billingham in 7th.
c Fouled out for Willoughby in 8th.
d Grounded out for Carroll in 9th.
e Flied out for Miller in 9th.
f Grounded out for Doyle in 9th.

Double—Carbo. Home Run—Perez. Stolen Bases—Griffey, Morgan. Sacrifice Hit—Geronimo, Double Plays—Doyle to Burleson to Yastrzemski, Burleson to Doyle to Yastrzemski, Concepcion to Morgan to Perez. Wild Pitch—Gullett. Left on Bases—Cincinnati 9, Boston 9. Umpires—Frantz, Colosi, Barnett, Stello, Maloney, Davidson. Attendance—35,205. Time of Game—2:52.

1st Inning
Cincinnati
1 Rose flied to shallow right.
2 Morgan struck out on a 3-2 pitch.
3 Bench grounded to short.
Boston
  Carbo doubled high off the left field wall.
1 Doyle flied to right.
2 Yastrzemski grounded to second, Carbo advancing to third.
3 Fisk struck out.

2nd Inning
Cincinnati
1 Perez grounded to short.
  Foster singled off the left field wall
2 but was out trying to stretch the hit into a double, Carbo to Doyle.
3 Concepcion grounded to short.
Boston
  Lynn walked.
1 Petrocelli struck out.
2 Evans fouled to Rose.
3 Burleson flied to right.

3rd Inning
Cincinnati
  Griffey lined a single to right-center.
1,2 Geronimo hit into a double play, Doyle to Burleson to Yastrzemski.
  Gullett singled to right.
3 Rose forced Gullett at second, Lee to Doyle.
Boston
1 Lee struck out.
  Carbo walked on a full count.
  Doyle singled to right, Carbo racing to third.
  Yastrzemski singled to right, scoring Carbo as Doyle went to third.
  Yastrzemski took second on the throw to third.
  Fisk got an intentional pass, loading the bases.
2 Lynn struck out.
  Petrocelli walked, forcing in Doyle.
  Evans walked on four pitches, forcing in Yastrzemski.
3 Burleson struck out.

4th Inning
Cincinnati
  Morgan beat out a bunt down the first base line.
1 Bench flied to Lynn in deep right-center.
  Morgan stole second.
2 Perez flied to right.
3 Foster fouled to Fisk.
Boston
  Lee chopped a single past Perez.
  Lee went to second on a wild pitch.
1 Carbo grounded to second, Lee going to third.
2 Doyle grounded to third, Lee holding.
3 Yastrzemski fouled to Morgan at the first base line.

5th Inning
Cincinnati
  Concepcion beat out a hit to first.
  Griffey safe on Doyle's error, Concepcion going to third.
1 Geronimo took a called third strike.
2,3 Rettenmund, pinch-hitting for Gullett, hit into a double play, Burleson to Doyle to Yastrzemski.
Boston
  For Cincinnati—Billingham now pitching.
1 Fisk struck out.
  Lynn walked.
  Petrocelli drilled a single to left, Lynn stopping at second.
2 Evans flied to deep center, Lynn going to third after the catch.
  Burleson walked to fill the bases.
3 Lee flied to deep center.

6th Inning
Cincinnati
  Rose singled to right.
1 Morgan flied to right.
2 Bench forced Rose at second, Burleson to Doyle. Bench was safe on Doyle's wild throw to first for the double play.
  Perez hit a two-run homer over the left field wall. His third of the Series.
3 Foster flied to right.
Boston
1 Carbo grounded to first.
2 Doyle flied to shallow left.
3 Yastrzemski grounded to second.

7th Inning
Cincinnati
  For Boston—Miller now playing in left.
1 Concepcion grounded to short.
  Griffey walked.
  For Boston—Moret relieved Lee, who had developed a blister.
2 Geronimo popped to short.
  Griffey stole second.
  Armbrister, pinch-hitting for Billingham, walked.
  Rose singled to center, scoring Griffey as Armbrister went to third, Rose taking second on the throw home.
  Morgan walked on a full count, loading the bases.
  For Boston—Willoughby came in to pitch.
3 Bench fouled to Fisk.
Boston
  For Cincinnati—Carroll now pitching.
1 Fisk struck out.
2 Lynn grounded out, Perez to Carroll.
3 Petrocelli grounded to short.

8th Inning
Cincinnati
1 Perez popped to third.
2 Foster grounded to short.
3 Concepcion grounded to third.
Boston
  Evans walked.
1,2 Burleson hit into a double play, Concepcion to Morgan to Perez.
3 Cooper, batting for Willoughby, fouled to Rose.

9th Inning
Cincinnati
  For Boston—Burton pitching.
  Griffey walked.
1 Geronimo sacrificed Griffey to second, Petrocelli to Yastrzemski.
2 Driessen, batting for Carroll, grounded to second, Griffey going to third.
  Rose walked.
  Morgan blooped a single to center, scoring Griffey as Rose went to third. Morgan took second on the throw to third.
  For Boston—Cleveland came in to pitch.
  Bench walked, loading the bases.
3 Perez flied to right.
Boston
  For Cincinnati—McEnaney pitching.
1 Beniquez, batting for Miller, flied to right.
2 Montgomery, pinch-hitting for Doyle, grounded to short.
3 Yasterzemski flied to center.

1975 WORLD SERIES COMPOSITE BOX

	Wins	Composite Line Score	
Cincinnati Reds (N.L.)	4	2 0 0 6 7 5 3 2 3 1 0 0	- 29
Boston Red Sox (A.L.)	3	5 1 3 5 0 2 7 3 3 0 0 1	- 30

Manager	Regular Season W	L	Pct.	G. Ahead	
Sparky Anderson	108	54	.667	20	(defeated Pittsburgh in playoffs)
Darrell Johnson	95	65	.594	4.5	(defeated Oakland in playoffs)

BATTING AND FIELDING

WORLD SERIES STATISTICS

	Pos	G	AB	R	H	2B	3B	HR	RBI	BB	SO	SB	BA	SA	PO	A	E
CINCINNATI REDS																	
Tony Perez	1b	7	28	4	5	0	0	**3**	**7**	3	**9**	1	.179	.500	**66**	5	1
Joe Morgan	2b	7	27	4	7	1	0	0	3	5	1	2	.259	.296	17	**28**	0
Dave Concepcion	ss	7	28	3	5	1	0	1	4	0	1	**3**	.179	.321	12	23	1
Pete Rose	3b	7	27	3	**10**	1	**1**	0	2	5	1	0	**.370**	.481	7	8	0
Ken Griffey	rf	7	26	4	7	**3**	**1**	0	4	4	2	2	.269	.462	10	1	0
Cesar Geronimo	cf	7	25	3	7	0	**1**	2	3	3	5	0	.280	**.600**	23	1	0
George Foster	lf	7	29	1	8	1	0	0	2	1	1	1	.276	.310	13	1	0
Johnny Bench	c	7	29	5	6	2	0	1	4	2	4	0	.207	.379	44	6	0
Marv Rettenmund	ph	3	3	0	0	0	0	0	0	0	1	0	.000	.000	0	0	0
Ed Armbrister	ph	4	1	1	0	0	0	0	0	2	0	0	.000	.000	0	0	0
Darrell Chaney	ph	2	2	0	0	0	0	0	0	0	1	0	.000	.000	0	0	0
Terry Crowley	ph	2	2	0	1	0	0	0	0	0	1	0	.500	.500	0	0	0
Dan Driessen	ph	2	2	0	0	0	0	0	0	0	0	0	.000	.000	0	0	0
Doug Flynn		Did not play															
Bill Plummer		Did not play															
Don Gullett	p	3	7	1	2	0	0	0	0	0	2	0	.286	.286	0	0	0
Jack Billingham	p	3	2	0	0	0	0	0	0	0	0	0	.000	.000	0	2	0
Rawly Eastwick	p	5	1	0	0	0	0	0	0	0	0	0	.000	.000	0	0	0
Will McEnaney	p	5	1	0	1	0	0	0	0	0	0	0	1.000	1.000	0	0	0
Pedro Borbon	p	3	1	0	0	0	0	0	0	0	0	0	.000	.000	0	0	0
Pat Darcy	p	2	1	0	0	0	0	0	0	0	1	0	.000	.000	0	1	0
Gary Nolan	p	2	1	0	0	0	0	0	0	0	0	0	.000	.000	1	0	0
Fred Norman	p	2	1	0	0	0	0	0	0	0	0	0	.000	.000	0	0	0
Clay Carroll	p	5	0	0	0	0	0	0	0	0	0	0	—	—	2	0	0
Clay Kirby		Did not play															
team total		7	244	29	59	9	3	7	29	25	30	9	.242	.402	195	76	2

Double Plays—8
Left on Bases—50

	Pos	G	AB	R	H	2B	3B	HR	RBI	BB	SO	SB	BA	SA	PO	A	E
BOSTON RED SOX																	
Cecil Cooper	1b-ph	5	19	0	1	1	0	0	1	0	3	0	.053	.106	40	1	0
Denny Doyle	2b	7	**30**	3	8	1	**1**	0	0	2	1	0	.267	.367	12	23	**3**
Rick Burleson	ss	7	24	1	7	1	0	0	2	4	2	0	.292	.333	9	20	1
Rico Petrocelli	3b	7	26	3	8	1	0	0	4	3	6	0	.308	.346	7	14	0
Dwight Evans	rf	7	24	3	7	1	**1**	1	5	3	4	0	.292	.542	23	1	0
Fred Lynn	cf	7	25	3	7	1	0	1	5	3	5	0	.280	.440	23	1	0
Carl Yastrzemski	lf-1b	7	29	7	9	0	0	0	4	4	1	0	.310	.310	36	1	0
Carlton Fisk	c	7	25	5	6	0	0	2	4	**7**	7	0	.240	.480	37	3	2
Juan Beniquez	lf-ph	3	8	0	1	0	0	0	1	1	1	0	.125	.125	6	1	0
Bernie Carbo	ph-lf	4	7	3	3	1	0	2	4	1	1	0	.429	1.429	1	1	0
Rick Miller	lf	3	2	0	0	0	0	0	0	0	0	0	.000	.000	1	0	0
Doug Griffin	ph	1	1	0	0	0	0	0	0	0	0	0	.000	.000	1	0	0
Bob Montgomery	ph	1	1	0	0	0	0	0	0	0	0	0	.000	.000	0	0	0
Tim Blackwell		Did not play															
Bob Heise		Did not play															
Jim Rice		Not eligible for Series—Injured															
Luis Tiant	p	3	8	2	2	0	0	0	0	2	4	0	.250	.250	0	4	0
Bill Lee	p	2	6	0	1	0	0	0	0	0	3	0	.167	.167	0	1	0
Reggie Cleveland	p	3	2	0	0	0	0	0	0	0	2	0	.000	.000	0	0	0
Rick Wise	p	2	2	0	0	0	0	0	0	0	0	0	.000	.000	0	0	0
Roger Moret	p	3	0	0	0	0	0	0	0	0	0	0	—	—	0	1	0
Jim Willoughby	p	3	0	0	0	0	0	0	0	0	0	0	—	—	1	0	0
Jim Burton	p	2	0	0	0	0	0	0	0	0	0	0	—	—	0	0	0
Dick Drago	p	2	0	0	0	0	0	0	0	0	0	0	—	—	0	0	0
Dick Pole	p	1	0	0	0	0	0	0	0	0	0	0	—	—	0	0	0
Diego Segui	p	1	0	0	0	0	0	0	0	0	0	0	—	—	0	0	0
team total		7	239	30	60	7	2	6	30	30	40	0	.251	.372	196	72	6

Double Plays—6
Left on Bases—52

REGULAR SEASON STATISTICS

	Main Pos	G	AB	R	H	2B	3B	HR	RBI	BB	SO	SB	BA	SA
CINCINNATI REDS														
Tony Perez	1b	137	511	74	144	28	3	20	109	54	101	1	.282	.466
Joe Morgan	2b	146	498	107	163	27	6	17	94	**132**	52	67	.327	.508
Dave Concepcion	ss	140	507	62	139	23	1	5	49	39	51	33	.274	.353
Pete Rose	3b	162	662	**112**	210	**47**	4	7	74	89	50	0	.317	.432
Ken Griffey	of	132	463	95	141	15	9	4	46	67	67	16	.305	.402
Cesar Geronimo	of	148	501	69	129	25	5	6	53	48	97	13	.257	.363
George Foster	of	134	463	71	139	24	4	23	78	40	73	2	.300	.518
Johnny Bench	c	142	530	83	150	39	1	28	110	65	108	11	.283	.519
Marv Rettenmund	of-ph	93	188	24	45	6	1	2	19	35	22	5	.239	.314
Ed Armbrister	ph-of	59	65	9	12	1	0	0	2	5	19	3	.185	.200
Darrell Chaney	ss-2b	71	160	18	35	6	0	2	26	14	38	3	.219	.294
Terry Crowley	ph	66	71	8	19	6	0	1	11	7	6	0	.268	.394
Dan Driessen	1b-of-ph	88	210	38	59	8	1	7	38	35	30	10	.281	.429
Doug Flynn	3b-2b	89	127	17	34	7	0	1	20	11	13	3	.268	.346
Bill Plummer	c	65	159	17	29	7	0	1	19	24	28	1	.182	.245
Don Gullett	p	22	62	5	14	1	1	0	9	2	15	0	.226	.274
Jack Billingham	p	33	65	5	7	0	0	0	4	8	22	0	.108	.108
Rawly Eastwick	p	58	15	0	1	0	0	0	0	0	8	0	.067	.067
Will McEnaney	p	70	14	0	0	0	0	0	0	0	5	0	.000	.000
Pedro Borbon	p	67	24	4	7	1	0	0	2	0	4	0	.292	.333
Pat Darcy	p	27	47	1	4	1	0	0	1	0	27	0	.085	.106
Gary Nolan	p	32	68	10	12	1	1	0	7	7	29	0	.176	.221
Fred Norman	p	34	60	3	7	1	0	0	4	3	19	0	.117	.133
Clay Carroll	p	56	19	1	0	0	0	0	0	0	6	0	.000	.000
Clay Kirby	p	26	32	3	6	1	0	0	2	2	15	0	.188	.219
team total		162	5581	**840**	1515	278	37	124	**719**	**691**	916	**168**	.271	.401

John Vukovich (ph-3b), Don Werner (c), Tom Carroll (p), and Tom Hall (p) also played for the Reds during the season.

	Main Pos	G	AB	R	H	2B	3B	HR	RBI	BB	SO	SB	BA	SA
BOSTON RED SOX														
Cecil Cooper	dh-1b	106	305	49	95	17	6	14	44	19	33	1	.311	.380
Denny Doyle	a 2b	89	310	0	96	21	2	4	36	14	11	5	.310	.429
Rick Burleson	ss	158	580	66	146	25	1	6	62	45	44	8	.252	.329
Rico Petrocelli	3b	115	402	31	96	15	1	7	59	41	66	0	.239	.334
Dwight Evans	of	128	412	61	113	24	6	13	56	47	60	3	.274	.456
Fred Lynn	of	145	528	**103**	175	**47**	7	21	105	62	90	10	.331	.566
Carl Yastrzemski	1b	149	543	91	146	30	1	14	60	87	67	8	.269	.405
Carlton Fisk	c	79	263	47	87	14	4	10	52	27	32	4	.331	.528
Juan Beniquez	of-dh	78	254	43	74	14	4	2	17	25	26	7	.291	.406
Bernie Carbo	of	107	319	64	82	21	3	15	50	83	69	2	.257	.483
Rick Miller	of	77	108	21	21	2	1	0	15	21	20	3	.194	.231
Doug Griffin	2b	100	287	21	69	6	0	1	29	18	29	2	.240	.272
Bob Montgomery	c	62	195	16	44	10	1	2	26	4	37	1	.226	.318
Tim Blackwell	c	59	132	15	26	3	2	0	6	19	13	0	.197	.250
Bob Heise	3b	63	126	12	27	3	0	0	21	4	6	0	.214	.238
Jim Rice	of-dh	144	564	92	174	29	4	22	102	36	122	10	.309	.491
Luis Tiant	p	35	1	0	0	0	0	0	0	0	0	0	.000	.000
Bill Lee	p	41	0	0	0	0	0	0	0	0	0	0	—	—
Reggie Cleveland	p	31	0	0	0	0	0	0	0	0	0	0	—	—
Rick Wise	p	35	0	0	0	0	0	0	0	0	0	0	—	—
Roger Moret	p	36	0	0	0	0	0	0	0	0	0	0	—	—
Jim Willoughby	p	24	0	0	0	0	0	0	0	0	0	0	—	—
Jim Burton	p	29	0	0	0	0	0	0	0	0	0	0	—	—
Dick Drago	p	40	0	0	0	0	0	0	0	0	0	0	—	—
Dick Pole	p	18	0	0	0	0	0	0	0	0	0	0	—	—
Diego Segui	p	33	0	0	0	0	0	0	0	0	0	0	—	—
team total		160	5448	**796**	**1500**	**284**	44	134	**756**	565	741	66	**.275**	.417

a—from California

Kim Andrew (2b), Tony Conigliaro (dh), Steve Dillard (2b), Butch Hobson (3b), Buddy Hunter (2b), Deron Johnson (1b), Dick McAuliffe (3b) Tim McCarver (ph-c), Andy Merchant (c), Steve Barr (p), and Rick Krueger (p) also played for the Red Sox during the season.

PITCHING

WORLD SERIES STATISTICS

	G	GS	CG	IP	H	R	ER	BB	SO	W	L	SV	ERA
CINCINNATI REDS													
Don Gullett	3	**3**	0	**18⅔**	19	9	9	**10**	**15**	1	**1**	0	4.34
Jack Billingham	3	1	0	9	8	2	1	5	7	0	0	0	**1.00**
Rawly Eastwick	**5**	0	0	8	6	2	2	3	4	**2**	0	**1**	2.25
Will McEnaney	**5**	0	0	6⅔	3	2	2	2	5	0	0	**1**	2.70
Gary Nolan	2	2	0	6	6	4	4	1	2	0	0	0	6.00
Clay Carroll	**5**	0	0	5⅔	4	2	2	2	3	1	0	0	3.18
Pat Darcy	2	0	0	4	3	2	2	2	1	0	**1**	0	4.50
Fred Norman	2	1	0	4	8	4	4	3	2	0	**1**	0	9.00
Pedro Borbon	3	0	0	3	3	3	2	2	1	0	0	0	6.00
Clay Kirby	Did not play												
team total	7	7	0	65	60	30	28	30	40	4	3	2	3.88
BOSTON RED SOX													
Luis Tiant	3	**3**	**2**	**25**	**25**	**10**	**10**	8	12	**2**	0	0	3.60
Bill Lee	2	2	0	14⅓	12	5	5	3	7	0	0	0	3.14
Reggie Cleveland	3	1	0	6⅔	7	5	5	3	5	0	**1**	0	6.75
Jim Willoughby	3	0	0	6⅓	3	1	0	0	2	0	**1**	0	0.00
Rick Wise	2	1	0	5⅓	6	5	5	2	2	1	0	0	8.44
Dick Drago	2	0	0	4	3	1	1	1	1	0	**1**	0	2.25
Roger Moret	3	0	0	1⅔	2	0	0	3	1	0	0	0	0.00
Jim Burton	2	0	0	1	1	1	1	3	0	0	**1**	0	9.00
Diego Segui	1	0	0	1	0	0	0	0	0	0	0	0	0.00
Dick Pole	1	0	0	0	0	1	1	2	0	0	0	0	∞
team total	7	7	2	65⅓	59	29	28	25	30	3	4	0	3.86

REGULAR SEASON STATISTICS

	G	GS	CG	IP	H	ER	BB	SO	W	L	Pct	SV	ShO	ERA
CINCINNATI REDS														
Don Gullett	22	22	8	160	127	43	56	98	15	4	.789	0	3	2.42
Jack Billingham	33	32	5	208	222	95	76	79	15	10	.600	0	0	4.11
Rawly Eastwick	58	0	0	90	77	26	25	61	5	3	.625	**22**	0	2.60
Will McEnaney	70	0	0	91	92	25	23	48	5	2	.714	15	0	2.47
Gary Nolan	32	32	5	211	202	74	29	74	15	9	.625	0	1	3.16
Clay Carroll	56	2	0	96	93	28	32	44	7	5	.583	7	0	2.63
Pat Darcy	27	22	1	131	134	52	59	46	11	5	.688	1	0	3.57
Fred Norman	34	26	2	188	163	78	84	119	12	4	.750	0	0	3.73
Pedro Borbon	67	0	0	125	145	41	21	29	9	5	.643	5	0	2.95
Clay Kirby	26	19	1	111	113	58	54	48	10	6	.625	0	0	4.70
team total	162	162	22	1459	1422	546	487	663	**108**	54	**.667**	**50**	8	3.37
BOSTON RED SOX														
Luis Tiant	35	35	18	260	262	116	72	142	18	14	.563	0	2	4.02
Bill Lee	41	34	17	260	274	114	69	78	17	9	.654	0	4	3.95
Reggie Cleveland	31	20	3	171	173	84	78	52	13	9	.591	0	1	4.43
Jim Willoughby	24	0	0	48	46	19	16	29	5	2	.714	8	0	3.54
Rick Wise	35	35	17	255	262	112	72	141	19	12	.613	0	1	3.95
Dick Drago	40	2	0	73	69	31	31	43	2	2	.500	15	0	3.84
Roger Moret	36	16	4	145	132	58	76	80	14	3	.824	1	1	3.60
Jim Burton	29	4	0	53	58	17	39	19	1	2	.333	1	0	2.89
Diego Segui	33	1	1	71	71	38	43	45	2	5	.286	6	0	4.82
Dick Pole	18	11	2	90	102	44	32	42	4	6	.600	0	1	4.42
team total	160	160	62	1437	1463	636	490	720	95	65	.594	31	11	3.98

Total Attendance—308,272   Average Attendance—44,039   *Winning Player's Share—$19,060   *Losing Player's Share—$13,326
*Includes Playoffs and World Series

1976
Almost All the Way Back

In 1976 the New York Yankees reembraced the traditions of their history. After two years in exile in Shea Stadium, the Yanks returned to the rebuilt Yankee Stadium and welcomed fans back to the Bronx with their first pennant since 1964. Owned by George Steinbrenner since 1973 and managed by Billy Martin since mid-1975, the Yankees emerged from their dark ages on the strength of general manager Gabe Paul's crafty dealing. At the end of last season, he made trades which brought Mickey Rivers and Ed Figueroa from the Angels; Willie Randolph and Dock Ellis from the Pirates; and Doyle Alexander, Ken Holtzman, and Grant Jackson from the Orioles. At the heart of the New York lineup was catcher Thurman Munson, whose clutch hitting and defense won him the MVP award in the American League. Graig Nettles and Chris Chambliss joined Munson as the major run-producers, while Rivers, Randolph, and Roy White used their speed to set the table for the power hitters. Catfish Hunter, the former Oakland ace who joined the Yankees in 1975 as a free agent, led a pitching staff that also featured reliever Sparky Lyle. The Yankees got to the Series by running away with the A.L. East title and then beating the Kansas City Royals in the fifth game of the playoffs on a ninth-inning homer by Chambliss.

In the Series the Yankees would meet the defending champion Cincinnati Reds. Manager Sparky Anderson had strong hitters up and down his lineup. Joe Morgan won his second straight MVP award with his batting, power, speed, and defense; while George Foster, Ken Griffey, and Pete Rose were crowning outstanding hitting seasons. The other starters were Tony Perez, Cesar Geronimo, Johnny Bench, and Dave Concepcion—none of them easy outs. With the designated-hitter rule in effect in the Series for the first time, Anderson found a place in the lineup for young Danny Driessen. The pitching staff was deep, with seven men in double figures for victories. The Reds came to the Series fresh from a three-game sweep of the Phillies for the N.L. pennant.

The Reds relied on lefty Don Gullett, their ace who had come back from mid-season arm troubles, to start game one at Riverfront Stadium. Because Hunter had started against Kansas City only three days earlier, Martin sent Doyle Alexander to the mound. The Reds flexed their batting muscle right away when Morgan belted a first-inning homer. New York tied the game with a run in the second inning, but Gullett then settled into his groove and iced the Yankee bats. The Reds got to Alexander for a run in the third and another in the sixth before knocking him out in the two-run seventh inning. With the Reds ahead 5–1, Gullett injured an ankle in the eighth inning and left Pedro Borbon to finish the game.

The Reds had another lefty ready for the Yankees in Fred Norman, while Catfish Hunter started for New York in game two. Played on a cold Sunday night, this game was the closest of the Series. The Reds scored three times in the second inning on two walks, four hits, and a sacrifice fly. The Yankees reached Norman for a run in the top of the fourth on singles by Munson, Chambliss, and Nettles. With Hunter retiring the Reds without trouble, the Yankees tied the score in the seventh inning. Randolph led off with a single and scored on a double by Fred Stanley, the Yankees's underrated shortstop. After Rivers flew out, White singled Stanley to third. After Jack Billingham replaced Norman, Stanley scored the tying run on a grounder by Munson. But in the bottom of the ninth, after Hunter retired the first two batters, Griffey reached second on Stanley's throwing error. After Morgan was intentionally walked, Perez lined to left to win the game 4–3.

Ahead two games to none, the Reds kept up the pressure in game three in New York. They banged Dock Ellis for three runs in the top of the second inning and another in the fourth on a solo homer by Driessen. Although New York scored once in the fourth and again in the seventh, Will McEnaney relieved Cincinnati starter Pat Zachry in the seventh and permitted no scoring the rest of the way for the 6–2 victory.

After one day off because of rain, the Reds were ready for the kill. Although the Yankees jumped out to the early lead with a first-inning run off Gary Nolan, the Reds scored three times in the fourth off Figueroa, featuring Bench's two-run shot into the left-

field stands. The Yanks closed the gap to 3–2, but four Cincinnati runs in the top of the ninth blew the game open and triggered an emotional outburst by Billy Martin that caused his ejection from the game. McEnaney again saved the game in relief as the Reds became the first N.L. team since 1922 to repeat as World Champions. For individual honors, Johnny Bench could point to his .533 average, while Thurman Munson posted a .529 average, with hits in his final six trips to the plate.

Game 1 October 16 at Cincinnati

N.Y.	010 000 000
Cin.	101 001 20x

New York	Pos	AB	R	H	RBI	PO	A	E
Rivers	cf	4	0	0	0	3	0	0
White	lf	4	0	1	0	4	0	0
Munson	c	4	0	1	0	5	1	0
Piniella	dh	3	1	1	0	0	0	0
b May		1	0	0	0	0	0	0
Chambliss	1b	3	0	1	0	4	0	1
Nettles	3b	3	0	1	0	1	3	0
Maddox	rf	2	0	1	0	0	0	0
c Gamble		1	0	0	0	0	0	0
Randolph	2b	2	0	0	0	3	2	0
Stanley	ss	1	0	0	0	2	3	0
a Velez		1	0	0	0	0	0	0
Mason	ss	0	0	0	0	0	1	0
Alexander	p	0	0	0	0	0	1	0
Lyle	p	0	0	0	0	0	0	0
Totals		29	1	5	1	24	8	1

Pitching	IP	H	R	ER	BB	SO
New York						
Alexander (L)	*6	9	5	5	2	1
Lyle	2	1	0	0	0	3
Cincinnati						
Gullett (W)	7⅓	5	1	1	3	4
Borbon	1⅔	0	0	0	0	0

*Pitched to 2 batters in 7th

Cincinnati	Pos	AB	R	H	RBI	PO	A	E
Rose	3b	2	0	0	1	2	2	0
Griffey	rf	4	1	0	0	2	0	0
Morgan	2b	4	1	1	1	3	4	0
Perez	1b	4	0	1	1	11	0	0
Driessen	dh	4	0	0	0	0	0	0
Foster	lf	3	1	2	0	5	1	0
Bench	c	3	1	2	1	5	1	0
Geronimo	cf	3	0	1	0	2	0	1
Concepcion	ss	3	1	1	0	2	3	0
Gullett	p	0	0	0	0	0	1	0
Borbon	p	0	0	0	0	0	0	0
Totals		30	5	10	4	27	12	1

a Struck out for Stanley in 7th.
b Flied out for Piniella in 8th.
c Fouled out for Maddox in 9th.

Doubles—Piniella, Perez, Geronimo. Triples—Concepcion, Maddox, Bench. Home Run—Morgan. Stolen Base—Griffey. Sacrifice Flies—Nettles, Rose. Double Plays—Alexander to Randolph to Chambliss, Randolph to Stanley to Chambliss, Morgan to Concepcion to Perez, Morgan to Perez. Hit by Pitcher—Chambliss (by Gullett). Wild Pitch—Lyle. Left on Bases—New York 6, Cincinnati 4. Umpires—Weyer (N), DiMuro(A), B. Williams(N), Deegan(A), Froemming(N), Phillips(A). Attendance—54,826. Time of Game—2:10.

1st Inning
New York
1 Rivers struck out.
2 White grounded out off Rose to Concepcion to Perez.
3 Munson struck out.
Cincinnati
1 Rose flied to center.
2 Griffey lined to left.
Morgan hit a home run into the lower right field seats.
Perez singled to left-center.
3 Perez caught trying to steal, Munson to Stanley.

2nd Inning
New York
Piniella lined a double to right.
1 Chambliss grounded to second, Piniella advancing to third.
2 Nettles hit a sacrifice fly to deep center, scoring Piniella.
3 Maddox grounded to third.
Cincinnati
1 Driessen flied out to Rivers in deep right-center.
Foster walked.
2,3 Bench grounded into a double play, Alexander to Randolph to Chambliss.

3rd Inning
New York
1 Randolph grounded to short.
2 Stanley took a called third strike.
3 Rivers grounded to second.
Cincinnati
1 Geronimo popped to third.
Concepcion lined a triple to the left-center field wall.
2 Rose hit a deep sacrifice fly to center, scoring Concepcion.
3 Griffey popped to third.

4th Inning
New York
1 White lined to third.
2 Munson flied to short right.
3 Piniella grounded to first.
Cincinnati
1 Morgan flied to White in left-center. Perez doubled down the third base line.
2 Driessen lined to White in left-center.
3 Foster was credited with a single when his grounder hit Perez. Perez was automatically out with the putout to Nettles.

5th Inning
New York
Chambliss singled to left.
1,2 Nettles hit into a double play, Morgan to Concepcion to Perez. Maddox tripled down the left field line.
3 Randolph flied to deep center.
Cincinnati
Bench singled to center.
1,2 Geronimo hit into a double play, Randolph to Stanley to Chambliss.
3 Concepcion grounded to Stanley, making an excellent play on the slow bouncer.

6th Inning
New York
Stanley walked.
1 Rivers forced Stanley on a bunt, Gullett to Concepcion.
2 Rivers caught stealing Bench to Morgan.
White got safely to second when his liner to Geronimo was dropped.
Munson singled to right, White stopping at third.
3 Piniella lined to Morgan in short center.
Cincinnati
Rose walked.
1 Griffey forced Rose, Stanley to Randolph.
2 Morgan struck out, while Griffey was stealing second.
Perez singled to left, Griffey scoring.
3 Driessen fouled to Munson.

7th Inning
New York
Chambliss was hit by a pitch.
1,2 Nettles grounded to Morgan, who tagged Chambliss and threw to Perez for the double play.
Maddox walked.
Randolph walked.
3 Velez, batting for Stanley, struck out.
Cincinnati
For New York—Mason playing short.
Foster singled to left.
Bench tripled off the right field wall, scoring Foster.
For New York—Lyle now pitching. Bench scored on a wild pitch. Geronimo blooped a double to left-center.
1 Concepcion struck out.
2 Rose grounded to short, Geronimo moving to third.
3 Griffey struck out.

8th Inning
New York
1 Rivers fouled to Bench.
White singled to left.
For Cincinnati—Borbon came in to pitch.
2 Munson rolled out to Borbon, White going to second.
3 May, hitting for Piniella, lined to right.
Cincinnati
1 Morgan lined to second.
2 Perez struck out and was tagged by Munson after dropping the strike. Driessen safe on a fumble by Chambliss.
3 Foster flied to short left.

9th Inning
New York
1 Chambliss grounded to Perez, unassisted.
2 Nettles lined to Perez.
3 Gamble, pinch-hitting for Maddox, fouled to Rose.

Game 2 October 17 at Cincinnati

New York	Pos	AB	R	H	RBI	PO	A	E
Rivers	cf	5	0	0	0	6	0	0
White	lf	3	0	1	0	6	0	0
Munson	c	4	1	1	1	7	1	0
Piniella	rf	4	0	2	0	1	0	0
Chambliss	1b	4	0	2	0	2	0	0
Nettles	3b	4	0	1	1	2	1	0
Maddox	dh	3	0	0	0	0	0	0
a May	dh	1	0	0	0	0	0	0
Randolph	2b	4	1	1	0	2	0	0
Stanley	ss	3	1	1	1	0	0	1
Hunter	p	0	0	0	0	0	1	0
Totals		35	3	9	3	x26	3	1

Pitching	IP	H	R	ER	BB	SO
New York						
Hunter (L)	$8\frac{2}{3}$	10	4	3	4	5
Cincinnati						
Norman	$6\frac{1}{3}$	9	3	3	2	2
Billingham (W)	$2\frac{2}{3}$	0	0	0	0	1

N.Y.	000	100	200
Cin.	030	000	001

Cincinnati	Pos	AB	R	H	RBI	PO	A	E
Rose	3b	4	0	0	0	0	0	0
Griffey	rf	4	1	0	1	1	0	0
Morgan	2b	4	0	2	0	6	3	0
Perez	1b	5	0	2	1	8	1	0
Driessen	dh	4	1	2	0	0	0	0
Foster	lf	4	0	1	1	2	0	0
Bench	c	4	1	2	0	3	0	0
Geronimo	cf	2	1	0	0	4	0	0
Concepcion	ss	4	0	1	1	2	3	0
Norman	p	0	0	0	0	0	1	0
Billingham	p	0	0	0	0	1	0	0
Totals		35	4	10	4	27	8	0

a Grounded out for Maddox in 8th.
x Two out when winning run scored.

Doubles—Bench, Driessen, Stanley. Triple—Morgan. Stolen Bases—Concepcion, Morgan. Sacrifice Fly—Griffey. Double Play—Concepcion to Morgan to Perez. Left on Bases—New York 7, Cincinnati 10. Umpires—DiMoro, Williams, Deegan, Froemming, Phillips, Weyer. Attendance—54,816. Time of Game—2:33.

1st Inning
New York
1 Rivers flied to center.
2 White popped to Morgan in short center.
3 Munson flied to Griffey in short right-center.
Cincinnati
1 Rose lined to deep left.
2 Griffey flied to White in deep left-center.
Morgan singled to center.
Morgan stole second.
3 Perez popped to Nettles near the mound.

2nd Inning
New York
Piniella beat out a grounder to deep short.
1 Chambliss flied to deep center.
2 Nettles flied to Foster in left-center.
3 Maddox struck out.
Cincinnati
Driessen doubled to deep center.
Foster singled to center, Driessen scoring.
1 Foster caught trying to steal second, Munson to Randolph.
Bench doubled to left-center.
Geronimo walked.
Concepcion blooped a single to right-center, Bench scoring, and Geronimo going to third.
Concepcion stole second.
Rose walked, loading the bases.
2 Griffey hit a sacrifice fly to short center, Geronimo scoring after the catch.
3 Morgan fouled to Munson, making a good catch near the Yankees' dugout.

3rd Inning
New York
1 Randolph flied to center.
Stanley walked.
2 Rivers grounded to first, Perez unassisted, as Stanley went to second.
3 White popped to Morgan.
Cincinnati
Perez singled to right.
Driessen beat out a high bouncer to first, Perez stopping at second.
1 Foster struck out.
2 Bench flied to left.
Geronimo walked, loading the bases.
3 Concepcion struck out.

4th Inning
New York
Munson beat out a grounder to third.
1 Piniella flied to left.
Chambliss singled to left, Munson stopping at second.
Nettles singled to center, Munson scoring and Chambliss going to third.
On the throw to third Nettles took second.
2 Maddox struck out, Bench making the tag for the out.
3 Randolph bounced to short.
Cincinnati
1 Rose lined to deep left.
2 Griffey flied to deep center.
Morgan tripled to left-center.
3 Perez flied to Rivers in short right-center.

5th Inning
New York
1 Stanley popped to short.
2 Rivers grounded to short.
White walked.
3 Munson tapped out to the mound.
Cincinnati
1 Driessen flied to left.
2 Foster grounded to third.
3 Bench struck out.

6th Inning
New York
Piniella singled to left.
Chambliss singled to center, Piniella going to second.
1 Nettles fouled to Morgan behind first.
2,3 Maddox hit into a double play, Concepcion to Morgan to Perez.
Cincinnati
1 Geronimo popped to third.
2 Concepcion lined to left.
3 Rose struck out.

7th Inning
New York
Randolph singled to center.
Stanley doubled into the left field corner, scoring Randolph.
1 Rivers flied to center.
White singled to left advancing Stanley to third.
For Cincinnati—Billingham replaced Norman on the mound.
2 Munson forced White at second, Morgan to Concepcion, as Stanley scored.
3 Piniella forced Munson, Morgan unassisted.
Cincinnati
1 Griffey flied to shallow center.
2 Morgan fouled to Munson, who made a spectacular catch.
3 Perez popped to second.

8th Inning
New York
1 Chambliss grounded to second.
2 Nettles lined to Perez.
3 May, pinch-hitting for Maddox, grounded out, Perez to Billingham.
Cincinnati
1 Driessen flied to Rivers in right-center.
2 Foster struck out.
Bench singled to left.
3 Geronimo tapped back to the mound.

9th Inning
New York
1 Randolph took a called third strike.
2 Stanley popped to second.
3 Rivers bounced out, Perez unassisted.
Cincinnati
1 Concepcion flied to shallow center.
2 Rose flied to left.
Griffey got safely to second when Stanley threw his slow grounder into the Red dugout.
Morgan got an intentional pass.
Perez lined a single to left, Griffey scoring the game-winner.

Game 3 October 19 at New York

Cincinnati	Pos	AB	R	H	RBI	PO	A	E
Rose	3b	5	1	2	0	1	1	0
Griffey	rf	4	0	1	0	0	0	0
Morgan	26	4	1	1	1	2	0	1
Perez	1b	4	0	0	0	7	2	0
Driessen	dh	3	2	3	1	0	0	0
Foster	lf	4	1	2	2	4	0	0
Bench	c	4	0	2	0	8	0	0
Geronimo	cf	4	1	1	1	3	0	0
Concepcion	ss	4	0	1	1	1	2	0
Zachry	p	0	0	0	0	0	2	1
McEnaney	p	0	0	0	0	1	0	0
Totals		36	6	13	6	27	7	2

a Flied out for Stanley in 4th.
b Grounded out for Gamble in 8th.
c Struck out for Mason in 9th

Doubles—Driessen, Foster, Morgan. Home Runs—Driessen, Mason. Stolen Bases—Driessen, Geronimo. Double Plays—Stanley to Randolph to Chambliss, Nettles to Chambliss, Nettles to Randolph to Chambliss, Perez to Concepcion. Left on Bases—Cincinnati 4, New York 11. Umpires—Williams, Deegan, Froemming, Phillips, Weyer, DiMuro. Attendance—56,667. Time of Game—2:40.

Cin.	030	100	020
N.Y.	000	100	100

New York	Pos	AB	R	H	RBI	PO	A	E
Rivers	cf	4	0	2	0	1	0	0
White	lf	3	0	0	0	1	0	0
Munson	c	5	0	3	0	6	2	0
Chambliss	1b	5	1	1	0	11	1	0
May	dh	4	0	0	0	0	0	0
Nettles	3b	2	0	0	0	1	4	0
Gamble	rf	3	0	1	1	2	0	0
b Piniella	rf	1	0	0	0	0	0	0
Randolph	2b	4	0	0	0	4	4	0
Stanley	ss	1	0	0	0	1	2	0
a Hendricks		1	0	0	0	0	0	0
Mason	ss	1	1	1	1	0	1	0
c Velez		1	0	0	0	0	0	0
Ellis	p	0	0	0	0	0	0	0
Jackson	p	0	0	0	0	0	3	0
Tidrow	p	0	0	0	0	0	0	0
Totals		35	2	8	2	27	17	0

Pitching	IP	H	R	ER	BB	SO
Cincinnati						
Zachry(W)	$6\frac{2}{3}$	6	2	2	5	6
McEnaney(SV)	$2\frac{1}{3}$	2	0	0	0	1
New York						
Ellis(L)	$3\frac{1}{3}$	7	4	4	0	1
Jackson	*$3\frac{2}{3}$	4	2	2	0	3
Tidrow	2	2	0	0	1	1

*Pitched to three batters in 8th.

1st Inning
Cincinnati
Rose blooped a single to right.
1 Griffey bounced to first, Rose going to second.
2 Morgan rolled out to first, Rose advancing to third.
3 Perez popped to Randolph in short right.
New York
Rivers safe on Zachry's bad throw to first on his bunt.
1 Rivers was picked off first, Zachry to Perez.
2 White popped to Rose near the plate.
Munson singled to center.
3 Chambliss struck out.

2nd Inning
Cincinnati
Driessen beat out a high bouncer off of Ellis and fielded too late by Randolph.
Driessen stole second.
Foster got a ground-rule double when his blast to right-center bounced over the wall, scoring Driessen.
Bench beat out a liner, which Chambliss leaped for and deflected to Randolph, Foster stopped at third.
1 Geronimo forced Bench, Stanley to Randolph, Foster scoring.
Geronimo stole second.
Concepcion blooped a single to left, scoring Geronimo.
2,3 Rose bounced into a double play, Stanley to Randolph to Chambliss.
New York
1 May grounded to first.
Nettles walked.
2 Gamble lined to center.
3 Randolph flied to left.

3rd Inning
Cincinnati
1 Griffey tapped to third.
2 Morgan bounced to second.
3 Perez fanned.
New York
1 Stanley tapped back to the mound.
2 Rivers struck out but had to be tagged when Bench dropped the third strike.
White walked.
3 Munson flied to center.

4th Inning
Cincinnati
Driessen homered on a liner into the right-center field stands.
1 Foster grounded to second, Randolph making a great fielding play.
Bench singled to right.
For New York—Jackson came in to pitch.
2 Bench was picked off first, Jackson to Chambliss to Stanley.
3 Geronimo lined to right.
New York
Chambliss singled to center.
1 May struck out.
Nettles again walked.
Gamble lined a single to center, Chambliss scoring, with Nettles stopping at second.
2 Randolph fouled to Bench.
3 Hendricks, pinch-hitting for Stanley, flied to Foster in left-center.

5th Inning
Cincinnati
For New York—Mason playing shortstop.
1 Concepcion struck out.
2 Rose tapped out, Munson to Chambliss.
3 Griffey flied to White in left-center.

5th Inning (continued)
New York
Rivers blooped a single to left.
White walked.
1,2 Munson lined into a double play, Perez to Concepcion.
3 Chambliss struck out.

6th Inning
Cincinnati
1 Morgan struck out.
2 Perez grounded back to the pitcher.
Driessen got his third hit, a double on a soft fly to center that fell in front of a diving Rivers.
3 Foster flied to shallow right.
New York
1 May flied to center.
2 Nettles struck out.
3 Gamble popped to Morgan in short right.

7th Inning
Cincinnati
1 Bench was out on an excellent stop of his grounder by Jackson who threw him out at first.
2 Geronimo struck out.
3 Concepcion flied to center.
New York
1 Randolph struck out.
Mason lined a homer into the lower right field stands.
Rivers walked.
2 White forced Rivers at second, Rose to Morgan.
Munson singled to right, White stopping at second.
For Cincinnati—McEnaney now pitching.
3 Chambliss bounced out, Perez to McEnaney.

8th Inning
Cincinnati
Rose singled to center.
Griffey singled to right, Rose going to third.
Morgan doubled down the right field line, Rose scoring with Griffey stopping at third.
For New York—Tidrow came in to pitch.
1 Perez bounced to Mason, and Griffey got caught in a rundown, Mason to Munson to Nettles to Munson. Morgan got to third and Perez to second.
Driessen intentionally walked, loading the bases.
Foster lined a single to left, Morgan scoring and the bases still loaded.
2,3 Bench bounced into a double play, Nettles to Chambliss.
New York
1 May grounded to short.
Nettles safely to second as Morgan booted his grounder.
2 Piniella, batting for Gamble, grounded to short, Nettles moving on to third.
3 Randolph flied to Foster in left-center.

9th Inning
Cincinnati
For New York—Piniella playing in right.
Geronimo singled to left.
1,2 Concepcion bounced into a double play, Nettles to Randolph to Chambliss.
3 Rose struck out.
New York
1 Velez, pinch-hitting for Mason, struck out.
Rivers singled to right.
2 White fouled to Perez.
Munson got his third hit, a single to right as Rivers stopped at second.
3 Chambliss flied to left.

Game 4 October 21 at New York

Cin.	0 0 0	3 0 0	0 0 4
N.Y.	1 0 0	0 1 0	0 0 0

Cincinnati	Pos	AB	R	H	RBI	PO	A	E
Rose	3b	5	0	1	0	3	0	0
Griffey	rf	5	0	0	0	2	0	0
Morgan	2b	3	1	1	0	2	3	1
Perez	1b	3	1	0	0	6	1	0
Driessen	dh	3	1	0	0	0	0	0
Foster	lf	3	1	1	1	8	0	0
Bench	c	4	2	2	5	2	1	0
Geronimo	cf	4	1	2	0	3	0	0
Concepcion	ss	3	0	2	1	1	3	1
Nolan	p	0	0	0	0	0	1	0
McEnaney	p	0	0	0	0	0	0	0
Totals		33	7	9	7	27	9	2

Pitching	IP	H	R	ER	BB	SO
Cincinnati						
Nolan (W)	6⅔	8	2	2	1	1
McEnaney (SV)	2⅓	0	0	0	1	1
New York						
Figueroa (L)	*8	6	5	5	5	2
Tidrow	⅔	3	2	2	0	0
Lyle	⅓	0	0	0	0	0

*Pitched to two batters in 9th.

New York	Pos	AB	R	H	RBI	PO	A	E
Rivers	cf	5	1	1	0	4	0	0
White	lf	5	0	0	0	2	0	0
Munson	c	4	1	4	1	3	3	0
Chambliss	1b	4	0	1	1	9	2	0
May	dh	3	0	0	0	0	0	0
b Piniella	dh	1	0	0	0	0	0	0
Nettles	3b	3	0	2	0	2	3	0
Gamble	rf	4	0	0	0	1	0	0
Randolph	2b	4	0	0	0	4	2	0
Stanley	ss	1	0	0	0	1	2	0
a Hendricks		1	0	0	0	0	0	0
Mason	ss	0	0	0	0	1	0	0
c Velez		1	0	0	0	0	0	0
Figueroa	p	0	0	0	0	0	1	0
Tidrow	p	0	0	0	0	0	0	0
Lyle	p	0	0	0	0	0	0	0
Totals		36	2	8	2	27	13	0

a Fouled out for Stanley in 6th.
b Flied out for May in 8th.
c Struck out for Mason in 9th.

Doubles—Chambliss, Concepcion, Geronimo, Rose. Home Runs—Bench 2. Stolen Bases—Geronimo, Morgan, Rivers. Double Play—Stanley to Nettles to Chambliss to Randolph. Wild Pitch—Figueroa. Left on Bases—Cincinnati 4, New York 9. Umpires—Deegan, Froemming, Phillips, Weyer, DiMuro, Williams. Attendance—56,700. Time of Game—2:36.

1st Inning
Cincinnati
Rose lined a ground-rule double into the stands down the left field line
1,2 Griffey bounced to Stanley, and Rose was caught in a rundown, Stanley to Nettles, who threw to Chambliss, and Griffey was tagged out. The play went from Stanley to Nettles to Chambliss to Randolph.
3 Morgan grounded to first.
New York
1 Rivers popped to short.
2 White grounded to second.
Munson blooped a single to right-center.
Chambliss doubled to left-center, Munson scoring.
3 May grounded to short, Concepcion making a fantastic stop behind second.

2nd Inning
Cincinnati
1 Perez grounded to first.
2 Driessen flied to short left.
Foster walked.
3 Foster out trying to steal second, Munson to Randolph.
New York
1 Nettles tapped back to the mound.
2 Gamble popped to Rose near the pitcher's mound.
3 Randolph flied to center, Geronimo making a shoestring catch.

3rd Inning
Cincinnati
1 Bench popped to second.
Geronimo singled to left-center.
Geronimo stole second.
Concepcion walked.
2 Rose forced Concepcion at second, Chambliss to Stanley, as Geronimo advanced to third.
3 Griffey just out when his grounder was deflected from Figueroa to Randolph, who threw to first.
New York
Stanley walked on four pitches.
1 Rivers flied to short left.
2 White flied to Griffey in deep right-center.
Munson singled to right with Stanley stopping at second.
Chambliss was safe on Morgan's fumble, loading the bases.
3 May lined to left.

4th Inning
Cincinnati
Morgan walked.
1 Perez lined to Rivers in left-center. Morgan stole second.
2 Driessen fouled to Munson.
Foster singled to left, scoring Morgan.
Bench blasted a two-run homer just inside the left field foul pole.
3 Geronimo just nipped as Stanley made a great stop and throw of his grounder.
New York
Nettles singled to right-center.
Gamble safe at first and Nettles at second when Concepcion dropped a throw from Perez.
1 Nettles was trapped off second when Randolph missed a pitch during an attempted bunt. The play went from Bench to Concepcion to Rose.
2 Randolph took a called third strike.
3 Stanley lined to right.

5th Inning
Cincinnati
1 Concepcion bounced to third.
2 Rose flied to left.
3 Griffey fouled to Nettles.
New York
Rivers singled to right.
1 White flied to short left.
Rivers stole second.
Munson singled to center, Rivers scoring. Munson's fifth straight hit.
2 Chambliss lined to Foster in left-center.
3 May grounded to second.

6th Inning
Cincinnati
Morgan lined a single to left-center.
1 Perez rolled to third, Morgan advancing to second.
2 Driessen popped to second.
3 Foster struck out.
New York
Nettles singled when his high bouncer went over Morgan's head.
1 Gamble popped to second.
2 Randolph flied to center.
3 Hendricks, pinch-hitting for Stanley, fouled to Perez.

7th Inning
Cincinnati
For New York—Mason playing shortstop.
1 Bench flied to short right.
2 Geronimo called out on strikes.
Concepcion lined a single to center.
3 Concepcion caught trying to steal second, Munson to Mason.
New York
1 Rivers flied to Foster in short left-center.
2 White flied to Geronimo, making a running catch in short center
Munson got his sixth successive hit on a single to center.
For Cincinnati—McEnaney replaced Nolan on the mound.
3 Chambliss rolled to second.

8th Inning
Cincinnati
1 Rose flied to Rivers in left-center.
2 Griffey tapped out, Munson to Chambliss.
3 Morgan flied to Rivers in deep right-center.
New York
1 Piniella, pinch-hitting for May, lined to left.
Nettles walked.
2 Gamble flied to Foster in left-center.
3 Randolph forced Nettles at second, Concepcion to Morgan.

9th Inning
Cincinnati
Perez walked.
Perez went to second on a wild pitch.
Driessen walked.
For New York—Tidrow came in to pitch.
1 Foster flied to center, with Perez advancing to third after the catch.
Bench lined a three-run homer into the left field seats. His second homer in the game.
Geronimo got a ground-rule double when his hit down the first base line was touched by a fan.
Concepcion also got a ground-rule double when fans touched his hit down the third base line. Geronimo scored.
For New York—Lyle now pitching.
2 Rose bounced to second, Concepcion moving over to third.
3 Griffey grounded to first.
New York
1 Velez, pinch-hitting for Mason, struck out.
2 Rivers lined to third.
3 White flied to Foster in left-center. **This was Foster's eighth putout, tying a Series record set by Edd Roush in 1919.**

1976 WORLD SERIES COMPOSITE BOX

	Wins	Composite Line Score		Regular Season			
			Manager	W	L	Pct.	G. Ahead
Cincinnati Reds (N.L.)	4	1 6 1 4 0 1 2 2 5 - 22	Sparky Anderson	102	60	.630	10
New York Yankees (A.L.)	0	1 1 0 2 1 0 3 0 0 - 8	Billy Martin	97	62	.610	10.5

BATTING AND FIELDING

CINCINNATI REDS

	Pos	G	AB	R	H	2B	3B	HR	RBI	BB	SO	SB	BA	SA	PO	A	E
Tony Perez	1b	4	16	1	5	1	0	0	0	0	0	0	.313	.375	32	4	0
Joe Morgan	2b	4	15	3	5	1	1	1	2	2	2	2	.333	.733	13	10	2
Dave Concepcion	ss	4	14	1	5	1	1	0	3	1	3	1	.357	.571	6	11	1
Pete Rose	3b	4	16	1	3	1	0	0	1	2	2	0	.188	.250	6	3	0
Ken Griffey	rf	4	17	2	1	0	0	0	1	0	1	1	.059	.059	5	0	0
Cesar Geronimo	cf	4	13	3	4	2	0	0	1	2	2	0	.308	.462	12	0	1
George Foster	lf	4	14	3	6	1	0	0	4	2	3	0	.429	.500	14	0	0
Johnny Bench	c	4	15	4	8	1	1	2	6	0	1	0	.533	1.133	18	2	0
Dan Driessen	dh	4	14	4	5	2	0	1	1	2	1	0	.357	.714			
Doug Flynn		Did not play															
Mike Lum		Did not play															
Ed Armbrister		Did not play															
Bob Bailey		Did not play															
Bill Plummer		Did not play															
Joel Youngblood		Did not play															
Don Gullett	p	1	0	0	0	0	0	0	0	0	0	0	—	—	0	1	0
Gary Nolan	p	1	0	0	0	0	0	0	0	0	0	0	—	—	0	1	0
Pat Zachry	p	1	0	0	0	0	0	0	0	0	0	0	—	—	0	2	1
Fred Norman	p	1	0	0	0	0	0	0	0	0	0	0	—	—	0	1	0
Will McEnaney	p	2	0	0	0	0	0	0	0	0	0	0	—	—	1	0	0
Jack Billingham	p	1	0	0	0	0	0	0	0	0	0	0	—	—	1	0	0
Pedro Borbon	p	1	0	0	0	0	0	0	0	0	0	0	—	—	0	1	0
Santo Alcala		Did not play															
Rawly Eastwick		Did not play															
Manny Sarmiento		Did not play															
team total		4	134	22	42	10	3	4	21	12	16	7	.313	.522	108	36	5

Double Plays—4
Left on Bases—22

NEW YORK YANKEES

	Pos	G	AB	R	H	2B	3B	HR	RBI	BB	SO	SB	BA	SA	PO	A	E
Chris Chambliss	1b	4	16	1	5	1	0	0	1	0	2	0	.313	.375	26	3	1
Willie Randolph	2b	4	14	1	1	0	0	0	0	1	3	0	.071	.071	13	8	0
Fred Stanley	ss	4	6	1	1	1	0	0	1	3	1	0	.167	.286	4	7	1
Graig Nettles	3b	4	12	0	3	0	0	0	2	3	1	0	.250	.250	8	8	0
Oscar Gamble	rf	3	8	0	1	0	0	0	1	0	0	0	.125	.125	3	0	0
Mickey Rivers	cf	4	18	1	3	0	0	0	0	1	2	1	.167	.167	14	0	0
Roy White	lf	4	15	2	2	0	0	0	0	3	0	0	.133	.133	13	0	0
Thurman Munson	c	4	17	2	9	0	0	0	2	0	1	0	.529	.529	21	7	0
Lou Piniella	dh-rf-ph	4	9	1	3	1	0	0	0	0	0	0	.333	.444	1	0	0
Carlos May	ph-dh	4	9	0	0	0	0	0	0	1	0	0	.000	.000			
Otto Velez	ph	3	3	0	0	0	0	0	0	0	3	0	.000	.000			
Jim Mason	ss	3	1	1	1	0	0	1	1	0	0	0	1.000	4.000	1	2	0
Elliott Maddox	rf-dh	2	5	0	1	0	0	0	0	1	2	0	.200	.600	0	0	0
Ellie Hendricks	ph	2	2	0	0	0	0	0	0	0	0	0	.000	.000			
Sandy Alomar		Did not play															
Fran Healy		Did not play															
Catfish Hunter	p	1	0	0	0	0	0	0	0	0	0	0	—	—	0	1	0
Ed Figueroa	p	1	0	0	0	0	0	0	0	0	0	0	—	—	0	1	0
Doyle Alexander	p	1	0	0	0	0	0	0	0	0	0	0	—	—	0	1	0
Grant Jackson	p	1	0	0	0	0	0	0	0	0	0	0	—	—	0	3	0
Dock Ellis	p	1	0	0	0	0	0	0	0	0	0	0	—	—	0	0	0
Dick Tidrow	p	2	0	0	0	0	0	0	0	0	0	0	—	—	0	0	0
Sparky Lyle	p	2	0	0	0	0	0	0	0	0	0	0	—	—	0	0	0
Ken Holtzman		Did not play															
Ron Guidry		Did not play															
team total		4	135	8	30	3	1	1	8	12	16	1	.222	.282	104	41	2

Double Plays—6
Left on Bases—33

REGULAR SEASON STATISTICS — CINCINNATI REDS

Main Pos	G	AB	R	H	2B	3B	HR	RBI	BB	SO	SB	BA	SA
1b	139	527	77	137	32	6	19	91	50	88	10	.260	.452
2b	141	472	113	151	30	5	27	111	114	41	60	.320	.576
ss	152	576	74	162	28	7	9	69	49	68	21	.281	.401
3b	162	665	130	215	42	6	10	63	86	54	9	.323	.450
of	148	562	111	189	28	9	6	74	62	65	34	.336	.450
of	149	486	59	149	24	11	2	49	56	95	22	.307	.414
of	144	562	86	172	21	9	29	121	52	89	17	.306	.530
c	135	465	62	109	24	1	16	74	81	95	13	.234	.394
1b-of	98	219	32	54	11	1	7	44	43	32	14	.247	.402
inf	93	219	20	62	5	2	1	20	10	24	2	.283	.338
of	84	136	15	31	5	1	3	20	22	24	0	.228	.346
of	73	78	20	23	3	2	2	7	6	22	7	.295	.462
of-3b	69	124	17	37	6	1	6	23	16	26	0	.298	.508
c	56	153	16	38	6	1	4	19	14	36	0	.248	.379
of-inf	55	57	8	11	1	1	0	1	2	8	1	.193	.246
p	25	44	2	8	0	0	0	3	1	7	0	.182	.182
p	34	79	1	8	0	0	0	3	3	33	0	.101	.101
p	38	62	1	7	0	0	0	2	3	25	0	.113	.113
p	33	50	1	7	0	0	0	1	1	9	0	.140	.140
p	55	6	0	1	0	0	0	0	2	4	0	.167	.167
p	34	59	4	14	3	0	0	4	3	12	0	.237	.288
p	69	18	2	4	0	0	0	0	0	4	0	.222	.222
p	30	43	5	6	1	0	0	2	2	26	0	.140	.163
p	71	17	0	0	0	0	0	0	1	10	0	.000	.000
p	22	7	0	0	0	0	0	0	0	1	0	.000	.000
	162	5702	857	1599	271	63	141	802	681	902	210	.280	.424

Don Werner(c), Joe Henderson(p), Pat Darcy(p) and Rich Hinton(p) also played for the Reds during the season.

REGULAR SEASON STATISTICS — NEW YORK YANKEES

Pos	G	AB	R	H	2B	3B	HR	RBI	BB	SO	SB	BA	SA
1b	156	641	79	188	32	6	17	96	27	80	1	.293	.441
2b	125	430	59	115	15	4	1	40	58	39	37	.267	.328
ss	110	260	32	62	2	1	1	20	34	29	1	.238	.273
3b	158	583	88	148	29	2	32	93	62	94	11	.254	.475
of	110	340	43	79	13	1	17	57	38	38	2	.232	.426
of	137	590	95	184	31	8	8	67	13	51	43	.312	.432
of	156	626	104	179	29	3	14	65	83	72	31	.286	.409
c	152	616	79	186	27	1	17	105	29	38	14	.302	.432
of-dh	100	327	36	92	16	6	3	38	18	34	0	.281	.394
a dh	87	288	30	80	11	2	3	40	2	32	1	.278	.361
of-inf	49	94	11	25	6	0	2	10	23	26	0	.266	.394
ss	93	217	17	39	7	1	1	14	9	37	0	.180	.235
of	18	46	4	10	2	0	0	3	4	3	0	.217	.261
b c	26	53	6	12	1	0	3	5	3	10	0	.226	.415
inf-dh	67	163	20	39	4	0	1	10	13	12	12	.239	.282
c c	46	120	10	32	3	0	0	9	9	17	3	.267	.292
p	36	1	0	0	0	0	0	0	0	0	0	.000	.000
p	34	0	0	0	0	0	0	0	0	0	0	—	—
b p	19	0	0	0	0	0	0	0	0	0	0	—	—
b p	21	0	0	0	0	0	0	0	0	0	0	—	—
p	32	0	0	0	0	0	0	0	0	0	0	—	—
p	47	0	0	0	0	0	0	0	0	0	0	—	—
p	64	0	0	0	0	0	0	0	0	0	0	—	—
b p	21	0	0	0	0	0	0	0	0	0	0	—	—
p	7	0	0	0	0	0	0	0	0	0	0	—	—
	159	5555	730	1496	231	36	120	682	470	616	163	.269	.389

a—from Chicago(A) b—from Baltimore c—from Kansas City
Rick Dempsey(c), Cesar Tovar(dh), Gene Locklear(of), Juan Bernhardt(of), Larry Murray(of), Kerry Dineen(of), Rich Coggins(of), Mickey Klutts(ss), Ron Blomberg(ph), Terry Whitfield(of), Rudy May(p), Tippy Martinez(p), Jim York(p), Dave Pagan(p), and Ken Brett(p) also played for the Yankees during the season.

PITCHING

CINCINNATI REDS — WORLD SERIES STATISTICS

	G	GS	CG	IP	H	R	ER	BB	SO	W	L	SV	ERA
Don Gullett	1	1	0	7.1	5	1	1	3	4	1	0	0	1.23
Gary Nolan	1	1	0	6.2	8	2	2	1	1	1	0	0	2.70
Pat Zachry	1	1	0	6.2	6	2	2	5	6	1	0	0	2.70
Fred Norman	1	1	0	6.1	9	3	3	2	2	0	0	0	4.26
Will McEnaney	2	0	0	4.2	2	0	0	1	2	0	0	2	0.00
Jack Billingham	1	0	0	2.2	0	0	0	0	1	0	0	0	0.00
Pedro Borbon	1	0	0	1.2	0	0	0	0	0	0	0	0	0.00
Santo Alcala		Did not play											
Rawly Eastwick		Did not play											
Manny Sarmiento		Did not play											
team total	4	4	0	36	30	8	8	12	16	4	0	2	2.00

NEW YORK YANKEES — WORLD SERIES STATISTICS

	G	GS	CG	IP	H	R	ER	BB	SO	W	L	SV	ERA
Catfish Hunter	1	1	1	8.2	10	4	3	4	5	0	1	0	3.12
Ed Figueroa	1	1	0	8	6	5	5	5	2	0	1	0	5.63
Doyle Alexander	1	1	0	6	9	5	5	2	1	0	1	0	7.50
Grant Jackson	1	0	0	3.2	4	2	2	0	3	0	0	0	4.91
Dock Ellis	1	0	0	3.1	7	4	4	0	1	0	1	0	10.80
Dick Tidrow	2	0	0	2.1	5	2	2	1	1	0	0	0	7.71
Sparky Lyle	2	0	0	2.2	1	0	0	0	3	0	0	0	0.00
Ken Holtzman		Did not play											
Ron Guidry		Did not play											
team total	4	4	1	34.2	42	22	21	12	16	0	4	0	5.45

REGULAR SEASON STATISTICS — CINCINNATI REDS (PITCHING)

G	GS	CG	IP	H	ER	BB	SO	W	L	Pct	SV	ShO	ERA
23	20	4	126	119	42	48	64	11	3	.786	1	0	3.00
34	34	7	239	232	92	27	113	15	9	.625	0	1	3.46
38	28	6	204	170	62	83	143	14	7	.667	0	1	2.74
33	24	8	180	153	62	70	126	12	7	.632	0	3	3.10
55	0	0	72	97	39	23	28	2	6	.250	7	0	4.88
34	29	5	177	190	85	62	76	12	10	.545	1	2	4.32
69	1	0	121	135	45	31	53	4	3	.571	8	0	3.35
30	21	3	132	131	69	67	67	11	4	.733	0	1	4.70
71	0	0	108	93	25	27	70	11	5	.688	26	0	2.08
22	0	0	44	36	10	12	20	5	1	.833	0	0	2.05
162	162	33	1471	1436	573	491	790	102	60	.630	45	12	3.51

REGULAR SEASON STATISTICS — NEW YORK YANKEES (PITCHING)

G	GS	CG	IP	H	ER	BB	SO	W	L	Pct	SV	ShO	ERA
36	36	21	299	268	117	68	173	17	15	.531	0	2	3.52
34	34	14	257	237	86	94	119	19	10	.655	0	4	3.01
19	15	3	137	154	50	39	41	10	5	.667	0	2	3.28
21	2	1	59	38	11	16	25	6	0	1.000	1	1	1.69
32	32	8	212	195	75	76	65	17	8	.680	0	1	3.18
47	2	0	92	80	27	24	65	4	5	.444	10	0	2.64
64	0	0	104	82	26	42	61	7	8	.467	23	0	2.25
21	21	10	149	165	69	35	41	9	7	.563	0	2	4.17
7	0	0	16	20	10	4	12	0	0	—	0	0	5.63
159	159	62	1455	1300	516	448	674	97	62	.610	37	15	3.19

Total Attendance—223,009   Average Attendance—55,752   Winning Player's Share—$26,366   Losing Player's Share—$19,935

1977
Leaving the Squabbles Behind

The New York Yankees were often called "the best team money could buy." Out of the first reentry draft for free agents, owner George Steinbrenner signed slugger Reggie Jackson for a $3 million package and lefty pitcher Don Gullett for $2 million. The Yankees also picked up shortstop Bucky Dent and pitcher Mike Torrez in trades. Added to last year's A.L. championship squad, these newcomers gave the Yanks a look of inevitable victory. But a lackluster first half of the season was remarkable only for public reports of ill will between manager Billy Martin, Jackson, and Thurman Munson; and for repeated rumors of Martin's impending dismissal. A late burst of 38 victories in the last 51 games, however, saved Martin's job and edged the Red Sox and Orioles for the A.L. East crown. Despite the presence of many big-name stars, Yankee fans were most charmed by Ron Guidry, a skinny, hard-throwing lefty who came out of the bullpen early in the season to star as a starting pitcher. To get into the Series, the New Yorkers came up with three runs in a heroic ninth inning to beat Kansas City 5–3 in the fifth game of the A.L. Playoff.

Facing the Yankees in the Series were the Los Angeles Dodgers, managed by first-year skipper Tom Lasorda. The Dodgers had an unprecedented four 30-home-run hitters in Steve Garvey, Reggie Smith, Dusty Baker, and Ron Cey, who supported a deep pitching staff headed by 20-game winner Tommy John. The Dodgers won 22 of their first 26 games to take charge in the N.L. West and eliminated the Phillies in four games in the playoffs.

The Dodgers called on Don Sutton to pitch the first game in Yankee Stadium against Don Gullett, who had been plagued with a bad shoulder. The Dodgers jumped on Gullett for two runs in the top of the first, but the Yanks responded with one in the bottom of the inning. A homer by Willie Randolph tied the score in the sixth. In the bottom of the eighth, Munson doubled Randolph home to put New York ahead 3–2. In the ninth, however, a single by Baker and a walk to Steve Yeager finished Gullett and brought on ace reliever Sparky Lyle. Pinch hitter Lee Lacy drilled a single off Lyle to tie the score, which sent the game into extra innings. The Yankees finally broke the game in the twelfth inning against Rick Rhoden on a double by Randolph and a single by defensive replacement Paul Blair.

The second game gave the world an unappetizing look at Catfish Hunter. Plagued by assorted injuries all season, Hunter had not pitched in a month, but answered Billy Martin's call to help a mound staff worn down by the Kansas City series and thinned by injuries. The Dodgers pounded Catfish for three homers in less than three innings and coasted to a 6–1 victory, evening the Series for its journey to California.

The media reported uncomplimentary remarks by Martin and Jackson about each other during the travel day, but the Yanks put their bickering aside as soon as game three began. They roughed up Tommy John for three runs in the top of the first on hits by Mickey Rivers, Munson, Jackson, and Lou Piniella. Mike Torrez pitched strongly for New York but made a mistake to Dusty Baker, who belted a three-run homer to tie the score in the third. In the top of the fourth, the Yanks scratched out a run to go ahead 4–3; a walk to Jackson plus hits by Piniella and Chris Chambliss in the fifth gave New York an insurance run. Outside of Baker's shot, the Dodgers could not touch Torrez and fell behind two games to one.

They fell almost to the brink of extinction by losing game four 4–2 to the four-hit pitching of Ron Guidry. Reggie Jackson contributed a double to a three-run New York second inning and belted a homer in the sixth to round off the Yankee scoring.

But the Dodgers fought back in game five by jumping on the shopworn Yankee pitching. They sent Gullett to an early shower with an offensive attack that rolled up a final 10–4 score. The key Dodger blow was a three-run blast by Yeager in the fourth inning. Reggie Smith added two runs on a sixth-inning homer, while the Yanks got back-to-back home runs by Munson and Jackson in the eighth.

The travel day back to New York produced some more off-the-field news. Yankee pitcher Ed Figueroa had been scheduled to pitch game six, but Martin scratched him because of a sore side and an injured finger. Figueroa jumped the club for a few hours, but returned in time to watch the Yanks win their first World Championship since 1962 with an 8–4 victory. Torrez pitched in Figueroa's place and allowed the Dodgers to score twice in the first inning. In the bottom of the second, however, with Jackson on first, Chambliss sent a shot into the bleachers to tie the score off Burt Hooton. A Smith homer put the Dodgers ahead 3–2 in the third, but then Reggie Jackson took center stage. In the fourth, with Munson aboard, he sent Hooton's first pitch into the right field stands to put the Yanks ahead. In the next inning, he connected with Elias Sosa's first pitch for another two-run shot to right. And in the eighth inning, with the Yankees comfortably ahead and already in a festive mood, Jackson launched Charlie Hough's first knuckleball into the center-field bleachers 450 feet away. The only other player in Series history to hit three home runs in a game was Babe Ruth, who did so on two separate occasions, game 4, 1926, and game 4, 1928. Jackson's five homers for the Series set a record, and the Yankees returned to their fame as the best team in baseball in October.

1977

Game 1 October 11 at New York

L.A.	200	000	001	000				
N.Y.	100	001	010	001				

Los Angeles	Pos	AB	R	H	RBI	PO	A	E
Lopes	2b	5	1	0	0	4	2	0
Russell	ss	6	1	1	1	4	3	0
Smith	rf	4	0	1	0	2	1	0
Cey	3b	3	0	0	1	3	2	0
Garvey	1b	4	0	1	0	8	3	0
Baker	lf	4	1	1	0	2	0	0
Burke	cf	3	0	1	0	2	0	0
a Mota		1	0	0	0	0	0	0
Monday	cf	1	0	0	0	0	0	0
Yeager	c	3	0	0	0	4	1	0
c Landestoy		0	0	0	0	0	0	0
Grote	c	1	0	0	0	3	3	0
Sutton	p	2	0	0	0	1	1	0
Rautzhan	p	0	0	0	0	0	1	0
Sosa	p	0	0	0	0	0	0	0
b Lacy		1	0	1	1	0	0	0
Garman	p	0	0	0	0	0	0	0
d Davalillo		1	0	0	0	0	0	0
Rhoden	p	0	0	0	0	0	0	0
Totals		39	3	6	3	*33	17	0

a Flied out for Burke in 9th.
b Singled for Sosa in 9th.
c Ran for Yeager in 9th.
d Grounded out for Garman in 12th.
* None out when winning run scored.

Doubles—Munson, Randolph. Triple—Russell.
Home Run—Randolph. Sacrifice Hits—
Gullett 2. Sacrifice Fly—Cey. Hit by
Pitcher—Baker (by Gullett), Jackson (by
Sutton). Left on Bases—Los Angeles 8,
New York 12. Umpires—Chylak(A), Sudol(N),
McCoy(A), Dale(N), Evans(A), McSherry(N).
Attendance—56,668. Time of Game—3:24.

New York	Pos	AB	R	H	RBI	PO	A	E
Rivers	cf	6	0	0	0	8	1	0
Randolph	2b	5	3	2	1	2	4	0
Munson	c	4	1	2	1	9	1	0
Jackson	rf	2	0	1	0	1	0	0
Blair	rf	2	0	1	1	1	0	0
Chambliss	1b	5	0	1	1	11	1	0
Nettles	3b	4	0	0	0	0	4	0
Piniella	lf	5	0	2	0	3	0	0
Dent	ss	5	0	2	0	0	3	0
Gullett	p	1	0	0	0	1	1	0
Lyle	p	2	0	0	0	0	0	0
Totals		41	4	11	4	36	15	0

Pitching	IP	H	R	ER	BB	SO
Los Angeles						
Sutton	**7	8	3	3	1	4
Rautzhan	⅓	0	0	0	2	0
Sosa	⅔	0	0	0	0	1
Garman	3	1	0	0	1	3
Rhoden(L)	***0	2	1	1	1	0
New York						
Gullett	8⅓	5	3	3	6	6
Lyle (W)	3⅔	1	0	0	0	2

**Pitched to two batters in 8th.
***Pitched to three batters in 12th.

1st Inning
Los Angeles
Lopes walked.
Russell tripled to the left-center field wall, scoring Lopes.
Smith walked.
1 Cey hit a sacrifice fly to Piniella in deep left-center, Russell scoring after the catch.
2 Smith got trapped in a rundown trying to steal, Munson to Randolph to Chambliss to Randolph to Gullett.
Garvey walked.
3 Baker forced Garvey at second, Nettles to Randolph.
New York
1 Rivers grounded to second.
2 Randolph grounded to third.
Munson singled to left.
Jackson blooped a single to center, Munson going to third.
Chambliss singled to right, scoring Munson, with Jackson stopping at second.
3 Nettles grounded to short.

2nd Inning
Los Angeles
1 Burke struck out.
2 Yeager bounced to short.
3 Sutton struck out.
New York
1 Piniella flied to Burke in deep left-center.
2 Dent grounded to third, Cey making a good one-handed grab.
3 Gullett struck out, but Yeager, dropping the third strike, had to throw him out.

3rd Inning
Los Angeles
1 Lopes took a called third strike.
2 Russell flied to Rivers in deep right-center.
Smith singled to left.
Cey walked.
3 Garvey flied to deep center.
New York
1 Rivers flied to left.
2 Randolph called out on strikes.
3 Munson also struck out.

4th Inning
Los Angeles
Baker was hit by a pitch.
1 Burke flied to center.
2 Yeager rolled to second, Baker advancing to second.
3 Sutton bunted out to Gullett.
New York
1 Jackson popped to third.
2 Chambliss popped to Lopes in short center.
3 Nettles bounced out, Garvey to Sutton.

5th Inning
Los Angeles
1 Lopes grounded to third.
2 Russell flied to deep left.
3 Smith took a called third strike.
New York
1 Piniella struck out.
Dent singled to center.
2 Gullett sacrificed Dent to second, Garvey to Lopes.
3 Rivers lined to right.

6th Inning
Los Angeles
1 Cey flied to deep left.
Garvey beat out a bunt down the third base line.
2 Baker flied to short center.
Burke singled to right-center. Garvey tried to score from first but was
3 out, Rivers to Munson.
New York
Randolph hit a home run into the left field stands.
1 Munson bounced to second.
Jackson was hit by a pitched ball.
2 Chambliss lined to right.
3 Nettles flied to Burke in right-center.

7th Inning
Los Angeles
1 Yeager fouled to Chambliss.
Sutton walked.
2 Lopes struck out.
3 Russell forced Sutton at second, Nettles to Randolph.
New York
Piniella singled to right-center, but
1 was out trying to stretch it into a double, Smith to Russell.
Dent beat out a slow roller to Cey.
2 Gullett again sacrificed, Sutton to Lopes covering first.
3 Rivers fouled to Cey.

8th Inning
Los Angeles
1 Smith flied to right.
2 Cey struck out.
3 Garvey grounded to short.
New York
Randolph walked.
Munson lined a double into the left field corner, scoring Randolph.
For Los Angeles—Rautzhan relieved Sutton on the mound.
Jackson walked.
1 Chambliss forced Munson on a bunt, Rautzhan to Cey.
Nettles walked, filling the sacks.
For Los Angeles—Sosa now pitching.
2 Piniella struck out.
3 Dent forced Nettles at second, Russell to Lopes.

9th Inning
Los Angeles
For New York—Blair playing right field.
Baker singled to left.
1 Mota, pinch-hitting for Burke, flied to short right.
Yeager walked on four pitches.
For New York—Lyle came in to pitch.
Landestoy ran for Yeager.
Lacy, batting for Sosa, singled to left. Baker scored, with Landestoy stopping at second.
2 Lopes flied to Rivers in short right-center.
3 Russell lined to center.
New York
For Los Angeles—Garman pitching, Grote catching, and Monday in center field.
1 Lyle struck out, bunting foul on the third strike.
2 Rivers struck out.
3 Randolph grounded to short.

10th Inning
Los Angeles
1 Smith flied to Rivers in deep left-center.
2 Cey bounced to short.
3 Garvey struck out.
New York
Munson walked on four pitches.
1 Blair forced Munson on an attempted sacrifice, Grote to Russell.
2 Chambliss forced Blair at second, Garvey to Russell.
3 Nettles rolled out in front of the plate, Grote to Garvey.

11th Inning
Los Angeles
1 Baker bounced to third.
2 Monday struck out.
3 Grote popped to first.
New York
Piniella singled to center.
1 Dent, attempting to sacrifice, forced Piniella, Grote to Russell.
2 Lyle struck out.
3 Rivers flied to short left.

12th Inning
Los Angeles
1 Davalillo, pinch-hitting for Garman, grounded to second.
2 Lopes flied to short center.
3 Russell grounded to second.
New York
For Los Angeles—Rhoden now pitching.
Randolph doubled into the left field corner.
Munson intentionally passed.
Blair singled to left, Randolph scoring the game-ending run.

1977

Game 2 October 12 at New York

L.A. 2 1 2 0 0 0 0 0 1
N.Y. 0 0 0 1 0 0 0 0 0

Los Angeles	Pos	AB	R	H	RBI	PO	A	E
Lopes	2b	4	0	0	0	2	1	0
Russell	ss	4	1	1	0	0	4	0
Smith	rf	3	2	2	2	2	0	0
Cey	3b	4	1	1	2	1	1	0
Garvey	1b	4	1	2	1	6	1	0
Baker	lf	4	0	0	0	2	0	0
Monday	cf	3	0	1	0	0	0	0
Burke	cf	1	0	0	0	5	0	0
Yeager	c	4	1	2	1	9	0	0
Hooton	p	3	0	0	0	0	0	0
Totals		34	6	9	6	27	7	0

a Struck out for Tidrow in 5th.
b Flied out for Dent in 7th.
c Flied out for Clay in 8th.

Double—Smith. Home Runs—Cey, Garvey, Smith, Yeager. Double Play—Garvey to Russell to Garvey. Left on Bases—Los Angeles 2, New York 4. Umpires—Sudol, McCoy, Dale, Evans, McSherry, Chylak. Attendance—56,691. Time of Game—2:27.

New York	Pos	AB	R	H	RBI	PO	A	E
Rivers	cf	4	0	0	0	4	0	0
Randolph	2b	4	1	1	0	2	2	0
Munson	c	4	0	1	0	3	3	0
Jackson	rf	4	0	0	0	0	0	0
Chambliss	1b	4	0	0	0	11	2	0
Nettles	3b	2	0	1	0	0	6	0
Piniella	lf	3	0	1	0	4	0	0
Dent	ss	2	0	1	0	0	1	0
b Johnson		1	0	0	0	0	0	0
Stanley	ss	0	0	0	0	1	0	0
Hunter	p	0	0	0	0	0	0	0
Tidrow	p	1	0	0	0	0	0	0
a Zeber		1	0	0	0	0	0	0
Clay	p	0	0	0	0	1	1	0
c White		1	0	0	0	0	0	0
Lyle	p	0	0	0	0	0	0	0
Totals		31	1	5	0	27	15	0

Pitching	IP	H	R	ER	BB	SO
Los Angeles						
Hooton (W)	9	5	1	1	1	8
New York						
Hunter (L)	2⅓	5	5	5	0	0
Tidrow	2⅔	3	0	0	0	1
Clay	3	0	0	0	1	0
Lyle	1	1	1	1	0	0

1st Inning
Los Angeles
1 Lopes lined to center.
2 Russell lined to left.
Smith lined a double off the left-center field wall.
Cey hit a two-run homer over the left field fence.
3 Garvey grounded to second.
New York
1 Rivers fouled to Cey.
2 Randolph struck out.
3 Munson struck out.

2nd Inning
Los Angeles
1 Baker grounded to third.
2 Monday bounced out, Chambliss to Hunter.
Yeager homered into the left field seats.
3 Hooton grounded to third.
New York
1 Jackson took a called third strike.
2 Chambliss also took a called third strike.
3 Nettles lined to second.

3rd Inning
Los Angeles
1 Lopes bounced to second.
Russell lined a single to left.
Smith hit a two-run home run into the right-center field bleachers.
For New York—Tidrow relieved Hunter.
2 Cey fouled to Munson.
Garvey beat out a slow roller to short.
3 Garvey caught trying to steal, Munson to Randolph.
New York
Piniella singled to right.
1 Dent struck out.
2 Tidrow was called out on strikes.
3 Rivers bounced to second.

4th Inning
Los Angeles
1 Baker flied to shallow center, Rivers making a running catch.
Monday singled to center.
Yeager blooped a single down the right field line, Monday going to third.
2 Monday was trapped on an attempted squeeze, Munson to Nettles to Munson.
3 Hooton struck out.
New York
Randolph beat out a grounder to deep short.
Munson singled to center, Randolph racing to third.
1,2 Jackson grounded to Garvey, who threw to Russell to trap Munson off of second. Garvey made both putouts as Randolph scored on the DP.
3 Chambliss grounded to short.

5th Inning
Los Angeles
1 Lopes flied to Rivers in deep left-center.
2 Russell grounded to third.
3 Smith grounded to first.

5th Inning (continued)
New York
Nettles singled to center.
1 Piniella forced Nettles at second, Russell to Lopes.
Dent singled to right, Piniella stopping at second.
2 Zeber, pinch-hitting for Tidrow, took a called third strike.
3 Rivers flied to left.

6th Inning
Los Angeles
For New York—Clay now pitching.
1 Cey grounded to short.
2 Garvey grounded out, Chambliss to Clay.
3 Baker flied to left.
New York
1 Randolph bounced to third.
2 Munson grounded to short.
3 Jackson struck out.

7th Inning
Los Angeles
1 Monday flied to left.
2 Yeager bounced to third.
3 Hooton flied to left.
New York
For Los Angeles—Burke came in to play center field.
1 Chambliss flied to Smith in deep right-center.
Nettles walked.
2 Piniella flied to deep center.
3 Johnson, batting for Dent, also flied to center.

8th Inning
Los Angeles
For New York—Stanley playing short.
1 Lopes tapped back to the mound.
2 Russell flied to center.
Smith walked.
3 Cey forced Smith at second, Randolph unassisted.
New York
1 White, pinch-hitting for Clay, flied to Smith in short right-center.
2 Rivers flied to Burke in deep right-center.
3 Randolph lined to Baker in the left field corner.

9th Inning
Los Angeles
For New York—Lyle pitching.
Garvey homered into the left field stands.
1 Baker popped to Stanley in short left.
2 Burke rolled out, Munson to Chambliss.
3 Yeager grounded to third.
New York
1 Munson fouled to Yeager.
2 Jackson flied to Burke in left-center.
3 Chambliss flied to short center.

Game 3 October 14 at Los Angeles

N.Y. 3 0 0 1 1 0 0 0 0
L.A. 0 0 3 0 0 0 0 0 0

New York	Pos	AB	R	H	RBI	PO	A	E
Rivers	cf	5	1	3	1	4	0	0
Randolph	2b	4	0	0	0	1	2	0
Munson	c	5	1	1	1	9	0	0
Jackson	rf	4	0	0	0	0	0	0
Blair	rf	1	0	0	0	1	0	0
Piniella	lf	3	0	2	1	2	0	0
Chambliss	1b	4	0	1	1	8	1	0
Nettles	3b	4	1	1	0	1	4	0
Dent	ss	3	0	1	0	1	2	0
Torrez	p	3	0	0	0	1	1	0
Totals		35	5	10	5	27	10	0

Pitching	IP	H	R	ER	BB	SO
New York						
Torrez (W)	9	7	3	3	3	9
Los Angeles						
John (L)	6	9	5	4	3	7
Hough	3	1	0	0	0	2

N.Y. 3 0 0 1 1 0 0 0 0
L.A. 0 0 3 0 0 0 0 0 0

Los Angeles	Pos	AB	R	H	RBI	PO	A	E
Lopes	2b	4	0	0	0	1	4	0
Russell	ss	4	0	0	0	2	4	0
Smith	rf	3	1	1	0	2	0	0
Cey	3b	3	0	0	0	1	1	0
Garvey	1b	4	1	2	0	9	1	0
Baker	lf	4	1	2	3	1	0	1
Monday	cf	4	0	0	0	3	1	0
Yeager	c	4	0	2	0	9	1	0
John	p	2	0	0	0	0	0	0
a Davalillo		1	0	0	0	0	0	0
Hough	p	0	0	0	0	0	0	0
b Mota		1	0	0	0	0	0	0
Totals		34	3	7	3	27	11	1

a Hit into Force out for John in 6th.
b Struck out for Hough in 9th.

Doubles—Munson, Rivers 2, Yeager. Home Run—Baker. Stolen Bases—Lopes, Rivers. Sacrifice Hit—Torrez Double Play—Garvey to Russell to Garvey. Hit by Pitcher—Piniella (by John). Left on Bases—New York 8, Los Angeles 7. Umpires—McCoy, Dale, Evans, McSherry, Chylak, Sudol. Attendance—55,992. Time of Game—2:31.

1st Inning
New York
Rivers blooped a double to right.
1 Randolph grounded to second, Rivers advancing to third.
Munson doubled into the right field corner, scoring Rivers.
Jackson singled to left, Munson scoring. Baker bobbled the ball, and Jackson got to second.
Piniella singled to center, Jackson scoring.
2 Chambliss struck out.
3 Nettles grounded to second.
Los Angeles
Lopes walked.
Lopes stole second.
1 Russell took a called third strike.
2 Smith tapped to third, Lopes going to third.
Cey walked.
3 Garvey grounded to second.

2nd Inning
New York
1 Dent bounced to third.
2 Torrez struck out.
Rivers got another double down the right field line.
Randolph walked.
3 Munson struck out.
Los Angeles
Baker singled to center.
1 Monday struck out.
Yeager doubled to right, Baker stopping at third.
2 John struck out.
3 Lopes bounced out, Chambliss to Torrez.

3rd Inning
New York
1 Jackson struck out.
Piniella was hit by a pitch.
2,3 Chambliss hit into a double play, Garvey to Russell to Garvey.
Los Angeles
1 Russell grounded to third.
Smith singled to right.
2 Cey lined to Rivers in right-center. Rivers made an excellent running catch.
Garvey singled to center, advancing Smith to third.
Baker hit a three-run homer into the bull pen beyond the left field fence.
3 Monday took a called third strike.

4th Inning
New York
Nettles singled to right-center.
Dent singled on a soft roller off of Cey's glove, Nettles stopping at second.
1 Torrez sacrificed, advancing both base runners, Yeager to Lopes.
2 Rivers grounded to second, Nettles scoring with Dent going to third.
3 Randolph flied to right.
Los Angeles
1 Yeager flied to short center.
2 John again struck out.
3 Lopes grounded to short.

5th Inning
New York
1 Munson grounded to short.
Jackson walked on four pitches.
Piniella singled off of John's glove, Jackson going to second.
Chambliss singled to right, scoring Jackson, with Piniella racing to third.
2 Nettles struck out.
Dent walked, loading the bases.
3 Torrez struck out.
Los Angeles
1 Russell grounded to short.
Smith walked on four pitches.
2 Cey flied to Piniella in left-center.
Garvey beat out a high bouncer to third, Smith stopping at second.
3 Baker forced Garvey at second, Nettles to Randolph.

6th Inning
New York
1 Rivers grounded to second.
2 Randolph grounded to short.
3 Munson struck out.
Los Angeles
1 Monday flied to deep left.
Yeager singled to center.
2 Davalillo, hitting for John, forced Yeager, Randolph to Dent.
3 Lopes tapped back to the mound.

7th Inning
New York
For Los Angeles—Hough now pitching.
1 Jackson struck out.
2 Piniella popped to Russell in short left.
3 Chambliss grounded to short.
Los Angeles
For New York—Blair replaced Jackson in right.
1 Russell lined to third.
2 Smith struck out.
3 Cey flied to short center.

8th Inning
New York
1 Nettles lined to right.
2 Dent flied to short left.
3 Torrez flied to center.
Los Angeles
1 Garvey flied to center.
2 Baker struck out.
3 Monday grounded to first.

9th Inning
New York
Rivers singled to center.
1 Randolph flied to short center.
Rivers stole second.
2 Munson struck out for the third time.
3 Blair lined to Cey, making a diving catch.
Los Angeles
1 Yeager tapped to third.
2 Mota, batting for Hough, struck out.
3 Lopes took a called third strike.

Game 4 October 15 at Los Angeles

| N.Y. | 030 001 000 |
| L.A. | 002 000 000 |

New York	Pos	AB	R	H	RBI	PO	A	E
Rivers	cf	4	0	1	0	3	0	0
Randolph	2b	4	0	0	0	3	2	0
Munson	c	4	0	1	0	8	1	0
Jackson	rf	4	2	2	1	2	0	0
Blair	rf	0	0	0	0	0	0	0
Piniella	lf	4	1	1	1	2	0	0
Chambliss	1b	3	1	1	0	8	0	0
Nettles	3b	3	0	0	1	1	3	0
Dent	ss	3	0	1	1	0	2	0
Guidry	p	2	0	0	0	0	0	0
Totals		31	4	7	4	27	8	0

Pitching	IP	H	R	ER	BB	SO
New York						
Guidry (W)	9	4	2	2	3	7
Los Angeles						
Rau (L)	*1	4	3	3	0	0
Rhoden	7	2	1	1	0	5
Garman	1	1	0	0	0	0

*Pitched to three batters in 2nd.

Los Angeles	Pos	AB	R	H	RBI	PO	A	E
Lopes	2b	2	1	1	2	3	6	0
Russell	ss	4	0	0	0	1	5	0
Smith	cf	4	0	2	0	1	0	0
Cey	3b	4	0	0	0	0	0	0
Garvey	1b	4	0	0	0	14	1	0
Baker	lf	4	0	0	0	1	0	0
Lacy	rf	2	0	0	0	1	0	0
Yeager	c	3	0	0	0	4	2	0
Rau	p	0	0	0	0	0	0	0
Rhoden	p	2	1	1	0	1	1	0
a Mota		1	0	0	0	0	0	0
Garman	p	0	0	0	0	0	0	0
Totals		30	2	4	2	27	15	0

a Flied out for Rhoden in 8th.

Doubles—Cey, Chambliss, Jackson, Rhoden. Home Runs—Jackson, Lopes. Stolen Base—Lopes. Sacrifice Hit—Guidry. Double Plays—Russell to Lopes to Garvey, Lopes to Russell to Garvey. Left on Bases—New York 1, Los Angeles 4. Umpires—Dale, Evans, McSherry, Chylak, Sudol, McCoy. Attendance—55,995. Time of Game—2:07.

1st Inning
New York
Rivers singled to right.
1 Randolph popped to first.
2,3 Munson hit into a double play, Russell to Lopes to Garvey.
Los Angeles
Lopes walked.
Lopes stole second.
1 Russell struck out.
2 Smith grounded to third, Lopes holding second.
3 Cey struck out.

2nd Inning
New York
Jackson doubled inside the third base line.
Piniella singled to right, Jackson scoring.
Chambliss doubled to left, Piniella stopping at third.
For Los Angeles—Rhoden relieved Rau.
1 Nettles grounded to second, Piniella scoring with Chambliss going to third.
Dent singled to right, scoring Chambliss.
2 Guidry sacrificed Dent to second, Yeager to Lopes.
3 Rivers struck out.
Los Angeles
1 Garvey popped to first.
2 Baker flied to deep right.
3 Lacy struck out.

3rd Inning
New York
1 Randolph bounced to short.
2 Munson struck out.
3 Jackson flied to left.
Los Angeles
1 Yeager fouled to Munson.
Rhoden got a ground-rule double when his liner down the left field line bounced over the fence.
Lopes hit a two-run homer over the center field fence.
2 Russell grounded to short.
3 Smith took a called third strike.

4th Inning
New York
1 Piniella grounded to short.
2 Chambliss grounded to second.
3 Nettles grounded out, Garvey to Rhoden.
Los Angeles
1 Piniella robbed Cey of a home run as he leaped to the top of the wall to make the catch.
2 Garvey struck out, but was tagged by Munson as the third strike was in the dirt.
3 Baker grounded to third.

5th Inning
New York
1 Dent grounded to second.
2 Guidry grounded to second.
3 Rivers grounded to deep short.
Los Angeles
1 Lacy flied to left.
2 Yeager grounded to deep short.
3 Rhoden flied to deep center.

6th Inning
New York
1 Randolph popped to first.
2 Munson struck out.
Jackson homered into the left-center field pavilion.
3 Piniella struck out.
Los Angeles
Lopes walked.
1 Russell flied to shallow center.
2 Lopes caught trying to steal second, Munson to Randolph.
3 Smith grounded to third.

7th Inning
New York
1 Chambliss grounded to first.
2 Nettles bounced back to the mound.
3 Dent flied to deep left.
Los Angeles
Cey singled off Nettles' glove.
1 Garvey struck out.
2 Baker popped to second.
Lacy walked.
3 Yeager forced Cey on a bouncer to Nettles.

8th Inning
New York
1 Guidry struck out, Yeager to Garvey.
2 Rivers popped to second.
3 Randolph flied to right.
Los Angeles
1 Mota, pinch-hitting for Rhoden, flied to short right.
2 Lopes grounded to second.
3 Russell struck out.

9th Inning
New York
For Los Angeles—Garman the new pitcher.
Munson singled to right.
1 Jackson flied to Smith in left-center.
2,3 Piniella grounded into a double play, Lopes to Russell to Garvey.
Los Angeles
For New York—Blair playing right.
1 Smith popped to Randolph in short right.
Cey doubled down the left field line.
2 Garvey grounded to second, Cey advancing to third.
3 Baker flied to center.

Game 5 October 16 at Los Angeles

| N.Y. | 000 000 220 |
| L.A. | 100 432 00x |

New York	Pos	AB	R	H	RBI	PO	A	E
Rivers	cf	4	0	0	0	4	0	0
Randolph	2b	4	0	1	0	3	1	0
Munson	c	4	1	2	1	5	0	0
Johnson	c	0	0	0	0	0	0	0
Jackson	rf	4	2	2	1	1	0	0
Chambliss	1b	4	1	2	0	8	0	0
Nettles	3b	4	0	2	1	0	3	1
Piniella	lf	4	0	0	0	3	0	1
Dent	ss	4	0	0	1	0	3	0
Gullett	p	1	0	0	0	0	1	0
Clay	p	0	0	0	0	0	0	0
a Zeber		1	0	0	0	0	0	0
Tidrow	p	0	0	0	0	0	1	0
b White		1	0	0	0	0	0	0
Hunter	p	0	0	0	0	0	0	0
d Blair		1	0	0	0	0	0	0
Totals		36	4	9	4	24	.9	2

Pitching	IP	H	R	ER	BB	SO
New York						
Gullett (L)	4⅓	8	7	6	1	4
Clay	⅔	2	1	1	0	0
Tidrow	1	2	2	2	0	0
Hunter	2	1	0	0	0	1
Los Angeles						
Sutton (W)	9	9	4	4	0	2

Los Angeles	Pos	AB	R	H	RBI	PO	A	E
Lopes	2b	5	1	2	0	2	5	0
Russell	ss	5	1	2	1	1	1	0
Smith	cf-rf	4	2	1	2	6	0	0
Cey	3b	4	0	0	0	0	2	0
Garvey	1b	4	0	2	0	9	0	0
Baker	lf	4	2	3	2	2	0	0
Lacy	rf	3	1	2	1	1	0	0
Burke	cf	2	1	0	0	3	0	0
Yeager	c	2	1	1	4	2	0	0
c Oates	c	1	0	0	0	1	0	0
Sutton	p	4	0	0	0	0	0	0
Totals		37	10	13	10	27	8	0

a Struck out for Clay in 6th.
b Popped out for Tidrow in 7th.
c Flied out for Yeager in 7th.
d Flied out for Hunter in 9th.

Doubles—Garvey, Nettles, Randolph. Triple—Lopes. Home Runs—Jackson, Munson, Smith, Yeager. Sacrifice Fly—Yeager. Left on Bases—New York 5, Los Angeles 5. Umpires—Evans, McSherry, Chylak, Sudol, McCoy, Dale. Attendance—55,955. Time of Game—2:29.

1st Inning
New York
1 Rivers grounded to second.
2 Randolph lined to center.
Munson blooped a single to left-center.
3 Jackson flied to center.
Los Angeles
Lopes tripled off of the bull-pen gate in left.
Russell singled to left, Lopes scoring.
1 Smith rolled out to third, Nettles making a bare-handed stop to the left of the mound, Russell moving to second.
2 Cey struck out.
3 Garvey struck out.

2nd Inning
New York
1 Chambliss bounced to second.
2 Nettles grounded to first.
3 Piniella popped to second.
Los Angeles
1 Baker flied to center.
Lacy singled to left.
2 Yeager popped to Randolph behind first.
3 Sutton struck out.

3rd Inning
New York
1 Dent lined to center.
2 Gullett lined to center.
3 Rivers grounded to second.
Los Angeles
1 Lopes lined to center.
2 Russell grounded to short.
3 Smith grounded to short.

4th Inning
New York
1 Randolph flied to center.
2 Munson grounded to short.
3 Jackson flied to Lacy making a running catch in short right.
Los Angeles
1 Cey flied to deep left.
Garvey doubled to the right-center field wall.
Baker singled to left, scoring Garvey.
Baker got to second when Piniella fumbled the hit.
Lacy was safe at first on Nettles' fumble as Baker held second.
Yeager hit a three-run homer deep into the left field stands.
2 Sutton took a called third strike.
Lopes singled to center.
3 Russell tapped back to the mound.

5th Inning
New York
Chambliss singled to right.
1 Nettles flied to Smith in right-center.
2 Piniella grounded to third, Chambliss moving to second.
3 Dent lined to left.
Los Angeles
Smith walked.
1 Cey flied to right.
Garvey singled to right, Smith advancing to third.
For New York—Clay relieved Gullett.
Baker singled off Dent's glove, Smith scoring, with Garvey stopping at second.

5th Inning (continued)
Lacy singled to right-center, Garvey scoring with Baker going to third.
2 Yeager hit a sacrifice fly to Rivers in shallow left-center, scoring Baker.
3 Sutton grounded to second.

6th Inning
New York
For Los Angeles—Smith moved to right and Burke came in to play center.
1 Zeber, pinch-hitting for Clay, struck out.
2 Rivers flied to center.
Randolph doubled to right-center.
3 Munson popped to Lopes in short center.
Los Angeles
For New York—Tidrow pitching.
1 Lopes tapped back to the mound.
Russell singled to right-center.
Smith hit a two-run homer into the right-center field bleachers.
2 Cey flied to left.
3 Garvey grounded to short.

7th Inning
New York
Jackson singled to center.
Chambliss singled to right, Jackson going to third.
Nettles doubled into the left field corner, Jackson scoring, with Chambliss stopping at third.
1 Piniella flied to short right.
2 Dent grounded to second, Chambliss scoring and Nettles going to third.
3 White, pinch-hitting for Tidrow, popped to short.
Los Angeles
For New York—Hunter the new pitcher.
Baker singled to left.
1 Burke forced Baker at second, Nettles to Randolph.
2 Oates, batting for Yeager, lined to center.
3 Sutton struck out for the third time.

8th Inning
New York
For Los Angeles—Oates stays in as catcher.
1 Rivers flied to left.
2 Randolph grounded to third.
Munson hit a home run into the left-center field bleachers.
Jackson also hit a home run, hitting the right field foul pole.
3 Chambliss grounded to second.
Los Angeles
1 Lopes grounded to short.
2 Russell flied to Piniella in left-center.
3 Smith popped to second.

9th Inning
New York
Nettles singled to short right when Smith lost the ball in the sun.
1 Piniella flied to deep left.
2 Dent fouled to Oates.
3 Blair, pinch-hitting for Hunter, lined to center.

Game 6 October at New York

| L.A. | 201 000 001 |
| N.Y. | 020 320 01x |

Los Angeles	Pos	AB	R	H	RBI	PO	A	E
Lopes	2b	4	0	1	0	0	4	0
Russell	ss	3	0	0	0	1	4	0
Smith	rf	4	2	1	1	1	0	0
Cey	3b	3	1	1	0	0	1	0
Garvey	1b	4	1	2	2	13	0	0
Baker	lf	4	0	1	0	2	0	0
Monday	cf	4	0	1	0	3	0	0
Yeager	c	3	0	1	0	4	2	0
b Davalillo		1	0	1	0	0	0	0
Hooton	p	2	0	0	0	0	0	0
Sosa	p	0	0	0	0	0	0	0
Rau	p	0	0	0	0	0	0	0
a Goodson		1	0	0	0	0	0	0
Hough	p	0	0	0	0	0	0	0
c Lacy		1	0	0	0	0	0	0
Totals		34	4	9	4	24	11	0

Pitching	IP	H	R	ER	BB	SO
Los Angeles						
Hooton (L)	*3	3	4	4	1	1
Sosa	1⅓	3	3	3	1	0
Rau	1⅓	0	0	0	0	1
Hough	2	2	1	1	0	3
New York						
Torrez (W)	9	9	4	2	2	6

*Pitched to three batters in 4th.

New York	Pos	AB	R	H	RBI	PO	A	E
Rivers	cf	4	0	2	0	1	0	0
Randolph	2b	4	1	0	0	2	3	0
Munson	c	4	1	1	0	6	0	0
Jackson	rf	3	4	3	5	5	0	0
Chambliss	1b	4	2	2	2	9	1	0
Nettles	3b	4	0	0	0	0	0	0
Piniella	lf	3	0	0	1	2	1	0
Dent	ss	2	0	0	0	1	4	1
Torrez	p	3	0	0	0	1	2	0
Totals		31	8	8	8	27	11	1

a Struck out for Rau in 7th.
b Beat out a bunt for Yeager in 9th.
c Popped out for Hough in 9th.

Double—Chambliss. Triple—Garvey.
Home Runs—Chambliss, Jackson 3, Smith.
Sacrifice Fly—Piniella. Double Plays—Dent
to Randolph to Chambliss, Chambliss to
Dent to Chambliss. Passed Ball—Munron.
Left on Bases—Los Angeles 5, New York 2.
Umpires—McSherry, Chylak, Sudol, McCoy,
Dale, Evans. Attendance—56,407.
Time of Game—2:18.

1st Inning
Los Angeles
1 Lopes grounded to short.
2 Russell grounded to second.
 Smith safe on Dent's fumble.
  Smith went to second on a
  passed ball.
 Cey walked.
 Garvey lined a triple into the right
  field corner, scoring Smith and Cey.
3 Baker took a called third strike.
New York
1 Rivers fouled to Baker, leaning into
  the stands in short left.
2 Randolph grounded to short.
3 Munson rolled to short.

2nd Inning
Los Angeles
1 Monday bounced to first.
2 Yeager struck out.
3 Hooton flied to short right.
New York
 Jackson walked on four pitches.
 Chambliss hit a two-run homer into the
  right-center field bleachers.
1 Nettles grounded to first.
2 Piniella flied to Smith in short
  right-center.
3 Dent grounded to second.

3rd Inning
Los Angeles
1 Lopes bounced back to the mound. Torrez
  threw poorly to Chambliss but Chambliss
  got the poor throw by a step.
2 Russell grounded to short.
 Smith blasted a home run into the
  right-center field bleachers.
 Cey singled off Nettles' glove.
3 Garvey flied to deep center.
New York
1 Torrez struck out.
2 Rivers bounded to second.
3 Randolph flied to short center.

4th Inning
Los Angeles
1 Baker flied to Jackson in deep
  right-center.
 Monday blooped a single to left.
 Yeager singled off the left field wall
2 and was out trying for a double,
  Piniella to Randolph. Monday stopped
  at third.
3 Hooton struck out.
New York
 Munson singled to left.
 Jackson lined the first pitch into the
  right field stands for a two-run home
  run.
 For Los Angeles—Sosa relieved Hooton
  with a 2–1 count on Chambliss.
 Chambliss doubled on a Texas-leaguer
  between Russell and Baker.
1 Nettles grounded to second, Chambliss
  going to third.
2 Piniella hit a sacrifice fly to left,
  scoring Chambliss.
 Dent walked.
3 Torrez grounded to short.

5th Inning
Los Angeles
1 Lopes flied to short left.
 Russell walked on four pitches.
2,3 Smith hit into a double play,
  Dent to Randolph to Chambliss.
New York
 Rivers singled to center.
1 Randolph forced Rivers on a bunt,
  Yeager to Russell.
2 Munson lined to short center.
 Jackson again blasted the first pitch
  into the right field stands for a two-
  run homer. His fourth of the Series.
 For Los Angeles—Rau relieved Sosa.
3 Chambliss grounded to first.

6th Inning
Los Angeles
1 Cey struck out.
2 Garvey flied to Jackson in short
  right-center.
3 Baker flied to left.
New York
1 Nettles struck out.
2 Piniella flied to deep center.
3 Dent grounded to short.

7th Inning
Los Angeles
1 Monday grounded to second.
2 Yeager bounced back to the mound.
3 Goodson, pinch-hitting for Rau,
  struck out.
New York
 For Los Angeles—Hough now pitching.
1 Torrez struck out.
 Rivers singled to right.
2 Randolph grounded to third, Rivers
  going to second.
3 Munson struck out but had to be
  thrown out Yeager to Garvey.

8th Inning
Los Angeles
 Lopes singled to center.
1 Russell lined to right.
2,3 Smith grounded into a double play,
  Chambliss to Dent to Chambliss.
New York
 For the third successive time Jackson
  blasted the first pitch for a home
  run, this one into the center field
  bleachers. **Three in one game ties the
  record of Babe Ruth in 1926 and 1928.
  His 5th homer also sets a new World
  Series' record.**
1 Chambliss grounded to second.
2 Nettles struck out.
3 Piniella fouled to Garvey.

9th Inning
Los Angeles
1 Cey took a called third strike.
 Garvey beat out a hit to deep short.
 Baker singled to left, Garvey
  going to second.
2 Monday flied to deep right, Garvey
  advancing to third after the catch.
 Davalillo, pinch-hitting for Yeager,
  bunted down the third base line.
 Nettles threw to Munson, but not in time
  to get Garvey, as Baker stopped at
  second.
3 Lacy, pinch-hitting for Hough, popped
  up a bunt to Torrez.

1977 WORLD SERIES COMPOSITE BOX

	Wins	Composite Line Score				
New York Yankees (A.L.)	4	4 5 0	5 3 2	2 4 0	0 0 1	- 26
Los Angeles Dodgers (N.L.)	2	7 1 8	4 3 2	0 0 3	0 0 0	- 28

Manager	Regular Season W	L	Pct.	G. Ahead
Billy Martin	100	62	.617	2.5
Tommy Lasorda	98	64	.605	10

BATTING AND FIELDING

NEW YORK YANKEES

	WORLD SERIES STATISTICS															
	Pos	G	AB	R	H	2B	3B	HR	RBI	BB	SO	SB	BA	SA	PO	A	E
Chris Chambliss	1b	6	24	4	7	**2**	0	1	4	0	2	0	.292	.500	55	5	0
Willie Randolph	2b	6	25	5	4	**2**	0	1	1	2	2	0	.160	.360	13	14	0
Bucky Dent	ss	6	19	0	5	0	0	0	2	2	1	0	.263	.263	2	15	**1**
Graig Nettles	3b	6	21	1	4	1	0	0	2	2	3	0	.190	.238	2	20	**1**
Reggie Jackson	rf	6	20	**10**	**9**	1	0	**5**	**8**	3	4	0	**.450**	**1.250**	9	0	0
Mickey Rivers	cf	6	**27**	1	6	**2**	0	0	1	0	2	1	.222	.296	24	1	0
Lou Piniella	lf	6	22	1	6	0	0	0	3	0	3	0	.273	.273	16	1	**1**
Thurman Munson	c	6	25	4	8	**2**	0	1	3	2	**8**	0	.320	.520	40	5	0
Paul Blair	rf-ph	4	4	0	1	0	0	0	1	0	0	0	.250	.250	1	0	0
Cliff Johnson	ph-c	2	1	0	0	0	0	0	0	0	0	0	.000	.000	0	0	0
Roy White	ph	2	2	0	0	0	0	0	0	0	0	0	.000	.000			
George Zeber	ph	2	2	0	0	0	0	0	0	0	2	0	.000	.000			
Fred Stanley	ss	1	0	0	0	0	0	0	0	0	0	0	—	—	1	0	0
Fran Healy		Did not play															
Mickey Klutts		Did not play															
Mike Torrez	p	2	6	0	0	0	0	0	0	0	4	0	.000	.000	2	3	0
Don Gullett	p	2	2	0	0	0	0	0	0	0	2	0	.000	.000	1	2	0
Ron Guidry	p	1	2	0	0	0	0	0	0	0	1	0	.000	.000	0	0	0
Sparky Lyle	p	2	2	0	0	0	0	0	0	0	2	0	.000	.000	0	0	0
Catfish Hunter	p	2	0	0	0	0	0	0	0	0	0	0	—	—	1	0	0
Dick Tidrow	p	2	1	0	0	0	0	0	0	0	1	0	.000	.000	0	1	0
Ken Clay	p	2	0	0	0	0	0	0	0	0	0	0	—	—	1	1	0
Ed Figueroa		Did not play															
Ken Holtzman		Did not play															
team total		6	205	26	50	10	0	8	25	11	37	1	.244	.410	168	68	3

Double Plays—2
Left on Bases—32

		REGULAR SEASON STATISTICS													
		Main Pos	G	AB	R	H	2B	3B	HR	RBI	BB	SO	SB	BA	SA
Chris Chambliss		1b	157	600	90	172	32	6	17	90	45	73	4	.287	.445
Willie Randolph		2b	147	551	91	151	28	11	4	40	64	53	13	.274	.387
Bucky Dent		ss	158	477	54	118	18	4	8	49	39	28	1	.247	.352
Graig Nettles		3b	158	589	99	150	23	4	37	107	68	79	2	.255	.496
Reggie Jackson		of	146	525	93	150	39	2	32	110	75	129	17	.286	.550
Mickey Rivers		of	138	565	79	184	18	5	12	69	18	45	22	.326	.439
Lou Piniella		of-dh	103	339	47	112	19	3	12	45	20	31	2	.330	.510
Thurman Munson		c	149	595	85	183	28	5	18	100	39	55	5	.308	.462
Paul Blair		of	83	164	20	43	4	3	4	25	9	16	3	.262	.396
Cliff Johnson		dh-c-1b	56	142	24	42	8	0	12	31	20	23	0	.296	.606
Roy White		of	143	519	72	139	25	2	14	52	75	58	18	.268	.405
George Zeber		2b	25	65	8	21	3	0	3	10	9	11	0	.323	.508
Fred Stanley		ss	48	46	6	12	0	0	1	7	8	6	1	.261	.326
Fran Healy		c	27	67	10	15	5	0	0	7	6	13	1	.224	.299
Mickey Klutts		3b	5	15	3	4	1	0	1	4	2	1	0	.267	.533
Mike Torrez	a	p	35	0	0	0	0	0	0	0	0	0	0	—	—
Don Gullett		p	22	0	0	0	0	0	0	0	0	0	0	—	—
Ron Guidry		p	36	0	3	0	0	0	0	0	0	0	0	—	—
Sparky Lyle		p	72	0	0	0	0	0	0	0	0	0	0	—	—
Catfish Hunter		p	22	0	0	0	0	0	0	0	0	0	0	—	—
Dick Tidrow		p	49	0	0	0	0	0	0	0	0	0	0	—	—
Ken Clay		p	21	0	0	0	0	0	0	0	0	0	0	—	—
Ed Figueroa		p	32	0	0	0	0	0	0	0	0	0	0	—	—
Ken Holtzman		p	18	0	0	0	0	0	0	0	0	0	0	—	—
team total			162	5605	831	1576	267	47	184	784	533	681	93	.281	.444

a—from Oakland.
Carlos May(dh), Jim Wynn(dh), Del Alston(dh-ph), Ellie Hendricks(ph), Dave Kingman(dh), Dave Bergman(1b), Larry McCall(p), Marty Perez(ph), Gene Locklear(of), Gil Patterson(p), Stan Thomas(p), and Dock Ellis(p) also played for the Yankees during the season.

LOS ANGELES DODGERS

	WORLD SERIES STATISTICS															
	Pos	G	AB	R	H	2B	3B	HR	RBI	BB	SO	SB	BA	SA	PO	A	E
Steve Garvey	1b	6	24	5	**9**	1	**1**	1	3	1	4	0	.375	.625	**59**	6	0
Davey Lopes	2b	6	24	3	4	0	**1**	1	2	**4**	3	**2**	.167	.375	12	**22**	0
Bill Russell	ss	6	26	3	4	0	**1**	0	2	1	3	0	.154	.231	9	21	0
Ron Cey	3b	6	21	2	4	1	0	1	3	3	5	0	.190	.381	5	7	0
Reggie Smith	rf-of	6	22	7	6	1	0	3	5	**4**	3	0	.273	.727	14	1	0
Rick Monday	cf	4	12	0	2	0	0	0	0	0	3	0	.167	.167	5	0	0
Dusty Baker	lf	6	24	4	7	0	0	1	5	0	2	0	.292	.417	11	0	**1**
Steve Yeager	c	6	19	2	6	1	0	2	5	1	1	0	.316	.684	32	6	0
Lee Lacy	ph-rf	4	7	1	3	0	0	0	2	1	1	0	.429	.429	2	0	0
Glenn Burke	cf	3	5	0	1	0	0	0	0	0	1	0	.200	.200	10	0	0
Vic Davalillo	ph	3	3	0	1	0	0	0	1	0	0	0	.333	.333			
Manny Mota	ph	3	3	0	0	0	0	0	0	0	1	0	.000	.000			
Ed Goodson	ph	1	1	0	0	0	0	0	0	0	1	0	.000	.000			
Gerry Grote	c	1	1	0	0	0	0	0	0	0	0	0	.000	.000	3	3	0
Johnny Oates	ph-c	1	1	0	0	0	0	0	0	0	0	0	.000	.000	1	0	0
Rafael Landestoy	pr	1	0	0	0	0	0	0	0	0	0	0	—	—			
Don Sutton	p	2	6	0	0	0	0	0	0	1	4	0	.000	.000	1	1	0
Burt Hooton	p	2	5	0	0	0	0	0	0	0	2	0	.000	.000	0	0	0
Rick Rhoden	p	2	2	1	1	1	0	0	0	0	0	0	.500	1.000	1	1	0
Tommy John	p	1	2	0	0	0	0	0	0	0	2	0	.000	.000	0	0	0
Charlie Hough	p	2	0	0	0	0	0	0	0	0	0	0	—	—	0	0	0
Mike Garman	p	2	0	0	0	0	0	0	0	0	0	0	—	—	0	0	0
Doug Rau	p	2	0	0	0	0	0	0	0	0	0	0	—	—	0	0	0
Elias Sosa	p	2	0	0	0	0	0	0	0	0	0	0	—	—	0	0	0
Lance Rautzhan	p	1	0	0	0	0	0	0	0	0	0	0	—	—	0	1	0
team total		6	208	28	48	5	3	9	28	16	36	2	231	.413	165	69	1

Double Plays—3
Left on Bases—31

		REGULAR SEASON STATISTICS													
		Main Pos	G	AB	R	H	2B	3B	HR	RBI	BB	SO	SB	BA	SA
Steve Garvey		1b	162	646	91	192	25	3	33	115	38	90	9	.297	.498
Davey Lopes		2b	134	502	85	142	19	5	11	53	73	69	47	.283	.406
Bill Russell		ss	153	634	84	176	28	6	4	51	24	43	16	.278	.360
Ron Cey		3b	153	564	77	136	22	3	30	110	93	106	3	.241	.450
Reggie Smith		of	148	488	104	150	27	4	32	87	104	76	7	.307	.576
Rick Monday		of	118	392	47	90	13	1	15	48	60	109	1	.230	.383
Dusty Baker		of	153	533	86	155	26	1	30	86	58	89	2	.291	.512
Steve Yeager		c	125	387	53	99	21	2	16	55	43	84	1	.256	.444
Lee Lacy		of-2b	75	169	28	45	7	0	6	21	10	21	4	.266	.414
Glenn Burke		of	83	169	16	43	8	0	1	13	5	22	13	.254	.320
Vic Davalillo		of-ph	24	48	3	15	2	0	0	4	0	6	0	.313	.354
Manny Mota		ph	49	38	5	15	1	0	1	4	10	0	1	.395	.500
Ed Goodson		ph-1b	61	66	3	11	1	0	1	5	3	10	0	.167	.227
Gerry Grote	b	c	18	27	3	7	0	0	0	4	2	5	0	.259	.259
Johnny Oates		c	60	156	18	42	4	0	3	11	11	11	1	.269	.353
Rafael Landestoy		2b	15	18	6	5	0	0	0	0	3	2	2	.278	.278
Don Sutton		p	33	73	3	11	2	0	0	8	8	21	0	.151	.178
Burt Hooton		p	32	67	1	11	2	0	0	3	2	15	0	.164	.194
Rick Rhoden		p	32	78	8	18	3	0	3	12	0	13	0	.231	.385
Tommy John		p	31	79	3	14	1	0	1	4	3	14	0	.177	.228
Charlie Hough		p	70	22	1	4	0	0	1	2	1	2	0	.182	.318
Mike Garman		p	49	7	0	0	0	0	0	0	0	2	0	.000	.000
Doug Rau		p	32	71	4	10	1	0	0	2	5	11	0	.141	.155
Elias Sosa		p	45	4	1	1	0	0	0	0	0	1	0	.250	.250
Lance Rautzhan		p	25	1	0	0	0	0	0	0	0	1	0	.000	.000
team total			162	5589	769	1484	223	28	**191**	729	588	896	114	.266	.418

b—from New York(N)
Bob Castillo(p), Al Downing(p), John Hale(of), Jeff Leonard(of), Dennis Lewallyn(p), Teddy Martinez(inf.), Kevin Pasley(c), Boog Powell(ph), Joe Simpson(of), Stan Wall(p), Ron Washington(ss), and Henry Webb(p) also played for the Dodgers during the season.

PITCHING

	WORLD SERIES STATISTICS													REGULAR SEASON STATISTICS														
	G	GS	CG	IP	H	R	ER	BB	SO	W	L	SV	ERA		G	GS	CG	IP	H	ER	BB	SO	W	L	Pct	SV	ShO	ERA
NEW YORK YANKEES																												
Mike Torrez	**2**	**2**	**2**	**18**	16	7	5	5	**15**	**2**	0	0	2.50	a	31	31	15	217	212	92	75	90	14	12	.538	0	2	3.82
Don Gullett	**2**	2	0	12.2	13	**10**	**9**	**7**	10	0	**1**	0	6.39		22	22	7	158	137	63	69	116	14	4	.778	0	1	3.59
Ron Guidry	1	1	1	9	4	2	2	3	7	1	0	0	**2.00**		31	25	9	211	174	66	65	176	16	7	.696	1	5	2.82
Sparky Lyle	**2**	0	0	4.2	2	1	1	0	2	1	0	0	1.93		**72**	0	0	137	131	33	33	68	13	5	.722	26	0	2.17
Catfish Hunter	**2**	1	0	4.1	6	5	5	0	1	0	**1**	0	10.38		22	22	8	143	137	75	47	52	9	9	.500	0	1	4.72
Dick Tidrow	**2**	0	0	3.2	5	2	2	0	1	0	0	0	4.91		49	7	0	151	143	53	41	83	11	4	.733	5	0	3.16
Ken Clay	**2**	0	0	3.2	2	1	1	1	0	0	0	0	2.45		21	3	0	56	53	27	24	20	2	3	.400	1	0	4.34
Ed Figueroa	Did not play														32	32	12	239	228	95	75	104	16	11	.593	0	2	3.58
Ken Holtzman	Did not play														18	11	0	72	105	46	24	14	2	3	.400	0	0	5.75
Team total	6	6	3	56	48	28	25	16	36	4	2	0	4.02		162	162	52	1449	1395	581	486	758	100	62	.617	34	16	3.61
LOS ANGELES DODGERS																												
Don Sutton	**2**	**2**	1	16	**17**	7	7	1	6	1	0	0	3.94		33	33	9	240	207	85	69	150	14	8	.636	0	3	3.19
Burt Hooton	**2**	**2**	1	12	8	5	5	2	9	1	**1**	0	3.75		32	31	16	223	184	65	60	153	12	7	.632	1	2	2.62
Rick Rhoden	**2**	0	0	7	4	2	2	1	5	0	**1**	0	2.57		31	31	4	216	223	90	63	122	16	10	.615	0	1	3.75
Tommy John	1	1	0	6	9	5	4	3	7	0	**1**	0	6.00		31	31	11	220	225	68	50	123	20	7	.741	0	3	2.78
Charlie Hough	**2**	0	0	5	3	1	1	0	5	0	0	0	1.80		70	1	0	127	98	47	70	105	6	12	.333	22	0	3.33
Mike Garman	**2**	0	0	4	2	0	0	1	3	0	0	0	0.00		49	0	0	63	60	19	22	29	4	4	.500	12	0	2.71
Doug Rau	**2**	1	0	2.1	4	3	3	0	1	0	**1**	0	11.57		32	32	4	212	232	81	49	126	14	8	.636	0	2	3.44
Elias Sosa	**2**	0	0	2.1	3	3	3	1	1	0	0	0	11.57		44	0	0	64	42	14	12	47	2	2	.500	1	0	1.97
Lance Rautzhan	1	0	0	.1	0	0	0	2	0	0	0	0	0.00		25	0	0	21	25	10	7	13	4	1	.500	2	0	4.29
Team total	6	6	2	55	50	26	25	11	37	2	4	0	4.09		162	162	**34**	1475	1393	**528**	438	930	98	64	.605	39	13	**3.22**

Total Attendance—337,708 Average Attendance—56,285 Winning Player's Share—$27,758 Losing Player's Share—$20,899

1978
Many Comebacks in One

Although the Yankees and Dodgers returned to the World Series, neither had the dignified stroll of a reigning monarch. Both had to scramble to make it back. The Yankees were out on their feet during the heat of July. They trailed the Boston Red Sox by 14 games in mid-July wracked by pitching injuries and open hostility between manager Billy Martin and slugger Reggie Jackson. On July 17, Martin was replaced as manager by Bob Lemon. While injuries and fatigue caught up with the Red Sox in late summer, the Yankees won 48 of 68 games under Lemon's easygoing leadership. They finished the regular season in a dead heat with Boston and met the Sox in a one-game playoff for the A.L. East title on October 2. The Yanks won the game 5–4 behind the pitching of ace lefty Ron Guidry and a three-run homer by Bucky Dent. The Yanks had an easier time of it in the A.L. championship series, sinking the Kansas City Royals for the third straight year.

In the N.L., the Dodgers played sluggish ball during the summer, falling 6½ games behind the San Francisco Giants. Unlike the openly feisty Yankees, the Dodgers were known as a close-knit bunch led by an affectionate manager in Tom Lasorda. But Steve Garvey and Don Sutton had a shoving match in the clubhouse before a game, showing the world that all was not peaches and cream with the All-American Dodgers. The incident fired up the Dodgers and brought them together for a stretch run in which they captured first place in the N.L. West. In the playoffs, they repeated last year's drubbing of the Philadelphia Phillies.

The Dodgers wore black armbands to dedicate the Series to coach Jim Gilliam who died from a brain hemorrhage two days before the Series began.

When the Series began in Los Angeles, the Dodger bats roughed up Yankee pitching for 15 hits and an 11–5 victory.

The next night, Burt Hooton started for the Dodgers against Catfish Hunter, whose late-season renaissance sparked the Yankee pennant drive. Ron Cey belted a three-run homer off Hunter in the sixth inning to put the Dodgers ahead 4–2. The Yanks closed to 4–3 in the seventh, then threatened in the ninth. With one out, the Yankees put men on first and second against Forster. Lasorda then brought in rookie Bob Welch, a fastballing righty. Thurman Munson hit a soft liner to right for the second out, and then Reggie Jackson ran the count to 3–2. With the crowd on its feet, Jackson fouled off four straight pitches before fanning for the third out.

Trailing two games to none, the Yanks asked Ron Guidry to turn the Series around in New York. Guidry had enjoyed one of the best pitching years since the prime of Sandy Koufax, but the star of the day was Yankee third baseman Graig Nettles. In a show reminiscent of vintage Brooks Robinson, Nettles turned in four sparkling plays that broke the back of the Dodger attack. He saved a run with a backhand grab of a shot by Reggie Smith with two out in the third inning. In the fifth, he knocked down another line drive by Smith over the base and turned it into an infield single. Then, with the bases loaded and two out, he speared a hot smash by Steve Garvey to end the inning. Again, in the sixth inning, a stunning play on a shot by Lopes over the bag extinguished another Dodger rally. With Nettles taking care of the defense, the New York lineup got to Don Sutton for a 5–1 victory.

The fourth game began as a match-up of opening-game pitchers John and Figueroa. Reggie Smith reached Figueroa for a three-run homer in the fifth, while the Yanks answered with two runs in the sixth. Jackson singled home the first run, putting men on first and second with one out; Lou Piniella hit a grounder to shortstop Bill Russell, who stepped on second and threw to first to try for a double play. Jackson, who was already forced out, was hit by Russell's throw, with the Dodgers claiming that he deliberately stuck his hip in the way. At any rate, the second Yankee run scored while the Dodgers chased the ball. Munson doubled in the tying run in the eighth off Forster. Welch came on to end the Yankee rally, but ran into trouble in the tenth inning. Roy White walked with one out. After Munson popped out, Jackson earned revenge by singling off the rookie. Piniella then singled to win the game 4–3.

Now in full throttle, the Yanks blew the Dodgers away 12–2 in game five. The Yankee attack notched 18 hits and had a fistful of heroes. Munson drove in five runs and White three. Mickey Rivers had three hits despite a sore hip; so did Bucky Dent and Brian Doyle, the light-hitting infielders at the bottom of the lineup.

Although the Dodgers hoped to recover when the teams reconvened in Los Angeles, it was too late to stop the Yankee juggernaut. The Yanks captured the Series with a 7–2 victory in game six. Dent and Doyle combined for six hits and five RBI's, and Jackson avenged himself by lashing a homer off Welch. Coming alive after a slow start, the Yankees became the first team ever to lose the first two games of the Series and come back to win it in six.

Game 1 October 10 at Los Angeles

New York	Pos	AB	R	H	RBI	PO	A	E
Rivers	cf	4	0	0	0	4	0	0
Blair	cf	1	0	0	0	1	0	0
White	lf	4	0	1	0	2	0	0
Munson	c	4	1	0	0	4	1	0
Jackson	dh	4	1	3	1	0	0	0
Piniella	rf	4	2	1	1	2	0	0
Nettles	3b	4	0	1	1	0	2	0
Chambliss	1b	4	1	1	0	5	0	0
Stanley	2b	2	0	1	0	4	1	0
b Johnson		1	0	0	0	0	0	0
Doyle	2b	0	0	0	0	1	0	0
Dent	ss	4	0	1	2	1	3	1
Figueroa	p	0	0	0	0	0	0	0
Clay	p	0	0	0	0	0	0	0
Lindblad	p	0	0	0	0	0	0	0
Tidrow	p	0	0	0	0	0	0	0
Totals		36	5	9	5	24	7	1

Pitching	IP	H	R	ER	BB	SO
New York						
Figueroa (L)	1⅔	5	3	3	1	0
Clay	*2⅓	4	4	3	2	2
Lindblad	2⅓	4	3	3	0	1
Tidrow	1⅔	2	1	1	0	1
Los Angeles						
John (W)	7⅔	8	5	3	2	4
Forster	1⅓	1	0	0	0	3

*Pitched to two batters in 5th.

N.Y.	000	000	320
L.A.	030	310	31x

Los Angeles	Pos	AB	R	H	RBI	PO	A	E
Lopes	2b	5	2	2	5	1	2	1
Russell	ss	5	1	3	0	3	5	1
Smith	rf	5	0	1	1	1	0	0
Garvey	1b	5	1	2	0	14	0	0
Cey	3b	4	1	1	0	0	4	0
Baker	lf	4	2	3	1	1	0	0
Monday	cf	2	2	1	0	0	0	0
a North	cf	1	1	1	2	0	0	0
Lacy	dh	3	0	1	1	0	0	0
Yeager	c	4	1	0	0	7	0	0
John	p	0	0	0	0	0	4	0
Forster	p	0	0	0	0	0	0	0
Totals		38	11	15	10	27	15	2

a Doubled for Monday in 7th.
b Struck out for Stanley in 8th.

Doubles—Monday, North, Russell, Stanley. Home Runs—Baker, Jackson, Lopes 2. Double Plays—Lopes to Russell to Garvey, Dent to Stanley to Chambliss, Munson to Doyle, Wild Pitch—Clay. Left on Bases—New York 6, Los Angeles 6. Umpires—Vargo(N), Haller(A), Kibler(N), Springstead(A), Pulli(N), Brinkman(A). Attendance—55,997. Time of Game—2:48.

1st Inning
New York
1 Rivers grounded to second.
White walked on a full count.
2,3 Munson hit into a double play, Lopes to Russell to Garvey.
Los Angeles
1 Lopes fouled to Chambliss.
Russell blooped a single to right-center.
2 Smith flied to short right.
Garvey singled to left, Russell racing to third.
3 Cey flied deep to Piniella against the right field wall.

2nd Inning
New York
Jackson singled through John's legs into center.
1 Piniella flied to right.
2 Nettles grounded to Garvey, unassisted, as Jackson went to second.
3 Chambliss grounded to short.
Los Angeles
Baker hit a home run just over the left field wall.
Monday doubled to left-center, Rivers just missing a shoestring catch.
Lacy walked on a 3–1 pitch.
1,2 Yeager bounced into a double play, Dent to Stanley to Chambliss, as Monday went to third.
Lopes hit the first pitch over the left field wall for a two-run homer.
For New York—Clay came in to pitch.
3 Russell popped to short.

3rd Inning
New York
Stanley doubled into the left-center field gap.
1 Dent grounded out, John to Garvey, as Stanley advanced to third.
2 Rivers grounded to short, as Stanley held third.
3 White struck out.
Los Angeles
1 Smith took a called third strike.
2 Garvey rolled out to short.
Cey walked.
3 Baker forced Cey at second, Nettles to Stanley.

4th Inning
New York
1 Munson struck out.
2 Jackson grounded to third.
3 Piniella grounded to short.
Los Angeles
Monday walked on a full count.
1 Lacy flied to deep center.
Yeager reached safely to first and Monday to third as Dent threw low to second after a great stop.
Lopes hit his second homer of the game, a three-run shot over the left-center field wall.
Russell singled up the middle.
2 Smith out, Chambliss unassisted as Russell went to second.
3 Garvey struck out.

5th Inning
New York
1 Nettles grounded to first.
2 Chambliss flied to Baker in short left-center.
Stanley walked.
3 Dent forced Chambliss at second, Cey to Lopes.

5th Inning (continued)
Los Angeles
Cey beat out a chopper to third.
Baker singled to right, Cey going to third.
Cey scored and Baker went to second on a wild pitch.
For New York—Linblad now pitching.
1 Monday struck out.
2 Lacy flied to Rivers in short left-center.
3 Yeager lined to center.

6th Inning
New York
1 Rivers bounced back to the mound.
2 White again struck out.
3 Munson grounded to third.
Los Angeles
1 Lopes grounded to short.
2 Russell flied to left.
3 Smith lined to Rivers in left-center.

7th Inning
New York
Jackson blasted a long homer to right.
Piniella singled to right.
1 Nettles struck out.
Chambliss reaches safely to first on Lopes' high throw to Russell on a grounder.
Piniella safe at second.
2 Stanley grounded to third, both runners advancing.
Dent singled to left, scoring both Piniella and Chambliss.
3 Rivers grounded to first.
Los Angeles
For New York—Blair now in center field.
Garvey looped a single to left.
1 Cey popped to Stanley in short right.
Baker singled to right, Garvey going to third. On the throw to third, Baker took second.
North, hitting for Monday, bounced a double over Nettles' head, scoring Garvey and Baker.
Lacy singled to left, North scoring.
For New York—Tidrow now on the mound.
2 Yeager flied to left.
3 Lopes forced Lacy, Nettles to Stanley.

8th Inning
New York
For Los Angeles—North playing center.
White singled to left.
1 Munson forced White, John to Russell.
Jackson singled to right, Munson racing to third.
2 Piniella forced Jackson, John to Russell, with Munson scoring. Russell's throw to first was wild and Piniella got safely to second on the error.
Nettles singled to right, Piniella scoring.
For Los Angeles—Forster relieved John.
Chambliss blooped a Texas-League single into short center, Nettles to second.
3 Johnson, batting for Stanley, struck out.
Los Angeles
For New York—Doyle playing second base.
Russell got a ground-rule double to right.
Smith singled to right, scoring Russell.
1,2 Garvey struck out and Smith was doubled trying to steal, Munson to Doyle.
3 Cey flied to center.

9th Inning
New York
1 Dent grounded to short.
2 Blair struck out swinging.
3 White struck out for the third time in the game.

Game 2 October 11 at Los Angeles

N.Y.	002	000	100
L.A.	000	103	00x

New York	Pos	AB	R	H	RBI	PO	A	E
White	lf	5	2	2	0	1	0	0
Thomasson	cf	3	0	1	0	2	0	0
a Blair	cf	1	0	1	0	2	0	0
Munson	c	4	1	1	0	3	1	0
Jackson	dh	4	0	1	3	0	0	0
Nettles	3b	4	0	0	0	3	3	0
Piniella	rf	4	0	2	0	2	0	0
Spencer	1b	4	0	1	0	8	1	0
Doyle	2b	3	0	1	0	2	1	0
b Johnson		1	0	0	0	0	0	0
Stanley	2b	0	0	0	0	0	0	0
Dent	ss	4	0	1	0	0	1	0
Hunter	p	0	0	0	0	1	0	0
Gossage	p	0	0	0	0	0	0	0
Totals		37	3	11	3	24	7	0

Los Angeles	Pos	AB	R	H	RBI	PO	A	E
Lopes	2b	4	1	1	0	3	4	0
Russell	ss	4	0	1	0	2	1	0
Smith	rf	4	2	1	0	3	0	0
Garvey	1b	3	0	1	0	6	1	0
Cey	3b	3	1	2	4	1	1	0
Baker	lf	3	0	0	0	2	0	0
Monday	cf	3	0	0	0	1	0	0
North	cf	0	0	0	0	0	0	0
Lacy	dh	3	0	0	0	0	0	0
Yeager	c	3	0	1	0	8	1	0
Hooton	p	0	0	0	0	1	0	0
Forster	p	0	0	0	0	0	1	0
Welch	p	0	0	0	0	0	0	0
Totals		30	4	7	4	27	9	0

Pitching	IP	H	R	ER	BB	SO
New York						
Hunter (L)	6	7	4	4	0	2
Gossage	2	0	0	0	0	0
Los Angeles						
Hooton (W)	*6	8	3	3	1	5
Forster	$2\frac{1}{3}$	3	0	0	1	3
Welch (SV)	$\frac{2}{3}$	0	0	0	0	1

*Pitched to one batter in 7th.

a Doubled for Thomasson in 7th.
b Hit into double play for Doyle in 8th.

Doubles—Blair, Jackson, Munson. Home Run—Cey. Stolen Base—White. Double Plays—Nettles to Spencer, Cey to Lopes to Garvey. Hit batter—Jackson (by Hooton). Wild Pitch—Hooton. Left on Bases—New York 10, Los Angeles 2. Umpires—Haller, Kibler, Springstead, Pulli, Brinkman, Vargo. Attendance—55,982. Time of Game—2:37.

1st Inning
New York
1 White lined to Smith near the right field line.
Thomasson singled to center.
2 Thomasson out over-sliding second on a steal attempt he had beaten, Yeager to Lopes.
Munson doubled off the left field wall.
3 Jackson struck out.
Los Angeles
1 Lopes fouled to Nettles.
2 Russell grounded to short.
3 Smith popped to first.

2nd Inning
New York
1 Nettles grounded to second.
2 Piniella flied to Smith in deep right, Smith making an over-the-head catch on the warning track.
Spencer singled between first and second.
3 Doyle flied to center.
Los Angeles
1 Garvey flied to center.
2 Cey grounded to third, Nettles making a good backhand stop.
3 Baker flied to Piniella in deep right-center.

3rd Inning
New York
1 Dent popped to short.
White singled to right-center.
2 Thomasson flied to left.
White stole second.
Munson walked.
Jackson doubled down the right field line, scoring White and Munson.
Munson scored when he eluded Yeager who had come up the line to field Smith's throw.
3 Nettles struck out.
Los Angeles
1 Monday struck out.
2 Lacy lined to right.
Yeager beat out a roller to third.
Nettles made a diving stop in the hole but his throw was not in time.
3 Lopes flied to deep center.

4th Inning
New York
1 Piniella flied to left.
2 Spencer popped to second.
Doyle singled to right.
3 Dent grounded to short.
Los Angeles
Russell singled to left.
1 Smith forced Russell at second, Nettles to Doyle.
Garvey singled down the third base line. Smith to second.
Cey singled to center, Smith scoring as Garvey stopped at second.
2,3 With Garvey and Cey running on a 3–2 pitch, Baker bounced to third. Nettles tagged Garvey and threw to first to complete a double play.

5th Inning
New York
1 White popped to short.
2 Thomasson grounded out, Garvey to Hooton.
Munson struck out but reached safely to first as the pitch was wild.
Jackson hit on the right arm by a pitch.
3 Nettles struck out.
Los Angeles
1 Monday grounded out, Spencer to Hunter.
2 Lacy popped to second.
3 Yeager struck out.

6th Inning
New York
Piniella beat out a hit to deep short.
1 Spencer fouled to Cey.
2 Doyle grounded to second, Piniella advancing to second.
3 Dent struck out on a full count.
Los Angeles
Lopes singled to left.
1 Russell foul bunted to Spencer.
Smith singled to right, Lopes getting to third.
2 Garvey fouled to Munson.
Cey hit a three-run home run into the left field stands.
3 Baker fouled to White.

7th Inning
New York
White singled to left on a 3–2 pitch.
For Los Angeles—Forster now pitching.
Blair, pinch-hitting for Thomasson, hit a ground-rule double over the left field wall. White stops at third.
1 Munson struck out.
2 Jackson grounded to second, scoring White, with Blair going to third.
3 Nettles struck out.
Los Angeles
For New York—Gossage came in to pitch and Blair stays in at center.
1 Monday grounded to second.
2 Lacy lined to third.
3 Yeager rolled out, Munson to Spencer.

8th Inning
New York
For Los Angeles—North playing center.
Piniella singled to right-center.
1 Spencer struck out.
2,3 Johnson, pinch-hitting for Doyle, hit into a double play, Cey to Lopes to Garvey.
Los Angeles
For New York—Stanley playing second.
1 Lopes flied to center.
2 Russell flied to center.
3 Smith grounded to first.

9th Inning
New York
Dent singled to left.
1 White out on a slow bouncer to Forster, Dent going to second.
Blair walked.
For Los Angeles—Welch relieved Forster.
2 Munson flied to right.
3 Jackson struck out.

Game 3 October 13 at New York

L.A.	001	000	000
N.Y.	110	000	30x

Los Angeles	Pos	AB	R	H	RBI	PO	A	E
Lopes	2b	5	0	1	0	3	2	0
Russell	ss	4	0	2	1	2	3	0
Smith	rf	4	0	1	0	2	0	0
Garvey	1b	4	0	1	0	4	2	0
Cey	3b	3	0	0	0	0	1	0
Baker	lf	3	0	2	0	5	0	0
Lacy	dh	4	0	1	0	0	0	0
North	cf	3	1	0	0	5	0	0
Yeager	c	1	0	0	0	2	1	0
a Mota		0	0	0	0	0	0	0
Grote	c	0	0	0	0	0	0	0
Ferguson	c	1	0	0	0	0	0	0
Sutton	p	0	0	0	0	0	0	0
Rautzhan	p	0	0	0	0	0	0	0
Hough	p	0	0	0	0	1	0	0
Totals		32	1	8	1	24	9	0

New York	Pos	AB	R	H	RBI	PO	A	E
Rivers	cf	4	0	3	0	2	0	0
b Blair	cf	0	0	0	0	0	0	0
White	lf	3	2	1	1	2	0	0
Munson	c	4	1	1	1	4	1	0
Jackson	dh	3	0	1	1	0	0	0
Piniella	rf	4	0	1	1	1	0	0
Nettles	3b	4	1	1	0	2	5	0
Chambliss	1b	3	0	1	0	8	0	0
Doyle	2b	4	0	0	0	7	2	0
Dent	ss	4	1	1	1	0	5	1
Guidry	p	0	0	0	0	1	1	0
Totals		33	5	10	5	27	14	1

Pitching	IP	H	R	ER	BB	SO
Los Angeles						
Sutton (L)	$6\frac{1}{3}$	9	5	5	3	2
Rautzhan	$\frac{2}{3}$	1	0	0	0	0
Hough	1	0	0	0	0	0
New York						
Guidry (W)	9	8	1	1	7	4

a Walked for Yeager in 6th.
b Ran for Rivers in 7th.

Double—Garvey. Home Run—White. Stolen Bases—North, Piniella. Double Plays—Nettles to Doyle to Chambliss, Dent to Doyle to Chambliss. Left on Bases—Los Angeles 11, New York 7. Umpires—Kibler, Springstead, Pulli, Brinkman, Vargo, Haller. Attendance—56,447. Time of Game—2:27

1st Inning
Los Angeles
1 Lopes flied to center on the first pitch.
Russell blooped a single to center.
2 Russell out attempting to steal second, Munson to Doyle.
Smith walked on a full count.
3 Garvey forced Smith at second, Dent to Doyle.
New York
Rivers singled to center.
1 Rivers out trying to steal, Yeager to Russell.
White homered down the right field line into the seats on a 3–2 pitch.
2 Munson called out on strikes.
Jackson walked with a full count.
3 Piniella flied to North in deep right-center.

2nd Inning
Los Angeles
1 Cey struck out.
Baker walked on a full count.
2,3 Lacy hit into a double play, Nettles to Doyle to Chambliss.
New York
Nettles singled through Lopes.
Chambliss walked.
1 Doyle forced Chambliss at second, Russell to Lopes, as Nettles went to third.
2 Dent forces Doyle at second, Cey to Lopes, Nettles scored as Dent just beat the throw to first.
Rivers singled to right, Dent advancing to second.
3 White grounded to second.

3rd Inning
Los Angeles
North walked.
North stole second.
1 Yeager grounded to short, North going to third.
2 Lopes lined to third.
Russell just beat out a grounder to deep short, scoring North.
3 Smith grounded to third, a great stop by Nettles.
New York
1 Munson struck out.
2 Jackson grounded to second.
Piniella blooped a single over second.
Piniella stole second.
3 Nettles flied to North in right-center.

4th Inning
Los Angeles
1 Garvey blooped a bunt foul over the third base line to Guidry.
Cey walked on four pitches.
2 Baker flied to right.
3 Lacy took a called third strike.
New York
Chambliss singled on a smash to third, Cey made a great stop saving a sure double.
1 Doyle flied to Baker in left-center.
2 Dent grounded to first, Chambliss going to second.
3 Rivers flied to deep left.

5th Inning
Los Angeles
1 North out on bunt back to Guidry.
Yeager walked with a full count.
Lopes singled to left, Yeager stopping at second.
2 Russell popped to second.
Smith only singled over third as Nettles got a glove on it to save an extra base hit, loading the bases.
3 Garvey forced Smith at second, Nettles to Doyle.
New York
White walked.
1 Munson flied to Smith in right-center.
2 Jackson forced White, Garvey to Russell.
3 Piniella flied to deep left.

6th Inning
Los Angeles
1 Cey flied to Rivers in left-center.
Baker singled to left-center.
Lacy singled to center, Baker to second.
2 North, on a full count, flied to deep left. Baker to third after the catch.
Mota, batting for Yeager, walked on four pitches, loading the bases.
3 Lopes forced Mota at second on a fabulous stop by Nettles to Doyle.
New York
For Los Angeles—Grote the new catcher.
1 Nettles flied to deep right.
2 Chambliss flied to deep center.
3 Doyle flied to left.

7th Inning
Los Angeles
1 Russell grounded to short.
2 Smith flied to left.
Garvey doubled over Rivers' head and went to third on Dent's error for failing to handle the throw in.
3 Cey fouled to Nettles on a full count.
New York
Dent singled to left.
Rivers beat out a bunt, Dent moving to second.
For New York—Blair running for Rivers.
1 White forced Blair at second, Russell to Lopes, with Dent going to third.
Munson singled to third, scoring Dent, with White going to second.
For Los Angeles—Rautzhan replaces Sutton on the mound.
Jackson singled to left, scoring White, with Munson racing to third.
2 Piniella grounded to short, scoring Munson and sending Jackson to second.
3 Nettles flied to deep center.

8th Inning
Los Angeles
For New York—Blair stays in to play center.
Baker, on a full count, blooped a single to left.
1,2 Lacy grounds into a double play, Dent to Doyle to Chambliss.
3 North grounded to Short.
New York
For Los Angeles—Hough now pitching and Ferguson catching.
1 Chambliss grounded out, Garvey to Hough.
2 Doyle flied to center.
3 Dent flied to left.

9th Inning
Los Angeles
1 Ferguson struck out.
2 Lopes grounded to third.
Russell walked on a full count.
3 Smith struck out.

1978

Game 4 October 14 at New York

```
L.A.   000  030  000  0
N.Y.   000  002  010  1
```

Los Angeles	Pos	AB	R	H	RBI	PO	A	E
Lopes	2b	4	1	0	0	0	4	0
Russell	ss	5	0	2	0	3	4	1
Smith	rf	4	1	1	3	1	1	0
Garvey	1b	4	0	0	0	15	0	0
Cey	3b	4	0	1	0	0	4	0
Baker	lf	4	0	0	0	0	0	0
Monday	dh	2	0	0	0	0	0	0
North	cf	4	0	0	0	2	0	0
Yeager	c	3	1	1	0	5	0	0
a Davalillo		1	0	0	0	0	0	0
Grote	c	0	0	0	0	3	0	0
John	p	0	0	0	0	0	0	0
Forster	p	0	0	0	0	0	0	0
Welch	p	0	0	0	0	0	0	0
Totals		35	3	6	3	x29	13	1

Pitching	IP	H	R	ER	BB	SO
Los Angeles						
John	*7	6	3	2	2	2
Forster	⅓	1	0	0	0	0
Welch (L)	2⅓	2	1	1	1	3
New York						
Figueroa	5	4	3	3	4	2
Tidrow	3	2	0	0	0	4
Gossage (W)	2	0	0	0	1	2

*Pitched to one batter in 8th.

New York	Pos	AB	R	H	RBI	PO	A	E
Blair	cf	4	1	2	0	2	0	0
c Rivers		1	0	0	0	0	0	0
White	lf	3	2	1	0	4	0	0
Munson	c	3	1	2	1	8	0	0
Jackson	dh	4	0	2	1	0	0	0
Piniella	rf	5	0	1	1	5	1	0
Nettles	3b	4	0	0	0	2	1	0
Chambliss	1b	4	0	0	0	4	1	0
Stanley	2b	3	0	0	0	1	1	0
b Spencer		1	0	0	0	1	0	0
Doyle	2b	0	0	0	0	0	0	0
Dent	ss	4	0	1	0	4	2	0
Figueroa	p	0	0	0	0	0	0	0
Tidrow	p	0	0	0	0	0	0	0
Gossage	p	0	0	0	0	0	0	0
Totals		36	4	9	3	30	6	0

a Flied out for Yeager in 9th.
b Struck out for Stanley in 9th.
c Fouled out for Blair in 10th.
x Two out when winning run scored.

Doubles—Munson, Yeager. Home Run—Smith. Stolen Bases—Garvey, Munson. Sacrifice Hit—White. Double Play—Piniella to Chambliss to Dent. Hit Batter—Jackson (by Forster). Left on Bases—Los Angeles 7, New York 8. Umpires—Springstead, Pulli, Brinkman, Vargo, Haller, Kibler. Attendance—56,445. Time of Game—3:17.

1st Inning
Los Angeles
1 Lopes flied to right on a full count.
  Russell beat out a bunt for a hit.
  Smith walked.
2,3 Garvey lined to Piniella in right;
  he threw to Chambliss, but Smith
  got back. Chambliss threw to Dent
  who doubled up Russell.
New York
  Blair beat out a dribbler along the
  third base line.
1 White grounded to second, Blair
  going to second.
  Munson singled to right. Smith threw
2 to Yeager getting Blair trying to
  score.
3 With a full count Jackson grounded
  to first.

2nd Inning
Los Angeles
  Cey singled to center.
1 Baker popped to short.
  Monday walked on 4 pitches.
2 North flied to center, Cey going to
  third after the catch.
3 Yeager popped to short.
New York
1 Piniella grounded to third.
2 Nettles grounded to second.
3 Chambliss grounded to short.

3rd Inning
Los Angeles
1 Lopes lined to third, Nettles making
  a superb catch.
2 Russell flied to Stanley in short
  left.
3 Smith called out on strikes.
New York
1 Stanley flied to short center.
  Dent singled to left-center.
  **Time was called due to rain and
  the game was delayed 40 minutes
  before resuming.**
2 Blair popped to short.
3 White flied to right.

4th Inning
Los Angeles
  Garvey walked.
  Garvey stole second.
1 Cey grounded to short, Garvey holding.
2 Baker flied to left. Garvey went to
  third after the catch.
3 Monday popped to short left.
New York
  Munson got a base on balls.
1 On a full count, Jackson struck out
  as Munson was stealing second.
2 Piniella grounded to third, Munson
  holding.
3 Nettles grounded to short.

5th Inning
Los Angeles
1 North grounded to short.
  Yeager doubled to right-center.
  Lopes walked.
2 Russell struck out.
  Smith hit a three-run homer into the
  right field seats.
3 Garvey, on a full count, flied to
  deep right.
New York
1 Chambliss popped to Yeager in front
  of the plate.
2 Stanley grounded to third, a good
  play by Cey.
3 Dent also grounded to Cey, making
  another good play.

6th Inning
Los Angeles
  For New York—Tidrow pitching.
1 Cey struck out.
2 Baker struck out.
  Monday singled to center.
3 North grounded to second.
New York
1 Blair struck out.
  White singled to center.
  Munson walked on a full count.
  Jackson singled to right, scoring
  White, with Munson stopping at second.
2 Piniella hit a perfect double-play
  ball right to Russell who stepped on
  second to force Jackson. Russell's
  throw to first to get the double
  play hit Jackson and caromed toward
  right field. Munson scored and
  Piniella was safe on Russell's
  error.
3 Nettles grounded to Lopes.

7th Inning
Los Angeles
1 Yeager struck out.
2 Lopes flied to right.
  Russell blooped a single to center.
3 Smith flied to right.
New York
1 Chambliss grounded to second.
2 Stanley grounded to short.
3 Dent grounded to short.

8th Inning
Los Angeles
1 Garvey flied to deep left.
2 Cey grounded to third.
3 Baker struck out.
New York
  Blair singled to left.
  For Los Angeles—Forster relieved John.
1 White sacrificed Blair to second,
  Garvey unassisted.
  Munson doubled to left (with a two
  strike count), scoring Blair.
  Jackson was hit by a pitch.
  For Los Angeles—Welch replaces Forster
  on the mound.
2 Piniella popped to Garvey in short
  right (with a full count).
3 Nettles struck out.

9th Inning
Los Angeles
  For New York—Gossage pitching.
  Monday walked on a full count.
1 North, attempting to sacrifice, pop
  bunted to Nettles.
2 Davalillo, pinch-hitting for Yeager,
  flied to left.
3 Lopes popped to Dent in short center.
New York
  For Los Angeles—Grote catching.
1 Chambliss struck out.
2 Spencer, pinch-hitting for Stanley,
  also struck out.
3 Dent flied to center.

10th Inning
Los Angeles
  For New York—Doyle playing second.
1 Russell flied to center.
2 Smith struck out.
3 Garvey struck out, Gossage
  retiring the side on just ten
  pitches.
New York
1 Rivers, batting for Blair, fouled
  to Grote.
  White walked on a full count.
2 Munson popped to short.
  Jackson singled to right, White
  stopping at second.
  Piniella singled to center, knocking
  in White with the game-ending run.

1978

Game 5 October 15 at New York

L.A.	1 0 1	0 0 0	0 0 0					
N.Y.	0 0 4	3 0 0	4 1 x					

Los Angeles	Pos	AB	R	H	RBI	PO	A	E
Lopes	2b	4	2	2	0	3	5	0
Russell	ss	5	0	2	1	1	4	1
Smith	rf	4	0	1	1	2	0	1
Garvey	1b	4	0	1	0	10	0	1
Cey	3b	3	0	1	0	0	0	0
Baker	lf	4	0	0	0	2	0	0
Monday	cf	3	0	0	0	2	0	0
Lacy	dh	4	0	0	0	0	0	0
Yeager	c	2	0	1	0	1	0	0
a Oates	c	1	0	1	0	3	1	0
Hooton	p	0	0	0	0	0	0	0
Rautzhan	p	0	0	0	0	0	0	0
Hough	p	0	0	0	0	0	0	0
Totals		34	2	9	2	24	10	3

New York	Pos	AB	R	H	RBI	PO	A	E
Rivers	cf	5	2	3	1	0	0	0
b Blair	cf	1	1	0	0	0	0	0
White	lf	5	2	2	3	2	0	0
Johnstone	rf	0	0	0	0	1	0	0
Munson	c	5	1	3	5	8	1	0
Heath	c	0	0	0	0	0	0	0
Jackson	dh	3	0	1	0	0	0	0
Piniella	rf	4	0	1	1	4	0	0
Thomasson	lf	1	0	0	0	0	0	0
Nettles	3b	5	0	1	0	1	2	0
Spencer	1b	4	2	1	0	6	0	0
Doyle	2b	5	2	3	0	5	1	0
Dent	ss	4	2	3	1	0	2	0
Beattie	p	0	0	0	0	0	1	0
Totals		42	12	18	11	27	7	0

a Walked for Yeager in 7th.
b Ran for Rivers in 7th.

Doubles—Dent, Munson, Russell. Stolen Bases—Lopes, Rivers, Russell, White. Double Plays—Russell to Lopes to Garvey, Lopes to Russell to Garvey, Nettles to Doyle to Spencer. Wild Pitches—Hough 2. Passed Ball—Yeager. Left on Bases—Los Angeles 9, New York 10. Umpires—Pulli, Brinkman, Vargo, Haller, Kibler, Springstead. Attendance—56,448. Time of Game—2:56.

Pitching	IP	H	R	ER	BB	SO
Los Angeles						
Hooton (L)	2⅓	5	4	3	2	1
Rautzhan	1⅓	3	3	3	0	0
Hough	4⅓	10	5	5	2	5
New York						
Beattie (W)	9	9	2	2	4	8

1st Inning

Los Angeles
Lopes hit a Texas League single to right.
Lopes stole second.
1 Russell flied to left.
Smith singled to right, scoring Lopes. Smith went to second on the throw to the plate.
2 Garvey grounded to short, Smith holding at second.
3 Cey struck out.

New York
Rivers singled to right.
White reached safely to first and Rivers to second when Russell bobbled White's hard grounder to short.
1 Munson flied to deep center. Both runners tagged up and advanced after the catch.
Jackson intentionally walked to load the bases.
2,3 Piniella grounded into a double play, Russell to Lopes to Garvey.

2nd Inning

Los Angeles
1 Baker fouled to Spencer.
Monday walked on four pitches.
2 Monday caught trying to steal, Munson to Doyle.
3 Lacy called out on strikes.

New York
1 Nettles grounded to second.
2 Spencer flied to right.
3 Doyle grounded to short. Garvey made a leaping catch of Russell's high throw.

3rd Inning

Los Angeles
1 Yeager flied to deep right, Piniella crashing into the wall as he made the catch.
Lopes singled through the middle.
Russell lined a double to left, Lopes scoring.
2 Smith struck out.
Garvey beat out a smash between short and third that Nettles was just able to stop and hold Russell to third.
3 Cey bounced to third.

New York
Dent walked on four pitches.
Rivers singled to left, Dent stopping at second.
White lined a single to right, Dent scoring and Rivers going to second. Rivers and White pulled off a double steal as Yeager could not hold a low outside pitch.
Munson lined a single to right-center, scoring both Rivers and White. Smith's throw to the plate was late and wild and bounced into the stands, Munson getting to third on the error.
1 Jackson struck out.
Piniella singled to left, scoring Munson.
For Los Angeles—Rautzhan relieved Hooton on the mound.
2,3 Nettles grounded into a double play, Lopes to Russell to Garvey.

4th Inning

Los Angeles
1 Baker popped to third.
2 Monday popped to second.
3 Lacy struck out.

New York
1 Spencer grounded to first.
Doyle singled between first and second.
Dent singled on a hard smash off Russell's glove. Doyle took third and Dent went to second on the throw to third by Baker.
Rivers bounced a single (his third) between first and second, scoring Doyle with Dent stopping at third.
2 White grounded to Garvey, who stepped on first and then threw wildly to home trying to get Dent. Rivers went to third on the error. (An RBI to White on the play.)
For Los Angeles—Hough came in to pitch.
Munson singled to right, scoring Rivers.
Jackson walked.
3 Piniella flied to center.

5th Inning

Los Angeles
Yeager singled to left.
1 Lopes flied to deep right.
Russell singled to right, Yeager advancing to third.
2 Smith flied to short right. Russell stole second, unchallenged.
3 Garvey struck out.

New York
Nettles singled to center.
1 Spencer popped to second. Nettles went to second on a passed ball.
2 Doyle lined to right.
Dent beat out a hard smash off Russell's glove. Nettles stopped at third.
3 Rivers grounded to second.

6th Inning

Los Angeles
Cey walked on a 3-2 pitch.
1 Baker lined to left.
2 Monday grounded to Spencer, Cey going to second.
3 Lacy flied to right.

New York
1 White grounded to short.
2 Munson flied to deep left.
Jackson singled off Garvey's glove into right.
3 Piniella flied to Baker in deep left-center.

7th Inning

Los Angeles
Oates, pinch-hitting for Yeager, walked.
Lopes walked on a 3-2 pitch.
1 Russell struck out.
2 Smith popped to second.
3 Garvey struck out on three straight curve balls.

New York
For Los Angeles—Oates catching.
1 Nettles lined to second.
Spencer looped a single to center.
Doyle singled to right, Spencer stopping at second.
Both Spencer and Doyle advanced on base on Hough's wild pitch.
2 Dent struck out.
Rivers struck out swinging on an outside knuckle ball that rolled all the way to the screen. Spencer scored, Doyle went to third and Rivers to first on the second wild pitch of the inning.
For New York—Blair running for Rivers.
White singled to right, scoring Doyle, as Blair stopped at second.
Munson doubled (his third hit) to deep left-center, scoring Blair and White.
3 Jackson grounded to second.

8th Inning

Los Angeles
For New York—Blair playing center, Johnstone in right (batting second), and Thomasson playing left (batting fifth).
Cey singled on a bouncer over Nettles' head.
1 Baker struck out.
2 Monday flied to right.
3 Lacy forced Cey, Dent to Doyle.

New York
1 Thomasson struck out swinging.
2 Nettles struck out swinging.
Spencer walked.
Doyle singled (his third hit) to right, Spencer stopping at second.
It was the Yankees' 16th single of the game creating a new Series' single game record.
Dent doubled (also his third hit) down the third base line, scoring Spencer, with Doyle stopping at third.
3 Blair struck out, but had to be thrown out by Oates.

9th Inning

Los Angeles
For New York—Heath catching.
Oates singled to center.
1,2 Lopes hit into a double play, Nettles to Doyle to Spencer.
3 Russell grounded back to the pitcher.
Beattie's first complete game in the major leagues.

Game 6 October 17 at Los Angeles

N.Y.	030	002	200					
L.A.	101	000	000					

New York	Pos	AB	R	H	RBI	PO	A	E
Rivers	cf	4	0	0	0	1	0	0
Blair	cf	1	0	0	0	0	0	0
White	lf	4	1	1	0	4	0	0
Thomasson	lf	0	0	0	0	1	0	0
Munson	c	5	0	1	0	6	1	0
Jackson	dh	5	1	1	2	0	0	0
Piniella	rf	4	1	1	0	0	0	0
Johnstone	rf	0	0	0	0	0	0	0
Nettles	3b	4	1	1	0	0	5	0
Spencer	1b	3	1	0	0	9	1	0
Doyle	2b	4	2	3	2	2	3	0
Dent	ss	4	0	3	3	3	3	0
Hunter	p	0	0	0	0	1	0	0
Gossage	p	0	0	0	0	0	0	0
Totals		38	7	11	7	27	13	0

Doubles—Doyle, Ferguson 2. Home Runs—Jackson, Lopez. Stolen Base—Lopes. Sacrifice Hit—Davalillo. Double Plays—Doyle to Dent to Spencer, Nettles to Doyle to Spencer. Wild Pitch—Sutton. Left on Bases—New York 6, Los Angeles 3. Umpires—Brinkman, Vargo, Haller, Kibler, Springstead, Pulli. Attendance—55,985. Time of Game—2:34.

Los Angeles	Pos	AB	R	H	RBI	PO	A	E
Lopes	2b	4	1	2	2	0	2	0
Russell	ss	3	0	1	0	0	3	0
Smith	rf	4	0	0	0	2	0	0
Garvey	1b	4	0	0	0	9	0	0
Cey	3b	4	0	1	0	1	2	0
Baker	lf	3	0	0	0	2	0	0
Monday	cf	3	0	0	0	2	0	0
Ferguson	c	3	1	2	0	11	0	1
Davalillo	dh	2	0	1	0	0	0	0
Sutton	p	0	0	0	0	0	0	0
Welch	p	0	0	0	0	0	0	0
Rau	p	0	0	0	0	0	1	0
Totals		30	2	7	2	27	8	1

Pitching	IP	H	R	ER	BB	SO
New York						
Hunter (W)	*7	6	2	2	1	3
Gossage	2	1	0	0	0	2
Los Angeles						
Sutton (L)	5⅓	8	5	5	1	6
Welch	1⅓	2	2	2	1	0
Rau	2	1	0	0	0	3

*Pitched to one batter in 8th.

1st Inning
New York
1 Rivers grounded to second.
   White singled to left.
2 Munson grounded to short, White going to second.
3 Jackson bounced to short.
Los Angeles
   Lopes hit his third home run of the Series into the left field seats.
   Russell singled to right-center.
1 Smith struck out looking on three pitches.
2 Russell caught trying to steal second, Munson to Doyle.
3 Garvey struck out.

2nd Inning
New York
1 Piniella grounded to third.
   Nettles singled to right-center.
   Spencer walked.
   Doyle doubled over Baker's head, scoring Nettles, with Spencer stopping at third.
   Dent singled to center scoring both Spencer and Doyle. Dent went to second when the throw in got by Ferguson.
2 Rivers grounded to second, Dent moving to third.
3 White flied to left.
Los Angeles
1 Cey flied to deep left.
2 Baker grounded to short.
3 Monday grounded to second.

3rd Inning
New York
1 Munson struck out.
2 Jackson struck out.
3 Piniella grounded to first.
Los Angeles
   Ferguson doubled off the right-center field wall. Piniella ran into the wall trying for the ball.
1 Davalillo sacrificed Ferguson to third, Spencer to Hunter.
   Lopes singled to center, scoring Ferguson.
   Lopes stole second.
   Russell walked.
2,3 Smith hit into a double play, Doyle to Dent to Spencer.

4th Inning
New York
1 Nettles flied to Monday in left-center.
2 Spencer took a called third strike.
   Doyle singled off Sutton's glove.
   Dent looped a single into center, Doyle stopped at second.
3 Rivers lined to left.
Los Angeles
1 Garvey grounded to third.
2 Cey popped to Dent in short left.
3 Baker grounded to short. Dent made a great stop.

5th Inning
New York
1 White struck out.
2 Munson grounded to third.
3 Jackson struck out.
Los Angeles
1 Monday struck out.
2 Ferguson flied to center.
3 Davalillo grounded to third.

6th Inning
New York
   Piniella after 4 fouls singled to left.
1 Nettles flied to right.
   Piniella went to second on a wild pitch by Sutton.
2 Spencer struck out and was tagged by Ferguson, Piniella moving to third.
   Doyle singled to center, Piniella scoring and Doyle going to second on the throw to the plate. This was Doyle's third hit for the second consecutive game.
   For Los Angeles—Welch relieved Sutton.
   Dent also got his third hit, a bloop single over short, scoring Doyle.
3 Rivers struck out.
Los Angeles
1 Lopes grounded to third.
2 Russell flied to left.
3 Smith grounded to third.

7th Inning
New York
   White walked on four pitches.
1 Munson struck out.
   Jackson blasted a two-run home run, on the first pitch, high up in the left field stands.
2 Piniella flied to Monday in right-center.
3 Nettles flied to right.
Los Angeles
1 Garvey flied to left.
   Cey singled to left.
2 Baker flied to left.
3 Monday popped to short.

8th Inning
New York
   For Los Angeles—Rau the new pitcher.
1 Spencer foul to Cey.
2 Doyle bounced back to the mound.
3 Dent grounded to short.
Los Angeles
   For New York—Blair playing center.
   Ferguson got a ground-rule double when his hit bounced over the center field fence.
   For New York—Gossage relieved Hunter on the mound.
   Davalillo beat out a bouncer to second, advancing Ferguson to third.
1 Lopes struck out.
2,3 Russell hit into a double play, Nettles to Doyle to Spencer.

9th Inning
New York
1 Blair struck out.
2 White struck out.
   Munson beat out a dribbler down the third base line.
3 Jackson struck out for the third time in the game.
Los Angeles
   For New York—Thomasson playing left field and Johnstone playing right.
1 Smith flied to deep left on the first pitch.
2 Garvey took a called third strike.
3 Cey fouled to Munson.

1978 WORLD SERIES COMPOSITE BOX

	Wins	Composite Line Score										
New York Yankees (A.L.)	4	1	4	6	3	0	4	13	4	0	1	- 36
Los Angeles Dodgers (N.L.)	2	2	3	3	4	4	3	3	1	0	0	- 23

Manager	Regular Season W	L	Pct.	G. Ahead
Billy Martin, Dick Howser, Bob Lemon	100	63	.613	Won playoff over Boston
Tommy Lasorda	95	67	.586	2.5

BATTING AND FIELDING

NEW YORK YANKEES

WORLD SERIES STATISTICS

	Pos	G	AB	R	H	2B	3B	HR	RBI	BB	SO	SB	BA	SA	PO	A	E
Chris Chambliss	1b	3	11	1	2	0	0	0	0	1	1	0	.182	.182	17	1	0
Brian Doyle	2b	6	16	4	7	1	0	0	2	0	0	0	.438	.500	17	7	0
Bucky Dent	ss	6	24	3	10	1	0	0	7	1	2	0	.417	.458	8	16	2
Grain Nettles	3b	6	25	2	4	0	0	0	1	0	6	0	.160	.160	8	18	0
Lou Piniella	rf	6	25	3	7	0	0	0	4	0	0	1	.280	.280	14	1	0
Mickey Rivers	cf-ph	5	18	2	6	0	0	0	1	0	2	1	.333	.333	7	0	0
Roy White	lf	6	24	9	8	0	0	1	4	4	5	2	.333	.458	15	0	0
Thurman Munson	c	6	25	5	8	3	0	0	7	3	7	1	.320	.440	33	5	0
Reggie Jackson	dh	6	23	2	9	1	0	2	8	3	7	0	.391	.696			
Paul Blair	cf-ph-pr	6	8	2	3	1	0	0	0	1	4	0	.375	.500	5	0	0
Jim Spencer	1b-ph	4	12	3	2	0	0	0	0	2	4	0	.167	.167	23	2	0
Fred Stanley	2b	3	5	0	1	1	0	0	0	1	0	0	.200	.400	5	2	0
Gary Thomasson	cf-lf	3	4	0	1	0	0	0	0	0	1	0	.250	.250	3	0	0
Cliff Johnson	ph	2	2	0	0	0	0	0	0	0	1	0	.000	.000			
Jay Johnstone	rf	2	0	0	0	0	0	0	0	0	0	0	—	—	1	0	0
Mike Heath	c	1	0	0	0	0	0	0	0	0	0	0	—	—	0	0	0
Willie Randolph	Not eligible for Series—Injured																
Catfish Hunter	p	2	0	0	0	0	0	0	0	0	0	0	—	—	2	0	0
Jim Beattie	p	1	0	0	0	0	0	0	0	0	0	0	—	—	0	1	0
Ron Guidry	p	1	0	0	0	0	0	0	0	0	0	0	—	—	1	1	0
Ed Figueroa	p	2	0	0	0	0	0	0	0	0	0	0	—	—	0	0	0
Rick Gossage	p	3	0	0	0	0	0	0	0	0	0	0	—	—	0	0	0
Dick Tidrow	p	2	0	0	0	0	0	0	0	0	0	0	—	—	0	0	0
Ken Clay	p	1	0	0	0	0	0	0	0	0	0	0	—	—	0	0	0
Paul Lindblad	p	1	0	0	0	0	0	0	0	0	0	0	—	—	0	0	0
Sparky Lyle	Did not play																
team total		6	222	36	68	8	0	3	34	16	40	5	.306	.383	159	54	2

Double Plays—9
Left on Bases—47

REGULAR SEASON STATISTICS

		Main Pos	G	AB	R	H	2B	3B	HR	RBI	BB	SO	SB	BA	SA
Chris Chambliss		1b	162	625	81	171	26	3	12	90	41	60	2	.274	.382
Brian Doyle		2b	39	52	6	10	0	0	0	0	0	3	0	.192	.192
Bucky Dent		ss	123	329	40	92	11	1	5	40	23	24	3	.243	.317
Grain Nettles		3b	159	587	81	162	23	2	27	93	59	69	1	.276	.460
Lou Piniella		of-dh	130	472	67	148	34	5	6	69	34	36	3	.314	.445
Mickey Rivers		of	141	559	78	148	25	8	11	48	29	51	25	.265	.397
Roy White		of-dh	103	346	44	93	13	3	8	43	42	35	10	.269	.393
Thurman Munson		c	154	617	73	183	27	1	6	71	35	70	2	.297	.373
Reggie Jackson		of-dh	139	511	82	140	13	5	27	97	58	133	14	.274	.477
Paul Blair		of	74	125	10	22	5	0	2	13	9	17	1	.176	.264
Jim Spencer		dh-1b	71	150	12	34	9	1	7	24	15	32	0	.227	.440
Fred Stanley		ss	80	160	14	35	7	0	1	9	25	31	0	.219	.281
Gary Thomasson	a	of	53	116	20	32	4	1	3	20	13	22	0	.276	.405
Cliff Johnson		dh-c	76	174	20	32	9	1	6	19	30	32	0	.184	.351
Jay Johnstone	b	of	36	65	6	17	0	0	1	6	36	10	0	.262	.308
Mike Heath		c	33	92	6	21	3	1	0	8	4	9	0	.228	.283
Willie Randolph		2b	134	499	87	139	18	6	3	42	82	51	36	.279	.357
Catfish Hunter		p	21	0	0	0	0	0	0	0	0	0	0	—	—
Jim Beattie		p	25	0	0	0	0	0	0	0	0	0	0	—	—
Ron Guidry		p	37	0	1	0	0	0	0	0	0	0	0	—	—
Ed Figueroa		p	35	0	0	0	0	0	0	0	0	0	0	—	—
Rick Gossage		p	63	0	0	0	0	0	0	0	0	0	0	—	—
Dick Tidrow		p	31	0	0	0	0	0	0	0	0	0	0	—	—
Ken Clay		p	28	0	0	0	0	0	0	0	0	0	0	—	—
Paul Lindblad	c	p	7	0	0	0	0	0	0	0	0	0	0	—	—
Sparky Lyle		p	59	0	0	0	0	0	0	0	0	0	0	—	—
team total			163	5583	735	1489	228	38	125	693	505	695	98	.267	.388

a—from Oakland b—from Philadelphia(N) c—from Texas
Del Aston(ph), Ron Davis(p), Rawly Eastwick(p), Damasco Garcia(2b), Don Gullett(p), Fran Healy(c), Ken Holtzman(p), Bob Kammeyer(p), Mickey Klutts(3b), Larry McCall(p), Andy Messersmith(p), Dave Rajsich(p), Domingo Ramos(ss), Dennis Sherrill(3b), and George Zeber(2b) also played for the Yankees during the season.

LOS ANGELES DODGERS

WORLD SERIES STATISTICS

	Pos	G	AB	R	H	2B	3B	HR	RBI	BB	SO	SB	BA	SA	PO	A	E
Steve Garvey	1b	6	24	1	5	1	0	0	0	1	7	1	.208	.250	58	3	1
Dave Lopes	2b	6	26	7	8	0	0	3	7	2	1	2	.308	.654	10	19	1
Bill Russell	ss	6	26	1	11	2	0	0	2	2	2	1	.423	.500	11	20	3
Ron Cey	3b	6	21	2	6	0	0	1	4	3	3	0	.286	.429	2	12	0
Reggie Smith	rf	6	25	3	5	0	0	1	5	2	6	0	.200	.320	11	1	1
Rick Monday	cf-dh	5	13	2	2	1	0	0	0	4	3	0	.154	.231	5	0	0
Dusty Baker	lf	6	21	2	5	0	0	1	1	1	3	0	.238	.381	12	0	0
Steve Yeager	c	5	13	2	3	1	0	0	0	1	2	0	.231	.308	23	2	0
Lee Lacy	dh	4	14	0	2	0	0	0	1	1	3	0	.143	.143			
Bill North	ph-cf	4	8	2	1	1	0	0	2	1	0	1	.125	.250	7	0	0
Joe Ferguson	c	2	4	1	2	2	0	0	0	0	1	0	.500	1.000	11	0	1
Vic Davalillo	ph-dh	2	3	0	1	0	0	0	0	0	0	0	.333	.333			
Manny Mota	ph	1	0	0	0	0	0	0	0	1	0	0	—	—			
Jerry Grote	c	2	0	0	0	0	0	0	0	0	0	0	—	—	3	0	0
Johnny Oates	ph-c	1	1	0	1	0	0	0	0	1	0	0	1.000	1.000	3	1	0
Teddy Martinez	Did not play																
Tommy John	p	2	0	0	0	0	0	0	0	0	0	0	—	—	0	4	0
Don Sutton	p	2	0	0	0	0	0	0	0	0	0	0	—	—	0	0	0
Burt Hooton	p	2	0	0	0	0	0	0	0	0	0	0	—	—	1	0	0
Charlie Hough	p	2	0	0	0	0	0	0	0	0	0	0	—	—	1	0	0
Bob Welch	p	3	0	0	0	0	0	0	0	0	0	0	—	—	0	0	0
Terry Forster	p	3	0	0	0	0	0	0	0	0	0	0	—	—	0	1	0
Doug Rau	p	1	0	0	0	0	0	0	0	0	0	0	—	—	0	1	0
Lance Rautzhan	p	2	0	0	0	0	0	0	0	0	0	0	—	—	0	0	0
Rick Rhoden	Did not play																
team total		6	199	23	52	8	0	6	22	20	31	5	.261	.392	158	64	7

Double Plays—4
Left on Bases—38

REGULAR SEASON STATISTICS

		Main Pos	G	AB	R	H	2B	3B	HR	RBI	BB	SO	SB	BA	SA
Steve Garvey		1b	162	639	89	202	36	9	21	113	40	70	10	.316	.499
Dave Lopes		2b	151	587	93	163	25	4	17	58	71	70	45	.278	.421
Bill Russell		ss	155	625	72	179	32	4	3	46	30	34	10	.286	.365
Ron Cey		3b	159	555	84	150	32	0	23	84	96	96	2	.270	.452
Reggie Smith		of	128	447	82	132	27	2	29	93	70	90	12	.295	.559
Rick Monday		of	119	342	54	87	14	1	19	57	49	100	2	.254	.468
Dusty Baker		of	149	522	62	137	24	1	11	66	47	66	12	.262	.375
Steve Yeager		c	94	228	19	44	7	0	4	23	36	41	0	.193	.276
Lee Lacy		of-inf	103	245	29	64	16	4	13	40	27	30	7	.261	.518
Bill North	d	of	110	304	54	71	10	0	0	10	65	48	27	.234	.266
Joe Ferguson	e	c	67	198	20	47	11	0	7	28	34	41	1	.237	.399
Vic Davalillo		ph	75	77	15	24	1	1	1	11	3	7	2	.312	.390
Manny Mota		ph	37	33	2	10	1	0	0	6	3	4	0	.303	.333
Jerry Grote		c	41	70	5	19	5	0	0	9	10	5	0	.271	.343
Johnny Oates		c	40	75	5	23	1	0	0	6	5	3	0	.307	.320
Teddy Martinez		inf	54	55	13	14	1	0	1	5	4	14	3	.255	.327
Tommy John		p	33	66	2	8	2	0	0	6	3	13	0	.121	.152
Don Sutton		p	34	72	1	6	0	0	0	3	4	22	0	.083	.083
Burt Hooton		p	32	67	4	10	1	0	0	2	7	15	0	.149	.164
Charlie Hough		p	55	12	1	4	1	0	0	2	0	2	0	.333	.417
Bob Welch		p	23	29	3	5	1	0	0	1	0	7	0	.172	.207
Terry Forster		p	47	8	1	4	1	0	0	2	0	0	0	.500	.625
Doug Rau		p	30	63	3	9	1	0	0	5	2	13	0	.143	.159
Lance Rautzhan		p	43	4	0	0	0	0	0	0	0	1	0	.000	.000
Rick Rhoden		p	30	52	5	7	1	0	0	4	3	14	0	.135	.154
team total			162	5437	727	1435	251	27	149	686	610	818	137	.264	.402

d—from Oakland e—from Houston
Glenn Burke(of), Mike Garman(p), Pedro Guerrero(1b), Bradley Gulden(c), Gerry Hannahs(ph), Enzo Hernandez(ss), Rudy Law(of), Dennis Lewallyn(p), Joe Simpson(of), Dave Stewart(p), Dick Sutcliffe(p), and Myron White(of) also played for the Dodgers during the season.

PITCHING

NEW YORK YANKEES

WORLD SERIES STATISTICS

	G	GS	CG	IP	H	R	ER	BB	SO	W	L	SV	ERA
Catfish Hunter	2	2	0	13	13	6	6	1	5	1	1	0	4.15
Jim Beattie	1	1	1	9	9	2	2	4	8	1	0	0	2.00
Ron Guidry	1	1	1	9	8	1	1	7	4	1	0	0	1.00
Ed Figueroa	2	2	0	6.2	9	6	6	5	2	0	1	0	8.10
Rich Gossage	3	0	0	6	1	0	0	1	4	1	0	0	0.00
Dick Tidrow	2	0	0	4.2	4	1	1	0	5	0	0	0	1.93
Ken Clay	1	0	0	2.1	4	4	3	2	2	0	0	0	11.57
Paul Lindblad	1	0	0	2.1	4	3	3	0	1	0	0	0	11.57
Sparky Lyle	Did not play												
team total	6	6	2	53	52	23	22	20	31	4	2	0	3.74

REGULAR SEASON STATISTICS

		G	GS	CG	IP	H	ER	BB	SO	W	L	Pct	SV	ShO	ERA
Catfish Hunter		21	20	5	118	98	47	35	56	12	6	.667	0	1	3.58
Jim Beattie		25	22	0	128	123	53	51	65	6	9	.400	0	0	3.73
Ron Guidry		35	35	16	274	187	53	72	248	25	3	.893	0	9	1.74
Ed Figueroa		35	35	12	253	233	84	77	92	20	9	.690	0	2	2.99
Rich Gossage		63	0	0	134	87	30	59	122	10	11	.476	27	0	2.01
Dick Tidrow		31	25	4	185	191	79	53	73	7	11	.389	0	0	3.84
Ken Clay		28	6	0	76	89	36	21	32	3	4	.429	0	0	4.26
Paul Lindblad	c	7	1	0	18	21	9	8	9	0	0	—	0	0	4.50
Sparky Lyle		59	0	0	112	116	43	33	33	9	3	.750	9	0	3.46
team total		163	163	39	1461	1321	516	478	817	100	63	.613	36	16	3.18

LOS ANGELES DODGERS

WORLD SERIES STATISTICS

	G	GS	CG	IP	H	R	ER	BB	SO	W	L	SV	ERA
Tommy John	2	2	0	14.2	14	8	5	4	6	1	0	0	3.07
Don Sutton	2	2	0	12	17	10	10	4	8	0	2	0	7.50
Burt Hooton	2	2	0	8.1	13	7	6	3	6	1	0	0	6.48
Charlie Hough	2	0	0	5.1	10	5	5	2	5	0	0	0	8.43
Bob Welch	3	0	0	4.1	4	3	3	2	6	0	1	1	6.23
Terry Forster	3	0	0	4	5	0	0	1	6	0	0	0	0.00
Doug Rau	1	0	0	2	1	0	0	0	3	0	0	0	0.00
Lance Rautzhan	2	0	0	2	4	3	3	0	0	0	0	0	13.50
Rick Rhoden	Did not play												
team total	6	6	0	52.2	68	36	32	16	40	2	4	1	5.47

REGULAR SEASON STATISTICS

	G	GS	CG	IP	H	ER	BB	SO	W	L	Pct	SV	ShO	ERA
Tommy John	33	30	7	213	230	78	53	124	17	10	.630	1	0	3.30
Don Sutton	34	34	12	238	228	94	54	154	15	11	.577	0	2	3.55
Burt Hooton	32	32	10	236	196	71	61	104	19	10	.655	0	3	2.71
Charlie Hough	55	0	0	93	69	34	48	66	5	5	.500	7	0	3.29
Bob Welch	23	13	4	111	92	25	26	66	7	4	.636	3	3	2.03
Terry Forster	47	0	0	65	56	14	23	46	5	4	.556	22	0	1.94
Doug Rau	30	30	7	199	219	72	68	95	15	9	.625	0	2	3.26
Lance Rautzhan	43	0	0	61	61	20	19	25	2	1	.667	4	0	2.95
Rick Rhoden	30	23	6	165	160	67	51	79	10	8	.556	0	3	3.65
team total	162	162	46	1440	1362	499	440	800	95	67	.586	38	16	3.12

Total Attendance—335,304 Average Attendance—55,884 Winning Player's Share—$31,236 Losing Player's Share—$25,483

1979

Once Again Walking the Plank

The memory still ate at Earl Weaver. His Orioles had won the first two games of the Series in 1971, only to lose to the Pirates in seven. The great Roberto Clemente had inspired Pittsburgh to that comeback championship. With this year's rematch, Weaver could exorcise the ghosts of that near-miss. The Orioles had no super-stars, only a deep array of long-ball hitters and savvy pitchers. They had won easily in the A.L. East and in the ALCS against the Angels.

The Pirates, on the other hand, had to scratch their way to the N.L. East title. They bumbled in the early going and straightened out only after getting Tim Foli and Bill Madlock to play the infield. Manager Chuck Tanner juggled an undistinguished pitching staff masterfully. The key ingredient in the Pirate mix was 38-year-old Willie Stargell, the spiritual successor to Clemente. His booming bat and clubhouse bonhomie kept the Pirates loose through a tight divisional race and a surprise sweep of the Reds in the NLCS. The Bucs sincerely billed themselves as a family, built around Pops Stargell.

The Pirates got a rude welcome to Baltimore's Memorial Stadium. In the bottom of the first inning, the Orioles chased Bruce Kison with five runs. Cy Young winner Mike Flanagan went all the way, retiring Stargell in the ninth with the tying run on third. Veteran aces Jim Palmer and Bert Blyleven dueled the next day in game two. After eight innings, the score was 2–2 and both starters were gone. Bill Robinson led off the Pirate ninth with a pinch single off Tippy Martinez. Earl Weaver waved Don Stanhouse to the mound. Stanhouse was Weaver's bullpen stopper despite a nasty habit of putting men on base in key situations. After a pinch runner was thrown out stealing and Madlock flied out, Stanhouse began his high-wire act. He allowed an infield hit to Ed Ott, then walked Phil Garner. His dangerous living caught up with him this time; pinch hitter Manny Sanguillen drove Ott home with a single to right. Pittsburgh reliever Kent Tekulve eschewed the dramatics and retired the Orioles in order.

The Pirates found Scott McGregor's curves easy at the start of game three, taking a 3–0 lead after two innings. McGregor, however, settled down, while Pirate starter John Candelaria blew up. The Orioles touched him for two runs in the third and five in the fourth. The key hit was a based-loaded triple by Kiko Garcia, who went four-for-four. McGregor went all the way for an 8–4 victory. The fourth game could have easily sunk the Pirates' high spirits. The Bucs led 6–3 at the end of seven, then watched the bullpen torch the lead. Pinch hits by John Lowenstein and Terry Crowley fueled a six-run Baltimore eighth and put Pittsburgh at death's door.

With his pitching staff chewed up, Tanner chose little-used Jim Rooker to start game five. Rooker turned in five strong innings and left with Baltimore ahead 1–0. Blyleven relieved him and kept the Oriole bats muffled. The Pirates meanwhile got to Flanagan and his relievers, scoring seven times in their final three licks. The teams then traveled to Baltimore for a resolution.

The Oriole bats snoozed on in game six. Candelaria pitched six shutout innings, succeeded by a near-flawless Tekulve. Jim Palmer kept the game scoreless through six innings but could not keep the pace. The Pirates scored twice in both the seventh and eighth innings for a 4–0 victory, which evened the Series.

Scott McGregor and Jim Bibby carried the weight of starting game seven. In the third inning, Rich Dauer brought the crowd to its feet by lining a shot into the left-field seats. The Pirates pinch-hit for Bibby in the top of the fifth and entrusted the game to the bullpen. McGregor scattered hits harmlessly until the sixth, when Bill Robinson singled and Pops Stargell launched a rocket over the right-center field fence. Staked to a 2–1 edge, relievers Don Robinson, Grant Jackson, and Tekulve kept the Orioles quiet. Two ninth-inning runs off five Baltimore relievers clinched the game and left Earl Weaver in a déjà vu nightmare.

Game 1 October 10 at Pittsburgh

Pittsburgh	Pos	AB	R	H	RBI	PO	A	E
Moreno	cf	5	0	0	0	4	0	0
Foli	ss	5	1	1	0	1	3	1
Parker	rf	5	1	4	0	3	0	0
B. Robinson	lf	5	1	1	0	2	0	0
Stargell	1b	5	1	1	2	7	0	1
Madlock	3b	3	0	0	0	0	1	0
Nicosia	c	4	0	0	0	4	1	0
Garner	2b	4	0	3	2	3	2	1
Kison	p	0	0	0	0	0	1	0
Rooker	p	1	0	0	0	0	2	0
a Sanguillen		1	0	0	0	0	0	0
Romo	p	1	0	0	0	0	0	0
b Lacy		1	0	0	0	0	0	0
D. Robinson	p	0	0	0	0	0	0	0
c Stennett		1	0	1	0	0	0	0
Jackson	p	0	0	0	0	0	0	0
Totals		40	4	11	4	24	10	3

Pitching	IP	H	R	ER	BB	SO
Pittsburgh						
Kison (L)	⅓	3	5	4	2	0
Rooker	3⅔	2	0	0	1	2
Romo	1	0	0	0	2	0
D. Robinson	2	0	0	0	1	1
Jackson	1	1	0	0	0	1
Baltimore						
Flanagan (W)	9	11	4	2	1	7

Baltimore	Pos	AB	R	H	RBI	PO	A	E
Bumbry	cf	4	1	1	0	3	0	0
Belanger	ss	3	1	0	0	1	4	1
Singleton	rf	3	0	1	0	2	0	0
Murray	1b	2	1	1	0	12	1	0
Lowenstein	lf	4	1	0	1	1	0	0
Roenicke	lf	0	0	0	0	0	0	0
DeCinces	3b	3	1	1	2	0	4	2
Smith	2b	2	0	1	0	1	3	0
d Dauer	2b	1	0	1	0	0	1	0
Dempsey	c	4	0	0	0	7	0	0
Flanagan	p	4	0	0	0	0	2	0
Totals		30	5	6	3	27	15	3

a Grounded out for Rooker in fifth.
b Reached first on error for Romo in sixth.
c Singled for D. Robinson in eighth.
d Singled for Smith in eighth.

Doubles—Parker, Garner. Home Runs—DeCinces, Stargell. Stolen Base—Murray. Sacrifice Hit—Bumbry. Double Play—Madlock to Garner to Stargell. Wild Pitch—Kison. Left on bases—Pittsburgh 10, Baltimore 8. Umpires—Neudecker, Engel, Goetz, Tata, McKean, Runge. Attendance—53,735. Time of Game—3:18.

1st Inning
Pittsburgh
1 Moreno bounced to second.
2 Foli flied to left.
Parker doubled down the right field line.
3 Robinson struck out.
Baltimore
Bumbry singled to left on the first pitch.
Belanger walked.
1 Singleton bounced back to the pitcher, both runners advancing.
Murray walked, loading the bases.
Lowenstein safe on Garner's throwing error to second, scoring Bumbry and Belanger as Murray went to third.
Murray scored and Lowenstein went to second on a wild pitch.
DeCinces hit a two-run homer into the left field bleachers.
Smith singled to right.
For Pittsburgh—Rooker came in to pitch.
2 Dempsey lined to Foli, who threw wildly to first trying for the double play. Smith went to second.
3 Flanagan tapped in front of the plate, thrown out by Nicosia.

2nd Inning
Pittsburgh
1 Stargell struck out.
2 Madlock grounded to third.
3 Nicosia grounded to second.
Baltimore
1 Bumbry bounced back to the mound.
2 Belanger called out on strikes.
Singleton beat out a grounder to third.
Murray singled to center, Singleton stopping at second.
3 Lowenstein struck out.

3rd Inning
Pittsburgh
1 Garner called out on strikes.
2 Rooker bunted out to the mound.
3 Moreno flied to center.
Baltimore
DeCinces walked.
1,2 Smith grounded into a double play, Madlock to Garner to Stargell.
3 Dempsey grounded to second.

4th Inning
Pittsburgh
Foli singled to center.
Parker singled to right, Foli advancing to third.
1 Robinson grounded to third, Foli holding third as Parker went to second.
2 Stargell grounded to second, scoring Foli with Parker going to third.
Madlock walked.
3 Nicosia forced Madlock, Belanger to Smith.
Baltimore
Flanagan safe on Stargell's error.
1 Bumbry sacrificed Flanagan to second, Rooker to Garner, covering first.
2 Belanger flied to center.
3 Singleton flied to Parker in deep right-center.

5th Inning
Pittsburgh
Garner doubled to left.
1 Sanguillen, pinch-hitting for Rooker, grounded to short, Garner holding second.
2 Moreno struck out.
3 Foli bounced to third.

5th Inning (continued)
Baltimore
For Pittsburgh—Romo pitching.
Murray walked.
1 Lowenstein flied to center.
2 DeCinces flied to right.
Murray stole second.
Smith intentionally walked.
3 Dempsey flied to left.

6th Inning
Pittsburgh
Parker singled to center.
Robinson singled to right, Parker stopping at second.
1 Stargell struck out.
2 Madlock flied to right.
Nicosia safe on DeCinces' bobble, loading the bases.
Garner singled to left, scoring Parker and Robinson, with Nicosia stopping at second.
Lacy, batting for Romo, was safe on DeCinces' fumble, his second error of the inning, loading the bases.
3 Moreno flied to center.
Baltimore
For Pittsburgh—Don Robinson pitching.
1 Flanagan struck out.
2 Bumbry grounded to Foli.
3 Belanger also grounded to short.

7th Inning
Pittsburgh
1 Foli grounded to short.
2 Parker grounded to third.
3 Robinson flied to right.
Baltimore
Singleton walked.
1 Murray flied to center.
2 Lowenstein flied to left.
3 DeCinces flied to Parker making a fine running catch in right-center.

8th Inning
Pittsburgh
For Baltimore—Roenicke playing left.
Stargell homered into the right field stands on a 2-and-2 pitch.
1 Madlock flied to center.
2 Nicosia struck out.
Garner beat out a high bouncer to third when DeCinces lost the ball in the lights. Stennett, pinch-hitting for D. Robinson, looped a single to right, Garner going to third.
3 Moreno took a called third strike.
Baltimore
For Pittsburgh—Jackson now pitching.
Dauer, batting for Smith, singled to center.
1 Dempsey flied to center.
2 Flanagan struck out.
3 Bumbry forced Dauer, Foli to Garner.

9th Inning
Pittsburgh
For Baltimore—Dauer playing second.
1 Foli grounded to short.
Parker singled to center for his fourth hit of the game.
Parker went to second on a pick-off attempt when Belanger dropped Murray's throw for an error.
2 Robinson grounded to second, Parker going to third.
3 Stargell flied to Belanger in short left.

Game 2 October 11 at Baltimore

Pittsburgh	Pos	AB	R	H	RBI	PO	A	E
Moreno	cf	5	0	1	0	1	0	0
Foli	ss	4	0	1	0	0	5	1
Parker	rf	4	0	1	0	1	1	1
Stargell	1b	4	1	1	0	12	0	0
Milner	lf	3	1	1	0	3	0	0
d B. Robinson		1	0	1	0	0	0	0
e Alexander	lf	0	0	0	0	0	0	0
Madlock	3b	4	0	2	1	0	4	0
Ott	c	3	1	1	1	6	0	0
Garner	2b	2	0	1	0	4	6	0
Blyleven	p	2	0	0	0	0	0	0
a Easler		0	0	0	0	0	0	0
D. Robinson	p	0	0	0	0	0	1	0
f Sanguillen		1	0	1	1	0	0	0
Tekulve	p	0	0	0	0	0	0	0
Totals		33	3	11	3	27	17	2

Pitching	IP	H	R	ER	BB	SO
Pittsburgh						
Blyleven	6	5	2	2	2	1
D. Robinson (W)	2	1	0	0	3	2
Tekulve (S)	1	0	0	0	0	2
Baltimore						
Palmer	7	8	2	2	2	3
T. Martinez	*1	1	0	0	0	1
Stanhouse (L)	1	2	1	1	1	0

*Pitched to one batter in 9th.

Pitt.	020	000	001
Balt.	010	001	000

Baltimore	Pos	AB	R	H	RBI	PO	A	E
Bumbry	cf	5	0	0	0	5	0	0
Belanger	ss	3	0	0	0	1	2	0
c Crowley		0	0	0	0	0	0	0
T. Martinez	p	0	0	0	0	0	0	0
Stanhouse	p	0	0	0	0	0	0	0
Singleton	rf	4	1	1	0	1	0	0
Murray	1b	3	1	3	2	10	2	0
DeCinces	3b	4	0	0	0	0	6	1
Lowenstein	lf	3	0	1	0	1	0	0
Smith	2b	4	0	0	0	3	0	0
Dempsey	c	3	0	1	0	4	2	0
Palmer	p	2	0	0	0	1	1	0
b Kelly		0	0	0	0	0	0	0
Garcia	ss	1	0	0	0	1	0	0
Totals		32	2	6	2	27	13	1

a Walked for Blyleven in 7th.
b Walked for Palmer in 7th.
c Walked for Belanger in 7th.
d Singled for Milner in 9th.
e Ran for B. Robinson in 9th.
f Singled for D. Robinson in 9th.

Double—Murray. Home Run—Murray. Sacrifice Fly—Ott. Double Plays—Murray to Palmer, Madlock to Garner to Stargell, Murray to Belanger to Smith, Parker to Ott, Foli to Garner to Madlock to Garner. Wildpitch—Palmer. Left on Bases—Pittsburgh 7, Baltimore 8. Umpires—Engel, Goetz, Tata, McKean, Runge, Neudecker. Attendance—53,739. Time of Game—3:13

1st Inning
Pittsburgh
Moreno singled up the middle.
1,2 Foli fouled to Murray who threw to Palmer, covering first doubling up Moreno.
3 Parker grounded to third.
Baltimore
1 Bumbry grounded to second.
2 Belanger flied to deep left.
3 Singleton bounced to second.

2nd Inning
Pittsburgh
Stargell singled to right.
Milner singled to center, Stargell stopping at second.
Madlock singled to right-center, scoring Stargell as Milner advanced to third.
1 Ott hit a sacrifice fly to center, scoring Milner.
2 Madlock out trying to steal second, Dempsey to Smith.
3 Garner grounded to short.
Baltimore
Murray homered into the right field seats on a 1-and-1 pitch.
1 DeCinces grounded to third.
Lowenstein walked.
2 Smith lined to second.
Dempsey singled off Foli's glove, moving Lowenstein to third.
3 Palmer struck out.

3rd Inning
Pittsburgh
1 Blyleven lined to center.
2 Moreno struck out.
Foli singled to right.
Foli took second on a wild pitch.
3 Parker grounded to third.
Baltimore
1 Bumbry flied to left.
Belanger safe at second when Parker muffed his soft pop for an error.
2 Singleton grounded to second, Belanger advancing to third.
Murray walked on four pitches.
3 DeCinces grounded to short.

4th Inning
Pittsburgh
1 Stargell flied to left.
2 Milner popped to Murray.
3 Madlock grounded to third.
Baltimore
Lowenstein singled off Garner's glove.
1,2 Smith bounced into a double play, Madlock to Garner to Stargell.
3 Dempsey grounded to short.

5th Inning
Pittsburgh
1 Ott out bunting back to the pitcher, Garner singled to center.
2,3 Blyleven bunted into a double play, Murray to Belanger to Smith.
Baltimore
1 Palmer flied to left.
2 Bumbry grounded to third.
3 Belanger flied to center.

6th Inning
Pittsburgh
1 Moreno bounced to third.
2 Foli flied to center.
Parker singled to center.
3 Stargell grounded to third.
Baltimore
Singleton singled to left.
Murray lined a double to left-center, scoring Singleton.
1 DeCinces grounded to short, Murray advancing to third.
2,3 Lowenstein lined to Parker and Murray was doubled up on a perfect throw to the plate, Parker to Ott.

7th Inning
Pittsburgh
1 Milner flied to center.
Madlock beat out a hit to DeCinces, whose throw sailed over Murray's head for an error as Madlock took second.
2 Ott struck out.
Garner was intentionally walked.
Easler, batting for Blyleven, walked to load the bases.
3 Singleton struck out.
Baltimore
For Pittsburgh—D. Robinson pitching.
1 Smith popped to first.
Dempsey walked.
Kelly, pinch-hitting for Palmer, walked.
2 Bumbry struck out.
Crowley, batting for Belanger, walked loading the bases.
3 Singleton struck out.

8th Inning
Pittsburgh
For Baltimore—Garcia playing short and batting ninth, T. Martinez now pitching.
1 Foli flied to right.
2 Parker grounded to third.
3 Stargell took a called third strike.
Baltimore
Murray blooped a single to center.
DeCinces bunted and Murray was safe at second when Foli dropped the throw from Robinson.
1,2 Lowenstein hit into a double play, Foli to Garner for the force at second and to Madlock back to Garner for the tag on Murray.
3 Smith grounded to second.

9th Inning
Pittsburgh
B. Robinson, batting for Milner, singled to left.
For Baltimore—Stanhouse came in to pitch.
Alexander running for Robinson.
1 On the first pitch Alexander out trying to steal, Dempsey to Garcia.
2 Madlock flied to deep center.
Ott singled on a bouncer off Smith's chest.
Garner walked.
Sanguillen, batting for D. Robinson, singled to right, scoring Ott as Garner went to third.
3 Moreno lined to second.
Baltimore
For Pittsburgh—Tekulve pitching and Alexander playing left.
1 Dempsey struck out.
2 Garcia took a called third strike.
3 Bumbry grounded to short.

Game 3 October 12 at Pittsburgh

Baltimore	Pos	AB	R	H	RBI	PO	A	E
Garcia	ss	4	2	4	4	0	4	0
Ayala	lf	2	1	2	2	0	0	0
a Bumbry	cf	2	1	1	0	2	0	0
Singleton	rf	5	0	2	1	4	0	0
Murray	1b	4	0	0	0	7	1	0
DeCinces	3b	5	0	0	1	0	1	0
Roenicke	cf-lf	5	0	1	0	5	1	0
Dauer	2b	5	1	1	0	2	3	0
Dempsey	c	5	2	2	0	7	0	0
McGregor	p	3	1	0	0	0	0	0
Totals		40	8	13	8	27	10	0

a Hit by pitcher for Ayala in 4th.
b Lined out for Jackson in 7th.

Doubles—Garcia, Moreno (2), Garner, Dauer, Stargell, Dempsey. Triple—Garcia. Home Run—Ayala. Sacrifice Fly—Parker. Wild Pitch—Romo. Balk—McGregor. Hit by Pitcher—Bumbry (by Romo). Left on Bases—Baltimore 9, Pittsburgh 4. Umpires—Goetz, Tata, McKean, Runge, Neudecker, Engel. Attendance—50,848. Time of Game—2:51

Balt.	002	500	100
Pitt.	120	001	000

Pittsburgh	Pos	AB	R	H	RBI	PO	A	E
Moreno	cf	4	1	2	0	2	1	0
Foli	ss	4	0	0	0	0	6	1
Parker	rf	3	0	0	1	2	0	0
B. Robinson	lf	4	0	1	0	4	1	0
Stargell	lb	4	2	2	0	8	1	1
Madlock	3b	4	0	1	1	0	0	0
Nicosia	c	4	1	1	0	8	0	0
Garner	2b	4	0	1	2	2	1	0
Candelaria	p	1	0	1	0	0	0	0
Romo	p	1	0	0	0	0	1	0
Jackson	p	0	0	0	0	0	0	0
b Lacy		1	0	0	0	0	0	0
Tekulve	p	0	0	0	0	1	0	0
Totals		34	4	9	4	27	11	2

Pitching	IP	H	R	ER	BB	SO
Baltimore						
McGregor (W)	9	9	4	4	0	6
Pittsburgh						
Candelaria (L)	*3	8	6	5	2	2
Romo	$3\frac{2}{3}$	5	2	2	1	4
Jackson	$\frac{1}{3}$	0	0	0	0	0
Tekulve	2	0	0	0	0	1

*Pitched to four batters in 4th

1st Inning
Baltimore
Garcia doubled down the right field line.
Ayala bloop singled to center, Garcia stopping at third.
1 Singleton struck out.
2 Murray lined to second.
3 DeCinces struck out.
Pittsburgh
Moreno doubled to center.
Moreno went to third on a balk.
1 Foli fouled to Dempsey.
2 Parker hit a sacrifice fly to center. Moreno scoring after the catch.
3 Robinson struck out.

2nd Inning
Baltimore
1 Roenicke grounded to short.
2 Dauer grounded to short.
3 Dempsey grounded to short.
Pittsburgh
Stargell singled to center.
1 Madlock took a called third strike.
Nicosia singled to left, Stargell stopping at second.
Garner doubled to left-center, scoring Stargell and Nicosia but was trapped
2 in a rundown trying to make third, Roenicke to Garcia to DeCinces to Murray to Dauer.
Candelaria singled to left.
3 Moreno grounded to second

3rd Inning
Baltimore
1 McGregor fouled to first.
Garcia walked.
Ayala hit a two-run homer over the left field fence.
Singleton singled to center.
Murray walked.
2 DeCinces flied to left.
Roenicke singled to left but Singleton
3 was out trying to score, Robinson to Nicosia.
Pittsburgh
Rain caused a 67 minute delay.
1 Foli flied to center.
2 Parker struck out.
Robinson singled to left.
3 Stargell struck out.

4th Inning
Baltimore
Dauer doubled to left-center.
Dempsey singled to right, Dauer moving to third.
Dauer held third as Foli booted McGregor's grounder, loading the bases.
Garcia tripled to right-center, clearing the bases.
For Pittsburgh—Romo came in to pitch.
Bumbry, batting for Ayala, was hit by a pitched ball.
Singleton singled to center, scoring Garcia as Bumbry went to third.
1 Murray flied to right.
2 DeCinces forced Singleton, Foli to Garner, scoring Bumbry.
DeCinces advanced to second on a wild pitch.
3 Roenicke struck out.
Pittsburgh
For Baltimore—Bumbry playing center as Roenicke moved to left.
1 Madlock flied to right.
2 Nicosia flied to right.
3 Garner grounded to short.

5th Inning
Baltimore
1 Dauer struck out.
2 Dempsey took a called third strike.
McGregor walked.
Garcia singled to left, McGregor stopping at second.
Bumbry beat out a grounder to Garner, loading the bases.
3 Singleton flied to center.
Pittsburgh
1 Romo flied to right.
Moreno doubled down the left field line.
2 Foli flied to Roenicke.
3 Parker flied to the fence in right.

6th Inning
Baltimore
1 Murray flied to left.
2 DeCinces bounced back to the mound.
3 Roenicke flied to left.
Pittsburgh
1 Robinson struck out, tagged by Dempsey.
Stargell doubled to right-center.
Madlock singled to center, scoring Stargell.
2 Nicosia flied to very deep center.
3 Garner flied to the left field wall.

7th Inning
Baltimore
1 Dauer flied to center.
Dempsey doubled to right-center.
2 McGregor struck out.
Garcia looped a single to center, scoring Dempsey. Moreno's throw had Garcia trapped off first, but was safe when Stargell's throwing error hit him in the back as he broke for second.
For Pittsburgh—Jackson now pitching.
3 Bumbry flied to left.
Pittsburgh
1 Lacy, batting for Jackson, lined to second.
2 Moreno took a called third strike.
3 Foli flied to Roenicke.

8th Inning
Baltimore
For Pittsburgh—Tekulve now pitching.
1 Singleton grounded to second.
2 Murray grounded out, Stargell to Tekulve.
3 DeCinces grounded to short.
Pittsburgh
1 Parker grounded to second.
2 Robinson grounded to short.
3 Stargell popped to first.

9th Inning
Baltimore
1 Roenicke struck out.
2 Dauer grounded to short.
3 Dempsey fouled to Parker.
Pittsburgh
1 Madlock grounded to short.
2 Nicosia grounded to second.
3 Garner flied to center.

Game 4 October 13 at Pittsburgh

Balt.	003	000	060
Pitt.	040	011	000

Baltimore	Pos	AB	R	H	RBI	PO	A	E
Bumbry	cf	5	1	1	1	1	1	0
Garcia	ss	5	2	2	2	6	5	0
Belanger	ss	0	0	0	0	0	0	0
Singleton	rf	5	0	3	1	0	0	0
Murray	1b	5	1	0	0	8	1	0
DeCinces	3b	1	1	0	0	2	0	0
Roenicke	lf	3	0	0	0	2	0	0
c Lowenstein	lf	2	1	1	2	1	0	0
Dauer	2b	3	0	1	0	1	2	0
d Smith	2b	0	1	0	0	0	0	0
Skaggs	c	3	1	1	0	2	2	0
e Crowley		1	0	1	2	0	0	0
f Dempsey	c	0	1	0	0	3	0	0
D. Martinez	p	0	0	0	0	0	1	0
Stewart	p	1	0	0	0	1	2	0
a May		1	0	0	0	0	0	0
Stone	p	0	0	0	0	0	0	0
b Kelly		1	0	1	0	0	0	0
Stoddard	p	1	0	1	1	0	2	0
Totals		37	9	12	9	27	16	0

Pittsburgh	Pos	AB	R	H	RBI	PO	A	E
Moreno	cf	5	0	2	1	2	0	0
Foli	ss	4	2	3	0	1	5	0
Parker	rf	5	0	2	1	1	0	0
Stargell	1b	5	1	3	1	8	0	0
Milner	lf	3	1	2	1	2	0	0
D. Robinson	p	0	0	0	0	0	0	0
Tekulve	p	0	0	0	0	0	0	0
g Easler		1	0	0	0	0	0	0
Madlock	3b	3	1	2	0	1	1	0
Ott	c	5	0	1	2	8	0	0
Garner	2b	4	1	2	0	5	7	0
Bibby	p	3	0	0	0	0	0	0
Jackson	p	0	0	0	0	0	0	0
B. Robinson	lf	1	0	0	0	0	0	0
Totals		39	6	17	6	27	13	1

a Struck out for Stewart in 5th.
b Singled for Stone in 7th.
c Doubled for Roenicke in 8th.
d Intentionally walked for Dauer in 8th.
e Doubled for Skaggs in 8th.
f Ran for Crowley in 8th.
g Flied out for Tekulve in 9th.

Pitching	IP	H	R	ER	BB	SO
Baltimore						
D. Martinez	1⅓	6	4	4	0	0
Stewart	2⅔	4	0	0	1	0
Stone	2	4	2	2	2	2
Stoddard (W)	3	3	0	0	1	3
Pittsburgh						
Bibby	6⅓	7	3	2	2	7
Jackson	⅓	0	0	0	0	0
D. Robinson	⅓	2	3	3	1	0
Tekulve (L)	1⅔	3	3	3	2	1

Doubles—Madlock, Ott, Garcia, Singleton, Stargell, Milner, Parker, Lowenstein, Crowley. Home Run—Stargell. Stolen Base—DeCinces. Double Plays—D. Martinez to Garcia to Murray, Dauer to Garcia to Murray, Foli to Garner to Stargell (2), Garner to Foli to Stargell. Left on Bases—Baltimore 6, Pittsburgh 10. Umpires—Tate, McKean, Runge, Neudecker, Engel, Goetz. Attendance—50,883. Time of Game—3:48.

1st Inning
Baltimore
1 Bumbry grounded to second.
2 Garcia struck out.
3 Singleton struck out.
Pittsburgh
1 Moreno grounded to short.
  Foli singled to center.
2,3 Parker hit into a double play, D. Martinez to Garcia to Murray.

2nd Inning
Baltimore
1 Murray struck out.
  DeCinces walked.
2 While Roenicke struck out, DeCinces stole second.
3 Dauer popped to second.
Pittsburgh
  Stargell homered over the center-field fence on a 2-and-2 pitch.
  Milner singled to right.
  Madlock hit a ground-rule double into the Pirate bullpen in left, Milner going to third.
  Ott's long drive bounced over the fence in center for another ground-rule double, scoring Milner and Madlock.
  Garner singled to center, Ott was
1 trapped in a run down when he tried to score, Bumbry to Murray, to Skaggs to DeCinces, Garner went to second.
  For Baltimore—Stewart came in to pitch.
2 Bibby lined to Stewart, who threw the ball into center trying to double Garner at second. Garner stayed at second.
  Moreno singled to center, scoring Garner.
3   Moreno was picked off first, Stewart to Murray.

3rd Inning
Baltimore
  Skaggs safe on Madlock's throwing error.
1 Stewart struck out.
  Bumbry singled to center, advancing Skaggs to second.
  Garcia doubled to left center, scoring Skaggs and Bumbry.
  Singleton doubled to left center, scoring Garcia.
2 Murray struck out.
3 DeCinces flied to left.
Pittsburgh
  Foli beat out a dribbler to third.
1 Parker flied to center.
  Stargell doubled into the right field corner, Foli stopping at third.
  Milner intentionally walked, loading the bases.
2,3 Madlock grounded into a double play, Dauer to Garcia to Murray.

4th Inning
Baltimore
1 Roenicke grounded to third, a good play by Madlock.
  Dauer singled to left.
2,3 Skaggs hit into a double play, Foli to Garner to Stargell.
Pittsburgh
1 Ott lined to left.
  Garner singled to left.
2 Bibby forced Garner on an attempted sacrifice, Stewart to Garcia.
3 Moreno forced Bibby at second, Garcia unassisted.

5th Inning
Baltimore
1 May, pinch-hitting for Stewart, struck out.
2 Bumbry flied to left.
3 Garcia flied to center.
Pittsburgh
  For Baltimore—Stone on the mound.
  Foli walked.
  Parker singled to left, Foli stopping at second.
1 Stargell popped to third.
  Milner doubled just inside the foul line in right, scoring Foli as Parker stopped at third.
  Madlock intentionally walked to load the bases.
2 Ott flied to short left.
3 Garner forced Madlock at second, Garcia to Dauer.

6th Inning
Baltimore
  Singleton singled to center.
1,2 Murray hit into a double play, Garner to Foli to Stargell.
  DeCinces walked.
3 Roenicke flied to right.
Pittsburgh
1 Bibby struck out.
2 Moreno grounded to second.
  Foli singled to right.
  Parker looped a double to left, scoring Foli.
3 Stargell struck out.

7th Inning
Baltimore
1 Dauer flied to center.
  Skaggs singled past third.
  Kelly, batting for Stone, beat out a bouncer to Stargell.
  For Pittsburgh—Jackson came in to pitch.
2,3 Bumbry grounded into a double play, Foli to Garner to Stargell.

7th Inning (continued)
Pittsburgh
  For Baltimore—Stoddard pitching.
1 Milner popped to short.
  Madlock walked.
2   Madlock out trying to steal second, Skaggs to Garcia.
3 Ott grounded off Stoddard's leg to Murray who stepped on first.

8th Inning
Baltimore
  For Pittsburgh—Don Robinson pitching and batting fifth and Bill Robinson playing left and batting ninth.
  Garcia singled to right.
  Singleton singled to left, Garcia to second.
1 Murray forced Singleton, Foli to Garner as Garcia went to third.
  DeCinces again walked, loading the bases.
  For Pittsburgh—Tekulve came in to pitch.
  Lowenstein, pinch-hitting for Roenicke, drilled a double to left, scoring Garcia and Murray with DeCinces going to third.
  Smith, batting for Dauer, was intentionally walked, loading the bases.
  Crowley, batting for Skaggs, doubled into the right field corner, scoring DeCinces and Lowenstein with Smith stopping at third.
  Stoddard singled to left, scoring Smith as Crowley stopped at third.
  Dempsey ran for Crowley.
2 Bumbry forced Stoddard, Foli to Garner, as Dempsey scored.
3 Garcia struck out.
Pittsburgh
  For Baltimore—Lowenstein playing left, Smith playing second and Dempsey catching.
1 Garner bounced to the mound.
2 B. Robinson struck out.
  Moreno singled to left.
3 Foli grounded to short.

9th Inning
Baltimore
1 Singleton grounded to second.
2 Murray grounded to second.
  DeCinces walked for the fourth time.
3 Lowenstein grounded to second.
Pittsburgh
  For Baltimore—Belanger came in to play short.
1 Parker took a called third strike.
  Stargell singled up the middle.
2 Easler, batting for Tekulve, flied to left.
  Madlock singled to center, Stargell moving to third.
3 Ott struck out.

1979

Game 5 October 14 at Pittsburgh

Balt. 000 010 000
Pitt. 000 002 23x

Baltimore	Pos	AB	R	H	RBI	PO	A	E
Garcia	ss	4	0	0	0	2	1	0
Ayala	lf	1	0	0	0	2	0	0
b Bumbry	cf	1	0	0	0	1	0	0
Singleton	rf	4	0	0	0	0	0	0
Murray	1b	4	0	0	0	7	1	0
Roenicke	cf-lf	4	1	1	0	2	0	0
DeCinces	3b	4	0	2	0	1	4	0
Dauer	2b	3	0	0	0	2	1	0
d Lowenstein		1	0	1	0	0	0	0
Dempsey	c	3	0	2	0	7	0	0
e Crowley		1	0	0	0	0	0	0
Flanagan	p	1	0	0	0	0	2	0
c Kelly		1	0	0	0	0	0	0
Stoddard	p	0	0	0	0	0	1	1
T. Martinez	p	0	0	0	0	0	0	0
Stanhouse	p	0	0	0	0	0	0	1
Totals		32	1	6	0	24	10	2

Pitching Baltimore	IP	H	R	ER	BB	SO
Flanagan (L)	6	6	2	2	1	6
Stoddard	⅔	2	2	2	0	0
T. Martinez	*⅓	2	1	1	0	0
Stanhouse	1	3	2	2	2	0

*Pitched to one batter in 8th.

Pittsburgh	Pos	AB	R	H	RBI	PO	A	E
Moreno	cf	4	1	0	0	3	0	0
Foli	ss	4	2	2	3	3	7	0
Parker	rf	4	1	2	1	1	0	0
B. Robinson	lf	3	1	1	1	2	0	0
Stargell	1b	3	1	1	1	10	0	0
Madlock	3b	4	1	4	1	0	1	0
Nicosia	c	4	0	0	1	5	0	0
Garner	2b	4	1	2	0	3	3	1
Rooker	p	1	0	1	0	0	1	0
a Lacey		1	0	1	0	0	0	0
Blyleven	p	1	0	0	0	0	0	0
Totals		34	7	13	7	27	12	1

a Singled for Rooker in 5th.
b Flied out for Ayala in 6th.
c Struck out for Flanagan in 7th.
d Singled for Dauer in 9th.
e Flied out for Dempsey in 9th.

Doubles—Robinson, Roenicke, Dempsey, Parker. Triple—Foli. Sacrifice Hits—Robinson, Blyleven. Sacrifice Fly—Stargell. Double Plays—Garner to Foli to Stargell, Blyleven to Garner to Foli to Stargell. Left on Bases—Baltimore 7, Pittsburgh 9. Umpires—McKean, Runge, Neudecker, Engel, Goetz, Tata. Attendance—50,920. Time of Game—2:54.

Pitching Pittsburgh	IP	H	R	ER	BB	SO
Rooker	5	3	1	1	2	2
Blyleven (W)	4	3	0	0	1	3

1st Inning
Baltimore
1 Garcia lined to Rooker, making a great catch.
2 Ayala grounded to short.
3 Singleton flied to center.
Pittsburgh
1 Moreno struck out.
2 Foli flied to center.
3 Parker struck out.

2nd Inning
Baltimore
1 Murray flied to right.
2 Roenicke popped to first.
3 DeCinces struck out.
Pittsburgh
1 Robinson grounded to third.
2 Stargell flied to center.
Madlock singled off of DeCinces' glove.
3 Nicosia flied to deep left.

3rd Inning
Baltimore
1 Dauer popped to first.
2 Dempsey bounced to third.
3 Flanagan flied to center.
Pittsburgh
1 Garner bunted out to the pitcher.
2 Rooker took a called third strike.
3 Moreno fouled to Garcia.

4th Inning
Baltimore
1 Garcia grounded to short.
Ayala walked.
2 Singleton called out on strikes.
3 Murray popped to second.
Pittsburgh
1 Foli grounded to third.
2 Parker struck out.
Robinson doubled to right-center.
3 Stargell grounded to second.

5th Inning
Baltimore
Roenicke doubled to left-center.
DeCinces singled to right, Roenicke stopping at third.
1,2 Dauer grounded into a double play, Garner to Foli to Stargell, as Roenicke scored.
Dempsey singled to left.
Flanagan walked.
3 Garcia forced Flanagan, Foli to Garner.
Pittsburgh
Madlock singled up the middle.
1 Nicosia struck out.
2 Garner flied to deep left.
Lacy, pinch-hitting for Rooker, beat out a hit to third as Madlock stopped at second.
3 Moreno struck out.

6th Inning
Baltimore
For Pittsburgh—Blyleven pitching.
1 Bumbry, pinch-hitting for Ayala, flied to left.
2 Singleton grounded to second.
Murray safe on Garner's error.
3 Roenicke struck out.

6th Inning (cont.)
Pittsburgh
For Baltimore—Bumbry playing center as Roenicke moves to left.
Foli walked.
Parker singled to center, Foli stopping at second.
1 Robinson sacrificed, Flanagan to Murray, advancing both runners.
2 Stargell hit a sacrifice fly, Foli scoring after the catch and Parker going to third.
Madlock singled to center, scoring Parker.
3 Nicosia grounded to third.

7th Inning
Baltimore
1 DeCinces struck out.
2 Dauer grounded to short.
Dempsey doubled to center.
3 Kelly, pinch-hitting for Flanagan, struck out.
Pittsburgh
For Baltimore—Stoddard now pitching.
Garner beat out an infield hit to short.
1 Blyleven forced Garner on a bunt, Stoddard to Garcia.
2 Moreno forced Blyleven, Garcia to Dauer.
Moreno went to second on Stoddard's wild pick-off attempt.
Foli tripled to right-center, scoring Moreno.
For Baltimore—T. Martinez pitching.
Parker doubled to left-center, scoring Foli.
3 Robinson grounded to third.

8th Inning
Baltimore
1 Garcia bounced to short.
Bumbry walked.
2,3 Singleton's grounder deflected by Blyleven to Garner to Foli to Stargell for a DP
Pittsburgh
Stargell singled to right.
For Baltimore—Stanhouse pitching.
Madlock singled to center, Stargell advancing to third.
1 Nicosia flied to Dempsey.
Garner singled to left, scoring Stargell with Madlock stopping at second.
2 Blyleven sacrificed up both runners, Murray to Dauer covering.
Moreno intentionally walked, loading the bases.
Foli singled up the middle, scoring Madlock and Garner with Moreno stopping at second.
Both runners advanced on a wild pick-off throw by Stanhouse.
Parker intentionally walked, loading the bases.
3 Robinson popped to third.

9th Inning
1 Murray flied to center.
2 Roenicke popped to short.
DeCinces singled to left.
Lowenstein, batting for Dauer, singled to right, DeCinces stopping at second.
3 Crowley, pinch-hitting for Dempsey, flied to left.

Game 6 October 16 at Baltimore

Pitt. 000 000 220
Balt. 000 000 000

Pittsburgh	Pos	AB	R	H	RBI	PO	A	E
Moreno	cf	5	1	3	1	4	0	0
Foli	ss	5	1	2	0	0	5	0
Parker	rf	4	0	1	1	3	0	0
Stargell	1b	4	0	1	1	8	0	0
Milner	lf	3	0	0	0	0	0	0
Tekulve	p	1	0	0	0	0	0	0
Madlock	3b	4	0	0	0	1	2	0
Ott	c	4	1	2	0	6	0	0
Garner	2b	4	1	2	0	4	2	0
Candelaria	p	2	0	0	0	0	1	0
a Lacy		1	0	0	0	0	0	0
B. Robinson	lf	0	0	0	1	1	0	0
Totals		35	4	10	4	27	10	0

a Struck out for Candelaria in 7th.
b Flied out for Roenicke in 7th.
c Singled for Dauer in 7th.
d Struck out for Palmer in 8th.
e Flied out for Garcia in 8th.
f Grounded out for Ayala in 8th.

Doubles—Foli, Garner. Sacrifice Flies—Stargell, Robinson. Hit by Pitcher—Garner (by Palmer). Double Plays—Madlock to Stargell, Foli to Garner to Stargell. Left on Bases—Pittsburgh 10, Baltimore 5. Umpires—Runge, Neudecker, Engel, Goetz, Tata, McKean. Attendance—53,739. Time of Game—2:30.

Baltimore	Pos	AB	R	H	RBI	PO	A	E
Garcia	ss	3	0	1	0	1	2	0
e Kelly		1	0	0	0	0	0	0
Belanger	ss	0	0	0	0	0	0	0
Ayala	lf	3	0	0	0	2	0	0
f Crowley		1	0	0	0	0	0	0
Stoddard	p	0	0	0	0	1	0	0
Singleton	rf	4	0	3	0	1	0	0
Murray	1b	4	0	0	0	5	1	0
DeCinces	3b	4	0	0	0	1	3	0
Roenicke	cf	2	0	0	0	4	0	0
b Bumbry	cf	1	0	0	0	2	0	1
Dauer	2b	2	0	1	0	1	1	0
c Smith	2b	1	0	0	0	0	0	0
Dempsey	c	3	0	1	0	7	0	0
Palmer	p	2	0	0	0	1	0	0
d Lowenstein	lf	1	0	0	0	1	0	0
Totals		32	0	7	0	27	7	1

Pitching Pittsburgh	IP	H	R	ER	BB	SO
Candelaria (W)	6	6	0	0	0	2
Tekulve (S)	3	1	0	0	0	4

Pitching Baltimore	IP	H	R	ER	BB	SO
Palmer (L)	8	10	4	4	3	5
Stoddard	1	0	0	0	0	0

1st Inning
Pittsburgh
Moreno singled up the middle.
Foli doubled off DeCinces' glove, Moreno stopping at third.
1 Parker grounded to third, both runners holding.
2 Stargell fouled to DeCinces.
3 Milner bounced to Palmer who touched first for the putout.
Baltimore
Garcia singled to center.
1 Ayala flied to center.
Singleton singled to left, Garcia stopping at second.
2,3 Murray hit into a double play, Madlock who stepped on third to Stargell.

2nd Inning
Pittsburgh
1 Madlock grounded to third.
2 Ott grounded to short.
Garner singled to center.
3 Candelaria struck out.
Baltimore
1 DeCinces bunted and was out, Candelaria to Stargell.
2 Roenicke flied to center.
3 Dauer flied to center.

3rd Inning
Pittsburgh
1 Moreno flied to center.
2 Foli grounded to short.
3 Parker took a called third strike.
Baltimore
Dempsey singled to center.
1 Palmer struck out.
2 Garcia flied to right.
3 Ayala lined to second.

4th Inning
Pittsburgh
1 Stargell flied to center.
Milner walked.
Madlock walked.
2 Ott forced Madlock at second, Dauer to Garcia, Milner going to third.
Garner was hit by a pitch, loading the bases
3 Candelaria struck out.
Baltimore
Singleton singled to center.
1 Murray grounded to third, Singleton going to second.
2 DeCinces grounded to short as Singleton held second.
3 Roenicke popped to Garner.

5th Inning
Pittsburgh
1 Moreno lined to second, super catch.
2 Foli fouled to Dempsey.
Parker walked.
3 Stargell struck out.
Baltimore
Dauer singled to center.
1,2 Dempsey hit into a double play, Foli to Garner to Stargell.
3 Palmer struck out.

6th Inning
Pittsburgh
1 Milner bounced to short.
2 Madlock flied to deep right.
Ott looped a single to left.
3 Garner flied to center.
Baltimore
1 Garcia flied to center.
2 Ayala grounded to short.
Singleton singled to left.
3 Murray forced Singleton, Foli to Garner.

7th Inning
Pittsburgh
1 Lacy, pinch-hitting for Candelaria, struck out.
Moreno singled to right.
Foli beat out an infield hit over second, Moreno stopping at second.
Parker singled past Dauer, scoring Moreno as Foli advanced to third.
2 Stargell hit a sacrifice fly to left, scoring Foli, and Parker advancing to second after the catch.
3 Milner flied to center.
Baltimore
For Pittsburgh—Tekulve pitching and batting fifth and Robinson playing left and batting ninth.
1 DeCinces grounded to short.
2 Bumbry, batting for Roenicke, flied to right.
Smith, batting for Dauer, singled to right.
3 Dempsey struck out.

8th Inning
Pittsburgh
For Baltimore—Bumbry playing center and Smith stayed in to play second.
1 Madlock flied to center.
Ott singled to deep right.
Garner's long drive bounced over the left field fence for a ground-rule double, Ott going to third.
2 Robinson lined to left, Ott scoring after the catch.
Moreno singled to center, scoring Garner, and went to second when Bumbry fumbled the ball.
3 Foli fouled to Dempsey.
Baltimore
1 Lowenstein, batting for Palmer, struck out.
2 Kelly, batting for Garcia, flied to left.
3 Crowley, batting for Ayala, bounced to second.

9th Inning
Pittsburgh
For Baltimore—Stoddard pitching and batting second, Belanger playing short and batting first, and Lowenstein stays in to play left.
1 Parker flied to center.
2 Stargell flied to deep left.
3 Tekulve grounded out, Murray to Stoddard.
Baltimore
1 Singleton struck out.
2 Murray flied to right.
3 DeCinces struck out.

Game 7 October 17 at Baltimore

Pitt.	000 002 002
Balt.	001 000 000

Pittsburgh	Pos	AB	R	H	RBI	PO	A	E
Moreno	cf	5	1	3	1	4	0	0
Foli	ss	4	0	1	0	3	1	0
Parker	rf	4	0	0	0	2	0	0
B. Robinson	lf	4	1	1	1	2	0	0
Stargell	1b	5	1	4	2	6	1	0
Madlock	3b	3	0	0	0	2	1	0
Nicosia	c	4	0	0	0	6	1	0
Garner	2b	3	1	1	0	1	2	0
Bibby	p	1	0	0	0	1	0	0
a Sanguillen		1	0	0	0	0	0	0
D. Robinson	p	0	0	0	0	0	0	0
Jackson	p	1	0	0	0	0	0	0
Tekulve	p	1	0	0	0	0	0	0
Totals		36	4	10	4	27	6	0

a Grounded out for Bibby in 5th.
b Struck out for Lowenstein in 7th.
c Walked for McGregor in 8th.
d Ran for May in 8th.
e Announced for Garcia in 8th.
f Grounded out for Ayala in 8th.
g Flied out for Dempsey in 9th.

Doubles—Stargell (2). Garner. Home
Runs—Dauer, Stargell. Sacrifice Hit—Foli.
Hit by Pitcher—Parker (by T. Martinez),
B. Robinson (by D. Martinez). Double
Play—Belanger to Murray. Left on
Bases—Pittsburgh 10, Baltimore 6.
Umpires—Neudecker, Engel, Goetz, Tata,
McKean, Runge. Attendance—53,733. Time
of Game—2:54.

Baltimore	Pos	AB	R	H	RBI	PO	A	E
Bumbry	cf	3	0	0	0	0	0	0
Garcia	ss	3	0	1	0	0	5	1
e Ayala		0	0	0	0	0	0	0
f Crowley		1	0	0	0	0	0	0
Stoddard	p	0	0	0	0	0	1	0
Flanagan	p	0	0	0	0	0	0	0
Stanhouse	p	0	0	0	0	0	0	0
T. Martinez	p	0	0	0	0	0	0	0
D. Martinez	p	0	0	0	0	0	0	0
Singleton	rf	3	0	0	0	1	0	0
Murray	1b	4	0	0	0	11	0	0
Lowenstein	lf	2	0	0	0	2	0	1
b Roenicke	lf	2	0	0	0	1	0	0
DeCinces	3b	4	0	2	0	3	3	0
Dempsey	c	3	0	0	0	3	0	0
g Kelly		1	0	0	0	0	0	0
Dauer	2b	3	1	1	1	4	2	0
McGregor	p	1	0	0	0	1	2	0
c May		0	0	0	0	0	0	0
d Belanger	ss	0	0	0	0	1	1	0
Totals		30	1	4	1	27	14	2

Pitching	IP	H	R	ER	BB	SO
Pittsburgh						
Bibby	4	3	1	1	0	3
D. Robinson	⅓	1	0	0	1	0
Jackson (W)	2⅔	0	0	0	2	1
Tekulve (S)	1⅓	0	0	0	1	2
Baltimore						
McGregor (L)	8	7	2	2	2	2
Stoddard	⅓	1	1	1	0	0
Flanagan	*0	1	1	1	0	0
Stanhouse	*0	1	0	0	0	0
T. Martinez	*0	0	0	0	0	0
D. Martinez	⅔	0	0	0	0	0

*Pitched to one batter in 9th.

1st Inning
Pittsburgh
Moreno singled to center.
1 Foli sacrificed Moreno to second,
McGregor to Murray.
2 Parker popped to third.
3 Robinson popped to third.
Baltimore
1 Bumbry grounded to Stargell who tagged
him out sliding into first.
2 Garcia bounced to second.
3 Singleton grounded out, Stargell to
Bibby.

2nd Inning
Pittsburgh
Stargell singled to left and continued
on to second when Lowenstein bobbled
the ball for an error.
1 Madlock grounded to short, Stargell
holding second.
2 Nicosia fouled to DeCinces.
Garner was intentionally walked.
3 Bibby grounded to Dauer who threw to
McGregor covering first.
Baltimore
1 Murray struck out.
2 Lowenstein struck out.
DeCinces singled to center.
3 Dempsey grounded to third.

3rd Inning
Pittsburgh
1 Moreno lined to right.
2 Foli grounded to short.
3 Parker struck out.
Baltimore
Dauer lined Bibby's first pitch into the
left field stands for a home run:
1 McGregor bounced to short.
2 Bumbry popped to short.
Garcia singled to right.
3 Garcia was out trying to steal second,
Nicosia to Foli.

4th Inning
Pittsburgh
1 Robinson popped to Dempsey.
Stargell blooped a double into left.
Madlock was safe when he grounded to
Garcia but Garcia's throw to DeCinces
was wild, allowing Stargell to get to
third.
2 Nicosia lined to second.
3 Garner popped to Murray and was called
out for interference when he collided
with Murray while inside the foul line.
Baltimore
1 Singleton flied to right.
2 Murray struck out.
3 Lowenstein fouled to Madlock.

5th Inning
Pittsburgh
1 Sanguillen, batting for Bibby, bounced
back to the mound.
2 Moreno lined to left.
3 Foli lined to left.
Baltimore
For Pittsburgh—D. Robinson pitching.
DeCinces singled to center.
1 Dempsey flied to right.
2 Dauer flied to center.
McGregor walked.
For Pittsburgh—Jackson came in to pitch.
3 Bumbry fouled to Madlock.

6th Inning
Pittsburgh
1 Parker grounded to second.
Robinson singled to left.
On the first pitch Stargell hit his
third homer of the series over the
right field fence.
2 Madlock grounded to third.
3 Nicosia grounded to short.
Baltimore
1 Garcia popped to second.
2 Singleton flied to deep center.
3 Murray fouled to Stargell.

7th Inning
Pittsburgh
1 Garner grounded to third.
2 Jackson grounded to short.
Moreno singled to right past a diving
Dauer.
3 Foli forced Moreno, DeCinces to Dauer.
Baltimore
1 Roenicke, pinch-hitting for Lowenstein,
struck out.
2 DeCinces flied to center.
3 Dempsey flied to left.

8th Inning
Pittsburgh
For Baltimore—Roenicke stays in at left.
1 Parker struck out.
2 Robinson flied to left.
Stargell doubled off the left field wall
for his fourth hit of the game.
Madlock intentionally walked.
3 Nicosia forced Madlock, Garcia to Dauer.
Baltimore
1 Dauer popped to short.
May, batting for McGregor, walked.
Belanger ran for May.
Bumbry walked.
Ayala was announced for Garcia.
For Pittsburgh—Tekulve came in to pitch.
2 Crowley batted for Ayala and grounded to
second, both runners advancing.
Singleton walked intentionally to load
the bases.
3 Murray flied to deep right.

9th Inning
Pittsburgh
For Baltimore—Belanger playing short and
Stoddard pitching (batting second).
Garner doubled to left.
1 Tekulve bunted out, Stoddard to Dauer,
Garner holding.
For Baltimore—Flanagan came in to pitch.
Moreno singled to center, scoring Garner.
For Baltimore—Stanhouse now pitching.
Foli singled to left-center, Moreno
advancing to third.
For Baltimore—T. Martinez took over on
the mound.
Parker was hit by a pitch, loading the
bases.
For Baltimore—D. Martinez now pitching.
Robinson was hit by a pitch, forcing
in Moreno with the bases still loaded.
2,3 Stargell grounded into a double play,
Belanger to Murray.
Baltimore
1 Roenicke struck out.
2 DeCinces struck out.
3 Kelly, batting for Dempsey, flied to
center.

1979 WORLD SERIES COMPOSITE BOX

	Wins	Composite Line Score	
Pittsburgh Pirates (NL)	4	1 8 0 1 1 8 4 6 3	- 32
Baltimore Orioles (AL)	3	5 1 6 5 1 1 1 6 0	- 26

		Regular Season		
Manager	W	L	Pct.	G. Ahead
Chuck Tanner	98	64	.605	2
Earl Weaver	102	57	.642	8

BATTING AND FIELDING

WORLD SERIES STATISTICS

PITTSBURGH PIRATES

Player	Pos	G	AB	R	H	2B	3B	HR	RBI	BB	SO	SB	BA	SA	PO	A	E
Willie Stargell	1b	7	30	**7**	**12**	**4**	0	**3**	**7**	0	6	0	.400	**.833**	59	2	2
Phil Garner	2b	7	24	4	**12**	**4**	0	0	5	3	1	0	**.500**	.667	21	23	2
Tim Foli	ss	7	30	6	10	1	**1**	0	3	2	0	0	.333	.433	8	**32**	**3**
Bill Madlock	3b	7	24	2	9	1	0	0	3	**5**	1	0	.375	.417	3	10	1
Dave Parker	rf	7	29	2	10	3	0	0	4	2	**7**	0	.345	.448	13	1	1
Omar Moreno	cf	7	**33**	4	11	2	0	0	3	1	**7**	0	.333	.394	20	1	0
Bill Robinson	lf-ph	7	19	2	5	1	0	0	2	0	4	0	.263	.333	11	1	0
Steve Nicosia	c	4	16	1	1	0	0	0	0	0	2	0	.063	.063	23	2	0
Ed Ott	c	3	12	2	4	1	0	0	3	0	2	0	.333	.417	20	0	0
John Milner	lf	3	9	2	3	1	0	0	1	2	0	0	.333	.444	5	0	0
Lee Lacy	ph	4	4	0	1	0	0	0	0	0	1	0	.250	.250	—	—	—
Manny Sanguillen	ph	3	3	0	1	0	0	0	1	0	0	0	.333	.333	—	—	—
Mike Easler	ph	2	1	0	0	0	0	0	0	1	0	0	.000	.000	—	—	—
Renny Stennett	ph	1	1	0	1	0	0	0	0	0	0	0	1.000	1.000	—	—	—
Matt Alexander	pr-lf	1	0	0	0	0	0	0	0	0	0	0	—	—	0	0	0
Jim Bibby	p	2	4	0	0	0	0	0	0	0	1	0	.000	.000	1	0	0
Bert Blyleven	p	2	3	0	0	0	0	0	0	0	0	0	.000	.000	0	1	0
John Candelaria	p	2	3	0	1	0	0	0	0	0	2	0	.333	.333	0	1	0
Kent Tekulve	p	5	2	0	0	0	0	0	0	0	0	0	.000	.000	1	0	0
Jim Rooker	p	2	2	0	0	0	0	0	0	0	1	0	.000	.000	1	2	0
Grant Jackson	p	4	1	0	0	0	0	0	0	0	0	0	.000	.000	0	0	0
Enrique Romo	p	2	1	0	0	0	0	0	0	0	0	0	.000	.000	0	1	0
Don Robinson	p	4	0	0	0	0	0	0	0	0	0	0	—	—	0	1	0
Bruce Kison	p	4	0	0	0	0	0	0	0	0	0	0	—	—	0	1	0
Dave Roberts	Did not play																
team total		7	251	32	81	18	1	3	32	16	35	0	.323	.438	186	79	9

Double Plays—12
Left on Bases—60

REGULAR SEASON STATISTICS

Player		Main Pos	G	AB	R	H	2B	3B	HR	RBI	BB	SO	SB	BA	SA
Willie Stargell		1b	126	424	60	119	19	0	32	82	47	105	0	.281	.552
Phil Garner		2b-3b	150	549	76	161	32	8	11	59	55	74	17	.293	.441
Tim Foli	a	ss	133	525	70	153	23	1	1	65	28	14	6	.291	.345
Bill Madlock	b	3b	85	311	48	102	17	3	7	44	34	22	21	.328	.469
Dave Parker		of	158	622	109	193	45	7	25	94	67	101	20	.310	.526
Omar Moreno		of	162	**695**	110	196	21	12	8	69	51	104	77	.282	.381
Bill Robinson		of	148	421	59	111	17	6	24	75	24	81	13	.264	.504
Steve Nicosia		c	70	191	22	55	16	0	4	13	23	17	0	.288	.435
Ed Ott		c	117	403	49	110	20	2	7	51	26	62	0	.273	.385
John Milner		of-1b	128	326	52	90	9	4	16	60	53	37	3	.276	.475
Lee Lacy		of-ph	84	182	17	45	9	3	5	15	22	36	6	.247	.412
Manny Sanguillen		ph	56	74	8	17	5	2	0	4	2	5	0	.230	.351
Mike Easler		ph	55	54	8	15	1	1	2	11	8	13	0	.278	.444
Renny Stennett		2b	108	319	31	76	13	2	0	24	24	25	1	.238	.292
Matt Alexander		of	44	13	16	7	0	1	0	1	0	0	13	.538	.692
Jim Bibby		p	34	45	3	8	1	0	2	5	0	25	0	.178	.333
Bert Blyleven		p	38	70	1	9	1	0	0	3	0	33	0	.129	.143
John Candelaria		p	33	68	0	9	4	0	0	6	1	18	0	.132	.181
Kent Tekulve		p	94	15	3	2	0	0	0	1	1	8	0	.133	.133
Jim Rooker		p	19	33	1	4	0	0	0	0	1	13	0	.121	.121
Grant Jackson		p	72	9	0	0	0	0	0	1	0	2	0	.000	.000
Enrique Romo		p	84	12	0	2	0	0	0	1	0	2	0	.167	.167
Don Robinson		p	29	49	4	10	0	0	0	3	3	9	0	.204	.204
Bruce Kison		p	37	55	6	8	2	0	1	6	1	19	0	.145	.236
Dave Roberts	c	p	21	5	0	0	0	0	0	1	1	0	1	.000	.000
team total			163	5661	775	1541	264	52	148	710	483	855	180	.272	**.416**

a—from N.Y. Mets. b—from San Francisco. c—from San Francisco.
Dale Berra (ss-3b), Frank Taveras (ss), Alberto Lois (pr), Doe Boyland (ph), Gary Hargis (ph), Ed Whitson (p), Joe Coleman (p), Dock Ellis (p), and Rick Rhoden also played for the Pirates during the season.

WORLD SERIES STATISTICS

BALTIMORE ORIOLES

Player	Pos	G	AB	R	H	2B	3B	HR	RBI	BB	SO	SB	BA	SA	PO	A	E
Eddie Murray	1b	7	26	3	4	1	0	1	2	4	4	**1**	.154	.308	**60**	7	0
Rich Dauer	2b-ph	6	17	2	5	1	0	1	1	0	1	0	.294	.529	10	10	0
Kiko Garcia	ss	6	20	4	8	2	**1**	0	6	1	3	0	.400	.600	10	17	1
Doug DeCinces	3b	7	25	2	5	0	0	1	3	**5**	5	**1**	.200	.320	7	21	**3**
Ken Singleton	rf	7	28	1	10	1	0	0	2	2	5	0	.357	.393	9	0	0
Al Bumbry	cf-ph	7	21	3	3	0	0	0	1	2	1	0	.143	.143	14	1	1
Gary Roenicke	lf-cf-ph	6	16	1	2	1	0	0	0	0	6	0	.125	.188	14	1	0
Rick Dempsey	c-pr	7	21	3	6	2	0	0	0	1	3	0	.286	.381	38	2	0
John Lowenstein	lf-ph	6	13	2	3	1	0	0	3	1	3	0	.231	.308	6	0	1
Billy Smith	2b-ph	4	7	1	2	0	0	0	0	2	0	0	.286	.286	4	3	0
Benny Ayala	lf-ph	4	6	1	2	0	0	1	2	1	0	0	.333	.833	4	0	0
Mark Belanger	ss-pr	3	6	1	0	0	0	0	0	1	1	0	.000	.000	3	7	1
Terry Crowley	ph	5	4	0	1	1	0	0	2	1	0	0	.250	.500	—	—	—
Pat Kelly	ph	5	4	0	1	0	0	0	0	1	1	0	.250	.250	—	—	—
Dave Skaggs	c	1	3	1	1	0	0	0	0	0	0	0	.333	.333	2	2	0
Lee May	ph	2	1	0	0	0	0	0	0	1	1	0	.000	.000	—	—	—
Mike Flanagan	p	3	5	0	0	0	0	0	0	1	2	0	.000	.000	0	4	0
Scott McGregor	p	2	4	1	0	0	0	0	0	2	1	0	.000	.000	1	2	0
Jim Palmer	p	2	4	0	0	0	0	0	0	0	3	0	.000	.000	2	1	0
Tim Stoddard	p	4	1	0	1	0	0	0	1	0	0	0	1.000	1.000	1	4	1
Sammy Stewart	p	1	1	0	0	0	0	0	0	0	1	0	.000	.000	1	2	0
Tippy Martinez	p	3	0	0	0	0	0	0	0	0	0	0	—	—	0	0	0
Dennis Martinez	p	2	0	0	0	0	0	0	0	0	0	0	—	—	0	1	0
Don Stanhouse	p	3	0	0	0	0	0	0	0	0	0	0	—	—	0	0	1
Steve Stone	p	1	0	0	0	0	0	0	0	0	0	0	—	—	0	0	0
team total		7	233	26	54	10	1	4	23	26	41	2	.232	.335	186	85	9

Double Plays—5
Left on Bases—49

REGULAR SEASON STATISTICS

Player	Main Pos	G	AB	R	H	2B	3B	HR	RBI	BB	SO	SB	BA	SA
Eddie Murray	1b	159	606	90	179	30	2	25	99	71	78	10	.295	.475
Rich Dauer	2b	142	479	63	123	20	0	9	61	36	36	0	.257	.355
Kiko Garcia	ss	126	417	54	103	15	9	5	24	32	87	11	.247	.362
Doug DeCinces	3b	120	422	67	97	27	1	16	61	54	68	5	.230	.412
Ken Singleton	of	159	570	93	168	29	1	35	111	109	118	3	.295	.533
Al Bumbry	of	148	569	80	162	29	1	7	49	43	74	37	.285	.376
Gary Roenicke	of	133	376	60	98	16	1	25	64	61	74	1	.261	.508
Rick Dempsey	c	124	368	48	88	23	0	6	41	38	37	0	.239	.351
John Lowenstein	of	97	197	33	50	8	2	11	34	30	37	16	.254	.482
Billy Smith	2b	68	189	18	47	9	4	6	33	15	33	1	.249	.434
Benny Ayala	of	42	86	15	22	5	0	6	13	6	9	0	.256	.523
Mark Belanger	ss	101	198	28	33	6	2	0	9	29	33	5	.167	.217
Terry Crowley	dh	61	63	8	20	5	1	1	8	14	13	0	.317	.476
Pat Kelly	of-dh	68	153	25	44	11	0	9	25	20	25	4	.288	.536
Dave Skaggs	c	63	137	9	34	8	0	1	14	13	14	0	.248	.428
Lee May	dh	124	456	59	116	15	0	19	69	28	100	3	.254	.412
Mike Flanagan	p	39	0	0	0	0	0	0	0	0	0	0	—	—
Scott McGregor	p	27	0	0	0	0	0	0	0	0	0	0	—	—
Jim Palmer	p	23	0	0	0	0	0	0	0	0	0	0	—	—
Tim Stoddard	p	29	0	0	0	0	0	0	0	0	0	0	—	—
Sammy Stewart	p	31	0	0	0	0	0	0	0	0	0	0	—	—
Tippy Martinez	p	39	0	0	0	0	0	0	0	0	0	0	—	—
Dennis Martinez	p	40	0	0	0	0	0	0	0	0	0	0	—	—
Don Stanhouse	p	52	0	0	0	0	0	0	0	0	0	0	—	—
Steve Stone	p	32	0	0	0	0	0	0	0	0	0	0	—	—
team total		159	5371	757	1401	258	24	181	717	608	**847**	99	.261	.419

Larry Harlow (of), Wayne Krenchicki (3b, 2b), Mark Corey (of), Bob Molinaro (of), Tom Chism (1b), Ellie Hendricks (c), Dave Ford (p), John Flinn (p), Jeff Rineer (p) also played for the Orioles during the season.

PITCHING

WORLD SERIES STATISTICS

PITTSBURGH PIRATES

Player	G	GS	CG	IP	H	R	ER	BB	SO	W	L	SV	ERA
Jim Bibby	2	**2**	0	$10\frac{1}{3}$	10	4	3	2	10	0	0	0	2.61
Bert Blyleven	2	1	0	10	8	2	2	3	4	**1**	0	0	**1.80**
Kent Tekulve	**5**	0	0	$9\frac{1}{3}$	4	3	3	3	10	0	**1**	**3**	2.89
John Candelaria	2	**2**	0	9	14	6	5	2	4	**1**	**1**	0	5.00
Jim Rooker	2	1	0	$8\frac{2}{3}$	5	1	1	3	4	0	0	0	1.04
Don Robinson	4	0	0	5	4	3	3	**6**	3	**1**	0	0	5.40
Grant Jackson	4	0	0	$4\frac{2}{3}$	1	0	0	2	2	**1**	0	0	0.00
Enrique Romo	2	0	0	$4\frac{2}{3}$	5	2	2	3	4	0	0	0	3.86
Bruce Kison	1	1	0	$\frac{1}{3}$	3	5	4	2	0	0	**1**	0	108.00
Dave Roberts	Did not play												
team total	7	7	0	62	54	26	22	26	41	4	3	3	3.19

(difference in E Runs due to rule 10.18(i) in game 3.

REGULAR SEASON STATISTICS

Player	G	GS	CG	IP	H	ER	BB	SO	W	L	Pct	SV	ShO	ERA
Jim Bibby	34	17	4	138	110	43	47	103	12	4	.750	0	1	2.80
Bert Blyleven	37	37	4	237	238	95	92	172	12	5	.706	0	0	3.61
Kent Tekulve	**94**	0	0	134	109	41	49	75	10	8	.556	34	0	2.75
John Candelaria	33	30	8	207	201	74	41	101	14	9	.609	0	0	3.22
Jim Rooker	19	17	1	104	106	53	39	44	4	7	.364	0	0	4.59
Don Robinson	29	25	4	161	171	69	52	96	8	8	.500	0	0	3.86
Grant Jackson	72	0	0	82	67	27	35	39	8	5	.615	14	0	2.96
Enrique Romo	84	0	0	129	122	43	43	106	10	5	.667	5	0	3.00
Bruce Kison	33	25	3	172	157	61	45	105	13	7	.650	0	1	3.19
Dave Roberts	21	3	0	39	47	14	12	15	5	2	.714	1	0	3.23
team total	163	163	24	**1493**	1424	566	504	904	**98**	64	**.605**	**52**	7	3.41

WORLD SERIES STATISTICS

BALTIMORE ORIOLES

Player	G	GS	CG	IP	H	R	ER	BB	SO	W	L	SV	ERA
Scott McGregor	2	**2**	**1**	**17**	16	6	**6**	2	8	**1**	**1**	0	3.18
Mike Flanagan	3	**2**	**1**	15	**18**	**7**	5	2	**13**	**1**	**1**	0	3.00
Jim Palmer	2	**2**	0	15	**18**	6	**6**	5	8	0	**1**	0	3.60
Tim Stoddard	4	0	0	5	6	3	3	1	3	**1**	0	0	5.40
Sammy Stewart	1	0	0	$2\frac{2}{3}$	4	0	0	1	0	0	0	0	0.00
Don Stanhouse	3	0	0	2	6	3	3	3	0	0	**1**	0	13.50
Dennis Martinez	2	1	0	2	6	4	4	0	0	0	0	0	18.00
Steve Stone	1	0	0	2	4	2	2	2	2	0	0	0	9.00
Tippy Martinez	3	0	0	$1\frac{1}{3}$	3	1	1	0	1	0	0	0	6.75
team total	7	7	2	62	81	32	30	16	35	3	4	0	4.35

REGULAR SEASON STATISTICS

Player	G	GS	CG	IP	H	ER	BB	SO	W	L	Pct	SV	ShO	ERA
Scott McGregor	27	23	7	175	165	65	23	81	13	6	.684	0	2	3.34
Mike Flanagan	39	38	16	266	245	91	70	190	**23**	9	.719	0	**5**	3.08
Jim Palmer	23	22	7	156	144	57	43	67	10	6	.625	0	0	3.29
Tim Stoddard	29	0	0	58	44	11	19	47	3	1	.750	3	0	1.71
Sammy Stewart	31	3	1	118	96	46	71	71	8	5	.615	1	0	3.51
Don Stanhouse	52	0	0	73	49	23	51	34	7	3	.700	21	0	2.84
Dennis Martinez	40	**39**	**18**	**292**	**279**	119	78	132	15	16	.484	0	3	3.67
Steve Stone	32	32	3	186	173	78	73	96	11	7	.611	0	0	3.77
Tippy Martinez	39	0	0	78	59	25	31	61	10	3	.769	3	0	2.88
team total	159	159	52	1434	1279	520	467	786	**102**	57	**.642**	30	**12**	**3.28**

Total Attendance—367,597 Average Attendance—52,514 Winning Player's Share—$28,264 Losing Player's Share—$22,114

1980
After the Dues, Redemption

Tug McGraw had been here before, and so had the Phillies. For neither had there been joy. When the Mets had won the Series in 1969, McGraw had ridden the bench from start to finish. Despite his screwball and his cheerleading, the Mets had lost to Oakland in 1973. Now he was back with the Phillies, losers in their only two previous Series. The Phils traveled a hard road to this meeting. They sizzled in September and snatched the N.L. East title from Montreal by one game. They then emerged from a grueling LCS with Houston; four of the five games went into extra innings, with the Phillies coming from behind for three victories. In his first full season, manager Dallas Green had a Cy Young winner in Steve Carlton, an MVP in Mike Schmidt, and an untouchable reliever in the enthusiastic Tug McGraw.

The Kansas City Royals also had a freshman manager in Jim Frey. His club cruised home atop the A.L. West, then evened an old score by sweeping the Yankees in the LCS. George Brett drew headlines all summer as he flirted with the sacred .400 mark, finally settling for a mortal .390. The unquestioned heart of the Royals, he came into the Series tortured by a bad case of hemorrhoids.

Brett was in the lineup as the Series began in Philadelphia. The Royals jumped out to a 4–0 lead after two and a half innings, with Willie Aikens hitting a two-run homer. K.C. starter Dennis Leonard got his lumps in the bottom of the third. Bake McBride belted a three-run homer as part of a five-run Philly outburst. The Phils boosted their lead to 7–4 before another Aikens home run brought K.C. to within one run. Into the fray came McGraw, whose two innings of work sealed a 7–6 victory.

The second game matched experienced lefties, Steve Carlton and Larry Gura. The Phillies scored first in the fifth inning, building three hits into two runs. The Royals got onto the scoreboard with one in the sixth, then jumped on a troubled Carlton in the seventh. Suddenly out of control, Carlton walked the bases full. Amos Otis seized the opportunity with a two-run double. A sacrifice fly by John Wathan put K.C. ahead 4–2. Frey entrusted the lead to Dan Quisenberry, whose submarine delivery had saved 33 games during the regular season. He did not save this one. After a leadoff walk, the Phils pounded him for four hits and four runs. Schmidt drove in the go-ahead run with a double. The Royals retreated to Kansas City down by two games, hopeful of a midwestern turnaround.

Brett used the day off to undergo minor surgery, then celebrated his relief with a first-inning home run off Dick Ruthven. The Phillies pulled even in the second and did so every time the Royals scored. Tied at 3–3 after nine, the Royals won it in the tenth off McGraw with a walk, a stolen base, and an Aikens single.

The Royals squared the Series in game four. They drove starter Larry Christenson from the mound in the first with a four-run barrage, led by Brett's triple and Aikens's home run. Outside of another Aikens homer, the Philadelphia relievers kept the Royals in check while the offense inched back. Dennis Leonard rehabilitated himself with seven good innings, and Quisenberry did the same by holding the 5–3 lead to the end.

For the pivotal fifth game, Dallas Green turned to Marty Bystrom, a talented but inexperienced rookie. Frey relied on the veteran Gura. After eight innings, the Royals clasped a 3–2 lead. Quisenberry was on the mound for the third straight day. After Schmidt led off with a single, Del Unser bashed a liner down the first-base line to score Schmidt. After two men went out, Manny Trillo's single scored Unser and put the Phillies ahead 4–3. Tug McGraw ran the gauntlet in the ninth, walking the bases full before fanning Jose Cardenal to end it.

With Carlton on the mound, the Phils expected to wrap it up in game six. A 4–0 lead after seven innings put the taste of victory on Philadelphia's lips. A touch of fatigue sent Carlton off in favor of McGraw, who survived one more untidy ninth. The Royals loaded the bases with one out. Frank White lofted a foul pop near the first-base dugout. The ball plopped into catcher Bob Boone's glove, only to squirt out immediately. Before it hit the ground, Pete Rose grabbed the ball for the second out. McGraw then whiffed Willie Wilson and leaped for joy on the mound.

Game 1 October 14 at Philadelphia

K.C.	022 000 020
Phil.	005 110 00x

Kansas City	Pos	AB	R	H	RBI	PO	A	E
Wilson	lf	5	0	0	0	2	1	0
McRae	dh	3	1	1	0	0	0	0
Brett	3b	4	1	1	0	0	2	0
Aikens	1b	4	2	2	4	13	0	0
Porter	c	2	1	0	0	5	1	0
Otis	cf	4	1	3	2	1	0	0
Hurdle	rf	3	0	1	0	1	0	0
a Wathan	rf	1	0	0	0	1	0	0
White	2b	4	0	1	0	0	5	0
Washington	ss	4	0	0	0	1	6	0
Leonard	p	0	0	0	0	0	0	1
Martin	p	0	0	0	0	0	0	0
Quisenberry	p	0	0	0	0	0	0	0
Totals		34	6	9	6	24	15	1

a Grounded into double play for Hurdle in 8th.

Doubles—Boone 2, Brett. Home Runs—Otis, Aikens 2, McBride. Stolen Bases—Bowa. Sacrifice Fly—Maddox. Hit by Pitcher—Rose (by Leonard), Luzinski (by Martin). Wild Pitch—Walk. Double Play—Bowa, to Trillo to Rose. Left on Bases—Kansas City 4, Philadelphia 6. Umpires—Wendelstedt, Kunkel, Pryor, Denkinger, Rennert, Bremigan. Attendance—65,791. Time of Game—3:01

Philadelphia	Pos	AB	R	H	RBI	PO	A	E
Smith	lf	4	0	2	0	3	1	0
Gross	lf	1	0	0	0	1	0	0
Rose	1b	3	1	0	0	7	2	0
Schmidt	3b	2	2	1	0	2	3	0
McBride	rf	4	1	3	3	3	0	0
Luzinski	dh	3	0	0	0	0	0	0
Maddox	cf	3	0	0	1	2	0	0
Trillo	2b	4	1	1	0	1	2	0
Bowa	ss	4	1	1	0	0	3	0
Boone	c	4	1	3	2	6	0	0
Walk	p	0	0	0	0	0	0	0
McGraw	p	0	0	0	0	0	0	0
Totals		32	7	11	6	27	11	0

Pitching

Kansas City	IP	H	R	ER	BB	SO
Leonard (L)	3⅓	6	6	6	1	3
Martin	4	5	1	1	1	1
Quisenberry	⅓	0	0	0	0	0

Philadelphia	IP	H	R	ER	BB	SO
Walk (W)	*7	8	6	6	3	3
McGraw (S)	2	1	0	0	0	2

*Pitched to two batters in 8th.

1st Inning
Kansas City
1 Wilson struck out.
  McRae walked.
2 Brett foul-popped to Schmidt.
3 Aikens flied to Maddox.
Philadelphia
1 Smith grounded to second.
2 Rose grounded to short.
3 Schmidt struck out swinging.

2nd Inning
Kansas City
  Porter walked on a full count.
  Otis homered to left on a 2-1 pitch.
1 Hurdle flied to Smith in deep left-center.
2 White flied to right.
3 Washington grounded to Rose, who flipped to Walk covering.
Philadelphia
1 McBride grounded to short.
2 Luzinski flied to deep left.
3 Maddox grounded to third.

3rd Inning
Kansas City
1 Wilson grounded to second.
  McRae singled to center.
2 Brett struck out.
  Aikens hit a two-run homer to right-center on a 1-2 count.
  Porter walked.
  Otis beat out a high chopper to third, Porter stopping at second.
  Hurdle singled to left, but Porter was
3 out trying to score, Smith to Boone.
Philadelphia
1 Trillo grounded to short.
  Bowa singled through the middle.
  Bowa stole second.
  Boone doubled into the left field corner, scoring Bowa.
  Smith singled to left, Boone stopping at third, but scored when Smith got
2 caught in a rundown, Wilson to Brett to Washington to Aikens.
  Rose was hit by a pitch.
  Schmidt walked on a 3-1 count.
  McBride lined a 3-run homer over the right field fence.
3 Luzinski struck out swinging.

4th Inning
Kansas City
1 White grounded out, Rose to Walk.
2 Washington grounded to short.
3 Wilson grounded to third.
Philadelphia
1 Maddox struck out swinging.
  Trillo beat out a bouncer up the middle.
  Trillo took second on Leonard's wild pick-off throw.
2 Bowa grounded to second, Trillo advancing to third.
  Boone doubled into the right field corner, scoring Trillo.
  For Kansas City—Martin came in to pitch.
3 Smith flied to right.

5th Inning
Kansas City
1 McRae flied to deep right.
2 Brett flied to Maddox, making a leaping catch at the wall.
3 Aikens struck out swinging.
Philadelphia
1 Rose grounded to short.
  Schmidt walked.
  McBride singled to left, Schmidt stopping at second.
  Luzinski was hit by a pitch to load the bases.
2 Maddox hit a sacrifice fly to left, scoring Schmidt.
3 Trillo popped to Aikens.

6th Inning
Kansas City
1 Porter fouled to Schmidt.
2 Otis flied to right.
3 Hurdle grounded to short.
Philadelphia
1 Bowa fouled out to Porter.
2 Boone grounded to second.
  Smith beat out a bouncer to third.
3 Smith out trying to steal, Porter to Washington.

7th Inning
Kansas City
  White singled up the middle.
1 Washington lined to left.
  White stole second.
2 Wilson flied to left.
3 McRae grounded to third.
Philadelphia
1 Rose grounded to second.
  Schmidt beat out an infield hit.
  McBride singled to right, Schmidt stopping at second.
2 Luzinski struck out swinging.
3 McBride flied to center.

8th Inning
Kansas City
  For Philadelphia—Gross playing left.
  Brett doubled to left-center.
  Brett to third on a wild pitch.
  Aikens hit his second two-run homer of the game over the right field fence.
  For Philadelphia—McGraw came in to pitch.
1 Porter flied to left.
  Otis singled to left.
2,3 Wathan, pinch-hitting for Hurdle, hit into a double play, Bowa to Trillo to Rose.
Philadelphia
  For Kansas City—Wathan playing right.
1 Trillo flied to right.
2 Bowa grounded to second.
  Boone singled to right.
  For Kansas City—Quisenberry came in to pitch.
3 Gross grounded to short.

9th Inning
Kansas City
1 White grounded to third.
2 Washington called out on strikes.
3 Wilson struck out swinging.

Game 2 October 15 at Philadelphia

K.C.	000	001	300	
Phil.	000	020	04x	

Kansas City	Pos	AB	R	H	RBI	PO	A	E
Wilson	lf	4	1	1	0	1	0	0
Washington	ss	4	0	1	0	0	3	0
Brett	3b	2	0	2	0	2	2	0
Chalk	3b	0	1	0	0	0	1	0
c Porter		1	0	0	0	0	0	0
McRae	dh	4	1	3	0	0	0	0
Otis	cf	5	1	2	2	5	0	0
Wathan	c	3	0	0	1	2	0	0
Aikens	1b	3	0	1	0	6	0	0
LaCock	1b	0	0	0	0	2	0	0
Cardenal	rf	4	0	0	0	3	0	0
White	2b	4	0	1	0	3	3	0
Gura	p	0	0	0	0	0	0	0
Quisenberry	p	0	0	0	0	0	0	0
Totals		34	4	11	3	24	9	0

Philadelphia	Pos	AB	R	H	RBI	PO	A	E
Smith	1f	3	0	0	0	0	0	0
a Unser	cf	1	1	1	1	0	0	0
Rose	1b	4	0	0	0	7	1	0
McBride	rf	3	1	1	1	2	0	0
Schmidt	3b	4	1	2	1	1	1	0
Moreland	dh	4	1	2	1	0	0	0
Maddox	cf	3	1	1	0	1	1	0
b Gross	lf	1	0	0	0	0	0	0
Trillo	2b	2	0	0	1	6	3	1
Bowa	ss	3	0	1	1	0	6	0
Boone	c	1	1	0	0	10	1	0
Carlton	p	0	0	0	0	0	1	0
Reed	p	0	0	0	0	0	0	0
Totals		29	6	8	6	27	14	1

Pitching	IP	H	R	ER	BB	SO
Kansas City						
Gura	6	4	2	2	2	2
Quisenberry (L)	2	4	4	4	1	0
Philadelphia						
Carlton (W)	8	10	4	3	6	10
Reed (S)	1	1	0	0	0	2

a Doubled for Smith in 8th.
b Grounded into double play for Maddox in 8th.
c Struck out for Chalk in 9th.

Doubles—Maddox, Otis, Unser, Schmidt. Stolen Bases—Wilson, Chalk, Sacrifice Hit—Washington. Sacrifice Flies—Trillo, Wathan. Wild Pitch—Carlton. Double Plays—Bowa to Trillo to Rose 3, Washington to White to Aikens, Maddox to Rose to Schmidt, Washington to White to LaCock. Left on Bases—Kansas City 11, Philadelphia 3. Umpires—Kunkel, Pryor, Denkinger, Rennert, Bremigan, Wendelstedt. Attendance—65,775. Time of Game—3:01.

1st Inning
Kansas City
1 Wilson struck out, but was thrown out Boone to Rose.
2 Washington grounded to short.
Brett bounced a single to center.
McRae singled to right, Brett stopping at second.
3 Otis forced McRae, Schmidt to Trillo.
Philadelphia
1 Smith flied to center.
2 Rose flied to center.
3 McBride popped to third.

2nd Inning
Kansas City
1 Wathan popped to first.
Aikens walked.
2 Cardenal took a called third strike.
White struck out but was safe on a wild pitched third strike, Aikens stopping at second.
3 Wilson struck out swinging.
Philadelphia
1 Schmidt grounded to third.
2 Moreland lined to left.
3 Maddox struck out swinging.

3rd Inning
Kansas City
1 Washington took a called third strike.
Brett singled to right.
McRae singled to left, Brett going to second.
2,3 Otis grounded into a double play, Bowa to Trillo to Rose.
Philadelphia
1 Trillo flied to center.
2 Bowa fouled to Brett.
3 Boone flied to center.

4th Inning
Kansas City
1 Wathan flied to right.
Aikens singled to center.
2,3 Cardenal grounded into a double play, Bowa to Trillo to Rose.
Philadelphia
1 Smith struck out swinging.
2 Rose lined to center.
3 McBride lined to second.

5th Inning
Kansas City
1 White grounded to short.
2 Wilson struck out swinging.
Washington singled to center.
Brett walked on four pitches.
3 McRae struck out swinging.
Philadelphia
1 Schmidt grounded to third.
Moreland singled to deep short.
Maddox doubled into the left field corner, Moreland stopping at third.
2 Trillo hit a sacrifice fly to right, scoring Moreland with Maddox going to third after the catch.
Bowa lined a single to left, scoring Maddox.
Boone walked.
3 Smith flied to right.

6th Inning
Kansas City
Otis lined a single to center.
Wathan walked on four pitches.
Aikens safe on Trillo's throwing error, Otis scoring and Wathan getting to third.
1 Cardenal struck out swinging.
2,3 White hit into a double play, Bowa to Trillo to Rose.

6th Inning (continued)
Philadelphia
For Kansas City—Chalk playing third.
1 Rose flied to right.
McBride walked on a full count.
Schmidt singled to center, McBride stopping at second.
2,3 Moreland grounded into a double play, Washington to White to Aikens.

7th Inning
Kansas City
Wilson walked on four pitches.
1 Washington sacrified Wilson to second, Carlton to Trillo covering.
Wilson stole third.
Chalk walked.
Chalk stole second with Wilson holding third.
McRae walked, loading the bases.
Otis doubled down the left field line, scoring Wilson and Chalk as McRae stopped at third.
2 Wathan hit a sacrifice fly to center, McRae scoring after the catch, but Otis
3 was out at third, Maddox to Rose to Schmidt.
Philadelphia
For Kansas City—Quisenberry replaced Gura on the mound.
1 Maddox grounded to third.
2 Trillo grounded to short.
3 Bowa grounded to second.

8th Inning
Kansas City
1 Aikens struck out swinging.
2 Cardenal flied to deep right.
White grounded a single to left.
Wilson lined a single off of Rose's glove, White stopping at second.
3 Washington struck out swinging.
Philadelphia
For Kansas City—LaCock playing first.
Boone walked on a full count.
Unser, batting for Smith, lined a double to left-center, scoring Boone.
1 Rose grounded to first, Unser advancing to third.
McBride singled to right, scoring Unser.
Schmidt doubled to wall in right-center, scoring McBride, and took third on the play at the plate.
Moreland lined a single to center, scoring Schmidt.
2,3 Gross, pinch-hitting for Maddox, hit into a double play, Washington to White to LaCock.

9th Inning
Kansas City
For Philadelphia—Unser playing left, Gross playing center, Reed pitching.
1 Porter, pinch-hitting for Chalk, was called out on strikes.
McRae bounced a single to center.
2 Otis forced McRae at second, Bowa to Trillo.
3 Wathan struck out swinging.

Game 3 October 17 at Kansas City

Phil.	010	010	010	0
K.C.	100	100	100	1

Philadelphia	Pos	AB	R	H	RBI	PO	A	E
Smith	lf	4	0	2	1	0	0	0
b Gross	lf	0	0	0	0	0	0	0
Rose	1b	4	0	1	1	11	0	0
Schmidt	3b	5	1	1	1	3	3	0
McBride	rf	5	0	2	0	1	0	0
Moreland	dh	5	0	1	0	0	0	0
Maddox	cf	4	0	1	0	3	0	0
Trillo	2b	5	1	2	0	2	6	0
Bowa	ss	5	1	3	0	1	3	0
Boone	c	4	0	1	0	8	1	0
Ruthven	p	0	0	0	0	0	0	0
McGraw	p	0	0	0	0	0	0	0
Totals		41	3	14	3	29	13	0

Kansas City	Pos	AB	R	H	RBI	PO	A	E
Wilson	lf	4	1	0	0	3	0	0
White	2b	5	0	0	0	4	2	0
Brett	3b	4	1	2	1	0	3	0
Aikens	1b	5	1	2	1	7	1	0
McRae	dh	4	0	2	1	0	0	0
Otis	cf	4	1	2	1	9	0	0
Hurdle	rf	4	0	2	0	1	0	0
a Concepcion		0	0	0	0	0	0	0
Cardenal	rf	0	0	0	0	0	0	0
Porter	c	4	0	0	0	4	0	0
Washington	ss	4	0	1	0	1	2	0
Gale	p	0	0	0	0	0	1	0
Martin	p	0	0	0	0	0	0	0
Quisenberry	p	0	0	0	0	1	1	0
Totals		38	4	11	4	30	10	0

Pitching	IP	H	R	ER	BB	SO
Philadelphia						
Ruthven	9	9	3	3	0	7
McGraw (L)	$\frac{2}{3}$	2	1	1	2	1
Kansas City						
Gale	$4\frac{1}{3}$	7	2	2	3	3
Martin	$3\frac{1}{3}$	5	1	1	1	1
Quisenberry (W)	$2\frac{1}{3}$	2	0	0	2	0

a Ran for Hurdle in 9th.
b Sacrificed for Smith in 10th.

Doubles—Trillo, Brett. Triple—Aikens. Home Runs—Brett, Schmidt, Otis. Stolen Bases—Hurdle, Bowa, Wilson, Sacrifice Hit—Gross. Double Plays—White to Washington to Aikens, Bowa to Trillo to Rose, White (unassisted). Left on Bases—Philadelphia 15, Kansas City 7. Umpires—Pryor, Denkinger, Rennert, Bremigan, Wendelstedt, Kunkel. Attendance—42,380. Time of Game—3:19.

1st Inning
Philadelphia
Smith singled to right.
1 Rose struck out on a foul tip.
Schmidt walked on a full count.
2 McBride flied to left.
3 Moreland flied to center.
Kansas City
1 Wilson grounded to second.
2 White grounded to third.
Brett homered into the right field seats on a 1-1 count.
3 Aikens grounded to second.

2nd Inning
Philadelphia
1 Maddox grounded to third.
Trillo singled off Gale's foot.
Bowa singled to right, Bowa stopping at second.
Boone walked, loading the bases.
2 Smith lined back to Gale who threw him out at first, scoring Trillo.
Rose walked to again load the bases.
3 Schmidt flied to center
Kansas City
1 McRae fouled to Rose.
Otis beat out a hit to short.
2 Hurdle forced Otis at second, Bowa to Trillo.
3 Porter forced Hurdle at second, Bowa unassisted.

3rd Inning
Philadelphia
McBride singled to right.
1 Moreland called out on strikes.
2 Maddox forced McBride at second, Brett to White.
Trillo doubled down the right field line, Maddox advancing to third.
3 Bowa grounded to third.
Kansas City
1 Washington lined to Maddox in short left-center.
2 Wilson struck out swinging.
3 White grounded to third.

4th Inning
Philadelphia
1 Boone flied to center.
2 Smith flied to center.
3 Rose grounded to second.
Kansas City
1 Brett fouled to Schmidt.
Aikens tripled to left when Smith missed a diving catch.
McRae lined a single to right-center, scoring Aikens.
2 Otis grounded to second, McRae advancing to second.
3 Hurdle grounded to second.

5th Inning
Philadelphia
Schmidt hit a 2-1 pitch into the left field bullpen for a home run.
1 McBride took a called third strike.
Moreland singled to left.
For Kansas City—Martin now pitching.
Maddox singled to short, Moreland stopping at second.
2,3 Trillo grounded into a double play, White to Washington to Aikens.
Kansas City
1 Porter grounded to second.
2 Washington flied to center.
3 Wilson struck out swinging, his 7th of Series in only the 3rd game.

6th Inning
Philadelphia
Bowa singled to center.
1 Boone flied to center.
Smith singled to center, Bowa stopping at second.
2 Rose struck out swinging.
3 Schmidt forced Smith at second, Washington to White
Kansas City
1 White struck out swinging.
2 Brett flied to center.
3 Aikens struck out swinging.

7th Inning
Philadelphia
1 McBride flied to center.
2 Moreland flied to center.
3 Maddox flied to right.
Kansas City
1 McRae grounded to third.
Otis hit a 1-1 pitch over the right field fence for a home run.
Hurdle singled to right.
2 Porter struck out swinging, as Hurdle stole second.
3 Washington fouled to Schmidt.

8th Inning
Philadelphia
1 Trillo flied to left.
Bowa beat out a roller to the mound.
2 Boone flied to center.
Bowa stole second.
Smith walked.
Rose singled to right-center, scoring Bowa with Smith advancing to third.
For Kansas City—Quisenberry came in to pitch.
3 Schmidt flied to center. **A World Series record for Otis with 9 put outs.**
Kansas City
1 Wilson grounded to short.
2 White struck out swinging.
Brett lined a double to right-center.
3 Aikens took a called third strike.

9th Inning
Philadelphia
McBride singled to left.
1 Moreland flied to deep left, McBride going to second after the catch.
Maddox intentionally walked.
2 Trillo grounded out Aikens to Quisenberry, covering first as both runners moved up.
3 Bowa bounced out back to the mound.
Kansas City
McRae singled to left.
1,2 Otis grounded into a double play, Bowa to Trillo to Rose.
Hurdle beat out a hit to short.
Concepcion running for Hurdle.
3 Porter flied to right.

10th Inning
Philadelphia
For Kansas City—Cardenal playing right.
Boone singled to center.
1 Gross, batting for Smith, sacrificed Boone to second, Aikens unassisted.
Rose intentionally walked.
2,3 Schmidt lined to White, stepping on second to double up Boone.
Kansas City
For Philadelphia—Gross stayed in to play left as McGraw came in to pitch.
Washington singled to left.
Wilson walked.
1 Washington out stealing, Boone to Schmidt.
2 White struck out swinging.
Wilson stole second.
Brett intentionally walked.
Aikens singled to left-center, Wilson scoring the game-ending run.

Game 4 October 18 at Kansas City

Philadelphia	Pos	AB	R	H	RBI	PO	A	E
Smith	dh	4	0	0	0	0	0	0
Rose	1b	4	1	2	0	8	2	0
McBride	rf	3	0	1	0	3	0	0
Schmidt	3b	3	0	1	1	2	0	0
Unser	lf	4	0	1	0	1	0	0
Maddox	cf	4	0	1	0	2	0	0
Trillo	2b	4	2	1	0	0	6	0
Bowa	ss	4	0	2	1	1	1	0
Boone	c	3	0	1	1	6	0	0
Christenson	p	0	0	0	0	0	0	1
Noles	p	0	0	0	0	1	0	0
Saucier	p	0	0	0	0	0	0	0
Brusstar	p	0	0	0	0	0	0	0
Totals		33	3	10	3	24	9	1

Pitching	IP	H	R	ER	BB	SO
Philadelphia						
Christenson (L)	1/3	5	4	4	0	0
Noles	4 2/3	5	1	1	2	6
Saucier	2/3	0	0	0	2	0
Brusstar	2 1/3	0	0	0	1	0
Kansas City						
Leonard (W)	*7	9	3	2	1	2
Quisenberry (S)	2	1	0	0	0	0

*Pitched to one batter in 8th.

Phil.	010	000	110
K.C.	410	000	00x

Kansas City	Pos	AB	R	H	RBI	PO	A	E
Wilson	lf	4	1	1	0	4	0	0
White	2b	5	0	0	0	2	4	1
Brett	3b	5	1	1	1	0	7	0
Aikens	1b	3	2	2	3	13	0	0
McRae	dh	4	1	2	0	0	0	0
Otis	cf	4	0	2	1	1	0	0
Hurdle	rf	2	0	1	0	3	0	0
Porter	c	3	0	0	0	2	1	0
Washington	ss	4	0	1	0	2	3	1
Leonard	p	0	0	0	0	0	0	0
Quisenberry	p	0	0	0	0	0	0	0
Totals		34	5	10	5	27	15	2

Doubles—McRae 2, Otis, Hurdle, McBride, Trillo, Rose. Triple—Brett. Home Runs—Aikens 2. Stolen Base—Bowa. Sacrifice Flies—Boone, Schmidt, Wild Pitches—Leonard, Saucier, Double Play—Brett to White to Aikens. Left on Bases—Philadelphia 6, Kansas City 10. Umpires—Denkinger, Rennert, Bremigan, Wendelstedt, Kunkel, Pryor. Attendance—42,363. Time of Game—2:37.

1st Inning
Philadelphia
1 Smith grounded to third.
Rose singled to White and went to second when White threw past Aikens.
2 McBride flied to left.
3 Schmidt struck out swinging.
Kansas City
Wilson singled to left.
Wilson went to third when Christenson's pickoff throw went past Rose.
1 White flied to shallow right.
Brett tripled down the right-field line, scoring Wilson.
Aikens hit an 0-1 pitch into the right field waterfall for a 2-run homer.
McRae doubled to center.
Otis doubled off the wall in right-center, scoring McRae.
For Philadelphia—Noles came in to pitch.
Hurdle walked on four pitches.
2 Porter struck out swinging.
Washington beat out a grounded to Bowa, loading the bases.
3 Wilson grounded out, Rose to Noles on a very close play.

2nd Inning
Philadelphia
1 Unser flied to left.
Maddox singled to right.
2 Trillo forced Maddox, White to Washington and went to second on Washington's throwing error to first.
Bowa singled to left, scoring Trillo and advances to second on the throw to the plate.
3 Boone grounded to third.
Kansas City
1 White flied to center.
2 Brett grounded to second.
Aikens hit a 2-1 pitch deep into the right field bullpen for his second homer of the game and fourth of the Series.
McRae doubled to right-center.
3 Otis flied to right.

3rd Inning
Philadelphia
1 Smith grounded to third.
2 Rose flied to left.
McBride walked.
3 McBride out trying to steal second, Porter to White
Kansas City
Hurdle doubled to left.
1 Porter fouled out to Schmidt.
2 Washington grounded to second, Hurdle advancing to third.
3 Wilson struck out.

4th Inning
Philadelphia
Schmidt beat out a bunt.
1 Unser flied to center.
2 Maddox grounded to Aikens, who tagged him, advancing Schmidt to second.
3 Trillo flied to right.
Kansas City
1 White fouled to Rose.
2 Brett struck out.
3 Aikens struck out swinging.

5th Inning
Philadelphia
1 Bowa flied to right.
Boone singled to center.
2,3 Smith hit into a double play, Brett to White to Aikens
Kansas City
1 McRae struck out swinging.
Otis singled up the middle.
Hurdle walked on a full count.
2 Porter took a called third strike.
3 Washington fouled to Schmidt.

6th Inning
Philadelphia
1 Rose grounded to third.
McBride doubled off the left-center field wall.
2 Schmidt grounded to third, McBride holding at second.
McBride went to third on a wild pitch.
3 Unser struck out swinging.
Kansas City
For Philadelphia—Saucier pitching.
Wilson walked.
1 White flied to right.
2 Brett flied to left.
Wilson went to second on a wild pitch.
Aikens walked.
For Philadelphia—Brusstar replaced Saucier on the mound.
3 McRae forced Aikens, Rose to Bowa.

7th Inning
Philadelphia
1 Maddox popped to short.
Trillo doubled to the right field wall.
Bowa singled to left, Trillo stopping at third.
2 Boone hit a sacrifice fly to deep left-center, caught on a fine play by Wilson, Trillo scoring after the catch.
Bowa stole second.
3 Smith grounded to short.
Kansas City
1 Otis flied to center.
2 Hurdle grounded to second.
Porter walked.
3 Washington grounded to second.

8th Inning
Philadelphia
Rose doubled to the left field wall.
For Kansas City—Quisenberry came in to pitch.
1 McBride grounded to second, Rose running to third.
2 Schmidt hit a sacrifice fly to deep right, scoring Rose.
Unser singled to right.
3 Maddox grounded to short.
Kansas City
1 Wilson grounded to short.
2 White grounded to second.
3 Brett grounded to second.

9th Inning
Philadelphia
1 Trillo grounded to third.
2 Bowa grounded to second.
3 Boone grounded to short.

Game 5 October 19 at Kansas City

Philadelphia	Pos	AB	R	H	RBI	PO	A	E
Rose	1b	4	0	0	0	7	1	0
McBride	rf	4	1	0	0	2	1	0
Schmidt	3b	4	2	2	2	1	1	0
Luzinski	lf	2	0	0	0	1	0	0
a Smith	lf	0	0	0	0	0	0	0
c Unser	lf	1	1	1	1	0	0	0
Moreland	dh	3	0	1	0	0	0	0
Maddox	cf	4	0	0	0	2	0	0
Trillo	2b	4	0	1	1	3	5	0
Bowa	ss	4	0	1	0	0	2	0
Boone	c	3	0	1	0	10	0	0
Bystrom	p	0	0	0	0	1	1	0
Reed	p	0	0	0	0	0	0	0
McGraw	p	0	0	0	0	0	1	0
Totals		33	4	7	4	27	12	0

Pitching	IP	H	R	ER	BB	SO
Philadelphia						
Bystrom	*5	10	3	3	1	4
Reed	1	1	0	0	0	0
McGraw (W)	3	1	0	0	4	5
Kansas City						
Gura	6 1/3	4	2	1	1	2
Quisenberry (L)	2 2/3	3	2	2	0	0

*Pitched to three batters in 6th.

Phil.	000	200	002
K.C.	000	012	000

Kansas City	Pos	AB	R	H	RBI	PO	A	E
Wilson	lf	5	0	2	0	2	0	0
White	2b	3	0	0	0	2	6	0
Brett	3b	5	0	1	1	1	2	1
Aikens	1b	3	0	1	0	10	1	1
d Concepcion		0	0	0	0	0	0	0
McRae	dh	5	0	1	0	0	0	0
Otis	cf	3	1	2	1	3	0	0
Hurdle	rf	3	1	1	0	3	0	0
b Cardenal	rf	2	0	0	0	0	0	0
Porter	c	4	0	2	0	2	0	0
Washington	ss	3	1	2	1	2	2	0
Gura	p	0	0	0	0	2	4	0
Quisenberry	p	0	0	0	0	0	0	0
Totals		36	3	12	3	27	15	2

a Ran for Luzinski in 7th.
b Flied out for Hurdle in 7th.
c Doubled for Smith in 9th.
d Ran for Aikens in 9th.

Doubles—Wilson, McRae, Unser. Home Runs—Schmidt, Otis. Stolen Base—Brett. Sacrifice Hits—White, Moreland. Sacrifice Fly—Washington. Double Plays—White to Aikens to Gura, Gura to Aikens. Left on Bases—Philadelphia 4, Kansas City 13. Umpires—Rennert, Bremigan, Wendelstedt, Kunkel, Pryor, Dinkinger. Attendance—42,369. Time of Game—2:51.

1st Inning
Philadelphia
1 Rose bounced back to the mound.
2 McBride flied to center.
3 Schmidt flied to left.
Kansas City
1 Wilson struck out swinging.
2 White grounded out, Rose to Bystrom.
Brett singled to right.
Brett stole second.
3 Aikens called out on strikes.

2nd Inning
Philadelphia
1 Luzinski took a called third strike.
2 Moreland flied to right.
3 Maddox called out on strikes.
Kansas City
1 McRae grounded off of Bystrom's glove to Trillo who threw to Rose.
2 Otis struck out swinging.
3 Hurdle grounded to short.

3rd Inning
Philadelphia
1 Trillo flied to center.
Bowa singled to center.
2,3 Boone flied to White in shallow right with an over-the-shoulder catch. He threw to Aikens who threw to Gura at first to double up Bowa.
Kansas City
Porter singled to right.
Washington bunted to Schmidt and got a single when no one covered first.
1 Wilson flied to center.
2 White popped to second.
3 Brett grounded to second.

4th Inning
Philadelphia
1 Rose grounded off Gura's glove to White who threw to Aikens for the out.
McBride safe on Aikens' error on a throw by Gura.
Schmidt homered on a 2-2 pitch over the wall in deep right-center.
2 Luzinski grounded to third.
3 Morehead popped to third.
Kansas City
Aikens singled to center.
1 McRae flied to right.
Otis singled to left, McRae stopping at second.
2 Hurdle struck out swinging.
3 Porter lined to Rose.

5th Inning
Philadelphia
1 Maddox flied to left.
2 Trillo lined to right.
3 Bowa flied to Otis in deep left-center.
Kansas City
Washington singled to center.
Wilson singled to the left of Schmidt, Washington advancing to second.
1 White sacrificed up both runners, Schmidt to Trillo, covering first.
2 Brett grounded to second, Washington scoring and Wilson going to third.
Aikens walked.
3 McRae fouled to McBride against the wall in deep right.

6th Inning
Philadelphia
Boone singled to right-center.
1,2 Rose lined to Gura who threw to Aikens to double up Boone.
3 McBride foul popped to Washington.

6th Inning (continued)
Kansas City
Otis homered over the wall in left.
Hurdle singled to right-center.
Porter singled to right, Hurdle advancing to third.
For Philadelphia—Reed on the mound.
1 Washington hit a sacrifice fly to left, Hurdle scoring after the catch.
Wilson doubled off the wall in right,
2 but Porter was out trying to score, McBride to Trillo to Boone.
3 White fouled to Schmidt.

7th Inning
Philadelphia
1 Schmidt flied to right.
Luzinski walked on a full count.
Smith ran for Luzinski.
Moreland safe on a deep hit to short as the force at second failed.
For Kansas City—Quisenberry relieved Gura on the mound.
2 Maddox forced Moreland at second, Washington to White, Smith to third.
3 Trillo forced Maddox, White to Washington
Kansas City
For Philadelphia—Smith stays in to play left with McGraw now pitching.
1 Brett struck out swinging.
2 Aikens called out on strikes.
McRae doubled to the left field corner.
Otis intentionally walked.
3 Cardenal, batting for Hurdle, flied to center.

8th Inning
Philadelphia
For Kansas City—Cardenal stays in to play right field.
1 Bowa grounded to second.
Boone got safely to second on Brett's throwing error.
2 Rose grounded to second, Boone advancing to third.
3 McBride grounded to second.
Kansas City
1 Porter grounded to second.
2 Washington struck out swinging.
3 Wilson bounced back to the pitcher.

9th Inning
Philadelphia
Schmidt singled off Brett's glove.
Unser, pinch-hitting for Smith, doubled down the right field line, scoring Schmidt.
1 Moreland sacrificed Unser to third, tagged out by Aikens.
2 Maddox grounded to third, Unser holding.
Trillo singled off Quisenberry's glove, scoring Unser.
3 Bowa grounded to short.
Kansas City
For Philadelphia—Unser in left.
White walked.
1 Brett took a called third strike.
Aikens walked on four pitches.
Concepcion ran for Aikens.
2 McRae forced Concepcion at second, Bowa to Trillo, White advancing to third.
Otis walked on four pitches, loading the bases.
3 Cardenal struck out.

Game 6 October 21 at Philadelphia

K.C.	000 000 010
Phil.	002 011 00x

Kansas City	Pos	AB	R	H	RBI	PO	A	E
Wilson	lf	4	0	0	0	3	0	0
Washington	ss	3	0	1	1	2	4	0
Brett	3b	4	0	2	0	1	1	0
McRae	dh	4	0	0	0	0	0	0
Otis	cf	3	0	0	0	2	0	0
Aikens	1b	2	0	0	0	6	0	1
a Concepcion		0	0	0	0	0	0	0
Wathan	c	3	1	2	0	4	1	0
Cardenal	rf	4	0	2	0	4	0	0
White	2b	4	0	0	0	2	1	1
Gale	p	0	0	0	0	0	0	0
Martin	p	0	0	0	0	0	0	0
Splittorff	p	0	0	0	0	0	1	0
Pattin	p	0	0	0	0	0	0	0
Quisenberry	p	0	0	0	0	0	0	0
Totals		31	1	7	1	24	8	2

a Ran for Aikens in 9th.

Doubles—Maddox, Smith, Bowa.
Sacrifice Fly—Washington. Double
Plays—Bowa to Trillo to Rose, Bowa
to Rose, Splittorff to Washington to
Aikens. Left on Bases—Kansas City 9,
Philadelphia 7. Umpires—Bremigan,
Wendelstedt, Kunkel, Pryor, Denkinger,
Rennert. Attendance—65,838. Time of
Game—3:00.

Philadelphia	Pos	AB	R	H	RBI	PO	A	E
Smith	lf	4	2	1	0	1	0	0
Gross	lf	0	0	0	0	0	0	0
Rose	1b	4	0	3	0	9	0	0
Schmidt	3b	3	0	1	2	0	0	0
McBride	rf	4	0	1	1	2	0	0
Luzinski	dh	4	0	0	0	0	0	0
Maddox	cf	4	0	2	0	1	0	0
Trillo	2b	4	0	0	0	2	3	0
Bowa	ss	4	1	1	0	3	3	0
Boone	c	2	1	1	1	9	1	0
Carlton	p	0	0	0	0	0	2	0
McGraw	p	0	0	0	0	0	0	0
Totals		33	4	9	4	27	9	0

Pitching	IP	H	R	ER	BB	SO
Kansas City						
Gale (L)	*2	4	2	1	1	1
Martin	2⅓	1	1	1	1	0
Splittorff	**1⅓	4	1	1	0	0
Pattin	1	0	0	0	0	2
Quisenberry	1	0	0	0	0	0
Philadelphia						
Carlton (W)	***7	4	1	1	3	7
McGraw (SV)	2	3	0	0	2	2

*Pitched to four batters in 3rd.
**Pitched to one batter in 7th.
***Pitched to two batters in 8th.

1st Inning
Kansas City
1 Wilson took a called third strike.
2 Washington struck out swinging.
3 Brett grounded to second.
Philadelphia
1 Smith grounded to second.
  Rose singled to left.
2 Schmidt popped to short.
3 McBride lined to shallow left.

2nd Inning
Kansas City
1 McRae flied to short right.
  Otis walked on a full count.
  Aikens walked on a full count.
2,3 Wathan hit into a double play,
  Bowa to Trillo to Rose.
Philadelphia
1 Luzinski struck out swinging.
  Maddox doubled to right-center.
2 Trillo flied to right, Maddox
  going to third after the catch.
3 Bowa foul popped to Wathan.

3rd Inning
Kansas City
1 Cardenal flied to Smith in deep
  left-center.
2 White struck out swinging.
3 Wilson struck out swinging on three
  pitches.
Philadelphia
  Boone walked on four pitches.
  Smith safe on White's throwing error,
  which pulled Washington off of the bag.
  Rose beat out a bunt down the third
  base line, loading the bases.
  Schmidt singled to right center, scoring
  Boone and Smith with Rose advancing to
  third.
  For Kansas City—Martin replaced Gale
  on the mound.
1 McBride fouled to White.
2 Luzinski lined to third.
3 Maddox flied to right.

4th Inning
Kansas City
  Washington singled deep in the hole.
1,2 Brett grounded into a double play,
  Bowa to Rose.
3 McRae grounded to short.
Philadelphia
1 Trillo popped to Wilson behind second.
2 Bowa grounded to third.
3 Boone flied to shallow right.

5th Inning
Kansas City
1 Otis struck out swinging.
2 Aikens took a called third strike.
  Wathan singled up the middle.
3 Cardenal popped to Trillo in right.
Philadelphia
  Smith doubled on a grounder to left-
  center.
1 Rose flied to deep center, Smith going
  to third after the catch.
  Schmidt walked.
  For Kansas City—Splittorff replaced
  Martin on the mound.
2 McBride topped a roller to Washington,
  Smith scoring with Schmidt advancing
  to second.
3 Luzinski grounded to short.

6th Inning
Kansas City
1 White popped to short.
2 Wilson bunted to Carlton.
3 Washington struck out.
Philadelphia
  Maddox lined a single to left.
1,2 Trillo grounded into a double play,
  Splittorff to Washington to Aikens.
  Bowa doubled over Wilson's head in left.
  Boone lined a single to center,
  scoring Bowa.
3 Smith flied to Otis in right-center.

7th Inning
  For Philadelphia—Gross playing left.
  Brett singled to right.
1 McRae fouled to Bowa.
2 Otis flied to very deep right.
3 Aikens grounded back to the pitcher.
Philadelphia
  Rose singled off Brett's glove.
  For Kansas City—Pattin now pitching.
1 Rose out trying to steal second,
  Wathan to White.
2 Schmidt called out on strikes.
  McBride safe on Aikens' bad throw
  to Pattin.
3 Luzinski called out on strikes.

8th Inning
Kansas City
  Wathan walked.
  Cardenal singled to left, moving
  Wathan to second.
  For Philadelphia—McGraw relieved
  Carlton on the mound.
1 White fouled to Rose.
  Wilson walked to load the bases.
2 Washington hit a sacrifice fly to
  center, scoring Wathan as the other
  runners held.
  Brett beat out a one-hopper to again
  load the bases.
3 McRae grounded to second.
Philadelphia
  For Kansas City—Quisenberry pitching.
1 Maddox fouled to Wilson.
2 Trillo grounded to short.
3 Bowa flied to right.

9th Inning
Kansas City
1 Otis called out on strikes.
  Aikens walked on a full count.
  Concepcion running for Aikens.
  Wathan singled to right, Concepcion
  stopping at second.
  Cardenal lined a single to center,
  loading the bases.
2 White foul popped in front of the Phillie
  dugout, the ball popping out of Boone's
  glove to Rose.
3 Wilson struck out—**a World Series record
  of 12 strikeouts.**

1980 WORLD SERIES COMPOSITE BOX

	Wins	Composite Line Score
Philadelphia Phillies (NL)	4	0 2 7 3 5 1 1 6 2 0 - 27
Kansas City Royals (AL)	2	5 3 2 1 1 3 4 3 0 1 - 23

Manager	Regular Season W	L	Pct.	G. Ahead
Dallas Green	91	71	.562	1
Jim Frey	97	65	.599	14

BATTING AND FIELDING

PHILADELPHIA PHILLIES

WORLD SERIES STATISTICS

Player	Pos	G	AB	R	H	2B	3B	HR	RBI	BB	SO	SB	BA	SA	PO	A	E
Pete Rose	1b	6	23	2	6	1	0	0	1	2	2	0	.261	.304	49	6	0
Manny Trillo	2b	6	23	4	5	2	0	0	2	0	0	0	.217	.304	14	**25**	1
Larry Bowa	ss	6	24	3	9	1	0	0	2	0	0	**3**	.375	.417	5	18	0
Mike Schmidt	3b	6	21	**6**	8	1	0	2	7	4	3	0	.381	.714	9	8	0
Bake McBride	rf	6	23	3	7	1	0	1	5	2	1	0	.304	.478	13	1	0
Garry Maddox	cf	6	22	1	5	2	0	0	1	1	3	0	.227	.318	11	1	0
Lonnie Smith	lf-pr-dh	6	19	2	5	1	0	0	1	1	1	0	.263	.316	4	1	0
Bob Boone	c	6	17	3	7	2	0	0	4	4	0	0	.412	.529	49	3	0
Greg Luzinski	dh-lf	3	9	0	0	0	0	0	0	1	5	0	.000	.000	1	0	0
Keith Moreland	dh	3	12	1	4	0	0	0	1	0	1	0	.333	.333	—	—	—
Del Unser	ph-cf-lf	3	6	2	3	2	0	0	2	0	1	0	.500	.833	1	0	0
Greg Gross	ph-lf	4	2	0	0	0	0	0	0	0	0	0	.000	.000	1	0	0
Ramon Aviles		Did not play															
George Vukovich		Did not play															
John Vukovich		Did not play															
Steve Carlton	p	2	0	0	0	0	0	0	0	0	0	0	—	—	0	3	0
Dick Ruthven	p	1	0	0	0	0	0	0	0	0	0	0	—	—	0	0	0
Tug McGraw	p	4	0	0	0	0	0	0	0	0	0	0	—	—	0	1	0
Bob Walk	p	1	0	0	0	0	0	0	0	0	0	0	—	—	2	0	0
Marty Bystrom	p	1	0	0	0	0	0	0	0	0	0	0	—	—	1	1	0
Dickie Noles	p	1	0	0	0	0	0	0	0	0	0	0	—	—	1	0	0
Warren Brusstar	p	1	0	0	0	0	0	0	0	0	0	0	—	—	0	0	0
Ron Reed	p	2	0	0	0	0	0	0	0	0	0	0	—	—	0	0	0
Kevin Saucier	p	1	0	0	0	0	0	0	0	0	0	0	—	—	0	0	0
Larry Christenson	p	1	0	0	0	0	0	0	0	0	0	0	—	—	0	0	1
team total		6	201	27	59	13	0	3	26	15	17	3	.294	.403	161	68	2

Double Plays—8
Left on Bases—41

REGULAR SEASON STATISTICS

Player	Main Pos	G	AB	R	H	2B	3B	HR	RBI	BB	SO	SB	BA	SA
Pete Rose	1b	162	655	95	185	**42**	1	1	64	66	33	12	.282	.354
Manny Trillo	2b	141	531	68	155	25	9	7	43	32	46	8	.292	.412
Larry Bowa	ss	147	540	57	144	16	4	2	39	24	28	21	.267	.322
Mike Schmidt	3b	150	548	104	157	25	8	**48**	**121**	89	119	12	.286	**.624**
Bake McBride	of	137	554	68	171	33	10	9	87	26	58	13	.309	.453
Garry Maddox	of	143	549	59	142	31	3	11	73	18	52	25	.259	.386
Lonnie Smith	of	100	298	69	101	14	4	3	20	26	48	33	.339	.443
Bob Boone	c	141	480	34	110	23	1	9	55	48	41	3	.229	.338
Greg Luzinski	of	106	368	44	84	19	1	19	56	60	100	3	.228	.440
Keith Moreland	c	62	159	13	50	8	0	4	29	8	14	3	.314	.440
Del Unser	ph-1b-of	96	110	15	29	6	4	0	10	10	21	0	.264	.391
Greg Gross	of	127	154	19	37	7	2	0	12	24	7	1	.240	.312
Ramon Aviles	ss	51	101	12	28	6	0	2	9	10	9	0	.277	.396
George Vukovich	of	78	58	6	13	1	1	0	8	6	9	0	.224	.276
John Vukovich	3b	49	62	4	10	1	1	0	5	2	7	0	.161	.210
Steve Carlton	p	38	101	7	19	1	0	0	6	1	21	0	.188	.198
Dick Ruthven	p	33	68	7	16	5	1	0	8	2	22	1	.235	.338
Tug McGraw	p	57	8	0	2	0	0	0	1	0	2	0	.250	.250
Bob Walk	p	27	50	5	7	1	0	0	2	4	20	0	.140	.160
Marty Bystrom	p	6	14	1	1	0	0	0	1	1	9	0	.071	.071
Dickie Noles	p	48	13	1	4	0	0	0	2	0	5	0	.308	.308
Warren Brusstar	p	26	1	0	0	0	0	0	0	0	1	0	.000	.000
Ron Reed	p	55	10	0	3	1	0	0	0	0	2	0	.300	.400
Kevin Saucier	p	40	8	0	0	0	0	0	0	0	4	0	.000	.000
Larry Christenson	p	14	19	6	7	0	0	1	4	3	9	0	.368	.526
team total		162	**5625**	728	1517	272	54	117	674	472	708	140	.270	.400

Luis Aguayo (2b), Jay Loviglio (2b), Bob Dernier (of), Tim McCarver (ph), Orlando Isales (of), Don McCormack (c), Ossie Virgil (c), Randy Lerch (p), Nino Espinosa (p), Sparky Lyle (p), Scott Munninghoff (p), Mark Davis (p), Lerrin LaGrow (p) and Dan Larson (p) also played for the Phillies during the season.

KANSAS CITY ROYALS

WORLD SERIES STATISTICS

Player	Pos	G	AB	R	H	2B	3B	HR	RBI	BB	SO	SB	BA	SA	PO	A	E
Willie Aikens	1b	6	20	5	8	0	**1**	**4**	**8**	**6**	8	0	.400	**1.100**	**55**	2	**2**
Frank White	2b	6	25	0	2	0	0	0	0	1	5	1	.080	.080	13	21	**2**
U. L. Washington	ss	6	22	1	6	0	0	0	2	0	6	0	.273	.273	8	20	1
George Brett	3b	6	24	3	9	2	**1**	1	3	2	4	1	.375	.667	4	17	1
Clint Hurdle	rf	4	12	1	5	1	0	0	0	2	1	1	.417	.500	8	0	0
Amos Otis	cf	6	23	4	**11**	2	0	3	7	3	3	0	**.478**	.957	21	0	0
Willie Wilson	lf	6	**26**	3	4	1	0	0	0	4	**12**	2	.154	.192	15	1	0
Darrell Porter	c-ph	5	14	1	2	0	0	0	0	3	4	0	.143	.143	13	2	0
Hal McRae	dh	6	24	3	9	**3**	0	0	1	2	2	0	.375	.500	—	—	—
Jose Cardenal	ph-rf	4	10	0	2	0	0	0	0	0	3	0	.200	.200	7	0	0
John Wathan	ph-rf-c	3	7	1	2	0	0	0	1	2	1	0	.286	.286	7	1	0
Onix Concepcion	pr	3	0	0	0	0	0	0	0	0	0	0	—	—	—	—	—
Dave Chalk	3b	1	0	1	0	0	0	0	0	1	0	1	—	—	0	1	0
Pete LaCock	1b	1	0	0	0	0	0	0	0	0	0	0	—	—	2	0	0
Rance Mulliniks		Did not play															
Jamie Quirk		Did not play															
Larry Gura	p	2	0	0	0	0	0	0	0	0	0	0	—	—	2	4	0
Dennis Leonard	p	2	0	0	0	0	0	0	0	0	0	0	—	—	0	0	1
Dan Quisenberry	p	6	0	0	0	0	0	0	0	0	0	0	—	—	1	1	0
Renie Martin	p	3	0	0	0	0	0	0	0	0	0	0	—	—	0	0	0
Rich Gale	p	2	0	0	0	0	0	0	0	0	0	0	—	—	0	1	0
Paul Splittorff	p	1	0	0	0	0	0	0	0	0	0	0	—	—	0	1	0
Marty Pattin	p	1	0	0	0	0	0	0	0	0	0	0	—	—	0	0	0
Ken Brett		Did not play															
Jeff Twitty		Did not play															
team total		6	207	23	60	9	2	8	22	26	49	6	.290	.469	156	72	7

Double Plays—8
Left on Bases—54

REGULAR SEASON STATISTICS

Player	Main Pos	G	AB	R	H	2B	3B	HR	RBI	BB	SO	SB	BA	SA
Willie Aikens	1b	151	543	70	151	24	0	20	98	64	88	1	.278	.433
Frank White	2b	154	560	70	148	23	4	7	60	19	69	19	.264	.357
U. L. Washington	ss	153	549	79	150	16	11	6	53	53	78	20	.273	.375
George Brett	3b	117	449	87	175	33	9	24	118	58	22	15	**.390**	**.664**
Clint Hurdle	of	130	395	50	116	31	2	10	60	34	61	0	.294	.458
Amos Otis	of	107	394	56	99	16	3	10	53	39	70	16	.251	.383
Willie Wilson	of	161	**705**	**133**	**230**	28	**15**	3	49	28	81	79	.326	.421
Darrell Porter	c	118	418	51	104	14	2	7	51	69	50	1	.249	.342
Hal McRae	dh	124	489	73	145	39	5	14	83	29	56	10	.297	.483
Jose Cardenal (a)	of	25	53	8	18	2	0	0	5	5	5	0	.340	.377
John Wathan	c-of	126	453	57	138	14	7	6	58	50	42	17	.305	.406
Onix Concepcion	ss	12	15	1	2	0	0	0	2	0	1	0	.133	.133
Dave Chalk	ss-2b	69	167	19	42	10	1	1	20	18	27	1	.251	.341
Pete LaCock	1b	114	156	14	32	6	0	1	18	17	10	1	.205	.263
Rance Mulliniks	ss-2b	36	54	8	14	3	0	0	6	7	10	0	.259	.315
Jamie Quirk	3b	62	163	13	45	5	0	5	21	7	24	3	.276	.399
Larry Gura	p	36	0	0	0	0	0	0	0	0	0	0	—	—
Dennis Leonard	p	38	0	0	0	0	0	0	0	0	0	0	—	—
Dan Quisenberry	p	75	0	0	0	0	0	0	0	0	0	0	—	—
Renie Martin	p	32	0	0	0	0	0	0	0	0	0	0	—	—
Rich Gale	p	32	0	0	0	0	0	0	0	0	0	0	—	—
Paul Splittorff	p	34	0	0	0	0	0	0	0	0	0	0	—	—
Marty Pattin	p	37	0	0	0	0	0	0	0	0	0	0	—	—
Ken Brett	p	8	0	0	0	0	0	0	0	0	0	0	—	—
Jeff Twitty	p	13	0	0	0	0	0	0	0	0	0	0	—	—
team total		162	**5714**	809	**1633**	266	**59**	115	766	508	709	**185**	**.286**	.413

a—from N.Y. Mets.

Rusty Torres (of), Jerry Terrell (util.), Bobby Detherage (of), Steve Braun (of), Manny Castillo (3b), German Barranca (pr), Ken Phelps (1b), Steve Busby (p), Rawley Eastwick (p), Craig Chamberlain (p), and Mike Jones (p) also played for the Royals during the season.

PITCHING

PHILADELPHIA PHILLIES

WORLD SERIES STATISTICS

Player	G	GS	CG	IP	H	R	ER	BB	SO	W	L	SV	ERA
Steve Carlton	2	**2**	0	**15**	**14**	5	4	**9**	**17**	**2**	0	0	2.40
Dick Ruthven	1	1	0	9	9	3	3	0	7	0	0	0	3.00
Tug McGraw	4	0	0	$7\frac{2}{3}$	7	1	1	8	10	1	1	**2**	1.17
Bob Walk	1	1	0	7	8	6	6	3	3	1	0	0	7.71
Marty Bystrom	1	1	0	5	10	3	3	1	4	0	0	0	5.40
Dickie Noles	1	0	0	$4\frac{2}{3}$	5	1	1	2	6	0	0	0	1.93
Warren Brusstar	1	0	0	$2\frac{1}{3}$	0	0	0	1	0	0	0	0	0.00
Ron Reed	2	0	0	2	2	0	0	0	2	0	0	1	0.00
Kevin Saucier	1	0	0	$\frac{2}{3}$	0	0	0	2	0	0	0	0	0.00
Larry Christenson	1	1	0	$\frac{1}{3}$	5	4	4	0	0	0	1	0	108.00
team total	6	6	0	$53\frac{2}{3}$	60	23	22	26	49	4	2	3	3.69

REGULAR SEASON STATISTICS

Player	G	GS	CG	IP	H	ER	BB	SO	W	L	Pct	SV	ShO	ERA
Steve Carlton	38	**38**	13	**304**	243	79	90	**286**	**24**	9	.727	0	3	2.34
Dick Ruthven	33	33	6	223	241	88	74	86	17	10	.630	0	1	3.55
Tug McGraw	57	0	0	92	62	15	23	75	5	4	.556	20	0	1.47
Bob Walk	27	27	2	152	163	77	71	94	11	7	.611	0	0	4.56
Marty Bystrom	6	5	1	36	26	6	9	21	5	0	1.000	0	1	1.50
Dickie Noles	48	3	0	81	80	35	42	57	1	4	.200	6	0	3.89
Warren Brusstar	26	0	0	39	42	16	13	21	2	2	.500	0	0	3.69
Ron Reed	55	0	0	91	88	41	30	54	7	5	.583	9	0	4.05
Kevin Saucier	40	0	0	50	50	19	20	25	7	3	.700	0	0	3.42
Larry Christenson	14	14	0	74	62	33	27	49	5	1	.833	0	0	4.01
team total	162	162	25	1480	1419	564	530	889	91	71	.562	40	8	3.43

KANSAS CITY ROYALS

WORLD SERIES STATISTICS

Player	G	GS	CG	IP	H	R	ER	BB	SO	W	L	SV	ERA
Larry Gura	2	**2**	0	$12\frac{1}{3}$	8	4	3	3	4	0	0	0	**2.19**
Dennis Leonard	2	**2**	0	$10\frac{2}{3}$	15	**9**	**8**	2	5	1	1	0	6.75
Dan Quisenberry	**6**	0	0	$10\frac{1}{3}$	10	6	6	3	0	1	**2**	1	5.23
Renie Martin	3	0	0	$9\frac{2}{3}$	11	3	3	3	2	0	0	0	2.79
Rich Gale	2	**2**	0	$6\frac{1}{3}$	11	4	3	4	4	0	1	0	4.26
Paul Splittorff	1	0	0	$1\frac{2}{3}$	4	1	1	0	0	0	0	0	5.40
Marty Pattin	1	0	0	1	0	0	0	0	2	0	0	0	0.00
Ken Brett	Did not play												
Jeff Twitty	Did not play												
team total	6	6	0	52	59	27	24	15	17	2	4	1	4.15

REGULAR SEASON STATISTICS

Player	G	GS	CG	IP	H	ER	BB	SO	W	L	Pct	SV	ShO	ERA
Larry Gura	36	36	16	283	272	93	76	113	18	10	.643	0	4	2.96
Dennis Leonard	38	**38**	9	280	271	**118**	80	155	20	11	.645	0	3	3.79
Dan Quisenberry	**75**	0	0	128	129	44	27	37	12	7	.632	**33**	0	3.09
Renie Martin	32	20	2	137	133	67	70	68	10	10	.500	2	0	4.40
Rich Gale	32	28	6	191	169	83	78	97	13	9	.591	1	1	3.91
Paul Splittorff	34	33	4	204	236	94	43	53	14	11	.560	0	0	4.15
Marty Pattin	37	0	0	89	97	36	23	40	4	0	1.000	4	0	3.64
Ken Brett	8	0	0	13	8	0	5	4	0	0	.000	1	0	0.00
Jeff Twitty	13	0	0	22	33	15	7	9	2	1	.667	0	0	6.14
team total	162	162	37	1459	1496	621	465	614	97	65	.599	42	10	3.83

Total Attendance—324,516 Average Attendance—54,086 Winning Player's Share—$34,693. Losing Players Share—$32,212

1981
Despite Everything, It Mattered

The Yankees and Dodgers crackled with tradition, opponents now for the eleventh time. But tradition had been trashed this summer by a two-month players' strike. When play resumed in August, fans welcomed the return of baseball ambivalently and fumed with angry resentment. To compensate for the gutted schedule, the owners set up playoffs capped by a World Series that had hung in the balance all summer.

The Dodgers got here by beating Houston and Montreal in the playoffs. Manager Tom Lasorda had bolstered his strong hitting and pitching with two young players. Pedro Guerrero moved into the starting lineup with his steady bat, and on the mound, Fernando Valenzuela was the talk of the country with his prestrike heroics. His cool use of a wicked screwball won his first eight games, five of them by shutout. The Mexican rookie cemented the L.A. rotation and won the Cy Young Award.

The Yankees relied more on experience and a feisty attitude. Team owner George Steinbrenner added outfielder Dave Winfield to the squad with a contract worth $21 million over 10 years. The Yanks had a strong lineup, terrific left-handed starting pitchers, and premier reliever Goose Gossage.

In the Series opener, the Yanks jumped out to a 5–1 lead after seven innings in New York. The Dodgers made their move in the eighth. In relief of Ron Guidry, Ron Davis walked the first two batters. Gossage came in and immediately yielded a run-scoring single to Jay Johnstone. A sacrifice fly made the score 5–3 with one out and one man on. Steve Garvey then ripped a shot down the third-base line that Graig Nettles miraculously speared in a headlong dive. The catch ended the Dodger threat. The next night, Tommy John and Gossage combined for a four-hitter, which put the Dodgers at a two-game deficit heading back to L.A.

Two rookies started game three, Valenzuela and Dave Righetti. Both began unsteadily. Ron Cey bopped a three-run home run in the bottom of the first, while New York scored twice in the second. A two-run shot by Rick Cerone in the third put the Yankees ahead 4–3. Valenzuela settled down after that and allowed no further scoring. Los Angeles went to the offense in the fifth against reliever George Frazier. After Garvey led off with a single, Cey walked. Guerrero then doubled Garvey home. Frazier walked Monday intentionally, then left in favor of Rudy May. Mike Scioscia hit into a double play, but the go-ahead run scored. When the Yankees threatened in the eighth, a diving grab of a bunt by Cey broke the rally.

The Dodgers pulled even the next day. The Yankees led 6–3 in the middle of the sixth. In the bottom of the sixth, Johnstone pinch-hit a two-run homer off reliever Davis. Dave Lopes then lofted a fly ball to right. Reggie Jackson, sidelined by a calf injury in the first three games, played it into a two-base error. Bill Russell cashed in with a game-tying single. With the score 6–6, Frazier was back on the mound for New York in the seventh. Dusty Baker reached on an infield hit. Monday then popped into short right-center field, only to reach second base when Bobby Brown misplayed the ball. Frazier once again issued an intentional pass and departed. Tommy John came into this urgent situation and allowed two runs on a sacrifice fly, a sacrifice bunt, and a scratch single. A solo home run by Jackson in the eighth couldn't change the outcome.

The Yankees suffered more in game five. Guidry nursed a 1–0 lead into the seventh, only to give up back-to-back homers by Guerrero and Yeager. Reuss pitched all the way for the 2–1 victory, which brought L.A. to the verge of the title. After the game, Steinbrenner got into a brawl with two fans in a hotel elevator, then left for New York with his left hand in a cast.

The Yankees tried to stem the tide with John on the mound. The score was knotted at 1–1 in the fourth when the Yankees put two men on base. Lemon decided to pinch-hit for John despite the early inning. The Yankees did not score, then turned to the star-crossed Frazier for relief. The Dodgers immediately scored three in the fifth and four in the sixth to clinch the title.

Game 1 October 20 at New York

Los Angeles	Pos	AB	R	H	RBI	PO	A	E
Lopes	2b	3	1	0	0	3	1	0
Russell	ss	3	0	0	0	2	1	0
c Johnstone		1	0	1	1	0	0	0
Stewart	p	0	0	0	0	0	0	0
Baker	lf	2	0	1	1	3	0	0
Garvey	1b	4	0	1	0	5	0	0
Cey	3b	4	0	1	0	0	1	0
Guerrero	cf	3	0	0	0	3	0	0
Monday	rf	4	0	0	0	4	0	0
Yeager	c	3	1	1	1	3	0	0
d Landreaux		1	0	0	0	0	0	0
Reuss	p	1	0	0	0	0	1	0
Castillo	p	0	0	0	0	0	2	0
Goltz	p	0	0	0	0	0	0	0
a Sax		1	0	0	0	0	0	0
Niedenfuer	p	0	0	0	0	0	0	0
b Thomas	ss	0	1	0	0	1	1	0
Totals		30	3	5	3	24	7	0

Pitching	IP	H	R	ER	BB	SO
Los Angeles						
Reuss (L)	2⅔	5	4	4	0	2
Castillo	1	0	1	1	5	0
Goltz	⅓	0	0	0	0	0
Niedenfuer	3	1	0	0	0	0
Stewart	1	0	0	0	1	0
New York						
Guidry (W)	7	4	1	1	2	6
Davis	*0	0	2	2	2	0
Gossage (SV)	2	1	0	0	0	2

*Pitched to two batters in 8th.

New York	Pos	AB	R	H	RBI	PO	A	E
Randolph	2b	3	0	0	0	3	3	0
Mumphrey	cf	3	2	2	0	3	0	0
Winfield	lf	3	0	1	0	1	0	0
Piniella	rf	4	1	2	1	4	0	0
Watson	1b	3	1	2	3	8	0	0
Nettles	3b	3	0	0	1	1	3	0
Cerone	c	3	0	0	0	8	0	0
Milbourne	ss	4	1	0	0	0	2	0
Guidry	p	2	0	0	0	0	0	0
Davis	p	0	0	0	0	0	0	0
Gossage	p	0	0	0	0	0	0	0
Totals		28	5	6	5	27	9	0

a Flied out for Goltz in 5th.
b Walked for Niedenfuer in 8th.
c Singled for Russell in 8th.
d Grounded out for Yeager in 9th.

Double—Piniella. Home Runs—Yeager, Watson. Stolen Bases—Mumphrey, Piniella. Sacrifice Hit—Guidry. Sacrifice Fly—Baker. Passed Ball—Cerone. Double Play—Thomas to Garvey. Left on Bases—Los Angeles—5, New York—6. Umpires—Barrett, Colosi, Cooney, Harvey, Garcia, Stello. Attendance—56,470. Time of Game—2:32.

L.A. 000 010 020
N.Y. 301 100 00x

1st Inning
Los Angeles
1 Lopes grounded to third.
2 Russell grounded to short.
3 Baker popped to second
New York
1 Randolph grounded to second. Mumphrey singled to right.
2 Winfield struck out swinging. Piniella lined a ground-rule double down the right field line, Mumphrey taking third. Watson hit a 3-run home run to right-center on a 1-2 pitch.
3 Nettles flied to deep right.

2nd Inning
Los Angeles
Garvey lined a single off of Nettle's glove.
1 Cey popped to first.
2 Guerrero struck out swinging.
3 Monday struck out swinging.
New York
1 Cerone grounded to short.
2 Milbourne bounced back to the pitcher.
3 Guidry struck out swinging.

3rd Inning
Los Angeles
1 Yeager struck out swinging.
2 Reuss struck out swinging.
3 Lopes grounded to short.
New York
1 Randolph grounded to first. Mumphrey lined a single to center.
2 Winfield flied to Baker in deep left-center. Mumphrey stole second. Piniella singled to left, scoring Mumphrey. For Los Angeles—Castillo came in to pitch. Piniella stole second. Watson walked on four pitches.
3 Nettles flied to right.

4th Inning
Los Angeles
1 Russell grounded to third. Baker lined a single to left.
2 Garvey flied to deep center.
3 Cey flied to right.
New York
Cerone walked on four pitches.
1 Milbourne forced Cerone at second, Castillo to Russell.
2 Guidry sacrificed Milbourne to second, Castillo to Lopes covering first. Randolph walked on a full count. Mumphrey walked on four pitches, loading the bases. Winfield walked forcing in Milbourne. For Los Angeles—Goltz relieved Castillo
3 Piniella popped to second.

5th Inning
Los Angeles
1 Guerrero flied to deep center.
2 Monday grounded to second. Yeager homered to right on the first pitch. A towering blast.
3 Sax, pinch-hitting for Goltz, flied to center.

5th Inning (continued)
New York
For Los Angeles—Niedenfuer now on the mound.
Watson lined a single to right.
1 Nettles flied to right.
2 Cerone popped to short.
3 Milbourne forced Watson at second, Cey to Lopes

6th Inning
Los Angeles
1 Lopes grounded to second.
2 Russell flied to right. Baker walked.
3 Garvey struck out swinging.
New York
1 Guidry flied to center.
2 Randolph flied to deep left.
3 Mumphrey flied to left.

7th Inning
Los Angeles
Cey lined a single down the left field
1 line but was out trying for second, Winfield to Randolph. Guerrero walked.
2 Monday struck out swinging.
3 Yeager flied to right.
New York
1 Winfield popped foul to Yeager.
2 Piniella flied to deep center.
3 Watson flied to right.

8th Inning
Los Angeles
For New York—Davis relieved Guidry. Thomas, pinch-hitting for Niedenfuer, walked. Thomas went to second on a passed ball. Lopes walked on four pitches. For New York—Gossage relieved Davis. Johnstone, pinch-hitting for Russell, lined a single to right, scoring Thomas with Lopes going to third.
1 Baker hit a sacrifice fly to right, scoring Lopes.
2 Garvey lined to Nettles, making a super dive.
3 Cey forced Johnstone at second, Nettles to Randolph.
New York
For Los Angeles—Thomas stays in playing short with Stewart the new pitcher.
Nettles walked on a full count.
1 Cerone flied to center
2,3 Milbourne grounded into a double play, Thomas to Garvey.

9th Inning
Los Angeles
1 Guerrero struck out swinging on a full count.
2 Monday took a called third strike.
3 Landreaux, pinch-hitting for Yeager, grounded to second.

Game 2 October 21 at New York

Los Angeles	Pos	AB	R	H	RBI	PO	A	E
Lopes	2b	3	0	0	0	7	3	1
e Monday		1	0	0	0	0	0	0
Howe	p	0	0	0	0	0	0	1
Stewart	p	0	0	0	0	0	0	0
Russell	ss	4	0	1	0	0	5	0
Baker	lf	4	0	0	0	0	0	0
Garvey	1b	3	0	2	0	6	0	0
Cey	3b	4	0	0	0	0	3	0
Guerrero	rf	4	0	0	0	4	0	0
Landreaux	cf	3	0	0	0	4	0	0
Yeager	c	2	0	0	0	1	0	0
b Johnstone		1	0	0	0	0	0	0
Scioscia	c	0	0	0	0	1	0	0
Hooton	p	2	0	0	0	0	1	0
Forster	p	0	0	0	0	0	1	0
c Smith		1	0	1	0	0	0	0
d Sax	2b	0	0	0	0	0	0	0
Totals		32	0	4	0	24	12	2

Pitching	IP	H	R	ER	BB	SO
Los Angeles						
Hooton (L)	*6	3	1	0	4	1
Forster	1	0	0	0	1	0
Howe	⅓	2	2	2	0	0
Stewart	⅔	1	0	0	1	1
New York						
John (W)	7	3	0	0	0	4
Gossage (SV)	2	1	0	0	1	3

*Pitched to two batters in 7th.

L.A.	000 000 000
N.Y.	000 010 02x

New York	Pos	AB	R	H	RBI	PO	A	E
Mumphrey	cf	2	0	0	0	1	0	0
Milbourne	ss	4	0	1	1	1	3	1
Winfield	lf	4	0	0	0	1	0	0
Gamble	rf	2	0	0	0	2	0	0
f Piniella		1	0	1	0	0	0	0
g Brown	rf	0	1	0	0	0	0	0
Nettles	3b	4	1	2	0	1	5	0
Watson	1b	4	0	2	1	13	0	0
Cerone	c	2	0	0	0	7	0	0
Randolph	2b	2	1	0	1	1	3	0
John	p	1	0	0	0	0	2	0
a Murcer		0	0	0	0	0	0	0
Gossage	p	1	0	0	0	0	0	0
Totals		27	3	6	3	27	13	1

a Sacrificed for John in 7th.
b Flied out for Yeager in 8th.
c Singled for Forster in 8th.
d Ran for Smith in 8th.
e Struck out for Lopes in 8th.
f Singled for Gamble in 8th.
g Ran for Piniella in 8th.

Double—Milbourne. Sacrifice Hits—John, Murcer. Sacrifice Fly—Randolph. Double Play—Russell to Lopes to Garvey. Left on Bases—Los Angeles 6, New York 9. Umpires—Colosi, Cooney, Harvey, Garcia, Stello, Barnett. Attendance—56,505. Time of Game—2:29.

1st Inning
Los Angeles
1 Lopes lined to center.
2 Russell grounded to second.
3 Baker grounded to second.
New York
Mumphrey walked.
1 Milbourne forced Mumphrey at second, Russell to Lopes.
2 Winfield forced Milbourne at second, Cey to Lopes.
Gamble walked.
3 Nettles took a called third strike.

2nd Inning
Los Angeles
1 Garvey grounded to third.
2 Cey grounded to third.
3 Guerrero grounded to short.
New York
Watson lined a single to right.
1 Cerone flied to right.
2 Randolph forced Watson at second, Cey to Lopes.
3 John grounded to second.

3rd Inning
Los Angeles
1 Landreaux grounded back to the pitcher.
2 Yeager grounded to short.
3 Hooton struck out swinging on 3 pitches.
New York
1 Mumphrey flied to right.
2 Milbourne flied to center.
3 Winfield grounded to short.

4th Inning
Los Angeles
1 Lopes grounded to second.
2 Russell grounded to short.
3 Baker struck out swinging.
New York
1 Gamble popped to second.
Nettles lined a single to left.
2 Watson forced Nettles at second, Cey to Lopes.
3 Cerone forced Watson at second, Russell to Lopes.

5th Inning
Los Angeles
Garvey grounded a single to center.
1 Cey grounded to third, Garvey moving to second.
Guerrero safe on Milbourne's throwing error, Garvey going to third.
2 Landreaux struck out swinging.
3 Yeager lined off John's glove and was thrown out by John.
New York
Randolph safe on Lopes' error.
1 John sacrificed Randolph to second, Hooton unassisted.
2 Mumphrey flied to center.
Milbourne doubled down the left field line, scoring Randolph.
3 Winfield grounded to second.

6th Inning
Los Angeles
1 Horton struck out swinging.
2 Lopes grounded to third.
Russell singled down the left field line.
3 Baker forced Russell at second, Nettles to Randolph.
New York
1 Gamble flied to center.
2 Nettles flied to right.
3 Watson grounded to short.

7th Inning
Los Angeles
Garvey singled to left.
1 Cey flied to deep right.
2 Guerrero lined to short.
3 Landreaux flied to left.
New York
Cerone walked.
Randolph walked on four pitches.
Murcer pinch-hitting for John.
For Los Angeles—Forster now on mound.
1 Murcer sacrificed up both runners, Forster to Garvey.
Mumphrey was intentionally walked.
2,3 Milbourne hit into a double play, Russell to Lopes to Garvey.

8th Inning
Los Angeles
For New York—Gossage came in to pitch.
1 Johnstone, batting for Yeager, flied to deep right.
Smith, batting for Forster, singled to right.
Sax ran for Smith.
2 Monday, pinch-hitting for Lopes, struck out swinging.
3 Russell popped foul to Nettles.
New York
For Los Angeles—Scioscia catching, Sax stays in to play second and Howe now pitching.
1 Winfield flied to center.
Piniella, batting for Gamble, lined a single to center.
Brown ran for Piniella.
Nettles looped a single to center, Brown stopping at second.
Watson singled to left, scoring Brown with Nettles stopping at second.
Both runners advanced when Stewart threw a pick-off attempt to second into center field.
Cerone intentionally walked, loading the bases.
2 Randolph hit a sacrifice fly to deep right, scoring Nettles.
3 Gossage struck out on three pitches.

9th Inning
Los Angeles
For New York—Brown stays in playing right field.
1 Baker grounded to first.
Garvey walked on a full count.
2 Cey took a called third strike.
3 Guerrero also called out on strikes.

Game 3 October 23 at Los Angeles

New York	Pos	AB	R	H	RBI	PO	A	E
Randolph	2b	2	0	0	0	5	3	0
Mumphrey	cf	5	0	0	0	2	0	0
Winfield	lf	3	0	0	0	2	0	0
Piniella	rf	5	1	2	1	0	0	0
Watson	1b	4	1	2	1	9	0	0
Cerone	c	4	2	2	1	5	1	0
Rodriguez	3b	4	0	2	0	1	3	0
Milbourne	ss	3	0	2	1	2	4	0
Righetti	p	1	0	0	0	0	0	0
Frazier	p	1	0	0	0	0	0	0
May	p	0	0	0	0	0	0	0
c Murcer		1	0	0	0	0	0	0
Davis	p	0	0	0	0	0	0	0
Totals		32	4	9	3	24	11	0

Pitching	IP	H	R	ER	BB	SO
New York						
Righetti	*2	5	3	3	2	1
Frazier (L)	**2	3	2	2	2	1
May	3	2	0	0	0	2
Davis	1	1	0	0	0	1
Los Angeles						
Valenzuela (W)	9	9	4	4	7	6

*Pitched to two batters in 3rd.
**Pitched to four batters in 5th.

N.Y.	022 000 000
L.A.	300 020 00x

Los Angeles	Pos	AB	R	H	RBI	PO	A	E
Lopes	2b	4	1	2	0	7	3	1
Russell	ss	5	1	2	0	3	0	0
Baker	lf	4	0	0	0	2	0	0
Garvey	1b	4	1	2	0	7	1	0
Cey	3b	2	2	2	3	2	3	0
Guerrero	cf-rf	3	0	1	1	0	0	0
Monday	rf	2	0	1	0	0	0	0
b Thomas	cf	1	0	0	0	0	0	0
Yeager	c	1	0	0	0	2	0	0
a Scioscia	c	3	0	1	0	4	1	0
Valenzuela	p	3	0	0	0	0	1	0
Totals		32	5	11	4	27	12	1

a Grounded out for Yeager in 3rd.
b Hit into double play for Monday in 7th.
c Bunted into double play for May in 8th.

Doubles—Lopes, Cerone, Watson, Guerrero. Home Runs—Cey, Watson, Cerone. Sacrifice Hits—Righetti, Lopes. Hit by Pitcher—Guerrero (by Righetti). Double Plays—Randolph to Watson, Milbourne to Randolph to Watson, Russell to Lopes to Garvey, Cey to Lopes. Left on Bases—New York 9, Los Angeles 9. Umpires—Cooney, Harvey, Garcia, Stello, Barnett, Colosi. Attendance—56,236. Time of Game—3:04.

1st Inning
New York
Randolph walked on a full count.
1 Mumphrey forced Randolph, Cey to Lopes.
Winfield walked on four pitches.
2,3 Piniella grounded into a double play, Russell to Lopes to Garvey.
Los Angeles
Lopes doubled down the left field line.
Russell bunted for a single, Lopes going to third.
1 Baker popped to second.
2 Garvey struck out swinging.
Cey hit a three-run home run to left on a 2-2 pitch.
Guerrero was hit by a pitch.
Monday had an infield single to deep first, Guerrero advancing to third.
3 Yeager popped to first.

2nd Inning
New York
Watson homered to center on an 0-1 pitch.
Cerone lined a double off the left field fence, nearly a home run.
1 Rodriguez flied to right, Cerone advancing to third after the catch.
Milbourne lined a single to right, scoring Cerone.
2 Righetti sacrificed Milbourne to second, Garvey to Lopes.
Randolph walked.
3 Mumphrey grounded to the pitcher.
Los Angeles
Valenzuela walked.
1 Lopes sacrificed Valenzuela to second, Cerone to Randolph.
2 Russell grounded to second, Valenzuela going to third.
3 Baker popped to first.

3rd Inning
New York
1 Winfield struck out swinging.
Piniella lined a single to center.
2 Watson popped to second.
Cerone hit a two-run home run to left-center on a 1-0 pitch.
Rodriguez beat out an infield hit and got to second on Lopes' throwing error.
Milbourne walked intentionally.
3 Righetti struck out swinging.
Los Angeles
Garvey singled to center.
Cey walked.
For New York—Frazier relieved Righetti on the mound.
1 Guerrero struck out swinging.
2 Monday flied to left.
3 Scioscia, batting for Yeager, grounded to short.

4th Inning
New York
For Los Angeles—Scioscia catching.
1 Randolph grounded to short.
2 Mumphrey grounded to second.
Winfield walked on a full count.
3 Piniella lined to left.
Los Angeles
1 Valenzuela grounded to short.
2 Lopes grounded to third.
Russell singled to left.
3 Baker forced Russell at second, Rodriguez to Randolph.

5th Inning
New York
Watson hit a ground rule double down the right field line.
1 Cerone struck out swinging.
2 Rodriguez grounded to second, Watson advancing to third.
Milbourne walked intentionally.
3 Frazier struck out swinging on three pitches.
Los Angeles
Garvey chopped a single to deep third.
Cey walked on a full count.
Guerrero doubled over third, scoring Garvey as Cey stopped at third.
Monday intentionally walked, loading the bases.
For New York—May relieved Frazier.
1,2 Scioscia hit into a double play, Randolph to Watson, with Cey scoring and Guerrero going to third.
3 Valenzuela grounded to short.

6th Inning
New York
Randolph walked on a full count.
1 Randolph caught attempting to steal second, Scioscia to Lopes.
2 Mumphrey took a called third strike.
3 Winfield grounded to third.
Los Angeles
Lopes lined a single to left.
1 Russell flied to left.
2 Baker struck out swinging.
3 Garvey popped foul to Rodriguez.

7th Inning
New York
1 Piniella flied to right.
2 Watson flied to left.
3 Cerone popped to second.
Los Angeles
Cey lined a single to center.
1 Guerrero struck out swinging.
2,3 Thomas, pinch-hitting for Monday, hit into a double play, Milbourne to Randolph to Watson.

8th Inning
New York
For Los Angeles—Guerrero moved to right as Thomas stayed in playing center.
Rodriguez lined a single to left.
Milbourne singled off Lopes' glove, Rodriguez going to second.
1,2 Murcer, batting for May, popped a foul bunt to Cey who threw to Garvey doubling up Milbourne.
3 Randolph grounded to Cey, who put out Rodriguez unassisted.
Los Angeles
For New York—Davis now pitching.
Scioscia singled to right.
1 Valenzuela forced Scioscia at second, Rodriguez to Milbourne.
2 Lopes struck out on a foul tip held by Cerone.
3 Russell popped to short.

9th Inning
New York
1 Mumphrey grounded to second.
2 Winfield flied to Guerrero.
3 Piniella struck out swinging.

Game 4 October 24 at Los Angeles

N.Y.	2	1	1	0	0	2	0	1	0
L.A.	0	0	2	0	1	3	2	0	x

New York	Pos	AB	R	H	RBI	PO	A	E
Randolph	2b	5	3	2	1	2	2	0
Milbourne	ss	4	1	1	1	1	3	0
Winfield	cf-lf	4	0	0	0	4	0	0
Jackson	rf	3	2	3	1	2	0	1
Gamble	lf	4	1	2	1	2	0	0
c Brown	cf	0	0	0	0	1	0	0
f Piniella	lf	1	0	0	0	1	0	0
Watson	1b	3	0	1	2	5	0	0
Cerone	c	5	0	2	1	7	0	0
h Robertson		0	0	0	0	0	0	0
Rodriguez	3b	4	0	2	0	0	3	0
g Foote		1	0	0	0	0	0	0
Reuschel	p	2	0	0	0	0	0	0
May	p	1	0	0	0	0	1	0
Davis	p	0	0	0	0	0	0	0
Frazier	p	1	0	0	0	0	0	0
John	p	0	0	0	0	0	0	0
i Murcer		1	0	0	0	0	0	0
Totals		39	7	13	7	24	7	1

Los Angeles	Pos	AB	R	H	RBI	PO	A	E
Lopes	2b	5	2	2	2	5	2	0
Russell	ss	5	0	1	1	2	5	1
Garvey	1b	5	1	3	0	5	1	0
Cey	3b	5	0	2	2	1	5	0
Baker	lf	5	1	1	0	4	0	0
Monday	rf	3	1	1	0	2	0	0
Thomas	cf	1	0	0	0	3	0	0
Guerrero	cf-rf	3	0	2	0	2	1	0
Scioscia	c	1	1	0	0	2	0	0
e Yeager	c	0	0	0	1	1	0	0
Welch	p	0	0	0	0	0	0	0
Goltz	p	0	0	0	0	0	0	0
a Landreaux		1	1	1	0	0	0	0
Forster	p	0	0	0	0	0	0	0
b Smith		1	0	0	0	0	0	0
Niedenfuer	p	0	0	0	0	0	0	0
d Johnstone		1	1	1	2	0	0	0
Howe	p	0	0	0	0	0	1	1
Totals		36	8	14	8	27	11	2

Pitching New York	IP	H	R	ER	BB	SO
Reuschel	**3	6	2	2	1	2
May	1⅓	2	1	1	0	1
Davis	1	2	3	1	2	1
Frazier (L)	***⅔	2	2	2	1	0
John	2	2	0	0	0	2

Los Angeles	IP	H	R	ER	BB	SO
Welch	*0	3	2	2	1	0
Goltz	3	4	2	2	1	2
Forster	1	1	0	0	2	0
Niedenfuer	2	2	2	2	1	0
Howe (W)	3	3	1	1	0	1

*Pitched to four batters in 1st.
**Pitched to two batters in 4th.
***Pitched to three batters in 7th.

a Doubled for Goltz in 3rd.
b Struck out for Forster in 4th.
c Ran for Gamble in 6th.
d Hit home-run for Niedenfuer in 6th.
e Hit sacrifice fly for Scioscia in 7th.
f Grounded out for Brown in 8th.
g Struck out for Rodriguez in 9th.
h Ran for Cerone in 9th.
i Reached on error for John in 9th.

Doubles—Milbourne, Landreaux, Garvey,
Monday. Triple—Randolph. Home
Runs—Randolph, Johnstone, Jackson.
Stolen Bases—Lopes 2, Winfield.
Sacrifice Hits—Milbourne, Scioscia,
Howe. Sacrifice Flies—Watson, Yeager.
Left on Bases—New York 12, Los
Angeles—10. Umpires—Harvey, Garcia,
Stello, Barnett, Colosi, Cooney.
Attendance—56,242. Time of Game—3:32.

1st Inning

New York
Randolph lined a triple down the right field line.
Milbourne doubled down the right field line, scoring Randolph.
Winfield walked.
Jackson lined a single to left to load the bases.
For Los Angeles—Goltz relieved Welch.
1 Gamble flied to center, the runners holding.
2 Watson hit a sacrifice fly to left, scoring Milbourne.
3 Cerone forced Jackson at second, Lopes unassisted.

Los Angeles
1 Lopes grounded to third.
2 Russell grounded to third.
Garvey lined a single to right.
3 Cey lined to center.

2nd Inning

New York
1 Rodriguez struck out swinging.
2 Reuschel took a called third strike.
Randolph hit a home run to right-center.
3 Milbourne grounded to second.

Los Angeles
1 Baker lined to short.
2 Monday lined to left.
Guerrero blooped a single to center.
3 Scioscia lined to left.

3rd Inning

New York
1 Winfield grounded to second.
Jackson singled to center.
2 Gamble forced Jackson at second, Russell to Lopes.
Watson walked.
Cerone singled to left, scoring Gamble with Watson stopping at second.
Rodriguez singled to deep short, loading the bases.
3 Reuschel forced Rodriguez at second, Russell to Lopes.

Los Angeles
Landreaux, pinch-hitting for Goltz, doubled inside the first base line.
Lopes lined a single to right, scoring Landreaux.
Lopes stole second.
1 Russell took a called third strike.
Garvey beat out a roller to third, Lopes advancing to third.
2 Cey grounded to short, scoring Lopes with Garvey going to second.
3 Baker struck out swinging.

4th Inning

New York
For Los Angeles—Forster on the mound.
Randolph walked on a full count.
1 Milbourne sacrificed Randolph to second, Cey to Lopes covering first.
2 Winfield safe on a fielder's choice when Randolph went out Russell to Cey.
Winfield stole second.
Jackson walked on a full count.
Gamble grounded a single to deep second, loading the bases.
3 Watson forced Gamble at second, Russell to Lopes.

Los Angeles
Monday walked on four pitches.
Guerrero singled to left, Monday stopping at second.
For New York—May relieved Reuschel.
1 Scioscia sacrificed up both runners, May to Randolph covering first.
2 Smith, pinch-hitting for Forster, struck out swinging on three pitches.
3 Lopes grounded to short.

5th Inning

New York
For Los Angeles—Niedenfuer pitching.
1 Cerone flied to center.
2 Rodriguez popped to short.
3 May fouled to Baker.

Los Angeles
1 Russell flied to right.
Garvey doubled down the left field line.
Cey singled to left, scoring Garvey.
For New York—Davis replaced May.
2 Baker called out on strikes.
3 Monday struck out swinging.

6th Inning

New York
Randolph safe on Russell's throwing error.
1 Milbourne fouled to Baker.
2 Winfield flied to deep left, Randolph taking second after the catch.
Jackson intentionally walked.
Gamble lined a single to right-center, scoring Randolph with Jackson advancing to third.
Watson lined a single to left, scoring Jackson, Gamble going to third.
Brown ran for Gamble.
3 Cerone flied to right.

Los Angeles
For New York—Brown playing center with Winfield moving to left.
1 Guerrero flied to center.
Scioscia walked.
Johnstone, batting for Niedenfuer, blasted a two-run homer to right-center.
Lopes was safe at second when Jackson dropped his fly down the right field line.
Lopes stole third.
Russell lined a single to left, scoring Lopes.
For New York—Frazier relieved Davis.
2 Garvey flied to left.
3 Cey flied to left.

7th Inning

New York
For Los Angeles—Howe on the mound.
Rodriguez singled to left-center, but
1 was out trying to take second, Guerrero to Russell.
2 Frazier grounded to first.
3 Randolph flied to right.

Los Angeles
Baker beat out a slow roller to short.
Monday blooped a double to center, Baker taking third.
Guerrero intentionally walked, loading the bases.
For New York—John relieved Frazier.
1 Yeager, pinch-hitting for Scioscia, hit a sacrifice fly to right, scoring Baker.
2 Howe sacrificed up both runners, Rodriguez to Randolph covering first.
Lopes beat out a high chopper to third, scoring Monday with Guerrero advancing to third.
3 Russell grounded to short.

8th Inning

New York
For Los Angeles—Yeager catching, Guerrero moved to right as Thomas came in and went to center.
1 Milbourne lined to center.
2 Winfield flied to deep center.
Jackson hit a home run to right-center, his third hit of the game.
3 Piniella, pinch-hitting for Gamble, grounded to the pitcher.

Los Angeles
For New York—Piniella stays in to play left with Winfield moving back to center.
1 Garvey struck out swinging.
Cey lined a single to right.
2 Baker flied to center.
3 Thomas struck out swinging.

9th Inning

New York
1 Watson grounded to short, Garvey making the tag after being pulled off the bag.
Cerone singled to center.
2 Foote, batting for Rodriguez, struck out swinging on three pitches.
Murcer pinch-hitting for John.
Robertson ran for Cerone.
Murcer safe when his grounder taken by Garvey was muffed by Howe, Robertson going to second.
3 Randolph flied to deep center.

Game 5 October 25 at Los Angeles

N.Y. 010 000 000
L.A. 000 000 20x

New York	Pos	AB	R	H	RBI	PO	A	E
Randolph	2b	3	0	0	0	0	0	0
Milbourne	ss	4	0	1	0	1	1	0
Winfield	cf-lf	4	0	1	0	4	0	0
Jackson	rf	4	1	1	0	0	0	0
Gossage	p	0	0	0	0	0	0	0
Watson	1b	3	0	0	0	6	0	0
Piniella	lf-rf	4	0	2	1	3	0	0
b Brown		0	0	0	0	0	0	0
Cerone	c	4	0	0	0	8	1	0
Rodriguez	3b	3	0	0	0	2	3	0
Guidry	p	3	0	0	0	0	0	0
Mumphrey	cf	0	0	0	0	0	0	0
Totals		32	1	5	1	24	5	0

Pitching	IP	H	R	ER	BB	SO
New York						
Guidry (L)	7	4	2	2	2	9
Gossage	1	0	0	0	1	0
Los Angeles						
Reuss (W)	9	5	1	1	3	6

Los Angeles	Pos	AB	R	H	RBI	PO	A	E
Lopes	2b	3	0	0	0	3	3	3
Russell	ss	4	0	0	0	0	7	0
Garvey	1b	4	0	1	0	12	1	0
Cey	3b	2	0	0	0	0	2	0
a Landreaux	cf	0	0	0	0	1	0	0
Baker	lf	4	0	0	0	2	0	0
Guerrero	rf	3	1	1	1	1	0	0
Yeager	c	3	1	2	1	7	0	0
Thomas	cf-3b	3	0	0	0	0	0	0
Reuss	p	2	0	0	0	1	2	0
Totals		28	2	4	2	27	15	3

a Ran for Cey in 8th.
b Ran for Piniella in 9th.

Doubles—Jackson, Yeager. Home Runs—Guerrero, Yeager. Stolen Bases—Lopes, Landreaux. Hit by Pitcher—Cey (by Gossage). Double Plays—Russell to Lopes to Garvey, Lopes to Garvey. Left on Bases—New York 7, Los Angeles 6. Umpires—Garcia, Stello, Barnett, Colosi, Cooney, Harvey. Attendance—56,115. Time of Game—2:19.

1st Inning
New York
1 Randolph grounded out, Garvey to Reuss.
2 Milbourne grounded to second.
3 Winfield struck out.
Los Angeles
1 Lopes struck out.
2 Russell popped to third.
Garvey singled to center.
Cey walked.
3 Baker lined to Piniella who made a running catch dropping to his knees.

2nd Inning
New York
Jackson's base hit down the left field line rolled into the field decorations for a ground-rule double.
Watson safe as Lopes dropped his ball for an error, Jackson going to third.
Piniella singled to deep short, scoring Jackson as Watson stopped at second.
1,2 Cerone hit into a double play, Russell to Lopes to Garvey, Watson advancing at second.
3 Rodriguez grounded to short.
Los Angeles
1 Guerrero flied to center.
Yeager doubled off the top of the wall in left-center.
2 Thomas flied to Winfield making a spectacular diving catch after mis-judging the ball.
3 Reuss took a called third strike.

3rd Inning
New York
1 Guidry called out on strikes.
Randolph walked.
Milbourne singled to left, Randolph stopping at second.
2 Winfield forced Milbourne at second, Cey to Lopes as Randolph went to third.
3 Jackson struck out.
Los Angeles
1 Lopes flied to center.
2 Russell grounded to third.
3 Garvey struck out.

4th Inning
New York
Watson walked.
Piniella grounded to Lopes who bobbled it and threw it into the dugout.
Watson got to third and Piniella to second, with Lopes charged with two errors.
1 Cerone grounded to short, both runners holding.
Rodriguez intentionally walked, loading the bases.
2 Guidry's bunt forced Watson, Reuss to Yeager.
3 Randolph grounded to first.
Los Angeles
1 Cey called out on strikes.
2 Baker struck out.
3 Guerrero struck out.

5th Inning
New York
1 Milbourne bounced to the mound.
Winfield singled to left.
2,3 Jackson grounded into a double play, Lopes to Garvey.
Los Angeles
1 Yeager popped to third.
2 Thomas struck out.
Reuss walked.
3 Lopes grounded to short.

6th Inning
New York
1 Watson grounded to short.
2 Piniella flied to right.
3 Cerone flied to left.
Los Angeles
1 Russell flied to Piniella making a running catch in deep left-center.
2 Garvey struck out but had to be thrown out, Cerone to Watson.
3 Cey grounded to third.

7th Inning
New York
1 Rodriguez grounded to short.
2 Guidry struck out.
3 Randolph grounded to short.
Los Angeles
1 Baker struck out.
Guerrero homered into the left-center field bleachers.
Yeager homered into the left-center field bleachers also.
2 Thomas flied to center.
3 Reuss lined to short.

8th Inning
New York
1 Milbourne grounded to third.
2 Winfield struck out.
3 Jackson flied to left.
Los Angeles
For New York—Gossage relieved Guidry on the mound (batting 4th), Mumphrey playing center (batting 9th), Winfield moved to left, Piniella moved to right.
Lopes walked.
1 Russell's bunt was popped to Watson.
2 Garvey flied to right.
Cey was hit by a Gossage fastball on the left side of the helmet. After several minutes he left the field on his own power.
Landreaux ran for Cey.
Lopes and Landreaux pulled off a successful double steal.
3 Baker grounded to third.

9th Inning
New York
For Los Angeles—Landreaux playing center as Thomas moves to third.
1 Watson grounded to short.
Piniella singled to center.
Brown ran for Piniella.
2 Cerone flied to center.
3 Rodriguez struck out.

Game 6 October 28 at New York

L.A. 000 134 010
N.Y. 001 001 000

Los Angeles	Pos	AB	R	H	RBI	PO	A	E
Lopes	2b	4	2	1	0	1	2	1
Russell	ss	4	0	2	1	0	5	0
Garvey	1b	4	1	1	0	9	0	0
Cey	3b	3	1	2	1	1	1	0
b Thomas	3b	2	1	0	1	0	0	0
Baker	lf	5	2	2	0	2	0	0
Guerrero	cf-rf	5	1	3	5	6	0	0
Monday	rf	3	0	1	0	1	0	0
Landreaux	cf	1	0	0	1	0	0	0
Yeager	c	5	0	1	1	6	0	0
Hooten	p	2	1	0	0	0	0	0
Howe	p	2	0	0	0	0	0	0
Totals		40	9	13	9	27	8	1

a Flied out for John in 4th.
b Hit into force out for Cey in 6th.
c Ran for Nettles in 6th.
d Announced for Reuschel in 6th.
e Singled for Gamble in 6th.
f Struck out for May in 8th.

Doubles—Nettles, Randolph. Triple—Guerrero. Home Runs—Randolph, Lopes, Russell. Stolen Bases—Randolph, Lopes, Russell. Sacrifice Hit—Russell. Left on Bases—Los Angeles 10, New York 12. Umpires—Stello, Barnett, Colosi, Cooney, Harvey, Garcia. Attendance—56,513. Time of Game—3:09.

1st Inning
Los Angeles
1 Lopes grounded to third.
2 Russell grounded to second.
Garvey lined a single to center.
Cey singled to left, Garvey to second.
3 Baker flied to right.
New York
Randolph walked on a full count.
Randolph stole second.
1 Mumphrey flied to center.
2 Winfield lined to Baker, making a good backhand catch.
3 Jackson struck out on a full count.

2nd Inning
Los Angeles
1 Guerrero flied to deep right.
2 Monday grounded to short.
Yeager safe on Milbourne's throwing error.
3 Hooton grounded back to the mound.
New York
1 Watson grounded to third, super play by Cey.
2 Nettles grounded to second.
3 Cerone grounded to short.

3rd Inning
Los Angeles
1 Lopes grounded to third.
Russell singled to right.
2 Russell caught trying to steal second, Cerone to Randolph.
3 Garvey flied to center.
New York
1 Milbourne grounded to first.
2 John grounded to center.
Randolph homered into the left field bleachers on a 1-0 pitch.
Mumphrey grounded a single inside the first base line.
Winfield walked on four pitches.
3 Jackson flied to left.

4th Inning
Los Angeles
1 Cey struck out swinging.
Baker lined a single to center.
2 Guerrero lined to left.
Monday singled through Watson's legs, Baker stopping at second.
Yeager singled to left, scoring Baker with Monday stopping at second.
3 Hooton struck out swinging.
New York
1 Watson grounded to short.
Nettles lined a double down the right field line.
2 Cerone struck out swinging on 3 pitches.
Milbourne intentionally walked.
3 Murcer, batting for John, flied to deep right.

5th Inning
Los Angeles
For New York—Frazier pitching.
Lopes bounced a single to left.
1 Russell sacrifices Lopes to second, Watson unassisted.
2 Garvey flied to left.
Cey bounced a single to center under Randolph's glove, scoring Lopes.
Baker singled to short center, Cey racing to third.
Guerrero tripled to left-center, scoring Cey and Baker.
3 Monday struck out.
New York
Randolph doubled to the wall in left.
1 Mumphrey lined to third.
2 Winfield foul popped to Yeager.
3 Jackson grounded to second.

New York	Pos	AB	R	H	RBI	PO	A	E
Randolph	2b	3	1	2	1	2	2	0
Mumphrey	cf	5	0	1	0	2	0	0
Winfield	lf	4	0	0	0	2	0	0
Jackson	rf	5	0	0	0	3	0	0
Watson	1b	5	0	0	0	10	0	0
Nettles	3b	3	0	2	0	1	2	1
c Rodriguez	3b	1	1	1	0	0	2	0
Cerone	c	3	0	0	0	7	2	0
Milbourne	ss	2	0	0	0	0	3	1
John	p	1	0	0	0	0	0	0
a Murcer		1	0	0	0	0	0	0
Frazier	p	0	0	0	0	0	0	0
Davis	p	0	0	0	0	0	0	0
Reuschel	p	0	0	0	0	0	0	0
d Gamble		1	0	0	0	0	0	0
e Piniella		1	0	1	1	0	0	0
May	p	0	0	0	0	0	0	0
f Brown		1	0	0	0	0	0	0
LaRoche	p	0	0	0	0	0	0	0
Totals		35	2	7	2	27	10	2

Pitching	IP	H	R	ER	BB	SO
Los Angeles						
Hooten (W)	5⅓	5	2	2	5	2
Howe (SV)	3⅔	2	0	0	1	3
New York						
John	4	6	1	1	0	2
Frazier (L)	1	4	3	3	0	1
Davis	⅓	1	3	2	2	1
Reuschel	⅔	1	1	0	2	0
May	2	1	1	1	1	2
LaRoche	1	0	0	0	0	2

6th Inning
Los Angeles
For New York—Davis relieved Frazier.
1 Yeager struck out.
Hooten walked.
Lopes walked.
Russell singled to left, scoring Hooten with Lopes stopping at second.
For New York—Reuschel now pitching.
Lopes and Russell pulled off a good double steal.
Garvey walked intentionally.
2 Thomas, batting for Cey, forced Russell at third, Nettles unassisted, Lopes scoring with Garvey going to second.
Baker safe on Nettles' bobble to load the bases.
Guerrero singled to center, scoring Garvey and Thomas, Baker taking third and Guerrero second on the throw.
Monday intentionally walked.
3 Yeager grounded to short.
New York
For Los Angeles—Thomas playing third, Guerrero moved to right and Landreaux playing center.
1 Watson grounded to short.
Nettles grounded to second.
Rodriguez ran for Nettles.
Cerone walked.
Milbourne walked, loading the bases.
Gamble, batting for Reuschel.
For Los Angeles—Howe relieved Hooten.
Piniella, batting for Gamble, singled to center, scoring Rodriguez.
2 Randolph lined to right.
3 Mumphrey lined to right.

7th Inning
Los Angeles
For New York—Rodriguez playing third and May pitching.
1 Howe struck out swinging.
Lopes walked on four pitches.
2 Russell grounded to second.
3 Garvey flied to center.
New York
1 Winfield grounded to short.
2 Jackson struck out.
3 Watson grounded to short.

8th Inning
Los Angeles
1 Thomas grounded to second.
2 Baker popped to second.
Guerrero homered into the left-field bleachers on a 2-1 pitch.
3 Landreaux called out on strikes.
New York
Rodriguez singled to left-center.
1 Cerone flied to right.
2 Milbourne popped to second.
3 Brown, batting for May, struck out.

9th Inning
Los Angeles
For New York—LaRoche now pitching.
1 Yeager flied to right.
2 Howe struck out.
3 Lopes struck out but had to be thrown out, Cerone to Watson.
New York
Randolph walked.
1 Mumphrey struck out.
2 Winfield flied to right.
Jackson safe on Lopes' fumble, Randolph stopping at second. **Lopes sixth error of the series.**
3 Watson flied to center.

1981 WORLD SERIES COMPOSITE BOX

	Wins	Composite Line Score									
Los Angeles Dodgers	4	3	0	2	1	7	7	4	3	0	- 27
New York Yankees	2	5	4	5	1	1	3	0	3	0	- 22

Manager	Regular Season W	L	Pct.	G. Ahead
Tom LaSorda	63	47	.573	—
Bob Lemon	59	48	.551	—

BATTING AND FIELDING

LOS ANGELES DODGERS

WORLD SERIES STATISTICS	Pos	G	AB	R	H	2B	3B	HR	RBI	BB	SO	SB	BA	SA	PO	A	E
Steve Garvey	1b	6	24	3	**10**	1	0	0	0	2	5	0	.417	.458	44	3	0
Davey Lopes	2b	6	22	**6**	5	1	0	0	2	4	3	**4**	.227	.273	26	14	**6**
Bill Russell	ss	6	**25**	1	6	0	0	0	2	0	1	1	.240	.240	4	**26**	1
Ron Cey	3b	6	20	3	7	0	0	1	6	3	3	0	.350	.500	4	11	0
Rick Monday	rf-ph	5	13	1	3	1	0	0	0	3	**6**	0	.231	.308	9	0	0
Pedro Guerrero	cf-rf	6	21	2	7	1	**1**	**2**	**7**	2	**6**	0	.333	**.762**	17	1	0
Dusty Baker	lf	6	24	3	4	0	0	0	1	1	**6**	0	.167	.167	13	0	0
Steve Yeager	c-ph	6	14	2	4	1	0	**2**	4	0	2	0	.286	**.786**	20	0	0
Derrel Thomas	ph-ss-cf-3b	5	7	2	0	0	0	0	1	1	2	0	.000	.000	4	1	0
Ken Landreaux	ph-cf-rf	5	6	1	1	1	0	0	0	0	2	1	.167	.333	6	0	0
Mike Scioscia	c-ph	3	4	1	1	0	0	0	0	1	0	0	.250	.250	7	1	0
Jay Johnstone	ph	3	3	1	2	0	0	1	3	0	0	0	.667	1.667	—	—	—
Reggie Smith	ph	2	2	0	1	0	0	0	0	0	1	0	.500	.500	—	—	—
Steve Sax	ph-pr-2b	2	1	0	0	0	0	0	0	0	0	0	.000	.000	0	0	0
Jerry Reuss	p	2	3	0	0	0	0	0	0	1	2	0	.000	.000	1	3	0
Burt Hooton	p	2	4	1	0	0	0	0	0	1	3	0	.000	.000	1	0	0
Fernando Valenzuela	p	1	3	0	0	0	0	0	0	1	0	0	.000	.000	0	1	0
Steve Howe	p	3	2	0	0	0	0	0	0	0	2	0	.000	.000	0	1	1
Tom Niedenfuer	p	2	0	0	0	0	0	0	0	0	0	0	—	—	0	0	0
Dave Goltz	p	2	0	0	0	0	0	0	0	0	0	0	—	—	0	0	0
Terry Forster	p	2	0	0	0	0	0	0	0	0	0	0	—	—	0	1	0
Dave Stewart	p	2	0	0	0	0	0	0	0	0	0	0	—	—	0	0	1
Bobby Castillo	p	1	0	0	0	0	0	0	0	0	0	0	—	—	0	2	0
Bob Welch	p	1	0	0	0	0	0	0	0	0	0	0	—	—	0	0	0
Alejandro Pena		Did not play															
team total		6	198	27	51	6	1	6	26	20	44	5	.258	.389	156	65	9

Double Plays—6
Left on Bases—46

REGULAR SEASON STATISTICS	Main Pos	G	AB	R	H	2B	3B	HR	RBI	BB	SO	SB	BA	SA
Steve Garvey	1b	**110**	431	63	122	23	1	10	64	25	49	3	.283	.411
Davey Lopes	2b	58	214	35	44	2	0	5	17	22	35	20	.206	.275
Bill Russell	ss	82	262	20	61	9	2	0	22	19	20	2	.233	.282
Ron Cey	3b	85	312	42	90	15	2	13	50	40	55	0	.288	.474
Rick Monday	of	66	130	24	41	1	2	11	25	24	42	1	.315	.608
Pedro Guerrero	of	98	347	46	104	17	2	12	48	34	57	5	.300	.464
Dusty Baker	of	103	400	48	128	17	3	9	49	29	43	10	.320	.445
Steve Yeager	c	42	86	5	18	2	0	3	7	6	14	0	.209	.337
Derrel Thomas	3b-ss	80	218	25	54	4	0	4	24	25	23	7	.248	.321
Ken Landreaux	of	99	390	48	98	16	4	7	41	25	42	18	.251	.367
Mike Scioscia	c	93	290	27	80	10	0	2	29	36	18	0	.276	.331
Jay Johnstone	ph-of	61	83	8	17	3	0	3	6	7	13	0	.205	.349
Reggie Smith	ph	41	35	5	7	1	0	1	8	7	8	0	.200	.314
Steve Sax	2b	31	119	15	33	2	0	2	9	7	14	5	.277	.345
Jerry Reuss	p	22	51	3	10	0	0	0	3	0	18	0	.196	.196
Burt Hooton	p	23	42	3	8	3	0	0	3	4	13	0	.190	.262
Fernando Valenzuela	p	25	64	3	16	0	1	0	7	1	9	0	.250	.281
Steve Howe	p	41	1	0	0	0	0	0	0	1	1	0	.000	.000
Tom Niedenfuer	p	17	0	0	0	0	0	0	0	0	0	0	—	—
Dave Goltz	p	26	17	0	1	0	0	0	2	1	9	0	.059	.059
Terry Forster	p	21	2	0	0	0	0	0	0	0	0	0	.000	.000
Dave Stewart	p	32	5	2	2	0	1	0	1	1	0	0	.400	.800
Bobby Castillo	p	34	9	1	4	2	0	0	1	0	2	0	.444	.667
Bob Welch	p	23	45	3	10	0	1	0	2	1	16	0	.222	.267
Alejandro Pena	p	14	6	0	0	0	0	0	0	0	6	0	.000	.000
team total		110	3751	450	984	133	20	**82**	427	331	550	73	.262	.374

Pepe Frias (inf.), Ron Roenicke (of), Joe Ferguson (ph), Mike Marshall (1b, 3b), Gary Weiss (ss), Candy Maldonado (of), Bobby Mitchell (of), Mark Bradley (of), Jack Percante (ph, 2b), Jerry Grote (c), Rick Sutcliffe (p) and Ted Power (p) also played for the Dodgers during the season.

NEW YORK YANKEES

WORLD SERIES STATISTICS	Pos	G	AB	R	H	2B	3B	HR	RBI	BB	SO	SB	BA	SA	PO	A	E
Bob Watson	1b	6	22	2	7	1	0	**2**	**7**	3	0	0	.318	.636	**51**	0	0
Willie Randolph	2b	6	18	5	4	1	**1**	**2**	3	**9**	0	1	.222	.722	13	11	0
Larry Milbourne	ss	6	20	2	5	**2**	0	0	3	4	0	0	.250	.350	5	16	2
Aurelio Rodriguez	3b-pr	4	12	1	5	0	0	0	0	1	2	0	.417	.417	3	9	0
Lou Piniella	rf-ph-lf	6	16	2	7	1	0	0	3	0	1	1	**.438**	.500	7	0	0
Jerry Mumphrey	cf	5	15	2	3	0	0	0	0	3	2	1	.200	.200	6	0	0
Dave Winfield	lf-cf	6	22	0	1	0	0	0	1	5	4	1	.045	.045	13	1	0
Rick Cerone	c	6	21	2	4	1	0	1	3	4	2	0	.190	.381	42	4	0
Reggie Jackson	rf	3	12	3	4	1	0	1	1	2	3	0	.333	.667	5	0	1
Graig Nettles	3b	3	10	1	4	1	0	0	0	1	1	0	.400	.500	3	10	1
Oscar Gamble	rf-lf-ph	3	6	1	2	0	0	0	1	1	0	0	.333	.333	4	0	0
Bobby Murcer	ph	4	3	0	0	0	0	0	0	0	0	0	.000	.000	—	—	—
Bobby Brown	pr-rf-cf-ph	4	1	1	0	0	0	0	0	0	1	0	.000	.000	1	0	0
Barry Foote	ph	1	1	0	0	0	0	0	0	0	1	0	.000	.000	—	—	—
Andre Robertson	pr	1	0	0	0	0	0	0	0	0	0	0	—	—	—	—	—
Dave Revering		Did not play															
Ron Guidry	p	2	5	0	0	0	0	0	0	0	3	0	.000	.000	0	0	0
Tommy John	p	3	2	0	0	0	0	0	0	0	0	0	.000	.000	0	3	0
Rudy May	p	3	1	0	0	0	0	0	0	0	0	0	.000	.000	0	1	0
Goose Gossage	p	3	1	0	0	0	0	0	0	0	1	0	.000	.000	0	0	0
George Frazier	p	3	2	0	0	0	0	0	0	0	1	0	.000	.000	0	0	0
Rick Reuschel	p	2	2	0	0	0	0	0	0	0	1	0	.000	.000	0	0	0
Ron Davis	p	4	0	0	0	0	0	0	0	0	0	0	—	—	0	0	0
Dave Righetti	p	1	1	0	0	0	0	0	0	0	1	0	.000	.000	0	0	0
Dave LaRoche	p	1	0	0	0	0	0	0	0	0	0	0	—	—	0	0	0
team total		6	193	22	46	8	1	6	22	33	24	4	.238	.383	153	55	4

Double Plays—2
Left on Bases—55

REGULAR SEASON STATISTICS		Main Pos	G	AB	R	H	2B	3B	HR	RBI	BB	SO	SB	BA	SA
Bob Watson		1b	59	156	15	33	3	3	6	12	24	17	0	.212	.385
Willie Randolph		2b	93	357	59	83	14	3	2	24	57	24	14	.232	.305
Larry Milbourne		ss	61	163	24	51	7	2	1	12	9	14	2	.313	.399
Aurelio Rodriguez		3b	27	52	4	18	2	0	2	8	2	10	0	.346	.500
Lou Piniella		of-dh	60	159	16	44	9	0	5	18	13	9	0	.277	.428
Jerry Mumphrey		of	80	319	44	98	11	5	6	32	24	27	13	.307	.429
Dave Winfield		of	105	388	52	114	25	1	13	68	43	41	11	.294	.464
Rick Cerone		c	71	234	23	57	13	2	2	21	12	24	0	.244	.342
Reggie Jackson		of-dh	94	334	33	79	17	1	15	54	46	82	0	.237	.428
Graig Nettles		3b	103	349	46	85	7	1	15	46	47	49	0	.244	.398
Oscar Gamble		of-dh	80	189	24	45	8	0	10	27	35	23	0	.238	.439
Bobby Murcer		dh	50	117	14	31	6	0	6	24	12	15	0	.265	.470
Bobby Brown		of	31	62	5	14	1	0	0	6	5	15	4	.226	.242
Barry Foote	a	c	40	125	12	26	4	0	6	10	8	21	0	.208	.384
Andre Robertson		ss	10	19	1	5	1	0	0	0	0	3	1	.263	.316
Dave Revering		1b	76	206	20	48	5	2	4	17	22	32	0	.233	.335
Ron Guidry		p	23	0	0	0	0	0	0	0	0	0	0	—	—
Tommy John		p	20	0	0	0	0	0	0	0	0	0	0	—	—
Rudy May		p	27	0	0	0	0	0	0	0	0	0	0	—	—
Goose Gossage		p	32	0	0	0	0	0	0	0	0	0	0	—	—
George Frazier		p	16	0	0	0	0	0	0	0	0	0	0	—	—
Rick Reuschel	b	p	12	0	0	0	0	0	0	0	0	0	0	—	—
Ron Davis		p	43	0	0	0	0	0	0	0	0	0	0	—	—
Dave Righetti		p	15	0	0	0	0	0	0	0	0	0	0	—	—
Dave LaRoche		p	26	0	0	0	0	0	0	0	0	0	0	—	—
team total			107	3529	421	889	148	22	100	403	391	434	46	.252	.391

a—from Chicago Cubs b—from Chicago Cubs

Bucky Dent (ss), Dennis Werth (1b), Jim Spencer (1b), Johnny Oates (c), Mike Patterson (of), Steve Balboni (1b), Tucker Ashford (2b), Doug Bird (p), Gene Nelson (p), Bill Castro (p), Tom Underwood (p), Dave Wehrmeister (p), Andy McGaffigan (p) and Mike Griffin (p) also played for the Yankees during the season.

PITCHING

LOS ANGELES DODGERS

WORLD SERIES STATISTICS	G	GS	CG	IP	H	R	ER	BB	SO	W	L	SV	ERA
Jerry Reuss	2	**2**	**1**	11 2/3	10	5	5	3	8	**1**	1	0	3.86
Burt Hooton	2	**2**	0	11 1/3	8	3	2	**9**	3	**1**	1	0	1.59
Fernando Valenzuela	1	1	**1**	9	9	4	4	7	6	**1**	0	0	4.00
Steve Howe	3	0	0	7	7	3	3	1	4	**1**	0	0	3.86
Tom Niedenfuer	2	0	0	5	3	2	0	1	0	0	0	0	0.00
Dave Goltz	2	0	0	3 1/3	4	2	2	1	2	0	0	0	5.40
Terry Forster	2	0	0	2	1	0	0	3	0	0	0	0	0.00
Dave Stewart	2	0	0	1 2/3	1	0	0	2	1	0	0	0	0.00
Bobby Castillo	1	0	0	1	0	1	1	5	0	0	0	0	9.00
Bob Welch	1	1	0	0	3	2	2	1	0	0	0	0	∞
Alejandro Pena	Did not play												
team total	6	6	2	52	46	22	19	33	24	4	2	0	3.29

REGULAR SEASON STATISTICS	G	GS	CG	IP	H	ER	BB	SO	W	L	Pct	SV	ShO	ERA
Jerry Reuss	22	22	8	153	138	39	27	51	10	4	.714	0	2	2.29
Burt Hooton	23	23	5	142	124	36	33	74	11	6	.647	0	4	2.28
Fernando Valenzuela	25	**25**	**11**	**192**	140	53	61	**180**	13	7	.650	0	**8**	2.48
Steve Howe	41	0	0	54	51	15	18	32	5	3	.625	8	0	2.50
Tom Niedenfuer	17	0	0	26	25	11	6	12	3	1	.750	2	0	3.81
Dave Goltz	26	8	0	77	83	35	25	48	2	7	.222	1	0	4.09
Terry Forster	21	0	0	31	37	14	15	17	0	1	.000	0	0	4.06
Dave Stewart	32	0	0	43	40	12	14	29	4	3	.571	6	0	2.51
Bobby Castillo	34	1	0	51	50	30	24	35	2	4	.333	5	0	5.29
Bob Welch	23	23	2	141	141	54	41	88	9	5	.643	0	1	3.45
Alejandro Pena	14	0	0	25	18	8	11	14	1	1	.500	2	0	2.88
team total	110	110	**26**	997	904	333	302	603	63	47	.573	24	**19**	3.01

NEW YORK YANKEES

WORLD SERIES STATISTICS	G	GS	CG	IP	H	R	ER	BB	SO	W	L	SV	ERA
Ron Guidry	2	**2**	0	**14**	8	3	3	4	**15**	**1**	1	0	1.93
Tommy John	3	**2**	0	13	**11**	1	1	0	8	**1**	0	0	**0.69**
Rudy May	3	0	0	6 1/3	5	2	2	1	5	0	0	0	2.84
Goose Gossage	3	0	0	5	2	0	0	2	5	0	0	**2**	0.00
George Frazier	3	0	0	3 2/3	9	7	**7**	3	2	0	**3**	0	17.18
Rick Reuschel	2	1	0	3 2/3	7	3	2	3	2	0	0	0	4.91
Ron Davis	**4**	0	0	2 1/3	4	**8**	6	5	4	0	0	0	23.14
Dave Righetti	1	1	0	2	5	3	3	2	1	0	0	0	13.50
Dave LaRoche	1	0	0	1	0	0	0	0	2	0	0	0	0.00
team total	6	6	0	51	51	27	24	20	44	2	4	2	4.24

REGULAR SEASON STATISTICS	G	GS	CG	IP	H	ER	BB	SO	W	L	Pct	SV	ShO	ERA
Ron Guidry	23	21	0	127	100	39	26	104	11	5	.688	0	0	2.76
Tommy John	20	20	7	140	135	41	39	50	9	8	.529	0	0	2.64
Rudy May	27	22	4	148	137	68	41	79	6	11	.353	1	0	4.14
Goose Gossage	32	0	0	47	22	4	14	48	3	2	.600	20	0	0.77
George Frazier	16	0	0	28	26	5	11	17	0	1	.000	3	0	1.61
Rick Reuschel	12	11	3	71	75	21	10	22	4	4	.500	0	0	2.66
Ron Davis	43	0	0	73	47	22	25	83	4	5	.444	6	0	2.71
Dave Righetti	15	15	2	105	75	24	38	89	8	4	.667	0	0	2.06
Dave LaRoche	26	1	0	47	38	13	16	24	4	1	.800	0	0	2.49
team total	107	107	16	948	827	305	287	**606**	59	48	.551	30	**13**	**2.90**

Total Attendance—338,081 Average Attendance—56,347 Winning Player's Share—Not released Losing Player's Share—$28,845

1982

Herzog's Potent Brew

The clash of styles promised a gourmet meal. The Milwaukee Brewers played in snug County Stadium on a traditional grass field. Their powerful lineup led the major leagues in home runs, with shortstop Robin Yount the MVP in an array of stars. Pete Vuckovich won 18 games and the Cy Young Award, while Rollie Fingers regularly bailed out the starting pitchers. With a 23–24 mark on June 2, the Brewers replaced manager Bob Rodgers with coach Harvey Kuenn. His relaxed manner turned an uptight team into the freewheeling Harvey's Wallbangers. The Brewers sizzled through the hot months to amass a sizable lead. When Fingers tore an arm muscle in September, the Brewers fell on hard times. They regrouped to beat Baltimore on the final day of the season for the A.L. East title. After losing the first two games of the LCS to the Angels, they again made like Lazarus and won the next three in a row.

The Cardinals, on the other hand, had streaked in September and swept the Braves in the LCS. Manager Whitey Herzog had tailored his club for the spacious artificial turf of Busch Stadium. The Cards hit the fewest homers in the majors but thrived on line drives, speed, defense, and wonderful relieving by Bruce Sutter.

In game one, 53,723 fans filled Busch Stadium in anticipation. They sat in quiet shock as the Brewers pounded out a 10–0 laugher. Mike Caldwell threw a three-hitter as Paul Molitor and Yount combined for nine hits at the top of the Brewer lineup. After two and a half innings of game two, the Brewers led 3–0. The Cards finally awoke in the bottom of the third, turning three hits into two runs. A two-run double by Darrell Porter in the sixth tied the game at 4–4. St. Louis went ahead in the bottom of the eighth. Milwaukee lefty Bob McClure walked leadoff batter Keith Hernandez. After George Hendrick hit into a force play, Porter singled. Kuenn had lifted McClure in favor of stocky Pete Ladd. He walked Lonnie Smith on a close 3–2 pitch, possibly a strike, then walked pinch hitter Steve Braun on four pitches to force the go-ahead run across. Sutter nailed down the 5–4 victory with 2 1/3 scoreless innings.

In Milwaukee, Willie McGee starred in game three, won by the Cardinals 6–2. He robbed Molitor of an extra-base hit in the first with a catch in deep center field. In the fifth, he broke a scoreless tie by swatting a three-run homer off Vuckovich. He hit another home run in the seventh, then took a homer away from Gorman Thomas with a leaping catch in the ninth.

After six innings of game four, the Cardinals had a 5–1 lead. Thomas fouled out to begin the Milwaukee seventh. Ben Oglivie then reached on an error by pitcher Dave LaPoint. After Don Money singled, Charlie Moore popped up for the second out. The dam burst as Jim Gantner doubled, Molitor walked, Yount singled, Cecil Cooper singled, Ted Simmons received an intentional pass, and Thomas singled. Jim Slaton and McClure finished the 7–5 victory.

The Brewers pulled ahead in game five with great defense and dogged pitching by Mike Caldwell. Although touched for 14 hits, Caldwell was not relieved until the ninth on the way to a 6–4 victory. Defensive gems were turned in by Moore in the fifth, Cooper in the seventh, and Molitor in the eighth. The Brewers even got to Sutter for two insurance runs in the eighth.

In dire straits, the Cardinals took control in game six. John Stuper threw a four-hitter while the Brewer defense fell apart. Oglivie and Yount made bad plays in the two-run Cardinal second. A two-run homer by Porter in the fourth opened up a comfortable lead, which ballooned to 13–1 at game's end.

Vuckovich and Joaquin Andujar started the final game. The Cards scored first on three singles in the bottom of the fourth. The Brewers scored once in the fifth on an Oglivie homer and twice in the sixth on two hits and a throwing error by Andujar. Staked to a 3–1 lead, Vuckovich allowed leadoff hits to Ozzie Smith and Lonnie Smith in the sixth. With his shoulder aching, Vuckovich left in favor of McClure, thrust into the sort of spot tailored for the injured Fingers. Gene Tenace wangled a walk, then Hernandez tied the game with a base hit. Hendrick singled to put St. Louis ahead 4–3. The Brewers tried in vain to score off Andujar in the seventh and Sutter in the last two frames. The 6–3 triumph gave St. Louis its first world title in 15 years.

Game 1 October 12 at St. Louis

Milw.	2 0 0	1 1 2	0 0 4
St. L.	0 0 0	0 0 0	0 0 0

Milwaukee	Pos	AB	R	H	RBI	PO	A	E
Molitor	3b	6	1	5	2	0	2	0
Yount	ss	6	1	4	2	1	1	0
Cooper	1b	4	1	0	0	14	3	0
Simmons	c	5	1	2	1	3	0	0
Oglivie	lf	4	1	0	0	0	0	0
Thomas	cf	4	0	1	1	2	0	0
Howell	dh	2	0	0	0	0	0	0
a Money	dh	2	1	1	1	0	0	0
Moore	rf	5	2	2	0	4	0	0
Gantner	2b	4	2	2	2	0	7	0
Caldwell	p	0	0	0	0	3	1	0
Totals		42	10	17	9	27	14	0

a Flied out for Howell in 7th.

Doubles—Moore, Yount, Porter. Triple—Gantner. Home Run—Simmons. Sacrifice Hit—Gantner. Hit by Pitcher—Howell (by Forsch). Double Play—Hernandez to O. Smith to Hernandez. Left on Bases—Milwaukee 10, St. Louis 4. Umpires—Weyer, Haller, Kibler, Phillips, Davidson, Evans. Attendance—53,723. Time of Game—2:30.

St. Louis	Pos	AB	R	H	RBI	PO	A	E
Herr	2b	3	0	0	0	2	5	0
L. Smith	lf	4	0	0	0	2	0	0
Hernandez	1b	4	0	0	0	14	1	1
Hendrick	rf	4	0	0	0	1	0	0
Tenace	dh	3	0	0	0	0	0	0
Porter	c	3	0	2	0	3	0	0
Green	cf	3	0	0	0	2	0	0
Oberkfell	3b	3	0	1	0	0	4	0
O. Smith	ss	3	0	0	0	3	3	0
Forsch	p	0	0	0	0	0	0	0
Kaat	p	0	0	0	0	0	0	0
LaPoint	p	0	0	0	0	0	0	0
Lahti	p	0	0	0	0	0	0	0
Totals		30	0	3	0	27	13	1

Pitching	IP	H	R	ER	BB	SO
Milwaukee						
Caldwell (W)	9	3	0	0	1	3
St. Louis						
Forsch (L)	5⅔	10	6	4	1	1
Kaat	1⅓	1	0	0	1	1
LaPoint	1⅔	3	2	2	1	0
Lahti	⅓	3	2	2	0	1

1st Inning

Milwaukee
1 Molitor grounded to second. Yount singled on a full count. Cooper walked on four pitches.
2 Simmons was called out on strikes. Oglivie safe on error by Hernandez, scoring Yount with Cooper going to third. Thomas beat out a grounder to deep short, Cooper scoring and Oglivie stopping at second. Howell was hit by a pitch on the right arm, loading the bases.
3 Moore fouled to Hernandez.

St. Louis
1 Herr grounded to short.
2 L. Smith grounded to third.
3 Hernandez grounded to second.

2nd Inning

Milwaukee
1 Gantner flied to center. Molitor just beat out a hit to short. Yount singled to center, Molitor stopping at second.
2 Cooper popped to short.
3 Simmons popped to second.

St. Louis
1 Hendrick flied to center.
2 Tenace popped to first. Porter doubled to right-center.
3 Green lined to first.

3rd Inning

Milwaukee
1 Oglivie bounced to second.
2 Thomas grounded to third.
3 Howell grounded to second.

St. Louis
1 Oberkfell grounded to second.
2 O. Smith grounded to second, Gantner making a good play.
3 Herr popped to short.

4th Inning

Milwaukee
Moore doubled down the left field line.
1 Gantner sacrificed Moore to second, Hernandez unassisted. Molitor hit a broken-bat single to short center, scoring Moore, but was
2 out trying for second, O. Smith to Herr.
3 Yount grounded to third.

St. Louis
1 L. Smith struck out swinging.
2 Hernandez grounded to second.
3 Hendrick grounded out, Cooper to Caldwell.

5th Inning

Milwaukee
1 Cooper flied to left. Simmons hit a home run to left on a 1–1 pitch.
2 Oglivie grounded to second.
3 Thomas rolled out to first.

St. Louis
1 Tenace bounced to the mound.
2 Porter grounded out, Cooper to Caldwell.
3 Green bounced to third.

6th Inning

Milwaukee
1 Howell grounded to first.
2 Moore grounded to short. Gantner lined a single to right. Molitor singled to left, Gantner stopping at second. Yount blooped a double just inside the right field foul line, scoring Gantner and Molitor. For St. Louis—Kaat relieved Forsch.
3 Cooper struck out.

St. Louis
1 Oberkfell grounded to second.
2 O. Smith flied to center. Herr walked on a full count.
3 L. Smith struck out swinging.

7th Inning

Milwaukee
Simmons singled to center.
1,2 Oglivie hit into a double play, Hernandez to O. Smith to Hernandez. Thomas walked on four pitches.
3 Money, pinch-hitting for Howell, flied deep to Hendrick who made a good running catch in right-center.

St. Louis
1 Hernandez grounded out, Cooper to Caldwell.
2 Hendrick grounded to second.
3 Tenace called out on strikes on a full count.

8th Inning

Milwaukee
For St. Louis—LaPoint came in to pitch.
1 Moore flied to left.
2 Gantner bounced to third. Molitor got his fourth hit on a deep grounder to a diving O. Smith. Yount got his fourth hit also, a single to right, Molitor stopping at second.
3 Cooper forced Yount at second, Herr to O. Smith.

St. Louis
Porter bounced a single to center for only the Cards' second hit, both by Porter.
1 Green flied to deep right, Moore catching the ball over his head on the warning track. Oberkfell grounded a single to center, Porter stopping at second.
2 O. Smith flied to right.
3 Herr flied to right.

9th Inning

Milwaukee
1 Simmons flied to center. Oglivie walked on four pitches.
2 Thomas bounced to third, Oglivie advancing to second. Money singled through the hole in short, scoring Oglivie. For St. Louis—Lahti came in to pitch. Moore high chopped a single over the mound, Money stopping at second. Gantner tripled to deep right-center scoring Money and Moore. Molitor singled to deep short, scoring Gantner **and setting a World Series record with his fifth hit in the game.**
3 Yount took a called third strike.

St. Louis
1 L. Smith flied to right.
2 Hernandez grounded to second.
3 Hendrick foul popped to Cooper.

Game 2 October 13 at St. Louis

Milwaukee	Pos	AB	R	H	RBI	PO	A	E
Molitor	3b	5	1	2	0	0	1	0
Yount	ss	4	1	1	1	4	3	0
Cooper	1b	5	0	3	1	9	2	0
Simmons	c	3	1	1	1	5	0	0
Oglivie	lf	4	0	1	0	2	0	1
Thomas	cf	3	0	0	0	1	0	0
Howell	dh	4	1	0	0	0	0	0
Moore	rf	4	0	2	1	3	0	0
Gantner	2b	3	0	0	0	0	3	0
Sutton	p	0	0	0	0	0	0	0
McClure	p	0	0	0	0	0	0	0
Ladd	p	0	0	0	0	0	0	0
Totals		35	4	10	4	24	9	1

a Struck out for Iorg in 7th.
b Flied out for Oberkfell in 7th.
c Walked for Green in 8th.

Doubles—Moore, Herr, Yount, Porter, Cooper. Home Run—Simmons. Stolen Bases—Molitor, McGee, Oberkfell, O. Smith. Wild Pitches—Stuper 2. Double Play—Hernandez to O. Smith to Hernandez. Left on Bases—Milwaukee 8, St. Louis 7. Umpires—Haller, Kibler, Phillips, Davidson, Evans, Weyer, Attendance—53,723. Time of Game—2:54

Milw.	0 1 2	0 1 0	0 0 0
St. L.	0 0 2	0 0 2	0 1 x

St. Louis	Pos	AB	R	H	RBI	PO	A	E
Herr	2b	3	1	1	1	2	1	0
Oberkfell	3b	3	1	2	1	0	3	0
b Tenace		1	0	0	0	0	0	0
Ramsey	3b	0	0	0	0	0	0	0
Hernandez	1b	3	0	0	0	7	2	0
Hendrick	rf	3	2	0	0	0	0	0
Porter	c	4	0	2	2	8	1	0
L. Smith	lf	3	0	0	0	1	0	0
Iorg	dh	2	0	1	0	0	0	0
a Green	dh	1	0	0	0	0	0	0
c Braun	dh	0	0	0	1	0	0	0
McGee	cf	4	1	0	0	4	0	0
O. Smith	ss	4	0	2	0	5	3	0
Stuper	p	0	0	0	0	0	0	0
Kaat	p	0	0	0	0	0	0	0
Bair	p	0	0	0	0	0	0	0
Sutter	p	0	0	0	0	0	0	0
Totals		31	5	8	5	27	10	0

Pitching	IP	H	R	ER	BB	SO
Milwaukee						
Sutton	6	5	4	4	1	3
McClure (L)	1⅓	2	1	1	2	2
Ladd	⅔	1	0	0	2	0
St. Louis						
Stuper	*4	6	4	4	3	3
Kaat	⅔	1	0	0	0	0
Bair	2	1	0	0	0	3
Sutter (W)	2⅓	2	0	0	1	1

*Pitched to one batter in 5th.

1st Inning
Milwaukee
1 Molitor bounced to third.
Yount walked.
Cooper lined a single to left, Yount running to third.
2,3 Simmons grounded into a double play, Hernandez to O. Smith to Hernandez.
St. Louis
1 Herr flied to left.
2 Oberkfell flied to right.
3 Hernandez flied to right.

2nd Inning
Milwaukee
1 Oglivie struck out swinging.
Thomas walked on four pitches.
2 Howell forced Thomas at second, Hernandez to O. Smith.
On a wild pitch Howell went to second.
Moore lined a double to the wall in left-center, scoring Howell.
3 Gantner flied to center.
St. Louis
1 Hendrick struck out swinging.
2 Porter grounded to second.
3 L. Smith grounded to short.

3rd Inning
Milwaukee
Molitor singled to center.
Molitor stole second.
On Stuper's second wild pitch, Molitor went to third.
1 Yount grounded to second, Molitor scoring.
2 Cooper popped to short.
Simmons homered into the right field stands on a 2-2 count.
Oglivie singled to right.
3 Thomas forced Oglivie at second, Oberkfell to Herr.
St. Louis
Iorg bounced a single to right.
1 McGee forced Iorg at second, Cooper to Yount.
McGee stole second.
2 O. Smith grounded to short, McGee advancing to third.
Herr hit a ground-rule double to right-center (on one bounce), McGee scoring.
Oberkfell singled to right just past a diving Gantner, scoring Herr.
3 Hernandez fouled to Oglivie.

4th Inning
Milwaukee
1 Howell struck out swinging.
2 Moore grounded to third.
Gantner walked on four pitches.
3 Molitor struck out swinging.
St. Louis
1 Hendrick popped to first.
2 Porter grounded to second.
3 L. Smith bounced to third.

5th Inning
Milwaukee
Yount doubled off the left field wall.
For St. Louis—Kaat relieved Stuper.
Cooper singled to left-center, driving in Yount.
1 Simmons flied to center.
2 Oglivie popped to short.
For St. Louis—Bair relieved Kaat.
3 Thomas struck out swinging.

5th Inning (continued)
St. Louis
1 Iorg grounded to second.
2 McGee popped to short.
3 O. Smith grounded to short.

6th Inning
Milwaukee
1 Howell struck out swinging on 3 pitches.
2 Moore flied to center.
3 Gantner popped to short.
St. Louis
1 Herr took a called third strike.
Oberkfell lined a single to right-center.
Oberkfell stole second.
2 Hernandez flied to right, Oberkfell tagged up and went to third after the catch.
Hendrick walked on a full count.
Porter lined a double into the left field corner, scoring Oberkfell and Hendrick. Porter took third on Oglivie's throwing error.
3 L. Smith struck out swinging.

7th Inning
Milwaukee
1 Molitor struck out swinging on a full count.
2 Yount flied to left.
Cooper looped a double to right.
For St. Louis—Sutter came in to pitch.
Simmons intentionally walked.
3 Oglivie bounced out over the mound to a racing-in O. Smith.
St. Louis
For Milwaukee—McClure now pitching.
1 Green, batting for Iorg, struck out swinging.
2 McGee struck out swinging.
O. Smith lined a single to center.
O. Smith stole second on a pitchout.
Herr walked on a full count.
3 Tenace, batting for Oberkfell, flied to center.

8th Inning
Milwaukee
For St. Louis—Ramsey playing third.
1 Thomas foul popped to Porter.
2 Howell struck out swinging.
Moore bounced a single over third.
3 Gantner grounded to first.
St. Louis
Hernandez walked on four pitches.
1 Hendrick forced Hernandez at second, Cooper to Yount.
Porter lined a single to center, Hendrick stopping at second.
For Milwaukee—Ladd replaced McClure.
L. Smith walked on a full count, to load the bases.
Braun, pinch-hitting for Green, walked on four pitches forcing in Hendrick.
2 McGee lined to short.
3 O. Smith got credit for a single when his grounder hit Braun for the out. Putout goes to Cooper.

9th Inning
Milwaukee
Molitor beat out a bunt down the first base line.
1 Molitor out trying to steal second, Porter to Herr who picked up the low throw.
2 Yount grounded to short.
3 Cooper flied to center.

Game 3 October 15 at Milwaukee

St. Louis	Pos	AB	R	H	RBI	PO	A	E
Herr	2b	5	0	0	0	1	3	0
Oberkfell	3b	4	0	0	0	1	1	0
Hernandez	1b	4	0	0	0	8	0	1
x Hendrick	rf	2	1	1	0	3	0	0
Porter	c	4	0	0	0	6	0	0
L. Smith	lf	4	2	2	0	1	0	0
Green	lf	0	0	0	0	0	0	0
Iorg	dh	4	1	1	0	0	0	0
McGee	cf	3	2	2	4	6	0	0
O. Smith	ss	3	0	0	1	1	3	0
Andujar	p	0	0	0	0	0	1	0
Kaat	p	0	0	0	0	0	0	0
Bair	p	0	0	0	0	0	0	0
Sutter	p	0	0	0	0	0	0	0
Totals		33	6	6	5	27	8	1

Pitching	IP	H	R	ER	BB	SO
St. Louis						
Andujar (W)	6⅓	3	0	0	1	3
Kaat	⅓	1	0	0	0	1
Bair	*0	0	0	0	1	0
Sutter (SV)	2⅓	1	2	2	1	1
Milwaukee						
Vuckovich (L)	8⅔	6	6	4	3	1
McClure	⅓	0	0	0	0	0

*Pitched to one batter in 7th.

St. L.	0 0 0	0 3 0	2 0 1
Milw.	0 0 0	0 0 0	0 2 0

Milwaukee	Pos	AB	R	H	RBI	PO	A	E
Molitor	3b	4	0	0	0	1	0	0
Yount	ss	3	1	0	0	5	5	0
Cooper	1b	4	1	1	2	14	0	1
Simmons	c	4	0	1	0	1	1	1
Oglivie	lf	4	0	0	0	4	0	0
Thomas	cf	4	0	1	0	2	0	0
Howell	dh	2	0	0	0	0	0	0
a Money	dh	1	0	0	0	0	0	0
Moore	rf	3	0	0	0	0	0	0
Gantner	2b	3	0	2	0	0	6	1
Vuckovich	p	0	0	0	0	0	2	0
McClure	p	0	0	0	0	0	0	0
Totals		32	2	5	2	27	14	3

x Awarded first base on catcher's interference.
a Walked for Howell in 7th.

Doubles—Gantner, L. Smith, Iorg. Triple—L. Smith. Home Runs—McGee 2, Cooper. Double Play—Herr to O. Smith to Hernandez. Left on Bases—St. Louis 4, Milwaukee 6. Umpires—Kibler, Phillips, Davidson, Evans, Weyer, Haller. Attendance—56,556. Time of Game—2:53.

1st Inning
St. Louis
1 Herr popped to short.
2 Oberkfell flied to left.
3 Hernandez grounded to second.
Milwaukee
1 Molitor flied to a leaping McGee at the 402 foot mark on a full count.
2 Yount flied to right.
3 Cooper grounded to second.

2nd Inning
St. Louis
Hendrick beat out a two-hopper to third.
1 Porter bounced back to the mound, Hendrick moving to second.
2 L. Smith bounced to short, Hendrick advancing to third.
3 Iorg bounced back to the pitcher.
Milwaukee
1 Simmons bounced to Andujar on a full count.
2 Oglivie lined to right.
3 Thomas struck out swinging.

3rd Inning
St. Louis
1 McGee grounded to short.
2 O. Smith grounded to short.
3 Herr grounded to second.
Milwaukee
1 Howell bounced to short.
Moore walked on four pitches.
Gantner doubled to right, Moore going to third.
2 Molitor struck out swinging on a 3-2 pitch.
3 Yount grounded to second.

4th Inning
St. Louis
1 Oberkfell foul popped to Molitor.
2 Hernandez fouled to Oglivie.
Hendrick walked.
3 Hendrick caught trying to steal second, Simmons to Yount.
Milwaukee
1 Cooper flied to center.
2 Simmons flied to right.
3 Oglivie struck out swinging on a 3-2 count.

5th Inning
St. Louis
1 Porter called out on strikes.
L. Smith doubled to left-center.
Iorg safe when Cooper booted his grounder, L. Smith going to third.
McGee blasted a three-run homer to right on the first pitch.
2 O. Smith flied to center.
3 Herr grounded to second.
Milwaukee
1 Thomas popped to second.
2 Howell grounded to third.
3 Moore grounded to short.

6th Inning
St. Louis
1 Oberkfell popped to short.
2 Hernandez grounded to second.
3 Hendrick grounded to short.
Milwaukee
Gantner lined a single to right.
1 Molitor flied to center.
2,3 Yount grounded into a double play, Herr to O. Smith to Hernandez.

7th Inning
St. Louis
1 Porter popped to short.
L. Smith tripled to right-center and scored when Gantner's throw went into the dugout.
2 Iorg flied to center.
McGee hit another home run into the right field stands on a 1-0 pitch.
3 O. Smith popped to short.
Milwaukee
1 Cooper flied to center.
Simmons blasted a single off of Andujar's knee. Andujar was carried off the field and replaced by Kaat.
2 Oglivie took a called third strike.
Thomas lined a single to left, Simmons stopping at second.
Money announced as pinch-hitter for Howell.
For St. Louis—Bair relieved Kaat.
Money walked, loading the bases.
For St. Louis—Sutter relieved Bair.
3 Moore fouled to Oberkfell on the top step of the dugout.

8th Inning
St. Louis
1 Herr grounded to second.
2 Oberkfell flied to left.
3 Hernandez grounded to short.
Milwaukee
1 Gantner flied to left.
2 Molitor fouled to Porter.
Yount walked.
Cooper hit a two-run home run to right on a 0-1 pitch.
3 Simmons grounded to first.

9th Inning
St. Louis
Hendrick awarded first on catcher interference when Simmons tipped his bat for an error.
1 Porter popped foul on a bunt to a diving Cooper.
2 L. Smith flied to deep left.
Iorg hit a ground-rule double when his drive to right was touched by a fan, Hendrick had to stop at third.
McGee was intentionally walked.
O. Smith walked, forcing in Hendrick.
For Milwaukee—McClure on the mound.
3 Herr grounded to second.
Milwaukee
For St. Louis—Green playing left field.
Oglivie safe on error by Hernandez.
1 Thomas flied to deep left-center where McGee robbed him of a home run above the fence.
2 Money called out on strikes.
3 Moore flied to shallow center.

Game 4 October 16 at Milwaukee

St. Louis	Pos	AB	R	H	RBI	PO	A	E
Herr	2b	4	0	0	2	1	1	0
Oberkfell	3b	2	2	1	0	0	2	0
b Tenace		1	0	0	0	0	0	0
Hernandez	1b	4	0	0	0	8	1	0
Hendrick	rf	4	0	1	1	1	0	0
Porter	c	3	0	1	0	5	0	0
L. Smith	lf	4	1	1	0	2	0	0
Iorg	dh	4	0	2	1	0	0	0
a Green		0	0	0	0	0	0	0
McGee	cf	4	1	1	0	4	0	0
O. Smith	ss	3	1	1	0	3	1	0
LaPoint	p	0	0	0	0	0	2	1
Bair	p	0	0	0	0	0	0	0
Kaat	p	0	0	0	0	0	0	0
Lahti	p	0	0	0	0	0	1	0
Totals		33	5	8	4	24	8	1

Pitching	IP	H	R	ER	BB	SO
St. Louis						
LaPoint	$6\frac{2}{3}$	7	4	1	1	3
Bair (L)	*0	1	2	2	1	0
Kaat	*0	1	1	1	1	0
Lahti	$1\frac{1}{3}$	1	0	0	1	0
Milwaukee						
Haas	$5\frac{1}{3}$	7	5	4	2	3
Slaton (W)	2	1	0	0	2	1
McClure (SV)	$1\frac{2}{3}$	0	0	0	0	2

*Pitched to two batters in 7th.

St. L.	1 3 0	0 0 1	0 0 0
Milw.	0 0 0	0 1 0	6 0 x

Milwaukee	Pos	AB	R	H	RBI	PO	A	E
Molitor	3b	4	1	0	0	1	0	0
Yount	ss	4	1	2	2	3	3	1
Cooper	1b	4	1	2	1	10	0	0
Simmons	c	2	0	0	0	6	0	0
Thomas	cf	4	0	1	2	4	0	0
Oglivie	lf	3	1	1	0	1	0	0
Money	dh	4	2	2	0	0	0	0
Moore	rf	4	0	1	0	0	0	0
Gantner	2b	4	1	1	1	1	5	1
Haas	p	0	0	0	0	1	2	0
Slaton	p	0	0	0	0	0	0	0
McClure	p	0	0	0	0	0	0	0
Totals		33	7	10	6	27	10	2

a Ran for Iorg in 8th.
b Struck out for Oberkfell in 9th.

Doubles—Oberkfell, Money, L. Smith, Iorg, Gantner. Triple—Oglivie. Stolen Bases—McGee, Oberkfell. Sacrifice Fly—Herr. Wild Pitches—Haas, Kaat. Double Plays—Herr to Hernandez, O. Smith to Hernandez, Gantner to Yount to Cooper, Gantner to Cooper. Left on Bases—St. Louis 6, Milwaukee 6. Umpires—Phillips, Davidson, Evans, Weyer, Haller, Kibler. Attendance—56,560.
Time of Game—3:04.

1st Inning
St. Louis
1 Herr called out on strikes on three pitches.
Oberkfell doubled down the right field line.
2 Hernandez struck out swinging on a full count.
Hendrick singled off Yount's glove into short center, scoring Oberkfell.
Porter bloop singled to right, Hendrick stopping at second.
3 L. Smith forced Hendrick at third, Molitor unassisted.
Milwaukee
1 Molitor grounded to third.
Yount bounced a single to third.
2,3 Cooper lined to Herr who doubled up Yount, Herr to Hernandez.

2nd Inning
St. Louis
1 Iorg flied to center.
McGee singled through the hole at short.
McGee stole second.
O. Smith walked.
Both runners moved up one base on a wild pitch by Haas.
2 Herr hit a sacrifice fly to deep center, both McGee and O. Smith scored when Thomas slipped on the warning track.
Oberkfell walked.
Oberkfell stole second.
Hernandez was safe on a smash through Gantner's legs for an error, Oberkfell scored and Hernandez got to second.
3 Hendrick popped foul to Cooper
Milwaukee
1 Simmons struck out swinging.
2 Thomas flied to center.
Oglivie tripled off the wall in left-center.
3 Money struck out swinging.

3rd Inning
St. Louis
1 Porter bounced out to the pitcher.
2 L. Smith lined to the mound.
3 Iorg popped to short.
Milwaukee
1 Moore flied to center.
2 Gantner bounced to third.
3 Molitor struck out swinging.

4th Inning
St. Louis
1 McGee grounded to short.
O. Smith beat out a bunt toward third.
2 Herr flied to center.
3 O. Smith was picked off first, Haas to Cooper.
Milwaukee
1 Yount bounced back to the mound.
Cooper singled to deep short.
Simmons walked.
2 Thomas fouled to Porter.
3 Oglivie grounded to first.

5th Inning
St. Louis
1 Oberkfell grounded to second.
2 Hernandez grounded to short.
3 Hendrick flied to center.
Milwaukee
Money doubled to left-center.
Moore blooped a single to shallow center, Money stopping at third.
1,2 Gantner grounded into a double play, O. Smith to Hernandez, scoring Money.
3 Molitor flied to center.

6th Inning
St. Louis
1 Porter struck out swinging on a full count.
L. Smith lined a double into the left field corner.
Iorg doubled to right-center, scoring L. Smith.
For Milwaukee—Slaton came in to pitch.
2 McGee flied to left field.
O. Smith safe on an error by Yount, who pulled Cooper off the bag, Iorg going to third.
3 Herr lined to short.
Milwaukee
1 Yount one-hopped back to the pitcher.
2 Cooper flied to right.
3 Simmons flied to center.

7th Inning
St. Louis
Oberkfell walked on a full count.
1,2 Hernandez hit into a double play, Gantner to Yount to Cooper.
3 Hendrick grounded to second.
Milwaukee
1 Thomas fouled to Porter.
Oglivie safe on an error by LaPoint who dropped the throw from Hernandez.
Money looped a single to right, Oglivie stopping at second.
2 Moore popped to short.
Gantner lined a double to right-center, scoring Oglivie as Money went to third.
For St. Louis—Bair relieved LaPoint.
Molitor walked, loading the bases.
Yount hit a check-swing single to right, scoring Money and Gantner with Molitor advancing to third.
For St. Louis—Kaat relieved Bair.
Cooper lined a single off the glove of a diving Oberkfell, scoring Molitor with Yount stopping at second.
Both runners moved up on a wild pitch by Kaat.
For St. Louis—Lahti replaced Kaat with a 2-1 count on Simmons.
Simmons intentionally walked, loading the bases. Walk charged to Kaat.
Thomas singled to left-center, scoring Yount and Cooper with Simmons going to third and Thomas to second on the throw to third.
Oglivie intentionally walked.
3 Money flied to left.

8th Inning
St. Louis
Porter walked on a full count.
1 L. Smith struck out swinging.
Iorg singled to center, Porter racing to third.
Green ran for Iorg.
For Milwaukee—Slaton now pitching.
2,3 McGee hit into a double play, Gantner to Cooper.
Milwaukee
1 Moore bounced back to the mound.
2 Gantner lined to short.
3 Molitor flied to left.

9th Inning
St. Louis
1 O. Smith grounded to second.
2 Herr called out on strikes.
3 Tenace, pinch-hitting for Oberkfell, struck out swinging.

Game 5 October 17 at Milwaukee

St. Louis	Pos	AB	R	H	RBI	PO	A	E
L. Smith	dh	5	0	2	0	0	0	0
Green	lf	5	2	2	0	2	0	0
Hernandez	1b	4	1	3	2	5	1	0
Hendrick	rf	5	0	3	2	1	0	0
Porter	c	5	0	1	0	5	1	0
b Ramsey		0	0	0	0	0	0	0
McGee	cf	5	0	1	0	4	0	0
Oberkfell	3b	4	0	3	0	0	2	0
a Tenace		1	0	0	0	0	0	0
Herr	2b	4	0	0	0	3	2	1
O. Smith	ss	3	1	0	0	3	2	0
Forsch	p	0	0	0	0	1	0	1
Sutter	p	0	0	0	0	0	0	0
Totals		41	4	15	4	24	8	2

Pitching	IP	H	R	ER	BB	SO
St. Louis						
Forsch (L)	7	8	4	3	2	3
Sutter	1	3	2	2	1	2
Milwaukee						
Caldwell (W)	$8\frac{1}{3}$	14	4	4	2	3
McClure (SV)	$\frac{2}{3}$	1	0	0	0	1

St. L.	0 0 1	0 0 0	1 0 2
Milw.	1 0 1	0 1 0	1 2 x

Milwaukee	Pos	AB	R	H	RBI	PO	A	E
Molitor	3b	4	1	1	1	2	5	0
Yount	ss	4	2	4	1	3	3	0
Cooper	1b	4	0	1	1	8	2	0
Simmons	c	3	0	0	1	4	1	0
Oglivie	lf	4	1	2	0	1	0	0
Thomas	cf	4	0	0	0	3	0	0
Money	dh	3	1	0	0	0	0	0
Moore	rf	4	1	2	1	1	0	0
Gantner	2b	4	0	1	1	4	4	1
Caldwell	p	0	0	0	0	1	1	0
McClure	p	0	0	0	0	0	0	0
Totals		34	6	11	6	27	16	1

a Flied out for Oberkfell in 9th.
b Ran for Porter in 9th.

Doubles—Hernandez 2, Yount, Moore, Green. Triple—Green. Home Run—Yount. Stolen Base—L. Smith. Double Plays—Porter to Herr, Oberkfell to Herr to Hernandez, Molitor to Cooper. Left on Bases—St. Louis 12, Milwaukee 7. Umpires—Davidson, Evans, Weyer, Haller, Kibler, Phillips. Attendance—56,562.
Time of Game—3:02.

1st Inning
St. Louis
L. Smith singled off Caldwell's glove.
1 Green struck out swinging, as L. Smith stole second.
2 L. Smith was caught trying to steal third, Simmons to Molitor.
Hernandez singled to right.
3 Hendrick forced Hernandez at second, Molitor to Gantner.
Milwaukee
1 Molitor flied to center.
Yount lined a single off Forsch's ankle.
Cooper lined a single to right, Yount stopping at second.
Forsch threw the ball into center trying to pick off Yount as both runners moved up one base on the error.
2 Simmons grounded to first, Yount scoring and Cooper going to third.
3 Oglivie flied to center.

2nd Inning
St. Louis
1 Porter grounded to second.
2 McGee grounded to third.
Oberkfell singled to center.
3 Herr forced Oberkfell at second, Yount to Gantner.
Milwaukee
1 Thomas flied to deep center.
2 Money grounded to short.
3 Moore lined to short.

3rd Inning
St. Louis
1 O. Smith lined off Caldwell's glove to Gantner who threw to first for the out.
2 L. Smith grounded to short, good play by Yount.
Green tripled to short right as Moore tried to make a diving catch.
Hernandez doubled to left-center, scoring Green.
Hendrick singled up the middle, a great stop by Gantner saved a run as Hernandez stopped at third.
3 Porter grounded to second.
Milwaukee
1 Gantner popped to short.
Molitor walked on four pitches.
Yount doubled down the left field line, Molitor stopping at third.
2 Cooper grounded out, Hernandez to Forsch as Molitor scored and Yount went to third.
3 Simmons flied to left.

4th Inning
St. Louis
1 McGee grounded to third.
Oberkfell singled to right.
Herr safe when Gantner booted his grounder, Oberkfell going to second.
2,3 O. Smith bounced into a double play, Molitor to Cooper.
Milwaukee
Oglivie singled to center.
1,2 Thomas struck out and Oglivie was caught trying to steal, Porter to Herr.
3 Money took a called third strike.

5th Inning
St. Louis
1 L. Smith lined to Moore making an outstanding diving catch.
2 Green flied to center.
Hernandez walked.
3 Hendrick flied to Thomas in right-center.

5th Inning (continued)
Milwaukee
Moore doubled down the left field line.
1 Gantner grounded to second, Moore moving to third.
Molitor lined a single to left, scoring Moore.
Yount singled to third, Molitor stopping at second.
2 Cooper flied to right.
Simmons walked, loading the bases.
3 Oglivie struck out.

6th Inning
St. Louis
1 Porter struck out swinging.
McGee lined a single to right.
2 Oberkfell forced McGee at second, Gantner to Yount.
3 Herr forced Oberkfell at second, Yount unassisted.
Milwaukee
Thomas safe on Herr's error.
1,2 Money grounded into a double play, Oberkfell to Herr to Hernandez.
3 Moore bounced to third.

7th Inning
St. Louis
O. Smith walked on a full count.
L. Smith singled to right, O. Smith stopping at second.
1 Green flied to center.
2 Hernandez forced L. Smith at second, Cooper to Yount with O. Smith advancing to third.
Hendrick singled to center, scoring O. Smith and sending Hernandez to second.
3 Porter grounded out, Cooper to Caldwell. A diving play by Cooper.
Milwaukee
1 Gantner popped to short.
2 Molitor fouled to Green.
Yount lined a home run into the right field bleachers **to become the first player in Series history to have two four-hit games.**
3 Cooper flied to center.

8th Inning
St. Louis
1 McGee struck out.
Oberkfell singled to left.
2 Herr forced Oberkfell at second, Yount to Gantner.
3 O. Smith forced Herr at second, Gantner unassisted.
Milwaukee
For St. Louis—Sutter came in to pitch.
1 Simmons struck out swinging.
Oglivie singled to center.
2 Thomas struck out swinging.
Money walked on four pitches.
Moore singled to right-center, scoring Oglivie and Money running to third.
Gantner singled to right, scoring Money and sending Moore to third.
3 Molitor forced Gantner at second, O. Smith to Herr.

9th Inning
St. Louis
1 L. Smith bounced to third.
Green bounced a double over Molitor's head.
Hernandez doubled to right-center, scoring Green.
Hendrick singled up the middle, scoring Hernandez.
For Milwaukee—McClure on the mound.
Porter singled to right, Hendrick stopping at second.
2 McGee struck out on three pitches.
Ramsey came in to run for Porter.
3 Tenace, batting for Oberkfell, flied to left.

Game 6 October 19 at St. Louis

Milw.	000	000	001	
St. L.	020	326	00x	

Milwaukee	Pos	AB	R	H	RBI	PO	A	E
Molitor	3b	4	0	1	0	0	0	0
Yount	ss	4	0	0	0	0	3	2
Cooper	1b	4	0	0	0	8	2	0
Simmons	c	2	0	0	0	4	0	0
Yost	c	0	0	0	0	1	0	0
Oglivie	lf	4	0	1	0	5	0	0
Thomas	cf	3	0	0	0	0	0	0
a Edwards	cf	0	0	0	0	0	0	0
Money	dh	3	0	0	0	0	0	0
Moore	rf	3	0	1	0	2	0	0
Gantner	2b	3	1	1	0	3	2	2
Sutton	p	0	0	0	0	1	2	0
Slaton	p	0	0	0	0	0	0	0
Medich	p	0	0	0	0	0	0	0
Bernard	p	0	0	0	0	0	0	0
Totals		30	1	4	0	24	9	4

St. Louis	Pos	AB	R	H	RBI	PO	A	E
L. Smith	lf	3	1	1	0	1	0	0
Green	lf	1	1	0	0	0	0	0
Oberkfell	3b	5	1	0	0	1	4	1
Hernandez	1b	5	2	2	4	8	0	0
Hendrick	rf	5	2	2	1	3	0	0
Porter	c	4	1	1	2	2	0	0
Brummer	c	0	0	0	0	0	0	0
Iorg	dh	4	3	3	0	0	0	0
McGee	cf	4	1	1	1	5	0	0
Herr	2b	3	1	2	2	1	2	0
O. Smith	ss	4	0	0	0	5	3	0
Stuper	p	0	0	0	0	1	1	0
Totals		38	13	12	10	27	10	1

a Ran for Thomas in 8th.

Pitching	IP	H	R	ER	BB	SO
Milwaukee						
Sutton (L)	$4\frac{1}{3}$	7	7	5	0	2
Slaton	$\frac{2}{3}$	0	0	0	0	0
Medich	2	5	6	4	1	0
Bernard	1	0	0	0	0	1
St. Louis						
Stuper (W)	9	4	1	1	2	2

Doubles—Iorg 2, Herr, Gantner. Triple—Iorg. Home Runs—Porter, Hernandez. Stolen Base—L. Smith. Sacrifice Hit—Herr. Wild Pitches—Medich 2, Stuper. Balk—Sutton. Double Plays—Oberkfell to Herr to Hernandez, Herr to O. Smith to Hernandez. Left on Bases—Milwaukee 4, St. Louis—3. Umpires—Evans, Weyer, Haller, Kibler, Phillips, Davidson. Attendance—53,723. Time of Game—2:21.

1st Inning
Milwaukee
1 Molitor popped to short.
2 Yount lined back to the pitcher.
3 Cooper flied to left.
St. Louis
1 L. Smith called out on strikes.
2 Oberkfell flied to right.
3 Hernandez grounded out, Cooper to Sutton.

2nd Inning
Milwaukee
Simmons walked.
Oglivie singled to center, Simmons stopping at second.
1 Thomas flied to center.
2,3 McGee grounded into a double play, Oberkfell to Herr to Hernandez.
St. Louis
1 Hendrick struck out swinging on a 3-2 pitch.
2 Porter grounded to second.
Iorg doubled into the left field corner off Oglivie's glove.
McGee safe at first when his grounder went through Yount's legs, scoring Iorg.
Herr doubled off the right field wall, scoring McGee.
3 O. Smith grounded to short.

3rd Inning
Milwaukee
Moore singled to left-center.
1 Gantner struck out swinging.
2,3 Molitor hit into a double play, Herr to O. Smith to Hernandez.
St. Louis
L. Smith safe at first when Gantner muffed his grounder.
Smith stole second.
1 Oberkfell popped to second.
2 Hernandez grounded to second, Smith advancing to third.
3 Smith caught trying to steal home, Sutton to Simmons.

4th Inning
Milwaukee
1 Yount flied to right.
2 Cooper popped to short.
3 Simmons flied to right.
St. Louis
Hendrick singled to left-center.
Hendrick went to second on a balk.
Porter belted a two-run home run to right on a 1-1 pitch.
Iorg lined a triple down the right field line.
1 McGee grounded to short, Iorg holding.
2 Herr squeezed in Iorg on a perfect bunt, Sutton to Cooper.
3 O. Smith grounded to first.

5th Inning
Milwaukee
1 Oglivie flied to center.
2 Thomas struck out swinging on a 3-2 count.
3 Money grounded to third.
St. Louis
L. Smith blooped a single to right.
1 Oberkfell grounded back to the mound, Smith moving to second.
Hernandez blasted a two-run home run into the right-center field bleachers.
For Milwaukee—Slaton relieved Sutton.
2 After a 26-minute rain delay, Hendrick popped to second.
3 Porter flied to left.

6th Inning
Milwaukee
For St. Louis—Green playing left field.
1 Moore lined to short.
2 Gantner flied to right.
3 Molitor grounded to third.
St. Louis
For Milwaukee—Medich pitching.
Iorg doubled to left center.
Iorg to third on a wild pitch.
McGee singled to right, scoring Iorg.
Herr blooped a single to left, McGee stopping at second.
McGee and Herr both advanced on another wild pitch.
1 Smith grounded to first, both runners holding.
After a long rain delay of two hours and thirteen minutes, Green walked to load the bases.
2 Oberkfell forced McGee at the plate, Cooper to Simmons, bases stay loaded.
Hernandez singled to right, scoring Herr and Green with Oberkfell advancing to third.
Hendrick singled to right, scoring Oberkfell. Hernandez went to third and Hendrick to second on Moore's throw to third.
Porter safe when Gantner muffed his grounder with Hernandez and Hendrick scoring.
3 Iorg, up for the second time in the inning, lined to left.

7th Inning
Milwaukee
1 Yount grounded to short.
2 Cooper grounded to short.
3 Simmons grounded back to the mound.
St. Louis
For Milwaukee—Yost replaced Simmons as catcher.
1 McGee flied to left.
2 Herr flied to left.
3 O. Smith flied to left.

8th Inning
Milwaukee
1 Oglivie flied to center.
Thomas reached safely on a throwing error by Oberkfell.
Edwards ran for Thomas.
2 Money popped to short.
3 Moore popped to third.
St. Louis
For Milwaukee—Edwards stayed in to play center and Bernard became the new pitcher.
1 Green called out on strikes.
Oberkfell safe on Yount's throwing error.
2 Hernandez flied to right.
3 Hendrick forced Hernandez at second, Yount to Gantner.

9th Inning
Milwaukee
For St. Louis—Brummer replaced Porter as catcher.
Gantner doubled into the left field corner.
Molitor singled to center, Gantner advancing to third.
Gantner scored and Molitor went to second on a wild pitch.
1 Yount grounded to third with Molitor holding second.
2 Cooper flied to center.
Yost walked.
3 Oglivie flied to center.

Game 7 October 20 at St. Louis

Milw.	000	012	000	
St. L.	000	103	02x	

Milwaukee	Pos	AB	R	H	RBI	PO	A	E
Molitor	3b	4	1	2	0	0	1	0
Yount	ss	4	0	1	0	4	1	0
Cooper	1b	3	0	1	1	8	1	0
Simmons	c	4	0	0	0	5	0	0
Oglivie	lf	4	1	1	1	0	0	0
Thomas	cf	4	0	0	0	3	0	0
Howell	dh	3	0	0	0	0	0	0
Moore	rf	3	0	1	0	3	0	0
Gantner	2b	3	1	1	0	1	6	0
Vuckovich	p	0	0	0	0	0	0	0
McClure	p	0	0	0	0	0	0	0
Haas	p	0	0	0	0	0	0	0
Caldwell	p	0	0	0	0	0	0	0
Totals		32	3	7	2	24	9	0

St. Louis	Pos	AB	R	H	RBI	PO	A	E
L. Smith	lf	5	2	3	1	4	0	0
Oberkfell	3b	3	0	0	0	1	5	0
a Tenace		0	0	0	0	0	0	0
b Ramsey	3b	1	1	0	0	0	0	0
Hernandez	1b	3	1	2	2	12	2	0
Hendrick	rf	5	0	2	1	1	1	0
Porter	c	5	0	1	1	4	0	0
Iorg	dh	3	0	2	0	0	0	0
c Green		0	0	0	0	0	0	0
d Braun	dh	2	0	1	1	0	0	0
McGee	cf	5	1	1	0	1	0	0
Herr	2b	3	0	1	0	1	5	0
O. Smith	ss	4	1	2	0	2	2	0
Andujar	p	0	0	0	0	1	1	1
Sutter	p	0	0	0	0	0	1	0
Totals		39	6	15	6	27	17	1

a Walked for Oberkfell in 6th.
b Ran for Tenace in 6th.
c Announced for Iorg in 6th.
d Grounded out for Green in 6th.

Pitching	IP	H	R	ER	BB	SO
Milwaukee						
Vuckovich	$5\frac{1}{3}$	10	3	3	2	3
McClure (L)	$\frac{1}{3}$	2	1	1	1	0
Haas	2	1	2	2	1	1
Caldwell	$\frac{1}{3}$	2	0	0	0	0
St. Louis						
Andujar (W)	7	7	3	2	0	1
Sutter (SV)	2	0	0	0	0	2

Doubles—Gantner, L. Smith 2. Home Run—Oglivie. Sacrifice Fly—Cooper. Left on Bases—Milwaukee 3, St. Louis 13. Umpires—Weyer, Haller, Kibler, Phillips, Davidson, Evans. Attendance—53,723. Time of Game—2:50.

1st Inning
Milwaukee
1 Molitor flied to right.
2 Yount grounded to third.
3 Cooper grounded to third.
St. Louis
1 L. Smith flied to right.
2 Oberkfell struck out, swinging.
Hernandez beat out a high bouncer to second.
3 Hendrick fouled to Simmons.

2nd Inning
Milwaukee
1 Simmons flied to left.
2 Oglivie grounded to third.
3 Thomas flied to center.
St. Louis
1 Porter called out on strikes.
Iorg singled on a grounder that Gantner dove for.
2 McGee flied to center.
Herr walked.
O. Smith bounced a single over the mound, loading the bases.
3 L. Smith flied to right.

3rd Inning
Milwaukee
1 Howell grounded out, Hernandez to Andujar.
2 Moore grounded to second.
3 Gantner grounded to short.
St. Louis
1 Oberkfell grounded to first.
Hernandez walked.
Hendrick singled to left, Hernandez stopping at second.
2 Porter flied to deep right, Hernandez going to third and Hendrick to second, after the catch.
3 Iorg grounded to second.

4th Inning
Milwaukee
Molitor singled to right.
1 Yount forced Molitor at second, Oberkfell to Herr.
Cooper singled to right, Yount was out
2 trying for third, Hendrick to Oberkfell.
3 Simmons popped foul to Porter.
St. Louis
McGee singled to center.
Herr singled to right center, McGee advancing to third.
1 O. Smith popped to second.
L. Smith singled to deep short, McGee scoring with Herr stopping at second.
2 Oberkfell forced L. Smith at second, Cooper to Yount as Herr advanced to third.
3 Hernandez struck out swinging.

5th Inning
Milwaukee
Oglivie homered deep into the right field bleachers on the first pitch.
1 Thomas flied to deep left.
2 Howell grounded to third.
3 Moore grounded to second.
St. Louis
1 Hendrick grounded to short.
2 Porter popped to short.
Iorg singled when his bouncer hit second base.
3 McGee flied to center.

6th Inning
Milwaukee
Gantner doubled to right-center.
Molitor beat out a sacrifice bunt toward third fielded by Andujar whose throw hit Molitor in the back. Gantner scored and Molitor to second on the error.
Yount beat out a high bouncer between first and second, Molitor going to third.
1 Cooper hit a sacrifice fly to deep left, Molitor scoring after the catch.
2 Simmons forced Yount at second, Hernandez to O. Smith.
3 Oglivie forced Simmons at second, Herr to O. Smith.
St. Louis
1 Herr grounded to third.
O. Smith singled to left.
L. Smith doubled into the left field corner, moving O. Smith to third.
For Milwaukee—McClure relieved Vuckovich on the mound.
Tenace, pinch-hitting for Oberkfell, walked to load the bases.
Ramsey ran for Tenace.
Hernandez singled to right-center, scoring O. Smith and L. Smith with Ramsey going to third.
Hendrick singled to right, scoring Ramsey with Hernandez stopping at second.
2 Porter forced Hendrick at second, Gantner to Yount as Hernandez went to third.
Green was announced as pinch-hitter for Iorg.
For Milwaukee—Haas came in to pitch.
3 Braun, batting for Green, rolled to second.

7th Inning
Milwaukee
For St. Louis—Ramsey playing third.
1 Thomas struck out swinging.
2 Howell flied to deep left where L. Smith made a lunging catch.
Moore singled to deep short.
3 Gantner bounced back to the pitcher.
St. Louis
1 McGee grounded to second.
2 Herr lined to short.
3 O. Smith grounded to second.

8th Inning
Milwaukee
For St. Louis—Sutter came in to pitch.
1 Molitor grounded to short.
2 Yount struck out swinging.
3 Cooper grounded to second.
St. Louis
L. Smith got a ground-rule double down the right field line.
1 Ramsey, trying to sacrifice, bunted the third strike foul for a strikeout.
Hernandez intentionally walked.
2 Hendrick flied to center.
For Milwaukee—Caldwell relieved Haas.
Porter lined a single to right, L. Smith scoring with Hernandez going to third.
Braun singled to center, Hernandez scoring as Porter stopped at second.
3 McGee grounded to second.

9th Inning
Milwaukee
1 Simmons bounced to the pitcher
2 Oglivie grounded to second.
3 Thomas struck out swinging.

1982 WORLD SERIES COMPOSITE BOX

	Wins	Composite Line Score									
St. Louis Cardinals	4	1	5	3	4	5	12	3	3	3	- 39
Milwaukee Brewers	3	3	1	3	1	5	4	7	4	5	- 33

Manager	W	L	Regular Season Pct.	G. Ahead
Whitey Herzog	92	70	.568	3
Harvey Kuenn	95	67	.586	1

BATTING AND FIELDING

WORLD SERIES STATISTICS

	Pos	G	AB	R	H	2B	3B	HR	RBI	BB	SO	SB	BA	SA	PO	A	E
ST. LOUIS CARDINALS																	
Keith Hernandez	1b	7	27	4	7	2	0	1	**8**	4	2	0	.259	.444	62	7	2
Tommy Herr	2b	7	25	2	4	2	0	0	5	3	3	0	.160	.240	11	19	1
Ozzie Smith	ss	7	24	3	5	0	0	0	1	3	0	1	.208	.208	22	17	0
Ken Oberkfell	3b	7	24	4	7	1	0	0	1	2	1	**2**	.292	.333	3	21	1
George Hendrick	rf	7	28	5	9	0	0	0	5	2	2	0	.321	.321	10	1	0
Willie McGee	cf	6	25	**6**	6	0	0	**2**	5	1	3	**2**	.240	.480	24	0	0
Lonnie Smith	lf-dh	7	28	**6**	9	**4**	**1**	0	1	1	5	**2**	.321	.536	11	0	0
Darrell Porter	c	7	28	1	8	2	0	1	5	1	4	0	.286	.464	33	2	0
Dane Iorg	dh	5	17	4	9	**4**	**1**	0	1	0	0	0	**.529**	**.882**	—	—	—
David Green	cf-ph-dh-lf-pr	7	10	3	2	1	**1**	0	0	1	3	0	.200	.500	4	0	0
Gene Tenace	dh-ph	5	6	0	0	0	0	0	0	1	2	0	.000	.000	—	—	—
Steve Braun	ph-dh	2	2	0	1	0	0	0	2	1	0	0	.500	.500	—	—	—
Mike Ramsey	3b-pr	3	1	1	0	0	0	0	0	0	1	0	.000	.000	0	0	0
Glenn Brummer	c	1	0	0	0	0	0	0	0	0	0	0	—	—	0	0	0
Julio Gonzalez		Did not play															
Joaquin Andujar	p	2	0	0	0	0	0	0	0	0	0	0	—	—	1	2	1
John Stuper	p	2	0	0	0	0	0	0	0	0	0	0	—	—	1	1	0
Bob Forsch	p	2	0	0	0	0	0	0	0	0	0	0	—	—	1	0	1
Dave Lapoint	p	2	0	0	0	0	0	0	0	0	0	0	—	—	0	2	1
Bruce Sutter	p	4	0	0	0	0	0	0	0	0	0	0	—	—	0	1	0
Jim Kaat	p	4	0	0	0	0	0	0	0	0	0	0	—	—	0	0	0
Doug Bair	p	3	0	0	0	0	0	0	0	0	0	0	—	—	0	0	0
Jeff Lahti	p	2	0	0	0	0	0	0	0	0	0	0	—	—	0	1	0
John Martin		Did not play															
Steve Mura		Did not play															
team total		7	245	39	67	16	3	4	34	20	26	7	.273	.412	183	74	7

Double Plays—8
Left on Bases—49

	Pos	G	AB	R	H	2B	3B	HR	RBI	BB	SO	SB	BA	SA	PO	A	E
MILWAUKEE BREWERS																	
Cecil Cooper	1b	7	28	3	8	1	0	1	6	1	1	0	.286	.429	**71**	10	1
Jim Gantner	2b	7	24	5	8	**4**	**1**	0	4	1	1	0	.333	.583	9	**33**	**5**
Robin Yount	ss	7	29	**6**	**12**	3	0	1	6	2	2	0	.414	.621	20	19	3
Paul Molitor	3b	7	**31**	5	11	0	0	0	3	2	4	1	.355	.355	4	9	0
Charlie Moore	rf	7	26	3	9	3	0	0	2	1	0	0	.346	.462	13	0	0
Gorman Thomas	cf	7	26	0	3	0	0	0	3	2	**7**	0	.115	.115	15	0	0
Ben Oglivie	lf	7	27	4	6	0	**1**	1	1	2	4	0	.222	.407	13	0	1
Ted Simmons	c	7	23	2	4	0	0	**2**	3	**5**	3	0	.174	.435	28	2	1
Don Money	ph-dh	5	13	4	3	1	0	0	1	2	3	0	.231	.308	—	—	—
Roy Howell	dh	4	11	1	0	0	0	0	0	0	3	0	.000	.000	—	—	—
Marshall Edwards	pr-cf	1	0	0	0	0	0	0	0	0	0	0	—	—	0	0	0
Ned Yost	c	1	0	0	0	0	0	0	0	1	0	0	.000	.000	1	0	0
Mark Brouhard		Did not play															
Rob Picciolo		Did not play															
Ed Romero		Did not play															
Mike Caldwell	p	3	0	0	0	0	0	0	0	0	0	0	—	—	4	2	0
Pete Vuckovich	p	2	0	0	0	0	0	0	0	0	0	0	—	—	0	2	0
Don Sutton	p	2	0	0	0	0	0	0	0	0	0	0	—	—	1	2	0
Moose Haas	p	2	0	0	0	0	0	0	0	0	0	0	—	—	1	2	0
Bob McClure	p	5	0	0	0	0	0	0	0	0	0	0	—	—	0	0	0
Jim Slaton	p	2	0	0	0	0	0	0	0	0	0	0	—	—	0	0	0
Doc Medich	p	1	0	0	0	0	0	0	0	0	0	0	—	—	0	0	0
Dwight Bernard	p	1	0	0	0	0	0	0	0	0	0	0	—	—	0	0	0
Pete Ladd	p	1	0	0	0	0	0	0	0	0	0	0	—	—	0	0	0
Rollie Fingers		Did not play															
team total		7	238	33	64	12	2	5	29	19	28	1	.269	.399	180	81	11

Double Plays—4
Left on Bases—44

REGULAR SEASON STATISTICS

		Main Pos	G	AB	R	H	2B	3B	HR	RBI	BB	SO	SB	BA	SA
ST. LOUIS CARDINALS															
Keith Hernandez		1b	160	579	79	173	33	6	7	94	100	67	19	.299	.413
Tommy Herr		2b	135	493	83	131	19	4	0	36	57	56	25	.266	.320
Ozzie Smith		ss	140	488	58	121	24	1	2	43	68	32	25	.248	.314
Ken Oberkfell		3b	137	470	55	136	22	5	2	34	40	31	11	.289	.370
George Hendrick		of	136	515	65	145	20	5	19	104	37	80	3	.282	.450
Willie McGee		of	123	422	43	125	12	8	4	56	12	58	24	.296	.391
Lonnie Smith		of	156	592	**120**	182	35	8	8	69	64	74	68	.307	.434
Darrell Porter		c	120	373	46	86	18	5	12	48	66	66	1	.231	.402
Dane Iorg		of-ph	102	238	17	70	14	1	0	34	23	23	0	.294	.361
David Green		of	76	166	21	47	7	1	2	23	8	29	11	.283	.373
Gene Tenace		c-ph	66	124	18	32	9	0	7	18	36	31	1	.258	.500
Steve Braun		ph	58	62	6	17	4	0	0	4	11	10	0	.274	.339
Mike Ramsey		inf	112	256	18	59	8	2	1	21	22	34	6	.230	.289
Glenn Brummer		c	35	64	4	15	4	0	0	8	0	12	2	.234	.297
Julio Gonzalez		3b	42	87	9	21	3	2	1	7	1	24	1	.241	.356
Joaquin Andujar		p	38	95	3	15	1	1	0	4	0	44	1	.158	.189
John Stuper		p	23	42	1	5	0	1	0	0	1	24	0	.119	.167
Bob Forsch		p	36	73	7	15	3	1	0	3	3	20	0	.205	.274
Dave Lapoint		p	42	38	2	2	0	0	0	1	1	18	0	.053	.053
Bruce Sutter		p	70	8	1	1	0	0	0	1	0	1	0	.125	.125
Jim Kaat		p	62	12	0	0	0	0	0	0	1	4	0	.000	.000
Doug Bair		p	63	13	0	1	0	0	0	0	0	3	0	.077	.077
Jeff Lahti		p	33	13	0	1	0	0	0	0	0	8	0	.077	.077
John Martin		p	24	11	1	1	0	0	0	0	1	3	0	.091	.091
Steve Mura		p	35	53	3	3	0	0	0	3	1	10	0	.057	.057
team total			162	5455	685	1439	239	**52**	67	632	569	805	**200**	.264	.364

Tito Landrum (of), Orlando Sanchez (c), Kelly Paris (inf.), Gene Roof (of), Andy Rincon (p), Jeff Keener (p), Eric Rasmussen (p) and Mark Littell (p) also played for the Cardinals during the season.

		Main Pos	G	AB	R	H	2B	3B	HR	RBI	BB	SO	SB	BA	SA
MILWAUKEE BREWERS															
Cecil Cooper		1b	155	654	104	205	38	3	32	121	32	53	2	.313	.528
Jim Gantner		2b	132	447	48	132	17	2	4	43	26	36	6	.295	.369
Robin Yount		ss	156	635	129	**210**	**46**	12	29	114	54	63	14	.331	**.578**
Paul Molitor		3b	160	**666**	**136**	201	26	8	19	71	69	93	41	.302	.450
Charlie Moore		of	133	456	53	116	22	4	6	45	29	49	2	.254	.360
Gorman Thomas		of	158	567	96	139	29	1	**39**	112	84	143	3	.245	.506
Ben Oglivie		of	159	602	92	147	22	1	34	102	70	81	3	.244	.453
Ted Simmons		c	137	539	73	145	29	0	23	97	32	40	0	.269	.451
Don Money		dh	96	275	40	78	14	3	16	55	32	38	0	.284	.531
Roy Howell		dh	98	300	31	78	11	2	4	38	21	39	0	.260	.350
Marshall Edwards		of	69	178	24	44	4	1	2	14	4	8	10	.247	.315
Ned Yost		c	40	98	13	27	6	3	1	8	7	20	3	.276	.429
Mark Brouhard		of	40	108	16	29	4	1	4	10	9	17	0	.269	.435
Rob Picciolo	a	2b	22	21	7	6	1	0	0	1	1	4	0	.286	.333
Ed Romero		2b	52	144	18	36	8	0	1	7	8	16	0	.250	.326
Mike Caldwell		p	35	0	0	0	0	0	0	0	0	0	0	—	—
Pete Vuckovich		p	30	0	0	0	0	0	0	0	0	0	0	—	—
Don Sutton	b	p	7	0	0	0	0	0	0	0	0	0	0	—	—
Moose Haas		p	32	0	0	0	0	0	0	0	0	0	0	—	—
Bob McClure		p	34	0	0	0	0	0	0	0	0	0	0	—	—
Jim Slaton		p	39	0	0	0	0	0	0	0	0	0	0	—	—
Doc Medich	c	p	10	0	0	0	0	0	0	0	0	0	0	—	—
Dwight Bernard		p	47	0	0	0	0	0	0	0	0	0	0	—	—
Pete Ladd		p	16	0	0	0	0	0	0	0	0	0	0	—	—
Rollie Fingers		p	50	0	0	0	0	0	0	0	0	0	0	—	—
team total			163	**5733**	**891**	1599	277	41	**216**	**843**	484	714	84	.279	**.455**

a from Oakland Athletics b from Houston Astros c from Texas Rangers
Kevin Bass (of), Larry Hisle (dh), Bob Skube (of-dh), Randy Lerch (p), Jerry Augustine (p), Doug Jones (p), Chuck Porter (p) and Jamie Easterly (p) also played for the Brewers during the season.

PITCHING

WORLD SERIES STATISTICS

	G	GS	CG	IP	H	R	ER	BB	SO	W	L	SV	ERA
ST. LOUIS CARDINALS													
Joaquin Andujar	2	**2**	0	$13\frac{1}{3}$	10	3	2	1	4	**2**	0	0	**1.35**
John Stuper	2	**2**	**1**	13	10	5	5	**5**	5	1	0	0	3.46
Bob Forsch	2	**2**	0	$12\frac{2}{3}$	18	10	7	3	4	0	**2**	0	4.97
Dave Lapoint	2	1	0	$8\frac{1}{3}$	10	6	3	2	3	0	0	0	3.24
Bruce Sutter	4	0	0	$7\frac{2}{3}$	6	4	4	3	**6**	1	0	**2**	4.70
Jim Kaat	4	0	0	$2\frac{1}{3}$	4	1	1	2	2	0	0	0	3.86
Doug Bair	3	0	0	2	2	2	2	2	3	0	1	0	9.00
Jeff Lahti	2	0	0	$1\frac{2}{3}$	4	2	2	1	1	0	0	0	10.80
John Martin	Did not play												
Steve Mura	Did not play												
team total	7	7	1	61	64	33	23*	19	28	4	3	2	3.39
MILWAUKEE BREWERS													
Mike Caldwell	3	**2**	**1**	$\mathbf{17\frac{2}{3}}$	**19**	4	4	3	**6**	**2**	0	0	2.04
Pete Vuckovich	2	**2**	0	14	16	9	7	**5**	4	0	1	0	4.50
Don Sutton	2	**2**	0	$10\frac{1}{3}$	12	**11**	**9**	1	5	0	1	0	7.84
Moose Haas	2	1	0	$7\frac{1}{3}$	8	7	6	3	4	0	0	0	7.36
Bob McClure	**5**	0	0	$4\frac{1}{3}$	5	2	2	3	5	0	**2**	**2**	4.15
Jim Slaton	2	0	0	$2\frac{2}{3}$	1	0	0	2	1	1	0	0	0.00
Doc Medich	1	0	0	2	5	6	4	1	0	0	0	0	18.00
Dwight Bernard	1	0	0	1	0	0	0	0	1	0	0	0	0.00
Pete Ladd	1	0	0	$\frac{2}{3}$	1	0	0	2	0	0	0	0	0.00
Rollie Fingers	Did not play												
team total	7	7	1	60	67	39	32	20	26	3	4	2	4.80

*individual earned runs do not add to team total because of rule 10.18(i) being applied in game 4.

REGULAR SEASON STATISTICS

	G	GS	CG	IP	H	ER	BB	SO	W	L	Pct	SV	ShO	ERA
ST. LOUIS CARDINALS														
Joaquin Andujar	38	37	9	266	237	73	50	137	15	10	.600	0	5	2.47
John Stuper	23	21	2	137	137	51	55	53	9	7	.563	0	0	3.36
Bob Forsch	36	34	6	233	238	90	54	69	15	9	.625	1	2	3.48
Dave Lapoint	42	21	0	153	170	58	52	81	9	3	.750	0	0	3.42
Bruce Sutter	70	0	0	102	88	33	34	61	9	8	.529	**36**	0	2.90
Jim Kaat	62	2	0	75	79	34	23	35	5	3	.625	2	0	4.08
Doug Bair	63	0	0	92	69	26	36	68	5	3	.625	8	0	2.55
Jeff Lahti	33	1	0	57	53	24	21	22	5	4	.556	0	0	3.81
John Martin	24	7	0	66	56	31	30	21	4	5	.444	0	0	4.23
Steve Mura	35	30	7	184	196	83	80	84	12	11	.522	0	1	4.05
team total	162	162	25	1465	1420	549	502	689	**92**	70	**.568**	47	10	3.37
MILWAUKEE BREWERS														
Mike Caldwell	35	34	12	258	269	112	58	75	17	13	.567	0	3	3.91
Pete Vuckovich	30	30	9	224	234	83	102	105	18	6	**.750**	0	1	3.34
Don Sutton	7	7	2	55	55	20	18	36	4	1	.800	0	1	3.29
Moose Haas	32	27	3	193	232	96	39	104	11	8	.579	1	0	4.47
Bob McClure	34	26	5	173	160	81	74	99	12	7	.632	0	0	4.22
Jim Slaton	39	7	0	118	117	43	41	59	10	6	.625	6	0	3.29
Doc Medich	10	10	1	63	57	35	32	36	5	4	.556	0	0	5.00
Dwight Bernard	47	0	0	79	78	33	27	45	3	1	.750	6	0	3.76
Pete Ladd	16	0	0	18	16	8	6	12	1	3	.250	3	0	4.00
Rollie Fingers	50	0	0	80	63	23	20	71	5	6	.455	29	0	2.60
team total	163	163	34	1467	1514	649	511	717	**95**	57	**.586**	**47**	6	3.98

Total Attendance—384,570 Average Attendance—54,939 Winning Player's Share—$43,280 Losing Player's Share—$31,935

1983
The Rise of the Stooges

The Orioles were a perfect Earl Weaver team, managed perfectly by Joe Altobelli. After almost 15 years in charge, Weaver had retired to the broadcasting booth. Even-tempered Altobelli orchestrated the diverse Oriole talents with restrained flair. Cal Ripken and Eddie Murray both played like MVPs, with Ripken ultimately winning the award. Around these twin pillars, Altobelli had a deep corps of platoon players adept at the long ball. Strong pitching, solid defense, and attention to fundamentals rounded out a team that won the A.L. East comfortably and whipped the White Sox in four games in the LCS.

Facing them were the Philadelphia Phillies, back for the fourth time in history. In 1950, they had won the pennant with a young cast known as the Whiz Kids. This year, key contributions by oldsters earned the sobriquet of the Wheeze Kids. The Phils were tied for first place in the N.L. East on July 18 when G.M. Paul Owens fired manager Pat Corrales and took over in the dugout himself. A 22–7 record in September broke open a close divisional race, followed by a four-game victory over the Dodgers in the LCS.

Scott McGregor started game one for the Orioles, with Cy Young winner John Denny on the mound for the Phils. Denny had won 13 of his last 14 decisions, and he kept his rhythm with a 2–1 victory. Denny and reliever Al Holland gave out only five hits, with the one run coming on a first-inning homer by Jim Dwyer. McGregor pitched nearly as well, but he unfortunately allowed two homers, by 40-year-old Joe Morgan in the sixth and by Garry Maddox in the eighth.

Their offensive failure in the first game worried the Orioles. Because the DH rule was not in effect that year, Ken Singleton's bat was out of the lineup. Rich Dauer, Todd Cruz, and Rick Dempsey batted sixth through eighth and had been dubbed the Three Stooges for their weak hitting. In game two, each of the Stooges contributed to a 4–1 Baltimore victory. Both teams started rookies, Mike Boddicker for Baltimore and Charles Hudson for Philadelphia. Boddicker pitched a three-hitter and allowed only an unearned run. The Orioles staged the winning rally in the bottom of the fifth. John Lowenstein led off with a home run that tied the score at 1–1. Dauer singled, and Cruz then beat out a bunt. Dempsey honored stooges everywhere by doubling to right for another run. Boddicker lofted a sacrifice fly for the third run of the inning.

When play resumed in Philadelphia after a day off, Owens caused a stir by benching Pete Rose, his 43-year old spark plug. The Phils turned to their money pitcher, Steve Carlton, to face Mike Flanagan. After five innings, the Phils led 2–0 on homers by Gary Matthews and Morgan. Dan Ford put the Orioles on the scoreboard with a solo homer in the sixth. With two outs, Dempsey doubled in the top of the seventh and scored on Benny Ayala's pinch single. Owens then relieved his ace starter with Al Holland, his ace reliever. John Shelby greeted Holland with a single, and Ford then hit a hard grounder to short. When Ivan DeJesus botched the play, Ayala scored the go-ahead run. Sammy Stewart and Tippy Martinez preserved the 3–2 victory for Jim Palmer, who had pitched the fifth and sixth innings in relief.

Owens brought Denny back in game four, while Altobelli turned to young Storm Davis. The Orioles grabbed a 2–0 lead in the fourth on singles by Dwyer, Ripken, Murray, and Dauer. Restored to the lineup, Pete Rose doubled in the bottom of the fourth and scored on a double by Joe Lefebvre. The Phillies went ahead 3–2 in the fifth on a double by Bo Diaz, a single by Denny, and another double by Rose. The Orioles struck back in the sixth. With one out, Lowenstein singled and Dauer doubled. An intentional pass to pinch hitter Joe Nolan loaded the bases. Altobelli then sent Singleton up to hit for Dempsey; Denny promptly walked the tying run home. Willie Hernandez went to the mound and allowed the go-ahead run on a sacrifice fly by pinch hitter Shelby. A double by Dwyer and single by Dauer added a key Baltimore insurance run in the seventh. Stewart and Martinez again kept the lead despite a ninth-inning Philly rally.

Ahead three games to one, the Orioles moved in for the kill. McGregor kept the Philadelphia batters off balance all night, shutting them out on five hits. The Baltimore batters, meanwhile, had their long-ball strokes working. Murray led off the second with a solo homer, and Dempsey did the same to open the third. When Murray belted a two-run shot in the fourth, the outcome was apparent. Earl Weaver had led the Orioles to one world championship; Joe Altobelli had quickly matched him.

Game 1 October 11 at Baltimore

| Phil. | 000 001 010 |
| Balt. | 100 000 000 |

Philadelphia	Pos	AB	R	H	RBI	PO	A	E
Morgan	2b	4	1	2	1	1	5	0
Rose	1b	4	0	1	0	11	0	0
Schmidt	3b	4	0	0	0	0	1	0
Lezcano	rf	3	0	0	0	0	0	0
d Hayes	rf	1	0	0	0	0	0	0
Matthews	lf	4	0	0	0	4	0	0
Maddox	cf	3	1	1	1	3	0	0
Diaz	c	3	0	0	0	7	0	0
DeJesus	ss	3	0	0	0	1	5	0
Denny	p	3	0	0	0	0	0	0
Holland	p	0	0	0	0	0	0	0
Totals		31	2	5	2	27	11	0

Baltimore	Pos	AB	R	H	RBI	PO	A	E
Bumbry	cf	4	0	1	0	4	0	0
Stewart	p	0	0	0	0	0	0	0
T. Martinez	p	0	0	0	0	0	0	0
Dwyer	rf	3	1	1	1	2	0	0
c Ford	rf	1	0	0	0	0	0	0
Ripken	ss	4	0	1	0	1	4	0
Murray	1b	4	0	1	0	8	0	0
Lowenstein	lf	3	0	1	0	2	0	0
e Roenicke		1	0	0	0	0	0	0
Dauer	2b	3	0	0	0	3	1	0
Cruz	3b	3	0	0	0	0	3	1
Dempsey	c	2	0	0	0	6	1	0
a Shelby	cf	1	0	0	0	0	0	0
McGregor	p	2	0	0	0	0	0	0
b Nolan	c	1	0	0	0	1	0	0
Totals		32	1	5	1	27	9	1

a Struck out for Dempsey in 8th.
b Grounded out for McGregor in 8th.
c Flied out for Dwyer in 8th.
d Grounded out for Lezcano in 9th.
e Flied out for Lowenstein in 9th.

Double—Bumbry. Home Runs—Dwyer, Morgan, Maddox. Double Play—Ripken to Dauer to Murray. Left on Bases—Philadelphia 2, Baltimore 4. Umpires—Springstead, Vargo, Clark, Pulli, Palermo, Rennert. Attendance—52,204. Time of Game—2:22.

Pitching	IP	H	R	ER	BB	SO
Philadelphia						
Denny (W)	7⅔	5	1	1	0	5
Holland (S)	1⅓	0	0	0	0	1
Baltimore						
McGregor (L)	8	4	2	2	0	6
Stewart	⅔	1	0	0	0	1
T. Martinez	⅓	0	0	0	0	0

1st Inning
Philadelphia
  Morgan safe when Cruz dropped his pop behind the mound.
1 Morgan caught trying to steal second, Dempsey to Dauer.
2 Rose struck out swinging.
3 Schmidt lined to center.
Baltimore
1 Bumbry lined to center.
  Dwyer homered over the right field wall on a full count.
2 Ripken grounded to short.
  Murray singled to left.
3 Lowenstein struck out swinging.

2nd Inning
Philadelphia
1 Lezcano lined to short.
2 Matthews flied to center.
3 Maddox struck out swinging.
Baltimore
1 Dauer struck out swinging.
2 Cruz struck out swinging.
3 Dempsey grounded to short.

3rd Inning
Philadelphia
1 Diaz grounded to third.
2 DeJesus struck out swinging.
3 Denny flied to left.
Baltimore
1 McGregor grounded to second.
2 Bumbry flied to left.
3 Dwyer grounded to second.

4th Inning
Philadelphia
  Morgan singled to center.
1 Rose forced Morgan at second, Cruz to Dauer.
2 Schmidt flied to deep center.
3 Lezcano struck out swinging.
Baltimore
  Ripken singled to right.
1 Murray forced Ripken at second, DeJesus to Morgan.
2 Lowenstein flied to left.
3 Dauer bounced to short.

5th Inning
Philadelphia
  Matthews singled to left.
1,2 Maddox hit into a double play, Ripken to Dauer to Murray.
3 Diaz flied to center.
Baltimore
1 Cruz grounded to short.
2 Dempsey grounded to third.
3 McGregor grounded to second.

6th Inning
Philadelphia
1 DeJesus flied to right.
2 Denny took a called third strike.
  Morgan homered over the right field fence on a 1-2 pitch.
3 Rose grounded to short.
Baltimore
1 Bumbry flied to center.
2 Dwyer fouled to Diaz.
3 Ripken struck out looking.

7th Inning
Philadelphia
1 Schmidt struck out swinging.
2 Lezcano grounded to short.
3 Matthews flied to right.
Baltimore
1 Murray bounced to first.
  Lowenstein singled to right.
2 Dauer flied to center.
3 Cruz grounded to second.

8th Inning
Philadelphia
  Maddox homered into the left field stands on the first pitch.
1 Diaz flied to Lowenstein, who robbed him of a home run with a leaping catch.
2 DeJesus grounded to short.
3 Denny grounded to third.
Baltimore
1 Shelby, batting for Dempsey, struck out swinging.
2 Nolan, batting for McGregor, grounded to second.
  Bumbry doubled off the right field wall. For Philadelphia—Holland relieved Denny.
3 Ford, batting for Dwyer, flied to left.

9th Inning
Philadelphia
  For Baltimore—Shelby playing center, Nolan catching, Ford playing right, and Stewart on the mound.
1 Morgan popped to first.
  Rose singled to right.
2 Schmidt struck out swinging.
  Hayes announced for Lezcano.
  For Baltimore—T. Martinez relieved Stewart.
3 Hayes grounded to first.
Baltimore
  For Philadelphia—Hayes in right field.
1 Ripken foul popped to DeJesus.
2 Murray struck out swinging.
3 Roenicke, pinch-hitting for Lowenstein, flied to deep left.

Game 2 October 12 at Baltimore

Philadelphia	Pos	AB	R	H	RBI	PO	A	E
Morgan	2b	4	1	1	0	1	1	0
Rose	1b	4	0	0	0	7	1	0
Schmidt	3b	4	0	0	0	0	3	0
Lefebvre	rf	2	0	1	1	1	0	0
Matthews	lf	3	0	0	0	2	0	0
G. Gross	cf	3	0	0	0	5	0	0
Diaz	c	3	0	1	0	5	1	0
c Samuel		0	0	0	0	0	0	0
Virgil	c	0	0	0	0	1	0	0
DeJesus	ss	3	0	0	0	1	1	0
Hudson	p	1	0	0	0	0	0	0
b Hayes		1	0	0	0	0	0	0
Hernandez	p	0	0	0	0	1	0	0
Andersen	p	0	0	0	0	0	0	0
d Perez		1	0	0	0	0	0	0
Reed	p	0	0	0	0	0	0	0
Totals		29	1	3	1	24	7	0

Pitching	IP	H	R	ER	BB	SO
Philadelphia						
Hudson (L)	4⅓	5	3	3	0	3
Hernandez	⅔	0	0	0	1	1
Andersen	2	3	1	1	0	1
Reed	1	1	0	0	1	1
Baltimore						
Boddicker (W)	9	3	1	0	0	6

Phil.	000 100 000
Balt.	000 030 10x

Baltimore	Pos	AB	R	H	RBI	PO	A	E
Bumbry	cf	2	0	0	0	2	0	0
a Shelby	cf	2	1	1	0	1	0	0
Ford	rf	3	0	1	0	1	0	0
Ripken	ss	3	0	1	1	1	6	0
Murray	1b	4	0	0	0	13	1	1
Lowenstein	lf	4	1	3	1	0	0	0
e Landrum	lf	0	0	0	0	0	0	0
Dauer	2b	4	1	0	0	2	2	0
Cruz	3b	4	1	1	0	0	3	0
Dempsey	c	3	0	1	1	6	1	0
Boddicker	p	3	0	1	1	1	2	0
Totals		32	4	9	4	27	15	1

a Struck out for Bumbry in 5th.
b Struck out for Hernandez in 6th.
c Ran for Diaz in 8th.
d Grounded into double play for Andersen in 8th.
e Ran for Lowenstein in 8th.

Doubles—Lowenstein, Dempsey. Home Run—Lowenstein. Stolen Bases—Morgan, Landrum. Sacrifice Flies—Lefebvre, Boddicker. Hit by Pitcher—Ford (by Hernandez). Double Play—Dauer to Ripken to Murray. Left on Bases—Philadelphia 2, Baltimore—8. Umpires—Vargo, Clark, Pulli, Palermo, Rennert, Springstead. Attendance—52,132. Time of Game—2:27.

1st Inning
Philadelphia
1 Morgan struck out swinging.
2 Rose struck out looking.
3 Schmidt grounded to short.
Baltimore
1 Bumbrey tapped out, Diaz to Rose.
2 Ford grounded to third.
3 Ripken flied to right.

2nd Inning
Philadelphia
1 Lefebvre struck out swinging.
2 Matthews grounded to third.
3 Gross grounded to second.
Baltimore
1 Murray flied to center.
Lowenstein doubled into the right-center alley.
2 Dauer flied to left, Lowenstein advancing to third after the catch.
3 Cruz flied to center.

3rd Inning
Philadelphia
1 Diaz popped to third.
2 DeJesus grounded to short.
3 Hudson rolled to the pitcher.
Baltimore
1 Dempsey popped to second.
2 Boddicker called out on strikes.
3 Bumbry struck out looking.

4th Inning
Philadelphia
Morgan singled to deep short.
Morgan stole second.
1 Rose out bunting, Dempsey to Murray, Morgan holding at second.
Schmidt safe at first on a grounder to Ripken, whose throw was dropped at first by Murray. Morgan went to third.
2 Lefebvre hit a sacrifice fly to center, Morgan scoring and Schmidt going to second after the catch.
3 Matthews flied to center.
Baltimore
1 Ford struck out swinging.
2 Ripken flied to center.
3 Murray grounded to third.

5th Inning
Philadelphia
1 Gross grounded to short.
2 Diaz took a called third strike.
3 DeJesus grounded out, Murray to Boddicker.
Baltimore
Lowenstein homered over the center field fence on a 2-0 count.
Dauer singled to left.
Cruz beat out a bunt single to third, when Schmidt had no one to throw to at first.
Dempsey doubled into the right field corner, scoring Dauer with Cruz going to third.
1 Boddicker lined a sacrifice fly to left, Cruz scoring after the catch.
For Philadelphia—Hernandez replaced Hudson on the mound.
2 Shelby, batting for Bumbry, took a called strike.
Ford was hit, beaned by a pitch.
Ripken walked, loading the bases.
3 Murray flied to center.

6th Inning
Philadelphia
For Baltimore—Shelby stayed in to play center.
1 Hayes, pinch-hitting for Hernandez, struck out swinging.
2 Morgan grounded to first.
3 Rose grounded to third.
Baltimore
For Philadelphia—Andersen pitching.
1 Lowenstein grounded out, Rose to Andersen.
2 Dauer lined to short.
3 Cruz grounded to third.

7th Inning
Philadelphia
1 Schmidt flied to right.
2 Lefebvre grounded to first.
Matthews singled to right.
3 Gross forced Matthews at second, Cruz to Dauer.
Baltimore
1 Dempsey struck out.
2 Boddicker grounded to short.
Shelby beat out a grounder to second.
Ford singled to right, Shelby advancing to third.
Ripken singled to right, Shelby scoring and Ford racing to third.
3 Murray grounded to second.

8th Inning
Philadelphia
Diaz singled to right.
Samuel ran for Diaz.
1 DeJesus forced Samuel at second, Ripken to Dauer.
2,3 Perez, batting for Andersen, grounded into a double play, Dauer to Ripken to Murray.
Baltimore
For Philadelphia—Virgil catching with Reed on the mound.
Lowenstein singled to left.
Landrum ran for Lowenstein.
1 Dauer struck out as he fouled off a third strike bunt attempt.
Landrum stole second.
2 Cruz fouled to Rose.
Dempsey walked intentionally.
3 Boddicker flied to center.

9th Inning
Philadelphia
For Baltimore—Landrum stays in to play right field.
1 Morgan flied to deep center.
2 Rose bounced back to the mound.
3 Schmidt struck out.

Game 3 October 14 at Philadelphia

Baltimore	Pos	AB	R	H	RBI	PO	A	E
Shelby	cf	4	0	2	0	5	0	0
Ford	rf	3	1	1	1	1	0	0
Ripken	ss	3	0	0	1	3	0	0
Murray	1b	4	0	0	0	10	0	0
Roenicke	lf	4	0	0	0	1	1	0
Dauer	2b	4	0	0	0	4	2	0
Cruz	3b	3	0	0	0	0	4	1
Dempsey	c	4	1	2	0	5	2	0
Flanagan	p	1	0	0	0	0	0	0
a Singleton		1	0	0	0	0	0	0
Palmer	p	0	0	0	0	0	0	0
b Ayala		1	1	1	1	0	0	0
Stewart	p	1	0	0	0	1	0	0
T. Martinez	p	0	0	0	0	0	0	0
Totals		33	3	6	2	27	13	1

Pitching	IP	H	R	ER	BB	SO
Baltimore						
Flanagan	4	6	2	2	1	1
Palmer (W)	2	2	0	0	1	1
Stewart	2	0	0	0	1	3
T. Martinez (SV)	1	0	0	0	0	0
Philadelphia						
Carlton (L)	6⅔	5	3	2	3	7
Holland	2⅓	1	0	0	0	4

Balt.	000 001 200
Phil.	011 000 000

Philadelphia	Pos	AB	R	H	RBI	PO	A	E
Morgan	2b	3	1	1	1	5	2	0
Lezcano	rf	4	0	1	0	1	0	0
Hayes	rf	0	0	0	0	1	0	0
Schmidt	3b	4	0	0	0	0	4	1
Matthews	lf	3	1	1	1	0	0	0
Perez	1b	4	0	1	0	8	0	0
Maddox	cf	4	0	0	1	0	0	0
Diaz	c	3	0	2	0	11	0	0
c Lefebvre		0	0	0	0	0	0	0
d Rose		1	0	0	0	0	0	0
DeJesus	ss	3	0	2	0	0	5	1
Carlton	p	3	0	0	0	0	0	0
Holland	p	0	0	0	0	0	0	0
e Virgil		1	0	0	0	0	0	0
Totals		33	2	8	2	27	11	2

a Struck out for Flanagan in 5th.
b Singled for Palmer in 7th.
c Announced for Diaz in 9th.
d Grounded out for Lefebvre in 9th.
e Grounded out for Holland in 9th.

Doubles—Dempsey 2. Home Runs—Matthews, Morgan, Ford. Double Plays—DeJesus to Morgan to Perez, Morgan to Perez. Left on Bases—Baltimore 6, Philadelphia 7. Umpires—Clark, Pulli, Palermo, Rennert, Springstead, Vargo. Attendance—65,792. Time of Game—2:35.

1st Inning
Baltimore
1 Shelby called out on strikes.
2 Ford bounced to short.
3 Ripken struck out.
Philadelphia
1 Morgan grounded to second.
2 Lezcano grounded to short.
3 Schmidt flied to center.

2nd Inning
Baltimore
1 Murray struck out.
2 Roenicke grounded to short.
3 Dauer grounded to short.
Philadelphia
Matthews homered over the left-center field fence on the first pitch.
Perez singled to center.
1 Maddox flied to center.
2 Diaz flied to center.
DeJesus singled to right, Perez safe at third when Cruz dropped the throw for an error as DeJesus got to second (Ford an assist on the play).
3 Carlton grounded to third.

3rd Inning
Baltimore
Cruz walked.
1,2 Dempsey hit into a double play, DeJesus, making a good backhanded stop in the hole, to Morgan to Perez.
3 Flanagan took a called third strike.
Philadelphia
Morgan homered over the right field wall on a 2-1 pitch.
1 Lezcano flied to right.
2 Schmidt grounded to third.
Matthews walked, first walk given up by Orioles staff in the Series.
3 Perez flied to left.

4th Inning
Baltimore
Shelby singled to center.
Ford walked.
Ripken walked, loading the bases.
1 Murray popped to Morgan.
2,3 Roenicke hit into a double play, Schmidt to Morgan to Perez.
Philadelphia
1 Maddox struck out on a pitch in the dirt, thrown out Dempsey to Murray.
Diaz singled down the left field foul line but was out trying for second, Roenicke to Dauer.
DeJesus beat out a hard grounder to second.
3 Carlton grounded to second.

5th Inning
Baltimore
1 Dauer grounded to third.
2 Cruz grounded to third.
Dempsey doubled into the left field corner.
3 Singleton, batting for Flanagan, took a called third strike.
Philadelphia
For Baltimore—Palmer pitching.
1 Morgan popped to second.
Lezcano singled to right-center.
2 Schmidt fouled to Dempsey.
3 Matthews forced Lezcano at second, Cruz to Dauer.

6th Inning
Baltimore
1 Shelby struck out.
Ford homered over the left field wall on the first pitch.
Ripken safe at first on Schmidt's throwing error to first.
2 Murray struck out.
3 Roenicke forced Ripken at second, DeJesus to Morgan.
Philadelphia
1 Perez flied to Shelby who made a running catch in right-center.
2 Maddox grounded to short.
Diaz bounced a single off the plate over the mound with no play at first.
Diaz went to second on Palmer's wild pitch.
DeJesus walked.
3 Carlton struck out.

7th Inning
Baltimore
1 Dauer flied to right.
2 Cruz grounded to third.
Dempsey doubled to deep left-center.
Dempsey went to third on Carlton's wild pitch.
Ayala, batting for Palmer, lined a single to left, scoring Dempsey.
For Philadelphia—Holland relieved Carlton.
Shelby singled to left, Ayala stopping at second.
Ford safe when DeJesus booted his grounder into left, Ayala scoring. Shelby went to second.
3 Ripken flied to center.
Philadelphia
For Baltimore—Stewart pitching.
Morgan walked.
1 Lezcano struck out looking after missing two bunt attempts.
2 Morgan out trying to steal, Dempsey to Dauer.
3 Schmidt struck out.

8th Inning
Baltimore
For Philadelphia—Hayes playing right.
1 Murray flied to right.
2 Roenicke struck out swinging.
3 Dauer struck out swinging.
Philadelphia
1 Matthews struck out swinging.
2 Perez popped to Ripken in short left.
3 Maddox grounded to third.

9th Inning
Baltimore
1 Cruz popped to second.
2 Dempsey called out on strikes.
3 Stewart struck out swinging.
Philadelphia
Lefebvre announced for Diaz.
For Baltimore—T. Martinez pitching.
1 Rose, batting for Lefebvre, grounded to third.
2 DeJesus flied to center.
3 Virgil, batting for Holland, grounded to short.

Game 4 October 15 at Philadelphia

Baltimore	Pos	AB	R	H	RBI	PO	A	E
Bumbry	cf	3	0	0	0	3	0	0
e Ford		1	0	0	0	0	0	0
Stewart	p	1	0	0	0	0	0	0
T. Martinez	p	0	0	0	0	0	0	0
Dwyer	rf	5	2	2	0	0	0	0
Landrum	rf	0	0	0	0	0	0	0
Ripken	ss	5	1	1	0	0	1	0
Murray	lb	4	0	1	0	9	0	0
Lowenstein	lf	4	1	1	0	2	0	1
Dauer	2b-3b	4	1	3	3	3	2	0
Cruz	3b	2	0	1	0	0	1	0
a Nolan	c	1	0	0	0	2	0	0
Dempsey	c	1	0	0	0	3	0	0
b Singleton		0	0	0	1	0	0	0
c Sakata	2b	1	0	0	0	2	2	0
Davis	p	2	0	0	0	0	1	0
d Shelby	cf	1	0	1	1	3	0	0
Totals		35	5	10	5	27	7	1

a Intentionally walked for Cruz in 6th.
b Walked for Dempsey in 6th.
c Ran for Singleton in 6th.
d Hit sacrifice fly for Davis in 6th.
e Struck out for Bumbry in 6th.
f Grounded out for Reed in 7th.
g Singled for Lefebvre in 8th.
h Ran for Perez in 8th.
i Grounded out for G. Gross in 9th.
j Ran for Diaz in 9th.
k Singled for Andersen in 9th.

Doubles—Lefebvre, Diaz, Rose, Dauer, Dwyer. Sacrifice Fly—Shelby. Wild Pitch—Davis. Balk—Stewart. Double Plays—Dauer to Murray, Ripken to Sakata to Murray, Andersen to DeJesus to Morgan. Left on Bases—Baltimore 8, Philadelphia 6. Umpires—Pulli, Palermo, Rennert, Springstead, Vargo, Clark. Attendance—66,947. Time of Game—2:50

Balt.	000	202	100
Phil.	000	120	001

Philadelphia	Pos	AB	R	H	RBI	PO	A	E
Morgan	2b	5	0	0	0	1	1	0
Rose	1b	3	1	2	1	5	3	0
Schmidt	3b	4	0	1	0	0	0	0
Lefebvre	rf	3	0	1	1	2	0	0
g Perez		1	0	1	0	0	0	0
h Samuel		0	0	0	0	0	0	0
Lezcano	rf	0	0	0	0	1	0	0
Matthews	lf	3	0	1	0	3	0	0
G. Gross	cf	3	0	0	0	3	0	0
i Maddox		1	0	0	0	0	0	0
Diaz	c	4	1	2	0	7	0	0
j Dernier		0	1	0	0	0	0	0
DeJesus	ss	4	0	0	0	2	1	0
Denny	p	2	1	1	1	3	1	0
Hernandez	p	0	0	0	0	0	0	0
Reed	p	0	0	0	0	0	0	0
f Hayes		1	0	0	0	0	0	0
Andersen	p	0	0	0	0	0	1	0
k Virgil		1	0	1	1	0	0	0
Totals		35	4	10	4	27	7	0

Pitching	IP	H	R	ER	BB	SO
Baltimore						
Davis (W)	5	6	3	3	1	3
Stewart	$2\frac{1}{3}$	1	0	0	1	2
T. Martinez (SV)	$1\frac{2}{3}$	3	1	1	0	0
Philadelphia						
Denny (L)	$5\frac{1}{3}$	7	4	4	3	4
Hernandez	$\frac{1}{3}$	0	0	0	0	0
Reed	$1\frac{1}{3}$	2	1	1	1	3
Andersen	2	1	0	0	0	0

1st Inning
Baltimore
1 Bumbry grounded out, Rose to Denny.
2 Dwyer grounded to second.
3 Ripken flied to deep left.
Philadelphia
1 Morgan struck out swinging.
2 Rose struck out swinging.
3 Schmidt struck out looking.

2nd Inning
Baltimore
1 Murray flied to right.
2 Lowenstein lined to center.
3 Dauer grounded to the pitcher.
Philadelphia
1 Lefebvre flied to center.
2 Matthews grounded to third.
3 Gross grounded to the pitcher.

3rd Inning
Baltimore
Cruz singled over the mound.
1 Dempsey flied to center.
2 Davis struck out attempting to bunt.
3 Bumbry lined to left.
Philadelphia
1 Diaz popped to Dauer in shallow right.
2 DeJesus flied to center, good catch.
3 Denny lined to left.

4th Inning
Baltimore
Dwyer lined a single to right.
Ripken singled to left, Dwyer to second.
Murray singled to right, bases loaded.
1 Lowenstein struck out swinging.
Dauer singled to right, Dwyer and Ripken scoring with Murray advancing to third.
2 Cruz struck out swinging.
Dempsey intentionally walked to again load the bases.
3 Davis called out on strikes.
Philadelphia
1 Morgan flied to center.
Rose lined a single to center.
Schmidt blooped a broken-bat single to left, Rose advancing to third.
Lefebvre doubled into the right field corner, scoring Rose as Schmidt stopped at third.
Matthews walked, loading the bases.
2,3 Gross grounded into a double play, Dauer to Murray.

5th Inning
Baltimore
1 Bumbry grounded out, Rose to Denny.
2 Dwyer grounded out also, Rose to Denny.
3 Ripken popped to first.
Philadelphia
Diaz doubled down the left field line.
1 DeJesus lined to first.
Diaz to third on a wild pitch.
Denny singled to left, scoring Diaz and went to second on Lowenstein's throwing error to the plate.
2 Morgan grounded to first, advancing Denny to third.
Rose lined a double to left-center, scoring Denny.
3 Schmidt flied to Lowenstein, making a good catch in left-center.

6th Inning
Baltimore
1 Murray flied to center.
Lowenstein lined a single to center.
Dauer doubled down the left field line, advancing Lowenstein to third.
Nolan, batting for Cruz, was walked intentionally loading the bases.
Singleton, batting for Dempsey, walked, forcing in Lowenstein.
Sakata ran for Singleton.
Shelby announced for Davis.
For Philadelphia—Hernandez replaced Denny on the mound.
2 Shelby hit a sacrifice fly to Matthews, making a super leaping catch against the wall, scoring Dauer.
Ford announced for Bumbry.
For Philadelphia—Reed relieved Hernandez.
3 Ford struck out on a foul tip.
Philadelphia
For Baltimore—Nolan catching, Sakata at second, Shelby in center, Dauer moved to third as Stewart came in to pitch.
1 Lefebvre flied to center.
Matthews singled to center.
2 Gross lined to center.
Matthews went to second on a Stewart balk.
3 Diaz took a called third strike.

7th Inning
Baltimore
Dwyer doubled to the gap in left-center.
1 Ripken called out on strikes.
Murray walked.
2 Lowenstein struck out swinging.
Dauer singled to center, scoring Dwyer with Murray stopping at second.
3 Nolan popped to DeJesus with an over the shoulder catch in short left.
Philadelphia
1 DeJesus struck out swinging.
2 Hayes, batting for Reed, grounded to first.
3 Morgan flied to center.

8th Inning
Baltimore
For Philadelphia—Andersen pitching.
1 Sakata flied to right.
Shelby singled to right.
2,3 Stewart bunted into a double play, Andersen to DeJesus to Morgan.
Philadelphia
Rose walked on four pitches.
1 Schmidt foul popped to Dauer.
For Baltimore—T. Martinez relieved Stewart on the mound.
Perez, pinch-hitting for Lefebvre, singled to center, Rose stopping at second.
Samuel ran for Perez.
2,3 Matthews hit into a double play, Ripken to Sakata to Murray.

9th Inning
Baltimore
For Philadelphia—Lezcano in right.
1 Dwyer grounded to first.
2 Ripken lined to right.
3 Murray grounded to first.
Philadelphia
For Baltimore—Landrum playing right.
1 Maddox, batting for Gross, grounded to second.
Diaz lined a single to right.
Dernier ran for Diaz.
2 DeJesus grounded to third, Dernier going to second.
Virgil, batting for Andersen, singled to center, scoring Dernier.
3 Morgan lined to second.

Game 5 October 16 at Philadelphia

Baltimore	Pos	AB	R	H	RBI	PO	A	E
Bumbry	cf	2	0	0	1	3	0	0
c Shelby	cf	1	0	0	0	1	0	0
Ford	rf	4	0	0	0	3	0	0
Landrum	rf	0	0	0	0	1	0	0
Ripken	ss	3	1	0	0	3	0	0
Murray	1b	4	2	3	3	6	0	0
Lowenstein	lf	2	0	0	0	0	0	0
b Roenicke	lf	2	0	0	0	1	0	0
Dauer	2b	4	0	0	0	2	1	0
Cruz	3b	4	0	0	0	0	6	0
Dempsey	c	3	2	2	1	7	0	0
McGregor	p	3	0	0	0	0	0	0
Totals		32	5	5	5	27	7	0

a Flied out for Bystrom in 5th.
b Struck out for Lowenstein in 6th.
c Flied out for Bumbry in 8th.
d Grounded out for Hernandez in 8th.

Doubles—Dempsey, Maddox. Triple—Morgan. Home Runs—Murray 2, Dempsey. Sacrifice Fly—Bumbry. Wild Pitch—Bystrom. Double Play—Cruz to Dauer to Murray. Left on Bases—Baltimore 2, Philadelphia 6. Umpires—Palermo, Rennert, Springstead, Vargo, Clark, Pulli. Attendance—67,064. Time of Game—2:21

Balt.	011	210	000
Phil.	000	000	000

Philadelphia	Pos	AB	R	H	RBI	PO	A	E
Morgan	2b	3	0	1	0	0	1	0
Rose	rf	4	0	2	0	3	0	0
Schmidt	3b	4	0	0	0	1	2	0
Matthews	lf	4	0	0	0	6	0	0
Perez	1b	4	0	0	0	5	1	0
Maddox	cf	4	0	2	0	3	0	0
Diaz	c	2	0	0	0	7	0	1
DeJesus	ss	3	0	0	0	1	2	0
Hudson	p	1	0	0	0	0	0	0
Bystrom	p	0	0	0	0	0	0	0
a Samuel		1	0	0	0	0	0	0
Hernandez	p	0	0	0	0	1	0	0
d Lezcano		1	0	0	0	0	0	0
Reed	p	0	0	0	0	0	0	0
Totals		31	0	5	0	27	6	1

Pitching	IP	H	R	ER	BB	SO
Baltimore						
McGregor (W)	9	5	0	0	2	6
Philadelphia						
Hudson (L)	*4	4	5	5	1	3
Bystrom	1	0	0	0	0	1
Hernandez	3	0	0	0	0	3
Reed	1	1	0	0	0	0

*Pitched to one batter in 5th.

1st Inning
Baltimore
1 Bumbry lined to short.
2 Ford struck out swinging.
3 Ripken lined to Matthews making a lunging back-handed catch in left.
Philadelphia
1 Morgan struck out swinging.
Rose singled to center.
2 Schmidt flied to right.
3 Matthews also flied to right.

2nd Inning
Baltimore
Murray homered over the right field wall on a 2-2 pitch.
1 Lowenstein flied to deep right.
2 Dauer flied to short center.
3 Cruz struck out swinging.
Philadelphia
1 Perez struck out swinging.
2 Maddox flied to center.
3 Diaz foul popped to Murray.

3rd Inning
Baltimore
Dempsey homered over the wall in left on the first pitch.
1 McGregor flied to right.
2 Bumbry grounded to short.
3 Ford struck out swinging.
Philadelphia
1 DeJesus flied to right.
2 Hudson struck out swinging.
Morgan walked.
3 Rose popped to short.

4th Inning
Baltimore
Ripken walked.
Murray hit a two-run homer into the right-center field stands on a 0-1 pitch.
1 Lowenstein popped to third.
2 Dauer flied to left.
3 Cruz flied to left.
Philadelphia
1 Schmidt grounded to third.
2 Matthews struck out swinging.
3 Perez flied to center.

5th Inning
Baltimore
Dempsey doubled off the left-center field wall.
For Philadelphia—Bystrom relieved Hudson on the mound.
McGregor safe at first when Diaz dropped his bunt for an error. Dempsey stayed at second.
Both runners advanced one base on a Bystrom wild pitch.
1 Bumbry hit a sacrifice fly to left, Dempsey scoring after the catch.
2 Ford grounded to short, McGregor holding at second.
3 Ripken struck out looking

5th Inning (continued)
Philadelphia
Maddox looped a single to right-center.
Diaz walked on four pitches.
1,2 DeJesus grounded into a double play, Cruz to Dauer to Murray, with Maddox going to third.
3 Samuel, batting for Bystrom, flied to center.

6th Inning
Baltimore
For Philadelphia—Hernandez the new pitcher.
1 Murray struck out swinging.
2 Roenicke, pinch-hitting for Lowenstein, also struck out swinging.
3 Dauer grounded out, Perez to Hernandez.
Philadelphia
For Baltimore—Roenicke playing left.
1 Morgan popped to short.
Rose singled to right.
2 Schmidt struck out swinging.
3 Matthews forced Rose at second, Cruz to Dauer.

7th Inning
Baltimore
1 Cruz grounded to third.
2 Dempsey flied to left.
3 McGregor bounced to second.
Philadelphia
1 Perez called out on strikes.
Maddox doubled off the left-center field wall.
2 Diaz fouled to Dempsey.
3 DeJesus grounded to third.

8th Inning
Baltimore
1 Shelby, pinch-hitting for Bumbry, flied to center.
2 Ford struck out swinging for the third time in the game.
3 Ripken lined to right.
Philadelphia
For Baltimore—Shelby stayed in to play center, Landrum replaced Ford in right.
1 Lezcano, batting for Hernandez, grounded to third.
Morgan tripled down the right field line.
2 Rose flied to left, Morgan retreated back to third after he fell down.
3 Schmidt grounded to third.

9th Inning
Baltimore
For Philadelphia—Reed pitching.
Murray singled to right.
1 Roenicke flied to deep center.
2 Dauer flied to left.
3 Cruz grounded to third.
Philadelphia
1 Matthews flied to right.
2 Perez flied to center.
3 Maddox lined to short.

1983 WORLD SERIES COMPOSITE BOX

	Wins	Composite Line Score
Baltimore Orioles	4	1 1 1 4 4 3 4 0 0 - 18
Philadelphia Phillies	1	0 1 1 2 2 1 0 1 1 - 9

Manager	Regular Season W	L	Pct.	G. Ahead
Joe Altobell:	98	64	.605	6
Paul Owens	90	72	.556	6

BATTING AND FIELDING

BALTIMORE ORIOLES

	Pos	G	AB	R	H	2B	3B	HR	RBI	BB	SO	SB	BA	SA	PO	A	E		Main Pos	G	AB	R	H	2B	3B	HR	RBI	BB	SO	SB	BA	SA
	WORLD SERIES STATISTICS																		REGULAR SEASON STATISTICS													
Eddie Murray	1b	5	20	2	5	0	0	2	3	1	4	0	.250	.550	46	1	1		1b	156	582	115	178	30	3	33	111	86	90	5	.306	.538
Rich Dauer	2b-3b	5	19	2	4	1	0	0	3	0	3	0	.211	.263	14	8	0		2b	140	459	49	108	19	0	5	41	47	29	1	.235	.309
Cal Ripken	ss	5	18	2	3	0	0	0	1	3	4	0	.167	.167	6	14	0		ss	162	663	121	211	47	2	27	102	58	97	0	.318	.517
Todd Cruz	3b	5	16	1	2	0	0	0	0	1	3	0	.125	.125	0	17	2	a	3b	81	221	16	46	9	1	3	27	15	52	3	.208	.299
Dan Ford	ph-rf	5	12	1	2	0	0	1	1	1	5	0	.167	.417	5	1	0		of	103	407	63	114	30	4	9	55	29	55	9	.280	.440
Al Bumbry	cf	4	11	0	1	1	0	0	1	0	1	0	.091	.182	12	0	0		of	124	378	63	104	14	4	3	31	31	33	12	.275	.357
John Lowenstein	lf	4	13	2	5	1	0	1	1	0	3	0	.385	.692	4	0	1		of	122	310	52	87	13	2	15	60	49	55	2	.281	.481
Rick Dempsey	c	5	13	3	5	4	0	1	2	2	2	0	.385	.923	27	4	0		c	127	347	33	80	16	2	4	32	40	55	1	.231	.323
John Shelby	ph-cf	5	9	1	4	0	0	0	1	0	4	0	.444	.444	10	0	0		of	126	325	52	84	15	2	5	27	18	64	15	.258	.363
Jim Dwyer	rf	2	8	3	3	1	0	1	1	0	0	0	.375	.875	2	0	0		of	100	196	37	56	17	1	8	38	31	29	1	.286	.505
Gary Roenicke	ph-lf	3	7	0	0	0	0	0	0	0	2	0	.000	.000	2	1	0		of	115	323	45	84	13	0	19	64	30	35	2	.260	.477
Joe Nolan	ph-c	2	2	0	0	0	0	0	0	1	0	0	.000	.000	3	0	0		c	73	184	25	51	11	1	5	24	16	30	0	.277	.429
Ken Singleton	ph	2	1	0	0	0	0	0	1	1	1	0	.000	.000	—	—	—		dh	151	507	52	140	21	3	18	84	99	83	0	.276	.436
Benny Ayala	ph	1	1	1	1	0	0	0	1	0	0	0	1.000	1.000	—	—	—		of	47	104	12	23	7	0	4	13	9	18	0	.221	.404
Lenn Sakata	pr-2b	1	1	0	0	0	0	0	0	0	0	0	.000	.000	2	2	0		2b	66	134	23	34	7	0	3	12	16	17	8	.254	.373
Tito Landrum	pr-lf-rf	3	0	0	0	0	0	0	0	0	0	1	—	—	1	0	0	b	of	26	42	8	13	2	0	1	4	1	0	0	.310	.429
Scott McGregor	p	2	5	0	0	0	0	0	0	0	0	0	.000	.000	0	0	0		p	36	0	0	0	0	0	0	0	0	0	0	—	—
Mike Boddicker	p	1	3	0	0	0	0	0	1	0	1	0	.000	.000	1	2	0		p	27	0	0	0	0	0	0	0	0	0	0	—	—
Sammy Stewart	p	3	2	0	0	0	0	0	0	0	1	0	.000	.000	0	0	0		p	58	0	0	0	0	0	0	0	0	0	0	—	—
Storm Davis	p	1	2	0	0	0	0	0	0	0	2	0	.000	.000	0	1	0		p	34	0	0	0	0	0	0	0	0	0	0	—	—
Mike Flanagan	p	1	1	0	0	0	0	0	0	0	1	0	.000	.000	0	0	0		p	20	0	0	0	0	0	0	0	0	0	0	—	—
Tippy Martinez	p	3	0	0	0	0	0	0	0	0	0	0	—	—	0	0	0		p	65	0	0	0	0	0	0	0	0	0	0	—	—
Jim Palmer	p	1	0	0	0	0	0	0	0	0	0	0	—	—	0	0	0		p	14	0	0	0	0	0	0	0	0	0	0	—	—
Dennis Martinez	Did not play																		p	32	0	0	0	0	0	0	0	0	0	0	—	—
Tim Stoddard	Did not play																		p	47	0	0	0	0	0	0	0	0	0	0	—	—
team total		5	164	18	35	8	0	6	17	10	37	1	.213	.372	135	51	4			162	5546	652	1492	283	27	168	761	601	800	61	.269	.421

Double Plays—5
Left on Bases—28

a—from Seattle b—from St. Louis
Leo Hernandez (3b), Aurelio Rodriguez (3b), Mike Young (of), Glenn Gulliver (3b), John Stefaro (c), Bob Bonner (2b), Dave Huppert (c), Allan Ramirez (p), Bill Swaggerty (p), Paul Mirabella (p), Dan Maragiello (p), and Don Welchel (p) also played for the Orioles during the season.

PHILADELPHIA PHILLIES

	Pos	G	AB	R	H	2B	3B	HR	RBI	BB	SO	SB	BA	SA	PO	A	E		Main Pos	G	AB	R	H	2B	3B	HR	RBI	BB	SO	SB	BA	SA
Pete Rose	1b-ph-rf	5	16	1	5	1	0	0	1	1	3	0	.313	.375	26	4	0		1b	151	493	52	121	14	3	0	45	52	28	7	.245	.286
Joe Morgan	2b	5	19	3	5	0	1	2	2	2	3	1	.263	.684	8	10	0		2b	123	404	72	93	20	1	16	59	89	54	18	.230	.403
Ivan DeJesus	ss	5	16	0	2	0	0	0	0	1	2	0	.125	.125	5	14	1		ss	158	497	60	126	15	7	4	45	53	77	11	.254	.336
Mike Schmidt	3b	5	20	0	1	0	0	0	0	0	6	0	.050	.050	1	10	1		3b	154	534	104	136	16	4	40	109	128	148	7	.255	.524
Sixto Lezcano	ph-rf	4	8	0	1	0	0	0	0	0	2	0	.125	.125	2	0	0	c	of	18	39	8	11	1	0	0	7	5	9	1	.282	.308
Garry Maddox	ph-cf	4	12	1	3	1	0	1	1	0	2	0	.250	.583	7	0	0		of	97	324	27	89	14	2	4	32	17	31	7	.275	.367
Gary Matthews	lf	5	16	1	4	0	0	1	1	2	2	0	.250	.438	15	0	0		of	132	446	66	115	18	2	10	50	69	81	13	.258	.374
Bo Diaz	c	5	15	1	5	1	0	0	0	1	2	0	.333	.400	37	1	1		c	136	471	49	111	17	0	15	64	38	57	1	.236	.367
Tony Perez	ph-1b	4	10	0	2	0	0	0	0	0	2	0	.200	.200	13	1	0		1b,ph	91	253	18	61	11	2	6	43	28	57	1	.241	.372
Greg Gross	cf	2	6	0	0	0	0	0	0	0	0	0	.000	.000	8	0	0		of	136	245	25	74	12	3	0	29	34	16	3	.302	.376
Joe Lefebvre	ph-rf	3	5	0	1	1	0	0	2	0	1	0	.200	.400	3	0	0	c	of	101	258	34	80	20	8	8	38	31	46	5	.310	.543
Von Hayes	ph-rf	4	3	0	0	0	0	0	0	0	1	0	.000	.000	1	0	0		of	124	351	45	93	9	5	6	32	36	55	20	.265	.370
Ozzie Virgil	ph-c	3	2	0	1	0	0	0	1	0	0	0	.500	.500	1	0	0		c	55	140	11	30	7	0	6	23	8	34	0	.214	.393
Juan Samuel	pr-ph	3	1	0	0	0	0	0	0	0	0	0	.000	.000	—	—	—		2b	18	65	14	18	1	2	2	5	4	16	3	.277	.446
Bob Dernier	pr	1	0	1	0	0	0	0	0	0	0	0	—	—	—	—	—		of	122	221	41	51	10	0	1	15	18	21	35	.231	.290
Kiko Garcia	Did not play																		inf	84	118	22	34	7	1	2	9	9	20	1	.288	.415
John Denny	p	2	5	1	1	0	0	0	1	0	1	0	.200	.200	3	1	0		p	36	77	7	13	1	0	0	2	2	16	2	.169	.182
Charlie Hudson	p	2	2	0	0	0	0	0	0	0	1	0	.000	.000	0	0	0		p	27	54	4	5	0	0	0	3	2	32	0	.093	.093
Steve Carlton	p	1	3	0	0	0	0	0	0	0	1	0	.000	.000	0	0	0		p	37	97	9	19	5	0	0	1	2	20	0	.196	.247
Willie Hernandez	p	3	0	0	0	0	0	0	0	0	0	0	—	—	1	0	0	d	p	63	13	2	5	0	0	0	1	0	5	1	.385	.385
Larry Andersen	p	2	0	0	0	0	0	0	0	0	0	0	—	—	1	1	0		p	17	2	0	0	0	0	0	0	0	0	0	.000	.000
Al Holland	p	2	0	0	0	0	0	0	0	0	0	0	—	—	0	0	0		p	68	7	0	0	0	0	0	0	0	5	0	.000	.000
Ron Reed	p	3	0	0	0	0	0	0	0	0	0	0	—	—	0	0	0		p	61	6	0	1	0	0	0	0	0	2	0	.167	.167
Marty Bystrom	p	1	0	0	0	0	0	0	0	0	0	0	—	—	0	0	0		p	24	38	2	9	1	0	0	4	2	14	0	.237	.263
Kevin Gross	Did not play																		p	17	33	1	3	1	0	0	1	1	14	1	.091	.121
team total		5	159	9	31	4	1	4	9	7	29	1	.195	.308	132	42	3			163	5426	696	1352	209	45	125	649	640	906	143	.249	.373

Double Plays—3
Left on Bases—23

c—from San Diego d—from Chicago Cubs
Larry Milbourne (2b), Len Matuszek (1b), Bob Molinaro (ph), Steve Jeltz (inf.), Bill Robinson (1b), Jeff Stone (pr-ph), Alex Sanchez (of), Tim Corcoran (1b), Luis Aguayo (ss), Darren Daulton (c), Sid Monge (p), Tug McGraw (p), Porfi Altomarino (p), Larry Christiansen (p), Steve Comer (p), Tony Ghelfi (p), Dick Ruthven (p), Don Carman (p) and Ed Farmer also played for the Phillies during the season.

PITCHING

BALTIMORE ORIOLES

	G	GS	CG	IP	H	R	ER	BB	SO	W	L	SV	ERA	G	GS	CG	IP	H	ER	BB	SO	W	L	Pct	SV	ShO	ERA
	WORLD SERIES STATISTICS													REGULAR SEASON STATISTICS													
Scott McGregor	2	2	1	17	9	2	2	2	12	1	1	0	1.06	36	36	12	260	271	92	45	86	18	7	.720	0	2	3.18
Mike Boddicker	1	1	1	9	3	1	0	0	6	1	0	0	0.00	27	26	10	179	141	55	52	120	16	8	.667	0	5	2.77
Sammy Stewart	3	0	0	5	2	0	0	2	6	0	0	0	0.00	58	1	0	144	138	58	67	95	9	4	.692	7	0	3.62
Storm Davis	1	1	0	5	6	3	3	1	3	1	0	0	5.40	34	29	6	200	180	80	64	125	13	7	.650	0	1	3.59
Mike Flanagan	1	1	0	4	6	2	2	1	1	0	0	0	4.50	20	20	3	125	135	46	31	50	12	4	.750	0	1	3.30
Tippy Martinez	3	0	0	3	3	1	1	0	0	0	0	2	3.00	65	0	0	103	76	27	37	81	9	3	.750	21	0	2.35
Jim Palmer	1	0	0	2	2	0	0	1	1	1	0	0	0.00	14	11	0	77	86	36	19	34	5	4	.556	0	0	4.23
Dennis Martinez	Did not play													32	25	4	153	209	94	45	71	7	16	.304	0	0	5.53
Tim Stoddard	Did not play													47	0	0	58	65	39	29	50	4	3	.571	9	0	6.09
team total	5	5	2	45	31	9	8	7	29	4	1	2	1.60	162	162	36	1452	1451	585	452	774	98	64	.605	38	15	3.63

PHILADELPHIA PHILLIES

	G	GS	CG	IP	H	R	ER	BB	SO	W	L	SV	ERA	G	GS	CG	IP	H	ER	BB	SO	W	L	Pct	SV	ShO	ERA
John Denny	2	2	0	13	12	5	5	3	9	1	1	0	3.46	36	36	7	243	229	64	53	139	19	6	.760	0	1	2.37
Charlie Hudson	2	2	0	$8\frac{1}{3}$	9	8	8	1	6	0	2	0	8.64	26	26	3	169	158	63	53	101	8	8	.500	0	0	3.35
Steve Carlton	1	1	0	$6\frac{2}{3}$	5	3	2	3	7	0	1	0	2.70	37	37	8	284	277	98	84	275	15	16	.484	0	3	3.11
Willie Hernandez	3	0	0	4	0	0	0	1	4	0	0	0	0.00	63	0	0	96	93	35	26	75	8	4	.667	7	0	3.29
Larry Andersen	2	0	0	4	4	1	1	0	1	0	0	0	2.25	17	0	0	26	19	7	9	14	1	0	1.000	0	0	2.39
Al Holland	2	0	0	$3\frac{2}{3}$	1	0	0	0	5	0	0	1	0.00	68	0	0	92	63	23	30	100	8	4	.667	25	0	2.26
Ron Reed	3	0	0	$3\frac{1}{3}$	4	1	1	2	4	0	0	0	2.70	61	0	0	96	89	37	34	73	9	1	.900	8	0	3.48
Marty Bystrom	1	0	0	1	0	0	0	0	1	0	0	0	0.00	24	23	1	119	136	61	44	87	6	9	.400	0	1	4.60
Kevin Gross	Did not play													17	17	1	96	100	38	35	66	4	6	.400	0	1	3.56
team total	5	5	0	44	35	18	17	10	37	1	4	1	3.48	163	163	20	1462	1429	542	464	1092	90	72	.556	41	10	3.34

Total Attendance—304,139 Average Attendance—60,690 Winning Player's Share—$65,488 Losing Player's Share—$43,280

1984
A Logical Conclusion

Joylessly, everyone predicted a mismatch. On the one hand, the Tigers had led the A.L. East nonstop from day one, then swept the Royals in the LCS. Sparky Anderson had built a team with classic strength up the middle. Lance Parrish, Lou Whitaker, Alan Trammell, and Chet Lemon all combined great defense with potent bats. Right fielder Kirk Gibson added to the mix with the best hitting of his career. The trio of Jack Morris, Dan Petry, and Milt Wilcox anchored the starting rotation, while Willie Hernandez and Aurelio Lopez saved games with astounding regularity. Anderson had managed the Reds to two World Championships; he now aimed to do the same with an American League team.

San Diego manager Dick Williams had won with the Oakland A's and had beaten Anderson's Reds in 1972. His Padres had opened up a big lead in the N.L. West in July, only to straggle home with a 28–28 record after August 1. They had taken three straight from the Cubs in the LCS after losing the first two games. Young slugger Kevin McReynolds broke his left wrist in game four of the LCS, and the San Diego starting pitchers had been chewed up by the Cubs. Williams had three Series veterans in Steve Garvey, Graig Nettles, and Goose Gossage, the latter two new arrivals from the Yankees. Tony Gwynn developed into the N.L. batting champ, while a sterling bullpen held the mound staff together.

Bereft of his best pitches, Jack Morris nevertheless went all the way for a 3–2 triumph in game one. The Tigers scored in the top of the first off Mark Thurmond with a Whitaker double and a Trammell single. A two-run double by Terry Kennedy put the Padres ahead 2–1 in the bottom of the first. Larry Herndon responded with a two-run homer to right in the fifth for a 3–2 Tiger lead. The Padres began the sixth with singles by Nettles and Kennedy. Bobby Brown tried to bunt and wound up striking out. Morris then fanned Carmelo Martinez and Gary Templeton to end the threat. Utilityman Kurt Bevacqua went from hero to goat in seconds as he opened the Padre seventh with a double to right and was thrown out trying for a triple.

In game two, Padre starter Ed Whitson lasted 2/3 of an inning, bombed for three runs in the top of the first. The Padres scored a run in the first on a bunt, a walk, and two sacrifices. Two singles and a ground out brought another home against Dan Petry in the fourth. In the fifth, Nettles walked with one out. Kennedy reached on a smash that took a vicious hop at Whitaker. Still smarting from his base-running gaffe in game one, Bevacqua shot a three-run homer to left to put San Diego ahead 5–3. Flawless San Diego relief pitching evened the Series at one game apiece.

The Padres reverted to pumpkins in game three. With one out in the second, Lemon singled off Padre starter Tim Lollar. Marty Castillo rose to the occasion with a two-run blast to left. Lollar walked Whitaker, then Trammell doubled for a run. After Gibson walked, Parrish reached on an infield hit. Into the game came Greg Booker, who immediately walked Herndon for another run. Booker walked three more men in the third inning to load the bases; Greg Harris entered and promptly hit Gibson in the foot for another run. Eleven walks in the first five innings paved the way to Detroit's 5–2 victory.

The Padres stayed true to form in game four, getting horrid starting pitching and wonderful relieving. In the bottom of the first, Whitaker reached on an error by Alan Wiggins. Trammell then launched an Eric Show pitch into the left-field seats for a 2–0 lead. Kennedy narrowed the gap with a solo homer in the second. In the Detroit third, Whitaker singled, and Trammell hit another homer off Show. With Jack Morris in top form, the two homers stood up for a 4–2 victory.

Thurmond started game five for the Padres and failed to get out of the first inning. The Tigers scored three times on five hits, including a two-run homer by Gibson. The Padres climbed back to a 3–3 tie in the fourth. Gibson began the Tiger fifth with a single off Nettles's glove. Two walks moved him to third with one out. On a pop to short right field, Gibson alertly dashed home after the catch by Wiggins. When Williams called on Gossage for relief, the magic spell was ripped. Homers by Parrish and Gibson ran the score to 8–4 and set the Motor City dancing in the streets.

Game 1 October 9 at San Diego

Det.	1 0 0	0 2 0	0 0 0
S.D.	2 0 0	0 0 0	0 0 0

Detroit	Pos	AB	R	H	RBI	PO	A	E
Whitaker	2b	4	1	1	0	3	3	0
Trammell	ss	5	0	2	1	0	2	0
Gibson	rf	4	0	0	0	1	1	0
Parrish	c	3	1	2	0	9	1	0
Herndon	lf	3	1	2	2	1	0	0
Garbey	dh	4	0	0	0	0	0	0
Lemon	cf	4	0	1	0	2	0	0
Evans	1b	3	0	0	0	4	1	0
c Bergman	1b	0	0	0	0	3	0	0
Castillo	3b	2	0	0	0	1	0	0
b Grubb		0	0	0	0	0	0	0
d Brookens	3b	1	0	0	0	0	2	0
Morris	p	0	0	0	0	3	0	0
Totals		33	3	8	3	27	10	0

a Ran for Nettles in 6th.
b Announced for Castillo in 8th.
c Ran for Evans in 8th.
d Flied out for Grubb in 8th.

Doubles—Whitaker, Kennedy, Parrish, Bevaqua. Home Run—Herndon. Stolen Bases—Trammell, Gwynn. Double Plays—Whitaker to Evans, Garver unassisted. Left on Bases—Detroit 9, San Diego 6. Umpires—Harvey, Barnett Froemming, Garcia, Runge, Reilly. Attendance—57,908. Time of Game—3:18.

San Diego	Pos	AB	R	H	RBI	PO	A	E
Wiggins	2b	4	0	1	0	1	2	0
Glynn	rf	2	0	1	0	3	0	0
Garvey	1b	4	1	1	0	9	2	0
Nettles	3b	2	1	2	0	3	1	0
a Salazar	3b	1	0	0	0	0	0	0
Kennedy	c	4	0	2	2	3	0	0
Brown	cf	4	0	0	0	3	0	0
Martinez	lf	4	0	0	0	3	0	1
Templeton	ss	4	0	0	0	2	2	0
Bevacqua	dh	3	0	1	0	0	0	0
Thurmond	p	0	0	0	0	0	2	0
Hawkins	p	0	0	0	0	0	1	0
Dravecky	p	0	0	0	0	0	0	0
Totals		32	2	8	2	27	10	1

Pitching	IP	H	R	ER	BB	SO
Detroit						
Morris (W)	9	8	2	2	3	9
San Diego						
Thurmond (L)	5	7	3	3	3	2
Hawkins	2⅔	1	0	0	3	0
Dravecky	1⅓	0	0	0	0	1

1st Inning
Detroit
Whitaker doubled to center.
Trammell lined a single to left, scoring Whitaker.
1 Trammell was picked off first, Thurmond to Garvey to Templeton.
2 Gibson flied to left.
Parrish beat out a hit to deep third.
Herndon singled on a high hopper to Nettles, who had no throw, Parrish advancing to second.
3 Garbey forced Parrish at third, Nettles unassisted.
San Diego
1 Wiggins struck out.
2 Gwynn flied to right.
Garvey singled to right.
Nettles lined a single to left, Garvey stopping at second.
Kennedy doubled into the right field corner, scoring Garvey and Nettles. Kennedy went to third on the throw to the plate.
3 Brown bounced out, Evans to Morris.

2nd Inning
Detroit
1 Lemon grounded to third.
2 Evans grounded to second, great grab.
3 Castillo flied to center.
San Diego
1 Martinez grounded to deep short.
2 Templeton struck out.
3 Bevacqua flied to deep left.

3rd Inning
Detroit
1 Whitaker flied to left.
Trammell singled to left.
2 Gibson struck out as Trammell stole second.
Parrish walked on four pitches.
3 Herndon forced Trammell at third, Nettles who stepped on the bag.
San Diego
Wiggins singled up the middle.
Gwynn walked.
1,2 Garvey grounded into a double play, Whitaker tagging Gwynn and throwing to Evans as Wiggins went to third.
Nettles walked.
3 Kennedy flied to center.

4th Inning
Detroit
1 Garbey grounded to first.
Lemon got safely to second on his liner to left that Martinez muffed.
2 Evans grounded to second, Lemon going to third.
Castillo walked.
3 Whitaker flied to center.
San Diego
1 Brown popped to Morris on an attempted bunt.
2 Martinez struck out.
3 Templeton grounded to short.

5th Inning
Detroit
1 Trammell flied to right.
Gibson walked.
2 Gibson picked off and thrown out trying for second, Thurmond to Garvey to Templeton.
Parrish doubled down the left field line.
Herndon homered into the right field bleachers on a 3-1 pitch.
3 Garbey struck out.
San Diego
1 Bevacqua flied to center.
2 Wiggins lined to second.
Gwynn singled to center.
Gwynn stole second.
3 Garvey grounded to second.

6th Inning
Detroit
For San Diego—Hawkins now pitching.
Lemon singled to left.
1,2 Evans grounded to Garvey who made a leaping catch and stepped on first to double up Lemon.
3 Castillo popped to third.
San Diego
Nettles singled to center.
Kennedy singled to center, Nettles stopping at second.
Salazar running for Nettles.
1 Brown struck out.
2 Martinez struck out.
3 Templeton struck out.

7th Inning
Detroit
For San Diego—Salazar playing third.
Whitaker walked.
1 Trammell flied to right.
2 Gibson popped to first.
3 Parrish flied to left.
San Diego
Bevacqua doubled into the right field
1 corner but was out trying for a triple, Gibson to Whitaker to Castillo.
2 Wiggins tagged out by Morris on an attempted bunt.
Gwynn walked.
3 Gwynn caught trying to steal second, Parrish to Whitaker.

8th Inning
Detroit
Herndon walked.
1 Garbey grounded out off Hawkins' glove to short, Herndon going to second.
2 Lemon flied to center.
Evans intentionally walked.
Grubb announced for Castillo.
For San Diego—Dravecky came in to pitch.
Bergman ran for Evans.
3 Brookens batted for Grubb and flied to right.
San Diego
For Detroit—Bergman playing first and Brookens playing third.
1 Garvey struck out.
2 Salazar grounded to third.
3 Kennedy struck out.

9th Inning
Detroit
1 Whitaker struck out.
2 Trammell popped to second.
3 Gibson grounded to short.
San Diego
1 Brown struck out.
2 Martinez grounded to third.
3 Templeton grounded to first.

Game 2 October 10 at San Diego

Detroit	Pos	AB	R	H	RBI	PO	A	E
Whitaker	2b	4	1	1	0	2	1	0
Trammell	ss	4	1	2	0	3	2	1
Gibson	rf	4	1	2	1	1	0	2
Parrish	c	3	0	0	1	3	2	0
Evans	3b-1b	4	0	1	1	4	1	0
Jones	lf	2	0	0	0	2	0	0
a Herndon	lf	2	0	0	0	0	0	0
Grubb	dh	1	0	1	0	0	0	0
b Kuntz		1	0	0	0	0	0	0
Lemon	cf	3	0	0	0	5	0	0
Bergman	1b	2	0	0	0	4	1	0
c Brookens	3b	1	0	0	0	0	1	0
Petry	p	0	0	0	0	0	1	0
Lopez	p	0	0	0	0	0	0	0
Scherrer	p	0	0	0	0	0	1	0
Blair	p	0	0	0	0	0	0	0
Hernandez	p	0	0	0	0	0	0	0
Totals		31	3	7	3	24	10	3

Pitching	IP	H	R	ER	BB	SO
Detroit						
Petry (L)	$4\frac{1}{3}$	8	5	5	3	2
Lopez	$\frac{2}{3}$	1	0	0	1	0
Scherrer	$1\frac{1}{3}$	2	0	0	0	0
Blair	$\frac{2}{3}$	0	0	0	0	1
Hernandez	1	0	0	0	0	0
San Diego						
Whitson	$\frac{2}{3}$	5	3	3	0	0
Hawkins (W)	$5\frac{1}{3}$	1	0	0	0	3
Lefferts (SV)	3	1	0	0	0	5

Det.	300	000	000
S.D.	100	130	00x

San Diego	Pos	AB	R	H	RBI	PO	A	E
Wiggins	2b	5	1	3	0	2	1	0
Gwynn	rf	3	0	1	0	2	1	0
Garvey	1b	3	0	0	0	7	0	0
Nettles	3b	1	1	0	1	1	4	0
Kennedy	c	4	1	1	0	9	0	0
Bevacqua	dh	4	2	3	3	0	0	0
Martinez	lf	3	0	0	0	1	0	0
Templeton	ss	4	0	3	0	4	0	0
Brown	cf	3	0	0	1	0	0	0
Salazar	cf	1	0	0	0	1	0	0
Whitson	p	0	0	0	0	0	0	0
Hawkins	p	0	0	0	0	0	0	0
Lefferts	p	0	0	0	0	0	0	0
Totals		31	5	11	5	27	6	0

a Flied out for Jones in 7th.
b Struck out for Grubb in 7th.
c Struck out for Bergman in 8th.

Home Run—Bevacqua. Stolen Base—Gibson. Sacrifice Hit—Garvey. Sacrifice Flies—Parrish, Nettles. Balk—Petry. Double Plays—Gwynn to Garvey, Parrish to Whitaker. Left on Bases—Detroit 3, San Diego 8. Umpires—Barnett, Froemming, Garcia, Runge, Reilly, Harvey. Attendance—57,911. Time of Game—2:44.

1st Inning
Detroit
Whitaker lined a single to left-center.
Trammell singled to left, Whitaker moving over to third.
Gibson lined a single to right-center, Whitaker scoring and Trammell advancing to third.
Gibson stole second.
1 Parrish fouled deep to Martinez, Trammell scoring and Gibson to third after the catch.
Evans looped a single to left, scoring Gibson.
2 Jones popped to short.
Grubb singled through the hole into left, Evans racing to third.
For San Diego—Hawkins came in to pitch.
3 Lemon grounded to third.
San Diego
Wiggins dragged a bunt single past the mound.
Gwynn walked.
1 Garvey sacrificed up both runners, Petry to Bergman.
2 Nettle hit a sacrifice fly to left, Wiggins scoring and Gwynn moving to third after the catch.
3 Kennedy foul popped to Evans.

2nd Inning
Detroit
1 Bergman flied to right.
2 Whitaker bounced to first.
3 Trammell struck out swinging.
San Diego
1 Bevacqua bounced to third.
2 Martinez flied to center.
Templeton singled up the middle.
On a balk Templeton went to second.
3 Brown took a called third strike.

3rd Inning
Detroit
1 Gibson grounded to second.
2 Parrish lined to short.
3 Evans popped to third.
San Diego
Wiggins singled on a soft fly to left.
1 Wiggins out attempting to steal second, Parrish to Trammell.
2 Gwynn grounded to second.
Garvey safe on Trammell's error.
Nettles walked.
3 Kennedy forced Nettles at second, Trammell unassisted.

4th Inning
Detroit
1 Jones popped to short.
2 Grubb grounded to third.
3 Lemon grounded to third.
San Diego
Bevacqua singled through the hole into left.
1 Martinez called out on strikes.
Templeton singled to right, Bevacqua advancing to third.
2 Brown forced Templeton at second, Trammell to Whitaker as Bevacqua scored.
Wiggins singled to right, Brown stopping at second.
3 Gwynn flied to right.

5th Inning
Detroit
1 Bergman popped to Templeton in short left.
2 Whitaker struck out swinging.
3 Trammell struck out swinging.
San Diego
1 Garvey flied to deep center.
Nettles walked.
Kennedy singled on a one-hopper off Whitaker's chest, Nettles to second.
Bevacqua hit a three-run homer into the left field bleachers on an 0-1 count.
For Detroit—Lopez now pitching.
Martinez walked.
Templeton singled to right and both runners advanced on Gibson's bobble.
2 Brown popped to third.
3 Wiggins lined out to short center.

6th Inning
Detroit
For San Diego—Salazar took over in center field.
Gibson lined a single to left.
1 Parrish popped to second.
2,3 Evans lined to Gwynn and with Gibson running he was easily doubled off first, Gwynn to Garvey.
San Diego
For Detroit—Scherrer now pitching.
Gwynn beat out a perfect drag bunt.
1 Garvey flied to left.
2 Gwynn was picked off trying to steal, Scherrer to Bergman to Trammell.
3 Nettles flied to center.

7th Inning
Detroit
For San Diego—Lefferts came in to pitch.
1 Herndon, pinch-hitting for Jones, flied to center.
2 Kuntz, pinch-hitting for Grubb, struck out.
3 Lemon bounced to third.
San Diego
For Detroit—Herndon playing left field.
Gibson misplayed Kennedy's foul ball near the Tiger's bullpen for an error.
1 Kennedy grounded to first.
Bevacqua lined a single to left.
For Detroit—Bair on the mound.
2,3 On a third strike to Martinez, Bevacqua was caught trying to make second, Parrish to Whitaker.

8th Inning
Detroit
1 Brookens, batting for Bergman, struck out.
2 Whitaker fouled out to Kennedy.
Trammell singled to left.
3 Gibson struck out.
San Diego
For Detroit—Hernandez pitching, Evans moves to first with Brookens playing third.
1 Templeton flied to shallow center.
2 Salazar grounded to third.
3 Wiggins grounded to short.

9th Inning
Detroit
1 Parrish took a called third strike.
2 Evans struck out swinging
3 Herndon foul popped to Wiggins.

Game 3 October 12 at Detroit

San Diego	Pos	AB	R	H	RBI	PO	A	E
Wiggins	2b	5	1	2	0	4	1	0
Gwynn	rf	5	1	2	0	2	0	0
Garvey	1b	5	0	1	1	7	0	0
Nettles	3b	2	0	0	1	0	2	0
Kennedy	c	3	0	0	0	5	0	0
Bevacqua	dh	4	0	1	0	0	0	0
Martinez	lf	4	0	1	0	0	0	0
Templeton	ss	4	0	2	0	1	3	0
Brown	cf	3	0	0	0	5	0	0
a Salazar		1	0	1	0	0	0	0
Lollar	p	0	0	0	0	0	0	0
Booker	p	0	0	0	0	0	1	0
Harris	p	0	0	0	0	0	0	0
Totals		36	2	10	2	24	7	0

Pitching	IP	H	R	ER	BB	SO
San Diego						
Lollar (L)	$1\frac{2}{3}$	4	4	4	4	0
Booker	1	0	1	1	4	0
Harris	$5\frac{1}{3}$	3	0	0	3	5
Detroit						
Wilcox (W)	6	7	1	1	2	4
Scherrer	$\frac{2}{3}$	2	1	1	0	0
Hernandez (SV)	$2\frac{1}{3}$	1	0	0	0	0

S.D.	001	000	100
Det.	041	000	00x

Detroit	Pos	AB	R	H	RBI	PO	A	E
Whitaker	2b	3	1	0	0	3	4	0
Trammell	ss	3	1	2	1	3	1	0
Gibson	rf	2	0	0	1	1	0	0
Parrish	c	3	0	1	0	6	0	0
Herndon	lf	4	0	1	1	1	0	0
Garbey	dh	5	0	0	0	0	0	0
Lemon	cf	5	1	2	0	4	0	0
Evans	1b	2	1	0	0	3	1	0
Bergman	1b	0	0	0	0	3	0	0
Castillo	3b	4	1	1	2	2	2	0
Wilcox	p	0	0	0	0	1	1	0
Scherrer	p	0	0	0	0	0	0	0
Hernandez	p	0	0	0	0	0	0	0
Totals		31	6	7	5	27	9	0

a Singled for Brown in 9th.

Doubles—Wiggins, Trammell, Garvey. Home Run—Castillo. Stolen Base—Gibson. Sacrifice Fly—Nettles. Hit by Pitcher—Gibson (by Harris). Wild Pitch—Lollar. Left on Bases—San Diego 10, Detroit 14. Umpires—Froemming, Garcia, Runge, Reilly, Harvey, Barnett. Attendance—51,970. Time of Game—3:11.

1st Inning
San Diego
Wiggins doubled down the third base line.
1 Gwynn bounced back to the mound, Wiggins holding.
2 Garvey struck out.
Nettles walked.
3 Kennedy grounded to second.
Detroit
1 Whitaker flied to short right.
Trammell walked.
2 Gibson grounded to second, Trammell moving to second.
Parrish walked.
3 Herndon flied to center.

2nd Inning
San Diego
1 Bevacqua lined to second.
2 Martinez struck out.
Templeton singled off Whitaker's glove.
3 Brown flied to right.
Detroit
1 Garbey grounded to short.
Lemon singled to right.
Lemon to second on a wild pitch.
2 Evans flied to deep center, Lemon moving to third after the catch.
Castillo hit a two-run homer into the upper deck in left on a 1-2 pitch.
Whitaker walked on a full count.
Trammell doubled into the left field corner, Whitaker scoring.
Gibson walked.
Parrish singled on a hard smash to third off of Nettles' glove, loading the bases.
For San Diego—Booker relieved Lollar.
Herndon walked, forcing in Trammell.
3 Garbey flied to center.

3rd Inning
San Diego
Wiggins blooped a single to center.
Gwynn singled to right, Wiggings advancing to third.
1 Garvey forced Gwynn at second, scoring Wiggins, Whitaker to Trammell.
2 Nettles fouled to Parrish.
3 Kennedy grounded to second.
Detroit
1 Lemon grounded to third.
Evans walked.
2 Castillo hit a tapper back to the mound, Evans taking second.
Whitaker walked.
Trammell walked to load the bases.
For San Diego—Harris relieved Booker.
Gibson was hit by a pitch, forcing in Evans.
3 Parrish flied to center.

4th Inning
San Diego
Bevacqua singled to center.
1 Martinez took a called third strike.
Templeton beat out a slow hit down the third base line, Bevacqua going to second.
2 Brown forced Bevacqua at third, Castillo unassisted.
3 Wiggins forced Brown at second, Whitaker unassisted.
Detroit
Herndon singled off Nettle's glove.
1 Garbey forced Herndon at second, Templeton to Wiggins.
2 Lemon struck out.
Evans walked.
3 Castillo flied to center.

5th Inning
San Diego
1 Gwynn struck out.
2 Garvey grounded out Evans to Wilcox.
3 Nettles fouled to Castillo
Detroit
1 Whitaker took a called third strike.
2 Trammell popped to second.
Gibson walked.
Gibson stole second.
Parrish walked.
3 Evans popped to short.

6th Inning
San Diego
Kennedy walked.
1 Bevacqua fouled to Parrish.
Martinez singled off a diving stab by Castillo, Kennedy advancing to second.
2 Templeton flied to center.
3 Brown flied to left.
Detroit
1 Garbey called out on strikes.
Lemon beat out a grounder to short with a head-first dive.
2 Evans struck out.
3 Castillo popped to second.

7th Inning
San Diego
For Detroit—Scherrer came in to pitch, Bergman now playing first.
1 Wiggins grounded to third.
Gwynn singled off Scherrer's glove.
Garvey doubled when Herndon missed a shoe-string grab, Gwynn advancing to third.
2 Nettles hit a sacrifice fly to center, Gwynn scoring and Garvey going to third after the catch.
For Detroit—Hernandez came in to replace Scherrer.
3 Kennedy lined to deep center where Lemon raced back to make a spinning grab.
Detroit
1 Whitaker was called out on strikes.
Trammell beat out a bunt down the third base line.
2 Gibson grounded to first, but Garvey's throw was not in time to double up Trammell at second.
3 Parrish popped to second.

8th Inning
San Diego
1 Bevacqua bounced to third.
2 Martinez grounded to short.
3 Templeton popped to second.
Detroit
1 Herndon grounded to short.
2 Garbey grounded to third.
3 Lemon flied to right.

9th Inning
San Diego
Salazar, pinch-hitting for Brown, lined a single over Whitaker.
1 Wiggins popped to short.
2 Gwynn forced Salazar at second, Whitaker to Trammell.
3 Garvey flied to center.

Game 4 October 13 at Detroit

S.D.	010 000 001
Det.	202 000 00x

San Diego	Pos	AB	R	H	RBI	PO	A	E
Wiggins	2b	3	0	0	0	2	2	1
d Summers		1	0	0	0	0	0	0
Roenicke	lf	0	0	0	0	0	0	0
Gwynn	rf	4	0	1	0	1	0	1
Garvey	1b	4	1	1	0	8	0	0
Nettles	3b	4	0	0	0	1	4	0
Kennedy	c	4	1	1	1	8	1	0
Bevacqua	dh	3	0	1	0	0	0	0
Martinez	lf	2	0	0	0	1	0	0
c Flannery	2b	1	0	1	0	1	0	0
Templeton	ss	3	0	0	0	0	3	0
Brown	cf	3	0	0	0	2	0	0
Show	p	0	0	0	0	0	0	0
Dravecky	p	0	0	0	0	0	0	0
Lefferts	p	0	0	0	0	0	0	0
Gossage	p	0	0	0	0	0	0	0
Totals		32	2	5	1	24	10	2

Detroit	Pos	AB	R	H	RBI	PO	A	E
Whitaker	2b	4	2	2	0	3	7	0
Trammell	ss	4	2	3	4	2	1	0
Gibson	rf	4	0	1	0	1	0	0
Parrish	cf	4	0	0	0	1	0	0
Evans	3b	2	0	0	0	1	1	0
Brookens	3b	1	0	0	0	0	0	0
Grubb	dh	1	0	0	0	0	0	0
a Garbey	dh	2	0	0	0	0	0	0
Jones	lf	1	0	0	0	1	0	0
b Herndon	lf	2	0	1	0	0	0	0
Lemon	cf	2	0	0	0	2	0	0
Bergman	1b	3	0	0	0	11	2	0
Morris	p	0	0	0	0	2	1	0
Totals		30	4	7	4	27	12	0

Pitching	IP	H	R	ER	BB	SO
San Diego						
Show (L)	2⅔	4	4	3	1	2
Dravecky	3⅓	3	0	0	1	4
Lefferts	1	0	0	0	0	0
Gossage	1	0	0	0	0	0
Detroit						
Morris (W)	9	5	2	2	0	4

a Hit into force out for Grubb in 3rd.
b Struck out for Jones in 4th.
c Singled for Martinez in 8th.
d Struck out for Wiggins in 8th.

Doubles—Bevacqua, Whitaker, Garvey. Home Runs—Trammell 2, Kennedy. Stolen Bases—Gibson, Lemon. Wild Pitches—Morris 2. Double Plays—Kennedy to Nettles, Templeton to Wiggins to Garvey. Left on Bases—San Diego 3, Detroit 4. Umpires—Garcia, Runge, Reilly, Harvey, Barnett, Froemming. Attendance—52,130. Time of Game—2:20.

1st Inning
San Diego
1 Wiggins out on a bunt back to the mound.
2 Gwynn grounded to second.
3 Garvey grounded to second.
Detroit
Whitaker safe at first on Wiggins' throwing error.
Trammell belted a 2-0 pitch into the lower deck in left for a two-run homer.
1 Gibson flied to center.
2 Parrish grounded out deep to Nettles.
3 Evans fouled to Kennedy.

2nd Inning
San Diego
1 Nettles grounded to second.
Kennedy homered into the upper deck of the right field bleachers on an 0-1 count.
Bevacqua doubled past third into the left field corner.
2 Martinez took a called third strike.
3 Templeton grounded to second.
Detroit
1 Grubb grounded to first.
2 Jones called out on strikes.
3 Lemon struck out.

3rd Inning
San Diego
1 Brown bounced out, Bergman to Morris.
2 Wiggins fouled to Evans.
Gwynn singled to right.
3 Garvey forced Gwynn at second, Trammell to Whitaker.
Detroit
1 Bergman grounded to second.
Whitaker lined a single to right and went to second on Gwynn's error.
Trammell again belted a two-run homer into the upper deck in left on a 1-1 pitch.
Gibson singled to center.
2 Parrish fouled to Garvey.
Gibson stole second.
Evans walked.
For San Diego—Dravecky relieved Show.
3 Garbey, pinch-hitting for Grubb, forced Evans at second, Nettles to Wiggins.

4th Inning
San Diego
1 Nettles popped to second.
2 Kennedy flied to left.
3 Bevacqua fouled to Bergman.
Detroit
1 Herndon, pinch-hitting for Jones, struck out.
Lemon walked.
Lemon stole second.
2,3 Bergman struck out and Lemon was thrown out trying to steal third, Kennedy to Nettles.

5th Inning
San Diego
For Detroit—Herndon playing left field.
1 Martinez grounded to third.
2 Templeton struck out.
3 Brown popped to short.
Detroit
Whitaker doubled to left.
Trammell singled to left, Whitaker moving to third.
1 Gibson struck out.
2 Parrish hit a bouncer to Nettles who threw to Kennedy for the out on Whitaker, Trammell stopping at second.
3 Evans struck out.

6th Inning
San Diego
1 Wiggins grounded out, Bergman to Morris.
2 Gwynn grounded to second.
3 Garvey popped to short.
Detroit
1 Garbey flied to right.
Herndon singled to right.
2,3 Lemon one-hopped into a double play, Templeton to Wiggins to Garvey.

7th Inning
San Diego
1 Nettles bounced to first.
2 Kennedy flied to center.
3 Bevacqua took a called third strike.
Detroit
For San Diego—Lefferts now pitching.
1 Bergman flied to center.
2 Whitaker grounded to short.
3 Trammell flied to deep left.

8th Inning
San Diego
For Detroit—Brookens playing third.
Flannery, batting for Martinez, singled to center.
1 Templeton flied to center.
2 Brown popped to second.
Flannery went to second on a wild pitch.
3 Summers, batting for Wiggins, struck out.
Detroit
For San Diego—Flannery playing second, Roenicke in left and Gossage pitching.
1 Gibson popped to second.
2 Parrish grounded to third.
3 Brookens grounded to short.

9th Inning
1 Gwynn bounced to second.
Garvey doubled off the left field fence.
2 Nettles grounded to second, Garvey advancing to third.
Garvey scored on Morris' second wild pitch.
3 Kennedy lined to right.

Game 5 October 14 at Detroit

S. D.	0 0 1	2 0 0	0 1 0							
Det.	3 0 0	0 1 0	1 3 x							

San Diego	Pos	AB	R	H	RBI	PO	A	E
Wiggins	2b	5	0	2	1	4	0	1
Gwynn	rf	5	0	0	0	4	0	0
Garvey	1b	4	0	1	1	3	1	0
Nettles	3b	3	0	1	0	2	1	0
Kennedy	c	4	0	0	0	5	1	0
Bevacqua	dh	3	2	1	1	0	0	0
Martinez	lf	4	0	2	0	2	0	0
d Salazar	cf	0	0	0	0	0	0	0
Templeton	ss	4	1	1	0	1	3	0
Brown	cf-lf	2	1	1	1	3	0	0
e Bachy		1	0	1	0	0	0	0
f Roenicke		0	0	0	0	0	0	0
Thurmond	p	0	0	0	0	0	0	0
Hawkins	p	0	0	0	0	0	1	0
Lefferts	p	0	0	0	0	0	0	0
Gossage	p	0	0	0	0	0	1	0
Totals		35	4	10	4	24	7	1

Detroit	Pos	AB	R	H	RBI	PO	A	E
Whitaker	2b	3	1	1	0	4	3	0
Trammell	ss	4	1	0	0	3	0
Gibson	rf	4	3	3	5	1	0	0
Parrish	c	5	2	2	1	8	0	1
Herndon	lf	4	0	1	0	4	0	0
Lemon	cf	3	0	2	1	2	0	0
Garbey	dh	1	0	0	0	0	0	0
a Grubb		0	0	0	0	0	0	0
b Kuntz		0	0	0	1	0	0	0
c Johnson		1	0	0	0	0	0	0
Evans	1b	4	0	0	0	6	1	0
Bergman	1b	0	0	0	0	1	1	0
Castillo	3b	3	1	2	0	0	1	0
Petry	p	0	0	0	0	1	0	0
Scherrer	p	0	0	0	0	0	1	0
Lopez	p	0	0	0	0	0	0	0
Hernandez	p	0	0	0	0	0	1	0
Totals		32	8	11	8	27	11	1

Pitching	IP	H	R	ER	BB	SO
San Diego						
Thurmond	⅓	5	3	3	0	0
Hawkins (L)	4	2	1	1	3	1
Lefferts	2	1	0	0	1	2
Gossage	1⅔	3	4	4	1	2
Detroit						
Petry	3⅔	6	3	3	2	2
Scherrer	1	0	0	0	0	0
Lopez (W)	2⅓	0	0	0	0	4
Hernandez (SV)	2	3	1	1	0	0

a Hit by pitch for Garbey in 4th.
b Hit sacrifice fly for Grubb in 5th.
c Reached first base on error for Kuntz in 7th.
d Ran for Martinez in 8th.
e Singled for Brown in 9th.
f Ran for Bochy in 9th.

Double—Templeton. Home Runs—Gibson 2, Parrish, Bevacqua. Stolen Bases—Wiggins, Parrish, Lemon. Sacrifice Hits—Whitaker, Trammell. Sacrifice Flies—Brown, Kuntz. Hit by Pitcher—Grubb (by Hawkins). Wild Pitch—Hawkins. Double Play—Garvey to Templeton. Left on Bases—San Diego 7, Detroit 9. Umpires—Runge, Reilly, Harvey, Barnett, Froemming, Garcia. Attendance—51,901. Time of Game—2:55.

1st Inning
San Diego
Wiggins singled to center.
1 Gwynn struck out as Wiggins stole second, and continued to third when Parrish's throw went into center field.
2 Garvey bounced to second, Whitaker threw to the plate to retire a sliding Wiggins. Garvey safe at first.
3 Nettles grounded to second.
Detroit
Whitaker singled to right.
1 Trammell forced Whitaker at second on a very close play, Templeton to Wiggins. Gibson hit a two-run homer into the upper deck in right-center on the first pitch.
Parrish singled to left.
Parrish stole second.
Herndon singled to center, Parrish advancing to third.
Lemon singled through the hole into left, Parrish scoring with Herndon stopping at second.
For San Diego—Hawkins relieved Thurmond.
2 Herndon caught trying to steal third, Kennedy to Nettles, with Lemon going to second.
Lemon took third on a wild pitch.
3 Garbey popped to second.

2nd Inning
San Diego
1 Kennedy bounced out Evans to Petry.
2 Bevacqua lined to left.
Martinez singled to left.
3 Templeton grounded to first.
Detroit
1 Evans flied to deep right.
2 Castillo took a called third strike.
3 Whitaker flied to short center.

3rd Inning
San Diego
Brown beat out a chopper to short.
1 Wiggins bounced to second, advancing Brown to second.
2 Gwynn grounded to short, Brown going to third.
Garvey beat out a smash to deep short, Brown scoring.
Nettles walked.
3 Kennedy forced Nettles at second, Trammell to Whitaker.
Detroit
1 Trammell flied to Gwynn in right-center.
Gibson walked.
2 Parrish flied to left.
3 Herndon grounded out to deep short, a good play by Templeton.

4th Inning
San Diego
Bevacqua walked.
1 Martinez struck out.
Templeton doubled to left-center as Herndon fell, Bevacqua going to third.
2 Brown lined a sacrifice fly to center, Bevacqua scoring after the catch.
Wiggins singled to center, Templeton scoring and Wiggins going to second on the throw to the plate.
For Detroit—Scherrer came in to pitch.
3 Gwynn flied to Gibson in deep right.
Detroit
1 Lemon lined to third.
Grubb, pinch-hitting for Garbey, was hit by a pitched ball.
2 Evans flied to right.
Castillo singled to right, Grubb advancing to second.
Whitaker walked on four pitches, loading the bases.
3 Trammell flied to center.

5th Inning
San Diego
1 Garvey flied to center.
Nettles blooped a single to center.
2 Kennedy tapped back to the mound, Nettles advancing to second.
For Detroit—Lopez relieved Scherrer on the mound.
3 Bevacqua struck out.
Detroit
Gibson singled off Nettles' glove.
1 Parrish flied to the wall in left, Gibson going to second after the catch.
Herndon walked.
For San Diego—Lefferts now pitching.
Lemon walked, loading the bases.
2 Kuntz, pinch-hitting for Grubb, hit a sacrifice fly to Wiggins in short right. It seemed Gwynn lost the ball in the lights.
3 Evans took a called third strike.

6th Inning
San Diego
1 Martinez called out on strikes.
2 Templeton lined to left.
3 Brown took a called third strike.
Detroit
Castillo singled to deep short as he just beat Templeton's throw.
1,2 Whitaker high chopped to Garvey who stepped on first and threw to Templeton who tagged a sliding Castillo at second.
3 Trammell's liner bounced off of Nettles' glove to Templeton who threw to first.

7th Inning
San Diego
1 Wiggins called out on strikes.
2 Gwynn flied to left.
3 Garvey bounced to third.
Detroit
1 Gibson took a called third strike.
For San Diego—Gossage relieved Lefferts.
Parrish lined a home run into the lower deck in left on an 0-1 pitch.
2 Herndon flied out deep to Gwynn who made a leaping catch at the wall.
Lemon singled to center.
Johnson batted for Kuntz.
Lemon stole second.
Johnson safe when Wiggins bobbled his grounder, Lemon going to third.
3 Evans flied to center.

8th Inning
San Diego
For Detroit—Hernandez came in to pitch, with Bergman taking over at first.
1 Nettles popped to Whitaker in short right-center.
2 Kennedy lined to Whitaker, making a leaping catch.
Bevacqua homered into the upper deck in left on an 0-1 pitch.
Martinez singled to left.
Salazar ran for Martinez.
3 Salazar was picked off and caught stealing, Hernandez to Bergman to Whitaker.
Detroit
For San Diego—Salazar stays in to play center and Brown moves to left.
Castillo walked.
Whitaker safe on a sacrifice when Nettles had nowhere to throw, Castillo went to second.
1 Trammell sacrificed up both runners, Gossage to Wiggins covering first.
Gibson blasted his second home run of the game, a three-run shot into the upper deck in right on a 1-0 count.
2 Parrish struck out.
3 Herndon also struck out.

9th Inning
San Diego
1 Templeton grounded to short.
Bochy, pinch-hitting for Brown, singled to left.
Roenicke ran for Bochy.
2 Wiggins fouled to Parrish.
3 Gwynn flied to left.

1984 WORLD SERIES COMPOSITE BOX

	Wins	Composite Line Score	
Detroit Tigers	4	9 4 3 0 3 0 1 3 0	- 23
San Diego Padres	1	3 1 2 3 3 0 1 1 1	- 15

	Regular Season			
Manager	W	L	Pct.	G. Ahead
Sparky Anderson	104	58	.642	15
Dick Williams	92	70	.568	12

BATTING AND FIELDING

DETROIT TIGERS

WORLD SERIES STATISTICS

	Pos	G	AB	R	H	2B	3B	HR	RBI	BB	SO	SB	BA	SA	PO	A	E
Darrell Evans	1b-3b	5	15	1	1	0	0	0	1	4	4	0	.067	.067	18	5	0
Lou Whitaker	2b	5	18	**6**	**5**	**2**	0	0	0	4	4	0	.278	.389	15	**18**	0
Alan Trammell	ss	5	20	5	**9**	1	0	**2**	6	2	2	1	**.450**	.800	8	9	1
Marty Castillo	3b	3	9	2	3	0	0	1	2	2	1	0	.333	.667	3	3	0
Kirk Gibson	rf	5	18	4	6	0	0	**2**	**7**	4	4	**3**	.333	.667	5	1	**2**
Chet Lemon	cf	5	17	1	5	0	0	0	1	2	2	2	.294	.294	15	0	0
Larry Herndon	lf-ph	5	15	1	5	0	0	1	3	3	2	0	.333	.533	6	0	0
Lance Parrish	c	5	18	3	5	1	0	1	2	3	2	1	.278	.500	30	3	1
Barbaro Garbey	dh-ph	4	12	0	0	0	0	0	0	0	2	0	.000	.000	—	—	—
Dave Bergman	pr-1b	5	5	0	0	0	0	0	0	0	1	0	.000	.000	22	4	0
Johnny Grubb	ph-dh	4	3	0	1	0	0	0	0	0	0	0	.333	.333	—	—	—
Tom Brookens	ph-3b	3	3	0	0	0	0	0	0	0	1	0	.000	.000	0	3	0
Ruppert Jones	lf	2	3	0	0	0	0	0	0	0	1	0	.000	.000	3	0	0
Rusty Kuntz	ph	2	1	0	0	0	0	0	1	0	1	0	.000	.000	—	—	—
Howard Johnson	ph	1	1	0	0	0	0	0	0	0	0	0	.000	.000	—	—	—
Doug Baker		Did not play															
Jack Morris	p	2	0	0	0	0	0	0	0	0	0	0	—	—	5	1	0
Dan Petry	p	2	0	0	0	0	0	0	0	0	0	0	—	—	1	1	0
Milt Wilcox	p	1	0	0	0	0	0	0	0	0	0	0	—	—	1	1	0
Willie Hernandez	p	3	0	0	0	0	0	0	0	0	0	0	—	—	0	1	0
Bill Scherrer	p	3	0	0	0	0	0	0	0	0	0	0	—	—	0	2	0
Aurelio Lopez	p	2	0	0	0	0	0	0	0	0	0	0	—	—	0	0	0
Doug Bair	p	1	0	0	0	0	0	0	0	0	0	0	—	—	0	0	0
Juan Berenguer		Did not play															
Dave Rozema		Did not play															
team total		5	158	23	40	4	0	7	23	24	27	7	.253	.411	132	52	4

Double Plays—2
Left on Bases—39

REGULAR SEASON STATISTICS

		Main Pos	G	AB	R	H	2B	3B	HR	RBI	BB	SO	SB	BA	SA
Darrell Evans		dh-1b	131	401	60	93	11	1	16	63	77	70	2	.232	.384
Lou Whitaker		2b	143	558	90	161	25	1	13	56	62	63	6	.289	.407
Alan Trammell		ss	139	555	85	174	34	5	14	69	60	63	19	.314	.468
Marty Castillo		3b-c	70	141	16	33	5	2	4	17	10	33	1	.234	.383
Kirk Gibson		of	149	531	92	150	23	10	27	91	63	103	29	.282	.516
Chet Lemon		of	141	509	77	146	34	6	20	76	51	83	5	.287	.495
Larry Herndon		of	125	407	52	114	18	5	7	43	32	63	6	.280	.400
Lance Parrish		c	156	613	72	175	42	1	22	101	41	120	2	.285	.443
Barbaro Garbey		1b-3b	110	327	45	94	17	1	5	52	17	35	6	.287	.391
Dave Bergman		1b	120	271	42	74	8	5	7	44	33	40	3	.273	.417
Johnny Grubb		of-dh	86	176	25	47	5	0	8	17	36	36	1	.267	.432
Tom Brookens		3b-ss	113	224	32	55	11	4	5	26	19	33	6	.246	.397
Ruppert Jones		of	79	215	26	61	12	1	12	37	21	47	2	.284	.516
Rusty Kuntz		of	84	140	32	40	12	0	2	22	25	28	2	.286	.414
Howard Johnson		3b	116	355	43	88	14	1	12	50	40	67	10	.248	.394
Doug Baker		ss	43	108	15	20	4	1	0	12	7	22	3	.185	.291
Jack Morris		p	35	0	0	0	0	0	0	0	0	0	0	—	—
Dan Petry		p	35	0	0	0	0	0	0	0	0	0	0	—	—
Milt Wilcox		p	33	0	0	0	0	0	0	0	0	0	0	—	—
Willie Hernandez		p	80	0	0	0	0	0	0	0	0	0	0	—	—
Bill Scherrer	a	p	18	0	0	0	0	0	0	0	0	0	0	—	—
Aurelio Lopez		p	71	0	0	0	0	0	0	0	0	0	0	—	—
Doug Bair		p	47	0	0	0	0	0	0	0	0	0	0	—	—
Juan Berenguer		p	31	0	0	0	0	0	0	0	0	0	0	—	—
Dave Rozema		p	29	0	0	0	0	0	0	0	0	0	0	—	—
team total			162	5644	**829**	1529	254	46	**187**	**788**	602	**941**	106	.271	.432

a from Cincinnati Reds
Dwight Lowry (c), Rod Allen (dh), Scott Earl (2b), Nelson Simmons (of-dh), Mike Laga (1b), Glenn Abbott (p), Randy O'Neal (p), Sid Monge (p), Roger Mason (p) and Carl Willis (p) also played for the Tigers during the season.

SAN DIEGO PADRES

WORLD SERIES STATISTICS

	Pos	G	AB	R	H	2B	3B	HR	RBI	BB	SO	SB	BA	SA	PO	A	E
Steve Garvey	1b	5	20	2	4	**2**	0	0	2	0	2	0	.200	.300	**34**	3	0
Alan Wiggins	2b	5	**22**	2	8	1	0	0	1	0	2	1	.364	.409	13	6	**2**
Gary Templeton	ss	5	19	1	6	1	0	0	0	0	3	0	.316	.368	8	11	0
Graig Nettles	3b	5	12	2	3	0	0	0	2	**5**	0	0	.250	.250	7	12	0
Tony Gwynn	rf	5	19	1	5	0	0	0	0	3	2	1	.263	.263	12	1	1
Bobby Brown	cf-lf	5	15	1	1	0	0	0	2	0	4	0	.067	.067	13	0	0
Camelo Martinez	lf	5	17	0	3	0	0	0	0	1	**9**	0	.176	.176	7	0	1
Terry Kennedy	c	5	19	2	4	1	0	1	3	1	1	0	.211	.421	30	2	0
Kurt Bevacqua	dh	5	17	4	7	**2**	0	**2**	4	1	2	0	.412	**.882**	—	—	—
Luis Salazar	pr-3b-cf-ph	4	3	0	1	0	0	0	0	0	0	0	.333	.333	1	0	0
Bruce Bochy	ph	1	1	0	1	0	0	0	0	0	0	0	1.000	1.000	—	—	—
Tim Flannery	ph-2b	1	1	0	1	0	0	0	0	0	0	0	1.000	1.000	1	0	0
Champ Summers	ph	1	1	0	0	0	0	0	0	0	1	0	.000	.000	—	—	—
Ron Roenicke	lf-pr	2	0	0	0	0	0	0	0	0	0	0	—	—	0	0	0
Andy Hawkins	p	3	0	0	0	0	0	0	0	0	0	0	—	—	0	1	0
Craig Lefferts	p	3	0	0	0	0	0	0	0	0	0	0	—	—	0	0	0
Mark Thurmond	p	2	0	0	0	0	0	0	0	0	0	0	—	—	0	2	0
Greg Harris	p	1	0	0	0	0	0	0	0	0	0	0	—	—	0	0	0
Dave Dravecky	p	1	0	0	0	0	0	0	0	0	0	0	—	—	0	0	0
Goose Gossage	p	2	0	0	0	0	0	0	0	0	0	0	—	—	0	1	0
Eric Show	p	1	0	0	0	0	0	0	0	0	0	0	—	—	0	0	0
Tim Lollar	p	1	0	0	0	0	0	0	0	0	0	0	—	—	0	0	0
Greg Booker	p	1	0	0	0	0	0	0	0	0	0	0	—	—	0	1	0
Ed Whitson	p	1	0	0	0	0	0	0	0	0	0	0	—	—	0	0	0
Luis DeLeon		Did not play															
team total		5	166	15	44	7	0	3	14	11	26	2	.265	.361	126	40	4

Double Plays—5
Left on Bases—34

REGULAR SEASON STATISTICS

		Main Pos	G	AB	R	H	2B	3B	HR	RBI	BB	SO	SB	BA	SA
Steve Garvey		1b	161	617	72	175	27	2	8	86	24	64	1	.284	.373
Alan Wiggins		2b	158	596	106	154	19	7	3	34	75	57	70	.258	.329
Gary Templeton		ss	148	493	40	127	19	3	2	35	39	81	8	.258	.320
Graig Nettles		3b	124	395	56	90	11	1	20	65	58	55	0	.228	.413
Tony Gwynn		of	158	606	88	**213**	21	10	5	71	59	23	33	**.351**	.444
Bobby Brown		of	85	171	28	43	7	2	3	29	11	33	16	.251	.368
Camelo Martinez		of	149	488	64	122	28	2	13	66	68	82	1	.250	.395
Terry Kennedy		c	148	530	54	127	16	1	14	57	33	99	1	.240	.353
Kurt Bevacqua		inf	59	80	7	16	3	0	1	9	14	19	0	.200	.275
Luis Salazar		3b-of	93	228	20	55	7	2	3	17	6	38	11	.241	.329
Bruce Bochy		c	37	92	10	21	5	1	4	15	3	21	0	.228	.435
Tim Flannery		inf	86	128	24	35	3	3	2	10	12	17	4	.273	.391
Champ Summers		ph	47	54	5	10	3	0	1	12	4	15	0	.185	.296
Ron Roenicke		of	12	20	4	6	1	0	1	2	2	5	0	.300	.500
Andy Hawkins		p	36	41	2	8	0	0	0	1	1	14	0	.195	.195
Craig Lefferts		p	62	17	1	5	1	0	0	0	0	6	0	.294	.353
Mark Thurmond		p	32	58	1	11	1	0	0	4	3	10	0	.190	.207
Greg Harris	b	p	19	8	3	3	1	0	0	0	0	1	0	.375	.500
Dave Dravecky		p	50	41	3	4	2	0	0	3	3	8	0	.098	.146
Goose Gossage		p	62	22	0	4	0	0	0	0	1	8	0	.182	.182
Eric Show		p	32	69	7	17	3	0	3	10	0	23	0	.246	.420
Tim Lollar		p	31	68	6	15	1	1	3	15	6	21	0	.221	.397
Greg Booker		p	32	7	1	2	1	0	0	0	0	2	0	.286	.429
Ed Whitson		p	36	61	0	3	0	0	0	1	1	12	0	.049	.049
Luis DeLeon		p	32	4	0	0	0	0	0	0	0	3	0	.000	.000
team total			162	5504	686	1425	207	42	109	703	472	810	154	.259	.371

b from Montreal Expos
Kevin McReynolds (of), Mario Ramirez (inf), Eddie Miller (of), Doug Gwosdz (c), Sid Monge (p), Floyd Chiffer (p) also played for the Padres during the season

PITCHING

DETROIT TIGERS

WORLD SERIES STATISTICS

	G	GS	CG	IP	H	R	ER	BB	SO	W	L	SV	ERA
Jack Morris	2	**2**	**2**	**18**	13	4	4	3	**13**	**2**	0	0	2.00
Dan Petry	2	**2**	0	8	**14**	**8**	**8**	5	4	0	**1**	0	9.00
Milt Wilcox	1	1	0	6	7	1	1	2	4	1	0	0	1.50
Willie Hernandez	**3**	0	0	$5\frac{1}{3}$	4	1	1	0	0	0	0	**2**	1.69
Bill Scherrer	**3**	0	0	3	5	1	1	0	0	0	0	0	3.00
Aurelio Lopez	2	0	0	3	1	0	0	1	4	1	0	0	0.00
Doug Bair	1	0	0	$\frac{2}{3}$	0	0	0	0	1	0	0	0	0.00
Juan Berenguer	Did not play												
Dave Rozema	Did not play												
team total	5	5	2	44	44	15	15	11	26	4	1	2	3.07

REGULAR SEASON STATISTICS

	G	GS	CG	IP	H	ER	BB	SO	W	L	Pct	SV	ShO	ERA
Jack Morris	35	35	9	240	221	96	87	148	19	11	.633	0	1	3.60
Dan Petry	35	35	7	233	231	84	66	144	18	8	.692	0	2	3.24
Milt Wilcox	33	33	0	194	183	86	66	119	17	8	.680	0	0	4.00
Willie Hernandez	**80**	0	0	140	96	30	36	112	9	3	.750	32	0	1.92
Bill Scherrer	18	0	0	19	14	4	8	16	1	0	1.000	0	0	1.89
Aurelio Lopez	71	0	0	138	109	45	52	94	10	1	.909	14	0	2.94
Doug Bair	47	1	0	94	82	39	36	57	5	3	.625	4	0	3.75
Juan Berenguer	31	27	2	168	146	65	79	118	11	10	.524	0	1	3.48
Dave Rozema	29	16	0	101	110	42	18	48	7	6	.538	0	0	3.74
team total	162	162	19	1464	1358	568	489	914	**104**	58	**.642**	**51**	8	**3.49**

SAN DIEGO PADRES

WORLD SERIES STATISTICS

	G	GS	CG	IP	H	R	ER	BB	SO	W	L	SV	ERA
Andy Hawkins	**3**	0	0	12	4	1	1	**6**	4	1	**1**	0	**0.75**
Craig Lefferts	**3**	0	0	6	2	0	0	1	7	0	0	1	0.00
Mark Thurmond	2	**2**	0	$5\frac{1}{3}$	12	6	6	3	2	0	**1**	0	10.13
Greg Harris	1	0	0	$5\frac{1}{3}$	3	0	0	3	5	0	0	0	0.00
Dave Dravecky	1	0	0	$4\frac{2}{3}$	3	0	0	1	5	0	0	0	0.00
Goose Gossage	2	0	0	$2\frac{2}{3}$	3	4	4	1	2	0	0	0	13.50
Eric Show	1	1	0	$2\frac{2}{3}$	4	4	3	1	2	0	**1**	0	10.13
Tim Lollar	1	1	0	$1\frac{2}{3}$	4	4	4	4	0	0	**1**	0	21.60
Greg Booker	1	0	0	1	0	1	1	4	0	0	0	0	9.00
Ed Whitson	1	1	0	$\frac{2}{3}$	5	3	3	0	0	0	0	0	40.50
Luis DeLeon	Did not play												
team total	5	5	0	42	40	23	22	24	27	1	4	1	4.71

REGULAR SEASON STATISTICS

	G	GS	CG	IP	H	ER	BB	SO	W	L	Pct	SV	ShO	ERA
Andy Hawkins	36	22	2	146	143	76	72	77	8	9	.471	0	1	4.68
Craig Lefferts	62	0	0	106	88	25	24	56	3	4	.429	10	0	2.13
Mark Thurmond	32	29	1	179	174	59	55	57	14	8	.636	0	1	2.97
Greg Harris	19	1	0	37	28	11	18	30	2	1	.667	1	0	2.70
Dave Dravecky	50	14	3	157	125	51	51	71	9	8	.529	8	2	2.93
Goose Gossage	62	0	0	102	75	33	36	84	10	6	.625	25	0	2.90
Eric Show	32	32	3	207	175	78	88	104	15	9	.625	0	1	3.40
Tim Lollar	31	31	3	196	168	85	105	131	11	13	.458	0	2	3.91
Greg Booker	32	1	0	57	67	21	27	28	1	1	.500	0	0	3.30
Ed Whitson	31	31	1	189	181	68	42	103	14	8	.636	0	0	3.24
Luis DeLeon	32	0	0	43	44	26	12	44	2	2	.500	0	0	5.48
team total	162	162	13	1460	1327	565	563	812	92	70	.568	44	**17**	3.48

Total Attendance—271,820 Average Attendance—53,364 Winning Player's Share—$51,381 Losing Player's Share—$42,426

1985
Brett and Bret: The I-70 Series

The Big Apple hoped for a Subway Series. Southern California ached for a Freeway Series. When October 19 rolled around, however, America pulled up a chair for the I-70 Series, pitting the Cardinals and Royals in an all-Missouri affair. The two teams had much in common besides geography. Both played in spacious ballparks with hard artificial turf. Both relied on speed, defense, and pitching more than on the long ball. The top four men in the Cardinal lineup sparked a perpetual-motion offense. Rookie Vince Coleman stole 110 bases with disarming ease. Willie McGee, Tommy Herr, and Jack Clark followed with a barrage of line drives. Ozzie Smith anchored the defense, and a platoon of unheralded relievers ably replaced the departed Bruce Sutter. Completely astounding the baseball world was John Tudor, a 31-year-old lefty obtained from Pittsburgh in a winter trade. After a feeble 1–7 start, he found the groove of a lifetime. He won 21 of 23 decisions from June 1 through the LCS victory over the Dodgers. The biggest loss of the LCS was Coleman, pinned under an automatic tarp machine before game four and sidelined with a bone chip.

The Royals had won the A.L. West with a late-season rush, then had come from behind to beat Toronto in the LCS. The Royal offense didn't impress people, particularly with DH Hal McRae on the bench. The backbone of the team was third baseman George Brett, a superstar still at his peak. Dan Quisenberry still reigned in the bullpen, while manager Dick Howser assembled a talented young pitching staff. Bret Saberhagen led the way with a 20–6 mark, blending a good fastball with poise far beyond that of the normal 21-year-old.

In Kansas City for game one, the Royals dropped a 3–1 decision. Even with Tudor off his game, the Royal offense failed in several key spots. The Cards strung together three solo runs for a sedate victory. The next night, the Royals led 2–0 after eight innings. K.C. starter Charlie Leibrandt had a two-hit shutout in progress with three outs to go. McGee led off with a double, but then Smith and Herr made harmless outs. Clark and Tito Landrum followed with tantalizing seeing-eye hits. Leibrandt then walked Cesar Cedeno to load the bases. In a flash, Terry Pendleton dropped a soft liner down the left-field line for a three-run double, sending K.C. to a brutal 4–2 loss.

After heading east on I-70, the Royals pulled together for a 6–1 victory in game three. Saberhagen tossed a masterful six-hitter, while Lonnie Smith and Frank White got the key hits. In game four, however, the Royals tasted vintage Tudor. He threw a five-hit shutout, with home runs by Landrum and McGee the big hits in a 3–0 victory. With the champagne on ice, both teams scored in the first inning. With one out in the top of the second, left fielder Landrum turned Jim Sundberg's fly ball into a double. Buddy Biancalana then singled Sundberg home. Minutes later, Wilson smacked a two-run triple to right. The 6–1 Royal victory sent the Series back to Kansas City.

Both Leibrandt and Danny Cox pitched superbly in game six. The Cardinals scored first in the eighth on a pinch single by Brian Harper. The Royals came up for their last licks against Todd Worrell, a strapping young reliever. Leadoff man Jorge Orta bounced to first baseman Clark, who tossed to Worrell at first. In a palpably bad call, the umpire called Orta safe. The next batter, Steve Balboni, then lofted a pop foul that Clark let drop untouched. Balboni then singled to left. Trying to sacrifice, Sundberg bunted into a force play at third. With McRae at the plate, a passed ball moved the runners up. Worrell then passed McRae to load the bases. Pinch hitter Dane Iorg then arched a blooper into short right field. Sundberg chugged around third and scored the winning run in a dusty headfirst slide.

Tudor faced Saberhagen in the finale. Darryl Motley tagged Tudor for a two-run homer in the bottom of the second. While Saberhagen mowed the Cardinals down, the Royals chased Tudor in the third, then routed the Cards with six runs in the fifth inning. The Cards came unraveled in those tortured moments, dragging that fifth inning out with two frantic rhubarbs. Whitey Herzog and Joaquin Andujar were ejected and got to watch the end of the 11–0 debacle from the clubhouse. For the Royals, living so long on the brink made their title that much sweeter.

Game 1 October 19 at Kansas City

St. L.	0 0 1	1 0 0	0 0 1
K.C.	0 1 0	0 0 0	0 0 0

St. Louis	Pos	AB	R	H	RBI	PO	A	E
McGee	cf	4	0	1	1	1	0	0
O. Smith	ss	3	0	0	0	1	2	0
Herr	2b	4	1	1	0	3	3	0
Clark	1b	4	0	1	1	6	2	0
Landrum	lf	4	1	2	0	3	0	0
Cedeno	rf	3	0	1	1	3	0	0
Worrell	p	1	0	0	0	0	0	0
Pendleton	3b	2	1	0	1	1	4	1
Porter	c	3	0	1	0	7	2	0
Tudor	p	1	0	0	0	0	2	0
Van Slyke	rf	2	0	0	0	2	0	0
Totals		31	3	7	3	27	13	1

Pitching	IP	H	R	ER	BB	SO
St. Louis						
Tudor (W)	6⅔	7	1	1	2	5
Worrell (SV)	2⅓	1	0	0	1	0
Kansas City						
Jackson (L)	7	4	2	2	2	7
Quisenberry	1⅔	3	1	1	0	2
Black	⅓	0	0	0	2	1

Kansas City	Pos	AB	R	H	RBI	PO	A	E
L. Smith	lf	3	0	1	0	0	1	0
Wilson	cf	4	0	1	0	0	1	0
Brett	3b	4	0	1	0	1	3	0
White	2b	4	0	0	0	3	5	0
Sundberg	c	3	0	1	0	11	0	0
Motley	rf	3	1	0	0	0	0	0
d Sheridan		1	0	1	0	0	0	0
Balboni	1b	4	0	1	0	11	0	0
Biancalana	ss	1	0	0	0	0	1	0
a Jones		1	0	1	0	0	0	0
Quisenberry	p	0	0	0	0	0	0	0
Black	p	1	0	0	0	0	0	0
e Orta		1	0	0	0	0	2	0
Jackson	p	2	0	0	0	0	0	0
b McRae		0	0	0	0	0	0	0
c Concepcion	ss	0	0	0	0	0	2	0
f Iorg		1	0	0	0	0	0	0
Totals		32	1	8	1	27	15	0

a Tripled for Biancalana in 7th.
b Hit by pitch for Jackson in 7th.
c Ran for McRae in 7th.
d Doubled for Motley in 9th.
e Flied out for Black in 9th.
f Flied out for Concepcion in 9th.

Doubles—Landrum, Cedeno, Sundberg, McGee, Clark, Sheridan. Triple—Jones. Stolen Base—O. Smith. Sacrifice Hit—Tudor. Hit by Pitcher—McRae (by Tudor). Double Play—Pendleton to Porter. Passed Ball—Porter. Left on Bases—St. Louis 6, Kansas City—8. Umpires—Den Kinger, Williams, McKean, Engel, Shulock, Quick. Attendance—41,650. Time of Game—2:48.

1st Inning
St. Louis
1 McGee struck out swinging.
2 Smith grounded to deep short.
3 Herr bounced to Brett, racing in.
Kansas City
1 Smith popped to Cedeno in short right.
2 Wilson flied to right.
3 Brett struck out swinging.

2nd Inning
St. Louis
1 Clark lined softly to first.
2 Landrum lined to second.
3 Cedeno struck out on a checked swing.
Kansas City
1 White tapped out, Porter to Clark. Sundberg walked on a full count. Motley singled to left, Sundberg stopping at second.
Balboni singled a single to center, scoring Sundberg, Motley to third on Pendleton's fielding error.
2 Motley caught trying to steal home on attempted squeeze, Porter to Pendleton to Tudor to Smith. Balboni to third on the run down.
Biancalana walked on a full count.
3 Jackson struck out swinging.

3rd Inning
St. Louis
Pendleton walked.
Porter singled to right, Pendleton racing to third.
1 Tudor sacrificed Porter to second as Pendleton held third, Jackson to White covering first.
2 McGee grounded to second, Pendleton scoring with Porter going to third.
Smith walked.
Smith stole second.
3 Herr bounced out to the mound.
Kansas City
Smith singled to left.
1 Smith picked off trying to steal, Tudor to Clark to O. Smith to Clark to Herr.
2 Wilson popped to second.
Brett beat out a hit to deep short.
3 White grounded to first.

4th Inning
St. Louis
1 Clark took a called third strike.
Landrum looped a double down the right field line.
Cedeno ripped one over third for a double, scoring Landrum.
2 Pendleton grounded to second, Cedeno advancing to third.
3 Porter took a called third strike.
Kansas City
Sundberg lined a double just inside the third base bag.
1 Motley flied to deep right, Sundberg going to third after the catch.
2,3 Balboni foul popped to Pendleton in short left who threw to Porter to double up Sundberg trying to score.

5th Inning
St. Louis
1 Tudor called out on strikes.
McGee doubled into the gap in right-center but out trying for third, Wilson to White to Brett.
3 Smith grounded to second.
Kansas City
1 Biancalana grounded to short.
2 Jackson struck out.
3 Smith struck out.

6th Inning
St. Louis
1 Herr bunted out to Brett.
2 Clark flied to right.
3 Landrum foul popped to Sundberg.
Kansas City
Wilson singled to left-center.
1 Brett popped to second.
2 White flied deep to Landrum in left-center.
3 Sundberg grounded to third.

7th Inning
St. Louis
1 Cedeno blooped out foul to Balboni.
2 Pendleton struck out swinging.
3 Porter struck out swinging.
Kansas City
1 Motley flied to left, fine catch.
2 Balboni struck out swinging.
Jones, batting for Biancalana, tripled down the right field line.
McRae, pinch-hitting for Jackson, was hit by a pitch.
Concepcion running for McRae.
For St. Louis—Worrell pitching and Van Slyke playing right (batting 9th).
Smith walked on a full count, loading the bases.
3 Wilson fouled to Landrum.

8th Inning
St. Louis
For Kansas City—Concepcion playing short with Quisenberry now pitching.
1 Van Slyke took a called third strike.
2 McGee slowly bounced to second.
3 Smith grounded to short.
Kansas City
1 Brett flied to deep right, Van Slyke made a leaping catch at the wall.
2 White foul popped to Porter.
3 Sundberg grounded to third.

9th Inning
St. Louis
Herr singled to center.
Clark lined a double deep to left,
1 scoring Herr but Clark hung up and out Smith to Concepcion to Brett to White.
Landrum lined a single to right.
2 Worrell strikes out trying to bunt. Landrum went to second on a passed ball.
For Kansas City—Black came in to pitch.
Pendleton intentionally walked.
Porter walks, loading the bases.
3 Van Slyke again called out on strikes.
Kansas City
Sheridan, pinch-hitting for Motley, doubled into the right field corner.
1 Balboni grounded to first, advancing Sheridan to third.
2 Orta, batting for Black, flied to short center.
3 Iorg, pinch-hitting for Concepcion, flew out to right.

Game 2 October 20 at Kansas City

| St. L. | 000 000 004 |
| K. C. | 000 200 000 |

St. Louis	Pos	AB	R	H	RBI	PO	A	E
McGee	cf	4	1	1	0	2	0	0
O. Smith	ss	4	0	0	0	3	3	0
Herr	2b	4	0	0	0	1	5	0
Clark	1b	3	1	1	1	10	0	0
Landrum	lf	4	1	2	0	2	1	0
Cedeno	rf	3	1	0	0	0	0	0
Lahti	p	0	0	0	0	0	0	0
Pendleton	3b	4	0	2	3	1	2	0
Porter	c	3	0	0	0	7	0	0
Cox	p	2	0	0	0	1	2	0
a Harper		1	0	0	0	0	0	0
Dayley	p	0	0	0	0	0	0	0
b Van Slyke	rf	1	0	0	0	0	0	0
Totals		33	4	6	4	27	13	0

Pitching	IP	H	R	ER	BB	SO
St. Louis						
Cox	7	7	2	2	3	5
Dayley (W)	1	1	0	0	0	1
Lahti	1	1	0	0	0	0
Kansas City						
Leibrandt (L)	8⅔	6	4	4	2	6
Quisenberry	⅓	0	0	0	1	0

Kansas City	Pos	AB	R	H	RBI	PO	A	E
L. Smith	lf	4	0	2	0	4	0	0
Jones	lf	0	0	0	0	2	0	0
Wilson	cf	4	1	2	0	3	0	0
Brett	3b	4	1	1	1	1	5	0
White	2b	3	0	3	1	0	4	0
Sheridan	rf	4	0	0	0	1	0	0
Quisenberry	p	0	0	0	0	0	0	0
Sundberg	c	4	0	0	0	7	0	0
Balboni	1b	4	0	1	0	12	0	0
Biancalana	ss	1	0	0	0	1	4	0
c Orta		1	0	0	0	0	0	0
Leibrandt	p	2	0	0	0	0	2	0
Motley	rf	0	0	0	0	0	0	0
Totals		31	2	9	2	27	11	0

a Flied out for Cox in 8th.
b Flied out for Dayley in 9th.
c Hit into double play for Biancalana in 9th.

Doubles—Brett, White 2, McGee, Landrum, Pendleton. Stolen Bases—White, Wilson. Sacrifice Hit—Leibrandt. Double Plays—Herr to Smith to Clark 2, Cox to Smith to Herr. Left on Bases—St. Louis 5, Kansas City 6. Umpires—Williams, McKean, Engel, Shulock, Quick, Denkinger. Attendance—41,656. Time of Game—2:44.

1st Inning
St. Louis
1 McGee grounded to short.
2 Smith foul popped to Brett.
3 Herr grounded to third.
Kansas City
Smith lined a single to left.
1,2 Wilson bounced into a double play, Herr to Smith to Clark.
3 Brett grounded to first.

2nd Inning
St. Louis
1 Clark struck out swinging.
2 Landrum took a called third strike.
3 Cedeno bounced to short.
Kansas City
White bunt singled down third base line. White stole second.
1 Sheridan called out on strikes.
2 Sundberg struck out swinging.
3 Balboni struck out swinging.

3rd Inning
St. Louis
Pendleton blooped a single to right.
1 Porter struck out swinging.
2 Cox called out on strikes.
3 McGee flied to deep center.
Kansas City
Biancalana walked.
1,2 Leibrandt bunted into a double play, Cox to Smith to Herr.
3 Smith grounded to third, a diving stop.

4th Inning
St. Louis
1 Smith grounded out to the pitcher.
2 Herr grounded to short.
Clark walked on a full count. Landrum singled to right, Clark advancing to third.
3 Cedeno lined to short.
Kansas City
Wilson singled to right.
Brett doubled down the right field line, Wilson scoring.
White lined a double over O. Smith's head into left-center, scoring Brett.
1 Sheridan grounded to first, White moving to third.
2 Sundberg again struck out swinging.
3 Balboni flied to deep center.

5th Inning
St. Louis
1 Pendleton grounded to third.
2 Porter called out on strikes.
3 Cox also again struck out.
Kansas City
1 Biancalana grounded to second.
2 Leibrandt popped foul to Pendleton.
3 Smith flied to left.

6th Inning
St. Louis
1 McGee bounced back to the mound.
2 Smith flied to deep center.
3 Herr grounded to third, Brett making a diving stop and throw.

6th Inning (continued)
Kansas City
Wilson beat out a slow roller to second.
1 Brett flied to left.
Wilson stole second. Herzog argued and the replay shows Wilson out.
White walked.
2 Sheridan struck out swinging.
3 Sundberg tapped back to the mound.

7th Inning
St. Louis
1 Clark foul popped to Sundberg.
2 Landrum grounded to short.
3 Cedeno grounded to third.
Kansas City
1 Balboni grounded to third.
Biancalana walked.
2 Leibrandt sacrificed Biancalana to second, tagged out by Cox.
Smith singled between short and third
3 but Biancalana thrown out at the plate, Landrum to Porter.

8th Inning
St. Louis
For Kansas City—Jones playing left.
1 Pendleton grounded to first.
2 Porter flied to deep left.
3 Harper, batting for Cox, flied to left.
Kansas City
For St. Louis—Dayley on the mound.
1 Wilson grounded to second.
2 Brett struck out swinging.
White doubled off the left field wall.
3 Sheridan grounded to second.

9th Inning
St. Louis
McGee doubled over Brett into left.
1 Smith grounded to third, McGee holding.
2 Herr flied to right.
Clark singled to left, scoring McGee. Landrum punched a double down the right field line, Clark going to third. Cedeno walked intentionally, loading the bases.
Pendleton doubled down the left field line, scoring all three runners.
For Kansas City—Motley in right (batting 9th), Quisenberry relieved Leibrandt (batting 5th). Porter walked intentionally.
3 Van Slyke, pinch-hitting for Dayley, popped to center.
Kansas City
For St. Louis—Lahti now pitching with Van Slyke playing right.
1 Sundberg flied to center.
Balboni safe on an infield hit that bounced slowly down the third base line.
2,3 Orta, pinch-hitting for Biancalana, grounded into a double play, Herr to Smith to Clark.

Game 3 October 22 at St. Louis

| K. C. | 000 220 200 |
| St. L. | 000 001 000 |

Kansas City	Pos	AB	R	H	RBI	PO	A	E
L. Smith	lf	5	0	2	2	1	0	0
Jones	lf	0	0	0	0	1	0	0
Wilson	cf	5	0	2	0	3	0	0
Brett	3b	2	2	2	0	2	3	0
White	2b	4	2	2	3	1	3	0
Sheridan	rf	5	0	0	0	1	0	0
Sundberg	c	2	1	1	0	8	2	0
Balboni	1b	4	0	1	0	9	0	0
Biancalana	ss	5	1	2	1	1	1	0
Saberhagen	p	3	0	0	0	0	0	0
Totals		35	6	11	6	27	9	0

a Grounded out for Campbell in 5th.
b Grounded out for Horton in 7th.

Doubles—L. Smith, White. Home Run—White. Stolen Bases—Wilson, McGee. Sacrifice Hit—Saberhagen. Balk—Horton. Double Plays—Herr to Clark, Sundberg to Brett. Left on Bases—Kansas City—11, St. Louis—5. Umpires—McKean, Engel, Shulock, Quick, Denkinger, Williams. Attendance—53,634. Time of Game—3:00.

St. Louis	Pos	AB	R	H	RBI	PO	A	E
McGee	cf	4	0	1	0	1	0	0
O. Smith	ss	4	1	1	0	1	5	0
Herr	2b	3	0	1	1	2	1	0
Clark	1b	4	0	1	1	9	0	0
Van Slyke	rf	4	0	0	0	1	0	0
Pendleton	3b	4	0	1	0	0	1	0
Porter	c	4	0	0	0	8	1	0
Landrum	lf	3	0	1	0	4	0	0
Andujar	p	1	0	0	0	0	1	0
Campbell	p	1	0	0	0	0	0	0
a Jorgensen		1	0	0	0	0	0	0
Horton	p	0	0	0	0	1	0	0
b Harper		1	0	0	0	0	0	0
Dayley	p	0	0	0	0	0	0	0
Totals		32	1	6	1	27	8	0

Pitching	IP	H	R	ER	BB	SO
Kansas City						
Saberhagen (W)	9	6	1	1	1	8
St. Louis						
Andujar (L)	*4	9	4	4	3	3
Campbell	1	0	0	0	1	2
Horton	2	2	2	2	2	1
Dayley	2	0	0	0	2	2

*Pitched to two batters in 5th.

1st Inning
Kansas City
1 Smith called out on strikes.
Wilson grounded a single to left.
Wilson stole second.
Brett walked intentionally.
2,3 White grounded into a double play, Herr, making a nice play, to Clark.
St. Louis
McGee singled to left.
1 Smith popped foul to White in right. McGee stole second.
Herr walked.
2,3 Clark took a called third strike and McGee thrown out trying to steal, Sundberg to Brett.

2nd Inning
Kansas City
1 Sheridan flied to center.
Sundberg singled to right.
2 Balboni blasted one to the left field wall.
3 Biancalana flied to left.
St. Louis
1 Van Slyke grounded to third. Pendleton beat out an infield hit to second.
2 Porter flied to left.
3 Landrum grounded to first.

3rd Inning
Kansas City
1 Saberhagen struck out swinging.
Smith singled to right-center.
2 Smith out trying to steal second, Porter to O. Smith.
Wilson singled to short.
Brett singled to right, Wilson going to third.
White walked, loading the bases.
3 Sheridan struck out swinging.
St. Louis
1 Andujar struck out swinging.
2 McGee struck out swinging.
3 Smith grounded to third.

4th Inning
Kansas City
Sundberg walked.
1 Balboni lined hard to left.
Biancalana credited with an infield single to the mound when no one covered first, Sundberg to second.
2 Saberhagen sacrificed up both runners, Andujar to Herr.
Smith doubled to right in front of a diving Van Slyke, scoring both Sundberg and Biancalana.
3 Wilson flied to left.
St. Louis
1 Herr grounded to short.
2 Clark took a called third strike.
3 Van Slyke struck out swinging.

5th Inning
Kansas City
Brett singled to right.
White hit a two-run homer over the left field fence.
For St. Louis—Campbell relieved Andujar.
1 Sheridan grounded to first.
Sundberg walked.
2 Balboni struck out swinging.
3 Biancalana struck out swinging.

5th Inning (continued)
St. Louis
1 Pendleton grounded to second.
2 Porter flied to center.
Landrum singled to right.
3 Jorgensen, pinch-hitting for Campbell, bounced out, catcher to first.

6th Inning
Kansas City
For St. Louis—Horton now pitching.
1 Saberhagen grounded to short.
2 Smith grounded to short.
3 Wilson called out on a check-swing.
St. Louis
1 McGee popped to third.
Smith singled to center.
Herr singled to right, Smith stopping at second.
Clark singled to center, Smith scoring with Herr stopping at second.
2 Van Slyke blooped to center.
3 Pendleton lined to right.

7th Inning
Kansas City
Brett walked.
On a pick-off attempt Horton balked Brett to second.
White doubled to deep left, scoring Brett.
1 Sheridan grounded to short, White holding second.
2 Sundberg lined to the pitcher.
Balboni intentionally walked.
Biancalana singled to right, driving in White with Balboni going to third. Biancalana went to second on the throw to the plate.
3 Saberhagen grounded to short.
St. Louis
1 Porter popped to short.
2 Landrum struck out swinging.
3 Harper, pinch-hitting for Horton, grounded to second.

8th Inning
Kansas City
For St. Louis—Dayley now pitching.
1 Smith struck out swinging.
2 Wilson took a called third strike.
Brett walked on a full count.
3 White foul popped to Clark.
St. Louis
For Kansas City—Jones came in to play left.
1 McGee grounded to second.
2 Smith grounded to third, Brett making a nice play from in the hole.
3 Herr lined to center.

9th Inning
Kansas City
1 Sheridan grounded to short.
Sundberg walked on a full count for the third time in the game.
2 Balboni flied to deep right.
3 Biancalana popped to first.
St. Louis
1 Clark struck out swinging.
2 Van Slyke struck out swinging.
3 Pendleton flied to left.

Game 4 October 23 at St. Louis

K.C.	000 000 000
St. L.	011 010 00x

Kansas City	Pos	AB	R	H	RBI	PO	A	E
L. Smith	lf	4	0	0	0	1	1	0
Wilson	cf	4	0	1	0	1	0	0
Brett	3b	4	0	1	0	0	3	0
White	2b	4	0	0	0	2	3	0
Sundberg	c	4	0	1	0	7	1	0
Motley	rf	4	0	0	0	0	0	0
Balboni	1b	2	0	1	0	11	1	0
Biancalana	ss	2	0	0	0	0	4	0
b McRae		1	0	0	0	0	0	0
Concepcion	ss	0	0	0	0	1	2	1
Black	p	1	0	0	0	0	0	0
a Wathan		1	0	0	0	0	0	0
Beckwith	p	0	0	0	0	0	0	0
c Jones		1	0	1	0	0	0	0
Quisenberry		0	0	0	0	1	1	0
Totals		32	0	5	0	24	16	1

Pitching	IP	H	R	ER	BB	SO
Kansas City						
Black (L)	5	4	3	3	3	3
Beckwith	2	1	0	0	0	3
Quisenberry	1	1	0	0	2	0
St. Louis						
Tudor (W)	9	5	0	0	1	8

St. Louis	Pos	AB	R	H	RBI	PO	A	E
McGee	cf	3	1	2	1	2	0	0
O. Smith	ss	3	0	0	0	0	0	0
Herr	2b	3	0	1	0	1	2	0
Clark	1b	3	0	1	0	10	0	0
Landrum	lf	4	1	1	1	1	0	0
Cedeno	rf	3	0	0	0	4	0	0
Van Slyke	rf	0	0	0	0	0	0	0
Pendleton	3b	3	1	1	0	1	2	0
Nieto	c	1	0	0	1	9	0	0
Tudor	p	3	0	0	0	0	1	0
Totals		25	3	6	3	27	5	0

a Struck out for Black in 6th.
b Grounded out for Biancalana in 7th.
c Doubled for Beckwith in 8th.

Doubles—Herr, Jones. Triple—Pendleton. Home Runs—Landrum, McGee. Sacrifice Hits—Nieto, O. Smith. Wild Pitch—Quisenberry. Double Play—Black to White. Left on Bases—Kansas City 6, St. Louis 5. Umpires—Engel, Shulock, Quick, Denkinger, Williams, McKean. Attendance—53,634. Time of Game—2:19.

1st Inning
Kansas City
1 Smith popped a bunt foul to Nieto. Wilson singled to center.
2 Brett grounded to first, Wilson going to second when Wilson kicked the relay out of Smith's mitt.
3 White flied to right.
St. Louis
1 McGee grounded to third. Smith walked.
2 Smith picked-off trying to steal, Black to Balboni to Biancalana to Sundberg.
3 Herr struck out swinging

2nd Inning
Kansas City
1 Sundberg flied to right.
2 Motley struck out swinging.
3 Balboni grounded to third.
St. Louis
1 Clark struck out swinging. Landrum hit a line drive home run over the right field fence.
2 Cedeno grounded to short.
3 Pendleton grounded to second.

3rd Inning
Kansas City
1 Biancalana called out on strikes.
2 Black took a called third strike.
3 Smith struck out swinging.
St. Louis
Nieto walked on a full count.
1,2 Tudor popped a bunt into a double play, Black to White covering. McGee homered over the left field fence.
3 Smith grounded to short, Biancalana made a diving stop.

4th Inning
Kansas City
1 Wilson grounded to first.
2 Brett struck out swinging.
3 White grounded to second.
St. Louis
1 Herr grounded to third. Clark singled to left, but was out
2 trying for a double, Smith to White.
3 Landrum grounded to short.

5th Inning
Kansas City
1 Sundberg flied to Cedeno, making a good running catch.
2 Motley grounded to third. Balboni singled to left.
3 Biancalana flied to shallow right.
St. Louis
1 Cedeno popped to first. Pendleton tripled to left-center. Nieto squeeze bunts for a sacrifice, scoring Pendleton, and on Black's bad throw to the plate, Nieto got to second.
2 Tudor struck out swinging. McGee walked intentionally.
3 Smith flied to left.

6th Inning
Kansas City
1 Wathan, batting for Black, struck out swinging.
2 Smith popped to first.
3 Wilson popped to first.
St. Louis
For Kansas City—Beckwith pitching. Herr doubled to right.
1 Clark struck out swinging.
2 Landrum grounded to third, Herr holding second.
3 Cedeno flied to center.

7th Inning
Kansas City
For St. Louis—Van Slyke playing right. Brett singled to left.
1 White flied to deep center. Sundberg singled to right, Brett stopping at second.
2 Motley flied to left. Balboni walked to load the bases.
3 McRae, batting for Biancalana, grounded to Pendleton who stepped on the bag to force Sundberg.
St. Louis
For Kansas City—Concepcion took over at shortstop.
1 Pendleton grounded to second.
2 Nieto struck out swinging.
3 Tudor struck out swinging.

8th Inning
Kansas City
1 Jones, pinch-hitting for Beckwith, doubled to left.
1 Smith struck out swinging.
2 Wilson grounded to second, Jones advancing to third.
3 Brett struck out swinging.
St. Louis
For Kansas City—Quisenberry now on the mound. McGee looped a single to left.
1 Smith sacrificed McGee to second, Quisenberry to Balboni. Herr intentionally walked. Both runners advance on a wild pitch
2 but McGee was out trying to score, Sundberg to Quisenberry with Herr going to third. Clark walked.
3 Landrum grounded to second.

9th Inning
Kansas City
1 White grounded back to the mound.
2 Sundberg foul popped to Clark.
3 Motley flied to center.

Game 5 October 24 at St. Louis

K.C.	130 000 011
St. L.	100 000 000

Kansas City	Pos	AB	R	H	RBI	PO	A	E
L. Smith	lf	4	2	2	0	2	0	0
Jones	lf	0	0	0	0	0	0	0
Wilson	cf	5	0	2	2	2	0	0
Brett	3b	4	0	1	0	1	1	0
Pryor	3b	0	0	0	0	0	1	0
White	2b	5	1	0	1	2	2	0
Sheridan	rf	5	0	2	1	2	0	0
Balboni	1b	4	0	1	0	11	1	0
Sundberg	c	4	2	1	0	6	0	0
Biancalana	ss	3	1	2	1	1	5	0
Jackson	p	4	0	0	0	0	2	1
Totals		38	6	11	5	27	12	2

Pitching	IP	H	R	ER	BB	SO
Kansas City						
Jackson (W)	9	5	1	1	3	5
St. Louis						
Forsch (L)	1⅔	5	4	4	1	2
Horton	2	1	0	0	3	4
Campbell	1⅓	0	0	0	0	2
Worrell	2	0	0	0	0	6
Lahti	2	5	2	1	0	1

St. Louis	Pos	AB	R	H	RBI	PO	A	E
McGee	cf	4	0	2	0	0	0	0
O. Smith	ss	3	0	0	0	1	1	1
Herr	2b	4	1	1	0	2	1	0
Clark	1b	3	0	1	1	5	2	0
Landrum	lf	4	0	1	0	1	0	0
Cedeno	rf	4	0	0	0	1	0	0
Pendleton	3b	3	0	0	0	1	4	0
Nieto	c	4	0	0	0	14	1	0
Forsch	p	0	0	0	0	1	0	0
Horton	p	1	0	0	0	0	0	0
Campbell	p	0	0	0	0	1	0	0
a DeJesus		1	0	0	0	0	0	0
Worrell	p	0	0	0	0	0	0	0
b Harper		1	0	0	0	0	0	0
Lahti	p	0	0	0	0	0	0	0
Totals		32	1	5	1	27	9	1

a Flied out for Campbell in 5th.
b Struck out for Worrell in 7th.

Doubles—Herr, Clark, Sundberg, Sheridan. Triple—Wilson. Stolen Base—L. Smith. Double Play—Pendleton to Herr. Left on Bases—Kansas City 9, St. Louis 7. Umpires—Shulock, Quick, Denkinger, Williams, McKean, Engel. Attendance—53,634. Time of Game—2:52.

1st Inning
Kansas City
Smith singled to left. Wilson singled to left, Smith going to second.
1 Brett flied to left, both runners advancing after the catch.
2 White grounded to short, Smith scoring as Wilson held.
3 Sheridan struck out swinging.
St. Louis
1 McGee grounded back to the mound.
2 Smith lined to center. Herr got a ground rule double when his blast bounced into the bullpen in right. Clark doubled in the gap in right-center, scoring Herr.
3 Landrum fouled to Balboni.

2nd Inning
Kansas City
1 Balboni flied to right. Sundberg lined a double to left. Biancalana singled to right, scoring Sundberg on a very close play, and advanced to second on the throw home.
2 Jackson took a called third strike. Smith walked on a full count. Wilson blasted a triple into right-center, scoring Biancalana and Smith. For St. Louis—Horton relieved Forsch.
3 Brett grounded out, Clark to Horton.
St. Louis
1 Cedeno popped to second.
2 Pendleton grounded to second.
3 Nieto grounded to short.

3rd Inning
Kansas City
1 White struck out swinging. Balboni walked.
2 Sheridan struck out swinging.
3 Sundberg forced Balboni, Herr to Smith.
St. Louis
1 Horton struck out swinging. McGee singled to center. McGee went to second on Jackson's wild pick-off throw over Balboni's head. Smith walked.
2 Herr popped to first. Clark walked, loading the bases.
3 Landrum foul popped to Brett.

4th Inning
Kansas City
Biancalana walked.
1 Jackson bunted foul for a strike out. Smith singled to right, advancing Biancalana to third. Smith stole second.
2 Wilson struck out but had to be thrown out at first, both runners holding. Brett walked intentionally. For St. Louis—Campbell relieved Horton on the mound.
3 White struck out swinging.
St. Louis
1 Cedeno grounded to short.
2 Pendleton also grounded to short.
3 Nieta flied to left.

5th Inning
Kansas City
1 Sheridan grounded out, Clark to Campbell.
2 Balboni struck out swinging.
3 Sundberg grounded to third.

5th Inning (continued)
St. Louis
1 DeJesus, batting for Campbell, flied to right. McGee singled to left.
2 McGee picked off, Jackson to Balboni to Biancalana. Smith safely to second on error by Brett.
3 Herr flied to left.

6th Inning
Kansas City
For St. Louis—Worrell now pitching.
1 Biancalana struck out swinging.
2 Jackson struck out swinging.
3 Smith struck out swinging.
St. Louis
1 Clark fouled to Sundberg.
2 Landrum grounded to second.
3 Cedeno grounded to third.

7th Inning
Kansas City
1 Wilson struck out swinging.
2 Brett struck out swinging.
3 White struck out swinging—6 straight.
St. Louis
Brett missed Pendleton's foul but fell down the dugout steps.
1 Pendleton struck out swinging.
2 Nieto called out on strikes.
3 Harper, batting for Worrell, struck out swinging.

8th Inning
Kansas City
For St. Louis—Lahti on the mound. Sheridan singled to left-center. Balboni singled to left, Sheridan stopping at second.
1,2 Sundberg hit into a double play forcing out both runners, Pendleton to Herr. Biancalana singled to center, Sundberg stopping at second. Jackson safely on first due to error by O. Smith, Biancalana scoring and Sundberg going to third.
3 L. Smith took a called third strike.
St. Louis
For Kansas City—Jones goes in to play left field.
1 McGee called out on strikes.
2 Smith flied to deep center, Wilson making a great catch running backwards.
3 Herr grounded to short.

9th Inning
Kansas City
1 Wilson grounded to first. Brett singled to right.
2 White forced Brett at second, Pendleton to Herr on a great stop by Pendleton. Sheridan doubled to left, driving in White.
3 Balboni grounded to third.
St. Louis
For Kansas City—Pryor replaced Brett at third base.
1 Clark grounded to third. Landrum beat out an infield single to third.
2 Cedeno flied to right. Pendleton walked.
3 Nieto forced Pendleton at second, Biancalana to White.

Game 6 October 26 at Kansas City

St. L.			
St. L.	000	000	010
K.C.	000	000	002

St. Louis	Pos	AB	R	H	RBI	PO	A	E
O. Smith	ss	3	0	0	0	2	3	0
McGee	cf	4	0	0	0	4	0	0
Herr	2b	4	0	0	0	1	2	0
Clark	1b	4	0	0	0	5	0	0
Landrum	lf	4	0	1	0	1	0	0
Pendleton	3b	4	1	1	0	1	1	0
Cedeno	rf	2	0	1	0	1	0	0
b Van Slyke	rf	0	0	0	0	0	0	0
Porter	c	3	0	1	0	10	1	0
Cox	p	2	0	0	0	0	0	0
a Harper		1	0	1	1	0	0	0
c Lawless		0	0	0	0	0	0	0
Dayley	p	0	0	0	0	0	0	0
Worrell	p	0	0	0	0	0	1	0
Totals		31	1	5	1	25	8	0

Kansas City	Pos	AB	R	H	RBI	PO	A	E
L. Smith	lf	4	0	1	0	0	0	0
Wilson	cf	3	0	1	0	3	0	0
Brett	3b	4	0	0	0	3	4	0
White	2b	4	0	1	0	2	2	0
Sheridan	rf	3	0	1	0	2	0	0
d Motley		0	0	0	0	0	0	0
e Orta		1	0	1	0	0	0	0
Balboni	1b	3	0	2	0	9	1	0
f Concepcion		0	1	0	0	0	0	0
Sundberg	c	4	1	1	0	6	0	0
Biancalana	ss	3	0	1	0	1	4	0
g McRae		0	0	0	0	0	0	0
h Wathan		0	0	0	0	0	0	0
Leibrandt	p	2	0	0	0	1	0	0
Quisenberry	p	0	0	0	0	0	0	0
i Iorg		1	0	1	2	0	0	0
Totals		32	2	10	2	27	11	0

Pitching	IP	H	R	ER	BB	SO
St. Louis						
Cox	7	7	0	0	1	8
Dayley	1	0	0	0	1	2
Worrell (L)	$\frac{1}{3}$	3	2	2	1	0
Kansas City						
Leibrandt	$7\frac{2}{3}$	4	1	1	2	4
Quisenberry (W)	$1\frac{1}{3}$	1	0	0	0	1

a Singled for Cox in 8th.
b Ran for Cedeno in 8th.
c Ran for Harper in 8th.
d Announced for Sheridan in 9th.
e Singled for Motley in 9th.
f Ran for Balboni in 9th.
g Walked for Biancalana in 9th.
h Ran for McRae in 9th.
i Singled for Quisenberry in 9th.

Double—L. Smith. Sacrifice—Leibrandt. Passed Ball—Porter. Double Plays—Biancalana to White to Balboni, Herr to Smith to Clark. Left on Bases—St. Louis—5, Kansas City—9. Umpires—Quick, Denkinger, Williams, McKean, Engel, Shulock. Attendance—41,628. Time of Game—2:48.

1st Inning
St. Louis
1 Smith grounded to third.
2 McGee flied to short center.
3 Herr struck out swinging.
Kansas City
Smith doubled down the left field line.
1 Wilson grounded to second, Smith going to third.
2 Brett took a called third strike.
3 White grounded to short.

2nd Inning
St. Louis
1 Clark popped to third.
2 Landrum flied to short right.
3 Pendleton grounded to third.
Kansas City
1 Sheridan struck out swinging.
Balboni singled to left-center.
2 Sundberg called out on strikes.
3 Biancalana forced Balboni at second, Smith to Herr.

3rd Inning
St. Louis
1 Cedeno struck out swinging.
2 Porter foul popped to Brett.
3 Cox grounded out, Balboni to Leibrandt.
Kansas City
1 Leibrandt struck out swinging.
2 Smith flied to deep center.
3 Wilson flied to left.

4th Inning
St. Louis
1 Smith fouled to Sundberg.
2 McGee grounded to short.
3 Herr grounded to third.
Kansas City
1 Brett flied to deep right.
White bunted safely toward third.
2 White out attempting to steal second, Porter to Smith.
Sheridan singled to right.
3 Balboni flied to center.

5th Inning
St. Louis
1 Clark popped to White in shallow center.
2 Landrum flied to right.
3 Sheridan grounded to third.
Kansas City
Sundberg singled to left.
1 Biancalana flied to center.
2 Leibrandt sacrificed, Clark unassisted.
3 Smith grounded to third.

6th Inning
St. Louis
Cedeno singled to left.
Porter singled to right, Cedeno stopping at second.
1 Cox out on a popped-up bunt to Brett.
2,3 Smith grounded into a double play, Biancalana to White to Balboni.
Kansas City
White singled to right.
1,2 Brett hit into a double play, Herr to Smith to Clark.
3 White struck out swinging.

7th Inning
St. Louis
1 McGee grounded to short.
2 Herr grounded to short, another fielding gem by Biancalana.
3 Clark struck out swinging.
Kansas City
1 Sheridan struck out swinging.
Balboni walked.
2 Sundberg struck out swinging.
Biancalana singled to right, Balboni going to second.
3 Leibrandt struck out swinging.

8th Inning
St. Louis
1 Landrum flied to center.
Pendleton singled to right.
Cedeno walked.
2 Porter took a called third strike.
Harper, pinch-hitting for Cox, dropped a single just beyond second, scoring Pendleton with Cedeno stopping at second.
Van Slyke ran for Cedeno.
Smith walked, loading the bases.
For Kansas City—Quisenberry came in to pitch for Leibrandt.
Lawless ran for Harper.
3 McGee forced Smith at second, White to Biancalana.
Kansas City
For St. Louis—Van Slyke playing right with Dayley pitching.
1 Smith struck out swinging.
Wilson walked.
2 Brett struck out swinging.
3 White flied to center.

9th Inning
St. Louis
1 Herr grounded to first.
2 Clark struck out swinging.
Landrum beat out a bounce hit in front of the plate.
3 Pendleton flied to center.
Kansas City
Motley announced as pinch-hitter for Sheridan.
For St. Louis—Worrell came in to pitch.
Orta, pinch-hitting for Motley, beat out an infield roller to first on a very controversial play (the replay shows an out).
Balboni singled to left, Orta going to second.
Concepcion ran for Balboni.
1 Sundberg bunted and forced Orta at third, Worrell to Pendleton, Concepcion to second.
Both runners moved up a base on a passed ball by Porter.
McRae intentionally walked to load the bases.
Wathan ran for McRae.
Iorg, batting for Quisenberry, singled to right, scoring both Concepcion and Sundberg with the game-ending runs.

Game 7 October 27 at Kansas City

St. L.			
St. L.	000	000	000
K.C.	023	060	00x

St. Louis	Pos	AB	R	H	RBI	PO	A	E
O. Smith	ss	4	0	1	0	2	2	0
McGee	cf	4	0	0	0	5	0	0
Herr	2b	4	0	0	0	2	2	0
Clark	1b	4	0	1	0	4	1	0
Van Slyke	rf	4	0	1	0	5	0	0
Pendleton	3b	3	0	1	0	1	1	0
Landrum	lf	2	0	1	0	0	0	0
Andujar	p	0	0	0	0	0	0	0
Forsch	p	0	0	0	0	0	0	0
a Braun		1	0	0	0	0	0	0
Dayley	p	0	0	0	0	0	0	0
Porter	c	3	0	0	0	4	0	0
Tudor	p	1	0	0	0	0	0	0
Campbell	p	0	0	0	0	0	0	0
Lahti	p	0	0	0	0	0	0	0
Horton	p	0	0	0	0	0	0	0
Jorgensen	lf	2	0	0	0	1	0	0
Totals		32	0	5	0	24	6	0

Kansas City	Pos	AB	R	H	RBI	PO	A	E
L. Smith	lf	3	2	1	2	3	0	0
Jones	lf	1	0	0	0	1	0	0
Wilson	cf	5	1	2	1	7	0	0
Brett	3b	5	2	4	0	2	0	0
White	2b	4	1	1	1	0	5	0
Sundberg	c	3	1	1	1	2	0	0
Balboni	1b	4	2	2	2	7	0	0
Motley	rf	4	1	3	3	3	0	0
Biancalana	ss	3	0	0	0	2	1	0
Saberhagen	p	4	1	0	0	0	0	0
Totals		36	11	14	10	27	6	0

Pitching	IP	H	R	ER	BB	SO
St. Louis						
Tudor (L)	$2\frac{1}{3}$	3	5	5	4	1
Campbell	*$1\frac{2}{3}$	4	1	1	1	1
Lahti	$\frac{2}{3}$	4	4	4	0	1
Horton	**0	1	1	1	0	0
Andujar	***0	1	0	0	1	0
Forsch	$1\frac{1}{3}$	1	0	0	0	0
Dayley	2	0	0	0	0	1
Kansas City						
Saberhagen (W)	9	5	0	0	0	2

*Pitched to one batter in 5th.
**Pitched to one batter in 5th.
***Pitched to two batters in 5th.

a Flied out for Forsch in 7th.

Double—L. Smith. Home Run—Motley. Stolen Bases—L. Smith, Brett, Wilson. Wild Pitch—Forsch. Double Plays—Pendleton to Herr to Clark, Herr to Smith to Clark. Left on Bases—St. Louis 5, Kansas City—7. Umpires—Denkinger, Williams, McKean, Engel, Shulock, Quick. Attendance—41,658. Time of Game—2:46.

1st Inning
St. Louis
1 Smith flied to short center.
2 McGee flied to short center.
3 Herr popped to Biancalana in short left.
Kansas City
1 Smith popped to short right.
2 Wilson grounded to short.
Brett singled to right.
3 White flied to deep center.

2nd Inning
St. Louis
Clark lined a single to right.
1 Van Slyke struck out swinging.
2 Pendleton flied to short center.
3 Landrum popped to third.
Kansas City
1 Sundberg flied to center.
Balboni walked.
Motley hit a two-run homer just fair of the left field foul line on a full count.
2 Biancalana lined to third.
3 Saberhagen struck out swinging.

3rd Inning
St. Louis
1 Porter flied to short left.
2 Tudor struck out trying to bunt.
3 Smith grounded to second.
Kansas City
Smith walked.
1 Wilson flied out foul to Van Slyke.
Brett check-swings a single past the mound, Smith stopping at second.
Smith and Brett pulled off a double steal.
White walked, loading the bases.
Sundberg walked, forcing in Smith, the bases still loaded.
For St. Louis—Campbell relieved Tudor.
Balboni singled to left, driving in Brett and White with Sundberg going to second.
2 Motley grounded to first, advancing both runners.
Biancalana walked to again load the bases.
3 Saberhagen struck out, swinging.

4th Inning
St. Louis
1 McGee grounded to second.
2 Herr flied to Smith in left-center.
3 Clark grounded to short.
Kansas City
1 Smith flied to short right.
Wilson singled to center.
Brett singled to left, Wilson stopping at second.
2,3 White grounded into a double play, Pendleton to Herr to Clark.

5th Inning
St. Louis
1 Van Slyke flied to center.
2 Pendleton flied to left.
Landrum singled to left.
3 Porter flied to short center.
Kansas City
Sundberg singled to right.
For St. Louis—Lahti came in to pitch.
Balboni singled a bouncer to left, Sundberg stopping at second.
Motley lined a single into right, scoring Sundberg with Balboni stopping at second.

5th Inning (continued)
1 Biancalana struck out swinging.
2 Saberhagen bunt forced Motley at second, Clark to Smith with Balboni going to third.
Smith blasts one down the left field line for a double, scoring Balboni and Saberhagen. Smith went to third on the throw.
Wilson beat out a chopper to second, Smith scoring.
For St. Louis—Horton relieved Lahti.
Brett singled to center, Wilson racing to third. Brett's 4th hit of the game.
For St. Louis—Andujar pitching (batting 7th); Jorgensen in left field (batting 9th).
White lofted a single over Pendleton, scoring Wilson, Brett racing to third.
Herzog ejected as he argued a call that Andujar did not like.
Sundberg walked to load the bases.
Andujar ejected when he charged Denkinger on the 4th ball call. He is held all the way to the dugout.
For St. Louis—Forsch pitching.
Brett scored, White went to third and Sundberg to second on a wild pitch.
3 Balboni flied to center.

6th Inning
St. Louis
For Kansas City—Jones playing left.
1 Jorgensen grounded to second.
Smith singled to left.
2 McGee flied to Motley in right-center.
3 Herr popped to short.
Kansas City
Motley singled to center.
1,2 Biancalana grounded into a double play, Herr to Smith to Clark.
3 Saberhagen called out on strikes.

7th Inning
St. Louis
1 Clark flied to the wall in left.
Van Slyke singled to right.
Pendleton singled to right, Van Slyke stopping at second.
2 Braun, pinch-hitting for Forsch, flied to center, Van Slyke advances to third after the catch.
3 Porter flied to right.
Kansas City
For St. Louis—Dayley now pitching.
1 Jones flied to right.
2 Wilson flied to deep center.
3 Brett flied to center.

8th Inning
St. Louis
1 Jorgensen grounded to first.
2 Smith foul popped to Brett.
3 McGee grounded to second.
Kansas City
1 White flied to left.
2 Sundberg popped to second.
3 Balboni flied to right.

9th Inning
St. Louis
1 Herr grounded to second.
2 Clark flied to center.
3 Van Slyke flied to deep right.

1985 WORLD SERIES COMPOSITE BOX

	Wins	Composite Line Score
Kansas City Royals	4	1 6 3 4 8 0 2 1 3 - 28
St. Louis Cardinals	3	1 1 2 1 1 1 0 1 5 - 13

Manager	Regular Season W	L	Pct.	G. Ahead
Dick Howser	91	71	.562	1
Whitey Herzog	101	61	.623	3

BATTING AND FIELDING

WORLD SERIES STATISTICS

KANSAS CITY ROYALS	Pos	G	AB	R	H	2B	3B	HR	RBI	BB	SO	SB	BA	SA	PO	A	E
Steve Balboni	1b	7	25	2	8	0	0	0	3	5	4	0	.320	.320	**70**	3	0
Frank White	2b	7	28	4	7	**3**	0	**1**	**6**	3	4	1	.250	.464	10	**20**	0
Buddy Biancalana	ss	7	18	2	5	0	0	0	2	5	4	0	.278	.278	6	**20**	0
George Brett	3b	7	27	5	10	1	0	0	1	4	7	1	**.370**	.407	10	19	**1**
Pat Sheridan	rf-ph	5	18	0	4	2	0	0	1	0	7	0	.222	.333	6	0	0
Willie Wilson	cf	7	**30**	1	**11**	0	**1**	0	3	1	4	**3**	.367	.433	19	1	0
Lonnie Smith	lf	7	27	5	9	**3**	0	0	4	3	8	2	.333	.444	7	2	0
Jim Sundberg	c	7	24	**6**	6	2	0	0	1	**6**	4	0	.250	.333	47	3	0
Darryl Motley	rf-ph	5	11	1	4	0	0	**1**	3	0	1	0	.364	.636	4	0	0
Lynn Jones	ph-lf	5	3	0	2	1	**1**	0	0	0	0	0	.667	1.667	4	0	0
Jorge Orta	ph	3	3	0	1	0	0	0	0	0	0	0	.333	.333	—	—	—
Dane Iorg	ph	2	2	0	1	0	0	0	2	0	0	0	.500	.500	—	—	—
Hal McRae	ph	3	1	0	0	0	0	0	0	1	0	0	.000	.000	—	—	—
John Wathan	ph-pr	2	1	0	0	0	0	0	0	0	1	0	.000	.000	—	—	—
Onix Concepcion	ss-pr	3	0	1	0	0	0	0	0	0	0	0	—	—	0	2	0
Greg Pryor	3b	1	0	0	0	0	0	0	0	0	0	0	—	—	0	1	0
Jamie Quick		Did not play															
Bret Saberhagen	p	2	7	1	0	0	0	0	0	0	4	0	.000	.000	0	0	0
Charlie Leibrandt	p	2	4	0	0	0	0	0	0	0	2	0	.000	.000	1	2	0
Danny Jackson	p	2	6	0	0	0	0	0	0	0	5	0	.000	.000	0	4	**1**
Bud Black	p	2	1	0	0	0	0	0	0	0	1	0	.000	.000	1	2	**1**
Dan Quisenberry	p	4	0	0	0	0	0	0	0	0	0	0	—	—	1	1	0
Joe Beckwith	p	1	0	0	0	0	0	0	0	0	0	0	—	—	0	0	0
Steve Farr		Did not play															
Mark Gubicza		Did not play															
team total		7	236	28	68	12	2	2	26	28	56	7	.288	.381	186	80	3

Double Plays—3
Left on Bases—56

REGULAR SEASON STATISTICS

KANSAS CITY ROYALS		Main Pos	G	AB	R	H	2B	3B	HR	RBI	BB	SO	SB	BA	SA
Steve Balboni		1b	160	600	74	146	28	2	36	88	52	166	1	.243	.477
Frank White		2b	149	563	62	140	25	1	22	69	28	86	10	.249	.414
Buddy Biancalana		ss	81	138	21	26	5	1	1	6	17	34	1	.188	.261
George Brett		3b	155	550	108	184	38	5	30	112	103	49	9	.335	**.585**
Pat Sheridan		of	78	206	18	47	9	2	3	17	23	38	11	.228	.335
Willie Wilson		of	141	605	87	168	25	**21**	4	43	29	94	43	.278	.408
Lonnie Smith	a	of	120	448	77	115	23	4	6	41	41	69	40	.257	.366
Jim Sundberg		c	115	367	38	90	12	4	10	35	33	67	0	.245	.381
Darryl Motley		of	123	383	45	85	20	1	17	49	18	57	6	.222	.413
Lynn Jones		of	110	152	12	32	7	0	0	9	8	15	0	.211	.257
Jorge Orta		dh	110	300	32	80	21	1	4	45	22	28	2	.267	.383
Dane Iorg		of	64	130	7	29	9	1	1	21	8	16	0	.223	.331
Hal McRae		dh	112	320	41	83	19	0	14	70	44	45	0	.259	.450
John Wathan		c	60	145	11	34	8	1	1	9	17	15	1	.234	.324
Onix Concepcion		ss	131	314	32	64	5	1	2	20	16	29	4	.204	.245
Greg Pryor		inf.	63	114	8	25	3	0	1	3	8	12	0	.219	.272
Jamie Quick		c	19	57	3	16	3	1	0	4	2	9	0	.281	.368
Bret Saberhagen		p	32	0	0	0	0	0	0	0	0	0	0	—	—
Charlie Leibrandt		p	33	0	0	0	0	0	0	0	0	0	0	—	—
Danny Jackson		p	32	0	0	0	0	0	0	0	0	0	0	—	—
Bud Black		p	33	0	0	0	0	0	0	0	0	0	0	—	—
Dan Quisenberry		p	84	0	0	0	0	0	0	0	0	0	0	—	—
Joe Beckwith		p	49	0	0	0	0	0	0	0	0	0	0	—	—
Steve Farr		p	16	0	0	0	0	0	0	0	0	0	0	—	—
Mark Gubicza		p	29	0	0	0	0	0	0	0	0	0	0	—	—
team total			162	5500	687	1384	261	49	154	657	473	840	128	.252	.401

a from St. Louis Cardinals
Omar Moreno (of), Dave Leeper (of), Jim Scranton (ss), Bob Hegman (2b), Mike Jones (p), Mike LaCoss (p), Mark Huissman (p), Larry Gura (p), Tony Ferriera (p), and Dennis Leonard (p) also played for the Royals during the season.

WORLD SERIES STATISTICS

ST. LOUIS CARDINALS	Pos	G	AB	R	H	2B	3B	HR	RBI	BB	SO	SB	BA	SA	PO	A	E
Jack Clark	1b	7	25	1	6	2	0	0	4	3	**9**	0	.240	.320	49	4	0
Tommy Herr	2b	7	26	2	4	2	0	0	0	2	2	0	.154	.231	11	13	0
Ozzie Smith	ss	7	23	1	2	0	0	0	0	4	0	1	.087	.087	10	16	**1**
Terry Pendleton	3b	7	23	3	6	1	**1**	0	3	3	2	0	.261	.391	6	14	**1**
Cesar Cedeno	rf	5	15	1	2	1	0	0	1	2	2	0	.133	.200	9	0	0
Willie McGee	cf	7	27	2	7	2	0	**1**	2	1	3	1	.259	.444	15	0	0
Tito Landrum	lf	7	25	3	9	2	0	**1**	1	0	2	0	.360	**.560**	12	1	0
Darrell Porter	c	5	15	0	2	0	0	0	0	2	5	0	.133	.133	36	4	0
Andy Van Slyke	rf	6	11	0	1	0	0	0	0	0	5	0	.091	.091	8	0	0
Tom Nieto	c	2	5	0	0	0	0	0	1	1	2	0	.000	.000	23	1	0
Brian Harper	ph	4	4	0	1	0	0	0	1	0	1	0	.250	.250	—	—	—
Mike Jorgensen	lf	2	3	0	0	0	0	0	0	0	0	0	.000	.000	1	0	0
Steve Braun	ph	1	1	0	0	0	0	0	0	0	0	0	.000	.000	—	—	—
Ivan DeJesus	ph	1	1	0	0	0	0	0	0	0	0	0	.000	.000	—	—	—
Tom Lawless	pr	1	0	0	0	0	0	0	0	0	0	0	—	—	—	—	—
Vince Coleman		Did not play															
John Tudor	p	3	5	0	0	0	0	0	0	0	4	0	.000	.000	0	3	0
Danny Cox	p	2	4	0	0	0	0	0	0	0	2	0	.000	.000	1	2	0
Ken Dayley	p	4	0	0	0	0	0	0	0	0	0	0	—	—	0	0	0
Todd Worrell	p	3	1	0	0	0	0	0	0	0	1	0	.000	.000	0	1	0
Joaquin Andujar	p	2	1	0	0	0	0	0	0	0	1	0	.000	.000	0	1	0
Bill Campbell	p	3	0	0	0	0	0	0	0	0	0	0	—	—	1	0	0
Ricky Horton	p	3	1	0	0	0	0	0	0	0	1	0	.000	.000	2	0	0
Jeff Lahti	p	3	0	0	0	0	0	0	0	0	0	0	—	—	0	0	0
Bob Forsch	p	2	0	0	0	0	0	0	0	0	0	0	—	—	0	0	0
team total		7	216	13	40	10	1	2	13	18	42	2	.185	.269	184	60	2

Double Plays—9
Left on Bases—38

REGULAR SEASON STATISTICS

ST. LOUIS CARDINALS		Main Pos	G	AB	R	H	2B	3B	HR	RBI	BB	SO	SB	BA	SA
Jack Clark		1b	126	442	71	124	26	3	22	87	83	88	1	.281	.502
Tommy Herr		2b	159	596	97	180	38	3	8	110	80	55	31	.302	.416
Ozzie Smith		ss	158	537	70	148	22	3	6	54	65	27	31	.276	.361
Terry Pendleton		3b	149	559	56	134	16	3	5	69	37	75	17	.240	.306
Cesar Cedeno	b	of	28	76	14	33	4	1	6	19	5	7	5	.434	.750
Willie McGee		of	152	612	114	**216**	26	**18**	10	82	34	86	56	**.353**	.503
Tito Landrum		of-ph	85	161	21	45	8	2	4	21	19	30	1	.280	.429
Darrell Porter		c	84	240	30	53	12	2	10	36	41	48	6	.221	.413
Andy Van Slyke		of	146	424	61	110	25	6	13	55	47	54	34	.259	.439
Tom Nieto		c	95	253	15	57	10	2	0	34	26	37	0	.225	.281
Brian Harper		ph-of	43	52	5	13	4	0	0	8	2	3	0	.250	.327
Mike Jorgensen		1b-ph	72	112	14	22	6	0	0	11	31	27	2	.196	.250
Steve Braun		ph-of	64	67	7	16	4	0	1	6	10	9	0	.239	.343
Ivan DeJesus		ph-3b	59	72	11	16	5	0	0	7	4	16	2	.222	.292
Tom Lawless		2b	47	58	8	12	3	1	0	8	5	4	2	.207	.293
Vince Coleman		of	151	636	107	170	20	10	1	40	50	115	**110**	.267	.335
John Tudor		p	37	94	9	13	3	2	0	2	5	25	0	.138	.213
Danny Cox		p	35	79	3	12	1	0	0	6	4	24	0	.152	.165
Ken Dayley		p	57	5	0	2	0	0	0	0	0	1	0	.400	.400
Todd Worrell		p	17	1	0	0	0	0	0	0	0	1	0	.000	.000
Joaquin Andujar		p	38	94	2	10	2	0	0	8	5	50	3	.106	.128
Bill Campbell		p	50	6	2	2	0	0	0	1	3	2	0	.333	.333
Ricky Horton		p	49	16	1	1	0	0	0	0	3	5	0	.063	.063
Jeff Lahti		p	52	9	0	0	0	0	0	0	0	5	0	.000	.000
Bob Forsch		p	34	45	3	11	2	1	1	4	0	10	0	.244	.400
team total			162	5467	**747**	1446	245	**59**	87	**687**	**586**	853	**314**	**.264**	.379

b from Cincinnati Reds
Kurt Kepshire (p), Randy Hunt (c), Mike Laveilliere (c), Curtis Ford (of), Art Howe (1b-3b), Lonnie Smith (of), Neil Allen (p), Joe Boever (p), Andy Hassler (p), Pat Perry (p), Matt Keough (p), and Doug Bair (p) also played for the Cardinals during the season.

PITCHING

WORLD SERIES STATISTICS

	G	GS	CG	IP	H	R	ER	BB	SO	W	L	SV	ERA
KANSAS CITY ROYALS													
Bret Saberhagen	2	2	**2**	**18**	11	1	1	1	10	**2**	0	0	**0.50**
Charlie Leibrandt	2	2	0	$16\frac{1}{3}$	10	5	5	4	10	0	**1**	0	2.76
Danny Jackson	2	2	1	16	9	3	3	5	12	1	**1**	0	1.69
Bud Black	2	1	0	$5\frac{1}{3}$	4	3	3	5	4	0	**1**	0	5.06
Dan Quisenberry	**4**	0	0	$4\frac{1}{3}$	5	1	1	3	3	1	0	0	2.08
Joe Beckwith	1	0	0	2	1	0	0	0	3	0	0	0	0.00
Steve Farr	Did not play												
Mark Gubicza	Did not play												
team total	7	7	3	62	40	13	13	18	42	4	3	0	1.89
ST. LOUIS CARDINALS													
John Tudor	3	**3**	1	**18**	**15**	**6**	**6**	**7**	**14**	**2**	**1**	0	3.00
Danny Cox	2	2	0	14	14	2	2	4	13	0	0	0	1.29
Ken Dayley	**4**	0	0	6	1	0	0	3	5	1	0	0	0.00
Todd Worrell	3	0	0	$4\frac{2}{3}$	4	2	2	2	6	0	**1**	**1**	3.86
Joaquin Andujar	2	1	0	4	10	4	4	4	3	0	**1**	0	9.00
Bill Campbell	3	0	0	4	4	1	1	2	5	0	0	0	2.25
Ricky Horton	3	0	0	4	4	3	3	5	5	0	0	0	6.75
Jeff Lahti	3	0	0	$3\frac{2}{3}$	10	**6**	5	0	2	0	0	**1**	12.27
Bob Forsch	2	1	0	3	6	4	4	1	3	0	**1**	0	12.00
team total	7	7	1	$61\frac{1}{3}$	68	28	27	28	56	3	4	2	3.96

REGULAR SEASON STATISTICS

	G	GS	CG	IP	H	ER	BB	SO	W	L	Pct	SV	ShO	ERA
KANSAS CITY ROYALS														
Bret Saberhagen	32	32	10	235	211	75	38	158	20	6	.769	0	1	2.87
Charlie Leibrandt	33	33	8	238	223	71	68	108	17	9	.654	0	3	2.69
Danny Jackson	32	32	4	208	209	79	76	114	14	12	.538	0	3	3.42
Bud Black	33	33	5	206	216	99	59	122	10	15	.400	0	2	4.33
Dan Quisenberry	**84**	0	0	129	142	34	16	54	8	9	.471	**37**	0	2.37
Joe Beckwith	49	0	0	95	99	43	32	80	1	5	.167	1	0	4.07
Steve Farr	16	3	0	38	34	13	20	36	2	1	.667	1	0	3.11
Mark Gubicza	29	28	0	177	160	80	77	99	14	10	.583	0	0	4.06
team total	162	162	27	1461	1433	566	463	846	91	71	.562	41	**11**	3.49
ST. LOUIS CARDINALS														
John Tudor	36	36	14	275	209	59	49	169	21	8	.724	0	**10**	1.93
Danny Cox	35	35	10	241	226	77	64	131	18	9	.667	0	4	2.88
Ken Dayley	57	0	0	65	65	20	18	62	4	4	.500	11	0	2.76
Todd Worrell	17	0	0	22	17	7	7	17	3	0	1.000	5	0	2.91
Joaquin Andujar	38	38	10	270	265	102	82	112	21	12	.636	0	2	3.40
Bill Campbell	50	0	0	64	55	25	21	41	5	3	.625	4	0	3.50
Ricky Horton	49	3	0	90	84	29	34	59	3	2	.600	1	0	2.91
Jeff Lahti	52	0	0	68	63	14	26	41	5	2	.714	19	0	1.84
Bob Forsch	34	19	3	136	132	59	47	48	9	6	.600	2	1	3.90
team total	162	162	**37**	1464	1343	505	453	798	**101**	61	**.623**	44	20	3.10

Total Attendance—327,494 Average Attendance—46,785 Winning Player's Share—$76,342 Losing Player's Share—$54,922